Roger's Profanisaurus
TURTLESHEAD REVISITED

First published in 2024 by
Diamond Publishing Ltd
Part of the Metropolis Group,
4th Floor, Harmsworth House,
13 – 15 Bouverie Street, London
EC4Y 8DP

ISBN 978-1-9164219-6-7
© 2024 Fulchester Industries/
Diamond Publishing Ltd.

A CIP catalogue record for this book is
available from the British Library.

Compiled and edited by Graham Dury,
Simon Thorp & Alex Morris.

Roger's PROFANISAURUS

TURTLESHEAD REVISITED

Britain's Favourite Swearing Dictionary

— 2024 Edition —

diamondpublishing

A Foreword by Roger Mellie OBE

AS THIS BOOK – which is by my reckoning the sixth or possibly seventh edition of my *Profanisaurus* – finally heads off to the printers, my mind goes back to something that happened to me many years ago.

I was a young man with no idea what I wanted to do with the rest of my life. I had tried my hand at various dead-end jobs – van driver, window cleaner, male model.

Walking through the park one day, idly thinking about nothing in particular, I sat down to enjoy the late summer sun. After a while, I became aware of a figure sitting nearby, throwing stones at some swans. His broad-brimmed hat cast a deep shadow over his face, so it was difficult to make out his appearance. When the grizzled stranger spoke, however, I recognised his voice in an instant.

"You look like a young man with no idea what he wants to do with the rest of his life," the drifter drawled. "That's right, sir," I replied.

"I was like you once," he continued, sagely. "At the start of this great adventure. But if I've learnt anything down the years, it's this…"

"…There's a definite gap in the market for a really thick book containing thousands upon thousands of definitions and euphemisms for sex acts, private parts and things that people do in the toilet," he said.

I shook my head incredulously, and the stranger chuckled. "You may not believe me now, but in the year 2024, you'll find yourself editing an enormous, disgusting lexicon of the foulest words in the English language," he said. "770 pages of utter filth that you would be quite rightly ashamed to show to your own mother."

That mysterious stranger was right. As I sit here with the finished pages of *Turtleshead Revisited* on my desk waiting to go off to the printers, my mind goes back to that moment all those years ago. And that sage old-timer's prophetic words ring through my mind.

And do you know who that mysterious stranger in the park was? That man was former Leeds United and Scotland midfielder (later Leeds and Doncaster manager) Billy Bremner. Or certainly someone who looked very like him.

pp.
Roger Mellie OBE.

Roger Mellie OBE

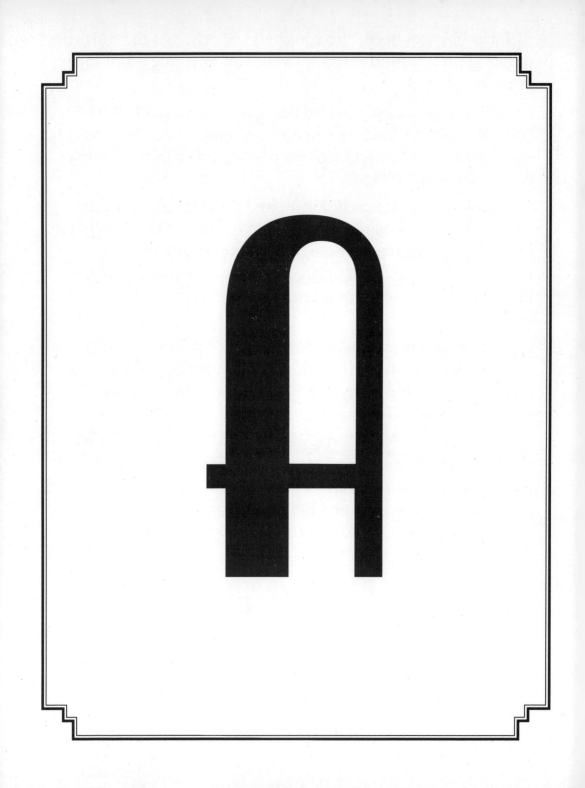

AA *adj.* The smallest size of commercially available brassiere, suitable for *espressos*. Low voltage *tit pants* furnished with *FA cups. Stit pants.*

aaaand action! *exclam.* Cecil B deMille-style announcement made – possibly through a megaphone – before loudly *breaking wind*. Also *and in local news; attention all shipping; let off some steam, Bennett; listen, I think I hear a horseshoe bat etc.*

AA-lister *1. n.* An alcoholic celebrity. *2. n.* A flat-chested celebrity. *Miss Lincolnshire, surfboard, jugless Douglas.*

AA man *1. n.* A *piss artist* in a yellow van. *2. n.* A fellow who gets a jumpstart off *birds* with *bangers like two aspirins on an ironing board.*

AA member *n.* A battery-powered *neck massager* with lifelike wiggly veins up the side, a side-mounted *clit* stimulator, and a big *bobby's helmet* on the end. A *fiddlestick, dildo, dolly dagger, slot machine, twat rattler* or *vagimix.*

aard on *n.* An uncircumcised *Dutch salute* that resembles the twitching snout of a peckish South African earth pig (*Orycteropus afer*), eager to get stuck into a tempting mound that is crawling with arthropods.

aard vark *exclam.* How somebody with a gobful of hot chips might say "hard work".

aardvarks' gasmasks, pair of *n. Tit pants* of the sort worn by women whose *shoe shiners* have migrated south over the years. Also *spaniels' earmuffs, wombles' noses.*

aardvark's nose *n.* A *kindling limb* with an intact *fiveskin*. An *anteater, tickle tackle, windsock, Kenny's hood. 'Then God spake unto Abraham in a loud voice, saying, Any uncircumcised male, who has still got an aardvark's nose, will be cut off from his people, for he has broken my covenant.'* (from *The Book of Marillion*, 6:3).

abacab *n.* Attempting to *do the dirty* with a somewhat *big-boned* or hairy lass. From the chorus of the eponymous Genesis song of the early eighties, *viz.* "Well, there's a hole in there somewhere. Yeah, there's a hole in there somewhere."

abandoned shit farm, face like an *sim.* A poetic phrase describing one whom the good Lord has seen fit to bless with aesthetically unconventional features. Also *lovely personality, a mush like a spat out toffee, welder's bench, bulldog licking piss off a nettle, bag of slapped twats* or *Thai stripper's scrotum.*

abandon ship *v.* To leave a long, wide *ever given* turd in the *shitpot* without flushing. See also *King Canute, Nemo's boot, panjammer, crowd pleaser,* *plumber's bonus.*

abattoir floor *n.* A particularly untidy *snatch*. Slightly grimmer than a *butcher's dustbin;* much grimmer than a *butcher's window*. Also *stamped bat, split bag of mince, kicked over trifle* or *the bottom of a ratcatcher's mallet.*

abba *1. n.* Swedish pop band with a cracking blonde in it. As well as two lady singers and a bloke with a beard who played the piano. *2. abbrev.* A *forbidden pleasure;* Area Between Balls and Arse. Also *taint, tintis, notcher, great.*

abba bladder *n.* A fellow who, when out *on the pop, breaks the seal* early. From the lyrics of the eponymous group's 1980 chart-topper *Super Trouper;* one who is constantly "feeling like a number one".

abbatar *1. n.* Hi-tech performing hologram as used in the erstwhile Scandinavian Eurovisionists' twenty-first century "live" performances. *2. n.* Any virtual reality means used to simulate the amorous company of Anna-Frid or Agnetha (or Bjorn and Benny for that matter) in their pomp; most likely a shop mannequin in a red or blonde wig, and a swimming armband.

ABC/abc *abbrev.* The Anus Bollock Connector or male perineum. See also *abba, ploughman's, Finsbury Bridge, scruttock, landing, no man's land etc.*

abdickate *v.* To retire gracefully from performing one's connubial obligations. *'Mrs Simpson abdickated about half way through the first night of our honeymoon and went off with von Ribbentrop.'*

Abdul's special sauce *n.* A thin, red, oddly metallic-tasting liquid that is found in *badly packed kebabs,* and which usually ends up smeared round the mouths of hungry gents after closing time on Saturday nights.

Aberdare tic-tac *n.* An anabolic steroid tablet. Named after the South Wales town where, it is said, every young man between the ages of nineteen and twenty-four eats them like sweets.

ABFAB/abfab *1. abbrev.* Common contraction of the title of the TV comedy show *Absolutely Fabulous. 2. n. abbrev.* A lady who has such a *lovely personality* that, when she is viewed from the waist down, it is impossible to tell which way she is facing. Unless you can see her feet. Arse Both Front And Back.

Abi habit *euph.* A married man's compulsion to fire up his computer and search out the buxom Miss Titmuss's famous home movie the moment his *bag for life* toddles off to the shops, or to bed, or turns her back in order to make a cup of tea.

a bit more choke and she would have started *exclam.* Humorous expression to be used after one has just launched a particularly loud and/or prolonged *air biscuit. Also a confident appeal by the Australians there.*

Abi Tumnus *n. prop.* A lady that on first sight seems very pleasing on the eye but who, upon closer scrutiny, is revealed to have hairy, unkempt, goat-like legs, a beard, and cloven hooves.

abject jizzery *n.* Haunting sense of remorse, shame and sadness that strikes immediately following a successfully concluded act of *gentlemanly relaxation*. An extreme and chronic form of *wangst.* Also *wanguish, tugger's remorse, crying over spilt milk, wank hangover, cumdown.*

abnormal load *n.* An *arse* so large it necessitates a motorcycle outrider. See also *beeps while reversing.*

abominable slowman *n.* That member of any party of drinkers *on the lash* who, at the point when his fellows have sunk their pints and are ready to move on, has only *budgie-supped* two inches of his own beverage.

abra-kebabra *n.* A magical illusion performed at the end of a night *on the piss,* whereby a traditional Turkish delicacy is made to disappear down the performer's throat, only to miraculously reappear a short time later on the back of a taxi driver's head. See also *rubber kebab.*

abroadie *adj.* (əˈbrɔːd-ee) Theatrical version of the Geordie accent unaccountably adopted by Newcastle folk after they move away from the north east, even if they didn't have much of an accent before.

abrowsal *n.* Embarrassing state of penile semi-hardness seen in the trousers of fellows casually flicking through *jazz mags* while laughing and shaking their heads or when ironically browsing the top shelf *art department* in a newsagent or motorway services.

abseiling *n.* The act of masturbating while simultaneously using a *dildo* in your *anus.* From the similarly coordinated two-handed action which is (apparently) required in both disciplines, not to mention the fact that there is a good chance the emergency services may have to be called out to rescue you at any moment.

absolute discharge *1. n.* Legal procedure whereby the defendant is found guilty, but no further action is deemed necessary by the court. *2. n.* In s*x, the situation that obtains when a beastly male is able to *empty his nuts* up a lady without let or hindrance, because she is on the pill, post-menopausal, already pregnant, abroad or whatever.

ACAB/acab *1. acronym.* Popular knuckle and forehead tattoo amongst members of the urban underclasses. All Coppers Are Bastards. *2.*

acronym. NZ. Association of Community Access Broadcasters; a popular forehead and knuckle tattoo amongst staff of local radio stations.

acafella *adj.* Descriptive of an unaccompanied *act of personal entertainment. 'No groupies in tonight, lads. We'll just have to go acafella.'* (The Flying Pickets, overheard in the dressing room, Ebbw Vale Leisure Centre, 1983).

accessories *n. Tits. 'Miss Winslet's outfit is set off with a lovely set of accessories.'*

access time *1. n.* In computing, the time taken between requesting and receiving data. *2. n.* In foreplay, the time taken for a woman's *blip tap* to produce sufficient *moip* to allow a randy swain to penetrate her smoothly without feeling like he is scraping his *giggling stick* on the Great Barrier Reef.

accidental floss *n.* Impromptu deep cleansing of one's interdental spaces when removing stray theads of *gorilla salad* from the front teeth.

accident brown spot *n.* A health & safety hazard where one is quite likely to *crap* oneself, *eg.* Turn 13 of the Olympic bobsleigh track at Whistler Sliding Centre, Vancouver, or the *nipsy*-testing southbound A167(M)/A1058 turning near Jesmond, Newcastle.

accordian, the *n.* Playfully slapping one's better half's buttock cheeks into each other while *scuttling* her from behind. And then sending a monkey with a cup to collect loose change from passers-by.

accstellarate *n.* To greatly increase your rate of *wifebeater* consumption in order to catch up with drinking companions who arrived at the pub before you did.

ace *1. n.* In tennis, a powerful point-winning serve that the receiver's racquet does not touch, of the sort that Boris Becker used to hit, and thus *2. n.* A sexual encounter that is over in a single stroke, *eg.* Boris Becker's broom cupboard dalliance with Angela Ermakova in 1999. *3. n.* A man with one *bollock. 4. n.* £1.49 for eight tins.

ace in the hole *1. phr.* In an argument or legal case, a decisive or overwhelming fact that is kept in reserve until needed. *2. phr.* Encomium in praise of a skilled sexual partner. *'Say what you like about the vicar, but he's ace in the hole.'*

ace of arse *n.* The patch of dark skin around the *nipsy,* reminiscent of the ace of spades symbol, which forms the target of cosmetic bleachers. The *arisola.*

ace of hearts *n.* An alarmingly sanguinary sheet of used *bumwad* that informs the wipee that his *Michael Miles* have unfortunately been ruptured by an excessively large or firm *Bungle's finger.*

achtung Spitfire! *1. exclam. WW2.* Teutonic shout of alarm typically heard when a German airfield came under RAF attack in the film *Battle of Britain. 2. exclam.* Cheery cry after hearing a *hurricane on one's tail.*

acid splashback *n.* When *stooling* on a recently disinfected *khazi,* a sudden spout of *turd*-propelled Domestos that brings tears to all three eyes. See *ring sting, anal bleaching.*

Acker Bilk *1. n. prop.* Neatly goateed, bowler-hatted Jimmy Hill-lookalike yokel clarinettist who rose to prominence during the trad boom of the 1960s, releasing eleven Top 50 singles, including the plaintive, chart-topping *Stranger on the Shore.* For more details, see his 1962 autobiography *Acker Bilk,* by Gordon Williams and Acker Bilk. *2. n.* A meticulously well-kept *minge* of the sort often seen in *jazz mags.* A *snapper mat* that is trimmed to a sharp point.

Acker Bilk's beard *n.* An anonymously deposited, above-the-waterline mini *skidmark,* where an *ocean-going lobster* has nudged the porcelain on its way to *Shanks Bay.* A *stranger on the shore.*

ACNB *abbrev.* Adequately endowed *penilistically* speaking, but with little or nothing to offer in the *clockweights* department. All Cock No Bollocks.

acne carriage *n.* The preferred conveyance of the sort of spotty-complexioned, tracksuited scallywags who effect backward-facing caps. Usually a Vauxhall Corsa or Citroen Saxo *with fourth party insurance.* Also *estate car, Aldi TT.*

a confident appeal by the Australians there *exclam.* Phrase which should be amusingly delivered in the clipped voice of Richie Benaud following a raucous *shout from down under.* An Antipodean twist on *a bit more choke and she would have started; speech!; you're only supposed to blow the bloody doors off etc.*

acorn *n.* Nestling forlornly in the *shrubbery* of a fat German naturist, a little *bell end* that looks unlikely to ever grow into a mighty oak.

acorn antique *n.* A small piece of knobbly *woodwork* that has seen better days and may no longer be of much practical use. May have a few age-related marks and show severe patination, worm damage, mildew, and foxing.

acrotwat *n.* An experimental Darwinian who, after copious consumption of *giggle water,* becomes possessed by the spirit of The Great Wallenda and is compelled to attempt feats of derring-do upon scaffolding, public statuary, tower cranes *etc.* Usually with comically tragic results.

AC Slatering *n.* The act of taking a *crap* while

facing the wrong way round on the *chod bin.* From the character AC Slater in the utterly, utterly *crap* 1980s US teen sitcom *Saved by the Bell,* who always had to turn his chair round the wrong way before sitting on it.

action man eyes *n.* The surreptitious, commando-style sideways glance – initiated by a small, well-concealed lever – that an eagle-eyed chap gives to the top shelf *noddy comic* section as he leaves a newsagent or petrol station.

action man's hand *n. medic.* A debilitating condition, symptomised by manual paralysis, brought about by excessive or prolonged masturbation.

action man's toboggan *n.* A substantial and fast-moving, lozenge-shaped *Sir Douglas,* not dissimilar in size & texture to the popular doll's gravity-assisted snow-traversing accessory.

action man syndrome *n. medic.* Suffered by male cyclists who find that, following a long bike journey, their genitalias have gone all numb in the style of the popular *fruitbowl*-free boys' dolls.

action respray *n.* A Pekinpah-esque slow-motion *bolt-shooting* sequence in a big budget *bongo* movie. A *bollockbuster.*

active pork assist *n.* Derived from the similarly-named car technology, a skilful hand that gently manages to guide a chap's *ragtop* into the smallest space without *bumping the kerb* or *scuffing the rim.*

activitity *n.* A "hands on" style of *mammary management.* Also *come in Tokyo, finding Radio Hilversum, etch-a-sketch, safe cracking.*

act of decommissioning *1. n.* 1990s Northern Irish peace process. *2. n.* Blocking a public convenience and rendering it unusable. *'I wouldn't go in there if I was you, Mr McGuinness. Ian Paisley's just been in and carried out an act of decommissioning.'*

Acton foreplay *n.* A thick finger jabbed into one's chest as a prelude to getting well and truly *fucked.* A particularly common practice in the hostelries of this salubrious West London suburb.

Adam Ant, give her an *1. v.* To inscribe a white line across a lady's face using one's *naughty paintbrush,* in a style reminiscent of the briefly popular eighties pistol-waving dandy highwayman's makeup. To *lob ropes* over the bridge of the missus's nose. *2. v.* To lob a car starter motor through a *bird's* front window.

Adam Ant shit *n.* An act of defecation performed in a *bog* with a broken seat, *viz.* When one is forced to "stand and deliver".

Adam Richman's chod bin, as full as *sim.* Said of something that is comprehensively packed to the gunwales. A reference to the state of the eponymous *Man vs Food* presenter's *bum sink* following one of his frequent televised gustatory challenges on the Food Channel. *As full as a ~fat bird's shoe, ~parson's sack, ~wanker's fist, ~bull's bum, ~seaside shithouse.*

Adam's bridge *n.* The bit of skin between a lady's *gash* and her *freckle*. The *tinter, carse, taint, twernt, Humber bridge etc.*

add a dash of lime *euph.* To *piss* in the bath, thus adding a charming splash of colour and piquancy to one's evening soak.

additional feature *euph.* A *bongo vid.* From the discreet way in which pay-per-view *stick flicks* were described on the hilarious parliamentary expenses claims submitted by former Home Secretary Jacqui Smith. Eeh, remember that?

address the Nuremberg rally *n.* To excitably perform *cumulonimbus* on a *bird* with a *Hitler tash*, while simultaneously fondling her left *churn* and *nip-nop* with one's extended right hand; the overall effect calling to mind the erstwhile Führer's infamous pose while addressing the masses in 1938, albeit rotated through about 90°.

address the speaker of the house *v.* To *suck off* the *honourable member for Pantchester.* To engage in *horatio.*

add-to-basket bride *n.* A lifelong partner and soul-mate acquired *via* a touchingly romantic and secure internet transaction. *'Have you met my add-to-basket bride, vicar? Her name escapes me for the moment, but I'm pretty sure it begins with a vowel.'*

add to the ambience *euph.* To release a particularly fragrant *bottom burp.* *'There's a couple coming round to view the house, and I've just enough time to put a pot of coffee on, bake a loaf of bread and add to the ambience before they get here.'*

add to the horror *phr.* To follow someone into the *powder room* when your need is too great to stand on ceremony. *'I'd give it five minutes if I was you, Mrs Patmore.' 'I can't wait. I've got to add to the horror, Mr Carson.'*

add to your story *euph.* 1. *v.* To post some *shit* on a popular social networking site. 2. *v.* To *drop a log.*

ADIDAS/adidas *acronym.* Conditioned Pavlovian response of those who were potty-trained the old fashioned way. After Dinner I Do A Shit. Also, for those of a lexicographical bent, the letters may be reversed to spell *SADIDA, ie.* Soon After Dinner I Do Another.

adidas shit *n.* A satisfying *dump* that leaves three stripes, as opposed to a single swoosh, at the bottom of the *pan* after flushing.

administration *n. Paperwork* done in the *back office*; the cleansing of the *nipsy* after *emptying the boot.*

admiral's in port, the *exclam.* Phrase shouted aloud when one finds that someone has left an unattended *dreadnought* wallowing at anchor in the *chod bin.*

Adrian Chiles 1. *n. prop.* Cushion-faced former presenter of *The One Show.* 2. *n. rhym. slang.* Haemorrhoids. Also Harry Syles, Kurt Weills, Rockfords. *'Ooh, me Adrian Chiles aren't half giving me some gyp this morning, nan.'*

adult 1. *adj.* Descriptive of something to have *one off the wrist* at, on or over *eg. Adult* channel, *adult* magazine, *adult* phoneline, *adult* text messages, *adult movie.* 2. *adj.* Descriptive of the sort of talk that would have made Mary Whitehouse *shit* her *fucking* pants. *'The following programme contains adult language.'*

adultery tax *n.* The exorbitant cost of buying breakfast in a Little Chef handily located adjacent to a discreetly situated Travelodge. *'I'm afraid you can't claim your adultery tax back as a legitimate business expense, Mr Giggs.'*

Advanced British Standard 1. *n.* Baccalaureate-style qualifications for 16 to 19 year olds that will apparently replace A-levels and once again make everything wonderful forever. 2. *n.* Post-Brexit alternative to the *British Standard Handful*, ushering in a nationwide utopia of traditional Barbara Windsor-sized norks.

advance to Pall Mall *v.* To be given the opportunity to *move straight to pink.* See also *go back to Old Kent Road.*

adventure bay 1. *n. prop.* A fictional location on kids' show *Paw Patrol.* 2. *n.* Fishy harbour where, from time to time, the *skin boat* is wont to dock and unload its sticky cargo. *The Bermuda triangle, pearl harbour.*

ADW *abbrev.* All Day Wank. A 24-hour trip to the *Billy Mill Roundabout* with no hand signals. Something to do if you're a lighthouse keeper, crane driver on a foggy day, an Apollo Command Module pilot at a loose end on the dark side of the Moon, while trapped under a collapsed building following an earthquake, or when an elderly and much-loved member of the royal family dies and they put the telly off.

aerial assault *n.* An act of *horatio* given to a man while he is standing on a chair, due to the lady being unable to kneel down, *eg.* When she is wearing party clothes, a wedding dress, a spinal brace *etc.*

Aero-dynamic *adj.* Used when referring to a *salad-dodging bird*'s body that would not fare particularly well, one might suppose, in a wind tunnel test.

aeroplane blonde *n.* A dark-haired female who bleaches her *barnet, ie.* She who is equipped with a "black box".

aerosoil *n.* The fine faecal spray which typically accompanies a blast that is, with the best will in the world, unlikely to freshen the air.

afcanestan *n.* A fungal warzone situated in the *dunghampers* of a somewhat unclean lass.

Afghan *1. n.* A long, silky-haired *fanny.* Named after the long, silky-haired dogs which were briefly fashionable in the 1970s. *2. n.* A mouldy, tangled *fanny.* Named after the mouldy, tangled coats which were briefly fashionable in the 1970s.

A for apple *n.* A *Thora Hird* that splashes down in the water, resulting in a wet *bomb-bay.* Named after the scene in the film *Dambusters* when the eponymous Lancaster releases a bomb that bounces too high and brings down the plane. (Although that was bollocks because the real A for Apple successfully caused a small breach in the Mohne dam before being shot down over the Dutch coast on its return flight). An *own goal.*

afterburner *1. n.* A hot blast of *sulphur dibaxide* left to bake for an hour inside a car on a sweleringly hot day as a surprise treat for the wife when she gets in to go shopping. *2. n.* A pyroflatulatory *anal announcement.* A *blue streak, St. George's ruin, go for throttle up.*

after dinner bint *n.* A *bird* who only lets you *fuck* her after you have taken her out for a meal.

after dinner cigar *n.* An aromatic cheroot pushed out of the *Cambridge entrance* by food going in at the other end of the alimentary canal. *'If you will excuse me, gentlemen, following that third helping of steak and kidney pudding, I fear I must retire forthwith to smoke an after dinner cigar in the cludgie.'*

after dinner speech *n.* A hearty bout of flatulence following a particularly large repast. A noisome peroration delivered without reference to notes. Delivering an *after dinner speech* is considered good etiquette in some cultures, such as Humberside.

afterdrop *1. n. medic.* In first aid, a situation where body temperature continues to fall, even when the casualty has reached a warmer environment. *2. n.* When standing up on a hot day, the phenomenon of a cheap *bog* seat clattering down after sticking to the sweaty backs of the legs.

after eight mince *1. n.* The exaggeratedly flamboyant gait affected by one who has recently taken a gallon of booze on board and is concentrating extremely hard on not falling over. *2. n.* The uncomfortable filling of a drinker's *tackle hammock* as a consequence of his unwise decision to have *one for the road. 'Fancy another pint, Dr Williams?' 'Better not, Dr Sentamu. I'm doing a royal wedding in the morning and I've already got a full serving of after eight mince here.'*

after froth *n.* The scummy remnants of ejaculation which are still to be found lingering in the *hog's eye* ten minutes after the main event.

afternoon wood *n.* The equivalent of *morning wood* for students, people who are actively seeking employment, professional musicians and members of the royal family. Post-meridian priapism.

aftershave, tramp's *n.* The manly and sexy aroma which wafts out of a pub at eight o'clock in the morning, and drives the bag ladies wild.

aftershock *n.* The second *sit down toilet adventure* of the day, experienced a couple of hours after the main seismic eruption.

after spaff *n.* That extra splodge of *spooge* that drops out of the *aardvark's nose* ten minutes after *Elvis has left the building.* Also the *missing fish, post bolt, jitlag, after froth.*

afterthought *n.* A very short clearing of the *nether throat* emitted after a much longer and richer *anal announcement,* much like a full stop marking the end of a sentence.

Agamemnon *1. n. prop.* In classical mythology, one of the principle protagonists in Homer's *Iliad*; the commander of the Greek forces during the siege of Troy. Don't say we never fucking learn you anything. *2. n.* An unimaginative gift purchaser; "the King Of Argos".

Agatha Christie *n.* A silent, putrid *arse crime* committed by someone in this very room, and at this stage only one person knows whodunnit. (If it's anything like *The Mousetrap,* it's the bloke who comes in through the window on skis (who says he's a policeman but isn't, whilst the real policeman – who knows that the bloke who comes in through the window on skis isn't a policeman, but is himself pretending he *isn't* a policeman – says nothing and allows him to continue with his nefarious carryings on. Jesus, it's bad)).

Agatha Wristie *n. prop.* A detective drama that unexpectedly puts *lead* in a fellow's *pencil. 'Did you see that Agatha Wristie last night with Peter Ustinov, Bette Davis and Angela Lansbury? Phwooar!'*

aggrophobic *n.* One who is afraid of fighting; a *yitney.*

aginda *n.* A clearly set out plan to stay in on your own and drink three quarters of a bottle of Tanqueray, before laughing and crying yourself to sleep on the floor. And then doing *any other business* in your pants.

agony ants *n.* Aggressive, stinging insects of the order *Hymenoptera* that commonly inhabit the *tea-towel holders* of reluctant wipers. Sufferers with particularly angry infestations can be identified by their frequent squirming from cheek to cheek. Also known as *cleftermites, Indian killer bees* or *arse wasps*.

a good shit would kill him/her *exclam.* Said of someone who is *as thin as a vegan's dog*.

a great fire burns within me, but no one stops to warm themselves at it, and passers-by only see a wisp of smoke *1. exclam.* Profound statement made by monaural post-impressionist Vincent Van Gogh. *2. exclam.* Slightly less profound statement made the night after a prawn vindaloo and eight cans of Skol.

AG2R, sign for *1. v.* In professional cycling circles, to join the only team that wears brown shorts, and thus *2. v.* To *papper* one's *kegs*. *'How's it going, Sir Bradley?' 'Not bad Cav, but if I don't get to a shitter soon I'll be signing for AG2R.'*

ahad *adj.* NE. On fire. *'Ah shite, the chip pan's went ahad again, mutha.'*

ah, bisto! *exclam.* A witty interjection uttered by a *beneficiary* when he detects the beefy aroma of a warm *meat feast* at an *air buffet*.

ahead on pints *adj.* In an advanced state of inebriation after ten rounds, but still standing, just.

AHIAO *abbrev.* Used in reference to an exceptionally accommodating young lady. Any Holes In Any Order. *'Whatever "in love" means. She's AHIAO, so that's something, one supposes.'*

a hot water bottle and a bottle of Bovril *phr. onomat.* The sound made by a substantial sub-aquatic *bottom burp*. Also known, variously, as a *blooper, tottle, Edward Woodward, bottle of olives,* or *Bill Oddie*.

ah, smell that fresh country air *exclam.* Something to be said after dropping a ripe *guff*. See also *sew a button on that; anybody hurt?; speak on, sweet lips that never told a lie*.

aim Archie at the Armitage *euph.* To *point Percy at the porcelain*.

aiming juice *n.* The beverage of choice for a darts or snooker player back in the old days; beer. *'Another twenty pints of aiming juice, Mr Werbeniuk?'*

air baby *n.* A Bakewell tart that takes a great deal of effort to deliver and of which one feels enormously proud. *'What's that appalling whiff?' 'Ah, that would be my brand new air baby. It's a beauty, isn't it? Anyway, you may call your next witness, Mr Rumpole.'*

airbag *n.* A budget airline stewardess who looks like she's parachuted out of the ugly plane and hit every cloud on the way down. See also *trolley tubby*.

air bags *n.* Huge, pneumatic breasts which can leave you seeing stars and temporarily deaf. *Oomlaaters, cajooblies*. See *dead heat in a zeppelin race*.

air biscuit *n. Fart, botty burp.* A floating body of *trouser gas* that could ruin your appetite between meals.

air biscuit guitar *n.* When suffering from flatulence, using one's cupped right hand to "pluck" pockets of one's gaseous foulage out of the air before propelling it nosewards, while holding one's left arm outstretched as if fingering an ear-shredding solo on an imaginary fretboard.

airblade *1. n.* A high-powered, wall-mounted hand drying device found in pub toilets, which more or less obviates the need to rub your wet hands on the front of your trousers following a *piss*. *2. n.* A *trouser cough* of such violence that it feels as if your *arsehole* has had a big axe embedded in it by a short-sighted Tudor executioner.

airblade *n.* A loud and forceful post-urinational blast of hot air optimistically sneaked out under the noise of a hand dryer.

airborne toxic event *1. n.* Five-piece US rock band from Los Feliz, Los Angeles, it says here. *2. n.* A *Ming the merciless*, following which one would be well advised to keep all doors and windows tightly shut until the all-clear has sounded.

airbrakes, disengage the *v.* To release the first *horse & cart* of the morning.

air buffet *n.* A lingering, gaseous meal which is more nourishing than an *air biscuit*, and to which one may make several return visits.

airburst *n.* A *Jedi knight* that explodes on contact with the atmosphere, *foulage* that *comes out like bats at dusk*, leaving the *pan* with the texture of a Wall's Feast ice lolly. A *flock of pigeons*, a *space shuttle*.

air corridor *n.* The *back passage* or *VIP entrance*.

airhorn *n.* On a *wank holiday*, the eighteenth *Barclays* of the morning, after which you have *wanked* your *bollocks* dry, so you can just pull up your *trolleys* and walk away. Assuming you still have any strength in your legs.

air lingus *n.* A sexual position adopted by soft porn *jazz mag* lesbians, where one of them is just about to lick the other one's *twat*. Not to be confused with *cunnilingus*, which is the Irish national airline.

air of the dog *n.* A mephitic stink that follows you about *the morning after*, and cannot be shaken off;

a pungent morning-after *touch of the vapours* of which Rover would be proud. Also *air of the log.*

air onion *n.* A *Lionel Bart* that makes the eyes water.

air sick *1. adj.* Afflicted with nausea on a flight. *2. n.* An empty *bowk* where you don't bring anything up, perhaps while looking at a selfie of Ian Botham.

air sitar *n.* A twangy *trouser cough* with distinct Bollywood overtones.

air tattoo *n.* A *shit* image of a *cabbage brown* butterfly stencilled onto the *fairy hammock* of the *dunghampers.* A *wind sketch.*

air tulip *n.* A delightfully fragrant *gut,* of the sort that would be *dropped* by Lady Di, Audrey Hepburn or Grace Kelly. But not, you might suppose, by Ricky Tomlinson.

airwolf *1. n.* 1980s helicopter-based TV series that was indistinguishable from 1980s helicopter-based TV series *Blue Thunder. 2. n.* A terrible howling sound heard after a night *on the pop.* A particularly predatory *jam tart.*

air your guts *v.* To *puke, spew, barf etc.* To *shout soup.*

aisle of shite *n.* The centre row in a budget supermarket that is piled high with cheap socket sets, slippers and car accessories. The *man magnet.*

Ajax, like *sim.* Descriptive of a large *Simon Cowell* movement which dissapears, in the words of the late Molly Weir, "clean around the S-bend" Usually followed by a *glory wipe.* Without scratching. Actually, come to think of it, Molly Weir did the Flash ads, not Ajax, didn't she.

AKAWKFA/akawkfa *abbrev.* A gobshite who is always spouting off in the pub on subjects of which he has no discernible comprehension or expertise. A Know All Who Knows Fuck All.

AK farty-seven *n.* A loud and powerful fusillade of *shite* – caused by pockets of *sulphur dibaxide* becoming trapped between the *faceeshusses* in one's *back body* – which sounds and feels not unlike the discharge of a crudely constructed Albanian assault rifle. *'I crouched down and took out my underpants with an AK farty-seven.'*

Alabama hot pocket *n.* An act so vile that, in the unlikely event that it exists and anybody's ever done it, it makes a *Boston pancake* look like a vicarage tea party. *'Welcome to the Yellowhammer State, Home of the Alabama Hot Pocket.'*

Aladdin's rug *n.* An inch-thick mat of *shit tickets* laid upon the water's surface before embarking on one's *dirty business,* with the intention of leaving the *shark's mouth* spotlessly clean after flushing.

Aladdin's slippers *n. Magic lamps* that turn up pertly at the end, of the sort usually found on

yummy mummies. Scoopies.

Alan Johnston's vegetable patch *n.* A *ladygarden* that isn't as bad as *Terry Waite's allotment* by any means, but would nevertheless benefit from an afternoon's work with the shears to bring it up to snuff. From the BBC journalist who was kidnapped in the Gaza Strip back in 2007, and spent several months chained to a radiator while his parsnips went to seed.

Alans *n. rhym. slang.* Ladies' *undercrackers.* From Alan Whickers = knickers. *'Come on, love, fair's fair. I've bought you six pints of Younger's and a bag of scratchings, so get your Alans off.'*

Alan Sugar's beard *n.* A straggly, threadbare *fanny,* not hugely dissimilar to the one sported by Glenda Jackson in *The Music Lovers.* A *Ho Chi Minge, fufu manchu, minge the merciless.*

alanysis *n.* In television sports punditry, a trite statement of the blindingly obvious that is presented as insightful, expert scrutiny, typically on a Saturday evening.

à la récherche du tug perdu *phr. Fr.* Expression describing a fellow's bittersweet, nostalgic longing to rediscover fondly remembered scenes of *Frankie Vaughanography* on the internet. Possibly involving a lady called Madeleine. And a bloke called Arnold Schwarzenpecker.

alarm clock, tramp's *n.* A loud, early morning *Bakewell* that would rouse its progenitor from the deepest slumber, and may even cause him to leap out of the bed and change the sheets.

alarm cock *n.* Apparatus which springs into action first thing every morning, and can be used by a man to wake up his spouse. Usually by prodding her in the back with it, or, if that fails to do the trick, sticking it up her *arse.*

alarm plop *n.* An early morning wake up call courtesy of the previous night's tea.

Alaskan bush people *1. phr.* Title of a Discovery Channel docudrama-style reality show depicting the tribulations of a family and large TV crew surviving in the US northern territories. *2. n.* Those who prefer their *beartrapper's hats* in a wild and woolly, off-grid style.

Alaskan pipeline *n.* Ice docking. *Ninety-nine flake.*

Albany Street phone box, as busy as the *sim.* Descriptive of any person or establishment that is particularly over-active or rushed off its feet. Named in honour of the popular public telephone kiosk at the top of the eponymous Hull thorough-fare, which is famous for the freelance herb and spice merchants who ply their trade there. *'That Phil Schofield's never off the telly these days, is he?*

He's as busy as the Albany Street phone box, him.'

albatross *1. n.* A large seabird with a twelve-foot wingspan that is said to bring good luck, or possibly bad luck, to sailors. *2. n.* A *grumble flick* sexual position featuring five men and one woman flapping about, which was the inspiration for a popular Fleetwood Mac instrumental in 1968.

Albers pitstop *n.* Leaving the toilet with your *cock* still hanging out of your trousers. From the farcical episode halfway through the 2007 French Grand Prix at Magny-Cours when Spyker driver Christijan Albers exited the pit lane with half the fuel rig still hanging off his car.

Albert dock *1. n.* Famous Liverpool maritime location named in honour of the Victorian Prince Consort's ironmongery-bedecked *bellend*, from where Richard and Judy used to do their show; now a lively shopping and food district. *2. n.* Possibly made-up s*xual act whereby a chap's pierced *lid* is tucked inside a pal's *fiveskin*.

Albert Pierrepoint's rope, as tight as *1. sim.* Used to describe someone who is not overly generous; a reference to the celebrity noosemonger of the early twentieth century. See also *tight as a nun's cunt, ~ a bullfighter's pants, ~ a shark's arse, ~ a teenage wanker's curtains. 2. sim.* Descriptive of constricted *ladyparts* that afford little room for manoeuvre. See also *tighter than a worm's belt, ~ a penguin's nutsack, ~ OJ's glove etc.*

albino gecko *n.* A white thing with sticky legs that a lady may suddenly find creeping down her face. *'Sorry about that, love. I was galloping the lizard and I must've accidentally let the albino gecko out.'*

album track *n.* A workmanlike and thoroughly unmemorable *J Arthur* of approximately four minutes' duration.

alcofrolic *n.* A frivolous yet ultimately regrettable act of *carnival knowledge* which is embarked upon while *heavily refreshed. 'I'm sorry, love. She meant nothing to me. It was just an alcofrolic.'*

alcoholiday *n.* A sojourn from which one doesn't bring back any memories.

alcohologram *n.* A fascinating multi-dimensional optical illusion which usually occurs round about the eleventh pint of *wifebeater.*

alcohorlicks *n.* Warming, malty beverages drunk during the morning to aid restful sleep during the afternoon.

alcopocalypse *n.* The morning after a smashing night *on the pop* when one feels like one has been strafed by helicopter gunships.

alcopoop *n.* The loud, smelly, life-affirming *shit* you have the next morning after a heavy night *on the razz*, which quite often contains your hangover.

An *escape sub.*

alco-Popeye *n.* A bloke who, after imbibing one too many WKDs, takes on the persona of the famously incoherent, monocular maritime cartoon mentalist and wants to fight everyone in sight.

alcopopscotch *n.* The nimble pavement-hopping gait required to avoid stepping in brightly hued vomit when proceeding down Preston Road, Hull, or similar streets throughout the land, on a Friday night.

alcorithms *n.* Little understood process by which pints of beer mysteriously affect the male metabolism. *'Sorry I didn't get home last night, my darling, but me alcorithms was on the blink.'*

alcotroll *n.* A woman who looks *fugly* even through high-powered *beer goggles.*

alcozheimers *n. medic.* State of advanced mental befuddlement occasioned by excessive and/or prolonged *top shelf drinking*, which is typically symptomised by forgetting what you are doing, aimlessly wandering up and down and periodically soiling yourself.

alcuracy *n.* The increasing level of confidence in your ability to play darts or pool that accompanies each successive beer. Also *pinpint accuracy.*

al dente *1. adj.* From the Italian, meaning "to the tooth" or "to the bite". A poncy way of saying "just so", when referring to the precise way that pasta should be cooked. Not a problem that arises, of course, if one gets one's spaghetti out of a dented tin from the supermarket Whoops aisle, and eats it cold with a spoon because one's gas has been cut off. *2. adj.* Middle class, but *well hard.*

Aldi TT *n.* Any ageing coupe, usually of Korean manufacture, bought by folk whose motoring aspirations sadly outstrip their modest budget by a considerable margin. A two-door *estate car* or *Lidl red Corvette.*

ale force winds *n.* The toxic sciroccos which blow through *cack canyon* the morning after a night spent getting *hammered* on brown beer. *Ale force winds* which measure highly on the *Beaufart scale* and are occasionally accompanied by an unexpected fall of *ale stones.*

alehouse ball *n. sport.* In Sunday League football, a mindless punt which is lumped vaguely forward with no clear idea as to its purpose or intended recipient. *'And a right alehouse ball from Ronaldinho, there. A complete waste of... Fuck me! The buck-toothed cunt has scored!'* (John Motson, June 2002).

alehouse cock *n. medic. Brewer's droop*, a tragic affliction which makes the erotic act of congress feel like *stuffing a marshmallow in a piggy bank*. See also *poking fog up a hill with a sharp stick*.

alehouse tan *n.* The healthy, florid complexion and broken facial veins sported by the dedicated *turps nudger*, eg. Tramps, regional television newsreaders and sundry eminent Premiership football club managers.

alehouse whisper *n.* An attmpted *sotto voce* utterance rendered *molto fortissimo* by booze. *'Fuck me Dave, I'd love to shag big Eric's missus.' 'Keep it down a bit, Paul. You've got a touch of the alehouse whisper there, and Eric's coming over.'*

alements *n. medic.* Any lacerations, abrasions and contusions discovered following an evening *on the pop*. *Binjuries, UDIs*.

alert all commands, deploy the fleet! *1. exclam.* Catch-all order issued by various disposable Imperial officers in *The Empire Strikes Back*. *2. n.* An amusing vocalised overture performed immediately prior to the delivery of a noisy *Chewbacca's call*. Also *I'm just going to exercise my constitutional right, now back to Davina etc.*

alesheimer's disease *n. medic.* Premature senility and loss of memory brought about by intemperate imbibition of *bed glue*. See also *alcozheimers*.

ale stones *n.* Noisy cascade of marble-sized *tods* after a night spent quaffing Younger's Scotch Bitter.

alestorm *1. n. prop.* A Scottish Pirate Metal band. *2. n.* A rather nasty case of the *beer slime* the morning after a session on the brown booze, that leaves you blind in one eye and in need of a new crutch.

Alexa, open a window *exclam.* An up-to-the-minute, modern day riposte uttered in the aftermath of a *guff*. See also *thank-you for the opportunity, Lord Sugar*.

Alexa, play music by Ed Sheeran *exclam.* An amusing quip to make before *dropping one's guts*.

Alfgarnetstan *n. geog.* Hostile zone in the *Middle East End* populated by intolerant, violent people who dress strangely and talk funny.

Alfie male *n.* An ageing man who still, for some inexplicable reason, proves remarkably attractive to young women notwithstanding his antediluvian vintage, wrinkles and plumbing issues. *'Born on this day: The Minstrel, Canadian racehorse, 1974; Street Cry, Irish racehorse, 1993; Rupert Murdoch, Alfie male, 1906.'*

Alfred *n.* An itchy *cock*. Named after the "master of suspense" film director Alfred Itchycock. *'(As MARGO re-enters the room with the turkey on a trolley, TOM has got up from his seat and is frantically pulling at his trousers. MARGO looks horrified, then turns away, shielding her face.) MARGO: Barbara, Jerry, don't look now, but I think Tom's having a wank. BARBARA: Do you mind, Tom? You're making Margo uncomfortable. TOM: I'm sorry Margo. But I can't help it, Barbara. These longjohns we made on the loom are giving me a terrible Alfred.'* (script for *The Good Life Christmas Special, 1977*).

alfresco diner *n.* A cosmopolitan *Harold Ramp*.

Alf's nose *euph.* Term used to describe the state of a fellow's *giggle stick* following prolonged immersion in water. From the sad, wrinkled proboscis of the 1980s TV alien puppet. *'I've got a right Alf's nose after that swim, I can tell you.'* (Captain Matthew Webb, Calais, 25th August 1875).

Ali *n.* A *dropped gut* of the *silent-but-deadly* variety, named in honour of the erstwhile late pugilist because it "floats like a butterfly and stings like a bee". See also *gaseous clay*.

Alice Roberts' nails, as dirty as *euph.* Descriptive of a lady who is mostly posh and well spoken but also a bit *mucky*. From the pulchritudinous BBC4 palaeopathologist.

alien *n.* The sort of *Tom tit* that rips you apart in an attempt to get out, in a similar style to the space monster that exits John Hurt half way through his pudding in the film of the same name. Though not through your chest, obviously. The opposite of a *lager log*.

alien has woken up, the *exclam.* The painful, twisting feeling in the guts that presages a foul monster exploding out of your body. *'I'm afraid I must pay an urgent visit to the little boy's room, your highness, only the alien has woken up and I don't want to papper my kegs.'*

aliens, abducted by *euph.* Excuse proffered by one who finds himself afflicted with terrible, unexplained anal injuries the morning after an evening that he is unable to recall.

A-list *1. n.* An index of top celebrities known to the man in the street, *eg.* Kylie Minogue, Elton John, Pippa Middleton. *2. n.* Mental catalogue of people the man in the street would like to *do up the shitter, eg.* Kylie Minogue, Pippa Middleton.

alisthair darling *n.* A *bird* with mis-matched plumage, *viz.* One whose *barnet* colour contrasts with her *pube* colour, in a style reminiscent of the unsettling eyebrow/hair hue combination of the late ventriloquist's dummy-esque Chancellor of the Exchequer and Member of Parliament for Edinburgh South West. An *aeroplane blonde*.

Al Jizzera *n.* Any satellite television channel whose monodextrously inclined viewers' interests are focused principally around issues related to the gulf. *'You coming to bed, love?' 'In a minute, dear. I'll just sit up and watch Al Jizzera for a bit.'*

alka-seltzer *n.* The involuntary fizzing of a female's *parts* when she becomes aroused. Not really a great play on words, if we're being competely honest.

alkie seltzer *n.* An effervescent drink taken to settle the stomach following a night *on the lash.* The hair of the dog. *'Christ, my guts are fucking rotten this morning, but I'll be right as rain after a few cans of alkie seltzer. You seen my pilot's cap anywhere, love?'*

alkizeimers *n. medic.* Drink-related forgetfulness. Also *alcozheimers.*

alkytraz *1. n.* The police station drunk tank. *2. n.* Any Saturday night spent incarcerated on the salubrious Welsh island of Barry.

all at sixes and fours *adj.* Descriptive of a happily mixed-up *man at C&A* who is equally content with a portion of *rice or chips.* Bisexual, derived from the scoring opportunities available to a snooker player who doesn't really care whether he pots the *pink* or the *brown.*

all-black *n.* A woman who; when performing an act of *horatio,* starts off impressively but invariably loses her nerve and chokes at the finish, in the style of the well-known New Zealand national rugby team, who are notoriously bad at sucking *cocks.*

all cisterns go! *exclam.* A hearty cry from the toilet cubicle after the launch of a particularly hefty *escape sub.* Often to be heard the day following a heavy session *on the hoy.*

all fart and no poo *phr.* Said of something of little or no substance; full of hot air. *'That four percent Stella is fucking rubbish. It's all fart and no poo, if you ask me. What do you think, Oz? Oz, wake up.'* Also *all fart and no shite. 'That fucking thing's never going to get into space. The beardy twat's all fart and no shite.'*

all guns blazing, go down with *v.* To simultaneously *shit* and *piss* yourself while out on a major session. *'You've got to hand it to the bishop, mother superior. He went down with all guns blazing.'*

all inclusive *n.* An unfeasibly large *Thora Hird* that is passed while on holiday, comprising the remnants of an array of exotic and unfamiliar foodstuffs.

all mouse and no pussy *phr.* Descriptive of someone whose love life is mainly conducted *via* an internet broadband connection these days.

all mouth and no trousers *1. phr.* Gobby. *'...a poor player that struts and frets his hour upon the stage and then is heard no more. It is a tale told by an idiot, full of sound and fury, signifying nothing. He's all mouth and trousers, that cunt.'* (from *Macbeth* by William Shakespeare). *2. phr.* Descriptive of a

brash, yet odourless *arse trumpet;* a *Bakewell* that values style over substance, if you will.

allotment *n.* Anywhere that isn't the allotment, *eg.* The pub, the bookies, the dog track. *'I'm off to the allotment, love. Have you done me a clean shirt?'*

allotment pie *1. n.* A rather bland-sounding dish of garden vegetables, slugs and compost, that was slightly more popular than the Blitz. *2. n.* A hard-to-digest and past-its-sell-by-date *haddock pastie* found mouldering in the midst of *Arthur Fowler's allotment.* See also *blast from the past.*

alloy welder *n.* A *happy shopper, switch hitter* or *half rice half chips* fellow who is *all at sixes and fours* and who happily *drinks from both taps.* Derived from the AC/DC welding machine which is required when joining aluminium alloys, as opposed to the fully heterosexual DC-only equipment typically employed when joining ferrous metals.

all porned out *adj.* Of a male who is *working from home,* suffering from over-exposure to internet *grot* and therefore unable to summon sufficient enthusiasm to continue his research. A temporary situation.

all quiet on the breast an' cunt *phr.* Somewhat contrived exclamation which is, nevertheless, descriptive of a lady who has retreated from the front line in the *sex war. 'Seen that Germaine Greer recently?' 'Aye mate, it's definitely all quiet on the breast an' cunt there.'*

all quiet on the western front *1. n.* Title of a famous Oscar-winning film of 1930, depicting the horrors of trench life in the 1914-1918 War, *based on a novel originally published in Germany,* which is a bit rich because they probably started it. *2. phr.* Something to say when a chap fails to rise to the occasion down south. *'How's that, Pele? Owt stirring yet?' 'Sorry, Mrs Pele. It's all quiet on the western front, I'm afraid. I'd best have another handful of them Bongo Bill's banjo pills.'*

all rib and dick *adj.* Of a male, decidedly thin. *'I never took to that David Tennant as Dr Who you know, Mother Superior. He's all rib and dick if you ask me.'*

all round to Mrs Brown's *1. n.* Saturday night television entertainment show that, you might imagine without actually going through the ordeal of watching it, is a bit like *Noel's House Party* only with an elderly female impersonator shouting "Feck!" every ten seconds or so, with all the production values of the last sketch in an episode of *Crackerjack.* *2. euph.* That wonderful moment when a chap's *bag for life* intimates that some *backdoor action* might just possibly be on the cards.

all-seeing eye, the *n.* As featured on American dollar bills, a triangular symbol of (depending on your point of view) divine providence or the shape-shifting Illuminati lizards of the New World Order. *'I was hoping for a shot on the missus's all-seeing eye for me birthday, but it turns out I'm in the dog house again.'*

all shout and no shit *phr.* An urgent lavatory trip that turns out to be just a lot of hot air. Descriptive of an *arse* that is *writing cheques it cannot cash.*

all stand for the French national anthem *phr.* A humorous introduction to be declaimed before performing a rousing fanfare on the *botty bugle.* Also *unleash the benefits of Brexit!*, *Siri play me some James Blunt etc.*

all the shit *n.* See *shit, all the.* Go on, you're not going to get the definition here, you'll have to flick half way through the fucking book for this one.

all threes *n.* Naturally assumed *self abuse* position, balanced on one hand and two knees, adopted when one's *noddy book* is placed on the edge of a bed or sideboard.

all tit *adj.* Descriptive of a smaller female who is somewhat *over-qualified.*

all you can shit buffet *n.* The unfortunate consequence of gluttonous over-indulgence at a favoured oriental eatery.

almond *1. rhym. slang.* Penis. From almond rock = cock. Almond rock? *2. n. rhym. slang.* Socks. *3. n.* An imperial measure of *sailor's ale,* approximately one stomach full. Derivation unknown. *4. n.* A lightweight drinker, *ie.* One who has to be rushed to hospital for a stomach pump after necking a pint-and-a-half. Derivation also unknown.

almond flakes *n. Mandruff, dried taddies.* Also *mammary dandruff.*

almond smoothie *n.* A generous (approximately a pint and a half) serving of *man milk.* Derivation unknown and, indeed, completely without foundation.

almosturbate *v.* To stop halfway through an act of sinful *self-pollution,* either to avoid being caught or as part of an attempt to summon up a modicum of enthusiasm for a *poke* when one really isn't in the mood. To practise *wankus interruptus;* to *stir the tanks.*

alpenfahrt *1. n.* A walk up a Swiss mountain. A word that would probably benefit from some umlauts if we knew how to find them on the keyboard. *2. n. Following through* with cereal grains after an over-enthusiastic *guff.*

alright for toast *phr.* Descriptive of a stale *slice* that exhibits questionable visual appeal and freshness,

as well as small patches of mould, but which might be just about worth *sticking the naughty fork* in and *buttering up* if there's nothing more appetising on offer.

alright, put your cock away *exclam.* A useful put-down phrase when someone has been hogging the limelight for too long, *eg.* By going on about his car, his salary or an international sporting event he more or less successfully had something to do with organising about a dozen years ago. *'Alright Seb, put your cock away, there's a good lord.'*

also-ran *n.* Residual, self-pitying trickle of *jizz* that settles in the *scuds* long after the main *bolt* has been *shot* and the *strides* have been pulled up & buckled.

alter birthday *1. n.* The fictional birth date two years after their actual birth date that a teenager has to memorise in order to get a half fare on the train. *2. n.* The fictional birth date two years prior to their actual birth date that a teenager has to memorise in order to buy white cider at the *offie.*

alternative milk *1. n.* What ethical modern hipsters add to their hot drinks; gritty liquids made from ground mung bean husks and the like. *2. n.* What Piers Morgan typically drinks in his tea. See *caterer's tribute, jerk sauce.*

alternative, the *n.* The *arse.* *'And David sent messengers, and took Bath-Sheba: and she came in unto him, and it was her unclean time so he done her up the alternative.'* (from *2 Sam. 11:3*).

al Tesco *adj.* Descriptive of the modern, metropolitan, open-air dining experience, whereby gourmands purchase their delicacies from a supermarket and consume them while walking between social engagements or sitting outside like in Europe. But sat on some *pissy* steps instead of at a ritzy cafe table by the Trevi Fountain.

altitude thickness *n. milit.* Helicopter pilot's airborne equivalent to the more earthbound condition of *convoy cock.*

always has the prawn starter *euph.* Said of a lady who eschews uncomfortable footwear, *likes walking holidays,* and *does her own heavy lifting.*

amateur juggler *n.* A person who is prone to occasional flatulence, from the fact that he or she "drops one every now and then".

amateur night *n.* See *Black Eye Friday.*

Amazon basin *n.* The parcel-filled area at the foot of the tree on Christmas morning.

Amazon-esia *n. medic.* Condition whereby the postie turns up with a pile of brown packages and you have no memory whatsoever of ordering any of them.

ambassador's hedge *n.* An immaculately trimmed *bush*.

ambassador's reception *euph.* A visit to the toilet involving the expulsion of a tetrahedral pile of small, nutty *rabbit tods,* similar in appearance to the famous all-night-garage-gift chocolates which were popular with visiting foreign dignitaries in the 1980s.

Amber *n. rhym. slang.* An excretious deposit or *Douglas.* See also *Amber warning. 'She was great in the fart sack, vicar. But I couldn't believe she left a dirty great Amber under the duvet.'*

amber gambler *1. n.* An impatient motorist who takes the opportunity to drive through the lights even as they turn to red or just before they turn to green, thus leaving themselves open to prosecution. *2. n.* Likewise, any male who *cops off* with a young *goer* of dubious vintage. *'Today's birthdays: Fran Zwitter, Slovenian historian and rhyming slang, 1905; Robin Day, phlegmatic British political interviewer and television presenter, 1923; (name, type of guitar played and identity of former rock band removed on legal advice) and amber gambler, 1936.'*

Amber warning *n.* A *log dropped* in a partner's bed; a subtle sign that a romantic relationship may just possibly be heading for trouble. Named in honour of Johnny Depp's estranged squeeze, *viz.* Amber Heard = Douglas Hurd.

ambient drop *1. n.* In daytime TV quiz *Tipping Point,* counters that fall into the win zone between rounds and are then "voided from the machine". *2. n. Breaking cover* inadvertently whilst going about your daily business. *'Sorry vicar. That was an ambient drop. Start again from "Through this holy anointing…".'*

ambisextrous *adj.* Descriptive of a *Betty both,* that Is to say one who is able to *bat for both teams.* Half rice half chips.

Amelia Earhart *1. n. prop.* Famous US aviatrix who disappeared in 1937, although the *Daily Mail* is forever announcing they've found her glasses or her teeth or her knickers on some godforsaken Pacific island somewhere. *2. n.* Nickname bestowed upon a lady who, after being wined and dined, announces she's going to the *bog* and flies off into the night, never to be seen again.

Americano *1. n.* Hot water with a dash of espresso; what you get these days when you ask for a cup of fucking coffee. *2. n. Following through* accidentally while reclining in a warm bath and essaying a relaxed, bubbly *Edward Woodward.*

American tip *1. n.* A piece of handy advice given

by someone from the USA. *2. n.* A short *rubber johnny* that just covers the *herman gelmet* and prevents the *wanked-up spunk* going on the hotel sheets.

American trombone *n.* A *spit roast.* A *horny* band comprising two men – usually Premiership footballers – and one woman, who plays the *pink oboe* of one of them, while the other *does* her up the *brass section.*

amidships *euph.* A polite term used by cricket commentators, vicars and public school nurses to describe the *knackers* and *cock. 'Ooh, Aggers! That delivery was pitched long, swung back in from middle and off and caught him squarely amidships.' 'Yes, Johnners. The poor cunt must be in fucking agony. More cake?'* (*Test Match Special,* Radio 3).

amnesic dysentery *n. medic.* A hangover. *'Oliver Reed, the British actor who appeared in Tommy, Women in Love and the Mike Aspel Show, died today following a long battle with amnesic dysentery. He was 61.'*

amsterdamage *n.* Serious destruction or impairment of one's mental, physical, marital and financial faculties that begins five minutes into a no-frills flight to the Dutch debauchery capital with your mates, and persists long after your ignominious deportation back to Blighty.

Amsterdam roulette *n.* A *glory-hole*-based game of chance where everyone loses.

Amsterdam uppercut *n.* The "wrist deep" action employed by one skilled in the art of *fisting. 'Palmolivia was powerless to resist. The oily mechanic's eyes burnt into hers like sapphires. She felt his muscular arms enfolding her softly yielding body as she was literally swept away in a whirlwind of passion behind a pile of old tyres. Yearning for his manly touch, she lay down and yielded her most precious treasure to him. 'Do it now, Swarfego,' she breathed. 'Give me an Amsterdam uppercut.'"* (from *The Lady and the Exhaust Fitter* by Barbara Cartland).

amstradivarius *n.* A poor quality thing dressed up as a good quality thing, *eg.* One of them Chinese cars they do disastrous crash tests on, Emma Thompson's eighties solo comedy series, or Channel 5 Select.

amuse bouche *1. n. Fr.* In *cordon bleu* parlance, a bite-size *hors d'oeuvre* at a posh dinner party or restaurant; a small, intricate starter dish aimed at arousing a gourmand's taste buds prior to sampling the main course, *eg.* A sausage roll, small Scotch egg or cheese football. *2. n.* A pre-*coitus* meat-based snack *noshed* by a lucky lady. Often served with a couple of *nuts* and a side order of *gentleman's relish. 3. n.* A piquantly appetising little something nibbled at when *dining at the Y.*

amuse bush *n.* Sophisticated term for foreplay; a fiddly entrée prior to the main course of *pork in cider*, typically finishing with a yoghurt-themed dessert. *Frigmarole, defrosting the freezer, firkyfoodling.*

amuse douche *n. Fr.* Something that makes you *piss yourself* with laughter.

anal announcement *n. Fart, chuff, beefy eggo, trouser cough.* A rousing *rumpet voluntary.*

anal bleaching *1. n.* Having the skin around one's *nipsy* lightened to improve its aesthetic appearance, although to be frank, the words "silk purse" and "sow's ear" spring to mind. *2. n.* A *Neptune's kiss* from a *jobby engine* which has recently been cleaned and still contains a strong solution of Harpic.

anal boot *n. milit.* A National Service army barracks forfeit whereby members of a platoon spit into a glass of beer before another stirs it with his *cock*, after which it is poured down the cleft of another's *arse* into the mouth of the unlucky loser of a wager. *'Permission to speak, sir! When we was fighting the Pathans on the north-west frontier, I got the anal boot off the lads in the 37th Lancers.'*

anal delight *1. n.* A soft, light, fluffy chocolate-, strawberry- or butterscotch-coloured pudding served in a large porcelain bowl. *2. n.* Pleasures taken in *tradesman's practices.*

anal distancing *n.* Restriction designed to prevent breathing difficulties.

analgesic *n.* Partial relief from a hangover provided by the passage of a good *tom tit.* See also *alcopoop, escape sub.*

anal glaucoma *n. medic.* Debilitating illness, often prevalent among heavy drinkers and the long term unemployed, whereby the sufferers "cannot see their arses getting out of bed today". *'Sorry Mr Jenkins. Unfortunately, I have been unable to look for work this week as I have been suffering from a severe case of anal glaucoma.'*

analog *n.* A written record of every time the missus lets you *do* her up the *wrong 'un.*

analogue to digital conversion *1. n.* The electronic process by which a current or voltage is changed from a continuous, varying signal into a series of discrete numbers. *2. n.* An unwanted consequence of using insufficiently robust *lavatory tissue, viz.* Getting all *shit* on your fingers when wiping your *arse.*

analogy *n.* The comparison of a lady's *derriere* to another thing, such as a peach or the back end

of a bus.

analversary *n.* Once-a-year bash at the *bag for life's freckle.* Something a married man never forgets, bizarrely.

analweiss *n.* A small, pungently aromatic brown flower that greets us every morning, looks happy to see us, and is often accompanied by the sound of music.

anchor man *1. n.* A puce-faced, be-wigged alcoholic who reads the news from behind a desk because he is in no fit state to leave the studio and file a report while standing up. *2. n.* The first link in a multi-person *bum chain.*

anchovy alley *1. n.* Name of a Teenage Mutant Ninja Turtles "Pop-Up Pizza Playset" that was once, apparently, the must-have gift for the nation's toddlers over Christmas. A Tracey Island *de nos jours,* if you will, now to be found at car boot sales and landfill sites up and down the country. *2. n.* A narrow, fishy ginnel up which cheese-topped things other than pizzas might occasionally pop. Also *Henrietta Street.*

anchovy's fanny *n.* The *fishiest* of all possible *suppers.*

ancient wristory *n.* A nostalgic *ham shank* over an old flame. Also *tosstalgia, pasturbation, quimsy.*

and aweeeee! *1. exclam.* Said in the soft Scottish accent of the Lowland shepherd; an instruction to a favoured sheepdog to set off to the right. *2. exclam.* Expression of blessed relief when finally finding a discreet spot or council-sanctioned facility to *strain one's greens. 3. exclam.* Whispered whilst discreetly *treading on a duck.*

and Bully's special prize... *1. exclam.* Comical preamble to announce the impending arrival of something that sounds more like a motorboat than it does a caravan (although, if you remember, Bully's Special Prize was for hitting the bullseye in the *Prize Board* round, and was usually a drinks trolley or electric drill, something that would of cost Central Television about thirty quid out the Argos catalogue, and which couldn't easily be shared between two blokes who knew each other from the pub darts team. The motorboats and caravans were for getting 101 or more with 6 darts in the *Star Prize Gamble*). Also *gentlemen start your engines, I'll name that tune in one. 2. exclam.* Drunken birthday announcement by a partner who is bending over and inviting a fellow to *throw the meat dart at the brown bullseye.*

and everyone who knows me *exclam.* A wireless-quiz-contestant-style witticism to be delivered after *dropping* a cacophonous *gut.* See also *one year out!*; *you can't stop there, Mr Derek*; *what's that, Sweep?*; *an excellent theory, Dr Watson*;

fer-fetch a cloth, Granville and so on.

and I commend this statement to the house *1. exclam.* Traditional vocal flourish at the end of a lengthy parliamentary speech, typically greeted by barks of approbation from the *twats* on the same benches as the speaker and cries of "Shame!" from the opposition. *2. exclam.* Said in a statesmanlike manner after *dropping the order paper.* See also *a confident appeal by the Australians there; and you can't say fairer than that; well that's the end of that bottle of HP etc.*

and if you listen... that sounds like a golf *exclam.* A carefully timed two-part gnomic epigram to be delivered with a solid, German-engineered *backfire* in the middle. An obscure reference to a TV car advert that hasn't been on for a good few years now.

and if you've just joined us *exclam.* Said as if addressing an unseen camera on a topical chatshow. A convenient phrase which can be used to fill in awkward conversational silences, for example during a tea party to which Chrissie Hynde, Bernard Matthews, Simon Weisenthal, David Irving, Germaine Greer and John McCririck have been invited.

and in local news... *phr.* Announcement immediately prior to a dispiriting report from our air pollution correspondent.

and I thought they smelled bad on the outside *exclam.* Quote from *The Empire Strikes Back* that can be uttered when having a cheeky sniff of your *fish fingers.*

and it's live! *exclam.* Excited preamble to *whistling down the Y-fronts,* spoken in the style of erstwhile Sky football commentator Martin Tyler.

and just like that a new star is born *exclam.* To be intoned using the voice of the late Professor Stephen Hawking following a *mass colonal ejection event.*

and now a word from our sponsor *exclam.* Said just before playing a catchy *ring jingle.* Also *our survey said; and this is me; my next guest needs no introduction; Siri, pull my finger; please be upstanding for the President of the United States of America.*

and now for something completely different *exclam.* Jocular, Pythonesque catchphrase employed in an attempt to lighten the mood when flipping one's wife/girlfriend/sister-in-law/next door neighbour over onto their front in preparation for a *Spanish inquisition.*

and now it's time for the news where you are *1. exclam.* Stock introduction used at the end of glamorous national news broadcasts to announce the drab, plebeian local headlines about cats stuck up trees, chip shop fires and whatnot, read by a bitter alcoholic. *2. exclam.* Humorous preamble to a *muckraking* soundbite from an anonymous source.

and now on BBC4... *phr.* Humorous and poignant precursor to a didactic *Exchange & Mart.*

and now over to Laura Kuenssberg for the latest from Westminster *exclam.* News anchor-style announcement prior to the arrival of a very urgent *poosflash.* See also *and the thunderball is, going once going twice, prisoner... show yourself!, and now a word from our sponsors etc.*

and now over to our Brussels correspondent *exclam.* Announcement of the imminent launch of a Vitamin B6-infused salvo from the *postern gate.*

and one from the bottom, please Rachel *exclam.* Humorous announcment to be uttered, for maximum comic effect, immediately before the delivery of a quick *teatime teaser.*

and/orgasm *n.* A questionable *fanny bomb.* 'How was it for you, darling?' 'A bit of an and/orgasm, if I'm honest, Lord Archer, and that's putting it kindly. Anyway, can I have my two grand in a brown envelope now?''

Andover overdraft *euph.* A dirty protest carried out in the foyer of one's bank.

and please give a warm welcome to our special gust *exclam.* A jovial, Michael Parkinson-style introduction prior to *dropping one's guts.* A round of *thunderous applause* or *toast to the Queen* (or *King*).

Andrea Leadsom has tabled an amendment *exclam.* Announcement that something stinks and a lot of cleaning up will shortly be required.

Andreas *n. prop.* A *tug, toss, Hilary.* A *ham shank.* Named in honour of briefly-famous German ski-jumper Andreas Wank, who, for the avoidance of doubt, can be looked up on the internet. But probably best not if you're at work.

André Rieu's encore *1. n.* In the world of the performing arts, after you've just sat through an enormous pile of *shite* and you think it's all finished, the dispiriting realisation that there is still a bit more *shite* to go before you can get up and leave. A reference to the pensioners' favourite *two-bob* Michael Bolton-lookalike fiddle maestro. *2. euph.* The same sort of thing, but you're sat on the *bog.* See also *curtain call, second sitting, epilog, double jeopardy* and *Mexican wave.*

andrexia nervosa *n. medic. psych.* The state of mild, ironically bowel-loosening panic that sets in after one has imprudently sat down on the *chod bin* and opened up the *clackervalve* before remembering to check if there is any *arse paper* left on the roll.

Andrex index *n.* Rating system that graphically indicates the artistic merits or otherwise of a particular *grumble flick*. *'The plot is, at best, contrived, the direction, dialogue and camerawork are, to put it kindly, barely adequate and the acting is wooden to the point where I feared that several of the leading characters could at any moment succumb to an attack of Dutch Elm disease. Nevertheless, these shortcomings are more than made up for by the frequent, graphic, hardcore sex sequences where you really can see it going right in, not to mention out and off. It earns a stonking five on the Andrex index, and that's why Double Facial Cum Guzzling Anal Sluts 8 is my Movie of the Week.'* (Jonathan Ross, *Film 2009*, BBC1).

Andrex puppy nose *n.* An unexpectedly moist, brown finger end which one finds protruding through a square of toilet tissue after inadvertently *shaking hands with the French* while dandifying the *rear deck*. Also known as a *Kermit's collar* or *brown ballerina*.

Andrex runway *n.* Stretching from *pubes* to throat on a *relaxing gentleman's* prone body, the long carpet of *arsewipe* that provides a convenient landing strip for his airborne *jizz*. A *wank runway, Fred carpet*.

Andrex sandwich *n.* The horizontally stratified result of two successive bouts of defecation, the second occurring directly after the toiletee has wiped themselves clean but before they have had the opportunity to flush. Prevalent in the lavatories of East Coast Main Line trains and domestic post-*cuzza* situations but, inexplicably, rarely depicted in TV adverts involving labrador puppies. See also *bangers and mash, lasagne turd*.

Andrex worthy *adj.* Descriptive of a highly satisfying *dump* that one has deemed worthy of a superior wipe; a *number two* that is far too upmarket for any of that 1-ply supermarket-branded nonsense.

and that's all I have to say on the matter *exclam.* Humorous statement following an emphatic *trump*. Also *an excellent theory, Dr Watson; what's that, Sweep?; anybody injured?*

and that's all I have to say on the matter *exclam.* Uttered in an authoritative manner after letting a ferocious gust escape from one's *BBQ Hula Hoop*. See also *a bit more choke and she would have started, there goes another pair of trousers, you'll have to buy that now, you've ripped it etc.*

and that's raced away to the cover boundary *exclam.* Spoken in the manner of a *Test Match Special* pundit, preferably John Arlott, Henry Blofeld or Brian Johnston, when someone *slips* one through at the *gasworks end*. See also *another brutal forehand there by Sharapova.*

and the dirt is gone! *exclam.* What Barry Scott probably says after he *steps on a frog.*

and then the guns fell silent *exclam.* Something to be said during a period of uneasy calm following a furious fusilade of *bumshots.*

and there goes Nigel Mansell! *exclam.* Post-flatulatory announcement, ideally to be delivered in the excitable style of erstwhile late Formula 1 commentator Murray Walker.

and the thunderball is… *exclam.* Chucklesome pre-*trump* announcement. Also *listen to this, too good to miss, da-da da-da da.*

and this is Daddy Pig! *exclam.* Proclamation made prior to the *dropping* of a particularly violent *hat*, reminiscent of the thunderous "oink" produced by Peppa's paterfamilias in the introductory section of the long-running porcine cartoon.

and tonight's lottery numbers are… *exclam.* Something to announce before *dropping a bonus ball.*

and to think… I hesitated *exclam. Hellbound: Hellraiser 2*-inspired pronouncement following a transdimensionally diabolical message from the *chamber of hell* that smells like an attic full of corpses and will almost certainly necessitate the destruction of your mattress.

Andy Dufresne *n. prop.* An odourless *guff;* a *dropped gut* that does not smell. From the escaping convict character played by Tim Robbins in *The Shawshank Redemption*, who crawls through a tunnel of *shit* and somehow manages to come out nipping clean at the end.

Andy Dufresne's hammer *n.* A *tool* that is worn down to the nub. A reference to the the utensil the named character used to tunnel through his cell wall to escape. *'How was your holiday in Frinton-on-Sea, vicar?' 'Delightful, Mrs Trubshaw. Some amount of fanny, I can tell you. I've come back with a dick like Andy Dufresne's hammer.'*

Andy Murray's arm clutching an apple, like *sim.* Descriptive of a very large, thick, veiny, and angry-looking *cock.*

and you can't say fairer than that *exclam.* A jocose locution to be employed following a loud *suggestion from Councillor Brown.*

anecdon't *n.* A tale that you really ought to keep to yourself. *'Our vicar's got some great anecdon'ts, like that time when he shat his trousers during a funeral service.'*

anecscrotal evidence *n.* Any thoroughly trustworthy and reliable information gleaned at second, third or fourth hand regarding a lady's shameful bedroom shenanigans. *'You know her who sometimes reads the Six O'Clock News? Well there is strong anecscrotal evidence to suggest that she takes it up the wrong 'un.'*

an excellent theory, Dr Watson *exclam.* Another humorous quip which can be used immediately after someone has *dropped* a very loud *Exchange & Mart.* Also *a confident appeal by the Australians there; you'll have to buy that now, you've ripped it.*

angel *1. n.* Spin-off series from *Buffy the Vampire Slayer. 2. n.* A passive *puddle jumper.* One who bends over while another *gives it six nowt* up their *arse.*

angel of the morning *1. n.* Much-loved Radio 2 80s favourite by the suitably named Juice Newton. *2. n.* Considerate lass who provides morning *oral* or *hand relief* without too much prompting.

angel's Charlies *n.* Offensively sexist term for a pair of heavenly *front buffers,* sported by a bit of high quality *blurtch.*

angel's delight *n.* Female *beef dripping* prior to a bout of *how's your father.* Also *bird's custard.*

angel's kiss *n.* A *botty burp* that is so sweet, so tender, and so inoffensive in its piquantly beefy egginess that even one's *better half* would smile indulgently at it.

anger farmer *n.* A social media *smallholder* who cultivates gammon for a living.

anger jam *n.* The sticky substance ejected from a fellow's *slag hammer* while watching a German *art film* with one clenched fist, a red face and gritted teeth.

anger nectar *n.* Any lager that, if drunk responsibly, engenders feelings of generalised enmity. *'Leave him, your holiness. He's been on the anger nectar all afternoon.'*

angle grinder *n.* A multiple-participant circular *bum chain;* a challenging yet rewarding sexual free-for-all engaged in by public schoolboys in their dormitories, monks in the cloisters of the Monastery at Zakynthos, and leather-capped *book readers* in Richard Littlejohn's fevered imagination. Also known as *Pierre's delight, the pink spider, the Dutch cartwheel* or *monkey cuddle.* It is believed that seasoned experts can perform the *angle grinder* with as few as three practitioners, when it is apparently called a *tricorn.*

angry *adj.* Of a gentleman, to be aroused into a state of tumescence. Having, if you will, a *bone on. 'Exhausted by writing of the Great Fire of London, I decid'd to retire early to my bedchamber, whenceforth I perchanced upon Flossy the maid, bent over the counterpane of my four poster bed. The sight of her thus did inflame the most base of* my passions, and I fast became as angry as a rolling pin.' *(The Diary of Samuel Pepys,* 1666).

angry bike, on the *euph.* A term used to describe a red-faced woman who is vigorously pedalling her menstrual cycle. *'Take no notice of my wife. She's on the angry bike.'*

angry cat *n.* A *turd* which leaves your *nipsy* hanging in tatters, like an old wind sock or a joke cigar, and it feels like you have just *crapped out* a Lego castle.

angry cossack *n.* Upon sitting down for a *Tom tit* when the *bog* seat is missing, the exuberant and energetic Slavic folk dance that must be performed in order to prevent one's *bum cheeks* accidentally touching the porcelain.

angry one *n.* Descriptive of the hostile body language employed by a gentleman lost in the act of *self love. 'If Kelly Brook wanted to lift the nation's spirits during these uncertain times, she could get them out again, and we could all have a simultaneous angry one at 8 o'clock. I'm done with this, sorry, goodbye.'* (Piers Morgan, *Good Morning Britain*).

angry pirate *n.* An unlikely sounding and quite possibly illegal sexual act whereby a bloke *shoots his mess* into his ladyfriend's eye and then kicks her in the shin. For some reason.

angry rabbi *n.* A sticky zip on pair of jeans.

angry squid, squirting like an *sim.* Said of an over-excitable woman who will shortly have to put her knickers back on and get the Vax out.

angry turds *n.* A frustrating game enjoyed opportunistically on the *shit pot.*

an heave offering unto the Lord *1. phr.* Biblical command (*Numbers etc.*) to bestow a portion of your bread to a priest, who will presumably pass it along to the Lord in due course. *2. phr.* Bodily command, typically following extensive drinking, to vouchsafe a portion of one's recently consumed *catbab* to the tarmac.

animal crackers *n. rhym. slang.* The male *clockweights.* From the Shirley Temple song of the same name, but you wouldn't necessarily want them in your soup.

ankle chaingang *n.* A crowd of middle-aged ladies out on the town. See also *M&Ms, poon squad.*

ankle spanker *1. n.* An extremely long *cock. 2. n.* A normal-sized *cock* on a man with extremely short legs.

ankle splasher *n.* Following a bout of *self help,* a *gypsy's kiss* that tends to sprinkle everywhere but in the *bum sink* bowl. Completely different from all the other *pisses* a man has, then.

Anne Frank *v. rhym. slang.* To masturbate. While

hiding in a cupboard for five years.

Anne Frank's drumkit, as much use as *sim.* Used to describe something utterly useless that merely takes up space. Also ~*Kate Moss's chip pan*. *'That (insert name of current England manager here) is about as much use as Anne Frank's drumkit. They should never have got rid of (insert name of last-but-one England football manager here).'*

Anne Swithinbank's fingernails, as mucky as *sim.* Descriptive of the type of young woman who takes a refreshingly flexible approach to sexual morality. Also *zoo keeper's boot*, ~*cow doctor's glove*. *'As his marriage to Diana crumbled, Charles found himself more and more searching out the company of his old flame Camilla. He told Jonathan Dimbleby: "Mrs. Parker-Bowels is a great friend of mine. What's more, she's as mucky as Anne Swithinbank's fingernails."'*

Anne Winters *n. prop.* Where the missus buys her frosty underpinnings.

annex the Sudetenland *v.* To seriously befoul the air. *'Best avoid the bunker en suite for the next thousand years, Eva. I've just annexed the Sudetenland in there.'*

Annie and Clarabel *n.* The sort of thing you see on *Jeremy Kyle*; two subservient girlfriends of a domineering male, who live in full knowledge of each other's existence and are indeed happy to engage in regular three-way activities. From Thomas the Tank Engine, who enjoyed a similar freewheeling *ménage à trois* with his two carriages.

announce the piss *v.* To *blow off* while standing at a public house urinal in the style of a butler loudly declaiming the arrival of a dowager duchess at a grand ball.

Ann Summers *euph.* Descriptive of any poor quality band, television programme or performance which is "pretty pants". *'How was your Happy Mondays gig?' 'It was Ann Summers, but on the bright side they were only on for less than an hour.'*

annual sex *n.* That special time of year when your better half forgets herself and consents to intercourse. Your *fannyversary*.

anointing the faithful *1. n.* In a church, when the vicar drops holy water onto the faces of his kneeling congregation. *2. n.* In a *grumble flick*, when the leading male thespian drops *spaff* onto the faces of his kneeling co-stars. *3. n.* In church, where the vicar drops *spaff* onto the faces of his kneeling congregation. Admittedly, not in many churches, but it probably does happen.

anoraksic *adj. & n.* Descriptive of the malnourished, unhealthy and gaunt demeanour of a young swain who spends a lot of time in his bedroom avoiding fresh air and sunlight, subsisting on a diet of pot noodles, pop tarts and Dairylea dunkers.

another brutal forehand there by Sharapova *exclam.* Humorous phrase that can be employed, expressed in the style of a Wimbledon tennis commentator, when someone's *rear end* serves up an unnecessarily loud grunt. Depending on the precise pitch and timbre of the said *heart to heart*, the expression *another brutal forehand there by Venus Williams/Elena Dementieva* or even, in extreme circumstances, *Michelle Larcher de Brito etc.* may be substituted. See also *a bit more choke and she would have started; answer the door, Lurch; anybody hurt?*

another man's gravy *n.* While *dining at the Y*, an inadvertent taste of a previous customer's *special sauce*.

another pair of trousers, there goes *exclam.* A humorous interjection after *stepping on a duck* in a cacophonous fashion.

another slice of swan Camilla? *exclam.* Remark after one has audibly *vented to atmosphere*. See also *answer the door, Lurch*; *can I quote you on that?* and *what's that Skippy? The miners are in trouble?*

Ant & Dec *euph.* The phenomenon of one *clockweight* looking slightly bigger than the other, especially on a Saturday night. The *oddball couple*.

Ant & Decs *1. phr.* Popular *art pamphlet* photographic studies, wherein the model displays her well-trimmed *minge* and *anus*, ie. A half-bald *twat* and a little *arsehole*. *'Right love, that's the hamburger shots finished. Now roll over and I'll take a couple of Ant & Decs to finish off the film.' 2. n. prop. rhym. slang. Dunghampers, undercrackers, poopcatchers, kicksies, thunderbags, squirrel covers, tacklebags, scads, scuns, shreddies etc.* Underpants. From Ant & Decs = Bill Grundies. *'Oi, Maggie! Throw us up another pair of Ant & Decs, will you? I've shat this one.'*

antanddecstrous *adj.* Of a fellow, blessed with the miraculous ability to feel two *twats* at the same time. *Firky-bifoodlidacious. 'Look at Lembit with the Cheeky Girls. How does he do it, Vince?' 'The bent-faced josser's antanddecstrous, Nick.'*

ant burners *n.* Powerful, jam-jar-style spectacles. *'Your majesty, I'd like to introduce you to Sir Mervyn King, the Governor of the Bank of England.' 'Bugger me, Lord Chancellor. Check out the fucking ant burners on this cunt.'*

anteater *n.* See *aard on*. It's probably on the first page.

anteater's gasmasks, pair of *n.* See *aardvarks'*

gasmasks, pair of.

ant fanny *n.* Smaller than a *mouse's ear* but bigger than a *paper cut.*

antflaccid *n.* Viagra. *Bongo Bill's banjo pills, my-coxafloppin, blueys etc.*

anticibation *n.* The hopeful, *half-a-teacaked* wait of an excitable young man while he is watching a late night foreign film on BBC2 or Film 4, in the knowledge that these minority channels aren't averse to showing *tits, bums* and *fannies* as long as they are integral to the plot and there's subtitles and people drinking wine to make it look all meaningful and artistic.

anti-cockwise *adj.* Descriptive of the changed sexual orientation of a previously heterosexual woman who has gone a bit *lezzy. Off solids. 'I see that Samantha Fox has went and turned all anti-cockwise, then.'*

anti fatter *n.* A woman with such *big bones* that even necking a pint of medical disinfectant alcohol won't make her seem attractive. An *alcotroll* with a *lovely personality.*

antiques roadshow *1. n.* Popular BBC Sunday teatime TV show featuring Fiona Bruce slumming it with the unwashed hordes, while cupidinous members of the public have their heirlooms valued "for insurance purposes" by well-spoken men in stripy blazers and women called Bunty. *2. n. Gilf* night at the local discotheque. *3. n.* Granny porn. *4. n.* A Saga holiday, possibly involving coach travel with repeated stops for the lavatory.

antiques scroteshow *n.* Any car-boot-sale-quality treasure-valuation-based daytime television programme, *eg. Flog It!, Dickinson's Real Deal, Cash in the Attic etc. 'I took your grandad's medals down the antiques scroteshow at the civic centre, and I got eight quid.'*

anti-roll bar *n.* A nocturnal *diamond cutter* that prevents a chap from rolling over to lie on his stomach in bed. Also *motorcycle kickstand, daily beast, morning glory, slumber lumber.*

anti-waxxers *n.* Name given to those ladies who prefer to neither mow their *ladygardens* nor trim their underarm hedges, as seen in certain German video productions, *eg.* Nena singing her 1983 hit *99 Red Balloons.*

ant-man *1. n. Marvel* comic book superhero who uses shrinking technology to go right small or some such similar *bollocks. 2. n. Nom de guerre* of an ugly fellow who, when it comes to women, "pulls three times his own weight".

anus *n.* An offensive term for the *council gritter, brass eye or nipsy.*

anus calling! *phr.* Said brightly when suddenly gripped by an urge to *drop a big load of shopping.* From the formerly popular make-up catalogue slogan, *viz.* "Ding dong! Anus calling!".

anus horribilis *n.* An *arse* that looks like it hasn't been wiped for a year, *eg.* HM The Queen's, during the notorious twelve-month butlers' strike of 1992.

anusthetic *1. n.* A type of knockout gas. *Carbon dibaxide. 2. n.* A feeling of numbness in the lower body experienced following a protracted period spent sat on the *porcelain throne* reading the *Autotrader* or an anthology of Jeremy Clarkson columns.

anvil *1. n.* Romantic term for the marital bed. Also *cock block. 2. n.* A woman with an impressive tally of notches wrought on her headboard; one who has "had some hammer". *'Born on this day: Daniel Gabriel Fahrenheit, temperature inventor, 1686; Jacob Rees Mogg, twat, 1969; Cynthia Plaster Caster, anvil, 1947.'*

anvil tipper *n.* A tumescent *slag hammer* of such magnitude that it could upend a blacksmith's percussive working surface.

anybody injured? *exclam. interrog.* Humorous interjection following a particularly loud *horse and cart.* See also *an excellent theory, Dr Watson; what's that, Sweep?*

any old pork in a storm *n.* The "last resort" chap that a desperate lady brings home after suffering a prolonged *sausage* drought.

any sword's a reward *phr.* The female equivalent of the gentlemanly aphorism that "any hole's a goal".

anything further from the prosecution? *exclam.* Asked of a party who has, in the words of Geoffrey Chaucer, "let fly a great fart, the like of a thunderdent". Whatever a thunderdent is.

anyway the wind blows *1. phr.* The final lyric in Queen's ubiquitous hit song *Bohemian Rhapsody. 2. exclam.* Something to say over the whooshing of a nice, gentle *apple tart.*

Anzac biscuit *n. Aus.* A *turd* full of disturbingly recognisable lumps of food, slightly less appetising than the WW1 oat comestible of the same name.

AOCB *1. abbrev.* The final item on the agenda of a committee meeting, *viz.* Any Other Competent Business, apparently. *2. abbrev.* The gentlemanly equivalent of a lady *rinsing her lettuce,* that is, a perfunctory, hurried wash in anticipation of imminent sexual activity, *viz.* Arse, Oxters, Cock and Balls.

AONB *1. abbrev.* Area of Outstanding Natural Beauty; any venue to which an abundance of high quality *tussage* seems inexorably and inexplicably drawn, *eg*. The Players' Lounge at Old Trafford, the Strangers' Bar at the Houses of Parliament or Mick Jagger's bedroom. *2. abbrev.* A view that takes one's breath away. A UNESCO World Heritage Sight. Arse of Outstanding Natural Beauty.

A1 ring *1. n.* Austrian Grand Prix motor racing circuit. *2. n.* A smashing *bonus tunnel* with a tricky chicane at turn 2. Not to be confused with *glans hatch.*

apache *1. n.* Sex without a *jubber ray*; *riding bare-back*. *2. n.* Popular instrumental hit by 60s guitar combo The Shadows.

apache hammock *n.* Stealthy and cunning technique of putting a *crash mat* of paper down the *bog* before taking a *number two* in order to avoid noise and *splashback*. Named in honour of the Native American tribe who were famed for their stealth and cunning. Also *pap baffle, turd raft, dump proof course.*

apathy *n. medic.* Constipation. Demonstrated by an *arse* that "doesn't give a shit". *Brown drought.*

apeshit *1. n.* That which is flung at your granny in a zoo. *2. adj.* In a state of mental perturbation. *Fucking radgy. 'Born on this day: Evel Knievel, human crash test dummy, 1938; Peter Stringfellow, fanny magnate, 1940; Gregg Wallace, apeshit greengrocer, 1966.'*

apollo 13 *1. euph.* A rapid release of gas in a confined space that causes the occupants to retreat to a safer place. *'Houston, we have a problem. Fred's done an Apollo 13.' 2. n.* An unexpected and disastrous venting of gas, which necessitates the abandoning of all plans, and an emergency return trip home. An *Apollo 13* crisis is only averted once a safe *splashdown* has been achieved. And one's trousers and underpants have been put out for the binman. From the slapstick Moon mission starring Tom Hanks.

apologies from my end *exclam.* Another post-flatulatory *mea culpa*. Something to say after *coughing a dead rat*. See also *sorry, I just need to pop down and change the barrel.*

apoology *n.* Something you proffer to your other half after badly befouling the *bumsink*. *'I'd give it ten minutes if I was you, love, before going in to clean that bastard. I think I must have had a dodgy pint. Please accept my profound apoologies.'*

appeals to a different set of visual criteria *euph.* Extremely *fugly. 'I'm afraid we were unable to offer your daughter a prize in the Bonny Baby competition, Mrs Widdecombe. Only it seemed to the judges that she appeals to a different set of visual criteria.'*

appendix tickler *n.* A *kidney stroker*. A bout of *backdoor work* up the missus's *chamber of horrors. 'Turn over, love. I fancy giving you an appendix tickler tonight. You'll like it. Not a lot, but you'll like it.'*

apple *n.* A Special Constable or Police Community Support Officer. Because they're "not a PC". A *Happy Shopper copper* or *potted plant. Also Mr Plobby, doppelclanger, quorn sausage, fakeon.*

applecatchers *n.* Generously proportioned *dunghampers* for the more generously *arsed* lady.

apple cunt *n. pej.* A spoilt little *shit* who, no matter how much money you spend on them, always wants more. Based on the popular phone company who do things like changing their charger connection, replacing the headphones socket *etc.*, just so you have to buy their own, expensive stuff instead of the Poundland alternative, when it breaks.

apple daft *adj.* Descriptive of the state of cerebral confusion achieved by *Harry Ramps* following *al fresco* consumption of cheap white cider.

apple grumble *n.* American *tug pamphletry.*

appleptic *adj.* Insensible to one's surroundings due to an elegant sufficiency of White Lightning or Frosty Jack.

appointment *n.* A euphemistic drinking opportunity. *'I know I promised to put those shelves up tonight, love, but I've got an urgent appointment at eight.'*

approach Dresden *v.* To experience a strong feeling in the *back body* that one will shortly be opening the *bomb bay doors,* in the style of a World War II pilot flying a fully loaded Avro Lancaster towards the popular RAF target city. Possibly accompanied by the ominous sound of ack-ack, warning sirens and a certain amount of hot shrapnel.

approach shot *1. n.* In golf, a pitch from fairway to green. *2. n.* In sex, an unfortunate premature ejaculation just as a chap is getting near the *hole. Spending your money before you get to the shop, potting the black on the break, pressing send too soon, falling at Beecher's.*

April *n. rhym. slang.* The fundament. From April in Paris = Aris; Aristotle = bottle; bottle and glass = arse. *'Careful leaning on that bar, Delboy. You might end up falling on your April.'*

April stool *n.* An *Eartha Kitt* that doesn't turn up after one has dashed to the gents certain that there's *a mole at the counter. 'My client was convinced that he had one in the departure lounge, your honour, but it turned out it was just an*

April stool.'

apron lifter *n.* One with a penchant for the *bigger-boned* woman. Also *gastric bandit, chubby chaser, blob jockey, bouncy hunter.*

aquafresh *1. n.* A *skidmark* created on the inside of the trousers of someone wearing a G-string, *ie.* Three stripes of two different colours. *2. n.* The thin, breath-freshening red stripe down the length of a *Tom tit*, caused by a bleeding *clackervalve.*

aqualung, tramp's *n.* A 3-litre bottle of cheap cider.

Arabian goggles *n.* The saucy act of sitting on a woman's forehead and resting your *bollocks* in her eyes while being *noshed off*. Quite possibly anatomically impossible, but it might be worth a try nevertheless. *Egg-cupping.*

Arabians *rhym. slang.* The *Gladyses*. From Arabian nights = Earthas. The *Brad Pitts.*

Arab stallion, hung like an *sim. Donkey-rigged, well-endowed.*

Arbroath smokie *n. Scots.* A particularly strongly-flavoured *haddock* delicacy.

archaeologist *n.* A curious gentleman with a preference for poking his *tool* about in historical *trenches*. One who is not averse to *meating the ancestors*. A *biddy fiddler, mothball diver, old dear hunter, granny magnet* or *OAP-dophile.*

archaeologist's tailor *euph.* Any person, object or event that is utterly unfit for purpose. From the manifest ineptitude of those who typically clothe the sartorially challenged trench-dwellers as seen on *Time Team*, BBC4 *etc.*

arch-angeling *n.* The miraculous act of *knocking up* a virgin while giving false credentials in order to avoid the unwanted attentions of the CSA.

archerfish *1. n.* A *brown trout* which, upon impact, generates a high-speed jet of water that accurately strikes the still-closing sphincter. Or knocks a fly off an overhanging branch. *2. n.* Any sea creature that writes *shit* novels, goes with *prossies* and commits perjury.

archer's window, fanny like an *sim.* An archaic description of a woman's *parts of shame* that are particularly tight, from their supposed resemblance to a medieval *balistraria*. *'Praise the Lord, Mother Superior. You've got a fanny like an archer's window.'*

'ardly *n.* A somewhat diminutive *ball snorkel*; one that is "so small it is 'ardly worth mentioning".

area 51 *1. n.* A secret facility within Nevada's Edwards Air Force Base, where the US authorities store all the crashed flying saucers from outer space and the bodies of aliens and that. It's true. You just look on the internet. *2. n.* A mysterious region of the female anatomy to which access is extremely limited.

area 51s *n.* Large swinging breasts. From the previously mentioned air base, which is widely believed to contain "massive hangers".

areola borealis *n.* An enchanting, ethereal phenomenon, occasionally glimpsed around the poles on a *bird's northern hemispheres.*

are you in there, Mr Hill? *exclam.* A jocular remark made to put people at their ease when someone has passed *flatus* which smells like the late comic Benny Hill's flat did after the police broke down the door.

are you not entertained? *1. exclam. rhet.* Line delivered by ancient Roman Australian Maximus Decimus Meridius in that film *Gladiator*. *2. exclam. rhet.* Witty riposte following a *trumpet involuntary.*

Argos *euph. n. prop.* Nickname given to the a married bloke's *bag for life* when she's had "no interest for 36 months". That'll be on their third anniversary, then.

Argos biro, hung like an *sim.* Of a gentleman, to be furnished with a *gut stick* the size and shape of one of the famous catalogue shop's customer-insulting ballpoint pens. Descriptive of a chap who has a *cock like a bookie's pencil*. *eg. The Rt Hon Jack Straw MP.*

Argos it *v.* After splitting up with your significant other, to mentally leaf through your back catalogue of past sexual relationships because you simply can't be *arsed* to go out *on the pull*. From the famous advertising slogan of the endlessly depressing high street store; "Don't shop for it, Argos it."

argosm *n.* A joyless, spirit-sapping orgasm achieved using a catalogue.

argue with the colonel *v.* To suffer from gastric complications following a visit to a famous Kentucky-based fried chicken restaurant. *'Are you okay, love? You've been in there nearly three hours.' 'I'll be fine. I'm just arguing with the colonel.'*

argument from design, the *1. n.* A philosophical rationale for the existence of a creator deity, positing that living organisms are too well designed to have originated by chance. *2. n.* Definitive proof that there can be no God, based on the fact that it is anatomically possible for a man to sit upon – and crush – his own *ballbag*. Not to mention the empirical evidence of how difficult it is to have a *piss* in the dark with a raging *boner* at four in the morning.

Argyll sweater *1. n.* Diamond-patterned knitwear popular with celebrity golfers in the 1970s. *2. n. Big-boned* Scottish lassie running to catch last orders at the Buchanan bus station Greggs.

aris *n. rhym. slang.* Convoluted rhyming slang for *shitter.* From Aristotle = bottle, bottle and glanus = anus.

arisola *n.* The darker patch of skin which forms a decorative escutcheon around the *rusty bullet hole.* The *ace of arse.*

aris tweed *n.* Tough, hard-wearing, matted *third eye* hair from which you could weave a pair of Highland gamekeeper's trousers. Also *glarsefibre.*

Ark Royal landing deck *n.* Descriptive of the state of the *skid pan* U-bend in a student house *crapper.* Also *the starting line at Brands Hatch* or *thrush's chest.*

Arkwright *n.* A lady of easy affections and loose knicker elastic. One whose *twat*, like the Balby corner shop in the popular situation comedy, is "open all hours".

Arkwright's till *1. euph.* Descriptive of an unpredictable and over-aggressive woman, who snaps at the slightest provocation and takes all one's money. Named after Ronnie Barker's dangerous-looking counter-top prop in *Open All Hours.* *2. n.* A dangerously volatile *snatch.* *'Every time Jacob Rees-Mogg appears on the telly, my fanny slams shut like Arkwright's till.'*

armadillo *n.* The characteristic shape formed by the rolls of adipose tissue around a lardy lass's shoulders, hips and back while she is being *scuttled* from behind.

arm and hammer *1. n.* Trade name of a brand of inexplicably expensive toothpaste which contains baking powder in case you want to make some fluoride-flavoured muffins. *2. n.* The two components required by a *wanksmith* before he gives a length of hot *pink steel* what-for on his scrotal anvil.

armani & navy *n.* Poorly made imitation designer clothes purchased from *world of inferiors. Scrote couture.*

arm beer *n.* Heroin.

armbreaker *euph.* A particularly vicious *hand crank. 'What with excellent browsing and sluicing and a couple of armbreakers and what-not, my afternoon passed quite happily.'* (from *Wooster Wanks Himself Daft*, by PG Wodehouse).

armchair angler *n.* One who gets his *tackle* out in order to enjoy a spot of *indoor fly fishing.*

armed knobbery *n.* Use of the *single-barrelled snotgun* to effect a sudden withdrawal from the *wank bank.*

Armitage blanks *n.* A fruitless shootout at the *shark's mouth.* See also *stage fright, stall shy.*

armpits, cock, arse, and out the door *phr.* Efficient morning ablutions regimen when running late. *'And how did you enjoy your kedgeree this morning, your holiness?' 'Never got to try it, cardinal. Me alarm didn't go off so it was a case of armpits, cock, arse, and out the door.'*

armtits *n.* Bingo wings, dinner lady's arms.

army and navy *adj.* Descriptive of one who likes his *bread buttered both sides. Half rice half chips.*

Arnie *n.* A *Tom tit* that is, for whatever reason, cut short and thus leaves one with the chilling impression that, like the sinister, right wing Austrian muscle man, it'll "be back".

aroma diffuser *1. n.* A scientific device that breaks "essential oils" down into smaller molecules, dispersing them into the air for a pleasant or calming effect on the gullible. *2. n.* The *arsehole.*

aromatherapy *n.* The head- and room-clearing therapeutical effects of a ripe *treacle tart.*

around the world *n.* Sexual practice which lasts considerably less than eighty days and costs about £25. *Anilingus, bog snorkelling, backdooral* or *rimming.*

arrange the orchestra *v.* To make adjustments to one's *horn, woodwind, string* and *brass* sections. To rearrange the *fruitbowl* through the trouser pockets. Also *wind the clock, nip and roll, sort out the boys, tune the banjo, stir the stew, pop the mouse back in the house.*

arresting a pissed tramp, like *sim.* The frustrating act of trying to manhandle a flaccid, spent *old man* into some sort of standing position.

arse *1. n.* The *Gary Glitter, chuff, nick, tradesman's, chamber of horrors.* The *an*s. 2. exclam.* A negative reply, expressing denial. *'Did you or did you not, on or about the night of June the twelfth 1994, feloniously and with malice aforethought murder Nicole Brown Simpson and Ronald Goldman?' 'Did I arse.' 3. v.* To do, up the arse. *'Have you seen the new girl in accounts? I'd give her a right good arsing, I would.' 4. n.* A silly fellow.

arse about *v.* To have a bit laugh and carry on.

arse about tit *adj.* Somewhat muddled. *'Ladies and gentlemen, this is your captain speaking. I'd like to apologise for that slightly bumpy landing, only I've been drinking since we took off and I got the controls all arse about tit on the final approach.'*

arse-and-a-half of full cream milk *phr.* A gentlemanly exclamation of approbation upon seeing a comely female backside. *'Anneka! The clue is in the windmill! It's somewhere in the windmill! Get out of the helicopter and run up the... Wow! That's an arse-and-a-half of full cream milk right there!'*

arse angel *1. n.* The dark, spreadwinged patch of

perspiration on the back of a jogger's shorts, or a driving instructor's trousers. *2. n.* The symmetrical, seraphim-shaped pattern that appears on a cow's backside when it uses its tail as a fly whisk while taking a *shit.*

arse antlers *n.* That Celtic tattoo that dodgy *birds* seem to think is a classy thing to have growing out of the top of their *bum crack.*

arse ants *n.* Nominal cause of an itchy *ringpiece.* *'Are you free, Mr Lucas?' 'Not now, Captain Peacock. I need to deal with me arse ants.'*

arse baby *n.* A *ring ripper,* a *dreadnought.* A huge *turd.*

arse balm *n. milit.* Any emollient skin preparation applied to a squaddie's *south mouth* to avoid chaffing prior to a 20-mile route march in full kit, *eg.* Nivea, cocoa butter, Stork SB.

arse banter *n.* Generic term for the cheeky conversational repartee that eminates from the *nipsy.* *'Don't take offence, your holiness. That's just a bit of arse banter.'*

arse bar *n.* Unappetising *bum toffee* confection following which you would be well advised not to lick your fingers clean.

arse barnacles *n.* Unremovable *winnets* on which the fingers of the right hand can be keelhauled. *Miniature heroes.*

arsebestos *n.* The remarkable heat-resistant substance from which an inveterate *Ruby Murray* enthusiast's *cigar cutter* is fabricated.

arsebidextrous *adj.* Gifted with the ability to lean over onto either *bum cheek* in order to *let one rip.* *'What very few people realise is that the Princess Royal is also arsebidextrous, as this clip of her elegantly dropping a gut during the dressage section of the Badminton Horse Trials shows.'* (Nicholas Witchell, narrating *Princess Anne – Sixty Years of Being Absolutely Marvellous,* BBC TV).

arse biscuit *n.* A chocolate-chip *turd* that is suitable for dunking.

arse bra *n.* A pair of heavily elasticated ladies' *dunghampers. Harvest festivals* which exhibit a high coefficient of isotropic homogeneity.

arse bucket challenge *n.* To gird one's loins manfully and use a public *Rick Witter* that is already befouled with *bangers and mash.* And then upload the footage to Facebook.

arse burner *n.* A pair of *piabetics shagging* in the standard missionary style, whereby the person on top risks scorching their buttocks on the bedroom lightbulb.

arse candle *n.* A *shirt raiser* which is so protracted and gaseous that, were one to apply a lighted match, it would sustain a flickering, votive-like flame.

arse chimes *n. medic.* Piles. Also *Chalfonts, Dukes, farmers, Emmas, four minute miles, Kurts, Bernards, Michaels, nauticals, Nurembergs, seig heils, polaroids, Rockfords, ceramics* or *lever arches.*

arse clock *n.* The comforting familiarity of the regular and predictable movements of the *Simon Cowells.* A delicate mechanism that can be thrown askew by illness, a change of time zone, or several pints of real ale followed by a scorchingly hot curry.

arse code *n.* The random cascade of dots and dashes the day after one has consumed a lamb phaal and ten pints. See also *arse-2D2.*

arse confetti *n.* The mixed assortment of small, curly hairs and, apparently, grit typically left scattered across the toilet seat by a previous occupant. *Bumdruff, arse tobacco.*

arsecons *n.* Of e-mails and phone texting, resourceful use of punctuation to illustrate the condition of someone's *jacksie, eg.* Normal *arse* (-!-) lard *arse* (-!-) tight *arse* (!) sore *arse* (-*-) slack *arse* (-0-) *etc. Arse* icons, probably superseded these days by emojis or some such *bollocks.*

arse crackers *1. n.* Unnaturally pendulous *clock-weights* that belabour the *farting clappers* when one is forced to run in loose shorts. *2. n.* Notably unsuccessful brand of crispbreads, launched by McVitie's in 1975.

arse cress *n.* Spindly anal vegetation that doesn't get much light. The hairs that attach the *winnets* to *Dot Cotton's mouth.*

arse croutons *n.* Small wads of rolled up *chod wipe* found nestled betwixt the ample *bummocks* of a *salad dodger.*

Arse Cunt Balls Dick *phr.* Useful mnemonic to remember the correct sequence of answers when playing Fastest Finger First on *Who Wants to be a Millionaire?*

arse curtains *n. Undercrackers* as worn by a well-upholstered female whose glands have eaten all the pies.

arsed *adj.* The state of being bothered. *'CEDRIC: Come onto the balcony, Lavinia. The moon is so terribly, terribly enchanting this evening. The stars are twinkling like the lights in your eyes when you laugh. LAVINIA: (off stage) In a bit. I can't be arsed at the minute.'* (from *Don't Put your Daughter on the Game, Mrs Worthington* by Noel Coward).

arse de triomphe *n.* A particularly impressive *derriere,* with a load of red-faced Frenchmen driving round it in circles, honking their car horns and smoking Gitanes.

arse d'oeuvres *n. Fr.* Bite-sized unappetizers prior

to a substantial *air buffet.*

arse fairy *n.* A bit like the tooth fairy, only instead of removing milk teeth from under your pillow and leaving small amounts of cash wrapped in toilet paper behind, she miraculously changes the missus's smashing, firm bottom into a flabby, wide one when you're not looking. *'Bloody hell, love. The arse fairy's been, so I'm leaving you.'*

arse feta *n.* The barely edible cheese that forms inside a driving instructor's trousers on a hot day.

arse fuse *n.* The first *tab* of the morning, the lighting of which precipitates a sudden and breath-taking pyrotechnic display. The pin on a *bum grenade.*

arse gargle *n.* An horrendously wet *clearing of the nether throat* that is performed over the *bum sink* every morning.

arse gasket *n.* One of those paper *bog seat* covers that you get in the USA to stop you getting germs on your *nipsy* while a big *shite's* coming out of it.

arse glue *n.* A particularly spicy *cuzza* that, once eaten, has the unique property of sticking one's buttocks to the *chod bin* for most of the following day.

arse gout *n. medic.* High class flatulence fuelled by rich foodstuffs. *'Another helping of venison and port trifle, Sir Terry?' 'I shouldn't really, Heston. It gives me terrible arse gout.'*

arse grapes *n. medic.* Haemorrhoids, *farmers, Chalfonts, Emmas, ceramics, Bonny Marys, Adrians.*

arsehole *1. n.* The *dirtbox, tea towel holder. 2. sim. pl.* Measure of the roughness of someone or something. *'That Jordan is as rough as arseholes without her make-up on. Mind you, when she's got it on she's as rough as fuck.' 3. n.* Contumelious epithet. *'Born on this day: Julie Burchill, helium-voiced contrarian, 1959; Tracey Emin, shitted bed artist, 1963; Julian Assange, arsehole, 1971.'*

arseholed *adj.* Completely *wankered. Shit-faced.*

arsehole farm *n.* A golf course.

arsehole survivor *n.* That single small *tod* that floats around, hanging on and defying further flushes in the hope of rescue by a passing helicopter, after all its mates have been *sent to the beach.*

arsehole to breakfast time, bollocked from *phr.* Descriptive of loud, prolonged and vicious admonishment following a mild infraction. *'After Ozzy's latest bout of infidelity, he was summoned to the family home & bollocked from arsehole to breakfast time.'* (*Court Circular* column in *The Times,* August 2016).

arseholitaire *n.* The only game in town for the friendless *arsehole.* *'What you doing for Christmas, Nigel?' 'The usual. Microwave meal-for-one and a few games of arseholitaire.'*

arseholitude *n.* Self-inflicted loneliness.

arseimonious *adj.* Descriptive of someone who buys budget *bogroll.*

arsejection moulding *n.* The kind of *sit down toilet adventure* that requires you to tease your *nipsy* back into roughly the right shape afterwards. A *humpty dumpty* that changes the way you walk. See also *(like a) hedgehog through a cheesegrater.*

arse juggler *n.* A *celery rinser* who prefers to travel on an alternative means of municipal public transport to that which might otherwise have been expected. A *book reader* or *puddle jumper.*

arse Karcher *n.* A bidet.

arse ker-plunk, play *v.* To squeeze an *Exchange & Mart* out when you know there is a danger of *following through* at any moment. To *pull out a straw* and hope you don't *drop a marble.*

arse labour *v.* The agonising cramps which indicate it is time to give birth to *Meat Loaf's daughter.* *'Was I really going that fast, officer? I'm terribly sorry, only we've been out for a couple of arse glues at a well-known Newcastle upon Tyne curry restaurant, and my wife has gone into arse labour.'*

arse lag *n.* The annoying situation following a long haul flight whereby your *Simon Cowell* movements fail to revert to their regular, accustomed routine, and you have to go for your daily *dump* just before bedtime instead of first thing in the morning. Or vice versa.

arse like a brake light *sim.* Of one's *ringpiece,* to be enjoying the benefits of last night's *Ruby Murray.* *'Come to the Curry Capital, Bigg Market, Newcastle upon Tyne. You'll get a warm welcome, a hot curry and an arse like a brake light the next morning – or your money back!'* (Speech to the United Nations by the late Abdul Latif, Lord of Harpole).

arse like a Tetley tea bag *sim.* Descriptive of a *ringpiece* the morning after sinking a powerful vindaloo. From the old television advert in which, to the accompaniment of a voiceover by Barnsley's greatest son Brian Glover, a tea bag was suspended in mid-air, boiling water was poured onto it, and red hot, steaming brown liquid flooded out. An *arsehole* that feels like it's got "two thousand perforations".

arse like a wind sock *sim.* A well-*bummed shitter.*

arse like the top of a sauce bottle *sim.* A less-than-clean rectum. A *nipsy* where slight spillages and leaks have dried *in situ,* and which will have to be picked clean.

arsemada *n.* A menacing flotilla of small *turdlets* which resembles the Spanish fleet. Probably doesn't resemble it very much, if truth be told.

arsemageddon *n.* An apocalyptic rectal meltdown that feels like the end of the world as we know it. An *arse like a broken ice cream machine, three pile island.*

arse man *n.* One whose *boat* is *floated* by ladies' *dirtboxes* in preference to their *gams, quims* or *thruppennies.* '*I'm going to refer you to the consultant proctologist at the hospital, Mrs Smith. He's one of the country's leading arse men.*'

arsematic *n. medic.* One who makes it difficult for others to breathe.

arse memories *n.* Turds. '*Fucking Nora. I just trod in one of next door's cat's arse memories again, June.*'

arsenal *n.* The public toilet fixture that isn't the urinal. The *bum sink* or *jobby engine.*

Arsenal are at home *euph.* Said when a lady is *up on blocks*, *chasing the cotton mouse, dropping clots, smoking short cigars etc.* Arsenal can be replaced with the name of any football team who play in red, *eg.* Manchester United, Liverpool, Spartak Moscow, the 1966 England World Cup squad, Wisla Krakow.

Arsenal sock, fanny like a *sim.* Descriptive of one of those 2-foot long, bright red, knitted vaginas that smell of feet and liniment.

Arsenal's 2017 cup run, easier than *sim.* Said of a young lady whose *knickers are off quicker than the Happy Mondays.* Also *easier than ~ junior scrabble; ~ a two-piece jigsaw puzzle.*

arse on, (have an) *v.* To *have a monk on.* To be in a huff or bad humour. '*There once was a man with an arse on / Who went to take tea with the parson / He was in such a mood / He refused all his food / That stroppy old cunt with an arse on.*' (from *The Book of Fucking Nonsense* by Edward Lear).

arse over tit, go *v.* To fall comprehensively. '*Eeh, mother. Come and look at this video on the internet of some bloke in a football kit going arse over tit down a London Underground escalator.*'

arseovoir *n.* The little indent just above a builder's buttock cleft that holds about half a pint of foetid sweat. The *bum cruet.*

arse parcels *n.* The goods which fall out of a *ripped shopping bag.*

arse parchment *n.* A rare scroll of paper upon which many a sorry tale may be inscribed.

arse-patcho *n.* A thin anal soup; a delicately balanced consommé of partially digested *catbab* meat, exotic spices, crisps, pork scratchings and farmhouse cider.

arsepeggio *n.* An act of flatulence performed with such masterful control that a distinct series of musical notes can be identified. Achieved by

mastering the embouchure of one's *nipsy.*

arse pips *n. Winnets, tagnuts, dangleberries.*

arse piss *n.* Diarrhoea. Also *fizzy gravy, rusty water, anal fire water, hoop soup, Montezuma's revenge etc.*

arse-ritis *1. n. medic.* Affliction affecting long-term jobseekers which is characterised by stiffness in the buttocks and legs. Usually caused by sitting down all day watching *Railroad Alaska, Alaska: The Last Frontier, Edge of Alaska, The Last Alaskans* and *Wheeler Dealers* on the Discovery Channel. And then again an hour later on Discovery +1. *2. n. medic.* Debilitating medical condition whereby one simply cannot be *arsed* to get up and do things.

arse scratcher *n.* A *treacle tart* so powerfully emitted and mysteriously coarse-grained that it soothingly abrades one's itchy *nipsy* on its way past. Also *Roy Castle's kettle.*

arseshot *n.* If someone hears another person's *dropped gut*, then they are in *arseshot.*

arse-souls *n.* Nebulous, noisome wraiths that glide from the *jacksie*, often accompanied by groans, moans, and the rattling of chains. And a *fucking ronk.*

arse spider *n.* A tenacious, well-knotted *winnet* that cannot be removed without bringing eight spindly hairs with it.

arseterisk *n.* A brown punctuation mark left on the back of the *bog seat* by a previous inconsiderate or overweight sitter.

arseterity measures *n.* Taking all your *dumps* while you are at work to save on the expense of buying your own *brown shield stamps.*

arsetex *n.* Public lavatory bowl render. Also known as *fartex* or *ploppydex.*

arsethetically pleasing *adj.* Of a set of *mud flaps*, easy on the eye. '*Yes, the blonde one out of Abba was always, to my mind, particularly arsethetically pleasing. And his missus wasn't bad either.*'

arse tobacco *n.* The unpleasant collection of colonic detritus, anal effluvium, faecal flotsam and pubic jetsam left on the *bog* seat after wiping. So called because it is "a mixture of ready-rubbed and flake".

arse Tourette's *n. medic.* Comedy disorder of the lower alimentary canal characterised by sudden, repeated *Simon* movements and uncontrollable, involuntary anal vocalisations. Particularly prevalent amongst the elderly, the infirm, and recent visitors to the Curry Capital Restaurant, Bigg Market, Newcastle upon Tyne.

arse tramp *n.* A *cleft*-dwelling vagrant who hangs around in the bushes long after his pals have been moved on by the prudent use of *bumwad.* A tenacious *dangleberry.*

arse vinegar *n.* The acidic condiment found in the *arseovoir.*

arse wasps *n.* A swarm of aggressive, imaginary insects that attack and sting your *brown eye* after a particularly spicy meal. *Indian killer bees.*

arse weasel *n.* A long, flowing *cack* that tickles the *nipsy.*

arse-whipped *adj.* Said of a bloke who'd do anything for a sniff of *back door action* off his missus. *Under the bum.*

arse whisperer *1. n.* One who has the magical and rare ability to quieten down a lift full of people by silently *dropping a gut.* *2. n.* One who utters words of encouragement at their own *fundament* whilst in the act of *fouling*, in a style reminiscent of a megaphone-toting rowing coach cycling along a towpath, using stock phrases such as "Come on, ya bastard!", "You beauty!" and "Ten more of those!"

arsewidth *n.* Scientifically measurable degree to which one can be *arsed.* *'I know something's got to be done about the current mispricing of liquidity in the corporate loan market, Prime Minister. But I'm doing me Wordle at the moment, so I simply don't have the arsewidth to deal with it.'*

arsewife *n.* A *bag for life* who's not averse to letting her hubby have the occasional rummage round her *chutney locker.*

arse wig *n.* The *tagnutty* halo of hair around the *gammon ring.* Also *poopée.*

arsewipe *1. n.* Bathroom tissue, *bumwad, shit scrape, brown shield stamps.* *2. n. pej.* Contumelious epithet for a *tosser.*

arsicle *n.* A frozen *turd* hanging out of the bottom, discovered upon waking up at the conclusion of a refreshing, post-pub, drunken snooze on the *jobby engine.* A *stalacshite.*

Ars Magna *1. n.* A 16th century Book by mathematician Girolamo Cardano which introduces the concept of imaginary numbers when dealing with the square roots of negative integers. *2. n.* A right big *muckspreader.*

art department *n.* The newsagent's top shelf, where the proprietor keeps his *pornucopia* of periodicals of particular interest to connoisseurs of the undraped female form.

artful as a supermarket butcher *sim.* Descriptive of a woman who makes the best of her limited assets by presenting herself in an appealingly packaged manner while simultaneously concealing what lies beneath. From the similar skills of a superstore meat vendor, who takes a slab of old mutton and, with careful manipulation, disguises the fat,

hairy, gristly bits so that it looks like a tasty bit of succulent fillet.

art homework *n.* Back in the dark ages before the internet, that crusty pamphletry which was binned by an adolescent youth's mother when she tidied his bedroom.

Arthur Fowler's allotment *euph.* An unkempt, riotously overgrown *ladygarden* which looks like it has not been tended since May 1996.

artisan/artisanal *adj.* Descriptive of any product or service that is cackhandedly manufactured or supplied by someone who used to do it as a hobby.

artist of the Wessobrunner school *1. n.* A craftsman creating elaborate Baroque stuccowork in the manner of the late seventeenth/early eighteenth century Bavarian style. *2. n.* A German *home video* performer catering for the *bukkake* end of the market. An *abstract expressionist.*

art pamphlet *n.* A *jazz magazine, bongo periodical* or *noddy book.* Any one-handed reading material.

art room sink, face like an *sim.* Said of a lucky lady who has been the more or less simultaneous recipient of the romantic attentions of several generous gentlemen. Also known as a *plasterer's radio, quattro formaggio, Dracula's candle* or *cock mess monster.*

asboranto *n.* Grunt-based language used by those of low breeding when communicating with each other. *'What's happening on Jeremy Kyle?' 'Search me. I don't speak asboranto.'*

asbo spumante *n.* The alcoholic beverage of choice for the fiscally-challenged youngster.

ascertain *1. v.* To determine or discover conclusively. *2. v.* To entertain with one's anus. *'Phwooarr!!! Frumpy Kate's nipsylicious sister Pippa certainly put the "hot" into patri-hot-ic as she ascertained the horny crowds outside Westminster Abbey in her nipsy-hugging frock.'* (picture caption from *The Daily Telegraph,* April 30th 2011).

Asda rollback *n.* A crafty *self-harm* opportunity taken advantage of by a *tescosexual* during the *wank window* while his missus is out at the supermarket shopping for his tea.

Asdas, legs like *sim.* Expression which can be used waspishly when referring to a lady who is generous with her favours, ie. One whose legs, like those of the sexually promiscuous supermarket, are "open twenty-four hours".

Ashford and Simpson *euph.* A *motion* that is, in the words of the eponymous Motown duo's 1984 single, "solid as a rock".

Ashley Young *euph.* A random Bruno Fernandez-style tumble to the ground when no one else is around, named in honour of the ex-Watford

& Aston Villa winger, currently falling over for Everton. *'Hello? Can you send an ambulance? Me nan's had a nasty Ashley Young down the stairs.'*

asking Edward Scissorhands for a wank, like *sim.* Describing an arguably sub-optimal choice of person to perform a particular job. *'You voted for Liz Truss to run the country? That's like asking Edward Scissorhands for a wank.'*

Aslan *n.* Offensively sexist, male chauvinist description of a woman who has the hair of a lion, the face of a witch and the body of a wardrobe, *eg. Fugly,* frightening, feminist icon the late Andrea Dworkin.

Aslan is on the move *1. exclam.* A popular line from one of them Narnia books, in which the presence of a big lion is announced. *2. exclam.* Something to say the day after a big curry, when your stomach emits a huge roar and you have to run to the *crapper* before your entire digestive system ends up in your underpants like a big steaming pile of wildebeest entrails.

Aslan's breath *n. medic.* A case of *dung lung* so noisome that it instantly renders one's *old chap* flaccid. From *The Lion, the Witch and the Wardrobe* in which, by breathing on them, the lion un-petrifies people who have previously been turned to statues by the White Witch.

as one door closes another one opens *phr.* An optimistic philosophical apophthegm of the sort espoused by glass-half-full types, which can be propounded at the missus's monthly *times of adversity. 'Sorry Terry, not tonight. I've got the painters in.' 'Don't be downhearted, June. You know what they say; as one door closes another one opens.'*

aspartame daddy *n.* Bloke who pretends to be rich in order to *get his end away.* A fake *sugar daddy.*

aspect ratio, change in *euph.* A person's sideways enlargement due to weight gain, *eg.* From 4:3 to 16:9. *'Christ, look at this picture of Marlon Brando in Apocalypse Now. That's quite a change in aspect ratio since On the Waterfront, isn't it?'*

ass *n. US.* That part of the body the metaphorical *whupping* of which indicates a comprehensive victory, that is often altruistically put on the line by police commanders and of which the invitation to kiss is often rhetorically proffered.

Assange tan *n.* The wan complexion of a *human rhubarb* who hasn't been getting out much lately.

assess for flesh *v.* To perform a high-speed visual scan across a page of social media photo album thumbnails, such as like what might be found on the internet, in order to identify and locate surreptitious *t & a.* And *c.* What BBC News 24 presenters are doing when you think they're checking their laptops for the latest developments in a breaking story.

assets *n. journ. Charms, qualifications, references, vested interests.*

ass, gas or grass? *phr. interrog.* Question asked by American rednecks when picking up hitch-hikers.

asspresso *n.* A short but powerful burst of *liquid darkness.*

asspurger's syndrome *n. medic.* Upsetting condition suffered the morning after an excess of brown beer and strongly seasoned comestibles.

assquatch *n.* Abominable cryptozoological monster that is occasionally spotted emerging from its dark cave with a great deal of moaning. A post-constipation *Meat Loaf's daughter.*

asstrash *n. US.* Rectal garbage.

asstrocity *n.* A *shit* so unpleasant as to constitute a breach of the Geneva Convention. A crime against humanity. *'I wouldn't go in there for ten minutes or so if I was you, Mr Boutros Boutros-Ghali. Me nan's just committed a terrible asstrocity.'*

asstronome *n.* One who has a predilection for *rimming.* A *truffle-hunting* connoisseur with a relish for exotic flavours from *around the world.*

asstro-turf *n.* The matted foliage visible in a *carpet fitter's smile.*

Astra map pocket, fanny like a *sim.* Large but at the same time surprisingly tight.

astronomical with the truth *exclam.* Descriptiive of a top class *bullshitter.*

aswad *1. n. prop.* 80s reggae group, featuring Brinsley Forde out of off of Here Come *the Double Deckers.* *2. n.* A folded ream of lavatory tissue stuffed down the *kegs* in case of faecal accidents. Also *manpon.* *3. acronym.* A Slash, Wank And Dump. A multi-tasking *chod bin* visit. *3. n.* A woman who is, architectuarally speaking, far more attractive when viewed from a rear elevation than a frontal one. A *back beauty.* From the previously mentioned band's only chart-topping hit single *Don't Turn Around.* Also known as a *golden deceiver.* *4. abbrev.* A Single Wank A Day. A sensible ration for a growing lad if he is to avoid excessive stunted growth, hairy palms, blindness and insanity.

at a loose end *euph.* Descriptive of a fellow who is *relaxing in a gentleman's way. 'Why is there spunk all over the walls, floor and ceiling, Damien?' 'Sorry Prime Minister, I was at a loose end.'*

Atatürk's revenge *n.* A heavy flock of semi-viscous, lumpy *mocking birds* and lots of liquid, experienced after a heavy night on the raki and prescription-strength döner kebabs with all chilli sauce on. Named in honour of the father of modern Turkey and his win at Gallipoli during the first lot.

ATC *1. abbrev.* Air Training Corps: the RAF's youth wing. *2. abbrev.* Air Traffic Control. *3. abbrev.* All To Cock; When any situation is irrevocably *fucked up*. *'Is is fair to say, Prime Minister, that your plans for the economy are ATC?' 'You've hit the nail on the head there, Peston, right on the fucking head.'*

Athanasian *n.* A woman of *easy virtue*. From the start of *The Athanasian Creed* (which almost certainly has nothing to do with St. Athanasius, for what it's worth) which, like many ecclesiastical writings, is often known by the beginning of the text in Latin, and thus is also referred to as the "quicunque vult". Which is Latin for "whoever wishes". Don't say we never learn you anything.

athlete's flute *n. medic.* A *happy rash* affecting the *pink oboe* in the aftermath of a romantic encounter with *a lady of easy virtue*. *'Mr Speaker. Could the honourable gentleman the minister please explain to the house why he was scratching himself down there all through the Queen's speech?' 'Not that it's any of the honourable lady's business, Mr Speaker, but I've got a touch of athlete's flute, as it happens, following my recent trade delegation to Amsterdam.'*

athlete's foot *n.* A twelve-inch erection brought about by illegal performance-enhancing pharmaceuticals.

athlete's fud *n. medic.* A yeasty infection of the *minnie moo*. Thrush, *gash rash, Lady Chalk of Bilingsgate*.

at it *adj.* To be engaged in copulation like knives. The use of this term is restricted to disapproving neighbours. *'Tssch. Sounds like those two next door are at it like knives again.'*

Atkinson diet, the *n.* English food, eaten in preference to any of that bloody foreign muck. Named after robustly opinionated *independent thinker* and therefore former television football pundit Ron.

at lagerheads *euph.* Said of a couple having a lively exchange of philosophical opinions while *heavily refreshed*.

ATM *1. abbrev.* A cashpoint. Probably an abbreviation of Automatic Till Machine or something like that. We could look it up, but who cares? *2. abbrev.* Anal To Mouth. A self-explanatory grumble video trope. *3. abbrev.* Similarly, a dirty *trollop*. From Arse Then Mouth. It's Automated Teller Machine, by the way.

at my signal, unleash hell! *exclam.* A rather ominous thing to say before *letting off* a *guff* that is capable of slaying a large force of warriors. A quote from *Gladiator* or *Braveheart*, something like that.

atomic mutton *n.* A mature woman trying to look much younger than she obviously is. *'Or will he choose number three – our cackling piece of atomic mutton from Essex, who has been round the fucking block a few times and was best before 1985?'*

atomic tortoise *n.* Any superficially innocent-looking pastry product which conceals a filling hotter than the sun. For example, a meat pie bought from a particular pie shop which, bizarrely, we are unable to name due to legal restrictions in Cardiff. The pie shop's in Cardiff, not the legal restrictions.

attack of the mallards *phr.* Descriptive of the experience of being followed around by a noisy duck. With bad breath. *'I do apologise, Ken. I seem to be having an attack of the mallards.' 'No problem, Janice. We'll just put it down to nerves. Now let's play Popmaster!'*

attack of the vapours *1. n.* Nervous state or hysterical fainting fit that might overcome a Victorian woman or Ann Widdecombe after inadvertently catching sight of a piano leg. *2. n.* Being blindsided by a *fart* so vile it causes one to collapse on to a chaise longue like Valeria in Wilkie Collins's *The Law and the Lady*. Also *a touch of the vapours*.

Attenborough's passport, fanny like *sim.* Description of a lady's *bodily treasure* which is distinctly dog-eared and well-thumbed, in the style, one would imagine, of the erstwhile globe-hopping naturalist and national treasure's travel documents. *'Christ almighty, I knew she had quite a few miles on the cock, but when I got down there she had a twat like Attenborough's passport.'* (Wedding day speech by HRH the Prince Andrew, Duke of York).

attention all shipping *exclam.* An urgent *gale warning* issued prior to a passage of potentially harmful *wind*. See also *and now for something completely different*; *and Bully's special prize...*; *gentlemen start your engines*; *let off some steam, Bennett.*

attic full of Rolf Harris paintings, like an *sim.* Said of a financial speculation which hasn´t paid off as handsomely as one might have originally hoped. *'Yeah, just before the bubble burst, I sold everything and put it into Bitcoin. To be frank with you, my investment has performed like an attic full of Rolf Harris paintings. Do you want any ketchup with that?'*

Atticus Pund *n. prop.* Anagram of "a stupid

c***" (cunt). From the cheekily named fictional detective character in Anthony Horowitz's *Magpie Murders*.

attitude adjustment *n*. A *wank*. *'Och Paw, stop being so grumpy with the bairns and take yirsel' aff tae the but'n'ben fir a wee attitude adjustment.'*

Audi driver *n*. Someone who appears desperate to get *up your arse*. From the customary road manners exhibited by drivers of the stupid-fairy-light-bedecked German motor cars.

audience with Brian Blessed, an *euph*. A lady's moment of quiet reflection prior to wielding the shears and tackling *Terry Waite's allotment*.

auditioning the finger puppets *n*. A single act, one woman show which is not suitable for children. *Gusset typing, Kit-Kat shuffling*.

auditors in, have the *euph*. A stockbroker's version of *having the decorators in*, whereby "everything seems to be in the red."

Augustus *n*. A caller at the *tradesman's entrance*. From the Roald Dahl book *Charlie and the Chocolate Factory*, where Augustus Gloop got "stuck up the chocolate pipe".

auld lang syne *n*. A frankly unlikely crossed-hands *circle jerk* in a *Frankie* cinema.

aunteater *n*. *Biddy fiddler, old dear hunter, bone shaker, relic hunter, granny magnet, mothball diver, tomb raider, resthomosexual* or *OAP-dophile*.

auntie *1. n*. Affectionate term for the BBC coined by the BBC. *2. n*. An elderly *gentleman* who is *good with colours*.

auntie climax *n*. A *milfish* piece of posh *totty* presenting a history programme on the BBC who causes a young cove to sit on the couch with a cushion covering his embarrassment when watching TV with his parents. *'Did you see the new Dr Alice Roberts documentary about the plague? Frankly, I thought it was a bit of an auntie climax.'*

auntie freeze *n*. During an act of *gentlemanly relaxation*, a involuntary suspension of erotic inspiration engendered by thinking about an elderly female relative. *Nanaphylactic shock*.

auntie magnetic *adj*. Tending to attract *vintage bintage*.

auntie matter *n*. *Olive oil, Mabel syrup, olden syrup*.

auntie's round *exclam*. Euphemistic reference to a *visit from Aunt Flo*.

aunt Mary *n*. A lady's hairy *fadge*. A *Judith, Bluto's beard* or *Lord Winston's moustache*.

au pair's toothbrush *euph*. The male *manhood*. From the punchline to the famous *New Yorker* cartoon of a child in a Sex Education class, *viz*. "My Dad's got two of those, miss. A small one for pissing and the other big one is for cleaning the au

pair's teeth when Mom's out."

aurora biriani *n*. The flickering, multi-coloured phosphorescent glow from one's *chocolate starfish* the morning after a particularly aggressive takeaway. Also the *northen shites, Hawaiian sunrise, aurora tandooralis*.

au snatchurel *phr. Fr*. Descriptive of an un-tended *ladygarden*. *'Struth, it's like a toasted cheese sandwich that's been dropped on a barber's floor down here, Germaine.' 'Yes, I've been keeping it au snatchurel, cobber.'*

Aussie kiss *n*. Similar to a *French kiss* but performed *down under*.

Austen Tourette's *n. medic*. Male psychological condition characterised by the reflexive making of sarcastic and disparaging comments while sat with one's wife/spouse/girlfriend watching a *Pride and Prejudice*-style costume drama on the television. Treatment usually consists of the sufferer being walloped with a scatter cushion and banished from the room until the poncey bonnet-wearing nonsense has finished.

austerity night *n*. A curtains-closed evening in with a *pot noodle and a wank*.

author! author! *exclam*. Cry of appreciation after a *dropping of guts*.

auto-bography *n*. A memoir of negligible literary merit that is kept for reading whilst on the toilet. *'I'm halfway through Jeremy Clarkson's auto-bography, vicar.' 'Well can you hurry up? I'm dying for a piss out here.'*

autoglass repairman *n*. A peripatetic tradesman who spends his days injecting his *special resin* at high pressure into dubious *cracks* of various shapes and sizes.

autograph the gusset *v*. To allow the newly born *turtle's head* to countersign one's *bills*.

autoproctologist *n*. One who is up his or her own *arse* all the time.

avoids PC World *euph*. Said of someone who would rather that their hard drive was not professionally examined.

avril *n*. The lavatory. Named after the semi-popular Canadian chanteuse Avril Latrine.

avuncular *adj*. Seventies media description of a family entertainer who is now behind bars.

awaken the bacon *v*. To sexually arouse a *bird's gammon flaps*. To get the *lady fat* sizzling prior to an oleaginous *Dutch breakfast*.

away and take your face for a shite *exclam*. Dismissive rejoinder towards one prone to fabricating stories or speaking nonsensically. There's a crisp tenner waiting here for the first panellist (or audience member) on *Question Time* to use this phrase.

away end *n.* The anus. Also *fifties teatowel holder, freckle, rusty sheriff's badge etc.* *'That Princess M_____ of K___ is a right goer, your majesty. I'm gonna take her up the away end this Saturday.'*

away win *n.* An adulterous episode which happily goes undetected.

awkward-on *1. n.* Descriptive of socially unacceptable and maladroit *tumescence* in the *trouser department.* *'Good Lord, what is that protruding from your breeches?' 'Don't worry, it's just my awkward-on. Keep on going with the investiture, your Majesty.'* *2. n.* The uncomfortable post-ejaculatory situation whereby a fellow is is obliged, for whatever reason (*eg.* roommate's unexpected return, Amazon delivery, presenting a daytime television show, *etc.*), to quickly pull up his strides, tuck his *wood* behind his belt, and carry on regardless.

AWOL *1. euph.* When a fellow has no energy or man porridge left. From All Wanked Out Love. *2. abbrev. milit.* Absent Without Official Leave. *3. abbrev.* A Wank On my Lonesome. Difficult to imagine how it might be used. *4. acronym.* Females who are disposed, when particularly emotional or suitably drunk on Prosecco, to disappear off together. Acquaintances With Occasional Lezzing.

a wreath was laid, but I don't think I was involved *exclam.* An exculpatory phrase to be optimistically proffered following a *bottom burp.*

axis powers, the *euph.* The male genitalia, comprising the Italian *meatballs,* the *Jap's eye* and the *herman jelmet.*

axle grease *n.* A budget lubricant used in *grumble flicks.* *Hockle flobbed* onto a *cock* before it gets pushed in.

Axminster spinster *n.* A single *lady in comfortable shoes, ie.* One who has not done a great deal of *rug munching* lately. Also *Wilton widow, Axminster Annie.*

Ayers Rock *n. rhym. slang. Aus.* Something large, red and *in the South.* *'Oi, Germaine. When you've finished burning your bra, come over here and have a nosh on me Ayers Rock.'*

Aztec two-step *n.* Diarrhoea dance along the lines of the *Tijuana cha-cha, Turkish two-step.* or *sour apple quickstep.* *'Tonight, Tess, Anton will be performing the Aztec two-step, as he bought some dodgy boil-in-the-bag prawn chimichangas at a car boot and had them for his lunch.'*

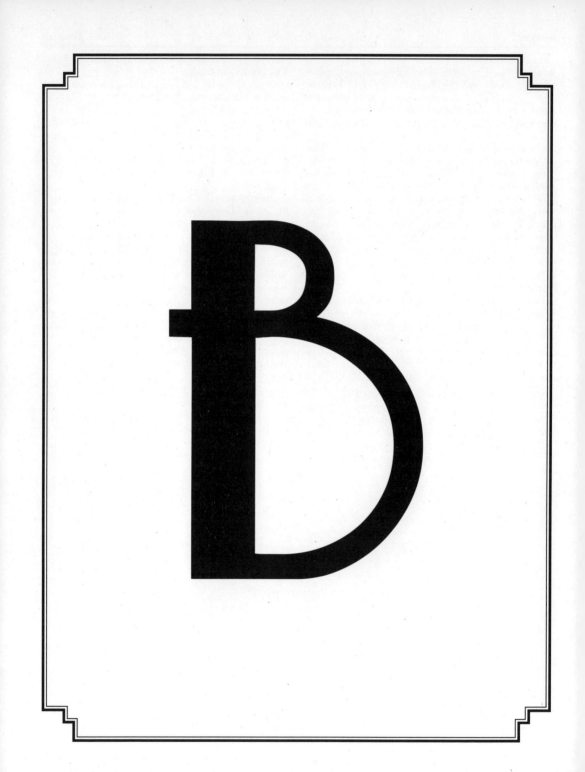

babber *v.* A term popular in the delightful South Yorkshire hamlet of Barnsley and its environs, meaning to *shit* oneself involuntarily. To *papper.* *'Ayup, why's Dickie in his football shorts, Brian?'* *'He babbered hissen, Geoffrey.'*

Babel fart *n.* A stench so strong and foul that it causes onlookers to involuntarily swear in a different language.

Babenfreude *n. Germ.* Literally, the frisson of mischievous delight a fertile person experiences when posting their baby photos on Facebook for their barren friends to peruse.

babia majora *exclam. US.* Phrase uttered by Americans upon sighting a gaggle of *flange* or a *flange* of *quim* at a public gathering, such as a senior prom, clambake or lynching.

babnride *n.* Colloquial contraction/elision of the words "kebab" and "taxi-ride", used when referring to certain late-opening establishments where food and a cab may be simultaneously requisitioned. *'And that completes the shipping forecast. Ace, that's me finished for the night. I'm off for a babnride at the Trojan takeout.'*

babooning *n.* In *dogging* circles, inadvertently breaking the windscreen wipers off a car while engaging in vigorous sexual congress across the bonnet. Also known as *doing a Whipsnade.*

baby birding *n.* In the world of *grumbular* cinematography, the jostling of two or more *stick vid* starlets who are hungry to get a mouthful of the same tasty *worm.*

baby drowners *n.* Unfeasibly humungous *assets* that could prove hazardous to a neonate.

baby eating a Twix, arse like a *sim.* Descriptive of one who leaves something to be desired in the *back body* hygiene department.

baby gap *n.* A vagina. Also *Barbie gap, Toblerone tunnel, Cumberland gap, Foyston gap.*

baby gerbil pictures *euph.* Extreme close-up photographs of a woman's *parts of shame* that are fuzzy and predominantly pink.

baby gravy *n. Spaff, speff, spongle, spungle, spangle, heir gel. 'Would you care for a splash of baby gravy on your pie, Mother Superior?'*

baby parrot's hatching, the *exclam.* Warning that the *turtle's head* is crowning. *'It's lovely to bump into you, vicar, but the baby parrot's hatching and I really have to run."*

baby's arm *n.* Boastfully descriptive of a substantial *kindling limb, ie.* One that is a good ten inches long with a bend in the middle. Sometimes covered in jam and usually "holding an apple".

baby's dinners *n.* Assets, air bags, norks.

baby-sham *n.* The weedy ejaculate of a vasectomy victim. *Decaff spaff.*

baby shower *1. n.* Some sort of party they have in American sitcoms, during which pregnant women are given gifts and childless, needy thirty-something characters played by actresses like Courtney Cox get all broody. *2. n.* The act of splashing *bairn brine* onto an accommodating ladyfriend.

baby stingray *sim.* A term used to describe the *downstairs accoutrements* of a woman with disproportionately extensive *Keith Burtons. 'For fuck's sake Camilla, it looks like a baby stingray when you pull them apart like that.'*

baby, tramp's *n.* A large bottle of white cider nursed tenderly in the crook of a *professional outdoorsman's* arm as he reclines in the *Scotsman's lounge.*

bacardi bruiser *n.* An inebriated lady who elects to fight rather than to cry.

bacardigan *n.* Tart *fuel* version of the *beer coat. 'Are you sure you'll be warm enough walking along Whitley Bay seafront during a blizzard in November wearing just those skimpy Kylie shorts and a spangly boob tube, nan?' 'Oh yes. I don't notice the cold when I've got me bacardigan on.'*

Bacardi geezer *n.* A bloke who quite inexplicably chooses *bint sauce* as his favourite tipple.

bacca *n.* Named in honour of the big *Star Wars* dog, a *"chewie"*, possibly accompanied by pained, throaty warbling.

Baccus Marsh *n. Aus.* A *dobber* or *lazy lob-on.* From the spongy area halfway between *Melbourne* and *Ballarat.*

baccy pouch *n.* An overgrown *mapatasi.* A *pant moustache, St. Bruno.*

Bach *n.* A female's *dropped hat,* named in honour of the eponymous composer's most famous classical hit *Air on a G-String* out of of off of the Pure New Wool adverts. Which was actually Pachelbel's *Canon,* but all that stuff sounds the same.

bachelor camo *n.* The pungent, insect-attracting remnants of meals-gone-by that decorate the T-shirts and jeans of male singletons.

bachelor's arm *n. medic.* Temporary condition experienced following a quick bout of unexpected exercise. See also *Ennis elbow, student's elbow.*

bachelor's boomerang *n.* A rock-hard sock found under the bed or sofa cushion of one who is not in a steady relationship. *A midget's surfboard, Mother Shipton's sock* or *crunchie.*

bachelor's bostik *n.* Organic adhesive used on magazine pages and computer keyboards. Also *sement, jazz glue, Aphrodite's evostick, prick stick, man mastic, glunk, grotspangle.*

bachelor's collar *n.* Unbroken ring of *cheese* round the neck of the *bell end,* indicative of enforced sexual continence, poor genital hygiene, or most likely a combination of both. *Cliff's ruff.*

bachelor's goodnight kiss *n.* The touching, smooching sound of an uncircumcised *fiveskin* being squeezed clean after a pre-slumber *prong-throttle.*

bachelor's heft *n.* Involuntary tumescence experienced by a single fellow who isn't *getting any*. Not entirely dissimilar to *middle-aged heft*; which is involuntary tumescence experienced by a married man whose missus has "had enough of that sort of thing".

bachelor's lifestyle *euph.* A foetid, woe-filled *Playboy pad* piled high with empty pizza boxes, discarded lager cans and well-thumbed pornographic magazines, not to mention a lavatory that has been blocked with *bangers and mash* since shortly after the householder's last girlfriend left him, several years ago.

bachelor's newsletter *n.* A *tug pamphlet.*

back beauty *n.* A woman who appears to be attractive from behind, but when seen from the front is a bit of a horse. *Back beauties* form a staple joke in Benny Hill's humorous televisual oeuvre, whereby an apparently sexy *piece* in a discotheque would generally turn round and be Henry McGee or Bob Todd in a wig. Either that or they'd be Anna Dawson with a couple of teeth missing. *A backstabber, golden deceiver.*

backbench rebellion *n.* A rectal revolt, often experienced following a night at the Curry Capital, Bigg Market, Newcastle upon Tyne. *'I thought you said you were ready to leave.' 'Sorry love, I've just had an unexpected backbench rebellion. I might be another ten minutes.'*

backbone *n.* An excited *John Thomas* that makes its presence felt in the *bag for life's* lumbar region while spooning or during a Heimlich manoeuvre.

back brace *1. n. medic.* A *Meat Loaf's daughter* of such length, girth and consistency that, prior to its delivery, you are unable to bend or flex your spine and are forced to adopt a standing posture and facial expression reminiscent of an outraged Frankie Howerd. *2. n. medic.* Gentleman's orthopaedic device employed in order to ameliorate the debilitating effects of over-optimistically attempting a *thirty-four-and-a-halfer. 'Excuse me, do you have any back braces in stock?' 'I'll just go and have a look, Lord Archer.'*

back-burner *1. n.* Notional thing upon which plans are put in order to avoid ever having to do them. *2. n.* The inevitable result of a delicious hot curry. *'Will you be attending the ambassadorial reception this evening, your majesty?' 'No, I'll probably just*

have a few cans and a back-burner in front of the snooker.'

back catalogue *1. n.* A *bongo mag* for the more *dirt-box*-obsessed peruser. *2. n.* A list of people you have of had, or would like to have of had, *done up the dirtbox.* Also *A-list. 3. n.* Material which one has brought out before. And is still plastered all over the bowl of one's *chod bin* with loads of flies buzzing round it.

"Back Door" *n. prop.* Notional middle name of any female celebrity who might be deemed worthy of *getting her back doors smashed in, eg.* Kylie "Back Door" Minogue, the late Kathy "Back Door" Staff, or The "Back Door" Saturdays.

backdooral *n.* A type of unhygienic behaviour involving bottoms and mouths. *Around the world, rimming, nipsilingus, truffle hunting.*

backdoor arrangement *n. US.* A friendly and amicable exchange of goods between parties, especially one made via a *rear entrance.*

back door boogie *n.* The theme tune for *Pot Brown,* played by Russ Conway.

backdoor diplomacy *1. n.* The practice of clandestine or underhand negotiation in order to secure an international agreement. *2. n.* Clandestine negotiations, invariably underhand, to secure the agreement of a lady to let one *do her up the wrong 'un.*

backdoor pilot *1 n.* An episode of a current television show that serves to surreptitiously pitch a spin-off series, *eg.* The 1976 episode of *Bouquet of Barbed Wire* during which Prue heard a Swanee whistle in the attic, that spawned *Rentaghost. 2. n.* A *rear gunner.*

backdraft *1. n.* The sudden and disastrous ignition of superheated gases, a fire-fighting term made famous by the 1991 film of the same name. *2. n.* A dangerously high concentration of *carbon dibackside,* which renders the immediate vicinity bereft of breathable oxygen. *3. n.* The rousing fanfare that precedes a good *shit.* The *Bakerloo breeze.* See also *please stand clear from the platform edge, the next train to pass through this station is not scheduled to stop here.*

backeye *n.* The *brown eye, red eye* or *brass eye.* You know, the *jacksie.*

backfire *v.* A *blow on the ragman's trumpet* with sufficient volume to startle a police horse.

back forest gateau *n.* A well-baked *chocolate cake* from the *bum oven,* served up steaming on a pan of white porcelain with a Guinness glaze, following a good evening out. May be accompanied by cherries.

back garden *n.* That place, situated at the rear

of the premises, where the more vertiginously inclined horticulturalist may till the soil, sow his seed and keep a selection of rusty bicycles. The *podex* or *council gritter.*

back gwats *n.* See *back tits.* It's only another twenty-one definitions from here.

backhander *n.* A *gypsy's kiss* of such explosive ferocity that the unfortunate individual using the next *shark's mouth* can feel the sprayback on the back of their hand.

back it in here driver *exclam.* An order to a sexual partner to reverse onto one's *big rig.*

back lane bandit *n.* A local youth behind the wheel of a souped-down *chaviot* who knows the serpentine country roads along which you are travelling like the back of his hairy-palmed hand and therefore drives right up your *chuff.*

back one out *v.* To *reverse park your breakfast,* a tricky process which usually involves much looking over the shoulder, grunting and sweating.

back on solids *1. euph.* Descriptive of a woman who has recently been *drinking from the hairy goblet,* but who is now back eating *beef on the bone. 2. euph.* Descriptive of a *fan of musical theatre* who has taken a brief excursion into the world of heterosexual relations, but is now happily *puddle jumping* again.

back on 3s and 4s *adj. medic.* Assessment of one who has returned to a state of defecatory normality following a (possibly curry-induced) period of gastric upset. This is based on the Bristol Stool Form Scale, which doctors use to fit their patients' *Brads* into one of seven categories. 3 and 4 are considered healthy and normal.

backpacking *n.* Placing a folded-up sheet of toilet paper – also known as a *manpon* – into the *bum* crevice as a precaution against self befoulment following a heavy night on the pop.

back passage *n.* A rear exit and/or entrance at which tradesmen are wont to knock.

back pocket rocket *n.* A *turd* that shoots out of your *arse* at speed and disappears round the bend, leaving no trace whatsoever and making you wonder whether you actually did do a *crap* at all or if you just imagined the whole thing. A *ghost shit* or *poodini.*

back projection *1. n.* Crude special effects technique used in old movies and *Z-Cars. 2. n.* A powerful jet of hot *feeshus* that exits the *rusty sheriff's badge* like water from a fireman's hose.

back scuttle *1. v.* To *scuttle* from the back. *2. n.* A *scuttle* from the back. *3. n.* A crematorium furnace receptacle in which vertebrae are kept.

back seat driver *1. n.* Car passenger who offers useful advice and helpful tips to the driver. *2. n.* Gentleman who puts his *sixth gearstick* up someone else's *exhaust pipe.* A *botter* rather than a *bottee.*

backside disaster *1. n.* A bare radical skate/snowboarding trick performed on the lip of a gnarly half-pipe, whatever the fuck that's supposed to mean. *2. n.* The result of *gambling and losing.*

backsident *n.* A *follow-through* that comes as a complete shock to its progenitor. An unexpected *pitch invasion.*

backstabber *n.* A *stegular* woman who peforms the *witch's trick* on innocent men. A *back beauty* or *golden deceiver.*

backstage pass *1. n.* In the showbiz world, a token which allows one privileged access to the behind-the-scenes areas of a theatre or similar place of entertainment, usually obtained by *sucking off* a fat, bearded man in a Hawkwind T-shirt. *2. n.* Permission from the *bag for life* to *access all areas.*

backstop *1. n.* That place where a person's back reaches a stop and thus becomes their *ringpiece.* The *Blue Peter Italian sunken garden. 2. n.* The rear upper surface of the lavatory pan which – somewhat mysteriously – often seems to get *shat* on.

back teeth are floating, my *phr.* An expression of a person's urgent need to pass water. *'You couldn't point me towards the nearest gurgler, could you, Carson? Only I've had six cups of Earl Grey this morning and my back teeth are floating.'*

backter *rhym. slang.* A lady's *front bottom.* From back to front = cunt. *'Oi, Fatty. Careful near me backter with that champagne bottle.'*

back tits *n.* On the more pie-loving lady, the folds of fat which spill over the rear panels and fastenings of her brassiere, giving her the appearance of having *knockers* on her back. *Back gwats.*

back to bed Peppa! *exclam.* An amusing thing for a chap to say after *stepping on a duck.* Also *thank-you for the music; a bit more choke and she would have started; better an eviction than a bad tenant; ease springs.*

back to handcranking *phr.* Expressive of the unfortunate situation whereby a chap is forced to *fall back on his own resources. 'It's a terrible business. The missus is on life support after getting dragged into the works of that escalator at the Arndale Centre, so it's back to handcranking for me.'*

backwards burp *n.* Fart, air dump, tree monkey.

backwards compatible *1. adj.* In the world of computers, a term guaranteeing that one bit of equipment or software will work with another, older piece of equipment or software. Not that it will. *2. adj.* In the world of *anabatic geoponics*, prepared to be the wheelbarrow rather than the earthy chap pushing it from behind.

back wheels *n. Bollocks, balls. 'What a gob, your royal highness. You've even managed to get my back wheels in.'* (Peter Sellers overheard behind a hedge at Kensington Palace).

backwoodsman *1. n.* An unkempt, feral type with a Davy Crockett hat and a blunderbuss, who subsists on a diet of gophers. *2. n.* A *woodsman* with a natural bent towards the *exhibition position.*

backyard fireworks *n.* An exciting display of *rear end affection* after dark. *'I made her jump last night with some backyard fireworks.'*

backyard safari *1. n.* Four-episode wildlife series from 1981, hosted by late hirsute naturist David Bellamy. *2. n.* A spot of *anal.*

bacne *n. medic.* Dorsal pustules, spinal *zits. 'Excuse me, Lord Archer. Would you like me to scrub your bacne for you?' 'No thank you, Mr Big.'*

bacon bazooka *n. Pork sword, spam javelin, mutton musket.* Basically, take a type of meat and add some sort of weapon to it. The *chopper.*

bacon belt *n.* The perennially unstylish lardy spare tyre visible between the fashionable hipster jeans and modish crop top of a fat *bird. Muffin tops.*

bacon factory *n.* The feminine *pig bite.*

bacon mudguards *n.* The lateral escutcheons on a woman's *spam hatch.*

bacon powder *n.* Illicit, particulate condiment found in the cruets of media types. Also known as *showbiz sherbet, charlie, dickhead dust, Bolivian marching powder, Keith Richards' dandruff, sniff. 'The ambulance has just pulled up outside. Quick, hide the bacon powder.'*

bacon slicer *n.* A metaphorical dieting apparatus. *'Her off Emmerdale that was on Strictly, she could do with a go on the bacon slicer.'*

bacon spunk *n.* That hot white stuff that appears in the pan when you have a fry-up.

bacon strips *n.* Female external genitalia, presumably with the word 'DANISH' printed on in blue ink. The lapels on a *ragman's coat, bliffage.*

bactress *n.* A *scudflick* starlet who is typically photographed from the rear only. See also *STA.*

badass *1. adj. US.* A street term descriptive of the sort of splendid terpsichorean moves made by an accomplished dancer. *2. adj. US.* A street term descriptive of the excellence of a *motherfucker. 3. n. US.* Street term describing a *freckle* which is afflicted with *farmers.*

bad Blakey *n.* A face pulled, reminiscent of the erstwhile misanthropic *On the Buses* inspector,

when a rank *Judi Dench* hits the nostrils

bad blood *n.* The feeling of seething resentment felt by a bloke who has organised a romantic getaway only to find that his inamorata's *pussy* is devouring *cunt mice* at a rate of knots.

bad crisp, a *euph.* Cause of vomiting after a night out.

Bader's balance *n.* The semi-leaning, stiff-legged stance adopted by a *relaxing gentleman* as he approaches the successful climax of a *Hilary.*

Baders, the *v. medic.* Temporary legular paralysis brought on by sitting reading the *Autotrader* on the *chod bin* for an excessive time. A complaint named after the tin-legged World War II fighter pilot Sir Douglas Bader. Often accompanied by *Bombay birthmarks.*

badge *n.* One's coital colours. *'I went to Brian's house-warming party last night. Pinned my badge on his sister.'*

badger *n.* A *minge* you could pluck and make into shaving brushes.

badger baiting *n.* Deliberately tormenting one's better half while she's *up on blocks* by doing things that will cause her to go into a *blob strop, eg.* Leaving the *bog* seat up, placing a dirty cup on the floor, breathing too much.

badger gas *n.* Noxiously toxic fumes experienced while evacuating the *Simons* the morning after a surfeit of rough cider and *catbabs.*

badger loose *euph. RAF.* An Air Force issue *air biscuit. '"I say, Ginger," cautioned Biggles, sniffing the air. "Smells like number two engine is on fire." "No, that's me," confessed Algie. "I've just let a badger loose."'* (from *Biggles Follows Through*, by Capt. WE Johns).

badger's ballbag, face like a *sim.* Phrase used to describe something or someone not very attractive. *'I wouldn't say my wife's ugly, ladies and gentlemen, but when they were designing the Royal Wedding stamps, the Post Office accidentally printed a picture of a badger's ballbag on them instead of her portrait, and no-one noticed.'* (HRH the Prince of Wales addressing the Royal Institution of British Architects Annual Dinner at the Mansion House, 2005).

badger's drift *n.* The *smelly bridge, notcher* or *taint.*

badger the witness *v.* To *wank.* During a recess in court.

badly packed kebab *n.* An untidy *fadge* that only starts to look appetising after 10 pints. A *butcher's window, ripped sofa, stamped bat, smashed up plum pudding* or *full Turkish.*

badly rolled cigarette *euph.* An untidily hairy *biffer* stuffed into a pair of overly small, white *dunghampers. Loose baccy, Rhodes Boysons.*

bad plumber's mop, wetter than a *sim.* Said of a woman who is *dripping like an egg sandwich*, caused by either sexual activity or a shoe shop sale. Also *wetter than a cod's wetsuit, wetter than an otter's pocket, wetter than a fat bird's armpit, wetter than Meat Loaf's hankie, wetter than Lee Evans's suit, wetter than a turfer's knee, wetter than a window cleaner's cuff* or *wetter than Whitney Houston's last joint.*

bad thrower *n.* Not the marrying kind.

badunkadunk *n.* onomat. A big *arse*.

bag *n.* A rough *dollymop*.

bagbird *n.* An attractive young *bag lady*.

bag fee *1. n.* Excess charge levied on air travellers who wish to take heavy luggage on a flight. *2. n.* The price of a marriage licence. *3. n.* An unwanted bill wrought by a fellow's *happy sack, viz.* A divorce settlement or child support payment.

bag for life *1. n.* A revolutionary twenty-first century device for carrying your organic groceries out of the supermarket and hoisting them into the boot of your hybrid-powered Lexus 4x4; similar to an old-fashioned shopping bag but with the added advantage that it combats global warming, reverses El Ninos and thus prevents polar bear cubs from drowning in the Gulf Stream. *2. n.* What a gentleman receives after his wedding vows. The strange phenomenon of instantaneous female personality change that occurs the moment that matrimonial formalities are successfully completed. *3. n. rhym. slang.* The missus.

baggage boy *n.* The opposite of a *pillow biter*. A *backseat driver*.

baggage handler *n.* Unpleasantly sexist term for a fellow who is not too fussy about the quality of his *cockwash* arrangements. Also *dog handler* which, if anything, is even more unpleasantly sexist.

baggage handler's arm, cock like a *sim.* To have a *chafed chap* due to excessive *self discipline* or sexual intercourse. From the similarity to the injuries suffered by airport luggage operatives as they poke their forearms through the zips of partly opened suitcases feeling for cigarettes, booze, cameras, wallets, porn, ladies' underwear *etc.*

bagged salad breathe for a while, likes to let his *euph.* Said of a chap who *eats fancy cakes*.

bagging *v.* Discreet public lavatory *cottaging* technique involving one participant standing in a shopping bag to mislead any *tit-head* peering under the cubicle door looking for *botters*.

bagging area *n.* The dance floor of any club or bar whenceforth, at the end of the evening, a gentleman may find himself leaving with an "unexpected item".

Baghdad, she's been shot over more times than *sim.* Humorously said of a *plasterer's radio*.

bag it up *v.* To perform the preliminary preparations for a *posh wank* on one's *old fella*; that is to say, to don a *jubber ray* or *American tip*. *'Have you seen my dunkies, mother? I'm going to bag it up in plenty of time for Bridgerton.'*

bag ladies' period *sim.* A rhetorical measure of unpalatability. *'Don't buy Mrs Timpkin's home made jam, vicar. I've tasted nicer bag ladies' period.'*

bag of beef *n.* A capacious *butcher's dustbin* which is not suitable for vegetarians. See also *box of cow tongues, slack mabbut, hippo's mouth.*

bag of chips off the old block *euph.* Cruel and accurate descriptor of a daughter who is as adept at bending spacetime as was her mother before her.

bag of fertiliser *n.* The *scrotum*. Also *happy sack, raisin bag.*

bag of knickers *n.* Scampi fries. *'Two pints of Newton & Ridley's and a bag of knickers please, Mrs Turpin.'*

bag of Lego *euph.* Descriptive of the experience of intimacy with a lady devoid of womanly curves. *eg. 'Fuck me, I wouldn't fancy fucking that Kate Moss much. It would be like humping a bag of Lego.'*

bag of pennies *euph.* A faecal motion. *'I'd give it a few minutes if I was you, love. I've just dropped a bag of pennies in there.' 'Right you are, Bamber.'*

bag of slapped twats, ugly as a *sim.* Not conventionally attractive, facially inept. Descriptive of one who looks like *she's fallen off the bells at Notre Dame.*

bag of slugs *n.* A particularly slimy *mingepiece*. *'Jeeves answered on the first ring. "What-ho, old chap," I said. "Fish out those French letters from my dressing table, there's a fellow. I'm taking afternoon tea with the Duchess of Worcester and I've just got my fingers off her." "I should imagine, sir," replied the sage retainer, "it was not unlike inserting your hand in a bag of slugs."'* (from *I'm Coming, Jeeves!* by PG Wodehouse).

bag of spinach *n.* A *membrum virile* which, immediately upon being exposed to warmth and moisture, wilts dramatically. *'Come on, Terry. I'm dripping like a gravel lorry at the lights here.' 'Sorry June, I've got a bag of spinach again.'*

bagpeel *n. medic.* Condition suffered by men on hot days that is symptomised by the *ball bag* glueing itself to the inner thigh, necessitating awkward, Jack Douglas-style leg spasms to separate the two.

bagpipe *v.* To have armpit sex, or engage in an *Hawaiian muscle fuck.* See also *(take someone)* *under one's wing, huffle.*

bagpuss *n.* An old, fat, furry *cunt; a* saggy, old, cloth-like, red and white *fadge* that has a few whimsical stories to tell.

Bagshot *1. n.* A small commuter town in Surrey that is handy for the M3. *2. n.* An ejaculation that completely empties the scrotum *like a punched icing bag.*

bagsy *v. legal.* An assertion of claim upon something, based solely upon the legal precedent that the one who speaks first has primary rights of ownership. *'Right. Bagsy me the Sinai. Yous lot of had it since the Six Day War in 1967. It's not fair.'* (Anwar Sadat, Israeli-Egyptian Summit, 1978).

bahdumb bahdish *1. n. onomat.* The sound of a bored houseband drummer pointing the punchlines out to the studio audience during the host's opening monologue on an American chatshow. *2. n. onomat.* The sound of a *Sir Douglas Hurd* leaving your *nipsy* and momentarily later hitting the water in the *pan.*

bahookie *n.* Scots. Arse. *'Jings, crivens, paw! A've got a braw thistle stuck in ma bahookie.' 'Ah'm not yir paw, Jimmy. Ah'm yir husband.'*

BAIB/baib *acronym.* Notional accolade awarded by male office workers to the female colleague whom they consider to be in possession of the most aesthetically pleasing anterior elevation, shortly before they are all fired. Best Arse In Building.

baibhe *n.* Gaelic. A furfuraceous old *slapper.*

Bailey's comet *n.* The spectacular plume of sickly Irish cream liqueur arcing across the night sky out of the mouth of a young drinker.

Bailey's mouthwash *n.* Of a lady, to *horate* a gentleman friend with her gob full of ice cubes.

bailiff's banquet *n.* The assorted detritus that is found once a court-appointed official takes possession of a property, *eg.* An artificial Xmas tree, a pair of *shitted undercrackers,* a well-thumbed copy of the June 1985 *Reader's Wives Bums Special,* 20,000 cannabis plants *etc.*

bairn brine *n.* Baby gravy, population paste, heir gel.

bairn's sock, it's like trying to get a roll of carpet into a *sim.* A somewhat hyperbolic excuse for not wearing a *dunky.*

baked Alaska *1. n.* An improbably depraved act involving clingfilm, the freezer and a fresh-ly-baked *arse pudding. 2. n.* A steaming *dump* taken in an outside bog during a cold snap. Also *Arctic roll.*

bake off *n.* A game played by bored workmates in adjacent *crapper* cubicles, whereby they judge each others' steaming efforts.

bake one *v.* To not go for a *shit* when you really

ought to. *'How was Glastonbury, dear?' 'I'll tell you when I come out the shitter, mum. Only I've been baking one since last Wednesday'.*

Bakerloo breeze *1. n.* The pungent wind that precedes the London underground train moments before it exits the tunnel. *2. n.* The pungent *wind* that precedes the *cocoamotive* moments before it exits the *bonus tunnel.*

baker's ache *n. medic.* Chronic stomach cramps resulting from keeping an *arse cake* in one's *dirty oven* for too long. *'We had been digging through the hot sand day and night for almost a whole week before we finally reached the door of Tutankhamun's tomb. Amidst all the excitement, there had been no opportunity for me to attend to my most basic human needs and as a result I had the baker's ache something chronic. Putting aside my discomfort, with trembling hands I made a tiny breach in the upper left hand corner of the entrance. Widening the hole a little, I inserted the candle and peered in. At first I could see nothing, the hot air escaping from the chamber causing the candle to flicker. Presently, details of the room emerged slowly from the mist, strange animals, statues and gold – everywhere the glint of gold. Jesus though, I didn't half need a shit, I can tell you.'* (Howard Carter, November 26th 1922).

baker's impatience *n.* See *potter's wheel.*

Baker's scarf *n.* The crusty gathering of fluff, dander and *smeg* that collects under a chap's *fiveskin,* vaguely reminiscent of the substantial knitted tippet famously sported by the eponymous fourth Doctor.

Baker Street irregulars *1. n.* Team of Cockney urchin spies employed by Sherlock Holmes. *2. n.* Medical term for temporary *back body* problems suffered by a lady following a *last minute platform alteration* between Regent's Park and Marylebone.

bakes a light cake *euph.* Said of a chap who *likes to let his bagged salad breathe for a while. 'It's no good. I can't keep living this lie any longer. I'm going to just come out and say it. Mum, dad, I bake a light cake.'*

Bakewell *rhym. slang.* A *dropped hat.* From Bakewell tart = Exchange & Mart.

bald-headed hermit *n.* A long-winded way of saying *cock.* Also *bald man.*

bald man *n.* Kojak, Captain Picard, Spurt Reynolds *etc.* The penis, *old man, chap.*

bald man in a boat *1. n.* A lady's *clematis.* The *wail switch, bean bag, little red riding hood. 2. n.* A hairless fellow ensconced in a waterborne craft.

Baldwin, a *n.* A fellow who mistakenly believes he

is *firing blanks*. Derivation unknown.

baldy hof incha *n. Glasweg.* Literally "hairless half incher", a phrase much used when Celtic and Rangers fans convene to discuss Bobby Davro's penis.

Balham ballet *n.* The intricate, yet graceful movements of an inebriated tramp on any South London high street.

Balkans *n.* In British *Carry On* films, a vague euphemism for the testicles, *bollocks.* Also the *Urals*, the *Balearics.*

ball *1. v. US.* To *poke, nob* or *bang, esp.* a "chick". *2. n.* A singular *clockweight.*

ballacks *exclam.* Mild curse, named after the eponymous German football captain and Chelsea midfielder, who contrived to achieve runner-up status in three major footballing competitions within the space of a mere five weeks.

Ballarat *n. Aus.* A fully erect penis. See also *Lake Wendouree, Baccus Marsh. 'Are you ready yet Bruce?' 'Almost there, Sheila. I'm nearly at Ballarat.'*

ball bag *n.* Bag in which the *balls* are kept. The *nadsack, knackersack* or scrotum.

ball bags breakfast *1. phr.* A recent, unfortunate BBC news headline when Zoe Ball was announced as the new Radio 2 morning programme host. *2. phr. sim.* Used, albeit with an added apostrophe, when suffering a particularly dispiriting hangover. *'And how are you doing this morning, your holiness?' 'Fuck me. I feel like a ball bag's breakfast.'*

ballbearings in a condom *sim.* Descriptive of an older woman's saggy *knee shooters* while she's on top. *Dick tits.*

ball bumpers *n.* Cosmetically enhanced lips, as worn by Brian's late mum off *Coronation Street* and, less attractively, by former Homebase ad queen Leslie Ash.

ball buster *1. n.* Unpleasant neighbour who puts a garden fork through your football when you kick it over the fence. *2. n.* A sexually aggressive female who puts a garden fork through your *scrotum.* A *cock chomper.*

ball butter *n.* Rich, cheesy spread produced by giving one's *man milk* a good old churn.

ball control *1. n.* In football, skillful footwork in the style of Lionel Messi, Eden Hazard or Danny Mills. *2. n.* A gent's ability to withhold his *seed* and delay his *pop shot. 'Say what you like about George Best, he had great ball control.'*

ballcuzzi *n.* An improvised whirlpool bath for the *pods*, apparently consisting of a teapot filled with warm (not boiling) water, to which bath oil and/or salts are added. The gentleman then lowers his *chicken skin handbag* into the water

while his partner blows gently down the spout to create a swirl of soothing bubbles. That could work, but probably best not try it in the café at Wetherby Services.

ballet, the *euph.* Where the wife assures you she's going when, in fact, she's off to watch a ropey Chippendales knock-off in some bar, where she intends to tug an oily *tassel* or two while screeching herself hoarse while drinking Lambrini.

ballfro *n.* A cool 70s-style halo of hair around the *happy sack.*

ball glaze *n. medic.* The clear, colourless solution secreted by the *clockweights* which gives the *tadpoles* something to swim in. Also *guardsman's gloss, perseverance soup, dew on the lily.*

ballistics *n.* The science of *jizzbolts.*

balloon animal boobs *n.* Amusing, squeaky, odd-shaped breasts.

balloon knot *n. Ringpiece, chocolate starfish, Dot Cotton's mouth.* A puckered *gazoo.*

balloon technician *n. medic.* A cosmetic surgeon; one who adjusts the amount of air in women's *cans.*

ballpaper *n.* Tissue used to catch *jizz* after one has *stroked the parsnip.*

ballpaper paste *n.* Viscous glue which causes *ballpaper* to adhere firmly to the carpet.

ballroom clitz *n.* A bulbous, *vajazzled vajayjay* that looks not unlike a glitterball in a 1970s discotheque.

ballroom dancing *n.* A quick knees-bent jig done by a chap to free up his *clockweights. 'You alright there, Anton? You look a bit uncomfortable.' 'Just doing a spot of ballroom dancing, Tess.'*

ballrooms *rhym. slang.* Diarrhoea. From the Sweet song Ballroom Blitz = the Brads. *'Over to you Esther.' 'Actually Cyril, can you do the next bit with the potato that looks like a cock as well? Only I've got the ballrooms.'*

balls *1. n.* The miniature, spherical *spunk* factories a gentleman keeps in his *chicken skin handbag. 2. n.* Courage, guts, spunk. *'I like him. He's got balls.' 3. exclam.* Denial. *'Has he balls got balls!' 4. exclam.* Rubbish, nonsense, poppycock. *'Balls! Of course he's got balls.' 5. n.* Round things you play football with. *6. n.* Grand dance parties. *'Excited ingenue who has been invited to a fancy society event, addressing the host: Oh, Lord Ponsonby! I do so love your splendid balls! Lady Ponsonby (who has inadvertently overheard this unfortunate double entendre): Fucking cheeky slag. Madam's long-suffering maid (holding her by the shoulders): Leave it, your ladyship. She's not worth it.'* (cartoon by George du Maurier, Punch,* 1888).

ballsackmic vinegar *n.* The final, toe-curlingly good dressing added by an eager cook to *culturally* *unique national treasure* Piers Morgan's chips. *Chef's special sauce.* Also *ballsackmic dressing.*

balls applause *n.* The self-congratulatory clapping sound that often coincides with an impressively athletic display of *knackrobatics.*

balls deep *adj.* Of a *pork sword,* buried up to the hilt. The maximum *length* which it is possible to *slip* someone. In a *sausage and doughnut situation,* the greatest extent to which the *sausage* can *fuck* the *doughnut. In up to the apricots, in up to the maker's nameplate etc.* In Jack Straw's case, that's about an inch-and-a-half in.

ballseye *exclam.* Director's cry of approbation heard on a pornographic film set when the featured male thespian (or *stunt cock*) manages to successfully *chuck his muck* directly into the eyeball of his lady co-star. *'Well done, Gunther. Ballseye!'*

ballshoop alley *n.* The *gooch, tintis, taint, notcher.*

balls like bats' wings *sim. medic.* Deflated, leathery testicles; a condition often accompanied by insanity, blindness and stunted growth. *Knackers* that have been *wanked* flat.

ball snorkel *n.* The male penis.

balls-on *adv.* Used primarily as the adverbial function of adjective modifier, usually in the superlative, *eg. 'My Porsche is balls-on fast.'* or *'Have you tried Red Bull? Man, that shit is balls-on!'*

ball soup, sitting in *euph.* A polite way of saying that someone has very *sweaty bollocks.* Also *~scrotum soup. 'By the end of his cross-examination at the hands of the Liaison Committee, Mr Sunak appeared to be sitting in about three pints of ball soup.'*

balls think my cock's been cut, my *phr.* Exclamation bemoaning a protracted period of celibacy. *'Look, your holiness, I've not had a wank since the fifties. My balls think my cock's been cut.' 'Tell me about it, Cliff. You're singing to the fucking choir here, mate.'*

ball swipe *n.* While *dogging,* the act of resting your *cods* on a fellow *dogger's* windscreen and requesting that they turn on their wipers at high speed to smack them from side to side while you *pleasure* yourself. It is, apparently, recommended that the *dogger* should receive a jet of cold screenwash every five minutes or so to soothe irritation. Also, keep the engine ticking over to prevent a flat battery.

ballsworth *n.* An imperial measurement of *spunk* volume, approximately half an ejaculation or one-fortieth of an *almond* avoirdupois.

ball tampering *1. n.* During a test match, an evil, despicable act performed by unscrupulous bowlers upon the seam of the ball which could well lead to the downfall of civilization. *2. n.* Evil, despicable

act performed upon the seam of your scrotum which could well lead to being placed on the sex offenders' register.

bally heck *exclam.* Wartime form of *bloody hell* used when swearing was rationed. Strong expletives and eggs were reserved for soldiers on the front line. *'SHORTY: Bally heck! A doodlbug's just blown Lavinia's head off. What rotten luck. FREDA: Never mind, eh? I'll put the kettle on and make us all a nice brew.'* (from the screenplay for *In Which We Serve,* 1944).

balm before the storm *n.* The clear seminal secretion that heralds, to the observant *merchant banker,* the imminent onset of a full-on *yoghurt drop. Pre-cum, ball glaze, knacker lacquer, knuckle varnish.*

Baloo *n. prop.* The most *well hung* man attending a mature orgy. The *king of the swingers.*

baloobas *n.* See *bazoomas.*

Balotelli's fireworks *n.* A particularly explosive burst of *tommy tits* that wrecks the bathroom.

Balrog wants his dinner *1. exclam.* Quote from the eponymous character as featured in the cult 1990s beat-em-up computer game *Street Fighter.* It says here. *2. exclam.* Humorous riposte to an abrupt, growling *anal announcement* that melds indignance with a wet sense of superiority.

balsa *n.* A semi-erect penis, resembling the soft texture of the popular model aeroplane construction material, the opposite of *hickory dick.*

bampot *n. Scots.* Survivor of the mental health system. A *mentalist, headbanger* or *heed-the-baall* who always sits next to you on the bus.

banal sex *n.* Pedestrian lovemaking in the *missionary position. 'Sorry love, I don't do banal.'*

banana *n. rhym. slang.* Hampshire rhyming slang for *feeshus.* From banana split = shit.

banana hammock *n.* A skimpy pair of *undercrackers* or swimming trunks. The male equivalent of *genital floss.*

banana steamer *1. n.* A speciality coffee-based beverage. *2. n.* A large, crescent-shaped and pungent *Sir Douglas.*

banana yoghurt *n.* Not particularly healthy breakfast alternative to *porridge,* to either swallow or spit according to personal preference. Rich in *Vitamin S.*

band aid *1. n. prop.* Charitable supergroup headed by Bob Geldof who raised lots of money with *Do They Know It's Christmas? 2. n.* Heightening pleasure by putting a rubber band* around your *clockweights* and *wanking yourself off.* Or, indeed, having it done to you by someone else in a generous act of charity. (*Interestingly, the same technique that farmers use to get sheep's tails to fall off).

B&B bungee jump *n.* During a torrid night of boarding house passion, an accident caused by the parting of two single beds at a crucial moment causing one of the participants to plunge to the floor, restrained only by an insecure, rubbery connection in the crotch area. *'Andrew Flintoff has withdrawn from the third Test against Pakistan at Edgbaston after suffering a groin strain in a B&B bungee jump accident at a guest house in Ramsbottom. A local woman is in Intensive Care.'*

bandit bandits *n.* Universally despised, friendless individuals who goal-hang near pub fruit machines waiting for an opportunity to step in and win the jackpot.

B&Q *n.* A hurried act of furtive intercourse enjoyed in the spare room of one's girlfriend's parents' house. A *B&Q* is performed with a sock inserted in the lady's mouth, with a view to maintaining radio silence during the entire sorry, sordid business. From Brief and Quiet.

bandsome *adj.* Said of an aesthetically ill-favoured fellow who is rendered inexplicably attractive by his proximity to a microphone, electric guitar *etc.* *'Eeh, that Mick Hucknall's a bandsome devil, isn't he?'*

B&T *abbrev.* Cheap thrills which may be taken with a slice of lemon. *Bum* and *Tit.*

bandy *adj.* Of a female, to have a bit of a *froth on.* *'That Issey Miyake after-shave stinks like shite, but it knocks the birds bandy, I can tell you.'*

bang *v.* To copulate like a *shithouse* door in the wind.

bang a nail in that *exclam.* Said of a *dropped gut* so thick that it could be affixed to the wall of a suitably robust structure.

bang! and the dirt is gone! *exclam.* What Barry Scott shouts when he done a *ghost shit* on the toilet.

bangaroo *n.* A *scuttle* exhibiting an elevated coefficient of restitution. A bouncy *spaceclopper.*

banger hangar *n. Sausage wallet, cock wash.*

bangers *1. n.* Things you probably shouldn't stick up cats' *arses.* *2. n.* Good, old-fashioned *Carry On*-style *milkers.* *3. n.* Old cars. Which also probably shouldn't be stuck up cats' *arses.*

bangers and gash *n.* A filling portion of *tits* and *fanny* with all *baby gravy* on them.

bangers and mash *1. n.* The flushed heaps of half-dissolved bumwad, human excrement, used *fanny nannies* and what-have-you which are often to be seen adorning the tracks at railway stations. Not, as a passenger, that you get the impression anyone has ever managed to successfully flush a train toilet. *Rat's banquets, Radcliffe's sleepers.* *2. n.* The contents of a well-used but badly flushed *bog,* the *bangers* being the *turds* and the mash being the *bumwad.* Usually found in the public conveniences of pubs, campsites and non-stop coaches to Spain. *'"Cinders and ashes, Thomas, your coaches are a disgrace!" cried the Fat Controller. "There are used tickets on the floor, there's soot all over the windows, and Clarabelle's cludgy is full of bangers and mash."'* (from *Thomas and the Dyno-Rod Man* by Rev. W Awdrey).

banging on the big bass drum *n.* The act of *shagging* a fat *bird* from behind while lustily slapping her *arse* in a playful manner in the style of a circus parade percussionist parading down the high street.

banging the cutlery drawer, like *sim.* A delightful trope describing sexual intercourse with an unacceptably scrawny woman, with all her knobbly knees, sharp elbows and jutting hips and that.

Bangkok handbag *n.* Dubious hotel-wardrobe-based solitary sexual practice enjoyed by many now-deceased celebrities.

Bangkok 2am rule *n.* Unwritten legal statute that anything that happens in the family-friendly Thai holiday resort after two in the morning doesn't count. Also *Wanchai goggles, Blok M fever.* *'Was that a ladyboy you ended up with last night, then, grandad?' 'Yeah, but I was completely rat-arsed, so I invoked the Bangkok 2am rule.'*

Bangladeshi bagpipes *n.* Distressingly discordant *wind* instruments played in curry house *crappers* throughout the land. Also *Bombay bagpipes, dhansakbutt.*

bangles *1. n.* All-female pop group of the 1980s or thereabouts, fronted by Susanna Hoffs. Ah … Susanna Hoffs. *2. n.* Particularly delicate parts of the *crown jewels.* The *orbs,* rather than the *sceptre.* *'Ooh, doctor. I've caught me bangles on some barbed wire.'*

bangover *1. n.* The post-*piss-up* headache that, temporarily vanquished by the *act of love,* returns with all its mates at the moment of *stackblow.* *2. n.* Those morning feelings of sluggishness, listlessness and lethargy induced by an over-exuberant bout of *horizontal jogging* (that's *fucking a lady* up the *cunt*) the night before.

banjo *1. n. US.* Musical instrument played by inbreds in the American deep south, that makes a tinny, twanging sound when plucked. *2. n.* The thin ridge of skin on the penis connecting *Kojak's roll-neck* to the *bobby's helmet,* that makes a tinny, twanging sound when plucked. The *guy-rope*.

banjo bolt *1. n.* A perforated hollow fitting used for pressurised fluid transfer, commonly found in automotive fuel, oil and hydraulic systems. We knew that, by the way. We didn't look it up. *2. n.* A great big stainless steel self-tapper knocked through a gentleman's *membrum virile*.

banjo cleaner *n.* Of female dentition, that gap between the two upper front incisors which effectively scrapes detritus from a chap's *banjo* during *horatio*. At one time, Guy Ritchie was renowned for having one of the cleanest *banjos* in showbusiness.

banjoed *adj.* Of the late Oliver Reed, nearly drunk enough to go on Michael Aspel's chatshow and sing a song. *Pissed-up, wankered, arseholed, shitfaced, rat-arsed.*

banjo pie *n.* Any food product whereby the first bite causes debris to fall down your front, so you hold it at a safe distance while brushing pastry crumbs from your shirt front with a rapid strumming motion.

banjo pills *n. medic.* Viagra. *Cock drops, mycoxafloppin.* Also *blueys, pork pills, Bongo Bill's banjo pills.*

bank *exclam.* Monosyllabic ejaculation enunciated in best *Weakest Link style* when a bloke spots an attractive lady and wishes to store the image in his *mammary banks* for later use. Also *file under W.*

banker *1. n.* The unseen producer of *Deal or No Deal*, who talks to Stephen Mulhern via an old-fashioned telephone. *2. n.* A lady, espied upon entry to a nightclub, who a chap thinks will be a certainty should all other attempts to *pull* fail.

banker's draught *n.* Eminently civilised flatulence emitted from the *aniii* of pinstriped city gents. Also *dropped bowler hat.*

bank holiday weekend, wetter than a *sim.* An impressively *batterlogged* state of feminine arousal. See also *wetter than a window cleaner's cuff, as wet as Dermot O'Leary's shirt, wetter than a cod's wetsuit, wetter than an otter's pocket, wetter than a fat bird's armpit, wetter than Meat Loaf's hankie, as wet as Rod Hull's roof, wetter than Lee Evans's suit, as wet as a snail's doorstep, wetter than a turfer's knee* or *wetter than Whitney Houston's last joint.*

banking engine *1. n.* An additional rear locomotive that helps push a train up a steep incline. *2. n.* In a *bumming conga* or *human shuntipede*, the final link who brings up the rear. The *anchor man* or *caboose.*

bank of chance *n.* Bookmakers.

bannistered *adj.* To be in a state of extreme *refreshment*, to the extent that one has to be carried home by two friends. Derived from the state that record-breaking athlete Roger Bannister got himself into after crossing the finish line after running the world's first sub-four-minute mile.

bannocks *1. n.* Unappetising Scottish bread buns. *2. n.* Unappetising Scottish *knackers*. *3. exclam.* Expression of anger or frustration. *'Aw Bannocks! A've just dropped a fuckin' ha'penny doon the drain. Bang goes oor dinner, children.'* (cartoon by Phil May, *Punch*, 1896).

banshee *n.* A terrifying, wailing act of flatulence with Steve Severin on bass and Budgie on the drums.

BANT/bant *acronym.* Big Arse No Tits.

banty *n.* One who nods at *stoats*.

bapdog *n.* An ugly *bird* with a cracking pair of *tits, ie.* One who has *hefferlumps.*

bap happy *adj.* The stunned, bemused mental state that one enters having overdosed on *meat vids, bongo mags* or broadband internet *grumble.*

bapjism *n.* The very first *pearl necklace* that a young lady receives.

bappuccino *n.* A cup of coffee made using the frothy contents of a lactating lady's *milk jugs.*

baps *1. n.* Soft bread rolls that you could stick a sausage in. *2. n.* Tits with a similar aptitude.

BAPS/baps *acronym.* Bollocks And Pits. *'I only had time for a quick shower so I just washed my baps.'*

bapset *n.* A lady's matching underwear outfit. A useful term for those who are unsure of the correct pronunciation of the word "lingerie". *'I like your bapset, Dita. Get that in Matalan, did you?'*

baptising Mr Brown *n.* Repeated futile attempts to flush away a particularly recalcitrant *arse baby* that shows no signs of budging.

baptism *1. n. Chestular rope-lobbing.* The act of sprinkling *holy water* across a pair of heavenly *bazongers*. *2. n.* Psychological term for a defining stage in the development of a chap's *headlamp* fixation. *'Patient Z first developed his taste for large breasts during lactation, and has thenceforth gained excitation throughout his life from both seeing, sucking and fondling large breasts. I call this moment his 'baptism' as a bubby man or bap-fancier.'* (from *Das Psykologikken Geprinkipelschaft auf den Stonkenjubblies* by Sigmund Freud).

baptop *n.* A portable computing device maintained for the purpose of accessing the *bapternet*. Also *filth machine, faptop, dirty mac, porn pump, flaptop, cumputer. 'I'm just popping into town to get my baptop fixed, luv.' 'Okay Gary. See you in about thirty years.'*

Barack Obamas *n. prop. rhym. slang.* Haemorrhoids. From Barack Obamas = farmers. *'Ooh,*

I'll tell you what. These bleeding Barack Obamas aren't half giving me some gyp this morning, I can tell you. And now here's Carol Kirkwood with what the weather's got in store for us today.'

barbecue alone *v.* To engage in a solitary bout of *meat manipulation* while drinking lager in the garden.

barbecue sauce *n.* Cheap, yet strangely potent, bottled lager swilled down by the man of the house in order to keep cool when bending over a tray of blazing charcoal lumps in the back yard, while wearing a humorous apron with a cartoon drawing of *tits* on it. *'Ooh, me guts are rotten this morning, love. I don't know whether it's all them half-cremated, half-frozen chicken thighs and raw sausages I ate last night or the twenty bottles of barbecue sauce I necked while I was cooking them.'*

barbepoo *n.* The unmistakeable *foulage* that results from the standard British summer *al fresco* diet of charred, half-cooked half-frozen sausages, ketchup, and lager, consumed while experiencing the early stages of drizzle-induced hypothermia.

barber of Savile *n.* A gents' hairdresser who typically purveys the sort of *sex case* coiffures favoured by *philanrapists*, trainspotters and 1970s television personalities.

barber's bin *n.* A particularly badly kempt and unruly *snatch*. A *pieman's wig*. *'I'm sorry but I'm not doing that again, Germaine. It was like sticking my head in a barber's bin.'*

Barber's Bridge *1. n.* A small town in Gloucestershire that was the site of the first intermediate station north of Gloucester on the old Ledbury & Gloucester Railway, as is well known. *2. n.* The small tuft of hair left on a lady's nethers after a *Brazilian* wax.

barber's floor *n.* An exceptionally hairy *quim*, with a glum, sixteen-year-old on the minimum wage disinterestedly pushing a brush round it. Yeah, *dis*interestedly. So what?

barber's lather pot *sim.* A generously filled *snatch*. Also a *billposter's bucket, St. Bernard's chin*. A very, very, very *well-buttered bun*. *'My daughter is a groupie for So Solid Crew.' 'Good heavens, vicar! She must have a twat like a barber's lather pot.'*

barber's lolly *1. n.* In childhood, a reward given for sitting still while one's hair is cut. *2. n.* In adulthood, a reward given in return for performing any unpleasant task. *'Suck that? Alright, but you'll have to buy me an expensive barber's lolly afterwards, Mr Hefner.'*

barber's pole *1. n.* The stripy result of *parting the whiskers* while the *painters are in*. An *eggy soldier*. *2. n.* Tricky male masturbatory technique entailing

a helical clockwise twist on the upstroke.

barber's sandwich *n.* A badly pruned *muff*, from its resemblance to a buttered bap inadvertently dropped onto the unswept lino in a hairdresser's.

Barbie gap *n.* The alluring aperture between the tops of a woman's legs. Also *Toblerone tunnel, Cumberland gap, Foyston gap*.

Barbie's dildo, a knob like *sim.* Descriptive of an individual who is *hung like a Chinese mouse*. Also *bookie's pencil, Argos biro. 'You may be the former Justice Secretary and a member of the Privy Council, Jack. But you've still got a knob like Barbie's dildo.'*

Barbie's minge *sim.* Something with a particularly difficult or troublesome mode of entry. *'Gentlemen, make no mistake. The castle will be heavily guarded. I warn you now, it will be like getting into Barbie's minge.'*

Barclays *rhym. slang.* A *J. Arthur.* From Barclays Bank = ham shank.

Barclays premier league *n.* Notional society of top-ranking, record-breakingly prolific masturbators. *'He's Barclays premier league material, he is. No wonder the BBC used to pay him six million quid a year.'*

bare-arsed boxing *n.* The s*xual act.

barely got the smell off one's fingers *phr.* Said of a chap who moves swiftly from one ladyfriend to the next. *'Rolling Stone Ronnie Wood certainly wasn't allowing the moss to gather under his feet last night as he stepped out with new Brazilian supermodel girlfriend Macarena Parasol, 20, just days after being dumped by his previous girlfriend, Brazilian supermodel Copacabana Maracas, 21. A close pal of the wrinkly rocker, 105, commented: "This is the real thing. Ronnie's head over heels about Macarena, even though he's barely got the smell off his fingers from Copacabana."'* (from *The Daily Mail*, every day).

bare that in mind, I'll *exclam.* Said by a cheeky chap when he espies an attractive lady about whom he intends to later fantasise *in the rik* while manually stimulating his penis.

barf *v.* See *bark at the ants*.

barf bag *n.* Sick bag, as found on an aeroplane. Also a useful alliterative insult.

barf, Turkish *n.* A *puked-up* doner-based delicacy that the pigeons can have a good wade around in the following morning.

bargain *rhym. slang.* A *cuntish* fellow. From the popular daytime TV show, *Bargain Hunt*, which was originally hosted by popular orange *bargain* David Dickinson, then by that spivvish *cunt* with a bow tie.

bargain bucket *1. n.* An over-employed and overstretched *clopper*. A *Mary* like a *welly top*. 2. *n.* What one may eat when over-*refreshed* at the *arse-end* of a night out. An unappetisingly large and greasy *fish supper* festooned *with batter bits*.

bargain cunt *n.* Upon purchasing a new item, for example a television set, ipod or washing machine, that acquaintace who always maintains that you should have come to him first as he could have got it for you for half what you just paid. However, when put to the test, the *bargain cunt* is invariably unable to obtain anything on the cheap because their "mate is away" or some such similar lie.

barge-arse *n.* A lady of rotund posterior aspect.

bargoyles *n.* Hideously ugly female pub fixtures.

bargument *n.* Like a normal argument but with added drink and the threat of glassing.

bariatric buggy *n.* Chariot of choice for the *big-boned* when trundling to the shops for pasties, pies and diet pop. A *council go-kart*.

baristard *1. n.* A coffee snob who believes he can brew up a better macchiato in his £19.99 Argos filter machine than the tax-averse professionals can. *2. n.* A barista who looks down his nose when you ask for just a cup of normal coffee.

bark at the ants *v.* See *barf.*

bark carrots *adj.* See *bark at the ants.*

barker's egg *1. n.* Any *hound cable,* and especially *2.n.* A poodle *shite*. Canine *foulage* so old that it has gone white and crumbly, like a log of fancy cheese at a 5-star eaterie.

barker's truffles *n.* Pedigree *dog eggs* of the type you might expect to step in on such rarefied thoroughfares as Mayfair or Pall Mall, but would rarely encounter on Botchergate in Carlisle.

barking spider *n.* The *ringpiece, freckle, chocolate starfish, rusty sheriff's badge, nipsy.*

bark is worse than its bite, its *exclam.* Said of a large and noisy *treacle tart* which, luckily, has no olfactory teeth to speak of.

barmageddon *n.* The least genteel drinking establishment in a charmingly earthy estate or town; typically a flat-roofed pub. A *hostilery* where one is likely to suffer serious injury for merely being there, *eg.* A certain pub in North Shields, which is affectionately known by its clientele as "The Flying Stool".

barmaid on her first shift, like a *sim.* Disparaging description of a sexually inexperienced lady clumsily attempting to furnish a gentleman with a *hand shandy*. See also *sink plunger, double dragback*. *'Fucking hell love, what are you doing down there? You're like a barmaid on her first shift.'*

bar medicine *n.* Self-prescribed treatment for a variety of chronic existential malaises.

barnacle *n.* An inconsiderate pub-goer who prevents others from replenishing their drinks by obstinately guarding his position at the bar all night, nursing a single pint of the cheapest lager available. From bar + nacle.

Barnacle's nosh box *1. n.* A world-famous £2.40 variety "meal deal" at the eponymous Stockton-on-Tees fish & chip shop. *2. n.* A manky *haddock pastie licked out* behind a Teesside fish & chip shop, for about £2.40 including *scranchions.*

Barnes Wallis *n.* A bouncing *tallboy* released from the *bomb bay* which sends a splash of water onto your *undercarriage*. A *panbuster, A for apple.*

Barney *1. n.* An instant *diamond cutter*. Named after the not-at-all-*Colwyn Bay* children's dinosaur that grows from something small and harmless into a large purple-headed monster in the blink of an eye. *2. n. prop. rhym. slang.* A *feeshus*. A reference to the famous Trumpton fire brigade roll call, intoned whenever they were called out to rescue the mayor's hat from up a tree, remove a tin of paint from the Town Hall clock or hose the remains of a suicide victim off the front of Lord Belborough's train. From Barney McGrew = poo. *3. n.* A *pagga.*

barney rubble *n.* That which, during the course of a good-natured exchange of political viewpoints, is torn up from pavements, walls *etc.*, and *hoyed* at the *tit-heads.*

Barney Rubble's car *n.* A pile of *logs*. *'Have you seen the potato masher anywhere? Barney Rubble's car's double-parked in the shitter.'*

Barnsley *n.* An unexpected *semi*. From the eponymous South Yorkshire football team's surprising performance in the 2008 FA Cup, when they made it into the final four. *'Eeh by gum. Yon forward defensive prod from young Ernie Sheepshanks were textbook, weren't it Geoffrey?' 'Aye, Dickie. It were that good I've got a Barnsley.'*

Barnsley bidet *n.* Cosmopolitan, European-style *nipsy* freshen-up technique whereby one remains seated while flushing the *bum sink.*

Barnsley blastmark *n.* Stain on an interior door caused by pressing one's naked buttocks against it so as to amplify its glorious resonance when *blowing off.*

Barnsley blow job *n.* During sexual congress in the *missionary position,* when the lady *drops a gut* with sufficient gusto to blast her suitor's *balls* up his *arsehole.*

Barnsley briefcase *n.* A Netto, Aldi or Kwiksave carrier bag carried into work each day by one who is employed as a professional call-centre operative in the salubrious South Riding metropolis. The typical contents of a *Barnsley briefcase* include a triangular, pre-packed sandwich, a bottle of Oasis, a copy of the *Sun* and a biro which pokes out the bottom of the bag. Not to be confused with a *Basingstoke briefcase*, which is a carrier from Waitrose, Sainsbury's or some other upper class establishment.

Barnsley caviar *n.* Mushy peas. Also *Geordie hummus, Scouse guacamole.*

Barnsley chops *1. n.* Type of lamb cutlets served to guests at the Brooklands Hotel in the glitzy Yorkshire resort. *2. n.* South Yorkshire *Keith Burtons* that look like Colin Welland's sideburns in *Kes.*

Barnsley moustache *n.* A tide mark of *fanny batter* resembling the facial hair sported by youths of the eponymous northern beauty spot. Caused by an accumulation of *blip* during vigorous *cumulonimbus.*

Barnsley reindeer *n.* The Toys R Us lorry.

Barnsley shag *n.* An act of sexual intercourse which climaxes not with an orgasm, but with the bloke falling asleep *on the job* due to a surfeit of Whitbread Trophy bitter.

Baroness Trumpington *1. n. prop.* Much-respected former Bletchley Park intelligence operative, agriculture minister and Mayor of Cambridge. *2. n.* A young lady with a tendency towards flatulence.

barrel fever *n. medic.* The *shakes*, whereby the first pint of the day has to be held with both hands to prevent spillage. See also *hatties.*

barren land, the *euph.* That special place between the *clockweights* and the *poopchute*, medically known as the perineum. So-called because because "nothing grows there and no one ever goes there". Also sometimes called the *memorable inch* because "if someone does take the time to tinker, you will remember them forever". See *barse.*

barren trump *n.* A useless *Exchange & Mart* that has no sound or smell and thus provides no satifaction or entertainment value whatsoever.

Barrington Road glitter *n. Northumb.* Horse *shite*. Also *road apples.*

Barry Gibb *n.* The *centre console* or *carse*. Because it used to be situated between a *cunt* and an *arsehole.*

barryjuana *n.* Bargain basement variety of cannabis, which comes in a browny-green lump containing additives such as rubber. Smoked in large quantities by the tracksuited inhabitants of Barry – the delightful South Wales beauty spot made famous in the television series *Gavin and Stacey.*

Barry Scott! *exclam.* A humorous rejoinder issued after either *passing wind*, doing a great big *shit*, or *blowing one's beans*. Named in honour of the erstwhile shouty Cillit Bang ad personality's inadvertently kitsch catchphrase "Bang! And the dirt is gone!".

barse *n.* The little bit of skin between a chap's *bannocks* and his *freckle*. The *great.*

barse broth *n.* One part *wet fart* and a generous portion of hot *wedding vegetables* mixed well in the *undercrackers* results in a family size helping of *barse broth*. Serve with or without croutons, according to taste.

barsed, can't be *euph.* Somewhere between not being *arsed* and not having the *balls* to do something. *'That big man just called me a slag, Rupert. If you were any sort of a man you'd defend my honour.' 'I'm sorry love, but I simply can't be barsed.'*

barseley *1. n. prop.* Small town in South Yorkshire. *2. n.* A perinaceous herb known for its powerful aroma; *taint hair* on the *garden bridge.*

barse mallow *n.* A light, pink, fluffy substance that forms spontaneously in a *salad dodger's tintis*. A sweet-toothed counterpart to the more savoury *arse feta.*

barsicle *n.* A *stalacshite.*

barsley sauce *n.* Arse vinegar.

bar stool *n.* An habitual drinker's *turd*, typically a thin, sickly *arse weasel* that slides out and lies forlornly in the water feeling very sorry for itself.

barter in the fish market *euph.* Of a lady, to *play the invisible banjo.*

Barthez *1. n.* Former Manchester United goalkeeper. *2. n.* A bald *twat.*

Bartlett's dilemma *n.* A gentleman's happy bedtime conundrum. From the scene in *The Great Escape* when Squadron Leader Bartlett (played by Richard Attenborough) has to decide which of the three tunnels to send his chaps down.

barumph *v.* To sniff a lady's bicycle seat. To *snurgle, shramp, quumf* etc.

BAs *n. rhym. slang.* The testicles. From the name of the aviophobic *A-Team* character played by Mr T (real name Mysterious Teapot) who, notwithstanding his fierce appearance, was famously compassionate towards the imbecilic, *viz.* Bosco "Bad Attitude" Baracus = knackers.

baseball shot *n.* A pornographic photo trope whereby the *catcher* uses two fingers to signal to the *pitcher* what to throw.

base pissing *n.* The extreme sport of urinating from a great height for the purporses of entertainment, *eg.* Off a cliff into the sea, off a bridge into a river, or out of a tree onto a cow.

bash *n.* The feminine *parts of shame.* *'That's it Sharon. Uncross your legs so we can get a quick flash of your bash.'*

bashful *adj.* Inclined towards *self-help.* *'I'm afraid Jonathan's not coming out to see you, vicar. He's feeling a bit bashful.'*

bashing booth *n.* A small room or cubicle where a gentleman may sit in quiet, solitary contemplation of a live *jazz* performance. With his trousers round his ankles and his stinking, red raw *chopper* in his hand. The working environs of a *jizz mopper.*

bash the bishop *v.* To *pull the Pope's cap off, box the Jesuit.* To *bank with Barclays.*

bash Wednesday *n.* An important annual event in the ecclesiastical calendar that is celebrated by all members of the clergy worldwide. On this special day, ecumenical matters are put to one side, affording the cleric in question time alone in the vestry to contemplate the ineffable mysteries of creation while quaffing large quantities of communion wine and *spilling his seed* upon the stony ground. And possibly the curtains too.

Basil *n. rhym. slang.* A lady's *Kate.* From TV fox puppet Basil Brush = bush. A *front garden* with a delicious herbal aroma.

Basildon bagpipe *n.* An Essex-based development of the *trombone,* whereby the lady sucks the gentleman's *clockweights* while *tossing* his *Charlie* with one hand and fingering his *freckle* with the other, causing him to emit a series of shrill squeaks and an unpleasant droning sound.

Basildon bidet *n.* A cold, wet smacker on the *trumpeter's lips* that fortuitously obviates the need for wiping. *Neptune's kiss.*

Basildon Brazilian *n.* An economical bikini wax technique espoused by local maidens intending to vacation in sunnier climes, which involves a box of Tesco Chablis, a wooden tent peg to bite on and a roll of duct tape.

Basildon water feature *n.* A skip half-full of rusty water.

basket making *v. arch.* Medieval sexual intercourse. *Coccupational therapy.*

bass cleft *n.* The *arse crack, carpet fitter's smile, bumline* or *home baking aisle.*

bastard *n.* A football referee.

BAST/bast *acronym.* Big Arse Small Tits.

baste *v.* Of a professional sportsman, to pull out mid-*roast* and *toss* hot *man fat* onto a *bird*'s back.

baste the turkey *v.* To squeeze men's *bulbs* so that hot *baby gravy* shoots out the end of their *cocks.*

bateau mouche *n. Fr.* A *dreadnought* that is so

satisfyingly large one could easily imagine it being used to to take tourists along the Seine. A *pleasure steamer.*

bath bomb *1. n.* A ball of effervescent salts which fizzes when dropped into the water. *2. n.* An unfortunately timed *evacuation* which can quite take the shine off an otherwise pleasant soak in the tub.

bath jack *n.* In the tub, putting a clenched fist at the bottom of the spine to allow a discreet chap to *wax the dolphin* without making splashes.

bath merkin *n.* The tangled cake of *pubes, arsecress,* muck and other assorted gribbly bits of effluvium that gathers in the plughole and could, in extreme and frankly implausible circumstances, be pressed into service as an *ersatz* pubic wig.

bathroom broadband *n.* The installation of a lengthy and unsightly dark brown or black *cable* in the bottom of the toilet bowl. A substantial *download* that is certainly not *superfast.*

bathroom nutmeg *n.* During a *sit-down lavatory adventure,* the unfortunate practice of unknowingly *wazzing* through the gap between the seat and the porcelain, thus creating an awful mess on the floor that must be surreptitiously and swiftly cleared away.

bathroom origami *n.* The ancient and beautiful oriental art of folding a single sheet of *bumwad* into complex geometric folds, pleats and creases in order to avoid getting all *shit* on one's fingers.

bathturbate *v.* To *polish the lighthouse,* play *up periscope.* To masturbate in the bath. Derivation unknown.

bat in the cave *n.* A precariously suspended *bogie* that hangs upsettingly in someone's nostril. *'I'm sorry, your royal highness, but before we start the interview I thought I'd mention that you've got a bat in the cave there.' 'Thanks Emily, that could have been embarrassing.'*

batmanning *1. n.* In the world of rock-climbing, cheating by using the belay rope to hoist oneself up. It says here. *2. n.* Super-heroic act performed by those returning home from the pub, *ie.* Crawling along on all fours in a manner reminiscent of the not-very-special effect used to make Adam West and Burt Ward appear to scale a vertical wall in the quasi-eponymous television series of the 1960s.

Batman on the side of the Palace, like *sim.* Descriptive of something which sticks out a mile, such as Sharron Davies's terrific *chapel hat pegs* during the Athens 2004 Olympic coverage.

Batman's bomb *n.* When *caught short* while out and about, an explosive *bum grenade* that is disposed of safely just in the nick of time. *'I'll be a bit late getting to you, only I had to stop off at the services and drop Batman's bomb.'*

Batman's cave *euph.* A lady's *secret entrance* which is difficult to locate due to an over-abundance of *bush.*

Batman's parents, feel like *v.* To experience an uncomfortable sensation of impending doom while travelling on foot through a rough part of town in a state of overdress, *eg.* Wearing a coat or socks in Newcastle.

batmobile, arse like the back end of the *sim.* Descriptive of the state of one's *brass eye* after a particularly hot *Ruby Murray.* *'I had a real ring stinger at the Curry Capital last night. My arse is like the back end of the fucking batmobile this morning. Five stars.'* (*Guardian* food critic Victor Lewis-Smith, 2005).

bat on a sticky wicket *v.* To be the second man to the *crease*; to *stir* another's *porridge*; partake of a *buttered bun* or have *sloppy seconds.* Also *bat on a wet wicket.*

baton rouge *n.* After a visit to the *deep south* when the *levees have broken*, the resultant state of one's *Dr John.* A step further than *gypsy week*, but probably not as extreme as a *scrapheap challenge.* *Barber's pole, vampire wick end, blood sausage.*

baton twirler *1. n.* A performer, such as a majorette, who twirls a short, decorative wand or staff, using manual techniques such as the thumb toss and the elbow roll. *2. n.* A *rub-a-tug shop* employee, *tossteopath.* *3. n.* A keen devotee of *monomanual self-improvement.*

bats at dusk, to come out like *sim.* Of loose *stools*, to exit the *clay pit* at a ferocious rate. Descriptive of a *flock of pigeons, fall of shoes from the loft* or the *splatters.*

bat signal *1. n.* A warning of imminent *evil-doings* that calls for immediate action. *'Excuse me, Mrs Turpin. I'm afraid you'll have to bury him yourself, only I've just had the bat signal.'* *2. n.* The picture of the mother or mother-in-law that appears on your mobile phone that alerts you to carefully put it down in case you answer it by mistake.

batter catcher *n.* That small tuft of hair tucked under the bottom lip, which enables its owner to trap some of that pungent *clam chowder* for later. *'And would you like your batter catcher trimmed as well, Sir Trevor?'*

battered kipper *n.* A frothsome *gash* on your old *trout.* A *blippy mackerel* that makes a nice *fish supper* for a *lip-licking gashtronome* with a healthy *flappetite.*

Battersea hand warmer *n.* A freshly-scooped *dog dirt* in a bag; a useful alternative energy device allowing a *shit machine* walker to keep his mitts nice and toasty on the coldest of mornings. *"My dear Watson,"* expostulated the great detective. *"Have you not noticed? Rarely do we observe the owner of a St. Bernard wearing gloves in this chilly weather."'* (from *The Hound Rope of the Baskervilles* by Sir Arthur Conan Doyle).

battery flattener *n.* A confirmed spinster's prolonged and ultimately unsuccessful session on the *neck massager.*

battery horse *n.* An exceptionally powerful *fanny hammer* that goes through PP3s like there's no tomorrow.

battery tits *n.* Affectionate epithet for a *bird* with *knockers like two aspirins on an ironing board.* From the tiny battery and comedy bra size AA. See *FA cups.*

batting for both sides *euph.* Bowling from both *ends*, as opposed to just the *gasworks end.*

batting for Darrington *euph. Good with colours.* From Ambridge's perennial opponents in the Whit Monday Single Wicket Competition for the Mark Hebden Memorial Trophy in *The Archers.* *'Your Freddie still not got himself a nice girlfriend, then, Mrs Mercury?' 'No, he's batting for Darrington these days, Mrs May.'*

battle cry *n.* A loud and stirring *rumpet voluntary*, signalling a declaration of war against a particularly troublesome *Thora.*

battleship rivets *n.* Stupendous iron-rich nipples. *Chapel hat pegs, JCB starter buttons, blind cobblers' thumbs.*

battleships, just like playing *sim.* Trying to engage genitals with a lardsome *piabetic*, whereby they repeatedly update you regarding your lack of progress by saying: "Missed... Missed... Missed...".

battleshits *1. n.* Large *dreadnoughts* that create a menacing blockade, and thus prevent the passage of any further ocean-going *steamers.* *2. n.* A decibel-based competition against an anonymous foe ensconced in the next cubicle.

batty-boy *n. W. Indies.* A *tail-ender.*

batty-crease *n.* The line of whiting or chalk on a cricket pitch which defines the position of the batter.

batulence *n.* Extremely high-pitched *farting*, which only creatures of the order *Chiroptra* are able to hear. Also known as *Galton's whistle*, named after the ultra high-pitched device used by dog football referees on *That's Life.*

bat wing *n.* When *John Wayne's hairy saddlebag* is stuck to the inner thigh and forms a stretched, leathery bracket not dissimilar to the veiny aeronautical appendage of the flying titmouse.

bat wings *n. pl.* Thin, leathery, nocturnal flaps. *Beef curtains* that Ozzy Osbourne might have inadvertently take a bite out of in years gone by.

Baumgartner's balloon, more air than *sim.* Suffering from an excess of *carbon dibaxide*; a reference to fizzy-pop-fuelled right-wing Austrian daredevil Felix and his supersonic parachuting shenanigans back in 2012. And yes, it was helium in his balloon, before you get the Basildon Bond out.

Bavarian, the *n. Passing wind* in a series of releases whilst walking, thus giving the impression that you are being followed by a small, malodorous oompah band. Also known as a *duckwalk, string of pearls, ugly duckling* or *one-stroke cylinder engine.*

baw bag *n. Scots.* Oor Wullie's scrotum. A Mc*Chicken skin sporran.*

bawd *n. arch.* Old-fashioned term for a *rub-a-tug shop* proprietress, like what that Cynthia Payne was. Also *madam.*

bawhair *1. n. Scots.* A single *pube.* *2. n. Scots.* A *de minimis* unit of measurement. *'A quick look oer the shoulder a'fore ye pull awa frae the kerb, indicate tae pull oot, let the clutch oot a bawhair an' awa' ye go.'*

Bay of Pigs *1. n.* Some sort of Cuban monkey-business in the 1960s, involving Russian missiles and President Kennedy bringing the world to the brink of nuclear Armageddon in between *fucks* with Marilyn Monroe. *2. n.* A humorous reference to the state of Hornsea beach in the summer; a harmless quip which will nonetheless no doubt fall foul of the so-called "politically correct" lobby.

bay window over a tripe shop *n.* The *gunt.*

bazongers *n.* Gravity-defying, surgically enhanced, hemispherical breasts that explode in aeroplanes. *'Look out the window, Warren or Dane or Teddy or Dwight or Gareth or Matt or Scott or Peter or Alex or Danny or Leandro or Gavin or Kieran or Carl. The people on the ground look like ants. Oh shit, me bazongers of blown up.'*

bazooka wound in a yak *euph.* A poetic phrase which can be used to describe a woman's unkempt *nethers.* Also *ripped sofa, cut on a bear's arm, butcher's dustbin, stab wound in a gorilla's back.*

bazoomas *n.* See *begonias.*

BBBA *abbrev. medic.* The Bit Between the Bollocks and the Arse. The *barse, ploughman's, scruttock, ABC* or *great.*

BBC *1. abbrev.* Big Brother Contestant. A person who appears pleasant enough at first, but who

quickly turns out to be a right *custard.* *2. abbrev.* Popular webular search term when *buying a present for the wife.*

BBQ/bbq *abbrev.* A Bodleian Beauty Queen. A woman in a workplace populated by socially inadequate males (*eg.* A monastery, trainspotter's clubhouse, Maplins shop, university library), who, notwithstanding her limited appeal in the wider world, becomes an object of lust for the habitués of said establishment.

BBW/bbw *1. abbrev.* Big Beautiful Women to internet users whose *boat* is *floated* by that sort of thing. *2. abbrev.* Big Bloated Whales to those whose *boat* isn't *floated* by that sort of thing.

BC and AD *abbrev.* Before Crap and After Dump. Relating to the times preceding – and subsequent to – the miraculous birth of *feeshus.*

BDF/bdf *abbrev.* A post-festive *own goal*, brought about by excessive consumption of rich foodstuffs, a surfeit of sprouts and too much ale. A Boxing Day Fart with all the trimmings.

beach baby *1. n.* Title of a 1974 song by one-hit-wonders The First Class. Try and remember that; it'll come up in a pub quiz. *2. n.* One of the *kids* that has been *sent to the beach* but has inconveniently returned to shore, intact, on the next tide. *2. n.* A brown *sea trout. 'The sands are usually pristine but sometimes, due to the close proximity of the council shite pipe, beach babies can be found on the foreshore.'*

beach body ready *1. adj.* Of a woman, slim, toned and buff, and therefore able to venture out in her bikini without sickening other holidaymakers. *2. adj.* Of a gentleman, equipped with mirrored sunglasses and therefore able to saunter down the beach while discreetly checking out the *tussage.*

beachcomber's nightmare *n.* A woman with such a *bubbly personality* that "even the tide wouldn't take her out".

beached ready *adj.* Looking whale-like in swimwear. *'Next on the catwalk we have John McCririck, looking beached ready in a pair of high-cut microbriefs by Kiniki.'*

beach hutt *n.* A magnificently lardiferous sunbather, looking remarkably like the eponymous Tatooine-based *Star Wars* space gangster and David Mellor-a-like. Also *pizza hutt*: similar but scoffing a stuffed crust meat feast with no salad.

bead *v.* To exude *balm before the storm* from the *hog's eye* during moments of arousal. *'I tell you, Alan, I was that excited I was beading before I'd even parked the Range Rover.'* (Stan Collymore, Radio 5Live).

bead curtains *n. Dangleberries, toffee strings, mud-*

buttons, tagnuts, behind which you might expect to find a fortune teller. Also *beaded curtain.*

bead in your bellend, have a *euph.* To be grumpy. *'And now we head over to Ambridge for tonight's episode of the Archers, where Jack's got a bead in his bellend after finding a pair of Nigel Pargetter's spunked underpants in Peggy's handbag.'*

beadle *n.* A small drinks can of the sort given out on planes. *'Can I have six beadles of tomato juice and three vodkas, please?' 'Of course, Captain.'*

Beadle's fist *n.* A tightly shrivelled or retracted scrotum.

beagle break *n.* A five-minute recreational interval at one's place of work which is spent puffing on a *coffin nail* on the *cancer verandah.*

beagling *n.* Posh *dogging.* Having a *gang-bang* over the bonnet of a 4x4 while wearing a Barbour jacket, puce cords and Hunter wellies.

beaked up *adj.* Gifted with extreme confidence whilst under the influence of *jazz talc.* *'They've fired him now, but my grandad watches it and he says he always looked well beaked up when he was on. You could see it up his nostrils, apparently.'*

Beaker's mouth *n.* The involuntary movement of the vaginal lips when an erotic actress is being *done* up the *bonus tunnel,* as seen in many a *grumble flick.* Reminiscent of the movements of the Muppet laboratory assistant "me-mo-ing".

beanbag *n.* The *clematoral hood;* fleshy awning that keeps the rain off a female's *wail switch.* Also *toucan's bill, little red riding hood.* *'Up a bit, up a bit further. That's it, Roy. Just there. You've got your finger right on me beanbag.'*

beanbagging *n.* A very specific form of *teabagging,* in which either Sean Bean, Judge Roy Bean, astronaut Alan Bean or Rowan Atkinson lower their *pods* into the mouth of a recumbent partner.

bean buddies *n. Tennis fans* who are wont to stash their *comfortable slippers* under the same *wanking chariot.*

bean counter *1. n.* A parsimonious fellow. *2. n.* A promiscuous *lesbo.*

beanfeast *1. n.* Annual dinner laid on by a company for its employees. *2. n.* A "delicious alternative to meat" made by Batchelors. *3. n. Lesbo* group carryings-on; a televisual spectacle much enjoyed by bachelors. A sapphic orgy. A *carpet munchers'* all-you-can-eat buffet.

bean flicker *n.* She who is *in the hockey team.* A wearer of *comfortable shoes, lady golfer* or *tennis fan*

bean grinder *1. n.* Motorised device frequently used by busy baristas. *2. n.* Motorised device frequently used by busy spinsters. Also known as

a *battery flattener.*

beanis *n.* A confusing, fleshy protuberance found in some underpants that is, one might think, just slightly too big to be a *clematis,* whilst paradoxically also much too small to be a *cock.* *'What's that?' 'It's my beanis, Melania.'*

bean protein *1. n.* Foodstuff obtained by processing various legumes for human or animal consumption (eg. Tofu obtained from soya) that gives vegans their healthily pale, skinny appearance. *2. n.* The goodness in a farmer's *legumes. Spunk.*

beans on toast *1. n.* A quick and yet satisfying snack. *2. n.* A quick and yet satisfying *tug.* *'Can you get someone else to read the news? I'm just going to nip home for beans on toast.'*

bear *n.* A big, fat, grizzly *Colwyn Bay* who looks like Garry Bushell.

bear bile *n.* Descriptive of any food or drink that is particularly unpalatable. *'Betty, this hotpot is like fucking bear bile, I said bear bile.'*

bear cave *phr.* The performance of s*xual congress whilst trying to make a minimal amount of noise. From the imagined reality of taking shelter from a storm or other threat only to find yourself surrounded by sleeping grizzlies. *'Gran's in the next room and mum and dad are still up, so we're going to have to bear cave this, Mother Superior.'*

Bear chod *n.* When camping, an excruciating *al fresco* evacuation of the *Simons,* caused by the binding nature of your diet of grubworms, raw fish, and pine needle tea, as recommended by hardened, hotel-dwelling outdoorsman Grylls.

bear claw *n.* Late night, drunken and clumsy pawing at a ladyfriend's *honey pot,* possibly resulting in torn garments.

beard *1. n. arch.* Fulsome *twat-thatch, mapatasi.* *2. n.* A woman who is married to a *batty-boy* in an attempt to conceal his true sexuality. See *whiff of lavender.* *'Do you reckon that Sophie's a beard then, or what?'*

beard bait *n.* Artisanal, locally-sourced, farm-to-table *bollocks* designed to attract the skinny-jeans-and-man-bun crowd.

bearded bank robber *n.* A lass with a particularly hairy *biffer* who wears nylon tights but no *undercrackers.*

bearded clam *1. n.* An edible mollusc. *2. n. Aus.* An edible *fish mitten.*

bearded clamcorder *n.* Equipment used by a 1970s *grumble* film-maker. *'Quick, fetch the bearded clamcorder over here, Clive. You can see it going in.'*

bearded dragon *n.* A menopausal, *over the pill* spouse, complete with hot sweats, facial hair and sudden mood swings.

bearded ninja *n.* A frustratingly fleeting glimpse of a *fuzzy peach* in a film, *eg.* Sharon Stone's in *Basic Instinct,* Jenny Agutter's in *Logan's Run* or Doris Hare's in *Mutiny on the Buses.*

bearded squid *n.* A *fanny* that will bite your face off.

beard, tramp's *n.* A hairy, unwashed and unkempt *furry hoop.* With all bits of food stuck in it.

Bear Grylls pills *n.* Any drink or drugs taken on board by a man which may cause him to act in a more courageous and/or foolhardily fisticuffsome manner than might be good for his health. *'Please pay no attention to my companion, Mr McLean. He's been on the Bear Grylls pills.'*

Bear Grylls's picnic table *euph.* Descriptive of a village football pitch, the pavement outside a flat roof pub, or the sandpit of a school long jump, liberally furnished with *survivalist luncheon snacks* by local dog owners. *'Watch your slippers in the vicarage garden, your holiness, it's like Bear Grylls's picnic table out there.'*

bear's cave *euph.* A rather scary *arsehole* with brown claw marks around the entrance.

bear's paw, the *1. n.* Pressing sense of urgency that grips one immediately prior to an apocalyptic *bempty.* *'Mr Howard, did you threaten to overrule him?' 'Okay, yes, I did. Are we done? Only I've got the bear's paw here. Where's the fucking bogs?'* *2. n.* A big hairy *twat* that leaves you spitting hairs out of your mouth.

bear trap *1. n.* A big *cludge,* strong enough to snap a man's ankle if he put his foot into it. One might imagine that Pat Butcher out of *EastEnders* had a *bear trap* in her knickers, for example. *2. n.* A spring-loaded pair of the *bag for life*'s undies, lying sunnyside up on the floor.

bear trapper's hat *n.* An excessively hirsute *front bottom.* A *biffer* or *Davy Crockett hat.* *'Put my ladder up to the flat / Saw a nun with a bear trapper's hat / I get a wank out of things like that / When I'm cleaning windows.'* (from *The George Formby Song Book,* 1945).

beast in black *1. n.* A heavy metal pop combo from Finland, whose toe-tapping pop stylings include *Zodd the Immortal, Die by the Blade* and *From Hell With Love.* *2. n.* That horrendous black sludge you get in the *bog* the morning after a heavy night *on the black stuff.* See also *Irish bhaji, Guinness rope.*

beast of chod bin *n.* A massive jet-black *turd.*

beast with one back, make the *v.* To perform an act of s*xual intercourse while experiencing a fifty percent personnel shortfall.

beast with two backs *n.* A strange, grunting animal with two heads and four legs, commonly found in Newcastle bus shelters, back alleys and taxi queues after midnight.

beast with two cracks, the *euph.* An unconvincing display of feigned *girl-on-girl action.* Still, better than nothing.

beast with two sacks *n.* Visually off-putting *chicken skin handbag*-based *Newton's cradle* situation typically experienced by a pair of professional footballers engaged in a spot of *Dorothy Perkins.*

beat a donkey out of a bog *sim.* NI. A Northern Irish expression useful when painting a word picture of something with roughly similar dimensions and proportions to a shillelagh. *'Have ye seen the size of the Pastor's cock, Michael? You could beat a donkey out of a bog with that fecker, so you could.'*

beaten like a ginger step-child *adj.* Descriptive of a particularly ferocious and merciless thrashing, for example, off a bouncer at a nightclub, off a policeman in a cell, or off Bjork at Bangkok Airport. *'This is dreadful. I don't think Hawking can take much more of this punishment. Bruno's raining the blows down now, left right left right. I can't look, this is terrible. Hawking's being beaten like a ginger step-child.'* (Harry Carpenter, commentating on a charity boxing match, *BBC Children in Need,* 1998).

beatifying the cardinal *n.* A more extreme version of *bashing the bishop.* *'Cup of tea, your holiness?' 'Give me ten minutes, will you? I'm just beatifying the cardinal.'*

beating eggs *n.* A charmingly lyrical evocation of the sound made by a lady washing her *parts of shame* with soap while squatting in the shower.

beating the veal *1. n.* An important process in the preparation of Wiener schnitzels. *2. n.* Feminine *self pleasure.* Also *tickling the scampi.*

beatlejuice *n.* Fanny *batter* brought about by the arrival of a boy band. Usually accompanied by deafening screaming and tears. *'Half the seats in the theatre were ruined after the Rollers had been on. And we couldn't even burn them because they were soaked through with beatlejuice.'*

beat off *v.* To *rub one out, knock one out, crack one out, bust off.* To commit a *monomanual act of self delight.*

beat sheet *1. n.* A document used by American television writers when planning and sequencing their stories, so that their profound prose fits neatly round the adverts for heartburn medicine, second hand and incontinence wear. *2. n. arch.* Back in the days when the information superhighway was but a gleam in Tim Berners Lee's eye, a tattered page torn from the *Freeman's Catalogue titpants* section to help a young fellow *chuck* *his muck.*

beat the buzzer *v.* To impregnate one's missus in the week prior to the divorce coming through.

beat the meat *v.* To avail oneself of a *ham shank*, perform the *five-knuckle shuffle, pull your pud, fire the one o'clock gun etc.* To mash your *cock* flat on the kitchen work surface with a wooden mallet.

beautifat *adj.* Descriptive of one of those females who has a lovely *boat race* and a *lovely personality* to match.

beaver *1. n. US.* Female pubic hair. *Gorilla salad. 2. n. coll. US.* An offensively sexist term used when referring to a group of *birds.* Also *blart, mackerel, fanny, tussage, knob fodder. 3. n.* One who relishes nibbling *wood.*

beaverage *n.* The refreshing brew that is quaffed from the *hairy goblet* when *dining at the Y. 'Another beaverage, Mr Dover?' 'Yes please. I'll just use the same furry cup, save you washing it.'*

beaver bait *n.* A sturdy length of bark-covered *log* that can be found damming the bottom of the U-bend.

beaver cheese *n.* Stale *man milk* fermenting on a woman's *badger. Chuffdruff, gusset sugar, blick.*

beaver cleaver *n.* Primitive wooden *weapon.*

beaver dam *1. n.* Ladies' personal feminine hygiene requisite. *Jam rag, fanny nanny, blobstopper,* large pile of tree trunks. *2. n.* A bath plughole, when blocked up with the flotsam and jetsam of the wife's *minge.*

beaver-dammed *adj.* Female equivalent of *cock-blocked, viz.* Prevented from enjoying a spot of *carnival congress* by forces outside one's control.

beaver lever *n.* A *flapjack. 'Wait there with your feet in the stirrups, Mrs Robinson. I'll just go and fetch a beaver lever.'*

beaver paddle *n.* Bizarre act performed by a man mid-way through committing sexual intercourse with a lady, when he unexpectedly pulls out his *meat flute,* grips it in his hand and then slaps it repeatedly against her *bodily treasure.* From the similarity to the way that the eponymous Ken Dodd-toothed rodent of the genus *Castor* slaps its scaly tail against the water for a cheap sexual thrill.

beaver's guts *n.* In the world of *art pamphlet* photography, that which is visible in a *close up pink* study. An *untidy sock drawer.*

beaver tails *n.* Long, flat *thru'penny bits* which resemble the relatively unerotic, scaly tails of the eponymous timber-chompers. Also known as *socktits, spaniels' ears, NGTs, nan-chukas, shoe shiners, Gandhi's flip-flops.*

be bog *n.* Free-form atonal public lavatory jazz, improvised on *brass eye* instruments, *eg.* The *trouser trumpet. Pan pipes, pot music, acrapella.* See also *tuning up.*

because you're worth it *exclam.* Waggish phrase to be used by a gentleman as he rubs his recently dropped *spooge* into his ladyfriend's head and shoulders. Also known as a *Persian shampoo.*

Bechamel bullet *n.* A high velocity, savoury slug of *gentleman's spendings* which could be used to garnish a *parmo.*

Beckham, do a *v.* To fail to *score,* despite being given every opportunity to do so.

Beckham penalty *n.* A *piss* which combines high speed and inaccuracy, hitting everywhere except its intended target. Often results in a *Queen Mum's smile.*

becksfart *n.* Brand-specific lager hangover flatulence. Has an aroma a bit like egg mayonnaise.

Becks ray specs *n.* *Beer goggles* with expensive German optics.

bed *v.* A tabloid term, to *sleep with,* to *fuck. 'I went out with Tracey last night and ended up bedding her up the arse in the bus shelter.'*

bed & buckfast *n.* A sojourn in Glasgow during which one samples the local culture and has a fight in Cowlairs Park.

bed bellows *n.* The action of a semi-somnolent *guffer,* who lifts and lowers his leg in order to flap the quilt up and down and thus bring the benefits of his rectal largesse to the attention of his partner. Or partners if it's an orgy.

bed blocker *1. n.* In a hospital, a long term convalescent who annoys staff by neither being particularly ill nor having the decency to drop dead in order to free up a bit of space on the ward. A bit like Sid James in *Carry On Doctor.* Also known as a *gomer. 2. n.* A person with whom one has been intimate in the past but whose charms have faded and who continues to defy all efforts to kick them into touch.

bed coin *n.* An unexpected nugget of flattened *feeshus* discovered amongst the sheets while making the bed.

bed flute *n.* Woodwind instrument closely related to the *pink oboe* that responds well to double tonguing.

Bedford diff *euph.* A female rear end that has succumbed to the ravages of time. *'Bloody hell Fred, did you see that lass's arse? It was hanging down like a Bedford diff.'*

Bedfordshire clanger *1. n.* Type of heavy, suet-based pie, also known as a Trowley dumpling or bacon badger. *2. n.* Piquant, gaseous titbit prepared loudly in a *Dutch oven. 3. n.* A proper *pan cracker* or *gorilla's breakfast,* also known as a

Trowley dumpling or *bacon badger*.

bed glue *n*. Liquid that adheres people firmly to their mattresses, especially students. Beer.

bedknobs and broomsticks *1. n*. Film starring her out of *Murder She Wrote* and that bloke out of *Mary Poppins* who looks like her out of *Murder She Wrote* wearing a false moustache, which stirs up Pavlovian feelings of boredom, resentment and uninterest in any poor cunt who ever sat through an episode of *Screen Test* in the 1970s. *2. n*. The early morning result of a low fibre diet.

bed muscle *n*. The *old fella*.

bed of rice *n*. A *bog* in a curry house that has been plied with a surfeit of *shit scrape* by a previous occupant such that it will not flush.

bedroom popadoms *n*. Large, dried *wankerchiefs. Porn crackers, wankers' crisps*.

bedroom tax *1. n*. Welfare reform intended to cut the amount of benefit that poor people can claim if they are considered to have a spare bedroom that could, conceivably, be let out to a paying lodger. Whose rent would presumably then count as income, so they wouldn't be able to claim any other benefits either. *2 n*. The cost of a meal in a fancy restaurant that paves the way to the boudoir.

bedruggled *adj*. Describes the appearance of one who has aged beyond their years due to an heroic intake of illicit pharmaceuticals and/or booze, *eg*. Ozzie Osbourne, Keith Richards, the late Shane McGowan.

bedside sock, tough as a *sim*. Said of an overdone steak, say, an intractable diplomatic problem, or a particularly *nails* cage fighter. See also *hard as Tarzan's feet*; *hard as Elvis's last turd*; *hard as Captain Scott's last morning stiffy*; *hard as a cyclist's nipsy*; *hard as a goat's toe etc*.

beef *n*. A hearty *brew*. A high cholesterol *eggo*.

beef baubles *n*. Testicles. *'The bad news, Evel, is that you failed to clear the row of 16 double decker buses. The good news, however, is that one of your beef baubles did.'*

beef bayonet *n*. Bacon bazooka, mutton musket, lamb cannon, luncheon meat howitzer.

beef box *n*. A container into which the *tubesteak* is put. Also *meat safe*.

beef cloud *n*. A *fart* that smells like one has just opened a very old, leaky tin of Butcher's Tripe Mix dogfood or a fresh packet of Bernard Matthews' honey roast ham.

beef curtains *n. medic*. The *piss flaps*. Also *Keith Burtons, steak drapes, Vulcan bomb doors*. See *chippy's toolbag*.

beef curtain, the *n. geopol*. The imaginary line running along the borders of European countries of Holland, Germany, Austria and Hungary where *knocking shops* are legal, separating them from their more prudish neighbours. *'A beef curtain has descended over Europe. Can anyone change me this ten bob note into Guilders?'* (Winston Churchill addressing the Hague Congress, 1948).

beef dripping *n*. The spreadable extract found in a *butcher's window*, traditionally used in the preparation of well-*battered fish suppers*.

beef encounter *1. n*. A romantic, one-off *bang*. A *hit and run*, a *none night stand. 2. n*. In a public place, for example on a railway platform, a short-lived romantic dalliance of the sort in which Trevor Howard and Celia Johnson are unlikely ever to have indulged.

beef jerky *1. n*. Inexplicably popular delicatessan snack that is indistinguishable from chewing a dog treat or watch strap steeped in bleach. *2. n. One off the wrist*.

beef olive *n*. A *sausage* wrapped in *beef*.

beef or salmon *1. n*. Name of the much-fancied horse which nevertheless ran a nightmare in the 2006 Cheltenham Gold Cup. *2. phr. rhet*. Question asked of a person of indeterminate proclivities in order to ascertain whether they eat *meat* or *fish*.

beef piston *1. n*. A crowd-pleasing pro-wrestling move, probably. *2. n*. Nickname of *glans*-headed pro-wrestler-turned-thesp "Dwayne Johnson" (real name Thelwell Rockingham).

beef slider *1. n*. A *bijou* American-style hamburger sandwich for those with a small appetite that is often served with cheese and sauerkraut. *2. n*. A *Bully's special prize* that leaves an incriminatory trail of *bisto skids* on the ledge of the *shitpot* just above the waterline, necessitating swift and judicious use of the *chodbin* brush before the *bag for life* clocks the mess. *3. n*. A particularly well-lubricated *todger* that is not often served with sauerkraut.

beef teabag *n*. A set of *knackers* dipped in a rich stock and then popped into a lucky recipient's mouth. *'We boiled up snow and ice to make hot, beefy Bovril, then gave Sherpa Tensing a beef teabag.'*

beef wellington *1. n*. Dish originally popularised by 19th century military hero the Duke of Beef. *2. n*. A rubber prophylactic device placed over a gentleman's *meat flute* to prevent babies and/or *the clap. 3. n*. A *wizard's sleeve, clown's pocket* or *trawlerman's sock*. A voluminous *mimsy* of such epic proportions that one might wonder whether one's entire lower leg might comfortably fit in it.

beefy eggo *n*. A pungently carnivorous *Exchange & Mart*.

Bee Gees bite *n*. The first mouthful of an extremely

hot foodstuff, such as a Pop Tart or McDonald's apple pie, that causes the eater to involuntarily perform the falsetto "ah-ha-ha-ha-" intro to *Stayin' Alive*.

Bee Gee Tips *n.* A cup of scalding hot tea.

beekeeper's apprentice, face like a *sim.* A good-natured reference to one blessed with a less than perfect complexion, *viz.* A person who looks like they have been *bobbing for apples in the deep fat fryer*. *'Born on this day: Bruce Lee, dead martial arts star, 1940; Tony Green, late Bullseye scorer, 1939; Steve Bannon, alt-right beekeeper's apprentice, 1953.'*

Beelzebum *n.* A particularly evil dose of the *squirts* accompanied by the acrid stench of brimstone.

beeory *n.* A ludicrously ill-informed hypothesis on any subject that is formulated under the influence of brown booze. *'Mr Johnson gave a speech to the Monday Club, setting out his economic beeory.'*

beerache *n. medic.* The painful afliction of the eardrum usually experienced after returning home *pissed* and late. Like tinitus, but with an annoying woman's voice ringing out instead of bells.

beer angel *n.* The unseen guiding force that watches over and keeps safe the inebriated as they stagger across all six lanes of the North Circular at chucking out time.

beer armour *n.* The invisible protective clothing that prevents injury on the way home from the pub by shielding the body from all sensation of damage on contact with the pavement.

beer baby *n.* A large, booze-induced gut. A *Foster's child, verandah over the toyshop*. What a gent acquires after years of *refreshment*. See also *beerby, kebabby*. *'Eeh, have you seen Jezza lately? He's blooming. He looks as if he's having a beer baby.'*

beer badly *adj.* A popular turn of phrase in the Barnsley area. Suffering the malign after-effects of *refreshment*. *'What's up wi' thee?' 'Shut it, cock. Ah'm beer badly, tha knows.'*

beer bollocks *n.* Courage-filled *cojones* grown by a usually timid man after he has imbibed several pints of strong lager. *'Where's Terry?' 'He's lying down on the pavement outside. He grew some beer bollocks and decided to take on all four of the bouncers.'*

beer buggy *n.* A shopping trolley found abandoned at the side of the road.

beer callipers *n.* Miraculous leg splints which enable *wankered* stragglers to make their way home at closing time.

beer cancer *n. medic.* The sort of hangover that not only makes you feel utterly *shit*, but lasts so long that you suspect you may be genuinely ill.

beer coat *n.* An invisible, yet warm outer garment worn when walking back from a club at three in the morning.

beer compass *n.* Homing device that ensures your inexplicably safe arrival home after a heavy night *on the pop*.

beer cones *n.* Invisible contraflow system surrounding a drunkard meandering up the road, allowing traffic to move freely around him.

beer degree *n.* A qualification attained after a sufficient intake of alcohol, which enables one to talk at length and with complete authority on any given topic. *'Toby got his beer degree at Oxford, don't you know.'*

beer facelift *n.* Subjective cosmetic surgical procedure which is only visible to *pissed up* men. *'Have you seen Barry's new bird? He met her when she'd had a beer facelift and now he can't shake her off.'*

beer gas *n.* An extremely potent odour that can be used to disperse crowds.

beergasm *n.* The moment of pure pleasure experienced upon taking the first sip of bitter at the end of a hard day at work or watching television, marked by a tingly sensation all over and the release of a low moan.

beer goggles *n.* Booze-fuelled optical aids which make *hounds* look like *foxes*. *Pint glasses*.

beer googles *n.* Recognition of the fact that, throughout the course of an evening, the quality and tone of the *grumble* being searched out by a web user is inversely proportional to the amount of alcohol he has consumed.

beer halo *n.* Alcohol-induced self-righteousness.

beer hunter *1. n.* A jolly drinking game whereby Chris Evans's employees are forced to open cans of beer into their ears from a six-pack, one tin of which has been shaken vigorously. *2. n.* A demented person who ransacks the house in the early hours, searching for the smallest drop of booze. As Chris Evans has been known to do.

beer infection *n. medic.* Debilitating complaint commonly suffered the morning after a night *on the sauce*. Symptoms include headache, dizzyness, upset stomach, tiredness and aching limbs, and the sufferer can be left bed bound. *'Time to get up, dear. It's Sunday morning and we're going to the garden centre.' 'Sorry love, I'll have to give it a miss. I seem to have caught a beer infection.'*

beeriod *n.* Twice-weekly malady suffered by men after a night *on the lash*. Symptoms include headache, mood swings and a bloated stomach.

'Leave me alone, woman, me beeriod started this morning.'

beer lag *n.* The disruption to normal sleep patterns encountered after intense lunchtime drinking. *Beer lag* can leave one unable to keep one's eyes open for *Antiques Roadshow*, but then wide awake at two in the morning.

beerlarious *n.* Amusing only when drunk; specifically, putting a traffic cone on a statue's head.

beer lever *n.* The right elbow, or left elbow if you happen to be left-handed. Also known as the *drinking lever* or *wank crank*.

beerlimic *n.* A *one-pint wonder*. He who drinks *rubber beer.*

beer lingual *adj.* Able to understand the incoherent ramblings of the thoroughly *wankered*. *'BBC Television is seeking to recruit an experienced, enthusiastic and fully beer-lingual typist to provide live subtitling for the popular, late night This Week political discussion show hosted by Andrew Neil.'*

beer lobe *n.* Abdominal appendage that characteristically develops in mid-life.

beerloom *n.* Any item that one wouldn't ordinarily touch with a bargepole, but which suddenly seems irresistible when you go on eBay *pissed* out of your skull in the wee small hours. *'A Madness fruit machine? What on earth possessed you? How much did you pay?' 'Nearly three hundred quid. It's a fucking beerloom.'*

beer me out *exclam.* Plea issued whilst presenting an unconventional view in the pub, in the hope of being allowed a more open-minded reception than sober minds might offer. *'I know it sounds a bit mad, but beer me out, lads. In some ways, Liz Truss was quite a good Prime Minister.'*

beer miles *1. n.* Earned off the missus by doing dodgy DIY around the house and garden. *2. n.* Easy, cheap, long-distance travel made possible by the consumption of large quantities of ale.

beer-mint wino *n.* A worker who consumes large amounts of Tic-Tacs or Polos in an effort to to disguise their alcoholic breath when returning from "lunch."

beer monkey *n.* Mythical simian creature which, during a drunken slumber, sneaks into your bed, ruffles your hair, steals your money and *shits* in your mouth.

beermuda triangle *n.* The triangulated geographical space defined at its vertices by three public houses, within the boundaries of which Euclidean polygon a drinker may be lost for days, if not indefinitely. In Sydney, Australia, there is a particularly potent *beermuda triangle* between The Lord Nelson, The Palisades and The Hero of Waterloo.

beer muffs *n.* Invisible ear defenders that attach themselves to a man's head after several pints, rendering him unable to hold a conversation without shouting or to watch TV at anything but full volume.

beer mugger *n.* The unseen assailant you discover has hit you over the head and taken £35 out of your wallet the morning after you "nip out for a swift couple of pints".

beero *n.* One who, fortified by several pints, is prepared to engage in acts of incredible heroism, *eg.* Squaring up to doormen on the other side of the street, gesticulating at others in an abusive manner from inside a taxi travelling at speed.

beer plugs *n.* Alcoholic sound level inhibitors which occasion a total lack of response to any form of auditory stimulus. *Beer plugs* allow a *pissed* individual to remain happily and soundly asleep in the midst of such high volume disturbances as nightclub PA systems, burglar/fire alarm sirens and the *filth* with dogs kicking his door in.

beer pressure *1. n.* A benevolent psychological influence applied by drinking companions, encouraging one to consume more alcohol than one feels comfortable drinking. *2. n.* The irresistible temptation to do something one ordinarily wouldn't consider on the way home from the pub, such as having a fight, scaling a tower crane or stripping naked and sitting on the roof of a police car.

beer queer *1. adj.* Of a normally heterosexual person, to be tempted to go *half rice half chips* when fuelled by sufficient quantities of *dizzyade*. *Booze bent. 2. n.* A temperance type who has taken the pledge to eschew strong liquor. A *teapot sucker* or teetotaller.

beersay *n.* Gossip of a highly dubious nature, spread by a *piss artist* down the pub, *viz.* "You know that Sue Lawley…" *etc.*

beer scooter *n.* Miraculous method of transport employed when leaving the pub after drinking an *elegant sufficiency* of alcohol. So-called because one returns home seemingly in no time and at incredible velocity. Also *beer taxi.*

beer shoes *n.* Gloves.

beer sniper *n.* An invisible marksman who silently "takes out" drunkards causing them to unexpectedly collapse in the street, fall off bar stools, go *arse over tit* while addressing Norwich City fans *etc.*

beer stretcher *n.* A magical post-*sesh* St John's Ambulance service. When *fully refreshed* and lying down in the *Scotsman's lounge,* ditch or on the pub toilet floor, one is immediately whisked home on the *beer stretcher* to the comfort of one's own bed, to awaken refreshed and re-invigorated in the morning with absolutely no memory of the journey. *'I came home on the beer stretcher, only I must have stopped off at the all-night garage because when I woke up there was a 50+ wank mag and an empty Scotch eggs packet on the bed.'*

beer tent *n.* A professional darts player's shirt.

beer thinners *n.* The pint of water one forgets to consume at the end of a long evening *on the pop*.

beer trumpet *n.* Primitive, alcohol-powered hearing aid which causes users to laugh uproariously at a statement which, in the cold light of day, can be seen to contain not even a homeopathic quantity of humour.

beer whistle *n.* At a football match, the signal given 10 minutes before half time that causes a mass exodus of gentlemen going for a pint, a pie, a *piss* or a simultaneous combination of the three.

beerwolf *n.* One who wakes up in unfamiliar surroundings with torn clothes, aching limbs, the taste of blood in his mouth and suffering from nightmarish flashbacks to terrible events which occurred the previous evening.

beer wood *n.* The thing that feels like an erection, but isn't, when attempting sexual congress under the influence of alcohol.

bee's bollocks *phr.* The dog's knees. *'For more than 95 years, Bentley has created exceptional automobiles in constant pursuit of the exquisite, the powerful and the individual. And today's line-up is now joined by the Bentayga, a vehicle that really is the bee's bollocks, taking exquisite refinement into new territory, challenging preconceptions of what a luxury sports utility vehicle can be. NB. No riff-raff.'*

bee's dick *n.* The incredibly small distance, or period of time, which is needed in order to achieve an important outcome. *'I nearly finished the exam. I was only a bee's dick short of answering the last eight questions.'*

bee stings *n.* Small *tits*. Chestnuts, stits, tisn'ts, Dutch Alps, lung warts.

Beethoven's fifth *n.* A stirring *movement* which may leave its begetter hard of hearing.

beetle bonnet *n.* The female pubic mound as viewed through tight garments. From the design of the iconic VW car beloved of hippies and nazis. *Camel's foot, camel's lip,* visible *knicker sausages.*

begging Jock *n.* A tired, weathered *cludge* resembling nothing so much as the cupped, beseeching hands of a middle-aged Scottish *gentleman of the road.*

begone, demon Lord of Karanga! *exclam.* Powerful oath which is invoked when attempting to flush away a particularly obstinate *shite*. Taken from the fantasy novel *Demon Lord of Karanga* by David Eddings. Us neither.

begone foul beast! *exclam.* Something to declaim, Peter Cushing-style, after *dropping a diabolical monster.*

begonias *n.* See *bejonkers.*

beg to move the motion, I *1. exclam.* What an MP says when they want to open a debate in the House of Commons. *2. exclam.* What a MP says when desperately restraining *a mole at the counter* but all of the parliamentary *shitters* are occupied.

behind with the rent *euph.* A discreet way of explaining that a person is a *good listener.*

be-hymen *n.* A person's *anal virgin string,* that may be be snapped inadvertently when falling awkwardly onto a milk bottle while wearing a loose-fitting dressing gown, to pick an example entirely at random.

Beijing smog mask, filthy as a *sim.* Said of a right dirty woman who'll do anything. *'See her reading the news? You wouldn't think it to look at her, but I have it on the very good authority of a bloke whose dad used to work with her boyfriend's brother that she's as filthy as a Beijing smog mask.'*

Beijing traffic jam *n.* A particularly intractable bout of constipation that lasts several days, and which results in high levels of noxious pollution.

bejonkers *n.* See *bouncers.*

Bela Lugosi's gob *n.* An *axe wound* which drips with fresh blood on a regular basis. A *jam sandwich.* See also *Dracula's teabag.*

belching beaver *1. n.* An American craft beer brewery located in San Diego. *2. n.* A particularly uncouth *sea breeze* blowing from a *lass's front bottom.*

belching fluid *n.* Draught lager. *'Excuse me sir, but you were driving very erratically as you left the pub car park.' 'Well I can assure that I am as sober as a fucking judge, officer. I've only been drinking belching fluid.'*

Belfast key *n.* A fired earthenware block which can grant the owner entry through any glazed door or window. A brick. *'Aw shite. I've locked meself out of the house again.' 'Never mind, mother. I've got a Belfast key here.'*

Belfast taxi *n.* Battery-powered shopping scooter for the old, the infirm and those who are too fat or idle to walk. A *Disneyworld dragster, bariatricycle* or *Frinton Ferrari.*

Belfast tickle stick *n.* A baseball bat, iron bar, length of four-by-two, *etc.*

Belgian *1. adj.* Of chocolates, twice as expensive as normal. *2. n.* In the world of sex, a spot of *ESD* or

ATM. Hot karl.

Belgian biscuit *n.* Sexual practice of Flemish origin that costs over £100, although that price has went up post-Brexit. Not to be confused with *Belgian bun.*

Belgian bun *n.* Walloon-based deviant behaviour which presently comes in at about £75. Not to be confused with *Belgian biscuit.*

Belgian curl *1. n.* Delicious and sweet pastry treat. *2. n.* A firm *bum cigar* rolled and cut in the Flanders region.

Belgian letterbox *n.* A *backdoor* aperture that typically gets rattled by the postman early in the day. *'I don't suppose you'd have a quick shufty at my Belgian letterbox, would you, doctor?'*

belgrano *n.* A lady who looks irresistibly *fuckable* from behind.

Belisha beacon *n.* Flashing orange globe on a black and white pole, named after the British Transport Minister in 1934, Leslie Hore-Beacon.

bell *n.* A lady's *clit.* The *devil's doorbell* or *wail switch,* generally found just above the *snail's doorstep.* Somewhere round there, anyway. Nobody *really* knows.

bell clapper *n.* An humungous dangling *turd* that tolls the *bummocks* as one tries to swing it loose.

belle-end *n.* The hindquarters of an attractive *femme.* From the French, who know that sort of thing when they see it.

bellefire *1. n.* A crappy manufactured girl group. Couple of records in the hit parade, but nowt special. *2. n. medic.* A *herman*-based symptom of *cock rot.*

bellegend *n.* A legendary bellend. From bellend + legend. *'Born on this day: John Dillinger, US criminal, 1903; Meryl Streep, Oscar-winning actor, 1947; Alastair Stewart, broadcasting bellegend, 1952.'*

bellegend *n.* Someone who has achieved celebrated status at being a *bellend.* *'Born on this day: Michael Portillo, twat, 1953; Miles Davis, trumpeter, 1926; Laurence Fox, broadcasting bellegend, 1978.'*

bell end *1. n.* An amusingly named tent. *2. n. medic.* The glans of the male penis. Also *bellend, bellender.* The *bobby's helmet* or *bishop's mitre.*

bell end brie *n.* Brimula, fromunder, knacker barrel.

bellendium *n.* A list of people one finds annoying or contemptible. See also *twatalogue.*

bellendrical *adj.* Shaped like the end of a chap's generative member. *'How would you like your hair done this week, Miss Widdecombe?' 'Bellendrical please, Sandra.'*

bellendry *n.* The art or craft of being a *bellend.* *'Quick, put This Week on. Let's enjoy a bit of late night bellendry with our cocoa.'*

bellendsleydale *n.* Full fat, matured Yorkshire *knob cheese* that goes nice on a cracker. *'A bit of ripe bellendsleydale on that, Mr Martin?'*

bellend warmer *n.* A *piss.*

belle of the dole *n.* A recently dumped thirty-something mother who gets all done up to the nines to sign on.

bell housing *1. n. mech.* The flywheel/clutch cover on a car. *2. n.* The *fiveskin* on a gentile's genital.

bell mop *n.* A chap's intimate wipe.

bellooning *n.* The gentlemanly art of pinching the tip of the *prepuce* while having a *piss* in order to give the *farmer's hat* a good sluice out.

bell rag *n.* A cloth with the specific designated purpose of removing *spodge* from *under the bridge.* The raw material from which *bedroom poppadoms* are forged by *wanksmiths.*

bellringer *n.* A bruising blow on the *Herman jelmet* from a precariously fitted *chod-bin* lid, that clangs like the intro to *News at Ten.*

Bells *n.* A child of questionable parental lineage, that is to say one who is descended from a blend of various *manly liquors.* *'Well, he's got the coalman's nose, the postman's eyes, the gas man's ears and the 1992-1993 Division Two Premiership-winning Featherstone Rovers squad's hair. He's definitely a Bells.'*

Bellshill baker *n.* Scottish equivalent of a *Cleveland Steamer;* a *broon baguette* enjoyed hot and fresh, straight from the *mud oven.*

bells of Bacchus *euph.* The soothing jingle of multiple bottles of beer or wine in a GP's trolley as he wheels it over the supermarket car park bumps.

Bells palsy *n. medic.* A type of sudden onset muscular paralysis causing a whisky connoisseur to lose control of all but the most basic cognitive and motor functions, particularly affecting the ability to speak coherently and walk to his car in a fairly straight line.

bell-swagged *adj.* To be endowed with a large *bishop's hat* on a contrastingly small *Jesuit. Mushroom-rigged.*

bell tower *1. n.* A campanile. *2. n.* A leaning *knob shaft.*

bell wringing *v.* A harmless pastime that builds up the arm muscles, and has been popular with monks for the last two thousand years.

belly-brothers-in-law *n.* Two – or more – gentlemen who are related by the fact that they have had sexual relations with the same lady. A literal translation of the Swedish word "buksvåger". See also *custard cousins, brothers quim, twatmates.*

'Did you know that Ingmar Bergman and Gene Simmons out of Kiss are belly-brothers-in-law? They have both apparently slept with the actress Liv Ullman.' 'That's very interesting, but could you direct me to the Billy Bookcases please, pal?'

belly flopper *n.* A clumsy *brown trout* whose graceless, Penny Mordaunt-style entry into the water causes splashing of the *arse.*

belly full of swimmers *n.* Delightfully alluring phrase used by the charming ladies of Bristol when they are planning to start a family. *'Come home with me and give I a belly full of swimmers.'*

belly porridge *n. Shit.*

belly warmers *n.* Big, droopy *tits. Overblaaters.*

belly welly *n.* A non-specific cleftal area in a well-upholstered lady's abdomen. *'She was so fat I didn't know if it was a yeti's welly or a belly welly I was humping, your holiness.'*

belongings *n.* Used in the badly translated subtitles of an un-named Dutch/German *bongo vid* to describe the leading gentleman thespian's *nether parts. 'That's right you whore. Take his belongings and put them in your mouth.'*

below the line comments *1. n.* Readers' comments on social media or on a newspaper website. *2. n.* Crafty *skidders* underneath the *chodbin* water surface that are difficult to remove with the *yellow toilet brush.*

belt-fed mortar, bangs like a *sim. milit.* A measure of the sexual enthusiasm of a lady. See also *shithouse door in the wind, kangaroo shagging a space hopper. 'Have you met our regimental goat, Field Marshall? She bangs like a belt-fed mortar.'*

belt fed wombat, goes like a *sim.* Used to describe a physically vigorous woman. From the nickname of the army's 84mm recoil-less rifle of the 1970s, typically to be found mounted on an aged 432 armoured fighting vehicle. Also *bangs like a chip shop back gate.*

belt loosener *n.* A substantial *flatus* which, once released, reduces one's waist size by several inches. *'Just time for a quick belt loosener before your Christmas day address to the nation, your majesty.'*

belt-tightener *n.* A *shit* of such epic magnitude that the cincture must afterwards be pulled in by a notch to prevent the trousers declevitating.

belvita breakfast biscuit *n.* An early morning *trump* that completely puts you off food until at least lunchtime.

BEMHO/bemho *abbrev.* A standard issue *boner.* Basic Early Morning hard-on.

bempty *n.* A right proper *clear out*; a ground-up spring clean of the *Simon Cowells.* From bum +

empty. *'I am just going outside for a bempty and I may be some time.'* (Last words of Captain Oates, March 17th 1912).

Ben Brown is coming in to bat *exclam.* An announcement that egestion is imminent. See also *the wolf is at the door; there's a pig at the back gate; Mr Johnson is approaching the despatch box etc.*

benchmark *n.* Stigmata on a *Harold Ramp's arse* after he has sat in the park for an extended period.

bender *1. n.* A prolonged drinking spree. An *all-dayer* or *Leo Sayer. 2. n.* A crustie's tent. *3. n.* A *pinch of snuff.*

bender with Dame Sally, go on a *v.* To have a quiet, alcohol, cigarette and takeaway-free night in, as recommended recently by Dame Sally Davies, the Government's Chief Medical Officer, in the hope of avoiding cancer, diabetes and heart disease long enough to fully savour and enjoy your inevitable, horrific decline into senility, penury and physical decrepitude.

bend my back over it, I'd *exclam.* A glowing endorsement given by a chivalrous gentleman as to the desirability of, purely for example, a given Antipodean former soap actress and pop-star, any Brazilian Olympic beach volleyball player, or maybe a female member of the extended royal family.

bend one in *v.* To manage to *get your leg over. 'She sounds well fit. I'd like to bend one into her, Paul.'*

bend the elbow *v.* To go for a *beer goggles* fitting.

bend the knee *euph.* Westeros slang for the performing of *horatio* or *cumulonimbus.*

bendy bully *n.* The male *member* in its semi-flaccid state after scoring 180 and stepping back from the oche, ready to be roughly pushed into a pewter beer tankard by Jim Bowen.

benefactor *n.* Of *farts* and *farting*, the selfless altruist who supplies it. Also known as the *donor.*

beneficiaries *n.* Those who reap the rewards of a *benefactor's Lionel Bart.*

benefit buddies *n.* The group of lonely OAPs and unemployable misfits who gather outside the Post Office half an hour before it opens in the morning just to talk to one another.

benefit buffet *n.* In supermarkets, the shelves situated close to checkouts that bear a mouth-watering array of dented tins, loaves of bread with torn packaging, crushed crisps and almost out of date meat.

benefit of the stout *phr. 'I wasn't sure at first because she had a face like a bulldog having a tricky shit, but in the end I gave her the benefit of the stout.'*

Bengal tiger *n.* An Indian beast that growls ominously in one's guts. *'Fuck me, what the* *fucking fuck was that?' 'Pardon me, your holiness. My Bengal tiger appears to have awoken.'*

Benghazi *1. n.* Usually beleaguered town in Libya. *2. n. rhym. slang.* The lavatory. From Benghazi = khazi. *'How much longer you going to be in that Benghazi, your majesty?'*

Ben Hur *v.* To *take a lady from behind* while using her arms as chariot reins. Also *Ben her, the charioteer.*

Benidorm tan *n.* The sickly, yellow complexion with which an all-inclusive holidaymaker returns to England at the conclusion of a fortnight spent trying to reduce his liver to pâté.

Benito's hat *1. n.* Chain of popular Mexican eateries serving fresh burritos and, it says here, world famous margaritas. *2. n.* A latex prophylactic *Ted Heath* that sits tightly atop the bald head of a chap's *angry dictator.*

Benjamin Button *n.* A *one pump chump* who is *up and over like a pan of milk.* A fellow who, like the character in the eponymous Brad Pitt film, "finishes right at the start".

Ben Jones *euph.* An act of *horatio.* A *chewie,* a *BJ.* Named after the Virgin Radio presenter. Also *Billy Joel, Boris Johnson, Brian Johnston.*

Benny Hill *rhym. slang.* A form of oral contraception. *'It's nothing to do with me, Mrs Gamp. You told me you was on the Benny Hill.'* (from *Nicholas Nickelby,* by Charles Dickens).

Ben's despair *1. n.* On a television quiz show (for example that one with the giant tu'ppenny waterfalls to pick one entirely at random), the fleeting moment when the most attractive contestant is eliminated from the game and the crestfallen host has to play the final jackpot round with his arm around the shoulders of a 24-stone builder. And thus *2. n.* The moment when all of the attractive clientele have left the pub and the remaining customers are a right bunch of *mingers.*

Bensham tuxedo *n.* The pyjamas. Smart/casual wear for exclusive soirées in the salubrious Gateshead garden suburb.

bent *1. adj. Good with colours* as a nine bob note. *2. adj.* Descriptive of a dishonest *scuffer.*

bentertainment *n.* The sort of TV programmes that only girls and *botters* watch, *eg. What Not to Wear, Sex & the City, Coronation Street, Real Housewives of Cheshire etc.*

bento box *1. n.* A compact and attractive package of pickled, salty and fishy treats, from the Land of the Rising Sun, and thus, *2. n.* A Geisha girl's *clopper.*

bepalmed *adj.* Of a jobseeker or student, to be marooned in that awkward hour or so when he's already *wanked* his *knackers* flat as a pancake, but it's arguably too early to open a can.

Beppe's beard *n.* A severely but neatly trimmed *bush,* named after the severely but neatly trimmed chin growth of the former *EastEnders* character, who was written out in 2002. A *clitler, Mugabe muff.*

berk *n.* See *Berkeley Hunt.*

Berkeley Hunt *rhym. slang. Cunt.*

Berlin Wall *1. n.* Heavily policed strip of no-man's land formerly dividing the forbidden East and free West halves of the German city. *2. n.* The *taint, tinter, notcher, carse, biffon, scran, twernt, Humber Bridge etc.*

Bermuda triangle *n.* A mysterious area where *skin boats* full of *semen* seem to disappear with suspicious regularity.

Bernard Manning's ghost *n.* The foulsome scent of a big fat *shite* that can be detected upon entering a small, airless room or cubicle after some wag has *farted and departed.*

Bernd Schuster *1. n. prop.* German International footballer of the 1980s, who had the distinction of playing for both Barcelona and Real Madrid. *2. n.* Description of one's *back passage* the morning after scarfing down a particularly spicy lamb vindaloo.

Bernie Clifton, the *euph.* The naked, *cock*-bobbing walk to answer a knock on one's door when in a state of "comedy-ostrich-neck"-style arousal.

berry *1. n.* A sexual deviant, a kinky person. A goddam prevoit. *2. n.* One who has *carnival knowledge* of animals. *'Today's birthdays: Bruce Forsyth, big-chinned late tap-dancer, 1928; Sir John Mills, iconic late film and stage actor, 1902; Eric Gill, late artist and berry, 1882.' 3. n.* A lady with a great body, but a less-than-pleasing face, *eg.* The body of Halle, but the face of Chuck. A *bobfoc.*

Bertie *1. n.* A male homosexual. *2. n.* A *charlie. 3. adj.* Of a woman, to be blessed with morals as *slack as a brewer's cock.* From the spoonerism Bertie Ditch = dirty bitch. *'...or should he go for saucy number three, who sounds well Bertie and says she takes it up the council?'*

Bertie Bassett's hat *n.* The small, unsatisfying, sticky nugget of dark excrement that drops to the bottom of an otherwise empty toilet bowl. *'No sign of Bertie, but he's dropped his hat.'*

Berwick Rangers' goalmouth *1. n.* The badly churned-up sea of mud between the posts at Shielfield Park. *2. n.* The badly churned-up sea of mud in the back of a pair of *shitted undercrackers.*

besoms *n.* An old maid's *spaniel's ears* which now swing so low that they can be used to brush things up off the floor.

bespectable *adj.* Respectable in glasses, *eg.* The late Richard Wattis. You remember him, he was Eric and Hattie's neighbour in *Sykes.* Used to be in everything.

bespoke poke *n.* An act of s*xual congress enjoyed in relatively refined surroundings, such as in a posh hotel bedroom with ensuite bathroom facilities on hand for post-coital ablutions. As distinct from, say, in a Glasgow phonebox with vomit on the floor or across the bonnet of a Ford Focus in the Hog's Back layby just off the A31.

best friend I can't keep my hands off, a *1. phr.* Form of words used by women on dating apps, to denote their ideal male companion. *2. euph.* From a male perspective, the *John Thomas.* Also *partner in crime, travel buddy.*

be still my beating cock *exclam.* An exclamation of excitement upon meeting the subject of one's amorous aspirations.

bet Freds *n.* A tight group of loud, Lynx-deodorant-smelling, thirty-something men – who only refer to each other by nicknames – hanging around the bar in a momentarily trendy establishment.

bet middler *n.* A woman who looks like an odds-on favourite "from a distance", but all bets are off when you get close-up.

bet she can shit! *exclam.* Uttered to your mate under your breath as you pass a particularly keen *avoider of leaf vegetables.*

better an empty house than a bad tenant *exclam.* Amusing, aphoristic Wildean apophthegm, proffered as a riposte to someone evicting a sproutsome anal squatter. See also *a bit more choke and she would have started; a confident appeal by the Australians there; an excellent theory, Dr Watson; anybody injured?; don't tear it, I'll take the whole piece; how much?; keep shouting sir, we'll find you; more tea vicar?; someone let him in; someone's tinkered with Herbie; speak on, sweet lips that never told a lie; speak up caller, you're through; taxi for Brown; that's working, now try your lights; well struck sir!; what's that, Sweep?; you'll have to buy that now, you've ripped it; sew a button on that; catch that one and paint it blue; good health!; pin a tail on that; you're only supposed to blow the bloody doors off* and *there goes the elephant.*

Betty both *euph.* A *happy shopper* or *switch hitter.* *'Yes, he is. I've heard he's a Betty Both and so is his wife.'* (Paul Lavers, unintentional live broadcast, Friendly TV, 2003).

Betty Swollocks *n.* Polite term for *knacker* discomfort. *'Forgive me, Your Majesty, while I adjust my doublet and hose. I have sailed the seven oceans these last six months and have not changed my codpiece since we left the New World. I fear I have the most awful Betties.'* (Sir Walter Raleigh, Audience with Queen Elizabeth I, 1584).

between cocks *euph.* Said of a woman who is currently single.

between two stools. *1. phr.* Term coined by slap-headed mystic GI Gurdjieff to describe the agony of one who has experienced a taste of a higher consciousness but cannot maintain it. *2. euph.* Descriptive of someone who has had an unsatisfactory *shit*, and feels a follow-up *sit down toilet adventure* is imminent.

between worlds *adj.* Said of an *alloy welder* who is not sure if they have gone fully *over to the other side.* Also *half rice half chips, ambisextrous, army and navy.*

Beverley *n. rhym. slang.* A lady's rigorously depilated *bush.* Named after the formerly popular singer Beverley Craven = shaven haven. *'I couldn't believe my luck, nan, when I stuck my hand up her frock and she'd got a Beverley.'*

Beverly Hills *n.* Ridiculous, Californian-style silicon-stuffed *churns.*

bevvy *1. n.* A portion of *booze.* A quantity of drink. *2. n. coll.* A number of beauties, although that might be spelled differently, come to think of it.

bevy *n. coll.* Ah, yes it is, look.

bezzing *1. n.* Vigorous chewing of the face after nibbling one too many *disco biscuits.* *'Shit, these beans are good. I'm bezzing me tits off!'* *2. n.* The act of dancing like a drunken gibbon, in a similar fashion to virtuoso maracasist Bez (real name The Hon. Beswick Ffitzherbert-Cholmondeley) out of the Happy Mondays.

BHM *1. abbrev.* IATA code for Birmingham International Airport. *2. abbrev.* The *ne plus ultra* of ladies who prefer it *au naturelle*; Big Hairy Minge. Also *biffer, Davy Crockett hat, Terry Waite's allotment.* *'Blimey, Germaine. That's quite the BHM you've got there, cobber.'*

bible, chav *n.* The Argos catalogue.

Bic arse *euph.* Lavatory adventure postscript in which *drawing an ace* proves impossible, as the brown ink refuses to run out.

BICFIL/bicfil *abbrev.* Body Is Cracking, Face Is Lacking. The sort of dreadfully sexist "banter" that unreconstructed "lads" might utter when presented with a shapely woman with a *face like a fucking welder's bench.* Also *bobfoc, butterface, double barker* or *foffof.*

biddeos *n. Scud vids* in which the actresses look somewhat younger on the packaging than they do in the film itself.

biddy bait *n.* The use of Union Jack graphics and the word "British" on supermarket products (for example cat food, Brussels sprouts, incontinence wear) in order to snare patriotic *gimmers* as they bumble around the supermarket looking for the few products still on the shelves after they voted for Brexit.

biddy bouncer *n.* A *Vi-curious* chap who enjoys more mature feminine company. An *OAP-dophile, biddy fiddler, archaeologist, resthomosexual, mothball diver* or *tomb raider.*

biddy fiddler *n.* A fellow who prefers the company of ladies who are of sufficient maturity that they can ride the bus for free during off-peak periods. A *granny magnet.*

bidet *n.* A "shower of arseholes". *'Slapstick prime minister Liz Truss today appointed a veritable bidet to top positions in her new cabinet.'*

biff *n.* Poetic epithet for a lady's *bodily treasure.* *'Cross your legs again, will you Sharon? The camera missed your biff that time.'*

biff boff *1. n.* An expulsion of air from a lady's *front bottom.* A *gash guff. 2. n.* A mobile phone network.

biffer *n.* A particularly hairy *minge* or *Judith.* *'Gaw, you've got a right old biffer on you there, Mother Superior.'*

biffie *n. Bog, shitter, dunny, cludgy. 'I'd give the biffie ten minutes if I was you, nan.'*

biffin *n.* Perspiration which condenses in the *biffin bridge* area during *coitus.*

biffin bridge *n.* See *barse.*

biffing plate *1. n.* The *beetle bonnet* or *monkey's forehead. 2. sim.* That which is flat. *'Christ! This lager's as flat as Kate Moss's biffing plate.'*

Biffo *n.* A female who wears dungarees despite not actually being *on the bus to Hebden Bridge.* A *lesbisn't.*

biffon *n.* That part of the female anatomy between the *council gritter* and the *fadge,* which the man's *clockweights* "biff on" during intercourse. The *taint, tinter, twernt, Humber bridge.*

biffy giro *n.* Government-provided funds that allow a resting gentleman to purchase the intimate attentions of an hirsute odalisque.

bi-furious *adj.* A man who flies into a hystrionic rage at the slightest suggestion that he may *know what's in his flowerbeds.*

big allotment challenge *1. n.* Tedious BBC2 programme in which green-fingered folk compete to grow plants. *2. n. Dining at the Y* on the produce from *Terry Waite's allotment.*

big arse and gastric band *n.* A *pie-abetic*

northern ensemble.

big bad wolf *n.* Someone who likes to *eat* grandmas. An *OAP-dophile, biddy fiddler.*

big bamboo *1. n.* A chap's *old man. 2. n.* In the film *Chitty Chitty Bang Bang,* a rousing, knockabout song performed by Dick Van Dyke. About his *cock.*

Big Ben *1. n.* A large bell in the Elizabeth Tower of the Houses of Parliament, London. *2. n.* An enormous *erection,* possibly with Robert Powell hanging off it for dear life.

big bluey storage *n.* A reliable bachelor friend with whom a man can temporarily deposit his lifetime's accumulation of *grot mags, stick vids, split kipper* Polaroids of his ex and other items of sentimental value, when he is about to commence cohabiting with a new *significant other.* A *porn buddy.*

big boned *1. adj.* Of thin people with corpulent skeletons, suffering from an unfortunate medical condition that makes it look like they eat forty cakes a day. Also *glands. 2. adj.* What *donkey-rigged* men are, when they've got a *horse's handbrake.*

big brother is watching you *phr.* The *wood-*felling realisation, while watching a *scruff* video, that there is a photo of a grinning sibling on top of the TV set which must be laid face down before one can continue *relaxing in a gentleman's way.*

big brown dog barking at the back door *euph.* A substantial *digestive transit* that is desperately scratching to be let out.

big cock day *n.* A day, quite possibly in spring, the arrival of which is greeted with the *dawn horn,* and throughout which the sap continues to rise. *'As he wrestled himself into his shreddies, Mr Darcy knew it was going to be a big cock day.'* (from *Pride And Prejudice* by Jane Austen).

big dame hunting *n.* A night out on safari in the hopes of bagging a *big-boned* trophy.

big five, the *n.* Immediately prior to his commencing a night on the town, the immutable fixtures in a with-it gentleman's ablutory regimen, *viz.* Shit, shave, *shuffle,* shower and shampoo. *The shushes.*

bigfoot's back *euph.* A particularly hirsute patch of *gorilla salad* round a *yeti's welly.*

biggest balls in his bedroom, he's got the *phr.* Said of keyboard warriors and chatroom moderator types. *'Saw that tweet from your son the other day, Mrs Watson. He must be right tough.' 'Oh yeah, he's got the biggest balls in his bedroom, him.'*

biggie smalls *n.* Fat lasses' *scads.*

biggie smells *n.* The pungent aroma given off by a heavily perspiring *salad dodger,* probably due to their glands.

Biggles's scarf *n.* Unusually long *Keith Burtons*.

big gulp, the *1. euph.* The Bob Monkhouse-style water level rise in the bog that precedes the dispatch of Boxing Day *foulage. 2. n.* Impressively large soft drink consumed by hyperactive American toddlers.

big in Japan *euph.* Said of niche musical acts who barely manage to scrape into the UK charts but somehow shift *shitloads* of records in the Land of the Rising Sun.

big Jimmy! *1. exclam.* A long, passionate, strained cry from Kevin Rowland that cues in long-term Dexys Midnight Runners collaborator "Big" Jimmy Paterson's trombone solo during the song *Liars A to E. 2. exclam.* A long, passionate, strained cry just before a foot-stomping *brass eye fanfare*.

big mac *1. n.* A disappointing *hamburger*, consisting of two tired, grey pieces of meat, random, sorry-looking vegetation and traces of unidentified mayonnaise-like liquid. *2. n.* A high street fast food that looks and tastes like *1. 3. n.* A carefully chosen, artfully lit and meticulously composed photograph of the sort used by a rough female on a social networking site to ensure that her image is as misleadingly attractive to the eye as possible. Named after the laughably unrealistic burger photographs displayed above the counters of certain litigious fast food restaurants, which bear scant resemblance to the dishevelled, unappetising objects their customers find in the box after purchase.

big muck *n.* A hearty, blood pressure-raising *dump* enjoyed several hours after gorging on fast food.

big O, the *n.* See *O, the big.*

big parade *n.* A rousing *brass-eye* fanfare that sounds like "seventy-six trombones".

big rip, the *1. n. Phys.* Scientific theory that the universe is expanding due to so-called "dark energy", with galaxies moving further and further away from each other or something. It's on Wikipedia if you fancy a slightly more detailed explanation. *2. n.* A sudden and cataclysmic expansion of *ignoble gases* in "your anus".

big ted's leg *n.* A man-size *shite. 'Do you know what sort of things can block the toilet? Let's watch a man break up big ted's leg with his potato masher… through the arched window.'*

big V-buster *1. n.* Oddly-titled weapon of attack featured in the acclaimed children's programme *Kyuukyuu Sentai GoGoFive* which, needless to say, we never miss. *2. n.* One of those huge novelty *dildos* they have on display in sex shops "just

for laughs".

bi jovi *n.* A *bone Jovi*, unexpectedly encountered in somewhat *puddle-jumpy* circumstances, which might surprise a fellow to the extent that his monocle falls out.

bike *n.* A frequently *ridden* woman; one who has had thousands of gentlemen swing their legs over her. *'You don't want to go near her, mate. She's the office/factory/London Symphony Orchestra and Festival Chorus bike.'*

biker foreplay *n.* The romantic practice of *kick-starting the motorbike* next to one's *significant other*, and then holding her head under the covers so that the potent *exhaust fumes* can get her in the mood. A *Dutch oven*.

biker's Highway Code, thin as a *sim.* Reference to something which is notably slight. *'Strewth Marvin, I saw Tim Henman's grand slam record today, and it is as thin as a biker's Highway Code.'*

bike shed *n.* A *meat market*.

bike shed butcher *n.* A popular lass who's handled a few pounds of sausages in her time.

bikini burger *n.* A *vertical bacon sandwich*. See *hairy pie*.

Bilbo Baggins' foot *n.* An hirsute vagina, resembling the hairy toes of a hobbit.

Bilbo Baggins' sock drawer *euph.* A particularly commodious *clout*.

bile mile *n.* The finishing straight of a marathon *spewing* session, where one's gallbladder is going flat out to produce something worth *yoffing*, but is frankly fighting a losing battle.

bilge tanks *n.* The "double gut" effect caused by an overly tight belt on an overly large belly.

bilious fog *n.* Any cloud of dense, sulphurous, boiled-egg-and-Brussels-sprout-induced vapour emanating from *cack canyon*, so thick that a safe passage may only be negotiated through it by means of a machete or chainsaw.

bilious Fogg *n.* A loud and boring workmate who recounts the particulars of his exotic round-the-world peregrinations in such mind-numbing detail that it makes you want to retch.

Bill Grundies *rhym. slang.* Undies, trolleys, dunghampers.

Billingsgate banjo *n.* Something that a lady strums and which smells of fish. That'll be her *twat*, then.

Billingsgate box *n. Minge.* Based on a comparison between the smell of a cockney seafood market and a cockney *fadge*.

Bill Oddie *n. prop. onomat.* A short, sharp *Edward Woodward* in the bath.

billposter's bucket *sim.* Large paste-filled *snatch. 'I was stationed in Scutari Hospital for six months,* *the only woman amongst thousands of soldiers. By the end of my first shift I had a twat like a billposter's bucket.'* (from *My Poor Cunt – The Crimean Wartime Memoirs of Florence Nightingale*).

bills *n.* Shreddies, bills, dunghampers.

Bill Wyman *rhym. slang.* A lady's *virgin string.* Named after (the rest of this sentence has been deleted following an urgent letter to the printworks from our lawyer)ones bassist. From Bill Wyman = hymen.

Billy Bowden's bunny *n.* An extremely small and bent *middle peg,* reminiscent of the erstwhile New Zealand cricket umpire's famously crooked "finger of doom."

Billy Bunter *1. n. prop.* The erstwhile, hamper-crazed "fat owl" of Greyfriars School. *2. n. rhym. slang.* A prostitute's customer. From Billy Bunter = punter. *'Oh yes, Jeffrey's been my most loyal Billy Bunter for years.'*

Billy Connolly's beard *n.* A *ragweek fanny.*

Billy Dainty *n.* The awkward, foward-leaning, *arse*-out posture that a chap has to adopt in order to mask a *bone on* when making his way, for example, to the pub bogs. Named after the *priapismic* Happy Shopper Max Wall who played the brown-coated cameraman on *Emu's Broadcasting Company.*

billy goat's chin *n.* A gruff *muff under the bridge* with a distinctly coarse beard of *arse cress.*

billy goat's mouth *n.* An exceptionally loose *fadge.* With bits of the mayor's hat sticking out of it.

Billy Joel *1. n. prop.* Scrotum-faced New York singer/songwriter who is, bizarrely, friends with robustly opinionated Fitzwilliam-born bat-swinger Geoffrey Boycott. *2. n.* A *Boris Johnson.*

Billy Mill roundabout *n.* Climactic point of a bout of masturbation. From the formerly climactic point of the A1058 Coast Road near Newcastle, which is tragically now just a junction with loads of traffic lights. The *vinegar strokes.* *'My mum walked in just as I was coming up to the Billy Mill roundabout.'*

Billy munter *n.* A female *with a lovely personality.*

Billy no mates *1. n.* A lonely little buoyant *turd* that remains hanging around in the *chod bin* after all the others have gone to the beach. *2. n.* A person bereft of close acquaintances.

Billy Smart *n. rhym. slang.* A *Bakewell* equipped with a top hat and a red tail-coat.

Billy Two-Mirrors *n.* Affectionate nickname for one whose bones are so big that they need to double their allocation of looking glasses in order to fully encompass their reflection. Also *Bessie Two-Mirrors. 'Oi, Billy Two-Mirrors. You forgot my*

McFlurry, you fat cunt.'

Billy Wright *n. rhym. slang.* Legendary Wolverhamtpon Wanderers footballer who married Vera Lynn or the Andrews Sisters or someone, latterly immortalised as rhyming slang for *shite. 'Aw. Who's done a Billy Wright in my shoe?'*

bilp *n.* Blip, milp, truffle butter.

bilper *n.* Full fat *man milk, spaff, Harry monk, jitler, jism, chef's special sauce.* Good old-fashioned *spunk.*

Bilston kiss *n.* Christened in honour of the eponymous town of the same name, a Midlands version of a *Glasgow Kiss,* with the added feature that the victim gets his nose bitten off at the same time.

biltang *n.* Dry, tough and chewy *beef curtains.* From biltong + poontang.

biltrum *n.* The *chin rest.* See *wannocks.*

bimbo *n.* A *tit-for-brains.*

bimbo bakery *n.* The tanning salon.

binalot *n.* 'Value' dogfood, or indeed the contents of any bargain basement meat product. *'A pint of cookin', please landlord, and one of your binalot pies.'*

bincess *n.* A rough *piece* dolled up to the sevens.

bindow *n.* An open car window that is used as a handy receptacle for refuse. *'Where should I put all this McDonald's rubbish, dad?' 'Pop it in the bindow, son. Don't want it messing up the car.'*

binegar *1. n. prop.* Excellently named small village and civil parish in Somerset, England, located on the A37, 4 miles (6.4 km) east of Wells, between Shepton Mallet and Chilcompton. *2. n.* The vile-smelling condiment at the bottom of the kitchen waste receptacle. *Bin juice.*

binge wanker *n.* A fellow who concentrates his week's quota of *self delight* into the period between 6pm on a Friday and 10pm on a Sunday, but "never on a school night".

bingo armour *n.* The excessive amounts of tawdry jewellery worn by flabby-armed ladies enjoying a night frantically crossing out numbers in a former cinema. *Blingo, bingo clink.*

bingo band *n.* A tattoo originally applied halfway around the arm of a slender lady, which doesn't reach halfway round her arm any more.

bingo baps *n.* Shrivelled, pendulous *socktits* that hang down to an *old biddy's* waist. *Knee shooters, nan-chukas, toe polishers, basset hounds' ears, beaver tails, Gandhi's flip-flops, stalactits.*

bingo bollocks *n.* The danglesome *clockweights* of a senior citizen. Also *crown green bollocks, low hanging fruit.*

bingo bongo *1. exclam. zool.* The mating call of the

male silverback western lowland gorilla *(Gorilla gorilla gorilla).* 2. *n.* Granny porn. *'Oi, mister. Give me a pack of Scotch eggs and a bingo bongo mag, will you? I'm off me face.'*

bingo caller *n.* A male who likes to *dip his wick* in the dry wells of the elderly.

bingo dabbers *n.* The enlarged nipples of a pregnant lady. *'They used to look like raspberries, but ever since she's been up the duff, they've looked more like bingo dabbers.' 'There's no room at the inn, but it's warm and dry in the stable, with a manger for a bed.'*

bingo doors *n.* An old, well-battered set of *cat flaps*. *'My next guest needs no introduction, except to say that even well into her seventh decade her bingo doors would be well worth bashing in. Ladies and gentlemen, Dame Helen Mirren.'*

bingo ink *n.* Unnecessarily judgemental name given to tattoos. See also *council camouflage, tramp stamp, whoremark, everlasting jobstopper, bingo band etc.*

bingo ninja *n.* A formidable old *bird* in a leopard-print onesie, dripping with rose gold jewellery and chain-smoking Superkings, as seen outside bingo halls throughout the UK on most evenings.

bingo partner *n.* A man who is currently engaged in a romantic dalliance with a somewhat more mature lady.

bingo top *n.* A feminine upper body garment, cut in such a way as to encourage men to cast their "eyes down" in expectation of a glimpse of *nork* and/or *Bristol Channel. 'I couldn't help it, love. She was wearing her bingo top.'*

bingo wing commander *n.* A chap with a penchant for the company of more mature females. *'Today's birthdays: Robin Day, erstwhile political interviewer, 1923; Ronnie and Reggie Kray, entrepreneurs, 1933 ; Wayne Rooney, Premiership footballer and bingo wing commander, 1985.'*

bingo wings *n.* Upper-arm adipose underhangs found on post-menopausal ladies of a common bent. *Arm tits.*

bin juice *1. n.* The aromatic liquid found at the bottom of refuse receptacles. *2. n.* The distillate syphoned off an unkempt lady's *growler.*

binjuries *n.* Ailments acquired while in a drunken stupor, *eg.* Griddle burns on the *arse* cheeks caused by falling onto an electric fire on Anglesey, to pick an example entirely at random.

binked *adj.* Descriptive of one who has fallen victim to an *etch-a-wretch* and will bear the shameful scars forever. From Badly + Inked. *'That's very touching the way he's got his kid's name binked in*

an arch over his arsecrack in Olde English capitals.'

Bin Laden's beard *n.* A particularly luxuriant, yet unruly *stoat.* The antithesis of a *Hitler tash.*

bin lid penny *euph.* A more extreme version of *half a crown thru'penny bit* for the more anally flexible frightened person. *'I bet it was bin lid penny for Nick Ross every time the doorbell rang until they arrested Barry George. And after that too.'*

bin lids *n.* The areolae round a lady's nippular bits.

binman's belch, less finesse than a *sim.* Descriptive of a person who exudes a frankly substandard level of class, panache and dignity. *'Outrageous. The brand new fragrance by Kerry Katona, the star with less finesse than a binman's belch.'*

binorkulars *n.* Sunglasses as worn by an observant fellow at the beach. *Perv windows.*

bin ripper *n.* An *alcoholic womble.* One who finds his treasure amongst the things everyday folk leave behind. A *Harold Ramp.*

bins out the back of a dead fanny factory, smells like the *phr. sim.* A telling phrase descriptive of a fruity fragrance, for example the honk off the Wildriggs feed plant enjoyed by the populace of Penrith. *'Would you like to sample some perfume, madam? It's Fantasy by Britney Spears.' 'Jesus, that smells like the bins out the back of a dead fanny factory. How much is it?'*

binstipation *n.* When the kitchen binliner only comes out after a substantial amount of straining and profanity-enriched vocal encouragement.

bint *n.* Derogatory term for a *butcher's daughter.*

bintage year *n.* A period of twelve months frittered away *putting it about* with *ladies of easy virtue.*

bintcoins *n.* Alternative form of currency; specifically Next vouchers.

binter *n.* On programmes such as *Loose Women,* the pointless, shrill and utterly inconsequential gossip about *The X-Factor, Strictly Come Dancing* or *Big Brother* that passes for conversation. *Fanny banter.*

binterfering *n.* When some Doris sticks her nose in unnecessarily.

binternet *n.* The world-wide electronic network which, it is whispered, can apparently be used to view titillating pictures of young ladies in various states of undress.

binterrogation *n.* An onslaught of awkward and unwelcome questions from the *bag for life* that commences immediately upon entering the front door, four hours late and in a state of extreme *refreshment.*

binterruption *n.* An unwarranted wifely reminder to keep one's counsel.

binterview *n.* Evaluation of a prospective

employee, conducted by a man, for a position open to all suitably qualified and experienced applicants of any gender, whereby in reality the best looking piece of *blart* to walk through the door will likely be the one that gets hired. *'I have to pop into town to buy a low-cut top as I've got an important binterview tomorrow.' 'Right you are, Sister Wendy.'*

bint imperials *n. Rocks* so hard that your *bird* could break her molars on them. But without the breath-freshening qualities of their confectionery almost-namesakes.

bint sauce *n.* Any beverage which is particularly appealing to a bar's distaff clientele. *Tart fuel, knicker oil, bitch piss. 'Pint of Exhibition, three bags of scratchings and half a dozen pickled eggs for me, and a small bint sauce for the missus, please.'*

bin tumescence *n.* The way a full black bag becomes sexually excited and swells up to an unlikely and disturbing volume as it is removed from its container.

bio bling *n. Jelly jewellery. Pearl necklaces, spunky earrings* and the like. Also *Jizzie Duke.*

bio-break *1. n.* Term used by business *wankers* when they need to have a five minute interregnum between meetings in order to answer *the call of nature. 2. n.* A *monkey's fag-break.*

biography bus *n.* The first public transport service of the day that runs after the time that pensioners' free travel passes become valid, on which every seat is occupied by some old *gimmer* recounting their life story to anyone who will listen.

biological cock *n.* Shortly before a young swain is due to get married, the feeling he gets that he must *tup* as many women as possible before his time to do so runs out for ever.

bi-pod *n.* The MP3 player of someone with un-accountably diverse and eclectic musical tastes, where a predominantly macho selection of music (*eg.* Heavy metal, punk, brass bands *etc.*) is inexplicably intertwined with tracks such as *It's Raining Men, YMCA* and *Kay Why* by Brothers Butch.

bipper *n.* A lady's *clematis.* The *starter button* or *wail switch.*

bips *n.* Fucking enormous hips, like those you see on them American monsters in the queue for the turkey legs at Disneyworld. From beast + hips. *'Oi, Steve! Come through here and check out this woman's bips on this Youtube clip of Jerry Springer!'*

bird *n.* Outdated, offensively sexist way of referring to a woman. *'Phoar! Is this your new bird? She's a bit of alright, ain't she? Fantastic tits. What does she go like, then?' 'None of your business, vicar.'*

bird feeder *1. n.* A rigid tube, through which birds

empty the nuts. *2. n.* A rigid tube, through which *birds* empty the *nuts. 'There were a couple of swallows on my bird feeder this morning. And I also got my bollocks nibbled by a cheap whore behind a skip, which was nice.'*

bird flu *n. medic.* Pre-*women's things* irritability. *Early onset rag radge, strawberry mivvie.*

bird food *n.* Muesli, lettuce, cous-cous, brown bread, salad, vegetables *etc.*

birdie dance *n.* Arm-flapping terpsichorean routine performed while hovering above the *crapper* trying to lay an *egg.*

bird on the wire *1. n.* Title of a track on Leonard Cohen's 1969 album *Songs from a Room,* which was later re-recorded by Judy Collins and, we reckon, Aaron Neville. *2. n.* A female who is *highly strung* due to *a visit from aunt Flo.*

bird sanctuary *n.* A place where women of the opposite gender can congregate, safe from the reaches of male gentlemen, *eg.* The bingo, the hairdressing salon, the toilet cleaning products aisle at Tesco's.

bird scarer *1. n.* A visual or audible device designed to deter avian creatures from congregating at airports or agricultural areas. *2. n.* A *copper's torch* of sufficient magnitude to alarm a conventionally *fannied* female, *eg.* The one belonging to the former MP for Ealing North Stephen Pound. A *bride frightener.* Also *Scots. Boaby dazzler.*

bird scarer *n.* A particularly long or girthsome, or long *and* girthsome, *stench hammer.*

birds' custard *1. n.* A sweet, gloopy substance that comes out of a tin. *2. n.* A savoury, gloopy substance that comes out of a lady's *clout. Blip, bilp, fanny batter, moip, milp. 3. n.* What you get on your hair and shirt when walking beneath a place where avians congregate. *4. n.* What you get on your hair and shirt when walking beneath a place where middle-aged women congregate to watch Michael Bolton.

birdseed *n. derog.* Nickname for a henpecked fellow.

bird's eye view *n.* Your girlfriend or *bag for life*'s totally objective opinion of your many wrongdoings, based upon impartial evidence gathered from her entirely dispassionate perspective.

birds' nest *1. n.* In nature, where a load of chicks hang around open-mouthed, all eager to get a fat worm in their mouths. *2. n.* In pornography, and the real life of the lead singer of Saxon, much the same thing. Only without Bill Oddie watching through binoculars, you would hope.

birds' nests *n. rhym. slang. Whammers.* From birds' nests = ladies' breasts.

birds' nest soup *n.* The contents of lady's *drip tray;*

considered a savoury delicacy in some cultures. *Clop slop.*

birds of pray *n.* Fit nuns.

bird's trifle *1. n.* Popular proles' pudding containing several fingers and a lot of jelly, topped with custard and cream but frequently missing the cherry. *2. n.* A dirty lady's *letterbox.*

birdstrike *1. n.* In aeronautical circles, a high altitude pigeon or similar avian hitting the whirring fanblades of a jet engine, leaving everything covered with blood, minced guts and feathers. *2. n.* One's wife or girlfriend's monthly *moon juice* session, when she wheels her *under-carriage* into the hangar for a week's essential *flap* maintenance.

bird table *n.* Unpleasantly sexist term for an otherwise attractive lady who is spoiled by a dearth of *knockers.* From the fact that "it would look great with a couple of tits on it".

Birkenhead confetti *n.* Gravel.

birminger *n.* A Brummie *bird* who is a minger. From Birmingham + minger.

Birmingham booty call *n.* The West Midlands hobby of setting one's mobile phone to vibrate before inserting it up a lady's *fundament* and ringing it. The *Birmingham booty call* became even more popular when the original 1983 Motorola 8000 "brick" was superseded by more modern, streamlined units.

Birmingham botox *n.* Budget cosmetic procedure, available in most Black Country pubs, which leaves one's face looking not unlike that of Sylvester Stallone's late mom. A sound *pasting.*

biroglyphics *n.* The mysterious and generally un-attributed ideographs which are commonly found adorning overused lecture hall tables, telephone kiosks and public lavatory cubicle walls, where they offer fascinating insights into more primitive cultures. *'I'm afraid I can't read a word of these biroglyphics on the cludgy door, Lord Carnarvon.'*

birthmark *n.* Clinging tenaciously to the side of the *chodbin* after flushing, a sepia smudge that signifies the recent arrival of a newly born *arse baby.*

birth marks *n.* The two red welts atop a male's knees after he has been reading the *Autotrader* on the *crapper* for a long period while *dropping a box of shoes from the attic.*

biscuit *n.* A *turd. 'Would you like a biscuit to dunk in your tea, Mr Farage?'*

biscuit barrel *n.* A *big-boned* fellow with a sweet tooth.

biscuits *1. n. UK.* the contents of the stomach after a heavy night's drinking. *'Get me a bucket quick,*

your honour, I'm gonna chuck me biscuits.' 2. n. US. Tight *buns.* Attractive *ass cheeks,* a *sweet fanny.*

bisexual *adj.* See *half-rice half-chips.*

Bishopbriggs Sports Centre, dirtier than *sim.* Said of a lady who will do anything for her man. In reference to East Dunbartonshire's former flagship leisure centre which has, we understand, seen better days and is now a stranger to a bottle of bleach and a scrubbing brush.

bishop rage *n.* A *monkey spanking* performed with such vigour that the perpetrator takes on the appearance of one of thirsty artist Francis Bacon's famous screaming Popes.

bishop's dick, stiff as a *sim.* Descriptive of the muscular and joint rigidity experienced following a 20-mile hike. *'With Striding Edge safely negotiated, I wearily descended the Victorian pony track down Birkhouse Moor with its fine views across to St. Sunday Crag. At the foot of the slope I crossed Grisedale Beck and joined the tarred road for the difficult last eight miles, finally entering Patterdale as stiff as a bishop's dick.'* (from *Coast to Coast the Miserable Way* by Alfred Wainwright).

bishop's licence *n.* That which is granted to a man left home alone by his wife, enabling him to *wank* himself blind at his leisure.

bishop's minger *n.* A woman so plain that she has to marry a vicar.

bishop's mitre *n.* A *bobby's helmet.*

bishop's move *n. Pissing* diagonally from one pub urinal into an adjacent one, in the style of chess grandmaster Gary Kasparov when he goes for a *piss.*

bishop's waltz *n.* Keeping one's threadbare old t-shirt held up over the chest with the chin and one's soiled tracksuit bottoms held out at the waist with the thumb of one hand, the other wrist dripping with fresh *kebab fat,* while waddling awkwardly to the toilet following an act of mid-morning *self pollution.* Also known as a *spangle dash.*

bi-spurious *adj.* Of a D-or-lower list female celebrity, feigning *lesbitious* tendencies for the purposes of courting publicity. *'I see that bird with the big lips off TOWIE or Made in Chelsea has announced she's gone bi-spurious, then. Ooh, she's got a new perfume out, look.'*

Bisto kids *n.* The products of *lady golfer* couples' judicious use of the gravy baster.

Bisto skids *n.* The beefy stains left down the back of the *pan* after a night *on the sauce. Toilet snail* trails.

bit, a *1. n.* An imperial unit of *the other,* slightly less than an entire *portion. 2. n.* Unspecified quantity of *crumpet,* usually partaken *on the side.*

bitch piss *n.* Alcopops. *'For myself, please barlord, a foaming pint of your finest Old Jack's Tipple, and a small bottle of bitch piss for the missus.'*

bitch tits *n.* Large, flabby breasts found on overweight males of any age. Particularly amusing when sported by an obese American president playing golf in a polo shirt. *Triple-hearters, dog udders, moomlaaters, Trump's toppers.*

bitchwhore *n. pej.* An unpopular female.

bite and shite *n.* A double whammy whereby a gentlemen visits his local hostelry to enjoy a nice bit of *scran* followed by a pleasant *sit down bob.*

bite off more than you can poo *v.* To overeat.

bite the mango *v.* To chomp on a particularly moist *flange*, such that the juice dribbles down the muncher's chin. One of your five-a-day.

biting point *n.* The first tingly inklings down amongst the loins that a prolonged bout of *self help* might just possibly be about to prove worthwhile after all. *Fringles.*

biting the butter *n.* Going down to commit an act of *cumulonimbus* on a *plumper's clunge,* only to find the experience akin to that of biting into a warm, salty slab of Lurpak.

bit of fluff *n.* A singular piece of *totty.*

bit of grey *euph.* Davina McCall's mum's *badger.*

bit of rough *n.* A sexual partner, usually male, from a lower social echelon. One who wouldn't think twice about wiping his *cock* on a *bird's* curtains, *eg.* Mellors in *Lady Chatterley's Lover,* or HM the late Queen's *tit*-feeling bedtime interloper Michael Fagan.

bitten by the brewer's horse *euph.* As *refreshed* as a newt.

bitterflies *n.* Mythical intestinal insects that flutter in the stomach when it's knocking off time and one can almost taste the first pint.

bitter truth, the *1. n.* Title of a 2003 William Lashner novel featuring a "jaded Philadelphia lawyer" which has three-and-a-half stars on Amazon, where it is available used from £1.54. *2. phr.* The working man's equivalent of "In Vino Veritas". Setting the record straight when *pissed up* on Tetleys.

BJLs *abbrev.* Blow Job Lips. See also *DSLs*

Bjork *v. onomat.* To vomit in Iceland (country or supermarket).

blaaters *n.* Oomlaaters.

black and blue menstrual show *n.* An unprovoked assault accompanying a particularly disputatious *tammy huff.* A bruising *blobstrop* encounter of noteworthy pugnacity, tempestuousness

or excitability.

Blackbeard's ghost *n.* A triangular, white, spooky apparition occasionally glimpsed by the *one-eyed lookout* in the *crow's nest.* A mature lady's once-raven *mapatasi.* A *fanny badger.*

blackboard Friday *n.* The extra loud evening in July when pubs and clubs fill up with teachers who cannot hold their drink, who are celebrating the start of their six week summer holidays. Which they will be spending marking homework, thus explaining their excitement.

black country gateau *euph.* The back alley leavings of a Dudley-based vagrant.

black country urgency *n.* The performance of a task with dizzying slowness and ineptitude, in the style of Dave Hill out of Slade.

black eye Friday *n. NI.* The Friday immediately preceeding Christmas, on which Ulsterfolk of all sexes, ages and mental capabilities descend upon drinking establishments to celebrate with each other the anniversary of the birth of Our Lord Jesus Christ. The traditional end result of this festive gathering incorporates (in no particular order of preference) violence, molestation, vomiting, crying, marital breakdown and pregnancy. Also known as *amateur night.*

blackfish *1. n.* A nickname given to killer whales. *2. n.* A Guinness *shite* or *burnt tyre.* See also *Irish alarm clock.*

black forest gateau *n.* A luxuriant and filling *knicker pudding. Hairy pie.* £3.95.

black forest shateau *n.* An overly rich mountain of *feeshus* of the sort produced the morning after an evening out on the stout.

black gates, the *1. n.* In *The Lord Of The Rings,* the entrance to the Land of Mordor where the evil forces of the dark Lord Sauron reside, or some such *bollocks. 2. n.* A Guinness drinker's *arsehole* on a Saturday morning.

black hole of cal-cutlery *phr.* Mysterious place where one's favourite bowl, plate, knife and/or fork disappears for days on end. The dishwasher.

black lodge *1. n.* An extradimensional place that features in David Lynch's cult TV series *Twin Peaks. 2. n.* The state of the *crapper* when one has *unleashed the dobermans* the morning after a night drinking stout.

Black Magic box, I bet she knows the secrets of the *exclam.* Said of a woman *with a lovely personality.*

black mamba *n.* The horrifically toxic aftermath of a night spent knocking back something that is supposed to be good for you, curled up waiting to strike in the *chod pan.*

Blackpool cock *n.* A pink, sticky erection upon

which one's missus could break her teeth. And which would probably make her feel sick before she was even half way through eating it.

Blackpool cocktail bar *euph.* Any drinking establishment whose clientelle, it could be argued, might be somewhat lacking in poise, refinement and sophistication, *eg.* Sneaky Pete's in Edinburgh before it got shut down after one too many murders.

Blackpool jellyfish *n.* Any floating carrier bag/*dunky*/*fanny nanny* found washed up along the famous Golden Mile.

blackpoo log fumes *n.* The rank miasma emanating from a Guinness and blood-pudding-fuelled *Eartha*.

black saffron *euph.* Excuse given by a chef when one of his *pubes* is discovered in a meal. *'What's this in my Hay-aged Dover Sole Coulibiac with Celeriac and Perigord Truffle, Mr Blumenthal?' 'Ah yes, that's a frond of black saffron, madam. It's an acquired taste.'*

blacksmith's apron *n.* A mature lady's substantial, leathery *front bottom*.

blacksmith's cramp *n. medic.* Lower right arm complaint suffered by those who do a lot of hammering.

black winds of death *1. n.* Toe-tapper by German pirate band Running Wild. Us neither. *2. n.* Particularly nasty flatulence caused by over-enthusiastic consumption of Guinness.

bladder adder *n.* The *trouser snake*. *'Bugger. I've just caught me bladder adder in me zip. Here's Sally Traffic with the travel.'*

bladdered *adj.* See *blitzed*.

bladdertorial combat *n.* Vicious man-to-man duel, whereby a man attempts to drink more pints of booze than his comrades before having to relieve himself. See *break the seal*.

bladdiator *n.* A fellow who engages in *bladdertorial combat*.

bladoosh! *n. onomat.* The satisfying noise of a solid *number two* hitting the water dead centre.

blamestorming session *n.* A round-the-pub-table discussion which incorporates forcefully expressed opinions.

blancmangerie *n.* Plus-size women's *funderwear* that halves in price on February the fifteenth.

blandersnatch *n.* A *mingepiece* that has been *fannicured* to resemble a Barbie part; one that is devoid of uniqueness, personality and *gorilla salad*.

bland job *1. n.* Being *tossed off* by a lass while so *pissed* that one can hardly feel it. See *no job 2*. *n.* Run-of-the-mill *manual relief* administered by a frankly uninterested partner. A *bland job* is

normally considered better than *pulling yourself off*, but only just.

blandsome *adj.* Supposedly good-looking. Descriptive of the sort of man that society attempts to condition women into finding attractive, *eg.* That muscly *twat* off *Poldark* that gets them all *frothing like bottled Bass*, as opposed to the pot-bellied and flatulent, half-*pissed*, *Viz*-reading blokes that women truly desire.

blandstand *n.* An erectivation of the *membrum virile* that is arguably more than a *semi*, but is certainly not a *diamond cutter*.

blank canvas *n.* A lovely, freshly cleaned toilet.

blanket drill *n. milit.* An early morning *mutton musket* practice that results in the loss of the *officer's mess*.

blanket ripper *n.* Back-draught in a *Dutch oven*.

blanket starch *n.* That which stiffens a bachelor's sheets.

blanket welding *n.* Under-the-covers heavy manual work involving *pink steel*, which can lead to blindness.

blart *1. n.* Vagina. *2. n. coll.* Women, *totty*. *'Golly gosh! This nunnery is heaving with blart'*.

blart attack *euph.* A strange feeling, starting in the *pills* and spreading down the right arm, upon finding oneself surrounded by a large quantity of top flight *cabbage. Acute vangina.*

blart gallery *n.* A pub containing wall-to-wall *totty*.

blarticulate *adj.* Silver-tongued; able to charm the *dunghampers* off the ladies.

blartifacts *n.* Items of used ladies' *intimate apparel* stolen from washing lines in, to pick an example entirely at random, the town of Barnoldswick in Lancashire, or bought from vending machines by *bespectable* Japanese businessmen.

blartist *n.* One who demonstrates unrivalled skills in the field of *blartistry. 'Titian remains among the foremost blartists of his era, and few would dispute that the sublime nudes of his oeuvre constitute an unrivalled array of proper little minge winkers.'* (Brian Sewell, *Titian's Tiffins*, review in the *Evening Standard*, August 2002).

blartphone *n.* A smartphone whose main use is to look at *grumble* sites and text photographs of the owner's engorged genitalia to women to whom the owner has just been introduced. *'Can I borrow your charger, Ian?' 'Not at the moment. Me blartphone's plugged into it.'*

blast from the past *1. n.* In disc jockey *hyperbole*, any record that is not currently in the charts. *2. n.* A not particularly appetising *whiff of last night's supper. 3. n.* A senior citizen's *dropped gut,* still bearing vestigial traces of his or her quondam wartime diet of powdered egg, Woolton pie and snoek. *'Ooh, I definitely got a sniff of steamed mutton there, nan. It was a real blast from the past.'* 4. *n.* A crafty *one off the wrist* fuelled by saucy recollections of an erstwhile conquest.

blat splatter *n.* Female ejaculate. *'Persil Bio simply lifts stains out of clothes, even on the cold water cycle. Mud, ketchup, red wine or dried-on blat splatter are no match for Persil, which leaves your clothes lemon fresh and with a new, bluey-whiteness you'll love.'*

blazing saddles *1. n.* Title of Mel Brooks's spoof Western, one scene of which involved a great deal of farting. *2. n.* The *ringpieces* of a group of men who have enjoyed a surfeit of *Edwina* the previous night, and consequently do a lot of farting. And *shitting* blood. *3. n. medic. Four minute miles.*

BLBP *abbrev.* A ring of *bumwad* wrapped around the front rim of a public *crapper* seat to ensure that a well-endowed fellow's *pride and joy* does not accidentally come into contact with the danger zone. Big Lad Buffer Pad.

bleach bum *n.* Horseshoe-shaped chemical burn upon the buttocks resulting from use of a privy that has recently been doused with industrial-strength caustic chemicals.

bleachy head *n.* The unmistakable post-ejaculatory *honk* of ammonia coming off of one's *old man.*

bleeding the brakes *n.* Carefully releasing the *turtle's breath* without engaging its *head.*

bleeding the heat valve *n.* The dispiriting business, typically a symptom of middle age when men tend to develop *leaky washers*, of being compelled to take a minuscule little *piss* (hopefully) following a hot bath.

bleed the lizard *v.* See *syphon the python.*

bleed the radiator *v.* To commit an act of flatulation in which one would be well advised to hold a rag over one's *brass eye* to prevent sludge going all over the wall. A bit like when you have to sort out your central heating, only you don't have to spend twenty minutes emptying out the fucking kitchen drawer looking for that little brass key.

Bleep & Booster *1. n.* Vaguely remembered black and white *Blue Peter* science fiction series, voiced by the same bloke who did *Captain Pugwash. 2. n.* The *ringpiece.*

bletherskate *n. Scots. Shit-for-brains, fuckwit, twat.* Literally meaning *sporran of shite.*

blick *n.* Pubic scurf, *muffdruff.*

bliff *n. Minge, front bottom.*

bliffage *n.* Very generously cut *bacon strips.* Also *gruffage, quimmage.*

bliff mag *n.* A *top shelf* periodical. *Rhythm journal,*

art pamphlet, noddy book. *'Do you want anything from the shops, Jonathan?' 'A couple of bliff mags please, Jane.'*

blighty wound *1. n.* In the WW1 trenches, a non-lethal injury a soldier hoped to receive in order to be repatriated. *2. n. Shitting your grundies* after mistaking a *fart* for a *solid*, and getting sent home early.

blimp *v.* To surreptitiously ogle ladies' breasts and *arses* from behind a pair of mirrored sunglasses.

blimpic games *n.* Annual mass participation sporting event occurring at the very start of each new year, in which every *big-boned piabetic* in the country dons skin-tight lycra and takes to the streets to get in shape.

blimplants *n. Knockers*, surgically enhanced to comic proportions, as sported by the likes of Jordan (from time to time) and the late Lolo Ferrari. *Bazongers.*

blimp my ride *phr.* Rueful expression descriptive of the process whereby the missus undergoes rapid and frighteningly unpredictable ballooning straight after the ink is dry on the marriage certificate.

blind cobbler's thumbs *n.* Large, well-hammered *nipples. Pygmies' cocks, chapel hat pegs, fighter pilots' thumbs.*

blind dirt snake *n.* A malodorous, legless lizard inhabiting *cak canyon*, which migrates south every morning as you spark up the day's first Superking. A *Richard the Third.*

blind man's buffet *n.* A *fanny* that can be located by the olfactory senses alone. *Blind man's muff.* A stanksome *snatch.*

blind man's porn *n.* Explicit sexual noises, usually coming from an adjacent room, tent or house. A *horn chorus.*

blind man's wank *n.* Once to the left, once down the middle then once to the right and repeat, in the style of a visually-impaired fellow finding his way across the street with his stick in a WC Fields film.

blind sitter *n. medic.* A fellow who presents himself at his local A&E department with a foreign object firmly lodged up his rectum and an accompanying flimsy excuse, *viz.* He "sat on it whilst wearing a loose-fitting dressing gown". *'Better break out the rubber gloves, nurse. We've got another blind sitter in the waiting room.*

blind skateboarder's elbow, cock like a *sim. 'But you must believe me when I tell you that I have found it impossible to carry the heavy burden of responsibility and to discharge my duties as King as I would wish to do without the help and support of* *the woman I love. And I tell you what, I've loved her that much recently I've got a cock like a blind skateboarder's elbow.'* (Abdication speech of King Edward VIII carried live on the *Ed Stewpot Stewart Show*, BBC Home Service, December 11th 1936).

bling *n.* Tasteless bijouterie of the sort worn by Bet Lynch, Liberace, or Lewis Hamilton.

blinglish *n.* Street language spoken by rappers and bishop's son DJ Tim Westwood.

blinkered *adj.* Wearing one's *trolleys* back to front in order to deliberately impair the *beast's* vision.

blip. *1. n.* A momentary deviation on a graph. *2. n.* The watery substance of female love. *Fish cream, nog juice, moip, bilp, sloom.*

blip fountain *n. medic.* The Bartholin's gland that secretes vaginal lubrications. The *batter tap.*

blistered pisspot, face like a *sim.* Useful phrase to describe the appearance of a woman who has fallen out of the *lovely personality* tree and hit every branch on the way down. And then landed in a pile of broken glass. *'Ladies and gentlemen, here to perform her latest single is a singer who needs no introduction. She sings like a cat having barbed wire pulled out of its arse and she's got a face like a blistered pisspot so let's give a big Summertime Special welcome to Bonnie Tyler.'*

blistering barnacles *1. exclam.* Mild oath ejaculated by Captain Haddock in the popular *Tintin* stories. *2. n.* Badly scalded *clockweights*, caused by showering in foreign hotels with unfathomable tap operation systems. *3. n.* Sun-dried *love tomatoes* as found on British nudists who have fallen asleep on a Mediterranean beach (and also on spivvish TV rag & bone man David Dickinson). *Dry roasted nuts.*

blisters on your racket hand *1. n.* What that Emma Raducanu had at the Australian Open, when friction burns on her palm impeded her playing performance. *2. euph.* Symptom often inexplicably suffered by male viewers of the ladies' tennis.

blit *n.* See *blivvet.*

blitzed *adj.* See *wankered.*

blitzkrieg plop *n.* A full rectal assault on the porcelain, characterized by the deployment of short, fast, powerful bursts of locally concentrated firepower.

blitzscaling *1. n.* In business, descriptive of a company that is doing whatever is necessary to get big quickly. *2. n.* Necking a mitful of *Bongo Bill's banjo pills.*

blivvet *n. coll. Mackerel, blart, fanny, tussage.*

blizzarding *n. Breaking wind* mid-*felch.*

bloatee *n.* The type of carefully toped beard favoured by the chubbier male in the vain hope that it will demarcate his chin from his neck and thus indicate where his face stops. As sported by hopelessly optimistic *pie shifters.*

bloatox *n.* Food-based facial rejuvenation system, whereby one's *mug* looks firmer, tighter and younger after using "fillers", *viz.* An intense programme of Greggs pasties, chicken nuggets and chips to create the effect of a youthfully bloated visage.

blob *1. n.* Condom. Also known as a *French safe, French letter, rubber Johnny, spooge Scrooge, dunky. 2. v.* To inadvertently make pregnant. *"You look a little green around the lemon, old chap. Bad news is it?" I enquired, as Jeeves continued to study the letter. "I'm afraid so Sir," he replied gravely. "I attended a party of the downstairs staff of Brokenbury Manor, and I am afraid things got a little out of hand. To cut a long story short, Sir, it appears that I have blobbed the cook."'* (from *Use the Back Door, Jeeves* by PG Wodehouse).

blob blimp *n.* A post-coital cabaret in which a used *jubber ray* is inflated and knotted for the amusement of one's ladyfriend.

blob it *v.* To oversleep. *'Jesus, Phil, look at the time. Get up, quick! I'm being coronated in half an hour and we've blobbed it.'*

blob jockey *n.* A gentleman with a penchant for the fuller-figured, Rubenesque lady. A *chubby chaser, gastric bandit.*

blobnoxious *adj.* Stroppy due to *women's things. 'In his autobiography, Burton claimed that his sixth divorce from Taylor was due to her blobnoxious behaviour on the set of Who's Afraid of Virginia Woolf.'*

blob, on the *adj.* See *on the blob.*

blobseekers allowance *1. n.* Loose change frantically excavated from the depths of his pockets by a drunk man swaying optimistically in front of the prophylactic machine in a pub *shitter. 2. n.* Permission to *plough* his *bird's back forty* granted to a man after he has proved his *boner fides* by gallantly scrambling the streets to locate a *Jimmy hat* after closing time.

blobsleigh *n.* Unexpected barefoot skid on last night's discarded sheath. The *spunky-footed luge.*

blobstopper *n.* A *fanny mouse*, a *slim fanatella* or *jam rag.* Put crudely, a feminine hygiene product.

blobstradamus *n.* A woman who peers into the future to predict the state of her *things* during a particular date range. *'So are you and your piece off to Ayia Napa the first week in June, then Dave?' 'No. Blobstradamus says she'll be up on blocks* *that week.'*

blobstreperous *adj.* Of a lady, rendered irrationally unreasonable after *falling to the communists*.

block of flaps *n.* A multi-storey pile of *lady golfers*. With a broken lift. For example, the fondly remembered "Razzle Stack" that was regularly featured in the hedge-dwelling *bongo pamphlet* of the same name.

Blofeld *n.* A *biddy fiddler, mothball diver, tomb raider, OAP-dophile* or *granny magnet*. Named after the erstwhile James Bond villain in honour of his habit of "stroking a white *pussy*".

Blofeld brunette *n.* A natural blonde who dyes her hair dark to feign intelligence. However, inspection of her lap reveals a, wait for it, here it comes again, "white *pussy*". And draft plans for world domination.

Blofeld's kiss *n.* The tell-tale facial pillow scar left by a drunken night's sleep. *"And for God's sake wash your face, 007," added M. "You can't meet the Swedish Ambassador sporting a Blofeld's kiss."'* (from *James Bond and the Blustery Day* by Ian Fleming).

blonde bombsite *n.* The distressing prospect that often greets a chap upon waking after a night of loud *banging* in the dark. The very antithesis of a blonde bombshell; "more Marilyn Manson than Marilyn Monroe", if you will.

blonde herring *n.* A woman who looks like she ought to be a nice bit of *mackerel* from the back, but who turns out to be an *old trout* from the front. A *golden deceiver* or *back beauty*.

blongle *n. medic.* Seminal fluid containing traces of blood. *Blunk, blism, blimphet*. That's right, there's four words for it. And that's just the ones beginning with "bl".

blood and custard *1. n.* Humorous, sex-case/train-spotter parlance for the cream and maroon livery in which British Railways coaching stock was painted in the 1950s and 1960s. *2. n.* The sort of curse that a soft pirate like Captain Pugwash might have uttered when he discovered that Cut-throat Jake had beaten him to the treasure of the San Fandango. *3. n.* The evidence left on the sheets after one has *done* it with a lady during her *unclean time*.

blood bachelor *n.* Married man undergoing the monthly interruption to his conjugal privileges while his missus is *on the mop*.

blood brothers *n.* Any group of men cast out to the pub while their wives, whose *women's things* have magically synchronised, sit at home throwing crockery at the walls.

blood diamond jubilee *n.* A dense, semi-precious

Fabergé dog egg which takes a sphincter-splitting hour of agony to force out. A celebration of an inglorious sixty minutes *on the throne*.

blood diamonds *1. n.* Painfully hard *turds. n. 2. n.* The testicles. An unprepossessing bag of *dirty stones* that is handed over into a young lady's care in the middle of the night.

bloodhound's jowls *1. n.* Oversized *beef curtains* that could track an escaped convict across Dartmoor. *2. n.* A mature *bird's funbags* during the later stages of collapse.

blood in your undies, here's *exclam.* Heart-warming oath in the style of "bottoms up" or "cheers" which can be used when raising a glass amongst company. *'And now I would like to propose a toast: To the President of the Arab Republic of Egypt, Anwar al-Sadat, and to the Prime Minister of the State of Israel, Menaham Begin; to the great peoples they serve, the people of Egypt and the people of Israel, now joined together in hope; and to the cause we all serve: here's blood in your undies.'* (Former US President Jimmy Carter, on the occasion of the signing of the Egyptian-Israeli Peace treaty, March 26th 1979).

blood muppet *n. Jam dam, cotton mouse, gash mop, Dracula's teabag.* A *women's things* thing.

blood orange *n.* The *arsehole* after it has been savaged by a particularly vicious *chocolate shark*. A *Japanese flag*.

blood slide *n.* A *scuttle* during *blob week*.

bloodsports *n. Salsa dip.*

bloodstick *n.* A fellow's erectivitated *membrum virile*.

blood wank *n.* The ill-advised and possibly life-threatening act of *gentlemanly relaxation* that takes the day's tally into double figures. Regularly achieved by certain second year physics students at Manchester University and all bus drivers.

bloody *adj.* Swearword.

bloody sundae *1. n.* An act of *cumulonimbus* performed on a lady who is *up on blocks. 2. n.* A U2 song about an act of *cumulonimbus* performed on a lady who is *up on blocks*.

bloomers *1. n.* A voluminous item of women's *no-funderwear. 2. n.* Large loaves of bread. *3. n.* Unfunny and self-indulgent "mistakes" made on camera which are later transmitted as part of tiresome BBC "comedy" compilations.

blooper *1. n.* ITV version of *bloomer. 2. n.* A sub-aquatic *trouser cough* or *bottle of olives.* Also *tottle, Edward Woodward, old faithful* or *Bill Oddie*.

bloo-tac *n.* A *feeshus* that is sufficiently malleable and ductile that small pieces could be rolled between thumb and forefinger and applied to the four corners of a poster.

blootered *adj. Blotto, wankered, shitfaced. 'I'm afraid Mr Reed can't go on your show in this condition, Mr O'Connor. He's not nearly blootered enough.'*

blot bang rub *1. phr. milit.* Skin decontamination procedure used by HM armed forces following a nuclear, biological or chemical attack. *2. phr. milit. Nipsy* decontamination procedure used by HM armed forces the day after a particularly delicious curry from the Curry Capital, Bigg Market, Newcastle upon Tyne.

blotox *n.* Characteristic *fellatrix's* trout-pout. Those ludicrously over-developed lips sported by the type of girl who has *cooked plenty of socks* in her time. *'Oi, Gillian. Have you had your gob done?' 'No, it's just a bit of blotox, Geoff.'*

blotto *adj. Bleetered, wankered, shitfaced.*

blottopilot *n.* Inbuilt male homing device which secures a safe return to one's house after a night *on the sauce,* whatever one's level of inebriation. Often fitted to one's *beer scooter.*

blotto voce *adv. Lat.* As spoken indiscreetly by one who has imbibed an excess of *brown sauce.* It's just the beer talking. *'(A burly builder MR O'SHAUGHNESSY exits the pub and finds TOM in his car, throwing toys into the street). MR O'SHAUGHNESSY: Oi. What the fuck do you think you're doing in the back of my fucking car? TOM: I'm the Bishop of Southwark. It's what I do.'*

blotty *n. coll. Pissed-up tussage, soused mackerel.* From blotto + totty. *'There's a nice bit of blotty at the bar, Sid.'*

blouse browse *n.* A swift, casual surf for *skirt* on the web.

blouse hounds *n. Shirt puppies* which are getting a bit long in the tooth.

blouse lifter *n.* A *skirt lifter, Victorian photographer, lady golfer.*

blow a dog off a chain *v. Aus.* To *let off* with a severity sufficient to strip canines from their moorings.

blowback *1. v.* Of drug addicts, to puff smoke from a *Devil's lettuce* joint into another drug addict's mouth. *2. n.* A gobful of one's own *spangle* thoughtfully passed on by a *nosher.* A snowball. *3. n.* A potentially fatal *blue dart* ignition mishap.

blow ballast! *1. exclam. nav.* Order shouted by a submarine captain to surface the vessel. *2. exclam.* Shouted by a person about to let loose a rip-roaring fanfare on the *trouser trumpet.* See also *I'll name that tune in one, please hold for the president, our survey said.*

blowbot wars *n.* Couple's under-the-quilt *farting* competition. Possibly accompanied by an over-ex-

citable commentary from Jonathan Pearce.

blowd *n.* A strange brown haze at the bottom of the *lavvy* made by a *turd* that has successfully resisted the flushing process. *Poo tea, PG shits.* From brown + cloud.

blow diddley *n.* An unsuccessful conclusion to an evening of wooing; a familiar experience, you would imagine, for Ernie Bishop when he started going out with Emily. A *blowout.*

blow dry *1. n.* Getting *sucked off* until your *nuts* resemble a *bat's wing. 'Fancy a blow dry?' 'Okay. I'll just pull up on the hard shoulder.' 2. v.* Of a dirty lady, to repeatedly *suck off* a fortunate male professional footballer, pop musician or stand-up comedian until his *pods* are exhausted of *men's spendings.*

blower's buttonhole *n.* A small, white fascinator left on the lapel following unscheduled or interrupted *horatio. 'I like your blower's buttonhole, Gillian.'*

blowflake *n.* A fastidious old maid who just won't.

blowhole *1. n.* Nostril-like orifice used by whales to expel foul air and attract Japanese scientists with harpoons. Often accompanied by what looks like steam but is actually fine water droplets. *2. n.* Orifice used by land-based mammals to expel foul air after a night spent consuming large amounts of beer, kebabs, chicken vindaloos *etc.* Often accompanied by what looks like steam and is, in fact, actual steam. *3. n.* The *hog's eye* or *meatus. 4. n.* A *nosher's* mouth.

blowing the knobwebs away *phr.* Descriptive of the first *nosh-off* a bloke receives following a particularly prolonged *dry spell,* during which spiders have made their homes in and around his *farmyard.*

blowing the sousaphone *euph. Sucking off* an obese partner whilst carrying him in a fireman's lift.

blowjob *n.* Dangerous sex act whereby the female inflates the male's testicles like balloons by blowing air into his penis. Also *blow job.*

blow jobbie *n.* A *nosh-off* enjoyed, if that is the right word, whilst taking a *shit.* Or, arguably, a *shit* enjoyed while being *noshed off.*

blowjob off Emu *n.* A *wank.*

blowjob off Zippy, like getting a *sim.* The risky act of allowing a dentally disturbed person, or one with braces, to perform the act of oral *horatio* on your *John Thomas.* From the Norris-off-*Corrie*-soundalike trouser-fastening-gobbed puppet who featured on low-rent 1970s kids' show *Rainbow. 'Sorry Janet. Not today, it would be like getting a blowjob off Zippy.'*

blow jobsworth *n.* Any person who refuses to *suck*

off a fellow for a petty reason.

blowjob tickets *n.* Cash.

blowjob week *n.* A once-monthly, seven-day *nosh fest* while *the tomato boat is docked.* *'Now your life doesn't have to stop just because blowjob week starts.'*

blowlamp *n.* A *fart* which is strong enough to fetch old paint off a door or caramelise the sugar on a crème brûlée.

blow mud *v.* To noisily expel a loose stool, *crop spray* or *pebbledash;* to release a *flock of pigeons.*

blown tail pipe *n. medic.* Damaged exhaust system. *'I'm afraid the Duchess will be unable to attend your reception tomorrow, as she has a blown tail pipe.'*

blow off *v.* To *pump.*

blow off steam *1. v.* Of a steam engine or highly strung person, to get rid of pent-up energy. *2. n.* To sound a high pressure *brass section* fanfare.

blow on the ragman's trumpet, a *euph.* A long and tuneless blast on the *botty bugle.*

blow poke *1. n.* A multi-function fireplace implement made infamous as the suggested murder weapon on Netflix series *The Staircase.* *2. n.* A *chewie* with an additional finger interpolated up the *coalhole* for good measure.

blow sisters *n. Lesbidaceous* nuns, often to be seen shopping for candles, sharing baths and riding tandems along cobbled streets.

blow the bogpipes *v.* To produce a howling, ear-drum-shattering drone from the vicinity of one's sporran while *crapping* in the *but'n'ben.*

blow the elephant's nose *v.* To wrap a piece of tissue around the end of one's *trunk* in order to absorb any outgoing *man mucus* which may flob out of it for any reason.

blow the shit back up your arse, it's windy enough to *exclam.* A quaint and somewhat hyperbolic way of describing a breezy bout of weather. *'"Fuck this, Piglet, I'm getting out of these woods," said Winnie. "It's windy enough to blow the shit back up your arse."'* (from *Winnie the Pooh and the Blustery Day* by AA Milne.)

blowtox *n.* Simple cosmetic procedure, usually performed by a female, which plumps up a fellow's *old man*, temporarily removing visible lines and signs of ageing by up to 100%.

blow up the Death Star *euph.* To successfully target a small thermal exhaust port right below the main port.

blow winds and crack your cheeks *exclam.* A quote from Act 3, Scene 2 of Shakespeare's *King Lear* that may be orated when a "sulphurous and thought-executing" breeze sits in the shoulder of your sail. Also *what's that, Sweep?; fer-fetch a cloth*

Granville; an excellent theory, Dr Watson.

blow your arse *v.* To inadvertently void the *nether throat* while forcibly clearing your sinuses.

blow your biscuits *v.* To *puke*, yawn in technicolour, *sing a rainbow, yoff.*

blow your own trumpet *1. euph.* To boast about your own abilities, for example at a job interview. *2. v.* To commit an auto-erotic act of *horatio* upon one's own *horn.* Probably something to leave off your CV.

BLT+ community *euph.* Brickies, taxi drivers, bouncers *etc.*

blubber beret *n.* The *pie hider*, when worn as an *ad hoc* Frank Spencer-style hat by a chap *licking out* his *double chalker* lass.

blubber Johnny *n.* One who *lives life in the vast lane*; a person whose sheer bulk effectively prevents copulation.

bludger *1. n.* One of two balls in the Harry Potter *bollocks* broomstick cricket game Quidditch. *2. n.* A *stool* of the very firmest consistency imaginable. A *pan-cracker.*

blue *1. adj.* Of comedians and jokes, a little bit near the knuckle. *"Ere no, lady. This one's a little bit blue. I was up a mountain last week, walking along a narrow path and I met a gorgeous naked woman coming the other way. Well, I didn't know whether to wank myself off or fuck her up the cunt.'* (Max Miller, *Max at the Met*, 1951). *2. adj.* Of films, to have a different relationship to the knuckle altogether.

blue ball *n.* The *taint.* Because it is "between the pink and the brown".

blue balls *1. n. pl. Bollocks* which are fit to burst through lack of use. *DSBs, Sir Cliff's plums, nuts like two tins of Fussell's Milk, monks' nuts. 2. n. medic.* Painful medical condition in young men caused by not *getting any* off their *significant others.*

bluebottle banquet *n.* A freshly laid *al fresco tom tit*, which instantly attracts a swarm of ravenous flies. Familiar to farmers, festival-goers, boy scouts and 1982 World Professional Darts champions.

bluecoat *n.* A lady who favours s*x *via* the *tradesman's entrance.* From the practice in greyhound racing whereby the dog in the blue coat is traditionally run from "trap two".

blue cock *n.* A tight-fisted *wanker. 'Oh! But he was a mean and miserable hand at the grind-stone, Scrooge! A squeezing, wrenching, grasping, scraping, clutching, covetous, old blue cock!'* (from *A Christmas Carol* by Charles Dickens).

blue dart *n.* That brief but exciting pyrotechnic display achieved by igniting one's *air biscuits.* An *afterburner, blue streak.*

blue deceiver *n.* Flaccid fellow who secretly consumes *Bongo Bill's banjo pills* prior to a night of passion to give his date the misleading impression that he is some sort of latter day Errol Flynn.

bluelight blues *n.* Feelings of misery and inadequacy in a young fellow caused by nocturnal overuse of his *blartphone.* Also *wangst.*

blue notes *n.* The mellifluous, jazzy sounds produced by a fellow the moment a dirty lady starts to blow a few double-tongued arpeggios on his *purple-reeded sex clarinet.*

Blue Peter badge *n. rhym. slang.* The feminine *bower of bliss*; the *vadge, fadge etc. 'Love, I've emptied the bins, cleaned the car and mowed the lawn. Do I get a Blue Peter badge tonight then, or what?'*

Blue Peter bird cake *1. n.* Half a coconut shell filled with a solid paste of lard and old seeds. *2. sim.* Descriptive of a right full old *growler. 'Up betimes and feeling heavy of nodgers I made my way to Mrs Fitzgibbon's bordello on Threadneedle Street to see darling Bess. However, to my dismay I found she had done good business this day, and indeed, when I remov'd her scads did find that her cunny resembled naught but a Blue Peter bird cake. I was forced to demand back my shilling.'* (from *The Diary of Samuel Pepys*).

Blue Peter tortoise has come out of hibernation, the *exclam.* Said when one has the *turtle's head,* especially after Val Singleton has woken it up by wafting a limp lettuce leaf near *Dot Cotton's mouth.* Also *there's a brown dog scratching at the back door.*

blue Sky thinking *n.* During a meeting, fondly casting one's mind back over the previous night's ten-minute freeview offering on a well-known satellite television channel.

blue spinach *n.* Slang term for the blue pills that have the same effect on the *trouser muscle* as the eponymous stringy vegetable used to do on Popeye's arms. *Bongo Bill's banjo pills. 'Bloody hell. Look at your cock, Edson. There's big anvil shapes bulging out the side and the bell end is ringing like a Test Your Strength machine.' 'Aye pet. I've just had me blue spinach, you see.'*

blue-veined junket-pump *n.* Technical name for the *penis.*

blue-veined piccolo *n.* Like a *bed flute,* only smaller.

blue-veined throbbosis *n. medic.* Serious condition of the genitals which occurs when a chap's *giggling pin* has been tumescent for such a long period that it starts to ache like a new mother's *udders.* The symptoms are usually accompanied by *blue balls.*

blue waffle *n.* One of those things on the internet, like "two girls one cup", "tub girl" and "lemon party", that should never *ever* be typed into Google with the Safesearch button "off".

blue wail *n.* A *grumble* thespian's overly melodramatic soliloquy, delivered as he *spouts.*

bluey *1. n.* A *bongo movie. 2. n.* A *mycoxafloppin* tablet, a *dick-tac. 'Are you going to be much longer on the shitter, June? Only I popped my bluey half an hour ago and it's starting to wear off.'*

blumpkin *n. US.* An American rock *groupie* speciality, for some unfathomable reason. To administer a *gobbie* to an artiste while the latter is *dropping his kids off at the pool.* Being *duggled,* or indeed *duggling.*

blunderbarse *n.* A *nipsy* which sprays a cone of high-speed feculent matter out in every direction, rather in the manner of one of them old-fashioned Elmer Fudd-style farmer's shotguns with the end of a trombone welded onto the barrel. A *twelve bore shitgun.*

blunderguff *v.* To expel an horrendous-smelling *fart* only to realise that the tastiest *dish* in the office is fast approaching.

blunderpiss *n.* A haphazardly scattered *wazz* that lacks accuracy at long range due to a flared muzzle.

blunk *1. n.* Blongle. *2. n.* Scabrous, multi-layered jewellery of the type purveyed by Elizabeth Duke *etc.* From bling + junk.

blurt *n.* Splod.

blurtch *n. medic.* The female reproductive organs, taken as a whole. *'Congratulations, your majesty. You have been delivered of an heir to the throne of England, Great Britain, and her Commonwealth Dominions. I'll just stick a couple of stitches in your blurtch and you'll be as right as ninepence.'*

blurtch engine *1. n.* A streaming video website where *presents for the wife* can be sourced. *2. n.* A search tool used as an alternative to Google in order to locate *artistic photography* on the internet, in order to keep the Autofill results on the former clean and family-friendly.

blurter *1. n. Aus.* The *chocolate starfish, ringpiece. 2. n.* A little fishy that thou shalt have on a little dishy.

blut *n. medic.* A lady's *snapper.*

Bluto's beard *1. euph.* A spectacularly hirsute *Judith,* resembling the vigorous chinny hair of Popeye's thick-necked, Gary Bushell-looky-likey nemesis. A *biffer. 'Pistacchia was powerless to resist. Macadamio's eyes burnt into hers like sapphires. His muscular arms enfolded her softly yielding body as she felt herself being swept away in a whirlwind of passion. Tenderly, she tugged down her silken bloomers to reveal the womanly* *treasure she had longed to yield to him ever since the first time they met at the confectionery counter of Fortnum & Mason. "Bloody hell, love," he cried. "Have you never heard of waxing? Your blurtch looks like Bluto's beard."'* (from *The Lady and the Liquorice Salesman* by Barbara Cartland). *2. n.* The dark ring of fluff found festooned around the *aardvark's nose* after wearing black *undercrackers*.

Blyton-Karloff syndrome *n. medic.* Affliction that strikes women for up to one week in four, turning them with terrifying speed from chirpy Milly Molly Mandys into pale-featured, sunken-eyed, murderous beasts. *Women's things.*

BNB *abbrev.* A *one night stand* whereby the chap sneaks out the bed and *fucks off* before his slumbering coital partner awakes. Bed Not Breakfast.

boabie *n. Scots.* Glaswegian term for the male *member.*

boabie lard *n. Scots. Population paste. 'Och, maw. Gran'paw's bin surfin' yon internet on ma wee laptoppie again, and the glaikit auld fud's left boabie lard a' awa the keyboard.'*

boa constrictor digesting a horse, like a *sim.* Descriptive of a *generously-skeletoned* woman who has somehow poured herself into a dress that is several sizes too small.

boak *v.* See *bowk.*

boarding house tap, arse like a *sim.* A rattling *nipsy* with an intermittent supply of hot, rusty water. Also *arse like a Tetley tea bag. 'I went to Heston Blumenthal's for my tea on Tuesday night. It's now Saturday and I've still got an arse like a boarding house tap.'*

BOAT/boat *acronym.* Someone who is a Bit Of A Twat. Also *boater.*

boatswain's whistle *n. nav.* Stiff pipes that sailors blow into while cupping the spheres below with their hands. An act customarily performed as a *rear admiral* comes onto their *poop deck*, whatever that means. Also *bo'sun's pipe.*

Boba Fett's hemet/Bobba Fett's hat *1. n.* A well-battered *helmet* that has seen plenty of action. From the legendary *Star Wars* bounty hunter's battle-scarred *titfer. 2. euph.* A battered old *mug* with a few *shots* messing it up a bit.

bob a job *euph.* The art of urinating onto a *floater* left by a previous visitor, such that it "bobs" about, charmingly, like something out of *Swallows and Amazons.*

bober fret *n.* When in somebody else's house, the blind panic and rising anxiety felt after unloading a massive *Thora*, which – despite repeated

flushes – refuses to disappear.

bobber job *n.* A buoyant *Richard the Third* that resolutely refuses to go down the *shit pan*, and which remains floating about no matter how many times you flush. A *pond skater, bog bean, playful dolphin.*

bobbery *n.* Female-on-male *strap-on*-assisted *arse-banging. Pegging.*

bobbing for apples *n.* Alternately applying and relaxing light pressure to the back of a lucky fellatrix's head while she enjoys a *drink on a stick*, thus allowing her the welcome opportunity to take a short gasp for air between *noshes.*

BOB/bob *1. acronym.* Cabin crew slang for the most attractive passenger on an aeroplane. Best On Board. *2. acronym.* A *neck massager, dildo, twat rattler.* From Battery-Operated Boyfriend.

bobby bath *n.* A chap's perfunctory rinse of his *fruit bowl* in the *bum sink* prior to a sexual encounter. Probably not something that Nigel Havers would do, as a rule.

Bobby Charltons *n.* Rogue *fuckwhiskers* trapped under the *fiveskin* that stick themselves across the dome of your *bell end*, in the manner of the late centre-forward's final few remaining noggin hairs. *Robert Robinsons, Demond Morrises, Frodo's harp, Old McDonald's combover.*

Bobby Davro eyes *n.* Descriptive of a cold, soul-less, miserable stare on the face of one who is doing something that is meant to be fun, for example appearing in a pantomime.

bobby dazzler *1. n.* Any item of pottery bought at an antiques fair with £100 of licence payers' money which is later sold for £3 at an auction. *2. n.* A rather gorgeous young lady who, when in one's hotel room, turns out to be a *babylicious trolley dolly.* A *tiptop, trap, flipper* or *cockbird.*

bobby's anorak *n. Kojak's roll-neck, cock collar, Wilfrid's jumper.* The prepuce.

bobby's helmet *n. Bell end.* From the distinctive shape of the traditional British police constable's hat which manages to look like a *tit* and a *cock end* simultaneously.

Bobby Splithead *n. prop.* Affectionate term for the *herman gelmet. 'Say hello to Bobby Splithead.'*

Bob Dylan's guitar, fingered more times than *sim.* Said of a lady with loose morals and even looser *scad* elastic. Also *fingered more times than the Sun Hill ink pad.*

BOBFOC/bobfoc *acronym.* Body Off Baywatch, Face Off Crimewatch. Having a *welder's bench* inexplicably mounted on top of a finely carved *rack and pegs.*

BOBFOK/bobfok *acronym.* Interchangeable

variant of *bobfoc* (see above), to describe a woman blessed with a comely figure but cursed with a *boat race* resembling Fred Dibnah *shitting* a coathanger. Body Of Barbie, Face Of Ken.

bobhouse *n.* The *shit box.* *'My darling Bobo, I will not take no for an answer – you simply MUST come to Chatsworth. Just imagine, the ballroom is the longest of any house in Europe! The dining room has a table that can seat 200! And there are 120 bedrooms! Can you believe it? And each one with its own en-suite bobhouse!'* (Letter to Jessica Mitford, from her sister Deborah, Duchess of Devonshire).

Bob Ross's brush *1. n.* Unwanted male arousal at an inappropriate event resulting in the extreme action of whacking the offending *member* off a wall, fencepost, altar rail or crematorium doorframe in the style of the late artist "beating the devil" out of his bristly painting implement. *2. euph.* A thoroughly ruined *tool* after a thirty-minute session of stippling and a plunge into a liquescent vessel, before being hastily withdrawn and slapped vigorously from side to side. A reference to the late, frizzy-barnetted and *fanny-chopped* televisual landscape artiste Bob Ross cleaning his painterly bristles.

Bodmin bidet *n.* The act of a *bird* hanging her *arse* over the edge of the bath and washing her *ringpiece* with the shower head in anticipation of a session of a *brown love* tryst. Named after the Cornwall town where, according to local folklore, "the girls only get pregnant when it slips out and goes in the right hole".

bodybuilder's clit *n.* Something that is surprisingly larger than you might expect. *'Have you seen these antibiotics I'm on, granny? They're fucking huge, like bodybuilders' clits.'*

bodycam *1. n.* Metropolitan Police-issue apparatus to prevent apprehended offenders getting a black eye whilst falling down the stairs. *2. n.* Videographer employed at SA20 Cricket matches to find scantily clad *birds* in the crowd.

boff *v.* See *bonk.*

boffee break, taking a *n.* The act of manually *relieving tension* at one's place of work. *'Where's Ben? He's supposed to be filming the final double cumshot scene in Yummy Mummies 16.' 'He'll be back in five minutes. He's just taking a boffee break.'*

boff licence *n.* A shop vending an intriguing and comprehensive selection of international *art pamphletry.* *'I'm just popping down the boff licence. Anyone want anything?'*

BOFO/bofo *acronym.* Term used by cheeky artisans, such as those who were employed in the 1970s British motor car industry and members of the House of Lords, who can think of better things to do with their time than carrying out the work for which they are paid. Book On Fuck Off. Also *COFO*; Clock On Fuck Off. Also *SISO,* ie. Sign In Sod Off.

BOFOFOB/bofofob *acronym.* An existential conundrum upon entering the *khazi*; you know you need to go, but the outcome is uncertain. From Block Of Flats Or Flock Of Bats? Half an hour of trying to pass an incalcitrant *copper bolt* or thirty seconds of *squirting rusty water.*

Bofors bum *euph. medic.* Condition of the lower *Enochs* whereby *flatus* is forcefully expressed in a regular rhythm, thus imitating the firing of the famous WW2 40mm anti-aircraft gun, in four-round bursts, two rounds per second, until the ammo runs out or all enemy planes are downed. See also *string of pearls, duck walk, the Bavarian etc.*

bog *n.* The *shit house* or lavatory.

bog bang, the *n.* A sudden, massive expansion of primordial matter from a dark point of singularity.

bog banksy *n.* An *art brut*-style bowl-side decoration. Also *gut graffiti, turds and pictures, doodle-loo etc.* *'Have you seen that bog banksy in the end trap, Melvyn?' 'Yes, it's a load of crap.'*

bog barnacle *n.* A cheap plastic *bum sink* seat that remains firmly stuck to the back of one's legs upon rising.

bog bean *1. n. bot. Menyanthes trifoliata,* a species of marsh-dwelling wild flower. *2. n.* A robust, fun-sized *floater* that bobs around in the *pan* like a buoyant Robert Maxwell and can prove surprisingly resilient to flushing. Also *Duncan, humming turd, playful dolphin.*

bog beavers *n.* Shy denizens of the U-bend who busy themselves making *arse paper* dams to trap *brown trout.*

bog bib *n.* Tucking your T-shirt under your chin to avoid splashback during a *sit-down toilet adventure.*

bog body *n.* A substantial and leathery *Richard the third* that's the approximate size, texture and colour of the mummified human remains regularly found buried in peaty areas of Ireland and Scandinavia.

bog busking *n.* Humming, whistling or singing while having a *number two* to alert others to your presence if there is poor lighting, a broken lock on the door, or to keep yourself amused while waiting for a shy *Richard the Third.*

bog clogger *n.* A prodigious *feeshus* that prevents the efficient function of a *chod hopper.* *'Holy Mary, mother of God, is it yourself who's responsible for* *that bog clogger, Cardinal, or was it one of the choirboys again?' 'I'm sorry to be sure, Sister, but these new communion wafers are having a powerful effect on me holy guts, so they are.'*

bog croc *n.* Enormous and girthsome *Thora* which lies full-length along the *pan* with only the tip of its nostrils above water. Distinguishable from the smaller *bog gator* by the visible sweetcorn teeth in its lower jaw.

bog dice *n.* The small cubes of disinfectant that are rolled down the trough using *piss* instead of a croupier. Used to replace the smell of stale urine with one of stale urine and disinfectant. *Kola cubes.*

bog egg *n.* A fellow's free range *pride*, freshly laid in his porcelain nest.

bog eye *n.* The *anus* of the rectum. The *ringpiece.*

bogey spoon *n.* A fingernail.

bog food *n.* Brownish-tinted goodness from the *rear serving hatch. A German buffet.*

bogging *n.* A lavatorial version of *dogging*; visiting public toilets in order to watch people defecate. That'll most likely be the Germans doing that, you mark our words.

boggy style *adj.* Descriptive of romantic congress enjoyed in a municipal convenience.

boghogger *n.* One who spends an inordinate amount of time ensconced in the *smallest room.*

boghorn *n.* A sonorous warning trumpet which is automatically sounded when the atmospheric conditions in the *sweet wrapper* become hazardous to shipping.

bog jockey *n.* An altruistic person who, to avoid unpleasant odours from contaminating the bathroom for other users, reaches behind himself to press the flush lever at the exact moment their *foulage* leaves the *starting gate*, thus keeping to an absolute minimum the time its surface is exposed to the air that others have to breathe (also useful for masking unpleasant splashing noises). So called as the toilet user assumes the position of a jockey astride his mount while thrashing its *arse* with a riding crop.

bog leg *n. medic.* Deadening of the lower limbs caused by reading a magazine/book/cornflakes packet on the *shitter,* which results in temporarily impaired standing and walking ability.

bogleian library *n.* The selection of reading material kept within easy, seated reach of a chap's *crapper. 'Professor Tolkien was highly esteemed by his peers at Oxford, many of whom emulated his morning routine of drinking a cup of strong coffee before spending a tranquil hour studying in the bogleian library.'*

bog library, the *n.* Selection of reading material that builds up around the toilet of a bachelor. *Shiterature, loo reads.*

bog mallet *n.* That which wallops a fellow square in the face as he enters a recently vacated *inspiration room.*

bog-mess monster *n.* A legendary brown beast that curls its body out of the water in at least two places. May be a *brown trout* or a *dead otter.*

bog moth *n.* A persistent *cottager,* drawn like one of the eponymous poor man's butterflies to the sordid, dingy lightbulbs of public lavatory cubicles.

bog oak *1. n.* Dark, heavy timber that has been submerged in moist conditions for centuries. *2. n.* Dark, heavy *Peter O'Toole*s that are thick and dense enough to cause distress when being passed. *3. n. Throne bone.* Lavatorial *wood.*

BOGOF *1. abbrev.* An unexpected bonus when buying UPVC replacment windows. Buy One Get One Free, and hence *2. abbrev.* An unexpected bonus when *dropping one's guts.*

bog of eternal stench *1. n.* Scene from the movie *Labyrinth*, which starred David Bowie in his rather tight, *bollock*-hugging jeggings. *2. n.* The toilets on a Virgin train.

bog origami *n.* The ancient art of folding *shit tickets* into artistic shapes whilst perched upon the *jobby engine,* attempting to *evict* an uncooperative *bad tenant.*

bogosphere *n.* The air quality in a lavatory cubicle or bathroom. *'I'd give it ten minutes if I was you, your holiness. I had apricot Chicken Tonight and a spotted dick for me tea yesterday, so the bogosphere's a bit rich in there at the moment.'*

bog ostrich *n.* A person who spends the latter part of an evening of drink and merriment with their head buried in the lavatory.

bog rake *n.* Last chance *dash for gash* at a *meat market* having missed the *two am bin rake.* That is to say, loitering near the ladies' *khazi* in the hope of *pulling* a desperate lovely who has just been for a *shit.*

bog salmon *n.* An agile *turd* that, despite being flushed down river, manages to swim against the current back to its birthplace. A *poomerang.*

Bogside barbecue *n. NI.* From the salubrious area of Derry, a social gathering of locals enjoying cans of lager around a smouldering Ford Escort.

bog's jellyfish *n.* Dangerous yet passive aquatic creature found floating in the *bum sink* when an excess of *arsewipe* traps an air bubble therein. A bog's jellyfish rolls around in the murky water after the first flush only to be discovered hours later by unsuspecting bathers. A *Welsh man o'war.*

bog snorkelling *n. Around the world* or *dirtbox diving. Anilingus.*

bogstopper *n.* A *dreadnought* so humungous that the *shitpot* has trouble chewing it up and swallowing it.

bog treacle *n.* The utterly predictable result of eating a whole bag of Pontefract cakes in a single sitting.

bogwarts *n. medic.* Embarrassing ailment caught off a public *cludgy* seat. Also known as *brothel sprouts.* '*We've got the results of your tests back, and I'm afraid it's bogwarts again, Lord Archer of Weston-super-Mare.*'

bogzilla *n.* An unfeasibly large and frightening monster that emerges from the water to terrorise the populace.

boh! *exclam.* The noise made by a man after a particularly heavy woman has bounced up too far and sat down hard-on his *gut stick,* breaking it in two. Reportedly Prince Albert's last utterance.

BOHOF *acronym.* In the style of, say, World War 1 flying ace Albert Ball or speedway's Barry Briggs. Balls Out, Hair On Fire. '*Liz is planning to run a real BOHOF administration.*'

boiled eggs for four *n.* Visual impairment enjoyed by two reciprocating *horatiolists* in the *69* position. A *double Dutch blindfold.*

boiler *n.* An ugly woman who gets *serviced* once a year by the gas man.

boilerdom *n.* The state of being a *boiler* into which many *fugly ducklings* pass directly upon reaching puberty.

boiler maintenance *euph.* The flowers, Ferrero Rochers and repeated apologies needed to keep one's *bag for life* operating efficiently.

boilermaker's daughter *euph.* A young lady equipped with a splendid brace of *ship's rivets.*

boiler room *n.* An unacceptably sexist term for any quarters where two or more *tripe hounds* congregate.

boiler ticket *1. n.* Ten-year safety certificate issued for a pressure vessel on a steam locomotive. *2. n.* A nominal *free pass* for sexual congress with anything that happens to be available. See also *pink ticket, free hit, ticket to Tottieville, token for the cockwash, vadge visa.*

boiling beetroots *euph.* Of a lady, *up on blocks.* '*Sorry, not tonight, love. I'm boiling beetroots.*' '*Oh. Can I kick your back doors in instead, then?*'

boil your eggs *v.* To place your testicles over the *gazoo* of a flatulent naked woman who is standing on her head, for three minutes or so. A sexual practice that, if anyone has ever performed

it, which let's face it is fucking unlikely, will undoubtedly have proved to be not worth the fucking bother.

bojazzle *n. Nadbag-*based equivalent of a *vajazzle,* usually achieved through a combination of alcohol, glitter and Pritt-stick.

bolecule *n.* Tiny particle of matter emanating from the *clockweights* that might find itself deposited variously on bedsheets, inside socks, wiped on curtains or, very occasionally, in a *fanny.*

bolitics *n.* The practice of talking utter *bollocks* about politics. Often performed by drunks in pubs, students in halls of residence and Michael Gove.

bolivious *adj.* So *off your tits* on South American *nose sherbet* that you don't know what you're saying, what you're doing or how your actions are being perceived by others. '*I asked him for a Blue Peter badge but he just seemed completely bolivious of my presence.*'

bollicules *1. n.* Microscopically small testicles. '*Okay, Mr Davro, I'd like you to cough for me while I've got my hand under your bollicules. '2. n.* One who appears to be lacking in *cojones, ie.* A coward or eunuch.

bollock ballast *n. Man custard.*

bollock-blind *adj.* Said of a lady who totally ignores the *clockweights* when administering *hand shandies,* performing *horatio* or indeed *tromboning.* The opposite of a *clackerwitch.*

bollock boiler *n.* A hot bath. '*So, you've been in the jungle for the best part of two weeks. What's the first thing you're going to do when you get back to the hotel, Nadine?*' '*I'm going to have a shit on a proper toilet and run meself a nice bollock boiler, Ant.*'

bollock brunch *n.* An 11am *ham shank.*

bollock dangler *euph.* A day of very hot weather. '*So, in summary, tomorrow there will be showers in the west, clearing and becoming brighter later, while in the east expect a real bollock dangler with temperatures expected to reach 32 or 33 celsius.*'

bollock goatee *n.* The fashionable, jazz-style beard of *plums* that appears on a woman's chin while she is *smoking a gadgee.*

bollock hockey *n.* An aggressive and boisterous alternative to *pocket billiards,* with a simpler scoring system.

bollock in each pocket, a *exclam.* Said of a fellow whose trouser frontage might be considered somewhat too well-fitted. *Squirrel cheeks.* '*Jesus, them jeans are a bit tight. You look like you're carrying a bollock in each pocket, if you don't mind me saying so, Mr Plant.*'

bollocking the budgie *euph.* Ruffling the feathers

on one's own perky little *cock*.

bollock jockeys *n.* See *bollock rats*.

bollock limpets *n. medic.* Tenacious pubic lice. *'Bad news, I'm afraid dear. We've got bollock limpets.'*

bollock lounge *n.* A well-ventilated, spacious pair of boxers, affording one's *clockweights* the light and air they need to relax and recharge.

bollocknaise *n.* The heavily seasoned *sauce* that film director Michael Winner was, you might imagine, served in every restaurant he ever sat down in. *'More bollocknaise on your spaghetti, Mr Morgan?'*

bollocko *adj. milit.* Naked, *in the nip*; to quote Alan Partridge, *completely Billy bollocks*.

bollock pond *n.* A pair of egg-cups filled with warm water, used as a miniature bidet for a bloke's *clockweights*. It would take some organising, but it could happen.

bollock rats *n.* See *willipedes*.

bollocks *1. n.* Nonsense. *'That's utter bollocks, that is.'* 2. *n. Knackers, balls. 'Oi, missus. Look at me bollocks.'* 3. *exclam.* Denial. *'Did you expose your bollocks to Mother Teresa?' 'Did I bollocks.'* 4. *exclam.* Dismay. *'You're under arrest for exposing your bollocks to Mother Teresa.' 'Oh, bollocks.'*

bollocks, do one's *1. v.* To spend all one's money on something. *'I done my bollocks on the fucking gee-gees on Saturday, your holiness.'* 2. *v.* To knock oneself out. *'I done my bollocks loading that fucking piano into the lorry on my own, your holiness.'*

bollock service *n.* To make a withdrawal from *Barclays*. *'Tell you what, Hank, my balls are blue. It's about time I had them in for a bollock service.'*

bollocks in a sack *phr.* A crude variant of "peas in a pod". *'Have you seen them Jedward twins? They're like two bollocks in a sack.'*

bollocks, lose your *phr.* Rhetorical admonition of a forgetful fellow. *'You'd lose your bollocks if they weren't in a bag.'*

bollock sluice *n.* A bath containing about two inches of water, sufficient only for washing the *nads*. Which, let's be honest, is generally all that's needed.

bollock spider, the *euph.* The rapid tickling of a chap's *egg sack* by a close acquaintance's upturned five fingers.

bollock zombie *n.* A mindless, groaning, stumbling, glassy-eyed automaton who's just taken a good swift blow to the *clockweights*.

bollonary *n. medic.* A sort of mild heart attack suffered while emptying an over-full *pod purse*. A *hardiac arrest*.

bolloquialism *1. n.* Any commonly used, region-specific exclamation which actually means *bugger all*, eg. "Howay the lads" (Newcastle), "Chum ed la" (Liverpool), "Ee by gum" (Yorkshire), "Och the noo" (Wales) *etc.* 2. *n.* A particularly irritating figure of speech, *eg.* "Touch base", "Know what I mean?", "Does what it says on the tin", "Simples" *etc.*

bolly odour *n.* The spicy aroma one's *back body* develops following a night on the *Ruby Murrays*.

bollywood *n.* Penile tumescence achieved while watching a sexy screen starlet who hails from the Indian subcontinent, such as Priyanka Chopra, Padma Lakshmi or Barbar Bhatti.

bolt *1. v.* Of a horse, to suddenly gallop off. 2. *v.* To suffer from extremely premature ejaculation. *'I got that bird from the Feathers who looks like Rachel Riley back to my flat last night.' 'Did you give her a good sorting, mate?' 'Did I fuck. As soon as she got her tits out I bolted.'*

bolt from the blue *n.* A nostalgic, Viagra-fuelled *yoghurt drop*.

bolt from the brown *n.* A sudden and unexpected appearance made by a *bum cigar*. A *break for the border* or *charge of the shite brigade*.

boltmaker *n.* Any foodstuff that results in tougher than average *feeshus*. *'I do like half a dozen Scotch eggs, but they are terrible boltmakers.'* (Nigella Lawson on *Simply Nigella*, BBC2).

bolt on *1. n.* A large bore exhaust pipe strapped to the rear of an *estate car* by a *twat*. 2. *n.* A *boner* that is achieved with seemingly impossible speed, but which appears to soften up just before the end.

Bolton alarm clock *n.* The convoy of police cars, ambulances and fire engines which charges through the streets of the delightful Lancashire resort at precisely 9.05 each morning.

Bolton dipstick *n.* The middle finger of a gentleman's right hand. See *Bolton dip test*.

Bolton dip test *n.* A quick check of a lady's *under-carriage* to make sure that she is well-oiled and ready for sexual intercourse. *'Heliotrope could smell Fandango's musty male aroma as he held her in his muscular Cruft's judge's arms. She could feel his hands as they eagerly explored every inch of her lithe, pedigree labrador breeder's body. Then he reached down for a quick Bolton dip test.'* (from *Pedigree* by Jilly Cooper).

Bolton lemsip *euph.* Putting on two jumpers and having a *wank*.

Bolton shotput *n.* A sport played by Lancashire nightclub bouncers in which their clients are grabbed firmly under the chin and shoved as hard as possible into the road, against a wall or through a shop window.

Bombay bad boy *1. n.* A "spicy curry" Pot

Noodle which, one might safely imagine, Jacob Rees-Mogg has never tried. *2. n.* A fruit machine that might be found in a flat roof pub. *3. n.* A proper morning-after *pancracker.*

Bombay birthmarks *n.* The red patches evident just above the knees of someone who has spent the last hour ensconced on the *shitter* reading the *Autotrader* from cover to cover. Twice.

Bombay mix *1. n.* Dried, spicy snack. *2. n.* What spatters the *chod-bin* following a beery repast at the Curry Capital, Bigg Market, Newcastle upon Tyne, formerly the Rupali. When it was there, that is, obviously.

Bombay roll *n.* Like a sausage roll, but with *tits* instead of pastry and a *cock* instead of a sausage. And it costs £25 instead of 30p. But you could probably still get it at Greggs if you asked the woman behind the counter nicely.

bomb bay *n. medic.* The final lock on the alimentary *shit* canal. The *turtle's parlour* or rectum.

bomb bay bedbath *n.* A *crapped* bed consequent upon a pleasant night of curry and lager.

bomb bay duck *n.* A *dog's egg* that quacks to let one know it wants to hatch out.

bomb-bay fuck *n.* Earning one's *brown wings.* Especially when the *fish course* is a bit dry.

bomb-bay ivory *n.* Tell-tale copious display of teeth in the smile of a *chod-bin*-bound person, burdened by a full-to-bursting *back body*, but in the full knowledge that the delights afforded by a copious *bombing run* are imminent.

bomb bay mix *n.* A single lavatorial sitting that produces a veritable smorgasbord of stool consistencies; everything from *copper bolts* to a *rusty water geyser*, and all points in between. *Shitterish Allsorts, variety cack.*

bomb-bay mix-up *n.* Accidentally licking the wrong hole during an amorous encounter and getting an unexpected taste of the previous evening's takeaway.

bomb bay sapphire *n.* A *turd* which has been baked for so long in the *shit pipe* that it exhibits a hardness comparable to that of a precious stone.

bomb China *v.* To release your *payload* over the *Yellow River*. To do a *Billy Wright* while ensconced on the *porcelain throne.*

bomb on a short fuse *n.* The *shit* that causes one to sprint around looking for a *chod bin* in the manner that Adam West ran around the pier looking for a safe place to throw an incendiary device in the 1966 film *Batman.*

bombs away! *exclam.* A humorous exclamation after *dropping one's payload* into the lavatory.

bomb scare *n.* A supermarket *shit* of such stenchful intensity that it clears the shop.

bomb threat *euph.* A *suspicious package* which looks like the owner has stuffed socks, vegetables, sausages *etc.* into his *scads* in order to make his *explosive payload* look bigger. *'Nice bomb threat there, Mr Plant.'*

bonafido *n.* A genuine dog's *lipstick.* *'And you're absolutely sure that this photograph exists?' 'Oh yes, it's bonafido alright.'*

Bonanza, arse like the start of *sim.* A reference to the title sequence of the popular American cow-boy-based television show, which featured a ring of fire repeatedly burning through a paper map. *'Fuck me. That's the last time I order a Chinese curry from the kebab van out the back of Matalan. I've got an arse like the start of fucking Bonanza here, Evan. And now Thought for the Day with Anne Atkins.'*

bone *v. US.* To *fuck.*

bone broth *1. n.* The sort of thing your toothless, rickets-ridden old nan was raised on before there was Findus Crispy Pancakes and Angel Delight; a savoury, nutrient-dense, and collagen-rich stock that is beneficial for digestion and gut health. It says here. *2. n.* Bean protein. Also *crotch broth, smut butter.*

bone call *n.* A telephonic duologue during which at least one participant is engaged in a filthy act of *self pollution,* of which his co-conversationalist may or may not be aware. *'Mr Watson, come here. I want to see you.' 'Hang on a mo, pal. I've got my hands full at the minute making a bone call to that nurse who lives down the hall.'*

bone collector *1. n.* Film starring Angelina Jolie. *2. n.* A woman of easy affections.

bone dry *adj.* Of a chap, unable to get his *chap* even mildly damp.

bone folder *1. n.* An essential tool for those engaged in bookbinding and paper-based craft in general. *2. n.* An aesthetically challenged female. *'Well, I think it's time to re-stitch this rare first folio of Shakespeare's Sonnets between blind-stamped buckram boards.' 'Have you brought your bone folder?' 'I've left her in the car.'* (*Bamforth's Bookbinding Chuckles* postcard by Donald McGill, 1928).

bone idyll *n.* What many a red-blooded male enjoys when his significant other is called away unexpectedly and he is left to his own devices at home, *viz.* A blissful period of time spent half-naked, unwashed, watching internet *scud*, and *wanking his balls flat.*

bone jovi *n.* A *semi-on.* A somewhat grudging erection that is, in the words of the song made famous by the semi-eponymous spandex-clad poodle-rockers, "halfway there". A *Tim Henman* that is living on a prayer.

bonekickers *1. n.* Extraordinarily well-researched, realistic and popular drama starring that fat bloke out of *Downton Abbey. 2. n.* Extraordinarily grotesque harpies whose appearance in a nightclub, bar, Agora amusement arcade *etc.*, may have a somewhat adverse effect on any latent priapism. See also *lumberjills, frombies.*

boneless banquet for one *1. n.* A joyless bucket of fried chicken purchased by a single person to take back to their gloomy, damp bedsit where they will sit and eat it by the cold light of a flickering television set. *2. n.* A female feast of *self-pleasure.* *'After a hard day working at the Stock Exchange, Jan could think of no better way to unwind than a takeaway, a glass of Chardonnay and a boneless banquet for one.' 3. n.* The situation that obtains when a gentleman finds himself unable to *rise to the occasion* and must entertain his ladyfriend purely by *dining at the Y.*

boneless box *1. n.* A last resort family meal purchased from a popular fake-colonel-based high street dead chicken franchise. *2. n.* A *lezzer's cludge,* because it contains plenty of *batter* but rarely has a *bone* in it.

bone marrow *euph. 'It's that Mr Cummings on table eight, chef. He's sent back his pea and ham soup.' 'Get your trolleys off, Greg. We'll spice it up it with a couple of helpings of bone marrow.'* See also *caterer's tribute, chapioca, jazz potatoes, jerk sauce, lemon jizzle cake* and *smut butter.*

bonemeal *1. n.* A white fertilizer made from ground-up cattle skeletons which is used to grow vegetarians' food. *2. n.* A nourishing, meaty snack for the ladies, served with a cheese topping on a bed of nuts.

bone of contention *n.* An erection that sparks a stonking argument, *eg.* One that arises while watching beach volleyball with the wife.

bone on *n.* A *panhandle, wood, string. 'Aye, if you pause it there, I'm pretty sure he's got a bone on.'*

bone prone *adj.* Of a gentleman, susceptible to spontaneous tumescence at inopportune moments. *Bone proneness* is a social handicap that may force the unfortunate sufferer to avoid medical examinations, family funerals, royal garden parties, live television interviews with Sophie Raworth *etc.*

boner *1. n. US.* A daft mistake or cock-up. *2. n. US.* That which is used to *bone* someone with. A *bone on.*

boner bus *n.* A particular public transport route whereby one's omnibus driver is forced to navigate several cobbled streets, the vibrations thus experienced furnishing male passengers with *half a teacake* on their daily commute. Also *double dicker, Coronation treat, national sexpress.*

bonersaurus *n.* An erection of such gargantuan magnitude that it wouldn't look out of place on a plinth in the foyer of the Natural History Museum.

bonership *1. n.* The utterly misguided proprietorial feeling that a dreadful sexist pig develops regarding the lady he is currently *knobbing* up the *snatch. 'Dave, you know your sister, the one with the big tits? Anyone got bonership, or am I in with a chance?'*

bone shaker *1. n.* An early type of bicycle. *2. n.* A gentleman who favours the more mature lady. A *biddy fiddler, oap-dophile, tomb raider, granny magnet* or *mothball diver. 3. n.* An expert *woodburner,* who goes at your *twig* like Ray Mears starting a fire. *4. n.* A *ride* that has to be finished by hand. *5. n.* A lass whose sexual repertoire is limited to *manual relief.'*

bone stone *n.* A viagra tablet. A *bluey* or *Bongo Bill's banjo pill.*

bone up *1. v.* To revise prior to an important school or college exam for which one has not done nearly enough work. *2. v.* To furiously rub your penis until it achieves a turgid state of tumescence, also prior to an important school or college exam for which one has not done nearly enough work.

bone weary *adj.* Incapable of fulfilling one's marital obligations due to having a tired *Hampton.*

bone xylophone *n. medic.* Gynaecological term for the interior of a woman's rib cage. Her *slats. 'Oi, Heather. Let's go play the bone xylophone.'*

bone yard *n.* A secluded, often overgrown place in which *stiffs* are buried.

Boney M, do a *v.* To proudly put one's freshly laid excrement on public display. From the lyrics to the ersatz recording group's 1978 hit *Brown Girl in the Ring, viz.* "Show me a motion".

bon flapetite! *exclam.* Muttered by a *gashtronome* before he tucks into a *fish supper.*

bong covid *n. medic.* A protracted bout of wheezing and breathlessness caused by reckless inhalation of *the devil's lettuce.*

Bongo Bill's banjo pills *n. medic.* Pharmacological requisites for the older chap. *Antflaccids, mycoxafloppin.*

bongo bush *n. bot.* A plant which bears torn-up pornographic fruits. Common in the 1970s.

bongo fury *1. n.* Title of a 1975 album by Frank Zappa and Captain Beefheart which has got three-and-a-half stars on AllMusic. *2. n.* Furious and frenetic bout of *debugging the hard drive* following a temporary internet outage.

bongo mag *n. Rhythm literature, spangle book, bliff mag.*

bongular *adj. Pornographic.*

bonk *1. v.* Soft tabloid term for *fuck*, which is "knob" spelled backwards, for what it's worth. *2. n. W. Mids.* Obscene term meaning hill.

bonkers conkers *n.* Ecstasy tablets. *Disco biscuits, egg rolls, beans.*

bonk holiday *n.* An otherwise sexually timid female's cultural sojourn to visit some of the more well-trodden destinations of the Greek or Spanish Islands, where she behaves like a complete *hose monster* until it's time to get back on the plane. *'Hello Emily, I've not seen you in the Rovers for a while.' 'You won't have, Rita. I've been away for a bonk holiday break in Aiya Napa.'*

bonk on *n.* A splendidly tumescent member. *'A copy of Splosh and a box of tissues please, Mr Newsagent. I've got an almighty bonk on and I fancy a wank.'*

bonk shock *n. medic.* Unruly hair, glazed-over eyes, wobbly legs, slurring and inability to communicate lucidly following excessive s*xual activity. *'It's one of the worst cases of bonk shock I've ever seen, Sister.' 'Well, as long as he can still shuffle out onto the balcony to wave at the crowds a bit, nobody will be any the wiser, doctor.'*

Bonny Marys *n. medic. rhym. slang.* Haemorrhoids. From the Robbie Burns poem Bonny Mary of Argyles = Adrian Chiles.

bonobo's breakfast *n.* An early morning *lamb shank.* From the famous sex maniac chimpanzees you sometimes see *pulling themselves off* left, right and centre on TV nature documentaries. Dirty little buggers.

bonological order *n.* The prioritised sequence in which a person would, hypothetically, *have it off* with individual members of a pop group, *eg.* The Spice Girls (Posh last), The Coors (the drummer last), Lieutenant Pigeon (the piano player first) *etc.*

bonus ball *n.* The unheralded faecal pebble that drops in the gusset after an unsuccessful punt on the *fart lottery.*

bonus wank *n.* An unexpected opportunity to *relax in a gentleman's way. 'I'm just popping to the shops, luv. Do you want anything?' 'Yes, I'll have me a bonus wank while you're out.'*

BOOAFT/booaft *acronym. US. milit.* Barked One Out And Followed Through. *'6th June. Normandy coast. Guts really bad following ill-advised Scotch egg in Portsmouth cafe before embarking for Normandy. On bridge of heavy cruiser Augusta,*

supervising naval bombardment of heavily fortified Omaha Beach, in ultimately unsuccessful attempt to break down the German defences and allow Allied Infantry to land safely. Guns deafening, firing incessantly from ship's main battery. Decided to take opportunity to break wind under covering fire. BOOAFT.' (extract from the diary of Lieutenant General Omar Bradley, 1944).

boobery *n.* A place where *boobs* are kept.

boobies *n.* See *boobs.*

boobie trap/booby trap *1. n.* The irresistible allure of a fun night in with a *shirt-filling* maiden, only to find oneself confronted with *chicken fillets* and a couple of *wasp stings* when things are starting to get interesting. An apparently alluring pair of *norks* that's actually a push-up bra full of padding. *2. n.* A glimpse of the *twins* that causes rational decision making to go out of the window. A momentary *sneaky peek* of cleavage that ensnares a man and ultimately proves to be his undoing.

boobs *n.* See *boobies.*

booger sugar *n. US.* Cocaine, *Bacon powder. 'And now Richard's going to show you how to make your own Tracey Island out of an old breakfast cereal box, a couple of washing up liquid bottles, three lolly sticks, a lottery ticket wrap of booger sugar and some sticky-backed plastic.'*

book a table at the Cock Tavern *1. v.* To make a reservation at a recently gone-upmarket Smithfield boozer. *2. v.* To plan a night in with a compliant ladyfriend.

bookend *1. v.* To *spitroast* someone in a library. *2. n.* The fellow at either end of an *SVSO. 'It is estimated that up to 85% of professional footballers have, at some time in their career, been bookends.'*

bookie's biro *sim.* Descriptive of the reduced, chewed-up state of one's *old man* after a prolonged session of *horatio.* A *well-chomped chopper. 'I came back from my weekend in Amsterdam with a suitcase full of souvenirs, a head full of happy memories and a charlie like a bookie's biro.'* (Jim White, *BBC Holiday Programme*).

bookie's bog *euph.* Descriptive of something that is a right old mess. *'Beckham now. Steps forward to take the penalty that could see England go through to Euro 2004. He looks composed, but he must be feeling the pressure. Starts his run up and oh my word. He's made a complete bookie's bog of that one.'*

bookie's carpet, face like a *sim.* A worn, dirty, fag-burnt physiognomy, like on that woman with the scraggy blonde hair who always seems to be shouting "Leave it!" at someone when you sit on the remote control and accidentally put

EastEnders on for five seconds.

bookie's favourite *n.* A surefire *ride*, even when *the going is soft.*

bookie's pencil *n.* Descriptive of a dismally short, stumpy *cock*. *'He sings, he tells jokes, he does impressions and he's got a cock like a bookie's pencil. Ladies and gentlemen, put your hands together and give a warm welcome to Mr Bobby Davro.'* (Jimmy Tarbuck, 1988 Royal Variety Performance).

bookie's tip *n.* A John McCririck-style sequence of tic-tac twitches, flinches and flapping arms that signals to a favourite *fellatrix* that it's odds on she's about to hit the jackpot and get a mouthful of *spooge*.

book reader *euph.* In the days before our present frank, outspoken terminology, *book reade*r was Hollywood gossip column code for an actor who was *good with colours.* Also *sensitive.* *'Born on this day: Henry Fonda, Grapes of Wrath star, 1905; Margaret Sullivan, Shop Around the Corner star, 1909; Liberace, litigious ivory-tinkling book reader, 1919.'*

bookwanker *n.* Someone who disparages film or TV adaptations because they are not exactly the same as their source material. *'Well actually, I think you'll find that in the books Tyrion loses his whole nose at the Battle of the Blackwater.' 'Have you ever known the touch of a lover, you bookwanker?'*

boomerang *n.* A sock that has been masturbated into so many times that it is hard enough stun a passing wallaby before returning to the thrower. A *womble's toboggan, crunchie.*

boomerwang *n. Aus.* A bent *cock* that presumably *comes* back into your hand remarkbly quickly after being *tossed.*

booster shot *n.* Of a *grumble flick* actress, to take on a third gentleman's *membrum virile*, when a brace of *pricks* has failed to provide sufficient coverage.

boot *n.* A mature female *with a lovely personality.*

boot advantage points *n.* Brownie points scored with the *bag for life* by behaving in a more or less civilised manner, *eg.* Getting home before last orders, not *pissing* in the wardrobe while *well-oiled*, smiling and nodding at the correct moments when her uninteresting friends are round for a meal *etc.*

booty *1. n. coll.* Pirates' treasure. *2. n. coll.* Rappers' treasure.

booty call *n.* A telephonic dialogue whereby either or both of the participants is having a *strum.* Until *the pips go.*

booty diggers *n. US.* Unattractively worn-down fingernails. *'Camera two, zoom in on the trifle while Fanny's putting the almond flakes on top, so we get a good shot of her booty diggers.'*

booze control *n.* The exceptionally cautious way a regional television newsreader drives home from the pub after he's had a proper *skinful*, so as not to draw unwelcome attention to himself from the *scuffers, ie.* Keeping one wheel safely on the pavement, the headlights off and never venturing above five mph.

booze flu *n.* A non-viral ailment that strikes suddenly after an evening at the pub and causes the sufferer to take the next day off work. Symptoms include staying in bed and feeling like *shite. Beer cancer.*

booze fuse *n.* A *cock* suffering an outage following exposure to alcohol. *Tragic wand.*

boozemaid *n.* A fellow *gentleman of the road* who altruistically offers one an invigorating early morning shot on his can of *tramps' treacle.*

boozeman's barrage *n.* Haphazard, acrid bombardment of *wazz* fired in the general direction of the toilet (or the back of the wardrobe) from the unwanted *bone-on* of a scantly awake drunkard.

booze rouge *n.* The pink, glowing complexion of a drunk lady. *'You going to the Norwich match tonight, Delia? Don't forget to slap your booze rouge on.'*

booze snooze *n.* An alcohol-induced siesta taken in the pub, the pub *bogs* or in a layby or hard shoulder.

booze tardis *n.* A four-dimensional *beer scooter* that can transport a *wankered* person through both space and time. *'How did you get home from Parliament, Michael?' 'In my booze tardis, I think.'*

boozoms *n.* Self-inflicted, public house-induced man breasts. *Beerjugs, daddaries, moobs.*

borderline Frenchman *adj.* Politically incorrect and unacceptably xenophobic expression descriptive of terrible body odour. *'Fair enough, it's a hot day and everyone is sweating. But that bloke who just carried the filing cabinet up the fire escape is frankly borderline Frenchman.'*

bored dog's balls, cleaner than a *sim. 'In order to avoid the transmission of puerperal fever between patients, it is important that, before making examinations, doctors ensure that their hands are cleaner than a bored dog's balls.'* (from *Etiology, Concept and Prophylaxis of Childbed Fever* by Ignaz Semmelweis).

boredom stroke *n. medic.* Involuntary face spasm suffered whilst enduring an interminable anecdote in the pub, or a joke where you've already guessed or heard the punchline, whereby you feel a yawn approaching and try to keep your mouth shut, and end up looking like you're in a Soundgarden video. Also known as *bellend's palsy*.

boregasm *n.* A disinterested act of *self-pollution* for want of anything else to do.

Boris *1. n.* An act of premature *spangulation*. Named after the incident in a restaurant cupboard that turned out to be the most expensive five seconds of tennis ace Boris Becker's life. *2. n.* Term used by females for their *farmyard area*, apparently.

Boris bridge *1. n.* Scheme to build a fixed road link between Britain and France, a crackpot suggestion put forward by the eponymous Honey Monster-style slapstick ex-*bolitician*. *2. n.* The *barse, notcher, twernt, tintis.*

Boris cocktails *euph.* Generously offered to reporters waiting outside, cups of tea that one has dipped one's *cock* in.

Boris Day *n. prop.* Woman whose abundant blonde tresses cannot completely disguise the fact that she bears an uncanny resemblance to an overweight, middle-aged man lately burdened by the offices of state.

Boris Johnson *n.* An act of oral *horatio, a nosh* or *blow job*. From the similar initials of the former bumbling newspaper columnist turned bumbling comedy MP turned bumbling comedy Lord Mayor of London turned bumbling comedy Foreign Secretary turned bumbling comedy Prime Minister turned bumbling newspaper columnist.

Boris Johnson cycling down the South Bank, like *sim.* Descriptive of a windswept blonde *mingepiece*, a reference to the guilefully dishevelled, Gerard Hoffnung-channelling, parliamentary Pantaloon.

Boris minor *n.* A child of uncertain parentage. *'There are estimated to be several dozen Boris minors still on the roads around Downing Street.'*

born again fistian *n.* One who has recently become single and is once again spending the majority of his time *praying for milk*.

born again pissed-ian *n.* One who has recovered from a bout of temperance and rediscovered the joys of the malted hop and the fermented grain.

born slippy *1. n.* Title of a 1995 instrumental by electronic band Underworld which is, of course, not to be confused with its B-side *Born Slippy. NUXX*, which features vocals by Karl Hyde. *2. adj.* Descriptive of a *true grit* that feels like it's a case of the *Brads*, but turns out to be a completely solid *otter off the bank*.

borp *n.* A *dropped hat*. From bottom + burp. *'Don't you know it's rude to borp, Mother Teresa?'*

borrage *v.* To *reshuffle the cabinet via* the trouser pocket. *'I've been expecting you, Mr Bond. Please take a seat.' 'With you in a second, pal. I'm just* having a quick borrage. I don't want to squash me knackers.'

borzoi ballet *n. Unconventionally attractive* females dancing *en masse* around their handbags.

bosch *v.* Of bishops and farmers – to drill a *glory hole* between cubicles in a public lavatory for the purpose of spying on – or making their *peniii* available to – the farmer or bishop in the adjacent *trap*.

Bose shit *n.* Named in honour of the compact-yet-expensive speakers, a small *turd* that nevertheless produces a rich, room-filling smell. With plenty of trouser-flapping bass. See also *woofer, brown noise*.

bosphorus *n.* The bit that connects the fishy pleasures of the Mediterranean with the exotic mysteries of the Black Sea. The *taint, tinter, notcher, biffon etc.*

boss fart *n.* The final – and most deadly – blast that concludes a session of flatulence. *'Sorry dear, that was the boss fart on the blower. I've got to go and take care of some paperwork.'*

Boston pancake *n.* There's no easy way to say this. If you're of a nervous disposition, it might be best to look away now: It's a *shit* done on someone's chest, which is patted down flat with the buttocks and then *jizzed* on. Bloody hell.

Boston tea party *n.* When three or more men take turns dipping their *chicken skin handbags* into a willing pal's mouth. They have to make their own entertainment in Lincolnshire.

boswellox *1. n.* An unlikely sounding wrinkle-cream ingredient. *2. n.* Utter bollocks, *eg.* The claims made in wrinkle-cream adverts.

Bosworth field *euph.* A messy battle fought on the *Quintin Hogg* the morning after a heavy night on the ale and curry. After a protracted period of unpleasantness, it ends with the death by drowning of *Richard the Third*.

bot activity *1. n.* International propaganda shenanigans whereby shady, state-employed malefactors set up fake social media accounts in order to influence political opinion. *2. n. Fucking* someone *up the arse*.

BOTBLATRIT/botblatrit *abbrev.* A woman whose impressive *busty substances* are her only redeeming feature. Big Old Tits But Look At The Rest (of) It. See also *fugly but juggly*.

botcaps *n.* Plugs of *shit roll* placed in their *aniii* by overweight driving instructors to prevent *skids* on hot days. *Manpons, manitary towels, mantipads, mantiliners, Tompax.*

bot-holing *n.* Weekend pursuit of mud-covered chaps who don't mind getting trapped in narrow crevices.

Botley interchange *1. n.* Section of Oxfordshire thoroughfare that connects the A34 to the A420 and thus *2. n.* The section of the female anatomy which separates the *front* from the *back bottom*. The *carse, tinter, taint, notcher, snarse, biffin bridge* and so on and so forth.

bot noodles *1. n.* A lipsmacking mixture of boiling water, savoury sludge and spicy sauce that stops thankfully short of the *pan*'s "fill level". *2. n.* Blades of grass, worms, bits of wool and other undigested miscellanea dangling from a dog's *nipsy* after it has taken a *Tom tit*.

bot pourri *n.* A *foulage* whose pleasant aroma is as rich and flavoursome as the meal from which it was spawned. Also a *gorilla's breakfast*.

bot shots *n.* Small, rapid-fire *Richard the Thirds* released in quick succession. *Kak-ak*.

Botson strangler *n.* A *poo* that is half in and half out of the *nipsy* at the moment the *cigar cutter* reflex kicks in.

bott *v.* What a *botter* does to a *bottee*.

bottanical garden *n.* Any place where *al fresco fruit-feelers* are wont to flock.

botta nova *n.* Rhythmic, seated, circambulatory movement of the *bummocks*, performed in order to dislodge a *brown trout*.

bottee *n.* One who is *botted* by a *botter*.

botter *n.* One who *botts* a *bottee*.

botter brush *n.* A *book reader*'s hairy *giggle stick*.

bottery barn *n.* Public convenience frequented by gentlemen with *nice nails*. A *cottage*.

bottled Bass, frothing like *sim.* Descriptive of the lubricity of a *stoat*. *'You may be knocking on a bit, love, but your granny's oysters are frothing like bottled Bass.'*

bottle mottle *1. n.* Finish achieved following an inexpert application of fake tan. See also *Dickinson holiday, glamourpotamus, creosort*. *2. n.* *Hammered* finish achieved following consumption of alcoholic beverages over many years, typically by an expert, *eg*. Wine taster, head brewer, regional television presenter *etc*.

bottle of olives *onomat.* The sound a *fart* makes in the bath. Named after late actor Edward Woodward. Also *tottle, Bill Oddie*.

bottle opener *n.* A particulary strong and robust *blurtch*. Presumably with a little metal hook at the top.

bottom *n.* The part of the *bottee* which is *botted* by a *botter*.

bottom bracket *1. n.* Where the cranks fit on your bike. *2. n.* Where your *crank* fits on the local bike. The *clout, minge, fanny, flange, growler, front*

bottom, ladygarden or *quimpiece*.

bottom brambles *n. medic.* Bonny Marys, Jeremy Kyles, Adrians. *'Pass the Preparation H will you, Carson? Me bottom brambles are giving me some right fucking gyp. I should never of took part in the Easingwold Point to Point at the weekend.'* *'Certainly, Lady Mary.'*

bottom cork *n.* The last firm *Peter O'Toole* that pops out before the fizzy torrent of *beer slime*. The *pace car*.

bottom-end tidy-up *1. n.* An automotive engineering term for a procedure that will leave a motorist's wallet up on blocks. *2. n.* What is required after a few day's without access to modern bathroom facilities, *eg*. At the end of a long weekend spent at a pop festival or a National Express coach trip from Leeds to London. *'Ladies and gentlemen, we will shortly be arriving at Leicester Forest East services, where you will be able to avail yourselves of horribly overpriced hot snacks and drinks, and enjoy a bottom-end tidy-up in the bogs.'*

bottom feeder *n.* An *anal linguist* or *rimmer*. A *round the world bottsman*.

bottomist *n.* A chap who studies and performs experiments on, other people's *fundaments*. A student of *bumcraft*.

bottom line *1. n.* Some sort of financial thing on a balance sheet that would probably be of interest to one of them entrepreneur types on *Dragon's Den*. *2. n.* A *screecher* or *skidmark* left behind on the bedsheets as a naked (or kilt-wearing) gentleman slides off his *wanking chariot* when he's got an urgent *appointment at the Kensington Executive*..

bottom line *1. n.* The final total of an account. *2. n.* The *arse crack*.

bottom log *n.* A scuttled *dreadnought* that hits the sea bed while still exiting the *windward passage*. Also *bridger, earthing cable*.

bottom of a ratcatcher's mallet, fanny like a *sim.* A poetic turn of phrase which can be used to describe a particularly messy *snatch* when in polite company, for example on Radio 4's *Midweek* programme, while sitting on the Booker Prize judging panel or when taking afternoon tea with the Dowager Duchess of Grantham.

botto voce *adj. Lat.* Descriptive of a barely audible *anal* aside. From the 18th century Italian; voce = voice & botto = nipsy.

botty burp *n.* A burp from the *botty*, believe it or not. A *trouser cough* or, indeed, *fart*. Also *bottom burp*.

bounce out *1. n.* In darts, when your arrow doesn't stick in the board due to it hitting the wire instead. *2. n.* In s*x, when your *willy* doesn't stick in the *fanny* or *arse* due to it hitting the *notcher* instead, followed by Tony Green saying "unlucky".

bouncers *1. n.* Unsportsmanlike, short-pitched deliveries in cricket aimed at intimidating the batsman. *2. n.* Muscle men, *ripped to the tits* on *Aberdare tic-tacs*, who keep the riff-raff out of pubs and clubs. *3. n.* Big, wobbly *tits*. *4. n.* Big, wobbly *knackers*.

bounce that on your cock a few times and see how it feels *exclam.* Offensively sexist phrase for use when pointing out a tasty bit of *blart* to a mate. Can be accompanied by the qualifier *Phwooar!* for greater emphasis, if required.

bouncy castle *1. n.* A large, fat, rubbery *snatch*, where you've got to take your shoes off before you have a go on it. *2. n.* A larger *bird*, endowed with *tits* like leaking, floppy turrets, who is fun to jump onto after spending the afternoon drinking Woodpecker, until you start feeling a bit sick

bouncy hunter *n.* Gentleman aficionado of the more generously endowed female physique, who is wont to *slap the fat and ride the waves*. Also *chubby chaser, gastric bandit, blob jockey*.

bouquet fanny *n.* Pronounced "bucket". A lady who puts on lots of airs and graces, but is, in reality, a right *goer, eg.* Her royal hi(the rest of this entry has been obscured on legal advice)rk.

bouquet of beans *n.* A high fibre *borp*.

bourbon *n.* Someone who is really good at *horatio* or *cumulonimbus*. A "fancy licker" who is *like a dog with a plate of gravy*.

Bournemouth beefburger *n.* After a sunseeker is caught short in the middle of a beach with no open public *crappers* nearby, the unappetising contents of his hastily improvised, handheld *pap baffle* made from a styrofoam burger box.

Bournville boulevard *n. The arse, fudge tunnel, choclate starfish. 'What the witness says is true. My client has been known to occasionally stroll up Bournville boulevard, your honour.'*

Bovril bullets *n.* Stools, excrement, foulage. *Feeshus.*

bovvercraft *n.* A vehicle that slews across in front of you in traffic but you resist the temptation to remonstrate because it is driven by a bald, thick-necked *hard case*.

'bow Derek *n.* A *bird* who looks like a *perfect ten* only after one has imbibed a surfeit of cider.

bowel buckaroo *n. medic.* The Tom tits.

bowel buddies *n.* Two people who work in the same building who only know each other due to always having their morning *Donald* in adjacent cubicles at exactly the same time each day.

bowel bugle *n.* A rousing early morning reveille

performed on the *trouser trumpet*. A *stinky rooster.*

bowel howl *n.* Fearsome wailing of a *botty banshee*, the *sound of your supper.*

bowel jowls *n.* The hangdog *dirt curtains* of a *mud-plugger.* A droopy set of *mudflaps* that could probably do a good impression of Walter Matthau.

bowel pager *n.* A *fart.*

bowel towels *n. Shit tickets. 'Mam! Can you throw us up some bowel towels?'*

bowel trowel *n.* One of a selection of tools at the disposal of the *uphill gardener.* See also *cheesy wheelbarrow, trouser rake, one-eyed purple-headed blue-veined hairy secateurs.*

Bowie stare *n.* The unsettling sight of a knickerless stripper's *brown eye* and *pink eye* as she turns her back on a chap and bends over. Named after the late wonky-eyed *half rice-half chips* crooner David.

bowk *v.* To *barf, vomit, spew, yak, hoy up, bake a pavement pizza.* Also *bowk up.*

bowl constrictor *n.* An enormous *blind dirt snake* that suffocates its victims by choking the breath out of them.

bowler's grip *n.* Manually pleasuring a ladyfriend with your thumb in her belly button and the remaining four fingers tucked inside her *twat.* While wearing a pair of tight, luridly coloured shoes that are crawling with someone else's verruca germs.

bowl from the pavilion end *v.* To *bott*, travel on *the other bus.*

bowl-huggingly refreshed *adj.* Descriptive of the state of a callow youth at the end of an afternoon session in their local 'Spoons.

bowling ball *n.* A woman who loves nothing more than getting *fingered* down an alley.

bowling like Imran Khan *sim.* Running into a *pagga* and attempting to join in with a wild, overhead swing.

bowling partner *n.* A person in whom one inserts two fingers and a thumb.

bowling shoe, fanny like a *sim.* A particular-ly well-worn and ill-fitting *clopper. 'Leia was powerless to resist. C-3PO's eyes burned into hers like light-emitting diodes. His strong metal arms enfolded her body as she felt herself being swept away on an Imperial battle cruiser of passion. After they had made love, and he had shot his electronic muck, they lay together in the twin moonlight. 'How was it for you?' she asked. 'To be perfectly honest, highness,' answered the droid, 'it was a bit of a let down. Jabba the Hutt was right. You've got a fanny like a fucking bowling shoe.'* (from *The Space Princess and the Gold Protocol Droid* by

Barbara Cartland).

bowling underarm *1. n.* Wiping one's *arse. 'Jesus, that's the last time I buy a lamb biryani at a pound shop. I've been bowling underarm all fucking day. Anyway, let's see what treasures the people of Aberystwyth have brought for our experts to see today.'* 2. *n.* Of a man, *driving from the lady's tee,* viz. Sitting down for a *whizz.*

bowl mole *n.* A small Cindy Crawford-style beauty spot on the side of the lavatory pan that resists all attempts at removal by *yellow toilet brush* and has to be picked off with a fingernail.

bowl winder *n.* A long, unbroken, helical *potty python.* Often requires disassembly with a coat hanger or other improvised *poo horn* in order to facilitate disposal. A *coil pot, bowl constrictor.*

bowser trouser *n.* A fellow with a *wet penny in his pocket.* From the portable drinking water containers which are suddenly a common sight on the streets of flooded towns.

bowsprit *1. n.* In the maritime world, a mast or spar running forwards from a ship's bow, to which are fastened stays. *2. n.* In the world of *bone ons,* the sort of *diamond cutter* which points ahead as one walks and could, if one weren't careful, *poke a hole in a cheap door.*

'bow tiddly *adj.* A little unsteady on one's feet after a morning quaffing an excess of the famous Herefordshire apple drink.

box *1. n.* The vagina. *'I wouldn't mind getting into her box.'* 2. *n.* In cricket, a gentleman's protective device worn around the *undercarriage. 'Ooyah me pods! I wish I'd worn a box.'*

box biter *n.* Politically incorrect, offensive terminology for a *rug muncher.*

box brownie *1. n.* A cheap, simple camera, manufactured by the Eastman Company, which brought photography to the man in the street. *2. n. nav.* A maritime souvenir. A *feeshus,* saved and kept on a velvet cushion in an hermetically sealed container by a resourceful matelot after a visiting VIP (such as the late Princess Margaret, to take an example completely at random) has taken a *dump* in the *head* of his ship (such as HMS Ark Royal, to take yet another example, also completely at random). All we're saying is, it's the sort of thing that *could* happen.

box bulge *n.* The *poond, gunt, fat hat, blubber beret* or *FUPA.*

boxcar willy *n.* Involuntary priapism occasioned by the steady, low-frequency throb of a large diesel-engined vehicle. Also known as *bus driver's knob, travel fat, traveller's marrow, diesel dick, routemaster* or a *Varney teacake.* Named after the

erstwhile, dead country & western singer of the same name who always got a *hard-on* while sat on his tour bus.

box cutter *1. n.* A multi-functional tool with a sharp, retractable blade that is popular with violent criminals. *2. n.* An enormous male *member* which would cause untold damage to a normal *flange* but probably wouldn't touch the sides of (name removed in anticipation of forceful legal advice)'s.

box doc *n. medic.* A gynaecologist or *fanny mechanic.* Also *doctopussy, cunt dentist, cloptician.*

boxer's eye *n.* A puffed-up, swollen *fanny* whose owner ought to *throw in the towel. Bugner's eye.*

boxer's punchball *n.* The acorn of *shit* that hangs off the *toffee strings* and resists all attempts to *tap the ash off,* simply bouncing around like a pugilist's exercise equipment.

box girder *n.* A sturdy and rigid erection wrought from *pink steel* of an exceptionally high tensile strength.

box gutter *1. n.* Means of removing rainfall from a building. *2. n.* The *banny, gunt, fupa, blubber beret, fadgida, pie hider, fat hat* or *poond.*

box hedge *n.* A meticulously toped *landing strip* resembling the hairstyle sported by *The A Team*'s Mr T.

boxing day jobby, denser than a *sim.* Descriptive of someone *fuckwitted.* Also *thick as a ghurka's foreskin/ Welshman's cock/ brickie's wrist* etc. As *thick as Jim Bowen's glasses.*

boxing day sale *n.* That traditional post-festive colonic clearance event where "everything must go". Usually follows the traditional, ill-thought-through over-ordering of comestibles for the Christmas season. Also *Christmas clearout.*

boxing day turd, denser than a *sim.* Said of a *fuckwit* who is *as thick as a bull's dick.*

boxing glove on a spring, like a *sim.* Descriptive of a noisomely miasmatic *stoat.* A stinky *fanny. 'I pulled down her pants and the honk hit me in the face like a boxing glove on a spring. And now over to John Sopel for the latest developments from Washington DC.'*

box jellyfish *n.* A used *pie-liner.*

box of assorted creams *n. Aus.* She who has recently been over-accommodating to a number of gentlemen. A promiscuous female with a *twat like a billposter's bucket.*

box of cow tongues *n.* An unpleasantly graphic *snapper.* A *butcher's dustbin, fishmonger's dustbin, Norwegian's lunchbox.*

box office *1. n.* A brothel, *rub-a-tug shop.* 2. *n.* A *good time girl's bodily treasure* with a £3 handling fee. *3. n.* A *porn* shop.

box on standby *1. phr.* Statement that one's televisual receiving apparatus is more or less powered up although currently inactive. *2. phr.* Said of a lady who is more or less permanently *up for it.*

boxpok *1. n.* A steam locomotive wheel made using box sections instead of solid spokes, it says here. *2. n.* medic. An infectious condition afflicting a lady's *front bottom. 'Hang on, what's this?' 'It's a boxpok, love. Can't you just work round it?'*

box set *n.* A multi-part *Eartha* to be enjoyed in a single sitting. A *binge shit.*

box the Jesuit *v. 17thC.* How Friar Tuck may have referred to *strangling the parson* behind a bush in Sherwood Forest. Also *pulling the Pope's cap off.*

box to box action *1. n.* Football commentator speak for an exciting match that is, if you will, "end to end stuff". *2. n.* Something that is always a welcome sight in any half decent *lezzer* vid.

Boycott shits *n. medic. The runs.* It just takes you longer to get them.

Boy George's hat *n.* A ludicrously prominent *nip-nop.*

Boy George's radiator *euph.* Any appliance, fixture or fitting showing severe signs of damage, as if it has been pulled, rattled or yanked hard in order for someone to release themselves from it. Derivation unknown. *And that's a huge crash for Button as he exits the tunnel. The good news is the marshals have got him safely out, but his Honda looks like Boy George's radiator after that 185mph sideways impact with the tyre wall.*

boyner *n. NI.* A lady who appears to be about sixteen when seen from the back, but looks ninety when viewed from the front. From the Battle of the Boyne, the pivotal military engagement during the Irish Williamite Wars fought between the armies of King James and King William in July 1690. Twenty-six years worse than a *Kronenberg.*

boy scout's penknife *n.* The tell-tale bulge in an adolescent's pocket that gives away the location of his favourite whittling implement.

BPS *n. abbrev.* A more modern version of the traditional *beer compass;* an inbuilt system that safely guides you home when lost and *wankered* in an unfamiliar metropolis. Beer Positioning System.

brabarian *n.* A fellow who finds the tricky act of unfastening the catches on a his missus's *tit pants* overly cerebral and tiresome, and prefers to simply pull the *knockers* out of their cups and go at them like that, a bit like how you'd imagine

Brian Blessed would.

brace *rhym. slang.* To defecate. From brace and bit = shit.

brace position, adopt the *v.* To place the *bummocks* against a solid or resonant object when *breaking cover* in order to achieve the maximum volume, timbre and thus comedic effect.

Brad *rhym. slang.* A *dump.* From Brad Pitt = Donald Trump. *'Give me the paper, I'm off for a Brad.'*

Bradford dishwashing *n. Pissing* in the sink.

Bradford fountain *n.* A burst water main or sewer.

Bradley Biggins *n.* A *big-boned* lycra-clad cyclist on the *Tour de Greggs.*

Bradman *1. n.* An extended session of *relaxing in a gentleman's way,* involving a lot of stroking one's *balls* under the covers. *2. n.* A prolonged *cumulonimbus* marathon. A long time at the *crease.* From the famous Australian cricketer Sir Donald Bradman (1908 – 2001), who used to spend a lot of time *wanking* and *licking out* his missus.

Brads, the *n. medic. The Earthas. 'Can you pass me some moist wipes in? I've got a bad case of the Brads.'*

Brahms and Liszt *adj. rhym. slang.* Convenient euphemism for *shitfaced,* which was much used by the writers who penned the lyrics for the Two Ronnies' comedy songs.

Braille end *n.* A *bobby's helmet* afflicted with sufficient warts, polyps and calluses to enable one familiar with tactile writing to discern a word, or even an entire phrase, while *wanking it off.*

Braille tits *n.* Tiny, raised *knockers* that allow a blind man to read a woman's chest over and over again. *Stits, fried eggs, chest warts, bee stings.*

brain donor *n.* An intellectually challenged person.

brake fade *1. n.* Motoring term for a loss of performance in the braking system of a vehicle caused by heat build-up, loss of friction, or water in the brake fluid. *2. n.* The terrifying feeling that you are about to *shit* your *applecatchers* before you make it to the *jobby engine* due to a build-up of *rusty water* in the *sump* and concomitant loss of grip in the *snippit valve.*

branaconda *n.* A high-fibre *bumsnake* of the sort typically found nesting in a vegetarian's *khazi.*

Brando's butter/Brando butter *n.* Any *ad hoc* product pressed into service in order to facilitate the insertion of something into a *nipsy.* From the scene in *Last Tango in Paris* when the eponymous *big-boned* actor spreads a knob of butter on his *nob* prior to *doing* Maria Schneider up the *Rick Witter.*

brandy dandy *n.* A chap who sports more logos

than an F1 driver at a post-race press conference.

brandy snap *n.* The *pubal area* of a russet-haired lady. A ginger *minge, Cuddles's mouth.*

branflake *n.* A small disc of dried-out *roughage* left clinging to your *cornhole,* typically after spending a bit too much time perusing the *Autotrader* while *dropping the kids off at the pool.*

bran in the pan, put the *v. Parking your breakfast* as a matter of some urgency. *'Come on, Posh! You've been in there twenty minutes.' 'Belt up, Dave. I'm putting the bran in the pan.'*

Bransholme lighthouse *n.* Nickname for the Humberside Police helicopter, owing to the fact that it spends most nights illuminating the exclusive Bransholme Estate in Hull.

branstorming *n.* Taking a little time out of the day to *paint the porcelain* courtesy of yesterday's high fibre breakfast cereal.

bra snack *n.* A nourishing, opportunistic, *pub grubby* ogle of the barmaid's *knockers* while ordering drinks. *Nork scratchings.*

brasserie *1. n.* A posh brothel. From brass (Latin for knocking) + erie (Greek for shop). *2. n.* A retail purveyor of *funderwear.*

brass eye *n. Brown eye, red eye, chocolate starfish, rusty sheriff's badge, panda's eye.* The *fifties tea towel holder,* if you will. *'Have you ever got a milk bottle lodged up your brass eye? Here's one I did earlier.'*

brass horn *n.* Steadily mounting level of male randiness that can only be relieved by a visit to the local *rub-a-tug shop* or red light district for some *executive relief. 'Where are you off to, Jerry?' 'I'm just popping out for half an hour or so to get rid of this brass horn I've got while watching Barbara planting her runner beans, Margo.'*

brassical music *n.* Stirring, methane-rich repertoire performed on the sofa following consumption of a greens-rich Sunday lunch.

brass rubbings *n.* Rusty finger paintings found in a gentleman's *undercrackers* following a good scratch of his poorly wiped, sweaty *arse crack.*

bratmobiles *n.* People carriers.

bra trek *n.* An unnecessarily long detour undertaken by a desperate, *full-nutted* young fellow in the vague hope that he might catch a cheeky glimpse of some red hot *totty,* a snippet of visible underwear or some other similar groin-tingling titbit.

bravefart *n. Letting some of the air out of the balloon* while you are the only passenger in a lift, gambling that no-one will get in before you get out.

Braveheart visit *n.* A *sit-down toilet adventure* enjoyed while wearing a dressing gown, such

that one drops one's *trolleys* and throws the back of the garment up before performing one's ablutions in a style reminiscent of the theatrical act of disrespect to the English depicted in the eponymous film starring popular multiculturalist Mel Gibson. A *concert pianist shit.*

braydar *n.* The uncanny ability of a suspicious wife to sniff out and home in on her hubby's secret stash of donkey porn.

Brazilian rocket *n.* A gentleman who *explodes while still on the launchpad.* One who *stamps on the toothpaste* before he's got his pants off. A *no-push charlie.*

Brazilian variant *1. n. medic.* South American P1 strand of the Covid-19 virus that was definitely nothing to worry about and happily has been replaced as a "variant of concern" by delta and omicron instead. *2. n.* Any new style in *ladygarden* topiary.

Brazilian wax *n.* A bald *monkey's forehead.* A *shaven haven, Beverley Craven* or *Barthez.*

Brazillian deforestation *n.* The change from a tufted *landing strip* to the full *baby Kojak.*

Brazil nuts *n.* Shaven *clockweights* with a thin strip of *plum fluff* left down the middle.

brazzers grip *n.* The technique of grabbing another person by the throat that is apparently favoured by adult performers on the aforementioned *adult* website. Also popular with bouncers at chucking out time and advertising moguls having playful tiffs with their loved ones outside London fish restaurants.

breacher *n.* Malfunction in a pair of boxer shorts whereby the fly annoyingly allows the *old fella* to poke through, giving a man the disconcerting sensation that he is continuously exposing himself. *'The vicar regretted wearing those scads to the funeral because they gave him a distracting breacher right the way through the service.'*

breach of the peach *n. Kicking in* the missus's *back doors* while shouting "Sweeney!".

breach of the piss *n.* Fixed penalty offence common in South Ayrshire, whereby the unfortunate miscreant has no choice but to go for a *gypsy's kiss* in a public place after all the pubs and takeaways have shut because the council, in its infinite wisdom, has decided to lock up all the municipal *cludgies* after dark.

breach the hull *v.* To poke one's digit through inferior quality *bumwad* when wiping one's *arse. Push through. 'Day 82, and the men are getting restless. Squabbles are beginning and tempers are short. John Norton handed out the ship's biscuits, but Mr Christian refused to eat, accusing him* *of breaching the hull and then not washing his wanking spanners.'* (from *The Log of HMS Bounty* by William Bligh, 1764).

bread crumbing *n.* Hansel and Gretel-style *duckwalking, viz.* Dropping a small *air biscuit* on every forward step in order to enable those behind you to follow your trail.

bread knife *rhym. slang.* The *bag for life.* *'Quick. In the wardrobe, Stormy. It's the fucking bread knife, whatever she's called.'*

breadlocks *n.* The nutritious foody entanglements of a tramp's beard.

break a cock *exclam.* Hardcore *grumble* actor's pre-performance version of "break a leg".

break America, trying to *1. euph.* Phrase used by PR companies and showbiz columnists to describe that phenomenon whereby home-grown British celebs like Robbie Williams, Chris Evans and Lieutenant Pigeon vanish to LA for six months and signally fail to get arrested. *2. n.* Signing on. *'What are you doing in William Hills at three in the afternoon?' 'I'm at a bit of a loose end at the moment, I've been trying to break America, you see.'*

break company *v.* To disrupt a gathering of *beneficiaries* by the release of a *McArthur Park.*

breakfart *n.* An early morning *botty burp* that sets you up for the rest of the day.

breakfast at stiffany's *euph.* Early morning *horatio.*

breakfast at Timothy's *phr.* Practice of middle-aged-and-older Brexiteers who turn up bright and early for morning *refreshment* at the 8am opening time of their local Wetherspoon's.

breakfast at wiffany's *euph.* An all-you-can-eat *seafood smorgasbord* served when *dining at the Y. Egg McMuffing.*

breakfast finished and my dinner began, didn't known when my *exclam.* Said by one enthralling his listeners with an entertaining reminiscence regarding a memorably chronic bout of the *Tijuana cha-chas.*

breakfast in bed *n.* A rousing matutinal *Bakewell tart* that sets one up for the rest of the day. A *dawn chorus* that flaps the quilt.

breakfast maker *n.* An early morning *dropped hat* which is so smelly that the missus has no choice but to get out of bed and make the breakfast.

breakfast of champions *n.* A *beef dripping*-rich *full English* eaten the morning after *putting the wife to the sword.*

breakfast podcast *1. n.* Helpful community service formerly provided by the BBC, whereby it was possible to download news content onto one's MP3 player. *2. n.* A sordid act of ante-meridian *self pollution* brought to a successful conclusion while a *horny* BBC Breakfast Programme presenter is on the screen. *'What's that on the screen?' 'It's a breakfast podcast. Best fetch a cloth, mother.'*

breakfast, tramp's *n.* A *docker's omelette.* A pavement *greb, prairie oyster.*

breakfast, Turkish *1.n.* Coffee, a cigarette and a bit of *anal.* *2. n.* The foul gases emitted as a *bottom burp* first thing in the morning after a large *catbab with all the shit,* which sets one up nicely for a busy day of sitting in a darkened water closet, sweating and gently sobbing.

break for the border *1. n.* A risky dash made by a beastly male's hand for a woman's *dunghampers* when he is uncertain of her reaction, half expecting a slap or possibly a court case. *2. v.* Of a *shit,* to catch one unawares by suddenly *darting south* as one is casually looking for something to read. A *charge of the shite brigade.*

breaking biosecure protocols *euph.* Enjoying a spot of *back door action* during a lockdown.

breaking the swan's neck *n.* The cruel technique employed when it is necessary to urinate through a *boner.*

break the crust *v.* The morning after an evening fuelled with hot food and brown beer, to *pinch off* the day's first *loaf,* an act which is shortly thereafter followed by an uncontrollable pyroclastic flow of hot brown lava from the *jacksie.* See also *kakatoa.*

break the ministerial code *1. v.* To infringe parliamentary rules and standards; a breach of trust which would get the rest of us sacked and possibly imprisoned, but for government ministers typically leads lead to promotion and a peerage. *2. v.* To *break wind* loudly. *'Was that you, Ant?' 'Yes, Dec. I was trying to sneak one out quietly while the Takeaway Truck was on, but I'm afraid I inadvertently broke the ministerial code.'*

break the seal *v.* To partake of one's first *piss* at the pub, usually after three or four pints. Return visits to the toilet are thereafter required every fifteen minutes throughout the evening.

break the siege *v.* To enjoy a long overdue *dump* following a bout of constipation.

breastaurant *n.* One of those eateries where the waitresses are hired based on their *impressive qualifications, eg.* Hooters, Mugs'n'Jugs, the Heart Attack Grill and the Honey Shack. But not necessarily Betty's Tea Rooms in Harrogate.

breastbone *1. n.* The sternum. *2. v.* To sail your *skin boat* up the *Bristol Channel.*

breastfallen *adj.* Deflated and downcast after discovering that a new squeeze's *mams* are not quite up to the quality that might have been hoped or expected.

breast fest *n.* Those summer months during which women sunbathe topless.

breasticles *n.* Particularly small, wrinkly bosoms of the type you'd expect Pat Coombs to have. Well certainly these days anyway.

breastimate *v.* To assess the size of a woman's *shirt potatoes* using one's skill and judgement.

breastitute *1. adj.* Descriptive of a lady who hasn't got two *thruppennny bits* to rub together. Also *Miss Lincolnshire, jugless Douglas. 2. n.* A busty pro.

breast nest *n.* A brassiere. Also *tit pants, kitten hammocks, rascal sacks, knocker hoppers.*

breathalising the wife *n.* On the way home after a night of heavy drinking, explaining to your *bread knife* that you are just going to pop something in her mouth and you would like her to keep blowing until you're happy.

breather ring *n.* An anular indentation on a long *turd,* indicating where the *cable layer* has had to pause for breath, allowing the *nipsy* to partially contract. A faecal aneurism. *'Fuck me! That was a mammoth battle. I left the bastard with three breather rings on it.'*

breath of fish air, a *phr.* A *queef* reminiscent of the last gasp of an expiring halibut.

breathwork *1. n.* Relaxation method recommended for anxious people, taught at an evening course down the local library. *2. n.* The odd-but-soothing way that a rude lady will periodically disengage from *horatio* to blow softly on her chap's *clock-weights*; a technique probably taught in an evening course down the local library.

breezer geezer *n.* A gentleman whose drinking habits reveal his *sensitive* nature.

brevilled *adj.* Sliding cosily between the covers of a warm bed which has recently been impregnated with a toasty *bottom burp.*

brew *n.* A nice refreshing *air biscuit* to dunk in one's tea.

brewdini *n.* A friend who magically disappears when it is his turn to get a round of drinks in.

brewer's droop *n. medic.* Marshmallowing of the penis due to excessive *turps nudging.* Also *the droop, knob of butter.*

brewer's fart *n.* A particularly sulphurous and malty *bowel howl. 'Jesus, he's just dropped a brewer's fart, grains and all.'*

brewer's fayre *n.* A pre-9.00am works *bogs* quorum.

brewer's flu *n.* A nasty hangover. *Beer cancer.*

brewer's poop *n.* Slurry-like morning *dump* that has the exact volume, consistency and aroma of the six pints of real ale that was consumed the

night before.

brewicide *n.* The act of drinking yourself unconscious/to death on *trampagne.* Thirsty former pig bladder-bothering Irishman George Best committed *brewicide* in 2005, as did fighty, barrel-chested thesp Oliver Reed in 1999.

brewnami *n.* A disastrous spillage of tea or similar hot beverage which causes devastation out of all proportion to the amount of liquid in the cup.

brew one up *v.* To be *burbulent,* to *bake an air biscuit. 'For your own safety step back please ladies, I'm brewing one up over here.'*

brexbox *n.* Preferred leisure pursuit of those who voted Leave in the 2016 EU referendum; a caravan. *'When he wasn't travelling round Britain's hospitals fucking corpses, Sir Jimmy liked nothing more than staying in his foetid brexbox on Scarborough cliffs.'*

brexhaustipated *adj.* So tired of all this Brexit *bollocks* that you don't give a *shit* any more.

brexit *1. n.* A potentially catastrophic *air biscuit* launched in the overly optimistic hope that it will be "better out than in". *2. n.* Sudden, premature departure from the breakfast table due to the rapid onset of a morning *dreadnought.*

Brexit Arms *n.* Wetherspoon's.

Brexit, I blame *exclam.* A statement issued in order to blithely deflect blame after the stench of a dropped *air biscuit* reaches the nostrils of others in the surrounding area.

brexit pint *n.* Quick visit to the pub for a drink which descends into an endless, messy *piss-up* with no end in sight.

Brian *1. n.* A cockney lady's *bits,* named in honour of erstwhile *Playschool* presenter Cant. The *twat-shaped window. And likewise 2. n.* A contumelious epithet which can be applied, Ray Winstone-style, to a person whom one is inclined to disparage.

Brian Blessed on mute *n.* A particularly hirsute and gaping *growler,* reminiscent of the *fanny-chopped,* shouty crackers actor/mountaineer with the sound turned down. *Bluto's beard.*

Brian Blessed's whisper *n.* A sly *Exchange & Mart* that one intends to squeeze out silently during a harpsichord recital, job interview, Trappist monastery breakfast *etc.,* but which erupts from one's *clacker* with such sudden, deafening ferocity that it can cause hearing loss and tinnitus in anyone caught within a one-mile radius of *browned zero.* An attempted silent *Lionel Bart* in polite company that ends up setting off car alarms three streets away.

Brian May's plughole, a fanny like *sim.* A lady's

badger which is so hirsute that it resembles the bath drainage outlet of the veteran Queen plank-shredder-turned-astrologer.

brice *v. Vict.* To engage in a sexual act in which one party is tied to a large stake known as the *bricing post.*

bricee *n.* Party who is *briced* by a *bricer.*

bricer *n.* One who *brices* a *bricee.*

bricing post *n.* Stake to which a prospective *bricee* is tied by a *bricer*, shortly before being *briced.*

brickie's bucket *n.* Used in the *wet trades.* Can be filled with *tools* and *filthy concrete.*

brickie's wrist, thick as a *sim.* A girthwise measurement of a man's penile endowment.

Brick Lane *1. n.* Bustling London thoroughfare running between Whitechapel High Street and Bethnal Green Road, which includes many exotic eateries amongst its attractions. *2. n.* The narrow skin isthmus connecting the *ringpiece* with the *knackers*, which generally experiences peak traffic flow shortly after visits to the aforementioned establishments. Also *tornado alley, smelly bridge, tintis etc. 'Emergency hotline. Which service do you require?' 'Ambulance please, operator. There's been a terrible accident on Brick Lane.'*

bricks and mortar *n.* A sit down toilet visit of sundry miscellaneous consistencies. *Bomb bay mix.*

brick shithouse, built like a *sim.* Resembling a Leeds Rhinos prop forward. Heavy set, stocky. *'Is that your missus? Fucking hell, she's built like a brick shithouse.'*

brick-teaser *n.* Builder who starts jobs but never finishes them. That'll be a builder, then.

bricky *n. Scots.* A huge, *hard as fuck diamond cutter. 'Yon's a muckle braw bricky ye've got there, if ye don't mind me sayin' so Dr Cameron.' 'Thank-you Janet. I was just havin' a wee wank before auld Jock McTavish comes in with his septic anal fistula.'*

bride & gloom *n.* A matrimonial couple, one of whom is not necessarily quite as happy at the prospect of getting hitched as is the other. *'And here come the bride and gloom now, to wave to the crowds from the balcony of Buckingham Palace.'*

bride frightener *n.* A *mighty Wurlitzer*, such as that famously sported by former MP Stephen Pound.

bride of wankenstein *n.* A "perfect woman" conjured forth mentally by combining the features of various different females. See also *Fuckinstein.*

Brideshead *1. n.* A second trip to the lavatory for a *dump*, named – as all students of classic English literature ought to know – after Evelyn Waugh's famous novel *Brideshead Revisited*, in which she wrote about someone posh going for two *shits*. *2. n.* To mark a significant anniversary (such as 1st, 10th, or golden), an attempt by a married couple to re-enact in detail the *horatio*-based shenanigans they recall fondly from the first night of their honeymoon.

bridesmaid's lunch *n.* A *cheesy nibble* with *plum sauce* followed by a *drink on a stick*, courtesy of the best man.

bridge of doom *n.* The female *perineum*. Also *carse, tinter, taint, biffon, butfer, gooch.*

bridger *n. Bottom log.*

bridge the gap *v.* See *TUBFUF.*

Bridlington tan *euph.* A measure of extreme improbability. *'A Windows computer still running at full speed more than a fortnight after being purchased? It's like a Bridlington tan. Technically, it could happen, I suppose, but I've been an IT professional for thirty years and I've never seen it.'*

brigadier *1. n.* Military officer ranking immediately below a Major General. *2. n.* A three-course meal for one's *cock* consisting of the *pink*, the *brown*, and a *chewie*, in that order. A *holy trinity.*

bright eye *n.* One's *ringpiece* the morning after a heavily spiced meal at which moment it is, in the words of the eponymous Art Garfunkel leporid-based ballad, "burning like fire". A *Johnny Cash, Wigan rosette.*

Brightlingsea bidet *n.* The act of depositing a wet wad of *hockle* onto a square of bathroom tissue before wiping one's *freckle*, as an aid to personal daintiness. Named in honour of the notorious dearth of functioning toilet facilities in the delightful Essex seaside resort.

Brighton *n. rhym. slang. On the other bus, a bit Llandudno.* From Brighton pier = Colwyn Bay.

Brighton breakfast *n.* A morning act of *felching* with perhaps a side dish of poached eggs.

brill ain't *n.* Sneakily antonymical conversational response. A phrase that sounds like "brilliant" while expressing the diametrically opposite sense.

Brillo pad *sim.* Coarse vaginal foliage. A *brandy snap*. A red-headed Scottish lassie might be described as having *'a mott like a rusty Brillo pad'.*

brim *n.* That soffited wainscotting around the base of the *helmet*. The *wankstop* or *sulcus.*

brimula *n.* Spreadable *knob cheese.*

bring down the gavel *1. phr.* What an auctioneer on *Bargain Hunt* does in order to bring everyone's suffering to a close. *2. n.* The highly audible sound made by the toilet seat when it releases itself from the back of the thighs, indicating the conclusion of someone's *duties. 'Ah, it sounds as though the Lord Chamberlain has brought down the gavel at last. Although I'd give it ten minutes if I was you.'*

bring home the bacon *1. v.* Of a heavily *refreshed*

fellow, to return to his domicile with a *right pig* after a night out. 2. *v.* To perform the selfless, yet pointless, unnecessarily fiddly and time-consuming act of enabling a female companion to achieve an *organism.*

bring off *v.* To cause someone to *drop their yoghurt.*

bring the beat back *1. exclam.* Something a hippity-hoppity "MC" – such as Grandmaster Flash, Roots Manuva or Jive Bunny – might say during a break in a song when announcing the return of a temporarily muted rhythm track. *2. exclam.* Something to announce before dropping a *Lionel.*

bring the safety car out *1. v.* The spoilsport action of Formula 1 organisers attempting to prevent exciting high-speed pile-ups occurring in dangerous conditions. *2. v.* A gentleman's attempt to prevent early *crashing of the yoghurt truck* in an exciting situation, *eg.* By thinking about abandoned puppies, football scores or the late Ivy Tilsley. *Summoning Moira.*

bring your backstory to life *1. phr.* Slogan used by Ancestry.com to encourage members of the public to discover that their utterly unremarkable ancestors apparently couldn't spell their own fucking surname the same fucking way twice in a fucking row. *2. phr.* To allow a romantic partner to *do* you *up the wrong 'un.*

bring your dinner to work *euph.* To wait until you get to your place of employment before retiring to the *Boss Hoggs* to enjoy your morning *dump.*

brink *n.* The *taint, tinter, carse, Humber Bridge, crontis.* So called because it rests between the *brown* and the *pink.*

brinks job *n.* To successfully *bang* the boss's wife without getting caught.

brioche cigar *n.* A *happy Havana* that stinks out the house and necessitates a home visit from the emergency plumber.

Bristol buckshot *n.* An amount of *Harry Monk* hitting the back of the throat with the same force and power as a shotgun blast.

Bristol Channel *n.* The cleavage, *LVC* or *sausage dock.*

Bristol cream *n.* A warming splash of *man milk* across the *bread knife*'s *fat rascals.*

Bristol meth *n.* Incredibly strong scrumpy that transports the drinker into *ciderspace. Electric lemonade, Tone Vale tonic.*

Bristols *n. ryhm. slang. Tits.* From Bristol Cities = titties. And Bristol dockers = knockers. And Bristol passive nests = massive breasts.

Bristols rover *n.* A man with wandering hands who is fond of fondling *norks. 'Watch out for the archbishop when you're in the vestry signing the register, Kate. he's a right Bristols rover, that one.'*

Bristol suspension bridge *1. n.* Elaborate, elevated wrought iron structure linking two headlands across the Bristol Channel. Also known as the Clifton Suspension Bridge. *2. n.* Elaborate, elevated lace structure linking two *knockers* across the *Bristol channel.* A bra. See also *titpants, knocker hoppers, rack sack, two-ring circus etc.*

Bristol therapy *n. medic.* Alternative holistic treatment whereby an ailing man is revived and soothed by exposure to a massive pair of *oomlaaters.*

BritBox and shitbox *phr.* How a gentleman spends his evening; an arguably less classy version of "Netflix and Chill" or "Amazon Prime and quality time".

Britney's chuff *euph.* A situation when a much-anticipated reality in no way matches up to what you'd imagined it would be like, to the point that you begin to wish you'd never seen it. *'I got the Sky Sports so I could watch the Ashes series. A right Britney's chuff that turned out to be.'*

broadband blister *n.* A callus that appears on a chap's *stench hammer* shortly after his internet download speed increases.

broadside *1. n.* A forceful verbal attack, like you might get off Jonathan Swift, Thomas Paine or Vinnie Jones. *2. n.* A performative act of flatulence achieved by leaning over onto one *arse* cheek and *farting* sideways. *'Jeremy Corbyn last night aimed a devastating broadside at Prime Minister [insert name here]'s economic record whilst wheeling his bike into his porch.'*

broat *n.* See *vurp.*

broboe *n.* The male member. *'Entering the room very softly, I had a view of Mr Rochester before he discovered my presence. He sat in his chair leafing through his mam's Grattan Catalogue, his countenance downcast as he tugged listlessly at his broboe.'* (from *Jane Eyre* by Charlotte Brontë).

brobs *n.* Overwhelmingly large *tits.* From the giant Brobdingnagians in *Gulliver's Travels.* Opposite of *lils.*

brofession *n.* Career or occupation that appears – despite the Equality Act – to remain the privileged preserve of the male of the species. For example, bin man, tarmac layer, fighting dog trainer, F1 driver, Chancellor of the Exchequer.

brofiterole *n.* Tonsorially speaking, a small man-bun. *'Nice brofiterole, Mr Mamoa.'*

brogueing *1. n.* A proper kicking received off a hoodlum who takes pride in his appearance, like what you might get off one of them Peaky Blinders or a Kray twin. *2. n.* Looking up a lady's skirt or Scotsman's kilt by virtue of one's highly polished shoes.

brokeback breakfast *n.* Any non-fried, continental-style, vegetarian-friendly foodstuff, such as yoghurt, fruit, muesli or brown bread with seeds, tomatoes or olives, such as might be nibbled in the morning by a man who *throws a light dart*.

brokeback mounting *n.* Sexual congress attempted by a couple of such disproportionate size or of such advanced age or frailty that one or both of them risks severe physical injury and possible paralysis.

broken arrow *1. n.* In Cold War parlance, an atomic weapons accident that does not create a risk of nuclear conflict. *2. n.* In the Vietnam War, an American unit being overrun and in need of air support. *3. n.* A 1996 film staring John Travolta as a baddy. *4. n.* A big morning *dump* that can't be extracted in one go and requires a follow-up visit to the *shite house* before lunchtime. *5. euph.* Someone who is utterly ineffectual within their place of work but who is impossible to get rid of due to the vagaries of employment law. So called because "they cannot be fired".

broken biscuits *euph.* Alliterative *damaged goods*. Descriptive of someone who's a bit off-kilter.

broken candy floss machine, fanny like a *sim.* Often used to describe the somewhat run-to-seed *bower of bliss* to be found in the *applecatchers* of a more mature conquest. A *twat* that resembles something you'd pull out of a blocked Henry hoover.

broken catflap *n.* A *knackered nipsy*. A term apparently coined by cheeky Scotch funnyman Frankie Boyle in his humorous routine at the 2019 Royal Variety Performance. *'A German married to a Greek for sixty years? You must have an arse like a broken catflap, ma'am.'*

broken deckchair, fanny like a *sim.* A lady's *front bottom* which proves very difficult, if not impossible, to successfully sort out. *'Sorry, love. I did me best, but in the end I just had to give up. You've got a fanny like a broken deckchair.'*

broken heart *n. rhym. slang.* A *treacle tart*. From broken heart = Exchange & Mart.

broken ice cream machine, arse like a *sim.* Symptom of major gastro-intestinal meltdown which results in a day off work that is spent sitting on the *chod bin* reading the local *Autotrader* and moaning.

broken washer *n.* The bit of a gent's plumbing that inevitably deteriorates with age, leading to intermittent dripping that keeps him up at night.

brolex *n.* Bejewelled chronometer the size and shape of a World War II limpet mine, attached to the wrist of a young man-about-town.

bromance *n.* A special, completely manly relationship between a pair of one hundred percent heterosexual men that involves a lot of hugging and intimate conversations, and which baffles and discomfits their other friends, wives and girlfriends.

Bromley tickle *n.* Digital titivation of a lady's *undercarriage* to gauge whether *congress* is on the cards or what. Named after the South London high street in which the technique was perfected, the *Bromley tickle* often precedes a *Bolton dip test*.

bromp *n. onomat.* A man-size *guff* that is delivered *con brio* and is felt by the person sitting next to you on a government bench, trireme galley or bus seat.

Brompton *1. n.* An over-elaborate and expensive fold-up bicycle used by serious, *bespectable,* architect types who like to block up the train doors on their way into work, standing there with their fucking beards, their fucking round glasses and their fucking helmets. *2. n.* An upper middle class *bike* who gets ridden on while her serious, *bespectable,* bearded architect husband is on the train into work.

Bronx cheer *n. arch.* Obsolete term for a *fart* used exclusively by Whoopee cushion manufacturers. Usually "a real Bronx cheer".

bronze medal *1. n.* Sporting decoration awarded for third place. *2. n.* Nominal honour bestowed on one who has gone up the *brass eye*. *Brown wings*. *3. n.* The *dot*.

broomstick *n.* Any small runaround car aimed specifically at female drivers, *eg.* Renault Clio, Ford Fiesta, Nissan Micra. Or historically the Hillman Imp or Riley Elf.

broomsticking *n.* Intercrural sexual practice common amongst leg fetishists and visitors to Japanese brothels, in which the lady grasps the bloke's *todger* between her thighs and rides it, much like a demented wiccan on her enchanted besom. Also known as the *Oxford Rub*.

broon baboon *n. Scots.* A *skidmark* in the stygian depths of a Hibernian *gurgler*. *'Frae Stornaway tae Ullapool, Kingussie an' Dunoon / The rain fell a' the mornin' and it was michty foggie / I borrow'd next door's lavatory brush tae clean a broon baboon / That ma darlin' Mary hod left theer in ma boggie.'* (from *Ode tae a Haggis Bought frae the Auchtermuchty Rugby Club Car Boot* by Rabbie Burns).

broon Hilda *n. prop.* A heftily-built woman who gets very loud and boisterous when *blootered* on the popular Zoeterwoude, Netherlands-brewed

Newcastle Brown ale.

brotein *n.* Orally-administered *oil of goolay*, reliably understood to be a cure for all known feminine ailments. The active ingredient in *Vitamin S. 'I know what her problem is. She's not getting enough brotein in her diet.'*

brothel sprouts *n. medic.* An attack of genital herpes following a visit to a *house of ill repute.* *'What's that on your cock, Lord Archer?' 'Oh that? It's nothing, just a few brothel sprouts, that's all. I've got them all up my back as well, you know. Do you want £2000 in a brown envelope?'*

brothelyser *n.* Following a lads' weekend away, an investigative *nosh* administered by a suspicious missus, whereby any failure to meet the required standard will lead to terrible consequences.

brother *n. Bean flicker, tuppence licker, carpet muncher, scissor sister.* A lesbian.

brother, email my *euph.* To masturbate. From the US baseball player Carlos Zambrano, who was put on the Chicago Cubs injured list because of a sore wrist caused by spending four hours a day on the internet "emailing his brother".

brothers quim *n. Twatmates* who are related solely by the fact that they have enjoyed intimate relations with the same woman (usually at different times). *Custard cousins* who have *stirred the paint in the same tin, eg.* Sir Donald Campbell and Selwyn Froggitt, Mick Jagger and Nikolas Sarkozy, Marvin Hamlisch and Simon McCoy.

brown admiral *n. zoo.* The common and far from beautiful butterfly that can be found in the *dunghampers* of someone who has failed to *draw an ace. A gusset moth, tiger's face* or *wind sketch.*

brown album, the *1. n.* LP released by the American rock band Primus. No, us neither. *2. n.* A *tosstalgic* rollcall of all the *A-listers* that a chap has *done up the wrong 'un.*

brown Atlantis *n.* A gargantuan, semi-solid land mass that with one flush is lost for all eternity.

brown ball *exclam.* Delivered in the tone of a Sheffield Crucible snooker referee confirming a player's choice of colour to pot, immediately prior to producing a breathtaking *cannon shot.*

brown ballerina *n.* The "tutu" effect achieved when one's index finger pierces cheap bathroom tissue while wiping one's *ringpiece. Also Kermit's collar.*

brown baubles *n.* The tightly knotted bags of *dog eggs* with which thoughtful pet owners decorate the trees in the countryside while out walking their *shit machines. Also fairy shites, Leeds baubles, Warrington baubles.*

Brownbeard's hammock *n.* A useful, suspended cotton receptacle in which to keep a roll of arsewipe handy while *dropping the kids off at the pool, ie.* Your *underkegs* round your ankles.

brown bear's nose *n.* A cute little round *turd* that hibernates at the bottom of the *grizzly bear pit.*

brown Betty *n.* The mess that can result from *back door love* with someone with a full or disturbed bowel.

brown-blooded shotgun victim, the *n.* Stomach-turning Sam Peckinpah-style crime scene found in one's lavatory bowl after a particularly loose *Simon Cowell* movement, usually following a *cuzza* or a night of chronic alcohol abuse.

brown bobsleigh *n.* A term used to describe the speedy downhill movement of a *digestive transit* that involves impossibly tight turns and feelings of terror and impending disaster. A *brown knuckle ride, the Cresta runs.*

Brown bounce *1. n.* Journalistic catchphrase describing the surprising resurgence in popularity of the former government following the then Prime Minister's level-headed response to the 2008 global financial crisis. That didn't last long. *2. n.* When a *bird* sticks your *cock* up her *arse* and rides it like she's on a spacehopper. That is to say, halfway up the path at the side of your house before falling off and grazing one of her knees. *3. n.* Upon dropping a rather large *brown trout* into the *Rick Witter*, the phenomenon of it disappearing reassuringly from view, only for it to disconcertingly bob back up to the surface. Usually happens when *laying a cable* at someone else's house.

brown brakelight *n.* A visible warning that the person in front of you may have slammed on the *anal anchors* slightly too late, and that as a consequence it may be best to steer a wide berth around them.

brown break *n.* An extra period of rest taken during the working day when an employee retires to a cubicle for a good twenty minute sit-down. *'That's all the national news headlines. Now I'm off for a brown break while you find out what's been happening in your own regions.'*

brown bullet-hole *n. Bumhole, barking spider.*

brown bunting *n.* The celebratory, *foulage*-smeared *bumwad* that adorns laybys frequented by cut-price staycationers. Also *Bear Grylls's tinsel.*

brown candle, light a *v.* To go for a *number two.*

brown chicks have fledged, the *phr.* Confirmation that one's *mocking birds* have left the nest. *'Well, Chris, I'm happy to report that the brown chicks have fledged and gone to the beach.'*

brown cough *n.* A *shart* or *follow-through.*

brown cuckoo *n.* A small *Richard the Third*, to

quote Ronnie Barker's cockney vicar, that pops in and out at regular intervals until a suitable landing area becomes available. An inquisitive *turtle's head*.

browndabout *n.* The *nipsy*.

brown daisy *n.* An unpleasantly scented flower which attracts bluebottles instead of bees and butterflies. A *bronze eye*.

brown derby *1. n.* Epithet of an ultimately unsuccessful Wimpy's restaurant dessert from the 1970s, named for some unfathomable reason after a stiff-brimmed felt hat. *2. n.* A mass *bumfest*, involving a multitude of muddy runners and riders. *3. n.* A sprint to the lavatory while suffering from a *farmer's protest*. *3. n.* A small sepia bowler hat worn by the *excitable trouser man* after he's been up the *wrong 'un*.

brown dog *n.* Similar to Winston Churchill's famous "black dog" of depression, a looming presence of foreboding and despair that can be remedied with a bit of blood, toil, tears and sweat in the *cludgie*.

brown drought *n. medic.* Constipation. A *delay on the Bakerloo line*.

brown dwarf *n.* The tiny, superdense, hard-to-find nugget of highly compressed *barker's egg* hiding somewhere on the sole of one's shoe.

brown eagle has landed, the *exclam.* Something to say whilst trotting back from the *crapper* with a satisfied grin on your face. '*You look pleased with yourself, Mother Teresa of Calcutta.' 'And so I should, my child, for the brown eagle has landed.'*

browned zero *n.* The epicentre of a particularly catastrophic anal detonation. '*I'd avoid trap two if I was you, Bamber. It's browned zero in there.'*

brown eraser *n. Shitting* on top of an existing *skidmark* only to find, upon flushing, that the blemish has been miraculously rubbed away.

brown extender *n.* At B&Q, a device for raising the height of an existing fence.

brown eye *n.* The *ring* through which the *brown trouts* jump on their daily migration to the sea. Also *brass eye*.

browneye lashes *n.* Glamorous hairs that surround the *balloon knot*. Often caked in a brown, mascara-like substance.

browneye points *n.* Favour accumulated in one's better half's eyes by means of doing chores, putting up shelves, not *crapping* in the kitchen sink *etc.* Nominal credits awarded by a fellow's ladyfriend which he may – in the fullness of time – redeem against *wrong'un*-based shenanigans. '*There was another dead pigeon in the water tank this week, so I went up and fished it out to earn myself a few browneye points.'*

brownfield site *n.* Area of common grassland where dog walkers take their hounds for an empty.

brown fingered *1. adj.* Somewhat inept at gardening. *2. adj.* Somewhat inept at *arse*-wiping.

brown finger poncho *n.* The square of *arsewipe* through which the digit pushes when one *breaches the hull*.

brown fingerprint *n.* Simulacrum of a badly wiped *Ena Sharples' mouth* left on the bedspread after putting on your socks. Also *nipsy's kiss, ringerprint, sheet toffee, bottom line*.

brown flower in the window, have a *euph.* Expression of one's need to defecate. '*Sorry, love, I'll get a fire engine off to you as soon as I can, but I've got a brown flower in the window here and it needs putting in some water.'*

brown foam *n.* When the tank of a seemingly terminal case of the *Earthas* is running dry, and what feels like air being blown through a thin milkshake is all that's left.

brownfriars bobby *n.* A small, buoyantly devoted *feeshus* that refuses to leave its owner's side no matter how many times he flushes. *Mrs Brown's boy*.

brown glow *n.* That lovely feeling of wellbeing after enjoying a nice big *shit*. '*You do look well, gran. You've got that lovely brown glow about you.'*

brown hatter *n.* A *bottsman* with *shit* on his helmet.

brown helmet *n.* An award presented to a man by his girlfriend or wife to commemorate the day she metaphorically *shits* on his head by leaving him. '*And it came to pass that Naboth had journeyed to the shops and his wife Bathsheba was left alone in his tent. And David came unto her in the tent of Naboth and knew her twice. And she took up her chatels and went to live in the tent of David amongst the Gibeonites. And Naboth did return to his tent and found that Bathsheba was gone. And he went to the inn with his mates Mephibosheth and Jonadab son of Shimeah, and he wailed and gnashed his teeth saying, I always did my best for her, no man could have done more. Yet she gives me the brown helmet. And great was his sorrow, even unto the twelfth pint.'* (from *Epidydimis*, Ch. 6 v. 12-16).

brown herring *n.* Alarming intestinal rumblings, pops and gurgles that imply the urgent need to *drop anchor in Shanks Bay*, but once one is seated on the *porcelain throne* reveal themselves to be nothing more substantial than a soggy *air biscuit*.

brown hole radiation *n.* Flatulent equivalent of black hole radiation like what Steven Hawking invented in 1973. Except involving *fartons* not photons.

brownhouse gases *n.* Environmentally harmful emissions of *carbon dibaxide* from a *tail pipe.*

brownian motion *1. n.* The apparently random movements of minute particles immersed in a fluid, discovered by physicist Richard Brown. *2. n.* The frequent and painful visits to the *throne room* experienced by one who has recently enjoyed a delicious meal at the Curry Capital.

browning off in the pan *1. phr.* A culinary term for quickly frying a steak to seal it. Or sear it. *2. phr.* Applying a non non-stick coating to the *pot*; having a *poo.*

Brownington-on-Sea *euph. Vict.* Name of a mythical town used by discreet nineteenth century types when broaching the embarrassing subject of *snipping off a length of dirty spine* in polite company. *'Pray kindly excuse me, your majesty. I most earnestly crave your indulgence while I take my leave, for I have a somewhat pressing engagement in Brownington-on-Sea.' 'I quite understand, Mr Disraeli, but check the maid's left a new roll of shitscrape in the crapper before you park your breakfast, won't you. Only I had to use the fucking cardboard tube to wipe my arse on when I went this morning.'*

browning your meat *euph.* Enjoying a spot of *bum fun* in the *back kitchen.*

brown jack *n. milit.* World War II artillery expression for what comes out of your *nipsy* when you are confronted by World War II Germans.

brown jewels *n.* The monarch's *winnets.* The *dangleberries* of state.

brown laser *n.* A beam of hot, liquid *shite* that exits the *brass eye* at the speed of light, and which could easily cut a secret agent in two.

brown latrine limpet *n.* Larger, stickier Pacific Rim cousin of the *bogpan barnacle*, that exists in a symbiotic relationship with the *chocolate starfish.*

Brownlee'd, a bit *adj.* In such a state of *over refreshment* from the drink that you need a friend to support you on your way to the taxi rank or car park, in the style of the eponymous Olympic triathlete Jonny who had to be helped across the finishing line by his brother Alistair at the Rio games.

brown light district *n.* Any area frequented by those who *prefer their peas minted.*

brown light, get the *euph.* When a fellow gets the nod to make his way up the *back lane.*

brown light's flashing *euph.* Emergency warning sign of a toiletry nature. *Umber alert. 'Can you hang the washing out for me, dear?' 'Sorry love.*

Brown light's flashing, with you in five.'

brown lilo *n.* A buoyant *Tom tit* that, if left alone, will eventually float out to sea and be eaten by a cod or cross-channel swimmer.

brownloading *n.* Surfing the internet on a smartphone whilst taking a *dump.*

brown map *n.* The virtual atlas that includes pubs and bars where one can *deal with the queue at the trade counter* in reasonable comfort during a night out. *'It was nice in there, with very little piss on the seat. Definitely one for the brown map.'*

brown maverick *n.* The *stooling* stage which comes immediately prior to *touching cloth.* The *turtle's head, winking at Calvin, Yoffy's finger.* From the lyrics to the Rodgers & Hammerstein standard *Oh, What a Beautiful Mornin', viz.* "Oh the cattle are standin' like statues / Oh the cattle are standin' like statues / They don't raise their heads as they see me ride by / But a little brown maverick is winkin' her eye."

brown men on swings *n.* See *miniature heroes.*

brown mile, the *euph.* The abject, seemingly endless waddle home a person endures after having *sharted.*

brown noise *1. n.* The hubbub produced by Brownian motion, as everyone knows. A sound whose spectral density is inversely proportional to the square of its frequency (come on, this is basic stuff). *2. n.* Sound emanating from the *chamber of horrors* whose volume is directly proportional to the quantity of curry and lager consumed by the person producing it.

brownout *n.* After a heavy night on the tiles, the distinctly unpleasant consequence that is one stage further than a blackout. *'Aw, bloody hell, June. The dog must've climbed in the bed and done a dirt in my pyjama bottoms last night, look. Again.' 'You can't fool me, Terry. We haven't even got a dog. You've had another one of your brownouts, haven't you?'*

brown owl *n.* A sizeable *log. Meat Loaf's daughter, a dead otter.*

brown panther, the *n.* Mythical anti-hero who strikes in staff toilets, leaving them in a disgraceful mess, with bits of *shite* on the seats & occasionally full *turds* on cistern tops or the floor. *'Remember Cato, the brown panther always leaves his calling card.'*

brown paratroopers *euph. Loose stools,* whereby one can imagine the sergeant shouting "Go! Go! Go!" as they pile out the moment that the *bomb bay doors* open over the *drop zone.* The complete opposite of *frightened skydivers.*

brown party *n.* See *yellow party* and make the

imaginative leap yourself.

brown peacock *n. medic.* A serious case of the *Brads* whereby one small twitch of the *back body* produces an impressive rooster tail of sepia plumage from the *rusty sheriff's badge.*

brown ping pong ball *n.* A remarkably natatorial *plop* which refuses to go to the beach, no matter how many times you flush it. One of them really annoying ones that raises your hopes by going round the U-bend, only to dash them when it bobs back to the surface a few seconds later like Glenn Close in *Fatal Attraction.* A *brown zombie.*

brown pipe engineer *n.* An *arse mechanic* who not surprisingly plies his trade at the *tradesman's entrance.*

brown pocket *n.* A smuggler's receptacle that allows him to spirit contraband through customs. *'Did you bring anything back from Amsterdam, Phil?' 'Yes. I've got some clogs and cheese in my suitcase and a lump of squidgy black in my brown pocket.'*

brown room *n.* Departure lounge for *turd class travellers.* The noisome vestibule of the *dirt bakery.*

brown roulette *n.* A game of chance with potentially disastrous consequences whereby one *shoots rabbits* through an *arse* over which one has little control. To risk a *fart* while suffering with the *squits. Twisting on nineteen.*

brown sky thinking *1. v.* A state of mind attained by a sage fellow when his or her mind wanders to thoughts of a defecatory nature. *2. v.* The state of mindfulness one experiences in the moments after *the bugler sounds the retreat.*

brown smile, the *n.* The grimace made when pushing a parcel of excrement out through *Ena Sharples's mouth.*

brown Spartan *n.* n. The exact opposite of a *brown trout,* in that rather than one's gleaming *captain's log* gliding effortlessly down the *slipway,* the tenacious *fucker* requires the combined efforts of a Persian army to be forced through the *nipsy,* including risking dislocated eyeballs and hip joints, together with a ruptured *porthole.*

brown stab vest *n.* Any item placed between the *ringpiece* and the *grundies* in an effort to prevent unwanted blotting when one lacks confidence in the tautness of one's *nether throat.*

brown sunrise *n.* While ensconced on the *throne,* the majestic sight of a *Thora Hird* gradually emerging from behind the knackers as one watches with the head between the knees. A sign that it's time to buy some Andy Capp books to keep on the cistern.

brown-tak *n.* A pliable, adhesive compound used by prisoners to stick posters to the wall. Also known as *scat-tak* and *bloo-tak.*

brown tap *n.* A particularly non-viscid bout of the *Mexican screamers.* The *gravy rocket.*

brown ticket *n.* Scatological equivalent of a *pink ticket,* giving a bloke free reign to produce the most joyously noxious *Bakewells* and *bog*-blocking *Earthas* whenever he likes while his better half is away. *'Yeah, she's in the infirmary for a month having a hysterectomy so I've got a brown ticket. Result.'*

brown tie *n.* The dirty mark left between a lady's *jugs* by a man having a *sausage sandwich* immediately after taking her up the *council gritter. Shit tie.*

brown time *n.* Getting paid for having a *shit* while at work, *taking one in the company's time. 'Leading psychologists suggest that it is vital we make the most of our brown time.'*

brown triathlon *n.* A difficult *crap* which consists of constipation, *skitters* and normal, all in the same visit. *'Jesus. You look terrible, mate.' 'I'm not surprised. I've just finished a brown triathlon. I feel like I've just done ten rounds with Henry Pooper.'*

brown trout *n.* A turd, big job, shite.

brown trout pond *n.* The lavatory bowl.

Brownville *euph.* A *dump. 'Must dash, your majesty. I've got to catch the last train to Brownville.'*

brown voyage *exclam.* Said after doing – but not flushing – a *number two* just before leaving the house on a long holiday.

brown whale's blowhole, like a *sim.* Descriptive of when *fizzy gravy* is erupting from one's *hoop. 'I'm afraid I can't do today's press conference, Dominic. My arse is like a brown whale's blowhole.'*

brown-whipped *adj.* Like *pussy-whipped* but in thrall to the *wrong 'un* instead. *'My mate Dave is definitely brown-whipped. He's in the middle of a 10-hour box set of Hugh Grant romcoms at the moment in the vague hope of some backdoor action later.'*

brown wings *n.* The honour bestowed on one who has performed *bumilingus* on a lady Hell's Angel. The *bronze medal.*

brown zero *n.* The ravaged epicentre of a catastrophic *exchange & mart.* Also *browned zero.*

brown zombie *n.* A *Douglas* that refuses to *go to the beach* and keeps on coming back in increasingly decrepit form after every flush.

Bruce Lee *n. prop. euph.* A term used by a chap conceding defeat on a *pulling night* and falling back instead on his conjugal rights, *viz.* Going home to "enter the dragon".

Brucie *n.* A *fart* which is performed while adopting the silhouetted "Thinker" stance made famous by the late Bruce Forsyth on *The Generation Game*, followed by a camp little kick forwards.

Brucie bonus *n.* An act of *self pollution* achieved after summoning the image of saucy *Question Time* ma'am Fiona into the mind's eye. *Puddle jumpers* may substitute Radio 2's mid-morning hunk Ken, if necessary.

Brummie orgasm *n.* A plangent, discordant and cacophonous sound. *'As the giant iceberg tore through the mighty liner's hull, in that same dread moment the ship's cat was tipped into a pan of boiling cooking fat and the palm court orchestra was caught in the deadly whiplash of the broken steel cables. It sounded like a Brummie orgasm.'*

brush his dick, he needs to *exclam.* Said of a fellow who has relaxed his hygiene regimen somewhat.

brush up on one's Punjabi *v.* To lick a lady's *bodily treasure. 'Virginia looked resplendent as she descended from the Sao Paolo steamer, quite bronzed and elegant in the London mist. After taking tea at Claridge's we took the charabanc to my rooms at Oxford, where I relished the opportunity to brush up on my Punjabi.'* (from *The Diaries of Evelyn Waugh*).

brush with stardom *euph.* During sexual relations whilst in a state of drunken disrepair, an arguably unwitting attempt to enter *via* the *back door*, before being hastily redirected towards the missus's preferred entrance. See also *French fancy.*

Brussels sprout *1. n.* Member of the *Gemmifera* group of cabbages (*Brassica oleracea*), that is cultivated for its edible buds. *2. n.* A member of the family who is seen once a year at the Christmas dinner table, despite the fact no-one likes them.

brut *1. n.* Man musk peddled by an unlikely alliance of bald former prize-fighters, motorcycle racers and popcorn-haired future football managers who found themselves sharing a bathroom mirror in the 1970s. *2. n.* The predictable end scene of a *grumble flick* when the lady participant encourages her male co-star to "splash it all over". And she's not talking about his aftershave. She's talking about his *spunk. 'Any chance of a Christmas bunk-up, Pauline?' 'Piss off Arthur, I'm stuffed. Tell you what though, I'll get my tits out so you can have a Brut 33.'* (from *EastEnders*, Christmas afternoon 1985). *3. n.* A great-smelling *gypsy's kiss* that gets "splashed all over" the *bog* seat, cistern, wall *etc.*

Bryan Adams relationship *euph.* A saucy liaison sustained for a strictly limited time. A "summer of '69".

Bryant and May *adj. rhym. slang. Colwyn Bay. 'Haven't you heard? The marriage is over. He's come in last week and told her straight, he's Bryant and May and he has been since they got married.'*

BS *abbrev. US.* Nonsense, balderdash, *wank.* See *bull.*

BSH *abbrev.* British Standard Handful. The Imperial unit by which *knockers* were measured in the good old days of *Confessions* films.

BTB *abbrev.* Very nearly, but not quite, absolute *shite.* Better Than Brookside. *'Look at this BTB gadget I bought for twenty pee at the car boot. It's like a telephone, but it's got a little screen so you can send and receive emails on it too.' 'You got that for twenty pee? They must have seen you coming, mate.'*

BT infinity *euph.* An emergency *poo, eg.* As a policeman is approaching the bank doorway where one is ensconced with one's trousers round one's ankles. From the fact that, according to the adverts, one "completes a download in seconds".

bubbies *n.* Coy term for *breasts*, much beloved of writers of cod-Victorian pornography. *"Ooh, zur! What does you think of moi bubbies, then?'* asked Molly the milkmaid, as she unzipped Squire Bowman's heaving breeches.'* (from *A Roll in the Hay*, by Jeffrey Archer).

bubble and squeak *1. n.* A budget meal usually cooked and eaten by students, consisting of ageing mashed potatoes, cabbage and various other unappetising plate-scrapings. *2. n.* An *apple tart* emitted following a meal constaining a high proportion of re-heated, left-over brassicas.

bubble and squeak – best take a peek *exclam.* Amusing couplet declaimed after a particularly liquid-sounding *treacle tart*, prior to a discreet investigation to ensure that undergarments have not been irreparably besmirched.

bubblebum *n.* An unfortunate release of *burbulent gas* through moist *buttocks,* the resulting sound being eerily reminiscent of Leonardo di Caprio's final words in *the film Titanic.*

bubble mix *n.* A playful term for *fanny paste.*

bubble poo *n.* Fizzy gravy.

bubbletrumps *n. medic.* The *shits.*

bubblin' crude *n.* The hot, treacly liquid that starts to seep from the *fifties tea towel holder* about twelve hours after a good session on the stout, whether or not you've got out of bed by then. Also *black tar, Tipperary tea.*

bubbly *adj.* Fat, overweight.

bubblyduck *n.* A particularly loud, prolonged, and wet *fart.* Named because the sound is identical to that of an agitated mallard being drowned in a bucket of custard.

bubes *n.* Those occasional curly hairs that ladies sometimes find sprouting around their *puppies' noses.* The legs of the European *hunchback* *spider. Hariolae.*

bucket fanny *n.* A spacious or roomy vagina. *A tardis twat, cathedral* or *welly top.*

bucket list *1. n.* An inspirational inventory of things you would like to do before you die, typically including things like seeing the fucking Taj Mahal, doing a fucking parachute jump, running with the fucking bulls at Pamplona, seeing the sun rise over the fucking pyramids and fucking swimming with fucking dolphins. *2. n.* A distinctly uninspirational inventory of *easy* women with whom you have had *carnival relations.*

bucket of snot *euph. Manc.* An extremely well-oiled box. Also *bag of slugs, splinge, snail's doorstep.* '*Mother Teresa was powerless to resist. The Pope's eyes burned into hers like Swarovski crystals. His strong papal arms enfolded her slight, nunnish body as she felt herself being swept away on a runaway palanquin of passion. Tenderly, he slipped his hand up her habit and into her fevered dunghampers. "Bloody hell, it's like a bucket of snot down there!" he exclaimed.*' (from *The Nun and the Pontiff* by Barbara Cartland).

Buckfast bravery *n.* Instances of incredible courage manifested by ruddy-faced Caledonian outdoorsmen, *eg.* Strolling across four lanes of traffic without looking left or right, sleeping on a railway level crossing, fighting a police horse *etc.*

Buckfast breakfast *n.* The first meal of the day for many a heather-dwelling *Angus McRamp.*

Buckfast in bed *n.* A luxurious, warming treat for a Glaswegian fellow who doesn't have to get up for his *Tennents Association* meeting until later.

buckie *n. Scots.* Affectionate nickname given to the health-giving tonic wine traditionally produced by the monks of Buckfast Abbey, Devon, for Glaswegian tramps and the students of Queen's University, Belfast.

buckle bunny *n. US.* A *cock*-hungry *bird.*

Buddha's earlobes *euph.* A particular type of *beef curtains* that dangle around a lady's thighs and resemble nothing so much as the pendulous lower pinnae of the eponymous rotund spiritual leader. Often found on Australian females. '*Fuck me, Daphne. I never noticed how low your piss flaps hang. They're like Buddha's fucking earlobes.*' (Des Clarke, *Neighbours*, 1988).

buddy breathing *1. n.* In SCUBA diving, where two frogmen share a mouthpiece in an emergency situation, taking it in turns to suck on the same oxygen supply. *2. n.* In *jazzular cinematography,* a trope whereby two actresses share a *cheesepipe,* taking it in turns to suck on the same *spongle* supply. *Baby birding.*

budget hairline *n.* The economical alternative to having a hair transplant. A *syrup* or *Irish jig.*

budget spunk *n. medic.* The fluids that a gentleman expels after undergoing a *walnut whip. Decaff spaff.*

budgie smugglers *n.* Extremely tight bathing trunks. *Noodle benders, nut chokers.*

budgie's nostril, fanny like a *sim.* A snug and restrictive *ladypart.* Also *miser's fist, archer's window, butler's cuff, mouse's ear, OJ's glove, grandad's coin purse, paper cut, worm's belt.* '*I tell you, every time she uncrosses her legs, you can see that the honoroubale lady's got a fanny like a budgie's nostril.*' '*Order! The prime minister – whoever that might be at the moment – must refrain from such unparliamentary language.*'

budgie's tongue *1. n.* Descriptive of the female erectile bit, particularly when her *clunge* has climbed a little plastic ladder to ring a bell. *2. sim. As dry as ~* Said of a *fruity slice* that turns out to be slightly less moist inside than one might have hoped. Also *dry as a moth sandwich.* '*She was cheap, I'll give her that. But she was as dry as a budgie's tongue, your honour.*'

budgie supping *v.* The act of pitifully amateur beer drinking performed by men who aren't used to it, *eg.* A terrified Tony Blair pecking at a pint for the benefit of TV cameras in Sedgefield Labour Club or London Mayoral candidate Zac Goldsmith's desperate photo opportunity behind the bar of an East End pub in 2016, where it looked like the poor *twat* had never seen a pint glass before.

budmiser *n.* The unusually quiet member of a lad's night out who waits until he has downed four rounds of drinks before revealing that he has come out without any cash.

buff *v.* To engage in the removal of the *poo*/sweat mix which accumulates in a chap's *arse cleft* during a long drinking session, or perhaps while moving filing cabinets up and down a fire escape on a hot and humid day, by the vigorous application of copious amounts of *bumwad.* '*That'll just buff out.*'

buffage *n. US.* Hurtful, offensive and sexist term used by women to describe men. '*Hey girls, check out the buffage in here.*'

buffalo soldier *euph.* A man who is nearing the *vinegar strokes* but desperately fighting a rearguard action trying to hold off *blowing his stack.* From the lyrics to the eponymous Bob Marley song of the same name, one who is "fighting on arrival".

buffalo wings *1. n.* Chicken wings that have been deep fried in a hot sauce. *2. n.* Plus-sized *bingo wings.* Bariatrically challenged *dinner ladies' arms.*

buffer *v.* To pause, motionless, for 10-15 seconds

during a *scuttle* in order to delay the inevitable and thus prolong sexual pleasure. From the message that often appears onscreen when watching *grumble* online *via* a low bandwidth internet connection. Apparently.

buffering *n*. The *treading water* strokes required to maintain a gentleman's posture while awaiting for videographic stimulation to load on his *faptop*.

buffers *n*. A pair of large, solidly sprung buttocks. *'Sorry Kim. I can't get it any further in from here. I've hit the buffers.'*

buffeting *n*. The disturbing half-gulping, half-choking carry-on that precedes a *psychedelic yawn*. A *frogs' chorus*.

buffet on Jeremy Kyle, like the *sim*. Descriptive of any offering of foodstuffs that is supposed to provide diners with a well-balanced meal, but instead presents them with an artery-hardening array of comestibles stuffed with vast amounts of sugar, salt, pig fat and cocoa solids, *eg*. The menu on offer at any student refectory or school canteen when Jamie Oliver isn't there filming it.

buffet slayer *n*. A female *lard of the manor*. A lady with a penchant for eating more than her fair share of free food.

buffing *n*. *Gusset typing*. The act of female masturbation.

buffing your eggs *1. n*. Technical jargon for cleaning chicken eggs. It says here. We're not looking it up. *2. n*. An intimate act of *personal delight* performed by a female *fingersmith*.

buffty *n*. *Scots*. A gay fellow. A *Gordon*.

bug fix *1. euph*. An app update that results in no noticeable improvement, and thus *2. euph*. A visit by the missus to the hairdressers.

bugger *1. n*. He who pokes animals, *arseholes* or animals' *arseholes*. A *berry*. *2. v*. To break or damage. To *fuck*. *3. exclam*. A cry of dismay. *'PC World phoned up while you were out, Gary. They said they'd managed to get your laptop going again, and you can pick it up any time tomorrow from the Police Station.' 'Bugger.'*

bugger all *n*. *Nowt, fuck all*.

buggeralls *n*. Your birthday suit. *'How was I to know the missus had planned a surprise party for me? In she bursts with all my friends, my mother, the vicar and all the girls from the office, and there's me sat watching Television X in me buggeralls.'*

bugger lugs *1. n*. Frankly peculiar north country term of endearment. *2. n*. Unsightly *Adrians* surrounding a well-hammered *balloon knot*.

buggernaut *n*. A large and forbiddingly armour-plated *dirtbox*.

bugger's grips *n*. Sideburns. Any tufts of facial

hair on the cheeks, as seen on Spiders from Mars bass player Trevor Bolder, late Victorian headmaster-style Tory MP Rhodes Boyson, and motorcycle racer "Rocket" Ron Haslam. *Bugger's handles, face fannies*.

buggy balm *n*. *Spooge, heir gel*.

bugler sound the retreat *exclam*. Rousing, military-style announcement of a *trumpet involuntary*.

Bugner's clinch *n*. The dance performed by a pair of knackered *heavyweights* at the end of the evening in a nightclub, where they lumber sweatily about in a circle while clinging to each other for support. Named after Hungarian/British/Australian ex-boxer Joe.

Bugner's eye *n*. Flapless female genitalia, resembling the ex-pugilist's closed-up eye in every fight he had.

build a lighthouse on it, they'd better *exclam*. The proud boast of a *master chocolatier* upon the launch of a particularly sizeable *dreadnought*. *'Crikey your majesty. If that one makes it out into the channel they'd better build a lighthouse on it.'*

build a log cabin *v*. To pass a series of sturdy motions.

builder *n*. An unresponsive sexual partner, *ie*. Someone that "never *comes*". Also *gasman, Initial City-Link van driver, Colin the fucking plumber*.

builder's airbag *n*. The 6-inch-thick layer of tabloids, empty crisp packets, pork pie wrappers and other assorted detritus perched on a white van's dashboard.

builder's breakfast *n*. A hearty, cholesterol-laden, no-nonsense *all-you-can-eat pant buffet* that services the early morning nourishment needs of the nations's bricklayers, chippies and plasterers.

builder's bum *n*. The protrusion of fat, sweaty *arse* cheeks above the sagging waist of the jeans. Common amongst bricklayers, council workmen and the *haute couture* customers of late fashion designer Alexander McQueen. *Bricky's crack, Dagenham smile*.

builder's cleavage *n*. The sweatily alluring *cleft* revealed by the low-slung jeans of a tradesman when he crouches to grout something.

builder's dashboard *n*. An unkempt and dishevelled *hillbilly's hat*, from its apparent similarity to to the upper fascia of an artisan construction worker's vehicle. *'Fuck me, Germaine. It's like a builder's dashboard down here.'*

builder's pencil *n*. A short, worn down and useless *membrum virile*. As found in well-chewed condition behind the ear/in the trousers of tradesmen worldwide.

builder's piss *n*. A quick trip to the toilet for a *number one* which suddenly, without warning, develops into a far bigger job than was originally anticipated.

builder's rubble tub, twat like a *sim.* A somewhat disparaging reference to the supposed capaciousness of a woman's *blurtch*. *'Feet up in the stirrups then, Mrs Medford. Excellent. Now approximately how far apart are the contractions..? Fuck me, no offence, Mr Medford, but your missus has got a twat like a builder's rubble tub.'*

builder's thumb *n.* A large, bright purple *clematis* that "never turns up".

builder's wink *n.* A *brickie's crack* that's frankly gone too far. *'The plasterer was bent over when I walked in and I got a full-on builder's wink.'*

building the trust *n.* A tentative series of exploratory mini-*farts* of varying intensity, used to gauge sphincter strength and reliability after a recent, unexpected *follow-through. 'I haven't really been sure of my arse since it went behind my back after the office party. We're still just, you know, building the trust at the moment.'*

build up some charge on the Van de Graaff generator *v.* In an action familiar to anyone who has studied physics beyond O-Level, to rub up and down on a piece of equipment that consists of a long pole with a shiny dome on the top.

buke *v.* To burp up a mouthful of sick. Also *rebuke* ~ to burp up another mouthful of sick.

bukhaki *n. milit.* Nocturnal military manoeuvre involving a billetful of other ranks masturbating onto the face of their sleeping brother in arms, who has returned to his barracks in a state of critical *refreshment. 'Bukhaki's happened in the night / The soldier wakens in his bunk / His eyes don't open to the light / They're all gummed up with squaddies' spunk.'* (from *Conscious* by Wilfred Owen).

bukkake *1. n.* Saucy carry-on whereby a load of randy blokes *tip their filthy concrete* onto a delighted *plasterer's radio. 2. adj. Jap.* Descriptive of dishes, such as bukkake-udon and bukkake-soba, where fresh soup-like toppings are poured on top of noodles. *3. adj.* In Britain, descriptive of dishes about to be served to an outspoken newspaper restaurant critic such as Giles Coren, onto which a group of kitchen employees – not to mention other customers – have *emptied their nuts.*

bukkake labrador *n.* A dalmatian.

bukkankle *n.* An unlikely activity from the Victorian era involving a lady's lower leg and a circle of easily-excited gentleman with mutton-chop whiskers.

bulimia amnesiac *n. medic.* One suffering from a condition whereby they binge eat, then forget to throw up. A *salad dodger, lard arse,* one who is a

martyr to their glands.

bull *n. US. Bullshit.*

bull bars *n.* The type of no-nonsense hostelries frequented by *tin-snip sisters.*

bulldog chewing a wasp *sim.* Descriptive of a lady's face that does not conform to conventional ideals of beauty. Also *bulldog licking piss off a nettle, blistered pisspot, welder's bench, stripper's clit.*

bulldog eating porridge *sim.* Poetic evocation of a *lady's bodily treasure* in the aftermath of an act of love. *'When I'd finished with her, she had a fanny like a bulldog eating porridge, I can tell you.'*

bulldog having a tricky shit, face like a *sim.* Physiognomically unconventional, *eg.* Any photograph of Theresa May trying to look like a normal person, eating chips, smiling *etc.*

bulldog's tail *n.* A *turtle's head.*

bulldog with its head out of a car window *n.* A dauntingly oversized, drooling *clopper* that's blowing in the wind.

bulldyke *n.* A butch, masculine or aggressive *fanny nosher.*

bulletproof monk *n.* A resilient blob of *jitler* that resists all usual methods of removal using tissues, socks or KFC lemony-fresh wipes. *'It's no good, I'm going to have to use a pan scourer to get this bulletproof monk off my laptop screen.'*

bullet-proof vest *1. n. milit.* Armoured clothing designed to minimise injury from incoming gunfire. Usually worn by TV reporters trying to look butch in conflict zones. *2. n.* Reinforced clothing designed to minimise the impact of outgoing nipples. Usually worn by females in cold conditions.

bullet train *n.* A *ride* that is over far too quickly.

bullet wound *n.* The unfortunate situation whereby a *relaxing* man *empties his clip* into his navel and then proceeds to scuttle to the lavatory to sort himself out a bit while hunched over, clutching his stomach and thus, to a casual bystander, creating the impression that he has been shot.

bull fiddle *1. n.* What Jack Lemmon calls his double bass in *Some Like it Hot. 2. n.* A spot of *firkyfoodling* on a *heffer* with *a lovely personality.*

bullfrogging *1. n.* A specialised variation on the act of *horatio*, whereby the *nosher* takes not only the *noshee's tallywhacker* but also both his *magic beans* into his or her mouth, thus creating the effect of the Missouri state amphibian (*Lithobates catesbeianus*), complete with its swollen throat and guttural, retching call. *2. n. Farting* against a closed door from the outside, so that the occupants of the room believe that a large batrachian is about to enter.

bullfruit *n.* A *tailgunner* who is a bit *rock*.

bullgina *n.* A big hairy *quim* that could chase a Spaniard down a cobbled street.

Bullimore *n. prop.* An extremely buoyant bit of *cack,* which refuses to drown. Named after extremely buoyant round-the-world yachtsman Tony Bullimore, who spent three days being lashed by storms under his capsized boat in 1996.

bulling *1. n. milit.* The act of a new recruit who is forced to spend endless hours adding layers of polish to his boots in order to achieve an almost mirror-like shine he can see his face in, and thus *2. n.* the act of a new recruit to the world of hardcore *grumble* who feels compelled to invest a similar amount of effort attempting to get a similar glossy finish on his *little soldier's helmet.*

bulljob *n.* An aggressive, drunken *nosh* off an aggressive, drunken lady, possibly with a ring through her nose.

bull queen *n.* A large, butterfingered prison inmate who cannot keep hold of the soap in the shower, and who instructs other, smaller, prisoners to bend over and pick it up for him. Then he sticks his *cock* up their *arse.*

bull's dick, thick as a *sim.* Somewhat unintelligent, *fuckwitted. 'I knew him at school and he was as thick as a bull's dick.'*

bullseye *n.* Successfully going *straight for the kill* in the bedroom, without foreplay or any of that mullarkey.

bullshit *1. n. Feeshus* of male cattle. *2. n.* Rubbish, nonsense, *bollocks. 3. v.* To lie, deliberately mislead, talk rubbish to. *'Don't you bullshit me now, you hear, bitch, or I'll cut yo' jive-ass face wide open.'* (Sir Neville Chamberlain to his wife, after she informed him that Hitler had invaded Poland).

bull's nostril, fanny like a *sim.* A moist, steaming *blurtch* with a *curtain ring* stuck through it.

bully in the bathroom *n.* A distressing fight to deliver a *mud child* in the smallest room, often leaving the victim in tears and sometimes even with a bloody nose. *'Jesus, you look awful. What happened?' 'I went to take a quick dump and I met a bully in the bathroom. I'll be okay in a bit.'*

Bully's Prize Board *1. n.* Part of the popular darts gameshow *Bullseye,* where guests could win various prizes announced by the late Tony Green in the following distinctive manner: *"HHHHIN One!...HHHHIN Two!..."* etc., and thus *2. n.* An ultimately unsatisfying and prolonged toilet visit while suffering from a *log jam,* when it would be a good idea to settle down, find your rhythm etc. *'Sorry I'm late, ladies and gentlemen. I've*

been stuck on Bully's Prize Board.' (HRH Prince Charles, addressing the Board of Architecture and National Heritage, 1987).

Bully's special prize *1. n.* A speedboat, caravan or beige Talbot Samba. *2. n.* An extra large, beefy *shit. 'I'd give it ten minutes before you go in there, your majesty. I've just won Bully's special prize.'*

bum *1. n.* Arse, bottom, poop-chute. The *back body. 2. n. US. Harold Ramp, pan handler.* A homeless person. *3. v.* Of cigarettes, to scrounge, scavenge. *4. v.* To *bott. 5. adj. US. legal.* Of *raps,* to be unjust, unfair. *6. n.* Trebor mint preservation apparatus. *7. adj.* Of steers, misleading or inaccurate. *8. adj. mus.* Of notes played or sung, out of tune. *9. adj. leg.* Of raps at the point of arrest, poorly thought out.

bumanizer *n.* A fellow who boasts an impressive tally of conquests in the field of *countergradient horticulture.*

bum bandit *n.* A robber, outlaw or highwayman who steals people's bottoms.

bum bar *n.* A richly textured item of *arse chocolate. 'Take the helm, Captain Hardy, I'm off down the poop deck to unwrap a bum bar.'*

bumbardment *n.* A brutal, *nipsy*-shredding attack of the *galloping plopsy. Pony express, hoop soup.*

bumbats *n. medic.* Source of loud flapping noises in the small hours. *'Sorry to keep waking you up, pet, only the bumbats are flying tonight. But it's your own fault. I told you not to give me that veggie mince cottage pie.'*

bum baubles *n. medic.* Big, round, shiny *farmers* that your missus and the doctor can see their faces in.

bumbay mix *n.* Unappetising array of small, brown, dry objects despatched from the *back passage* when either ill, severely hungover, or both.

bum beater *n.* A chap's *tool. 'And Onan knew that the seed should not be his; and it came to pass, when he went in unto his brother's wife, that he spilled it on the ground, lest that he should give seed to his brother. And the thing which Onan had done with his bum beater displeased the LORD: wherefore he slew him also.'* (from *Genesis 38:9*).

bum beaver *n.* An *arse* where the *cress* has grown out of control. A *botty beard,* a *DLT.*

bum bees *n.* Anal discomfort suffered after a mild curry, for example a Bhuna. *'Rest assured you'll never get bum bees if you eat at the Rupali Restaurant, Bigg Market, Newcastle upon Tyne. It's a whole nestful of furious arse wasps every time or your money back.'*

bumberland sausage *n.* A giant *Richard the Third* that resembles the distinctive coil shape of the

Lake District speciality banger, and which should ideally be pricked with a fork before pulling the chain.

bum bhaji *n.* A deep-fried, spicy rectal *fritter.*

bum bile *n. medic.* Diarrhoea. *'I'm afraid the Earl of Grantham can't come to the telephone right now, your grace, only he's had bum bile summat rotten all morning.'*

bumbilical cord *1. n.* A length of *cable* that is so firmly attached to the bottom that one's partner has to fetch a pair of scissors to complete the birthing process. *2. n. Uphill gardening string.*

bumbino *n. It.* A *bottom baby* which can be dandled affectionately upon the knee.

bumblebee dance *1. n.* Action performed by bees in which they shake their abdomens to indicate to other members of the hive in which direction the pollen lies. *2. n.* The waggling of the buttocks in order to dislodge a reluctant *geetle* from the *dot.* A *logarhythm.*

bumble bee pants *n.* Nethergarments which have been worn for so long that they are "yellow at the front and brown at the back".

Bumbledore *n. prop.* Someone in possession of a particularly long, straggly *underbeard*, such as might trail in one's soup.

bumblefuck *n.* Person in a workplace who tries to look as busy as a bee but who is actually doing *fuck all.* *'Hey Dave, you bumblefuck, do some fucking work.' 'Yes prime minister.'*

bumbling *adj.* Descriptive of a somewhat inept or heavy-handed attempt to gain access *via* the *back door.*

bumboozled *1. adj.* Innocently beguiled into a state of mental disorientation by a passing, shapely *peach pie.* *2. adj.* Of an otherwise resolutely heterosexual fellow, to be drunkenly tricked into a spot of *puddle jumpery.*

bum boulder *n.* A giant, exit-blocking *chod* that rolls down your large intestine sending all screaming before it, like that one off of *Indiana Jones.*

bum brake *n.* The *cigar cutter* or *nipsy.*

bum brusher *n. Vict.* A schoolmaster. From the good old days before political correctness when there was nothing wrong with a spot of wholesome, *arse*-based corporal punishment which never did red-faced ex-military men who write to the *Daily Telegraph* any harm. A term which is quite possibly still in current usage on the Isle of Man, where it is still the 1950s.

bum carpet *n.* Luxuriant deep-*pile* region of *winnety* hair cultivated around the *gammon ring.*

bum carrot *n.* A mythical lure dangled in front of a hapless chap's face in order to coerce him into performing an undesired chore on the bogus promise of a bit of *wrong 'un* based shenanigans. *'Why's Joe spending the day taking his mother-in-law to the bingo?' 'I guess his missus must've dangled the bum carrot again.'*

bum chain *n.* A rather intimate version of the Conga, danced around the streets at the end of a *brightly coloured* party. See also *anchor man.*

bum chums *n.* Primary school term for any two boys who always sit next to each other.

bum cigar *n.* In after dinner conversation, a *stool.* *'Well, if you'll excuse me ladies, I think I shall retire to the bathroom and light a bum cigar.'*

bumclutter *n.* The rubble, dreck and general spoilage that must be cleared from the *bag for life*'s *back passage* before you attempt to take her *up the chip shop.*

bum conkers *n.* Shiny, brown, spherical agglomerations which hang off the *arse strings*, and can be baked in the oven or soaked in vinegar.

bumcraft *n. Uphill gardening, cable laying* and *stepping on ducks.* The wholesome celebration and enjoyment of all things *bumular.* You could probably get a badge for it in the Scouts.

bum crumbs *n. Kling-ons* which have ceased to cling on. Usually found in the bed or in the gusset of the *trolleys.*

bum custard *n.* The thick yellow, school dinners-style excreta that emerges from the *dot* the morning after a heavy night *on the lash.* Possibly also has a bit of a skin on it.

bumdelicious *adj.* Descriptive of a female in possession of a particularly fine *arse.* *'It is a truth universally acknowledged, that a single man in possession of a fortune, must be in want of a bumdelicious wife.'* (from *Pride and Prejudice* by Jane Austen).

bumdinger *n.* A particularly excellent *poo*, usually one of significant size or piquancy. A proper *door handle biter.*

bumdruff *n.* The *anal scurfage* and general buttock effluvium left on the back of the *bog* seat after one has been for a *digestive transit. Arse confetti, bumdreds and thousands.*

bum drummer *n.* A *bad thrower.*

bum drums *n.* Rhythmic tympanic paradiddles from the trouser department that announce the imminent arrival of *Lord Brown of Shitechester.* *'How is one supposed to address the nation with that awful noise going on, Mr Attenborough?' 'Sorry your Majesty, only I've got the bum drums today. Can we start recording again after I've went for a shit?'*

bum fingers *n. medic.* Haemorrhoids. Also *arse*

grapes, Keith Floyds, Chalfonts, Emma Freuds, ceramics etc.

bumfire night *n.* After eating a surfeit of spicy foodstuffs, an evening of loud bangs that could upset the dog.

bumfit *1. n.* "Fifteen" in the bizarre counting system operated by Cumbrians, where counting on the fingers isn't an option unless you want to use base 12. *'Forty bumfit. Federer only has to hold this serve to take the tethera set.' 2. n.* A spectacular and unheralded attack of the *Tom tits* that leaves the victim shaking on the floor. *3. adj.* Well fit in the *bum* area.

bum fluff *n.* Risible pubescent attempt to grow a moustache.

bumfoolery *n.* Light-hearted action centred loosely around the *Bleep & Booster. Good with colours* in a *Carry On* film stylee.

bumfounded *adj.* Struck mute by the sight of a particularly attractive *arse. 'Sorry Colin, I didn't get a word there. I was so bumfounded when Rachel bent over to pick up that dropped consonant that I forgot where I was and what I was doing.'*

bumfucker hot *adj.* Measure of the spiciness of a foodstuff that subsequently occasions acute discomfort in the *back body. 'What relish would you like on your kebab Sir?' 'Bumfucker hot please, my good man.'*

bum goblin *n.* A gnarled, malevolent *jobbledehoy* that jumps out from behind you, casting a painful spell on your *ringpiece.*

bum grapes *n. medic.* Agonising, juice-filled purple fruits which grow well in the moist, shady regions of the *Khyber Pass.*

bum gravel *n.* A scree-like accumulation of anal detritus found in the bed after one has *raked one's arse out. Bum crumbs.*

bum gravy *n. medic.* Diarrhoea, *rusty water, hoop soup.*

bum grenade *1. n.* A short *anal fuse* that can be initiated with the day's first cup of coffee, cigarette, or letter from the tax office. *2. n.* An incendiary bomb which is lobbed into the *pan,* causing the grenadier to beat a retreat with the greatest possible alacrity.

bum gum *n.* The twitching, inquisitive nose of a feculent *motion* that gets chewed when *cable-laying* is unavoidably delayed for any reason.

bum gums *n. medic.* Sphincter that *chews a brick.*

bumice *n.* Floating anal jetsam in the *shit pan.* Similar to the porous volcanic rock pumice, which floats because of trapped gases.

bum in a bucket, like a *sim.* Description of a person with fat cheeks in a crash helmet. *'Please,*

someone, anyone, tune in the same time next week to see Matt LeBlanc looking like a bum in a bucket as he takes the new Ferrari Testosterossa round the Top Gear test track with all smoke coming off the tyres.'

bumjela *n.* Pile cream. Also known as *turtle wax, bummolene, preparation arse.*

bum jumble *n.* Bits and bobs of excrement. *'Fucking hell, Brendan. Paula's left some bum jumble in the road again.'*

bum lungs *n.* Additional, apparently rectally situated, breathing apparatus which allows members of the fairer sex to speak for extended periods of time without pausing for breath.

bummange *n.* A light, fluffy *arse* dessert. *Anal delight.*

bummer *1. n.* One who *bums.* *2. n.* A disappointing situation. Such as being stuck on a beach for the whole summer, after missing a charabanc.

bummer's toe *n. medic.* Fungal infection of a *good listener's* cuticle caused by his foot getting trodden on repeatedly during vigorous *uphill gardening.*

bummery *n. coll.* A rather pleasing collective term for all things *anus*-related, *viz. Bottery, fisting, felching, grapeshot, rimming etc.* Also *bumcraft, arseyology.*

bummifier, the *n.* Lonely, off-white/grey, well-used, cardboard-like *undercarriage* wash-flannel that gets lost in the depths of the washing basket, and proceeds to *bummify* all future garments placed in there. *'What's that foisty smell in the bathroom, Camilla?' 'That'll be the bummifier, Charles.'*

bummocks *n.* The buttocks of the *bum.*

bummolene *n. medic.* Mythical *arse*-soothing ointment. *'So, Prue, was Tim's Carolina Reaper chilli sponge cake a winner for you?' 'Christ, Paul, there were consequences. I've got through seven tubes of Bummolene since I had a slice.'*

bummous *n.* Paste-like, savoury substance found between the *buffers* after a long plane journey, a drive down the M6 in heavy traffic on a hot day with no air conditioning, or a *shart.*

bummy *adj.* Ripe. *'Have you washed any undies yet, Kate? Only I've had these ones on for three days now and they're getting a bit bummy.'*

bummy mummy *n.* A milf whose *back doors* you'd quite like to *kick in.* A *milb, milfuta.*

bumnugget *n.* A *number two,* consisting of an accretion of many smaller *number twos.* A *number six/eight/ten etc.*

bump *v.* To *bum* your *significant other* immediately prior to dumping her. From bum + dump.

bum pasty *n.* A steaming, crusty *arse pie,* fresh out

of the *mud oven*. A *Cornish nasty.*

bumper *n.* A *Richard the Third* of such firmness, solidity and density that one can hear it knocking about through the alimentary canal while making its way to freedom, occasionally setting off bells and buzzers like a ball in a pinball machine.

bumpies *rhym. slang. Fun bags.* From bumpy bits = tits.

bumpkin factory *n.* Any woman of childbearing age from the West Country or the Fens.

bumpkin pie *n.* Derogatory term for a lady who is *as thick as Norfolk pig shit* but nevertheless extremely warm, friendly and comforting.

bumplings *n.* A single *digestive transit* cut up into separate chunks by involuntary abdominal spasms while on the *bum sink.*

bum plums *n. medic. Arse grapes* that possibly contain stones you could break your teeth on.

bump start *n.* An invigorating, pre-breakfast bout of *self-pollution.*

bump the kerb *v.* Of a *heavily refreshed* Casanova, to make a series of ineffectual attempts to steer his *cock* into the *hairy parking space.* A repeated failure to score a *hole-in-one.* 2. *v.* To deliberately on purpose nudge the wife's *wrong 'un* with the *pit prop. 'Sorry June. I seem to have bumped the kerb there.' 'You cheeky cunt, Terry.'*

bum puppy *n.* A friendly, over-eager *Bakewell tart* that leaps and gambols around you, and licks your face.

bum-roll *1. n.* Toilet tissue, *arsewad.* 2. *n.* A rumbling *Lionel Bart* which builds up anticipation and tension preceding the imminent arrival of a *Peter O'Toole.* Followed by a splash.

bum rope *n.* Shit. *'Has anybody seen the Autotrader? I'm just going to snip off some short lengths of bum rope.'*

bum rudder *n.* Richly poetic description of a fellow engaged in a spot of *back door work. 'I scored with Eliza the other night. What a filthy cow, she even let me put it in her blooming arsehole. You should've seen me, I was hanging out the back of her like a bum rudder, Professor Higgins.'*

bumscare *n.* Severe pressure in the lower abdominal region prior to a controlled explosion.

bum scum *n.* The unpleasant residue on an improperly wiped *fifties tea towel holder.*

bumseye *n.* Bully's special prize in the *mud darts.*

bumshee *n.* A blood-curdling howl of anguish coming from a lavatory cubicle. See also *bogpipes.*

bumsick *n. medic.* Rapid, liquid, *back door* vomit experienced when poorly or the morning after a *bad pint.* Often accompanied by nausea and cramps. The *shits.*

bum sink *n.* The lavatory.

bum slugs *n.* Soft, slimy *feeshus* that leave a muci- laginous trail on the *nipsy*, and it probably might be in order to pour a bit of salt on them.

bum sneeze *n.* A loose, flatulence-propelled *Simon Cowell* movement that leaves the bowl peppered with brown flak.

bumsong *n.* A long, tuneful and mellifluous solo on the *botty bugle.*

bum soup *n. Ad hoc* savoury consommé cooked up between the *mudflaps* of catering staff working in hot kitchens. *'Another bowl of bum soup for Mr Coren on table six.'*

bum spuds *n.* Faecal tubers. Human *Peter O'Tooles.*

bumstruck *adj.* Rendered speechless by the sight of a particularly shapely and alluring *shitlocker.*

bum sweets *n. medic.* Anal suppositories to treat *Emma Freuds. 'You'd be surprised how common this condition is, Miss Middleton. I'm going to prescribe you a course of bum sweets and it should clear up in a couple of weeks.'*

bumtags *n. Dangleberries.*

bum tongue *n.* A large piece of *ordure* hanging from *Dot Cotton's* mouth just before it licks the bowl.

bum-uppance *n.* Just desserts reserved for those people who, in the process of hanging curtains in their kitchens while wearing loose-fitting dressing gowns, somehow slip and end up with a foreign object, such as a potato or a milk bottle, stuck up their *arse.* Various well known people have famously got their *bum-uppance*, including (name removed on legal advice), (name removed on legal advice) and Lord Archer of Weston Super Mare.

bum vinegar *n.* The sweat found between the *arse* cheeks in general, and in particular during or after vigorous exercise, such as moving a filing cabinet up a fire escape on a hot day, to pick an example completely at random. A condiment that goes well with *arse feta. Sarsehole.*

bumwad *n.* Lavatory tissue, *shitscrape, bottery tickets.*

bumwipers *n.* Drivers of German motor cars, par- ticularly Audis, who gets so close to your *ringpiece* they could probably reach out and give it a quick buff and polish.

bum worm *n.* A tiny *poo* poking its head out between your cheeks to take the air.

bum yawn *1. n.* A putrid early morning utterance to greet the new day. 2. *n.* A frequently glimpsed phenomenon in certain high quality *grumble flicks.*

bunch *n.* A mid-day session of *dining with the Askwiths.* A *nooner* for those who *know what's in their flowerbeds.* From bumming + lunch.

bunga bunga *adj.* Type of party enjoyed by

fun-loving former/future/current/he's dead now Italian Prime Minister/convict/corpse Silvio Berlusconi during which, in preference to playing pass the parcel and musical chairs or bobbing for apples, the honoured guests were invited to *have it off* with teenage prostitutes.

bunga bungalow *n.* A *fur trapper's cabin* wherein sundry off-colour practices are undertaken. Also *shag pile, stabbin' cabin.*

bung hole *n.* The *fadge*, at which a dirty lady *fizzes.*

bunglasses *n.* Like *binorkulars*, but pointing slightly lower down.

bungleballs *phr.* A complete absence of the male *family jewels*, for example after swimming in cold water. From the big bear in *Rainbow*, who lacked *meat* and, indeed, *two veg*. Though it would have been a bit weird, even back in the seventies, if they'd given him an anatomically accurate *cock* and *knackers.*

Bungle fever *n. psych.* An attraction to hairy women. See also *Bungle's wallet, collie's chest.*

bunglefuck *n.* A *furry* act of *coitus* enjoyed while dressed as an animal.

Bungle's finger *n.* A short, stocky *turd*, named after the stumpy digits of the 70s ursine simpleton.

Bungle's jungle *n.* An unruly clump of *muff pubes*, of the sort often featured in old 70s *Frankie Vaughan* vids, according to those who have seen them.

Bungle's wallet *n.* An untidily hirsute *steak purse.*

bun in the oven, to have a *v.* To be pregnant, *up the stick, in the club, in trouble, up the pasture*. 'Guess what, love. I've got a bun in the oven.' 'That's nice. Is my tea ready yet?'

bunion ring *n.* An old lady's *jacksie.*

bunko booth *n.* The late Paul Daniels's *shithouse*. A water closet cubicle.

bunk up *1. n.* A utility *poke*. 'Darling, you look beautiful tonight. Any chance of a bunk up?' *2. n.* Assistance in climbing. 'Shit. I'm so pissed I can't get onto the bed. Any chance of a bunk up?'

bunk-up badge *n.* A love bite, usually found on really ugly people's necks to prove they have a love life. Or a at least access to a bicycle pump. A *hickie, bub* or *shag-tag.*

bunnet brie *n. Scots. McHelmetdale*. 'Whit's yon stink, maw?' 'Och, Wullie. It's jist Granpaw's bunnet brie, son.'

bunnet cheese *n. Glasweg*. The piquantly cheesy deposits which accumulate around the brim of the *haggis farmer's hat*. 'My thoughts hovered over all varieties of mortal edible, and finally settled on a Porterhouse steak with a Welsh rabbit to follow. After picking listlessly at my bunnet brie whilst

longing hopelessly for these dainties, after a few minutes I drifted off to sleep.' (from The Sixty-Nine Steps by John Buchan).

bunny-boiler *n.* A determined woman who misinterprets a one-off drunken *scuttle* as the overture to a deep and lasting relationship, then tries to win your affections when you go back to the missus by boiling your kids' pets and in the end you have to drown her in the bath but she's not even dead. *A pork 'n' stalk.*

bunny rub *n.* A *tit wank, diddy ride, Bombay roll.*

buns *1. n.* Regional variation of *baps*. *2. n. US*. *Ass* cheeks. *3. n.* Bread rolls or small cakes. 'Nice buns, Mary.'

bunt *1. n.* A disease of wheat caused by the *Tilletia* fungus. *2. n.* The bulging part of a fishing net or a ship's sail. *3. v.* To greedily steal hampers of tuck from one's fellow public schoolboys. *5. n.* On a *salad dodging* lady, where the stomach seamlessly merges into the pudendums. From belly + cunt. Also known as the *super-poond, FUPA* or *gunt*. *4. v.* In baseball, to bat a pitched ball very gently so that it rolls into the infield close to home plate. Whatever that means. *5. v.* Of a goat or calf, to push with the horns or head. *6. n.* The perineum; that bit between the *bum* and the *cunt*. Also known as the *carse, notcher, transporter bridge, tinter, taint, tisnae, tissent, crunk* and *Luton-to-Dunstable busway.*

bunting *n.* Church fete-style strings of *jizz* looped around a *grumble flick* actress's *mush.*

bun to sausage ratio *n.* Female/male quotient, assessed at a party, gathering or office.

Bunty club *n.* Any organisation or institution which is exclusively dominated by women. A *flangocracy.*

bunty or twinkle? *exclam. interrog.* A polite question, ostensibly alluding to the titles of girls' comics from the 1970s, asked in order to ascertain whether a lady acquaintance who is off to *powder her nose* will be *dropping the kids off at the pool* or merely *splashing her boots.*

buppy fat *n. Cheb*-fuelled *teacaking* of the *giggle stick.*

Burberry apes *n.* Designer-clad football hooligans.

Burberry shitbomb *n.* The delightful smell of perfume in the water closet after one's girlfriend or wife has been in to *drop the kids off at the pool*, viz. Air freshener on lead guitar and vocals, with excrement on bass and drums.

burbulence *n.* The uncomfortable alimentary rumbling which precedes the breakage of wind. 'Over Nova Scotia I finished the last of my egg sandwiches. Half an hour later I hit a pocket of burbulence, and had to fasten my seat belt and *extinguish all lights.'* (from *My Flight Across the Atlantic* by Amelia Earhart).

burger nips *n.* Large aereolae that are similar in size, shape, texture (and possibly flavour) to the comestibles typically found in a tin of Goblin-brand beef patties.

burglar's dollop *n.* An episode of trouser-soiling through fear or nerves. *'Theresa May takes the stand for her keynote address to the Tory Party Conference in Manchester. It's a real burglar's dollop moment for the embattled Tory leader.'* (Nick Robinson, *BBC News 24*).

burial at sea *n.* The dignified commital of a *dead otter,* without *splashback.* The opposite of a *depth charge* or *belly flopper.*

burlesque *1. n.* Type of ironic striptease show that it's alright for blokes to go and see. *2. adj.* Similar to Burl Ives.

burly *n. Bum wipe,* toilet paper, *chocolate shark bait, turd tokens, shit tickets. 'Mam! Can you throw us up a new roll of burly?'*

burly-esque *adj.* Descriptive of a lady who *does her own heavy lifting.*

BURMA/burma *acronym. milit.* Secret code used on wartime correspondence – Be Upstairs Ready My Angel. See also *Norwich, polo.*

burn bad powder *v. arch. milit.* Of *trouser trumpetry,* to *light a tyre,* emit a *fyst.*

burning bush *n.* Cystitis.

burning dufflecoat, pull me through with a *exclam.* A jocular cry uttered upon producing a particularly malodorous *Bakewell* while in polite company, *eg.* When appearing on Radio 4's *Law in Action* or taking afternoon tea with the chief economist of the Bank of England.

Burnley taxi *n.* A police car.

Burnley tea *n.* A 4-pack of beer and a scratchcard.

Burnley wallet *n.* Rough and ready Lancashire street punishment technique referred to in *Phoenix Nights,* which involves pulling the victim's scrotum up under his chin before performing some sort of horizontal cut across *Sir Cliff's neck.* The sort of thing they do in the UK's first town to make regular rainfall measurements.

burn off a digestive *v.* To use up approximately the same number of calories as there are in a wheaten sweetmeal biscuit by *having one off the wrist.*

burnout *1. n.* In the world of dragster racing, a short burst of wheelspin on the starting line which leaves impressive, black, smoking stripes on the tarmac and is intended to warm up the racing slicks. *2. n.* In the world of *diddy-riding,* an unfortunately exposed *arse crayon* which leaves a thick stripe of brown residue on one's ladyfriend's

torso. And a strong smell of burning tyres.

burn out the arse clutch *v.* To fail to avoid defecating into one's *hoggers* while standing up having a *piss.*

Burnside drawer *n.* The bottom drawer in a fellow's office desk, which contains contraband material, *ie.* Alcohol, cigarettes and pornography. Named after no-nonsense, good old-fashioned copper Detective Chief Inspector Frank Burnside out of off of *The Bill.*

burnt fence, teeth like a *sim.* Descriptive of poor dentition. *English teeth, mouth like a locksmith's back pocket.*

burn the bacon *v.* To *go at* one's ladyfriend so enthusiastically that her *gammon flaps* chafe, and you have to open a window and waft her *snatch* with a newspaper in case the smoke alarm goes off.

burnt picket fence, teeth like a *sim.* A poetic evocation of the sort of quirky, charming and characterful half-timbered pearlies typically found in the mouths of *dentally handicapped* Brits.

burnt tyre *n.* An acrid, black, semi-vulcanised section of *dirty spine* passed through the *back body* following a heavy night on the Guinness.

burnt up in the atmosphere, it must have *phr.* When what feels like a *ring-splitting arseteroid* turns out, after much pushing and shoving, to be a tiny, smoking pebble.

burp the worm *v.* To *choke the chicken.*

burst couch *euph.* A well-used *clopper* which has had all the stuffing *fucked* out of it.

burst crate of tomatoes, arse like a *sim.* A phrase illustrative of the state of a traumatised *ringpiece.* *'I wish I could tell you that Andy fought the good fight, and the Sisters let him be. I wish I could tell you that – but prison is no fairy-tale world. The Sisters kept at him – sometimes he was able to fight 'em off, sometimes not. Every so often, Andy would show up with an arse like a burst crate of tomatoes.'*

burst ravioli *n. Pudenders* that have seen more miles than a London bus.

burst sausage *n.* A female *salad dodger* who has somehow squeezed her porky frame into a frock which is several sizes too small to accommodate it.

burst the brown balloon *v.* To do a *windy pop* at the end of a child's birthday party.

burtains *n. medic. Labia majorcas. Gammon flaps, Keith Burtons, bacon shutters.* From beef + curtains.

bury a king *v.* To surreptitiously deposit a *Richard the Third* in a car park. In Leicester.

bury a quaker *v.* To dispense with the contents of one's rectum. *To crimp one off, lay a cable,* release a payload from the *bomb bay*.

bury bad news *v.* To disguise one's flatulent emissions by making clever use of one's environment. From the government's cheeky habit of releasing bad figures and/or unpopular legislation on days when the headlines are dominated by other, more dramatic news. For example, to *pump* out a vile, sulphurous *trouser cough* just after you start the car so that the miasma is masked by the eggy whiff from the catalytic converter; to *drive over cats' eyes* while driving over cats' eyes; to open a packet of ham while *opening a packet of ham*; to *cut the cheese* while cutting cheese.

bury the hobbit *v.* To lose *Bilbo Bellend* in the *wizard's sleeve*.

bus bender *n.* A *bubbly* female who is so *well-nourished* that, if she were to be involved in a road traffic accident, she would cause more damage to the vehicle that ran into her than she would incur herself.

bus door *n.* An *airbrake* released with a satisfying hiss.

busdriver's chair, like a *sim.* A beautiful, poetic expression used to describe a well-used and stinking *clopper* which has had all the stuffing knocked out of it.

busdriver's knob *n. medic.* A state of almost permanent semi-priapism suffered by corporation omnibus operators who sit on a vibrating seat all day, eyeing up their *horny* female passengers. A long lasting *semi-on, Varney's teacake, rootmaster.*

bush *1. n.* The *gorilla salad* on a good old-fashioned hairy *minge. 2. n. coll.* Talent, totty, crumpet. *'Plenty of bush in tonight, eh lads.'*

bus hailer *n.* A tube of paper, filled with tobacco, which, when exposed to the flame of a lighter in the vicinity of a bus-stop, precipitates a long-awaited public transport vehicle to instantly arrive.

bush babies *1. n. zool.* Cute, nocturnal, tree-dwelling primates. *2. n.* Leftover blobs of *jizz* left in the *ladygarden undergrowth* following a hasty withdrawal.

bushcraft *1. n.* Self sufficiency in the boondocks, as practised by roly poly twig-nibbler Ray Mears. *2. n.* The gentle art of seduction, as practised by Rod Stewart. *3. n.* The mysterious and fabled skills required to *pleasure* a lady between the sheets, as practised by Paul (Leo) out of the Floaters. *4. n.* The art of clipping a lady's *garden hedge* into various decorative shapes, *eg.* A *heart, club, Robert Mugabe, Jimmy Edwards etc.*

bush doctor *1. n.* A rural medic in Australia. *2. n.* Title of a 1978 album by reggae star Peter Tosh, with a scratch 'n' sniff cover that smelled

of cannabis. Or it could have been fox *piss. 3. n.* Polite term for a gynaecologist. Also *cunt dentist, fanny mechanic, mingineer* or *snatch quack.*

bushell *1. n.* An imperial measure of grain equivalent to 2219.36 cubic inches, under which one can hide one's light. *2. n.* A hairy *cunt.*

bushey troughs *1. n.* Whence locomotives scooped up water into their tenders during the days of steam power. *2. n.* The deep, wet *bowers of pleasure* to be found on larger lasses.

bush kangaroo *n.* Fellow who skips from one intimate liaison to another.

bushman's hankie *n. Aus.* Term given to the process whereby mucus is expelled from the nose by placing a finger over one nostril and blowing. Popular amongst professional footballers, tennis players and *Newsnight* presenters at 10.29pm. Also known as a *single barrelled snot gun* or *oyster.*

bush meat *n.* Meat found under *bushes.* Usually *vertical bacon* or *mutton shutters.*

bushmonk *n.* A saucy freelance penitent who hides or secretes himself in an item of shrubbery for the purposes of *knocking himself about a bit,* especially near the bowling green in Heaton Park, Newcastle upon Tyne.

bush pig *n.* A slightly more polite term for a *swamp hog.*

bush pilot *1. n.* A lugubrious Australian aviator who delivers canned lager to sweating, pithily monosyllabic, outback-dwelling, cork-hatted men in television adverts. *2. n.* A fellow gifted with the almost uncanny ability to instinctively navigate his way round a *Sheila's map of Tasmania.*

bush tents *n.* Ladies' *applecatchers.*

bushtucker *1. n.* Anything on the menu when *eating out down under. 2. n.* Al fresco Frankie Vaughan.

bushtucker challenge. *1. n.* Particularly unpalatable *hairy fish and chips. 2. n.* A trial of manliness undertaken while out on a morning constitutional whereby a fellow attempts to *pull himself off* over a *bongo book* found discarded in the undergrowth without being detected by passers-by, parkies, police, clergy *etc.*

bushtugger man *n.* A gentleman of the road *relaxing himself daft* amidst the municipal shrubbery.

bushwhacked *n.* Knackered as a result of sexual intercourse. *'Fancy a game of table tennis, Ben?' 'Not tonight, Linzi. I'm proper bushwhacked.'*

bushwrinkle *n. Mummy's toolshed.* The *vaginis horribilis.*

business lacumen *n.* A singular display of poor decision-making ability. *'Oh yeah, I've got great business lacumen. After my disastrous foray into the Video 2000 system, I sank what remained of* *my family fortune into the Rabbit CT2, Mercury Callpoint and Zonephone telephone networks. Anyway, as I was saying, have you got ten pence for a cup of tea, pal? I'm auditioning for the Apprentice this afternoon.'*

busker's hat *n.* The pocketful of change left over from a night *on the lash,* that feels like about twelve quid, but when emptying it into one's hand to buy a bottle of blue Powerade the next morning, turns out to be about thirty-six pence worth of one and two pees.

busker's hat, doormat like a *sim.* The coin-be-strewed state of a chap's porch following a difficult navigation home from the pub using the popular *fancy walking* method.

bus knob *n. medic.* Involuntary *lob on* brought about by the gentle, but insistent, vibration provided by the engine of a passenger service vehicle, transmitted to the sufferer's *lunchbox* through his seat. Especially if he's wearing loose trousers and sitting next to a fat-*titted* Swiss backpacker. *Diesel dick, travel fat, hard-on the buses.*

bus lane bollards *n.* Unexpectedly prominent *nip-nops* which, one might fondly imagine, sound a warning klaxon while becoming erect. *Pygmies' cocks, Scammel wheel nuts, chapel hat-pegs, fighter pilot's thumbs.*

busman's jollyday *n.* The habit of public transport drivers who pair up at the depot so that they can give each other *blow jobs* at the end of their journeys. Particularly enjoyed, it says here, by those fellows working the 170 Roehampton to Victoria route.

busted sofa *n.* A plump-lipped *shaven haven* that looks like formerly alive but now definitely dead Dead or Alive singer Pete Burns's *pie-hole.*

busted teabag *euph.* A *chod bin* containing hundreds of small fragments of *shite* swirling around after the previous occupant has flushed it with somewhat limited success.

busted wheelbearing on a '63 DAF truck, moaning like a *sim.* Descriptive of the sounds made by a particularly vocal *piece* enjoying a *length.* From the characteristic orgasmic-lady-style sound produced by troublesome Swedish HGV wheelhubs which is well known to vintage lorry mechanics. *'Lady Chatterley was powerless to resist. Mellors's eyes burnt into hers like created tanzanites. His strong gamekeeper's arms enfolded her tender body as she felt herself being swept away on a supercellular mesocyclone of passion. Before long, they were in the throes of passion on the floor of his rude hut, and Connie couldn't stop herself moaning like a busted wheelbearing on a '63 DAF truck*

every time he pushed his working class knob up her frothing upper class cludge.' (from *The Lady and the Gamekeeper* by DH Lawrence).

busting low *1. n.* Formerly popular and frankly inexplicable fashion whereby young *fancy Dans* walked about with their trousers hanging off their *arses.* These days they wear tight drainpipes that are three inches too short, and slip-on shoes with no socks. Twats. *2. n.* Reaching the final, desperate stages prior to a full-scale *crapping* of the *applecatchers.* See also *growing a tail, the turtle's head, riding a brown pony along a bumpy track, kettling.*

bustman's holiday *n.* A topless beach.

bust off *v.* To masturbate, *knock oneself about a bit, relax in a gentleman's way.*

busy *1. adj.* Descriptive of a T-shirt that's got its hands full. *2. adj.* Of a gentleman, *light on his feet. 'How come your eldest lad's not got himself a nice girlfriend yet then?' 'Oh, he's got no time for girls, my Colin; he's always so busy, see. Cottaging and bumming, mainly.'*

butch as a fitter's dog, as *sim.* Phrase descriptive of a particularly masculine-looking *tuppence-licker.*

butcher emptying out his offal bin, like a *sim.* Descriptive of a proper *rectal clearout* when one is *in receivership* and *everything must go.* See also *bempty, next sale.*

butcher's best cut *n.* Bespoke, fuly-lined *beef curtains.*

butcher's cock, stiff and sore as a *sim.* Said of something swollen and painful, and sometimes pustular. *'Did the Thai massage help with your back problem, your highness?' 'No, I'm still stiff and sore as a butcher's cock.'*

butcher's daughter *1. n.* A woman who has had unlimited access to the pastie counter throughout her upbringing. A *salad dodger. 2. n.* A woman who has had "more than her fair share of sausages", *eg.* Her late royal highness, the Princess Margaret. A *trollop.*

butcher's dishcloth *sim.* A delightful expression descriptive of the *sump* of a lady's knickers when *the fleet is in.*

butcher's dog, to lie like a *sim.* Descriptive of the bedtime arrangements of a typical married man. To sleep "within reach of the beef while forbidden to touch it".

butcher's dustbin *n.* A sight grimmer than a *butcher's window.* The *bottom of a ratcatcher's mallet.*

butcher's fist *n.* The male equivalent of the *camel's toe,* as regularly spotted at the Tower Ballroom in Edgbaston, Birmingham's premier over-sixties nitespot. Also *hamster's mouthful, packet, Darcy*

Bussell's footrest, munge.

butcher's kiss *n.* Evidence left on the bedsheet that a fellow has been *porking* his wife during *cricket week.*

butcher's pie *n.* A recently exercised set of *beef curtains* that are pink on the inside with plenty of jelly and a flaky crust on the outside.

butcher's string *n.* Skimpy underwear on a fat lass.

butcher's turd *sim.* Descriptive of the richness of something. *'Do have some more gateau, Mr Darcy.' 'Well perhaps just a little slice, Mrs Bennet. It's as rich as a butcher's turd.'* (from *Pride and Prejudice* by Jane Austen).

butcher's window *n.* An appetizing display of raw genitalia.

butfer *n.* An amusing term for the female perineum. The *carse*, the *tinter*. *'NORFOLK: She has the most agreeable butfer. BISHOP: The butfer, sir? Wherefore is it called thus? NORFOLK: Sir, butfer that, thou wouldst be in the shit.'* (from *The Merry Readers' Wives of Windsor* by William Shakespeare).

butler in the pantry *n.* A polite *Thora* which knows its place and remains discreetly below stairs, occasionally coughing until summoned.

butler sauce *n.* A rich *man gravy.* *'"I say, Jeeves," I expostulated. "What's this bally sticky custard stuff in my kedgeree? Dash it all, old chap, it's all over my toast, and floating in my Earl Grey too!" The sage retainer barely looked up from ironing my spats. "It is butler's sauce, sir," he replied. "I just wanked on your breakfast."'* (from *Stick It Up Your Arse, Jeeves!* by PG Wodehouse).

butler's cuff *n.* A tightly buttoned vagina, the opposite of a *wizard's sleeve*. A *twat like a mouse's ear.*

butler's revenge *n.* A silent but deadly *fart. SBD.*

butler's ringpiece *adj.* Descriptive of something that is nipping clean. *'"What can you see, Holmes?" I expostulated, as the great detective peered into his microscope. "I'm examining the handle of this dagger of unusual oriental design in the hope of finding a speck of tobacco of a sort only available from one shop in London, or a hair from a rare species of Patagonian chinchilla," he replied. "However, I fear our murderer has wiped it as clean as a butler's ringpiece."'* (from *The Brown Hatted League* by Sir Arthur Conan-Doyle).

butta blockers *n.* As beta blockers regulate blood flow, so *butta blockers* regulate *arse* flow. *'I've been on the butta blockers all day after the trip to the Rupali Restaurant, Bigg Market, Newcastle upon Tyne and 15 pints of Guinness last night.'*

butt butter *n.* The *arse grease* left in the *hob* after a good *grill-rattler. Satan's prune juice.*

butt chuckle *n.* A tittersome *rump rasp.*

butt cutlet *n.* A wholesome organic *loaf* cooked up in the *dirt bakery.* A vegetarian's *rump steak.*

buttella *n.* Feculent the consistency and colour of chocolate ganache, often found spread across the *pans* in your local Wetherspoons; a viscous, gummy substance that you definitely wouldn't want to spread on your crêpes.

butter-bags *n.* Churns.

butter balls *n.* A careless ejaculator whose lack of due diligence when *blowing his beans* leads to regular mishaps. Also known as a *butter bollocks* or *pram filler.*

buttered bun *n.* A well-used *snatch.* A *box of assorted creams.*

butterface *n.* A woman with a great figure, yet the physiognomy of a darts player's wife. From the phrase "She's got a good body, but her face…" A *bobfoc.*

butterfly *n.* A *pink admiral* with widely spread wings.

butterfly chicken *n.* Named after a popular item from the Nandos menu, a descriptive term for a particularly well-used and ugly *lady-badge.*

butterfly effect *n.* A disastrous *grime bubble* encased in a cocoon of hot liquid that forms a lepidopterous brown smudge between the *buttock* cheeks. A blast of wind so chaotic and unpredictable in its effects that it may well change the course of events for the rest of your day.

butterfly enthusiast *n.* A connoisseur of *close-up pink wingspans.*

butterfly with tits *euph.* Hyperbolic figure of speech pertaining to a particularly unlikely state of events. *'You'll never guess who come in the Albion for the meat draw on Friday, Dave. That Stella McCartney.' 'Oh yeah? Is that right, is it? Well I was in the park yesterday and I seen a butterfly with tits.'*

butter's choice *n.* Second hand tobacco in discarded *cancer stick* remnants, harvested outside the supermarket by thrifty *Harry Rag* fans.

buttery *n.* A bar frequented by men who *don't eat their crusts.*

butter your cheeks *v.* To *fart* and *follow through.*

buttflood *n.* The *squirts*, the *Earthas.*

but there's a 'U' in 'cunt' *exclam.* Correct response to the office *twat* who, fresh from a round of managerial buzzword bingo, comes out with the phrase "there's no 'I' in 'team'…"

butt nuggets *n.* Jeremies.

buttock *n.* Fifty percent of a whole *arse.*

buttock broker *n.* A controller of prostitutes, a pimp. Also *titty farmer, pussy farmer, gash baron, fanny magnate.*

buttock hall *n. Meat market.* A pub or club where a

fellow can satiate his *slappetite.*

buttock jig *n.* A close, horizontal dance that typically takes place after chucking out time. *Making the beast with two backs.*

buttocknut squash *n. medic.* Traumatic injury sustained when a man with pendulous *clock-weights* sits down too rapidly on the *chod-bin.*

button *n.* A lady's *clematis.* The *devil's doorbell, wail switch, bald man in a boat.*

button groove *n. Hairy axe wound, snapper.*

buttonhole *v.* To *bang* a *RFHTFH* right in the belly button. Or thereabouts.

button mushroom resting on a spacehopper, like a *sim.* Descriptive of a gent whose relative lower proportions are somewhat out of whack. A *cheese wagon*; the opposite of *ACNB. 'What do you think of that, then, Una?' 'Ooh, Cliff. It's like a button mushroom resting on a spacehopper.'*

button on a fur coat, like a *sim.* A less-than-impressive *endowment.* A tiny *knob. 'What do you make of that then, doctor?' 'Ooh, the Right Honourable Mr Straw MP. It's like a button on a fur coat.'*

button view *n.* A tantalising *sneaky peek* of a woman's *ta tas* and/or *tit pants* viewed through the gap in between the buttons of her shirt or blouse.

butt plug *n.* A medical appliance used to prevent water from the bath going up your *arse.*

butt purr *n.* A rumble emanating from the *back passage*, suggesting nothing so much as the contented murmurings of a *Felis catus domesticus* having its ears tickled.

butt putty *n.* Akin to a type-4 *feeshus* on the UK Standard Bristol Stool chart, and used primarily as a sealing agent.

buttress *1. n.* A *grumble flick* actress who makes a speciality of performing in *back door action* productions. *2. n.* Any lady who prefers it *up the wrong 'un.*

butt's fizz *n.* Celebratory *bubble poo.*

butt slammers *n. US.* Members of the gay community, who tend to accidentally catch their bottoms in the door in their eagerness to go out and be homosexual.

butt sneeze *n. US. Fart.*

butt tumbler *n.* A *fruit feeler* or *mudflapper.*

butt wood, chop some *v.* To *hack off* a large, knotty *log*, possibly while shouting "Timber!" *'Those were lean years on Walton's Mountain. Work was hard to find, and we often went hungry. But throughout that harsh and bitter time we were sustained by the love, warmth and laughter that filled our family home. The house in which we were born and raised is still there, and on the winds that sigh along those misted Blue Ridge Mountains, the sound of Grandma chopping her morning butt wood echoes still.'*

buy a headache *v.* To purchase a strong alcoholic beverage. *'What are you going to do with your share of the auction profits?' 'I'm going to buy meself a headache, Christina.'*

buying your better half an anniversary present *euph.* *Flogging on* to the *binternet* while the missus is out of the house. From the subtle "eight second demos" television advert for Windows 7 back in 2009, *viz.* "Buying your better half an anniversary present and you don't want her to find out? Turn on Private Browsing. Do your thing, clickety-click and no-one knows what you've been up to." See also *do your thing, clickety-click.*

buy one get one free *euph.* Forgetting to scan every other item at the self service till in your local supermarket.

buysexual *n.* A fellow who pays for *it.* Buysexuals in their natural habitat can commonly be observed in the Zeedyjk area of Amsterdam. And again two weeks later, sitting on uncomfortable plastic chairs outside the GUM clinic of their local hospital. Next to Lord Archer of Weston-super-Mare.

Buzz lightbeer *1. n.* A mate who drinks *vicar's piss* rather than proper beer like a real man, thereby remaining relatively sober instead of going to "incapacity and beyond". *2. n.* A *two-pot screamer* or *half-pint Harry* who gets *banjoed* after a pitifully small amount of liquor.

BVH *abbrev.* Blue Veined Hooligan. A hard, six-inch tall, one-eyed, purple-faced *skinhead.*

BWR *abbrev.* Beeps When Reversing. Code used between considerate men to identify, yet save the feelings of, a lady who has failed to achieve an acceptable level of thinness. A *barge arse* or *double sucker.*

by George, she's got it! *exclam.* Said in the style of Rex Harrison as Professor Henry Higgins whenever one's fair lady *drops a consonant.* Also *there goes the Maldives; there's Bully – you're out of time; what year is it?! Who's the president?!*

Byker button *n.* A safety pin. Named after the exclusive Newcastle upon Tyne locale made famous by TV's PJ and Duncan, Ant and Dec.

Byker plug *n.* An anally inserted wad of *bog paper* reputedly favoured by habitual drinkers of Newcastle Brown as a means of preventing spontaneous bowel evacuations.

Byker tea cake *n.* A *Glasgow kiss.* A headbutt. *'Fuck me! Did you see that? Fucking Zidane just give fucking Materazzi a fucking Byker tea cake!'* (John Motson, commentating on the 2006 FIFA World Cup Final).

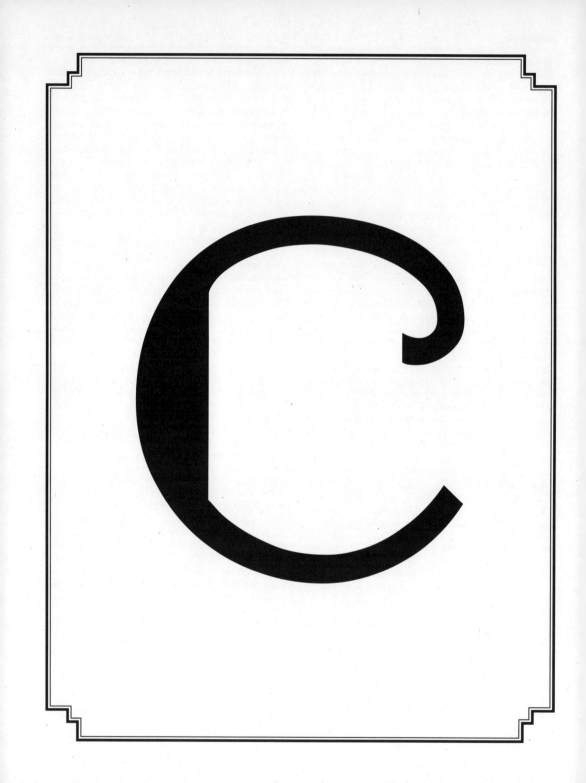

cabbage *n. coll.* Girls, *totty, blart, tussage, beaver.* *"What-ho, Jeeves!" I ejaculated. "I've just been down to the Pink Flamingo club. Never seen so much cabbage in all my born pecker."'* (from *Achtung, Jeeves!* by PG Wodehouse).

cabbage brown *n.* The delicately traced sepia image of a rare butterfly found stencilled into the gusset after one has absent-mindedly *got engaged.* See also *nickertine stains, phartoshop, wind sketch.*

cabbage fart *n.* An *old dog's alarm clock.* A *dropped back* that smells of rotting vegetation.

cabbage gas *n.* Naturally occurring renewable fuel which powers *Dutch ovens. Carbon dibaxide.*

cabbie's doorbell *n.* A car horn, used to inform a whole street that their neighbour's 3.00 am taxi has arrived.

CAB/cab *acronym.* The male genitalias, *viz.* Cock And Balls. Alternatively, in cold weather, after swimming or when Bobby Davro, known as a *minicab.*

cab hookers *n.* Taxi drivers who hang around on the streets outside nightclubs in the early hours, soliciting for business by pulling their trouser legs up.

cabin doors to manual *1. exclam.* Shouted as you run to the toilet upon sensing the onset of a severe attack of diarrhoea. From standard aircraft taxiing procedure (British Airways Pilot's Manual Section 4: What to shout when the pilot's about to shit his trousers). *2. exclam.* Aeronautically-themed quip a gentleman may make as he embarks on his *final approach. 3. euph.* Taking matters into one's own hands, if you will. *'The missus is away to stay with her sister, so it's cabin doors to manual for me this week, vicar.'*

cabinet re-shuffle, carry out a *v.* To re-arrange one's *honourable members, wind the clock. 'Your honour, my client was merely carrying out a cabinet re-shuffle when he was caught in the bushes behind the nurses' home.'*

cable & wireless *euph.* Browsing the internet while on the throne. *Poogling.*

cable laying *n.* The excretion of lengths of *copper bolt.*

cable stitch *1. n.* A knitting term describing yarn which has been looped to resemble a twisted rope. *2. n.* A sharp, stabbing pain in the side caused by excessive exertion while trying to expel a recalcitrant length of *dirty rope.*

cable water *n.* The *piss* you suddenly realise you need after *dropping a copper bolt,* even though you've already zipped up your trousers, put your coat on and are halfway back to the bar.

cab man's rests *rhym. slang.* Bristols, thru'penny bits.

caboose *n.* The *anchor man* in a *bum train.* Lucky *Pierre's* rear attendant.

cacafeugo *1. n. prop.* A Spanish ship captured by Sir Francis Drake on March 1st 1579. *2. n. Shit fire.* Red hot *squirts,* often experienced following a deliciously spicy repast at the Curry Capital, Bigg Market, Newcastle upon Tyne.

cack *1. n. Shit,* excrement, *feeshus. 2. v.* To *papper,* usually one's *trolleys.* Also *cacka, cak. 3. exclam.* Expression of disappointment. *'Mr President. The House Judiciary Committee has instigated articles of impeachment against you for obstruction of justice, abuse of power and contempt of Congress.' 'Oh cack.'*

cackaccino *n.* An invigorating brown potful topped with a "froth" of unflushed *bumwad,* invariably found upon entering the *Rick Witter* on a train.

cack-ack/cack-ak *n. onomat.* Repeated volleys of hot excrement that pepper one's *chod-bin* bowl with smoking shrapnel. *Cack-ak* fire can be particularly intense following a meal of vegetarian food that is rich insoya, peas, beans and pulses.

cacking vocals *n.* The diverse melodic sounds that accompany the successful production of a *number two:* grunts, groans, squeaks, and sighs. Similar to – but not to be confused with (and, indeed, arguably more tuneful than) – any British entry to the Eurovision Song Contest.

cack-in-the-box *n.* A large, unflushed *railway sleeper* which startles you when you lift the lid.

cackophony *n.* The jarring, discordant sound of a really noisy *German Bight. Musique concrète.*

cack shack *n.* The *crapper* or *shit house. 'The throne room is out of order, your majesty. Her royal highness Princess Michael of Kent done a Meat Loaf's daughter in it earlier on and then his royal highness Prince Michael of Kent blocked it with bangers and mash trying to flush it away for her, the daft twat. I'm afraid you'll have to use Camilla's cack shack instead.'*

cacrobatics *n.* Breathtakingly ambitious faecal smearing. *Abstract excrementism, grimnastics.*

Cadbury *n.* One that can't handle his beer. A *two-pot screamer, half-pint Harry, almond* or *one can Van Damme.* From the fact that he can only accommodate "a glass and a half".

Cadbury alley *n. Bourneville boulevard.*

Cadbury's production line, seen more fingers than a *euph.* Said humorously of a loose-moralled *hosebag* whose *undercrackers* have been made light work of by many hands. Also (*see more* *fingers than a) Kit-Kat factory conveyor belt.*

caddy *n.* One who takes care of the *shaft* and *balls* and is worth their weight in gold.

cadge-ual *adj.* Of an occasional smoker, prone to the habit of "cadging" *coffin nails* off the nearest available source, often making an insincere offer of a ten pee coin in recompense or promising to buy a pack of twenty at some yet-to-be-confirmed future date.

caesar salad *euph.* A messily carnal combination, whereby the gentleman brings the *cheese* and *salad dressing* while the woman is responsible for providing the *lettuce* and a hint of *anchovy*.

cafartic *adj.* Descriptive of the feeling of relief you get following a particularly satisfying *pump*.

café hag *1. n.* A popular brand of decaffeinated coffee. *2. n.* A *fit* woman whom, upon returning to your flat for coffee following a night out, and seen under the harsh fluorescent lights of your kitchen while waiting for the kettle to boil, is revealed to be neither *fit* nor womanly.

cafetière, the *n.* The ethically dubious motion of pushing a lady's head *south* against a certain amount of resistance. Also known as a *French press.*

CAFID/cafid *acronym.* The first *digestive transit of the day.* Coffee And Fag Induced Dump.

CAFOD/cafod *acronym.* Said of a *bad thrower.* Clearly A Friend Of Dorothy.

Cain & Abel *n. rhym. slang.* A *Vince* of biblical proportions, ironically not named after the hugely *shite* Jeffrey Archer potboiler.

cajooblies *n. Oomlaaters.*

cakebowling *n.* The act of *licking someone out* with more enthusiasm than usual.

cake detector *n.* A portly person who does need to ask directions to the nearest Greggs. A *salad dodger, piabetic, double fare, barge arse.*

cake magician *n.* Showman with the gift of being able to make the dessert course disappear without trace. *'Born on this day: Desmond Llewelyn, Q, 1914; Greg Gutfeld, foghorn-voiced contrarian, 1964; Barry White, soul singer and cake magician, 1944.'*

cakeover *n.* That staple of daytime television where they take a plain, fat lass, give her new clothes, make-up and hair, and she comes out at the end of the show looking like a plain, fat lass with new clothes, make-up and hair.

caker *n.* One with a healthy appetite; a dough-nut-quaffing *fat fuck.*

caker's dozen *n.* Thirty several. *'How many chicken wings would you like?' 'Just a caker's dozen for*

me, love.'

cakey *n.* Said of a slightly larger person, complete with *bingo wings, cankles* etc. Named for their self-evident love of baked confections. *'Born on this day: Raymond Baxter, futurologist, 1922; John Cooper Clarke, skeletal poet, 1949; Demis Roussos, cakey warbler, 1946.'*

calamari ring *n.* An unappetisingly rubbery, battered *nipsy.*

calcium cannons *n.* Breasts, *norks, milkers. 'Big smile over here for the Guardian, your royal highness! Get your calcium cannons out!'*

Calcutta croissant *n.* Angst-inducing mid-morning treat, hot from the *shatisserie.*

Calcutta rinse *n.* Using an inverted showerhead to cleanse one's *rusty bullethole* when bereft of *shit tickets.*

Calcutta splutter *n.* A rousing, Neddy Sea-goon-style *ringpiece raspberry* blown the morning after an inadvisably piquant *cuzza.* Also *Bombay spray.*

California tan *n.* An extreme sexual peccadillo practised by those who inhabit the wilder shores of scatological experimentation, the folk who consider *Cleveland steamers, Boston pancakes* and *Belgian biscuits* to be a little mundane, not to say jejune, if you will. Without going into too much detail, you will need a supply of laxatives, a sieve and a new carpet.

call down for more mayo *v.* To *jack the beanstalk.*

call Huey *v.* To vomit, *puke.* Also *call Ralph, call Ruth, call God on the great white telephone* etc.

calling for cock *n.* Of a lady, yawning.

call in the bomb squad *v.* To successfully defuse a particularly dangerous *false start* at an awkward social event.

call Joseph Bazalgette! *exclam.* Shocked response to encountering foul air in a *water closet,* having ignored the previous occupant's advice to leave it ten minutes if them was you. A reference to the Victorian king of piping *shite* out of the home (and, somewhat ironically if you think about it, the great-great-grandfather of the bloke who made *Big Brother*). *'Call Joseph Bazalgette please, love. There's a Great Stink in our downstairs shitter.'*

call of duty *1. n.* A space invaders game on the computer. *2. n.* A sudden urge to *drop the kids off at the pool.* A pig at the gate, mole at the counter, Mr Brown at the back door.

call Radcliffe *n.* To leave halfway through something you know you won't be finishing, *eg.* A crap pint, a bad relationship, an Olympic long distance race, a men-only charity ball at the Dorchester. *'How did you like Vera Drake?' 'Jesus*

Christ. I called Radcliffe on it after the first half hour, mate. Went to see Spongebob instead.'

call the hotline! I smell gas! *exclam.* Excitable announcement following the *passing of wind*, in line with the instructions on British Gas vans.

call the midwife *1. n.* Title of a gentle television drama series enjoyed by girls. *2. exclam.* A desperate plea yelled from the *Rick Witter* by someone giving breach birth to *Meat Loaf's daughter. 3. exclam.* Cry of alarm reserved for the most severe cases of flatulence, when there is a genuine risk of one's *brown waters* breaking.

call to prayer *n.* An early morning, wailing *horse and cart* which indicates that it is time to rise. A *breakfast mecca.*

Callum Plank *1. n. prop.* Founder of Scotland's leading auto-salvage haulage company. *2. rhym. slang.* An act of auto-erotic delight. *'I'm just off for a Callum Plank over the bra pages of your Damart catalogue, nan.'*

calm down Arthur *exclam.* On light-hearted TV series *Peaky Blinders*, a phrase often spoken by Thomas Shelby to his homicidal maniac of a brother, which could also be essayed in a vain attempt to avoid unnecessary unpleasantness after inadvertently bumping into anyone in a Wetherspoon's after 10:30 in the morning.

calve *v.* To have a difficult delivery on the toilet. To attempt to pass an exceptionally toublesome *Peter O'Toole* where, in extreme cases, it may be necessary to tie a rope around it and get someone to pull it out. A *Herriot turd.*

Cambridge entrance *n.* An access route popular with pupils of the country's leading boarding schools; the *cigar cutter.*

Cambridgeshire Council employee car park on a Friday, as empty as *sim.* Descriptive of something with a lot of unoccupied space in it. *'Blimey, Mr Souness. This trophy cabinet is as empty as Cambridgeshire Council employee car park on a Friday.'*

Cambridge Smith! *exclam.* A mildly amusing response to a *starter for ten.* Spoken urgently in the excitable style of Roger Tilling's nerd-naming voiceover on BBC2 boffin quiz *University Challenge.* Also *there's no taste like Hovis; Congratulations, it's a boy.*

camel's foot *n. Twix lips, beetle bonnet, monkey's forehead.* The pediments of the *toblerone tunnel.*

camel tongue *n.* The outline of a man's *Johnson* in an overly tight pair of *strides. 'Nice camel tongue, Mr Plant. Big smile for the Cambrian News.'*

camera toe *n.* When a woman inadvertently and unknowingly reveals her *lady bits* through her clothing in a photograph. *'Big smile and a camera*

toe over here for the Daily Express, Lady Diana? That's right, love. Keep the sun behind you.'

Camillas *n.* The *guts.* From Camilla Parker-Bowells = Simon Cowells.

camoufart *n.* A voluble *gut dropped* in order to disguise the sound of a possibly Covid-related cough.

camouflage fart *n.* A noisome *guff* dropped in a situation where there's no chance of it being detected, *eg.* On a farm, in an old folks' home, while changing a nappy or standing anywhere within fifty feet of the *bogs* on a Virgin train.

camouflush *n.* In a public *crapper,* the act of concealing the embarrassing sound of plops, splashes and *Lionel Barts* from your fellow cubicle-dwellers by repeatedly pulling the chain.

camp *adj.* As butch as Kenneth Williams.

Campbell *v.* To inadvertently utter the *c-word* in inappropriate circumstances, such as while hosting an early morning programme on a national radio station. A term coined by Andrew Collins and Richard Herring, which refers to 5Live host Nicky's unfortunate habit of repeatedly saying the *c-word* while presenting his early morning programmes on a national radio station.

Campbell's condensed *n.* A small volume, double-strength *brew* which, when diluted with air, can feed a whole room.

camper's kebab *n.* A *dump* taken in one's hat when one would rather not leave the tent. *'It was blowing a terrible blizzard last night. Indeed, it was so cold that when nature called, Bowers decided not to expose himself to the risk of frostbite and instead ordered a camper's kebab. After living on nothing save penguin fat, rancid Pemmican and seal blubber for the last six months, the smell was too much for Oates, who called him a dirty cunt and went outside to get some fresh air. He ventured out into the blizzard and we have not seen him since.'* (from the handwritten entry for March 18th, 1912, found in a *Lett's Antarctic Explorer's Diary* on the body of Captain Robert Falcon Scott).

campshite *n.* An endearingly back-to-basics UK camping facility which provides hardy staycationers with a nostalgic time-travel experience of the 1970s; a windswept field with rudimentary toilet and washing facilities surrounded by a muddy swamp.

CAMRA angle *n.* Real ale *brewer's droop.* About 165° off the vertical.

CAMRA cripple *n.* A *pissabled* chap who suffers difficulty walking after spending the afternoon enjoying the wares on offer at a beer festival.

can *1. n. US. Bottom. 2. n. US.* A quantity of *Bob*

Hope, marijuana. 3. n. US. Prison. *4. n. US.* Toilet, shithouse. *'They put me in the can after I was caught in the can sticking a can up my can.'*

canadin *n.* Proprietary medicine available in supermarkets and off-licences throughout the land; a cure for all life's ills.

canal no. 5 *n.* Perfume bought from a pound shop.

can anyone smell burning? *exclam. interrog.* Uttered in an alarmed fashion in a crowded elevator just after delivering a *silent-but-violent letter from Mr Shit.* See also *the president has landed, better an eviction than a bad tenant, they call the wind Mariah, back to bed Peppa! etc.*

cananza *n.* A veritable feast of tin-based supping at home. A housebound *Leo Sayer. 'I'm not gannin' oot the day, like. Just having meself a cananza in the hoose, Camilla.'*

canaraderie *n. Fr.* Alcohol-induced bonhomie.

canary killer *n.* A *fart* that smells like a 1960s cokeworks.

canary, send in the *exclam.* Old mining term now appropriated by folk who have just befouled the atmosphere in the *bobhouse. 'Fuck me. Send in the canary before you use that shitter, your majesty. I just done a right stinky dump in there.'*

cancelling the milk *n.* Taking a post-ejaculatory *piss*, to *clear the pipes* and prevent later seepage.

cancer shop *1. n.* A charitable retail outlet selling corpses' trousers, Mantovani records and damp, mouldy copies of *Readers' Digest. 2. n.* A high street tanning studio. The *bimbo bakery.*

cancer steam *n.* The pungent and highly visible exhalations of vapour that hang around doorways where *douche flautists* congregate to suck on their *robot dicks.*

cancer veranda *n.* The *al fresco* area around an office building entrance to which *snoutcasts* are exiled.

c and c *abbrev. Clips and cunts.* Generic term for any television programme consisting of nothing but clips from other televison shows/films/ads/ videos interspersed with hilarious, insightful and profound comments from assorted *cunts* whose only reason for existing appears to be appearing on *c and c shows.*

candle wax *n.* Drips of *population paste* that have been left to solidify on an area of laminate flooring in front of a bachelor's home computer.

candy floss *1. n.* A large, fluffy fairground snack which is impossible to finish, damages the teeth and invariably leaves one feeling slightly nauseous. *2. n.* A large, fluffy *bush* which is impossible to finish, damages the teeth and invariably *etc., etc.*

candy rush *n.* A hurried, frantic bout of *self help.*

From the space invaders game Candy Crush in which "you have thirty moves to get your fruit out".

candy twist *1. n.* A term local to the potteries of Stoke-on-Trent; a stylish flourish when pulling a handle for a cup, beaker or jug. *2. n.* A deft twist of the *helmet* when *pulling yourself off,* a term also local to Stoke-on-Trent.

can flu *n. medic.* A crippling aliment brought on by an over zealous-session *on the sauce.* Also *beer cancer* or a serious *yeast infection.*

can I have a quick word? *1. exclam. interrog.* Ominous manager-speak invitation that presages a proper *bollocking* off the boss. *2. exclam.* Semi-formal means of introducing an *Exchange & Mart.*

can I have that in writing? *exclam.* A humorous post-*air-biscuit* exclamation. See also *ET phone home; you were only supposed to blow the bloody doors off; be not afeard, the isle is full of noises; move along, nothing to see here; I second that motion and add a turd.*

can I quote you on that? *exclam. interrog. rhet.* Another one of those useful phrases to drop into the awkward silence which follows a voluble *botty burp.* See also *my, that duck's got bad breath, can I have that in writing? etc.*

cankle *n.* On a lady *with a lovely personality*, where the calf is indistinguishable from the ankle. Derivation unknown.

canned laughter *n.* The bouncing *enbonpoint* of a tittersome female or Lord Owen of Plymouth.

cannonball *v.* Of a happily flexible gentleman who never leaves the house, to perform a *thirty-four-and-a-halfer.* To administer *self-horatio.*

cannonball express *n.* A big *turd* that comes "a-steamin' and a-rollin'" out of the *brown engine shed*, before jumping the points and de-railing into the *porcelain buffers.* From the rollicking theme tune to the 1960s children's programme *Casey Jones* (which was already ten years old then).

cannon trousers *n.* An amusing epithet bestowed upon one who is suffering from high-calibre flatulence.

cannon wheels *n.* The testicles. *'Have you got the end in yet, Bobby?' 'Aye, I'm in up to me cannon wheels you cheeky cow.'*

canoe *n.* A streamlined *poo* which is shaped perfectly to ensure anal comfort throughout its expulsion from the *dirt bakery; ie.* One that tapers to a point at both ends like a shuttle off a powerloom.

can of farts *euph.* Baked beans. *'What would you like for breakfast, Lady Bellamy?' 'One lightly* *poached egg, one piece of toast and half a can of farts please, Hudson.'*

canorama *n.* A horizon-to-horizon widescreen prospect of beer tins. A student's window ledge.

CANRA *acronym.* The Campaign for Neurologically Reactive Ale. A loose amalgamation of unshaven beer enthusiasts who typically gather on town centre benches, in parks and around war memorials to discuss the relative merits of their preferred tinned brews, shout at passers by, and occasionally foul themselves.

cans, chav *n.* Big, gaudy headphones with inferior sound quality.

can tan *n.* The healthy, bronzed skin tone achieved by gentlemen who sit on the *shandy sunbed* all day, supping from tins of 9% lager. *Tramp's tan.*

can't-can't, the *n.* Ill-advised, *pissed-up* dances of the sort essayed by red-faced, sweating uncles at wedding discos, typically ending up with them falling through the bride's table, the cake or a plate glass window, garnering them a £250 cheque from *You've Been Framed* in the process. *'Get the video camera out, mam. Uncle Cedric's had nine Stellas and he's getting up to do the can't-can't to Bad Manners.'*

can't fart fairer than that *exclam.* Said after waiting until your wife has finished a phone call to her boss before unleashing a rambunctious *ripper.*

can't understand new technology *exclam. acronym.* Phrase which can be usefully dropped into conversation during meetings with patronising IT personnel, or encounters with smart-arsed salesmen in electrical stores, when you are being bombarded with technical bullshit. *'Yeah, the way I see it, your choice is between the Canon Powershot SX730 with 20.3 megapixels and a 40X optical zoom and the Bosch SMS24AW01G, which does twelve place settings and has an adjustable top shelf for tall glasses. Do you want to take out the five year extended warranty?' 'Eeh, sorry, mate. Can't understand new technology.'*

canvas cashpoint *n.* On a festival campsite, an illicit source of money, cameras, mobile phones, car keys, iPods, drugs *etc.* Someone else's tent.

canwankerous *adj.* Descriptive of someone who is both cantankerous and a *wanker.* From cantankerous + wanker.

can you leave the fat on mine? *exclam.* Humorous response to a particularly high cholesterol *beefy eggo* from the *trouser grill.*

can you put that into an email for me please? *exclam. interrog.* Said after someone *drops a gut* in the office, preferably during a very important meeting.

can you smell what the arse is cooking?! *exclam. interrog.* Something to be bellowed in the style of a rabble-rousing WWE wrestler before *letting off* a blast of *country air* capable of immobilising Giant Haystacks.

can you stick a flake in that? *exclam. sarc.* Addressed caustically to one's bartender when a lager is poured which is more head than beer.

cappuccino fanny *n.* When the *furry cup* has reached its maximum state of effervescence. *Frothing like bottled Bass, wetter than a fat bird's armpit, wetter than Lee Evans's suit etc.*

cappuchinos *n.* A pair of bubblepoo-lathered casual slacks. *'Nice cappuchinos, Lord Archer.'*

captain *1. n.* A sadly under-endowed fellow. From the 1979 song where Tennille sings to her pseudymously-ranked husband: "Do that to me one more time. Once is never enough with a man like you." *2. n.* The penis. *'Don't be shy, love. Pop your head below decks and say hello to the captain.'*

Captain Birdseye *n.* A fellow who doesn't seem to have too much trouble getting *fish fingers.* *'Today's birthdays: Linda Lovelace, late movie knob gobbler, 63; Eddie Cheever, US racing driver, 54; Rod Stewart, gravel-voiced Captain Birdseye, 67.'*

Captain Birdseye's chin *n.* Something hairy and haddocky. *'Fucking hell, love. It's like Captain Birdseye's chin down here.'*

Captain bugwash *n.* A squeegee-wielding *twat* who lunges at your windscreen when you stop at the lights for four seconds in inner London traffic.

Captain Caveman *n.* A yodelling *biffer.*

Captain Caveman's club *euph.* A stout length of *dirty spine* which, during passing, causes one to make unintelligibly loud exclamations and, upon later inspection, resembles the titular troglodyte's timber weapon of choice.

Captain Caveman's nose *n.* The *clematis* or *wail switch.*

captain, do a *v.* To display one's *buttocks* through the back window of a coach, usually to a couple of nuns in a Morris Minor. To do a *moonie.*

Captain Hogseye *n.* Curly-bearded seafarer with a shiny, bald, purple head who trawls in *cod cove.* And spits a lot.

Captain Hook *n.* A fellow proficient in the gentle art of using his crooked index finger to haul the gusset of his ladyfriend's *bills* safely out of the way, for whatever reason.

Captain Kirk's fingers *n.* The discomfiting result when you economise by purchasing cheap *bumwad* and your digits "boldly go where no man has gone before".

Captain Oates, do a *v.* To altruistically leave the pub early when struggling with the pace, so as not to hold your more manly fellow drinkers back.

captain on the bridge *1. exclam.* Announcement made when Kirk steps out of the Enterprise lift. *2. exclam.* Something a gentleman says as he hopefully prods his *significant other* with the end of his plasma cannon. *3. exclam.* In American war movies, a command which causes all crew members to snap rigidly to attention. *4. euph.* When making one's way urgently to the *poop deck* to *launch a brown torpedo* at short notice, a sudden, urgent need to stand up straight with the buttocks tightly clenched.

Captain Scott's last morning stiffy, as hard as *sim. Nails.* From the intrepid Arctic/Antarctic explorer's final, frost-bitten night under canvas. Also *as hard as Elvis's last turd.* '*Careful, Phil. I wouldn't flick any more peanuts at that nutter by the bar if I was you. He's as hard as Captain Scott's last morning stiffy.*'

captain's helmet *n.* A *Thora Hird* so long that it hits the *sump* while still having half-an-inch poking out above the *Plimsoll line,* like the Titanic's gaffer's *titfer* after he drove it into that iceberg.

captain's pie *1. n.* Tasty *slice* caught fresh and filleted by Captain *Hogseye.* A *haddock pastie* or *hairy pie. 2. n. milit.* Of naval catering, that pastry-cased comestible which belongs to the officer in charge.

captain underpants's mandolin *n.* A diminutive yet satisfying *one-stringed instrument* that is typically *strummed* solo.

caramel keg *1. n.* A much-loved, self-explanatory chocolate in a box of Cadbury's Roses. *2. n.* A lady with a *pint glass figure, eg.* Her with the red face and the glasses who used to show off at the front of Les Dawson's tap-dancing troupe the Roly Polys. Mo Moreland, she was called, and she *pegged it* just in time for Christmas 2023.

Caravaggio *1. n. prop.* Hell-raising Oliver Reed-style painter of the Italian Renaissance, who actually murdered someone. *2. n. It.* The act of *copping a swift feel* in the back seat of an Italian car just before the wiring goes *tits up,* the doors fall off and it dissolves into a pile of rust.

caravanner *n.* A slender gentleman hitched to a distinctly more sizeable spouse, *ie.* One who is used to towing a large, ungainly *load* around.

car bar *n.* When attending, for example, a wedding reception, sneaking your empty glass out into the car park to fill it up with your own beer from your boot; a practice that is expressly forbidden at Judge's Hotel in Yarm. Although, just possibly, it might not be quite so prevalent amongst their clientele if they weren't charging £4.75 for a fucking can of Guinness.

carbonara excuse, the *phr.* Tried and trusted *pisspoor* palliation proffered to a husband/wife/the lady at the launderette, *eg.* "It was a very sloppy pasta sauce", when handing over a dress/shirt/hat that has quite clearly been *spunked up* on.

carbon arseprint *n.* A measure of an individual's contribution to global warming or climate change caused by a release of *brownhouse gases* so powerful that it leaves a sooty residue in the *dunghampers.*

carbon bumprint *n.* The deleterious effect upon the environment that is a direct consequence of any given visit to the *smallest room* for a *number two.*

carbon cockprint *n.* Scientific measure of how many offsprings you have and thus the future potential environmental impact of your filthy carnal urges. '*What? You're going all the way to Stockholm just to shag that bird? Your carbon cockprint will be massive.*'

carbon dating *n.* Consorting romantically with a partner who is considerably more superannuated than oneself. '*Still carbon dating, eh, monsieur Macron?*'

carbon dibaxide *n.* Chemical name for *arse gas.* The principle chemical constituent of *anusthetic.*

carbon fuckprint *1. n.* The total environmental, infrastructural, sartorial and psychological damage caused by any sexual event.

carbon fuckprint, reducing your *phr.* Saving fuel by *getting your leg over* a lady in your own street or village. Or, in Lincolnshire, your own home.

carbon hatprint *n.* Damage done to the environment by flying your favourite hat halfway round the world on a jumbo jet. '*Have you not considered your feckin' carbon hatprint at all there, Bono?*'

carbon manoxide *n. Sci.* The foul miasma of *ignoble gas* that envelopes a fellow the morning after a night on the strong ales, spiced comestibles and pickled eggs. What kills you if you decide to gas yourself in a *Dutch oven. Carbon dibaxide, poopane, knockout gas.*

carbon neutral *adj.* Descriptive of an escape of *flatus* from the *back door* that is neither loud nor particularly odorous.

carbon offset *n.* Opening a window, striking a match, or spraying around some Lynx in the aftermath of a particularly noisome *Exchange & Mart.*

car boot table *n.* Something or someone that looks good from a distance but when you get up close, it's a right pile of *shit.* See also *low resolution fox, tramp l'oeuil, good from far but far from good, fabric softener.*

car bootylicious *adj.* Descriptive of those rough *bints* one sees on *Dickinson's Real Deal,* wearing *saggy-arsed* velour tracksuits and *bingo clink* whilst trying to flog their dead nan's wedding ring for a couple of tenners. Also *aldilicious.*

carb unloading *n.* The process of *doing* a nice big *duty.*

car cock *n. medic.* Involuntary *travel fat.* *'Sorry kids, we can't sit inside Crunchy Fried Chicken today. We'll have to go to the drive-through because daddy's got car cock.'*

car crash flash *n.* A rubbernecker's *sneaky peek* when a woman with *big bones* sits down in a very short skirt. Something a fellow really doesn't want to look at, but nevertheless feels strangely compelled to.

cardie muffins *n. Tits* of the sort you would expect a spinster librarian to have.

Cardiff grandmother *n.* A lady whose own children have flown the nest and who is now, at the age of twenty-eight or so, out *on the pull* again.

Cardiff market carrot, as soft as a *sim.* Descriptive of an *overly-refreshed* chap's *Mr Snout* following a *Leo Sayer* in the land that time forgot. *'Do you want anything while I'm out, dear?' 'Yes. Can you bring me six bottles of blue Powerade and a big pack of extra strong Bongo Bill's Banjo pills please? Me Charlie's as soft as a Cardiff Market carrot.'*

cardinal's cap *n. medic.* A swelling and reddening of the *herman* brought on by chronic *bishop rage. Fireman's helmet.*

cardington *n.* A vast bra for the storage of vast *knockers.* Named after the Bedfordshire airfield where two enormous airship hangars were constructed side by side in 1917. *'Lot 456. Substantial Playtex cardington, formerly the property of the television impressionist Faith Brown. May be of interest to circus freakshow exhibitors, or could possibly be cut down and used to carry oversized piles of loose coal, roadstone or sharp sand. Estimate £30-£35.'* (from Christie's Showbiz Memorobilia Auction Catalogue, October 2003).

car door khazi *n.* A discreet, improvised roadside toilet created by opening the nearside front and rear doors of one's landaulette in a layby – the doors thus conveniently forming the sides of a vehicular *pissoir,* if you will. The sort of thing Bernard Manning would do when he was *caught*

short whilst out in his Roller or his Cadillac.

cardswipe *n.* The groove on a *bird's* frontage.

card table *n.* A position whereby a lady engages in simultaneous oral/vaginal pleasures with two gentlemen who could, should they wish, play a game of cards on her back. Admittedly an unlikely scenario. *A spit roast, corn on the cob.*

carefree bachelor *n.* Bloke in a tracksuit, living the playboy lifestyle and enjoying (if that's the right word) a breakfast of lager and crisps in a Wetherspoon's.

careless accountant *n.* One who "fails to keep track of the pounds". A *salad dodger, seasoned diner, three-pegger.*

careless whisper *euph.* A disastrous attempt at a *one cheek sneak* that results in *dropped Maltesers. Following through* in the style of an 80s pop tune.

caretaker's keys *euph.* Being granted *access all areas* for a sexual encounter on a special occasion. Also known as a *backstage pass. 'It's my birthday and she's lent me the caretaker's keys.'*

cargle *v.* Of a dirty lady, to gargle with a gentleman's *erotic spendings.* Like they do. From cum + gargle.

cargo pants *n.* A *barge arse* who *beeps while reversing.*

cargoyle *n.* A person with such *a lovely personality* that all dates with them are spent in the car to avoid the possiblity of being spotted in their company.

Carling darling *n.* One whose attractiveness only becomes apparent after you have had a few lagers. A *ten pinter, gallon girl.*

Carlsberg colonic *n.* A full rectal auto-irrigation carried out conveniently while one sleeps off a fair few cans of what is probably the best super-strength *wreck the hoose juice* in the world.

Carlsberg expert *n.* A philanthropically didactic bar-dwelling gentleman who, having consumed more than a few pints of the eponymous Danish lager, becomes a generous fount of all knowledge & wisdom. See also *gintellectual.*

carnival *n.* A sexual game whereby a woman sits on a man's face and he has to guess her weight.

carnival knowledge *n.* Biblical phrase meaning to have sex. *'And it came to pass that Mary was up the spout, yea though Joseph had not lain with her, and certainly had not carnival knowledge of her.'* (from *St. Paul's Letters to the Gas Board,* Chapter 6, *v.* 3-5).

carniwhore *n.* A *speciality film* actress with a real taste for *meat.*

Carolgees' cuff *n.* Having one's *wanking spanner* lodged wrist deep in a hairy *biffer.*

Carol Vorderman, do a *v.* To sit on the *Rick Witter* doing what the erstwhile *Countdown* mathematician is famous for, *viz.* "Working one out". To *do* *the numbers round, one from the bottom.*

car park interview *n.* A robustly-opinionated exchange of *ad hominem* arguments between two *heavily-refreshed* public house patrons.

car park karaoke *n.* A post-drink entertainment where women *pissed up* on *tart fuel* take turns on the *purple-headed microphone.*

carpark sutra *n.* Variety of gymnastic positions that can be used by a couple *banging* on the back seat of an Astra. Usually while parked round the back of Shire Oak Miners' Welfare and surrounded by a crowd of enthusiastic *onanists* staring through the windows.

car park, to *v.* To kick seven shades of *Brad Pitt* out of someone. To *take them outside.*

carpenter's dream *n.* A sexually promiscuous woman. From the fact that she is "flat as a board and easy to screw".

carpentry *euph.* Lesbism, *viz.* "A spot of tongue & groove".

carpetbagger *1. n. US.* In the Reconstruction period (1863 – 1877) that followed the American Civil War, a northern migrant to the defeated south. *2. n.* A *teabagger* blessed with a pair of very large, very hirsute *clockweights*. *3. n.* A voracious *woman in comfortable shoes*, who has a lusty appetite for *rugs*. A *KD lady* who is at the *box biter* – as opposed to the *lettuce licker* – end of the lesbidatory spectrum.

carpet duster *n.* A dense, heavier-than-air cloud of *carbon dibaxide* which forms a thin yet potent layer over the whole floor surface.

carpet fitter's knee, like a *sim.* Any well-bashed part of the body. *'Bloody hell, Ulrika. Your biffing plate is like a carpet fitter's knee.'*

carpet muncher *n.* She who wolfs down *gorilla salad*, but turns her nose up at *meat and two veg.*

carpet tiles *rhym. slang. medic.* Bumgrapes, Adrian Chiles, Michael Miles.

carrot bladder *n. medic.* Secret internal organ situated just beside the pyloric sphincter from where diced carrots magically appear when you vomit. (© Billy Connolly Ltd. 1978).

carrot knackers *n.* Affectionate term for a ginger-haired fellow. *'Oi, carrot knackers. There's a picture of you in a nazi armband on the front of the Sun.'*

carrot snapper *n.* A lady with the sort of protruding front teeth that would do a rabbit proud. A *bunny girl. 'Born on this day: Johannes Kepler, astronomer who correctly explained planetary motion, thereby becoming the founder of the science of celestial mechanics, 1571; Louis Pasteur, scientist and discoverer of the theory that infectious diseases are*

caused by germs, whose pioneering work became the foundation of the science of microbiology, and hence a cornerstone of modern medicine, 1822; Janet Street Porter, screeching carrot snapper, 1946.'

carrot sorbet *n.* A refreshing, palate-cleansing *chunder* enjoyed in the middle of a drinking session.

Carry On conundrum, the *n.* Specifically, when confronted by a woman with luxuriant *undergrowth*, does one prefer *Up The Jungle* or *Up The Khyber*? Also known as the *Sherlock Holmes Two Pipe Problem.*

carry out, to have a *v.* To *cack* oneself and have to walk to the nearest convenient spot for a *scrape out.*

carry your bat *1. v.* In the world of cricket, to return to the pavilion, having remained at the crease throughout your team's entire innings without getting out. *2. v.* In the world of *having it off*, to abandon a drunken act of sexual intercourse after giving it your best shot.

carse *n.* The female equivalent of the *barse. Biffon, Humber bridge, tinter, fanoose.*

Carsten Janker *rhym. slang.* A *wanker.* From the bullet-headed footballing teuton who taunted the crowd after putting Germany 1-0 ahead at the start of their 5-1 trouncing by En-ger-lernd, En-ger-ernd, En-ger-lernd! En-ger-lernd, En-ger-lernd, En-ger-lerrr-ernd! in 2001. We beat them in 1966 too.

carte brune *n. Fr.* The nominal licence afforded one who enters a cubicle in an otherwise empty public lavatory, to *release the chocolate hostage* with as much noise, fury and gusto as he sees fit, protected as he is by the cloak of anonymity.

cartholic *n.* A motorist who eschews the usual safety precautions as recommended in the *Highway Code*, preferring to simply "pull out and hope for the best."

cartman *n. medic.* A small *stool.* From the little *shit* in the popular children's cartoon series *South Park.*

carumpfing *n.* Automobile-based *snurging* of ladies' car seats. *Carbooning. 'Yes miss, we've done the full 10,000 mile service. Your car needed four gangle pins, trumpets all round and a new glibshaft. The lads are just carumpfing it and it'll be ready to collect any time after four-thirty.'*

carvery arse *n. medic.* Distressing tirade of exceptionally vile *Lionels* suffered after polishing off a king-size plate at the Toby, with extra Yorkshire pud and bonus chipolatas. *'Mrs McCririck was admitted to hospital on Tuesday after her husband* *suffered a serious attack of carvery arse.'*

carwash *n.* View of the vagina while performing *cumulonimbus*. The hair of the *muff lips* looking like them big whirly brush things that knock your wing mirrors off.

Casanova's rubber sock *n.* Condom, *blob, dunky, French letter, Coney Island whitefish*. *'Anything for the weekend, sir?' 'Yes, a pack of three Casanova's rubber socks please.'*

case of the creaks *n.* An excuse typically made by those suffering from loud flatulence. *'Fetch the WD40, dear. The kitchen door's got a case of the creaks.' 'And even that racket hasn't covered up the sound of your horrendous trumps.'*

Casey Stoner *n. rhym. slang. Aus.* Named after the two-time MotoGP champion motorbicyclist; an erection. From Casey Stoner = boner. *'I was watching this video last night of some bird with her Mick Grants pulled down flicking her Barry Sheene and it gave me a proper Casey Stoner, I can tell you. And now over to Darren Bett for the weather.'*

cashanova *n.* One who doesn't waste his money, but invests it wisely on prostitutes. A chap who pays for his love. A *punter*, a *John*, a *buysexual*.

cash crash *n.* A deliberate car accident that is intended to enrich the perpetrator *via* insurance and injury claims.

cash for gash *euph.* A stop at the bank machine on the way out *on the pull*.

cashier number two please *exclam.* An amusing utterance to warn the denizens of neighbouring *traps* about the impending splash as a length of *dirty spine* hits the water.

cash in the attic *1. n.* Daytime TV programme in which gullible homeowners are bullied into selling their worthless heirlooms for the entertainment of semi-comatose students, professional comedians and the unemployed. Exactly like *Flog It! 2. v.* To perform a *money shot* into a *bird's* mouth.

cash out *1. v.* To *bottle it* on a bet, for whatever reason, and settle for a lesser payout. *2. v.* To *bottle it* on a *scuttle*, for whatever reason, and settle for a *hand shandy* instead.

cashpoint cripple *n.* One who has to park as close as possible to the ATM when nipping to get some money, even if it means stopping their car on a double yellow line or restricting traffic.

cashtrate *v.* To cut off a person's financial assets. *'Coming down the pub tonight, Bob?' 'No mate. The wife's taken the lot, even the penny jar. I've been totally cashtrated.'*

cashtration *n.* The horrific act of buying a house, which renders the subject financially impotent for an indefinite period.

casino, chav *n.* A betting shop, turf accountancy practice or amusement arcade.

Casper the friendly gust *n.* A childishly inoffensive passing of gas.

cassoulet anglais *n. Fr.* A *can* full of sausage and beans. How a modern languages undergraduate might refer to the state of a blocked *shite house pan* in shared student accommodation.

cast a bronze *n.* To drop-forge a *copper bolt* using the lost wax method. *'Stay stood like that, Mademoiselle Claudet. Don't move. I'm just off to the crapper to cast a bronze. I'll be gone more than half an hour.' 'Right you are, Monsieur Rodin.'*

cast Churchill's reflection *v.* To perform an historical political impression involving a porcelain bowl with water in the bottom, your *arse* and a *bum cigar*.

casting spells *n.* What a young man does with his *magic wand* when left alone in the house for a prolonged period. Or even a short period.

casting your pearls before swine *1. idiom.* Offering something valuable to an ungrateful person. *2. euph.* Rubbing one out over a proper *vet's dustbin* in *Readers' Wives*.

Castleford cocktail *n.* Named after the delightful West Riding locale of the same name, any cheap drink that is a mixture of a spirit and a non-alcoholic liquid, *eg.* Vodka and Coke, creme de menthe and Tizer, gin and Cresta, the purchaser of which beverage then struts around like they've just purchased a bottle of £1000 Champagne.

castle on the queen side *1. v.* In chess, to perform the risky strategy of castling on the opposite side of the board from the usual default manoeuvre of castling on the king's side. Whatever that means. *2. v.* Of a man, to be prone to a spot of *aerobatic puddle avoidance.*

cast no shadow *1. n.* Track off of the album *What's the Story Morning Glory?* by Mancunian monkey-walkers Oasis. *2. euph.* Of *crimping off* and *dumping*, a *glory wipe* or the miraculous act of *drawing an ace.*

Casualty moment *n.* During the course of your everyday activities, a sudden realisation that the action you are performing resembles the sort of thing typically seen in the opening sequences of the hospital-based BBC tea-time calamity-fest. Carrying a pan of hot fat through a room full of toddlers playing marbles, preparing to perform an unrehearsed fire-breathing act at the opening of a posionous snake zoo, cutting the hedge with an electric circular saw while drunk and standing on a swivel chair, deciding to change into your swimming trunks while driving at high speed into a fog-bank near Beachy Head are all examples of *Casualty moments.*

Catalan custard *n.* Strange, viscous deposit found in the gusset of one's *grundies* after a heavy night *on the piss* in Barcelona. A discovery accompanied by unnerving, nightmarish flashbacks to an unpleasant interlude set on a seedy strip club stage which involves a blindfold, a man dressed in a monkey costume and a cheering crowd. *'What's up, Tom?' 'I've found some Catalan custard in my gusset, Barbara.'*

catalob *n.* The involuntary semi-*erection* which pops up while innocently browsing the *funderwear* section of a mail order catalogue.

catbab *n.* An exotic snack containing unidentifiable meat of questionable provenance, usually sold out of the window of an old ambulance.

catch a brown edge *v.* To accidentally inhale the dying aroma of somebody else's *air biscuit* just as the *dirt oven* door is closed. *'Fuck me, Mother Teresa. I just caught a brown edge off that!'*

catcher's mitt *1. n.* A contraceptive diaphragm, a *fuck-plug, babe roof. 2. n.* The use of one's spare hand to catch the *jitler* when *pulling the Pope's cap off.*

catch-fart *n. 17thC.* Someone who follows their master so closely that they are in the firing line for more than they bargained for. Also *brown noser, toady, arselick,* or *suckhole.*

catchment area *1. n.* The geographical radius from which a hospital's patients or a school's pupils are drawn. *2. n.* The region throughout which an *Exchange and Mart* can be smelled. *'Please accept my apologies in advance, your majesty. I think you may have inadvertently strayed within my catchment area.'*

caterer's tribute *euph. Spunk.* From the touching, little-known ceremony performed to mark the passing of the late Michael Winner, when *masturchefs* across the country gravely *spunked* up into whatever they were cooking in memory of the *jizz*-necking "film" director, gourmand and bon viveur.

catering for cyclists *adj.* A scene often found in parks during the summer when a generously proportioned lady lies on her back to sunbathe and thus unwittingly creates an ample facility in which to trap the front wheel of one's velocipede.

CAT F/cat F *abbrev.* Rating of the severity of a traffic jam where there is no good reason for it to have formed, so that one is forced to blame the tailback on "(some) Cunt At The Front".

cat five *1. abbrev. RAF.* Classification of an aircraft

that is considered beyond repair following a crash, which you would assume would be most aircraft that have had a crash. *2. abbrev. RAF.* Classification of a *chod bin* that is considered beyond use following a *dirty bomb.*

cat flap, fanny like a *sim.* Said of a notably fecund woman. *'That Queen Victoria had nine kids in seventeen years, you know, vicar.' 'Christ, she must of had a fanny like a fucking cat flap.'*

cat flaps *1. n.* Means by which a cute little pussy can enter the house. *2. n.* Means by which a *cock* can enter a cute little *pussy.* Labia minora, Keith Burtons.

Catford bunch *n.* An inexpensive floral offering to a ladyfriend, hand made from the flowers taped to the railings and lamp-posts of South London in memory of the recently stabbed.

catfunt *n.* Spooneristic epithet for one who does not conform to popular norms regarding body mass.

cath-arse-is *n.* A dramatic *Simon Cowell* movement of such magnitude that it triggers a vicarious emotional purgation (see Aristotle's *Poetics* for further details).

cathedral *sim.* Describing an oversized vagina which is too echo-y for a satisfactory *organ recital.* A *bucket fanny.*

Catherine wheel *n.* A person afflicted with spectacular food poisoning, who is spinning around not knowing which end to point towards the toilet, in the style of the popular 1970s firework.

Catholic condom *n.* Approved by the Pontiff, an elastic band around the base of the *pope's hat* and both sets of fingers and toes tightly crossed.

catholic tastes *1. n.* Wide-ranging interests, from the word "catholic" meaning "universal". *2. n.* Narrowly focused interests, specifically those pursued by certain members of the *left-footed* clergy which revolve principally around the contents of their prepubescent choirboys' surplices.

cat one incident *1. n.* Term used by employees of the Environment Agency to describe pollution that kills loads of fish and stuff. *2. n.* Term used to describe a really big *Eartha* that blocks the *bogs* at the Environment Agency offices. *'I wouldn't go in there if I was you, Stuart. There's a cat one incident in trap two.'*

cat on the bed *euph.* Descriptive of the sensations transmitted through the mattress that a gentleman feels when his fellow bedlady is *playing the invisible banjo. 'Can you feel something, Melania?' 'It's just a cat on the bed, Donald. Now go back to sleep in* *your big nappy.'*

cat's brain *n.* An unpleasantly shrivelled scrotum. As if there were any other sort available.

Cat's call *n.* A five second warning issued to those in one's immediate vicinity that an *air biscuit* is about to be released. From the lyrics to Cat Stevens's 1972 hit *Can't Keep It In, viz.* "Oh I can't keep it in / I can't keep it in / I've got to let it out".

cat scarer *n.* An unsuccessful haircut. A coiffure so bad that the victim's own moggy doesn't recognise them and runs off.

cat's cock hair *n.* The tiniest of margins, rhetorically speaking. Also *bawhair, midge's dick. 'I see the Mackems have avoided relegation by a cat's cock hair, Gary.'*

cat's cradle *n.* The globulous, sticky spoils strung between the fingertips of a *crane driver.*

cat's face *n.* Mrs Slocombe's *cunt.*

cattle *rhym. slang.* To engage in *coitus.* From cattle truck = fuck. Also *trolley* (& truck), *Friar* (Tuck) or *Russian* (duck).

cat with a strawberry-flavoured arse, like a *sim.* Descriptive of the happy demeanour of those who cannot believe the extent to which Heaven appears to have smiled upon them, *eg.* A rollover lottery winner, a dog with two *cocks* or any 1970s showbiz personality who has not so far been called in for questioning by detectives from Operation Yewtree.

cat with its throat cut, like a *sim.* Humorous term used to describe an alarmingly hirsute *front bottom.* Also *like a cat with its head cut off. 'Put your applecatchers back on will you, Germaine. There's no way we're printing a picture of that bloody thing in the magazine. It's like a cat with its throat cut.'*

caught in the cross hairs *1. adj.* About to end up like Abraham Lincoln, JFK or Tim Westwood's *arse. 2. adj.* Experiencing difficulty penetrating *Terry Waite's allotment.*

caught white handed, to be *phr.* To lose a game of *rushin' roulette.*

cauliflower *1. n.* S*x. *'Hey! Your missus gave me a bit of cauliflower while you were at work last night.' 2. n. 18thC.* Lettuce.

cauliflower beanbag *n.* The *hanging brain. 'Excuse me officer, I wonder if you'd be so good as to direct me to the nearest casualty department, only I appear to have inadvertently caught my cauliflower beanbag in the nozzle of this Hoover Dustette vacuum cleaner.'*

cauliflower biff *n. medic.* A *clout* that has had a right good *banging.* A *blurtch* that looks like one

of Bill Beaumont's ears.

cauliflower cheese *n.* Smegma.

cauliflower cunt *n.* Somewhat coarse description of an extremely well used *ladygarden* which looks like it's just done ten rounds with Rocky Marciano.

cauliflower rear *n. medic.* Distressing condition of a *dunny funnel* that has been *bashed in* too often; a rectal prolapse. Also *pink sock, arse tulip.*

caulker's J-Cloth, face like a *sim.* Descriptive of a *plasterer's radio.* See also *Jackson Pollock's shoes, quattro formaggio, Spaphrodite.* See also (face like an) *art room sink.*

caustic wit *n. rhym. slang.* A *shit. 'Born on this day: Evel Knievel, motorcycle stunt rider, 1938; Peter Stringfellow, fanny magnate, 1940; Toby Young, caustic wit, 1963.'*

cavalier *n.* An uncircumcised penis. With a wide *brim,* a big smile and a feather stuck rakishly in the top.

cavalry caviar *n. milit.* In armed forces circles, a highly prized, piquantly flavoured and salty delicacy that is traditionally served on a digestive biscuit or cream cracker. *Officer's Mess.*

caveman knickers *n.* A large and unruly *muff,* not unlike a mammoth fur undergarment. *The pieman's wig.*

caveman's necklace *n.* The haphazard dentition witnessed in persons hailing from less genteel urban environments. Also *teeth like a crossword, English teeth, a pan of burnt chips* or *a mouth like a locksmith's back pocket. 'Sit back in the seat and open wide please, Mr MacGowan, and I'll take a look at your caveman's necklace.'*

cave paintings *1. n.* Mysterious and multicoloured daubings of dinosaurs, which date from the upper Palaeolithic period after the last ice age. Found extensively decorating the inside walls of limestone caves in France and Spain during the 19th century. *2. n.* Mysterious and multicoloured daubings dating from a night after protracted consumption of draught Bass. Found comprehensively decorating the insides of *undercrackers* and bed linen the length and breadth of the UK on most weekend mornings.

caviar *1. n.* Expensive delicacy made from fish *women's things. 2. n.* Web-speak for scatological *grumble,* apparently.

cavity insulation *n.* Deliberately soiling yourself in a desperate attempt to keep warm. The sort of thing Bear Grylls probably does when he has to spend the night kipping in the woods after losing the key to his room at the local 5-star hotel.

C-biscuit *n.* An *air cookie* which inadvertently slips off the front of a lady's *plate.* Also *queef,*

Lawley kazoo, flap raspberry, a hat dropped forwards. Also made into a moving film about a champion racehorse suffering from chronic vaginal flatulence.

cboobies *n.* A television channel that dads watch once their kids have gone to bed.

C-breeze *n.* A gentle gust, fragranced with the scents of the ocean. *Queef, kipper kazoo, crumpet trumpet, Seagoon's last raspberry, fishmitten's bark.*

c-commerce *1. n.* Modern buzzword descriptive of companies "engaging with consumers" *via* messaging apps and other such bollocks. *2. n. Good time girls'* core speciality. Also *fanny farming, knocking shopwork.*

C-cut *1. n.* Curve cut; a trendy hairstyle with the bottom of the hair describing an elegant arc like the letter 'C', making the hair appear longer than it is. Not dissimilar to Jennifer Aniston's 'Rachel cut', it says here. *2. n.* High-maintenance *twat thatch.*

ceci n'est pas une pipe *phr. Fr.* A classy, Magritte-inspired way to let a lady know she's *put a rocket in your pocket. 'Ceci n'est pas une pipe, ma cherie.' 'Anyway, as I was saying, about the flower arrangements in the nave, vicar...'*

cedar burp *n.* A small outbreak of *chocolate thunder.*

celeberating *n.* The practice, typically espoused by the denizens of the gutter press, of featuring so-called celebrities in their pages in order to attack and generally humiliate them. Famous people who have been widely and unfairly *celeberated* include *pointy-titted* scrawnbag Madonna and *baldy-quimmed* mentalist Britney Spears.

celebrate too early *1. v.* Of a sportsperson, to whoop it up prematurely, that is to say before the ball crosses the line, reaches the boundary, makes its way over the net *etc. 2. v.* To be *up and over like a pan of milk.* See also *let the passengers off the bus before the stop. 'Sorry Monica. I think I might have celebrated a bit too early there. That'll just sponge off.'*

celery rinser *euph.* A chap who *sews his own buttons, bakes a light cake, lijkes to let his bagged salad breathe* and is *first on the dancefloor.*

cellulike *n.* A *chubby chaser.*

Celtic reminder *n.* When enjoying an illegal Sky Sports broadcast, the discombobulating moment when the advert shows Dominos Pizza prices in euros and you realise that you're watching an Irish stream.

cementimetre *n.* Approximate unit of measurement between any two adjacent bricks.

cement the relationship *v.* To *tip your filthy concrete* up a lady's *crevice. 'Kate caught William's eye at a St. Andrews student fashion show, but the young Prince didn't cement the relationship until several weeks later, behind a skip outside the university Geography Department.'*

cemetery gates *n.* An old lady's *muff minders. Granny's oysters, world of leather, opera curtains.*

Cemetery Junction *1. n.* A lacklustre film starring screeching autocachinnator Ricky Gervais. *2. n.* The lacklustre area of scrub between a woman's *front bottom* and *back bottom.* The *taint, tinter, twernt, blue zone etc.*

censorsnip *n.* Any pixelation or other digital spoiling tactic used to ruin an otherwise tasteful picture of a lady's *fun bags* in a low quality/price newspaper or magazine. *'The Daily Mail operates a strict censorsnip policy on all the photographs of scantily-clad barely legal teenagers flaunting themselves on private property that it snaps using extremely powerful telephoto lenses.'*

central reservation *1. n.* Area separating opposing lanes of traffic on a divided carriageway. *2. n.* The sparsely vegetated, somewhat weed-strewn region betwixt the missus's *arse* and her *fanny.*

centre console *1. n.* On an aeroplane, the control panel situated between the pilot's and the co-pilot's seats. *2. n.* How airline personnel refer to the *butfer, gooch, barse etc.,* from the punchline to a joke which is popular amongst trolley dollies, *viz.* "What do you call the bit between the cunt and the arsehole? The centre console." *'When his plane the Spirit of St. Louis landed at Le Bourget Field at the end of his epoch-making trans-Atlantic solo flight, Lindbergh had been tightly strapped into his cramped, pressed-steel pilot's seat in the unheated cockpit of the Ryan monoplane for more than thirty-three hours. He later recalled that it was not until two days later that he finally regained some feeling in his centre console.'*

centre parting *n.* Highly enjoyable form of solo *balloon knot* sport whereby the practitioner sits on a sturdy, solid chair or bench and then forcibly breaks wind while leaning forward at an angle of forty-five degrees, thus causing the emitted *trouser cough* to shoot straight up the middle of his or her back, like a sort of gaseous Evel Kneivel going up a ramp. HRH the Duchess of York is said to be an enthusiastic *centre parter* and, during Christmas dinners at Balmoral often demonstrates her skills by knocking a paper crown off the top of her own head.

cereal material *n.* Any ale at or below 4% ABV, that is to say a *breakfast beer* fit only for one's cornflakes.

Cerutti beauty *n.* A lady who appears to be 18 but

who, when viewed from the front, looks at least 81. From the eponymous manufacturer's mens' fragrance "1881". Similar to a *Kronenberg, boyner, George Orwell* or *nana Kournikova.*

cervix charge *n.* The hidden costs incurred when *getting one's leg over, eg.* Flowers, meal, taxi home, changing locks *etc.*

cesar geezer *n.* A gent who cultivates a close relationship with his pet hound, by the simple expedient of smearing the eponymous dog food upon his *bone* and inviting said canine to partake. *'Born on this day in history: George Washington, wooden-toothed first president of the United States, 1732; Heinrich Rudolf Hertz, German physicist and car hire entrepreneur, 1857; Eric Gill, British sculptor, typographer, wood engraver, and cesar geezer, 1882.'*

CF Bundy *abbrev. medic.* Doctors' shorthand written on the charts of terminally ill patients. Completely Fucked But Not Dead Yet.

CFCs *1. n.* Chlorofluorocarbons; the greenhouse gases in aerosols and fridges which used to damage the environment. *2. n.* Huge 4-wheel-drive vehicles required by people in Chelsea and Wilmslow when shopping and collecting the kids from school. Cars For Cunts.

CFN *abbrev.* A *ringpiece* which flies in the face of the Kyoto agreement and burns at tremendous temperatures, belching out toxic fumes and clouds of particulates which are harmful to the ozone layer and one's underpants. A *heavy smoker,* an *arse* with a huge *carbon dibaxide* footprint. Coal Fired Nipsy.

CGI *1. abbrev.* The City and Guilds Institute. *2. abbrev.* Cunt Gap Index. A measurement on a scale of finger widths of the size of a woman's *Toblerone tunnel.*

chag *n.* A *chav* who is also a *slag.* Someone who would probably *do it* with anyone in return for a swig of Frosty Jack or a shot on an e-cigarette.

chagrin *n.* Slightly embarrassed post-*coital* smirk.

chain reaction *n.* Upon rising from the *chod bin* and prior to flushing, the involuntary act of retching and/or, *in extremis,* the *blowing* of one's *chunks* as a result of the aromatic miasma of one's own foetid *digestive transits.*

chair envy *n.* Being jealous of a piece of furniture when an attractive woman is sat on it.

chairslider *n.* A man so dishy that he effectively reduces a bird's coefficient of friction. *'Did you see the new guy in Accounts?! He's a complete chairslider.'*

Chalfonts *rhym. slang.* Piles, *bum grapes.* From the town of Chalfont St.

Gemerrhoids, Buckinghamshire.

Chalfont Thunderer *1. n.* The sort of fictional steam train that might hurtle through a picturesque station run by Will Hay in *Oh Mr Porter,* while Graham Moffatt blows a whistle and Moore Marriott waves a little flag. *2. n.* A first class early morning *d'Oyly Carte* that chugs out of the *nipsy,* rattles the pots on the shelf and vibrates a fellow's *arse grapes.*

challenge oneself *v.* To engage in a spot of *five against one.* To *knock yourself about a bit.*

chamber of commerce *n.* Any orifice which is leased to the public for financial gain.

champagga *n.* A fight fuelled by expensive beverages, as opposed to Special Brew. A brawl one may see once in a blue moon outside a brasserie.

Champagne cork *1. n.* That last solid *nipsy* stopper that pops out forcefully after a night on the beer, to be followed by a frothy explosion. The *pace car, doorman* or *gatekeeper.* *2. n.* Bullet-hard *nipple* that pops out of the *tit pants* with enough force to take your eye out. *An organ stop, JCB starter button* or *chapel hat peg.*

champagne shit *n.* A sit-down toilet visit where one strains for some time to *pop a cork,* but once it goes it is followed by a magnum of fizzy brown liquid. A *champoo.* See also *Willy Wonka's river.*

champion bullwanker *n.* A woman with large arms, typically either a school dinner lady or Russian shotputter.

Champion the wonder log *n.* An heroic, thoroughbred *feeshus* that leaves its begetter walking like they've just ridden Red Rum up and down Southport sands for an hour.

Champney shit *n.* An epic evacuation session that erupts with bubbles, like a spa. Lovely image.

Chancellor of the Exchequer will now read a short statement, the *exclam.* Declared as a jocular means of announcing imminent flatulence. Also *please welcome to the stage Nickleback/Peter Kay/ Skrillex; live from Norwich.*

chancellor's briefcase *n.* A particularly dry, red, leathery, weathered *clopper* that only gets opened one or twice a year.

Chanel No.2 *euph.* The distinctive, delicate perfume of the alimentary canal. Hopefully not sniffed off your wrist. *Oh de toilette.*

change ammo *v. milit.* To empty one chamber of the *mutton musket,* thus readying the *firing piece* for the next shot. To take a last minute *gypsy's kiss* prior to a *bang.*

change at Baker Street *v.* During intercourse, to decide to *play the B-side.* From the only station on the London Underground where it is possible to change from the Pink line (Hammersmith & City) to the Brown line (Bakerloo).

change at Edgware Road *euph.* When engaging in the *act of concubinage* with a *salad dodger*, a transfer from the *pink* to the *brown* line which, rather than being a very quick adjustment (as in a *change at Baker Street*), in fact requires one to come out to the surface, re-orientate one's position, and then re-descend.

change at Oxford Circus *v.* Similar usage to *change at Baker Street*, but for *monthly* ticket holders. *Going from red to brown.*

change lanes *v.* To switch, mid-romp, from vaginal to anal penetration or vice versa. *'When on the job, it is good practice to signal one's intentions before changing lanes so as not to take anyone by surprise.'* (from *The Joy of Sex for Learner Drivers* by Dr Alex Comfort).

changer a Châtelet *v. Fr.* To *change at Baker Street* with a French *oiseau*. Named after the Paris Metro station situated in the 1st Arrondissement where one can change from the *rose* line (7) to the *brun* (11). That might be the last underground railway line-based definition. Fingers crossed anyway.

change rain *n.* The shower of coins which falls from the trouser pockets when a gentleman is attempting to undress quietly and not wake his slumbering wife.

change your ringtone *v.* To get one's *wazoo* bleached.

changing of the guard *1. n.* A stirring show of manual ambidexterity when one hand has been overused. *2. n. Women's thing* replacement, a ceremony occurring shortly after *trooping the colour.*

changing one's ringtone *n.* Anal bleaching.

changing the washer *n.* Remedial action required to address the issue of post-curry *ring* leakage. In the event of the *balloon knot* failing to keep one's *rusty water* sufficiently at bay, furtive trips to the water closet are required to make good the faulty orifice using an index finger swathed in toilet tissue. *'During an Atlantic crossing on a glamorous ocean liner, incognito ballet star Peter Peters (Fred Astaire) falls for showgirl Linda Keene (Ginger Rogers), but their burgeoning romance is hampered when Peter inadvertently eats an Eccles Cake that is six weeks past its best before, and keeps having to slip away to change the washer in the midst of romantic trysts on deck, leading Linda to believe he has a secret girlfriend who he's meeting in the bogs.'* (synopsis of *Shall We Dance*, 1937).

Chan it *v.* To take unnecessary risks in mundane situations while under the delusion that if shortarsed martial arts hero Jackie can do it, then so can you. Examples include running between two buses, escaping an attacker on your bicycle and fending off an assailant with an umbrella. *'Yeah, he Channed it. alright. You should have seen him go.' 'Is that why he's in a neck brace and he's eating through a tube?' 'Oh yes.'*

channy *n.* The lower mandibular adornment sported by many a modern male who cannot be *arsed* to shave. From chin + fanny.

chanson *n.* Any tacky trinket purchased at a fleamarket on *Bargain Hunt* or ornament adorning an elderly *gimmer*'s mantelpiece or sideboard. From the Manhattan Transfer song, which seemed to be performed on *The Two Ronnies* every week for about fifteen years, whose lyrics went; "Chanson d'amour / Tat! Tat! Tat! Tat! Tat!"

chanus *n. medic.* Technical term describing that deep dimple some people – such as Kirk Douglas, John Travolta and Robert Mitchum – have in their chins. We just looked it up and it's called the "mental cleft" apparently. From chin + anus.

chap *1. n.* The *Charlie. 2. v.* To gently slap your *old fella* in the face of a sleeping wife, friend or party guest, take a photograph and leave it in a place where they are bound to come across it, *eg.* On a fridge door, car windscreen, the world wide web.

chapel hat pegs *sim.* Large, erect *nips. Pygmy's cocks, Scammell wheel nuts, fighter pilot's thumbs*.

chapel of rest *n.* The snug bar of the Northumberland Hussar pub on Sackville Road, Heaton, Newcastle upon Tyne.

chapioca *n. Merry monk.* *'Everyone in the kitchen and all the other guests and several passers-by were very sorry to hear about your colleague Mr Winner's recent demise, Mr Coren. Here is your chapioca pudding.'*

chapkin *n.* A protective cloth placed over a fellow's stomach and chest in order to soak up any salty spillages which may accidentally occur for any reason while he is lying on his back.

chappatio *n.* The flattish remains of a very good night out on a section of path outside the front of the house, *ie.* An Indian-themed *pavement pizza*.

chap rag *n.* A baby-wipe used to clean the *balls*.

chap's eye *n.* A politically correct alternative to a certain other outdated and offensive term, which can be used to describe the male urethral opening when in polite company.

chapstick *n.* An implement with which a lady moistens her dry lips.

chapstick on the lips, I need a bit of *exclam.* What a keen *gobbler* might mutter during a long, cold, barren winter.

character actress *euph.* A kind way to describe a lass who, if she were a thesp, with the best will in the world would likely rarely be cast as the romantic lead in a movie. A right *minger.*

charcoal chimney *1. n.* A device used to light a barbecue. *2. n.* The *arsehole.* Which may also, in extreme circumstances, be used to light a barbecue.

charge of the light ale brigade *n.* The stampede of builders, roofers and scaffolders to the pub at 2pm on a Friday. Or any other day that a drop of rain has fallen. Or it looks like it might rain later. Somewhere in the British Isles.

charge sheet, the *n.* In a marriage, the seemingly endless list of misdemeanours committed by the husband.

charge the Rolex *euph.* To *knock yourself about a bit.* From the rapid wristular oscillations that are required to wind the kinetic mainspring of an exclusive Swiss timepiece. Also *wind your watch, charging the watch battery.*

charge the skin dynamo *n.* To *pull oneself off.* *'What are you doing in there, Damien?' 'Just charging my skin dynamo, Prime Minister.'*

charging the brush *n.* The act of sneakily dampening the finger just south of a lady's *devil's doorbell.*

charging the watch battery *euph.* Having *one off the wrist.* See *charge the Rolex.* *'I was watching Countdown and I just had this irresistable urge to charge my watch battery. That Nick Hewer's gorgeous.'*

charioteer, the *n.* Self explanatory sexual position involving a woman with long hair who's down on all fours, and a man with very short legs pretending to be Charlton Heston. A *ben her.* Also *attempting to enter the gates of Rome.*

chariots of ire *n.* Pestiferous mobility scooters that creep up silently around your heels on the high street or when you are ensconced deep in the convoluted floorspace of a pound shop.

charity work *n.* The altruistic act of buying a drink for – or flirting with – an aesthetically challenged woman out of pity. *'Where are you off to?' 'I'm just going to go on the dance floor to do a bit of charity work with fat Lisa from accounts.'*

Charles's pen *n.* A cock that *goes off* too quick and makes a mess.

Charley, go all *v.* To begin talking unintelligible, garbled *shite* after downing ten pints of *wifebeater,* like the cheaply-animated cartoon cat in the 1970s public information films.

Charlie *1. rhym. slang.* Cunt. From "Charlie Hunt".

'You look a right charlie'. 2. n. Showbiz sherbet. 3. n. Hampton Wick, the penis.

Charlie and the chocolate factory *1. n.* A well known children's book by Roald Dahl. *2. euph.* Sex up the *cocoa channel.* *'Oh, Go on, June. It's my birthday tomorrow. How about showing Charlie round the chocolate factory?' 'But I've already got you some new golfing gloves, Terry.'*

Charlie Cairoli's hat *n.* A lady's *minge,* brimful of *spoff.* From the erstwhile clown's perpetually blancmange-filled bowler.

Charlie Dimmock's nipples *n.* Term used by vicars to describe the hat-pegs in their chapels.

Charlie foxtrot *1. exclam. milit.* In the radio operators' phonetic alphabet, an abbreviation for an unfortunate sequence of events, *viz.* "CF" – a *clusterfuck. 2. n.* The ludicrous nightclub dancefloor gyrations of a children's television presenter who is under the influence of a *conkful* of *bacon powder.*

Charlie in the chocolate factory *n. Bolivian marching powder* snorted in a public *shithouse eg.* The *crappers* at the Groucho Club.

Charlie potatoes *n.* One who labours under the misapprehension that he all that when he ain't. Someone who thinks he's the *bollocks.* *'Look at that cunt swaggering about like he's Charlie Potatoes.'*

Charlies *n.* 1970s *assets.*

Charlies' angels *1. n.* See *tit fairies. 2. n.* Women who appear attractive to a man as a consequence of him having taken a *toot* of *Keith Richards' dandruff* on board. A Class-A variation on the term *five pinter.*

Charlie sheen *n.* The characteristic glow and sweaty forehead that a children's television presenter gets after enjoying a quick sniff of *Bacon powder.*

Charlie 3 *n.* A *chuftie plug,* named in honour of our newly appointed monarch's previously stated desire to be Camilla's *dangermouse.* He did say, though, that it would be "(his) luck to be chucked down a lavatory and go on and on forever swirling round on the top, never going down" presumably due to the size of his ears.

Charlie two-dinners *n.* A gentleman whose glands eschew salads in favour of pies, sausages and more pies. A *double sucker.*

charlimingus *n.* Technical term for *double bassing.*

Charlton Heston *n. prop.* Nickname given to an inveterate *self harmer.* One whose cold dead hands have to be peeled from around his *fouling piece.*

charms *n.* In British tabloid journalism, a coy way of referring to the breasts. Usually prefixed "ample". *'Lovely Lisa, 21, who hails from Hyde in*

Cheshire, loves detective stories, but it would be a criminal waste to "hide" away her ample charms! Not to mention her pink nipples and the areolae which radially delineate the extent of the lactiferous ducts in her mammary tissue.'

charm the snake *1. v.* To perform a public entertainment act whereby a king cobra is encouraged to rise and dance mesmerically before eventually spitting its venom. *2. v.* To perform a personal entertainment act whereby a *membrum virile* is encouraged to rise and dance mesmerically before eventually spitting its venom.

charva *n. Charver, chav.* A *scratter, pog* or *ned.*

charva cava *n.* Substandard *trampagne.* White cider.

chasbo *n.* A *burberry ape, scratter* etc. The proud owner of a legal document awarded for bad conduct and anti-social behaviour. And five As at A-level, these days.

chaser *n.* Shortly after having *carnival knowledge* of a lady, a fellow's self-*pulled hand shandy* in the shower to thoroughly void his *clockweights.*

chase the cotton mouse *v.* To have the *painters in, flags out, surf the crimson wave,* be *up on blocks.*

chase the dragon *1. v.* To "snort" a syringe full of marijuana cigarettes up your bottom through a burnt spoon. *2. n.* To attempt to get a good whiff of one's own *dropped back* in an attempt to acheive the ultimate high.

chasing a clearance *n.* The act of *raking out the cage* in a single sitting while playing a snooker-based game on a smartphone.

Chas'n'Dave, do a *euph.* Of a saucy strumpet, to "get her knees up".

chastity patch *n.* A small smear of excrement surreptitiously wiped on the back of one's girlfriend's neck before she goes on a lasses' night out, the aim of which is to deter any would-be suitors.

Chatham crow *n.* The classy corvoid *tartoos* that ladies of the eponymous historic Kent municipality typically sport on their lower backs just above their *arse cracks. Chatham crows* are usually displayed to best advantage by a pair of jeans or sweatpants that are three sizes too small. *Arse antlers.*

Chatham pocket *n.* A prisoner's rectum, where contraband goods, such as Class A drugs, lighters, tobacco and mobile telephones may be stashed.

chat noir *1. n.* A popular early 20th Century French art nouveau poster design by Theophile Steinlen, like what they used to sell at Athena before they went *tits up. 2. n.* Sinister black deposit in the *khazi* following a night on the stout.

chatting with Moses *euph.* Women's downstairs unpleasantness, *eg.* Thrush or whatever. A reference to Moses and his "burning bush" from *Exodus 3:1.*

chat with the chef *euph.* Excuse used by a diner when returning to a restaurant table following a prolonged and unexplained absence. *'Where have you been, Jay? You were gone half an hour there and you look half a stone lighter.' 'Sorry. I've just been for a chat with the chef.'*

chauffeur's glove *n.* A tight-fitting *flunkey.* Possibly with three buttons on the back.

chav *n.* A member of the lower orders. The sort of person who, all things considered, would have been unlikely to turn up on *Ask the Family* in the 1970s. *Also charver, charva,* and any other spellings you can think of.

chavalanche *n.* A terrifying Burberry-clad cascade of *scratters.*

chavalcade *1. n.* A town centre procession of souped-out, clapped-up Astras, Corsas and XR3is driven by a motley assortment of be-tracksuited *ratboys. 2. n.* A pram-pushing convoy of the above on their way to Greggs.

chavalry *1. n.* Mobile units of these halfwit youths on toddlers' BMX bicycles you get on the pavements these days, easily recognised by their uniform of shellsuit trousers, hoopy pullovers, leather gloves and peaked caps.

chavarium *n.* A public house filled with members of the urban underclasses drinking away their economic woes. A hostelry where one would be unlikely to bump into Lucy Worsley, Jacob Rees-Mogg, Simon Sebag Montefiore or Princess Michael of Kent.

chavatar *n.* A cyberspace representation of an autochthon of the lower social strata. *'Aw bloody hell, some fucking chavatar's nicked me quest point cape.'*

chavelin *1. n.* A housebrick, broken bottle or *shitty* stick *etc.*, launched airwards athletically by a playful youth *2. n.* Semi-olympian sport played by the denizens of the urban underclass. Darts.

chavelodge *n.* Budget accommodation for young folk vacationing at his majesty's pleasure.

chavenue *n.* A boulevard favoured by promenading *scruburbanites.* From charming + avenue.

chaviar *n.* Supermarket own-brand baked beans.

chaviot of fire *n.* A burnt out Clio, Astra or Citroen AX on a rough estate. A *fourth party insurance* write-off.

chavity *n.* Altruistic donations solicited by *asbopolitan* burghers for drink, drugs *etc. 'Hey mate, have you got fifty pence for chavity? I'm desperate for a cup of tea. And a fix.'*

chav-nav *n.* Ankle-mounted hi-tech electronic device which ensures that young scallywags can find their way home before 8pm each evening. Also *Romford Rolex*.

chavoy, the *1. n.* A guesthouse that is the holiday destination of choice for the budget conscious traveller, *eg.* The Airport Britannia Hotel, Manchester. 2. *n.* An elite food establishment, *eg.* Spudulike, Greggs Moments, the Fat Duck.

chavrons *n.* The trendy, angular shapes cut into the Action Man-style hair on a young ASBO laureate's head.

chav-tank *n.* Spa.

CHBB *abbrev. medic.* Debilitating condition akin to *arseritis* or *exhaustipation*. Can Hardly Be Bothered. *'Come on, we're due at my mother's for the church group sobriety lunch, and you know how much she looks forward to it.' 'Sorry love, I don't think I can manage a trip out today. The old CHBB is flaring up again.'*

cheapies *n.* Adolescent sexual thrills. *'Miss Pollard bent down to pick up the chalk and gave William his cheapies.'* (from *William Stirs Below* by Richmal Crompton).

cheating nipsy *euph. medic.* Haemorrhoids. *'Darling, I'm just taking the dog for a walk. Do you fancy coming along?' 'Sorry, I can't, darling. My nipsy's cheating on me.' 'How can you be sure?' 'I found lipstick on my gusset.'*

chebs *n.* Tits, norks, headlamps. Breasts.

check *n.* On a person with a *lovely personality*, where the chin is indistinguishable from the neck. From *chiropodist* + *poopdeck*.

checking for seatbelts *euph.* Police motorway patrol officers' excuse for ogling women in passing cars.

checking for stowaways *euph. naut.* The act of rummaging in the *grundies* following a suspected *follow-through*, rather in the same manner as sea-faring folk make sure there are no non-paying passengers lurking below deck. *'For fuck's sake, William! Get your mitts out of your strides. The ambassador will be here in a minute!' 'Sorry Kate. That last one felt a bit lumpy so I'm just checking for stowaways.'*

checking in at the Furchester *1. n.* Reference to a CBBC show about Muppets that run a hotel. Us neither. 2. *euph.* Pleasuring a woman *orally*. *'Will you be joining us down the pub later, Dave?' 'Sorry lads. The girlfriend's coming round, so I'll be checking in at the Furchester instead.'*

checking the lottery *euph.* The number one reason that subscribers give to their Internet Service Provider when requesting that "premium" services are unlocked. *'I got so excited while I was checking the lottery that I spunked up all over*

my laptop.'

checkmate *n.* The abrupt ending of a *wank* due to one's laptop battery running out of juice at a critical moment.

check one's emails *v.* To search for *grumble* on the interweb, for the purpose of fuelling a sordid and shameful act of *self harm*. *'Hurry up there, son. I want to check my emails. Into a sock.' 'Alright dad. Can I just finish off my homework first, though? Into a sock.'*

check on the kittens *v.* To pop back home to *fire the six o'clock gun* before a night out with the lads. *'Coming for a pint after work?' 'Okay, but I've just got to go home and check on the kittens first.'*

check on the scones *v.* To *turn one's bike around*, have a *Chinese singing lesson, strain the potatoes, see a man about a dog.* To relieve oneself, *have a slash.*

checkout time *n.* The period that elapses while the heady aroma of an *air biscuit* percolates its way out through the layers of one's clothing.

checkout trauma *n.* while carrying out a *Bolton diptest* on a new ladyfriend, finding an *unexpected item in the bagging area.* An unsettling experience typically suffered by western males while sojourning in far-eastern fleshpots, when they accidentally *cop off* with *flippers.*

check the house for moles *euph.* When in company, to vanish for an extended period of time in order to rid the premises of burrowing brown creatures. *'You haven't seen the Autotrader or my glasses anywhere, have you? I'm just off to check the house for moles.'*

check the oil *v.* To pop your *cock* in some *bird's dirtbox* before pulling it out, inspecting, it and wiping it with a cloth.

check the roast *v.* To see whether what you've been *baking* in *the devil's kitchen* is ready to come out. To go for a *shit.*

Cheddar apple *n.* A very large, savoury *bell end.*

Cheddar gorge *n.* A malodourous, *cheesy twotsit.* A curdled *cream pie.*

Cheddar ledge *n.* The ripe *brim* of the *farmer's hat.* The *cheese ridge, wank stop* or sulcus.

cheek flapper *n.* A *cedar burp* which registers highly on the *beaufart scale.* A *clapper rattler,* a *drive on the cats' eyes.*

cheeky caravan club *n.* That happy, permanently vacationing section of society who supply pegs and tarmac.

cheeky hando's *euph.* A quick and spontaneous *five-knuckle shuffle.*

cheerful Charlie *n. rhym. slang.* Sausage fat. From the dour-faced *Minder* detective played on screen by Patrick Malahide, *viz.* DS Cheerful Charlie Chisholm = jism.

cheese and wine gathering *1. n.* A discreet business meeting. *2. n.* An enormous bring-your-own-bottle *piss-up* during which the kids' swing gets *fucked.*

cheese board *n.* In a public convenience, the inside front rim of the toilet bowl against which your *Wilfred* brushes while you perch uncomfortably atop the lavatory seat.

Cheeseboard Charlie *n.* Amusing pejorative term used to describe an individual who is excessively accustomed to big restaurant sessions. *'Oi, Cheeseboard Charlie, shut your fucking pie hole. Let Shirley Maclaine get a fucking word in edgeways will you, you fat twat.'* (Michael Parkinson interviewing Peter Ustinov, BBC TV, 1978).

cheese chowder *n.* Soupy evidence of romantic carryings-on between a *gentleman of the road* and a saucy baglady. Commonly left on the floor in bus shelters, on the arm rests of park benches *etc.*

cheese cracker *n.* A pungently savoury *custard tart.* An air *snack* rather than a *buffet.*

cheese cutter *1. n.* A wiry tangle of matted *arse cress* that adds immeasurably to the trials and tribulations of a *digestive transit.* A *log splitter. 2. n. medic.* A rogue *pube* caught in the *fiveskin* while still attached to the body. Results in two-fold agony; simultaneously cutting into *Captain Picard's head* while trying to tear itself out at the root. Also known as *Bobby Charltons, Old MacDonald's combovers, Robert Robinsons, Desmond Morrises.*

cheese drawer *1. n.* A pungent receptacle in one's fridge where diseases spawn. *2. n.* A *bird*'s undercrackers after she's had a bloody good *seeing to.*

cheese fog *n.* The pervading noisomely foetid atmosphere found in a *self-polluting* teenager's room on a particularly rampant *twelve wank Wednesday.* *'Fetch the Febreze up, mother. There's such a thick cheese fog in here I can't see my hand in front of my face.'*

cheesegrater special *n.* An aggressive *wank* carried out using nails. *'At noon home to dinner, where my wife still in a melancholy fusty humour, and crying; and doth not tell me plainly what it is, but I by little words find that she hath heard of my going to plays and carrying on with darling Deb every day in her absence; and that I cannot help. After supper, we retired to bed where I felt decidedly amorous and got the mummy's arm. However, my wife's cantankerous humour was decidedly not improved at all and although I did kiss her and touch her thing she was against it and laboured with much earnestness, and yet at last I did beseech her to take me in her hand but the rotten cow gave me a cheesegrater special.'* (from *The Diary of Samuel Pepys*, March 18th 1668).

cheese Gromit, cheese! *exclam.* Humorous and excited exclamation at the discovery of a build-up of *helmetdale* or *organzola* underneath the *fiveskin.*

cheesemaker *1. n.* A fromagier, *eg.* The Aldi Happy Farmer, Dairylea, Alex James out of Blur. *2. n.* A fellow who hasn't washed his *John Thomas* for a fortnight. (A chap who doesn't bathe for three weeks is a *French cheesemaker.* And if it's four weeks-plus, he's known as *the full Stilton with a crust, eg.* Alex James out of Blur.)

cheese map *n.* Protein-based staining often to be found on the front of a young man's lower nightwear. *'Mums know that new Azox 2-in-1 will remove 99% of all household stains even on the cold water cycle. Dried-on food on the baby's bib, grass and mud on Janet's hockey skirt, oil and grease on dad's overalls or cheese maps on the vicar's pyjama bottoms… none of them can stand up to Azox's magic new non-bio formula.'*

cheesepipe *n.* The tubular organ that secretes spreadable *willydelphia.*

cheesepipe clingfilm *n.* A condom or *child catcher.*

cheese ridge *n.* That fertile area of the *wankstop* where *dream topping* is matured for weeks and months. The *brim* of the *lid.* A fellow's *sulcus.*

cheese wagon *n.* The phenomenon of a huge *ballsack* and a tiny penis. Also *button mushroom sitting on a spacehopper, spacehoppers and seafood.*

cheese whistle *n.* The marvellous musical instrument kept in a fellow's tweeds. The *pink oboe* or *bed flute. Toot meat.*

cheese wrapper *n. rhym. slang.* How a Cockney would refer to a proper *hosebag, hingoot* or enthusiastic *sausage grappler.* From cheese wrapper = slapper.

cheesy moments *1. n.* A discontinued bar-snack alternative to Mini Cheddars. Interestingly, a change.org petition begging Walkers to bring them back has been running for four years and currently stands at nearly 5000 signatures, so they are clearly much-missed. *2. n. Noshing off* a poorly maintained *elephant gun.*

cheesy wheelbarrow *n.* A self-explanatory sexual position adopted by two breathless *uphill gardeners* during sports day.

cheesy wotsit *1. n.* A pungent mouthful that leaves the fingers unpleasantly stained. *2. n.* A sort of cross between a fat crisp and the residue from an indoor firework.

cheetabix *n.* Any cheaper, supermarket-own-brand ersatz variety of the real thing.

cheeto *n.* Descriptive of the withered, Judith

Chalmers-hued state of a *self-employed* fellow's *privates* following an apathetic act of *self flagellation* essayed while listlessly eating a family-sized bag of Wotsits or similar. As they do.

cheezer *n.* That which is a cross between a *chick* and a *geezer*, *eg.* Sir Richard Branson.

chef d'emission *n. Fr.* Any disgruntled employee in a catering establishment who takes the opportunity to add his own *secret ingredient* to, picking an example entirely at random, *Times* restaurant critic Giles Coren's dinner. A *masturchef.*

chef's arse *n.* An uncomfortable, perspiring, smelly *bum cleft*. From the condition's prevalence amongst busy catering professionals, *eg.* Gordon Ramsay, Anthony Worrall-Thompson and Nigella Lawson.

chef's special sauce *n. Spunk.* 'Here is your steak, Mr Morgan. And chef wanted you to know that he enjoyed your interview with the president so much, he's put you an extra helping of his special sauce on there.'

chelm *v.* To rub one's cheesy *herman gelmet* on the rim of a drinking vessel or bottle for the purpose of adding a *soupçon* of extra piquancy for the unwitting imbiber. 'I wouldn't touch that, Holly if I was you. Gino chelmed it while you were chopping the onions.'

Chelmsley Wood foreplay *n.* Any form of domestic violence or spousal abuse. Named after the Chelmsley Wood area of Solihull, West Midlands, which is known to be somewhat rough.

Chelmsley Wood lie detector *n.* A West Midlands Police Force truncheon.

Chelmsley Wood pill *n. Anal sex.* Also *UTBNB*, one up the bum, no harm done. A *Colchester condom* or *dodgy corner.*

Chelsea physio *n.* A right *hottie* who turns up in a place where you'd never expect it, such as a *Star Wars* convention, the opening ceremony at a tram museum or a railway memorabilia auction in Sheffield. Possibly a reference to the rather fetching ex-wielder of the magic sponge at Stamford Bridge, Dr Eva Carneiro rather than the current incumbent, Stuart Vaughan.

Cheltenham smile *n.* The most miserable face imaginable; the typical mien of the eponymous Cotswold town's woebegone *flaneurs.*

Chelyabinsk Oblast *n.* A huge flash and bang that shatters windows and panics citizens over a wide area.

chemi-khazi *n.* What one commits when entering a portable lavatory cubicle at a music festival. *Pooicide.*

cheps *n. Chebs.*

cheques, chavellers' *n.* Giros.

Cherie Blair's cake hole *n.* A strangely convoluted and, frankly, frightening *snapper.* A wide mouth conducive to group *horatio*. A *Carly Simon*, a *three-dick gob, Wallace.*

Cherie's smile *n.* Scary-lipped part of the anatomy of a lady who's been around a bit, for example one of those *not-particularly good time girls* commonly to be seen disporting themselves in windows near the Holiday Inn, Nuremberg.

cherknobyl *n.* A *love-length* that accidentally blows up with little or no warning.

Chernobyl *euph.* The situation that obtains when cleaning up your *nipsy* takes significantly longer than the split-second explosion that originally necessitated such a course of action.

cherries *n.* The hanging male testicles, which resemble nothing so much as a pair of fruits on a fruit machine. The *plums.*

cherry *1. n.* An intact *virgin string.* A *Bill Wyman* that has not been *popped.* *2. n.* One's virginity generally.

cherry boy *n.* A crimson, hormone-filled adolescent male with an intact *virgin string*, on whom a dampened finger will sizzle.

cherry on! *phr. Yorks.* Shouted at someone who looks embarrassed in order to put them at their ease, accompanied by mimed licking of the fingers, dabbing and hissing.

cherubimical *adj. Wankered*; an expression noted by Enlightenment polymath Benjamin Franklin in a treatise of 1737. 'Leave him, Mifflin. He's cherubimical as a fucking newt.'

chess champion *n.* A socially maladroit person who is so gifted and special that they are still, at the age of thirty-seven, living at home and allowing their mum to choose their wardrobe, thus killing any hope they may have once harboured of ever *popping their cherry.*

chest dogs *n.* Fully grown *shirt puppies.*

Chesterfield necklace *n.* A double chin. Also *meat scarf, pelican's beak.*

chest freezer *n.* A sports bra.

chest furniture *n. Tits, hooters, headlamps.*

chesticulating *n.* Jiggling one's *jugs* to summon a barman or waiter without the need for hand signals or words. A technique used most successfully by young, full-*bosomed* ladies and Lord Owen of Plymouth when he's trying to catch the Lord Chancellor's eye in the Upper House.

chestimate *v.* To use your skill and judgement to gauge the size of a lady's *sweatermeat*. Also *n.* A remote assessment of *tit pants* size.

chest measles *n.* Flat *tits*.

chestnuts *n.* *Stits, juglets.*

chest pains *n. medic.* Aching feelings induced by the sight of a *well-qualified* female. *'I was just watching Carol Kirkwood do the weather, doctor, and I suddenly got short of breath and started getting these chest pains.'*

chest pillows *n.* *Chebs* again. Also *dirty pillows, rib cushions.*

chest tuners *n.* The symmetrical dials on a lady's *frontage* that enable a gentleman to find Radio Luxembourg. *Nips.*

Chewbacca after a fight *sim.* Descriptive of an untidy *biffer.*

Chewbacca's belly button *n.* A particularly hirsute *snatch.*

Chewbacca's calling *exclam.* A long, protracted *fart* that brings to mind the strangulated guttural mewings of the famous *Star Wars* dog.

Chewbacca's growl *n.* The involuntary shrieks and groans released when one passes a *bum spud* as wide as a *footballer's tie knot.*

Chewbacca's knackers *sim.* An area of notably unkempt and overgrown *gorilla salad.* *'Bloody hell. I bet that Lorraine Kelly's clout's hairier than Chewbacca's knackers.'*

chewie *n.* An act of *horatio*, a *gobbie*, gobble, *nosh* or *Boris Johnson.*

chewing a Revel *n.* The discomfiting sensation upon finishing an unsatisfactory, or otherwise incomplete, *sit down lavatory adventure.* *'I thought I was all done there, but I'm still chewing a Revel.'*

chewing a toffee *n.* The unpleasant sensation of anal chafing and squelching when walking out of the *bog* following insufficient wiping of the *freckle.*

chewing on a brick *n.* Of *logs* and *logging*, that desperate point when the *turtle's head* – and indeed its *shoulders* – protrude, and the *arse* is left gumming away at a *dirt* like a toothless pensioner finishing off the toffee pennies in a box of Quality Street.

Chicago shuffle *n.* An entirely imaginary sexual act whereby a lady traps a gentleman's *member* under her arm before shuffling a pack of cards. A *Las Vegas bagpipe* or *Monte Carlo musclefuck.*

chichis *n. Mex. Tits, knockers.*

chic-hole *n.* A town oversubscribed with artisan markets, craft fairs, boutique coffee shops and Tudorbethan mansions. *'Today on Bargain Hunt we're in the Kent chic-hole of Sevenoaks.'*

chicken *n.* Young male who *takes his own bags to the supermarket.* A *botter's apprentice.*

chicken breasts *1. n.* A big, fat, alluringly shaved

snatch. *2. n. Blimplants.*

chickenhawk *n.* The time-served *botter*, to whom several *botter's apprentices* are indentured at any one time.

chicken lickin' *n.* A bout of *horatio* performed in the exuberant, strutting style of erstwhile cartoon rooster Foghorn Leghorn. A *throatbanger.*

chicken penny *n.* A small piece of chewy meat that some people are inexplicably prepared to eat. The *arsehole.*

chicken skin handbag *n.* *The scrot, nadbag.*

chicken's napper *n.* The pink, dangly bits of the female *parts of shame.* So-called due to their resemblance to the battery cage-dwelling egg-layers' pink, dangly, useless, *bonce* appendages.

chicken wings *n. medic.* The anatomical spare skin underneath the upper arms of a *Duchess of Giblets,* so called as they resemble the contents of a KFC Zinger burger. *Bingo wings, dinner ladies' arms.*

chicktionary *n.* A fellow's *little black book,* containing the telephone numbers of his past inamoratae. *'Hi Shaz, it's Baz. I hope you don't mind me phoning you up, only I found your number in my chicktionary. Anyway, my missus is in a coma so I was wondering if you fancied meeting up to suck me off some time later this week.'*

child catcher *1. n.* Menacing character in *Chitty Chitty Bang Bang*, played by Robert Helpmann. *2. n.* A *rubber Johnny* or, if you're in luck, a mouth or *Bristol Channel.*

children of the underworld *1. n.* Title of a song by US Death Metal band Deicide, recently covered by Daniel O'Donnell on his album *A Picture of You. 2. n.* Small, brown *Richard the thirds.*

Chilean mineshaft *n.* A dark, narrow, dirty tunnel; the *trap two* version of a *mouse's ear.*

chilistytis *n. medic.* A chance to experience all the fun and games of a serious urinary tract infection by forgetting to wash your hands after preparing a habanero chili and going for a *gypsy's kiss.* Also *jalapenis, Scotch bunnet.*

chill the husband's salad *v.* Of a lady, to position herself such that a cold blast from the air conditioning goes up her frrock, thus keeping her *lettuce* crisp and fresh. The opposite of *warming the husband's supper.*

Chimbonda *n. prop.* A lady with *big-boned pins* wearing leggings that are far too tight. Named after the diminutive, muscly legged, Guadeloupe-born Skelmersdale United right back Pascal Chimbonda, who has a penchant for wearing tights under his shorts. *Two pounds of shit* *in a one pound bag.*

chimera *n.* A monstrous *turd* that – similar to the creature from Greek Mythology that consisted of parts from a host of different animals – comprises a mixture of types from the Bristol stool scale.

chimney sweep *1. n.* A soot-covered man who cleans your chimney and brings good luck. *2. n.* A soot-covered man who dances on the roof after *banging* you up the *dirtbox.*

chimney sweep's brush *n.* Dick Van Dyke's penis.

chimpanzee's elbow *n.* A distressing nipple, surrounded on all sides by thick hair. See also *hunchback spider.*

chimp grooming for ticks, like a *sim.* Reminiscent of a person rummaging through the *gorilla salad* looking for croutons.

chimping *1. n. Spanking the monkey* while grinning from ear to ear. And having a cup of PG Tips. *2. n.* The frankly unlikely (though you wouldn't put it past the Germans) act of *shitting* into your hands and throwing it at your partner, for your mutual pleasure. *'Mature professional gentleman, married, 52, seeks discreet, elegant, educated lady, 35-45, for long walks in the country, fine wine and food, trips to the theatre and sophisticated classical music concerts. Must be into chimping.'*

chimp oneself red *v.* To furiously *relax in a gentleman's way,* to have *one off the flipper.*

CHIMPS/chimps *acronym.* Somewhat ungenerous police station terminology referring to Community Support Officers. Completely Hopeless In Most Policing Situations or Can't Help In Most Police Situations. Also *potted plants, apples. 'Hello, is that the Emergency Services? There's a naked, blood-soaked, axe-wielding lunatic screaming and masturbating in my living room.' 'Unfortunately there are no proper policemen available to help you due to health and safety stroke public liability insurance issues. We're sending a couple of chimps over, but their mum says they've got to be home for their tea no later than six.'*

chimps' fingers *n.* Particularly dry, thin stools, often with distinct knuckles. *'Twenty six days at sea, and the men are wracked with stomach cramps. Regular bowel motions are naught but a memory. I myself have not passed solids for nigh on two weeks, and that was but a couple of chimps' fingers 200 miles SSE of Christmas Island.'* (from *The Journal of Captain Bligh,* 1765).

chin *v.* To successfully belabour an opponent in a bout of fisticuffs. *'I could fucking chin him, easy.'*

chin airbag *n.* A phantom double chin on a non-fatty. Usually associated with *pissed,* impromptu group photographs on a night out, especially common late on during wedding receptions when wearing a collar and tie and leaning slightly backwards. *'Fucking hell! It's a great photo of everybody, but look at me! It looks like my chin airbag has gone off.'*

chinamite *n.* Any illegally imported firework that laughs in the face of the Pyrotechnic Articles (Safety) Regulations 2015, British Standards BS 7114 to 4/7/17 and BS-EN 15947-2015, and exhibits the sort of explosive strength normally reserved for blasting railway tunnels through mountains.

Chinese algebra, harder than *sim.* Descriptive of the magnificent tumescence of a right *diamond cutter. 'You're a lucky lady tonight, love. This bugger's harder than Chinese algebra.'*

Chinese fire drill *n.* A scene of utter disorder and pandemonium. *'Emergency services were today called out to the Dover branch of Netto after staff reduced to price of own brand baked beans to 1p a tin. In the Chinese fire drill that followed, 17 people were trampled to death and another 68 were detained in hospital after suffering crush injuries'.* (BBC News 24, Jan 3rd 2003).

Chinese firework *n.* The *Charlie* of a *one pump chump, ie.* One that *goes off* almost instantaneously.

Chinese gravy *n.* Something with a foul flavour. *'I was dining at the Y the other night and my fish supper tasted worse than Chinese gravy.'*

Chinese helicopter pilot *sim.* A bloke sitting up and operating his *chopper.*

Chinese junk *rhym. slang. Jitler, pineapple.*

Chinese mouse, hung like a *sim.* Opposite of *hung like an Arab stallion.*

Chinese singing lesson *n.* A *gypsy's kiss.* A *piss.*

Chinese tool *n.* A feeble penis, *ie.* One that is barely up to the job in hand.

Chinese wordsearch, hard as a *sim.* A good way to describe a particularly tumescent erecticulation of the *gentleman's parts;* that is to say, when one's *on* is very *hard* indeed. *'I woke up this morning and I was as hard as a Chinese wordsearch, your majesty.'*

chinge *n.* An unsightly beard. From chin + minge. *'It's about time Lewis Hamilton shaved that chinge off.'*

chin hammock *n.* A Covid facemask worn by someone who doesn't understand how breathing works.

chin music, play a little *v.* To give some wiseguy a fourpenny one up the bracket.

chinny merkin *n.* A sexy old lady's wispy beard.

chinny reckon *v.* To evince scepticism.

chin omelette *n.* A concoction of briskly whisked *man-egg-white* served warm onto a lucky recipient's lower mandible. A *cumbeard, St.*

Bernard's chin.

chinook position *n.* Coital congress arrangement often practised behind skips, up back alleys and round by the wheelie bins at the back of the kebab house, wherein the female participant is supported betwixt her partner's *virile member* and a wall. So called because it involves being lifted off the ground by a powerful *chopper.* Also known as a *fork lift truck* or *flying buttress.*

chinook, the *n.* When two gents simultaneously *willycopter* a lady in the face. Named after the dual-rotored vehicle used by the RAF to safely transport Princes William and Harry to stag parties on the Isle of Wight.

chin rest *n. Duffy's bridge.*

chinseed oil *n. Spoff* that escapes from a *sword swallower's* mouth and dribbles down their chin. A common saucy trope of the pornographic oeuvre.

chin splash *n.* Condition caused by trying on a *pearl necklace* in a clumsy manner.

chinstrap *n.* The small piece of skin which holds the *German helmet* safely in place. The *banjo, Tarzan cord* or *guyrope.*

chin tinsel *n. Sloom*-based decorations dangling from the mandibles of a *messy eater.*

chin varnish *n. Perseverance soup, tomato varnish, knacker lacquer.*

chinwag *n.* The side-to-side use of one's lower jaw, preferably with a few days' growth of stubble, in the style of a ruminating *heffer,* to stimulate a lady's *barnyard foliage.*

chip and dip *euph.* Ripping a corner off of the cardboard *shitscrape* tube to wipe your *ringpiece* in the desperate hope of *getting the last bit of salsa out the jar.*

chipnosis *n. psych.* A mesmeric state of mind brought about by a night *on the sauce,* whereby you find yourself in a takeaway restaurant craving food that has been fried in a suspicious brown liquid of dubious origin.

chipolata *n.* A Mexican lady *con los huesos grandes.* A *greedy Gonzales.*

chip pan alley *n.* The sort of high street which only contains fast food outlets interspersed with the occasional tattoo parlour. Not Knutsford, then, probably.

chip pan winkle *n.* A somnolent, heavily *refreshed* fellow whose kitchen catches fire at about 2 am.

chip-panzee *n. Scratter, ned, pog, Kyley.* A bloke who scratches himself under the arms whilst consuming French fries.

chipper *1. n.* A smaller version of a *chopper. 2. n. Scots.* The *snatch* of an enthusiastic and experienced lady, from the cautionary remon-

strance "She'll tak ye in as tatties and spit ye oot as chips".

Chipperfield *n.* A proper leathering you get off a bouncer for no good reason.

chippie's toolbag *n.* Of women's *bodily treasures,* the *labia majorcas.* The *beef curtains, mutton shutters, Deputy Dawg's ears. 'Mary was powerless to resist. Bert the Sweep's eyes burnt into hers like sapphires. His muscular arms enfolded her softly yielding body as she felt herself being swept away by an umbrella of passion. Tenderly, his sooty hands tugged down her silken bloomers to reveal the womanly treasure he had so long longed to behold. "Caw bloimey, missus," he cried in his authentic cockney voice. 'No offence loike, but you've got piss flaps like a chippie's toolbag."* (from *The Edwardian Sweep and the Nanny* by Barbara Cartland).

chippopotamus *n.* A generously proportioned lady who honestly just eats like a mouse but whose glands scoff vast quantities of deep-fried spuds.

chippy lippy *n.* Tell-tale traces of tomato sauce on one's face and clothing after a night on the town. *'Me missus went nuts because she thought I'd been gobbing off with some bird. Turns out it was just chippy lippy.'*

chippy tits *n. medic.* Physical condition cultivated by builders, plumbers and electricians who prefer to eat the packed lunch lovingly prepared by their other half for their *ten o'clocks* before adjourning to the nearest chip shop two hours later for some decent grub.

chips & gravy *euph.* Tickety boo. *'From here on in, treacle, it's all fucking chips & gravy.'* (HRH the Duke of Windsor to his new bride, Mrs Wallis Simpson on the occasion of their marriage, June 3rd 1937).

chip shop back gate, bangs like a *sim.* A rhetorical reference to the performance of an enthusiastic sexual partner. Also *bangs like a belt-fed mortar* or *bangs like a shit-house door in a gale.*

chip shop, taken up the *euph. Done up the wrong 'un.*

chip shovels *n.* The hands of a *big-boned* person.

chips'n'hame *phr. Scots.* The observed state of someone's failure to *score* and their resulting departure from the pub or club. *'Wee Angus has had nae luck the neet.' 'Aye, Hamish. It's chips'n'hame for him.'*

chipster *n.* A rotund, bearded fellow to be seen hanging round the Hoxton branch of Cooplands.

chips that pass in the night *n.* A post-pub takeaway repast that makes its presence felt in one's bed several hours later.

chipwreck *n.* A person who has unaccountably

failed to lose weight despite clearly putting a lot of time and energy into nimbly *dodging salad*. Ironically, *chipwrecks* typically adhere to the government's healthy eating injunction to eat five or more portions of fruit or veg each day, concentrating particularly on regular portions of the vegetable *Solanum tuberosum*.

chirp on *n.* The sort of good-natured, non-threatening erection that Kenneth Connor would have got in *Carry On Cruising* when Liz Fraser bent over to pick up a quoit. Not so much Esma Cannon. A *stiffy* that causes one to slap the back of one's neck and pull one's collar out while rubbing one's right leg up and down one's left calf.

chirpy scouser, as popular as a *sim.* Very unpopular indeed. *'Houston, we have a problem. I just dropped a really bad fart in my spacesuit, and let me tell you it's about as popular as a chirpy scouser. Oh yeah, the oxygen tank's just exploded and all.'* (Commander James A Lovell, transmission to Mission Control from onboard Apollo 13, April 13th 1970).

chisel a gargoyle *v.* To *hammer your nail* into a *ten pinter* in the grounds of a religious establishment such as Salisbury Cathedral, York Minster or St. George's Church, Unsworth, Bury. To pick a location entirely at random.

chizz *n.* The gloopy white gunk found inside packs of fresh chicken pieces that appears not to be poultry-meat-related, but one hopes that it is when all is said and done. From chicken + jizz.

chlorinate the pool *v.* To *spill one's seed* in a public bathing facility.

chlorine cock *1. n. medic.* When visiting the public baths, a stiffening of the male member which is caused by the chemicals in the water. *2. n. medic.* When visiting the public baths, a diminution of the male member "like a frightened turtle" which is caused by the coldness of the water. *Shrinkage, Obi-Wan's cape, a cock like a salted slug.*

choad *n.* A *penis;* specifically one that is wider than it is long. Or, if you prefer, shorter than it is wide. Also *chobe*.

chocnose *v.* A traditional end of party trick whereby a guest drops his trousers and rubs his *arse* on the nose of a comatose friend for the amusement of the other guests. *'August 3rd. Opening night party for Cavalcade at The Savoy. Kit [Hassall], Gerty [Lawrence] and Fanny [Brice] were all in attendance. Ivor [Novello] passed out on the chaise longue after drinking far too much Bolly, and Jimmy [Clitheroe] chocnosed him, poor dear. How we laughed!'* (from *The Diary of Noel Coward*).

chocolate air biscuit *n.* A *Lionel Bart* with extra topping.

chocolate bobsleigh *n.* A sizable *Thora* that leaves the same sort of alarming *skidmarks* on the *pan* that John Noakes's crash helmet did down the Cresta Run.

chocolate chip *n.* Special type of dark, shiny residue which is generally found spattered on the bowls of the lavatories at international airports. *Chocolate chip* can only be removed using products which are so astringent that they can not be sold to the general public.

chocolate eclair *n.* A *Cleveland steamer*.

chocolate eggs *n.* *Bollocks* coated in *beer-slime splashback* after a particularly loose *dump*.

chocolate eye *n.* The *bronze eye, brass eye, red eye, backeye* or *brown eye*. The *bumhole*.

chocolate fountain *n.* A spectacular anal, upside-down firework ignited in the lavatory to celebrate having a belly full of beer and a dodgy curry the night before.

chocolate helicopter *n.* When a dangling *turd* refuses to nip off and you have to do a *logarhythmic* shimmy to send it on its way. More like a chocolate hover mower, really.

chocolate hiccups *n.* Flatulence that can be stopped by holding your *bum-breath*, or pouring a glass of water backwards up your *shitter*.

chocolate iceberg *n.* Giant *Sir Douglas* sitting in the *pan*, nine tenths of which remains below the surface. A *growler*.

chocolate Jabba *n.* A forceful movement of the *Simon Cowells*.

chocolate knob, to have a *v.* Of a fortunate fellow, to experience little or no difficulty in persuading ladies to perform *horatio*.

chocolate lab *n. 1.* A brown-coated breed of dog. *2. euph.* A person's *dirt bakery*; the foul-smelling back-stairs Porton Down-style research facility where toxic confections of various strengths, aromas and consistencies are brewed.

chocolate meerkat *n.* A sizeable *Peter O'Toole* which protrudes from the water in the lavatory pan as if scanning the locale for predators.

chocolate mince *n. medic.* Diarrhoea. What one might expect after downing a family size bar of Dairy Milk and a curry to line the stomach, followed by ten 660ml bottles of assorted beers of the world.

chocolate money *n.* The currency of choice when persuading the missus to take it up the *dung tunnel*. *'Here's a bit of chocolate money, love. Go and buy yourself some new shoes.'*

chocolate porridge *1. n. milit.* A tasty and energy-giving mixture of rolled oats and chocolate powder cooked up from an old ration pack. *2. n.* Whilst on manoeuvres, the result of eating a surfeit of salad and a pack of cheese & onion rolls before knocking back a big plastic bottle of cheap cider.

chocolate quilting *n.* The considerate public lavatory practice of covering a floating *Bullimore* with a duvet of *lavatory tissue* so as to avoid startling the next toiletee.

chocolate smoothie *n.* The kind of *otter off the bank* that slips into the water with minimal fuss and, at best, requires merely a cursory wipe. The kind of *Richard the Third* you would kill for after a night of ale and spicy Indian cuisine. Also known as a *plop tart* or *7am angel.*

chocolate speedway rider *n.* Purple-helmeted, *muck*-spattered star of the *dirt track.*

chocolate starfish *n. Rusty sheriff's badge, Bovril bullet hole, fifties tea towel holder.* The *clackervalve.*

chocolate Sunday *n.* A day of rest spent sat on the *chodbin* following a Saturday night of *heavy refreshment* and an unwise intake of dodgy solids.

chocolate swirl *1. n.* Soft-centred confection usually offered out of guilt. *2. n.* An unimpressive and ultimately ineffective flush on a train *chod bin.*

chocolate thunder *n. Tail wind, trouser typhoon.* Also *under thunder.*

chocolate wink *n.* A gentleman's cheeky treat for the special lady in his life whereby, when exiting the shower, he bends forward, reaches back and parts his buttocks, momentarily exposing his momentarily cleanish *bronze eye.*

chocolate workshop *n.* An intense session of *doing* a loved one up the *tradesman's entrance.*

chocolate yodel *n.* A particularly musical *trouser blaster* that ends with a bonus soft-centred deposit.

chocwaves *n.* Tangible surges of pressure emanating from a sub-aquatic anal eruption. *'Jez shat the jacuzzi but luckily we managed to get out during the first chocwaves.'*

chod bin *n.* The lavatory bowl or *bum sink.*

chod bin chicken *n.* Light-hearted game of "dare" played by thrillseeking commuters on rush hour trains equipped with automated toilets, in which players must shuffle from the *Rick Witter* in order to close the electronically opened door in full view of a crowd of their fellow travellers standing in the gangway.

chod botherer *n.* Someone who knocks on the *bog* door at an awkward moment. Also *Jehovah's shitness.*

chodcast *n.* Altruistically sharing the sonic delights of a noisy *Simon Cowell* evacuation with an ac-

quaintance, via the skilful in-bowl deployment of a mobile phone. A firm grip is recommended.

chod conkers *n.* Glossy, reddy-brown nuggets that float in the *crapper,* resembling seeds of the genus *Aesculus. Arse chestnuts.*

choddbins *n.* Cistern-based can storage solution.

chodder *n. Knob cheese.* Also *helmetdale, brimula, fromunda, Fred Leicester, Lymeswold etc.*

chode-stool *n.* A shiny red *ball-bag* under a tiny *Hampton.* Quite possibly toxic if ingested.

chod hop *v.* To move with increasing desperation from cubicle to cubicle in a municipal *crapper,* searching for an acceptable toilet to use, *ie.* One which is not covered in diarrhoea or *piss,* has a lock on the door or a seat *etc.* To play a *game of thrones.*

chodrell bank *n.* The *bog,* especially one that looks like a radio telescope.

chods away! *exclam.* Shouted, pioneering aviator-style, as the first *easement* of the day is undertaken.

chod's law *n.* The immutable axiomatic principle which states that, after you have stayed in and waited eight hours for a home delivery, the driver is guaranteed knock on the door at the precise moment you sit down and start to *drop the kids off at the pool.* Unless he's from Initial City-Link, in which case he won't bother knocking. Or even leaving a card. Especially since Initial City-Link apparently ceased trading in 2015. Not that you'd be able to tell.

chodzilla *n.* A *Douglas* of such gargantuan proportions that it could snap a Tokyo bus in two.

choir of angels *n.* A cloud-parting zephyr of heavenly *wind* that rises in pitch, timbre and volume, bringing a lump to the *nether throat* and a tear to the eye.

choke a brown dog *v.* To apply the *bum brake* too early. To nip off a *shite* halfway through.

choke out, got the *euph.* Slow to sparkle the morning after a night of unseemly alcohol consumption. *Flooded. 'You won't get much sense out of Judy this morning. She's still got the choke out.'*

choke the chicken *v.* To masturbate.

choke the goose *v.* To masturbate again.

choking hazard *n.* A man "with *small parts".* Ironically.

cholesterol farmer *n.* A *pie-abetic.*

cholesterol special *n.* A Byronic breakfast, *ie.* One that is "swimming in grease".

chollocks *1. n.* On a lettuce-averse male, where the double chin and gut merge seamlessly into a single continuous surface down to his *clockweights.* From chin + bollocks. *2. n.* A pair of roundish mounds either side of the cleft chin of a well-fed chap.

chomit *v.* Following a *refreshing* evening *on the sauce*, to stand up while on the *Rick Witter* in order to *shout soup* onto a freshly laid length of *dirty spine*. From chod + vomit.

chommie *n.* The *barse*.

chomping at the dog bowl *euph.* Enthusiastically performing the *oral s*x, viz.* Head down, bum in the air, furiously and frantically "licking one's chum".

chomping at the shit *n. Turtling*, having *ringside seats*, when *Mr Brown at the back door* or there is *a mole at the counter.*

chong my dong *exclam.* A response to an invitation to do something that one would rather not. *'Oi, baldy. You can chong my dong if you think I'm going to be sixth in line to the throne. Me and the missus are off to get a Netflix deal and a big fuck-off house in California instead.'*

choosing a horse *n.* The act of taking a newspaper to peruse at length while ensconced on the *jobby engine. 'Why does dad always take the Sun to the bathroom, mummy?' 'He's just choosing a horse, dear. And he also likes to wipe his arse on Tony Parsons's column.'*

chooza *n. NZ.* A *choad.*

choozies *n. Aus.* Breasts.

chop *v.* To *wallop your wood*, practise karate while holding a *weapon* in the hand. To *turn Japanese.*

chope the chicken *v.* To masturbate furiously over a photograph sneakily taken up a lady's skirt.

chopper *1. n.* Penis. *'That (insert name of striker currently having a run of bad form) couldn't score in a brothel with a £50 note wrapped round his chopper.' 2. n.* Fancy orange bike that fat kids owned in the 1970s. *3. n.* Helicopter. *4. n.* Axe. *5. n.* Nickname of anyone with the surname Harris. *6. n.* A tooth. *'Fuck me, that Rob Beckett's got some choppers on him.'*

choreplay *n.* Tiresome pre-sex ritual required by selfish women. *Frigmarole.* See also *defrost the freezer.*

chortlies *n.* The sort of *Confessions* film-style *top bollocks* that are guaranteed to bring a smile to a passing chap's face, result in a vicar/hedge cycling incident or cause a randy ambulance driver to spit out his pastie.

chorus from Mama Jo's bongos *n.* An early morning *fart* that sounds like someone from *Scooby Doo* running on the spot before scarpering from a ghost. *Morning thunder.*

Christmas balloons at Easter, tits like *sim.* Particu-

larly sad *spaniel's ears*. Dangling off the architrave.

Christmas clacker *n.* A forlorn and foetid *dump valve* after twelve days of eggnog and rich festive fodder.

Christmas 1914 *euph.* A period of unnatural calm and tranquility between the beginning of something and the moment when the full horror of what has been set in motion becomes apparent. The *grace period* between the consumption of a hot meal and the inevitable bloody trauma that ensues.

Christmas spirit *n.* An essentially altruistic approach to oral sex adopted by generously inclined ladies. *'Mr Pickwick had taken quite a shine to his landlady Mrs Bardell, as she displayed the Christmas spirit in abundance, noshing him off three times a day and never asking for anything in return.'*

Christmas vegetables *n.* The *trouser department*; that is to say, "two sprouts and a parsnip".

Chris Whittys *n. rhym. slang. Titties*, named in honour of the government's charismatic Chief Medical Officer at the time of the hoo-ha.

Chris Witty's suit, a fanny like *sim.* Descriptive of a massive *minge*. A reference to the eponymous boffin's generously tailored work *threads.* Also *horse's collar, melted welly, clown's pocket, kangaroo pouch, hippo's mouth.*

chrome-dome *n.* A *slap head, baldy.*

chrome plated crow *n.* A nasal piercing.

chronically understaffed *1. adj.* Descriptive of insurance company call centres, NHS hospitals and – these days – the Chuckle Brothers. *2. n.* Descriptive of the state of having a diminutive *wang.*

chubasaurus *n.* A monstrous *pant pointer.* A mammoth *dobber.*

chubber necking *n.* Crashing your car/moped/ shopping trolley while distractedly staring at a *bariatrically challenged* passer-by.

chubblies *n.* A fat *bird's choozies.*

chubby bullet, take the *v.* To distract and occupy the *lettuce-averse* mate of a fit *bird* your friend is attempting to chat up. To act selflessly, like a soldier who throws himself on a grenade to save his comrades, or a CIA agent who dives into the path of an assassin's bullet. *'Thanks for taking the chubby bullet, mate.'*

chubby checker *n.* A pornographic film-set technician responsible for monitoring and maintaining the leading man's state of penisular tumescence. A *fluffer. 'Cut! Either we've got the wrong lens on the camera or Gunther's losing string. Quick, somebody fetch the chubby checker out*

141

the bookies.'

chubby dart, throw a *v.* To get a ladyfriend to kneel down and *toss off* your *bendy bully,* possibly while simultaneously knocking back several pints of beer. More accomplished *chubby dart* throwers can do it with a crafty thumb and three fingers, just like Eric Bristow.

chubby hole *n.* A cosy, snug cavity where an inebriated man can place his *old fella* without fear of it rattling around like the *last hot dog in the tin.*

chubby nudgers *n.* The mammoth *milky swingers* of a lady who is *unenthusiastic about fruit,* specifically their unsettling predisposition to invade the personal space of others in their vicinity. *'Madam, would you kindly keep your chubby nudgers to yourself. I'm trying to land a fucking Zeppelin here.'*

chuckamuckaccino *n.* The sort of thing a disgruntled barista might serve to a habitually non-tipping customer or TalkTV presenter. Although how he manages to *crack one out* behind the counter is anybody's guess. They do it somehow.

chuck flick *n.* An artistic cinematographic production that eschews narrative arc, character development and dialogue in favour of action, *eg. European Cum-Bath 26.* A *stick vid* or *grumble flick.*

chuckies *n.* Balls. *'"Ow! Right in me chuckies," said Pooh.'*

chucking out time *1. n.* Following drinking up time at your local, that final moment when you are reluctantly herded towards the door by an impatient licensee who is theatrically looking at their watch. *2. n.* The period following the above, when you are bent double in the pub car park, *honking* your kidneys up.

chucking up your footprints *euph.* Extreme vomiting. *'The ambergris tartlet and popping candy terrine were a triumph, although the razor clam trifle may arguably have been a touch under-flambéed, as my companion was shitting through the eye of a needle and chucking up her footprints all night.'*

chuckle brother *1. n.* Either of the male participants in a *spit roast.* From the children's TV comedy northerners' catchphrase "To you, to me". *2. n.* Of two men engaged in a simultaneous romantic dalliance with a young lady, the act of passing her back and forth between them. *'Tell you what, Supersonic, let's phone Pat Coombs and see if she fancies a quick chuckle brother in the Blue Peter Italian Sunken garden.'*

chuckle grapes *n.* Adrians, farmers, ceramics. *'The LORD will smite thee with the botch of Egypt, and with the chuckle grapes, and with the scab, and with the itch, whereof thou canst not be healed.'* (from Deuteronomy 28:27).

chuckle vision *n.* The stirring, panoramic view of rolling *glandscape* experienced while taking a breather during an act of *cumulonimbus* on a fat lass.

chuck out special *n.* Leftover fried chickens, and portions thereof, that have been sweating all day, available for next to no money from USA Fried Chicken in Witney, Oxfordshire at around 2am.

chuck salt *v.* The consequences of masturbating again, after already masturbating oneself dry once.

chuck up *v.* To vomit, *honk up, barf, sing a rainbow.*

chucky cheese *n.* Vomit-inducing tangy cheddar matured in unwashed *fiveskins.*

chuck your muck *v.* To *lose your mess, spend your wad, tip your filthy concrete, blow your beans etc.* To ejaculate.

chud *n.* A small, uncomfortable, and embarrassing nub of *poo* in the *undercrackers,* caused by the *cigar cutter* slamming shut while trying belatedly, not to mention fruitlessly, to arrest a *follow through* in its tracks. A neatly severed *rat's nose, geetle* or *bumbob.*

chudleighs *n.* Chuds, chebs, charlies, charms, chichis, choozies. Ladies' *tits.*

chuff *1. v.* To *pass wind, shoot a bunny rabbit.* *'Oops! Best open a window, vicar. I'm about to chuff.'* *2. n.* Vagina, *front bottom.* *3. n. zool.* An exiguous *anus,* usually of a gnat.

chuffage *n. coll.* A *rats' banquet, bangers and mash, Radcliffe's sleepers.* Railway track faecal detritus.

chuff chaser *n.* Diminutive chin beard cultivated in the style favoured in the 1960s by celebs such as Acker Bilk, Jimmy Hill or Kenny Ball. *'Nice chuff chaser, Anne.'*

chuff chowder *n.* A pungent soup served as a first course when *dining at the Y.* Hopefully without croutons.

chuffdruff *n. Muffdruff.* Residual flakes of desiccated *mess* and *fanny batter* found on the *mapatasi.* Pubic equivalent of *mammary dandruff.*

chuffinch *n.* The tiny, superfluous island of *Rubiks* often left at the top end of a bird's shaven *snapper.* Also *Hitler 'tache, shreddie, Blakey.*

chufflink *n.* A piece of over-elaborate *clitoral* ironmongery of the sort often sported by loose women in *bongo vids. Cuntlery, curtain ring, mufflink.*

chuff mountain *n.* A surfeit of *cabbage* at a party.

chuff muncher *n.* A *woman in comfortable shoes* with a penchant for chowing down on other ladies' *Jacky Dannies.*

chuff-nuts *n.* Dangleberries.

chuftie plug *n. Cotton pony, fanny mouse.* Tampon.

chug *v.* To *choke the chicken, spank the monkey, burp the worm.*

chugg boots *n.* Ersatz sheepskin-style footwear as worn by members of the lower orders.

chugger *n.* A clipboard-wielding charity collector who stalks the pavement wearing a luminous bib and relieving passers by of their valuables, loose change, spare time *etc.* From charity + mugger.

chugnuts *n.* Extremely big *Chalfonts.* 'A cushion, Mrs Bennet, a cushion! I fear the frivolities at Lady Marchmain's ball have brought down my chugnuts no end.' (from *Pride and Preludice*, by Jane Austen).

chumbawumbas *onomat.* A rather predictable use of a pop group's name as slang for breasts. Other examples of this phenomenon are; *Bananaramas* (penises), *Wurzels* (testicles) and *Bee Gees* (hairy twats).

chumblies *n. medic.* Nuts, knackers, clockweights.

chum bucket *1. n.* Underwater burger restaurant in the children's cartoon series *Spongebob Squarepants*, which is in competition with Bikini Bottom's other sub-aquatic fast food outlet the Krusty Krab. *2. n.* A lady's *snatch* with all the aromatic qualities of a pail of live fish bait. *3. n.* The result of a penetrative romantic assignation when the *sharks are sniffing.*

chum fart *n.* A foul, meaty stench that manifests while a fellow is relaxing in his armchair after Sunday lunch, whether or not he owns a dog.

chumhole *n.* The bit of a *bottee* that gets *botted* by a *botter.* The *freckle, dot* or *nipsy.*

chumley warning *1. n.* The signal a gentleman gives to a fussy *nosher* to tell her that *Elvis is about to leave the building.* *2. n.* The signal a lady gives to a *nosher* to warn him that she is about to *step on a frog.*

chunder *v. Aus.* To *chunk, shout soup.*

chunder and lightning *n.* Drinking oneself sick on white cider in a park, aged thirteen.

chunderbirds *n.* Binge-drinking teenage girls full to the brim with *tart fuel* and screwtop wine, who stagger around parks and town centres *hoying up* and crying. *'It's seven pm on a Friday and Chunderbirds are GO!'* (voiceover from Police surveillance video footage of Chappelfield Park, Norwich on Fair night).

chunderbolt *n.* A sudden bolt of *spew* from the blue.

chunder flash *n.* The moment when a life-threateningly *refreshed* young lady *eats her chips backwards*, and simultaneously, inadvertently exposes her

chebs, arse, fanny, or all of the aforementioned. A phenomenon frequently seen in binge-drinking documentaries, *Daily Mail* articles about New Year's Eve and outside nightclubs up and down the country at 3am on a Sunday morning.

chunderwear *n.* Lingerie that has an emetic, rather than an erotic, effect on the viewer, *eg.* A size 48 *throng* on a size 52 *arse.*

chunk *v.* To vomit. Also chunder, *blow chunks.*

chunky, that was *exclam. Aus.* An antipodean phrase describing a proper *pub clearer. 'I sentence the prisoner in the dock to five years and nine months in prison. Jesus, that was chunky, Rolf.'*

chunt *n.* A more-than-usually aggressive *chugger*, who refuses to take no for an answer. From charity + cunt. *'You off down Greggs again, Camilla?' 'No, too many chunts on the high street today. I'll order a pizza instead.'*

Churchill *n.* A *bum cigar* of such monstrous dimensions that, when it finally makes its way through the London sewage system and proceeds to travel down the River Thames at a funereal pace, all the cranes in the East End lower their arms in sorrow at its passing.

Churchill bulldog *1. n.* A heavily be-jowelled *10-pinter.* *2. n.* A girl who loves to say "Oh, yus" in the back of a car.

Churchill's ashtrays *n.* Massive *nip-nops* that look like the erstwhile wartime leader has been stubbing out his trademark *Romeo y Julieta* cigars on someone's *tits.*

church roof foof *euph.* Description of a *gash* that is *dripping like a gravel lorry at the lights.*

churn one's bollock butter *v.* To *relax in a gentleman's way, bash the Bishop, pull oneself off. 'Forgive me father, for I have sinned. I keep churning my bollock butter while I'm watching Countdown.' 'I know what you mean, my son. That Colin Murray gives me the proper horn and all.'*

churns *1. n.* Proper *milkers.* *2. n.* Testicles. *3. n.* Seemingly any vessel containing white fluid.

chutney Chuckle brother *n.* See *dirty Sanchez.* Also known as a *Stinky Selleck.*

chutney ferret *n.* A *chocolate speedway rider.*

chutney locker *n. medic.* The *bomb bay*, the rectum. See *dirt bakery.*

chwank, on *euph.* Charging a mobile device for the sole purpose of accessing *Mexican weather forecasts. 'I've got me phone on chwank, because I only had five percent on it and I need at least ten minutes for a decent tug. And now here's Tomasz Schafernaker with the weather.'*

cidercafe *n.* A town centre bench or war memorial

from which *ciderspace* can be accessed.

ciderdown *n.* A *piss*-stained duvet used to keep an *apple-happy* gentleman of the road or bag lady warm in a shop doorway. Any warming effects brought on by drinking a surfeit of *Welsh Champagne* prior to retiring for a cosy night's kip in the park. Also known as an *electric lemonade blanket*.

ciderfects *n.* The unpleasant results of a night drinking *yokel anaesthetic*. Symptoms may vary from mild headache or nausea to permanent blindness, insanity and death.

cider lolly *n.* The portion of one's disposable income that is reserved for the purchase of White Ace and other delicious beverages. *'Excuse me mate, you couldn't spare some change could you? Only I don't get me cider lolly till next week when me parliamentary expenses claim comes through.'*

cidersense *n.* Superhuman state of enhanced mental acuity experienced as a consequence of drinking White Lightning or Frosty Jack.

ciderspace *n.* A virtual multidimensional world inhabited by *Harold ramps*.

cider terrorism *n.* Unlawful attacks and threats of attack against fellow drinkers at the end of a long sesh *on the 'bow*.

cider visor *n.* Fruit-based *beer goggles* for the younger street drinker.

cigar butts *n. JCB starter buttons, blind cobblers' thumbs, chapel hat pegs.*

cigar clipper *1. n.* An exceptionally tight *clopper*. A *mouse's ear* or *paper cut. 2. n.* The *nipsy*.

Cillit *euph.* Someone who scares off all the fruity ladies. Named after the popular detergent's shouted TV ad slogan, *viz.* "Bang and the dirt is gone".

Cincinnati bowtie *n.* A particularly dapper form of *Boston pancake*, suitable for formal occasions.

Cinderella *n. prop.* A person who leaves the party before midnight with only one shoe.

Cinderella story, a *n.* Identifying the perpetrator of the foul smell from the next lavatory cubicle by recognising their shoes under the gap. Or, if it's Sandie Shaw, their bare feet.

circle game, the *phr. 1.* n. Title of a wistful song by Joni Mitchell on her 1970 album *Ladies of the Canyon. 2.* n. Another name for the *soggy biscuit game*, as played by squaddies, public schoolboys, and members of the elite Bullingdon Club.

circle jerk *n.* A communal *hand shandy* session. A *milk race, daisy chain, auld lang syne, monk's chain. Ten off the wrist.*

circuit breaker *1. n.* A short, strict Covid lockdown that the government had neither the *balls* nor

the organisational *chops* to organise effectively. *2. n.* An emergency *J Arthur* aimed at preventing oneself from doing something inadvisable at a works Christmas party, a family wedding, or during a visit to a pet shop.

circular luxury *1. n.* Introducing a token element of recycling into the la-di-dah world of high fashion. *2. n.* The simple, spine-spraining pleasure of *auto-fellatio*; a *thirty-four-and-a-halfer. 'Don't bother your grandad. He's in his allotment shed enjoying a bit of circular luxury.'*

circumcisors *n.* A prodigious set of gnashers that could quite conceivably remove a gentleman's *turtleneck jumper* with surgical precision during a particularly vigorous *horatio* session. *'Careful down there with them circumcisors of yours, Janet.' 'Right you are Normski.'*

cistern chapel *n.* The porcelain font where *Meat Loaf's daughter* is baptised.

cistern full of piss, he's about as much use as *sim.* Said disparagingly of a somewhat ineffective person. Also *~ a Glaswegian's salad drawer, ~ Kate Moss's chip pan, ~ tits on a fish etc.*

city centre slalom *n.* The expertly executed, meandering route taken by metropolitan office workers on their lunch, whereby they maintain a safe gap between themselves and oncoming *Terence Stamps* and charity *chuggers*.

city trader *n.* A fellow who is adept at studying multiple screens concurrently, *eg.* Watching *Match of the Day* on his television while simultaneously viewing *grumble* on his laptop.

clabby *adj.* Exceptionally pink. Used to describe *bacon strips. 'Fuck me, love. You've got some clabby bacon strips on you, I'll give you that. And I've seen a few cunts in my time, what with being a consultant gynaecologist and obstetrician.'*

clacker *1. n.* Half of a popular child-maiming playground toy of the early 1970s. *2. n. coll.* Easy women *en masse. 'Plenty of clacker in the Red Lion tonight, lads.' 3. n.* The *quimpiece. 4. n.* A singular *clockweight*. Fifty percent of the contents of the *clackerbag*.

clackerbag *n.* A leathery receptacle for *clockweights*.

clacker lacquer *n. medic.* Shameful secretion from the *blip tap* up a lady's *snapper. Love juice, moip, fanny lube, bilp, parsley sauce.*

clackervalve *n.* The *nipsy, ringpiece, arsehole. 'Porphyria was powerless to resist. His eyes burned into hers like sapphires. His muscular arms enfolded her body as she felt herself being swept away in a whirlwind of passion. Tenderly, Sven lay her down on the ottoman, whipped off her scads and stuck his thumb up her clackervalve.' (from The Lady and* *the Football Manager* by Barbara Cartland).

clacker whacker *n.* Any hand-held, anatomically formed object used by a woman to relieve stress. A *neck massager, AA member.*

clackweed *n.* Perennial pubic hair.

Clacton chinwag *n.* Tender moment that takes place between a man and a kneeling woman who has had a couple of bottles of *tart fuel.* A *blow job.*

Clacton nesquik *n.* A swift, frothy-topped *milkshake* whipped up by a stereotypical Essex-based female.

clad the impaler *v.* To put on a *jubber ray, dress for dinner.*

clagnet *n.* A net-like tangle of *arse cress* which forms over the *freckle,* leading to a sensation similar to that felt when one defecates through a pair of fishnet tights. One would imagine.

clagnuts *n. Dangleberries, tagnuts, miniature heroes.*

clag rag *n.* Bathroom tissue. Also *shit tickets, arsewipe, brown shield stamps.*

claim to shame *n.* Any past feat, act or performance which, at the time, caused feelings of great pride and achievement but which now, due to the way fate has intervened, creates exactly the opposite emotions. Recipients of such an award might include all big game hunters, former cast members of the *Black and White Minstrel Show* and past contestants on *Stars In Their Eyes* who opted to impersonate Gary Glitter or Rolf Harris.

Claire Goosebumps *n.* Smashing *Gert Stonkers* of the type sported by the popular former *Casualty* actress. *Tits* which are capable of *"Waking the Dead".*

clamateur *n.* A clumsy, naive male who is inexperienced in the workings of the fairer sex's *farmyard apparatus.* A *batterfingers.* 'Honestly Jet, it was nothing. He had no idea what he was doing down there. He was a total clamateur.'

clambake *1. n.* One of them teenagers' beach parties they have in 1950s American films with all surfboards on the car roof. *2. n.* A room full of women. The female equivalent of a *sausage fest. 3. n.* A ladies only event at a sauna.

clambition *n.* Hopes and aspirations of becoming familiar with a young lady's *oysters.* Or even an old wrinkly lady's *oysters,* if such is your whim.

clam bunting *n.* Lacy intimate feminine apparel. 'Oh bugger. Someone's nicked me clam bunting off the line again.'

clamchop *n.* The tasty cut of *beaver mutton* found in a lady's knickers.

clamcorder *n.* Video camera used for close-up work in low-budget *nutflix* productions.

clamdestine *adj.* Of sex, surreptitious-

ly enjoyed while the wife is drunk, asleep or otherwise unaware/preoccupied.

clamdruff *n.* The dried *jitler, fanny batter* and general downstairs effluvium and detritus that accumulates around the *bodily treasure* of a lady who is less than attentive in the ablutionary department. *Pornflakes, chuffdruff, spandrels, men overboard, hundreds and thousands.*

clam dunk *n.* A spectacular all or nothing shot at the *furry hoop.* A *break for the border.*

clamembert *n.* Female equivalent of *helmetdale. Fanny cheese.*

clam jousting *n.* A *fur-bumping* encounter between two *scissor sisters* who are *Siamese quims.* Also *velcro fastening, pasty bashing, carpet bumping.*

clammed up *euph.* The situation whereby a female simultaneously and instantly goes both quiet and *gooey in the fork* when in the company of someone that she finds attractive.

clamouflage *n.* Thick, impenetrable *bush* which makes the target impossibly hard to spot at first glance. The *pubes* on a *biffer.*

clampage *1. n.* A night out spent in frenzied pursuit of a *seafood supper. 2. n. coll.* A quantity of clamps.

clam ram *n.* A *gut stick, cock, cheesepipe, prong.* 'Ow! I've caught me clam ram in me zip again, your majesty.'

clams casino *1. n. prop.* American hippity-hop producer best known for his use of unorthodox female vocal samples and work with Lil B and A$ap Rocky. Yes, him. *2. n.* A seafood dish prepared with bacon and breadcrumbs. *3. n.* A *lesbidaceous* niterie.

clam shandy *n.* A lady's version of a *hand shandy.* A few scales on the *invisible banjo.*

clam 69 *n. Soixante-neuf* performed by a pair of *lesbidacious* females.

clam slam *n.* Feminine version of a *teabagging.*

clam smacker *n.* A *bean flicker.*

clam-wrestling *n.* The saucily lesbidaceous act of *tribadism. Bumping haddock.*

clange *n.* A Scottish *minge.* Also *jockflap, Edinburgh fringe, fud, flingel.* 'Och, put awa' yir clange, Morag. Dinnae ye ken it's the sabbath?'

clanger *n.* An audible, swooping, Swanee whistle-style *Bakewell* that is reminiscent of the consonant-free melodic language spoken by the knitted 70s space rodents. 'I'm not having that home-made broccoli soup of yours again, Idris. Last time you gave me a bowl I was dropping clangers for a week.'

clanger's nose *n.* The sorry state of a man's *membrum virile* after a heavy night or while he is feeling unwell.

clank *v.* To *relax in a gentleman's way* over a *site* *of special interest* along the information super-highway. From click + wank. *'Gaw! That sounds fucking filthy. Three jizz-hungry birds going good on one guy, I'm gonna go clank that, just as soon as I can find my credit card. Meanwhile, now over to Daniel Corbett for tomorrow's weather.'*

clankers *n. onomat.* The same as *clinkers,* only louder.

clapometer *n.* Imaginary medical instrument used by doctors to diagnose venereal disease. *'Don't touch her, mate. I hear she scores ten on the clapometer.'*

clap oneself in on the home straight *v.* To spurt to victory by a short neck in a *milk race.*

clapper *n.* The *clematis, devil's doorbell, panic button, tongue punchbag, bald man in a boat, shark's nose, clown's hat, starter button* or *wail switch.* Named after the wiggly bit inside a bell.

clappers *1. n. pl.* In *farting,* the buttocks. *'Christ! That one didn't half rattle the clappers.'* *2. n.* Those parts of a bell like which a sexually enthusiastic lady *goes.*

clapping fish *n.* Female genitalias.

clapping sea lion *n.* The sound that a woman's *jugs* make when they slap against each other during vigorous physical activity, *eg.* Cutting through a cast iron drainpipe with a junior hacksaw, playing the congas, clubbing a seal, spanking a POTUS with a rolled-up copy of *Forbes* magazine.

clap, the *n. medic.* Any sexually transmitted disease, but usually gonorrhoea. Or syphilis. Or non-specific urethritis. *Cock rot.*

Clapton *n.* A nicely paced *Jodrell,* such as a gent might enjoy when his wife is out for the evening, or in hospital. After eponymous plank-spanker Eric's nickname "Slowhand". *'It was a normal Thursday night, your honour. The missus had gone out with the girls so I put Jenna Jameson on the video, opened the hand cream and settled down for a Clapton.'*

claptrap *1. n.* Nonsense. *2. n.* A lady of loose morals and even looser hygiene standards from whom an unsuspecting swain is likely to catch a dose of *happy rash.*

claque *n.* The unsightly residue formed on the banks of a single man's *brown trout pond.* Very difficult to shift, even with vigorous brushing or scratching with the nails. From cack + plaque.

Clara Dawes *n.* An extremely hairy *mott.* A *Judith.* From the *parts* of the actress playing the part of Clara Dawes in the recent TV adaptation of *Sons and Lovers.*

claret mouse *n. Dracula's tea bag.* A spent *jamrag.*

Clarkson's cock *n.* Anything small, based on the commonly held assumption that men, such as the outspokenly irreverent, curly topped, fighty, motorhead petrol-mouth former *Top Gear* presenter, only feel the need to drive round in big-engined sports cars in order to mask some deficiency in their *trouser departments. 'You couldn't even swing Clarkson's cock in here.'*

Clarkson, the full *n.* A male *poond.*

Clarkson with a hammer, as happy as *sim.* A reference to DIY enthusiasm that lasts the length of the demolition stage only. *'How's your new bathroom coming on Enid?' 'Don't ask, Ethel. He started off like Clarkson with a hammer on day one, but nothing's happened since. We're still pissing in a bucket.'*

clarse-hole *n.* A posh person who behaves like a *ringpiece.* An *aristo-twat.* *'Born on this day: Smokey Robinson, American singer and songwriter, 1940; Ray Winstone, roly poly cockney thespian, 1957; Andrew Albert Christian Edward, Prince Andrew, Duke of York, golfing clarse-hole, 1960.'*

clarts *n.* Tacky excrement, such as would cling to the lavatory bowl above the water line rather than slip below the surface.

clarty goalmouth *n.* A *muff* one could lose a boot in.

clash of clams *euph.* Popular mobile phone diversion.

clash of the titans *n.* An epic pair of *norks* clattering around in Lord Owen of Plymouth's shirt.

class A dugs *n.* A *Bristolian display* of such magnificence that it can cause a chap to lose his senses. *Norkotics. 'I tell you what, Lord Owen of Plymouth. Those are class A dugs you've got there.'*

Clattenburg *n.* Heavily edited hardcore pornography *ie.* Where it obviously *goes in,* but you don't see it. Named after the hapless referee in the famous 2005 Mendes goal incident, where it obviously went in, but he didn't see it. Also known, since the 2010 World Cup Finals, as a *Mauricio Espinosa,* after the hapless linesman in the England/Germany match.

clatter *1. n.* A verbal retort from pals of a Scottish gent after he has let off a worrying *trouser cough* that may conceivably have resulted in *clatteral damage. 2. v.* To *pleasure* someone, *esp.* from behind. *'I'd love to spend a minute or two clattering into the back of that.'*

claw, the *n.* The grotesque contortions of a *jitler*-covered hand that a fellow is forced to employ in order to avoid spilling any *splinkle* onto his mum's soft furnishings while making his way to the toilet following a successful bout of *self help.*

claypit *n.* Source of the raw material for making

coil pots. The *arse*.

cleach *n.* The small strip of skin between a *bird's front bottom* and her *back bottom*. Scientifically referred to as the *taint, tinter, carse, snarse, Niftkin's bridge, clutch* or *biffon*, but more crudely called the perineum.

clean and jerk *1. n.* Standard sort of weightlifting method, also sometimes known as the clean and press. *2. n.* Seizing the opportunity for a spot of *self improvement* while taking a bath. *Waxing the dolphin, polishing the lighthouse, up periscope, burping the sea slug*.

clean behind the curtains *v.* To perform thorough *cumulonimbus* on a young lady's *split bag of mince*

cleanis *n.* A *veiny bang stick* that is freshly laundered, lint free and lemon fresh, straight from the shower; a situation which, on average, lasts for about a minute a day.

clean the au pair's teeth *v.* To receive the *oral sex*.

clean the guttering *v.* Following a post-*Ruby Murray* downpour, to pay extra attention to the process of wiping the *turtle guillotine*.

clean up on aisle one *exclam.* What a gentleman says to his missus when he has successfully *dropped his yoghurt*. Also *clean up required in aisle two*, for the more romantically adventurous.

clean up on aisle two *1. exclam.* That second visit to the *shitter*, about ten minutes after a somewhat softish *download*, when you realise that more wiping of the *marmite pot* is needed. A situation that is often announced over the tannoy in supermarkets. *2. exclam.* Said after a *Greek-style yoghurt* has been *dropped*.

clean workspace *n.* A *shaven haven*.

clean your golf clubs *v.* To buff up your *one wood* in the garage. *'Where are you going, darling?' 'I'm just off to clean my golf clubs, dear. I'm going to do it over this brand new issue of Razzle I've just brought back from the newsagent so none of the polish goes on the floor.'*

clear a backlog *v.* Following a period of relative inactivity in the *back office*, a series of rapid manoeuvres carried out in an attempt to make up lost ground.

clear one's head *v.* To have a *wank*.

clearout *n.* The last and thus the most satisfying of the multitudinous morning *Peter O'Tooles* enjoyed after a night of beer, curry and *catbabs*. *'And how are you feeling this morning?' 'Well, I've been on and off the shitter since seven, but I've just had a proper clearout and I think my insides are more or less returning to normal now.' 'That's good to hear, doctor.'*

clear smear *n. Perseverance soup, guardsman's gloss, knuckle varnish, ball glaze*.

clear the custard *v.* To enjoy a long overdue *hand shandy*. *'I've got ten minutes before I have to take mass. I'll just nip upstairs and clear the custard.'*

clear the lobby! *exclam.* Bellowed in the stentorian tones of erstwhile short-*arsed* House of Commons speaker John Bercow, when one needs to urgently *pass a motion* or *step on a* quite possibly constitutionally damaging *frog*. Also *division! clear the lobby!*

clear your scroat *v.* To relieve oneself of a viscous build-up by means of a tactical *wank*. *'What are you doing in there Cliff? You're going to be late for Una.' 'I'll be out in a moment, Bruce. I'm just clearing my scroat.'*

cleavadge/cleavag *1. n.* The pronounced knuckles in a *camel's foot*. The twin-mound protuberance visible in the overly-tight pantular area of a lycra-clad lady. Also the *beetle bonnet, twix lips, monkey's chin* or, even more charmingly, *pig's trotter. 2. n.* Not to put too fine a point on it, when a *bird's* top is cut so low you can almost see her *twat*.

cleaverage *n.* A self-advancement strategy utilised by *well-qualified* women; the use of their *competitive advantages* to put themselves into more advanageous positions. *'Having suffered a downturn in her pension, my nan used her considerable powers of cleaverage to negotiate a drink at the bar.'*

cleftal horizon *n.* Technical term for the *crack* of the *arse*. *'ROY: Just to the left of the cleftal horizon. BARRISTER: In layman's terms please Mr. Tenneman. ROY: Just to the left of the bumline.'* (from *The IT Crowd* by Graham Linehan).

cleft-handed *adj.* Somewhat prone to touching people's *arses*. *'Your honour, my client is not, as has been alleged by his many victims, an opportunist pervert and inveterate sex attacker, he is merely cleft-handed, and has been since the sixties.'*

cleftovers *n. Food in the beard.* Also known as *clinkers, winnets, tagnuts, bum rubbish, miniature heroes, brown jewels* and *fartleberries*.

clegma *n.* A tenaciously noisome deposit lurking under a *bell end*.

clems *n.* The *clockweights, swingers, nads, cods. 'Ow, I've got one of me clems caught in me zip!'*

Cleopatra's barge *n.* A stately, lavatorial vessel of considerable length that appears to be unsinkable. However, once broken up, *Cleopatra's barge* can easily be floated out to sea.

Cleopatra's needle *n.* A huge, pock-marked and veiny, granite-hard phallus that tapers towards the top.

C-level *1. n.* Modern *bollocks*-y buzzword denoting

sundry high-ranking executive job titles in a business, *eg.* CEO, CFO, CTO. *2. n.* Service offered – along with *O-* and *A-levels* – by a *working girl* advertising her professional *oeuvre* in a London phone box. If there's any phone boxes left in London. *3. n.* A notional datum line used to measure the length of a frock or skirt. *'Phwoar! Fuck me! Look at them legs. And that skirt can't be any more then two inches below C-level. And a consonant please, Rachel.'*

Cleveland steamer *1. n.* A merchant cargo vessel operating on Lake Erie. *2. n.* A sexual act much favoured by your average Teuton that doesn't bear thinking about. Also *chocolate eclair.*

click and drag *euph.* The act of *farting* and then walking to another location while "dragging" the aroma behind you so that everyone you pass can enjoy your largesse.

cliff chicken *n.* Seagull.

cliffclangers *n.* Heavily swollen *bollocks, eg.* The sort that might be owned by an ageing Christian rock and roll singer who has yet to find the right girl. Also *cliffhangers.*

Clifford *n.* A measurement not exceeding two-and-a-half inches. Named after late *sexcase* publicity guru Max, whose jury had to be sent out of court for laughing after hearing evidence that he had a freakishly small *cock. 'That carpet's a couple of Cliffords short of the wall.'*

cliff Richard *n.* An *al fresco turd* which is discreetly deposited over the edge of a bank.

climb on *v.* The culmination of a romantic evening. *'Lavinia was powerless to resist. His eyes burned into hers like rubies. His strong arms enfolded her tender body as she felt herself being swept away on a tidal wave of passion. Then he dropped his trolleys and climbed on.'* (from *The Lady and the Gentleman* by Barbara Cartland).

clinkers *n. onomat. Aus.* Tenacious particles of feculent welded onto the *arse spider's* legs; *toffee strings, winnets, cling-ons, dangleberries, bum conkers.*

clint *n.* The fibrous flotsam, jetsam, effluvium and detritus that inevitably gets caught in the labyrinthine recesses of a lady's *clown's pocket.* From clematis + lint. *'What's that on your top lip, dad?' 'Just a bit of clint, son.'*

Clint squint *n.* A super-tight *dirty Harry,* named after the trademark inpenetrably narrow eyes of eponymous man with no name Clinton Eastwood Junior.

Clio lane *n.* The inside lane of a motorway or dual carriageway.

clippage *n.* The brown mark at the back of the *chod bin* seat caused by inept *arsal* positioning when dropping the shopping. *'Lot 345. A rhinestone-encrusted lavatory seat removed from the Graceland Mansion, Memphis, Tennessee, formerly the personal property of Elvis Presley (1935-77). Signs of use. Some clippage. Est. $50,000 – $75,000.'*

clip the cigar *v.* To dextrously use one's *nipsy* to cut short a thick, brown smoking object.

C-list *n.* Female version of the *wank bank.* The buff celebrities, neighbours, lexicographers and workmates that a woman thinks about while *auditioning the finger puppets.*

clit *n. medic.* The female *wail switch.*

clit and run *n.* A light-hearted indecent assault whereby one makes a playful grab for *Captain Caveman's* nose followed by a swift getaway into the crowd.

clitarosaurus *n.* A *devil's doorbell* of such terrifying magnitude that it would take a catastrophic meteor strike to wipe it out.

clitbait *n.* Clickbait of a more specialised nature, that is estimated to make up to 90% of the internet. *2. n.* Trite photographs and stories on *Mail Online* that are designed to attract the interest of lunching office workers.

clit bang *n.* Generic feminine hygiene product, *eg.* Sprunt, Febreze, Toilet Duck *etc.*

clit car *n.* A once desirable motor vehicle that has been rendered undesirable as a consequence of its own popularity, *eg.* The Subaru Impreza, them Minis, or the Fiat 500. From the fact that, like a *clematis,* "every cunt's got one".

cliterate *adj.* Said of one who knows his way very well around the *bongo* sites on the worldwide web. From computer + literate. *'He's surprisingly cliterate, that Jonathan Ross.'*

cliterati *n.* A dazzling array of *grumble flick* starlets. Perhaps attending some sort of *bongo* convention, an adult video awards ceremony or a presidential *clambake* at Mar-a-Largo.

cliterature *n. One-handed reading* matter.

clit-hanger *n.* A lady's nail-biting fear that her over-eager beau is going to fail to stay the course.

clitler *n.* A fashionably stamp-sized *downstairs* moustache, as seen on female erotic movie artistes who leave a daft little tuft. A *toothbrush muff, mufftache, muffgabe.*

clit lit *n.* Any book which is taken up and read by a bloke with the sole purpose of instigating conversation with members of the opposite *you know what,* with the ultimate aim of getting into their knickers, *eg. A Short History of Tractors in Ukranian, Girl with the Dragon Tattoo* or anything by Jane Austen.

clitmitten *n.* The non-string bit on a particularly

small G-string. Presumably the G.

clitmus test *n.* The various fondlings, fiddlements and gropages undertaken by a conscientious chap in order to establish whether his ladyfriend is ready for him to *slam in the lamb*. Also *Bolton dip test*.

clitney shears *n.* Intimate feminine shaving apparatus. *The ambassador's hedgeclippers*. See *west country trim*.

clitoral flow test *n.* Simple evaluation carried out to determine whether a *minge* is sufficiently lubricated. An appraisal – performed with a finger, tongue, or nose – of whether there is *dew on the lily*.

clitoris allsorts *n.* The array of delicacies on display in the windows along a typical Amsterdam street.

clit over tit *phr.* Descriptive of when a *bird* goes *arse over bollocks*, for example on a hen night after fourteen proseccos. Also *arse over tit*. *'And Torville's gone clit over tit there on the triple salco. That's going to cost them points.'*

clittybashing *n.* while pleasuring a lady doggy-style, the 180 degree longitudinal oscillation of the *clockweights* along the axis of motion that rattles her *clematis*.

clitty litter *1. n.* The snail-like trail of perfume and glitter left on a fellow's knee by a stripper's *bits*. *2. n.* Vaginal flotsam and jetsam in the *drip tray* of a lady's *dunghampers*.

clit whittler *n.* A sex-change surgeon. *'Now just relax, sir or madam. Dr Woudstra is one of the most eminent clit whittlers in the business.'* See also *TCGR, tranny cranny etc.*

clivanus anvaclit technique *n.* The semi-skilled action of tonguing a lady's *wail switch, bodily treasure* and *back body* in one smooth, continuous motion, and then performing the same erotic trifecta in reverse. *'Make £££s performing the clivanus anvaclit technique on bored housewives. I can show you how!'* (advertisement for the Buster Bloodvessel School of Oral Sex, Margate, in the *International Herald Tribune*, August 1986).

cloacal chords *n.* The organs of anal speech which are located in the *nether throat* and occasionally, – particularly after a visit to the Curry Capital (formerly the Rupali Restaurant), Bigg Market, Newcastle upon Tyne (now probably closed) – manage to achieve a high falsetto which could shatter a crystal wine glass or drive a collie dog mad.

clock *1. n.* One who swings like a pendulum do. A *happy shopper* or *switch hitter*, one who is *half rice half chips*. *'Born on this day: Penelope Keith, posh actress, 1940; Paul Gambaccini, walking top twenty encyclopedia, 1949; Hans Christian Anderson, Danish clock, 1805.'* *2. n.* Something that is smaller than a *cock* but larger than a *clit*. *'Nice clock, Lord Archer.'*

clocker *n.* A lady who has done a somewhat higher mileage than advertised.

clock off *v.* To *wank* yourself to sleep. To have a *knuckle nightcap*.

clock springs *n.* Very strong, curly pubic hairs usually spotted on the *clockweights* or coiled tightly around the top of the *belltower*. Often found stuck onto bars of soap or in cheap sandwiches.

clockweights *n.* Onerous *millstones* that have to be *cranked* at least once every eight days. The testicles.

clodge *n.* The *spadger*.

clodger *n.* A female tenant who defrays part of her rent by sub-letting her *clodge* to her landlord. Or, for that matter, in these modern times of lesbians and equal opportunities and what-not, her land*lady*.

clogmaker's hammer, arse like a *sim.* Descriptive of the buttocks of a 33rpm gentleman who appears to be *banging* his *old boot* at 78.

clootie dumpling *1. n.* A traditional desert pudding from Scotland. *2. n.* An overweight, suetty woman of the type commonly to be spotted after dark in takeaway food outlets north of the border.

clop *v. onomat.* To slap another man in the face with one's *old fella* when the opportunity presents itself.

clopper *n.* A romantic term for the female genitalias. *'Ocarina was powerless to resist. His eyes burned into hers like topazzes. His strong arms enfolded her body as she felt herself being swept away on a hailstorm of passion. 'Take me, Abdul, take me', she gasped. 'I'm fizzing at the clopper''.* (from *The Dowager and the Sheik* by Barbara Cartland).

clopper castle *n.* A heavily crenellated house of ill repute. *'Just off to clopper castle, love. You couldn't lend me twenty quid, could you?'*

cloppercino *n.* A foaming *furry cup*. A bit more frothy than a *twatte*. *Flappuccino*.

clopperganda *n.* The false image propagated by the *grumble* industry, that every lady has an aesthetically-pleasing and more-or-less hygienic *mimsy*, not unlike that of a young Bavarian shepherdess. Also known as *vagitprop*.

clopper slip *n.* KY jelly. Also *fuck butter, WD over-40, I can't believe it's not batter, pork pie jelly, phoney batter, shammy batter, trout jelly*.

cloppicing *n.* The clearing of overgrown *twat thatch* for lumber.

clop slop *n. Moip, blip, fanny batter, sloom, trawler's bilge, parsley sauce, clacker lacquer, crème de* *la femme, girlpop, jungle juice, vagoline, beef dripping etc.*

cloptician *n.* A gynaecologist. See also *box doc, cunt dentist, dirty dentist, snatch quack, doctopussy, mingineer*. *'The cloptician will see you now, Mrs Trubshaw.' 'Ooh, good. Me fanny's been giving me some proper gyp lately.'*

close, but no bum cigar *exclam.* A consolatory retort to a noisy *parp*, in the style of *another turn and I'm sure she would have started.*

closedown *n.* The sudden loss of a fellow's energy, joie de vivre and speech that occurs mere seconds after *spaffing*, and may last anything from five minutes to twenty-seven years.

close the deal *v.* To *butter up* some *crumpet.*

close to his mother *euph.* Of a fellow, *sensitive, good with his hands* or *style conscious*. Not to put too fine a point on it, *light on his feet.*

close-up pink *n.* Medically explicit *clabby cliterature*. Erotica that wouldn't look out of place in a gynaecology textbook.

closing ceremony *euph.* A disappointing or embarrassing end to an otherwise enjoyable experience, *eg.* A failure to achieve *organism* or a non-existent or tiny *Thora* at the end of a prolonged bout of hearty *guffing*. Derivation unknown.

closing time donner *n.* A well-worn *grotter* that looks like a rushed and messily prepared *cat sandwich*. A *badly packed kebab. 'Lady Emma was powerless to resist. His eye burned into hers like a marble. His muscular arm enfolded her body as she felt herself being swept away in a gale of passion which measured a good five on the Beaufort wind force scale. She felt a thrill of forbidden pleasure run through her like a whippet as the Admiral pulled down her bloomers. "Take me, Fellatio," she cried. "Take me now!" "Bloody hell, love," said Lord Nelson, peering at her fanny through the wrong end of his brass telescope. "What have you been up to while I've been away at sea engaging Napoleon's war fleet at Aboukir Bay in the Battle of the Nile? Your blurtch looks like a closing time donner."'* (from *The Wife of the Ageing British Envoy and the 18th century Naval Hero* by Barbara Cartland).

clot hammock *n.* A feminine hygiene requisite for the management of *women's things. 'And get us some extra-large clot hammocks while you're out, will you? I'm bleeding like a fucking stuck pig here.'*

clothes horse *euph.* When copulating with a lady who is blessed with an aesthetically unconventional appearance, to drape a towel, bed sheet or dust mat over her back so that you can only see the *back doors.*

clothes peg on a beanbag, like a *sim.* Insult directed at a chap whose *slag hammer* is disproportionately smaller than his *chumblies.*

clothestrophobic *adj.* Someone with a psychological aversion to normal garment wearing, *eg.* Naturists, strippers and female patrons of the Bigg Market, Newcastle upon Tyne.

cloth tit *n.* The least far a gentleman can get in a sexual encounter with a lady. *Outside tops. 'Did you get your hole?' 'No, I only got my cloth tit.'*

clot mops *n.* Feminine napkins. *Dangermice.*

clotted cream *n. Semenolina* with a dollop of jam.

cloud babies *1. n.* A charming BBC children's television programme. *2. n.* Air biscuits. *'Jesus Kate, what's that stench?' 'Sorry Wills, I've just given birth to a couple of cloud babies.'*

cloudy with a chance of meatballs *phr.* Forecast of high wind and *alestones* after enjoying ten pints of *cooking lager*, several bags of scratchings and a *catbab* the night before.

clout *1. n. Clunge. 2. n.* South African female rock band whose hit song *Substitute* was originally recorded by the Righteous Brothers.

clout atlas *n.* A particularly graphic *bongo book. 'Eeh, just look at all those pink bits in the clout atlas.'*

clout round the head with a brass hand, he wants a *exclam.* Said of one whose conduct arguably leaves something to be desired.

cloven hoof *n. Camel's foot, camel's mouth, camel's lips*. In fact, any part of a camel. *'Did you see Madonna at Live Earth? I was right at the back of the stadium and I couldn't get a view of the big screen, but even I could see her cloven hoof. And I've got cataracts.'*

clown car *1. n.* A *flangepiece* that is on the point of imminent collapse due to the excessive number of men clumsily clambering in and out of it every evening. *2. n.* Stuffing your *Johnson* and the boys into your ladyfriend's mouth, so that steam comes out of her nose and her ears fall off. *3. n.* A short, violent anal expulsion which sounds like a troop of comical circus entertainers has just rocked up in a small, back-firing automobile.

clowns' buckets, spunk *v.* Of single gentlemen who have spent the day *challenging themselves* repeatedly, to eventually conjure forth nothing more than a sharp wince.

clown's clog *n.* An oversized *dump* in your *ring* that makes you walk funny.

clown's flower *n.* Amusing phenomenon that occasionally occurs when a fruity gentleman ventures *down south* for a spot of *funny fingers* and *cumulonimbus on his ladyfriend* and he accidentally stimulates her *magic bean*, causing her to *wazz* in his face in the style of a big top funnyman's booby-trapped buttonhole.

clown's hat *n.* A *bald man in a boat*. A *clematis* with all wallpaper paste shooting out the top of it.

clown's pie *n.* A very, very wet *clodge*. *'Finding ourselves alone in the shooting lodge at Balmoral, her majesty bade me descend to her ladygarden. After fifty years of widowhood, I found her to be be considerably aroused. It was like being hit in the face with a clown's pie.'* (from *The Memoirs of Queen Victoria's Ghillie* by John Brown).

clown's pocket *sim.* To describe the bigger, baggier and perhaps yellow and red checkered vagina. *'May I introduce my wife, your worship? She has a fanny like a clown's pocket.'*

clown's smile *n.* Facial make-up donned when performing at the *red ring circus. Mexican lipstick, pasata grin, rag pudding.*

clubbed seal, raw as a *sim.* The state of a lady's *nether pelt* after she's been *banged* senseless with a substantial *giggle stick.*

Club sandwich *n.* The practice of discreetly secreting a *fine art pamphlet* between two crusty highbrow journals when making one's way to the *throne room.*

cluck off *exclam.* Parting words to a *one night stand* whom you don't wish to see again but would ideally like to do a spot of washing up and push the Hoover around a bit before they leave. An amalgamation of "clean up" and "fuck off".

clud *n.* The residue that can be found on the *barber's pole* after intercourse with a lady who happens to be *on the blob*. Also *blunk, blongle, blism, blimphet.*

cludger *n.* A lower class lass from the north west of England, specifically Bolton.

cludgy *n. Shite house,* lavatory, *thunderbox.* The *khazi.*

clump *n. coll. Blart, fanny, tussage. 'I tell you what, mother superior, this nunnery of yours is absolutely fucking crawling with clump.'*

clumper *n.* The *nipsy, clackervalve, cigar cutter.*

clumsy beekeeper, face like a *sim.* Descriptive of a lady with a *lovely personality*. A *homely* wench who has a mug like a *stripper's clit* or is *as ugly as a Thai stripper's scrotum.*

clunge *n.* The *clout, furry hoop, hairy goblet.*

clunge gunge *n. Blip, bilp, milp, moip, fanny batter, bird's custard, clacker lacquer, parsley sauce, beef dripping.*

clunge huggers *n.* Particularly brief shorts, typically denim, that only just keep a lady's *junk in the trunk*, and almost leave the *arse* cheeks exposed. See also *cooter cutters, Daisy Dukes.*

clungent *adj. Moipish, fentsome, sloomy.* See also *fanny's haddock.*

clunge sponge 1. *n.* Any handy textile item pressed hastily into service post *coitus* by one's ladyfriend to stop the *Harry Monk* leaking out of her *James Hunt*. 2. *n.* A beard. See also *batter catcher. 'There was an old man with a beard, who said, "It is just as I feared! Two owls and a hen, four larks and a wren, have all built their nests in my clunge sponge!".'* (from *Edward Lear's Book of Fucking Nonsense*).

clungie *n.* A lady's intimate *nether-regional* self portrait. *'I've got this bird on social media, and I think I'm in love with her. We haven't actually met yet, but she has sent me a clungie.'*

cluster buster 1. *n.* Forfmer comedy PM's project to tackle localised disease outbreaks. 2. *n.* A good kick in the *knackers.*

clusterfuck 1. *n.* A group of people who are unable to make a simple decision, *eg.* Cartoonists standing on a pavement outside a pub in London wondering where to eat, a group of PC World salesmen on a team-building course trying to construct a raft out of oil drums, planks and rope, or the United Nations Security Council. 2. *n.* A *gang bang.*

clutch *n.* The piece of skin between the anus and the vagina. So called because it works like its namesake component on a car, *ie.* "It helps you to slide your gear in smoothly". The *carse, tinter, notcher, Humber Bridge etc.*

clutch Bungle *v.* To be in dire need of a *Tom tit. 'Honest, I'd love to come on the pitch and play, only I'm clutching Bungle at the moment, Mr Robson.'*

clutteris *n.* A lady's *on-switch* surrounded by so much knotted hair that you couldn't find it if you wanted it. An unkempt *lady garden* feature, obscured by matted *gorilla salad, fanny batter bits,* stray Rice Krispies *etc. 'Keep rooting about, your royal highness. I'm pretty sure there's a perfectly servicable cluttoris hidden in there somewhere.'*

CND *abbrev.* A troublesome neighbour or *ball buster.* Cunt Next Door. *'The CND wants to know if she can borrow a cup of sugar, mam.' 'Tell her to fuck off.'*

coach driver's gusset, bouquet like a *sim.* Oenophile's description of a somewhat substandard bottle of wine.

coal hole *n.* Any grubby little aperture around the back of something. A popular entry point for burglars and tradesmen.

coalminer's hanky, dirtier than a *sim.* She who approaches the carnal buffet with a refreshingly open mind. Also *dirtier than a train toilet, ~a taxi floor, ~the office microwave, ~John McCririck's wanking pants.*

coal scuttle, polish the *v.* To indulge in a foul act

of *self-pollution, bleed the hydraulic system, stab the cat etc.* To have a *wank. 'Bless me holy father, for I have sinned. On Friday, I committed the sin of envy when my brother bought himself some new shoes. On Saturday I committed the sin of sloth when I fell asleep during the qualifying session for the Grand Prix. Then this morning I'm ashamed to say I had impure thoughts about polishing the coal scuttle over the bra pages of the Freeman catalogue.' 'Sorry my son, what was that again? I was just busy polishing the coal scuttle over the bra pages of the Freeman catalogue and I missed what you said.'*

coat hangers *n.* Large, erect *nipples* that can double up as an emergency car aerial.

coats the tongue *phr.* Said of a particularly noisome aroma. *'Fuck me, who's been in there?' 'I know what you mean, vicar. Rather coats the tongue, doesn't it?'*

cobbing *n.* Espying a piece of sweetcorn stuck to your *brown hat.*

cobblers *n. ryhm. slang. Bollocks.* A dismissive rejoinder much used by Albert Steptoe. From cobbler's awls = balls. *'This is the main Dr Martens workshop, where over a thousand professional shoe and bootmakers work.' 'What a load of cobblers.'*

cobbler's dummy, like a *sim.* Said of a gentleman whose arm is in perpetual rhythmic motion.

cob on *n.* A foul temper, usually displayed by a *werecow.* Also *blob strop, monk on.*

cobs *n. Nads, pills, pods.* Testicles. *'Ooyah! Go and fetch a cloth, our Ashley. I've caught me cobs, I say me cobs, in the bacon slicer again.'*

coccupied *adj.* Of a desirable woman, to already have a boyfriend. *'Phwooar, I really fancy that Sienna Miller. If she wasn't already coccupied and if I didn't have another 60 hours of my community service nightshift rodding the drains at the offal plant to go, I'd be up her like a rat up a drainpipe, I'm telling you.'*

cock *1. n.* Penis, *willy, knob. 2. n.* A person to whom a chirpy cockney wishes to speak, often prefixed by "Wotcha..." *3. n.* A gentleman chicken. *4. v.* Something that you can do to a snook. *5. n. Yorks.* The hardest kid in the school playground, typically a self-appointed position. *"'I'm warning you, Jennings, keep clear of Venables," said Darbishire, nodding owlishly behind his round glasses. "He's the cock of the school and he'll kick your fucking teeth in."'* (from *Jennings Gets His Fucking Teeth Kicked In* by Anthony Buckeridge).

cockado *n.* App where a *bad thrower* might meet other *light darts* enthusiasts; Gaydar or Grindr.

cock-a-doodle-poo *n.* The *shit* that, needing to come out, wakes you up at *sparrowfart* in the morning. *Alarm cack.*

cock-a-fanny *n.* Hiding one's *wedding tackle* between one's legs to give the appearance of having female genitals. Popularised by Damned guitarist Captain Sensible (real name Raymond Ian Sensible), the murderer out of *The Silence of the Lambs* and East German shot-putters of the 1970s.

cockage *1. n.* Extra fee levied upon women attending a show featuring male strippers. *2. n.* Generative organs seen *en masse. 3. n.* Obscene juvenile graffiti featuring repeated *three-line puds. 'I don't know who's responsible, but there's a lot of cockage on the downstairs bog wall and that's the one you use, your holiness, is all I'm saying.'*

cock-a-hoop *1. adj.* The metaphysical state of mind produced by advantageous circumstances. *'I just won a million on a scratchcard. I'm cock-a-hoop.' 2. adj.* The state of one fellow who is engaged in an act of *brown love* with another. *'I just managed to get my glans up your nipsy. Frankly, I'm cock-a-hoop.'*

cock and can, the *n.* The perfect evening in for a single gent. *'You fancy coming to the Red Lion, Baz?' 'Nah, it's the cock and can for me tonight, Dave.'*

cockapoo *1. n.* A popular cross between a spaniel and a poodle. *2. n.* A messy attempt at *bum sex.*

cock around the clock *n.* A twenty-four hour marathon *rhythm and blues* session.

cockasins *n.* Uncomfortable *applecatchers* that are not fit for purpose.

cockass *n.* West Country slang describing a person who is a bit of a *cock*, and also a bit of an *ass*; a commonly used endearment that can be used without causing offence in respectable company such as at a loved one's funeral or across a supermarket Tannoy system.

cock au van *n.* An impatient delivery driver with a propensity for driving up one's *arse.* Not to be confused with the delicious French meal of the same name.

cockbait *n.* A subgenre of clickbait that tricks chaps into believing that a film or book is about something manly, such as football, boxing or motorsports, when it is really about soppy girly things like relationships, *eg. The English Game* on Netflix.

cock block *n. Shag slab, wanking chariot,* bed. *'God knows, I wouldn't mind lying that on me cock block.'* (Archbishop of Canterbury Dr Robert Runcie speaking at the Marriage of Prince Charles and Lady Diana Spencer, 1981).

cock-blocked *adj.* Prevented from *getting one's end*

away by forces outside one's control.

cock book *n.* Literature which encourages a chap to whip up a quick *cheese-based white sauce*. *'I wish you wouldn't tidy my bedroom while I'm out, nan. Where have you put all me cock books?'*

cock-bottling *n.* Notorious 1950s practice at certain dairy depots, whereby new apprentices would be tied down naked by the female employees and made to put their *old fellas* inside bottles, before being churned until completion. *'But a woman's needs are manifold, and Sue she married Ted. But strange things happened on their wedding night, as they lay in their bed. Was that the trees a rustling, or the ticking of the clock? Or just a ghostly bottle getting wanked round Ernie's cock?'* (from *Ernie (the Fastest Cock-Bottler in the West)* by Benny Hill).

cock buskers *euph.* Your local lapdancing club. *'That's last orders, lads. Anyone fancy the casino or cock buskers for a couple more pints?'*

cockbuster *1. n.* A video shop, or indeed work colleague, specialising in the commercial hiring and distribution of *grumble vids*. *2. n.* Descriptive of a *big-boned* lady who, whilst engaging enthusiastically in a *reverse cowgirl* or similar ambitious manoeuvre, manages to snap her partner's *knob*.

cockchafer *1. n.* A boiled-sweet-sized beetle from the *Scarabaeidae* family, also known as the maybug. *2. n.* An especially snug *fadge*.

cockchops *n. pej.* A pernicious, malicious, seditious fool. A *fuckwit*, an *idiot*. *'Armstrong: 'That's one small step for man, one giant leap for mankind.' (Beep) Aldrin: 'Oi, cockchops. That should have been "one small step for A man." I knew they should of let me go fog out the rocket.'* (from NASA transcript of Apollo 11 mission, 1969).

cock clamp *n.* A *'v' cramp* or *mouse's ear*. A tight *muff*.

cock clock *n.* The positioning of twelve gentleman's *fun trumpets* around the face of an eager *grumble* actress. That doesn't sound very hygienic. See also *cocktopus*.

cock collar *n.* The *fiveskin*. Also *aardvark's nose, windsock, Kenny's hood, bell housing*.

cock doily *n.* Something worn as a fashion accessory by an over-dressed, affected, fop, *eg.* Them flouncy cuffs that dangle out the end of Laurence Llewellyn-Bowen's sleeves, Rees Mogg's fucking double-breasted 1930s sideshow giant's suit, Sunak's toddler trousers that come halfway up his little calves.

cockdown *n.* A desperate situation whereby no sexual activity whatsoever is allowed. That'll be from about a week after you get married to when they push you into the burner at the crem, then.

cock drops *n. Blueys.* Viagras. *Bongo Bill's banjo pills.*

cock duster *n.* A handlebar moustache sported by the sort of leather-clad Village People-style *bad throwers* who people the explicitly graphic fantasies that keep Richard Littlejohn tossing all night. Also *scrotum tickler.*

cock eggs *n. medic.* Clems, swingers, clockweights. Testicles. Also *knob eggs*. *'Vasectomy is a simple, routine procedure carried out under a local anaesthetic during which the surgeon makes a small inscision in the scrotal sac, through which he severs the cock eggs from their clacker strings.'* (Family Planning Leaflet published by The Marie Stopes Foundation).

cock-ends than weekends, she's seen more *euph.* Said of a woman who has *had more sausage than a fat German butcher*. Also (had) *more loads than Dot Cotton's washing machine*; *more men up her than the Statue of Liberty etc.*

cockerel, chav *n.* The raucous dawn chorus of banging, shouting and swearing that rouses estate dwellers at 4am on a Sunday as their neighbours return home after a heavy night on the *Nelson*.

cockery book *n.* A *self-help pamphlet* that is an indispensible source of inspiration for the bed-sit-dwelling single man who wishes to quickly whip up something satisfying of an evening.

cockfest *n.* A *joystick*-heavy pornographic film.

cockforest *n.* A pub with plenty of *wood* but not enough *bushes*.

cockfoster *1. n.* A warm and welcome, albeit temporary, home for one's *baby's arm*. *2. v.* To lovingly nurture *half a teacake* until it becomes a full *stonk on*, perhaps while travelling in a crowded London Underground carriage.

cock Fosters/cockfosters *n.* Fizzy yellow *piss*.

cock had been caught by a fisherman, like his *sim.* Description of the buttock-clenched, pelvis-thrust-forwards way a chap sprints to the khazi during a sudden *shit rush*. *'"Heathcliffe must have the runs again," sighed Cathy. "Only this morning I saw him running to the crapper like his cock had been caught by a fisherman."'* (from *Wuthering Shites* by Charlotte Brontë).

cock hair *n.* Imperial unit of measurement used in engineering, equivalent to 2.32 *gnat's cods*. *'It seems that the O-ring failed 45 seconds after take off, allowing a jet of superheated gas just a cock hair wide to penetrate the main solid fuel booster.'*

cock harp *n. medic.* Condition of the male *wedding vegetables* whereby two or more pubic hairs become trapped in the brim of the *farmer's hat*, resulting in a tightly strung scrotal guitar which plays at a pitch only audible to dogs, Bee Gees and bats. Also known as a *foreharp* or *Frodo's banjo*. See also *Bobby Charltons*.

cock heavy *adj.* Descriptive of a drinking establishment blighted by a serious dearth of *buffage*. Also *sword heavy*.

cock her into it *v.* To cajole a lady with whom one is sharing a bed into *coitus* by means of persistent and relentless nudging and *frottering*. *'The missus told my client she had a headache, but he managed to cock her into it anyway, your honour.'*

cock holster *n.* A romantic term for a lady's mouth. *'Felicity was powerless to resist. His eyes burned into hers like amethysts and his strong arms enfolded her tender body as she felt herself being swept away in a whirlwind of passion. Then, she knelt before him and he stuck his eight-inch charlie right in her cock holster.'* (from *The Secret Millionaire Officer and the Gypsy Duchess* by Barbara Cartland).

cockidex *n.* Gloopy adhesive in a handy pump dispenser, which is nevertheless difficult to apply neatly. *Pyjama glue, sement, jazz glue, Aphrodite's evostick, gonad glue, prick stick, man mastic.*

cock-in-a-box *n.* Any magical surprise involving an erect penis as the revealed object. Possibly leads to a custodial sentence.

cock in a cunt shop, as happy as a *sim.* Contented. *'If we can but prevent the government from wasting the labours of the people, under the pretence of taking care of them, they must perforce become as happy as a cock in a cunt shop.'* (Thomas Jefferson).

cock in a top hat, sticking one's *v.* Unfulfilling *futtering* up a slack *snapper.*

cockjaw *n.* The open-mouthed expression adopted by *Frankie Vaughan* queens after they've quaffed a gobful of *manpop.*

cock knocker *n.* A gentleman who *bangs* at the *back door.*

cock knot *n.* The machine head of the *one stringed banjo;* the *frenum.*

cock krill *n.* Spunk, *jitler.*

cockleganger *n.* In movie and television production, a stand-in *generative member* brought on set when an artiste is either reluctant to get his *Charlie* out in front of the cameras or somewhat lacking in manly vigour when he does so. A *stunt cock.*

cockle's headpiece *n.* The female *clematis.*

cockless pair *n.* A particularly athletic-looking lesbian couple.

cock lodger *n.* An idle man who persuades a gullible single mum to let him move in and sit on her sofa all day watching DVDs in exchange for the odd *scuttling*. *'This is Boris, my cock lodger.'*

cock mess monster *1. n.* A *grumble flick* actress, transformed by a small fortune in *money shots*. A *plasterer's radio*. *2. n.* A cryptozoological beast occasionally sighted floating round the bath after *playing up periscope.*

cock monkey *1. n.* A lady who does a lot of jumping about, squealing and general circus-like activity in the *fart sack*, especially when presented with a banana. *2. n.* A film set technician who keeps the gentleman lead thespian erect during set changes, drug runs, *spunk* mopping *etc.* A *fluffer.* *3. n.* A *loose* woman who mimics her simian namesake by swinging from *giggle-twig* to *giggle-twig* in the style of a gibbon, making sure she has a firm hold of the next one before releasing her grip on the last.

cock moss *n.* The cobwebby bryophytes which slowly grow on fallow, fallen *wood.*

cock Ness monster *n.* A *lazy lob on* in the bath that is reminiscent of a cryptozoological Scottish plesiosaur poking its head out of the water and having a bit of a look about.

cockney *1. n.* A pearly buttoned, colourfully opinionated person born within the sound of Bow Bells, who either drives a taxi or sells fruit on a market and doesn't have a bad word to say about Ronnie and Reggie, as they loved their mum and only ever killed their own. *2. n.* A person of indeterminate gender. From cock + fanny.

cock nostril *n.* The *hog's eye*, from which *cock snot* is occasionally ejected under some force.

cocknuckle *n.* The sixth metacarpophalangeal; that which always comes at the top of the deck in a *five knuckle shuffle*. The *glans.*

cockofadge *n.* A very butch woman, or possibly a slightly effeminate man. "Did you see that, Tommy? Couldn't tell if it had a cock or fadge."

cock off *1. n.* Of a *grumble* actor, to leave work at the end of a hard day *at the orifice*. Having *cocked on* in the morning, obviously. *'You're home early, Ben.' 'Yeah. I fancied getting a round of golf in before me tea, so I cocked off early.' 2. v.* To suspend one's working day in order to enjoy a protracted recess of *gentlemanly relaxation*. *'Cabinet sources allege that at the height of the pandemic, Mr Johnson was regularly cocking off halfway through the afternoon.'*

cock of the bingo *n.* An old dear of advanced years who is *built like a brick shithouse* and displays a physically intimidating demeanour.

cockoholic *n.* One who is addicted to cockohol. *'Mate of mine used to work as a roadie for Abba. Reckoned that blonde bird was a fucking cockoholic.'*

cock on the block, put your *phr.* Figure of speech comparable to "put your neck on the line". *'Earlier *on today, apparently, a woman rang the BBC and said she heard there was a hurricane on the way. Well, if you're watching, I'm going to put my cock on the block and say don't worry, there isn't.'* (Michael Fish, BBC weather forecast, October 15th 1987).

cock opera *n.* A *scudflick* where all the female performers break into melismatic vocal outbursts, usually while being *banged* from behind.

cock or ball? *n.* Name of a game, similar to Hangman or I Spy, which can be used to pass the time during long train journeys, dull wedding services or parliamentary debates, whereby the interlocutor requires their neighbour to identify a flap of nondescript skin poking through his trouser fly.

cock o' van *n.* When a seemingly normal bloke gets behind the wheel of a white Transit and immediately drives about like a *fucking prick.*

cock patience *n.* A solitary pursuit whereby one whiles away the hours with one's favourite *gash 'n' gary* mags arranged in a circle around oneself. Also *wank crescent, pornorama.*

cockpit *n.* The piece of skin between the *devil's bagpipes* and the *German shepherd's winkhole.* The *barse.*

cock pocket *n.* Any orifice frequented by the excitable *sausage man.*

cock porridge *n.* A messy load of hot oats fired from the *porridge gun.*

cock puppet *n.* A notably malleable *grumble* performer being flopped about by a selection of male co-stars. Also known as a *throwabout.*

cock rock *1. n.* A variety of popular music performed by *rock poodles* such as *Whitesnake, Van Halen etc.* *2. n.* The substance that *knobs* are made of that is able to go from marshmallow limp to diamond hard at the thought of a pair of *tits.*

cock rot *n. medic.* VD, a dose. *"'Jane, my little darling (so I will call you, for so you are), you don't know what you are talking about; you misjudge me again: it is not because she is mad I hate her. It is because she gave me cock rot.'"* (from *Jayne Eyre* by Charlotte Brontë).

cocks and rubbers *n.* The shameful extra-curricular sexual exploits of amateur sleuths attending weekend murder mystery parties.

cock sedative *n. medic.* Alcohol. *'Don't wait up, love. I'm going for a few pints of cock sedative.'*

cocks in hands, put *phr.* An expression used by film directors and magazine editors hoping to widen their products' appeal to the male market. *'Okay Miss Cruz, Miss Johannsen, that's a wrap on the lez-up. Right, people, that ought to put cocks in hands. I suppose we'd better start working on a plot*

or something.'

cock's length *n.* A small measure of distance. *'Blimey, that tampon/pint glass/dog shit missed me by a cock's length.'*

cocksmith *1. n.* A tradesman skilled in the forging of lengths of *pink steel.* A pornographic thespian. *2. n.* One who is prone to *pulling his wire.* A *wanker.*

cock smock *n.* An old T-shirt laid across the stomach while *hand-jiving,* in order to catch any passing *spunks.* A *chapkin.*

cock smoker *n.* A lady who doesn't mind a puff on one's *Whitehouse cigar* after dinner. An inveterate *fellatrix.*

cock snot *n.* That which is sneezed out of the *cock nostril.*

cocks orange pippin *n.* Apple that is typically on the end of a *baby's arm.*

cock star *n.* A virtuoso solo performer on that most challenging of instruments – the *pink oboe.*

cocksucker *n.* A motorist who cuts you up.

cocksucker's doormat *n.* Facial hair growth favoured by the ageing male attempting to hide his jowls. A goatee beard, *bloatee.*

cocktail shaker *n.* An upmarket *piss artist.* *'Born on this day: Roy Hattersley, slapstick politician, 1932; Dame Maggie Smith, cross actress, 1934; Keith Floyd, cocktail shaker, 1943.'*

cock tease *n.* A woman who wears *fuck me shoes* and then swiftly changes into *fuck off slippers* when you get back to her place.

cocktoberfest *n.* Pejorative epithet that can be given to any *sausage-heavy* gathering. *'Fuck me, Dr Welby. This General Synod's a bit light on pussy, isn't it.' 'You can say that again, Bishop. It's like cocktoberfest in here.'*

cocktopus *n.* In a *grumble video* clip, the slimy, colour-changing face at the centre of eight, pulsing, tentacle-like appendages. A *plasterer's radio* or *cock mess monster* who looks like *Jackson Pollock's shoes.*

cock typing *n.* Sending multiple text messages, for example during a sporting event, which are hastily written and hence full of mistakes, such that they appear to have been clumsily tapped in using one's penis.

cockular, go straight for the *v.* Of a *cougar* or other mature predatory female homing in on her quarry, to aim for immediate copulation without any delay, foreplay, or time for her prey to give adequate consideration as to his actions or the ultimate consequences thereof.

cockumentary *n.* A serious-minded factual film exploring issues surrounding the adult entertainment industry broadcast at 11 o'clock in order to educate and inform viewers. While they *pull themselves off*. The sort of programme that should be sponsored by Kleenex. A *masturmentary, sockumentary, rudimentary*.

cockupational therapy *n*. Repetitive exercises that ease stiffness, aid relaxation and can help restful sleep. That'll be *wanking*, then.

cockupied *adj*. Engrossed in an *act of personal delight*. *'Derek, what are you doing in there?' 'I am currently cockupied, Mavis. Put the kettle on.'*

cockusoap *n*. A television serial drama, the cast of which contains a disproportionate amount of high quality *tussage*, eg. *Hollyoaks* but not *Last of the Summer Wine*.

cock venom *n*. *Spaff, spodge, spooge*, etc. *Spunk*.

cockwash *n*. The *punani*. See also *token for the cockwash, municipal cockwash*. *'My Charlie's absolutely filthy. I think I'll stick it through the cockwash on Sunday morning.'*

cockwasher *n*. A *fellatrix* who takes it *up to the back wheels*. A *deep throater* or *pork sword* swallower. A woman with a *bollock goatee*.

cockweb *n*. A post-ejaculatory gossamer thread of *jipper* between the *trout's mouth* and the thigh, upon which a bluebottle might become ensnared.

cockweiler *n*. A *boner* that is all bark and no bite; not as hard as you would think. A *big softie*.

cock-whittle *n*. A *fadge* with sufficient tension and friction to reduce a fellow's *twig* to a mere stub.

cock witch *n*. The hideous mental crone summoned into the mind's eye of a fellow when he wishes to *keep the wolf from the door. Also globstopper, auntie freeze*.

cockwomble *n*. An easily pleased male who is prone to wander, particularly around the common end of the *meat market*, in order that he might mingle with "the things that the everyday folks leave behind".

cockwood *euph*. Building trade argot for a six-inch length of timber which is customarily offered to the lady of the house by a labourer in the hope of gaining her favour. *'Where's Gary disappeared to?' 'Don't know, boss. Last time I seen him he was down by the skip gathering cockwood to light the fire.'*

cocoa channel? *phr. interrog*. Asked with one eyebrow raised. Ostensibly the sort of query that a charmer like Nigel Havers, Peter Bowles or Dean Gaffney might put to his ladyfriend about her perfume preferences, but which is in fact a subtle enquiry as to whether she takes it up the *council gritter*.

cocoa sombrero *n*. A Mexican *brown hatter*.

coconut husk *n*. In erotic photography, the soft

mound of *clocksprings* which becomes visible when a lady *assumes the position*.

coconut minge-mat *n*. Pubic hair you could wipe your feet on. A *welcome twat*.

coco plops *n*. Pieces of post-curry *bowl fodder* that are "so chocolatey they turn the water brown". See also *rusty copper bolts*.

coco-pops *n*. *Winnets*, known briefly as Choco Krispies.

cod *adj*. Extremely *Swiss*. Fucking rubbish. *Mouse, pants*. *'This Swiss watch you got me off the Turkish market is fucking cod.'*

cod cove *n*. A *fish mitten* or *Grimsby box*.

codel *n*. To *break wind* sufficiently loudly that one risks setting off an avalanche. From colon + yodel.

cod piece *1. n*. A sort of historical thong favoured by King Henry VIII and the singer out of Cameo. *2. n*. One of Birdseye's less popular frozen fish products. *3. n*. A feminine undergarment with a distinct maritime odour. *'Please excuse my wife, your worship. She has been watching a George Clooney film and now she needs to change her cod piece.'*

codpiece yoghurt *n*. Soured, semi-solid *man milk*. *'Fancy a bowl of codpiece yoghurt, Una?' 'I'll go and get me spoon, Cliff.'*

cods *n*. *Cobblers*. Often prefixed "a kick in the...".

cod's mouth *n*. The shaven *part* of a mature lady who is attempting to ape the appearance of a younger *piece down there*, such that it looks like the mouth off the lead singer of Aerosmith has been transplanted between her *gams*. See also *trout's mouth*.

cod snot *n*. Naturally occurring feminine lubricant. *Milp, blip, Fiona Bruce, truffle butter*.

cod's wetsuit, wetter than a *sim*. Descriptive of a woman's *bits and bobs* when she's *dripping like a fucked fridge*. Also *otter's pocket, turfer's knee*.

cod wallet *n*. A *Billingsgate banjo*.

coffee bagging *n*. Sexual practice similar to *teabagging*, only there's more sediment present.

coffee bean *n*. The back view of a dirty lady's *Gareth* as she bends over on all fours. *Coconut husk, reverse peach, teazle*.

coffee, chav *n*. A can of energy drink. *Baseball cappuccino, nedscafe*.

coffee turtle *n*. The first *turd* of the day, powered on its way by the first cup of Nescafé of the day.

coffin-dodger *n*. Affectionate term for an incontinent, elderly relative. An *oxygen thief* or *morgue cheater*.

cogging *n*. It's like *dogging*, but on your push-iron.

coiling point *n*. The exact scientific instant at which *touching cloth* becomes *touching socks*.

coilus interruptus *n. Lat.* Method employed by God to prevent the birth of *Meat Loaf's daughter* whereby the Jehovah's Witnesses ring the doorbell just as you are about to start laying the foundations of a *log cabin*.

coin bouncer *n.* A pubic area of such verdant bushiness that if you dropped half a crown on it, it would simply rebound off.

coin-flipper *1. n.* An habitual numismatic fidgeter, eg. George Raft. *2. n.* An habitual *monomanualist* or *wanker.*

coins of the realm *n.* Trouseral *piss spots* of various sizes sported by gentlemen leaving public house lavatories.

cointreauception *n.* Middle class *brewer's droop* caused by over-indulgence on orange-flavoured triple-sec apéritif.

coital efficiency *euph.* Clever way to make being a *two-push Charlie* sound like a good thing. Also *Johnny jibber, potting the black on the break, spending your money before you get to the shop.*

coitus *n. Lat.* S*xual interc*urse.

coitus binterruptus *n. Lat.* Any act of congress which is disturbed half-way through by the unexpected return of the *bag for life*.

cojones *1. n. Span.* Balls. *2. n. Span.* Guts, spunk. But not the sort of spunk that comes out of your *cojones*.

coke zero *n. Bacon powder* that contains little or no genuine *sniff*.

Colchester condom *euph. milit.* Anal sex, *one up the bonus tunnel; a* phrase used by squaddies in the not-at-all-rough garrison town. *'Please be careful, Field Marshal'. 'Don't worry, sweet tits, I'll be using a Colchester condom.'*

Colchester crimson *1. n.* Deep carmine red hue used historically, as we all know, for a number of trains on the Great Eastern Railway. *2. n.* The paint scheme applied to a fellow's *John Thomas* during a *rag week* rendezvous east of Romford.

cold jerky *n.* The process by which a particularly frantic *self harmer* rekindles his love for the real thing by enduring a prolonged period of abstinence from his monomanual vice.

coldplay *1. n.* Sexual practice whereby the saucy participants smear each other with cold human excrement. *2. n.* A pop group. *'Fancy a bit of Coldplay?' 'Unless you mean the sexual practice whereby the saucy participants smear each other with cold human excrement, then no. I do have my standards.'*

cold shower, like wanking in a *sim.* Descriptive of an energy-sapping, chaffing, and ultimately unrewarding task or activity.

cold starter *n.* When several abortive attempts must be made to have a *Tom tit* before a satisfactory *cable* can be laid.

cold tea bag *n.* The feeling a person gets in their underpants a couple of minutes after *gambling and losing*.

Cole Porter *n. prop.* A person of dubious moral standing for whom, in the words of the eponymous songwriter's 1934 Broadway ditty, "anything goes."

Colgate smile *1. phr.* Catchline from the toothpaste advertising campaign of the 1970s. *2. n.* Giving one's *Herman gelmet* a cheeky little rub with something minty prior to *brushing the au pair's teeth.*

colimbo *n.* That desolate time of day occurring in the afternoon and heralded by the appearance onscreen of Peter Falk's squint-eyed, dirty-rain-coated supersleuth, when the jobseeker/person *working from home* realises that not only is there nothing new worth watching on Sky, but it's also as yet still too early to start drinking.

Colin the caterpillar *n. prop.* A *shite* of such epic proportions that it resembles the cake – and nutritional cornerstone – of all children's birthday parties. Also *Cuthbert, Wiggles, Cecil, Charlie, Clyde* and so on, legal action notwithstanding.

collagen biospheres *n. Knockers* which miraculously iron the wrinkles out of a fellow's *twig*.

collanders *n.* Ill-fitting *applecatchers* that may *strain one's vegetables.*

collar and cuffs *euph.* Matching hair colour, up top and down below. *'See that blonde? Do you reckon her collar matches her cuffs? If you think you can help, contact Tyne and Wear CrimeStoppers on the number at the bottom of the screen. Our team of detectives is waiting to take your call.'*

collect a debt *v.* To *beat your meat* like it owes you money.

colliders *n.* Proper airbag-style *lady bumps*, as immortalised in the famous Lennon and McCartney number where they warble about "the girl with colliders goes by."

collie's chest, fanny like a *sim.* Descriptive of the more hirsute ladygarden. *'This is the tale of Bertha Boot / Who's bought a brand new bathing suit / When she wears it in the water / You see things you didn't oughta / On the beach at Whitley Bay / Her knockers show up clear as day / But down below the view is best / Her fanny's like a collie's chest.'* (from *Odd Odes* by Cyril Fletcher).

collie's ear, fanny like a *sim.* Descriptive of a battered old *minge* that the vet might poke a torch inside while tutting.

colly wobbles *n.* The strange, unnerving feeling that one is being watched while *having it off*. Possibly by a *wanking* ex-Premiership footballer.

colon burger *n.* A *shit* weighing in at a quarter of a pound uncooked.

Colonel's breath, the *euph.* Dropped approximately 25 minutes after consuming a portion of food from the popular high street fried chicken franchise, a finger-lickingly pungent *trouser cough* that is redolent of ex-military man Sanders's secret blend of eleven herbs and spices.

colonic fatigue syndrome *n. medic.* Condition whereby the sufferer is so exhausted by a taxing *digestive transit* that they have to go for a lie-down lasting several months.

colonsequences *n.* Blanket term for *Simon Cowell*-related problems experienced as a result of over-indulgence. *'Christ, I had a skinful the night before the wedding. Tell you what, though, I was suffering the colonsequences the next day. I had to run off to the bog three times during the wedding service or else I would've shat meself. Sometimes I wonder if I'm really cut out to be a vicar, you know.'*

colour in the koala *euph.* To enjoy a particularly messy *bomb bay* clearance in the smallest room. From the effect that prolonged wiping produces on heavily marsupial-embossed Cushelle *bumwad*.

Columbian flush *n.* Tell-tale double or triple toilet evacuation procedure used by *showbiz sherbet* enthusiasts to conceal the preparation and consumption of their favourite powdery foodstuffs.

Columbian hay fever *n. medic.* Specific form of allergic rhinitis triggered by sensitivity to the pollen of the *Erythroxylum coca* plant. *Columbian hay fever* is chiefly characterised by symptoms such as red eyes and a runny nose, and is suffered to a disproportionate degree by people working in the advertising, music and children's television businesses.

Columbian oranges *n.* A refreshing line of *sniff* enjoyed in the *bogs* at half time.

Columbo *n.* Named after the monocular, raincoat-clad TV detective, a seemingly ineffectual *epilog* that suddenly stops you in your tracks as you're walking out of the front door, by needing "just one more thing..." Also *Jimmy Cricket*.

Columbo's coat *1. n.* A tatty and creased-up *fanny* that looks like an aged basset hound might use it for a bed. Not to be confused with a *Columbo's mac* which is, of course, a tatty and creased-up *fiveskin* that looks like an aged basset hound has spent the morning chewing it behind the sofa. *'Oops. I think my Columbo's mac has got caught in your Columbo's coat.'* *2. n.* A rumpled prepuce that is much too long for the *one-eyed bobby* it covers. Columbo's coat, *Delaney's overcoat*.

Colwyn Bay *1. n.* Welsh seaside resort famous for its multi-storey Morrisons and its elephant-less zoo. *2. rhym. slang.* Homosexual, *Whitley Bay*. *'This is your cellmate, Lord Archer. Try not to drop anything on the floor, only he's a bit Colwyn.'*

combat jack *euph. US. milit.* Marines Corps slang describing a *wank* in a warzone, and thus *2. euph.* Any risky workplace act of *monomanual self delight. 'Sorry, you caught me in the middle of a combat jack there. Anyway, here's Darren Bett with the weather.'*

combo *n.* One in the *goo*, then *one* in the *poo*. To *pot the brown* after the *pink*, though not at the Crucible, Sheffield.

combover *n.* A swope. *'Why don't you combover and see me some time?'* (Mae West propositioning Robert Robinson).

combover cuffs *n.* Hairy hands, like what flocculent, banterous sports commentator Richard Keys has.

combustoflatulation *n.* Anal flame-throwing. *Pyroflatulation, blue streak.*

come *1. v. Cum. "Did you come on your bicycle, mother superior?' 'Yes, vicar. It must have been the cobbles down the high street stimulating my clit."* (Bamforth's *Seaside Chuckles* postcard by Donald McGill, 1931). *2. n. Cum.*

come-atose/cumatose *adj.* Of a male, unconscious shortly following the *shooting* of his *wad*.

comeback skid *n.* A *Richard the Third* which – having been flushed – makes an unexpected and messy return around the U-bend to the *stadium of shite* just as the *crappeur* employs the bogbrush to eliminate streaky evidence of dirty deeds, leading to stubborn bristle soiling. Also used to describe the unwelcome return of an undesirable previously assumed to have permanently fled the scene.

come in Tokyo *n.* Manipulating both a lady's *dials* at the same time in the manner of a World War II radio operator. *Finding Radio Luxembourg.*

come like a bishop *sim.* Of a man, to ejaculate in an explosive style, to *go off like a punched icing bag*, as one would imagine a long-term celibate does every now and again.

come on in, the water's lovely! *exclam.* A phrase used by professional footballers to indicate to their opposite numbers that they wish to change ends while *spitroasting* blonde women.

come to bathroom eyes *euph.* A seductive Teutonic figure of speech. *'Achtung, Eva's giving me them* *come to bathroom eyes again, Heinrich.'*

come to bed pies *1. n.* Pastry-based foodstuffs presented to a *hopper arse* in exchange for a *bunk up. Pork for pork. 2. n.* The alluring display in Greggs's window that has ensnared many a *salad dodger.*

come to bunkbed eyes *n.* Miscollimated ocular organs; one of which is looking at you, while the other is looking for you.

comfortable *adj.* Of shoes, having "lick me" written all over them.

comfortably numbs *n.* Tight yoga pants or leggings worn by ladies as casual or clubwear. So named because, like in the lyrics of the Pink Floyd song, "your lips move but I can't hear what you are saying". Also *mumblers.*

comforts *n. Yorks.* Casual visitors, because they just "come for t'day".

comfort wipe *n.* Having a quick *bumwad* swab at the *gammon ring* during a *stand up visit* to the water closet, just in case an earlier *Exchange & Mart* was *loaded.* An act that brings a certain peace of mind to the anxious *guffer.*

command module *n. Bell end*, glans, *bishop's mitre, purple pearler.*

commercial sex *n.* A hurried act of penetrative congress enjoyed during the advertisement break in a television programme, for example the three-minute long intermissions that punctuate *Coronation Street.*

commercial shake *n.* An act of *self harm* carried out by a TV viewer during the ads, so as not to interrupt his appreciation of the programme. The volume of the transmission is helpfully increased during the adverts so that they can be heard from the *smallest room.*

commission a ship *v.* To take a *dump*, from the spectacular splash caused when the prow of a freshly launched *dreadnought* hits the water.

committed goth *euph.* One who is deceased. *'In a very real sense, he is not dead. Try to think of him more as a committed goth. Now let us pray.'*

committee shitty *n.* A *motion* that is unexpectedly seconded after the paperwork is complete. A *council dump.*

commode dragon *n.* A venomous species of unflushable U-bend-dwelling monster, characterised by its giant size and mottled, angry appearance.

commodore *n.* A woman who is "three times a lady" – *ie.* She makes full use of the trifecta of available orifices when engaging with a male acquaintance.

commodore, the *1. n.* A sexual act whereby an en-thusiastic female allows her sexual partners to make full use of all available orifices; thus being, in the words of the famous song by the eponymous group, "once, twice, three times a lady". *2. n.* For a similar reason, one who is blessed with a *lovely personality,* but cursed with ravenous glands.

Commodus *n. prop.* A name given to a reluctant hero who always seems to turn up after a scrap with the immortal line from the film *Gladiator, viz.* " Am I too late? Have I missed the battle?"

communists in the funhouse, there are *phr.* Humorus Danish saying used during *rollover week,* when *the painters are in.*

community chest *n.* A pair of *Charlies* that the whole estate has had a *go* on.

commuting *n.* Choosing to live in an area within a convenient distance of a place where one confidently expects to find ugly women to *tup. 'We are delighted to welcome to the market this deceptively delightful 1 bedroom studio flat which would make an ideal starter home for the single, semi-skilled gentleman. The property is deceptively delightfully situated within easy commuting distance of Newcastle's Bigg Market, with its many amenities. £95,000 ono.'*

competent at ironing *euph.* Sensitive. *'You know that bloke off that thing on the telly? He's as competent at ironing as a nine-bob note.'*

competitive advantage *euph.* Big *tits, first impressions, qualifications, references,* high capacity *juggage. 'I know her criminal record, history of drug use and non-existent educational attainments perhaps count against her, but I felt as soon as she walked into the room that she had a competitive advantage over the other candidates.'*

completed Pornhub *euph.* Having spent a whole day *rubbing oneself raw* to internet *grumble* (previously *completed X-Hamster*). *'Hi Mick. Did you have a good day off?' 'Aye boss, cracking. I stayed in bed and completed Pornhub.'*

completion fluid *1. n.* In the oil industry, a salty solution that is piped under pressure into the production zone during the final stages of drilling. *2. n. Spaff.*

compliments to the chef *n.* The drunken, unintelligible, Marlon Brando-style ramblings of a lucky woman immediately after she has completed a successful act of *horatio* on an accommodating gentleman friend.

compliment the chef *v.* To *drop one's guts* after a meal. Good manners in some countries and Humberside, but if in any doubt, it's probably best to check first with your host.

compose one's thoughts *euph.* Polite phrase often

used by snooker commentators to describe the actions of players who leave the table in between frames. To defecate, take a *shit, drop the kids off at the pool, light a bum cigar, crimp one off etc.* *'It's all square in the Embassy World Snooker Championship finals and you could cut the atmosphere here at the Crucible with a knife. And as referee Len Ganley prepares the table for the all-important deciding frame, Ray Reardon's just leaving the arena for a moment to compose his thoughts. Let's hope he washes his hands after he wipes his arse.'*

composing hut *1. n.* A place of reflection and solitude, in which an artist can hide from the world and focus on creating delightful sounds. Favoured by the likes of Grieg and Mahler. *2. n.* Likewise, a locked *khazi* the morning after a nice lamb tindaloo.

compost mentis *adj. Lat.* Descriptive of a *fuckwitted* person; a *shit-for-brains* or *bufflehead.*

compression stroke *n.* When seated upon the *jobby engine*, that part of the defecatory cycle that is characterised by downward thrusts and gaseous emissions.

con *n. Fr. Le jardin de la femme, fanoir.*

Conanism *1. n.* The act of *wanking* oneself *off* so frequently that one develops a right arm like right wing, muscle-bound, execution-happy California State Governor Arnold Schwarzenegger. *2. n. Pleasuring yourself* in an unspeakably barbaric way, *eg.* While wearing a butcher's chain mail glove.

con artiste *n. Fr.* A *cunning linguist, muff diver, Jacky Danny Cousteau, puba diver.*

concentrate on the matter in hand *v.* To commit a beastly sin of the flesh that will result in stunted growth, blindness and hairy palms.

concert pitch, getting to *n.* The dissonant *trumping, brumping* and *frapping* sounds, ostensibly similar to those of a brass band tune-up, which emanate instead from hostel dorm rooms where large groups of males are sleeping off a heavy night *on the fizz.*

conclusion fluid *n.* The viscous matter squirted over the face of a startled *Frankie Vaughan* actress in the back of a vehicle that is, you might safely assume, not a real taxi.

concraptions *n.* The agonising stomach twinges experienced before giving birth to an *arse baby.* *'I'd best get to the khazi, love. My concraptions are only a minute apart and I'm three centimetres dilated. Call the mudwife, and tell her to be quick.'*

concrete donkey *n.* A *horse's handbrake* or *diamond cutter.*

conditioning, chavlovian *n.* The token bit of trite moral instruction proffered by the host at the end of *scratter*-baiting talk shows such as *Jeremy Kyle.*

conduct the ragtime band *v.* To wave one's *baton* in a rousing performance of the Russian national anthem when *Arsenal are playing at home.*

cones *n.* Pointy, orange, dayglo breasts found alongside the M25 or in Madonna's vest.

cones are out *euph.* A warning that there is only one lane in use and it's *blow job week.*

conflatulations *1. n. interj.* A term of praise accorded one by one's friends after one has *stepped on* a spectacular *duck*. *2. n.* Title of Cliff Richard's unsuccessful 1968 Eurovision Song Contest entry.

congrafellation *n.* The act of giving a lucky lady an appreciative pat on the head after she has performed a decent *nom de plums.*

congratulatio *n.* Celebratory *blojos.*

congress tart *n.* Pastry-based confection with a layer of raspberry jam and a moist coconut topping.

conjaculations *1. n.* Mutual expressions of appreciation following a satisfactory conclusion to a bout of genital intercourse. *2. n.* Title of Cliff Richard's unsuccessful 1968 Eurovision Song Contest entry.

conkers *n.* See *hairy conkers.*

conkers deep *adj.* To be in a state of total intromission. *In up to ~ the back wheels, ~ the maker's nameplate, ~ the apricots.*

conker water *n.* Spangle, spooge, spadge, gunk.

conscious uncoupling *1. n.* How him out of that group and her out of them films chose to describe the end of their ten-year marriage. *2. n.* Crapping out a right *Elvis killer.*

consider it licked *exclam.* A *sotto voce* compliment paid to an attractive young lady one has just clapped eyes on in the street, nightclub or a railway carriage *etc.*

consider the matter closed, I *1. exclam.* Magic words, often uttered by politicians, that make all embarrassments simply evaporate into thin air. For a few minutes. *2. exclam.* Said after *sharting* in order to preclude any embarrassment.

consolitis *n. medic.* Sudden and debilitating disease, symptomised by a croaky voice and melodramatic coughing that seems to strike down half the office the day after an eagerly awaited new Playstation or XBox game gets released.

consonant dodger *n.* Disparaging term for a member of the lower orders who eschews stops, fricatives, nasals, bilabial articulants, pulmonic egressives, ejectives and implosives while speaking.

constipation constellation *n.* The situation whereby one has to bear down on a breached *dreadnought* with such force that one sees stars.

constitutional 1. *n.* Old-fashioned term for a daily walk taken for health reasons. *'Just off for your morning constitutional, Oates?'* 2. *n.* A brisk spot of daily *cottaging* that a city gent might perform in the *bogs* at Liverpool Street.

constitutional change *n.* When your usual daily appointment to *drop the kids off at the pool* is missed because of disruption to your usual routine, *eg.* When travelling. Also known as *getting up before your arsehole.*

consult Clarkson *v.* To adjourn to the bathroom for a sit-down perusal of yet another *shite*-sized chapter of the *Top Gear* petrolmouth's cistern-busting semi-literary *oeuvre.*

contactless 1. *adj.* Modern method of paying with a credit card that has been, one would imagine, a boon for credit card thieves. 2. *adj.* A term used to describe a top *shagger* who routinely gives the wrong phone number to his romantic conquests. *'Don't you worry all these birds you're tupping are going to catch up with you, Callum?' 'No chance mate, I've gone contactless.'* 3. *n.* A more efficient and hygienic alternative to the *gash card* or *hairy cheque book*, whereby a lady gets herself out of a missed deadline at work, parking ticket or speeding fine with anything from a smile and a quick flash of her *norks* to letting a bloke give himself a *Nescafe handshake* in front of her. 4. *n.* A *wad* that is *spent* without any physical connection. A *two-pump chump*'s *money shot.*

contact rear *exclam. milit.* When out on patrol, a squaddies' warning of imminent danger coming from behind. Also *our survey said.*

containment and delay 1. *phr.* Strategy – if it can be called that – employed by the British government during the 2020 Covid-19 outbreak. 2. *n.* Rearguard action strategy, employed by a *buffalo soldier* indulging in a *monomanual act of personal delight*, involving the summoning up of an horrific, *cock*-shrinking mental image when he feels his *milk shake* starting to bubble a bit.

contemplation pit *n.* The *khazi*. *'Jesus Christ, archbishop. Was you the last in the contemplation pit? It fucking stinks in there.'*

continental breakfast *n. milit.* The humorous squaddie's pastime of having a dig around in his *Marmite pot* before inscribing a *dirty Sanchez*-style moustache onto the top lip of a slumbering comrade. *'Quadrangle trench was somewhat shallow and left us exposed to enfilade fire from the woods to the South. Boothby had found a German shovel and spent the afternoon digging for all he was worth. By dusk he was exhausted by his efforts*

and fell thankfully into a deep sleep. Lieutenant Cholmondeley took the opportunity to give the poor fellow a splendid handlebar continental breakfast.' (from *Memoirs of an Infantry Officer* by Siegfried Sassoon).

continental shelf *n.* Feature of foreigners' barbaric *jobby engines,* providing a place in the *throne room* where one's stinking *royal decrees* can pile up to be admired before being flushed away.

contractions are four minutes apart *exclam.* In medical terms, the explanation for increasingly regular *Bakewells* prior to the arrival of a bouncing *mud baby.*

contraflow *n.* A spot of *backdoor work, ie.* Going against the prevailing traffic.

control alt delete *phr.* The amusing way in which an IT worker announces that he is about to *log out. 'Where are you going, Iain?' 'I'm off to control alt delete.'*

controlled explosion 1. *n.* How experts dispose of unwanted ordnances and dead cetaceans. 2. *n.* When a fellow cannot be completely sure that what feels like flatulence waiting to come out is entirely gaseous and, as a precaution, he makes sure he is safely situated over a *crapper* before relaxing his *balloon knot.* 3. *n.* A small, tightly squeezed test-*fart* detonated in order to establish the risk of personal befoulment. 4. *n.* Detonating your *suspicious package* in advance of a date in order to avoid a *schoolboy error. Taking the edge off, putting a wank in the bank.*

controlled explosion in the number two reactor *euph.* An unexpectedly lively *dump* of toxic material, which may occasion the imposition of an exclusion zone.

conulingus *n. Licking out* a ladyfriend on the spurious assumption that she will later reciprocate on a *quid pro quo* basis, only to be left with dangerously *blue balls.*

convent porridge *n.* Hot, steaming *spunk* ladled out of a cauldron by a smiling Mother Superior. *Nuns' porridge, jizz.*

convict lenses 1. *n.* High powered *funglasses,* as commonly worn by men who have recently been released following a prolonged period of incarceration at His Majesty's Pleasure. Or, conversely, 2. *n.* Metaphorical astigmatic optical apparatus sported by the sort of woman who sees a conviction for armed robbery or murder as an attractive secondary sexual characteristic in a suitor.

convict's shuffle *n.* The "chaingang"-style gait one adopts when looking for *bumwad* while manacled round the ankles by one's lowered *grundies*.

convivial setting *euph.* The office *bogs*. *'The Sun are reporting that Suranne Jones got her kit off on Dr Foster. I think I'll go and peruse that story in a more convivial setting.'*

convoy cock *n. milit.* A squaddie's *travel fat*.

cooch *n. US.* A Yankee *poon*.

cooint *n.* A variation on a terrible swearword, used in the quaint picture-postcard village of Barnsley, South Yorkshire.

cookie monster's eyes *n.* A poorly-executed set of *blimplants* reminiscent of the Yoda-voiced *Sesame Street* biscuit enthusiast.

cooking a grenade *1. n.* Tactic favoured by US Marines and *Call of Duty* players whereby the pin on a grenade is pulled, but throwing it is delayed, reducing the time to detonation once thrown. *2. n.* Deferring the act of *laying a cable*, resulting in a *Meatloaf's daughter* capable of peeling the glaze off the porcelain.

cooking at both ends *adj.* Of the eater of a spicy *cuzza*, descriptive of the burning sensations experienced first in his throat and then, about an hour later, when his *bottom hob* gets lit. *'Come to the Curry Capital, Bigg Market, Newcastle upon Tyne, where we'll prepare you a meal that will have you cooking at both ends in no time.'*

cooking lager *n.* Utility pub booze, as drunk by Selwyn Froggatt. *Wallop.* Also *cookin'.*

cooking on gash *1. phr.* Turn of phrase employed by a gentleman who is confident that he has a cast iron guarantee of getting *on the nest*. *'I couldn't wait for the Remembrance Day ceremony to get finished so I could get cooking on gash with that bird from the office back at my Grace & Favour apartment in Whitehall.'* *2. n.* A fellow who is enjoying an extremely good run pulling the ladies, in the style of Robin Askwith in the *Confessions* films, *viz.* *'Hey Mick, I heard you were out shagging again last night.' 'Yes, Keith. I'm cooking on gash at the moment. As indeed I have been pretty much constantly since about 1963.'*

cook off *1. v. milit.* Of ammunition, to detonate spontaneously due to excessive heat. *2. v.* Of a bachelor, to detonate spontaneously in his trousers due to excessive lap-dancing.

cooldown *n.* Ten minutes of viewing normal *grumble* featuring simply men and women naked and *shagging*, in order to wind down and re-orient oneself after several hours of viewing extreme double fisting, gonzo scrotal inflation and man-on-dog sploshing videos on the internet. A *cooldown* is advisable just as the sun is rising and it's getting towards time to go to work. *Decompression.*

cool down a transformer *v.* An old Southern Electric Board term; to have a crafty *piss* in an electricity sub station, usually altruistically performed against the side of an overheating piece of voltage conversion equipment.

cooling off period *n.* A certain amount of time, usually a week, before a brand new, pristine mobile device is sullied by the viewing of internet *grumble* videos.

cooter *1. n. prop. US.* A character from *The Dukes of Hazzard.* *2. n.* The visible contents of Daisy Duke's shorts in the *Dukes of Hazzard. The gorilla's knuckle.*

cooter cutters *n. US.* The type of shorts worn by Daisy Duke in *The Dukes of Hazzard,* in which – as was quite obvious to viewers – she kept her *cooter.*

cop a feel *v.* To get one's *tops* or *fingers*. Or *tops and fingers.*

copalotapus *n.* A sexually accomplished and very active dinosaur who, in spite of his advancing vintage, would put a lot of younger *pork swordsmen* to shame, *eg.* Ben Dover, Rod Stewart, Young Mr Grace *etc.*

coping mechanism *n.* A self-administered therapy regime to enable recovery from a distressing situation, *eg.* Loneliness, relationship problems, employment worries, nothing on the telly. A *wank.* Also *nature's hangover cure.*

copperation *n.* A nerve-shredding game whereby a fellow opportunistically *cops a feel* of his snoozing partner's *bodily treasures* in the hope that he won't set her buzzer off and make her nose flash.

copper bolt *v.* A very heavy or dense *sweaty morph.* With a clockwise thread.

copperdantic *adj.* Unnatural mode of speech used by members of the constabulary to lend import, gravitas and false precision to the everyday, the mundane and the completely made-up.

copper's knock *n.* An unnecessarily brusque *back-scuttling* attempt which is abruptly initiated at 6.00am, while the missus is still half asleep.

copper's torch *n.* A large, heavy, *bell-swagged schlong* dangling disturbingly between the legs of a skinny old man. A *schlepper.* *'What's the matter, your holiness? Are you wrestling with an intractable theological conundrum, such as the concept of original sin?' 'No, cardinal. I've just went for a slash and I've been and caught me copper's torch in me zip.'*

copper wire *n.* A stray *pube* that appears, somewhat embarrassingly, in a handful of loose change.

copy twat *n.* An acquaintance that always gets the same clothes, car, phone, mailorder bride *etc.*

as oneself.

coq au vag *n. Fr.* The main course after an evening spent warming up a saucy *chick* of Gallic extraction.

coquefort *n. Knobcheese*. Also *mancheesegoo, fludge, cauliflower cheese, knacker barrel, fromunder, stinking bishop* or *willydelphia*.

cordless bone *n.* A *bobby's helmet* without the *roll-neck* and *cheese-slicer* apparatus.

cordless driller *n.* A *battery operated boyfriend.* A *twat mallet* owned by your neighbourhood *friggit Jones.*

cordon bleugh *n.* The sophisticated sort of cuisine whizzed up on their bedsit mini-hobs by sad bachelors, *eg.* A pot noodle sandwich, bubble and squeak made from the remains of an uneaten pot noodle sandwich, a bubble and squeak leftovers sandwich, cornflakes and lager.

corgi registered *1. euph.* Descriptive of a lady who makes friends very quickly and is happy to be certified *gas tight* in a secluded car park or layby. *2. euph.* Humorously said of a man who is fully qualified at *servicing boilers.*

corked *1. adj.* Of a fine vintage wine which has been spoiled by the tannins in the bottle stopper. Which is the reason the real experts like to stick to a nice drop of screwtop or the stuff you get in a box. *'Mr Coren's sent his 1978 Montrachet back. He says it's corked.' 2. adj.* Of a lady, *up on blocks. 'How was your week in Tenerife, Dave?' 'Shit, mate. Me bird was corked the whole time we was there.' 3. adj.* Of *spaff,* to be contaminated with bits which render it unpalatable. *'Mr Coren's sent his soup back. He says the spunk in it is corked.' 4. n.* Of a *trouser cough,* having bits in it. *'Yes, yes, I'm somewhat of a connoisseur and just by sniffing it I can tell you that it is definitely corked. Please take this pair of underpants back.'*

corks *1. n.* Nipples. *2. exclam.* 1950s schoolboy cry of surprise. *'"Corks!", cried Darbishire. "I've just seen Matron's corks. Anyone for a daisychain?"'* (from *Jennings and the Sticky Sheets* by Anthony Buckeridge).

corn *rhym. slang.* The *chopper.* From corn on the cob = knob.

cornbeef cudgel *n.* Short, thick *trouser stick* that a chap might take up in order to *relieve tension,* and so aid restful sleep. The *spam baseball bat.*

cornbeef gash *n.* A *school dinner* that has quite clearly been pulverised to a gristly shadow of its former glory but is, nevertheless, a cheap, sure thing. Especially when prepared with plenty of *batter.*

cornbeef lighthouse *n.* Big thing that flashes to attract sailors' attention.

cornbeef sandwich *n.* Filling starter when *dining at the Y.*

cornfakes *n.* Any supermarket own-brand rip-off breakfast cereal. See also *cheetabix.*

cornhole *1. n. US. Brass eye, ring, balloon knot. 2. v.* To shove one's *cock* up the same.

Cornish chuff *1. n.* A wrongly spelled crow-like bird (*Pyrrhocorax pyrrhocorax*) which is native to the Cornish coast and characterised by its red beak, red legs and high-pitched, excitable "chiow" call, it says here. *2. n.* Pastie-powered act of flatulation which could cause a stampede in a tin mine.

Cornish internet *n.* Ceefax, teletext. The *skinternet.*

Cornish nosebleed *euph.* The consequences of a young lady suffering a coughing fit at a critical moment while enjoying a *drink on a stick.*

Cornish payrise *n.* An increase in remuneration vouchsafed with one hand while being simultaneously taken away with the other. *'In his budget speech, Mr Hammond confirmed that he would be offering pensioners an index-linked Cornish payrise of 0.03%, on top of the 1p a week he had already promised them in his Autumn statement.'*

corn on the cob *n.* A *spitroast,* where two professional footballers revolve a hot lady in a shallow dish of melted butter.

corn on the nob *n.* A niblet on a *bottsman's lid.*

corn on the swab *n.* Telltale *shitscrape* evidence of previous sweetcorn consumption.

cornucopia *n.* A *horn* of plenty. A *cock* with all grapes, wine and fruit coming out of the end. *'Look at the size of the norks on that one, Dr Spillsbury. She's given me a proper cornucopia.'*

corona check *euph.* A quick post-*fart* sniff to check that one's sense of taste and smell is still intact, thus confirming a Covid-19-free diagnosis. *'You've got a bit of a runny nose and a temperature, Boris. Shall I phone 111?' 'No worries, Carrie. I just did a corona check and I fucking stink.'*

coronal mass ejection *1. n.* In astrophysics, a huge burst of solar wind, plasma and electromagnetic radiation which is periodically released into space by the sun. *2. n.* A spectacular forward blast caused by the consumption of an excess of Mexican lager. *'Thanks for lending me your suit, Dave. I had a bit of a coronal mass ejection down the front of it, but I reckon that'll just sponge out.'*

Corona virus *n. medic.* Condition which leaves sufferers feeling like *shit* the morning after imbibing a surfeit of Mexican lager that was inexplicably going cheap in the supermarket.

coroner's cloth *n.* A piece of lavatory tissue tactfully placed over *skidmarks, pebbledashing* or any other discomfiting debris one has left in the toilet bowl, in the same way that Police scene-of-crime officers would cover up a dead body or other such unpleasantness from the gaze of passers-by. *Chocolate quilting, papering over the cacks, Turin shroud.*

corporate dogging *n.* Standing by and watching your workmates getting *shafted* by the management.

corporation *n.* The *gock*; a seamless merging of the belly and upper genital areas of a male.

corpse in a carpet *n.* A *Sir Douglas* of such huge dimensions that it resembles a lorry driver's victim rolled up in a length of Axminster with all flies buzzing round it.

corpsing *1. n.* Of an actor, getting the giggles. *2. n.* Of a *wanker* or Sir Jimmy Savile, *pulling himself off* with freezing cold hands.

corpy *adj.* Of household fittings and suchlike, distinctly *council*. *'Ooh, I wouldn't buy one of them onyx-effect dessert trolleys, your royal highness. They're a bit corpy.'*

correctile dysfunction *n.* A tendency to mansplain (which, for the benefit of any female readers, is the tendency of men to explain things to women in a condescending or patronising manner).

corridor of uncertainty *euph.* As a rude lady lowers herself towards a bloke's erectivitated member, those tantalising few seconds when, were you to enquire of him whether he is expecting to be *potting the pink* or *the brown*, he really couldn't answer you with any degree of confidence.

cortina, the *euph.* The deeply erotic, although physically improbable, act of inserting both fists into a partner's anal or vaginal orifice before "turning the wheel" left and right as if driving along a slippy road in a 1970s Ford saloon with crossply and radial tyres mixed on the same axle. Also known as the *fist and twist* or *steering into the skids.*

corybungo *n.* Arse, fundament, backside. *'The tomato boat's just docked, so you'll have to do me up the corybungo.'*

cosif *n. medic.* The *tinter,* the *taint.* The perineum. *"'Cos if"* it wasn't there, her guts would fall out.

cossie fog light, arse like a *sim.* One's *nipsy,* following a difficult digestive transit.

costume drama *n.* The frantic behaviour of an hysterical woman who cannot decide what to wear for a party.

cottage *v.* To visit a thatched public lavatory with climbing roses round the door looking for a bit of *Colwyn Bay* action.

cottage cheese pastie *n.* A well-*shagged hairy pie.* A box of assorted creams.

cottage kex *n.* Type of gentlemen's trousers with an elasticated waist, enabling them to be lowered or raised at extremely short notice and with the minimum of fuss. For whatever reason. *'Lot 38. Pair of bespoke cottage kex tailored by Ede & Ravenscroft, Savile Row, for Sir Alec Guinness in 1946. est. £65,000-£75,000.'*

cottage pie *1. n.* A wholesome dish made of minced beef and vegetables in gravy, topped with mashed potatoes and served with relish and other sauces. *2. n.* A mess of sodden tissues, sticky with *gentleman's relish, uncle mustard* and other savoury condiments, left in a *bottery barn* following a vigorous session.

cottager's pentathlon *n.* A long walk, some hide and seek, a brief spot of wrestling, a protracted *swordfight,* and then a 400 metre dash when the *dibble* shows up.

cottager's waddle *1. n.* The tell-tale gait of a man who has just, successfully, been *looking for badgers. 2. n.* A small village in Dorset. Possibly.

cottage spy *n.* An inquisitive gent in a pac a mac who stands uncomfortably close by while one is taking a *Chinese singing lesson* in a public lavatory. A *willy watcher.*

cottage upright *1. n.* A small pianoforte typically dating from the late nineteenth century. *2. n.* A convenient and *nicely poised* amorous liaison.

cottaging bag *n.* A public *cludgie* portmanteau, in which a chap and/or his chum discreetly stand while they get up to their saucy antics, to avoid being spotted under the door by a nosy *tit-head.*

cottaging hat *n.* A baseball cap, beanie or equivalent headgear that offers partial disguise when filmed on CCTV. *'I like your new cottaging hat, vicar.'*

cottaging tax *n.* The 30p entry fee for the *bogs* at large railway stations.

cottagopolis *n.* London, with particular reference to the central area bounded by Hampstead Heath on the north, Clapham Common in the south, the City in the east and Kensington in the west.

cotton bullet *n.* A *cotton mouse.*

cotton eclipse *n.* The rare, fleeting opportunity for a *sneaky peek* that a fellow gets when a woman or Scotsman sitting opposite him sits down or crosses their legs. A *brief encounter, the rabbit's tail, scholar's bonus.*

cotton kennels *n.* The cups of a *brassiere, ie.* Where a young lady "keeps her puppies warm and secure".

cotton mouse *n. A cotton pony.*

cotton pony *n. A cotton bullet.*

couch chains *n.* The crippling and binding effects of ten cans of *black eye juice* that prevent a fellow getting up off the settee. *Bed glue. 'I'd come and help you bring the shopping in, love, but I'm trapped by these couch chains.'*

cougar *n. US.* Sexist and offensive American slang term for an older woman in pursuit of a younger man, *eg.* Mrs Robinson in the film *The Graduate*.

cough a dead rat *v. To drop a gut, to step on a duck.* To flatulate.

cough and drop nurse *n.* A comprehensive school health visitor who checks whether or not adolescent schoolboys' *nuts* wobble while they are clearing their throats.

coughart *v.* To attempt to disguise a loud *exchange & mart* with a theatrical clearing of the throat. Or vice versa, for that matter.

cough cabbage water *v. To tread on the gloy bottle.*

cough drop *1. n.* Technique used by a woman to empty her *front bottom* of *cock hockle*. *2. n.* Technique used, usually unsuccessfully, in a public lavatory cubicle to mask the sound of a *load of old shoes falling out of the loft*. *3. n.* An accidental *back room clearout* while clearing the throat.

coughy morning *1. n.* The first full-tar *Harry Wragg* of the day, which creates a refreshing wave of nausea before setting off an invigorating fit of violent hemoptysis. *2. n.* The result of an occasional smoker having too many *cancer sticks* the night before.

cough your filthy yoghurt *euph.* A romantic expression for ejaculation. To do a *money shot*. *'Ursula was powerless to resist. His eyes burned into hers like sapphires. His strong arms enfolded her tender body as she felt herself being swept away in a whirlwind of passion. Then he dropped his trolleys and coughed his filthy yoghurt in her hair.'* (from *The Gentleman and the Lady* by Barbara Cartland).

couldn't get laid in his own wet dream, he *phr.* An unfortunate chap who is consistently unlucky in love, a situation that would remain sadly unchanged even if he was in a women's prison with a handful of free pardons tied round his *Charlie*.

couldn't hit his own cock with a slipper *euph.* Said of a footballer whose kicking has lately exhibited a marked dearth of accuracy. *'Why the fuck didn't he let Carroll take that penalty?' 'Because Carroll couldn't hit his own cock with a slipper, your highness.'*

couldn't hit his undies with a fart *exclam.* Said of a striker whose accuracy in front of goal is sub-optimal. *'I tell you what, Gary, that Richardson couldn't hit his undies with a fart.'*

couldn't pull a greasy stick out of a dead dingo's arse *phr.* A disparaging reference to a fellow's perceived merits. *'Fuck me, what are we going to do with him? He's utterly useless. He couldn't pull a greasy stick out of a dead dingo's arse.' 'I know. let's make him Health Secretary.'*

could someone shut the back door please? *exclam. rhet.* Phrase uttered when a noisome vapour from an unknown source is detected. See also *who let the ducks in?*

could you repeat that, Donald? *exclam.* Said after someone *steps on a duck*. See also *speak up caller, you're through; taxi for Brown; what's that, Sweep?; sew a button on that; mighty fine words, preacher.*

could you repeat that in English, please? *exclam.* There's another one.

council *1. rhym. slang. The bumhole.* From *council gritter = shitter*. *2. adj.* General purpose dismissive term for anything or anyone deemed somewhat lacking in class. *Two bob. 'Mummy, can I go and play with Jade and Kylie?' 'No, sweetheart, you can't. They're a bit council.'*

council camouflage *n.* Tattoos.

council catwalk *n.* A public place in which *fugly birds* congregate or otherwise disport themselves, normally wearing skimpy tops two sizes too small, the better to show off their *muffin tops* and collections of prison *tats*.

council cock *n.* A genital which is unemployed and living on *handouts*.

council diamonds *n.* Sparkling pavement residue found, for example, following a collision between a *Vauxhall Chavalier* and a telephone box.

council estate landmine *n.* A *dirty bomb* left not particularly covertly on the pavement in an area with a high *SPSM* quotient.

council facial *n.* The steamy blast that greets you when opening the dishwasher at the end of its cycle.

council FM *n.* The medley of *shite* music that is played at extreme volume levels out of the windows of homes on your estate, mainly during the summer.

council futon *n.* Piece of dual-purpose street furniture which is used for sitting on during the day and sleeping on at night. A park bench, *shandy sunbed* or *tramp grill*.

council go-kart *n.* A mobility scooter. Also known as a *Belfast taxi, Disneyworld dragster, Frinton Ferrari, Mansfield motorcycle* or *nanbretta*.

council gritter *rhym. slang. Gary Glitter, apple fritter,* *pint of bitter, shitter.* The anal aperture, is what it is.

council house lava lamp *n.* A bottle of Sainsbury's Flanders beer with some cashew nuts dropped in it.

council liposuction *n.* Short-term weight loss following a violent attack of the *Engelberts.*

council pop *n.* Water. Also *tapoline.*

council Sky *euph.* Free-to-air digital television.

council suitcase *n.* A binliner.

council tax *n.* A weekly levy paid in manageable £1.50 instalments over the fag counter at the newsagent or Spar, which funds the Royal Ballet.

council twat *n.* A scraggy, utility *clout.* Not very good quality, but it does the job.

countdowning *n.* The custom of selecting from the more obscure and volatile liquors on offer in a hostelry in the hope that this will accelerate the intoxicatory process, *viz.* "Three from the bottom shelf, two from the top shelf please, Rachel."

counting the pennies *phr.* Determining how many days a bath towel has been in use by assessing the number of brown circle-marks left while drying your *ringpiece* every morning. *'Do you need a new towel for after your shower, Charlie?' 'Hang on, Camilla. I'll just count the pennies.'*

Count of Monte Wristo *n.* Any male between the ages of 13 and 25 who has a lot of time on their hands in which to plot *acts of revenge* on whomsoever has *got his blood up.*

country air *n.* The smell of a *fart* dropped while driving past a field. *'Mmmm. Just smell that country air, children.'*

countryfile *1. n.* Title of a BBC programme about trees and shit. *2. n.* Person with a perverted desire to indulge in sexual activity in the open air.

countryman *1. n.* An impractically small estate car of the 1970s with bits of wood nailed round the back. *2. n.* A *crap* enjoyed in the great outdoors. *'I wandered lonely as a cloud / That floats on high o'er vales and hills / I stopped to drop a countryman / Amongst the golden Daffodils.'* (from *Daffodils* by William Turdsworth).

country supper *n.* Something regularly enjoyed in Chipping Norton by David Cameron and Rebekkah Brooks.

count, the *n.* Letting out a big *Donald* whilst lying in bed, reaching around and feeling a moist *ringpiece*, and then having to pull your dressing gown around your shoulders like a cape to prevent spreading *shite* everywhere.

coup de tat *n. Fr.* A sudden and unexpected takeover of a previously classy high street by pound shops, Wilkinson's, and *scratter*-filled amusement arcades. *'Head for the hills, everyone.*

There's been a coup de tat in Leamington Spa.'

course I loves thee, fucks thee dunn I? *n.* West Country gent's riposte to the question put by his girlfriend: "Do you love me?"

court Madam Knuckle *v.* To woo your right hand. See also *Madam Palm and her five daughters, Palmela Handerson.*

court martial from Sergeant Bash, receive a *v.* To subject oneself to a furious act of anger-fuelled *self-indulgence. 'Can you keep an eye on the milk pan, dear? I'm going upstairs to receive a court martial from Sergeant Bash.'*

Covent Garden nun *n.* A *fuckstress* or *Fulham virgin.* A *ho'.*

Coventry climax *1. n.* Innovative West Midlands fire pump manufacturers who provided engines for racing cars, buses and tanks before being absorbed into the doomed British Leyland group in the 1980s. *2. n.* A sad phantom of an ejaculation – in the words of the Coventry-based ska group The Specials's 1981 hit – "coming like a ghost town". *3. n. One off the wrist* on the *huffy bed* in the spare room after some minor indiscretion has rendered one *persona non grata* in the marital bedchamber.

covered wagon *1. n.* Method of holding the *tassel* in which the thumb is on the underside of the *shaft* and the fingers form a canopy like the top of a cowboy's wagon. A style much favoured by the street-urinating drunkard. *2 n.* Driving your old heffer under canvas after you've had a bellyful of beans. A *Dutch oven.*

covering fire *n.* The act of waiting for someone in a public toilet to turn on the taps or hand-driers before defecating in order to conceal the deafening *fall of old shoes from the loft* that accompanies the release of one's *flock of pigeons.*

COVID playoff beard *n.* Grizzly Adams-style facial hair grown during the 2020 lockdown, cultivated in order to project a sense of barbarian, survivalist desperation, as if a fellow had been cast out into the deep wilderness with only his wits and a sharpened piece of obsidian, rather than just sitting inside watching re-runs of *Antiques Roadtrip.*

cowboy walk *n.* Broad, rolling, John Wayne-style gait required when walking to the *bog* with the *turtle's head.*

cow doctor's glove, dirty as a *sim.* Sexually adventurous. *'See her reading the news? You wouldn't think it to look at her, but I have it on the very good authority of a bloke whose dad used to work with her boyfriend's brother that she's as dirty* *as a cow doctor's glove.'*

Cowell movement *n.* A cod-musical, tuneless, screeching *arse ballad* involving a surfeit of ostentatious, Mariah Carey-style arpeggiation and faux-soulful grimacing, which brings tears to the eyes of anyone unlucky enough to hear it.

Cowell movement *n.* Poptastical music, regularly dumped on the nation's airwaves and streaming services *via* the eponymous pop impresario's TV talent shows, that is basically *shit*. *'Coming up: Dimelo by Rak-Su – another Cowell movement entering the charts, fittingly, at number two.'*

cowelloke *n.* Plastic singing, as practised by the sort of talent-free *cunts* who appear on *pleb*-fleecing primetime telly *shitfests*.

cowgirl *n.* A sexual position popular with the choreographers of American *grumble flicks*, involving a lazy man and a bow-legged woman. A *fucking bronco.*

cow parsley *n.* The salad first course eaten by a *barge arse* as an antidote to the three-cake blowout they will shortly shovel down their fat face for dessert.

cow pissing on a flat rock, like a *sim.* A poetic turn of phrase to evoke heavy rainfall, particularly in built-up areas. *'And don't forget to take a brolly with you if you're heading out in West Wales later this afternoon, because there's a band of heavy cloud moving in from the Irish Sea and it's going to be like a cow pissing on a flat rock.' 'Thank-you Carol.'*

cow's cunt, flatter than a *1. sim.* Perfectly horizontal or otherwise free of contours. *'It occurred to me that if it were possible to flow a ribbon of liquid glass freely onto a bath of molten tin, the resulting sheet of continuous "float glass", once cooled with sufficient care, would be flatter than a cow's cunt.' 2. sim.* Exhausted or otherwise bereft of vim or vigour. *'You couldn't give me a jump start off your Popemobile could you, your holiness? Only the battery on me Bedford Rascal's flatter than a cow's cunt.' 3. sim.* Out of tune. *'Bloody Nora, have you heard the bloke out of Toto singing these days? He's flatter than a cow's cunt.'*

cow's stomachs *n.* The effect of an ill-fitting bra on an over-endowed lady, giving the appearance of four udders instead of two.

coxo *n. Baby gravy.*

coyote *euph.* A woman who you would chew your own arm off to get away from in the morning.

coyote gulch *n.* A searingly hot and dry *wizard's sleeve.*

crabalanche *n.* Sudden outpouring of latero-per-ambulatory seafood from a dirty *bird's drip tray.*

crabe *n.* A measure of *shite*, thought to equal about

two crates full.

crabitat *n.* Pubic hair.

crab ladder *1. n.* The *male* penis. *2. n.* The hairy line that links the top of the pubes to the belly button. *Crab trellis, pubic footpath.*

crab paste *n.* A deposit of *fanny batter,* especially on a cucumber. *'This salad tastes funny, nan.' 'Eat it up, it's just a bit of crab paste.'*

crab picker's fingers *n.* The malodorous result of consorting with a lady of relaxed bathing habits, a happenstance that results in digits scented similarly to those of a manual labourer employed in a crustacean processing facility.

crabs *n. Bollock jockeys, mechanical dandruff,* pubic lice. What a young man catches under the pier.

crabstick *1. n.* An unappetising, savoury pink mouthful that is often touted round the pub. *2. n.* An unappetising, savoury pink mouthful that is often touted round the pub.

crack *1. n. Minge, fanny,* as famously owned by a young lady from Ealing. *'Close your legs, honey. Folks will see your crack.'* (Ronald Reagan at his presidential inauguration, 1980). *2. n.* Pointless *bollocks* spoken after four pints of Guinness in Irish theme pubs. *3. n.* The cleft of the *arse* cheeks. The *bottom line* or *cleftal horizon.*

crack a boiling egg *euph.* Descriptive of the aftermath of a bathtime act of monomanual pleasure, whereby the bather is surrounded by bobbing white flotsam, similar to the stringy albumen leaked by a cracked egg into a pan of water.

crack addict *1. n.* A fellow who has a penchant for the *wrong'un. 2. n.* A fellow who has a penchant for the *right 'un.*

crack a fat *v.* To achieve a *bone on.*

crack a moistie *v. Aus.* Of a *rude lady,* to become aroused in the *downstairs department.* To get a *wide on.*

crack and bone man *n.* A bisexual or *happy shopper.* *'Honestly, I'm not fussy. I'm a crack and bone man.'*

crackaratti *n.* The luminaries that make up the cream of the Glaswegian narcotics community, who convene their daily *salons philiosophiques* outside the Renfield Centre at around 5.30pm to take advantage of the free soup.

crack a stiffy *v.* To *crack a fat.*

crackcident *1. n.* A slip whereby *it* accidentally goes in *the wrong hole* during a romantic assignation. *2. n.* A slip where a liquid accidentally comes out instead of a gas. *Jacksident.*

crackerjacks *n.* Testicles. *'It's Friday, it's five to five, and I'm off upstairs to whack me crackerjacks.'*

crack hanger *n.* The inverted coat-hanger-shaped

triangle of thong visible on women bending over in hipster jeans. Also *top triangle.*

crackler *n.* A particularly satisfying *dump* that crackles like somebody gently crumpling a kettle chips bag as it exits the *nipsy.*

crackling *1. n.* According to your dad, the best bit of a Sunday roast. *2. n.* According to your dad, the best bit of *Top of the Pops,* when Pan's People came on.

crack maggot *n.* See *man overboard.*

crackne *n. medic.* A profusion of spots in or around the *arse* cleavage; a condition sometimes exhibited by actors in pornographic videos, apparently.

crack of doom *1. n.* A term lifted from the Good Book and Shakespeare that is, apparently (we wouldn't know without looking it up), descriptive of a portentous trumpet blast signalling the Day of Judgement. *2. n.* The ominous sound of a loud fanfare from the *brass eye. 3. n.* The *event horizon.*

crack one's back *v.* To commence a long overdue *Ingrid, ie.* Where one's spinal column sounds like it is breaking up and is about to emerge through one's *clackervalve.*

crack one's nuts *v.* To empty your *pods.*

crack open the bubbly *v.* To splash diarrhoea everywhere, although, all things considered, there's precious little cause for celebration.

cracksuit *n.* Convenient form of leisure clothing favoured by chemically dependant members of the urban underclasses. A *smacksuit.*

crack the flags *v.* A vigorous, no nonsense *gut drop* that makes a fresh, crisp sound.

crack the pan *v.* To lay a massive *egg, chip the china.*

crackuum *n.* A person who sucks all the "crack" out of a room. Typically someone who talks about work or any other matter not relating to football, beer, cars or *fanny. 'Today's deaths: William the Lion, Scottish King, 1214; Tamanishiki San'emon, Japanese sumo wrestler, 1938; Benjamin Britten, British crackuum, 1976.'*

cradle of filth *n.* Any *ad-hoc* contrivance fashioned from *bog roll* that allows a person in a less-than-sanitary public *shitter* who is *snipping off a length of dirty spine* to do so without fear of splash-back from the AIDS-riddled water below.

cradock *1. n.* A *cock-a-fanny. 2. n.* An old *cunt* with wonky, bright red lips. Named after the famous TV chef of the 1960s and 1970s, Fanny Cradock, who was an old *cunt* with wonky, bright red lips.

craft ale fan *euph.* An alcoholic. Someone who quaffs 8.5% lager at lunchtime because of the "hoppy" flavour or whatever.

CRAFT/craft *1. acronym. medic.* Doctor's notes terminology for a geriatric patient exhibiting

symptoms of the onset of senile dementia. Can't Remember A Fucking Thing. *2. acronym.* Term used by educationalists on school records to describe the learning potential of their less academically gifted pupils.

craftsmanshit *n.* Badly constructed flat-pack furniture. *'What do you think of my Billy bookcase, Doreen?' 'Pure craftsmanshit, Kevin. Maybe you should have read the instructions.'*

crafty *n.* A discreet act of *self pollution. 'The inspector completely over-reacted when he caught our Steve having a crafty on the bus. He says they might take his PSV licence off him.'*

crafty ant *n.* Awkwardly instantaneous occurrence of *ringpiece* itchiness which happens at the exact moment when it would be most unsuitable to give it a good scratch. Also *wire spiders.*

crafty butcher *n.* A man who likes to "take his meat around the back."

crafty cuckoo *n.* A cheeky chappie who fertilises a *bird's* eggs and then leaves them to be raised by another. *'Today's deaths: Michael Hordern, Paddington actor, 1995; Barbara Castle, Mrs Slocombe-like UK politician, 2002; Hughie Green, TV presenter and crafty cuckoo, 1997.'*

crafty Damien *n.* An opportunistic *wank* at work. Derivation unknown.

crafty fisherman *n.* An hermaphrodite, *ie.* One who carries around "a spare set of *tackle".*

cranberry dip *n.* A special sauce for sausages only available during *rag week. Tomato boat ketchup.*

crane operator *n.* A *stick vid* actress with a *joy stick* in each hand, the motion of which gives the appearance that she is positioning a crane or wrecking ball. Also *Madam two-swords, downhill skier.*

crank *1. n.* Penis. *2. rhym. slang.* To have a *wank* in the style of someone attempting to start a vintage car. A *ham shank. 3. n.* A bathroom multi-tasking exercise. A *crap* and a *wank* performed simultaneously by someone with an extremely busy schedule. *4. v.* To cry and masturbate at the same time.

crankenstein *n.* A *Charlie* with all bolts stuck through its neck. *'What's the matter, Justin? You're white as a sheet.' 'I was just stood next to Evan in the bogs having a piss and I accidentally caught a glimpse of his crankenstein out the corner of my eye, Rabbi.'*

crankshaft *n.* The bit of a man that must be vigorously *tugged* in order to get him going.

crank up Old Savage and blaze one out! *1. exclam.* As – apparently – used by a character in *Breaking Bad* on being introduced to a chum's epic new sound system. *2. euph.* To have a *wank*. *'Wow! That is so cool, man, it makes me want to crank up Old Savage and blaze one out!'*

crap *1. n. Shit. 2. v.* To *shit. 3. adj. Shit. 4. exclam. Shit.*

crapalanche *n.* A sudden, violent, downhill *Simon Cowell* movement that can be set off by a loud noise.

crapaplegic *n.* One who finds himself unable to walk after spending far too long reading *auto-bog-raphies* on the *shitter.* A *crapple.*

crap apples *n.* Plastic bags filled with *dog-toffee* found hanging on tree branches and hedgerows.

craparazzi *n.* Photographers assigned to the *shitterati, eg.* Snapping former *Big Brother* contestant Cameron Stout leaving a launderette in Arbroath for a six-page spread in *Heat* magazine.

crapas *n. Sp.* A selection of small *turds* which vary considerably in texture and colour, deposited into the *bum sink* the day after a suspiciously good value all-you-can-eat buffet.

crap-au-chino *n.* The act of *shitting* one's pale strides after a strong cup of roast coffee.

crape diem *phr. Lat.* A wise motto that will stand one in good stead throughout one's life: Literally, to seize any and every opportunity that arises to take a *dump. 'Crape diem. The wise man goes for a shit when he can, the foolish man when he must.'* (Aristotle).

crap flaps *n.* The doorstep of the *nipsy.* The insides of the cheeks of the buttocks of the *arse.*

crapidation *n.* In a public lavatory, the fear of the appalling horrors about to be exposed when lifting the lid. *'With a trembling hand and much crapidation, Roderick made to lift the lid. What he saw plastered in the bowl made the blood freeze in his veins. It was a sight that was to cast a black shadow over his soul for the rest of his life.'* (from *The Fall of the Shithouse of Usher* by Edgar Allan Poe).

crapier-mâché *n.* Those little bits of *bumwad* that gather around one's *dot* after a severe wiping. A *wasps' nest.*

crap in hand *phr.* Late to an important event that you had forgotten all about until ten minutes before the off, carrying a gift that has very evidently been hurriedly procured from whichever shop or petrol station was open *en route* to the party/church/crematorium.

crapiphany *n.* A *Boxing Day log* of such stubborn staying power that it remains *in shitu* until well into Plough Monday.

crapitulate *v.* To give in to the urge to let loose a *crappachino with chocolate sprinkles* in hostile circumstances, *eg.* At the in-laws', or your significant other's after a first sleepover. *'I'd managed to hold off until the Sunday morning at Glastonbury, but I had to crapitulate in the end or I was never going to make it through Van Morrison's set.'*

crapitus *n. Lat. medic.* The creaking noise emitted by overstretched or broken *farting strings* as a *Meat Loaf's daughter* forces its way out of the *chamber of horrors,* sounding similar to the noises made in days of yore by a galleon wallowing at anchor.

crapkins *n.* Fast food restaurant paper serviettes which, when pilfered in handfuls, act as free *shitscrape.* Popular amongst cash-strapped students.

crap nap *n.* A refreshing alcohol-induced siesta taken in a pub gents cubicle, when one is overcome with sudden tiredness at the effort of pulling down one's trousers and sitting on the *throne. Shitwinks, farty winks.*

crapocalypse *n.* A *crapaclysmic shit* of such harrowingly biblical proportions that it can only be interpreted as a herald of The End, as prophesied in the *Book of Revelations* and the *Daily Express.*

crapodile *n.* A large and very unpleasant surprise that lurks in the water, waiting to prey on unwary visitors who visit remote public lavs. Usually only the top part of the beast is visible.

crap of honour *n.* The last piece of foulage that resists the urge to *go to the beach* with the rest when the *bog* is flushed, and does half a dozen clockwise circuits before following its colleagues. Also *bob-a-jobbie, humming turd, non-mover at number two.*

crapostrophe *n.* A trip to the toilet that punctuates an otherwise dull working day.

crappaging *n.* Packaging that is virtually impossible to open without giving yourself a hernia, severing a main artery and/or destroying the product you are trying to access.

crapper *1. n.* The lavatory. Named after the inventor of the self-cleaning water closet, Thomas Shitehouse. *2. n.* A *crap rapper.* From crap + rapper. *'Today's birthdays: Lev Demin, Soviet cosmonaut, 1926; Mohammed Abed Elhai, Sudanese writer and academic, 1944; Daz Sampson, British crapper, 1974.'*

crappetiser *n.* A *pony & trap* taken to make a bit of space for your tea.

crappetite *1. n.* An insatiable hunger for the *jobby engine. 'That Mexican/Thai sausage curry from the Chinese last night has given me a fierce crappetite this morning, I can tell you.' 2. n.* A penchant for more proletarian comestibles, such as Scotch eggs, Pot Noodles, KFC chicken poppers, Rustler's burgers, pickled onion Space Raiders and Angel Delight.

crapple *n.* An apple of disappointing quality. Derivation unknown.

crappling hook *n.* Any convenient tool, usually one's fingers if truth be told, used to fish out the floating remnants of a recently chopped *dead otter* to avoid the embarrassment of your host/ colleagues/cellmates discovering any telltale evidence of your recent, unflushable efforts.

crapprehension *n.* Ironically *Simon Cowell*-loosening anxiety that a forthcoming *dropped gut* may result in a *code brown* situation.

crappuccino *n.* A particularly frothy form of diarrhoea which one only gets while abroad. See *kexpresso.*

crappy ending *1. n.* In a British massage parlour, a disappointing conclusion to proceedings. *2. n.* In a German massage parlour, a thoroughly successful conclusion to proceedings.

crappy salad *n. Scots.* Token leafy foodstuffs, including lettuce and that. *Gastroturf.* *''Whit's the matter, Wullie? Ye look like ye've seen a ghostie.' 'Jings, hoots and crivens m'boab, Angus! Some bampot's left a wee bit o' crappy salad in the box next tae ma deep-fried pizza.'*

craprobat *n.* One who performs incredible feats of physical flexibility when *parking their fudge.* Like the dirty *bastard* who famously managed to leave his mark up every door and wall of the *bogs* at the entrance to Tsavo East National Park in Kenya, and even managed to hit the ventilation fan high on the ceiling, plus every window.

craps *n. US.* A shit game with dice.

crap's cradle *n.* A Möbius strip of *arsewipe* positioned in the *Rick Witter* bowl prior to defecation in order to minimise embarrassing *ploppage.*

craptain Webb *n.* A long *turd* that "dips its toe" in the water before diving in and embarking for France. A *bridger* or *bottom log.*

craptivating *adj.* Descriptive of something completely *shit,* yet strangely fascinating, *eg. All New TV's Naughtiest Blunders,* (2004), presented by Steve Penk.

craptocurrency *1. n.* Sound investments advertised via *Frankie* sites and spam email. Obscure clones of Bitcoin "into" which "the smart money" is, apparently, "getting". *2. n.* Scottish banknotes tendered south of the border.

craptop *n.* The temporary replacement computer that you are forced to use while your usual machine is at the menders or being examined by the police.

crapture *n.* The semi-ecstatic afterglow of a successful *sit down toilet adventure.*

crash land the helicopter *v.* To engage in a particularly stressful, two-handed battle with your *chopper* that ends messily.

crash mat *n.* A *pap baffle, turd raft, pilo.*

crash one's pants *v.* To momentarily lose control of one's *motions* leading to a *pile up* in one's *garnies.* *'I was so scared when Derek went into his trance, I nearly crashed my pants, I can tell you.'* (Yvette Fielding, *Most Haunted Live,* Living TV, Oct 31st 2003).

crash the yoghurt truck *v.* To *shed your load* at the *Billy Mill roundabout. Empty the wank tanks.*

crate of shame *n.* A council-supplied glass-recycling box in full view of one's judgemental neighbours, overflowing with damning evidence of the previous week's consumption of beer, wine and spirits. With a token coffee jar on the top in an attempt to cover up the ignominy. Also *sound of shame n.* The thunderous noise of crashing beer bottles, wine bottles, vodka bottles, gin bottles, *trampagne* bottles and so on, as they are dumped into one's bin, preferably in the dark.

cravate de notaire *n. Fr.* Literally, a *solicitor's tie.* Version of *pearl necklace* from France, where lawyers in courtrooms have all *spunk* down their shirt fronts.

crazy log *n.* A little *shit* that produces an annoying crescendo of high-pitched *ringtones.*

creaking gate *n. medic.* Doctors' terminology for a person who has been in bad health for some time but who *refuses to buy the farm.*

cream *v.* To *drop your yop, esp.* in your pants. To *milm.*

creama-donna *n.* The *creme-de-la-femme, moip, fanny batter, love juice* – call it what you will – of a dirty lady who finds herself in a state of se*ual arousal, most likely whilst watching that bit in *Pride and Prejudice* where Mr Darcy walks out the pond in his wet *dunghampers.*

cream egg *n.* A rather sickly treat for a *felcher*; a *snowdrop* with a chocolate coating.

cream geez *n.* Affectionate term for *love butter* that's been left in the *wank tanks* too long; an alternative to *ballpaper paste* that goes nice on a *cracker.*

creaming into the void *euph.* Descriptive of a lonely act of *onanism,* or perhaps an unkind comment a fellow might make after *plastering* a particularity wide *hallway.*

cream, over-whisking the *n.* Excessive indulgence of one's *egg white cannon. 'You've got a distinctive hobble in your step, Watson. You've not by any chance been over-whisking the cream since the* *missus left, have you?'*

cream pie *n.* In the world of erotic cinematography or photogravures, a *blurtch* or *freckle* getting all *spoff* shot up it, with all *spoff* up it and/or with all *spoff* dripping out of it. We truly live in a wonderful age.

cream rinse *n.* A bubbly hair-care product that is often provided gratis with a *facial.* A *spermanent wave.*

cream tea *1. n.* An elegant afternoon treat that a thoughtful gentleman might provide for a ladyfriend. *2. n.* A couple of generously proportioned *nipplecakes*, topped off with a healthy dollop of *squirty cream. Iced baps. 3. n.* A posh *bird's* cuppa into which a *milk monitor* has *jaffed.* Over the back of a spoon.

crease grease *n. Arse vinegar. 'Amazing. New Azox non-bio even lifted the ingrained crease grease out of this thirty-stone driving instructor's nylon Y-fronts after a long summer's day on the road with a nervous driver in a Citroen C2 with broken air conditioning and jammed windows.'*

creative juices flowing, get one's *euph.* To *crack one out* first thing.

credit crunch *1. n.* An international economic meltdown which caused the price of Tesco's 26p oranges to go up to 29p. *2. n.* In masturbatory management, the critical point when a man who has been single for a prolonged period finds that he has insufficient collateral in his *wank bank* to fund his increasingly impoverished efforts at *self abuse.*

credit cruncher *n.* An opportunistic *Max Planck* enjoyed as a result of whichever fiscal downturn is currently occurring, *eg.* While at home due to reduced hours, being laid off or made redundant, or perhaps during a leisurely visit to the *bogs* at work because it is quiet.

credit cunt *n.* One who has come out of the present worldwide economic meltdown in markedly better circumstances than when they went into it.

credit munch *n.* A *drink on a stick* or *vertical bacon sandwich* enjoyed while temporarily mired in reduced circumstances.

credit score *n.* Getting a sexual favour off the other half in return for notably good behaviour, such as painting the kitchen, not *pissing* in the wardrobe too much. Cashing in your *pink shield stamps.*

creme de la femme *n. Moip.*

creme de month *n.* Bi-fortnightly *egg nog* that tastes anything but refreshingly minty.

creosort *n.* A woman who has overdone it with the fake tan.

crepitate *v.* To discharge a noxious fluid accompanied by a slight explosive sound. How Stephen Fry would describe *following through.*

crescent wank *n.* To arrange one's favourite *jazz periodicals* in a half-moon display, before kneeling down to perform a five finger exercise on the *spunk trumpet.*

cresta cunt *n.* A state of extreme female arousal. From the 1970s fizzy drink slogan, *viz.* "It's frothy, man".

crevice ticks *n. Winnits, freckle maggots, mudlice.*

cribbage *n. Doing* someone *up the wrong 'un* with a phallic object; *pegging.* From the traditional maiden-aunt-friendly game's traditional scoring system.

cricket ball wrapped in Brillo pads, like a *sim.* An extremely dense, heavily-compacted and knobbly *Andrew* that passes about as smoothly as a Chubby Brown corporate gig for the Festival of Light.

cricketer's tea *n.* A liquid lunch of the sort formerly favoured by thirsty Ashes hero Freddie "Andrew" Flintoff.

cricket week *n.* A five-day test, when a gentleman must *bowl from the gasworks end* while his wife is *padded up.*

cri de curry *n. Fr.* The plaintive, anguished howl (*eg.* "Fire in the hole!") of a person who has over-indulged in the culinary delights of the Orient the previous evening, and whose *fundament* is now paying the inevitable bill. Plus tips.

crimbo crawler *exclam.* A postman, binman, milkman *etc.*, who acts like a miserable *bastard* all year round, but suddenly starts being nice just before Christmas in the hope of getting a festive gratuity.

crimping off a length *n. milit.* Naval slang for *dropping a depth charge, laying a cable.*

crimping the walnut *phr.* Physically twitching the *brass eye* to prevent the *rat's nose* poking out. *'Watch Sky News Political Correspondent Adam Boulton crimping the walnut on live TV. You won't believe what happens when he sneezes!' (Buzzfeed).*

crimson rambler *n.* A bold and adventurous fellow who refuses to be put off his stride simply because his missus is *dropping clots.*

crimson wave *n.* Also *crimson tide.* See *surfing the crimson wave.*

Cringer & Battle-Cat *1. n.* Something off *Masters of the Universe;* He-Man's tiger horse thing that he rides round on and its alter-ego, or something, probably the other way round. *2. n.* The two extreme states of male genitalias.

crinkle cuts *n. medic.* The large, crenellated *scallop lips* that protrude from a salty *bag. Real McCoy's,* *turkey's wattles*, a *doctor's signature.*

crinkles *n. Cock* wrinkles. *'Q: What's the first thing to come out of a man's penis when he gets an erection? A: The crinkles!'* (from The *Jim'll Fix It Joke Book*, BBC Publications 1975).

crinkly wrapper *1. n. rhym. slang.* The *brass eye.* That from which one *floats an air biscuit on the shite market. 2. n.* An ageing hip-hop artiste.

cripple shit *n.* A desperate urge to *drop off the shopping* that leaves one physically debilitated.

crips and bloods *1. n.* Rival Los Angeles-based street gangs. True dat. *2. n.* A post-curry *shite* that combines the twin qualities of galloping *squits* and a bleeding *nipsy.*

crisping *n.* The result of being so distracted while ensconced on the *jobby engine* that any residual ordure remaining around the *nipsy* dries to a consistency that means wiping is no longer required and a brisk brush off or stamp of the feet should suffice.

crispy pocket *n.* The genteel art of *wanking* into the hotel bathrobe pocket, leaving it so it looks untouched as a cheeky surprise for the next guest.

Croatian windsock *n.* The sorry state of a chap's *quiver* when he has *lost his darts. 'Sorry love, we'll have to give it a miss tonight. I've got a cock like a Croatian wind sock.'*

crockstick *n.* A crutch, especially when used by someone whose injury obviously healed months ago. *'I see your Jim's still on his crocksticks.' 'Yes. He's been off work six months now waiting for his compo to come through for that big bag of Quavers that fell on his foot in the canteen.'*

crofting *n.* Rugged, tweedy, north Scottish form of *cottaging*, possibly taking place in a granite but'n'ben.

crone bone *n.* A state of somewhat unsettling sexual arousal brought on by an unlikely stimulus, *eg.* A picture of Camilla Parker-Bowels in jodhpurs.

Crone's disease *n. medic.* Tragic condition that turns fruity *milfs* and *cougars* into embittered witches and harridans.

cronk *v. rhym. slang.* To do a *shite.* Named after the late US broadcaster Walter "and that's the way it is" Cronkshite.

crop spraying *v.* See *pebble dashing.*

crosshair *n.* A stray *pube* lying horizontally across the *hog's eye*, thus creating a handy, sniper-like scope during the act of micturition, allowing one to aim accurately at the seat and floor.

crossing the streams *1. phr.* A reference to something that happens in *Ghostbusters* (1984) that we have neither the time nor the inclination to bother looking up. *2. n.* An amusing but

non-sexual (usually) *watersport* which takes place between two chaps at the urinal and typically results in wet feet.

cross sector expertise *euph.* Bisexuality.

crosswebber *n.* Someone who lies about their gender on the internet.

crosswind *n.* A violent or angry *trouser cough* which could make changing lanes difficult.

crossword, teeth like a *sim.* Descriptive of the off-putting appearance of horrendous dentition, liberally strewn with gaps and cavities. Along with a sexy *bird* taking off her sunglasses to reveal that she was cross-eyed, and another one turning round and revealing herself to be Henry McGee with a bubble perm, a girl smiling and having *teeth like a crossword* was the third situation that Benny Hill encountered while trying to chat up women in unrealistic, speeded-up discotheques on his show. *English teeth, a pan of burnt chips.*

crotch broth *n. Scots.* Semen, *manfat etc.* *'Och, help m'boab, Morag. Oor Wullie's got all crotch broth matted in his sporran again.'*

crotch crickets *n.* Crabs, cockhoppers.

crotch eggs *n.* Hairy *knackers.*

crotch fruit *n.* Affectionate name for one's offspring. Also *fuck trophies, cuntburps.*

crotch gremlins *n. medic.* Any genital ill humour of the sort which is typically contracted from dodgy foreign *pieces* or Skegness toilet seats. *Pox, cock rot, clap,* the *Val Doonican.*

crotch opera *n. Aus.* Classy *grumble*, shot using a tripod.

crouching tiger, hidden dragon *n.* Ancient Chinese sexual position. *Doggy-style* sex with a woman so *fugly* that a chap can't bring himself to look her in the face.

Crouch's leg *n.* A long, thin, pale, pasty, sorry-looking penis with which its owner, contrary to all outward impressions, just keeps on *scoring.*

crouton *n.* An erection that floats in one's soup.

crow *1. n. US.* That *muck* which has been *chucked*, esp. onto the *mapatasi.* Post-*porking* residue on the *hairy clam. Muffdruff. 2. n.* Nostril carrion. A *bogie, greb, greenie*, particularly when wiped on a wall.

crowbar *n.* An erection which is hard enought to force a sash window. A *jemmy-on.*

crowd control *n.* The purpose of underwear items that are designed to hold ladies' *thronging masses* in check. *'Even with them safety pins, Liz Hurley's really struggling with crowd control in that frock. Sandy Gall, News at Ten, Leicester Square.'*

crowd pleaser *n.* Unusual or noteworthy *movement* which one feels an urge to show off to someone before flushing it away.

crowd sauced *adj.* Descriptive of a lucky adult entertainment actress who has achieved *full funding* from a large group of willing backers. See also *twenty-one gun salute, plasterer's radio.*

crowdsaucing *n.* Multi-participant *cake icing.* Bukkake. See also *iced by a blind baker.*

crowning glory *n.* A *mole at the back door* that promises to perfectly top off a thoroughly successful day.

crown jowls *n.* The baggy bit of excess skin that hangs off the end of the *grub screw. Kenny's hood.* The *fiveskin.*

Crown St. Princess *n.* A scrawny *good time girl* who works on Crown Street, which is apparently the red light district of Liverpool. A Scouse *mattress-back, Covent Garden nun.*

crow poacher *n.* An inveterate nose picker.

crow's nest *n.* A particularly ramshackle *snatch* in which a *one-eyed pirate* might feel at home. Also *worzel gusset.*

Croydon national anthem *n.* The sound of sirens, which causes the populace of the popular Surrey town to stand. A *Bolton alarm clock.*

Croydon plaque *n.* A temporary police notice commemorating a recent newsworthy event, and appealing for witnesses to come forward. Named after the bullet-riddled South London beauty spot, where such lively street furniture is a commonplace addition to the lively urban *aceldama.*

Cruella de Vil *n. prop.* A tonsorial flourish typically bestowed upon raven-haired *adult* actresses at the culmination of a scene; a dramatic flash of white *heir gel* across their coiffure. *'Just fast forward to the last bit where he gives her a Cruella de Vil, granddad.'*

Cruft's jellies *n.* The uniquely bouncing *shirt potatoes* of the *well-nourished* matrons who canter around the show ring of the famous *shit machine* festival.

cruise at periscope depth *n.* To walk about in the morning with your twitching *Kilroy* poking over the waistband of your *grundies.*

cruiser and tug *n.* The common phenomenon of a stunning female who is always accompanied by an *homely* little fat pal.

crumpa lumpa *n.* A tubby, *cake-worrying* lady with an orange hue that suggests that she frequents a cheap *bimbo bakery* or, alternatively, that she is exhibiting the symptoms of a beta carotene overdose.

crumpee *n.* A non-gender-specific affliction affecting those in the autumn years of their lives,

whereby they cough, *trump* and *pee* almost simultaneously. *'Fetch a mop, mam. She's done another crumpee.'*

crumpet *1. n.* A traditional Scottish cake made of soft, light dough, eaten toasted and buttered, and much craved by the late Sid James. *2. n.* 1970s *blart.*

crumpet batter *n.* Gentleman's *erotic spendings.*

crumpeteer *n.* A fellow who has a way with the ladies. An expert in the science of *crumpetology, eg.* Rod Stewart, Mick Jagger, Les Dennis.

crumpet trumpet *n.* An involuntary release of air from a young lady's *front bottom.* A *vulvuzela, forward hat drop, queef, snatchaphone* or *Lawley kazoo.*

crumpet voluntary *n.* A *fannyfare* or *flap raspberry.* See also *frampton, sea breeze, queef, C-biscuit.*

crunchie *1. n.* A tasty confectionary snack. *2. n.* A brittle sock worn on the foot a day or two after one has *wanked* into it. A *bachelor's boomerang.*

crunk *n.* The *taint, barse, tintis, tinter.*

crustard *1. n.* A sweet mixture of cream and custard for use on desserts, it says here. *2. n.* The slightly less palatable substance often found under a poorly maintained *fiveskin. 'Another dollop of crustard on your apple pie, Mr Coren?'*

crusties *1. n.* Dog-on-a-string-owning soapophobes. *2. n.* Over-worn *bills* somewhat lacking in "April freshness". *Dunghampers* with a dirty *drip tray.*

crystal bollock *euph.* After seriously *pissing off* a significant other, the prognostical ability to foresee that you will not *get your end away* for many weeks.

Crystal Gayle *1. n. prop.* Long-haired, lightweight US country performer of the 1970s. *2. n.* A prison-based sexual act which may (in fact, almost certainly will) "make your *brown eye* blue". *'He walked into the shower block / Of Reading's dreadful gaol / And stooping to pick up the soap / The prisoner's face turned pale / As a voice behind him whispered / "How about a Crystal Gayle?"'* (from *The Ballad of Reading Gaol* by Oscar Wilde).

crystal maze, go *v.* To find oneself unable to perform a simple task due to pressure, *eg.* A learner being unable to get the car out of reverse gear during their driving test, Eamonn Holmes being unable to competently present a television programme when the cameras are on. To go all *cunty booby.*

crystal skull *1. n.* A Damien Hirst masterpiece consisting of a human cranium adorned with over eight billion pounds' worth of Swarovski crystals, like something from a Cheshire car boot sale or the window of Collectables. *2. n.* A young lady's head bejewelled with several *pods'* worth of *jelly jewellery.*

CSB *abbrev.* Default hairstyle setting for young lady *scratters.* From Chav Scrape Back.

C-section *1. n.* The use of surgery to deliver infants; a procedure dating back to Roman times and that. *2. n.* Roped off area of a Wetherspoon's wherein a stag-do or hen-night is being hosted.

CSI *abbrev.* The post-crime damage surveillance done in a room where a violent act of *self harm* has occurred. Cum Scene Investigation.

CT scan *n.* Act performed by men in public areas. A quick glance at passing ladies' *Toblerone tunnel* areas to check for the presence of *camels' toes.*

Cuban wank *n.* A *diddy-ride, Bombay roll* or *tit-wank.*

cubble *n.* A way of insulting someone in the vilest possible terms without resorting to the language of the gutter. From cunt + bubble. See also *kingbast, funt.*

cubicle clown *n.* That person in the next lavatory cubicle who sounds like he is making balloon animals.

cubicle grin *n.* A sly smirk on one's face while standing at the public lavatory hand basin as an unsuspecting victim walks in and enters one's recently vacated defecatory paralleliped where he will encounter the full, foetid stench of the recent *porcelain massacre* that has occurred therein.

cubism *1. n.* An early twentieth century school of painting typified by the works of Picasso and Braque which amalgamated multiple viewpoints into a complex surface of geometrical planes. *2. n.* A harmless gentleman's hobby which involves sneaking into a cubicle in the female toilets of a pub, club or department store and listening in to the action in the neighbouring "cubes".

CUBs/cubs *acronym. Aus.* Cashed Up Bogans: an Antipodean expression to describe people with lots of money but very little taste.

cuckold *n.* A man whose wife allows another man to lay his *cock eggs* in her *box.*

cuckoo *n.* A scoundrel who moves in on a *bird's nest* when someone else has nipped to the bar after doing all the groundwork.

cuckoo cable *n.* A scuttled *dreadnought* abandoned in someone else's *bog pan,* such that it becomes their responsibility.

cuckoo clock *n.* A *cottage* where the patrons pop out from the door every quarter of an hour in the hope of drumming up a bit of business. *'Where are you off to, George?' 'I'm just off down the cuckoo clock in the park, Andrew.'*

cuckoo fart *n.* The act of *dropping one's hat* in the presence of another person in such a manner that they believe the resulting miasma to be their own dirty work.

cuckoo nest *n.* Stuffing loads of *bog roll* into a public *crapper* in order to construct a cosy roost for one's *bum eggs,* where they can be admired *in situ* by the next lucky occupant.

cuckoo shit *n.* A *log* laid in another man's *pot.*

cucumber blight, touch of the *euph. medic.* Cockrot, happy rash. *'I've got the results of your tests here, Lord Archer, and I'm afraid you've got a touch of the cucumber blight.'*

cuddle *n. rhym. slang.* A *slash.* From cuddle and kiss = *piss. 'Excuse me, vicar. Do help yourself to another rich tea. I'm off to the shitter for a quick cuddle.'*

cuddle puddle *n.* The wet patch left on the bed after an *adult episode.. 'Fucking hell. This mattress is soaking. Have you pissed the bed again?' 'No, that's just the cuddle puddle is that. Fancy swapping sides?'*

Cuddles's mouth *n.* A particularly free-moving set of *lady lips,* framed by an enormous clump of gingery fuzz. Named after the late Keith "Orville the Duck" Harris's less successful, though equally annoying, *gobshite* monkey companion.

cuddle the monkey *v.* After a bout of *chimping* (or even half way through one), to fall asleep while still grasping *half a teacake.*

cue rest *n.* A keen *fellatrix's* well-worn chin cleft.

cuff guff *n.* A boilersuit-clad workperson's method of sneakily deploying a *trouser cough* in a colleague's direction by *dropping one* and then squatting and pointing a sleeve, thus propelling the *beefy eggo* into their face.

cuff stinks *n.* The malodorous end result of an unfortunate shirt mishap suffered when wiping one's *nipsy* following a messy *Douglas.*

cuff the dummy *v. US. milit.* To wank, scrub the cook, box the Jesuit.

Culturally Unique National Treasure *acronym. euph.* The sort of people whose endearing charm captures the hearts of folk at home and abroad. *'That Piers Morgan is such a Culturally Unique National Treasure, isn't he?'*

cum *1. v.* A sexiness-enhancing mis-spelling of *come* used by the authors of *bongular* literature to describe male ejaculation. *2. n.* A sexiness-enhancing mis-spelling of *come* used by the authors of *bongular* literature to describe male ejaculate. *3. n.* A sexiness-enhancing mis-spelling of *come* used by Noddy Holder in the title of his band Slade's 1972 hit *Cum On Feel the Noize.*

cumbalina *n.* A female of diminutive stature who

demonstrates a marked penchant for *pork lollies*. A *throwabout* or *laptop*.

cumbeard *n*. A white, coagulated sperminiferous goatee worn by one who has greedily helped themselves to a double portion of *spangle*.

Cumberland curl *1. n*. A somewhat off-puttingly designed helical Wetherspoon's pub sausage which presents a convincing simulacrum of a *shite*. *2. n*. A somewhat off-puttingly designed *shite* which presents a convincing simulacrum of a Wetherspoon's pub sausage. *2. n*. A gentleman's *porky banger*. Also *Cumberland*.

Cumberland gap *1. n*. A repetitive, annoying skiffle song by late banjoist Lonnie Donegan which topped the hit parade in 1957. *2. n*. The triangular gap at the top of a lady's thighs which arouses curiosity as to whether the old *Cumberland curl* could fit through. The *quedge*.

cumber-queue *n*. A fresh selection of vaguely cylindrical groceries lined up on a table, waiting to be pressed into use in a nightmarish, home-made *grumble-flick*.

cumbilical cord *n*. A string of *jizz* dangled between a bloke's *herman jelmet* and his missus's *snatch*.

Cumbledore *n. prop*. A *plasterer's radio* whose chin is adorned with a long, white beard in the fashion of the late Hogwarts headmaster. Although his was made out of hair rather than *jitler*.

cumbleweed *n*. Crispy, crinkly leafed flora which proliferates under the beds of teenage boys, bachelors, students and jobseekers, becoming particularly abundant immediately after each time the household's broadband download speed improves. *Cumcabbage, bedroom popadoms, porn crackers*.

cumbrellas *1. n. Dunkies. 2. n*. Oversized false lashes, worn by sexually promiscuous ladies to protect their eyes from low-flying *jism*.

cumchugger *n*. A *bird* who enjoys guzzling *spadge*.

cumcrete *n*. A naturally occurring *rock*-based aggregate which, once set, has sufficient tensile strength to bond hairs together in a vice-like manner. *'Oi, Eric. What's this stuff all up the dog's back? I can't get his brush through it.' 'Cumcrete, Ethel.'*

cum cunnus semper cunnum *phr. Lat*. A learned, pithy response to an aggravating person, who will be impressed by one's effortless access to an ancient language much employed by scholars and persons of letters. "Once a cunt, always a cunt."

cumdown *n*. That feeling of soul-crushing worthlessness that follows a *Sherman* as inevitably as night follows day. See also *wangst* and *wank hangover*.

cum duster *n*. Whichever unfortunate object happens to be conveniently at hand for the post-*coital* or post-*wank* clean-up.

cumersault *n*. An acrobatic ejaculation performed without the aid of a safety net.

cum/fart zone *n*. A *boomerang-socked* bachelor's foetid bedroom or, even worse, his *Dutch oven*.

cumglum *adj*. Feeling sadness deep in one's soul after yet another *one off the wrist*. *'A cumglum Mr Johnson stood up and announced the latest Covid figures to cheers from the Tory back benches.'*

cumjunctivitis *n. medic*. Unpleasant, sticky eye infection which is an unavoidable complication following careless *telescoping*.

cummed up *adj*. Curdled with *heir gel*. *'Bloody hell, love you should have kept your glasses on. Your eyes are all cummed up.'*

cummingtonite *1. n. chem*. A metamorphic amphibole mineral with the chemical composition $(Mg,Fe2+)2$ $(Mg,Fe2+)5Si8O22(OH)2$; being magnesium iron silicate hydroxide. Don't say we never learn you anything. *2. n*. A romantic fallow period; an equivalent to Superman's Kryptonite that leaves a gentleman prone to being *up and over like a pan of milk*.

cumoflage *n*. Putting one's crusty *Womble's toboggan* at the bottom of the laundry pile in the hope that it blends in with the respectable washing and one's mum/wife doesn't notice.

cum on one's faggots *v*. To put one's future prospects in jeopardy as the result of a foolhardy action. To *piss on one's chips* or *fart on one's Weetabix. eg*. A jewellery firm boss jocularly referring to his company's products as "crap", or a butcher being exposed in his local paper for masturbating on his rissoles.

cumpilation *n*. A snappily edited compendium of the best bits from a variety of *grumble vids*. A *top of the popshots* chart rundown, if you will, but preferably without a running commentary from Bruno Brookes.

cum powder *n*. The ammunition with which an elderly gentleman's failing *weapon* is cocked. *'I fear the Duke will want to shoot all over my Bristols.' 'Don't worry, dear. He is so old the only thing he can fire is a bit of cum powder.'*

cumputer *n*. An old PC used solely for the perusal and storage of *grumble* from the world wide web. A *filth machine, dirty Mac* or *faptop*.

cum shields *n*. Ladies' spectacles. *'Go and put your cum shields on, Dierdre. I'm feeling right randy tonight.'*

cumster *n*. A small, hamster-like female who fills

her cheeks with *nuts.*

cum to mind *v.* Of a person or favoured memory, to appear as a mental image in the imagination of one embarking on the *vinegar strokes. 'These days I find it's often Kylie Minogue who cums to mind when I'm poking the missus.'*

cum to one's senses *v.* To experience feelings of self loathing and disgust immediately upon ejaculation when, all of a sudden, one experiences a Damascene conversion and wearing the girl-friend's lingerie, *poking* a Bangkok *ladyboy* or *having one off the wrist* into Carol Decker's wardrobe no longer seem a such a good idea.

cum tree *1. n. bot. Pyrus calleryana* – the Callery pear that has an aroma like *spunk.* Particularly so if a load of dendrophiles have wanked up it. *2. n.* An *adult* performer – or a keen amateur for that matter – who has been in the firing line for a substantial barrage of *money shots.* An artiste with a *face like a St Bernard's chin.*

cumulonimbecile *n.* Someone who is ignorant of how to pay *lip service* to a lady. Also *clamateur.*

cumulonimbus *n. Lat.* Oral sex. Tongular stimulation of a lady's *wail switch.*

cumuppance *n.* Finally getting caught *pulling the pope's cap off* on the sofa by the missus/mother/partner/Alison Hammond and a live *This Morning* camera crew.

cum whip *n.* The act of grasping one's *todger* at a critical point during a bout of *self harm* and enhancing the *muck chucking* experience with a rapid, Indiana Jones-style snap of the wrist.

cunch *n.* A satisfying midday snack furnished by, or comprising of, the secret *girly parts* of an obliging ladyfriend. Derivation unknown.

cundensation *n.* The glistening droplets of *moip* that start to form on a previously cold *minge* when it comes into contact with something warm, *eg.* A cheeky finger, a sizeable *diamond cutter,* or the washing machine on its spin cycle.

cunk *n. Blip* that's well past its sell-by date. *Cunt gunk.*

cunker *n.* Romantic term for one of a lady's *bodily treasures.* The *snatch.*

cunnichingus *n.* Stimulating the female genitals with your chin in order to give your tongue a wee rest.

cunnifungus *n. Lat.* Female equivalent of *knob cheese'n'mushroom.*

cunnilingual *n.* Sufficiently fluent in a foreign tongue that one can seduce that country's women. Not all of them, obviously.

cunnimingus *v.* The act of orally pleasuring a lady

with personal hygiene issues. *Licking a nine volter.*

cunny *n. Lat. Fadge,* vagina. From the Latin *cunnus* = shagpipe.

cunny delight *n.* Highly-flavoured sticky juice imbibed from a *furry cup. Blip, bilp, milp.*

cunny dew *n.* Early morning *fanny batter.*

cunnylicious *adj.* Descriptive of any woman, or part thereof, demanding to be chomped down on.

cunny money *n.* That notional currency which is kept in the *gash register.*

cunshine *n.* The frustrating reflections which invariably hinder full enjoyment of the glossy *whacknicolour* photographs in *art pamphlets.* Also *porn glare, razzle dazzle.*

cunt *1. n. 14thC. medic.* Polite term for lady's genitals. *2. n. 21stC.* Impolite term for lady's genitals. *3. n.* How a person in the Cotswolds might refer to a mole. *'The cunts have dug up the lawn again, the little cunts.' 4. n.* A traffic warden.

cuntage *n.* Acts of profound idiocy. *'There's a lot of cuntage going on out there on the M25 today.'*

cuntan *n.* The pale complexion sported when returning from a holiday abroad by a lucky gentleman who has been unavoidably detained in his hotel bedroom throughout his sojourn.

cuntankerous *adj.* Of a *splitarse, showing off* while the *tomato boat is docked in tuna town. Blob stroppy.*

cuntawallah *n.* A professional purveyor of *ladies of the night.* Also *fanny farmer, fanny magnate, spunkawallah, flapmonger, gash baron, mackerel, ponce* or *pimp.*

cuntbitten *adj.* Of a gentleman, to have contracted *Val Doonican* from a dirty lady. To be struck down with a *dose* of clappage.

cunt book *n.* The *dog house. '16th August 1945. Went down the Feathers with Joe and Dwight to celebrate winning the War. Back to Downing Street 4am. Lost keys. Climbed up drainpipe and fell into bins. Woke kids up. Clementine came down to let me in. I reckon I'm in the cunt book for at least a fortnight.'* (from The Diary of Sir Winston Churchill).

cunt bread *n.* A yeast infection on a lady's *ninja's toe.*

cunt bubble *1. n.* An air lock up the *blurtch,* often leading to a *Lawley kazoo. 2. n.* Whoever designed the traffic system for getting in and out of the short-stay car park at Newcastle Central Station.

cunt bunting *n.* A washing line saucily festooned with bikini briefs, tangas and thongs. *'I see your nan's back from Brid then, Dave. She's got her cunt bunting out.'*

cunt buster *1. n.* An enormous erection. A *diamond cutter. 'Olivia was powerless to resist.*

His eyes burned into hers like sapphires. His strong arms enfolded her softly yielding body as she felt herself being swept away in a whirlwind of passion. Then he dropped his trolleys revealing a right cunt buster.' (from *The Lady and the Gypsy* by Barbara Cartland). **2.** *n.* A large baby.

cunt candle *n.* An outstanding idiot amongst men, one who stands out like a shining beacon of utter imbecility, *eg.* Whoever designed the traffic system for getting in and out of the short-stay car park at Newcastle Central Station.

cuntcloth *n.* A more offensive version of a *toerag.* *'It is the Crown's case that Mr Clifford is a right cuntcloth, m'lud.' 'Good point. Guilty. Eight years. Take him down.'*

cunt conkers *n. Love eggs* up a bird's *Ho Chi Minge.* *'I stopped off at the sex shop on the A1 and got you some cunt conkers for your birthday, nan.'*

cunt corks *n.* Term used in chemist's shops when one is too embarrassed to ask for a box of *women's things.*

cunt dentist *n.* A gynaecologist. *Snatch quack.*

cunteen *n.* A number which is larger than twelve but smaller than twenty, and is used to describe the size of a group of things that one dislikes, *eg.* *'There were cunteen fucking TV chefs.'*

cunt envelope, pushing the *euph.* Used to describe someone whose behaviour is frankly testing the bounds of *twattishness to destruction and beyond. 'Do we have to invite Uncle Andrew to the reception? Only he's really been pushing the cunt envelope recently.'*

cunterbery tales *euph.* Any gathering of males where they boast of recent – mostly imaginary – sexual conquests.

cuntestant *n.* A type whose chance to grab their allotted fifteen minutes of fame consists of an appearance on *Bargain Hunt, Tipping Point* or any one of a number of similar shows that make relatively few demands on their participants' intellect.

cuntext *n.* The manner in which a swear word is used, determining the degree to which the recipient should take offence. *'Is it ever acceptable to call a cabinet minister a cunt?' 'It all depends on the cuntext, Prime Minister.'*

cunt farm *n.* A posh school. *'He attended one of the country's top cunt farms before being awarded a demyship at Magdelen College, Oxford.'*

cuntfetti *n.* Small, decorative pieces of *lavatory tissue* adorning a lady's *messtuarine delta. Cunting.*

cunt flump *n.* A monthly feminine requisite, named after the furry, absorbent, wooly hat-wearing, garden-loving children's television characters

of the 1970s. *'I would be quite happy – as, I am sure, would other honourable members – if the Government regarded women's wotsits as being free of VAT. Cunt flumps are not a luxury; they are essential items in a lady's budget.'* (Stephen Pound MP, reported in *Hansard*).

cunt fruit *n.* A baby or small child. Also *fanny apple. 'How was the party? Any fitties?' 'Jimmy's sister was there, but as usual she brought her cunt fruit.' 'Who brings their cunt fruit to a party?'*

cunt gravity *n.* The invisible force whereby smaller, satellite *twats* are drawn into the orbit of a really big *cunt. 'So, how did you end up as a member of Chris Moyles's breakfast show posse?' 'I don't know really. I just drifted into it due to cunt gravity, I suppose.'*

cunt grunt *n.* A politer term for a *fanny fart.* Also a *queef,* a *hat dropped forward,* a *Lawley kazoo, Seagoon's last raspberry, cunt guff, vulvuzela.*

cunt guff *n.* The *dropping forwards of a lady's hat.*

cunt hair *n.* An Imperial unit of measurement used in carpentry, equal to about three sixteenths of a *whiff-waff. 'Just take a cunt hair off that door, Steve, and it'll fit like a cock up a puppy's arse.'*

cunt-harness *n.* A *G-string, shit splitter* or *box hammock.*

cuntherd *n.* Person employed to try and prevent a group of raucous, self-centred individuals from getting on everyone else's *tits eg.* A nightclub bouncer dealing with a hen party, a teacher on a school field trip, or the Speaker of the House of Commons.

cunt hook *n.* Any stylish car such as a VW Lupo or Daewoo Matiz with oversized wheels, blacked-out windows and rear spoilers, which impresses discerning ladies. A *fanny magnet. 'Fiesta XR2, red, D reg, 312k, 1 new tyre, some history, MOT October, a real cunt hook £120 ono. First to see will buy. No tyre kickers in case the wheels fall off.'*

cuntilever *n.* A small protuding structure held upright by two suspended counterweights.

cuntinental *adj.* Descriptive of anyone who sits outside a cafe in Britain drinking coffee and eating croissants whenever the drizzle lets up for ten minutes.

cuntinental breakfast *n.* An insubstantial early morning *meal at the Y* which leaves the diner wanting more.

cunting **1.** *n.* A lady's bestest *harvest festivals,* brought out to decorate the *quaynte* on special occasions. **2.** *n.* The bits of general paper effluvium and detritus decorating a woman's *minge.*

cuntingency plan *n.* An emergency arrangement for the provision of alternative *fanny* in case the usual supply dries up for any reason. *Plan C. 'Colonel Biffinbridge? I'm afraid I've got some bad news for you. Your wife has been run over by a steam roller and killed. Is there anybody who could come over to stay with you tonight? Would you like me to get in touch with someone?' 'No, I'll be fine, officer. I've got a cuntingency plan. The wife's sister's a bit of a goer.'*

cuntispiece *n.* The explicitly illustrated leaf which precedes the title page of a *bongo book*.

cuntistry *n.* The art of being a *cunt. 'Say what you like about those Trump boys, you've got to admire their consummate cuntistry.'*

cuntitude *n.* A *cuntish* attitude.

cunt juggler *n.* A man with a variety of girlfriends on the go. And possibly a wife, too. Also *cunt shuffler.*

cuntlashed *adj.* Twice as drunk as *shitfaced.*

cuntlery *1. n.* Delicate ironmongery found when rummaging in *drawers. Curtain rings, chufflinks. 2. n.* Infuriating items of crockery, cutlery or glassware that turn up just after you've put on the dishwasher or finished washing up. Someone should sell that one to Michael McIntyre.

cuntlery *n.* Any utensil or digit used to assist when *dining at the Y*. For example, fingers, lolly sticks, clothes pegs or spoons *etc.* used to hold back the *beef curtains.*

cuntlifters *n.* An elderly lady's *dunghampers. Granny's bills, oyster catchers.*

cunt mumps *n. medic.* That condition which causes a female to instantly reject the conversational gambits of a potential suitor.

cunt munch *n.* A term of endearment used by a woman in reference to her significant other. *'Come on, cunt munch, put one of your uniforms on. We've got to open Parliament or something.'*

cunt off *v.* To dismiss or ignore someone in an unpleasant manner. *'The minister was met by a large group of protestors as he made his way into the conference, but he completely cunted them off.'*

cunt of Monte Cristo *n.* Someone who gets *pissed* on cheap sherry and makes a *twat* of theirself at a family occasion. *'Don't take any notice of your Uncle Gerald, children. He's the cunt of Monte Cristo.'*

cunt of the litter, the *n.* The member of a famous sibship who is particularly notorious for their egregious personality and behaviour. For example, Prince Andrew, Liam Gallagher, Diana Mitford.

cuntomers *n.* Extremely annoying customers. *'I'm sorry. I'm dealing with a cuntomer at the moment.'*

cuntometer *n.* A giant-faced, multi-dialled wristwatch of the sort worn by fighter pilots, racing drivers and powdered egg salesmen. See also *cuntograph.*

cunt on one's sleeve, wear one's *euph.* To be a massive, unapologetic, obvious *cunt. 'Say what you like about Piers, the cunt wears his cunt on his sleeve, and you've got to give the cunt credit for that.' 'I suppose so, Susanna. And now here's Laura with the weather.'*

cuntourage *n.* The cohort of *twats* who accompany a radio DJ on his metropolitan peregrinations. *'Don't go in the bar, whatever you do. Chris Evans is in there with Aldo Zilli and the rest of his cuntourage.'*

cuntpany *n.* Any business that falls into disfavour for any reason.

cunt plank *n.* An electric scooter.

cunt pole *n.* A selfie stick. The handle on a *twat mirror*. Also *narcicisstick.*

cuntproof *adj.* Very simple; literally impossible to *fuck up. 'Just imagine it, Lord Mandelson, to celebrate the new millennium we'll build a giant dome and fill it with zones such as "Shared Ground" made of recycled card, a "Faith festivals" calendar and something called the "Childhood Cube". And here's the really clever bit – we won't have a car park. I tell you, it cannot fail. This scheme is absolutely cuntproof.'*

cuntrarian *n.* A person who gets great pleasure in taking a contrary position or attitude. *'Born on this day: Gus Grissom, test pilot and astronaut, 1926; Eddie Murphy, US actor and comedian, 1961; Nigel Farage, cuntrarian, 1964.'*

cuntrepreneur *n.* A successful business person. *'Born on this day: Will.I.Am, American singer or something, he's got funny glasses, 1975; Alan Bean, test pilot and astronaut, 1932; Sir Philip Green, yachted cuntrepreneur, 1952.'*

cuntrified *adj.* Of a public house, to have been turned into a ritzy wine bar by the addition of a DJ, bowls of olives on the bar and a bunch of *twattish,* braying media types.

cunt rope *n.* A polite term for pubic hair. *'I say, Prue. I just found some cunt rope in my vol-au-vent.'*

cunt ruffler *n.* A man who enjoys provoking ladies who have *fallen to the communists* because he finds their mood swings amusing. Easily recognised by his black eyes, missing teeth and stab wounds.

cunt rug *n.* A *muff, merkin.* A pubic *syrup.*

cunt saboteur *1. n.* A woman's monthly *period drama. 2. n.* A wife who insists on accompanying her hubby to a works do that he confidently expects will be heaving with single, eligible *flange.*

cunt scratchers *n.* Humorous term for hands. *Wanking spanners, dick skinners. 'You need cunt scratchers / To hold someone you care for / You* *need cunt scratchers / To show that you're sincere.'* (lyric by Max Bygraves).

cuntsistency *n.* Achieving an *cuntsistent* level of *cuntishness* which does not vary greatly in quality over time. *'Say what you want about Katie Hopkins, vicar, but she is always cuntsistent with her shittily twattish opinions.'*

cuntslab *n.* Wobbly paving stone which, when stepped upon, fires a jet of mucky water up one's trouser leg (also see *affpuddle* in *The Meaning of Liff*). *'Have you pissed your kecks, Lord Nelson?' 'No, Lady Hamilton. Stepped on a fucking cuntslab, didn't I?'*

cuntsman *n. US.* A *cocksman, stickman, crumpeteer.* A Don Juan type, highly skilled in the pursuit of *poontang.*

cuntspeak *n.* Workplace terminology overused by office middle managers to make themselves sound more important than they actually are.

cuntstipated *adj.* Suffering a lack of *fanny* action. *'How's it going, Cliff?' 'Still cuntstipated, Hank. That's eight decades now.'*

cuntstruck *adj.* Besotted, hopelessly in love.

cuntsultant *n.* In business, an expert who is hired at huge expense by one's boss to evaluate working practices from an outsider's perspective.

cunt-tinted glasses, wear *v.* To hold an unnecessarily negative opinion of another person one has only just met and against whom one has taken a wholly unjustified animus.

cuntuppance *n.* Well-deserved humiliation following some sort of *fanny*-related behaviour. *Lust desserts. 'I see Darren Day's got his cuntuppance again.'*

cuntural anthropology *n.* while on holiday, intercourse performed with the exotic denizens of other lands.

cuntwank *n.* A one-sided, loveless, no-nonsense bout of intercourse. A *hands free. 'I've just seen that Victorian lesbo drama on the telly. Phwooar! So I'm off upstairs for a cuntwank off the missus.'*

cuntweep *n.* The *bird's custard* found in a lady's *Alan Whickers* after she has sat in the office all day chatting about Robert Pattinson, whoever he is. Not Robert Robinson, anyway.

cunty booby *adj.* To be in a state of confusion. *'I don't pretend to understand the universe – when I start thinking about it I go all cunty booby, me.'* (from *Latterday Pamphlets Number 6,* by Thomas Carlyle).

cuntylinctus *n. Milp, blip, fanny batter.*

cup-a-poop *n.* The art of catching a *guff* in the palm of the hand and then passing it on to an unsuspecting victim so he/she can share its wholesome,

warming (and hopefully crouton-free) goodness. See *cupcake*, it's just there look, after *cupboard love.*

cupboard love *1. n.* A reference to an animal, usually a cat, who shows you affection only because you feed it. *2. n.* Said of someone who is irresistably attracted to biscuits. *'That Gemma Collins is a big girl, isn't she Dave?' 'Yes mate. I'm afraid she has a case of cupboard love.'*

cupcake *n.* A small quantity of *fart* gas caught between the palms of the hands and released in a person's face. An *amuse nez, cup-a-poop.*

cup cracker *n.* A *cabman's rest* which is too large for the *titpant* to which it has been allotted.

cup final *n.* A female who promises "a great deal of action at both ends".

cupidity *n.* An extreme form of stupidity, from the famous, *cunt*-based family entertainment spoonerism much employed by Kenny Everett on prime-time BBC1 back in the 1980s.

Cupid's measles *n. medic.* Victorian terminology for *cock rot.*

Cupid's toothpaste *n.* Oral *gunk.*

cuprinol *euph.* A virtuoso *fellatrix,* on account of the fact that – in the words of the timber preservative's ad campaign – "no-one does wood more good". *'Born on this day: Halle Berry, X-Men actress, 1966; Earvin "Magic" Johnson, basketballist, 1959; Gillian Taylforth, EastEnders cuprinol, 1955.'*

c-urchin *n.* Somewhat off-putting state of a woman's *clam* after it has been shaved and then allowed to grow back, so that the newly emergent *pubes* resemble – somewhat off-puttingly – the spines of the similarly named marine echinoderm.

curd *n.* Jizz.

cure for piles *n.* Any person who *noshes* a fellow *off* with such power that any extraneous protruberances from the fundament get sucked safely back inside.

curious otter *n.* An elongated *Peter O'Toole* lying contentedly with its nose just above the waterline.

curler *1. n.* A lump of excrement. *2. n.* Something in Olive off of *On the Buses*'s hair. *3. n.* A lump of excrement in Olive off of *On the Buses*'s hair.

curler's knee *n. medic.* Temporary numbness in the leg joints that, one might imagine, afflicts winter athletes and also those who have spent too long reading the *Autotrader* on the *jobby engine.*

curler's rest, the *1. n. prop.* Pleasant drinking establishment in Hillhead, Glasgow. *2. n.* Pause between passing difficult *shits* taken to avoid bursting another blood vessel in the eye.

curl one in *v.* To achieve a showboaty *fuck* from a

difficult starting position.

curl one off *v.* To carefully deliver a *mudchild.*

currant in my tooth, I've a *exclam. euph.* Phrase used by one who is suffering from *sweetcorn itch.*

curricane *n.* A huge swirling vortex of foetid, high temperature *guff* that could carry one away to the magical land of Oz.

curry butty *n.* Occurrence whereby, following a particularly potent *Ruby Murray,* a restaurant *crapper* furnishes insufficient *bumwad* to finish the clean-up operation, *viz.* Wedging what remains of the cardboard roll between your *arse cheeks* and waddling to an adjacent cubicle in search of fresh supplies. See also *chip 'n' dip.*

curry fever *n. medic.* A particularly virulent form of dysentery brought on by the previous evening's consumption of well-seasoned viands of dubious provenance.

curry hurry *n.* The increasingly hasty homeward bound trot of one who has recently partaken of some sort of exotic foodstuffs which are already *touching cloth* in high-temperature, quasi-viscous form.

curry McFlurry *n.* A soft, whipped-up delight with chili and chicken sprinkles, conjured forth from the *back end of the Batmobile* by the previous night's feast of brown booze and piquantly spiced Asiatic sweetmeats. Not quite as spectacular as a *rooster tail.*

curry morning *euph.* A day when it is "wet and windy".

curryoakie *n.* An enthusiastic but tuneless solo performance from *the nether throat* after sinking a gallon of bitter and an Indian meal. A *blanket ripper.*

curry polka *n.* The short-stepped mince towards the lavatories one perforce adopts following a delicious overdose of spicy sweetmeats at the Rupali Restaurant (formerly Curry Capital, and then before that the Rupali again, now probably closed, let's face it), Bigg Market, Newcastle upon Tyne.

curry slurry *n.* The mixture of semi-liquified excrement, intestines and internal organs left in the pan of the *chod bin* the morning after a particularly hot Madras. *'I'd give it ten minutes if I was you, dear. I just did a bit of a curry slurry in there. Oh, and can you call an ambulance. And a priest.'*

curse *n.* The perineum of either sex. Also *Humber bridge, taint, tinter, notcher, carse, biffon, scran, twernt, Berlin Wall, Botley Interchange, Barry Gibb, Bosphorus, brink, crontis, clutch, joy division, Potsdamer Platz, butfer, snarse, biffin bridge, Checkpoint Charlie, varse, Dutch canal, Wirral peninsula, scrincter, stinker's bridge, scran, gisp, barse, tintis, great, notcher, ABC, gooch, Finsbury bridge, isnae, scruttock, Perry Como's lip, tornado alley, scranus, smelly bridge, Brick Lane* or *crunk.* Origin unknown.

curtain *n.* Jason Donovan's *fiveskin.* From his 1992 song about *wanking* entitled *Any Dream Will Do,* which contained the lines "I close my eyes / Draw back the curtain (ah-ah-ahh)".

curtain call *n.* A return to the lavatory for an *epilog.* A *second sitting.*

curtain critic *n.* A fellow who is *good with colours.* *'Oh the vicar's definitely a curtain critic. You've only got to see the way he walks up to the pulpit in them arseless chaps each Sunday. It's his wife I feel sorry for.'*

curtain drop *n. Cat flap* length. The size of a woman's *beef curtains.*

curtain rings *n.* Labial ironmongery.

curtain rod *n.* A stout length of *pink steel.*

curtain twitchers *n. Tennis fans, lady golfers.*

curvy *adj. UK. journ.* Of women, having large breasts and/or *arses.*

cushion creeper *n.* An upholstery-muffled *Exchange & Mart.*

custard *1. n.* A sweet sauce made from eggs and milk that goes well with rhubarbs. *2. n.* Someone who is simultaneously a bit of a *cunt* and a bit of a *bastard. 3. Rhym. Slang.* A *Bakewell.*

custard cannon *n. Lamb cannon, mutton musket, pork sword, beef bazooka, spam blunderbuss, etc, et fucking cetera.*

custard cousin *n.* The relationship a fellow has with others who have shared the same *slice* of *pie. eg.* Bryan Ferry and Mick Jagger are *custard cousins,* likewise Bill "Selwyn Froggitt" Maynard and speed ace Donald Campbell.

custard muscle *n.* Subcutaneous body fat. *'You cheeky cow. That's solid custard muscle is that.'*

custard pie *n.* A pre-*spoffed fadge.* Referred to in various blues songs, including 1947's *Custard Pie Blues* by Brown McGhee. Also forms the basis of the Led Zeppelin song *Custard Pie,* in which Robert Plant exclaims: "Save me a slice of your custard pie", apparently implying that he would later like to re-*poke,* and indeed *nosh* on, his ladyfriend's aforementioned *jitler-*filled *clopper.*

custard skin *n.* The remains typically left in a *fairy hammock* at the conclusion of a proper session on the back seat of a Saxo.

custard steps *euph.* Brisk means by which a gentleman wearing a wrist-mounted fitness tracker can achieve his allocated daily walking target without leaving the house. A *three-minute mile.*

custardy battle *1. n.* A fight to resist the temptation to push one's *bellend* into a trifle. *2. n.* A Japanese *art film* featuring extended scenes of competitive *spoffage*, the like of which no respectable man in his right mind would care to witness.

custody tart *n.* An arrested woman who *sucks off* the duty sergeant, or performs similar act *in lieu* of bail.

customer deflection *1. n.* In the 'science' of operating a website or call centre, the practice of a business hiding its phone number or otherwise making things so awkward that punters give up trying to make contact. *2. n.* In the older and nobler art of being a *good time girl*, using a deft body movement to avoid receiving a *wet signature*.

customer service 69 aisle x *exclam.* Phrase called out over supermarket tannoys to alert male staff of the presence of a fit *bird* in aisle x, so they can go over and *sneak a peek* while pretending to run a price check or look at some tins or something.

custurd *n.* A *feeshus* that is the same colour, temperature and consistency as the popular dessert topping.

cut and paste *1. n.* In the world of education, a process used by students when "researching" their essays and dissertations on Wikipedia. *2. v.* In the world of journalism, what investigative reporters do to press releases in their tireless quest to expose the truth. *3. n.* A method used by internet-surfing politicians when compiling telling dossiers in order to justify taking a country to war. *4. n.* In the world of motion picture *grumble* drama, the act of withdrawing from a lady's *minge* in order to deposit the contents of one's *clackerbag* on her face or *thru'penny bits.* '*Hurry up Gunther, we're running out of tape. It's time for a cut and paste.*' *5 v.* To practise *coitus interruptus.* To *get off at Edge Hill.*

cut and shuteye *euph.* The peculiar yet familiar phenomenon of falling asleep on the sofa halfway through a BBC4 documentary about French art, the Agrarian Revolution, or the architecture of castles, and waking up two hours later halfway through one about UB40, the Severn bridge or Raleigh bikes, with your drowsy brain attempting to link the disparate subjects together and make you think it's the same programme.

cut an onion *v.* To *drop a gut* so potent and nasty that it brings tears to your eyes.

cut a rug *1. v.* In World War II, to take to the dancefloor and impress onlookers by jitterbugging energetically, especially with an American airman. *2. v.* To *split a kipper, part the whiskers etc.*

To make sweet, penetrative love to a *piece* who works in a munitions factory.

Cuthbert *n. prop.* Someone or something that is "cringe-worthy". From the so-named character in *The Bash Street Kids, eg.* Accidentally putting *Embarrassing Bodies* on, Joey Barton agreeing to appear on *Question Time*, or MP Sara Teather's stand-up comedy routine about Peter Hain at the 2011 Liberal Democrat Conference in Birmingham.

cut 'n' shut *1. n.* A second hand car, skillfully engineered from the front and back of two insurance writeoffs. *2. n.* A woman, seemingly constructed of two ill-matched donor women, *eg.* A fantastic body, but a *minger;* a cutie, but built like a bus; or a flat-chested bonebag sat on a big *arse* and tree trunk legs.

cut on a bear's arm *n.* A particularly hairy *growler.* A *ripped sofa.*

cut price spice *n.* A lady who models herself on Victoria Beckham, but does so on a much tighter budget. Sits next to *David Peckham* on trips in his *estate car.*

cut the cheese *v.* To *open the ham.*

cut the cord *v.* To break the link between one's *arsehole* and an invisible, yet highly noticeable cloud of recently expelled *gut gas* by means of rapid, short wafting motions of the hand.

cut through the red tape *v.* To ignore received wisdom and *swim when the red flags are flying.*

cutting open a binbag full of livers, like *euph.* Doing a big, nasty *shit.* '*Christ, I feel better for that, your holiness. It was like cutting open a binbag full of livers. Mind, I'd give it ten minutes if I was you. Make it a couple of hours.*'

cutty sark *n.* A large *floater* that stings the *clippers.*

cuzza *n.* A *Ruby Murray.*

c-worthy *adj.* Descriptive of a shipshape *stonk-on* that is ready to sail into *tuna town.*

cyber clap *n.* The embarrassing situation whereby your home computer becomes riddled with viruses as a result of *buying your better half an anniversary present.*

cyberia *n.* The frigid temperature in the marital bedroom after a fellow's *bag for life* goes through his text messages and/or internet search history.

cybernating *n.* Socially dormant whilst preoccupied visiting certain seedy domains along the information superhighway.

cybertranny *n.* Man or woman who pretends to be of the opposite sex in internet chat rooms, *eg.* 16-year-old Brenda turns out to be a 35-stone tattooed American man called Jim-Bob. Wearing his mother's skin as a suit.

cyclist's nipsy, as hard as a *sim.* Said of a particularly robust gentleman or ladywoman. *'Did you see that video of Ross Kemp? He's as hard as a cyclist's nipsy, him.'*

Cyclops *n.* A legendary purple-headed monster with a single *hog's eye*. And two big hairy *bollocks* dangling underneath.

Cyclops-boxing *n.* A particularly pugilistic bout of fisticuffs against a polyphemous opponent.

Cyclops' hoof *1. n.* The ungulate toe of an Homeric monster as imagined by Ray Harryhausen in the popular *Sinbad* films. *2. n.* A Cinerama *camel's foot*, as often seen in Nottingham city centre on Friday and Saturday nights.

Cyprus manoeuvre *n.* Removing the penis during *doggy sex* and re-entering "accidentally" up the *bonus tunnel*. The *Limasol slip*, invented in 1972 by Greek scientists.

Cyril Smith's legs, I could shit between *exclam.*

Said by one whose loose *duties* would rate an easy 7 on the Bristol Stool Scale. A reference to the famously roly-poly late Rochdale MP and ennobled *nonce-nugget* profferer.

Cyril Sneer *1. euph.* Named after the *dong*-nosed, cigar chomping villain in eighties cartoon romp *The Racoons*, a fellow's *old chap*. *2. n.* A smear test. *'Where's your nan?' 'She's gone to see the quim quack for a Cyril, grandad.'*

Cyril Sneer's sneck, cock like *sim.* A man's wrinkly, bedraggled *tackle* following a no-nonsense bout of penetrative affection.

Czech book *n.* A *twatalogue* featuring undraped studies of sultry young ladies from the former East European state. *'I fancy banking at Barclays, but I can't find me Czech book anywhere, mum.' 'Have you looked on top of your wardrobe? That's where your dad keeps his noddy books.'*

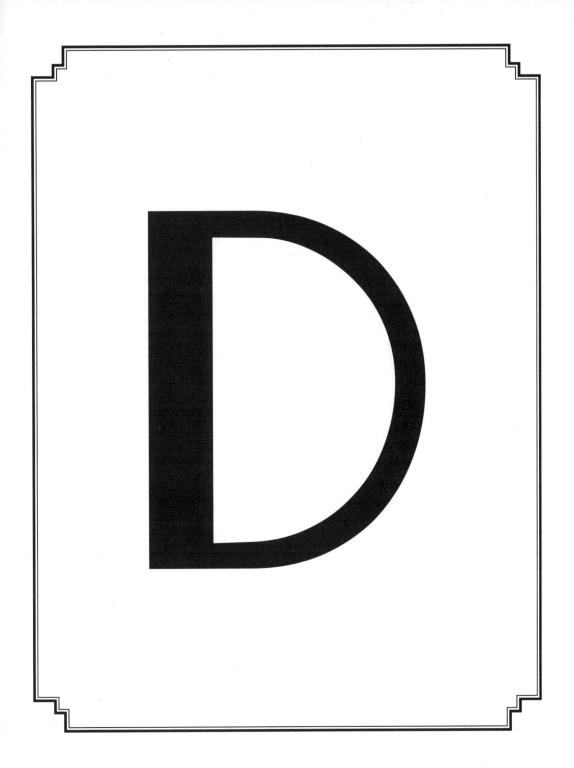

DA *abbrev.* 1950s "Teddy boy"-style haircut, so-called because of its supposed resemblance to an American District Attorney.

dabble in the Yakult *v.* After *relaxing in the way that only a gentleman can,* to find that the *bumwad* has failed to catch all the *spoff* and you have just trodden in a dollop.

dab the wound *v.* Of a lady, to gently *audition the finger puppets, dial Australia,* practise scales on the *upside down piano.*

daddaries *n.* Male version of mammaries. *Mannery glands, mantits, moobs, moomlaaters. 'Phwoar. I bet you don't get many of those daddaries to the pound, Lord Owen.'*

dad dressed as Brad *n.* The male counterpart of a *Whitney dressed as Britney.*

daddy longlegs *n.* A particularly firmly anchored, stubborn *winnet* that, when extracted, takes a bunch of uprooted *coil springs* with it, thus resembling the eponymous lampshade-dwelling household pest.

daddy long-legs squatting on a wasp, like a *sim.* Descriptive of a sexual act between two participants of vastly differing heights, *eg.* Sophie Dahl and Jamie Cullum, Peter Crouch and Abby Clancy or Ian Krankie and Wee Jimmy.

daddy's sauce *n.* Baby gravy, pineapple chunk, heir gel.

daddy wrong legs *n.* A *heavily-refreshed* gentleman of advancing years, throwing shapes on the dancefloor at a wedding reception while completely oblivious to the mortification of everyone present.

dadvert *n.* Any form of sexually provocative advertising that grabs a family man's undivided attention, *eg.* Them chocolate flake commercials of the 70s.

Dagenham *adj. Mad as a lorry.* "Two stops past Barking".

Dagenham handshake *n.* Sexual practice whereby the gentleman inserts a finger in the *pink,* a finger in the *brown,* then uses a third to ring the *devil's doorbell.* See also *shocker.*

Dagenham smile *n. Builder's bum, bricky's crack.*

dagenite *n.* A *Bakewell tart* that smells like a dropped 70s Ford car battery.

dagger, Turkish *n.* A curved *Thora* with a jewel-encrusted handle that one wouldn't, frankly, fancy holding in one's teeth.

dags *n.* Shepherd-speak for sheep's *dangleberries.*

daily beast, the *1. n.* An American news website founded by Tina Brown. Or something. We lost interest halfway through the first paragraph on Wikipedia. *2. n.* A fellow's *morning glory* or *dawn horn.* The *motorcycle kickstand.*

dairy bags *n.* Proper old-fashioned *churns* of the sort Nurse Gladys Emmanuel would have stuck in Arkwright's face while plumping up his pillows, causing him to blow his cheeks out and blink amusingly.

Daisy *n. prop.* A *bisexual made for two.* From the popular song.

daisy chain *n.* An *AC/DC* circuit. The sort which only occurs in *bongo films,* Richard Littlejohn's most feverish imaginings and public school dormitories.

daisy cutter *n.* A heavyweight *fart* in breach of the Geneva Convention, that leaves nothing standing within a wide radius.

dakkery doo *n.* A relaxing concurrent *shit* and a *Harry Rag.* From the German word Dak = cigarette. *'His holiness will be with us presently, Cardinal. He's just went for a dakkery doo.'*

Dalai lager *n.* In a public house, a *gobshite* who, when suitably *bitten by the brewer's horse,* spouts endless words of wisdom. Also *Carsberg expert, gintellectual, smarty pints, Budwisah.*

dalek *n.* An erection which is reminiscent of a forehead-mounted sink-plunger, with bollocks made out of Morris Minor indicators, which is best viewed from behind the sofa.

Daley *n.* Named after Olympic diving sensation Tom, a streamlined *otter off the bank* which leaves the *wrinkled penny* and enters the water without making a splash, possibly fitting in a triple somersault and a half-pike during its graceful descent.

dalhoonies *n. Gazungas.*

Dalton *n.* A small and unimpressive *Douglas* that, judging from the immense straining it took to produce, you might have expected to be an absolute *dreadnought.* From the bouncer character played by Patrick Swayze in the 1989 film *Road House,* who is constantly told by other characters: "I thought you'd be bigger".

daltons *n.* The *nuts. 'Ooh, me daltons!'*

damaging gusts *1. n. met.* In weather forecasting circles, a warning of wind likely to cause harm to buildings. *2. n.* In curry-loving circles, the onset of the sort of *nipsy burbulence* which could easily dislodge a nearby chimney pot or take the roof off the shed.

dambuster *n.* A lavatory brush.

Dan Brown novel *euph.* "Shit on paper", and hence soiled *bumwad. 'I would submit that the defendant never looked back after dropping the kids off at the pool and hence didn't notice that he had left an entire Dan Brown novel floating in there,* *your honour.'*

dance card *n.* A list of all those one is actively *seeing to* at any one time. Throughout the 1980s, Mick Hucknall consistently had the longest *dance card* in showbusiness.

dance of the flaming arseholes *n. milit.* Squaddies' entertainment designed to while away those long dark nights in the barrack room. A volunteer is selected, his hands tied at chest height and a six foot taper of newspaper inserted rectally. Once in place, the farther end of the paper is lit and the volunteer released. Much hilarity ensues as he attempts to remove said taper from his *nipsy* before the flames reach a critical area or the Sergeant Major comes in in his dresssing gown to ask why everyone isn't fast asleep. The game is apparently particularly popular amongst the Scots Guards.

dance of the seven ales *n.* Unbalanced, faux-seductive Terpsichorean moves essayed in nightclubs by *pissed* revellers of either gender in a misguided attempt to secure some *floor sweepings* before the *ugly lights* come on.

dancer's lance *n.* An unwelcome *dalek* that appears when dancing closely with a lady. A *Saturday night lever, St. Vitus pants.*

dance the blanket hornpipe *v.* To perform a *sailor's jig* in one's hammock. To have *all hands on dick.*

dance the horn pipe *v.* To attempt to disguise a state of arousal by walking about like a half-shut penknife, in the style of Groucho Marx. During his 1970s heyday, Michael Parkinson was an expert at *dancing the horn pipe*, especially when welcoming pulchritudinous actresses such as Helen Mirren onto his chatshow.

dancing bear *n.* A grizzly brown monster surrounded by a cloud of flies that stands on its end in the *pan* and refuses to be flushed away unless hit with a stick.

dancing like Andy Pandy *n.* The nervous, light-footed gait employed by a person urgently looking for the nearest *Rick Witter* while *touching cloth.*

dancing on bubblewrap, like *sim.* Phrase descriptive of the snap, crackle, pop sound emitted by one's *chocolate starfish* following a particularly fruity *Ruby Murray*. *'Jesus man. I spent most of last night sat on the bog sounding like S-Club 7 dancing on bubblewrap. I'm never going to Curry Capital, the Bigg Market, Newcastle upon Tyne again. Especially since, as we've already established, it's been shut for years.'*

dancing with the captain *n.* Masturbation. Wearing a bowler hat. See *grandma's party.*

dang *1. n.* Penis. *2. exclam. US.* Expression of annoyance. *'Dang them pesky Al Qaeda varmints.'* (George W Bush, State of the Nation Address, 2002). *3. n.* A word which, together with "ding" and "dong", features prominently in the lyrics of many Eurovision Song Contest entries.

dangermouse *n.* A tampon or *slim fanatella.*

danger UXB *1. n.* Title of a 1970s ITV drama series about wartime bomb disposal experts, where they would wipe away a bead of sweat before clipping through a wire and then the ticking would stop. *2. n.* The banging, fizzing and gurgling that is the nerve-wracking overture to a life-changing *Simon Cowell* movement.

danger wank *n. Self-abuse* technique whereby you shout your parents from downstairs, and then try to *blow your tanks* before they get to your bedroom.

dangerzone *1. n.* Lyrical roadbound destination of Kenny Loggins, who is now well into his seventies, so these days he's probably got one of them tartan shopping trolleys. *2. n.* A chap's fourth pint over lunch.

dangleberries *n. Winnets*; excrement adhering to the *arse cress* around an inefficiently wiped *ringpiece. Fartleberries, toffee strings, bead curtains, kling-ons, clinkers, miniature heroes.*

dangle me in dogshit! *exclam.* Somewhat hyperbolic, one would hope, exclamation proffered when confronted with a surprising remark. *'In this condition, at auction, this Ming vase could be worth upwards of fifty thousand pounds.' 'Well dangle me in dogshit! We keep it on a shelf in the outside crapper.'*

dangler *n.* A dangling *donger, a copper's torch. 'Oi missus, look at me dangler.'*

danglers *n.* Hairy conkers. *'Oi missus, look at me me danglers.'*

dangly ham *n. Beef curtains, bacon strips, gammon goalposts.*

Dannii Minogue *n. prop.* The pointless bit of flesh that sits between a *cock* and an *arsehole*; from Kylie's sister's job sitting between Brian McFadden and Kyle Sandilands (no, us neither) on *Australia's Got Talent*. Also *tintis, taint, BBBA, scrincter, stinker's bridge, scran, gisp, barse, great, notcher, ABC, gooch, Finsbury bridge, isnae, scruttock, Perry Como's lip, tornado alley, scranus, smelly bridge, Brick Lane* or *crunk.*

Danny Fishcharge *n.* Spooneristic vaginal *gleet.*

Danny's delay *euph.* The sensation of thinking that you are fully ready to pay a fruitful visit to the *netty*, only to find that your *copper bolt* is not quite ready to quit the *mud oven* just yet, thus prolonging your time *on the throne*. Named after Flt. Lt. Danny

Velinski, played by Charles Bronson in the film *The Great Escape*, who suffered a sudden bout of claustrophobia which held up his exit from the dirt tunnel for a few minutes.

Dan Pallet *1. n. prop.* Charismatic and erudite sports reporter on BBC Midlands News. *2. n.* Pieces of wood roughly nailed together to form a platform on which Daniels can be stacked for ease of transport or storage. *3. n.* A *double penetration* or *DP*, if you will. Also *man at C&A, Dorothy Perkins, double decker.* *'Hello-o. Fancy a quick Dan Pallet with me and Barry, love?'*

DAPPAG/dappag *acronym.* A reference to a pea-nut-bladdered fellow, such as a Premiership footballer or Bobby Davro, for example. Drink A Pint, Piss A Gallon.

darb *v.* To *shag, bonk, bang.* *'I shit you not, in that film where it looks like he's darbing her, he actually darbed her.'*

dark end of the street *1. n.* Soul ballad written in less than half an hour by William "Spooner" Oldham and Chips Moman that was in that film *The Commitments. 2. euph.* The *tradesman's entrance* or *back passage.*

darkest hour is just before the porn, the *1. phr.* Those angst-ridden moments as a teenager wonders whether his mam is ever going to nip down the shops. *2. phr.* Those angst-ridden moments as an adult man wonders whether his missus is ever going to nip down the shops.

dark fart *n.* A *dropped gut* that contains a spot of unexpected *shopping.*

dark matter *1. n.* A mysterious substance that purportedly constitutes up to 80% of the mass of the universe. *2. n.* Mysterious *bum rubbish* that emerges from your *arse* the morning after a heavy night on the *black stuff.*

dark passenger *1. n.* The homicidal alter-ego of US TV's *Dexter. 2. n.* Malicious *turdlet* that clings to the perianal area during a *Tom tit, before* releasing its grip and surreptitiously falling into your under-garments as you stand up.

dark star *n.* Black, or rather brown hole from which the *pink Darth Vader* might emerge wearing a *shitty* helmet. *Uranus.*

darkthrone *1. n.* A seminal Norwegian black metal band who have released ground-break-ing albums such as *A Blaze in the Northern Sky, Under a Funeral Moon* and *Transylvanian Hunger.* Us neither. *2. n.* The *crapper* the morning after a surfeit of Guinness.

darned hole in a jumper *sim.* Descriptive of a tightly gathered *ringpiece.*

dart blart *n. coll.* The relatively attractive females who escort overweight *tungsten ticklers* to the stage during high profile televised events.

darted animal *n.* A *heavily refreshed* fellow who is reeling along and staggering from side to side, just prior to falling over in the gutter in a style strongly reminiscent of a rogue rhinoceros which has just been shot with a tranquiliser gun.

Dartford double, the *n.* Inserting both fists into somebody's *nipsy.* For whatever reason.

Dartford hotel *n.* A mattress or rug found in the undergrowth.

Darth Maul's lightsabre *n.* A projectile explosion of nastiness from both ends, mimicking the dou-ble-ended weapon belonging to the face-paint-ed baddie from one of the less good *Star Wars* movies. See also *Catherine wheel.*

Darth Vader's dog *n.* An in-bred pedigree hound who apparently suffers from the same pneumatic breathing difficulties as the Dark Lord/Green Cross Code man.

Darth Vader's hat stand *n.* A sinister, six-foot tall, wheezing *cock.*

Darth vulva *n.* The act of eating a *fish supper* with such gusto that it makes a sound not unlike Luke Sywalker's evil nemesis/long lost father trying to consume a squid without taking his helmet off.

Darwen fortnight, wetter than a *sim.* A state of extreme female arousal. A proper *slop on.* Named in honour of the small Lancashire town that is renowned for its annual mid-July holiday wash-out. Also *wetter than Lee Evans's suit, wetter than a turfer's knee, wetter than Whitney Houston's last joint* or *wetter than a window cleaner's cuff, wetter than a fat bird's armpit.*

dash-cam Van Damm *n.* An otherwise unremarka-ble fellow – typically lacking martial arts, special forces, or tactical weapons training – who nev-ertheless, following minor road traffic incidents, takes it upon himself to become a low budget vigilante. Presumably with the intention of getting his GoPro camera violently shoved up his *chuff.*

dash for gash *n.* The desperate last half hour before *chucking out* at a night club. The *2 am bin rake.*

dashing white sergeant, the *1. n.* A traditional ballroom dance that is popular with old people. Or possibly was popular with old people in the past, before young people started getting old. *2. n.* Hot beads of *love piss* fired at high velocity across the face and *churns.* Not necessarily quite so popular with old people.

das U-bend Boot *n. Germ.* Especially large, streamlined and submarine-proportioned *dumpage* that lurks silently in the depths of the plumbing as it is assaulted by *depth charges* from above. Putting one in mind of the terror and claustrophobia suffered by WW2 sub crews as portrayed in Wolfgang Petersen's 1981 knockabout favourite *Das Boot*.

datebomb *n.* A revelation uttered during the course of a romantic evening that instantly blows a burgeoning relationship out of the water. Something that, on reflection, would probably have been better left unsaid.

date locker *n.* Rectum, *bomb bay*.

date palm *1. n. bot. Phoenix dactylifera*, a tree cultivated for its sweet, edible fruits. *2. n.* The last resort of the fruity bachelor with an empty diary.

dating *euph. Aus.* Indulging in *bum games*. *'Yeah, Sheila and I were dating last year. But then I got hepatitis C.'*

Dave Narey *adj. rhym. slang. Scots.* Descriptive of one who would benefit from a major *waxing session, eg.* Brian Blessed, Anne Robinson. Named after the Dundee United footballer who famously scored with a 25-yard toe-poke against Brazil in the 1982 World Cup.

David Coulthard's chin *euph.* A gentleman's disturbing experience of glancing in the mirror midway through an *act of personal delight* and noticing that his lower mandible is stuck out in a style reminiscent of the box-faced ex-Formula One never-quite-was-been's.

David Davis eyes *1. euph.* The puffed-up, swollen lids of one who looks like he has just gone ten rounds. In the pub. *2. n. Harry Redknapp's eyelids.*

David Peckham *n.* A young man who aspires to look like the professionally famous former England captain, but lives a very different lifestyle, *ie.* He has bleached, slicked-up hair, but wears *Armani and Navy* and drives a G-Reg Astra.

davrossing *n.* From the sedentary creator of the Daleks, having a drunken *wank* while sitting immobile in a chair, waving one's free hand about and ranting about one's enemies. *'Don't go in the sitting room, mother. Our Justin's in there, davrossing.'*

Davy Cannons, I've got the *phr.* Splattering the porcelain so badly it could break windows. Named in honour of the Northumbrian farmer who, in 1995, famously registered his displeasure with something or other by spraying *shite* over his local NatWest bank and council offices in Morpeth.

dawn horn *n.* An early morning *tent pole, bed flute, morning wood.* See also *big cock day*.

dawn lumberjack *n.* A *woodsman* who is partial to taking his *chopper* in his hand at *sparrowfart*.

dawn patrol *1. n.* The somnolent truckers, amphetamine-crazed taxi drivers and insomniac *Daily*

Mail readers who used to tune in and listen to thirsty presenter Sarah Kennedy's surreal, early hours ramblings on Radio 2 in the old days. *2. n.* In the world of *gentlemen's entertainment* venues, the collection of circus sideshow freak strippers who take over from the *A-team* at about half past four in the morning. Named, appropriately enough, after the marching group of elephants in Disney's *Jungle Book*.

dawn raid *n.* The surreptitious act of a gentleman who has woken up next to his still-sleeping partner and, for want of anything better to do, attempts to *cop a feel* without waking her up. Typically repelled with an elbow to the ribs and possibly a court order.

dawn star *n.* The desirable lady who is currently taking a leading role in the torpid erotic reveries of a tumescent fellow at the time his morning alarm goes off. Also *pole star.*

daydrammer *n.* One who enjoys flights of fancy due to regular day-time *turps-nudging, eg.* A regional television presenter. Also *daydram*; a refreshing draft enjoyed between breakfast and tea.

day in the wife, a *n.* A long-awaited Sunday afternoon *scuttle.* *'Can't come down to the boozer, lads. I'm spending a day in the wife.'*

daylighting *1. n.* Construction industry term describing the appearance of a tunnelling machine or driven pipe emerging from a soil face. *2. n. Touching cloth, turtling.*

daylight rubbery *euph.* A quick *one off the wrist* whilst the missus has popped out to the corner shop. Or to make a cup of tea in the kitchen. *Daylight throbbery, Opportunity cocks, fifty wrist, striking while the iron is hot.*

day-nighter *1. n.* In limited-overs cricket, a match started mid-afternoon and completed under floodlights well into the evening. *2. n.* A less-than-attractive *good time girl* who nonetheless offers very reasonable hourly rates.

day of wrist *1. n.* Any non-working day, usually a Sunday. Unless you're a vicar, in which case it's the other six. *2. n.* A day when one's missus is indisposed, *eg. Up on blocks,* giving birth, in a coma *etc.,* enabling one to spend the day celebrating the invention of superfast broadband in a suitably *gentlemanly fashion.*

Daz moment *n.* The exact time that a *MILF* reaches her sexual peak. From the quondam washing powder advertisement slogan: "Get out the dirty, even at thirty".

dazzle *1. n.* Op-art-style geometric paint scheme used by wartime ships to confuse enemy submarines about their size, tonnage and course.

2. *n.* Similarly styled clothing worn by *homely* lasses with deception in mind.

DCAF *abbrev.* Pronounced "de-caff" like the pointless coffee, a term used to describe a woman walking in front of you whose rear aspect is so sexually attractive that you would be prepared to enjoy *carnival liaisons* with her even if she turns round and looks like Bob Todd in a wig. Don't Care About the Face.

dead cat bounce *1. phr.* In topical stockmarket and economic parlance, an unexpected improvement in prospects which is swiftly followed by a further fiscal downturn. *2. phr.* Following a heavy night *on the sauce*, waking up feeling improbably chipper, only for your condition to inevitably and rapidly go downhill as the morning progresses.

dead dog *n.* A *Thora* of stupendous proportions that is attracting flies.

dead German hanging out of a window *euph.* A proper *copper's torch* of a *cock*. *'Jazz turns round and says, in the thickest Glaswegian accent you ever heard: "Neil, I've seen it. It's fucking huge. Like a dead German hanging out of a window."'*

dead heat *n.* The situation whereby the urge to defecate comes to glorious fruition at the exact moment when the buttocks touch the *bog seat*.

dead heat in a Zeppelin race *sim.* Large *tits, knockers, bazookas, oomlaaters, Gert Stonkers* that cause you to shout "Oh, the humanity!".

dead herring *n.* A female woman in a pub or club who looks as filthy as a pornstar but turns out to be as frigid as a deceased fish.

deaditor *n.* One who immediately rushes to alter all the tenses on a famous person's Wikipedia entry immediately after their demise is announced; a word coined by Dutch internettist Hay Kranen. *'I see the deaditors have been out in force on your mam's page, Charles.'*

deadliest snatch *n.* A *crab*-filled *minge* with an odour reminiscent of below-decks on a North Sea trawler.

dead man's handle *1. n.* Safety cut-out switch on a piece of machinery, such as a train or industrial guillotine, which must be depressed in order for it to operate. *2. n.* A cheeky – not to mention borderline illegal – use of one's partner's *wanking spanner* while they are asleep in order to *make the bald man cry*. *3. n.* The life-saving "Stop" button on a DVD remote control, over which a gentleman's left thumb constantly hovers while he is enjoying an artistic videographic presentation.

dead man's panhandle *n. medic.* The pointlessly impressive *lob-on* resulting from death due to auto-erotic asphyxiation.

dead man's wellies *n.* The often colourful but highly repulsive used prophylactics which pepper festival campsites and pub car parks following bank holiday discos.

dead midget *n.* Politically incorrect term for a dimensionally challenged, pathetic-looking *lob on*. A *French horn* that couldn't even be used to clear ear wax. From the fact that it is "Just a little stiff".

dead otter *n.* A single stool of substantial proportions.

dead possum with its tongue hanging out, like a *sim. Aus.* A poetic Antipodean turn of phrase describing a badly maintained and unsightly *stamped bat*.

dead rubber *1. n.* In cricket, when a series is won but there is still one nothing-at-stake match remaining. *2. n.* A used *dunky*.

dead semen scrolls *n.* The paper tissues deployed to mop up a gentleman's *suicidal tadpoles*. Also known as *spankerchiefs, prawn crackers* and *wanker's crisps*.

dead sparrow *n.* A small amount of *foulage* that has fallen into an area of the *shark's mouth* beyond the reach of advancing toilet flushes and must be left there until the missus volunteers to do something heroic.

deaf wish *n.* What a married man desires most when listening to *her indoors* droning on.

dealer's choice *1. n.* In card games, the situation whereby the player controlling the pack is permitted to dictate the rules of the game and the specific variant that is played. *2. n.* In a relationship, the situation whereby the gentleman is privileged to choose the sexual favours that he requires as a consequence of some propitious circumstance, such it being his birthday or his partner wanting something. *'I'm sorry, love, but if you want that new kettle it's up the wrong 'un and no buts. I'm calling dealer's choice.'*

deal or no deal *n.* Bloke's nightclub quandary; whether to turn down the offer of a certain *legover* from a below-par *banker* early in the evening in the hope that he can get a higher calibre *box* later on, and thus risking ending up with *fuck all* at the end of the night.

dealt a Beadle, to be *v.* While playing cards, to receive a totally *shit* hand.

deal with the queue at the trade counter *v.* To excuse oneself in order to sort out *the shopping*.

Deansgate tornado *n.* Invisible yet severe, alcohol-fuelled, destructive cyclone which invariably strikes Manchester town centre between 11pm and 3am on Friday and Saturday nights. So named because it leaves irreparable carnage throughout the area, with people staggering about in torn clothes and clinging to lampposts to retain their balance. A *Whitley Bay whirlwind*.

dearache *n. medic.* A chronically painful and uxorially initiated infection that only affects the air-filled space and tiny vibrating bones behind the left eardrum of family saloon-driving husbands.

dearotica *n.* Type of DVD ordered from a Nigerian porn site that costs the hapless purchaser the entire contents of his bank account. And his marriage. And it's not even that good.

death by chocolate starfish *1. n.* An incredibly disgusting *McArthur Park*. *2. n.* A chronic attack of the *Earthas*.

death nest *n.* Estate-agent-speak for the smaller house that elderly people buy late in life.

death penalty *1. n.* Lynch-mob-style justice meted out by bloodthirsty American states. *2. n.* Dramatic coming together of boot laces inside the 18-yard box (or outside if you're a Wolves defender) resulting in the striker going to ground as if sniped from row Z of the main stand by Lee Harvey Oswald.

death rattle *n.* The satisfying noise made when one shakes a packet of *cancer sticks* to ascertain roughly how many are left.

death row *1. n. US.* The section of a prison where the Texan authorities keep simple-minded black men prior to their execution for crimes which they have usually not committed. *2. n.* A retirement home or sheltered housing complex.

death star *n.* An especially malodorous *ringpiece*. A stenchsome *nipsy*.

debone *1. v.* To lackadaisically prepare a piece of fish for consumption by an elderly and much-loved member of the royal family. *2. v.* To break off relations with a girlfriend or wife. *3. v.* To *pull out* at the last minute, play *Vatican roulette*.

debris on the westbound runway *exclam.* Warning of the presence of a series of messy *skids* in the bowl. See *dunghill slalom*.

debt Fred *n. prop.* A social outcast who is always skint because of a disability that means he can't walk past a betting shop, and is always looking for a *tap*. A gambling addict. '*Hide your wallets, lads. Debt Fred has just walked in and it's the Grand National tomorrow.*'

debtors' dish *n.* Satellite television broadcast receiving apparatus. Disparaging term used by bailiffs and debt collectors who know that their indolent quarry will probably be at home watching advertisements for loan companies on the *shit pump*.

decadong *n.* A male *membrum virile* which, when roused to anger, achieves a length of ten inches in the old money. One like Burt Reynolds had, by all accounts.

decafathon *n.* A gruelling day-long test of stamina, during which you consume only things that are good for you. '*Battered sausage, chips and soapy peas please love, and a big bottle of Tizer. I'm doing a decafathon tomorrow.*'

decanter, tramp's *n.* A used soft drinks bottle into which neat spirits can be poured so that a *thirsty* fellow can get discreetly *refreshed* in an inappropriate or otherwise awkward situation without undue risk of detection. A *coach driver's flask*.

decant sediment *v.* To inadvertently *follow through*. '*Could you fetch me a clean pair of plus-fours please, Carson? I appear to have decanted sediment into these fuckers.*'

decent chippy *euph.* Something that is open most nights, and where one is certain of getting a tasty *fish supper* with plenty of *batter*.

declaration to the house *n.* When living in shared premises, the statement delivered to other tennants who might enter a *dumping shed* which you have recently vacated, explaining that you have nothing to do with the foul stench within.

declare *v.* To call off a *scuttle* and *retire from the field* early doors as soon as one has successfully hit one's better half's *wail switch*. '*If it's alright with you, Trudie, I'm going to declare there. I've got to be up early in the morning to tune my lute.*'

declare early *v.* To be *up and over like a pan of milk*.

decompression *n.* See *cooldown*.

decompression guff *n.* A small *Bakewell* let out in order to grant oneself a little breathing space while desperate for the *crapper*.

decorate the downstairs loo *v.* To *plaster the toilet*.

decoy bait box *n.* Petite packed lunch container holding a dainty sandwich or crackers, carried by a huge fat *lass* into her workplace canteen in order to disguise the fact that she's just eaten two bacon butties, a family bag of crisps and a whole packet of Jaffa cakes in the car park.

decrapitation *n.* The act of cutting the head off a *Richard the Third* in order to answer the door, get the phone or present *Thought for the Day* on Radio 4.

deep cut *1. n.* A seldom-played album track, B-side or other musical rarity. Appreciated only by a true connoisseur. *2. n.* An *Exchange & Mart* comprised of rare gases, fusing yesterday's Chicken Tindaloo with last Wednesday's Monster Munch. Appreciated, again, only by a true connoisseur.

deep fat friar *n.* A bald man who has pledged himself to a life of poverty, chastity, obesity and dedication to his local chippy.

deep vein throbnosis *n. medic.* An uncomfortable *chob-on* that is worryingly difficult to shift.

deep vein thronebosis *n. medic.* Loss of feeling and temporary paralysis in the lower legs due to extended periods spent ensconced on the *shit pan* reading this.

deep vein trombonist *n.* Musical type who likes to play *The Flight of the Grumblebee* on a lucky fellow's instrument.

deerstalker *n.* A lady's *bodily treasure* with tweedy *flaps* and a pipe stuck in it. Also known as a *Basil Rathbone.*

defaecated coconut *n. medic.* A stool of such girth and gnarliness that it resembles the drupe of the Coco palm *(Cocos nucifera)*, both in appearance and in the effect of its transit through the *brown eye.*

defarture lounge *n.* The vestibule of the *dirt bakery,* where *exhaust gases* gather in order to build up to maximum pressure. '*Fuck me, your majesty. I've got a right beauty brewing up in the defarture lounge, I don't mind telling you.*'

defecacious *adj.* Having had a particularly satisfying start to one's day, leaving one lighter of step and with a powerful sense of achievement, confident that no matter what the day ahead might bring, one will *ace it* like a boss, Mary Poppins-stylee.

deffocated *adj.* Absolutely, one hundred percent sure you've *shit* them.

deflate *v.* To *suck off.* '*Oi, Gillian. Deflate this for me, will you?*'

defrosted Austin Powers, face like a *sim.* A bird with her mush covered in *spooge.* From the scene in Mike Myers's *International Man of Mystery* movie, in which his secret agent character is covered in a strange type of goo whilst thawing out following 30 years of space-bound suspended animation.

defrosting the fridge *1. n.* Something attempted by most married couples once or twice a year, and thus *2. n.* Foreplay. Also *defrost the freezer.*

defuel *1. v.* In the aviation industry, to release excess liquid through your hose from an overfull tank, and thus, *2. v.* On the way back from the pub, to release excess liquid through your *hose* from an overfull tank. Usually in a bank or building society doorway.

deglaze the pan *1. v.* In cookery, to add liquid to a cooking vessel in order to loosen stuck-on food particles. *2. v.* To add a generous helping of hot liquid to the *gravy bowl,* typically following a dozen pints of real ale and a *catbab* of dubious provenance. *3. v.* In the *khazi,* to hose down *pebbledashed* porcelain using a carefully directed

stream of *gypsy's kiss.* The *yellow toilet brush.*

dehorn *1. v. agric.* In farming, to remove the horns from livestock in order to make them into little trumpets. *2. v.* To render flaccid.

de-icer *1. n.* Motorists' windscreen-clearing solution, typically a bottle containing a poisonous-looking blue mixture of ethyl alcohol and low molecular weight glycol. *2. n.* Any drink bought for a woman by a man in the hope of de-frosting her *snatch,* typically a bottle containing a poisonous-looking blue mixture of ethyl alcohol and low molecular weight glycol.

de-ice the flaps *1. v.* In aeronautical circles, to carry out various procedures on an aeroplane which ensure that ice deposits on the wings do not impair the operation of the control surfaces and mechanisms. *2. v.* Of a frigid lady, to make use of her *muff* following a substantial lay-off.

Deirdre's neck *1. n.* The knotted strings supporting the *nadbag* that are under immense tension. *2. n.* The stringy tendons, ligaments and sinews that pop out of a fellow's neck as he reaches the *vinegar strokes.* Named after the high-tension, harp-like structures which anchored Ken Barlow's gravel-voiced late missus's head onto her shoulders in *Corrie.*

déja poo *1. n. Fr.* The peculiar feeling that you've had a particular *shite* before, or in a dream or something. Usually happens on a Sunday, if that's any help. *2. n. Fr.* An eerily familiar *non-mover at number two* that reappears after the first flush. A *poomerang.* *3. phr. Fr.* The feeling that you've heard this *shit* before.

déja thru *n. Fr.* Weird, other-worldly feeling experienced when *gambling and losing* in the same location on more than one occasion, *eg.* On the N21 Angel bus, to select a completely hypothetical example purely at random.

delay on the Bakerloo line *euph.* Constipation. '*"Sorry I'm late. There was a delay on the Bakerloo line." "Have you tried eating a bowl of prunes?"*' (*Bamforth's Seaside Chuckles* postcard by Donald McGill, 1918).

delete some cookies *v.* To nip upstairs for a sly *Max Planck.* '*Evening, love. I've had a very busy day, so I'm just off upstairs to delete some cookies.*'

delete your wristory *v.* To purge one's *filth machine* of all incriminating evidence.

Delhi belly *n. medic.* Delicate stomach condition leading to the *Eartha Kitts.*

Delia *n.* At a social engagement, the cringeworthy performance of an embarrassingly loud and drunken partner. From tired and emotional TV chef Delia Smith's motivational half-time address at the Norwich versus Man City game on February 28th 2005. *'Oh Christ. She's had half a dozen Bacardi Breezers on an empty stomach. Give it ten minutes and she'll be doing a Delia on me.'* 2. *n.* Following excessive alcohol intake, a floppy male *member* at which its owner may be reduced to shouting "Where are you? Let's be having you!"

delicate sound of thunder 1. *n.* 1988 Pink Floyd live double album that goes on a bit. 2. *n.* An attempted silent *soup cooler* that rattles windows within a two-mile radius.

deli counter *n.* A fragrant bit of *butcher's pie; a* display of *beef* with a gamey aroma, similar to the experience of walking past the charcuterie in your local supermarket.

Delilahs *n.* Stickily sweatsome *plums* which attach themselves to the side of the leg, and require hip-swivelling moves of the sort favoured by leather-faced, leather-trousered Welsh *scads* magnet Tom Jones to dislodge.

delivery from the coalman, take a *v.* To have a grubby chap empty his *sack* in your *back passage* on a regular basis.

delivery room *n.* The *Rick Witter.* Place where many a *bum baby* first sees the light of day. *'Call the mudwife and get me to the delivery room, dear. My brown waters have broken.'*

dell 1. *n.* 16th C. Prostitute, *Tom.* 2. *n.* Former Hampshire venue of Southampton F.C.'s annual relegation battle.

demaritalized zone 1. *n.* Following a row before bedtime, the rigorously policed ten-inch no-man's land imposed between a couple. 2. *euph.* Another name for the *no glans land* which sits between the *pudenders* and the *freckle.* Also known, variously, as the *Dutch canal, scrincter, stinker's bridge, scran, gisp, barse, tintis, great, notcher, ABC, gooch, Finsbury bridge, isnae, scruttock, Perry Como's lip, tornado alley, scranus, smelly bridge, Brick Lane* and *crunk.*

demonstruation *n.* Oestrogen-fuelled mass *tammy huff* involving a gaggle of women, usually directed at some poor bloke who has made the innocent mistake of holding a door open because it was how he was brought up or jokingly slapping a bottom, also because it was how he was brought up.

Denis Norden, do a *v.* To chat up a piece of *clump* in an unnecessarily long-winded and tiresome way instead of just asking for a *poke.* From the way that the late erstwhile antediluvian *It'll be Alright on the Night* host used to bore the liver out of everyone for ten minutes before each batch of funny clips.

Dennis Thatcher's earwax *euph.* Something *nagged*

to fuck.

Dennis Wise *n. prop.* In golfing circles, a short yet daunting putt. "A nasty little five-footer".

dentally handicapped *adj.* Blessed with *English* teeth. *'My cousin's dentally handicapped, you know. He's got a gob like a burnt fence.'*

dented bells, face like a bag full of *sim.* Unconventionally attractive. *'Born on this day: Gerard Depardieu, French actor and pissed-up cultural ambassador, 1948; Lily Cole, big-eyed frock model with A-levels, 1987; Janet Street-Porter, screeching TV presenter with a face like a bag full of dented bells, 1946.'*

dented tin *n.* A *bargain basement babe*; a woman who, at first glance, appears to be a total stunner but who is rendered affordable by a subtle fault, *eg.* Bad breath, an obsessive compulsive disorder, a small prehensile tail *etc.*

dentist, at the *euph.* Of an accommodating lady, to put her head back and open wide, though possibly not to spit afterwards. *'Good date, Mike?' 'Oh aye. She pretended she was at the dentist.'*

department of smelly noises *n.* The *freckle.*

depleting the Amazon *phr.* Said of a *shite* of such vast proportions that a rainforest-worth of *bumwad* is required to deal with it adequately.

depoomidifier *n.* The air-freshening act of opening the bathroom window after *making room for seconds.*

Deptford wives *n.* An *ankle chaingang* of women of uncertain breeding, staggering under the weight of their *bingo clink* on a night out. Often to be seen lifting their tops to expose their *noinkers* on news coverage of New Year's Eve.

depth charge 1. *n.* A large or heavy *Peter O'Toole; a copper bolt.* Also *belly flopper, Admiral Browning, Maxwell.* 2. *n.* An explosive *bouquet of beans* in the bath that would easily take out a U-boat, in the frankly unlikely event that one happened to be lurking under the bubbles.

deputy dog *n.* Unacceptably sexist term to describe the *hound* who is typically seen shadowing a *fox.*

derection *n.* The opposite of an erection, usually obtained by thinking about something unerotic. See *summoning Moira.*

Dermot *n. rhym. slang.* A loose-fitting *quim, Big Daddy's sleeping bag, clown's pocket, trawlerman's sock etc.* From former English cricketer Dermot Reeve = wizard's sleeve.

Dermot O'Leary's shirt, as wet as *sim.* Sopping. From the cuddly *This Morning* presenter's past unfailing willingness to offer his shoulder as a tear-sponge to blubbing, over-emotional *X-Factor* hopefuls who'd just had their dreams stamped into the dust by Simon Cowell.

derren *adj. medic.* Of a man, sterile. From the mentalist magician Derren Brown who, in a TV Russian Roulette stunt, was found to be *firing blanks*. *'No, we don't need a blob, love, I'm derren. But if you're really worried, I'll slip it in your brown pocket.'*

Deryckk Guyler's washboard *1. n.* A rattly clangor from the *nether throat* reminiscent of the eponymous peculiarly spelled late heavily brylcreemed Fenn Street school caretaker's 1970s variety show novelty percussionist act. A reference for the youngsters there. *2. n.* Something that gets *fingered* rapidly and without a great deal of finesse.

descent into five finger gully *1. phr.* Classic navigational error when descending off the summit of Ben Nevis. *2. phr.* Interfering with a lady blessed with a notoriously capacious *wizard's sleeve.*

designated troll *n.* A *fugly* employee hired to make an unattractive employer look more attractive by comparison.

designer vagina *n.* Any *muff* which has been nipped and tucked, or trimmed into an unusual shape, *eg.* A heart, a *Hitler tash*, the Netto logo or Craig David's beard. *Armani fanny, Versnatche.*

desk lifter *n.* An attractive lady teacher who, on bending over to pick up some chalk can cause 30 desklids to be raised simultaneously.

desktop dusting *n.* A fellow's daily ritual of deleting the numerous *male interest* images and thirty-second video clips from his Desktop, Recent Documents and Internet History folders, and thus leaving his computer as *clean as a gay bloke's flat.*

desktop dykes *n.* The sort of aesthetically pleasing *lipstick lesbians* found in huge quantities on a healthy young man's hard disk, but are much more rarely encountered in real life.

Desmond Three-Three *n. prop.* A *Tommy Top-It*; one who always feels the need to go one better than everyone else. See also *Elevenerife, four ball Paul.*

desolation of smeg *n.* The long, dark twenty minutes of a single fellow's soul following the *dropping of his yoghurt.*

despatch master *n.* One who has achieved a high level of expertise in the art of loud and/or noxious *trouser coughage.*

desperate Dan *n.* A stubbly *cow pie* covered in spots that gives the impression it has been shaved with a blowtorch.

dessert boot *n.* A lady whose impressive devotion to puddings has somewhat compromised her looks.

detail *1. v.* To deep-clean every part of a motor vehicle to make it look better than new; what Biff Tannen does for a living in certain episodes of *Back to the Future.* *2. v.* In toilet situations, the exact opposite, *viz.* To give every part of the *biscuit wrapper* a liberal spray of *feeshus*, including under the seat and on the *bog* handle. *'Eeeew! Some twat's detailed the only working khazi! They've even hit the light and the door lock. Oh well, needs must, I suppose.'*

detesticles *n.* Like regular *clockweights*, but hateful to look at. Just like regular *clockweights*, then.

detox *v.* To go for a *number two*; the only way your body gets rid of nasty stuff (along with *piss*), despite what the adverts might tell you. *'Eugh! Some filthy bastard's detoxed on the doorstep again, mum.'*

Detroit Cities *n. rhym. slang. US.* Big softly sprung *headlamps* that soak up the bumps like a 1970s Cadillac Fleetwood Eldorado.

Dettori, do a *v.* Of a bloke, to leave the scene preveniently following the successful conclusion to an act of congress. Named after the "flying dismount" made famous by jockey (and father of five) Frankie Dettori MBE who, whenever he's *ridden a winner,* immediately jumps off, smiling.

developing the pink *1. euph.* In snooker, how John Virgo would describe using the cue ball or other balls to move the pink into a more pottable position. *2. n.* Readying the *veiny bang stick* for a bout of *self help.*

Devil clears his throat, the *exclam.* A witty, *post hoc* statement meant to lighten an atmosphere which has just been noisily befouled by guttural rumblings from the bowels of hell, accompanied by a sulphurous stench of Hades. Also *and there goes Nigel Mansell!*

devil's bagpipes *n.* A chap's *meat and two veg.*

devil's chimney *1. n.* Geological tourist attraction in the absence of anything else to look at on the Isle of Wight. *2. n.* The *shitter.*

devil's doormat *n.* The front of a lady's *twangers.*

devil's doughnut *n.* A huge, perfectly circular *Cumberland curl.*

devil's dumplings *n.* The *chesty substances* found on ladies' fronts.

devil's dustbin *n.* A lavatory bin overflowing with used *Dracula's teabags.*

devil's dust caps *n.* Nipples.

devil's elbow, the *n. medic.* That cursed segment of the *membrum virile* which refuses to firm up.

devil's evacuate *n.* Piping hot *bum slurry* fermented in the depths of Hades. Diarrhoea.

devil's handshake *n.* A Roman Catholic *wank.* A means of reserving oneself a place in the eternal lake of fire.

devil's inkwell *n.* A gentleman's post *bust off* navel, brim-full with his sinfully onanistic yield.

devil's kiss *n.* A *heart to heart* released during sex in the *69* position. *Hell's mouth.* On the plus side, it's probably not quite as bad as a *Satan's banquet.*

devil's kitchen *n.* The *chamber of horrors* or *sludge factory.*

devil's lasagne *n.* A layer of *shit*, followed by a layer of *shit tickets*, followed by another layer of *shit*, followed by a further layer of *bum-wad*, and so on *ad excretum.* The type of horrific sight found in a festival *mobile throne* cubicle. See also *Andrex sandwich, bangers and mash, Viennetta.*

devil's laundry *n.* The diabolical aftermath of a cacodemonic *Tom tit* that has been followed up with a distinctly spendthrift wiping operation; a slap-up feed of *bangers and mash.* The typical contents of a Virgin train lavatory.

devil's lettuce, the *euph.* Marijuana, *hippy salad.*

devil's magnum, the *n.* A heavily used *bog brush* that is so caked with old *feeshus* and bits of paper that it resembles the eponymous lolly. Though probably without the ice cream filling.

devil's motorboat *n.* A release of *flatus* like *the death rattle of a bull elephant.*

devil's pâté *n.* Feeshus, foulage.

devil's pew *n.* A heavily befouled public *bog* seat that is sat upon in a dire emergency when needs must.

devil's playground *n.* A sulphurous pit. The *arse* or *wrong 'un.*

devil's pocket, the *n.* A lady's *bower of bliss.*

devil's pulpit, the *1. n.* Beauty spot in the Wye Valley. *2. n.* Beauty spot in the *Y-valley.*

devil's revels *n.* Small brown morsels of faecal matter with a motley variety of fillings.

devil's thumbprints *n.* The intriguing dimples usually found on the lower backs of erotically inclined women. Also *Dirk Diggler's thumbprints.*

devil's whisper *n.* The absolutely last *exchange & mart* it is possible to let out before you really do have to go for a *shit.*

devo-max *1. n.* A Scottish model for maximum independence while still remaining in the union. *2. n.* A married man's model for maximum independence from his *bag for life* while still remaining within the union, *viz.* Separate bank accounts, living in the garden shed, and furtively obtaining sexual release from a pile of well-thumbed *jazzmags* he keeps behind some tins of paint in the garage.

Devonport decking *n. Piss*-stained mattresses, burnt-out cars *etc.* which form attractive front garden terracing features throughout the lively Plymouth locale.

dewing up *n.* Of a dirty woman, *creaming her dunghampers.* *'Bless me father, for I have committed the sin of impure thought. I got front row tickets for Michael Bolton at the Arena and I was dewing up before he even come on the stage.'*

dew on the lily *1. euph.* A lubricated *flange. 2. n.* Knob glaze, pre-cum. Perseverance soup, knuckle varnish.

dew point *1. n. meteorog.* Speaking psychrometrically (yes, that's the right spelling), the temperature to which air must be cooled in order to become saturated with water vapour. *2. n.* In a romantic dalliance, the moment – following protracted wooing, negotiations and light rubbing of the inner thigh – at which *her indoors* becomes amenable to a game of *hide the sausage.*

Dewsbury refurb *euph.* Hasty method of recovering the insured value of loss-making premises, involving barbecue lighter fluid, matches and running like fuck. *'Tonight on Corrie, Ken bemoans the size of these new ten pee pieces and Leanne carries out a Dewsbury refurb on her failing restaurant Valandro's.'*

dew south *n.* The condition of a young lady's *parts* when she is in a state of arousal, for example while watching Marino scratch his *nuts* on *Love Island.*

dew tube *n.* A pleasantly moistened *snatch* on a bright spring morning.

dexys, do a *v.* Of a sexist male, to sober up in the night and realise that the dolly *bird* he thought he'd pulled has turned into a right *hound.* To do a *midnight runner.*

DFKDFC *abbrev. medic.* Used in patients' notes during diagnosis – Don't Fucking Know, Don't Fucking Care. *'Patient: Female. Age: 72. Presented: Hot flushes, swollen tongue, racing heart, low blood pressure, tingling down right side, loose finger nails. Diagnosis: DFKDFC. Treatment: Amoxyl 3 times a day.'*

DFS *1. abbrev.* A well known furniture shop where, it would seem, you would be hard pressed to ever pay full price for a sofa. *2. abbrev.* Used to describe a partner who is averse to imbibing *gentlemen's relish.* Doesn't/Didn't Fucking Swallow. *3. abbrev.* An elephantine *Andrew* the size of a well stuffed, brown leather sofa. From Double Flush Situation. *4. euph.* One who is constantly having *massive clearances.*

dial Australia *v.* Of a lady, to *reach down under* using her digits. To *gusset type* or do the *front bum shimmy.*

dialog *n.* A feeshus of mixed consistency, *viz.* one

that is neither diarrhoea nor solid. One that cannot decide whether it is *a flock of bats or a block of flats.* See also *monolog, one point five.*

diamond cutter *n.* The hardest erection known to man. *Pink steel, number one wood, third rail.*

diamond dogs *1. n.* Title of an album by late *half-rice half-chips* rocker David Bowie. *2. n.* An offensively sexist and unacceptably misogynistic expression describing a gaggle of *fugly munters* with *vajazzled hoo-has.*

diamond head *1. n.* A notably unsuccessful heavy metal band from Stourbridge who have apparently been plugging away for more than forty years, the poor sods. *2. n.* A *blowjob* that results in a *stiffy* that could *poke a hole through a cheap door.*

diamond in the muff *n.* A genuinely attractive woman in a *grumble flick.*

Diana's dashboard *euph.* A *Kurt Cobain's ceiling.* A tasteless turn of phrase used to describe a messy pair of ladies' *scrods* during *rag week* which we certainly wouldn't include in a respectable book such as this.

Diana, to do a *v.* To collide at a spot between two *tunnels* when having sex. To hit the *taint* with one's *bell end.*

diary buster *1. n.* Annoying business-speak for a sudden, utterly pointless three-hour meeting at which attendance is obligatory. *2. n.* A prolonged emergency visit to the *smallest room* to evacuate a *Douglas* the size of a Californian Redwood, thus necessitating the cancellation of all previous appointments.

dibble *1. v. 14thC.* To *shag. 2. n.* Cartoon police officer in Top Cat. *3. v. onomat.* To playfully prod around at the *hangar doors.*

Dibnah dick *n.* A sudden loss of erectile strength causing the *skin chimney* to collapse as if its foundations have been destroyed by the late eponymous Bolton steeplejack and traction engine enthusiast. Can be brought on by catching a whiff of badly wiped *arse* when *changing at Baker Street,* or accidentally glancing at the telly when Ann Widdecombe's on.

diccolo *n.* A smaller, more shrill version of the *flesh flute,* producing a higher tone when *blown.*

dick *1. n. US.* Penis, *pud, plonker. 2. n.* Idiot, *plonker.* *'Rodney, you fucking dick.'* (*Only Fools and Horses Christmas Special,* 1955) *3. v.* To *fuck.*

dick and dom *euph.* A perfect bachelor's night in, *viz.* A *wank* followed by a pizza.

dick beaters *n.* Hands. Also *wanking spanners, dick skinners, spunky wrenches, cunt scratchers.*

dickclipse *n.* The predictable phenomenon whereby a middle-aged man's genitalia becomes progressively obscured by his beer gut.

dick-do *n. US.* Light-hearted epithet used to describe a *salad-dodger.* Based on the assumption that "their gut probably sticks out more than their dick do". *'Deaths; Peter Ustinov, polyglot dick-do, 82.'* (from *The International Herald Tribune,* March 29th 2004).

dick doc *n.* The bloke's equivalent of his missus's *snatch dentist.* *'Excuse me, nurse, I've caught my bellend in my zip. I'd prefer to see a man dick doc, if that is at all possible, as I am uncomfortable about the idea of a woman getting excited at the sight of my pitifully small, bleeding, septic prepuce.'*

dick docker *n.* A rabbi.

dick duster *n.* A hairy top lip on a lady. *'Anne, we'll have to do that wink again. You've got something on your dick duster.'*

Dickens cider *euph.* Saucily humorous phrase that can only really be used effectively in response to a very narrow range of questions, preferably posed by a red-nosed man in a pub on a garishly illustrated seaside postcard, *eg.* *'What'll your missus be having tonight, Dave?' 'Hopefully she'll have a Dickens cider, Bob.'*

dick frost *n.* The sparkly residue found on the *pizzle shaft* the morning after a night of *frottage.*

dickhead *n.* Fool, *joskin, shit-for-brains.* An idiotic fellow.

dickhead dust *n.* White powder which, when snorted through a rolled-up banknote, turns even the nicest individual into a complete *twat.* Cocaine, *showbiz sherbert, Bolivian marching powder etc.* *'One of the Sunday newspapers reported that a Blue Peter presenter had been seen taking dickhead dust. I believe that he has not only let himself and the Blue Peter team down, including the dogs and tortoises and the Italian sunken garden, but he's also let all of you down badly. He himself agrees with me that, in the circumstances, he can no longer continue as a presenter on the programme. However, he'll be back in a couple of years doing phone-ins on Radio 5 and then he'll get Simon Mayo's gig.'* (On-air apology by Lorraine Heggessey, head of BBC Children's Television, 1999).

dickie dido *n.* Part of a lady, the hairs on which come down to her knees.

dickie light *n. Aus.* In a brothel bedroom, a fluorescent bulb at crotch level which allows a shrewd *good time girl* to examine her prospective customer's *fruit bowl* for any particularly untoward boils, warts, rashes or *cockrots.*

dickie seat *1. n.* On a veteran motor car, pop-up rear passenger accommodation that is intended for occasional use. *2. n.* A spinster's chair that has been handily equipped with a *neck massager.*

Dickinson holiday *1. n.* A bottle of fake tan which makes the wearer look like a fucking satsuma. Named after bright orange cheeky TV auction wideboy David Dickinson. *2. n.* A spell behind bars for fraud.

dick leave *n.* Time taken off work by a fellow to ease the embarrassment of having sent a photo of his genitalia to a colleague who has then shared it around the office. *'I'm sorry, his worship is on six weeks' dick leave at the moment. I can put you through to the town clerk's office if you like.'*

dick like a Wolves first half *sim.* Descriptive of something limp and flaccid. *'That Jeffrey Archer was trying to bang me round the back of a skip for money the other day. Honestly, he's got a dick like a Wolves first half.'*

dickling *n.* Sympathetic term descriptive of a fellow believed to have been short-sold in the *trouser department*. *'Born on this day: Habib Bourguiba, Tunisian politician, 1903; Jonas Savimbi, Angolan politician, 1934; Jack Straw, British dickling, 1946.'*

dick mist *n.* At the end of a *grumble* marathon, the white foam that gathers around the *brim* of a chap's *helmet* like the graveyard fog on the front of *Bat Out of Hell.*

dick on a stick *1. n.* A really bad barbecue offering. *'How's your marinated lamb kebab, vicar?' 'It's a dick on a stick, Mrs Antrobus. Fucking disgusting.'* *2. n.* Someone who just cut you up in the car.

dick on backwards, sorry I had my *exclam.* Said after having a disastrously badly aimed *piss* whilst drunk, half asleep, tired or just careless. *'Bloody hell, Piers! You've got it all over your trousers. And the wall and the ceiling. And in your hair.' 'Sorry luv, I had my dick on backwards.'*

dickorations *n.* Festive bits of metal knocked through one's *cockshaft, bellend* and *scrotbag.* *'Oh, Evan! What delightful dickorations.'*

dick phlegm *n. Cock hockle.*

dick pic *n.* An excessively personal smartphone snap sent to a casual female acquaintance. A *meat tweet.* *'Nice dick pic, Christian. That reminds me, I've got to buy some chipolatas.'*

dickram yoga *n.* The subtle art of *pissing* while balancing on one leg, with your other leg fully extended behind in order to hold the broken door shut.

dick-skinned *adj.* Exhibiting a blasé attitude toward the plight of those less fortunate than oneself, whilst outraged by the terrible things reported on the front pages of the *Daily Express.* *'Your grandad's furious about this ban on bendy bananas and powerful toasters, you know, not that*

he ever eats bananas or toast. Mind, he's always been very dick-skinned has your grandad.'

dick skinner *1. n. prop.* British disc jockey who used to be on Radio 1 and Sheena Easton. *2. n. medic. US. Wanking spanner, cunt scratcher.* Hand.

dicksmith *n.* A time-served, no-nonsense, workmanlike prostitute.

dick's never dry, I bet his *phr.* Said of a chap whose record of success with the fairer sex implies that his member has insufficient time between romantic conquests to return to a dry state. *'That Robin Askwith out of them Confessions films is a lucky bastard. He may have a face like Patricia Hayes but I bet his dick's never dry.'*

dick-spittle *n.* Dew on the lily, perseverence soup, guardsman's gloss.

dick splash *1. n.* Urine on trousers or suede shoes caused by shakage or *splashback.* See also *forget-me-nots.* *2. n. US.* Contumelious epithet for an unworthy person. Named after Senator Richard Splash, Vice President under Jimmy Carter.

dicksy chicks *n.* Ladyboys. Also *bobby dazzlers, rotten peaches, Gwendolens, flippers, shims, tiptops* or *trolley dollies.*

dick-tac *n.* A *bluey* or *Bongo Bill's banjo pill.*

dick tits *1. n. Top bollocks* which are eminently suitable for the provision of *diddy-rides*, and unhelpfully *2. n. Headlamps* which hang down like copper's torches. Knee shooters, sock tits.

Dick Turpin, do a *n.* To defecate from a non-seated position, to "stand and deliver". *'What's mithering you, Rita? You're all of a pother.' 'I've just been in th'Rovers for a shit, Mavis. And th'traps in there were that mucky I had to do a Dick Turpin.'*

Dick Turpin's flintlock, cocked more times than *phr.* Said of a vintage *piece* that has been *rogered more times than a policeman's radio, banged more times than an auctioneer's gavel, fucked more times than a Goodmans stereo.*

Dick Turpin's hat *n.* A good, old-fashioned, three-cornered, hairy *blurtch* that would make the *old fella* "stand and deliver".

dick van dyke *n.* A *strap-on cockney.* A lesbotic *twat rattler*, dildo or *Mary pop-in.*

dick weed *n. US.* A goldang *melon farming fuckwit.*

dick wheat *1. n.* Male pubic hair. *2. n. prop.* Presenter of NBC's most popular late night chat show throughout the 1960s.

dickwit *1. n.* Probably a character from a Charles Dickens novel. *2. n.* A bloke who thinks with his *Charlie.* *3. n.* A foolish person.

diddies *n. Scots.* Ladies' tits.

diddy man *1. n.* A jam butty miner. *2. n.* An

embonpoint enthusiast.

diddy ride *n. Scots.* A deep-fried *sausage sandwich.*

didgeripoo *n.* Any *Simon Cowell* movement that is accompanied by a low-pitched and sustained *jam tart,* as if Rolf Harris is lurking nearby with his instrument in his hands. Which, before he died, wasn't beyond the realms of possibility.

did you ever hear your name whispered on the wind? *exclam. rhet.* To be said while cupping one ear just before expelling a loud blast of *flatus.* Also *our survey said; please hold for the president; listen to this, too good to miss, da-da da-da da.*

Dierdre's specs *n.* Large *aereolae.* Also *saucepan lids, wagon wheels.*

diesel dyke *n. US.* A butch *tennis fan.* Also *bulldyke, fanny nosher.*

diet choke *n.* A refreshing, low-calorie *drink on a stick* which is rich in *vitamin S.*

diet cloak *n.* Garment employed to reassure others that you are not a *bat fastard.* *'Does my bum look big in these hotpants?' 'Just slip your diet cloak over the top, nan. No-one will notice.'*

diet fart *n.* A loud clearing of the *nether throat* that sounds dangerous but actually has no smell and is ultimately harmless. The opposite of a *silent but deadly.* *'No need to open the window, your majesty. It was just a diet fart.'*

difficult brown *n.* Tricky option in *bum games.* See also *Irish, snookered behind the red.* *'I'd rather take the easy pink than the difficult brown.'*

difficult child *n.* One who, once *dropped off at the pool,* refuses to go into the water and clings onto the side.

difficunt *n.* A difficult *cunt.* From difficult + cunt.

Digby *n. prop.* A big, ugly woman. From the 70s children's film *Digby, the Biggest Ugly Woman in the World.*

Digby's collar *euph.* A *wizard's sleeve,* named in honour of the capacious, leathery neck restraint worn by the famous *Screen Test* sheepdog.

digestively overqualified *adj.* Fat. *'I am afraid that you are somewhat digestively overqualified for the position of chief coach to the UK Olympic Heptathlon squad, Eamonn.'*

digestive transit *1. n.* Advert-speak for a big, steaming *crap. 2. n.* Lightweight commercial vehicle which delivers biscuits.

dig for victory *v.* To deliver a two-fingered Churchillian salute up a lady's *front* and *back gardens.*

dig in the whiskers *n. Aus.* A spot of *beard-splitting.*

digital breach *1. n.* A cyber attack – usually as a result of an employee innocently clicking on a link while performing "internet research". *2. n.* A right good *fingerbanging. 3. n.* Unpleasant experience when wiping the *teatowel holder* with sub-standard *arsewad.* *'Sorry about your toastie, Mr Rayner. Only Heston's had a digital breach and we've been that busy he's not had time to wash his hands yet.'*

digital Coventry *n.* A pub table full of ignorant *twunts* all staring at their fancy phones.

digital detox *1. n. Guardian*-esque term for keeping away from your smartphone for a few minutes in order to focus on reading f novels, decorating your second home in Cornwall and making jam. *2. n.* A variant of the *grummer holiday,* whereby a fellow eschews the unlimited possibilities of modern-day online *cyberscud* in favour of the simpler, ancient ways of softcore *hedge-porn,* as found in *Knave, Razzle* and *New Cunts.*

digital download *1. n.* Electronic means of acquiring a document, file or software package. *2. n.* Using the fingertips to dislodge a stubborn nugget of *feeshus* when *cleaning out your recycle bin.* See also *last Malteser in the packet, Linda Bellingham's fingertips, mechanic's nails.*

digitally enhanced *adj.* Fingered.

digitally remastered *adj.* The mental image of a *homely* girl that has been miraculously enhanced in the fevered mind of a masturbating admirer.

digitoflatal reflex *n. medic.* A primitive physiological response whereby the release of *bum gas* through the *fifties tea towel holder* is initiated by a small force applied by a third party longitudinally to the e*xtensor indicus proprius.*

dignity curtain *n.* When having an hirsute male dog's coat clipped, a lower abdominal pelmet of hair which discreetly obscures any dangling bits, thus sparing his blushes.

dig up a badger and bum it *exclam.* Phrase used when in a state of extreme sexual frustration. *'I tell you what, Olivia. I'm that horny I'd happily dig up a badger and bum it.'*

dik tuk *1. n.* A popular mode of transport in Thailand. *2. n.* A popular mode of penile concealment in Thailand.

dildo *n.* Practice version of the *pork sword.* A *bob, neck massager, dolly dagger.*

dildo chicken *n.* A vegetarian-friendly poultry substitute, *eg.* Quorn, Fricken and so on. So-called because it "replaces the cock".

dildole *n.* Source of income for attractive ladies who work from home entertaining lonely men with broadband internet connections and plenty of tissues.

dill *1. n.* An unpleasant thing put in burgers by the staff at McDonald's. *2. n.* A type of pickle.

dillberries *n. Dangleberries, wufflenuts.*

DILLIGAF/dilligaf *abbrev.* Disinterested rhetorical

response to a question or enquiry, *viz.* Do I Look Like I Give A Fuck?.

dilm *n.* Unpleasant-tasting spermicidal lubricant on a *dunky.*

dilmah *n. Aus.* An amusing party entertainment whereby the performer bounces his *knackers* on the forehead of the first person to fall asleep. Named after an Australian brand of tea bag and the similar dunking action associated with them.

diminished responsibility *phr.* Plea used by men upon waking to their partner complaining that they had spent the night *dropping their guts* horrendously whilst remaining asleep the entire time; a legal loophole open to abuse by those who want to *let one go* but aren't quite asleep yet.

diminishing returns *n.* The series of about twenty *wanks* that a fellow must have after his vasectomy operation before he eventually begins to produce 100% *decaff spaff.*

dimmock *1. v.* Of a lady, to create a *water feature.* See *squat 'n' squirt.* *2. v.* Of the *fighter pilot's thumbs* on a lady's *Charlies,* to pop out like car cigarette lighters.

dine at Grimsby docks *v.* To have a *fish supper.* *'The wife let me have Greek on my birthday, so for hers I had to promise to dine at Grimsby docks.'*

dine at the Marriott's buffet *v.* To succumb to a bout of alimentary unpleasantness. Named after Tottenham Hotspur's meek last-match-of-the-season capitulation to West Ham in 2006, after the team's players were (our lawyer wishes to make clear) definitely not poisoned by dodgy comestibles consumed at the plush five-star hotel the previous evening. *'Uh-oh, and if our helicopter camera high above Tower Bridge could just zoom in there....yes, it looks like Radcliffe's been dining at the Marriott's buffet again, Sue.' 'Yes, Steve. She's definitely shat herself alright.'*

dine out *v.* To *eat out* away from home, *eg.* With the woman next door, the wife's sister, a bus clippie *etc.*

dine with Spongebob *v.* To *don the beard, impersonate Stalin, dine at the Y.* From the eponymous, geometrically pantalooned cartoon character, who has an insatiable appetite for *crabby patties.*

ding-a-ling *n.* Chuck Berry's late *cock.* With two silver bells hanging off it on a string.

ding! dong! *exclam. arch.* Caddish expression of delight when Terry-Thomas spotted a woman with *dunce's hats.*

dingleberry roast *n.* A lighted *fart,* an *afterburner, a blue streak.*

dingo's breakfast *n. Aus.* A *piss* and a bit of a look around.

dining at the 8 *euph.* A somewhat more outré alternative to *dining at the Y,* served round the back. Probably have a couple of mints after, eh?

dining at the eye *n.* Enjoying a *drink on a stick.*

dining out at the clitz *n.* Engaging in *cumulonimbus* with a female who is well above average.

dining with the Askwiths *euph.* Illicit or surreptitious *puddle jumping.* From the deliberately misleading excuse offered to his missus by flamboyant Victorian playwright Oscar Wilde when he was late home for his tea; *viz.* That he was going for a meal with *Confessions* film actor and Patricia Hayes-lookalike Robin Askwith and his family.

dinky-rigged *adj.* Antithesis of *donkey-rigged. Hung like a Chinese mouse, short-staffed. 'Born on this day: Joseph Paxton, landscape gardener, 1803; Elisha Otis, lift pioneer, 1811; Jack Straw MP, dinky-rigged former Home Secretary, 1946.'*

dinner at Hugh Fearnley-Whittingstall's, worse than *sim.* A phrase descriptive of an event or occurrence that is even more unpleasant than dining at the double-barrelled chef's gaff on a menu of poached weasel in a piquant hedgehog vomit sauce, fricasée of camel's arsehole and crispy stoat gonads, with *pigshit* ice cream for afters.

dinner lady's arms *1. n. medic.* Bingo wings. *2. sim.* Large, but nonetheless unhealthy-looking *cocks.* A lardy *tallywhacker* that looks like it might have a heart attack at any moment.

dinner masher *n.* A *botter.*

dino-rod *1. n.* A megafauna-sized *membrum virile* used to clear out a partner's pipes. *2. n.* A megafauna-sized *dump* used to clear out your own pipes.

dinosaur eggs *n.* Big, hard *babies' dinners.*

dinosaur frightener *n.* A particularly horrible *arse. 'I was accosted by some youths the other day, but I ended the fracas by yanking down my kecks and showing them my dinosaur frightener.' 'Well done, gran.'*

dinosaur's ball bag, face like a *sim.* Said of a person with a particularly haggard, careworn physiognomy. *'That Keith Richards. Fuck me, he's got a face like a dinosaur's ball bag, him.'* Or indeed *'That Tyrannosaurus. Fuck me, he's got a face like Keith Richards's ball bag.'*

dino-whore *n.* A *good time girl* who hasn't been a girl for a good long time. A *pro-AP.*

diplomatic cable *1. n.* A top-secret, urgent message sent between embassies. *2. n.* A top-secret, urgent *Donald* taken at the house of a friend or in-law, typically conducted in complete silence and followed by a clean-up procedure that is distinctly more thorough than usual. 3. *n*. A potentially embarrassing *Sir Douglas* deposited by a politician or similar public figure. *'Boris has left another diplomatic cable blocking the crappers, Monsieur Juncker.'*

dip 'n' dazzle *n*. A humorous epithet used to describe one whose ocular organs are so far out of whack as to be reminiscent of badly adjusted headlights. An *Isaiah*. *eg*. The late Marty Feldman or that Kit Williams who done the book with the rabbit.

dipping a worm in a bucket *v*. Engaging in unsatisfying sexual congress. *The last hot dog in the tin.*

DIPS/dips *acronym*. Paris Hilton's car wing mirrors. Drunken Impact Protection System.

dip the clutch *v*. To elongate or otherwise flex the left leg while in one's motor car, in order to lift the corresponding buttock cheek off the driver's seat and thus ease the release of *brownhouse gases* from the *exhaust pipe*.

dip your bread in this! *exclam*. Something to be said before *letting off*. See also *name that tune; our survey said; let's see if you're right and if so, how many people said it.*

dip your nib in the office ink *euph*. To partake in a romantic liaison with a female work colleague. To *shit on your own doorstep*. *'What am I going to do, Tony? The News of the World's caught me dipping me nib in the office ink again.'*

dip your wick *v*. To slip your vinegary *dill* into the *hamburger*.

diquid *1. n*. Spunk, cum, jizz, spaff, spooge. *'Eurgh! There's all diquid in me knicker drawer, Monsieur Poirot.'* 2. *n*. The unhappy combination of ejaculate and water. Also *cock mess monster*.

directors commentary *n*. The disconnected, self-obsessed *sotto voce* ramblings of bitter-sodden tramps.

director's cut *n*. The point in an 18th generation *jazz video* where a previous *Chinese helicopter pilot* has inadvertently pressed "Record" instead of "Pause", leaving the viewer with a four-second clip of *Panorama* circa 1994.

Dirk Diggler's thumbprints *n*. Them dimples on a *bird's* lumbar region.

dirt angels *n*. Miraculous brown U-bend stigmata in the shape of celestial wings.

dirt bakery *n*. That part of the human anatomy where *holemeal loaves* are freshly manufactured around the clock. The *chamber of horrors*.

dirtbox *n*. *Date locker*, rectum. Source of delights

for devotees of *bumcraft*.

dirt diggler *n*. A *poo* of unnatural length and girth.

dirtier than your browsing history *sim*. Said of something that could, if we're being honest, do with a good scrub with a wire brush and a liberal squirt with the bleach. Also *dirtier than ~ a taxi floor; ~ a coalminer's hanky, ~ John McRirick's wanking pants, ~ an office microwave*. *'Don't let the dog on the sofa, Frank. He's been rolling in cow shite again and he's dirtier than your browsing history.'*

dirt penny *n*. An unwiped *dot*. *'It's a very simple, straightforward procedure. I'm just going to put a glove on and pop my finger up your dirt penny, Paul. Then, after the break, Gino d'Acampo will be here to bake a chocolate and jam cake with almond sauce and we'll be talking to TOWIE's Gemma Collins about her battle with piles.'*

dirty air *1. n*. The region behind a Formula One racing car which is affected by aerodynamic turbulence, thus making it difficult to overtake. 2. *n*. The region behind a flatulent person which is affected by *arseodynamic burbulence*, thus making it difficult to breathe.

dirty back scratcher *n*. Toilet brush.

dirty bee *n*. A long and high-pitched blast on the *kazoo* which sounds like a honey-making insect trapped in a tin can.

dirty Beppe *n*. A *dirty Sanchez*, but with coverage extended to the chin.

dirty bomb *1. n*. A crude explosive device containing radioactive material designed to contaminate an area, making it uninhabitable. 2. *n*. A *dropped back*, the fallout from which makes the immediate vicinity uninhabitable for the foreseeable future, *eg*. One detonated by Jocky Wilson at a cocktail party. 3. *n*. An explosion of *shite* that peppers the bowl with bio-hazard shrapnel.

dirty Bristow *n*. A sexual act performed by a lady whereby she kneels behind a standing gentleman and licks his *anus* while reaching through his legs to stimulate his penis. Occasionally stopping to swig a pint of lager. *Tromboning*.

dirty chips *n*. One distinctly unappetizing result of not pulling your string vest up properly when going for a *sit-down lavatory adventure*. You'll be needing that string vest washed and all.

dirty cornflakes *n*. Pressed and dried *jizz* spots on a pillow case after a *facial*.

dirty dentist *n*. *Fanny mechanic, snatch doc, box doc, cunt dentist*. A consultant gynaecologist. *'I'm having a bit of bother with me clopper, love, so I'm off to the dirty dentist for a scrape.'*

dirty devil *n*. An under-duvet *dropped gut* that tests one's relationship to breaking point. *'Sorry about *that dirty devil, love. Anyway, it's your turn on top, isn't it? Then you can stick the kettle on when you're on your way out.'*

dirty divination *n.* The mystic art of studying your soiled bathroom tissue in an attempt to see what the bowels foretell, rather in the same manner that a fortune teller might glance into the tealeaves.

dirty dust *n.* The heady waft of a well-toasted *air crumpet*.

dirty end of the bridge *n.* The *shitty* extreme of the *biffon*; a condition suffered by *forward wipers*.

dirty fart *n.* A *Lionel Bart* with delusions of grandeur. A *follow through*.

dirty Groucho *n.* Like a *dirty Sanchez*, but including a pair of dark-rimmed spectacles. And probably a cigar.

dirty hitchhiker, the *euph.* Sticking a thumb up the *council* of an intimate partner in order to get a much needed lift.

dirty lolly *n.* A girl whom one is tempted to *pick up* and lick, but who is probably covered in germs.

dirty onion *n.* The overture to an act of *backdoor romance* that is performed with such unexpected vigour by the *bummer* that it brings tears to the eye of his *bummee*.

dirty parachute *1. n.* A piece of *bog roll* that gets stuck up the *ringpiece*. *2. n.* When air gets trapped under discarded *arsewipe* and it floats. Also *Welsh man o' war.*

dirty penguin, walk the *v.* To waddle in a shameful, short-stepping manner designed to ameliorate the unpleasant consequences of *gambling and losing* while out and about.

dirty phonecall *n.* Any telephone conversation undertaken while ensconced on the *jobby engine*. *'Did you hear Popmaster this morning? I'm sure the second round was a dirty phonecall. You could tell from the acoustics. Luckily, I don't think the contestant noticed.'*

dirty piñata *n.* A plastic bag containing *hound cable*, thoughtfully left dangling off a tree branch by a passing *shit machine* walker. Also known as a *biz bat*.

dirty protest *n.* The result of placing a bowl of baked beans in the microwave without covering it up, creating – in miniature – the *shit*-smeared decor of a late 1970s H-Block prison cell.

dirty Sanchez *1. n.* Quondam television programe in which a group of intellectually challenged Welshmen dared each other to drink *piss*, set fire to their *bell ends*, nail their scrotums to double decker buses *etc.* *2. n.* Sticking one's finger up a lady's *back bottom* during *doggy-style* sex. Then

drawing a moustache on her top lip, apparently.

dirty satisfaction *n.* The mixed feeling of shame, relief and joy felt immediately after passing a *King Kong's finger* that is three sizes too big for your *leather bagel*.

dirty scarecrow *n.* When roped in by a partner to help change the bedsheets, the charming, amusing and affectionate act of *dropping a gut* into an empty pillowcase, forcing it over their head and gathering it around the neck. It is estimated that *dirty scarecrows* are the cause of more than 40% of marriage failures in Britain. *'The eighteenth time the couple divorced, Burton claimed that Taylor had done the dirty scarecrow on him whilst the couple were honeymooning in an exclusive Botswana game lodge.'*

dirty seahorse *n.* A partial *floater* which is suspended mid-tank after being birthed. *'It's a dirty seahorse, here to feed on bits of sweetcorn and other local flora.'* (David Attenborough, *The Brown Planet*, BBC 2001).

dirty secret *n.* A pungent *back biscuit* left by a surreptitious *benefactor* as he innocently sidles away from a group. *'I knew I was going to get fired when I got called into the boardroom. Mind you, at least I managed to leave a dirty secret for Alan, Karen and Tim as I got up to leave.'*

dirty song but someone's got to sing it, it's a *1. phr.* Lyric from the Faith No More song *We Care A Lot*. *2. exclam.* Witticism after *dropping* a rather tuneful *hat*.

dirty spine, snip a length of *v.* To *lay a cable, drop a copper bolt*.

dirty Stilgoe *n.* A variation on the *dirty Sanchez,* but this time with the full beard drawn on, in order to create the effect of the erstwhile *Nationwide* topical songsmith known, variously, as Archie Slogdirt, Dr Gloria Ethics *and* Giscard O'Hitler (anags).

dirty ticket *n.* A very easy lady. *'I must say, when I first met Sarah at Klosters, I thought she was a bit of a dirty ticket. However, she's put all that behind her now, and I think she's going to make an excellent Duchess.'* (Prince Philip, wedding reception speech, 1986).

dirty Titchmarsh, do a *v.* To perform a rudimentary garden makeover without the owner's knowledge, a process that typically involves adding a used *jubber* and a pair of discarded *scads* to the existing landscaping arrangement. See *incapability brown*. *'You know that lass I was talking to in the pub? The one who was feeling sick so I took her outside for some fresh air? After she spewed up we got talking, and to cut a long story short, we ended up doing a* *dirty Titchmarsh in a garden round the corner.'*

dirty Triffid *n.* A *daisy-chain* of *felchers.* Like something out of that saucy skinflick *The Human Centipede.*

dirty U-boat *n.* The (probably non-existent, though if it does exist, it'll be very popular in Germany) act of doing a *poo* in the bath for sexual gratification.

dirty waffle *n.* A *shite* placed in a sock and then inserted into your hotel trouser press in order to fill the air with the aroma of hot, baking *turd.* 'The Br(name of Britannia Airport Hotel, Manchester obscured on legal advice)er is the perfect location for pleasure and business. Each room comes with dirty windows, ensuite manky bathroom and a complimentary dirty waffle.'

dirty water *n. medic.* A medical term for seminal fluid. *Bollock bile.*

disabilitits *n. Funbags* which are so large that they become a hindrance. Impressionist Faith Brown was apparently entitled to a parking permit because of her terrible *disabilitits.*

disabler *n.* Very obvious and prolonged penile tumescence during office hours that more or less permanently prevents one from getting out of one's chair.

disappinted *adj.* Descriptive of the emotional state of one who has inadvertently been left out of a round at the pub. *'I'm not upset, your royal highness. I'm just disappinted, that's all.'*

disasturbate *v.* To suffer onanistic bad fortune, *eg.* Your mum coming in the room with a cup of tea, falling off a chair as you reach the *vinegar strokes,* or suddenly realising you're being filmed with a hidden camera for a live *Gotcha* on *Noel's House Party.*

discharge papers *1. n.* Documents issued following cessation of service from the armed forces. *2. n. Wankerchiefs* used by a fellow to clean up following *compulsory service.* See also *papier splâché, porn crackers, wanker's crisps.*

disco fanny *adj.* The full strength flavour achieved by a vigorous evening of giving it *six nowt* on the dance floor.

disco light beauty *n.* A woman who looks cracking when viewed from the DJ booth, but is revealed in all her hideous glory when the *ugly lights* go on.

disco nap *n.* A spot of mid-afternoon shut-eye that ensures you will be able to stay awake while clubbing until the early hours.

disco tits *n.* Out, loud and proud *dairy arrangements.*

discovery channel *n.* Any satellite television station used by teenagers in the pursuit of *self improvement. Al Jizzera.*

disembowelmovement *n.* A *Thora* so girthsome

that, when it is finally passed, it creates a powerful vacuum that threatens to suck your *Camillas* right out through your *cigar cutter.*

disfabled *adj.* Claiming invalidity benefit on dubious grounds, *eg.* That copper who was off work with stress, but bravely managed to referee a Premiership football match.

dishonourable discharge *1. n. milit.* The shameful result of knocking the *little general's helmet* off. *2. n.* An act of *self delight* performed in a morally questionable location, *eg.* In the toilets of your nan's nursing home, at a funeral parlour or into a knicker drawer belonging to the un-named vocalist of a late 1980s power-pop combo while she is on stage singing *China in Your Hand.*

dish the dirt *1. v.* To reveal or spread scandalous gossip. *2. v.* To *pebbledash* the *bum sink* during a particularly comprehensive *sit down toilet adventure.*

disnae channel, the *n. Scots.* The *rear entrance* of a shy lassie who has yet to succumb to the shameful delights of *backyard action.*

disneyland *n.* A woman of whom it takes an inordinate amount of time and a large amount of money to *enter,* although once you do, all the *rides* are free. Also *legoverland.*

dispatch war rocket Ajax *euph.* To have a nice big *shit,* from the bit in that *Flash Gordon* film. *'Will you cover me for 10 minutes please, Priti? I'm off to dispatch war rocket Ajax.' 'No problem, Boris.'*

display model *n.* An impressive bit of *morning wood* that's just for show and, despite everyone's best efforts, refuses to *go off.*

disrackted *adj.* Diverted by a *well qualified* lady. *Titnotised.*

disrupting yourself *1. n. Wanky* business-speak term for radically making yourself over to achieve personal mastery, or some such similar *bollocks. 2. n.* Having an unusually intense *J Arthur* that takes you out of your comfort zone.

distance yourself from that! *exclam.* Exclaimed after *dropping your guts* during a pandemic.

disturbance in the force *1. n.* An uneasy feeling experienced after unleashing the destructive power of your *death star. 2. n.* Horrible gut pains you get before having a massive *Tom tit. Concraptions. 'What's the matter, Obi-Wan?' 'It's nothing, Luke. Just a disturbance in the force. I'll be right as rain after I've dropped me shopping.'*

ditch one in the Hudson *v.* On the way home from the pub, curry house or Fat Duck, to suddenly get the *two minute warning* while still a considerable distance from the safety of one's own *dumper* and be forced to make an emergency *final approach* and *splash landing* in a nearby quiet thoroughfare. To suffer a *turd strike*.

ditch pig *n.* An affectionate, lighthearted epithet for a girl *with a lovely personality*.

dive my brave hawk-men! *exclam.* Something to bellow at the top of your lungs, in the style of *shouty crackers* thesp Brian Blessed, accompanied by a *shit-eating grin* as the first *chod* is released from the *bomb bay doors*.

dive on the barbed wire *v.* To *take the chubby bullet*.

divine wind *1. n.* Usual translation of the Japanese word *Kamikaze*, used to describe the typhoon which destroyed a Mongol invasion fleet in the 13th Century and which was later applied to suicide pilots in WWII. *2. n.* Tuneful and fragrant *botty pops* released by highly skilled geishas during the final stage of congress.

diving bell *n.* A notably cold, hard *muff* which clangs when you *bang it*.

diving for pearls *n.* Post-poke truffling in the *bearded clam*.

divot *n.* A particularly hairy *placket* that ideally should be replaced.

dixi *exclam. Lat.* The classical phrase "I have spoken" – normally used at the end of a speech or argument by someone who had an expensive education. *2. exclam. Lat.* An erudite, post-flative quip; the sort of thing that the Archbishop of Canterbury might say after *dropping his guts*.

dixy's midnight runs *n. medic.* The overwhelming urge to empty one's *Enochs* during the penultimate hour of the day, felt shortly after consuming any form of vaguely poultry-based sustenance prepared at the popular north-western fast food franchise.

DIY *euph.* A single-handed job done around the house at the weekend using one *tool* and a small bag of *nuts*.

dizzyade *n.* Beer. Also *dizzy pop*.

Dizzy Gilespie *n.* A formidable blast on the *spunk trumpet* where the lady's cheeks puff out like a bullfrog's, and it would be a good idea for the man to stick a mute up his *arse* to keep the noise down.

DM *1. abbrev.* Direct Message – a personal missive sent *via* social media platforms such as Twitter and that, typically with an attached low-angled photograph of one's *nadbag* and *scrank*. *2. abbrev.* Doctor Marten – a type of boot worn by policemen, Buster Bloodvessel and Tony Benn. *3. abbrev.* Dog Message – to post a parcel of canine foulage through an enemy's letterbox. *'You take granny's Corgis home, Meghan. I'm just going to DM Piers Morgan.'*

DMITO *abbrev.* Seen in veterinary surgery records.

Dog More Intelligent Than Owner.

DMJ *abbrev.* A smart sportscoat or blazer bought in a charity shop. Dead Man's Jacket. *'You'll never get into the Royal Enclosure dressed like that.' 'Not a problem. I'll just nip into Action Cancer and get meself a smart DMJ.'*

DNAise *n.* The savoury condiment most often served to *Times* food critic Giles Coren with his chips, spread on his sandwiches or stirred into his soup. *Baby gravy, plum sauce.* Also *DNAisse*.

DNF *1. abbrev.* In Formula 1, a form of letters which indicates a car that failed to successfully complete the full distance of a grand prix. Did Not Finish. *2. abbrev.* Following a date, a form of letters which denotes that a gentleman failed to bring his evening to a successful conclusion. *'How did you get on with all them stewardesses in the hotel last night, James?' 'Not so well, Murray. Just eighteen pole positions and twenty-three DNFs.'*

D-notice *1. n.* Government order requiring news editors not to publish certain sensitive information for reasons of national security. *2. n.* Official warning served on the missus that, all things being well, she will be in receipt of a good *dicking* later that day, *eg.* Flowers, chocolates *etc.*

do *v.* To *fuck* someone. *'I'd do her.'*

do a West Ham *sim.* To *score* and *stay up* when you haven't really got it in you. Formerly *do a Southampton, do an Everton*.

dobber *1. n.* A *rubber johnny*. *2. n.* A semi-erect *dill*. A lazy *lob on*. *3. v.* To cheat someone out of something, to rip off. From a bloke called Dobber Bailey from Coventry who famously, twenty years ago, got ripped off buying an engine for his Triumph TR7. *'I tried to buy a genuine Nigerian Breitling off the internet but I got dobbered.'*

dobgob *v.* To *spooge up* when only half *stonked*. Also *dobglob*.

Doc Brown, do a *v.* To delete all the *left-handed websites* from one's computer's history file, an act usually carried out between 12.30am and 1.00am, after the wife has gone to bed. Named after the eccentric inventor in the *Back to the Future* films, who was not averse to meddling with the past when the need arose.

dock *1. n.* Arse. The polite term by which horsey types refer to their steeds' *fudge tunnels*. *2. v.* To *shag*. Up a horse's *arse*. Possibly while standing on your motorcycle helmet.

docker's knuckle *n.* A particular gnarly *chocolate starfish*. *"Jesus, your nan must have an arsehole like a docker's knuckle, Jennings,"* said Darbishire, *as he rifled feverishly through the envelope of photographs that Venables had hidden behind the* cistern.' (from *Jennings Drops His Hymn Book* by Anthony Buckeridge).

docker's omelette *n.* A glistening gobbet of rubbery phlegm with remarkable anti-traction properties. A *gold watch*, a *Rolex prairie oyster*.

docker's tea break *sim.* Descriptive of something very long. *"'Oh, what a tiny little man," laughed Verruca Salt as she saw the Oompah Loompah with his bright orange skin and green hair. "He may be small," cautioned Mr Wonka as he turned briskly on his heel, "but he'll have a cock as long as a docker's tea break."'* (from *Charlie and the Chocolate Sandwich* by Roald Dahl).

docker's thumbs *n.* Nipples so hard one could hang a soaking wet duffle coat off them. *Scammell wheelnuts, JCB starter buttons, Dimmocks, cigar butts, fighter pilot's thumbs.*

dock fairy *n. E Yorks.* A mysterious siren who flits about the cosmopolitan harboursides of Goole, guiding the inebriated matelots of Vladivostok and Murmansk to warmer quarters.

docking *n.* The rolling of one's *fiveskin* over another chap's *hat*. A *clash of heads*.

docking station *n.* A *puddle jumpers'* hostelry where copious amounts of *fairy liquid* are quaffed.

dockyard cat, fanny like a *sim.* Descriptive of a particularly unkempt, semi-feral *snatch*. *Max Clifford's allotment, Rolf Harris's windowbox, Stuart Hall's front lawn.*

dockyard rivets *n.* Cigar butts, pygmies' cocks.

dockyard shithouse, abused like a *sim.* Said of something or someone that has to put up with a lot of *crap* on a daily basis.

doctopussy *n.* A consultant gynaecologist. Also *fanny mechanic, snatch doc, box doc, cunt dentist.* *'I'm having a bit of bother with me clopper, love, so I'm off to the doctopussy for a scrape.'*

doctor doom *n. coll.* Any online medical self-diagnosis website. *'Well, I've had a look on doctor doom for you, and it's bad news, nan. You've only got three weeks to live.'*

doctor's signature *n.* A particulary wiggly pair of *beef curtains* resembling a GP's illegible scrawl at the bottom of a prescription.

dodd *v.* To *shit* oneself in public. Named after a certain James Dodd who *shit* himself on the way to work and then phoned in to say he couldn't come in because he had *shit himself.*

Dodd finger *n.* An exploratory digit that tickles a lady's *tradesman's entrance* during the *warm-up exercises*, in order to ascertain whether she's up for a spot of *rearguard action*. From the late, dentally challenged tax-averse Scouse jam butty magnate's famous between-the-legs tickling stick.

'I say. What a lovely day, madam, what a lovely day for sticking a Dodd finger up your arse and saying, "How's that for something to bring Tears to your eyes?".'

Dodd job *n.* A *nosh* administered by the more toothsome lady, or perhaps one who likes to bite. *'Fancy another Dodd job, Normski?' 'No thanks, Janet. By the way, have you seen the TCP anywhere?'*

dodger's conscience *n.* The ridiculous purchase of a diet drink after a *Duke* or *Duchess of Giblets* has ordered a large pie and chips, two pickled eggs, a battered sausage and "a saveloy while I'm waiting".

dodgy corner *n.* Anal sex. "He's taken it, and it's gone behind".

dodgy prawn *euph.* Rogue crustacean often found at the bottom of the tenth pint glass to be drained in an evening. *'It's definitely not a hangover dear, I must have had a dodgy prawn.'*

dodgy starter motor *euph.* Lots of noise and spluttering before any *movement*.

doesn't fart in bed *n.* Said of a gent who *keeps his coins in his wallet*.

doesn't play poker *euph.* Said of a fellow who *knows what's in his flowerbeds*. *'You know him who does the weather on the BBC? He doesn't play poker, you know. I seen it in the Daily Mail.'*

doesn't really follow football *euph.* Descriptive of a chap who *is not really interested in cars*. *'See that bloke over there getting banged up the shitter off the big hairy man in leather shorts? Well, apparently he doesn't really follow football, if you get my drift.'*

doesn't skip like a boxer *euph.* Said of a chap who *bakes a moist sponge*.

does the prisoner have anything to say before I pass sentence? *exclam.* Solemn introduction for an *air biscuit*. See also *on my command unleash hell; listen to this, too good to miss, da-da da-da da; did you ever hear your name whispered on the wind? etc.*

doff one's cap *1. v.* To exhibit cringing deference to one of an arbitrarily higher social rank as a mark of respect. How the farmers in *Downton Abbey* treat Lord Grantham, even though he's just pretending to be really posh. *2. v.* To ejaculate one's filthy *man-muck* onto a posh *tart's tits. 3. v.* To have a *quickie. 'The gas man didn't have time to stop and chat, nan. He just doffed his cap and left.'*

D of the dung *exclam.* The exact moment that the buttocks touch the *bog* seat, triggering an explosive defecation that could blow your eardrums inside out.

dog *1. n.* A woman who, according to a balding, flatulent man leaning on the bar with his gut hanging over the belt of his *pissy* trousers, fails to reach an acceptable standard of physical attractiveness. A *steg*. 2. *n.* A male prostitute. 3. *v.* To hang around in car parks at night, in the pretence of walking the family pet, in order to join a selection of retired footballers, minor television personalities, soap actors and politicians spying on courting couples and *watching it going in* while frantically *searching for loose change* in their pockets.

dog at broth, like a *sim.* Descriptive of a desperate sexual act, usually *cumulonimbus*. *'After returning from war service, Prince Philip was like a dog at broth when introduced to her majesty's front bum.'* (from *Prince Philip Duke of Edinburgh: How Very Marvellous and Wonderful He Was* by Nicholas Witchell).

dog beers *n.* Any ale quaffed by one who is unable to handle their drink. Downing one *dog beer* leaves the average *two-pot screamer* feeling and looking like he has drunk seven.

dogblossom *n.* Drooping, pungently scented blooms, usually blue or black, commonly found hanging in the lower branches of parkland or urban trees. *Brown baubles, Warrington baubles.*

dog bomb *n.* A discarded squeaky toy that is inadvertently trodden on in the hallway while tiptoeing to the toilet at 3am for a *piss*, thus waking up the entire house and Fido, who now thinks it is playtime.

dog catcher *n.* A man who goes looking for unwanted *hounds* in a nightclub after all the pedigree *blart* has been collared. A *munter hunter, rat-trapper.*

dog chalk *n.* The elusive white canine excrement that was everywhere in the 1970s. If lightly gripped, *dog chalk* could be used by youngsters to draw on pavements.

dog coffin *n.* An unwanted jumper, worn once at Christmas and then put aside until a shroud is required for a deceased best friend.

dog deaf *n. medic.* Selective hardness of hearing which affects *shit machine* owners, rendering them unable to hear their beloved pets barking all day and night, also rendering them aurally insensate to desperate entreaties from their neighbours to keep the bastard things quiet.

dog eat dog *n.* Poor quality lesbidaceous *soixante-neuf.*

dog eating hot chips *sim.* A crude and voracious, yet effective, *horatio* technique. *'Lusitania was powerless to resist. His eyes burned into hers like garnets. His muscular arms enfolded her body as she felt herself being swept away in a force 10 gale of passion. Slowly, she fell to her knees, unzipped*

Signor Giuseppe's breeches and went at his bellender like a dog eating hot chips.' (from *The Countess and the Lion Tamer* by Barbara Cartland).

dog egg brown *n.* An even more prosaic and functional colour than duck egg blue. *'And all up here next the stairs we're doing it dog egg brown, Kirsty.'*

dog eggs *n. Turds,* often laid on the pavement. Also known as *lawn sausages.*

dog egg theory *n.* Scientific *blart* hypothesis; *viz.* "The older it is, the easier it is to pick up".

dog fat *euph.* Puppy fat that has reached maturity.

doggee *n.* A person who altruistically transacts their romantic assignations, often in a *sylvan* setting, for the amusement and pleasure of passers by. And gets *spunked* on by them all.

dogger bank *n.* A receptacle containing *jipper*-filled tissues and *jubber rays,* found in a lay-by along a quiet rural road.

Doggerland *1. n.* Name given by geologists to the former landmass connecting Great Britain to mainland Europe until around 6200 BC. 2. *n.* Present-day Essex.

dogger's rust *n.* The corrosion found on vehicles belonging to suburban *park and ride* enthusiasts, caused by a build-up of salty deposits around the key holes, door handles and window surrounds.

doggie chalks *n.* White canine excrements. *Poodle shit.* See also *dog chalk, barker's egg.*

doggies *n.* Intercourse performed in the position favoured by *hounds,* usually near some dustbins.

dogging *n.* The saucy behaviour of those who *dog.*

dogging bag *n.* Prophylactic sheath put over one's *pork sword* to prevent *seasoning your hamburger* with another *gentleman's relish* while enjoying shared recreational activities with anonymous strangers in a local park, wood or layby. *'Right, I'm just going to take Fido for a quick walk round the Thicket Roundabout.' 'Don't forget your dogging bags, dad. Or Fido.'*

dogging in Dubai *sim.* The rhetorical *ne plus ultra* of unlikelihoods. *'I tell you, mate. You've about as much chance of getting in her knickers as you have of going dogging in Dubai.'*

doggy style *adj. Doing it* from the back. Or up against a visitor's trouser leg.

dog handler *n.* Offensively sexist term for a man who is prepared to *cop off* with with a right *fugly* old *ditch pig.*

dog in a bath *n.* An ethically dubious bedroom game similar to *rodeo sex. 'The missus was setting the video last night and I was on me vinegar strokes when I called her by her sister's name. It was like* *trying to keep a dog in a bath.'*

dog in the fog, like a *sim.* Descriptive of one who vanishes unexpectedly at some point during an all-day drinking session. *'Where's Dr Welby gone? He just disappeared like a dog in the fog.'*

dog left in the kennel *euph.* An unimpressive single *Thora* discovered in the *pan* after what felt like a serious session on the *bum sink.*

dogler effect *n.* The scientific phenomenon of a *long range fox* who looks attractive from a distance who, as she get nearer is revealed to be a bit of a *hound* but then, as she walks away again, gradually gets more attractive again. Also known as *dogler shift.*

dog lime *n.* Dog eggs, canine feculent.

dog-locked *adj.* Stuck in a compromising position due to an unlikely muscular spasm, usually in the back of a car in a *Confessions* film. Also known as a *dog's lock-in.*

dogmanay *n. Scots.* Traditional Glaswegian festival of *al fresco nookie*, celebrated up and down Sauchiehall Street shortly after closing time.

dognose *v.* To disturb one's slumbering wife following a *slash* in the small hours by touching her on the leg or buttocks with a cold, wet *bell end.*

dog owner's slipper, tits like a *sim.* Said affectionately of an old *slapper*'s well-chewed *fun bags.*

dog's arse *adj.* To be troubled with flatulence. *'Excuse the wife. I'm afraid she's got a dog's arse today, your serene highness.'*

dog's back *n.* See *Bilbo Baggins' foot.*

dog's bollocks *n.* The *ne plus ultra* of something; the very best. Bee's knees, *donkey's knob, monkey's nuts, cat's knackers etc. 'This garage pasty you done in the microwave is the dog's bollocks, Elon.'*

dog's cock *n.* The number sixty. From darts slang, where a treble-twenty is called a "lipstick", it says here. *'Excuse me, miss. How much would you charge me for a blow job behind that skip?' 'Thirty quid, or you can have unprotected anal for a dog's cock, Lord Archer of Weston super Mare.'*

dog scratching at the back door, I've got a *exclam.* Announcement to the room that you are off for an *Eartha Kitt.* Also *(the) Blue Peter tortoise has come out of hibernation, there's a pig at the gate etc.*

dog section *1. n.* Division of the constabulary that uses highly trained alsatians to apprehend people who run around with quilts tied to their right arm, firing starter pistols into the air. *2. n.* Sexist and offensive police station slang for the corner of the canteen where the WPCs who least resemble strippagrams (and therefore are least likely to turn up at a rowdy stag do and be mistakenly

invited to disrobe) congregate to eat.

dog shagging a football, rumped up like a *sim.* Said of someone with notably poor posture. *'Okay, cut. That was great, Sister Wendy, really good. Absolutely perfect. But can we just try it once more, please, and this time could you try not to be all rumped up like a dog shagging a football?'*

dogshit in a field, like *sim.* Descriptive of something which is very common. *'Yes, well the good news is it's a traditional Chinese blue and white bowl decorated with Daoist emblems. It was made during the reign of the first Qing emperor Shunzhi, so it dates from the mid-fifteenth century, and it's in exceptionally good condition. The bad news is, unfortunately, that these things are like dogshit in a field. You literally can't give the fuckers away. For insurance purposes I'd value it at about a fiver tops.'*

dog shit on toast *euph. milit.* A bad situation. Also *dog shit on toast with ginger hairs on top* – A bad situation that is deteriorating.

dog's legs *n. medic.* Temporary weakness in the male thighs following a spot of *back-scuttling* with a *dirty lady.*

dog's lipstick *n.* A shimmery pink, retractable cosmetic. *'What's that you've got on your mouth, Debbie?' 'It's some dog's lipstick, Paul.'*

dog slobber *n. Electric spaghetti.*

dog slug *n.* The act of licking around, and indeed inside another person's *rusty sherrif's badge.* A *trip round the world*, a *rim job.*

dog's marriage *n.* A twenty-minute *al fresco back scuttle* that only ends when the neighbours throw a bucket of water over you.

dog's match *n.* A sexual encounter in a public place, *eg.* In a bush, golf course bunker, doorway, taxi queue or hospital casualty cubicle.

dog toffee *n.* Tacky pavement deposit that readily adheres to the sole of a shoe or supports an upright lollipop stick.

dog toffee liqueur *n.* A length of *hound rope* that looks firm and solid until trodden on, when it reveals its rich, liquid filling.

dog toss *n.* Grinding against a woman's leg in an over-eager fashion while dancing at a nightclub, school disco, or wedding reception. *'Any more of those dog tosses, and I'm throwing you out, Mr Gove.'*

dog track *n.* The song (usually *Lady in Red*) played at ten to two in a nightclub, that precipitates a last-attempt mad dash onto the dancefloor by all remaining *hounds* on the premises. A *desperate dance.*

dog with a bike, like a *sim.* When you are admiring a *classy piece* from afar and "You could bark at it, but you couldn't ride it".

dog with a plate of gravy, like a *sim.* Descriptive of one who is a seriously hardcore *Jacky Danny Cousteau*. A *bourbon*.

dog with two dicks, like a *sim.* Descriptive of a *tomcat with three balls*. Said of or by one who is incredibly pleased with himself. *'That's one small step for man, one giant leap for mankind. I'm on the fucking Moon and I'm as happy as a dog with two dicks, me.'* (Neil Armstrong, July 1969).

Doherty's kitten *euph.* Not to be confused with Delaney's donkey, a person of either gender who regularly partakes in a spot of *cumulonimbus*. *'I tell you what, our vicar's licked more crack than Doherty's kitten.'*

doing your own research *1. n.* Autodidactically relying on social media posts and videos for one's information on politics, medical science, the shape of the Earth, how to spell "autodidactically" *etc. 2. n.* Staying indoors watching hours and hours of internet *grummer*.

Dolby yawn *n.* Yawning until your hearing pops into a crystal-clear audio quality you never realised you'd lost.

dole-ite hours *n.* The period that elapses between the end of *Bargain Hunt* and nightfall, during which the great unwashed masses venture out to sign on and pick up their Rizlas, crisps and Special Brew.

dole model *n.* An inspirationally indolent figurehead or exemplar. *'Prince Edward's been my dole model ever since he did an afternoon's work thirty-five years ago.'*

dole pole *n.* A walking stick used as a prop by an enterprising able-bodied person while attempting to claim extra social security benefits. See also *social sticks*. *'Eeh. Look at the time. I'll have to run or I'll be late for my appointment at the DSS.' 'Don't forget your dole pole, son.'*

doleslaw *n.* Unloved piles of shredded lettuce, cabbage, onion, cucumber and tomato, as found adorning polystyrene kebab boxes on bus stop benches throughout the country.

dolesmith *n.* One who makes a living by practising the traditional British craft of collecting state benefits.

doles Royce *n.* Name given to a mobility vehicle of a *big-boned* incumbent arriving at the Post Office to cash their Giro.

doley grail *n.* A pot noodle in its elegant vessel.

doley's blackout *n.* A mid-afternoon session of *self-abuse* snatched during a lull in daytime television. Achieved by shutting the curtains after

Quincy for a quick *tug*.

Dolita *n.* A young *piece* who will never have to work a day in her life.

dollar up a sweep's arse, as clean as a *sim.* Something that is very clean indeed. *'The Armstrong-Rockwell P1600 Superatmospheric Autoclave uses high pressure steam super-heated to 121°C to sterilize surgical instruments, leaving scalpels, retractors and forceps as clean as a dollar up a sweep's arse.'*

dolly dagger *n.* A *bob, dildo, AA member.*

dolly filler *n.* Sticky white putty that is useful for filling *cracks*.

dolly grip *1. n.* A person employed on a film set to hold toys still. *2. n.* A firm and unyielding grasp of the hind-quarters; a hold of the sort that a dodgy sheep farmer might employ.

dollymop *n.* An amateur or inexperienced prostitute or slattern.

Dolly Parton's tits *euph.* The holy grail of things you will never get to see.

dolmio day *n.* The first seventh of *rag week.*

dolphin pods *n.* Immaculately presented and glossily hairless scrotal sacs, as sported by the likes of Richard O'Brien, Duncan Goodhew and R Kelly. It says here.

dolphin skin *n. medic.* The epidermis of the *herman gelmet.*

do-me do-you *n.* A double-headed rubber or plastic device that can be shared by any pair of consenting adults who have a refreshingly open-minded attitude to *the other.*

dominos effect *n.* Being a fat *bastard* due to eating too many cheesy takeaways.

Donald *1. n. rhym. slang.* Fuck. From Donald Duck. *2. adj. rhym. slang.* Irretrievably broken or ruined, a term derived from the name of the erstwhile speech-impaired, bad-tempered Disney cartoon fowl. From Donald Ducked = fucked. *'What's up, Cliff?' 'I snapped me banjo string and now me cock's Donald, Hank.'*

Donald *n.* A *trump* that could blow the hair on the back of your *noggin* up and forward over your forehead.

Donald Campbell *n. prop.* At the end of a long and unproductive visit to the toilet, the eventual arrival of some sort of relief. From the famous last words of the speed ace as his motorboat Bluebird K7 flipped over at approximately 300mph during a world record attempt on Coniston Water in 1967, and he *shat* himself, *viz.* "I'm going, I'm going, I've gone!"

Donald, do a *v.* To expel methane gas from your

rectal cavity. To *fart, drop your guts, trump.*

Donald ducking *n.* The practice of wearing a shirt and no trousers, in the style of the popular cartoon fowl. *'It'd be a lovely view out the front of the caravan, if it wasn't for that big fat man in the three-berth Elddis who insists on Donald Ducking when he takes his turd hopper down the chemical toilet sluice every morning.'*

Donald junior *1. n.* A small and ineffectual – but nevertheless angry-seeming – *bellend.* *2. n.* A small, unflushable *shite.*

Donald, take a *v. rhym. slang.* To take a *shit.* From Donald J Trump = dump.

Donald Trump's Twitter, a shitter like *sim. rhet.* Descriptive of an *arse* that is liable to make attention-grabbing and highly obnoxious pronouncements at any time of day or night. *'Pardon me, ambassador. I was out at the Rupali Restaurant, Bigg Market, Newcastle upon Tyne last night and I've got a shitter like Donald Trump's Twitter today.'*

donating a kidney *n.* High pressure expulsion of *wazz* following a prolonged period of restricted access to lavatory facilities. *'How far is it to Scotch Corner Services, cardinal? I'm anxious to donate a kidney.'*

Doncaster delicatessen *n.* A kebab shop.

Doncaster market, I bet she buys her knickers on *exclam. Yorks.* Said of a woman with a *lovely personality* who has successfully managed to circumvent salad for many years.

done 'is dinner *exclam.* A Scottish expression for when someone has been a bit sick. *'Ach no, Wullie! Gran'paw's bin watchin' Twa Lassies One Cup on yon internet, an' he's been an' done 'is dinner again!'*

dong *n.* The sound of Big Ben in the *News at Ten* opening titles.

dong covid *n. medic.* A lengthy illness leading to desuetude of the *willy,* or erectile dysfunction conveniently blamed on post-viral fatigue. Also *schlong covid, organ failure, lack of composure in front of goal. 'Sorry love, this has never happened to me before. It must be dong covid, I did give it a bit of a pasting during self-isolation, come to think of it.'*

donger *n.* Whanger, pork sword, dill.

dongloids *n.* Telltale globlets of *jizz* found on the marital duvet following a *game of singles.*

donk bin *n.* The metal waste receptacle typically found in the viewing area cubicles of peep-show booths for the convenience of sneezing patrons. Named after the noise that heavily laden tissues make when hitting the sides.

donkey *1. n.* A clod-hopping footballer, such as Titus Bramble off of Wigan Athletic or St.

Johnstone's Michael Duberry. *2. n.* A male prostitute, derived from the onomatopoetic fact that he is a "he-whore".

donkey kisser *n.* An inexperienced osculatrix. A lady who *snogs* like a burro chewing an apple.

donkey punch *n.* Of *bum games,* to knock your partner out cold with a blow to the back of the head while in the *vinegar strokes.* Has the same aphrodisiacal effect as slamming a goose's neck in a drawer while committing bestiality. Results in inceased orgasmic intensity and a custodial sentence.

donkey rigged *adj.* Of a man, blessed with a sizeable *stick of rock.*

donkey's earhole *n.* A particularly large, flappy, twitching vagina. A *hippo's mouth,* a *clown's pocket.*

donkey style, do it *v.* To copulate up the *wrong 'un, ie. In the ass.*

donkified *adj.* Having a *horse's handbrake,* in a state of *tumescence. On the bonk.*

Don King in a headlock *sim.* Descriptive of a foreign lady's armpits.

donner *n.* An unattractive romantic prospect, a *ten pinter, ie.* Someone one wouldn't fancy too much when sober.

donner meat *n.* Sundry lumps and slices of greasy flesh hanging from the *clunge* of a dumpy *piece.*

donny burns *n.* The tan achieved when standing in the away end at Doncaster Rovers on a hot day, when only half of your body is exposed to the blistering rays of the scorching South Yorkshire sun.

donor *n.* One who believes it is better to give than to receive, flatulence-wise. See *benefactor.*

don't believe me just watch! *exclam.* Room-rousing cry delivered immediately before a massive *guff* which sounds remarkably similar to the horn break in *Uptown Funk.*

don't fly a helicopter over that *1. exclam.* Warning given following the Chernobyl nuclear reactor accident, for example. *2. exclam.* Advice proffered to one entering a recently vacated lavatory where a catastrophic meltdown has occurred.

don't forget to hit that Like button *exclam.* A polite request from a female encouraging a paramour to concentrate attention on her *giggle switch.*

don't forget to leave a review on iTunes *exclam.* Another fun thing to say after someone has just *stepped on a duck.* See also *I would like to say thank you on behalf of the group and ourselves and I hope we've passed the audition; that's a penalty! etc.*

don't look at it Marion! *exclam.* To be cried, Indiana Jones-style, shortly before spraying one's *milm* into the face of a loved one. Usually results in something resembling the melted *mush* of a WWII Nazi officer.

don't look, Marion! Keep your eyes shut! *exclam.* Based on Indiana Jones's shout to his *piece* when the Nazis open the Ark of the Covenant; a humorous phrase when someone suffers a face-melting bout of flatulence.

don't speak ill of the dead *exclam.* Admonition delivered with the head bowed solemnly when someone dares to criticise a person who has recently *passed wind*.

don't tear it, I'll take the whole piece *exclam.* Ancient, humorous, rag trade-based phrase used in response to an extremely dry, raspy *trouser cough. See also anybody injured?; well struck Sir!*

don't tell him Pike *1. exclam.* The country's favourite comedy line, shouted out just before Delboy fell through the bar. *2. exclam.* An order delivered in the clipped tones of Captain Mainwaring following a loud *dropped gut.* See also *we're doomed.*

doodlebugs *n.* Heavy *Gert Stonkers* which, when released from their restraining *tit pants,* dive earthwards suddenly and silently without any warning, leaving smoking craters where they strike the ground. *Metatarsal breakers.*

doofa *n.* A *ten-to-two-er.* From the phrase "She'll do for me".

dooking for fritters, looks like he's been *sim.* Amusing Caledonian expression used to describe a youth with a *plooky* face, who looks like he might have been *bobbing for chips in a deep fat fryer.*

doom bar *1. n.* Popular Rock Brewery ale named after the sand bank in the mouth of the Camel Estuary. *2. n.* A pub or social club that is so filled with miseries and *gloomers* that one feels suicidal after just a couple of jars. See also *chapel of rest.*

doom box *n.* Any wireless when tuned in to *The Today Programme* or *PM.*

doomsday book *n. Toilet literature* perused between sobs while suffering an apocalyptic rectal breakdown. Usually the *Autotrader* or an anthology of Jeremy Clarkson articles.

Doonicans *n.* Assorted *claps,* NSUs and *doses.* From the initials of late bejumpered Irish rocking chair croonster Val.

doorbell *n.* A small button above the *snail's doorstep* that is so difficult to find that it is often easier to use the *knockers.* The *clematis.* Also *devil's doorbell.*

door handle biter *n.* A large and painful stool.

doorknob *n.* Humorous epithet for a nightclub bouncer which one would do well to keep to oneself, all things considered.

doorman *n.* A daunting *feeshus* that is as broad as it is long, very dense, and hard, and which can leave a chap lying on the floor, clutching his stomach and crying uncontrollably.

doorman, have a word with the *v.* To butter up the *bald headed bouncer* in order to be allowed into the premises he is guarding. To *cumulously nimbate* the *clematis.*

doormat basher *1. n.* One who whacks their partner's *fanny* on the back yard wall to get the dust off it, whatever that means. *2. n.* A *lesbo.*

door-opener *1. n.* In *wanky* sales talk, something that gets you access to the company bigwigs who actually make purchasing decisions. *2. n.* A *Lionel* that necessitates an immediate supply of fresh air.

doorstep darts *n.* The vain and laborious process of repeatedly trying to find the keyhole at the conclusion of a serious night *on the sauce.*

doors to manual *1. exclam.* Aircraft crew instruction given so that the escape slide will not deploy when the door is opened. *2. euph.* The empleasurement option available to a lady who finds herself unexpectedly single once more.

doos *n.* Tits.

doosra *1. n. Urdu.* In cricket, a particular type of offspin delivery that "turns the other way", and hence *2. n.* A fellow who is *fond of shopping, doesn't skip like a boxer,* and bowls from the *pavilion end.*

doppelbanger *n.* A *porkswordsman* who has, somewhat disconcertingly, elected to *do the dirties* on a regular basis with a female who looks exactly like himself.

doppelganger dick *n.* A *hard-on* of such intensity, that one's own face is seen reflected in the shiny head, affording it the appearance of a miniature double. A *mini me.*

doppelginger *n.* The red-headed offspring of an otherwise normally *barnetted* couple. Yes, him for example.

doppelwänger *n.* A penis that is indistinguishable from your own, fortuitously spotted while watching an *artistic* film.

dopper *n.* A *dork.*

Doppler shit *n.* A *twintone bum siren* that gradually changes in pitch and clarity, before suddenly – and alarmingly – dropping an octave.

doppling *n.* The act of a member of a superannuated rock group who *spoffs up* onto an unsuspecting member of the public from an upper-storey window, multi-storey car park or hotel balcony. Also *seagulling. 'What shall we do after the concert, Rick?' 'I fancy a couple of pints and then a spot of* *doppling, Francis.'*

Doris *adj. rhym. slang. On the other bus.* From the name of the famous Hollywood musical actress who, in the 1950s and 60s, starred in a series of light romantic comedies with *Doris* actor Rock Hudson; Doris Domosexual.

doritoes *n.* Exceptionally cheesy feet.

dork *n.* A *dopper.*

dork scratchings *n.* The crispy, flaky fragments which collect in the underthings of those who habitually *work from home. 'I'd like your cheapest service wash on these Dorito-stained shirts and jogging bottoms please, and can you hoover the worst of the dork scratchings out of me Y-fronts?'*

Dorothy gherkins *n.* Horrendous, cheap green leggings that show off the wearer's cellulite lumps and bumps in all their horrific glory.

Dorothy Perkins *n.* DP or double penetration. Of a lady, to simultaneously have *gentlemen callers* at her front and back doors. Also a *man at C&A,* a *double decker. 'In the cinema, one so-called film featured a man using disgusting sexual language. Another showed a lady baring her bosoms in the most provocative manner. A third film showed two well-hung men giving a woman a right Dorothy Perkins while she repeatedly took the Lord's name in vain. I was so disgusted that I vomited into my handbag. I think Mr Muggeridge next to me felt ill too, as he was groaning and rummaging frantically in his trouser pockets for a handkerchief.'* (Mary Whitehouse's report on a fact-finding trip to Amsterdam's Red Light District, 1968).

dorsal fin *n.* The sharp ridge or crest, consisting of raw cornflakes, which painfully slices lengthways down the *clackervalve* during a *sit down visit* to the water closet to *park one's breakfast.*

dossier *n. Fr.* A Parisian vagrant. *'Zut alors. Un dossier a fait un grand merde sur la chaise d'autobus. Donc je dois m'asseoir sur le siège à côté.'*

Dot Cotton *1. n. prop.* Seemingly immortal chain-smoking *EastEnders* embodiment of Munch's *The Scream.* Played by actress June Brown, who died in 2022. *2. v.* The urinary equivalent of *touching cloth.*

Dot Cotton's washing machine, had more loads than *phr.* Said rhetorically of a woman of easy affections who has been *rogered more times than a police radio.* Also *cocked more times than Davey Crockett's rifle, had more sausage than a fat German butcher, been fucked more times than an Amstrad word processor* etc.

do the clam *1. n.* Title of a song performed by Elvis Presley in his 1965 feature film *Girl Happy,* and later covered by The Cramps. *2. n.* To *finger/lick out/poke* a *minge.*

do the decent thing *v.* Of a lady who is *up on blocks,* to dutifully empty her husband's *bins* by means of an act of *horatio.*

do the dirty *v.* To engage in the filthy act of *you know what.*

do the motorcycle *v.* When in urgent need of the facilities, to be faced with what passes for a *shitpot* in Italy, comprising of two foot places and a hole in the floor, thus being forced to assume the posture of a motorcyclist when doing one's business, while being careful not to *drop a toffee* into one's pantaloons.

do the rubbish *v.* To *take it up the wrong 'un.* Named, aparently, after a girl working in a certain Glaswegian Italian restaurant, who not only took out the refuse but happily *took it* up the *council gritter* too. *'That bird last night was a right dirty cow, mam. She did the rubbish.'*

dottle knocker *n.* A level of penile rigidity so impressive that a gentleman could use it to dislodge the tobacco remnants from his bent apple.

double adapter *1. euph. AC/DC* man equipped with a *one pin plug* at the front but also having the benefit of a fully functioning *single pin socket* at the back. A *switch hitter. 2. n. Lucky Pierre.*

double Barker *n.* A woman blessed with the body of Sue in her prime, but cursed with the face of Ronnie in his. A *bobfoc.*

double bassing *v.* To have sex from behind, fiddling with the lady's left nipple with your left hand and twanging away at her *clematis* with your right – a position similar to the one adopted when playing the upright bull fiddle, although the sound is completely different. To perform *charlimingus.*

double bluff *n.* Cunning jape played on the public by supermarket shelf stackers whereby they place the fresh bread at the front.

double booked *adj.* Of a lady, to be romantically entertaining two gentlemen at the same time. A *man at C & A.*

double bouncers *n.* Value for money *tits* that resonate at twice the frequency of their owner's gait. *ie.* Two bounces per step taken.

double chalker *n.* Someone so morbidly *big-boned* that if they were found murdered, it would take two pieces of chalk to draw a line around them. *'Today's birthdays: Roy Orbison, US singer-songwriter, 1936; Ed Stewart, Junior Choice DJ, 1941; Michael Moore, US polemicist double-chalker, 1954.'*

double chinsters *n.* Those with an evident penchant

for pies and pastries.

double cream *n.* Someone who is "tasty but rather thick". *'The awards ceremony was enlivened by a dash of double cream in the form of our glamorous compere, known to all off her appearances in TOWIE.'*

double cuffs *n.* The excessively large *chinstraps* on a *bear trapper's hat.*

double deluxe *n.* The right royal act of simultaneously *shouting soup* and *shitting* oneself. See also *Catherine wheel.*

double dipper *1. n.* One who, unable to decide between *rice and chips,* has half a portion of each. A *switch hitter, happy shopper.* A bisexual. *2. n.* One who does a bit of *double dipping* (see below).

double dipping *1. n.* The social *faux pas* of returning a previously bitten tortilla chip, for instance, into a communal bowl for a second portion of sauce, as seen in the *Seinfeld* episode *The Implant. 2. n.* The social *faux pas* of tramping your *naughty boot* through all the *muck* in your ladyfriend's *back yard* before waltzing in through her *front door* and leaving *shit* on the *snail's doorstep.*

double doors *n.* Beef curtains, cat flaps, hangar doors.

double dragback *1. n.* The Marseille turn. An impressive football trick as perfected by the likes of headbutt-happy Frenchman Zinédene Zidane. *2. n.* A painful *wanking* accident whereby an inexperienced masturbatrix loses rhythm, resulting in one downward stroke being immediately followed by another, thus causing severe *one string banjo* trauma. An ineptly syncopated *Barclays.*

double dunk *n.* A full and comprehensive act of *teabagging,* incorporating the full *meat and two veg.*

double Dutch *1. n.* Unintelligible or garbled speech or language uttered by, for example, Stanley Unwin, Alf Ippititimus or Donald Trump. *2. n.* Toe-tapping song about skipping recorded by punk boutique manager Malcolm Mclaren. *3. n.* Bedtime flatulence enjoyed by two people sharing a bed.

double duty dump *n.* A *shite* so explosive and effervescent that afterwards one doesn't just have to wipe one's *rusty bullet hole* but also the *pan* as well.

double entry book keeping *n.* The compilation, by an overly optimistic fellow, of a mental catalogue of potentially accommodating partners.

double fare *n.* One whose big *arse* takes up two seats on a train or bus. A *salad dodger, barge-arse, fat fuck.*

double feature *euph.* A second, supplementary *Tom tit which* appears after a young man has spent too long *on the pot* in the *smallest room* watching videos, browsing social media, and playing games on his mobile telephone.

double flapper *n.* Badge of honour worn by a festival goer after he deposits a *load of shopping* in the *bogs* that is so large as to cause the Portaloo flap to oscillate twice.

double flusher *n.* A recalcitrant *re-offender* that refuses to leave until one has pulled the chain at least twice.

double glazing *n.* Something that the late Ted Moult would almost certainly not have approved of or, indeed, endorsed in a long-running television advertising campaign. Two blokes *blowing their beans* over one *bird* at the same time.

double hatting *1. n.* Typically *bollocks* business term, that means "doing two jobs at once due to general workplace disorganisation." *2. n.* Wearing one *French letter* over another upon one's *John Thomas,* out of an excess of caution. *'You sure about this, your holiness?' 'Don't worry, love. I'm double hatting.'*

double header *n.* Of a *grumble flick* thespienne, the intriguing act of performing simultaneous *horatio* on two *lip stretchers.*

double-jabbed *adj.* Of a lady who has been *poked* both at the front and *up the council* in the last 28 days. *'Yeah, me nan's been double-jabbed.'*

double jeopardy *n.* Unexpected secondary *stoolage.* A *second sitting, epilog.*

double jobbing *1. n.* Holding down two careers simultaneously, for example whilst working from home or being the Prime Minister. *2. n.* A *second sitting, epilog* or *double rollover.*

double or shits *n.* Game of chance whereby a jalfrezi will either sort you out or cause all manner of horrors.

double rollover *n.* That exhilarating feeling of complete emptiness, when you know you've already done tomorrow's *foulage* today.

double scoop *1. n.* Two generous helpings of ice cream in the same cone. *2. n.* A generous helping of *snatch* followed by a generous helping of *wrong 'un.*

double slit experiment *1. n.* Famous demonstration of wave/particle duality that was first performed by Thomas Young in 1801. *2. n.* An attempt to persuade two ladyfriends into joining a *three-in-a bed romp* that demonstrates the fundamentally probabilistic nature of quantum mechanical phenomena.

double stacking *1. phr.* In Formula 1, when two cars from the same team come in for a pit-stop on the same lap. *2. n.* Typically 24 hours after missing your daily *thunderbox* appointment, a routine unloading of an *Amber Heard* is shortly followed by an urgent "Box box box!" from the *Simon Cowells*.

double the melt *v.* To give a lady not one, but two portions of hot stringy cheese in her *hambuger*. To squirt a second portion of filling into a *vertical bacon sandwich* with one's *cheddar apple*.

double trap champion *n.* A colleague who has the ability to render both of the works *bogs* cubicles uninhabitable with a single *copper bolt*.

double velvet *n.* A particularly keen *ginger beer, ie.* Someone who "loves your bum".

double-wristing *1. n.* Fashionable trend of wearing two watches on one arm, or a watch on each arm. We've not seen it, but it sounds distinctly *twattish*. *2. n.* Swapping hands to share the load during an extended period of *gentleman's relaxation*.

double-yolked eggs, balls like *sim.* Of testicles, wrecked by over-exertion. *'Careful there, Precious. If you try to lift that fucker, you'll end up with balls like double-yolked eggs.'* (John Noakes, *Blue Peter*).

double yolker *n.* A pornographic actor blessed with the elusive ability to *fire off* two consecutive *pop shots* without pausing for a sit down and a cup of tea in between. It is not known whether this happens in civilian life. See also *twice off the same hard*.

doubtfit *n.* Set of clothes that a lady somewhat over-optimistically purchases to "slim into". *'I'm just off out to drop these doubtfits off at the Oxfam shop, love. Do you want anything from Greggs while I'm in town?'*

douche flute *n.* A high-tech e-cigarette that is so large and complicated it looks like its vaper is fellating a robot.

Dougal *1. n.* The agitated, easily animated, Tony Hancock-soundalike cylindrical dog from The *Magic Roundabout. 2. n.* A hairy *fanny* that has really gone to seed.

doughnut puncher *n.* A *dinner masher*.

doughy hood *1. n.* Character in *The Archers* played by Arnold Ridley, better known as Private Godfrey from *Dad's Army. 2. n.* A *women's thing* that can probably be fixed with a tub of natural yoghurt.

dove's chest *n.* A plump *front lump* or *beetle bonnet*. Also *monkey's chin, monkey's forehead, grassy knoll, collie's chest* or *proud Mary*.

dowel *1. n.* In carpentry, a piece of wood that can be tapped gently into a hole. *2. n.* In sex, a piece of *wood* that can be tapped gently into an *a-hole*.

Dow Jones *n. prop.* A fellow who is expert in the art of *footsie*.

downhill skier *n.* A person who *pulls off* two blokes

at once, one on either side, on a Sunday tea-time. A *crane operator.* See also *skiing position*, but you'll not learn anything else.

download festival *1. n.* Annual musical jamboree held at Donington Park that normally involves a large crowd and a lot of mud. *2. n.* Weekly lavatorial jamboree held in the works *shitters* at about 9.30 on a Monday morning, that normally involves a large crowd and a lot of mud.

download from plopbox *v.* To install a *wireless cable. 'Can you sort your XL Bullie out? It's got me by the throat again.' 'Give me fifteen minutes, love. I just need to download a large file from plopbox.'*

download the brownload *v.* To *excretiate. 'Where've you put the Exchange and Mart, nan? I'm off to download the brownload.'*

downstairs filter *1. n.* Something essential that must be wired into your satellite system in order for shopping channels, Achtüng Sexy and Bloomberg to reappear on your television screen. *2. n.* A pair of ragged underpants. *'They're barely a downstairs filter, them.'*

downstairs nose *n.* The male penis. *'Where's Heston?' 'He's just blowing his downstairs nose into Piers Morgan's soup.'*

down the dustpipe *1. n.* Title of a 1970 Status Quo single that reached number twelve in the hit parade; the first record to feature the band's soon-to-be-trademark boogie shuffle. *2. euph. Up the arse.*

downtime *1. n.* The period which elapses between ejaculation and rearousal. In most men, *downtime* is around 20 minutes, though in the case of Cliff Richard it is now about 6 decades and counting. *2. n.* That moment just after a chap's *significant other* has popped out to the shops, and it's "down with the pants" to interfere with himself. *'How will you spend your time, Mr Johnson, now that you've been booted out of number ten for a catalogue of failings?' 'With plenty of downtime. Much the same as when I was in number ten.'*

down to one's last bead *adj.* Having an empty *sack, balls like bats' wings*. Bereft of *men's spendings, wankrupt.*

dowsing rod *n.* A *twig* that involuntarily twitches when approaching an area of great wetness.

doxy *n. arch.* Whore, *good time girl.*

do ya want some? *exclam. interrog. rhet.* Threatening phrase used by one who is about to *flatulate.*

doylem *n.* A foolish fellow, bufflehead or *bellend. 'You are an utter fucking doylem, Kwasi. I'm going to appoint you to the post of Chancellor of the Exchequer.'*

D'Oyly *n. rhym. slang.* From D'Oyly Carte = heart

to heart.

do you need a gravy jug for that? *exclam. interrog.* Enquiry made of someone who has just dropped a very wet and bubbly *bottom burp.*

do your thing, clickety-click *euph.* To have a *wank* over internet pornography. See also *buying your better half an anniversary present.*

do you want fries with that? *exclam.* Said after someone drops a *beefy eggo* that could be served up in a bun with a bit of limp lettuce and a slice of gherkin. Also *Alexa, open a window.*

do you want that breaded or battered? *exclam.* Humorous quip to break the awkward silence after *her indoors queefs* mid-way through a romantic *fish supper.*

DP *acronym.* Double Penetration. Especially *one up the arse, one up the fanny.* Often leads to a professional footballer-based *Newton's cradle.*

Dracula's allotment *n.* An overgrown *radar trap* with *the painters in.*

Dracula's candle *n.* The half-melted tallow sconce that inevitably makes an appearance at some point in a Hammer film, which bears a striking resemblance to the star performer at the end of a *bukkake* scene in a *grumble flick.* A *plasterer's radio, quattro formaggio, art room sink, white witch, cock mess monster.*

Dracula's coffin, open *v.* To produce a sinister, high-pitched and prolonged *Bakewell* that sounds like the creaking lid of Christopher Lee's casket being lifted in a horror movie. Or, indeed, in real life these days, as he's *carked it.*

Dracula's door *n.* A protracted *Tony Hart* which rises and falls in pitch, resembling nothing so much as the sound of ancient Transylvanian castle hinges.

Dracula's tea bags *n.* Used *dangermice.*

drag and drop *1. phr.* In computing, the ingenious method whereby, thanks to the use of a graphical user interface, PC users can move icons between folders or create shortcuts on their desktop. *2. phr.* The first cigarette of the day which, when combined with coffee, can lead to a cataclysmic opening of the *Camillas. Embassy number two.*

dragging a wardrobe up a concrete ramp, like *sim.* A phrase descriptive of a particularly cavernous and rasping act of flatulation.

dragging like a seal's ringpiece *sim.* Descriptive of something that seems to last forever, *eg.* Being chained to a radiator next to Brian Keenan in Beirut, waiting for a Pink Floyd song to reach a bit of tune you recognise, watching a *Mrs Brown's Boys* Christmas Special.

dragon food *n.* Placatory chocolates bought for the *bag for life* when one is in the *cunt book.* 'Shit, I've been out on the piss for three days. I'd better stop by the garage and pick up some dragon food before I get home.'

dragon's claw *n.* A Welsh *camel's hoof.* 'Look you, Mrs Llwwyydd, that's some dragon's claw you got there in your jeggings, isn't it?'

dragon's nostril *n.* The state of the *ringpiece* after a piquant *Ruby Murray* or a vigorous *St George.* A *Japanese flag.*

dragon's snout *n.* A particularly grotesque *turtle's head* which is accompanied by blasts of fiery breath, and may cause damsels to become distressed.

dragon wagon *n.* The sorry-looking rusty white van typically parked at the side of major commuting routes, or along the road back from the pub, which sells *shit* bunches of flowers to appease fire-breathing missuses. 'Sorry I missed the kids' nativity play, love, only something came up at work. But look, I brought you these from the dragon wagon.'

drag strip *1. n.* A damp track on the toilet seat left by *well hung* lady who has went and got up without having a wipe first. *2. n.* An unusually long, smoking *skidmark.*

drain your spuds *v.* To urinate. To have a *gypsy's kiss, turn your bike around, slash, wazz, whizz.*

dramafications *n.* Massive over-reaction to a relatively minor incident. 'Kindly ignore my wife's dramafications, your holiness. She's on her rags this week.'

drambo *n. Scots.* Someone who will fight anyone in the room after a few shandies. Also *two can Van Damme, half pint Harry, tinny mallet.*

drat strap *n.* A G-string worn underneath the sheer outer garmentry of a young, nubile bit of *crackling.* Named after the cry of frustration and disappointment it elicits from an intending pervert.

draughtsman *n.* A fellow whose only apparent skill is the ability to regularly *tread on ducks.* A *backsmith.*

draughty front door *euph.* A way to refer to a *front bottom burp* or *queef* when in polite company. 'I do beg your pardon, your holiness. I've got a bit of a draughty front door today.' 'Think nothing of it, Sister Assunta. Mother Teresa come for a look round the Sistine Chapel yesterday and her fish mitten was barking like a fucking border terrier at a rabbit show.'

draw a cock over it *v.* To do a shoddy job or *cunt* something *off.* 'England certainly didn't turn in a particularly impressive performance against Germany this afternoon, eh Alan?' 'No Gary. They *pretty much drew a cock over the entire game.'*

draw a map of the Bakerloo Line *v.* To leave a long, thin tube-shaped *motion* across the lavatory bowl. Substitute Northern Line if a Guinness drinker or Central Line if suffering from chronic *Adrians.*

draw an ace *v.* When wiping one's *chocolate starfish* thoroughly, to eventually have an unsoiled piece of paper which indicates that the process has been more or less successfully completed.

drawing a curve on an Etch-A-Sketch *euph. Tuning into Radio Luxembourg.* To manipulate both of a ladyfriend's *jockey's whips* at the same time. Also *come in Tokyo, safecracking.*

drawing board *n.* A good-sized *rack* upon which a fellow can express himself artistically.

drawing with a brown crayon *n.* An extended and frustrating session of post-*sit down toilet adventure nipsy*-husbandry, whereby one inscribes a sepia line across fifty sheets of *bumwad* before finally achieving an acceptably clean sheet. Or giving up. See also *arse like a marmite pot. 'Sorry I was in there so long, your worship. I was drawing with a brown crayon.'*

draw mud from the well *v.* To *follow through. 'I've just drawn mud from the well, so it's back to Evan in the studio.' 'Thank-you Kirsty.'*

drawn-on durex *n.* A biro line sketched around the base of the penile shaft by a scurrilous fellow with the intention of fooling a drunken lady into thinking he has taken sensible precautions.

drayhorse's bottom lip *sim.* A big, floppy, whiskery *snatch.* Full of carrots.

dreadlocks, Scouse *euph.* Any haircut longer than a grade 0 all over. See *Geordie curls, Geordie affro, Wallsend trim.*

dread logs *n. Winnets* you could use to batter down a door.

dreadnought *n.* Even bigger than a *dead otter.* A veritable *battleshit, U-boat, woodwork chewer.*

dreamboat body, shipwreck face *n.* A jaunty, nautical alternative to *bobfoc* when describing your local *prawn.*

dreamcatcher *1. n.* North American Indian cultural artifact available in the airport gift shop. *2. n.* A youth's pyjama bottoms, *wank sock* or paper tissue.

dream cream *n.* That which is frequently to be found spread across the inside of a young gent's night-time pantaloons. *'What's this all over your jimjams, our Terry?' 'That's just dream cream, mum.'*

dream topping *n.* Night *spongle,* whipped up somnobulistically in the *farmer's hat* during por-

nographic REM sleep.

drecktory *n.* Any catalogue that comes with the *Mail on Sunday* or is pushed through the door by a middle aged man in a plastic mac. A dispiriting compendium illustrating a huge range of must-have gadgets, *eg.* Electronic crossword puzzle solvers, illuminated magnifying glasses, plug-in rodent deterrents, chair-arm remote control pockets *etc.*

dredge *v.* To slowly and systematically trawl through the furthest, murky, Stygian recesses of nightclubs in search of female companionship.

Dremel cock *n.* A small *tool* which takes considerably longer to do its job than a normal-sized one would.

dressed for church *euph.* Descriptive of a bleary-eyed young lady in the early hours of Sunday morning, tottering about the streets in her best frock and one shoe.

dressing the wound *n.* The sneaky act of disguising a peskily unflushable *dead otter* with a tasteful shroud of *bumwad.*

dress-messer *n.* A gentleman with a *hair trigger.* A two-push Charlie or *speaking clock.*

drier than prince Andrew's armpit *sim.* Something exceptionally dry, despite appearances suggesting otherwise. *As dry as a budgie's tongue, as dry as a moth sandwich, as dry as an old dog's nose. 'Come on, luv. Make a bit of an effort, will you? I've been rubbing away for a good ten minutes here and you're drier than Prince Andrew's armpit.'*

drink balls *n.* Physical courage that becomes manifest after about six pints of lager, meaning that ordinary men become invincible superheroes who can beat bouncers in a fight. See also *beer bollocks, Buckfast bravery. 'Oh dear. It looks like Jarvis's drink balls have just dropped.'*

drink from both taps *v.* To be a *double dipper,* to bend both ways. See *half rice half chips.*

drinking cap on *euph.* Said of one whose thought processes have been severely disrupted as a result of taking alcoholic beverages on board. *'The Merthyr and Wales number 8, who evidently had his drinking cap on, was arrested at the motorway service station shortly after 5.30am.'*

drinking for two, I'm *phr.* A jocose apophthegm, typically accompanied by gentle rubbing of the stomach, declaimed by a portly gentleman in response to comments regarding his possibly excessive alcohol intake. Also used by pregnant, smoking women outside any pub that sells two breezers for £1.50.

drinking hamster, like a *sim.* Descriptive of a thirsty fellow who goes at his missus's *snatch* like a stumpy-*arsed* rodent licking its water bottle.

drinking lever *n.* The right elbow or, if left-handed, the left elbow.

drinking medal *n.* Unexplained scar or bruise acquired on the Saturday night town centre battlefield.

drinkles *n.* Characterful lines and crows' feet on a regional television presenter's face, following an heroic lifetime of knocking back *top shelf booze* like it's the end of the world.

drink my kids *exclam.* Informal variant of *"suck my penis"*, usually used in a declamatory sense, rather than a genuinely sexual one.

drink on a stick *n.* A spot of *pancreatitis therapy*. *'Pull over in this layby, Geoff. I fancy a drink on a stick.'*

drink outside the box *v.* To imbibe liquor somewhere out of the ordinary, *eg.* A real ale *twat in* a trendy wine bar, a shiny-suited estate agent in an old man pub or in a traffic jam while listening to *Ken Bruce's Popmaster* on Greatest Hits Radio.

drink shame *euph.* Tabloidese phrase dreamt up by purple-nosed hacks with *livers like King Tut's ballsack*. Making someone feel bad just because they like a couple of fucking beers in the morning.

drink straight from the tap *v.* To perform a *Boris Johnson*.

drinks under the dartboard, looks like she *sim.* Of a lady who possesses a face that does not necessarily conform to classical standards of beauty. *A face like a blistered pisspot.*

drinkypoos *n.* The body's way of rewarding a fellow for spending an evening *on the pop*. See also *alestorm, fall of old shoes from the loft.*

drip mat *n.* Three sheets of *bum wad* used to soak up *dew from the lily* during a sordid act of *self pollution.*

dripping gravy *euph. medic.* Touching cloth while suffering from the raging *trots*. *'How are you feeling, Gary? Are you up to playing tonight?' 'I think so, Bobby. I've been dripping gravy all day, but I should be okay unless I have to stretch for the ball.'*

dripping like a fucked fridge *sim.* Of a lady, to be sexually aroused. *'I'm in the mood for love / Simply because you're near me / and whenever you're near me / I drip like a fucked fridge.'* (Song lyric, *The Mood for Love* by Cole Porter).

dripping like a George Foreman grill *sim.* Descriptive of a *bird* who is *fizzing at the bung hole* or *frothing like bottled Bass.*

dripping like an egg sandwich *sim.* Of a lady, *frothing at the oysters.*

drips in the tap, a few more *phr.* Excuse given by a gentleman who is returning from the pub *bogs*

with a *wet penny in his pocket*. *'Look at that. I put it away too early when there was still a few more drips in the tap. Anyway, where was I? Oh yes, your grandad's operation. Well, I'm afraid there were complications during surgery. I think you should prepare yourselves for some bad news.'*

driptease *n.* Erotically enticing prelude to a session of *watersports*. *'Do you want your golden shower now, Terry?' 'No thanks June, just a driptease to get me going at the moment, please.'*

drip tray *n.* The often crusty *sump* in a pair of lady's *dunghampers.*

drive from the ladies' tee *v.* Of a man, to sit down in order to *turn his bike around.*

drive in the slipstream *euph.* To be the *botter* rather than the *bottee*. To *bring up the rear* in the style of an *Audi driver.*

drives a small car *euph.* Said of a chap who *likes musicals* and *prefers his peas minted* and his *salad rinsed.*

drive stick *1. v. US.* To be capable of driving a motor car equipped with a manual gearbox. *2. v. US.* To be a lady in *uncomfortable shoes*, to not *like tennis*. To be a non-*lezza.*

drive the porcelain bus *v.* To pay a kneel-down visit to the lavatory during which one holds the rim like a Routemaster steering wheel while doing a spot of *psychedelic yodelling.*

driving miss daisy *euph.* Attempting intercourse when less than fully *stonked up*. Playing snooker with a piece of string, poking fog up a hill with a sharp stick, pushing a marshmallow into a moneybox, putting toothpaste back in the tube.

driving on the cats' eyes *v.* To emit a long, low, rumbling *fart* that sounds like it's going to damage your suspension.

driving range *n.* The perineum, *snot, tinter*. Where one hits one's *balls* when swinging one's *wood.*

driving test *n.* The act of seeing how far it is possible to wind up the missus. Often ends in an *emergency strop*. See *badger baiting.*

drizzle drawers *n.* Underclothing that is worth its weight in gold when a fellow is wearing a light-coloured trouser.

drooping the colour *n.* When a chap's *guardsman* fails to stand to attention. *'Any chance of a quick punch up the whiskers?' 'I'm afraid not, luv. I'm drooping the colour this morning.'*

droopon coupons *n.* The various clues left around, for example bits of *jamrag* packaging in the bathroom bin, that inform a chap that his wife is *up on blocks* and therefore conjugally indisposed.

droop photo *n.* Following a series of pleasingly stiffening shots of a potential inamorata viewed on a dating app, an unexpectedly ugly (*ie.* less artfully arranged, cropped and photoshopped) image of someone with a face like *she's sucking on a piss-flavoured gobstopper* that results in the immediate and catastrophic collapse of a chap's *chap*.

drop a clot *v. medic.* To menstruate. *'It was Mr Darcy who spoke first. "Your disdain takes me somewhat aback, Miss Bennet. I fear I might have acted in some way inappropriately to cause you such offence." "No, Mr Darcy, your behaviour has been impeccable, and the fault lies with me. I am dropping clots at the moment and find myself in the foulest of humours," she replied.'* (from *Pride and Prejudice* by Jane Austen).

drop a cork *n.* To launch a remarkably buoyant *dreadnought*. To excrete a *jack-in-the-box, brown ping-pong ball, poomerang* or *repeat offender. 'What are you doing in there, Mr Smith? Shouldn't you be up on the bridge, steering the boat?' 'I just dropped a cork, Mrs Ismay. I've flushed it six times, but ninety gallons of Atlantic seawater haven't been enough to take the bastard off yet. God himself could not sink this shit.'*

drop a deuce *euph. Lay a cable,* do a *number two,* do a *duty,* defecate. Phrase popularised in the US comedy show *My Name is Earl.*

drop a Dibnah *v.* Following an exceptionally smelly *botty burp,* to enquire, in the style of the late traction engine-driving chimney demolisher, "Did you like that?"

drop a dress size *v.* Of a lady, to do a really big *digestive transit. 'You're looking well this morning. Have you had your hair done or something?' 'No, I just dropped a dress size I've been baking for a couple of weeks, that's all.'*

drop a gut *v.* To *step on a duck.*

drop a link *v. milit.* To *do a duty.* From the practice of armoured units, who apparently sometimes have to remove a short section from their tank tracks when they become slack. *'Field Marshal Montgomery, we're ready to start the battle of El Alamein. Are you coming out?' 'With you in a minute. I'm just dropping a link.'*

drop anchor *v.* To become aroused in the *trunks department* while doing the breast stroke. See *chlorine cock.*

drop anchor in bum bay *v.* To arrive at the *rear admiral's* favourite port of call. To wash up on *spice island.*

drop a pebble *v.* To erroneously emit a *rabbit tod* while attempting to *shoot a bunny.* See also *follow through.*

drop a tadpole in her beer *v. Aus.* To make a lady pregnant. *'Her Majesty the Queen is pleased to announce that after several years of trying, HRH Prince Edward, the Duke of Wessex has finally succeeded in dropping a tadpole in the Rt Hon Sophie, Countess of Wessex's beer.'* (Official notice, Buckingham Palace Gates, May 2003).

dropbox *1. n.* A cyber portal for uploading and downloading large files. *2. n.* The *crapper.*

drop dead gormless *adj.* Descriptive of one who has fallen out of the ugly tree and landed on their head.

drop Einstein's dinner *v.* To produce *feeshii* that resemble the unpalatable contents of the can of food served to Doc Brown's dog at the start of *Back To The Future.*

drop fudge *v.* To *pinch a loaf, crimp one off.*

drop her yoghurt *v.* Of a lady, to have an *organism* in her *parts* for whatever reason. *'And when the bloke on the scaffolding outside her office took his vest off, she dropped her yoghurt there and then.'*

drop off a calling card *n.* To politely deposit an *air biscuit* on a silver tray while visiting an acquaintance in their home.

drop one *v. Let off, drop your hat, drop a gut, step on a duck, cut the cheese.*

drop one's back *v.* Likewise, to enflatulise the atmosphere around one's *gammon ring.*

drop one's revels *v.* To suffer an unfortunate chocolate-based *follow through* experience while *clearing one's nether throat. 'It's no good. I can't finish this Olympic Marathon, I've dropped me Revels.'*

drop one's yop *v.* To ejaculate messily in a manner reminiscent of a bottle of the popular drinkable yoghurt being dropped onto the tiled floor of a petrol station. *'What's the matter, Cliff?' 'I just dropped my yop, Sue. Best get the Vax out.'*

dropout *n.* Underpant condition whereby a *knacker* protrudes from the bottom of the *shreddies,* or famously in Peter Beardsley's case, football shorts.

dropped glockenspiel, teeth like a *sim.* Descriptive of a person who may benefit from a course of corrective orthodontistry. Also, variously, *teeth like a burnt picket fence, pan of burnt chips, crossword,* or *a mouth full of sugarpuffs. English teeth.*

dropped in like the Google earth man *euph.* Disorientated and alone in an unfamiliar location due to excessive fluid intake.

dropped lollipop, head like a *sim.* The *noggin* of a balding man who refuses to shave the remaining hair off his head, resulting in a scalp with similar amounts of hair on it to sticky confectionery retrieved from the living room carpet. *'I can't believe you paid £180 for that haircut, Wills. You've* *got a head like a dropped lollipop.'*

dropped pie, face like a *sim.* To resemble one who has been *bobbing for chips in a deep fat fryer. 'Who's that newsreader I'm thinking of? You know the one. He's got a face like a dropped pie.' 'John Sergeant.'*

dropped tripe *n.* A particularly "offal" *exchange & mart.* See also *pedigree hum, piping out the haggis, give Rover his breakfast.*

dropping a McWhirter *euph.* Producing a *dreadnought* of such epic proportions that you feel the need to phone the *Guinness Book of Records* and alert the coastguard. Squeezing out a proper *fuck-off U-bend blocker.*

dropping a perpendicular *1. n.* Trigonometrical method of calculating the angles of a non-right-angled triangle or creating a right angle without the use of a protractor, like you would if you were stranded on a desert island with just a ruler and a pair of compasses. *2. n.* On the *crapper, laying a cable* so long and rigid that one end is in the *pan* and the other half is up your *council gritter*, giving the sensation of riding a bike with no saddle.

dropping a weight division *1. n.* In boxing, a fighter losing sufficient poundage so as to be able to compete in a lower weight category, thus enabling him to take on a larger number of opponents in the ring. *2. n.* In *shitting*, the act of expelling such an impressive quantity of *feeshus* that you could conceivably make the move from heavy to cruiserweight or, if you've got amoebic dysentery, junior flyweight.

droppings, chav *n.* Paper cups, polystyrene burger boxes and chip wrappers, neatly wrapped in paper bags and excreted via the passenger window of a Saxo/Corsa at very high speed.

dropping some copper in your piggy bank *n.* Having a *poo* in the *bum sink.*

dropping the jackpot *n.* A violent cascade of *loose change* which requires little or no effort to expel from the *bomb bay*; a big win on the *potty slot*, usually as a result of heavy refreshment and curry the previous night. Also *a flock of pigeons* or *a load of shoes falling from the loft.*

dropping the kids off at the waterpark *euph.* Like *dropping them off at the pool*, but more extreme as the result of eating over 2kg of Frosted Shreddies the previous evening.

dropping the shopping *euph.* See *drop the kids off at the pool.*

drop shot *n.* An expertly executed *hockle while sat on the Rick Witter*, neatly nutmegged between the thighs, the rim of the *shit-pan* and the *Autotrader.* *'Great drop shot there, Sir Noel.'*

drop the competitors off at the Aquatic Centre
euph. To go for a *dump* of Olympian proportions. To pass a *digestive transit* so impressive you could hang a medal round its neck and give it a bunch of flowers.

drop the hymn book *v.* To *guff* in church.

drop the kids off at the pool *euph.* To defecate out of your bottom into the toilet.

drop your guts *v.* To break wind. *'"Fossilised fish hooks," croaked Venables. "Which one of you beanfeasters has dropped his guts?"'* (from *Jennings Makes a Daisy Chain* by Anthony Buckeridge).

drop your hat *v.* To *fart.* Also *drop a bomb, drop your handbag, drop a gut.*

drop your hat forwards *v.* To *fanny fart, muff chuff, queef.* To play the *Lawley kazoo*, blow a *Harry Ramsden's raspberry. 'Just as I was donning the beard, she dropped her hat forwards.'*

drop your tank *1. n.* Term which is apparently used by firefighters when they need to empty four hundred gallons of fluid quickly from their pump. *2. n.* Successfully concluding a romantic encounter by quickly emptying a large quantity of fluid. *'(ALEX pulls DAN towards her and starts tugging at his flies.) ALEX: Come on, Dan. Make love to me now, here in the elevator. You know you want to. You've wanted to since the first time you saw me. DAN: No, you're alright love. I've already dropped me tank, thanks.'* (from the screenplay for *Fatal Attraction*, 1987).

dropzone four please, Ben *exclam.* Said when faced with a choice of portaloos at an outdoor event. From the hit ITV quiz show *Tipping Point*, in which contestants drop overly thin metal discs into a giant amusement arcade coin-pusher machine in the hope of winning cash. Also *fire up dropzone two; let's go, Peloton; bring the thunder!; may I introduce…; let's meet the chaser; Phillip Schofield here.*

drout *n.* A dried-up *fanny.* From drought-ridden + clout.

drown a copper *v.* To give birth to a *dead otter.*

drown a duck *v.* To float an *air biscuit* while in the shower. Descriptive of the noise produced by a quivering *ringpiece* in the presence of flowing water.

drowning motorbike *n.* A particularly wet *Exchange and Mart.* A *bubbly duck, gargling custard.*

drown some kittens *n.* To pass a litter of small *Peter O'Tooles* which nobody wants to give a home to. Then throw them off a canal bridge in a sack.

drown the chocolate slugs *v.* Alternative to *lighting a bum cigar* for those anticipating a somewhat looser stool.

DRS enabled *1. phr.* In Formula 1, a reference to

some sort of flaps that open up. *2. phr.* When *feeding the pony,* a reference to some sort of *flaps* that open up.

drug dealer's doorbell, in and out like a *sim.* Descriptive of a *shagger*'s *arse* or, for that matter, a *fiddler's elbow.*

drugly *adj.* Withered and wizened due to a penchant for narcotics.

drugs bust *n.* Simultaneous entry of two *bobbies' truncheons* through the front and back doors. Also *police raid, SVSA.*

drug smuggler's wait *n.* An interminable period of lavatorial pandiculation which involves sitting on the *bog* waiting for one of them *shits* that take ages to come down, like when you've ate too much meat or tons of eggs.

druncle *n.* A male relative who generally stinks of *refreshment.* *'Do something, dear. Your Druncle George has just dropped the baby onto the barbecue again.'*

drunk's piss, as clear as *sim.* Descriptive of something which is perfectly transparent. From the fact that a *heavily refreshed* fellow's urinary emissions are often so dilute that he can get away without rinsing the sink clean after he's done the *Bradford dishwashing.*

dry bath *n.* A right pummelling. *'Christ. What happened to you?'* *'I said hello to Björk at the airport and she gave me a dry bath.'*

dry bob *1. n.* A public schoolboy who doesn't row. *2. v.* Fully clothed sex, leading to *milmed undercrackers.* *3. n.* A bankrupt *money shot,* a *spaffless stack blow.*

dry clean, Scouse *n.* The act of removing a dirty item of clothing from the laundry basket or *floordrobe* and spraying it with deodorant, aftershave – or, in extreme circumstances fly spray – in order to facilitate another day's wear.

dry docked *adj.* Lack of lubrication situation where a low tide of *blip* prevents the *skin boat* sailing smoothly into *tuna town.*

dry dream *n.* An irksome reverie during which you are trying to *have it off* with your missus but she is having none of it. *'Somewhere over the rainbow / Skies are blue / And the dry dreams you dare to dream / Really do come true.'*

dryer's remorse *euph.* The trail of shame left on a bathroom towel after ineffectively scouring the *nether regions* whilst showering. *'When it comes to dryer's remorse, Persil mums know best.'* (TV ad, 1978).

dry eye in my pants, there wasn't a *phr.* Descriptive of a situation where the protagonist has experienced a level of visual stimulation such that

an involuntary *yoghurt drop* has ensued. *'Did you see that Kirsty Gallacher doing the tango on Strictly last night? Jesus Christ, there wasn't a dry eye in my pants. And now it's back to you in the studio, Sian.'*

dry firing *1. n.* The action of cycling the bolt and firing mechanism of a rifle without having a round in the chamber. *2. n.* The inevitable result of a gent who is *working from home*'s attempt to beat his own long-standing *personal best.* A *ghost cough, fat-free yoghurt drop* or popless *popshot.*

dry heat *1. n.* Early means of sterilisation. *2. n.* Following a spicy *Ruby Murray* or Chinese, a piping hot *dropped hat* which burns on the way out.

dry lining *n.* Workmanlike use of *shit tickets* laid around the *bum sink* to ameliorate *acid splashback* when *releasing the chocolate hostage.*

dry riser *1. n.* Some kind of water supply for fire-fighting or central heating. *2. n.* A *snipped* but otherwise more or less fully functioning *pintle.* *3. n.* An erection that erectivitates without any stimulation, either visual or tactile. See *busdriver's knob.*

dry roasted *adj.* Entered simultaneously at either end by a pair of professional footballers, without the benefit of lubrication (also a sort of peanut).

dryrrhoea *n. medic.* An uncontrollable and alarming-sounding – yet ultimately harmless – bout of flatulence.

dry run *1. n.* An ill-advised and risky, although happily successful, attempt to *kick start the Harley Davidson* when one is blighted with a bout of the *Eartha Kitts.* *2. n.* A trip to the toilet cubicle, complete with a fifteen minute sit-down with the trousers and *grundies* round the ankles, taken with no intention whatsoever of *laying a cable.* A half-holiday enjoyed during the working day which has all the benefits of a lavatory break with none of the *nipsy*-based palaver and aggravation that usually accompanies such a visit. *3. n.* Sex with a spinster whose *box* is as moistureless as *Gandhi's flip-flops.*

dry sit down *n.* A nice ten-minute skive in the works *Rick Witters.*

DSB *abbrev.* Dangerous Sperm Build-up. To have two tins of Fussell's Milk. *'I'm sorry, Sir Cliff, but you are suffering from DSB. As your doctor, the only course of treatment I can prescribe at this stage is an ADW.'*

DSL *abbrev.* Dick Sucking Lips.

DSSneyland *n.* The Gurnos Estate, Merthyr Tydfil. See also *giropractor, dole model.*

dub *n.* "Duck" in Flowerpot Men language. See *flub.*

Dublin buffet *n.* Two packets of crisps opened

up for a whole pub table to share. Also known as a *Scouse buffet, Geordie buffet, Glasgow buffet, Barnsley buffet* or *Todmorden tapas,* depending on from whence one hails.

Dublin office *euph.* The pub. *'I'm terribly sorry, he can't speak to you now. He's in the Dublin office.'*

duck bread *n.* A lady who is past her prime.

duck butter *n. Aus.* Assorted smegmalogical effluviums accumulating under the *fiveskins* of the unclean.

duck dastardly *n.* The perpetrator of a particularly noxious *exchange & mart* that is heralded by an audible warning resembling nothing so much as the call of a domestic wildfowl.

duck fat *exclam.* A quasi-spooneristic exclaimation of denial, disdain or non-cooperation that may safely be employed within the hearing of elderly aunts, prospective mothers-in-law, papal envoys *etc.*

Duckhams, do a *v.* To *tip your filthy concrete* after just a couple of pushes. Wittily named after the popular "two stroke" engine oil.

ducking *n.* Aquatic version of the popular erotic hobby known as *dogging,* which takes place not in a car park, but in a boatyard, harbour or along a quayside. A practice which presumably involves a scandal-ridden Premiership footballer in a raincoat walking along the side of a river accompanied by a mallard on a lead, waiting for the opportunity to watch a pair of tabloid newspaper reporters pretending to *have it off* in a cabin cruiser while he *tosses himself off* inside his trousers for the benefit of a nearby photographer with a long lens.

duckles *n.* The indentations in the backs of a fatty's hands where their knuckles should be. From dimples + knuckles.

duck sandwich *n.* Prominent *pudenders* visible through the tight leggings of fat-thighed ladies. *Knicker sausages.*

duck sausage *n.* A filling gourmet meal which is best eaten in a crouched position. *'I'm glad you got to meet Val Doonican after the concert, nan.' 'Aye, but I had to have three portions of duck sausage off his roadies to get backstage.'*

duck's breakfast *1. n. Welsh.* Early morning *sausage* and *split kippers.* Accompanied by gentle quacking and a flurry of feathers. *2. n.* Phrase used to describe how poor people, for example students, start their day. That is to say "a drink of water and a shit."

duck slippers *n.* That acoustical effect sometimes heard when a post-*coital* lady waddles across the landing to relieve herself of a load of *plum duff,*

and a gentle quacking noise emerges from her *bills* with each step.

duck smuggler *n.* A *Glen Miller;* one who produces a *string of pearls,* as if trying to smuggle a small avian fowl past customs by hiding it up his *arse.* One who lets out a sequence of "quacks" while walking.

ducks on the stairs! *exclam.* Something a person might usefully shout to clear a path while charging towards the *crappers* in Tesco while experiencing a bout of explosive diarrhoea.

duck soup *n.* The products of a *follow through.* The sixth Marx Brother, *Skiddo.*

duck-stepping *n.* A variation on goose-stepping whereby the marcher releases a gentle *quack* with each step. As famously practised by flatulent late rock'n'roller/*scat* enthusiast Chuck Berry. Also *duck walk, ugly duckling,* a *string of pearls, the Bavarian.*

Duckworth-Lewis method *n.* Means of *getting a result* when it's getting late and all else has failed.

dude ranch *n.* A light-coloured, tangy dressing that can be *tossed* onto a lady's *lettuce. Gentleman's relish, semen mayo, man-egg mayonnaise.*

duel fuel *n. Fighting water.*

duelling banjos *1. n.* A female dormitory *wank race,* perhaps in a nurses' home or nunnery. *2. n.* The vigorous *Scruggs-style* double-tug motion of a *meat vid crane operator. 3. n.* The situation that occasionally obtains when two uncircumcised males are having sex with the same woman, and the undersides of their *tuning pegs* catch on each other.

duel with the pink Darth Vader *n.* A *Hand Solo.*

duff *1. n.* Bum, arse. *2. n.* Fadge, minge, twat, clopper.

duffle coat *n.* A reusable thick-skinned *fucksock. 'I've still got my grandad's old duffle coat, you know. It's still going strong.'*

duffle coat toggles *n.* JCB starter buttons, pygmy's cocks, chapel hat pegs, organ stops, dockers' thumbs, blind cobblers' thumbs, Scammell wheelnuts, cigar butts.

duffy's bridge *n.* The *biffin bridge, tinter, taint, barse.* The perineum of either gender.

Dufresne-ian *adj.* Descriptive of any DIY/home improvement project that takes as long to complete as the escape tunnel dug by Tim Robbins's character in *The Shawshank Redemption.*

Dufresne's hammer, a cock like *sim.* A *tool* that has, over the course of several decades of nightly *Shawshanks,* been worn down nearly to the nub.

DUFTO/dufto *acronym.* Any old *bird* at a film premiere who has a whiff of mothballs around her. Dug Up For The Occasion.

duggle *v.* To receive or perform an act of oral *horatio* while *crimping off a loaf.* To take part in a *blumpkin.*

dugs *n. Baps, paps.* Olde worlde version of *jugs*, still in use amongst yokel folk.

dug with a new slipper, like a *sim. Scots.* Enthusiastically (dug = dog). *'Help m'boab, Wullie! Look at thae baps. I'd be a' awa them like a dug with a new slipper.'*

Duke of giblets *n.* A *salad dodger.*

Duke of Kunt *n.* A proper aristocrat amongst *culturally unique national treasures, eg.* Piers Morgan.

Duke of York's award *1. n.* Some sort of prize for "digital excellence", whatever that is, named in honour of the late Queen's *cunt of the litter. 2. n.* Rival certificate to the Duke of Edinburgh's Award, earned by those who can complete the 28-minute rail journey from Woking to central London without breaking a sweat.

Dukes *1. n. rhym. slang. Charms, shirt potatoes, headlamps.* From Grand old Duke of Yorks = norks. *'I see the Duchess has went and got her Dukes out in the paper, then.' 2. n. rhym. slang. medic.* Haemorrhoids. From Duke of Argyles = piles.

dumbbell diva *n.* A fellow who, when utilising a gymnasium, emits excessive grunting to give the impression that he is lifting huge weights in order to impress the female patrons who could easily lift twice as much without making a sound.

dumbocracy *n.*The reckless exercise of an ill-informed plebiscite.

Dumbo's ears *n.* The large, sometimes grey, flaps of meat found in a lady's *dunghampers.*

dump *1. n.* A 40-minute reading session in the *dunny. 2. v.* To *curl one off.*

dump and burn *1. v. milit.* RAF term for the act of jettisoning fuel behind engines on afterburn, resulting in a spectacular display of rumbling noise and flames. *2. n.* Going for a *Tom tit* after consuming unhealthy levels of spicy food, resulting in a spectacular display of rumbling noise and flames.

dump dew *n.* The glistening pool of sweat left on the *bog* seat after *laying* a particularly troublesome *cable.*

dumperature *n. medic.* A hot *shit* or *ring roaster.* *'I'll be a while love, I reckon. Last night's kebab has given me a dumperature.'*

dump grump *n.* Melancholic woe brought on by constipation or the lack of an opportunity

to defecate.

dumpling *1. n.* A solitary, suety *splutterbean* floating in a *pan* of *bum stew. 2. n.* A woman who is blessed with such a *lovely personality* that you would have to "roll her in flour to find her wet bits".

dumplings *1. n. pl.* Baby *dumps. 2. n.* Particularly filling breasts that go well with *meat and two veg.*

dump proof course *n.* Layer of *bog* paper laid across the water surface in the *pan* by a careful camper prior to *dropping the kids off at the pool*, in the hope of obviating *splashback* and a chilly *Neptune's kiss.* See also *crash mat, pap baffle, turd raft* and *pilo.*

dump station *n.* The *chod bin.*

dump stump *n.* When you're just about to leave for work or an important appointment and suddenly you need a *shit*, handily causing an increased level of anxiety that you will be late.

dump valve *1. n.* A thing that a baseball-capped youth might attempt to somehow fasten to his car engine so it makes a loud whooshing noise between a couple of gear changes before breaking down catastrophically at the side of the road.. *2. n.* The *nipsy.*

Duncan *n.* A *floater.* From buoyant former Olympic sportsman Duncan Goodhew.

dunce's hats *n.* Them conical pointed *tits* found underneath woollen sweaters in 1950's America. *Twin peaks.*

Dundee cake, like half a *sim.* Term used when describing a particularly large *trophy* left in the bottom of the *shitter* by the previous user. *'I would avoid trap two if I was you, your majesty. The Archbishop of Canterbury was in there just now and he flushed it twice but it still looks like half a Dundee cake down there.'*

Dundee hold-all *n.* A plastic carrier bag. Good for carrying a cargo of cheap *pisswater* lager back from the shops. Also *Barnsley briefcase, Glasgow suitcase, Doncaster portmanteau.*

Dundee suitcase *euph. Scots.* A bin bag. *'Police have been called after a dog walker found a large quantity of builder's rubble and dogshit dumped in a Dundee suitcase on wasteground near Kinblethmont.'*

dune buggy *n.* A woman who engages in amorous activity in the secluded areas at the rear of Southport beach. Also known as a *builder's skip* due to the large amount of loose sand shovelled up her *arse* by her companion's *bollocks* during a typical act of intercourse.

dung dreadlocks *n.* Haile Selassie's *beaded*

curtains. Laid-back *tagnuts.*

dung funnel *n. medic. Fudge tunnel.*

dunghampers *n. Undercrackers, trolleys, bills.*

dunghill slalom *n.* The near vertical slope at the back of the *jobby pan* which can get encrusted to a substantial depth after Vindaloo, whisky and Cuban cigars. *'Are you alright in there, Winston? It's been forty minutes.' 'I'm just cleaning the dunghill slalom with a chisel thank-you, Clemmie.'*

dung lung *n. medic.* Descriptive of one who has been *necking turds.* A halitosis sufferer.

dung puncher *n.* A gentleman homosexual. A *doughnut puncher* or *spud fumbler.*

dungsten carbide *n.* The material from which the forward end of certain, particularly firm *Douglas Hurds* appears to be forged, with which they could drill their way through the most tightly pursed *fifties teatowel holder* like the Mole out of Thunderbird 2. *'Bloody hell, mother. That one had a tip of pure dungsten carbide on it. It's completely de-burred me nipsy.'*

dung trumpet *n.* A melodic refrain on the *botty bugle* which brings to mind nothing so much as the plangent opening bars to the signature tune of *Johnny Briggs* or *Open All Hours.*

dunk *1. v.* To dip a biscuit in a cup of tea. *2. v.* To throw a basketball downwards through the hoop. *3. v.* To dip one's *wick* into a *billposter's bucket.*

dunking a Bourbon *n.* Delivering a massive *bridger* that has its head in the water whilst still attached to your *ringpiece.* Also *earthing cable, craptain Webb.*

Dunkirk *euph.* A tactically critical and hastily planned toilet visit for a swift and full emergency *evacuation.* Often brought about quickly following a seriously dodgy pint or *Ruby Murray,* and necessitating a *piss, shit* or *chunder* – or indeed, any two or all three at the same time. See also *grand slam, operation dynamo etc.*

dunky *n.* Protective rubber *franger* worn when *dunking* to prevent the penis going soggy and falling off into the *hairy goblet.*

dunny *n. Aus.* Toilet, *netty, cludgy, shite house.*

dunny budgie *n. Aus.* A fly buzzing round an Australian *bog.*

dunny funnel *n. Aus.* The *anus* of the *back bottom.*

dunnylingus *1. n. Aus.* A romantic *nosh* at a *vertical bacon sandwich* enjoyed in a public lavatory cubicle. *2. n.* A *trip around the world.*

durashit *n.* Faecal matter of such stickiness and viscosity that it can adhere to porcelain despite multiple flushes and applications of bleach.

dusk till dawn *n. rhym. slang. Porn.* *'By the way, I tidied your bedroom for you while you were out, our Frank.' 'Aw bloody hell, mam. You'd better not have*

thrown all me dusk till dawn out again.'

dusk tusk *n.* Twilight counterpart of *dawn horn,* a cause of insomnia which can usually be remedied by loosening off your *nuts* with a suitably sized *wanking spanner.*

dustbin teeth *euph.* Said of one who has lost many of the burnt chips out of their dental *pan.* So-called because there is "one in every yard". *'Don't forget to brush both your dustbin teeth before you go to bed, Wilfrid.'*

dustette *n.* Obsolete hand-held Hoover vacuum cleaner which proved very popular with bachelors who needed to suck the dust off sausages.

dusting between earthquakes *euph.* The soul-destroying and laborious practice of wiping one's *arse* after *spending tuppence in ha'pennies and farthings,* only to be subjected to a second wave of *loose change* that immediately undoes all of one's hard work.

dustman's library *n.* An archive of vintage, recycled *niff mags* usually found in the cabins of dustcarts, or in the portacabin at the local civic amenity site.

dustman's lorry *n.* The rumblings that wake a fellow at 6am on a Wednesday morning. *'The dustman's lorry's just pulled in, dear. I'd better go and put out the bins.'*

dustman's ruler *1. n.* A short and stubby measuring tool, only of sufficient length to allow a council refuse operative to judge that your wheelie bin lid is open 1mm beyond the statutory limit so he won't legally be able empty it, much as he would like to. *2. n.* A risibly short *manhood.* *'Oi Rishi! Is that a dustman's ruler in your pocket or are you just pleased to see me?'*

dustman's special *n.* A *fart* containing such a high concentration of methanethiol and other sulphur compounds as to be reminiscent of the scent of rotting garbage. *'Gaw, is the wind blowing in from the landfill site again, June?' 'No Terry. Great Aunt Lucy just dropped a dustman's special.'*

dust mite *n.* An habitual cocaine user. *'Born on this day: Gustav Kirchhoff, German physicist, 1824; Wally Schirra, American astronaut, 1923; Pete Doherty, English dust mite, 1979.'*

dust puffer *n.* A male who is no longer able to *jizz up* following overuse of his *old boy.*

dust sucker *n.* A woman who prefers to take her romantic pleasures with a more mature gentleman caller.

dust the duvet *v.* To *hitchhike under the big top, starch the sheets.*

Dusty Klatt *1. n. prop.* Young Canadian motocross racer. *2. n.* A lady's *parts of shame* that have never done anything to be ashamed of. A *furry hoop* that has seen less use than Jeffrey Archer's honesty box. *3. n.* A redundant *fanny* that won the West 125cc Motorcycle Championship in 2005.

Dutch *n.* *Sausage sandwich, tit wank, diddy ride.* Also *Dutch fuck.*

Dutch afterburner *n.* The romantic act of having your girlfriend *fart* in your mouth, then blowing it up her nose. That's going to take some arranging.

Dutch Alps *n.* Small breasts, *fried eggs, stits, patsies, bee stings.* Also *Lincolnshire Cairngorms.* As scaled by a *Dutch mountaineer.*

Dutch arrow *n.* A *woody shaft* that twangs up the *bonus tunnel.*

Dutch astronomy *euph.* Scouring the internet for hours on end looking for ever better and higher definition pictures of ladies' *brown stars.*

Dutch auction *n.* Process of negotiating services and costs with two or more rival *good time girls,* especially when using an awkward combination of English, French, German, and charades.

Dutch baby *1. n.* What the Americans appear to call a Yorkshire pudding. *2. n.* The spawn of a badly misjudged *Dutch oven.*

Dutch bellows *n.* A *blanket ripper.*

Dutch blast *n.* Accordian-like effect achieved at the open end of the quilt when one wants to sample or indeed share the fragrant fruits of a bedtime *rumpet voluntary.*

Dutch blindfold *n.* In the *69* position, with the woman underneath and the gentleman's *clock-weights* fitting nicely in her eye sockets. All things considered, it's probably just as well she can't see anything.

Dutch boy *n.* A lady in *comfortable shoes,* a *tennis fan,* a lesbian, *ie.* One who always "has their finger in a dyke".

Dutch breakfast *n.* Something you have after *awakening the bacon* that will set you up for the day.

Dutch brogues *n.* A pair of plain suede shoes decorated with delicate traceries of *piss* spots. *Flush puppies.* '*Hey, I like the Dutch brogues, Ken.* '

Dutch brylcreem *n.* A glutinous product that you don't particularly want in your coiffure. *Gunk, heir gel.*

Dutch canal *n.* That nameless bit between a chap's *balls* and his *arsehole,* variously known as the *scrincter, stinker's bridge, scran, gisp, barse, tintis, great, notcher, ABC, gooch, Finsbury bridge, isnae, scruttock, Perry Como's lip, tornado alley, scranus, smelly bridge, Brick Lane* or *crunk.*

Dutch cap *n.* An extremely tight-fitting rubber hat worn in Holland.

Dutch cappuccino *euph. Felching.*

Dutch conclave *n.* A particularly impressive form of *Dutch oven* in which a foul-smelling smoke is emitted from the end of the quilt, reminiscent of the moment when the College of Cardinals announces the election of a new Pope by *farting* up the Vatican chimney.

Dutch decongestant *n.* Noxious vapours that occasionally rise up when *back-scuttling* a person with a somewhat relaxed personal hygiene regimen, causing the sinuses to burn and the eyes to run.

Dutch door *n.* A *bird* who *swings both ways.*

Dutch floor polish *n.* *Spunk.*

Dutch flowers *n.* Fannies. *'We were right on the front row at Stringfellows. You could really smell the Dutch flowers.'*

Dutch gasmask *n.* The heroic and selfless act of a fellow who launches a *Dutch hand grenade,* only to clasp his hand over his own mouth in order to spare the nasal sensibilities of all nearby.

Dutch grill *n.* The cheeky act of *blowing off* into your partner's pillow so that when they get into bed and lie down, their head is cooked with slow-release *cabbage gas.*

Dutch hand grenade *n.* A *beefy eggo,* caught in the hand and then detonated under an unsuspecting person's nose. A *cupcake.*

Dutch helm disease *n. medic.* Form of *Doonican* acquired on a weekend visit to some of the more specialist tourist attractions in De Walletjes. Also *vice crispies, athlete's flute.*

Dutch hiccups *n. medic.* The involuntary eructations of an enthusiastic *fellatrix* who has swallowed a chap's *old fella* right *up to the maker's nameplate.*

Dutch jellyfish *n.* The free-swimming result of a *five knuckle shuffle* in the bath.

Dutch lilo *n.* A *Tom tit* that is left floating about in a swimming pool. As seen in infamous scenes in *Caddyshack, Benidorm* and Ingmar Bergman's *Cries and Whispers.*

Dutch look *n.* An uncomfortably detailed examination of the range of unappetising products produced by the *dirt bakery.*

Dutchman's dessert *n.* Following the main course, the afters kept warm in a *Dutch oven.*

Dutch Marathon *n.* The hasty, yet seemingly never-ending walk home after purchasing a new selection of *fleshmags* from a specialist newsagent.

Dutch milkman *1. n.* Fan at a rock festival who *pisses* in a bottle and throws it at the band on stage. *2. n.* One whose job it is to wipe down the video booths in Amsterdam sex shops after the empty-*nutted* punters leave. *3. n.* A premature ejaculator. *'Oh, never mind. I see the Dutch milkman has already been, Jeffrey. While I was at the shops.'*

Dutch miracle *n.* The magical appearance of *art pamphlets* under a mattress or on top of a wardrobe in a hotel bedroom.

Dutch mustard *n. Jitler. 'More Dutch mustard on your caviar, Mr Morgan?'*

Dutch oven *n.* The act of cooking one's partner's head beneath the bedclothes using *cabbage gas.* Also *covered wagon.*

Dutch oyster *n.* An exotic mouthful of the contents of one's own *winkle.* One probable consequence of a *Swiss kiss.*

Dutch pedicure *n.* A specialist continental affectation whereby a chap *chucks his muck* onto someone else's feet.

Dutch postman *n.* Someone who delivers something you don't want. For example, next door's dog that does a *crap* on your lawn.

Dutch reach *1. n.* In the latest edition of the *Highway Code,* a new way to open your car door so as not to knock down passing cyclists. *2. n.* Something a fellow might receive from an Amsterdam-based *trombonist.* Not entirely dissimilar to a *Basildon bagpipe. 3. n.* Some sort of unspeakable act, probably in the final throes of copulation, involving a Stroopwaffle, a bicycle, a pair of wooden shoes, a piece of Gouda, a spliff and a liberal disposition.

Dutch roundabout *1. n.* A traffic island wherein vehicles entering or leaving must give way to both pedestrians and cyclists, who have their own, clearly-demarcated lanes by which they can safely cross in front of waiting traffic. *2. n.* A continental orgy the nature of which – were it to actually take place – would almost be sufficient reason for this country to withdraw from the European Economic Union. *3. n. Dew on the lily* and a pre-greased *bonus tunnel,* aiding efficiency in transiting between *exits.*

Dutch rudder *n.* For want of anything better to do, having someone complete your act of *monomanual self delight* for you by pulling up and down on your forearm while you hold your own penis.

Dutch salute *n. Irish toothache.* An erection.

Dutch sandwich *1. n.* Shifty tax avoidance scheme used by sinister mega-global corporations to rip off the general public. *2. n.* Continental version of a *posh wank* where the *pork sword* is encased in a thin slice of gouda and a couple of pieces of rye bread. *3. n.* A *ménage a trois* undertaken in Amsterdam; two tourists with an accomodating

local resident in the middle.

Dutch satay *n.* The epilogue of a *stick vid* where the starlet sucks on the leading man's rapidly softening phallus after she's been *front* and *back fucked* with it, and had it smear *spunk* all over her *tits.*

Dutch sauna *n. Drowning a duck* while sharing a hot shower cubicle with one's spouse. An aquatic *Dutch oven.*

Dutch souvenir *n.* A little something brought back in the urethra to surprise the wife and help you remember Amsterdam.

Dutch strawberry *n.* The *herman gelmet.* With *cream.*

Dutch submarine *n.* Large *jubber ray* full of *spunk,* sorry, *semen.* It doesn't really work written down. A *Coney Island whitefish.*

Dutch teabreak *n.* The act of *relaxing in a gentleman's way* while at work. Taking a *monkey's fag break.*

Dutch tilt *1. n.* In photography, a composition whereby the camera is set at an angle so that the vertical lines are out of kilter with the side of the frame. *2. n.* A *pissed up* gait whereby an individual who has recently been drinking Continental lager is set at an angle such that his vertical axis is out of kilter with the walls of nearby buildings. Although presumably he'd look vertical in a *Dutch tilt* photograph.

Dutch timeout *n.* Two fingers up the *chocolate windmill.*

Dutch trading company *1. n. prop.* Name of an early 17th century global business organisation; one of the first examples of a multinational corporation. Don't say we never fucking learn you anything. *2. n.* Any 21st century business, dodgy corner shop or scraggy *ratboy chav* from whom one can purchase hardcore *Frankie* and/or class B drugs.

Dutch traffic *n.* The queue of *wanking* gentlemen at a *gang bang. 'I would've come earlier, only the Dutch traffic was terrible.'*

Dutch travel agent *n.* A *sex worker* who gets you where you need to go with a friendly attitude and a smile.

Dutch tuba *n.* Receiving a *nosh* while sat on the *crapper* enjoying a euphonious *digestive transit* and making low-pitched moans and groans like the opening theme to *Hancock's Half Hour.*

Dutch tug *n.* A no-nonsense commercial *hand-job.* Do not pay more than £10.

Dutch welcome mat *n.* A stain on the carpet which indicates where a *feeshus* has been inefficiently expunged from the weft at some point in the past.

Dutch wife *1. n.* How people in Japan refer to their sex dolls. *2. n.* How people in the Netherlands refer to their missuses.

Dutch wink *n.* The flashing of the *bacon rasher* when crossing and uncrossing the legs. *'The film has action, drama, suspense and a superb Dutch wink from Sharon Stone.'* (Barry Norman, reviewing *Basic Instinct*).

duty, do a *v.* To *stool.*

duty jury *n.* Those who are called upon by an outraged colleague to view and judge some humungous *brown trout* discovered in the works *Rick Witters.*

duvet charming *n.* The mythical eastern art of consuming *musical vegetables,* then falling asleep and causing the counterpane to rise mystically to the plangent whinnying of your *arse flute.*

duvet dive *n.* The act of a fellow who rapidly heaves up the bedclothes and pretends to be fast asleep when he hears his wife approaching the bedroom door halfway through his morning *hand shandy.*

duvet raiser *n.* A particularly spicy meal. *'Let's have a curry tonight. I fancy a real duvet raiser.'*

DVDA *abbrev.* Double Vaginal, Double Anal. The Holy Grail of *bongo video* acts, presumably involving four India-rubber men and one uncomfortable woman.

DVDADO *abbrev.* We spoke too soon.

dye your dinner *euph.* To finish off the evening by imbibing a hefty quantity of stout.

dying man's handshake *n.* A tragically loose *minge.* *'How was it for you, Liam?' 'Like a dying man's handshake, Patsy.'*

dyke *n.* Lesbian, *tuppence licker, carpet muncher, lady golfer, tennis fan, three wheeler*; a woman who is *on the other bus,* most likely the 596 *to Hebden Bridge.* See also *diesel dyke, bulldyke.*

dyke differential *n.* The notable discrepancy between the attractiveness of the sort of lesbians depicted in *grumble vids, seed catalogues etc.*, and the sort actually encountered in real life.

dykey likey *n.* A straight man who is befriended by *ladies in comfortable shoes.* The male version of a *fag hag.*

Dylan *n.* A tangled, matted, unkempt mess of a *bush,* resembling the hairstyle of grizzled singer-songwriter Bob. A *Terry Waite's allotment.*

dynamic growth corridor *1. phr.* Expression coined by then Chancellor of the Exchequer Philip Hammond to describe the area between Milton Keynes and Oxford that is, he said, ripe for expansion. *2. phr.* Polite way to refer to one's *back passage* when a Brobdingnagian *poo* is imminent.

Dy-na-mi-tee, I'm Miss *phr.* Strident refrain from one's better half in the run-up to her monthly *cow's week.* *'Now feel my flow you get me though, I'm Ms. Dy-na-mi-tee!'*

dynamite week *n.* Dangerous period of time when one's *bag for life* is particularly volatile and has a small fuse hanging out of her *box.*

dysenterested *adj.* Descriptive of the face you make when someone is talking *shit.*

Dyson *n.* A *bird* with a right good suck on her.

dysparpsia *n. medic.* A gastric dysfunction that manifests itself in a series of strident anal announcements. *'Listen to that. there must be a circus in the next field. I can hear a troupe of performing seals tuning up their car-horns while the brass band practises clown music on a selection of trombones, euphoniums and sousaphones.' 'No, that's me, dear. I'm suffering from a spot of dysparpsia. Oh no, the caravan door's jammed shut.'*

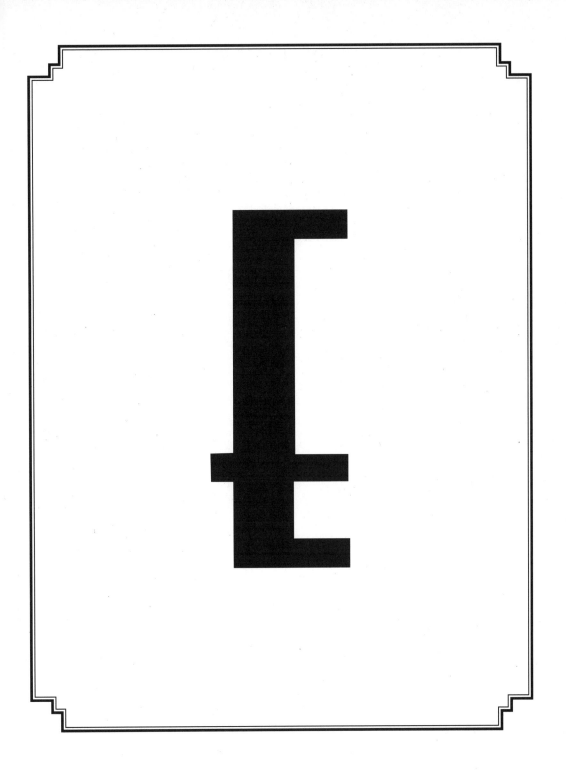

ear chafers *n.* Ladies' stocking tops, *giggle bands.*

Earl Brown, going for an *euph.* Enjoying a refreshing cuppa and a *shit.*

earlids *n.* Invisible, soundproof flaps of skin which descend over a gentleman's ears when he is being conversed at by his lady wife. *Beer muffs.*

early barf *n.* A premature end to a night of drinking, caused by an individual's inability to hold his or her *sauce, eg.* Late former US President George Bush, who spewed up and fell on the floor after just half a pint of weak shandy when out on a pub crawl with Japanese Prime Minister Kiichi Miyazawa in 1992.

early day motion *1. euph.* Political term for *shitting* the bed. *'When I heard that Andy Coulson had been arrested, I immediately tabled an early day motion.'* (Rt Hon. David Cameron MP, quoted in *Hansard*, July 9th 2011). *2. n.* A *turd* break taken as soon as one arrives at work.

early gurning centre *n.* A place to which one can see under-age revellers displaying the characteristic facial tics and spasms associated with consumption of *disco biscuits, eg.* The Pier, Cleethorpes.

early morning dip *n.* To make love to a woman while she is still asleep. A romantic act that can carry a 15-year prison sentence.

early riser *n.* One who is prone to *debilitating stiffness* in the morning.

early shart, get an *v.* Of busy go-getter types, to rise from their slumbers at an earlier hour than usual because they have *shat* themselves. Normally due to a semi-conscious gamble and its consequent failure to pay-off. *'Five-thirty on day two of the microwave curry task, and at the house the members of Team Graphene get an early shart.'*

early taxi? *exclam. interrog.* A witty riposte which can be employed when someone has *passed* a particularly noxious *wind*. *'Will you be needing an early taxi, Archbishop Welby?'*

earn brownie points *v.* Of a gentleman, to perform selfless acts of kindness, like doing the dishes or a spot of ironing in the hope that one's partner will express her gratitude with a game of *mud darts.*

ear of Sauron, the *n.* The *bag for life*'s all-hearing shell-like, which sends her scurrying downstairs as soon as a fellow cracks open a beer or flicks on a *gentleman's entertainment channel* whilst she is upstairs in the *Tower of Mordor.*

ear pie *n.* A right *bollocking* a woman gives a man when he stays too long in the pub, forgets her birthday, *fucks* her sister, *etc*. Also *GBH of the ear-hole.*

Eartha Kitts *rhym. slang. Shits,* diarrhoea.

Also *Brads.*

earthing cable *n.* An elongated *copper bolt* that touches down safely in the *chod bin* water before it has fully exited the *nipsy.* A *bridger* or *bottom log.*

earth wind & fire *1. n.* Critically acclaimed US disco/funk band founded in Chicago in 1969, whose hits include *Got To Get You Into My Life, September* and *Fantasy. 2. n.* The truly woeful digestive after-effects of an evening spent drinking copious amounts of real ale, topped off with a vindaloo. And some lager. And a kebab on the way home.

ease springs *1. exclam. milit.* In the armed forces, an order to move the working parts of a weapon forwards into a safe position after firing. *2. exclam.* An amusing announcement to make after a particularly mechanical-sounding burst of flatulence. Also *back to bed Peppa; a confident appeal by the Australians there; an excellent theory, Dr Watson; anybody injured?; fer-fetch a cloth, Granville.*

easing of lockdown *1. n.* The lifting of certain restrictions on travel, shopping *etc.* during the coronavirus outbreak. *2. n.* A post-constipation *shit.* Something which causes traumatic times.

Eastbourne, on the way to *euph.* Of an ageing lady's *Davy Jones's lockers*, heading south for a well-earned retirement.

Eastenders, an *n.* Eight *basso profundo* blasts from the *brass section*, ending on a real tea-time cliffhanger.

Easter egg on legs, like a *sim.* Unpleasantly judgemental phrase which nevertheless perfectly describes the puce-faced woman in glasses who appeared to be the principal dancer in Les Dawson's Roly Polys. You know the one, she used to be the Mighty Atom out of the Mighty Atom and Roy.

Easter Island statue with an arse full of razor blades *sim. Aus.* A permanently grave, sour countenance. A phrase that describes the full range of actor Jimmy Nail's facial expressions to a T.

East Hull loan *euph.* A short term financial advance arranged by altering and kindly cashing other people's benefits cheques. *'How did you pay off the fine you got for that War Widows Pension fraud, Dave?' 'I took out an East Hull loan.'*

east wind *1. n.* A meteorological air current that blows in a westerly direction. *2. n.* A harsh, bracing breeze that blows in the aftermath of a particularly strong *ring burner*. *'There's an east wind coming all the same, such a wind as never blew on England yet. It will be cold and bitter, Watson, and a good many of us may wither before its blast. But it's God's own wind none the less and a cleaner, better,* *stronger land will lie in the sunshine when the storm has cleared. Now pull my finger.'* (from *Sherlock Holmes and the Mysterious Case of the Lamb Phall* by Arthur Conan Doyle).

Eastwood *n.* A *clit* which is a real fistful.

Easyjet eardrum *n. medic.* Severe tympanic pressure felt when returning from the pub *shitfaced* and *her indoors* starts *giving it this.*

Easyjet seat pocket, fanny like a *sim.* A *wizard's sleeve.* From the fact that the seats of the older models of jet departing from Luton have huge, overstretched flaps on the back of them, from years of accommodating all manner of bulky goods.

easy jetters *n.* British girls on holiday, so-called because they arrive by budget airline, they're *easy* and after a week in the sun they've turned orange.

easy now *exclam.* Humorous post-flatal shout-out, delivered in a drum'n'bass stylee. Also *ET phone home; you were only supposed to blow the bloody doors off; be not afeard, the isle is full of noises; move along, nothing to see here; I second that motion and add a turd.*

easy peelers *1. n.* Tart fruits with an easily shed exocarp and rind. *2. n.* WPCs with evidently loose morals, who turn up at strip shows and get their *kits* off. *3. n.* Fruity *tarts* with easily shed garmentry. *4. n.* Summer shorts that allow a man, *via* a minor adjustment of leg position, to break his *chicken skin handbag*'s sweaty bond from his thigh, thus letting it swing free in the cooling breeze.

eat *v.* To perform a "despicable" (© *The Sun* newspaper, 2008) mouth-based sexual act on the *pudenders* of another. To *nosh* someone, either *off* or *out.*

eat breakfast backwards *v.* To *drive the porcelain bus, yoff, barf, sing a rainbow.*

eat cockroaches *1. v. 18thC.* To engage in the filthy, disgusting act of *self-pollution. 2. v.* To engage in the filthy, disgusting act of appearing on *I'm a Celebrity Get Me Out of Here.*

eat fancy cakes *v.* Of a gentleman, to have a tendency towards the *craftier* end of *butchery.* To *jump puddles*, to be a *ginger beer. 'It's a disgrace that the perfectly good word "gay" has been taken from us. Well I for one will not be joining the politically correct brigade and using polite euphemisms to describe these people and the things they get up to. There's no getting away from it, they eat fancy cakes, pure and simple.'* (letter from a Colonel in the *Daily Telegraph*, 2010).

eat humble cock *v.* Of a lady who has been involved in a disagreement with a gentleman friend, to acknowledge in the time-honoured manner that she may not have been right after all.

eating catfood by seven *phr.* A humorous way of describing the often embarrassing and regrettable outcome of acting on ill-thought-out *highdeas* entertained during the early hours of a pharmaceutically deranged social evening.

eating out of your gland *euph.* Descriptive of a second party who is docile enough to eat from an outstretched part of the body. *'You've got Mother Teresa eating out of your gland there, your holiness.'*

eating sushi off a barbershop floor *sim.* Performing *cumulonimbus* on a *pieman's wig.*

eatin' me's spinach, I's *exclam.* Useful phrase which can be uttered out of the side of the mouth while passing a *Thora* of such a massive circumference that one's face takes on the assymetrical physognomial mien of squint-eyed, steroid-abusing, pipe-smoking cartoon sailor Popeye for the duration of the process.

eat one's greens *v.* To do something one would really rather not do just to earn *brownie points* from a female partner, *eg.* Listen to her go on about her day, put some shelves up, pretend to turn down the volume on the Grand Prix.

eat out *1. v.* To consume a wide pizza served by a short Chancellor of the Exchequer in front of a gaggle of coughing photographers. *2. v.* To *lap fanny, dive muff, cumulonimbulate, don the beard, dine at the Y.*

eat out to help out *1. phr.* A government scheme to boost the country's Covid figures by encouraging the public to frequent disease-ridden restaurants at a temporarily discounted rate *2. n.* Philanthropically munching on a middle-aged neighbour's *ladygarden* to boost her self-esteem following a long-winded divorce.

eau de colon *n.* Rusty water, fizzy gravy.

eau de public toilette *n.* A piquant aroma. A perfect *farting gift* for a loved one.

eau de toilet duck *phr.* The classy aroma of a boot fair-bought fragrance pervading the air of such cultural hotspots as Newcastle's Bigg Market on a Friday night.

e-bagging *n.* Dangling your *scrotal portmanteau* in front of a web-cam to virtually *tea-bag* someone. *'Today's birthdays: Alphonso, Earl of Chester, 1273; Bev Bevan, ELO tub-thumper, 1944; Sir Ian Botham, e-bagger and UK trade ambassador, 1955.'*

eBaids *n.* The virulently infectious, deadly germs that must be scrubbed off the disease-ridden things bought on online auction sites before they can be used. From eBay + Aids. *'I like your new china tea service, Audrey.' 'Yes, it's Crown Derby. But we're not using it at the moment because I* *haven't got round to cleaning the eBaids off it yet.'*

Ebdon slide *1. n.* In snooker, careful positioning of the fingers on the table while cueing. *2. n.* In sex, careful positioning of the fingers on the lady's *bits* in order to expose the *Alien's face*.

Eccles cake *n.* A casually discarded *Eartha*. Named after local newspaper hack (name removed following legal advice) of the *Sussex Express* who, after a night on the strong cider, *shat* himself in the pub and shook it out of his trousers before ordering another pint of Biddenden's 9-percenter.

Eccles snake *n.* A penis with warts.

EC flags *n.* Big nipples. Also *bingo dabbers, blind cobbler's thumbs, chapel hat pegs, organ stops* and so on and so forth.

e-chimping *n.* Hurling *shit* at people electronically, *via* emailed corporate newsletters, press announcements, endless fucking reminders to leave "feedback", requests to wish people you barely know happy birthday, repeated invitations to join cunting LinkedIn *etc.*

eclipse girl *n.* A female lady in a pornographic film or magazine who, if you stare at her for too long, will make you go blind.

econnoisseur *n.* A budget-conscious erotic epicurean, who appreciates the benefits of the Freeman's catalogue bra pages and Smartprice tissues.

Ecosser *n.* A patriotic Scottish person who proudly declaims his national identity by affixing a French language sticker to the back of his Japanese car.

Eddie *n.* See *Stobart*.

Eddie Jordan gridwalk *n.* A prolonged and agonising period of social and/or conversational uncomfortableness. Named after the Old Man Steptoe lookalike Channel 4 F1 pundit's mortifyingly awkward and fruitless attempts to find anybody prepared to talk to him before a Grand Prix.

Edinburgh fringe *n. Scots. rhym. slang.* Minge. *'Demerara was powerless to resist. His eye burned into hers like a sapphire. His muscular tentacles enfolded her softly yielding body as she felt herself being swept away in a tempest of passion. 'It's no good, I can't hold on any longer,' Fernando whispered urgently, as he shot his thick black ink up her Edinburgh fringe.'* (from *The Lady Deep-sea Diver and the Octopus* by Barbara Cartland).

editing suite *n.* The part of a man's brain that is able to instantly store and arrange stock sexual imagery for future reference. The *mammary bank, wank bank. 'Look at the jugs on that filly, Hudson.' 'Yes Mr Bellamy sir, that's certainly one*

for the editing suite.'

e-dophile *n.* A web chatroom *nonce.* An internet *diddler. 'When I took my laptop in for repairs because I got custard in the keys, they did me for being an e-dophile and I ended up on Savile Row.'*

e-dummy *n.* A millennial's pacifier, *viz.* Their smartphone.

Edward II *euph.* A fiery, post-*Edwina ringpiece,* combined with severe stomach cramps, internal haemorrhaging and ice cold sweats. From the similar experience of the famous historical king, who was *arsed* with a red-hot poker by his wife's boyfriend, a situation which unsurprisingly led, shortly thereafter, to his demise.

Edward jizzer hands *n.* A man who keeps his *wanking spanners* busy.

Edward Woodward *onomat.* A bathtime *fart* named in honour of the deceased *Callan* thesp. A *bottle of olives, tottle, Bill Oddie, old faithful.*

Edwina *n.* A curry that is a real pain in the *arse.*

eel out of a welly, like shaking an *sim.* Phrase which can be used to describe the experience of having a *shit* that takes very little effort. An *otter off the bank. 'How was it for you, Mother Teresa?' 'Like shaking an eel out of a welly, your holiness.'*

effluent *adj.* Wealthy, but also a bit *shit. 'Brentwood in Essex has been named Britain's most effluent town.'*

E45 wank *n.* An act of *self pollution* utilising the popular low-friction dermatological unguent. An *E45 wank* has the added benefit of moisturising the *pink oboe,* especially important if one is suffering from a dry, chapped *cock* or eczema on or around the *farmer's hat.*

e-gasm *n.* A *web-grumble*-assisted *stack blow.*

egg and spooge race *n.* The rush to the doctor or chemist for an emergency *Vince Hill* the morning after an ill-judged liaison.

egg banjo *n.* The characteristic pose adopted when hot yolk spills out the bottom of an egg sandwich, with one hand holding the sandwich and the other making a strumming motion to cool it down.

egg-bound *1. adj.* Blocked of *dung-funnel,* constipated, *shit shy. 2. adj.* On your way to see an egg.

egg drop soup *n.* Home-made version of the classic Chinese dish, prepared by gentlemen in the bath.

egg hole *n.* The *fanny, quim, blurtch, clunge* or *clopper. 'Artist Gustave Courbet scandalised the French art establishment in 1866 when he unveiled his painting The Origin of the World. The controversial canvas, which is now on display at the Musée d'Orsay in Paris, is a graphic, close-up depiction of his muse and lover Joanna Hiffernan's egg hole.'*

(from *Civilisation* by Kenneth Clark).

egg in the nest *n.* A bald *noggin* which is still surrounded by a halo of hair, *eg.* The hemispherical glasses-strewn pate of late *Great Bald Head Race* scientist Professor Heinz Wolff.

egg in your pants *euph.* Discreet phrase used by a polite fellow when attempting to ascertain the last time a lady-friend *fell to the communists.* '*I'm sorry pet, but before this date goes any further, I simply must enquire as to the last time you laid an egg in your pants.*'

egg mcmuffin *n.* When a *bird guffs* up your nose while you are *dining at the Y.*

egg mcwhiff *n.* A particularly sulphurous mid-morning *air buffet* produced after breakfasting at a fast food restaurant.

egg sandwich anyone? *exclam. interrog.* Humorous and polite utterance following the *dropping of a gut.* See also *another scone vicar?; that hinge needs oiling etc.*

egg sandwich, dripping like an *sim.* Of a lady, to be sexually enfrothulated. Also *gooey at the fork, fizzing at the bung hole, dripping like a fucked fridge, dripping like a George Foreman grill, frothing like bottled Bass, wet as Dermot O'Leary's shirt, wetter than a cod's wetsuit, wetter than an otter's pocket, wetter than a fat bird's armpit, wetter than Meat Loaf's hankie, wetter than Lee Evans's suit, wetter than a bad plumber's mop* or *wetter than a turfer's knee.*

egg sandwich?, who fancies an *exclam. interrog.* A witty warning to neighbours or workmates that a foulsome miasma will shortly be expressed from one's *nether throat.* And that perhaps it might be worth opening a window.

egg sarnies, make *v.* To *relax in a gentleman's way.*

eggs Benidorm *n.* Thoroughly scrambled and fertilised ova following a *Spanglish* holiday *fuck-for-all.*

egg-tapping *n.* Form of mild sado-masochism in which the *clockweights* are struck lightly with a teaspoon.

egg timer *n.* Shortly before a sulphurous *dropped hat*, when inner rumblings begin to herald the start of the countdown.

egg white cannon *n.* A 4-inch *blue-veined blunderbuss* loaded with two leaden *balls.*

eggycentre *n.* The source of a cataclysmic posterior detonation. *Browned zero.*

eggy pop *1. n.* A brief, yet pungently sulphurous, *air omelette* that could seriously vitiate a bystander's lust for life. *2. n.* Any beer that has a proven impact on one's *Camillas, eg.* Robinson's Unicorn

Best Bitter..

eggy soldier *n.* The result of taking a *dip* while the *red flag is flying.* A *barber's pole.*

egotestical *adj.* Descriptive of one who is prone to talking *bollocks* about himself.

e-gret *adj.* A feeling of self-reproach experienced following any ill-considered internet transaction. '*E-grets, I've had a few.*' (Pete Townshend, song lyric).

e-gypsy *n.* A person who can't make up their mind which ISP to use, resulting in your e-mails to them always being returned. A wandering nomad on the information superhighway.

Egyptian PT *1. n. milit.* Sleep. *2. n.* Masturbation.

eh?-lister *n.* A celebrity you've never heard of. Usually a "Hollyoaks star".

Eiffel Tower, do the *v.* Of a pair of professional footballers engaged in a *spitroast* with a lucky young lady, to make eye contact and exchange a high five, thus creating the characteristic outline of the famous Parisian pylon.

eighteen spoker *n.* A particularly hairy woman's *arsehole* that resembles a tiny bicycle wheel, hopefully without a derailleur gear in the middle.

eighteen wheeler *n.* A *turd* of such length that it runs a significant risk of jack-knifing in the *pan.* A *Stobart, brown Sovine.*

eight-seven-two *euph.* Manchester colloquialism for the *filth*, based around their erstwhile telephone number 0161 872 5050.

e-jac *n. Relaxing in a gentlemanly way* with the help of electronic technology.

ejacisfaction *n.* The momentarily blissful, tranquil feeling experienced following *one o'er the thumb.* Just before the self-loathing, crushing shame, and *wangst* kicks in.

ejacu-early *n.* The opposite of *ejacu-late.* That which is *spaffed* into their Y-fronts by those over-excitable unfortunates who typically *spend their money before they get to the shop, pot the black on the break, let the passengers off the bus before the stop etc.*

e-jaculate *v.* To discharge the *mutton musket* over some form of computerised *grumble.* '*What's good for getting e-jaculate out of a Macbook keyboard?*'

ejaculater seat *n.* Computer chair.

ejaculatte *n.* A cup of coffee made by a young male barista which takes a little longer than usual. Also *fappuccino.* '*Here's your ejaculatte, Mr Coren. Sorry for your wait, only I was doing my trousers back up.*'

ejaculee *n.* He whom has *spoff-offed.*

ejamulation *n.* The inadvertent release of a sudden, premature spurt of jam when biting into a doughnut.

ejector seat *n.* A violent early morning evacuation that exits the *arsehole* with such force that it causes one to lift vertically off the seat and smash into the ceiling. A *neckbreaker* or *U-bend straightener.*

elbow *euph.* The sad and desperate situation a man can find himself in when hitched to a lady with a low sexual appetitie. From the eponymous pop band's lyric, *viz.* "Throw those curtains wide, one day like this a year would see me right."

elbow bender *n.* A *bar fly*, a *boozer.*

elderflower *1. n* An ingredient put into cordial. *2. n* An old maid's mothy *clopper.*

Eleanor Rigby's funeral *euph.* A mutually unsat-isfying sexual encounter, *ie.* One at which, in the words of the famous Beatles song, "nobody came".

electric chair *1. n.* A device used by the authorities to keep the number of black men with special educational needs in Texas at a manageable level. *2. n.* The last resort seat in a pub next to the most crashing bore in the establishment.

electric lemonade *n.* A hallucinogenic, West-coun-try scrumpy cider. Also known locally as *Tone Vale Tonic,* after the former Somerset County Asylum that housed many of its devotees.

electric relaxation *1. n.* Title of a 1993 song by hip-hop group A Tribe Called Quest. *2. n.* Solitary leisure time activity for someone in possession of a battery-powered *neck massager* until it goes flat.

electric soup *n. Scots.* Nourishing home-brewed beverage made by bubbling coal gas through milk.

electric spaghetti *n. Spunky string.*

electric twitch *n.* Involuntary jerk of the head displayed by *grumble flick* starlets upon receiving a faceful of *jitler.* Named after the similar reflexive spasm which can be achieved by stroking the bars of an electric fire.

elepants *n.* Jumbo-sized ladies' trunks.

elephant gun, the *n.* When a *fellow* has manfully managed to abstain from firing off his *single-bar-relled snot gun* for a week prior to an amorous engagement, the redoubtable blast of fermented, cheesy *spluff* that hits his lucky *nosher* squarely between the eyes shortly after – or, indeed, just before – she begins operations.

Elephant Man's hat *sim.* Descriptive of a very spacious *fanny.* A *clown's pocket, hippo's yawn, donkey's earhole.*

elephant nudging a tree, like an *sim.* Phrase used to describe the act of doggedly persisting with sexual relations despite suffering from *brewer's droop.*

elephants *adj. rhym. slang. Refreshed as a fart.* From elephant's trunk = drunk.

elephant's ears *n.* Enormous, grey, flappy flaps.

Huge *Keith Burtons.*

elephant's eyelashes *n.* The vigorous, jumbo-sized nasal hairs which Mother Nature inexplicably deems an essential *bird*-pulling accoutrement for males once they reach the age of thirty or so.

elephant's foot *1. n.* Nickname given to a highly radioactive, hardened mass of corium found in the basement of the Chernobyl power station following the nuclear reactor's meltdown in 1986. *2. n.* A potentially lethal *Andrew* with a long half-life that is passed the day after a heavy session on the ale. *'I'd give that toilet 10 minutes if I were you, love. I've just done an elephant's foot in there.'*

elephant's funeral, farting like an *sim.* When trying to *fire up dropzone two* quietly and discreetly, such as at a new ladyfriend's house, but your *bum gums* tighten up from nerves so all that is emitted is a long, mournful, trumpeting wail, of the sort that might be uttered by a recently bereaved pachyderm.

elephant shit in the in the room, the *euph.* A problem that everyone is aware of yet no-one mentions, that has really started to stink.

elephant's kneecap, fanny like an *sim.* Useful phrase that can be used when describing the *pudenda* of a female who has attained the twilight years of her life. *'Fucking hell, your majesty. No offence, like, but you've got a fanny like an elephant's kneecap.'*

elephant's leg *n.* The sweating grey thing revolving behind the counter in a kebab shop.

elephant's toenails *n.* Big, brown, crusty nipples on a *high miler* who, one might reasonably surmise, has been round the block a few times.

elephant stopper *n.* A massive *fowling piece.* A *member for Ealing North.*

elephant, the *n.* Penile puppetry diversion. An amusing and charming simulacrum of the popular grey-skinned, gampstand-footed pachyderm achieved using a chap's *generative member* and his pocket linings pulled inside out. A great way to break the ice at parties or, indeed, to get yourself placed on the sex offenders' register.

Elevenerife *n. prop.* The fictitious holiday destination of the sort of *twat* who always has to go one better than everyone else. *'Been on your holidays, Claude? Where'd you go, then?' 'We had a week in Tenerife, Sir Alan.' 'Oh yeah? I just flew back from a fortnight in Elevenerife. In a solid gold jumbo jet. And my suitcases are made of diamonds. Can't you lower your chair any more?'*

eleven-pointer *n.* An altogether successful date.

Red, pink, brown (mouth, *fanny*, *freckle*).

Elsa, do an *v.* To *befoul* oneself, down below and round the back. From the words sung by Queen Elsa in *Frozen*, *viz.* "Let it go, let it go, can't hold it back any more", shortly after constructing her magnificent ice palace which appears to contain no lavatory facilities.

Elsie Tanner Montana *n.* Another phrase for an ageing woman who adopts the fashions of someone much younger. Also *atomic mutton*, *nana Kournikova*, *Thora bird*.

Elton John *n.* A *Dutch oven*. From the lyrics to the former Reginald Dwight's 1983 single *I Guess That's Why They Call it the Blues*, *viz.* "Rolling like thunder / Under the covers".

Elton John with a fanny, he's like *sim.* Descriptive of someone who obviously doesn't know what they are doing. *'Have you seen that (insert name of unpopular footballer here)? He's like Elton John with a fanny.'*

Elvis *n.* A *shit* that requires so much effort to force out that one almost has a stroke. The oppposite of a *life affirmer*. *'Are you okay? You look terrible, your majesty.' 'I'll be fine, Bishop. That Boxing Day Elvis just took it out of me, though.'*

Elvis impersonator *1. n.* A person who passes himself off as the late king of rock'n'roll. *2. n.* One engaged in an epic fight to the death with a *knotsplitter*. *3. n.* One who disappears into the lavatory for a worryingly long time.

Elvis killer *n.* A big old breached *toilet baby.*

Elvis's collar, stiffer than *sim.* A measure of the rigidity of a *diamond cutter.*

Elvis's last turd, as hard as *1. sim.* An estimation of a person's toughness. *See also hard as a policeman's knock; hard as Captain Scott's last morning stiffy; hard as Tarzan's feet. 'I reckon I could take that Mike Tyson now he's an old cunt.' 'Bollocks mate. He may be old but he's still as hard as Elvis's last turd.' 2. sim.* Difficult. Also as hard as *Steven Hawking's homework* or hard as *a Chinese wordsearch.*

Elvis's leg *n.* The onset of the *vinegar strokes* while *fucking* upright in a doorway, bus shelter or taxi queue. Often accompanied by an "Uh-huh-huh" vocalisation and involuntary curling of the lip.

Elvis's legs *n.* Spasmoidal, numb-shanked gait affected after being sat on the *bum sink* for an hour or two perusing the *Autotrader.*

embalmer, the *n.* Specialised wrestling move whereby one's good lady's stomach gets covered with *sex wee.*

embark on an epic journey of self discovery *v.* To

have a *Barclays.*

Embassy No. 2 *1. n.* A cigarette/defecation combination performed in workplace toilets up and down the country. *'Keep an eye on runways six to fourteen for me, will you, Mrs Depledge? I'm just nipping out for an Embassy No. 2.' 2. n.* An urgent *shit*, usually prompted by the first puff one takes on the first *Harry Rag* of the day.

embooziasm *1. n.* Dynamic fervour for a project consequent upon a certain amount of strong liquor having been taken on board. Also *embooziastic*. *'The minister was originally very embooziastic that these negotiations could be successfully concluded with the minimum of fuss, but now he's sobered up and decided to resign.' 2.* n. The sudden urge, having consumed half a glass of sherry, to drink to excess. *'This whole quarantine business has given your father a renewed embooziasm for metal polish, children.'*

embuggerance *n.* Anything that causes obstruction or annoyance. *'And Peter Sallis's underpowered Austin A30 is going to be a real embuggerance for Jenson Button as the Mercedes driver attempts to put in a quick lap to get his car on the front row in tomorrow's race.'*

emergency entrance *n.* The *back passage*, utilised when the missus has *got mice*. Also known as *The Flying Horse.*

emergency handbrake *n.* The act of suddenly bringing an act of frenzied *relaxation* to a halt while watching such programmes as *Hollyoaks* or *Neighbours*, when the shot cuts from a *fit* piece of *tussage* to a *vinegar Joe* such as Jack from the Dog in the Pond, or Harold from the General Store.

emergency stop *1. n.* In a driving test, the moment when the candidate is required to bring his vehicle to a sudden halt while maintaining full control at all times. *2. n.* The act of suddenly pressing the *dead man's handle* upon hearing the missus's key in the front door while watching a *noddy film*. It would be a good idea to pull your trousers up too, if sufficient time is available. *3. n.* A dramatic and impressive skid down the side of the bowl. Typically accompanied by a strong smell of burning rubber.

emergency stop button *n.* The *bollocks.* From the fact that a sharp blow to the *knackers* will instantly render any man into a state of agonised immobility, whatever he happens to be doing. *'Welcome to Fight Club. The first rule of Fight Club is: you do not talk about Fight Club. The second rule of Fight Club is: you DO NOT talk about Fight Club! Third rule of Fight Club: don't kick anyone in* *the emergency stop button. It's just not nice.'*

emergency strop *n.* An unexpected fit of menstrual temper. A *tammy huff, tamtrum* or *blobstrop*. *'Jesus, Dave, how did you get your black eyes, broken nose, missing teeth, stitches and whiplash?' 'The missus done an emergency strop when I wasn't expecting it.'*

Emersons *n. prop. medic. rhym. slang.* Chalfonts, named in honour of late prog rock keyboardist Keith. From Emerson Lake & Palmers = farmers. *'Jeez mate, I'm having problems here. Me Emersons are hanging down further than Rick Wakeman's cape.'*

emissionary position *n.* A coital arrangement which is guaranteed to bring things to some sort of conclusion when all else has failed and both participants are starting to get bored. *'It's no good, June, me spigot's starting to go soft again. And I think me back's about to give out too.' 'Okay Terry. My old lobster pot's had enough as well. Let's just switch to the good old emissionary position so you can tip your filthy concrete and we can get off to sleep.'*

emission control *n.* Any deliberately unerotic mental countdown practised in order to prevent a premature *blast off*. *'Why do you keep muttering that list of the various team sheets and scores from Celtic's 1970 European Cup run, Rod?' 'It's just a bit of emission control, Penny.'*

Emmas *rhym. slang.* Nobbies, farmers, ceramics, lever arches. From Emma Freuds = Adrian Chiles.

Emmerdale undertaker, busier than an *sim.* Said of someone who never sits still. From the popular early evening ITV soap opera set in a sleepy Yorkshire hamlet with a higher murder rate than Caracas.

emmeroids *n.* *Adrians* suffered by the sort of people who sit around watching re-runs of old soap operas on daytime TV. From Emmerdale + haemmorhoids.

emotional crotch *n.* A girlfriend.

empathy flush *n.* A rare and touching gesture of solidarity amongst men ensconced in adjoining lavatory cubicles, whereby a fellow responds to a courteously applied *sympathy flush* with one of his own, to indicate support for the original flusher in his time of difficulty.

Emperor Minge *euph.* One who is a wow with the ladies, *eg.* The late Hugh Hefner, the late Peter Stringfellow, Rod Stewart, Ken Barlow. A man who seems to *have a chocolate knob.*

empire of dirt *n.* A lifetime's accumulation of *mucky books, eg.* The contents of Philip Larkin's attic.

emptier than Orville's arsehole *sim.* Vacant,

unoccupied. *'I went in the Dog and Hammer for last orders and the place was emptier than Orville's arsehole.'*

empty headlock, fanny like an *sim.* Said of a cavernous and accommodating *clunge* that is reminiscent of the empty void left when a wrestler frees himself from the eponymous underarm hold. Also *arse like an empty headlock*. *'What can I say about my next guest? She's one of the last great stars from the golden age of Hollywood and after nine husbands, she must have a fanny like an empty headlock. Ladies and gentlemen, please give a big Pebble Mill at One welcome to Miss Zsa Zsa Gabor.'*

emptying the handbag *n.* A particularly satisfying rectal *clear-out* following a prolonged bout of constipation. Named after the television laxative advert in which a *backed-up* young lady smilingly tips a load of food out of her reticule before heading off to a party.

emptying the spam folder *v.* A spot of single-handed *hard-drive* maintenance.

empty legs *1. euph.* Figure of speech used by cyclists to describe fatigue. *2. phr.* Said by one who has *wanked* himself to a standstill, *eg.* During a protracted session of *online research* whilst *self-isolating*.

empty movement *1. n.* Railway terminology; running a train with no passengers in order to get it to where it needs to be for the next journey. *2. n.* When you sit down to give birth to a stout *mudchild* but all you get is a load of gas and air.

empty nester *1. n.* A shattered husk whose kids have grown up and left home. *2. n.* A light-footed fellow returning from the *bogs* after *dropping* the 3lbs of *shopping* which has been festering in his colon for days.

empty one's back *v.* To *crimp off a tail*, to *drop a length of dirty spine*.

empty one's beer sack *v.* To go for a *piss* in a pub.

empty the bins *v.* To *go off*. *'The Holy Father condemns as anathema all artificial forms of contraception. The only means of birth control allowable within the Roman church is the practice of ejaculatio extra-vagio. That is, to whip the Charlie out at the vinegar strokes and empty the bins onto the missus's gunt.'* (Papal Edict, 1988).

empty the boot *v.* To *drop off the shopping*.

empty the brown bin *v.* To perform a dolphin-unfriendly act of waste disposal on the same day. Except if it's a bank holiday.

empty the caboose *v.* To excrete, pass motions, *drop the kids off at the pool etc.*

empty threat *n.* A terrifyingly loud *fart* that mysteriously fails to assault one's nasal passages. The opposite of an *SBD*.

Emu's beak *n.* A *bird's snapper* that can suddenly, and unexpectedly, turn ugly. And make your shoe fall off.

enamel bucket *n.* A big, dry, cold, rattly *fanny*.

Ena Sharples' mouth *n.* A disapproving and puckered *rusty bullet hole*. Commonly seen on *grumble mag* models bending over a snooker table. Also *Dot Cotton's mouth*, the *fifties tea towel holder.*

enchilardarse *n.* Someone who has achieved *plumper* status through enthusiastic consumption of spicy Mexican comestibles.

encore une fois! *exclam.* A rousing francophone announcement in the style of the famous sample featured in the 1997 song of the same name by *twattish* German band Sash, to be uttered after a healthy *René Descartes.*

encumbered *adj.* Hampered by an unwieldy *mancumber.* '*Mr Faraday, kindly switch off your electromagnet at once. Prince Albert is so encumbered by its electromotive flux that he can barely fucking walk.*'

encyclopaedo *n.* A childless adult with a suspiciously comprehensive knowledge of the *High School Musical* films, *Glee*, the life and works of Justin Bieber, or any other bollocks that you really shouldn't know anything about if you're more than twelve.

end-of-level wank *n.* An act of filthy *self pollution* undertaken in order to calm the nerves sufficiently to proceed past a particularly tricky portion of a console game. '*I must have tried a hundred times to complete that section, but as soon as I had an end-of-level wank it was like taking candy from a baby.*'

end of terrace *n.* A less-than-partial *panhandle.* An erection that shares many of the attributes of a *semi*, but lacks some of its street credibility.

end of that bottle of HP, well that's the *exclam.* Phrase to be used following the production of an exceptionally squirty-sounding *heart to heart,* that may or may not have resulted in a *follow through.* So called from its audible resemblance to the noises made by the final dregs of a heavily depleted sauce bottle being squeezed over a *cholesterol special.*

end of the Morning Fresh, sounds like the *1. exclam.* Phrase used when running out of the eponymous cheapo washing up liquid, as one squeezes the last of the nasty yellow stuff through the nozzle. *2. euph.* Phrase used typically following a visit to Newcastle's world-famous Curry Capital restaurant, as one forces the final drops of nasty yellow liquid through one's *nozzle.* Unlikely

to be accompanied by a wholesome aroma of lemony freshness.

enemy at the gate *n.* A particularly insistent *copper bolt* which makes its presence felt at a somewhat inconvenient time, *eg.* When one is getting married, going in for a job interview or about to lay siege to Stalingrad in 1942. '*Do you, Diana Frances take Charles Philip Arthur George as your lawfully wedded husband, to have and to hold from this day forward, for better, for worse, in sickness and in health, to love and to cherish, till suspicious death do you part in about sixteen years or so?*' '*Sorry bish, got to dash. I've got an enemy at the gate.*'

energy saver *n.* A *wet dream*, because it furnishes the mental stimulation of full intercourse without any of the sweat. All the benefits of VR *Frankie* without the cost or *twattish* apparel.

en garde! *exclam. Fr.* Said (whilst lifting one's arm D'Artagnan-style to mimic the raising of a sword) to warn an opponent to take a defensive position prior to *letting one fly.*

Engelberts *rhym. slang. Eartha Kitts*, squirts.

English batsman *n. Aus.* Someone who doesn't spend very long at the *crease.* A *two push Charlie,* a *two stroke joke,* a *one pump chump.*

English disease, the *n.* Homosexuality, as defined by the French.

English lit *n. rhym. slang.* A *caustic wit.* '*I'm off for an English lit. Here's Garry with the sport.*'

English overcoat *n.* The French equivalent of the English *French letter.* A *Coney Island whitefish, cheesepipe clingfilm, jubber ray.*

engorgement ring *n.* A mythical item of betrothal jewellery promised to a lady in return for getting one's *nuts* emptied.

engorgeous *adj.* Sexually alluring. '*I hope you don't mind me saying so, but I think you're absolutely engorgeous. As a token of my esteem, kindly accept this bouquet of flowers and a photograph of my cock and balls. Please don't call the police as I am already on a caution. Yours sincerely, Lord Archer of Weston super Mare.*'

engorgeous *adj.* Sufficiently alluring as to engender tumescence in the *membrum virile.*

engrossed in the ladies' tennis final, I'm *exclam.* An urgent, panic-infused rejoinder to the wife/children/in-laws/neighbours/fire brigade that they must not, under any circumstances, enter the room in which a fellow is currently ensconced. An injunction that is typically delivered in a rather high-pitched, strained voice and is often accompanied by the muffled sound of trousers being pulled back up and frantic wrestling with a zip. A variation on *enjoying the Hollyoaks*

Omnibus. 'Darling, where are you? I want to show you my new Manolos.' 'I'm in my study, darling. But don't come in, I'm engrossed in the ladies' tennis final.' 'Is that all? For a moment there I thought you were having a wank.'

enhammered *adj.* Finding someone sexually attractive, even though they look like a *bag of knuckles*, purely because one has consumed a life-threatening amount of alcohol.

enjoy nature *v.* To take a slow, relaxed *dump* with the exhaust fan switched off. To wallow in the *country air.*

Ennis elbow *n. medic.* Type of right arm-based repetitive strain injury suffered by a male who has been *relaxing in a gentleman's* way in seven different styles during the course of a single day's viewing of the Olympic women's heptathlon competition.

Enoch bowels/Enochs *n. medic.* The *runs, two bob bits* or *fizzy gravy* mixed with "rivers of blood" from an internal pile issue or a particularly robust curry. Named in honour of the horrible late pensioners' favourite 1970s politician.

enormity of the situation *euph.* A *pan handle.* *'Come on, love. Why can't you grasp the enormity of the situation?'*

enormous fan of Eurovision *euph.* A fellow who *sews his own buttons.*

enough to make one's blood run beige *phr.* A nonplussed reaction to something deeply dull or bland. *'This exhibition of watercolour landscapes by the King is enough to make my blood run beige, it really is.'*

en-pointe *1. adj. Fr.* Classical ballet term whereby a dancer supports all their body weight on the tips of their fully extended feet. *2. adj.* Descriptive of the female equivalent of the male *jester's shoes*; an involuntary stretching of the toes heralding the onset of the feminine *organism. 'Zoom in on Roxxy for the money shot, camera two. She's going en pointe.'*

en pointe piss *n.* A public *Rick Witter gypsy's kiss* taken in the tippy-toed style of Rudolf Nureyev in an attempt to avoid the trouser cuffs coming into contact with the half-inch deep lake of orange *wazz* in front of the trough/urinal.

'Enry's 'ammer *n.* A *diamond-cutting* erectivita-ton of such proportions that it deprives the brain of blood and leaves the owner in a semi-coma-tose state, as if he had been hit around the head by deceased boxing champ Henry Cooper's trademark left hook. About forty years ago.

ensure the juices are running clear *v.* On a game *bird,* to perform a handy check that her *meat* is ready for *eating.*

ENT *1. abbrev.* Hospital department specialising in audiometry, tympanonometry, electronysta-mography, mastoid disease treatments and sinus problems. *2. n.* A *shit* or *fart* that attacks the ears, nose and throat.

Enterprise transporter accident *euph.* A nice looking *bird* with lousy *knockers* accompanied by a ugly *bird* with great *knockers.*

entertainment system *n.* One's ladyfriend's *tits, arse* and *fanny. 'What's that in your bag, Dr Von Hagens?' 'Just an entertainment system. I'm taking it home for the weekend.'*

enthusiagasm *n.* An expression of overly effusive ardor. *'Did you see the Great British Bake-Off? Paul Hollywood had an enthusigasm over a lemon meringue pie.'*

entrance exam *n.* The general prodding, rubbing, squeezing, poking, pinching, sniffing *and what-have-you* that a fussy lady carries out on a prospective paramour's *giggle stick* before eventually allowing him *on the nest.*

entwanglement *n.* The unfortunate entrapment of a chap's *matrimonial equipment* when he rolls over in bed, or wears supermarket jeans on a car journey of more than 15 minutes.

Ephraim Monk *1. n. prop.* The fictional brewery that owns the Woolpack pub in *Emmerdale.* *2. rhym. slang.* Gentleman's spendings. From Ephraim Monk = pineapple chunk.

epilog *1. n.* Just when you think you've finished *dropping the kids off the pool* and cleaned up after them, then another one emerges as if from nowhere: that's the *epilog.* A *second sitting.* *2. n.* A large calibre, late night *flashing light* that feels like it may induce a seizure.

epissany *n.* Inexplicable solution to a hitherto unanswerable pub quiz question, unexpectedly arrived at by someone just returning from the toilets. *'Yeah, I had an epissany in there. I was idly looking at my smartphone when it suddenly came to me that the theme to The Man with the Golden Gun (1974) was composed by John Barry and Don Black, and performed by Lulu.'*

equipment *n.* Either a lady's *headlamps* or a gentleman's *unmentionables,* and occasionally both. *'Would it be it alright if I stuck my equipment between your equipment, love?' 'No you can't stick your equipment between my equipment. Now, you've already got your eight favourite records, the Bible and the complete works of Shakespeare. Which other book are you going to take to your Desert Island?'*

erasure *1. n.* British synth-pop band of the 1980s,

who may or may not have been the same as Yazoo. *2. n.* The act of female masturbation, *viz.* "rubbing one out".

erectile vomiting *n.* *Shooting* your *load,* a lot.

e-rection *n.* Tumescence achieved via the medium of internet *Frankie.*

erection section *n.* The top shelf of a newsagents, where the *pornucopia* is kept.

erectoral fraud *n.* The duplicitous practice of stuffing one's undies or codpiece with socks, vegetables, Swiss rolls *etc.,* in order to give a misleading impression of one's natural endowment.

erector scale *n.* Scientific system for the measurement and classification of the intensity of male arousal. Similar to the Richter scale but with *bone-ons* instead of earthquakes.

erectory enquiries *n.* Tentatively prodding one's slumbering missus in the small of the back with the *motorcycle kickstand* in order to ascertain the probability of *a bit of the other.*

Eric Liddle's home straight *euph.* The final, agonising moments of the *vinegar strokes,* when a *self harmer* throws back his head and opens his mouth wide in a style which is eerily reminiscent of the 1924 Olympic 400 metres Champion, as immortalised in the film *Chariots of Fire.*

Eric Pickle's running shoes, seen less action than *sim.* Description of an enforced and prolonged period of celibacy. Also *Eamonn Holmes's rowing machine, Bamber Gascoigne's swearbox.*

Ernie *n.* A lucky chap blessed with the ability to ejaculate within seconds of commencing sexual intercourse. Coined in honour of Benny Hill's famous comedy song about "the fastest milkman in the West".

Eros *n.* The pose that must be struck when *pissing* in a toilet with no lock on the door, precariously balancing on one leg with the other holding the door shut. *Dickram yoga.*

escape from alcotramp *v.* To suddenly spot something fascinating in a shop window across the street when approaching an animated *Harold Ramp.*

escape sub *n.* A technologically advanced brown, sea-going vessel in which an evil hangover makes its getaway. An *alcopoop.*

escort vehicle *n.* A *rabbit tod* with flashing yellow lights that precedes an *underpantechnicon.* Also *pace car, champagne cork.*

ESD *abbrev.* Eat Shitty Dick. To *smoke a pink cigar* fresh from *kak canyon. Hot karl, ATM.*

eskiho*n.* A girl who wears *puggboots* and a mini-skirt, an unacceptably sexist and offensive term which has no place in a respectable publication.

eskimoing *n.* Ice docking.

eskimo's glove *n.* Warm, furry mitten that smells of fish and can accommodate one's whole hand. Not unlike a large vagina.

eskimo's hotpot *n.* A steaming, freshly baked *shit* in deep snow. *'I'm just going outside for an eskimo's hotpot. I may be some time.'*

espresso *n.* A *quickie* gratefully received from a stranger in a lay-by or motorway service station, which wakes up a fatigued lorry driver, traffic policeman or commercial traveller so that he can continue his journey with a smile on his face.

espressos *n.* Petite *boobs* requiring only a brassiere furnished with "small cups". Traditionally topped with creamy foam.

essential maintenance *euph.* What a gent undertakes regularly to ensure that all his vital functions are in working order. A *wee* and a *wank.*

Essex breakfast *n.* The morning after pill.

Essex gap *n.* The *Toblerone tunnel* at the top of a pair of knock-off leggings. The *Dartford Tunnel.*

Essex tartan *n.* Burberry.

estate car *n.* Acne carriage.

estibate *v.* To perform a rough calculation as to whether one has enough time for a *wank.*

estimate the birth girth *v.* To perform the first act of *coitus* following childbirth. *Stirring the paint with a toothpick,* post-natal *last hotdog in the tin.*

Eston tuxedo *n.* An item of clothing reserved for special occasions (weddings, court appearances *etc.*), as sported by inhabitants of the eponymous district of the Teesside Riviera. See also *Merthyr threepiece.*

ET *euph.* When your *earthing cable* hits the water while still connected to your *fifties tea towel holder.* Possibly a reference to the fictional Gail-faced alien's long finger, but who knows? Also *bridger, bottom log.*

etch-a-sketch *v.* To attempt to draw a smile on a woman's face by simultaneously twiddling both of her nipples. *Finding Radio Luxembourg, come in Tokyo.*

etch-a-wretch *n.* A tattooist. *'That's a horrible tattoo you've got there off the etch-a-wretch in the precinct, Shane. But don't worry. I think I should be able to cover it up with a big swastika.'*

eternity leave *n.* The sack. *'My boss caught me photocopying some woman's arse on the office Xerox machine, and sent me on eternity leave. What's more, she says she's going to make sure I never get a job in a mortuary ever again.'*

Ethel *1. n. rhym. slng.* An act of *self abuse.* From Ethel Merman = Sherman tank = wank. *'Where* *is he? He's due on the balcony to bless the crowds in thirty seconds.' 'Don't worry, cardinal. He's just went in the bog for a quick Ethel over the letters in the Daily Sport.'* 2. *euph.* A person in your circle of friends who is known to be under-endowed in the *trouser department.* From the *EastEnders* character of the same name, who never stopped going on about her "little willy". Until she died in 2005, obviously. *'Born on this day: Haystacks Calhoun, American wrestler, 1934; Sir Terry Wogan, Irish radio and television presenter, 1938; Jack Straw MP, Parliamentary Ethel, 1946.'*

Ethelbrown the Ready *n.* A pretender to the *porcelain throne.* A *King Richard* in waiting.

ethically sauced 1. *adj.* Inebriated after consuming Fairtrade organic biodynamic wines, as opposed to Diamond White. 2. *adj.* Inebriated after consuming *trampagne,* but having actually purchased it as opposed to stealing it. *'Say what you like about those unconscious twelve-year-olds in the park, vicar, but at least they're ethically sauced.'*

ethics girl *n.* The kind of girl who doesn't *fuck* on a first date, won't *do it* in a car or shop doorway and wouldn't *swallow* even if one could get her to suck it in the first place. The antithesis of an Essex girl.

E3 3JY 1. *phr.* Postcode for Bromley-by-Bow in the East End of London; the location of "Bow Locks" on the River Lee Navigation, and hence 2. *n.* Nonsense. *'Don't talk a load of old E3 3JY, you fucking cock-end.'*

eticlit *n.* The observance of rules of correct decorum when *dining at the Captain's table.*

Eton leapfrog *n. Bottery.*

ET's finger *n.* A long, knobbly *bot dog.*

euphemersity *n.* An educational institution which has been promoted beyond its abilities. *'There's absolutely nothing to worry about. Your surgeon has a diploma from Treforest Tech, one of the country's leading euphemersities.'*

euphijism *n.* A word so laden with erotic potency that it has a young gentleman's *Harry Monk up and over like a pan of milk* left on a high flame. For example, the word "blow" when Lauren Bacall done it in *To Have and Have Not* (1944).

eureka fingers *n.* The condition of the digits following a *breakthrough* in the bathroom. Also known as a *brown ballerina* or *Kermit's collar.*

event horizon *n.* Something to do with black holes and dark matter. You can make this one up yourselves.

ever given turd *n.* Named in honour of the Panama-registered container ship that ran aground perpendicular to the flow of traffic within the Suez Canal in March 2021 (it was only stuck

there a week, it says here), causing a blockage of the inland waterway that impacted world trade, a lengthy *Sir Douglas* jammed across the *Denis Howells.*

everlasting bog stopper *n.* A *Meat Loaf's daughter* so gigantic that it permanently blocks the U-bend and you have to sell the house.

everlasting gobstopper 1. *n.* Strange confection invented by fictitious, health & safety-averse chocolate magnate Willy Wonka. 2. *n.* Ten inches of thick, choking *cock.* 4. *n.* Something that someone could break their teeth on. The *clockweights, knackers, plums.*

everlasting job-stopper *n.* A facial tattoo.

everlasting, the 1. *n.* A song from the Manic Street Preachers's 1998 album *This Is My Truth Tell Me Yours.* 2. *n.* A *shite* that is still stinking out the house a full five hours after it was *sent to the beach.*

everybody likes a wank but nobody likes a wanker *exclam.* A wise epigram that sounds even better in Latin: "glubere omnes amant, gluptores autem oderunt".

every dark clout has a silver lining *prov.* An optimistic phrase that reflects on the fact that even the most hirsute *beaver* can nevertheless prove copacetic.

everyone's a critic *exclam.* A waspish apophthegm to celebrate a raucous *Bronx cheer* from the *nether throat.*

everything but the girl 1. *n.* Hull-based 90s pop duo who hit the *Billboard Hot 100* in 1995. 2. *n.* A sophisticated act of *relaxation* incorporating low lights, soft music and a bottle of wine. *Romancing the bone, one-man orgy.*

everything everywhere all at once 1. *n.* Title of an Oscar-winning 'absurdist comedy-drama' film. 2. *n.* An *airtight.* See also *join in the applause, Popeye.*

Eve's pudding 1. *n.* A British dessert made with apple and sponge cake, which is traditionally eaten with custard. They do a nice one at Marksies. 2. *n.* A Biblical term for a lady's *undercarriage,* which is also traditionally eaten with custard.

eviction notice 1. *n.* Legal warning of an imminent tenancy termination, before you get thrown out by your landlord. 2. *n.* A legally enforceable *Bengal tiger* stirring in the guts. *'I've just received three minutes' Eviction Notice on yesterday's chicken bhuna. Now here's Carol with today's weather.'*

evil Mr Whippy machine *euph.* Descriptive of when one's *cigar cutter* becomes the diabolical equivalent of an industrial ice cream dispenser, typically the morning after a night on export strength lager and a sizeable *Ruby Murray,* dispensing a potent, hot, caustic, coiled *length* *of dirty spine* into the *pan* followed by a couple of chocolate flakes and a generous dollop of monkey blood.

exam shits *n. medic.* Excessive diarrhoea caused by a student's examinations week diet of Red Bull, Pro-Plus and cups of tea. Examples can be found in varsity *crappers* throughout the land, not least those in the basement of the John Rylands Library at the University of Manchester.

exasturbate *v.* To make an already difficult situation even more fraught through an involuntary deposit in the *wank bank*. *'I already got the massive horn every time she spoke to me, but the other lunchtime she exasturbated things by talking about her tits for a whole hour. Jesus, my nuts were like two tins of Dulux Brilliant White all afternoon. So I just sign here do I, officer?'*

excalibird *n.* A magnificent *piece* that a chap manages to *pull* successfully, against all the odds.

excalibur *1. n.* A magic *turd* of legendary proportions that rises eerily out of the water in a mist-shrouded toilet. *2. n. prop.* A mythically potent *pork sword* that is too large for a dirty lady to draw forth from her lover's flies in one go.

excalibut *n.* Gentleman's Mach 3 razor clogged up with his girlfriend's *trouser twiglets.*

excessorise *v.* To adorn oneself with a plethora of bangles, chains and dangly earrings *etc.*, in a vain attempt to distract attention from one's *fugly* face.

Exchange & Mart *1. n.* A magazine with too many adverts, if you can imagine such a thing, which hasn't been printed since 2009. *2. v. rhym. slang.* To *drop a gut. 3. n. rhym. slang.* A *dropped gut.*

excremation marks *n.* The tell-tale *skidmata* left on one's gusset following a spot of extra-*grundular moonraking.*

excretoire *1. n.* A writing desk of very poor quality. *2. n.* A perfectly serviceable desk upon which writing of very poor quality is executed. *'Lot 316. An early 18th century excretoire. Having a cushion-moulded map drawer above a fielded panelled fall, enclosing a marquetried walnut interior of small drawers, the lower section with four short drawers within a rebated oak frame. Formerly the property of Lord Archer of Weston-super-Mare.'*

excused shorts *phr.* Of a *well-endowed* school-lad or scoutmaster, who might be embarrassed by his *todger* dangling out there for all to see. *'You're excused shorts, Larkin.'*

executive relief *euph.* How *getting pulled off* is described in small ads.

executive time *1. n.* Daily intervals included in comedy President Donald Trump's official White House timetable, during which he conducted important business. *2. n.* When *working from home*, carefully scheduled telly watching, naps and *wanks. 'Sorry I didn't get to the phone there. I was just having a bit of executive time.'*

exercise my constitutional right, I'm just going to *exclam.* Announcement immediately prior to a forceful and pungent *bowel bugle* fanfare.

exercise the ferret *1. v.* To pull something thin and hairy from one's trousers and pop it into a muddy hole in the hope of catching something. *2. v.* To pull something thin and hairy from one's trousers and pop it into a muddy hole in the hope of *not* catching something.

ex files *n.* A *wank bank* folder containing the most filthy memories of sexual depravities enjoyed with previous partners.

exhaustipated *adj.* So tired that you don't give a shit. *'Sorry madam, your three-year-old son may well have swallowed three bottles of headache tablets, been savaged by a pitbull and pulled a pan of hot chip-fat onto himself, but I've been at work since sparrowfart on Thursday and frankly I'm exhaustipated. Might I suggest that if you are in any way dissatisfied with the prescription for a course of mild antibiotics I have just filled in and handed to you, you might care to take your custom to another hospital.'*

exhaust pipe *n.* The *bumhole, fudge tunnel, back box.* Also *tailpipe.*

exhaust pipe engineer *n.* One who tinkers with *exhaust pipes.*

exhibition position *n.* Variation on *doggy-style* sex. The man takes the kneeling position from behind, places one hand on the lady's back and the other jauntily on his hip. Then turns and smiles at an imaginary audience, pretending to be a moustachioed German *Frankie Vaughan* star. A *Rigsby shag.*

exit music *n.* An epic and glorious *quackfest* of a symphonic nature.

exit, pursued by a bear *1. phr.* Famous stage instruction from Shakespeare's *Twelfth Night. 2. phr.* Leaving a room with a lot of grizzly growling in one's wake. See also *blow winds and crack your cheeks.*

exit stage centre *exclam.* Phrase declaimed loudly and theatrically in the style of late noted thesp Sir Donald Sinden after one breaks wind in front of an audience.

exit wound *n.* The state of the *freckle* after a particularly fierce *Len Murray.*

exorcist *n.* One who is gifted with the power to rid a place of spirits, especially the top shelf behind the bar. *'Born on this day: Stuart Hall, It's* *a Cockout sexcase, 1929; Jesus Christ, son of God, 0; Shane MacGowan, late dentally handicapped exorcist, 1957.'*

expecting a harsh winter *euph.* Putting on weight or over-eating. *'She's stuffing her face with eclairs. She must be expecting a harsh winter.'*

expecting arselforce *euph.* State of agitation in anticipation of an *express delivery*, typically days after it was originally due.

expellianus! *exclam.* Cod-Latinesque conjuration uttered when someone *drops* a magical *gut.*

ex-pert *adj.* Saggy.

explaining a joke to a German *phr.* Descriptive of a task that is both pointless and fruitless.

exploding cigar *n.* A solid piece of faecal matter splattered jokily across the *jobby engine* bowl by excess gas.

explosion in the quarry *n.* Following a warning shout of "Fire in the hole!", an uncontrollable eruption of female *love wee*, if you believe in that sort of thing.

explosive decompression *1. n.* When an air-tight seal on an aircraft breaks and pressurised gas and debris is forced out. Mind, they did it on *Mythbusters* and it was nothing to write home about, if we're honest. *2. n.* When the air-tight seal on your *balloon knot* breaks and pressurised *carbon dibaxide* and *bum crumbs* are forced out.

expresso bongo *1. n.* A *crap* film from the 60s starring Sir Cliff Richard. *2. n.* The fast forwarding through the uninteresting bits of the sort of films which almost certainly do not star Sir Cliff Richard.

expresso pongo *n.* The first strong coffee of the day that awakens one's peristaltic urges. *'Can you do the sports news, Louise? I've just had an expresso pongo.'*

extra-Caligula activity *euph.* Any saucy peccadillo of such depravity that it would make even the famously debauched Roman Emperor blush. *'Fetch me a live goose, a twenty-foot length of washing line, a tub of coleslaw and a small chest of drawers, my dear. I'm going to indulge in a little extra-Caligula activity.'*

extras *1. n.* On *Coronation Street*, those slightly awkward people in Dev's shop who pay for their groceries, nod and leave without saying a word. *2. n.* Something one tentatively asks for while winking at a masseuse or osteopath. The *tugging* as opposed to the *rubbing* in a *rub-a-tug shop.*

ex ungue lionem *1. phr. Lat.* Classical wordage: "to know the lion by its claw", whereby one recognises a genius by their work. Perhaps uttered whilst reading *Beyond Reasonable Doubt* by Jeffrey

Archer. *2. n.* Uttered in the wake of a particularly pungent *Bakewell.*

eyeball straightener *n.* The *hair of the dog.* An alcoholic tincture that restores the health the morning after a *bad pint.* A *heart starter.* *'On behalf of the crew and myself, I'd like to welcome you aboard this Icarus Airlines flight into the side of Mount Erebus. Captain Plywood has completed his pre-flight checks and had his morning eyeball straightener, so please fasten your seatbelts and secure all baggage underneath your seat or in the overhead compartments and make sure your table trays are stowed in the upright position for take-off.'*

eyeburns *n.* Where the eyebrows on an hirsute chap's *mug* continue seamlessly into his sideburns. Also *sidebrows.*

eye cabbage *n.* The opposite of *eye candy.* An ugly *piece* you leave at the side of your plate.

eyeful of both ends, an *n.* A *sneaky peek* down a lady-friend's *tit pants* and up her skirt, all accomplished during the same swift movement, *eg.* When she bends to tie her shoelaces, falls down an escalator, gets grabbed by an enraged elephant *etc.*

eyehooks *n.* Things that monopolise a fellow's attention. *'Did Carol Kirkwood say what the weather was going to be like today?' 'She might have done. I was watching her eyehooks.'*

eye magnets *n.* Dazzling *searchlights* at which any red-blooded man could not resist the temptation to *sneak a peek.*

eye of Horus *1. n.* In Egyptian mythology, a symbol of rebirth. *2. n.* On Victoria Coren's highbrow *Blockbusters* quiz *Only Connect*, the name of one of the sets of so-called questions that the speccy misfits get to choose from. *3. n.* The *ringpiece*, from which many a *mud baby* is spawned into the netherworld.

eye of Sauron *1. n.* In JRR Tolkien's *Lord of the Rings*, a "lidless eye wreathed with flame" with which the Lord Sauron watched over Middle Earth, and thus *2. n.* A lidless, fiery *brown eye* which is the inevitable consequence of dining at the Curry Capital, Newcastle upon Tyne. A *Johnny Cash, Japanese flag, Wigan rosette.*

eye of the fart *n.* The region of uncannily fresh air which can be found at the centre of a strong *Exchange & Mart.* Also *eye of the storm.* *'Fuck me, your holiness, was that you? It fucking stinks.' 'Sorry, cardinal. I can't smell anything, me, because I'm sitting in the eye of the fart.'*

eye-opener *1. n.* An alcoholic beverage consumed in the morning. A *Kentucky breakfast* or *eye-straightener. 2. n.* A brisk spot of *cottaging* before elevenses. *'I'm just popping out to Liverpool*

Street bogs for an eye-opener, dear.'

eyes bigger than his penis *phr.* Said of a bloke who's *bitten off more than he can screw.*

eyes down for a full house *1. exclam.* A popular phrase used by bingo callers to begin another life-sapping game for their *oxygen-thieving* clientelle. *2. exclam.* Said by a chivalrous fellow to discreetly draw the attention of his associates to a particularly allluring *embonpoint* or *décolletage* that has heaved into view.

eyes like a shithouse rat *sim.* Descriptive of one with extraordinary visual acuity. *'Check my collar for lipstick will you, Edwina. Only my Norma's got eyes like a fucking shithouse rat.'*

eyes like sheeps' cunts *n. medic. David Davis eyes.* Self-explanatory symptom of an extremely bad hangover. See also *feel Welsh.*

eyes wide shit *phr.* Reference to a terrifying defecatory event that is wrought through with the fear of rectal tearing.

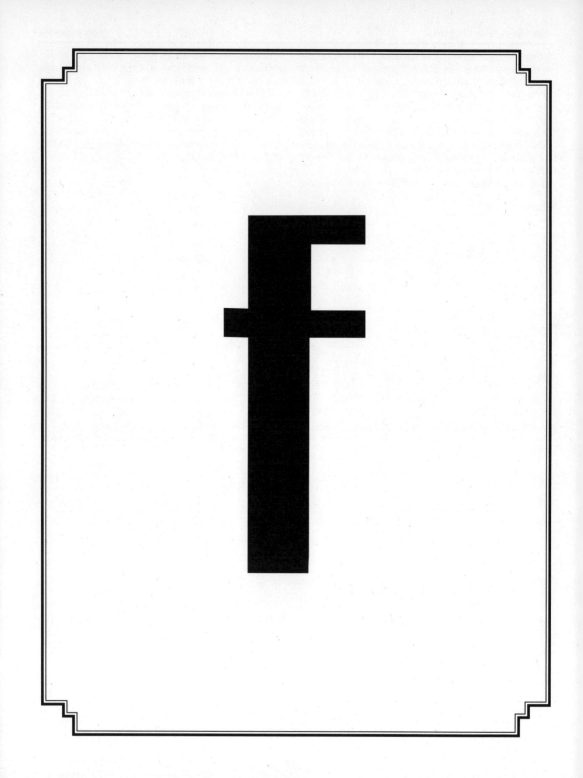

Fabergé egg *n.* A large oval *dump* which comes out encrusted in red jewels as a result of *famers* or a ripped *nipsy*. A *limited edition*.

FAB/fab *1. n.* Expression meaning "yes" made famous in the string-heavy children's series *Thunderbirds*. *2. acronym.* Standardised weighting order for assessing the quality of a piece of *crumpet*, *viz.* Face; Arse; Baps. *3. acronym.* The unpleasant olfactory combination of Feet, Arse and Balls encountered when entering a young man's bedroom, a prison cell or a monastery. *'This room smells FAB, Brother Dominic.' 'Yeah, sorry about that. I haven't washed my feet, arse or balls for a month.' 4. n.* The soap bar in the shower, one end of which a person has used to lather-up their *dung funnel* in anticipation of a good, hygienic rake-round with the fingertips, such that it now resembles the spaceship-shaped 1970s ice lolly. Though that was apparently called a Rocket, not a Fab.

fabric softener *n.* A *low resolution fox* who takes a chap's *giggle stick* on an erotic rollercoaster ride from a state of *diamond cutting* tumescence to marshmallow softness as she comes within range, thus relieving pressure on his trouser frontage.

facadebook *n.* A social medium whereby individuals project a misleading image of the person they want to be seen as, rather than the person they actually are.

facebonk *v.* To *sleep with*, or indeed *fuck*, someone you met *via* a social networking site. To *poke*.

facebook street *n.* A lurid virtual soap opera played out through a series of posts on social media, during the course of which a vague acquaintance's life falls apart for your vicarious entertainment.

face fannies *n. Bugger's grips*, sideburns. As sported by the singer out of Supergrass, the late Dr Rhodes Boyson and Anne Robinson.

face fart *n.* A burp or belch. Particularly one that smells of *shit*.

face for HD, not got a *sim.* Aesthetically unconventional. *'That Evan Davis hasn't really got a face for HD, has he mother?'*

face, front and forks *euph. milit.* A *whore's bath*, taken when there's no time, opportunity or inclination for a shower. Flannelling the face, chest, groin and armpits. *'You're due on set in five minutes, Miss Collins.' 'Right you are. I'm just doing me face, front and forks.'*

face grating *n.* Performing the act of *cumulonimbus* upon a woman with advanced *five o'clock fanny*.

facehugger *1. n.* That thing off *Alien* that looks a bit like a wet lobster with a long tail. *2. n.* The stuff of nightmares; a truly horrific *Bakewell tart* that seems to lay its eggs down your throat.

facemuck *n. Man mess* produced when idly browsing photos of female friends on social networking sites.

face painting *v.* To adorn one's spouse with *jelly jewellery*.

facerucking *n.* Engaging in confrontational behaviour on a social networking site, usually at the conclusion of a smashing night *on the pop*.

face saver *n.* An early morning taxi which removes a less-than-attractive female from one's house before the neighbours awaken.

face that could make a test tube flaccid *euph.* Said affectionately of a notably unattractive lady. *'I wouldn't say my first guest is ugly, ladies and gentlemen, but she's got a face that could make a test tube flaccid. No, but seriously though, folks, let's give it up with a big Any Questions welcome for former shadow Secretary of State for Health Ann Widdecombe.'*

face the fast bowlers *v.* To increase the strength of your drinks in order to attain your target of getting *out* more quickly.

face the spinners *v.* To turn to a more lady-like-strength drink in an attempt to stop getting *out* quite so quickly.

face-time *1. n.* The period that you actually spend talking directly to someone, rather than by phone or email. *2. n.* Time spent *dropping your yogurt* into, or onto, someone's face. *'If you want me to be closer to your family, dear, I suppose I could always face-time your ma.'*

facial awareness *n.* Male medical condition closely linked to penile *dementia*; a lowered ability to discern the physiognomical features of a spectacularly *well-qualified* woman to whom a fellow has been introduced. *'I'm sorry, Jodie. Have we met before? I'm afraid I don't have very good facial awareness.'*

factor fuck all *euph.* Sunburn protection utilised by topless building site workers during the summer months.

factory AIDS *n.* The miscellany of invisible, yet ever present, bits of dirt, snot, *spunk* and *turd* which is present on all new culinary purchases. *'Trevor, can you pass me one of those new lunchboxes so I can pack the kids' turkey twizzlers?' 'Hang on, luv. I'm just rinsing the factory AIDS off them.'*

factory whistle, the *n.* A distinctive, high-pitched klaxon warning a worker that he will shortly be required to clock in for a taxing shift at the *municipal sludge works*.

factory wipe *1. n.* A thorough reset of a computer back to a pristine system state. *'There you go, Mr*

Glitter. I've done a full factory wipe. There's no way anybody could find anything incriminating on there.'. 2. n. After clearing out the cupboards in *the Devil's kitchen*, spending ten minutes longer than usual on *paperwork*, and getting through three times the normal amount of *bumwad* while doing so. *'There, I've done a full factory wipe. You could eat your dinner off my arsehole now, your majesty.'*

FA cups *1. n.* Perennially annual English football knockout competitions. *2. n.* Consolation prizes offered as sops to whingeing children. *Fuck All* cups. *2. n.* Those with which *Miss Lincolnshire*'s brassiere is furnished.

fadge *1. n.* A cross between a *fanny* and a vagina. *2. n.* How the late Queen pronounced the word "fudge". *'Would you like a chew on my fadge, Lord Carnarvon?'*

fadge hook *n.* A Bic razor. From the Norfolk "fagging hook" – a slashing device used to remove troublesome undergrowth and slash the earth beneath. *'You'm left that fadge hook o' yars on the sink yisty, nan.'*

fadgida *n.* The flabby stomach of a *chubster* that effectively conceals her *fadge. Also pie hider, fat hat.*

fadgie *n.* A *front tuck* up the *quimpiece.* From fadge + wedgie. *'Every time Daisy was on set, just before the cameras rolled, them cotton pickin' Duke boys would lift her up by her goldarn belt loops and give her a proper old fadgie.'*

FADS/fads *abbrev.* From the motor trade, descriptive of something worthless, *eg.* The trade-in value of any Citroen over 3-months old. Fuck All Divided by Six.

fad sucker *n.* A spooneristic epithet describing a person whom one disparages, *eg.* Farage all alone watching the Queen's Speech stood by his microwave on Christmas Day.

faecal expression *n.* The contorted and gurning physiognomical expression of one who is struggling to lay a particularly tricky section of *clay pipe.*

faecal position *n.* The delicate, round-shouldered and slightly curled posture adopted by someone who has been caught short some distance from lavatory facilities.

faecal recognition *n.* Form of artificial intelligence by which means the lady of the house always knows which family member has left an unflushed *Thora* in the *pan.*

faecal tart *n.* Like a *treacle tart,* but not quite so cloyingly sweet.

faecal touch *n.* Opposite of the Midas touch, *ie.* Everything this person lays a finger on turns to shit. *'Sir Clive really did have the faecal touch.'*

faecal treacle *n.* Viscous *squits, runs,* diarrhoea. *Molarses, bum toffee.*

faeceasy *n.* The designated lavatory in your home that is situated away from living quarters and is thus somewhat difficult for a guest to find in a hurry. This is the toilet where the lady of the house prefers *number twos* to be executed. *'We only use that one for best, your holiness. If you're planning on having a number two, you'll have to use the outside faeceasy next to the coal bunker.'*

faecebooking *n.* Social networking while ensconced on the *jobby engine.*

faeces pieces *n.* Nutty nuggets in a chewy coating.

faequel *n.* A *crap* sequel or prequel, *eg. The Fly II, Jaws The Revenge, Jaws 3-D.*

FAF *acronym.* Fan Assisted Fart. When sitting in the office or at home, lifting a *bum-cheek* to *let rip* whilst simultaneously sneakily turning your desk fan on and pointing it in the direction of an unsuspecting victim.

FAFCAM/fafcam *acronym.* Fit As Fuck, Common As Muck.

faff *1. n.* A lady's *front bottom. 2. v.* To *fart about. 'Stop faffing and make the incision, Dr Barnard.'*

faffro *n.* An overly fussy hairstyle which has clearly entailed a great expenditure of effort and expense by the hairee while yielding *shite* results.

FAFTAF/faftaf *acronym.* A woman who is extremely attractive but who unfortunately failed her rocket science exams. Fit As Fuck, Thick As Fuck.

FAFTAS/faftas *abbrev.* Likewise, a lady that a sexist pig would happily *empty his cods* up but would be unlikely to pick as his "Phone a Friend" choice on *Who Wants to be a Millionaire?*. Fit As Fuck, Thick As Shit.

fag *1. n.* An 8-year-old boy at a public school who has to fetch tea, fetch toast and *fetch off* prefects. *2. n. Tab, ciggie,* a *cancer stick. 3. n.* A tiresome chore, *eg. Fetching off* prefects at a top public school. *4. n. US.* One who *sews his own buttons.*

fag burn in a fur coat, he would shag a *phr.* Said of a resourceful chap who displays a willingness to avail himself of whatever recreational facilities might fortuitously present themselves. One who would *dig up a dead badger and bum it. 'I wouldn't share a taxi with Toulouse Lautrec, if I was you, Madame Foret. That mucky little bastard would fuck a fag burn in a fur coat.'*

fag fireworks *n.* The brief, but nonetheless impressive night-time pyrotechnic display given to motorists following behind vans driven by smokers.

fag hag *n.* A wizened old woman who prefers the

company of homosexuals.

fagnet *n.* A man who, when out clubbing, only manages to attract *spud fumblers.*

fagnolia *adj.* The rich, yellowy-creamy-brown hue, somewhere between Lemon Punch and Honey Mustard on the Dulux paint card, which used to be found on the interior walls and ceilings of betting shops and pubs but is now restricted to the homes of chain smokers.

fagnostic *n.* One who either doesn't know or hasn't quite made his mind up which way he wants to swing.

fagpie *n.* Predatory pest who always scavenges a *coffin nail* when others are lighting up but never buys their own.

fagriculture *n. Uphill gardening* and its associated lifestyle. *Bumcraft.*

fag shack heater, arse like a *sim.* Descriptive of a *nipsy* that is glowing red hot for whatever reason a *nipsy* might end up glowing red hot. *'Come to the Rupali Restaurant, Bigg Market, Newcastle upon Tyne where you're guaranteed a warm welcome, a delicious curry and an arse like a fag shack heater to remember us by.'*

FAGUAC *exclam. abbrev.* Of someone attempting to *dine at the Y* but having difficulty locating the *bearded clam* due to an excess of adipose tissue in the vicinity; "Come on, Vanessa. Fart and give us a clue."

Fahrt zum Hades *1. n.* Title of an 1817 Franz Schubert song (D526) about journeying into Hell, not to be confused with the similarly titled AC/DC record. *2. n.* A diabolically sulphurous *guff.*

fail one's driving test *1. v.* To prove unable to reach a required level of ability when driving a motor vehicle. *2. v.* To prove unable to steer a *horse and cart* around a *brown bollard.* To *gamble and lose, follow through.*

failure to launch *1. phr.* A form of words with which Elon Musk is overly familiar. *2. phr.* An inability to *fire one off.* A form of words with which many middle aged men are overly familiar.

faint on *n. medic.* A devastating condition affecting certain males who are *hung like rogue elephants.* When a *fat is cracked,* the shaft drains the body of its blood, causing the patient to become light-headed or even unconscious.

faint rustle of taffeta *euph.* A vague *whiff of lavender* about a chap whom one suspects may be harbouring a *long-standing interest in fashion.* *'Hmm. He may have won all them medals, but there's still the faint rustle of taffeta about him if you ask me.'*

fairground air rifle, she's had more cocks than *sim.* Said of a woman who has been *rogered more times than a policeman's radio.* Also *(she's been) cocked more times than Davey Crockett's rifle.*

fairy goblet *n.* Bronzed chalice favoured by the more *style-conscious* gentleman about town. *Spice island.*

fairy hammock *n.* A *trollop's dunghampers.*

fairy liquid *n. Tart fuel, lady petrol, knicker oil.* Soft drinks such as WKD and Bacardi Breezers and that.

fairy wings *n.* The charming, gossamer tracery of *arse* sweat left on the seat when a lardy chap gets up off the *bog* on a warm day.

faith invaders *n.* Well-meaning *God botherers* knocking at your door selling the word of the Lord.

fajita *1. n.* Mexican stuff piled on a flour or corn tortilla. *2. n.* A discreet way to refer to a *lady in comfortable shoes.* *'Today's birthdays: Charlie Parker, American jazz musician, 1920; James Hunt, British racing driver, 1947; Jeanette Winterson, Yorkshire fajita, 1959.'*

fakeon *1. n.* A bacon substitute eaten by *Guardian*-reading types. *2. n.* A Community Support Officer or *Happy Shopper copper.* *'Don't worry, man. They is not real pigs, they can't even arrest you. They is just fakeon.'*

falconer's gauntlet *n.* A *wanking sock* so encrusted and infused with dried *spoff* that it would doubtless prove impenetrable even to the razored talons of a bird of prey.

falconer's glove, the *n.* Carrying a *man custard*-covered hand to the bathroom after a *thrap. The claw.*

Falklands Islands princess *n.* A lone woman placed in a *cock heavy* environment, such as an oil-rig, a men's prison or an Antarctic research station, thus finding herself suddenly the cynosure of all eyes despite looking like the Elephant Man's less attractive sister. A *Bodleian beauty queen.*

fall at Beecher's *v.* To *come off* several furlongs before reaching the finishing post. To *last as long as Gemma Collins's easter egg, celebrate too early.*

fallen off her bike *euph.* A monthly *cycle accident* leaving a woman bleeding from the *saddle area.*

fallen to the communists *euph.* Of a woman who has *fallen off her bike,* had a visit from Aunt Irma. *'Any luck last night?' 'No. She's fallen to the communists.' 'So? She's got a fuckin' mooth, hasn't she?'*

falling down juice *n.* Beer, according to the witlessly humorous. Also *fighting water, bed glue, dizzyade.* *'Ah, splendid. I'll take a refreshing tankard of the old falling down juice if I may, my good man.' 'You're barred.'*

fall of soot *n.* The messy result of a failed *driving* *test.* A *follow through, lost gamble.*

fallopian tube strike *euph.* Inconvenience on the *Hammersmith & City line* occasioned when the missus is *bottling beetroots*, although, with luck, a *replacement bust service* will have been laid on.

fall out the officers! *exclam.* Piece of light-hearted badinage which traditionally greets a loud blast on the *botty bugle.*

false fart *n.* An *ill wind* that blows nobody any good. Except someone who runs an underpants shop. *'I'm afraid I'll have to rush to the bathroom, your majesty, as it appears I've had a false fart.'*

false flag incident *1. n.* When a country artificially creates the impression that it has been attacked by a foe, *eg.* The Soviets' "Operation Trust" in 1921, "Operation Northwood"s in the Cuban Revolution and various other examples mentioned on Wikipedia. *2. n.* When a drunken *toileteer* inspects his *bumwad* and finds it clean, and unwisely surmises he is good to pull up his *scads* when in fact he has completely missed an ongoing disaster area around his *teatowel holder.*

false start *1. n.* In sport, a movement made by a participant before the starter has fired their pistol. *2. n.* When you accidentally fill your *grundies* with *shite* on the way to the *bog.*

false start *n.* Following a night of heavy *refreshment*, the counter-intuitively happy beginnings of the next day when the subject mistakenly feels that they have escaped miraculously unscathed, only to start getting shaky, sweaty and nauseous as the morning wears on.

false tart *1. n.* Some vegan, gluten-free object masquerading as a cake. *2. n.* A *sex doll.* Also known as a *Dutch wife* or *plastic bag.*

false tart *n.* An apparent female who turns not to be. A *shim, tiptop, trolley dolly, bobby dazzler* or *ladyboy. 'My holiday in Bangkok got off to a bit of a false tart and I ended up with egg on my face. And a sore bottom.'*

family fartunes *n.* Post-Sunday-lunch symphony of *guffing*, belching and snoring as the entire family sleep it off in front of the *idiot lantern.*

family jam *1. n.* A delicious homemade preserve, often received at Christmas from an elderly relation who can't be *arsed* to go out and buy you a proper present from a shop. *2. n. Population paste, gentleman's relish.*

family jewels *n.* Priceless heirloom *knackers. 'Oof! Right in the family jewels, Harry! And Bowe's knackers are going to be hurting now.'*

faminge *n.* An extreme scarcity of *buffage;* a dearth of *fanny.* From famine + minge.

famous five go to Brighton *1. n.* Title of an Enid Blyton bedtime story, probably. *2. n.* Allowing one's digits to venture South for an adventure after lights out.

fancy wank *v.* To use an ugly *bird's blurtch* to save wear and tear on your wrist. *Hands free,* the *cock wash.*

fandruff *n. Fanny* dandruff. *Muff-druff, scurf 'n' turf.*

fanfare for the common man *1. n.* Song by English progressive rockers/Yeovil-based solicitors Emerson, Lake and Palmer. *2. n.* The *brass section* accompaniment ringing out from the gents toilet cubicles at any motorway services.

fanic *n.* State of alarm when one is about to *step on a frog* while scared that one's flatulence may contain a *free gift*, for example after drinking several pints of beer and eating a big curry. This problem may be alleviated by retiring to a convenient *fanic room* and taking suitably sensible precautions.

fanipulation *n.* The ancient female practice of using the promise of *fanny* to influence the behaviour of men. *'She fanipulated me into putting them shelves up, and then she said she had a headache.'*

fanity *n.* A lady's excessive pride in the appearance of her *growler. 'Had I been in love, I could not have been more wretchedly blind. But fanity, not love, has been my folly.'* (from *Pride and Prejudice* by Jane Austen).

fanjita *n.* A *tuppence con queso fresco.*

fankle *n.* The bit on a *digestively overqualified* lass's leg that comes between the calf and the foot. From fat + ankle. Also *cankle.*

fannaemia *n. medic.* Debilitating affliction suffered by single men whose diet incorporates insufficient quantities of *mackerel.*

fannanigans *n. Women's things.* From fanny + shenanigans.

fannicure *n.* A pampering of the *bush.* A *quim-trim,* eg. A *Hitler tash* or a *Jimmy Edwards.*

fannished *adj.* Suffering an almost vampiric hunger for a serving of *quim.*

fannitary towel *n.* A *jam rag, gash plaster, chuftie plug.*

fanny *1. n. UK. Snatch, snapper, quim, cunt, puh-seh.* Female genitals, ladies' *pudenders. 2. n. US. Arse, backside* (confusingly). *3. n. prop.* Fictitious Great Aunt. *4. adj.* Like a fan.

Fanny Adams, sweet *phr. Fuck all, eg.* What you get offered when part exchanging a French car.

fanny alley *n.* A scenic diversion that takes a gentleman from his office desk to the lavatory cubicles via the secretarial pool.

fanny apple *n.* A neonate. A new born baby. *'Births: Smith. At the Portland Hospital. To Evadne and Captain George Everard, a boy, Spartacus, brother* *to Troy and Elgin. Mother and fanny apple doing well. Deo Gracias.'*

fannyarse *n.* A *crafty butcher* whose *dirtstar* has been *lubbocked* to the extent that it resembles a lady's *quim.*

fanny badger *n.* See *Blackbeard's ghost.*

fanny bag *1. n.* US. What would be called a "bum-bag" on this side of the Atlantic, on account of they call their *arses* "fannies" in America. And a "bum" is a tramp, apparently. You couldn't make it up. *2. n.* A relatively unattractive woman that a callous man retains as a low-maintenance *bang* during periods of sexual drought. Men are beasts. *'No, your worship. To be fair, she's more of a fanny bag than a girlfriend.'*

fanny banter *n.* Female conversation, such as that enjoyed on programmes like *Lorraine* and *Loose Women.*

fanny batter *n.* The substance which leaves one's chin greasy after a *fish supper. Sloom, blip, bilp, moip.*

fanny battering ram *n.* A stout length of *wood* used to burst *Mary Hinges.* A *crowbar.*

fannybelly *n.* The *gunt, poond.*

fanny bib *n.* A sanitary towel.

fanny bitter *n. medic.* The piquant flavour of bacterial vaginosis. *Bitter batter.*

Fanny Bloom *1. n. prop.* Delightful French-Canadian chanteuse. *2. n. medic.* A not-particularly-delightful dose of *gash rash.*

fanny bomb *n.* The female organism. *'How was it for you, pet? Did the old fanny bomb go off?'*

fanny bowser *n.* Any vehicle, for example a stretch Hummer or Lincoln Towncar, filled to the brim with *heavily-refreshed*, libidinous ladies on a night out. Also *bunga bus, quimousine.*

Fanny Burney *1. n. prop.* Noted 18th century author, famed for novels such as *Evelina. 2. n. medic.* The *clap* on a young lady's *entrance.*

fanny by gaslight *1. n.* Post-discotheque back-alley congress; A *chinook* or *fork lift truck*, if you will. *2. n.* Title of a 1944 Gainsborough Studios melodrama starring Phyllis Calvert as the daughter of a Cabinet Minister who is unknowingly employed by her father, Lord Manderstoke (James Mason), as a servant, and gets *fucked* in a back alley by Harry Somerford (Stewart Grainger) shortly after chucking out time.

fanny chamois *1. n.* UK. A feminine wipette. *2. n.* US. A moist washlet.

fanny clamp *n.* Vice-like grippage from a dirty lady's inner *bacon sarnie* as she has an *organism.*

Fanny Cleaver *1. n. prop.* Bad-backed character in Charles Dickens's book *Our Mutual Friend,*

who wisely chooses to go by the soubriquet Jenny Wren. *2. n.* A geet big muckle *wullie.*

Fanny Cradock's mincemeat omelette *1. n.* A genuine recipe by the eponymous 1970s culinary TV harridan, and thus *2. n.* Something which is unspeakably unpalatable. *'I nearly banged that (name of former MP and Privy Councillor removed on legal advice) last night, but when she got her kit off, it was like Fanny Cradock's Mincemeat Omelette down there.'*

fanny famine *n.* A period of time during which a chap's *meat and two veg* are left to lie fallow. *Fanny famines* of varying durations are typically experienced by divorcees, Catholic clergymen and Peter Pans of pop.

fannyfare *n.* A brassy *flap raspberry* that could make a room full of Chelsea Pensioners rise to their feet and salute.

fanny farm *n.* A *knocking shop.* A brothel, *trollbooth* or *maison de tolerance.*

fanny filter *n.* The "safe content" option on an internet search engine which prevents teenage boys and office workers locating pictures of the one thing they would like to find on the worldwide information superhighway.

fanny fit *n.* A *bird's* unnecessary histrionic episode. A *tammy huff, blob strop* or *showing off.*

fanny flange *n.* The vaginal escutcheon.

fanny flump *n.* A *women's things* thing. A *chuftie plug, cotton pony* or *dangermouse.*

fanny fog *n.* A gentleman's inability to make even the most routine decision when surrounded by *blart. 'Okay, we've completed our deliberations and let me tell you, it certainly wasn't easy in that fanny fog. But I'm delighted to announce that the winner of this year's competition is ... ooh, it's gone again.'*

fanny footprint, reducing your *n.* Deleting text messages, pictures and call logs, in order to prevent the world collapsing round you.

fanny fright *n. medic.* Nervous condition affecting some macho men who suddenly find themselves unable to have *a bit* when presented with an opportunity. *Lack of composure in front of goal.*

fanny full *euph.* A building site term used to describe a small quantity of something, for example casting plaster mixed up in a margarine tub to fill the gaps between sections of coving. *'How much plaster do you want, dad?' 'Just a fanny full, son.'*

fanny gallops *n.* In a lady, the early rumblings of sexual excitement at the sight of a Calvin Klein Y-fronts poster or George Clooney flogging coffee capsules. The *hots*.

fanny hammer *n*. A *bob*.

fanny hockle *n*. The product of a post-*scuttle fadge cough*.

fanny hopper *1. n*. A 2-foot diameter inflatable orange *minge* with handles at the top. *2. n*. A springy *crumpeteer* who hops from one *fanny* to another like a cricket. A *stickman*, a *skippy*, eg. Darren Day, Mick Jagger, John Prescott.

fanny jabber *n*. Women's talk, *binter*. '*Coleen Nolan, Jane Moore, Janet Street-Porter and Jamelia are joined by former Coronation Street actress Sherrie Hewson for a load of high-pitched fanny jabber and shrieking. Subtitles and the off button available for those with sensitive hearing.*'

fanny licker *n*. A small dog, such as a Yorkshire Terrier or Pekingese, which is best-suited to sitting on a lady's lap. '"*Oh God. Tricky-Woo's got worms,*" *wailed Tristram as he put down the phone. "Tricky-Woo?" I said. "Who, or indeed what, is Tricky-Woo?" "My dear James, it's Mrs Pomfrey's fanny licker,*" *laughed Siegfried, as he stuck his arm up yet another cow's arse.*' (from *Some Vets Do 'Ave 'Em* by James Herriot).

fanny loaf, baking a *euph*. Suffering from an acute yeast infection. Also *cunt bread*.

fanny magnate *n*. A commercial purveyor of ladies' favours, pornographer or strip club owner. A *pimp, fanny farmer*.

fanny magnet *n*. Something or someone to which top drawer *blart* is inexplicably drawn, *eg*. A Ferrari, a Rolex watch, Mick Hucknall.

fanny mechanic *n. medic*. One who performs *MOTT tests*; a *box doc, snatch quack, scrape doctor, cunt dentist*. A gynaecologist.

fanny mower *n*. A bikini-line grooming device. '*Wills, have you seen my fanny mower? I've got a biffer like Brian Blessed's chin here.*' '*It's in the cupboard under the sink, Kate.*'

fanny nanny *n*. A feminine napkin, *fanny bib*.

fanny nosher *n*. A *woman in comfortable shoes* who takes the *other bus* to *dine at the Y*. A *tennis fan, lady golfer, carpet muncher*.

fanny out *adj*. Self-explanatory description of a male exotic entertainment venue. '*I like going to Blue Velvet, me. It's not just a titty bar, you see, archbishop. It's fanny out.*'

fanny paddy *n*. A *muff huff* or *blob strop*. A *monty*.

fanny rat *n*. A sexually promiscuous male. A *skippy* or *bed hopper*. '*Today's birthdays: David Mellor QC, former Conservative politician and fanny rat, 68.*'

fanny shrinker *n*. A natty little sports car driven by a woman of a certain vintage in an attempt to compensate for her sagging bodywork and gaping

shutlines. A *milf float*.

fanny swill *n*. The frothy, post-coital substance exuded from a lady's *pig bite* after a good session.

fannytastic *1. adj*. Anything wonderful to do with the female genitals. *2. adj*. Descriptive of a thing which is so excellent that it can only be compared with a *minge*. '*Have you been watching the X-Factor this year?*' '*No, I've got cataracts and burst eardrums and it's been fannytastic.*'

fanny tax *n*. Surcharge paid on drinks in a bar staffed by top class *blart*.

fannytosis *n. medic*. Bad breath as a result of *cumulonimbus*.

fanny turd *n*. A child. '*Births: Chocmonockly Ffeatherstonehaugh. On February 17th, at the Portland Hospital. To Rupert and Rowenta (nee Ponfrit-Cake), a 6lb 8oz fanny turd, Parkinson Cowan. A brother for Tefal, Moulinex and Tarpaulin. Deo Gracias.*' (from *The Times*, Feb 12th 2004).

fannyversary *n*. The single, once-a-year *fuck* off his missus to which a husband is legally entitled. *Annual sex*.

fanny whisperer *n*. A ladies' man. '*Born on this day: Aleksay Nikolayevich Tolstoy, Russian author, 1828; George Foreman, banjolele-playing boxer and heavyweight grill manufacturer, 1949; Rod Stewart, gravel-voiced fanny whisperer, 1945.*'

fan of soft furnishings *euph*. A *bad thrower*.

fanoir *n*. Fr. French insult. '*Porthos a dit, "Que vas-tu utiliser pour un visage quand ma grand-mère veut retrouver son fanoir, Monsieur D'Artagnan?"*' (from *The Three Musketeers* by Alexander Dumas).

fanoose *n*. The *tinter, taint, twitter, Humber Bridge, twernt etc*.

fanopy *n*. Overhanging *gunt* that protects the *bald man in the boat* from sunburn or rain. From fanny + canopy.

FANTA/fanta *acronym*. A one night stand, *beef encounter, overnight bag*. Fuck And Never Touch Again.

fanta Lucia *n. prop*. Appellation bestowed upon a woman who has evidently chosen a self-tanning product at the ocherous end of the tonal spectrum.

fanta pants *n*. A light-hearted term used to describe a woman with an orange *bush*. '*The Red Shoes (UK, 1948) Ground-breaking expressionist fantasy directed by Michael Powell and Emeric Pressburger, starring fanta pants ballerina Moira Shearer.*' (from *Halliwell's Film Guide 2001*).

fantasturbation *n*. Any unlikely sexual scenario dreamt up by someone *relaxing in a gentleman's way* as an aid to the process, *eg*. Imagining saving a Hollywood starlet from being kidnapped by space aliens and she's so grateful that she lets him do absolutely anything he wants to her. Right there in the street.

fanticipation *1. n.* Surge in excitement felt by young pop devotees just as they are about to see their idols walk on stage for the the the first time. *2. n.* Surge in excitement felt by blokes just as they are about to see their new *bird*'s *fanny* for the first time.

fantimagnetic *adj.* Not particularly attractive to members of the opposite sex. *'Until I won the Euromillions, I was positively fantimagnetic. Now I can't beat the buggers off with a shitty stick.'*

Fanuary *n.* A month during which a woman neglects her neatly *fanicured ladygarden* and allows it to grow into a magnificently unkempt *bush.*

fan your arse *v.* To perform a male courtship display; masculine showing off. *'Well you can tell by the way I fan my arse / I'm a woman's man, with a sweaty barse.'* (Song lyric, *Stayin' Alive* by The Bee Gees).

fapathetic *adj.* Impotent; not in the mood for even a quick *one off the wrist*. *'Seeing Ann Widdecombe on telly is enough to turn even the most virile lad utterly fapathetic.'*

FAP/fap *1. acronym.* The Portuguese Air Force or *Força Aérea Portuguesa.* 2. *acronym.* The Peruvian Air Force or *Fuerza Aérea del Peru.* 3. *n. onomat.* A term apparently popularised on the internet for the sound made by a single stroke of gentlemanly *self improvement.* Also *fap fap fap;* an exclamation of red-blooded approval for the pulchritudinousness of a female. *'Romeo: See, how she leans her cheek upon her hand! Oh that I were a glove upon that hand, that I might touch that cheek! Fap fap fap!'* (from *Juliet does Verona and Mantua* by William Shakespeare).

fapier mâché *n.* Following a spot of *do-it-yourself*, the creative by-product of a careless clean-up of spilt *population paste* using cheap *shitscrape.*

fapkin *n.* Like a napkin, but not used for cleaning up after a nap.

fappetite *n.* The desire to *crack one out.* *'That Carol Vorderman off Countdown really whets my fappetite, I can tell you. No, not Carol Vorderman. Silly me, she doesn't do it any more, does she? I mean Nick Hewer.'*

faptism *n.* A lad's first successful *one off the wrist* as a teenager.

faptism of fire *n.* A grown man's first *one off the wrist* following a stag weekend in Amsterdam.

Farage's bank account *euph.* An old man's genitals, *viz.* Once full to the brim, with rapid growth potential and something many people would like to get their hands on, but now virtually

empty, attracting little interest and prone to scorn and rejection.

Farage's suit jacket, messier than *sim.* The result of intentionally *chucking one's milkshake.* *'By gum, Miss Lovelace. You're messier than Farage's suit jacket.'*

Farage's 'tache *n.* A feeble outcrop of *bumfluff* on a *twat.*

faralytic *adj.* In such a state of extreme *refreshment* that one lies down and refuses all offers of assistance. From the incident when Mo Farah finished second in the 5000m final of the 2017 London IAAF World Championships. *'When he was spotted lying on the pavement in Danglemah on Monday night, passers by said Nationals MP Barnaby Joyce, 56, appeared to be faralytic.'*

farce *1. n.* A play which involves Brian Rix hiding in a wardrobe and his trousers falling down in front of the vicar. *2. n.* The *snot, tinter, snotter etc.* Also *farse.*

farewell thunder child *1. exclam.* The plaintive, valedictory cry of Manfred Mann's Chris Thompson on epic progressive rock concept album *Jeff Wayne's Musical Version Of The War Of The Worlds*, lamenting the passage of the eponymously named battleship as it slowly sinks beneath the waves after being attacked by a Martian war machine. *2. exclam.* The plaintive cry of a gentleman lamenting the passing of a Brobdingnagian *dreadnought* as it slowly sinks beneath the waves and round the U-bend.

farkle *n.* A lady's *queef* from the *front bottom.* A bit like a *fart*, but with extra sparkle. A *muff puff.*

farm bent *adj.* Descriptive of a *berry* who finds himself quadruped inclined to romance as a consequence of enforced rural remoteness. *'GRAMS: Wine bar. Int. Day. FX: Door opens. EDDIE GRUNDY: Nelson! Come quickly! There's trouble in five acre field! NELSON GABRIEL: What on earth? EDDIE GRUNDY: It's your dad, Nelson. He's gone farm bent. NELSON GABRIEL: Oh no, not again. GRAMS: Dissolve to ext. day. FX: Distressed cow. WALTER GABRIEL: Ooh, yeah. Take that Daisy. You know you want it right up you, you dirty bitch. FX: Particularly loud moo.'* (from *The Archers*, BBC Radio 4, October 3rd 1983).

farmers *rhym. slang. Emmas.* From Farmer Giles = piles.

farmer's bike, fanny like a *sim.* A young lady's dusty and battered *private parts.*

farmer's breakfast *n.* A *shit* and a drink of water.

farmer's broth *n. Spiff, spodge, sprangle etc.*

farmer's footprint *n.* A huge *skidmark.* *'That's the last time I let Meat Loaf in to use the Sistine*

Chapel shitter. The fat bastard's left a right farmer's footprint in the U-bend, your holiness.'

farmer's frisbee *n.* A cowpat.

farmer's omelette *n.* A particularly infirm, runny, yellow motion. *'Apologies, Lady Grantham. I must perforce retire upstairs for a farmer's omelette.'*

farmer's protest *n.* An outbreak of chronic *ooh-aarrhoea* which pebbledashes the *chod bin* bowl with semi-liquid *shit.* From the universal habit of agricultural types who register their objections to unfair service charges by spraying thousands of gallons of cow *crap* all over the front of their local bank.

farmer sutra *n.* The ancient Dutch treatise on the art of erotic *barnyard love.* With a comedy soundtrack.

farm farts *n.* The smell of the countryside. *Country air. 'Ah, farm farts. Breathe that in, children.'*

farn't *n.* An *air biscuit* that, no matter how hard one tries, cannot be *floated.* A *fart* that can't. *Flatulisn't.*

FARO/faro *acronym.* A gentleman's post-intercourse afterplay. Fart And Roll Over.

farogenic *adj.* Descriptive of a female who appears to be attractive from a distance, but proves to be a great disappointment when viewed at closer range. *Nice from far but far from nice.*

farse *n.* The narrow isthmus of skin that separates a lady's *fadge* from her *arse.* Derivation unknown. Also many other words.

farsehole *n.* One who is not only fat, but an *arsehole* to boot. From fat + arsehole. *'Born on this day: 'Jessica Lange, King Kong actress, 1949; Luther Vandross, late soul singer, 1951; The Rt Hon Sir Eric Pickles MP, farsehole, 1952.'*

fart *1. n.* A *bottom burp*; an expulsion of foul air from the *chamber of horrors* that causes the *clappers* to vibrate musically like a tuning fork. A *beefy eggo,* a *poot,* an *air biscuit. 2. v.* To *drop* one of the above, *step on a duck. 3. n.* An ineffectual or wet fellow.

fart about *v.* See *faff.*

fartache *n.* After eating a meal of dodgy canned chilli beans, lingering pangs of regret that keep you tossing, turning, and crying through a sleepless night.

Fartacus *n. prop.* A hero who takes responsibility for a *duck* on which they didn't *step.* From the Roman slave of the same name who was crucified on the Appian way for *letting off* in the presence of Julius Caesar.

fart & depart *n.* At a social gathering, *dropping a gut* before swiftly moving away to allow someone

else to take the credit for your gaseous *largesse.*

fart an' give us a clue *exclam.* Said to put a *bariatrically-challenged* partner at ease while attempting to locate the way in.

fart bathing *n.* Sitting in a cloud of your own *arse gas* and enjoying it.

fart blanche *n. Fr.* The opportunity to freely *drop a Tommy Squeaker* without fear of detection, *eg.* In a noisy ham-packing factory, in the pits at a stock car race, or when nursing one's great uncle back to health from a near-death diarrhoea mishap.

fartbreak ridge *n.* The rugged, windswept anatomical scarp that runs from the *anus* to the *nutsack* or *fanny,* upon which *gusty zephyrs* sometimes break. The *biffin bridge.*

fart buffer *n.* The methane safety cushion which presages a *turd* and allows one a little extra time to reach the lavatory. The *turtle's breath. 'I'm afraid I must dash, your holiness. I've used up my fart buffer and I'm touching cloth here.'*

fartburn *n. medic.* A stinging blast of *cuzza* gas that could set the *fairy hammock ahad.*

fart button *n.* The "mute microphone" control in video conferencing software such as Zoom and Microsoft Teams. *'Sorry. I was a bit late with my fart button there, Lord Sugar.'*

fart catcher *1. n.* Fruit feeler. *2. n.* Derogatory term for one who waits on another person, *eg.* A valet, footman, flunky. *3. n.* A fawning BBC News "royal correspondent" like Nicholas Witchell. *4. n.* In cricket, the wicket keeper.

fart chair *n.* A lavatory. *'Where's your grandad?' 'He's in his fart chair, mam.'*

fart curtain *n.* A barrier *dropped* in an open doorway that is unlikely to keep flies out.

farte blanche *n. Fr.* The comfortable stage in a relationship when a chap is able to *step on a duck* in bed without fearing any retribution, or any reaction whatsoever for that matter, from his *significant other.*

fartefact *1. n.* The product of an unexpected *follow-through.* An *objet d'arse. 2. n.* An old *dropped gut* discovered still lingering upon re-entry to a previously vacated room. *'With trembling hands, I inserted the candle and peered in. At first I could see nothing, the ancient fartefacts escaping from the chamber causing the candle to flicker. Presently, details of the room emerged slowly from the mist, strange animals, statues and gold. Everywhere the glint of gold.'* (from *An Account of the Discovery of the Tomb of Jimmy Savile on Scarborough Cliffs* by Howard Carter).

farter *n. Aus. milit.* A sleeping bag. *'Tuesday, December 18th, 1912. Ate last of the pemmican in* *the night. Heavy snow again. Found Bowers dead in his farter. There is no hope for us now.'* (from *The Journal of Captain Scott*).

farters' market *n.* A busy works *bogs.*

fartex *n.* Trade name of that tasteless swirly material with lumpy bits which is loudly pebble-dashed round the inside of one's lavatory, and which can adversely affect the value of one's property. *Fartex* is applied by means of a portable high-pressure spray system and is available in a wide range of brown shades. Or black if you've been eating liquorice or have intestinal bleeding. Also *arsetex.*

fartface *n.* Someone with facial features that look as if they are permanently engulfed in someone else's *bum gas*, eg. Ex-*Countdown* host Nick Hewer. Although that might have been Susie Dent's fault.

fart factory *n.* The local Indian restaurant. *'Come to the Rupali, formerly Curry Capital and before that the Rupali again, Newcastle's best fart factory (now closed).'*

fart filter *n.* A pair of underpants. Also *dunghampers, undercrackers, overscrotes, tacklebags, Alans.*

fart for the day *n.* The first, life-affirming, *arse*-rattling, *guff* of the morning; a deep, almost poetic/ traumatic/life-changing experience. *'And now it's time for fart for the day, with Anne Atkins.'*

fart Friday *n.* A weekly happening in office premises across the country whereby pre-weekend lunchtime pints result in much flatulence and mirth in the afternoon. For example, on the 7th floor of the Kings House in Harrow, to pick an example entirely at random.

fart fuel *n.* Food consumed for the sole purpose of creating flatulence. For example, a breakfast of spam fritters, black pudding and tabasco baked beans, scarfed down before heading to the in-laws' for the day.

fart funnel *n.* The *rumpet.*

fartgargle *n.* A frothy expulsion of literary *air biscuit*, typical of the biographies of weapons-grade bellend AN Wilson.

fartgazing *n.* Distracted expression assumed when releasing a prolonged *chuff.*

fartglow *1. n.* The cosy llumination produced when a *guff* is ignited, short but somehow lingering, like a guttering tallow candle. *2. n.* The warm feeling a bloke gets after winkling out a particularly shy and reluctant *brew.*

fart grabber *n.* An habitually acquisitional type, who, were you careless enough to *drop a gut* in their presence, would snatch your *flatus* while your back was turned and make off with it in the hope it might have some value. An opportunist thief of the lowest kind. *'Born on this day: Elizabeth Montgomery, fragrant Bewitched actress, 1933; Claudia Cardinale, fragrant Once Upon a Time in the West actress, 1938; Lord Archer of Weston super Mare, perjurous fart grabber, 1940.'*

fart higher than your arse *euph.* To have an inflated opinion of oneself. To think oneself *all that when one ain't.*

farticles *n.* The crumbs of an *air biscuit*, often found in the sheets after *breakfast in bed.*

fartification *n.* The lid of a *Dutch oven*, held down firmly to prevent the egress of noxious *cooking smells.*

fartificial *adj.* Said of something that sounds like someone *stepping on a duck*, while having an altogether different explanation. *'Did you just step on a duck, Chris?' 'No, that noise was fartificial, Michaela. I actually just stepped on a duck.'*

fartillery *n.* A rousing *passage of wind* worthy of inclusion in a grand performance of Tchaikovsky's *1812 Overture*. Possibly with large calibre rounds used.

fart in colour *v.* To *chase the wind* or *follow through.* To suffer a *knickerbocker gory.*

farting against thunder *phr. meteorog.* Descriptive of a hopeless task that will inevitably end in failure. *'I may be farting against thunder here, Mr Howard, but if you'll excuse me I'm going to be frightfully rude and ask you the same fucking question for the thirty-eighth fucking time. Did you or did you not threaten to over-rule him?'*

farting around the poo *phr.* An expression which describes a person who isn't doing a job properly, in the style of someone who really needs a *shit* but is putting it off and instead simply passing gas around the *turd* in their *bomb-bay. 'I would like to assure the public that this company is certainly not farting around the poo here. We recognise the urgency of the situation in the Gulf only too well. On Monday afternoon, we intend to have a meeting to discuss starting to think about the basis of a possible plan to plug the break in the pipeline with old table tennis balls, shredded Wellington boots, broken fountain pens and discarded tea-bags.'*

farting bracket *n.* A footrest found to the left of the brake pedal in luxury motor vehicles equipped with automatic transmission, which enables the driver to lift one buttock and *let one go* without taking his attention off the road. *'Once again, the Merc has an extensive range of eye-wateringly costly dealer-fit options. But in this price range, goodies like air conditioning, heated seats and a farting* *bracket really should come as standard.'* (Jeremy Clarkson, *Sunday Times*).

farting clappers *n. medic.* Small, fragile, castanet-like bones up one's *nick* that resonate at particular frequencies, producing an unexpectedly loud "braaap!" sound in polite company.

farting crackers *n.* Trousers. *'When invited to a black tie function, the correct mode of attire for gentlemen is; white dress shirt and collar, cummerbund, black shoes, a black dinner jacket and matching farting crackers.'*

farting gift *n.* The evocative, lingering scent of *eau de colon* someone secretly leaves behind following a sharp exit from a lift or shared cab.

farting on eggshells *n.* Very carefully and delicately *easing springs* when one fears that there is a distinct possibility of *following through.*

farting point, the *n.* The inevitable stage in any relationship at which one partner brings an end to the practice of *farting* covertly and begins *blowing off* in an audible and olfactorily detectable manner.

farting shot *n.* A valedictory *brown dog's bark* emitted a few moments before leaving a room/elevator/meeting. *'Jesus, what's that? It fucking ronks.' 'I think it's Heseltine's farting shot, prime minister.'*

farting sideways *v.* To have a bad case of the *Badminton trials.* *'"Do please sit down, Mr Willoughby," Lady Marchmaine invited. "Thank you, madam," he replied, diffidently. "But if it is all the same with you, I shall remain standing. I rode a fox to earth over three counties yesterday and consequently I fear I shall be farting sideways for the foreseeable future."'* (from *Sense and Sensibility* by Jane Austen).

farting strings *n. medic.* Tendons or ligaments in the *lisks* which are prone to snapping during periods of excessive mirth. *'In a landmark court case, a Birmingham pensioner with an IQ of 6 is suing the BBC after snapping her farting strings laughing at the sitcom Mrs Brown's Boys.'*

fartive *adj.* To behave in a stealthy manner designed specifically to avoid the detection of one's *dropped guts* by others.

fart juggler *n.* One gifted with the ability to hold and queue *dropped hats* when in a potentially embarrassing situation, for example in a lift, and then fire off a *repeater* when at a safe distance. An *air traffic controller, stacker.*

fart knocker *1. n. Bum bandit, fudge nudger. 2. n.* One who criticises another's *air biscuits.*

fartle *1. v.* To startle yourself from sleep with a morning *bugle call*, in the style of a flatulent boxer dog. *'Fartled myself awake pretty betimes after too*

much veggie mince the night before and thence to the office, doing something towards our great account to the Lords Commissioners of the Treasury, and anon the office sat, and all the morning doing business.'* (from *The Diary of Samuel Pepys*). *2. v.* To creep behind a work colleague who is concentrating on a task and silently *drop one* before slipping quietly away.

fartleberries *n.* Dangleberries, winnets, chocolate raisins.

fartled *adj.* Shocked or surprised by an unexpected *bark from a brown dog.* *'You fartled me, Mr Tomlinson.'*

fart of the furniture *exclam.* Blaming a creaky sofa for an anal misdemeanour.

fart on a naan *phr.* A somewhat rhetorical reference to after-curry *arse gas* which smells exactly the same as the meal that created it. See also *gorilla's breakfast.* *'Christ, that smells so much like last night's dinner I could just fart on a naan and have it again.'*

fart on one's weetabix *euph.* To spoil one's chances. A less vulgar version of *piss on one's chips* or *cum on one's faggots.*

fartoodeetoo *n.* An amusing, burbling, polyphonic *gut drop* that sounds not unlike the indecipherable burblings of the *Star Wars* Dusty-Bin-a-like droid. *Far-2D2.*

fartopsy *n.* Scientific investigation to determine the cause of a surprisingly foul *ronk* that one's *freckle* has emitted. From fart + autopsy *'Fuck me, that one came out of nowhere. I don't recall eating tinned meatballs and I've had no strong ale, so I'm going to have to perform a fartopsy.'*

fartosophical *adj.* Descriptive of that moment of peaceful contemplation that follows a satisfying *trouser trumpet.* *'It was in a fartosphical mood that I opened the window and began wafting the Daily Mirror.'*

fart probation *n.* After taking up a new employment position, the time elapsed until it is deemed acceptable to *drop a gut* in front of one's colleagues. *'How's the new job, Sajid?' 'It's okay. The boss is a bit of a dick but my fart probation was only two weeks so I can't complain.'*

fartriloquist *n.* Old time variety performer who *steps on a frog* in one place while making it sound like it came from further away.

fart round corners, can *phr.* Said of a *backsmith* of such low talent that their only claim to fame is the ability to make your eyes water while not in your direct line of sight.

fart sack *n.* The bed, *scratcher, shag slab.* *'Malaria was powerless to resist. His eyes burned into hers* *like Swarovski crystals. His strong arms enfolded her body as she felt herself being swept away on a monsoon of passion. Tenderly, Pablo took her by her heaving shoulders, pulled her scads down and did her on his king-sized fart sack.'* (from *The Countess and the Matador* by Barbara Cartland).

fart sauce *n.* A *raspberry coulis* that is served with *arse cress*. The rancid *jus* accompanying a wet *poot*.

fart scissors *n.* Imaginary implements which would prove useful when a chap has retired to a discreet antechamber to *cut the cheese*, only to discover that his *shit shadow* is following him back into the room like an over-affectionate stray puppy.

farts council *n.* A row of toilet cubicles where each occupant is noisily passing a tricky *motion*. Also *privy council, rump parliament*.

fart sharer *n.* A tandem bicycle. *'It won't be a stylish marriage / I can't afford a carriage / But you'll look sweet / upon the seat / Of a fart sharer built for two.'*

fartsome *adj.* Description of one with a right *shitbox* on them. *'She's a fartsome filly alright, Captain, and no mistake.'*

fart sponge *n.* A cushion.

fartsteps, follow in [someone]'s *v.* To be forced into using an office *Rick Witter* that has been miasmatically befouled only seconds previously by a co-worker. *'It's a great honour to follow in your fartsteps, Sir Alan.'*

fart sucker *n.* A sycophantic *arse licker, gravy taster* or *shirt fly, eg.* Piers Morgan "interviewing" Donald Trump.

fart to a shit fight, bring a *v.* In a competitive situation, to be seriously overmatched. *'And Dunn really has brought a fart to a shit fight here, Harry.'*

fart to your bum's content *phr.* An expression that is descriptive of the happy freedom now enjoyed by millions of home workers who know that tapping the spacebar mutes their Zoom microphone.

fart transplant *n.* Turning your back on your partner in bed and *dropping your guts* against their *back doors* in order to send the *flatus* up their fundament.

fart-2D2 *n.* A burst of flatulence from the *death star* that is characterised by its randomness of tone, squeak and squelch. Also *arse-2D2, fartoodeetoo*.

fartwa *n.* A never-ending sentence which was issued against his customers at the Rupali Restaurant, Bigg Market, Newcastle upon Tyne, by the late Abdul Latif, Lord of Harpole.

fart wire *n.* The rear string of a thong which bisects the buttocks and, like a cheese-wire cutting through a truckle of Cheddar, will effortlessly slice through the densest *trouser cough*. *Officer's laces.*

fart with a skin on it, face like a *sim. Aus.* Useful expression which can be used when referring to a person with an unhappy or dissatisfied *mien*. *'Cheer up, Julian. You've got a face like a fart with a skin on it this morning.'*

farty time *n.* The moment in a new relationship when it seems acceptable to *drop your guts*. *'Oops, pardon me, Meghan.' 'Don't worry, Harry. It's well past farty time.'*

farty winks *n.* A flatulent and refreshing post-prandial nap usually taken on a Sunday afternoon in order to let one's guts settle after a big dinner. *'Jesus. Is the dog ill?' 'No, it's your dad. He's just having farty winks in front of the Grand Prix.'*

fast and furious *n.* A quick *lamb shank* – the opposite of a *Clapton*.

fast food foxtrot *n.* The forward-leaning, open-legged, side-to-side prance one assumes when trying to eat a kebab on the hoof without getting any chili sauce on one's chinos.

fast roping *n.* Unlikely sounding masturbation technique which involves poking your *arse* with your left thumb while *tugging yourself off* with the other hand. So named as it is evidently not dissimilar to the method employed by the military for getting down a crag quickly. *Abseiling, pokey bott wank*

fasturbation *n.* Emergency, hurried *self abuse*.

fatbastarditis *n. medic.* Condition characterised by a variety of symptoms such as aches, pains and agues, experienced generally by middle-aged people whose lives have been led by their tastebuds. *'I'm sorry to be the bearer of bad news, Mr Clarkson, but this is the worst case of fatbastarditis I have seen in forty years of private medicine.'*

fat bird's armpit, wetter than a *sim.* An expression used by meteorologists when talking about excessive precipitation. *'Northern areas, which we have represented on this weather map at an angle so that the distance from Nottingham to Aberdeen occupies the same amount of screen space as the gap between Exeter and Plymouth, can expect a mild, dry morning, with scattered sunshine. However, don't organise any barbecues just yet, because during the early afternoon this large area of moist air moving in from the Atlantic will meet this high pressure front over the Pennines, and by teatime the whole fucking country will be wetter than a fat bird's armpit.'*

fat bird's shoe, full as a *sim.* Descriptive of a something or someone which is stuffed to bursting point, *eg.* A former glam-rock star's hard disk, a postman's wardrobe, Jim Davidson's skin. *'More spooge, Marc?' 'No thanks, lads. I'm as full as a fat bird's shoe.'*

fate, faecal finger of *phr.* Expression describing

that awful moment when the wet strength of your toilet tissue is not quite up to the job in hand.

fatellite *n.* A puny little bloke caught in the gravitational tug of a *curvy lass*.

fat food *n.* Lipid-heavy *scrote cuisine* favoured by the sort of folk who prefer to eschew such frankly bourgeois dining accoutrements as cutlery, tables, plates, vegetables *etc*. *'They say fat food's not healthy but my dad ate nowt but pies all his life and he lived to be seventy-eight stone. He died when he were twenty-six.'*

fath *n.* A male moth.

fat hat *n. Blubber beret.*

fathletics *n.* Darts, snooker, pool *etc*. The less physically demanding sports, as enjoyed by the *big-boned*. From fat + hletics.

fatic electricity *n.* Charge of several million volts that builds up between the thighs of a big girl on her way to Greggs in spray-on jogging bottoms.

fat kid on a see saw, goes down like a *sim.* Affectionate reference to a lady who is generous with her oral favours; an *Ikea bulb, Titanic, taxi driver's clutch.*

fat lady's flip-flop, as flat as a *sim.* Said waggishly of a catastrophically overworked *ballbag* or a poorly presented glass of cider. Also *flat as a plate of cold piss, flat as a kipper's dick, flat as a witch's tit.*

fat lass sarnie *n.* A shameful, yet hugely satisfying sandwich that must be consumed out of the view of one's mates on account of its embarrassing nature, *eg*. A crisp, mayonnaise and tomato ketchup bap.

fat lass's biscuit tin, as empty as a *sim.* Barren, vacant. *As empty as Tim Henman's trophy cabinet. 'I've had a good rummage about in your Y-fronts, Piers, but as far as I can tell they're as empty as a fat lass's biscuit tin.'*

fat lollies *n.* The sort of high denomination seventies-style *thru'penny bits* often to be seen on a cockney criminal's *bird* when he is being arrested mid-*job* on *the Sweeney. Fat lollies* were also the default *jug* setting on negligee-clad women who typically answered the door to milkman/plumber/mobile gynaecologist Robin Askwith in the *Confessions* films.

fatman scoop *n.* The use of a cupped hand to ladle one's sweating genitals out of the *bollock consommé* that accumulates in the groin on a hot day.

fat man's salad *n.* Pouring a bag of nuts into a bag of crisps to make an additional side dish accompaniment for a pint of lager. That'll be two of your

five-a-day right there, then.

fatmobile *n.* A shopping scooter driven by a *big-boned* type. A *Mansfield motorcycle, pie chomper's chariot, council go-kart. 'Holy sausage rolls, Robin, I'm starving. To the fatmobile!'*

fat nav *n.* The inbuilt homing system which allows the more copiously skeletoned to find their nearest branch of Greggs.

fat rascals *n.* Playful *titties.*

fat rash *n. medic.* An area of inner thigh soreness on a *salad dodger,* caused by the severe chafing which occurs when running to the pie shop as closing time approaches.

fattery *1. n.* Derogatory comments which will get you nowhere with the *lettuce averse*. *2. n.* Complimentary comments aimed at the *big-boned* with the intention of charming them out of their enormous *applecatchers, eg.* "You don't sweat much for a fat lass."

fatties' loft insulation *n.* Home exercise equipment; gym mats, pink dumbbells, exercise balls *etc.,* which are pressed into service lining the attics of *gustatory athletes* about a week or so after the Argos January Sale.

fattitude *n.* Self belief and *chutzpah* exhibited by someone sat on a bench in a precinct, chomping their way through a family pack of Scotch eggs.

fattle *n.* Collective term for women whose glands are well versed in brassica avoidance techniques.

fattoo *n.* A permanent ink design applied to a *double sucker. 'Ooh, Is that your new fattoo, Michelle. What's it of?' 'It's a life-size copy of Raphael's School of Athens.' 'Nice. And what are you going to have on the other buttock?'*

fatty *n.* An erection; something that causes much hilarity in the school showers. Unless it's the PE teacher's.

fatty acid *n.* Beer.

fatty clappers *n.* Good old-fashioned no-nonsense *knockers*. The sort of *devil's dumplings* that would make Kenneth Connor have a sort of minor epileptic fit. *Fat lollies, milky swingers, bouncers.*

fatty, crack a *v.* To get a *stonk on* or *bone up. 'Right, into the showers, lads. I've cracked a fatty and I don't want to waste it.'*

FATWA/fatwa *abbrev.* A non-verbal means of expressing one's opinion on another person's attitude, behaviour or beliefs. Fart And Then Walk Away.

faulty O-ring *euph.* That which causes an unexpected and terminal explosion thirty seconds into the mission, when a man *goes for throttle up. 'Sorry Monica. It must've been a faulty O-ring. I'm* *sure most of that will just sponge off.'*

faunacate *v.* To commit consensual lascivious behaviour with a saucy member of another species that's been giving you a come-hither look, *eg.* A sheep, dolphin, hamster *etc.*

faux-caine *n.* Particularly poor quality *marching powder* of the sort that a cash-strapped local television personality might snort up his or her nose through a rolled scratchcard or bus ticket.

faux job *n.* A pantomimic act of simulated *horatio* in a soft-core *stick vid* production.

faux pair *n. Fr.* Artificially augmented *jubblies. Beverly hills. 'I like your faux pair, missus. They're a right tidy sight.'*

faux parp *n.* The *passing of gas* in a sophisticated social setting. *'I'll never forget the first time I had to serve her majesty with a cup of tea in her Balmoral quarters. I was so nervous that I committed an horrendous faux parp while I was bending over her bed to get the bag out the cup and she nearly spewed.'* (from *She Told Me I Could Have Them Dresses, Honest – The Memoirs of a Royal Butler* by Paul Burrell).

faux pie *n.* Not a real pie. One of those bloody microwaved abominations you get in chain pubs, consisting of a misleadingly small amount of gristle casserole the temperature of molten glass hidden under a four-inch thick duvet of puff pastry.

faux-pwa *n.* A slip of lap-dancing club etiquette. To *milm* one's *kex* when fishing for a tenner to stuff in a bored dancer's *dunghampers.*

fauxtrot *n.* Of a woman crossing the street, the act of escalating the frequency of her footsteps while not actually increasing her velocity, with the purpose of creating the illusion that she is getting a *fucking* move on.

fauxvid *n. medic.* A mild illness starting on a Monday morning with an almost imperceptible dry cough and the slightest of headaches which is guaranteed to get you a week off on full pay while you catch up on some much needed telly time.

fawn *v.* To *reach the Billy Mill Roundabout. 'The Russian Queen was powerless to resist. Rasputin's eyes burned into hers like sapphires. His monkular arms enfolded her body as she felt herself being swept away in a whirlwind of passion. Then he whipped out his Charlie and fawned all down her dress.'* (from *The Lady and the Cossack* by Barbara Cartland).

fawnication *n.* Sex (possibly illicit) with a young deer.

f-duct *1. n.* An aerodynamic channel between the legs of a Formula One racing driver. *2. n.*

An aerodynamic channel between the legs of a woman. *Toblerone tunnel, Foyston gap.*

fearless broadcaster *n.* A self-important *cunt. 'Piers is a fearless broadcaster, and everyone here at ITV hopes the operation to remove his tongue from the former President's nipsy is a complete success.'*

feastender *n.* A fat cockney *piece.*

feasting with panthers *n.* Oscar Wilde's coded reference to his scandalous carryings-on with jockeys and what-not. Doing a bit of *the love that dare not speak its name.* See *Zorba.*

feathering the clutch *euph.* When ensconced in a public convenience, skilfully and delicately controlling one's *nipsy* when defecating, to minimise the noise and embarrassment.

feather spitter *n.* An over-enthusiastic *pillow biter.*

Featherstone wedding cake *n.* A pork pie, a post-matrimonial delicacy which is popular amongst the denizens of the delightful West Riding beauty spot.

fecal treacle *n.* The sort of ultra-adhesive *bum toffee* that clings tenaciously to the side of the *shit pot* with the same force as No More Nails. *Pooperglue, fartex, ploppydex.*

feck *1. exclam. Ir.* Not quite *fuck.* Popularised by Fathers Ted and Jack. *2. n.* That quality which a feckless person is lacking.

feckfast *n. Ir.* An act of ante-matitudinal congress involving *cumulonimbus,* which delays the perpetrator to such an extent that he is forced to forgo his morning muesli and subsist until his elevenses on the nourishment he can obtain from the *fanny batter* in his beard and eyebrows.

fecorations *n.* Useful conflation of "fucking" and "decorations" which can be muttered by one not wholly imbued with a spirit of seasonal goodwill when venturing into the attic in early December in search of a damp box of knotted green wire, broken glass, mouse shit, dead bats and spiders.

feeder hand *1. n.* In the sport of darts, the non-throwing *wanking spanner* that passes the arrows to the throwing hand. *2. n.* That with which a chap *feeds a tired horse.*

feeders' wives *n.* The specialist section of a *bongo mag* which is devoted to amateur photographs of *pillow-smuggling* beauties.

feeding me rabbits *euph.* Having a *wank.* From the character Lucien in Liverpudlian sitcom *The Liver Birds,* who would stay home alone all day and answer the door looking dishevelled, explaining *"I was just feeding me rabbits".*

feeding time at the trout farm *euph.* The crowded view that greets one after *dropping off* a three- or four-day collection of *mudbabies at the pool* after *breaking the siege* following an enforced period of *brown drought.*

feed it a bun *phr.* Term used to emphasise the enormousness of a male member. *'I didn't know whether to suck it or feed it a bun.'*

feed the beavers *v.* To *drop a log* into the *yellow river.*

feed the cat *euph.* An excuse used when popping out for a spot of extra curricular activity. *'Sorry Fizz, I can't see you tonight. I've got to feed the cat. Have you seen my blobs anywhere?'*

feed the chicks *n.* To regurgitate. *'I'm just off outside to feed the chicks. Get us another pint and some more crabsticks, will you?'*

feed the ducks *v.* To *wank.* From an apparent similarity in hand movements to a man on a park bench *wanking.* Also *spill your seed.*

feed the fish *v. nav.* To vomit over the side of a ship, *bury one's biscuits* at sea. A nautical *honk.*

feed the fishes of the Thames, I have to *exclam.* Expression of a need to go to the bathroom and release *foulage* that will more-or-less immediately end up in a nearby waterway.

feed the otters *v.* To enjoy a *sit-down lavatory adventure.*

feed the oyster *v.* To engage in vaginal intercourse. To *do the dirty.*

feed the pony *v.* To *frig* a lady's *front bottom.*

feed the prawns *v.* To take a *shit.*

feejit *n.* An acceptable way of calling someone a "fucking idiot" when in polite company.

feel-good movie *n.* A film which, notwithstanding its minimal plotting and rudimentary dialogue, gives the audience a pleasantly warm feeling.

feel like Andy Warhol looks *v.* To *feel Welsh.*

feel the ghost of Freddie Mercury *n.* Mid-way through the act of *horatio,* to realise that the missus is well overdue a lip wax.

feel Welsh *v.* To be hungover, feel none too chipper. To have *eyes like sheeps' cunts.*

feely-touchy, a bit *adj.* Touchy-feely but not in a good way. Practically everybody in showbiz during the 1970s, it seems, was a bit *feely-touchy.* *'Is it, your honour, such a crime to be a bit feely-touchy?'*

feeshus *n.* Excrement. *'Come on, someone own up. Who's left a feeshus in me shoe?'*

feet seeking pissile *n.* A wayward *gypsy's kiss,* typically but not exclusively the first one of the day, that goes everywhere but into the lavatory bowl. Wearers of suede shoes are particularly vulnerable to *feet seeking pissile* attack.

fe fi fo fum *acronym. exclam.* A frustrated ululation: Fuck Everything, Fuck It, Fuck Off, Fuck Ur Mum.

felch *v.* The tender act whereby a gentleman orally retrieves his *spoff* from his partner's *arsehole.* Also *feltch, snowdrop.* *'Birds do it / Bees do it / Even educated fleas do it / Let's do it / Let's felch some spunk.'* (Song lyric *Let's Do It* by Cole Porter).

felchmeister *n. Germ.* A man in lederhosen and with a shaving brush in his hat who is particularly adept at "Vanillepudding aus dem Farbtopf holen".

Fellaini's flannel *euph.* A decidedly unkempt *ladygarden,* named in honour of the wild-barnetted Belgian former midfielder.

fellation *n.* The feeling of sublime joy a gentleman feels when having the immoral act of *horatio* performed upon his turgid person.

fellationship *n.* A loosely maintained romantic dalliance in which a bloke occasionally gets *gobbled off* in a pub *bog,* behind a skip, or in the Oval Office *shitter.*

fellatio ratio *n.* Out of the total number of people in the room, the proportion whom one might allow to *nosh off* one's *slag hammer.* *'Alan, you can't fire another woman this week. The producer says we've got to keep the fellatio ratio up.'*

fellatrix flick *n.* Special skill demonstrated by experienced *muck-vid* actresses whereby with a rapid, mid-*blow-job* turn of the head and neck, they tuck their flowing locks behind one ear to enable the director of cinematography unfettered camera access to the action without interrupting their bobbing rhythm.

fellowship of the ring *n.* A highly improbable circular formation involving an unknown number of *bad throwers.* A felicitous consequence of such an unlikely happenstance is that every participant would be a *lucky Pierre.* A *monks' chain.*

fellow-tio *n.* A chap *sucking the poison out* of another chap's *zoob.*

felmet *n. medic.* The point where the *fiveskin* is connected to the *bell end.* The *bobby's chinstrap, banjo, guyrope, Tarzan cord, Ordsall chord.*

felt a great disturbance in the Force, I *exclam.* Intoned in a shocked voice as if millions of voices cried out in terror, and were suddenly silenced by a planet-shatteringly loud *Lionel Bart.* Also *Alexa, open a window.*

felt tip 1. *n.* A marker pen *stool* that protrudes from the *nipsy* and keeps drawing lines on one's *bumwad.* The *brown crayon.* 2. *n.* A *tip* that has just been *felt.*

fem *n.* A highly photogenic species of *lady golfer.* Commonly found on TV *Frankie Vaughan* channels, reclining in pairs on the sofa. Also *femme.*

female pattern baldness *euph. Ladygarden* topiary

of whatever stripe, *eg.* A *shaven haven, clitler, Jimmy Edwards, Beppe's beard* or whatever.

femme brûlée *n.* A creamy *minge* where you need a spoon to crack your way through the crispy topping.

femme fartale *n. Fr.* A scarlet woman who is prone to expel wind more often than is strictly decorous.

femme fatale *n.* A *clopper* that could prove deleterious to one's health.

femme fraîche *n. Fr.* A *fanny* soured with a bacterial culture; pH approximately 4.5.

femtex *n.* Hormone-based explosive which becomes dangerously unstable once a month.

fenchested *adj.* Of a lady, to be sadly lacking where it counts. Named after the horribly flat, unsexy Fenland area of eastern England. See also *Dutch Alps, stits.*

feng shit *n.* Mystical process in which everything in the smallest room must be just right to ensure the most auspicious energy flow through one's nether channels. The routine undertaken by a defecator to ensure that a big *turd* comes out and doesn't go back up again. *'Answer the doorbell will you, love. I'm having me crap and the interruption ain't half upsetting me feng shit.'*

fent *n.* The erotic perfume of a woman's *clout.* Estate agent's tip: if a worn pair of ladies' pants is draped over a steaming kettle, the room will soon be filled with the alluring aroma of *fent.*

fent-a-ghost *n.* The strange aroma of *fent* left in your duvet, which lingers no matter how many times you change the bedding, normally experienced after *shafting* a regular *pie eater.* Humorously named after the utterly *shit* 1970s children's television programme *Rent-A-Ghost,* starring Nadia Popov from *Coronation Street* who is Gail Tilsley's gold-digging mum Audrey who was Joan in *The Fall and Rise of Reggie Perrin* who used to be married to Alf Roberts who fell off the car park in *Get Carter* starring Michael Caine who was in *The Battle of Britain* with Paul Angelis, whose real-life brother Michael used to be married to Audrey's on-screen daughter Gail.

fenticing *adj.* Descriptive of the thrilling aroma of a fresh *blurtch.*

fentilator *n.* A pair of *the missus's* – or next door neigbour's – used *grundies* worn on the head by a pervert while he is *boxing the Jesuit.* A *musk mask.*

Fenton *n. prop.* Named after the famous Youtube pooch, a predatory *biddy fiddler.* That is to say, one who chases "old dears" around the park.

fer-fetch a cloth, Granville *exclam.* A humorous phrase to be uttered in the immediate aftermath of a resonant *dropped hat.* From the catchphrase

of stuttering Doncaster shopkeeper Arkwright in the 1980s sitcom *Open All Hours.* Also *ease springs; don't tear it, I'll take the whole piece; how much?; keep shouting sir, we'll find you; more tea vicar?; I'm Peppa Pig.*

Fergie frown *n.* The milk-curdling expression assumed by a bloke's betrothed when he returns home *blind refreshed* after being unavoidably detained at a licensed tavern. From the side-splitting repertoire of comedy faces utilised by former Manchester United supremo Sir Alex Ferguson when his team were being comprehensively outplayed, like when they got dumped out of the FA Cup by Leeds United.

Fernbridge, a bit *euph.* The parliamentary equivalent of being *a bit Yewtree, eg.* The Rt Ho(The rest of this entry has been deleted following an urgent intervention from our lawyer)MP.

fernougle *n. Scots.* A Scotsman's *heated handrail* of humungous proportions. A *sporran splasher. 'Just got in from the Isle of Skye / My fernougle's lang but my kilt's cut high / The ladies shout as I go by / 'Donald where's yer troosers?''* (Sir Harry Lauder, traditional Scottish song).

Ferrari pitstop *n.* An ill-judged *splash and dash,* in which a gentleman leaves the *bogs* with his *cock* still hanging out and spilling fuel along the floor.

Ferris Bueller, the *n.* Self-satisfied pose adopted by a fellow while his *handy shandular* needs are being manually administered to by another. From the eponymous *wanker*'s picture, grinning smugly with his hands behind his head, on the poster for the film *Ferris Bueller's Day Off.*

ferry fucker *n.* A none-too-considerate lover whose personal *Kama Sutra* involves little more than "rolling-on and rolling-off."

fertle *v.* To *feed a lady's pony* through her *bills.*

festival flange *n.* Extra premium export strength *minge. Disco fanny* that has been baked in the sun and hasn't been washed for three days. The Special Brew of *twats.*

festival hot dog *n.* A hand-held *pap baffle.* As used by the artists Gilbert & George in the preparation of their shitty pictures.

festival knickers *1. n.* The undergarmentry worn by young ladies at open air pop concerts, *ie.* Crispy *shreddies* with a long weekend's worth of excitement evident in the gusset. *2. n.* The lower undergarmentry worn by middle aged ladies at Tom Jones concerts, *ie.* None at all.

festive perineum *n.* The famously nondescript bit between Christmas and New Year. *'What are you doing over the festive perineum?'*

festive period *n.* That which makes the missus

grumpy & unpredictable over Christmas.

fetch n. & v. *Spunk.* And indeed to *spunk up.* Also *fetch up.* '*Have you seen my other trousers anywhere, Bates? There's fetch down the front of these.*'

fetch hot water and towels! *exclam.* A jocose exclamation to be uttered in the style of James Robertson Justice after someone's *wind has broken,* heralding the imminent delivery of a *bouncing mud child.*

fetching off n. The gentle art of *tipping your concrete* into a lady's knicker drawer while she's out of the room. '*Hurry up fetching yourselves off, you lot. Carol Decker out of T'Pau's just finishing her encore and she'll be back any moment.*'

fetch the shovel, Mildred! *exclam.* Cry of mock panic upon rising from the *chod bin* and being confronted with the horrors one's *nipsy* has wrought. Also *go get the mongoose!, alert the coastguard!*

FFBB *abbrev.* Fart, Fanny and Bad Breath. The stench in – for example – Richard Burton and Elizabeth Taylor's bedroom the morning after one of their dozen-or-so tempestuous marriages.

FFFA *abbrev.* A reference to the sort of worthless *nonebrities* who rock up on the television these days. Famous For Fuck All.

FFTBBB *abbrev.* The inevitable converse of a *bobfoc.* A girl who possesses a face pretty enough to be rendered by a Renaissance great, but who has a body resembling a medieval vision of Hell. Face From Titian, Body By Bosch.

fiarrhoea n. *medic.* Volcanal eruptions following a night on the vindaloo. '*Hollywood movie stars, world leaders and the crowned heads of Europe have all got fiarrhoea after a slap-up feed at the Rupali Restaurant, Bigg Market, Newcastle upon Tyne.*'

fib tits n. Breasts that cause disappointment when removed from their enhancing *tit pants,* when they prove to have been *economical with the truth* about their proportions and/or pertness all along. '*How did you get on with that cracker from the Feathers with the great knockers?*' '*Crap mate. Turns out she had fuckin' fib tits.*'

fiddler crab 1. n. In the world of human *relaxation,* a gentleman who has *relaxed* so much that one forearm is the size of Popeye's while the other has practically withered away. 2. n. In the world of marine biology, the South eastern Atlantic crustacean *Uca pugnax, Uca pugilator* or *Uca minax,* distinguished by the fact that one of its arm nipper things is much larger than the other as a result of too much *wanking.*

fiddler's mittens n. Lady's hands. '*You can tell Madonna's older than she looks, though. You've only got to look at her fiddler's mittens.*'

fiddlestick n. An electronic leisure device for adults, a *neck massager, selfie stick, bob, AA member* or *dolly dagger.*

fiddle with the controls v. To *relax in a ladylike manner.*

fiddle yard 1. n. A concealed part of a model railway enthusiast's layout where he stores his toy trains and manipulates them away from the gaze of the general public. 2. n. A concealed part of a model railway enthusiast's layout where he stores his toy trains and *wanks himself off.*

fidge n. *Santorum, sexcrement, shum, toffee yoghurt.*

fidget spinner n. A lady's *clematis,* which can be used to exercise the fingers.

fidl n. A budget-conscious *strum* over a cheap'n'cheerful *bongo mag,* such as *Razzle* or *Exchange and Mart.*

fido fudge 1. n. Branded American peanut butter and bacon snack for dogs. 2. n. A length of *hound rope* somewhat lacking in structural integrity, lying in wait for the inattentive perambulist. '*Ah, fuck! I've trod in some fido fudge. Quick, pass me a matchstick whilst I find a puddle.*'

field trip n. The inevitable consequences of any *al fresco* sojourn which involves the consumption of psilocybin mushrooms or other illicit narcotic comestibles. Usually while one's students are occupied filling in worksheets that will later be shredded and used as bedding for the school gerbils.

fiery flue-brush n. A spicy vindaloo which carries all before it and transits the digestive tract without pausing to exchange pleasantries. Also known as a *light curry supper.*

fiery surprise n. To receive a brand spanking new electric fire that one never knew about.

fifth Marx brother n. Faecal residue left on the gusset of the *undercrackers* as a result of insufficient wiping. From "Ginger Marx". *Skiddo Marx, duck soup.*

fifty-fifty, go 1. v. On a popular television quiz programme, to have the computer randomly and unerringly remove the two less likely answers, leaving the same pair of possibilities the contestant previously told Clarkson they were toying with. 2. v. To risk releasing a *Bakewell tart* into one's *trolleys,* despite the fact that there is a very real possibility it will be accompanied by half a cup of tea and a chocolate eclair.

fifty-one week Methodists *euph.* Those mysterious members of the community who you never see in your local *boozer,* yet suddenly take over the fucking place for the last week of every year.

fifty shades of brown *euph.* A phrase used to describe a particularly varied morning of explosive diarrhoea following a hefty *sesh*.

fifty shades of gravy *n.* Descriptive of the multi-hued *fairy hammock* on an unkempt lass's *dunghampers*.

fifty wrist *n.* A frantic, blurred *knob-strangling* session opportunistically enjoyed during the narrow *wank window* while the missus pops out to the corner shop for a twenty Benny Henny.

fig *n.* A lady's pudendum. *'If you freeze it just there, grandad, you can see her fig.'*

fight a turkey *v.* *Choke a chicken*. To strangle your *cock*.

fighter pilot's thumbs *n.* *Chapel hat pegs, JCB starter buttons*.

fight fire with fire *v.* Of a bearded fellow, to perform *cumolonimbus* on an hirsute *flange* in the style of that bloke in *The Joy of Sex* who looks like he's got his chin stuck in Jeremy Beadle's disguise box.

fight fire with fire *v.* To heroically drink through a raging hangover.

fighting a boozing battle *n.* A familiar sight outside late bars and nightclubs. Young men wearing white, short-sleeved shirts, exchanging blows while under the influence of alcohol. *'Where's Harry?' 'Last time I saw him he was outside on the steps fighting a boozing battle with a photographer, Meghan. He said he'd see you back at the Chinook.'*

fighting dog's ear, fanny like a *sim.* A phrase that could be used in polite company when referring to the state of a female's *bits* after a right good hammering. *'Arachnaphobia was powerless to resist. His eyes burned into hers like hot toast. His muscular arms enfolded her body as she felt herself being swept away in a dual cyclone of passion which reached every nook and crevice of her being and which seemed to last for hours. When he had finished doing her, he rolled off, dropped his guts and lit a Woodbine. 'How was it for you, darling?' he whispered. 'Did the earth move?' 'Not half,' she replied. 'You've left me with a fanny like a fighting dog's ear here.''* (from *The Egyptian Concubine and the Cheesemonger* by Barbara Cartland).

fighting patrol, teeth like a *sim. milit.* Amusingly said of one with substandard dentition, *viz.* "All blacked out with five metre spacing".

fighting water *n.* *Falling down juice, wreck the hoose juice, Spesh*.

fight or flight turd *n.* A monster lurking in your lower *Simon Cowell* that is of such proportions that you can't make your mind up whether to run

away and hide, or to face it like a man.

FIGJAM/figjam *abbrev. Aus.* Antipodean phrase used when referring to a colleague who believes himself to be the *dog's bollocks* when he is, in reality, a *tosser*. Fuck I'm Good. Just Ask Me.

file a report *n.* To almost soil your *nutchockers* when dropping a *sneaky blinder*. A near miss that you may be obliged to bring to the attention of the Civil Aviation Authority.

file for wankruptcy *v.* To use the last vestiges of your strength to reluctantly put away your stash of *art pamphlets* after *emptying Barclays' vaults*.

file under W *phr.* To store in one's *mammary banks* an erotic image to which you intend to later refer for a nefarious purpose. *'Crikey, she's got enormous norks. File under W.'*

Filey fanny *n.* The knees-apart, *up-bloomers* seated posture adopted by elderly northern ladies on deckchairs at the seaside. Believed to be a means of keeping the flies off their ice creams.

FILF/filf *1. n. acronym.* The object of a *chubby chaser's* affections; Fatty I'd Love to Fuck. *2. n. acronym.* The gay or bisexual equivalent of *milf. 3. acronym.* Feminist I'd Like to Fuck. You'd think they'd be flattered. *4. n.* An erotically alluring *old biddy.* Fossil I'd Love to Fuck. Also *filfy adj.*

Filipino palm vinegar *1. n.* A popular recipe ingredient in western Pacific cuisine. *2. n.* A popular lubricating unguent liberally dispensed wherever *happy endings* are sold.

filleting knife *euph.* A particularly ugly woman or *lumberjill*. One who swiftly and efficiently "removes the bone from your meat".

fillet-o-fish *n.* A *haddock pastie* that is on the menu, but for which one has to wait four minutes while it is prepared. While your chips go cold and your McFlurry melts.

fill in *v.* Of a gentleman, to pass on the benefits of things he has discovered while browsing the internet to his *significant other*. *'Goodness gracious me. I had no idea that Lindsay Lohan's figure was quite so Junoesque. I'd better go and fill in the missus.'*

fill the dishwasher *v.* To have sexual intercourse with one's missus. Bit sexist, that one.

fill two birds with one bone *phr.* Descriptive of the sort of *ménage à trois* George Best would have had, back in the sixties when they were all *at it*. And he was still alive, obviously.

fill your boots *v.* To make the most of a sexual opportunity. Often prefaced "go on son".

film four *n.* The act of having to stay awake till four in the morning in order to *enjoy* a meaningful French art film on the obscure *wankers'* movie channel.

filofucks *n.* Notches on a young buck's bedpost, by which means he records and tabulates his miscellaneous romantic escapades.

FILTH/filth *n. acronym.* Larger boned ladies who make it into a fellow's *wank bank*; Fatties I'd Love To Hump.

filth machine *n.* An old computer which is kept purely for the purpose of surfing porn. A *dirty mac* or *faptop.*

filth of Saruman is washing away, the *phr.* A remark that can be uttered out loud, or even thought to one's self, as one *pisses skidmarks* off the the *bum sink.* A line uttered by the big tree man in *Lord of the Rings.*

filthy Ned *n. Dirty Sanchez's* brother.

final ball of the over *1. n.* The last of six legal deliveries bowled from one end of a cricket pitch. *2. n.* The last *scuttle* of a relationship that is *on its last legovers.*

final demand *n.* A "last warning"-style twitch from the *Camillas* which signals that one must drop everything in order to *park the fudge* immediately. A *final demand* usually arrives from the *gasworks* when one has been putting off a *poo* in anticipation of a forthcoming commercial break. *'I'm just going to pause this here, nan, only I've just had a final demand.'*

final warning shot *n.* The last blast of *pump gas* before the *monkey's toe* makes an appearance. A fusilade so unspeakably pungent that it can only mean the next report will be *live ammunition.*

final whistle *n.* A *fart* that comes in three loud, controlled blasts, causing half the assembled crowd to jump up and cheer.

final word *n.* Lavatorially speaking, the short, sharp toot on the *botty bugle* that announces to anyone in the vicinity that a bloke's *python* has been well and truly *syphoned.* A *foul stop.*

finding a peanut in a kebab *euph.* Descriptive of the difficulty encountered when a gentleman attempts to locate the *wail switch* during foreplay.

finding Nemo *n.* Taking the *big allotment challenge. Dining at the Y, licking out.*

find the key to the pie cabinet *v.* To become significantly larger than in former years.

find the lady *1. n.* Nigh-on impossible street gambling game, in which one must identify the genuine Queen of Hearts before the police arrive. Typically ends with one being cunningly tricked, milked dry and thoroughly *rogered. 2. n.* Nigh-on impossible task on a night out in Thailand, in which one must identify the genuine female amongst all the *flippers.* Typically ends

with one being cunningly tricked, *milked dry* and thoroughly *rogered.*

finger blessing *v.* Firkyfoodling sans *dunghampers.*

finger buffet *n.* An all-you-can-eat *fadge.* Also *otter's dinner, beanfeast, smorgasbord, breakfast of champions.*

finger discipline *n.* The skilful manual dexterity exhibited by a *wankered Glasgow piano* virtuoso. *'You've got to hold the two lemons and nudge that cherry, your holiness. Oi, oi, oi, watch your fucking finger discipline.'*

fingered by Wolverine *euph.* Suffering from a particularly heavy *women's things.*

finger food *n.* Something small and delightful you pick up at a party, but which leaves your hands smelling.

fingerhut *n.* A small, rude dwelling for the digits, typically found amongst the undergrowth while exploring a magically overgrown *ladygarden.* A *moss cottage.*

fingering her like Steve Harris plays his bass *phr.* Descriptive of a rapid-fire *finger-banging* technique reminiscent of the way Iron Maiden's bassist plucks the strings of his Fender Precision guitar.

finger in several pies, have a *v.* To be up to one's neck in *tussage. 'Stewart admitted he could see little prospect of the Faces reforming any time soon, but said he had a finger in several pies at the moment.'*

finger of fudge *n.* The consequences of *breaching the hull.* A *taxi driver's tan.*

finger pie *n.* A *handful of sprats,* a *pony feeding session.*

fingers *n.* One step beyond *tops. "Smell them!', cried Jennings 'Pwoar!' sniffed Darbishire. 'What an ozard ronk. What have you been up to?' Jennings grinned conspiratorily. 'I just got my fingers off Venables' sister in the prep room and I'm never going to wash my hand again."* (from *Jennings and the Strange Urges* by Anthony Buckeridge).

fingers, as sticky as a Scouser's *sim.* Descriptive of an unkempt *clunge. 'Jesus, woman. Your clout's as sticky as a scouser's fingers.' 'I know. But to be fair, I only came in to have my root canal done.'*

fingers in the sparkle jar *1. n.* Title of the autobiography of much-loved BBC punk naturalist Chris Packham. *2. n.* Firkyfoodling a *vajazzled beaver.*

fingersmith *1. n.* A disgusting *self-polluter* of either gender. *2. n. Piss-poor* BBC costume drama about Victorian *carpet-munching,* which disappointed thousands of sofa-bound *fingersmiths* across the country.

fingertip grip *1. n.* In the world of snooker, holding the butt of one's cue with the very ends of one's digits in order to better control a tricky shot. *2. n.* In the world of somewhat desperate late-night-television-fuelled *gentleman's relaxation,* to chalk your *naughty cue* at the sight of BBC snooker presenter Hazel Irvine. Presumably while hoping against hope that the whole sordid, dismal transaction will be successfully completed before John Virgo appears on the screen and sets you back a good ten minutes or so.

finished off more miners than Thatcher, she's *exclam.* Affectionate description of one north-east lady who has apparently been *on the batter* behind a skip outside Ashington Conservative Club since the mid-90s. Famous for her £3 *hand-job* special.

finisher *n.* The favourite page of an *art pamphlet* saved for the climax of a *cat stabbing* session.

finishing the dishes *1. n.* That deflating experience when you discover that the fucking dishwasher has not cleaned its contents properly so you have to complete the fucking job yourself, wondering all the while what was the fucking point of getting the fucking bastard thing in the first place. *2. n.* Resorting, following a disappointing or regrettable *poke,* to a dispiriting act of *monomanual labour. 'When the Lord saw what Onan had wrought He was sore displeased and great was His anger, and he spake unto Onan in a loud voice saying Onan, you did lie in your tent with your wife Tamar and yet while she slept did you then take yourself in your hand and thus did spill your precious seed all upon the ground and everywhere which was exceedingly sinful in mine eyes. And Onan waxed sorrowful for he saw that he had indeed sinned before the Lord, begging forgiveness from Him saying, O Lord, I am sorely repentant for my wickedness but yea, I was only finishing the dishes.'*

finishing touches *1. n.* In a *rub-a-tug shop,* the closing manoeuvres of the latter service as opposed to the former, typically costing the client an extra five quid or so. *2. n.* The final few flicks of the *naughty paintbrush* when *painting the ceiling.*

finish in traffic *1. v.* In basketball, to score despite one's route to the basket being crowded with opposing defenders. *2. v.* Of a male *grot* performer, to *shoot* cleanly across multiple actresses' *hoops* under pressure.

Finnan haddie *1. n.* Gastronomically speaking, a high class fish supper, *viz.* Haddock which has been smoked over peat. *2. euph. Gashtronomically* speaking, a high class *fish supper.* From the lyrics to the Cole Porter song *My Heart Belongs to Daddy,* as saucily performed by Julie London, Marilyn Monroe and Eartha Kitt, and somewhat less suggestively by Herb Alpert, *viz.* "If I invite / A boy some night / To dine on my fine Finnan haddie / I just adore his asking for more / But my heart belongs to daddy."

Finnegan's wake *n.* Descriptive of one's face upon waking in the morning after a heavy session *on the turps* and a poor night's sleep. Characterised by grey pallor and puffyness around the eyes. *David Davis eyes.*

Finsbury bridge *n.* The *barse.*

FIOFI/fiofi *acronym.* A tough-looking, unattractive woman. From (would you rather) Fuck It Or Fight It.

Fiona Bruce *n. prop. rhym. slang. Blip, milp.* From BBC newsreader Fiona Bruce = fanny juice.

fire alarm *n.* When all hell breaks loose from all your emergency exits as you are settling down for a nice quiet *Betty Boo.* A burning backdraft of *arsepiss, Wallace* and collapsing girders.

fire and forget *phr.* A miraculous *how do you do* that *shows a clean pair of heels* and doesn't require any wiping. A *future shit, happy Havana, Hollywood ending* or *miser's shite.*

fire cover *1. n.* What an heroic soldier requests from his comrades prior to single-handedly storming an enemy machine gun nest. *2. n.* A request made to the wife when on holiday and staying in a tiny hotel room, after you have consumed a dodgy paella and a plethora of *pedro's piss. 'My guts are rotten, love. I've got to go to the bog. Put the telly on, will you? Give me some fire cover.'*

firecracker *n.* A lady who is only worth a single *bang.*

fire down below *exclam.* An announcement signifying the discovery of a genuine redhead.

fire flap *1. n. nav.* Precautionary measure intended to prevent a conflagration at sea. *2. n.* A lady's *downstairs region* that is carrying *the gift that keeps on giving, viz. Happy rash.*

fire in the hole! *exclam.* A somewhat plaintive warning shout issued from the water closet after a night on the pop and Vindaloo, possibly at the Curry Capital, Bigg Market, Newcastle upon Tyne. When it was open.

fire into the brown *1. phr.* When shooting; to aim your barrel indiscriminately into a flock of birds. *2. phr.* To *shoot your load* indiscriminately up your partner's *jacksie.*

firelighter *n.* An exceptionally dry *turd* that has a low flash point.

fireman's blanket *n.* A precautionary *plop*-catching mat of *brown shield stamps* laid on the *bog* water surface, with the intention of preventing noise and/or *splashback.* Also *crash mat, pap baffle, turd raft, pilo.*

fireman's ladder *n.* An extremely proud and

extendable erection that gathers an anxious crowd.

fire off some arse chaff *v.* To *drop a gut* in order to get rid of someone who is following you around.

fire off some knuckle children *v.* Of a healthy young man, to *sow his wild oats* on the ground/ into a tissue/into a sock/up the dog's back/into a lady's knicker drawer/onto Giles Coren's risotto.

fire one across the bows *v.* A *navel engagement* whereby the *pirate of men's pants* withdraws from the battlezone just before the *egg white cannon* shoots its payload into *cod cove*. See also *pull out and pray, Vatican roulette*.

fire snakes *n.* Venomous post-curry or post-chili *Peter O'Tooles* that rattle out the *arse* at a fair old lick.

fire the early morning gun *1. v.* To *drop anchor, lay a cable, take a sounding.* To enjoy an ante-mati-dudinal *shit. 2. v.* To *dance the blanket hornpipe.*

fire, throw a log on the *v.* To *shit* oneself while attempting to light a *fart.*

fire up dropzone two *1. phr.* Said by host Ben Shephard when a player wants to drop a coin into the second area during giant tuppenny water-fall-based *doleys'* TV gameshow *Tipping Point. 2. phr.* An announcement prior to going off to *drop a length of dirty spine. 'Fire up dropzone two. Ooh, the £10,000 jackpot counter's teetering on the edge. I can't take the excitement. Fire up dropzone two.'*

firewood *n.* The state of penisular arousal whereby nothing and nobody is going to stop it *going off*, not even your gran knocking on the shed door with a cup of tea. *Vinegar string.*

firing blanks *v.* Post-*snip spoffing. 'You can put the ticklers away, love, I'm firing blanks.'*

firing on both cylinders *euph.* When an accommodating young lady entertains two gentleman callers simultaneously. *Man at C&A, Dorothy Perkins, double decker, the beast with two sacks.*

firing on one cylinder *euph.* A deep, rumbling *trouser trumpet* with "put-put" noises at the end, reminiscent of a 1950s British motorbike being revved and then allowed to stall.

firing the one o'clock gun *1. n.* Act performed every day at around thirteen hundred hours from the parapets of Edinburgh Castle in order to make all the American tourists in Auld Reekie *shit* their brand new tartan troosers. *2. n.* Act performed by a man upon returning home during a lunch-break while his flat-mates, kids *etc.* are out. *'Well, that's all the lunchtime news from me Martyn Lewis. I'll be back with the main headlines at six, but meanwhile I'm nipping off home to fire the one o'clock gun.'*

firing up the Quattro *euph.* Getting into something that may have looked and felt great in the

eighties, but which has since arguably lost some of its former allure. *Milfing.*

firkin *1. n. arch.* An Imperial measure of ale capacity, equal to nine gallons or half a kilderkin. *2. n.* The *firkwitted* epithet for half the *firkin* pubs in Britain.

firkyfoodling *n. arch.* Tudor foreplay. *'Dearest Maid Miriam. Until lately did my husband Henry be a most wonderful and caring lover. But forsooth I am most sad to relate that of recent times he wanteth naught but most hasty coupling with me and he spendeth no time on the firkyfoodling. Yea I fear that my tastes for the courses of love hath declined as a consequence. And now he hath vouchsafed to cut my head from my shoulders. Five wives hath he taken already before me, and of two hath he separated their heads from their shoulders. What am I to do? Pray, pray, pray help me. C. Parr, London.'* (Letter to the *Daily Mirror*, 1545).

first half shat-trick *n.* A fine achievement by any working man; the *laying* of three *cables* before midday.

first impressions *n.* Breasts. *Competitive advantages, impressive CVs. 'Well I must say, first impressions are certainly positive, Lord Owen of Plymouth.'*

first load *n.* That which is flushed down the *chod pan* prior to that second round of lower intestinal grumbling which heralds the arrival of a bonus *drop of shopping.*

firstly are you okay? I hope so *exclam.* Question posed in the immediate aftermath of an *airborne toxic event*, delivered in the glib, insincere style of a daytime TV presenter.

first mud *n.* The *popping* of a *brown cherry*. Earning your *bronze medal.*

first on the dancefloor *euph.* Of a gentleman who *knows what's in his flowerbeds*; being *good with colours, sensitive*, prone to supra-puddular aerobatics and what-have-you. *Colwyn Bay as a nine bob note.*

first task of the day *euph.* A *wank. 'Well that's the first task of the day completed, dear. Time for a short nap, then I'll clean the car.'*

first two inches are cold, the *exclam.* A cry to indicate the urgency with which one requires a lavatory. *'I answered the urgent hammering on the door. It was Holmes, in the guise of a one-legged Greek Admiral, and possessed of a wild expression the likes of which I had never seen upon his countenance before. "What is it, Holmes?" I expostulated, wiping the sleep from my eyes. "Why, it's three in the morning!" "There is no time for explanations, Watson," he gasped as he pushed past me* *towards my water closet. "The first two inches are cold."'* (from *The Case of the Great Big Shit* by Sir Arthur Conan Doyle).

firtle *v.* To cut a hole in a poster of one's favourite pop star, film actress or politician, and *fuck* it.

fish *1. n. prop.* Former lead singer out of Marillion, real name Derek Penis or some such. *2. adj.* Not very good. *Crap, Swiss, pants, mouse, fucking rubbish. 'The lead singer out of Marillion is fish.'*

fish box *n.* A lady's *twat. Billingsgate box, fish mitten.*

fishcake *n.* The feminine art of cupping a *queef* and presenting it to an unsuspecting victim. Distaff counterpart of the *cupcake,* also available with batter.

fish drowner *n.* A *clown's pie.*

fisherman's blues *1. n.* Title of a 1988 Waterboys album which reached number thirteen in the UK charts. *2. n.* The deep disappointment and resentment felt by a chap who has successfully *licked out* his missus when she fails to return the favour. See also *conulingus.*

fisherman's jumper *n.* A damp, overly hairy *cunker,* smelling not too dissimilar to a deep sea trawler captain's wool sweater after hauling in a net full of haddock. *'Having been accustomed all my life to ideals of a feminine nakedness gleaned from classical antiquities, I was somewhat taken aback on my wedding night to find that my young bride had a right old fisherman's jumper between her legs.'* (from *The Memoirs of John Ruskin,* 1819-1900).

fisherman's sock, pull her on like a *sim.* No-nonsense method of sexual intercourse. *'Concertina was powerless to resist. His eyes burned into hers like zirconium. His muscular arms enfolded her body as she felt herself being swept away on a tsunami of passion. They stood before each other naked, until he could wait no longer to slake his ardour. Roughly, he grasped her by the waist and pulled her on like a fisherman's sock.'* (from *The Lady and the Independent Financial Adviser,* by Barbara Cartland).

fisherman's swig *n.* A well deserved sup from the *hairy goblet* at the end of a hard day's work.

fish fingers *n.* The lingering odour experienced after performing the *cat and the fiddle* on a rude lady's *landing gear.* Hopefully without ketchup.

fish flakes *n.* The dried scraps of *kipper sauce* left in a gentleman's *rubiks* after a night of passion.

fish from the other bank *v.* To be *on the other bus* or *good with colours.* To *jump puddles.*

fish fryer's cuff *sim.* Descriptive of a pair of well-worn knickers with a heavily *battered* gusset.

fish-hook shit *n.* A *turd* containing a sharp object that snags the *nipsy, eg.* A peanut, a filling, the

wife's *clit ring.*

fishing nets *n.* Mesh *undercrackers* infused with the ripe *fent* of seafood.

fish mitten *n.* A *muff* that keeps the fingers and thumb of one hand warm.

fishmitten's bark *n.* An audible release of *clam gas. A queef, fanny fart, hail Mary.*

fishmonger's dustbin *n.* A very flavoursome and aromatic *kipper* that could attract seagulls from miles around. A *blind man's muff, Norwegian's lunchbox.*

fishmonger's flakjacket *n.* Protective apron or bib donned when *going down* on an *unkempt growler. 'With you in a minute, Germaine. I'm just looking for my fishmonger's flakjacket.'*

fish mouth *n. medic.* The *meatus* or *hog's eye. 'Without warning, the somnolent peace of the dorm was broken by an ear-splitting cry from Jennings's bunk. "Ooyah! Someone call matron!" he screeched. "What on earth…?" yawned Darbishire, clumsily groping in the darkness for his spectacles and knocking his tooth mug onto the linoleum. The light clicked on and there stood Mr Wilkins, purple-faced in his dressing gown and slippers. "What is the meaning of all this noise?" he blustered. "Sorry sir," said Jennings. "But I've somehow got a biro refill stuck in me fish mouth."'* (from *Jennings Sticks a Ballpoint Pen Down his Cock-end* by Anthony Buckeridge).

fish peach *n.* A recently shaven *haven* with three days of stubble. Combines the texture of the eponymous furry fruit with the bracing zest of a bank holiday in Whitby.

fish slice *n.* The seam on a pair of tight-fitting ladies' jeans which occasions an uncomfortable intrusion down the centre of the *captain's pie.*

fish slipper *n.* A more voluminous version of the *fish mitten,* into which a gentleman is wont to slip *half a foot* with not inconsiderable relief at the end of a trying day.

fish spa *1. n.* A currently fashionable pedicure treatment whereby women dip their weeping corns into a stagnant fishbowl full of other people's verruca germs. *2. n.* A female version of the *gentleman's wash,* carried out in a pub toilet sink, a *gash splash.*

Fish Street *1. n.* The female vagina. *2. n.* A narrow, damp and cobbled thoroughfare in central Shrewsbury, accessed *via* Grope Lane and Bear Steps. *'I was in Grope Lane, but I never made it to Fish Street'.*

fish supper *1. n.* A grease-laden Friday night feast with the tang of the sea and plenty of batter. *2. n.*

Fish and chips.

Fishwick *1. n. prop.* A small Scottish village 4 miles west of Berwick upon Tweed. *2. n.* The bit of braided string that hangs out of a *kipper* that has *fallen to the communists*. A *mouse's tail.*

fissure kisser *n.* A person who will do anything to get ahead, including snogging the boss's *arse*. *'Wanted: Young business entrepreneurs to audition for a role in the BBC's forthcoming Apprentice series. No qualifications required but applications from owners of overly tight suits and avid fissure kissers are welcomed.'*

fist *1. v.* Of boxers, to punch someone in the ring. *2. n.* Of *competent ironers*, to punch someone in the *ring*. *3. n.* Of heterosexuals, to punch someone in the *quim* or the *ring*.

fisticuffs *n. Knocking oneself about a bit. 'How did your quiet night in go, then, your holiness?' 'I'm afraid it descended into fisticuffs, as usual.'*

fistival *n.* A carnivalesque jamboree of *fisting*, for want of a better explanation.

fist magnet *n.* Someone who attracts punches to his face.

fist of fury *n.* Of a gentleman with a restricted *wank window*, for example while his missus has just nipped next door for a cup of sugar, a mindlessly violent act of *self abuse* carried out in a sort of masturbatory red mist. An *armbreaker, bishop rage, power wank.*

fist of used tenners, fanny like a *sim.* Descriptive of a *well-stuffed*, if somewhat dry, *sausage wallet.*

fistorian *n.* A fellow who maintains a keen and active amateur interest in vintage *grumble.*

fist pump *1. n.* A celebratory victory gesture as favoured by British tennis players when they occasionally win a point. *2. n.* Exhibition standard *onanism* as practised by former British tennis players.

fistress *n. Madam Palm,* with whom a man might be tempted to cheat on his missus.

fist sitting *n.* The act of supporting the buttocks on one's clenched hand while engaging in a bathtime *dolphin waxing* session, thus preventing the tell-tale splashing, squeaking noises that are unavoidable as the pace picks up towards the *vinegar strokes.*

fisty-cuffs *1. n.* A *pagga* or *Barney*. *2. n. Tadpoles in cream* deposited on the lower sleeve of a shirt following a bout of *pud-pulling.*

fit *adj.* Attractive, worthy of *one.*

fitbin *interj.* The rudest word in the English language, so rude that its meaning has been encased in 500 tons of concrete and dumped in the Irish Sea.

fitbit 10K *n.* Fireworks, vibrations and other celebrations from an exercise wristband when it confuses a protracted session of *gentleman's relief* with a health-giving jog round the park.

fitbot *n.* A sweat-inducing, 15-minute *Simon Cowell* workout so strenuous that it registers as a cardiovascular activity on one's wrist-based step counter, often leading to a 'Goal Achieved' notification.

fit for fucking, fat for cooking *exclam.* An expression of an unacceptably sexist attitude that we would not in any way endorse or repeat. Having a *hottie* on the side while maintaining one's *salad-dodging bag for life* because she makes a lovely Sunday roast.

fitting a kitchen *euph.* Taking a week off work to indulge in a *DIY* marathon. *'Dave, you look knackered mate considering you've just had a holiday.' 'I am Tom, I've had no rest at all. I've been fitting a kitchen.'*

five a day, getting one's *phr.* Euphemistically said of an idle chap sitting at home all day *relaxing in a gentleman's manner. 'Doctor: 'You look quite drained, Mr Jones. Have you been getting your five a day?' Patient: 'I certainly have doctor. Me plums are as flatter than a cow's cunt.''* (Bamforth's Seaside Chuckles postcard by Donald McGill, 1928).

five against one *n.* A very one-sided but nonetheless enjoyable game of wrestling in which *Madam Palm and her five sisters* attempt to *strangle Kojak*. The game ends when someone *makes the bald man cry.*

five bar *n.* A toilet with good phone reception.

five card stud with the gangster of love, play *v.* To *shuffle one's deck. 'Can I borrow your Grattan Catalogue, dear? I'm just off down the shed to play five card stud with the gangster of love.'*

five day test *n.* A pointless *Ethel* that never really gets going and typically has no prospect of a satisfactory conclusion.

five finger death punch *1. n.* Popular USA alt-rock combo. No, us neither. *2. n.* Five sticks of Peperami between two slices of thickly buttered white bread, all washed down with tea with four sugars and a Capstan Full Strength; the breakfast of champions. *3. n.* A no-nonsense spot of *fisting.* Also *Amsterdam uppercut, a fiver in.*

five finger spread *n.* Counter-productive attempt to suppress *a yoff* with the hand. A *chuckspreader, yawn sprinkler.*

five knuckle shuffle *n.* Dealing yourself a *good hand. Cock patience.*

five man army, the *1. n.* Title of a 1969 spaghetti western set during the Mexican Revolution, directed by Don Taylor and starring that bloke out of *Mission Impossible*. Not the *short arse* off *Top Gun* who believes in space aliens, him off the telly version who was the pilot in *Airplane*. 2. *n.* Title of the fifth track on Massive Attack's 1991 album *Blue Lines*. 3. *n.* Those noble soldiers who engage in *hand to gland combat* with the *purple-helmeted little soldier.* The fingers; *Palmela Handerson's five sisters.*

five o'clock fanny *n.* A stubbly *ladygarden*. A *Flintstone fanny* or *face grater.*

five o'clock fart *n.* The raucous and often terrifying consequence of sitting in an office all day unable to *let rip* until home-time.

five pee fifty pee *sim.* Anal/numismatical comparison descriptive of the rapidly alternating diameter of one's rectal sphincter at moments of extreme nervousness. *Bin lid penny, half a crown thru'penny bit. 'Did you see the match last night?' 'Yeah, the last ten minutes were proper five pee fifty pee.'*

five-pinter *n.* An ugly woman who a fellow would only deign to chat up after five pints of *dizzyade*. A *St. Ivel lass.*

five pint facelift *n.* A subjective improvement in one's partner's appearance after imbibing 62.5% of a gallon of booze.

fiver *n.* A diet-conscious individual, who sensibly foregoes the government-recommended "five a day" for the much more modest "five a year".

fiver in, a *1. phr.* Levy paid in order to gain entry to a public house or similar. *'How much is it to get into the Hare and Hounds on New Year's Eve?' 'It's a fiver in.' 2. n.* A *fisting.* *'Are you going to (name of formerly popular entertainer's name removed on legal advice)'s party after chucking-out time? It's a fiver in.'*

fiver, Scottish *n.* A *bird* who leaves a gent wondering whether or not she's *legal tender.*

fives *n.* A traditional Etonian game played with four fingers, a thumb and a *cock.*

five shades of grey *n.* A half-hearted suburban couple's attempt at kinky *slap and tickle.*

five six *exclam.* A gent's means of announcing to his companions that he has espied a buxom young lady in the vicinity. From the erstwhile nursery rhyme "Five six, stick out tits". See also *eyes down for a full house.*

fiveskin *n. Fourskin.*

five-to-two-er *n.* A *bird* who is five minutes uglier than a *ten-to-two-er.*

fivetune *n.* A considerable amount of money. *'The government last night admitted that it had spent an absolute fivetune on sub-standard PPE, purchased*

from some twat Matt Hancock met at the pub.'

five-wheeled snurglar *n.* An office-based *snufty* who eschews bicycle saddles, preferring instead to *quumf* the seat fabric of swivel chairs that have been recently occupied by attractive female co-workers.

fizzing at the bung hole *adj.* Descriptive of effervescent sexual arousal in a woman. *Dripping like a fucked fridge, frothing like bottled Bass.*

fizzle *n.* A gentle or quiet *arse firework* to which it would be unwise to return.

fizz pan *n.* The *chod bin, poop tureen, asserole dish.*

fizzygoth *n.* Woman who becomes a foul-mouthed, rampaging monster after an evening on the Prosecco.

fizzy gravy *n.* Diarrhoea, *rusty water, champoo, fizzy gravy, hoop soup* and so on.

fizzyjizz *n.* Aerated semen caused by over-enthusiastic *cat stabbing. Bubblecum.*

fizzy knickers *n.* A proper *froth on.*

flabattoir *n.* A *fanny like a kicked-over raspberry trifle.*

flabdomen *n.* A *gustatory athlete's party seven.* Also *flabdominals.*

flabia *1. n.* Fat *labia. 2. n. prop.* Fainty character in *The Prisoner of Zenda.*

flabia *n.* A fat *cunt.*

flabia *n.* The fleshy escutchions on a fat *bird's badge.*

flaboteur *n.* An overweight woman, tempting her slimmer friends and colleagues with cake in order to spoil their figures.

flabstinence *n.* The involuntarily celibate state forced upon the *salad-shy* by their physical condition.

flabulous *adj.* Term applied to *big-boned birds* who over-compensate for their excessive surface area by presenting to the world a raucously upbeat personality. *'I'm 38-stone and I feel flabulous!'*

flabwank *n.* An act of personal satisfaction carried out into an area of soft tissue located somewhere on a *lettuce dodger's* capacious frame, *eg.* Into a *bingo wing*, the *under-gunt* or flabby upper-thigh mass.

flaccid acid *n. Droop juice* that hinders a chap's performance to a certain degree. *Los lobos.*

flaccid flashback *euph.* A thought or mental image that is so utterly disturbing and repugnant by its nature that it immediately turns a *horse's handbrake* into a *floppy, eg.* Nan burping after eating too much stuffing, topless uncle mowing the lawn, Olive off *On The Buses*, that bit in *Oh Lucky Man!* with the man's head sewn onto a pig's body, that pops into one's head during sex, causing one to deflate like one of Richard Branson's transatlantic balloons. *'What's the matter, love? Your*

Charlie's like a dead budgie.' 'Sorry luv. I just had a flaccid flashback of Ann Widdecombe on Strictly.'

flaccid reflux *n. medic.* Post-*wank* seepage.

flaccid trip *n.* Any experience that leaves a person feeling thoroughly deflated. *'Wow. I just watched Mumford and Sons headlining on the Pyramid Stage. What a flaccid trip, man.'*

flaccinating *adj.* Descriptive of a distracting quality or feature in a sexual partner that – once noticed – cannot but lead to a marked loss of turgidity in the *membrum virile. 'Your voice, Janet. It's… it's flaccinating.'*

Flacido Damingo *n. prop.* Affectionate nickname bestowed upon the owner of a disappointingly limp Spanish *cock.* A form of politely humorous abuse used by British girls holidaying on the Costa del Sol, traditionally shouted after the interjection "Oi!".

flackets *n. medic.* Beef curtains.

fladge and padge *abbrev.* Of *rub-a-tug shop* services, getting a bit of *Mr Whippy* off a *good time girl* in a nurse's outfit. From flageantry and pageantry. *'Bit of fladge and padge today, I think.' 'That'll be fifty pounds, Lord Archer.'*

flag bravo *n. nav.* A large red pennant unfurled atop a ship's masty thing to warn others of any dangerous activity which may be taking place. 2. *euph. nav.* A term used by female members of the Royal Navy to describe their monthly period of confinement. *'Ooh, Admiral. I wouldn't go munching on me oggie if I was you. I've got me flag bravo hauled up.'*

flag hags *n.* Deluded, grinning, toothless old *oxygen thieves* who wave Union Jacks at the monarch as he gets whisked past in the back of a Rolls-Royce that is hermetically sealed to keep their germs out.

flag of Guernsey, flying the *euph. medic.* Finding the colours red, yellow and white emblazoned across one's lavatory tissue. *'Please convey to his majesty my apologies, I will be unable to attend his investiture as I'm presently flying the flag of Guernsey.'*

flags are out *exclam. Wet paint* warning when the fixture list shows *Arsenal are playing at home.*

flail *n.* The *twitter.* Also *tinter, taint, biffin's bridge, Humber bridge, carse, scran, Barry Gibb, Bosphorus, Botley interchange, brink, butfer, cleach, clutch, snarse, cosif, crunk, fanoose,* or *farse.* "The bit between a lady's flower and her tail".

flally *n.* A flaccid *willy;* a problem in the bedroom but not in the supermarket. From flaccid + willy.

FLAMALAP/flamalap *acronym.* A lady that looks way hotter from behind than she does from the front. Face Like A Man, Arse Like A Peach. Also

golden deceiver, back beauty, backstabber, witch's trick, nolita, kronenberg, boyner or *ASWAD.*

FLAME/flame *abbrev.* Fanny Like A Mouse's Ear. An expression typically accompanied by a workmanlike rubbing together of the hands and a Mike Reid-style Jack-the-lad neck-thrust.

flamingoland *n.* Any watering hole with a high density of *Yorkshire flamingos.*

flamingo's flip-flops, wetter than a *sim.* Comical description of something, or rather someone, who is is a high state of sexual arousal. Also *otter's pocket, fish drowner, mermaid's flannel* or *clown's pie.*

flamingo up *n.* Like a *cock up,* only much, much bigger. *'Well, that was quite a flamingo up, Kwasi.'*

Flanders poppy *sim.* A *ringpiece* that has been through the wars, *ie.* One that is "bright red and shot to pieces".

flange 1. *n.* A *fish mitten.* Also *muff, beaver, minge.* 2. *n. coll.* Not a word to describe a group of baboons. The correct term for a group of baboons is "troop" or "congress". So there. 3. *n. coll. Fanny, blart, tush, buffage.*

flange bandit *n.* A fellow who slopes off with a lady to make *the beast with two backs* after you have done all the ground work; the nightclub equivalent of a goal hanger mooching round the *box.* Also *cuckoo.*

flangepiece *n.* Slang term used when referring to someone as a dolt or buffoon. *'Oi, Menuhin, put your fucking bow down. This movement's supposed to be fucking pizzicato, you fucking flangepiece.'* (Sir Edward Elgar, 1927).

flange squeal 1. *n.* Ear-splitting, high-pitched noise that occurs when the wheels of railway rolling stock slip laterally on the rail when transiting a curve, due to the lack of a differential. 2. *n.* Ear-splitting, high-pitched noise that occurs when large *member* slips into a *flange,* much to the delight of the lady concerned.

flangina 1. *n. medic.* Any form of physical or emotional pain caused to a man by the nagging of his female partner. *'I know I said I'd be back by ten and now it's Tuesday, but for fuck's sake give it a rest will you, woman. You're bringing on my flangina.'* 2. *n. medic.* Women's things.

flangineer *n.* A *muff doctor* or *fanny mechanic* who doesn't mind rolling his sleeves up and getting stuck in.

flangipane *n. Nutty custard,* often found in *tarts* and open *pies.*

flannelled *adj.* The state of one's face after *going down* on a *fish drowner.*

flap acid *n.* The acrid fluid leaking from a well-used

sump that is capable of taking the enamel off one's teeth.

flap a herring *v.* To *fart* in a wet and audible manner, such that the *cheeks* of the buttocks clap together. Also *drown a duck*.

flaparazzi *n. coll.* The gutter-dwelling photo-vultures who wait outside nightclubs in the hope of snapping *upskirt* pictures of knickerless celebrities to sell to the *Daily Telegraph*.

flapas bar *n.* A continental drinking establishment where a bachelor might find himself more likely than usual to secure the attentions of a female companion for the evening.

flap dabbling *n.* In the world of *masturbating* ladies, to *gusset type* in a uninterested fashion. From flap + dabbling.

flap dance *n.* A Terpsichorean performance in a gentleman's club which involves a little more *close up pink* than is customary in the circumstances.

flapdoodle *1. n.* Dismissive term for meaningless nonsense and waffle. *2. n.* A tattoo on a lady's *Keith Burtons*. Also *twattoo*.

flap-flops *1. n.* onomat. The shoes commonly worn by old ladies in naturist resorts. *2. n.* onomat. The *tits* commonly worn by old ladies in naturist resorts.

flapier mâché *n. Fr.* A crafty piece of moist toilet paper sometimes found hiding whilst one is performing the act of *cumulonimbus*.

flapjack *1. n.* A dense, syrupy cake, a bit like concentrated guinea pig *shit* mixed with muesli, that has pretentions to healthiness. *2. n. medic.* A *quim quack's* tool for jacking *flaps* apart. A speculum. *3. n.* A device, usually in the form of a small gift, given by a suitor to his intended in the hope that it will help him *get some cabbage* off her. *4. n.* The frankly unhealthy act of *freeing the tadpoles* over one's good lady's *parts of shame. 5. n.* In women's football, a ball passed through an opposing player's legs.

flapjacking *n.* Two tasty ladies having a nibble at each other's *sticky bits.* *'Come and look at this, your holiness. There's a new flapjacking vid on ScrewTube.'*

flapkin *n.* A *fairy hammock* for the *haddock pastie.* *'Do you want anything from the shops, Posh?' 'Aye, Dave. Fetch us a box of flapkins.'*

Flapland *n.* Permissive locale where *artistic* films are made, *eg.* The San Fernando Valley, Los Angeles or the Thicket Roundabout, Maidenhead.

flap like a slack fanny in a breeze *v.* Of a goalkeeper, to perform poorly and ineffectually during a football match. *'You've got to say, Gary, David James has flapped like a slack fanny in a breeze when the crosses come in.'*

flapmates *n.* A pair of cohabiting *curtain twitchers* or *tennis fans.*

flapmonger *n.* One who mongs *flaps.* A *tart farmer, fanny magnate, pimp, buttock broker, mackerel.*

flap oil *n.* Aftershave. The fragranced liquid applied to a male's neck prior to a *cunt hunt* or during a *Scouse dry-clean. Slagbait, snogging water, fuck oil.*

flapper *1. n.* A young *piece* in the 1920s, who affected bobbed hair and a short skirt, and who would listen to jazz on a gramophone and do that dance where her legs went out at the sides. *2. n.* A lady with heavily swagged *Keith Burtons* like an Edwardian dowager's drawing room.

flappetite *n.* A healthy appetite for *flaps.* From flap + appetite. *'Our Mick's got an insatiable flappetite, you know.' 'Is that right, Mrs Hucknall?'*

flappocks *n.* The confusing yet strangely intriguing in-between-style genitalia of a *trolley dolly* who is half way through a programme of gender reassignment surgery, in either direction.

flap's eye *n.* The female urethral opening; that which occasionally gives a chap an encouraging *hairy wink.*

flapsidermy *n.* The art of preparing, *mounting* and *stuffing* a bird.

flap snack *n.* A quick *fish burger* or *vertical bacon sandwich.* Elevenses at *the Y.* Token *cumulonimbus* that shouldn't adversely affect your *flappetite.*

flap snap *n.* Frankly improbable female equivalent of the *dick pic.* Also *twat snap.*

flap snapper *1. n.* A photographer who specialises in the depiction of feminine beauty. A *flaparazzo.* *'Born on this day: Lucy Davis, TV actress spawn of Jasper Carrott, 1973; Jim Bakker, scandal-ridden US televangelist, 1940; David Bailey, top drawer flap snapper, 1938.' 2. n. medic.* In the world of gynaecology and obstetrics, a firstborn infant which weighs in at more than 9lbs in the old money. A *cuntbuster.* *'Births: Haystacks. On March 9th at Halifax Maternity Hospital. To Mavis and Horace, a bouncing, bearded 38lb flapsnapper, Giant.'* (from *The Yorkshire Post*, March 11th 1946).

flap snot *n. medic. Danny Fishcharge. Lizzie dripping, clam jam. Gleet.*

flap the kipper *n.* Practice indulged in by lady rowers. Probably not as entertaining as it sounds.

flaptisement *1. n.* A first-time *downstairs tongue-snorkelling* for a new belle. *2. n.* A *businesslady's* postcard placed in a phone box.

flaptop *n.* A portable computer equipped with wireless *binternet* access for the on-the-move bachelor. A *dirty mac.*

flaptulence *n.* The *dropping forwards* of a *lady's hat. Queefage, fanny farting.*

flapuccino *n.* A highly aroused *quim* on a dirty lady, whereby a cocktail of sundry miscellaneous *below-stairs* fluids have been whisked up into a froth against the *golfer's divot.* With a sprinkle of chocolate powder on the top and one of them little biscuits in a plastic bag.

FLARP/flarp *acronym.* That unfortunate situation whereby a young lady has allowed her *fusewire* to go the way of a neglected dog's fur. As is well known to viewers of daytime television programmes such as *Animal Rescue Live*, the only remedy in such situations is the application of agricultural shearing equipment in order to completely remove the hopelessly matted fleece. Fanny Like A Rescue Poodle. Also *noodle knickers, Percy Thrower's lawn, Ricky Tomlinson's beard.*

flarting *n.* *Piping out the haggis* in front of a someone you fancy and then give them a cheeky wink. Quite possibly the technique that makes Bryan Ferry such a hit with the fairer sex. From flirting + farting.

flash *v.* To treat a lucky victim to a surprise private viewing of one's *fruitbowl.*

flasher *n.* An eccentric gentleman who frequents municipal parks wearing a mac, beret, little round glasses and with his trouser bottoms tied round his knees with string. See *referee's coin, cock like a.*

flash in the pan *1. n.* A *man glue*-free *step on the gloy bottle*; even less less *mess* than a *slap and trickle.* A cashless *money shot. 2. n.* The act for which the late George Michael was arrested in a Beverly Hills *cottage* on April 7th 1998.

flash the ash *exclam.* A gentle reminder of a person's social responsibility to share his cigarettes with others in their peer group. *'Oi, fuck face! Flash the ash, you tight-fisted cunt.'*

flash the upright grin *v.* To expose the female genitals, *flash the gash. 'Okay, Sharon. When I shout 'Action!' flash the upright grin.'*

flash to bang *1. n. milit.* In ballistics, the time interval between the observed flash of an explosion and the arrival of the sound, thus enabling the observer to calculate the distance from ground zero. *2. n.* The time lapse between *dropping a gut* and observing the first twitching nostril of a nearby work colleague.

flat as a fat fuck's flip-flop *sim.* Colloquial tongue-twister. *'How's your pint of bitter, Miss Widdecombe?' 'It's as flat as a fat fuck's flip-flop.'*

flat as a kipper's dick *adj.* Bidimensionally

homologous. Descriptive of unleavened *baps.*

flative *adj.* Of food, that which induces flatulence, eg. Cabbage, sprouts, *musical vegetables.*

flatliner *n.* A sequence of regularly spaced *air biscuits* of equal length and volume, followed by one long, sustained release of *brown air.* From the rhythmic similarity to the sound made by TV hospital drama heart monitors just before a fashionably stubbled surgeon reluctantly stops pumping the patient's chest, looks at the clock, then pulls off his rubber gloves and flings them away.

flatprint *n.* The triangular-shaped imprint of sweat remaining left on the back of the toilet seat by a hairy backside. Due to its distinctive hair patterning, the *flatprint* is unique to every individual and may be used by detectives for identification purposes.

flat slag *n.* A previously rotund lady who has lost a lot of weight, resulting in an excess of skin.

flat Stanley *n.* A sexual encounter involving a very large *piece.*

flat, straighten up the *v.* Of a closeted *puddle-jumping* couple, to hang a *Hollyoaks* calendar on their wall in order to disguise the *whiff of lavender* in the air.

flattened some grass in her time, I bet she's *phr.* Said mischievously of a lady who has a "certain look" about her that might lead a casual observer to (possibly – indeed most probably – erroneously) suppose she might have had more than a few *rolls in the hay* over the years, although that may not be the case and we are certainly not suggesting it is. Far from it. *'Eeh, I bet that Nigella Lawson has flattened some grass in her time.'*

flatter than a plate of piss *1. sim.* Topographically or otherwise planar, *eg.* Lincolnshire, Jemini's performance of the UK entry *Cry Baby* in the 2006 Eurovision Song Contest, Kate Moss's *biffing plate. 2. n.* Insufficiently effervescent. *'Oi, landlord. Get us another pint, will you. This fucker's flatter than a plate of piss.'*

flatter than hammered shit *sim.* Descriptive of very small *chebs* indeed. *'My next guest needs no introduction. She rose to international fame in the Pirates of the Caribbean, and has since cemented her reputation with a series of blockbuster performances in films such as Atonement, Never Let Me Go and The Imitation Game. And she's done all this with a chest that's flatter than hammered shit. Please give a big hand to Miss Keira Knightley.'*

flattery *n.* A slight, unexpected splatter consequent upon a *trouser cough*, which "gets you nowhere", especially during a job interview or while modelling *haute couture* silk underpants halfway down the runway at a Paris fashion show.

flatty, crack a *v.* To suffer an unfortunate erectile dysfunction in the *trouser department.*

flatue *n.* A comical shape – for example the one-legged, poised stance of the Angel of Christian Charity at Piccadilly Circus, Michelangelo's Dying Slave, Rodin's Thinker or Anthony Gormley's Angel of the North – "thrown" by one who is about to noisily *drop a gut.*

flatulence *n.* The whole kit and kiboodle of *dropping a gut.* From the Latin *flatus; to start & lentus;* a cold tractor.

flatulentriloquism *n.* The miraculous art of "throwing" a highly audible *triffid wilter*, thus causing all blame to be directed at someone else.

flatusfaction *n.* The feeling of blissful, fulfilling contentment experienced while casually depositing a crisp *calling card* as one leaves a crowded lift.

flaunt *v.* Of a young woman, to inadvertently allow herself to be photographed by a *Daily Mail* smudger armed with an enormous telephoto lens. See also *show off, pose. 'After leaving the Ritz Hotel last night, the Princess of Wales flaunted her curves for Parisian photographers while being cut out of the wreckage of her crashed limousine.'*

flavour of the month *n.* The savoury tang of *moon juice.* The *twaste* left in the mouth following a *scrapheap challenge.*

flavour saver *n.* The jazzy tuft of hair betwixt a chap's bottom lip and his chin. The *moip mop, unpleasantness, blip bib, batter catcher* or *chuff chaser. 'Usual is it, Mr Ball?' 'Just a little off the top and sides, if you would, and sharpen the sides and corners on my flavour savour, please. And the same for my jazzmen. Oh, and seven packets of ribbed Johnnies for the weekend.'*

fleahive *n.* A filthy approximation of a beehive-style haircut, which can make you start to itch if you so much as look at it.

fleegle *n.* Of a lady's *pudenders*, that portion of giblets which protrudes beyond the *lobelia Majorcas* in the manner of the eponymous *Banana Splits* character's tongue. One for our younger readers there.

fleemail *n.* A rapidly scribbled note of thanks, including a false name and address, left on the pillow of a *munter* by a long-gone *fanny hopper* who woke up and couldn't find his *beer goggles.*

fleg *n. medic.* What Norfolk *good time girls* cough up in the morning; a viscid amalgam of phlegm and smegma. *'Careful where you'm tread, Zebediah. Your ma/sister/cousin's left a gert pile of fleg on the step.'*

flembrandt *n.* A distinctive piece of pavement art seen adorning a walkway. *Lung paint, gold watch, docker's omelette, hockler's draught, Old Leigh oyster, Dutch pikelet etc.*

fleshback *n.* A Proustian *recherche de temps perdu* experienced during s*xual relations when, due to a familiar position, feeling or groan, you are suddenly reminded of when you were *fucking* someone else.

fleshbombs *n.* Two large wads of *jubbly gelignite* packed inside a pair of bulging *tit pants. 'Phwooar! Nice fleshbombs, Lord Owen.' 'Thank-you, Mr Speaker.'*

flesh lettuce *n.* Crinkly downstairs *lady bits.*

flesh tones *n.* The sweet music played on the *bed flute.* The lyric-free theme tune *to the old meat whistle test*, teased out of the *Devil's bagpipes* by a skilled *pink oboist.*

flesh wallet *n.* The *hairy cheque book, pubic purse.* Somewhere to keep one's *money shots.*

fleshy flugelhorn *n.* Tuneful continental variation on the *bed flute, pink oboe, spunk trumpet, beef bassoon* or *pork euphonium.*

flex, have a *v.* To *bust off* or *rub one out.*

flexitarian *n.* One who flip-flops with regard to their sexual preferences, choosing at various junctures to eat both *fish* and *meat*; a bisexual. See also *switch-hitter, alloy welder, happy shopper, all at sixes and fours.*

fliar *n.* One who is economical with the truth. From fucking + liar.

flickbait *1. n.* Flirty hair-toying on reality TV. *2. n.* Playing the *gusset piano* with a come hither look; *buffing your eggs.*

flick chick *n.* An habitual *gusset typist.*

flicker book *n.* An *art pamphlet* for a lady; an *invisible banjo* players sheet music. *'You going past the Oxfam shop today? Only I've got a binbag full of your nan's old flicker books to get rid of.'*

flick finger *n. medic.* The digit with which a woman presses the *devil's doorbell* whilst watching Colin Firth paddling about in his shirt.

flick lit *n.* Erotic fiction aimed at the feminine gender, *eg. Fifty Shades of Grey, Fifty Shades Darker, Fifty Shades Freed, Fifty Shades Strikes Back, Return of the Fifty Shades of Grey, Episode VII The Fifty Shades Awakens etc.*

flies' dinner gong *n.* A entemologically Pavlovian *custard tart.*

flight safe mode *1. n.* Setting on a laptop or mobile phone that means it will not interfere with the pilots' cockpit apparatus, on which they are currently attempting to do today's Wordle. *2.*

n. Following a weekend of excessive beer and foreign food, taking a large dose of Imodium prior to boarding a plane in order to survive the journey without *shitting* oneself. *'How's your arse, your holiness? Are you going to last the journey?' 'I think I'll be alright now thanks, Mother Teresa. I've been down to Boots and put myself in flight safe mode.'*

flik *n.* Dried up *spoff* found on curtains, furniture, foreheads, shrouds *etc*. *'I felt so betrayed when the President denied we had had a relationship. Then my friend Linda Tripp reminded me that I still had the dress with his flik all over it in the cupboard.'* (Monika Lewinsky, Statement to the US Senate Impeachment Committee, 1999).

flinge *n. coll. Blart, tussage, flap.* From flange + minge. *'Come on. Let's go and find some flinge.'*

flingel *n. rhym. slang.* Vagina. From the instrumental hit *The Rise and Fall of Flingel Bunt* by The Shadows. *'Come on, Hank. Let's go and find some flingel.'*

flinging in the rain *n.* Masturbating in the shower.

fling string *v.* To *jizz* via air mail. To *lob ropes.*

flip chart *n.* Record of one's previous convictions for assault and breach of the peace.

flip-flaps *n.* Big old meaty, low-hanging *Keith Burtons* that make a slapping sound while walking.

flip flop *1. n.* A poor quality shoe substitute worn by people who can't afford heels. *2. n.* A *tug* administered while one is so unenthusiastic about life that one can't even muster up a *semi-on.*

flipper *1. n.* A Taiwanese *ladyboy of the night* that fools a gagging *punter* to the extent that he thinks: "Fuck it. I've paid me money, I'll just flip her over". *2. n.* One of those porpoise-like *chods* that is so aquatically dynamic and buoyant that it could possibly jump back out of the *pan*, flip through a hoop and dance backwards across the surface on its tail.

Flipper's beak *n.* A *shaven haven*, often to be seen poking out of the water and making a clicking sound before wrestling a pistol out of a bank robber's hand.

Flipper's burp *n.* A *ladygarden* with a pungent maritime fragrance.

flipping pancakes *n.* The practice of frantically *tossing* one's eggs prior to sending *batter* arcing up into the sky. One Tuesday a year.

flips *n.* Facial smackers that have been surgically enhanced in an attempt to make the owner's pout more trouty. From fish + lips. *'Nice flips, Kylie.'*

flits *n.* Flat *tits.* From flat + tits. *Tisn'ts.*

float an air biscuit *v.* To *enable cookies.*

floater *1. n.* A *Duncan* in the *pan* which will not

flush away. *2. n.* A member of the *crap* 70s soul band, *eg.* Larry (Cancer), who likes a woman that loves everything and everybody, who *pegged it* in 2019.

floater coater *n.* A layer of material, such as bathroom tissue, that is placed over a *bob-a-jobbie* in order to facilitate it being *sent to the beach* in a respectful manner. *'Pass me another bog roll under the door, would you Cardinal? I don't have enough left on this one for a floater coater and I'm on me third flush here.' 'Certainly your holiness.'*

floating point *1. n.* In computing, arithmetic using formulaic representation of real numbers as an approximation in order to support a trade-off between range and precision. Don't say we never learn you anything. *2. n.* The happy state familiar to semi-turgid gentlemen in the tub, whereby his *clockweights* are submerged whilst his *love truncheon* remains buoyantly bobbing at the surface.

floats like a butterfly and stings like VD *phr.* Below-the-belt boxer's apophthegm.

flock of bats or a block of flats *phr.* Said prior to going to the *smallest room* when unsure as to the consistency of *foulage* that may be produced. *'Jesus, my guts are rotten this morning. I don't know whether I'm going to have a flock of bats or a block of flats. And now here's the Reverend Fergus Butler-Gallie with Thought for the Day.'*

flock of pigeons *n.* The sound of a loose *Camilla* movement. *A fall of old shoes from the loft.*

flock of sparrows, coming out like *sim.* Descriptive of the more urgent *digestive transit.* *'I was on the toilet all night. It was coming out like a flock of sparrows. Cyril?' 'Thank-you Esther.'*

flog cabin *n.* A fortress of solitude where a chap can ponder on the meaning of life, admire nature, and *toss his knackers flat.*

flogging on *v.* Accessing the internet in search of *left-handed websites.*

flog'n'bog *v.* To multi-task by having a *shit* and a *wank* at the same time. To *shank.*

flog pocket *n.* The front flap of a pair of Y-fronts, useful when a fellow needs rapid access to his *old chap* for whatever reason.

flog roll *n.* Toilet paper to *jizz* on or to *jizz* in. *'Mam! Can you lob me up another flog roll? Grandad's used the last sheet on this one.'*

flog the log *v.* To *whup one's wood, spank the plank.*

flogtograph *n.* A surreptitious snap of an attractive lady that is taken by a member of the *faparazzi* to be perused later in private.

Flo job *n.* A toothless *nosh* off a senior citizen.

floodgates *n.* The well-greased *sluices* on a woman

who is *as wet as a window cleaner's chamois pocket.*

floor chimes *n.* The collection of empty cans and bottles under the driver's seat of a regional television presenter's Jag, which roll together and produce a soothing jingle-jangle sound when he drives round a corner, up a kerb or over a bicycle.

floordrobe *n.* The clothing receptacle most used by students, teenagers and men home from the pub.

floorish *adj.* Said of an alcoholic beverage which renders one unable to walk. *'Ooh, this Buckies is so floorish. Pour me another, ambassador.'*

floor is lager, the *n.* Similar to the lava-based kids' game and hit Netflix series in which participants avoid various pitfalls to earn a cash prize. The Wetherspoons-based challenge involves avoiding slipping *arse over tit* on a floor awash with cheap booze in order to make it to the bar for the reward of a flat pint.

flop flaps *n.* A frankly disappointing pair of *labias.*

flopfuck *n.* A *scuttle* essayed while less than fully tumescent. *Playing snooker with a piece of string, poking fog up a hill with a sharp stick, pushing marshmallows into a moneybox, putting toothpaste back in the tube, trying to open an oyster with a bus ticket.*

flop out *n.* Condition whereby the flaccid *sex pipe* protrudes through the bottom of the *underkegs,* this often occurring during the transfer from a sitting to a standing position.

floppy red cup *n.* The *hairy goblet, furry cup.*

floppy seconds *n.* All that is left for the next lady in line after she has been beaten to the *main course.*

floptician *n.* A medical expert who specialises in the field of erectile dysfunction. *Bongo Bill.*

floptimistic *adj.* Over-confident regarding one's amatory abilities when *heavily refreshed. 'Died on this day: Fidel Castro, Cuban revolutionary, 2012; Bernard Matthews, Norfolk-based turkey magnate, 2010; George Best, perennially floptimistic footballer, 2005.'*

flop to pop *n.* A standard interval used to assess *blowjob* efficacy. The time taken for an experimental subject to *lose his mess* from a flaccid start. *'Egbert was powerless to resist. Her eyes burned into his like sapphires. Her ladylike arms enfolded his masculine body as he felt himself being swept away in a whirlwind of passion. Then she knelt down in front of him and took him from flop to pop in three minutes flat.'* (from *The Officer and the Gypsy* by Barbara Cartland).

floral sex *n.* How a lady might show her appreciation when presented with a bunch of daffs from the all-night garage.

Florida fartbox *n. US.* An *abnormal load* on the back, albeit quite normal in the Sunshine State. An *Orlando dirtbox* seen in the queue to get into Cosmic Ray's Starlight Café.

florins *n. ryhm. slang.* The *shits.* From the pre-decimal coins known as *two bob bits.*

flossing the squirrel *n.* Of a lady, sporting a thong-styled underpant.

flotation tank *1. n.* A device in which a person with too much money sits in order to relax, meditate and find their inner self. *2. n.* The *bog,* which does the same job for nowt.

floury bap *n. rhym. slang. NI.* How a Belfast baker would refer to a *crap. 'Hold the shop for me a while there, will you? I'm off in the back room for a wee floury bap into that bucket behind the raisins. And while I'm there, I may as well start them flapjacks.'*

flower duet *1. n.* Rather touching operatic piece for soprano and mezzo-soprano. From the first act of *Lakmé* by Delibes, which, as we all know, saw its debut at the Paris Salle Favart in 1883. *2. n.* Delicate *scissoring.*

flower, Scouse *n.* A dog egg. *'Careful not to tread in the Scouse flowers, vicar.'*

flowstopper *n.* A *Sir Douglas* of such impressive length and girth that it stands proud, tall and clear of the *chodbin* water whilst effectively blocking the U-bend.

floydian slip *n.* An inappropriate and unexpected remark made at a dinner party after indulging in one too many aperitifs. Named after the late, robustly opinionated, deceased, perpetually *wankered* TV chef Keith.

flub *1. n. onomat.* The sound of a *fanny fart. 2. v. Fuck* in Flowerpot Men language. See *dub.*

flubberghasted *adj.* Overcome and struck speechless at the sight of a person who evidently lives *life in the vast lane. 'We went to DisneyWorld and quite frankly we were flubberghasted. I mean, the missus is thirty-five stone, but compared to some of that lot in the line for Splash Mountain she looked like Lorraine fucking Chase's thinner sister.'*

flu, chavian *n. medic.* Any of a range of difficult-to-disprove ailments which are fortuitously contracted by a long term jobseeker, entitling the sufferer to graduate from the dole to sickness benefit. *'I would go out to work, Jeremy, only I've been struck down with chavian flu for the last eight years. Some days I've barely been able to muster enough energy to sit on the sofa and watch your programme.'*

fludge *n. Olde Eng.* Smegma. The pungent creamy detritus found between a gentleman's *bell end* and his *shaft,* under the *brim* of the *wank stop.* From fiveskin + sludge. Also variously known as *cauliflower cheese, duck butter, knacker barrel, fromunder, moy, ridge paste, trollop snack, stinking bishop* or *willydelphia*.

fluent Guinnish *n.* Descriptive of one spouting *bollocks* and gibberish at the culmination of a stout night spent *dyeing his dinner.* '*I can't understand a feckin word he's saying, your holiness. He's speaking fluent Guinnish.*'

fluff *n. nav.* A maritime *blow off.*

fluffer *n.* In a *bongo vid* studio, a professional *fellatrix* employed between takes to ensure the tumescence of the male actors.

fluffit *n.* The sweetest name in common use for a maiden's *cunt.*

fluff on the needle *euph.* A polite way of intimating that someone or something may have done a *windy-pop.* '*What's that smell, your majesty?*' '*Well, I'm not pointing the finger, but it's either one of the corgis or Philip. Somebody's definitely got fluff on the needle.*' (transcript from *Royal Family* fly-on-the-Chippendale-wainscotting documentary, 1969).

fluffy nut crunch *n.* Tasty and nutritious breakfast cereal made from the debris shaken out of an upturned armchair.

fluid art *1. n.* Making abstract pictures with runny paints, most likely done by geniuses at art school as a preparation for putting a motif on your flat white after they graduate. *2. n.* A *wet signature* applied with creative *panache.* Also known as a *Jackson Bollock.*

fluid situation *n.* An unfortunate predicament whereby one's personal continence may be somewhat compromised.

flum *n.* Snatch thatch, pubes, rubiks, fusewire.

flump *1. n.* A cylindrical marshmallow sweet. *2. n.* An offensive and hurtful term used by sexist women to describe the limp penis of a man who, for all they know, may be suffering from serious medical problems. *3. v.* To *thumb in* a less than tumescent member when attempting sexual congress with some *tart* while completely *hammered.*

flumpert *n.* The enlarged *mons pubis* of a mature, salad-averse female, which is reminiscent of the proboscis of a bull elephant seal (*Mirounga angustirostris*).

flunge *n. coll.* Attractive women with whom you are already acquainted. '*There's no chance of pulling in here tonight, it's full of flunge.*'

flunkey *1. n.* A Royal slave, one who fawns on a *nob, eg.* Nicholas Witchell. *2. n.* A *dunky.*

flush back *n.* The psychologically upsetting re-appearance of a buoyant *Tom Daley* after an initial pull on the chain fails to send it to the beach. See

also *flushbacks.* Oh, look, there it is next.

flushbacks *n.* Repeated, nightmarish toilet visits in the wake of an ill-advised chilli-based repast.

flush hour *n.* In a workplace, the period of time after morning coffee during which there is even a queue for the gents' *shitter.*

flushing a dirty buffer *1. n.* In computing, the synchronisation process used when the data on disk and the data in memory are not identical. *2. n.* Some sort of filthy Teutonic carry-on.

flushin' roulette *n.* High stakes game played by festival-goers as they steel themselves to open the porta-loo door.

flush mob *n.* That group of inconsiderate people who always seem to be occupying the *shitter* cubicles when you are desperate to *drop off the shopping.*

flush out the brown rabbit *v.* To introduce your *pink ferret* to the missus's *front warren* and thus elicit an evacuation from her *back warren.*

flush puppies *n.* Dalmatian-spotted suede shoes that have been standing too close to a urinal.

flushstration *n.* The sense of increasing annoyance felt when a *faecee* one has just excreted refuses to disappear down the U-bend, despite repeated cranks on the handle.

flute *n.* An Irish term meaning the male penile *knob.* '*May I introduce you to my wife, your worship? She's a keen flute player.*' *2. n.* A complete *tool, eg.* Another driver that cuts you up. '*What a fucking flute.*' '*We've reported him to the stewards, Max.*'

flute player's lips *n.* Descriptive of the pursed *ringpiece* ejecting last night's curry and beer.

fluting *n.* Like *playing the pink oboe*, only sideways and with your *significant other* running their fingers up and down your *prodder.*

flutter *n.* Of a lady, to urinate charmingly, that is to say without *blowing off* like a backfiring Ford Zephyr halfway through.

flux capacitor *1. n.* The invention that allows a 35-year-old Michael J Fox to play a teenager in the *Back to the Future* trilogy. *2. n.* The Y-shaped vein on the shaft of the *tallywhacker.*

fly farmer *n.* A person whose approach to personal hygiene might, one could imagine, be found wanting in polite company. A *tramp's mate.* '*Born on this day: Jonny Bairstow, Yorkshire and England wicky, 1989; Serena Williams, Wimbledon champeen, 1981; Ricky Tomlinson, Brookside fly farmer, 1939.*'

fly feast *n.* An *al fresco* act of *cable laying*, usually up an alleyway or behind some bushes.

flying dirty *1. adj.* Description of an aircraft which has its gear and flaps lowered while airborne. *2.*

adj. Description of a lass who has her *gear* and *flaps* lowered. Possibly behind a skip at closing time.

flying her Chinook *euph.* One in the pink and one in the stink, gyrating in circular movements. If that's even possible. No, it isn't.

Flying Horse, the *euph.* Anal s*x. From the name of the alternative hostelry utilised by the residents of *Coronation Street* when their preferred venue of the Rover's Return is rendered unavailable/ unusable for whatever reason. *'Fancy a quickie, Hilda?' 'Sorry Stan, I'm up on blocks. It'll have to be the Flying Horse tonight, I'm afraid.'*

flying pastie *n.* Excrement wrapped in newspaper and thrown into a neighbour's yard for whatever reason. See *pyropastie.*

flying Scotsman *n.* A highly complicated sex act that doesn't sound like it's worth the bother.

flying squatsman *euph.* One who has reached top speed in his desperate search for a *chod bin.* With all high pressure steam coming out his *arse,* and making chuff-chuff noises.

flying squirrel *n.* Genital manipulation amusement guaranteed to break the ice at social events. *Farmyard* animal impression involving the stretching of one's scrotal leather almost to breaking point, in the style of the wing-like membranes on the popular airborne rats of the genus *Pteromys.*

fly in the eye *n.* An itchy *Roy Castle's kettle* relieved by vigorous scratch. An *angry wasp.*

fly's eyes *n.* A gentleman's party trick whereby the shorts or bathers are pulled tight between the legs so that the *clockweights* bulge out on either side of the *fairy hammock. 'August 6th. We all go down to Cliveden for the weekend. Gerty [Laurence] and Fanny [Brice] were there as usual. Ivor [Novello] entertained us all by singing King's Rhapsody by the pool, and followed it by doing fly's eyes. How we all shrieked. Benjamin [Britten] laughed so much he shat himself, poor dear.'* (from *The Diaries of Noel Coward,* 1938).

fly's graveyard *n.* The *nutsack* netherworld situated on the dorsal side of the *chicken skin handbag* which to this day remains unseen by human eyes.

fly sheet *n.* A *fiveskin.*

fly spray *n.* Male spendings; *spunk, jism, jitler, nut butter, baby gravy* etc. *'She wasn't on the pill so I covered her face in fly spray instead.'*

fly spy *n.* A charming family game. A freshly lain dog's egg is covered in superglue and left in a hot, sunny space. At the end of thirty minutes, the person whose guess is closest to the actual number of bluebottles stuck to it is the winner.

fly the coop *v. rhym. sl.* Another roundabout way to describe having a *Tom tit.* From fly the coop = poop. *'And now, a little earlier than usual as I have to fly the coop, here's Owain with the weather.'*

fly the flab *v.* Of a *salad dodger's bingo wing,* to flap back and forth during a frantic act of *self improvement.*

fly the flag *v. NZ.* To *zuffle.*

fly tipping *n.* The act of rewarding a fly for excellent service in a soup restaurant.

FMBD *abbrev.* An expression of mild exasperation, viz. Fuck My Black Dog.

fnarr! fnarr! *exclam.* Suppressed childish exclamation of amusement uttered after a double entendre. Also *k-yak! k-yak!*

foaming at the bung hole *adj.* Frothing at the *gash, glistening.*

foam javelin *1. n.* Safety version of the popular school sports equipment, primarily designed to prevent having someone's eye out. *2. n.* A *sheathed weapon.* See also *posh wank.*

FOBAT/fobat *abbrev.* Leaving the theatre during the interval when one realises that going home and doing the ironing is preferable to sitting through the second half of (to pick a musical entirely at random) Sting's Broadway hit *The Last Ship.* Fuck Off Before Act Two.

fob watch chain *n.* Thin thread of *spooge* that on occasion dangles between a gent's *herman jelmet* and his *wank clamp* immediately after he has enjoyed an act of *monomanual self delight.* See also the *Devil's drawbridge, the gerbil's washing line.*

fodder *n.* Collective term for the mental images of pulchritudinous young ladies that a gentleman files away in his *mammary banks,* to be retrospectively reviewed in those future moments when he needs to *relax.*

FOFFOF/foffof *abbrev.* Fair Of Figure, Foul Of Face. *Bobfoc.*

FOFGIRL/fofgirl *abbrev.* Funny On Facebook, Git In Real Life.

FOFO/fofo *abbrev.* Acronymic game played by beastly males, preferably from the safety of a *tithead* patrol car with the windows wound all the way up, and involving the instant answering of a paraphrased version of the following question, viz. "Would you care to partake in sexual relations with the indicated young lady, or would you rather prefer to request her instantaneous departure?" That is to say, expressed somewhat more succinctly, "Fuck Or Fuck Off?"

FOG/fog *abbrev.* The sort of stare that one gives to a *coffin dodger* at a bus stop in order to avert the possibility of them attempting to strike up a conversation about the weather, the paucity of the old age pension or the size of these new five pence pieces. Fuck Off Granny.

foggles *1. n. RAF.* Wrap-around glasses used in pilot instrument training, which are frosted except for a section at the bottom, so as to restrict the pilot's view to his instrument panel only. *2. n.* A phenomenon whereby, on meeting a lady, one's attention is focused on her lower features to the exclusion of anything above shoulder level. *'She was a blonde, or perhaps a brunette. She might have been ginger. I can't remember, officer. I had my foggles on.'*

fog on the Tyne *1. n.* Title of a song released firstly as a single in 1974 by erstwhile Geordie boy band Lindisfarne, and later in 1990 with thirsty, poultry-toting, plastic-*titted* siege negotiator Paul Gascoigne on lead vocals. *2. n.* The dense, noxious fumes produced by habitual imbibers of Newcastle's eponymous Yorkshire/Netherlands-brewed brown ale.

fog up *adj.* Of *train pulling*, to be the driver, as opposed to the *porridge stirrer* in the *guard's van*. *'Bagsy me fog up. I don't want any of you lot's sloppy seconds again.'*

folder *n.* One whose good breeding, manners and culture have instilled in them the proper way of preparing toilet paper for smudging the *chocolate starfish*.

following the science *euph.* A catch-all explanation offered in an attempt to avoid further interrogation in the absence of any reasonable excuse. *'Why the fuck are you pissing in the kettle at 3am? You said you were only going out for a quick one.' 'Sorry, love. I'm just following the science.'*

following wind *n.* An *arse bark dropped* whilst out for a stroll with a brisk breeze blowing from behind, resulting in it wafting directly into your path, causing you to retch on your own foul odour.

follow-on *1. v.* In the game of cricket, a team who batted second and scored significantly fewer runs than the team who batted first may be forced to follow-on; to take their second innings immediately after their first. *2. n.* To have two consecutive and separate visits to the toilet where you need a *number two*, with no visits to just *have a wazz* in between.

follow through *v.* To accidentally soil one's *undercrackers* while attempting to release a bubble of *carbon dibaxide*. To create *russet gusset*, drop a pebble, truffle, butter your cheeks.

fomp *v. US.* To engage in sexual foreplay,

to *firkyfoodle.*

fondleberries *1. n.* Testicles. *2. n. Sweaterfruit.*

fond of shopping *euph. Good with his hands.*

fond of walking holidays *euph.* A *woman in comfortable shoes, tennis fan* or *tuppence licker.*

F1 finish *euph.* Fitting climax to a piece of cinematographic *grumble.* Three sweating guys spraying frothy liquid all over each other after a long hard afternoon in the *cockpit.*

Fonzie, the *n. Thumb-blasting* two women at once, whilst going "Heeeey", and somewhat similarly…

Fonz, the *n.* Sexual act involving a man being *noshed off* while his *nosher* simultaneously sticks both thumbs up his *rusty sheriff's badge* and attempts to say "Heeeey".

food baby *n.* A bouncing, ten-pound bundle of joy that is safely delivered the day after a big meal. A massive *Meat Loaf's daughter* that repeatedly wakes you up all through the night and leaves you with bags under your eyes.

food in the beard *euph.* A symptom of insufficient wiping after a *Tom tit.* To have *winnets* in the *crackers.*

food miles *n.* The length of the journey that a meal takes through a person's alimentary canal before once more emerging into daylight. According to experts, Mussels Vindaloo travels remarkably few food miles.

food outlet *1. n.* Building or structure used primarily for the preparation and sale of comestibles and non-alcoholic beverages. *2. n.* The *balloon knot.*

food's ghost *n.* An invisible, eerie presence accompanied by a low humming sound and the stench of death. A *McArthur Park.*

foofbrush *n.* A toothbrush reserved exclusively for use after performing *cumulonimbus.*

foo fighter *n.* A female who regularly has to defend herself from the unwanted attentions of amorous *lady golfers.*

foogle *n.* A *twat* who thinks they are a world authority on a subject after googling it and scanning halfway through the top paragraph on the first page that comes up. Also *wikiot. 'With us to talk about the new variant virus is one of the country's leading Coronovirus foogles.'*

foolerize *v.* Quite simply to dupe, hornswoggle or beguile someone. *'There's an old saying in Tennessee, I know it's in Texas, probably in Tennessee, that says, foolerize me once, shame on, shame on you. Foolerize me, you can't get foolerized again.'* (President George W Bush).

fool's gold *1. n.* The mineral pyrite – also known as iron sulphide. *2. n.* Song by baggy Manc band The Stone Roses. *3. n.* Glittering nuggets of undigested sweetcorn in one's *tods. 4. n.* The false sense of sexual optimism felt by a gentleman upon entering an event where initial appearances suggest a wall-to-wall *crumpetfest,* but where further inspection reveals the majority of attendees to be *on the bus to Hebden Bridge, eg.* A Tracy Chapman gig or comfortable shoe convention.

fool's overture *1. n.* Title of a track from the 1976 album *Even in the Quietest Moments,* by whiny prog-rockers Supertramp. *2. n.* The ominous first few seconds after deciding to *twist on nineteen.*

foop *n. onomat.* The sound of a penis being removed from an anal passage, presumably a similar noise to when you blow across the top of an empty milk bottle.

footballer's business card *euph.* A tasteful portrait of a premiership star's *cock* and *balls* sent via a camera-phone or webcam. Also known as a *ChatRoulette friendly hello.*

footballer's tie-knot, wide as a *sim.* An expression that describes something that is wider than it ought to be. *'Thank you, your grace, but I'd rather not sit down. I done a cack this morning and the bastard was as wide as a footballer's tie knot, believe me.'*

foot fetishist *n.* One with a highly developed special interest in 'Big' John Holmes (or 'Big' Stephen Pound MP)-sized male genitalia. Also known as a *feet footishist.*

foot high club *n.* A more affordable version of the *Mile High Club* for the lower orders. Usually involving a park bench, the back seat of a car, a shop doorway or the cage in a police van.

FOOTLIP/footlip *abbrev.* Someone who is careful with their money. First Out Of Taxi, Last In Pub.

footlong *n.* Exceptionally lengthsome *bog mess monster* that protudes out of the water. Normally produced after eating the sandwich of the same name. Also *chocolate meerkat, bogzilla.*

footloose and fanny free *euph.* *'Perennial bachelor boy Cliff simply hasn't found the right girl yet. Now a disarmingly youthful-looking ninety-two and after more than seventy years at the top of the showbusiness tree, he's as footloose and fanny free as ever.'*

footloose and panty free *phr.* Descriptive of a somewhat carefree time in a girl's life. *'Of course, Pippa was still footloose and panty free in those days.'*

footstool *1. n.* An Imperial *dreadnought* of impressive length. *2. n.* Pavement toffee, barkers' eggs and the like, when trodden on.

footwell flavour *n.* The soul-destroying aroma of *footstool* that appears three minutes after turning on the car heater.

foraging *n.* Woodland-based *cottaging;* "looking for a fungi to fill you up". Yes, well done. It's a plural.

foraging for wood *euph. Dancing with the captain* whilst in the World of Minecraft.

Forbsy drop, the *n.* The act of taking a full pint to the pub toilet and returning with it empty in an attempt to look like a hardened drinker. Named after a lawyer from St. Albans who can't take his beer. *'Heavily made-up Prime Minister Tony Blair today visited the Labour Club at his Sedgefield constituency and performed several Forbsy drops for the benefit of television news cameras, before announcing his intention to resign and leave Gordon Brown well and truly in the shit.'*

force choke *1. n.* The Green Cross Man's famous death-grip punishment. *2. n.* Donald Trump's signature move on his limousine bodyguard. *3. n.* A potent *apple tart* that instantly causes everyone nearby to start gagging.

forced-air *1. n.* A system of heating, common in North America, which uses air as its heat transfer medium and a furnace (usually gas-fired) to circulate warm air through a building. Don't say we never learn you anything. *2. n.* The sudden, unexpected, release of a *humdinger* from the *bomb bay,* which occurs as a result of an over-exertion, *eg.* Moving a piano up a fire escape, stretching in a quiet yoga class or standing up after being knighted. Usually accompanied by a short, sharp ripping noise and a red face.

force field *n.* A thick *fart* that clings to the warp, woof and weft of one's *duds,* preventing anyone from coming within six feet for a good ten minutes. A *Velcro guff.*

force is strong in this one, the *exclam.* Amusing utterance preceding a *bottom burp,* to be spoken in the voice of James Earl Jones. Also *our survey said; please hold for the president; I'll name that tune in one.*

force log-off *1. n.* Disconnecting a user from a computer system and terminating the session by over-riding the manual process. *2. n.* Finishing off a slow *Tom tit* in a hurry.

Ford egoboost *n.* Gargantuan utility vehicle equipped with everything necessary – other than a .50 calibre machine gun bolted to the roof – for deployment on the front line in Ukraine. Driven by a baseball-cap-wearing shelf-stacker from Telford.

FORD/ford *abbrev. medic.* Casualty doctors' notes terminology. Found On Road Drunk.

foregasm *n.* A *stack* which is *blown* while still trying to *light the fire.* When a gentleman *spends his* *money* before he's even got *into the shop*. Going *up and over like a pan of milk* before the niceties of *frigmarole* have been satisfactorily completed. A *Pope-shot*.

foreigner *1. n.* A person from another country in this country. Or a person from this country in another country. Or a person from another country in another country (other than the other country that they are from). Or a 1970s *poodle rock* band. *2. n.* A private job unofficially done using the facilities of one's business. *3. n.* A *dump* made uncomfortable due to the fact that it is being performed on someone else's *chod pan*

foreploy *n.* Any unscrupulous gambit used to get a woman into bed, *eg.* Claiming to be an airline pilot, member of the SAS, employee of the month at Burger King *etc.*

foreporn *n.* The token, exaggerated, wooden acting preceding the *spaff candy* of a *grumble vid*. Usually viewed on fast forward.

fore-skin conclusion *n.* Much like a foregone conclusion, but specifically applied to sexual situations; a turn of phrase employed in those circumstances when a chap considers he is one hundred percent guaranteed to *get his end away*. *'Are you off to decorate that lass's house tonight then?' 'Yep.' 'Reckon you'll get a shag out of it?' 'It's a fore-skin conclusion, mate.'*

foreskin jogging *n.* The act of *bashing the bishop* at a leisurely, gentle pace so as not to get out of breath or peak too early. *Treading water.*

foreskinzola *n.* A pungent, unappetising, mature *knob cheese, bunnet brie.*

forespray *n.* A *frigmarole*-avoiding alternative to foreplay consisting of a quick squirt of *WD over 40.*

forest dump *n.* An *ad hoc* and indeed *al fresco* expulsion of *feculent* during which you basically always know what you're going to get. A *flies' banquet.*

forest gunt *n.* An unkempt *pie hider.*

forewood planning *n.* The process of getting everything ready for a *wank, viz.* Tissues to hand, living room door secure, volume on laptop muted *etc.*

forgetiquette *n.* To inadvertently forget one's manners, *eg.* When taking a mobile phone call during Earl Spencer's speech at Lady Di's funeral or scratching one's *arse* and sniffing your fingers just prior to shaking the monarch's freakishly oedematous hand backstage at the Royal Variety Performance.

forget-me-mott *n.* An unkempt bed of *gorilla salad,* which could do with a bit of judicious pruning.

forget-me-nots *n.* The final notes in a *Chinese singing lesson.* Droplets which form a tiny but embarrassing wet patch on your trousers. *Dicksplash, a wet penny in the pocket.*

forget the password *v.* To suffer from constipation. To repeatedly fail in your attempts to to *log on.*

forgive me...forgive me *exclam.* Uttered in the style of a shambolic premier shuffling through speech papers after dropping a foul-smelling *guff.*

fork lift truck *n.* An exotic sexual position performed in back alleys and shop doorways, whereby the female participant is hoisted clear of the ground by the thighs in order to keep her *arse* clear of *piss,* vomit, broken glass and spent *jubbers.* A *chinook.*

forklift truck driver in Marks & Spencer's warehouse *sim.* Backhanded compliment such as might be made about an extremely *theatrical* type of gentleman. *'I bet he's lifted more shirts than a forklift truck driver in Marks & Spencer's warehouse.'*

form *1. n.* Means of judging horses by statistical comparison, before *pissing your money up the wall* at the bookies. *2. n.* Somewhat sexist means of judging *birds* by statistics: *Fitness, fuckability, prodworthiness.*

formula one *n. medic.* Patent medicine that is proven to cure Sunday afternoon insomnia.

formula one pit lane, like a *sim.* A toilet bowl lightly decorated with skid marks. See *the starting line at Brands Hatch.*

formula two *n.* Smoking *skidmarks* right round the bend. Also known as a *Stirling Moss, Lewis Hamilton, Jackie Stewart, the starting grid at Brands Hatch, wheelspin, Mr Brown's fingerprints etc.*

ForP?/forp? *phr. abbrev. interrog.* Useful coded word which may be exchanged between gentlemen on a night out, when questioning the circumstances of a lass with a *nice personality, viz.* Fat or Pregnant?

Forth bridger *n.* An irritable and cantankerous woman who appears on TV cultural discussion programmes and seems to *have the painters in* all year round, *eg.* Germaine Greer, Bonnie Greer; basically any woman called Greer.

fort knockers *n.* Highly reinforced and practically impenetrable *titpants* of the sort that nuns, librarians and Ann Widdecombe might wear.

forty-eight volter *n.* Even more shocking than a *nine volter.* A *minge* which, when licked, generates an electrifying effect similar to that obtained by applying one's tongue to an array of forklift truck batteries wired up for maximum current.

forty stone alone *euph.* A forlorn and lonely

pie enthusiast.

forty wanks *n.* An impromptu and refreshing afternoon *shuffle.*

for what we are about to receive may the Lord make us truly thankful, Amen *exclam.* See also *our survey said; Alexa open a window; listen to this, too good to miss, da-da da-da da; ladies and gentlemen, my next guest needs no introduction; and now a word from our sponsor etc.*

Fosbury flop *1. n.* An energetic release of the *manhood* from the flies prior to taking a *whizz.* *2. n.* The act of "flopping" your *todger* over a slightly-too-high fence in order to urinate on the other side, thus avoiding unpleasing dead spots on your own lawn. Named after the famous US high-jumper of the 1960s, who is sadly deceased and therefore not in any position to object.

Fosbury plop *n.* An *arse baby* of such proportions that the delivery method involves arching the back.

Fosbury's disease *n. medic.* Condition chiefly characterised by flaccidity in the male reproductive organ. Named in honour of the erstwhile American athlete who won a gold medal in the 1968 Mexico Olympic Games high-jump competition, using the revolutionary back-arching technique that is named after him, Dick Flop. The symptoms of *Fosbury's disease* are usually ameliorated by the administration of a dose of *mycoxafloppin, mydixadrupin* or *bongo Bill's banjo pills,* taken three times a day after meals.

fossil fuel *1. euph.* Meals on Wheels, Werther's Originals *etc. 2. n.* The kind of alcoholic beverages which light the passions of *gilfs* and other sexually active pensioners, *eg.* Cream sherry, Warnink's advocaat, Pernod and black, half a stout. *'Another fossil fuel for you, is it, Ena?' 'Yes, Minnie. I'm on a mission tonight.'*

FOTBOAL shirt *n.* Any item of fashionwear purchased from a street vendor at a significantly lower price point than which its manufacturer recommends, and consequently with little or no regard as to the legitimacy of its provenance. Fell Off The Back Of A Lorry.

fough *n.* An inadvertent puff of *turtle's breath* when clearing one's throat. Derivation unknown. Possibly from Frank + Bough.

foul and a miss, Dennis Taylor four *exclam.* See also *you won't find that one on the setlist tonight; a confident appeal by the Australians there; speech!; a bit more choke and she would have started etc.*

foul and the frame Steve Davis *exclam.* A call from the referee when a snooker player bends over the table and *drops a long brown.* Also *not at all vicar,*

thank-you for coming.

fouled hand *1. n.* In poker, a selection of cards that is ruled unplayable because of some irregularity, *eg.* That it contains too many or too few cards. *2. n.* When an accidental rip in one's lavatory tissue results in *Kermit's collar.*

fouled nets *1. n.* The dread moment on a trawler when the nets drag up something other than fish, such as a WW2 mine, the conning tower of a Russian submarine or the bloated, water-logged corpse of Robert Maxwell. *2. euph.* The dread moment on holiday when you check the lining of your new swimming shorts after an ill-advised night of strong lager and spicy comestibles and then, for whatever reason, decide to dive off your balcony into the hotel swimming pool.

foul papers *1. n.* In the world of Shakespearean scholarship, manuscripts bearing abandoned drafts of the bard's work. *2. n.* Soiled *bumwad.*

foul Paulo *n.* An Italian *Dirty Sanchez.* A faecal moustache.

found footage *1. n.* Somewhat tired horror flick genre, whereby some *fuckwit* keeps filming while being attacked by zombies, monsters or ghosts. *2. n.* A truly horrific feature of the modern, technologically-enabled drinking binge, whereby videos shot on your camera phone fill you in on exactly what you did the previous night, *eg.* Dancing like a *twat,* sitting naked on the roof of a police car and prank-calling your new boss at 3am before throwing up over your mate's new sofa.

four ball Paul *n.* A *bullshitter* who, if you told him you had three testicles, would have to go one better. Also *raconteur, twat o'nine tales, Bertie big bollocks, two shits.*

four-fifty at Newbury, like the *sim.* Poetic metaphor, referring to the last race of the day, conveying the state of an aroused female's undergarments when the going is soft to heavy. *'Alright Sheila, can I offer you a seat?' 'Best not. I've just been watching that Aidan Turner without his shirt on in Poldark and my knickers are like the four-fifty at Newbury.'*

four-flusher *1. n. US.* When playing cards, a person who makes empty boasts or bluffs when holding a four flush, whatever that is (we could look it up, but we can't be arsed). *2. n.* A *Thora* which takes some persuading to *go to the beach.* Also *arsehole survivor, beach baby, Billy no mates, brown ping-pong ball, non-mover at number two.*

four-man bob *n.* A large, speedily ejected *turd.* Possibly rocking backwards and forwards two or three times before coming out.

four minutes *rhym. slang.* Haemorrhoids. From

four minute miles = piles.

four-pint Farage *n.* A person whose politics shift markedly to the right after a few ales. A *half-gallon gammon.*

four seasons in one day *1. n.* Heartfelt ballad by Kiwi art-popsters Crowded House, about the decay of a romantic relationship, or something. *2. n.* The aftermath of a night of cheap ale and dubious *catbabs,* resulting in alternating *trots, non-movers at number two, stickle-bricks* and *pebble-dashing.*

four seasons total landscaping *n.* The *taint, notcher* or *ploughman's,* named in honour of that car park in Philadelphia where Rudy Giuliani did his press conference. That'll be "the bit between the sex shop and the crematorium".

four sheets to the wind *1. euph.* A nautical metaphor meaning extremely drunk. *2. euph.* An *ale force ten follow-through* of such strength that it will take at least the specified quantity of *bog-roll* to temper the effects.

four-sit-shitter, the *n.* In the morning, the number of goes it takes to successfully despatch the results of a fat curry from the night before.

four-stroke baron *1. n.* Progressive metal trio from Nevada. They sound good. *2. n.* A lad on a *hair trigger.* Half as bad a *dress messer* as a *two-push Charlie.*

fourth base *1. n. US.* Something to do with baseball or American football or something. *2. n.* The *anus.*

fourth party *adj.* The type of motor insurance favoured by the council *estate car* driver, *ie.* None. *'It's alright, mate. That'll just polish out. Anyway, I've got full fourth party insurance. You stand there and I'll just get back in my car to write down my details.'*

four tissue fantasy *n.* The object of a romantic young swain's desire.

fox at a bin bag, like a *sim.* Descriptive of the way a romantically-inclined damsel might go at a boulevardier's *knob* in an alleyway. Also *like a dog eating hot chips.*

fox licking shit off a wire brush, face like a *sim.* Phrase which is useful when one is referring to someone of a notably miserable mien.

fox's yawn *n.* A *wide-on* that could scare a chicken.

foxtail soup *n.* Vaginal exudate from only the most refined of sources, with a delicate bouquet prized by connoisseurs from the *snurgling, barumphing* and *garbooning* communities.

foxymoron *n.* A lady whose incredible physical attractiveness is matched only by her marked lack of intellect. *'Famous people born on November 23rd: John Wallis, influential English mathematician,* *1616; Franklin Pierce, 14th President of the United States, 1804; Manuel de Falla, greatest Spanish composer of the last century, 1876; Kelly Brook, wonky-titted foxymoron, 1979.'* (from *Schott's Oh Fuck Oh Fuck Oh Fuck the Deadline's Tomorrow Book,* 2005).

Foyston Gap *n.* The space at the top of a woman's thighs, a term peculiar to Greatfield, Kingston upon Hull, East Yorkshire. The *Toblerone tunnel, f-duct.*

FPM/fpm *abbrev.* A measure of the noxiousness of the atmosphere in a crowded lift, taxi cab or Space Shuttle. Farts Per Million.

FQI *abbrev.* A *Hart to Hart* which rises in pitch towards the end, as if posing a query. Fart Question Intonation.

fracking *1. n.* A popular means of extracting gas from under the desolate wastes of northern England. *2. n.* Performing *juggery pokery*; an act that typically concludes with a *pearl necklace.* From fuck + rack. *3. n. Blowing off* while on the job.

fraggle in the frazzle *n.* A penis hiding in a clump of unruly pubic hair.

Frampton *1. n. prop.* 1970s singer/plank-spanker with a voice like Steven Hawking. *2. n.* A *fanny fart.*

Francis *n. US.* A lady's *arse.*

franger *n. Dunky, English overcoat, blob, jubber ray.* A gentleman's prophylactic sheath.

frankenfiver *n.* A unit of currency which has been craftily customised by a previous handler, consisting of either a torn five pound note sellotaped back together, two torn five pound notes joined together to create a new one or, more spectacularly, a piece of genuine legal tender which has been hybridised by the skillful addition of Monopoly money. Usually issued as change from a larger denomination note, the *frankenfiver's* status as legal tender is a source of lively debate and discussion, especially amongst the taxi drivers to whom it is subsequently proffered.

Frankenstein's feet *sim.* The illusion of having another person's feet stiched onto one's legs, caused by the serrated indentations left by tight socks around the ankles.

frankenswine *n.* Selected cuts of value pork formed together to make something mildly resembling a slice of ham. *'Frankenswine is now just 48p for 36 slices at Finefare, Lady Bellamy.'*

frankentits *n. Knockers* which exhibit baseball-stitch-style scarring from their implant operations, leaving them looking like something knocked up by Peter Cushing in his laboratory. *Beverly hills* are usually revealed as *frankentits* when viewed from underneath. We should be so lucky.

frankfurter water *1. n.* Salty, meat-flavoured fluid in which a slippery sausage has been steeped. *2. n.* Salty, meat-flavoured fluid which has just come out the end of a *slippery sausage*.

Frankie *rhym. slang.* Grumble, *scud* material. From Frankie Vaughanography = pornography.

Franklin *n.* The urethra. *'Me Franklin burns when I piss, doctor.'*

Franz Klammer *1. n. prop.* Famous Austrian ski racer of the 1970s. *2. n.* An unkind epithet applied to a woman whose looks are fading. From the fact that she is "going downhill fast".

frap *v. onomat.* To *break company* through the *snippit valve*.

frappers *n. Fr. Knockers.* From the French word "frapper", meaning "to knock". *'Zut alors, tout le monde! Caisse de supermarché les frappers smashants on that oiseau at le bus-stop.'*

frappuccino *1. n.* A pretentious and expensive cross between coffee and Angel Delight, a bit like a caffeine-enriched slush puppy, but costing about eight quid at Starbucks. *2. n.* The creamy head cooked up by a lady's *cabbage* when in a state of high arousal. *'I was on form last night, I'll tell you. By the time I got down for me fish supper, she was frothier than a frappuccino. And now over to Daniel Corbett for tomorrow's weather.'*

Frasier, getting a *euph.* Having your ladyfriend *toss your salad* while at the same time *scrambling your eggs*, as per the theme tune to the erstwhile US sitcom, recently revived to apparently little effect.

frass *n.* Caterpillar *shite*, as trod in by centipedes.

fraudband *n. Thinternet.* *'Eeh, now what was the name of that company that used to do them adverts with Maureen Lipman? You know, the ones where she was on the phone to her grandson talking about "ologies". I simply can't bring the name of the company in question to mind.' 'Why don't you look it up on your fancy new laptop?' 'I would do, Granny, but the fraudband's gone down again. And even when it's on, it only runs at a tiny fraction of the 20Mbps download speeds promised in the publicity material.'*

fraudcaster *n.* A TV or radio presenter whose only apparent talent is being a right *twat*, yet who is for some reason deemed bankable by the telly companies.

fraud escort *n.* A young woman who, after being legally contracted to provide personal services of an intimate nature, turns out to be neither young nor, possibly, a woman.

fraud fiesta *n.* Mode of vehicular transport favoured by the uninsured young drivers who populate the Dicky Bird (Chesham Fold) estate in Bury. A fraud fiesta is easily identifiable by its massively loud stereo, bald tyres and an exhaust pipe the size of a wizard's sleeve.

frauditorium *n.* The room in which a parliament sits.

frazzle *n.* Any *bongo mag* catering exclusively for readers with a taste for *the biddy beautiful.*

freckle *n. Aus.* Arse, brown eye, chocolate starfish, dot, fifties tea towel holder, quoit or hoop. *'What's up, vicar?' 'I've got a milk bottle stuck up my freckle, Mrs Antrobus.'*

freckle freshener *n.* Moist, sewer-blocking *shite*-cloth for buffing the *fifties teatowel holder* to an effulgent shine.

freckle-heckle *v.* A loud and critical comment from the *back passage.*

freckle maggots *n.* Rolled-up pieces of 3-ply *shit ticket* which congregate around the *balloon knot* after it has been given a right good wipe.

Fred *n. rhym. slang.* Sprongle. From the famous golfer Fred Funk, whose name rhymes with *spunk.*

Fred Astaire *n. prop.* An uncomfortable fellow with a poorly wiped *cleft* who "dances cheek to cheek".

Fred Dibnah *euph.* A woman with a *face like a bag of chisels* who, during intercourse, is capable of "bringing the largest erection crashing down".

Fred Dibnah's chimneys, goes down like one of *sim.* Descriptive of the impressive enthusiasm with which a keen *fellator/fellatrix* goes about their sordid business.

Freddie Cougar *n.* A scary, sharp-fingered older woman who interferes with blokes while they sleep.

Freddie Frinton, a *euph.* A gentleman's night to himself, whereby he can imbibe any substance that takes his fancy, free from judgement, ridicule or a police investigation. Named after the largely forgotten comedian. (Except by the Germans, who inexplicably watch the late comic's humour-free slapstick sketch *Dinner for One* every New Year's Eve. Incidentally, if you watch it on Youtube, correct us if we're wrong here, but the off-colour punchline appears to be that the *pissed* butler's going to go upstairs and *fuck* the old lady.)

Fred Leicester *n.* Pungent *knob cheese* cultivated in the *brim* of the *bishop's hat.*

free beauty treatment *n.* A *Vitamin S*-enriched *facial*, involving the application of copious amounts of *heir gel* and *oil of goolay*. *'Congratulations love. You've just won a free beauty treatment.'*

freebird *n.* A flatulent *dawn chorus* that goes on for much longer than is necessary.

free hit *1. n.* In one-day cricket, an opportunity

for a batsman to take a shot without the risk of dismissal. *2. n.* The chance for a man to *bank at Barclays* without the fear of getting told off by his significant other, for example if she's away on business, staying at her mother's or trapped under a fallen wardrobe. A *pink ticket.*

free jazz *1. n.* Bewildering and seemingly chaotic subgenre of improvised music, supposedly enjoyed by men effecting berets, black polo neck jumpers and beards. *2. n.* Complex and out-of-control internet-based masturbational procedure, in which multiple windows containing different competing forms of *grumble* are kept open simultaeously on the desktop. Sometimes foolishly combined with a work conference call.

freelancer *n.* A short, hairy-palmed man with thick glasses who *works from home.*

Freeman's disgrace *euph.* The ignominious experience of *shitting* oneself while seated at a table in a curry house. Named after a certain Mr Neil (surname removed on legal advice), who shamefully soiled his tweeds after sampling one spoonful of Curry Hell, the world's hottest curry, at the Curry Capital Restaurant (formerly the Rupali), Bigg Market, Newcastle upon Tyne.

Freemans handshake *n.* A secret *one off the wrist* while browsing through the *tit pants* section of the famous mail order catalogue.

freemason's handshake, fanny like a *sim.* A tight *flingel,* particularly one which applies unusual pressure to the second knuckle of one's right hand.

free of the carbonite *euph.* A reference to that bit where Han Solo gets released from that big block of cold rock over Jabba the Hutt's mantelpiece; finally being in receipt of *a bit* off the missus after a long period of being frozen out due to some minor past indiscretion.

free range eggs *n.* Muscular *knackers* that can propel a blast of *man gravy* over an impressive distance. *Seven league bollocks.*

free runner *1. n.* A *bellend* who prances about on Youtube doing forward rolls and jumping over various urban obstacles instead of getting the fucking bus. *2. n.* A chap who stands in the pub drinking until it's his round, when he *fucks off.*

free spin *n.* Contraceptive-free *how's your father* with a *bird* who is already *up the pasture.*

free the Middleton two *v.* To drive over speed bumps at an excessive velocity in the hope of getting one's ladyfriend's *Gert Stonkers* to bounce right out of her low-cut top. Named after the Leeds area which is richly blessed with both traffic-calming street furniture and *big-titted* single mothers.

free the tadpoles *v.* To liberate the residents of one's *wank tanks*; have a *tug.*

free to a good home! *exclam.* Yet another in the long line of amusing responses to an audible *jam tart. Also that sounded like the call of the Scotch woodcock; what's that Sweep?; now we know what killed the dinosaurs.*

free Tommy *euph.* To have a *shit. 'Hold my pint, love. I'm off to the bogs to free Tommy.'*

Freetown fart *n.* A catastrophic *follow-through.* Named after the capital city of Sierra Leone, a metropolis renowned for its magnificent National Railway Museum, the grandeur of its Cathedral of St. George and the unrivalled opportunities it affords to visitors of catching amoebic dysentery. "It's a brave man who drops a gut in West Africa." – Dr Livingstone.

freeview and fuck? *exclam. interrog.* A candid alternative to *Netflix and chill?* for the modern male on a budget.

freight-only *n.* A railway route normally only used for low-key, mundane traffic, which is pressed into service when the normal line is undergoing maintenance. See also the *bonus tunnel, the flying horse, the wrong 'un.*

French *n.* Popular coital position whereby the man sits and sells onions astride a bicycle while the woman perches on the handlebars and inflates his testicles.

French accordian player *n.* A gent who is inexperienced in the art of romancing a lady, who believes the best way to go about things is to press and squeeze everything he can find as quickly as possible. A *clamateur* musician.

French cough *n. medic.* The gagging, retching noise a woman makes when she has *sucked off* more than she can chew. *'Yes, you thought she was in a Range Rover parked in a layby near Wetherby, but she's travelled over two hundred miles to be with you tonight. It's the owner of that distinctive French cough… Gillian Taylforth.'*

French cricket, play *1. v.* To improvise a simple, two participant ball game using a tennis ball and racquet. *2. v.* To improvise a simple, one participant *ball* game using the contents of one's underpants and one's right hand.

French cup *n.* In a gent's monomanual act of onanistic *self delight,* a cupped left *dick skinner* in which the *family jewels* rest while the sinful deed is undertaken. Or vice versa for a left-handed *Barclays,* obviously. *'Jonathan, could you keep at least one hand on top of your desk at least while you're interviewing Dita Von Teese?' 'Sorry John, no can do. You'll just have to film me from the shoulders up, I'm afraid, only I'm doing the French* *cup as well.'*

French door *1. n.* An exit on the back of a building that is ideal for running away through. *2. n.* The *arsehole. 'Apparently, Brando was such a method actor that when Bertolucci shouted 'Action!' he just grabbed a nob of butter and did her through the French door.'*

French fringe *n. rhym. slang.* The *foofoo* or *hoo-ha.* From French fringe = minge.

French have been involved, the *phr.* A term from the motor trade when something mechanical is either totally *fucked* or is devoid of any logical method of repair. *'I'm terribly sorry but I had to fail it on the hydropneumatic suspension, pal. The French have been involved, I'm afraid.'*

French hedge *n.* A badly executed bit of vaginal topiary. *'Qu'est-ce que c'est censé être, Brigitte? Il ressemble à une haie du jardin française.' 'C'est la moustache de Monsieur Hitler, Emmanuel. Je me l'ai découpé avec des ciseaux fond d'écran tout en regardant dans le miroir.'*

French horn *1. n.* Brass orchestral instrument, distinguished by its rotary valves, narrow conical bore and large, flared bell. *2. n.* Sexual position in which the female sits on the male's lap and he gets a mouthful of *tit* and four fingers in her *letterbox. 3. n.* A *bone on.*

French injury *n. medic.* Any accidental trauma involving something utterly improbable becoming lodged in your *Samantha.* From the pitiful explanation typically proffered to medical staff, *viz.* "I Fell".

French letter *n.* A *durex* or *English overcoat.*

Frenchman's guff *n.* A silent, two-fingered salute.

Frenchman's shoe *n.* An item of footwear liberally covered in dog *feeshus. 'Please come in your holiness.' 'I'm afraid I can't, your majesty, as I'm wearing a Frenchman's shoe. Have you got anything I can scrape the shit off with?'*

French palm *n.* Secret sexual technique which quite possibly explains why our Gallic cousins are widely regarded as the world's greatest lovers. Not to put too fine a point on it, the use of a cupped hand on a lady's *front bottom,* rather in the style of those coarse youths at swimming pools who make *farting* noises under their armpits.

French polish, to *v.* To *buff up one's wood* till you can see your face in it. And all *spadge* comes out the end. To have a *Tom Hank.*

French safe *n.* A secure *box* that can be cracked open by fiddling with a little button at the top. Usually found behind a hinged oil painting on the front of a woman's *trolleys.*

French sickness *n. medic.* Any *cock rot* caught from prostitutes advertising their services in phone boxes for £20 or less.

French snuff *n.* The pungent particles of *shit* which are inhaled from the end of the index finger after it has just scratched the *rusty bullet hole. Farticles.*

French tickler *1. n.* Some sort of Ken Dodd-style comedy prophylactic available from pub bogs vending machines in the 1970s. *'What a lovely day, madam, what a lovely day for rolling a contraceptive sheath equipped with wobbly protrusions ostensibly intended to heighten sexual pleasure onto Jacques Derrida's erect penis and saying "How's that for a French tickler?"' 2. n.* A *cock* with a significant amount of stubble covering it.

French wank *n.* A *posh wank.*

French water feature *euph.* An *al fresco gypsy's kiss. 'Hurry up, Henry. The taxi's here.' 'I'll be with you in a moment. I'm just constructing a French water feature in the NatWest doorway.'*

French week *n.* A long and demanding day at work which is probably equal to the amount of effort expended by our gallic cousins from Monday to Friday. *'How was work today?' 'Crazy, I put in a French week.'*

frenchy *n.* Rubber carrying case for a *French horn.*

fresh air *n.* The thing that smokers say they're going for when they step outside for a fag.

fresh prince of bell end *n.* A contumelious epithet.

Freudian slip *n.* An inadvertent slip of the tongue revealing subconscious sexual desires. Named after crack-headed, *motherfucking* psychoanalyst Sigmund.

friar's chin *n.* To tuck one's vest/shirt/jumper under one's chin to keep it out of harm's way while *pulling the Pope's cap off* over a *Tijuana bible.* See *bishop's waltz.*

friar's weeds *n.* A holy unkempt garden of *13 amp fusewire.*

Friar Tuck *rhym. slang.* An act of coition. A *Donald Duck.*

friction bairns *n.* The offspring of a *trouser bandit.* So called because the *lavender* father *shoots his load* solely as a result of the resistance caused by one surface rubbing against another. *'Ere, did you know that Julian Clary's missus has just had twins?' 'Friction bairns, them.' 'And that Graham Norton's got eight kids, you know.' 'Aye. Them lot's all friction bairns and all.'*

Friday foal *n.* One who, late on a Friday evening, proceeds to take on the ambulatory characteristics of a new-born baby deer. A *beer Bambi.*

Friday night gamble *n.* Rejecting the advances of a perfectly acceptable bit of *tussage* on the chance that one might pull something even better later on in the evening. *Twisting.*

Friday's foam *1. n.* The creamy scum found on top of select cocktails at TGI Friday's. *2. n.* The creamy froth produced at the end of a barren week off.

fridge magnet *1. n.* A low-Gauss decorative geegaw – typically a souvenir of someone else's holiday – that falls off and slides under the front of one's refrigerator. *2. n.* A fat *bastard* who counts their daily steps between the settee and where the pies and trifle are kept.

fridge magnet *n.* A man whose successive girlfriends' sexual appetites are a source of disappointment to him. *'Trish won't take it fudgeways either. What am I, a fridge magnet?'*

fridgilante *n.* One who regularly takes things – specifically the contents of the refrigerator – into their own hands.

fried chicken *n.* A sweaty, greasy, shaven *bargain bucket*, as seen on a drunken young lady who's been dancing all night. Also *disco fanny.*

fried eggs *n.* Small *baps, titterlings, stits.*

fried eggs and bacon *euph.* The inexplicable phenomenon of morbidly obese women who still manage to somehow have no *shirt potatoes* whatsoever.

fried egg sandwich *n.* A *diddy ride* off of *Miss Lincolnshire.* Also *sausage pizza.*

Friedrich Von Trapp *1. euph.* A Bavarian alternative to *dropping the kids off at the pool.* Named after the older boy in *The Sound of Music*, whose line in the song *So Long, Farewell* is "Adieu, adieu, to you and you and you." *2. n. Bav. rhym. slang.* A *Sir Douglas.*

friendly fire *1. n. milit.* The actions of US armed forces against journalists, ambulances, wedding parties and anyone who fights alongside them. *2. n.* An unexpectedly powerful *jizz bolt* that overshoots the belly and hits a *self-abuser* in the face. *3. n.* Of a gentleman *jazz flick* actor, to be caught in the line of fire of a fellow thespian's *pop shot. 4. n.* Small residue of urine ejected from the *tallywhacker* when one is trying to put it back into one's flies following a *scoot.* Usually when wearing light-coloured trousers.

friend of Dorothy *n.* Politically correct terminology for a chap who *throws a light dart.*

friend of Jimmy's *euph.* A chap who prefers the company of the younger generation.

friends reunited *1. n.* A momentarily mildly-interesting website that was very popular for about a week in 2005, but which nobody has looked at for at least the last decade. *2. n.* The glorious and romantic moment when a man, while cleaning out

a cupboard, discovers a long-forgotten cache of *art pamphlets.*

friends with benefits *1. n.* Acquaintances who maintain a sexual realtionship without becoming emotionally involved. *2. euph.* A polite term for the urban underclasses. *'I see there's some more of our friends with benefits on the Jeremy Kyle show, your majesty.'*

frig *v.* To *frotter, wank,* esp. a lady's *squidge.*

frig brig *n.* The bedroom. *'Is your David playing, Mrs Baddiel?' 'I'll just shout him down, Frank. He's up in his frig brig.'*

frig-freezer *euph.* The feminine equivalent of the male *wank-bank.* Somewhere a woman can keep a sexual memory fresh, ready for later use. *'I see Tom Hardy is reading a bedtime story on CBeebies again. That'll be something to put in your frig-freezer, nan.'*

frigger's freeze *n. medic.* The feminine version of *wanker's cramp.*

friggit Jones *n.* A spinster of the parish who seems to buy an awful lot of batteries.

friggonometry *n.* The precise science involved in selecting and arranging one's fingers at the correct angle while *diddling* a rude lady's *devil's doorbell.* The *Ebdon slide.*

friggy pudding *n.* Any sort of post-*frotter* residue which a young chap might find on his fingers after giving a *friggonometry* lesson to a female accomplice. *Frappuccino.*

fright *n. coll.* Collective term for a group of ugly women. *'Right, so that's agreed. Susanna's going to be the lead singer. Now we just need a fright of birds to stand behind her and play the instruments.'*

frightened skydivers *sim.* Descriptive of *Andrews* that are reluctant to exit the *bomb bay doors. 'I think I'm going to have to try All Bran. My turds are like frightened skydivers.'*

frigmarole *n.* Unnecessarily time-consuming foreplay performed on a missus. *Choreplay.*

frigmata *n.* Sanguinous marks on the hands of one who has been *flicking the bean* of a woman when *Aunt Flo is visiting.*

frigment of one's imagination *n.* A subject conjured up in the mind to oil the wheels of *self abuse.*

frigor mortis *1. n. medic.* Momentary paralysis experienced by a *bird* who has just had her *devil's doorbell* rung by the milkman. *2. n. medic.* State of stiffness in one's *old chap.*

frigorous *adv.* With regard to *playing the invisible banjo*, notably forceful and energetic. *Scruggs-style.*

frig roll *n.* Feminine version of the popular *soggy*

biscuit game, if such a thing is even possible.

frigspawn *n.* *Cock eggs* in the bath.

friguratively *adv.* Descriptive of someone talking a load of *wank.*

fringe-parter *n.* A gusty *fanny fart* during a session of *cumulonimbus.* A *lip rattler.*

frink *v.* To simultaneously think and drink; with the expectation of hitting upon a scheme of breathtaking clarity and potential, although typically ending up being conducted to melancholic excess. *'What's up with Dave? I think he's been frinking about his ex-wife too much.'*

Frinton Ferrari *n.* A pensioner's mobility vehicle. A *Holland-on-Sea hotrod.*

frist *n.* The unique joint between the arm and hand of one who suffers from *cake retention.* From fat + wrist.

frit *1. n.* A piece of laboratory glassware for filtering liquids. *2. v.* To *jill off.* From frig + clit. *3. adj.* Scared. *'Honestly, there's absolutely nothing to be frit of. We've taken every safety precaution we can think of on this whirly wheel challenge.'*

fritter *1. n.* NZ. A hot, *batter-coated morsel.* *2. n.* An item of food cooked in a frying pan.

fritzkreig *n.* The early morning nabbing of every sunlounger on the premises by German hotel guests.

frock *n.* Cosmetic husband in a *lavender marriage.* The male equivalent of a *beard.*

Frodos *1. n.* Annoying little *turds* that cling to the *ring. Geetles* that force one to *tap the ash.* *2. n. medic.* The unpleasant symptoms of a surfeit of spicy foodstuffs, whereby the patient feels as if his *ring* has been dropped into the fiery furnace of Mount Doom. *'After eating all them cheese-stuffed jalapeños last night at the Masonic Lodge buffet, I've got the Frodos something chronic, doctor.'*

Frodo's banjo *n.* See *cock harp.*

frog, catching the *n.* The act following a successful *peel and polish,* whereby a lady cups her hands to collect her manfriend's expelled *baby gravy.*

frog eye *n.* Male *camel's toe. Also hamster's mouthful, packet, Darcy Bussell's footrest.*

frogging *1. n.* Gallic *dogging.* Possibly a mildly racist entry, but it's only the French. *2. n.* Towpath-specific form of *dogging,* practised by boggle-eyed men crouching next to moored canal boats with insufficiently tightly drawn curtains. *Ducking.*

froggy style *n.* Type of sexual congress performed in the style of the popular warty green amphibians, ie. *Back-scuttling* their lass, then pulling out at the last moment and *spunking* up her back.

frog's chin *n.* The saggy *bag of tripe* that hangs over and obscures the *furry bike stand* of an unaccept-

ably curvaceous lady. The *gunt, bunt, poond, fupa, fat hap, blubber beret.*

frogspawn valdez *n.* A bathtime *tug* that is an environmental disaster to clear up.

frombie *n.* A lady who is blessed with such a *lovely personality* that the only way a gentleman could bring himself to *do her* would be "from behind".

from dashboard to airbag *phr.* The miraculous surgical transformation of a *Miss Lincolnshire* into a *double D tit queen* that may leave one disorientated, seeing stars and suffering from ringing in the ears.

from Devizes *euph.* Descriptive of a lady who either has one *nork* larger than the other or, alternatively, one *nork* smaller than the other. Or both. From the famous limerick by Poet Laureate John Masefield, *viz.* "There once was a girl from Devizes / who had knockers of differing sizes. / One breast was small, and of no use at all / but the other was large, and won prizes".

fromunder *n.* Type of pungent cheese cultivated by the less hygiene-conscious elements of male society. Also *helmetdale, brimula, knacker barrel.*

frontal forelimb *n.* A prehensile *dobber.* A *middle stump, third leg, prodder.*

frontal losnotomy *n.* One of them bogies which brings out a substantial part of your brain with it.

frontbone *n.* Not the backbone.

front bottom *n.* Ladies' *parts of shame.*

front bummer *n.* A woman in *comfortable shoes* who is *fond of walking holidays.*

front-bum rocket *n. Jampax.*

front bum trumpet pump *n.* A *cunt grunt, queef, kweef, cunt guff, muff chuff, Harry Ramsden's dinner gong, Seagoon's last raspberry, frampton, hat dropped forward, Lawley kazoo, muff chuff, crumpet trumpet* or *fanny fart.* See also *vulvuzela.*

fronted adverbials *n. Bollocks.* *'Earlier today, I kicked the education minister in his little fronted adverbials.'*

front-end developer *1. n.* Someone who works with computers or something. *2. n.* Professional title of the person who "prepares" the male actors in the *Frankie* industry; a *fluffer.*

front end of a butcher's mincer *euph.* Any lower bodily orifice that has recently taken a right hammering.

front loaded date *n.* A social engagement where the male party's sophisticated and gallant veneer gradually slips away, until by the end of the evening he is revealed in all his boorish glory.

front parlour *euph.* A space kept clean and tidy and reserved only for entertaining particularly special guests, such as the vicar.' *When Mr. Percy visits, Miss*

Haversham always makes sure he is well entertained in the front parlour. Ordinarily she wouldn't dream of letting him in via the tradesman's entrance.'

front weights *euph. Lancs.* Breasts. A Lancashire farmers' term, more usually spoken when referring to the counterbalances fitted to the front of a tractor. *'By heck, that young piece of tuppence has a champion set of front weights on her.'*

front wiper *n.* A person whose *bones are so big* that they have to wipe their *arse* from before instead of aft.

froot *n.* The "front boot" of a car, especially one of one them new-fangled electric ones, where they're showing off because they don't need an engine, and accordingly *2. n.* A young lady's *beetle bonnet.* Hopefully not on fire at the side of the road.

frosticles *1. n.* From Roy Wood's 1973 not-chart-topper, a frosty icicle. From Frost + Icicle. *2. n.* Cold *knackers.*

frostitute *n.* A lady of the night who gives her clients a service without a smile.

frosty biscuit *n.* A variation on the *soggy biscuit* game, as played by mountaineers and Arctic/ Antarctic explorers. *'I'm just going outside, I may be some time.' 'Right you are Oates. But don't stay out there too long, we're having another round of frosty biscuit in a minute, just as soon as Bowers can feel his fingers again.'*

frosty John *n.* The act of *interfering with oneself* at the urinals after getting ditched by your date. *'After long-lens paparazzi pictures of Sarah's topless tryst with a Texan millionaire appeared in tabloid newspapers, a troubled and humiliated Andrew was reportedly seen having a frosty John in the Buckingham Palace bogs.'* (from *The Yorks: A Royal Love Story* by Nicholas Witchell).

frosty milkman's finger *n.* The tip of a fellow's *purple pearler* when he awakens following an unexpected *snoregasm.* *'"How dare that cheeky cow say I am impotent?" roared Henry to his assembled courtiers. "Why, only the other night I had the milkman's frosty finger twice!"'* (from *Fourth Time Lucky – The King's Beloved Sister* by Jean Plaidy).

froth cloth *n.* Female *wank sock.*

frothing at the gash *adj.* See *frothing at the South.*

frothing at the South *n.* Of a lady, being in a state of preternatural sexual excitement. Also *fizzing at the bung hole, gagging for it, frothing like bottled bass, dripping like a fucked fridge.*

frott *v.* To *frotter.*

frottage *1. n.* The act of deriving pleasure by rubbing one's clothed genitals on any convenient surface, *eg.* A door jamb, a fridge, someone else'e *arse* on

a crowded tube train. *2. n.* A thatched building with roses round the door where someone goes to *frott.*

frottage cheese *n.* The sticky end product of a successful act of *frottage.*

frotter *1. v.* To *frott. 2. n.* One who *frotts, frotters* or commits an act of *frottage.* A *frotterer.*

frotterer *n.* One who indulges in *frottage, ie.* One who *frotts* or *frotters.* Also *frotter.*

frozen mop *n.* A *boner* covered with a frosty layer of dried *mandruff.* *'I fell asleep halfway through the second half, had a dream about a spit roast with Dwight and Jordan and then woke up with a frozen mop. Now, Alan, what did you think of Arsenal's second goal?'*

frozen points *n.* The *chapel hat pegs* of a sexually excitable woman that are often the cause of delayed train services.

frube *v.* After an act of *self harm,* to squeeze the remaining drops of *spodge* out the end of one's *giggle stick,* as one would the *frottage frais* from one of those yoghurt-filled tubes.

frubing *n.* Sucking *jism* from a used *blob.* Usually done by a silent bystander hiding in the bushes, after a mad *dogging* session when all the participants have left to go home for tea. We're going to hell in a handcart.

frugal frube *n.* A *yop*-filled *dunky.*

frugalhorn *n.* Getting the job done before the ten-minute preview on the *mucky channel* ends.

fruit *n.* A chap who is not particularly good at throwing.

fruit & flowers *euph.* How drugs are referred to on television production accounting sheets.

fruit and veg stall, body like a *sim.* Said of a lady who has firm goods on display at the front and keeps all the saggy stuff hidden round the back.

fruit bowl *n.* Two plums and a banana. The collective term for a gentleman's *wedding tackle.* The *orbs and sceptre* of the *family jewels.*

fruit feeler *n.* A gentleman who is *light on his feet,* and who tends to *fumble spuds.*

fruit fly *n. Fag hag.*

fruit machine Freddy *n.* A chap who is well known to the local damsels for his lack of *staying power.* From the fact that, like a one-armed bandit, "they would be lucky to get three nudges out of him". One who is *up and over like a pan of milk.* Also variously known as a *two push Charlie, speaking clock, Timmy two stroke, one pump chump, two stroke poke, Brazillian rocket, English batsman, two stroke joke, Ernie, minute man, point & squirt merchant, Peter two pumps* or *SISO.*

fruit salad *n.* A small lady blessed with a big *top*

bum, ie. A small *peach* with a large pair. Works better spoken out loud than when written down, not that that's saying much.

fruits du nez *Fr.* How a waiter in a posh restaurant would refer to his *greenies*. *'Plat principale: Foie gras de cygne avec saumon fumé, haricots verts, huitres et fruits du nez du Maître d'hôtel; 300 euros.'*

fruit shoot *n.* The *spendings* of a fellow who is *good with colours.*

fruit up *v.* To *toss* someone else *off*, in a public school dormitory for example. *'"What's going on in here?" thundered Mr Wilkins as he burst into the showers. "Please, Sir," announced Venables, "I gave Jennings a ten shilling postal order to fruit me up. Now he says he's sprained his wrist during Latin prep, and he won't give it back."'* (from *Suck THIS, Jennings* by Anthony Buckeridge).

frum *v.* To *frig* a *bum.*

frump *v.* To sniff your girlfriend's fruity younger sister's *bills*. *'Not going away with the bird's family, mate?' 'No, I'm looking after the house for them. Wouldn't miss out on all that frumping for a big clock.'*

fruttocks *n.* The cheeks of the spare *arse* that certain *salad dodging* ladies possess around the front. The *bilge tanks, front buttocks.*

frying chips *n.* The sound a lady makes when she is seated on a *thunderbox, splitting her whiskers* and *putting out a fire.*

fry the onions and garlic *v.* To engage in a sizzling spot of foreplay before *browning the meat.*

FSH/fsh *abbrev.* A fellow's criminal record. Full Skirmish History.

FT *1. abbrev.* Customary contraction for the *Financial Times* or, more entertainingly, the *Fortean Times. 2. abbrev. pej.* Family friendly online shorthand for Fuck Them/Fuck That which can be used with impunity in newspaper comments sections.

FTSE *1. abbrev.* Financial Times Stock Exchange. An index of the performance of the top 100 companies that allows people with pension funds to work out how much they have lost that day and how long they are going to have to keep working in B&Q before the welcome release of death. *2. abbrev.* A *pappering of the kex.* Follow Through, Shit Everywhere.

fubble *n.* While sat in traffic on a hot day, a dense, caustic *Bronx cheer* bubble that makes its way into the outside world *via* the *taintal crevice.*

fubes *n.* 13 amp, usually ginger, *pubes*. Contraction of fusewire + pubes.

fucculent *adj.* Moistly voluptuous, like a

well-roasted *bird*.

fuck *1. n.* A single act of copulation. A *bang, scuttle* or *poke. 2. v. intrans.* To *have it off. 3. v. trans.* To *poke, nob,* or *shag* someone, or something, up the *cunker,* up the *dirtbox* or in any other available orifice. *4. v.* To comprehensively beat someone in a bout of fisticuffs, *esp.* a member of the constabulary. *'Come on, let's fuck a copper!' 5. v.* To break or damage something beyond repair. *'Ah, Mr Knievel. I've examined your X-Ray and I'm sorry to tell you that every bone in your body is fucked. And that includes them really little ones in your ears.' 6. v.* To dismiss something with contempt, particularly for a game of soldiers. *'There's a Health & Safety presentation about using the photocopier starting in five minutes.' 'Fuck that for a game of soldiers. I'm off for a fag and a wank.' 7. interj.* An exclamation of disappointment. *'I've just won two tickets to see Syd Little's gospel show.' 'Oh, fuck!' 8. exclam. interrog.* Slightly stronger version of "on earth" when used in a question. *'What the fuck happened here?' 9. exclam. rhet.* A forceful refutation. *'Did you fuck my wife?' 'Did I fuck!'. 10. n.* That which is given by a person who cares. *'Isn't it dreadful about the Queen Mum dying?' 'Personally, I couldn't give a fuck'. 11. n.* The flying thing that one who doesn't care could not give to a rolling doughnut. *12. exclam.* When used reflexively as a purely rhetorical invitation, an expression of incredulity at a thing, such as an unexpected turn of events or a piece of news. *'Well madam, you may be pleasantly surprised to learn that if this vase, in its present condition, were to come to auction today, I am confident that it would fetch at least twenty-five thousand pounds. You should insure it for at least thirty thousand pounds, possibly forty thousand.' 'Fuck me!' 13. phr.* A rhetorical concept that is in receipt of knowledge not given to oneself. *'And where is your brother now?' 'Fuck knows, your honour.'*

fuckabulary *n.* Those twenty words which, skilfully combined and recombined, make up the entire dialogue of all the *Frankie Vaughan* movies ever made. Also *cockabulary, hairy pialogue.*

fuckadillo *n.* A quirk or peccadillo in a person's sexual life. *'She always liked to do it with a Bourbon cream gripped between her knees. It was just a fuckadillo of hers.'* (Arthur Marshall being interviewed about the late Duchess of Argyll on the *Russell Harty Show,* LWT 1978).

fuck a frog if I could stop it hopping, I would *exclam.* An expression of male sexual frustration said by a man who would *shag a fag burn in a fur coat.* A less coarse version of *I would dig* up a badger and bum it for use in refined social situations. *"'Dash it all, Jeeves," I expostulated to the sage retainer. "I've not had any company of the female persuasion for weeks and it's really starting to rag my pip. I tell you, I'd fuck a frog if I could stop it hopping."'* (from *Bend Over and Brace Yourself, Jeeves!* by PG Wodehouse).

fuck all *n.* Nowt. *Fanny Adams*. 'Did you fuck her last night at all?' 'Did I fuck. I got fuck all all night.'

fuck all in a five-year plan *adj. Can.* An attempt to justify an extravagant purchase. *'I know strictly speaking we don't need a subwoofer on the stereo, but 800 quid is fuck all in a five-year plan. Now put them scissors down, love.'*

fuckall Paul *n. prop.* That pub scrounger who – having proffered all kinds of "can't fail" financial advice – then can't afford a round as all of his liquid capital is tied up in his investments. *'Quick lads, finish up! Fuckall Paul's just walked in and we are out of here.'*

fuck à l'orange *n.* A saucy act of penetrative affection performed up one of them *birds* covered in all fake tan, like what you get on *The Only Way is Essex* or *Geordie Shore.*

fuck an air fanny *v.* To *relax in a gentleman's way*. To *have it off* with a *ghost rider.*

fuckanory *exclam.* An extension of the word *fuck*, used to express extreme shock, disappointment or annoyance. *'Fuckanory, have you seen what he's tweeted today?'*

fuckard *n. arch.* Someone who was no rocket scientist a full five hundred years before rockets were invented. Except in China. A 15th century *Johnny No-Stars*. A *dolt, fuckwit* or *dotard.*

fuck barrel *n.* An affectionate term for one's *bag for life.*

fuck biddy *n.* A *friend with benefits*. And a pension.

fuck bumpers *n.* Energy absorbing buttocks.

fuckbus *n.* An accommodating lady who looks like she's got room for a few passengers up on top. A *double dicker.*

fuck butter *n.* KY jelly. *I can't believe it's not batter, WD over-40.*

fucked as a Blackpool donkey *sim.* Expression to confirm that one's physical condition is rather worse than desired, particularly after an evening of heavy *refreshment*. *'A message for the best football supporters in the world. We need a twelfth man here. Where are you? Where are you? Let's be 'avin' you! Come on! Sorry for shouting, only I've got to be honest with you. I'm as fucked as a Blackpool donkey here.'*

fucked fanny, dripping like a *sim.* Descriptive of the condition of a faulty refrigerator.

fucked more than Micheal Owen's knee, she's been *sim.* An unpleasantly sexist comment about a woman who's been *cocked more times than Davy Crockett's rifle*. A reference to the footballer who retired more than a decade ago. Also *(she's) had more sausage than a fat German butcher, been rogered more times than a policeman's radio, had more pricks than a second hand dartboard* etc.

fucked with his own cock *euph.* Having brought misfortune upon oneself with one's own foolish actions. *'In his summing-up, the coroner said that, in jumping from the flyover while drunk and wearing a home made rocket suit, the deceased had been reckless as to his own and others' safety, and recorded a verdict of fucked with his own cock.'*

fucker *1. n.* A disagreeable, overweight person, often prefixed "big fat". *2. n.* Anything at all. *'Fucking hell, look at the size of that fucker!'* (Sir Christopher Wren on seeing the dome of Saint Peter's in Rome).

fuckfoods *n.* Any provocatively shaped or saucily textured comestibles that could, in an extreme emergency, be pressed into impromptu service by the enterprising shopper who finds him or herself feeling a bit frisky in Tescos. Examples include, but are not limited to, cucumbers, corncobs, oven-ready chickens, bananas, curly wurlies, gourds and liver.

fuck her shadow on a gravel path, I'd *exclam.* A romantic compliment expressing a gentleman's romantic longing for the object of his affections.

fuck her while she's still warm! *exclam.* Light-hearted cinema/theatre audience heckle to be shouted from the stalls immediately following the on screen/stage demise of a female character in the hope – at a live performance – of making the actress in question laugh. *'Juliet, my wife! Death, that hath suck'd the honey of thy breath hath had no power yet upon thy beauty.' 'Fuck her while she's still warm, Larry!'*

fuck hutch *n.* A small flat kept as a discreet venue for illicit liaisons. *Stabbin' cabin, bunga bungalow.*

fucking a dying man's handshake , like *sim.* A charmingly poetic turn of phrase said of sexual congress up a not particularly well-toned *wizard's sleeve*. *'Did the earth move for you, darling?' 'Not really, darling. It was like fucking a dying man's handshake.'*

fucking the night *sim.* Copulating with a *yeti's welly.*

Fuckinstein *n. prop.* A mythical fantasy woman fashioned from various parts of desirable *pieces*; the plans for such a wonder usually formulated by an alcohol-fuelled committee. *'Right, so it's agreed;*

Our Fuckinstein will have Kylie's arse, Susannah Reid's legs, Charlize Theron's face, and Sharon the barmaid's tits. Now that's sorted, we can get on with this year's Nobel Prize nominations shortlist.'

fuckit list *n.* Personal inventory of all the things you can't be *arsed* to do before you die. *'You going to the away match at the weekend, then?' 'Nah. That one's going on the fuckit list.'*

fuck juice *n.* Jitler.

fucklings *n.* Little treasures, the fruit of one's loins.

fuck me shoes *n.* Footwear worn by a *Martini girl* who will *do it* "any time, any place, anywhere".

fuck muck *n.* Spodge.

fuck 'n' chuck *n.* A lady with whom a gentleman has had a *whirlwind one-night romance,* and then does the decent thing by leaving him alone afterwards. The opposite of a *bunny boiler.* A *hump 'n' dump.*

fucknuts *exclam.* Multi-purpose oath. *'Oh fucknuts, the humanity!'*

fuck off *1. exclam.* A request for someone to leave. *2. adj.* Of a price, quote or estimate for goods or services, an over-inflated figure intended to put the customer off when the supplier doesn't want the business. *'He wants me to clean his gutters out, but I don't fancy going up there. I'll give him a fuck off price.' 3. adj.* Descriptive of anything that is exceptionally large or intimidating. *'He came to clean me gutters out, and turned up with a big fuck off ladder. And he only charged £250. Well you wouldn't catch me going up there for that money.' 4. exclam.* An expression of incredulous stupefaction. *'Here, you'll never guess who come in here the other day and bought an Eccles cake and some rubber bands. Elton John! Stood right where you're stood he was, plain as day, in them big shoes he had in Tommy. Paid with a million pound note, he did, and told me to keep the change.' 'Fuck off!'*

fuckofferer *n.* A nasty piece of work whose sole purpose is to discourage visitors on behalf of the management of the institution that employs them, *eg.* A nightclub bouncer, security guard or doctor's receptionist. Also *doorknob.*

fuck off moment *n.* During a person's morning commute, the point at which they decide enough is enough, mutter a foul-mouthed imprecation and switch off the radio. It is estimated that up to 80% of listeners to BBC Radio 4's *Today* programme experience a simultaneous *fuck off moment* at approximately 7.45am each day.

fuck oil *n.* Aftershave. Also known as *snogging water* or *slagbait.* *'Happy Christmas, granddad. I've got you a bottle of fuck oil off the indoor market.'*

fuckonathon *n.* When an easy task becomes hard work. *'What took you so long? I thought you were just nipping out to change the headlight bulb on your Rover 75.' 'Don't ask. It was a right Fuckonathon.'*

fuckophany *n.* Pointless hoo-ha. *'Life's but a walking shadow; a poor player, that struts and frets his hour upon the stage, and then is heard no more: it is a tale told by an idiot, a fuckophany full of sound and fury, signifying nothing.'* (from *Macbeth* by William Shakespeare).

fuck oven *n.* A polite euphemism for a lady's *bower of delight.* *'Did you see that strippagram at Rishi's leaving do? She was absolute class. She managed to fit a whole coke bottle in her fuck oven.'*

fuckoven *n.* The household appliance from which, after significant pre-heating, may spring forth a freshly baked *cuntling.*

fuckpond *n.* A little post-coital pool that forms in a depression on the bottom sheet, usually full of *taddies.* A *fuckpuddle.*

fuckpouch *n.* The overhanging lump of *ladyflesh* which casts a shadow over the main event. The *poond, blubber beret, fat hat.*

fuck reins *n.* A woman's *barnet* fashioned into lengthy pigtails such that a gentleman friend can grasp them firmly, *Ben Hur*-style.

fucksaw *n.* A *dildo* attached to a mains-powered reciprocating saw. Frankly, it's an accident waiting to happen, is that. They should do a Public Information Film.

fuckshitfuckshitfuckshit *exclam.* Imprecation uttered when driving a car through a particularly tight space at too high a speed.

fucksock *n.* The sort of condom your granny would knit.

fuck stick *n.* A short, stout piece of *wood* used for *fucking* something. A chap's *twig.*

fucksticks *exclam.* An expression of mild impatience. *'Fucksticks. I've left the communion wafers in the vestry again.'*

fuckstrated *adj.* US. Having a severe case of *DSB.*

fuckstruck *adj. Cuntstruck, betwatted* or *muffled.*

fucktagon *n.* A situation so bad that "it's fucked whatever angle you look at it". Nothing springs immediately to mind.

fucktangular *adj.* Descriptive of a situation that is complicated and messy in multiple unpleasant and difficult ways.

fucktastic *adj.* Evidently better than fantastic, but neither *fucking fantastic* nor *fan-fucking-tastic.* From fuck + tastic.

fuck the dog *1. v. Can.* To do absolutely nothing. *'Busy day at the office, dear?' 'Not really. Made a few calls in the morning, went to the pub at dinnertime, PMQs, then fucked the dog in the afternoon.' 2. v.* How the English Arts & Crafts sculptor, typeface designer and printmaker Eric Gill (1882-1940) occupied his spare time when he wasn't sculpting, designing typefaces or making prints. Well, you had to make your own entertainment in them days.

fuck trophy *n.* A baby. Usually applied to the progeny of ugly couples who need proof of their ability to achieve congress.

fuck truck *1. n.* Erstwhile "UK Amateurs" film production that was unlikely to win the Best Cinematography prize at the Academy Awards. Or even a BAFTA. *2. n.* A filthy van with a mattress in the back, used for location filming in the same.

fuck trump *1. phr.* Content of a foul-mouthed speech made by Robert De Niro in which he somewhat disparaged the eponymous comedy 45th POTUS. *2. n.* A noise produced inadvertently while *having it off.* A *queef, flap raspberry, Harry Ramsden's dinner gong, Neddy Seagoon's last raspberry, front bum trumpet pump, frampton, hat dropped forward, Lawley kazoo, muff chuff, crumpet trumpet, vulvuzela* or *fanny fart.*

fuckulties *n.* Notional allure retained by an older woman to whom a generously disposed fellow would be prepared to *give one. 'I tell you what, she may be kicking eighty, but that Helen Mirren's still got all her fuckulties, your holiness'*

fuckupied *adj.* Descriptive of a cubicle that is out of service due to *shaggers. 'The first inch was already cold, but the only cubicle was fuckupied. Do you think you can get these Y-fronts clean?'*

fuckwhiskers *n.* Pubes. The charming thatch on a *moss cottage.*

fuckwit *n.* A simpleton, fool, one of little intelligence. A *bollock brain, Johnny No-Stars, eg.* Whoever designed the traffic system for getting in and out of the short-stay car park at Newcastle Central Station.

fuck with the cock you've got, you can only *exclam.* Useful get-out clause for men defending themselves against accusations of inadequacy. *'Well, we made the wrong tyre choice at the start of the weekend and our new rear diffuser package is still not delivering the downforce on the slower corners. Still. you can only fuck with the cock you've got, so eighth is quite a reasonable result at the end of the day.'*

fucky dip *n.* The randomized means of selecting oneself a *special friend* for the duration of a swingers night, *eg.* Picking a set of car keys from a bowl on a coffee table in a suburban semi with pampas grass in the front garden. In a 1970s film starring Linda Bellingham, Bob Todd, John Junkin

and Cardew Robinson. Also *quimbola, twottery.*

fucsimile *n.* Any high-end realistic sex-doll or *Dutch wife. 'Our Jeffrey bought one of them fucsimiles out the back of Knave and he's already had to send off for a replacement anus.'*

fud *n. Scots. Berkeley Hunt.* A *flingel.*

fuddle *v.* To *chuck your mess* or *tip your filthy yoghurt. 'G-G-G-Granville, f-fer-f-fetch a cloth, will you? I've f-fer-f-fuddled me t-ter-t-trousers again watching n-nurse Gladys Emmanuel bend over.'*

fudge *v.* To lie in the 'spoons' position with one's partner, and *fart* romantically so that it vibrates on their person. Also *love puff.*

fudge drums *n. Blunderguffs. 'That pasty at the General Synod lunchtime buffet has had me on the fudge drums all afternoon, your grace.'*

fudge factor *n.* Scientific assessment of how much a chap is *au fait with Doris Day.*

fudge factor five *euph.* The state of *sitting on a shire horse's head.*

fudge icing *n.* The decorative coating found on the bowls of portable *shitters* towards the end of Glastonbury Festival, for example.

fudge packer *n.* One who packs fudge for a living, for example in the despatch department of a fudge factory.

fudge tunnel *n.* A tunnel made out of, or for the underground transportation of, fudge.

fudge up *v.* To *pebbledash* the toilet bowl. *'Bloody hell, Camilla. You've fudged up the shit-pot again.'*

fudgeways *euph. Up the council.*

fudgina *n.* The *rusty bullet hole. 'Sorry pet. Genuine mistake. I thought you said fudgina.'*

fud slush *n.* Scottish *milp,* usually smeared on a chap's ginger chops while he's tucking into a *haddock pastie.*

FUFAD/fufad *acronym.* Feet Up Fuck All Done.

fuffoon *n.* An affectionate term for a lady's *pleasure centre. 'And look, your holiness. When you freeze the frame as she crosses her legs, and zoom right in, you can definitely see her fuffoon.'*

fufu *n.* The main female *part of shame.*

fufu flour *n.* The principal ingredient in a batch of *fanny batter.*

fufu manchu *n.* A sinister, long, straggly *underbeard.*

fug *n.* A friendly hug that an unscrupulous fellow hopes will eventually lead to a *fuck.*

fuggit *exclam.* Ancient Egyptian curse uttered when denied a British passport.

fug horn *n.* Low frequency audible alert emitted from the *botty bugle* as a warning to those in the vicinity that atmospheric conditions are about to change, and not necessarily, one might reasonably suppose, for the better.

fugly *adj.* Fucking ugly.

fugly but juggly *euph.* A bird who was at the back of the line when looks were being given out, but who evidently pushed right to the front of the queue at the *knockers* counter. See also *botblatrit.*

FUKT/fukt *acronym.* Post Office acronym for any parcel marked "fragile", which has come open as a result of being kicked around by bored sorting office staff playing football. Failed Under Kinetic Testing.

fulfil your destiny *v.* To ejaculate. After *wanking* so hard it feels like your hand has fallen off.

Fulham handshake *n.* A friendly greeting exchanged between two gentlemen in a public lavatory cubicle. A *WC Handy.*

full as a bull's bum *sim.* Absolutely stuffed. Also *full as a fat bird's shoe, full as a parson's sack, full as a seaside shithouse. 'Another cucumber sandwich, Reverend Latimer?' 'No thank-you, Mrs Antrobus. I'm as full as a bull's bum.'*

full A13, the *euph.* An adventurous session of *hanky-panky* that is analogous to a journey from London to the coast along the said thoroughfare, *ie.* A gentleman performs a *Dagenham handshake,* his ladyfriend returns the favour via a *Basildon bagpipe,* and the whole sordid shenanigans culminates in a visit to her "South end".

fullbeams *n.* Ladies' *headlamps* which really ought to be dipped in order to avoid dazzling oncoming males. *Searchlights.*

full Belgian *n.* The opposite of a full *Brazilian.* A large, untidy *muff.* A *Judith, biffer* or *Terry Waite's allotment.*

full Bristol, the *n.* When an intense and possibly traumatic *sit down toilet adventure* produces a bowl of *bum trifle* that spans the entire spectrum of the eponymous West-Country-based medics' Stool Chart.

full cuntal lobotomy *n.* A loss of reason found in men when they are presented with the opportunity to have s*x.

full emu, the *n.* Being *fisted* up to the elbow; a right good *gut-smashing.* See also *muppeting, lung-grabber, Amsterdam uppercut, the Sooty show.*

full English *1. n.* A particularly greasy early morning *bang,* often followed by a big *shit* and a cup of tea. *2. n.* The *undercrackers* of the doubly incontinent after they've been *given it with both barrels. 'Can you give these a wash please, nan? I'm afraid they're the full English.' 3. n.* Following a spell on foreign shores, the delivery of one's first non-*skittery Tom tit* that has no "foreign muck" sullying it. *'Sally, we've been back on British soil*

eight days and I swear that's my first full English.' 'Excellent news, dear. And even better, we're nearly at the front of the Customs queue now.'

full English breakfast *n.* A very untidy vagina that is frankly too much to face just after you get up. A big plateful of *knicker sausages, bacon strips,* fried mushrooms and baked beans.

full English, she/he eats a *1. euph.* Said of a person who shows a healthy appetite for a *Byronic breakfast. 2. n.* Said of a person of either gender who likes their *bacon* as much as their *sausage.* Subtly descriptive of the proclivities of an *alloy welder.*

full frontal prudity *n.* A marked reluctance to appear *in the rik* in the bedroom, locker room or on a nationally broadcast television dating show. Common amongst *plumpers* and *needle dicks.*

full funnel marketing *1. n.* Stupid business-speak for the revolutionary concept of "telling loads of people about something and then hoping some of them buy it". *2. n.* Those little cards in London phone boxes that advertise pulchritudinous ladies who *do everything.*

full Monty, the *1. n.* Any male strip performance where the artiste goes the whole hog and gets his *Charlie* and *knackers* out. *2. n.* A *hard-on.*

full Nelson *n.* When *wrestling oneself,* a hold involving one hand, one eye, and a funny-shaped hat. And possibly an impressive column.

full Roger McGuinn, the *euph.* An extensive set of genital ironmongery that "jingle jangles" like the eponymous Byrds plank-spanker's trademark Rickenbacker 12-string guitar. See also *Sam Spoon's rhythm pole. 'Ooh, Evan. I didn't realise you had the full Roger McGuinn.'*

full service history *n.* A married fellow's detailed knowledge of who has previously messed about under his wife's *beetle bonnet.*

full set of valves and sockets *euph.* Complimentary reference to a nubile young lady, when she excites concupiscence in a passing swain. *'Gwooar, fuck me. I tell you what, that Konnie Huq's got a full set of valves and sockets. And now over to Daniel Corbett for tomorrow's weather.'*

full spatchcock, go the *v.* To do something you never thought was possible. *'Look at how wide her legs have went, your holiness. How does she do that?' 'She's went the full spatchcock, cardinal. You'd never of thought she could do that, would you of, when you seen her doing her good works in the Calcutta slums?'*

full stack engineer *1. n.* In software development, a boffin who is adept in handling a wide range of disciplines from the back end via the middleware to the front end. Or whatever. *2. n.* A highly qualified person adept at *servicing* all of a *bird's* various *bodily treasures*. A chap who can keep a fairly hefty pair of *norks* suitably entertained. While, perhaps, simultaneously dealing with network interface issues *down below*. *'Born on this day: Linda Lovelace, grumble artiste, 1949; Pat Benatar, warbler, 1953; Rod Stewart, full stack engineer, 1945.'*

full theatre tour *n.* Access to all areas of a ladyfriend, *ie.* Starting off in the *upper circle*, then moving into the *lower circle* before finishing off in her *private box* with some Maltesers. May also include a *backstage pass* and a photo.

full throttle for take off *exclam.* The only way of having a *gypsy's kiss* when in possession of a *diamond cutter.*

full Trumpton *n. onomat.* A lengthy recital on the *rear end trumpet* which sounds eerily reminiscent of Captain Flack calling his Fire Brigade register, *viz.* "Pugh! Pugh! Barney McGrew! Cuthbert! Dibble! Grubb!". A *full Trumpton* may also continue with the sound of a tappetty vintage Fire Engine being cranked into reluctant life with a starting handle.

fumble bags *n.* Good value *knockers. Jamboree bags, fat rascals.*

fumble mitten *n.* A fellow's trouser pocket when used as a means to vigorously *wind the clock*. *'Lot 347: A pair of well-used mid-1970s Farah hopsack slacks in fawn, formerly the property of TV presenter Jess Yates (1918-1993). Rusty zip, some staining around the crotch, and extensive wear to left and right fumble mittens. Est. £600-£650.'*

fumbling with your change *euph.* Surreptitious act of *self pollution* at a lap dancing club. *'Is your mate having a wank there, pal?' 'Nah, I think he's just frantically fumbling with his change.'*

fumidor *n.* An airtight container for keeping *bum cigars* in tip-top condition. Often stored in the fridge prior to an appointment with the proctologist.

funbags *n.* Breasts, *jugs, thru'pennies.*

funbagtastic *exclam.* Upon seeing a glorious pair of *fleshbombs*, one might utter: *'Funbagtastic!'*

fun boy three *1. n.* Novelty pop act of the early 1980s; a sort of Ska/New Wave Wurzels. *2. n.* The *fruit bowl*. The *meat and two veg, fishing tackle, hanging salad. 'Ooh! Right in the fucking fun boy three! Let's hope David Gower remembered to put his box on before he came out to bat, Geoffrey.'*

fun bucket *n.* An unacceptably sexist and offensive way of referring to the *village bike.*

funburn *n. medic.* Painful reddening on the skin

around the elbows, knees and buttocks, after *having it off* on a cheap nylon carpet.

funch *n.* Sex during your lunch hour, from fuck + lunch. Also *nooner.*

funcle *n.* The same-sex civil partner of a *comfortably shod* aunt. From female + uncle.

fun cushions *n. Dirty pillows.*

fun custard *n.* A clown's *ejaculate*. Should you find yourself using this expression, rest assured your life has gone down a very inauspicious path indeed.

funderwear *n.* Erotic but impractical lingerie. Purchased at great psychological expense by red-faced husbands, only to be returned to the shop the next day by thunder-faced wives. *Gash garnish,* any *bapset* bought from Ann Summers.

fundungeon *n.* A lady's *below-stairs* accommodation.

fun extractor *n.* A sour-faced woman sitting in the corner of a room, sucking all the enjoyment out of the atmosphere. *'Jesus, we went round to Tez's but he had the fun extractor turned on and it was a shit night.'*

fungry *adj.* More than a little peckish. From fucking + hungry. Also *bungry, cungry.*

fun junction *n. medic.* The area in a young lady's *soft undercarriage* between the *front* and *rear bottoms*. Upon arrival, a fellow might exclaim: *'Which way along the fun junction tonight, dear?'*

funky gibbon *n. medic.* Distressing condition whereby a chap involuntary sings the rousing three-note choral overture from the eponymous 1975 Goodies hit after crushing his *hairy saddlebags* between his thighs.

funky hammer juice *n.* The *clam bisque* which, it is rumoured, sometimes sprays from a *Judy Drench's blurtch* while she is being *nimbed* on her *cumulus. Oyster juice.*

funky spingers *n.* Spooneristic *knuckle glitter.*

funny bone *n.* An inexplicable erectivitation of the *membrum virile* that occurs during a comedic performance. *Stand-up, heckler's lump.*

funny girl *n.* A *trolley dolly* who has that little bit extra. Often found in Thailand and in unreliable anecdotes about a friend of a friend who went on holiday to Thailand. A *tiptop, false tart.*

fun size *n.* A very small *tod*. But bigger than a *miniature hero.*

fun sock *n.* An *English overcoat. 'Anything for the weekend, Mr Straw?' 'Aye. I'll have a packet of fun socks, please. Extra small size.'*

fun sponge *1. n.* A personality vacuum; one who hates fun and radiates cheerlessness. *'Born on this day: Julio Iglesias, Spanish crooner, 1943; Cherie Blair, venttriloquist's dummy-faced legal eagle,*

1954; Nicholas Witchell, BBC News *fun sponge,* 1953.' *2. n.* The *banana cupboard.* '*Up on the table please, Mrs Leadbetter. Let's have a butchers at your fun sponge.*'

funt *1. n.* The *bodily treasure* revealed beneath a fold of *flubber.* From fat + cunt. *2. n.* An inveterate *double fare.* From fat + cunt. *3. n.* An obsolete Russian unit of currency. From fat + cunt.

funtan *n.* A short-lived, healthy glow in a gent's face following a spot of *self-discipline.*

fun tube *n.* A *rubber Johnny.* '*Three fun tubes please, chemist.*' '*I'm afraid we only have extra small in stock, Mr Davro.*' '*Oh, bugger. That's no use to me. Don't you have anything smaller?*'

FUPA/fupa *abbrev.* Fat Upper Pussy Area. The bloated lower belly of a woman. See *gunt.*

fur burger *n. Minge, hairy pie, vertical bacon sandwich.*

fürburgring *n.* An interminable and hazardous circuit around a particularly byzantine *clopper.* The missus's *southern loop.*

furbutt dib-dab *n.* Unwelcome fluff contamination while cleaning up after a *sit-down toilet adventure.*

furgle *1. n. prop.* Christian name of the lead singer of the Undertones. *2. v.* To copulate rudely, crudely or noisily, like you would imagine a village idiot would with a milkmaid.

furloined *adj.* After being granted an involuntary leave of absence, with reduced income and no prospect of impressing a mate, to somewhat neglect one's *bush admin.*

furlong *n.* Imperial unit of pubic hair length.

fur on it, it's got *exclam.* Phrase used to describe a *grizzly* that has been maturing in the *chamber of horrors* for far too long. '*So, Audrey, that's a very generous offer from the banker. Is it deal or no deal?*' '*I'll tell you in a minute, Noel. I'm just off to the shitters to strangle a Mars Bar. I've been baking this fucker in that long it's got fur on it.*'

furred game *n.* That which a *cuntry gent* hunts on a Friday night. *Hair pie,* the game meat in a *country supper.*

furry bicycle stand *n.* A *hoop* that is set into concrete outside the library.

furry godmother *n.* A whiskery old *trout.*

furry handbag *n.* An out of shape, floppy *fanny,* with all lipsticks and keys falling out of it.

furry hoop *n.* A hairy *biffer. Sweep's brush.*

furry letterbox *n.* An eight-inch wide, spring-loaded horizontal *clapping fish* that traps the postman's fingers.

furry muff *exclam.* A ribald alternative to saying "fair enough" when speaking to an elderly relative, someone in a call centre on the other side of the world, or giving evidence in court.

furt *1. n.* A painful passing of wind, possibly following the consumption of several pints of Guinness and a quantity of pickled eggs. From fart + hurt. *2. n.* A furtive fart, and thus *3. v.* To *step on a duck,* surreptitiously.

fur trader *n.* A *tennis fan.*

fur trapper's cabin *n.* A city centre dwelling, such as a flat or bedsit, which is retained by a married man solely for the purpose of midweek *beaver-hunting* expeditions.

FuSBAC *acronym.* A handy composite swear word comprising Fuck, Shit Bugger, Arse, and Cunt.

fusewire *n.* A ginger person's *thirteen amp gorilla salad. Fire down below.*

Fussell's milk *1. n.* A thick, sweet condensed milk. *2. n.* The contents of the male *churns* after prolonged abstinence from sexual activity. '*Throw me a bone, love. Me bollocks are like two tins of Fussell's milk here.*'

fussell your Russells *euph.* Of an over-excitable young man, to be *up and over like a pan of milk* into his *Russell Grants.* '*Are you trying to seduce me, Mrs Robinson?*' '*Yes, but it looks like I'm too late. You appear to have fusselled your Russells, Dustin.*'

fussy about wallpaper *euph.* Said of a fellow who *throws a light dart.*

futtering *n.* A *trip to Hairyfordshire.* A bout of *front door work.*

futurehead *1. n.* In popular music, any member of the eponymous Sunderland-based 4-piece beat combo who, if their Wikipedia page is anything to go by, haven't exactly found themselves overwhelmed by work recently. *2. n.* The tungsten-tipped head of a *Thora* which announces its impending arrival by burrowing through the *nipsy* like the Mole out of Thunderbird 2.

future shit *n.* A space age *dump* that requires no wiping, like everyone will do in the year 2030.

futz *n. US.* The vagina.

fuzzbox *1. n.* A guitar effects unit popular in the late seventies. A *big muff. 2. n.* A *minge* that is going to get used.

fuzz lite *n.* A Community Support officer. A *potted plant.*

fwank *v.* To desperately stimulate the *ivory tower* while trawling through a female friend/colleague/ vague acquaintance's profile pictures on a popular social networking site, in the hope of happening upon some vaguely enticing bikini snaps.

fyst *n. arch.* A 15th century, foul-smelling *fart.*

fysticuffs *n. arch.* Getting punched by ungrateful *beneficiaries* after *scaring the cat.*

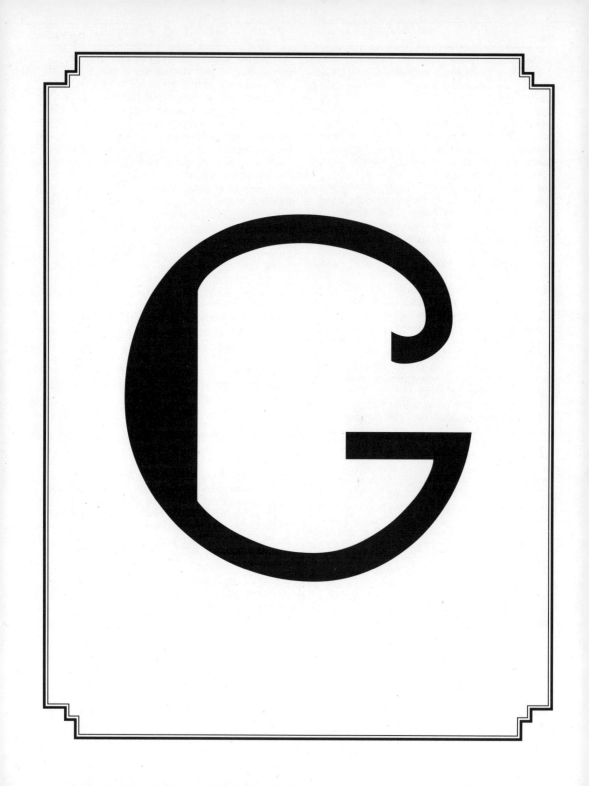

Gabrielle *n.* A semi-successful *Velma*. A *King Harold.* Occluding one of your ladyfriend's eyes with a well-aimed *jizzbolt.* Also *spoff monocle, German eyebath.*

gaby *n.* The offspring of a pair of same-sex parents. *'Congratulations, Mr and Mr John. It's a beautiful, bouncing gaby.'*

gadders *n. Notts.* Stockings and suspenders. Nottinghamshire schoolboy *stiffy*-maker from the seventiess. *'Phwooar! Look, Graham! She's got gadders on! You can see the clips through her habit!'*

gag *1. n.* A pre-*spew* spasm, often cause by a blockage in the throat – what Mama Cass supposedly did on a sandwich and Steve Peregrin Took did on a cocktail cherry, but Linda Lovelace didn't do on a *cock. 2. v.* What women are doing *for it* when they *want it up 'em. 3. n.* A joke sold to a stand-up comedian or adult comic for five bob in the old money.

gagfluff *n.* The savoury little *clockspring rolls* of smegma, *pubes* and underpant fibres that a lady encounters under her chap's *fiveskin* while she is performing *horatio.* Also the fragments of *bogroll* and *dessicated blip* found amongst a lady's *flaps* by a fellow performing *cumulonimbus.*

gag hag *n.* An unfussy woman who is prepared to *have it off* with stand-up comedians. A comedic *groupie.*

gag reflex *n. medic.* The ability to tell a joke on any subject at the drop of a hat. Barry Cryer, for example, had a very highly developed *gag reflex.*

gak *1. n.* Springle, sprongle, sprungle. *2. abbrev.* Grade A Knobhead.

Gallagher *n. prop.* The stylised *horatio* technique employed by one who is too vertically challenged to reach the *giggle stick* using conventional methods. Named after the distinctive stance taken by singer Liam, now performing with his own Oasis tribute band Beady Eye, whereby he tilts his head back and mouths upwards into the microphone.

gallic *n.* Stimulating a partner's *balloon knot* with the tongue. Probably doesn't do a lot for fresh breath confidence. *Rimming, round the world, nipsilingus.*

gallon girl *n.* An Imperial-quantity-specific *gifwid.* A proper *eight-pinter.*

galloping knob rot *n. medic.* VD, any painful *Doonican* resulting in the production of *gleet* and the *pissing* of razor blades. *Dutch helm disease, crotch gremlins, happy rash, vice crispies.*

gallop the lizard *v.* To *relax in a gentlemanly manner.*

gam *1. n. US.* Lady's leg. *'Hot Diggety! Check out the gams on that swell broad, Bub.' 2. v.* To *gamahuche.*

gamahuche *v.* To *lick out, eat out, impersonate Stalin.*

gamble and lose *v.* The secret vice of a *man of the cloth* who has *put it all on brown.* To *fart* and *follow through.*

gamble crack *n.* When *working from home,* the chink in the living-room curtains that enables a *groin-thumper* to see if someone is coming up the path but also, conversely, affords that someone coming up the path the chance of catching them in the act. *'We know you're in, Mr Brown, we saw you through the gamble crack. If you're not going to come to the door, we'll just push a copy of the Watchtower through the letterbox.'*

gambler's squint *1. n.* A red-blooded chap's cheeky peek at a bit of *sideboob. 2. n.* While standing at a public urinal, a cheeky peek at what your opponent has in his hand.

gamechanger, the *n.* When one is bloated and suffering gastric discomfort, a doomsday *trouser cough* of devastating power that brings instant relief but should, on account of its formidable potency, only be unleashed following a thorough check that the coast is clear and no innocent civilians are within its range. An anal watershed.

game of thrones *1. n.* Title of a fantasy series on the telly that's based on some books. *2. n.* Upon realising too late that there is no *bumwad* in your public convenience *trap,* the undignified and crab-like shuffle around the other stalls in a desperate attempt to find some.

gammon and pineapple *n.* Ham-on-ham.

gammon-bacon-bacon-gammon sandwich *euph.* A meaty *vadge.* See also *butcher's window, mutton shutters etc.*

gammon flaps *1. n.* Hole in a farmhouse door through which pigs are able to come and go at will. *2. n.* Beef curtains, bacon strips, Barnsley chops. The swinging saloon doors on a *bird's blurtch.*

gammon fodder *n.* Any sort of political statement, social media post or other behaviour that causes a purple-faced GBNews viewer to froth at the mouth and type aggressively in the *Daily Mail* comments section, *eg.* An athlete taking the knee in support of BLM, a statue of a Georgian racist being taken down or any Twitter post by Sadiq Khan.

gammonite *n.* Descriptive of those spam-faced, round-cheeked right-wingers you see applauding Richard Littlejohn in the *Question Time* studio audience or production gallery.

gammon ring *n.* The *nipsy.*

Gandalf's hat *1. n.* The grey headwear favoured by Tolkein's heroic wizard. *2. n.* The lop-sided fungus that can flourish atop the *bell end* of a less-than-scrupulously hygienic *lord of the ring*. Also *pith helmet*. 3. *euph.* Almost, but not quite tumescent, *viz.* Mainly upright but a bit floppy at the top.

gander's neck *n.* An extremely long, thick *clam ram* which hisses menacingly if one gets too close.

gang bang *1. n.* A *shit* song by Black Lace, which featured in the splendid film *Rita, Sue and Bob Too*. *2. n.* A nightmarish sexual free-for-all in a tastelessly decorated living room. *'Anybody fancy another Scotch egg or shall we start the gang bang?'*

gaping gill *n.* The state of an unfortunate *grumble flick* actress's *ringpiece* just after the male lead has withdrawn his *slag hammer*. Named after the famous North Yorkshire pot hole, that is 50m across and 200m deep. But not full of *spunk*. Also *granny without her teeth in, gaper*. See also *foop*.

gap lapper *n.* A *tennis fan*. Or possibly a person who runs repeated circuits around a clothes shop.

garage *euph.* The obliging lady that a chap visits when he needs his *big end* serviced.

garbonzas *n. Gazungas.*

garboon *n.* One who *barumphs. A snufty* or *snurglar.*

garden bridge *1. n.* Tragically cancelled scheme to build a prestigious new river crossing for the oft-neglected town of London; a project which somehow ran up a £43 million bill in return for a couple of fanciful artist's impressions and a swish logo. *2. n.* An hirsute *taint.*

Gardener's Question Time *1. n.* Achingly dull Radio 4 programme on which middle-aged women from Harrogate ask Kathy Clugston whether their compost needs pruning if there's going to be a late frost or something. *2. n.* A series of discreet enquiries made by a herb enthusiast while attempting to procure a certain type of home-grown foliage which is a popular filling for roll-up cigarettes.

Gareth *n. rhym. slang.* Named after the late *New Avengers*/Nescafé ad/*Call My Bluff* star; the *clopper*. From Gareth H*nt = cunt. *'The duchess was kind enough to let me lick out her Gareth.' ' Me too, vicar. Small world.'*

Gareth or Gary? *interrog. rhym. slang.* Politely encoded enquiry towards an agreeable lady who is evidently equally receptive to any locus of penetration, *viz. Either* in her *Gareth Hunt* or her *Gary Glitter.*

garfunkel *1. v.* To cover a public lavatory seat with paper in order to avoid contamination of one's posterior. The late *Carry On* star Kenneth Williams was by all accounts a keen *garfunkellist* when forced to evacuate his troublesome *Simons*

in any toilet other than his own. To *scump*. *2. n.* Any *ad hoc* protective paper structure created in or on a municipal *chod bin*, "like a bridge over troubled water".

garlogies *n. Bell end* bogies.

Garrity dance *n.* Making your way across the landing, knees together, after taking a *Brad* and finding nothing with which to wipe your *balloon knot*. Named after the stupid dance popularised by the now deceased lead singer of Freddy and the Dreamers, who was always running out of *shitscrape*. See also *game of thrones.*

Gary Glitter *n. prop. rhym. slang. Council gritter.* Named after the 'seventies glam rock *sexcase*. Also *Gary.*

Gary Neville's managerial career in Spain *euph.* Something that is over almost as soon as it starts. See also *Rio Ferdinand's boxing career; Up and over like a pan of milk etc.*

gas an otter *v.* To sneak a *cushion creeper* past an unsuspecting mustelid while he's snoozing in his burrow.

gas baby *n.* A *fart*. *'Contractions started at the end of Sunday dinner, and after a difficult labour Brian gave birth to a healthy gas baby. We wish him and his partner well as they begin this exciting new chapter in their lives.'*

gaseous anomaly *1. n.* The sort of sparkly cloud frequently seen attacking the USS Enterprise in *Star Trek*. *2. n.* A *silent but deadly shirt raiser*. *'I wouldn't go into that turbo lift Mr Scott. I think Spock's left a gaseous anomaly in there.'*

gaseous clay *n.* A bowel movement in which the sufferer passes flatulence-assisted *stools* which look like something from a school pottery lesson and which, upon hitting the pan, '"float like a butterfly". However, because of their high exit velocity, they also "sting like a bee".

gas finger *n.* When one has *a pig at the back gate*, a particularly rasping *fart* that does a sterling job of scratching an itchy *ringpiece*. Also *quack scratch, arse scratcher, Roy Castle's kettle.*

gas giant *1. n.* A large planet that is not composed of solid matter such as rock; your Neptunes, Jupiters, Saturns and so on. *2. n.* An impressive outburst of *carbon dibaxide* from your *anus* (pronounced "ˈjʊərməs").

gash *1. n.* Hairy *axe wound* between a woman's *lisks*. The vulva. *2. n. coll. Totty, blit, bush, talent, blart*. *'Plenty gash in tonight, Mr Speaker.'*

gash and Gary *n.* Of *jazz periodicals*, a comprehensive *below stairs* photograph of a lady in which both her *front* and *back doors* are on display.

gashback *1. n.* Reward points earned by buying

flowers, chocolates *etc.*, which can be redeemed at the *fish counter.* As opposed to *brownie points,* which can be cashed in *up the arse.* 2. *n.* A sudden, spontaneous recollection of what you managed to *pull* at the weekend, which will result in a sudden urge to either nip to the bog for a quick *ham shank,* or accelerate into a tree on the drive to work. 3. *n.* A *grumble* flashback, that is to say the experience of spotting a person you think you recognise, then realising it's because you've seen someone who looks like them in a bit of *Frankie* recently

gash badger *n.* A voracious *rug muncher* who is not in the slightest put off by thick pile.

gash baron *n.* A merchant trading in women of questionable repute. A *tart farmer, flapmonger, pimp.*

gash brown *n.* A female who thinks outside the box and elects to wipe from back to front.

gash card *n.* A female only method of payment for goods and services. Accepted by taxi drivers, milkmen and pizza delivery boys. *Hairy cheques.*

gash crash 1. *n.* A motor accident, usually in early spring, caused when drivers are distracted by appealingly attired females. See also *rear ender.* 2. *n.* An *early bath* for a *one pump chump.*

gashes to ashes *phr.* Intoned by a soon-to-be-ex-bachelor over the symbolic burning of his lifetime's collection of *top shelf material* and Freeman's catalogues whose pages have somehow become terribly stained and/or stuck together.

gash factory *n.* A strip club, *box office.*

gash feathers *n.* The plumage on a *bird's nest.* Female pubic hair.

gash giant *n.* An humungous Glaswegian *fud.*

gash guzzler *n.* An enthusiastic sipper of the *hairy cup.*

gash in hand *euph.* Traditional form of tax-free payment for goods and services. Definitely not contactless.

gash in the attic 1. *n.* Every dad's secret roofspace stash of 1970s *grumble.* 2. *n.* A fortuitous bundle of *bongo mags* found stashed in the loft of a newly acquired property. *Ceiling whacks.* 3. *n.* A sweet, silver-haired old *crack.*

gashion pages *n.* The section of a *haute couture* magazine where the models are actually worth a look, as opposed to the freaky-looking, miserable skellingtons in all the other pictures.

gash leak *n.* A monthly emergency in one's domicile where the most insignificant spark could result in a huge explosion.

gash mark six *n.* A state of feminine arousal. *'A lady's hairy oven must be heated to gash mark six before the gentleman slams in his lamb.'* (from *Bedroom Management* by Mrs Beeton).

gash mask *n.* A woman who sits atop a man's face in order to prevent him breathing in any harmful odours.

gash matter *n.* Remnants of a *fish supper* on the chins of a *diner at the Y.* An *11 o'clock shadow,* dried *sloom, scraps.*

gashmere *n.* The soft, downy strands of *gorilla salad* which form the warp, woof and weft of an upper class *wizard's sleeve.*

gashmina *n.* A posh *jam rag.*

gash pastie *n.* A particularly flaky vagina. *'She was so dry down there it looked like a gash pastie.'*

gashpatcho *n. Spanish soup,* which is on the menu for a few days each month. Also *tomato boat ketchup, cranberry dip, moon juice, egg nog, lunar mess* or indeed *fanny jam.*

gash plaster *n.* A feminine napkin, *jam rag* or *dangermouse.*

gashpoint *n.* Handy ATM machine in the locality of a red light district or near a brothel.

gashquatch *n.* A particularly hirsute *growler.*

gash rash 1. *n. medic.* A light-hearted ladies' *downstairs thing, eg.* Thrush, *athlete's fud.* 2. *n.* Gentleman's post *lick-out* irritation of the chops.

gash splash *n.* The distaff equivalent of a *gentleman's wash.* *'Bloody hell, Barbara. I just popped next door to borrow Jerry's watering can and I caught Margot having a gash splash in the kitchen sink.'*

gash station *n.* A nightclub or bar where less-than-discerning gentlemen are able to *cop off* with *welly-topped slappers.*

gashtag *n.* The string off a tampon; a *cunt mouse's tail, pantypopper, misery cord.*

gash tash *n.* That which tickles your top lip when you are *donning the beard.*

gashtray *n.* The *fairy hammock* of a lady's *farting crackers.*

gashtric band *n.* A device designed to drastically reduce a gentleman's consumption of *hairy pie.* A wedding ring.

gashtronaut *n.* An intrepid explorer who boldly goes where no man has gone before.

gashtronome *n.* A connoisseur of *haddock pasties.* A *fish supper* gourmand.

gaslighting 1. *n.* Using sinister psychological methods to manipulate someone into questioning their own sanity, like what Charles Boyer does to Ingrid Bergman in that film. 2. *n.* Igniting one's own methane supply.

gas man *n.* In a *grumble flick* production, a *corgi registered* actor whose responsibility is to look for potential leaks in an actress being *spit-roast-*

ed and to plug them up, rendering the said lucky lady *gastight.*

gasman's olive *n.* The result of *back door work* whereby the male *member for Pantshire*, once withdrawn, brandishes a tell-tale *chutney collar* resembling a copper 'olive' of the sort used in the plumbing trade. *'The Archbishop regrets that he will be unable to attend the service this morning, as he's came down with the gasman's olive.'*

gas mask *n.* A scented wet wipe strategically placed over one's *freckle*, in order to disguise what would otherwise be a rather unpleasant aroma.

gassenger *n.* A person who is travelling in an automobile, bus, train, aeroplane, or other conveyance, and keeps stopping to *pump gas.*

gasset *n.* When a lingering *beefy eggo* impregnates the material of one's *twangers.* Also known as a *velcro guff* or *force field.*

gas skirt *n.* Trousers that are puffed out due to wind, like what Dutchmen wear.

gastight *adj.* Of a *stick vid* actress, to be simultaneously bunged up in all available orifices.

gastric bandit *n.* An unscrupulous *chubby chaser.*

gastric broadband *n.* A form of extreme bariatric surgery reserved for only the most dedicated of *salad dodgers.*

gatekeeper *n.* An obstinate *turd*, firmly ensconced across the *nipsy*, that bars the way and stubbornly prevents others from passing. Also *pace car, doorman.*

gaucho growler *n.* A short back and sides on a *velcro triangle.*

Gavin, going for a quick *n. rhym. slang. Scots.* A brisk *act of self delight* or over-shaking the *little fella* during a work-based *piss* break. Named in honour of former Arbroath midfielder Gavin Swankie.

Gaviscon deluxe *n.* Baileys/Cointreau cocktail.

gay *1. adj.* Descriptive of a day when one might require the door to be shut. *2. adj.* Of retired colonels who write to the *Daily Telegraph*, a perfectly good word for happy or brightly coloured. *3. adj.* Synonym for "bad", according to gay disc jockey Chris Moyles.

gay and display *1. n.* *Puddle-jumping* carryings-on in car parks. *2. n.* A gentleman who behaves in an overly camp manner, *eg.* Him off Channel 4 with the glasses and the teeth who sounds like Dierdre Barlow hyperventilating sulphur hexafluoride.

gay as a summer's fair, as *sim. On the other bus. 'Mam, dad, it's time you knew. I'm as gay as a summer's fair.' 'Elton, this has come as such a shock.'*

gay blob *n.* An unexpected case of the *Brad Pitts* which effectively puts the kybosh on the evening's planned *mudlarks. 'Any chance of a bit of backdoor action tonight, love?' 'Sorry Dave, I can't. I'm on the gay blob.'*

gay by *n.* A road-side area where *fruit-feelers* can congregate to *look for badgers.*

gay church *n.* That which *spud fumblers* attend religiously. The gym.

gaydar *n.* A remote imaging process developed during the war at Bletchley Park which was able to detect Judy Garland records at substantial distances.

gaylord *n.* A good-natured term of homophobic abuse used by schoolboys to refer to anyone who is not gifted at sport or who wears glasses.

Gaza strip *n. Skidmark* that looks like the aftermath of several decades of military conflict.

gazebo *n.* A substantial erection in the garden.

gazoo *n. Arse, bum.*

gazungas *n. Gert Stonkers.*

Gazza strip, the *n.* Gateshead/Low Fell. An area of historically disputed territory situated between Newcastle and Sunderland, where a number of public houses are used by rival fans of both teams on derby days, leading to outbreaks of sporadic violence and damage.

gearbox *1. n.* The *anus. 'Molly was powerless to resist. His eyes burned into hers like anthracites. His strong arms enfolded her body as she felt herself being swept away on a squall of passion. Then, in a single move Buzz pulled down her clouts, bent her over the ironing board and stuck his Charlie up her gearbox.'* (From *The Cornish Milkmaid and the Astronaut* by Barbara Cartland). *2. n.* The female *bell housing.*

gearbox trouble *euph.* Said of a woman who needs a *fanny mechanic* to have a poke round her leaky *sump.*

gear goggles *n.* When buying six tubs of ice cream at 3am, *Bob Hope*-assisted optical aids which make the woman who works in the 24-hour petrol station look attractive.

gearstick gargler *n.* A popular and talented young lady who is able to fully accommodate a *meat endoscopy* from a well-made gent without *honking up* her kebab onto his *clockweights.*

gee gee *1. n.* Childish expression for horse used, usually in its plural declension, by gambling types. *'I'm going to put a few quid on the gee gees.' 2. n.* A girl who is pretty much definitely going to *suck you off.* A Guaranteed Gobble.

geek *n.* Someone who knows too much about a subject that it isn't worth knowing anything about, *eg.* Computers, PlayStation cheat codes, railway trains. A *human rhubarb*.

geek's sheath *n.* A nerd's means of preventing the transmission of viruses onto his computer while visiting sexual sites on the web. An internet prophylactic of the sort manufactured by McAfee, Norton Utilities *etc.*

geek yoghurt *n.* Amatory residue left across his laptop keys by a spotty youth after he has completed imaginary intercourse with the remote object of his desires.

geek yoghurt *n.* The chronic accretion of seminal fluid in a socially inept male's bedsheets, underwear, socks, curtains *etc.*

geetle *n.* The little pointed bit of *shit* that hangs outside one's *nipsy* after one has had a *Gladys*. A *bumbob*.

geeze bag *n. Wind bag, fartpants.* A prolific *pump* artist.

geezerbird *n. Gadgy wife, half-a-gadge.* A butch-looking woman.

Geldof *v.* To impose a fairly woeful performance on an unwilling audience who feel it would be impolite not to indulge you. *'Go and find your grandad's mouth organ. He's allowed a little Geldof on Christmas Day.'*

Gemma Collins's easter egg, last as long as *sim.* To *blow one's tanks* somewhat prematurely. *'How did you get on with that new blonde bird you got off the internet, Dave?' 'Terrible. I lasted as long as Gemma Collins's easter egg. Never even got me strides off.'*

Gemma Collins's knicker elastic, stronger than *sim.* A description of something or someone that is really tough or potent. Also *stronger than a pig farmer's aftershave. 'Would you like another glass of Buckfast, reverend?' 'Not for me, thanks. That stuff's stronger than Gemma Collins's knicker elastic.'*

gender bender *n.* An effeminate, flowery male of indeterminate or obscure sexual orientation.

gender blender *n.* A person whose physical and facial appearance offer no clue as to which sex they actually belong to, if any.

gender fluid *1. adj.* Androgynous. *2. n. Blip. 3. n. Spoff.*

Gene Hunt *n. prop. rhym. slang.* Named after the character in that *Life On Mars* thing that everyone went on about fifteen years ago. Fucking hell. *'Pull your habit down, Sister Asumpta. The monks can see your Gene Hunt.'*

gene pool *n.* The puddle of *heir tonic* that is wont to collect in a gentleman's navel following a supine act of *self respect*. The *devil's inkwell*.

generation game *n. Having it off* with one's partner's parent, grandparent, great grandparent or worse; as performed on a daily basis by the delightful guests on daytime telly chat shows. Bring back Peter Ustinov or Jacob Bronowski.

genetically modified fruit *euph.* Well-hoofed *plums.* See also *emergency stop button.*

genetic make-up *1. n.* The entirety of an organism's hereditary information. *2. n.* Strands of viscous, white DNA decorating a woman with a *face like an art room sink. Spaghetti bollocknaise.*

Genevieve *n. prop.* An *old banger* from whom you might expect to get an uncomfortable *ride*.

genie rub *n.* Buffing up a *skin lantern* until you are granted three sticky wishes.

genis *n.* Where the flesh around the base of a *salad dodger's slag hammer* becomes indistinguishable from his general *beergut* area. The male equivalent of the *gunt*. Also *gock*.

genital floss *n.* A skimpy bikini bottom or thong. *Arse floss.*

genital husbandry *n.* The timeless craft of *winding the clock. Re-setting the crown jewels, re-shuffling the cabinet, nip & twist.*

genitalia failure *n.* Marshmallowing of the *cock*. The *droop*. Something inexplicable that has never happened before, usually.

genitalman *n.* A chap who lets his *hanging brain* do his thinking for him.

Genk *1. n. prop.* Belgian city located on the Albert canal between Antwerp and Liege which, as you know, is famous for its Ash Wednesday carnival. *2. n.* Foreskin residue found on the *bell-ends* of gentlemen with a less than satisfactory *brimula* hygiene regimen.

gentertainment *n.* A gender-specific videographic *divertissement. 'There's a bloke, walks right into a flat / Sees a bird, who is rubbing her twat / No need to guess, what comes after that / That's gentertainment!'* (from *That's Gentertainment!*, song by Howard Dietz and Arthur Schwartz).

gentle giant *n.* A *shit* so big that it brings tears to your eyes, but which gently kisses you on the cheek just before it leaves. A *French lodger*.

gentleman's cure-all *n.* Something that brings ease and comfort in any given circumstance. *Coccupational therapy.*

gentleman's espresso *euph.* Vigorously *grinding your beans* in order to produce a disappointingly small amount of liquid.

gentleman's excuse me *1. n.* A popular *meat flick* scenario in which several blokes take it in turns to *push a lady's guts in. 2. n.* The gallant post-nightclub practice of assisting a *plumper* with whom one has inadertently *copped off* into a taxi, gallantly shutting the door for her and then *running like fuck*.

gentleman's gel *n.* A soothing facial/breast unguent for ladies which doubles as a hair styling product. *Heir cream.*

gentleman's inconvenience *euph.* A spontaneous *semi-* or full *erection* that occurs at an inappropriate or troublesome time.

gentleman's jacket *n.* A piece of toilet roll laid in the *pan*, Walter Raleigh-style, to prevent unnecessary *splash-back* when launching a *dreadnought*. Also *crash mat, pap baffle, turd raft, pilo.*

gentleman's machinery *n.* Polite phraseology for a fellow's *rude mechanicals.*

gentleman's reading room *n.* The one room of the house where one may comfortably kick back and peruse the *Autotrader* from cover to cover. The *water closet.*

gentleman's relish *1. n.* A polite term for *jizz*, such as what might be used by society folk at a Buckingham Palace Garden Party. *2. n. Fucking* horrible-tasting paste that comes in a nice pottery pot.

gentleman's toe pump *n.* The frantic but pleasurable wiggling of the toes, about 15 seconds after the *jester's shoes,* that helps to squeeze out the last drops of *jitler.*

gentleman's wash *n.* A hurried cleansing of the male genitals (usually in a pub toilet sink) in anticipation of some forthcoming sex action.

gentlemen's ensuite *euph.* The kitchen sink. *'The gentlemen's ensuite's blocked again, Camilla.' 'Where've you put the potato masher, Charles?'*

gentlemen's quarterly *1. n.* Full name of door-stopping poncey lifestyle mag *GQ*. *2. n.* An infrequent but nevertheless luxurious *J. Arthur* of the sort practised by aristocrats and likely the Pope.

gentlemen start your engines *exclam.* Witty preamble to the kick-starting of an un-silenced, high-revving, methane-powered *lump.*

Gently Mentally *n. prop.* An affectionate nickname bestowed upon a local *nutjob* who is not harmful to humans. *'It's Gently Mentally from down the road. He wants to know if he can borrow your chainsaw and your ice hockey mask.'*

geocaching *1. n.* GPS-based outdoor fun; locating "treasure" in a remote location *2. n.* Technologically advanced rural *dogging.*

Geoff Hurst! *exclam.* A gentleman's exclamation at the *point of no return*. An homage, if you will, to the classic Kenneth Wolstenholme commentary in the 120th minute of the 1966 World Cup Final. Also *they think it's all over. It is now!.*

geogashing *n.* The noble tradition of stashing bin-bags full of *scud mags* amongst woodland undergrowth, to be discovered and enjoyed by future generations of *oil tankers*. Usually because an irate partner found them in the loft.

Geordie Alka-Seltzer *n. A wank.* In former times, a popular hangover cure in north-eastern dockyards, now often used on budget flights back from Prague by young men who have over-imbibed.

Geordie curls *euph.* See *scouse dreadlocks.*

Geordie foix gras *n.* Pease pudding. Also known as *Geordie hummus, Yorkshire caviar, Barnsley caviar* and *Scouse guacamole.*

Geordie hummus *n.* Pease pudding. See also *Yorkshire caviar.*

Geordie overcoat *n.* A vest or sleeveless T-shirt as donned by the entire male population of Newcastle-upon-Tyne during periods of particularly cold weather.

Geordie sauna *n.* A kitchen with all the doors and windows closed and the oven on full power with its door open. And the chip pan on.

Geordie's passport *n.* A bus ticket. Also *Scouse visa.*

Geordie sterling *n.* Greggs gift cards.

George *1. v. US.* To *roger. 2. n. rhym. slang.* Phlegm. From George Lucas = mucus.

George Best undercoat *n.* The pint of milk drunk "to line the stomach" prior to going out on a drinking binge lasting several days. *'I can't be over the limit, officer. I may have necked 10 pints, but I had a George Best undercoat before I came out.'*

George Formby, a wanking arm like *sim.* A right arm that is just a blur of split, triple and fan strokes.

George Herbert *euph. Horatio.* From the poem *Love Bade me Welcome* penned by the eponymous Welsh-born poet, orator and priest (1593-1633), which contains the line "'You must sit down', Says Love, 'and taste my meat', So I did sit and eat." Once again, don't say we never fucking learn you anything.

George Orwell *n.* A girl who looks "19" from behind but "84" from the front. Named after the eponymous author's famous book *The Road to Wigan Pier. A Kronenberg.*

George yesterday *exclam.* Heartfelt felicitations typically mumbled by counter staff after minor retail transactions. Translation: "Enjoy the rest of your day".

German *n.* Sexy carryings-on where the participants *shit* on each other like pigs.

German ambassador *n. A pastry chef.* From the amusing fact that the German word for an ambassador is Botschafter.

German breakfast *n.* An erection. Also *Irish toothache*, a *Zebedee*, a *chirp on*, a *crowbar* or a *Dutch salute*.

German buffet *n.* One of those continental *bogs* which, when flushed, fills the bowl before emptying, thus giving you a full-on inspection of the tempting delicacies within.

German cornflake *n.* A herpes scab on one's *herman gelmet*.

German eyebath *n.* A *spoff monocle*. Also *Gabrielle, St. Valentine's Day mascara, King Harold*.

German padlock, the *n.* Inserting the *bald avenger* up one's own hindquarters. *'Tonight! On the stage of the Lyceum Theater, Broadway! The wonder of the age: Mr Houdini will attempt his infamous milk churn escape, extricate himself from a steel bank safe AND finally attempt a German padlock in full view of the audience.'*

German pit crew *euph.* The furry underarm area of a European *piece*, for example her who done that song about red balloons.

German pop *n.* Urine.

German rigger *n.* Theatrical term for one who prefers his *rigging* done in the German fashion.

German's eye *n. Jap.* The frankly racist way the *hog's eye* is referred to in Japan (ドイツの目). So called because "it never smiles".

German wings *1. n.* A budget Teutonic airline which offers regular flights from Berlin, Stuttgart and Cologne. *2. n.* The first time you get *shat on* by a *good time girl* in one of Hamburg's more cosmopolitan tourist districts. The peer-reviewed honour bestowed on one who has just enjoyed their debut *scat* experience. Not the bollocks Cleo Laine-style jazz singing kind, neither. *'Did you have a successful business trip, Jeffrey?' 'Yes Mary. I managed to catch the Hamburger Symphoniker performing Lohengrin at the Laeiszhalle Musikhalle, signed a seven-figure pan-European paperback deal for my new novel and, even better than that, I got my German wings too.'*

gerotica *n.* What one gets indelibly burned into one's hard disk the moment one logs onto a specialist *biddy-fiddling* website. An XXX-rated version of Ena Sharples, Minnie Caldwell and Martha Longhurst in the Rovers snug.

gertie *1. n. Fanny, minge. 2. n. coll.* Women, *blart.*

gert stonkers *n.* Gonzagas.

gesundheit *n. Ger.* A simultaneous, albeit unintentional, sneeze and *brown trout* in the trousers. A cause for congratulations in Germany, that is.

get *n. Bastard, twat.* Often applied to children, prefixed "You cheeky little…" and accompanied by a playful swipe to the back of the head.

get a click *v.* To *score, pull, tap off*, with a view to *getting boots.*

get boots *v. US.* To *get it on, get your end away, get your leg over, get your hole.*

get engaged *v.* To scratch at your *rusty bullet hole* in public, *ie.* To "pick your ring".

get in the hole *1. exclam.* A hilarious shout from American golf fans whenever Dustin Johnson hits the ball *2. exclam.* A rib-tickling shout whenever a flatulent golfer accidentally *lowers his handicap* while bending over to pick up a dropped glove. *3. exclam.* Cry of encouragement whenever Tiger Woods drops his plus fours.

get it on *v.* To *get off.*

get it up *v.* To erectivitate. *'It's no good, love. I can't get it up.'*

get off *v.* To *get it on* with someone. Or some*thing*.

get off at Edge Hill *v.* To do a *coitus interruptus*, to withdraw before *spangling*. From Edge Hill, which is the last railway station before Liverpool Lime Street. Similarly *Haymarket* (Edinburgh), *Gateshead* (Newcastle), *Marsh Lane* (Leeds) *etc.*

get off at Lambeth North *euph.* To *change at Baker Street* and then disembark slightly before the terminus. *Getting off at Edge Hill* while *riding the brown line*, typically done for stylistic effect.

get on at Baker Street without a ticket *euph.* To do a spot of *caboose work* without first obtaining the necessary authority. You could end up getting prosecuted, and quite right too.

get one's sovereigns on *v.* while preparing for a *pagga*, to adorn one's hands with cheap *clink*, thereby creating a budget knuckle duster effect. To *put up your Lizzie Dukes. 'Best get your sovereigns on, Mrs Walker. Albert Tatlock's in the snug and he's got the red mist again.'*

get out and walk *exclam.* Disparaging parting remark, made over the shoulder to a retreating *air biscuit.*

get out of shag free card *n.* An excuse used by a person to avoid taking part in an act of sexual union. *'I'm absolutely gutted. The missus has got multiple compound fractures in each femur, had both her hips dislocated, broken her coccyx in six places and shattered her pelvis after falling into the mechanism of a escalator on the London Underground. No doubt she'll be using that as this week's get out of shag free card.'*

gets about more than Dominic Cummings in a pandemic *exclam.* Said of a right *goer.*

gets a four pack in for the weekend *euph.* Said of a chap that *bakes a light sponge.*

get some blood in it *v.* To have the early stages of a

bonk-on, half a teacake.

get the dick *phr.* Used when things go badly awry, particularly as a result of bad weather. *'The cricket's got the dick again, I see, vicar.'*

get the key in the lock *v.* To manage, miraculously, to engage in some vague sort of penetrative intercourse with one's better half while thoroughly *blootered.*

get the keys out before reaching the car *v.* To be *up and over like a pan of milk; spend your money before you get to the shop; press send too soon.*

getting a shoulder ride off of Leo Sayer, looks like she's *exclam.* Said of a lady with a large *ladygarden.* A reference to the famously frizzy tonsure of the erstwhile singer/songwriter/*shortarse.* *'Seen this old picture of Germaine Greer, your holiness? She looks like she's getting a shoulder ride off of Leo Sayer.'*

getting one's hair cut for charity *n.* Giving the appearance of being legitimately occupied while someone else is, in fact, doing all the work. Doing *fuck all.*

getting your step count up *euph. Working from home* whilst wearing a smartwatch on your rapidly reciprocating *relaxation* wrist.

Gettysburg address *n.* The act of *cumulonimbus.* From the view afforded to an hirsute lady when she looks down, of what appears to be a *fanny-chopped* President Lincoln delivering his famous oration. Especially if her hubby is wearing a top hat.

get up them stairs *exclam.* A gentleman's romantic suggestion to his wife which indicates that he has finished eating, drinking and watching football, and now wishes to retire to the bedroom to make an ungainly and flatulent attempt at sexual intercourse.

get wood *v.* To attain a full state of tumescence, *get string.* *'Quick, Heinz! Roll the camera. Gunther's got wood.'*

get-you-home spare *n.* A substandard, low performance woman picked up at the end of a frankly deflating night.

get your end away *v.* To *get your leg over* and *fill your boots.*

get your leather *v.* To *have it off, get your hole.* *'How did you get on with that pissed-up bird I saw you arresting last night? Did you get your leather in the back of the van?' 'Certainly not, your honour. I only got my cloth tit.'*

get your nose in *v.* To have been in the *bogs* for a length of time sufficient to have become immune to the foul stench left by a previous occupant. *'Jesus Carol, it fucking reeks in here.' 'Give it a few minutes, Tomasz. You'll soon get your nose in.'*

get your numbers up *v.* Of an individual who is soon to be wed, to work round-the-clock to increase his tally of partners before the prohibition of marriage cramps his style somewhat.

get your oats *v.* To enjoy a bit of *slap and tickle* while wearing longjohns, like Peter Butterworth does in *Carry On Follow That Camel.*

get your own back *v.* To *sup at the furry cup* after leaving some *hot fish yoghurt* inside the *snail's doorstep,* assuming you've not fallen asleep, that is.

GFS *abbrev. medic.* Doctor's notes terminology used to indicate that the patient may be talking out of their *arse.* Gesticulating From Sacrum.

Ghandi's flip flops *1. adj.* Descriptive of the dryness of a nun's *cunt. 2. n.* Spaniel's ears.

ghee whizz *n.* A buttery, sludgy *piss* taken by a chap stricken with a urinary tract infection.

gherkin out of the burger, take the *exclam.* To remove a *mouse* from a lady's front *skirting* in order to gain unobstructed access.

Ghislaine Maxwell's diary, as much use as *sim.* Descriptive of something which has no use. See also *~ as Anne Frank's drum kit, ~ as a Glaswegian's salad drawer etc.*

ghostbuster *n.* An eminently successful act of single-handed *exorjism.* From the lyrics of the theme song from the 1984 film starring Dan Ackroyd, Bill Murray and the other one who had glasses, who may be dead. *viz.* "Bustin' makes me feel good."

ghost drop *1. n.* In twopenny waterfall-based daytime TV quiz show *Tipping Point,* what they call a counter that sticks to the wall on its way down. *2. n.* A *back pocket rocket* that has inexplicably vanished into thin air when you turn round to admire it in the *chod pan.* Also *poodini.*

ghost in the latrine *euph.* Overpowering sense that someone or something has been here before, leaving nought behind it but an ethereal smell from beyond the grave and a feeling of evil.

ghost jizz *n.* The non-existent result of a *flash in the pan.* A *map of Atlantis.*

ghost milk *n. Perseverance soup, guardsman's glaze, knuckle varnish, dew on the lily, tomato varnish, balm before the storm, wrist oil, tatty watta.*

ghost of Christmas past *1. n.* An allegorical character out of off of Charles Dickens's *A Christmas Carol. 2. n.* A turkey and Brussel sprout-scented *guff.*

ghost of Christmas presents *n.* The mysterious, silent and invisible parcel delivery driver who flits unseen and unheard up the drive and stealthily puts a "While you were out" card through the door while you are in.

ghost rider *n.* The beautiful, fictitious and weightless young lady that a prostrate young man imagines to be astride him during a bout of *self delight*. A *frigment* of a *tugster's* imagination.

ghost shit *n.* Stool or *dump* of which there is no trace when one stands up and turns to admire it. A *poogitive, poodini, Lord Loocan.*

ghost sighting *euph.* The nominal cause of soiled nether apparel amongst thoroughly *wankered* gentlemen making their way home from country locals. *'Looks like you've had another ghost sighting in the churchyard, vicar.' 'Yes officer. It was very frightening, as you can see.'*

ghost wank *n.* When the gentleman of the house mysteriously rises from the marital bed, floats downstairs and starts groaning.

gib *1. v.* To bullshit. *2. v.* To gatecrash. *3. v.* To stick your *old man* up a goose's *arse* and slam its head in a drawer. As you do.

gibble *v.* To have a giggle while giving a *gobble*.

gibbon gristle *n.* A funky penis.

giblets *n.* A *club sandwich*, a *ragman's coat*.

Gibraltese backhand *n.* A masturbatory act carried out in the characteristic style of the monkeys on the famous Spanish rock. The *Gibraltese backhand* involves a lazily inverted reverse grip and is typically performed while sitting on the bonnet of your car with your tongue hanging out.

gick *n. Ir. Shit.*

Gideon gumboot *n.* A used *blob* found pressed in a Bible in your hotel/motel bedside cabinet.

gifted *1. adj.* Of a schoolchild, annoying. *2. adj.* Of a lady, in possession of an impressive set of *qualifications.*

gift that keeps on giving *1. n. medic.* The *trots, Indian mustard, jungle jitters, hoop soup. A load of old shoes falling out of a loft. 2. n.* That last *teggat* of *feeshus* that seems to require a whole *bog roll* to wipe.

gift to womankind *n.* An early morning *tent pole* in the *fart sack;* a phrase used by the late Ian Dury in the song *Let Me Hit Your Twat with My Rhythm Stick.*

GIFWID/gifwid *acronym.* A plain lass who becomes the object of a gentleman's affections when he has taken an elegant sufficiency of *booze* on board. Girl I Fancy When I'm Drunk.

giggidy bytes *n.* From the catchphrase of *Family Guy's* Quagmire, the hard drive space taken up on a red-blooded fellow's computer by his erotic material.

gigglebiscuit *n.* Name given to the sort of irritatingly shallow woman who uses the pursuit of chocolate as the basis for her humour, *viz.* "Shall I have another chocolate biscuit? Oooh, shouldn't. Naughty! Giggle, giggle".

gigglers *n.* Suspender belt. *Giggle band.* 'Get past there and you're laughing'.

giggle stick *n.* The *twig, giggling pin.*

giggling pin *n. Mr Happy.*

Giggs boson *n.* A vanishingly small, dense point of intelligence which may be present between the eyes of a professional footballer, although such a particle's existence is as yet unproven.

gilbo *n.* The kind of *George Lucas* eructated during a cold, after drinking cream soda, or when afflicted with a serious chronic disease of the bronchial tract. *Gold watch, dockers' omelette, greb, gilbo.*

GILF/gilf *acronym.* Granny I'd Like to Fuck. A sexually alluring older woman, *eg.* Marie Helvin, Helen Mirren, Blanche off *Corrie* (before she died).

gilgai *1. n. Geol.* In the world of earth science, micro-relief characterised by small hummocks separated by shallow troughs, and hence *2. n.* A *diddy ride* on *Miss Lincolnshire.*

gillespie *n.* A diminutive male generative member. From the well-known graffito on the toilet wall in Wirral Grammar school depicting a small penis with the caption "Gillespie's dick x 4".

Gillette Fusion girl *n.* A dirty *trollop* who is prepared to go at it like a bull at a gate, thus ensuring that her gentleman friend does not feel the need to *see to his own needs* at all. From the eponymous depilatory product's television advert, which stated that use of said razor resulted in "no pulls or tugs".

Gillian McKeith's Tupperware cupboard, smells like *sim.* Something that is distinctly malodorous, based on the completely untrue rumour that the eminent fully qualified dietician takes home all the stools she examines on her telly programmes and then secretly eats them.

gimp *n.* A giant, masked *bummer* kept in a box in the basement of a gun shop.

gimp mask *n.* A tightly fitting facial covering worn exclusively by giant *bummers* kept in boxes in the basements of gun shops.

gin bin *n.* A lady who has imbibed more than her fair share of *the water of life* down the years, to the detriment of her physical appearance. *'Fuck me, camera two, the gin bin's got the shakes again. Best cut to Richard.'*

gin buddies *n.* Any gang of *pissed-up* middle class women.

gincident *n.* Any alcohol-related mishap. *'I'm*

terribly sorry, officer. There appears to have been a gincident involving my automobile and a bus queue.'

Ginderella *n. prop.* A pretty princess who is – after imbibing quantities of *crying juice* – transformed in dawn's early light into a ragged scullery maid of low bearing, wearing one shoe.

ginger beer *rhym. slang.* A fellow who is *Colwyn Bay.*

gingerbread man *n.* A rejuvenated chap emerging from a lavatory cubicle with a spring in his step. From the lyrics of the Sammy Davis Junior song, *viz.* "Fresh out of the pan / Sweet gingerbread man".

ginger wheelspin *n.* A great big *shit stripe* up the back of the *pan* making your *Rick Witter* look like a bmx track.

gingina *n.* A carrot-topped bird's *rusty fusewire, gorilla salad, fire down below.*

gingle *adj.* The forlorn state of being ginger and single.

gink *n. Geek.* A short-sighted Colonel in a checked suit and bowler hat.

ginkled *n.* Raddled due to the effects of heavy *top shelf drinking* on the skin and face, *eg.* Princess Margaret, Sid James *etc.* From gin + wrinkled.

ginsignia *n.* The dishonourable marks of a lifetime spent imbibing copious amounts of *mother's ruin, viz.* Red nose, broken facial capillaries, *Hatties,* prison record *etc.*

Ginster's crust *n.* The unfunny, puckered result of catching the end of one's *windsock* in one's flies while doing them up too fast, for example when a policeman appears.

Ginster's finest *n.* A *twat* that looks, smells and tastes like an out-of-date Cornish pastie. Often eaten by long distance lorry drivers and commercial travellers.

Ginster's paradise *n.* Any purveyor of cheap mass-produced beige food, typically frequented by the *big-boned.*

gintellectual *n.* A barstool-dwelling philosopher, whose words of wisdom are typically prefixed "Apparently… " or "I know a bloke who… ". A *gobshite.*

gintelligence test *n.* A challenging general knowledge quiz administered after midnight by one's significant other, containing questions such as "What time do you call this?", "Where the hell have you been until four in the morning?" and "Why didn't you answer your phone?".

ginvalid *n.* One who has tragically lost the use of their legs following a long battle with the Gordon's.

gip *n.* The sensation at the back of the throat

heralding the arrival of *Hughie and Ralph.*

gipper *1. n.* Legless American footballer played by former late US president Ronald Reagan (now deceased) in the inspirational film *Bedtime for Bonzo.* *2. n.* A *bird* who is as filthy as the bait bucket on a fishing boat.

giraffe piss *n.* The standard method of urination when in possession of a *panhandle, ie.* To stand with one's legs wide apart and angle the *tent pole* down towards the bowl in the manner of a long-necked cameleopard drinking at a water hole. *Full throttle for take-off.*

giraffe shit *n.* Any passed stool which causes one to stretch one's neck to get away from the smell.

giraffe's neck, cock like a *sim.* A description of an impressive *male member.* See also *baby's arm clutching a Jaffa* or *Pringles tube with a sheep's heart on top.* *'Goodness gracious, Mr Pound MP. You've got a cock like a giraffe's neck.'*

giraffiti *n.* Vandalism which is spray-painted very, very high up.

girlfriend experience *n.* A chargeable extra service which is sometimes offered by *rub-a-tug-shop* masseuses, *ie.* A bit of kissing and tenderness prior to a short, low-esteem, guilt-ridden *bang* on a wipe-clean sheet.

girlpop *n. Moip, blip, fanny batter.* Secretions of the *Bartholin's* gland.

Girlsberg *n.* Lightweight beer. *'Fancy a Stella, Colin?' 'Better not. I'll just have a Girlsberg, only I'm driving the hearse this afternoon.'*

girls' night in *n.* An internet-assisted evening at home enjoyed by a solitary bachelor. Also *ladies' night.*

girly goatee *n.* A lady's pubic effusion, which can be rubbed and tugged at thoughtfully during moments of contemplation.

girobics *n.* The regular fortnightly exercise a long term social sciences graduate gets every other Thursday when he lifts his *arse* off the sofa and ventures forth to collect his *beer tokens.*

girocopter *n.* Favoured method of urban transport for the less athletically inclined sports clothing wearer. A *council go-kart* or mobility scooter.

giro d'Italia *1. n.* One of the three Grand Tours of cycling that mainly takes place on the roads and through the mountains of Italy. *2. n.* An individual who informs the Department of Work & Pensions he is unfit or unable to work during the day, and is then seen delivering pizzas on his moped in the evening.

giro jolly *adj.* Subject to the euphoric mental state attained by the unemployed on Thursdays.

gironaut *n.* A long term supplementary

income claimant.

giropractor *n.* One with a wealth of expertise in the manipulation of the state benefits applications system, available for consultation in the Gurnos Social Club, Merthyr Tydfil from 10.30am to 12.30pm Monday to Sunday.

giroscope *1. n.* A satellite dish. *Debtors' dish.* *2. n.* A television set that is rarely switched on before 2pm.

girotica *n.* The restricted range of *relaxation* material which is affordable on the restricted budget of a chap who is searching for gainful employment, *eg.* Repeats of *Baywatch* on UK Gold, viewed from his foetid bed in the middle of the afternoon.

girthmark *n.* Evidence of wear and tear on the *old-fashioned fifties tea towel holder.*

gisp *n. medic.* A term used by doctors in North Wales to describe the *bit between the balls and the arsehole. The barse, tintis, great, ABC, BBBA.*

github *1. n.* A code-sharing platform for developers. Whatever the fuck that means. *2. n.* Where the office *arseholes* congregate. *'Has anyone seen Nigel and Piers?' 'Yes. They're brown-nosing each other at the github.'*

gi' us a squint of yer pooper *exclam.* A poetic romantic injunction which, apparently, rarely fails to oil the wheels of love in the West Country.

give blood *v.* To *release the chocolate hostages* while afflicted with galloping *chuckles and smiles.*

give it to me one more time! *1. exclam.* The last lyrics of the Queen song *Hammer to Fall,* which are quickly followed by a large crash of cymbals and guitar. *2. exclam.* "When you've just got time to say your prayers" immediately prior to a catastrophic *trouser cough.*

give Ronaldo a rub down *v.* Celebrity slaphead *wanking* terminology. *Strangle Kojak, take Captain Picard to warp speed, polish Telly Savalas up and down until spunk comes out of his head.*

give Rover his breakfast *v.* To unleash a particularly rich and pungent cloud of tripe fumes.

give the benefit of the doubt *v.* To have a *wank* over someone. *'I saw Nigella on her new cookery show last night, your holiness.' 'Ah, I haven't given her the benefit of the doubt in a while, I can tell you. Print out a picture of her, and I'll make amends after evensong.'*

give the bog its breakfast *v.* To defecate. *'My husband will be with you in a moment, vicar. He's just giving the bog its breakfast.'*

give the dog a bone *v.* To sexually satisfy a female before one goes rolling home.

give the dog a gravy bone *1. v.* To treat man's best friend to a meaty treat. *2. v.* To pop a *meaty treat* into *Dot Cotton's mouth.*

give the sock drawer a good seeing-to *euph. milit.* To embark upon a sustained bout of frenzied masturbation while a member of the Household Cavalry.

give Thumper a reprieve *euph.* To decide to have *one off the wrist* instead of *copping off* with a putative *bunny boiler.*

give yourself a big hand *v.* To celebrate after achieving a personal goal. This may include applauding, splashing out on a gift, treating yourself to a slap-up meal, or having a *wank.*

giving it the gun *n.* The act of going down on one knee in front of your girlfriend, mate's wife, wife's sister, or occasionally the wife, while holding your hand like a Magnum 45 and pushing it in and out.

Gladstone *arch. rhym. slang.* Victorian rhyming slang for a *fuck.* From Gladstone bag = shag. *'Her Majesty (at the conclusion of a long perinambulation upon a diminutive horse, accompanied by her faithful ghillie Mr John Brown Esquire): "We have much enjoyed our post-prandial equine constitutional, Mr Brown. Notwithstanding, we observe that your sporran is twitching in a most curious fashion." John Brown: "Och aye the noo, hoots mon and help m'boab, Ma'am. Ye dinnae fancy a quick Gladstone in yon bracken, by any chance, do ye?"'* (cartoon by Sir John Tenniel, *Punch*, 1887).

glad to get that off my nuts *exclam.* Laddish expression of relief uttered after *tipping* an overdue and psychologically burdensome *load of concrete.*

Gladys *rhym. slang.* To defecate. From Gladys Knight = Turkish delight.

glam-jams *n.* Fashionable "show" pyjamas worn when nipping to the shops or on the school run. Commonly accessorised with *pugg boots* and a high performance outdoor jacket.

glamoflage *n.* The use of materials such as paint, filler and illuminants, as well as injectable morphological agents, to render an *aesthetically unconventional* visage more in keeping with accepted standards of beauty. *'Got yer glamoflage on, then, Simon?'*

glamourpotamus *n.* A lady with a *lovely personality* who wears *shit-loads* of make-up, fake tan and worryingly high heels.

glanda padana *n.* A posh Italian *knob cheese.* Also *bellendsleydale, willydelphia, hedam, mozzerfella, veinish blue* and many, many more.

gland canyon *1. n.* A breath-takingly vast vagina. *2. n.* A spectacular cleavage. The *Bristol channel.*

glandcester *n.* An unknown, casual *shagger* who appears in one's family tree. Also *glandmother,* *glandfather, glandchildren etc.*

gland designs *1. euph.* When trying to seek the affections of another who is way out of your league, overly ambitious plans to *punch way above your weight* and budget. Long term, expensive, *loinal* projects that typically end in abject disappointment, bankruptcy and the sale of one's home. 2. *n. Tittoos, eg.* "Mild" and "Bitter", "This" and "That" *etc.*

gland grenades *n.* Hairy, wrinkled *spunk* bombs that have a tendency to *go off* in one's hand if they are not *tossed* far enough.

glandicap *n.* Measure of a person's potential to inspire a *boner*. Similar to a golfer's handicap. Actually, not too similar, if you think about it. *'My wife plays off a glandicap of twenty-two, vicar.'*

glanding gear *n.* Rusted *flaps* located on the missus's *undercarriage. Bomb doors.*

glandlord *n.* The owner of a property who prefers his tenants to pay the rent with their *hairy chequebook.*

gland national *n.* A *grumble flick* sequence featuring a *bit of bush* with a large number of sweating stallions *jumping* over it. A *three way* event. Also *glans national.*

gland of hope and glory *n.* A magnificent *custard cannon* which, at the rousing climax to a performance, would bring the crowd to its feet at the Royal Albert Hall, just before you were bundled off the stage, sectioned under the Mental Health Act and put on the Sex Offenders Register.

glandrail *n.* The raised rim area of the *glans* that stops a gentleman punching himself in the face during *self help*. The *wankstop* or, if you want to get all technical, the *sulcus.*

gland rover *n.* A 4x4 driven by a *cock. 'Just park your gland rover wherever you like, your royal highness. Sorry, your highness, I should have said.'*

gland sanitizer *1. n.* Liquid alcohol used to decrease infectious agents on the male *membrum virile* in anticipation of a *nosh, viz.* A dip in a pint in a pub toilet. *2. n.* The curtains.

glandscape *n.* The breathtaking *panhandloramic whacknicolour* vista that opens up before a chap's *hog's eye* while he is enjoying a *crescent wank.*

gland slam *1. euph.* Sitting alone at home, watching women's tennis. Or looking through Rumbelows' window for that matter. *2. n.* A notable sexual conquest.

glandstand *n.* A Saturday afternoon erection, starting 5 minutes before *World of Spurt.*

gland to mouth existence *n.* A living eked out using acts of *horatio* as currency.

gland tour *n.* The act of servicing three sweaty

cocks at the same time. Derivation unknown.

glandular fervor *n. medic.* A disease affecting men which causes them to masturbate like nobody's business.

glandular fever *n. medic.* Condition that makes a fellow hot and bothered while in the company of a woman with phenomenally huge breasts. Also *penile dementia, mamnesia.* It is not widely known that Michael Parkinson battled with chronic *glandular fever* throughout his glory years as a BBC chat show host, suffering a particularly bad attack when he interviewed Bette Midler in 1979.

glandwash *n.* The hasty use of handwash to give your *love stick* a quick once over in the kitchen or bathroom sink when the wife indicates an impromptu bout of *Horatio* might be in the offing. Which it won't be, obviously.

glans end to John O'Scrotes, from *phr.* A reverse *cock lick* from *soup to nuts.*

glans free *adj.* Said of a lady who eschews uncomfortable cordwainery.

glans gargle *n.* A swift enfreshenment of the *Johnson* using mouthwash.

glans hatch *n.* How members of the motor racing fraternity refer to a lady's *clopper. 'She needs more of ze punishment I zink. I'll smack her arse for a bit before sticking me floppy old frankfurter up her glans hatch. Then we'll have a nice cup of tea in the kitchen.'*

glansular fever *n. medic.* Condition affecting adolescent males whereby the *Piers Morgan* is continually swollen.

glarsefibre *n.* The badly matted yet rust-proof *shite/arsecress* matting effect achieved on a catastrophically ineptly wiped *freckle*. From the resultant disaster area's resemblance to a crudely repaired body panel on a crashed vehicle.

Glasgow hankie *n.* Technique employed by professional footballers and gentlemen of the road, whereby one nostril is held closed while its companion is evacuated onto the pavement or turf by means of a sharp nasal exhalation. Also known as an *oyster* or *bushman's hankie.*

Glasgow marathon *n.* A walk to the chip shop, tobacconist or off licence in your pyjamas, slippers and a coat. *'Kerry Katona runs Glasgow Marathon!'* (headline from *International Herald Tribune*, June 8th 2008).

Glasgow piano *n.* A fruit machine. Also *Scouser's cashpoint, scaffolder's laptop.*

Glasgow postman *n.* A thief. After the remarkable frequency with which birthday cards, parcels and giros go missing in the Glaswegian postal sorting system, it says here. *'Nobody move. One of the* *people in this very room is the Glasgow postman.'*

Glasgow salad *n.* Chips. See also *Yorkshire caviar, Geordie hummus.*

Glasgow shower *n.* A quick swipe of underarm deodorant used as an alternative to washing when in a hurry or Glaswegian.

Glasgow suitcase *n.* A carrier bag. Also *Barnsley briefcase.*

Glasgow tapas *n.* Half a bag of chips.

Glasgow toothpaste *n.* An extra-strong mint.

glassback *n.* A person with a poor health record at work. One whose constant illnesses keep them from work, but don't prevent them going to the pub at night or refereeing Premiership football matches at the weekend. A *sicknote.*

glassblower's pinch *n.* Final and desperate act of urine retention. Last ditch effort before turning your pantaloons into *tramp's trousers.*

glastoenteritis *n. medic.* Bad case of the *Earthas* brought about by an expensive weekend of £10 burgers and questionable lavatory provisions.

Glastonbury khazi *euph.* A celebrity who is "full of shit and constantly engaged."

Glastonbury main stage *euph.* The state of the *chod bin* following a harrowing post-Curry Capital visit, when it is left looking like the torrential-rain-soaked muddy fields of the popular alternative culture festival. Also *Ray Mears's dinner, Berwick Rangers' goalmouth.*

Glastonbury tailback *n.* The uncanny ability of some fussy people, usually women, to *squeeze their fig* for five days when lavatorial conditions are not quite to their liking.

Glaswegian siesta *n.* A night in a police cell.

Glaswegian's salald drawer, as much use as a *sim.* A disparaging comparison. Also *Anne Frank's drumkit, Kate Moss's chip pan, tits on a fish.*

glaze a knuckle *v.* To wank.

glaze the bacon *1. v.* To baste a joint of meat with a sugar-based coating in order to create an attractive shiny effect on the surface. *2. n.* To lacquer a ladyfriend's *gammon flaps* with *baby gravy* in order to create an attractive shiny effect on the surface.

glaze the ham *v.* To *shoot your load* onto a *piece of crackling*'s upturned buttocks.

glebe end *n. Lincs.* A quaint colloquial expression for the *herman gelmet*, the origins of which are lost in the mists of time.

glee *n. Spoff, spadge, spunk.* *'Blimey, when that Victoria Coren comes on telly, I can hardly contain my glee.'*

gleet *n. medic.* Unpleasant mucopurulent discharge caused by *cock rot. 'Blimey, when that Victoria*

Coren comes on telly, I can hardly contain my gleet.'

glenquidditch *n.* Chaotic sport that involves running around with a broom between your legs after not enjoying single malt whisky responsibly.

Glenshane pass *n. rhym. slang.* Alternative to the *Khyber*, up which a *bumsex*-fixated Northern Ireland resident could take his missus. *'Don't take me up the Glenshane Pass tonight, Ian. It's giving me terrible piles.'*

gliffet *n.* The scrotal *oxter.* That warm, moist channel between a gentleman's *nadsack* and his inner thigh, where a particularly piquant variety of sweaty cheese matures in the dark.

glimpsess *n.* A female who appears attractive when glanced momentarily, but whose appeal doesn't hold up at all well under more stringent ocular scrutiny. See also *low resolution fox, good from far but far from good, tramp l'oeuil.*

glist *1. n.* Dishwasher tablets that they don't make any more. *2. n. Ball glaze.*

glistening for it *adj.* Of a lady, sexually aroused, *fizzing at the bung hole. '"And we know for a fact, that Lady Marchmaine could not have killed the Bishop," added Miss Marple waspishly. "She had ridden from Barnchester to the Manor House in twenty minutes. When she arrived she was absolutely glistening for it and spent the afternoon with the Brigadier in his quarters. So YOU, Nurse Hatpin, must be the murderer!"'*

glitter-ati *n.* A loosely organised cabal of celebrity *nonces* from the 1970s.

glitter ball *n.* An under 16s disco.

glitter eggs *n.* Festive holiday decorations left by the dog after it eats a box of toffees, foil wrappers and all.

glitter slugs *n.* Lubed-up *Keith Burtons.*

glob *v.* To emit a viscous fluid slowly and rhythmically out the end of the *bride frightener.*

global warming *n.* The generally agreeable testicular sensation experienced by a fellow occupying a public transport seat that has been recently vacated by an attractive female.

globes *n.* Hanging objects of joy.

GLOB/glob *acronym.* Good Looking Old Bird. *Globs* depend on thick make-up, hair dye and powerful support hose in order to lure unwary young men close enough for them to pounce.

globstopper *n.* A mental image of a negatively attractive person or scenario that is summoned in order to *keep the wolf from the door*, so to speak.

gloke *n.* A woman who exhibits pseudo-blokish behaviour such as watching football, drinking beer, farting, smoking a pipe *etc*, in the mistaken belief that this will result in her being regarded as one of the lads. A *ladette.*

gloop the loop *v.* To create a flamboyant *curtain ring.* To *zuffle* with artistic *élan, éclat* and, indeed, *joie de vivre.*

glorification of the chosen one *n.* A quintessentially cosmopolitan *J. Arthur* with Stravinsky's *Rite of Spring* playing in the background.

glorious Goodwood 1. *n.* Some sort of yearly horse-racing event they seem to get very excited about on Radio 5. **2.** *n.* An erection of particular noteworthiness that they probably wouldn't get very excited about on Radio 5. In fact, likely as not, if you phoned Naga Munchetty up to tell her about it, she'd cut you off.

glory hole *n. US.* In a *cottage,* that conveniently *cock*-sized aperture *bosched* in a cubicle wall.

glory wipe *n.* The token single-sheet polish required after passing one of those rare but pleasant motions which slip out *like an otter off the bank,* leaving no trace of *Sir Douglas* on or around the *balloon knot.*

gloss drop *n.* A salon-quality moisturising serum, enriched with *Vitamin S and* applied to a lady's hair and/or face.

Glossop tapas *n.* A tempting smorgasbord of urine-sullied bar snacks, typically including dry roasted peanuts, mini cheddar crinkles, and them jalapeno pretzel bits, all mixed up by unwashed fingers.

glovebox 1. *n.* Another name for a lady's *parts of shame.* Usually containing bits of tissue, tampons, travel sweets *etc.* **2.** *n.* A warm, capacious *muff* into which five fingers can be comfortably inserted.

glow-worm 1. *n.* A long, thin, shiny *shite* produced after a really hot curry, that lights up the *pan.* **2.** *n.* Someone who the boss reckons has got the sun shining out of their *arse.*

gloy *n. Mess,* semen. From the paper glue used in schools. *'Oops! I think I've just trod on the gloy bottle. Ladies and gentlemen, Miss Barbara Dickson.'*

gloyster *n.* Barked into the basin as part of one's morning ablutions, a particularly sticky *hockle* which cannot be loosened even when one resorts to the hot tap on full pelt and the *breadknife's* toothbrush.

gluebook *n.* A well-read *art pamphlet* that is no longer openable.

glue flower *n.* The dried imprint left on clothing/sheets/curtains *etc.* which have been screwed up and used to wipe up *joy gloy* following a romantic interlude.

glue gun *n. Tool* used to stick the pages of *niff* mags together.

glue lagoon, the *euph.* The name given to the sticky, damp patch left on the bed, couch, car seat, woolsack *etc.,* by a partner who is *dripping like a gravel wagon at the lights.*

glunk *n.* Improvised, viscous adhesive used by students to affix torn wallpaper back in place in the minutes prior to a landlord's inspection. From glue + spunk.

glutes, thumbs and tongue workout *euph.* The physical activity undertaken by the majority of folk in modern gyms, *viz.* Sitting on their *arse,* playing on their mobile phones and talking.

Gnasher's loot *n.* A promiscuous woman's sexual history, *ie.* "A long string of big sausages".

gnat's cock hair *n.* A standard Imperial measure equal to approximately one and a quarter eighty-eighths of a sixteenth of an inch. A phrase often used to describe any small distance. Often shortened to a *gnat's.* Also *bawhair., cat's cock hair, midge's dick. 'How far do you want this filing cabinet moving, Mr Rees-Mogg?' 'Oh, just a gnat's cock hair towards the wall, that's all.'*

gnawgasm *n.* A female climax, achieved orally.

gnome's hat, like a *sim.* The appearance of the summit of one's *faceeshus* poking out of the water following a long stint on the *bum sink. 'If you think that's impressive you should've been here on Boxing Day, Mr Carson. Her shite was sticking out the pan like a fucking gnome's hat.'*

gnomon 1. *n.* Obscure word known only to the likes of Stephen Fry and Robert Robinson, describing the little sticky-up bit which casts a shadow on a sundial. **2.** *n.* The little sticky-up bit which casts a shadow on an under-endowed man, *eg.* The Rt Hon Jack Straw MP.

gnomosexual *n.* A short *puddlejumper.*

gnosh 1. *v.* To suck a penis in an enthusiastic and extremely noisy fashion. **2.** *n.* A blowjob.

go ahead London *exclam.* A humorous term used to break the ice when tweaking the *chapel hat peg* of a woman one has only just been introduced to. 6 months probation, if you're lucky.

goal hanger *n.* An annoying, predatory male friend who allows you to work your midfield magic on a girl in a nightclub before stealing your glory by nipping *in the box* for a simple tap in.

goalless drawers *n.* Ladies' undergarments that are designed to make it impossible to *score.*

go all the way to Cockfosters *v.* To have a *full portion of greens* with plenty of *summer cabbage.*

goalmouth scramble *n.* A hugely exciting, writhing mass of arms and legs which includes lots of intimate contact, but doesn't end up with anyone actually *scoring.* Frantic *heavy petting.*

goal scuttle *n.* The heaving, homo-erotic mass

of footballers' bodies that cavorts in a rampant orgiastic display whenever someone scores in a Premier League football match.

go around *1. phr.* When landing an aircraft, a warning from the control tower that the angle of approach is entirely wrong and the pilot must circle round and re-attempt the manoeuvre. *2. phr.* When taking a lady *up the council*, a similar admonishment.

goat's eye *n.* The "come hither" *tradesman's entrance* on a well-*bummed grumble queen.*

goatshagger's tickle *n.* A firm handshake. From the strong grip required when doing bestiality. *'My, that's quite a goatshagger's tickle you've got there, Mr Gill.'*

goat's toe, as hard as a *sim.* See also *as hard as Captain Scott's last morning stiffy; Elvis's last turd; Tarzan's feet; a policeman's knock; a Chinese wordsearch; Stephen Hawking's homework.* *'He said he was just shopping online for a present for his missus, but he had his lad in his hand and it was as hard as a goat's toe.'*

gob *1. n.* The *North and South. 2. v.* To spit, *hockle. 3. n.* A body of *lung butter* so propelled. A *greb*, a *greenie.*

gobbie *n.* See *gob job.*

gobble *n.* Noise made by turkeys wen they're *sucking you off.*

gobble bobble *n.* A hairband worn by a saucy minx to keep her *barnet* out of her eyes while *playing the pink oboe.*

gobbledegook *n.* The unintelligible, Soup Dragon-style utterances of a person in the throes of performing *horatio.*

gobbler *n.* An eager *fellator/fellatrix.* One who frequents a particular Gulch on Hampstead Heath.

gobbler's cough *n. medic.* Condition arising from the build up of genital detritus in the throats of over eager *noshers. White owl pellets.*

gobbler's notch *n.* The pronounced gap between the front incisors on a saucy piece of *crumpet.* Also known as the *banjo cleaner.*

gobble stopper *1. n.* A shaped piece of plastic which, when placed in the dog's bowl, stops it from wolfing down its kibble or meat too quickly. *2. n.* A piece of gold or platinum which, when placed on a woman's finger, stops her from *gobbling* a fellow's *meat*, full stop. A wedding ring.

go behind the red button *v.* To access a woman's *interactive features.*

gob job *n.* A *chewie, nosh, horatio.*

goblet of fire *n.* A *furry cup* from which one would be well advised not to sip.

goblin-cleaver *1. n.* A mythical sabre featured in *The Hobbit. 2. n.* The *pork sword* of a bloke with a very low *plain threshhold.*

goblin's wattle *n.* A distended *chicken skin handbag* not unlike the jowly excrescence sported by the character portrayed by Barry Humphries in the film *The Hobbit.*

gobshite *n.* Someone who talks *crap. eg.* Any contributor to *Thought for the Day*, but particularly Anne Atkins.

gobzilla *n.* A horrible foghorn-voiced monster of a person who you can hear coming from miles away.

gobzilla *n.* A person of monstrous dentition. *'Today's birthdays: Sissy Spacek, American actress, 1949; Dildo, British singer-songwriter, 1971; Shane McGowan, deceased Irish-born gobzilla, 1957.'*

go catholic *v.* To pull out of something at the very last minute. *'Bad news, Lord Coe. G4S have gone catholic on our arses.'*

go chimpy *v.* To exhibit anger; baring the teeth, screaming, jumping up and down, and possibly hurling excrement *etc.* *'The wife found that picture of her sister on my phone last night, and she's gone chimpy. So that's why I'm sleeping in the shed for a few days. But enough about my troubles, let's play Popmaster.'*

gock *n.* The male version of the *gunt.* Unsightly lower abdominal protuberance filled with residual beer, crisps and pies. From gut + cock. *'What's that on the top of your head, Gillian?' 'It's your gock, Geoff.'*

go Columbo *v.* To walk around in public without underwear, but still wearing a dirty overcoat; how your typical municipal *weeenie waggler* dresses on any given day. *'After Prime Minister's Questions, I shall meet with several of my constituents, and then spend the rest of the afternoon going Columbo in Regent's Park.'*

go commando *v.* To *freeball.* To go out *undercrackerless.*

go contactless *euph.* To have a *shite* whilst hovering above a *piss*-coated municipal toilet seat.

go cunt up *phr.* Go *arse over tit*, pear-shaped, badly awry. *'Houston, Houston, we have a problem. There's blowback in Challenger's solid rocket boosters. It looks like things could go cunt-up.'* (Silus T Oysterburger, Mission Controller, KSC Florida).

Godfather Part 2 *1. euph.* When the second *wank* of the day unexpectedly turns out to be more enjoyable than the first. *2. n.* A highly praised and critically acclaimed second *bang* off the same *wood.*

God goggles *n.* The imaginary optical accessories created by decades of religiously inspired celibacy, which cause a priest to get a raging *diamond cutter* when he sees a sixty-year-old nun with a moustache.

god of thunder *1. n. prop.* Title of a song by cartoon rock band Kiss, on their album *Destroyer*. *2. n.* Someone who *drops their guts* a lot. *'Ladies and gentlemen, please put your hands together and give a big Pebble Mill at One welcome to the god of thunder himself, Gene Simmons.'*

God's hands *n.* A bra. *'Relax. They're in God's hands now, Babs.'*

godshite *1. n.* Excessively vocal religious proselytiser. *2. n.* Religious carryings-on. *'And now it's time for some godshite with Jess Yates in Stars on Sunday.'*

God's sleeping tablet *n.* The natural way to induce restful sleep. In men, *cracking one off*; in women, *strumming the invisible banjo. Wanker's cocoa, temazepalm, a knuckle nightcap.*

Godzilla *n.* A ferocious burp, accompanied by clawing motions with the hands.

Godzilla's tail *n.* A *poo* that, when flushed, rears angrily out of the water as onlookers watch in horror.

goes for the vegetarian option *euph.* Said of a *well-manicured* chap who *knows what's in his wardrobe.*

go faster stripe *n.* A *fanny bush* shaved into a more aerodynamic design. *Pires's chin.*

go for poke *v.* To commit all one's available resources towards the sole aim of achieving some sort of sexual congress.

GOFPU/gofpu *abbrev.* A Good Old Fashioned Piss Up.

gogglefox *n.* A lady that looks ravishing in a pair of *geps, eg.* Olive off *On the Buses.*

going clear *1. n.* Title of 2015 documentary film about *hatstand* Scientologists purging their imaginary alien spirits while raking in cash from barmy celebrities. *2. n.* Engaging in so many bouts of *gentlemanly relaxation* that one drains one's *spunk* reserves to nought. Dropping from *full fat man milk* to skimmed UHT in a single afternoon.

going down *1. v.* Doing the oral s*x on someone, *giving head. 2. exclam. interrog.* The sort of thing some saucy Russian spy with all red lipstick on would say to James Bond when he gets in a lift, making him raise an eyebrow and adjust his tie.

going down on Hetty Wainthropp *n.* Horrific mental image summoned up in order to quell an untimely *bone on, eg.* When on the bus or tube, just as you have to stand up after being knighted, or seconds before you are called to the *Mastermind* chair by

Cliuve Myrie.

going for a McShit *v.* Visiting the *bogs* in fast food restaurants when one has no intention of buying the food. If challenged by a suspicious manager, the assurance of a food purchase after relieving oneself is known as a *McShit with lies.*

going for a thong *n.* The act of habitually manoeuvering yourself behind women who are sitting down and leaning forward such that there is a gap between their trousers and their underwear, in the vain hope of catching a glimpse of the tops of their *officers' laces.*

going forward *1. exclam.* How *wanky* business folk say "from now on". *2. phr.* Good old fashioned *coitus* up the *front bottom.*

going hydraulic *euph.* Strategic decision to forego the consumption of solid foodstuffs, thereby maximizing the invigorating effects of ale.

going live *1. n.* A former Saturday morning children's TV programme. *2. n.* Sex performed without a prophylactic appliance. *Riding bareback, a bath without wellies, skinnydipping.*

going off grid *1. n.* Nonsensical business-speak for taking a break away from one's computer whilst working at home. *2. n.* Taking a *monkey's fag break.* See *digital detox.*

going once...going twice... *exclam.* An announcement preceding a vigorously *dropped hat.* Also *the chancellor will now read a short statement, our survey said etc.*

going through one's expenses *euph.* Watertight and peevish excuse for spending an entire day working from home as, ostensibly, one struggles to find old taxi receipts and to work out how to claim back 5 euros of hotel tax from three days spent in Utrecht without it exploding the system. In reality, a *relaxing* day watching internet videos of the Sri Lankan ladies' netball team followed by some Uzbek balloon porn.

going to Paul's *exclam.* Phrase used to excuse oneself when leaving polite company to go and do a great big *shit.*

going to the judges *euph.* An indeterminate end to a bout of drunken *nookie.*

going to work for BT *n.* Laying a cable. *'I'm just going to work for BT for ten minutes, love. Can you put the kettle on? And open the window?'*

go interactive *v.* To *tickle* a lady's *bean.* From the BBC teletext instruction to "press the red button".

gokkasock *n. Dan.* An item of male hosiery pressed into service as a receptacle for *sploff* while *banking with Barclays. 'Do you want me to fetch you anything from the shops while I'm out, Mr Christian Anderson?' 'Yes, you can bring me some* *fresh gokkasocks. This lot have gone all crispy. It's like wanking meself off into a cheesegrater.'*

golden bogey *n.* A nose-stud.

golden deceiver *n.* A blonde *piece* who looks gorgeous from behind, but is actually a right *hound* from the front. A *backstabber, back beauty.*

golden eagle has shat, the *exclam.* The glorious moment when your wages appear in your bank account or pay packet. *'Are we having starters then, dear?' 'And a fucking pudding, love. For the golden eagle has shat.'*

golden fart, the *1. n.* The welcome *air biscuit* that announces the end of a bout of *bum gravy. 2. n.* Short-lived ITV Sunday teatime gameshow of the 1970s.

golden globes *1. n.* Happy Shopper television version of the Oscars ceremony, hosted by Ricky Gervais swigging from a can of Harp. *2. n.* Vintage *knockers*, which evoke fond remembrance of times past. *Old 'uns but good 'uns, lifetime achievement baftas.*

golden goal *1. n.* Highly popular innovation in football matches whereby, during extra time, the team that scores first immediately wins the match, thus leaving the opposition gutted. *2. n.* The act of *scoring* in extra time at the end of a night *on the razz*, thereby leaving your mates sick as parrots. After drawing a blank at the club and/or pub, pulling a proper *sixteen valve* on the bus home or at the kebab shop.

golden handjob *n.* Overly generous severance package whereby the payee receives a handsome consideration after making an absolute dog's dinner of the job they were originally hired to do. *Golden handjob* clauses are standard in contracts signed by football managers, investment bankers, cabinet ministers and BBC executives. *'Comedy PM Liz Truss is set to receive a substantial golden handjob after the influential 1922 committee of Tory MPs decided she'd fucked the economy enough.'*

golden handshake *n.* A rather sloppy *gypsy's kiss.*

golden rivet *n.* naval. The *freckle*, the *dot*, the apple of the *captain's* eye for *rear admirals* who *swab the poop deck. Spice island, bottery bay.*

golden shot *1. n.* Lethal, live, blindfold/crossbow-based gameshow that was on TV between 1967 and 1975, hosted by Jackie Rae (us neither), Bob Monkhouse, Charlie Williams and Norman Vaughan (you remember him, kids. He used to do the Cadbury's Roses adverts). *2. n. medic.* A heavy smoker's *jizzbolt.*

golden shower *n.* Getting *pissed* on for a saucy treat. *Water sports. 'The former President's apartment in Trump Tower is magnificently appointed. The 45th POTUS has a 24 carat toilet and bath, and also enjoys regular golden showers in his private suite.'*

golden shred *n.* A marmalade-coloured breakfast *piss* with all chewy bits in it. A *pipecleaner.*

golden slumbers *1. n.* Title of a ballad written by the 16th/17th century English poet and dramatist Thomas Dekker. *2. n.* Song penned by Paul McCartney, using copyright-free lyrics from *1.*, featured on some *shitey* John Lewis advert. *3. n.* Nocturnal micturition. *Pissing* the bed.

golden syrup *n.* The viscous amber mixture of *tweedledee* and *jipper* which has to be forced through the plumbing following any form of sexual activity.

golden ticket *1. n.* In Roald Dahl's *Charlie and the Chocolate Factory*, the magical token which allowed Charlie Bucket and his bone idle grandfather to visit Willie Wonka's fantastic confectionery works, and thus *2. n.* In a sexual relationship, permission to enter the wife's mysterious and exciting *chocolate factory*, though preferably without an elderly relative in tow.

Golden Wonder woman *n.* She who dodges the salad counter with a single bound.

goldfrapp *n.* A *Jonathan* executed while wearing a *jubber ray*. A *posh wank, French wank, boil in the bag.* A *birthday bash.*

goldibollocks *n. Hairy beanbags* which are neither too big nor too small, neither too hot nor too cold, and neither too soft nor too hard.

Goldilocks *1. euph.* Trying all three *holes* of a new romantic partner for a "perfect fit". *'Dad, I think this one's a keeper. She's got a breakfast bowl that Goldilocks would be proud of.' 2. n. prop.* A keen *nosher* who doesn't mind swallowing neither. From the fairytale character with a predilection for the taste of warm porridge.

Goldilocks dump *n.* A *poo* that is "just right" – one that is neither too sloppy nor too tough, and which subsequently leaves no mark upon the *arse paper.*

gold medal winner *n.* One who always *comes* first. A *one-push Charlie, minute man, siso* or *speaking clock.* A *Dutch milkman* who always *spends his money before he gets to the shop.*

gold watch *n.* A small clock or chronometer made of precious metal, which leaps from the throat after a cough. A *docker's omelette, greb, sheckle, prairie oyster.*

golf ball *n.* A pock-marked *clit* discovered lying in an area of rough.

golf ball arse *n. medic.* Condition of the *buttocks* after sitting for too long on a beaded car seat.

golfer's divot *n.* A shapeless clump of *pubage* flying through the air.

golf tees *n.* Chapel hat pegs.

Gollum column *n.* The pink, bald-headed trouser

disturbance occasioned by seeing a particularly attractive young lady and "we wantsss it".

gomer *acronym. medic.* Doctor slang for a *bed blocker.* From Get Out of My Emergency Room. Although these days, they generally *peg it* before the fucking ambulance turns up.

gonad glue *n. Gloy, gunk, wood glue.*

gonbut *n.* A person who stokes fond memories, especially when one is having a *Tommy tank, eg.* Marilyn Chambers and Mary Millington, but probably not Margaret Thatcher or Barbara Woodhouse.

gone broody *euph.* Said of one who is *sitting on eggs.* *'More tea, vicar?' 'Na, I'd best fuck off back to the vicarage. I've gone broody.'*

gone in sixty seconds *1. n.* Film about car thieves in sunglasses driving around with all smoke coming off their tyres. *2. phr.* Premature ejaculation. Also *Johnny jibber, spending your money before you get to the shop, falling at Beecher's, potting the black on the break.*

goner P-Popsie *1. exclam.* A radio transmission from Lieutenant Harold Brownlow Morgan Martin DFC, during the Dambusters raid, to confirm that he had launched his bouncing bomb towards the Möhne Dam. *2. exclam.* A retort made in the presence of an associate who has *dropped* a rather loud *Bakewell tart. 3. exclam.* Something to say after finally *emptying your handbag.*

gone southporn *phr.* A reference to a gentleman's decision to change his *relaxing* hand from right to left, perhaps after upgrading his broadband subscription. *'I just got 145Mb download speed and I was having a bit of trouble controlling the mouse, so I've gone southporn.'*

gone to Iceland *euph.* Crude, sexist expression used about a once more-or-less *satiscraptorily* attractive lady who has subsequently *relaxed her beauty regime, eg.* Former Atomic Kitten turned celebrity docusoap carcrash nightmare Kerry Katona.

gone to the bean *euph.* Said of a woman who has decided to *take the bus to Hebden Bridge* and eschew the tumescent male organ in favour of a *one bean salad* and *comfortable footwear.*

gonga *n.* A *docker's omelette* that occasionally has to be swallowed rather than served up on the pavement.

gonk *1. n.* A *shit* fairground prize, made out of stolen cats, that looks like a miniature cross between Gail Tilsley and Don King. *2. n.* A *rub-a-tug shop* punter. *'I'm sorry, Lord Archer. There's half a dozen gonks in the queue in front of*

you, so you'll just have to wait your turn.'

gonzagas *n. Guns of Navarone.*

Gonzo's nose *sim.* Descriptive of a gent's sorry-looking and unresponsive *trouser truncheon.* Named after the *Muppet Show* character. *'I'd love to give you one, darling, but I've had ten pints and I've got a cock like Gonzo's nose.'*

gonzo vid *n.* Low budget, unscripted *grumble* production where the cast wait until the cameras start rolling before going to the lavatory. An acquired taste.

goober *n. Aus.* Antipodean term for *cock venom.* *'Strewth, Rolf, what the billabong have you been doing? My knicker drawer's full of goober. I'm going to call the warden.'*

gooch *n.* The *barse, tintis, Finsbury bridge, great.* See also *goosh.*

goochy *adj.* Meteorological condition caused by a combination of moist ground and hot sun. *'Well, it's going to be exceptionally goochy today, with the ground wetter than a dog's nose and the sun hotter than a junkie's spoon. The Met Office has issued a a warning that barses are liable to become somewhat foisty, so drink plenty of water and rub a good wad of paper towels on it in the works restroom.'*

goochy fragrance *n.* The musky, manly aroma of a gymnasium locker room, rugby club changing area or wrestler's jockstrap launderette. *Eau de barse.*

good acting *exclam.* Praise that is uttered at the TV when an attractive lady thespian gets her *chebs* out. *'I liked that bit in Titanic where Kate Winslett has her portrait done. Very good acting in that scene, I thought.'*

good at wrapping presents *euph.* Said coyly of a fellow who, one suspects, is well appraised as to the contents of his flowerbeds.

good cop, bad cop *1. phr.* Of two gentlemen, faced with the classic *cruiser and tug* combination at the bar; they must chat up both, knowing that whilst one will achieve a good "cop", the other faces a less propitious outcome. *2. n. Cuffing the suspect,* but using both hands at different times.

good for the bees *exclam.* Said of a woman whose previously well cared-for *ladygarden* has been allowed to go wild. *'Well, at least it'll be good for the bees, I suppose, Germaine.'.*

good lenses, bad frame *euph.* A shallow judgement made of a person who possesses most of the important attributes that would make them a fine girlfriend/boyfriend but is let down by their outward appearance.

good listener *n.* A man who is *good with colours,*

light on his feet. One who *likes shopping.*

goodness of my dick, out of the *phr.* Explanatory statement of the male altruistic impulse. *'Alright, I'll put up your shelves, but I'm only doing it out of the goodness of my dick.'*

goodnight John-Boy *exclam.* Said after *breaking wind* in bed, shortly after turning out the lights.

good night out in Belfast *euph.* A fight.

goodnight sweetheart *1. n.* Woeful, ill-thought-out time travel *shitcom* featuring Nicholas "Rodney" "Plonker" out off of *Only Fools and Horses* Lyndhurst. *2. n.* The final, affectionate *anal announcement* of the day that a married man delivers before drifting off to sleep.

good nintentions *n.* That which you mean to do, *eg.* Household chores, DIY, tax return *etc.,* once you have completed your current video game level – but which you never quite get round to doing, despite staying up till four in the morning.

good pull through with a Christmas tree *euph. medic.* Notional treatment regime intended to cure a wide variety of ills. *'Patient: Female. Age: 46. Presented: Headaches, loose teeth, sweating, sore throat, nausea, ringing in the ears, bloodshot eyes, tremors, general lassitude. Treatment: good pull through with a Christmas tree.'*

good shag for a blind man *euph.* A somewhat frighteningly-countenanced woman with an otherwise delightful voice, *eg.* Mir(this name has been obscured on legal advice)es who did the voice of the Cadbur(so has this)ramel Bunny.

good stalking to *euph.* Sorting out the missus with a proper three-minute *scuttle.*

goods to declare, have *v.* To take the *red channel* at customs.

good time *n.* Street prostitute parlance for a fucking awful time.

good time to bury bad news *phr.* An opportune moment which presents itself in a crowded public place when one can offload a particularly noisy *Bakewell* without being detected, *eg.* At the start of a Formula 1 motor race, while Slayer are playing *Disciple,* during a low level, high-speed pass at a Red Arrows air display or while Janet Street-Porter is speaking.

good touch for a big man *phr.* Said of a chap with a particularly massive *slag hammer,* who proves deceptively tender and attentive during foreplay.

good with colours *adj.* Of a gentleman, adept at *jumping over puddles.*

good workout *n.* Wholesome aerobic activity that will cause you to break into a sweat and breathe hard for a while first thing in the morning. A

proper big *shit.*

gooey in the fork *phr.* Of a lady, to be not far short of *dripping like an egg sandwich.*

go off *v.* Of women, to pass their "best before" date.

go off like a punched icing bag *v.* Splendid phrase coined by thin-legged, high-haired funnyman Russell Kane on ITV2's *I'm a Celebrity's Little Brother,* during a comedic routine about ejaculation following an enforced period of celibacy.

go offroad *v.* To leave *Henrietta Street,* cross *Biffin's bridge* and drive oneself up a *dirt track.*

Goofy's ears *n.* Dangling labia; particularly pendulous *gammon flaps.*

goo gargle *n.* A hot *Vitamin S*-enriched protein mouthwash, which is spat out as opposed to being swallowed.

google *n. Spunk* produced as a result of internet *Frankie.*

googlewhack *v.* To type a bit of *crumpet*'s name into the popular internet search engine with the specific intention of *knocking oneself about a bit* over the resulting "hits".

goo goo muck *1. n.* Cramps song recently played by wireless weirdo Tom Ravenscroft. *2. n. Spunk* again.

goo gun *n.* A *pocket paste dispenser, jizz stick.*

goolie glue *n.* Man-made adhesive capable of bonding leg hair to skin and rigidifying all types of clothing, including socks, duvet covers and monks' habits.

goolies *n.* The colloquialism for *bollocks* least likely to offend a grandparent. *'Oi nan. Get your glasses on and I'll show you me shaved goolies.'*

goose *n.* A light-hearted sexual assault, often taken in bad spirit by po-faced women's libbers.

goose mechanics *euph.* The French. *'I see the goose mechanics have still got food in their supermarkets.'*

goose pumps *n.* Emissions of *flatus* that sound uncannily like a flock of bad tempered wildfowl.

goose, shit like a *v.* To suffer from a loose motion in the *back body. 'Don't drink that cloudy pint, Kirsty, or you'll be running off to shit like a goose all the way through Newsnight Late Review.'*

goose's tongue *n.* A lady's prominent and frankly unsettling *clematis.* Also *builder's thumb, clapper, starter button, clown's hat* or *magic jelly bean.*

goosh *n.* Yet another word for a chap's *tintis.* Also *gooch,* named in honour of the famous cricketer Graham Barse.

gooter/goother *n. Ir.* Dublin slang for a feisty, red-headed colleen's *front bottom.* A *mighty crack.*

gooze *v.* Of a *niff vid* actress, to make a big show of pretending to swallow her leading man's *milm* after a facial *money shot*. *'That bint ain't swallowin', she's just goozin'.'*

gorbie *1. n.* Red facial *stigmata* left after *donning the beard* during *rag week*. *2. n.* Red mark left on the brow after being hit with an elastic band.

gorblimey *adj.* A type of trouser popular among council flat tenants in the 1950s.

Gordon's alive! *exclam.* To be shouted in the style of *shouty crackers* thespian Brian Blessed following the release of a *merciless ming*.

goregasm *n.* A pleasant s**ual encounter with a lady who is *dropping clots*.

gorilla autopsy *n.* A large, untidy and hairy *clout*, such as the one on Lindsey from the Tartan Arms, Lloret de Mar, circa 2002.

gorilla biscuits *euph.* Descriptive of a lady with a *lovely personality*. *'I wouldn't say my wife's ugly, ladies and gentlemen, but she could get a job at the bakery pushing her face into the dough to make gorilla biscuits. My name's Tony Blair, I'm here all week.'*

gorilla salad *n.* Ladies' pubic hair. *Twat thatch, roughage.*

gorilla salad days *n.* Fond *tosstalgia* for the time before bikini line management became *de rigeur.*

gorilla's armpit *n.* A *snatch* which would daunt all but David Attenborough.

gorilla's breakfast *1. n.* A *shit* that smells good enough to turn around and eat again right out of the *pan*, as apes do in the wild on winter mornings. *2. n.* An affectionate name for an early morning *pan cracker.*

gorilla's eye *n.* A bird's *bodily treasure* that in some way slightly evokes the famous scene in *King Kong* where the *horny* ape looks through Fay Wray's bedroom window.

gorillas in the mist *1. n.* Boilers who, through an alcoholic fog, take on siren-like qualities. Can lead to *dances with wolves*. *2. rhym. slang.* Wankered.

gorilla's knuckles *n.* The *camel's lips*. A *Toblerone tunnel* cleft which is clearly visible through a lady's garmentry.

gorilla's pubes, thicker than a *sim.* Stupid. *'Bloody hell, nan. You're thicker than a gorilla's pubes. Have you ever thought about going on The Chase?'*

gorse *n. medic.* That un-named bit between the *gonads* and *arse*; the perineum. Also known, variously, as the *ABC, BBBA, great, gisp, gooch, Finsbury bridge, duffy's bridge, notcher, joy division, Perry Como's lip, kipper, the landing, stinky Mervin, tornado alley, twitter, wannocks, chommie, cockpit, grundle, scran, stinker's bridge, ploughman's, quiche, biffin bridge, taint, barse, tintis, scruttock,* *crunk* and *scranus*.

gory hole *n.* Like a *glory hole*, but infinitely more terrible, in an horrific scenario possibly involving a pair of loppers.

go set a watchman *1. n.* Title of the long-awaited sequel to Harper Lee's famous novel *To Kill a Mockingbird*, that no-one was really that fussed on when it come out, in the end. *2. v.* After using the works *bog*, to leave a *brown barge in the lock* overnight (or preferably over the weekend).

gossip column *n.* A cohort of chatting women moving slowly down a corridor. *'Sorry I'm late, only I got held up by a gossip column.'*

got football at ten-thirty *phr.* Useful Sunday morning escape phrase to be used when your *beer goggles* demist to reveal that you didn't *cop off* with Maria off *Coronation Street* but with her late neighbour Blanche instead. Works especially well when the football season is actually in progress.

go the whole log *v.* When visiting a public *crapper*, to make the impromptu decision to avail oneself of the facilities to a fuller extent than one had originally intended. *'Sorry to keep you waiting. I only went in to cut the end off a bum cigar, but once I'd got me trousers off I thought fuck it, and decided to go the whole log. Anyway, where was I? Oh yes. How do you find the defendant, guilty or not guilty?'*

go through the gears *v.* To perform a *fart* of continuous melody, going up in pitch every few seconds, making a sound like a London Routemaster bus pulling away.

go through the motions *v.* To indulge in the filthy German habit of carefully examining one's stools on the *jobby shelf* before flushing.

got it all to do *1. phr.* Woefully bullish statement of the situation from a football commentator or former manager when England concede a third goal in the eighty-fifth minute. *2. phr.* A hopelessly optimistic attempt to *take Captain Picard to warp speed* when you have a masturbatory mountain to climb, for example following ten pints of stout or over your granny's knitting catalogue.

got mice *adj.* Of a lady, to be *visited by Aunt Flo*. *Up on blocks.*

go to Barnsley *v.* To *scuttle* the *coal hole* of a lady. Named after the famous South Yorkshire tourist trap.

go to work on a Gregg *phr.* Rousing motto of the *bigger-boned* citizen.

go to work on an egg *v.* To start the day by emitting a series of rancid, brimstone-infused *botty burps*.

got the nose *phr.* Said of a preoccupied chap who's got a *mole at the counter* that point blank refuses to come out, possibly caused by eating too many eggs. *'The holy father can't talk to you at the moment, as he's got the nose.'*

gouch *n.* The *biffin bridge, chin rest, taint, tinter, notcher.*

go ugly early *v.* A nightclub or party gambit. To settle for a keen *swamp donkey* rather than chasing after something better and risking ending up with nothing at the end of the evening. To *stick at 15*. *'Good piss up last week, Gaz. I saw you went ugly early.'*

go up a grade *1. v.* In metal working or jewellery making, to change your abrasive paper from a coarse to a fine grade in order to create a smoother finish prior to the final polish. *2. v.* In the science of *bumwaddery*, to use a finer bathroom product in order to reduce friction on the *nipsy*, prior to the final polish. *'Pass the wet wipes over, please Carson. I think I need to go up a grade. This Izal is cutting my poor ringpiece to ribbons.'*

goutrage *n.* Anger exhibited by portly, red-faced gents who are so angry about things they have never bothered trying to understand that their monocles pop out.

gout throne *n.* A scooter or *fatmobile* used for trips to Greggs. Also *Belfast taxi, Frinton Ferrari*

Govan go-kart *n.* A shopping trolley, commandeered for joyriding purposes by the high-spirited youths of the eponymous Glaswegian garden suburb.

Govan tumbleweed *n.* Those blue and white-striped bags made of the thinnest imaginable plastic, available from corner shops, cheap off-licences and vendors of deep fried foods, that end up blowing around the streets of the self-styled Glasgow "borough of exceptional opportunity". *Govan tumbleweed* that ends up stuck in a tree is known as *Govan bunting.*

government artist *n.* A creative type whose sole artistic endeavor consists of "drawing the dole".

government constitutional *n.* A ministerially approved bout of exercise undertaken in the midst of a social distancing lockdown.

go viral *1. v.* Of a video, image, or story, to propogate quickly and widely on the internet through social media and email. *2. v.* To descend rapidly into a less than perfect state of health as a result of a long weekend in Amsterdam, a Friday night spent down the docks, or an evening *looking for badgers* in the woods. *'Sorry love. I think you should get yourself checked out again, only I've gone viral.'*

GPG/gpg *abbrev.* A statutory sexist measure of how much *horatio* a young lady will provide proportionate to the amount of *tart fuel* that a gentleman has purchased for her. Gobbles Per Gallon. Also

spg = swallows per gallon.

GPMG *abbrev. milit.* A lady who looks attractive at a distance but is not quite so alluring when viewed from nearby. Named after the army's General Purpose Machine Gun, which is "good at range but unbelievably messy close up".

grace period *n.* The few precious hours after a hot *cuzza* during which one can *tread on a duck* without the fear of *following through*. *'I tried Abdul Latif's Curry Hell, reputedly the hottest curry in the world. Upon the first taste, my eyes melted and my throat burst into flames, and with a grace period of just forty-five seconds I was straight off to the lavvy. On my 2-mile journey home I had to stop the car on 173 occasions, each time not knowing which end to point at the gutter.'*

Graham Norton's hair *n.* Descriptive of a person's *barnet* after being *seagulled* by a gentleman, or after walking under Status Quo's hotel room balcony.

grainspotter *n.* A real ale enthusiast.

gramble *n.* When a chap takes the chance of leaving his *grumble mags* on a high shelf in the spare room while he's out, betting that they are to high for his missus to find them.

grampire *n.* An octogenarian whose shrunken gums have long ago given up the ghost and thrown in the towel in the battle to accommodate their vintage dentures. Often seen on buses vainly attempting to wrap their 1950s Nye Bevan pearlies round a Werther's original.

granary *n.* A morally upright, dour loaf of bread with all seeds and bits of mouse *shit* in. *2. n.* A *rub-a-tug shop* full of *old biddies*. *'You been down the granary again, Wayne?'*

granary loaf *n.* Pungent, often nutty with a dark brown crust, and found in the beds of lazy octogenarians who can't be *arsed* to take a few small steps to the bathroom.

granbies *rhym. slang.* Term widely used in Leicestershire to describe the male *pods* or *clockweights*. From the now-defunct concert venue Granby Halls = orchestras. *'He'll be alright in a couple of minutes, your holiness. He's just had a kick in the granbies, that's all.'*

Gran Canaria *1. n. prop.* Somewhere people used to go on holiday back in the days when you could afford to go on holiday and could get through Passport Control. *2. n. prop.* Elderly relative who refuses to turn down the central heating, turning her home into a sweltering tropical paradise.

grandad erector *n.* A sight so sexually stimulating that it could raise the dead. *'Blimey, Kylie's new* *video is a real grandad erector.'*

grandad in my pocket *1. n.* Kids' television show in which James Bolam played a senior citizen who possessed the ability to shrink in order to escape from precarious situations. *2. n.* The wrinkly, perennially shrinking *old chap* who lives in your *undercrackers.*

grandad's coin purse *n.* A *growler* with a pair of tightly drawn *beef curtains*, which requires tough finger action at both ends in order to gain entry. Also variously known as a *butler's cuff, mouse's ear, paper cut* or *OJ's glove*. A *blurtch* that is tighter than a *worm's belt.*

grandalf *1. n.* A *Cumbledore* for the senior citizen. *2. n.* An old *bird* with a *wizard's sleeve.*

grandchav *n.* One who is blessed with grandchildren while still young enough to fully enjoy the experience. A *Cardiff grandmother. 'Mum. Could you help me with my homework, please?' 'Go and ask your grandchav, I've not finished mine yet.' 'But she's still doing hers too.'*

grandfather cock *euph.* A senior citizen with excessively pendulous *clockweights* that have to be laboriously raised each evening whilst pausing on the landing on the way to bed, Reverend Brontë-style.

grandma *rhym. slang.* An act of defecation. From the dimly remembered children's television character Grandma Flump = Donald Trump.

grandma's party *n.* A bout of masturbation. Wearing a bowler hat. See *reggae like it used to be.*

grandma's perfume *n.* The smell of *piss. Eau de toilette publique.*

grandmaster flash *n.* A tumescent mid-*lamb shank membrum virile*, typically being pushed ever closer to the edge by his *furious five.*

grandma's Wolseley *n.* The greying *minnie-moo* of an old dear which hasn't given anyone a *ride* since the 60s and won't start the next time someone puts his *key* in. Something with a pool on the floor under it, that smells of leather, dried grease and perished rubber.

grand national *n.* The aftermath of a booze- and meat-fuelled night out, after which it might be the kindest thing to shoot you. An *Eartha Kitt* so sticky that you need to get up into a half-squat and whip at it with a toilet brush, recreating the historic moment when AP McCoy triumphantly rode home his first winner, the appropriately named "Don't Push It".

Grand Old Duke of York *1. n.* A constantly frustrated ejaculation. A *pop shot* of *muck* – consisting of ten thousand eager homunculi – that is repeatedly marched to the top of the hill, only to be then marched back down again, occasionally finding itself stranded halfway up. *2. n.* An unconvincing erection, a mix of duty and apathy, one that is "neither up nor down". A *lard on*, a *dobber, half a teacake*. A *Prince Andrew*. *3. n. rhym. slang.* A *nork. 'Nice Grand Old Duke of Yorks, Felicity.'*

grand prix getaway *sim.* A heavily skidded U-bend. Also *starting grid at Brands Hatch, Ark Royal landing deck, thrush's chest.*

grand slam *n.* In the world of *salad dodging*, the fabled achievement of enjoying the holy quartet of takeaway meals in one day, *viz.* McDonald's for breakfast, Kentucky Fried Chicken for lunch, Burger King for tea and a dodgy kebab on the way home from the pub.

grand tour *1. n.* An historical voyage taken by wealthy young men in search of enlightenment, taking in Paris, Geneva, Milan, Munich *etc. 2. n.* A collection of cities visited by soon-to-be-broke young men in search of alcohol, drugs, *flange*, gambling and/or *ladyboys*, taking in Amsterdam, Hamburg, Bangkok, Las Vegas, Blackpool, *etc.* Also *gland tour. 3. n. Top Gear* in all but name.

gran flakes *n.* The contents of a nursing home Hoover bag.

granflan *n.* A slice of well-aged *hairy pie.*

Grange Hill sausage *n.* In the pornographic cinematographic milieu, a popular trope whereby something meaty appears unexpectedly, usually over the shoulder of an extremely surprised individual, hopefully without a fork stuck in it.

gran-house effect *n.* Build-up of noxious gases in the homes of the elderly causing a toxic atmosphere that shortens lives and drives families asunder.

granny bag *n.* A well-padded *mons pubis* resembling a pink bum-bag worn round the front.

granny batter *n.* KY jelly.

granny bollocks *n. Bingo wings* of the legs. *Meat jodhpurs.*

granny butter *n. prop. 1.* Nickname comedy Prime Minister Boris Johnson gave to his grandmother, who churned milk on a farm. *2. n.* Descriptive of a *granny magnet's farmer's broth. 'Wayne, I'm going to have o put these shorts through the wash again. This powder's not shifting the granny butter off them.'*

granny knot *n.* A wizzy, tangled mat of grey *pubes.*

granny magnet *n.* A male who, having had no luck finding a ladyfriend of his own age, is forced to *cop off* with a right old *crone, eg.* The *blotto* one with the incontinent laugh being held up by her mates in the kebab shop.

granny's attic *euph.* An unattractive lady, *ie.* One of whose cobwebby *clopper* it could humorously be said, "nobody's been up there in years".

granny's elbow *n.* An unpleasantly elongated *ball sack*. A *rantallion*.

granny's flannel *euph.* An extremely dry *Cradock*. *'How did you get on fucking that bird last night, Russell?' 'I did me best, Jonathan, but her cunt was like a granny's flannel and I couldn't get me cock in. Anyway, just before Sally Traffic with the travel news, it's time for the Radio 2 Record of the Week – On a Little Street in Singapore by everybody's favourite, Manhattan Transfer.'*

granny's hat, muff like your *sim.* Descriptive of a particularly hairy *otter's pocket*, possibly smelling strongly of mothballs, catfood and damp.

granny's kiss *n.* From a gentleman's perspective, the experience of performing *cumulonimbus* on a badly maintained *clopper*. Not unlike receiving a smacker from one's sloppy, pucker-lipped grandmother sporting a *Magnum PI* moustache and tasting like she's just eaten a gammon butty.

granny's laptop *n.* A cat.

granny's mouth *n.* A saggy, loose-lipped, whiskery *cunker*.

granny's oysters *n.* Elderly female genitalia.

granny's prawn *n.* Distinctly unappetising *seafood* dish which is well past its sell-by date.

granny's purse *n.* The condition of one's *farting clappers* after a comprehensive bowel evacuation, *ie.* Firmly snapped shut.

granny's thimble *euph.* Unsettling sensation when the end of one's *old chap* touches the cold, glazed interior of the *bum sink* during the course of a *sit-down toilet adventure*, causing an involuntary shudder. *A kiss from the witch's lips, porcelain tingle.*

gransformer *n.* An initially impressive show-room-fresh model that has turned into a right *old banger* by the morning.

grantanamo bay *n.* An elderly relative's residence, where one is subjected to hours of auditory torture in front of a television set turned up to maximum volume in lieu of hearing aids, with an effect on one's senses akin to sustained waterboarding.

Grantham's stalactites *n.* Vertical rivulets of dried *Melanie* on the back of a laptop computer. Named after the Dirty Den actor, amateur marksman and webcam exhibitionist Leslie.

Grant Shapps *n. rhym. slang. Piss-flaps, ladypetals etc.*, named in honour of the utterly unmemorable former Minister of, variously, Transport, Defence, Business, and Energy, and sometime Home Secretary. *'Her trousers were so tight I could see her Grant Shapps.'*

grape flicker *n.* A *trouser bandit* or *fruit feeler*.

grape smugglers *n.* Tight gentlemen's briefs, as worn by *grumble flick* stars in the 1970s. *Noodle benders.*

grapes of wrath *n. medic.* Vengeful haemorrhoids, Steinbecks. *'Fetch us some cream, love. Me grapes of wrath are stinging like a bastard and I've got an arse like a chewed orange.'*

graphic novel *n.* Art homework woven around a tenuous storyline.

grappling hooks *n.* The unyielding fasteners on a lady's *tit pants*.

grass art *n.* The Tony Hart-like placing of garden seats, picnic tables *etc.* on the lawn, so that by the end of the Summer one has created a humorous image in the turf, such as a pair of rudimentary *tits*, a *meat and two veg* or a simple four-letter expletive.

grass plucker *n.* A *Thora* that is roughly the consistency of houmous, so that the unlucky dogowner has to pull up fistfuls of turf in a bag-covered hand.

grassy knoll *1. n.* Site where the second gunman stood during the assassination of JF Kennedy. *2. n.* A fanny like two padded coat hangers.

grated carrot *n.* Coarse, ginger-coloured *gorilla salad*, suitable for a *vagetarian* diet. Rusty *fusewire*.

grating the cheddar *n. medic.* To accidentally scrape one's *lid* along the zip of one's *flies*. *"I say, Jeeves. Could you take these trousers to my tailor and have him replace the zip fastenings with good old fashioned buttons?' I croaked. 'I only bought them last week and I've grated the cheddar four times. My poor cock end is ripped to pip, don't you know."* (from *Swallow it All, Jeeves* by PG Wodehouse).

grattan *1. adj.* Descriptive of a state of ill-health. *'Shut the curtains will you, love? I must have had a bad pint last night and I feel right grattan.' 2. v.* To masturbate over desperate material in the absence of anything better to masturbate over. See also *grattanification*.

grattanification *n.* A young man's use of the *titpants* pages of his mum's catalogue in order to fuel his single-handed progress towards an *argosm*.

grave digging *n.* Resurrecting the deceased dog-ends in an ashtray in an attempt to make a functioning "Frankenstein"-style cigarette which is an abomination against nature.

gravel lorry at the lights, dripping like a *sim.* A bird who is *frothing like bottled Bass*. *'I wouldn't say she was gagging for it, but she was dripping like a gravel lorry at the lights.'*

Gravesend walking stick *n.* Any completely

unnecessary perambulatory aid, as used by virtually everyone in the eponymous North Kent locale as a means of backing up their incapacity benefit claims.

grave-sniffer *n.* A senior citizen. A *coffin-dodger, oxygen thief.*

gravy & mash *n.* Like *bangers and mash*, but without the chunks. A *bog* full of *arsewipe* and diarrhoea.

gravy bone *1. n.* An amusingly shaped, meat-flavoured dog chew. *2. n.* The result of attempting a spot of *backdoor work* with a lady who is suffering a gastric complaint.

gravy leg *n.* The result of *gambling and losing*, possibly – and indeed most probably – after ingurgitating a dubious, mollusc-based repast.

gravy taster *n.* An individual whose line of work leaves them with a permanently brown tongue. *A shirt fly* or *fart sucker. 'And now for the latest news from Buckingham Palace, let's go over to the BBC's chief gravy taster Nicholas Witchell.'*

greasebox *n.* A *quim.*

grease me up, I'm going in! *exclam.* The battle cry of a valiant gentleman who is about to go *over the top* into a dancefloor full of fatties.

greaser *1. n.* In aviation slang, a perfectly smooth landing. *2. n.* In lavatory slang, a perfectly smooth landing. *Like an otter off the bank, like shaking an eel out of a welly. 3. n.* A bloke who chins mods.

grease the runway *v.* To avail oneself of the first coffee or cigarette of the day, thus encouraging the appearance of an early doors *turtle's head.*

greasy as a butcher's prick *sim. 'Ooh, I don't trust that Paul Hollywood off the Great British Bake Off. He's greasy as a butcher's prick, that one, if you ask me.' 'Ooh, I know what you mean, Mrs Hollywood.'*

greasy stub *n.* The *clematis. 'Any plans tonight, mate?' 'No. I'll probably just stop in and flick the wife's greasy stub.'*

greasy waistcoat pocket *n.* A shallow, well-oiled *fanny* large enough for a thumb, gold watch or snooker player's cue tip chalk to be inserted.

Great British bake-off *euph.* The act of driving the full length of the A1 while absolutely *busting for a shit.*

Great British shake-off *n.* The sort of *wanking* competition that teenage boys occasionally indulge in during the odd moments when they aren't looking at their mobile phones with a glazed, gormless expression. Contrary to what the name might suggest, it has no connection with baked goods (unless a digestive biscuit enters the proceedings, of course).

great escape, the *euph. Dropping the shopping* – either accidentally or not – while fully clothed by discreetly shaking the *feeshus* down one's trouser leg and out past the ankles. From the scene in the eponymous movie where the Stalag Luft III tunnelers dispose of their soil in a like manner, right under the guards' noses.

greatest hits *1. n. rhym. slang.* The *shits. 'Bloody hell, Egon. You're a shadow of your former self. What happened?' I went for a delicious eight-course slap-up banquet at the Curry Capital, Bigg Market, Newcastle upon Tyne three weeks ago and I've had the greatest hits ever since. I tell you, I've a good mind to dock them a star in my next Good Food Guide.' 2. n. rhym. slang.* Chart-topping *tits.*

great hand-nob coordination, he's got *exclam.* Said admiringly of someone who demonstrates exceptional skills in *onanism. 'Say what you like about Mr Rees-Mogg, archbishop. But he's got great hand-nob coordination.'*

great, the *n.* That bit of the male anatomy which is between the back of the *gooch* and the front of the *barking spider.* The *barse, tintis, notcher* or, more crudely, the p*rineum. So-called because any time one's missus goes anywhere near it, one exclaims: "Ooh, that's great!"

great wall of china *n.* A row of Victorian urinals that is visible from space.

Great Yarmouth gnomes *n.* Washing machines, broken tellies and *pissed* mattresses used as garden ornaments in the *quaynte* Norfolk town.

greb *n. Hockle.*

Greek *n.* Any s*x games in which the *rusty bullet hole* is centrally involved. *Swedish.*

Greek biscuit *n.* An act in which one man kneads another man's *clackerbag*, as though preparing the dough prior to a spot of baking. Icing optional.

Greek courage, full of *adj.* Kebab-fuelled. For example, a pair of blokes having a fight on the pavement outside the Paradise Grill, Newcastle-under-Lyme, to pick an example entirely at random, could be described as being *full of Greek courage.*

Greek drum kit, play the *v.* While squatting on the facilities in a Mediterranean establishment, to operate the pedal bin in order to dispose of used *bumwad.*

Greeks, a touch of the *n. medic.* An explosive *Camilla* movement which sounds like your *back body* is spluttering out the name "Papadopoulos".

Greek sauna *n.* A *Dutch oven.*

Greek ship about, there must be a *exclam. nav.* Old merchant navy rejoinder to a matelot complaining about having an itchy *ring.*

Greek-style yoghurt *n.* The unpalatable mess found inside a recently *kicked-in back door. Santorum,* *shum, bummus.*

Greek tickle *n.* That which an erastes (ἐραστής) may perform with an eromenos (ἐραστής) behind a skip.

Greek tip *n.* A stray pubic hair adhering to coinage that is handed over in shops, restaurants, *etc. Copper wire.*

greenarse gases *n.* Pent-up methane which is damaging to the environment and a worry for those who inhabit it.

green goddess *1. n.* A middle-aged woman doing star jumps and running on the spot on breakfast telly in the 80s. *2. n.* One of those laughably ancient-looking emergency tenders which used to get brought out of mothballs regularly during the 80s to take the place of proper fire engines during strikes. *3. n.* A vintage, dumpy-looking *bird* who will *do the job* in the absence of a flashier, modern-looking model.

greengrocer's hotpot *n.* The steaming contents of a vegetarian's *pan.*

Greenland shark *1. n.* A massive, rough-skinned marine predator that lives approximately 1000ft beneath the waves and takes a long time to surface when caught. *2. n.* A large, *arse*-stingingly rough *copper bolt* that only appears from the depths of the *Simon Cowells* after ages of sitting *on the throne.*

Greenock laptop *n.* An 18-inch pizza box filled with with all manner of tempting deep-fried fare. See also *Scouse laptop, Barnsley briefcase.*

green Peter *n.* An exotic herbal cigarette which has been constructed and secreted about one's person before attending a social gathering. Should anybody – for example Michael Gove – later enquire as to the availability of any *jazz cabbage*, it can then be retrieved from its hiding place with a cheery cry of "here's one I prepared earlier".

green top *euph.* A partially-rigid male member. A *semi.*

green wings *n.* An unwanted accolade. Sex with a *clappy slapper.*

Greggarian calendar *n.* The daily diet variation of a *big-boned* fellow who alternates between steak and chicken bakes at the popular high street pastry emporium.

greggarious *adj.* Availed of many pies.

greggasaurus *n.* A loyally *omnomnivorous* customer of the high street baked comestibles outlet.

greggbound *adj.* Constipated following over-consumption of savoury comestibles.

greggcited *adj.* Of people who have *trouble with their glands*, unconscionably thrilled when approaching a branch of the popular high street treaterie.

greggetarian *n.* One who restricts their diet solely to the pastry-based sweeetmeats available from Greggs. *'Ooh no, he can't eat fruit or vegetables. He's a very strict greggetarian.'*

Gregg-handed *adj.* Caught in the act whilst gorging on tempting pies after telling everyone that you're on a diet.

greggings *n.* The seemingly standard lower-body attire of ladies about town who have, one might infer, a pechant for pastries.

gregglets *n.* Rotund children. Also *cub stouts, pork & beanie babies.*

Greggory's girls *euph.* A ravenous pod of cetacean-sized females encircling the entrance of the quasi-eponymous boulangerie.

Greggs and Co. *euph.* A troupe of heavily-overweight, pasty-fuelled dancing women. Also *Flan's People, sausage roly polys.*

Greggs baby *n.* The distended abdomen of a young lady, of whom it is difficult to determine whether she is with child or *with steak slice.*

Greggs bosons *n. phys.* The less-than mysterious particles that give *plumpers* their mass.

Greggs canapé *n.* A lower-class thing that has ideas above its station. *'I see that comic filled with crap jokes about wanking and shit is in the Tate Gallery, then. There's a real Greggs canapé if ever there was one.'*

Greggs confetti *n.* The pastry flakes that cascade off the savoury sweetmeats offered by the famous high street *bellicatessen.* Also *Greggs dandruff.*

Greggs dummy *n.* A chicken and mushroom-filled pacifier used by teenaged mums to soothe their teething infants.

Greggs, go to *v.* To pay a visit to an establishment that is full of *tarts* and *cream pies.*

Greggs hot shelf jackpot *n.* Any trifecta of heated delicacies purchased from the eponymous fooderie by a *bigger-boned* person, *eg.* A sausage roll, a Cornish pasty and a steak bake.

Greggs legs *n.* Chubby, cellulite-laden *pins* that ooze through the tears in a lady's "designer" ripped jeans with each shuffled step, like rising dough.

greggsodus *n.* A lunchbreak stampede to the nearest pie shop.

greggspectant *n.* Blooming as a result of pastry consumption rather than pregnancy. *Greggnant, greggspecting.*

Greggs revenge *n.* Descriptive of the delightfully rich aroma produced when one *steps on a duck* after consuming a steak bake.

greggstatic *adj.* The state of euphoria reached by a

big-boned person upon breathlessly reaching the front of the queue in a high street pie shop.

Greggs tie *n.* The vertical pastry-flake mess that adorns the front of your shirt, jumper or vest following the swift and careless consumption of a prolish comestible.

greggstra large *adj.* Of a T-shirt or sports top, a size measurement suitable for a person whose glands are full of pastry. *'We've got this shirt in XL, XXL, XXXL or there's this one in XXXXXL, Mr McCririck.' 'Hmm. It's still a bit tight under me bingo wings. Have you got any in greggstra large?'*

Greggs umbrella *n.* A carrier bag held over the head in order to keep off the rain.

greggulars *n. Seasoned diners, three-peggers, truffle hunters, cake detectors, piabetics.*

Gregg Wallace in a snood, like *sim.* Descriptive of an extremely engorged *clematis.*

Greggxit *n.* A swift waddle from the counter to the tables and reinforced chairs outside for a spot of *alfresco* gluttony. 2. *n.* Early death caused by an excessive penchant for baked sweetmeats.

greggy *adj.* The diametric opposite of leggy.

grenade *n.* A woman with a *lovely personality* in a nightclub, upon whom a selfless fellow throws himself to save his comrades.

grexit, vote for *v.* To eschew pastries made by the famous bakery chain. To go on a diet.

grey box *1. n. Eucalyptus microcarpa.* Type of tree with distinctively coloured bark which is endemic to the Antipodes. 2. *n.* The contents of an Australian feminist firebrand's *undercrackers,* you might imagine. And you'd be right.

greyer than Waitrose on a Tuesday morning *sim.* Descriptive of the preferred hair and clothing colours of the clientelle to be found in Britain's most exclusively priced supermarket. *'I pulled this right sexy milf last night, but when I went down on her, her muff was greyer than Waitrose on Tuesday morning.'*

grey flannel *n.* A pensioner's *opera curtains. Granny's oysters, biltong.*

Greyfriars Bobby *n. Edinb. rhym. slang.* A *feeshus.*

Greyfriars jobby *n. Scots.* A faithful, small, brown pal who refuses to leave and keeps on returning even after multiple flushes. A mournfully loyal turd which maintains a faithful, lonely vigil at its master's *food's grave.*

greyhound *1. n.* A very short skirt, *ie.* One that is "very close to the hare". 2. *n.* An hilarious rugby club changing rooms impression involving an erect *chopper* and a champagne wire.

greyhound griller *n.* A particularly scorned

bunny boiler.

greyhound's nostril *sim.* Descriptive of something which has been exposed to water and wind. *'How's the outside pool, Maureen?' 'Not as warm as it could be. Me twat's like a greyhound's nostril.'*

greyhound's snout *n.* Like the *turtle's head,* but a tad quicker out of the trap.

grey matter *n.* A gelatinous organic material intrinsically linked to the thought processes of the male human being. *Spunk.*

greyskull *n.* Affectionate term for an ageing *gimmer* or *biddy.*

grey wings *n.* The honour awarded to someone who has indulged in a *rumpular pumpular* act with a ladyfriend of more mature aspect. A medal for a chap who has bravely faced up to a spot of *gash in the attic.*

grief bacon *n.* Weight gained as a consequence of emotional turmoil. *'I tell you what, after her divorce she's really slammed on the cakes and hit the grief bacon.'*

Grifter handlebar grip, nob like a *sim.* When a fellow's been been *pulling skin wheelies* so often that his *todger* has indentations for his fingers to grip, similar to the erstwhile bicycle.

GRILF/grilf *acronym.* Grandma I'd Like to Fuck; a saucy bit of *prunetang, eg.* Joan Collins, that Purdey out of *The New Avengers* or any woman over the age of 32 from one of our country's less salubrious council estates.

grilled tomato *n.* A woman *with a lovely personality* that a gentleman puts off *having a go at* until all his other options are exhausted at the end of the evening. *'Shit. I fell over in the car park and broke both me hands so I can't even have a wank. I suppose I'll have to go and chat up that grilled tomato by the fruit machine now.'*

grimble *n.* Glossy, American marshmallow-hard *quornography* that looks like *Dynasty* with nipples.

grim-dins *n.* When you come home to find that all you have in the pantry is a tin of peas, a packet of spaghetti and some cold ham nearing its use-by date, and no amount of fucking Hellmans can "turn your nothing into something".

grime bubble *n. A fart, air biscuit.*

grime capsule *n.* A stack of 1980s *jazz mags* left behind by builders and discovered years later under the floorboards while renovating a house. A *Dutch miracle, basement jacks, empire of dirt.*

grim fairytale *n.* An incident of outdoor rural defecation; when *dropping them off at the pool* is impossible, due to the lack of a *pool,* sending the *kids* off into the forest to fend for themselves.

grimquims *n.* A collection of unsightly *butchers'*

dustbins, stamped bats, ripped sofas, ragman's coats and *badly packed kebabs*. *'Did you see last month's Razzle stack? What a bunch of grimquims.'*

grim reapedia *n.* Alternative name for Wikipedia, reflecting the online reference site's propensity for instantly recording celebrity deaths. *'I see the grim reapedeia has been at work. They only announced the poor fucker was dead a minute ago. The tenses in the main bit of the article are still wrong, mind.'*

grimsby *1. n.* A mingsome *minge*. *2. n.* An unidentified lump of gristle in a pie.

Grimsby meal *n.* An unpleasant northern *fish supper*.

Grimsby sauna *n.* Under the marital duvet, a hot, moist atmosphere with an overwhelming maritime bouquet.

grimshits *n.* A portmanteau term for faeces distinctly lacking in cohesion. *Fizzy gravy, bubblepoo* and *bicycle chains* are all *grimshits*.

grin and wear it *phr.* Descriptive of the closing scenes to be found at the end of certain genres of *bongo vid* whereby a *plasterer's radio* covered in *ejactoplasm* does her best to smile and wave bye-bye to the viewers.

grind *1. v.* To have sex with all the fervour of an old bus going up a steep hill in Lancashire. *ie,* If you stopped, you really wouldn't have it in you to start again. *2. v.* That which a stripper does when she is not *bumping*.

grinding the cotton *n.* Act of congress carried out without first taking the elementary precaution of removing one's clothing.

grin fucking *euph.* Activity of many people in a work environment who say "yes" when they have no intention – or indeed ability – to complete the task in question. *'Oi Hancock. Are you going to deliver a national Test and Trace programme by April or are you just grin fucking me?'*

grip lit *1. n.* Suspense novels. *2. n. Bongo mags.*

gripper *1. n.* More light-hearted heterosexual changing room horseplay, this time where somebody grabs hold of another's *arse cress* and gives it a great big yank. *2. n.* Unusual Christian name of a bully who featured in early series of the gritty school-based kids' soap *Grange Hill*. *3. n.* Midlands term for one who partakes of solitary hand-based pleasures.

gripping the lather *n.* The precise moment when a spot of innocently pleasurable bath-night self-soaping becomes an undeniable act of filthy beastliness. Again.

gristle gripper *1. n.* The female *mingepiece*.

gristle thistle *n.* Persistent purple-headed weed that commonly infests *moss cottage* gardens. *Turning Japanese knotweed.*

gristle whistle *1. n.* A "Swannee"-style *blow job*, performed on the *spam kazoo* while pulling the *Scotch eggs* up and down. *2. n.* The male generative organ.

gristle wielder *n.* A geriatric, old school *pork swordsman* such as Ben Dover, Hugh Hefner or Ming Campbell.

grit between the pillows *n.* Particularly crusty *men in the rigging* which lead to excessive chafing betwixt the *mudflaps*. *'CAPTAIN PEACOCK: Mr Humphries. Do you have to walk across the shop floor in such an affected fashion? MR HUMPHRIES: I'm sorry, Captain Peacock, only I spent the weekend camping in a quarry near Golders Green with a digger driver from Dumfries, and ever since I got back under me own duvet I've been suffering with terrible grit between the pillows.'* (*Are You Being Served?*, BBC TV 1978).

grizzly bear pit *n.* The *pan* of a blocked *chod bin*, viewed from above.

groaner *n.* A *Thora* that is so big that it cannot be expelled without vocal assistance. A *U-blocker.*

grobber *n.* That part of a person which allows evacuation of solid bodily waste. The *freckle, arse, rusty sheriff's badge, fifties tea towel holder, bumhole, etc.* *'CAPTAIN PEACOCK: You seem to be walking with some discomfort this morning, Miss Brahms. Is there a problem? MISS BRAHMS: Well, Captain Peacock. Last night I was expecting a candlelit meal and a romantic interlude off Mr Lucas, but all I got was a limp kebab and a dobber up me grobber.'* (*Are You Being Served?*, BBC TV 1978).

groglodyte *n.* One who drinks in the park and looks like *shit* despite enjoying an ostensibly healthy, outdoors lifestyle.

groinery *n.* The craft of *morning woodwork*, in which only one *handtool* is used.

groin grease *n.* The sweat that builds up around the inner thighs and *knackers* of a *salad dodger* on a hot day. *Arse feta.*

groin-join *euph.* A perfunctory act of *coitus*, devoid of romance or emotional significance. *'Subject: Meeting Wednesday about Covid etc. Could we push this back to 2pm? Trying to schedule some groin-join after PMQs.'*

grolly *v.* To do that thing professional footballers do where they cover up one nostril and blow *snot* out the other one. *'Can you believe that, Richard? Female linesman. Never mind the fucking offside rule – she probably don't even know how to fucking grolly.'* *'Course she don't, Andy. Daft cow probably* *thinks you do it down both fucking nostrils at once. Do me a favour, love. Still smash it, though.'*

Grolsch *n.* An under-lubricated *snatch, ie.* One that is "not ready yet" and needs another minute's brisk rubbing.

Grolsch washer *n.* An anal sphincter resembling the trademark orange rubber seal used on the bottle-tops of the popular Dutch beverage. *'That vindaloo I had at the Rupali Restaurant, Bigg Market, Newcastle upon Tyne last night has left my Grolsch washer in tatters, doctor.'*

gromble *n.* A chap who makes good use of the *bongo mags* that the everyday folks leave behind under bushes. A *grumble womble*.

grommet *n.* 1950s *totty.*

grond *1. n.* In the *Lord of the Rings*, the battering ram that shattered the gates of Minas Tirith, for any viewers who managed to stay awake that long. *2. n.* A *log* of terrifying proportions that could smash its way through even the most tightly clenched *ring.*

gronk *n. RAF.* A *shit.* *"'Bandits at three O'clock!" ejaculated Algy. "Great!"replied Biggles. "I've got half an hour to have a big smelly gronk!"'* (from *Biggles Drops his Fudge* by Capt. WE Johns).

gronk board *n. nav.* A panel in the mess where photographs of the ugliest women *banged* by sailors are displayed for the amusement of the entire ship's crew.

groodies *n.* How *charms* are referred to in the film *A Clockwork Orange.*

Groot's fingers *n.* An amalgamation of five gnarled *bum sausages* left in the *pan* in the wake of a particularly painful evacuation. Resembling the strange *Marvel Comics* arboreal creature's digits.

groovejet *1. n.* Turn-of-the-millennium dancefloor filler by Italian DJ Spiller, with vocals by her off *Blue Peter*'s girl. *2. n. medic.* A squirt of *the squits.*

groovement *n.* A cool *dung* taken while listening to your favourite funky jams.

groovy legs *n. med.* Post-prolonged *doggy-style* sex wobbly numbness in the lower limbs. *'I wasn't sure how long I was back-scuttling her, but it must have been ages, because when I stopped I had my groovy legs on.'*

G-rope *n.* A *G-string* for the fatter lass.

grope-atunity *n.* An unexpected and fortuitous, albeit morally dubious, chance for a bit of a *feel,* which comes knocking out of the blue. *'The missus turned over in bed last night so I took the grope-atunity to get me tops. And now over to Rob Bonnet with the sport.'*

grope fruits *n. Shirt potatoes, fat rascals.* Nice big pairs.

gross misconduct *n.* A harmless bout of workplace *self-improvement* that is quite possibly grounds for dismissal. *'Hold my calls, Moneypenny. I'm just off for a spot of gross misconduct in the photocopying room.'*

grot cotton *n.* Amusing nickname which can be applied to an actress/model who tends rather more towards the *bargain bucket* end of the erotic entertainment industry.

grotdog *n.* A lower-grade hotdog, of the sort which one might expect to purchase at Walthamstow Dog Stadium, to pick a location entirely at random.

grotenspiel *n.* An instrument for the entertainment of gents with a stiffness problem. And a subscription to *Hot Fanny Grannies.* A *faptop.*

grot slot *n.* The married man's 30-minute long internet pornography download window which occurs while his wife is at the shops.

grotspangle *n.* The adhesive residue found sticking together the pages of many second hand *rhythm mags. 'Lot 213, Recovered from on top of a wardrobe in the home of comedian David Baddiel, approximately 3500 items of adult literature consisting mainly of Whitehouse, Razzle, New Cunts &c, together with a substantial amount of Scandinavian scud. Good condition, but with evidence of grotspangle on most older issues. Est; £200-£500.'*

grotter *n.* The *snatch.*

grotweiler *n.* An unacceptably sexist and offensive term for an aggressive-looking, mangy old *growler* in a readers' wives-type publication.

groundhog lay *n.* A depressingly familiar intercourse routine between a man and his long term girlfriend or missus.

groundhog wank *1. n.* A dismal attempt at *self abuse* which repeatedly peters out, leaving the *wanksmith* with no choice but to start again. *2. n.* The overly familiar *tug* regimen of a *pornogamist* who only owns one *art pamphlet.*

groundsman's hut *n.* The *back door,* where one lodges a stiff complaint when the *turf* round the front is unplayable.

ground zero *n.* The *freckle* the morning after an evening of heavy *refreshment.* An *arse like a Japanese flag.*

group 4-skin *n.* Friction burns on the palms of the right hand, typically suffered by security guards on their long, lonely night shifts, with nothing to do but surf the internet and entertain themselves.

groupie sorbet *n.* A refreshing between-courses *amuse bouche* used by ladies to cleanse the palate when performing sex acts on several gentlemen in the same evening.

group-on *n. coll.* A gathering of erections.

group stages *euph.* A degree of genital tumescence so unimpressive that it fails to warrant classification as a *semi-* or even a *quarter-on.*

grouting *n.* The act of a horny-handed artisan applying a layer of thick paste between two raised areas for the purpose of aesthetic enhancement. *'Gunther, hurry up and finish the grouting. We still have the double anal scene to shoot before this car park starts getting busy.'*

Grove Hill decking *n. Al fresco* horizontal timber structures typically adorning the front and rear gardens of homes in one of the less affluent estates in Middlesbrough. Pallets.

grow a tail *v.* To defecate, *build a log cabin. Snip a length of spine.*

growl at the badger *v. Scots.* To noisily *nosh* a *beaver.* To loudly *nod at a stoat, gnosh.*

growler *1. n.* The sort of meat and potato pie sold from one of the various catering outlets inside the ground at Gigg Lane, Bury, in the mid-1980s. So-called because within 30 minutes of eating the pie, one's stomach would begin to grumble. A *Cornish nasty. 2. n.* The *shithouse. 3. n.* A semi-submerged *dreadnought,* nine tenths of which lies hidden below the surface. *4. n.* A big old hairy, slavering pitbull of a *minge.*

grown-up book *n. Self-help pamphlet, jazz mag, niff mag, noddy book, pop-up book.*

grub *n. Barse cheese.*

grubbery *n.* Almost extinct genus of thicket previously native to many roadside lay-bys and truck stops in the UK. These overgrown and often unremarkable looking plants could often yield massive quantities of discarded pornographic magazines, as well as free bottles of refreshing, bright orange, fizzy pop. See also *bongo bush, dredgerow.*

grubscrew *1. n.* An act of intercourse performed at work during a lunchbreak, perhaps in a store room or on a photocopier. *2. n.* A tiny, shrivelled *yang,* found on Egyptian mummies, Siberian nudists, Bobby Davro and the Rt Hon Jack Straw MP.

gruds *n.* Underpants. *'Do you want me to fetch you owt while I'm at the shops, Kanye?' 'Aye Kim. Can you get us another pair of Calvin Klein gruds? The elastic's gone in these.'*

gruffalo *1. n.* A monstrous, hairy character from the children's book of the same name. *2. n.* A particularly hirsute, nasty-looking *snatch.* A *wolf pussy. 3. n.* An unacceptable, unpleasant and misogynistic term which can be applied to a female who is blessed with a *lovely personality.* A *pig in knickers.*

gruffalo's hand *n.* Harsh and hairy *parts of shame.*

gruffle bag *n.* That strangely satisfying feeling of having *airy pillows* in your *undercrackers,* experienced just after you *cleave off* an *anal announcement.*

gruff nuts *n.* Them bits you can see hanging down between a woman's legs when she bends down to touch her toes. A somewhat less appetising-sounding version of the *reverse peach.*

Grumbelina *n. prop.* An actress who's had something inserted into her *chocolate starfish* and, for the benefit of the camera, is trying heroically to look sultry whilst enjoying it about as much as an ingrowing toenail.

grumbelows *n.* A retail purveyor of *seed catalogues.* A *bongo store.*

grumbilical cord *n.* The sturdy wire that linked one's satellite dish to one's Sky box, allowing ladies' *grotters* to appear on one's television screen.

grumble *1. n. rhym. slang.* The vagina, *quaynt, placket, Berkeley.* From grumble and grunt = Jeremy Hunt. *2. n.* Any form of *Frankie Vaughan* featuring *tits, arses and grumbles.*

grumble bee *n.* An indecisive chap circling the *niff mags* in a newsagents, unable to select a favourite *art pamphlet* as he flits from one to another.

grumbled *1. adj. Caught white-handed* mid-way through an act of *jazz-*fuelled onanism, when one's spouse returns unexpectedly early from a shopping expedition. *2. adj.* The unfortunate situation when one's mother/wife/cleaning lady stumbles across one's stash of *art pamphletry.* Caught in possession of pornography. *'Archbishop, I was cleaning your bedroom and I found 56 tons of hard core anal pornography on top of the wardrobe.' 'Oh, no! I've been grumbled!'*

grumblehound *n.* A creature whose nose, upon entering the newsagent, can be seen twitching in the direction of the top shelf.

grumble in the jungle *n. Rhythmic cliterature* found while taking the dog for a walk in the woods. The exotic fruits that are found under the *bongo bush. Grummer.*

grumbler *1. n.* A whinger or nay-sayer, if you will. *2. n.* A purveyor of *adult* entertainment. *'Today's birthdays: 1770 – Thomas Johann Seebeck, German physicist and discoverer of the thermoelectric effect; 1806 – Isambard Kingdom Brunel, British engineer, railway pioneer and steamship builder; 1926 – Hugh Marston Hefner, pyjama-clad US grumbler.'*

grumble sale *1. n.* A mass sell-off of second hand *gentleman's relaxation pamphletry* due to relocation, marriage or death. *2. n.* Any offer of cut-price merchandise in the window of a *monomanual requisites* retailer.

grumblestiltskin *n*. An ugly bloke who still somehow appears to get his fair share of *mackerel*, *eg*. Mick Hucknall, Ron Jeremy, Serge Gainsbourg.

grumble strip *n*. A well-pruned *minge* of the sort that would provide an attractive landing site for an experienced *bush pilot*.

grumbleweed *1. n*. A Syd Little lookalike, usually a *grumble video* director's brother, who manages to *poke* a selection of *cliterati* who would normally not even wipe their *arse* with him. *2. n*. A miraculous patch of undergrowth where discarded *rhythm books* can reliably be located. *3. n*. One who has masturbated so many times in a single session that he can no longer muster the strength to turn the pages of his *scud mag*; a fellow who has *wanked* himself into enfeeblement. *4. n*. A token *fluff tuft* on an otherwise clean-shaven porn starlet's *snatch*. A *clitler*. *5. n*. Any surviving member of the geriatric West Yorkshire-based comedy combo, specialising in gasmask-related songs and disturbingly accurate impressions of Sir Jimmy Savile. *6. n*. A puny little bloke who is reluctantly *up to his nuts* up some fat piece in a *wank mag*. *7. n*. Suspicious mould growth on the pages of discarded *Frankie Vaughanography*, probably not caused by natural elements.

grumbleweeds *n. pl*. The matted, sticky mess of *friar's weeds* which one is left with after surprising oneself with a startlingly copious payload of *spoff,* and which will require a good few yards of *shit scrape* to mop up.

grumbs *n*. The flakes of pastry-based confetti that accumulate throughout the day around the entrance to famous high-street bakeries. From Greggs + crumbs.

grummer *n. abbrev. Biff mags, art pamphlets*.

grummer holiday *n*. A voluntary or involuntary abstinence from online *scud*; at first painful, then engendering an increasing sense of liberation and euphoria. Followed by a catastrophic relapse into endless, sleepless hours of watching extreme *rimming, double fisting* and Venezuelan hardcore Dalek porn.

grump on *n*. Reluctant *wood*. An erection that has to be cajoled to tumesce. Prevalent amongst *jazz* actors, *slag night* male strippers and Peles.

grumpy pumpy *n. Carnival congress* when a fellow's *bag for life* is not *in the mood*, for reasons that he does not know and dares not ask. *Getting your oats* from a resentful conjugal partner.

grundle *n*. US. The *barse, tintis*.

grundleweeds *n*. The dispiriting amalgam of *clag,*

dangleberries and underpant fluff that forms on the *taint, grundle* or *biffin's bridge*.

grunge *1. n*. Style of rock music which emerged principally in the Seattle area during the 1980s, characterised by distorted guitars, quiet bits followed by loud bits, and the singer shooting himself through the mouth in mysterious circumstances. *2. n*. To put it crudely, a fat, hairy *twat*. *'Oi, Courtney. Put your fucking grunge away or I'll shoot meself.'*

grunt cake *n*. A *shit*.

grunter *n*. A much loved and well respected senior citizen who fought in two world wars *etc*., but who now cannot get off the sofa to pick the *Mail* up off the mat without grunting.

grunties *n. Jobbies*, faeces, *poo*.

grunting bunting *n*. Lavatory tissue. Also *shit scrape, arsewipe, bumwad. 'Throw us up another roll of grunting bunting, will you love?'*

grunts *n*. The type of *fugly boots* whose blurred Polaroid pictures appear on the readers' wives pages of *Tijuana bibles*.

G string, the *1. n*. The third string on a standard-tuned guitar. *2. n*. A notional geographical line running latitudinally south of the equator, bisecting both the magnetic and natural poles.

Guantanamo Bay *rhym. slang*. Said of one who prefers the company of "a few good men". Also *Colwyn, Whitley, Cardigan, Jessie J*.

guard dogs *n*. A pack of fierce *hounds* that accompany their attractive friend, preventing any bloke from trying his luck. *Tugs*.

guard fog *n*. A vicious *arse barker* unleashed in the hall immediately prior to going out, which hangs around waiting to catch an unsuspecting burglar and bite him on the nose.

guardsman's hat, fanny like a *sim*. Descriptive of an enormous black, hairy *snatch* that could, if one wasn't careful, slip down over one's eyes. Also, *busby berkeley*.

guard's parcel *n*. A present that turns out to be a disappointment. Derived from the advice given to those who live near a railway line frequented by freight trains, *ie*. Never pick up what looks like a discarded package near the tracks, it may contain the guard's excrement if he's been taken short. *'Pulling up Beattock, the guard needs a shite / But there's no bogs till Glasgow, much later tonight. / In time-honoured fashion he empties his arsehole / Into brown paper to make a guard's parcel.'* (from *The Shite Train* by WH Auden).

guard's van *n*. When *pulling a train*, the least desirable position in the queue. The last *pink carriage* into *fanny station*. *'Bagsy I'm not in the* *guard's van fellas.'*

guard's whistle *n.* A series of shrill blasts warning that the *brown train* will shortly be leaving *arse station*. *'I've got to dash, your holiness. That's the guard's whistle. I'll give you a bell some time in the week, yeah?'*

Guatemalan taco *n.* A sexual act which makes a *Cleveland steamer* or *Alabama hot pocket* seem positively *vanilla*.

gubbed *adj.* *Trousered, wankered, shitfaced, arseholed.*

gubbs *n.* *Thru'penny bits.*

guck *n. Muck, spod, gunk, mess, filthy concrete.*

gudders *n.* Excellent *qualifications*. From good + udders.

guff *v.* To *let one go, step on a frog.*

guff adder *n.* A large, brown and vile-smelling serpent that issues forth from one's *fissure*, hissing evilly at all and sundry. A bum *serpent* or *panaconda*.

guffaw *1. n.* A loud, spontaneous laugh, often heard after someone falls through a bar. *2. v.* To laugh forcefully. *3. n.* A sudden shout of amusement following a *Lionel*.

guff cloud *n.* The noxious, green *anusthetic* produced by *dropping one's hat. Carbon dibaxide.*

guff grenade *n.* A handful of *hot fog*, grabbed from the gusset area and lobbed over-arm in the direction of an enemy combatant.

guffnor, the *n.* That member of the household or workplace who produces the most *carbon dibaxide* and generally just stinks the place out. *'Who's the guffnor? I said, who's the fackin' guffnor?' 'You are, Mr Rees-Mogg. You're the guffnor.'*

guff-prone *adj.* Not confined to government ministers, the propensity to *blow off* loudly and often in public. *'Speaking to BBC news presenter Clive Myrie – who he repeatedly addressed as 'Sir Trevor' – guff-prone Education secretary Gavin Williamson last night apologised for mistaking Maro Itoje for Marcus Rashford.'*

guided muscle *n.* The *veiny bang stick.*

guide dog *n.* Leading a man round the shops on a Saturday afternoon, a woman who is so ugly that she calls into question his powers of visual acuity.

guide dogging *n.* The act of *dogging*, but involving a car with tinted windows, so it's difficult to *see it going in.*

guilt chip *n.* The single, token French fry left by a *salad dodger* after they have just troughed their way through three large Big Mac Meals.

guiltimatum *n.* An offer a chap can't refuse, whereby he is coerced by his significant other into shopping for children's shoes, attending a tedious family gathering or cleaning out the drains by being reminded of previous misjudgements he may have committed in the course of his relationship. *'Eeh. I never thought I'd see Chris de Burgh going round Ikea on a Bank Holiday Monday.' 'Yeah, apparently his missus gave him a guiltimatum when she caught him fucking the nanny.'*

guilt tip *n.* Any slightly over-the-top gratuity left at a restaurant or hotel following an un-admitted incident, for example a micturated hotel bed, *spew*-blocked basin, badly *zuffled* curtain or blocked *shitter.*

guilty pleasure *1. n.* In disc jockey *hyperbole*, a cheesy record that outwardly cool people can't help liking in spite of their better judgement. A floor-filler. *2. n.* An autoerotic act of sordid *personal delight.* A *sock-filler.*

Guinness elbow *n. medic.* Repetitive strain injury which principally afflicts keen imbibers of the popular Irish stout. *'What's afflicting you there, Michael?' 'Sure it's nothing. Just a wee touch of the old Guinness elbow, Patrick. Well, that and my usual alcohol-induced cirrhosis of the fecking liver.'*

Guinness pig *n.* Sexist terminology referring to an unattractive *bit of crack pulled* after a heavy night knocking back the popular altruistic Irish stout.

Guinness rope *n.* A length of dense *cable* which blocks the *pan* after a heavy feed of the black stuff. *'It takes 119 seconds to lay the perfect length of Guinness rope.'*

guinnets *n.* Jet black *dangleberries* that cling to the *arse* after a night drinking the famed stout. *Buoys from the black stuff.*

gullet mullet *n.* One of them *shitty* beards where the bit on the wearer's neck is all long and straggly.

Gumby theatre *n.* Any vexatious online political debate, perhaps on the subject of Brexit.

gumgam style *n. Horatio* performed following the considerate removal of the false teeth, possibly accompanied by up-tempo music.

gummy mix, drop one's *euph.* To accidentally do a little bit of inadvertent *shopping*, for example while out shopping.

gummy party *n.* A *nosh sesh* involving two or more toothless crones and a randy *bingo wing commander*, such as Wayne R(the remainder of this entry has been removed on legal advice)ooney.

gums around me plums, get your *exclam.* An irresistible romantic overture made by a male to a female.

gum shot *n.* The climactic finale of *granny horatio* caught on camera.

gun front *1. exclam. milit.* Term used by tank commanders when moving their vehicles' weapons into the forward elevated position prior to firing. *2. phr. milit.* Term used by squaddies when they *pitch a tent.*

gunge-tank *1. n.* Dismal, lowest common denominator television entertainment that Noel Edmonds considered the sort of thing that the plebs would lap up. And he wasn't far wrong, to be fair. *2. n.* A person who enjoys the romantic attentions of numerous men at more or less the same time.

gunghover *adj.* Excessively eager to resume drinking upon waking up after a heavy night on the *loony juice.*

gunning *n.* In a prison or similar secure facility, the light-hearted act of *cuffing the suspect* through the bars of one's cell at a passer-by. As seen in *Louis Theroux's Miami Mega Jail* and *The Silence of the Lambs.* *'What are you doing there, Lukewarm?' 'I'm just gunning at Mr Barraclough, Fletch.'*

gun slinger *n.* In a public lavatory environment, a *sharp-shooter* who manages to enter a neighbouring cubicle, empty his *chamber* and leave the saloon before you've managed to pull anything out of your *back holster,* let alone take aim or fire.

guns of Navarone *n.* Whoppers, tits, fleshbombs, milky swingers.

gunt *n. Can.* The *fupa, poond* or *blubber beret.*

Guntchester *n. prop.* A town full of fat *birds.* Also *Guntchester Rovers*: A group of fat women walking dogs; *Guntchester United*: Chubby *bints* playing football *etc.*

guntrification *n.* When a town or suburb gets taken over by over-sized, pie-snuffling *salad dodgers.*

guntstruck *n.* Infatuated with a *welly tubby. Stuck in orbit.*

gurgler *n.* The toilet, *shite pipe,* drain. *'Have you got a coat hanger? Only I was spewin' up last night and I've only gone and coughed me fuckin' falsies down the gurgler.'*

gurk *1. v.* To burp. *2. v. Aus.* To *guff.*

gurkha's sword *n.* A *hard-on* which has to be used before it can be put away. From the not necessarily true belief that a member of the tough Nepalese regiment must draw blood with his kukri before he is allowed to return it to its sheath.

gurning chimp *n.* A particularly expressive *fanny.*

gurniture *n.* Orthodontic bracery.

gurnturd *n.* A troublesome and stubborn *digestive transit,* the successful passing of which necessitates the pulling of a Popeye-style grimace. From the comedy facial gymnastics practised by toothless West Cumbrian drunks sticking their heads through horsecollars, as seen in endless patronising "local colour" pieces on *Nationwide*

back in the 1970s, and probably now on *The One Show,* if anyone ever watches it.

guru Palm and the five pillars of wisdom *n. Madam Palm and her five lovely daughters.* A *wanking spanner, cunt scratcher.*

gusher *n.* A dirty *Norris's* orgasmatromical *parts of shame* that would daunt Red Adair himself.

gusset *1. n.* The bottom of the *hoggers* area of a woman, the *fairy hammock's drip tray. 2. n. coll.* Flange, totty, fanny, blart. *'Any gusset in tonight, landlord?' 'Aye, plenty gusset.'*

gusset burger *n.* A meaty *camel's toe.*

gusset graze *n. medic.* The friction burn on the side of one's *old man* incurred when administering *a bit of the other* to an obliging young lady while tenderly riving her nethergarmentry to one side.

gusset icing *n.* The decorative crust which has fallen off a *bird's clown's pie,* giving her a *gusset like a fish fryer's cuff. Fanny batter, milp powder.*

gusset monkey *n.* A straggly *biffer* that on first glance looks like a freshly awoken marmoset with its tongue sticking out.

gusset nuzzler *n.* A *fanny nosher,* a *lady golfer,* a *lesbian.*

gusset pianist *n. Invisible banjo* player. *'I've heard she plays the gusset piano.'*

gusset ripple *1. n.* Corrugated indentations left in a pair of *scads* after the owner has been on the receiving end of a thorough *fingering. 2. n.* Unsuccessful chocolate bar of the 1970s.

gusset shot *n.* The thrilling glimpse of a young lady's *drip tray* with which an observant fellow is occasionally rewarded when watching *birds* dismounting from their bicycles. Perhaps while hiding in the bushes outside the nurses' home or a hall of residence with a pair of night vision binoculars. A *sneaky peek.*

gusset sugar *n.* Tooth-rotting *muffdruff. Batter bits.*

gusset typist *n.* A *bean flicker,* female *merchant, gusset piano virtuoso, touch typist.*

gustatory athlete *n.* One who sprints past the salad. Coined by the commentators on nightmarish US TV show *Gluttonbowl* to describe the parade of disgusting, *big-boned* inbreds taking part in their vile, albeit extremely entertaining, eating competition.

Gustaves *n.* Large breasts; literally "eye-fulls". Named after the architect of the famous Parisian pylon. *'Viewer numbers are falling. We've got to get Kendra under that waterfall with her Gustaves out... now!'*

gustbin *n.* A rather charming term used to describe the nether regions of a rather large lady.

gusto *1. n.* Enjoyment and enthusiasm in doing

something. *2. n.* Enjoyment and enthusiasm in doing something loud and smelly out of your *bum*.

gut beret *n.* Fat hat, as worn by a chap performing *cumulonimbus* on a *roll model*.

gutbutt *n.* Affectionate epithet for an extremely obese person, the folds of stomach hanging down out of their t-shirt, resembling nothing so much as a pair of extra, frontal *mudflaps*. Also *fruttocks*.

gutfucker II *n.* A dish comprising of four whole roasted beetroot (skinned), four whole black puddings (boiled, not fried), and four boiled duck eggs served on a bed of baked beans. Named after the effect this has on one's digestive function the following day.

gut full of arms and legs *euph.* Pregnancy. *'Our most excellent lady and mistress queen Jane, our noble and godly King Henry the Eighth's much beloved wife, hath conceived and hath a gut full of arms and legs.'*

gut grunt *n.* A burbulent rumbling in the viscera, or any subsequent anal emission.

gut instinct *n.* The timely sixth sense which enables a man to accurately predict that something bad is about to happen. *'My gut instinct is telling me it's time to open the window, love.'*

gut-smashing *n.* The saucy act of *fisting* someone up to the elbow, and beyond. *'Cor, the other day I was online watching one bird give another bird a right gut-smashing. And apparently that is inappropriate behaviour for the Cabinet Office, so I now need to start claiming Jobseeker's Allowance, please. Which forms do I need to fill in?'*

gut soup *n.* A bowl filled with particularly runny, steaming *foulage*.

gut spuds *n.* Spheroid *bum shrapnel*. *'Sorry mam. I dropped my gummy mix when I was out shopping so there's a few gut spuds in me kegs.'*

gutted hamster *n.* A *stamped bat*.

gutter butter *n.* The off-white stain of *blip* found in the *fairy hammock* of a *tart's applecatchers*.

gutter clutter *n.* Human detritus that collects at the side of the road in any large English town from midnight onwards on most Friday and Saturday nights, *eg.* A woman sat on the kerb with a broken shoe and her head in her hands, or a shirtless middle-aged man lying face down in pool of sick. *'It's 2am in Nottingham town centre, and Alpha Patrol are out tidying up the gutter clutter.'*

gutters *n.* An unattractive female. *'Have you seen the bird on page 3 today? Jesus Christ, what a fucking gutters.'*

gutter's shed *1. n.* A dockside building where fish are filleted. *2. n.* A particularly mingsome *minge*.

3. n. A *stabbin' cabin*.

gut the turkey *v.* To *tickle* the missus's *giblets*. To *firkyfoodle, feed the pony*.

guttocks *n.* The rolls of fat that obese women get on their stomachs which, when turned through 90°, look remarkably like their *arse. Fruttocks*.

gutton *n.* The shirt button that is subjected to the greatest level of strain, usually the third one up.

guybuprofen gel *n.* Warm, sticky balm copiously applied to the *breadknife's* lower back or *tits* in order to relieve stiffness.

guy dye *n.* Technique by which a fellow achieves a subtly psychedelic pattern on the front of his T-shirt over the course of a relaxing Sunday afternoon.

guyphone *n.* A young man's electronic communications device that is used solely for viewing *grot* and football. *'I've found his Holiness's guyphone in the Apostolic Palace khazi. Will you take it to him for me, Cardinal?' 'How do you know it belongs to the Holy Father, Bishop?' 'Liverpool FC and mature shaven havens?' 'Okay, I'll drop it off at his office.'*

guyrope *n.* The flap of skin connecting the *flysheet* to the *tentpole*. The *banjo, Tarzan cord*.

guzunda *n.* A potty or *pisspot*.

gwank *n.* A girly *wank*. A niftily fingered bout of boogie-woogie on the *gusset piano*.

Gwendolen *n. prop.* A superficially alluring bird who is packing a little bit extra in the *nest* department. A *rotten peach*. Named after the bar-room *bobby dazzler* inadvertently acquired by Crocodile Dundee in that film he done. A *flipper, shim, ladyboy, tiptop* or *trolley dolly*.

gwibble *n.* A dribbly, underpowered ejaculation; opposite of a *pwa*.

GWOAT/gwoat *1. acronym.* Greatest Woman Of All Time. *2. acronym.* Greatest Wanker Of All Time.

gymbo *n.* Those conniving, make-up-encrusted, marriage-wrecking *liebfraumilfs* who are apparently frequently to be found lurking in posh health and racquet clubs, where they do little or no training in case the perspiration ruins their *warpaint*. From gym + bimbo.

gym buddah *n.* An overweight woman in sportswear, with *overblaaters* and a huge *gunt*.

gymcrack *1. adj.* Shoddy, badly constructed. Like this spelling of the word "gimcrack". *2. n. medic.* Affliction affecting the nether regions of ladies who exercise vigorously while wearing tight-fitting clothing made from synthetic materials. The affected area may appear reddened and inflamed due to abrasion.

gymsniff *n. prop.* A fellow who attends the gym and who prefers to use the apparatus directly after sweaty young women in order to sniff the seat.

gynaecolumnist *n.* Any female journalist who uses her newspaper column to bang on about tampons and stuff.

gynaesty *n.* A dynastic succession of *cunts* from the same family who play a prominent role in film, entertainment, politics or another field.

gyno-rod *n.* Oversized plunger that could thoroughly rearrange a woman's plumbing. A *cock as long as a women's game of pool, bird scarer, bride frightener, kidney disturber, moundstretcher.*

gypsy clit *n.* A damned elusive *clematis*. One which, despite a fellow's best efforts to find it, never seems to be in the same place two nights running. A *Flying Dutchman in a boat, scarlet pimpernel.*

gypsy's curse *n.* The loss of *wood* before insertion, as a result of failing to buy some pegs at some point in the past 20 years.

gypsy's dog, like a *sim.* Descriptive of someone who looks like he could do with a square meal.

'Feargal Sharky? He's like a gypsy's dog, him. All ribs and bollocks.'

gypsy's eyelash *n.* The rogue *clockspring* in the *hog's eye* that causes the *piss* to go everywhere but in the *bog*. Common cause of *pan smile* or *Queen Mum's grin.*

gypsy's kiss *rhym. slang. Piss.* Usually abbreviated to gypsy's. *'Keep a look out for icebergs, will you? I'm just off below decks for a gypsy's.'*

gypsy week *n.* A *bird's* time of the month. *'DON JOHN: Marry, Borachio. How fared thee last night behind the tavern with thy wanton wench Margaret? Did'st thou fill thy boots? BORACHIO: I'faith, I did not the dirty deed. For by my troth, 'twas gipsy week. DON JOHN: Gipsy week, sayest thou? Wherefore is it called thus, sirra? BORACHIO: I'll vouchsafe you for wherefore 'tis called thus, my liege, for when I didst put my hand down her pants, I didst get my palm red.'* (from *Much Ado About Wanking* by William Shakespeare).

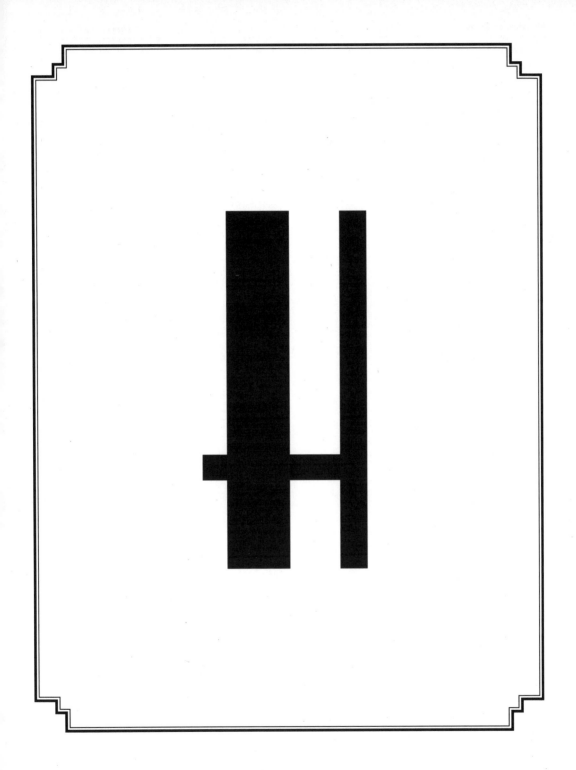

Haarlem tripwire *n.* An exceptionally loud, percussive blast on the *brass trumpet,* reminiscent of the sound of a Dutchman in clogs falling down the stairs.

habeas porcus *n.* Latin legal term, which literally means *getting off* with the fattest *bird* in the pub.

haberdashers' handshake *n.* A *banjo string* duet.

habergashery *n.* The *bling*-bedecked stall on the market that is frequented by Essex girls who are looking to *bejazzle* their *vajayjays.*

hackground *n.* A carefully arranged Skype backdrop featuring bookshelves and guitars, with all your *crap* shoved to the sides and out of shot.

Hackney air show *n.* The nightly, and often daily, helicopter aerobatic display performed by the *rozzers* as they hunt for burglars, rapists and terrorists in the eponymous metropolitan garden village.

Hackney bunting *n.* Police crime scene cordon tape, which is commonly used to decorate the streets of the delightful London borough.

Hackney diamonds *n.* Broken glass. Coined by local artist Jason Shulman and used as an LP title by grizzled octogenarian riffers the Rolling Stones in 2023.

hack off a lump *v.* To *crimp off a length.* To defeculate.

haddock pastie *n.* Hairy pie, captain's pie, Grimsby meal.

Hadley job *n.* An act of *horatio* during which the *noshatrix* handles your *tassel* in the foppish, effete manner that the lead singer of *Spandau Ballet* used to handle his microphone.

had more sausage than a fat German butcher, she's *exclam.* Said of a *bird* who's had *more cocks than Davy Crockett's rifle, had more loads than Dot Cotton's washing machine, had more men up her than the Statue of Liberty etc.*

had the dick *exclam.* Descriptive of something which is broken beyond repair. '"What-ho, Jeeves," I exclaimed. "Fetch the Frazer-Nash round to the front door, there's a good chap. I feel like taking a spin." "I'm afraid that may not be possible, Sir," he replied. "Your Aunt Millicent drove it to Ascot and back with the handbrake on, and I fear it has had the dick."' (from *For Fuck's Sake, Jeeves!* by PG Wodehouse).

haemogobbling *n.* Dining at the Y when the house wine is *moon juice.*

haemogoblin *n.* A gentleman who has a *fish supper* at the *all-night sushi bar,* despite the fact that it is closed for redecoration.

hag *n.* An ugly woman, *boiler, boot, steg, swamp donkey, ditch pig.*

hag do *n.* Linguistically speaking, a cross between a hen night and a stag do. Either way, it's a nightmarish booze-fuelled gathering of people you would rather not *have it off* with.

haggis *1. n.* Unappetising object consisting of meat and oats stuffed into a veiny skin bag. *2. n.* Unappetising object consisting of meat and oats stuffed into a veiny skin bag.

haggis rag *n.* A small piece of fabric, esp. towelling, used for wiping clean or drying the *haggis* after a bout of exercise.

hagnetism *n.* The mysterious, invisible force that makes certain men attract only ladies with *lovely personalities.*

hagover *n.* Saturday morning penile headache caused by an excess of s*x on Friday night. *'I knew I shouldn't of fucked that last slapper in the Red Lion. I've woke up with terrible hagover. Anyway, today's recipe is braised leg of mutton with caper sauce.'*

hag reflex *n.* Involuntary early morning retching caused by looking across at the lady occupying your bed and realising that what looked like Dannii Minogue last night now, in the cold light of day, looks more like Danny La Rue. And not in a good way.

Hagrid or Hermione? *exclam. interrog.* An inquiry as to whether a particular young lady possesses an unkempt, hirsute vagina, or a tidy, neatly clipped one. Named after the contrastingly haired characters out of *Harry Potter. 'I say, mister Roy. Mate of mine reckons he's seen a photo of Germaine Greer's cunt on the internet.' 'Really Basil? Was it a Hagrid or a Hermione?' 'Hagrid. Very much so, he said. Like a fucking collie's chest, it was apparently. Ha-ha! Boom! Boom!'*

Hagrid's hairbrush *n.* Term used to describe a particularly wild and unkempt *growler.* Also *fanny like a dockyard cat, Percy Thrower's lawn, Terry Waite's allotment, welder's shoelaces, Max Clifford's hedge.*

hail damage *n.* The vile, unsightly, dimpled skin found on the thighs of middle-aged celebrity women and brought to the world's attention by gleeful paparazzi. Cellulite.

hairache *n.* The mother of all hangovers.

hair across his arse *phr.* Descriptive of someone who has a permanent *cob on. 'That Antonio Conte always looks so fucking miserable. It's like he's had a hair across his arse for the last ten years.'*

hairdryer treatment, the *1. n.* A practice favoured by certain purple-faced football managers, *viz.* Shouting at close quarters to explain to a professional footballer where they might be able to improve their game. 2. *n. Farting* in someone's face at close quarters.

hair grip *n.* The distinctly uncomfortable sensation of getting a bit of *fusewire* tightly entangled under one's *fiveskin* and around the brim of the *farmer's hat*. A *cheese cutter* or *cock harp*.

hairigami *n.* The ancient art of folding a few extra-long strands of hair from round the sides and back of a *baaldy's noggin* into a convincing *simulacrum* of a coiffure. *'That's a magnificent bit of hairigami you have there, Mr President.' 'Door!'*

hairline crack *1. n.* A minor structural defect found in, for example, a motorway flyover or aircraft wing. *2. n.* A *minge* that has been shaved within an inch of its life.

hair of the dogging *n.* Any attempt to relieve residual feelings of guilt felt by an habitual car park *perv* who assuages his angst by going out and doing it again the next day. *'Where are you off to, Stan?' 'Just popping out for some hair of the dogging, love.'*

hair of the pig *n.* A full English breakfast or bacon sandwich that blocks the arteries and thus restores the humours the morning after a night of *heavy refreshment*.

hair trousers, to be wearing *v.* To be naked from the waist down.

hairy axe wound *n.* Vertical *gash*. The *mingepiece, quim, cock socket*.

hairy bath *n.* A *shag*. *'Did you get a noshing off that bird behind Lidl, then?' 'No, she'd got her braces in so she just gave me cock a hairy bath.'*

hairy beanbags *n.* Plumped-up, pink 1970s-style seating provided within the underpants for the exclusive use of *Kojak, etc.* Testicles. *John Wayne's hairy saddlebags*.

hairy brain *n. medic.* The small wrinkled organ, approximately the size of two plums, that governs a gentleman's thought processes. Also *hanging brain*.

hairy Champion *n.* An impressive *stench hammer* that should be on the Music Hall stage. Opposite of a *Little Titch*. One for the teenagers there.

hairy cheque book *n. Gash card, furry purse*.

hairy cod mother *n.* A heavily *battered fish supper*.

hairy conkers *n. Knackers, clockweights*.

hairy cornflake *1. n.* An affectionate name for former *shit* DJ Dave Lee Travis, coined and used exclusively by himself before...well, you know. *2. n.* Affectionate name for a small, dried crust of *poo* stuck firmly to the *arsecress*. *3. n.* An hirsute breakfast cereal that was expensively launched by Kellog's in 1976, but inexplicably failed to find favour with the public.

hairy cup *n. Hairy goblet, furry hoop*.

hairy doughnut *n.* An occasionally jam-filled confection, often dusted with *gusset sugar*.

hairy egg *n.* A testicle. *'What's up, Evel?' 'I've only gone and cracked me hairy eggs on the handlebars again.'*

hairy goblet *n. Hairy cup, front bottom, bodily treasure, parts of shame*.

hairy handshake *n.* A firm five-fingered greeting that costs £10 from a woman behind a skip, following which there are *no hard feelings*.

hairy harmonica *n.* Any blown or sucked *organ* that can be played without using the hands, producing a sequence of rising tones.

hairy heroes *n.* The *bollocks, clockweights, knackers;* the *gonk-faced Mother Teresa sisters* or *McSquirter twins*.

hairy knickers *n.* Descriptive of that situation when a lady removes her *farting crackers* and her thoroughly unruly *minge* makes it appear that she has yet to do so. A wall-to-wall carpeted *barber's floor,* a *Terry Waite's allotment*. An extreme *biffer* and *thighbrows* combination.

hairylea triangle *n.* A teatime treat that is not always easy to open and occasionally somewhat cheesy.

hairy mango and midge *n. Ladyparts. 'I shit you not. Freeze the frame and just as she crosses her legs you can definitely see her hairy mango and midge.'* (Barry Norman, *Film '92*).

hairy mits *rhym. slang.* Tits. *'Look at the hairy mits on that! I could do her through a hedge backwards. Anyway, back to the matter in hand. We are gathered here today to join these two people in holy matrimony.'*

hairy muff *exclam.* A light-hearted alternative to saying "fair enough", used by those life-and-soul-of-the-party types who make a point of asking "anyone fuck offy?".

hairy pants *n.* See *hairy knickers*.

hairy pie *n.* A *fur burger*.

hairy pint *n.* An unsuspecting person's alcoholic beverage that has been discreetly spiked with a small quantity of *pubes* for the amusement of onlookers.

hairy raisins *n. Hunchback spiders,* petite *chimpanzees' elbows*.

hairy saddlebags *1. n. Knackers 2. n. Pissflaps*. No confusion happening there, then.

hairy scallops *n. Bearded clams, mungo jerrys*.

hairy swingers *n.* Hirsute *man-sacks* containing the *hairy conkers*.

hairy toffee *n. Dangleberries, kling-ons,*

miniature heroes.

hairy tree *1. n.* A legendary, bewhiskered sapling in Girvan, Scotland, supposedly planted by erstwhile troglodyte cannibal Sawney Bean's daughter. Now the subject of an epic Holy Grail-style quest by former Ipswich Town, Coventry and Scotland forward Alan Brazil. See also *stumpy tower. 2. n.* A chap's moss-covered *twig and berries. 'Fancy a wee climb up the hairy tree, Morag? Thought not.'*

hairy violets *1. n.* Wildflowers of the genus *Viola*, often found on chalk downlands. *2. n.* Big hairy *gonads*, often found popping out of excessively tight swimming trunks.

hairy window *n.* That semi-translucent panel in the front portion of a pair of ladies' *scads*, occasionally to be glimpsed in the *funderwear* pages of your mam's catalogue, through which it is just possible to make out her *gorilla salad*, though not her *dangly ham.*

hairy wink *n.* A friendly twinkle of encouragement vouchsafed by a lady's *nether eye* to a novitiate *cumulonimbalist. 'A nun gave me the hairy wink / I got meself some close-up pink / What would the Holy Father think? / When I'm cleaning windows.'* (lyrics to *The Windowcleaner* by George Formby).

half a car battery *euph.* Descriptive of a place such as Skelmersdale which "has no positive side". No offence to Skelmersdale, obviously.

half a crown thru'penny bit *sim.* Pre-decimal version of *five pee fifty pee*, used to describe the rapid flexing of the *nipsy* during moments of severe anxiety. *Bin lid penny.*

half a jaffa *n.* That which may be glimpsed in the crotch area of a young lady wearing tight jeans. *Twix lips, beetle bonnet.*

half a lemon *n.* A paradoxical form of *lady golfer* who only fancies women who look like blokes.

half a nasty *n.* A *podge-on, dobber, grump on.*

half a spider *n. Feral Flynn*-style upper lip topiary of the type sported by the males of the urban underclass. A *joyrider's moustache* or *bum fluff wanker's badge.*

half a teacake *n.* Not quite a *fatty*, but definitely the beginings of an erection. The state you would like your *fruitbowl* to be in when a new paramour sees it for the first time.

half a wank *euph.* Any pointless task or activity. Something that's not worth doing, *eg.* Going for "a couple of pints".

half babies *n. Spuff, spingler, sprodd, spoddle, heir gel.*

half blood prince *1. n.* A chap's *member* after he's *had it off* with a woman during *rag week*. A less-than-rigid *barber's pole. 2. n.* A *cock* that is so floppy it would struggle to get into a *wizard's sleeve.*

half caff *n.* The strength of a fellow's *spooch* immediately post-vasectomy, *ie.* Before he's *crashed his yoghurt truck* the requisite twenty times to ensure he's completely *decaff.*

half-eaten Bison *n.* A *kebab* that has been exceedingly *badly packed.* A *fanny like the bottom of a ratcatcher's mallet.*

half Elvis, to do a *v.* To fall asleep, but not quite die, while having a *shit* on the toilet. Usually done by one in an advanced state of *refreshment.*

half-fat man-bat *n.* A semi-tumescent *gentleman sausage.*

half-glazed *1. adj.* Descriptive of a type of door. *2. adj.* Six pints in. The state Oliver Reed would be in on a chatshow and you'd say "He looks pretty sober tonight, to be fair."

half leapfrog *n. Having it off* in the *doggie position, setting the video.*

half marathon *1. n.* A challenging distance to run, requiring training and discipline; 13.1 miles. *2. n.* The average distance to a Wetherspoons pub toilet.

half-moons *n.* The type of super-short shorts that young ladies sport these days, causing thousands of vicars to cycle into hedges.

half nelson *1. n.* A grappling hold practised by both wrestlers and wrestlees. *2. n.* An unfinished act of *horatio.*

Halfords hero *n.* Motorist behind the wheel of a *noughtomobile*, who has kitted out his bottom-of-the-range hatchback with several hundred-weight of expensive tat, including alloy wheels, dump valves, ludicrous spoilers, an extremely loud stereo and an exhaust pipe like a fucking coal scuttle.

half rice half chips *adj.* Descriptive of a *switch hitter, alloy welder* or *happy shopper.* One who *drinks from both taps* or *bowls from both ends. AC/DC.*

half-roller *n.* A *sit-down toilet adventure* so messy that it will require the expenditure of at least half a roll of *shit tickets* to render one's *balloon knot* even vaguely acceptable in polite company. *'That left-over phal from last Friday is giving me big problems. I reckon it's at least a half-roller, but while you are waiting here's Moira with the news.'*

half shut knife *euph.* The characteristic stooping stance adopted by a man with an involuntary erection who has to walk across a room, *eg.* Michael Parkinson getting up to welcome a sultry young Helen Mirren onto his chat show in 1975 or Michael Parkinson getting up to welcome a sultry old Helen Mirren onto his chatshow in 2007.

half term rattle *n.* The ridiculously loud noise

one's wine-bottle-filled glass recycling bin makes after a week at home with the kids. It is possible to somewhat ease the embarrassment by shouting "We've sure eaten lots of jam just recently" to one's judgey neighbours while manoevering it down the drive.

half time, change ends! *exclam.* A humorous utterance when one does a *fart* closely followed by a burp, or *vice versa* for that matter.

half time talk *n.* In a *spitroast grumble flick*, the token dialogue which occurs between the two leading men while they change ends, eat orange segments *etc*.

halfturbating *n.* Absentmindedly rubbing the *old chap*, either under or over one's tracksuit bottoms, while watching or doing something completely unrelated.

halibut handshake *1. n.* A *fistful of mackerel, feeding the pony.* *2. n.* Traditional acknowledgement when two Billingsgate Market traders strike a deal over a box of flatfish.

halibutosis *n. medic.* A condition often affecting those who *quaff at the furry cup.*

Hallowe'en cake, face like a *sim.* Said of an aesthetically unconventional person. *'He's won seven Tony awards, three Grammy awards, one Oscar, fourteen Ivor Novello awards, seven Olivier awards and a Golden Globe. He's a giant of British musical theatre and he's got a face like a Hallowe'en cake. Put your hands together and give a rousing Over the Rainbow welcome to Andrew Lloyd Webber.'*

Halloween pumpkins *euph.* Bright orange luminous faces with teeth missing, seen in the clubs of Botchergate, Carlisle after midnight.

halopecia *n. medic.* Baldness caused by over-use of the XBox headset.

halved my BMI, I just *phr.* Polite way of announcing to dinner party guests that your prolonged absence from the table was due to the fact that you have just unloaded an humungous *digestive transit. Drop a dress size.*

ham and mustard gas *n.* Accurate description of an eye-watering act of *trouser trumpetry.*

hamazon, like going up the *sim.* A reference to paddling one's *skin boat* on a voyage of discovery up a particularly overgrown and swampy *messtuary*, which is possibly infested with leeches, fire ants and them really long millipedes.

ham bucket *n.* A *welly top.*

hamburger *n.* Of the female anatomy, that which can be seen in a *hamburger shot.* Something that really ought to have a *dill* stuck into it.

hamburger hill *n.* The large tor that frequently casts *stoat valley* into shadow on ladies of advancing years. A *gunt, fupa, poond.*

hamburger shot *n.* A rear view in a *scud mag* displaying a lady's *vertical bacon sandwich*, possibly with cheese. A *reverse peach, fillet-o-fish.*

ham clam *n.* A sturdily constructed yet juicy *snapper.* More compact than a *ham bucket.*

ham-fisted *euph.* Mid-wank. *'My mum came in and caught me ham-fisted the other night. The poor cow didn't know where to look.'*

ham-fisting *n. Gut-smashing*, but done inelegantly or inexpertly, if you can imagine such a thing.

ham flower *n.* The *anus. Analweiss, brown daisy.* That which is cultivated by an *uphill gardener.*

ham howitzer *n.* A *lamb cannon, beef blunderbuss, spam magnum.* Basically, any sort of meat + any sort of firearm.

Hamish blue *n.* Ripe, azure-tinted *knob cheese*, found north of the border and south of the sporran.

hamlet *n.* A half-hearted grade of erection, which can be found somewhere mid-way between a *flop on* and a *diamond cutter* on the universal scale of penile harditude. "2B or not 2B".

hammerfat *1. n.* The typeface familiar to pasty-faced, bedroom-bound players of old-fashioned Atari video games. *2. n. Wanked*-up *joff, jaff, spiff, spaff, spoff, spangle, spungle* or *spingle.* Something else that will be familiar to pasty-faced, bedroom-bound players of old-fashioned Atari video games.

hammer of the spods, the *n.* Adopting a manly, two-handed approach while beating out a length of *pink steel* on the scrotal anvil.

hammock *n.* Panty liner, *jam rag, sanitary towel, fanny napkin.*

Hammond's hat *n.* A *helmet* covered in *skidmarks.*

ham-on-ham *n.* Descriptive of the delightful sight of two ladies going at it *hammer and tongues. Gammon and pineapple.*

hampax *n.* The absorbent lining in the bottom of a packet of pork chops.

Hampstead grief *n.* The plight of a chap who *knows what's in his flowerbeds* who gets mugged by a scoundrel masquerading as a fellow *bottery barn* habitué.

Hampstead tube *1. n.* On the London Underground, the original nickname given to the western branch of the Northern Line, before the Northern Line became the Northern Line. *2. n.* The rectum. *'And you say you slipped whilst wearing a loose-fitting dressing gown, and that is how this milk bottle became lodged up your Hampstead tube, Mr P(name of 1970s children's television presenter removed following legal advice)?'*

Hampton *rhym. slang. Dick.* From Hampton

Weenis, a village in Essex with all wiggly blue veins up the side.

ham salad *n.* An unlikely sounding, yet ingenious, home-made masturbatory aid, consisting of a hollowed-out cucumber lined with ham and placed in the microwave prior to use. Even better, it counts as one of your five-a-day.

ham shank *rhym. slang.* A *Barclays, J Arthur, Max Planck*.

hamshank redemption *n.* A discreet *Sherman* enjoyed while desperately trying not to waken up one's cellmate.

ham slices *n.* Peeling the *chicken skin handbag* away from the inner leg on a particularly hot day. From the similarity to the process of peeling apart the layers of sweaty meat when opening a packet of Bernard Matthews Honey Roast Ham. *Bagpeel.*

hamsome *adj.* Porky. Used in the same way as *bubbly,* jolly or morbidly obese. *'My, that James Corden is a hamsome fellow, isn't he?'*

hamster's mouthful *n.* A man's *ball-sack camel's toe,* caused by comedically tight trousers, as demonstrated by Jamie Redknapp on *Sky Sports Super Sunday. 'Redknapp's looking very uncomfortable in the final third, Andy.' 'Yes Martin. What a hamster's mouthful. Take a bow, son.'*

Hancock's half hour *n.* A handy window in a fellow's busy work schedule that provides the opportunity for a quick *knee-trembler* with a colleague. See also *Matt finish.*

handbrake *1. n.* An unwanted and inexplicable thought or image that pops into a fellow's mind, bringing a sudden stop to an act of *self pollution, eg.* His late grandmother looking at him and tutting, his dead budgie lying on the bottom of its cage, the bit of the Zapruder footage where Kennedy's brains fall out the side of his head and his cranium goes skidding across the top of his car's boot, a puce-faced, sweating Buster Bloodvessel running on the spot in a diving suit on *Top of the Pops etc. 2. n.* That which hampers one's progress, slows one down and prevents one enjoying oneself. *'I'd love to stay out a bit later, lads, but the handbrake's had a hard day watching Jeremy Kyle and eating Hobnobs so she's feeling tired and wants to go home.'*

handbrake *n.* The *bag for life.*

hand brandy *n.* Like a *hand shandy* but with a higher abv.

hand Chandon *n.* A high-falutin' *crank* off a posh girl, who *pops your cork* with her thumbs under the *brim* of your *lid.*

hand Chandon *n.* A *wank* that ends in a style reminiscent of a Formula 1 Grand Prix podium

celebration, with *jizz* going all over your mechanics.

hand cock's half hour *n.* "Thirty minutes? That's very nearly an armful."

hand crank *n.* A manual means of imparting reciprocating motion to a shaft.

hand cuddle *n. Pulling a pint on the piss pump. 'I'm feeling a bit lonely, mum. I'm just nipping upstairs for a hand cuddle.'*

Hande hoch! *exclam.* The raising of an arm to 90 degrees in order to lean on the toilet wall, thus facilitating accurate targeting of the *drop zone.* See also *Dutch tilt.*

hand fanny-sizer *n.* Traditional method of determining the dimensions and pliancy of a prospective *enamorata's cludgepiece* by the insertion of the terminal portion of the human forelimb.

handful of sprats *n. 1950s.* A fistful of *fish fingers, rummage in the captain's pocket.*

hand grenade *1. n.* A palm-sized incendiary *squib* which detonates messily when *tossed. 2. n.* Somewhat unpleasantly, you would imagine, for all concerned, an act of *fisting* which culminates in an opening of the hand.

hand job *n.* Manual relief, one of the cheaper *extras* available at the *rub-a-tug shop,* or in the pub car park.

hand love *n.* The sordid act of *self-pollution.*

hand luggage *n.* The penis. *'Will your hand luggage fit in the overhead locker, sir?' 'I've not had any complaints yet, pet.'* (Bamforth's *Seaside Chuckles* postcard by Donald McGill, 1951).

hand luggage, Scottish *n.* The standard carry-on baggage of Caledonian air passengers, *viz.* A plastic carrier bag full of alcohol.

hand on the fox's tail, getting a *phr.* When excavating a particularly stubborn *bogie:* gaining enough traction to remove the offending article prior to wiping it on the underside of one's bus seat/ throne *etc.*

hand party *n.* An eyesight-wrecking festival of *self pleasure* enjoyed by a man whose *bag for life* is away for the weekend.

hand practice *n.* Solitary monomanual labour for the housebound bachelor who wishes to keep his wrist in. *'And have you done any work, paid or unpaid, since you last signed on?' 'No, I've just been shut in the house doing me hand practice.'*

hand pump *n. milit. Wanker, nut juggler etc. 'Oi! Windsor, you fucking hand pump. Get them fucking boots back on, your royal highness.'*

handrail for a battleship, she's had enough cock to make a *sim.* Said of a woman with a *lively romantic history. 'Our next special guest needs no* *introduction. The star of Cleopatra, Who's Afraid of Virginia Woolf and National Velvet, during her long and illustrious career she's won two Oscars, been married eight times and had enough cock to make a handrail for a battleship. Ladies and gentlemen, boys and girls, let's have a big Crackerjack welcome for Elizabeth Taylor.'*

handrex *n.* *Arsewipe* replacement for emergency use during any national panic-buying debacles. When one's hand is pressed into service in order to perform the various tasks that would usually be done by *bumwad*, ie. Blowing one's nose, mopping up a spillage of *Harry Monk*, and, of course, wiping one's *arse*. A practical and thrifty alternative which does however necessitate vigorous washing afterwards, so best get plenty of sanitizer in.

handruff *n.* Flaky deposits consisting of an amalgam of dried *potato fat, perseverance soup* and *helmetdale* found on the palms, thighs and soft furnishings of bachelors who have been watching a few episodes too many of *Desperate Housewives* without occasionally pausing to give the inside of the *friar's hood* a wash.

hands, face, space *1. phr.* Government-coined slogan intended to stop the spread of that Covid-19 they were always going on about a few years back. *2. phr.* Etiquette in a multi-person *custardy battle, i.e.* Stepping away politely after *going off* in order to allow the next fellow to *spaff*.

hands free *n.* See *fancy wank*.

hands free kit *1. n.* A neat system consisting of about 30 yards of wire draped around your dashboard that allows you to make and receive phonecalls on a mobile whilst weaving between lanes on a motorway and ramming into the back of other vehicles at high speed. *2. euph.* A lazy chap's female acquaintance who will happily *spanner him off* when he can't be *arsed* to do it himself.

hand shandroid *n.* A mechanical, robotic *wanking* device, such as one "Electrical" Entwhistle might have built out of a shop dummy and a lawnmower engine in *Last of the Summer Wine*.

hand shandy *n.* A frothy one, pulled *off the wrist*.

hands like cows' tits *sim.* Descriptive of one who is dextrously inept. An alternative to "butterfingers". *'I'm terribly sorry, Mrs Jones, but I accidentally cut through a major blood vessel near your husband's heart and he didn't survive the surgery. I'm afraid I was on the pop last night and I've got hands like cows' tits this morning. My bill will be in*

the post. The nurse will show you out. Good day.'

hand solo *n.* A solitary interlude of *self improvement*.

handsome *n.* Neither a threesome nor a twosome. A *one-in-a-bed romp* or *ménage à un.*

hand to gland combat *n.* A three-minute, one-man gladiatorial combat bout involving a *spam javelin.*

handular fever *1. n.* Condition suffered by those who *work from home*. *'Have you finished those reports yet, Dharmesh? The board needs them for the big presentation this afternoon.'* *'Sorry, I've had handular fever all week so I never got them done.'* *2. n. medic.* Excessive *self-abuse* whilst ill in bed with only your phone for company.

handycrap *n.* A *shit* taken by an able-bodied person who goes into *arse labour* only to discover that all the other toilets are occupied, out of order, or blocked with *bangers and mash,* and is forced to avail themself of the disabled facilities.

handyman *n.* A solitary sort of cove who *whacks off* a lot.

handy pandy *n.* A high risk *Ethel* taken over a particularly fetching children's TV presenter.

hang a rat *1. v.* To go to the lavatory for a *number two*. *'Where the fuck is he? He's supposed to be on the balcony blessing the multitude.'* *'Keep your fucking hair on, cardinal. He's just went to the khazi to hang a rat.'* *2. v.* To urinate whilst standing up (confusingly). *'I'm just off to hang a rat, but here's Carol with today's weather outlook.'*

hang a roll of flock wallpaper *euph.* A somewhat hyperbolic description of what one could do with a copious amount of thick *spoff.* *'"I say, Jeeves," I expostulated. "There's always capital fun to be had down at the Drones Club with old Fink-Nottle and the chaps, but hang it all if one doesn't sometimes hanker after a spot of female company." "Indeed sir," rejoindered the stalwart gentleman's gentleman. "The fragrant tenderness of the fairer sex is as balm to the soul. Who would deny that she is God's sublime creation, able to express more in a sigh than can a man in a sermon." "Yes, there is that, Jeeves old chap," I replied at length after pondering the sage retainer's wise words. "Plus which, you could hang a roll of flock wallpaper with what's brewing in my nads."'* (from *Stick It Up Your Hoop, Jeeves!* by PG Wodehouse).

hanging a portrait in the mahogany gallery *euph.* Depositing *jizz* in someone's *bumhole.*

hanging bacon *n.* A *club sandwich* which hopefully isn't held together with a cocktail stick.

hanging baskets *1. n.* Dangling areas of foliage which can look nice when properly tended but attract flies if allowed to run to seed. *2. n.* Blooming marvellous *tits* which sway in the breeze and look like they've been assiduously cultivated.

hanging brain *n.* A *coffin dodger's clockweights*, dangling out the leg of his shorts.

hanging chod *n.* A semi-detached *turd*.

hanging gardens, the *n.* The horrific rear elevation of a naked man bending over. Definitely not one of the Seven Wonders of the World.

hanging out the back of *adj.* Engaged in *doggy-style* sex with someone. See also *Rigsby shag, exhibition position.*

hanging salad *n. Wedding vegetables,* the *fruit bowl* or *family jewels.*

hanging the Mona Lisa in the North Point Arcade, like *sim.* A particularly Humberside-centric apophthegm, wittily referring to a good pair of *top bollocks* which are wasted on an ugly woman, from the fact that the situation is metaphorically akin to hanging a priceless Renaissance work of art in the cultural desert which is the North Point Shopping Arcade, Bransholme, Hull.

hang in the balance *v.* Of a fellow's *chap,* to float at the exact mid-point between a *lazy* and a *full lob.*

hangman's noose *n.* A capacious *seaside bucket,* big enough to push your head into. A *wizard's sleeve,* a *clown's pocket.*

hang on I'll get a plate *exclam.* Said during the aftermath of a notably fragrant *dropped gut.* Also *hold on caller, putting you through now; let's look at what you could have won.*

hangover Holmes *n.* A chap who uses all the evidence available to him about his person (*eg.* Bus tickets, cash machine receipts, stains, wedding rings, bruises, lovebites, missing fingers, *crabs*) in order to deduce what he got up to the previous night. See *Crimewatch reconstruction.*

hangover piss *n.* Descriptive of a healthy, bronzed urinary patina that brings to mind the hide of Judith Chalmers, Des O'Connor or David Dickinson.

hangsober *n. medic.* When you give up drinking for a few days and you feel worse than when you've been *on the lash.*

hang ten *1. v.* In surfing slang, to stand on the front of the board with all of one's toes curling over the edge. *2. v.* To be *masturbatricized* by one's partner using their feet rather than the more traditional *wanking spanners. 'Riding waves is really sweet / Catching tubes a real good treat / But best of all is hanging ten / With me knob between the missus's feet.'* (from *Wankin' USA* by the Beach Boys).

hangunder *n.* A feeling of generalised debility in an inveterate drinker, caused by underindulgence the previous night. *'Giz a shot on that White Lightning, pal. I've got a terrible hangunder and I*

just can't seem to shift it.'

hang up one's wank sock *v.* To get married. *'In 1848, at the age of twenty-nine, Ruskin met Euphemia Chalmers Gray and decided to hang up his wank sock.'*

hang your hole *v.* To *moon* or *do a captain.* At two nuns in a Morris Minor, as previously noted.

hanky panky *1. n. Slap and tickle,* a bit of the other, *nookie, how's your father.* Light-hearted *fucking. 2. n.* In the Madonna song of the same name, a bit of light *fladge and padge.*

Hannibal Lecter's breakfast *n.* The feast which awaits a man performing *cumulonimbus* on *Billy Connolly's beard,* and the ensuing *pasata grin* it leaves on his face. A *lick of paint.*

Hannibal tease *n.* The frustrating *horatio* technique of a lady who never really gets past the tip of a chap's *spam javelin* when *smoking the white owl.* A reference to the *A-Team's* Hannibal Smith whose trademark cigar somehow never burned down past the first quarter-inch.

Hans and Lotte *n. prop. rhym. slang.* The *fundament, back body,* or *arse;* a reference to 1950s TV scuba divers Hans and Lotte Hass. One for the teenagers there.

ha'penny *n.* Vagina. A *tuppence.*

happy camper *n.* A jolly fellow who *throws a light dart, eg.* Graham Norton, Duncan Norvelle, Peter Tatchell.

happy clappy *1. adj.* Annoyingly full of the love of God. *2. n.* Not really bothered about having *cock rot.*

happy ending *1. n.* In a film or novel, for example, a narrative denouement in which the various strands of the plot are drawn together in a satisfyingly felicitous manner, leaving the viewer or reader with a warm glow of pleasure. *2. n.* In a massage parlour, a denouement in which the customer gets *tossed off,* leaving him doing his flies back up with a feeling of dejection, despair and self-loathing while the masseuse disinterestedly wipes his grey *spunk* off her hand with some Tesco Discount Brand kitchen roll, And the first peron to write in and point out that the word "disinterestedly" is used wrongly in that sentence wins £5. (That prize has been claimed)

happy go mucky *adj.* Said of a person who is relaxed about being experimental and adventurous in the bedroom. *'Professional woman 50+, looking for companionship and maybe more. Hobbies include country walks, visits to museums, dinner dates and classical concerts. GSOH, happy go mucky, esp. chimping, Boston pancakes, ESD, DVDA, Alabama hot pockets, Kentucky meat showers etc.*

Box 6.'

happy Harry *n.* A semi-erect penis. A *dobber,* a *lard on, half a teacake.*

happy Havana *n.* A firm, rectilinear *bum cigar* of such pleasing proportions that it could almost have been rolled on the thigh of a sultry Latin American temptress, and requires little or no wiping to boot.

happy lamp *n.* The *sixth gear stick. 'I'm feeling right horny. Think I'll give my happy lamp a quick genie rub.'*

happy medium *n. Lucky Pierre.* The filling in a *spud fumbler* sandwich.

Happy Mondays, off quicker than the *sim. rhet.* An allusion to the Manchester-based band who, in our experience, when performing live certainly didn't outstay their welcome on stage. The *dunghampers* of a woman who is somewhat easy with her affections. *'Eh Dave, I got the bird from the Feathers back to the flat on Tuesday and her knickers were off quicker than the Happy Mondays.'*

happy paper *n. Beer tokens,* folding money.

happy rash *n. medic.* A light-hearted dose of the *pox.* A *Doonican.* Any non-fatal *STD.*

happy sack *n.* The scrotum, *clackerbag, chicken skin handbag, hairy saddlebags. 'Ooh, bugger. I just sat down awkwardly and squashed me happy sack. Anyway, where was I? Oh yes, I regard myself as a soldier, though a soldier of peace.'*

happy sealion, do the *v.* To enjoy vigorous *coupling,* the whole performance accompanied by a wet clapping sound, damp whiskers and a strong smell of fish. *'And there goes the Royal couple, leaving the Cathedral in the golden State Coach. And no doubt Prince William will be looking forward now to a lavish reception and banquet at Buckingham Palace, followed by a night of doing the happy sealion while fantasising about his sister-in-law's shitlocker.'*

Happy Shopper *1. n. prop.* A cheap 'n' cheerless grocery brand. *2. n.* A bisexual – one who *shops on both sides of the street.* A *half rice half chips* person or *switch hitter.*

Happy Shopper copper *n.* A community police support officer. *'I was too young to get a job as a lollipop man so I became a happy shopper copper instead.'*

Happy Shopper knockers *n.* No-frills *jugs.* Like proper *tits,* but with less filling. *Skimmed milkers.*

happytwat *n.* Any modern, upmarket sex shop, *ie.* One that doesn't smell of sweat, despair and *spunk.*

happy valley *1. n.* How the local police apparently refer to Calderdale in the West Riding of Yorkshire, because it is such a carefree locale. *2.*

n. The *taint, biffin bridge, tinter, carse etc. 3. n.* The *Bristol channel.*

happy valley *1. n. Last of the Summer Wine*-style crime drama series set in Yorkshire, starring Raquel off *Corrie. 2. n.* The *barse.*

happy valley *n.* The *biffin bridge, barse, carse, great, ploughman's, scruttock etc.*

happy vampire *n.* Something that rises at night and is full of blood. An erection of the *membrum virile.*

harbouring a known criminal *n.* Holding in a noisome *bottom burp* or suppressing a *baby's arm* while in an enclosed area or in close proximity to a lady.

harbour master *n.* A man who has piloted the course of a few *tugboats* in his time, he can tell you. A *stickman, fanny hopper, crumpeteer.*

hard as snails *adj.* Nowhere near as tough as it would appear, *eg.* The current King, who is Commander in Chief of the RAF with a chest full of medals yet has never sat further forward in a plane than the Club Class cabin. And let's not talk about his brother Edward.

hard as the knobs of Hell *sim.* Traditional Cheshire phrase for something that is very hard indeed. Also *hard as a Chinese wordsearch, hard as a policeman's knock, hard as Stephen Hawking's homework, hard as Captain Scott's last morning stiffy.*

hardbore *n. Grumble* that promises to be a real *meat vid* on the box, but when you get it home you find it's got Robin Askwith, Bill Maynard and Doris Hare in it. And Tony Blair's dead father-in-law.

hard hat *n.* A *stiffy,* or erection of the male parts. *'Fancy a spot of potholing under the bridge?' 'Not until I've got my hard hat on, love.'*

Hardly-Davidson *euph.* An unglamorous, slow and generally unimpressive mode of transport, *viz.* A moped. *'Is that Marlon Brando and his fellow members of the Black Rebels pulling up outside on their Triumph Thunderbirds?' 'No, it's your Auntie Joyce on her Hardly-Davidson.'*

hardly on *n.* A barely leavened *teacake.* Not quite three quarters of *half a soft on.*

hard of beering *euph.* Collective hearing disorder whereby groups of increasingly inebriated pub-goers gradually raise the level of their discourse throughout the evening until everyone in the gaff is yelling as loudly as possible in order to be heard over the fucking din.

hard off *n.* Something of a disappointment. *'After all the excitement of our last-gasp comebacks in the quarter and semi-final stages, I've got to admit that our four-nil defeat to Seville in the UEFA cup final in Eindhoven was something of a hard off, Adrian.'*

(Then Middlesbrough manager Steve McClaren speaking on BBC Radio 5, May 10th 2006).

hard-on *n.* *Wood*, a *bone on*, a *bonk-on*. A fully tumescent gentleman's part. *Irish toothache.*

hard sports *n.* What Germans get up to if left to their own devices with a glass coffee table in the room.

hardware *n.* Prophylactic sheathage.

hard work *exclam.* How somebody with a gobful of hot chips might say "aardvark".

hardy annual *1. n.* A plant which flourishes in summer and will, a year later, if the bulb is handled carefully, fail to emerge again. *2. n.* A gentleman prone to lengthy *interregna* between amorous episodes. *'Today's birthdays: Rod Laver, tennis player, 1937, Whitney Houston, thirsty warbler, 1963; Philip Larkin, hardy annual poet, 1922.'*

hardy perennial *1. n.* A plant which doesn't die in the winter or something. *2. n.* An ageing gentleman who is perpetually amorous, *eg.* Rod Stewart, Picasso.

hare's running, the *exclam.* Said upon discovering that all the *traps* are full in the works *khazi.*

haribone *n.* A *tool* which is frankly too soft and chewy for the job in hand.

hariolae *n.* The hairs that continental ladies cultivate around their *hunchback spiders*.

Harlem shuffle *n.* The facial gurning and involuntary neck spasms that beset a gentleman during the *vinegar strokes,* making him look like septuagenarian *harbour master* Sir Mickolas Jagger strutting about on stage. *'Quick, camera two, a close up of Gunther's cock. He's doing the Harlem shuffle.'*

harlet *n.* A young *slapper.*

Harley Davidson *n.* An act of lavatoryless defecation, in which the dumper is forced to cling to trees or railings in order to steady himself, thus adopting a position similar to that used when riding an impractically high-handle-barred American motorcycle. A *fatboy, soft-tail, breezy rider.*

harlot *n.* A scarlet woman, a wicked lady. A rumbustious *strumpet.*

Harlow pub quiz *n.* Entertainment regularly held at the Essex town's popular nightspots. The quizmaster usually asks one of two questions: "What the fuck are you looking at?" or "Do you fucking want some?", to which all the possible answers are wrong. *West Yorkshire Mastermind, Scotswood Only Connect, Glamorgan University Challenge.*

Harmison loosener *n.* An *explosive delivery* first thing in the morning which ends up anywhere but near to its intended target. *'Last night's chicken jalfrezi resulted in Derek sending down a ferocious Harmison loosener.'*

haroldite *n.* A super-gluey adhesive in a cylindrical tube which is invaluable for sticking the pages of *art pamphlets* together. Also *population paste, joy gloy, Aphrodite's evostick, jazz glue, prick stick, man mastic, pyjama glue* and *cockidex.*

harpooning *n.* *Having it off* with a blubbery old trout.

Harpo speaks *exclam.* Said following a loud honk that is reminiscent of the famously mute Marx brother sounding his horn.

harp strings *n.* Residual strands of *man mess* left hanging 'twixt the upper and lower jaws following a bout of oral tomfoolery.

harrisment *n.* Being touched by a popular 1970s entertainer in an inappropriate manner.

Harry *1. rhym. slang.* Jizz. From Harry Monk = spunk. *2. rhym. slang.* Hobo. From Harry Ramp = tramp *3. rhym. slang.* Cigarette. From Harry Rag = fag. *4. rhym. slang.* Lunchtime snack. From Harry Rees-Bandwich = cheese sandwich.

Harry Hill *n. rhym. slang.* The contraceptive pill. *'It's alright Boris, I'm on the Harry Hill.'*

Harry Rampsdens *n.* Discarded fish and chips, as feasted upon by cheery gentlemen of the road. *Tramps' truffles.*

Harry Ramsden's fingers *1. euph.* Descriptive of the state of the digits after fiddling with an excitable woman's *haddock pastie,* ie. "Covered in batter and smelling of fish". *2. n.* Title of Kim Carnes's less successful follow-up to *Bette Davis Eyes.*

Harry Ramsden's raspberry *n.* The combination of smell and sound to be endured during a dirty girl's *fanny fart.*

Harry Ramsden's skip *n.* A mingsome *snatch.* *'Kleptomania was powerless to resist. His eyes burned into hers like Swarovski crystals. His strong arms enfolded her body as she felt herself being swept away on a pontoon of passion. Gently, Tarpaulio's roughly hewn lumberjack's fingers teased down her bloomers as he got down on his knees to lick her out. 'Christ on a bike, love,' he cried. 'It smells like Harry Ramsden's skip down here.'"* (from *The Countess and the Tree Surgeon* by Barbara Cartland).

Harry Redknapp's eyelids *sim.* Descriptive of particularly hang-dog *beef curtains,* that look like they've been sat up all night playing on a Nintendo DS. *David Davis eyes.*

Harry's bar *1. n.* Sophisticated New York drinking establishment favoured by the Metropolitan elite for the consumption of fine wines and cocktails.

2. n. Outdoor area favoured by *Harold Ramp* and friends for the *al fresco* downing of White Lightning. The *tramp grill.*

Harry's challenge *n.* A daunting *fish supper* that is too much for one man. A big *kipper.* From the menu at the Yardley branch of Harry Ramsden's which offered a meal of that name, and where one was granted a certificate if the portion was finished.

harrystyle *n.* A hairline that's only going in "one direction".

Harry Styles *n. prop. rhym. slang.* Haemorrhoids. Also *Adrian Chiles, Emma Freuds, Bonny Marys.* An annoying pain in the *arse.*

harsepital *n.* The place to which a fellow shuffles off when, after attempting to *blow off* with vigour and gusto, he suffers an accident or emergency in the trouser department.

Hartlepool baguette *n.* Unpalatable, trouser-based, cheese-heavy *al fresco* snack which is popular with young ladies in the picturesque northern resort, particularly at chucking out time.

harvest festival *n.* Domestic state of play for the bachelor gentleman when, following a fortnight *on the lash*, he is reduced to living on out-of-date tinned food from the back of the cupboard.

harvest festivals *1. n.* One-night stands, *ie.* Ploughing the field before scattering. *2. n.* A pair of well-fitting but comfortable underpants where "all is safely gathered in".

Harvey Smith, more clear rounds than *sim. rhet.* Said of a chap who is a bit shy when it's his turn to get the drinks in. *'Fuck me, where's Dave gone? He's in the chair.' 'He's sloped off, mate. He's had more clear rounds than Harvey Smith, that cunt.'*

has anyone got any questions? *exclam.* Said prior to *letting off* a *Bronx cheer* that exhibits a rising, inquisitive intonation.

has a skin-care regime *euph.* Descriptive of a chap who *keeps his fingernails clean.*

hasbian *n.* A past-it *lesbian* whose *carpet munching* days are over.

hashtag *1. n.* Symbol used on the internet, found on the computer keyboard by calling out "Oi, luv. How do you get a fucking hashtag again?" *3. n.* A large *winnit* consisting of four *arse* hairs crossed and attached in the familiar manner.

Hastings jellyfish *n.* Semi-transparent gelatinous object that floats just beneath the water, or is seen washed up on the beach. A *dunky, Coney Island whitefish, Dutch man o'war* or *Thames trout.*

has to stand on a chair to brush his/her teeth *phr.* Said of a *short-arsed* person's difficulties in performing the simpleist of tasks. *'Eeh, I wouldn't*

say my husband's short, ladies and gentlemen, but he has to stand on a chair to brush his fucking teeth.' (Mrs Akshata "It's the way I tell 'em" Sunak, *Britain's Got Talent* auditions, 2019).

hatch a plot *v.* To enjoy an extended trip to the *shitehouse* in order to lament, machinate and scheme in peace while simultaneously taking the opportunity to drop a refreshing *copper bolt* or five.

hatchback *n.* A woman with prominent buttocks. *'Jesus. Look at the arse on that Mother Superior over there by Guercini's altarpiece of the Burial of St. Petronilla, your holiness. What a hatchback.' 'Indeed, cardinal. You could stand your pint on her parcel shelf.'*

hatch eggs *v.* To remain seated on the *chod bin* long after the last *turd* has been dropped. *'What are you doing in there? I've got the turtle's breath and a new Autotrader.' 'I'm hatching eggs.'*

hat full of cold piss *n.* Motor trade argot for an undesirable and worthless automobile. *'I know I told you that this hearing-aid beige Triumph Acclaim was a fast-appreciating prestige classic when I sold it to you for £8,000 last week, but the marque has fallen out of favour somewhat in the past couple of days and I'm afraid it's a hat full of cold piss now, sir. Tell you what, I'll give you two bob and a toffee apple for it, and I'm cutting my own throat.'*

hat rack *n.* Someone whose head is only of any use for the storage of hats. A *Johnny No-Stars, cunt candle, shit-for-brains. eg.* Bez out of The Happy Mondays, whoever designed the traffic system for getting in and out of the short-stay car park at Newcastle Central Station.

hatstand *adj.* Descriptive of one who is *differently mentalled.*

Hatties *rhym. slang.* Delirium tremens. A *turps nudger's* shakes. From *Carry On* actress Hattie Jelirium-Tremens. *'Take over the landing will you, Buzz? I've got the Hatties.'*

hat, tramp's *n.* A large, shapeless, sweaty and discoloured *clopper.*

hat trick *n.* A soiled pair of *trolleys* in the laundry basket, comprehensively befouled with faecal, urinary & seminal excrescences. *'Anything for the wash this morning, Donald?' 'Just these hat-tricks from the press conference, thanks Melania.'*

have a go at oneself *v.* To *stab the cat, feed the ducks, stab the ducks, feed the cat.*

haveagone hero *n.* That bloke in the pub who acts all tough, yet, when asked to step outside, vanishes faster than Usain Bolt.

have a wank on it *phr.* A procedure that any

gentleman should undertake when there is a big decision to be made in order to afford himself the opportunity to make his judgement with a clear mind. And *knackers*. '*I just don't know. I'd really like a Porsche Panamera, but on the other hand the missus needs that eye operation in Switzerland to stop her going blind.' 'Tell you what, sir. You go home and have a wank on it.*'

have it off *v.* To get *a bit*, have a *portion*, give somebody *one*. To get one's *leg over*.

have one's arse in one's hand *euph.* To be in a bad mood, to have a strop on. '*Arnie's BACK!... and this time he's got his arse in his hand!*' (Advertising poster for *Terminator 3*).

Havers, on the *adj.* Descriptive of the way certain blokes smarm up to members of the opposite sex in an overly charming way, *eg*. Kissing their hands, listening to them *etc.*, in the style of middle-aged charmer Nigel.

have the painters in *v.* To menstruate, be *on the blob, fall to the communists*.

have you ever heard the booming of a bittern? *1. exclam. interrog.* Question asked of Doctor Watson by Stapleton in Sir Arthur Conan Doyle's *The Hound Of The Baskervilles*. *2. exclam. interrog.* Question asked before releasing a loud *Exchange and Mart*, especially when out and about in the great outdoors. '*Have you ever heard the booming of a bittern, Michaela?*'

have you heard the new Coldplay single? *exclam. rhet.* Line delivered before letting off a particularly tuneless *Lionel*. Also *and now a quick word from our sponsors; speak to me O toothless one; our survey said; I'll name that tune in one; fire up drop zone two; I smell with my little nose, something beginning with*.

have you tried a shite? *exclam. interrog.* Question asked rhetorically of a person who is constantly *blowing off*. '*Have you tried a shite, Eamonn? We're getting complaints off viewers.*'

having a go at today's Wordle *euph.* To *light a bum cigar*, to *lay a cable*; to defecate. '*Where are you off to, William?' 'I'm off to the throne room for three quarters of an hour to have a go at today's Wordle, Kate.*'

having a Wilkie *n.* Sitting on the toilet with your hands cupped together and clenched, your face a picture of concentration, while trying to will your *brown ball* between the white porcelain posts of the *bum sink*. A somewhat contrived reference to the characteristic kicking stance of heavily constipated former part-time England rugby *glassback* Jonny Wilkinson.

having tea with Aslan *euph.* A fellow who is so

deep *in the closet* that he has taken to dining with the famous Narnia-based lion.

Hawaiian muscle fuck *n.* The act of *bagpiping*.

Hawaiian sunrise *n.* A glorious and uncomfortable orange, red, blue and purple aurora, which can be seen around one's *ringpiece* early in the morning after consuming spicesome comestibles.

Hawaiian waft *n.* To disperse the aroma after *stepping on a duck,* using an exotic hula-hula motion.

Hawick *onomat.* To *puke*. After the Scottish border town. '*I think I'm going to Hawick.*'

Hawley's gift *n.* Dispensation to perform an act of *horatio* upon his turgid person granted by a gentleman to his ladyfriend on the occasion of her birthday. From the line in the eponymous Sheffield-based crooner's song *For Your Lover Give Some Time, viz.* "It was your birthday yesterday. I gave a gift that almost took your breath away."

hay fever *n. medic.* A seasonal illness, whose sufferers are forced to convalesce at home during the summer months, with the windows and curtains shut to prevent "pollen" getting in. And also so that the neighbours/postman *etc.*, don't see them sat on the sofa *wanking* over the Wimbledon Ladies' heats.

haywain *1. n.* An instantly recognisable but ultimately tedious jigsaw puzzle from Waddingtons. *2. n.* A lady's recently mown beauty spot, preferably in Suffolk, of which one might remark "That's cunt stubble country."

HBYFC *abbrev.* Used by cheeky folk to efficiently wish friends many happy returns while light-heartedly abusing them in the foulest possible way.

HCH *abbrev.* A *big-boned* individual; also *salad dodger, lard arse, cake detector etc.* A High Calorie Human. '*Born on this day; Victoria Beckham, former Spice Girl and automobile technologist, 1974; Pete Shelley, Buzzcocks frontman, 1950; John McCririck, dead HCH, 1940.*'

HD ready *1. adj.* Of large, flatscreen television sets in electrical shops, descriptive of the fact that they are capable of displaying impressively detailed pictures of yachts, the Changing of the Guard and tropical fish. *2. adj.* A gentleman's assessment that his current feminine companion is sexually amenable, *ie.* That she is "ready for his Hot Dog".

head *n.* Something which is given by women to men, and is afterwards described as "good" by the recipient when talking to friends. A *chewie, nosh, gobbie*. Not to be confused with the Monkees' film of the same name which – come on, let's be honest – was anything but good.

head and breakfast *1. n.* A place where one can get

a *Thai at night*, and a *full English* in the morning. 2. *n.* A really good evening out that finishes up with a farewell *nosh-up* in a budget guesthouse. Also known as a *yawn and spawn.*

head and shoulders *euph.* *Deepthroat* that also includes the *knackers.*

head arse *n.* The cleft of skin visible on the lower cranium of *well-nourished* blokes who have elected to shave their heads, *eg.* The corpulent security officers in almost all supermarkets. Former late wrestler Mal "King Kong" Kirk had one of the best *head arses* in the business.

head for the hills *exclam.* Warning cry when forced to hide your *soldier* in the *Dutch alps,* because the *redcoats are in the valley.*

head in one's top pocket, to have *v.* To be so copiously *wankered* that your head cannot balance on your neck any more and seems to be falling into the top pocket of your shirt. An extreme form of *nodding.*

headlamps *n.* Bristols, jugs, charlies, assets. *'Phewf! I wouldn't mind giving her headlamps a rub.'*

head of dogshit *phr.* The most worthless position at any given workplace. *'Sorry John, I have no idea where they keep the bin liners. You'd be better off talking to the head of dogshit.'*

head off a nun, like trying to get *sim.* Descriptive of something very difficult to achieve. *Finding a pube in an afro.* *'And I'd like to reassure pensioners that I fully intend to bring in legislation on asylum that will make getting British citizenship like trying to get head off a nun before the next parliament.'*

head office *n.* The missus. *'You coming down the pub, Harry?' 'Hang on. I just need to check with head office.'*

head start *euph.* Oral foreplay. *'I gave her a head start but I still came first.'*

headwind *n.* The unfortunate release of a *bottom burp* while receiving *horatio. Devil's kiss, Hell's mouth.*

health stick *n.* A fruity penis, packed with the goodness of *nuts* and at least a teaspoonful of nourishing *Vitamin S.*

health worker clap *euph.* A *wank* enjoyed at 8pm on Thursdays during any lockdowns that might occur from time to time, so it sounds like your street is cheering you on. *'I'm going to have a health worker clap tonight.'*

hear me out, please just *exclam.* Soothing words uttered in the midst of a heated argument just before a fully developed *bon mot* from an unexpected quarter takes matters in an unexpected direction.

heart starter *n.* A bracing breakfast-time snifter,

for example a few cans of Special Brew, a couple of pints of cooking sherry or a bottle of Tesco Value gin, taken to invigorate one's semi-comatose body following the previous evening's merriment. An *eyeball straightener, Kentucky breakfast.*

hear ye! hear ye! *exclam.* A loud ecphonesis (look it up), possibly accompanied by the ringing of a handbell, made prior to dropping an almighty *poos headline* that the whole marketplace can hear.

Heather Mills! *exclam.* Incredulous declamatory response uttered when a third party makes a claim which is so outrageous and unlikely that a reasoned rejoinder is almost impossible. Named after Macca's hyperbole-prone, assymetrically limbed ex-missus. *Chinny reckon. 'I reckon Derby could still do it, you know. Man United are only sixty points ahead.' 'Heather Mills!'* 2. *n.* A descriptive exclamation used by players of ball sports such as pool or golf when a ball falls short of its target, because "it hasn't got the legs".

heat pump 1. *n.* Cunning way of stopping utilities companies from ripping you off with inflated gas prices. Costs between £10,000 and £20,000, plus installation, it says here. 2. *n.* The flatulent *back body.*

heat pump 1. *n.* 2. *n.* A warm and gaseous *digestive transit.*

heat pump 1. *n.* Device which transfers energy by circulating a refrigerant through a cycle of evaporation and condensation (like on the back of a fridge, you might suppose) and costs about fifteen grand to fit. 2. *n.* Long, drawn out, high temperature *trouser trumpetry* due to overdoing the chicken vindaloo the night before.

heavage *n.* A *Bristol Channel* that is only there thanks to cleverly engineered *tit pants.*

heave *v.* To vomit, *make a pavement pizza,* release a loud *technicolour yawn* or *shout soup.*

heave a Havana *v.* Grow a tail, take *a dump, light a bum cigar, cast Churchill's reflection.*

heave-ho 1. *n.* The *arse. 'She threw me out on my heave-ho.'* 2. *n.* The *Spanish archer. 'She gave me the heave-ho on my arse.'*

heavy dick *n.* The very first stirrings of erectivation. The beginnings of a *semi-on.* For example, that situation which occurs when one is on holiday abroad, whereby a combination of warm weather and semi-naked women leaves you feeling like you've got a sock full of sand in your pants.

heavy lifting, she does her own *euph.* Said of a comfortably-shod female who is *fond of the fish course.*

heavy of bollock *adj. arch.* Shakespearean term describing a swain who has had neither a *shag* nor a *tug* in some considerable time. *'York has* *returned from Ireland, my liege, to defend you from dupliticious Somerset; yet I fear his army are tired and heavy of bollock.'* (from *Henry VI Part 2, The Klumps*).

heavy shooter *n.* One whose *money shots* tend to be *pwas* rather than *gwibbles*.

heavy wetter *n.* An extravagant *spender*; a chap who produces an unfeasibly large amount of *heir gel* when he *goes off*. Also known as a *milkman, eg. Grumble* legend Peter "One Man Bukkake" North.

hebola *n. medic.* A terrible, debilitating disease exclusively afflicting the male population that is often misdiagnosed as the common cold.

hebrew *n.* Semen. *Sailor's ale.*

he considered the priesthood *euph.* An elliptically intriguing contemplation often featured in the biographies of men who *take their time shopping.* Also *he never married.*

he-dam *n. knob cheese, helmetdale, purple Leicester, brimula, Lymeswold etc.*

hedge coke *n.* Plastic bottles filled with fluid slightly too pale to be true cola, discarded on roadside verges by lorry drivers in order to tempt thirsty runners or cyclists in need of refreshment. *Trucker's tizer, kidney cider, Scania scotch.*

hedge funds *n.* The substantial deposits of crumpled *grumble* stashed in the hedgerows of suburban alleyways or scrublands by canny young *merchant bankers. Ray Mears's library.*

hedgehog *n.* A *ladygarden that was mowed* five days ago. A *face grater.*

hedgehog through a cheesegrater, like a *sim.* The polar opposite of *an otter off the bank, viz.* An extremely painful *shite* that seems takes ages to shift.

hedgehog under a floorboard, fanny like a *sim.* A none-too-freshly trimmed *bush* in a skimpy bikini.

hedge quimmers *n.* A *fannicurist's* lady shaver.

hee *1. n. Thai.* The *minge, hairy cheque book. 2. interj.* A noise made by laughing gnomes/laughing policemen.

hefty-clefty *n.* A *welly top*, a *horse's collar*, a *melted welly, spla welly.* A very wide *Mary.*

Heineken manoeuvre *n.* Life-saving first aid procedure.

Heinz jacuzzi *n.* The luxurious, self-indulgent pleasure to be had in any bath, courtesy of an earlier consumption of baked beans. *'I'd give it ten minutes if I was you, dear. I've just had a Heinz jacuzzi. And probably best not to light any tea-lights in there for a few hours, neither.'*

heir bag *n. medic.* The male scrotum or *shaggis.* The container where *liquid kids* are stored, which

handily prevents injury to the *barse* when a man is kicked between the legs. Something that goes off and leaves your ears ringing.

heir cut *n.* The *snip.*

heirdo *n.* A funeral.

heir flick *1. n. prop.* Comedy crank-legged Gestapo pervert out of nazi-based eighties family sitcom *'Allo 'Allo. 2. n.* A quick and deliberate flourish of the wrist at the termination of a monomanual act of *self delight* that is intended to lob a rope of DNA through the air in a pleasingly parabolic arc.

heir gel *n.* See *heir spray.*

heir loss *n.* Successful self abuse.

heir spray *n.* A man's volatile *baby juice. Spooge, spoff, spaff, spiff, jitler. Merry monk.*

heirspray *n.* Airborne *jizz* that probably harms the ozone layer.

heir to the throne *1. n.* The front runner in the royal line of succession; Prince William at the time of going to press, possibly a toddler by the time someone buys this in an Oxfam shop on the Moon in the future. *2. n.* The person at the head of the toilet queue.

held up by the fog *euph. Dropping one's hat* as one lowers one's *kecks* to open the *bomb-bay doors*, and sitting down into a dense cloud of *sulphur dibaxide* which then acts as a *general anusthetic. 'Sorry I'm late for breakfast dear. I was held up by the fog.'*

Helena Bonham *euph.* The *back passage.* From the charming English rose actress Helena Bonham-Farter.

helicopters, attack of the *n.* Drunken spinning of the head, a sudden reminder that you need to make an urgent call on the *great white telephone.* The *whirlies, wall of death.*

helicopter, the *n.* Post-rugby match entertainment: Whipping out one's *chopper* and whirling it around a bit at a high angular velocity.

helium balloon *n.* The unfortunate situation that sometimes obtains during a *cattle* up the *council*, when the woman *blows off* and inflates the gentleman's *chicken skin handbag*, causing him, at the very least, to talk like Joe Pasquale or, in extreme cases, to float helplessly out of the window and be pointed at by passing children.

helium heels *n.* Affectionate nickname for a woman who tends to end the evening with her legs in the air.

he'll be happy with that, it's landed on the green *exclam.* Humorous utterance delivered in the avuncular style of Peter Alliss after someone has *dropped a gut.*

hello Cleveland *exclam.* Phrase uttered by a

gentleman who is *doing* a lady from behind and inadvertently *pots the brown* rather than the *pink*. From the scene in *Spinal Tap* when the band find themselves in the wrong tunnel.

hello from the other side *1. phr.* Line from that Adele song. *2. phr.* Something a psychic medium might say before asking if anyone in the theatre knows anyone whose name contains an 'e', or it might be a 'w'. *3. euph.* A *botty burp*.

Hello, who just joined? *exclam. interrog.* Amusing conference-call-derived riposte to a voluble *Exchange & Mart*.

hell raising flour *n.* Cocaine.

helmet *1. n.* The *bell end, glans, bishop's mitre, purple pearler. 2. n.* A quantity of *fellatio*. An amount of *blow jobs*. *'My nan wanted to meet Roger Whitaker, and she had to give the roadies helmet to get backstage.'*

helmetdale *n.* A strong-smelling, mature *knob cheese*.

helmet mag *n.* A *stroke periodical, art pamphlet, noddy book.*

helmet pelmet *n.* The *fiveskin, Kojak's roll-neck.*

helmetscale *n.* Fully ossified *Lymeswold* that has to be chipped off the *Pope's cap* using a toothpick or, in serious cases, a Dremel. Found only on the most determined opponents of genital hygiene of the sort you might find hanging around in Maplin's.

helmet, to give it some *v.* To engage in an activity with some gusto. To give it *rice*, give it *welly*, give it *six-nowt*, go at it three cocks to the cunt. *'It may be necessary to apply a considerable amount of torque in order to loosen the wheel studs. Indeed, you may have to give the wheel brace quite a bit of helmet before they begin to yield.'* (from the *Austin Maxi Haynes Manual*, 1978).

help around the house *v.* To attempt to wash *shit* stains off the inside of the *bum sink* by half-heartedly aiming one's *piss* stream at them during the ad break in *Dickinson's Real Deal*.

helter skelter *n.* The urgent, churning sensation in the lower bowel which indicates the imminent arrival of a high-speed *mudchild* sitting on a metaphorical doormat with its boots sticking out forwards.

Hemingway sphinx *n.* A breed of hairless cat.

he must be taking a run-up *phr.* Jocosely optimistic assessment when a once urgent *turtle's head* inexplicably retreats back up the *bumhole*.

hench *adj.* Walking round like you've got two rolls of carpet under your arms.

Hench's revolver *n.* A small *fouling piece,* from the description of a murder weapon in Raymond Chandler's novel *The High Window, viz.* "...a belly

gun, with practically no barrel."

hen don't *n.* The sight which, when a chap walks into a bar in which are ensconced 15 *pissed-up* orange women wearing pink cowboy hats, causes him to turn on his heel and immediately walk straight back out again.

Hendrix on the high notes *sim.* Descriptive of the facial contortions of a gentleman in the final throes of the *vinegar strokes*, reminiscent of the late plank-spanker in full axe frenzy.

Henman *n.* An impotent fellow. Named after the former British tennis sensation Tim, who never managed to make it past the *semi* stage.

Henrietta Street *1. n.* An old, narrow, twisty thoroughfare in Whitby and thus *2. n.* An ageing, serpentine *clunge* with a strong aroma of kippers and haddock.

Henry *n. rhym. slang.* An act of *self pleasure*. From the name of the well known Yorkshire-based gun shop Henry Krank = Sherman tank.

Henry Moore *1. n. Philist.* A large pile of *shit* in a public place. *2. n.* A large reclining dog *turd* on the pavement.

Henry the Eighth *1. n.* A king amongst *farts,* that is to say one which will "do in the wife". *2. n.* A temporary, but nevertheless full-bodied, Tudor-style red beard formed on a man's chops after *dining at the Y* when *Arsenal are playing at home*.

he-nut butter *n.* Put crudely, the viscid liquid which contains spermatazoa, the male gametes or germ cells. In more scientific terms, *spaff, jitler, chalaza, baby batter etc.*

herbal essence *n.* The pulchritudinous likes of Helen Mirren, Lorraine Kelly and possibly, but probably not, Gillian Taylforth, who are "still giving you pleasure after 40 years". Actually, *definitely* not Gillian Taylforth.

Herbert Pocket *n.* The pocket that the *herbert* slips into. The *arsehole*. From the name of the character in *Great Expectations*, played in the 1946 film by Sir Alec Guinness, and the one that he gave to police upon his arrest for *cottaging*.

Herbie *n. medic.* The *clap*; the "love bug".

Herbie's bonnet *n.* A pleasingly curved *twat* with the number 53 stuck to it.

herbievore *n.* One who chows down exclusively on *beetle bonnets*.

here come the warm jets *exclam.* What Brian Eno says to his missus when he wakes up in the night with bad guts.

here's Donald! *exclam.* Articulated in the comedy horror style of Jack Nicholson in *The Shining*, just before, or immediately after, an extremely loud, noxious and offensive *exchange & mart.*

here's jobby! *exclam.* Similarly, an assertive interjection after a sinister entity forces its way through the *back door.*

here's one from my new album *exclam.* Something to say before *letting off*, typically garnering a reaction of palpable disappointment from one's audience.

here's one written by our drummer *exclam.* Something to say before counting in a rather tuneless and forgettable *rumpet voluntary.*

here's one you can warm yer hands on *1. exclam.* Often said by late *fanny-chopped* music legend Chas Hodges out of Chas & Dave when introducing one of his rockney combo's many hits. *2. exclam.* Said before rattling the beer bottles in the sideboard with a particularly gusty *knees-up*, which can subsequently be followed with a rousing cry of "Gertcha!"

here's what the critics are saying *exclam.* Announcement made just before you *drop your guts* in polite society. See also *and the thunderball is*, *and now on BBC4, our survey said, and now a word from our sponsor, please hold for the president etc.*

Hergest ridge *n.* An exceptionally unkempt and overgrown *biffin's bridge*, as immortalised by him who done the music for *The Exorcist* and *Blue Peter.*

Herman measles *n. medic. Cock rot.*

Herman's hermits *1. n.* Sixties English beat group fronted by Peter Noone. *2. n.* Pernicious species of *crab* native to the *herman jelmet* region. *'Dave had a lovely weekend in Amsterdam, but unfortunately he came back with Herman's hermits.'*

Hermione's handbag *n.* An endlessly capacious *kitten purse*, named after Hermione Granger out of Harry Potter, who cast a magical spell on her reticule so she could squeeze limitless quantities of stuff in it. *Mary Poppins's bag.*

hernobyl *n.* A bout of *rag week* meltdown, resulting in widespread, catastrophic damage to property, health and the environment.

heron's nest *n.* An even gnarlier *Terry Waite's allotment* with all twigs stuck out of it at funny angles. *A worzel gusset.*

herring under a fur coat *1. n.* A traditional Russian dish of fish with grated vegetables and fruit. *2. n. Sushi off the barbershop floor* enjoyed when *dining at the Y.*

Hershey highway *n. US.* Transatlantic *Bournville boulevard, Cadbury alley.*

Hershey highwayman *n. US.* An *ass bandit.*

Heskey *n.* A girl who *goes down* at the slightest touch.

he's lost a lot of blood *1. exclam.* Staple quote of many 1980s action movies, supposedly throwing into question whether or not the severely injured lead actor will pull through to the end of the film, whereas the whole audience knows perfectly well that of course he fucking will, on account of he's featured prominently on the posters and they'll need him for all the sequels. *2. exclam.* Something a gentleman might ruefully say to an unimpressed female companion, immediately preceding "this has never happened before".

hestrogen *n.* Hormone present in modern, cosmopolitan fellows.

heteroflexible *adj.* Said of a gent who is basically straight but occasionally hops onto *the other bus* for a couple of stops.

hettython *n.* The act of taking the day off work, closing the curtains and watching all five series of *Hetty Wainthrop Investigates.*

he VA glue *n.* Water-based, sticky white adhesive that, no matter how carefully it is used, invariably gets absolutely everywhere.

hey Google, what's this song? *exclam. interrog.* Something to say before whistling a familiar melody on the *poot flute.*

HGVino *n.* Name given to the bottles of alarmingly orange *piss* that are thrown out of passing lorries whose drivers are too lazy to stop at the services to *strain their greens.*

HGV positive *euph. medic.* Grave diagnosis made after running extensive tests on a lady with an *arse like the back end of a bus*, who *beeps when reversing.*

H-H-H-Hancock's half hour *exclam.* Said after a euphonious blast on the *trouser tuba.* Also *Ah … Ludwig, Sykes, you're a lady…I'm a man.*

hiatus symbol *n.* Any item flaunted by a woman as a signal that there'll be *none of that nonsense* tonight, *eg.* A box of *fanny napkins*, a packet of headache tablets on the bedside table, a wedding ring on the third finger of her left hand *etc.*

hibernating grizzly *n.* A big, hairy, brown *shit* asleep in the *claypit* that one would be foolish to rouse from its slumbers.

hickies *n. Slapper*-speak for love bites, *shag tags.*

hickory dick *n.* A *cock* so hard it would bend any nail that one might misguidedly attempt to drive into it.

hidden mucky *n.* A surreptitious *dump* essayed in a theme park.

hidden track *1. n.* An annoying, unwanted bit of music that suddenly comes on after a couple of minutes of silence at the end of an album. *2. n.* An extra bit of *turd* that unexpectedly makes its presence felt when you've already wiped your *dot* and pulled your *trolleys* up. A *Columbo. 3.*

n. A supplementary drip of *jitler* that drops out the end of the *giggle stick* about ten minutes after you've *crashed the yoghurt truck*. The *missing fish, post bolt*.

hide and squeak *n.* When in polite company, the desperate act of sneaking off to a quiet place in order to launch a loud *air biscuit* without reaping the social consequences.

hide the salami *n.* A bedtime game for two players, one *sausage* and a *hairy pie*. Also *sink the salami, bury the bratwurst, conceal the Cumberland.*

hiding denim *euph.* Exhibiting a *camel's toe.* *'Blimey, your nan's hiding a lot of denim today.'*

hiding policemen's helmets *adj.* Of a lady, to be *nipping out, smuggling peanuts.*

highbernate *v.* To enjoy a pleasant nap whilst *ripped to the tits.*

highdea *n.* A brilliant plan or scheme that is conceived while under the influence of stupefying intoxicants that, when viewed in the cold, sober light of day, is revealed to be a load of old *cack, eg.* Writing a sitcom about the funny things students say when stoned, building a floating city in the sky using helium-filled girders, or Fleetwood Mac's *Tusk* album. A West country equivalent is the term *cidea.*

highdrate *v.* To imbibe fluids with a view to getting drunk.

higher than a Jack! *1. exclam.* Bruce Forsyth's *Play Your Cards Right* catchphrase when a pair of contestants were, for example, endeavouring to win a bizarrely nondescript car. *2. exclam.* Foolhardy announcement made when *twisting on nineteen.* See also *brown roulette, Russian poolette, gamble and lose.*

high miler *n.* An *old banger* who looks like she's been round the clock a few times, but is still running, *eg.* Joan Collins, Shirley Bassey.

high pressure vein cane *n.* Short for the *nob.* Also *prick, tallywhacker, Hector the meat injector.*

high roller *n.* One who uses a startlingly large amount of toilet paper, due to either producing voluminous, low viscosity turds or having an inefficient *arse wiping* technique.

high speed rinse *n.* An act of *self pollution* committed in the shower. *Flinging in the rain.*

high street harpy *n.* The opposite of a *high street honey,* whatever that might be. A *chavtastic, scratter* woman of the sort that lurk in gangs in town centres, waiting for easily embarrassed, middle-aged men to pass, before yelling at them to show them their *cocks.*

high velocity trifle *n.* A soft *feeshus* fired from the *chocolate starfish* at great speed, which is instantly aerated into a smooth, frothy confection when it meets the outer atmosphere. The resultant fluffy material is ideal for pebble-dashing porcelain and has powerful adhesive properties when brought into contact with blankets, sleeping bags and quilts.

high vis jacket *n. medic.* A luminously-diseased *fiveskin* or syphilitic *bell-end.* Also known as a *whisky nose, ET finger* or *puffin beak.*

highway hock *n.* Half-full plastic bottles of *piss* ejected by lazy HGV drivers who can't be bothered to stop for a leak. Also *layby lager, trucker's tizer, kidney cider, scania scotch, hedge coke, wagon wine.*

hi-ho *exclam.* Half of the customary collective salutation employed by the vertically challenged when embarking on an ante-matitudinal journey to their subterranean place of employment.

Hilary *n. rhym. slang.* A *five knuckle shuffle.* From US actress Hilary Swank. *'I just seen that Carol Vorderman flogging loans on the satellite and I knocked out a quick Hilary there and then.'*

hillbilly's hat *n.* A particularly dishevelled *cock socket.* A *Clampett.*

hillbilly toothpick *n.* The bacula. A small, rod-like penis bone common to many mammals, such as skunks, raccoons and gophers. Typically used by inbred rural Americans to pluck corn dogs, chitterlings and hominy grits from what's left of their dentition prior to appearing on the *Jerry Springer Show.* Before he died, of course.

hill start *n.* The painstaking task of *pleasuring oneself* after a heavy drinking session, when reaching *biting point* can take hours.

Hilton breakfast *1. n.* A product or service which combines substandard quality with a premium price, facts which become apparent only when it is too late to change your mind and run away. Examples of *Hilton breakfasts* include poncy salon haircuts, Galloway pony treks and early morning meals at certain international hotel chains which will remain nameless for legal reasons. *2. n.* *Dining at the Y* on a badly lit *sextape.*

himbledon *n.* Fortnight long festival of *men's singles* enjoyed by sofa-bound bachelors watching the women's rounds of the famous All-England tennis tournament on television. With the curtains pulled tightly shut.

himlick manoeuvre *n. medic.* The urgent *rimming* of a choking man's *rusty bullet wound,* the sudden shock of which causes the victim to immediately cough up the offending item.

himulsion *n.* The white gloss which a keen *do-it-yourselfer* applies in a carefree manner to the ceiling, the walls, his wife's hair *etc.*, while flicking his *naughty paintbrush* about.

Hindenburg, hatch a *v.* To work up an incendiary abundance of highly inflammable *poopane gas* in the *rear hangar*, usually after eating broccoli. To release seven million cubic feet of explosive gas, causing onlookers to cry "Oh, the humanity!".

Hindenburg point *n.* The theoretical limit of *scrotal inflation*. Best avoided, we would imagine.

hind-shite *1. n. Post hoc* social media wisdom. *2. n.* Retrospective alimentary wisdom. *'With hindshite, I should never have eaten that second spicy chicken burger, your holiness.'*

hindsight *n.* The distraction of looking at an attractive, repulsive, or otherwise interesting posterior. *Hindsight* is estimated to be the cause of 95% of low-speed rear-end collisions on British high streets, and up to 99% of accidents involving straw-hatted vicars riding their bicycles into hedges. *'Sorry officer. In hindsight, I didn't pay enough attention to that red light. Or that bus queue.'*

hinging oan by a midge baa-hair *phr. Scots.* In a difficult position or with a vanishingly small chance of success. *'With such a slim majority, the Prime Minister is hinging oan by a midge baa-hair as she attempts to get this legislation through the Commons so that it can be rejected by the House of Lords next week.'*

hingoot *n. Scots.* A lady of easy virtue, a *slapper*, a *prossie*, a *good time girl*. Literally, a woman who has enjoyed so much *cock* that her fanny is "hinging oot".

hip-hop *1. n.* Rhythmical rap-based musical genre originally from the USA. *2. n.* Painful-looking street waddle performed by unfortunates at the wrong end of the NHS arthroplasty waiting list.

hippobotamus *n.* A large, out of proportion, lady's rear end, of the sort viewed when following Kerry Katona down the desserts aisle at Iceland. *Arse like a Toyota Rav-4.*

hippocrocapig *n.* A lady with the *loveliest personality* you could imagine.

hippo's ear *n.* A *hippo's mouth*. A *donkey's yawn*. A *fanny* like a fucking *bucket*.

hippo's ears *n.* Petite *nips* displayed on disproportionately large *milky swingers*, somewhat reminiscent of the tiny external auditory structures seen on the river-dwelling Moomin-faced ungulates.

hippo's jaw *n.* A large and over-extended *fadge* into which you could throw a bucket of buns. Also *donkey's earhole, clown's pocket.*

hippo's mouth *n.* Another large, unsightly,

gaping vagina.

hippo's saddle *n.* Something big, grey and leathery in a lady's *knickers. Elephants' ears.*

hipposuction *n.* Over-optimistic cosmetic surgical procedure carried out on the larger lady.

hipsies *n.* Tree-hugging new-age travellers who travel around in smoke-billowing old buses.

hipster blowing a kiss *euph.* A very hairy *arsehole.*

hipster's beard, fanny like a *sim.* A particularly well-groomed, hirsute *quim* that is prone to gentrification and can be tugged on while pondering.

hipster wank *n.* An artisan act of *onanistic self delight* performed over charmingly *tosstalgic* material such as the bra pages of a Kays or Grattan catalogue from the 1970s or Pan's People on a BBC4 re-run of *Top of the Pops*. Though not that one where they did *Monster Mash*.

hip tits *n.* Those flabby rolls of stomach blubber that hang down around the waists of those unbelievably fat Americans you see waddling around Disneyland. *Bilge tanks, jerry cans.*

his dark materials *1. n.* Popular TV series, based on the work of Philip Pullman, in which human souls take on animal form. *2. n.* A physical or digital stash of *grumble* that brings out a chap's baser, more bestial instincts, forcing him into having *one off the wrist. 3. n.* A *non-mover at number two* left for the missus to deal with, typically on a Saturday morning.

hissing Sid *n.* One's *one-eyed trouser snake.*

hit and miss *rhym. slang.* Piss.

hit and run *v.* To indulge in sexual intercourse with a *boiler* despite one's better judgement, then *leg it* before she wakes up.

hit a shit wall *v.* To saunter into a previously occupied lavatory where the stench of a previous incumbent's *gaseous clay* stops you dead in your tracks like Steven Hawking with a flat battery.

hitch-hiking under the big top *n.* Early morning *blanket drill; starching the sheets, polishing the tent pole.*

hitching to heaven *n.* More thumb-based *hand to gland* combat.

hit from the pong, a *n.* A bath-time *Lionel Bart* that bubbles up like a puff on a water pipe; a *shit-hole shisha.*

Hitler piss *n.* A braced, inadvertent nazi salute position from which to have a drunken *Chinese singing lesson* at the pub toilet trough.

Hitler's hat stand, seen more helmets than *sim.* Said of a woman who is *generous with her affections. 'I wouldn't say she's easy, but she's seen more helmets than Hitler's hatstand. Ladies and gentlemen, let's give a big Royal Variety Performance* *welcome to Sarah Ferguson, Duchess of York.'*

Hitler tash *n.* A *clitler, shreddie* or *Lamborghini*.

Hitler tods *phr.* Used to describe something unspeakably rotten. *'Have you listened to that album that Nick Knowles made? It's absolute Hitler tods.'*

Hitler wank *n.* An act of *self-pollution* performed in a shower with the right arm lodged firmly against the cubicle wall to prevent loss of balance.

hit the ground drinking *v.* Upon commencing a new challenge or activity, to put it off or give up almost immediately in order to get *shitfaced* instead. *'Within a few months of the Covid pandemic reaching our shores, and with Brits dropping like flies, the PM rolled up his sleeves and hit the ground drinking.'*

hit the sack *1. v.* To go to bed. *'Well, it's time to hit the sack, I suppose, dear.' 2. n.* To knock one out energetically, like a boxer at the gym. *'Ah well, the missus has hit the sack. Time to put Babestation on and hit the sack.'*

hit the snooze button *v.* To give oneself an extra fifteen sticky minutes in the old *wanking chariot* first thing. *'Sorry I'm late, only I hit the snooze button five times this morning. But thanks for the OBE anyway, your majesty.'* (Jonathan Ross, Buckingham Palace, 2005).

hit unmute *1. v.* Typically performed shortly after silently *dropping one's hat* during a virtual work meeting or live BBC News interview. *2. v.* To activate a partner's *wail switch* during a romantic assignation; *ring the devil's doorbell, hit the panic button* and so on.

HMP *abbrev.* A lady for whom only the finest things in life will do. High Maintenance Pussy.

HMS Brown Surprise *n.* A *dreadnaught* that is laid down and, despite being flushed out to sea, remains proudly lurking in the U-bend, just within eyeshot and ready to defend the *chod-bin* from enemy attack.

ho *n.* What a sexist rapper calls his *bitch.*

HOB *abbrev. RAF.* Hang Over Blanket. The comforting quilt from under which a chap spends the day watching Cartoon Network following a heavy night of *top shelf drinking.*

hobbit *n.* A small hairy thing.

hobbit dick *n.* A *penis* that is wider than it is long. A *tuna can cock, Welshman's cock, choad, chooza.*

hobble squat *n.* The locomotive technique employed by one who has just *released the chocolate hostage*, only to discover that there is a marked dearth of *shit tickets* in his *chod booth.* Also known as the *convict's shuffle, jailbreak,*

paperchase or *the penguin.*

hobgoblin *n.* A *bumgoblin.*

hobnail boots, that one wore *exclam.* A phrase shouted loudly in order to make the most of a volubly *dropped gut. 'In polite company, following another's audible act of flatulence, it is permissible to offer a comment. If the wind breaker was the wife of a Governor General, one might say 'One-nil to you, your Excellency'. If the younger son of a Duke has farted, a comment such as 'Fuck me, that one wore hobnail boots, my Lord,' would be perfectly acceptable.'* (from *Debrett's Etiquette*, 1928).

hobnob *1. n.* A big, dirty *ringpiece*, barnacled with such an excess of *winnetry* that it takes on the appearance of the much-loved, family biscuit. *2. v.* To engage in sexual congress on a kitchen work surface, especially the top of the cooker.

hobo latte *n.* A cosmopilitan pick-me-up as drunk by a merry gentleman of the road. *Spesh,* white cider, *sub-prime wine, electric soup.*

hobophobic *adj.* Averse to gentlemen of the road. *'Ooh no, Nigel never buys the Big Issue. He's violently hobophobic.'*

hobo slapiens *n.* An itinerant chap who is happy to engage in unarmed combat with all-comers and who can thus usually be discovered sitting in A&E with a bloody vest tied round his head by 2pm at the latest.

Ho Chi Minge *euph.* A straggly, unkempt *nether beard* on a female lady. From its likeness to the straggly, unkempt-*fanny*-like *face fungus* of the popular North Vietnamese leader. Also *Fufu Manchu.*

hockler's draught *n.* A slimy, green *prairie oyster* produced the morning after a night of brown beer and *Harry Wraggs.* A *docker's omelette, gold watch, greb, gilbo, sheckle, gonga, Old Leigh oyster, phlegm brûlée, tramp's breakfast, greeny* or *Dutch pikelet.*

Hockley Heath beef eater *n.* A sexual position much favoured in the West Midlands. Named in honour of a well known clandestine *shagging* hotel near the M42.

hockmagandy *n.* The one day of the year when Scotsmen *fuck* their wives. *McFannyversary, carpet burns night.*

hoeing the HP *v.* Uphill gardening on the *brown sauce allotment.*

HOFNAR/hofnar *1. n.* prop. A mid-nineties Seattle-based college band. *2. acronym. US.* Hard-On For No Apparent Reason.

hogans *n. US.* Heroic *Charlies, Gert Stonkers, Norma Snockers.*

hog line *1. n.* In curling, the visible red strip marking where a curler must release the stone. *2.*

n. The urethral opening in the *bobby's helmet.* The *chap's eye.*

hog roast *1. n.* An act of sexual congress involving two short-sighted centre forwards and an aesthetically challenged female. *2. n. Corn on the cob* featuring two young blokes and an older, chubby *bird,* usually at the behest of her camera-toting hubbie.

hog's eye *n.* The serving hatch through which *perseverance soup* arrives.

hog's eye hairpiece *n. Aus.* That long, piss-combed tuft of hair that seems to grow out the end of a dog's *unit.* Like on the top of Woody Woodpecker's head.

hogwarts *1. n.* Fictional school that would, one might reasonably suppose, fall foul of much current Health & Safety legislation that relates to educational premises. *2. n. medic.* A sexually transmitted infection that might well be picked up during the initiation ceremony for an exclusive Oxford University dining club.

hoho sapiens *n.* Risible human beings who populate most so-called "reality" television programming, noted for their fake tans, *trout pouts,* and meaningless tattoos. *'Come through here, vicar, and watch this fucking hoho sapiens on Married at First Sight.'*

hoist the vein sail *v.* To obtain a *stiffy.* To *round Cape Horn,* in the expectation of a faceful of salty spume.

hokey cokey *n.* A *grumble*-inspired *money shot*; one that goes "in, out, in, out, shake it all about", if you will.

hokey cokey relationship *n.* When the missus kicks you out and you go back and the missus kicks you out and you go back *etc.*

hold the foam *v.* To conjure up a mental image of an ugly person in an attempt to postpone ejaculation. To *bring the safety car out.*

hold your nerve *v.* To bravely *step on a duck* when suffering from a bout of the *runs.* To *twist on nineteen.*

hole *1. n.* Anything you can stick something up. *2. n.* The next category of sexual attainment up the scale after *cloth tit* and *tops* and *fingers.* *'Did you get your hole?' 'Ooh yes, I got me hole alright.'*

hole brothers *n.* Literal translation of the charming Japanese term *Anakyōdai,* describing two or more men who have had relations with the same lady. Also *custard cousins, twatmates, brothers quim.*

hole food *n.* Free-range *pork* that satisfies the appetites of revellers at a *polony party. Cock.*

hole hiccups *n. medic.* Flatulence. *'I do beg your pardon, vicar. My nan is suffering from hole hiccups at the moment.'*

hole in one *n.* Successful penile intromission without using the hand for guidance.

hole milk *n. Vitamin S.*

hole of the moon *1. n. 1985* Waterboys single taken from the group's 1985 album *This Is The Sea.* *2. n.* A *barking spider. 'I saw the rain dirty valley, you saw the hole of the Moon.'* *3. n.* The art of manually parting the buttock cheeks in order to give passers by a better view of one's *chocolate starfish* when *mooning. Hanging your hole, playing Brigadoon.*

holesale *n.* A generous discount offered by a *lady of the night.*

holeslaw *n.* Random bits of cabbage and suchlike protruding from the *rusty sheriff's badge.*

holiday money *n.* Male genitalia, the *family jewels, meat and two veg,* the *fruit bowl.*

holiday on rice *n.* Any trip to a foreign locale where the exotic cuisine sampled enthusiastically on the first day leaves one with such a bad case of the *shits* that one only dares eat boiled rice, or something equally bland, for the rest of one's stay. *'Oh yes, Sid had the tom yam goong as his starter and I had the pla nueng manao. For the main course he had chu chi pla kraphong, and I went for the suea rong hai and kaeng khae. For pudding, we both had the khanom bua loi. It really was absolutely delicious. The rest of the fortnight was a holiday on rice.'*

Holland Street hopscotch *n.* Light-hearted game played by residents of the eponymous East Hull boulevard, as they avoid the vast amounts of *hound rope* on the pavement while making their way to Fulton's Foods and Greggs.

hollyoats *n.* A leisurely Sunday afternoon bout of *personal pollution* enjoyed while watching the omnibus edition of the blonde-heavy Chester-based soap.

Hollywood ending *1. n.* A satisfying cinematic denouement in which good triumphs over evil and everyone goes home happy. *2. n.* A *Tom tit* that necessitates no wiping.

Hollywood halo *n.* A thoroughly waxed and bleached *ringpiece,* affording a glorious view replete with undoubted star quality to anyone approaching from the *gasworks end.*

Hollywood handshake *n.* A *wank.*

Hollywood loaf *1. n.* A high-quality, lovingly crafted and crusty cake of brown bread made to the exacting standards of Paul, top pastry chef star of *The Great British Bake Off.* *2. n.* A similarly high-quality and aesthetically pleasing *U-bend blocker* which has been lovingly baked for several hours. A proper *showstopper.* *3. n.* A *podge-on, half a teacake.* So named because of its popularity with male actors called upon to perform in the nude.

Hollywood wax *n.* A completely depilated *mingepiece*. A *Barthez*.

holmaphobe *n.* A person with an entirely rational hatred of *fat fuck* Eamonn Holmes.

holodeck 4, if anyone needs me I'll be on *exclam.* Quote from a *Star Trek: The Next Generation* episode entitled *The Perfect Mate*, when Fammke Jannsen tries it on with Riker, and he somehow resists temptation, makes his excuses and leaves. Having *one off the wrist* when you're really, really *on the horn*.

holy gust *n.* The third member of the sacred trinity, after *piss* and *shit*.

Holyhead ballgown *n.* An inexpensive, budget-branded polyester outfit of the style favoured by the elegant society ladies of the charming North Wales town.

holy shit *1. exclam.* Mild imprecation made by Batman's sidekick upon entering a Virgin Trains toilet. *2. n.* When moving into a new dwelling or property, the ceremonial *christening* of the *chod bin*.

holy trinity *1. n.* A scene in a *bongo movie* where a triumvirate of male thespians simultaneously enter a single actress via the three main access portals thoughtfully provided by Mother Nature. *2. n.* One twenty pound note, one tenner and one fiver destined for a quiet night down the pub. *3. n.* A *shit*, a shower and a shave, though not necessarily in that order. The *shushes*. *4. n.* Engaging in anal, oral and vaginal sex in one session.

homage *n. Knobcheese.* From the French *homme* + *fromage.* Also *foreskinzola, bunnet brie, Hamish blue, he-dam, helmetdale, purple Leicester, brimula, knacker barrel, Fred Leicester, peckerino, bellendsleydale, willydelphia, mozzerfella, veinish blue, Cheear, Lymeswold* etc.

hombrero *n.* A *titfer* that is worn for style reasons as opposed to practicality. A *twhat*.

homburger *n.* A vegetarian fast food option for *good listeners*.

home baking aisle *1. n.* The least popular section of the supermarket. *2. n.* The *arse crack*, where *air biscuits, chocolate logs* and *fudge loaf* are prepared.

home brew *1. n.* Laser-print quality *grumble mags* made from *cyber scud*. *2. n.* The offspring of an ill-judged value vodka-fuelled liaison between two members of the same family, usually – but not exclusively – to be seen having a shirtless punch-up on the *Jerry Springer Show*, or some such current daytime TV *prolefest*. *'Yeah, there's definitely a touch of the home brew about that one.'*

Have you seen the size of his fucking ears?'

home entertainment system *n.* A bachelor's pride and joy; his frequently polished genitals.

homegrown *n.* Hallucinogenic gases produced from one's own *gazoo*, courtesy of which it is reputedly possible to "get high on your own supply".

home office *n.* The ideal ergonomic set-up when *working from home, viz.* Drawn curtains, some tissues, a laptop and several cans of Monster energy drink.

homeopathic shandy *n.* Beer with 0.00000000000000001% lemonade in it. A pint.

home secretary *1. n.* His Majesty's Principal Secretary of State for the Home Department. *2. n.* The *breadknife*. *3. n.* In the specific circumstances whereby your missus is the Rt. Hon. Priti Patel MP between the years of 2019 and 2022, both.

hominous *adj.* Of events, about to turn a tad *Whitley Bay* with tragic consequences. *'I've just been invited back to a swimming pool party at the home of a popular comedian, all-round entertainer and quiz-show host.' 'That sounds hominous.'*

hommage *n.* Act of devotion performed in a kneeling position.

homnambulist *n.* Chap who gets an inexplicable urge to go walking about on Hampstead Heath in the wee small hours.

hom. sap. *1. n. abbrev.* Trendy shorthand for "Homo Sapiens". *2. n. Jism* that seeps out the end of the old *family tree*.

homversation *n.* Of males, the discussion of anything at all except cars and football, but particularly *Coronation Street*, clothes, hair and cottaging anecdotes.

honesty box bargain *n.* A *five fingered discount* available to the value-conscious shopper at railway station newsagents. Named after the express counter which used to be thoughtfully provided for the use of passengers who were in a hurry not to pay.

honey altar *n.* The sunken treasure that the *muff diver* goes in search of. The *pearly gates*.

honey bucket *1. n.* A song by alternative rock band The Melvins off their 1993 album *Houdini*. Us neither. *2. n.* A well-*milmed chuftie* with all bees buzzing round it.

honey glaze *n.* The shine on one's *pork sausage* the morning after a penetrative romantic assignation.

Honey Monster's eyelids *euph.* The visible top half of a buxom lady's *funbags* when she is sporting a strapless frock.

honeymoon period *1. n.* For a bloke, the happy, short-lived period between his bird's *rag weeks*. *2.*

n. A really frustrating post-matrimonial holiday.

honeypot *n.* A waxy *fanny* surrounded by bees.

Hong Kong Phooey's filing cabinet, banged more times than *sim.* See *fucked more times than Michael Owen's knee, rogered more times than a policeman's radio.*

Hong Kong Pooey *n.* A process of deduction undertaken while ensconced on the *throne* with a bad dose of the *Brads,* whereby the previous day's meals are pondered over in the style of the eponymous cheaply animated *shite* 1970s martial arts/janitor/dog/crimefighter cartoon series. "Was it the binding four-egg omelette for breakfast? No. Was it the cheese pastie and Scotch egg lunch? No. Was it the gallon of Guinness and chicken Madras supper? Could be!"

honkies *n.* Big *muckspreader* round back, thumb up *bum,* all business.

honk up *v.* To *hoy up, bowk.*

honourable member for Morningwood North, the *n.* How the Speaker of the House refers to his first *stiffie* of the day.

honour, Scouse *exclam.* Merseyside-based variation of Baden-Powell's famous oath of youthful trustworthiness. *'Yeah, no worries. I'll look after the till, mate. Scouse honour.'*

honour the crowd *v.* To *let rip* with such an evil smell that innocent bystanders are forced to stand and applaud. *'And Henman honours the crowd as he bends down to pick up his kit for his annual Wimbledon early exit, and gracious me, judging by the stains on his shorts, the poor fellow must have followed through.'* (Dan Maskell (deceased) BBC TV commentary).

hooberstank *n.* The first, and usually biggest, *fart* of the morning. *Morning thunder, reveille, dawn chorus.* A *full English breakfast maker.*

hoobs *1. n.* A bizarre set of Muppet aliens which used to appear on Channel 4 in the mornings. *2. n.* A particularly impressive set of *funbags* which, if they made a sound, which they do not, would make a sound not unlike blowing across the top of a jeroboam. From huge + boobs. Also *hoobies.*

hood *n.* An eager *horatialist,* named after the British battle cruiser that famously got sank off the Bismarck, and "went down in less than three minutes".

hoodwink *1. v.* To deceive, or mislead by falsehood, *eg.* When selling endowment mortgages or pension schemes. *2. v.* The act of squeezing the *fiveskin* over the *Dutch strawberry* in order to encourage the last few drops of *piss* to exit the *blow hole.*

hoofpaste *n.* A feminine hygiene product, *eg.*

Vagisil, Canestan, Jeyes or Sprunt.

hoo-ha *1. onomat.* Noise made by a person doing an impression of Al Pacino. *2. n.* The female *parts of shame.* *'Britney, for the last time will you put your fucking underkecks back on. No-one wants to see your hoo-ha.'*

hooker *1. n. US.* A *ho', pro* or *good time girl.* *2. n.* A bloke in a rugby scrum who performs sexual favours in return for money.

hooker porridge *n.* The wholesome, steaming, oaty contents of a *lady of the night* after a long shift.

hooker's toothpaste *n. Merry monk.*

hookie nookie *n.* A day spent indulging in penetrative *how's your father* with one's new special friend, while officially stricken down with "that one day tummy bug that's been doing the rounds lately". A *duvet lay.*

hooking fish *v. Feeding the ducks, stabbing the cat, playing the one-string banjo.*

hook, line and sphincter *phr.* A measure of the ardour with which an *arse man* falls head over heels for the crinkly object of his affections.

hoop *1. n.* The *twot.* *2. n.* The *dot.*

hoopage *n.* A spot of the old *bum sex.* *'The lotus floats upon the lake in the moonlight / Knickers off love and bend over / I fancy a bit of hoopage for a change.'* (from *Up the Bum No Babies – a Haiku Collection* by Matsunaga Teitoku).

hoop flogger *n.* A lady who is *on the batter.*

hoop, furry *n.* A *biffer* or *sweep's brush.*

hoop soup *n. medic.* The *runs, trots, squits* etc. Galloping diarrhoea. *'Sorry I had to rush off while you were talking to me just then, only I've had this terrible hoop soup for weeks, and I felt another bowlful coming on. Anyway, I'm back now. Can I finish taking your order?' I can particularly recommend the caramel mousse.'*

hoop stretcher *n.* A *crafty butcher* who hides his *salami* in a *tea towel holder.*

hootchie *n. US. Totty, blit, muff.*

hootchie cootchie *n. Hanky panky, how's your father.*

hooter *n. Conk, neb, sneck.* Nose. Not the singular of *hooters.*

hootermammy *n.* A former *Miss Lincolnshire* who receives a visit from the *titty fairy* during pregnancy. One who has *collected the baby bonus.*

hooters *n. Bazookas, baps, headlamps.* Not the plural of *hooter.*

Hoover's disease *n. medic.* Condition contracted by all women shortly after they get married, where they make a continual whining sound but "don't suck any more". Also *Dyson's syndrome.*

hoover up *v.* To try, usually unsuccessfully, to "sniff up" the smell of a recently dropped *fart* when one sees an attractive woman approaching.

hope and anchor *1. n.* Popular pub/live music venue in that London. *2. n. rhym. slang. Wanker.*

HOP/hop *acronym.* Hang Over Poo. Giant, exceedingly loose stool, the noisy passing of which is a significant milestone on the road to recovery from a hangover. An *alcopoop* or *escape sub. 'Ahh! I feel much better after that hop. Anyone fancy a pint?'*

hop into the horse's collar *v.* Nip to the *municipal cock wash*.

hop o'my thumb *1. n.* Fairy tale, written by Charles Perrault, about a tiny child who overcomes adversity and steals some boots off a giant. *2. n.* An unenthusiastic *third leg jump*, the issue from which which fails to clear one's opposable digit, thus temporarily precluding the possibility of one living happily ever after.

hopper arse *n.* A *forty guts* or *salad dodger*. A *big-boned* person, with really fat *glands* that can't stop guzzling crisps.

hoptical illusion *n.* A ropey *piece* who appears beautiful when viewed through *beer goggles*.

horatio *n.* Posh Latin term used by doctors, lawyers and police to describe a *chewie*.

horifice *n.* An horrifically unkempt, overgrown or otherwise offensive anatomical cleft.

horizontal jogging *n.* Hilarious golf club bar euphemism for sexual intercourse, used by blokes like Basil Fawlty's brother-in-law Roger, *esp.* "a bit of the old…".

horizontally accessible *adj.* Describing a young lady with *yoyo knickers*.

horizontally tall *euph.* Fat.

hornbag *1. n.* A bag for keeping horns in. *2. n.* An extremely attractive woman, *ie.* One who gives you *the horn*.

hornbeam *1. n.* Hardwood trees of the flowering plant genus *Carpinus*. *2. n.* A *fleshlight*. What used to be called a *pocket fanny*; a torch filled with swarfega.

horn breaker *n.* An overly-enthusiastic rider of the *horse's handbrake*.

horn chorus *n.* A very loud, early morning wakeup call from an adjacent hotel or halls of residence room, usually at around three am or, failing that, about half an hour after the local nightclubs kick out. The *horn chorus* is typically accompanied by the sound of squeaking bedsprings and/or a rhythmic thumping noise through the connecting wall.

horndog *n.* An extremely unattractive woman, *ie.* One who loses you the *horn*. A *derection, lumberjill*.

hornithology *n.* The non-scientific study of *birds*,

which is best, nevertheless, carried out from the safety of a hide.

horn of Gondor! *1. exclam.* A shout made by Legolas in *The Lord Of The Rings – The Fellowship of The Ring*, following an almighty blast from Boromir, played by Sean Bean (pronounced Sean Bean). *2. n.* An exclamation made after a *lord of the ringpiece* drops an almighty blast.

hornpipe *1. n.* In olden days, a lively rhythmical movement associated with sailors. *2. n.* See *1*.

horn, the *n.* Ceremonial symbol of a man's affection for a woman, paradoxically given by the woman to the man.

hornucopia *n.* Any *adult* video website which presents a temptingly wide selection of abstruse categories to peruse.

horny *1. adj.* The state of a man in possession of *the horn*, or indeed a woman who fancies a shot on it. *2. adj.* Descriptive of a woman who gives a man *the horn. 'Hey, that Kate Silverton on BBC News 24 is well horny.'*

horror express *n.* Taken after a night of beer and fast food, a long journey on a train with no functioning toilet facilities – that is to say most trains. Named after the 1970s movie starring Peter Cushing, Christopher Lee and Telly Savalas. Us neither.

Horse and Hound *1. n.* Glossily-produced magazine for people who live in the country and like animals and killing things. *2. n.* The "readers' wives" section at the less salubrious end of the *art pamphlet* shelf.

horse blowing after the Grand National, blowing like a *sim.* Suffering from stentorian flatulence; a reference to the similar sound produced by one of the few nags who survive to the end of the popular steeplechase/glue manufacturers' productivity drive.

horsebox *n.* Any "value" packet lasagne purchased in a supermarket.

horse curtains *n. Beef curtains* that are definitely not as advertised.

horse eating oats *sim.* Feeding the pony. *'And David went unto the house of Bathsheba and she had not known her husband Naboth for ages. And David did put his hand down her knickers and lo, it was like a horse eating oats.'* (*Deuteronomy 6:23*).

horse flu *n.* The HN-Bet365 virus that strikes down many an Irishman during the Cheltenham festival.

horse's collar *1. n.* A big old vagina. *2. sim.* Comparison implying generous *farmyard* proportions. *Cathedral, clown's pocket, hippo's mouth. 'I wouldn't say my wife's got a tight minge, ladies and gentlemen. That's because she's got a* *fanny like a horse's collar.'*

horse's doofers *n.* Superlative *mutt's nuts, dog's bollocks*, bee's knees. The *donkey's knob.*

horse's handbrake *n.* A *diamond cutter*, a *concrete donkey*; a raging *bone on* wrought from *pink steel.*

horse's head, sitting on a *phr.* Of people queueing for the *dunny*, suffering from a more extreme case of the *turtle's head*. *'Hurry up will you, your majesty. I'm sitting on a horse's head out here.'*

horseshoe, the *n.* The act of arranging one's favourite *technical manuals* in a semicircular fashion, each one opened at its most alluring double-page spread, before indulging in a session of frenzied *self pollution*. A *Dutch rainbow, crescent wank.*

horse's nose *n.* The early stages of a *Beverley Craven* being allowed to grow out. Noticeable when *feeding the pony*. *Five o'clock fanny.*

horse snout *n.* Of a lady of a certain age, sporting a "no hair" policy in the *farmyard area.*

horse startler *n.* A p*nis of such girth that it would cause severe distress if inserted into an equine. *'Oh do put your horse startler away, Eric. Lord Reith's coming round to look at your sketches for that sculpture you're doing on Broadcasting House.'*

horse that has been machine-gunned in a tunnel, fanny like a *sim.* A charmingly poetic figure of speech for an aesthetically displeasing *ladygarden* apparently coined by cheeky family entertainer Frankie Boyle. *'Births: Chumley. At the Portland Hospital, London. To Porphyria (née Fanshaw) and Aethelstan, quadruplets Atticus (10lb 6oz), Leander (11lb 3oz), Ulysses (12lb) and Dave (12lb 6oz). Babies doing well and mother nursing a fanny like a horse that has been machine-gunned in a tunnel. Deo gracias.'*

hosebag *n.* Woman of loose morals. She with a *twat* like a *paper hanger's bucket*. *A dollymop, slapper.*

hose job *n.* Blow job, chewie, horatio.

hose monster *n.* An ugly woman who cannot get enough hosepipes.

hosepipe ban *n.* A seasonal veto on *the other*, imposed by *her indoors.*

hospital button *n.* A particularly unhealthy looking *gold watch*. *'Call 999 love. I've just howked up a hospital button.'*

hoss piss *n.* A Cumbrian term for an extremely protracted act of micturition following a night of heavy drinking.

hostilery *n.* A flat roof pub which extends a less-than-wholehearted welcome to its patrons. See also *chapel of rest*, *eg.* The Flying Shuttle, Bolton.

hot *adj.* Condition which, in conjunction with

horny, was often used to describe tubby, bored women eating crisps and doing the *Take a Break* crossword on the end of expensive telephone sex lines, *eg.* *'Hot and horny bitches thirsty for your love seed. £1.80/min.'*

hot and cold running urinal *n. milit.* The sink. May also be used as an ashtray or even, in a dire emergency, somewhere to wash the hands. See *Bradford dishwashing.*

hotapotamus *n.* Politically correct term for a woman who is *big-boned* yet attractive.

hot arse flower *n.* A warm *brass section.*

HOTBOT/hotbot *acronym.* Expression of one's desire for a *dog's marriage*. Hang Out The Back Of That.

hot Brompton *n.* The romantic act of *snipping off a length of dirty spine* in your fair lady's cleavage and using her *whammers* to squash it. This country is going to the dogs.

hot circle *n.* Letting go of a particularly rancid *Exchange & Mart* and then walking round a (seated or standing) group of unsuspecting friends, thus imprisoning them in an invisible, sulphurous stockade from which there is no escape.

hot cross bun *n.* Pattern often seen iced across the face of certain actresses performing in artistic filmed dramas.

hot cup of tea with two lumps *n.* The practice of *teabagging*, but this time with the *teapot's* mouth full of hot water. *Warming the pod*, *PG lips*, *dick brew.*

hot daughter bottle *n.* An unsolicited gift (often alcoholic) given to the parents of a particularly pert bit of *tussage* by a suitor in a bid to ingratiate himself with them and thus ease access to the contents of their daughter's *tit pants* and/or *dunghampers*. *'Good evening Mr and Mrs Knightley. I've brought you a hot daughter bottle as a present. It's Ballycastle ... just like Baileys but only £3.99 in Aldi. Is your Keira in?'*

hot desking *1. n.* In business, the practice of several employees sharing the same workspace. *2. n.* In the lavatory, the uncomfortable sensation of sitting down on a toilet seat that is still warm from the previous patron. Also called a *Shoeburyness* in the *Meaning of Liff.*

hot dog *1. n.* An egg delicacy famously enjoyed by the cult actor Divine in the film *Pink Flamingoes* (Children's Film Foundation, 1977). *2. v.* To eat said morsel, freshly laid by a poodle. *3. v.* To slap one's *sausage* into a lady's *buns*, with plenty of onions.

hot-dog end *n.* The *turtle's head*. From the similarity to how a hot-dog sausage looks when poking out of the end of a bread roll. *'Hurry up in the shit house, gran. I've got a hot-dog end here.'*

hotel toast *euph.* Descriptive of a girl who's not as *hot* as she once was.

hot fish yoghurt *n.* Cream sauce filling for a *hairy pie.*

hot fog *n.* A *guff* with the unmistakeable, cloying aroma of oxtail soup.

hot fudge Sunday *n.* The inevitable aftermath of a *hot curry Saturday.*

hot glue gun *n.* A male *Frankie* star's *willy.*

hot hello *n.* The warm trickle down her leg that reminds a lady of the *monetary* deposit that was recently made into her *special bank.*

hot karl *n.* Post-anal sex *horatio.*

hot lunch *n.* See *Cleveland steamer.* Or better still, don't.

hot meat injection *n.* An inoculation with the *spam syringe.*

hot monocle *n.* Half a *Velma.* A *facial* which reduces the *bag for life*'s ability to see by fifty percent. Also *Gabrielle, King Harold.*

hot plate *n.* When a *lady of the night drops a log* on a customer's chest. Also something to cook your tea on, though you may well be off your food, all things considered. See also *Boston pancake.*

hot pocket *n.* Stomach-wrenching, high calorie, American *discomfort food* snack, conveniently designed for the *bigger-boned* individual. 2. *n.* A roll of blubber that one's *bendy bully* accidently slips into while romancing a woman *with a lovely personality.*

hot poo shuffle *n.* The troubled gait of one who is urgently, yet tentatively, making their way to the lavatory before a recent spicy meal manages to burn its way out.

hot, runny shit off a stainless steel shovel, like *sim.* Descriptive of something very rapid. *'Massa went to overtake, seemed to jink to the right into Perez, who seemed to be moving to the left to line up an overtake on Vettel, and the two of them speared off the track into the barriers like hot, runny shit off a stainless steel shovel.'*

hots, the *n.* What *birds* get for Spanish waiters.

hot stones *n.* The buckshot-like, high temperature slurry passed the morning after a spicy *cuzza.* The lumps that articulate the consonant sounds in a *Calcutta splutter.* Also *solar stones.*

hot tub *1. n.* A jacuzzi. 2. *n.* An alluringly *filfy plumper.*

hotty *n.* US. *Totty, blart. Hot patootie.*

hot water bottle *n.* An unattactive woman who is taken into a bloke's bed purely in order to keep it warm. *'I don't know what he sees in her.' 'She's a hot water bottle. He'll chuck her in the Spring.'*

hound *n.* Offensively sexist term for a *dog, steg, boiler.*

hound cable *n.* Barker's rope, footstool. Dog shite.

house of flying daggers *1. n.* 2004 Chinese action movie starring Ziyi Zhang, Dandan Song and Hongfei Zhao. No, us neither. 2. *n.* A man's home during the one week every month when his better half is *dropping clots.*

housewarming gift, leave a *v.* To make a deposit of *foulage* in the *biscuit wrapper* of a friend's house, but not pull the chain.

Houston we have a problem *exclam.* Internally voiced message of alarm after inadvertently *following through.*

hovercraft, the *n.* A *queef* causing a substantial set of *Keith Burtons* to billow outwards, the overall effect somewhat reminiscent of the bulging skirts on one of the popular air-cushioned comedy boats of the 1970s that, if we imagine them now, usually had Cilla Black or Shirley Bassey stood on them, belting out some song in a gale.

hovercrapt *n.* The acrobatical art of balancing above a *public bog crapper* in order to *lay a cable* without your clean *arse cheeks* touching the filthy, germ-ridden seat.

hovis *n.* A particularly tight *snapper.* A *butler's cuff.* From the bread advertising slogan: "White with all the goodness of brown."

how a cat's arse works, wants to know *phr.* Descriptive of someone who goes into a lot of unnecessary detail. *'That Unai Emery leaves nothing to chance at Aston Villa. He even wants to know how a cat's arse works.'*

Howard *n.* When an altruistic chap has *blown his beans* up his ladyfriend, but takes advantage of his last few seconds of penile hardness to generously give her a couple of extra pushes for good luck. A "little Xtra", named after former bespectacled building society mouthpiece Howard off of the Halifax adverts. If the pushes are administered up the *bird's dirtbox*, it is called a *Howard brown*, thus using the poor fellow's full name for a cheap comic effect.

Howard's Way *rhym. slang. Colwyn Bay.* From the *shit* BBC TV drama of the same name. *'Mum, Dad, I've got something to tell you. I'm Howard's Way.'*

how much? *exclam.* Amusing mock-shocked utterance from one who has just *broken wind.* *Don't tear it, I'll take the whole piece; that's working, now try your lights.*

how's your father *n.* Sex. Often prefixed "Fancy a quick bit of... ahem...?"

hoy *v.* To throw, lob, chuck, *esp.* beer down

one's neck.

hoy, on the *adj.* On the piss.

hoy up *v.* To *spew up, barf, esp.* beer up one's neck.

HP Lovecraft *euph.* A monstrous *turd.* From the eponymous author's habit of giving his books such stirring titles as *The Thing on the Doorstep, Lurker at the Threshhold, The Dunwich Horror etc.*

HPS *abbrev.* Horizontal Payment Scheme. Female method of remuneration accepted by taxi drivers, traffic wardens and drug dealers. Also *hairy cheque book, gash card.*

HP sauce *n.* Viscous fluid found in the *dunghampers* of excitable *birds.* A savoury condiment product of the *haddock pastie.*

HR department *1. n.* The Human Resources section of a business, whatever that means. *2. n.* An impressive set of *competitive advantages.* A *Huge Rack.* 'Phwooar! You've got a very impressive HR department there, Lord Owen. I bet you don't get many of them to the pound.'

HRTV *abbrev.* Any daytime television programe which is primarily aimed at bored, middle-aged housewives, *eg. This Morning, Loose Women, Doctors, Biker Buildoff etc.*

HSBC *1. abbrev.* The old Midland Bank as was, now Hongkong and Shanghai Banking Corporation Holdings plc. *2. n.* A special fellowship of those afflicted with *Chalfonts.* The Half Shit & Blood Club. *3. abbrev.* A discreet session of under-duvet *banking with Barclays.* Hand Shandy Below Covers.

HTC *1. abbrev.* Popular manufacturer of mobile telephones. *2. abbrev.* A *two-push Charlie* who always *spends his money before he gets to the shop.* One who is *up and over like a pan of milk.* Hair Trigger Cock.

http://www.p45.com *n.* Generic address of any website accessed during *wanking hours* which might be considered NSFW.

hubsidised *adj.* Of a married woman's ludicrous, loss-making business venture that is only kept afloat thanks to regular cash injections from *him indoors.*

huby *n.* A semi-erect penis, a *dobber, half a teacake,* a lazy *lob on.*

Huddersfield quidditch *n.* The traditional sport of running away from taxis without paying in the Cash Converter-riddled Yorkshire Shangri-La.

huffle *v.* To *bagpipe.* To take part in an *Hawaiian muscle-fuck.*

hug and chalk woman *n.* A female whose *bones are so big* that in order to cuddle her, it is necessary to reach as far as you can, make a chalk mark, then reach as far as you can again and so on until you have gone all the way round.

Hugh Hefner pool party, seen more cunts than a *phr.* Said of a fellow who has had more than his fair share of success with the opposite gender. 'Eeh, that Mick Hucknall's certainly got a way with the ladies. He's seen more cunts than a Hugh Hefner pool party.'

Hughie Green *n.* A swift *wank* taken when "opportunity knocks". *'Mr Pickwick closed the door behind Mrs Fezzyfelt, sat down behind his old oak desk, and took the turnip watch from his waistcoat pocket. "Oh my wig!" he shouted. "I have yet five minutes until Mr Sticklebrick arrives. Time enough for a swift Hughie Green."'* (from *The Pickwick Papers* by Charles Dickens).

Hughie Green face *euph.* The surprised, monocular expression of a lady whose consort has, "just for fun", elected to withdraw just prior to the conclusion of an act of *horatio,* thereby depositing his base spendings in one of her eyes. Also, variously, a *Gabrielle, Velma, King Harold, spoff monocle, German eyebath* or *St Valentine's Day mascara.*

Hugh Jackman *n. prop.* A *Hilary.* As Boris Johnson is to a *blow job,* so Hugh Jackman is to a *hand job.* From the initials of the *Wolverine* actor.

Hugo Boss *n.* The act of holding the wife's or girl-friend's head under one's quilt after *farting.* A *Dutch oven.* From the male perfume advertising slogan "Your fragrance. Your rules".

Hulk Höegarden *n. prop.* Someone who gets a bit lively after a relatively small amount of drink. Also *two can Van Damme, tinny mallet, drambo, two pint Tyson etc.*

hulk on *n.* An instant and unstoppably enthusiastic erection, that refuses to be calmed and threatens to burst through the slacks.

hulk spunk *n.* Snot.

hullaby *n.* Restful-sleep-inducing technique that is often utilised in the delightful East Yorkshire city on weekends. A headbutt, *Byker teacake* or *Glasgow kiss.*

Hull hen party *n.* A raucous gaggle of women *with lovely personalities.*

hum *1. v.* To *ming,* stink. *2. v.* To sing with the lips closed, or as near to closed as possible during a *hum job. 3. n.* A bad smell, *ronk* or *honk.*

human pacman *n.* The dispiriting experience of browsing furniture in DFS.

Humber Bridge *1. n.* Suspended estuary crossing which connects Grimsby to Hull and thus *2. n.* The thing on a lady which links the *fishy bit* to the *shitty bit.* The *taint, tinter, carse.*

humble grumble *n.* Poor man's porn, *eg.* Women's

Health Week leaflets pressed into service as *monomanual literature*. *Paupernography*.

Humble pie *n*. TV presenter Kate's *pudding*, served with lashings of hot sauce.

humbug *n*. A heavily be-*skidmarked* U-bend. A *tiger's back, Ark Royal landing deck*.

humdinger *n*. A *fart* which makes the wallpaper peel.

humidititty *n*. Sweat under the *boobs*.

humidors, tramp's *n*. The fag-bins outside drinking establishments which provide *paraffins* with their daily supply of fine smoking requisites.

hum job *n*. Vegetarian oral s*x involving no meat, just *two veg*. Accompanied by simultaneous humming of the musical variety.

hummer *1. n*. A large, macho military vehicle favoured by Californian hairdressers, hen parties and Arnold Schwarzenegger. *2. n. Arse, bum. 3. n.* A *humdinger*.

hummersexual *n*. One who finds himself so deficient in the *trouser department* that neither a sports car nor a vast Harley Davidson motorbike can furnish sufficient compensation, and so he is forced to climb behind the wheel of an absurdly oversized and comically butch 4x4 vehicle. '*Born on This Day in History: Honzhi, Emperor of China, 1470; Henry Ford, motor industry pioneer, 1863; Emily Brontë, novelist, 1818; Vladimir Zworykin, Russian physicist, 1889; Arnold Schwarzenegger, hummersexual Actor, 1947.*'

hummingbird, hung like a *adj*. Having a *cock* like a *Chinese mouse*.

hummingbird's wing *sim*. Descriptive of the speed of a naughy lady's fingers while interfering with her *bodily treasure*. '*I come home from the pub last night and caught the missus playing her banjo to an Enrique Iglesias video. Her fingers were going like a fucking hummingbird's wing, I can tell you.*'

humming turd *n*. A noisome *floater* that won't *bugger off* despite numerous flushings, and persists in hovering around, flapping its wings and generally being a nuisance. A *non-mover at number two*.

humousexual *adj*. Of or pertaining to a fellow who prefers to partake of light, effeminate dishes such as tofu, cous-cous, quiche, meringue, salad, fruit *etc*.

hump *1. v.* To *shag*, have sex in the style of an old labrador with its *lipstick* out. *2. v.* To carry heavy amplification equipment to and from a live music venue while one's *arse* sticks out the back of one's jeans.

hump and dump *1. v.* To behave in an ungentlemanly manner towards a young lady with whom you've *copped off*. See also *FANTA*. *2. n.* Unkind

name for the young lady concerned.

Humphrey *n*. An artistic U-bend *skidmark*. A piece of "bog art", named after the late actor Humphrey.

humpty *n*. The act of *humping*.

humpty dumpty *1. n.* Doomed, egg-shaped protagonist of the famous nursery rhyme. *2. n.* A *shite* taken while in bad humour.

hunchback spiders *n*. Ladies' hairy nipples.

hunch box *n*. The *bog*.

hunchie *n*. A particularly difficult *mudchild*, that leaves one contorted like a constipated red setter in the park.

hundred and thousands *n*. The left-over bits of toilet tissue often to be found sprinkled about a drunken lady's genitalia. *Spandrels, men overboard, croutons, tiger nuts*.

hundred handed one, the *1. n.* A creature in Greek mythology famed for undoing the thousand knots with which Hera had bound her lustful and unfaithful husband Zeus. Remember that one for when you're on *University Challenge* or *Only Connect*. We can guarantee it won't come up on *Tipping Point* or *Catchphrase*. *2. n.* An *overly-relaxed* gentleman who seems to defy time and biology with the number of *five knuckle shuffles* he manages to get through in a single day.

Hungarian, fluent *euph*. The utterly incomprehensible language which is evidently being spoken by one's drinking companions when one arrives late and stone-cold sober at a social engagement after being unavoidably detained *en route*.

Hungarian goulierash *n. medic. Knobrot* picked up on a cheap eastern European holiday.

Hungarian hopscotch *n*. A distinctly unlikely sounding *Barclays* banking technique, whereby the subject squats down, places his turgid *membrum virile* between his ankles and then hops up and down until he either *brings himself off*, breaks a hip or has a heart attack, whichever happens sooner. Or quite possibly all three at once.

hung like a hobbit *adj*. Said of a chap with a short, fat, hairy one.

hung like a mousetrap *adj*. Prone to sudden, premature ejaculation. '*Is that it, Lord Archer? Half a push?*' '*Yes. I'm hung like a mousetrap, but please don't tell anyone. Here's two thousand pounds in an envelope.*'

hungry arse *n*. Condition afflicting women whereby their *bills* disappear up the *crack* of their *hummers* as they walk. See also *hiding denim*.

hungry hippo *euph*. A woman who has "had a lot of balls in her mouth", and in the plural form...

hungry hippos *1. n.* Frantic and quickly broken 1970s board game for children. *2. euph.* Affectionate collective epithet for a herd of salivating, *salad-dodging* lasses in the queue for one's local *kebabulance* after a night on the *tart fuel*.

hunt for brown October *n.* The act of seeking out and destroying a *U-bend U-boat*. With a bog brush, stick or barbecue utensil.

hunt for red October *1. n.* Film starring Sean Connery as a Scottish/Russian submarine-captain, if memory serves. Or that might be *Gorky Park*, come to think of it. *2. n.* A saucy bedroom game whereby a lady who is *up on blocks* invites a lucky chap to seek out and remove her *blobstopper* using only his teeth. No, it was William Hurt in *Gorky Park*.

hunting the Bismarck *euph.* A lengthy and patient search for a troublesome nugget of floating *feeshus* after *following through* in a bubble bath

hunt will be through soon, the *exclam.* A grizzled response to a loud, lengthy and slightly wet toot on the *botty bugle*.

hurl *1. v.* To *hoy*. *2. v.* To *hoy up*. *3. exclam.* How a Geordie pronounces the word "hole".

hurr *v.* To breathe forcefully, theatrically and at close quarters onto an item of food or drink before temporarily leaving the room for whatever reason, in order to put off anyone who might otherwise be tempted to *scouse* it in your absence. *'And don't touch that lemon meringue pie while I'm on the shitter, Cora. I've hurred on it.'*

hurt locker *1. n.* 2008 movie starring Jeremy Renner, Anthony Mackie and Brian Geraghty. No, us neither. *2. n.* The *nipsy, dot* or *freckle* after any one of the following (or combination thereof); a portion of the late Abdul Latif's Curry Hell – the world's hottest curry, excessive/incorrect/overly vigorous wiping with cheap *arse paper*, *anal fisting* or the passing of a gargantuan *Thora*.

hurt yourself *v.* To vigorously *relax in a gentleman's*

way. *'Thanks for that new niff mag, mate. I'm going to go home now and hurt myself.'*

husband hole *n.* The *bag for life*'s *parts of shame* or *man cave*.

hushflush *n.* A pull of the chain in a public lavatory before sitting down in order to mask embarrassing noises.

hush puppies *n. Blouse hounds* so cute that all red-blooded men are rendered speechless in their presence.

hussy *n.* A shameless woman, a drunk and an unfit mother.

hydrothermal vent *1. n.* A fissure on the seafloor from which geothermally heated water discharges. *2. n.* A hot, gaseous and wet discharge from the *cleftal fissure*.

hyena has bit it, it looks like a *phr.* Descriptor for an upsettingly unruly *growler* of the sort that viewers of a sensitive disposition may care to look away from. A *butcher's dustbin, stamped bat, bottom of a ratcatcher's mallet* or *ripped out fireplace*.

hymen climbin' *n.* The act of being the first fellow to plant his *flagpole* up *Mount Venus*. Plucking a *bird's virgin string*.

hymen seek *n.* Going out *on the pull*.

hyperfentilation *n.* Mild dizzyness caused by deep breathing while wearing a *musk mask*.

hypnotits *n.* Export strength *hush puppies* that can lead to *norkolepsy*.

hypolybast *n.* A portmanteau term describing a politician. From hypocritical + lying + bastard. *'I'm voting for that hypolybast I seen on Question Time. He made a lot of good points, I thought, and I seen him waving a pint of bitter round on the news.'*

hypotesnooze *n.* A nap taken in a bed that is slightly too short, only made comfortable by lying along its diagonal.

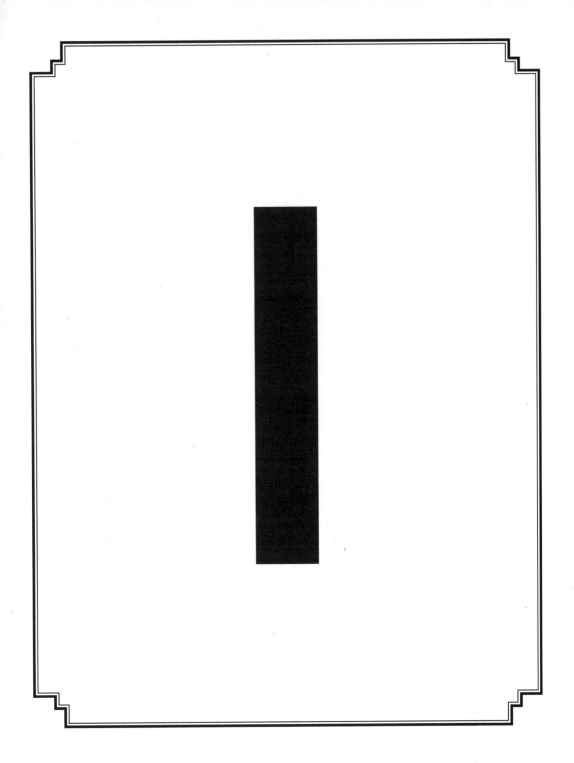

I admit fully that my judgement was probably coloured by my tendency to be too honourable *exclam.* An unconvincing apology essayed immediately after issuing a Krakatoa-level *shart*.

I 'ate that duck *exclam.* Said in the style of ventriloquist Keith Harris's comedy monkey Cuddles after someone emits a *botty quack*.

ibeerprofen *n.* A popular alcoholic painkiller, an overdose of which can lead to vomiting, memory loss and liver failure. *Canaesthetic, canadin.*

I bet that holds some shit! *exclam.* A charming compliment proffered to a *bird* with a big old *dirtbox* on her.

IBF *abbrev.* The more traditional form of fertilisation, *viz.* I've Been Fucked.

Ibiza itch *n. medic.* Any *happy rash* or minor *Doonican* contracted by one's *downstairs unmentionables* while holidaying on the popular nsu-kissed Mediterranean island. *'He's the man, the man with the Midas…Sorry Mr Broccoli, I've got to go and put some ointment on me clopper. I've got Ibiza itch something rotten.' 'I know, love. We could hear you scratching at it over the French horns.'*

IBM *1. n. prop.* A large computer company. *2. abbrev.* Itty Bitty Meat. A small *Hampton*. *3. abbrev.* Inches Below Muff. The units in which a *greyhound skirt* is measured.

IBS *1. abbrev. medic.* Irritable Bowel Syndrome, a condition of the *Camillas* chiefly characterised by abdominal pain, urgent bowel movements and diarrhoea, the cause of which remains fundamentally unknown. *2. abbrev. medic.* Irrational Bitter Skitters, a condition of the *Camillas* chiefly characterised by abdominal pain, urgent bowel movements and diarrhoea, the cause of which is *necking* too much brown beer. The *cask ale can-can* or *real ale rumba.*

I can feel it kick *exclam.* Said by one who is expecting an humungous *mudchild*.

I can keep the match ball now *exclam.* To be said when returning from the works *bog* following the third *Donald* of the day.

I can't believe it's not batter *n.* KY Jelly, *granny batter.*

I can't believe it's nut butter *exclam. 'Oi, waiter. What's this funny-tasting stuff spread on my bread rolls?' 'It's I can't believe it's nut butter, Mr Coren. And all the chefs have wanked into your soup too, you unpleasant bellend.'*

ICBM *acronym.* Of modern day state-of-the-art trouser weaponry, an Inter Cuntinental Ballistic Missile.

iced bun *n.* An old-fashioned ladies' hair-do that's all dripping in *spunk*. For whatever reason.

iced by a blind baker *euph.* Said of a *tart* that has been the subject of a saucy *bukkake* attack from several badly aimed *egg white cannons*.

iced fingers *n.* Bakers' confectionery-speak for the results of *glazing the knuckle*.

ice docking *n.* The saucy practice of titilating a lady using a *dildo* carved from a frozen *turd*.

Iceland buffet, as appetising as an *sim.* A sentiment familiar to any viewer familiar with the dubious comestibles traditionally hawked in close-up during the ad break bumpers on *I'm a Celebrity*; that is to say, not particularly appetising.

ice the cake *1. v.* To decorate a *tart* with *cream*. Often seen in European *grumble flicks. 'Gunther! There's only thirty seconds of tape left in the camera. Quick, ice that cake!' 2. v.* After *fouling* oneself, to squeeze the *crap* down the trouser legs and out of the turn-ups in order to deposit discreet chocolate rosettes on the floor, in the style of a baker decorating a gateau. With *shite* out of his *kegs*.

ice the log *n.* An environmentally sound toilet visit where one has a *wank* after a *shit*, thereby saving water on the flush and halting global warming.

icing bag *n.* Paul Hollywood's *knackersack*.

icing the eclair *n.* Challenging act of *self-abuse* administered while sitting on the *bog* after a *Donald*.

I closed my eyes and she slipped away *phr.* A phrase best employed when reflecting on a lengthy and emotional relationship with, and subsequent painful splitting-up from, a *power ballad* of monstrous proportions. From the 1976 Boston hit *More than a Feeling*.

icun *n.* One who is held in more or less universal low esteem yet still manages to retain a high profile in the media. An icon of *cuntishness. 'And on Celebrity Naked Attraction tonight. TV icuns Piers Morgan and Jeremy Kyle will be checking out ladies' fannies.'*

I cunt believe it *exclam.* Sarcastic utterance proffered *sotto voce* to a mate upon witnessing an act of galactic *twattery*.

idea shit *n.* Business speak for a poor quality brainstorming session. As if there were any other sort. *Crapping* out a load of ideas to see what floats and what gets flushed. *'Well, me and the lads in creative had an idea shit and we reckon we should put a free U2 album on everyone's computer, whether they want one or not.' 'Wooh! Let's do it.'*

I'd eat a pound of her shite for a fuck at her oxter *exclam.* Rhetorical asseveration made by Dundonian males when espying a particularly good looking lady.

idiot lantern *n.* A television set. The *shit pump.* *'What do you think of me new idiot lantern? Now I can watch Bargain Hunt in high definition 3-D widescreen with Dolby Pro-Logic 5.1 surround sound.'*

I'd like to leave you with something to remember me by *exclam.* A witty, farewell utterance made immediately prior to vouchsafing a *farting gift.*

I don't know who needs to hear this, but... *1. exclam.* Commonly used phrase at the start of a tweet pointing out something apparently obvious. *2. exclam.* Said just before violently *dropping a gut.* Also *sharing is caring; did you ever hear your name whispered on the wind?; listen to this, too good to miss, da-da da-da da; observe Mr Bond, the instruments of Armageddon!*

I don't remember that song having those lyrics *exclam.* An amusing thing to say after *blowing a fanfare on the muck trumpet* at a gig, preferably during a quiet song. See also *Judas!; ignore that, it's just a glitch in the matrix etc.*

I don't think anyone outside the Westminster bubble is interested in that *exclam.* Humorous, "Sir" Jacob Rees-Mogg-style response to a particularly long and audible *flatulisation.* See also *there goes the cockle train; would the in-store cleaner please make their way to the underwear department? etc.*

I'd recommend letting that breathe a little before dipping your nose in *1. exclam.* Thoughtful suggestion to one's welcoming host when handing over a mature bottle of red, presented in thanks for a generous lunch invitation. *2. exclam.* Thoughtful suggestion to one's welcoming host when departing their downstairs branch of the *bank of brown*, having made a substantial post-prandial deposit.

I'd stand upwind if I were you *exclam.* Health and safety advice/*apoology* issued to innocent folk who find themselves in the immediate vicinity prior to the *dropping of one's gut.* See also *these shares pay dividends; please hold for the president; I'll name that tune in one; it's been put into local lockdown etc.*

i-fart *n.* A *crowd pleaser* released while listening to a portable MP3 player on earphones which, in the *benefactor's* head was a stealthy, undercover *one cheek sneak* but which, to the other occupants of the carriage, was a veritable *call to prayer.*

I feel a song coming on *exclam.* A theatrical precursor to the imminent *sound of music*, possibly accompanied with a slap of the thigh.

if he'd played that with a bit more side, he'd be safely on the brown *1. exclam.* Incisive moment of snooker commentary from John Virgo, delivered during the Higgins *vs* Williams snooker final at the Sheffield Crucible. *2. exclam.* Waggish riposte to a robust *trouser cough.* See also *a confident appeal by the Australians there; lo, 'tis a raven sent from Winterfell; it's not…. human, Jim, etc.*

if it's up there I'll give you the money myself *1. exclam.* Caustic remark made by a bored prostitute following a drunken *punter's* third attempt to penetrate her. *2. exclam.* Witty preface to a twin-tone rasp from *Mr Babbage.* See also *please hold for the president, our survey said* and *who wants to be a millionaire.*

if that's not out I'm not playing *exclam.* A frankly Wildean post-flatulatory aphorism.

if you know the words sing along *exclam.* A Butlins Redcoat-style invitation to enjoy a tuneful volley of notes from the *brass section.* Also *our survey said; and now a word from our sponsor; ladies and gentlemen, please be upstanding for the President of the United States; incoming wounded!*

if you're selling that bike saddle... *exclam.* A light-hearted phrase shouted out by a jolly van driver to help boost the self-esteem of a comely female velocipedist.

Iggle Piggle's potty *n.* Rhetorical description of an area redolent of the stench of freshly deposited human excrement, named in honour of the formerly popular baby out of off of *In the Night Garden* (who is probably about forty now). *'I'd avoid the end trap if I were thee, mate. It kefs like Iggle Piggle's potty.'*

Iggy popshot *n. Whacking off* on a *TV's ass.*

ignoble gas *n. Carbon dibaxide, anusthetic.*

ignoranus *n.* One who is not only incredibly *fuckwitted*, but an *arsehole* to boot.

I haven't watched it but I've wanked it *exclam.* Said of a TV programme or film where a viewer has just skipped to the best bits.

I have the full backing of the Prime Minister *exclam.* Announcement made after *following through* catastrophically.

Ikea bulb *1. n.* A lady that *blows* the first time one turns her on. *2. n.* A *one pump chump* who is *up and over* like a pan of milk.

Ikeas *n. medic.* Loose stools.

I know a good cure for that *exclam.* A slightly unsympathetic reply given by a dispenser of *man medicine* to his girlfriend when she complains about an ailment of some sort.

I KNOW ya gonna dig this *1. phr.* Sample that was overused on late 1980s house records. *2. exclam.* Spoken refrain introducing a particularly toe-tapping *Lionel Bart.*

I'll bet he doesn't eat his crusts *exclam.* Said of a chap who, it would appear, is unlikely to wade his way through small bodies of standing water, has a penchant for *taking his peas minted* and who rarely, if ever, encounters significant difficulty when dealing with subjective chromatic variations.

illegally blonde *adj.* When the *beef curtains* do not match the *cuffs.* Or something.

I'll give it five *1. exclam.* Brummishly accented catchphrase coined by diminutive Wednesbury minx Janice Nicholls on *Thank Your Lucky Stars* in the 1960s. Another one for the teenagers. *2. exclam.* Catchphrase used in countless West Midlands homes on a Sunday morning, when the lady of the house wants to use the *bog* after her man.

I'll have a consonant please Rachel *exclam.* A request made of a female to carry out any arbitrary task, with the sole object of affording a sexist male the opportunity to observe her *arse.*

I'll have what she's having *1. exclam.* A famous line from the film *When Harry met Sally,* delivered by the director's mum after Meg Ryan fakes an *organism* in a diner. *2. n.* Something to say after a lady *drops her shopping.*

illigiterate *n.* An ignorant *bastard.*

I'll inform the Archbishop immediately *exclam.* While attending the General Synod, a suitable announcement following a thunderous *trumpet involuntary* in A-flat minor.

I'll just nip down to reception for a paper *exclam.* After spending a night in a hotel with a new partner, a lie proferred as an excuse to leave the room and find somewhere to *drop one's shopping,* thus saving oneself the embarrassment of saying "I'd leave that a few minutes if I was you."

I'll name that tune in one *1. exclam.* Said after a warm-up on the *trouser trumpet,* especially if Tom O'Connor's round for tea. Which would be surprising, all things considered. *2. n.* A game that can be played when listening to an unfamiliar Oasis record. *'I'll name that tune in one – it's Jean Genie mixed with Subterranean Homesick Blues.'*

I'll need a box of hankies for this film *1. phr.* Said by a woman when sitting down to watch a weepy, such as *The Time Traveller's Wife, Marley and Me* or *Beaches.* *2. phr.* Said by a man when sitting down to watch *Showgirls, Barbarella* or *Showgirls* again, after he's had a little nap.

I'll raise my leg to that *exclam.* A slightly more crude version of "I'll raise a glass to that", usually followed by a rasping *Lionel Bart.* See also *we interrupt this programme to bring you an important announcement; and the thunderball is; my next guest needs no introduction.*

I'll show my arse on Bury Market *exclam.* Lancs. Rhetorical riposte when being challenged with a highly unlikely event. *'If it falls to me to start a fight to cut out the cancer of bent and twisted journalism in our country with the simple sword of truth and the trusty shield of British fair play, so be it. And if these false, slanderous and calumnious charges that I have behaved in a way that was not completely above board are shown to have the slightest scintilla of truth in them, then I'll show my arse on Bury Market.'* (Jonathan Aitken MP, speaking in 1995).

I'll take that bid Mr Brown *exclam.* Said in the manner of a *Bargain Hunt* auctioneer after one *drops a lot off* at the sale room.

I love it loud *1. n. prop.* Title of a song by the rock band Kiss from their album *Creatures of the Night.* *2. exclam.* Something to say after *letting off* an almighty *heart to heart.* See also *my best work is behind me, I fear; they call the wind Mariah; two sniffs of that and you're greedy.*

I love the smell of methane in the morning *exclam.* Something to be said, Marlon Brando-style, after dropping the first apocalyptic *guff* of the day.

imagincy brake *n.* The invisible left pedal found in the footwell of a ladyfriend's car.

I'm a grow-er not a show-er *exclam.* A thoroughly convincing explanation of why a man's flaccid member may, at first glance, appear misleadingly risible.

I'm a lover, not a strimmer *exclam.* Humorous retort when confronted by a *ladygarden* that is more *Max Clifford's shrubbery* than *Beppe's beard.*

I'm declaring a climate emergency *exclam.* Said in the manner of a politician after a *chemical waste incident* that's been brewing all morning causes your fellow passengers to open the car windows in haste. Also *the great smell of Brut!; horn of Gondor! etc.*

I'm getting the word… *phr.* Said in the voice of famed psychic Clinton Baptiste just before a release of *erectoplasm* from the *third eye.*

I'm going to have to push you for an answer *exclam.* A warning of imminent unpleasantness. Also *our survey said, please hold for the president, now back to Davina* and *gentlemen start your engines.*

I'm going to have to stand up for this one, Cilla *1. exclam.* Uttered preceding a high-risk – and possibly ill-advised – release of anal gas. *2. exclam.* Uttered preceding a high-risk – and possibly ill-advised – left-turn in a pub anecdote. From the sadly missed Saturday night dating show, in which a contestant would rise from their stool with misplaced confidence to perform a high-risk, cringe-inducing party trick.

I'm not right *exclam.* Recognition that the noisome miasma from one's alimentary canal has ultimately proved too rich for one's olfactory senses. A reaction to the fact that the speaker has delivered a *stinker* that not even its own mother can love. *'Are you happy, my dear Albert?' 'Nein my leibchen Victoria, I'm nicht richt. It must of been them French eggs I had at the Great Exhibition.'*

I'm not sure you made it loud enough sir *1. exclam.* A witty comment passed by Batman's batman Alfred Pennyworth in *The Dark Knight* upon the shooting of a gun. *2. exclam.* A witty comment passed by anyone upon the *dropping* of a *gut.*

I'm Peppa Pig *exclam.* A humorous aphorism that can defuse the hostile atmosphere that sometimes obtains following a *lusty snort* from the *nether snout.* Also *fer-fetch a cloth, Granville; someone let him in; someone's tinkered with Herbie; speak on, sweet lips that never told a lie; I'm ready for the question, Noel.*

Imperial barge *n.* The male member. A particularly majestic *skin boat.* *'You should have seen how Mrs Eisenhower's eyes lit up when my nine-inch imperial barge heaved into view.'* (from *The Memoirs of Winston Churchill*).

impersonate Stalin *v.* To perform oral sex on a woman, *dine at the Y, eat hairy pie.* *'Hold tight up there love. You'll like this, I'm just gonna do a quick impersonation of Stalin.'*

imposter syndrome *n.* Modern, bourgeois affliction whereby one suspects that the eye-watering *Tony Hart* one has just emitted in a crowded room was actually done by another, more skilled individual.

impractical shoe *n.* The lesbidaceous equivalent of a *beard,* living in a symbiotic faux-relationship with a lady who *fits her own shelves.*

I'm ready for the question Noel *exclam.* Humorous interjection after someone *steps on a fortissimo frog.* Also *speak up caller, you're through; taxi for Brown; what's that, Sweep?; sew a button on that; mighty fine words, preacher; one year out.*

I'm selling this for a friend as he's not on eBay *phr. euph.* Once you've paid for this heap of *shite* you'll never find me.

I'm sorry, I didn't quite get that *1. exclam.* Response from Alexa devices when the electronic voice assistant has failed to comprehend what has been said. *2. exclam.* Witty rejoinder following an audible *windypop* or *bum chime.*

I'm sorry, I don't investigate crimes in the past *exclam.* Watertight exculpatory response to anyone who accuses one of being responsible for

several loud, liquid *sharts* a few seconds previously.

I'm with a client *exclam.* Said when someone knocks on the *bog* door when one is ensconced on the *shit hopper* in the *Kensington Executive.*

in and out like Hodgson's men, he was *phr.* Describing a male performance that was ludicrously brief, and which failed to satisfy in any way. Etymology unknown.

in a while, paedophile *exclam.* Witty response to the humorous valediction "see you later, masturbator."

inbetweeners *n.* *Turds* stuck in transition between *Camilla* and bowl with no chance of retraction. Also a Channel 4 teen comedy that, let's be honest, appears to be at least partly scripted by repeatedly sticking a pin into a copy of the *Profanisaurus.*

inbognito, go *v.* Somewhat in the style of late fugitive MP John Stonehouse, to discard your *shitted Alans* and stuff them in a public lavatory cistern before making good your escape.

in-box *1. n.* A deskbound office receptacle for messages, communiques, unpaid bills, blackmail threats and the like. *2. n.* A lady's *furry hoop.* *'What shall I do with this, Miss Pleasurecraft?' 'Oh, just stick it in my in-box.'*

inbreastigate *v.* To search out and examine the particulars of a subject. *'What are you looking at, love?' 'I'm just inbreastigating the actress Alex Kingston on Google Images, dear.'*

incapability brown *n.* A *shit* in the garden, left by a passing drunkard.

inch-high private eye *1. n. prop.* A diminutive cartoon private dick of the 1970s. *2. n.* A *beef bayonet* of laughably small proportions.

inchilada *n.* A spicy morsel of hot meat which smells of cheese.

incompotence *n. medic.* Inability to perform s*xually, solely due to ineptitude.

incontinental breakfast *n.* A meal which really doesn't agree with you, resulting in a sprint to the *khazi* with your finger up your *aris.*

independent thinker *n.* A *fucking mental.* *'Today's birthdays: Bob Holness, dead quiz show host and saxophonist, 89; Errol Brown, dead seventies slap-head, 69; Charles Manson, dead independent thinker, 83.'*

Indian mustard *n.* Diarrhoea.

Indian rope trick *1. n.* An impressive erection attained under seemingly impossible circumstances, *eg.* After twelve pints and/or six *wanks.* *2. n.* The process of having a *Tom tit* while standing on one's head, the object being to see how high you can raise your magical *cable* without it breaking up into individual *Bungle's fingers.*

indoor fishing *v.* A coarse form of *angling for tadpoles.*

indoor hobo *n.* One who lives inside, but looks like they should be living in a doorway, *eg.* Johnny Vegas, Ricky Tomlinson, Tracey Emin. A *tramp's mate.*

indoor league *1. n.* Show which was cheaply produced by Yorkshire Television between 1972 and 1977, in which pipe-smoking, cardigan-toting ex-cricketer Fred Trueman introduced coverage of such pub sports as shove ha'penny, skittles and arm wrestling. *2. n.* Code word for *cottaging* used in working class boozers throughout the north. *'I'll see thee in the toilets for a spot of indoor league.'*

indoorphins *n.* Feel-good chemicals produced by the body when you give your PayPal account a proper walloping whilst drinking wine. Also *spendorphins.*

indoor sports *n.* Exercise; specifically a workout for the right arm and wrist.

indoor toe *n.* The female erogenous zone, possibly the *wail switch.* *'You should have seen Mother Teresa's face light up when I tickled her indoor toe, your holiness.'*

induce labour *v.* To wipe your *nipsy* prior to a *Simon Cowell* movement with the intention of encouraging the delivery of *Meat Loaf's daughter.* *'Sorry I'm late, Paul. I was sat on the crapper for ten minutes, and in the end I had to induce labour to get the fucker out. Anyway, let's see what the contestants have baked.'*

inebriati, the *n.* Shadowy, secretive brotherhood united by a shared fondness for Communion wine, Communion white cider and Communion extra-strength lager.

infellation *n.* The rising cost of *Boris Johnsons.* *'Ooh, this infellation is terrible. I remember the days when you could get the bus into town, a slap up tea at the Lyon's Corner House and a whore to suck you off in a doorway afterwards, and you'd still have change from half a crown.'*

influencer *n.* One who can immediately alter the mood in a room by *dropping* an absolutely putrid *gut* and then probably blogging about it.

Ingrid *1. rhym. slang.* An act of anal excretion. Named after the luscious "tits out" *Hammer Horror* actress Ingrid Pitt. *2. rhym. slang. A lady's jubbly.* Named after the luscious "Ingrids out" *Hammer Horror* actress Ingrid Pitt.

inheritance *n.* A miasmatic bequest bequeathed to a toilet-goer by the previous occupant.

injured in the warm-up *euph.* Said of a footballer who *shits* himself and is forced to retire discon-solately from the field of play. *'Lineker there, he's got injured in the warm-up and he's gone for an early bath.'*

injury time *1. n.* The dying seconds of a football match where the losing side throw caution to the wind and take a shot at anything in a desperate attempt to score. *2. n.* The last song of the evening in a nightclub. The *2am bin rake.*

Inman strut/Inman's twitch *phr.* Rapid, short-stepped gait essayed whilst tightly clenching the buttocks to control a particularly excitable *turtle's head.* Named in honour of late *Are You Being Served?*'s Mr Humphries actor John.

in need of snookers *1. phr.* In a game of snooker, when one player is losing by more points than the combined value of the points left on the table. *2. phr.* When you are royally in the *shite* and needing a miracle, after forgetting your wedding anniversary or something else women care about, for example.

inner monolog *n.* One big *poo* in your guts.

innocent smoothie *n.* A nocturnal emission of *jitler.* *'I was having a dream about Jenny Agutter in Logan's Run and when I woke up I'd had an innocent smoothie.'*

in'n'out burger *n.* The act of calling in at a fast food restaurant for the sole purpose of laying a dog's egg. *'Keep your hair on, Mrs Trubshaw, I'm just stopping here for a quick in'n'out burger. I'm sure they wouldn't cremate your husband until you get there.'*

innubendo *n.* A particularly awkward – most likely physically impossible, come to think of it – sexual act.

in off *1. n.* In billiards and snooker, the potting of an intended ball following a felicitous ricochet. *2. n.* Also in billiards and snooker, the potting of an unintended ball following an infelicitous ricochet. *3. n.* In sexual relations the potting of a supposedly unintended *difficult brown* caused by a suspiciously felicitous ricochet while aiming for an *easy pink.* *'Sorry dear. I must have got an in off there.'*

inquisitive sea lion *n.* A *brown owl* lodged in the U-bend, leaving its snub-nosed end gently poking out curiously above the water's surface as if taking a look around for Sir David Attenborough or sardines.

in receivership *adj.* Involved in a toilet situation which necessitates a sudden complete *clearout of stock.* A *dump* where "everything must go". *'I'm afraid Sir Clive can't come to the phone right now as he is in receivership. If you're phoning to complain about the shitty rubber keys on your ZX81 computer,* *please press one. If you're phoning because your C5 battery has went flat after less than a hundred yards and you've been ran over by a bus, please press two. For all other enquiries, please press three.'*

inside burns *n.* *Thighbrows, judge's eyebrows, Rhodes Boysons.* Effusive lateral *pubage* out the sides of a young lady's *dunghampers.* *'I'm with you all the way on burning your bra and everything, Germaine. But could you do something about your inside burns? They're putting me off my stroke.'*

inside job *n.* A game of *pocket billiards.* Vigorously and rhythmically *looking for change* in your front pockets at a sophisticated lap-dancing establishment. An *IPW.*

insignificant other *euph.* A boyfriend or girlfriend who will do until something better comes along. *'Billionaire Rupe, have you met millionaire Mick, my insignificant other?'*

insomniwank *n.* *Tossing,* but not turning, when unable to get to sleep in the wee small hours.

installing Windows *n.* Excuse given to the missus when one intends to lock oneself in the spare room and *toss* one's *plums flatter than a bat's wings* over a series of hardcore internet *grumble* websites. *'What are you doing in there, Jerry? Tom and Barbara are waiting downstairs with a birthday cake for you.' 'Nothing Margot, just installing Windows. Could you push some more tissues under the door, please?'*

instant diet *n.* A huge *pony* that allows you to do up your belt a couple of notches.

instoolments *n.* The successive episodes of a *trilogy* or *mini-series.* *'I'm paying for that slap-up feed at the Rupali Restaurant, Bigg Market, Newcastle upon Tyne, in instoolments, you know.'*

in Swiss that's good morning to you! *exclam.* Lyric from the opening musical number of the 1938 Laurel & Hardy feature *Swiss Miss,* to be delivered following a *downstairs yodel.*

intelligent load shedding *1. n.* In electrical engineering, a technique used after a loss of generation to maintain supply by removing non-essential drains of power. *2. n. Rubbing one out* while watching something vaguely intellectual, such as Rachel Riley off *Countdown* or Victoria Coren on *Only Connect.* But rarely Richard Osman on *Pointless.*

intensely convivial *adj.* Descriptive of a fellow who is no stranger to the interior of licensed premises. *'He's been a fixture in here for years, you know. He's had three liver transplants now, and he's still as intensely convivial as he ever was.'*

intercourse work *n.* Modular weekend and evening

tasks typically researched online.

interior decorating *n.* Slapping a bit of white *himulsion* about the womb using the *naughty paintbrush.*

interior decorator *n.* In a *bukkake* session, the chap who actually gets to *do it* with the *plasterer's radio.*

interior monologue *1. n.* A stream of consciousness; a narrative trope in written fiction, if you will. *2. n.* The burbles, pops and gurgles emanating from a *salad dodger's hip tits* between his elevenses and half-elevenses.

international breeding programme *1. n.* Zoological project whereby examples of endangered species are paired with overseas counterparts in order to maintain a healthy gene pool. *2. n.* A cheap holiday in Tenerife.

internectuals *n.* Those people who consider themselves part of the academic elite as a consequence of their ability to look stuff up on Wikipedia.

internet ready *adj.* Descriptive of one who already *paddles the skin canoe* with their left hand.

internetty *n.* A lavatory cubicle which is within laptop wireless network range, allowing a computer literate toilet-user to browse the worldwide web for antiquarian books, to pick an example at random, while he is seated on the *thunder box* masturbating furiously.

interrogate the prisoner *v.* To *box the Jesuit, strangle the parson, choke the chicken, bash the bishop, pull the Pope's cap off, have a five knuckle shuffle, pull your pud, spank the monkey etc.* To interfere with oneself in the *farmyard area.* *'Richard, come down and get your tea.' 'I'll be right down, Judy. I'm just interrogating the prisoner. Into your shoe.'*

interview at Butlins *euph.* A *knock-up* during *cricket week,* from which one "comes out with a red coat".

in the club *adj.* *Up the duff,* pregnant, *preggers.* From *in the pudding club.*

in the hockey team *adj.* Lesbidaceous.

in the pink *adj.* In receipt of a healthy dose of whatever it is that women have in their *undercrackers.*

in the red, get *euph.* The thin streak of blood on your *shit tickets* that tells you that you've been wiping for long enough. *'After a night of curries and stout, I was in the toilet all the next morning. I used half a roll and eventually got in the red. It was a wake-up call, I can tell you. Coming up next, Springwatch.'*

in there like swimwear *euph.* Descriptive of one who ingratiates himself with ease. A reference to the way bathing togs have a marked tendency to go straight up your *arsehole*. *'Did you see Ronnie Wood with that busload of Eastern European waitresses who are young enough to be his daughters? He was in there like swimwear.'*

in the soft drinks aisle *euph.* Completely mental, as in "past crackers and nuts". *Mad as a Maltese roundabout.*

in the wet *adj.* Well and truly *cunt-struck*.

in through the out door *1. n.* Title of Led Zeppelin's not very good final album. *2. n.* How Robert "Percy" Plant might refer to a spot of *back door action; s*x* up the *shitpipe.* Which is probably the title of an Ivor Biggun LP.

intimidate the witness *v.* To browbeat and bludgeon one's *purple-headed deponent*, leaving you both crying, sore and remorseful.

introduce a topic *euph.* To unwrap an *air biscuit* that has a hazelnut in every bite.

introducing the band *euph.* The chorus of empty *guffs* that often precede a substantial *Robert Powell* movement. Named after the first track on Suede's album *Dog Man Star,* which is a short piece that precedes much more stout content.

intrumpitent *adj.* Used when referring to a person who involuntarily *wees* their pants while *dropping a gut*. From incontinent + trump (with trump sort of dropped into the middle of the word).

invasion of privacy *euph. The other. 'See that Ekin-Su Cülcüloğlu? I wouldn't mind invading her privacy.'*

inverse bare law *n.* Principle stating that the likelihood of a *bird* getting her *baps* out on the beach is inversely proportional to the desirability of her doing so.

investigating kung fu gangs *euph.* The deadly act of bizarre auto-erotic asphyxiation, in the course of which a fellow *chokes his chicken* furiously while strung up like a choked fowl in a butcher's window. After David Carradine's family's frankly unconvincing explanation for how the late actor met his grisly fate in a hotel wardrobe.

investment wanker *n.* One who forks out for a subscription *bongo* service from Sky television in the expectation of getting a substantial return on his *holding*.

invincibility cloak *n.* That drink-fuelled shield that gives a man the ability to fight like Tyson, escape from the police in a single bound and fall off scaffolding without harm.

in vino fertilisation *n.* The usual manner in which babies are conceived.

invisible marker pen *1. n.* Writing implement whose marks show up under fluorescent light. *2. n.* A small, hidden *teggat* of *foulage* – wedged in

layers of fat or hairs around the *arsehole* – that keeps on drawing on the *shit-scrape* even after protracted wipeage.

invisible nan *n.* The supernatural entity that is a source of unease for any chap engaging in such shameful acts as *relaxing in a gentleman's way,* betting on a dog fight, watching *Top Gear etc.* The uncomfortable sensation that his late grandmother's ghost might be watching from the other side, and tutting. Also known as a *handbrake*.

invisible wind factory *1. n.* A cutting edge live music venue in Liverpool where you're unlikely to see The Wurzels on their 'Drink Up Thy Cider' tour. *2. n.* The *arsehole*.

involuntary liquidation *1. n.* A formal insolvency procedure which results in a company being forcibly shut down. *2. n.* A wet dream. See also *snoregasm, energy saver.*

ipad from a panty pad, he/she doesn't know an *exclam.* Said of one who has difficulty distinguishing their *gluteus maximus* from their *cubitus*. *'I wouldn't say my fuckin' missus is thick, ladies and gentlemen, but she doesn't know an ipad from a panty pad.'* (King Charles III addressing the United Nations, 2023).

iPhear *n.* The sensations of dry-mouthed panic, horror and trepidation experienced by a chap when his missus picks up his iPhone and opens Safari.

iplod *n.* A speed camera.

ipod earphones *n.* Particular type of *jelly jewellery* furnished simultaneously by two generous gentlemen engaged in an act of *double glazing*. Stereophonic streams of *jitler* dribbling down from a lady's ears. *Shot by both sides.*

iprod *n.* Small portable device that annoys other passengers on crowded buses and trains.

Ipswich smile *n.* A *pasata grin, Mexican lipstick*.

iPud *n.* A portable, self-contained source of cheap entertainment which can be accessed via the trouser pockets and keeps nearby commuters smiling while the owner *shuffles his playlist*.

IPW *acronym.* The act of rummaging for change in one's *strides* while in a lap-dancing establishment. In-Pocket Wank; an *inside job, trouser browser.*

Irish *1. n.* Heterosexual anal sex, supposedly as a means of contraception. *UTBNB. 2. rhym. slang.* A hairpiece. From Irish coupé = toupée.

Irish alarm clock *n.* Ten pints of Guinness. From the fact that a night on the stout more often than not leads to horrific, involuntary bowel movements which cause one to wake early the next morning. *'I hope you don't sleep in tomorrow. You're piloting a Space Shuttle up to the Interna-*

tional Space Station, remember?' 'Don't worry, dear. I've set my Irish alarm clock.'

Irish appendectomy *n.* A dramatic *buoy from the black stuff* which feels like it contains an internal organ, or at the very least some sort of vestigial gland.

Irish backstop *1. n. medic.* Congestion of the *Camillas* caused by drinking too much Guinness. *2. n.* That sticky-out bit which stops a *butt-plug* from going up your *arse.*

Irish bhaji *n.* The sort of black, spicy, onion-smelling *Thora* which emerges from the *back body* the morning after one takes on board an excessive amount of Guinness.

Irish luggage *n.* Politically incorrect phrase used to describe the life's accumulations of a *paraffin lamp*, traditionally carted about in a picturesque knotted hankerchief on the end of a stick slung over his shoulder, but more usually in an old supermarket trolley filled with *shitty* bundles of carrier bags.

Irish shave *n.* A *dump.*

Irish toothache *1. n.* An erection, *bone on. 'Is that a gun in your pocket, or have you just got Irish toothache?' 2. n.* Pregnancy. *'Is that a spacehopper in your smock, or have you just got Irish toothache?'*

Irish tumble drier *n.* A cement mixer. A frankly racist and offensive term which we can categorically assure our readers would never find its way into a publication with such high editorial standards as what this one do. Has.

irn maiden *n. Scots.* A lassie with a healthy, natural skin tone hovering around the Pantone® 021C mark.

iron *n. rhym. slang.* A *crafty butcher.* From iron stealer = fruit feeler.

ironman time *1. n.* The time taken for an endurance athlete to complete a gruelling triathlon which comprises a 4km swim, a 180km cycle and a 42km run. *2. n.* When embarking upon a conversation with someone who's done an ironman triathlon, the period that elapses before they tell you about it. *'I met that Gordon Ramsay once.' 'Oh yeah? What's his ironman time?' 'About 35 seconds.'*

irons a sharp crease *euph.* Said of a chap who is *image conscious.*

irons his socks, I bet he *euph.* Said of a fellow who *knows what's in his flowerbeds.*

IRS *1. abbrev. US.* The Yankee taxman. *2. abbrev. medic.* Itchy Ring Syndrome. Irritating anal affliction caused by insufficient wiping of the *chocolate starfish*, or by inflammation of the *farmers.* Or both. Imagine that.

I say! *exclam.* Caddish expression of delight upon

seeing a pair of *dunces' hats.* See also *ding! dong!*

iScar *n.* A 9" long red welt on the upper abdomen, caused by the one-handed balancing of a tablet-style media device thereupon while *surfing the web for antiquarian books.*

I shat the sheriff *exclam.* Recognition of catastrophic tarnishing of a star-shaped *badge of office.*

I shot the sheriff *exclam.* A humorous rhetorical apopthegm uttered upon leaving the *crapper* after dropping a *U-bend straightener.* From the line in the eponymous Bob Marley song, *viz.* "One day the bottom will drop out".

i-shuffle *n.* The *self-harming* behaviour of a fellow watching a *pudcast* on his portable device. Also *i-wank.*

islands in the stream *1. n. prop.* Title of a song by Kenny Rogers and Dolly Parton that reached number 7 in the UK charts in 1983. *2. n.* Them unpleasant-tasting pineapple cubes in a men's urinal trough.

Isle of Wight *1. n.* A UK holiday destination made popular by Queen Victoria. *2. n. rhym. slang.* A load of rubbish. From Isle of Wight = pile of shite. *'That holiday we had on the Isle of Wight last summer was a complete Isle of Wight. We're going to Wales this year.'*

I smell like I sound *1. phr.* A somewhat strange lyric from Duran Duran's 1982 hit *Hungry Like the Wolf. 2. phr.* A humorous thing to say after *blowing off.*

I smell with my little nose, something beginning with *exclam.* Another one of those humorous, infantile preludes to a sonorous act of flatulation. Also *our survey said*; *the following report contains flashing images.*

isnae *n. Scots.* The *taint, tintis, ABC, scruttock.*

isolated warrior *1. n.* An action game released for the Nintendo Entertainment System in 1991. Us neither. *2. n.* A lone lump of *feeshus* that refuses to excuse itself from the *gravy pan* and stubbornly remains afloat even after several flushes.

issues with tissues *phr.* Euphemistical term used when speaking about someone believed to be a serial masturbator. *'Why can't we give him a knighthood, your Majesty? He presents one of the country's most popular radio programmes, after all.' 'Issues with tissues, Lord Chancellor. Issues with tissues.'*

is that Ziggy? *exclam.* Expression which can be used to lighten the mood when one has just *stepped on a duck* in polite company. A reference to the question commonly asked by cigar-chomping holographic sidekick Al when speaking into his multi-dimensional walkie-talkie in an attempt to get in touch with his 1999-based employer in the retrospectively bizarre TV series *Quantum Leap*.

is there a pulse in the end of that? *exclam*. Said to a chap with a proper *bride frightener*, *eg*. King Dong, "Big" John Holmes, Stephen Pound MP.

I stink therefore I am *exclam*. A deeply profound Cartesian philosophical adumbration, to be uttered as an angst-ridden existential reflection on the eternal plight of man, immediately following a *botty burp*.

Italian car/bike *euph*. A sleek, sexy *piece* who looks good and can be fine for a ride or a quick spin but who is ultimately a scarily expensive, high-maintenance, low-tolerance, highly-tuned "hard time waiting to happen." Also a *Venus fly-trap*.

Italian chipper *n*. A filthy dirty masturbating woman. From the fact that the Italian word for a deep-fat fryer is apparently *friggatrice*.

Italian enema *n*. The first strong coffee of the day, ensuring a smooth morning *dump*. Ex-laxpresso, Laxwell House, messcafé.

Italian job *1. n.* A finely balanced *bum cigar* teetering on the edge of a building site portaloo or a German *shitpot*, in the manner of the bus at the end of the eponymous film. *2. n.* As the closing credits roll, a massive, solid *shite* that hangs half in and half out of your *nipsy* and could go either back up the pipe or splash down into the bowl.

Italian jobbie *n*. A feculent motion with such a forceful stench that it "blows the bloody doors off".

Italian tune up *1. n.* Thrashing the hell out of one's old banger just before taking it for its MOT. *2. n.* Thrashing the hell out of one's *old banger* before a good session with a ladyfriend. *Putting a wank in the bank*.

it always helps when someone can speak the language *phr*. A humorous aphorism that effectively alleviates embarrassment after someone has audibly *dropped a gut*.

itch *n*. The feeling of mild sexual attraction towards his wife which a married man gets on average once every seven years.

itchypoo park *n*. The area around *spice island* during a bout of *IRS*.

itchy ring finger *1. n.* A good omen which may symbolise that one is soon to become engaged to be married. *2. n.* Digit attending to mild irritation in the *back body*.

it fits like a cock up a puppy's arse *phr*. '*I told you this garage was big enough for a Range Rover, and I was right. It fits like a cock up a puppy's arse, look. Careful you don't scratch the paintwork while

you're climbing out of the boot, nan.'*

I think I ate a clown *exclam*. Apologetic phrase issued from one's water closet cubicle after *dropping a particularly large pair of shoes out of the loft*.

I think it's Hawkins *exclam*. Announcement upon espying a particularly bloody *axe wound*. A quote from the movie *Predator*, typically accompanied by the sound of flies.

I think that barrel needs changing *exclam*. Something to say after a particularly malty *brew*.

it's a buoy! *exclam*. Useful expression which can be employed following the delivery of a sizeable, floating *battleshit*.

it's a good answer, but it's not right *exclam*. Said in a soft Ulster brogue in the style of Roy Walker following a polite, after-dinner *clearance of the nether throat*.

it's a knockout *n*. An amusing pub game where an individual with *legs like snapped candles* has to attempt to carry three brim-full pint glasses through a jostling, crowded hostelry from bar to table without spilling any.

it's all about the notes you don't play *exclam*. Sage response to a slow, sparsely orchestrated piece of *exit music*.

it's been put into local lockdown *exclam*. Humorous topical alternative to "I'd give it 10 minutes if I were you," vouchsafed when exiting *the smallest room*.

it's good but it's not Carling *exclam*. Said by a third party after a very disappointing *Exchange & Mart*.

it's his stag *exclam*. Phrase shouted by a merry fellow's intoxicated friends as he is roughly half-nelsoned into the back of a police van the night before his wedding. Possibly not acknowledged as a plea of mitigation in a court of law.

it's lights out and away we go! *exclam*. Pre-intercourse rallying cry said in the excitable manner of Formula One commentator David Croft at the start of a Grand Prix. See also *and that's it, the race has been red-flagged*.

it's not small, you're just a long way away *exclam*. A phrase that can be pressed into use by a gentleman when he sees an expression of disappointment on his inamorata's *fizzog*.

it's stop start to Knutsford *euph*. Something you often hear from that Lynn Bowles on Radio 2 when she does the traffic. Reference to a *ménage à moi* that is interrupted and then resumed.

it's the beer talking *exclam*. Phrase offered by way of an excuse when those killer *ale force winds* start blowing the morning after a night spent swilling *pop*.

it's trying to communicate with us, captain *exclam.* To be announced in the style of *Star Trek* science officer Mr Spock after breaking wind loudly.

it's what he would have wanted *exclam.* A phrase to help liven the mood at a funeral when someone *drops a gut*.

I've farted, so I'll finish *exclam.* Humorous riposte to the question, "How much longer are you going to be in there?".

I've got the bows up – I'm going! *exclam.* Enunciated through gritted teeth in the clipped style of late speed ace Donald Campbell, shortly before creating a splash of epic proportions.

I've got the hob on *exclam.* Said of a painfully hot *ring* experienced the morning after spending the night getting comprehensively *shitfaced*.

I've lost R2 *exclam.* Said following a particularly vigorous expulsion of faecal matter, which leaves the *shitter* traumatised by a wave of aftershocks. Taken from the destruction of the Death Star scene in the little known 1977 film *Star Wars*.

I've loved in it *exclam.* Humorous staff version of the popular fast food advertising jingle, usually sung while preparing or serving *McDonald's special sauce* on the minimum wage.

I've struck oil! *exclam.* Humorous utterance upon *following through* in public at the end of a smashing night on the black stuff.

ivory tower *n.* A night-time erectitivation of the *membrum virile*. A *dreaming spire*, a somnolent *dusk tusk*.

i-wank *n.* A bout of frantic self abuse fuelled by erotic images uploaded onto a portable video player or mobile phone. An *i-wank* is typically followed by a period of soul-destroying guilt and invariably concludes with the hasty deletion of all pornographic material from the aforementioned media device. Also *i-shuffle*.

I was born to walk against the wind *1. phr.* A lyric from the heavy metal band Manowar's song *Heart of Steel* on their album *Kings of Metal*. Us neither. *2. exclam.* Something to say after *death's bell rings*.

I was in Baghdad when you were in your dad's bag *exclam.* A more witty version of "I was doing this when you were still in short trousers", overheard in a warehouse in Warrington.

I wonder who's cock he/she has been sucking *exclam. interrog.* A rhetorical query on hearing of the unlikely promotion of someone to a position considerably beyond their training, knowledge or experience.

i-zooming *n.* The action of two fingers trying to pry open a lady's *hangar doors*, reminiscent of the pincer-like movement required to enlarge a picture on the screen of a mobile telephone. See also the *Ebdon slide*.

izzy wizzy let's get busy *exclam.* Words of self encouragement prior to an act of self pleasure while wearing a glove puppet. Also *jizzy wizzy~*; *izzy jizzy~* etc.

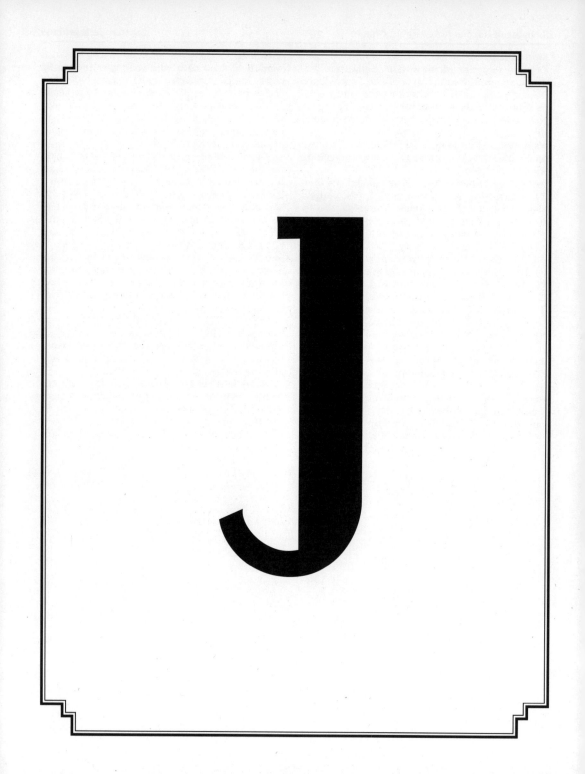

Jabba's cousins *n.* A pair of fat, saggy, unappealing *udders*. Named after the close family members of the erstwhile Tatooine crimelord, as introduced recently in *The Book of Boba Fett*. See also *triple-hearters, Trump's toppers*.

jabbernese *n.* Any language other than the Queen's English. That should probably be King's English these days, come to think of it.

jabsworth *n.* Overly officious marshal at a Covid vaccination centre.

JAC/jac *acronym.* Useful nickname for the sort of "celebrity" you've never ever heard of who rocks up on programmes like *Dancing on Ice, Celebrity Coach Trip, Celebrity Come Dine With Me, Celebrity Love Island* or *Celebrity Embarrassing Bodies*, who usually turns out to be off *Hollyoaks* or *TOWIE*. Just Another Cunt. See also *FFFA*.

jackage *n. coll.* Any materials used by a fellow for the purposes of *jacking off to, at, on* or *over. Jazz, grumble, grummer, Frankie Vaughan etc.*

jackal, the *1. n.* The mysterious assassin hired to bump off Charles de Gaulle in the novel by Frederick Forsyth, later played by Edward the Eighth in the film of the same name. *2. n.* The moustachioed seventies pornstar lookalike international terrorist from the days back when you didn't have to be that scared of terrorists. Him with the sunglasses off the front of the Black Grape album, who had a slight look of the bass player out of off of Dr Feelgood. *3. n.* A gentleman's covert delight; crouching down and sneaking forwards in order to gain proximity to a passing lady's bottom in order to catch a whiff of her *particulars*. An act characteristically accompanied by bared teeth and clawing motions with the hands.

Jack & Dani *n. prop. rhym. slang.* The female *love island*.

jackanory *1. n.* A piece of erotic fiction. *2. n.* A slow and gentle attempt at anal sex, involving a tub of marge, patience and repeated enquiries of "are you sitting comfortably".

jack cheese *1. n.* The stringy stuff they put on hamburgers in Britain to make them sound more authentically American. *2. n.* The stringy stuff chefs spread onto the food of unpopular customers. *'The chef's just wanking some jack cheese out of his knob onto your main course, Mr Coren'*

Jack Douglas *1. n. prop.* British film and television performer notable for wearing dungarees and a cap, whose Alf Ippatitimuss character was prone to sudden, spasmodic physical tics and hence *2. n.* Any violent, involuntary recoil from

something, *eg*. A pint of milk which has gone off, a blocked Virgin train lavatory swimming in urine and faeces, or accidentally seeing a second of *Embarrassing Bodies* while flicking through the TV channels.

jacked up *1. adj.* Celibate while suffering from a *dose*. *2. adj.* Of a woman, *up on axle stands*.

jack-in-a-box *n.* A thirsty-pet-frightening, Aristotle-confounding *digestive transit* that is, inexplicably, less dense than water, no matter how many flushes are thrown at it.

jack muscle *n.* One of those annoying little *dicks* that jumps up at visitors and leaves the lady of the house apologising to her friends: "Don't mind him, love. He's just being friendly."

jack of all trades *n.* One who can manage a *fish supper* and a *sausage dinner* in one sitting. A *happy shopper.*

jack off *v.* To *whack off, choke the chicken, jerk the gherkin, rub one out.*

jackoffanory *n.* A mucky narrative read down the phone by an understanding wife, partner, or casual acquaintance to a man suffering from the raging *horn* while away from home, who needs some fodder when *pulling off the Pope's hat* in his hotel bedroom.

jackpot counter *1. n.* Counter decorated with a with a large red star that is dropped into the machine at the start of the fourth round of Ben Shephard's daytime television quiz *Tipping Point*. *2. euph.* A sore *arse* with a large, red, glowing star in the middle.

jack roll *1. n. SA.* A gang bang. *2. n. US.* A mugging.

jack rustle *n.* The tell-tale sound of a fellow who is surreptitiously *wagging his tail*.

jackshit/jack shit *1. n.* What something worthless is, or indeed isn't, worth. *'Here on the Antiques Roadshow we see a lot of items that are worth much more than their owners expect, but I'm afraid, madam, that this coal scuttle is worth jackshit.' 'Eeh, and to think that all these years we've been keeping the coal in it.' 2. n.* A *turd* of such length and tensile strength that the toiletee is lifted off the *crapper* and left balancing with his or her feet off the ground. A *neckbreaker, U-bend straightener* or *ejector seat. 3. n. Bugger all, sweet FA,* zero, zilch. Nowt.

jacksie *n.* Polite word for *arse*, especially in the recepticular context. *'You can stick your fucking knighthood up your jacksie, mate. I paid for a peerage.'*

jacksie driver *n.* A motorist who seems keen to steer his car right up your *nipsy*. Probably in a fucking Audi. They usually are.

jacksie rabbit *n. Muddy funster.*

Jackson *n.* A truly disappointing breast. From the infamous "wardrobe malfunction" incident which occurred during the 2004 Super Bowl XXXVIII halftime show, when one of Janet's rubbishy *knockers* fell out when she was doing some sort of dance routine with Justin Timberlake.

Jackson Bollock *1. n.* That square of carpet situated between a bachelor's computer chair and his monitor which, were it to be illuminated using an ultraviolet lamp, would resemble nothing so much as a monochrome Abstract Expressionist painting. *2. n.* The artistic display of a chap's *man juice* across the flesh canvas of his partner's back, *arse* or face *etc.*

Jackson 5 concert, fanny like a *sim.* Said of a particularly bushy *ladygarden* that brings to mind nothing so much as the giant coiffures sported by the members of the erstwhile family singing group, *viz.* Michael, Tito, Jermaine, Merrill, Donny, Janet, Little Jimmy and Ken.

Jackson Pollock's shoes *euph.* A measure of the messiness of a *plasterer's radio.*

Jacksons *n. prop. rhym. slang.* Testicles. From Jackson Pollocks = cobblers.

jacksydent *n.* A trouser mishap, a *follow through.* From jacksie + accident. *'Paula Radcliffe has pulled out of the 10,000 metres final after suffering a nasty jacksydent during the Marathon.'*

jack the beanstalk *v.* To attempt to pull up the *purple-headed gristle thistle* by the roots.

Jack the lass *n.* A none-too-convincing *tiptop* or *Bobby dazzler.*

Jack the ripper *n.* A hard, thick, bloodthirsty *turd* that is *wider than a footballer's tie-knot,* which does its evil work in one's *back passage.* A *ring splitter.*

Jacky Danny *rhym. slang. James Hunt.*

jacobite *1. n.* A rebellious supporter of the deposed James ll or some such bollocks off *University Challenge.* *2. n.* The minimum amount of spare computer memory needed for a gentleman to enjoy himself in a right royal manner.

Jacob Marley *n. prop.* After a *sit down toilet adventure,* shuffling across the landing with your trousers round your ankles like chains in search of a fresh roll of *arse paper,* as if being punished for sundry past misdeeds.

Jacob Rees-Mogg *1. n. rhym. slang.* A long log draped over the porcelain in a style that is emetically reminiscent of the limp Leader of the House reclining louchely along the parliamentary front bench. *2. n. medic.* Erectile dysfunction.

Jacobs *rhym. slang.* Testicles. From Jacobs crackers = bollocks. Generally stored close to the cheese.

Jacob's ladder *n. medic.* The tearing of the stitches holding a recent mother's *joybox* together.

Jafaican *n.* The sort of ludicrous artificial Caribbean accent effected by middle class youths.

jaff *v.* To *wank.* In Norfolk. There's nothing else to do in Norfolk. *'Ooh, I just jaffed me twizzler behind the slaughterhouse. It was boodiful, really boodiful.'*

jaffas *n.* The *nuts* of the *fruit bowl.* The *orbs* of the *family jewels.* *'Ooh, that's it. Peck me jaffas. That's boodiful, really boodiful.'*

Jäger bum *n. medic.* Ailment brought about by over-consumption of the German cough medicine/energy drink, which may result in one befouling one's lederhosen.

Jagger's lips *euph.* Used to describe the distressing anatomical repercussions of a high-pressured *trouser cough.* *'That last fart left my arse feeling like Jagger's lips, your majesty.'*

jail bait *n.* Worms dug up by tunnelling prisoners and later, after their escape, used for fishing.

jailbird *1. n.* An habitual criminal, who accepts arrest as an occupational hazard, and presumably accepts imprisonment in the same casual manner, *eg.* "Lord" Jeffrey Archer. *2. n.* An unattractive lady of whom it might be said: "Christ. I'd rather do time than do her".

jailbreak *n.* Upon discovering that you have run out of *arse paper,* shambling out of the *bog* and across the landing in search of fresh supplies, with your trousers round your ankles like shackles. Also known as *the penguin, Jacob Marley, convict's shuffle* or *paperchase.*

jake *1. n.* A columnar monument erected in memory of a nice pair of *jamboree bags* one once saw, or a notable scene from a *meat vid.* *2. n. Scots.* An ugly woman, *horndog, lumberjill.*

jakery *n. Bumcraft.*

jalfrezi curse *n. medic.* An ancient oriental hex whereby, following a chilli-laden curry repast, the victim may travel no further than twenty feet from a lavatory for a period of 24 hours.

jam *n.* Sperm. *'Our Ethel came back from her boyfriend's with jam all over her face.'*

Jamaican chocolate volcano *n.* The exotic Caribbean cousin of the *Cleveland steamer,* fuelled by enthusiastic consumption of spicy jerk chicken and Red Stripe beer.

jamboree bags *n. Funbags, fat rascals,* proper *milkers.*

jambush *n.* A *blobstrop* that comes out of nowhere.

James *rhym. slang.* A *twat* in the pejorative rather than the gynaecological sense. From the inexplicably popular helium-voiced singer/songwriter

James Blunt.

James Bond pants/007 pants *n. Undercrackers* of a certain vintage that a bachelor sniffs in order to check if they'll "do another day".

James Browns *n.* The deeply upsetting noises which emanate from a row of office toilet cubicles during the daily 10.00am works *turd off.* From their similarity to the rambling squeals, incoherent grunts and random vocalisations which passed for lyrics in the songs of the hardest working corpse in showbiz.

James Cameron's camera *euph.* A subaquatic *Thora* which, despite repeated flushing, continues to inhabit the haunting depths of one's U-bend. Named after the deep-sea video equipment submersible that was used to provide footage of the sunken RMS Titanic and which, every time it landed on the wreck or sea-bed, caused a cloud of brown rust particles to swirl about. An *Alvin.*

James Corden's mid morning snack *euph.* One of those pub food challenges that involves a paving stone-sized piece of steak accompanied by 4lb of chips, with a free T-shirt or a photocopied certificate for anyone that can keep it all down.

James Hunt *n. rhym. slang. Jacky Danny.* Named after the late louche Formula 1 racing driver and heroic *crumpeteer.*

jam house *n.* The lavatory or *log cabin. 'Dr Livingstone, I presume?' 'No. He's in the jam house dropping off his shopping.'*

jammer *n. Carib.* A *pud.* See also *windjammer.*

jammet *n. Carib.* A West Indian term for a *slapper.*

jamming device *1. n.* James Bond-style Cold War espionage contraption, which is designed to prevent radio signals from reaching the enemy. *2. n.* Something rarely if ever encountered by agent 007; a feminine hygiene requisite. Also colloquially known as a *blobstopper, fanny mouse* or *Dracula's teabag.*

jammy dodger *n.* A married lady who uses the fact that the *tomato boat has docked* to avoid performing her wifely duty.

jammy todger *n.* Something you wouldn't get off a *jammy dodger.* A *barber's pole, eggy soldier.*

jampax *n.* A *clot mop, cotton pony.*

jam penny *1. n.* Apparently her late majesty's favourite sandwich; a circle of bread smeared with butter and jam. You can see why she was in charge. *2. n.* A lady's *bodily treasure* when *the fleet's in.*

jam rag *n.* A tampon, *fanny mouse, chuftie plug.*

jam raid *n. Crimson tidal* movement which leaves *tuna town* inaccessible by *skin boat* at certain times of the month.

jam salvage *n.* Retrieving a *fanny mouse* that has accidentally got pushed two or three inches up a lady's *clopper* during an *ad-hoc cricket week scuttle.*

jam sandwich *1. n.* A *tomato saucy* threesome. *2. n.* A *rag week snatch, ie.* One with two layers of crust and a sticky red filling. *3. n.* Unamusing CB-lingo for a police car, used by lorry drivers who think they are behind the wheel of a chrome-laden eighteen-wheeler running moonshine in *Smokey and the Bandit,* but are in fact driving a grimy 1988 Foden loaded with rancid chicken guts along the A515 between Sudbury and Yoxall looking for a *fat-titted* hitch-hiker to grope and possibly murder.

jam session *n.* An improvised *ragtime* duet.

jam tart *1. n. rhym. slang.* A *Bakewell.* From jam tart = Exchange & Mart. *2. n.* A rough *trollop* who has *got the painters in.*

Jan *n. prop. rhym. slang.* The *anus.* From Belgian footballer Jan Vertonghen = wrong'un.

Jane *1. n.* A ladies' lavatory. *2. n.* A *Mary.*

jang *n. Dong. 'Fuckanory. I've caught me jang in me zip. Court is adjourned.'*

janitorial pleat *n.* An unexpected *stiffy* or *tent pole,* named after the unique and unusually positioned design feature found only in the work trousers supplied to lecherous old school caretakers.

Japanese dismount *n.* Falling off something. From that far eastern gymnast who fell off the pommel horse and later claimed it was actually his dismount, thus costing the British team their Olympic silver medal. *'After landing well clear of the ramp, the front forks of the bike collapsed, and Knievel performed a Japanese dismount which left him with two broken legs, a shattered shoulder, four cracked vertebrae and compound fractures in both wrists, as well as a ruptured spleen, concussion and life-threatening internal injuries.'*

Japanese flag *n.* Appearance of the *arsehole* when blighted by *ring sting. Arse of the rising sun, Hawaiian sunrise.*

japarazzi *n.* Possibly mildly racist term for the crowds of far eastern tourists in the capital who insist on snapping every monument and tend to get in the way a bit when one is out and about.

jarred *adj.* Pissed, sloshed, wankered.

J Arthur *rhym. slang. Wank.* From the erstwhile British film distributor J Arthur Rasturbation.

Jasmine fanny *euph.* A lady of loose morals, a *right goer.* From the fact that "she's always got Aladdin."

Jason Donovan moment *n.* The *point of no return* when you are about to *cumulo* the *nimbus* of a less-than-alluring female. From the *Joseph and his Amazing Technicolour Dreamcoat* song lyric, as popularised by the eponymous former *Neighbours* hunk and Kylie beau, *viz.* "I close my eyes, pull back the curtains, a-a-aah!"

JAT sandwich, dry as a *sim.* Moistureless. A reference to the desiccated in-flight provender served on Serbia's national airline. *'Shall I just give up, love? Only I've been giving you the halibut handshake for half an hour now and you're still as dry as a JAT sandwich.'*

jaw warmer *n. Scots.* A threatened spot of *chin music* from a *doorknob. 'Get oot o' here noo, Jimmy, before I gie ye a jaw warmer.'*

jaxidermist *n.* A gentleman who has a penchant for stuffing bottoms.

jaywank *v.* To cross the *Billy Mill Roundabout* without due care and attention. To *change up into sixth gear* without regard to the sticky consequences.

jazz *1. n.* Improvised music characterised by syncopated rhythms. *2. n.* The *fadge, mott. 3. n.* Sex, intercourse, *the other. 4. n. Frankie Vaughanography.*

jazz cannon *n.* A man's *mutton musket* which, when ignited by *art pamphlets*, becomes the *one o'clock gun.*

jazz drummer, go at it like a *sim.* When eating, to hunch over one's plate and shovel food into one's mouth at an unseemly speed, in a style reminiscent of Gene Krupa or Buddy Rich giving it *three cocks to the cunt. 'Mate of mine says he saw John Prescott going at a big pork pie like a jazz drummer in the café at King's Cross Station.'*

jazz egg *n.* A little *spodge* of *spadge.* A *spoff* of *spuff, jot* of *jit.*

jazz festival *1. n. Jazz mags* spread across the floor, *jazz* on the laptop, *jazz* on the telly, *jazz* on your phone. Not to put too fine a point on it, a veritable plethora of *jazz.* A big *horn section. 2. n.* The purchase of two or more *noddy books* at one time.

jazz fusion *n.* The process by which the pages of a *scud mag* are cemented together.

jazz hands *1. n.* The action of displaying and agitating one's palms in time to a syncopated musical accompaniment; a thoroughly annoying, expressive hand movement originating in the delightful world of musical theatre. *2. n.* The action of shaking the *jitler* off one's *wanking spanners* following a vigorous rifle through the *rhythm section* of one's favourite *bongo book.* Messy outcome of *jaywanking.*

jazzholes *n. Arseholes* who affect to like the sort of free-form music which is so clever that it sounds like a piano, double bass and drum-kit being

kicked down a fire escape by a *farting* pensioner.

jazzma *n. medic.* Male condition which is characterised by shortness of breath; a symptom which typically presents when the patient's *bag for life* gets back from the shops unexpectedly early.

jazz mag *n.* A published pamphlet of artistic material, a *gentleman's interest journal.* Printed in *whacknicolour.*

jazz magnate *1. n.* A porn millionaire, one who who has benefited from a series of wristy investments, *eg.* The late Paul Raymond, the late Bob Guccione, the late Hugh Hefner, the late Larry Flynt. *2. n.* A short, blind, hairy-palmed lunatic who owns a substantial stash of *scud mags.*

jazz oyster *n.* A *bongo book snapper,* alluringly prised open to reveal the semi-precious giblets within.

jazz potatoes *n.* Spuds which have been *salted* at the kitchen staff's discretion. *Winner's dinners. 'And finally, Mr Coren, the piece de resistance, jazz potatoes.'*

jazz scavenger *n.* A fellow *working from home* whose wireless broadband router goes *tits up* in the middle of an important bit of *research*, forcing him to frantically search for a neighbour's signal onto which to piggy-back. A *jazz passenger.*

jazz stash *n.* A fellow's library of monomanual reference works. Usually kept on top of a wardrobe, but in Frank Skinner's case kept in several large warehouses on an industrial estate.

jazz talc *n.* Bolivian marching powder, showbiz sherbet, Keith Richards' dandruff.

jazz trumpeter's cheeks *sim.* Descriptive of a lady's well-rounded *arse.* Buttocks that look like Dizzy Gillespie going for a high C.

jazz vocalist *n.* One who encourages himself with erotic one-sided *acafella* conversations ("ooh, baby, yeah!" *etc.*) with the girls in his *biff mags* while practising *self-pollution.*

JB *n.* See *Jodrell.*

j-cloth *n.* A teenager's phenomenally absorbent underbed sock, used for cleaning up adolescent spillages. That item of hosiery which eventually ossifies into a *bachelor's boomerang.*

jeaneology *n.* The scientific study of young women's *arses* viewed through tight denim. A learned discipline which is principally practised by male motorists in neck-braces.

jebbs *1. n.* Manufacturer of crash helmets and hence *2. n.* Big round *knockers* which carry a BSI kitemark and comply with BS 6658.

J Edgar *n.* Like a *J Arthur* but using a vacuum cleaner. Possibly ends with a trip to A&E and the upstairs plugs fuse blowing.

Jedi knight *n. rhym. slang.* Shite. Also *Jedi*. *'I'll not sit down if it's all the same to you, your majesty, only I've got all Jedi Knight up the back of me kegs.'*

Jedi mind trick 1. *n.* Something that muppet in the *Star Wars* films does while someone's operating him from behind a rock. 2. *n.* The act of gaining advantage over someone by lying.

jeeving *n.* The act of *touching a lass up* under her clothing but over her underwear. *Tickling the pony's nose* while it's still got its nosebag on, if you will. *Cloth fingers*, probably.

Jeez they'd come last on Celebrity Mastermind *exclam.* Said about someone of exceptionally low intellect.

Jeffrey Dahmer's fridge *n.* A refrigerator, typically found in a student house, containing suspicious-looking meat products of indeterminate vintage.

Jehovah's stiffness *n.* In men, an unwelcome erection which arrives at the most inconvenient times and then refuses to leave. A *tiffter, Jake, Eric, watchtower.*

Jehovah's wetness *n.* In ladies, autonomic dampness *under the bridge* experienced at inopportune moments.

jelly bag *n.* The wrinkled retainer where a gentleman keeps his *Egyptian Halls*. The scrotum. *'How's that, DPM?' 'Sorry Tracey, nowt's happening yet. Try tickling me jelly bag for a bit. And make it snappy, will you. I'm speaking at a memorial service for the dead of two world wars in twenty minutes.'*

jelly bollocks *n. Yorks.* Affectionate term for a soft lad or daft 'apeth.

jelly hammock *n. Drip tray*. The *sump* of a pair of *scads*.

jelly jewellery *n.* The earrings, nose studs, fancy spectacles and other facial adornments the *bread knife* sometimes receives when she was expecting her partner to give her a *pearl necklace*.

jelly roll 1. *n. US. Snatch, muff, totty.* 2. *n.* A *fuck* off a barrelhouse jazz pianist who died in 1941.

jelly the pie 1. *v.* In the pastry industry, to inject, well, jelly into a pork pie. 2. *v.* In a loving relationship, to inject, well, *spunk* into a *hairy pie*.

jelly water mangos *n.* Large *knockers, gazunkas, bazingas.*

Jemima Puddlefuck *n. prop.* Nickname for a female wetness enthusiast. See also *Judy Drench*.

Jennifer Canestan *n. prop.* An attractive woman who is riddled with *gash rash*. *Lady Chalk of Billingsgate.*

Jenny 1. *n.* A female donkey. 2. *n. US.* Some

female *ass.*

Jeremy Beadle's thumb, hung like *sim.* An unacceptably tasteless and offensive way of referring to a fellow who is somewhat under-endowed *down there. Hung like a Chinese mouse.*

Jeremy Clarkson's eyebrows *euph.* A messily overgrown *Judith*, named in honour of the *hangrily* pugilistic ex-*Top Gear* motormouth's unkempt supercilia; a *fanny like a scrapyard cat.* Also *Arthur Fowler's allotment, Lord Winston's moustache, the full Belgian.*

Jeremy Kyle grand prix *n.* Several circuits of the aisles of a budget supermarket during which one overtakes a succession of individuals from a less elevated end of the social scale.

jerk 1. *n. US.* A stupid, dim or dull person. A *goddam dicksplash.* 2. *adj.* Type of chicken popular in the West Indies.

jerking from home *n.* Failing to watch any daytime television due to multiple sessions of *self delight.*

jerkin' the gherkin *n.* Jiggling a small cucumber round on the end of a string.

jerk off 1. *v. Jack off*, masturbate. 2. *n. US.* A *fuckwit*.

jerkolator *n.* An extremely noisy *blow job*, performed by someone who comes back for coffee.

jerk sauce 1. *n.* The special secret ingredient that is apparently added to the KFC Reggae Reggae Box Meal. 2. *n.* The special secret ingredient added to every meal that the late Michael Winner ever consumed, even when he'd made his own tea.

jerk seasoning *n.* A pot of hand cream kept next to the bed, to facilitate a smooth session of *reggae like it used to be.*

jerk station *n.* An old computer of limited function and nominal value, used principally to browse the web in search of erotica. A *filth machine, faptop* or *dirty mac.*

jerkwad *n. US. Tosser, fuckwit, wankipants.* A person to whom one might show the elevated *digitus medius* of one's right hand before rhetorically inviting them to swivel thereupon.

jerry in the trench *euph.* Phrase used when describing an itchy *ringpiece* when one is in polite company. Useful when one finds oneself suffering from an attack of *arse wasps* or *wire spiders* at Glyndebourne, the Hay-on-Wye Literary Festival or when commentating on the the the Queen Mother's funeral, for example.

Jersey royals 1. *n.* High quality potatoes noted for having plenty of eyes on them. 2. *n.* High quality *chest spuds* as seen through knitted clothing. 3. *euph.* Smallish, but pert and firm, *shirt potatoes* which are particularly good boiled with a bit of melted butter on. *Sara Cox's orange pippins.*

Jessie J *adj. rhym. slang. Colwyn Bay.* 'Fancy a quickie behind a skip, lover?' 'No thanks, madam. I'm a bit Jessie J.'

jessticles 1. *n. Knackers* that have been *wanked flat* while watching two consecutive days of women's Track and Field. 2. *n.* Amusing *plums.*

jester's shoes *n. medic.* The involuntary upward curling movements of the toes that herald the onset of the *vinegar strokes,* while lying on one's back *wanking.* 'Zoom in on Gunther for the money shot, camera two. He's got the jester's shoes.'

jet-lag 1. *n. medic.* Desynchronosis, jet syndrome, circadian dysrhythmia *etc.* Alan Whicker's perpetual state of mind between 1959 and 1994. 2. *n. medic.* The intense and sudden fatigue that follows the release of a spurt – or, more likely, trickle – of *Harry Monk.* Also *jit-lag.*

jet slag 1. *n.* A woman who is always *up for a bit* in the *crappers* on a plane. 2. *n.* A woman whose morals are somewhat looser than usual due to extreme tiredness brought on by travelling from a different time zone.

jet-washing the algae off the patio *euph.* Whilst coupling *doggy fashion,* the act of withdrawing and immediately ejaculating onto one's romantic partner's *nipsy,* to give it a deep and thorough clean. 'One of the advantages of Vatican roulette is that last night I totally jet-washed the algae off the missus's patio.'

jeweller *n.* A gifted manufacturer of *jelly jewellery* and *pearl necklaces.* A *heavy wetter.*

jewels *n.* The *wedding vegetables* that a paterfamilias keeps in his *fruit bowl.*

jibble *n.* The final, sad, leaking tears of *spangle* which drip out of one's *hog's eye* in those *wangst*-ridden moments of spiralling despair and self-loathing which apparently follow a bout of *self help.* From jizz + dribble.

jibbles *n.* The involuntary vibration of the *jester's shoes* just before the *custard pie gets thrown.*

JIF *acronym.* Any alcoholic beverage. Judgement Impairment Fluid.

jiffy bag *n.* A workmanlike *fuck buddy,* into whom a fellow might safely throw his *valuables.*

jig-a-jig *n.* It, *how's your father, the other,* when explained, possibly with the addition of a simple mime, to someone who doesn't speak English.

jigger *n. 18thC.* That tool with which a man commits *jiggery pokery.* The *fuck stick.*

jiggered 1. *adj.* In a state of fatigue or collapse. *Buggered, knackered, shagged out.* 2. *adj.* Something that a surprised person is confident that they will be.

jiggery pokery *n. Shenanigans,* assorted sexual goings-on. 'I'll have no jiggery pokery going on under my roof.'

jiggle physics *n.* The abstruse scientific laws governing the gravity-defying, non-Newtonian up and down motion of *birds' churns* in video games.

jiggle ring *n.* The larger lady's *muffin top* lifebelt, waved to attract the attention of a prospective partner. 'Don't look now, but that Billy at the bar is shaking her jiggle ring at you.'

jiggle show *n.* A somewhat titillating, but *chest tuner*-free early evening television show, *eg. Baywatch, Charlie's Angels.* 'Quiet, children. Your father is trying to watch his jiggle show.'

jiggle the jewellery *v.* To *box the jesuit,* rough up the suspect.

jiggly fruit *n.* A nice *pair,* especially when un-en-cumbered by *tit pants.*

jigsaw juice *n.* Any strong alcoholic beverage in-advertantly taken to excess, thus causing the memory to fail during or after consumption and setting the drinkee the puzzle of trying to piece together the events of the previous evening. *Milk of amnesia.*

jill off *v.* Female equivalent of *jack off;* to *paddle the pink canoe.* Until it starts leaking.

jimble *n.* Standard Imperial measure of fluid volume, specifically the amount of *sailor's ale* that lands between the thumb and finger at the conclusion to a successful *Thomas the tank.* Approximately equal to a thimble-full or one four-hundredth of an *almond.*

Jim Bowen's glasses, as thick as *sim.* Disparaging assessment of a person's intelligence. A reference to the powerfully bespectacled late *Bullseye* host/deputy headmaster. Also *thick as a bull's dick, thick as Norfolk pig shit, thick as a ghurka's foreskin etc.* 'I tell you what, that Piers Morgan is as thick as Jim Bowen's glasses.'

jim-jam wigwam *n.* A conical teepee pitched in one's nightwear, using a fleshy tentpole for support.

Jim Kardashian *n.* A convincingly *bootylicious tranny.*

Jimmy Cricket 1. *n. prop.* Northern Irish stand-up comedian whose 1980s ITV show, entitled *And There's More,* was ironically axed after 24 episodes. 2. *n.* A never-ending sit-down visit to the *bum sink.* Also known as a *magician's hankie, Columbo or hidden track.*

Jimmy Edwards *n.* Tufts of *pubage* protruding either side of a bikini bottom, resembling the handlebar moustache of the late *Whacko!*

star. *Thighbrows.*

Jimmy hat *1. n.* A latex prophylactic device designed to keep the head of the penis dry during intercourse. An *American tip.* 2. *n.* A piece of headwear designed for, or worn by, someone called Jimmy.

Jimmy Riddle *rhym. slang.* Vicar-friendly term for *turning your bike around.* *'I'm just going for a Jimmy Riddle, vicar.' 'Well don't forget to shake the end of your cock to get the last few drops of piss off it.'*

Jimmy sack *n.* School lavatory high jinks. During an act of urination, the *fiveskin* is pinched shut, creating a high-pressure bag of *wazz* at the end of the penis. This can then be used to chase people.

Jimmy Savile *1. n.* Yorkshire-born ex-coal miner, who went on to become a founding Radio 1 DJ, and hosted the first edition of *Top of the Pops* as well as *Jim'll Fix It.* He also appeared on several adverts for British Rail, *bummed* dead bodies and raised large amounts of money for charity in a series of sponsored marathons. 2. *n.* A *bum cigar* of such humungous proportions that it forces involuntary high-pitched warbling noises to issue from its begetter's mouth, in the style made popular by the erstwhile ennobled *Jim'll Fix It* presenter when fixing it for his young guests to mow the lawn in the *Blue Peter* garden, or some other such bit of low-budget BBC tomfoolery.

Jimmy Savile Row *Scrote couture* style of shell-suit tailoring sported by *scratters.* See also *Savile Row.*

Jimmy Savile's chair *n.* A once treasured item which is now worth absolutely *fuck all.*

Jimmy Savile's grave *euph.* A somewhat rumpled, knotted and tousled plot that has been left unattended for a long period of time. Since 9th November 2011 to be precise. See also *Terry Waite's allotment, Ken Dodd's hairbrush, Stuart Hall's windowbox, Percy Thrower's lawn, Rolf's window box, Max Clifford's shrubbery.*

Jimmy Savile's running shoes, colder than *sim.* A turn of phrase evidently coined in honour of the late unlamented cigar-chomping *sex-case.* *'Fuck me, shut those tent-flaps will you, Tensing. It's colder than Jimmy Savile's running shoes in here.'*

Jimmy White's brother *n.* The most boring member of any group of lads who turns up every night at the pub to sit in abject, oppressive silence. From the urban legend that when the famous snooker player's brother died, his friends broke into the undertakers to take his corpse out for one last *piss-up.*

Jimmy Wonkle *n.* The gentleman's *widdle tap.* *'Ow! I've caught me Jimmy wonkle in me zip,*

Mr Humphries.'

Jim Royle's beard *n.* A *Dylan, pieman's wig.*

jinker *n.* That up which one may be rhetorically invited to stick something. *'Can I interest you in today's special lunchtime menu at all, madam?' 'Stick it up your jinker, sonny.'*

jipper *n. Cod yoghurt, cock soup.*

jism *n.* Semen. Also *gism, jissom, jizz, jizzom.* Other spellings are available.

jitbag *n.* A *dunky, jubber ray.* *'Hey, I think I'm in here, Jeeves. Have you got any jitbags about your person?'*

jit gel *n. US.* The contents of a used *jitbag* once it has floated across the Atlantic.

jit gel rag *n. US.* Any available object upon which you wipe your *cock* after sex, *eg.* Tissues, underpants, curtains, tramp's beard.

jit lag *1. n. NZ.* State of exhaustion experienced by men who are suffering from a zinc deficiency. *'Can't make it to the pub tonight, lads. Only I've just got me broadband working and I'm suffering from severe jitlag.'* 2. *n.* The slimy, post-ejaculatory *jazz egg* that drops out the end of one's *Charlie* about 20 minutes after *stack blow.* The *post bolt, missing fish, David Davis's teardrop.*

jitler *n.* Spunk.

jive cunny *n. medic.* 1940s precursor of *disco fanny* and *festival flange,* typically suffered by a bob-by-socked dazzler brewing up some extra tasty *cunker chutney* while jitterbugging *three cocks to the cunt* at the local Lindy hop and clam bake.

Jizebel *n. prop.* A saucy Jezebel who likes being *jizzed* upon. A *plasterer's radio, quattro formaggio, cock mess monster* or *white witch.*

jizlas *n.* Thin sheets of paper used to mop up *tugwax.*

jizz *1. n.* Jism. 2. *v.* To *shoot one's load, lose one's mess.* 3. *n.* The type of music played by high-col-lared alien combo Figrin D'an and the Modal Nodes during the Cantina scene in *Star Wars: A New Hope.*

jizzabyte *n.* A unit of computer memory equivalent to approximately 1 million million gigabytes. 1 jizzabyte is defined as the approximate amount of hard drive space occupied by the pornography downloaded by an average teenage youth or vicar in a single calendar month.

jizzappointment *n.* The underwhelming experience suffered when a keenly anticipated *popshot* fails to live up to expectations.

jizzard *n.* A swirling blizzard of the wrong sort of *snow,* sufficient to stop a *train being pulled* in a *grumble flick.*

jizzaster *n.* The leaving of incriminating masturbatory evidence behind. *'That wad of spunk on the carpet was a fucking jizzaster. Not to mention the Fuck Truck tape in the video, or the circle of open wank mags on the living room floor. Or me lying unconscious in the middle of it all with my trousers round my ankles and my red-raw cock in my hand.'*

jizzazzle *v.* To *vajizzle.* To give the missus a temporarily sparkly, sticky decoration around the *downstairs area.*

jizzbags *n.* The lobes of the scrotal sac, *John Wayne's hairy saddlebags.*

jizzbib *1. n.* A sacrificial T-shirt placed over the stomach and chest to prevent seminal claggage of the chest hair during a horizontal *wank. 'Don't just throw out your old jizzbibs. Sell them on Vinted.' 2. n.* The goatee beard of one who *throws a light dart.*

jizzbolt *n.* A glob of ejaculate that leaves the *hog's eye* with enough force to put the television screen through. A *golden shot, Bernie the bolt* or *twelve-bore popshot.*

jizzbolt jury *n.* Any group of men watching and discussing the merits of a *stick vid, eg.* On an oil rig, in a fire station or in the cabinet office.

jizzdens *n.* Masculine reference material that a man consults studiously during *cricket week.*

jizz drive *n.* An external storage medium for *left-handed website* downloads.

jizzer mortis *n. medic.* The paralyzed, claw-like state of the missus's *wanking spanner* after it gets covered in *splooge* from a *tug job.*

jizzery *1. n.* The sense of inward loathing and malaise immediately following the *dropping of one's yoghurt. Wangst, wanguish. 2. n.* The sorrowful form of *monomanual delight* practised by a newly single man.

jizz funk *n.* The musical genre of which the soundtracks to 1980s *stick vids* are principally constituted.

jizz hands *euph.* Shaking sticky *Thelonious* from one's *wanking spanners* at the conclusion of a productive *five knuckle shuffle. 'So, Mr Coren's soup was on the way out of the kitchen when I suddenly realised that not a single employee had wanked into it.' 'Christ on a fucking bike, what did you do?' 'Only one thing I could do, Kirsty. I rubbed out a quick one and gave it the jizz hands over the bowl as the waiter went by.' 'And what is your fourth record?'*

jizziotherapy *n.* A three-minute, one-handed massage that relieves stiffness for up to half an hour.

jizz jar *n.* Girlfriend.

jizz juggler *1. n.* An enthusiastic *wankatrix. 2. n.* One of the less successful variety acts to audition

for *Britain's Got Talent.*

jizz lamp *n.* A special ultraviolet torch favoured by fictional crime scene investigators looking for feloniously deposited *man spackle* on mattresses.

jizzle *n.* In *dogging* circles, a mixture of *jipper* and light rain on a car windscreen. Thankfully, the intermittent wipe is usually all that is required to deal with a minor fall of *jizzle. 2. v.* To drizzle *jizz.* Derivation unknown. *'Just think, son, Status Quo are staying on the top floor of this hotel. Ooh, I think it's starting to jizzle.'*

jizzmopper *n.* A member of the honourable profession of peep show *wank booth* hygienist.

jizzmopper's cloth *1. n.* An absorbent rag used by a professional *wank booth* hygienist in the performance of their daily duties. *2. sim.* Descriptive of a *cockoholic's dunghampers.*

jizzness *n.* Tiring occupation of well-*whoreganised* peripatetic executive/commercial traveller types. *'I have just been to Amsterdam for the weekend on jizzness. My next jizzness trip is planned for Estonia. You get any of that Benzathine penicillin left over?'*

jizzn't *n.* The *decaff spunk* of a man who's either had a vasectomy or whose *tadpoles* aren't very good at swimming. *'I'm sorry to tell you I've had a look at your sample under the microscope and I'm afraid it's jizzn't.'*

jizz off a porn queen's face *sim.* A hardcore version of "water off a duck's back". *'Frankly, Clare Short's criticisms of Tony Blair's presidential style of government are like jizz off a porn queen's face to the Prime Minister.'* (Andrew Marr, Radio 4 *Today* programme, May 2003).

jizz ships *n.* The flotilla of small *egg drop soup* tankers and *friggits* which float about on the surface of the bath after a chap has played *up periscope.*

jizzumped *adj.* Thwarted when an unwelcome and intrusive thought arrives just before one *completes.*

jizzy rascal *n.* A cheeky chap who *starches the sheets* at every available opportunity.

jizzy royals *n.* Small, white, perfectly formed *shirt spuds.* Best served garnished with a soupcon of melting *nut butter.*

JJJ *abbrev.* When a lady stands up, holds her belt loops and walks on the spot to adjust her *cat flaps* in skintight jeans. Jegging Jingle Jangle.

J-lower *n.* A girl blessed with a substantially bigger and much more gravitationally challenged *council gritter* than Miss Lopez. See also *Sharon sixteen stone.*

J-No *n. prop.* A *bubbly* girl who believes she looks good in tight jeans or hipsters.

Joanie *n.* A voluminous, tight, curly permed *front*

bottom of the sort that one might imagine finding on Richie Cunningham's sister in *Happy Days*.

job *n*. A *feeshus*. *'Who's left a job on the front step?'*

job application forms *n*. Sheets of *bumwad* filled in with a *brown crayon* while visiting the *job centre*. *Shit tickets. 'Mam! Can you lob up another roll of job application forms onto the landing?'*

jobby, a big *n. Scots.* A *dreadnought*. That which is "wheeked".

jobbycentre *n*. A municipal toilet. *'Where are you off to, George?' 'I'm just off down the jobbycentre, Andrew.'*

jobby clock *n*. The natural rhythm and pattern of the digestive system that causes one to have to *lay a cable* every day at exactly the same time. The biological mechanism that governs the *men stool cycle*, which can easily become confused by a long haul flight, a holiday, a surfeit of hard-boiled eggs or a visit to a hard water area.

jobby engine *n*. The lavatory or water closet. The *shit pot, bum sink*.

jobby jewellery *n*. Sweetcorn.

jobby jouster *n*. A knight of *King Richard the Third*.

jobbymoon *n*. Post-*poo* high, which may or may not involve a romantic stroll along a beach.

jobby pocket *n. Scots.* Warm, brown, loose, *Thora Hird*-like meat and gravy encased in pastry; a steak bake. *'D'ye want onything while a'm oot gettin' the messages, Wullie?' 'Aye maw. Ye can fetch me a jobby pocket frae the bakers.'*

jobby well done *n*. The sense of pride one feels after serving up a *gorilla's breakfast*.

job centre *n*. The *crapper, chod bin, jobby engine*.

jobstacle *n*. A large pile of *hound rope* left in the middle of the pavement. *'The postman's going to need some real agility to negotiate that jobstacle course.'*

job strain *1. n.* Work-related stress. *2. n. medic.* Constipation (as opposed to a *jobby well done*). Also *brown drought, forgetting the password*.

jocaine *n. Showbiz sherbet* that's been mixed with baking powder or talc, and thus fails to come up with the goods when snorted through a rolled ten pound note in a lavatory by a sweating children's television presenter. *Salted sniff, faux-caine*.

jockanory *n*. A tale of woe proffered by a ruddily complexionned Scotsman who finds himself perennially short of just fifty pence for the train fare he requires to take him back to the rolling heather-covered glens of his homeland. Pal.

jockeys *rhym. slang.* Nipples. From jockeys' whips = nips.

jockey's bollocks, neck like a *sim.* Dysphemistic description of one whose *noggin* is somewhat unimpressively attached to their shoulders, *eg*. Multi-phobic, professional *turd*-sniffer Dr Gillian McKeith PhD.

jockey's breakfast *n*. A glass of champagne and a thin *shit*.

jockey's coffin *n*. An exceptionally small and snug-fitting *fluffit*. A *mouse's ear, paper cut, wormhole, Bugner's eye, hairline crack. 'And so it was that Mary was pure and had not known a man and had a snatch like a jockey's coffin, yet she was great with child.'* (Luke 1:4).

jockey's glance *n*. Whilst ensconced on the *biscuit wrapper*, a swift look over the shoulder to admire your handiwork, reminiscent of Bob Champion on Aldaniti, approaching the finishing line of the 1981 Grand National.

jockey's starting position *n*. The well-braced *arse-in-the-air* stance adopted by one who is shortly anticipating a *shot from the starter's gun*.

jockey yoghurt *1. n.* Brand of sweet-tasting fermented dairy produce which is popular in Europe. *2. n.* The *milm* decorating the insides of an eager fellow's *scads* after an evening of *searching for loose change* at a lap-dancing establishment, while travelling on a crowded tube train or hiding in the branches of a tree overlooking the local nurses' home. *'Do you think you can get the jockey yoghurt out of these Y-fronts, Mary?' 'Yes, Jeffrey. I'll put them on a boil wash.'*

jockflap *1. n.* A Scottish panic. *'Tommy, dinnae get yersel in such a jockflap. I'm sure they cannae prove it.' 2. n.* Scottish *ladyparts*.

Jodrell *n. rhym. slang.* A *J Arthur*. From the UMIST radio telescope Jodrell Wank.

Jodrell banquet *n*. Having *one off the wrist* while sitting on one's knees with all one's *jazz mags* laid out on the floor in the style of a parabolic array of radio telescopes. Also known as a *pornorama, wank crescent* or *glandscape*.

Joe Strummer *1. n. prop.* Legendary deceased singer/songwriter of the Clash popular music combo, real name John Graham Mellor. *2. n. prop.* Cotswold Rail locomotive 47828. *3. n.* Nickname given to an individual who is prone to engage in spontaneous bouts of *onanism*.

Joey pouch *n*. An accommodating Antipodean *ladygarden*.

joff *v*. To *milm* one's *grundies* without even being *tumescent*. Derived from Jizz On Flop. *'I joffed when I found my dad's bootleg Night in Paris vid behind some tins of paint in the garage.'*

jog for yoghurt *v*. To undertake a mild bit of *manly exercise*.

jogging behind a gritter *sim*. An unkind description

of a person blessed with a *face like a blistered pisspot*. *'Jesus Christ! She's got a face like she's been jogging behind a gritter. Where did you find her?'* *'She was jogging behind a gritter.'*

John 1. *n.* *Percy, Willie, John Thomas*. A male member. 2. *n.* A *tom*'s client, a *Hillman Hunter*. 3. *n. US.* A *crapper*.

John Bonham upgrade *n.* A change of status that is far from being an improvement. Named after the colourful Led Zeppelin drummer who famously, after *pissing it*, traded his seat in first class with a roadie in economy.

John Craven 1. *rhym. slang.* A *shaven haven, Beverley Craven.* 2. *n.* The act of drinking five pints of beer or lager without going to the toilet for a *piss* until the third pint is finished. Derivation unknown, but possibly a reference to a "spoof" article about newsreaders' drinking capacity in issue 28 of the downmarket magazine *Viz* which enjoyed a brief vogue in the last century. A three-pint total is known as a *Jan Leeming*, from the same supposedly "humorous" article.

John Darwin's canoe *n.* A *stool* that mysteriously vanishes in the water, only to inconveniently appear some time later. A reference to the erstwhile Hartlepool-based criminal mastermind, who paid off his hundred-grand mortgage by hiding behind the water tank in his loft for 7 years.

John Holmes *n.* A massive marijuana cigarette, named after the legendary saucy actor of the same name who reputedly had a large *tassel*.

John Lees *rhym. slang. Scots. Tits.* From noted dead blues groaner John Lee Hooker = sooker.

John McCririck's wanking pants, dirtier than 1. *sim.* Used by a mother to describe the unkempt state of a child's room. 2. *sim.* Said of a woman who has a refreshingly open-minded attitude to carnal matters. *Also dirtier than a coalminer's hanky.* *'Fuck me, that blonde piece doing the weather looks dirtier than John McCririck's wanking pants.'*

John Merrick's cap *n.* A vast, out of shape *fanny*.

Johnny *n.* A *dunky,* a *jubber ray.* *'Eurgh! I just found a Johnny in my sandwich.'*

Johnny cache *n.* The bedside drawer in which prophylactics are stored.

Johnny Cash 1. *n.* £2 for 3 from the machine in the pub *bogs.* 2. *n.* A *Wigan rosette, Japanese flag.* A *burning ring of fire.*

Johnny Cradock's collar *n.* A foulsome, unwashed *brim,* named in honour of the eponymous, monocled seventies lush, whose missus famously had to clean his filthy shirt neck by rubbing it with a bar of Fairy soap. Another one for the teenagers there.

Johnny in the Shining, like *sim.* Desperate to get into the bathroom. *'What have you done to my bloody bog door, Barry?'* *'Sorry Paul, I had the turtle's head so bad I was like Johnny in the Shining.'*

Johnny jibber *n.* To lose *wood* upon opening the *flunkey.* Premature ejaculation and *Johnny jibber* are thought to affect 1 in 4 males at some time in their life.

johnnylingus *n.* Oral stimulation of a *jubbered-up* member, for example off a fussy lady when one has a dose of *cock rot.*

Johnny no-stars *n.* A *dolt* or *fuckwit.* From the "star rating" system on the badges worn by staff at burger restaurants. One who occupies a place on the lower end of the evolutionary fast food chain.

Johnny Ramone strum *n.* A particularly aggressive *wanking* technique consisting solely of downstrokes.

Johnny Rotten 1. *n. prop.* Erstwhile iconoclastic lead singer of the Sex Pistols pop group turned anti-establishment butter salesman. 2. *n.* A *franger* that is befouled with excrement following a *backdoor visit.*

John O'Scrotes *euph.* Any seaside town characterised by a seasonal influx of pill-popping, lager-swilling, fornicating *ratboys* and *slappers,* eg. Salou, Magaluf, Ibiza or Frinton.

John Sargeant 1. *n.* A *fry-up face.* Refers to anyone with features resembling the former BBC Chief Political Correspondent turned ballroom dancer. 2. *n.* A great British fried breakfast of which, before commencing, one might say "Now over to BBC Chief Political Correspondent John Sargeant".

Johnson *n.* A thick, self-serving and superficial *member.*

Johnson's baby oil 1. *n.* Popular mild unguent for those with sensitive skin. 2. *n.* The former *hypolybast* for Uxbridge and South Ruislip's surprisingly fecund *jitler.*

John the Baptist 1. *n.* prop. Biblical character, a sort of Happy Shopper Jesus who got his head cut off at the request of some New Testament pole dancer or other. 2. *n.* A pungently prophetic *air biscuit*; one that speaks of "a greater one to come" (probably in solid form).

John Thomas *n.* How gamekeeper David Mellors referred to his *slag hammer* in the controversial novel *Lady Chatterley's Lover.*

John Waynes *n.* Walking like Mrs Thatcher, George Bush or Tony Blair when he was visiting George Bush, ie. That gait adopted after *giving birth to Meat Loaf's daughter.* Makes the walker look like they've been sitting on a horse for three days.

John Wayne's hairy saddle bags *1. n.* Jizzbags. *2. n.* Saloon doors.

John Wayne's safety catch, more time off than sim. In an office or workplace, descriptive of *glassbacked* employees who are constantly ill.

John Wayne toilet paper *n.* The shiny, ineffective school bog *bumwad* remembered with scant affection from childhood days, and still employed in public lavatories. From the fact that "it's rough, tough and don't take shit from no man".

John Zorn *1. n. prop.* Way-out, hardcore, experimental jazz musician. *2. n. prop. rhym. slang.* Way-out, hardcore, experimental *jazz.* *'Got any John Zorn, mate?' 'Yeah, I keep it in the back room, Mr Brown.'*

joie de beaver *1. n. Fr.* The name of a strip club in Thomas Pynchon's novel *Bleeding Edge.* Apparently. *2. n.* The uplift in a young male's spirits engendered by a bit of *stoat* or, indeed, the prospect of getting his *wood* nibbled.

join Dutch's unit *v.* To have a *wank.* From the scene in the film *Predator* when Arnie (Dutch) says: "General, my team works alone, you know that".

joiner's bag *n.* A battered, capacious *blurtch* with all hammers and spirit levels falling out of it. Also *chippie's toolbag.*

join giblets *v.* To do *thingy* with a bare lady.

join in the applause *v.* To make a lady *airtight. 'I went into my flatmate's room to borrow his weights. He was doing his girlfriend from behind and she's always up for it so I joined in the applause, bishop.'*

join the soil association *v.* To befoul one's *grundies. 'I do beg your pardon. I just bent over to tie my shoelace and accidentally joined the soil association. Where was I? Oh yes, Dogger, Fisher German Byte, rain, one thousand and six, good, rising slowly.'*

joint security area *1. n.* The heavily policed piece of no man's land between South and North Korea which apparently offers a unique touristic experience to those who dare to enter it and hence *2. n. Tinsley flyover, Baker Street concourse.*

joint statement *n.* A dumb, confused or goofy utterance delivered under the influence of a herbal cigarette. See also *highdea.*

jollies *1. n. Police.* In constabulary terms, trips to scenes of crimes. *2. n.* Women's breasts. *'Look at the jollies on that nun, your holiness.'*

jollup *n.* A dollop of *jizz.* From the Greek jollopus = dollop of jizz.

jolly brown giant *n.* An enormous *non-mover at number two* awaiting despatch after a prolonged *delay on the Bakerloo line.*

jolly green giant *n.* A virescent *dreadnought*

that appears as a result of the over-consumption of fresh liquorice. Unlikely to provoke much laughter.

jollyrancher *n. US.* One blessed with the cat-like ability to *cannonball, ie.* A man who never leaves the house but orders in a lot of breath-fresheners.

Jolson, the *n.* When you slap someone's *arse cheeks* on both sides – creating hand imprints – then get them to twerk, giving the impression of jazz hands.

Jonathan *rhym. slang.* A *Sherman tank,* a *Barclays,* from the masturbating TV presenter Jonathan Ross OBE = toss OBE.

jonk *v.* To *jizz, spaff, spunk up, spuff, spill the Brasso, tip one's filthy concrete, lose one's mess, shoot one's load, shoot one's bolt, shoot one's stack, shoot one's wad, drop one's yop, discharge the mutton musket, slime, chuck one's muck* or *empty the bins. 'What's the matter, Carol?' 'Someone's been in me dressing room and jonked in me undercracker drawer.'*

joombye *n. Scots.* Jism, jizz, McSpunk, deep-fried *vitamin S.*

joop *v.* To *release one's signature fragrance* in a very pungent manner. From the eponymous male perfume's advertising slogan, *viz.* "Joop, the scent that makes the man."

Jordan's toppers *1. n.* Wholesome breakfast bars, full of natural ingredients. *2. n.* The ludicrously proportioned *chestular assets* of Mrs (subs – please fill in current surname), stuffed full of artificial ingredients, E-numbers and synthetic additives.

Joseph's balls *n. medic. Nuts* that have not been evacuated for a long time. From the supernaturally cuckolded biblical carpenter's testicles. *'How's tricks, Cliff?' 'To tell you the truth, Hank, I've not had any since the late fifties, and it feels like I've got Joseph's balls in my pants.'*

joskin *n.* A country bumpkin, a rustic dolt, a *sheep shagger.*

josser *n. 19thC.* Fuckwit.

Jossy's giants *1. n.* Title of a popular 1980s children's television series about a Geordie football team, the Glipton Giants, written by late, over-educated TV darts commentator Sid "that was like throwing three pickled onions into a thimble" Waddell. *2. n.* Big *tits* on a Newcastle lass.

jostle book *n.* A *rhythm mag* or *art pamphlet. 'I'm not lending you any more of me jostle books, vicar. You've stuck all the pages together in this one.'*

jostle the chosen one *v.* To *pull the Pope's cap off,* to *box the Jesuit.*

jotter *n.* The *teatowel holder, loon pipe, council gritter, gazoo, balloon knot, raisin, chocolate starfish, Gary, rusty sheriff's badge, freckle, clacker valve, kakpipe, corn dot, ringpiece, crapper, aris, quoit, poop chute,* *panda's eye etc*. The *arsehole*. 'Palmolive was powerless to resist. His eyes burnt into hers like malachites. His muscular arms enfolded her body as she felt herself being swept away in a mistral of passion. "I love you, Alfonso,' she gasped. 'Take me now, I'm yours.' 'Drop your grundies and bend over then, love,' said Alfonso, unzipping his heaving slacks. 'If it's alright with you, I'm gonna slip you a quick length up the jotter."* (from *The Lady and the Travel Rep* by Barbara Cartland).

joy division *1. n.* Seminal indie band whose lead singer hanged himself in Macclesfield. Well, you had to make your own entertainment in them days. *2. n.* The *notcher, carse, barse, Humber Bridge, tinter, taint, tisnae, tissent, crunk etc. 3. n. medic. Banjo* trauma, that is to say the unthinkable consequences of an accident wherein "love has torn us apart".

joy plug *n.* The congealed remnant of a successful *ensponglement* that causes a momentary pause at the start of a *hit and miss*.

joyrider's moustache *n.* Light, *Feral Flynn*-style growth of top lip *bum fluff* popular with teenage delinquents.

joysluice *n. medic.* The missus's Skene's gland, which produces *parsley sauce*.

joystick *n.* Of *choppers*, the *cockpit* instrument or *knob*, which gets throttled. *Trouser toy, pant plaything*.

joy valve *n.* A lady's *sluices*.

J-pig *n.* Something *porky* seen when the SafeSearch is set to "Off".

jubblies *1. n.* Ice lollies made in an isosceles tetrahedron shape, of the sort fondly recalled from the 1970s by stand-up comedians, but still widely available in the fucking shops. *'Do you remember them lollies, what were they called, Jubblies? Eeh, do you remember them, eh? Jubblies? Do yer? Garlic bread? What's all that about? Garlic bread? Garlic bread?'* 2. *n.* Lovely breasts, *funbags, milky swingers, fat rascals*.

jubnuts *n. Bead curtains, dangleberries, dags*.

judges' eyebrows *n. Spiders' legs*.

judge the fudge *v.* To assess the state of one's health by examining the contents of the *pan* for evidence of disease.

judge the sludge *v.* To lean over to one side on the *chod bin* in order to look down and assess the prodigiousness and quality of your rectal wares. *'I'll be out in a minute Priscilla, I'm just judging the sludge. Christ almighty, this one looks like King Kong's cock.'*

Judi Dench *n. prop. rhym. slang.* A stench.

Judith *n.* A very dense, dark *fadge*, as sported by the character of the same name in *Monty Python's Life of Brian*. *'Bloody hell, love, you've got a right Judith on you. It looks like you've been hit between the legs with a bag of soot.'*

Judy Drench *n. prop.* A right proper *Norris McWhirter*. A *squirter, Norris*.

juggage *n.* Collective term for a lady's assets. *'Phwooar. Your missus carries a lot of juggage, don't she? Passports please.'*

jugged-mare *n.* An aesthetically challenged woman who is nevertheless worth a go due to her large *tits*. A *bapdog*.

jugged up *1. adj.* Of a happy fellow, to find himself well catered for in the *headlamps* department. *'Dave doesn't come out much since he met Double-D Denise. He's jugged up.'* 2. *adj.* Of a lady, to be generously endowed in terms of chestular glandage. *'Blimey, she's jugged up. She must have been re-racked, surely.'*

juggernaut juice *n.* Roadside *rusty cola* found in lay-bys, discarded alongside rolls of carpet containing strangled hitch-hikers. *Truckers' tizer, kidney cider, hedge coke, Scania scotch, wagon wine*.

juggernorks *n.* A huge pair of *Gert Stonkers* that come bearing down on you well ahead of their owner. *Stobarts, mammoets, norberts*.

juggery pokery *n.* An act of penile love performed amongst a woman's secondary sexual characteristics. A well-sprung *tit fuck*, if you will.

juggler's doughnuts *1. n. prop.* A popular themed fast food stall at Alton Towers. 2. *n. Shirt potatoes* when handled in the style of a circus performer tossing balls from hand to hand.

juggling slugs *euph.* Digitally titillating an aroused *fadge* and so getting your hand properly covered in mucousy exudate.

juggosaurus rex *n.* A monstrously large-breasted woman, as mentioned in *The Inbetweeners*.

juggstaposition *n.* The visual mismatch of two contrastingly sized pairs of *oomlaters* in close proximity, Trinny Woodall standing next to former Foreign Secretary Baron Owen of the City of Plymouth, for example.

jug jousting *v.* A *bunny rub*.

jugless Douglas *n.* A crude and offensively disparaging epithet which may be applied to any female with a boyish figure and no visible *nodgers*. Also *surfboard, Miss Lincolnshire. 'Fuck me, she's a right jugless Douglas. Her chest's flatter than a plate of piss. But nevertheless, I hereby pronounce you man and wife.'*

jugly *adj.* Ugly, but with big *knockers*.

jugs *n.* A lady's *top bum. 'Nice jugs, ma'am.'*

Jugsy Malone *n. prop.* Affectionate nickname for

any lady who boasts an impressive set of *assets*. *'Order! Order! The minister will give way to the right honourable lady. No, not you... Jugsy Malone there on the opposition front bench.'*

jugular *adj*. Large breasted. *'Have you met my wife? She's very jugular.'*

juice of hazard *n*. Any over-strong, export strength alcoholic beverage, *eg*. Methylated spirits, metal polish, Carlsberg Special Brew, *electric soup etc*., the prolonged consumption of which may lead to unruly and erratic driving, especially when attempting to outrun the police.

juices are running clear, the *1. phr*. Of a bird which has been removed from the oven, a check made to ensure that it is fully cooked and ready to be boned and eaten. *2. phr*. When the *painters* have left, and the missus is ready to be *boned* or *eaten*.

juicy flute *n*. A chewy, salty snack. The *gut stick*.

JULF/julf *acronym*. Jumped Up Little Fucker, a pushy *twat*.

Julies *n*. The female equivalent of the *goolies*.

jullet *n. medic*. The phenomenon of the breasts, upper chest and chins of a *salad-dodging* lady all being merged into the same wobbling mass of flesh, like on a bull sealion. The antipode of the *gunt*. From jugs + gullet.

jumble grumble *n*. Car boot sale-quality, desperate *self-help* material, *eg*. Razzle, Nuts, the bra pages of the Freemans catalogue, a knitting pattern. *Poornography, paupernography*.

jumble sale lawn sprinkler *n*. The first *piss* of the day, which sprays absolutely anywhere except in its intended direction.

jump *1. v*. To *have it off* with someone's bones off the top of a wardrobe. *2. v*. To *scuttle*. *3. n*. A *scuttle*.

jumper lumpers *n. Top bollocks, breasticles, puppies, chebs. Impressive qualifications* that sing cautionary little songs when you suffer a misadventure.

jumper tits *n*. Lady's *jugs* which appear impressive beneath a woollen sweater, but which mysteriously vanish once the garment is removed. Chimaeric *twin peaks*.

jumpfuck *n*. In a film or television production, a sudden and exponentially loud cut to the shouty finale of a romantic coupling. Usually occurs when you're watching something in the afternoon when the windows are open.

jumping Jack rash *n. medic*. The clap, *Val Doonican, galloping knob rot*.

jump on the grenade *v*. Of a man, to perform the noble and selfless act whereby he *cops off* with an ugly *piece* solely to enable his friend to *pull* her *fit*

mate. From the slightly less impressive story from World War I where a Private threw himself on an explosive ordnance to protect his comrades from the blast.

jump start *v*. To allow a mate to step in and do the hard work involved in getting your *ride*'s *knicker engine* fired up for you.

junction nine *n*. A ribald term for a folically challenged fellow. From the similarly named interchange on the M25, which *goes to Leatherhead*.

Junction x *euph*. A versatile, geographically specific insult to a *fugly* woman, depending on where she lives in relation to the nearest motorway interchange. *'Have you met my wife, vicar? I call her Junction [11] because she's the [Banbury] turnoff.'*

jungle butter *n. Spunk* in the *pubes*.

jungle jitters *n*. Term coined by *TOWIE* alumnus Mark Wright when he was a contestant on *I'm a Celebrity* to describe the sensation of being trapped in the dark heart of the Australian rainforest with nothing but platypus *fannies*, crocodile *bollocks* and kangaroo *nipsies* for sustenance. *2. rhym. slang*. Loose stools, diarrhoea. *'Ooh, I tell you what. I'm bad with the jungle jitters today, and no mistake. Not guilty, your honour.'*

jungle juice *n. Blip, moip, fanny batter*.

jungle junction *1. n*. Popular children's television programme featuring an entertaining selection of zany woodland characters. *2. n*. An unkempt *growler* found in a lady's *fork*.

jungle VIP *n*. A woman with pendulous breasts. From the apposite lines of the song performed by Louis, the orang-utan "King of the swingers" in Disney's *Jungle Book* that used to be on *Screen Test* every fucking week.

junior *n. US*. Penis, usually used in reference to one's own. *'Could I have an appointment with the doctor, please? Junior's had an accident with the Hoover Dustette.'*

junior hacksaw *n*. The act of *finger banging* a lady's *blurtch* in the rapid style of an impatient metalwork teacher cutting lengths of 10mm mild steel stock for a forthcoming lesson.

junior scrabble, easier than *sim*. Phrase which can be used when referring to an accommodating female who is quite prepared to allow gentlemen to have penetrative sexual intercourse up her without requiring the poor sods to jump through hoops first.

junk *1. n. coll*. The contents of the *fruit bowl*. *'"I say, Jeeves. Drat these new fangled flies in my plus-fours," I blustered. "I've just caught all my junk in the bally zipper mechanism."'* (from *Ooh, Yes! Just*

There! Don't Stop, Jeeves by PG Wodehouse). *2.
n.* The *ejaculate* that lobs out the end of the *cock*
part of the *above*. "'Launder these plus fours,
Jeeves, there's a fellow," I said. *"I'm meeting Aunt
Agatha for tea, and there's dried junk down the
front from where Dulcie Wegg-Prosser gave my old
chap a strop in the back of the Lagonda."'* (from
Fetch Some Tissues, Jeeves by PG Wodehouse). *3.
n.* A Chinese sailing vessel.

junkie's carpet, rough as a *sim.* Descriptive of one
who looks, smells and feels awful. And would
probably be sticky if you stepped on them. *'And
how are you this morning, Lady Bellamy?' 'I'm as
rough as a junkie's carpet, Hudson.'*

junkie's dog, hungry as a *sim.* Famished. *'Would
you like twenty pork pies, Lord Prescott?' 'Ooh aye.
I'm as hungry as a junkie's dog.'*

junkie's spoon, hotter than a *sim.* *'How was your
weekend cultural break in Amsterdam?' 'It was
really good, thanks. The museums and art galleries
over there are absolutely terrific. The only thing is,
ever since I got back, my piss has been hotter than a
junkie's spoon.'*

junk mail *n.* Any mis-aimed *pop shot* from the
spam javelin, eg. In the eyes, up the nose, over
the computer keyboard, into a fellow commuter's

pocket *etc.*

jurassic parp *n.* A bubble of fossilized *carbon
dibaxide* from the *tar pit* that could bring tears to
the eye of a brontosaurus.

just going to have a word with chef *euph.* Mid-meal
excuse proffered in order to *go and turn your
bike around.*

just passing through security *euph.* When
your dinner hasn't quite yet reached the
departure lounge.

just take a bit off the back and sides *1. exclam.*
A gent's instructions to his barber. *2. exclam.* A
chap's helpful suggestion when instructing his
missus on how best to clean the *pan* as he exits
the *smallest room* after *throwing his shoes out of
the loft.*

just take it for a walk, will you? *exclam.* A jocose
rejoinder to one who has a *brown dog scratching
at the back door.*

just visiting Salisbury Cathedral, I was *phr.*
Paper-thin alibi proffered when you've been
caught *red-arsed* committing chemical warfare
with a catastrophically noxious substance, but
care so little that you can't be bothered to make
up an even vaguely plausible excuse.

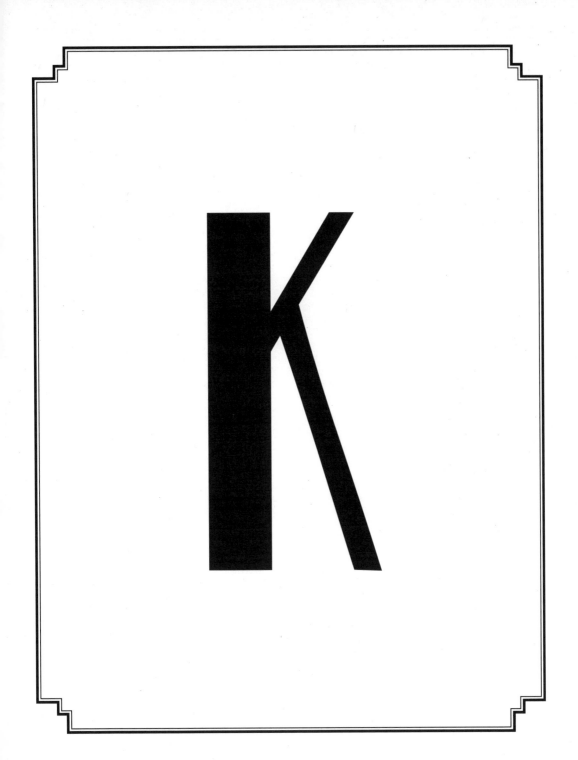

kack-in-the-box *n.* An unpleasant surprise encountered upon lifting the lid of the *gurgler*, such as a floating *teddy bear's arm*, a pile of *bangers and mash* or a *flock of dirty sparrows*.

kahoonas *n.* Large wobbly bosoms, *golden bodangers, kermungers, Gert Stonkers*.

kak *n. Keech, kaka, shite*. Feculent matter, to put it crudely.

kakatoa *n.* An earth-shattering anal explosion that can be heard half way round the world and which causes tidal waves and *poonamis* to sweep through the *chod bin,* devastating everything that lies in their path. Also *crackatoa, cackatoa*.

kak in the black *n.* A *number two* which, unsettlingly, has to be dropped in the pitch dark because the *bog* lights don't work. A *shit in the dark*.

kak klaxon *n.* The *rectal hooter* from which loud anal honks are emitted, together with the occasional *bonus ball*.

kakophany *n.* The noise of *a load of old shoes falling out of the loft*. A *flock of pigeons, musique concrète*.

kakpipe cosmonaut *n.* He who prefers to *dock* his *command module* in the *rear unloading bay*.

kalashnicock *n.* Overly complicated s*xual act where a *significant other* inserts a thumb up a fellow's *teatowel holder* whilst their fingers wrap around his *bag of fertiliser* like a pistol grip, with their trigger finger rubbing the *banjo string*, leading to several rounds of *friendly fire*.

kalashnikarse *n.* The unfortunate result of a poor dietary choice (*eg.* Large quantities of lager, peanuts and sweetcorn) while following a course of antibiotics.

kale force winds *n.* Brassica-assisted *trouser breezes*.

Kalihari bushman *n.* An expert at foraging through the undergrowth. A *deep sea muff diver, gashtronaut*.

kama-khazi *n.* Upon waking during the night with a *bone on* when one needs to urinate, forcibly pushing down on one's *Charlie* to point it vaguely in the direction of the toilet bowl like a Japanese pilot aiming his Mitsubishi Zero towards the deck of the USS Curtiss.

kama slutra *n.* Exotic repertoire of sexual positions practised in cars, in shop doorways and behind skips *etc.* on Saturday nights.

kami khazi *n.* A *depth charge* travelling at such speed, and with such little regard for its own safety and wellbeing, that it hits the water and is immediately carried round the U-bend and out of sight by its own momentum.

kangaroo pouch *n.* A large *granny fanny*, big enough to fit your head in. A *horse's collar, welly top*.

kangaroo shagging a spacehopper *sim.* Descriptive of the way a *shit house* door blows in the wind.

kanji *1. n.* An ancient form of Japanese writing. *2. n.* The *shit* that encrusts itself around the bowl of a student lavatory bowl, and would presumably provide something interesting to read for any ancient Japanese person who happened to pop in *to turn his bike around.*

Kaplinsky, suffer a *v.* To fail to hear some important information as one's attention is entirely focused upon the thighs or cleavage of the person speaking. Named after Natasha Kaplinsky, whose thighs and cleavage historically drowned out the news on BBC TV's Breakfast Programme.

Karen Carpenter's biscuit tin *n.* Something which is rarely used or in pristine condition. *'Winsome and Welshman are delighted to be able to offer this 1926 Rolls-Royce 20 HP landaulette with gleaming, original maroon coachwork by HP Mulliner. Formerly the property of the Maharajah of Kalahandi, this exceptional automobile has covered just 26 miles since new, and has been maintained in its original condition regardless of cost. Take our word for it, this truly stunning timewarp classic is a real Karen Carpenter's biscuit tin and is offered with new MOT and 6 months tax. £350 ono. No tyre kickers.'*

Karl Denver *1. n.* Famous singer, now desceased, whose voice ranged from a dark baritone to a powerful high-pitched yodel. Best known for singing the song *Wimoweh*. *2. n.* A chromatic *clapper rattler* produced while standing up from a chair. The *Karl Denver* begins in a lower key, but rises up the scale as the buttocks close, eventually achieving a powerful falsetto for the finale.

Karl marks *n.* Patches of reddened skin on the inner thighs of a lady who has spent the day being *licked out* by a *fanny-chopped* fellow. Or a bearded lady, if she's a lesbian who works in a circus. Every man or woman to their own goat, and all that. More power to everyone's elbows, we say.

Kate Bush *n.* A gargantuan *Aesop's fable* which proves so difficult to pass that it causes even the deepest-voiced male to cry out in a glass-shattering falsetto reminiscent of the eponymous Bexleyheath-born chanteuse at full chat. A *wuthering shite*.

Kate Humble's jumper, like *sim.* Said of the soft and downy *nether regions* of a lady.

Kate Moss's chip pan, as much use as *sim.* Said of something that is utterly useless and redundant, probably a footballer. Also *Anne Frank's drumkit, tits on a fish, a Glaswegian's salad drawer.*

Kate Nash *n. rhym. slang. Gash,* named after the Happy Shopper Lily Allen singer-songwriter. *'Get* *your Y-fronts off, Germaine, and I'll get a shot of your Kate Nash.'*

Katie Swunt *n.* Spooneristically cryptic expression; a refined, feminine version of *Betty Swollocks.*

Kay's mayonnaise *n.* A sticky, *argosmic* liquid typically found adorning the underwear pages of the popular mail order catalogue. *Freeman's sauce, Grattan glue.*

kazoo *1. n.* A tissue paper-covered aperture which *hums* tunelessly. *2. n.* A completely unmusical musical instrument. A *swannee whistle, gazoo.*

KD lady *n.* A *lezza.* Named after *comfortably shod* Canadian chanteuse KD Lang, who has yet to find the right young man.

Keats *n.* A bout of *self abuse* that one embarks upon, despite being physically debilitated. Named after the romantic poet John who, although struck down in his early years with galloping consumption, nevertheless managed a couple of *tugs* a day.

kebabarrhoea *n. medic.* What one suffers from the morning after. *'Are you all right in there, dear? It sounds like you are shooting the toilet up with an AK47' 'It's okay love, just a mild dose of Kebabarrhoea. Be a good wife and put the Andrex in the fridge, will you?'*

kebabble *n.* The incoherent mumblings and inept attempts at ordering food endured by the staff of greasy takeaway outlets after the pubs have closed.

kebabbledash *n.* The semi-durable rendering compound produced by the careful mixture of real ale and late-night *stomach fillers.* *'Oh no, I'm never going to make it up the stairs in time. I'll just have to stop here and kebabbledash the neighbour's front wall.'*

kebabby *n.* See *beerby.*

kebab compass *1. n.* Drunken navigation system which allows a chap to retrace his steps by following the trail of dropped salad along his "walk of shame". *2. n.* The hand-held device which late night revellers can be observed waving around on street corners in an attempt to get a bearing on their front door. See also *midnight mouth organ.*

kebabe *n.* A woman who looks incredibly tasty when one is *pissed* at two in the morning, but the thought of whom turns one's stomach in the sober light of day.

kebaberration *n.* A sudden, short and uncharacteristic *dump*, provoked by the previous night's *midnight mouth organ.* *'I can only apologise for what I have just done in your cludgie, ma'am. I*

would like to assure you that it was a kebaberration.'

kebab satnav *n.* A doner of dubious provenance, that is clutched by a drunkard and is mystically guiding him back home like a tom-tom. Also *kebab compass.*

kebab TV *euph.* The "adult" channels to be found on Channel 950 upwards on Sky that are typically viewed while *pissed as the Bishop of Southwark* in the early hours, when the prospect of ogling a muted ex-Page 3 girl with a floppy *boner* in your right hand and a floppy doner in your left seems perfectly proper.

kebabulance *n.* Late night emergency vehicle, such as the one parked on Christchurch Road, Reading or Link Road, Sawston.

keck cackler *n.* One with an easily amused *kazoo.* A person who exhibits *canned laughter.*

keck cougher *n.* He who *burps backwards,* or emits *under thunder* when *clearing his nether throat.*

kecks *n.* See *kegs.*

kecks telescope *n.* Rigid, highly polished cylindrical apparatus that extends after dark when heavenly bodies hove into view.

keech *n.* Crap, kak, kaka, keek. *'Bollocks, I've trod in a keech.'*

keel haul *v.* To drag one's tongue underneath a woman from *lip* to *ring.*

keema naan *n.* A shaved *fanny* with the very tip of the *bacon* sticking out.

keen student of military history *euph.* A nazi.

keepie-up with the Kardashians *euph.* Strumming along on the *one string banjo* while watching the eponymous heroes of the famous reality television spectacular, while hoping for a glimpse of Khloe in her nightwear or Kim bending over in a tight skirt.

keeping it on the clutch *n.* When *relaxing* through an erotic televisual broadcast, skillfully working a *Hilary* just below *boiling point* to see one through the adverts. *Treading water,* holding it at *the biting point.*

keeping Ted *euph.* Said of one who refuses to be drawn on the matter of their sexual orientation, despite the fact that it's overwhelmingly obvious. Originating from whisperings in Downing Street regarding an unnamed British Prime Minister of the 1970s.

keeping the green to regulation length *euph.* Performing an exceptionally close trim to the turf around the *flagstick* in order to prevent any entanglement.

keep one's powder dry *v.* To feign disinterest in a bout of sex with the *bag for life* to ensure one can give it to the girlfriend with both barrels in a later engagement.

keeps himself to himself *euph.* Said of a fellow who *looks after his own interests* while not necessarily being *master of his own domain.* *'That Jonathan Ross off the telly, he seems like the sort of chap who prefers to keep himself to himself.'*

keeps his coins in his wallet, he *euph.* Phrase which can be used when referring to a fellow who is *good with colours, sensitive, good with his hands, stylish, a good listener etc.*

keep shouting sir, we'll find you *exclam.* Humorous phrase uttered after someone has *dropped* a particularly loud *gut.* See also *how much?; taxi for Brown* and many more.

keep the cap on the sauce bottle clean *euph.* Said of a fellow who's a tad *left hand down a bit.* *'Keep it under your hat, but I have it on very good authority that that Liberace was apparently known to keep the top of his sauce bottle clean.'*

keep the change *exclam.* Invitataion to a lady to ingest a *money shot*, as opposed to expectorating it.

keepy-puppies *n.* *Knee shooters* so droopy they could be used for football practice. *Shoe shiners, low loaders.*

keepy-uppy *1. n.* A marathon ball control game practised by schoolboys in the park. *2. n.* A marathon *ball* control game practised by Sting in his wife. Tantric sex.

kegs *n.* See *kex.*

Keighley lullaby *n.* A soothing small hours *berceuse* enjoyed by the somnolent residents of the salubrious West Yorkshire Shangri-La, consisting of drunken shouting, breaking glass, sirens, and rights being read by arresting officers.

Keighley picnic *n.* A box of Stella Artois, for *al fresco* consumption.

Keighley wedding *n.* A punch-up.

keister *n. Nipsy, kazoo.*

Keith Burtons *n.* Spooneristic *beef curtains.*

Keith Harris, do a *v.* To get your hand so far up a *bird's hole* you could make her mouth move. From the formerly popular, now late, flightless duck ventriloquist. Also *do a Rod Hull, give it some Orville.*

Kelly Brooks *n.* An ill-matched pair of wonky *jugs.* Derivation unknown.

Kelly Smock *n. prop.* A jocose, spooneristically rendered epithet implying that the subject may have a relaxed attitude to personal hygiene. A name that could be used when writing a comment to be read out on the Jeremy Vine show. See also *Keith Burtons, Mary Hinge, Rob Knot, Bertie Ditch, Danny Fishcharge, Betty Swollocks, Norma*

Snockers, Mike Hunt etc.

Kemal *n.* A sexual act performed in a sordid or dirty location. Named after the *Big Brother 6* contestant who confessed on camera to *sucking someone off* in a skip. Not even behind a skip. IN a skip, for fuck's sake.

Ken Dodd *v.* To masturbate into your partner's hair while they are asleep, such that they awaken next morning with a hairstyle similar to that of the deceased, tax-averse Scouse comic.

Ken Dodd's hairbrush *n.* A particularly unkempt lady's *clunge.* From the fact that the late dentally challenged gagsmith's hairbrush probably looked like a scraggy *twat*, with all bits of unusually coloured hair stuck out of it at funny angles. *Terry Waite's allotment.*

Kennedy *n.* A sexual session which incorporates penetration in all orifices except the ears and nose. From the sex-mad American President John F Kennedy who once said: "you haven't finished with a woman until you've had her three ways". Also known as a *Berlin.*

Kennedys, the *n. prop.* The male genitalia; the *fruit bowl, meat and two veg, the boys.* Named after the famously ill-fated US political dynasty, *ie.* Jack and Bobby, and Ted in the middle with his big head.

kennel maid *1. n.* The hostess of a bargain basement massage parlour. *2. n.* A young woman whose unconventional looks have mitigated against her efforts to secure a suitable beau.

kennels *n.* The cups of the female brassiere; the place where the *puppies with pink noses* are kept safe and secure.

Kenny Lunt *n. rhym. slang.* A woman's *Jeremy Hunt.* Named after the spooneristically inopportune Hereford United football player, *viz.* Kenny "Lenny" Lunt = Chris Brunt = Jeremy Hunt.

Kensington spoff *n.* A yoghurt/milk amalgam used in *scud* movies where unnatural amounts of *population paste* are called for. Usually forced through a 14 inch *strap-on Larry* via a stirrup pump. Also known as *spunk double.*

Kent quake *n.* A gentle rumble followed by the release of an unimpressive amount of *arse gas* through one's *fissure.* A flatulent event which is low on the *sphincter scale*, but which could nevertheless cause a small amount of structural damage.

Kentucky battleship *n.* A not particularly seaworthy *tugboat.*

Kentucky breakfast *n.* A *heart starter* or *eyeball straightener.* A bracing, ante-meridian tincture, which might be followed by a short power-nap on a park bench or a refreshing *piss* in one's trousers.

Kentucky meat shower *1. n.* Famous incident which occurred near Olympia Springs on 3rd March 1876, when large lumps of raw meat fell out of the sky for several minutes. *2. n.* Something so foul it makes an *Alabama hot pocket* look like afternoon tea and scones with Sister Wendy. *'Welcome to the Blugrass State, home of the Kentucky meat shower.'*

Kentucky waterfall *n.* A mullet. *'Hot dang, Billy Ray. That sure is a mighty fine Kentucky waterfall you got yerself.' 'Gee thanks, your majesty.'*

Keown surgery *n.* A piece of maxillo-facial reconstruction (commonly a broken nose) performed by a no-nonsense centre-half during a Sunday League football match.

kerb-ab *1. n.* A park-dweller's late night snack from the *gutter buffet*. *'Do you know what'd just round the night off smashing after all them metal polishes? A nice kerb-ab.' 2. n.* A welcome pavement-borne repast for the 2 am reveller who has spent all his money on *Welsh champagne* and *disco biscuits* and thus find himself out of favour at his local takeaway.

kerbside quiche *n.* A *pavement pizza*.

Kermit *n. prop. rhym. slang.* The lavatory or *bum sink*. From Kermit the frog = bog. *'Oi Nigel, get me one in. I'm off to the Kermit for a Brad Pitt.'*

Kermits, the *n.* Of a sexist gent, the unwelcome situation of being constantly stalked and chatted up by a *pig* he would never wish to *fuck* in a million years.

kernt *n.* A works-email-friendly way of mentioning someone or something is a *culturally unique national treasure*.

kerplunking *1. n.* Playing a tabletop game, named after the sound of marbles tumbling to the base of a plastic tube before rolling onto the floor and crippling grandma. *2. n. onomat.* Dropping a titanic amount of *foulage* in the *chodbin* following a gustatory blowout at one's local *cuzza* house.

kerrangatang *n.* A large, hairy, heavy metal enthusiast.

kestrel GTX *n. Neck oil* that smooths the progress of *Harold Ramps*. A strong beer that can lubricate certain moving parts, if used in large enough quantities.

Kestrel manoeuvres in the dark *n.* The wayward shuffle of a *Harold Ramp* who has spent the whole day on the *wifebeater.*

ketchup *n.* Describing a girl like (name of former *tit model* removed on legal advice) that's "been on millions of sausages".

ketchup's nearly empty mother, the *exclam.* An amusingly exculpatory quip to shout after *treading*

on a duck.

kettle wank *n.* A gent's weekend morning five-minute *act of self delight*, typically prefaced with a request that his wife "just nip downstairs and make us a cup of tea, love."

kettling *1. adj.* Descriptive of the state of being in dire, immediate need of a *shit*. From the fact that a metal lid placed over one's *clackervalve* in such circumstances would rattle urgently, and possibly emit a high-pitched whistle to boot. *2. adj.* Of a sexually excited woman's *mingepiece*, *frothing* so vigorously that one could, if one were sufficiently ingenious and in possession of a length of suitable pressure hose, use it to power a "Mamod" traction engine across the bedroom floor or a small steam launch across Lake Windermere. *3. n.* Technique of high pressure demonstration control used by the Metropolitan Police which is intended to provoke anger in the crowd, thus giving the *scuffers* an excuse to crack some heads.

Kevin than Michelle, she's more *sim.* Said of a woman who more closely resembles ex-Newcastle United manager Kevin Keegan than she does ex-*Corrie sexpot* Michelle.

kevlar kleins *n. Shreddies* woven from material which possesses sufficient strength to withstand *botty burps* travelling at ballistic speeds.

kex *1. n. Shreddies, trolleys,* underpants. *2. n. Round-the-houses, kegs.* See **kecks.**

kexit *n.* Taking your *cock* out. A *kexit* can be either soft or hard, but generally leads to some form of unpleasantness for someone.

kexorcism *n.* The act of driving out an evil, demonic *food's ghost* from one's *chamber of horrors.*

kexpresso *n.* A type of diarrhoea produced by one who needed a *crappuccino*, but couldn't get to the toilet before it percolated through.

keyboard hero *n.* A lone wolf who is bravely prepared to engage in prodigious acts of personal courage that would normally entail the risk of a thorough kicking if he were not protected by the anonymity of an internet message board.

key change *1. n.* The bit, that occurs about two-thirds of the way through all Eurovision songs, when the writers depress the clutch and slam the orchestra into a higher gear in preparation for the final grind to the end. A *truck-driver's gear change. 2. n.* A change in the tone of a musical *rumpet voluntary* caused by unsuccessfully trying repress it mid-*guff*, which should hopefully garner it "douze pwa" from the Luxembourg jury.

key dropper *n.* A *bottee.*

Keyhole Kate *1. n. prop.* Voyeuristic comic book character from the olden days. *2. euph.* One who is blessed with a *twat like a mouse's ear.*

keyhole surgery *n.* The act of having a vigorous and satisfying dig around a particularly itchy *teatowel holder.*

key, Scouser's *n.* A crowbar, hammer, half a brick or anything used to open someone else's back door.

keystone *1. n.* In architecture, the wedge-shaped stone at the apex of an arch upon which the integrity of the entire structure is dependent. *2. n.* In multiple-participant-based sexual shenanigans, the crucial 5th or 6th man without whom a *daisy chain* is doomed to failure. *3. adj.* Of massed policemen, prone to falling over, hopping while rounding corners and being dragged along dusty roads behind charabancs while holding their hats on with one hand.

keys to the city *euph.* A striking *set of references* that are guaranteed to open doors and get their owner in anywhere.

K-FAD C-FAM *abbrev.* One who is apt to holding court on the day his JSA or wages are paid into his bank account. King For A Day, Cunt For A Month.

KFC *1. abbrev.* Something quick, spicy and filling involving a bit of greasy old *cock* and a *bucket of batter.* Knob Filled Cunt. *'I thought we'd stay in tonight, love. Fancy a KFC?' 2. n.* A girl who will cheaply provide a bit of breast, a bit of leg and a *box* to put your gristly *bone* in. *3. abbrev.* A Kiss, a Fuck and a Cuddle. *'I'm bored with this ambassador's reception. Fancy a KFC?'*

KGB *n.* Yet another amusing term for a lady's perineum. So named because "one slip of the tongue could land you in the shit".

KGB walk *1. euph.* Unusual gait employed by Vladmir Putin and other Chekists, in which the left arm swings normally but the right one stays still, close to their concealed weaponry. *2. n.* A similar style used by young men for playing *pocket billiards* whilst promenading.

khaki buttonhole *n.* The *chocolate starfish, rusty bullet hole.*

khaki plectrum, the *n.* The product of *arse-cheek* clenching while suffering from the *monkey's toe.*

khazi *n.* Shitter, bog, cludgie. NB. For best effect, this word should be spoken in the style of Wilfrid Brambell.

khazipan *n.* Soft, paste-like substance that is, all things considered, not suitable for cake decorating.

Khyber *rhym. slang.* Freckle. From Khyber Parse = arse.

kicked-in bait box, face like a *sim.* Used to describe an ugly person. *'Anne of Cleves was Henry's fourth wife, whom he chose to marry after seeing a portrait* of her painted by Hans Holbein. However, when the couple finally met in January 1540, the King was disappointed with his prospective bride and no longer wished the marriage to go ahead. "My lady is nothing so fair as she hath been reported," the King wrote to Archbishop Thomas Cranmer. "Indeed, she hath a fucking face on her like a kicked-in bait box."' (from The Eight Wives of Henry VI by Norman St. John-Stevas).

kicked over trifle, fanny like a *sim.* A term much used in Stoke-on-Trent to describe a lady's *bodily treasure* that is not particularly pleasing to the eye. *A butcher's dustbin, bottom of a ratcatcher's mallet.*

kick fart *v.* To initiate an act of *internal bumbustion* by raising one leg.

kicking the piper *n.* A bout of flatulence that sounds like a prolonged and violent attack on a traditional Scottish musician.

kick start the motorbike *v.* To lift one's leg prior to popping an anal wheelie.

kick the knackers out of *v.* To complete the majority of a piece of work. *'By the February of 1498, and after two full years of work in the refectory of St. Maria delle Grazie in Milan, Leonardo had just about kicked the knackers out of his Last Supper fresco.'* (from Vasari's *Lives of the Painters*).

kick with the left foot *v.* What players who arrive on the *other bus* tend to do, a football equivalent of *bowling from the pavilion end.*

kid in a sweat-shop, I feel like a *exclam.* Expression used when overwhelmed with unappealing options.

kid juice *n.* Baby gravy, heir spray., population paste.

kidney cider *n.* A discarded drinks container at the side of the road containing lorry driver's urine. *Trucker's tizer, Scania scotch.*

kidney disturber *n.* A bloke with an impressive endowment in the *trouser department,* such as might inadvertently interfere with the nephritic arrangements of a ladyfriend. *'Born on this day: Ken Russell, formerly purple dead film director, 1927; Fontella Bass, pipe-smoking dead female soul singer, 1940; Stephen Pound MP, kidney disturber, 1948.'*

kidney fizzer *n.* Uncomfortably biological hangover after a particularly heavy night of binge *refreshment,* characterised by bubbling sensations in the lower back. *Alcoseltzer.*

kidney prodder *n.* A notably impressive thrust during an act of sexual congress.

kidneys, shit one's *v.* To experience a traumatic *digestive transit* as a result of severe alarm or a particularly hot *Ruby Murray.* *'Come for a meal at the Curry Capital, Bigg Market, Newcastle upon*

Tyne, and if you don't shit your kidneys, I'll give you your money back'. (Abdul Latif, Lord of Harpole, short-lived Tyne Tees Television advertising campaign, 1996).

kidney wiper *n. Slat rattler.* See also *purple headed womb broom.*

kids have already got their trunks on, the *exclam.* Phrase uttered through the lavatory door at a recalcitrant sitter who fails to appreciate the urgency with which one needs to get in there and *drop the kids off at the pool.*

kid's piss *n.* A nightclub toilet act of urination whereby the *kex* and *bills* are lowered onto the shoes at the urinal by someone too *pissed* to attempt a penile extraction through the flies.

kid with an ice-cream, like a *sim.* Descriptive of the face of a lucky *niff flick* starlet after a series of well-aimed *pop shots.* A *plasterer's radio, quattro formaggio.*

kife *1. n. coll. Blart, totty, tussage, buffage, crumpet. 2. n. The other, crumpet.*

killer is in this very room, the *exclam.* A light-hearted remark used to cover one's embarrassment after *guffing* in public. Usually followed by an incredulous gasp from the assembled company.

killing a bear *n.* Passing a notably monstrous, grizzly, brown *arse brute.* *'Romeo, Romeo, wherefore art thou, Romeo?' 'Be down in a second, love. I'm just killing a bear.'*

kilt *1. n. coll. Skirt. 2. n. coll. Scots.* Blokes.

kilt lifter *n.* A Scottish fellow who is *good with colours,* a *McQueen,* a *gay Gordon.*

Kim *n. rhym. slang.* The anus. Named in honour of the despotically roly-poly and avunculacidal North Korean leader, *viz.* Kim Jong Un = wrong 'un.

Kim Karkrashians *n.* Psychologically unstable *Z-listers* of the sort who regularly suffer "breakdowns" on *Celebrity Big Brother, Celebrity Island with Bear Grylls, Celebrity Ghost Hunt Haunted Holiday* (which is a real programme, we shit you not) *etc.*

kinder *n.* A chocolate *dog egg* with a surprise inside, *eg.* Piece of Lego, foil, chewed-up tea towel *etc.*

Kinder fart *n.* A blast on the *muck trumpet* that comes with a surprise. A *shart.*

kinder surprise *n.* The gift of a smelly egg in the pants of a pre-school infant, found by a teaching assistant even while the father is sprinting up the path after depositing his child at the nursery.

kind regards *euph.* How one would sign off a work email to any member of management, or to a colleague for whom one has no respect. *Fuck off.*

kinell *phr.* Contracted bit of foul, four-letter language which is safe to deploy in front of a vicar, in-law, head of state, Mary Whitehouse's ghost, *etc.*

King Alfred's cakes *n.* Severely over-cooked products of the *dirt bakery.*

kingbast *n.* A sweary term that can be shouted in front of grannies, vicars, nuns *etc.*, without causing offence. Contraction of *fucking bastard.*

King Canute *n.* An enormous *Richard the Third* that blocks the U-bend and holds back the tide of the flush, causing the toilet to overflow.

King Charles, talk like *v.* To inadvertently find oneself imitating the strained, croaky speechifications of our capaciously auriculate monarch while attempting to pass a king-sized *door handle biter.*

King Charles the third *n. rhym. slang.* Turd. *'Pause the telly before they wheel the Queen's coffin in, nan. I really need a King Charles.'*

King Diamond with his bollocks caught in a mangle *phr.* Description of an unusually high-pitched voice. Named after the screeching lead vocalist of heavy metal band Merciful Fate, whose unusually high-pitched singing would no doubt be even more unusually high-pitched if his *bollocks* got caught in a mangle.

King for a day *euph.* To have a bad case of the *Brads, ie.* To spend all day *on the throne.*

King Kong attacks the lighthouse *euph. Relaxing in a gentleman's way* whilst taking a bath.

King Kong's finger *n.* A *turd* large enough to flatten a car or bring down a bi-plane. An *Elvis killer.*

King Kong's oven glove *n.* A huge and hot *Mary hinge.*

King Lear *n.* A stentorian, dramatic *flapper rattler* that will wow them in the back row of the Upper Circle. From, as everyone knows, Lear's line which opens Act III Scene 2 of the famous Shakespeare play, *viz.* "Blow, winds, and crack your cheeks!"

King leer *n.* Named in honour of the similarly-titled play; a sexist beast who is known to ogle the *tussage* after a few shandies.

King of the elephants *exclam.* An affectionate chorus, sung humorously in the street while pointing at someone with *big bones.*

King of the mountains *1. n.* In bicycle racing, the competitor who is the best at riding his bike up hills. In the Tour de France, the king of the mountains can be recognised by the fact that he wears a distinctive polka-dot jersey. *2. n.* A smug gentleman whose ladyfriend is blessed in the *headlamp* department. Can be recognised by the fact that he's usually to be seen on the front of *OK!* magazine, getting married, renewing his vows, having a christening, releasing a *shit* record, lounging in a swimming pool, recovering from a critical illness, bravely facing up to his divorce, battling for custody of his kids, bouncing back *etc.*

king of the mountings *euph.* A proper old school *stickman* who always *gets his cabbage*, while the other poor *sods* in the peloton get left behind.

King's College, Brown! *exclam.* Urgent announcement immediately after forcefully *dropping the clogs out the loft.*

King's Cross – St. Pancras *euph.* An elegant, sophisticated lady and her squat, mundane-looking constant companion. A *cruiser and tug.*

King Tut's ballsack, a liver like *sim.* The hepatic organ of a chap who likes to sip the occasional sweet sherry of an evening. *'I'm afraid it's not good news, Mr Best. We've had a look at your latest scans and, at the risk of using too much medical terminology, you've got a liver like King Tut's ballsack.'*

kinky! *exclam.* See also *can you leave the fat on mine?* and *ten points to Gryffindor.*

kipling triple *euph.* An exceedingly good *threes up* when a lady has an *eclair* in her mouth, a *cream horn* in the *gazunder* and something "ruddy 'ard" up the *shitter. 'To Cliveden for the weekend with dear Johnny [Geilgud], Ivor [Novello], and darling Kit [Hassall]. Ivor brought a crate of terrifically good Bolly down in the dicky seat of his laundalette and I'm afraid we all got a little tipsy over a plate of rather fine Whitstable oysters. Anyway, one thing led to another, the high jinks got a little out of hand and the four of us ended up doing a kipling triple on the croquet lawn.'* (from the Wartime Diaries of Hylda Baker).

kipper *1. n.* The *Billingsgate box, minge, captain's pie. 2. n.* That useful bit of skin that keeps the *plums* safely out of the *arse's* reach. The *barse, tintis, notcher. Perry Como's lip.*

kipper basting *v.* Shagging.

kipper carriage *n.* Any battery-powered contrivance employed by *old trouts* who are bent on terrorising pedestrians and sneering at children who dare to cycle on the footpath between their home and the cat-food shop.

kipper dinghy *n.* A lady's *secret bower of pleasure. 'Olympia is reminiscent in its subject matter of Ingres's Odalisque with a Slave. However, that is where the similarity ends, for in this case the artist does not present us with a depiction of an idealised nude. Instead, with his harshly direct lighting and his deliberate use of a limited colour palette and crude brush-strokes, Monsieur Manet has painted a naked courtesan, reclining on a chaise longue with*

her hand on her kipper dinghy.'

kipper for breakfast *n.* To rise early and go for a *horizontal jog*; an ideal cure for *dawn horn.*

kipper hamper for gentlemen *n.* An item in the Botham's of Whitby catalogue, consisting of Fortune's kippers, Landlord beer, fruitcake and some ginger & double chocolate biscuits.

kipper, like a tramp on a *sim. Con gusto. 'Will you lot fucking shut up, I'm trying to ironically watch Pan's People on BBC4 here. Phwooar! I tell you what, though, I'd be on that like a tramp on a kipper. Thirty-five years ago, obviously.* Pass me the tissues, nan.'

kipper's cunt *n.* Even more pungent than an *anchovy's fanny.* The *ne plus ultra* of fish-smellyness.

kipper's twat, fishy as a *sim.* Said of something distinctly questionable, eg. Channel 4 funny man Jimmy Carr's former tax arrangements.

Kirkcaldy kiss *n.* Wrinkled spot on a brand new roll of lavatory tissue, caused by some dirty *bastard* wicking their *dicky drops* on it.

kissed with Neptune's bitter tears *euph.* A romantically poetic reference to a spot of *splashback* while ensconced on the *jobby engine.*

kiss for granny *n.* The hermetically sealed, tightly pursed peck one gives one's girlfriend after *crashing the yoghurt truck* in her gob. A *nun's kiss, getting your own back.*

kissing tackle *n.* The north and south, *cakehole.*

kissing the tortoise *n.* Some sort of activity that doesn't bear thinking about, as performed by Ian McCulloch out of Echo and the Bunnymen, and subsequently sung about in that band's song *Seven Seas* on the 1987 album *Ocean Rain.*

kissing the tramp *n.* Performing cumulonimbus on a female with a ripe old *biffer* on her.

kiss it bigger *euph.* Oral assistance in getting the *right honourable member for Pantchester* to stand to attention.

kiss of light *n.* A pre-breakfast *Boris Johnson.* From the lyric of the 1977 Be Bop Deluxe song of the same name, which includes the line "Mine is to be her taste of the sea this morning".

kiss the Amish *v.* To perform oral sex upon a particularly *Dave Narey* pair of *catflaps.* To *lick out a bear trapper's hat, eat sushi off a barbershop floor.*

kiss the frog *v.* Of a lady, to perform *horatio.*

kiss the porcelain god *v.* To *talk on the great white telephone, drive the porcelain bus.*

Kit-Kat *v.* To stimulate a lady with four fingers at once, using a swift, forward thrusting, karate chop-type motion.

Kit-Kat shuffler *n. A masturbatress, weasel buffer,*

gusset typist.

kitten eyes *n.* Of a lucky lady who has just received a hefty load of hot *fish yoghurt* in her face, to have difficulty peeling her eyelids apart, in a manner reminiscent of a three-day-old baby cat opening its *minces* for the first time. *'Aw bless. She's got kitten eyes, look.' 'Quick. Freeze the frame, your holiness. I'm nearly there.'*

kitten hammer *n.* The penis. From the scientific fact well known amongst twelve-year-olds that every time they masturbate, a kitten dies.

kitten hammock *n. Tit pants.*

kitten purse *n.* Charming, feminine term for a lady's *cludge.*

kittens' noses *n. Puppies' noses, jockeys.* Nipples.

kitten-squeezes *n.* The distinctly odd, high-pitched, effete whimpers emitted by the women in Japanese *grumble flicks* while they are being *fingered, noshed* or *bonked.* Or *fucked* up the *shitter.*

kitty splitter *n.* A proper *bride frightener* of such gargantuan size that it ought to carry a Government Health Warning. A *clambuster.*

kiwi fruit *n.* A particularly hirsute *nadsack.* Named after the Chinese gooseberry, a fruit which exhibits a marked similarity to a hairy scrotum in both appearance and indeed flavour.

klatch *n. Drip tray* flotsam, *jelly hammock* jetsam. *Gusset effluvium.*

kleeneczema *n. medic.* The flaky skin condition contracted when a tissue sticks to a *wedding-milky* hand.

Kleenex, own shares in *euph.* A polite way to suggest that you think someone is a bit of a *wanker. 'If you ask me, that Sting looks like he owns more than a few shares in Kleenex.'*

kling-ons *1. n.* One of numerous races of *Star Trek* alien with Cornish pasty foreheads. *2. n. Winnets, dangleberries,* assorted anal hangers-on.

klutz *n.* A thickhead. From the German *for fuckwit.*

knack *1. v.* To break. *2. v.* To hit. *3. v.* To hurt. *'He knacked me with a baseball bat and knacked my shin. It fucking knacks, doctor.'*

knackatoa *n.* An unpredictable eruption of sticky magma from a fissure set above hot *rocks.*

knacker *1. n.* A single testicle. *2. n.* A *knobhead.* *3. v.* To tire out. *4. v.* To break.

knacker barrel *n.* Attractively packaged *smegma.*

knacker bilk *n.* A *player of the pink clarinet.* Possibly, but not necessarily, wearing a bowler hat.

knacker elastic *n.* The rubbery bands that hold the male *clockweights* in place within *John Wayne's* hairy *saddlebags.* The high tension suspension cords in *Dierdre's neck.*

knacker hammock *n.* A Covid-19 face mask worn somewhat lower on the person than was intended.

knacker lacquer *1. n.* Cheap, glossy paint sprayed onto decrepit old motor cars in an attempt to make them more attractive to less discerning punters. *2. n.* Inexpensive spray tan. *'David's looking a bit corpsey on camera two. Someone give him a quick blow-over with some knacker lacquer.'*

knacker lacquer *n.* The clear, vicous fluid secreted from Cowper's glands. Also *guardsman's gloss, pre-cum, clear smear, knuckle varnish, ball glaze, perseverance soup, tomato varnish, dew on the lily, wrist oil, balm before the storm, snake spit* or *French polish.*

knackernits *n. medic.* Crabs, *pissnits, mechanical dandruff.*

knackers *n.* Balls, nuts, plural testicles. *'Mmmm. Just taste that re-formed mixture of gristle, seagull shit and ground-up turkey knackers. Boodiful, really boodiful.'*

knacker tea *n.* That alarmingly dark yellow urine which has been mashing all night, becoming so concentrated that it could dissolve porcelain.

knackrobatics *n.* The vigorous and often spectacular manoeuvring of a gentleman's *John Thomas* during a bout of *bedroom gymnastics,* after being inspired while watching an educational *bongo vid* such as *Lovers' Guide 1, Lovers' Guide 2, Lovers' Guide 3* (eeh, remember them? They were a thing) or *Anal Assault 7.*

knee knocker *n.* An abnormally large *tallywhacker. 'I'm terribly sorry, Archbishop Welby, only the cat seems to have taken a liking to your knee knocker. Do let me know if he's bothering you at all and I'll put him out. More tea?'*

kneeling cushions *n.* Long, padded *tits.*

kneel meal *n.* A nourishing, *meaty treat on a stick.*

knees bent, arms stretched *exclam.* Something to say prior to letting off three rapid-fire cries from the *nether throat.*

knee shooters *n.* Large breasts with downward-pointing *jockeys.*

knee trembler *n.* Frightening intercourse while both parties are standing up. Often in a shop doorway or taxi queue.

knicker bacon *n.* Labial rashers.

knicker bandit *n.* A raider of washing lines, *Daz back doorstep challenger.*

knicker blocker glory *1. phr.* Malapropistical expression used on the back of an old postcard of the Golden Hind, as seen on the *Postcards from the Past* Twitter feed, *viz. 'We went out shopping today and had a lovely fish & chips dinner also a big Knicker Blocker Glory.' 2. n.* A big hairy *fadge,* like the one Germaine Greer used to flash at every opportunity she got.

knickerbocker glory *n.* A *back scuttle* effected while pulling the female's *anal floss* to one side.

knickerdropper glory *1. n.* A fruit-based treat served to one's inamorata as an aid to a beautifully romantic evening, *eg.* Half a bottle of orange *tart fuel* topped up with neat vodka. *2. n.* The best of all possible chat-up lines. Vouchsafed by God to to such *polyamorous* chaps as Mick Jagger, Rod Stewart and Tom Jones.

knicker giblets *n. Bacon strips* which can be boiled up to make a rich stock.

knicker oil *n.* Alcopops, *tart fuel.*

knickerpedia *n.* Youthfully well-thumbed reference section of your mam's Littlewoods catalogue.

knicker sausages *n.* Large *fanny lips.* Often found in *frying pants. Padded coathangers.*

knickers like Curt Cobain's ceiling *sim.* Telling phrase descriptive of the situation that sometimes obtains when a lady has taken insufficient precautions to protect her *fairy hammock* while she's *got the painters in.*

knickers like Jack the Ripper's hankie *sim.* Descriptive of the *dunghampers* of a woman who failed to *pad up* properly during *cricket week.*

knickertine stains *n. Skidmarks* off an *arse* that is a *heavy smoker.* See also *wind sketch.*

knife thrower's sleeve *n.* An unattractive vagina. *'Jesus, that bird I pulled last night was rough. Her minge was as ragged as a knife thrower's sleeve.'*

knight *v.* To bestow an honour on a lady with one's *pork sword* in recognition of her outstanding service in the kitchen. To *put to the sword*, to *fuck.*

knob *1. n.* The penis, *prick, John Thomas.* Also *nob. 2. v.* To engage in the romantic courses of physical love. *'I knobbed the arse off her.' 3. n.* About a *cock*'s worth of butter.

knobbledygook *n.* The incoherent gibberish spoken by a young lady at the height of sexual pleasure. Or perhaps while her mouth is full. Those two things are unlikely to happen at the same time.

knobbysox *n.* Relaxing and absorbent items of hosiery suited to accommodating the more sensitive portions of the male anatomy.

knob cheese *n. Smegma. Foreskin feta* found underneath *Kojak's roll-neck* and around the *banjo* or *cheese ridge.* Also *knob Stilton, knob yoghurt, Helmetdale, bell end brie, Lymeswold, brimula, fromunder.*

knob chopper *n.* Precariously balanced lavatory seat which falls down while one is having a *piss* and therefore must be held up manually. A *penis fly trap, willoutine..*

knob clocker *n.* An inveterately curious fellow standing at a public urinal who takes the opportunity to surreptitiously take a *gamber's squint* at the opposition. A *willy watcher.*

knobelisk *n.* A square-sectioned genital column that is thick at the base and tapers towards the top. *Cleopatra's needle.*

knobelty *n.* The joy of *having it off* with a fresh partner. Also known as *a bit of strange. 'Edwina, I'm afraid I'm going back to the missus. To be perfectly honest with you, the knobelty's worn off. Oh yes.'*

knob end *1. n.* The *herman gelmet. 2. n.* The extremity of a door handle. *3. n.* A *knobhead, jerk wad, horse's ass.*

knob fodder *n. coll. Blart, flange, tussage, fanny.*

knobhead *n. A fuckwit,* thickhead, oaf.

knob hinge *n. anat.* The point on the male anatomy where the lower abdomen meets the top of the *giggling pin;* the fulcrum point of a *bone on,* if you will.

knob jockey *n.* Someone who sits on a door handle while the door is in motion for sexual gratification.

knoblems *n. medic.* When a fellow's *womb broom* gets itself in a doozy of a pickle, *eg. Brewer's bugle, turtleneck entanglements, Dutch souvenirs etc.*

knob of butter *n. medic.* Softness in the *trouser department. Brewer's droop. Pele's cock.* Impotence.

knob scoffer *n.* Pejorative epithet implying that an individual likes to *smoke the white owl.*

knobseeker's allowance *n.* Funds self-allocated by proactive single females specifically for the provision of makeup, skimpy clothing, *boob jobs* and other items intended to make them more attractive to members of the opposite sex.

knob shiner *n.* Someone who is always prepared to polish a *pink oboe.*

knob snot *n. Cock hockle.*

knob socket *n.* Any orifice that a penis could be put into, *eg.* The neck of an oven ready chicken, a hole in a tree, a Hoover dustette, the wife's *fanny, etc.*

knobsolete *adj.* No longer of any sexual use, *eg.* A celibate male's privates, a laptop that no longer works.

knobstacle course *n.* Attempting sex while in a drunken stupor. See *labiarinth, Hampton Maze.*

knobtard *n.* One whose performance has failed to impress. Derivation unknown.

knob throb *n.* The pulsating surge of blood to the genital region which heralds the onset of a raging *diamond cutter.*

knobtical illusion *n.* An excuse given by a man for the apparently pitiful size of his *manhood. 'It only looks small because of the way the bathwater's bending the light. It's a knobtical illusion. It's* *making the ruler you're holding next to it look bigger too. That proves it.'*

knob toffee *n.* Sperm that could pull your missus's fillings out.

knobwebs *n.* Symptoms of a prolonged period of sexual abstinence, when fluff, dust and spider webs gather around a chap's *member. 'He said son, you are a bachelor boy / And that's the way to stay / Dusting the knobwebs off yo-ur old man / Until your dying day.'* (Song lyric by Cliff Richard, 1962).

knock and run *n.* A pesky *Thora Hird* which hammers urgently at the *old oak door*, only to disappear into the night once the customary posture is assumed upon the *bum sink*.

knocker hoppers *n. Tit pants, rascal sacks.*

knocker jockey *n.* A small woman with very big *jugs. A midget gem, tit kitten.*

knocker lockers *n. Titpants.*

knocker nest *n.* A bra. See also *over the shoulder boulder holder, kitten hammock.*

knockers *1. n.* Devices for banging on doors. *2. n.* Breasts. *'What a lovely pair of knockers, Lord Owen.' 3. n.* Of football punditry, those who have criticised a player in the past. *'Well Brian, the lad has certainly had his fair share of knockers.'*

knocking in the bat *1. n.* In cricket, the mysterious tradition of "seasoning" a new bat by beating it for six hours with a cricket ball or special magic mallet. *2. n. Self abuse.*

knocking one in *euph.* The female equivalent of *knocking one out.*

knocking shop *1. n.* Brothel, *rub-a-tug parlour. 2. n.* A pub or club where women go to be picked up. A *meat mart, buttock hall.*

knockin' on Heaven's door *1. n.* Title of a bad record by not-quite-*poodle rockers* Guns 'n' Roses, based loosely on quite a good song by Bob Dylan. *2. n.* The act of trying to penetrate a lady up her *tradesman's.*

knock off the bobby's helmet *v.* To engage in a fistfight with one's *little Kojak.*

knock once for yes *exclam.* Enunciated in the style of a spiritualist medium, just prior to the hair-raising manifestation of a nebulous cloud of gaseous *rectoplasm.*

knock one in *v.* The female version of *knock one out.* To *play the invisible banjo.*

knock one on *v.* To have it off. *'I've got five minutes before the wife picks me up, Miss Trubshaw. Do you fancy nipping into the stationery cupboard and knocking one on?'*

knock one out *v.* To have *one off the wrist. 'I've got five minutes before the wife picks me up, Miss Trubshaw. Do you fancy keeping lookout while I nip*

into the stationery cupbaord and knock one out?'

knock on wood *euph.* A *five knuckle shuffle.*

knock the back out of her *v.* Of a man, to have a very energetic *romp* up a lady.

knock the bottom out of *v.* To *bang the arse off* someone. *'How did you get on with that pissed up slapper you pulled last night, constable?' 'Great. I took her into the back of the van and knocked the bottom out of her, sarge.'*

knock the lid off the ark *v.* To release an *arse banshee* of biblical proportions that causes everyone in the room to disintegrate. From the climatic scene of the first *Indiana Jones* movie.

knock the table *v.* To suffer from constipation. From the conventional behaviour used by domino players to signify when they "can't go". *'I had a three goose-egg and black pudding omelette for my tea the Friday before last and I'm still knocking the table.'*

Knorr stockpot *euph.* A fat, meaty, ill-kempt *ladygarden.* So-called as it looks a bit like fat, meaty, ill-kempt chef Marco-Pierre White and, in the words of the old advert, "you can really smell the beef".

knot splitter *n.* A *toilet baby* of impressive, *nip-sy*-challenging girth. *'Gerry (alarmed): What was that scream, Margot? Are you alright in there? (Flush sounds. Toilet door opens. Margot appears, holding doorframe to steady herself) Margot: Get me a gin and tonic, Gerry, and make it a large one. Gerry (pouring drink): What's happened? Margot: That's the last time I eat a slice of Tom and Barbara's Broad Bean Flan. I've just done a knot splitter in there that's probably blocked the drains from Surbiton to Thames Ditton. (Tom appears at the French windows in wellingtons.) Tom: Have you just started the extractor fan in your bathroom, Margot? Margot: Yes. Why? Tom: Well, three of my pigs have just fainted from the smell. FX: 10 seconds of canned laughter. Cue theme music and end titles.'* (Extract from script of *The Good Life Christmas Special*, BBC TV 1978).

knotweed *1. n.* A invasive plant from the Far East which is practically impossible to get rid of. *2. n.* Nickname given to that chap in the pub who tends to join you without being invited, and is then resistant to all attempts to get him to *fuck off. 'Aw, shite, Ena. Knotweed has just walked in.' 'Don't look at him, Minnie, or we'll never get rid of the cunt.'*

know, in the Biblical sense *v.* To have *carnival knowledge* of or to *bang* someone. *'Last year at Club 18-30 I knew about forty birds in the Biblical* *sense, in eight days! And another six sucked me off.'*

knowledge, the *1. n.* Amongst London cabbies, a vast memorised account of all the streets in the capital which enables them to efficiently shaft wet-behind-the-ears out-of-towners. *2. n.* Amongst London *cottagers,* a vast memorised account of all the public *biscuit wrappers* in the capital which enables them to efficiently *shaft* wet-behind-the-ears out-of-towners.

Knowle facelift *n.* Budget cosmetic surgery, whereby bags under the eyes, wrinkles and even eyelids are flattened by the over-enthusiastic application of hair scrunchies.

knows her way around an engine *euph.* Said of a lady who eschews uncomfortable footwear. Also *good at reverse parking.*

knows his chintz *euph.* Said of a *pavilion-end bowler* who *puts from the rough.*

knows his way around Brighton *euph. Light on his feet.*

knows the heath like the back of his hand, he *exclam.* Said one of an *outdoorsy* fellow who *keeps his coins in his wallet.*

knows what's in his flowerbeds, he *euph. Good with colours. 'You know that bloke at number thirty-one? Well I was talking to Edna in the butchers and, well, not to put too fine a point on it, let's just say he knows what's in his flowerbeds, I'll put it no stronger than that.'*

knows what's in his wardrobe *euph.* Said of a young man who *knows what's in his flowerbeds* too.

knuckle down *euph.* To lock oneself in a dark study on the pretext of getting to grips with a pressing work engagement/novel deadline/political speech, belying one's true intention of indulging in an *ADW. 'How's it going working from home, then?' 'Well, you've just got to knuckle down and get on with it, haven't you?'*

knucklefucker *n.* An utter *wanker.*

knuckle glitter *n. Funky spingers.*

knuckle muck *n.* The product of a bout of *gentlemanly relaxation. 'I'll not shake hands with you, vicar. My hands are all covered in knuckle muck.'*

knuckle nightcap *n.* A late-night *Sherman* which aids restful sleep. *Forty wanks.*

knuckles, as blurry as a wanker's *sim.* Descriptive of something that is very out of focus. *'Despite intensive, round-the-clock investigations, police been unable to identify any suspects. Unfortunately, although the build-up to the murder, the hit itself and the gunman's escape through Fulham in a speeding car were all captured on numerous CCTV cameras, all the footage turned out to be as blurry*

as a wanker's knuckles.' (Nick Ross, *Crimewatch UK,* 1998).

koala bear's ears *1. n.* Tufts of female *puberage* sticking out the sides of *dunghampers. Judges' eyebrows, thighbrows. 2. n. Aus.* The *man flaps* that protrude round the sides of over-tight *noodle benders.*

Kojak's moneybox *n.* The *herman gelmet.*

Kojak's roll-neck *n. Foreskin.* Based on the slap-headed lolly sucking 1970s TV detective who always wore a cheesy-necked pullover.

KOKO/koko *acronym.* An exclamation coined by the Central Office of Information during World War II for the use of armed services personnel. Knickers Off, Knockers Out.

Kong-ga *n.* Song played by a wedding DJ towards the end of the evening to get all the *salad dodgers* up and dancing, *eg. It's Raining Men, Big Girls You Are Beautiful, Love Will Tear Us Apart* etc.

konz *n.* How a native Cornish speaker would refer to a *cunt. 'Oi, fetch us some more clotted cream and jam for my fucking cream tea, you konz.'*

kormatose *adj.* At the end of a refreshing night out, resting face down in the takeaway.

kosher dill *n.* A circumcised *gherkin.*

kraptonite *n.* A *shite* that gives off such an *ignoble gas* that it would bring Superman to his knees in his Fortress of Solitude.

krautside lane *n.* Outer division of the motorway which seems to be exclusively reserved for drivers of expensive German motor cars.

krispies *n.* A derogatory name for the type of *fuck-witted bellends* who ride around supermarket car parks in *Max Power*-style *naughtomobiles,* with the front seats lowered through the fucking floor so they can't see over the steering wheel. From the annoying "snap, crackle, and pop" of their bean-can exhaust pipes.

krispy kreme *n.* A flaky residue found on bedsheets, in ladies' hair, and in teenager's socks.

Kronenberg *n.* A lady who appears from behind to be about "16", but reveals herself to be about "64" when she turns round. From the famous "Young Bird Old Bag" lager made by the Kronenberg brewery.

Kruger *n.* A scary *hand job* from a woman with extremely long fingernails. A *Freddy.*

Krysten Ritter *1. n. prop.* Actress most renowned for playing the eponymous hero in the Netflix series *Jessica Jones.* No, us neither. *2. n. rhym. slang.* Cockney argot for the *rusty sheriff's badge. 'Ooh, I'll tell you what, me old China. I wouldn't mind Barry Tooking that Krysten Ritter up the*

Krysten Ritter.'

ku klux nan *n.* An otherwise outwardly benign grandparent who launches into an extended, extreme right-wing diatribe.

kumikaze attack *n.* A ruthless close-range assault on *pearl harbour.*

kung food *n.* Chinese comestibles.

kung-foolery *n.* Alcohol-induced martial art, involving much flailing of limbs and falling over, often resulting in broken bones.

kung fu farting *n.* Making exaggerated, Bruce Lee-esque martial arts-style movements and facial expressions while *dropping a gut. Kung fu farting* requires expert timing, but it can be a little bit frightening.

kung fu tits *n.* Anomalously proportioned *lady lumps* that require a fellow to adopt a braced, martial arts-style stance in order to tackle them front on.

Küntzkrümble *n. Germ.* Teutonic *fanny batter.*

Kuoni special *n.* A large *U-bend blocker*. From the fact that when it hoves into view at the local *shit farm*, the staff will clock up so much overtime whilst dealing with it that they will be able to book their holidays at the eponymous up-market charabanc tour organiser.

Kursk *n.* A giant *dreadnought* mouldering at the bottom of the *pan.*

Kurts *1. rhym. slang. medic.* The *squirts.* From German artist and typographer Kurt Schwitters = skitters. *2. rhym. slang. medic.* Haemorrhoids. From German composer of the Threepenny Opera Kurt Weills = piles. *'Ooh, doctor. These fucking Kurts aren't half playing havoc with me Kurts.'*

Kuwaiti tanker *rhym. slang.* A *merchant banker.*

Kwasi'd *adj.* Irretrievably broken during a hamfisted repair attempt. A reference to short-lived comedy Chancellor of the Exchequer Kwarteng, who competely *fucked* the economy despite only being in the job for about half an hour.

kweef *n. US.* A *pump* from the *front bottom*, a *forwards drop of the hat*, a *Lawley kazoo, vulvuzela.*

KY jelly *n.* Your pudding after a *fish supper* at *granny's oyster bar.*

Kyle style *n.* The fashions worn by denizens of the urban underclasses. *Scrote couture, Armani & Navy, Primani.*

Kyleys *n.* Literally, the sort of types who appeared on erstwhile ITV *scratter* parade the *Jeremy Kyle Show. 'I wouldn't leave my car there if I was you. The local Kyleys'll have the wheels off it the moment you turn your back.'*

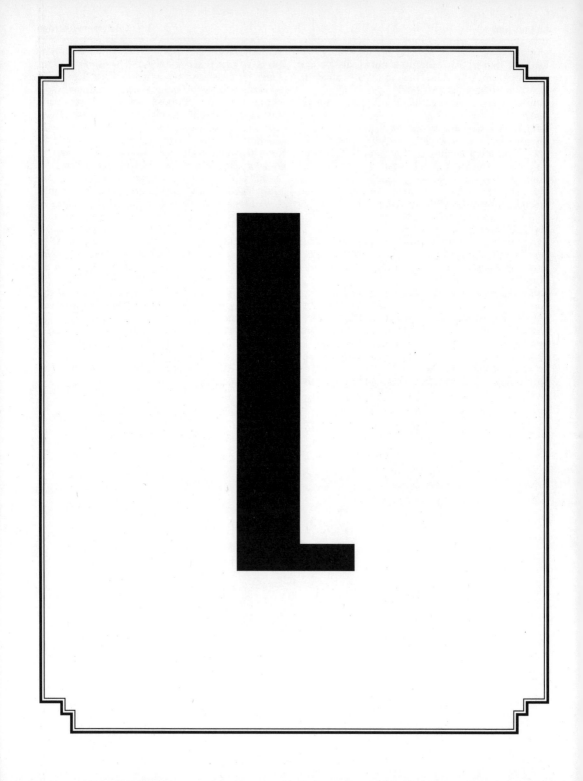

lab diamonds *1. n.* Artificially created gems that are apparently 60% cheaper than the ones a supermodel might get in a bag off a warlord. *2. n.* A vajazzle.

labia lard *n. Fanny batter, blip, beef dripping.*

labia majorca *n. medic.* A cheap and popular destination for lads on holiday. *Mutton shutters, Ibiza curtains.*

labia minorca *n. medic.* A slightly smaller holiday destination, though just as popular.

labia-rador *n.* An extremely hairy *growler* that smells of tripe.

labiarinth *n.* A term describing the unnecessarily complex design of a woman's *Hampton Maze.*

labiathan *n.* A dauntingly large and unwieldy *John Merrick's cap.* A step up from a *wizard's sleeve. Big Daddy's sleeping bag, a twat like a builder's rubble tub.*

lab kebab *n.* Ladies' donner labiums. A *vertical bacon sandwich* or *fur burger* that looks quite appetising when you've had a *skinful.*

labrador lipstick *n.* A dayglo pink *stalk on.*

labsag souchong *n.* Female labial *tea-bagging.* Could happen.

lab technician *n.* Someone with a workmanlike attitude to handling *knicker bacon.* A *twatsmith.*

lace curtain *1. n.* An exceptionally long *fiveskin, Serge Gainsbourg's mouth. 2. n.* A delicate gossamer fretwork of *helmetdale.*

La Chaviata *n.* Dramatic urban opera involving stolen Vauxhall Astras, two litre bottles of cider, lots of broken glass and police sirens.

lacking quality in the final third *euph.* Falling short in sexual allure above chest level. See also *bobfoc, missionary impossible, butterface.*

lack of composure in front of goal *1. n.* Syndrome suffered by footballers who fail to score when presented with a gilt-edged opportunity. *2. n.* A sudden lack of penile composure whereby one's *midfield playmaker* fails to rise to the occasion. *Falling at the final hurdle. 'Pele there, suffering from a rare lack of composure in front of goal, Brian.'*

lactose intolerant *adj.* Said of a frigid woman who refuses to imbibe the *milk of human kindness. 'My missus never swallows. She's lactose intolerant.'*

ladder legs *n. medic* Debility, tightness and cramping in a male's lower limbs caused by having to repeatedly stand on tip-toes while pleasuring a taller lady, or one wearing high heels. *'What's up, Bernie? Why have you stopped?' 'I've got ladder legs, Fabiana. You couldn't pop down to the kitchen and fetch me a chair to stand on, could you?'*

ladder of bastards *n.* A business's organisational structure of managers, toadies and charlatans as proudly displayed at Powerpoint staff briefings. *'Not that any of you give a shit, but here's the current ladder of bastards showing the new job titles we've all given ourselves and a quick glance at which back-stabbing sociopaths you need to avoid in the office.'*

ladies and gentlemen Miss Barbara Dickson *exclam.* Spoken in the style of the late Ronnie Corbett whilst introducing a warblesome interlude from the *nether throat.*

ladies' bridge *1. n.* A nickname for the Waterloo Bridge, which links London's posh theatreland with the more artsy and outre South Bank across the Thames. *2. n.* Accordingly, the *taint, Humber Bridge, Baker Street concourse, Tinsley Flyover, Luton-to-Dunstable busway, Potsdamer Platz, Joy Division, stinky Mervin etc.*

ladmin *n.* A young gentleman's workaday responsibilities, such as deleting *sexts* from ladies who may not be his *significant other.*

ladultery *n.* Cheating on your *bag for life* by convincing her that you have genuine work or family commitments that excuse your presence, when in fact you are sneaking off to the pub with your mates.

lady ache *n.* A more polite term for the *fanny gallops. 'Ooh, that Michael Fabricant doesn't half give me the lady ache, Lord Chancellor.'*

lady allotment *n.* Like a *ladygarden,* but less well tended.

ladyboy *n. ornith.* A confusing species of Thai *cock bird* with female plumage and *tits.* A *chickboy, shim, tiptop, trolley dolly, bobby dazzler.*

Lady Chalk of Billingsgate *n.* Thrush, a yeast infection of the *fadge. 'I regret to announce that Lady Chalk of Billingsgate is visiting at this present time, bishop. Could you pass the yoghurt?'*

lady cup *n.* The feminine *bower of bliss.* Also *cunt, twat, spunk oven.*

lady ga-garden *n.* A *front bottom* that has all big pieces of raw meat hanging off it. A *minge* blessed with pendulous *steak drapes.*

lady gagger *n.* A *membrum virile* of such prodigious dimensions that it would choke all but the most dedicated fellatrix.

ladygarden *n.* The small patch of scrubby turf in front of the *moss cottage.*

ladyglue *n.* Clear, viscous fluid exuded by ladies of the female variety before, during and after moments of peak sexual excitement, such as seeing Enrique Iglesias, Barry Manilow or Michael Bolton in concert.

lady golfer *n.* A *wearer of comfortable shoes.* A *carpet muncher, tennis fan, KD lady.*

lady graeme-garden *n.* A *front bottom* with big,

hairy sideburns and leather elbow patches.

lady in waiting *1. n.* Actress in a *meat movie* threesome who, temporarily, has nothing to do. A *grumble gooseberry,* a *ballflower. 2. n.* A reclining *grumble flick* actress anticipating the imminent arrival of several short flights from the *Greek Island of Testos. 3 n.* The lady in a *flesh mag,* who is sure to "do the job", but is held in reserve until the rest of the publication has been thoroughly investigated. A *finisher.*

Lady Jane *1. n.* In DH Lawrence's controversial 1928 allegory of love, lost innocence and the search for mind/body inegrity, what Mellors the gamekeeper calls Lady Constance Chatterley's *snatch. 2. n.* Named in honour of the famously short reign of Lady Jane Grey in 1553, a particularly brief spell *on the throne.* Also, variously, a *Louis XIX* (France); a *Luis II* (Portugal); a *Michael II* (Russia) and a *Sayyid Khalid bin Barghash* (Zanzibar).

lady killer *n.* A penis of such extreme length or girth that it could prove fatal. A *cunt buster,* a *kipper ripper, kidney wiper.*

lady log *n.* A substantial *dropping* from a female *Samantha,* which in the excretor's own mind allows her to believe she has shed at least one stone in weight.

Lady MacBreath *n. prop.* An amusing soubriquet for a *bag for life* who primarily dines on burgers from the well known "Scottish restaurant".

lady marmalade *n.* Patti Labelle's *fanny batter,* with bits of orange peel in it.

lady of leisurewear *n.* Perennially tracksuited female who, despite her taste in clothing, doesn't seem to care much for exercise or otherwise getting off her *arse* in general.

lady of the lake *n.* A mythical *brown trout* that reaches out of the pan as if looking for Excalibur before slipping down into the depths.

Lady Penelope's minge *n.* A *snatch* that is *boiling beetroots, ie.* One that has "a string attached".

ladypetals *n.* A demure and winsome soubriquet for the *pissflaps* of the *cunt.*

lady petrol *n.* Four star *tart fuel, unleaded bitch piss.* White wine.

lady philtrum *n.* The "bit between the lips and the area that smells" on a woman. Also, variously, the *Humber Bridge, taint, tinter, notcher, carse, biffon, scran, twernt, crontis, brink* or *clutch.* Really, you could open this book on any page and stick a pin in it and you'd likely find another name for it.

Lady Sa Ga *n. prop.* An old *hound* dressed up in outrageous and inappropriate clothing.

lady's bridge *1. n.* See *varse. 2. n.* Title of a Richard

Hawley album about his missus's *varse.*

lady's low toupée *n.* A *merkin,* a *cunt rug.* An all-weather *ladygarden.*

lady-tramp *n.* A woman of deceptively sophisticated appearance who lets herself down the moment she opens her mouth, *eg.* Denise Van Outen, Hylda Baker, Princess Margaret.

ladyturd *n.* The pervading miasma of perfume and deodorant after the missus has just *laid a cable* in the bathroom. Also known as a *Burberry shit bomb.*

lager bomb *n.* A strong-smelling *becksfart,* a symptom of *brewer's flu.*

lagerithmetic *n.* That niche branch of mental mathematics pertaining to the relationship between units of alcohol consumed and the hours elapsed before it is notionally "safe" to drive a motor vehicle. *'Your honour, before passing sentence I would ask you to stop and question whether my client – a regional news presenter of some standing in his community – is guilty of the offence as charged, or whether he is, as I would contend, merely the innocent victim of a simple error in his lagerithmetic, caused by the three bottles of Pernod he had inadvertently downed earlier in the afternoon.'*

lagerland *n.* The fairytale destination of a fellow who has become overly *refreshed,* where he imagines himself to be a witty raconteur, God's gift to women, an invincible warrior, an agile scaffolding acrobat *etc.* Also known as *ciderspace.*

lagerlepsy *n. medic.* Falling asleep suddenly when you have had one beer too many. *'My client would contend, your honour, that he was not drunk while in charge of his vehicle. Tragically, he suffers from a rare medical condition which is exacerbated by sitting down between the hours of 11.00pm and 5.00am, and had merely sunk into a lagerleptic coma while driving home from the pub.'*

lager log *n.* A sleek and smooth morning-after *feeshus* that slips into the water *like an otter off the bank.* The opposite of an *alien.*

lager of la mott *1. n.* 1980s lager-style beverage, famed (vaguely remembered by the elderly) for its somewhat overblown Sword & Sorcery-themed television advertisements. *2. n.* Any bitter liquid quaffed with relish from a *furry cup.*

lager than life *euph.* A nice way of saying that someone's habitually boisterous and outgoing nature is as a result of chronic alcoholism. *'I'll never forget him, out there in all weathers, shouting at the traffic in his pissed shell suit. He was a real lager than life character, your grandad. It's such a shame his third liver didn't take.'*

lager top *1. euph.* Adding some transparent,

relatively dilute liquid into a blocked urinal full of thick, amber *piss*. *2. n.* A market-bought polo shirt which is unsubtly decorated with the logotype of a leading designer who is unlikely to have benefitted financially from the few pounds its owner spent on it. As worn by the kind of young men who are typically seen drinking loudly outside pubs or on public transport. A *Ted Faker.*

lair of the white worm *1. n.* Title of a 1988 Ken Russell gothic horror film, so you know what to expect there. *2. n.* A chap's bedroom. Or the back of his Transit van.

lairy-focals *n.* Aids to double vision which make a bloke feel hard as nails while rendering all the ugly women he sees beauty queens. Particularly fighty *beer glasses.*

Lake Wendouree *n. Aus.* Ejaculation. From the very, very small, sticky lake at *Ballarat,* Australia.

lamb cannon *n.* A high-calibre arms development dating somewhere between the *mutton musket* and the *bacon bazooka.*

Lambeth walk, doing the *euph.* Sauntering down the *frog and toad* in handcuffs.

lamb hangings *n.* A none-too-appetising *butcher's window* display. *Mutton shutters, beef curtains, gammon goalposts, steak drapes, bacon strips, flackets.* A lady's *labia majorcas.*

Lamborghini *n.* A *cunt 'tache.* A small, pointless tufty outcrop of pubage remaining on a *shaven haven.* Named after the high performance Italian supercar the Lamborghini Jazz Fanny.

lambrini surprise *n.* The mischievous act of drinking a surfeit of fizzy wine, *pissing* in the empty bottle and leaving it in the park for a thirsty *professional outdoorsman* to happen upon. A *tramp trap.*

lambs are screaming, the *1. exclam.* In James Herriot film *The Silence of the Lambs,* the repressed childhood memories of agent Clarice Starling that result in emotional trauma in later life. *2. exclam.* Expression of an urgent need to evacuate one's *Simon Cowells* if emotional trauma in later life is to be avoided.

lamp a champion *v.* To squeeze out a much larger *shit* than you thought possible. To *punch way over your weight* in the *ring.*

Lampwick *n.* Of a person who has received a gent's *spendings* in their mouth, the Proustian recreation of the regurgitatory noises made by the late Dick Emery's old man character James Maynard Kitchener Lampwick, who sounded like he was juggling a mouthful of false teeth and *hockle* at the start of every utterance.

Lance Harmstrong *n.* Nickname given to a youth

who acts dead hard despite riding round on a toddler's mountain bicycle, tucking his tracky bottoms into girl's white socks and wearing an *Essex tartan* hat.

land ahoy! *exclam.* Another of the growing list of witty remarks to be uttered after *the wind changes.* Also *good point well presented, they have a range now Captain* and *ah, the mating call of the mallard.*

landing *n.* The area between the bedroom and the lavatory, or between the *shitter* and the *sack.* The *barse, ABC,* the perineum. A place where it's probably best to leave the light off, all things considered.

landing a shark *n.* Whilst spending a day *working from home,* the arduous wrist-and-spirit-sapping task of attempting one's fifth act of *procrasturbation;* a largely pointless exercise for any but the most dedicated *onanist.*

landing thrusters engaged *phr.* When you produce a powerful jet of hot liquid *shite* which hits the water and cushions the impact forces just before your *arsecheeks* settle on the toilet seat.

landlady's forearm *n. medic.* Ailment closely linked to *bingo wings,* suffered by fat, dumpy women, *eg.* Star Psychic Sally Morgan, her off *Wife Swap* and all dinnerladies.

landlord's supper *n.* An item in the Botham's of Whitby catalogue, consisting of a delicious Botham's fruitcake, served with real Wensleydale cheese and a bottle of Timothy Taylor's Landlord beer. Obviously, if Botham's would like this reference to their excellent products to be a bit bigger and more effusive in future editions of the *Profanisaurus,* they know where they can find us.

landmine *n.* A fresh *dog's egg* hidden in a suburban lawn. Landmines are often detonated by lawnmowers, leading to untold misery.

Lando *n.* A *clag, dangleberry* or *winnit.* Named after the *Star Wars* rebel character who was caught on the edge of the Sarlak pit and was thus forced to hang near its foul-smelling and gaping mouth until either picked clear by Han Solo or blasted off with the shower.

land of wank believe *n.* Image of a celebrity or pop star from when they were in their prime that is used for purposes of *monomanual self delight.*

land on your nads *phr.* To experience the opposite of landing on your feet. *'Did you hear about Trevor? He accidentally knocked up fat Annie from the Dog and Trumpet. Now he's had to marry her and take a job as a giblet puller's assistant in his father-in-law's abattoir.' 'Fuck me. He sure landed on his nads there, didn't he?'*

landslide victory *n.* A huge vote of confidence for

a sitting party.

langball *n.* Type of *dangleberry* which attaches itself to *John Wayne's hairy saddlebags.*

langer *n.* Penis.

langered *adj. Wankered, refreshed.*

language Timothy! *exclam.* Yet another humorous rejoinder to a person *letting some air out of the balloon,* spoken in the style of Ronnie Corbett's screen father Sydney Lumsden in *Sorry* – better known as *Coronation Street*'s Betty Driver, alias Betty Turpin's late fictional husband Cyril, who was, in real life, married to the late Mrs Slocombe out of *Are You Being Served?*, real name the late Mollie Sugden – William Moore (1916-2000).

lank *adj.* Late, as a result of going for a *wank.* *'Sorry I'm lank. Now here are the main headlines.'*

lapdog *n.* A Spearmint Rhino dancer with a *lovely personality.* A *4am girl.*

lap of honour 1. *n.* A fitting finale to a passionate night of lovemaking. The act of diving face first into where one has just dumped one's *liquid kids.* *'Oh Richard, that was amazing. How about a lap of honour?' 'You can fuck right off, Liz. I've just shot a month's worth up there, isn't it.'* 2. *n.* Going down on the missus when you really don't feel like it. See also *cuntractual obligation.*

LAPOS/lapos *acronym.* A *knob* sported by the less generously endowed gentleman. Like A Penis Only Smaller. *'STRAW, Jack, Lab., Blackburn (1979) b. 3 Aug. 1946. Ed. Brentwood Sch.; Leeds Univ.: Inns of Court Sch. of Law. Parliamentary Career: Contested Tonbridge and Malling 1974, succeeded Barbara Castle in this seat, Foreign Secretary (2001 – 2006), Lord High Chancellor of Great Britain and Secretary of State for Justice (2007 – 2010), Shadow Deputy Prime Minister (2010 –). Chairman All Party Lapos Group (1979 –).'* (from *Who's Who With a Really Really Small Cock*).

lapper *n. Hairy pie* eater, *bacon sandwich* connoisseur.

lapping paste 1. *n.* An abrasive grinding unguent used in engineering. 2. *n.* The creamy amalgam of frothing saliva and *fanny batter* on a well-licked *clout.*

lap poodle *n.* A gently bouffanted *minge,* of the sort that was much in fashion in the 1970s. A *Judith, Jackson, muffro.*

laptop *n.* A light, compact, perfectly formed *piece of kit* that can be booted up on your lap or table as desired. A *throwabout.*

laptop, chav *n.* An open takeaway pizza box. Also *scouser's laptop.*

laptop glue *n.* The viscous product of having *one off the wrist* when *buying a present for the wife.* See

also *he VA. 'Excuse me, do you have anything for getting dried laptop glue off a keyboard?'*

lard as nails *adj.* Fat as *fuck* but surprisingly tasty in a *pagga.*

lardcore *adj.* Type of explicit erotica principally concerned with the carryings-on of *chipwrecked* females.

larder lout *n.* A person *with a lovely personality* who can't stop grazing. Fridge clearances a speciality.

lardetarian *n.* A person who has no particular special dietary needs, as long as they get a gut-busting portion of something. *'I'm afraid my wife can't eat salad. Do you have a lardetarian option on the menu?'*

lardette *n.* A generously proportioned, pint-swilling, *salad-dodging bird* who engages in raucous behaviour when suitably *refreshed.*

lardigan *n.* Woollen outer garments worn knotted around the waist by larger ladies in a futile attempt to hide their big, fat *arses.*

lardi gras *n.* A Lizzie Duke-heavy festival of *cracksuit*-wearing, *digestively overqualified* types which takes place every Saturday afternoon in the shadow of the golden arches at a precinct near you.

lardlips 1. *n.* Cheeky nickname for a woman who has had excessive filler on her facial lips courtesy of the *mush-masher.* 2. *n.* A stout matron's outer *flabia.*

lard of the flies *n.* The male *membrum virile,* just fattening up nicely in the trousers.

lard of the manor *n.* The *piabetic* bloke who lives on your estate. A *Duke of Giblets.*

lard on 1. *n.* A pornographic journeyman's perfunctory *hard-on* which does the job, but only just. A *satiscraptory* erection. 2. *n.* The state of non-sexual excitement felt by a *bigger-boned* gentleman when approaching a Ginster's display. 3. *n.* The sort of small, heart-threatening erection experienced when looking at a *filfy plumper.* 4. *n.* Term used to describe the sort of high-cholesterol *boners* enjoyed by fat slobs like that *twat* who used to do the Radio 1 breakfast show.

lard rover *n.* A stoutly reinforced bariatric mobility scooter. Also *nanbretta, council go-kart, obeseicle.*

lard wimple *n.* A *pelican's beak, chin airbag.*

lardy dah 1. *adj.* Bald, thin and able to play the piano. 2. *n.* A lady *with a lovely personality* who has ideas above her social station.

large bag of brown coins, empty a *v.* To perform a particularly noisy and staccato *Robert Powell* movement in a public *Rick Witter,* creating such a cacophonous reverberation that a passer-by might imagine someone is emptying the tip-collection jars from several pubs into the *bum sink* while grunting and sobbing.

large hadron collider, like shooting electrons in a *sim.* Unsatisfying coital congress with a *bucket-fannied slapper. Also throwing a Woodbine up Northumberland Street* (Tyneside), *throwing a sausage up Briggate* (Leeds), *chucking a fag down Parliament Street* (Nottingham). *'I fucking tell you what, right, some of the birds I've fucked have twats so big it's like shooting electrons in a large hadron collider.'* (Russell Brand sitting in for Ken Bruce, BBC Radio 2).

large hard-on collider *n.* A fat lass who is capable of generating vast amounts of kinetic energy with her pelvis, possibly leading to a pair of bruised *Higgs bosons.* And a broken *cock.*

lark rise to camel foot *euph.* Waking up with a *stiffy* and getting *stuck in* straight away.

larrup *v. olde Eng.* To furiously flagellate one's flaccid *giggle stick* in the style of Mr Jorrocks in full pursuit of Mr Reynard, in the forlorn hope that something interesting might pop up.

larse *n. medic.* The lateral point of the upper thigh where the leg becomes the *arse.* The bit seen in *jazz mags* that remains white even though the model has spent many hours on a sunbed. *'... the femoral vein ascends behind the semi-tendinosus, where it joins the great saphenous vein just behind the larse and continues on to meet inferior vena cava half way between the tits and the fanny...'* (from *Andy Gray's Anatomy*).

lart *v.* To laugh so much that you *fart.* *'Mr Will Sommers did tell his Majestie a storie of two nunnes in a bath, and King Henry was verily amused, such thatte he did lart, whyche was the talk of the Court even until Michaelmas.'*

lasagne turd *n.* A *Tom tit* topped with a layer of *arsewipe,* followed by an unexpected bonus layer of *bum mince,* then finished off with an extra stratum of *shit tokens.* Parmesan optional. *Bangers and mash, Viennetta.*

lashing strap *1. n.* In the haulage industry, a 3-inch-wide belt and buckle arrangement with a breaking strain of 5 tons, used by lorry drivers to tie down heavy loads onto the backs of their trucks. *2. n.* The choice of thong or *tit pants* strap for the *bigger-boned* lass.

lash on, get a bit *v.* To find some female company. *'Howay, let's gan oot an' get a bit lash on.'* *'Very well, your grace.'*

lash technician *1. n.* A person trained in the application of eyelash extensions. *2. n.* A workmanlike *fladge and padge* practitioner; a spanker. *'Do you have the number of a good local*

lash technician?' 'I certainly do, Lord Archer of Weston-super-Mare.'

lass grease *n.* Generic term used to describe the vast range of creams, lotions, foams, balms, oils and unguents with which women stuff their bathroom cabinetry.

Lassie, buried more bones than, she's *sim.* Of a woman, to be velocipedically inclined, municipally speaking.

lass vegas *n.* A northern bingo hall.

last chopper out of Saigon, the *euph.* The first bus of the day on which pensioners are allowed to travel for free.

last drag on a rollup *euph.* The pained, one-eyed expression pulled by a guitarist hitting a high note or by a *grumble* actor going for the *money shot.*

last hotdog in the tin *sim.* Descriptive of penetrative sex with a lady possessed of a *wizard's sleeve. Wall of death, dipping a worm in a bucket, waving a stick in a field.*

last meat supper *n.* Final fling before marriage. It's all *fish suppers* thereafter.

last metrosexual *n.* A *sophistipated* person who, after failing to *cop off* in Newcastle's Bigg Market on a Friday or Saturday night, resorts to chatting up any old *floor sweepings* available on the "last Metro" train out of Monument Station in the hope of getting a bit *fiddle.*

last minute bookings *n.* The desperate and desperately unattractive *blart* that one is free to pull at 1.59 am after the *ugly lights* come up in a nightclub.

last minute platform alteration *n.* During a *brief encounter,* an unexpected announcement from the man that he is about to attempt a *tight brown* rather than an *easy pink. Changing at Baker Street, playing the B-side.*

last night's pizza *n.* Someone that was hot when you picked them up, but doesn't seem quite so hot the next morning. *Hotel toast.*

last of the shampoo, that's the *exclam.* What a lady says to cover up her embarrassment when she *drops a gut* in the shower. Or when she runs out of shampoo.

last orders *n.* The ring of an *arse bell* that causes a stampede of similar magnitude to that experienced at 10.50 pm in pubs up and down the land. *'Stand back, your holiness. I had three Scotch eggs and a pint of Bass for lunch, and I've just called last orders.'*

last orders at the pink bar *euph.* Announcements heralding the onset of the *vinegar strokes.* *'Are you on the pill, love, 'cos it's last orders at the pink bar?'* (Wilfred Hyde-White quoted in the *Memoirs of*

Joyce Grenfell).

last pearl, piss out the *v.* Following ejaculation, to visit a lavatory/sink/bath/telephone kiosk/ bank doorway in order to urinate and thus scour out any remaining *jelly jewellery* which may be nestling inside the brim of the *farmer's hat.* To have a *pipecleaner.*

last piece of the jigsaw, looking for the *euph.* To be unavoidably detained while wiping one's *Marmite pot. 'Your tawdry jubilee barge awaits, your majesty.' 'With you in a minute, pal. I'm just looking for the last piece of the jigsaw.'*

last pint in the barrel *n.* A particularly wet, sticky and unsatisfactory *shite.*

last post *n.* Ceremonial act of *standing to attention* while lowering a partner's *knickers* last thing at night.

last resort *n.* Light-hearted pet name for the *bag for life, ie.* That to which one reluctantly returns after a failed night *on the pull.*

last supper *n.* The final lard-filled blowout which *piabetics* invariably enjoy prior to going into hospital for their gastric band or stomach stapling surgery, after being told by their doctors to have a light meal on the evening before their operations to avoid dying while under the anaesthetic.

last turkey in Tesco *n.* An amusing gents' changing rooms cabaret impression, in which the *scrotal skin* is pulled up and over the *bollocks* to create a vivid simulacrum of a lonely, unloved fowl sat shivering in a fridge at the eponymous supermarket. Also *the last turkey in the shop, Bob Cratchitt's pantry.*

last turkey in the shop *n.* Yet another bit of *ad hoc* genital vaudeville that never fails to impress the ladies, although it typically finds somewhat less favour with one's probation officer. See also *the elephant.*

last week's lettuce *n.* An unappetising lady's *cludge,* from its similarity to an out-of-date salad, *ie.* Brown, limp, sweaty, and sticking to the side of the bag. *'Fancy a lick of last week's lettuce, Charlie?' 'No thanks, Camilla.'*

last whoreders *n.* The chaotic rush for *rashgash* in a *meat market* at ten to two. *The witching hour, two o'clock binrake.*

last year's hanging basket *n.* An untidy, straggly *mott. Kenn Dodd's hairbrush, Terry Waite's allotment, Stuart Hall's windowbox.*

latch lifter *n.* A borrowed fiver which enables one to enter a public house. *'Lend us a latch lifter till I get my giro,* will you?'

late runner *n.* Having cleansed one's *tea towel holder* with whatever material is close to hand, the dispiriting realisation there is another length of

dirty spine moving inexorably into the *bomb-bay.* Also *Columbo, Jimmy Cricket.*

lathered *adj. Pissed, plastered, langered.*

latrino *n.* Microscopic brown particle observed using a ceramic/porcelain detector.

latrino lover *n.* A romantic lothario who prefers to initiate his sexual liaisons in public facilities.

la tristesse durera *1. n.* Not at all pretentious title of a song by the Manic Street Preachers. *2. n.* A despairing *Tony Hart* that goes "from a scream to a sigh."

LATTOT/lattot *exclam. abbrev.* Derogatory term used towards a man who sports bigger *bazingas* than most women. Look At The Tits On That. *'You join us at the State Opening of Parliament, just as the Liberal Democrat peer Lord Owen of Plymouth takes his oath of allegiance. And as he steps forward… Fuck me! Lattot!'*

Latvian handshake *euph.* Getting *wanked off* in a shop doorway.

laugh at the carpet *v.* To *park a tiger.* To vomit.

laugh at the grass *v. Aus.* To release an *al fresco liquid guffaw* at a particularly amusing bit of floor. *'Where's Bruce, Bruce?' 'He's outside laughing at the grass, Bruce.'*

launch a fragrance *v.* To roll out your *signature scent. 'Jesus, Kylie. What's that smell? Has a platypus died under the floor?' 'Ah, that's me, Jason. I was bad on the Supershine last night and I've just launched a fragrance.'*

launch your lunch *v.* To *hurl one's biscuits.*

Laura Kuenssberg's husband, wrist muscles like *sim.* Said of a gentleman whose wife is seemingly never at home, and thus – one might imagine – has particularly well developed forearms. *'Next up on Indoor League is arm wrestling, and Andy Devey is taking on the undefeated champion Bill Richardson in the final. It's going to be a close match, because both these lads have been training hard and have wrist muscles like Laura Kuenssberg's husband. Ah'll see thee in part two.'*

Laurence Olivier *n.* The *ne plus ultra* of excrement; the definitive *Richard the Third.*

lava lamp *1. n.* A kitsch electrical appliance that was all the rage in the 1960s and could be again, especially according to the management of the Gadget Shop (which went into administration in 2005). *2. n.* The appearance of the bath after one has *waxed the dolphin* in it. *3. euph.* A female who is "very hot but not terribly bright".

lava lamp, guts like a *sim.* The unpleasant sensation that big, glowing, waxy bubbles of superheated gas are backing up one's large intestine. Possibly following a night *on the pop* or a delicious meal enjoyed at the Curry Capital, Bigg Market, Newcastle upon Tyne (now closed).

lavatory *n.* The *smallest room*, little house, *loo*, water closet, convenience, place of easement, *shithouse, crapper, privy, bog*, latrine, *cackatorium, temple of cloacina*, toilet, *khazi, thunder box, comfort station, meditation room, library, gentleman's reading room, shitter.*

lavatory dyscalcula *n. medic.* That condition by which a sufferer is afflicted when they attempt the *wrong number* in a lavatory. The upsetting discovery that, for example, a much-needed *number two* was only a *Lionel*, or worse, the realisation that a *number two* was, in fact, needed whilst halfway through a *number one* at the urinal.

lav child *n.* A bouncing *mud baby* delivered after a protracted period of agonizing *arse labour*.

lavender *adj.* Pertaining to *good listeners*.

Lavender Lodge, they live in *euph.* Coded reference to women who are *fans of walking holidays*. Named after the *lady golfer* residents of the eponymous address in in the village of Fawcett Magna, near Ambridge, in Radio 4 serial *The Archers*. See also *batting for Darrington*.

lavender marriage *n.* Any matrimonial coupling about which there is a whiff of *lavender*.

lavender milk *n.* The *plum juice* of a fellow who prefers to skip across small areas of standing water.

lavioli *n. It.* Small, meaty parcels smothered in a rich, steaming gravy.

lavitation *n.* The yogic exercise performed when hovering over a public *bog* seat so as to avoid direct contact when having a *shit*. The *birdie dance*.

lav technician *1. n.* A bloke who skives by spending as many hours as is feasible ensconced on the works *crapper. 2. n.* A *theatrical* chap who does most of his work *in the stalls*.

lav train *n.* The swarm of women that all go to the toilet together in pubs.

Lavvie Sifree *n.* A *Thora* of such monumental dimensions that "something inside so strong" is required to successfully expel it from the *Enochs*.

Lawley kazoo *n.* A *hat dropped forwards. Harry Secombe's last raspberry. A kweef.* Derivation known, but subject to legal restrictions.

lawn sausages *n. Park links, dog's eggs, dog toffee, hound cable.*

law of beverages *n.* The system of precisely defined scientific axioms that govern the effect of booze upon the human body. *'Look dear, I'd had a skinful. It's hardly surprising in the circumstances that I woke up in your sister again. It's the law of beverages.'*

Lawrence of A-Labia *n. prop.* Name for a not-

at-all-sinister bloke who hangs around on the sand, checking out the *camel toes* of the bikini-clad bathers.

Laws-on *n.* An erection which commonly springs into life whilst watching Nigella on the telly, but, for some inexplicable reason, rarely does so when her late dad or brother are on.

laxident *n.* A *slip of the bum* while dosed up on the sennapods.

lay *1. n.* Prospective or past sexual partner. *'I knew your wife many years ago. She was a terrific lay.' 2. v.* To *fuck* a woman with a small amount of cement and a trowel.

lay a cable *v.* To *build a log cabin, grow a tail, drop a copper bolt.*

lay a cuckoo's egg *1. v.* A party trick where a foreign *bogie* is introduced into an unconscious reveller's nostril for the amusement of the other guests. *2. v.* To get someone else's missus *up the duff. 'Pastimes: making cardboard buses, fluffing up hair to appear eccentric, laying cuckoo's eggs.'* (from *Who's Who 2022*: entry for Boris Johnson).

lay-and-display *n.* A type of European lavatory where the *twinkie* lands on a dry porcelain surface for inspection prior to being flushed away.

layby cham *n.* Bottles of fizzy *piss* left at the side of the road by HGV drivers. Also *truckers' tizer, kidney cider, hedge coke, juggernaut juice.*

laying the tarmac *n.* A *Boston pancake* that ends up costing much more than the original estimate.

lazy lob on *n.* A semi-erect penis, a *dobber*, half *a teacake.*

lazy man's wee *n.* A gentleman's sit-down *piss*, usually taken in the middle of the night when his aim cannot be trusted, sometimes even on the toilet. A *she-pee*.

lazy otter *n.* A slow, relaxing *Thora Hird*.

lazy Susan *n.* Lackadaisical *Boris Johnson* position whereby the woman reclines on her back with her head dangling over the end of the bed.

lead in your pencil, to have *v.* To be *on the stonk*. Not like one of those floppy, leadless pencils.

lead the children of Israel to safety *v.* To commit a Moses-esque act of *rag week cumulonimbus*. To *part the red sea.*

lead the llama to the lift shaft *v.* To point *Percy* at the vagina.

leafblower *n.* A cacophonous, yet feeble, food delivery scooter that comes with an L-plated top box, hand muffs and a blanket. *'Well I must say, the truffled mushroom gnocchi, Caprese salad and Hazelnut panna cotta with chocolate ganache look delicious, John!' 'Nah, Kebab meat and chips. Call* *the Leafblower, Lisa.'*

leaker *n. Aus.* A sexually alluring female, that is to say, one who "has holes that need to be plugged up".

leaks more than a poundshop bucket *sim.* Said of a chap who pays uncommonly frequent visits to the gents during an evening at the pub.

Leaky Cauldron, drink in the *1. v.* To frequent the famous wizards' *boozer* out of off of *Harry Potter*. *2. euph.* After an evening's drinking, to magically lose control of one's bladder and *piss* all over your trousers, the bed, next door's spaniel, a copper *etc.*

leap of filth *n.* The feeling of blind trust needed when buying *grumble* online. *'Mr Watt told us: "I feel badly let down. I made a twenty quid leap of filth and you can't even see it going in." Cyril...' 'Thank-you Esther.'*

leap round *n.* A round of drinks purchased by the slower drinker in the group, in which he does not buy a drink for himself, to prevent himself falling behind. Similar in concept to a leap year, only with a pint less rather than a day more.

leather cheerio *n.* The *anal sphincter.* Also *bum gums, Grolsch washer, snippit valve.*

leather hamster *n.* A very cold and shrunken *ball bag.* What happens to the male *chicken skin handbag* following a refreshing dip in the sea. *'At the conclusion of my historic natation of the English Channel, I had a leather hamster for a good three weeks.'* (from *The Memoirs of Captain Matthew Webb*, 1875).

leather on willow, like the sound of *sim.* A very pleasing *crack. 'Was her topiary in good order?' 'Leather on willow, mate. Leather on willow.'*

leatherspooned *adj.* The state of a fellow the morning after overindulging in cheap booze.

leave a message for Ray Mears *v.* To have a *shit* in the woods, behind a bush in the park, on a golf course *etc.*

leave a note in the guestbook *euph.* When you sign off with an almighty *skid-mark* in the *bog* after staying as a guest in another person's home – just to let your host know you've enjoyed all of the facilities. *'You always know when Mr Rees-Mogg has stayed over as he never fails to leave a charming note in the guestbook.'*

leave a wet load in the drum *v.* To perform a *cream pie*, often as the dramatic dénouement to a *stick vid*.

leave everything on the water *1. phr.* Cliché much used by Olympic commentators when referring to Olympic rowers expending maximum effort in order to win a race. *2. phr.* Doing an immense, personal best *shit.*

leave her on charge *v.* To deliberately keep the missus in a state of sexual anticipation. *'Me and the wife are going away for a lovely weekend without the kids tomorrow, so I'm not sure whether to give her a good seeing-to tonight or to just leave her on charge. What do the panel think?' 'Bob Flowerdew?'*

leave negative feedback *v.* To *fart* and walk away.

leave the brown barge in the lock *v.* To fail to flush properly. To leave a *night watchman* floating in the *chod pan.*

leave the handbrake on *euph.* The act of secretly having two or three *off the wrist* pre-*coitus* in order to extend the *cooking time. 'She was fit as fuck and dressed like a tart but luckily I'd left the handbrake on and was good for forty minutes. And now, boys and girls, here's Peter and Don to tell you all about the fascinating hobby of matchbox collecting.'*

lecher's nightmare *n.* At the seaside, a grisly underwear display given by Stilton-thighed elderly ladies when they sit in deck chairs. *Next month's washing.*

lechfast *n.* A young East European man's morning meal enjoyed straight out of the tin. From Lech – the name of a popular premium strength lager which is popular in Poland.

lech-tacles *n.* Sunglasses. Also *perv windows.*

lechture *n.* A forthright sermon delivered to no-one in particular while under the influence of Polish lager. *'Oh-oh. Nigel's in the saloon bar giving another one of his lechtures about the immigrants.'*

le cock spurtif *n. Fr.* An iconic, non-trademarked logo adopted by novice and expert graffiti artists alike. Frequently essayed in public toilets and textbooks, and drawn in the dirt on the backs of vans, it consists of a stylised ejaculating *membrum virile* set atop a cursory bi-lobed *happy sack.* Also known as a *three-line pud.*

Lecter's lunchbag *n.* A young lady's *farmyard area* that takes on the appearance of a bloody bag of nibbled lips and lobes once a month, when the *tomato boat is docked in tuna town.*

Lee Anderson's lunch, cheaper than *sim.* Descriptive of one who hasn't got a round in since it cost 30p to do so.

Leeds Christmas tree *n.* Roundhay Park shrubbery bedecked with tightly knotted bags of *lawn sausages.* Also *brown baubles, Warrington baubles.*

Lee Evans's suit, as wet as *sim.* Said of a sexually aroused lady at her moistest. *Dripping like a fucked fridge, frothing like bottled Bass, wet as Dermot O'Leary's shirt.*

leffargy *n.* Intense fatigue and inability to do anything the morning after a night spent quaffing premium Belgian lager.

left footer *n.* A *Whitley Bay* or Catholic person, but ideally one who is both.

left-glanded *adj*. Descriptive of a gentleman who dresses to the sinister side.

left hand down, a bit *adj. Good with colours*. *'Have you met Quentin? You'll like him, he's a bit left hand down a bit.'*

left-handed batsman *n*. Someone who prefers his *balls* delivered from the *pavilion end*.

left-handed dream *1. n*. Avant-garde 1981 electronic album by Ryuichi Sakamoto. *2. n*. The thing where you lie on your arm till it goes numb, and then have a *wank* while pretending it's being done by Miss Popov from *Rentaghost*. A *submariner's special*.

left-handed website *n*. A *cyberscud* internet site whose visitors tend to operate the mouse with their larboard *dick skinner.*

left legger *n*. A lady who particularly enjoys being *sorted out, Confessions* movie-style, on the front passenger seat of a car. Derived from the technique of hanging her left leg out the window, thus affording the driver unhindered access to her *cunker*, assuming he can avoid getting the gear lever stuck up his *arse*.

left luggage *n*. Traces of *feeshus* left in the toilet bowl even after flushing.

leftovers *1. n*. Food remaining uneaten at the end of a meal. *2. n*. When you think you're done and then a bit more *piss* gushes out unexpectedly – sometimes streaming down your pants if you've put them back on – and leaving a wet patch.

leftovers *1. n*. Food remaining uneaten at the end of a meal. *2. n*. When you think you're done with your *number one* but then it turns out you weren't. See also *bowser trouser, a few more drips in the tap, forget-me-nots, slashback etc.*

left the lid off the gluepot? who's *exclam. interrog.* Rhetorical device implying that someone smells of *merry monk*. *'Jesus, your majesty! Who's left the lid off the gluepot?'*

legacy *1. n*. The glorious bequest to the nation of a highly popular and successful Prime Minister. *2. n*. A stinksome *Thora* left by the previous incumbent of a water closet who couldn't be *arsed* to flush. *'Theresa, can you bring the plunger up, please? David's left a legacy in the upstairs cludgie.'*

leg bye *n*. When a *Harmison loosener* trickles down leg-side for some unexpected *runs*. Diarrhoea dribbling out of the *popping crease* and down the *leg gully* after one has failed to avoid the *follow through*.

leg elvising *n*. The frantic *Ed Sullivan Show*-style gyrations performed while trying to shake a bit of

follow through out the bottom of one's trouser leg.

leg iron shuffle *n*. The gait adopted by one suffering from the *turtle's head*, trying to make it to the *crapper* without *signing his bills*.

leg lifter *n*. *Benefactor*. Somebody who *breaks company*.

leg man *n*. One who prefers *gams* to *tits* or *arses*.

leg necklace *n*. An act of *cumulonimbus*.

Lego enema, less fun than a *sim*. Used in reference to something that is superlatively unpleasant, such as the Chicxulub asteroid impact of 66 million years BC, the bubonic plague or Robson & Jerome's cover version of the Drifters's *Up on the Roof*.

Lego garage, like I've shat out a *sim*. Turn of phrase spoken by one who has recently been delivered of an uncomfortably hard *arse baby*. *'Christ, I knew I should of chewed them fucking crisps up a bit more last night. I feel like I've shat out a Lego garage. Anyway, welcome to In Our Time. This week I'll be discussing the teachings of St. Thomas Aquinas with Dr Patrick Pending of Cambridge University, Sir Basil Herb, emeritus professor of Theology at Imperial College, London and the philosopher Alain de Bottom.'*

lego hand *n. medic*. A tertiary form of *wanker's cramp*. A condition afflicting the hand of one who has overindulged in *the monomanual vice*. From the similarity to the rigid, empty grasp of the Danish toy figures.

Lego pineapple *n*. An extremely knobbly and uncomfortable *Thora*. *'Now there's some sad things known to man / But ain't too much sadder than the tears of a clown / When he just crapped out a Lego pineapple.'* (from *The Tears of a Clown* by Smokey Robinson and the Bandits).

leg over *n*. A *sausage and doughnut situation*. *'Did you get your leg over?' 'No, but I got tops and three fingers.'*

legs not corresponding *euph*. Descriptive of a *well-refreshed* wobbly walk home from the pub.

leg tensing *n*. The act of tensing one's leg when having a *toss*. *'This wank is going nowhere. I'd better get a bit of leg tensing in.'*

legwarmer *1. n*. Pointlesss eighties fashion apparel. *2. n*. A *Tony Hart* delivered at point blank range whilst cuddling in bed. *3. n*. An *air biscuit* straight out of *Ena Sharples' mouth* which, due to external restraints, for example the seat of a chair, spirals its way down one's trousering, providing a fleeting but nonetheless pleasurable warming sensation. *4. n*. The *fiveskin* or *peparami wrapper.*

leisure facilities *n. medic*. Breasts, *competitive*

advantages, impressive CVs.

leisure trove n. A veritable Aladdin's cave of *relaxation-oriented literature*, such as might be discovered in the study of a recently deceased vicar by his startled family.

Lemmy's wart n. A particularly recalcitrant and unresponsive *clematis*.

Lemmy's warts n. pl. Off-puttingly big *champagne corks*.

lemon curd 1. n. Citrus spread. 2. n. A *Richard the Third* that exhibits a zesty fragrance.

lemon enders n. A variety of female nipple that may be squeezed onto pancakes.

lemon jizzle cake n. Unlikely-sounding bakery-based equivalent of *Winner's sauce*. The sort of dessert that glassy-eyed *GBBO* lothario Paul Hollywood might be served after mercilessly critiquing the soggy bottoms at his local *patisserie*.

lemon meringue n. The deeply unedifying sight of a bowl of bright yellow *piss* topped off with a frothy morning *flob* that the previous *bastard* has failed to flush. *'Fuck's sake, Posh. You've left a lemon meringue in the shit pot again.'*

lemon party n. A term that it isn't wise to type into Google Image Search with the SafeSearch function set to "Off". See also *blue waffle*. Or rather, don't.

lemon pizzle cake n. Urinal bleach-blocks. Also known as *wazz spangles, bog dice, urineapple chunks*.

lemon turd n. The smell that accompanies one's better half as she emerges from the water closet at the conclusion of her morning ablutions. A combination of *eau de colon* and industrial strength air freshener.

Lemsip and a wank n. A cure for whatever ails you. A *panhandle-acea*. After listening to one's tale of woe, divorce, sacking *etc.*, a mate might reply, *'Have a Lemsip and a wank and you'll soon feel better.'*

lend v. To *give*, in the *sausage* sense. *'Phwoar! Your mum's a bit of alright. I wouldn't mind lending her one'.'*

Lene n. prop. medic. A hark back to a person's heyday when they *sowed their wild oats* in the 70s and 80s; a long-standing genito-urinary infection that periodically flares up and causes embarrassment and misery in later life. A "love-itch", from the 70s weird song warbler. See also *Saturday night fever, clap, cockrot, happy rash*.

Len Goodman's seven paddle, her legs are in the air more than sim. Said humorously of a woman who, not to put too fine a point on it, loves it *up her.* In reference to the formerly alive *Strictly* judge's favourite score. *'I wouldn't say she's easy, ladies and gentlemen, but the Duchess's legs are in the air more often than Len Goodman's seven paddle.'* (The Archbishop of Canterbury addressing the congregation at the marriage of HRH Prince Andrew and Sarah Ferguson, July 23rd 1986).

length n. An Imperial saucy postcard unit of *the other*, as *slipped* to a woman by a man who works in a lino factory.

length underwater n. Aquatic feat performed in the hotel complex swimming pool at four in the morning with a fat lass from Barnsley called Tracey.

Lenovo lunch euph. A veritable feast of crumbs and dead skin obtained by turning your laptop upside down.

lentil health, suffering from poor euph. medic. Subject to a bout of rancid flatulence of the sort associated with the combination of an exclusively vegetarian diet and over-reliance on pulses as a source of protein.

Leonardo n. An annoying little piece of *shit* that refuses to go down the *pan* after the main *dreadnought* has sunk. Named after the little actor who annoyingly floated around, refusing to die quickly at the end of *Titanic*.

Leons n. medic. The *trots*. From Leon Trotsky (1879-1940), the Russian revolutionary and Marxist theorist who famously got an ice-pick that made his ears burn, and also suffered something rotten with the *Mexican screamers*.

leopard's back n. Worse than a *tiger's back*; a *chod bin* that has been peppered with *arse shrapnel*.

Leo Sayer n. rhym. slang. An *all dayer*, a prolonged drinking session. An all-day party during which you drink "More Than I Can Say".

lepers' finger buffet, like a sim. Said when something is a mess. *'Don't you think it's about time you tidied the house up a bit, dear? The boss is coming round for dinner tonight and the place is like a lepers' finger buffet.'*

Les Beau n. prop. A dandy fellow who enjoys the company of *three-wheelers*. A *dykey likey*.

lesbeen n. A *lesbidaceous* has-been. A *hasbian, wasbian*.

lesbian n. A *tennis fan*.

lesbiany adj. Appertaining to lesbism. *'Randy young man: 'Any chance of you and your mate doing something lesbiany?' Sexy girlfriend: 'Okay, we'll put some more comfortable shoes on and go for a walking holiday, how about that?'* (Bamforth's *Seaside Chuckles* postcard by Donald McGill, 1922).

lesbionage n. The furtive act of watching a couple of *carpet munchers* as they *munch* each others's *carpets,* perhaps while up a ladder and wearing infra-red night vision goggles you ordered out the back of *Exchange & Mart.*

lesbo *n.* A *tuppence licker, bean flicker, lickalotopus, lady golfer.*

lesbology *n.* The scientific study of lesbian activity. A branch of radical feminism studied almost exclusively by males and which involves painstaking scrutiny of video footage. *'Have you met my dad? He's a keen amateur lesbologist.'*

lesbro *n.* A heterosexual man who prefers the company of women who prefer the company of women. The male equivalent of a *fag hag.* A *rug hugger, dykey likey.*

Les Dawson Creek *n.* Any area populated by women who resemble the aesthetically challenged eponymous late comedian in drag. *'Wish me luck. I'm off on the pull at the disco in the downstairs bar at Brough Park dog track.' 'I wouldn't bother, mate. It's like Les Dawson Creek in there.'*

lesidue *n.* Pronounced "lezzy dew". The moisture that remains on the morning bedsheets of those ladies who choose to eschew cramped footwear.

Leslie gash *n.* A luscious-lipped trout-pouting *fanny.* After the Ivy Tilsley-*gobbed* former Homebase ad star.

lesuits *n.* Radical, evangelising wing of women who *do their own heavy lifting on the bus to Hebden Bridge.* Always on the lookout for converts. *'Oh no, the lesuits have got hold of her.'*

let off *v.* To *let rip, blow off, launch an air biscuit.*

let off a bit of cream *v.* To relieve one's *plumbago.*

let off some steam, Bennett *exclam.* Humorous preamble to a *gaseous emission,* to be delivered in the style of Arnold Scharzenegger in the film *Commando.* Or any other of his films, for that matter. He wouldn't have been very good in *Kind Hearts and Coronets,* would he?

let one go *v.* To *let off.*

let Percy in the playpen *euph.* Of a woman, to consent to *a bit of the other.*

let rip *v.* To *let one go* like someone trying to start a reluctant chainsaw.

let's get rrrrready for grumble! *exclam.* An ear-piercing cry, similar to that made by a boxing match announcer, shouted by a man when his wife has left the house and gone to her mother's for the weekend, thus affording him a rare opportunity to enjoy a period of uninterrupted quality time with his *art pamphlet* collection and high speed broadband router.

let's go, peloton! *1. exclam.* Advertising hook used to sell exercise bikes to *bellends. 2. exclam.* At the opposite end of the fitness spectrum, a plaintive cry coming from the downstairs *crapper* following another night of overindulgence.

let's have a record *exclam.* A conversation-restarting phrase, to be deployed after a sudden *dropped gut* has silenced the room. To be delivered in the manner of Kirsty Young (or Lauren Laverne these days) on Radio 4's *Desert Island Discs,* introducing the next tune after her guest has reminisced themselves to a standstill while re-living some childhood trauma or other.

let's play lingo! *1. exclam.* Catchphrase of ITV daytime quiz host Adil Ray, who used to follow us on Twitter but doesn't any more. *2. exclam.* Cheeky offer made to a lady in the hope of *licking her out/*getting *sucked off.* Or both at the same time; you never know your luck.

let's see if it's right; let's see how many people said it *exclam.* In the style of *Pointless* host Alexander Armstrong, something to say after someone has *let fly* with a *fanfare on the trouser trumpet.*

let's see who's got Covid! *exclam.* Witty announcement delivered immediately prior to a forceful *smell test* from the *botty bugle,* the result of which may have significant miasmic properties. See aso *punch it Chewie; now back to Davina; observe Mr Bond, the instruments of Armageddon!*

let's skip dessert *exclam.* During the course of a romantic assignation, a request to omit *felching.*

let's take that offline *1. exclam.* Standard business-speak response to an issue or question that is awkward, embarrassing and unplanned for. *2. exclam.* Comical meeting-room response to a loud *Exchange & Mart.*

letter from Mr Shit, a *euph.* An advance announcement that a visit from a long-awaited guest is imminent. A *custard tart.*

let that sink in *1. phr.* Form of words commonly used by social media pundits, pointing out a post that has been badly phrased by someone whose opinions they disdain. *2. phr.* Punchline of a practical gag by Elon Musk just after he bought Twitter, and turned up carrying a basin. He's missed a trick there, mind. We would've given him a tenner for that as a Crap Joke. *2. exclam.* Said immediately after *dropping a gut.*

let the cock see the fanny *phr.* A somewhat crude variation on the expression "let the dog see the rabbit." Something Paddy McGuinness might finally have got to say on the last edition of *Take Me Out.*

let the dog out *1. v.* To go for a really big, urgent *Donald Trump. 'Sorry I'm late, only I had to let the dog out. Anyway, I'm here now, so let's play Popmaster.' 2. v.* To nip home at lunchtime and *feed* *the ducks* after a frustrating morning surrounded by *office beaver. Fire the one o'clock gun. 'Hold all my calls, Miss Jones. I'm just nipping home to let the dog out.'* 3. *v.* To release a ferocious *arse barker* immediately upon waking. *'Sorry about that, love. I had to let the dog out, only it's been scratching at the back door all night.'*

let the drain take the strain *phr.* Said of a sizeable *Mister Magoo* that may well overwhelm the house's foulpipe.

let the passengers off the bus before the stop/let the passengers off the bus early *euph.* To *spend your money before you get to the shop*; a phrase used by Ellie and Izzie from Leeds on *Gogglebox.* To *declare early*, or otherwise go *up and over like a pan of milk.*

let the twins out *euph.* Of a lady, to remove her brassiere.

let the wife down *euph.* Of peripatetic musicians, *banging* groupies while on tour. *'Hello? Claridges Room service?' 'Yeah, could you send up a cine camera, a length of rope and a live mudshark to room 308 please? I'm about to let my wife down.' 'Certainly Mr Bonham.'*

lettuce *n.* The crinkly leaves underneath the *gorilla salad.* The *piss flaps.*

lettuce licker *n.* A *lezza.*

level 42 *euph.* The act of *jaffing* into both of someone's eyes at the same time. Well, more or less. From the lyrics to the eponymous Brit-funk combo's song *Love Games, viz.* "I can see the salt in your eyes".

lever arches *rhym. slang.* Haemorrhoids. From lever arch files = Chalfonts.

lezza *n.* A woman who is *fond of walking holidays.*

lezzarection *n.* Of a *carpet muncher,* seeing the light and going *back onto solids.* Or possibly the other way round.

lezzo boots *n. Aus. A*ny clumpy, unfeminine footwear worn by women. The opposite of *fuck me shoes. Fuck off slippers.*

liabetic *n.* Someone afflicted with the *bullshit* bug.

Liam Gallagher, the *n.* The swaggering, reclined, semi-horizontal walking style that a man adopts during his customary midnight stroll from bedroom to bathroom in search of toilet roll; his laid-back Mancunian gait adopted in order to negate the effects of gravity upon his nocturnal emissions, and thus protect the pile of his landing carpet. Also known as an *Ian Brown.*

liarrhoea *1. n.* Description of the *shit* spouted by a dissembling fellow. *2. n.* Excuse used for pulling a *sickie* at work after sinking your own bodyweight

in Boddingtons.

lib dem loafers *n.* Unsightly open-toed sandals of the sort typically worn with socks by balding *euphemersity* lecturers.

library of congress *n.* A fellow's complete bedtime repertoire.

libratory *n.* A *crapper* which is well stocked with *shiterature.* From library + lavatory. *'I'm just off to the libratory to take out Clarkson on Clarkson by Jeremy Clarkson, dear.'*

Libyan uprising *euph.* A morning of violence in the *Benghazi area.* A stinging dose of the *Dickie dirts* after a plethora of dark beer and piquant provender.

lick a bus battery *v.* To commit *cumulonimbus* on a lady who is 2.66 times skankier than a *nine-volter.*

lickalotopus *n.* Scientific name for an experienced *rug muncher.*

lick both sides of the stamp *v.* To be *AC/DC*; said of a *happy shopper, Betty both.* See also *half rice half chips.*

licker licence *n.* Permission to have a drink from the *hairy goblet.*

licking a nine-volter *n.* Dining out on a particularly skanky *snatch,* the eye-watering effect being not dissimilar to the experience of placing your tongue across the terminals of a PP3 battery.

lick of paint *n. Mexican lipstick, pasata grin, clown's smile, Robert Smith's gob.* Consequence of a late *licker licence.*

lick one's arse and call it chocolate *phr.* Expression used to bring a deludedly optimistic person down to earth. *'Mr Speaker, my Right Honourable friend the Chancellor has told the house that thanks to his government's prudent fiscal policies the economy is in a stronger position now than ever. He is entitled to take that view, of course, and he is likewise entitled, should he wish, to lick his arse and call it chocolate.'*

lick out *1. v.* That which is done by a small child to a bowl of cake mix. *2. v.* That which is done by a moustachioed *grumble* star to *the captain's pie.*

lick toes intolerant *adj.* Said of a chap who has no intention whatsoever of sucking his wife's feet. *'Sorry Sarah, no can do. I'm lick toes intolerant.'*

lick-twat *n. prop.* One who has the gift of tongues. A virtuoso on the *hairy harmonica.*

lid *n.* The bit above the *brim.* The *herman gelmet.*

Lidl checkout worker, like a *sim.* A particularly violent, no-nonsense *hand job. 'It was quite traumatic, to be honest with you, gran. She went at it like a Lidl checkout worker.'*

Lidl class *adj.* Aspirational but frankly a bit skint.

Lidl shop of horrors *n.* Unnerving trip to an East Europe-based supermarket where you return home with a car full of treasure from the central isles (telescopic ladder, car mats, Torx socket sets *etc.*) despite only going in for milk and *bogroll*.

lido shuffle *1. n.* Title of a popular 'seventies single by Boz Scaggs (real name Bosley Scagglethorpe). *2. n.* Popular 'seventies activity performed discreetly by gentlemen whilst admiring the view at outdoor swimming pools.

liebfraumilf *n.* On a Ryanair hen party flight to Berlin, the sort of coarse, drunken, foulmouthed, middle-aged maneater who might cause a respectable fellow in a nearby seat to tut disapprovingly, even though he secretly wouldn't mind a *go* on her.

lie-fi *n.* Free bus or train internet that simply doesn't work. See also *thinternet, fraudband.*

lie-kido *n.* Martial art practised by self-proclaimed pub hardmen, ex-SAS paratroopers and the like.

life affirmer *n. Shit* taken during the worst depths of a hangover or other depression which is of such magnitude that it restores one's vital signs. A *crap* which would make the late Fred Astaire dance down the street, occasionally bouncing his silver-topped cane off the kerb.

life and arsehole of the party *euph.* At a convivial social gathering, a guest who is about as popular as a *bellend* infection. A *pisswizard. 'Have you met my brother-in-law, Bishop? He really is the life and arsehole of the party.'*

life atwatic, the *n.* Your entire existence spent being a *cunt.*

liferafting *n.* Socially polite method of defecation that is mandatory in Swiss apartment houses after ten at night (it says here and we've no intention of looking that up to check it). Involves layering several sheets of *arsewad* upon the water in the *pan* before the evening's business is transacted.

lift and separate *n.* Named in honour of the erstwhile *tit pants* advertising slogan; a sophisticated, eco-friendly and modern *buttocks*-spread *shitting* technique that apparently saves a fortune in *arse paper.*

lifting the cheek *n.* The sly behaviour of a *cushion creeper.*

lift the latch *n.* To shift one's bodyweight onto a single cheek in order to facilitate a release of *shitrogen monoxide.*

light bender *n.* A person of such large proportions that their enormous bulk distorts space-time, causing light to warp around it, as explained in Einstein's *Theory of General Relativity.*

light curry supper *n.* A vast, Chernobyl-strength vindaloo consumed at the end of an heroic

night's drinking.

light duties *n. medic.* Diarrhoea. *'Buckingham Palace announced that her majesty, who has mild COVID symptoms, is expected to perform light duties all week.'*

lighthouse cat, rank as a *sim.* Descriptive of a gentleman who has experienced an excessively long period without getting his hands on any *tussage. 'Giz a shot on your blurtch, Una. I feel as rank as a lighthouse cat.'*

lighthouse keeper's forearm *1. n.* A muscular limb of the sort developed following a great deal of repetitive exercise, and thus *2. n.* Anything large and impressively-solid, *'Fuck me! That smarted. I've just passed a lighthouse-keeper's forearm, your holiness.'*

lighthouse keeper, wanking like a *phr.* Ferociously *pulling one's pud* more or less around the clock, a lifestyle that only only a long-term solitary chap is able to enjoy. *Living the dream.*

lightning in a bottle *n.* A photographic *art study* which catches the moment a gentleman *expels his custard* in a shot arcing majestically towards the face of a beautiful young lady. Named after the equally tricky task of photographing a high-voltage meteorological discharge. *'That, Mr Fox-Talbot, is a powerful image. You have captured lightning in a bottle.'*

light the afterburners *v.* In honour of *short-arsed* scientologist Tom Cruise's fly-by of the aircraft carrier control tower in the movie *Top Gun,* to release an enormously powerful *ass blast* which results in rattling windows, disorientated friends, spilled coffee, a bollocking from the boss and possibly, some time later, the death of a close friend.

light the brown touchpaper *v.* To initiate the *shitting* process. Usually achieved via the first smoke and coffee of the day, after which one should stand well back with one's fingers in one's ears. Also *pull the pin on the arse grenade.*

lignite prospector *euph.* One who digs deep in his search for *brown coal.*

ligraine *n. medic.* A fictitious headache that usually occurs midweek, rendering the sufferer unable to work but quite able to attend interviews for better-paid jobs, travel to race meetings and engage in *fuckathons* with the woman next door while her old man is out.

like a leaf on a breeze you blew away *exclam.* Post-*windy pop* apophthegm taken from the gloomy Justin Hayward dirge *Forever Autumn.*

likes her sportswear *euph.* Lesbidaceous. Said of a woman who *hasn't got a fucking clue what's in her* *flower beds.*

likes his kettle and toaster to match *euph.* Said of a chap who *knows the line-up for Eurovision* and *makes his own wicker baskets.*

like starting an outboard motor *sim.* Descriptive of the action required to lovingly remove a string of anal beads from one's inamorata's *rusty sheriff's badge.* A *Suffolk punch.*

lilies on the pond *n.* The artistic practice – popularised by impressionist painter Claude Monet – of laying sheets of toilet tissue on the water surface before *giving birth to a dead otter.* A *pap baffle.*

lil-let savage *n.* A gruff-voiced woman *showing off* while she's *on her rags.*

lils *1. n.* 1950s/60s *thru'penny bits. 2. n. Stits, lung warts, snitches, bee stings, Dutch Alps.* From Liliputians.

Lily Les Tez *n. prop. rhym. slang.* An act of monomanual self delight. From the names of the late presenters of *Blankety-Blank* = wank.

lime water *n. Semen, spunk, spooge, spangle, tweedle.*

limpeting *n.* The female version of *teabagging.*

limp home mode *1. n.* In a modern car, an ingenious innovation that suddenly reduces the vehicle's speed to a crawl when a faulty sensor detects an anomalous EGR valve reading just as you put your foot down to pull into the fast lane of the M6 in front of a juggernaut carrying six bulldozers. *2. n.* A desperate MC Escher-style trudge towards *orgasm* when the spirit is willing but the flesh is weak.

Lincolnshire poacher *1. n.* Jaunty traditional English folk song that formed the playlist of an eponymous radio station believed to be sending signals to British intelligence agents in the Middle East. *2. n.* Type of cheese. *3. n.* Man who pursues women with small *norks.*

Linda Bellingham's fingertips *n.* The result of *breeching the hull* as a consequence of either over-zealous wiping of the *rusty sheriff's badge* or the purchase of insufficiently robust *arse paper.* Or a combination of the two. From the state of the erstwhile gravel-voiced late Oxo mum's digits after a day spent crumbling her favourite stock-cubes into casseroles for her fictitious family's tea. Also known as *taxi driver's tan, mechanic's nails, finger of fudge, filter tip.*

line dancing *n.* A vigorous knees-up or other un-selfconscious Terpsichorean display fuelled by a toot of *Keith Richards' dandruff.*

lineman's pastie *n.* A very full disposable nappy thrown from a train window at loafing, orange-clad track workers.

line of duty *1. n.* A popular BBC police procedural series where it was apparently a *filth* what done it. *2. n.* The damning evidence left in one's *scads* as a consequence of inadequate wiping at the crimescene.

line of wank *n.* A blind spot in the garden where a chap knows he can safely *relax in a gentleman's way* without being spotted by next door pegging out her washing, number 47 changing a duvet by her back bedroom window or his missus washing the dishes.

linesman *1. n.* In association football, an assistant referee or other official empowered with assisting the referee in enforcing the Laws of the Game during a match. *2. n.* A fellow with a penchant for *jazz talc*: *'Born on this day: Mother Teresa, religious leader, 1910; Macaulay Culkin, Home Alone actor, 1980; Michael Gove, Conservative linesman, 1967.'*

lingam *n. Hindu.* Penis. From ancient *grumble book The Karma Sutra.*

lining paper *n.* When a fellow's *piss chisel* runs out of fuel before successfully clearing all the *skid marks* off the porcelain, the careful insertion of a single sheet of *bumwad* that just touches the water and uses capillary action to keep any remaining marks damp such that the next assault successfully clears the problem.

link-detatched *adj.* A bit better than a *semi*, but still not quite *the full Monty.*

links effect, the *euph.* The aromatic toilet visit which is enjoyed the morning after a night on the beer and *Ruby Murray,* when one's *arse* resembles a sausage machine as operated by a cack-handed contestant on *The Generation Game.*

lino munching *n.* The correct term for *rug munching* when the munchee's *pile* has been waxed off.

lion *n.* More *chod bin* contents terminology. A magnificent two-tone *poo*, in gold and brown. Often makes its appearance accompanied by a loud roar and a pride of smaller cubs.

Lionel Bart *n. rhym. slang.* A particularly musical *custard tart* that gets you out of bed and forces you to swing the windows open and take a deep, life-affirming breath.

lion's breakfast *n.* A particularly unkempt *gorilla's wallet* that looks like a *splayed zebra.*

lion tamer's corpse *sim.* Descriptive of the sorry state of one's *chap* after a *rag week romp. Barber's pole, Roy horn.*

lion walk *n.* Sticking your *balls* out backwards between your legs and – not surprisingly in the circumstances – roaring in the style of a big cat.

lip gloss *n.* The colourless substance secreted by

the male generative member for the purpose of easing ingress into the vulval opening. Also *ball glaze, guardsman's gloss, dew on the lily, perseverance soup, balm before the storm, wrist oil, knuckle varnish, snake spit* or *French polish.*

lippie *v.* Of a dog, to *frotter* on one's leg with its *lipstick* out. '"*Aw. He must like you, Dr Watson," expostulated the great detective, sucking on his pipe thoughtfully and adjusting the brim of his deerstalker with the handle of his magnifying glass while playing his violin. "He's trying to lippie your leg, look."'* (from *The Randy Hound of the Baskervilles* by Arthur Conan Doyle).

lip reading *1. n.* Observing women in tight pants who have the *camel's foot.* '*If she bends over any more I'll be able to read her lips from here.*' *2. n.* The intense concentration of a *grumble* watcher captivated by the massive pink *beef curtains* on his computer screen.

lip ring *n.* A lipstick line around the circumference of one's *sword* which enables one to gauge how far it has been *swallowed* while one's missus is in the next room being sick.

lip ripper *n.* A magnificently girthsome *charlie.*

lip service *1. n.* Hollow compliments that an unscrupulous *crumpeteer* gives to a piece of *blart* upon whom he has designs. *2. n.* Etiquette observed when *dining at the Y.* *3. n.* The *bag for life*'s visit to the *snatch dentist* for her annual *mot test.* *4. n.* A lacklustre act of *horatio* performed by a timid or blocked-nosed *nosher.*

lip sink *1. n.* Minneapolis-based disco band whose 1979/1980 single *Funkytown* rose to number 2 in the UK hit parade. *2. n.* The wash basin in the ladies' toilet of a pub in which *birds* have the female equivalent of a *gentleman's was*h when they have *pulled.*

lipstick *1. n.* A dog's *cock,* available in a variety of shimmery colours. *2. n.* The feminine version of *bagpeel.*

lipstick lesbian *n.* Glamorous, feminine female homosexual, commonly found on the Adult Channel or in a wet dream but rarely down the pub.

lipstick on the collar *n.* Unwelcome red marks on the paper following an over enthusiastic wipe of the *freckle* with whatever budget *arsewad* one has been able to find amid the wrecked, *Day After*-style post-Brexit badlands of the supermarket toiletries aisle.

lip stretcher *n.* A particularly girthsome *choad.* A *Pringle tube.* A challenge to a pair of *DSLs.*

lip-syncing *n.* The best bit of a televised *scissor sisters* performance.

liquid allsorts *n.* The non-viscous feculent miscellany that results from an ill-advised binge on the Bertie Bassetts or Pontefract cakes.

liquid bastards *n.* Enthusiastic spermatazoans.

liquid bookmark *n.* A homemade means of marking one's place in the pages of an *art pamphlet.*

liquid gas *1. n.* Believe it or not, gas which has been compressed (or cooled down) and turned to liquid. *2. n.* A wet *fart.*

liquid gold *n.* A cup of tea in Betty's Tearooms.

liquidiser *n.* A powerful eight-pint *piss* that turns a bowl of *bangers and mash* into *brown Windsor soup.*

liquidity trap *1. n.* A perilous financial phenomenon described by JM Keynes, which tends to occur following a stock market meltdown or something. We're probably in the middle of one at the moment. *2. n.* Even more perilously, being imprisoned on the *bog* for hours due to a marathon case of the *tom tits.*

liquid kids *n.* Spooge, spunk, heir gel, baby gravy.

liquid laughter *n.* Puke, psychedelic yodelling, laughing at the grass.

liquid mode *1. n.* "A better reader experience for PDFs on mobile devices," it says here. *2. n.* A dispiriting session of *bum gravy.* As if there were any other kind. '*Ooh, I've had a terrible day, Caroline. I was in liquid mode throughout the whole service.*'

liquid pretzel *n.* A salty, refreshing snack. A somewhat tangled *lobbed rope.*

liquid rage *n.* Fred Funk, merry monk.

liquid squirtilizer *n.* When the farmer's *stools* loosen up a bit. See also *crop spray, blow mud, I could shit between Cyril Smith's legs.*

liquorice allsort *n.* A dark haired woman who frequents both the tanning salon and the tooth-whitening clinic. From her resemblance to the popular Bertie Bassett confectionery homunculus.

liquor portal *n.* The hole in the space/time continuum found outside pubs which transports the inebriated to the safety of their hallways in the blink of an eye. A trans-dimensional science fiction *beer Tardis.*

lirthy *adj.* Both lengthy and girthy.

listening to one's inner convictions *euph.* The phrase Hitler used to explain why he so spent so many hours alone in his locked bedroom.

listen – I think I hear a horseshoe bat *exclam.* Witty form of words to be whispered just before *breaking bad.* Also *you'll probably smell it before* *you see it.*

listen to Smooth's playlist *1. n.* To enjoy the predictable and dismal collection of tedious songs from about four performers that are repeated *ad nauseam* between ads on the popular radio station, leaving the listener unfulfilled. *2. n.* To engage in typically dismal carnal relations with one's long term *significant other*.

listen to them, the children of the night! What music they make! *exclam.* What one should say (preferably in a Transylvanian accent like Bela Lugosi, and with a torch pointing up from under your chin) after *letting off* a gothically crepuscular *air biscuit.* Also *lo, 'tis a raven with a message from Winterfell!*

lite sabre *n.* Male weapon of modest proportions that is nevertheless waved around by its owner as if it were something special.

little & large show *1. n.* Early evening BBC1 series featuring the eponymous, contrastingly sized semi-alive double act, which unaccountably ran from 1978 to 1991. *2. n.* A pair of *Kelly Brooks* in a low-cut top or bikini.

Little Ben *n.* A small *Big Ben*.

little death/petit mort *n. Fr.* In a male, the post-*fuck* feeling of *shagged outity* which is symptomised by the polar opposite of rigor mortis.

little fluffy clouds *exclam.* A phrase which can be used to great effect in the immediate aftermath of a rousing *rumpet voluntary. S*poken in a girlish, nasally congested voice similar to that of Rickie Lee Jones with a heavy cold as heard on the eponymous record by The Orb.

Littlehampton, the Rt Hon member for *euph.* A minuscule and miserable looking *chopper*, as cruelly rumoured to be owned by red-faced, short-*cocked* backbench Tory MP Mark Francois.

little house on the prairie *n.* A *clematis* or *clown's hat.*

little pink bag of shit *n.* An alternative to the more clichéd "little bundle of joy" used to describe a *fanny apple. 'Births: Locksbottom. At the Portland Hospital, London. To Lady Fellatia (née Smegmeaux) and Sir Turdfrith, a boy, Stradivarius, brother to Bendibus and Clitorice. Mother and little pink bag of shit doing well. Deo Gracias.'*

little red riding hood *n. medic.* The *preperitum clitoridis.*

little tadpoles looking for mama *1. n.* Title of a 1960 Chinese animated film; the late Te Wei's first attempt to break away from Western-influenced animation and aim for a more painterly style, it says here. *2. n.* A mid-air *cumshot* on its

way to a lady's face, *tits, arse* and/or back.

liverdance *n.* The involuntarily rhythmic Terpsichorean movements of an extremely heavily *refreshed* reveller. A *dance of the seven ales.*

liver lapels *n. Beef curtains, labia majorcas,* as found on Ed Gein's home-made suit.

live round *n.* An unexpected *shit* when one was only expecting to *pump* out a *fart*.

live rounds in a training exercise, use *v.* To fire potentially dangerous *spammunition* into the field of battle when it might have been more sensible to keep your *bacon bazooka* safely muzzled, *eg.* While having a final *bang* with a departing ex or while enjoying a drunken penetrative *romp* up a chubby waitress with big *tits. 'Why the long face, Boris?' 'Ich bin caught auf using live rounds in ein training exercise, Des.'*

liver sock *1. n.* The *fanny. 2. n.* A *butcher's favourite.*

live streaming *n.* The highly unlikely act of *pissing* on an electric fence and giving oneself a nasty shock up the *hog's eye.*

livin' alright, that's *exclam.* Verbal accompaniment to the act of *spaffing* onto the missus's *poond.* From the Joe Fagin-performed theme tune to 1980s comedy drama *Auf Wiedersehen Pet,* in which he exhorted listeners to "send a little back to the wife".

Livingstone daisies *1. n. bot.* Attractive flowers that come out when the sun shines. *2. n.* Attractive *knockers* that come out when the sun shines, causing taxi drivers to mount the pavement, milkmen to fall down manholes and straw-hatted vicars to ride their bicycles into fruit barrows. *Monocle poppers.*

living will *n.* A binding legal agreement, such that upon any serious injury or sudden death, your executor (*eg.* Flatmate/school janitor, BBC office cleaner, church warden, chief whip) will discreetly remove and "dispose of" your gigantic collection of *jazz.*

lizard rag *n. Aus.* A scaly piece of bedside cloth used for wiping excess *spoff* and *moip* from one's *bloodstick* after *popping the turkey in the oven.*

lizard's lick *n.* A feeble ejaculation that barely clears the *hog's eye;* the unimpressive result of excessive *working from home.* A bankrupt *money shot.* A *gwibble.*

llama's top lip *n.* A *camel's toe.*

Llandudno handbag *n.* A colostomy bag.

Llewelyn-Bowen's cuff *n.* An over-elaborate vagina. A foppish *ragman's coat.*

LNS *abbrev.* Quality time spent peacefully communing with the world. A Late Night Shite.

load *1. n.* 1996 Metallica album. *2. n.* The quantity

of *cock hockle* blown, chucked or shot at the point of orgasm. *3. n.* That which is shed by a lorry driver, while *wanking* in a layby.

loaded *adj. Aus.* To be in need of a great big *shit*. To be *touching cloth.* *"'Curiouser and curiouser" thought Alice, as the white rabbit came scampering past. "I wonder where he's going in such a hurry." "Oh, my dear paws!" he cried. "Oh my fur and whiskers, I'm loaded. If I don't reach the lavatory soon I shall surely papper my grundies."'* (from *Alice's Adventures in Wonderland*, by Lewis Carroll).

loaded for bear *1. adj.* Hunting term, indicating that one is packing particularly impressive ammunition. *2. adj. Fucking* term, indicating that one is packing particularly impressive ammunition.

loading the mag *euph. milit. Thumbing in a slacky.* The act of easing a reluctant *lard-on* into a *Tony Hatch* in a *Frankie Vaughan* film.

load of old shoes falling out of a loft, like a *sim.* Descriptive of a heavy bout of loose, lively diarrhoea. A *flock of pigeons.*

load rage *n.* A violent confrontation in which a purple-faced *bald man* is struck viciously and repeatedly with a *wanking spanner* until he starts crying.

load the dishwasher *v.* Insensitive and offensively chauvinist term; to deposit your *gentleman's relish* inside your old trout's *chum bucket.*

loaf that dare not speak its name *euph.* A freshly baked, crusty *log* that could easily ruin a man-about-town's reputation.

lobcock *n.* A large, flaccid penis such as could be *lobbed* onto a pub table by its drunken owner the way that Michael Elphick hits that fish on the bar in *Withnail and I.*

lob on, lazy *n.* Half a teacake.

lob-on-tomy *1. n.* When a *hard-on*, even a *diamond cutter*, wilts at the thought of an unappealing image (make up your own – probably involving Ann Widdecombe – here). *2. exclam.* One of the late Bobby Ball's less successful catchphrases.

lobotomy bay *n.* Semi-mythical destination of any serious drinking binge.

lob ropes *v.* To *jizz* onto something through thin air, *eg.* A face, some hair, the windscreen of a minor television personality's Seat Alhambra *etc.*

location, location, location *n.* To make a visit to all three aspects a lady's property in one visit, *ie.* Upstairs, downstairs, and *round the back.* *'And now on Channel 4, Location, Location, Location.' 'Hey, I tell you what, love. No offence but I wouldn't mind going location, location, location with that Kirstie Allsopp.'*

lockdown *euph.* A marital *no-entry order*, imposed for any reason. *'Do you fancy another pint?' 'Yeah, why not. I've got nothing to rush home for. I'm on lockdown again after saying her sister looked nice.'*

lockdown cock *n. medic.* Strain or surface abrasion of the *endus bellus*, imparted by increased *frottage* during solitary social distancing.

locked out, Mrs Brown is *euph.* Having *followed through.* *'Apologies, your excellency, but I really must be excused. I've just opened the back doors and it appears that Mrs Brown is locked out again.'*

lockfrown *n.* The expression on a fellow's face, hopefully historically, when he realised he had to summon up the strength to have ten *wanks*, drink fifteen cans and eat twenty bags of crisps every day for the next three months.

lock'n'load *1. phr.* Said in innumerable action movies as the hero leaps into action and cocks his weapon. *2. phr.* Expression used by a saucy *slapper* as she primes a chap's *custard cannon* with a practised snap of the wrist. *3. phr.* Expression used by a jobseeker as he pulls the curtains shut at 8.30am, prior to his fifteenth *tug* of the morning.

lock on, achieve *v.* When mentally thumbing through one's *mammary banks* while *knocking oneself about*, to recollect a particularly debasing erotic episode, thus leading proceedings to conclude in a satisfactory manner.

locksmith *n.* A girl who has an impressive working knowledge of *knobs* and their operation.

locksmith's back pocket, mouth like a *sim.* A term which describes somewhat haphazard dentition. A *pan of burnt chips.*

lodger todger *n. medic.* Erectile dysfunction, *the droop.* Crippling inability to rise to the occasion due to one's mother-in-law or other close family member taking up temporary residence in the marital home.

lodging house cat, fart like a *v.* To *blow off* enthusiastically, repeatedly and malodorously.

loft insulation *n.* A layer of *jazz mags* and dried out *ballpaper*, laid to the required depth of between 250 to 270mm to afford adequate thermal protection in the roof space of a typical bachelor's abode.

log *n. Bum cigar, brown trout, copper bolt.* A *feeshus.*

logacy *n.* The long-lasting *Judi Dench* in a toilet cubicle that is left by a generous *benefactor* for future generations to enjoy.

Logan's run *n.* A particularly aggressive *fist of fury* that produces a telltale red mark on the palm of the hand.

logarhythm *1. n.* In mathematics, a word that

sounds like logarithm, *viz*. The exponent of the power to which a base number must be raised in order to equal a given number. Something like that, anyway. You had to use interpolation and them books by Frank Castle. *2. n.* In *shitting*, the regularity of one's motions. *3. n.* The shaking of one's *arse* in an attempt to break the neck of a persistently dangling *turtle*. The working out of a *simple harmonic motion*. *4. n.* One's regular time of the day on the *choddy clock*.

log book *n.* Literature kept in the smallest room that gives you something to read, in addition to the back of the talcum powder or bleach bottles, when ensconced there for a prolonged period. For whatever reason. Something to leaf through while *operating the 3D printer, eg. The Autotrader, Viz, The Best of Andy Capp.*

log burner *n.* A ferocious phall that provides a handy source of blistering heat around which the family can gather on cold evenings.

log cabin *1. n.* A portaloo. A wendy house for *Meat Loaf's daughter. 2. n.* The *khazi. 3. n.* A pile of *turds* in the *bum sink.*

logdown *n.* The satisying release of a *brown egg* from the *cocoa chute.*

logectomy *n. medic.* Compound word derived from the Latin log (copper bolt) and ectomy (drop). *'I'm pleased to tell you that this morning's logectomy was a complete success.'*

log fire *n.* The pain experienced in the *back body* the morning after eating a sumptiously spicy repast. *Ring sting, Johnny Cash.*

log flume *1. n.* Simultaneously defecating and urinating down the same leg of one's *kex. 2. n.* A *turd* in a pub *pissing* trough. *3. n. medic.* The alimentary canal. A *brown knuckle ride* with many twists and turns that culminates in a refreshing splash into cold water. *3. euph.* In plumbing, a soil pipe, especially a badly installed and complicated one that deviates from the traditional straight vertical drop into a sewer line.

logger's leap *n.* A notably large and forceful *digestive transit* that causes heavy *splashback* when it dives into the *jobby engine*. Named after the long-standing water ride at Thorpe Park amusements.

logging material *n.* Reading matter perused while *chopping butt wood* in the *libratory*. Also *shiterature, loo reads.*

log in *1. v.* To arrive at work, switch on your computer, then immediately disappear for a paid *shit, and similarly 2. v.* When arriving at your place of employment first thing in the morning, to switch on your computer before going for a relaxed *Donald Trump* while the *bastarding*

antiquated piece of *shit* boots up.

log in the woodburner, got a *euph.* A genteel expression of one's urgent need for a *sit down lavatory adventure*. *'And God said unto Noah, I will bring a great flood upon the earth to destroy the corruption and evil that I hath created. Make thee an ark of gopher wood; rooms shalt thou make in the ark, and the length of the ark shall be three hundred cubits, the breadth of it fifty cubits, and the height of it thirty cubits. And you shall fill it with all the animals of the earth; the fowls after their kind, the cattle after their kind and every creeping thing of the ground by his kind, two of every sort shall come unto you, to keep them alive, excepting of course all the kangaroos and that. And Noah said unto the Lord, I'll get it started in a minute, pal, only I've got a log in the woodburner at the moment.'* (from *Genesis* 6:13-15).

logistics *n.* The careful planning that goes into the first *poop* of the day.

log off *v.* To *drop the shopping.*

log of lamb *n.* A *pan-filler* the morning after a night of heavy drinking topped off with a large kebab with *all the shit.*

logo lout *n.* A *scrote* dressed in heavily be-trademarked garb.

log on *v.* To *park one's breakfast* on any suitable horizontal surface, for example the boss's desk after winning the lottery.

log pile house *1. n.* In the children's story *The Gruffalo*, the home of the snake. *2. n.* The *Rick Witter*; the home of the *blind dirt snake. 'Can you put the bins out for me please, love?' 'I'll do it in a minute. I'm just off to spend a well deserved half hour in the log pile house.'*

log splitter *1. n.* A rugged device consisting of hydraulic rams and a sharpened wedge, used to simplify and expedite the process of preparing firewood. *2. n.* An ossified mat of congealed *winnets. Rhino horn.*

logzilla *n.* A monstrous *duty* that causes onlookers to run away screaming.

lollipop lady *n.* A woman who is partial to the occasional *slice of cheesecake.*

LOL/lol *acronym.* Leathery Old Labia. *'I just bumped into your nan at the shops lol'*

lolly bag *n.* The male scrotum.

lollygagger *1. n.* A lazy person, slacker or ne'er-do-well, it says here. *2. n.* Lady blessed by Mother Nature with a tongue long enough to wrap right around the shaft of one's *pocket rocket*. Not that she'd want to, so it's all academic, really.

lolly stick *n.* Anything pointlessly, but intentionally added to a pile of *shite*. A *turd's barnacle*. *'Has* *anyone seen that Big Brother's Little Brother? What a fucking lolly stick that is.'*

lolo *1. v.* Internet abbreviation; to log off before logging on. *2. v.* Of a chap who has retired to the *throne room* anticipating a leisurely, sat-down perusal of the delights of the interweb, only to find the arrival of his movement is as swift as an *otter off the bank*, and has concluded before his device has even finished its start-up rigmarole.

LOMBARD/lombard *acronym.* Loads Of Money But A Right Dickhead, *eg.* A professional footballer, someone who owns a carpet warehouse or Jay Kay out of Jamiroquai.

London museum visitor *euph.* A fellow who is quite happy to use both the *front and rear entrances, viz.* One who is quite happy to spend his time "poking around in the V&A". See also *play your cards right and I'll take you up the V&A.*

loneliest sport, the *1. n.* Boxing. *2. n. Wanking.*

loneliness of the long distance drinker, the *n.* Falling asleep on public transport after a heavy session *on the piss* and waking up in unfamiliar surroundings. For example, nodding off on the tube on the way home from the Ealing Beer Festival and waking up in Stratford, to pick an entirely random example.

lonely Sanchez *n.* There's no nice way to put this. A finger up the *bum*, then wiped under the nose while masturbating. This country

lone piper *n.* A single, *wanking* Scotsman historically employed to wake up the Queen Mum at Balmoral.

Lone Ranger *n.* The act of wearing a craftily pilfered pair of the wife's/wife's sister's/next door neighbour's/next door neighbour's sister's *dunghampers* over the face, in the style of the masked 1950s television hero, while embarking on a voyage of *self discovery.* Also known as a *musk mask, Spider-man wank* or *fentilator.*

long bald *adj.* Descriptive of the sort of middle-aged man's coiffure consisting of a screamingly bald head flanked by longer but poorly-nourished, stringy hair, *eg.* That of Newcastle Theatre Royal panto stalwart Clive Webb.

long ball game *1. n.* In football, a series of aimless pokes in the direction of the box in the hope of scoring. *2. n.* In bed, a series of aimless *pokes* in the direction of the *box* in the hope of *scoring.*

long distance Clara *1. n.* Wholesome female lorry driver in erstwhile BBC children's series *Pigeon Street. 2. n.* A *lorry driver's lunchbreak, ie.* Having a *crap* in a lay-by. *'Come in Steady Eddie. When are you expected back at the depot?' 'Control, this is Steady Eddie. I'm currently on the A66 but I had*

a wick Ginsters for breakfast at Abingdon Services, so I'm going to need ten minutes for a long distance Clara in the Barnard Castle lay-by.'

long hard think *n.* Bout of *self-help* performed without recourse to visual stimuli. See also *pipe dream, frigment of the imagination. 'I'm going to go away and have a long hard think about that, your royal highness.'*

long haul fanny *n. medic.* Condition of the female *farmyard area* caused by prolonged sitting in a cramped, crowded space, chief symptom of which is a distinctly malodorous *quiff.* Also known as *frequent flyer fent* or *coach class crotch.*

long haul shite *n.* A challenging *red-eye* marathon, for example on Boxing Day. A good magazine and/or DVT flight socks are essential, and it is a good idea to get up occasionally and walk around the *log cabin* to keep the circulation going in the legs.

long in the tit *adj.* Descriptive of an ageing female (or Lord Owen). *'I tell you what though, vicar, even though she's a bit long in the tit now, I reckon I'd still give Dame Joan Bakewell one.'*

long march south *n.* Embarking on a gruelling, time-consuming expedition with the eventual aim of *buttering up* the missus's frigid nether regions.

long piss *euph.* A *shit* that you don't want people to know that you *shat. 'You were in the facilities a long time just then, your majesty.' 'I was just having a long piss, Archbishop. Just having a long piss.'*

longshanks *n.* One who is blessed/cursed with a very low-swinging *chicken skin handbag.* A *rantallion.*

long soak in the bath *euph.* A lady's massive *wank. 'Just off for a long soak in the bath, love.'*

long term economic plan *n.* A financial strategy put in place when you have no idea what you're doing. *'Honey, why have you spent all of our grocery money on beer, cigarettes and pornographic magazines again?' 'Don't worry, dear. It's all part of my long term economic plan.'*

lonk *v. Germ.* To *shit* oneself on orgasm.

Looby *n. rhym. slang.* A *Peter O'Toole.* From the companion of erstwhile television puppet character Andy Pandy (yet another one for the youngsters there); Looby-Lu = Barney McGrew.

loogistics *n.* Gathering together your phone and a copy of the *Autotrader*, checking the current status of your *bogroll*, air freshener, water, beer *etc.*, before you sit down to drop a massive *earthing cable.*

look after the stall *1. exclam.* Something a market trader in *EastEnders* says to another character approximately every thirty seconds. *2. exclam.*

Something somebody suffering a sudden attack of the *Earthas* shouts as they sprint for the *bog*.

look at *v.* To masturbate euphemistically. *'Did you look at that porn film I lent you yesterday?' 'Yeah, I had a quick look at it.'*

look at him getting plenty while the rest of us scrap for crumbs *exclam.* Whilst viewing a film or television sex scene, a frustrated announcement from a gentlemen who's *had none* in a good while. Typically uttered in the presence of his good lady in a thinly veiled – and fruitless – bid to spur her into *a bit*.

look at me when I'm talking to you boy! *exclam.* Something to say after *dropping a gut*.

look for badgers *v.* To cruise for gay sex. Also *stretch one's legs*.

look for Burt *v.* To yoff, hoy up, spew, speak Welsh, sing a rainbow. From the common call of "Buuur-rrrrtttttt" as one voids the stomach contents following over-enthusiastic consumption of alcoholic beverages and spicy sweetmeats.

look for Lord Lucan *v.* To walk into a pub while theatrically looking in every direction as if expecting to see a waiting friend, when in reality your sole purpose is to make it to the *bogs* unchallenged before *shitting* your pants.

looking at tractors *euph.* Surfing the worldwide web for *Frankie*. *'Neil doesn't work here any more. He was caught looking at tractors.'*

looking for a bean in 10lbs of bacon, like *sim.* Expressive of the level of difficulty typically encountered when attempting to locate *the bald man in the boat*. *'Deborah was powerless to resist. The successful entrepreneur's eyes burnt into hers like agates. His muscular businessman's arms enfolded her body as she felt herself being swept away in a Bex Bissell of passion. 'Touch me, Theo!' she cried. 'Touch me in that secret place where every woman yearns to be touched!' 'I would do, love,' he replied. 'But to be honest with you, it's like looking for a bean in 10lbs of bacon down here.''* (from *The Lady and the Dragon* by Barbara Cartland).

looking for a lost ball in the rough *euph.* Trying to find a *clematis* hidden in the tangled undergrowth on *Terry Waite's allotment*.

looking for change in the hairy purse *n.* Deep, middle finger coin-sorting movement popular with *gusset-typing* old ladies at supermarket checkouts.

looking for Pokemon *phr.* Plausible explanation proffered by someone caught *dumping* in a shop doorway, nicking tools from a garden shed, *pulling the pope's hat off* in park shrubbery, or stealing underwear from a washing line *etc.*

looks like he can throw a dart *euph.* Said of a proper fat *bastard*. *'That Prince Andrew looks like he can throw a dart these days.'*

looniform *n.* Characteristic garb of one who favours screaming at the traffic as an occupation, usually consisting of slippers, bobble hat, a 1970s jacket and trousers that clear the ankles by a good three inches. Also the sort of outfit that wows them on the catwalk at London Fashion Week.

loon pipe *n. Anus.*

loop the loop *v.* To order a *vertical bacon sandwich* to *eat out* and a *drink on a stick* for the lady, *No.69* on the menu.

loo read *n.* Any book or magazine best perused while defecating. *Shiterature.*

loose at the hilt *adj.* Having diarrhoea, *the Brads*.

loose cannon *n.* A seated chap's *light artillery*, exposed in the field due to the shortness of his shorts. *'A-hem, you've got a loose cannon there, vicar.'*

loose clacker *n. coll.* A herd of *ten-to-twoers*. Ropey *cabbage*. The group of girls remaining as yet unclaimed at night club chucking out time. *Floor sweepings.*

loose fries in the bag *euph.* Descriptive of a feeling of serendipitous sexual jubilation on discovering the *bird* one is *copping off* with has hidden extras, *eg.* She has a shaved *snatch*, is wearing stockings, is a *swallower.* From the joyous feeling experienced when, on finishing one's *Maccy Dee's*, one finds extra chips in the bottom of the bag.

loose lips *n.* Affectionate description of a woman who has been *cocked more times than Davy Crockett's rifle.*

loosener *1. n.* In cricket, a wayward first delivery of the morning session. *2. n.* In *shitting*, a wayward first delivery of the morning session, possibly as a result of a bad pint or dodgy *catbab.*

loose, on the *adj.* Of a *dirty lady*, frothing like bottled *Bass.* Having a *wide on.* *'Ooh, that new Michael Bublé record's really got me on the loose, Derek.'*

loose sausage meat *n.* A flaccid penis which cannot be funnelled into a condom. *Stuffing the marshmallow.* *'Sorry love, my sausage meat seems a bit loose this evening.'*

loose shunting *n.* A *dog's marriage* with a *clown's pocket. Fucking the night.*

loose the juice *phr.* Of a gentleman, to release his *spendings. 'What a fuckin' night! She stuck her finger up me balloon knot and I loosed the juice all over her tits!' 'That Mother Teresa is quite a girl, your holiness.'*

looviathan *n.* A *sea biscuit* of such gargantuan proportions that, once flushed, it forms the subject of myriad breathlessly recounted legends amongst grizzled sewermen.

loovuzela *n.* See *poopoozela*.

Lord Foulbowel *n. prop.* Honorary title for one whose *lower chamber* is a rich source of *brownhouse gases*, eg. A flatulent Coventry City fan who spends 72 hours in a car accompanied by 4 friends as they attempt to visit all 92 football league grounds to raise money for charity.

Lord of the fleas *n.* A gentleman of the road.

lord of the fries *n.* A morbidly corpulent chip shop regular.

Lord of the pies *n.* A *salad dodger*, a *double sucker*. One whose *big bones* and *glands* are always dragging him into Greggs.

lord of the rim *n.* A fabled *digestive transit* of such gargantuan proportions that it rears up out of the water to peer over the edge of the pan like an all-seeing eye.

Lord Winston's moustache *n.* A particularly hairy and poorly trimmed *biffer,* named after the exuberant face fungus of the popular ennobled telly boffin, test-tube *fanny apple* pioneer and former leading *twat mechanic* Dr Robert Winston. Also *Rhodes Boysons, whack-os.*

lordy *n.* A posh Geordie.

Loretta Swit *n. prop. rhym. slang.* A *Brad Pitt.* Named in honour of the *three-dick-gobbed* actress who played Major Margaret "Hot Lips" Houlihan in depressing and seemingly endless 1970s US situation comedy *M*A*S*H.*

lorry driver's breakfast, fanny like a *sim.* Descriptive of a *clopper* which is cheap, greasy and requires plenty of sauce before consumption.

lorry driver's lunchbreak *n.* A *crap* in a layby, a *long distance Clara.*

lose a slipper *v.* To evacuate one's *Camillas* with such ferocity that it causes one to walk funny until the body eventually rebalances its fibre levels.

lose a vote of no confidence *euph.* To end up with a messy outcome (and possibly get thrown out of your home) when *twisting on nineteen.*

loser cruiser *n.* Any form of public transport used predominantly by members of the urban underclass, *eg.* The Number 585 Otara to Central bus in Aukland, New Zealand. Also, somewhat judgementally, known as a *scum shovel.*

lose some weight *v.* To perform a *digestive transit, drop a dress size.* 'Sorry, Your majesty. I need to lose some weight. Could you point me at the nearest shitter, pal?'

lose the marathon *v.* To take a long time to complete an act of *excreeshus.* Derivation unknown. 'That crap took me so long I would've lost the marathon.'

lose the toss *1. v.* Of a sportsman, to be unsuc-cessful in a coin-based wager. *2. n.* Of a builder or other tradesman, to *spoff* into the lady of the house's *dunghamper* drawer while she is out.

lose your darts *v.* To become inexplicably impotent, or otherwise unable to *raise your throwing arm.* 'I don't quite know how to put this, doctor, but I seem to have lost my darts, if you know what I mean.' 'There's no need to worry, Mr Brown. This happens to a lot of men of your age, especially those who work in stressful occupations such as contract publishing and the Cornish fish restaurant business. I'll put you on a course of Bongo Bill's Banjo Pills.'

lose your manners *v.* To *step on a duck* in polite company.

lose your mess *v.* To ejaculate, *shoot your load, chuck your muck, blow your beans.*

lose your pearls *euph.* To *lose your mess.*

los lobos *n. Sp. Brewer's droop* caused by an excessive intake of San Miguel, Sol or some other cheap Spanish beer. 'Sorry dear, not tonight. I've got los lobos.'

lost deposit *1. n.* Forfeiture of an election payment as a result of winning insufficient votes. *2. n. Cracking one off* in a darkened room but the *jizz* is nowhere to be seen when you turn the lights on.

LOTIMTO/lotimoto *abbrev.* Lovely On The Inside, Minging On The Outside.

lottery wings *n.* Larger, looser version of *bingo wings.*

lotties *n. Lils, dugs.*

loudmouth soup *n.* Beer.

Louganis *n.* When *dropping the kids off at the pool,* an acrobatic *turd* that strikes its head on the rim of the seat in the course of somersaulting gracefully into the water. Named after American diving champ Greg, who suffered concussion when he *stotted* his *noggin* off the board while attempting a reverse 2½ pike at the 1988 Seoul Olympics.

Louis *v.* To squeeze out a large and stubborn piece of *bum rubbish* with such force that one pulls a face like Satchmo going for a top E, and then has to mop the top of one's head with a handkerchief. A *stretch Armstrong* that hopefully ends with one singing "Oh yeeeeah!".

lounge with the furniture removed, like a *sim.* A spacious *liver sock* into which one could momentarily fancy fitting a table tennis table.

love bat *n.* During a game of sexual intercourse, the short, stout implement with which the man strikes his wife's *cunker.* See also *slag bat.*

love beads *n. milit.* Road surface farm animal containment provision which provides exceedingly fleeting and intermittent sexual stimulation for squaddies in the backs of "rumpety-pumpety" army trucks. A cattle grid.

love bumps *n. Funbags, guns of Navarone.*

love cough *n.* The *dropping forwards* of a *lady's hat*. A *queef, Lawley kazoo, frampton, fanny fart.*

love gloves *n.* Condoms. Also *rubber johnnies, dunkys, blobs, child catchers.*

love hinge *n.* The area of a larger lady's lower stomach that has to be lifted out of the way, like the lid on a piano, before an act of personal intimacy can take place. The *poond, fupa, blubber beret* or *fat hat.*

love juice *n.* That liquid produced in the *Billingsgate box* upon which the *skin boat* sails. Often referred to as *luv jooz* in illiterate 1970s *scud literature.* As if we can talk. *Blip, moip.*

love lane *euph.* Poetic euphemism for a *bird's clopper. Henrietta Street,* the *bower of bliss.*

love lift *n.* A vertical *shaft* that should ideally be accompanied by the ringing of a little bell.

lovely personality, a *1. euph.* Fugliness. *2. euph.* Big bones.

love palace *n.* Coarse version of *cunt.*

love puff *n.* Gentle and romantic *air biscuit* launched in the direction of one's partner in bed, often the morning after a *Ruby,* in an attempt to cement the intimacy of the moment.

loves a good musical *euph.* Said of a chap who is a big fan of Eurovision. *'Well who'd have thought he'd be married with kids? I always had him down as loving a good musical.'*

love sausage *n.* Big pink *banger* served with *hairy love spuds.*

love socket *n.* The *fadge,* plugging-in point for the *main cable.* Also *rocket socket, serpent socket, spam socket.*

love spuds *n.* Starch-filled root vegetables cultivated in the *shreddies.*

love torpedo *n.* Something that *goes off* with a big bang at the moment of contact. A *one pump chump*'s weapon of choice.

love tripe *n.* The savoury folds of tender flesh around a *bird's goalmouth.* The *labia majorcas* and *minorcas. Goofy's ears.*

love truncheon *n.* A *copper's torch* or *dead German hanging out of a window.*

love tunnel *n.* That place in which *Percy the small pink engine* shunts his *load.* For about three minutes before he *blows his stack* and his *back wheels come off.*

love wind *n.* A *queef.*

lower decking *n.* Deliberately not flushing away a *dreadnought* in one's work toilets, then hiding in the adjoining cubicle to savour the next occupant's reaction.

lower yourself *v.* To *rub one out* over less classy *fodder* than that which you would normally have of done. *'Well, I think you've really lowered yourself there, PeeWee.'*

low hanging fruit *1. n.* Some office-based jargon that refers to easily achievable tasks, obvious redundancy candidates or some such load of *old wank. 2. n. polit.* Funding which can be cut back easily during a belt-tightening budget. *3. n. Nads* that hang out of badly designed shorts. *4. n.* Long, leathery *plums* as sported by old *gimmers* such as Mick Jagger. You would imagine. See also *bingo bollocks. 5. n.* Pendulous *knockers. Knee shooters.*

low key big hog *n.* A massive *donger* on someone who you wouldn't necessarily expect to be so blessed. Dappy out of N-Dubz has a *low key big hog,* if you believe what you hear from those in the know, such as Dappy out of N-Dubz.

low loaders *n.* Saggy breasts with a minimal amount of ground clearance. *Toe shooters.*

lowthario *1. n.* A *fanny rat* who will *cattle* any old *boiler. 2. n.* An amorous midget.

LRF *abbrev.* Low Resolution Fox – a female who appears to be attractive from a long distance, but is in fact unbelievably ugly close up. A *twenty-four sheeter.*

LTD *abbrev.* Theatrical digs shorthand used by travelling musicians to indicate accommodation where the rent may be reduced in return for sexual favours. Landlady Takes Dick.

Lübefraumilch *n.* Cheap German plonk that eases a fellow's way along love's causeway. *Knicker oil, pant stripper, WD69.*

lubricated Lockets *n.* Type of *lavatory adventure* enjoyed following a heavy night on the brown beer; simply sitting down on the *throne* and raising one's heels to fire a frictionless fusilade of cough-sweet-sized nuggets effortlessly into the *pan.*

Lucan *n. prop.* Name give to a *brown trout* which enters the water at such a velocity that it manages to escape round the bend, named after the well known homicidal nob who similarly, it would seem, entered the water and simply disappeared.

Lucifer's waterfall *n. Cranberry dip.*

lucky dip *n.* That fortunate, final wipe of one's *ring* which reveals a hidden *clod,* thus preventing *pappered pants* and an *autographed gusset.*

lucky Pierre *n.* In *botting* circles, the busiest link in a three man *bum chain*; the filling in a *shirt lifter* sandwich. A *botter* who is simultaneously a *bottee.* A *happy medium, double adapter.*

lullage *n.* The overhanging flab seen on fat lasses wearing trousers they fully intend to slim into. A *gunt, poond, muffin top.*

lulu *n.* A lady who is getting on a bit, but is still worthy of *lengthage.* A *gilf. 'Hey, that Lulu's a bit of a lulu, isn't she, eh, your honour, eh?'*

lumber *1. n.* A raft of tightly packed *turds* occluding the toilet water surface in a *chod bin* after an afternoon testing the "all you can eat" buffet at an Aberdeen Steak House. *2. n. coll.* A unspecified quantity of erect penii.

lumberjack's homework *euph.* The act of waiting till you get back from work before *dropping your logs. 'I'm dying for a shit, Dave. But I knock off in five so I may as well bake it a bit longer and do a spot of lumberjack's homework.'*

lumberjill *n.* A hatchet-faced woman that fells a fellow's *mighty redwood.*

lumpyjumper *n.* A witty, light-hearted, non-sexist epithet for a female colleague. *'Oi, lumpyjumper. Make us a cup of tea, will you.'*

lunch at South Mimms *euph.* An act of *cumulonimbus.*

lunchbox *n.* In British tabloid journalism, that conspicuous bulge in athlete Linford Christie's shorts, where he used to keep his sandwiches, a carton of Ribena, a Twix and an apple.

lunchboxing *n.* Unbelievably perverse sexual practice which makes a *Cleveland Steamer* sound about as rude as getting a peck on the cheek off Julie Andrews.

lunching at the Lazy Y *v. Dining out* cowboy style, on *hairy pie,* beans and coffee.

lunch 'n' learn *1. n.* Tedious work event which will ruin your midday meal and from which you will recall nothing. *2. n. Dining at the Y* under the friendly *O-level* tutelage of a more experienced ladyfriend.

lunchtime recital *n.* When a pair of *book readers* retire to the works lavvies for a prandial *pink oboe* duet.

lung butter *n.* Phlegm, *green smoking oysters.*

lung-grabber *n.* An act of James Herriot-style shoulder-deep *fisting,* which must be possible as there's loads of it to watch on the internet. Apparently.

lung hammers *n.* Peculiarly unpleasant *spaniels' ears.*

lung nog *n.* Following a cracking night *on the pop* and the *cancer sticks,* the frothy posset of yellow or green spume barked out first thing in the morning. A *prairie oyster.*

lung rocket *n.* A cigarette. Also *coffin nail, tab, cancer stick etc.*

lungry *adj.* Having an appetite for cigarettes. *'Giz a drag on that, your excellency. I gave up for new year and now I'm proper fucking lungry.'*

lung warmer *n.* A cigarette. *'You couldn't give us a shot on your lung warmer could you, pal? I'm fucking gasping here.'*

lung warts *n. Stits, fried eggs. Parisian breasts.*

lurpy *n. Can.* Heterosexual *horatio.*

lush puppies *n.* Those grey slip-on brogues or loafers worn with white socks by middle-aged, *turps-nudging* "oldest swinger in town" types. *'Oi, Ho-Chi Minh or whatever your fucking name is. Where've you put me lush puppies?'*

lusty glaze *1. n. geog.* A small but popular beach on the outskirts of Newquay, it says here. *2. n. Perseverance soup.*

Luton, a *n.* Pubic hairstyle named after the popular Bedfordshire airport. An amateurish attempt at a *landing strip,* but with patches of different length *bush* dotted around at random.

Luton-to-Dunstable busway *n.* The perineum or *twernt, tinter, taint, gooch, biffin bridge, notcher, smelly bridge, carse etc.* From the fact that "it's the route from a shithole to a stinkhole", *via* Houghton Regis.

luxury gap, the *1. n.* Title of a 1983 album by Sheffield synth-popsters Heaven 17, which includes the hit singles *Come Live with Me, Crushed by the Wheels of Industry* and *Temptation* (feat. Carol Kenyon). *2. n.* The *taint, Baker Street concourse, Tuns Lane interchange etc.*

LVC *abbrev.* A particularly impressive *Bristol Channel.* From the name of the famous Harry Fowler-lookylikey Spaghetti western actor Lee Van Cleavage.

lychees *n. Chinese gooseberries.*

lying in state *euph.* In the grip of an epic hangover which leaves one bedridden and suffering vivid hallucinations that hundreds of peasants are filing mournfully passed one's open casket, a bit like Lenin in the Kremlin but not looking quite so chipper.

lying king, the *n.* Name given to the *twat* in the pub who's has been there, seen that, and done it all; the guy who's *shagged* supermodels, knocked out Mike Tyson, drunk Oliver Reed under the table, *etc.,* but in reality has done *fuck all* and still lives with his nan.

Lymeswold *n.* Mild, blue, soft *knob cheese. Full fat fromunder, knacker barrel, Fred Leicester.*

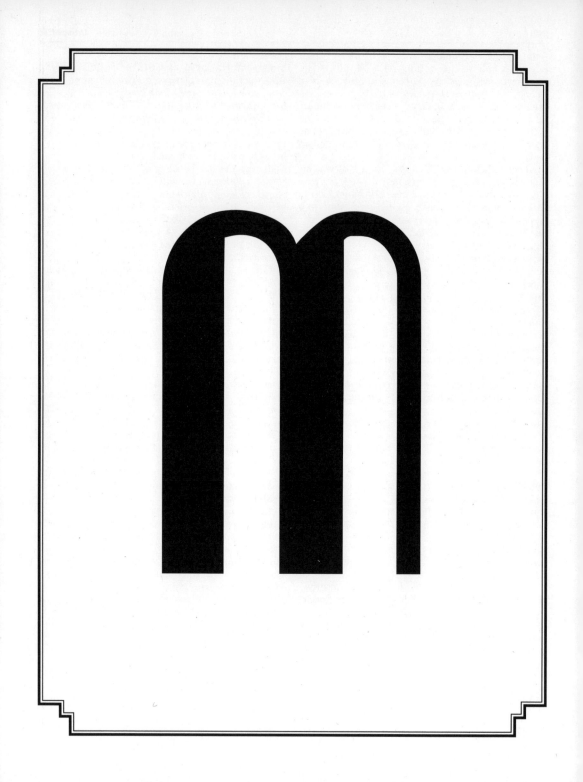

Mabel syrup *n.* Old *bird's flange juice. Olive oil, OAP soup, olden syrup.*

MacArthur Park *n.* An *arse cake* that's taken "so long" to bake and feels like it's never going to end.

Macaulay Culkin's catflap, an arse like *sim.* Extremely violent *rabbit tods*, akin to the air rifle pellets used by the eponymous youngster to thwart the burglars' first advance in *Home Alone.*

macaw smugglers *n.* "Big" John Holmes's *keks.*

Macbeth *n.* while sitting on the *bog* straining, the release of an apparently ferocious *windy pop* that comes to naught. A *dropped gut* that is "full of sound and fury, signifying nothing", as William Shakespeare had it in the famous toilet soliloquy from the Scottish Play. *Macbeth*, that is.

Maccy dees *n.* Affectionate nickname for a popular fast food restaurant, or comestibles purchased therefrom. *'Fancy a Maccy dees, Mr President?' 'Bigly. I'll have three and then shit myself for afters.'*

Maccy diesel *n.* The appetising, odorous fog of vaporised cooking oil that emanates from the popular chain of fast food restaurants and attracts packs of gourmandising customers from miles around.

Maccy pee *n.* Surreptitious use of the toilet facilities in a certain well-known fast food restaurant when you're busting for a *slash* but have no intention of purchasing food or drink. Also *McPiss.*

machelor *n.* A married bachelor, *viz.* A chap who plays the field, but keeps a little something at home for when all else fails. *'Today's birthdays: Maximilian Hell, Slovakian astronomer, 1720; Maria Reiche, German mathematician and archaeologist, 1903; Jeffrey Archer, athlete, author, politician, machelor, 1940.'*

mac in the bath, I wouldn't wear my *exclam.* Expression of a gentleman's unwillingness to don a prophylactic sheath on his *cock end.* Also *I wouldn't wear my wellies on the beach.* Coined in a *Viz Sid the Sexist* cartoon back in 1803.

mack *n.* A rumpled penis, *tadger.*

Mackem dandruff *n.* Pastry crumbs.

mackem-ole *n.* Mushy peas – as made famous by Peter Mandelson's visit to a north eastern chippy some years ago.

mackerel *1. n.* A *pimp*, controller of prostitutes. A *tart farmer, flapmonger, fanny magnate. 2. n.* The *tarts* he farms. *3. n. coll. Cabbage, crumpet, blart, tussage, knob fodder.*

mackerel microphone *n.* The bit of his missus that a fellow presses his lower face against, horse-racing-commentator-style, while carefully adjusting the settings on her *chapel hat pegs* when he is attempting to *call Radio Tokyo.* The *cleft, quacker* or *furry hoop.*

Madam Palm and her five sisters *n.* A hand when used for five minutes of harmless fun that will certainly result in its owner being cast into a Lake of Fire for all eternity by our infinitely merciful Lord. A *dick skinner.* Also *Palmela Handerson. 'I'm just nipping off to bed with Madam Palm and her five sisters.'*

madam's apple *n.* A warning sign that the stunning Thai temptress with a large *pair* you have picked up in a Bangkok bar may also turn out to be equipped with *plums* and a *tummy banana.*

Madam Twoswords *n.* A multitasking actress in a *stick vid* or *art pamphlet* who has a gentleman's waxy *Charlie* in each hand. A *crane operator, downhill skier.*

mad as a lorry *adj.* About as *radge* as it is possible to be. *In the soft drinks aisle.*

mad cow disease *1. n. medic.* Viral infection caught off cheap pies. *2. n. medic.* A monthly hormonal condition causing distress to married men's ears. *Rag rage, tammy huff, blob strop.*

made in Brighton *euph.* An object that leaves the observer in no doubt that its owner is *good with his hands, eg.* A leather cap, a man bag, a nearly empty tube of anal lube.

Madeley *n.* A bloke who feels comfortable talking about relationships, star signs, *Sex and the City, Ally McBeal* and *shit* like that.

Madeley's clipboard *n.* A flimsy defence put up in a vain attempt to hide a raging erection in the presence of, to pick an example entirely at random, a television studio full of swimwear models. Also *Parky's clipboard, Wossy's desk.*

Madeline Allbright *n. prop. rhym. slang. US.* An *excreeshus*, a *pop.*

madman's arse *euph.* Descriptive of an extremely unruly hairstyle, *eg.* That barnet sported by erstwhile gun-toting "Wall of Sound" murderer Phil Spector.

Madonna's nightie, up and down like *sim.* Phrase used by parliamentary sketch writers to describe the behaviour of over-eager MPs trying to get on the telly during Prime Minister's Questions.

mad woman's shit, all over like *sim.* Descriptive of something extremely disorganised and chaotic. *"'I really must apologise for the most dreadfully untidy state of my study, Mrs Fezzypeg," said Mr Pickwick as he anxiously cleared a bundle of papers off the chair nearest to the fire, motioning at his visitor to be seated. "Only my Tax Return is supposed to be in tomorrow and as usual, my bank statements are all over the room like mad woman's shit."'* (from *The*

Pickwick Papers by Charles Dickens).

MAFFNAR/maffnar *acronym.* Miserable As Fuck For No Apparent Reason. A female state of mind which can't be put down to being *on the blob,* menopausal or still miffed that you called her by her sister's name during an intimate moment. '*I don't understand it, mate. I stopped at the petrol station for a bunch of flowers and a box of Ferrero Rocher on the way home, but the mardy cow's gone all maffnar again. Fancy a pint?*'

mag dump *1. n.* Firing continuously at a target until your magazine is out of ammunition. *2. n.* Disposing of *grumble* continuously into a hedgerow until your backpack is out of *shooting fodder.*

Maggie *euph.* A woman who refuses to take it *up the shitter.* Named in honour of the late Mrs Thatch's famously side-splitting assertion, made at the 1980 Conservative Party Conference, that she was "not for turning".

magic carpet *n.* A small layer of cloth which prevents any distasteful *ball-on-ball action* from occurring when two professional footballers are *double teaming.*

magic carpet ride *n.* A *rattle* with a hairy lady that makes your slippers curl up at the ends.

magic circle *1. n.* A group of conjurors who never reveal their secrets. *2. n.* Dynamo's *nipsy.*

magic Harpic ride *n.* A mysterious journey of Oriental delight, sponsored by your local curry house. '*Come to the Curry Capital (formerly the Rupali), Bigg Market, Newcastle upon Tyne, and we promise you a magic Harpic ride which will last all night.*'

magician *euph.* A pal who *knows what's in his flowerbeds.* From the fact that, on a night out, he will often "disappear with a poof".

magician's hankie *1. n.* A *shite* that just keeps on going and going, like the endless knotted cloths pulled out of conjurors' hats, pockets, ears, and sleeves. *2. n.* A *botty burp* which, to the surprise of the assembled audience, continues to emerge over an astounding length of time, and in a multitude of audibly separate segments.

magician's knickers *n.* Pants that keep disappearing up one's *arse.*

magician, the *n.* The name given to the *knacker* in the pub who has the gift of making people disappear. '*Fuck me, Dave. Here's the magician. I'm off.*'

magic jelly bean *1. n.* Probably the title of a children's book. And if it isn't, it should be. Some stand-up comedian should write it. Come on, David Baddiel. *2. n.* The *clematis.* Also *wail*

switch, devil's doorbell, panic button, starter button.

magicking the beans *v.* The late Gareth Hunt's *wanking* action.

magic sheet *n.* Often seen in American TV movies, an enchanted blanket which clings to an actress through some invisible force, discretely covering her *fission chips.*

Magners Ver Magnusson *n.* A man of small stature who, once suitably *refreshed* on a small amount of cider, becomes convinced he is a twenty-stone Viking strongman. Also *two can Van Damme, Tinny Mallet, Cadbury, two pot screamer, half pint Harry, drambo* or *two pint Tyson.*

magnificent seven *n.* The frankly unlikely scenario of getting the opportunity to unload one's *weapon* in every available orifice on a casual *significant other.*

magnificent six *n.* The same act as above, but performed on Daniella Westbrook.

magnifiscent *adj.* Miasmatically splendid, specifically used when referring to a notably potent *dropped hat.* '*I say, your majesty. That Bakewell you just done was fucking magnifiscent. Now would you let me out of the sleeping bag?*'

magnifitits *n.* A remarkable pair of *top bollocks* found swinging around inside the T-shirt of a *Love Island* contestant or a Brazilian weather girl. '*Christ on drums, vicar. Check out the maginifitits on her!*'

magnify *v.* Of a gentleman, to trim back his pubic foliage in order to create the illusion that his *endowment* is more substantial than it actually is. '*Did you see the chopper on that stripper tonight, Ada?*' '*Aye I did, Dolly. But don't be too impressed – it was tied off and magnified.*'

magnolia *1. n.* A neutral, inoffensive wall-covering. *2. n.* A lady who "goes with anything".

mahogany chair leg *n.* An unusually wide, closely grained and uncomfortable *stool,* which appears to have been turned on a lathe by a Victorian craftsman in the days when things were built to last.

mahogany yacht *n.* A rudderless floating vessel constructed of faecal matter, common to the inshore areas of East Coast holiday resorts in the 1950s. '"*That's a piss-poor effort at the breast stroke, Dick,*" *chortled Julian.* "*And keep your mouth shut or you will swallow that mahogany yacht,*" *warned Anne.*' (from *Five Slum It in Southend* by Enid Blyton).

maidenhead *1. n.* Town in Berkshire. *2. n. medic.* A lass's *Bill Wyman, cherry* or *virgin string,* that can apparently be snapped by riding a horse, as it was in Catherine the Great's case.

mailed and sent *adj. rhym. slang. Whitley Bay* as a row of tents.

main cable *n.* A big single-pin *plug*.

maison de tolerance *n. Fr.* A brothel. Also *boutique frappante, maison de mauvaise réputation, magasin de frottage et remorqueur, ferme de Francoise.*

majesticles *n.* Regally magnificent *orbs*, perhaps presented on a velvet cushion by a cringing, liveried footman.

Major Morgan *1. n.* Early electronic handheld game which, if its grittily realistic television advertising was anything to go by, would cause an unpopular child to instantly become a sort of playground Pied Piper. *2. n. rhym. slang.* A gentleman's generative member. *'Oi Shirl, go and fetch the death and disasters. I've only been and caught me bleedin' Major Morgan in the Thousand Island dip on me Cliff Bennett and the Rabble Rousers again.'*

make a bald man cry *v.* To masturbate. *'Have you seen that Colombian triple jumper on the front page of the FT today? It's enough to make a bald man cry.'*

make a clog *v.* At the climax to an act of onanistic *self delight*, to discharge one's *custard rifle* into a sock. From the fact that, after being left for a few days, said item of hosiery becomes as rigid as a piece of traditional Dutch wooden footwear. *'What are you doing in the shed, Ruud?' 'Making a clog, dear.'*

make a cornet *v.* When you exhaust your supply of *bog roll* and are reduced to wiping your *freckle* with the remaining tube, like an animal. To *roll the crevice, chip and dip. 'I ran out of bum wad last night, so I had to make a fekkin' cornet and shove it down the back of the radiator.'*

make a pie out of that! *exclam.* Something to say after dropping a *beefy eggo*. Also *is that you, Elvira?; Harpo speaks; ah … Ludwig; I'll name that tune in one; there goes the cockle train etc.*

make babies *v.* To go *bone jumping*, to fornicate with the object of *dropping a tadpole in a young lady's beer.*

make friends with Nigel *v.* To attend to a lady's base *physical needs.* From the observation, made on BBC Radio 4's *News Quiz*, that *Shiver'n'Shake*-faced UKIP leader Nigel Farage's surname means *clopper* in Malay.

make like a Chinese helicopter pilot *v.* To indulge in an act of *self delight*; to frantically *waggle the joystick* from side to side.

makes a good quiche *euph.* Said of a gent who

knows what's in his flowerbeds.

makes good curtains *euph.* Wont to *fumble the odd spud. 'Friends of the minister said that he was happily married, and angrily rejected tabloid rumours that he makes good curtains.'*

make some room in your diary for this *exclam.* To be said just before unleashing an almighty *guff* during a meeting. Also *fire up dropzone two; has anyone got any questions?; now back to Davina.*

make something out of nothing *euph.* After *pulling,* to go to the bathroom and *put a bit of blood in it* before you get started in order to impress your conquest. To *get a head start. 'How did you get on last night, Dave?' 'I knew I'd be struggling at first, mate, on account of too much ale. Anyway, I managed to sneak off to the bog and make something out of nothing.'*

makes the hairs stand up on the palms of your hands *exclam.* Reference made by a gentleman to a particularly moving piece of *grumble.*

make the rounds *v.* To have one final late night grope of all the missus's *treasures* before falling asleep.

make the weigh-in *v.* To enter the toilet as a middleweight and come out half an hour later as a welterweight. To do a really big *poo, go on an instant diet, drop a dress size.*

makeunder *v.* The ongoing uglification process that flows from a surfeit of age, alcohol and street drugs.

make your shit hang sideways *v.* To be annoying. *'That fucking Eamonn Holmes really makes my shit hang sideways.'* (Bernard Levin, TV Review in *The Times*).

making empty threats *euph.* Said of a fellow who suffers from impotence.

making nylon *v.* An experiment in the bath resulting in the creation of viscous, stringy threads that stick to the hairs of one's legs.

making puppies *euph.* Engaging in "doggie-style" sex. *'They're making puppies again, Mrs Antrobus. Throw a bucket of water over them.'*

making the weight *1. n.* Something a boxer must do prior to a fight by sweating off as much excess weight as possible. *2. n.* Something a *big-boned* person must do prior to their weekly Weight-watchers meeting by having an enormous *dump* and putting on their lightest shoes.

making way for the lady *n.* An example of *toi-letiquette.* The innate sense of courtesy that seems to exist between urine and excrement whereby, during a *sit-down lavatory adventure, piss* invariably halts its stream to politely make way for the lady-like *Thora Hird,* before resuming its steady flow thereafter. *Crapping manners,* the *pisso doble.*

Makka Pakka's trumpet *n.* From *In the Night Garden,* if that's still a thing. The last *brass eye fanfare* of the day before drifting off to sleep.

malapriapism *n.* A mistaken *penile* intrusion into an orifice which is close by – but not the same as – another one, leading to an unintentionally amusing effect. A *cock up.*

male bag *n.* The *clockspring*-covered dangling sack in which the *clockweights* are kept.

malement *n.* A particularly nasty illness or affliction affecting only the bearers of XY chromosomes. See also *manthrax, he-bola etc.*

male pattern boredness *n.* while out shopping with his missus, the characteristic behaviour of an apathetic, lethargic bloke, *viz.* Ogling other women, staring abstractedly at lingerie mannequins, slashing his wrists *etc.*

male varnish *n.* Viscid fluid which is worn all over the hand, across the chest, and on one's la-dyfriend's face. Like nail varnish, but harder to remove from clothing. *Vitamin S.*

malfaeceance *n.* Legally speaking, an act that causes harm or distress to someone else, usually the next person to enter the *chodbin.*

MALLAM/mallam *acronym.* Middle Aged Loser Living At Mummy's.

malt loaf *n.* Pungently sweet-smelling *feeshus,* as dropped by a vegetarian or one whose diet sub-stantially eschews Haribos, sausage rolls and Ginster's pasties.

malty-tasking *n.* Male skill of drinking beer while simultaneously watching the telly.

mambas *n.* Mammaries, *mumbas.*

mambo number five *1. n.* An annoying novelty hit record which contains an instrumental line that sounds like a repetitive *fart. 2. n.* A repetitive *fart* that has all the makings of an instrumental line in an annoying novelty hit record. A *Rotterdam Termination Source.*

mamfest *1. n.* The stirring sight of a lot of ladies' breasts *en masse, eg.* At the beach, in a nightclub, through a hole drilled in the wall of a ladies' changing room in a *Carry On* film or Newcastle Polytechnic squash courts. Contraction of "mammary festival". *2. n.* A particularly fine and well presented pair of *bangers.*

mammarabilia *n.* Any impressive collection of vintage *smut,* including lovingly preserved antique *jazzmags* sourced from hedges in the 1980s and fuzzy VHS tapes that require the head cleaner treatment before each play.

mammaries *n.* Female secondary sexual character-istics. Also *tits, swinging pink milk churns, knockers.*

mammary dandruff *n.* Morning-after residue from a *sausage sandwich,* the dusty remnants of a *pearl necklace* dredged out of the *Bristol channel.*

mammary stick *n.* Convenient, pocket-sized electronic device for the storage of one's cybertronic *Frankie Vaughan* collection. A *sly pod.*

mammed up *adj.* Blessed in the *top bollocks* department. *'Fuck me, Terry. Have you seen that Jock weather bird on the telly? Proper mammed up she is. Her kids won't be going hungry.'*

mammogram *n.* An item of mail containing a few saucy snaps of his missus' bare *norks,* which is sent to a member of His Majesty's armed forces by his good lady and hopefully not by the milkman.

mammoth autopsy *n.* A *growler* that is far more hirsute, asymmetrical, and terrifying than a *rip on a gorilla's shin.*

mamnesia *n. medic.* A highly specific form of male memory loss. Upon seeing a fantastic pair of *norks,* the sufferer forgets key facts about himself, *eg.* That he is married, that he has four children, or that he is the presenter of a topical quiz show. Also *penile dementia.*

mam sandwich *n.* Two amply proportioned *bazingas* with the head of a happy gentleman wedged snugly between them.

manaconda *1. n.* A ludicrously oversized *dildo* of home manufacture, *eg.* Four tins of beans in a rubber sock. *2. n. Pant python, trouser snake, hissing Sid.* A *lirthy* male member.

manaesthetic *n.* Dextrous manual self-manipula-tion of a fellow's nether regions that brings on a state of pain-free slumber at the end of each day.

managlypta *1. n.* Peculiar raised relief effect observed on the walls of a *home worker* who is prone to acts of *self harm,* but who cannot be *arsed* to find a tissue, sock, pet *etc.* on which to deposit his *erotic spendings. Managlypta* is most commonly found decorating the surfaces immediately adjacent to a long term bachelor's computer desk. *2. n. Pearl drops.*

man at C&A *1. n.* A *DP* or *Dorothy Perkins. 2. n.* A chap who *enjoys shopping in both departments,* that is to say a bisexualist.

manatee's funeral *n.* A generous *Peter O'Toole* that is deposited from a ferry, or other sea-going vessel.

man bag *1. n.* A European-styled male handbag in which a modern beau-about-town keeps his iPad, Nick Hornby books and lipstick. *2. n.* A stylish leathery receptacle where a fashionable, modern chap keeps his *Alan Sugars* while he is out and about.

manbarassed *adj.* Descriptive of a fellow whose

bag for life has just proved him wrong about something, *'I'd sworn blind there was no patty de fwar grar in the cupboard, then Camilla goes and straight away she finds a tin at the back. I felt pretty manbarassed, I can tell you.'*

manberries *n.* Coarse term for the *clockweights, John Wayne's hairy saddlebags, knackers etc.* The testicles or *yongles.*

manberry sauce *n. Gentleman's spendings. Anger jam.*

man bleach *n. Pissinfectant* used for cleaning *skidmarks* off the *pot.*

man bollards *n.* After a night out, discrete piles of discarded clothes which have to be carefully negotiated on the way from the bedroom to the bathroom for a somnolent *gypsy's.*

mancakes *n. Heirbags* that have been *wanked flatter than a cow's cunt.*

man-catcher *n.* The *fanny.*

man cave *1. n.* A bloke's private area. *2. n.* A *bird's* private area.

manchild *1. n.* A chap with a massive, groomed *face fanny*, the kind a toddler would grow if they could. *2. n.* A fellow who unaccountably finds himself in a state of *heavy refreshment.* Taken from the 1989 Neneh Cherry hit of the same name, containing the lyrics "Manchild, will you ever learn? Manchild, look at the state you're in".

manchor *n.* A particularly weighty, hefty, solid *shite* that – once dropped – keeps its progenitor moored in the same spot indefinitely.

man conkers *1. n. Newton's cradle. 2. n.* A chap's *thirty threezers.*

man crèche *n.* A place for a wife to leave her husband, safely supervised and with plenty of entertainment on tap, while she spends hours anxiously trying on a selection of identical dresses and pairs of shoes before buying one which she will subsequently take back for a refund. The pub.

mancumber *n.* A male member of such cucurbitaceous dimensions as to satisfy the most capacious lady's *nugget bucket.*

Mancunian Way, walk the *1. v.* To make a stately progress along the A57(M), a picturesque 2-mile long stretch of the Manchester-Salford Inner Ring Road which links the M602 and M67. *2. v.* To adopt the semi-simian, rolling, swaggering gait reminiscent of Liam Gallagher out of off of Oasis or Ian Brown out of off of the Stone Roses.

Manc wag *1. n.* A spooneristic *bongo book. 2. n.* A north-western footballer's doxy. *3. n.* A witty Mancunian.

mancy *n.* A very girly fellow.

mandangles *n.* An older gent's *knackers.* Low

hanging fruit.

mandle *n.* A man's *handle.* *'Oi, love. Have a crank on me mandle, see if you can get me bollocks started.'*

M&Ms *1. n.* Sort of like an inferior American version of Smarties that taste faintly of vomit. *2. n. abbrev.* A colourful pack of cackling, drunken *cougars* out for a kill. From Middle-aged And Mucky.

mandruff *n.* Flakes of dried *lovepiss* found on one's wife's head and shoulders.

mands *n.* The large, shovel-like hands which are often the only warning to a holidaying lothario that he may be about to bite off more than he bargained for, so to speak, when he gets his latest conquest back to his hotel. From man + hands.

M&S low fat sausage, as dry as an *sim.* A *fanny* so moisture-free that it feels like it's lined with fine grade emery paper. Also *as dry as a moth sandwich; as an old dog's nose; as a budgie's tongue; drier than a spinster's Ginster's.*

M&S turd *euph.* A *shite* which is worthy of special attention due to its exceptional quality. "This is not just a turd, this is a five-day matured, chicken vindaloo with garlic naan and eight bottles of Cobra turd."

Mandy Jordache buying slabs, face like *sim.* Said of someone who is acting in a very suspicious manner. From the erstwhile *Brookside* character whose evil husband Trevor's disappearance coincided with the sudden decision to put a patio in at number 10. *'Did you see him coming out of the Ecuadorian Embassy? He had a face like Mandy Jordache buying paving slabs.'*

manecdote *n.* A dissembular vocalised narrative involving fighting, drinking, driving or sexual derring-do that is intended to enhance a fellow's standing amongst his peers.

man eggs *n.* Sperms, *taddies.*

man fanny *1. n.* A changing room entertainment whereby a bare swain impersonates a bare lady. A *cockafanny. 2. n.* A risible goatee beard sported by *euphemersity* lecturers and 45-year-olds who have just bought a motor bike.

manfat *n.* Semen. Also *man milk, cock snot.*

manflaps *n.* The tiny shutters surrounding the *fish mouth*, usually only visible when taking a much needed high pressure *piss.* The *hog's eyelids.*

manflesh, you shall taste *1. exclam.* The words uttered by Saruman to his prized fighting Orc as he is sent to hunt down the Fellowship of the Ring. *2. exclam.* A stirringly worded promise made to a casual acquaintance as a fellow drunkenly unzips his *kegs* behind a skip.

Manfred *n. prop. rhym. slang. Jitler, jism, spaff.* From the not-particularly famous-amongst-cockneys German philosopher Manfred Bunk = spunk.

Manfred Mann *1. n. prop.* South African keyboards player and progenitor of the popular earthband of the 1960s. *2. n.* An amusing way to describe a *spud fumbler* sandwich; ideally one which features a man called Fred as *lucky Pierre*.

mang *v.* Past simple of the verb "to ming". *'Did you shag that bird last night, Paul?' 'No, Barry. She fucking mang, so I just fingered her.'*

mange *n.* See *mangina*.

manger danger *n.* When walking down a high street at Christmas time, the ever-present possibility of an approach from a *God-botherer* inviting you to their church.

mangerine *n.* A fellow with sunbed-roasted skin. *'Born on this day: Heather Mills, altruistic unidexter, 1968; Melanie Jism, ex-Spice Girl, 1974; Des O'Connor, television mangerine, 1932.'*

mange tout, Rodders, mange tout *exclam.* Simultaneous cry of offence and exhortation issued by a young lady when her paramour draws back from *cumulonimbus* on encountering her piquantly *clinker*-ridden *maiden hair*. An exclamation best delivered in the style of Del Boy Trotter out of off of *Only Fools and Horses* and usually accompanied by an insistent thrusting of the poor chap's noggin back where it came from.

mangina *1. n.* The badly sewn Cornish pastie-like seam running along the underside of the scrotum that stops one's *clockweights* falling out and rolling under the fridge. *2. n.* The *nipsy* of one who is *good with colours*. *3. n.* Yet another name for the hilarious men's locker room jape of sticking one's *meat and two veg* back between one's legs to create a convincing simulacrum of a lady's *clout*. *3. n.* Old Greg's "downstairs mix-up" in the *Mighty Boosh*.

manging *adj. Minging.*

man-goo chutney *1. n.* A savoury relish typically found smeared round women's mouths after chucking-out time. *2. n.* Savoury condiment added to unpopular customers' food by disgruntled male catering industry personnel. *'More man goo chutney on your pork chops, Mr Morgan?'*

mangos *n.* See *jelly water mangos*.

mangrove *n.* The swampy, midge-infested male equivalent of a *ladygarden*.

mangry *adj.* Sexually frustrated. From man + angry. *'I've not had any action for two weeks now and I'm starting to get really mangry.'*

man ham *n.* The male generative equipment, including the *two veg*.

man handle *n.* The *bone on* that a store detective

gets upon apprehending a female shoplifter in anticipation that she may offer to *talk to the judge* in the stock room.

manhole cover *n.* A lady's bi-fortnightly requisite; a *Simon Cowell* or *smurf's hat*.

manhole inspector *n.* A chap who *bakes a light cake*.

manhood *n.* In British tabloid journalism, the male generative member.

man in the iron mask *n.* An extremely hirsute *snatch* trapped inside a pair of knickers. From the classic tale by Alexandre Dumas.

manitary towel *n.* An absorbent pad of folded lavatory tissue used to avoid embarrassing stains while suffering the effects of *Spanish plumbers*. Also *manpon, mantipad*.

manjack *n.* A *poo* which is so rigid that it starts lifting you off the *bog* seat when it hits the bottom of the *pan*. A *neckbreaker*.

mank bank *n.* Mental florilegium featuring *spunk-curdling* images of the most horrific episodes from a fellow's romantic career, brought to mind when he is attempting to stop his *milk from boiling over*.

mankee candle *n.* Distinctive scent noticeable in certain less high calibre residences; fragrance notes of chip pan, German shepherd and Lambert & Butler.

manker *n.* A *wanker* from Manchester. Morrissey, to pick an example entirely at random.

manky panky *n.* Sexual congress between tramps, crusties and sundry other unwashed sorts, usually attempted in a public park following the consumption of copious quantities of *spesh*, white cider and metal polish.

manmalade *n.* Sticky, tangy paste excreted from the business end of a gentleman's *fruit bowl*. Hopefully without any bits of peel floating round in it. *Anger jam, manberry sauce.*

man mastic *n.* Sticky white substance used for sealing ladies' eyelids *etc.*

man mayonnaise *n. Gentleman's relish, hanging salad cream, semen mayo.*

man medicine *n. Vitamin S*, administered via a *spam syringe.*

man meringue *n.* A light, crumbly nest of dried *milm* found on the inside of a gentleman's well-worn *Bill Grundies.*

man-milk of magnesia *n. medic.* A well-known cure for indigestion, or indeed any ailment currently being suffered by one's spouse or ladyfriend.

manna cotta *n.* A hand-prepared Italian *pud.*

mannequim *1. n.* A *sailor's favourite* or similar ersatz *spouse*. *2. n.* The carefully shaped and trimmed *face fungus* worn by every other *fucking* man in the street.

mannery glands n. A portly gent's *dugs*. *Bitch tits, moobs, moomlaaters.*

mannexe n. Any shed, garage, allotment, coal hole or other outside building where a chap can escape from *her indoors*.

manniseed balls n. The *nollies.*

manny n. The convincing illusion of womanhood achieved when a gentleman tucks his *giggling stick* and *knackers* back behind his legs. A *cockafanny*. A contraction of man + fanny. See *man fanny, mangina.*

Manny Cradock n. A hen-pecked bloke who does all the cooking in his house. Yes, only one 'd' in Cradock, since you ask.

mano a manhood n. Single-handed mortal combat with your *old fella.*

man of the cloth n. A holy *farter*, who, despite fervent prayer, finds that he has besoiled his raiments. A *through-follower.*

man on the inside euph. The stage of a *digestive transit* just before the *turtle's head*. 'Why's Colin walking so funny?' 'He's got a man on the inside.'

manopause 1. n. Man's mid-life crisis, characterised by the acquisition of a sports car, a ponytail, a motorbike and/or a girlfriend young enough to be his daughter. 2. n. medic. Hot and cold flushes, heart palpitations and a feeling of being 'spaced out', usually experienced by a gentleman following a night *on the piss* with a chicken jalfrezi to finish.

man overboard n. A *bald man in a boat* whom you fear has become detatched from his mooring, but who turns out to be a pellet of compressed *shit scrape.*

man pop n. *Spooge, jitler, baby gravy.*

man sandwich n. The opposite of a *spitroast*, that is to say two well-*buttered slices* with a *bacon filling*. Probably with some *special sauce.*

manscleaning. euph. Studied male incompetence in the field of domestic activity such that it really needs doing again to meet the missus's highest standards.

Mansfield motorcycle euph. Any form of assited mobility conveyance, eg. Shopping kart, electric scooter etc. Also *Morley moped, nanbretta.*

Mansfield tapas n. Greggs.

manshake n. A vigorous three-minute greeting for your best friend.

manshee n. One who could conceivably be a man or a woman.

man's makeup n. The light brown stripe left on a light-coloured bath towel by a chap's vigorous drying of his *potty slot*. Often blamed on his missus's foundation or bronzer. 'Terry, you dirty bastard. Why can't you wipe your arse properly? You've left man's makeup all over the towel again.' ' I've not done that, June, you fucking cow. It was you taking your slap off when you were pissed last night.'

manstruating adj. Of a male, being quick to lose one's rag at seemingly inoffensive comments regarding one's appearance, personality, behaviour or membership of Oasis. 'Take no notice of our Liam. He's manstruating this week.'

mantanamo bay n. The place your missus sends you when you are in the *cunt book*, from where you never know when you might be allowed to return home, and where you can find yourself subject to intense, hostile barrages of questions at any hour of the night or day.

mantap n. A fellow's *cock*. 'What is it this time, June? Can't you see I've got a bad back and my boss is coming for dinner unexpectedly and I'm pretending to have forgotten our wedding anniversary?' 'Really, Terry. Have you been running your mantap in the kitchen sink again? Only there's piss all over the fucking pots.'

manta ray, fanny like a sim. An overly large-winged *cludge* with a pointed nose poking out the top.

manties n. Women's underwear worn by a bloke who is firmly in denial about his true proclivities. 'Nah, I'm not wearing a G-string, these're manties. There is a difference.'

mantiliner n. See *mantipad.*

mantipad n. A folded piece of lavatory paper placed in a fellow's underbreeches in order to absorb any excess drips. Also *mantiliner, swedge, manpon, botcap, toffee rizla.*

man trap n. The female genitals, the *hairy love pit.*

mantrum n. A hissy fit thrown by a man. For example, the bit off that Elton John fly on-the-wall thing when he was in the south of France and the woman went "yoo-hoo" at him when he was playing tennis, remember, and he flounced back up to his hotel suite and started packing his suitcase? That was a mantrum.

manty pad n. Strategically placed in the front of one's underpants to prevent uncomfortable *men's things* dribblage after a *genie rub* during the working day, a sheet or two of folded-up *bumwad*. Also *manpon.*

manvestite n. A woman that looks like a man dressed as a woman. And we don't mean Danny La Rue.

manwich n. The lucky chap filling pressed between two slices of ladies.

man with a long neck, as happy as sim. Descriptive of one in a very chipper state of mind, comparable to a fortuitous fellow who is able to fulfill every gentleman's dearest dream. *'The Hull sewage worker who won this week's triple rollover Euromillions jackpot today told reporters that he was as happy as a man with a long neck.'*

man with nice nails *n.* One who is *good with colours.*

Manx plumbing *n.* The *third leg* in the middle, which points upwards or downwards depending on which function it is performing.

mapatasi *n. Aus. Minge.* From "Map of Tasmania", the small, *pube*-covered island off the south east Australian coast that smells of fish.

map of Africa *n.* The cartographical stain left on the bed sheet and often the mattress below after an exchange of bodily fluids. A splodge of *splooge.* Also *map of Ireland, map of Hawaii.*

maps of Europe *n.* Enormous *tits* that are covered in a network of blue and red veins.

marabou stork *n.* A *fixed bayonet, the old Adam.* An erection.

maracas *n. Knackers, clackers,* those things that swing beneath *tallywhackers* and make a rattling sound.

marble cake *n.* The swirly, variegated *excreeshus* of someone who's just had their *back doors kicked in.* Also *Swiss roll.*

marble gargler *n.* One who likes to *nosh nuts.*

marbleous *adj.* Very slightly senile. *'Oh yes, she's marbleous for her age, you know.'*

march of the penguins *1. n.* What passes for a nature film in America, narrated by him off *The Shawshank Redemption. 2. n.* An ungainly and seemingly endless waddle to the *crapper* while trying desperately to prevent the release of *Bully's special prize.*

mardigan *n.* A stout, passion-killing item of clothing worn by a vexatious woman who is *boiling beetroots.*

mardy *adj.* Moody, sullen, *esp.* describing an old *boot.*

Margaret's footpath *euph.* Inexplicably, the rarely seen space between a fellow's *ball bag* and his *bum hole. Also known as the landing, Luton-to-Dunstable busway, twernt, tintis, gooch, biffin bridge, notcher, barse, stinky Mervin, ploughman's, taint, scruttock* or *cockpit.*

marge *n.* A loose woman. From margarine, which "spreads easily". Also *Flora.*

Margot's mouth *euph.* A *nipsy* pursed so tightly that it resembles Penelope Keith's gob in *the Good Life* when her character tasted Tom's parsnip wine.

Marianas trench *1. n.* The deepest recorded sub-marinal depression on Earth, found in the Pacific ocean and reaching a depth of 35,839 feet below sea level. *2. n.* A *fanny* like a fucking bucket.

marinade *v.* To stick your *cock* in and just leave it there with absolutely no movement whatsoever. A pre-marriage practice that is popular amongst Mormons, apparently. *'I'll be your leprechaun and sit upon an old toadstool, I'll marinade you till I'm old and gray. I'll be your long-haired lover from Liverpool, you'll be my sunshine daisy from LA.'*

marine ply *n.* Pages of a favoured *bongo book,* stuck together with salty *pyjama glue* to form a tough, hard-wearing laminate.

Mario Kart piss *n.* A hurried *wazz* that must be successfully completed within a very short space of time. From the online game Mario Kart, where players must nip into the back garden and get their *scoot* in before the next race starts.

marks of Mecca *n.* Carpet burns on the knees caused by excessive worship at the *hairy temple.*

marks out of two? *interrog.* From one ogling male to another, to cue the reply "I'd give her one."

mark time *v.* Of a pornographic threesome's spare male participant, to half-heartedly perform *maintenance strokes* while his colleague is getting properly *serviced.*

mark your territory *v.* To *drop your guts* and walk away. To *leave negative feedback.*

Marlboro maracas *n.* The act of shaking random fag packets at a party in search of one that has one or two left in it.

Marley arse *n.* Accumulated *winnetage,* leading to *anal dreadlocks. Tagnuts* that have gone to pot.

Marley's chains *euph.* Breasts that, despite having headed south in a big way, must still be carried about by their owner. From the chain-dragging ghost of a former business partner that visits Scrooge in Charles Dickens's *A Christmas Carol.* Also *Ulrikas.*

marlin, fishing for *euph.* When you feel that your latest *cable laying* adventure may require you to strap yourself into a special chair and brace both feet firmly against the *poop deck. 'Don't bother your father, dear. He ate five kilos of liquorice allsorts yesterday and he's spending this morning fishing for marlin.'*

marmalade madam *n. 17thC.* A *Tom,* good time girl, *Covent Garden nun.* A prostitute.

Marmite driller *n.* One who *jumps over puddles* along the *Marmite motorway.*

Marmite kazoo *n.* The *litter tray* or *Bovril bagpipes.*

Marmite kofte *n.* The sort of viscous black *shite* that, instead of dropping into the *chod pan* in the traditional manner, chooses to smear itself around the *nipsy* like so much axle grease. The resulting

Augean Stables-style cleaning session only ever happens when one is in a hurry to catch a plane, train, last orders or read the closing headlines at the end of the *BBC Six O'Clock News*.

Marmite motorway *n.* A-road, *arse*, *back passage*.

Marmite pot, arse like a *sim.* A *ringpiece* which, after a particularly sticky *Brad Pitt*, seems to have a never ending supply of *shit* and the wiping of which will never *draw an ace*.

Marmite stripe *n.* Brown stain or *skidmark* found on unwashed *shreddies*. *Russet gusset*.

marooned on poo island *euph.* Sat forlornly on the *bum sink*, post-*fudge*, without any *arse wipe* to hand.

marrow *n.* The nutritious white substance that comes from inside your *bone*.

marrowless *adj.* Somewhat lacking vigour *in the trouser department*.

Mars bar *1. n.* A caramel, nougat and chocolate confection, which when eaten daily is a scientifically proven aid to labour, repose and recreation. *2. n.* A substantial and impressive *burnout*.

Mars bar party *n.* Any apocryphal celebration at the home of a member of the Rolling Stones which culminates in one of the guests eating the eponymous chewy confection out of the *nether parts* of another, while members of the Sussex constabulary kick the door down.

mars bra *n.* The common practice (in Germany anyway) of *dropping a length of dirty spine* onto your ladyfriend's *dirty pillows*.

martial farts *n.* The lethal, oriental skill of subduing an assailant by administering a short, sharp *kafarty chop* when their head is within range.

Martini girl *euph.* A woman of *easy affections*. A *trullion*, *slapper* or *bike*; from the tagline of the popular Vermouth ads of the 1970s, "Any time, any place, anywhere".

Martin! Martin! Martin! *exclam.* Phrase which can be shouted when standing next to someone whose repeated *gut dropping* implies that they may imminently *curl one off* all over the floor. From the zookeeper on *Blue Peter* who persistently called the name of his off-screen helper when Lulu the elephant tried to *shite* all over John Noakes' left foot.

Marty Feldmans *n.* On certain ladies, the lop-sided *tits*, where the nipples point up, down and all around. Named after the late comedian Marty Feldman, whose distinctive nipples pointed in different directions.

Marty Robbins *n.* An horrifically large poo; a proper *gorilla's breakfast*. Named after the late country and western artiste, whose 1959 chart-top-

per *El Paso* includes the following lines: "Just for a moment I stood there in silence / Shocked by the foul evil deed I had done."

Mary *1. n.* Sponge, pillow biter, angel. *2. n.* Bean flicker, carpet muncher. *3. n.* A liver sock.

Mary Berry's thumb *n.* A tiny but perfectly formed *boner*.

Mary Chipperfield *n.* A *wank* ie. A *monkey spanking* session. From the famous circus chimp dominatrix of the same name.

Mary Hinge *n.* Spooneristic *biffer*.

Mary Poppins *n.* A textbook *quim*. A fanny that is "practically perfect in every way".

Mary Poppins' bag *n.* A surprisingly roomy *snapper*. A *clown's pocket* out of which it would be possible to pull a mirror, a lamp and a large potted plant.

mash *v.* To fondle a lady's *shirt potatoes* as if testing them to destruction.

mash/map *acronym.* Morning After Shit or Morning After Poo. The *Douglas Hurd* that miraculously resolves one's residual hangover the morning after a night on the tiles. Also known as an *escape sub*, *arsepirin* or *manurofen*.

mashturbation *n.* Giving or receiving *manual relief* while intoxicated. The inherent flaccidity or loss of motor skills associated with alcohol often results in a mashing action whereby no end result is achieved. Also known as a *fat jogger* from the fact that "there is quantifiable motion but with no apparent effect".

masking scrape *n.* A prudent raft of *arse paper* employed to tactfully cover a recalcitrant *floater* that refuses to *go to the beach* even after several attempts at flushing. *Turin shroud*, *coroner's cloth*.

masonic handshake *1. n.* A secret signal surreptitiously passed between policemen, town planners and the shape-shifting lizards of the New World Order. *2. n.* Any act of *self help* which utilises an unusual grip.

massage parlour wank *1. sim.* Something that is performed quickly and efficiently. *'And the wheel change and refuelling was performed like a massage parlour wank by the Ferrari mechanics and Schumacher should exit the pit lane still in the lead.'* (Murray Walker). *2. sim.* Something that is expensive and over far too quickly, eg. The Pepsi Max ride at Blackpool, a Happy Mondays gig.

Massey Ferguson mudflaps *n.* Yet another colourful term relating to pendulous *lobelia majorcas*. Also *gammon goalposts*, *lamb hangings*, *steak drapes*.

massive heat signature!, that's a *1. exclam.* Oft-used phrase on Discovery Channel cryptozoology-caper *Expedition Bigfoot* (us neither) when something big, warm and unexpected shows up on the infra-red camera. *2. exclam.* Uttered following the release of a particularly pungent *Exchange & Mart*, possibly accompanied by the simultaneous appearance of something big, warm and unexpected.

masterfaece *n.* A *humming bird* of such epoch-defining magnificence that you briefly consider fishing it out of the bowl, putting it in a frame and hanging it in the nearest art gallery. Mind you, if you did you'd probably win the fucking Turner Prize. We're going to hell in a handcart, you couldn't make it up.

Mastermind wank *n.* An urgent bout of *self harm* during which the offender repeatedly mumbles "I've started so I'll finish".

master of ceremonies *1. n.* In this modern "hippy-hoppy" style of so-called music, a fellow in an ill-adjusted baseball hat who shouts about how super he is into a microphone. *2. n.* A red-faced, tail-coated man at a formal dinner who hits a wine glass with a spoon to get everyone's attention, before introducing some mercenary *twat* like Jimmy Carr who then gets up and makes a few lame cracks about the managing director's golf handicap in return for several thousand pounds and a free tea. *3. n.* One's *knob, todger, old man etc*. The male penis.

masturbair *v.* To mime an act of *personal pollution*, typically while comically exaggerating the dimensions of your *manhood*.

masturbatabase *n.* A gentleman's computerised repository of *relaxing* imagery. *'What's this folder here on your desktop, Terry? I can't open it. It seems to be password protected.' 'Oh that? It's nothing, June. Just some boring figures, that's all. It's my masturbatabase.'*

masturbatory *n.* A male homeowner's *wankatorium. 'Darling, I've had quite a day. Tell Carson I'm retiring to the masturbatory to rub a few out until dinner.'*

masturbbatical *n.* A break to allow one's wrist to recover from over-*relaxation*.

masturgrating *n.* The act of furiously grating cheese before your toast goes cold.

masturmates *n.* Public school dormitory chums.

masturmentary *n.* TV programme with a high *tit* and *fanny* count with a token bit of information thrown in to justify its showing, *eg.* A behind-the-scenes look at the pornographic film industry. The staple fare of late night satellite telly a few years back.

matelot's mattress *n. nav.* A thick piece of bedding

material provided to keep *Jack Tars* jolly in their bunks. A Wren.

mate-us symbol *n.* Where an otherwise unappealing gentleman buys an expensive car, watch, social media platform *etc.,* with the intention of impressing the ladies.

Mather & Platt *rhym. Lancs. Manc.* A lady's *bodily treasure.* Named after an old established Mancunian engineering company. *'I wouldn't mind getting me hands on her Mather & Platt, our Liam.'*

Mathias Rust, do a *v.* To indulge oneself in a *strawberry dip.* Named in honour of the young West German pilot who, in 1987, famously performed an "unauthorised landing in Red Square".

mathsturbate *v.* To have a vowel and three consonants while thinking about Rachel Riley or Nick Hewer. To practise one's *six-nowt times table.*

mating call *n.* The activation of pub toilet hand-driers as a deliberate attempt to impress any classy *birds* within earshot.

matted spam *1. n. prop.* Album track from ill-fated Swansea rockers Badfinger's eponymous 1973 LP. *2. n.* An overgrown *toasted cheese sandwich.*

Matteson's *euph.* In grumbular cinematography, the unfortunate outcome of a female protagonist missing her target by a centimetre or two when squatting down on her male co-star's *wankfurter,* causing it to bend into a shape which is disturbingly remniscent of the popular cheap sausage.

Matt finish *euph.* Spectacular hiccup in one's career caused by forgetting to paint over the office CCTV camera lens. See also *Hancock's half hour.*

mattress back *n.* A polyamorous lady who is generous with her romantic favours. A *bike.*

maturdity leave *n.* A period of rest, recuperation and convalescence after giving birth to *Meat Loaf's daughter.*

maven *n.* A male *shaven haven*, with the shrubbery trimmed back in order to make the *larch* look grander.

MAWBAB/mawbab *abbrev.* A woman who refuses to *make the effort* and effects short hair, corduroy trousers, comfortable shoes *etc.* Might As Well Be A Bloke.

Max Jaffa *n.* A solo *fiddle.* Live from Scarborough Spa.

max poo *phr.* Occurs when a rapidly ejected *feeshus* is moving at its fastest and the air density is at its highest. The air is pushing against the projectile with a lot of force, and this can cause it to buckle or break into messy, lavatory-clogging *chods* as its author shouts "Go for throttle up!"

may contain nuts *phr.* Notice which really should be displayed on the outside of a Thai temptress's *underkegs*, serving as a warning that there is a pretty good chance that she may turn out to be a *trolley dolly*.

mayor's hat *n.* A *howzat* often eaten by goats.

MBE *abbrev.* A sudden, colossal *dump*; a Massive Bowel Evacuation. Not be confused with the well known royal honour, *viz.* Member of the Most Excellent Order of the British Empire, *eg.* Paula Radcliffe MBE.

McArthur park *1. n.* A maudlin 1970s ballad by Richard Harris. *2. n.* A particularly evil *dropped gut* that gives the impression that "something inside has died".

McBusted *1. n.* Hard rocking supergroup made up out of former members of Busted and Fleetwood Mac. *2. exlam.* Mild oath used when accosted by fast food restaurant staff for going in to use the toilets without buying any of their muck. *'Oi! You there. Did you just come in to use the toilets and not buy any of our muck?' 'McBusted!'*

McCoys *n.* Flakes of dried, salty, starchy material found on a bachelor's bed linen, socks, carpet *etc.* Named after the popular snack's erstwhile advertising slogan, because they are "man crisps". See also *prawn crackers, porn crackers, popshot-tadoms, singlie rosettes* and *wanker's crisps.*

McDonald's farmyard *n.* The restaurant area of a high street fast food outlet, filled with sundry dullards, *scratters* and fatties grazing on burgers and fries while snorting appreciatively.

McEwan's exports *n.* Fiercely nationalistic Scottish people who take every opportunity to proudly declaim their love for their homeland, despite choosing to live in America. Or Australia. Or Spain. Or anywhere except Scotland, *eg.* Late veteran syrupped former milkman turned disciplinarian Sir Sean Connery.

McFadden transfer *n.* Upgrading to a better model, such as from Kerry Katona to Delta Goodrun, to pick an example entirely at random.

McGregor *n.* A *Mary* that is "torn between two lovers". *A Joy Division.*

McKeith *n.* A textbook *dump.* Named after excrement-obsessed TV gerbil Gillian McKeith.

McKeith's handbag, smells like *sim.* Anything that *ronks* of *shit,* as one imagines the previously mentioned comedy PhD-ed *turd*-tamperer's reticule must. Also *Oaten's briefcase.*

MCP *acronym.* Motorised Chav Pram.

McShurf *v.* To take advantage of a fast food chain's free wi-fi while having a *McShit.* From McDonalds

+ shit + surf.

McSlurry *n.* The fetid, hot and painful *grimshit* one experiences after dining for a week solely at a fast food restaurant. Also *McSplurry.*

McSquirter twins *n.* A gentleman's *clockweights.* Named after the identically dead, unconscionably right-wing pair of blazered *Record Breakers* co-hosts. The *gonk-faced Mother Teresa sisters.*

McSuck *n.* *Horatio* delivered with a force equivalent to that required to drink a newly poured McDonald's Thick Shake.

McWoman *n.* A *dish* who's not nearly as tasty as she appears in her photographs. From fast food chains' notorious habit of advertising their goods using pictures that bear little or no resemblance to the soggy, greasy, *flat-titted* meals they actually produce. *'Did you meet that bird you met on the internet?' 'Yes, but she turned out to be a right McWoman. And the meat was hanging out of the bun too.'*

MDF *abbrev.* A *dobber.* Medium Density Flop-on. Not quite *wood.*

me *n.* Personal pronoun used at the end of a sentence to emphasise preference. *'For all these wenches are beauteous fair, and I doth admire them all, me.'* (from *Romeo and Juliet* by William Shakespeare).

mea cunta *exclam. Lat.* An admission that one has acted like a complete *twat.*

meal deal *1. n.* A dispiriting bargain snack lunch comprising a sandwich, a bag of crisps and a carton of coloured liquid. *2. n.* A bargain date comprising a *hairy ham sandwich,* a *hot brownie* and a *hand shandy.*

meal memory *n.* A lamentable *Hart to Hart* that smells exactly like the last meal you consumed; the rectal equivalent of Charles Swann's Madeleine cake in Proust's *À la recherche du temps perdu.*

meanderthals *n.* The thick-headed people who aimlessly wander about in shops, getting in your bloody way.

meaningful votes *euph.* Repeated trips to the bog to unsuccessfully attempt to *curl one out. 'Hold my red case, would you, Sir Humphrey? I'm just off to the cludgy to hold another meaningful vote.'* (Jim Hacker MP, *Yes Prime Minister,* BBCTV).

means-tested benefits *1. n.* Sundry forms of state-funded supplementary income that are made available subject to the claimant not having a minimum set amount of money tucked away in their bank account. *2. n.* The criteria which a *gold-digger* applies when deciding to make her *assets* available to a particular chap, albeit a scheme predicated on a principle that is diametrically antithetical to the one applied by the Department of Work and Pensions.

meat and greet *phr. Scots.* A short, bleak and purely physical sexual encounter followed by a period of tearful self-loathing

meat and two vag *euph.* A ménage à trois. A *threesome* involving two ladies and a smiling man who keeps pinching himself.

meat and two veg *n.* A gentleman's *undercarriage.* A *pork sausage* and a couple of *love spuds.*

meat balloons *n.* Older boys' playthings, which do not stick to the wall even after protracted rubbing on a jumper. *Mumbas, large tits.*

meat banquet *n.* A drool-inducing array of *panhandles* for sexist women to ogle. Shame on them, quite frankly.

meatdusa *n.* A woman of such comely physical attributes that the *Hampton* of any man who looks at her instantly turns to stone.

meat feast *1. n.* Pizza topping. *2. n.* Scene in an *artistic* movie in which the female protagonist samples a veritable smorgasbord of *man salamis.* *3. n.* A calorie-rich cacation. A *three legged stool.*

meat flower *n.* Delightful, poetic term for a lady's *bodily treasure.*

meat flute *n. Pink oboe, spam clarinet.* Also *one-holed flute.*

meat-free diet *n.* A period of celibacy.

meat harp *n.* A vaguely fan-shaped instrument that a lady may choose to strum angelically from time to time. A *bird's fly trap.*

meat hook *n.* A swain's *pink steel prong*, as occasionally seen hanging about in the *butcher's window.*

meat injection *n.* An inoculation against virginity that is more often stuck in the *arse* than in the upper arm.

meat jodhpurs *n.* Well-developed *bingo wings* of the upper thigh. *'Blimey, your missus has got a right set of meat jodhpurs on her. Has her gym membership expired or something?'*

Meat Loaf, doing a *n.* Being denied a spot of *backdoor work* by the missus while being granted access to her other orifices. From the lyric of the song made famous by the fat, sweaty, late singer, *viz.* "Two out of three ain't bad."

Meat Loaf knickers *n.* Metaphorical *applecatchers* worn by prudish girls who refuse to indulge in any *chocolate speedway riding*, notionally emblazoned with the slogan "I would do anything for love" on the front, and "but I won't do that" on the back.

Meat Loaf's daughter *n.* A big boned *mudchild.* A gargantuan *dreadnought.*

meat market *n.* Bar or club where *Yorkshire flamingoes* with short skirts and blotchy legs dance round their handbags, waiting for a *pull.* A *meat rack, buttock hall.*

meat microphone *n.* Sensitive device on a very short lead into which drunken *car park karaoke* participants need little encouragement to vocalise.

meat moth *n.* A *spam butterfly* commonly attracted to the bright lights of a *grot mag* photographer's flashgun.

meat movie *n.* A *grumble flick.*

meat paste *1. n.* Something your mum puts on your sandwiches at school. *2. n.* Something disgruntled chefs put on Giles Coren's sandwiches.

meat petite *n.* Descriptive of a *Little Richard.*

meat platter *1. n.* An unappetizing raffle prize on offer in a working men's club. *2. n.* An unappetizing *clopper* on offer behind a skip a working men's club car park.

meat purse *1. n.* The steak handbag carried by Lady Gaga at the 2010 MTV Music Awards. *2. n.* The missus's lower naughty bits.

meat raffle *1. n.* A competition in a boozer to secure a sweaty platter of chops, sausages and bluebottle eggs. *2. n.* A competition in a boozer to strike up a meaningful relationship with a prospective *inamorata* or *lucky dip* drunken *tap-off* in a darkened nightclub.

meat safe *1. n.* Secure container for the storage of one's most prized *art pamphlets.* A *slime capsule, drawer of chests.* *2. n.* The *beef box.*

meat scarf *n.* A lipidinous accessory worn around the neck by the corpulent to ward off the cold. A double chin or *Chesterfield necklace.*

meatstroke *n. medic.* Exhaustion, torpor and sweaty palms caused by excessive *knuckling down.*

meat stub *1. n.* A rudimentary Wikipedia entry about some sort of butcher's produce, for example the article about haslet. *2. n.* A rudimentary male *pudender*, of the sort boasted by Bobby Davro or Jack Straw.

meat tarp *n.* A somewhat hyperbolic phrase descriptive of a lady's *nether parts* which are deemed sufficiently extensive as to be capable of covering a skip filled with building waste.

meat tenderiser *1. n.* A wooden mallet of the sort used by people who cook food on the television, but which has sat gathering dust in that pot of on your kitchen worktop for years now. *2. n.* A chap who *pounds his pork* with life-threatening ferocity, though hopefully not with a wooden mallet.

meat tie *n.* Formal pink neckwear for topless ladies. Tied with a shiny purple knot. With all *spunk* coming out the end. The sausage in a *sausage sandwich.*

meat tweet *n.* A personal snapshot sent by a man to

a friend he has just made on a social networking site; an image that eventually ends up being permanently downloaded onto the computer hard drive of his *bag for life*'s divorce lawyer. A *dick pic.*

meatus *n. medic.* The proper name for the *hog's eye*, apparently. *'Hello, doctor? This is Mr J Brown from Notting Hill. I'd like a confidential word about my meatus. I stuck a propelling pencil lead down it for an experiment and I think it's snapped.' 'I'm terribly sorry, you must have dialled the wrong number. This is Jeremy Vine on Channel 5. You're live on air.'*

meatus foetus *n. medic.* A gallstone.

meaty sweety *n.* A healthy snack that is rich in *Vitamin S* and takes a bit less chewing than a Curly Wurly.

meaty windchimes *n.* A dangling collection of sonorously resonant genitalia unencumbered by underwear. *'Although pictures of "Richard Hannay – Wanted for Murder" shouted out from the front page of every newspaper in Scotland, once I was dressed in the crofter's Tam o'shanter, bagpipes and kilt, nobody looked twice at me as I hurried to catch the Pitlochry omnibus, my meaty windchimes jangling melodiously in the crisp Highland air as I ran.'* (from *The Sixty-Nine Steps* by John Buchan).

mechanical dandruff *n.* Royal Air Force crabs, *willipedes*.

mechanic's bulge *n.* Arm muscle unavoidably cultivated by a chap who lies on his back *tightening his nuts* all day.

mechanic's nails *n.* Finger-end condition cause by *bumwad pushthrough. Taxi-driver's tan.*

medicinale *adj.* Descriptive of the traditional folk remedy of using many jars of *pub juice* to alleviate the symptoms of an ailment or injury, such as toothache, manic depression or liver failure. From medicine + ale. *'Darling, will you fetch me 8 cans of super strength back from the shop, please? Purely for medicinale purposes, you understand.'*

medicine balls *n.* Spherical glands containing *penis-sillin*, a tincture well known to cure almost all ailments from which one's wife or girlfriend may be suffering.

medicine stick *n.* The male *prodder*, from its infallible ability to relieve the symptoms of a host of feminine conditions. *'All she needs is a good seeing-to with the medicine stick.'*

medieval fireplace *sim.* A vast, gothic vagina with a big piece of pork slowly revolving in it.

Mediterranean Tetley *n.* When on a holiday, suffering from a dose of the *squitters*, and not minded to locate a foreign lavatory, going for a paddle with the intention of letting the bowels go through the perforated netting lining of one's swimming shorts. "Letting the flavour flood out" like one of the eponymous teabags.

medium bastard *n.* One who has laid off the pies for a while. An ex-*fat bastard.*

medophile *n.* One who has become so accustomed to participating in *saucy mesomes* that it has become his preferred form of sexual activity. One who is no longer *master of his own domain.*

mee-maw *n. onomat.* Of a young lady wearing spray-on leggings, the sound made by her *knicker sausages* moving in the *beetle bonnet* area as she sashays about. *'Just have a mee-maw over here, Khloe, and look at this massive pile of cash.'*

meerkat, have a *v.* To perform a surreptitious act of *personal pollution* while the missus is upstairs. So named because the beady-eyed malefactor maintains a heightened sense of alert throughout, in the style of one of the popular Go Compare desert weasels.

meerslap *n.* A clip round the ear off the missus after raising one's head to clock a bit of passing *clunge.*

meertwat *n.* An annoying little *cunt* who always pops up at the most inopportune moments.

meeting with the big man *n.* A session of *self-indulgence* while at work. *'Coming onto the cancer verandah, Dave?' 'No can do. I've got a meeting with the big man.'*

meet the villain of the evening *exclam.* Said in a voice mimicking no-nonsense *Life on Mars/Ashes to Ashes* copper Gene Hunt prior to hopefully getting one's *leg over.*

megraine *n.* Intermittent illness afflicting ladies and footballers when they realise they are no longer the centre of attention.

mehchuan 1. *n. Ch.* Mediocre Chinese food. From meh + szechuan. 2. *n.* A less-than-satisfying release following a so-so *hand shandy* at a dodgy acupuncture clinic.

me-jerk reaction *n.* Overwhelming desire to have *one off the wrist* that is brought on by an unexpected erotic stimulus, such as a photo of a swimwear-clad BBC4 documentary presenter (not Professor Jim Al-Khalili) in the *Radio Times*, or finding some old *jazz mags* in the shed.

Mekon 1. *n. prop.* The chief villain and leader of the Treens featured in Dan Dare's *Eagle* adventures of the 1950s, distinguished by his enormous cranium and little body, and hence 2. *n.* A badly poured pint which is "all head and fuck all else".

Melanie *n. prop.* Gentleman's spendings. From the name of the famous shellsuited singer and cartwheelist Melanie Jism. *Spurty spice.*

Melanied *adj.* Drunk, battered, *blatted.* From the surname of All Saints popsie Melanie Blatt. *'I'm sorry Eddie, but I can't let you go on air and read the news in that state. You're absolutely Melanied.'*

Melbourne *n.* A soft *cock.* The first part of that whole *Baccus Marsh … Ballarat … Lake Wendouree* thing.

melching *n. Minge felching.* From minge + felching.

melonade *n. Jizz, spunk, jitler.* From the proverb "When life gives you melons, make melonade."

meloncholy *n.* Disconsolate sadness and depression; a generalised malaise characterised by feelings of loss and longing for a past girlfriend who had humongous *chebbs* on her.

melon farmer *exclam.* The BBC-authorised, poorly dubbed version of *motherfucker* used in films such as *Die Hard* and the entire *Beverly Hills Cop* series. Also *ever-loving, muddy funster, piece of soot.*

melon refresher 1. *n.* An invigorating flavour of smoothie. 2. *n.* A *titwank* performed on a tired gentleman after a stressful day at work.

melons 1. *n.* Knockout female breasts. 2. *n. prop.* Middle name of the Duke and Duchess of Kent's daughter Lady Helen Windsor.

melted welly *n.* A poetic term describing a lady's *bodily treasure. 'Spatula was powerless to resist. His eyes burnt into hers like mamellated chalcedony. His muscular arms enfolded her body as she felt herself being swept away on a noctilucent cloud of passion. "Am I the first?" whispered Dartanyan. "Sort of," she vouchsafed in return, her voice quivering with unrequited passion. "I've not let the other two have a shot on me melted welly yet."'* (from *The Lady & the Three Musketeers* by Barbara Cartland).

melting pot 1. *n.* Blue Mink song from 1969, with a lyric they probably wouldn't include if they wrote it these days, referring to a huge crucible of sufficient capacity to render the world's population into a bubbling 310 million ton mass of hot blubber. 2. *n.* A *chodbin* that hasn't been flushed for some considerable time, *eg.* On a train.

Melvyn 1. *n. rhym. slang.* A cigarette. From Melvyn Bragg = fag. 2. *rhym slang.* Sexual intercourse. From Melvyn Bragg = shag. *'Me and the missus always light up a nice Melvyn after we've had a quick Melvyn.'*

member for trousers north, the right honourable *n.* One's *cock*; the *MP for Pantchester.*

memory foam *n.* Viscous fluid found on the mattress after a nostalgia-inspired bout of *self indulgence.*

memory stick *n.* While on holiday, giving a lucky lady a right *rogering* that she'll never forget for up

to several hours; an erotic episode that could also be filed away in one's *wank bank* for later use.

ménage à moi *n. Fr.* A three-in-a-bed romp where the two ladies fail to turn up. *One off the wrist.*

ménage artois *n.* An unconventional, yet loving, relationship struck up betwixt a gentleman and a well known brand of imported lager.

ménage à twat *n. Fr.* Sad state of affairs whereby a chap sets up house with the girl of his dreams only to find that she is the stuff of fucking nightmares.

ménage à un *n. Fr.* A saucy *mesome.*

men do *n.* A pre-nuptial celebration for a pair of *fruit feelers.*

men in the rigging *n. naval.* Small *tagnuts* trapped in the hairs of sailors' *arses. 'Six months since leaving Tahiti and no sign of land. We ate the last of the breadfruit weeks ago. Water and toilet paper strictly rationed. Crew growing restless, complaining of scrofula, scurvy and men in the rigging. Lord help us.'* (from *The Diary of Fletcher Christian*, 1789).

menoporn *n.* Faux middle brow, often historically set literary works aimed at ladies of a certain age, which feature phrases such as "She took him to her secret hidden place". *'Come on, love. We're going to miss the flight.' 'Hang on. I'm just getting myself a bit of menoporn to read by the pool.'*

mensleydale *n. He-dam, organzola, Fred Leicester.*

mensleydale *n.* Thick, crumbly Yorkshire *knob-cheese.*

men's spendings *n. arch.* Withdrawals from the *clackerbag. Money shots.*

men-stool cycle *n.* The short, yet happy period of a man's life when his *shit* appears at the same time every day.

menstrals 1. *n.* Confectionary choice of a lady during *cricket week.* 2. *n.* Chocolates purchased to soothe the missus when she's *showing off.*

menstrual arithmetic *n.* The reliably accurate calculations performed by a clued-up *left-footer* to decide whether it is safe to *shoot his load* up his missus, who is also the mother of his eighteen children.

menstrual breakdown *n.* A catastrophic *blob strop.*

menstrual cycle display team *n.* Any group of *birds* consisting of a moody one, a happy one, a normal one and a randy one.

mental elf *n.* A small, aggressive person. Also known as a *pub terrier.*

menziese *n. Minge.*

Mercedes badge *n.* A dog's *arse.*

merchant *n. rhym. slang. Kuwaiti tanker.*

merciless *adj.* Said of an aesthetically unconventional woman. A reference to the erstwhile despotic emperor of the planet Mongo in *Flash*

Gordon, who was, likewise, a "bit of a rotter".

merkin *n.* Man-made *mapatasi*, a *stoat syrup*, *pubic Irish*. An artificial *fanny bush*.

mermaid *1. n.* A *big-boned* lass with a pretty face, but nothing worth bothering with below the *tits*. *2. n.* A woman who is good to look at, but just won't open her legs.

mermaid, dripping like a *sim.* Said of a *bird* who is *gooey in the fork*, perhaps while watching a George Clooney movie. See also *dripping like a gravel lorry at the lights, frothing like bottled Bass, as wet as Lee Evans's suit, dripping like a metal teapot, wetter than Whitney Houston's last spliff* and so on.

mermaids *n. pej. Aus.* Australian truckers' slang for Department of Transport compliance officers who check that their lorries are not overladen by means of portable weighing machines which they set up at the roadside. So-called because they are "cunts with scales".

mermaid's cunt paste, thinner than a *sim.* A comment on a substance that exhibits little to no viscosity. *"'Ere, nan. This fucking gravy's thinner than a mermaid's cunt paste.'*

mermaid's flannel, wet as a *sim.* Descriptive of a very, very, very wet *fanny*. Also *otter's pocket, clown's pie, fish drowner.*

mermaid's kiss *n.* The soothing caress of dilute urine and toilet duck across the buttocks which occurs as a *dead otter* is consigned to Neptune's kingdom.

mermunter *n.* In swimming parlance, a lady who is much more attractive below the waterline than above it; quite the opposite of a mermaid.

merry monk *n. rhym. slang.* The happy result of *pulling the Pope's cap off.*

merryneum *n. Twixtmas*, that period between Christmas day and New Year, a term coined by potty-mouthed *Countdown* lexicographer Susie Dent.

Mersey trout *n.* A sweetcorn-eyed brown Scouse fish.

Merthyr minibus *n.* A white, multi-occupant vehicle of the sort found parked at the back of the Crown Court buildings on Glebeland Place every Friday afternoon, ready to ferry the local ne'er-do-wells to various secure institutions throughout the Glamorgan area.

Merthyr socialite *n.* A South Wales man-about-town who is often spotted in a giddy social whirl flitting between William Hills, The Windham and The DSS offices.

Merthyr three-piece *euph.* A tracksuit and trainers, as worn by the the townsfolk of the charming South Wales beauty spot on their regular visits to court.

mertis *n.* Gereral term for any unpleasant substance, such as an accumulation of white residue at the corners of an overweight cruise liner chef's mouth, something your dog lies in on a vet's back room floor while recovering from a general anaesthetic, or that sticky sediment you get between the fingers of a sweaty man who moves filing cabinets up and down fire escapes for a living. *'Montellimar supreme. A frothy concoction of delicious milk chocolate, with a tempting vanilla praline mertis filling, topped off with chopped hazelnuts and a dead bluebottle which must of fell in the machine at the factory.'*

mesome *n.* A *one-in-a-bed romp, ménage à un.* A wank. *'I'm off upstairs for a saucy mesome.'*

mess *n.* Semen, *gunk, cock hockle.* That which is *lost* when one *chucks one's muck.*

Messerschmitt knickers *n.* An *easy lady's scads, ie.* Pants which "come down without much of a fight".

MESS/mess *abbrev.* Spunk. Named after the chef's secret ingredient in McDonald's Extra Special Sauce.

messtuary *n.* A silty build-up of vaginal effluvium, genital detritus and *cludge sludge* in the *breadknife's delta of Venus,* which provides a welcome haven for yabbies, shrimps and mud crabs.

metabollock rate *n.* Scientific assessment of the speed of a chap's recuperation; specifically a measure of the time it takes for him to recover his ardour after *tipping his filthy concrete. 'Don't put your knickers back on yet, love, I'll be back on in five. I've got a very high metabollock rate, me.'*

metal gnu *n.* Female whose myriad of facial piercings fail to hide the fact that she looks like a wildebeest in a frock.

Metal Mickey/Minnie *n.* One who wears an inordinate amount of cheap *bling* in the forlorn hope that it will somehow help them look classy.

metal teapot, dripping like a *sim.* Of a friendly lady, to be romantically enthused to the point at which her *parts of shame* are discharging liquid much like a cheap pressed steel char dispenser in a garden centre café. Also *dripping like a fucked fridge; dripping like a gravel lorry at the lights; wetter than a turfer's knee; wetter than Whitney Houston's last spliff.*

meta-phwoars *n.* Those peculiar, coy words beloved of tabloid journalists when they are writing about *tits* but scared to use the word *tits*, eg. "Assets", "charms", "pink-tipped jelly earmuffs" *etc.*

metatarsal breakers *n. Headlamps* that look fantastic in their current *tit pants*, but which, once unclipped and subjected to the full force of gravity, fly to the floor where their impact may result in fractures to the footbones of their owner or innocent bystanders. *Toe shooters.*

metawank *n.* A self-referential form of masturbation following a protracted period of celibacy, whereby all that one can summon to mind for erotic inspiration is previously enjoyed *wanks.*

methane footprint *n.* An internationally recognised measure used to evaluate the potential environmental damage caused by an individual's emissions of *brownhouse gases.*

methane princess *1. n.* Name of the first ever ship built to transport liquefied natural gas. Don't say we never learn you anything. *2. n.* An attractive lady who drops incongruously foetid *silent-but-deadlies, eg.* HRH Pippa Middleton. Don't say we never learn you anything.

methane suitcase *n.* The *arse.* *'And did you pack this methane suitcase yourself, sir?'*

me-time *1. n.* Acronymic expression; Masturbating Energetically. *'I'm just going into my study for a bit of me-time while you write another one of them Kingsmen films, love.' 2. n.* The temporal period which a *gentlewoman* puts aside for the purpose of *relaxation.* See also *a long hot soak in the bath.*

me-too movement *n.* An unexpected second delivery of *feeshus* that makes an appearance just as the remnants of the first have been successsfully wiped from the *fifties tea towel holder.*

me trembler *n.* A furious, 45-second *wank* up an alley, while staring at a 3-inch screen.

metrobone *1. n.* The infectious, rhythmic, slapping disco beat created by the impact of buttocks and thighs during the act of *doggy-style* intercourse. *2. n.* Involuntary public transport tumescence. *Travel fat, diesel dick.*

mexcellent *adj.* Used to describe one of the several things that is both Mexican and excellent, *eg.* Tequila, Doritos, Ugly Betty's sister's *charms etc.*

Mexican aftershave *n.* The acrid tang of chili and garlic left in the *bog* after a rather nasty night of beer and spicy food.

Mexican barbecue *n. SVSASO.* A *Mexican pinic* with a *cock* stuck in the esposa's *gob* for good measure.

Mexican breakfast *1. n.* Any hearty, early morning meal which *pisses you up* for the day. A protein-rich dish such as huevos rancheros, combining eggs in a tomato sauce. *2. euph. Dining at the Y* during *rag week.* See also *take communion, pasata grin, Ipswich smile, red nose day, fish on Friday.*

Mexican lipstick *n.* The embarrassing, Robert Smith-ish *clown's smile* a fellow displays after

enjoying *Hannibal Lecter's breakfast.* A *pasata grin, Ipswich smile.*

Mexican omelette *n.* Alternative to a *Boston pancake,* but with extra salsa and a nice nap afterwards.

Mexican picnic *n. SVSA, a drugs bust.*

Mexican screamers *n. medic.* A gastroenterological disorder characterised by fiery liquid excrement. *Tijuana brass-eye, Mexican shat dance.*

Mexican suicide *n.* To die peacefully in one's sleep. *'It is announced with deep regret and sadness that Her Royal Highness Princess Margaret committed Mexican suicide at 6.32 this morning at St. George's Hospital.'*

Mexican wave *n.* The act of getting up off the *thunderbox* and then having to immediately sit back down again for a further, unexpected evacuation of the *Enochs.* From the similarity to the eponymous transverse, laterally displaced, periodical motion exhibited by bored sports crowds. A *second sitting.*

Mexican weather forecast *n.* Online *Frankie Vaughan.* A reference to the pulchritudinous Mexican meteorologist Yanet Garcia. *'Whatever you do, nan, don't come in. I'm just in the middle of checking the Mexican weather forecast.'*

Mexican yawn *n.* What happens when one person in a group yawns and then, one by one, everybody else does.

Mexidon *n. S. Yorks.* A Tyke with inaccurately collimated vision, *viz.* One eye looking towards Mexborough and the other looking towards Doncaster.

mezoomas *n. Pink velvet cushions* on which the *family jeweller* prefers to display a *pearl necklace.*

MFI *n.* A massive everything-must-go weekend *shit* enjoyed on a Sunday morning after downing eight or nine pints and a curry on Saturday evening.

Michael Heseltine's alsatian, a cock like *sim.* Said of a *man's best friend* that has had the life all but strangled out of it.

Michael McIntyre *euph.* A high velocity *Boris Johnson.* From the perceived similarity of a rapid *fellator's* head to the vibrating, blurred noggin of the eponymous, high-pitched TV comedy stalwart during one of his side-splittingly hilarious (to him at least), acutely observed routines.

Michael Owen's knee, a dick like *sim.* Something that goes pop within a minute. An *Ikea bulb.*

Michaels *1. n.* A fake pair of *tits* or "Bolt-ons". From the name of the popular crooner Michael Fakepairoftits. *2. n. rhym. slang.* Piles. From the 1970s TV game show host Michael Miles. *'These* nylon trolleys don't half chafe me Michaels.'

Michel n. prop. rhym. slang. Foulage. From boggle-eyed former *Masterchef* host and Nookie Bear lookalike Michel Roux = poo.

Michelin scar 1. n. A *skidmark* left on the *bum sink* bowl that looks like the sort of fancy swish or scrape of "jus" one might find on a plate in an upmarket restaurant. 2. n. The suturing marks left behind after a stomach stapling operation on a somewhat bibendulous person

Michigan splint 1. n. medic. A dental treatment from the US used to maintain and stabilise a centric relation prior to restorative work. 2. n. The romantic act of *doing a bird* up the *Myleene* with the exhaust system off a Dodge Ram truck.

Mickey 1. n. Ir. Dick. 2. adj. Mouse, Swiss. 'Sarah was a bit Mickey this morning. I think she was pissed again.'

Mickey money euph. Ir. Child allowance. From the Emerald Isle-ish slang term Mickey = cock.

Mick Jagger smoking a cigar, like sim. A mid-way point during the launch of a *bum torpedo*, when it is neither in the tube nor heading for the beach, but is somewhere in between. *Casting Churchill's reflection.* 'If I leaned forward now, Jeeves, it would look like Mick Jagger smoking a cigar.'

Mick Mills 1. n. prop. Former Ipswich and England footballer who regularly delivered excellent performances for the full ninety minutes 2. n. rhym. slang. Blue tablets that let middle-aged men do likewise. From Mick Mills = dick pills.

microbiome gentle 1. adj. Used on women's personal care products to indicate that they are safe to use on the purchaser's *minnie moo*. 2. adj. Descriptive of a gent who happens to be rather underendowed *in the trouser department*. 'Today's birthdays: Skin, slapheaded Skunk Anansie singer and guitarist, 1967; Tony Bennett, big band singer, 1926; Jack Straw, microbiome gentle politician, 1946.'

micro-chapped adj. Easily identified through having a small *Hampton*.

microslopic adj. Descriptive of a small *William Pitt* that is towards the runny end of the the UK Standard Bristol Stool Scale.

middle leg n. The penis. Also *middle stump, third leg*.

middle order collapse 1. n. Historically, an all too typical performance of the England cricket team when faced with the prospect of a victory or a draw in a test match. Or even just the slight possibility of not losing by an innings and six hundred runs for once. 2. n. A sudden want of vigour halfway

through a bout of penetrative affection.

Middlesbrough accent n. medic. A severe cough. *'The patient typically presents complaining of headache, high temperature, a productive Middlesbrough accent and nausea. Treatment – 200mg Amoxyl, three times a day' (Tuberculosis – a Guide for Doctors* – Health Department leaflet).

Middlesbrough salad, as lonely as a sim. Particularly isolated, like a forlorn green garnish sat untouched on a plate next to a parmo. 'Alone, alone, all, all alone / Alone on a wide wide sea! / No Middlesbrough salad there's ever been / Has been as lonely as me.' (from *The Rime of the Ancient Mariner* by Samuel Taylor Coleridge).

Middlesbrough vasectomy n. medic. A kick in the *bollocks*.

midfield playmaker 1. n. In football, an overpaid, prancing, centrally positioned player, eg. A *knob* like Glenn Hoddle. 2. n. A *knob*.

MIDF/midf acronym. The past tense counterpart to the conditional *MILF*. That is, a Mum-I-Did-Fuck.

Midgard serpent, the n. A *Thora* of such unfathomable dimensions that it may well presage Ragnarok.

midge's bawhair n. A metric division of length that can only be measured using an electron microscope and a magnifying glass at the same time. A hundred times smaller than a *bee's dick*. *'Fuck me, Henri. You'd better let me drive for a bit. I've had less than you and we were a midge's bawhair from hitting that white Fiat Uno, you know.'*

midge's dick euph. A very narrow margin. A reference to the small genitals of former Ultravox singer Ure, real name Midget Urine. Also *bawhair*. *'I was a midge's dick away from getting caught wanking by my mum last night.'*

midget gems n. Petite but perfectly formed *teats*.

midget porn n. Art pamphletry, videographic grumblery and interwebular erotica featuring the saucy carryings-on of little people, and usually featuring a coked-up woman dressed in a distinctly half-arsed Snow White costume, one would imagine. If it doesn't, they're definitely missing a trick there.

midget's surfboard n. A bachelor/teenager/ priest's *spongle*-hardened sock which has become petrified by a plethora of *emissions* and which is on the Home Office's list of approved weapons which can be used against household intruders. Also *Womble's toboggan, Mother Shipton's sock, bachelor's boomerang*.

midlife cricycle n. A high-powered motorbike bought by a 40-year-old man. Also *suicycle*.

mid-loaf crisis n. Anything that spoils the

enjoyment of a good *tom tit, eg.* A doorbell or telephone ringing, a dawning realisation that there is no *bumwad*, or a policeman approaching the shop doorway.

midnight cock wash *n.* An act of courtesy for a fellow's *significant other*. Pinching the *fiveskin* during a nocturnal *piss* in order to rinse *knob cheese* out of the *farmer's hat. Bellooning.*

midnight mouth organ *n.* A high- cholesterol instrument played with relish around kicking out time in town centres across the land. A kebab.

midnight organ fight *1. n.* Title of a 2008 album by Scottish indie rockers Frightened Rabbit. No, us neither. *2. n.* A post-pub *bang.*

midnight porridge *n.* A hefty helping of vomit on the pavement, usually served up round about *chucking out time. 'Look out Sister Wendy, there's some midnight porridge up ahead.'*

midnight proposal *n.* When going to the *porcelain throne* for a *gypsy's kiss* in the dark, getting down on bended knee to make sure your aim is accurate.

midruff *n.* The exposed area of torso between a young lady's cropped top and her low-cut jeans which may have been toned, tanned and firm a couple of years ago, but which now hangs over her waistband like so much uncooked bread dough. *Muffin tops,* the *jiggle ring.*

midstool *v.* Act of a chap who is so hopelessly lost in love that he would happily kiss the *clackervalve* of the object of his desire while they are half way through *dropping anchor* at *bum bay. 'FREDDY: You know what, Professor Higgins? Miss Doolittle's the one for me. I'm head over heels in love with the girl and I don't care who knows it. Dash it, old man, I think I'd even midstool Eliza if she asked.'* (from *Pygmalion* by George Bernard Shaw).

midwhiffery *n.* The professional skillset of a person assisting at the delivery of a malodorous *arse-baby, eg.* Opening a window, spraying a bit of Glade about, fetching hot water and towels *etc.*

midwife's knot *n.* The *cigar cutter, teatowel holder* or *Bovril starfish.* So-called due to its uncanny resemblance to the belly button of a working class child delivered in a pre-1960s British home or state hospital.

mid-wipe crisis *n.* Unavoidable moment of truth that immediately follows a *hull breach*; an urgent desire to take corrective action involving hot water, soap and a nail brush.

Miffy's mouth *n.* The *chocolate starfish*; a reference to the permanently pursed *gob* of the popular children's book Dutch rabbit.

mighty fine words, preacher *exclam.* Ecclesiastically apposite rejoinder following a rousing

sermon from the *brown pulpit.* Also *I'm ready for the question Noel; catch that one and paint it blue; good health!; pin a tail on that; you're only supposed to blow the bloody doors off; now I'm the king of the jungle.*

mighty mouse *1. n.* A Superman-style cartoon rodent, feebly animated by Paul Terry Studios from the 1940s onwards, and occasionally broadcast on British television in the 1970s and 1980s in the interests of disappointing and depressing the nation's children, who were hoping for a Tom & Jerry. *2. n.* Put politely, a *feminine hygiene requisite* of a sort suitable for the larger-*cunted* lady. A *tampaximum.*

mighty Wurlitzer *1. n.* An enormous organ. *2. n.* Reginald Dixon's *cock.*

migroine *n. medic.* Feeling of generalised cranial decrepitude after spending a little too long trapped in a *porn vortex. 'How was your day working from home, dear?' 'Er, fine love. I had to have a little lie down after lunch as I felt a migroine coming on.'*

Mike Bushell on a runaway horse, stiffer than *sim.* From the *BBC Breakfast* sports presenter's terrifying white-knuckle show-jumping experience from 2013, which left excited viewers wondering where and when his uncontrollable four-legged companion was going to unseat him. *'Well dear, either those three dozen oysters I've been eating every day are starting to work, or Susanna's skirts are getting shorter. I'm stiffer than Mike Bushell on a runaway horse this morning.'*

Mikes *n. prop. rhym. slang.* Convoluted testicular terminology. Mikes = (Michael) Jacksons = (Jackson) Pollocks = *bollocks. 'Nurse Dianne was powerless to resist, as the PM's Oxford-educated eyes burnt into hers like sapphires. His muscular arms enfolded her softly yielding body as she felt herself being swept away by a monsoon of exudate. Tenderly, her hands tugged at the bulging front of his rumpled trousers. "Get your langer out and I'll tickle your Mikes," she gasped in the throes of passion.'* (from *The Politician and the Nurse* by Nadine Dorries).

mild astegmatism *n. medic.* Bizarre ophthalmological phenomenon whereby the subjective attractiveness of a young lady decreases at a rate proportional to the amount of light ale one has imbibed. Like *beer goggles*, but in reverse.

MILDEW/mildew *acronym.* A *milf* for the more sexually adventurous lecherer. Mums I'd Like to Do Everything With.

mile cry club *n.* A desperate act of anguished, hung-over onanism performed in the cramped *bogs* of a budget airline *squeezyjet* flight while returning from an awful weekend stag-do in some godforsaken Eastern European industrial town.

mile high club *n.* Glamorous society of jet-setters who have attempted an uncomfortable, unsatisfactory *scuttle* in the *crappers* on an airliner.

mile high DIY *n.* An act of *self delight* carried out in the aeroplane *bogs* on the return flight from Corfu, for example. *'Captain, you're needed in the cockpit. Engine two is on fire and we've lost all aileron and elevator control. And the co-pilot's gone mad and is screaming about God.' 'With you in a tick, treacle. I'm just doing a spot of mile high DIY.'*

mile high grub *n.* An *art pamphlet* purchased at an airport newsagent.

mile high rub *n.* A *wank* on a plane.

mile 'I' club *n.* Similar to the *Mile High Club*, but for the solitary traveller. *Mile high DIY.*

Miles Davis? *exclam. interrog.* A chucklesome riposte to a melodious *trouser cough*. Voiced in the halting, uncertain tone of a contestant on *University Challenge* who, after having being played a brief burst of atonal trumpet jazz, is asked to identify its progenitor.

miles on the cock *euph.* Sexually experienced. *'That Patsy Kensit's been round the block a bit, you know. Bet she's got a few miles on the cock.'*

milfcake *n.* A beefy, robust *yummy mummy*. Commonly to be found herding children in an airport Burger King.

milf float *n.* A pretend sports car, such as the Peugeot 206CC, driven by an attractive young mother in an effort to recapture the carefree spirit of her lost youth.

milf grand prix *n.* The impressive grid line-up of gleaming four-wheel-drive sports utility vehicles which takes place on the pavements outside the gates of every posh secondary school in the country at 3.30pm.

MILF/milf *acronym.* Mum I'd Like to Fuck. *Yummy mummy.*

MILFO/milfo *n. acronym.* A *postpartum materfamilias* who is prone to parking her Landcruiser diagonally across two disabled spaces. Mum I'd Like to Fuck Off.

milfy way *n.* A constellation of nicely matured *crackers*.

MILILF/mililf *acronym.* A situation that was presumably unknown to the late great Les Dawson; that rare occasion when a fellow's *bag for life's* mum could also be doing with a good *seeing to*. Mother-In-Law I'd Like to Fuck.

MILILF/mililf *acronym.* Mother-In-Law I'd Like

(to) Fuck.

milk before the teabag *1. phr.* A common *faux pas* made by the uneducated when preparing a cup of the nation's favourite hot beverage. *2. phr.* When a gentleman gets so excited at the prospect of dunking his *knackers* in his partner's mouth that he *spunks* all over their face before he gets them in.

milkers *n.* Dairy bags.

milk frother *n.* Adult entertainment industry professional who *messes up*; an over-enthusiastic *fluffer* whose client *knocks off early*.

milking the ferret *n.* Urgent and vigorous masturbation that could leave your fingers bleeding.

milking the thistle *n. Scots.* Wanking.

milk maid *n.* A *grumble flick* actress who is there with an an obliging hand for her fellow thespians.

milkman *n.* That whistling chap who comes in the early morning, leaving yoghurt in your back passage.

milkman's bonus *n.* An unexpected gift after delivering a portion of *cream* to *Mrs Brown*. A *winnet on a stick*. See *shitty dick, kernel blink, poovenir.*

milkman's gait *n.* The walk adopted by someone who has *overshagged*.

MILK/milk *acronym.* A step down from a *milf*. Mum I'd Like to Know. A mature lady you like, but with the best will in the world, she isn't really worth *one*.

milk money *n.* Wages set aside to spend in *breastaurants* and strip clubs. *'I'm just going out for a walk, Mary.' 'Don't forget your milk money, Jeffrey.'*

milk monitor *n.* A breast man. *'Your grandad never misses Only Connect, you know. He's always been a milk monitor.'*

milk of human blindness *euph.* Jipper, Harry Monk, Thelonious, jitler, jizz, ejaculatte.

milk of human kindness *n.* See *liquid rage*.

milk race *1. n.* Adolescent *wanking* game for two or more youths. *2. n.* A barrack room *toss-up* to decide who eats a soggy cream cracker.

milk run *n.* The popular public school dormitory pastime of *wanking* into the open mouth of a sleeping fellow pupil, and running off before they wake up. *'"What's all this noise?" blustered a puce-faced Mr Wilkins, as he charged into the dorm, his eyes bulging with fury. "Don't you boys know it's past midnight?" "Please sir," volunteered Darbishire, "Cameron Minor gave Venables a five shilling postal order to do a milk run on Osborne." In his bunk, the blissfully unaware Osborne snored on, dreaming about a particularly large bowl of hot semolina pudding.' (from Jennings Whacks One*

Off by Anthony Buckeridge).

milk, Scottish *n.* Double cream.

milk shake *1. n.* The uncontrollable quaking caused by an imminent *stack blow. Elvis's leg, Cecil Parkinson's disease. 2. n.* The combination of wobbles, undulations and simple harmonic motions that a middle-aged woman's *bits* perform while she's riding her bloke. *3. n.* A dance favoured by *milfs* who are past the first flush of youth, involving an excess of alcohol and much swaying of the hips.

milk shower *n.* A form of soft-core dairy-based *watersports* that may be engaged in by a man and his lactating missus while she is enjoying a ride on his *solicitor general.*

milk the cow with one udder *v.* To be the only hand in the *farmyard area.*

milk the snake *v.* To practise *self abuse.*

milk tray *n.* A brassiere of the balconette style.

milkybar *1. n.* Popular white chocolate confection advertised by a heavily armed myopic toddler who claims they're "on him", but then you have to pay for them. *2. n.* A *smeg*-encrusted *Johnson.*

milky starfish *n.* A waxed and bleached *fifties teatowel holder.*

milky way, the *n. Titwanking* that does little to ruin one's *bappetite.*

millennium domes *n.* The contents of a Wonderbra, *ie.* Very impressive when viewed from the outside, but there's actually *fuck all* in there worth seeing. See *heavage.*

Millennium Falcon *n.* Epithet used when referring to a dodgy woman your mate has been *banging.* From the *Star Wars* film dialogue referring to Han Solo's spaceship; "You came in that thing? Wow, you're braver than I thought."

million pound drop *1. n.* A tense television gameshow that was broadcast between 2010 and 2015, in which contestants gambled large amounts of money on questions to which they did not know the answer, while Davina McCall shrieked at them. *2. n.* Following a night of brown beer and hot curry, a game of chance whereby a putative *man of the cloth* wagers his trousers that he has got the answer to the question: "Am I about to follow through?" correct. *3. n.* An absolutely enormous, weighty, solid *dreadnought.* Also *million pound drop live* ~ similar to *3* but experienced vicariously because you are ensconced in the next cubicle to the *dumper,* listening to, smelling and enjoying the whole exciting event as it unfolds.

Mills & Bone *n.* Erotic literature with plot pretensions for the red-blooded bachelor.

milm *v.* To cover something in *jism.* 'Oy, mum, I've

milmed me kex.'

milp pond *n.* A small, limpid pool of *bird's custard* found under a lady after her *bacon* has successfully been *awakened.*

miming slang *n.* The use of hand signals to order drinks at a busy bar, particularly when too *arseholed* to enunciate clearly.

mimsy *1. adj.* Descriptive of the state of the borogoves. *2. n.* A *clopper.*

mince medallions *n. Dangleberries, kling-ons.*

mince morsel *n.* An exceptionally pungent *Exchange & Mart* released in a confined area by an anonymous assailant.

mincident *n.* An unplanned and frankly unnerving encounter with a fellow adept at *jumping over puddles, eg.* When inadvertently sticking one's *cock* through a hole in a public lavatory cubicle wall.

mind over bladder *n.* While out *on the lash,* a conscious effort not to *break the seal. Willypower.*

mind over splatter *euph.* The repetition of a simple, powerful mantra – such as "I will not shit myself. I will not shit myself", during the last hundred yards or so of one's trip home from the pub. Sadly, the effort invariably proves to have been futile the moment one places the key in the door.

mind you don't slip on that *exclam.* A verbal warning that follows a particularly moist *stout-drinker's cheer.*

Minecraft beers *n.* In the pub, precious pints *skulled* in welcome peace and quiet after one's bored *sprogs* have been given a smartphone on which to play mindlessly for hours.

miner's arm *euph.* A brawny erection of the male *part* that could knock your teeth out in a pub.

miner's face, as filthy as a *sim.* Descriptive of a very accommodating lady who is eager to please in the bedroom. *Dirty as a zoo keeper's boot, filthy as a Beijing smog mask, dirty as a cow doctor's glove etc.*

miner's snot *n.* The liquid, stringy black *lav children* that can result from a night spent *sniffing the barmaid's apron.*

miner's sock *n.* A perspiring, debris-laden *clopper* after a hard day's graft.

minesweeping *n.* Behaviour which is widely practised at the conclusion of wedding receptions, funeral teas, parties and the like, whereby the band, waiters, undertakers and other sundry hangers-on comb the venue and consume any left-over food, booze, bridesmaids *etc.*

ming *1. v. Scots.* To emit a foul smell, to *hum.* 'Hoots mon, it's minging in here!' *2. n.* A foulsome miasma. 'Gaw, blimey! What's that blooming ming?' 'I'm *afraid Jocky Wilson has done a shit in your shoe, Mr Bristow.' 3. v.* To exude ugliness. *'That bellringer is minging.' 4. n.* The bill, the *scuffers*, the *bizzies*. *5. n.* A new marijuana cigarette made up from discarded ends. A tramp's *spliff, Frankenstein fag. 6. n. prop.* The evil Emperor of Mongo in *Flash Gordon. 7. n. coll.* A quantity of ugly women. *'Don't bother going to Simbas tonight. The place is heaving with ming.'*

ming dynasty *n.* A long, unbroken lineage of *mingers* evident through several generations of women from the same family, most usually on the *Jeremy Kyle Show*.

minge *n. Fanny, cludge, clopper, blurtch, quim.*

minge benefits *n.* The *snatch*-related rewards received by a man as a result of a selfless act performed for a loved one, *eg.* Cooking dinner, buying flowers or sitting through *EastEnders* without complaining too much.

minge binge *n.* The frantic *mackerel*-eating spree of the *gash gannet*.

minge bingo *n.* Pastime enjoyed while enduring a typically turgid rom-com with one's missus; the sly googling of any *fit*-looking actresses who appear in the movie to see if they've ever had their *gammon hangers* or *chest potatoes* out on camera or starred in an out-of-focus, pre-fame DIY *bongo vid*

minge fringe *n.* The hairiest part of a lady's *growler*, that a fellow is forced to brush out of the way repeatedly while he is enjoying a libation at the *blip tap.*

minge hinge *n. medic.* The female child-bearing pelvic area. *'This is the tale of Dora Duckett / Who had a minge hinge like a bucket / Her hubbie swore it was so wide / His charlie never touched the side / Despite her Albert Hall-like muff / He somehow got her up the duff / One night she cried out "Wake up Sid! / I think I'm going to have the kid!" / "Don't panic dear," her husband said / "I'll call the doctor from his bed" / The quack said "How d'you do" to Dora / And slipped his hand in to explore 'er / He stuck his arm right up her clout / As anxiously he felt about / "What's up?" Mr Duckett said / "Can you feel the baby's head?" / "Fuck the sprog," the doctor cried / "There's room for octuplets inside! / I've got my hand up your wife's crotch / Because I've lost my fucking watch."'* (from *Odd Odes* by Cyril Fletcher).

mingelicious *adj.* A *front bottom* alternative to the more *fat-arse*-centric term of approbation *bootylicious. 'That Kylie Minogue is right mingelicious isn't she, cardinal?'*

minge mat *n. Mapatasi, velcro triangle.*

minge miner *n.* A gynaecologist. Also *box doc,*

snatch doc, snatch quack, fanny mechanic, cunt dentist, dirty dentist.

minge mittens *n.* The digits following a spot of *firkyfoodling*. Fish fingers. *'I say, Miss Bennet, these fishcakes taste nice.' 'Take your minge mittens off, Mr Darcy. They're doughnuts.'*

mingeneering *n.* The science of *fanny mechanics. Snatch patching*, gynaecology.

mingerling *n.* To move and socialise amongst the less obviously attractive ladies in a nightclub after resigning oneself to the fact that one isn't going to pull a *looker. 'Well, looks like all the class blart has been snaffled. Better start mingerling, I suppose.'*

minge syringe *n. Pork sword;* a further addition to the words-that-rhyme-with-*minge* lexicon.

mingetout *n.* A *lesbitious* appetizer.

minge watching *n.* The excessive viewing of *box sets* while one's partner is out for the day.

minge winker *1. n.* A striptease artiste. *2. n.* She who flashes her *gash, eg.* While folding her legs. *'Today's birthdays – Sharon Stone, minge winker.'*

mingicle *1. n. Scots.* A frozen stalactite of Glaswegian *fanny batter. 'Och, Agnes. A told ye not tae go oot on the moors in yon greyhoond kilt. Yer mingicles are a' snaggled on yer applecatchers noo.' 2. n.* Stalactites dangling off *birds' snappers*, which form in northern climes when short-skirted young ladies go for a *gypsy's kiss* and then venture out into the freezing weather without first pausing in the *bogs* to *shake the lettuce*. Also known as *slicicles.*

mingineering *n.* Gynaecology. *'Today's birthdays: Rembrandt van Rijn, Dutch artist, 1606; Ian Curtis, British musician, 1956; Robert Winston, British mingineer, 1940.'*

mingivitis *n. medic.* Gum condition affecting those who have recently *motted out* a particularly *gipping blart*.

mingle *euph.* To *cottage* in a sociable manner. *'I'd love to stop and chat, your highness. But I really must mingle.'*

minglewank *n.* A surreptitious *tug* performed through the trouser pocket in a crowded place, *eg.* On a tube train, in a supermarket, at a funeral.

Ming the merciless *n.* An exceptionally foul-smelling *horse and cart*.

miniature heroes *1. n.* Small *fudge nuggets* which, even in the face of vigorous wiping, cling tenaciously to the *arse cress. 2. n.* Tiny *arse bars*.

miniaturist *1. n.* A meticulous painter of tiny artworks, such as Simon Bening or Hans Holbein the Younger, for example. *2. n.* One lacking in the trouser department, such as Bobby Davro or Jack

Straw, for example.

minihughie *n.* A mouthful of *spew* that can be discreetly swallowed back down. The *vurp's* slightly bigger brother.

mini series *1. n.* A troublesome *log* that requires several flushes to see it off. *2. n.* A pile of *shite* starring Jane Seymour or Jenny Seagrove.

minjury *n.* An accident that occurs to a lady's *foofoo*. *'Careful with that champagne bottle, Mr Arbuckle, you'll do someone a minjury.'*

mink *n.* A more up-market name for the wife's *beaver*.

minkle *n.* Hampshire term for a lady's *front pocket*. *'Fuck me, vicar. You can see her minkle.'* Can also be used as a friendly greeting; *'Hallo vicar, you fucking minkle.'*

mink's minge, soft as a *sim.* Descriptive of something which is very soft, *eg.* Fine velvet, silk pyjamas or the suspension in a French car. *'New Andrex Ultra. 50% longer, 50% stronger, but still as soft as a mink's minge.'* (Ad Campaign, Bartle Bogle Heggarty BBD DDP Needham Buggery Bollocks).

minky *1. n.* A French monkey. *2. n.* A species of whale. *3. n.* A *hornbag*. An attractive female.

minnie moo *n. Foofoo, fluffit.*

Minnie Ripperton *1. n.* American soul singer noted for her five octave range and best remembered for her 1975 hit single *Lovin' You*. *2. n.* A tiny, yet extremely high-pitched *Exchange & Mart* that could distract a sheepdog.

minotaur *1. n.* In Greek mythology, a monster with a man's body and a bull's head. *2. n.* In a night club, a monster with a woman's body and a face like a cow's *arse*.

minstrel cycle *n.* Monthly feminine occurrence principally symptomised by the sufferer taking to the sofa and scoffing endless bags of chocolates.

minuteman *1. n.* In the days of the Cold War, a sinister missile sitting in a silo somewhere in America, so-called because of its quick deployment time. *2. n.* A particularly *Judi Denchsome poo*, such that one might say: "I'd give it a minute if I was you" to the next person wishing to use the lavatory, especially if one didn't have a working knowledge of the subjunctive case. *3. n.* A *two-push Charlie* who is *up and over like a pan of milk.*

miracle baby *n.* The offspring of a deeply unattractive woman.

mirage *n.* A mystical pub that appears to be open after all the others are shut, but isn't.

Miranda *1. n. prop.* A pornographic actress who disconcertingly looks directly at the camera, thus breaking the so-called cinematic "fourth wall" and putting you off your stroke. A reference to TV's comedy faller-overer who habitually looks at the camera and puts you off your stroke. *2. n. rhym. slang.* An *air biscuit*. From Miranda Hart = Exchange & Mart.

misanthropissed *adj.* Drunk to a state of curmudgeonliness, like one of those blokes you see in your local Wetherspoon boozer, drinking heavily in silence.

miserbation *n.* The practice of *wanking* over free underwear catalogues, travel brochures and other sundry *humble grumble*, as indulged in by parsimonious bachelors who consider shelling out good money on a copy of *Razzle* to be a frivolous waste of money. *Ebenezer spooging.*

miser's coin bag *n.* A leathery old *scrotum* with some weight in it.

miser's fist *n.* A *bearded clam* that maintains a tight grip on a chap's *slag hammer*. The opposite of a *wizard's sleeve*. Also *fanny like an archer's window, butler's cuff, mouse's ear.*

miser's shite *n.* A miraculous *Enoch Powell* movement, the wiping of which causes no soiling of the first sheet.

miser's zoo *n.* Retail park mainstay Pets at Home; a chain of stores which inexplicably seem to remain profitable despite being visited principally by fathers bringing their young children to look at the animals while their wives pop into the shop next door to take back or exchange something. The pet shop was also referred to as the *cheap zoo* in *Flight of the Conchords.*

misery cord *n.* The bit of white string glimpsed protruding from the *bag for life's chuff* as she pulls her nightie on that tells a chap *the painters are in* and there will be no fun tonight. Also *fishwick, the mouse's tail.*

miss a gear, Davros? *exclam. interrog.* Humorous response to a short, rasping *Spanish lullaby* emitted during locomotion.

Miss Chaversham *n.* A female member of the lower orders who remains unmarried and without child at the advanced age of her early twenties and is hence consigned to madness and eternal spinsterhood.

Miss Chesterfield *n.* A buxom young lady. A well-upholstered *piece* with buttons on the ends of her *tits.*

Miss Hastings *n.* An ugly woman who is in fact the least ugly woman in one's environs. From the heavily be-uglywomanned Sussex seaside town.

missionary impossible *n.* A lady with a *lovely personality* who can only be *poked* in the *doggy* *position.* A *lumberjill*, a *bobfoc*, a *frombie.*

missionary position *1. n.* Sexual intercourse enjoyed when ensconced in a large cooking pot suspended over an open fire, while immersed up to shoulder level by bubbling water with all carrots in it. With a pith helmet on. *2. n. Having it off* with the man on top and the lady looking at the cracks in the ceiling, as recommended by the Pope.

missionary work *euph.* Of the fingers, entering into uncharted, and potentially extremely hostile territory for the first time.

mission creep *1. n.* Having a standing *piss,* before deciding to lower the toilet seat for a *shit. 2. n.* When a man – having foolishly taken his *bag for life* shopping with him – realises that the basket will have to be replaced with a wheeled trolley.

mission impissable *n.* Should you choose to accept it, the challenge of *wazzing* while on the *stonk,* requiring the individual to adopt a Tom Cruise-style near horizontal pose over the *pot.* Though if he was actually Tom Cruise he'd have to be up a ladder to get his *piss* over the rim.

Miss Lincolnshire *n.* Any woman with *spaniel's ears.*

Miss Pwllheli *n.* The ugliest female in any locale who could, should she wish, move to the north Wales town and win its annual beauty pageant by default.

Miss Selfridge shuffle *n.* The embarrassed, self-conscious little dance performed by a man left waiting in the *titpants* and *dunghampers* section of a department store while his wife is in the changing rooms.

missus button *n.* The control on the front of a desktop PC (often labelled "reset") which can be hit to remove all the vile, hardcore *grumble* from the screen when one's wife or partner returns home unexpectedly. The *top shelf destruct button.*

mistake chariots *n.* Prams.

misterectomy *n. medic.* Radical surgical procedure. The removal of a gent's *matrimonial components.* '*Come over here, Tiger. Me mum wants to give you a misterectomy.*'

mister Magoo *n. rhym. slang.* A *Scooby Doo.*

misty mountain top *n.* A *gnome's hat* which has been sat in the *chod pan* overnight, so that a light fog has begun to form around its summit.

Mitchells *n.* Huge pairs of *tits.* Termed after their resemblance to the bald heads of erstwhile *EastEnders* hard boys Phil and Grant. Also *Right Said Freds.*

Mitsubishi mud pie *n. Doggers'* take on the popular chain restaurant dessert, involving *anal* in the back of an Evo.

MIWIDS/miwids *abbrev.* Mum I Wish I Didn't Shag.

mixed grill *n.* A particularly unappetising *Fred Kite* of varying consistencies, colours and constitution. A *full German.*

mixed grill *n.* A sexual partner who "likes a bit of everything."

mixing the mud *phr.* In offshore engineering, to ream a cavity and fill it with viscous fluid in order to prevent a wall collapse.

mix your drinks *v.* To apocryphally indulge in the consumption of more than one individual's *pop* in a single, eclectic sitting. '*You been mixing your drinks again, Marc?*'

MOAB/moab *1. abbrev. milit.* Massive Ordinance Air Burst or, colloquially, the Mother Of All Bombs. Military shorthand for thermobaric devices that are more powerful than anything except nuclear weapons. *2. acronym.* Massive Ordinance Air Biscuit.

Mobe *n.* Abbreviation of Moby Dick. An epic *turd,* longer than a *mini series,* which may require harpooning with the lavatory brush to see it off.

mobese *adj.* Large-skeletoned. From morbidly + obese. '*Born on this day: James Last, beardy German bandleader, 1929; Victoria Beckham, sulky motor car designer, 1974; John McCririck, late mobese racecourse womble, 1940.*'

mobile bone *n.* Of a Gentleman who finds, for any number of reasons, at any time of the day or night, that he is sporting a pop-up *throbbing gristle kickstand* in the most inappropriate of places. '*Do excuse my mobile bone, Mother Teresa.*'

mobile spanking *n. Banking with Barclays* on a smartphone.

mobile throne *n.* A portable *shit house* that everyone avoids at pop festivals because the floor is two inches deep in *mocking birds.*

mockbuster *n.* Cunningly packaged *ersatz* DVD sold at a discount store to fool hurrying shoppers.

mockers *n. Moobs.* From man + knockers.

mocking birds *rhym. slang. Douglas Hurds.*

mocktail bar *n.* Licensed premises confusingly frequented by *flippers.*

mock turtle *1. n.* A character in *Alice in Wonderland,* written by antique *kiddie diddler* Lewis Carroll. *2. n.* Something that feels like a *shit,* but turns out to be a *fart.*

model T fart *n.* A *wind breakage* that sounds like one that is about to be run over by Laurel and Hardy.

MODO/modo *abbrev.* A *snatch* like a cheap pasty, that is to say one that is crusty on the outside and leaves a gamey aftertaste that lingers unpleasantly in the *gob* for hours. Meat Of Dubious Origin.

mod's parka *n.* A young lady's *clopper* of a particularly unattractive mien, resembling a sort of floppy funnel with a bit of flea-bitten fur stuck round the collar. Possibly encountered on Brighton beach while a youth in a leather jacket strikes it repeatedly using a stout length of pipe.

Moe Greene special *1. euph.* Named after the *Godfather* character, a gangland execution carried out by shooting someone in the eye. *2. euph.* The act of *blowing your stack* into a lucky ladyfriend's *mince.* *'I gave her a Moe Greene special and now she has to wear a pirate patch.'*

mofart *n.* A tuneful *magic poot flute* that would not disgrace the august surroundings of the Royal Albert Hall. Well, it would, though.

mofo *n. abbrev.* Abbreviation for *monkey feather.*

moggy style *adj.* Descriptive of sex in a neighbour's garden, performed at 3am by participants who don't necessarily like each other. Involves a lot of mewling and hissing, and usually ends with a bucket of water being thrown.

Mogwai *n.* An uncooperative *ladypart.* Named in honour of the famous gremlin out of that film, because "it's cute and furry, but no matter how much you play with it, you can't get it wet".

Mogwai's eye, fanny like *sim.* Descriptive of particularly bulbous *Keith Burtons.* Named after the eyelids of the gremlin, which resembled particularly bulbous *Keith Burtons.*

mohair knickers *n.* A large and unruly *minnie moo* with *Jeremy Clarkson's eyebrows* sticking out of it. A *biffer.*

moip *n.* Female genital lubrication. *Froth, fanny grease, vagoline, beef dripping, blip, bilp, sloom.*

moip mop *n.* A chap's beard used to soak up *sloom*, in the same way one would use a slice of bread to soak up gravy. *'Short back and sides, please. And could you trim the stray bits off my moip mop?'*

moist and meaty *adj.* Alliterating adjectives used extensively to describe the female and male genitals respectively, as well as dog food.

moisture in the charging port *1. n.* An error message, which appears when trying to charge a mobile phone after dropping it in the toilet. *2. n.* The state all shallow women get themselves into while watching Colin Thing in his shirt coming out that pond in *Pride and Prejudice. Gooey in the fork.*

molar coaster *n.* A thrill-packed, two-minute *chewie* off a toothsome *sword swallower.*

mole at the counter *euph.* A mammalian *turtle's head.* *'"From the imprint of his shoes, Watson, I deduce that our quarry is a left-handed doctor of unusually short stature, who has known prosperity but has lately fallen on hard times. And by the short, irregular length of his stride, it is apparent that he has a mole at the counter," said Holmes.'* (from *The Case of the Speckled Bowl* by Sir Arthur Conan Doyle).

molehilling *n.* When camping at night, *doing one's business* in a bag and then surreptitiously placing it under the groundsheet of a particularly annoying neighbour's tent.

mole in the back garden *n.* Small, brown animal that pops its head out for a second, leaving an unpleasant mound of soft dirt around the edge of its burrow.

mole's breath *1. n. Wanky* Farrow & Barrow paint colour that "Lord" David Cameron's shepherd's hut is probably painted in. *2. n.* A *queef.*

mole's eye *n.* A *fanny* which makes a *mouse's ear* look like a *horse's collar.* *'Consignia was powerless to resist. His eyes burnt into hers like ambers. His muscular arms enfolded her body as she felt herself being swept away on tradewind of passion. "Now, Fernando!" she gasped. "Take me now. All these years in the convent I've been saving myself for the right man, and now I've found you." "Fucking get in," breathed Fernando. "You must have a snatch like a mole's eye."'* (from *The Nun and the Windowcleaner* by Barbara Cartland).

moles' noses *n.* Extremely erect nipples.

mole with a wet nose *n.* A particularly moist *fart.* A *squench.*

molten brown *euph.* An unpleasant, morning-after-Vindaloo-style *digestive transit*, which melts the *balloon knot.* Named in direct contrast to the rather pleasant bathroom cosmetics manufacturer. A *rogan splosh, dump and burn.*

moment of clarity *n.* The instant following *stackblow*, when a *self-polluter* is assailed by intense feelings of disgust and self-loathing, and vows never to touch himself *down there* again. Just like he did half an hour previously. *Wangst, wanguish, tugger's remorse.*

moment of reflection *euph.* The time spent pleasantly staring into the middle distance while having a *shit.* *'As cathartic as this opera is, dear, I feel I must nevertheless adjourn for a moment of reflection.'*

Mona Lisa smile *1. n.* Title of a will.i.am song. *2. n.* The inscrutably rapturous expression on the face of a nun who has recently cycled down a cobbled street. Like they do.

Monday roast *n.* Following a substantial meal on the Sabbath, the next day's hearty morning *sit-down visit*, complete with *air biscuits* and gravy.

Monet bird *n.* A lady who, in reference to the

painted works of the renowned French impressionist painter Claude Monet (1840-1926), "looks better from a distance". A *low resolution fox*.

money goggles *n*. Notional optical aids that enable attractive young *pieces of crackling* to see past the aesthetic failings of much older, physically decrepit millionaires.

moneymoon *n*. The magical, albeit all too short, period of financial stability which one enjoys after a win on the horses or taking out a Payday Loan.

money pit *n*. A degrading term for the *patty* of a female that a fellow is courting, what with the exorbitant cost of chocolates and cinema tickets and all the other never-ending buttering-up *shit* required.

money shit, the *1. n.* The main event during a visit to the *Rick Witter*, usually preceded by the dropping of several, less satisfying *rabbit pellets*. *'Aaah. That's the money shit alright.'* *2. n.* The climactic scene in a German *grumble* film.

money shot *n*. The moment in a *bongo flick* where the leading man makes a small deposit from *Kojak's money box*, usually into the leading lady's face or onto her *rack*. A *pop shot*.

money tits *n*. The sort of smashing *Davy Jones's lockers* any man worth his salt would happily hand over his hard-earned wages to see unfettered, *eg.* The *fat rascals* fastened to the chest of leek-chomping warbler Charlotte Church.

mongrel *n*. A *dobber*, a *semi*, half a teacake. A *kindling limb* in a state of semi-turgidity that is neither one thing nor the other. A *Grand Old Duke of York* which is *on the bounce*.

Monica's eyes *euph*. A visibly *erectivitated* pair of *nip-nops*, named in honour of the protuberant ocular organs of scary *Masterchef* judge Monica Galetti. *Pygmies' cocks, Scammel wheelnuts, chapel hat pegs, JCB starter buttons*.

monkey *n*. The vagina. A *toothless gibbon*.

monkeybagging *n*. A man's means of heightening his pleasure while an act of oral *horatio* is being performed upon his *tummy banana*. *Monkeybagging* involves the simple act of tugging one's partner's ears perpendicularly away from their head, thus modifying the shape of their mouth and lips.

monkey bath *n*. A bath so hot that, when lowering yourself in, you go: "Oo! Oo! Oo! Aa! Aa! Aa!"

monkey cake *n*. A lady's *front bottom*.

monkey cum *n*. Any cream-based *tart fuel*, *eg.* Bailey's, that Aldi version of Bailey's. "Ballycastle", they call it.

monkey face *n*. The act of throwing a handful of carefully harvested *gorilla salad* trimmings onto

a romantic partner's physiognomy the moment after you have *whitened her teeth*.

monkey feather *exclam*. Bizarre substitute for *m*****f***** dubbed into Eddie Murphy films on BBC1 to avoid offending some stupid old cunt. Also *mother father, money farmer, melon farmer, muddy funster*.

monkey pie *1. n.* A chip shop delicacy heated to the temperature of the earth's core which, upon taking the first *Bee Gees bite*, causes its purchaser to cry out in a series of inarticulate, high-pitched simian shrieks and howls. *2. n.* A hairy, ill-mannered *clopper* that keeps blowing raspberries.

monkey run *n*. Half-sprinting, half-hobbling from the computer desk to the bathroom, an awkward trot performed by a web *grumble* enthusiast with the *jester's shoes* who has realised too late that all the socks are in the wash. A gait which brings to mind that of Clint Eastwood's ginger simian sidekick Clyde in the *Every Which Way but Loose* movie series. A *wounded soldier's walk, bishop's waltz*.

monkey's chin *n*. *Twix lips, beetle bonnet*, a prominent *mound of Venus*.

monkey's fag break *n*. Like slipping out for five minutes for a fag, but for a *ham shank* instead of a *Harry Rag*. A *wank* at work. *'Can the minister confirm that the forthcoming amendments to the bill will contain sufficient powers to tackle the proliferation of online pornographic material?' 'He'll tell you in a minute. He's just went for a monkey's fag break.'*

monkey's fist *1. n.* Large nautical knot traditionally used by sailors as a means of weighting the end of a rope to make it easier to throw or clobber someone with. *2. n. medic.* Uncomfortable post-coital condition whereby the *herman jelmet* retains its previous tumescence while the penile shaft withers back to its usual size. *'He looked uncomfortable on the final lap, I thought, Brendan.' 'Yes Steve. Speaking as someone who ran the 5,000 metres with a monkey's fist at Rome in 1974, it's no joke I can tell you.'* *3. n.* A small, brown *Richard the Third*. Found by a cockney vicar on the pavement.

monkey's forehead *1. n. Parts of shame*.

monkey's kneecap *n*. A scabby *quim* one could spend all day picking the fleas out of.

monkey's tail *n*. A small lick of *foulage* on the rear of the seat caused by sitting too far back while *dropping the kids off at the pool*.

monkey's toe *1. n.* A nipple big enough to peel a banana. A *Westminster Abbey hatpeg*. *2. n.* The *turtle's head*.

monkey strokes *n*. Like the *vinegar strokes*, but with added teeth-baring, cries of "Ooh! Ooh! Ooh! Aah! Aah! Aah!", and possibly a big blue *arse*.

monkey up the chimney, have a *1. v. arch.* To have a mortgage on one's house. *2. v.* To be in need of a massive *shit*.

monkey wank *n.* To masturbate oneself or another person using one's feet. While swinging in a tyre.

Monkhouse's syndrome *n. medic.* To vomit into the mouth and swallow it back down with a tortoise-like gulp and hand gesture, reminiscent of late comic Bob introducing a punchline on *Celebrity Squares*. *Bob's Full Mouth, vurp, broat.*

monk's chain *n. eccles.* An annulus or line of friars, public schoolboys or BBC football commentors interfering with each other's *parts of shame*. A *daisy chain*, a *circle jerk*.

monk's chunks *n.* The excess *smeg* build-up of a man who has given up caring any more.

monk's cowl *1. n.* A *wizard's sleeve, monk's hood*. *2. n.* A capacious *fiveskin*.

monks' trunks *n.* Underpants that are crunchy with dried *milk of human blindness*.

Monmouth banoffee *n.* When someone goes for a *shit* in a kettle. One of the less successful technical challenge rounds in the *Great British Bake Off.*

monolog *1. n.* A 1970s television play starring Thora Hird or Patricia Routledge that would cost *fuck all* to make and win Alan Bennett a BAFTA. *2. n.* A visit to the *smallest room* that achieves unqualified success in a single drop.

monolog *n.* The king of all *feeshii*. A single, unbroken length of *dirty spine* that slips into the water with the grace of an *otter off the bank*, leaving no *winnets* or *bum mince* in its wake.

monorailing *n.* What *Tomorrow's World* promised us would be commonplace by the year 2000; when a woman is on top and frictionlessly gliiding backwards and forwards along her fellow's *diamond cutter* rather than putting it in.

monster munch *1. n.* A popular snack that is unlikely to form part of your government-recommended five-a-day. *2. n.* A prolonged act of *oral delight* performed on one with a *lovely personality*, in order to avoid having to look at their face. Usually pickled onion flavour.

monsterpated *adj. medic.* So badly *backed up* that – when you finally manage to move your *Simons* – it feels like a raging Godzilla is trying to get out of your *arse*. Often accompanied by an enormous roar and tsunami-levels of *splashback* as the angry behemoth descends into the deep.

mons veneris *n.* The *beetle bonnet, tump, dove's chest*.

Montezuma's revenge *n. medic. Mexican screamers*,

the *shits. Tijuana cha-cha.* Named after the Aztec ruler Montezuma (1466-1520) who, following the conquest of his homeland by the Spaniard Hernán Cortés, vowed to exact his vengeance by giving a thousand generations of Europeans mild diarrhoea.

monthly wrench *n.* The variably sized *tool* which a chap employs in order to *tighten his nuts* while his *ride* is *up on blocks. Wanking spanner, dick skinner.*

Monty *n.* A *blopstrop* or *tammy huff.* Named in honour of Ryder Cup winner and perennial *mardy-arse* Colin Montgomerie.

Monty Don's fingernails, as filthy as *sim.* Exceptionally eager to please.

moo *n.* One of comedy racist Alf Garnett's less offensive insults, all things considered.

mooberty *n.* The stage in a man's life when the ripped, buff pectorals of his youth evolve into flabby *man tits*. Usually experienced after the age of thirty following excessive self-prescription of *bar medicine*.

moobs *n.* Flabby breast-like structures sported by non-sporting gentlemen whose only form of daily exercise is to jog past the salad in the works canteen. From man + boobs. *Man breasts, mannery glands, bitch tits.*

moody poo *n.* A *chocolate hostage* that, despite having banged loudly on the door earlier in the day when there was no opportunity to release it, refuses to come out later, when circumstances are more propitious. Also *sulker.*

mooey *n.* A *sausage wallet, minnie moo.*

mooing *n.* The self-pitying state of mind of one who has recently been dumped by a loved one, sat in their bedroom listening to James Blunt records.

moomlaaters *n.* Traffic-stopping *moobs.*

moo-moo land *1. n.* Fictitious location whither the KLF were apparently bound. *2. n.* A frankly disappointing *slag heap.*

moomph *1. v. Aus.* To sniff a lady's bicycle seat. *Barumph, snurgle. 2. n. Aus.* One who *moomphs. A garboon, snufty, snurglar.*

moon *v.* A rugby move, whereby the prop forward sprints around the defending back four to the rear of the bus and presses his naked *arse* up to the back window.

moon grease *n.* Sweaty *barse* juice, *arse vinegar. Driving instructor's suet.*

moonie *1. n. prop.* A follower of the Rev. Ying Tong Yiddel-I Moon. *2. n.* An act of *mooning. Hanging your hole.*

moon juice *n.* The liquid product of a lady's monthly discomfort. The cargo of the *tomato* *boat. Lunar mess, fanny jam.*

moon landing *n.* The slightly alarming moment which occurs at the precise moment that a person sits on another's face. *'I held my breath all the way through the moon landing.'*

moonlight shadow *n. medic.* Female constipation. From a lyric from the Mike Oldfield song of the same name, *viz.* "And she couldn't find how to push through". *'I tell you, your holiness. I shouldn't have had that six-egg omelette this morning, only I've got a touch of the moonlight shadow now.'*

moonraker *1. n.* One who is prone to scratch their *ringpiece. 2. n.* Space-based James Bond film in which, for the purposes of a particularly off-colour Christmas afternoon pun, a weightless Roger Moore apparently attempts to *thumb in a slacky* after already losing his *mess* up a scientist who is named to imply that she is a talented *cock-sucker.*

moonwalk *n.* The optical illusion of walking without moving achieved by someone trying to wipe a *dog's egg* off their shoes onto the grass.

moose *n.* Unkind way of referring to a *boiler* who's got *Don King in a headlock.*

moose knuckles *n. Can.* Camel's foot, Ninja's toe.

moosetrap *n.* The protracted, often expensive, and frankly unnecessary, efforts expended when attempting to seduce a right *boot* of a lass when, in reality, a simple "Fancy a bang?" would probably achieve the same outcome. Inspired by the popular charity shop 1970s children's boardgame *Mousetrap*, which featured an overly complicated contrivance for the purpose of entrapping a small plastic rodent that was frankly not going anywhere.

moped *n.* A *bubbly* woman. From the old joke that "it's fun to ride, but you wouldn't want your mates to know."

MOPILF/mopilf *acronym.* Member Of Parliament I'd Like to Fuck. *'Look at him, reclining on the front bench like Ingres' Odalisque. He's a real mopilf.'*

mop the fishmonger's floor *v.* To perform *cumulonimbus* on the *bag for life.*

Mordor march past *n.* The parade of spinsters that forms between a club and a kebab shop at closing time.

more cocks than a French textbook, he's/she's had *exclam.* Said of a well travelled person who has had a greater number of engorged male members in her than are to be found pencilled in the pages of a typical school primer. Also (*she's been*) *fucked more than Micheal Owen's knee, cocked more times than Davy Crockett's rifle, had more sausage than a fat German butcher, been rogered more times than a policeman's radio, had more pricks than a second*

hand dartboard etc.

more Ginster than gangster *adj.* Descriptive of the sort of portly *twat* with a shaved head, tracky pants, white polo shirt, lots of expensively cheap jewellery, and who has to use the roof of his ageing BMW in order to haul himself out onto the pavement before strutting off like an overweight Al Capone. *'The guy thought he was some kind of toughnut, but actually he was more Ginster than gangster.'* (from *The Pram in the Lake* by Raymond Chandler).

more lip than a cow's got cunt, you've got *exclam.* Something to say to someone with a cheeky disposition, *eg.* A double glazing salesman, a potty-mouthed Radio 2 presenter on the telephone or an overly insistent Jehovah's Witness on the doorstep. Also, for the more poetically inclined, *more front than a cow's got cunt.*

more Paul than Bamber *euph.* Not very bright.

more pricks than the Big Brother house, she's seen *exclam.* Somewhat waspish judgment of a lady of easy affections, who has been *cocked more than Elmer Fudd's shotgun.*

more rolls than Greggs bakery *sim.* A rhetorically witty description of a woman with a *lovely personality.*

more takeaways than Carol Vorderman, he/she's had *exclam.* Said of someone who is *big boned.* A reference to the TV mathematician/equity release scheme saleswoman's subtraction skills rather than her diet, one might imagine.

more tea vicar? *phr.* Faux-farcical attempt to distract a clergyman after the launch of an *air biscuit,* now widely used to diffuse post-*fart* tension. See also *keep shouting Sir, we'll find you; speak up caller, you're through; what's that, Sweep?; someone's tinkered with Herbie.*

more than three shakes is a wank *exclam.* Classic public toilet apophthegm that certain celebrities would have done well to heed down the years, all things considered.

Morgan *n. rhym slang.* Arse. From Morgan Stanley Dean Witter = shitter.

morgue cheater *n.* A senior citizen. A *coffin dodger, oxygen thief, grave sniffer* or *GBNews viewer.*

Mork *v.* To perform an act of sexual foreplay which involves simultaneously inserting four fingers from the same hand into two orifices on a lady, *two in the pink* and *two in the stink.*

Morley moped *n.* A mobility scooter. Also *Frinton Ferrari, Mansfield motorcycle, nanbretta.*

Mormon mini-van, the *n.* An extreme method of pleasing one's lady. Named in honour of the Latter Day Saints' fondness for large families.

Consisting of "two in the front" (fingers/*fanny*) and "five in the back" (fist/*arse*).

mornflakes *n.* Residue found in one's *pubes* after carelessly *relaxing in a gentleman's way* several times the previous evening.

morning after Pils *n.* Age-old remedy for easing the after-effects of a long session on the booze.

morning crackle *n.* The sound made by the *rusty sheriff's badge* when *opening the first post*.

morning finger *n. medic.* A malodorous digit at daybreak after going to bed with an itchy *arse*.

morning glory *n.* The appearance of a *tent pole* first thing in the morning. A *dawn horn, jake, motorcycle kickstand*.

morning has broken *exclam.* Something to exclaim joyfully after *dropping* the first *gut* of the glorious new day. Also *morning has broken wind.* '*Open a window, dear, for morning has broken.*'

morning level crossing *euph.* The first *hit or miss* of the day. From the fact that you have to wait for the barrier to go down before you can proceed. Even though, on a real level crossing, you have to wait for the barrier to go up before you can proceed, obviously. Unless you're a train driver.

morning line, the *1. n.* Erstwhile Channel 4 horse-racing programme hosted by Happy Shopper Steve Rider Derek Thompson and lamentable celebrity nose-picker John McCririck. *2. n.* The results left in one of them back to front German *shitters* when one *releases the chocolate hostage* after a breakfast of schnitzels, boiled cabbage and lager.

morning thickness *n.* A post-slumber state of erectivitation. Also *morning wood, morning glory, dawn horn*.

morning thunder *n.* The first, usually very powerful *fart* of the day. A *breakfast maker.*

morning wood *n.* Ante-meridian tumescence.

Moroccan woodbine *n.* A long, super-strength cigarette of the sort found in Amsterdam coffee shops.

morris dancer *n.* An excessively pierced woman who probably jingles as she *humps*, while at the same time showing great dexterity when batting your *whiffling stick*.

Morrissey's stag night, like *sim.* Descriptive of a public house peopled entirely by broken men of indeterminate age staring silently at their half-empty pint glasses. '*Shall we go to Yates's instead? It's like Morrissey's stag night in here.*'

Morse commode *n.* Long and short cryptic sound signals issued by the *Harris* while seated on a porcelain resonator. Audible *Morse commode*

patterns often signify distress.

mortal *adj. Refreshed* within an inch of one's life.

mortal combat *n.* Fighting between intoxicated fellows. Or occasionally, in the case of certain self-sufficient *Harold Ramps*, between a single intoxicated fellow.

mortar attack – dig in! *1. exclam.* The first bit of Talking Action Man dialogue when his string was pulled. *2. exclam.* Shouted warning upon emitting an explosive *Exhange and Mart*.

mortgage boy *n.* A high class *rent boy* with one foot on the property ladder.

mortgaged *1. adj.* In Monopoly, when a valuable property is turned red, and is therefore troublesome to land on for the foreseeable future. *2. adj.* Out of bounds during *rag week*.

mortgage eyes *n. medic.* The discollimated *peepers* of someone who is rather unhinged. That is, "one eye fixed and one eye variable". See also *wartime searchlights*.

Moscow centre *1. n.* Amongst Russian agents working abroad, the mysterious, omniscient source of orders, requests for status updates, and occasional summonses to return home to be interrogated and summarily shot. *2. n.* The *missus*.

Moses disease *n. medic.* The painful result of engaging in manual stimulation of the missus's *blurtch* after previously cooking with chillies, ie. "A burning bush". Also *Scotch bonnet*.

Moses effect *n.* What a seatbelt or bag strap does to a lady's *baps, ie.* Causing them to part like the Red Sea.

Moses fart *n.* A *blunderguff* of such foetid potency that it causes a navigable path to form through a sea of people. Particularly effective in a nightclub or when queuing to be served in a bank.

mosquito's tear *n.* An unimpressive quantity of ejaculate produced by a young man or bachelor at the conclusion of his ninth *pull* of the day, when the amount of *spuzz* issuing from his *hog's eye* is roughly equivalent to the quantity of liquid which drips onto the cheek of an insect of the family *culicidae* during the final scenes of *Love Story*, when Ali McGraw *carks it*.

Moss Bros hire trousers, more cocks in her than a pair of *sim.* Descriptive of a loose-moralled lady who boasts an impressively extensive sexual back catalogue. '*I tell you what, I wouldn't say she's easy, ladies and gentlemen, but she's had more cocks in her than a pair of Moss Bros hire trousers. So in conclusion, can we all raise our glasses and toast the bride and groom?' 'Thank-you, vicar. And now it's time for the best man's speech.*'

moss cottage *n.* The ideal home for *John Thomas*,

with all pubes round the door.

mosstril *n.* A single nasal aperture of the sort sported by celebrity types (*eg.* Daniella Westbrook) who have, at various times, found *Keith Richard's dandruff* a bit moreish.

Moston magpie *n.* White undergarments seen through the gossamer-thin black Primark leggings adorning the ample *muck spreaders* of women in the salubrious North Manchester suburb.

mothbait *n.* The cotton T-shirts on sale at Sports-Direct that at first glance would appear to be a bargain at three for a tenner.

mothball diver *n.* One who savours *granny's oysters*. A *biddy fiddler, OAP-dophile, old dear hunter.*

mothballed *1. adj.* Descriptive of a person possessed of such little courage or assiduousness that it is assumed his testicles would measure no greater than those of an insect of the order *Lepidoptera. 2. phr.* Used in reference to one who has shied away from a task requiring courage or effort. *'Cameron mothballed it once he realised Leave had won.'*

moth boy *n.* The member of a drinking party who, upon entering a pub, proceeds directly to the bandits, attracted by the flashing lights. *Fruit fly.*

mother and child reunion *n.* Having a massive *feeshus* which is immediately followed in the same sitting by a much smaller counterpart. From the eponymous song, containing the apposite lines "The mother and child reunion / is only a motion away", which was written after Paul Simon experienced just such an eventuality in the bogs at Widnes Railway Station.

motherfucker *n.* In filmic *oeuvre* of Quentin Tarantino, an unpopular person. A polite term which can be used in the place of obscene terms such as *melon farmer, monkey feather, money farmer etc.*

Mother Hubbard's dog *sim.* Descriptive of an underused *minge, ie,* Drooling and *gagging for a bone. 'It's noo a score and seven years since her beloved Bonny Prince Albert passed awa'. Today, while oot aside the loch, Her Majesty confided in me that she missed his big wullie affy bad, and that most o' the time, her wee royal badger was akin tae Mother Hubbard's dog.'*

mother load *n. Milf*-powered *spendings.*

mothership *n.* A massive *turd* floating in the *chod pan,* surrounded by a flotilla of assorted anal effluviums, jetsams and detritii.

mothership and a fleet of shuttles *euph.* In the world of defecation terminology, another way of describing that phenomenon whereby a large *dreadnought* is immediately followed by a flotilla

of smaller vessels which have been queuing behind it like nippy hatchbacks behind a tractor on a country road. A *pace car* situation.

Mother Shipton's kegs *n.* Petrified, crispy *undercrackers* found stuffed down the back of a bachelor's radiator. *Monks' trunks.*

mother's love *n.* The quality which alows one to re-enter the *cludgie* after *laying a cable* when others have deemed the *ming* too merciless to tolerate.

Mother Teresa's finger *n.* The opposite of a *Bungle's finger.* A pale, sickly, insipid *copper bolt* which resembles nothing so much as a digit from the hand of the erstwhile saintly Albanian bauble-hoarding nun. *'Best call the doctor and see if I can get an emergency appointment, love. I just done a Mother Teresa's finger.'*

moth sandwich, dry as a *sim.* Descriptive of something which is extremely deficient in the moisture department. *'What's the matter down there, Mr Elliott? Why have you stopped?' 'I'm going to have to go in the kitchen, I say the kitchen, for a glass of water, I say a glass of water, Mrs Bishop. Yon twat's as dry as a moth sandwich, I say a moth sandwich.'*

motion of no confidence *n.* A distinctly trepidatious *sit-down toilet* adventure. Also *motion of low confidence :* A runny *bum* due to nerves.

motion picture *n.* A "selfie" taken while ensconced on the *thunderbox.* A popular stag-do meme, it says here.

motion sensor *n.* The first tiny twitchings of the *cigar cutter* muscles sounding the alarm that a huge *dump* is about to enter the room.

motions, go through the *1. phr.* To perform an obligatory task but with no real effort or enthuisiasm. *2. phr.* To swim in the English sea.

motion sickness *n.* Nausea caused by doing a *Donald* so foul that it makes one gag.

motion thickness *n. Travel fat.*

motion to dismiss *1. n.* A party's request to a court to dismiss a case because of settlement, voluntary withdrawal, procedural defect or claim is one for which the law provides a remedy. Under the Federal Rules of Civil Procedure, Rule 41(a) [USCS Fed Rules Civ Proc R 41] a plaintiff may voluntarily dismiss the case. So now you know. *2. n.* When your flatulence is so ripe and frequent that those around you have no option but to insist you adjourn to the *little barrister's room* for further private negotiation.

motivational squeaker *n.* An extremely high-pitched yet piquant *guff* that will cause a great deal of sudden agitation, the opening of windows, waved order papers *etc.*

motorboat, the *n.* The act of placing one's face between a lady's *baps* and pushing them together from either side while making the noise of an outboard motor. A woman can thus be described as *motorboatable* if she possesses sufficient *motorboatability*. A *two-stroke man sandwich.*

motorcycle kick stand *n.* The morning erection that manifests itself while one is asleep on one's side, preventing one from rolling over onto one's stomach.

motorhead *1. n.* A famous heavily metallic popular music combo, famous for their jaunty ditties, including *Ace of Spades* and *Killed by Death*. *2. n.* An urgent *blowjob* delivered at breakneck speed behind a sleazy burger bar, cinema or skip.

motorway miles *phr.* Said about a woman of a certain vintage who has, nevertheless, retained some of her original showroom pizazz and sparkle. *'Fair enough, she's been round the clock a few times, but they're all motorway miles.'*

mott *1. n.* A lady from Cumbria. *2. n.* Part of a Norman fort from GCSE history. *3. n.* A *twat like a pair of padded coathangers.*

mottaging *n.* The female version of *cottaging*, if such a thing exists.

mott blotter *n.* A *fanny nanny* or *snatch patch.*

mott rot *n. medic.* Any malignant ailment caught off the missus's *quimpiece*. *'I've got the results of your tests back, Mr Douglas and it's bad news, I'm afraid. You've got mott rot.'*

mottzerella *n.* A stringy, warm substance with the appearance of melted cheese, found on a *smeesh* which has been somewhat neglected in hygiene terms. *Voodoo butter, chodder.*

mouldilocks *n.* An otherwise attractive woman who is let down by matted hair like off a *Harry Ramp.*

mound of the hound *1. n. prop.* Former name of Hounslow, western borough of That London. *2. n.* A *dog egg* or *Scouse flower.* Also *pavement roundabout, shoe pastry, Sunderland Easter egg.*

mound of Venus *n.* The craggy outcrop above *salmon canyon* usually hidden by a dense covering of *bush.* The *beetle bonnet, monkey's forehead, grassy knoll.*

moundstretcher *n. Wedding tackle* of truly gargantuan length and girth, observed swinging between the legs of porn stars, porridge-eating Scotsmen and the Rt. Hon. Stephen Pound MP.

moundville *n.* A set of coordinates corresponding to a locale that happens to be brimming with *quim, eg.* The local convent. *'I tell you, your holiness, you're going to have a great time at Mater*

Ecclesiae. That joint is moundville.'

mount *v.* To *hop on* for *a bit.*

mountain goat *n.* A gravity-defying *turd* (or section thereof), steadfastly clinging to the vertiginous porcelain slopes of the *crapper* bowl.

Mount Doom *n.* A curry restaurant where one goes to "burn one's ring".

Mount Fujis *n.* Uncannily conical tits as seen in 1950s American B films. *Twin peaks, sweatermeat, dunce's hats.*

mounting equipment *n.* The external genitalia of the male human. The *meat and two veg, three-piece suite, wedding tackle, fruitbowl, family jewels, wedding vegetables etc.*

mounting fluid *1. n.* Medium in which a sample is suspended on a microscope slide. *2. n. Blip, moip, milp, bilp.*

mourning wood *n.* An ante-matitudinal tumescence, weeping a salty tear from its *hog's eye.*

mouse *adj.* Descriptive of someone who is poor at what they do. *Swiss.* *'That Eamonn Holmes is a bit fucking mouse, isn't he?'*

mousemat *1. n.* A *jam rag.* *2. n.* A shredded wheat-style raft of dried *fanny batter.*

mouse meat *n.* Cheese.

mouse organ *1. n.* A rodent-based magical instrument that regularly used to turn up on *Bagpuss*. *2. n.* An unimpressive genital endowment. See also *tenis, grubscrew, snatch scratcher.*

mouse pissing on cotton wool, as quiet as a *sim.* *'Has your Andrew been isolating at the Pizza Express in Woking, ma'am? Only just lately, he's been as quiet as a mouse pissing on cotton wool.'*

mouser *n.* A *bird* who, when called upon to *do the decent thing*, nibbles rather than sucks. One would imagine that Mavis Riley, during her short, ill-fated marriage to Derek Wilton, was probably a *mouser*. In fact, that's probably what drove a wedge between her and Victor Pendlebury in the end.

mouse's ear, fanny like a *sim.* Descriptive of a tight *minnie moo*, a *butler's cuff.*

mouse's tongue *sim.* Descriptive of a very small penis. With a bit of cheese on the end.

mouse's waistcoat *sim.* *'Facility was powerless to resist. Mr D'Anus's eyes burned into hers like amethysts. His strong arms enfolded her tender body as she felt herself being swept away in a whirlwind of passion. Eagerly, she tore at his heaving breeches. "Take me, Mr D'Anus!" she gasped. "I've been saving myself for you." "Fucking get in!" he replied as he passionately rent her bloomers in twain. "You'll have a fanny tighter than a mouse's waistcoat."'*

(from *Pride and Prideability* by Jane Austen).

mousetrap *1. n.* Unbelievably bad Agatha Christie play which performs a sort of Care in the Community role for bad actors and has now been running in the West End for more than a hundred years. *2. n.* A bin found in the ladies' restrooms where women may discreetly dispose of their feminine hygiene products, such as *jamrags, fanny nannies,* and *chuftie plugs. 3. n.* One's wife's *minge* for the week or so each month when she is *dropping clots. 4. n.* A poorly balanced *chod hopper* lid that guillotines down onto the top of a fellow's *twig* while he's *straining his greens,* causing him to let go and make a grab for it, making *piss* go everywhere. Also *pivotal moment, golden handshake, Newton's curse.*

mouseturbation *n.* Any act of *self-pleasuring* which is powered by private-browser-window-generated stimuli.

moustaka *n.* A female lady's pubic hair which has been neatly parted down the centre in the style of a Wild West saloon bartender's moustache.

mouth muff *n.* A goatee beard sported by someone who mans an IT help desk and likes T'Pau. A *cocksucker's doormat.*

mouth-to-muff *n.* Lesbotic resuscitation technique. Also *quimlich manoeuvre.*

move the needle *1. v.* To invigorate one who is noticably undersized. *2. v.* To miraculously *get a rise* out of someone who exhibits *lack of composure in front of goal.*

move the phone *v.* To *break wind.* From the characteristic noise which a plastic telephone makes when moved across a wooden surface. *'Did you just move the phone, Sir Alan? It fucking ronks.'*

moving Blackbeard's eyepatch *n.* The time-saving practice of riving the gusset of a lady's *applecatchers* to one side in order to gain a swift entry to her *James Blunt.* Also *using the catflap, playing the violin. 'Lift your legs up, love. I can't get your knickers off.' 'Aw bloody hell. I'm really tired. can't you just move Blackbeard's eyepatch while I catch forty winks?'*

moving heavy furniture *euph.* An especially awkward and protracted evacuation of the *Denis Howells* which leaves the victim out of breath and sweating.

moving the girlposts *euph.* The proclivity of the fairer sex to abritarily adjust priorities or change their minds, leaving their menfolk utterly bewildered and possibly sleeping in the spare room.

moy *1. n.* Helmet cheese, *smegma. 2. adj. Shit, esp. dog's moy. 'Waterworld (1995. Dir. Kevin Costner)* starring Kevin Costner and Dennis Hopper. A visually striking, futuristic pile of high budget dog's moy.' (Halliwell's Film Guide).

mozzerfella *n. Hedam, bunnet brie.*

Mr Benn, to do a *v.* To get so *mullered* that you go into a toilet in a pub, and the next thing you remember is exiting the toilet of another pub with the strong suspicion that you have had a little adventure inbetween.

Mr Blobby *1. n. prop.* Much-hated TV personality and recording artiste from the mid-90s; part of Noel Edmonds's talent stable. *2. n.* A sexist epithet for a stroppy man, who appears to be *on the blob.* ''Born on This Day: Frankie Howerd, British comedian, 1917; Valentina Tereshkova, Russian cosmonaut, 1937; Alan Davies; tramp's-ear-chomping Mr Blobby, 1966.' 3. n.* A gentleman with full *gunk tanks* during the one week in four when he has to do without, due to his wife being *Mrs. Blobby.*

Mr Bond *n.* A particularly buoyant *turd* that returns to the surface of the water even after flushing. *'Ah, so we meet again, Mr Bond.'*

Mr Brown is at the window *euph.* To have the *turtle's head.* First used by Queen Victoria. *'Pray forgive us, Mr Gladstone, but we cannot receive you at the moment. Mr Brown is at the window, and we fear we may papper our kex.'*

Mr Brown's fingerprints *euph.* Forensic proof that a foul malefactor was present at the scene of a crime, *eg. Skidmarks* on an S-bend or gusset.

Mr Bum has his hand up *exclam.* A phrase used in polite company when one is forced to interrupt proceedings in order to *see a man about a brown horse. 'Doctor Hawley Harvey Crippen. You have been found guilty by this court of the charge that you did, with malice aforethought, murder your wife Cora on or about the thirty-first of January in the year of our Lord nineteen hundred and ten. Do you have anything to say before I pass sentence?' 'Indeed I do. As God is my witness, I am confident that if, in the future, haplotypes from the genetic material found buried under my cellar are compared with the mitochondrial DNA of my wife's relatives, it will be conclusively proven that... actually, could I please be excused for a moment, your honour? Mister Bum has his hand up.'*

Mr Happy's business suit *n.* An *English overcoat* or *rubber Johnny.*

Mr Hyde *1. n.* The uncontrollable, throbbing, dribbling, twitching, hairy beast into which Dr Jekyll transforms in the famous book and Russ Abbott sketch by Robert Louis Stevenson and Barry Cryer. *2. n.* The uncontrollable, throbbing, dribbling, twitching, hairy beast into which one's *knob* transforms when a particularly *fit piece* walks past.

Mr Johnson is at the dispatch box *1. phr.* Said when the former comedy PM prepared to do a turn in the Commons. *2. n.* Warning of a huge torrent of malodorous foulage is about to emerge. See also *a pig at the gate, mole at the counter, a brown dog scratching at the back door.*

Mr Jones *1. n. 19thC.* Penis. *2. n.* A butcher who frequently purports that "they don't like it up 'em".

Mr Kipling *n.* A "ruddy hard" *turd* that occurs after an excessive amount of time of having the *turtle's head*. An *arse cake* that has been exceedingly well baked.

Mr Plobby *n.* A comical character, reminiscent of the bungling and idiotic *Noel's House Party* prankster of yore, typically spotted staggering in an aimless, random manner along city streets, causing laughter amongst the public. A Police Community Support Officer. Also *doppelclanger, potted plant, quorn sausage, fakeon, happy shopper copper.*

Mr Sausage *n.* The excitable trouser man. Title of a *Mr Men* book that was hastily withdrawn from shops within an hour of going on sale in 1976.

Mrs Brown's boys *1. n.* A BBC comedy which is like an Irish amateur dramatic society version of Old Mother Riley where the leading character shouts "fuck" a lot. *2. n.* buoyant *rabbit toddlers* bobbing about in the *bum sink*.

Mrs Brown you've got a lovely daughter *1. n.* Title of a chart-topping single for Herman's Hermits in 1965. *2. phr.* To be exclaimed in the engaging, family-friendly style of Peter Noone after being delivered of a bouncing *mud baby.*

Mr Sheen *1. n.* Popular proprietary brand of furniture polish as used by discerning housekeepers across the UK. *2. n.* An Essex-specific colloquialism referring to a fellow's *chap* when it reaches such a state of glorious, turgid tumescence that one can see one's reflection in crystal clarity in the resultant mirror-like shine. *Mr Sheen* normally puts in an appearance during brisk *peel and polish* administered by the cleaner while the missus nips to the corner shop for bread or something.

Mrs Kipling *n.* A lady who, judging from her appearance, one could well believe was responsible for quality control and production line testing in a large cake factory.

Mrs Mills *euph.* A *wank* technique characterised by the use of a strong, rhythmic left hand, such that it feels like someone else, for example an overweight comedy piano player from the 1970s, is doing it.

Mr Softee *1. n. prop.* Popular ice cream van product, invented by Margaret Thatcher after she snatched all the milk. *2. n.* A gentleman who tragically finds himself unable to maintain penile rigidity due to age and/or excess *refreshment.*

Mr T'd *adj.* Getting absolutely *wankered* and passing out before taking an international flight and waking up in another country. Named after the actor who played the intellectually compassionate pteromerhanophobic character BA Baracus in *The A-Team.*

Mr Trebus's yard *sim.* Descriptive of a much-neglected, unhygienic and rat-infested *clopper.* With a couple of mopeds buried in it. From the late *Life of Grime* star's *shit-filled* garden.

Mr Tumble's spotty bag *1. n.* Prop owned by the eponymous, loveable CBeebies presenter. *2. n.* Unfortunate side effect of a dose of *Val Doonican. 'I knew I shouldn't have went with that lass from Geordie Shore, mother. Now I've got balls like Mr Tumble's spotty bag.'*

Mr Twix *n. prop.* Possibly mythical sex film industry employee claimed to have two penii.

Mr Whippy *1. n.* Semi-viscous ice-cream that comes out of a tap in a van. Also invented by Margaret Thatcher, interestingly enough. *2. n.* Flagellation, corporal punishment dished out at *rub-a-tug shops.* From £25. *3. n.* Semi-viscous *feeshus* that comes out of a tap in your underpants.

Mr Whippy's in town *exclam.* Declaration that all is not well in the *chamber of horrors.*

Mr Worf... fire! *exclam.* Announcement preceding a major blast from the *deflector dish.* Inspired by the cliffhanger line delivered by Commander Riker in *Star Trek: The Next Generation.*

M32 *n.* A *tit fuck,* ie. The most direct route for *coming* into the *Bristol* area.

muck *1. n.* Mess, baby bouillon, load, bolt. That which is *shot* from the *one o'clock gun.* *2. n. 'Have a look on Bravo, vicar. There's usually a bit of muck on there at this time of night.'*

muck button, the *n.* During a saucy romp, the judicious insertion of a crafty digit into a chap's *balloon knot* by his ladyfriend in the interests of bringing the whole beastly business to a mercifully swift conclusion.

mucker *1. n.* A close pal. *2. n.* One who messes things up by inappropriately *chucking his muck,* eg. Too early, too far or into your porridge.

muck-filled splatter puss *n.* The sort of well-used *minge* typically seen in the closing shots of a *gang bang grumble flick.* Let's see Chris Packham casually drop that one into an episode of *SpringWatch* without anyone noticing.

muck muscle *n.* The *cigar cutter*. *'Pass me the X-ray please nurse. Ah yes, it's a milk bottle alright, just as I suspected. And it's been pushed right up past your muck muscle, Lord Archer.'*

mucksavage *n.* A *bumpkin, buffle, cabbagehead* or *joskin*.

muck's chuck *n.* A distance considerably shorter than a stone's throw. *'You should call in on my brother. He only lives a muck's chuck from there.'*

muckspreader *1. n.* Part of a tractor that a big spray of *shite* flies out of. *2. n.* Part of a person that a big spray of *shite* flies out of. *3. n.* A purveyor of *adult-oriented* literature, *eg.* Messrs Hefner, Sullivan, Raymond, Desmond, Flynt *etc. 4. n.* A promiscuous man. Also *crumpeteer, fanny hopper, harbour master, pinksmith, sack artist.*

muck truck *n.* A late night emergency food vehicle parked at the side of the road near a pub or club at chucking out time, where the cuisine is often somewhat less than haute, but looks smashing after a gallon or so of *pop. A kebabulance.*

muck trumpet *n.* A tunefully farty *brass eye*.

muck turtle *n.* Mythical creature responsible for the laying of a *brown egg* one might find on the beach.

mucky *n.* Any item of a pornographic nature, book, video, *etc.* *'Have you got any mucky I can borrow?'* *'Yes, but don't get any spragg on it this time, vicar.'*

mucky dip *n.* A *scuttle* up the *coal hole*.

mud *1. n.* Excrement. *2. n.* Excrement 1970s pop group.

mudbound *1. n.* Critically acclaimed 2017 Netflix period drama charting the overlapping lives of two very different families in the American deep south. Yeah, we'll pop that on when we've finished binge-watching *Man versus Food. 2. adj.* Descriptive of a person who is *touching cloth* and, as such, is headed swiftly in the direction of the nearest *shitter*.

mud button *n.* Winnet, dangleberry, tagnut, clinker, *etc.*

mudchild *n.* A *sweaty Morph*. Also *mud child*.

mud darts *n.* The game of *anal love. Bum sex.*

muddy funster *1. n.* A *botter. 2. n.* A *melon farmer.*

muddy Rorschach *n. medic.* Analysing a mysterious brown pattern on a sheet of paper. Also *shitmus test*.

muddy thunder *n.* An ominous rumble that heralds the imminent eruption of a cataclysmic storm in your *dunghampers*.

muddy trickle, the *n. medic.* Diarrhoea. See also

arse piss, hoop soup, ballrooms etc.

muddy velcro *n.* When an unexpected dispatch of *bum gravy* settles beyond *biffin's bridge*.

muddy walnut *n. medic.* The prostrate gland. *'She had her finger so far up my dirtbox it was tapping my muddy walnut, your honour.'*

muddy welly *n.* A soiled prophylactic sheath which is best left by the *back door*.

mudeye *n.* Arse, ringpiece, one's old-fashioned *fifties tea towel holder*.

Mudgee mailbags *n.* Great big *norks*. Named after the remote Australian outback town of Mudgee, which gets its post delivered twice a year, apparently receiving it in large *tit*-shaped sacks. *'Strewth, you've got knockers like Mudgee mailbags, Camilla.'*

mud hole *n.* That *hole* from which one *blows mud*. The *crop sprayer, cable layer, nipsy.*

mudhole door *1. n.* The bottom of a steam locomotive boiler from where all the *shite* is riddled out from time to time. *2. n.* The *nipsy*.

mudlarks *1. n.* Horses which enjoy heavy ground. *Mudders. 2. n.* Historically speaking, people who hadn't paid enough attention at school and who were therefore forced to scrape a living scavenging for valuables in the *crap* along the banks of the River Thames. *3. n. Bumgames.*

mud mallet *n.* A forceful *shit*.

mud men *1. n.* Programme formerly on the History Channel starring ex-TV presenter Johnny Vaughan. *2. n.* A pair of gentlemen who like to stroll along *Bournville Boulevard*, taking their pleasures as they may.

mud oven *n.* The rectum of the *anus. 'Mitochondria was powerless to resist. His eyes burned into hers like haematites. His muscular arms enfolded her body as she felt herself being swept away in a pyroclastic flow of passion. Then he said those words of which she had dreamed so long, yet never dared hope to hear. "How much to give you one in the mud oven, then love?"'* (from *The Aged Prostitute and the Scouse Football Star who Got Signed by Manchester United for Twenty-Eight Million Quid and Then Went Back to Everton* by Barbara Cartland).

mud puppy *n.* An adorable *dog egg* that bites your ankles and fouls the carpet.

mudpussy *n.* The *arse*, when used by beastly heathens for purposes for which the Lord did not intend it.

mudskipper *1. n.* Fish of the family *Oxudercinae* which is able to emerge from the water and survive for prolonged periods in air. *2. n.* A *Peter O'Toole* that pops its head out the water to breathe.

mud smile *n.* A rusty grin in your *undercrackers*.

mud trumpet *n.* A prolonged, spluttering release of Jalfrezi vapor from *Dot Cotton's mouth*, which sounds like a sorrowful six-year-old Dizzy Gillespie sounding the Last Post for his recently departed hamster.

mud valve mechanic *n.* A *brown pipe engineer*, *exhaust fitter.*

mudweiser *n.* A glass of warm, American *piss*-like lager consumed at Glastonbury, which contains dried *cowshit* flakes that have fallen off your *crap*-caked face, but which you drink down anyway because it was seven *fucking* quid and you can't be *arsed* to start queuing all over again.

mud whistle *n.* A presidential *trump.*

mudwife *1. n.* A lady who regularly delivers *Meat Loaf's daughters* in the *birthing pool. 'I couldn't borrow your potato masher again, could I, Mrs Patmore? Only the mudwife's blocked the khazi in the east wing again.' 2. n.* One who assists another during the delivery of a particularly large, or breech, *Meat Loaf's daughter. 'Bobby Brown admitted on television last night that he has had occasion to act as a mudwife to his constipated missus Whitney Houston.'*

mud wrestling *n.* A long and messy battle on the toilet, involving much grunting and groaning, which usually ends in either a knock-out, a fall or a submission.

muellered report *n.* Slurred account of the amount and specifics of the evening's alcoholic ingestions.

muesli *n.* A sub-*pink* genre of close-up glamour photograph, depicting a tight-lipped *fish mitten*. From the description on at least two supermarket own brand boxes of muesli which state: "To open, slide finger under flap".

muff *1. n. Minge, fanny. 2. v.* To *shag,* have intercourse with. *3. v.* To fluff, miss an easy goal-scoring opportunity. *'Oh fuck! Emile Heskey has muffed it.' 4. n.* Stevie Winwood's brother, who played bass in the Spencer Davis Group. *5. v.* To *lick out. 6. acronym. coll.* Mums Up For Fucking.

muff diva *n.* A histrionic lady of sapphic inclination.

muff diver *n.* A footballer who misses an easy goal scoring opportunity, then falls over in an attempt to win a penalty kick.

muff diver's dental floss *n.* Female pubic hair.

muff diver's quickstep *n.* The spasmodic and frantic jerking of the legs of a gentleman who, while performing *cumulonimbus* on a ladyfriend, has his air supply cut off by the closing of her thighs as she approaches her desired level of enjoyment.

muff duffer *n.* A *joskin, fuckwit, buffle, mucksavage*

or *shit-for-brains. 'Today's birthdays: Ronnie Biggs, dead ex-train robber, 88; Chris Eubank, lisping fisticuffs dandy, 51; Brian Harvey, East 17 muff duffer, 43.'*

muffet *n. Fr. (pron.* muh-*fay)* A veritable all-you-can-eat feast of *hairy pie* for the casual *diner at the Y.*

muff huff *n.* Menstruational moodiness or PMT. A *period drama*, a *blob strop.*

muffia *n.* A collection of criminal women, or women who are married to criminals.

muffin *1. n.* Flour-based bakery product. *2. n. prop.* 1960s TV mule puppet – operated by Sir John Mills's sister, if memory serves – whose name remains a source of perpetual hilarity among the elderly and infirm.

muffin tops *n.* The pastry-like midriff overhang achieved by lasses wearing tight, low-slung *kex.*

muffle *v.* The female equivalent of *zuffle.*

muffled *1. adj.* Led by *muff*, shackled in the *salmon handcuffs*. Also *cuntstruck, fuckstruck. 2. adj.* Of ambient noise, subjectively abated as a consequence of a lady's thighs clamped tightly around the sides of a *cumulonimbalist's* head, thus occluding his *lugs*. Or, indeed, her *lugs* in these days of lesbians and what-not. And good luck to them, we say.

muffler *1. n.* A mute, used to modify the sound of a trumpet. *2. n. US.* What Americans call the silencer on a car exhaust. *2. n.* Device, fashioned from several layers of folded toilet tissue, which is popped in the back of the trousers to moderate the volume of the *botty bugle* when in polite company.

mufflinks *1. n.* Female genital jewellery. Pierced fanular silversmithery. *Curtain rings, cuntlery. 2. n. medic.* The stitches placed at either end of a knackered lady's *gammon mudflaps* after a painful childbirth during which the doctor got a bit scissor-happy due to baby having a head the size of a B&Q trolley.

muff nudge *n.* The light brushing of a female hairdresser's *beetle bonnet* against one's elbows when she leans forward to cut one's hair.

muffocation *n.* Inability to breathe when a *dirty lady* is sitting on your face.

muff pastry *n.* The flakes of dry *fanny batter* covering one's *pork sword* the morning after a good *scuttle. Clamdruff, hairy piecrust.*

muff riders *n. Clopper crabs.*

muffro *n.* Female pubic coiffure that resembles nothing so much as the popular hairdo which was famously sported by Jermaine Jackson in the seventies. On his head, of course, not his *blurtch.*

mufftash *n.* The stylish, Kevin Webster-style furry residue which adorns the upper lips of those who have but recently been *licking out* a lady's *mimsy*. A *Barnsley moustache*.

muff trumpet *n.* A *fanny fart* that would have a troop of soldiers standing by their beds.

muff tumbler *1. n.* A type of selectively bred fancy pigeon with feathered legs. *'Look at all the muff tumbler shit on Nelson's Column, nan.'* 2. *n.* Someone who often tumbles, face first, into a lady's *muff*. *'Born on this day: Joe Jackson, Michael Jackson's horrible dad, 1928; Lawrie McMenemy, football manager, 1936; Sir Mick Jagger, muff tumbler, 1943.'*

mufnstuf *n. onomat.* Absorbent wadding designed to stem the missus's monthly uncleanliness.

Mugabe *n.* A small, square, postage-stamp-sized patch of *Rubiks*. Preferred location – just under the nose.

mug-muffs *n.* Overpriced headphones. *'What do you think of my new electrostatic mug-muffs?'*

mugnet *n.* Something that is irresistibly attractive to the credulous; Hyde Park's "Winter Wonderland", for instance, to pick an example entirely at random.

mugshot *n.* A generous and warming faceful of hot'n'sour *bollock broth*.

mug stains *n.* Large, dark, flat *jockeys' whips* that often appear during pregnancy.

mukbang *1. n. Kor.* An internet fad, originally from Korea, where viewers watch *mukbangers* eating vast quantities of food. 2. *n.* A *scuttle* up the *Gary Glitter*. You could probably find that on the internet too, if you looked really hard.

mule's lip *n.* A large foreskin, like a sulky Frenchman's mouth.

muller *v.* To perform *horatio*. From the old advertising slogan of the popular yoghurt, *viz.* "Lick the lid of life".

mullered *1. adj.* Langered. 2. *adj. Sucked off.*

muller love *n.* The temporary amorous feelings one has towards a right *pig* as a result of being *mullered*. Finding someone attractive when looking at them through high ABV *beer goggles*.

mullet *n.* Inbreds' haircut favoured by country and western singers, the trailer-trash guests on the *Jerry Springer Show* and 1980s footballers.

mulligan *n. Aus.* Penis.

mull-over *n.* Trichologically speaking, a cross between a mullet and a combover; the sort of unsavoury, greasy hairdo sported by trainspotters, *kiddy-fiddlers* and those men you get in betting shops wearing shiny, wide-lapelled brown suits but no shirts.

multi-channel fulfilment *1. n.* The modern customer's ability to purchase goods instore, on the web or by mobile. 2. *n.* A modern, sexually liberated lady's *holy trinity*.

multi-task *v.* Of a romantic fellow, to treat his lucky inamorata to *fingers* and *tops* at the same time. When done from behind, this is known as *double bassing*, or the act of *charlimingus*.

mum-argh! *n.* When a chap is idly flicking through a sea of naked ladies, the psychologically damaging experience of happening upon a pornographic image featuring one who looks like his mother. Usually ends with the gentleman in question pulling up his trousers and going off to do something else for an hour, joining a monastery, or poking his eyes out.

mumbas *onomat.* Breasts. If *oomlaaters* made a noise, they would say "mumbas" in a deep, fruity baritone.

mumble *n.* Soft, badly written *Frankie* that women can casually read on the train without causing the kind of pursed-lipped outrage that a bloke leafing through an *art pamphlet*, for instance the November 1996 issue of *Readers' Wives Bums Special,* might expect to encounter. From mummy + grumble.

mumble in the jungle *n. Cunnibungalus.*

mumblers *n.* Tight women's bicycle shorts through which you "see the lips move but can't understand a word".

mumbleweed *n.* Female pubic hair that obscures the *lips*. See also *toasted cheese sandwich that's been dropped on a barber's floor.*

mummery glands *n.* The pectoral appendages adorning young mothers, perhaps set slightly lower than in previous years but nevertheless still admirable. *Mummery glands* give rise to excessive courteousness from male drivers waiting at zebra crossings.

mummy banana *n.* The extra portion of *fruit* in a *shemale's bowl.*

mummy returns *n.* A *brown zombie* that comes back wrapped in *shit tickets.*

mumph *onamat.* See *flub.*

Mumrah's cock *n.* The tissue wrappings placed around *Pharaoh's flute* to prevent any spillages of *kid juice* onto ceremonial robes *etc.* Particularly handy while re-enacting the ancient Egyptian creation myth of Atum, who had a swift *one off the wrist* on the Primordial Mound in the Void of Nu, and was surprised to discover that the first *wad* of supernatural *jitler* out of his *hog's eye* contained both the god Shu and the goddess Tefnut, who became the parents of all the other elements of the world. From the bandage-wrapped mummy in *Thundercats™*.

mumrar *n.* The act of sneaking up behind your mother and shouting "RAR!"

munch bunch *n.* A gang of *dykes* in a carpet warehouse.

munchy scrunchy *n.* An elasticated device which ensures that a *fellatrix's* hair does not fall into her eyes. Also *gobble bobble*.

mung *1. n.* Type of bean which is popular with *Guardian* readers. *2. n.* A particularly runny type of *arse feta*. *3. n.* That smell which emanates from within the fleshsome rolls of a *Duke of giblets*. '*Rik – I like what you did with the song, but I'm not sure that your interlude of vigorous breakdancing during the middle eight was such a good idea. There was a right fucking mung in here by the time you reached the last chorus. Dr Fox has had to open the window.*'

munge *n.* The male equivalent of the *camel's toe*. Darcy Bussell's footrest. '*Oh, just look at Nureyev dance, Dame Margot. Isn't he a wonderful mover?' 'Yes, and check out the fucking munge on him in them tights, Dame Alicia. It's like a butcher's fist.*'

Mungo Jerrys, the *1. n.* The comfortable mid-phase of a *shag* where one has settled into a relaxed, comfortable rhythm, prior to the more frantic mood of the *yabba dabbas*. Similar to the shuffling backing beat/heavy breathing vocal on the song *In the Summertime*. *2. n.* Hirsute *clodges* of the type typically featured in 1970s *grumble* fillums.

Mungos *n.* Great big sideburns as worn by Jerry Dorsey, lead singer of the above-mentioned combo. *Bugger's grips, face fannies.*

municipal cockwash *n.* A lady who is indiscriminate with her affections. The *town bike, box of assorted creams, buttered bun.*

munter gatherer *n.* A fellow who appreciates the company of women with *lovely personalities.*

munter punter *n.* A revoltingly chauvinistic, politically incorrect and unacceptably sexist term for a chap who habitually squires unconventionally attractive ladies. A *dog handler.*

muppet *n.* The sort of classy woman who loves it "up to the elbow".

muppet backing singer's mouth, fanny like a *sim.* Descriptive of a spacious *honeypot* that flaps open and shut with precious little subtlety.

muppet master *n.* She who pulls the strings. A fierce *bag for life* that leads her ineffectual husband around by the nostrils. Mildred out of *George and Mildred*, Mrs Thatch or Her late Majesty the Queen, for example.

muppet's mouth *n.* A *fanny* whose lips don't exactly follow the words its owner is speaking.

murder Tarka *v.* After releasing a particularly big

otter off the bank from your *ring of bright water*, to be forced to beat it senseless before you can flush away the evidence.

Murray walker *n.* One who enjoys an *al fresco Ruby* while meandering back from the pub. Named after the excitable Formula 1 motor-racing commentator Martin Brundle.

muscle Mary *n.* An extremely well-built *ginger beer.* A *canny hard puff.*

muscles sprouts *n. medic.* The boils, carbuncles, bubos and other nasty eruptions of the epidermis resulting from injudicious use of anabolic steroids, *Aberdare tic-tacs*, testosterone *etc.* by members of the bodybuilding fraternity. Also known as *roid rash.*

mush in the bush *n.* The kind of sex act that, one might imagine, Dick Van Dyke might perform on Julie Andrews. *Cockney cumulonimbus.*

mush-masher *n. medic.* A cosmetic plastic surgeon. See also *balloon technician*. '*I think your mam's been to see the mush masher again, Sly. Only she's suddenly got a hairy cleft chin.*'

mushy *n.* How Brazilian *working girls* refer to their *cloppers*. Apparently.

musical *euph. Good with colours* in Edwardian times. A subtle way of describing one with an *artistic temperament*; a *collector of delicate china.* '*I wonder if them jockeys are musical, Bosey. I'd love to give them all a right good bumming.' 'You will, Oscar. You will.*'

musical vegetables *n.* Baked beans, as eaten by cowboys and *trouser trumpeteers.*

musical wank *n.* A *strum* undertaken to the rhythm of some music, such as the "Just sold my car to we buy any car" jingle.

music of the night *n.* Drunken snoring, belching and farting by a bloke who's been on the ale all evening.

music of the spheres *1. n.* An ancient philosophical concept which purported to explain the movements of various celestial bodies, such as the planets and stars and that. *2. n.* An impressively orchestrated, multi-sensory onslaught from your anus (pronounced "Uranus"). *Top of the Plops.*

music room *n.* The lavatory. '*If you'll excuse me, your ladyship, I'm just going to the music room to play a few scales on my wind instrument.*'

musketeer duties *euph.* Said of a woman who is not averse to a spot of *dogging* with multiple partners. From the motto featured in Alexandre Dumas's famous historical novel, *viz.* "All for one and one for all." '*Are you coming down the Bingo tonight, Dolly?' 'No, Cissie, I can't. I'm on musketeer duties down the Thicket Roundabout.*'

musk mask *n.* A lady's *fenty undercrackers* worn as

a balaclava while *rubbing one out.*

mussel sarnie *n.* A fresh-smelling bivalvic snack. A *bearded clam.*

mussel soup *n.* *Hairy clam chowder* that is served *at the Y.*

mussy *n.* Prison slang for a fellow's *freckle.* A contraction of "man pussy". *'I don't suppose you could speak to the governor and get me a bit of ointment, could you Mr McKay? Only I dropped the soap in the showers and Luke Warm naffed me up the mussy.'*

mustang *n.* Of *shitty arses*, that stubborn *dangleberry* which cannot be shaken off.

mustard pie *n.* A *fanny* that's eye-wateringly pungent and acrid.

must get that floorboard fixed *exclam.* Another thing to say when someone *let's one go.* See also *a bit more choke and she would have started; a confident appeal by the Australians there; an excellent theory, Dr Watson; anybody injured?; don't tear it, I'll take the whole piece; how much?; keep shouting sir, we'll find you; more tea vicar?*

mutant hamster *n.* A rather unsightly and unkempt "butcher's dustbin", full of matted fur, sticky bits and strange protuberances.

mute button *n.* In a public lavatory, for example, the invisible remote control that you apparently operate upon entering, which renders any *trap* occupant completely silent until they have heard you wash your hands and leave the room.

mute reminder *n.* During a virtual meeting, a *bottom burp* that is loud enough to trigger the "you are on mute" notification.

mutilant *n.* One who is addicted to body art and piercings and thus being stopped at airport security for the rest of their life.

mutilation station *n.* A piercing studio.

Mutley chunter *n.* The act of voicing disapproval under one's breath when forced to perform an act under duress, in the style of Dick Dastardly's dog. Usually involves muttering "ratting, dratting," *etc.* through tightly clenched teeth.

…muttered Pooh *exclam.* An amusing way for a literate fellow to round off a bit of *back chat.* Likewise *…grumbled Eeyore, …said Thomas,* or *…commented Mr Rees-Mogg.*

mutton busting *1. n.* Rural event where young yokels compete to ride a sheep for as long as possible at a county show or in the back room of a remote Welsh pub. *2. n.* A competition in which *OAP-dophiles* compete to *ride* a shabby *old goat* for as long as possible. *Biddy fiddling, tomb raiding, old dear hunting, mothball diving etc.*

mutton dressed as kebab *sim.* Ugly women who doll themselves up and make themselves look even worse. Also *mutton dressed as spam.*

mutton dressed as ram *euph.* The more butch one out of a pair of *lady golfers.* A woman in uncomfortable, steel toe-capped *comfortable shoes* and smoking a pipe.

mutton musket *n.* A smaller, more portable field weapon than the *lamb cannon.* Also *mutton bayonet, mutton dagger.*

mutton tugger *n.* In a slaughterhouse, one whose job it is to pull the meat off the bones of old sheep.

mutt's nuts *adj.* Descriptive of something which is very good. The *dog's bollocks, the vicar's cock, donkey's knob, horse's doofers.*

muzzle *1. n.* A device applied to excitable puppies in order to apply a degree of control, and thus *2. n.* A sports bra.

my arse thinks my mouth's having all the fun *exclam.* Phrase used to excuse oneself from a conversation in order to go off and *drop the shopping.*

my best work is behind me, I fear that *exclam.* Said after dropping a *magnum opus* of a *dustman's special.* Also *I'm just raising the profile of the company; they call the wind Mariah; now we know what killed the dinosaurs.*

myclean arse *n.* *Pre-bumsex* hygiene regimen. Also, amusingly, a sort of aural anagram of the name of the classically trained former Hear'say singer turned daytime television *nonebrity.*

my cock was bigger than my balls *euph.* Remark when one admits they are no longer able to go on as long as they thought they could. *'Sorry, Stormy, we'll have to leave it there. My cock was bigger than my balls, I'm afraid.' 'Don't worry, Mr President, it happens to everyone at some time.'*

mycoxafloppin *n. medic.* The principal active ingredient in Viagra.

mydixadroopin *n. pharm.* Competitor product to *Mycoxafloppin.*

Myleene *rhym. slang.* The *anus.* From Myleene Klarsehole = arsehole.

my motion sensor must be switched on *phr.* Explanation given to his ladyfriend by a fellow who *does a Duckhams.* That is to say, "the slightest movement makes him go off".

my own right hand shall do it *1. exclam.* Sir Walter Scott's poetic declaration that he would pay off his debts by writing overlong books about kilts, Mel Gibson *etc. 2. exclam.* Poetic declaration of how one will remedy an overlong bout of *unemployment.*

mystic smeg *n.* Erectoplasm.

mystic steg *n.* A malevolently *fugly* presence which haunts you, asking you what your fucking star sign is.

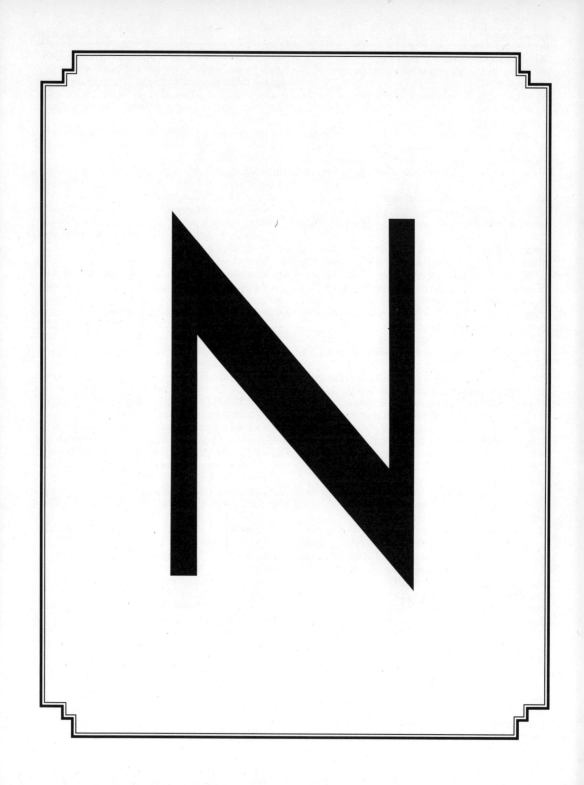

nables *n.* Fast-growing nose hairs which increase in girth and strength by the year. From nose + cables.

NABNUT/nabnut *abbrev.* A lady who is of ample posterior aspect yet slight of *bosomy substances.* Nice Arse But Nothing Up Top.

NACFOY/nacfoy *abbrev.* A lady who is, despite appearances to the contrary, over the legal age of consent. Not A Concern For Operation Yewtree. *'It's alright officer, she's completely nacfoy. Show the nice man your birth certificate, Janette.'*

Nadal *n. prop.* A *fart* that serves itself up with a long, noisy *follow through.* Named in honour of the eponymous, noisy, *arse*-picking tennis player of the same name.

Nadal rally *n.* A rowdily energetic marathon bout of lovemaking, characterised by the loud grunts which accompany each stroke.

nadbag *n.* The *nut sack, pod pouch, scrot sling, chicken skin handbag.*

nad break *1. n.* A mid-programme interval during which a viewer enjoys a swift spot of *gentlemanly relaxation. 'Stay tuned and we'll see you after this nad break. 2. n.* Any relaxing portion of a chap's daily television viewing schedule when he takes the opportunity to empty his *pods. 'I hope there's a nad break coming up, dear. My knackers are like two tins of Fussell's milk.' 'Don't worry. Nigelissima's on in a minute and she's cooking bananas.'*

nadger *n.* A *testee* which has been battered black and blue. *'I tell you what, she loves it rough. She's left me with a right pair of nadgers, Mother Superior.'*

nadgina *n.* A *cockney's plum purse,* which has been refashioned into a *cludge* by the skilled hands of a dextrous surgeon.

nadmin *n.* Regular *gonad*-related administration. *Paperwork.*

nad nogg *n.* Splod.

nadpoles *n. Jizzbag taddies. Spunks,* spermatozoan humunculi.

nads *n. Knackers,* testicles, *love spuds.*

Nagasaki tan *n.* A sunbed-induced glow of such ferocity that it appears that one was present an the detonation of an atom bomb, *eg.* One sported by Judith Chalmers, Jodie Marsh or David Dickinson.

nagativity *n.* The mental flaying of a subdued husband by the linguistic gnawing away of his resolve that begins within 48 hours of the exchange of vows.

nag for life *n. rhym. slang.* The missus. *'Have you met the nag for life, your holiness?'*

nagmatism *n.* The irresistible attractive influence emanating from the local pub. Triggered by repeated requests from the *nag for life* to mow the lawn, put shelves up *etc.*

nag nav *n.* In-car device that has no sense of direction or spatial awareness, but nevertheless manages to communicate its displeasure with any route taken.

nagony *n.* The psychological pain experienced by a hen-pecked gent.

nagpie *n.* A *bird* who brings sorrow.

nag-teamed *adj.* Worn down by a continuous verbal assault from the missus and the mother-in-law.

nail filler *n.* The unpleasant consequences of attempting to use a value brand of *shitscrape* to clean up in the aftermath of a difficult *sit down toilet adventure.*

nail gun *n.* A *cock* that goes off so quickly and so violently that it startles others in the vicinity.

nail through the end, all that's missing is the *phr.* An amusing thing to say to break the ice when making idle smalltalk with the fellow at the next urinal who appears to be wielding a caveman's club.

Nakasaki *n.* The ancient Japanese lady's erotic art of donning uncomfortable sex shoes and volleying her beloved in the *Jaffas.*

name that tune *exclam.* A humorous exclamation called out to draw attention to an amusing *dropping of the guts* at a middle class dinner party.

nam-pla *1. n.* Fish sauce, an essential Thai cooking ingredient. *2. n. Knob cheese,* an essential ingredient when cooking for Giles Coren.

nana dressed as Rihanna *euph.* The phenomenon of a mature female adopting unsuitably youthful attire of the sort favoured by the comely Barbados-born artiste behind such hits as *If it's Lovin' That You Want, Disturbia* and *Umbrella* (featuring J-Zee).

nana Kournikova *n.* A *bird* who appears to be *well fit* from the back, but who on turning round is revealed to be a pensioner. A *Kronenberg, Toyah, boyner.*

nana technology *n.* Electronic devices such as mobile phones, e-readers and television remote controls that feature big buttons and easy-to-read type, and are aimed at more mature consumers. *2. n.* The kind of products advertised by ageing cricketers and TV gardeners in the back pages of the *Radio Times* and the Sunday supplements. Usually purporting to alleviate or even completely eradicate some depredation of old age, *eg.* 5,000 candlepower reading lamps, walk-in bathtubs and electric foot spas.

nan bread n. Bingo wings, retired dinner ladies' arms.

nanbretta n. A mobility scooter.

nan-chukas n. Saggy lils that can be swung around the waist and shoulders, and used in extremis as offensive weapons. Extra-mobile knee shooters. Socktits with a billiard ball in the end.

nanecdote n. A long-winded and repetitive yarn as imparted by a superannuated female relative, with a soupçon of casual racism thrown in for good measure.

nangerine adj. The characteristic orange skin tone of biddies who over-winter in Tenerife.

nannie's crouch n. Unintended, squeaky air biscuit brought on by bending over.

nanny fanny n. That which fascinates and excites the inveterate biddy fiddler, and does exactly what it says on the rusty old tin.

nanny's wine n. The long-nosed bouquet of stale piss when you enter the home of a senior citizen.

nan's grin n. A toothless Beverley Craven.

nan's mattress, as pissed as your sim. To be in an extreme state of refreshment. 'Ladies and gentlemen, welcome aboard flight BA103 from Oslo. We would advise you to keep your safety belts fastened throughout the flight as it looks like it could be quite a bumpy ride. We're not expecting any turbulence, it's just that the captain is as pissed as your nan's mattress.'

nan's naans n. Baps over which the force of gravity has inexorably prevailed. Once three-dimensional and outwardly bound, now two-dimensional and downward-bound.

nansplaining n. Annoying stream of unsolicited parenting advice vouchsafed to the fathers of young children by little old ladies on the bus.

napalm n. A perfect example of a man's ability to multitask; the combination of a mid-afternoon doze with the act of self-love. Not necessarily in that order.

Napoleon fag n. A smoke enjoyed with one hand behind your back.

narcissistick n. Them poles that self-absorbed twats use to photograph themselves when they're not taking pictures of their fucking dinner.

Narnia, so far in the closet he's in euph. Of a man, to be in denial over how chromatically adept he is.

nasal chameleon n. The brightly-coloured string of snot that's ejected from a sneezer's nostril, resembling a lizard's tongue catching a fly.

nasal spray 1. n. Liquid medicine squirted into the olfactory passages. 2. n. A well-aimed popshot that goes right up the lucky recipient's nose.

NASA wank n. Any Cape Canaveral-style self-abuse session involving simultaneous use of two or more screens. A technological update of the traditional crescent wank. Also emission control.

NASCUA/nascua abbrev. Unpleasantly sexist way that a less politically correct man might refer a somewhat uptight lady. Needs A Stiff Cock Up Arse.

nastonbury n. Festival fanny. The ripe fent coming off a clout that hasn't been cleaned for four days.

nasty spumante n. Celebratory, foaming liquid squirted over a cheap woman when a fellow comes first.

national grottery, win the v. To be the lucky discoverer of a massive deposit of rhythm mags hidden under a bongo bush, in a skip or in a recently deceased vicar's study. To scoop the jack-off pot.

national service euph. Playing Call Of Duty or similar in one's bedroom solidly for two years in the prime of your life.

national treasure chest n. Much-loved celebrity whose rack, through a process of ingrained familiarity, frequent exposure or sheer brilliance, has achieved iconic cultural status, eg. Baron Owen of the City of Plymouth.

Nat King n. prop. rhym. slang. A penetrative relationship with a female member of the opposite sex, named after the velvety-voiced baritone crooner of the fifties and sixties, viz. Nat King Cole = hole. 'Did Kevin get his Nat King last night?'

nature's make-up n. A range of black and blue eye cosmetics favoured by the wives of certain British sportsmen, politicians and actors.

nature valley bar, drier than a euph. Descriptive of a marked lack of lubrication in any situation. 'Dave, pass that tub of grease, will you? These axles are drier than a Nature Valley bar.'

naughty Nazi salute n. A herman jelmet standing to attention.

nauticals n. rhym. slang. Piles. From nautical miles.

naval lint 1. n. Belly-button fluff. 2. n. Dried spunk at the top of a matelot's crab ladder.

navigator of the windward pass n. A rear admiral.

Navy cake n. milit. Army and Air Force term for the arse.

Navy gravy n. The salty spume found in a jolly Jack Tar's beard. Sailor's ale.

nawsome adj. Not awesome. A mild disparagement. 'What do you think about my new space rocket, guys?' 'It's nawsome, Richard.'

NBR abbrev. No Beers Required. A good-looking woman. Opposite of a five pinter or gallon girl.

NCP yoghurt n. The viscous off-white fluid spilled onto their grot mags by car park attendants *relaxing* in their booths. *'Excuse me, mate. Have you got any change for the ticket machine...? Eurgh. What's all that stuff on your hands, trousers and splashed across the open pages of your bongo book?' 'It's NCP yoghurt, that's all. And no, I don't have any change for the machine. Fuck off.'*

NDL *abbrev.* Nipples Don't Lie. Body language phenomenon that gives anthropologists an insight into how they are getting on (or how effective the air conditioning system is) when chatting up *birds* in the pub.

neapoli-tan *n.* A mixture of nut brown, sunburn red and pasty white flesh that makes you look like an Aldi dessert.

Neapolitan knickers *n.* The disgusting state of a proper old *slapper's gusset*. Vanilla, strawberry, chocolate, the lot.

Neapolitan shit *n.* Three different levels of excremental viscosity in a single sitting.

neard *n.* A nearly beard, of the sort worn by Formula 1's Lewis Hamilton.

near death experience *euph. Copping off* on *gr-ab-a-granny night* for *OAP-dophiles. Tomb raiding, biddy fiddling, relic hunting, mothball diving etc.*

near miss *euph.* A somewhat effeminate man, *eg.* One without neck tattoos.

necessary evil *n.* A zombie-esque hungover visit to the *chodbin*. A profoundly unpleasant experience, but a vital step on the road to recovery.

neckbreaker *n.* A *log* of such length, rigidity and tensile strength that it lifts the *shitter* vertically off the *pot*, crushing his or her neck against the ceiling. It is a little-known fact that Queen Victoria's death certificate gives her cause of death as "a neckbreaker occasioned by eating a plethora of black pudding, fruitcake and milk stout for her tea the day before."

neck-downer *n.* Any woman who is *as rough as rats* from the neck up.

necking turds *v.* Accusation made against one suffering from halitosis. *'Excuse me, madam, I don't wish to appear rude, but have you been necking turds?'*

neck tripe *n.* The unappetizing hanging flesh that adorns the throats of ageing ladies.

ned *n.* A Glaswegian *scratter.*

neddies *n. Nellies, knockers.*

ned zeppelin *n. Glasweg.* A piss-filled water balloon, hurled by a lively Scotch youth making his own entertainment.

needle dick *n.* Light-hearted, affectionate term of locker room banter describing a fellow with a small penis.

needlework *n.* Profitable fun with undersized men.

needs a lifejacket to eat soup *phr.* A disparaging assessment of a person's intellectual ability.

neeps and tatties *n. McKnockers.*

NEFFS/neffs *abbrev. medic.* Coded information often found on a *coffin dodger's* GP's notes, *viz.* Not Even Fit For Spares.

negative equity *1. n.* A financial trap whereby a homeowner has borrowed more money to buy their house than it is now worth. *2. n.* The feeling of having *crapped out* far more food out than you've consumed.

neither fish nor foul *euph.* Describing the nondescript bridge of skin between the *hell-hole* and the *kipper;* the *fun junction.* Also *butfer, carse, tinter, taint, notcher, snarse, biffin bridge, Humber Bridge* and so on and so forth.

nellegant *adj.* Gracefully elephantine.

nellies *n.* Knockers, tits, neddies, melbas.

Nelson *n.* A little bloke who gets *shat* on by loads of *birds.* Metaphorically speaking, you'd think, but these days you never know.

Nelson, do a *v.* When walking the dog, avoiding picking up an *egg* – especially one with a runny yolk – by turning a blind eye your pooch's activity. From Admiral Nelson's famously apocryphal battle cry, *viz.* "I see no shits".

Nelson Mandela *n. rhym. slang. Wreck the hoose juice, wifebeater.* Stella.

Nelson's column, a *n.* A profound tumescence. Something that is tall, hard as rock, has one eye at the top, and attracts filthy *birds.* And Japanese tourists with cameras.

Nemissus, the *n.* The wife. From the ancient Greek legends, a vengeful harpy who harries an individual to his fate. *"'It's alright, love," spake the mighty Zeuss, appearing to the Nymph in the form of a swan. "We can use my place up Mount Olympus. The Nemissus is out with the girls tonight.""from* Hesiod's *Theogony*).

Nemo's boot, like *sim.* A particularly weighty *Sir Douglas* that refuses to go to the beach, with the flush barely stirring it across the bottom of the *pan.*

Neptune's back massage *n.* The tickly journey a bubble of *carbon dibaxide* makes up the rear of a submerged diver or surfer's wetsuit, before emerging at the neck,

Neptune's delight *n.* Misuse of a jet of water from a bidet or other geyser-like device to act as an *ersatz* finger up the *fifties teatowel holder* while engaged in *carryings-on.*

Neptune's fury *1. n.* Some sort of ride at Hayling

Island Funland, whatever that is. We were going to watch a video of it on YouTube, but an advert came on first and we simply couldn't be arsed. 2. *n.* An underwater *fart*; specifically, a smelly, bubbly one in the bath.

Neptune's kiss *n.* A cold, wet smacker on the *russty sheriff's badge* caused by *splashback*. A *Basildon bidet.*

Neptune's pantry *1. n.* Fictitious chippy frequented by Richie and Eddie in *Bottom*. 2. *n.* A lady's *undercarriage*. Also *Bermuda triangle, adventure bay, anchovy alley, Barnacle's nosh box, Billingsgate banjo, chum bucket,* and so on.

Neptune's staircase *1. n.* Series of locks on the Caledonian Canal near Fort William. 2. *n.* The inner thigh of a lady, leading to *Neptune's pantry.*

nerd-on *n.* A spot of technology-driven tumescence. *'Ooh, I really like your new Ubuntu desktop environment, Brian. In fact it's giving me a right nerd-on.'*

Nescafé handshake *n.* An act of masturbation. A reference to the adverts where coffee granules used to appear in deceased *New Avengers* star Gareth Hunt's right hand after he pretended to have a *wank*. Also *magicking the beans.*

Nescafé quickstep *n.* The rather urgent visit to the *crappers* that typically occurs about half way through the first coffee of the morning. Also *ex-laxpresso, laxwell house.*

nesting *n.* Installing a floating mat of *bumwad* into the *pan* prior to taking a *dump,* in order to reduce the noise of the *cable* hitting the water and also to minimise the risk of any *splashback* up the *nipsy. Fireman's blanket.*

nest of skunks *n.* A rather hirsute and ripe old *ladygarden*. *'Germaine, will you please put your nest of skunks away? I'm trying to cook the tea.'*

net a serve *v.* To *fart* and *follow through,* perhaps while grunting like Maria Sharapova.

net curtains *n.* Old ladies' *drapes,* which tend to twitch over to one side when the neighbours come out.

netflick *n.* A broadband-fuelled *cat-stabbing* session.

nether eye *n.* That single *unseeing eye,* situated in the *nether region,* which cries brown, lumpy tears.

nether heather *n.* A Scotch lassie's under-kilt foliage.

netherseal *1. n. prop.* Village in southern Derbyshire where they buried Sir Nigel Gresley. 2. *n.* The *cigar cutter.*

nethersphere *n. medic.* Collective term for the female *parts*; the *hole caboodle.* Incorporating the *clunge/undercarriage,* the *Baker Street concourse,* and the lower third of the *arse.*

nether throat *n.* In *farting,* the *poot chute* or *botty*

bugle. *'Pardon me while I clear my nether throat, Mr Speaker.'*

Nether Wallop *1. n.* A picturesque small village in Hampshire. 2. *n.* A not-particularly picturesque *Barclays bank* performed in the frantic style of a desperate jockey in the final furlong of a steeplechase.

net pet *n.* Amongst the sort of people who habituate internet chatrooms, a boyfriend or girlfriend with whom many hours are spent flirting without actually ever meeting in the flesh. A useful rule of thumb is that a sexually adventurous blonde, 18-year-old *net pet* from the Home Counties will, more often than not, turn out to be a toothless 50-year-old Tennessee hillbilly with his dead mum in the fridge and an anorak made of *fannies.*

nettie/netty *n.* Outside loo, *clart cabin, shite house. Dunny, cludgie, growler, khazi.*

nettiquette *n.* Code of polite behaviour followed by lavatory users. From nettie + Rosanna Arquette.

Netto fabulous *adj.* Descriptive of one who eschews posh jewellers such as Tiffany's and Asprey's in favour of down market *blingmongers* like Price-drop.TV and Argos.

nettoflix *euph.* TV service for the budget-conscious. Freeview.

Netto ghetto *n.* A bijou shopping arcade consisting entirely of discount stores, *eg.* The Loreburn Centre, Dumfries.

Netto nosebag *n.* A plastic carrier from the popular discount chain, the handles of which are placed over the ears of a drunken car or coach passenger in an attempt to mitigate the effects of him *shouting soup.*

net zero *n.* The doomed emergency tactic of attempting to hurriedly breathe in one's own pungent *Exchange & Mart* before anyone else can smell it.

neuticles *n.* Trade name for an American brand of artificial *knackers* for castrated dogs.

never had time for a wife *euph. Not the marrying kind.* From the lyrics to the Billy Joel song *Piano Man*, which refer to Paul "the real estate novelist" who, despite being too busy working to get married, apparently has plenty of time to hang around in bars talking to sailors.

never never land *n.* Currys or DFS.

new age traveller's cheque *n.* A giro.

Newcastle cup run *euph.* Descriptive of that wistful feeling experienced by blokes looking down at their own erections and wishing they could *suck* themselves *off.* From the fact that they know "it's within reach, but it's never going to happen". Other football teams may be substituted depending on personal preference.

new entry! *exclam.* Said by a chap while boasting to his mates about being successful in *potting a tight brown* with his latest significant other.

New Orleans Rhythm Kings *1. n. prop.* Influential 1920s jazz band, sometimes abbreviated to the NORKs. No, it's true. And thus, *2. n.* A smashing pair of *dairy pillows*. *'New Orleans Rhythm Kings out for the cake-eaters!'*

Newport bus pass *n.* Of a young lady from the Heads of the Valleys, flashing her *top set* at the driver to get a free ride.

Newport chariot *n.* A rough-looking young shaver on a BMX being pulled along the A48 by a massive pitbull on a lead.

Newquay brown *n.* A floating *Thora* or other raw sewage doohickey, as sometimes encountered by surfers in the Cornish Riviera region.

newsagent hymens *n.* The small strips of sticky tape applied to top shelf *tug books* by canny retailers to stop them being read before purchase.

newsflash *n.* An exciting wink of *rabbit tail* glimpsed while watching breakfast telly. *'Did you see Susanna Reid's newsflash this morning?'*

new sheriff in town, there's a *exclam.* Phrase used when someone visiting one's home delivers an *air biscuit* which achieves hitherto unprecedented levels of pungency.

newsreader's shuffle *n.* When you're on the *crapper* and need to lean left to right and back again to get some momentum going.

new star soccer *n.* From the computer game of the same name; a very accurate *crap*, *viz.* a "precise curled effort". *'Come up and look at this, dear. That is some new star soccer right there.'*

newsteam assemble! *exclam.* Loud, *Anchorman*-style proclamation following a particularly powerful and sonorous anal fanfare.

Newton effect *n.* When struggling to pass a three *breather ring dreadnought*, the pleasing sensation as the force of gravity finally takes over.

Newton puzzlers *n. Tits* that seem to defy gravity.

Newton's cradle *1. n.* A still fashionable, chromed executive toy which, by means of colliding, suspended balls demonstrates Newton's third law of motion. *2. n.* The off-putting and often *timber-felling* image of two *grumble flick* actors or professional footballers banging their *knackers* together as they perform a *DP. 3. n.* A demonstration of the fundamental Laws of Motion that will be familiar to any man who has ever had access to a full-length mirror, *viz.* The hip-thrusting motion a fellow makes while standing with his legs apart to make his *meat and two veg* slap off his *gock*

and *barse*.

Newton's revenge *n.* The cruel effect of gravity upon aged *tits*.

Newton's turd law *n.* A physical reaction force created by an explosively released motion which momentarily lifts one's *bummocks* off the latrine.

Newtown hottie *n.* A young woman who, in a larger conurbation, would be scarcely worthy of a second glance, but in a small mid-Wales market town for instance, exhibits the comparitive va-va-voom of Marilyn Monroe in a wet vest.

next one's through the goods *exclam.* British Rail-based *farting* terminology, signifying that the next toot on the whistle heralds the arrival of the cargo.

next sale *n.* Twice-yearly incident where one is awoken at some ungodly hour to clear out a pile of unwanted *shit*.

next stop Cowcaddens! *exclam.* Ribald interjection following a notably pungent *Bakewell*. From the foetid methane smell that hits travellers approaching the eponymous station on the Glasgow Underground like a boxing glove on a spring.

next stop is Newark Castle, the *exclam.* Signifying the imminent arrival of a strong faecal smell. From the aroma experienced on the train when passing the sewage works just before Newark Castle station, which is typically strong enough to wake sleeping passengers, thus preventing them slumbering until Leicester.

NFF FFN *abbrev.* Nice From Far, Far From Nice. A lady who looks alright from a distance, but is a right *steg* close up. A *Thora bird*, a *golden deciever, lrf, Elsie Tanner Montana.*

NGTs *abbrev.* National Geographic Tits. Flat, pendulous breasts as sported by aged tribeswomen in the aforesaid school library *jazz mag. Spaniel's ears.*

Niagara balls *n.* An unusually fecund *big spender*. Also *heavy wetter, heavy shooter.*

niags *rhym. slang.* Nuts. From Niagara Festicles = testicles.

nice frames, bad lenses *phr.* Said of a woman with cracking *jubblies* that are let down by unsightly *nip-nops*.

nice hair, she's got *euph.* Description of a lady with a *lovely personality*, but without the *lovely personality. 'That Ann Widdecombe, she's got nice hair, hasn't she.'*

nicely poised *adj.* Of a gentleman, to be prone to *jumping puddles. Good with colours, on the other bus.*

nice nails, got *euph.* Stoke on Trent. *'That Michael*

Portillo, I bet he's got nice nails.'

nice piece of glass *n.* Comestible ordered by humorous types at the golf club bar. *'I'll have a nice piece of glass in a Stella sauce, please.'*

nichter scale *n.* Tabulated rating system used to articulate how much one would prefer not to *do* someone. *'Have a look at the fucking state of that. Christ on a fucking bike. She must register at least 9.5 on the nichter scale.'* (Sir Terry Wogan, introducing the Serbian entry to the 2007 Eurovision Song Contest).

nick bent *adj.* Temporarily travelling on the *other bus* while staying at His Majesty's pleasure.

nickles and dimes *1. n.* Low denomination US currency. *2. n.* A low denomination *grumble vid money shot.* A *stick flick lizard's lick.* *'Goddammit, Gunther. That was goddamn nickles and dimes.'* *'What do you expect? It's the fifth popshot I've done in two hours.'*

Nicko McBrain's drum skin *euph.* Descriptive of one who has a deficit of allure, calling to mind nothing so much as the percussive membranes of the instruments played by the Iron Maiden tub-thumper, who is himself no oil painting.

nick one to the wicketkeeper *v.* To fail to avoid the *follow-on* while wearing white trousers.

nick wax *1. n.* Proprietary brand of depilatory unguent applied to the nether regions by women seeking to achieve a smooth, hairless finish to the *batting crease.* 2. *n. prop.* Breakfast show DJ on Stoke hospital radio.

Nicky *n. prop. rhym. slang.* A lady's *fanny.* From Nicky Minaj = fadge.

niffler *n.* A handily capacious *minge* that can be used for storing large items; a reference to the cheeky, mole-like scamp from *Fantastic Beasts.* *'Get that kilo of coke up your niffler, love. I'll have it back when we've got through passport control and the heat is off.'*

niff mag *n. Bongo comic.*

niff up *v.* To render a locale's atmosphere unpleasant for one's fellow residents. *'This is your captain speaking. We are descending to five thousand feet as someone has niffed up the bog and we need to open a window.'*

niftkin's bridge *n.* Carse, tinter, Humber bridge. The *biffon.*

Nigella *n.* A feature of a person or thing that distracts you from its supposed purpose, *eg.* A hairy mole on a teacher, ridiculous graphics on telly news programmes, or a pair of splendid *knockers* housed in a low-cut dress sported by an absurdly flirtatious television chef.

Nigella express *n.* Nipping downstairs in the middle of the night for a quick *wank* by the light of the fridge.

Nigella's colander, dripping like *sim.* Descriptive of an erotically aroused lady. She who is *dripping like a gravel lorry at the lights.*

Nigella seeds *n. Bacon powder.*

Nigella shites *n.* The aftermath of eating upper class fodder.

Nigella sweller *n.* A cheeky *chubby-on* enjoyed while watching footage of busty, pan-rattling *sexpot* Lawson licking her finger after dipping it in a bowl of *(the rest of this sentence has been removed on legal advice).*

Nigella syndrome *n.* Psychological condition; An inability to fancy an attractive woman on account of having previously been familiar with her late father for many years.

night bus *1. n.* A cheap ride home after a night *on the sauce.* Usually stinks of fags and puke, and costs about two quid. *2. n.* A cheap *ride* at home after a night on the sauce. Usually stinks of fags and puke, and costs a Bacardi Breezer.

nightclub bouncers *n.* Pairs of burly *knockers* that are exposed to the public on Friday and Saturday nights. *'Fancy your chances with those nightclub bouncers, Dave?' 'Not really. To tell you the truth I think I'd rather get my head kicked in by those two big doormen instead.'*

night crap *n.* The *shite* you have before going to bed. *'I've had a simply enchanting evening, Lavinia. Fancy coming up to my flat for a night crap?'*

night in and a ready meal for one *1. n.* What the losing hosts on Channel 4's *Dinner Dates* received in lieu of a romantic slap-up feed with a real life woman in what appears to be a deserted local bistro at about half past ten in the morning. *2. euph.* The bachelor-about-town's evening-in of choice, *viz.* A pot noodle, a *wank* and a cry.

Nightingale toilet *n.* Anywhere – other than an actual lavatory – to *drop your clogs out of the attic* in an emergency. *'Owners of coastal premises up and down the country have failed to show that good old British blitz spirit, and have not offered up their front gardens to use as Nightingale toilets.'*

nightjar *1. n.* A bird of the feathered variety. *2. n.* Any convenient receptacle when *taken short* in the middle of the night.

night on the clown *n.* An evening during which a person consumes McDonald's comestibles. *'You cooking tonight, Heston?' 'Nah, I can't be arsed. Think I'll just have a night on the clown.'*

nightshift tranquiliser *n.* Practised mostly by males who work in the emergency services or 24-hour supermarket chains, an efficient means by which one who has just clocked off at breakfast time gets himself off to sleep when he gets home. *Relaxing in a gentleman's way.*

night watchman *n.* A nocturnal *copper bolt* that has failed to flush away and is discovered guarding the U-bend the next morning.

nikon *n.* A premature ejaculator with a *hair trigger.* From the Japanese manufacturer's popular automatic camera, *viz.* "the One Touch".

nil by south *phr.* Getting none.

NILF/nilf *1. acronym.* Nannies I'd Like to Fuck. Tasteless term used by sexist beasts to describe those eastern European beauties who look after middle class brats 22 hours per day in return for significantly less than the minimum wage and a company pram. *2. acronym.* Nurse I'd Like to Fuck.

nillionaires' row *n.* Name given to any run-down street in one of the country's less salubrious residential areas.

NIMBY/nimby *1. acronym.* Dismissive term for the sort of petty-minded little-Englanders who'd rather not have a tractor tyre burning plant, foghorn testing station or giant bluebottle farm built next to their home. From Not In My Back Yard. *2. acronym.* Members of the fairer sex who claim to be sexually adventurous, but turn out to be the worst sort of prudes when push comes to shove. A frigid person who habitually declines the invitation to engage in a game of *mud darts.* From Not In My Back Yard.

NIN *acronym. medic.* Normal in Norfolk. Doctor's shorthand implying that your physical and mental characteristics indicate that there is every chance that your mother is possibly also your sister, cousin, aunt and perhaps even your father.

nine-bob-note, as bent as a *1. sim.* Colwyn Bay. *2. sim.* Untrustworthy.

nine dart leg/ nine dart finish *1. n.* The successful completion of a game of darts using the minimum number of throws possible, a feat achieved notably on TV by Phil "The Power" Taylor during the 2002 World Matchplay Championship. *2. n.* The successful completion of a sexual encounter in the shortest possible time, usually achieved by a *one pump chump.*

ninety-nine *n.* After over-enthusiastic *nesting* on the *Morgan Stanley Dean Witter,* a *Sir Douglas Hurd* that sticks upright out of the paper at a jaunty angle, thus resembling the popular chocolate ice cream decoration. Hopefully without the monkey blood.

ninety-nine dalmatians *euph.* Of a lady, to be lacking a couple of *nice puppies.* 'She makes a

beautiful bride, don't you agree Mrs Danvers?' 'If you say so, Mr De Winter. It's just a shame she only has ninety-nine dalmatians.'

ninety-nine flake *n.* A particularly off-colour hybrid of *felching* and *ice docking* which frankly doesn't bear thinking about.

ninety-sixing *n.* A spot of *sixty-nining* that goes a bit wrong. For example, when one's partner *drops one* directly up one's nose, spoiling everything for ever.

ninja shit *n.* Upon entering a public lavatory cubicle for a *sit down visit,* to be met with a smell so foul that one has to pull one's jumper up over one's nose and mouth, in the style of the eponymous incognito Japanese fighters, before one can continue.

ninja's toe *n.* A *camel's foot, pig's trotter.*

ninth finger *n.* The *cock.*

nip and tuck *n.* The act of *nipping off* one of *Bungle's fingers* at the knuckle, with the result that the stump is retracted cleanly into the *bomb bay.* The correct response to a *mid-loaf crisis.*

nip balm *n. medic.* Any soothing condiment (*eg.* Preparation H, Anusol), intended to remedy particularly irritating *Harry Stiles. Bramble jelly.*

nipflix *n.* Small pieces of *shit* that flick up and adhere to the toilet wall during a vigorous *arse wipe.* 'You'll have to use your nails to get them nipflix off there, love.'

nipnosis *n.* Trance-like state induced by concentrating one's gaze on a pair of bobbing *milkers.* Often only ends when the *nipnotised* subject drives through a red light and broadsides a police car. *Titnosis.*

nip 'n' roll *n.* The dextrous art of relieving an itch in *John Wayne's hairy saddlebags. Sorting out the boys, re-shuffling the cabinet.*

nip on *n.* A nippular erectivation. A *hard-on* of the *chapel hat pegs.*

nipotism *n.* In the world of business, the discriminatory practice of hiring and promoting ladies on the basis of *first impressions,* to the detriment of the careers of their less *well qualified* counterparts.

nipping Christian *n.* A *cutpurse, Glasgow postman* or thief.

nipping the turtle *n. Crimping off a length, shutting the bomb bay doors after the copper has bolted.*

nipplecakes *n.* Appetising breasts that one wouldn't mind *icing. Baps.*

nipples in the fridge *phr.* Turn of phrase which can be usefully employed when referring to a person who has, to use Ann Widdecombe's telling comment about Michael Howard, "something of the night" about them. *'That Ann Widdecombe's* *a funny fish, I reckon she's got nipples in the fridge, me.'*

nipples north *euph.* Tits up. *'It's all gone nipples north, George. I'm going to quit and buy meself a shepherd's hut for £25,000.'*

nipplolatas *n. Chapel hat pegs* like cocktail sausages.

nippodrome *n.* Any place where a chap can go to enjoy a lively display of *milky swingers, eg.* A lap-dancing establishment, a nudist beach, the male squash court changing rooms at Newcastle Polytechnic where there used to be a *Carry On Camping/prison followed by* Sex Offenders Register-style hole drilled through into the ladies', apparently.

Nipsey Hussle *1. n. prop.* Erstwhile recently deceased Grammy-nominated rapper. *2. n.* Desperate rush to get sat down before stooling. *3. v.* To encourage someone to pay over the odds for a spot of *back door work. 4. n.* Wiggly hipped walk to relieve the itching from one's *rusty bullet wound. 5. n.* Surreptitious manoeuvre to secretly deal with a *fly in the eye,* usually attempted whilst waiting for the *bag for life* to try something on in New Look.

nipsy *n. medic.* The pincer-like muscle just around *Ena Sharples' mouth* that cuts one's *Bungle's finger* to a convenient length when contracted. The blade of the *cigar cutter.*

nipsy fodder *n.* A polite, almost charming epithet for *arse-wipe.*

nipsy mat *n.* That bit of skin between a man's *old fashioned fifties tea towel holder* and his *tennis pouch. 'I tell you, your holiness, my nipsy mat is that mucky Bear fucking Grylls would hesitate to put his hand down there.'*

nipsy's curse *n.* An extra hot curry, such as Curry Hell, formerly available at the Rupali Restaurant, Bigg Market, Newcastle upon Tyne (now closed), which causes one's *arsehole* to bear no children and die by drowning.

nipsy's kiss *1. n.* While carrying out the essential on-the-spot husbandry required following a *number two,* an inadvertent swipe of the shirt tails across the *chocolate starfish. 2. n. Ringerprints* left on the bedclothes after a naked person has sat on them. Also *sheet toffee, bottom line.*

nip/tuck *euph.* A lady who is not only blessed with *nipples like pygmies' cocks,* but also has a *front tuck* like a camel's hoof.

nitby *n.* Semi-acronymous term describing a baby born into the lower ecehlons of British society. Corruption of "Not in the Baby Book", from the unusual monikers given to *Greggs dummy*-sucking nippers, *eg.* Tiaamiii, Chardonnay, Beyonce,

Scratchcard, Bacardi *etc.*

NIYMFO/niymfo *acronym.* See *moped.* Not If Your Mates Found Out.

NKF *abbrev.* No Knickers Friday; an ancient tradition maintained by many young ladies in the historic city of Chester.

Noah's arse *n.* In the world of adult videography, a delightfully erotic tableau involving double anal penetration. From the fact that in the flood/boat fairy story detailed in the biblical book *Genesis,* the animals "went in two by two".

nob *1. n.* A hay clarse, hoity-toity person. A toff, probably wearing bright pink trousers, who enjoys *country suppers* at Rebecca's. *2. n.* A small piece of butter. *3. v.* To *fuck,* to penetrate with the *knob.*

nobbichoc *n.* A small brown chunk of *arse biscuit* or *clagnut* found adhering to one's *bald-headed hermit* following a *fall of soot* while *sweeping the back chimney.*

Nobbies *rhym. slang.* Haemorrhoids. From toothless 1966 World Cup-winning footballer Sir Norbert Staemorrhoids.

nobgoblins *n.* Those mythical creatures that make one's *meat and two veg* itch the second one finds oneself in polite company.

nobnoxious *1. adj.* Descriptive of the somewhat unpleasant aroma emitted by an unsanitary *cock. 2. adj.* Descriptive of highly objectionable and offensive behaviour from someone who is a bit of a *dick.*

Noboru, go for a *v.* To *snip off a length of dirty spine.* From the name of the late former Japanese Prime Minister Noboru Takeshita.

nobsessed *adj.* Of a girl, infatuated with a thoroughly unsuitable man who is, moreover, a bit of a *wanker.*

nob snob *n.* A lady who won't get into bed for less than ten inches.

nob snog *n.* A genteel term for an act of *horatio.*

nob snot *n. Cock hockle, gunk, mess, etc.,* wiped on one's sleeve.

nobsticle *n.* A *tallywhacker* so large it inhibits the owner from walking easily.

nob Tarzans *n. medic. Genital guests* who swing from *pube* to *pube* through one's underpant jungle. *Crabs.*

nob turban *n.* A crest of Kleenex adorning one's post-*wank helmet. Mumrah's cock.*

no, but you can roll it in glitter *exclam.* A pithily sagacious response to the aphorism "You can't polish a turd".

nocturdle *n.* A somnolent *number two* enjoyed during the hours of darkness, usually following curry and drinks.

nocturnal emission *n. medic.* The end result of a *wet dream.* What Henry the Eighth claimed to have had twice on his wedding night with Anne of Cleves, the dirty bastard.

nocturtle *n.* When you wake in the wee small hours to find you're *touching pyjamas.*

nodder *n.* A proudly tumescent *membrum virile* that bobs up and down as you walk, like the head of a comedy ostrich. See *Bernie Clifton.*

noddies *n.* The bikini overflow of an unwaxed lady, from its similarity to the effusive *bugger's grips* worn by 1970s rock legend Noddy Holder. *Thighbrows.* *'Cor, look at the noddies on that Bulgarian lass.'*

nodding donkey *1. n.* A type of mechanical hacksaw used in metalwork. *2. n.* An ugly damsel, usually with big teeth and ears, who doesn't often turn down the chance to *chew on a carrot.*

nodding terms *1. n.* That which a man is "on" with another man with whom he discusses football, politics and roadworks in the pub, even though he only knows his first name. *2. n.* That which a man is "on" with a woman who will give him a *gobble* in the car park round the back of the pub after he's bought her a couple of *knicker oils*, even though he only knows her first name.

noddy *n.* Condom, *French letter*, a cock *"holder".*

noddy book *1. n. Bongo mag. 2. n. Who's Crazee Now? My Autobiography* by Noddy Holder (Ebury Press, 1999).

noddy holder *n. prop.* An expression hailing from the English Midlands and meaning, quite simply, a brassiere.

Noddy Holder's sideburns *sim.* Descriptive of a particularly luxuriant ginger *bush,* the kind that Charlie Dimmock probably has. Or had. She's not been on the telly for a while.

no deal Noel *exclam.* Humorous idiomatic locution uttered in response to a loudly *dropped hat.* See also *you're only supposed to blow the bloody doors off, I'll give it five, what's that Sooty?* etc.

nodge *v.* To observe the sexual activity of others. To *voy,* ogle or *dog.*

nodger *n.* A *peeping Tom, voyeur.* A *merchant* who prefers "live" *grumble* rather than the recorded variety.

Noel Gallagher's high flying birds *n. rhym. slang. Feeshees.*

Noely *1. n.* Affectionate self-coined nickname for TV and radio un-personality Noel Edmonds. *2. n.* A *cunt* which is so small and tight that no-one can get any enjoyment out of it. Derivation unknown. *3. n.* A tightly pursed anal sphincter. A

crinkley arsehole.

no glans land *n.* The nether regions of a lady's nether regions. The *carse, taint, tinter, notcher, twitter, snarse* or whatever.

no hander *n.* A *Boris Johnson* performed upon one's person without any manual assistance, perhaps while swerving off the road into a shop frontage, reading the news or serving in a fish and chip shop.

no hard feelings *phr.* Failing to achieve *wood* despite being presented with a situation that would usually deliver a *pink steel diamond cutter.* *'I'm terribly sorry. This has never happened to me before. I've been with loads of prostitutes and I've always been able to get it up, more or less, even though it's very small.' 'No hard feelings, Lord Archer of Weston super Mare.'*

noinkers *n.* Jubblies, kahunas, shirt potatoes, boobs, sweater fruit, knockers, cab man's rests, baps, funbags, bumpies, neddies, chichis, mambas, dirty pillows, chebs, charlies, diddies, doos, cajooblies, jugs, bubbies, zeps, bazongers, headlamps, whammies, norks, bangers, tits, dumplings, hogans, thrupennies, assets, churns, whammers, yoinkahs, begonias, mumbas, pink pillows, top bollocks, melons, oomlaaters, nellies, choozies, chubblies, chumbawumbas, blimps, charms, baby's dinners, fun cushions, paps, bojangles, garbonzas, airbags, Gert Stonkers, puppies, Bristols. A lady's b*soms.

no job *n.* Being *sucked off* while so *pissed* one can hardly feel it. See also *bland job.*

no-legged stool *n.* Less common than the three-legged variety, a *sit down toilet adventure* requiring such a strong push that both legs come up in the air. See also *neckbreaker.*

nolita *n.* Yet another word for a woman who looks to be in her mid-teens from the back, but who turns out to be in her mid-50s from the front. Also *Kronenberg, boyner* or *back beauty.*

nollies *n.* Word used by posh southern ladies when referring to a gentleman's testicles. From nuts + bollocks + goolies. *'The Archbishop of Canterbury's shoes were so shiny that when he lifted his arms up to crown me Queen of Great Britain and all her Commonwealth Dominions, I could see his big hairy nollies reflected in them.'* (the late Queen, interviewed by Matthew Wright on *The Wright Stuff*, Channel 5).

nollocks *exclam.* A curse which can be used in polite company without causing offence. *'Don't talk fucking nollocks, vicar. Of course you want another cup of tea.'*

no man's land *n.* The disputed zone between a gentleman's *arsehole* and his *balls*, that is to say his perineum. Also *ABC, BBBA, great, gisp, gooch, Finsbury bridge, duffy's bridge, notcher, joy division, Perry Como's lip, kipper, the landing, stinky Mervin, tornado alley, twitter, wannocks, chommie, cockpit, grundle, scran, stinker's bridge, ploughman's, quiche, biffin bridge, taint, barse, tintis, scruttock, crunk* and *scranus.*

nom de plums *1. euph. Fr.* onomat. A *blow job. 2. n. Fr.* Polite Gallic slang for *bollocks.*

nom de spume *n.* The frankly unlikely stage names adopted by actors in *grumble vids, eg.* Dick Thrust, Ben Dover, Rod Steel, King Dong, Bob Todd *etc.*

no mow May *1. phr.* An annual environmental campaign during which garden owners avoid cutting their lawns for a month. *2. n.* A female who cultivates an untended and overgrown *ladygarden* as an environmental gesture. See also *Chewbacca's knackers, Jeremy Clarkson's eyebrows, Stuart Hall's windowbox, nest of skunks, getting a shoulder ride off Leo Sayer etc.*

no, Mr Bond, I expect you to die! *exclam.* Verbalised in a cod Latvian accent after loudly breaking wind.

no, my arse just blew you a kiss *exclam.* Reply to your significant other when they ask if you just farted.

nonads *1. n.* A fellow who is bereft of knackers, *eg.* A eunuch guarding a harem, a *castrato* in a nineteenth century Italian opera company, a member of the apocalyptic, phenobarbital-quaffing Heaven's Gate sect or Evel Kneivel following one of his less successful motorcycle stunt attempts in the 1970s. *2. n.* A chap who is fighty at the back of a crowd when he's *pissed* but who manages to keep his counsel when he's on his own.

non-album single *euph.* A small *Douglas Hurd* released between full-length *long players.*

non-brewed condiment strokes *n.* The *jester's shoes* of a fellow who's packing *seedless grapes*; the final few pushes before the *manfat-*free *custard pie* gets thrown.

nonce jotter *n.* The Sex Offenders Register. *'Just sign the nonce jotter here please, Mr Glitter. And then could you autograph this LP for my auntie Jean?'*

nonce nuggets *n.* Werther's Originals. Also *paedo pellets.*

nonce pocket *n.* A trouser pocket with a hole in it, topologically-speaking.

noncequences *n.* The fallout that befalls a celebrity after they are exposed as a bad sort. *'I see that bandy-legged gobshite is suffering some noncequences from the recent Channel 4 and Times revelations.'*

noncilitis *n. medic.* The rapidly degenerative

wasting illness that afflicts previously healthy celebrities when appearing in court on historic sex charges. Symptoms include extreme frailty, memory loss, confusion and bouts of indignation. *'I'm afraid my client is unable to answer that question, m'lud, on account of he is suffering from a very bad case of noncilitis.'*

nonebrity *n.* A pointless media figure who would love to rise up high enough to scrape onto the bottom end of the D-list. For example, that bloke off that thing with her who used to be in *Big Brother*, him who always seems to appear in those things with her off *Celebrity Love Island*, you know, that one who's living with her with the big *tits* off the adverts who used to go out with him out of Boyzone or was it Westlife.

no need to sieve that *exclam.* Humorous salutation to one's spouse when returning from a trip to the *water closet* for a bout of loose *foulage.*

none up, none down *euph.* The abode of a ruddy-faced professional outdoorsman, often located outside a railway station or supermarket. *'Where's druggy Dave living these days?' 'Oh, he's found himself a nice little none up, none down near some wheelie bins round the back of the 'Spoons on Shields Road.'*

nongratulations *n.* Token, nondescript acknowledgement made to someone who has failed to achieve anything particularly notable. *'As Prime Minister, I would like to offer my heartiest nongratulations to the UK entry in this year's Eurovision Song Contest.'*

non-mover at number two *1. euph.* Constipation. *'Alright, pop-pickers. There's a non-mover at number two, so it's time for a blast from the past. Here's Salt-n-Pepa with Push It. Not 'alf.' 2. n.* How Noel Edmonds might refer to a *floater* bobbing about in one of his hundreds of toilets.

nonnoisseur *n.* An uncultured oaf who is unable to tell the difference between Coke and Pepsi, Stork and butter, his *arse* and his elbow *etc.*

nonthener *n.* Septentrional version of a *mockney, viz.* One who moves south from the Midlands and theatrically adopts the flat vowels and dropped consonants of a true son of the hyperborean counties.

nontrepreneur *n.* A bloke who incessantly rabbits on about how he's going to make his millions with a business idea that he proceeds to do absolutely nothing about.

nontroversy *n.* A whipped-up confection of fake offence, bogus indignation and synthetic anger, typically propogated on social media, and then widely reported as if it is actually a thing. A *war* *of turds, eg.* Some smug *cunt* off breakfast telly pretending to get angry about a sausage roll that's been manufactured without slitting a pig's throat. *Nowtrage.*

noodle benders *n. Aus.* Close-fitting Speedo-style swimming trunks. Also *dick stickers, meat hangers.*

noodle knickers *n.* Affectionate epithet which can be applied to the *downstairs areas* of the more pubicly rampant lady. Also *tank driver's hat, Taz, wookiee hole, mary hinge, yak, superfuzz bigmuff deluxe edition, Judith, eskimo's glove, muff like your granny's hat, gruffalo, wolf pussy, fanny like a guardsman's hat, busby berkeley, hairy knickers, Lord Winston's moustache, Paddy McGinty's goat, Percy Thrower's lawn, Terry Waite's allotment, radar trap, barber's floor, beartrapper's hat, biffer, Bilbo Baggins's foot, black forest gateau, bushell, Clara Dawes, divot, Dougal* and *gorilla autopsy.* See also *FLARP.*

nook and cranny *euph.* The *front* and *back bottoms* – not necessarily in that order – of the more mature lady.

nookie *1. n.* Sex, only a *bit* of which it is advisable to have at any one time. *2. n. prop.* A humorous name for a ventriloquist's bear that looks like TV chef Michel Roux.

nooner *n.* See *funch.*

noose massoose *n.* A young lady skilled in *triggernobetry, viz.* One who can perform the *walnut manoeuvre. 'Have you met the Countess? She's a noose massoose, don't you know.'*

Nora Batty's cum face *euph.* Descriptive of someone whom the good Lord blessed with a *lovely personality. 'Have you seen the new barmaid? She looks rougher than Nora Batty's cum face!' 'Oi, that's my missus you're talking about. But yeah, you're right.'*

Norfolk *n.* A man-sized measure of vodka, *ie.* Six fingers. From the flat area of England where the folks keep themselves to themselves, if you know what they mean.

Norfolk wedding *n.* The union of a happy couple, surrounded by a scrum of enthusiastic onlookers, near the bogs at Roudham Heath, just off the A11. Apparently. *Dogging, geocaching.*

norkelling *1. n.* When on holiday, wandering along the beach to examine the wares on display. Preferably from behind a pair of *perv windows. 2. n.* The act of burying one's face so deeply into a pair of *funbags* that rudimentary breathing apparatus and possibly a session in a decompression chamber might be advisable.

norkestra *n.* A gathering of *well-qualified* ladies that deserves a standing ovation. A *string section.*

nork hammock *n.* Of female fashions, a halter neck top.

norkolepsy *n. medic.* A trance-like state in men caught in the beam of a fantastic pair of *headlamps, eg.* In the office, swimming pool, night club, church *etc. Titnotism, nipnosis.*

norks *n.* Knockers. Also *norkers, norgs, norgers.*

norks and mingey *euph.* The feminine triumvirate. A pointlessly laboured pun on the title of hyperactive lycanthropic late funnyman Robin Williams's 1978-1982 US sitcom *Mork and Mindy.*

norks drift *n.* What happens to a *fit lass's impressive qualifications* when she starts getting on a bit. See *on the way to Eastbourne.*

norkshire puddings *n.* A northern *bird's top bollocks. 'Do you want any gravy on them norkshire puddings, mother?'*

norks north *euph. Tits up. 'Put simply, Fiona, the fucking economy's gone norks north.'*

norkward silence *n.* Period of wordless embarrassment that ensues when a lady catches a gent peering furtively at her *chebs.*

Norman Cook *n.* A measure of alcohol which after being drunk can make a *Fat Bird Slim.* Approximately two *St. Ivels.*

Normanton frog brick, face like a *sim. Yorks.* Aesthetically unconventional. *'Fucking hell. That lass on the bus to Townville last night had a face like a Normanton frog brick.'*

Norman Wisdom's jacket, as tight as *sim.* Established metric for the expression of extreme level of snugness of a *vadge.* See also *as tight as a ~worm's belt; ~ bullfighter's pants; ~ shark's arse; ~ mouse's waistcoat; ~ teenage wanker's curtains.*

Norma Snockers *n.* Wieldy *bojangles.* See also *Gert Stonkers.*

Norris *1. n. prop. rhym. slang.* An overly excitable lady. Named in honour of the late *Guinness Book of Records* weirdo, *viz.* Norris McWhirter = squirter. *'I had a proper sexy night with big Janice from Accounts. Turns out she's a Norris. By the way, can I borrow your Vax?' 2. n. prop. rhym. slang.* Supplementary benefit. Named in honour of Emily Bishop's erstwhile busybody lodger at No. 3 Coronation Street, *viz.* Norris Cole = dole.

Norris on the spot *n.* An urgent *wank;* a reference to the deceased Guinness compendium editor's weekly against-the-clock slot on *Record Breakers.*

northern comfort *n.* Carlsberg Special Brew.

northern lights, going to see the *euph.* Taking one's beloved for a romantic evening drive to St. Mary's Lighthouse, Whitley Bay, to meet like-minded, headlamp-flashing incurable romantics in the car park.

northern rock hard *adj.* Descriptive of a chap who suddenly and unexpectedly suffers a catastrophic slump in his ability to maintain an acceptably large *endowment. Sub prime. 'I don't know what happened. Everything was going along fine, then suddenly I was northern rock hard. It was as though Janet Street-Porter had walked into the room.'*

Northern Rock moment *n.* The point at last orders, when you realise that you forgot to visit the cashpoint before you came out and are thus bereft of *liquid funds*, and are therefore reduced to grovelling round the pub, seeking a "lender of last resort". There's topical.

northerns *n. medic.* Haemorrhoids, *bum grapes.* From northern isles = St. Mary of Argyles.

north face *1. n.* Brand name of a clothes manufacturer which seems suspiciously popular amongst BBC News on-screen talent. *2. n.* Mountain climber's euphemism for the more difficult route up a lady. *'Gladys had the painters in on the South Col, so Alf decided to attempt the tricky north face.'*

north mountain *n.* The *shitter.* From Disney's *Frozen* when Elsa says to that Moose bloke: "I want you to take me up the north mountain."

North South divide *1. n.* Economic division across the UK. *2. n.* The *biffin bridge.* Also *stinky Mervin, notcher, carse, taint* and so on and so forth.

north/south divide *1. n.* The supposed marked disparities in wealth, opprtunity and housing that exist above and below Watford Gap. *2. n.* A description of the disparity between a woman's *rack* up top and her *pinnions* down below.

Norton commando *1. n.* A classic British motorbike with a pool of oil under it and its chain all in bits in the gutter. *2. n.* An inspiringly brave computer user who connects to the internet without first installing anti-virus software.

Norwegian hat *1. n.* Fleece headwear worn by Scandinavian types to keep their ears warm. *2. n. Fiveskin, Kojak's rollneck, monk's cowl etc.*

Norwegian's lunchbox *sim.* Descriptive of a *clopper* that smells like half a stone of whale blubber marinated in roll-mop herrings and sour milk.

Norwegian wood *1. n.* An erection achieved in a sauna. *2. n.* Title of a Beatles song, which John Lennon wrote after getting an erection in a sauna.

NORWICH *acronym. milit.* Cipher used on military correspondence – Knickers Off Ready When I Come Home. First used during World War I, when Norwich was known as Korwich.

no score drawers *n.* Unflattering ladies' undergarments worn when the *pools panel is sitting* and the dividend forecast is low.

nosebag *n.* An appetising *hairy pie* that looks worthy of a good *noshing*, in the enthusiastic style of Old Man Steptoe's horse Hercules tucking into his dinner.

nosebag on a chicken, fits like a *sim.* Said of something that snugly attaches to you like those tight trousers miniature former PM Rishi Sunak wears. *'Have you knobbed that new barmaid at the Bull yet, Walter?' 'Certainly have, Mrs Archer. Her fanny was that tight it fitted my cock like a nose bag on a chicken.'*

nosebleed *n.* A *fart* that is *fuck off* strong. An *air onion.*

nose, blow one's *v.* To wipe away the post-ejaculation *sprongle* from one's *hog's eye. 'I had to blow my nose on the back of her dress before pulling my pants back up.'*

nose fruit *n. Bogies.*

nose jizz *n. Snot, George Lucas.*

nose-seeking *adj.* Descriptive of a type of *Miranda* that actively hunts down the nearest nostril so that its full potency can be savoured almost immediately.

nosey porker *n.* An inquisitive, purple-faced *Hampton*, poking its snout out of a swain's breeches early in the morning following a night *on the sauce*, looking for the *Boss Hogg.*

nosh *n.* An act of *oral affection* which, according to Bill Clinton but perhaps not his missus, does not constitute sexual relations.

nosh box *n.* A lady's *parts of shame.*

noshferatu *n.* The sort of chap who doesn't mind *dining at the Y* while *the painters are in.* One who likes to take his *tuna* with plenty of *tomato sauce.*

nosh off *v.* To perform *philately* on a man.

nosh out *v.* To perform *cumulonimbus* on a woman. To *lick out, eat out.*

nosh pit *n.* Location under the boss's desk where less-talented employees go to negotiate rises, promotions, time off, workplace sexual harrassment claims *etc.*

noshtalgia *n.* Fond remembrance of particularly good tunes played on one's *pink oboe* in days gone by.

nosh the bosche *v.* To suckle on a chap's *German helmet.*

no sign of a struggle *euph.* When there's absolutely no mess on the paper after wiping one's *arse.* The opposite of *tickling the turtle's nose.*

nostaljerk *n. Knocking one out* for old time's sake over the *funderwear* section of a Littlewoods' catalogue.

no stranger to scatter cushions *euph.* Said of a

fellow who is *light on his loafers, good with colours, sews his own buttons etc.* An elliptical way of referring to one who *picks the chocolate dessert off the menu.*

Nostrildamus *n.* A prophet who is favoured with the ability to augur whether an impending *dropped gut* will be a proper crowd-disperser.

notcher *n. Biffin bridge.* The area of skin between the *clockweights* and the *starfish*, so called because it's "notcher" *bollocks* and it's "notcher" *arse. The great.*

not for a gold pig that shits diamonds *phr.* Rhetorical rejection of an offer to perform an unpleasant task. *'Rebecca, there's a boar in the barn that needs wanking into a bucket.' 'Not for a gold pig that shits diamonds. I'll have you know I'm a respectable model and media personality.' 'It's being filmed for the telly.' 'Which hand would you prefer me to use to bring it off?'*

not leftovers people *euph.* Fat.

not now, Bernard *exclam.* Humorous response to a *rectal retort*, also the title of a kids' book by the late, great David McKee. Actually, it was probably that first.

not now, Cato *exclam.* Phrase made popular in the Peter Sellers *Pink Panther* films, which can be used by a gentleman who is affected by an unwanted bout of *priapism, eg.* On a bus, while looking at the frozen foods in the Heaton, Newcastle branch of Safeway's in about 1990, or while blessing the masses from an open-topped Range Rover.

not on the programme, that one was *exclam.* Phrase employed in polite company by a *botty-bugle* soloist who has blown an impromptu *crowd-pleaser.* See also *encore une fois!*

not shy of colours *euph.* Said of a man who *sews his own buttons on* and *bakes a moist sponge.*

notstalgia *n.* Wistful memories of past things that are now regarded as a bit tired, *eg.* Finding an old copy of a *scud mag* that would once have got you *bashing the bishop* for all you were worth, but now seems a bit lame.

Notswolds, the *n.* Name given to any charmless, semi-rural part of England that is unlikely ever to count a Tory cabinet minister, cheese-making former pop star or *Top Gear* presenter amongst its residents, and where the only Range Rovers are driven by policemen. *'Welcome to Rochdale, heart of the Notswolds.'*

not the marrying kind *adj.* Descriptive of a fellow who is *nicely poised* or *good with colours. 'Has your Cedric found himself a nice girl and settled down yet?' 'No, well you know my Cedric. He's not the*

marrying kind.' 'Still a male prostitute then?' 'Yes.'

not very aggressive *euph.* Said of a fellow who *throws a light dart.*

not worth the paper it's written on *phr.* Said of A disappointingly small *shit* that is frankly a waste of *bumwad.*

nought and a one, a *euph.* Obsolete beardy-weirdy computer operator slang for a *gypsy's kiss.* From the fact that when operating an old fashioned ICL card-punching machine, pressing the nought and the one buttons at the same time encoded a *slash. 'Where are you going, Mr Babbage?' 'I'm just off for a nought and a one while my difference engine reboots.'*

noughtomobile *n.* A vehicle that occupies the lowest possible position on the *fanny-magnetism* scale, *eg.* A souped-up Daewoo Matiz with *Max Power* stickers, Zastava Yugo or Talbot Samba convertible.

nought to sixty *1. n.* Measure of acceleration time by which men in pubs judge the relative merits of various Lamborghinis, Ferraris and Aston Martins which they have never even seen, let alone driven. *2. euph.* An incredibly rapid erection which takes everyone around it by surprise. A *viagra sunrise.*

nourish bowl *1. n.* Hipster food, consisting of a colourful, flavor-packed pot of goodness; a perfect lunchtime pick-me-up *2. n.* A lady's *bodily treasure.*

nouveau obese *adj. Fr.* Said of a previously svelte person who has recently acquired unprecedented and extraordinary girth after *relaxing their fitness regime.*

novelty *adj.* In music, *shite.*

now back to Davina *exclam.* A humorous interjection or quip, to be made immediately prior to *letting off.* See also *gentlemen start your engines.*

now for the news where you are *exclam.* Announced before – or indeed after – a conspicuous *Lional Bart.*

now I'm the king of the jungle *exclam.* Cry of an alpha male after asserting his dominance with a forceful blast on the *botty bugle.* Also *mighty fine words, preacher; there goes the elephant; fall out the officers; thanks for that, now can you please throw something?; oh really sir, could you put that in writing?; now I'm no expert on cricket, but I'm pretty sure that's out.*

now is the time to heal *exclam.* Statesmanlike announcement following a particularly toxic *Donald.* See also *add that to your playlist.*

now let's hear from the audience *1. exclam.* Something *Question Time* presenter Fiona Bruce says after a politician, business leader or comedian on the panel has spoken for too long. *2. exclam.* A humorous rejoinder to a *trouser cough.* Also *now that deserves a Hollywood handshake.*

now pay attention 007 *exclam.* A phrase uttered prior to the release of an *apple tart* with a licence to kill.

now put your toys away *exclam.* Said in bed by an indifferent *bag for life* when she wants to pull her nighty down again and go to sleep. *'That's enough of that. Now put your toys away. I've got to get up at six.'*

no wrist for the wicked *exclam.* Uttered when forced to abandon plans for a *wank.*

nowt but cunt *phr. Yorks.* A swift and pithy character appraisal.

now we know what killed the dinosaurs *exclam.* A witty retort upon the release of a particularly piquant *Bakewell* that could be considered analogous to the meteor impact that did for all those big lizards during the Cretaceous-Paleogene extinction event. See also *keep shouting sir, we'll find you; more tea vicar?; someone let him in; someone's tinkered with Herbie; speak on, sweet lips that never told a lie; speak up caller, you're through; taxi for Brown* and *that's working, now try your lights.*

now we're sucking the right tit *exclam.* Phrase uttered when, in the course of a protracted attempt to successfully complete a difficult task, what appears to be a productive avenue of endeavour is felicitously happened upon. *'Goldarn it, Crick, look at this down my microscope. The paired nucleotide sub-units are exactly equal. The guanine and the cytosine, the adenine and the thymine.' 'By George, I do believe you're right, Watson. The length of each base pair is the same, so they fit exactly between the phosphate backbones of the molecule. Are you thinking what I'm thinking?' 'You betcha. If such a double helix structure were pulled apart, it is clear that each strand could then be used as a template for the assembly of a brand new base pair complementary strand. Hot diggity, now we're sucking on the right tit.'*

now you listen to me, and you listen good *exclam.* Something to be said just before *letting one rip,* in the style of Jimmy Cagney upbraiding a wiseguy.

NPC *abbrev.* Video game parlance for a Non Player Character. *2. n.* The kind of useless waste of space that occasionally gets *shat* into your workplace. Typically seen wandering about aimlessly and bumping into walls like an extra from *Grand Theft Auto* or Michael Gove.

N-POT/n-pot *abbrev.* A coded chap-to-chap reference to a passing lady's *assets,* such as might be used by a senior member of the Lords while observing a *fat-titted* researcher in the lobby of the Houses of Parliament. Nice Pair Of Tits.

NRP *abbrev.* Something to be enjoyed and savoured at one's leisure. A Nice Relaxing Poo.

NSFW *1. abbrev.* Internet warning that the content being linked to is Not Safe For Work. *2. abbrev.* Internet warning that the content being linked to is safe for work. Not Suitable For Wanking. *3. abbrev.* Not Safe For Wife. Can apply to incoming text messages or emails, as well as browser histories and pocket contents.

NSIT *abbrev. nav.* In naval parlance, said of a red-blooded chap who is prone to committing playfully indecent assaults on vulnerable women when the opportunity presents itself. Not Safe In Taxis.

NTL *euph.* An excessively long stay on the toilet reading the paper, philosophising *etc.* After the telecommunications company who spend months *laying* just one *cable.*

nubility, the *n.* A clique of high class young ladies that give a bit of *blue blood* to anyone driving past.

nudger *1. n.* A *Colwyn Bay* male. *2. n.* What a *fudge nudger* uses to *nudge fudge.*

nuffing *n.* The equivalent of *muffing,* but on a woman who has succumbed to the modern trend of Hollywood waxing.

nuggets *1. n.* Testicles. *2. n.* Any inedible part of a chicken or turkey, when coated in batter or breadcrumbs.

number one *euph.* A *penny, tinkle.*

number one wood *1. n.* A top-rated distance club for golfers. *2. n.* A rare, *diamond-cutting hard-on.* Pink steel. *'Call the doctor, will you love. I got a number one wood when I was shopping for antiquarian books on the internet and I've burst all the stitches in me bellend.'*

number six *n.* A *number two* that is three times the normal size, leading to the *John Waynes* and a possible hospital admission.

number threes *n.* Vomit.

number two *euph.* A *sit down, tuppence,* a *duty.*

nummghh *exclam.* The insulting noise made by pushing the tongue into the lower lip, usually directed at a person of low sense, or one who has inadvertently asked a foolish question. Regionally accentuated by either loose wristed hand waggles or transverse elbow-crested ear slaps.

numpty dumpty *n.* A person who manages to be both rotund and useless. An epithet coined by one or other of the sweary Scotch blokes in the film *In the Loop. 'Hello, I'd like to buy a return ticket to London King's Cross, please.' 'Please hold* *the line while I put you through to the next available numpty dumpty.'*

numpy pumpy *n.* Penetrative sexual intercourse engaged in by members of the lower orders, of the sort that keeps the Jeremy Kyle programme supplied with *scratters* who want DNA tests.

nunchucks *1. n.* Okinawan martial arts weapon consisting of two pieces of wood on a string that Bruce Lee used to whirl up under his arms and whack baddies with. *2. n.* Two pieces of *shite* held together by a string of undigested hair that helicopters out of a dog's bottom.

nunga munching *v.* The ganneting of *hairy pie*, *licking out* a lady's *cunker* with relish.

nunky *n. Notts.* A prophylactic sheath. *'Slim: You know you don't have to act with me, Steve. You don't have to say anything, and you don't have to do anything. Not a thing. Or maybe just whistle. You know how to whistle, don't you, Steve? You just put your lips together and … blow. Steve: Hang on. I'll just go down the bogs and get a pack of nunkies.'* (from the screenplay for *To Have and Have Not*, 1944).

nunnery *n.* Elizabethan name for a *rub-a-tug shop* from an age when nuns were widely believed to wear *yo-yo knickers*.

nun's clit, as sensitive as a *sim.* Reference to someone thin-skinned and liable to react badly to criticism. *'Whatever you do, don't mention Meghan to him. He's as sensitive as a nun's clit about that whole business.'*

nun's clit, clean as a *sim.* Descriptive of something that is vigorously and repeatedly washed on a regular basis, but rarely if ever used. *'You'll not find a better Harley Davidson Fat Boy Milwaukee Eight on the market, mate. I've had it three years and it's only done six miles from new, and that's moving it in and out of the garage to polish it. Honestly, it's as clean as a nun's clit.'*

nun's cucumber, wetter than a *sim.* See also *wetter than an otter's neck, wetter than a turfer's knee, wetter than Whitney Houston's last joint, wetter than a bad plumber's mop, wetter than Lee Evans's suit.*

nun's fanny *1. sim.* Descriptive of something that is extremely dry, *eg.* The Sahara desert, Jeremy Clarkson's throat. *2. euph.* Anything that is particularly tight, *eg.* Any space a lady attempts to park a car in, the glove that OJ Simpson didn't wear when he wasn't murdering his wife.

nun's knickers, dry as a *sim.* A jocular rhetorical flourish that can be employed when ordering a drink. Also *dry as a moth sandwich, dry as a budgie's tongue.*

nun's rug *euph.* A vintage item which is neverthe-less in absolutely mint, unused condition. *'For sale. L-registered Morris Marina in magnificent muconium beige livery with mouseback vinyl roof. This car has covered just 6 miles since new and has been kept in a dry, heated garage for the last thirty-two years, only being taken out once by its careful lady owner for a short run to the shops and back in 1973, after which it broke down and refused to restart. It still bears the original polythene seat-covers and has not even been run in yet. A real nun's rug of a classic which can only appreciate in value in the coming years. £18,500 ono.'*

nun's tits, pale as a *sim.* Descriptive of skin that doesn't get much exposure to sunlight. *'After answering his latest set of drugs charges, crack-guzzling Babyshambles frontman Pete Doherty stumbled down the courtroom steps looking pale as a nun's tits.'*

nun's tits, useful as a *sim.* Phrase used in reference to something, or someone, of no obvious utility whatsoever. *'Have you seen that (insert name of a newly signed expensive football player here)? He's about as useful as a nun's tits.'*

nun's twat, tighter than a *sim.* Descriptive of something requiring maximum torquage to loosen to a satisfactory level. *'How were your new school shoes, dear?' 'They're tighter than a nun's twat. I should have gone for the six-and-a-halfs, mum.'*

Nurembergs *n. rhym. slang.* Haemorrhoids. From Nuremberg Trials = piles. Also *Seig Heils, four minute miles.*

nurfing *n. Barumphing, snurgling, moomphing, quumfing.* Sniffing a lady's recently vacated bicycle saddle.

nurse! *phr.* Melodramatic exclamation made following a vicious *Exchange & Mart* that may, one fears, have necessitated an unplanned change of plus-fours.

nurse's apron, fanny like a *sim.* Either *a)* A pristine, starched, pressed set of lady's *nether bits*. Possibly with an upside-down watch pinned to them. Or *b)* A grubby, unwashed, bloody set of lady's *nether bits* that could well prove deleterious to one's health.

nurse's watch, clit like a *sim.* A jocose reference to a somewhat overgenerously proportioned *devil's doorbell*.

nut allergy *n. medic.* Potentially serious medical condition suffered by frigid women which, if left untreated, can lead to a severe *Vitamin S* deficiency.

nutbag shitty limits *n.* The late Ike Turner's *tintis*. There's a phrase that's going to come in handy.

nut butter *n.* A lightly salted dairy product served

hot from the male *churns* onto *baps*. *'Try not to get any of that nut butter on your tie, grandad.'*

nut chokers *n.* Gentlemen's tight *shreddies*. *Budgie smugglers, noodle benders.*

nutcracker *n.* This sounds unlikely. Inserting one of your *clockweights* into a ladyfriend's *winking walnut*, whereupon she clenches her buttocks. Also *ballbreaker.*

nutcrackers *n.* Unfeasibly tight "spray-on" *round the houses* sported by *rock poodles* such as Justin Hawkins out of now-defunct comedy band The Darkness.

nutcracker suite *n.* An hotel room with a good internet connection, a "Do not disturb" sign hung on the door and a plentiful supply of tissues.

nut custard *n. Banana yoghurt.*

nutcut *n. medic.* The small incision scar visible on a chap's *ostrich skin cheese bag* following a vasectomy. *'My husband went to get his balls chopped off last week, and the surgeon made a beautiful job. You've got to look really hard to spot his nutcut. More tea, bishop?'*

nut dust *n.* All that is left for a fellow to *jonk* after he has *worked at home* all day until his *knackers* are as *flat as bats' wings* and he is *chucking salt*. See also *weeze.*

Nutella knickers *n.* After an evening spent *rogering* the wife via the *back door*, her *Nutella knickers* may need to go in a boil-wash.

nut fangle *n.* Pre-*wank* prep work.

nutflix *n. Adult* interweb content enjoyed by *monomanualists*. The fruity television channel that a chap might casually flick to as soon as his *bag for life* has *fucked off* to bed. *C-boobies.*

nut flush *1. n.* Poker terminology used to describe the best possible flush hand on a board. Whatever that means. *2. n. Icing the log.*

nuthard *n.* A *fighter pilot's thumb* which sticks out as a result of inclement meteorological conditions.

Nutkin *1. n.* Of a man, the worst hairstyle it is possible to have, *eg.* Those worn by Phil Harding (*Time Team* yokel archaeologist), Bill Bailey (troll-like comedian) and Terry Mancini (has-been QPR footballer). Named after late TV animal trainer and former sealion's dinner Terry Nutkin. *2. n.* A Mick Miller-style scrotal *pube-do*, with a shiny bald bit in the middle and long strands hanging down round the sides.

nutmegs *n. Balls* that hang down right between a footballer's legs. *Granny's elbow.*

nut milk entrepreneur *1. n.* Risible profession of one of "Britain's best young business brains" who took part in the last series of *The Apprentice*. *2.*

n. Wanker.

nuts *1. n.* A fellow's *pods. 2. n.* Things your missus only eats as a special treat at Christmas. That'll be your *pods* again, then. *3. adj.* Mental. *'You should meet my brother, he's absolutely nuts. Seriously, he made a skin suit from his landlady and got sectioned under the 1971 Mental Health Act.'*

nutsack *n.* The scrotal sac or *nadbag.*

nutsack navigator *n.* A self-contained – yet potent – *air biscuit* that emerges in the vacuum of the *undercrackers* and makes its way gradually to the open air, charting a tortuous route around the *man bag* on its way. Also *trouser tickler.*

nutty slack *1. n.* A cheap fuel consisting of coal dust (slack) and small lumps of coal (nuts). *2. n.* The state of an octogenarian's *ball bag*. *'Alright, Sir Alan. We'll just have a quick check of your nutty slack and then we're done.'*

nut zero *phr.* The point in a bachelor's weekend when any further acts of *self delight* result in zero emissions. Typically well before 20.30 on the Friday night.

NWAW *abbrev.* Trade term for an antique item's lack of value or desirability, *viz.* Not Worth A Wank. Practically every item that any contestant or expert on *Bargain Hunt* or *Antiques Road Trip* has ever bought is *NWAW.*

NWW *abbrev.* The opportune short space of time between the departure of a partner to perform some rapid and mundane task and their expected return, *viz.* Narrow Wank Window.

nymph *1. n.* The caterpillar off a dragonfly. *2. n.* In a Laurence Alma-Tadema painting. a sexy young *bushless bird* wearing a diaphanous frock, possibly holding a jug or strumming a harp.

nympho *n.* Sex-crazed *bird* that's *gagging for it* 24 hours a day, 7 days a week. The sort who would answer the door to Robin Askwith in a see-through nightie because her hubbie was away working on an oil rig or in prison or whatever. A raving nymphomaniac who *loves it up her.*

nymphomation *n.* The insider data shared between a group of males about an unusually accommodating girl that one of them has had *carnival knowledge* of. *'Russell just gave me some great nymphomation about Georgina. I'm going to ring up her grandad and tell him straight away. But first, here's Cilla with Step Inside Love.'*

NYPD blue *n.* A *poke up the doughnut*, whereby the *pokee assumes the position* of a hoodlum being frisked by the Big Apple's finest, against the wall or across the bonnet of a car.

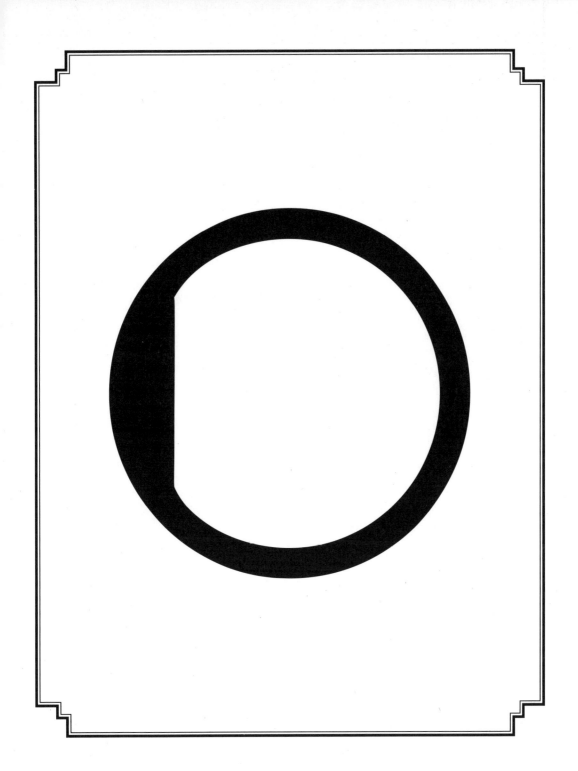

oakhampton *n*. A sturdy bit of *wood*. A *hard-on* you could mount on a lathe and turn the leg of a slate bed snooker table out of. Not to be confused with the Devon town of Okehampton, which is spelled differently and doesn't have as many wiggly veins going up the side.

OAP-dophile *1. n.* A *biddy fiddler, mothball diver, tomb raider* or *granny magnet*. *2. n.* A young woman who is inexplicably attracted to a (usually extremely wealthy) elderly man, *eg.* (Long list of names deleted on legal advice).

Oaten's briefcase, it smells like *sim*. Descriptive of a particularly unpleasant miasma. Derivation unknown. *'Did you have second helpings of that twenty-two bean casserole last night? It smells like Oaten's briefcase in here this morning.'*

oath, administering an *exclam*. Legal parlance for dropping a real *wig-lifter* in court.

oats *n*. A *portion* of that which one gets during sex with a Quaker. *Tiffin, crumpet.*

OBE *1. abbrev.* A memorable token of an evening out, awarded by a nightclub bouncer as one is ejected from his establishment. One Behind the Ear. *2. abbrev.* Order of the Brown Entrance. An honour bestowed on a gentleman for services to another's *shitter. Brown wings.*

obeast *n*. Someone who has a morbidly *lovely personality* and is also *bubbly* to boot.

obeastiality *n*. The frankly perverse practice of *fucking* unattractively overweight animals.

obeseicle *n*. Four-wheeled electric vehicle of the sort favoured, on their trips to the pie shop, by those who customarily eschew greens. *A bariatricycle.*

obesetiality *n*. Performing an act of penetrative intercourse on a *proper plumper. Slapping the fat and riding the waves.*

Obi-Wan's cape *euph*. Phrase used to describe the unfortunate occurrence of extreme flaccidity inside a chap's *grundies* (for example following immersion in cold water) to the extent that his *old man* completely vanishes, leaving in its stead an empty, crumpled, pink walnut whip. *Shrinkage.* From the scene in *Star Wars* where erstwhile Jedi Knight Sir Alec Guinness gets whacked with a neon tube by the Green Cross Man. Also the *Wicked Witch of the West. 'Not tonight, Josephine, I've just got out of the swimming pool and I've got Obi-Wan's cape.'*

oboe d'amore *1. n. Fr.* The "oboe of love", *viz.* A double-reeded woodwind musical instrument. *2. n.* The *spam clarinet, pink oboe.*

observation car *1. n.* On a scenic railway, a luxury train carriage with large windows. *2. n.*

At a *dogging* site, a carload of non-participating voyeurs parked over to one side. Tea, coffee and cake may be served.

observe Mr Bond, the instruments of Armageddon! *exclam*. A phrase to be said prior to letting of a series of *Lionels* so deadly they could spark a global thermonuclear conflict. See also *gentlemen start your engines; listen to this, too good to miss, na-na na-na na; over to you, Esther* and *now back to Davina.*

obstruction on the Humber Bridge *euph*. A strict no entry barrier to stop the *old feller* straying from the *Grimsby end* to the *Hull end.*

occulus rift *1. n.* Stupid name given to one of these new fangled virtual reality headsets. *2. n. Biffin's bridge.*

occupy the crease *1. v.* In cricket, to build a long innings without worrying unduly about anyone else's best interests. *'Geoffrey is a selfish cricketer, regularly occupying the crease with scant consideration for the needs of his team.'* *2. v.* To pleasure one's missus orally. *'Geoffrey is a selfish lover, seldom occupying the crease and showing scant consideration for the needs of his ladyfriend.'*

odds are good but the goods are odd *exclam*. Phrase which may be usefully employed on a Friday night when *picking up* women on Teesside.

odour toilette *n. Fr.* The less-than-alluring fragrance emanating from any freshly-abused *khazi.*

offalicious *adj*. Of genitalia, delicious-looking, resembling a juicy pile of glistening offcuts in a *butcher's dustbin.*

offal waffle *n*. A *raggy blart, ragman's coat, stamped bat* or what have you.

office and balcony *euph. Tops and fingers.* From ex-cabinet minister/celebrity jungle camel *cock*-chomper Matt Handcock's leaked WhatsApps. *'How bad are the pics?' 'It's a snog and heavy petting.' 'Did you snog her in the department?' 'Yes.' 'Where about?' 'Office and balcony.'*

office meerkats *n*. Groups of infantile male workers who repeatedly stand up and sit down between the hours of 11.00am and 1.00pm, in order to leer through their windows at attractive females going on their lunch.

office microwave, dirtier than an *sim*. Said of a carnivally adventurous woman. *'See her reading the six o'clock news there? Mate of mine's brother works with her boyfriend's dad and he says she's dirtier than an office microwave. Takes it up the shitter and everything.'*

officers' laces *n*. Ladies' string-like thongs buffed brown between their *arse cheeks. Fart wire.*

officer's mess *n. Spoff* deposited in a PC's trousers

after viewing a particularly unpleasant *Frankie Vaughan* flick seized as evidence during a raid on a suspect.

office, tramps' *n.* A conveniently located hub where *Balham ballerinas* hold meetings to decide on their future business strategies, core business criteria, mission statements *etc.* For example, a certain salubrious burger joint on the other side of Euston Road from Kings Cross and St. Pancras stations. The bit round the corner, from where the staff behind the counter can't see them.

off-piste *euph.* Sexual term whereby a gentleman ventures away from the officially sanctioned area and heads into more rugged and challenging terrain. '*Come on, love. I've cooked dinner and even helped with the washing up. How many more brownie points do I need before I can go off-piste?*'

offshite *euph.* Going for a *sit-down lavatory adventure* during working hours, or taking a *dump* at a location where you find yourself due to work commitments. '*Alright lads, just off for an offshite meeting although I'm not sure where the rooms are for it.*'

off-shore wanking business *euph.* An oil rig. '*Our Derek earns good money. He works in the off-shore wanking business, you know.*'

off the lay *adj.* Eggbound.

off the meaten track *euph.* Descriptive of a woman who is *off solids* or *on the turn.* In the early stages of *lesbitis,* thinking about getting *on the bus to Hebden Bridge.*

off the team *adj.* To be forbidden from playing on the *furry turf.* To be in your missus's *cunt book, in mantanamo bay.*

off to the diarrhoea room *euph.* Caught short by an urgent need to *paper the house.* '*Day 46 in the Celebrity Big Brother house, and after a night on the biryani, John McCririck's off to diarrhoea room again.*'

off your face *adj.* Ripped to the tits on the demon drink, *disco biscuits* or plant fertiliser.

off your trolley *adj.* Hatstand, *nuts, radio rental.*

oggle goggles *n.* Sunglasses. Also *perv windows, lech-tacles, binorkulars.*

oggles *n.* Eyewear used for watching *birds* swim underwater. The pool equivalent of *perv lenses.* '*I'm off to the baths, Rita.*' '*Don't forget your oggles, Len.*'

ogler's rest, the *n.* Nickname for any local pub famous for its fine collection of *blart.*

oh, a peacock! *exclam.* Uttered to a partner with glee, immediately after loudly *breaking wind* whilst wandering around the grounds of a country estate or stately home.

oh no-namism *n.* A man's sudden realisation that he has inadvertently left the living room curtains slightly agape when *staying up to watch Family Guy,* meaning there's a good chance the neighbours and several passers-by have seen him sat in front of *Al Jizzera* while furiously *pulling the Pope's cap off.*

oh pair *n.* A *well qualified* woman.

oh really sir, could you put that in writing? *exclam.* Also *now I'm the king of the jungle; is that Ziggy?; I'm Peppa Pig; you should put that on eBay; ooh, get her!*

oh, something I forgot to mention *exclam.* A comical introduction to an enormous *treacle tart.* Best said just as the team leader is wrapping up a mind-numbingly dull meeting.

oil & gas industry *euph.* Where an inveterate stout drinker works the day after a heavy night.

oil can *n.* A chap who is unable to satisfy his *ball and chain,* ie. "Two pumps and a squirt".

oil of goolay *n.* A white, sticky-type foundation cream which reduces the signs of ageing when applied to ladies' faces out the end of one's *cock.* Vitamin S-enriched emollient unguent produced in a chap's *milk churns.*

oil slick *n.* Viscous, floating *chatty watter* purged from the *sluices* after a an evening of spiced sweetmeats and dark beverages, which may prove harmful to seagulls and the marine ecosystem.

oil spill/oil spillage 1. *n.* An accidental release of petrochemical pollution into a body of water 2. *n.* Missing the *shark's mouth* and *pissing* on the bathroom floor. '*Sorry nan, you'll have to get your cloth out again. I've just had another oil spillage.*' 3. *n.* An *Eartha* that constitutes a health threat to marine life.

oil tanker *rhym. slang.* An *onanist, merchant banker, pole vaulter,* eg. Whoever designed the traffic system for getting in and out of the short-stay car park at Newcastle Central Station.

oil the bat *v.* To *polish the pork sword, wax the dolphin.*

oil the meat and not the pan 1. *phr.* Sage cooking advice proffered by celebrity chefs such as Rusty Lee. 2. *phr.* Sage *botting* advice offered by celebrity chefs such as (the rest of this sentence has been deleted on legal advice).

oil the truncheon *v.* To buff up the *bobby's helmet, collect kindling, wank.*

oily loaf *n.* A well-baked *Thora.*

oily rags *n. rhym. slang.* Cigarettes. '*Finish stitching up the patient will you, nurse? I'm just off outside* *for an oily rag.'*

oily seagull *euph.* The distressing state of a chap's *balloon knot* after a particularly claggy *Richard the third.*

OJ's glove *1. n.* The state of the hand after *finger banging* a lady during *ragweek. 2. n.* An extremely tight-fitting *liver sock. Grandad's coin purse.*

okay kids, runaround! *exclam.* A humorous quip to be used following a *windy pop.* Best delivered in gruff, cockney tones reminiscent of the late Mike Reid, but while he was alive. See also *you should put that on eBay.*

Okinawa hairline *euph.* Not completely bald but with one's coiffure "fallen back to a defensible position", in the style of the Japanese forces' Shuri Line in 1944. *'The usual is it, your royal highness? Short round the back and an Okinawa hairline on the top?'*

okra *1. n.* Tropical plant of the mallow family, *Hibiscus esculentus,* colloquially called "lady's fingers", and hence *2. n.* A dirty woman's act of *self pollution.*

oktoberpest *n.* Annoying little scrote that visits your house in the weeks leading up to Halloween and demands money with menaces. A trick-or-treater.

old Adam *n.* Onan's partner in Biblical crime.

old age traveller *n. Coffin dodger* with a rucksack who is taking advantage of their free bus pass to travel several miles to a remote market town to buy a small jar of coffee.

Old Bailey bird *n.* An embarrassingly unattractive ladyfriend who you would ideally like to smuggle into the house under a blanket, in a style reminiscent of the way that the police bundle particularly unpopular murderers into court buildings on the news.

old bangers *1. n.* Ancient cars fit for scrap. *2. n.* Pensioners' *knockers.*

old bat phone, the *n.* The house's landline telephone that is only ever called by one's mother-in-law.

Old Ben Kenobi *1. n. prop.* A fictitious character played by Sir Alec Guinness in *Star Wars* episodes 4, 5 and 6. *2. n. rhym. slang. Feeshus.* From Old Ben Kenobi = joaby. *'I've been very badly egg-bound all week. Four packets of Smints and an Old Ben Kenobi is my only hope.'*

old chap stick *n.* A handy applicator for soothing *lip balm.*

old cock throbbin' *1. phr.* The initial tingle or stirring that shows that the internet-sourced *pork pills* a chap took twenty minutes ago have started to kick in. *2. n.* That smug *fannychops* off the Viagra advert who has just "broken every code".

old cunt conga, the fucking *euph.* Any queue of senile lottery ticket purchasers and senior citizens standing between you and a supermarket till or post office counter. *'Aw shite. I'm right at the back of the old cunt conga again.'*

old dear hunter *n.* A *Vi-curious* gent with a penchant for the blue rinse brigade. A *biddy fiddler, tomb raider, Blofeld, Fenton, archaeologist* or *granny magnet.*

old dog's nose, dry as an *sim.* Descriptive of a *pink wafer.* A *moipless muff. 'What's up love? I've been tickling your wotsit for a good three minutes and you're still as dry as an old dog's nose.'*

old el paso doble *n.* Furtive and frantic feet movements while waiting for the toilet to be vacated, after overdosing on authentic faux-Mexican-style food the night before. Also the *Tijuana two-step, Montezuma's marimba.*

olden doubloons *n.* The *dunghampers* of a young lady who eschews *clackerfloss,* preferring instead *bills* of a more matronly cut. *Elepants.*

old enough to know batter *euph.* Knocking on a bit for a virgin. *'Eeh, I would have expected better of Sir Isaac. You'd think he was old enough to know batter.'*

oldest toad in the pond *n.* A particularly low, vociferous, grumbling *mariner's chart,* usually after eight pints of stout and a bar of Bournville.

old faithful *1. n.* A spectacular eruption of hot steam from a hole in the ground in Yellowstone National Park, USA, filling the area with a foul, sulphurous smell. *2. n.* A spectacular eruption of hot *spooge* from the mouth of an inexperienced *cock nosher,* particularly one lying on her back. *3. n.* A predictably regular blast of *carbon dibaxide* from a flatulent geezer with a *slow puncture. 4. n.* An acrid bathtime *Hart to Hart* which erupts through the suds with a foul, sulphurous smell. *'Shall I get in the bath with you, Charles?' 'I wouldn't, Camilla. I had a Pound Shop curry pot noodle and three bags of Quavers for tea, and old faithful is due to erupt any moment.'*

old fart cart *n.* A hearse complete with coffin.

old fashioned *1. n.* A Bourbon-based cocktail. *2. n.* A *wank* essayed without the use of the internet.

old fellow yellow *n.* A senior citizen's saffron-hued baby gravy. *Gold top, mellow yellow.*

Old Holborn *n.* The frayed edges of a *loosely packed tobacco pouch,* a *pant moustache. Spiders' legs* sticking out of a *heron's nest.*

oldie horn *n.* See *prunetang.*

Oldilocks *n. prop.* A *back beauty,* or *golden deceiver.* See also *witch's trick, backstabber, nolita, flamalap.*

Old Leigh oyster *n.* A particularly viscous phlegm delicacy which requires a bit more chewing than its slightly more aphrodisiacal bivalve namesake. *A docker's omelette.*

old London bus, fanny like an *sim.* A well-used *billposter's bucket* that lots of drunk blokes have made a mess in over the years.

old man *1. n.* Penis. Also *the old fella*. *'The old man's been out of work for six months. Most days we play pocket billiards to keep him occupied.' 2. n.* A refuse collector who wears *gorblimey* trousers.

old man with no teeth eating Weetabix, like an *sim.* Suggestively titillating description of the act of *cumulonimbus* like what you'd get in an erotic novel by Anaïs Nin, Emanuelle Arsan or Alan Titchmarsh.

Old McDonald's combover *n.* Stray *pubage* agonisingly trapped under the brim of the *farmer's hat. Bobby Charltons, Robert Robinsons, Desmond Morrises, Frodo's harp.*

old pink gristle test *n. Cumulonimbus. Donning the beard. Impersonating Whispering Bob Harris.*

old poacher's pocket, fanny like a *sim.* A capacious, gamey, saggy, tattered, well-used *growler* with all bits of blood, guts and fur stuck to it. One that's had plenty of fat *cocks* stuffed into it in a hurry, probably up against a tree in in the pitch black at 2 o'clock in the morning.

old shocker, the *n.* To surprise one's sexual partner by poking a cheeky *pinkie* up their *chuff* during intercourse. *"'I say, Bertie. You'll never guess what," gasped Piggy excitedly. "I've just been in a clinch with Marjorie in the rose garden. Just as I got to the vinegar strokes, she popped me the old shocker. Quite took me aback, don't you know."'* (from *Now Start Humming, Jeeves* by PG Wodehouse).

old traditional *euph.* A *hand shandy* given by a *lady of the evening* to a back bench member of Parliament. *'How much for an old traditional?' 'Ten quid, Mr* (surname of politician removed on legal advice)*, or I'll suck you off for fifteen.'*

old wank *n.* Usually *a load of~* or *a pile of~*. Nonsense, balderdash, poppycock. *'No offence, prime minister, but you're talking a load of old wank there.'*

old watch strap *euph.* Of one's *bag for life*, where after a few years of marriage and a couple of kids, where "the usual hole becomes too loose, but the adjacent hole is just too tight to be comfortable". *'My missus is like an old watch strap, your holiness. The front door is like punching a cloud, but the back door is like sticking me cock in a cigar clipper.'*

Olive oil *n. Mabel syrup, OAP soup, granny batter.*

Oliver *1. adj. rhym. slang.* Inebriated. From Oliver Twist = pissed. *'Please Sir, can I have some more?' 'Fuck off, you're already Oliver.' 2. n. rhym. slang.*

A *Hilary.* From Oliver Twist = one off the wrist.

Olympic flame *n.* One who "never goes out". *'Born on this day: Harrison Schmitt, American astronaut, 1935; Norman E Thagard, American astronaut, 1943; Julian Assange, Swedish Olympic flame, 1971.'*

Olympic lottery *euph.* A highly disappointing experience, such as applying for *sniffers' row* seats at the 2012 women's beach volleyball, only to end up with tickets for the men's shot put instead.

Olympic spurt *n.* The final frenzied push to *reach the finishing line* while carefully perusing YouTube videos of lithe sports personalities, *eg.* Colombian triple jumper Caterine Ibarguen, Jocky Wilson.

Olympic torch *n.* A solitary kernel of corn atop the *herman jelmet* following a spot of *Greco-Roman wrestling.*

Olympic village *n.* Any urban area with a disproportionate number of fat, unhealthy inhabitants trailing to Greggs in polyester-based sportswear.

omega sex *euph.* Making sure that your partner gets her daily allocation of *nuts* and *seeds.*

omelette maker *n.* A *tennis fan,* breaking eggs *on the bus to Hebden Bridge.*

omnibore *n.* A middle-aged man who is unable to hold anyone's attention when talking about any subject due to an extreme lack of personality.

Omo *euph.* Available for sex. From the habit of housewives who leave a box of the eponymous washing powder on their windowsill in order to advertise the fact that they are "On My Own" to passing tradesmen. A secret signal, similar in intention to, but slightly less elaborate than, that time when Lady Di got herself photographed in front of the Taj Mahal.

omosexual *n.* Any *randy* man who *has it off* with bored women whose husbands are out at work/on an oil rig/in prison for grievous bodily harm, *eg.* All plumbers, meter readers, milkmen, door-to-door brush salesmen *etc.*

on and off quicker than the Happy Mondays *sim.* A very brief and unsatisfactory performance. *'He's a right two push Charlie, nan. He was on and off quicker than the Happy Mondays.'*

onanism *1. n.* Incomplete sexual intercourse. *Vatican roulette,* where a father of twelve pulls out at the last minute. *2. n.* What the biblical *wanker* Onan the Barbarian did when he *spilled his seed* on the wainscotting in *Genesis. Strangling Kojak.*

Onan's razor *euph.* Similar to Occam's Razor, a simple, straightforward piece of no-nonsense *grot* that will allow a fellow to *chuck his muck* in the least amount of time.

Onan the librarian *1. euph.* Shabby Local

Authority employee who is noted for taking extra care when restacking the racier returns. 2. *n. prop.* Honorary title nestoweed on a curator of an extensive private collection of *self help manuals.*

once more unto the bleach! *exclam.* Rousing cry in the course of a ferocious battle against *Richard the Third.*

on crutches *euph.* Of a heavily inebriated person, supported on either side by a pair of marginally less *pissed* companions. *'I'm afraid the groom's going to be a bit late for the service, vicar. He's had a bit of a heavy morning and, to cut a long story short, he's on crutches.'*

one *n.* That which is proffered to a woman by a man. *'Did you give her one? I'd give her one.' 'I gave her one alright.'*

one-armed Scouse *n.* A feloniously adjusted fruit machine. An out-of-tune *Glasgow piano.*

one-armed taxi driver with crabs, busier than *sim.* Phrase used to describe a person who is rushed off their feet. *'That Romesh Ranganathan's never off the fucking telly these days is he? He's busier than a one-armed taxi driver with crabs.'*

one-bean salad *n.* A vagina. *'I had a one-bean salad at lunchtime and I'm still picking bits of it out of my teeth, vicar.'*

one brown mouse *1. n. prop.* Second track on side 2 of Jethro Tull's 1978 LP *Heavy Horses.* 2. *n.* A singular dollop of *feeshus* that is passed during a trip to the *bog.*

one cartridge, ignition off, clear out the cylinder *exclam.* Phrase used when performing a particular sort of explosive, underpant-wrecking *Exchange & Mart.* From the scene in the classic Sunday tea-time film *Flight of the Phoenix,* when pilot James Stewart uses up a precious ignition cartridge to clear engine debris, much to the annoyance of Teutonic modelmaker Hardy Kruger.

one cheek sneak *n.* A stealthy approach to *shooting bunnies.* From a sitting position, lifting one *buttock* in order to slide out an aurally undetectable *air biscuit.* A *cushion creeper, leg lifter.*

one-eared spacehopper *n.* Cliff Richard's genitals, you might imagine. A *panhandle* on someone with *DSB.*

one-eyed pant python *n.* A *cock* that could crush a pig to death.

one-eyed trouser snake *n.* A *spitting cobra* that is easily charmed by a *pink oboe* soloist.

one-eyed undertaker *n.* What Bob Dylan probably calls his *blind Willie McTell.*

one-eyed Willie *n.* The *pirate of men's pants,* desperate to get into the *crow's nest.*

one-eyed Willie's eye patch *n.* A condom, an

English sou'wester and *full-length kagoule.* With a hood full of *jitler.*

one-eyed zipper fish *n.* A cycloptic *trouser trout.* A *fly fisherman's tackle.*

one fart away from following through *phr.* An expression to be used when a person is in an angry state and is about to – possibly quite literally – "lose their shit". *'Keir Starmer told parliament that the new revelations about Mr Hancock's conduct at the height of the pandemic had left the entire Shadow Cabinet one fart away from following through.'*

one fart off a shit *1. phr.* Touching cloth. 2. *phr. lit.* On the cusp of malfeasance or disaster. *'All causes shall give way. I'm proper one fart off a shit and that.'* (William Shakespeare, *The Tragedie of Macbeth* III. 4.136–8, early First Folio draft).

one-fifty checkout, the exhibition way *1. n.* In darts, finishing by hitting three bullseyes instead of the more standard treble-twenty, treble-eighteen, double-eighteen route. 2. *n.* In the world of erotic cinematography, a thesp taking three *cocks* up the *arsehole* instead of the more clichéd *mouth, fanny, arse* trope.

one for Esther *1. n.* A *cock* shaped like a vegetable. 2. *n.* A vegetable shaped like a *cock.*

one for the dogs *euph.* A *fart* so high in pitch that it is to all intents and purposes inaudible to the human ear.

one four seven *1. n.* In snooker, a complete clearance during which the player empties the table in a single visit, scoring maximum points in the process. 2. *n.* In toiletry, a complete clearance in which the toiletee empties his *Camillas* in a single sitting, finishing with a black. *'Watch my pint, boys. I'm going for a one four seven.'* 2. *euph.* After *dropping the kids off at the pool,* finding that the first sheet of *arsewipe* is completely pristine after use. A *high break.*

one from the top, two from the bottom *euph.* During *Countdown, relaxing in a jobseeker's way* while simultaneously massaging your *clockweights* for extra stimulation. Hopefully not when Anne Robinson's on the screen.

one-handed mag *n.* Jazz magazine, rhythm read, art pamphlet. A *Frankie Vaughanographic* periodical as perused by a practiser of the monomanual vice.

one-handed yoga *n.* Gentle, rhythmic exercise that is used to relieve stiffness. *Pullates.*

one hand mode *1. n.* A setting on a smartphone that makes it easier to use. 2. *n.* A skill developed by male smartphone users enabling them to access filth *monomanually* whilst their other hand is busy.

one-holed flute n. A *pink oboe, blue-veined piccolo, purple headed* (insert name of vaguely cylindrical woodwind instrument here).

one in – one out *phr.* The direct, causal relationship that exists between drags on the day's first *Harry rag* and *farts*.

one in the pump, to have 1. v. To have the *hots* for a female. '*Phwooar! I've got one in the pump for her, I can tell you.*' 2. n. Drinking parlance for a pint paid for but not yet poured.

one man and his log n. A Sunday afternoon entertainment following a heavy lunch, whereby a ruddy-faced gent tries to force a large *flock of brown sheep* through a very narrow gate while whistling and emitting guttural cries.

one-man orgy n. A long-lasting and elaborate *cat stabbing* session involving assorted stimuli, speeds and positions. *Everything but the girl.*

one oar in the water *euph.* Descriptive of someone who is unlikely to forge a successful career in aerospace engineering or neurological medicine.

one o'er the thumb n. A *five knuckle shuffle.* '*Quite satisfied, Scrooge closed the door and locked himself in; double-locked himself in, which was his custom on these occasions. Thus secured against surprise, he took off his cravat; put on his dressing-gown and slippers, and his nightcap; and sat down before the fire with a copy of Enrazzlement for a quick one o'er the thumb.*'

one off the crossbar n. To be just not quick enough in dropping one's *scads* after being caught short by an unexpected visit from *Mr Whippy.* To *beskid* the waistband of your *shreddies.*

one off the wrist n. A *wank, hand shandy.* A *pint pulled off the piss pump.*

one on the down line *phr.* A railway industry term which track-workers use to inform each other of the approach of a fast-moving train or an imminent lavatory break during the working day.

onepack n. A *beer gut, party seven, Foster's child.*

one-percenter n. A celebrity *Z-lister* who, if encouraged to breed, would be responsible for diminishing the nation's average IQ by a solid hundredth.

one pint Viking n. A man who gets very fighty after a pitifully small amount of booze. A *two can van Damme, two pot screamer, drambo, half-pint Harry etc.*

oneplay n. Pre-masturbatory arousal techniques. *Self help.*

one point five n. A toiletry visit product that falls somewhere between a *number one* and a *number two.* A runny *shit.* Or, thankfully more rarely, a lumpy *piss.* A bicycle chain.

one pump chump n. He who *goes off* on the first prod. Twice as fast as a *two push Charlie.* Also known as an *English batsman.* See *up and over like a pan of milk.*

oner n. The line of condensed *arse cleft* perspiration left on a plastic seat after it has been sat on in the summer months. Upon exiting a taxi and preparing to pay, one might point to the seat and say, '*There's a oner, keep the change.*'

one-ring circus n. A long, sustained *bum roll* that terminates in a cymbal-like splash as the *Thora Hird* finally hits the water.

one shit wonder n. A popular musician or beat combo who has a brief, singular moment in the charts sun, despite being *crap, eg.* Falco, Chesney Hawkes, Vanilla Ice *etc.*

one shit wonder n. A very long, unbroken *poo.* An *earthing cable, monolog, bridger* or *tallboy.*

one shot one kill 1. n. Motto of snipers in the US Marines. 2. *phr.* Exclamation after unloading a particularly high calibre round from one's *pump action shit gun.*

one-string banjo n. A skin-covered instrument upon which a man might *strum* to his heart's content.

one-stroke cylinder engine n. A *Bakewell* released while walking that lasts for several paces. A *string of pearls, duckwalk, the Bavarian.*

one under the Metro n. A discreet commuter's surreptitious means of relieving tension beneath a strategically placed free newspaper while travelling on public transport.

one up the pipe *phr.* Touching cloth. '*What a pleasure to meet you, your majesty. Now if you'd excuse me for a moment, I have to nip to the Rick Witters, only I've had one up the pipe all morning.*'

one up two down 1. n. Some sort of cramped slum dwelling of the sort formerly occupied by a retrospectively happy elderly relative who preferred the olden days when they had Hitler, diphtheria and polio. 2. n. A *shit*, a *piss* and a *wank* enjoyed during the same *bog* break while at work.

one weekend Wiggins n. Overweight fortysomething who, inspired by the feats of the self-satisfied, *face-fannied* Tour de France winner, spends £3,000 on a state-of-the art roadbike which he takes for an awkward, unenjoyable ½ mile wobble on the roads near his house, during which the chain comes off six times, before putting it on eBay for a fraction of its value the following week.

one yank Frank n. A solo version of a *fruit machine Freddy.* An over-excitable masturbator who is *up and over like a pan of milk.*

one year out! *exclam.* Hollered in the style of affable mid-morning wireless host Ken Bruce when a *Popmaster* contestant narrowly fails to identify the correct year in which three named songs were in this week's chart. *2. exclam.* Hollered in the style of affable mid-morning wireless host Ken Bruce when he *blows off. Sew a button on that; that's the last of the shampoo etc.*

oneymoon *n.* A romantic week's break from the missus which affords the married man a welcome opportunity to enjoy an uninterrupted seven day period of luxurious *self abuse.*

oneymoon suite *n.* In an hotel, a room set aside for unaccompanied commercial travellers who do not wish to be disturbed; must include at least two *Frankie Vaughan* channels and a copious supply of quilted toilet tissue.

on final approach *1. euph.* Descriptive of an aircraft that is about to land, having lowered its undercarriage and fully extended its flaps. *2. euph.* Descriptive of a lady who is *dripping like a fucked fridge*, having lowered her *undercrackers* and fully extended her *pissflaps.*

on golden pond *1. n.* Title of a crushingly dull-looking film featuring, as far as you could tell, a lot of shots of Jane and Henry Fonda wearing floppy hats and squinting on a verandah. And Katharine Hepburn wearing a floppy hat and squinting on a verandah. And no exploding cars and machine gun fights. *2. euph.* Waking up on a tiled floor and realising that you have *relieved yourself* in the night without the benefit of plumbing. *Golden slumbers.*

on her dabs *adj.* Of a lady, to be menstruiferous. *Boiling beetroots, serving strawberry jam for tea, up on blocks, showing off. 'Did you see that clip of Björk attacking a reporter at Bangkok airport?' 'Yeah, she must've been on her dabs. And now here's Rabbi Lionel Blue with Thought for the Day.'*

onion bag *1. n.* Football pundit terminology for the goal, usually *'the old onion bag'. 2. n.* The male equivalent of a *camel toe.* Also *munge, butcher's fist, Darcy Bussell's footrest.*

onion bawji *n.* An aromatic, savoury handful delivered from the musky environs of one's sweaty *glandbag* direct to the nostrils of a lucky recipient. A *scrotal cupcake* that brings tears to the eyes.

onion ring *n.* A circle of battered hair found around the base of the *old chap* following vigorous intercourse with an hirsute partner.

on it like vomit *sim.* Doggedly pursuing a particular task. From the lingering smell and persistent, ineradicable stain associated with the popular regurgitated substance. *'"It seems to me that a careful examination of the room where the Colonel's body was discovered and the lawn outside*

the French windows where the dagger with the unusually carved ivory handle was dropped might possibly reveal some clues as to the identity of the mysterious vanishing Bishop," Miss Marple expostulated at length. "There is much evidence here for me to investigate, inspector, but do not worry. I am on it like vomit and I will unmask the miscreant after withholding a crucial piece of evidence from the readers until the second to last page."' (from *Murder at Barnton Manor* by Agatha Christie).

onk, on the *adj.* Of the male generative member, up and fighting. *'I popped a bluey, and half an hour later I was on the onk for the first time in twenty years.'*

on loan to United *euph. Up on blocks, fallen to the communists, on the blob, riding the menstrual cycle, on tow, packing string, chasing the cotton mouse, dropping clots, smoking short cigars, shooting jam, playing Arsenal at home.*

only connect *1. n.* A fiendishly difficult television quiz in which a team of nerdish brainboxes try to piece together a seemingly random set of clues in the form of words or pictures to see what links them together. *2. n.* An all-but-impossible puzzle in which a married man has to piece together a seemingly random set of clues, in the form of tearful outbursts, to see what his wife has got her fucking knickers in a twist about this time.

Only Connect wank *n.* An act that must be performed with impeccable timing such that one finishes while the host is on the screen, rather than when the camera is pointing at the motley assortment of Maplins fodder on either side of her. *'This is a very delicate bake, Prue. Leave it in the oven a fraction too long and it'll be burnt to a crisp, take it out too soon and it'll have a soggy bottom.' 'That's right Paul, they're going to have to time this showstopper like an Only Connect wank.'*

only shit with the arse you've got *phr.* Civil engineering expression bemoaning the provision of substandard tools and/or materials.

on my command, unleash hell *1. exclam.* Quote from the movie *Gladiator. 2. exclam.* A phrase to declaim in a stentorian fashion just before doing an humongously loud, clappy, *pump.*

on safari *euph. Not as other men.* Or, indeed, *ladies* for that matter.

on-sheet bathroom *n. Pissing* and/or *crapping* the bed. *'It had been a perfect evening. They laughed and drank until late, then made sweet love before falling asleep in each other's arms. Unfortunately, Mavis woke to discover Victor using the on-sheet bathroom.'*

on the batter *adj.* Of a lady, to be involved in the

practice of showing successive gentlemen good times behind a skip for £5. *'I think it's nice that she has her own career. She's been on the batter for years.'*

on the bench *adj.* After being *off the team*, to be optimistic that you may be given a late chance to *score*. To be temporarily out of the missus's *cunt book*. *'After the shameful episode with the exotic dancer I have alas been off the team these last six weeks. Today I bought my darling Victoria a bunch of flowers from the all-night garage, and I think I am on the bench.'* (from *Prince Albert's Journal*).

on the blob *adj.* Riding the menstrual cycle, fallen to the communists.

on the bonk *1. adj.* Fully turgid in the *trouser department*. *2. adj. W. Mids.* Standing on a hill.

on the bus to Hebden Bridge *adj.* Descriptive of a *woman in comfortable shoes*, or *tennis fan*. From the unusually large amount of *lady golfers* living in the West Yorkshire mill town.

on the green in two *euph.* Making rapid progress with a young lady to whom one has only recently been introduced. *'I was out with that gorgeous blonde from HR last night. She's a definite par 5 but I was on the green in two.'*

on the hoy *adj.* On the piss, on the razz, hoying it down one's neck, and then back up again onto one's shoes.

on the job *1. euph.* At it. Busying oneself with one's partner's *bits and bobs*. *'He's on the job at the moment. Can I get him to call you back in about ten minutes? Meanwhile, try to keep the patient's head elevated and his airways open.'* *2. euph.* Having a meeting in the Kensington Executive.

on-the-job straining *n.* Work time spent sat on the *bog* with a thick book or copy of the *Autotrader*.

on-the-job training *1. n.* A crucial aspect of developing competency in a given task. *2. n.* Being taught the ropes *in the sack* by a more experienced partner, so you can surprise your spouse with new tricks and techniques, leading to difficult questions and your belongings being thrown out of the window.

on the latch *adj.* Of a woman's *bodily treasure*, constantly pre-warmed, thus allowing for the ease of entry to be seen in most *stick flicks*. *'She'd been watching Monty Don all evening, so she was already on the latch.'*

on the menu *euph.* Of a pet, deceased. A reference to the offensive insinuation that veterinary surgeries are always situated next door to takeaways. *'How's Tricky-Woo, Mr Herriot?' 'Not good at all, I'm afraid Mrs Pumphrey. I let him out for a shit in the car park and Tristram reversed his MG over him. He's on the menu now.'*

on the money *1. phr.* Exact, spot on. *2. phr.* Descriptive of the experience of felicitously timing one's erotic *spendings* to coincide with those of the leading thespian in a *stick vid*.

on the mop *adj.* Of a lady, *showing off.*

on the nest *adj.* Treating your *bird* to a big juicy *worm* up the *fanny*.

on the nose *adj.* Exhibiting questionable hygiene. *'Fuck me, that bloke who just delivered all those filing cabinets up the fire escape was a bit on the nose.'*

on the other bus *adj.* Nicely poised, bowling from the Pavilion end.

on the pull *adj.* Fishing for *kipper*, on the salmon, on the sniff. *'He's on the pull at the moment. Can I get him to call you back in about ten minutes? Meanwhile, try to keep the patient's head elevated and his airways open.'*

on the slipway *adj.* Of stools and stool movement, having the *turtle's head*. *'Get out of that fucking bathroom will you, I've got a dreadnought on the slipway here.'*

on the sniff *adj.* On the pull, on the tap, getting a bit *lash on*.

on the soft *adj.* Less than tumescent. *'Look at that, your holiness. He's definitely on the soft, him. Hang on, I'll freeze the frame.'*

on the tug *euph.* An alternative to going out *on the pull* for the less confident male; Charging up one's *wank banks* by staring at scantily clad women on a night out, before heading home for a desultory *five knuckle shuffle*.

on tow *adj.* Of a woman, *up on blocks, smoking short cigars*. From the visible rope.

ooglewhack *v.* To have a much-needed *whack*, after having *oogled* an attractive lady.

ooh-aarrhoea *n. medic.* Farmer's *squirts*.

ooh, get her! *exclam.* Another waspish retort to one who has just *dropped their hat*, best delivered in a camp, Larry Grayson-style voice. Also *oh really sir, could you put that in writing?; well struck sir; speak up George; someone's moving in next door.*

ooh you are awful *exclam.* Said by a newly anointed *man of the cloth* as he takes his leave in the style of Dick Emery's famous sex-crazed blonde woman character, who was, apparently, named "Mandy" after Ms Rice-Davies out of off of the Profumo scandal. Don't say we never learn you anything.

oomlaaters *n.* Very large *chumbawumbas, mumbas*.

oomlattes *n.* Frothy, milky beverages supped from the missus's post-sprog *churns*. Also *bappuccinos, PG Tits*.

oomph! *n.* Sex appeal. *'By crikey, that Emily Bishop,*

477

she hasn't half got some oomph!'

oops something went wrong! *1. phr.* An annoyingly perky message that pops up on your computer screen when an app has crashed on you at a crucial time, wiping out hours of work. *2. phr.* A rather polite thing to say if you've just *blown off* and *followed through.*

oor wullie *n. Scots.* A communal double-ended *neck massager* kept in a drawer at the but 'n' ben.

oot on the tap *adj. NE.* Out *on the pull,* as opposed to *out on the hoy.*

OPE *abbrev.* A dazed and other-worldly sensation brought on by a visit to a mechanic, dentist, solicitor *etc.* Out-of-Pocket Experience.

open a packet of ham *v.* To *let off* a *beefy eggo.* From the practice of ham production line workers who *fart* into the packages of ham before sealing them. *'Who's opened a packet of ham? It fucking ronks in here.'*

open clam shots *n. Full-on oysters, close-up pink.* Artistic/medical *adult* camera work.

open door shit *n.* The pleasurably liberating experience of being able to enjoy *crimping off a length* with the *bog* door left wide open while the house is empty.

open Dracula's coffin *v.* To experience a protracted creaking noise that is accompanied by an ungodly stench. To *drop a McArthur Park.*

opening a bag of mozzarella, like *sim. 'I slid my hand into her knickers and she released the juice like opening a bag of mozzarella, your holiness.'*

opening the ark *euph.* A *Tony Hart* that could melt your face.

opening the pork scratchings *n. Letting off* a particularly meaty one.

opening up new pork markets *1. n.* Comedy Chuckle Brothers-quality ex-PM Liz Truss's erstwhile plan to fix the British economy. *2. euph.* Trying to access the wife's *wrong 'un.*

open or wrapped? *1. exclam.* Polite question asked by a chip-shop employee who is blithely pouring half a pound of salt onto your order. *2. exclam.* Polite enquiry concerning prophylaxis, made by a gentleman immediately prior to *sticking it in.*

open the bloodgates *v.* Of a woman, to shed the first tears that herald the commencement of *rag week.*

open the ham *v.* To produce a quiet, yet potent *gust.* In reference to the *beefy eggo* odour emitted by a newly breached packet of processed pigmeat.

open the hangar doors *v.* Of an experienced lady, to prepare herself for sexual intercourse. *'Wisteria was powerless to resist. His eyes burned into hers like amethysts. His muscular arms enfolded her body as she felt herself being swept away in a hurricane of passion. Gently, Renaldo laid her down on the silken ottoman in front of the roaring fire. Then, as he pulled her knickers off, she lifted her legs and opened the hangar doors.'* (from *The Lady and the South American Footballer* by Barbara Cartland).

open the oven door *v.* To stand up after having sat on a well baked *air-biscuit* for some time, thus giving those in the locale a second chance to enjoy its aroma. *'Watch your eyebrows, everyone. I'm about to open the oven door.'*

open the pod bay doors HAL *exclam.* An expression used by one who is severely *egg-bound.* To which one's *Enoch Powells* may well reply: "I'm sorry Dave, I'm afraid I can't do that."

open the shed door *v.* To *step on a frog* and produce a long squeaking sound. *'The Man Who Opened the Shed Door During the Three Minutes' Silence at the Cenotaph.'* (cartoon by HM Bateman, *Tatler & Bystander,* November 1936).

open your lunchbox *v.* To float an *air biscuit* reminiscent of yesterday's egg sandwiches.

opera house *n.* A large vagina with heavy pink safety curtains and great acoustics.

operate the spangle pump *v.* To express oneself onanistically. *'Oh bugger. The plumber's operated the spangle pump into my knicker drawer again.'*

operation chariot *n.* The act of ramming your *skin boat* into a ladyfriend's *dry dock.* A technique used, for example, when it's ten minutes till *Match of the Day* is on. Named after the famous British seaborne raid on St. Nazaire, on the night of March 28th 1942, when HMS Campbeltown was loaded with explosives and steered at high speed into the port's *piss flaps,* ten minutes before *Match of the Day* started.

operation mincemeat *1. n.* Wartime Secret Service plan to float a dead *Harold Ramp* into Portugal. *2. n.* Covert 2am visit to the *biscuit wrapper* following a night of *heavy refreshment* and *catbabs.* See also *Bonanza, arse like the start of.*

operation mincemeat completed *1. exclam.* Phrase uttered by the British WW2 submarine commander overseeing the deployment of the half-decayed corpse of a Welsh tramp carrying decoy documents intended to convince the Germans that the Allies were not planning to launch an invasion on Sicily. *2. n.* Phrase that can be uttered, using clipped, upper class diction, upon standing up at the conclusion of a *shit* and turning to survey the putrid, stinking remains bobbing about in the water.

operation mongoose *euph.* A ruthless plan of seduction adopted by a fellow with the intention of getting his *exploding cigar* into the mouth of a pretty woman. So called after the CIA's failed attempt to get a somewhat more lethally volatile smoking requisite into the *gob* of Cuban president Fidel Castro.

operation save big dog *1. phr.* Slapstick ex-Premier Boris Johnson's ultimately fruitless attempt to remain as Prime Minister by sacrificing a selection of hapless subordinates. *2. n. Jumping on the grenade.*

operation yellowhammer *1. n.* The codename used by the UK Treasury when referring to farcical, cross-government, civil contingency planning for the possibility of a no-deal Brexit, it says here. *2. n.* Cleaning up any *skids* on the bog using your *piss chisel.*

opportunity knockers *exclam.* Light-hearted phrase muttered to himself by a red-blooded chap upon encountering a *stacked* and available female. *'Tonight, for you, Rod Stewart, opportunity knockers.'*

opportunity knocks one out *phr.* Undertaking a fortuitous bout of *self-pollution* when the chance arises, no matter how brief, such as the missus turning over in bed while Mishal Husain is reading the news.

opportunity norks *n.* A sneaky boggle-eyed peek at a pair of *charms,* "just for fun".

optimetrist *n.* One who has high hopes that your new spectacles will work.

orange pippin *n.* A girl who loves "English cocks".

orangina *1. n.* Refreshing continental citrus beverage, made with real orange pieces. *2. n.* A particularly untidy ginger *clopper,* which wouldn't look out of place between the legs of Clint Eastwood's monkey's missus.

oranguman *n.* A colour-blind sun-worshipper with a healthy glow that registers 165 on the Pantone scale. *'Born on this day: Julie Newmar, Batwoman, 1933; Trevor McDonald, News at Ten man, 1939; David Dickinson, oranguman, 1941.'*

orang utan hang *n.* An *al fresco shit* in the woods where the *shittee* uses one arm to dangle from a tree.

orang utan salad *n.* Ginger *gorilla salad. Fusewire, grated carrot.*

orang utan's forehead, fanny like an *sim.* Charming turn of phrase which can be usefully employed when referring to a *brandy snap* which is liberally adorned with rufescent *fubes. 'Bloody hell, Rula. You've got a fanny like an orang utan's forehead.'*

orbs of joy *n.* Breasts of such full, rounded ripeness that any red-blooded man looking at them will experience feelings of almost religious calm,

contentment and elation.

orchestral manoeuvres in the dark *n.* The perilous process of taking a night-time *crap* when the lightbulb in the *biscuit wrapper* has blown.

orchestras *rhym. slang.* The testicles. From orchestra stollocks = bollocks.

ordering off-menu *1. n.* The sort of thing that self-important *twats* do when visiting restaurants. *'I always order off-menu, because I like the taste of spunk.' 2. n.* Of a bloke, asking his ladyfriend for some sort of unusual treat that she may not have previously considered laying on for him, such as letting him *jizz* in her hair, *scuttle* her up the *drainpipe* or watch while she *jills herself off* while dressed as a lady robot.

order of the bath *n.* A sticky white honour bestowed in a sash-like manner diagonally over a lady's well-soaped chest.

Order! Order! *exclam.* A voluble cry, delivered in the voice of John Bercow, or whoever it is these days, if one is interrupted by an unruly member of parliament or a *bottom burp.*

Ordsall chord *1. n.* Short rail link between the very posh and visible Manchester Piccadilly, and the less glamorous, not as accessible – and yet nevertheless curiosity-piquing – Manchester Victoria, and thus, as usual, *2. n.* The *taint, tinter, Humber Bridge* etc. *3. n.* The *banjo string* or *guyrope.*

oreo *n.* An inverse *chocolate sandwich.*

organ failure *1. n. medic.* Dysfunction of the liver, kidneys, spleen or similar, to such an extent that normal homeostasis cannot be maintained without resort to external clinical intervention. *2. n.* Dysfunction of the *giggling pin* to such an extent that normal tumescence cannot be achieved without resort to external clinical intervention. See also *Pele's knob, cock drop, lack of composure in front of goal.*

organ grinder *n.* A harmlessly eccentric public transport user who *frots* his groinal areas against other passengers.

organic sleeping pill *1. n. medic.* Some sort of herbal tablets from Holland & Barrett that contain a tincture of Valerian roots or some such bollocks. *2. n. medic.* A wank.

organise *v.* To penetrate, in a frankly sexual manner. *'Don't worry, mate. As best man, I will be happy to organise the bridesmaids.'*

organogram *1. n.* Business-*wank* term for a diagram showing organisational structure, including specialist areas and hierarchies. Christ, the hours must just fly by. *2. n.* A simplified artistic representation of the male genitalia. Also *three-line* *pud, spamogram, le coq spurtif.*

organ recital *n.* The competitive discussion of symptoms that begins within minutes of two women meeting.

organzola *n. Helmetdale.*

orgasm *1. n.* A *fanny bomb, stack blow, the Big O. 2. v.* To *ring the bell, shoot one's load, chuck one's muck.*

orgasm, multiple *n.* Something that makes women go cross-eyed and yodel.

origin of faeces *n.* The often perplexing challenge of finding out who has left a repulsive *brown trout* in the domestic or workplace *trap.*

Orion's belt *n.* Three *spoffs* of *jizz* across a woman's hip.

Orkney bathbomb *n. Dropping the kids off at the pool* whilst enjoying a bath. Enjoying it up to a certain point, presumably.

Ormskirk oyster *n.* A viscous, selenium-rich delicacy, best-swallowed whole.

Oscar *n. US.* The male penis.

Oscars night *n.* An unpredicted bout of heavy *women's things*, which leaves a *red carpet* from the front door to the *crapper.*

Oscar winner *1. n.* Typically, a long-drawn-out *shit* film that may eventually bring a tear to the eye before the blinking movie-goer finally leaves the pictures with a numb *arse. 2. n.* A long drawn out *shit* that may eventually bring a tear to the eye before the blinking toileteer finally leaves the *crappers* with a numb *arse.*

osteopornosis *n. medic.* Degenerate condition symptomised by skeletal atrophy, progressive hypermetropia, early onset pre-senile dementia and hairy palms.

O, the big *n.* See *the big O.*

other, a bit of the *n. How's your father, nookie.* Not *this* or *that.*

other place, the *1. n.* In parliamentary terminology, how Honourable Members refer to the chamber they eventually hope to end up in once they have resigned in disgrace. The House of Lords. *2. n.* In sexual shenaniganism, the *chamber* that dishonourable fellows hope their *members* will eventually end up in.

OTP? *abbrev. interrog. Aus.* On The Piss? The rhetorical question that is texted from one bloke to his various potential drinking partners.

otter *1. n.* An aquatic mammal. *2. n.* A bald male who has no particular interest in *beavers.*

Otterburn *1. n.* Small village in Northumberland where trainee soldiers learn to fire rifles. *2. n.* The fiery sensation in the *cigar cutter* when you've had a powerful *cuzza* (for example Curry Hell from the Rupali Restaurant (now closed), Bigg Market, Newcastle upon Tyne), and subsequently pass a hot *otter.*

otter off the bank, like an *sim.* Phrase used to describe a *Gladys* of particularly fine composition, which slips into the water from one's *bumhole* with a certain amount of panache.

otter's dinner, remains of an *sim.* A badly packed *beaver buffet,* from the fishy bones and shells left over after meals eaten by semi-aquatic weasels.

otter slide *n.* A brown, muddy *skidmark* down the side of the toilet bowl which looks like it could mark the eponymous animal's entry point into the water. *'I wouldn't go in that cubicle if I were you, Wilson and Keppel. Betty's left a massive otter slide.'*

otter's nose *n.* When getting *tops and fingers,* that which is felt by the latter. Something *under the bridge* that is wet and smells of fish. *'I got a result last night, mum. I touched the otter's nose.'*

our survey said *exclam.* Just for a change, something you can say *before* you *drop your hat. I smell with my little nose, something beginning with.*

our weapons have no effect! *exclam.* Warning shouted from the *water closet* when the air freshener is overpowered.

outbox, stuck in the *1. phr.* What happens to an email during a network outage. *2. n.* When, despite your best efforts, you just can't shift a particularly troublesome *dead otter* from your moribund *Simon Cowells.* See also *Beijing traffic jam, delay on the Bakerloo line etc. 'Jesus wept. I've got a non-mover at number two stuck in me outbox. I knew I shouldn't of ate that fucking ten-egg omelette for breakfast. And now here's Carol with the weather.'*

outcunt *v.* To manage to be a bigger *twat* than your rival. *'Jesus Christ, Barton has just gone in studs first there. He's even outcunted Pepe.'*

outer bull *n.* A *piss* into a toilet which hits only the porcelain around the puddle, thus keeping the noise down. The opposite of a *dad's piss,* named after the dartboard location that scores 25.

outeresting *adj.* The opposite of interesting. When someone says something so stupid, inane, or incorrect that one can only respond with, "Oh, that's outeresting."

outjumped *coll.* Situation whereby you realise that your friends, colleagues, neighbours and even in-laws are *getting their legs over* more often than you are.

outlet pipe from the Rugby Club washing machine, it looked like the *exclam. sim.* Description of a particularly loose *Simon Cowell* movement after a heavy night on rough cider.

out, Mrs Duck, and take your ducklings with you! *exclam.* To be said with considerable bravado after unleashing one particularly loud bum-quack followed by a number of smaller quacks.

out of botty experience *1. n.* A *dump.* *2. n.* The transcendental ability, when in the midst of a particularly difficult and troubling *digestive transit,* to float free above the noise and chaos below.

out of one's comfort zone *euph.* In one's discomfort zone. Right up the *council gritter.*

out on the slap *euph.* Of a lady of loose, questionable morals out looking for a good time. *'Where's yer nan?' 'She's out on the slap again.'*

outpouring of grief *1. n.* Communal expression of sadness in the wake of a tragic event, such as a natural disaster, the death of Lady Di or KFC running out of chicken. *2. n.* A torrent of boiling hot *shite* that leaves the ordinary person in the street bereft and sobbing. *'Following last night's prawn phaal, there's been a huge outpouring of grief. So I'd give it five minutes if I was you, vicar.'*

outrigger *1. n.* A thin, supplementary float that is rigidly fixed parallel and to one side of the main hull of a canoe, in order to minimise the risk of capsizing when filming the opening title sequence for *Hawaii Five-0,* for example. *2. n.* Prior to a routine, middle-of-the-night *tug,* a leg which a chap swings out of bed and uses to brace himself firmly against the floor in order to ensure that his *bag for life* isn't disturbed by any rhythmic mattress turbulence that may ensue.

outshat *euph.* The opposite of outshone. *'You've really outshat yourself there, Theresa.'*

out to the wing *exclam.* Comment typically made by older gentlemen before they *break wind.* So used because of the characteristic noise made by an old leather football when it was hoofed with a sturdy boot. *'Out to the wing.' 'Indeed your holiness. Shall I get a nun to open the window?'*

ovary action *n.* A *tampremental* female response to perfectly reasonable male behaviour. See also *showing off, period drama.*

over-active pieroid *n.* The female organ that is responsible for *big bones. 'It's not my fault. It's my glands. I've got an over-active pieroid.'*

overblaaters *n.* Pendulous *oomlaaters* which rest on a big round gut.

over-cheese the magpie *v.* To over-satiate something or someone notoriously greedy. *'So Admiral, did you stay at Lady Hamilton's last night?' 'Indeed, Mr Hardy, though I fear I may have over-cheesed the magpie, for the poor lass was sat on a bucket of ice*

when I left this morning.'

overclubbed *1. adj.* In golf, descriptive of an approach shot chipped towards the green which misses its intended target and tangles itself in the rough, eliciting groans from disappointed spectators. *2. adj.* In a *meat flick,* descriptive of a *pop shot* loosed off towards an actress's face which misses its intended target and instead tangles itself in her hair, eliciting groans from disappointed spectators.

over-egg the pudding *v.* To *buff the prong* in a somewhat spirited manner, resulting in friction burns. *'I'm afraid I won't be able to make it to the final meeting of the Synod, your grace, only I've over-egged the pudding, and walking in the procession would be a right bugger.'*

overfilled fajita, dripping like an *sim.* As sexually excited as a *fucked fridge.*

overhit a backpass *v.* To come dangerously close to *curling one* into one's own *onion bags.*

overjaculation *n. Relaxing in a gentleman's way* so much that nothing comes out but a puff of air. *Wanking yourself flat.*

overloaded *adj.* Blue-balled. *'Blimey, Cliff. You're well overloaded there. Your knackers look like two tins of Fussell's milk.'*

over Niagara in a barrel *phr.* The situation which occurs when flushing blocked toilets, for example the ones installed in Virgin Trains, whereby the water level rises up to the rim, causing any *floaters* to risk taking a death-defying plunge over the edge.

overnight bag *1. n.* An aesthetically unimpressive *one night stand. 2. n.* That which is humped sweatily across the foyer of a Travelodge by a commercial traveller.

overnight oats *1. n.* Poncey breakfast of cold porridge for people who can't be *arsed* to cook a proper fry-up of a morning. *2. n.* The dry, crusty flakes resembling oatmeal found all over the bedsheets and torso of an awakening *onanist* who has fallen into a deep and satisfying slumber following a healthy bout of *gentleman's relaxation* the night before.

overscrotes *n.* Underpants.

oversteer *1. n.* A phenomenon the contemplation of which occupies far more of Jeremy Clarkson's waking hours than is healthy for a grown man. *2. n.* A "loose rear end". *'Nothing like a bit of oversteer to grab your attention first thing in the morning.'*

over the air update *1. n.* Wireless delivery of new software or data to a mobile device. *2. n.* Letting the people around you know what you have been eating and drinking over the last few days via an *upload to the cloud* (also wireless).

over the lines, colour in *v.* To spray a lady with *knacker lacquer* after withdrawing from an orifice. To *crash the truck* outside the *yoghurt delivery bay.*

over the pill *adj.* Of a lady, post-menopausal. *'There's no precautions necessary, love. I'm over the pill so you can go ahead and fill your boots.'*

over the shoulder boulder holder *n.* An industrial-strength set of *tit pants*; heavy lifting apparatus for *jelly water mangos.* The sort of expression used by a *twattish* "office joker" sort.

overture *n.* A short episode of stomach gurglings, *bottom burps* and minor abdominal spasms that introduces the basic themes for an oncoming, prolonged and possibly symphonic *Tom tit.* A signal that it is time you got yourself seated for the show.

owl hoot *n. Fart* in the middle of the night that wakes one's partner due to its spooky, ethereal quality. Also *poltergust, food's ghost.*

owl movement *1. n.* A *Greyfriars Bobby* that is of much greater girth than is comfortable, thereby causing its progenitor's head to revolve and their eyes to widen in the manner of the eponymous nocturnal, mouse-skeleton-hockling bird of prey. *2. phr.* Sitting wide-eyed on the *crapper,* looking around the room while nonchalantly dropping pellets.

owl, the *n.* A 360 degree variation on the good old-fashioned *crescent wank*, in which a self-abuser arranges his favourite *bongo books* in a complete circle, before kneeling on a swivel chair in the middle and *pleasuring himself* while he spins round. Also known as the *Blair chair,* in honour of Linda Blair's rotating *noggin* in 1970s horror flick *The Exorcist.*

owner operator *n.* A lorry driver who *sheds his load* wherever the fancy takes him.

own goal *1. n.* A blast from the *gazoo* which is so obnoxious that even he who dealt it cannot stay in its presence and shuffles off the field of play shamefacedly. *2. n.* A trouser-bound *guff* which involves a *follow through.* From the Bomb Disposal Squad parlance for the premature detonation of a terrorist's bomb. At which point, presumably, said baddy *shits* himself. If he's got time.

owns an electric lawnmower *euph.* A fair indication that a man may *know his way around Brighton.*

own up *v.* After *breaking company*, to identify oneself as the *benefactor. Read the will.*

Oxford John *n.* A slow-braised *lamb shank.*

Oxford Road baptism *n.* The cool, soul-cleansing shower occasioned by the typically careless passage of a vehicle from one of Manchester's 25 different bus companies through one of the said student thoroughfare's countless vast, ankle-deep kerbside puddles.

OXO *n.* Inserting one's thumb into a lady's *back bottom* and a finger into her *front bottom,* before rubbing the two digits together as if crumbling the eponymous stock cube.

oxygen mask *n.* A cricket box humorously placed over the mouth and nose of an unsuspecting victim.

oxygen thief *n.* A senior citizen or *coffin dodger.* Also *morgue cheater, grave sniffer.*

oyster *n.* A *bushman's hankie.*

oyster catchers *1. n. Birds* that spend a great deal of time in pursuit of *bearded clams. 2. n.* Old *biddies' harvest festivals.*

oyster shelling *n.* Ejaculating into a cupped hand and immediately feeding the warm, salty contents to a partner.

oyster shot *n.* In the world of glamour photography, a carefully composed, lit and framed shot of a model's *clam* as she bends over, viewed from behind. An *oyster shot* can act as a powerful aphrodisiac.

oyster, tramp's *n.* A *hockled*-up *sheckle* on the pavement; a salty *al fresco* delicacy blessed with very few, if any, aphrodisiac properties. Also *tramp's breakfast, docker's omelette, greb, greeny, prairie oyster, gold watch, Dutch pikelet* or *Old Leigh oyster.*

ozone hole *n.* A *ringpiece* that is a continual source of worry for environmentalists.

Ozymandias, king of kings, look on my works, ye mighty, and despair; my name is *1. phr. lit.* Oft-quoted lines of the famous sonnet written by English romantic poet Percy Bysshe Shelley on the Colossus of Pharaoh Ramesses II. *2. exclam.* Rousing verse to be roundly declaimed following a successful *bottom burp.*

Ozzy ramble *n.* The shuffling, confused gait adopted by a man with a *horse's handbrake* and his trousers round his ankles, as he tries to manoeuvre around the sofa in order to secure a better angle to gain entrance to his good lady's *coconut husk.* From the shuffling, confused gait characteristic of shuffling, confused heavy metal pipistrelle gourmand Ozzy Osbourne, real name Oswestry Ostrichbourne.

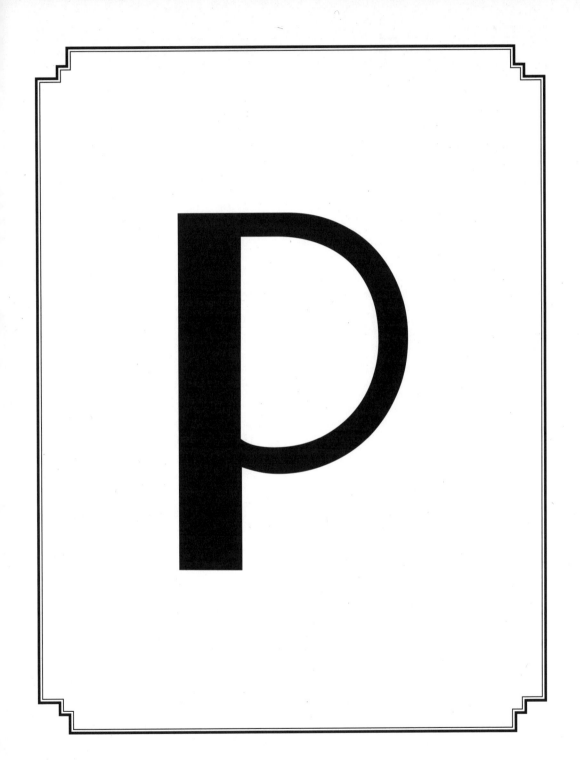

pace car *n.* When paying a *sit down visit*, the slow, unaerodynamic leading *turd* that gets out of the way to allow the fast, souped-up *botrods* behind it to put their foot down into the U-bend.

Pacific island *n.* A big *shite* in the *pan* with its top sticking out of the water, possibly with the remains of Amelia Earhart's Lockheed Electra half-buried somewhere on its slopes.

Pacific rimjob *n.* An act of *analingus* which is disastrously interrupted by a brown monster rising from the depths.

package holiday *euph.* A vacation for one's *package*. An extra-mural dalliance. *'Honestly, Colleen, it was nothing. Just a little package holiday.'*

packet *n.* The contents of the *kecks* visible in relief at the front of the *trolleys*. Male equivalent of the *camel's foot. Darcy Bussell's footrest, the lunchbox, butcher's fist.*

packet sniffer *1. n.* A computer program or dedicated hardware component that can intercept and log traffic passing over a digital network (or part of a network) to capture data packets and analyze content for system diagnostic purposes. Yup, we couldn't put it any better than that if we looked it up on the internet. *2. n.* A desperate middle-aged woman on a hen night, who has sat herself on the front row as close to the male stripper's *Betty Swollocks* as she can get.

packing flavour *adj.* When your *bottom burps* are full, rich, and heavily scented with *Channel no. 2.*

packing heat *euph.* Dropping a *Bongo Bill's banjo pill* before you go out, just in case. Also *putting a bullet in the chamber, tooling up.*

packing string *adj.* Up on blocks. Also *chasing the cotton mouse, dropping clots, smoking short cigars, boiling beetroots, on the blob, fallen to the communists, riding the menstrual cycle, on her rags, reading Cosmo, on tow.*

Paddington's turds, stickier than *sim.* Descriptive of something particularly viscous and adhesive, from the imagined gelatinous consistency and texture of the famous Peruvian ursine orphan's *chods*, consequent upon his simple diet of sandwiches made from white bread and marmalade.

paddle one's own canoe *v.* To enjoy a leisurely punt using a short pink pole. With all veins up the side. *'Dysphagia was powerless to resist. His eyes burnt into hers like soldering irons. His muscular arms enfolded her naked body as she felt herself being whisked away on a meringue of passion. "Ravish me now," she gasped. "Take me here on the chaise longue, I'm all yours." "Sorry ma cherie, I'd love to oblige," replied Toulouse-Lautrec. "But I've just spent all afternoon paddling my own canoe in sniffer's row at the Moulin Rouge, and now my clockweights are as flat as a crepe suzette."'* (from *The Artist's Model and the Short-arsed Post-Impressionist Painter* by Barbara Cartland).

paddle steamer *1. n.* Vintage pleasureboat employing a paddlewheel system for propulsion. *2. n.* A *Douglas* ejected in the safety of the sea during a splash about.

paddles with a gentle stroke *euph.* Said of a fellow who *prefers his spinach wilted, sews his own buttons on* and *irons his socks. 'Eeh, to look at him you'd think he paddles with a gentle stroke, wouldn't you?' 'You would. But he's been married, you know, to a woman. And he's swam the Channel.'*

paddle the pink canoe *v.* To *friggify*. Weekend recreational pursuit of the *gusset typist.*

paddling pool *n.* Male showertime entertainment whereby the *fiveskin* is pulled apart and the *porridge gun* is aimed up at the showerhead, causing the end of the barrel to fill up with water for whatever reason

Paddy *n. prop.* Affectionate nickname that might be applied to a male member of our valued and respected senior citizen community whose trouser line advertises the fact that he is a *Tena gent.*

Paddy McGinty's goat *1. n.* Hilarious song made famous by the late twinkle-toothed, sweater-wearing, sedentary crooner Val Doonican. *2. n.* A pungent, hairy *snatch* that could eat a mayor's hat. Also *Delaney's donkey, Gilligan's pony.*

Paddy Power *1. n. prop.* A "safe word" used when indulging in kinky, potentially painful erotic shenanigans in order to call a halt to proceedings. *2. n. prop.* A term used to describe the moribund sex life of a middle-aged married couple. *'We've been married for twenty-five years now. We still love each other, but frankly, our sex life is at the Paddy Power stage.'* From the eponymous bookmaker's advertising slogan: "When the fun stops, stop."

Paddy's hankie *n.* The hand.

paddywhack *v.* To *bang* a young lady who *has a lovely personality.* From the famous nursery rhyme chorus about an old man engaging in penetrative sexual intercourse with an ugly partner, *viz.* "Nick-nack paddywhack, give the dog a bone".

padlocks *n. Tits* that would be better off in a pair of socks than in a bra.

paedokyle *n.* A dodgy-looking male relative on a prole-baiting daytime telly show. *'It's clearly his baby, you can tell. He looks like a paedokyle to me, nan.'*

paedo lumps *n.* Raised areas of tarmac in the carriageway that cause motorists to drive slowly past primary schools.

paedo pan *n.* A man who never grew up, *esp. ~of pop.*

paedo pass *euph.* A successful CRB check.

paedo pellets *n.* Werther's originals, *nonce nuggets.*

paedophiladelphia *n.* A 1970s showbiz personality's *frottage cheese.*

paedophile's door *euph.* Anyone who combines a low income with constant high expenditure. *'MRS ALLONBY: They say, Lady Hunstanton, that Lord Illingworth finds himself perpetually penurious. Indeed, in that respect he is not dissimilar to a paedophile's door. LADY HUNSTANTON: Indeed Mrs Allonby? And why, pray tell, would that be? MRS ALLONBY: Because, Lady Hunstanton, he is always broke.'* (from *The Importance of Being Bummed by Jockeys* by Oscar Wilde).

paedo piano *n.* A Stylophone.

paedopiss *n. psych.* The unsettling, guilty feeling that occurs after having been forced to use a child's urinal at a busy airport or shopping mall.

paedorinal *n.* In a public lavatory, the *shark's mouth* which is situated alongside the shorter, small boys' version.

paedoscopes *n.* Those thick-rimmed National Health Service spectacles exclusively worn by trainspotters, scout masters and other assorted sexcases. *Paedospecs.*

paedo's helmet *n.* A flat cap or bobble hat. *'I'm just off train-spotting, then mum.' 'Don't forget your paedo's helmet, dear.'*

paedosmile *n.* A particularly sinister grin, the type that a *kiddie fiddler* might have, *eg.* Jimmy Savile on a British Rail poster.

PAFO *acron. medic.* Term used by consultants in Accident and Emergency departments to explain random cuts and bruises on their patients. Pissed And Fell Over.

pagafantas *n. Sp.* In Spanish, an older man who is unsuccessfully attempting to woo a much younger woman with whom he is in love. A sarcastic reference to the fact that he might end up fruitlessly buying the object of his unrequited affection lots of soft drinks. Literally "Fanta payer".

page three Stannah *n.* A scantily clad lady of advancing years, who nevertheless provides one with "a bit of a lift".

pagga *n.* A free-for-all no-holds-barred combat between anyone who wants to join in.

pagga starter *n.* A strong beer which breaks the ice at fights. *Supermarket smack, spesh.*

painted jizabel *n. prop.* An ancient heretic who decorates her *mush* with *spunk.* A woman with a face like Jackson Pollock's shoes.

painter & defecator *n.* A tradesman whose work is a load of *shit.* But he's cheap.

painting the ceiling *n.* Having a go with the *naughty paintbrush* and some *guardsman's gloss* while in a supine position.

paint the baby's bedroom *v.* To slap a bit of *managlypta* around the *bread knife's* vaginal walls.

paint the back door *v.* To drop a wet *fart, follow through, drop a bonus ball, butter your cheeks.*

paint the back of the house *v.* To *tupp* a lass from behind and then leave a *calling card* across her arse cheeks. Also *paint the spare room.*

paint the nursery *v.* To get *stuck up* a woman who is *up the stick. 'You coming out to the MOBO awards tonight Kanye?' 'Sorry lads, I can't. The missus says I've got to stay in and paint the nursery.'*

paint the town beige *v.* To indulge in an unambitious, lacklustre night out with one's mates. *'There's a quiz on at the Black Bull. What say we may a proper night of it and paint the town beige?'*

Paisley briefcase *n.* A thin blue plastic bag from a corner shop newsagent or convenience store that is filled with booze, carried by an economically inactive outdoorsman to his place of work, *viz.* The local *tramp grill.*

Paisley jogger *n.* A thief or shoplifter beating a hasty retreat through the streets of the popular Glasgow garden suburb.

Paisley removal *n.* Pointing *Percy* directly at an area of *pebbledashing* in order to amuse oneself during a *Chinese singing lesson.* See also *piss polo.*

palace gates *n.* Fanny lips, beef curtains, saloon doors.

palate cleanser *n.* The half-empty bottle of Listerine to be found in any self-respecting *good time girl's* bathroom cupboard.

palmageddon *n.* A disastrous act of *self delight* which leaves the perpetrator wishing the ground would open up and swallow him. For example, the one indulged in by Dirty Den in his *EastEnders* dressing room in May 2004, that was witnessed on the internet by a Sunday newspaper reporter calling herself "Halo Polisher".

palmalade *n.* A seeded sticky preserve produced in outhouses and other masculine dominions of solitude. *'Where's your Terry?' 'He's down the garden making palmalade in his shed.'*

palma sutra *n.* An exotic selection of positions in which a gentleman may enjoy solitary congress with his *dick skinner, eg.* The dying swan, the swooping dove, the *sticky belly flap cock.*

palmbidextrous *adj.* Gifted with the miraculous ability to *pleasure oneself* equally effectively with either hand. Or, indeed, with both hands at the same time.

palme d'or *1. n. Fr.* A prestigious prize offered at the Cannes Film Festival for the sort of arty flick you definitely wouldn't watch if it was on at the same time as *Carry On Cleo*. *2. n.* A notional accolade bestowed upoon one's current partner in recognition of a world class *wank*.

Palmela and her five sisters *n. prop.* The right *cunt scratcher*.

Palmela Handerson *n.* One's dream date to go out for a leisurely cruise in the *wanking chariot*.

palmesan *n.* The result of *pulling the Pope's hat off* repeatedly and excessively without pausing to perform the occasional spot of basic genital maintenance in between. Particularly rife amongst those presently seeking gainful employment. Also *dolecelatte, brimula, Lymeswold*.

palm export *1. n.* An amber Belgian beer that undergoes top fermentation. The taste is bittersweet with a strong hoppiness. *2. n. Spunk*.

palm fruit *n.* A lady's *chestular* offerings. A "large pair": two of your five a day.

palmikaze *n.* A suicidally reckless act of *turning Japanese, eg.* One where the intrepid pleasure-seeker thrashes himself into the *spin cycle* to the sound of his grocery-laden wife shouting "I'm home dear" from the front door.

palmistry *n.* A mystic art involving the flat of the hand and the *cock*. The skilled *palmist* is able to look a few minutes into the future and foresee a period of mopping up *jizz*.

palm oasis *1. n.* A picturesque tropical island or verdant watering hole. *2. n.* A lovely relaxing *wank* in the middle of a busy day.

palm oil *1. n.* An edible liquid derived primarily from the mesocarp of the fruit of the African oil palm *Elaeis guineensis*, the production of which is responsible for unsustainable levels of deforestation in third-world communities and a great deal of leafleting in British high streets. *2. n.* Any lubricant or emollient with a high melting point that is applied to the hand for the purpose of *self-improvement, eg.* Hand cream, Stork SB, WD40.

palmorama *n.* A late night "investigative" report into the American porn industry or similar, eagerly watched by single men who have a penchant for hard news or married men who are *staying up to watch Family Guy*. A *masturmentary, rudimentary, sockumentary*.

palmouflage *n.* Any form of *grumbular* disguise utilized when approaching the tills at the newsagent, *eg.* A copy of *The Economist* wrapped round *Razzle* or a copy of *Razzle* wrapped round

New Cunts 85. Or a copy of *New Cunts 85* wrapped round *Viz*.

palm sugar *1. n.* Catering industry sweetener made from the sticky sap of the coconut palm, *Cocus nucifera*. *2. n.* Catering industry savoury additive made from the sticky *sap* of an aggrieved kitchen worker's *nuts*, for the delectation of his more challenging clientele. *Chef's special sauce.*

palm sugar *euph.* A slightly dirtier, monomanualist's version of *eye candy*.

palm Sunday *1. n.* Christian feast day celebrated a week before Easter. *2. n.* Onanistic frenzy enjoyed when the *bag for life* goes to visit her mother or a shopping centre on the Sabbath. A relaxing *day of wrist* spent in one's own company in the absence of other weekend commitments.

palm ticklers *n.* Small, flat *lils* with protruding nipples. *Empire biscuits.*

palpootations *n.* Involuntary and unnerving contractions of the *nipsy* which make the heart beat faster the morning after a night *on the pop*.

pamper day *1. n.* An outpatient-style visit to an over-priced country hotel where big girls go to feel special, get their nails cut, sit in some mud, get their verrucas nibbled by goldfish *etc*. *2. n.* Following ten pints of Guinness and a curry the previous night, a day spent wearing an emergency underpant lining, such as an old sock, woolly hat or similar, as a precaution. *3. n.* Any 24-hour period that one spends in a heightened state of fear that one might inadvertently *soil one's bills.*

panaconda *n.* A South American *dirt snake* of enormous length, that suffocates its victims if they get too close.

pan au chocolat *n. Fr.* An unhealthily full *bog*.

pan au chocolat *n. Fr.* The result of a rather explosive session on the *bum sink*. '*I started with the part-seared scallops so I'll end with the pan au chocolat.*'

panavision *1. n.* Cinematographic company founded in 1953. *2. n.* The vertiginous, anamorphic vista across the porcelain expanses of *Shanks Bay* afforded to a fellow while he is attempting to cough up eight pints of stout, six bags of semi-digested pork scratchings and a *catbab* with *all the shit* which he swallowed less than half an hour ago without chewing.

pancake *1. n.* A disastrous, more-or-less planar *Tom tit* that pretty much covers the *chod bin*, the *dot* and possibly also the walls and ceiling. *2. n.* A hugely successful *toss* that covers the walls and ceiling.

pan-can, do the *v.* To raise or lower the *bog* seat in a public *Rick Witter* as if you were Nicole Kidman in *Moulin Rouge.*

panchromatic *1. adj.* Encompassing all the colours of the visible spectrum; usually descriptive of photographic film. *2.adj.* Descriptive of a dazzling, Technicolor *shite* in the *bog.*

panda's eye *n.* A *ringpiece.*

pandemic *n. medic.* A lavatory-based medical episode.

pander *1. v.* To act as a go-between in an act of sexual intrigue, *eg.* To go and buy a hamster and some parcel tape for that odd couple in the flat below. *2. n.* A large, impotent, bamboo-eating mammal.

P and O *euph.* A quick, perfunctory act of intercourse. A *roll on, roll off.*

Pandora's bog *n.* A public lavatory toilet with the lid down. Once opened, all the horrors of the world can invariably be found in *Pandora's bog.*

Pandora's box *1. n.* An artefact in Greek mythology which, when opened, unleashes all sorts of evils and curses. *2. n.* The *twat* of a lady who maintains a dubious personal hygiene regimen.

Pandora's box of holocausts *1. phr.* Typically overblown lyric from Marillion's 1984 single *Fugazi. 2. n.* Any budget supermarket shopping basket, wheeled or not, that is so irredeemably dirty it has to be a suspect in the search for the initial source of Covid19.

pandulum *n.* A long *motion* hanging out of the *arse* and swinging from side to side about an equilibrious position.

panelbeater *1. n.* Skilled workman who knocks the dints out of your car doors before spraying them a slightly different colour to the rest of your car. *2. n.* A *membrum virile* of large proportions, able to *bang* the dints out of a lady's *pink bonnet.*

panel pin *n.* A TV comedy quiz staple, such as that bald man with the "Laughing Cavalier" beard who shouts everything like he's trying to wake up someone who's been hit on the head by a falling tile, that thin Irish bloke in specs with the long hair, him who never opens his eyes, or the short, Scottish woman in a suit who talks about cats all the time.

pan for gold *v.* To strike it lucky in the water closet and do a runny *shite* containing numerous small fragments of treasure. See *one point five, bicycle chain.*

pan Gogh *n.* A piece of post-expressionist art left un-flushed in a public convenience to be appreciated by the next user of the cubicle.

panhandle *n.* An erect penis, a *stonk on.*

panhandle pipes *n.* A Peruvian sex act, whereby a woman blows across the top of several men's *cocks* of differing length arranged side by side.

Presumably in a shopping precinct.

panhandler's delight *n.* The little strip of tenacious *arse nuggets* that remain in the bottom of the U-bend after flushing away a particularly fibrous *feeshus.*

panic button *n.* The *wail switch, devil's doorbell* or *clematis.*

panicdote *n.* A hastily cobbled-together, inconsistent and poorly thought-out back story that stretches the bounds of one's spouse's credulity when it is deployed at short notice.

panjammer *n.* A stool that laughs in the face of the flush. A *U-blocker, plumber's bonus* or *crowd pleaser.*

pankled *adj.* Having one's pants pulled down to one's ankles. Derivation unknown.

panmax *1. n.* In shipping jargon, the largest vessel that the Panama Canal can accommodate. *2. n.* In *shitting* jargon, the largest *feeshus* a given convenience can accommodate. *'Excuse me your majesty, I've slightly misjudged the panmax. Can I borrow your sceptre for five minutes?'*

pan of burnt chips *n. orthodont.* Descriptive of dentition that leaves a lot to be desired. *'So in she comes with another fucking fishbone stuck in her craw. So she opens her mouth and it's like a pan of burnt chips in there. I know she's 102, but for Christ's sake, she should have had them manky pegs out years ago.'*

pan o'noir *n.* Dark coloured *feeshus* enjoyed after a night on the red wine.

pan pipes *n.* A simple wind instrument that plays haunting music in the *bob house.*

pan scourer *n.* A vagina covered in a coarse grade of *muff swarf. Brillo fanny.*

pan-seared *1. adj.* Something that happens to tuna steaks in gastro-pub kitchens in order to make them cost upwards of fifteen quid a pop. Plus another seven pounds for a small bowl of thick chips. *2. adj.* Of a toilet-goer's thighs, bearing the distinctive dark, lateral markings produced by a prolonged spell sat on the *casserollercoaster* reading the *Autotrader.*

pan smile *n.* The crescent-shaped *piss*-bleached patch of carpet that grins yellowly around the base of the *bum sink.* The *Queen Mum's smile.*

pan stick *1. n.* A cosmetic used for theatrical make-up. *2. n.* An *arse offering*, hastily snapped off and left floating in a municipal *shitter.*

pant anchors *n.* Your *bollocks*, specifically when they are placed above the elastic waistband of your *scads* to enable you to *piss* hands free without soaking your *kegs.* Used in pub toilets when texting, reading while standing up or propping yourself up to avoid falling over *etc.* What could possibly go wrong?

panta ray *n.* A widely spread area of feminine anatomy that exudes a distinct piscatorial aroma. A *stamped bat.*

pantballing *n.* An involuntary, messy but exciting sport, usually played on Saturday and Sunday mornings by men who were copiously *refreshed* on dark beers and a lethally hot *phall* the previous evening.

pantcakes night *n.* Soiling your *underbags* at the end of a smashing evening.

pantdruff *n.* Shedded skin, found in one's *grundies* after several days of wear. *'That's one small step for man, one giant leap for mankind. Ooh, this pantdruff's itching me knackers something rotten, Buzz. Over.'*

pant hamster *n.* Natural prey of the *one-eyed trouser snake.*

pantilever *n.* The *piss handle.*

pantler *n.* An inexpedient *stonk on* which looks like an accident-prone reindeer has run into a washing line.

pant moustache *n.* Effect achieved when the *mapatasi* extends symmetrically beyond either side of the *shreddies. Thigh brows, whack-os, Rhoydes Boysons, Jeremy Clarkson's eyebrows.*

pant music *n. Farts.*

pantography *n.* In the *action-romance movie* industry, the female artistes' obligatory panto-mime-like surprise at seeing something, *eg.* The size of the male performer's *cock-drop*-filled *giggling stick*; that his step-mother is *sucking him off etc.* Also *pornomime.*

pantomime horse dilemma *n.* Conundrum facing a pair of *chuckle brothers* when faced with a *man at C&A* situation after picking up a right mucky *scratter* outside a Leeds pub late on a Friday, *viz.* "Which end of the beast to take?"

pant poppet *n.* A small nugget of *Tom tit* that is inadvertantly ejected following a cough. So-called due to its similarity to the popular boxed chocolate treats of the 1990s.

pants *1. interj.* Exclamation of dismay. *2. adj.* Rubbish. *'This film is pants. It's not a patch on Jaws 4.'*

pant stripper *n.* Any fancy alcoholic drink that more or less guarantees free access to the *hairy pie. Knicker oil, WD69.*

panty climax *1. n.* Feeling of disillusionment and bathos experienced when you finally get to see the *damp squib* that a new partner has been squirrelling away in their undergarmentry. *2. n. Going off* in your *applecatchers. Spending your money before*

you get to the shops.

panty critter *n.* A hairy *beaver.*

panty floss *n.* A stray clump of pubic hair picked from a fairground worker's teeth.

panty liner *n.* A large ocean-going vessel full of young single ladies on a Club 18-30 style cruise. And whilst readers might expect this entry to include a reference to the presence of "plenty of seamen" on board, we're frankly not going to lower ourselves to that level.

pantymonium *n.* A flatulent charivari. A loud *trouser coughing fit* causing havoc in the *undercrackers.*

panxiety *n.* State of trepidation experienced in anticipation of a forthcoming *sit down toilet adventure.* Also *panxious (adj.).*

panzered *adj.* Fully *tanked up.*

pap baffle *n.* The scrunched-up piece of *shit scrape* placed in the *pan* which makes the person in the next *trap* genuinely believe that your foulage doesn't make a "plop" when it hits the water.

paperchase *1. n.* The athletic pursuit of *bumwad* from cubicle to cubicle with trousers and *grundies* around one's ankles. *2. n.* The manic sprint around the house trying to pick up all the in-criminating soiled tissues and *grot mags* one has strewn about before the wife returns from her shopping expedition.

paper cut *n.* Opposite of a *wizard's sleeve.* A *fanny* that is tighter than an *OJ's glove.*

paper hanger's bucket *n.* A big sloppy *twat* full of wallpaper paste. Also *billposter's bucket.*

paperless office *n.* An ecologically-sound *digestive transit* that requires no wiping. A *clean drop, future shit* or *Hollywood ending.*

paperless orifice *n.* The result of dropping a *crowd pleaser* where, given the immaculate condition of the *nipsy*, absolutely no *paperwork* is required.

paper over the cacks *v.* To discreetly drape unflushable, floating *Richard the Thirds* with *toilet tissue* in a vain attempt to mask their presence.

paper saver *n.* A *Simon Cowell* movement that leaves the bumwad clean straight off the tee.

paper scraper *n.* An *apple tart* so pungent that it can remove wallpaper and leave it in tiny pieces on the floor.

PAPFAP/papfap *acronym.* Pretty As a Picture, Fat As a Pig.

pap happy *adj.* No longer embarrassed to *fart* in front of a romantic partner. *'We very quickly reached that pap happy stage in our relationship, Cilla.'*

Papierkrieg *1. n. Germ. milit.* Literally "paper war"; a disparaging reference to report filing and record keeping. *2. n. Germ. milit.* The fruitless struggle to cope with a sausage, cabbage and beans-rich diet coupled with a fractured logistical system that regularly failed to provide adequate supplies of *shitscrape* to the stormtroopers at the front.

papier splâché *n. Fr.* Hardened tissues that litter the bedroom floors of teenage boys. *Popshotadoms, wankerchiefs, porn crackers, wanker's crisps.*

Papillon's purse *euph.* The rectal orifice when used as a repository for valuables, *eg.* When in a prison, boarding school or while negotiating the "Nothing to Declare" channel of a Turkish airport. From the film starring Steve McQueen in which the convicts stashed their cash "up the pipe".

papkin *n.* Like a napkin, but used by a young lady to wipe *spunk* off her *paps*.

pappalonia *exclam.* Outburst of appreciation for a woman with a massive set of *gazongers*.

papper *v.* To *shit*. *'Oh no, I think I might just of pappered me trolleys. So it's over to John Kettley for the weather while I have a look.'*

paps *1. n.* Celebrity-hungry photographers who murdered our Princess of Hearts. *2. n. arch.* Olde Worlde *Tittes*.

papsack *n.* A pair of *tit pants*, a *knocker hopper* or *brassiere*.

paps'n'flaps *phr.* Artful photographic pose that best showcases all of a young lady's manifold charms.

parachute in the trees *euph.* A lump of *Thora Hird* which, although it has successfully exited the *bomb bay doors*, has failed to clear the *arse cress* and is only discovered during the fateful first wipe. One should then proceed to the shower. A *man in the rigging.*

parade ground poo *n.* A *William Pitt* of such magnitude that the only fitting response is to hang a *bumrag* flag on it and salute as it passes out of the *chod-bin*.

parading the beef *1. n. nav.* A long-standing tradition in Admiralty circles, whereby a joint of meat is put on parade before being declared fit to eat by the Mess President. *2. n.* A long-standing tradition in northern nightclubs, whereby a gentleman promenades his *meat and two veg* in the not necessarily forlorn hope that a thoroughly *wankered* young lady will deem it fit to *nosh on.*

paradise pie *1. n.* A very succulent pudding served in restaurants. *2. n.* A *bird's trifle* that is mouth-watering to the eye.

paraffin *n. rhym. slang.* An itinerant gentleman of the road. From paraffin lamp = Harold Ramp.

paraffinalia *n.* The tools of the trade accumulated by a professional *hobo, eg.* Dozens of bags containing rubbish, an old pram, a greasy anorak

and a family size plastic bottle of white cider.

parallel parked *adj.* In bed together, *having it off.*

paralytically incorrect *n.* A consequence of heavy intoxication whereby one's easy-going, tolerant views are discarded in favour of a rather more robust manifesto.

pararoid *adj.* Absolutely *fucking* terrified of sitting down, *farting*, and/or standing up too quickly, for fear of rupturing your *farmers*.

parashite *n.* Annoying piece of used *arse wipe* that inflates with air during the flush and resists going down the pan.

parcel force *n.* Means of making *chod's law* work for you. Going to the toilet and pretending to have a *shit*, in order to fool the fates and cause the postman to make a package delivery at a time of your choosing.

parcel shelf *n.* The viewing platform provided in a German *jobby engine*, where one's *Atlantic Oceans* can be inspected at leisure prior to being flushed away.

pard-on *n.* An accidental *hard-on*. In order to defuse an awkward moment, a gentleman might say "Sorry, I have a pard-on," whilst pointing at his erectivitated member.

pard-on *n.* An unplanned *thumper* of such magnitude and conspicuousness that one feels obliged to excuse oneself to one's fellow lift users.

pardon my Dutch *exclam.* A humorous ejaculation to break the ice after *treading on a* particularly vile *duck.*

parfume de plop *n.* Acrid odour which accompanies a *twin tone* and heralds the arrival in the *turtle's den* of a *Peter O'Toole.*

Paris-chute *euph.* Something that rarely fails to open, as sported by the well known hotel-named socialite, chihuahua enthusiast and scrawny twilit internet *grumble* star.

parish lengthsman *n.* A horny-handed fellow employed to tend the *ladygardens* in a locale.

Parisian breasts *n.* See *lung warts.*

Paris Stilton *euph.* A lady who, from a distance and hidden behind her large sunglasses, make-up and handbag, looks reasonably appetizing – but who, on closer inspection turns out to be pock-marked, blue-veined and stinky. Also *lrf.*

park and ride *1. n.* Scheme run by one's local council. *2. n.* Scheme run by one's local prostitutes. *3. n.* Hurried intercourse in the back seat of a stationary car. A *rear-end shunt.* *4. euph.* Dogging at a convenient, out-of-town location, from the participating motorist's perspective.

parking sensor *n.* The satisfying crunching noise made by a lady's car (Or a man's, we'll have no truck with sexism here. Many women are able to drive almost as well as some men, as a matter of fact), to inform her that the rearward portion of a parking manoeuvre is complete.

park the bus *1. v.* Of a football manager, to put all your players behind the ball and in front of the goal in order to prevent the other team from scoring. *2. v.* To be delivered of a *feeshee* of such gargantuan proportions that one wouldn't be surprised to see pensioners disembarking from it and waiting at the side to get their suitcases.

park the custard *v.* To *laugh at the carpet*.

park the fudge *v.* To *shit, snip off a length of dirty spine, crimp off a length*.

park the pink bus *v.* To *slip* a lady a *length*. *'Time for bed. Come on, let's park the pink bus in the furry garage.' 'Okay. Then we can have a fuck.'*

park the tiger *v.* To puke, *yodel*, let out a *technicolour yawn*.

park viper *n.* A venomous *brown dirt snake* lying concealed in the grass, coiled and ready to strike at an unwary passer-by. *'Your grandad will have to join us later, I'm afraid. He's been bitten by a park viper.'*

park your breakfast *v.* To light a *bum cigar*, lay *a cable*.

parliament face *n.* Someone whose *mush* has been rearranged, either in a fight or by accident of birth, *viz.* "The eyes to the right, the nose to the left." *'Today's birthdays: Franki Valli, Four Seasons frontman, 1934; James Brown, Godfather of Soul, 1933; Douglass Carswell, parliament face, 1971.'*

parlour *n.* Place where one is only allowed on special occasions. The *bonus tunnel* or *wrong 'un*.

parmo *n.* A meat'n'cheese'n'egg-based Middlesbrough delicacy. See also *cholesterol special*.

parp *1. n. onomat.* A romantic foreplay technique whereby one squeezes a breast in the same way that a clown or sea lion would honk a car horn. *2. n. onomat.* A *heart to heart*.

parp baffle *n.* A *treacle tart* deployed under the cover of loud mechanical noise. Perhaps whilst exiting a 747 with its four RB211 engines spooling down after you've been fermenting your last meal for four hours in cramped conditions.

parpetrator *n.* One who supplied it, and then possibly denied it.

parpmaster *n.* An audible musical toot that allows those nearby to guess the intro of a popular music hit, *viz.* "Erm, I'm going to say Harold Faltermeyer and Axel F, Ken." "I'm afraid not, Janet. It was actually Def Leppard with Let's Get Rocked."

parson's sack *n.* The swollen state of a *scrotbag* which is as *full as a fat bird's shoe* following an enforced period of celibacy and/or masturbatory abstinence. *'Testicular pressure. The greatest internal pressure sustained in a pair of testicles is one of 65 atmospheres (995lb/ sq.in) or approximately 49,400mm of mercury at sea level, in the parson's sack of the pop singer Sir Cliff Richard (GB), following a 45-year build up of seminal fluid'.* (from *The Viz Sexist Book of Records*, Boxtree £4.99, or 3 copies for 10p at a car boot sale and a free seashell-covered TV-top thermometer thrown in).

part exchange *1. n.* A tempting deal offered by motor traders, whereby your current car is taken from you to be sold on at a huge profit, a minuscule amount is knocked off the price of the car you are buying (which they bought in a similar trade-in for fuck all), and you are invited to treat them as if they are doing you a favour. *2. n.* A saucy encounter.

particulars *n.* Of low budget British sex comedies involving police officers, ladies' *bills*, knickers. *'Excuse me, madam, but I may need to take down your particulars. And have a look at your cunt.'*

parting *n.* Pathetic *farting* which often results in such sweet sorrow.

parts of shame *n.* A God botherer's genitals.

party equipment *n.* Drink, drugs and what-have-you. *'Mr Gove, I've brought your party equipment.' 'Excellent, I'll deeply regret taking that later.'*

party popper *n.* When a chap's wife or mistress struts around the house naked with the tail of her *fanny mouse* hanging out of her *skirting board,* and he feels the urge to pull it and see if her *arse* flies off. See *time bomb fuse.*

party rings *euph.* As per the popular 1980s iced teatime biscuit, which you can still get, when your mate's mum bends over and offers both *the pink and the brown* on a plate.

party stick *n. Meatus erectus.*

party wall agreement *n.* Unwritten custom and practice contract entered into by the users of a *glory hole* or *snatch hatch.*

party willy *n.* The special form of blunderbuss-style penis wielded by houseguests. A *dick* that liberally distributes *wazz* on the seat and cistern, and also the floor, wall, and occasionally the ceiling, of your smallest room.

parvis *n.* Like an enclosed garden in front of a church or cathedral, where the monks and nuns play at dinner time (it's mentioned on the back cover, look).

pasata grin *n.* Mexican lipstick, *clown's smile* when one has *gone to work on an egg.*

passcode gruesome *adj.* The morning after a heavy

night *on the pop* when you look so monstrous that even your mobile phone's facial recognition software doesn't know who you are and you have to resort to tapping in a number before you can call the ambulance.

passing of King Joffrey, the *phr.* Over-exertion while attempting to evacuate a particularly grandiose, rotund and turgid *feeshus*. The resultant burst blood vessels in the eyes, veins popping out of the head and blood coming out of the nostrils bringing to mind nothing as much as the above-mentioned *Game of Thrones* character's face during his melodramatic death scene.

passion cosh *n.* A stout, six-inch, hand-held weapon. With all wiggly veins up the side. A *love truncheon*.

passion fingers *n. Aus. milit.* An Australian army term for a clumsy fellow, *ie.* Everything he touches he *fucks*.

passion flaps *n.* A more romantic alternative to *piss flaps*.

passion pit *n.* Bed, *fart sack, scratcher, wanking chariot*.

passion wagon *n.* Knackered van, usually a Ford Transit, with blacked-out windows and a *piss-*stained mattress and several empty beer cans in the back. Also *shaggin' wagon, spambulance, fuck truck, willibago*.

pass the hat round *1. v.* To collect money for the driver on a coach trip. *2. n.* To take part in a *gang bang*. *'On their tour bus going from gig to gig, the members of Motley Crue like to pass the hat around.'*

pass the mic *1. n.* A section from the woeful TV show *The Hitman and Her*, where a couple of drunken young women took it in turns to wail into a microphone. *2. v.* A scene in all decent *grumble flicks* where a couple of *niff* actresses take it in turns to suck the leading man's *charlie*.

paste paper basket *n.* A receptacle for the discreet disposal of used *mandrex*. *'MISS MARPLE: Archbishop. Can you tell me what you were doing when the murder took place? Specifically, where you were between the hours of nine and eleven on Sunday morning? ARCHBISHOP: Well, Miss Marple, my service at St. Mary's in the Field got cancelled and my wife got taken ill, so I decided to watch the Hollyoaks omnibus. MISS MARPLE: Do you have any proof of this? ARCHBISHOP: Well the paste paper basket in my study is full. You're more than welcome to have a rummage through it if you so wish.'* (*The Mousecrap* by Agatha Christie).

Pasteur's apron *n.* The last bacteria-ridden bit of roller towel left dangling down in the gents, upon which you dry your hands after washing them

assiduously for the required thirty seconds. Also known as *Darwin's apron* or *Darwin's bib*.

pastie baby/pasty baby *n.* An ear-ringed neonate sucking on a *Greggs dummy*.

pastie/pasty bashers *n.* Scissor sisters. Ladies in *comfortable shoes* who *bump haddock*. Also *pastie smashers, Siamese quims*.

pastieplasty *n. medic.* Procedure that has the opposite effect to liposuction, involving regular and excessive ingestion of pies.

pastie spumante *n.* A cheap, yet pleasingly effervescent, *quim*.

pastietute *n.* A *good time girl* whose idea of a good time involves a couple of steak bakes and a custard slice. A *good time girl* who is a good deal heavier than her *slagboard postcard* picture might suggest.

pastifier *n.* A savoury item stuffed into a baby's mouth to stop it crying during a Saturday morning trip to Primark. A *Greggs dummy*.

pasturbation *n.* Dwelling on earlier glories while *shaking hands with an old friend. Tosstalgia*.

Pat and Frank *n. rhym. slang.* A *wank*. Named after the erstwhile *EastEnders* couple of Pat and Frank Butcher. Also known as a *Patricia and Francis* in more socially elevated circles.

Pat Butcher ear-ring *n.* Item of *jelly jewellery* named in honour of the *EastEnders* character who, it says here, last appeared on the show in 2016 as a deathbed hallucination for Peggy Mitchell. Bet that was a side-splitting episode.

Pat Cuff *n. rhym. slang.* A *puddle jumper*. Named after the erstwhile Middlesbrough goalkeeper who, in the 1970s, spent ninety minutes every Saturday afternoon staring intently at ten arseholes.

pathfinder *1. n. milit.* A lone soldier who is sent ahead of his platoon in search of enemy activity or pockets of resistance. *2. n.* The first, brave finger to venture into the gusset region of a young lady's *dunghampers* in order to check whether the *Russians have invaded. 3. n.* An *air biscuit* that lets one know in no uncertain terms that it's time for a *Tom tit. 4. n.* A *pace car.*

PAT/pat *acronym.* Porn Assisted Tugfest. A marathon session of *self harm* fuelled by sundry miscellaneous *grot mags, grumble flicks*, bra catalogues *etc.*

Patrick Moore *n. rhym. slang.* How a cockney astronomer might refer to the door of his observatory. *'Fackin' nora, Sir Bernard. Shut the bleedin' Patrick Moore, will yer? I'm bent over me eighteen inch catadioptric Cassegrain trying to get a look at a large Magellanic cloud in the Crab's Head Nebula and there's a terrible Robert Kraft going* *right up me Willem de Sitter.'*

Patrick, pull a *1. v.* Of a man who is about to *tip his filthy concrete*, to effect an expression resembling that of the late Selsey-based stargazer, comedy glockenspiel player and *Sky at Night* presenter, with one eye half open and the other scrunched shut. *'Gunther, we're running out of tape here. Just pull a Patrick so we can all go home, will you.'* 2. *v.* To pull a boggle-eyed face after catching *Kojak's rollneck* in one's trouser zip.

pat the dog through the letterbox *n.* To *firkyfoodle* via the trouser flies. A phrase apparently overheard on a bus by *Guardian* cartoonist Posy Simmonds, and recounted by her in an interview, although the writer didn't explain exactly what it meant as it was in the *Telegraph.*

patty *n.* A posh lady's *snatch, ie.* What the current Queen Consort probably calls her *quim.*

Paula Radcliffe Way *1. n. geog.* A stretch of the A6 Clapham Bypass in Bedfordshire, named in honour of the athlete of the same name. *2. n.* A *shit* in the road.

Paul Daniels' hankie *sim.* Descriptive of a flaccid *member* being manually encouraged into a lady's *prickpocket*. From the "hankie in the fist" trick performed by the eponymous deceased magician. *Playing snooker with a piece of string, pushing marshmallows into a moneybox.*

Pauline *rhym. slang.* A *minge*. From late former *EastEnders* misery-guts Pauline Fowler = growler.

Paulsgrove street party *n.* A lively all day *al fresco* celebration which involves looting, drug runners, prostitutes, police armed response units, surveillance helicopters and general rioting. Named after a housing estate in Portsmouth that you are unlikely to see featured on *Location, Location, Location* any time soon.

Paul's house, go to *v.* To embark on a visit to the *smallest room* in order to do a *number two*. A reference to the popular Glade air freshener advert from the dim and distant past, *viz.* "I'm going to do a poo at Paul's".

pauncho *n.* A *poond* or *fat hat* that keeps a middle-aged man warm.

pavement melter *n.* A violent, vertical *backfire* that shoots down one's trouser leg at alarming speed, scalding the ankles before venting its super-heated fury on the concrete upon which one is standing.

pavement pizza *n.* The contents of your stomach as they appear after *barfing* in the street. A *parked tiger.*

pavement roundabout *n.* A *dog egg* on a public footpath that pedestrians must round before

continuing on their way. A *jobstacle course.*

pavement skating *n.* Sliding, Torville & Dean-style, on a moist *barker's egg* while running for a bus.

pavement snooker *n.* Bronchitis-based outdoor game played by coughing *Harry ramps* whereby different colours of *hockle* are gobbed out, *viz.* Greens, browns, yellows and, if you're really lucky, the odd red followed by a black.

Pavlov's cock/Pavlov's dick *n.* A keen *boner* drooling *dog slobber* in anticipation of being served a slap-up portion of *beef curtains.*

Pavlov's log *1. n. medic.* Conditioned reflex action causing one's *bomb bay doors* to start opening upon seeing a toilet. *2. n. medic.* The onset of defecatory cramps caused by the aroma of ground coffee or cigarette smoke. *3. n. medic.* The condition whereby the instant you are anywhere near a particular setting, such as pulling your car into your driveway after work, or arriving at a funeral, you inexplicably, and urgently, need a *shit.*

pawnbroker *n.* A lady whose *tits* are each roughly the same size and shape as her head.

Paxman's beard *n.* An unsightly, scraggy, grey *mott.* A *pieman's wig.*

pay and display *1. n.* Type of automated car park ticketing system whereby, typically, if it's eighty pee an hour and you've only got a pound coin, it fucking gives you one hour instead of the one-and-a-quarter hours you've fucking paid for. *2. n.* A high quality female escort, often sourced from eastern Europe, who is available at rates of between £1000-£2500 per evening to accompany gentlemen to social events, providing decorative companionship and thus impressing friends, colleagues and family friends.

pay at pump *euph.* The act of handing over the cash to a *good time girl* immediately after the *vinegar strokes.*

payday weekender *n.* After getting your wages on the Friday, the *shit* which you have on the Sunday, which resembles chocolate Angel Delight, has the texture of fresh tarmac, and smells like a Falaraki skip during a Greek heatwave.

pay in installments *v.* To be forced to make multiple lavatory visits to relieve the *Enochs* after a night of *Ruby Murray* and brown ales.

pay like Vegas *euph.* To pay for *the other* with chips. The sort of late night symbiotic commercial arrangement that is not unknown in the eponymous Nevada gamblers' paradise or, indeed, in the Bigg Market, Newcastle upon Tyne.

pay plop dollar *v.* To need a *shite* when one's only available option is to purchase a round of drinks in an overpriced establishment in order to use their toilet. To *pay through the arse*.

pay the gash bill *v.* To hand over money to a *good time girl* following a thoroughly unpleasant time. *'Where are you going with that brown envelope containing two thousand pounds in used notes, Lord Archer of Weston super Mare?' 'I'm just off to pay the gash bill.'*

PCC *1. abbrev.* The Press Complaints Commission. *2. abbrev.* Police and Crime Commissioner. *3. abbrev.* Post Coital Cigarette.

PCM *n. medic.* The anal sphincter or *snippit valve*. Poo Cutting Muscle.

peace pipe *n.* A *joint, reefer, spliff, bong* or *jazz cigarette*.

peach stone *n.* An hibernal scrotum, clenched tightly like a Scotsman's fist around his change.

peachy head *n. Horatio* performed by a particularly adept practitioner.

peacock *1. n.* A proud and resplendent ornamental fowl strutting across the lawn of a stately home, periodically making a noise like Sir Lenny Henry. *2. n.* An under-endowed gentleman who is *hung like an Argos biro*. Also known as a *dickling, Ethel*, or *miniaturist*.

peaky balders *n.* Demographic group of young adult males who, having gone bald early, draw attention to the fact by hiding their *slapheads* under 'newsboy' caps.

peaky blinders *1. n.* An apparently popular television programme about antediluvian Mancunian gangsters or something. *2. n.* A cracking pair of *shirt potatoes* of such remarkable shape and pertness that they could easily take someone's eye out

peal *n. coll.* More than one *bellend*. *'Look at that load of twats carrying that coffin. What a fucking peal.' 'Yes, vicar.'*

peanus butter *n.* A smooth and creamy product of the *nuts*, ideal in a *mam sandwich*, and somewhat disingenuously 'enjoyed' by the mucky ladies in *jazz magazines*.

peanut brittle *n. medic.* Condition of a hardened drinker whose only solid intake for some days has been items available at the bar. Symptoms include mental fragility and uncontrolled shaking. *'Harry froze as they spotted an unshaven Mr Snape slumped at the bar of the Black Cauldron. "We're done for now!" he cried. "No we're not," replied Hermione. "He's been drinking all weekend and he's completely peanut brittle."'* (from *Harry Potter and the Wizard's Sleeve* by JK Rowling).

pea pod *n.* A troublesome, lengthy stool that requires repeated flexing of the anal sphincter and lower bowel in order to expel it from the body, resulting in *breather rings* that give it a ribbed appearance similar to a pea pod, although hopefully not bright green. *'I'm just going upstairs to crimp out a pea pod, nan.'*

Pearl & Dean necklace *n.* A frankly unlikely sexual scenario, where one *jizzes* onto one's girlfriend in the pictures, presumably while shouting: "Pa-paa... pa-paa... pa-paa... pa-paa... pa-pa-pa... pa-paa... pa-paa... pa-paa... pa-pa... pow!"

pearl bracelet *n.* An item of *jelly jewellery* worn on the wrist.

pearl divers' lungs *sim.* The impressive ability of a man to *go down* for prolonged periods without the need to come up for fresh air.

pearl drops *n.* Scumbled *spunky* deposits found on the walls of gents' toilets, particularly in the south. *Managlypta.*

pearl grey tea *n.* Beverage which is customarily sipped in the afternoon with the little finger cocked elegantly.

pearl harbour *n. prop.* Scene of a messy navel engagement.

pearl in the oyster *n.* Not to put too fine a point on it, it's when a bloke gives a *bird* a *cream pie* and a drop of *nut muck* beads between her *piss-flaps*.

pearl necklace *n.* An item of *jelly jewellery*. One of those consequences of having a *sausage sandwich* at the *Billy Mill Roundabout* that so delight the ladies.

pearly dewdrops' drops *1. n.* Cocteau Twins song from the early eighties. *2. n.* Ball glaze, perseverance soup, guardsman's gloss, dew on the lily, knuckle varnish.

pearly gates *1. n.* What you knock on when you die. *2. n.* The sloppy *cat flaps* of a woman with multiple piercings in the *farmyard area*.

pebbledash *v.* To *crop spray* the toilet bowl with *clarts*, thus negatively affecting the value of your home.

pebbledashed semi *1. phr.* Expression used during Sir Keir Starmer's achingly sincere appeal to working class voters, *viz.* "That pebbledashed semi was everything to my family. It gave us stability through the cost of living crises of the seventies." *2. n.* Half a teacake getting sprayed in *foulage* after pulling out of a *ringpiece* in the middle of a *bum fun* session.

pecker *1. n. US.* Penis. *2. n. UK.* Nose.

pecker checker *n.* An enthusiastic amateur urologist who plies his trade in a public lavatory. He who does not obey the "eyes front" rule at a public urinal. A *willy watcher.* See also *gambler's* squint. *'Don't mind me, pal. I'm one of the country's most experienced consultant pecker checkers.'*

peckerino *n.* Particularly pungent *knob cheese.* Something you wouldn't necessarily want on your pizza, all things considered, but Giles Coren probably gets quite a bit of it on his. Also *palmesan, hedam, fromunder, foreskinzola, Fred Leicester.*

peckerino *n.* Rich, full fat Italian *knob cheese* that is traditionally shaved onto unpopular customers' pasta in Italian restaurants. *'Chef has seen you on television, so he's put extra peckerino on your spaghetti, Mr Clarkson.'*

pecker wrecker *n.* Ale, typically that with an ABV of 6% or above.

pecker wreckers *n.* A *bird's* corrective orthodontical scaffolding. *Gurniture.*

Peckham oysters *n.* Chicken wings.

pecking *v.* The head-nodding motion exhibited by one in such a *state of refreshment* that they can hardly keep awake.

pedal *n. rhym. slang.* To commit an act of *self-pollution.* From pedal and crank = Jodrell Bank.

pedalophile *n.* One who hires an item of holiday boating equipment, the better to practise a spot of ocean-bound *hornithology* while *cleaning his glasses.* A very specific epithet which you don't really get the opportunity to drop casually into the conversation very often, to be frank.

pedigree bum *n.* When your *farts* smell like *dog shite* or dog food. Not that there's a great deal of difference.

pedigree chum *n.* A *big-boned filf* you wouldn't mind a *go on.* From the 1970s pet food advertising slogan; "all meat and animal derivatives, a real treat".

pedigree hum *n.* A *dropped gut* that smells of offal and marrowbone jelly and gives you a lovely wet nose.

Pedro's piss *n.* Bland Spanish lager such as San Miguel, served lukewarm in plastic cups on the Costa del Sol. *'Eggo and chippos, please mate, plenty-o ketchup and another pint of Pedro's piss, por favor.'*

pee *1. v.* To *piss. 2. n.* Some *piss.*

peeing double *n.* Shooting out two calamitously divergent streams of *wazz.* A phenomenon usually caused by a *Bobby Charlton* adhered across the *hog's eye* or a plug of *jipper.* The *serpent's* (or *viper's*) *tongue, twin jets, stray spray.*

peek-a-poo/peekapoo *n.* A U-bend-hugging *Sir Douglas* that is reluctant to be flushed away. Also *deja poo.*

peel *1. v.* To strip, pose nude. *2. v.* When so doing,

to draw back the *beef curtains.*

peel and polish *n.* A swiftly administered, no frills blow job. *'Ten quid for full sex, fifteen for anal, three quid for a quick peel and polish.'*

peel and reseal *1. phr.* Tried and tested method used by food manufacturers to keep groceries, such as ground coffee and what-have-you, fresh. *2. phr.* Tried and tested method used by teenagers to keep their favourite *art pamphlets* far from fresh.

peeling a post-it note *euph.* The gentle manoeuvre separating the sides of the *chicken skin handbag* from the top of the thigh. An operation of increasing necessity with advancing age.

peeling the carrot *v. Spanking the monkey.*

peeling the midnight spud *n.* The semi-somnolent act of scratching one's sweaty *knackers* red raw. Also *boiling the midnight potatoes.*

peel myself back a bit *phr.* One of the reasons Oxford- and Cambridge-educated comedy Covid minister Matt Hancock gave for his decision to enter *I'm a Celebrity* for £300,000. *Relaxing in a gentleman's way.*

peel session *euph.* The late Mark E Smith having *one off the wrist.*

peels on wheels *n.* An independently peripatetic *good time girl* who is prepared, for a small fee, to drive round to gentlemen's abodes and *toss them off.*

peel the eel *v.* What Ray Mears does when he's all alone in the wilderness.

peel the furry prawn *v.* To manually attend to the *pudenders* of a young lady who is disinclined to wash.

peemale *n.* A man who urinates sitting down, possibly as a means of expressing solidarity with women, but more likely through alcoholic exhaustion. One who *drives from the ladies' tee.*

peen *v.* Having done a *number one.* Urinated. *'Tarquin, go to the toilet before our long car journey.' 'Don't worry mama, I've already peen.'*

peepage *n.* The shameful *dewdrop* of urine on the front of a chap's fawn slacks, caused by his *leaky washer.* *'Lot 346. Vintage pair of khaki trousers by Messrs Farah Ltd., formerly the property of Sir Cyril Smith MP. 82" waist, 19" inside leg. Heavy peepage, some rust and cheesy foxing to gusset. Est. £3000-£5000.'*

peep over the garden fence *v.* To attempt to conceal an unwanted erection by flattening it upwards against the stomach and tucking the *helmet* behind the waistband of the underpants. A *Kilroy,* a *Chad.*

peesouper *1. n.* The eye-watering, choking experience of having to use a train toilet several hours after the water for flushing has run out. That is to say, every time you use the toilet on a train. Even if you're the first person to use it when it has just rolled out of the fucking factory. 2. *n.* The practice, in environmentally or water bill-conscious households, of only flushing the *bog* once every several urinations, thus creating a thick and cloudy *piss* cocktail, as it were, of different family members' *wee wee* in the pan.

pee sticks *n.* A childish game played by male public convenience users, whereby *slash*-powered fag butts or matchsticks are raced down the urinal "canal".

peg *v.* Of a modern lady, to do a gentleman up the *council gritter* with a *strap-on.*

PEGOOMHS *abbrev.* The sudden psychological condition which manifests itself immediately after *chucking muck* up an *overnight bag.* Post Ejaculatory Get Out Of My House Syndrome.

PEGS/pegs *n. psych.* The sudden bout of angst suffered by a bachelor in that moment of cold lucidity after he *drops his filthy concrete.* Post Ejaculatory Guilt Syndrome. *Wangst.*

Pele's cock *n. medic.* An inability to maintain an erection, with reference to the deceased Brazilian goal ace's famous *cock drop* ads. Male sexual impotence.

pelican's beak *n.* A flappy double chin that is upsetting to look at, *eg.* That of the late Thora Hird or Hugh Lloyd.

pelican's yawn *sim.* A *fanny* big enough to hold 50lb of fish. A *hippo's mouth.*

pelmet *n.* A skirt so short that it "only just covers the top of the curtains".

pelmet helmet *n. medic.* Athlete's *half-a-foot* typically suffered by inveterate *zufflers. 'That's the worst case of pelmet helmet I've ever seen. Don't you ever wash your curtains?'*

pelt buckle *n.* An intimate piercing in an hirsute lady's *mimsy.*

pelt lapper *n.* A lady in *comfortable shoes*, a *tennis fan, rug muncher* or *lady golfer.*

penalty area *n.* An outsized and well-trodden *minge, viz.* "The six-yard box".

penalty pox *n.* A *clap* contracted from a bout of adulterous *futtery.*

pendolino *n.* An exceptionally large *brown trout.* Named after one of them technically advanced, state-of-the-art Class 390 tilting trains currently operated by Avanti on their West Coast Main Line route, because "it doesn't go round the bends as well as it should and it makes you an hour late for work".

pendulum *n.* A rather heavy and low hanging *willy*

that has to be hoisted up at least once a week.

Penelope shitstop *n.* The interruption of a car journey in order to let the *bag for life* take a *dump,* either at the motorway services or in the nearest roadside hedge, bush or ditch.

Penelope touch lamp *1. n.* Lighting device supplied by a well known high street retailer. *2. n.* Victorian name for the *clematis.*

penetrating oil *1. n.* A lubricating liquid of exceptionally low viscosity which is used to loosen tightly joined mechanical components and thus *2. n. Tart fuel, knicker oil, knickerdropper glory, lady petrol, WD Naughty.*

Penfold has drowned *exclam.* A witty warning made to one's housemates that there is a mole-like substance floating in the *shit pan.* From 1970s cartoon vermin Dangermouse's annoying *turd* of a sidekick.

penguin *1. v.* Act performed by a *good time girl* whereby, upon receiving payment but before providing service, she pulls the gentleman's trousers around his ankles and runs off down the alley. From the resemblance of the client's gait to that of the flightless Antarctic bird as he attempts to give chase, much to the amusement of onlookers. *2. n.* The trouser-ankled, cheeks-apart waddle adopted by one who has been surprised after *dropping the kids off at the pool* by a lack of *bumwad.*

penguin's back, as slick as a *sim.* Descriptive of an *otter's pocket. 'Fair was thys yonge nunne, and she was a ryte dirty lasse, hir flappes they dydd frothe like bottild Bass. When the Bishop finnly dydd gette her inn hys sacke, hir twatte itt was slycke as ann pengwynne's backe.'* (from *The Launderette Manager's Tale* by Geoffrey Chaucer).

penguin's nut sack, tighter than a *sim.* Not overly munificent. Also *tighter than*, variously, *a shark's arse, a bullfighter's pants, a teenage wanker's curtains.*

penile dementia *n. medic.* The effect a *panhandle* has on its owner in the company of a *hornbag*, causing him to temporarily forget about his wife and children.

penis *n.* A man's *old man,* a chap's *chap,* a gentleman's *gentleman.* The *veiny bang stick, slag hammer.*

Peniscola *1. n.* Town on the East coast of Spain, famed for its 13th century castle, picturesque old town and sandy beaches. *2. n.* Fizzy *spunk.*

penis de milo *n. medic.* Total debilitating paralysis in both arms, caused by excessive chipping away at one's *stonker.* Named after the famous armless Greek sculpture.

penis fingers *n. Aus.* In a workshop type scenario,

a bloke who "fucks everything he touches". *'Your faulty lawnmower has been serviced by our senior penis fingers, madam.'*

penis fly trap *n.* A precariously balanced toilet seat which stays vertical for a few moments before dropping upon unsuspecting *helmets* in its path. A *knob chopper, willoutine.*

penisn't *n.* A *micro cock, grubscrew* or *gnomon.*

penis pâté *n.* The spreadable *gentlemen's relish* obtained from under the *fiveskin* of a fellow who masturbates frequently and washes slightly less often.

penny dreadful *1. n.* A cheap, third-rate novel picked up when nothing else is available. *2. n.* A cheap, third-rate woman picked up when nothing else is available.

penny farthing *1. n.* An enormous bike, which is somewhat difficult to mount due to its enormous size, though surprisingly easy to ride once you get going. *2. n.* Yes, that's the way this one is going.

penny farthings *n. pl.* A comically mismatched set of breasts. With a man in a top hat bouncing up and down on top of them.

Penny Lane *euph.* The act of favouring a lady with a particularly heavy *load* of *filthy cement.* From the lyrics to the eponymous Beatles song, *viz.* "It's in my ears and in my eyes".

penny stamp *n. rhym. slang.* A happy-go-lucky, nomadic gentleman of the road, who answers to no-one as he takes his carefree pleasures where he may, merrily wandering the highways and byways of the land. *'Aw bloody Nora. A penny stamp's been and left a great big shit on the fucking steps again.' 'Can't you just step over it, your majesty?'*

penockle *n.* The underneath hinge-end of the male member. Where the *shaft* meets the *ball sack,* if you will. *Also a town in Cornwall, probably. 'It's a bit of a delicate matter, nurse. Do you think I could see a man doctor? Only I've got a nasty paper-cut on my penockle.'*

pen pidyn *n.* "Dickhead" in Welsh. When you walk in a pub in Caernarfon and the locals instanta-neously turn to their native lingo, this may be the first thing you hear. For the record, *cunt* and *bastard* are the same in both languages.

Penrith parking ticket *n.* A *shite* left on the windscreen of a vehicle that has been somewhat inconsiderately parked.

pensioner falling downstairs *sim.* Descriptive of the noises made by a series of solid motions hitting the water in quick succession. A *load of old shoes falling out of a loft.*

pensioner's banquet *n.* Free food samples in super-markets, *eg.* Bits of cheese that they've acciden-tally bought in far too much of, wafer-thin ham that's going off *etc.*

pensioner's leg *n.* A thin, pale, knobbly, varicose-veiny penis.

pensioner's tits, as low as a *sim.* Descriptive of something that is lower than one would reasonably expect. *'The ball pitched on middle and off and stayed as low as a pensioner's tits all the way to the stumps. A terrific delivery.'*

pent *n.* The male equivalent of *fent.* What you would smell if you stuck your face into Ian Botham's cricket bag.

pentathlon *1. n.* Athletics competition made up of five separate disciplines which are familiar to the sort of people who do pub quizzes. *2. n.* A marathon sex session involving five separate disciplines that are at best a distant memory to the sort of people who do pub quizzes. *'How do you want to do this then, Rod?' 'Manually, fanually, mammually and anually. Or are you up for a pentathlon, love?'*

people carrier *euph.* A decidedly unerotic, large capacity brassiere which has been designed with dull practicality in mind.

people porridge *n. Heir gel, baby gravy, population paste, pram fat.*

People's Lottery winner *euph.* A person with a *face that would make an onion cry.* From the intriguing observation that it never seems to be supermodels who enter these sorts of competitions.

peperami wrapper *n.* The *fiveskin* or *leg warmer.*

peppermint pig *n.* An unkind epithet for an inferior provincial lap dancing club.

percentage porn *adj.* A gentlemanly situation whereby, having embarked upon an act of *monomanual self-delight,* a fellow realises that the battery percentage left on his phone will not be enough to satisfactorily complete the job in hand.

Percy *1. n. UK.* Penis, especially Robert Plant's penis. *'I'm just off to point Percy at the porcelain.' 2. n.* A small green 0-6-0 saddle tank steam train named after the late Rev W Awdrey's small, green penis. *3. n.* 1971 comedy film about a man who gets a *knob* transplant, written by Robyn Hitchcock's dad.

Percy Thrower's lawn *n.* A *muff* that has been allowed to go to seed for years. A hairy, unkempt *wereminge. Terry Waite's allotment.*

perfect shat-trick *n.* Three quickfire *guffs,* one delivered whilst leaning on the left *arsecheek,* followed by one leaning on the right *arsecheek,* then a final one powered straight down the middle. The sort of swish, snappy and stylish flatulence you would expect from Gene Kelly,

Fred Astaire or Ricky Tomlinson.

perform Alkan's trois etudes op. 76 *1. v.* In the world of classical piano music, to play the three studies written by Charles Valentin Alkan in which the first movement is designated for the left hand alone, the second for the right hand alone, and the climactic finale is achieved with both hands working together. *2. v.* A virtuoso *Sherman* using first the left hand, then the right hand and finally both hands at once.

performing arse *n.* A distressing medical condition brought on by a surfeit of *musical vegetables*, whereby one's *wind section* performs repeated, unbidden, rousing renditions of the *rumpet voluntary*. May be eligible for a grant or possibly the Turner Prize.

perineum falcon *n.* One for whom the *tinter* holds a particular fascination.

perineum, the *n.* The stretch of drab days between Christmas and New Year. So called because they fall between two points of major excitement and activity. See also *taint week, festive perineum, merryneum, twixtmas.*

periniul herbs *n.* The cress which grows in the area between the testicles and the anus. Also known as *barsley, hardy periniuls, chuffodils.*

period costume *n.* Comfortable yet unflattering feminine leisurewear, such as a onesie, fleece or trackie bottoms, worn during *her indoors*'s *visits from Aunt Flo.*

period drama *n.* Moody and erratic behaviour of women at times of menstruation. A *blobstrop, tammy huff, showing off.*

period features *1. n.* Blocked fireplaces, draughty sash windows, warped panelled doors, paint-encrusted decorative mouldings and other sundry desirable architectural bits and pieces which allow thieving estate agents to bump up the prices of houses. *2. n.* In women, short temper, sore nipples, irrational behaviour and a propensity to throw sharp objects violently across the room.

periodic fable *euph.* Any one of the universal dissemblements used by a lady to indefinitely postpone a *scuttle* off her other half, albeit true for approximately four days per lunar month, *eg.* "Not tonight, I've got the painters in," "Not tomorrow night, I'll still have the painters in," and "I know I seem to have had the painters in every night for the last twenty years, but you just don't understand women's things," *etc.*

period pain *1. n. medic.* A dull, cramping ache in the ears and brain of an adult man which recurs regularly every twenty-eight days when the missus is *on the blob. 2. n. medic.* Blue balls.

period property *n.* Reference to any dwelling where the monthly mortgage payments bleed the owners white. *'Fuck me, Kev. This is turning out to be a right period property.'*

periperistalsis *n. medic.* The involuntary motions made by a *ringpiece* when its owner has but lately consumed an excess of spicy Portuguese comestibles.

periscope depth *n.* A particularly low level of bath water that allows a reposing fellow to narcissistically admire his own erect *todgepiece.*

perky blinders *n.* Name given to an extremely large set of *nip-nops* which could possibly have a fellow's eye out. See also *fighter pilots' thumbs, Scammel wheelnuts, pygmies' cocks, chapel hat pegs, duffle coat toggles, blind cobblers' thumbs, JCB starter buttons etc.*

permission to speak, sir *exclam.* A droll preface to an *anal announcement.* See also *if it's up there I'll give you the money myself; and now a quick word from our sponsors; our survey said; the chancellor will now read a short statement; gentlemen, start your engines; back to Davina in the studio.*

perousal *n.* The *frisson* of sexual arousal attained while flicking through a prospective purchase in *Grumbelows.*

perpetual motion *1. n.* Eating whilst sat on the pot *shitting.. 2. n.* A seemingly endless *number two.*

Perry Como *rhym. slang.* An easy-listening *crafty butcher.*

perseverance soup *n.* The tiny tears from the *hog's eye* which precede ejaculation. The clear secretion which lubricates the glans. That which comes out of the kitchen before the main course. *Dew on the lily, ball glaze, guardsman's gloss, knuckle varnish.*

Persian shampoo *n.* The act of *lobbing ropes* into your partner's hair and rubbing it in. Then rinse and repeat.

personal best *n.* A chap's proudest individual achievement; his tally of the greatest number of *wanks* in a day he's ever managed during his life.

personal development *1. phr.* Time allotted for training and education, allotted by employers to help staff in their roles. *2. n.* Time allotted to themselves by the self-employed to go and *crack one off.*

personal drainer *1. n.* A long-standing acquaintance who saps your mental energy. Someone who is a drag but with whom you seem to be lumped for life. *2. n.* One who saps your wallet, such as a wife, ex-wife, child, payday loan company, blackmailer *etc.*

personalities *euph.* Breasts. *Charms, assets, terrible*

497

arthritis. 'My, you've got a lovely pair of personali-ties, my dear. What are they, double-Ds?'

pert alert *n.* Appreciative, radar-like noises emitted by a man as a pair of smashing *top bollocks* comes in and out of range, *viz.* "Pert... pert.. pert. pert pertpertpert pert. pert.. pert... pert" *etc.*

pertfect *adj.* Of *knockers*, spot on *in the French style.*

pertigo *n. medic. psych.* Feeling of mild giddiness, light-headedness or generalised wobbliness experienced by a gentleman who is faced with a neat *tush* in a nightclub, office, at a funeral *etc.*

peruse-a-plop *n.* Game of carefully nudging open public lavatory doors to see which *trap* is the least horrific.

Peruvian num-nums *n.* The involuntary chewing noises emitted while turning over in one's sleep during the early hours of the morning.

pervanaut *n.* An intrepid internet explorer who boldly goes where few have gone before, usually after a can or two of Tennent's.

perveillance *n.* Surreptitiously surveying an area for local *talent. Perveillance* is most effectively carried out while strolling along a beach wearing mirrored sunglasses.

perviators *n.* Tinted eye protection for an observant fellow embarking upon his *summer assessments. Perv windows, lech-tacles, cunglasses.*

perviette *n.* A *chapkin*, as used for mopping up a fellow's sundry spillages.

perv view *n.* The scope of *kinks* in a person's sexual proclivity wheelhouse.

perv windows *n.* Sunglasses.

pescatarian *n.* A *lesbidacious bird*; one who consumes fish but not meat.

pesticles *n.* The *love spuds* of a *sex case.*

petal dick *n.* An amateur drinker who requires the toilet before his fifth pint. A *shandy pants, shandy pandy, peanut bladder.*

Pete feet *n.* Name given to a *bird* who arouses suspicion because of her abnormally proportioned bicrural extremities. Named after *Celebrity Big Brother* contestant, Colobos-monkey-coat-wear-ing, comedy-rubber-lipped, scouse *trolley dolly* and former Dead or Alive front-person Pete Burns, now simply dead. *'I only realised she was a Pete feet after I'd handed me cash over. After you with the anusol there, mate.'*

Peter O'Toole *n. rhym. slang.* A *Thora Hird*. From Peter O'Toole = Andrew Motion.

Peter Parker, a *n. Knocking yourself about a bit* with a pair of *women's scads* pulled down over your face. Named after Spider-Man's photographer alter-ego rather than the late head of British Rail,

one would hope.

Peter two pumps *n.* An inexperienced *swordsman.* A *two push Charlie, two pump chump, two poke joke.*

petit filou *n.* A *hairy yoghurt pot* so small that the *naughty spoon* has trouble getting in. A *mouse's ear, OJ's glove.*

petrol pump *n.* A post-curry *follow through* after which one would be well advised to avoid naked lights. A *ring-stinging* four star *backfire* from a fellow's *tailpipe* that would fail even the most cursory emissions test.

petrol stealer *n.* A woman who sucks like she's syphoning a couple of gallons of four star for her lawnmower.

pet the seal's nose *euph.* To *feed oats* to a moist-snouted *pony.*

petting zoo *n.* A low quality night club where it is nevertheless a racing certainty that you will manage to get your *tops and fingers.*

pezzle *n.* How a Cornish farmer probably refers to his *slag hammer.*

PFF *abbrev.* One who has opted to inject fillers into their face to look "younger". PolyFilla Features.

pfizer riser *n.* A serviceable *stiffy* powered by the eponymous blue *banjo pills.*

PFO *abbrev.* A diplomatically worded rejection letter from a prospective employer that is intended to spare the feelings of an unsuccess-ful job candidate. A typical *PFO* contains such phrases as "the standard of applicants was par-ticularly high" while making clear its somewhat blunter subtext, *viz.* "Please Fuck Off".

PFS *abbrev.* The magical peristaltic timing device that kicks in two minutes after getting home from a long weekend at an *al fresco* musical event, allowing one to finally move one's *Simon Cowells* and offload three days' build-up of *Loretta.* Post Festival Shit.

PG tits *1. n.* Comically conical brassieres of the sort worn by Madonna, which give the impression that the wearer has two pyramids growing out of their chest. *Witches' hats. 2. n.* Television "erotic movies" that are more-or-less suitable for family viewing or *Screen Test. 3. n.* A tannin-rich hot beverage alternative to an *oomlatte.*

phalactites *n.* Artex-style crust on a teenager's bedroom ceiling.

phallicopter, the *n.* A rotational exhibition of genital gymnastics (that looks more like a windowbox strimmer) performed upon his *chopper* by a gentleman in a vain attempt to impress his ladyfriend.

phallic thimble *n.* A gentleman's perfectly

respectable *endowment* that falls short of the overly-demanding standards set by *bucket-fannied* women.

phallitosis *n. medic.* Post-*horatio* breath.

phallucy *n.* Any statement made by a man about the size of his *third leg*, eg. In the readers' letters page of a *grumble book* or a small ad in a *greet & meat* mag.

phallusophical *adj.* Thinking a lot about *cocks.*

phallustrade *n.* An ornamental picketline of rigid *phalli*, such as might be seen in the opening scene of a particularly imbalanced *grumble flick.*

phantom farter *n.* An anonymous *benefactor.*

phantom load *1. n.* Mysterious electrical discharge into a device that is switched off; hence, your power is drained without providing its proper function. *2. n.* An apparently copious *drop of yop* of which there is, inexplicably, no sign when you have a look.

phantom menace *1. n.* After going into *arse labour*, rushing into the *crapper*, frantically dropping one's *trolleys* and sitting down, the disappointing package of noisome gas which emerges in place of a *turd. 2. n.* Fourth, that is to say first, installment in the *Star Wars* movie series, not to be confused with *A New Hope*, which was the actual first, that is to say fourth. *3. n.* A *ghost shit* that leaves you gasping for breath as if you were being strangled by the invisible hand of a Sith Lord.

phantom of the opera *n.* Appearance of a *stick flick* actress after her co-star has *crashed his yoghurt truck* copiously down the side of her face.

pharoah's tomb *1. sim.* Descriptive of a post-argument atmosphere. *2. rhym. slang.* The spare room.

phartoshop *n.* Airbrushing tool which applies diffuse ochre hues to the *underkegs* gusset at approximately 5% opacity. *'I like your wind sketch, dad.' 'Yeah, I did it in phartoshop.'*

phat *adj.* A modern "street" term used to denote excellence. Also *bad, badass, kickass. 'Shnizzle my pizzle, vicar, this new Flemish double manual harpsichord of yours is bare phat.'*

PhD *1. abbrev.* Pretty hard Dick. *'Where's Brian?' 'He's working on his PhD.' 2. acronym.* Pre-Hump Dump. A thoughtful concession to the olfactory sensitivities of one's romantic partner prior to embarking on a bout of *salami concealment.* Unless you fancy a bit of *German. 'Make sure you have a good PHD tonight, Gordon. Four hours of them guffs last night was enough to gag a maggot.' 'Okay, our Trudie. I'll even lay off the stout.'*

pheromone fart *n.* An *air biscuit* sneakily released at one's desk that, despite a total absence of women in the vicinity for the preceding 3 hours of the working day, appears to have a more instant summoning effect on the fairer sex than a gallon of *slagbait. The stynx effect.*

philanthrapist *n.* A *sex case* who raises a lot of money for charity in his spare time. From philanth + rapist.

philanthropissed *adj.* Drunk on someone else's money.

Phil Collins *1. euph.* An act of genital copulation committed without the use of a *jubber ray*, that is to say *bareback.* From the title of the erstwhile Genesis drummer's 1985 album *No Jacket Required. 2. n. prop. Making the bald man cry*, that is to say when one "can feel it, coming in the air tonight".

Phil Lynott's shoulders, like she's sitting on *sim.* Description of a notably impressive *biffer. 'Amongst the preparations which are being made for the big day, Kate is understood to be planning to undergo a Brazilian wax. According to Palace sources, after spending a year living on a remote air base in rural north Wales it's like Miss Middleton is sitting on Phil Lynott's shoulders down there. Nicholas Witchell, for BBC News, at Westminster Abbey.'*

Philly willy *n. medic.* A *todger* with a tasty nob of creamy cheese under the brim. And occasionally a bit of chocolate too.

philosopher's stone *n.* A *pebble* that emerges after a couple of hours' intense concentration.

phlegm brûlée *n.* A particularly creamy *docker's omelette* with a hard crust. Usually hocked up during a hangover.

phlegm fatale *n. medic.* The deadly affliction of man flu.

phlergm *n.* The frankly unpleasant, mucilaginous suspension of *cock hockle* and *black prairie oysters* coughed up by a thirty-fag-a-day *knob chomper.*

phloph *n. onomat.* The awful sound of a pair of heavily *beshitted scads* hitting the floor. In German it would have that two dot diacritical umlaut thingy over the "o", but we don't know where you find an on the keyboard and we're not looking it up. It was bad enough finding the circumflex and acute accents for *phlegm brûlée.*

phone ahead, a *n.* A *stool* of such volume and viscosity that one has a civic duty to call the water board to advise of its imminent arrival in order that they may make the necessary arrangements at the sewerage treatment works. *'Sorry treacle, I'll just be a moment. That was a phone ahead, so I'll just give Thames Water a quick bell and we'll be on our way.'*

phoney batter *n.* KY jelly. Also *I can't believe it's* *not batter, granny batter, fuck butter, pork pie jelly.*

phoney soprano *n.* One who has watched the eponymous New Jersey-based organised crime drama too many times and, as a result, believes himself to be a leading character thereof, despite actually working in Cash Converters, sellotaping the front covers of tattered, second-hand CDs back together.

phonography *n.* The sort of saucy mobile telephone video-clips which are popular with skint, squniting, *one-handed texters*.

photo dump *1. n.* A randomly assorted group of photos posted on social media. *2. n.* The act of peeking at grumble pics whilst on the jobby engine. Also *brownloading*. *3 n.* German erotica.

photo finish *1. n.* A session of *horizontal jogging* in which both contestants break the tape at the same time. Also *dead heat*. *2. n.* The frantic action of trying to leaf through your *jazz mag* to find your *finisher* when you're at the *point of no return*, desperately trying not to accidentally *spunk up* over an article about vintage cars.

photon torpedo *n.* *Star Trek* convention terminology for a *Tom tit* expelled with such force that it completely wipes out any *kling-ons* in the area.

photoshop it *phr.* The art of cleaning three day old *skidders* off the toilet bowl with one's bare hands, so called because it requires "creative use of a thumbnail". *'That shit's been on the side of the toilet for three days now, put some bleach down, will you?' 'It's alright love, I'll just photoshop it.'*

phuq *n. & v.* Ingenious alternative to the word *fuck* which, while remaining perfectly comprehensible, is able to evade the attentions of over-solicitous business e-mail censoring systems.

phwoarberries *n.* Big, ripe, juicy *tits*. With cream all over them. Breasts which, even when covered up, elicit a strangulated cry of "phwoar!" in the style of Kenneth Connor spotting Joan Sims in the shower in *Carry On Up the Jungle*.

phwoar games *n.* Hacking the security settings on the household PC in order to access a bit of *jazz*.

phwoar memorial *n.* An impressive erection produced as a result of a *trip down mammary lane.*

phwoartodidact *1. n.* A cultured man who has educated himself solely by watching documentaries presented by TV *hog's eye candy* such as bible boffin Dr Francesca Stavrakopoulou, classics crumpet Bettany Hughes or history hottie Dr Lucy Worsley. *2. n.* Likewise, a cultured woman who has educated herself solely by watching documentaries presented by TV hunks such as sexy scientist Dr Jacob Bronowski, raunchy royalist Dr

David Starkey or erotic egghead James Burke.

phyxasorbum *n. pharm.* A gentle gel for the relief of haemorrhoids, applied by a finger onto the affected area.

piabetic *n. medic.* A larger-boned fellow who risks falling into a coma if not kept regularly supplied with pastry-based products.

piano shifter *n.* Affectionate term for a woman with a *lovely personality, eg.* Shirley out of *EastEnders*.

Picasso arse *n.* A lady's *chuff* in knickers so tight that she appears to have four buttocks.

Picasso face *n.* Descriptive of a maiden who is certainly no oil painting.

Piccadilly advent calendar *n.* The hidden, surprising scenes revealed behind the semi-lockable doors in the lavatories at the eponymous Manchester terminus, *eg.* A middle-aged businessman engaged in a monomanual act of *self delight*, a *Harold Ramp* indulging in heroin or a spot of light *cottaging*.

pick a buttercup *v.* To *lift the latch*. *'Ew. Someone's just picked a buttercup.'*

pick-axe wound *n.* A bloodied rectum.

picket line copper *n.* The front man in a *bum chain*. From the way he is jostled about from behind, and has to hold onto his hat to stop it falling off, one would imagine.

picking the seam *1. n.* In cricket, the illegal activity whereby a fielder lifts the stitching on the ball in order to give his side an unfair advantage over their opponents. *2. n.* Thumb and forefinger method of relieving an itch present in a gentleman's *chicken skin handbag. Ball tampering.*

pick it up and run with it *1. exclam.* Desperate expression commonly used by ex-public school *rugger buggers* who have screwed up their lives by becoming media sales managers. *2. v.* To *cop off* with a *right howler* and get her out of the nightclub before any of your mates see her.

pickle bricks, that would *exclam.* A sentiment of muffled disdain offered in response to a sulphurous *arse cough. 'Sorry Philip, that'll be the swan's eggs.' 'Jesus Christ, Liz. That one'd pickle bricks.'*

pickle factory *1. n.* That which Eli and Nellie Pledge inherited in erstwhile situation comedy *Nearest and Dearest*. One for the youngsters. *2. n.* A problematic mate who is always getting you drawn into difficult situations.

pickle tray *1. n.* An appetiser taken before an Indian meal, eaten with popadoms, while you decide what to have for starters, main course, and something nice to finish off with. *2. n. Cloth tit, outside tops, inside tops and fingers.* But not *your* hole. *'How did you get on with Big Marge from Accounts?' 'She's frigid, that one. I didn't get past the pickle tray.'*

pickling the clam *euph.* Of a lady, *pissing* her *scads* and continuing to wear them. Very popular at festivals.

pick up the kids *v.* Upon encountering a faulty lavatory flush after *dropping the kids off at the pool*, to be forced into fishing them out of the water and improvising an alternative means of hygienic disposal. *'It was cheese and wine night at Dave and Sam's on Saturday. Half way through I nipped off to the crapper for a proper turn-out but I think the ball-cock was buggered because I couldn't get it to flush. In the end I had to pick up the kids and lob them out the first floor window.'*

picture but no sound *euph.* Descriptive of the wife's mood when one rolls in from the pub as *refreshed as a newt* with one's *earlids* pulled firmly down.

piddle *1. v.* To *pee. 2. n.* Some *pee.*

piddle paddle *n.* An unconvincing and unathletic "quick dip in the ocean" taken while at the seaside, where one ventures in only waist deep and emerges shortly thereafter with a refreshingly empty bladder. A *seawee.*

piddling pool *n.* Shallow body of water where small children can happily play for hours without, for some strange reason, demanding the toilet every five minutes.

pie & drive *phr.* A useful phrase when describing the hasty purchase and consumption of a hango-ver-killing pastie on the way to work the morning after a heavy night's drinking. *'You look like shit, love. Are you sure you'll be alright for work? You've got a dozen cataract operations to do today, remember.' 'I'll be cool. I'll just pie & drive.'*

pie and mighty *euph.* Any shop that caters exclusively for *bubbly* folk.

pie and pee supper *euph.* The joyfully Germanic sexploits of a fellow who takes pleasure in both *brown & golden showers. A biscuit and a cup of tea.*

piebald *1. adj.* Of a horse, white with black patches. *2. adj.* Of a lady, in possession of an exceptionally well-manicured *front lawn.*

piebery *n.* Corrupt practice of giving or accepting a pie in return for favours.

pie blight *n. Muff druff.*

piebrid *adj.* or *n.* Descriptive of someone who is no longer svelte, but has yet to become a fully qualified *plumper.* Mildly overweight.

piece of piss *n.* An easy thing. *'Hey, this show jumping thing is a piece of piss.'* (Christopher Reeve), *'Hey, adjusting television aerials is a piece of piss.'* (Rod Hull), *'Hey, fighting stingrays is a piece of piss.'* (Steve Irwin).

pieceps *n.* Bulging stomach muscles of the sort made famous by former Everton goalkeeper Neville Southall.

pie chart *1. n.* A circular diagram divided into sectors, the various sizes of which represent different quantities or amounts of pie. *2. n.* The centrefold pages of a gentleman's *artistic periodical.*

pie chomper's chariot *n.* An electric shopping scooter for the wantonly immobile. A *Holland-on-Sea hotrod.*

pie crust *n.* A crunchy topping on a stale *slice.* See *femme brûlée.*

pie curious *adj.* Descriptive of a person who, while not a full blown *Duke of Giblets,* is nevertheless not averse to a spot of sly *salad-dodging* from time to time.

pie-das touch *n.* A mythical curse on the *big-ger-boned,* causing anything they touch to turn to pastry.

pie dish *n.* A *bird* whom, notwithstanding her corpulence, remains sexually alluring to men, *eg.* One of them models in the plus-size *titpants* catalogue.

pied pooper *n.* A person who whistles a tune in order to charm out a particularly recalcitrant and troublesome *rat's nose.*

piedrated *adj.* Descriptive of one who has evidently had some success *dodging salads. 'Fuck me, your missus has put some right timber on. Is she eating for two?' 'No. She just likes to keep herself well piedrated.'*

pied up *adj.* Said of a person who has visibly *relaxed their fitness regime. 'Gosh, I've not seen you since your wedding. You've really pied up since then.'*

pie-eyed *adj.* What a *salad dodger* becomes at the point on his daily *porker's pilgrimage* when he rounds the corner and comes within spotting distance of his local high street bakery. *Greggcited.*

pie floater *1. n.* A weird Australian dish of a pie submerged in pea soup. Often eaten in the street by people with corks dangling off their hats. *2. n.* A tasty sweetmeat swimming in a surprisingly savoury sauce. The *wail switch, devil's doorbell* or *clematis.* Which is also often eaten by Australians in the street.

pie-hider *n.* A *gunt, bilge tank, muff pelmet.* The kind of overhanging gut that allows a lady to strip from the waist down while still retaining her modesty.

pie-lates *n.* Repetitive, ruminatory jaw exercises performed by those who harbour an antipathetic attitude towards cotyledonous vegetation.

pie-liner *n.* A femidom.

pieman's wig *1. n.* An artificial hairpiece worn by a purveyor of pastry-enveloped foodstuffs. *2. n.* An untidy *cunt-rug*.

pie-noceros *n.* See *chippopotamus*.

pie-Q *n.* A test of one's ability to purchase the maximum possible density of savoury baked products using the small change available in the pockets of one's jogging trousers.

pierexia *n. medic.* An elevation in a *salad dodger's* body temperature brought on by the excitement of an imminent opportunity to stuff his or her face.

Pierrepoint's rope, hung more than *sim.* Said of a gent who sports a proper *cuntbuster*. From the occupational cordage of erstwhile Mancunian publican and executioner Albert who, during his illustrious career, dispatched more than six hundred souls, a good number of whom may have actually been guilty.

Piers Morgan *n. rhym. slang.* An ineffectual *cock*. From the name of former *Daily Mirror* editor and utter *organ* Piers Morgan = ineffectual cock.

piesexual *adj.* Of a fellow with a romantic penchant for the more voluminously skeletonned lady.

pie shifter *n.* A *plumper* who can single-handedly clear the Ginster's display in their local petrol station.

pie shy, not *euph* Said of one who may be intimidated by salad. *'Judging by her fat arse, she's definitely not pie shy, your honour.'*

piet *n.* The staple dietary regime espoused by those with a marked penchant for pastries. *'I'm on a strict piet. In fact, I'm just off down the Pound Bakery for me five-a-day. You're welcome to walk alongside my shopping scooter if you like.'*

pig at a tatty, going at it like a *sim. Yorks.* To perform an act of oral pleasure with uninhibited gusto in Yorkshire. *'"Eeh, by gum, Cathy lass. Slow tha' sen dahn a bit", said Heathcliffe. '"Appen tha's going at it like a pig at a tatty."'* (from *Wuthering Heights* by Charlotte Brontë).

pig at the gate *euph.* A mole at the counter, Mr Brown at the window, a brown dog scratching at the back door.

pig bite *n.* A poetic term for the vagina. *'A daughter of the Gods, divinely tall / And with a pig bite like a horse's collar.'* (from *A Dream of Fair Women* by Alfred Lord Tennyson).

pigboard *n.* The rear wall of a metropolitan phonebox.

pigbox *n.* A Nissan Micra full of rough women, driving round a provincial town playing Destiny's Child and hunting for *cock*.

pigeon's breakfast *n.* Some sick. A *pavement pizza, roadside risotto, Scotch pancake*.

pigeon's chest *n.* The female swimsuit *lunchbox* standing proud. The *beetle bonnet, shark's fin*.

pig farmer's aftershave, stronger than a *sim.* See *Gemma Collins's knicker elastic*.

pig fart *n.* The erotic sound a *bit of crackling's* intimate parts may occasionally make while she is in the process of getting a good *stuffing*. A *queef.* See *screwly trumptious*.

piggy in the Lidl *n.* An *aldilicious* or *Netto fabulous* female of debatable exquisiteness who one might observe perusing the processed foodstuffs in the aisles of the popular budget supermarket.

piggy payback *n.* The momentary, vengeful blast of foetid *guff* that hits you in the face when opening a packet of wafer thin ham.

piggy style *n. Doggy style* but with more grunting, bristles and silage.

pig in a blanket *1. n.* A sausage wrapped in bacon. *2. n.* Affectionate term describing a woman *with a lovely personality* that a horrified chap wakes up next to after a night *on the lash. Hit and run. 3. n.* A man's – rarely appetising – *significant other*.

pig jizz *n.* The white stuff that collects in the pan after frying up some porky rashers. *'I was a vegetarian for twenty years, but in the end I just couldn't resist the lure of hot pig jizz.'*

pigpenning *n.* Sitting surrounded by – and stewing in – your own filthy, foetid smells because you simply can't be *arsed* to get up and move to safety. Named after the character in the long-running *Peanuts* cartoon strip who was constantly enveloped in a cloud of his own scribbled flatus.

pig's ears *n.* Bristly *gammon flaps* busting out around the gusset. *'An embarrassing exposure: while negotiating the low-slung running boards of her husband's Fraser-Nash landaulette outside the Café Royal, the Countess of Arbroath suffered an inadvertent mishap, whereby she unwittingly displayed an immodest prospect up her underskirts to the assembled photographers, one of whom managed to secure this surreptitious perspective wherein her pig's ears are clearly visible.'* (from the *Tatler & Bystander*, June 1926).

pigs in blankets *n. Bobbers* that have been lovingly covered with a sheet of *bumwad* to avoid embarrassment when the next *bogger* calls.

pigsticking *1. n.* Boar-hunting from horseback, using spears. A fine sport for lads. *2. n.* Going *on the pull* without any great expectations.

pig's tits *n. rhym. slang.* The *shits*. *'After you've been to the rub a dub, climb the apples and pears* to the Curry Capital, Bigg Market, Newcastle upon Tyne, for a Ruby Murray that will give you the pig's tits, or your money back.' (Advert in *Country Life* magazine).

pig's tits, fingers like *sim.* Said of a person who tends to operate their digits in a clumsy fashion. Examples of which could be Donald Trump typing "covfefe" rather than whatever the fuck he was trying to write, or King Charles trying to sign his name on his King application form and getting ink all over his sausages, and then blaming the pen.

pig's toe *n. The pig's trotter.*

pig's trotter, the *euph.* Prominent and well-defined labial *moundage* which is visible through a lady's leggings. A phenomenon also sometimes referred to as a *camel's foot, twix lips* or *knicker sausages. 'You'd best sit behind the desk to read the news tonight, Kirsty. You've got a right pig's trotter in them kecks.'*

PIK/pik *abbrev.* Pig In Knickers. An extremely unattractive, fleshly woman.

pile high club *1. n.* The notional society of fellows who have distinguished themselves by *pappering their trolleys* while seated. *2. n.* Exclusive brotherhood of those who have earned their *brown wings. 3. n.* Those who attend a free wedding buffet and wilfully abuse their hosts' generosity to the maximum. *4. n.* The not-particularly elite brotherhood of people who have had haemorrhoids in an aeroplane toilet.

pile of dead fannies, smells like a *sim.* Descriptive of something which gives off a foul, fishy odour. *'Bloody hell, Dr Von Hagens. What have you got in your garage? It smells like a pile of dead fannies.' 'It's a pile of dead fannies, mein dear chap.'*

PILF/pilf *1. acronym.* An alluringly glamorous female television personality. Presenter I'd Like to Fuck, and more explicitly *2. acronym.* An unpleasantly sexist reference to the sort of pulchritudinous academics who they get to present learned television documentraies these days. Professor I'd Like to Fuck.

pilgriminge *n.* An uncomfortably priapismic journey made by a man engaged in a long distance relationship.

pilgrim's pocket *n.* An exceptionally dry *clout. 'Edwina was powerless to resist. John's eyes burned into hers like semi-precious lapis lazulis. His strong arms enfolded her body as she felt herself being swept away on a mistral of passion. She gasped as she felt his powerful, but gentle fingers teasing at the moist flower of her secret sanctum. "Fuck me, your minge is sopping," he exclaimed. "Norma's*

twat's always dry as a pilgrim's pocket.'" (from *The Junior Health Minister and The Chief Whip,* by Barbara Cartland).

pillar to post, go from *v.* To dismount from one (typically smaller) *cock* in order to take a ride on another (typically larger) *cock.*

pillicock *n. arch.* A *tummy banana.*

pillock *n.* Possibly derived from *pillicock,* a tame, TV sitcom-friendly insult. *'Trigger, you fucking pillock.'*

pillow biter *n.* A *mattress muncher, feather spitter.*

pillow mint *1. n.* Small, inexpensive chocolate treat left on a guest's bed in better hotels in order to create the illusion that customer satisfaction is of the slightest importance to a management that would charge you £12 for a small bag of nuts that would cost 45p from the 24-hour garage round the corner. *2. n.* A hefty *feeshus* left in the *pan* with the express intention of offending the next occupant of the *shithouse.*

pills *n. Pods, knackers, niags.*

pilot drill *n.* A lesser-endowed professional footballer who is recruited to broach a blonde woman before his more impressively *tooled* team-mate steps in, in the style of an engineer who might utilise a smaller bit to assist with the boring of a larger hole in a piece of metal, for example. Charming.

pilot error *n.* A misjudged *joystick* move that causes an immediate tailspin.

pilot light *n.* An ex-socialite now restrained by the *pink handcuffs, ie.* One who "never goes out".

pilot's poke *n.* An emergency jettison of surplus fuel. *Roger and out.*

pilot the submarine *v.* To urinate nocturnally while too refreshed to find the light switch in the bathroom, thus being forced to direct one's stream solely by the sound it makes upon impact with the water/carpet/walls/dog/wardrobe/your feet. *Pissing by sonar.*

Pimm's limbs *n. medic.* Temporary lower body dysfunction typically suffered by attendees at the Henley Regatta, Lady's Day at Ascot *etc.,* causing sufferers to fall over and flash their *foo-foos* within telephoto range of a ravenous gaggle of amoral upskirt *smudgers* working for tabloid newspapers.

pimpleton *n.* A youthful *joskin* endowed with a surfeit of acne. Often to be seen driving his mother's Nissan Micra in a discourteous and aggressive manner while wearing a baseball cap.

pimp my ride *1. n.* Television programme in which knackered old bangers were given a new lease of life. *'Please, MTV, pimp my ride.' 2. v.* Surgical programme in which *knackered* old *bangers* are given a new lease of life. *'Please, doctor, pimp my ride. Paying special attention to her saggy tits, triple chin, beergut and flabby arse.'*

pinballing *v.* To make progress home from the *boozer* by a series of ricochets from one item of street furniture to the next. Accompanied by the ringing of bells and clunking noises.

pinball wizard *euph.* A chronic *self abuser*. From the libretto to the famous rock opera by the Who, *viz.* "He's a pinball wizard / There has to be a twist / A pinball wizard's / got such a supple wrist." One who has *relaxed in a gentleman's way* to such an extent that he is deaf, dumb and blind.

pinch a loaf *v.* To *curl one off.*

pinch and milk *n. Hand job* technique used by experienced masseuses to quickly bring matters to a *happy ending,* involving squeezing the penile base hard to increase blood flow while gently applying friction to the *bishop's hat.*

pinch of snuff *n. rhym. slang.* A *crafty butcher.*

pincushion *n.* A woman of *easy virtue. 'I've heard she was a bit of a pincushion, your holiness, notwithstanding all her good works in Calcutta.'*

pineapple *n. rhym. slang.* Something Giles Coren gets on his pizzas whether he wants it or not. From pineapple chunk = spunk.

pineapple rings *n.* Inverted *nip-nops* on a pair of *stits.*

Pingu having a tantrum, like *sim.* Descriptive of the sounds a bloke's sorry *arse* makes on a Sunday morning following a particularly vicious curry and ten pints of Theakston's Old Peculier on the Saturday night.

Pingu's walk *euph. onomat.* The noise of a gentleman enjoying some *alone time,* reminiscent of the slapping sound of the eponymous fictional penguin's flippers on the tundra.

pinhole *n.* A *Mary* that makes a *mouse's ear* look like a *hippo's mouth.*

pink *v.* Of a lady, to make a *fanny slug* on a window for the amusement and edification of passers by.

pink admiral *n. Spam butterfly.*

pink bat's face *n.* A nocturnal, high-pitched *spam butterfly* that eats *meat moths* for breakfast.

pink berets *n.* Large, flat breasts with stiff *nips.*

pink breathalyser *n.* The alternative drink-driving test offered to inebriated lady motorists by the more resourceful *scuffer. 'Could I ask you to blow into this pink breathalyser please, madam? I'll tell you when to stop.'*

pink cigar *n.* The *sex pipe.* Not to be confused with *bum cigar,* except in Germany. *'Tell me madam, do you perchance smoke the pink cigar?'*

pink Darth Vader *n. Knob.* From the wheezing *Star Wars* character with a *bell end* helmet.

pink floyd *1. euph.* A long and unnecessarily self-indulgent *solo* that takes ages to get going. See also *shandy tickler. 2. euph.* The act of entering the dark side of a lady's *moon. 'Fedora was powerless to resist. His eyes burned into hers like diamonites. His strong arms enfolded her body as she felt herself being swept away on a 930 millibar sea surge of passion. Suddenly, she felt Jalfrezi's hot breath on her cheek as he whispered in her ear. "Can I put Pink Floyd on tonight, love?" he asked. 'Alright then,' she replied. 'But only if you promise not to play any of your shit prog rock records while your cock's up my arse.'"* (from *The Woman Named After a Type of Hat and the Man Named After a Chicken Dish* by Barbara Cartland).

pink horror *1. n.* A daemonic character from the Warhammer fantasy universe. *2. n.* A rather unsightly *Readers' Wives*-style female *part* that's not unlike a *punched lasagne.* Also *bottom of a ratcatcher's mallet, stamped bat, kicked over trifle.*

pinkle *n.* A *minkle* that's been shaved within a millimetre of its life.

pink mist *n.* The priapismic haze that descends to cloud a man's better judgement. Also *penile dementia. 'Well, at the end of the day, Brian, I just seen Wayne's bird over there and the pink mist came down, basically.'*

pink oboe *n. Bed flute. 'Tell me madam, do you perchance play the pink oboe?'*

pink pillows *n.* Ladies' *fun cushions,* bosoms, *dirty pillows, cajooblies. 'Hello, is that reception? Could you send four pink pillows up to room 273 please?'*

pink pitta breads *n.* Elderly women's *jugs* that appear deflated like a burst tyre.

pink shit, have a *v.* The end of a romantic evening of *back door work.* The termination of the process of anal intercourse.

pinksmith *n.* One who is expert in *fannycraft.* A *crumpeteer, stickman, quim hopper.*

pink sock *n. medic.* Correct medical terminology for a catastrophic rectal prolapse or *arse tulip. 'And now this giant Icelander just has the final Atlas Ball to lift into place to take the title of World's Strongest Man … but what's this? I think he's pulling up. Something's wrong. He's not happy. He's not happy at all. He's pulling up and he's making the signal that he's got the pink sock.'*

pink steel *n.* Even harder than *wood.* Material used to forge *diamond cutters.*

pink, the *n.* A really good eyeful of the *Predator's face, esp.* in a *meat mag* or anatomical textbook. See *close-up pink.*

pink ticket *n.* Imaginary *vadge* visa issued to a

husband when he spends the night apart from his wife. *'Eureka! I've got my pink ticket for the conference on Tuesday.'*

pink velvet sausage wallet *n.* Short for *quim.*

pink wafer *n.* A *blurtch* which resolutely refuses to exude *fanny batter* even after being lovingly coerced for up to nearly several minutes by an attentive lover.

pink windmill *euph.* A *ménage a trois* with a couple of *filfs.*

pinot grigio pashmina *n.* Like a *bacardigan,* but for posh *birds* in Wilmslow or Alderley Edge; a warm yet invisible shawl consisting of several glasses of white wine.

pint glass figure *n.* Like an hour-glass figure, but with very little narrowing in the middle and some dimples.

pintle *n.* Olde Worlde *chopper. Pipe cleaner, pizzle.*

pint of Courage Tavern Ale, a *euph.* An act of *auto-erotic delight.* From the erstwhile beer advert slogan, *viz.* "It's what your right arm's for".

pint of mince *euph. Scots.* Any calorie-infused alcoholic beverage (Heavy, 80 Shilling, Guinness etc.) *'Bacardi and Coke, a Fruit Shoot and a pint of mince, barman! And a bag of Quavers for the dog.'*

pint of no return *euph.* The tipping point that takes a fellow from a state of jovial inebriation to being downright *wankered;* the drinking milestone passed by a fellow who has "just popped out for a couple", after which he becomes physically unable to moderate his alcohol intake; usually about his fourth pint. *'Oates got up, saying, "My dear friends, my time on this pub crawl expedition must come to an end. I have reached the pint of no return. I am going out now, I may be some time." And with that he staggered away into the night, looking for a shop doorway to have a piss in. That brave fellow made the supreme sacrifice so that we, the final few, may journey on.'* from *The Journals of Robert Falcon Scott* (Volume 3: the 1908 Swindon Stag-Do Expedition).

pint of prawns *n.* A gaping *quimpiece* that appears to contain more *seafood* than is anatomically possible. See also *pelican's yawn.*

pip *n.* An upper class *gut* of the kind one might imagine Penelope Keith *dropping.* A *top hat dropped forward.*

pipe *1. n. Fr.* An act of oral love. A *nosh, chewie, blow-job. 2. n. Cock.* From the old St. Bruno advertising slogan, *viz.* "Live in peace with your pipe". *3. n.* Pringles container.

pipe bomb *n.* An explosive *shit* that goes off without warning in the *pan,* causing massive collateral damage.

pipecleaner *1. n.* Furry wire used by children to make models in playschool. *2. n.* The first *piss* taken after committing an act of *self-pollution* or a *fuck. 3. n.* A *blood sausage.*

pipe dream *1. n.* An erotic reverie that causes a chap to wake up with a *pocket battleship* in his jim-jams. *2. n.* The often elaborately detailed and fanciful reveries a fellow conjures up in his imagination while contemplatively fingering his *skin flute.*

pipeline, something in the *1. phr.* What a showbiz person, *eg.* Richard Blackwood, might say when asked about the latest exciting developments in their career. *2. phr.* An expression of a person's imminent need for a *shit, eg.* Richard Blackwood on *Celebrity Colonic Irrigation Live.*

pipe of peace, smoke the *v.* Of a woman, to *do the decent thing* following an argument with her significant other.

piper at the gates of dawn *1. n.* An early Pink Floyd album. *2. n.* An early morning *turtle's head. Cock-a-doodle-poo.*

piper at the gates of porn *n.* The anticipatory semi-erection achieved involuntarily by a chap entering a newsagent with the intention of purchasing a *rhythm pamphlet.*

pipe smoker *1. n. US.* A bloke who *takes his time shopping. 2. n.* A person who smokes a pipe, *eg.* Fontella Bass, whose single *Rescue Me* peaked at number eleven in the UK charts in 1965.

piping *1. n.* The use of an icing bag to decorate cakes, as shown on the *Great British Bake Off. 2. n.* The act of *oral horatio. 'It's a great bake, love, but now get down there and show us what your piping skills are like.'*

piping in the haggis *1. n.* Traditional supper ceremony on Burns night. *2. n. Thumbing it in* after a surfeit of Scotch. *'Hold still, Morag. I'm piping in the haggis.'*

piping out the haggis *n.* Severe, discordant flatulence caused by the consumption of Scotland's finest offal-based comestible.

Pippa! *exclam.* A gentleman's howl of anguish emitted upon meeting his girlfriend's sister and immediately realising he has chosen in error.

Pippa pipe *n.* The *bonus tunnel. 'I took out Janice from the chippy last night. Only got as far as the bus shelter and she was begging me to do her up the Pippa pipe, the dirty cow.'*

pips have gone, the *exclam.* Inevitable situation that brings about a swift conclusion to a telephonic *booty call. 'Sorry love, got to go. The pips have gone.'*

PIP stick *n.* Variant of *dole pole,* required by

able-bodied persons when attending medical assessments for Personal Independence Payments. See also *social sticks.*

pipsy *n.* The penile *nipsy*, the *herring's eye* or meatus.

pirate *n.* A *breastitute* lady, *ie.* One with a "sunken chest".

pirate of men's pants *n.* A swashbuckling *jolly Roger.*

pirate's eye-patch *n.* A small, dark clump of neatly trimmed pubic hair in a lady's longjohns.

pirate's piss *n.* The *piss* you have with one eye shut to improve targetting after a long night *on the pop.*

pired *adj.* Tired after eating too many pies. *'Unfortunately, Eric Pickles is unable to join us on Question Time tonight, as he is apparently extremely pired.'*

Pires penalty *n.* An unsatisfying and embarrassing *dribble* instead of a *shot* which hits the *back of the net.* A *money shot* that's down to its last couple of coppers; a *gwibble.*

pishap *n.* A minor urination-related mishap, such as carelessly splashing one's shoes, dribbling a dewdrop down the front of one's tweeds or accidentally catching one's penis while removing it from an annoying neighbour's letterbox.

pish-planing *n. Scots.* Form of aqua-planing caused by entering the pub gents too quickly while wearing leather-soled brogues.

pisplaced *adj.* Descriptive of an item or items temporarily lost as a result of placing them in a safe place following a night *on the pop.*

piss *1. v.* To urinate. *2. n.* Some urine. *3. adv.* Extremely. *'That driving test was piss easy'. 'Your three-point turn was piss poor.'*

pissabled *adj.* A state of drunken infirmity whereby one is unable to walk upstairs, park one's car properly *etc.* Also *shandycapped.*

pissala *n.* A *slash* taken the day after a *cuzza*, where one's urine reeks charmingly of chicken tikka masala.

piss bib *n.* See *piss catcher.*

piss bliss *n.* The moment just before a long-awaited *scoot*, when a gentleman keeps it in for a couple of seconds longer, primarily for a cheap thrill when there's nothing to lose.

pisscalator *n.* Any stairway in a multi-storey car park that once ascends three times as fast as one would ordinarily, on account of the fact that it reeks of stale *wazz*. So that's every stairway in a multi-storey car park, then.

piss can alley *n.* A quorum of light-hearted *Harold Ramps* who convoke in the doorway of a shop or disused railway cutting.

piss catcher *n.* The absorbent, magnet-shaped furry rug which was installed around the plinth of many a typical home lavatory during the 1970s. Also known as a *pan smile* or, after it had been in place for a few months, the *Queen Mum's grin.*

piss catchers *n.* Piebald suede shoes worn by men standing at pub urinals. *Flush puppies. 'Alfonso is wearing a dayglo fringed bolero jacket by Monsieur Baguette at Debenhams (£578), PVC gimp vest by Trampant Sexcase (£2,350), calf-length pedal pushers from the Titchmarsh Collection at Milletts (£4.99) and bespoke nubuck piss catchers by Ffitzmaurice & Chocmonocley of Bond Street (£395.95).'*

piss chase *1. n.* Excuse for an *ad hoc* pub crawl, especially during cold weather. A game of *piss chase* involves going into a pub for a much needed *wazz*, and while there feeling morally obliged to have a pint. This results in one again being in urgent need of the lavatory a quarter of a mile further down the high street, and so on and so forth until closing time. Or indeed until death from old age, now that the pubs never shut. *2. n.* Popular playground game in Germany.

piss chisel *n.* A high-powered stream of micturant used to chip *skidmarks* of one's lavatory bowl. The *yellow toilet brush.*

pisscourse *n.* A drunken dialogue, typically conducted between a single person in a park.

pisscuits *n.* Urinal cakes. Also *wazz spangles, bog dice, urineapple chunks. 'Wee and pisscuits, vicar?'*

pissdain *n.* Expression of nonchalant contempt visited upon a disapproving passer-by when one is spotted midway through an act of public urination in a bank doorway.

pissdom *n.* The sort of mystic, booze-fuelled perception, sagacity and percipience exhibited by a *Dalai Larga.*

pissed *1. adj. UK.* As drunk as, variously, a newt, judge or *the president's mattress. 2 adj. US.* Annoyed. *'I'm real pissed at you, Mary-Ellen. That was John-boy's cookie and you took it, you greedy little asswipe.'*

pissed about more than a urinal cake *sim.* Description of a set of circumstances in which one has been excessively inconvenienced. *'Honestly, that's the last time I try to re-schedule a Yodel parcel delivery. I've been pissed about more than a urinal cake.'*

Pissedanbul or Cuntstantinople?, is it *exclam.* The moment around 9pm in the pub when a young man weighs up his prospects and decides if he's going to have a night *on the lash* with the lads or a night *on the pull.*

pissed as a tramp *adj.* To be so *refreshed* as to not particularly care where one sleeps.

pissed Gandalf *euph.* A poor manager. Because

"he is not in control of his staff".

pissed stop *n.* A drunken visit to an all night garage to buy biscuits, breakfast cereals and pornographic magazines.

pissed up *adj.* Descriptive of a fellow who is comprehensively *wankered*. Also *all pissed up*.

pissender *n.* The characteristic smell associated with old ladies – a mixture of *piss* and lavender – that would knock a fly off a bucket of *shit*.

pisses my tits off *phr.* An expression that indicates one is annoyed. *'These self-righteous bellends on my Facebook timeline are really starting to piss my tits off.'*

piss factory *n. Vict.* A public house.

piss family Robinson *euph.* An ebrious ménage of recreational drinkers whose booze-fuelled shenanigans help to keep the local constabularly in gainful employment.

piss fanfare *n.* A squeaky *trouser trumpet* that heralds the finale of a long and satisfying *slash*.

piss fit *adj. Aus.* Able to handle large amounts of alcohol as the result of regular heavy training sessions over a long period of time. George Best was, until his various livers let him down, one of the most *piss fit* people on the planet.

piss flaps *1. n. The mutton shutters* on *moss cottage,* Keith Burtons. *2. interj.* Exclamation of disappointment. *'Oh piss flaps! We haven't won the Euromillions again, Noel.'*

piss fork *n.* A post-coital bidirectional urine flow. *Twin jets.*

pisshead *n.* A thirsty fellow.

pisshead's calculator *n.* The act of totting up the the number of one, five and ten pence pieces in your pocket in order to deduce, via simple mental arithmetic, how many pints you purchased the previous evening.

pisshead's dozen *n.* Eighteen.

pisshead's labourer *n.* A barman.

pissible *adj.* Suddenly and unexpectedly within the bounds of probability due to one being under the influence of booze. *'Yes, looking at it from here, it should certainly be pissible for me to walk over the arch of the Tyne Bridge.'*

pissible *adj.* The frequently witnessed social phenomenon whereby the consumption of alcohol reduces a person's ability to make wise decisions. *'Is Dave gonna jump off that roof, then?' 'Well, he's had nine pints, so it's definitely pissible.'*

pissinfectant *n.* The use of a stream of forcibly directed *slash* in order to remove from the *bog* an area of stubborn *pebbledashery* left by the previous occupant, thus killing two birds with one stone.

Also known as the *yellow toilet brush, piss chisel.*

pissing in the wind *euph.* Wasting one's time, attempting the impossible.

pissing out of your arse *n. medic.* Suffering from violent, agonising dysentery. *'I opted for the delicious nitrogen-infused mussels with biscuit-reduced coconut and lemongrass curd, and it was delicious, although I was pissing out of my arse for a fortnight afterwards. 5 stars.'*

pissing peas *euph.* The feeling a gentleman has in his *love length* when afflicted with *galloping knob rot. 'I've caught a dose off that Elsie Tanner and I've been pissing peas all week, you know. And a rum for Uncle Albert as well please, Mrs Walker.'*

pissing through the letter box *euph.* When you sit down for a *shit* and inadvertently force *piss* out at an angle so it goes under the seat and straight into your strides.

pissing tic-tacs *n.* The peculiar sensation of urinating while suffering from a *clap* of some sort. Not quite as bad as *pissing razor blades.*

piss in the dark without getting it in his gob, he couldn't take a *exclam.* A jocose assessment pertaining to a clumsy, unintelligent or accident-prone fellow.

piss it *v.* To do something *piss* simple, *piss* easily. *'You watch this, I'm going to absolutely piss it.' 'Right you are, Evel.'*

piss it up the wall *v.* To fritter away something, *eg.* Money, talent, urine, your life.

pissive aggressive *adj.* Said of a *one can Van Damme* who challenges all comers to fisticuffs after half a pint of *duel fuel. Beer brave.*

piss Judas *n.* One who excuses himself in the middle of a delicate task, *eg.* Moving an upright piano up a narrow fire escape, syphoning the sediment out of a derelict septic tank, conducting a heart transplant *etc.,* in order to relieve himself.

piss kitten *n.* The completely redundant spare woman who follows her friend to the toilet for no other reason than to increase the length of the queue.

pisslexia *n. medic.* When texting at the end of a night in the *rub-a-dub*, a marked inability to spell properly or construct a coherent sentence.

piss like an American fighter pilot *v.* When extremely *Brahms*, to micturate in a haphazard and inaccurate fashion, *ie.* Spraying urine all over the floor, seat, shoes, journalists *etc.*

piss mist *n.* The fine fog that forms around a urinal trough at shin level when having a *gypsy's kiss.* Only noticeable when wearing shorts. *Wee fret.*

piss off *1. exclam.* A polite form of *fuck off. 2. v.* To annoy. *'The graphics on the BBC news really piss me off.'*

piss on your chips *v.* To put yourself at a long-term disadvantage through a foolhardy short-term action. *Fart on your Weetabix, cum on your faggots.* *'Of course, Nixon really pissed on his chips when he tried to fire independent prosecutor Archibald Cox.'*

pissoris *n. medic.* A well-hidden *pizzle* of such laughable size that it resembles nothing so much as a lady's *clematis*. A *button on a fur coat.*

piss, piece of *n.* A portion of easiness. *'Hey, flying this Concorde out of Charles De Gaulle Airport is a piece of piss.'*

pisspint *n.* A drink purchased "because it's only fair, isn't it", when calling in at a public house for the sole purpose of making use of the *bogs*.

piss polo *1. n.* Game of skill whereby disinfectant tablets are pointlessly manoeuvred in a urinal trough by the participants' *wazz* streams. *2. n.* A very unsuccessful flavour of sweet. Not quite as bad as the fruity ones, though.

piss porch *n.* The skin awning which protects a lady's *bald man in a boat* from the weather.

piss pot *1. n.* Lavatory bowl or *gazunder.* *2. n.* Idiot, fool. *3. n.* Old-fashioned motorcyclist's helmet.

pisspot control *n.* After a long-haul flight, muscular *Simon Cowell* contractions performed on arrival whilst searching for *Das Shitenhauser* at a foreign airport.

pisspotical *adj.* A state of confusion, disarray or disharmony. *'A cabinet spokesman yesterday denied claims of pisspotical in-fighting amongst ministers.'*

pisspour *n.* After the *luggage* has been packed away too hastily, an unfortunate dribble of leftover *innocent water* from *Gonzo's nose* which results in the appearance of a *trouserpatch*.

pisspraxia *n. medic.* Temporary neurological condition experienced by those who are busting for a *gypsy's kiss,* characterised by clumsiness which escalates at a rate exponentialy proportional to the proximity of the sufferer to the *khazi.*

piss pregnant *adj.* Suffering from a desperate need to micturate, for example on a tube train or while reading the news, as a consequence of earlier sinking nine pints of *neck oil*. *'Sorry about the state of my trousers, by the way. I was piss pregnant on the bus, and my waters broke just before I reached my stop. But to get back to your question; what qualities do I think I could bring to this position?'*

piss proud *adj.* Being the smug owner of a magnificent *dawn horn*; a *morning glory, motorcycle kick stand*.

piss rusty water *v.* To pass liquid *feculent.*

piss sauna *n.* The all-enveloping fog of urine steam in an outside pub lavatory on a cold winter's evening.

piss, shit and spunk *phr.* Salty alternative to blood, sweat and tears. *'We've put a lot of piss, shit and spunk into this HS2 project, prime minister.'*

piss switch *n. medic.* That intelligent part of a *toiletee's clackervalve* that tells the bladder that it's okay to release the *wazz* as soon as the *poop* is out of the *hoop*.

pissterical *adj.* In a state of uncontrolled alcohol-induced panic, anger or excitement. *'I would request that the members of the jury should pay no attention to Mr Doherty's pissterical outburst.'*

pissterious *adj.* Descriptive of strange and inexplicable phenomena that happen while under the influence of alcohol. (Hence also *pisstery n.*). *'"It's certainly most confounding, Holmes," I cried. "I don't remember getting all my hair cut off, having "Fuck the Pope" tattooed across my upper lip or losing three fingers off my right hand last night." The eminent detective listened to my words, then sat back in his leather armchair and lit his pipe. And played his violin. Afer a few moments he spoke. "Indeed, Watson," he expostulated. "It's certainly a bit pissterious, to say the least."'* (from *Sherlock Holmes and the Glaswegian City Break* by Sir Arthur Conan Doyle).

piss through a sheet of lead, I could *exclam.* Said by a dehydrated lorry driver, whose alarmingly dark, high-pH *cess* is extremely corrosive and can only be safely contained in an Irn Bru bottle.

piss through a stiffy *v.* To attempt that which is nigh on impossible. *'I'm going to try a simplify now, Philip. This is like trying to piss through a stiffy.'*

piss through a stiffy *v.* To attempt the impossible. *'"I say, Jeeves old chap," I ejaculated, "It really is dashed annoying. I mean, what's a bally chap supposed to do? I've been trying to catch the Hon. Celia Hunt-Fosbury's eye all week, but she always seems to have that dumpy chum of hers from Roedean in tow." "I take it, sir," replied the sage retainer, "that you are referring to the cigar-smoking young lady in tweeds…?" "That's the one!" I cried. "You've got her bang on the pip. What shall I do, Jeeves?" "I incline to the view, sir," the inestimable manservant continued, "that, in the circumstances, you should withdraw gracefully. I fear you may be trying to piss through a stiffy there."'* (from *Fuck Me Sideways, Jeeves!* by PG Wodehouse).

pisstine! *exclam.* Announced proudly when exiting the *smallest room* after successfully *wazzing* away all the previous users' *skidmarks*.

pisstrinos *n. Phys.* Those little bubbles of *wazz* that shoot off at near light speed along of the surface of the liquid when you *pee* into a cold stainless steel trough urinal.

pisstrol GTX *n.* A *number one* taken on a gradient, such that the gravity-driven flow of *tweedle* resembles the stream of engine oil in those Castrol adverts from the 1980s. Especially if it pools inside the jaws of a spanner.

pisstrone *n.* Cold, clear, tasteless soup served in a high class restaurant. *'And for your starter, sir ?' 'I think I'll try a bowl of the pisstrone.' 'Certainly, Mr Coren. That will be £35.'*

piss up *n.* An ale soirée; a social gathering of boozing companions.

pisswhacker *n.* A person who bumbles through life, without any evident purpose, rather as if they were thrashing pointlessly at a stream of urine with a stick. *'Born on this day: Sepp Blatter, football administrator, 1936; Sharon Stone, fanny actress, 1958; His Royal Highness The Prince Edward Antony Richard Louis, Earl of Wessex, Viscount Severn, Royal Knight Companion of the Most Noble Order of the Garter, Knight Grand Cross of the Royal Victorian Order, pisswhacker, 1964.'*

piss whip *1. euph.* The instantaneous moment when a drinker realises that they are *shitfaced.* The *cat of nine ales.* *'All of a sudden I'm absolutely mortal. It's like I've been lashed by the piss whip.'* *2. n.* The effect created by drunkenly waving one's *pezzle* up and down while having a *gypsy's kiss.*

piss whistle *n.* A *bed flute,* a *pink oboe.*

piss wicks *n.* One's shoelaces in a urine-flooded pub toilet.

piss with the lid down *v.* To do something very foolish, to make a schoolboy error. *'"Mr Paravicini's murderer is in this very room, and I'm afraid it is you, Brigadier Lewerthwaite!" cried Miss Marple. The room fell silent. "After murdering him, you dressed him in his pyjamas and carefully put his cufflinks on the dressing table to give the impression that the crime had been committed after bedtime, when you were playing bridge with myself and the Bishop. However, I'm afraid you pissed with the lid down, Brigadier," she said. "What the deuce do you mean?" Lewerthwaite blustered. "Simply this," she continued. "You placed the cufflinks on the right hand side of the dressing table when the position of the inkwell on his Davenport clearly showed him to have been left handed."*

pisswizard *n.* An *arsehole* of the highest order. A *cock-juggling thundercunt.* *'Born on this day: Ray Winstone, British actor and director, 1957; Beth Ditto, big-boned American singer, 1981; Prince Andrew, Duke of York and golfing pisswizard, 1960.'*

piss wrestling *n.* Tossing and turning in bed in order to fight the need to empty one's bladder for as long as possible.

pissy fit *n.* The kind of foul-tempered strop that can only be achieved when one is *blind refreshed.*

pisticuffs *n.* A comical, drunken attempt at combat, perhaps initiated outside a chip shop.

pisto *n.* Nasally abusive miasma prevalent in tower block lifts, multi-storey car park stairs or when sitting next to Gerard Depardieu on a plane. "Ah, pisto."

piston slap *1. n.* On a 1980s/90s Nissan or Ford motor vehicle, for example, when the mileage reaches a point such that the pistons have worn down so they slap the sides of the cylinder bores. *2. n.* An unsatisfactory act of *coitus* during which one's *tallywhacker* doesn't touch the sides. Caused by a overly capacious vaginal cylinder bore rather than an undersized piston, obviously.

pistorectomy *n. medic.* Vomiting up one's own internal organs while life-threateningly *merry.*

pistorious *adj.* Victorious in a contest of some sort while legless. *'We were pistorious in the pub quiz thanks to Lance looking up the answers on his iPhone.'*

pistory *n.* The oral anthology of dubious recollections and downright lies recounted by a young man after a night out *on the lash, eg.* "I'd already had thirteen pints when that bird started giving me the eye" and similar tosh.

pit bull *n.* A stocky, tenacious *brown bear's nose,* usually the final one of a *sit down lavatory adventure,* that hangs onto the *ringpiece* like grim death. An *angry monkey,* a *Harold Lloyd,* a *Robert Powell.*

pit cat *euph.* A little-used *clopper.* A *pussy* that never sees the light of day.

pitch a tent *v.* To get *wood* either beneath the bed linen, or conspicuously in your trousers. See *pit prop.*

pitch drop experiment *n.* An exceptionally difficult *digestive transit.* Named in honour of the scientific investigation into the viscosity of pitch which has been running at the University of Queensland for 84 years, during which time only eight drops have fallen from the neck of a funnel filled with semi-solid bitumen.

pitch inspection *n.* The checking of one's *bills* for any sign of a dropped *bonus ball* after a risky *Exchange & Mart.*

pitch invasion *1. n.* Entertaining 1970s football match behaviour in which the crowd unexpectedly leaves the stands and makes its way onto the field of play. *2. n.* Entertaining *farty-arse* behaviour in which a quantity of *feeshus* unexpectedly leaves the *arse* and makes its way onto the *gusset* of the *trolleys*. A *follow through*.

pitch invasion jacket *n.* One of those short tartan coats with a big fur collar, as worn by keen football fans and members of the Bay City Rollers in the 1970s.

pit clit *n. coll.* Gorgeous lycra-clad *crumpet* that used to stand around holding umbrellas on the starting grids of F1 races in the days before the sport got woke.

pit crew *n.* The unseen team of lubrication specialists, *arse*-technicians and bottom-douchers who prepare a *grumble flick* actress's *nipsy* in order to make it super-clean and effortlessly accommodating.

pit fillers *n.* Massive *thru'penny bits* which emigrate towards a *bird's* oxters when she's lying on her back.

pit of misery *n.* Any pub frequented by the sort of *twats* who shout "Dilly Dilly" as they neck their bottles of fizzy *piss*.

pit prop *n.* Strategic structural member found in a *passion pit*. A *tent pole*, a *dawn horn*.

PITS/pits *acronym.* What a polite guest does when going for a *slash* in the bathroom, so as not to stain the nice toilet floor or yellow the carpet. Piss In The Sink. Also *Bradford dishwashing*.

pitta tits *n.* Unleavened *baps* on a lady's chest. From their similarity to the unappetising Greek flatbreads seen in cosmopolitan retail emporia such as the Spar.

Pity Me incense *n.* The fragrance wafted from someone's tabs, named in honour of the bijou County Durham locale; *Eau de Lambert et Butler*.

pizzle *n. medic.* A sorry-looking *penis*, like one would imagine the Pope has. *Gonzo's nose*.

PJ playing paintball, like *sim.* Descriptive of a starlet's face at the climactic scene in a *grumble flick*, splattered with multiple pellets and wailing "I cannat see, man!" Not unlike that scene in *Byker Grove* where Ant or Dec or Dick or Dom got *jizzed* in the face at close range.

place of happy release *1. n.* In John Christopher's apocalyptic *The Tripods* novels, the facility where tired slaves go to die. *2. n.* In real life, one of those Thai massage places where a household name breakfast TV presenter used to go to get *wanked off*.

placket *n. arch.* A Medieval damsel's *cunt*.

PLAC lights/plac lights *n.* The hazard flashers on a white van blocking the thoroughfare. From Park Like A Cunt.

plamff *n. Scots.* One who, apparently bored of sniffing bicycle seats, opts to cut out the middle man and sniffs the gussets of ladies' soiled *bills* instead.

plan B *1. n.* A rap singer, of the sort you've no doubt seen on *The Top of the Pops*. *2. n.* A desultory *hand job* at the end of an *unfuckcessful* night.

plank *n.* A planned *wank*. From planned + wank. A useful entry in a stressed executive's diary for when his wife or girlfriend is absent which, during any subsequent inquisition into his scheduled assignations, can be explained away as a highly improbable trip to a local timber merchants to peruse their selection of stout battens.

planned engineering works *euph.* When the *bag for life's* up on blocks. *'I'm afraid certain services may be cancelled this weekend due to planned engineering works.'*

plant a tracking device *v.* In the style of a secret agent, to pick one's nose and surreptitiously stick one's *findings* to the underside of the nearest available horizontal surface. *'Finish planting your tracking device, Fiona. You're on air in five seconds.'*

Planter's hum *n.* The nauseating smell of *air croutons*. From the aroma of a freshly opened bag of dry-roasted peanuts.

planting out the onions *euph.* The point in the year, normally around springtime, at which the British male decides to ditch his winter clothes and opt for the summer dress code of knee-length shorts with no pants. *'After what had seemed like an impossibly long winter, the two days in April that had nudged the thermometer into double figures had convinced Malcolm that the time had come for him to plant out his onions'.*

plap *1. n. onomat.* The sound a *digestive transit* makes when it hits the *chod pan* water, particularly if it's one of them ones with the consistency of warm plasticine. *2. n. onomat.* An alternative to a *Peruvian num-num*. *3. onomat.* Upon waking, the noise made while testing that one's mouth still works first thing in the morning. *4. onomat.* Lip-based vocalisation indicative that one could murder a pint.

plasterer's radio *sim.* Descriptive of a lucky lady who is liberally adorned with *jelly jewellery*. Frequently found on Japanese and American cyber-scud.

plastic bag *n.* A lower end inflatable love companion.

Plastic Bertrand *1. n. prop.* Roger François Jouret – a French singer and old-age pensioner best known for the perennially popular 1977 punk-ish hit *Ça Plane Pour Moi*. *2. n.* Name given to a lady's *self-pleasuring* implement.

plastic cockney *n.* A *mockney*. A posh person who

affects to be an Eastender.

plastic flower, drink like a *sim.* When one of your mates is sipping at his pint very slowly. Also known as *budgie supping.*

plasticine hammer, knocking a nail in with a *sim.* Descriptive of the difficulty experienced when trying to *bang* a young lady who has signally failed to provoke a sufficient level of tumescence in one's *chap. Playing snooker with a piece of string.*

plate *1. n. arch. Horatio. 2. n. arch. Cumulonimbus. 3. n. arch.* A general purpose term for any sort of oral/genital shenanigans performed behind a Victorian skip. *'How much, love?' 'A penny for full, a farthing for hand or a ha'penny for plate, your grace. And if you want to slit me gizzard with a butcher's knife, it's half a crown.'*

platform twelve special *1. n.* ITV pop show from the 1950s. *2. n. Cottaging* slang for a public *bog* with generously appointed cubicles, as if designed for multiple occupants. From the delightfully spacious conveniences on the eponymous platform at Paddington station.

platignum jubilee *n.* Cut-price, half-hearted and dreary *al Tesco* celebrations to mark a royal anniversary, wedding, birth or tragic demisement. Generally consisting of a length of Home Bargains Union Jack bunting strung between a pair of wheelie bins, a pasting table sagging under the weight of a plate of egg sarnies, and a bouncy castle deflating in the drizzle. Named in honour of the digit-besmirching budget stationery brand.

plating *n.* The act of *going down* on a lady in the style of an enthusiastic gourmand licking his charger clean.

platty jubes *phr.* An exceptionally big *poo*; "seventy years on the throne".

play an octave *v.* To stretch one's hand, in the style of a stride pianist such as Erroll Garner, such that the thumb and little finger reach both of a lady's *chapel hat pegs* simultaneously.

play a sweet tune on the gristle-whistle *n.* To perform a rousing *hornpipe* on the *pink oboe*, perhaps in an attempt to relieve the symptoms of a severe *attack of pancreatitis.*

play a tune on the devil's clarinet *1. v.* To *interfere with yourself. 2. v.* To *suck someone off. 3. v.* borrow a woodwind instrument from the Lord of Hades, before knocking out a jazz standard on it.

playaway *n.* Masturbatory technique of chaps not overly endowed *in the trouser department.* From the song lyrics: "One finger, one thumb, keep moving".

play dough *n.* Disposable income, *beer tokens.*

play Drake *euph.* In a sexual engagement, to delay until the very last possible moment before *joining in the fray.* From the no doubt apocryphal story of olden days sailor Sir Francis Drake who, in 1588, waited until he had finished his game of bowls on Plymouth Hoe before addressing the imminent threat of the Spanish Armada. And then waited until he had defeated this waterborne invasion force before performing an act of penetrative vaginal intercourse up Queen Elizabeth I.

playful dolphins *n.* A situation arising when no amount of flushing and weighing down with two-ply will rid the *chod bin* of *floaters. 'Sorry gran, I flushed three times but there's still a couple of playful dolphins bobbing around in there.'*

play good cock/bad cock *v.* To perform a popular method of *self-interrogation* in which alternate violent and gentle strokes are employed to get the red-handed *suspect* to *spill his guts.*

Playhatch *1. n.* A charming hamlet in southern Oxfordshire, boasting a pub that dates from the 16th century. *2. n.* The female *undercarriage. 3. n.* The *wrong 'un. 4. n.* The non-existent gusset in a pair of saucy crotchless *dunghampers.*

playing at home to the Tampax Bay roadies *euph. Up on blocks*, suffering from *women's things.*

playing chopsticks *n.* A beginners' duet. Mutual masturbation.

playing off the seventeenth tee *euph.* A chap's choice when his missus is *up on blocks, ie.* When he has just "two holes left".

playing snooker with a piece of string *sim.* Trying to *sink a pink* with a *marshmallow cue. 'I'm sorry, pet, I've got the knob of butter. It's like playing snooker with a piece of string.'*

playing the accordian *v.* To alternately pull apart and squeeze together the cheeks of one's *arse* when perched on the *choddy hopper* in an effort to encourage the last bit of *shit* to drop off before polishing one's *nipsy.*

playing the bishop *n. Pissing* diagonally into the (hopefully vacant) adjoining urinal.

playing the bone-a-phone *v. Wanking,* pulling oneself a *hand shandy.*

playing the invisible banjo *v.* George Formby-esque female *touch typing* technique. *Scruggs style.*

playing the upside-down piano *1. sim.* The overture to the second movement of *hiding the sausage. Firkyfoodling. 2. sim. Stabbing the cat.*

playing track and field *euph.* Frantic female *friggonometry. Frottering* at such a frantic rate that it's like playing the popular eighties Sega classic.

playing with your nan's tits, better than *sim.* A version of the colloquial rhetoricism "better than a poke in the eye with a sharp stick" which can be used while in polite company.

play it out from the back v. To calmly and slowly release *greenarse gas* when more urgent and swift action may be required. *'And I think Lineker was trying to play it out from the back there, Brian. And you've got to say that's gone badly wrong.'*

plays both League and Union euph. Said of a *half-rice half-chips happy shopper* who espouses both codes.

play statues v. To stop suddenly in the street with a pensive look upon one's face when trying to determine whether one has just done a *guff* or a *poo*.

playsturbation n. Portmanteau term describing the activities of a single youth or temporarily home-alone husband who spends his time alternately playing action adventure games and *pulling himself off.*

play the Atari v. To waggle one's *joystick* furiously while poking one's tongue out with concentration and excitement, in the style of an 80s computer console gamer having a *wank.*

play the back nine v. *Irish golf.* To use one's *wood* to play into the bunker, to *get the dog in the bathtub.*

play the bacon kazoo v. To *nosh* noisily on a *badly packed kebab.*

play the bodhran v. To *beat one's meat* at the same tempo that Michael Flatley might dance a jig. From the similarity of an enthusiastic *chimper's* hand and wrist movements to those of a fellow knocking out a rhythm on the traditional Irish percussion instrument.

play the bottery euph. The morning after a heavy night's eating and drinking, to gamble the lot on a *fart*. See also *drop the jackpot, play the tuppenny waterfall.*

play the B-side v. To swap from the *missionary position* to the *doggie position. 'I got fed up with looking at her face while I was giving her one, so I flipped her over and played the B-side.'*

play the funky tuba v. To puff out the cheeks and produce a trouser-flapping bass note of 32Hz. *'I say June, how come none of the pictures on the wall are level any more?' 'That's me I'm afraid, Terry. I've been playing the funky tuba all morning.'*

play the long ball *1. v.* In football commentator parlance, to *twat* a leather spherule to the other end of the pitch. *2. v.* Of a pornographic actress, to lick and suck the larger of her male co-star's *knackers.*

play the ocarina n. To *trombone* a woman; a process which involves simultaneous *rimming* of the *freckle* and *firkyfoodling* of the *blurtch.*

play the pink oboe v. To perform oral sex on a man,

presumably with a thin reed sticking out of his *hog's eye*. Often used to denote homosexuality. *'I didn't know Freddie Mercury played the pink oboe. Who'd have thought it?'*

play the promotion flute v. To accelerate one's career prospects by *sucking off* the boss. See also *nosh pit, see the bishop.*

play the violin v. To scrape your *bow* against the missus's *G-string*. To make sweet music after merely pushing the *jelly hammock* of her *dunghampers* to one side.

play the whale v. To *spew.*

play your cards right euph. To engage in a spot of *tongue and groove work*, accompanied by enthusiastic cries of "Higher! Higher!" or "Lower! Lower!" until you *hit the jackpot.*

plead the duke euph. To claim that "the sun was low in the sky" as an excuse for your *cunt-witted* behaviour. A reference to the late Queen's late consort, and his famous motorised misunderstanding on the A149.

please hold for the president exclam. Yet another amusing statement to precede a *horse and cart*. Also *our survey said; and now a word from our sponsor; and the thunderball is.*

Please stand clear from the platform edge, the next train to pass through this station is not scheduled to stop here exclam. A timely warning issued immediately prior to the onset of a dangerously powerful *Bakerloo breeze.*

please take your items exclam. Go on, now *fuck off.*

pleasure v. Tabloidese, to *suck* or *wank off*. To perform a lewd act on oneself or on someone else.

pleasure trove n. A dazzling collection of *niff mags* found under a hedge or on top of an older brother's wardrobe. Also *gash in the attic.*

plebrities *1. n.* Distinctly non-effulgent stars of the sort often found frequenting ITVBe. Or ITV2. Or any ITV channel, come to think of it, these days. *2. n.* One who, no matter how famous they become, stays true to their roots.

pledge your allegiance to the king! exclam. Something to say before *dropping a right royal guff.*

plink plink fizz phr. onomat. Two *pathfinder marbles* followed by an explosion of *fizzy gravy* brought on by drinking Chinese herbal tea to treat constipation.

plinth v. Of a male *on the job*, to manoeuvre himself into a comfortable position for penetration.

plips n. *Pussy lips.*

plod n. A *half-on*. Half a teacake.

plod fodder n. coll. Highly arrestable individuals, usually found hanging round outside off-licences on dodgy estates.

plonker *1. n.* Penis. *2. n. Crap* put-down line from Britain's favourite tedious TV sitcom, usually delivered to screams of audience laughter just before someone falls through a bar or drops a chandelier.

plopapotamus *n.* A large, unsinkable *Douglas.*

plop art *n.* Bold designs left around the toilet bowl after a night at the local Balti house. *Fartex.*

plopathon *n.* An extended toilet break after which the *ploppee* may need to be wrapped in a foil blanket.

plop circle *n.* Mysterious and other-worldly condition that manifests when one has sat on the *bum sink* for an extended period after passing an *Andrew*, reading this book for example. There is, suddenly and as if by magic, a strange red ring around the backs of the legs and upper bottom. Also known as a *crap circle.*

plop corn *n.* Thrill-seeking undigested yellow foodstuff which rides your *log flume.*

plop dusting *n. Coughing a dead rat* while walking past a crowd or queue. *Carpet bombing, duck walking.*

plopmaster *n.* A well-timed morning *dump* that is taken while Ken Bruce plays a record between the two sets of questions on his famous music quiz. On Greatest Hits Radio these days, mind.

plopodopolus *n.* Polite term for the *smallest room. 'Excuse me, your majesty. You couldn't by any chance direct me towards the plopodopolus, could you? Only I'm busting for a shite here.'*

plop of the Irish *n.* A dark, foetid and loose length of *Guinness rope. 'Ah, you can't beat a plop of the Irish, so you can't, so you can't.'*

plopportunity *n.* A *poo-window* that may occur when a new partner nips out to the shops *etc*, meaning that you can *drop some bricks* at your leisure, assuming you're not having a *wank* instead..

plop socket *n. medic.* The anal sphincter. *'Phwooar! I'd love to give your sister one up the plop socket, Kate.' 'Could you just keep your opinions to yourself and get on with the service please, archbishop?'*

plopsy *n. medic.* Diarrhoea. Also *the skits, splurry, faecal treacle, jungle jitters, arse piss, rusty water* or *hoop soup. 'Doctor: I'm afraid your husband is suffering from the plopsy, Madam. Mrs Jones: Oh my. Do you have anything to clear it up? Doctor: Here, try this mop.'* (Bamforth's *Seaside Chuckles* postcard by Donald McGill, 1922).

plop tart *n.* A neat, no-need-to-wipe *cronk* enjoyed first thing in the morning. A *seven am angel.*

plop thickens, the *exclam.* Said of the restorative

effect of Immodium one one's post-*cuzza foulage.*

ploptician *n.* An expert who looks at your *turds* to tell if you're ill or not. *'Born on this day: Confucius, ancient Chinese philosopher, 551 BC; Thomas Crapper, not toilet inventor, 1836; Dr Gillian McKeith, ploptician, 1959.'*

ploughing the sand *1. euph.* A seemingly never ending and unrewarding job, *eg.* Painting the Forth Rail Bridge, checking Jeffrey Archer's novel manuscripts for spelling errors and grammatical mistakes. *2. euph.* Being *on the job* while far too *wankered* to *shoot one's stack.*

ploughman's *n.* The *barse, taint, notcher etc. 'Mr Kneivel's motorbike hit the last bus at an approximate speed of 120mph, before careering into several fruit machines and a tuppenny waterfall. He suffered severe internal injuries including fractured ribs, two broken legs and a fractured skull. He also ripped his ploughman's wide open on the petrol tank.'* (Attending physician's report, Las Vegas County General Hospital Accident & Emergency Department, 1978).

ploughman's lunch *euph.* A dirty *bird's all day breakfast*, from the fact that it "looks like beef, smells like cheese and tastes like a pickled onion".

plough the back forty *1. v.* Rural US slang for the act of tilling the lowest and muddiest acreage on the farm. *2. v.* Rural US expression for the act of tilling the lowest and muddiest part of the missus.

pluke *n.* A facial spot or carbuncle. A *zit.* Also *plook*, not that you'll ever need to write it down.

plumage *n.* Your chosen hairstyle for your plums, *eg. Ball-fro, Nutkin etc.*

plumbago *n. medic.* Painful ache in the *Gladstones* caused by over-revving the *spunk* engines without releasing the *horse's handbrake. Lover's nuts, blue balls.*

plumber's bag, go down like a *1. sim.* Of a professional footballer, to grasp any opportunity to secure a free kick. *2. n.* Of a plastic-*titted* lingerie model at Chinawhite's, to grasp any opportunity to secure a professional footballer.

plumber's bonus *n.* A *U-blocker* of such proportions that it has to be dealt with by someone who has served an apprenticeship. A *windfall* or *shitty & guilds.*

plumber's diary *n.* An item, or indeed person, that is entirely without use. *'Born on this day: Anna Lindh, Swedish politician, 1957; Christian Wulff, German politician, 1959 ; Alexander Boris de Falafel Johnson, plumber's diary, 1964.'*

plumber's drip tray, face/fanny like a *sim.* See also

art room sink, Dracula's candle.

plumber's lung *n.* A violent *arse bark.*

plumber's mate *n.* A bored housewife who entertains herself during the day by watching repeats of *Flog It* and *sucking off* sundry tradesmen who have called to fix the washing machine.

plumber's piss *n.* A post-ejaculation *pipecleaner,* probably taken in the hand basin.

plumber's privilege *n.* The ancient right granted to plumbers, which entitles them to relieve themselves into whichever appliance they have just installed, *eg.* Sink, bath, dishwasher *etc.*

plumber's shammy *n.* Clearing a blocked drain and getting a fistful of sodden *jam rags* for one's trouble.

plumber's tea *n.* A strong brown infusion in the *pot,* brewed overnight using cold water and a *dead otter.*

plumber's toolbag *1. sim.* Description of a follow-through. *'Jesus wept, I wish I'd not eaten that packet of ham I found in the back of my nan's fridge. My underpants are like a plumber's tool bag this morning. And now over to Carol for the weather.'* 2. *n. Furry bicycle stand, mott.*

plumber's wipe *n.* The art of shoving one's hand into a lady's *driptray,* and rubbing backwards and forwards, in the same way that a plumber would wipe a recently soldered joint.

plumbolic *adj.* In a state of significant disorganisation or disarray, caused by *fuckwitted* idiocy. Nothing springs to mind.

plum crumble *n.* A crusty old man's chewy testicular detritus, usually served up in a nylon *nut bag.*

plum duff *1. adj.* Barren in the trouser department. *'That woman next door's been married two years now and still no bairn. She says she doesn't want kids, but I reckon it's him and he's plum duff.'* 2. *n. rhym. slang.* A fellow who *bakes a light cake. 'That woman next door's been married two years now and still no bairn. She says she doesn't want kids, but I reckon it's him and he's a plum duff.'*

plumpa-lumpa *n.* A short, fat *bird* with a bright orange face. Also *Yorkshire flamingo.*

plumper *n.* A *buffet slayer.* A lady of ample proportions.

plump friction *n.* A jeggings-clad *salad dodger's* thighs rubbing together as she walks to the pie shop, creating enough static electricity to successfully revivify Frankenstein's monster.

plumping gloss *1. n.* A lip fattening brand of lipstick which delivers an instant, glamorous

Michael Gove-style trout pout. 2. *n. Vitamin S.*

plums *n. Knackers, balls,* testicles.

plum sauce *n. Crotch broth.*

plums to prunes *euph.* The before and after states of a chap's *hairy saddlebags. 'Jonathan was powerless to resist. His eyes burned into the centrefold's minge like quartzes. His hairy hand enfolded his battered Charlie as he felt himself once again being swept away on an onanistic whirlwind of passion. Then, all too soon it was over and he felt his ardour subsiding. "Bloody hell, that was fast,"he panted as he wiped his hand on the curtains. "I went from plums to prunes in less than a minute."'* (from *The ITV Chat Show Presenter and the Japanese Jazz Mag* by Barbara Cartland).

plumstruck *adj.* Incapable of speech following a soft glancing blow to the *chap equipment.*

plum tomatoes *n.* The state of a chap's *knackers* after he's carried out a *jam raid* on *tuna town.*

plunker *n. US.* A *blob, Trojan* or *jubber.*

Plymouth Argyles *n. rhym. slang. medic. Nurembergs.*

PMD *abbrev. psych.* Post Masturbation Depression. The overwhelming sense of guilt and hopelessness that ensues following a lengthy session with one's pants around one's ankles. *Wangst, tugger's remorse, abject jizzery.*

PMT *abbrev. medic.* Condition suffered by *gentlemen of the road* just prior to enjoying their first fruit-based beverage of the day. Pre Merrydown Tension.

poacher's folly *1. n.* In traditional countryside parlance, the act of shooting at rabbits and thereby scaring away the big game. *2. n.* In nightclub parlance, the act of chatting up the first rough *bird* one sees in a club and thereby scaring away the decent *tussage. Going ugly early, sticking at 15.*

poacher's glovebox, fanny like a *sim.* A somewhat gamey feminine receptacle.

poacher's pocket *1. n.* A fashion accessory favoured by illicit hunters and shoplifting television celebrities. *2. n.* A very large *sweep's brush* with a jar of coffee and some batteries stowed up it.

poaching an egg *n.* The correct manner of defecation when in earshot or noseshot of polite company. *Dropping anchor* into an already flushing toilet, thus whisking away all potential noises, miasmas and stipplings. *'When taken short while on state visits, her late majesty always poached an egg in case she left a tiger's back on the skidpan and caused a diplomatic incident.'* (Nicholas Witchell, BBC News 24).

poach your eggs *v.* To enjoy a scaldingly hot

monkey bath.

Pob lips *n.* The state of the *ringpiece* during an acute bout of diarrhoea. From the relentlessly low budget, Michael Gove lookylikey, spitting Welsh children's TV puppet of the same name.

pobolycwm *n. Welsh.* Literally "People who like quim".

pocket battleship *1. n.* A compact, heavily armed warship, such as The Graff Spee. *2. n.* A short, yet aggressive *hard-on*; a Bob Hoskins amongst erections. *3. n.* A short, rough *bint* you wouldn't want to meet in a dark alley.

pocket billiards *n.* A game for one player, two *balls,* and a *cock.*

pocket bonk-on *n.* Like pocket chess and pocket Scrabble, a genital erection that is for some reason smaller than usual, but still perfectly functional. Ideal for caravan holidays.

pocket fisherman *n.* He who plays with his *tackle* through his trouser pockets.

pocket frog *n.* A *fart, botty burp, windy pop.*

pocket jostle *n.* Surreptitious *inside job* essayed by a furtive *sex case* on a crowded bus or packed train.

pocket pinball *n.* A game where the testicles are fired up into the chest, where they ricochet from organ to organ while bells ring and one's eyes spin round.

pocket pinball wizard *n.* A fellow who may not be deaf or dumb, but is almost certainly blind.

pocket rocket *1. n.* A small, but powerful motorbike. *2. n.* A small, but powerful *knob.*

podcast *1. n.* A broadcast of digital content. *2. n.* A live stream of the *nadbag* contents. *3. n.* SI unit of measurement: approximately equal to 5cc of *spaff.*

podge-on *n.* A small *semi* which presents one's *old man* in a more favourable light than it deserves. *Half a teacake, dobber Grand Old Duke of York.*

podgerigar *n.* A fat *bird* with a taste for millet.

podiatrist *1. n.* A person who did something terrible in a previous life, whose job is to treat problems and diseases of people's feet. *2. n.* One who is employed to relieve excess pressure in gentlemen's *pods.*

podium finish *n.* To put a thumb over the *hog's eye* to make your *jaff* go further, like what race-winning Formula 1 racing drivers do. When they are having a *wank.*

pod purse *n.* Where the loose change for a *money shot* is kept.

pod race *n.* To *crack one off* in a high-pressure situation where time is of the essence, *eg.* While the missus is in the kitchen making a cup of tea or choking on a boiled sweet.

podsend *n.* A miraculous trove of quality *jackage*

which a man stumbles upon at his hour of greatest need.

poe *n.* The *fadge.* From the Gothic author Edgar Allen Minge.

poe slap *n.* A *fanny nanny, dangermouse.*

POETS day *abbrev.* Friday. From Piss Off Early, Tomorrow's Saturday.

poffle *v.* To *shart. Gamble and lose.*

pog *n. Ned.*

pogie *n. US.* The *Jacky Danny.*

POG/pog *acronym.* Having forgotten a locker coin at the baths or before going in the sea, leaving one's valuables under a towel with your upturned *scads* on top to discourage would-be thieves. Pants On Guard.

pogue mahone *exclam. Gael.* Original name of the Pogues. An anglicisation of the Irish "pog mo thoin", meaning "kiss my arse". A reasonable request, given the state of the late Shane MacGowan's mouth.

pointer sisters *n.* A slightly perkier version of the *Winslet twins.* A lovely pair of *twin peaks* that deserve a "slow hand".

point Percy at the porcelain *v.* To take Robert Plant to the toilet for a *wee wee.*

poisonality *n.* A toxic disposition, or a famous person blessed with same. *'Born on this day: James Burke, bald TV egghead, 1936; Maurice Gibb, dead Bee Gee, 1949; Noel Edmonds, television poisonality, 1948.'*

poison the pansies *euph.* Old Manx farming expression dating from prior to the invention of indoor *shitters. 'Thank you, Mrs Kelly. That was a fine pot of tea. Now, if you'll excuse me, I'll just pop outside and poison the pansies.'*

poke *v.* A thing that Facebook users used to do to their "friends".

poke holes in a cheap door *phr.* Property of a *diamond cutter. 'When Miss Bennet was near, Mr Darcy's heart raced, and he got a panhandle that could poke holes in a cheap door.'* (from *Pride and Prejudice* by Jane Austen).

poke in the eye for a kick in the bollocks, like swapping a *sim.* An alternative to "out of the frying pan and into the fire". *'Earl Stanhope said, with regard to the proposed ammendments to the Corn Laws, he hoped the House would attend to the wishes of persons out of doors, on a subject to which, he trusted, their lordships would feel it their duty to pay particular attention, and one that interested the individuals deeply. He cordially agreed in the opinion expressed by some, and these not merely distressed laborious persons, but persons in a most respectable line, that the change proposed to* *be made to the Act, would be like swapping a poke in the eye for a kick in the bollocks.'* (from *Hansard*, 6th March 1815).

pokelore *n.* Mythical yarns of erotic adventures spun to mates down the pub.

pokemon *n.* A sexual partner with multiple STIs, such that "you've gotta catch 'em all".

poker face *1. n.* In poker, a blank, emotionless expression that does not reveal anything about the cards being held by a player to his opponents. *2. n.* In *poking*, the frenzied, red-faced grimace of a chap who is on the point of *blowing his stack*.

poker hand *n.* A morning spent on the lavatory evacuating one's *Robert Powells*. A *running straight* followed by a flush; then a *full house* followed by a royal flush.

poke the spider's eye *v.* To dig at one's *claypit* through one's *farting crackers*.

pokey blinders *n. Nipples like pygmies' cocks*, that could take your fucking eye out if you're not careful.

pokey bott wank *n.* A two-handed act of *self gratification* which combines *wanking* with one grand hand while sticking a finger from the other one up your own *arse*. *Abseiling*. *'Are you coming up to bed, Tony?' 'In a minute, Cherie. I'm just having a pokey bott wank.'*

pokies *1. n.* Gambling machines, or one-armed bandits if you will. *2. n.* Ladies' *nips* when visible through their clothing. Ringo Starr's sister-in-law Daisy Duke out of *The Dukes of Hazzard* was well known for her *pokies*. By a spooky coincidence, the pilot episode of *The Dukes of Hazzard* was entitled *One-Armed Bandits*. Coincidence? We think not. *Chapel hat pegs, pygmies' cocks, blind cobblers' thumbs etc.*

poking fog up a hill with a sharp stick, like *sim.* The impossible task of attempting to *knob* a lady when afflicted with *brewer's droop. Pushing string, stuffing a marshmallow into a piggy bank..*

polar bear's arm *n.* A *fuck-off* bumper-size line of *Bacon powder*, of the sort typically enjoyed in the *bogs* of fashionable London clubs by sweating children's television presenters. *'And here's a polar bear's arm I snorted earlier. Get down spiders!'*

polaroids *1. n.* Old-school instant(ish), not-very-good photographs. *2. n. medic. Chalfonts* that "develop very quickly", caused by sitting on something cold. From polar + haemorrhoids. *'These are the worst polaroids I've ever seen, Mr Twisleton-Wykeham-Fiennes.'*

polestruck *adj.* A shallow woman who is erotically fascinated by firemen and their equipment.

pole tax *n.* A pecuniary sum or duty levied upon the patrons of *gentleman's entertainment* venues before the next performer deigns to appear on stage. Usually in the form of putting a quid into a pint glass or a hat.

pole vault *1. n.* Vagina, *stench trench*, strong room where the *spam sceptre* can be safely housed. For a couple of minutes. *2. n.* The mental repository of erotic imagery which is relied upon by ladies, or indeed gentlemen who are *close to their mothers*, to get them *over the line* during bouts of onanistic *self indulgence*. Similar to – albeit also the opposite of – the male heterosexual *mammary* or *spank bank*.

police horse fart *n.* A *change of heart* capable of dispersing an unruly mob.

policeman *n.* An amusing way of *dropping one's bait*, specifically the act of placing both hands behind the back and bending the knees out in a comical fashion as a prelude to the release of flatus. Can be accompanied by the words "'ello 'ello 'ello" or indeed "evenin' all", in the style of Dixon of Dock Green, according to personal preference. Another reference for the teenagers there.

policeman's dinner *n. US.* An *arsehole*.

policeman's knock, hard as a *1. sim.* Descriptive of a ne'er-do-well, for example, perhaps ensconced in a public house bar. *'I wouldn't mess with him, mate. He's as hard as a policeman's knock.'* *2. sim.* Descriptive of the physical resilience of an object. *'Lady Alexander caressed his thigh, slowly moving upwards and gasped. "My word, corporal," she said. "You're as hard as a policeman's knock!"'*

policeman's radio, rogered more times than *phr.* Said of a woman who's *had more cocks than Davey Crockett's rifle, more legs over her than a Blackpool donkey.*

policewoman's treat *n.* A *copper's torch*.

polike *n.* A "like" you place on a Facebook comment that you don't find in the slightest bit amusing or even vaguely interesting, posted purely out of politeness.

polish a turd *euph.* To fruitlessly attempt to dress up something *shite*, eg. The relaunch of the Morris Marina as the "Ital", or putting a baseball cap on William Hague.

polish one's spectacles *v.* To surreptitiously *masturbate* one's penis through the pockets, *eg.* When looking for change in a strip club or when sexually aroused on a tube train.

Polish surname, as long & hard as a *sim.* Descriptive of a proper *tongue twister* in the *trouser department*.

polish the lighthouse *v.* To *throttle Captain Birdseye* in the bath.

polish up on my German *phr.* Light-hearted slang expression for *pulling the Pope's cap off.* *'I'll catch you up at the palace, Liz. I'm just off to polish up on my German.'*

polish your own trumpet *v.* To commit an auto-erotic act *of self delight;* to *pull* oneself *a pint of Courage ale.*

politician's promise *euph.* A toilet session that involves a lot of noise and hot air, but which ultimately delivers very little in terms of solid output.

polony party *n.* A social gathering of two or more consenting adults where games include *hide the sausage, park the salami* and *split the kipper.* And one's party bag would contain a slice of cake and a dose of the *clap.* An orgy.

POLO/polo *acronym. milit.* Code used on military correspondence prior to coming home from a posting abroad. Pants Off, Legs Open. See also *NORWICH, BURMA.*

poltergust *n.* A sudden, eerie, pot-rattling presence emanating from *the other side.*

polyfella *n.* Thick white paste used for filling holes and cracks.

polygrot *euph.* An eminent expert in the field of *grumble* mags and vids. *'Born on this day: Ian Fleming, James Bond author, 1908; Martin Kelner, journalist and model, 1948; David Baddiel, polygrot, 1964.'*

pommel horse, an army surplus, she's had more jumps than *sim.* Descriptive of a woman who is slack in both the moral and vaginal senses. *'Or will lucky Benedict choose number three, the vivacious Mother Superior who loves to party and has had more jumps than an army surplus pommel horse?'*

Pompey pineapple *n.* The high tension raked-back hairstyle favoured by *bingo clink*-clad southern *trollops.*

Pompidou Centre *n.* A French lady's *foo foo* with all the plumbing on the outside. A badly packed *croque monsieur.*

pompom *n. Jam.* A furry thing waved by cheerleaders to entertain a crowd.

ponce *1. n.* A *pimp. 2. n.* A Brian Sewell soundalike; one who uses consonants when speaking. *3. v.* To borrow something with no intention of giving it back, *eg.* Cigarettes, garden tools, the Elgin Marbles. *4. n.* A right *Mary-Anne.*

ponce piss *n.* Champagne. *'In two! Pop your cork and enjoy your ponce piss from one of these diamond-cut Venetian crystal flutes.'*

poncilitis *1. n. medic.* Inflammation of the poncils. *2. n. medic.* Inflammation of nothing whatsoever,

but which nevertheless results in much pathetic whining from someone in rude health who is clearly a great big *ponce.*

ponderosa, the *n.* Place where a fellow can sit in quiet reflection of the day's events. *'Mam! There's no fucking arse paper in the downstairs ponderosa again!'*

pond-full *euph.* An impressively copious expulsion of *shittage.* *'Fuck me, that was a pond-full. Sorry vicar, where were we?'*

pondle *v.* To simultaneously ponder and fondle one's genitals while watching television or sitting in the park. As depicted in Auguste Rodin's slightly less popular statue *The Pondler.*

pond skater *n.* A particularly tenacious *floater* held in place by *chod bin* surface tension, resisting all attempts at flushing it away.

pond walrus *n.* A lengthsome, wrist-thick, fully coherent *Sir Douglas,* possibly with whiskers and tusks, which languishes half in and half out of the water in the *bum sink.* A *foot stool.*

pong *1. n.* The smell of a *poot. 2. n. onomat.* The sound of a service return in a game of table tennis.

pontdefecate *n.* To have a *shit* whilst thinking something over. Or think something over whilst having a *shit,* whichever is the most appropriate.

pontoon eyes *n. medic.* Where "one eye sticks and the other one twists".

pony *n. rhym. slang.* Shit. From pony and trap = crap. *'Just wait in the back of the cab, mate. I'm off into the rub-a-dub sweet-wrappers for a pony. Don't go anywhere, because I've left the meter running.'*

pony express *1. n.* An urgent *package* that always gets through. *2. n.* The galloping gait when rushing as quickly as possible for an urgent *appointment with Mr Brown.*

pony tales *n. Feeshee*-related reminiscences guaranteed to lighten the atmosphere at any gathering.

poo *1. exclam.* A word spoken with fingers on nostrils to describe an unpleasant odour. *2. n.* Shit. *3. v.* To do a *duty. 4. exclam.* Shout of alarm when a mingsome *ronk* becomes apparent. *5. abbrev.* Push One Out.

pooachute *n.* Raft of *bumwad* laid across the *chodbin* waters to prevent embarrassing splash noises of one's *dirty business* echoing around the home, office, high-street, train, or whilst perched akimbo atop the bonnet of the boss's Jag. Also *lilies on the pond, pap baffle, crash mat, poo cradle, pilo, shilencer, turd's nest, plopstop.*

pooaplegic *n. medic.* One who, having sat on the toilet for too long, has lost all feeling below the waist. A *crapple*.

poo bat *n.* The smell of someone else's *feeshus* which knocks you off your feet when you enter the *bog*. *'I'd give it ten minutes if I was you, Placido. Luciano's been off-loading his breakfast and believe you me, you don't want to get hit in the face with his poo bat.'*

poo bats *n.* Small, stout-coloured *farticulates* which leave their *nipsy* roost in order to fly and perch high up under the eaves of your toilet bowl.

poobicle *n.* The *underpantry*.

poobies *n.* A s*hit* pair of *tits*.

poobricator *n.* The first *oily rag* of the day after a night *on the sauce*, always immediately followed by the desperate need to defecate. See also *shitarette, drag and drop, Embassy number two, arse fuse, shit trigger.*

pooch coning *n.* A decidedly risky sexual pursuit which involves smothering *nut butter* over your privates, it says here, and then getting your next door neighbour's dog to lick it off. Nice to know that it's got a name at last.

poochi handbag *n.* A fashion-conscious lady's *Battersea hand warmer.*

Poocomknockerphilication *n. Cleveland steaming*, as performed by Ken Dodd.

poo cradle *n.* The floating raft of toilet tissue placed in the bowl before *dropping the kids off at the pool* in order to minimise the risk of *splashback*. Also *crash mat, pap baffle* or *pilo.*

poocrastination *n.* Spending way more time than necessary *on the throne* when you should be otherwise occupied. For instance, while at work, round at the in-laws *etc.*

poo credit *n.* When someone is on a diet and weighs slightly more than the previous day, but has not yet paid a visit to the *smallest room*. For a *shit*. *'I have put on half a pound darling, but it's okay. I'm still in poo credit today.'*

poocumber *n.* A long, cylindrical stool with little or no nutritional value.

poo day *n.* An occasional day off work, caused by one needing to do a lot of *duties*. Like a duvet day, but spent on the *shitter.*

poo dew *n.* The beads of liquid decorating the *arse* cheeks and the insides of the *grundies* after passing a wet *pop.*

poodini *n.* A rare *sweaty Morph* that magically escapes through the U-bend without any assistance whatsoever, even if you'd got a policeman to chain it up in a canvas bag first. A *ghost shit.*

poodle jumper *n.* A bestial *spud fumbler.*

pooetry *n. Shite* rhymes of the sort formerly exchanged between Ryan Giggs and

his ex-squeeze.

pooey Armstrong *n.* A stubborn *Thora* which causes one to puff one's cheeks out like a bullfrog while emitting ear-splitting *brass fartfare* noises. Pausing occasionally to mop one's brow with a handkerchief. So-called because, when it's all over, "you think to yourself, what a wonderful world".

poof *n.* A man who doesn't want another pint.

poo fairy *n.* Magical entity which regularly visits the female half of the population, resulting in the male half being under the handy illusion that ladies never need to *lay a cable.*

poof dust *n.* Phrase used by schoolboys to describe talcum powder in the days before there was such a thing as diversity training.

poo 45 *n.* A workplace *bogs shit* that is a sackable offence. *"Collect your poo 45, Mr Zahawi.'*

poof's pizza *n.* Quiche.

poofter *n. Aus.* An Australian man who doesn't want another ten pints.

poogasm *1. n.* Grunts and groans of pleasure and relief emanating from a cubicle in the blokes' *bogs*, typically followed by a large splash. *2. n.* The shiver of satisfaction that a chap gets when he knows he's got a cup of tea in one hand, a new copy of the *Autotrader* in the other, and he's just about to unleash a *yard of ale* out of his *arse.*

poogina *n.* A lady's back *front bottom.*

poogle *v.* To look something up on a smartphone while ensconced on the *shit pot*. *'What are you doing in there, dear?' 'Out in a minute, love. I'm just poogling the symptoms of irritable bowel syndrome.'*

pooh corner *n.* The smallest room in the house. The *Rick Witter, shite house.*

poo horn *n.* The kitchen utensil kept by the *chod bin* for easing *pan-blocker*s round tight-fitting U-bends, *eg.* Bread knife, scissors, egg whisk. *'Nip upstairs and fetch the poo horn down, will you love? The kids want an omelette.'*

pooing and froing *phr. medic.* A bad case of *bowel buckaroo* necessitating repeated trips to the *crapper* and back.

pookkake *1. n.* An explosive case of the *Earthas* that occurs at an inopportune juncture during a romantic dalliance. Or, presumably, at an opportune moment if you're going out with a German. *2. n.* The saucy act of *rubbing one out* onto a *bum goblin* left in a toilet.

poo lassoo *n.* Spraying air freshener around after stinking out the *crapper.* From the circular rancher-style action made overhead with the aerosol.

pool balls *n. medic.* A distressing affliction whereby the male genitalia seek refuge within the pelvic cavity, a condition common amongst wild swimmers who pursue their hobby in more inclement weathers. *Captain Webb's knackers.*

pooligan *n.* One who habitually *dumps his guts* in the *chod bins* of friends, family or casual acquaintences without giving a second's thought to the social embarrassment that the fallout from their actions will cause.

poolindrome *n.* A foodstuff that has the same physical characteristics both before and after *digestive transit*, *eg.* Veggie mince, sweetcorn, chili con carne. See also *gorilla's breakfast.*

pools for stools *euph. medic.* Descriptive of a patient who is suffering from the *Engelberts.*

pool table, stand out like a shit on a *v.* To fail notably to blend in with the herd. *'And do you see that man in this court today, Mrs Mousepractice?' 'Yes, it's him over there, the dirty old bastard in the red robes and the wig. He stands out like a shit on a pool table.'*

pooluted *adj.* Of an environment, rendered inhospitable due to *shite*; for example a recently *bombed-out* bathroom stall or a pleasant beach or woodland fouled by inconsiderate dog-owners. Or their pets.

poolystyrene *n.* One of them eager little fragments of buoyant *crap* that has broken away from the *mother shit* of a previous *chod bin* occupant, and simply cannot be flushed away.

poomerang *n.* A *turd* which is able to return from down under the U-bend with twice the force with which it was flushed away in the first place.

poomoania *n. medic.* An acute infection of the lower *arspiratory tract.* A condition which leads to repeated wheezing, coughing and sneezing from the *anus.*

poon *n. Fanny, crumpet, toosh. 'I guess, this means my poon days are over.'* (Abraham Lincoln after his inauguration in May 1776). *'Knickers off, this is poon city!'* (Bill Clinton after his inauguration in June 1993).

poond *n.* A *gunt, fupa, fat hat.* From the Geordie "a poond o' tripe".

poonder *v.* To mull things over on the *throne,* perhaps while reading the *Autotrader.*

pooning *n.* Sniffing ladies' bicycle seats. Also *snuft, snudge, shramp, quumf, scrunge, pringle, snerge, snedge, snaffle, snarze, snerk, snerdle, shniffle-piffle, nurf, moomph, barumph, garboon, poon, snarf, snood, snurdle* or *snurge.* An action more often named than actually done, you might suppose.

poon squad *n.* A pack of *cougars* out *on the lash,* hungry for *meat.* Working as a gang, they typically abduct the youngest, weakest male in a group, before taking him back to their lair, going *straight*

for the cockular and *fucking* him within an inch of his life.

poontang *1. n. US. A clopper. 2. n. US.* Some *clopper.*

poon town rat *n.* A f*m*n*ne hygiene requisite. Also *cunt mouse, chuftie plug, Dracula's teabag, tam rag, gash plaster, dangermouse, clot mop, jampax, snatch rat, jam dam, cotton mouse, gash mop, claret mouse, slim fanatella, gashmina, jammy dodger, twat rat, beaver dam, blobstopper, fanny nanny* or *jam rag.*

poo packer *n.* A confectionery factory employee who works in the fudge packaging department.

poopane *n.* Explosive, noxious gas emanating from the anal fissure. Highly flammable *carbon dibaxide.*

poop catchers *n. Knickers, dunghampers, bills.*

poop chute *n.* The *bumhole* or *arse,* up which parking tickets can be rammed.

poop deck *n.* The floor of the house upon which the bathroom is situated.

pooperglue *n.* Faecal *ejecta* that displays superior – not to say industrial-strength – adhesive properties. Removal is often only possible by using the *piss chisel,* thumbnail or blowtorch. *'Holy Mary, mother of God! The father's cludgee is daubed in fecking pooperglue again. Fetch a sister with good nails, and quick.'*

poopernova *n.* A sudden release of *dark matter* from Uranus (your anus).

poop hoop *n.* The back door of the *dirt bakery,* through which the *burnt chocolate cakes* are ejected.

poophoria *n.* The feeling of unalloyed bliss felt after *dropping a coachload of kids off at the pool.*

pooping cough *n. medic.* A highly debilitating smoker's condition which, when hacking away severely while *heavily refreshed,* causes one to *soil* one's own *rompers.* 2. *n.* Clearing one's throat melodramatically while ensconced in a public lavatory cubicle, in order to disguise the shameful fact that one is having a *shit.*

poopoo *1. v.* To idly disparage another's statement. 2. *n.* Poo.

poopoozela *n.* A loud, obnoxious, and unwelcome *botty bugle* fanfare, heralding the onset of a major event for the trumpeter, but simultaneously ruining the evening for everyone else. Also *loovuzela.*

poo pourri *1. n. Fr.* A pile of irregularly shaped, brown organic material, often found lying in a bowl and stinking the room out. 2. *n.* The stench of *feculent,* masked by the use of cheap air freshener. A *Burberry shitbomb.*

poo-pourri *n.* Plastic bags of fragrant *dog mud*

adorning trees and bushes.

poo preview *n.* An *air buffet*, a *mariner's chart*. The *turtle's breath* that serves as a trailer for a *mini series* that's coming soon.

pooquet *n.* The aroma of a well-aged *turd* – particularly when it exhibits secondary notes that linger on one's palate.

poorly ET *n.* Your next *Peter O'Toole* after using an Anusol pellet. Named after Hollywood's favourite space alien after he too was found lying limp and blanched in shallow water.

poor man's limo *n.* That feeling when you are the only passenger on a bus.

poor man's oyster *n.* When suffering from a cold, the salty mixture of blood, phlegm and mucus that must be swallowed after an aggressive sniff. If a *poor man's oyster* requires a lot of chewing, it is known as *Polish chewing gum*.

poorn *n.* A thankfully niche area of the continental *grumble* industry, concentrating principally on people who like to drop *copper bolts* on one another. Your Germans, that'll be.

poornography *n.* *Grumble* of a core which comes low on the Moh scale. The sort of soft-focus cotton wool-strength *grot* broadcast on Channel 5 in the good old days. (From poor + nography).

poor sense of direction, have a *v.* Of a man, to be *excellent with colours*.

poo-ruse *v.* To read at length, undisturbed, while sat on the *throne*. *'What are you doing in there, Melvyn?' 'I'm just poo-rusing the Man-Booker Prize shortlist.'*

poosex *n.* A charming word for *brown love*.

poosh *1. v.* A *shit* enjoyed in an upscale locale, *eg.* The Gents in Harrods, the Ziggu Camp loos at the Glastonbury Festival, in the middle of Claridge's Ballroom floor, or down a pair of exquisitely tailored Saville Row trousers. *2. v.* The amount of extra force required by the external sphincter muscle to evacuate a recalcitrant *stool*. *'Yotam, you've been in there an hour. Are you okay?' 'Just one more poosh and I'll have got rid of the last of those Turmeric braised eggs with tamarind dressing.'*

poo sledge *n.* A tissue laid carefully into the bowl to intercept *foulage* dropped from an offset *nipsy* and thus avoid leaving *Mr Brown's fingerprints*.

poosticks *n.* Game whereby lolly sticks are inserted into *barkers' eggs* by curious children. *'"What are you doing?" squeaked Piglet excitedly. "I'm pushing a lolly stick into a dog shit," replied Christopher Robin.'* (from *When we Were Alive* by AA Milne).

poot *1. v.* To perform a short *brass eye* fanfare, often sounded after eating *musical vegetables*. A good *poot* might, at best, push an average weight

man forward by about half a step. *2. n.* A *flies' dinner gong*.

poo tea *n.* An unrefreshing brown infusion made by allowing *logs* to brew in the pot for a long time. *PG shits, ty-poo. 'You only get an "eurgh!" with poo tea.'*

pooter *n.* The *bum* bellows with which a person *poots*. The *poot flute*. The preface to *diarrhoea of a nobody*.

poot flute *n.* *Trouser trumpet, singing ring, cornhole cornet, swannee whistle, pooter.*

poothulu *n.* A massive and otherwordly denizen of the *pan*.

pootonium *n.* A *turd* so toxic that sustained exposure to it can lead to hair loss, bleeding gums and ultimately death.

pootopia *n.* The blissful feeling upon opening the works *crappers* door and finding out the cleaners have just been. No *tiger's back*, no *arse baccie* or nowt.

pootube *1. n.* The flue on a *Dutch oven*. A tunnel created by the strategic lifting of part of the duvet, the purpose of which is to control the flow of *carbon dibaxide* in whichever direction a *benefactor* wishes. *2. n.* An internet video streaming site based in Germany, you would imagine.

poove *n.* A footstool at your auntie's house. *'We've ran out of chairs, our Terry. You'll have to sit on the poove.'*

poovenirs *n.* Keepsakes, such as sweetcorn kernels or bits of carrot debris, deposited on the *bellend* following a spot of *back door work*.

poovert *n.* A poo pervert or *scat man*. A *crothers*. Usually a Teuton, if truth be told. From poo + pervert.

poovery *n.* *Bumcraft.*

pop *1. n.* *Foulage*. A word used to great effect by Adam & Joe in those happy times when they used to be on the radio. *'Who's just walked this dog pop in on their shoes?' 2. acronym.* Post Orgasmic Piss. *'Thanks for the fuck, Monica. I'm just nipping behind that skip for a pop.'*

pop a knocker *v.* Of a lady, to overreact to a situation in a melodramatic fashion. *'Christ, love, it was only a chewie off your sister. There's no need to pop a knocker.'*

popazogalou *n.* A *chewie, gobble, blow job*. From the name of the landlord in the film *Personal Services* who accepted *payment in kind*.

pop down and change the barrel, sorry I just need to *exclam.* An anticipatory apology, uttered before – or possibly during – the release of a proper *brewer's fart*.

popemobile *n.* Sexual position favoured by

members of the *dogging* community. With the front seats folded fully flat, the man lies on his back and the woman sits atop him in the *reverse cowboy* position. Through the steamed-up two-inch thick spectacles of the casual passer-by *wanking* in his trousers, her erotic gyrations resemble nothing so much as the Pontiff waving to the adoring crowds from behind the two-inch-thick bulletproof glass of his trademark automobile.

Pope's hat *n.* A prophylactic sheath, *blob* or *dunky*. A *jubber ray*.

Pope's swear box, the *euph.* Something that has little or no contents. *'I can't come out this weekend, Paul. Me wallet's emptier than the Pope's swear box.'*

Popeye *1. n.* Term used to describe the gagging noise a woman might make during a particularly vigorous *Boris Johnson*. *2. n.* The state of a lady being *airtight* in all orifices. From the eponymous spinach-chomper's pre-punch-up catch-phrase "That's all I can stands and I can't stands no more."

Popeye eating spinach *sim.* To engage in enthusiastic *cumulonimbus*. With a pipe in one's mouth. *'And the husband of Bathsheba did venture forth for Regal Super Kings that numbered two score and did leave Bathsheba alone in the tent. And David did enter the tent and did know Bathsheba. And David did kneel before Bathsheba, and lo, he did go at it like Popeye eating spinach.'* (from *The Book of Clive* 6:3-5).

Popeye's laugh *n.* The involuntary, guttural, gagging noise made by a *fellatrix* who has *bitten off more than she can chew*. Coined due to the sound's similarity to the one-eyed, pipe-chomping, grotesquely distended-forearmed, spinach-powered cartoon sailor's trademark "uggug-gugguggugg" guffaw. A *French cough*.

Popeye spunk *n.* The thick, cloudy mixture found at the bottom of a bottle of olive oil when the temperature drops.

Popeye wipe *n.* The first, agonising attempt at a spot of *ringpiece* polishing after one has *dropped* a quantity of unruly, *screaming Mexican kids off at the pool*. From the resulting adoption of a facial expression resembling that of the eponymous monocular cartoon schizophrenic.

pop her cork *v.* To give a lady an *organism*. Presumably by shaking her up and down for twenty seconds and then pushing her *clit* up with your thumbs.

pop idle *adj.* Unable or unwilling to perform any useful role in society as a result of one's devotion to alcoholic beverages. *'Have you done any work,* paid or unpaid, since you last signed on?' 'No, I'm pop idle. You couldn't give us a sub until me giro comes through, could you, pal? Only I drank me last four cans of spesh before I come out and I'm shaking like a shitting dog here.'*

popmaster/popmastur *1. n.* One who can knock out *three in ten*. *2. n.* A chap who likes to *knock one out* at about twenty-five to eleven every morning. A chap whose bonus set of questions is on *wanking*.

pop pickers *1. n.* The erstwhile listeners to the late Alan "Fluff" Freeman's Saturday afternoon radio run-down of past hit parades. *2. n.* Girls of low morals that favour the company of older men (and why wouldn't they?).

poppycock *1. exclam.* Nonsense, *bollocks*. *'I just seen George Best at the bar buying a tomato juice.' 'Poppycock.'* *2. n.* Severe form of *the droop* suffered by those who have a penchant for *skag*.

pop shot *n.* Scene in a *noddy flick* in which a male actor is required to splash his *population paste* for the camera, after being suitably primed by the *fluffer*. Also *money shot*.

pop the brown balloon *v.* To *break cover* loudly in a fashion that could make a nervous person jump.

pop the brown champagne *v.* To uncork one's *rusty bullet hole* the morning after a night spent over-indulging oneself on booze, *'babs* and chili sauce. *'I'm feeling a bit better now, but fuck me, the first bog visit after I got up was like popping a bottle of brown champagne, I tell you. Meanwhile, over to Daniel Corbett for tomorrow's weather.'*

pop the night cork *v.* To perform the day's first evacuation of the *Simon Cowells* following a heavy night *on the sauce*, whereby an impacted, solid plug of *feeshus* is propelled outwards by a plume of *fizzy gravy*.

pop the turkey in the oven *v.* To pluck the feathers from one's penis and put it in a vagina at gas mark six, prior to getting one's father-in-law to self-importantly cut it into slices.

population paste *n.* *Joy gloy*, semen, *spunk*, *Aphrodite's evostick, jazz glue, prick stick*.

pop-up book *n.* A special type of reading matter where things magically spring into three dimensions as one leafs through the pages. A *bongo mag, art pamphlet, DIY manual*.

pop-up box *1. n.* Something utterly *shit* which cannot be avoided on the internet. *2. n.* Something utterly smashing which cannot be avoided on the internet. A lady's prominent pubular *mons veneris*. Also known as a *proud Mary, beetle bonnet, pig's trotter* or *pigeon's chest*.

pop-up panic *n.* The bowel-loosening fear that

comes from having to hurridly close down internet *grumble* sites one has been ogling due to the impending approach of a boss, spouse, parent or policeman, only to be suddenly assaulted by a barrage of obscene ad windows that multiply exponentially the more one tries to delete them.

pop-up pirate *1. n.* A game where one wrong move could cause the *one-eyed fella* to spring up out of his *barrel*. *2. n.* Likewise, a *stonk on.*

pop-up shop *1. n.* A temporary retail establishment of the sort run by *bellend Apprentice* contestants in Leadenhall Market, London, selling scented candles or artisanal sausages or some other such similar *bollocks*. *2. n.* A brothel, *knocking shop* or *box office.*

pop your cherry *v.* To lose your virginity, *break your duck*. *'Cliff: Hey, Hank. I just popped my cherry. Hank: Congratulations. Hey, that gives me an idea for a song.'* (screenplay for *Summer Holiday* (1963), by Samuel Beckett).

porcelain beard *n.* The stray *pubes* that befringe a public urinal.

porcelain bolt *n.* When caught short, a last-ditch attempt to make it to the *Rick Witter* before you *papper your grundies*; a sprint that even certain Jamaican athletes might struggle to keep up with.

porcelain pencil *n.* A *Richard the Third* that feels the need to express its artistic side while exiting the bowl, usually at a stranger's house. *'Some dirty bugger's had the porcelain pencil out, Mr Carson. There's more skids on that fucking bowl than on Count Zborowski's driveway.'*

porcelain shrine of Sister Bernardette *euph.* Small room on the ground floor of a public house (often labelled Disabled Toilets) whenceforth shameless penitents emerge miraculously able to walk.

porcelain tingle *n.* The cold shock that occurs when one's *bell end* touches the lavatory pan when sitting on the *throne*. A *harprick.*

porch pirates *n.* Charming scallywags who cruise the streets looking for parcels that a caring courier has decided to leave by your front door in plain view of the whole fucking world, and then considerately taking them in for safe keeping,

pork *1. v. Aus.* To *fuck*. *'I couldn't pork her because she had the painters in. And they were already porking her.'* *2. n. Aus.* The *spam javelin.*

pork and beans *adj.* A term to describe a *happy shopper*, or *Betty Both*. One who *bowls from both the pavilion and the members' end*. Half rice half chips.

pork chop *n.* Circumcision. *'The Lord spoke unto Moses in a loud voice, saying: If it should come to pass that a woman conceives and gives birth to a boy then on the eighth day he shall be given the pork chop.'* (from the *Book of Leviticus*).

porker's crisps *n.* The name given to the crusty remains found inside one's *undercrackers* the morning after *rodding someone's drains* in a nightclub *bog.*

porkfolio *n.* A photo gallery of erstwhile ladyfriends kept on a gentleman's mobile telephone and brought out to impress/disgust his drinking companions or prospective employers.

pork 'n' stalk *n.* A lady with whom one has had a whirlwind one-night romance, who continues to bombard one with texts, phone calls and cooked pets. A *bunny boiler.*

pork pie jelly *n.* Any lubricant that is applied to the *meat* in order to ease its insertion into the *hairy pie*, eg. KY jelly. Also *I can't believe it's not batter, phoney batter, granny batter, fuck butter,*

pork pie that's been trodden on *euph.* An *untidy slice*. A *ripped sofa, stamped bat, butcher's window, ragman's coat. The bottom of a ratcatcher's mallet.*

pork pills *n. pharm. Cock drops, blueys.* Viagras, *Bongo Bill's banjo pills.*

pork prescription *1. n.* A *bacon bazooka*, to be swallowed twice a day instead of meals. *2. n.* Doctor's authorisation for a *meat injection* when the patient is suffering from a *Vitamin S defiiciency.*

pork scratchings *n. medic.* Irritation of the *old chap* as a result of a misguided liaison with a promiscuous lady. A *dose. 'Excuse me, barman. But have you got pork scratchings?' 'Yes. I got them when I fucked your missus under the pier last week'.* (Bamforth's *Seaside Chuckles* postcard by Donald McGill, 1926).

pork served in three ways *1. n.* Something self-explanatory seen on the menu in poncy restaurants. *2. n.* One *cock* up the *fanny*, one up the *arse* and one in the mouth.

pork stalk *n.* The *veiny bang stick, spam javelin, bacon bazooka.*

pork stork *n. 'Dad, where do babies come from?' 'The pork stork, son.'*

pork string shit *n.* A *number two* that *hangs like a Tyburn villain*, refusing to drop. Sometimes caused by undigested butcher's cord that has been inadvertently ingested by an over-enthusiastic gourmand.

pork sword *n.* Penis, *tallywhacker, lamb cannon.* More of a pocket whittling knife than a mighty sabre.

Porky Pig, do a *v.* In the spirit of the stuttering, porcine Warner Bros. cartoon character, to walk or drive around town wearing only a shirt – with no trousers or underwear of any kind. Dirty fucking bastard.

porn actor arriving on set, as happy as a *sim.* Descriptive of someone who approaches life with an optimistic 'can-do' attitude. And probably a bad back.

pornado *n.* The situation where a computer user's desktop gets taken over by *Frankie Vaughano-graphic* pop-ups which are opening faster than he can close them. Also *girlwind, hairy pie-clone.*

pornaments *n.* *Gentlemen's literature* that adorns the tops of wardrobes and other "hard to reach" areas of furniture, that nevertheless gets dusted off on a regular basis.

pornaoke *n.* The humorous *Two Ronnies*-style art of putting obscene lyrics to much-loved popular tunes, *eg.* "Big blue vein" (*You're So Vain* by Carly Simon), "Wank You for the Music" (*Thank You for the Music* by Abba), and many more too numerous to mention.

pornbroker *n.* The man at work who can be relied upon to lend you a bit of *mucky* to see you through hard times. A *pornmeister,* a *jazz magnate. 'Let me introduce you to Maurice. He's our pornbroker here at Pan-Global Megacorp Inc.'*

porn buddy *n.* A *cliterary executor.* A single fellow's best friend who, in the event of his untimely death, is charged with the important task of removing and disposing of the deceased's stash of *grumble* before his grieving parents arrive to search through his effects for touching mementoes and stuff to put on eBay. If former Poet Laureate and lifelong *jazz* enthusiast Philip Larkin's *porn buddy* had managed to carry out the Hull University librarian's final wishes, it is estimated that the resulting bonfire of hardcore *art pamphlets* outside Pearson Park would have been visible from the Moon.

porn chorus *n.* The cacophony of *birds* that a gentleman hears when he opens his Windows in the morning. After his wife has gone to work.

porn cocktail *1. n.* In certain "niche" areas of saucy film making, a beverage concocted from the mingled *tadpoles* and *man mayonnaise* of a number of male performers which is ingested with a limited amount of relish by the female lead. *2. n.* Residue found on the bedsheets of frustrated teenagers.

porn cock tale *n.* An erstwhile explicitly exaggerated account of the dimensions of one's own *membrum virile* and the adventures that have befallen it, sent in to a *jazz mag.*

pornder *v.* To try to decide how best to spend the day productively before ending up online watching

MILF Norman as usual. *'Yes dear. I know the lawn needed mowing but after some serious porndering I decided against it.'*

porn dough *n.* Soft, sticky substance found adhering to *jazz mags* and laptops.

porner shop *n.* A convenient place where *wankers* go to purchase *biff books.* A small retail establishment which, despite intense competition from the internet, continues to purvey paper-based masturbatory materials in defiance of all economic principles. *'I'm just off to the porner shop, Dave. Do you want anything?' 'Aye. Get me twenty Benny Henny, a bag of Monster Munch and this month's Face Squatting Femmes.'*

porn flakes *n.* The crusty bits found on the sofa/sheets the morning after a late night *scruff video* session.

porn fuzz *n.* Characteristic picture quality of an 18th generation *bongo vid* that makes the performers look as if they are in the process of being incompetently beamed up to the Enterprise half the time. *Readybrek glow.*

porn glare *n.* A situation familiar to *trad jazz* enthusiasts; the cruel, frustrating shaft of light which partially obscures the spreadeagled *bird* on the double page spread of an *art pamphlet* as he strives for *vinegar. Razzle dazzle.*

pornhography *n.* *Grumblular* entertainment featuring female participants of notably poor quality.

porn horn *n.* A three-quarters-hard erection of the sort that is regularly seen being fed into the actresses in *scud films.* An *Indian rope prick.*

pornilingual *adj.* Of a fellow whose knowledge of other languages is derived solely from phrases heard while watching foreign *stick flicks.* Examples include the Japanese "Kimochee" (It feels good) and "Kau ga beta beta" (My face is all sticky), and the German "Ja, schmekt gut" (Yes, it tastes good) and "Jetzt mit der ganzen Faust" (Now with the whole fist).

porning realisation *n.* A gentleman's sinking feeling when sat at work or anywhere miles from home after an earlier bout of *blowing the elephant's nose,* when he suddenly remembers he has left a whole trail of filthy evidence for his wife to find upon her return home, *eg.* Crusty *porn crackers,* an array of foul *grumble* spread out in a semi-circle on the living room floor, a photo of her sister in a bikini from Benidorm last year all covered in spunk. And the photo all covered in *spunk* too.

pornithologist *n.* One who enjoys looking at pictures of *nests* and *tits* rather than going out and looking at them in the flesh. A *cock twitcher.*

pornithology *n.* The scientific study of two *birds at it like fucking knives. Lesbology.*

porn mauve *n.* Distinctive colour assumed by all male genitalia in *grumble vids,* a hue rarely if ever seen in real life.

porn mirage *n.* A cruel trick of the light, whereby a *tug*-hungry adolescent spots some *grummer* under a hedge, which on closer inspection turns out to be an Argos catalogue or the *Sunday Mirror* TV guide.

pornmower *n.* A *fanny mower* without the cutting length attachment.

porno cocktail *n.* A stimulating visual smörgåsbord of one-handed reading material, perhaps comprising editions of *Knave, Fiesta, Whitehouse,* something stronger and continental, and possibly a Freeman's catalogue opened at the lingerie section, all laid out in a semi-circle for easy reference.

porno curve *n.* A scientific term for the progressively fouler nature of the *grummer* viewed during the course of a four-hour *gland tour* of the internet. The graph typically reaches its highest point on the y-axis of grimness with women doing *scat* or Hungarian robot porn, before ultimately subsiding back to some palate-cleansing naked ladies. Progress along the curve can occasionally be interrupted by the wife preparing dinner, one's boss knocking on the office door or a call into the main chamber of the House to vote. Also known as a *wristogram* or *pie chart.*

pornogamy *n.* Amongst impoverished gentlemen, the practice of remaining continuously faithful to the same dog-eared *seed catalogue* for all their sexual and emotional needs over a number of years or even decades.

porno greygio *n.* The type of chilled wine which is an ideal accompaniment to a single lady's evening in with the curtains shut and one of them *mumble* books on her e-reader. The mucky slut.

porno grigio *n.* Soft adult material of a nature that would, one might suppose, be more appealing to the fairer sex.

pornoisseur *n.* A gentleman who appreciates only the finest things in one-handed life.

porno mouth *n.* An open-minded young lady whose coital utterances closely resemble the dialogue from *grumble flicks,* eg. "Split me in two with your big cock" *etc.*

porn on the fourth of July *sim.* Temporary Tom Cruise-style male lower body paralysis that occurs when attempting to stand up to make a cup of tea after loosing off several rounds from the mutton musket.

pornoquet *n. medic.* An emergency binding made from toilet paper, hastily wound around a *kindling limb* in an attempt to stem the flow of one's *life essences* during a *one-man battle* with the *purple-helmeted soldier.* See also *wank hat, nob turban.*

pornorama *n.* A magnificent, breathtaking array of *meat mags,* arranged in a vista to provide variety and spectacle while having a *tug.* A *wank crescent, glandscape.*

porno star, take it like a *phr.* Conciliatory and sympathetic expression uttered to one who has suffered poor luck, but needs to draw a line under it and carry on, *ie.* "Take it on the chin". *'Don't worry Theresa, some time we all have to take it like a porno star. There'll be other opinion polls.'*

pornowhack *n.* The act of entering an obviously filthy expression into Google, but unaccountably returning no "hits".

porn penguin *n.* A brisk, comical waddle across the living room in order to pause, rewind or fast forward through the plot-related bits of a *tug film* when the batteries have failed in your remote.

porn pipe *n.* One's broadband internet cable. *'The porn pipe's blocked. I can only assume that your father is downloading something enormous in his wankatorium.'*

porn pump *n.* A personal computer. Also *faptop, filth machine, dirty Mac.*

porn sacrifice *n.* A poorly hidden *stash* of low-quality *grumble* designed as a decoy to put your *bag for life* off the scent of the *export strength* stuff. A *blue herring, stalking horse.*

porn shui *n.* The mystic technique employed by a male office worker when deciding on the position of his workstation; an attempt to minimise the risk that a colleague may catch a glimpse of what he's actually looking at on his screen while pretending to ponder spreadsheets, check warehouse stock levels, do whatever it is you do with Powerpoint *etc.*

pornstache *n.* A luxuriant moustache of the sort sported by late *Department S* actor Peter Wyngarde, Times Radio presenter John Pienaar, and ennobled *cunt dentist* Lord Winston.

porn star balls *n.* Shaved *knackers,* usually viewed from the rear and between a *grumble* actor's legs as they repeatedly slap against the *tinter* of the object of his extremely temporary affection.

pornstarch *n.* The dried *man-milk* to be found in overused *wank socks* that makes them rigid enough to stand up and walk around on their own.

pornstar fartini *euph.* Effervescent eruptions that issue from a lady's *netherparts* as a consequence of sustained penetrative pounding in unusual positions.

porn star's fart *n.* A stealthy, raspless whooshing noise like that of a turbocharger.

porn sub *n.* A worthy and safe website that a fellow ensures he has running up and down the sidelines at the ready to, in an instant, conceal less family friendly internet material. While he's sat there with his trousers round his ankles and his *cock* in his hand.

porn trauma *n.* Upon reaching the *vinegar strokes* while watching an *art film* and finding the screen suddenly filled by a big, sweaty bloke with large sideburns, being too late to stop, and *gwibbling* to a disappointing finish. See *vinegar Joe.*

porn trumpet *n.* The male *Piers Morgan. 'Now I'm not one to blow my own porn trumpet.'*

pornucopia *n.* A seemingly endless supply of *jazz, eg.* On the top shelf of the magazine rack at Barton Park lorry services on the A1.

porn ultimatum *1. n.* The point at which the newsagent tells you to stop browsing and either buy a *bongo book* or get out of his shop. *2. n.* A pact made between two friends that each of them will clear his counterpart's house of any stashed adult material in the event of his death, in order to save the blushes of bereaved family members, ex-wives, the police *etc.*

porn vortex *n.* A whirling *Time Tunnel*-style fifth dimension where time has no meaning, encountered when browsing the worldwide web for *left-handed websites.* A chap could fall into a *porn vortex* and emerge ten minutes later to discover that three days have elapsed. A *burp-the-wormhole.*

pornytail *n.* The camera-friendly hairstyle of a *grumble flick* actress who thoughtfully ties her hair back to allow viewers an uninterrupted view of her *deep-throating* a *Charlie* like a baby's arm.

porpoise nose *n.* Like a *turtle's head*, but a bit more urgent. And making a clicking sound.

porridge gun *n.* Tool for distributing *population paste* quickly and efficiently.

port and starboard scran spanners *n. naval.* Knife and fork.

porthole pudding, have a *v.* To munch down hungrily on a *rusty sheriff's badge* with the fervour and enthusiasm of a pug licking a trifle bowl.

portion *n.* A large but non-specific quantity of *the other,* of the sort that Max Miller might talk about having. Remember him, kids? See also *one, a length, a bit. 'I'd give her a portion, and no mistake, missus.'*

PORT/port *abbrev.* A politically correct term for a

bird with small *tits.* Person Of Restricted Tittage, *eg.* Thirsty wine *gobshite* Jilly Goulden.

Portsmouth Harbour *euph.* The arrival of an attractive female and her ugly friends, in the style of a sleek ocean liner coming into port surrounded by a flotilla of tugboats.

Portuguese breakfast *n.* A hearty bowl-full to start the day. A watery, clotted *shit* that resembles the sort of thing they'd probably eat over there.

Portuguese man o' war *1. n.* Name given to a buoyant jelly fish, *Physalia atlantica,* characterised by the presence of one or more large air-sacs, by means of which it drifts about on the surface of the ocean. *2. n.* Swimming shorts so inflated with poisonous *carbon dibaxide* that they float above the surface of the pool, causing alarm to fellow swimmers.

Poseidon's fury *1. n.* A spectacular interactive adventure at Universal Islands of Adventure in Orlando, Florida. *2. n.* Like a *Neptune's kiss,* except you've recently put bleach in the *chod bin. Acid splashback* that leaves the victim dripping from the *barse.*

posharean *n. medic.* In obstetrics, a Caesarean section performed for no other reason than to keep the mother's *twat* nice and tight.

posh drive *n.* Wearing a Covid facemask whilst driving alone in a vehicle. Analogous to the onanistic act of the *posh wank* albeit not as hazardous when manoeuvring in traffic.

posh fag *n.* A cigarette outside under an umbrella when it's raining. *'I'm having a bit of a problem stitching this donor heart in here, due to tricuspid valve regurgitation. Do you fancy having a bash while I pop outside for a posh fag?'*

posh fart *n. Passing* wind following a bath or shower, and in the process drying one's own *nipsy.*

posh nosh *1. n.* Fancy foodstuffs, *eg.* Patty de fwar grar, caviar and chicken kievs. Basically, anything from the Tesco's "Finest" range. *2. n.* A *gobble* with a *rubber johnny* on. See also *posh wank.*

Posh Spice's smile, as much use as *sim.* A scathing equivalence. From Lady Beckham's happy face, which has apparently never been put into service by its owner. See also *as much use as ~Kate Moss's chip pan, ~a Glaswegian's salad drawer etc.*

posh Tetleys *n.* A ginger *snatch*, named after the said company's upmarket tea brand, *viz.* Red Bush. Also *brandy snap.*

posh wank *n.* Have they just sent you down here from *posh nosh*? A *mess*-free masturbatory manoeuvre undertaken while wearing a *dunky.*

Possil barbecue *n.* Burnt-out motor vehicle, usually found on gap sites in and around the eponymous leafy north Glasgow suburb.

posstitute *n.* A woman standing on a street corner who may be a *good time girl,* or may simply be waiting for a bus.

post and in *euph.* A *motion* that hits the bowl before sliding into the water. *'Fetch the bleach, Margot. I've just had a post and in.'*

post fartum depression *n. medic.* All-consuming melancholy upon hearing the cry of an unexpected *arse baby.*

postie's tip *n.* A birthday card with some money in it.

posting an omelette, like *sim.* Descriptive of a futile attempt at flaccid intercourse. *'Shall we just call it a day, Edson? This is like trying to post a fucking omelette.'*

post-it over the webcam, put a *v.* To take an elementary precaution when surfing the web, in order to prevent other internet users from inadvertently seeing you grappling with your *joystick.*

postman's arse *n. medic.* Condition caused by chronic chaffing of the *bum cheeks* and thus characterised by a painful red ring around the *tea towel holder* which afflicts those whose working day involves much walking and sweating.

postman's knuckle *n. medic.* An extremely painful hand condition suffered by mail delivery personnel who have to insert their fingers into their lady customers' cramped *slots* on a regular basis.

postman's nipsy *n.* Pavement jetsam discarded by a startled mailman *viz.* A rubber band.

postman's pocket, wetter than a *sim.* Of a lady in a highly excited state, *wetter than a turfer's knee, wetter than Whitney Houston's last joint. Frothing like bottled Bass.*

postman's sack *n.* A *fanny* that is "full of mail/ male". To be honest, that one works better said out loud than written down, and it doesn't even work that well said out loud.

postman's tickle *euph.* Two fingers inserted throught a *dirty letterbox.* After negotiating round a *growler.*

postman's wardrobe, fanny like a *sim.* A bulging *minge* that is stuffed to maximum capacity.

Post Office viagra *n.* A mailman's red elastic band applied to the base of the *giggling pin* to cut off circulation and thus preserve stiffness.

post-shit notes *n.* The handy stationery items with which a person wipes their *fifties tea towel holder* after passing a *Peter O'Toole.*

Post Traumatic Sex Disorder *n. medic.* Severe psychological condition suffered by a man who wakes up the morning after a heavy night *on the pop* to find himself in bed next to a right *fugly minger. 'I had a proper attack of Post Traumatic Sex Disorder*

until she turned over and I realised it was the wife.'

potato fat *n.* The starchy gloop that issues from a gentleman's *spuds* when he mashes them a bit. *Spunk, tattie watta, spud juice.*

pot brown *v.* To sink a long *pink* into the *herbert pocket.*

potch *v. Wales.* To partake of an extra-marital affair in the valleys. *'See that Jones the song? Well he's been potching for years, isn't it.'*

POTFO/potfo *abbrev.* Pointing Out The Fucking Obvious.

potholer *n.* An adventurous *mud child,* one end of which is connected to your *chuff* while the other has made its way round the U-bend, where its head pokes out through the meniscus in the trap to catch its breath, like a small, blind Loch Ness Monster. Also known as a *bumbilical.*

Pot Noodle horn *n.* Brewer's droop. A *cock like a wet noodle.*

pot pink *v.* To moor the *skin boat* in cod cove.

pots and pans *phr.* That phase of a night out when the drinks and empties are multivariate and double-parked on the table. *'I say, let's get on the dance floor.' 'Be there in a tick. I just need to do the pots and pans.'*

Potsdamer Platz *1. n. prop.* Area of no-man's land between dour, communist east and capitalist fun-loving west Berlin. *2. n.* The area of *no-man's land* between a lady's dour, communist *arse* and capitalist fun-loving *minge.* The *butfer, carse, tinter, taint, notcher, snarse, biffin bridge, Humber Bridge, niftkin's bridge* etc. *Checkpoint Charlie.*

potted plant *n.* An unkind epithet for a Police Community Support Officer. From the fact that they make the place look slightly better decorated while performing no discernibly useful function and using up space that could otherwise be put to better use. *'Hello? Emergency Services? Someone's trying to break into my car.' 'Don't worry madam. We'll send a potted plant round with some customer satisfaction survey forms to fill in tomorrow afternoon.'*

potter's wheel *1. n.* A thick, convoluted *blurtch,* sagging under its own weight such that it resembles a trouser-suited *joskin*'s attempt to throw a clay pot on the *Generation Game* in about 1975. *2 n.* Situation where a man carefully attempts to nurture a relationship with a lady over a period of time, only to ruin all his hard work by *copping a feel* too early. The *baker's impatience. 3. n.* The *cludgie.* A place for shaping *coil pots* using material retrieved from the *claypit. 'They say that everybody can remember where they were when they heard that Kennedy had been shot. I was sat on the* *potter's wheel reading a thirty-six-year-old copy of the Daily Mirror.'*

potting the black on the break *n.* A frustratingly premature ejaculation moments after handing over payment to a courtesan; forfeiting the game in the first ten seconds. *Spending your money before you get to the shop.*

pottle *1. n.* An old Imperial measure for liquids, equivalent to half a gallon. *'I'm not drunk, officer. I've only had a couple of pottles.' 2. n. onomat.* A single bubble of *carbon dibaxide* that breaks the surface of the bath water, rather ruining the effect that the scattered rose petals, candles, and romantic music was meant to achieve.

pottyfingers *n.* An inarticulate person who only shows up their lack of vocabulary by resorting to bad language when texting or writing emails, *eg.* Giles Coren.

potty-mouth *n.* US. A sweary *cunt.*

potty slot *n.* The *bum crack, bottom line, cleftal horizon.*

potty time *1. n.* Title of a weird 70s kids' television show hosted by Michael Bentine. *3. n.* When your *Donalds* smell of fresh foulage and it's time for a *sit-down visit.*

pouch *n.* An ageing, saggy *mott* that hangs between the legs like a sporran.

poundland *1. n.* High street discounter where the slogan is: "Buy cheap and you buy twice." *2. n.* Residence of a champion *pork swordsman*; *eg.* Ben Dover or Rocco Safredi's house. *3. n.* The foetid lair of an inveterate *wanker. 'This week, former journalist Piers Morgan invites Hello into his palatial Hampshire poundland.'*

poundland Pete *n.* That mate who is always bragging about what bargains he gets in the reduced aisle, who has just enjoyed a plate of Billy Bear ham for his dinner.

pound shop battery, less energy than a *sim.* Lethargic. *'Honestly, some days I can barely manage to drag meself out of bed to watch Jeremy Kyle or visit Greggs. I've got less energy than a pound shop battery. I sometimes wonder if I'm cut out to be a Kodo drummer.'*

pound shop Santa *n.* A less than generous person.

pound shop superglue, as sticky as *sim.* Descriptive as something which exhibits negligible adhesive properties.

poundstretcher *n.* An uncomfortably girthsome *arse baby* that weighs in at more than 454 grammes.

pound the pork *v.* Of sweating *pinksmiths*, to pummel a hot *pork sword* into shape. *Pound the pudding.*

poup pf the day *n.* When you forget to flush and find

that the unattended *bum spuds* have marinated to form a rich, brown pottage. *Farthouse broth.*

pouquet *n.* The olfactory signature of a good *Bakewell tart. 'Ah yes, this bottom burp has a very distinctive pouquet. It's a naive domestic dropped gut without any breeding, but I think you'll be amused by its presumption.'* (Cartoon by James Thurber in *The New Yorker*, 1937).

pour a pint for Bear Grylls *n.* To urinate.

pouring Pot Noodle *adj.* Producing an unappetizing, runny *poo*, though not quite unappetizing and runny enough to be described as Cup-a-Soup.

pour on the tip top *1. phr.* Advertising slogan for tinned cream with the great taste of modified tapioca starch from the 1970s (and still available today, amazingly enough). *2. v.* To *jizz* on someone's *arsegrapes.*

poutlet village *n. prop.* Any residential community in Cheshire blessed with beauty salons offering lip injectables.

povmiester *n.* The sort of cheap lager enjoyed by the underclasses that this nanny state government wants to take away from them, *eg.* Ace, Eiger, Jupiter.

powder one's nose *euph. 'Would the Secretary of State care to comment on the latest report on Housing and Communities?' 'He's just powdering his nose in the bogs, Mr Speaker.'*

powder room *1. n.* The ladies' WC where females go to dab their *conks* with talc (also to piss and shit) prior to attendance at a party. *2. n.* The gents' *bog* in a trendy London members' club, where lads' mag editors and children's television presenters go to snort *jazz talc.*

power ballad *n.* An *Elvis killer* of such colossal girth that, as it is passed, the victim raises his clenched fist into the air and pulls a face which calls to mind that of the lead singer of Boston during the chorus of *More than a Feeling*. A *Meat Loaf's daughter.*

power cake *n.* A turbo-charged *cupcake* which is unleashed in front of an electric fan.

power crap *n.* A refreshing, mid-afternoon *dump* that helps to split up a particularly tedious day at work.

power flower *n.* A *muscle Mary.*

power hour *n.* Self-improvement fad where you get up earlier and spend an hour on a planned activity. See also *hand cock's half-hour.*

power of Christ compels thee, the *exclam.* Incantation to exorcise the foul demons of the *chod bin* when the room becomes possessed by a particularly evil *out of botty experience*. Most effectively delivered while emptying a can of

Airwick in a North-South-West-East orientation, in a style reminiscent of a Papal blessing.

power to main thrusters *exclam.* Uttered before the *dropping* of a particularly highly-pressurised *hat,* the force of which causes the offender to rise vertically from their seat.

power trio *n.* A *piss*, a *shit* and a *wank*. The perfect way to start the day. Also *schwiss*.

powerwank *n.* A briskly efficient *tug* slotted into a busy work schedule. Often performed by politicians, captains of industry and de Vere Hotels bar staff on a fag break.

pox *n. medic.* Venereal disease, specifically syphilis. *Cock rot, clap.* Also *the pox*.

pox doctor's clerk, have a touch like a *v.* To be heavy-handed with something; to exhibit little or no finesse. *'The next contestant to take the stage at the Liszt-Garrison International Piano Competition is Mrs Mills, who is going to play a medley of Chopin's Polonaise-Fantaisie in A Flat Major, Ravel's Pavane pour une Infante Defunte and Jaromir Vejvoda's Roll Out the Barrel with all the touch of a pox doctor's clerk.'*

poxtrot *n.* A brisk visit to the VD clinic.

poxycillin *n. medic.* An antibiotic prescribed at the *clap clinic* for sorting out a dose of *happy rash*.

poxy resin *n.* Post *walnut whip man mastic*.

PPE *1. abbrev.* Piss Poor Excuse. Often in plentiful supply at times of crisis, *eg.* Pandemics and such. *2. abbrev.* Personal Protective Equipment for the wearing of. Not always in plentiful supply at times of crisis, and often supplemented with *1*.

PPP *abbrev.* The *pudenderage* of a mature lady that hasn't seen the light of day for a good long while, such that you have to break the crust & scoop out the jelly to get to the meat. Pork Pie Pussy.

practical classic *n.* A vintage *ride* in original condition, who looks like she'd start up a treat with a litle lube. *'Oh yes, she's a real practical classic. She goes like a train, outperforming many a newer model. Just lean in and smell that old leather.'*

practice protein *n.* The *vitamin-S*-based residue resulting from a session of *onanism*. A phrase coined by Mo Farah in them adverts for vegetarian meat he used to do.

practise social distancing *v.* To create two metres of clear space around you. *'Fuck me! Have you just practised social distancing, your holiness?'*

practising one's scales *1. euph.* A *cackaphonous rectal recital*; an overture of shortcrust *air biscuits* floated by the *Gary* to warm up before attempting a more challenging *musical movement*. *2. n.* Gusset piano fingerwork.

prairie dogging *v.* Of an *arse*, to have a stool poking in and out like an inquisitive gopher checking to see if the coast is clear. A mobile *turtle's head*.

prairie wind *1. n.* 2005 album by warblesome country rocker Neil Young; a moving song cycle of dreams, memories, family ties and the passage of time, if you will. *2. n.* A gently sulphurous zephyr that softly rustles the *arse cress* as it wafts across the barren *flies' graveyard*.

pram face *n.* A famous woman, perhaps a pop star or TV presenter, whose *mush* would more suitably adorn a sallow young mother pushing a pram around a council estate.

pram fat *n.* Plum sauce, heir gel, baby gravy.

pramland *1. n.* A shop on Hull's Holderness Road that sells baby paraphenalia. *2. n.* A certain Hull high school, whose pupils are allegedly amongst *1*'s biggest customers.

pram sauce *n. Jipper.*

pranny *n.* Fool, *arsehole, twat*. A form of insult popular amongst The Troggs pop group during recording sessions in the 1960s. Also *prannet*.

prat *1. n.* The *buttocks* of the *fundament* of the *arse*, onto which a slapstick comedian is wont to fall. *2. n.* A *pranny, fuckwit, arsehole*. A doltish sort.

prattle cruiser *n.* Large, slow-moving motor vehicle containing a wrinkled couple who talk blathering *crap* to each other, blissfully unaware of the miles of traffic stuck behind them.

prawn *n.* A girl with a fit figure, but an ugly face. From the edible crustacean, where the body is tasty, but the head is thrown away. A *bobfoc*.

prawn cracker *n.* Hot *patootie* with a fishy *minge*.

prawn crackers *n.* The crispy tissues found beneath a felow's bed. *Popshottadoms, wanker's crisps.*

prawn in an eagle's nest *n.* A curled-up pink *bollusc* surrounded by a particularly unkempt pubic *bush*.

prawn on a walnut *euph.* Tiny *tackle*. *'Fuck me, Maureen. I got him home, whipped his tweeds off, and it looked like a prawn on a walnut.'*

prawn penknife *n.* A tiny male *weapon*. A more diminutive version of a *pork sword*, possibly incorporating a small tool for removing stones from seahorses' hooves.

prawn sandwich *1. n.* Delicacy as famously served in the Directors' Boxes at Old Trafford. *2. n.* A lady being *roasted* by a pair of poorly endowed professional footballers.

praying to Atum *euph.* Masturbation: a reference to the ancient Egyptian creator god who *wanked* the universe into creation whilst feeling bored and lonely.

praying to chod *n.* The act of sitting with one's eyes closed while engaging in an act of anguished supplication to a greater force. *'Are you alright* in there, your holiness?' 'I'll be out in a minute, cardinal. I'm just praying to chod.'

prebound, on the *phr.* Realising your current relationship is doomed, the thoughtful act of beginning another one before finishing your old one, the better to facilitate a smooth changeover of services.

pre-chup *n.* That horrible watery stuff that drops onto your chips if you don't shake the ketchup bottle before pouring.

Precious McKenzie *n.* A small, but nonetheless very powerful, erection, capable of cleaning and jerking many times its own bodyweight. Named after the small, but nonetheless very powerful, Commonwealth Games gold medal-winning weightlifter of the 1970s.

pre-cum *n.* Substance often referred to in the letters pages of *jazz mags* but rarely mentioned elsewhere. It's certainly certainly not come up on *You and Yours* on Radio 4 very often. *Perseverance soup, dew on the lily, ball glaze, guardsman's gloss, preek.*

predate *1. v.* To exist or happen before another thing, sort of thing. *2. v.* To hunt, kill and eat another animal. *3. v.* To give your *cock* and *bollocks* a good rinse in anticipation of a bit of *how's your father.*

predator's face *n.* A somewhat unsettling vagina, which you would not mind swinging a stout length of *wood* into.

predictive pest *n.* A *wanker* who can't resist the urge to finish other people's sentences. *'Born on this day: George Martin, late Beatles producer, 1926; Dominic Wood, bungalow-dwelling television presenter, 1978; Justin Webb, Today programme predictive pest, 1961.'*

preek *n. medic.* A contraction of *pre-cum,* in case you want to tell someone about it and you're in a hurry.

pre-emptive strike *n.* The act of emptying one's *shot pouch* a couple of hours before going into action so as to make the ensuing battle last a bit longer.

prefer one's peas minted *euph.* Alluding to a *pastry chef* who *bakes a light sponge.*

prefers breaststroke to crawl *1. euph.* Said of one who *prefers his peas minted.* *2. phr.* Said of one who doesn't *prefer his peas minted.*

prefers his spinach wilted *euph.* Said of a chap who *knows what's in his flowerbeds* and is *competent with the pinking shears.*

pregnant pause *n.* A temporary hiatus in a bloke's marital relations as a consequence of his missus getting *up the duff.* This temporary pause can last anywhere from weeks to months to several years to decades.

pregnot *adj.* Of a lady, to look like she's *up the duff* when she is, in fact, just *big-boned.* Particularly the stomach bone. *Gregnant, up the pastry.*

prehab *n.* That extended period of being *heavily refreshed* which typically precedes a stopover in the Priory.

preheated Dutch oven *n.* A bed that has been comrehensively *trumped* in before a lucky young lass climbs into it and has her head stuffed under the covers.

preloved *1. adj.* Of a second hand motor car, on the point of a catastrophic mechanical failure. *2. adj.* Descriptive of a woman who has been *round the block* a few times. And got *fucked up the snatch* by loads of different blokes while she was on her travels.

Prelude in F minor *1. n. prop.* Piece by JS Bach; *"WTC1, BWV 857"* it says here. The sort of thing Robin Ray* would have recognised (*hint for our younger readers – he was Ted Ray's son. You remember Ted Ray, him from *Ray's a Laugh* – Patricia Hayes was in it); probably got used on an advert. *2. euph.* A particularly tunesome and mournful *dropped hat.*

premature pinch *n.* The snipping off of an unsmoked *bum cigar* when disturbed in the act, by an important telephone call for example, or a fucking Jehovah's Witness knocking on the fucking door.

prem de la crème *n. Fr.* One who is *up and over like a pan of milk.*

premium economy *n.* Guaranteeing oneself sole occupancy of a double seat on even the busiest of standard class train journeys by openly consuming a can of export-strength lager as the other passengers make their way up the aisle.

prepare for the wurst *exclam.* An expression of romantic fervour uttered to a lady by a gentleman just before he *slams in the lamb.*

prepare to meet thy doom! *exclam.* A grandiose utterance declaimed prior to letting off a stinky *guff.*

prepare yesterday's lunch *v.* To go for a *shit.*

preparing chunks *n.* Heading out for a post-pint curry and/or kebab. From the phrase that appears on the loading screen of the popular game *Minecraft.*

pre-poo *n.* Food.

prep the veg *v.* To rinse the soil off your *dangly bits* prior to sexual intercourse.

present from Margate, a *euph.* Any inanimate object which is introduced into the *back passage.*

From the famous, that is to say probably apocryphal, medical case of an unfortunate gentleman who was admitted to hospital with a pepperpot stuck up his *arse,* presumably following an incident involving falling backwards while dressed in a loose-fitting dressing gown. The medical record apparently stated: "On removal, the object was found to be inscribed with the words 'A Present from Margate'."

presents for a good boy *n. Tits.*

present your boarding pass *v.* To show the stewardess your *undercarriage,* in the vain hope of getting an in-flight upgrade to *dirty business class.*

pre-shite check *n.* The act of separating one's *bumcheeks* prior to contact with the *gurgler* seat in the belief that this will lead to significant economies in the consumption of *shitscrape. 'Are you going to be long in there, Martin?' 'Just doing my pre-shite check, dear.'*

president has landed, the *exclam.* An amusing announcement following a loud and deeply unpleasant *trump.* See also *better an eviction than a bad tenant; what's that, Sweep?; my, that duck's got bad breath* and many more.

presidential *adj.* In a similar vein, a tad *trumpy. 'Sorry about the smell, vicar. The dog ate a plate of left-over sprouts and he's been a bit presidential all day.'*

pre-soak *1. n.* Setting on a washing machine that helps make dirty clothes clean. Ask your mam. *2. n.* Pre-emptive eating of absorbent food in preparation for a long night *on the sauce.*

pressed ham *n.* The effect achieved by pushing one's naked *buttocks* onto the photocopier at the office Christmas party. In addition to *getting the sack.*

pressing matter *n.* An urgent *Tom tit. 'No time to open the new parliamentary session today I'm afraid, Lord Chancellor. I've got a pressing matter to attend to. By the way, you haven't seen this week's Autotrader anywhere, have you?'*

press send too soon *1. v.* When emailing, to tap the 'return' key prematurely, thus resulting in an incomplete or ill-considered message being sent. *2. v.* To *tip one's filthy concrete* somewhat earlier in the course of a romantic encounter than one would ideally have wished, all things being equal. *'Sorry about that, Monica. I must've pressed send too soon. I'm sure that spunk will just sponge off your frock.'*

press the devil's doorbell *v.* To *flick the bean.*

pressure washer *1. n.* German precision engineered device that removes all the *shite* from your driveway and deposits it up the side of your

neighbour's car. *2. n.* The *piss chisel.*

presuptual agreement *n.* Legally binding drinking itinerary agreed at the beginning of an evening, *eg.* "Right, so we start at the Black Bull, go on to the White Horse and finish at the Miner's Arms before having a magnificent Ruby Murray at the Curry Capital." As is the case with its ante-matrimonial contract counterpart, a *presuptual agreement* typically ends in a vicious fight and a costly court appearance.

pre wash *n.* Visual and olfactory inspection of a lady's *dunghampers* to ascertain whether bio or non bio powder, petrol or Nitromors is required to loosen stains on the *driptray* prior to laundering.

prexit *n.* The miracle of birth.

priapism *n. medic.* That condition affecting a fellow on *big cock day. 'Are you not going to stand for the national anthem, Mr Tatlock?' ''Appen I'll stay sat down, Mrs Walker. Only I'm suffering from an outbreak of priapism, tha knaws.'*

prick *1. n.* A penis. *2. n.* A *twat, fuckwit,* fool. *3. n.* A life-threatening finger injury often suffered by fairy tale princesses. *4. n.* A small doctor holding a hypodermic syringe on a seaside postcard.

prickipedia *n.* Unassailably true facts shared in the pub or on a GBNews bulletin.

prick lit *n. Rhythm literature.*

prickpocket *n.* A lady's hairy *box* into which a crafty fellow might dip his *artful todger.*

prick-stick *n.* A white DIY glue in a handy tubular dispenser used solely to stick the pages of *art pamphlets* together. *Man mastic, wood glue.*

prick tease *n.* A woman who goads one's *knob* by calling it names.

pricktionary *n. Burke's Peerage.*

priest's hole *1. n.* A cramped hiding place, usually behind the fireplace or under the floor in a large 17th century house, where fugitive Catholic clergymen could be concealed from the authorities. *2. n.* A choirboy's *nipsy. 3. n.* A *minge* that's a tight squeeze. A *paper cut, pinhole, mouse's ear.*

primadoner *n.* A substantial *trouser sausage* that looks like a sweaty elephant's leg, and makes the fat ladies sing at chucking out time.

Primark diet *euph.* A cheap, oversized fleece that covers a multitude of sins.

primarni *n.* The sort of extremely cheap off-the-peg/floor clothing that makes no bones about its lowly origins. *'What do you think of my new suit? It's primani. Only cost one ninety-nine, but you could easy pay three pounds or more for garb of this quality, you know.'*

primate *1. n.* A fellow from the lower echelons

of the evolutionary ladder who is clad in budget *couture*. 2. *n.* A bishop.

prime ribs *n.* A mouth-watering pair of luscious, *meaty steaks* that are practically falling off the bone.

prime the pump 1. *v.* A phrase – referring to government spending being used as a means to revitalise a sluggish economy, it says here – that dull-witted comedy US President Donald Trump claims to have coined despite irrefutable evidence to the contrary. 2. *v.* To have a judicious *hand shandy* prior to meeting a potential *score* to avoid going *up and over like a pan of milk*. 3. *v.* To kickstart a *bottom burp* by lifting one leg off the ground.

primordial soup 1. *n.* An ancient bubbling cauldron fecund with the building blocks of life from whence our ancestors emerged. 2. *n.* A bubbling wash basket in which socks previously imbued with the building blocks of life marinate into a hot, turbid mixture, thus infusing a fellow's laundry with a fresh, unmistakable aroma.

Prince Andrew 1. *n. prop.* Nickname given to a chap in the pub who uses the expression "no sweat" a lot, *eg.* "Don't worry, lads. I'll get the ale in, no sweat"; "I'll be there first thing, no sweat" *etc.* 2. *n. prop.* Honorary title bestowed upon a supplementary *backfire* delivered after the *benefactor* has exclaimed, "Let's try that again, shall we?" with the expectation that the room will rise as one to greet its arrival.

Prince Philip's funeral, as quiet as *sim.* When you organise a get-together and no-one turns up because there's a better party going on elsewhere. A reference to the low-key lockdown send-off for the late Duke of Edinburgh. *'Fuck me, Kier. This party's as quiet as Prince Philip's funeral.' 'I know, Jeremy. I hear they're all off doing Karaoke at number ten.'*

pringle 1. *n.* Yet another word for one who sniffs bicycle seats. A *snufty, snurglar, barumpher.* 2. *v.* To reach the *pint of no return* when drinking. From the famous eponymous saddle-shaped crisp advertising slogan, *viz.* "Once you pop, you just can't stop".

Pringle piss, have a *v.* To go for your inaugural first *wee* of the night when out on the ale, thus opening the floodgates to a lavatory visit every five minutes. From the previously mentioned ad tagline for the popular crisps which come in a cylindrical cardboard bag. To *break the seal.*

Pringles potette *n.* An improvised toilet utilising the popular cylindrical snack pipe. May impair the taste of your crisps, unless you're having Grilled Shrimp flavour.

printercourse *n. Having it off* on or against an item of office equipment at the works Christmas party. Hopefully not the shredder or an upturned stapler.

prints of darkness *n.* The result of *breaching the hull* after *parking your breakfast.*

prisoner… show yourself! 1. *exclam.* Dialogue from the 1973 Devil's Island-based movie *Papillon*: an order given by gaolers to convicts in solitary confinement. 2. *exclam.* Witty announcement prior to a noisy, stinky *trouser cough.* See also *our survey said; listen to this, too good to miss; my next guest needs no introduction* and *I'll name that tune in one.*

prison pussy *n.* The *anus, mud pussy,* up which a *lag* might be *naffed.*

prison-style workout 1. *n.* Series of plyometric exercises that can help maintain fitness and stamina in a confined space. 2. *n. Wanking.*

prison vision *n. medic.* A condition brought on by prolonged abstinence from female company, which causes the sufferer to lower his standards considerably, finding almost any woman attractive. *Porridge goggles, Camp X-ray specs. 'When I came out after 27 years of predominantly solitary confinement, I was suffering from terrible prison vision. Shortly after my release, I remember being entertained by Her Majesty the Queen at Buckingham Palace, and getting a bit of a chirp-on when her mum bent over to pat a corgi. Truly, incarceration is a terrible thing.'* (from *The Long Walk to Freedom* by Nelson Mandela).

private fur *n.* A lady's *secret squirrel.*

privates 1. *n.* Inoffensive unisex term for genitalia invented by the Women's Institute in 1904. At the opposite end of the rudeness scale to *fuckstick, hairy bollocks* and *cunt.* 2. *n.* A double entendre enabling *Carry On* scriptwriter Talbot Rothwell to humorously confuse low-ranking soldiers with their *meat and two veg* for comic effect.

pro-active 1. *n.* Yellow slime that claims to reduce cholesterol as long as you also live on salad and swim nine miles a day. 2. *adj.* Of a fellow who enjoys the company of *good time girls. 'Yes, Jeffrey's very pro-active, you know.'*

probe and drogue *n. RAF.* Repeated attempts, while drunk, to achieve penetration. Named after the floppy, dangling mechanism used for in-flight refueling.

probo *n.* One who makes a very comfortable living from vagrancy. A professional *Harold Ramp* with a mobile phone and a gold-plated Rolls Royce parked round the corner, of the sort only ever encountered by the puce-faced letter-writers in the *Daily Mail*.

proceed to secondary target *phr.* When a disgusting, unhygienic housemate has rendered the water closet unusable for any reason, to relieve one's bladder into the bathroom sink.

proclamation of the King *n.* Uncomfortable warning signs that a *Charles the Third* is on its way and you'd better make your way to the *throne room*.

procrapstinate *1. v.* To put off a trip to the *Rick Witter. 2. v.* To delay starting an important task by nipping off to *nip one off.*

procrasturbation *1. n.* The act of repeated, and often pleasureless *self-love* brought on by the need to stave off more weighty tasks. *'For heaven's sake, Lester, stop procrasturbating and get your tax return filled in.' 2. n.* The situation whereby a man is keen to partake in an *act of personal pleasure*, but is nevertheless entirely unable to decide which *bongo flick, left-handed website* or *grumble mag* to use for inspiration.

procreation ground *n.* Any public space that is transformed into an *al fresco dogging* or *cottaging* site as soon as darkness falls.

prodcast *n.* Hardcore internet *grumble. 'Our Kelvin, put down that Playstation for a minute and show your grandfather how to get Pamela Anderson's prodcast on his new iPad.'*

prodworthy *1. adj.* Of a fortunate young lady, deemed suitable for sexual relations by a man. *2. n. prop.* Surname of Augusta, the feminist town councillor played by June Whitfield in the film *Carry On Girls*.

profanigram *n.* The sort of selection of consonants and vowels which it would be nice to see Rachel Riley pull out during the letters round of *Countdown, eg.* Ssipflasp, sarsehloe, hingemair *etc*.

professional outdoorsman *n.* A Ray Mears-type who drinks metal polish. A *Harold Ramp.*

Professor Pissflaps *n. prop.* An epithet given to a female who thinks she is more intelligent than the average bloke. *'Alright, Professor Pissflaps, you've had your say. Let some fucker else get a word in edgeways.'* (David Dimbleby to Germaine Greer, *BBC Question Time*, March 2002).

Professor Plum *1. n.* The purple-bodied player in a game of *Cluedo. 2. n.* The purple-headed player in a variety of bedroom games.

profiterole model *n.* A woman whose *greggcitable* glands have a penchant for the pudding course. A *bus bender.*

prog log *n.* An *arse*-numbingly protracted *Simon Cowell* movement that features a twenty-minute keyboard solo from Rick Wakeman wearing a fucking wizard's hat.

proles' royce *1. n.* A stretch limousine with a screeching gaggle of drunken teenage girls hanging out of the window. *2. n.* A bus with a single passenger.

prolix *1. adj.* Of speech or writing, using, utilising or containing too many words; tediously lengthy, circumlocutious, long-winded or verbose; periphrastically pleonastic, and wearisomely logorrhoeic. *2. adj.* Going at a *nosh box hammer and tongues*; giving it *six-nowt* whilst *troughing out* the missus.

prolog *1. n.* The *turtle's head. 2. n.* A small *Sir Douglas* which is strategically expelled, thus allowing the passage of a series of much more weighty episodes thereafter.

prolog *n.* An impressive *stool.*

promance *n.* A sort of semi-regular relationship enjoyed with a specific *lady of the night.*

Prometheus has landed *exclam.* Muttered to oneself after a successful *touchdown.*

promise to oneself, on a *euph.* Of a gentleman, to be anticipating a spot of *rhythmic relaxation. 'Where are you off to, Otis? I thought we were going badger baiting.' 'Sorry lads, but I'm on a promise to myself.'*

promosexual *n.* A camp chap who is forever banging on about being *good with colours.*

prompt *1. n.* Involuntary *bottom burp* that slips out when using a urinal, giving the impression that an unseen, uncouth assistant has just cued-up the *piss-flow. 2. exclam.* Pre-*pump sotto voce* call delivered in the style of an old-fashioned stage actor who has forgotten his lines.

prongrat *n.* Hedgehog.

proof of purchase *n.* The sort of expensive, showy jewellery and expensive, showy vehicles bought for nubile blonde *pieces* by professional footballers.

prophylactic acid *n.* The tart contents of a used *dunky.*

prorogue *1. v.* Something that is done to parliament. *2. n.* A *pimp*, a *brasshouse*'s doorman.

prossie's start *n.* The advantage gained by a *good time girl* when running off with a *punter*'s money after failing to provide the contracted services, knowing that her unfortunate pursuer has his trousers around his ankles.

prostate polisher *n.* A chap who cruises up the *Bournville boulevard.*

prostitrout *n.* A *hingoot* who needs a bloody good wash.

prostitute experience, the *n.* The opposite of the *girlfriend experience*. When a chap's *ball and chain* behaves not in the chaste, frigid manner a regular girlfriend or wife would, but instead in the exuberant, taboo-busting and sheet-staining style of a sex worker. *'Let me tell you, she came out wearing suspenders and gave me the proper prostitute experience. I just about turned my nutsack inside out. And now over to Carol for the weather.'*

prostrate gland *n. medic.* Exocrine organ which develops during adolescence and makes the human male want to lie down all the time.

protein ear-rings *n.* Self-explanatory items of *jelly jewellery. 'I completely forgot the bag for life's birthday and the late night garage only had expensive flowers and them big boxes of Ferrero Rochers, so I made her some protein ear-rings instead.'*

protein shake *1. n.* Thickly textured sports drink, freshly prepared to help young men build muscle mass, and thus *2. n.* Gloopy *splod,* made from *plums* and thus rich in *vitamin S.*

Proud Mary *1. n.* A large Mississippi river boat. *2. n.* A lady's pronounced pubic mound. The *mons veneris, grassy knoll. 3. n.* A *bird's bits* that *keep on burnin'.* A *clapped-up clapping fish.*

proved *1. adj.* Term used by bakers to describe bread dough doubling in size due to the fermentation of yeast. *2. adj.* A polite and subtle way of saying someone's *bones have got bigger. 'Jesus, that Eamonn Holmes has definitely proved a bit lately, hasn't he.'*

prune juice *1. n.* Anal seepage. *2. n. Mabel syrup.*

prunetang *n.* A lady of considerably advanced years who has, by some unearthly means or other, managed to remain a bit of a looker, *eg.* Catherine Deneuve, Ginger Spice etc. A *gilf.* A witty corruption of *poontang,* an American word for *blart.*

pruning the roses *euph.* To have *hairache.* Once used by the late Brian Clough as an excuse for non-attendance at Nottingham Forest matches in the 1980s/90s.

prunt *n.* An obnoxious person of indeterminate gender, such that it is difficult to assign them the correct terminology.

Psalm 45 *euph.* The act of *praying for milk.* From the words of the famous biblical apophthegm: "Good luck have thou with thine honour; ride on, because of the word of truth, of meekness, and righteousness; and thy right hand shall teach thee terrible things."

Ps & Qs, mind your *exclam.* Politically incorrect advice for those bent on venturing into a venue frequented by the *puddle-averse.*

psychedelic yodelling *n.* Vocal projection of a *rainbow* out your *gob.*

PTSD *1. abbrev. medic.* Partial Tug Stress Disorder.

The mental confusion suffered by a gentleman whose wife unexpectedly arrives home from the shops ten minutes early, prematurely terminating his act of *self delight. 2. abbrev.* Post Traumatic Shit Disorder. The haunted look of a man silently emerging from the work toilets after thirty minutes.

pubby fat *n.* When a fellow discovers the finer things in life and trades in his chiselled six-pack for a well-rounded future. Also *beer-gut, jelly belly, one-pack etc.*

pubcast *n.* An endlessly repeated, dull, *pile of wank* story overheard by the unfortunate people who find themselves sitting near a public house bore as he regales each of his mates in turn with the same tale as they filter into the bar on a Friday night.

pube dude *n.* Schoolboy phrase used to describe the kid in the playground who had a hairy chest and 4 o'clock shadow by the age of twelve.

pube farmer *n.* An unemployed person. A *doley.*

pube in an afro, looking for a *sim.* A crude variation on "looking for a needle in a haystack". Also, *looking for a baw hair in an afro (Scot).*

pube lunch *n.* A tasty *bacon sandwich* with a token garnish of *gorilla salad,* served all day in a friendly atmosphere. *Cunch, fish dinner, haddock and lips.*

pube 'n' cigar *n.* A smoothly elongated, brown *floater,* finished off with an *arse* hair or two.

pub grub *n.* Cheap closing time/car park *cunnilingus. Licking out* the *floor sweepings.*

pubic bone *1. n. medic.* Ventral anterior bit of the pelvis. *2. n.* A male *membrum virile* stricken with body hair. Also *twig toothbrush, French tickler.*

pubic holiday *n.* An *ad hoc* day off that is taken to allow a fellow to *go to work* on his missus.

pubic library *n.* An array of *flesh books* kept on top of a wardrobe for easy reference.

pubik's cube *n.* A geometrical *Hitler 'tache.*

pubiquity *n.* The uncanny ability of stray strands of *gorilla salad* to turn up anywhere and everywhere, *eg.* On a bar of soap, between one's teeth, in the back of one's throat in the middle of the night, in McDonald's burgers, Mc-Donald's chicken nuggets, McDonald's thick shakes *etc.*

public hair *n.* The *smurf beard* appearing on each side of an unshaven *bird's* bikini bottom. Also *Jimmy Edwards, Noddy Holders, thighbrows.*

public purse *1. n.* Something that is evidently empty. *2. n.* Something that is probably quite full on a regular basis. The *quimpiece* on a lady of easy affections. A *postman's sack, box of assorted creams.*

pub muck *n.* Going for a *shit* in a pub. *'Where's Michael? It's his round.' 'He's went for a pub muck,* *prime minister.'*

pubonic plague *1. n. medic.* Acne. *2. n.* An annoying rash of teenagers, for example at the supermarket tills on a weekday lunchtime. *3. n. medic.* A *mechanical dandruff* infestation of *cupid's carpet.* *'How was your weekend away in Amsterdam, then nan?' 'Ooh, we had a smashing time until your grandad caught the pubonic plague off a big-cocked tranny in De Wallen.'*

pub scarecrow *n.* The inhabitant of one's boozer who has the uncanny ability to frighten away the *birds.*

pub singer *n.* A solo performer, grunting and yodelling in a cubicle while *laying a cable.*

pub terrier *n.* A breed of small, yappy, unpredictablen and aggressive though not necessarily dangerous, man whose presence makes one feel oddly uneasy. Found in most public houses in Britain.

pud *1. n.* The *willy.* That which was always *pulled* by Ivor Biggun (aka Doc Cox of *That's Life* rude vegetable fame), in his *Wanking Song. 2. n.* An economically drawn three-line graffito of the male genitalia. *3. acronym.* Post Urinal Drip. A *wet penny in the pocket.*

pudcast *n.* A spot of *Frankie Vaughan* downloaded onto a smartphone or tablet.

pudding burner *n.* Slatternly lady who frequents the pub on a Sunday lunchtime when she should really be at home cooking a hearty traditional meal for her husband.

pudding dagger *n.* The male penis. *'The statue of David, presently exhibited at the Accadamia de belle Arti in Florence, is widely recognised to be one of the greatest masterpieces of the Italian Renaissance. Sculpted from a single block of Carrara marble between 1501 and 1504, the symbolic nude figure of the Biblical hero stands over seventeen feet high. The grand and ambitious scale of the carving is quite remarkable; for example, in his memoirs, Michelangelo estimated that the statue's monumental pudding dagger weighed nearly a quarter of a ton, not including clackerbag.'* (from *Cocks of the Great Artists* by Giorgio Vasari).

puddism *n.* Philosophy that prizes dessert as life's ultimate goal. *Puddists* are notable for their slightly sweaty demeanour and Buddha-like bellies.

puddle, dropped in a *euph.* The state of a *bongo periodical* which has been subject to heavy and/or prolonged use. *'Christ. I wouldn't have lent you my Razzle if I'd have known it would come back in this state, George.' 'Yeah, I know. Sorry. I dropped it in a puddle.'*

puddle jumper *n.* A *fruit feeler, spud fumbler.*

pudenda benders *n.* Ladies' tighter-than-human-skin leggings that make the most *badly packed kebab* look like a nippingly trim mannequin's *front bottom.* Also *comfortably numbs, mumblers.*

pudendum *n.* Genital area. From the Latin pudes = meat pie & dendum = two potatoes.

pudoku *n.* Any number puzzle that can be successfully completed on the toilet by a man in the time it takes him to *lay a cable.* About an hour-and-a-half, then.

pud-whapper *n. US. Wanker,* jerkwad, an obnoxious person.

puff *1. v.* To exhale cigarette smoke. *2. n. prop.* Magic dragon that lived by the sea. *3. n.* A consumer *of fancy cakes.*

puffer fish *n.* A woman who inflates frighteningly to ten times her original size the very instant you pop a ring on her finger.

puff fluff *n.* An insufficiently malodorous *dropped hat,* which calls the *farter's* sexual orientation into question.

PUFO/pufo *acronym. milit.* An exhortation to remove oneself from a situation or otherwise abandon a current task. Pack Up: Fuck Off. *'Okay, Buzz and Neil. Eagle is go for pufo. Repeat, go for pufo. Over.'*

pugg boots *n.* Rip-off fashion footwear, made out of stray dogs and sold on markets up and down the country. Also *Dog Martens.*

pugwash *n. Aus.* Cleaning of the teeth using *tapioca toothpaste* and a *naughty paintbrush.* A *blow job.*

puh-seh *n. US.* A *grumble flick* vagina. Something that a more-or-less tumescent *meat vid* thespian seems generally keen to stick his *Hampton* up.

puke *v.* To spew, yoff, shout soup.

pukelele *n.* Any ukelele employed in a sickeningly twee manner, *eg.* When used to cover a classic rock song in a John Lewis Christmas advert, or to provide the omnipresent background burble on a navel-gazing YouTube vlog.

pull *1. v.* To *tap, pick up* a sexual partner. *'I pulled last night.' 2. n.* A spot of *self improvement. 'I didn't pull, so I went home, watched the free ten minutes of the Fantasy Channel and had a bit of a pull.'*

pullaby *n.* Something which, when accompanied by a rhythmical rocking motion, soon brings on a state of contented slumber.

pull a dirty *euph. US.* To *play the invisible banjo.* A phrase coined by sexually frustrated ex-Pussycat Doll Ashley Roberts on *I'm a Celebrity* after spending three weeks cooped up with Eric Bristow.

pull a fast one *v.* To have a quick, crafty *tug, eg.* A successful *Sherman* that is completed *from flop to pop* and back again during the opening titles of *Last Night of the Proms* while furiously thinking about Katie Derham and what she will be wearing that evening.

pull a late one *v.* To have a *wank* at work after everyone else has left.

pull a muscle *v.* To *relax in a gentleman's way* so much that you give yourself a limp.

pull an Askwith *v.* To leer or gawp lustily and suggestively over a woman. Named after the 1970s *Confessions* films *fanny magnet* actor and Patricia Hayes lookalike Robin.

pull a pint on the piss pump *v.* To pour oneself a 5ml *hand shandy*.

pull a sticky *v.* To phone in ill at work, when your intention is actually to spend the day *choking the chicken* or *stabbing the cat*.

pull a train *v.* To take turns at *stirring the porridge*, to participate in a *gang bang*.

pulled out of an Ecuadorian embassy backwards, looks like it's been *phr.* Descriptive of a hairy, unkempt *fanny* that is strangely reminiscent of hairy, unkempt Wikileaks founder Julian Assange as he was forcibly extracted from his *shite*-smeared diplomatic hideaway.

pulled pork *n.* A poor, alcohol-influenced choice of paramour with whom one *cops off* during the *2am bin rake* at a night club.

pulled the ripcord *euph.* Descriptive of a once svelte lady who has sadly ballooned like an inflatable raft and turned into a *bed breaker*.

pulletariat *n.* That class of society principally engaged in *monomanual labour*. The plebian social stratum that lives alone and watches *sockumentaries* while awaiting news of gainful employment. *Doleys, pube farmers,* students.

pullfilment *n.* The tired yet satisfied feeling a chap has after spending an evening perusing *seed catalogues* or watching *socktator sports*. *'Looking back, I've certainly got a lot of pullfilment from my life, Kirsty.'*

pulling power *n.* The strength of one's *fanny magnetism*.

pulling the goalie *1. n.* In hockey, replacing the goaltender with an extra attacking player in the final minute or so of a match that is being lost. Something along those lines anyway. *2. n.* Of a couple who are very much in love, discontinuing contraception in the hope of conceiving a screaming, vomiting, incontinent *anklebiter*.

pullman seat *n.* The comfortably crusty armchair in which a bachelor sits to *relax*.

pull my nightie down when you're finished *exclam.*

An instruction given by a lady who is somewhat less than enthusiastic about participating in her husband's epithalamic shenanigans.

pull off *1. v.* To manoeuvre a car away from the kerb. *2. v.* To drag a drunken friend away from a fight in which he has the upper hand, usually while shouting "It's not worth it" or "Leave it, he's had enough". *3. v.* To masturbate. *'I picked up a hitchhiker and she offered to pull me off in my cab. I was so disgusted that I pulled over, strangled her and rolled her up in some carpet. Then I pulled myself off.'*

pull out and pray *n.* A method of contraception that is also a test of faith. Birth control as used by people with dozens of children. *Vatican roulette, onanism.*

pullover *1. n.* Woolly garment *2. n.* Like a sleepover but involving frenzied masturbation.

pull pit *1. n.* Item of ecclesiastical furniture from which the bishop addresses the congregation. *2. n.* A foetid *wanking chariot* in which his grace might *pull the Pope's hat off.*

pull programme *n.* A jazz magazine, *niff book* or *boob brochure*.

pullseye *exclam.* Humorous ejaculation spoken by a fellow who has just successfully reduced his *bird's* field of vision by a factor of fifty percent.

pulltergeist *n.* The entity responsible for the sundry bumps and bangs heard while someone is using a muted laptop in another room of the house. See also *erectoplasm*.

pull the one-ended cracker *v.* To enjoy a monomanual yuletide festivity.

pull the pin out of the shit grenade *v.* To spark up the first *coffin nail* of the day, after which you have approximately ten seconds to find a *throne* to sit on. *Embassy number two, arse fuse, drag and drop.*

pull the plug *v.* To tentatively embark on one's morning *sit down toilet adventure* following a night *on the sauce*; a solid *dougie* that is the inevitable precursor to half a dozen bouts of hot *fizzy gravy*.

pull the Pope's cap off *v.* To *bash the Bishop, box the Jesuit*.

pull the skin back *euph.* A phrase to denote a thorough job well done. *'Myself and the other members of Team Serendiptous really pulled the skin back on this task, Lord Sugar.'*

pull the turkey's neck *v.* To *choke the chicken*. See *throttle the turkey*.

pull the whisks out with the mixer still running *v.* To splatter the bowl with *chocolate cake mixture*. To *pebbledash* the *chod bin*. *'Jesus, Camilla. What happened? It looks like you pulled the whisks out* *with the mixer still running.'*

pull the wool over one's eye *v.* To *wank* into a sock.

pull up to the bumper *v.* To *do* Grace Jones *up the shitter,* but only after she's asked you nicely.

pullympics *n.* Televised female sporting events that leave a certain type of male viewer in a somewhat more exhausted state than the participants, *eg.* Beach volleyball, ladies' tennis, nude jelly wrestling on the Playboy channel.

pull your pud *1. v.* To *wank.* 2. *v.* To drag a dessert along in some sort of trailer.

pull yourself together *1. phr.* To calm down. 2. *phr.* To *get your five a day.*

pulsar *1. n.* A celestial object, thought to be a rapidly rotating neutron star, that emits regular bursts of radio waves and other electromagnetic radiation at rates of up to one thousand pulses per second. Don't say we never learn you anything. *2. n.* A monster *stonk-on* throbbing like a *blind cobbler's thumb.*

PUMA/puma *1. acronym.* Pants Up My Arse. A specific reference to *cleftal* discomfort. *Hungry arse.* 2. *n.* North American wildcat. 3. *acronym.* An annoying, tailgating driver, generally at the wheel of an Audi. Prick Up My Arse.

pummel horse *n.* In a public house, that worn-out, leathery woman who is nevertheless accommodating to any of the regulars who fancy swinging their leg over her in return for a bag of Nobby's Nuts.

pump *v.* To *fart, poot, pass wind, shoot bunnies, drop a rose petal.* 2. *n.* A *dropped gut.*

pump action mottgun *n.* An advanced, rapid-fire development of the *mutton musket.*

pump and ceremony *n.* A *panfare for the common man.*

pump and circumstance *n.* A fart that *follows through. The last night of the pants.* '*Nobody does pump and circumstance like us British, Beryl.*'

pump and dump *1. n.* A form of penny stock fraud that involves artificially inflating the price of an owned stock through false and misleading positive statements. 2. *n. Following through* due to high liquidity.

pumper's lump *n. medic.* The condition of enhanced right forearm muscle due to excessive *jerking. Arnie's arms, hairy pieceps.*

pumpin' Duncan *1. n. prop.* Full-size mechanical sex doll marketed in the 1960s, with human hair and oscillating s*x parts (pause to have a quick look on eBay). 2. *n. prop.* Nickname for the bloke you work with who will *shaft* anything.

pumping gas *n.* Breaking wind while parking cars in San José. Probably best open the sunroof, Dionne.

pumping iron *n.* Beefily ferrous pre-*jobby*

raspberries after an evening on the stout.

pumping station *n.* A pornographic television channel. *Al Jizzera, discovery channel, C-Boobies.*

pumping up the tyres *v.* Involuntary movement of the leg during the *vinegar strokes. Elvis's leg, Elvis tremble.*

pump me tyres up, I'm just going to *exclam.* What the host says to his guest before going upstairs to *relax in a gentleman's fashion.*

pump room *1. n.* In a spa town, such as Harrogate, Bath or Leamington, a place where invalids and murder mystery authors used to go in order to take the waters. 2. *n.* Any designated area for the controlled release of noxious, sulphurous gases. The water closet. *'Excuse me, your holiness, I just need to pop over to the pump room.'*

pumps-a-daisy *n.* An *air biscuit* deployed on rear impact, for example when sitting down suddenly, when bending over to pick up a dropped hat, or after an emergency stop during a wedding conga line.

pump the brakes *v.* To tighten the vaginal muscles during intercourse when, for a variety of possible reasons, the penis is no longer being gripped with sufficient force to bring events to a satisfactory conclusion. *'Come on, love, throw me a bone. Pump the brakes a bit or something. I've got to be up first thing.'*

pump up the jam *v.* To take a *cranberry dip.* To *stir the paint.*

pump your roe *v.* To *tip your filthy concrete, cough your filthy yoghurt, squirt your dirty water pistol.* *'Stand back, Camilla. I'm about to pump my roe.'*

pumpy rumpy *n. Back-door* carryings on. *How's your farter, up the arse no babies.*

pum-vee *n.* A feminine *fannomenon* often resulting in *the camel's toe.* Pants Up My Vadge.

punami *n.* In a bar, a tidal wave of binge-drinking *flange* out on a *slag night.* From punani + tsunami.

punani *n.* A lady's *bits and bobs.*

punani granny *n.* A significantly older woman who is none the less still worth *one.* A *gilf, lulu.*

punch above one's weight *1. v.* In boxing, to come out on top in a bout against a superior fighter. 2. *v.* Of a plain gentleman, to succesfully *woo* a young lady whom he might ordinarily consider to be out of his class. *'Punching above your weight there, Rupe.'*

punched by the invisible man *euph.* On entering a freshly soiled toilet, being knocked off one's feet by an unseen force.

punched lasagne *n.* A *badly packed kebab* that has more miles on the clock than Postman Pat's van.

punched lasagne, fanny like a *sim.* A messy

place-setting when *dining at the Y. Bottom of a rat catcher's mallet. A* not entirely complimentary description of a lady's *funzone.*

punching a bucket of liver, like *sim.* Poetically erotic description of a young swain's innocent fumblings with an older, much more experienced lady, like in *The Graduate* or something. For example, his nan's mate from the bingo.

punching smoke, like *sim.* Having a pop at a *wizard's sleeve* while armed with equipment of insufficient calibre. *Throwing a woodbine up North-umberland Street* or *last hotdog in the tin. Dipping a worm in a bucket.*

punch its head in *v.* What a gentleman does to his *gentleman* when *relaxing in a gentleman's way.*

punch the clown *v.* To make *custard* shoot out the top of *Charlie Cairoli's* hat. To *pour oneself a hand shandy.*

punch the Spaniard *v.* To perform an act of *personal pollution.* To attempt to "knock Juan out".

punch up the whiskers *n.* A *knee trembler* or similar romantic encounter in a train lavatory, taxi queue, Radio 5 lift or Building Society doorway.

punctual plumber *euph.* A pornographic thespian playing the part of a washing machine repairman who, somewhat unconvincingly, *comes* on time.

punish *v.* To put one's ladyfriend *to the sword* in an enthusiastic manner. To administer a few strokes of the *old walking stick.*

punji stick *1. n. milit.* A jungle warfare booby trap, whereby an excrement-covered length of wood is hammered into a dark hole. *2. n. milit.* A squaddie's *membrum virile* following a bout of *bumcraft.*

punk cock *n.* A *hampton* adorned with multifarious piercings. A *knob* which is upsettingly bejewelled with chains, rings and pop rivets.

punks *rhym. slang.* Breasts. From punk rockers = knockers. *'Gonorrhoea was powerless to resist. His eyes burned into hers like topazzes. His strong arms enfolded her softly yielding body as she felt herself being swept away in a solar wind of passion. Before she had a chance to protest, he had whipped off her tit pants and started mucking about with her punks.'* (from *The Lady and the Powdered Egg Salesman* by Barbara Cartland).

punt from the Cambridge end *v.* To *do it* like they do in the Fens.

punting *n.* Sticking one's pole in the mud.

puppies *1. n. Bubbies.* Affectionate euphemism for *thru'penny bits.* Also *two puppies fighting in a bag. 2. n.* What emerges nine months after an act of *dogging. 'I'm just going to pick the puppy up from*

nursery, love.'

puppies' noses *n.* Little cold, wet, pink nipples that demand to be tickled.

PUP/pup *abbrev.* Pissed Up Purchase; an item purchased when on-line shopping late at night whilst thoroughly *refreshed, eg.* Splashing seven grand from the new kitchen savings to purchase a Japanese World War 2 motorcycle with machine gun mount. Collection only from Land's End.

puppy love *n.* An immature fondness for *funbags.*

puppy pedicure *n.* Inadvertently stepping into a fresh pile of steaming *hound rope* while wearing strappy high heels or sparkly flip-flops. Also applies to women.

pure as (name removed on legal advice)'s piss *sim.* Epithet applied to a *goer* whose reputation for chastity is absolutely beyond reproach.

purple-headed womb broom *n.* See *purple-headed yoghurt warrior.*

purple-headed yoghurt warrior *n.* See *purple-headed womb broom.*

purple heart *1. n.* US Military decoration. *2. n. rhym. slang.* A proper beefy *Bakewell. 3. n.* The *glans, bishop's hat.*

purple helmet *1. n. Pink Darth Vader's* headgear, *bobby's helmet, German helmet, Roman helmet, bell end. 2. n.* Any member of the former Rover Aerobatic display team.

purple pearler *n.* An extendable icing tool for decorating pink blancmanges.

purple rain *1. n. prop.* 1980s song/album/movie released by late, short-bottomed American popster Prince. *2. n.* Loose *foulage* suffered the morning after drinking far too much red wine.

purse *n.* A *snapper*

purse picked, get your *v.* To undergo the *walnut whip. 'Excuse me, do you sell extremely baggy trousers? I've just got my purse picked.'*

push back the chaser *1. phr.* Term used in the popular ITV game show *The Chase* where the quiz expert gets a question wrong and forfeits one place. *2. n.* Withdrawing the *turtle's head* back into the *bomb bay* when time is of the essence. *'Push back the chaser, Anne. They need you on set.'*

push gas *v.* To *poot, let rip.*

push her guts in *v.* To have sex with a lady. *'Oh Joan Hunter Dunn / With your strong legs in shorts / Your boyish good looks / Your excelling at sports / Your long golden hair / Your ruby red lips / Let me push in your guts / Twixt the council dump skips.'* (*Joan Hunter Dunn* by John Betjeman).

push her shite back a fortnight *phr.* To indulge in a bit of saucy penetrative anal intercourse with a lady.

pushing a wet mattress up a spiral staircase, like *sim.* Phrase descriptive of the effort which has to be expended when trying to constipate a relationship with an unresponsive woman.

pushing sauce *v.* The stage of *coitus* immediately after the *vinegar strokes, ie.* When the *yoghurt truck* has *crashed* and is in the act of *tipping out its filthy concrete.* Ejaculation. *'Bond and Fanny Akimbo made love on the silken sheets of the mini-sub's bed. Suddenly, the videophone crackled into life and the face of M appeared, seated at his familiar Whitehall desk. "Ah, there you are, 007. We've had reports that Blofeld is planning to blow up China with a big ray gun," he said gravely. Bond raised a quizzical eyebrow, and a sardonic smile played about his lips. "I'm afraid I have my hands rather full at the moment, sir," he said. "Call me back in about 10 minutes after I've pushed me sauce and zuffled me charlie on the curtains."'* (from *Goldtops and Goldfingers* by Ian Fleming).

pushing through the pain barrier *1. euph.* In gym parlance, completing a strenuous workout despite being in distress. *2. euph.* In toilet parlance, to tearfully continue pushing out a *Dame Thora* that feels considerably larger than the aperture through which it is being squeezed.

pushmi-pullyu *1. n.* Dr Dolittle's contrary beast with two heads at opposing ends of its body, and preumably no *arsehole. 2. n.* Deployment of the *khazi* flush mid-*Peter O'Toole* to suck a half-birthed *footlong* from one's *nipsy. 3. n.* A double-ended *dildo* that was rarely, if ever, the subject of a question on *Screen Test.*

push my finger *exclam.* Desperate, forlorn and ultimately futile post-partum plea made to friends, colleagues or the presiding judge when one has just *gambled and lost.*

push notification *1. n.* On a mobile phone, a message that is "pushed" from a back-end server or application to the user interface. Ah, yes. *2. n.* In *arse-wiping*, a nasty, soft sensation felt by the fingers; an unfortunate discovery that the *bog roll* is a bit saturated and/or on the thin side.

push the boat out *v.* To enjoy an exceptionally rich, fragrant and extravagant *launch* while ensconced on a very fancy *Kensington* executive.

push the envelope *1. v.* In test pilot circles, to explore the aeronautical limits of a prototype aircraft. *2. n.* In *pant shitting* circles, to *shit* one's *grundies.*

push through *n.* the consequence of buying "Economy Brand" *bumwad. '"Would you care for another scone, Father Brown" asked Lady Chelmshurst. "Bless you, but thank you no," replied the small priest, blinking owlishly and proffering a smelly digit towards his hostess's nose. "I've just been to lay a cable and I fear I had a push through."'* (from *Father Brown Points the Finger* by GK Chesterton).

pusstrated *adj.* Unable to burst a spot just before going on a big date.

pussy *1. n.* Of erstwhile British TV sitcoms set in quiet, heavily overstaffed department stores, a much-stroked pet cat frequently referred to by Mrs Slocombe. *2. n.* Molly Sugden's *cunt.*

pussycat trolls *n.* A group of unattractive females.

pussy knackers *n.* The male *camel toe* or *munge.* Also *butcher's fist, hamster's mouthful, Darcy Bussell's footrest.*

pussy pelmet *n.* A short mini skirt, a *greyhound skirt.*

pussy poof *n.* A *todger dodger, three wheeler* or *tennis fan.* She who is *fond of walking holidays* in preference to having a penis pushed up her vagina.

put a snake in a basket *v.* To go for a long, bendy *shit.* To *make a coil pot.*

put it all on brown *v.* To *gamble and lose. 'This is the man who wagered his pants on a dropped gut, just when the smart money put it all on brown.'*

put me off me bogies, enough to *phr.* Said of something sufficiently offputting as to put a *nose fruit* gourmand off their favourite delicacy. *'I don't think much of this internet that everybody's going on about. I seen that Two Girls One Cup the other day and quite frankly it was enough to put me off me bogies.'*

put one's mind to other things *euph.* To *give it six nowt on the old walking stick.* To masturbate. *'Once settled in my cell, and in some comfort, I put my mind to other things. Into a sock.'* (from *Borstal Boy* by Brendan Behan).

put on weight *v.* To get a *bone on. 'Have you put on weight?' 'No, I've got a bone on.'*

puts his tree up in November, he *euph.* Said of a fellow who has a habit of doing things earlier than is normally expected, *ie.* An *English batsman* who is *up and over like a pan of milk.* See *Rio Ferdinand's boxing career.*

put some fur around it *exclam.* A fellow's plaintive plea for help while attempting some sort of congress with his missus following a night *on the medicine.*

put some ketchup on that! *exclam.* Said after a loud *arse bark.* Also *wrap that in bread, you've got yourself a sandwich.*

puts seed out for the birds *euph.* Handy with herbs, on first name terms with the staff at Dorothy Perkins, not very aggressive.

put the baby to sleep *v.* To administer the rocking

action which is often required to get a restless *baby's arm* to settle down at night. Or at lunchtime. Or halfway through the afternoon, and again twice before tea-time for that matter.

put the brown bins out *v.* To divest oneself of a quantity of non-recyclable waste.

put the handbrake on *v.* To *hide your pride* during an act of *personal pollution* when rudely interrupted by an unwanted visitor, *eg.* Your mum, your granny, Noel Edmonds with a Gotcha! Oscar, the police, Jeff Brazier with a Postcode Lottery cheque for £25,000 *etc.*

put the oil where the squeak is *euph.* To temporarily silence one's nagging other half by applying a *gloss drop* of *Vitamin S* to the affected area.

put the red lights on *v. naval.* To have a silent *wank* in bed so as not to disturb one's wife. Also *silent running, American beauty.* See *outrigger.*

putting for the birdie *n.* The awkward, Douglas Bader-style stance adopted over the lavatory by a chap attempting to *strain his greens* while *on the stonk.*

putting from the rough *v.* Golfing equivalent of *bowling from the pavilion end.*

putting on the titz *n.* Getting a boob job. *'If your jugs are not unlike spaniels' lugs / Why don't you go and get them fixed? / Puttin' on the titz.'* (lyric by Irving Berlin from *Broadway Follies of '42DD*).

putting on the wrist *n.* Relaxing with a *shandy.*

putting toothpaste back in the tube *sim.* Descriptive of the difficulties encountered when attempting sexual congress while less than fully tumescent. *Thumbing in a slacky, playing snooker with string, pushing a marshmallow in a moneybox.*

put to the sword *v.* To make love to. *'From the Charing Cross Theatre, where I saw Mr Herbert give his Death of Icarus, to tea with the French Ambassador, and thence home to bed whereupon I put Mrs Pepys to the sword before settling down to sleep.'* (from *The Diary of Samuel Pepys*).

put your hands up for Detroit! *exclam.* Verbal retort after a partner emits a tuneful set of *parps* in the style of the squelchy bassline from the Fedde Le Grand song. Us neither.

put your tits into it *exclam.* Unacceptably sexist words of encouragement aimed at ladies who are undertaking physical tasks. *'Just the travellator to go now. Come on, Jet love. Put your fucking tits into it.'*

putz *n.* A *prick* in Yiddish. Also *schlong, schmuck, schmeckel, shvantz, shtupper.*

puyoled *adj.* Constantly sopping wet. Named after the former Barcelona footballer Carles Puyol, who spent every match *dripping like a fucked fridge.*

PWILF/pwilf *abbrev.* An alluringly expectant young lady. Pregnant Woman I'd Like to Fuck.

PWOM/pwom *abbrev.* Posh Wank On Me. The practice of sending one's mate a *bongo mag, rubber Johnny*, cigarette and match when he is laid up after an operation or industrial accident. Signed on an accompanying greetings card: *'Sorry to hear you're crook, have a PWOM.'*

pygmies' cocks *n.* Erect nipples. *'Did you see Sharron Davies on Olympic Grandstand? She had jockeys like pygmies' cocks.'*

pyjama glue *n.* A handy starch-based adhesive, particularly useful for bonding and stiffening cotton fabrics. Also good for sticking together the pages of *tit catalogues,* the wife's eyelids *etc. Prickstick, man mastic, haroldite.*

pyramid stage *n.* In a festival *crapper,* that final point in the evolution of a blocked *chodbin* when the *bangers and mash* are piled up into a great, stinking, conical pile, and some rotter has somehow managed to *curl one off,* in the most unlikely fashion, right on the summit. Maybe with a little flag in it.

pyroclastic flow *n.* In curryology, an explosive outburst in which dust, rock, lager, vindaloo and hot, sulphurous gas are ejected from one's *crinkly crater* at high temperature and speed.

pyroflatulate *v.* To light one's *farts.* See also *afterburner, blue streak.*

pyropastie *n.* Excrement wrapped in newspaper, then set alight on next door's doorstep in the hope that the occupant will stamp it out.

pyrrhic victory *1. n.* A military triumph obtained at arguably too great a cost to the winning side (from King Pyrrhus of Epirus's victory against the Romans in 279BC, where he won the battle but lost all his troops, a reference all *Viz* readers no doubt immediately spotted). *2. n.* Successfully *bringing yourself off* but getting all *spunk* in your eye.

PYSILF/pysilf *abbrev.* In honour of the Duchess of Cambridge's famously *bootylicious* sibling, as spotted on the day of the Royal Wedding, Princess's Younger Sister I'd Like to Fuck. Also *pysiltduta.*

Pythagoras piss *n.* Ancient Greek act of trigonometrical urination performed such that one's forehead is propped against the lavatory wall, and one's rigid body consequently forms the hypotenuse of a right-angled triangle.

Pythonesque *1. adj.* Of humour, in the distinctive surrealist style of the groundbreaking programme *Monty Python's Flying Circus. 2. adj.* Of a gentleman's *parts, fucking* massive.

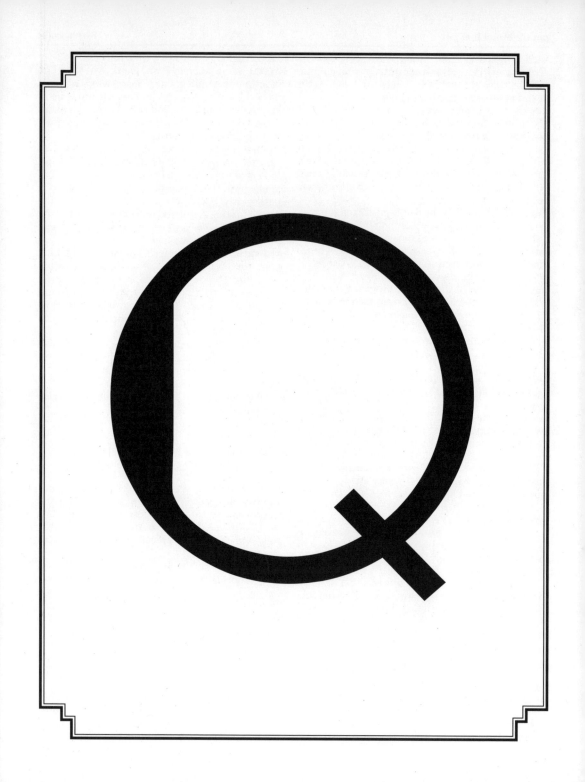

QALP/qalp *abbrev.* Quite A Large Poo.

QILF/qilf *abbrev.* In honour of our future monarch Kate Middleton, Queen I'd Like to Fuck. Charming. They'd have chopped your fucking head off for such *Lèse-majesté* in the olden days, and quite right too.

Q-tits *1. n. Fun bags* that are not what they appear to be, *ie.* Ones that have been artificially enhanced by the use of padded *tit pants,* leading to disappointment after *unwrapping the meat.* Derived from Q-ship, a term used to describe warships disguised as civilian vessels in 20th century naval warfare, so actually the opposite meaning if you think about it. *2. n. Knockers* that blow the wax out of your ears. *3. n.* Short-lived *Beano* adventure cartoon strip of the 1960s and 70s.

quack *n. onomat.* A sudden sound emanating from one's *bills* when one *steps on a frog.*

quackamole *n.* A smooth, greenish paste occasionally produced after an over-ambitious clearance of the *nether throat.* Not suitable for dipping nachos into.

quacker *n.* Poetic epithet for a lady's *garden of delight.*

quacker whacker *n.* A device for the maintenance of a neatly *fanicured lady garden.*

quack scratch *n.* A *bottom burp* which resonates at the perfect pitch to abrade an itchy *nipsy.* A proper *quack scratch* has a refreshing effect similar to a good pull-through with a bottle brush.

quacky races *n.* A desperate trolley dash to the last unoccupied *Rick Witter* cubicle.

quadruple *1. n.* In football, the ultimate achievement of winning three domestic and one European competition. *2. n.* In the *smallest room,* the ultimate achievement of *dropping a log* so large that it leaves skid marks on four sides of the *chodbin.*

quail *n.* A tasty young *bird* who's game for anything.

quakers *n.* Oats.

quaker, to bury a *v.* To *lay a cable. 'Do come in, Mr Darcy. Miss Bennet has just nipped upstairs to bury a quaker. Would you care to wait in the drawing room until she has wiped her arse?'* (from *Pride and Prejudice,* by Jane Austen).

qualifications *n.* Breasts, *first impressions, competitive advantages. 'Admittedly her CV looks a bit thin, and her interview responses were somewhat lacklustre, but she has some excellent qualifications.'*

quality assurance *n.* The act of looking between your legs to survey the *left luggage* in the *chodbin* before pulling the chain.

quality control *n.* The release of a small amount of *fart* to see how bad it is before releasing the rest.

Tasting the wine, sniffing the cork.

Quality Street, hitch-hiking up *euph.* Big muck-spreader round back, thumb up bum, all business.

quandong *1. n. Aus.* A difficult *lay,* a hard, as opposed to an easy, woman. One who wears armour-plated *knickers. 2. n.* A prostitute, *hooker, ho'.*

quank *1. n.* A quick *wank.* From quick + wank. *2. n.* A quiet *wank.* From quiet + wank.

quantitative easing *1. n.* In economics, increasing a country's money supply by printing a pre-determined quantity of new money, which is then used by the government to buy debts off itself, or something. So that's all clear, then. *2. n.* Emptying one's *Enochs* of a substantial build-up of toxic *feeshus. 3. n.* Discharging a pair of heavily overloaded *bollocks* following a prolonged period of celibacy. *'Are you still in there, Cliff? You're due in the Royal Box in less than thirty seconds to sing Congratulations to the Centre Court crowd.' 'I'll be with you in a moment, Sue. I'm just doing a spot of quantitative easing.'*

quantitty *n.* An amount of *knockers. 'I recently attended a stag do at Hooters Bar in Nottingham, and I am able confirm that there was an exceptionally high quantitty on show there, I can tell you.'*

quantum leap *n.* That mysterious lost period of time between lifting your last pint in the pub and waking up in bed the following day. Or the one after that if you're in hospital.

quantum wank *n.* An act of *personal pollution* performed while mentally re-living past sexual failures and "trying to right what once went wrong".

quarantini *n.* Experimental cocktail mixing, using whatever noxious *shit* you have left in the back of the cupboard. *'Do you fancy a quarantini, dear? It's that stuff in the elephant-shaped bottle we brought back from Morocco, with Stones Bitter, Advocaat and silver polish.'*

quart *n.* A *fart* which is too big for its dimpled container.

quarter pounder *1. n.* An unacceptably thin woman. *2. n.* An unacceptably fat *shit.*

Quasimodo's bell, as hot as *sim. 'How was Ibiza, Terry?' 'Great, Dave. There was loads of fanny and it was as hot as Quasimodo's bell.'*

quattro formaggio *1. n.* A pizza which has been topped with four different cheeses. *2. n.* A woman who has been topped with four different *knob* cheeses. A *plasterer's radio.*

quavering *n.* Licking around the pubic mound in

search of savoury, prawn-like flavours.

quaynte *n. arch.* A Chaucerian *placket*.

quaz *n.* An ugly *bell end* ringer. Abbreviation of Quasimodo.

Quebec Bravos *n.* Metropolitan Police phonetic radio code. QBs = Quality Breasts, used by bored *scuffers* on Saturday night city centre duty. *'Calling all units, calling all units. Quebec Bravos outside the 'Spoons in the High Street. Any units wish to assist? Over.'*

quedge *n.* The narrow space between the tops of a comely woman's thighs. The *Cumberland gap, Foyston gap* or *Toblerone tunnel.*

queef *n. Can.* A *Lawley kazoo, hat dropped forward,* or *flap raspberry.* Also spelled *kweef.*

queef curtains *n. Captain Birdseye's ear muffins.*

queef Lorraine *n.* A rather gamey *open pie* with more of a whiff of mushrooms, bacon and cheese about it, perhaps after interviewing someone hunky on the TVam sofa.

queef stroganoff *euph.* A slightly fishy *beefy eggo* released from the *Gareth Hunt.*

queef the beef *v.* To perform a violent act of feminine frontal flatulence which results in the ejection of the vaginal innards. *'Jerry! I've just queefed the beef.' 'Don't worry Margot, wait there and I'll fetch the wooden spoon.'*

queef Wellington *n.* A *front-bottom air biscuit* that is so meaty it could almost be wrapped in pastry and served with dauphinoise potatoes, petit pois and a light gravy.

queen *n.* A person who is raving *good with colours.*

Queen Amidala's lipstick *n. Chod bin* seat *skidmark* named after its resemblance to the *Phantom Menace* character's bizarrely applied *gob* make-up.

Queen Mary *n.* A particularly roomy *front bottom,* permanently moored at Long Beach, California.

Queen Mum's smile *n.* A *pan smile.* The staining on the lavatory carpet created by years of *pissing like an American pilot*

Queen's back catalogue, tits like *sim.* A pair of empty, saggy *udders* which have been chronically overmilked.

Queen's fart *n.* The gentle sigh of an expertly opened Champagne bottle.

Queen size mattress folded in a skip *euph.* The *camel's toe* of a larger lady in a trouser suit. *'Now let us meet the eight, who are going to generate. Jesus, missus. Your twat looks like a Queen size mattress folded in a skip. Like a Queen size mattress folded in a skip it looks.'*

Queensway *n.* A regular mammoth rectal stock clearance where "everything must go". *Next sale.*

queer *1. adj. pre-1960.* Odd, peculiar. *2. n. post-1960.* A *spud fumbler 3. adj. post-1960. Colwyn Bay.*

queerdo *n.* A strange *puddle jumper.*

quemi *n.* Half a *semi.* A *quarter pounder.*

queuebuster *1. n.* Permit which can be purchased at a theme park allowing its holder to skip to the front and experience the focussed, unalloyed rancour, enmity and animus of everyone else standing patiently in line. *2. n.* Low-slung top that allows a woman to get served at the bar with minimal waiting time.

queue jumper *n.* An *air biscuit* so foul that it clears the room in seconds.

quiche *1. n. Taint, notcher, barse,* whatever. *2. n. Puff's pizza.*

quick, Carruthers, the net! We've found one! *exclam.* Humorous riposte to a *rectal retort.*

quick coat of paint *euph.* An expeditious *legover.* *'I think the baby's room needs a quick coat of paint, love.'*

quickening, the *n.* Sudden, unexpected need for an immediate *shit* when you know that the nearest *chod bin* might not be close enough. *'I'm sorry officer. I know I should have waited and pulled off at the next services, but Scotch Corner is still seven miles away and I got the quickening something rotten just after the Bishop Aukland turning. By the way, do you have any paper or a clean pair of under-crackers in your patrol car, by any chance?'*

quick game of cup and ball *n.* The actions of a fellow getting into a *monkey bath, ie.* Lowering his *clockweights* slowly into the scalding water and then suddenly whipping them out again in the style of a Victorian child playing the repetitive nineteenth century parlour game.

quickie *n.* A swift bout of intercourse that one often fancies in the same way that one fancies a cup of tea. A hurried *one.* *'Oh, it's half time. Do you fancy a quickie, love?' 'Er… go on, then. But stick the kettle on first.'*

quick lick and a spit *1. n.* An effective personal hygiene procedure performed in the handbasin. A *gentleman's wash* or *vicar's bath. 2. n.* A somewhat rushed *bojo. 'Oh, alright then. But I'm reading the Shipping Forecast in ten minutes, so it'll just have to be a quick lick and a spit.'*

quick on the buzzer *1. adj.* Somewhat flatulent, suffering from a *slow puncture. 2. adj.* Up and over like a *pan of milk.*

quick release trousers *n.* Jogging bottoms which can be dropped in the blink of an eye, usually for *al fresco* or opportunistic bathroom/sexual purposes. *'Lot 456. Pair of gold lamé quick release* *trousers, formerly the property of Sir Jimmy Savile OBE, and worn by him while presenting Top of the Pops and working in the mortuary of Leeds General Infirmary. Estimate £300-£350.'* (extract from Christie's Showbiz Memorobilia Auction Catalogue, October 2013).

quick word from our sponsors, and now a *exclam.* A cheeky preface to an *arse jingle.*

quidders *n.* Pound shop patrons; the sort of folk who are unlikely to bid for Fabergé eggs at auction.

quidditch *1. n.* Fundamentally flawed game from them books. *2. n. medic.* The irritating ramifications of an assignation with a payday loan *pro.*

quiet firing *1. euph.* In business, the process of an employer encouraging an employee to resign. *2. euph.* Stealth bombing, arse whispering etc.

quiet Paul *n.* A silent but nonetheless powerful *treacle tart.* Named after Ed China's erstwhile mute assistant on *Wheeler Dealers*, who never utters a sound but is extremely strong. Also *SBD.*

quiet storm *n.* Broad radio format featuring slickly produced soul music, ranging from Smokey Robinson's 1970s output to Luther Vandross and Sade; a suitable accompaniment for cocktail parties, romantic evenings in, and perhaps very gentle *fisting.* *2. n.* A *silent-but-deadly* that your ears can just about pick up; a *Tandoori whisper.*

quiff *n.* A bad smell emanating from an unwashed *quim.*

quiffle *v.* To *strum* a willing lady's *Cumberland gap* as if it were Deryck Guyler's washboard; a dream of every teenage boy in 1950s Britain. From quim + skiffle.

quigley *n.* A hairy *minge.* From the *biffer*-like moustache of film actor Tom Selleck in the film *Quigley Down Under.*

quim *n.* Refined word for the *mapatasi* such as a gentleman might use at a hay clarse cocktail party. From the Welsh Cwm = Valley beneath the 13 amp fuse wire.

quimagination *n.* A mind's eye depiction of as yet unseen *parts of shame* *'In my opinion, Susannah's skirt was inappropriate for a show broadcast so early in the day, and left very little to this viewers' quimagination.'*

quimbargo *n.* A *nookie* ban imposed by a woman with a *nut allergy.*

quimbecile *n.* A stupid fellow who is also a *cunt, eg.* "Lord" Jeffrey Archer.

quimble *n.* A tremor of excitement in a *bird's snatch.* A *fanny gallop.* From quim + tremble.

Quimbledon *euph.* Any ladies' sporting event watched by gentlemen who are paying precious little attention to the scores. *'Where's me*

socks, love? Maria Sharapova's playing Serena at Quimbledon.'

quim bling *n.* Ladies' genital jewellery. *Mufflinks, curtain rings, cuntlery.*

quimbo *n.* Peculiar state of near-penetration. *No man's gland.*

quimby *n.* The middle person in a *threesome*, the filling in a *sex sandwich.* See also *lucky Pierre.*

quim chin *n.* *Muff mouth, cunty chops.* A bearded fellow. *'Did you see Noel Edmonds on telly last night? What a stupid fucking quim chin.'* (Ludovic Kennedy on *Did You See?* BBC2, 1983).

quim de la quim *n.* *Tussage* of the highest order. *'Well, that's the end of the evening dress section, and I think it's safe to say that the judges here at the Royal Albert Hall certainly have their work cut out tonight, because this year's contestants really are the quim de la quim. Now it's time for my favourite round, when we see them once again in their swimsuits, and I don't know about the viewers at home, but my cock's already got a bit of a twitch on and the girls haven't even come out yet.'*

quimegar *n.* An acidic condiment on one's *fish supper.*

quimff *n.* An overgrown, teddy boy-style *ladygarden.*

quiminals *n.* Prison lesbians. *Queen bees.*

quimle *v. onomat.* To eat *hairy pie.*

quimling *n.* A small but vexatious irritation; a child or teenager, a jumped up *arsehole* at work, or a pink-faced junior minister on a lunchtime politics show. A little *cunt.* *'Thank fuck for that. It's January and all the quimlings are back at school.'*

quimmery *n.* Any institution housing a quantity of naive young ladies. Also *crumpetry, ladygarden centre.* *'Oh shite. I must've left me step ladder round the back of the quimmery.'*

quimming trunks *n.* A gent's prize *Eddies*, usually worn when out *on the sniff.*

Quimper *1. n. prop. Fr.* Town in Western France best known as the ancient capital of the Bretons, whoever they were. *2. n. onomat.* The barely audible moan made at the moment of first contact between a chap's *pork sword* and his ladyfriend's *landing gear.*

quimper *n.* A quiet, feeble *fanny fart.*

quimple *n.* One of them chin dimples that looks quite like a *fanny.* As sported by Martin Kemp, Kirk Douglas and Katie Melua. From Quite like a fanny + Dimple.

quimpotent *adj.* Descriptive of a frigid lady who is unable to reach the required level of sexual arousal required by her beau.

quim pro quo *n. Lat.* An ancient Roman *blarter* system where goods and services are exchanged for *gash*. *Hairy cheque book.*

quim reaper *n.* A fellow who harvests more than his fair share of *meat harps*.

quim reaper, the *1. n.* A renowned *cocksmith*, *eg.* Sir Mick Jagger, Sir Rod Stewart, Sir John Betjeman. *2. n. Women's things*, to which they fall victim once a month.

quim skimmer *n.* A particularly short skirt. Also known as a *greyhound* or *pussy pelmet*.

quims on rims *n.* Female cyclists; the hapless prey of the *snurglar*.

quim strings *n.* Imaginary internal female organs that tighten in stressful situations. *'Bob Cratchit raised his glass. "To Mr Scrooge, the founder of the feast," he said cheerily. "Ha! Founder of the feast indeed," screeched his wife. "Why, I'll no sooner drink a toast to him that I would the devil himself, the mean-hearted, penny-pinching, tight-fisted old…" "Now, now, Sara," interrupted Bob. "Don't go snapping your quim strings. It's Christmas Day, and we shall drink to Mr Scrooge."'* (from *A Christmas Carol* by Charles Dickens).

quimsy *n.* The fond remembrance of *tussage* gone by. *Tosstalgia, pasturbation.*

quimtessential *adj.* Representing the most perfect or typical example of a quality or high class *front bum*.

quim vim *n.* A notably caustic detergent used to spruce up the overgrown paths round a neglected *ladygarden*.

quimwear *n.* Saucily skimpy clothing that covers up the *Ts & Cs* of beach-bound *pieces*. *Quimwear* – as recalled by more seasoned admirers of the female form – was often displayed in the likes of the *Freeman's Catalogue* before these modern days of internet *scat gangbangs, two girls one cups, tub girls* and *lemon parties* and so on. Your bikinis, microkinis, monokinis, thongs and what-have-you.

quimwedge *v.* To *do it* with a lady.

quince *1. n. Aus.* A mincing *queen. 2. n.* Something that owls and pussycats eat with a runcible spoon.

Quing *n. prop.* The current monarch. Often sung during the national anthem by folk who

forget that her maj *carked it;* "God save our gra-a-cious Qu…ing".

Quiros money *n.* Situation where you won a middling sum of money gambling on the little-known Spanish golfer to win a tournament several years ago and are, as far as the wife knows, still using those same winnings for betting. *'Oi! Shane, have you just been down the bookies again?' 'It's alright, love, I'm using the Quiros money.'*

qui tacet consentire videtur *exclam. Lat.* Classical parlance meaning "he who is silent is taken to agree". Stated to a room filled with nonplussed non-classicists before letting go with a *fucking ring-ripper.*

quite happy to wait in the fudge queue *euph. Good with colours.* Said of a chap *with a penchant for craft fairs.*

quoasis *n.* Humorous epithet which can be applied to any popular music combo whose new songs sound exactly the same as their previous oeuvre.

quoit *n. Ring, hoop, rusty sheriff's badge, balloon knot, tea towel holder.* That which gets *tossed* on a ship.

quornography *1. n.* Softcore vegetarian pornography, *ie.* No *meat. 2. n.* Any photographic or video imagery where the principal female subject is gaining pleasure from using a *fanny hammer,* that is to say a "meat substitute".

quorn sausage *n.* Yet another term for a police community support officer; because they're "not real pig". Also *apple, potted plant, chimp, happy shopper copper.*

quornucopia *n. coll.* A pasty sprig of vegetarians gathered in one place, with their eyes darting up and down a menu in search of the least tasty option, usually something with goats cheese and extra lettuce.

quumf *v.* To sit waiting outside a public library and take the opportunity to sniff ladies' bicycle seats as soon as possible after their owner has dismounted and gone inside. To *barumph, snurgle, moomph, scrunge.*

qwank *n.* A quick *wank.* Derivation unknown.

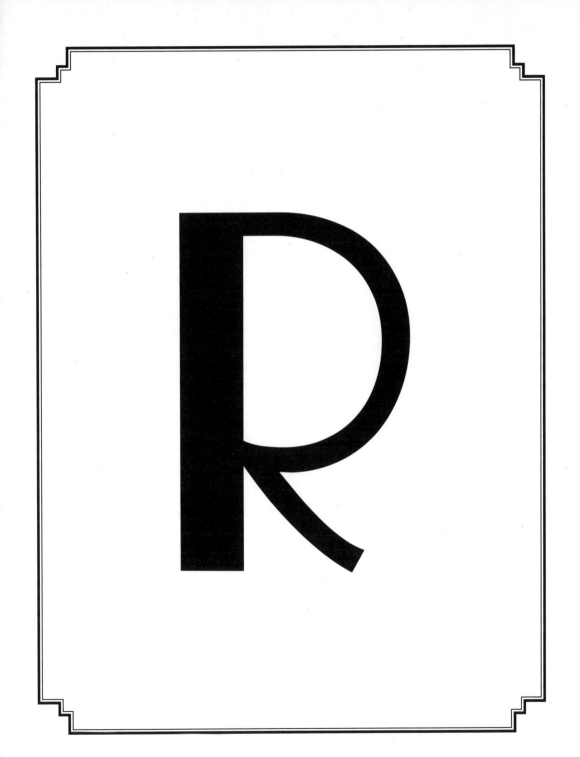

rabbit *n. Her indoors, giving it this.* Major cause of *GBH of the ear-hole.*

rabbit heart *n. medic.* The excessively rapid cardiac palpitations and atrial fibrillation typically experienced by a chap whose wife has come back unexpectedly early while he is *working from home.*

rabbit pie *1. n.* A woman's use of a lapine *fanny hammer* to *bring herself off* while she is getting ineffectually *banged* off a *poorly-endowed* man. *'Ooh, Mr Straw. This is the best rabbit pie I've ever had, it really is. You couldn't just nip out and get me some more AA batteries, could you?' 2. n.* The *faff.*

rabbit's chops, arse like a *sim.* Descriptive of the unsettling convulsions of the *blood orange* when one is in imminent need of an *Eartha Kitt.*

rabbit's fart, quiet as a *sim.* Descriptive of noise events registering between 0 – 10 on a standard decibel meter, *eg.* A CofE church on any Sunday other than Easter or Christmas, Tory backbenches when asked if there are any objections to raising the cap on bankers' bonuses, or Stuart Hall's booking agent's phone.

rabbit's nose, twitching like a *1. sim.* The behaviour of one's *gammon ring* following a particularly spicy *Pete Murray. 2. sim.* Poetic characterisation of the behaviour of a person's *nipsy* during moments of great stress. *Half a crown thru'penny bit* or, in extreme circumstances, *bin lid penny.*

rabbit's tail *n.* The split second flash of white cotton gusset caught in one's peripheral vision when a lady crosses her legs at the other side of a waiting room, railway carriage or international football stadium.

rabid dog, fanny like a *sim.* A *clown's pie, cappuccino twat, fish drowner.*

rabid fanny *n.* A dirty *snapper* which seems to have an aversion to water and spends a lot of time frothing at the lips.

race against slime *euph.* When a lady has to run to the *smallest room* before her beau's *muck* drips out of her *fanny* and onto the carpet/cat/dog/slippers.

race against the cock *n.* To rapidly *tug* yourself *off* before attaining full tumescence.

race against time *n.* When a fellow's missus has taken the kids out for an hour but he discovers his laptop has a flat battery.

race for pink *1. n.* TV coverage of the Giro d'Italia cycle race. *2. n.* CCTV coverage of the *2am bin rake* in nightclubs all over Britain.

race snails *v.* Of a football manager, to drive very slowly close to the kerb in order to ask directions from a prostitute after becoming lost in a red light district.

race to the bottom *1. n.* In economics, the lowering of taxes and lessening of worker/consumer protection by a government, encouraging other countries to cut standards even further and creating a vicious circle. *2. n.* Whilst watching a *jazz flick*, the use of the Fast Forward button until the first female star of the movie *takes it up the shitter.*

racing dog's bollocks on a frosty morning *sim.* Descriptive of the state of one's eyes the morning after a heavy night *on the turps.* Also *eyes like sheeps' cunts, David Davis eyes.*

racing Paula Radcliffe *euph.* When on a run, to have the additional stimulus of needing to get home before you *shit yourself* in public. *'Sorry Brendan. Can't stop to talk. I'm racing Paula Radcliffe.'*

racing tits *n.* Aerodynamic *boobs* with low wind resistance.

rack *n.* Female mammarial display, collectively the *tits, funbags. 'She's got a lovely rack on her. Very well presented. And nips like a fighter pilot's thumbs. She'll be a valuable addition to the board of directors.'*

rackattack *exclam.* Secret gentlemen-only phrase that can used to surreptitiously alert one's companions to an approaching feast of *eye magnets. 'You join us here at the Munich Geschwimmgeschplashenpond as the contestants line up for the Ladies' Olympic 200m breast stroke final…Fuck me, rackattack!'*

rackette *n.* The owner of an extremely pert *hat stand.*

rack of stolen watches *euph.* The resilient, hard-ridged residue which lines the inner surfaces of a bachelor's well-worn, unwashed housecoat. So named for its textural resemblance to the lining of a wartime spiv's illicit-chronometer-lined Crombie.

rack sack *n.* A *brasserie.* Also *tit pants, two ring circus, knocker nest.*

racunteur *n.* A teller of tales that are typically untrue and cast the teller in a role that dramatically boosts his own part in the story.

Radagast *n.* A successful *Lord of the ringpiece.* A *brown wizard.*

radar trap *n.* A hairy *fadge*, named after the popular speed enforcement devices of the sort often wielded by over-zealous *titheads* ensconced in the greenery, *ie.* "A cunt behind a bush".

Radcliffe *n.* A car that at first sight looks like a good runner, but ends up completely *fucked* at the side of the road after about fifteen miles.

Radcliffe, do a *1. v.* To fail to finish a pint. *2. v.* To give up three quarters of the way through a pub crawl, fall in a gutter, and have a bit of a cry.

Radcliffe respray *n.* Application of fresh layers of

fake tan, body glitter and deodorant in lieu of a wash prior to a night out; a technique espoused by the ladies of the quaint Lancashire hamlet.

radge 1. v. To become enraged, to lose one's *blob*. 2. n. A furious episode that a person "takes" or "throws" when they get the *red mist*. 3. n. adj. In a state of *radge*.

radgey n. One who is predisposed to taking or throwing *radges*.

Radio 4 funny adj. Any supposedly clever or jocular comment which elicits a false, humourless laugh.

radiohead n. An act of *oral horatio* administered while enjoying the erotically dulcet tones of a wireless presenter or *The Archers*, if livestock happens to be your thing.

radio rental rhym. slang. Radgy, hatstand, mental, *Mabel*.

RAF abbrev. Rough As Fuck. Particularly ugly or unattractive.

RAFCAM/rafcam abbrev. Rough As Fuck, Common As Muck.

raft n. Three or more *floaters*, arranged together in the *pan* more or less in parallel, a bit like them tethered alligators that bloke who looked a little bit like James Bond (from a distance) ran across in *Live and Let Die*.

ragamuffin man 1. n. Title of a 1969 hit for erstwhile British "beat" combo Manfred Mann. 2. n. A Ronald McDonald lookalike who evidently has no objection to *donning the beard* while the *tomato boat is docked* in *Tunatown Bay*.

rag and bone man 1. n. prop. Some sort of singer they have these days. 2. n. One who doesn't mind getting a *barber's pole* now and again; a chap who still *gets the horn* even when his *old nag* is *off games*.

rag doll n. A tasty-looking *tart* that is temporarily *off the menu*.

ragman's coat n. A *turkey's wattle*, a *raggy blart*, a *pound of liver*, a *club sandwich*. An untidily presented vagina.

ragman's trumpet n. A capacious *fanny*. *Big Daddy's sleeping bag*.

rag pudding 1. n. A traditional Lancastrian dish made of pastry, mince and onions. 2. n. *Dining at the Y* on a lady who is *up on blocks*. *Mexican lipstick, tasting the rainbow, haemogobbling*.

ragtime jazz n. The *clandestine* stash of *special interest literature* resorted to quad-hebdomadally by a gent while his *bag for life* is *reading Cosmo*.

ragtop 1. n. A convertible motor car. 2. n. An uncircumcised *Charlie* or indeed the *fiveskin* thereupon. The *aardvark's nose, monk's cowl*.

rag week 1. n. Seven days during which students

get *pissed* and behave like *cunts* in the name of charity. 2. n. Time of the month when the *flags are out. Blob week, cricket week, blow job week.*

railbird 1. n. In poker, a non-participatory spectator at a game. 2. n. In a pub or club, a *heavily refreshed* young lady who gives the impression that she has had a drink from every one of the optics on the rail behind the bar.

railway sleeper n. The largest, firmest and most angular *Thora* known to mankind, which makes a *dead otter* look like a minor *follow through*.

Rainbow Bridge of Bifrost, the 1. n. In Norse Mythology, a burning rainbow that reaches between Midgard (the world) and Asgard, (the realm of the Gods). 2. n. The *barse, notcher, carse, Humber, tinter, taint, tisnae, tissent, ABC* or *Joy Division*.

rainbow trout n. An aesthetically challenged *piece* who tries to disguise the fact by trowelling on vast quantities of multi-coloured *slap*.

rainbow yawn n. Puke, a *technicolour laugh, pavement pizza, pigeon buffet*.

raindance n. The Native American-style rhythmical stamping moves made by the feet of one with a full *beer sack* as he tries to get his keys in the front door following a night *on the pop*.

raining up a dog's ass euph. US. Descriptive of when the precipitation is hitting the pavement (or "sidewalk") so hard that it might bounce up a small canine's bottom. *'10-15 inches of rain fell across southern Alabama and western portions of the Florida Panhandle Sunday. Some localized areas of more than 20 inches of precipitation were reported in and near Pensacola, Florida. The Oceanic and Atmospheric Administration's National Weather Service warned of a high probability of flooding as it could continue raining up a dog's ass until at least Wednesday.'*

rainman n. A woman with phenomenal mental capacity, who can commit to memory every single male misdemeanor committed throughout the duration of a relationship. These are then re-gurgitated *ad nauseam* during arguments or for guilt trip purposes, emotional blackmail, court proceedings etc.

rainwater washdown n. A resourceful fellow's *al fresco* means of using any water which is available to him on his way back from a night out to rinse away unwanted perfume, make-up marks or *blip* from his person, prior to entering the house and encountering his eagle-eyed/nosed girlfriend or wife. During the more clement months, in the absence of convenient precipitation, morning dew or damp leaves can be successfully utilised to achieve a similar end.

raised manhole cover *n.* A particularly pronounced *front bottom.* A big *camel's foot* that could take your exhaust off.

raise 'n' gaze *n.* Charming male quirk. In the newsagents, the unavoidable and instinctive act of lifting one's eyes and checking out the top shelf *jazz periodicals. Action man eagle-eyes.*

raisin *n.* The *corn dot, freckle.*

raisin bag *n.* The *nut sack, clackerbag, hairy pod purse, John Wayne's hairy saddlebags.*

raisin factory *euph.* An old people's home. From the fact that senior citizens are left there to dry out and wrinkle before being shipped out in a small box.

rake the cage out *v.* To *build a log cabin*, give birth to a *Richard the Third.*

Ralph *v. onomat.* To vomit. Also *call Huey.*

Rambo'd *adj.* So *pissed* that one believes that one can take on any amount of people in the car park and win.

ram job *n.* Vatican-approved, conventional heterosexual sex, as opposed to a *blow job, hand job, Hawaiian muscle fuck* or *Boston pancake.* A *knob job.*

rammadanny *n.* An enforced monthly *Jacky Danny* fast.

Rammstein rag *n.* An extra thick *mousemat* for when a *bird's women's things* get really fucking heavy. Named after the really fucking heavy German metal combo.

rampette *n.* A raspy-voiced, middle-aged female cider taster.

ramp shot *1. n.* In cricket, a strike that deflects the ball over the batsman's shoulder; a shot that is, it says here, popular in the one day and T20 games. *2. n.* A rather intense and enthusiastic *pop shot* that flies over one's shoulder.

ram raiding on a scooter *adj.* Descriptive of a less than attractive young lady. *'She was a worthy woman, yette sore ugglie, with a face lyke shede been ramme-raidynge onn a scooter.'* (from *The Medical Receptionist's Tale* by Geoffrey Chaucer).

ram shackled *adj.* Engaged in the act of *botting.*

ram's horns, the *n.* An extreme example of the *jester's shoes*, marking the end of a protracted sexual drought at the moment of its quenching.

RAM sleep *n. abbrev.* The phase prior to deep sleep. Rapid Arm Movement.

Rancor's arms *n.* A collection of large, leathery *digestive transits* resembling the monster from *Return of the Jedi.*

randlord *n.* A perverted publican whose habitual gropery, *tit*-staring and constant stream of crude innuendo have inexplicably worn thin with his uptight and frigid female customers.

randy *n.* Cowboy version of *horny.*

randy as a panda *adj.* A jovial phrase describing one who is perpetually averse to sex. Also *frigid, allergic to nuts, married.*

randyvous *n.* A moonlit tryst arranged with purely carnal intentions.

range anxiety *1. n.* Unsettled sensation felt by electric car owners as their battery percentage dwindles whilst they drive fruitlessly from services to services looking for a working charger, or one with the right plug on it. *2. n.* Feeling of fear when wandering too far from the facilities during an attack of *rusty fire water. 3. n.* Felt when on the verge of *painting* a young lady's *kidneys* very early on during a romantic assignation. *4. n.* Feeling of hollow terror experienced by a *two-push Charlie*; will he reach his destination too quickly or can he hold out for a respectable time before *losing his charge?*

range is in use, the *euph. milit.* Army term denoting the fact that red (danger) flags are flying and thus a particular firing area cannot presently be entered, used by women when they've *got mice. Arsenal are at home, Aunt Irma is visiting, the tomato boat has docked etc.*

rangers returning! *1. exclam.* In *Game of Thrones*, the meaning of the Night's Watch sounding one long blast on the horn. Or something like that. *2. exclam.* In a *game of thrones* at the public lavatory, an amusing response to a long blast from an adjoining cubicle.

Rangoon ring *n. medic.* Curry-induced blistering of the *nipsy.* A *Wigan rosette, Japanese flag, Johnny Cash, Hawaiian sunrise.*

rank bank *n.* The opposite of a *wank bank*; an assiduously curated mental inventory of non-erotogenic material for the purpose of *keeping the wolf from the door.* See also *cock witch, globstopper, auntie freeze.*

rank outsider *n.* The foulest of *guts, dropped* outdoors and with an aroma so toxic it can be whiffed a furlong away.

rantallion *n. 18thC.* One whose *shot pouch* is longer than the barrel of his *fouling piece.* See also *longshanks, granny's elbow.*

rantrum *n.* An ill-tempered, inarticulate, rambling, ungrammatical and theatrical polemic, like what Donald Trump or Giles Coren would deliver.

rapid unscheduled disassembly *euph.* How Elon Musk describes it when another one of his experimental rockets explodes like a clown car.

rapier wit *n. rhym. slang. 'That Chubby Brown is a*

rapier wit.'

raptor, walk like a *sim.* The strange, careful gait of an *over-refreshed* female drinker in high heels, reminiscent of the smaller dinosaurs in the film *Jurassic Park.*

Raquel Belch *n.* A female with such a *lovely personality* that one tastes one's last meal again.

rascal wrapper *n. French letter, blob, rubber johnny, English overcoat.*

rash of the Titans *n.* A proper itch of the sort that would instill fear in the very Gods who dwell upon Mount Olympus.

raspberries in syrup *sim.* The consistency of *shit* after a night *on the hoy.* The kind that makes you pull a face like Kenneth Williams going "Ooh, Matron!"

raspberry *n. rhym. slang.* A *guff.* From raspberry tart = fart. *'Did you just drop a raspberry, vicar?' 'Yes. And when I bent down to pick it up, I farted and it fucking stinks.'*

raspberry beret *euph.* Getting *bobbed* up the *raisin* by a *bird* with a *strap-on.* From the song by erstwhile dead pop *short-arse* Prince, *viz.* "She went in through the out door, out door."

raspberry lavlova *n.* In the works place, the stench of *shite* subtly masked by a fruity vape.

raspberry pavlova *n.* Reams of unflushed, blood-stained *bumwad* left floating in the *pan* by a female when she is *dropping clots.* Or indeed, by her *Adrians*-afflicted hubby.

raspberry vinegar *n. Moon juice.*

rasper *n.* A lady who can't resist bringing her teeth into play when *playing the pink oboe.* 'How was she, then, Desmond?' 'Not bad, but she's a bit of a rasper.'

Rasputin *n.* An unkempt vaginal or anal beard of which it is a shame how it carries on.

rat *n.* A lady's *bodily treasure.* The *parts of shame.* *'Excreta was powerless to resist. His eyes burned into hers like sequins. His strong arms enfolded her tender body as she felt herself being swept away in an Aurora Borealis of passion. Then he said the words her heart had ached to hear for so long. "Giz a quick shot on your rat, love. I want to catch last orders."'* (from *The Lady and the Disgraced Former Manchester United and Northern Ireland Footballer* by Barbara Cartland).

rat arsed *adj. Shit-faced.*

ratarseholed *adj.* Simultaneously *ratarsed* and *arseholed.*

rat-a-tat-twat *n.* Someone who wakes you up by knocking on the door when you're trying to sleep in, or when you've been working nights, or who comes to the door to tell you they were just resurfacing your neighbour's drive and they've got some fucking tarmac left over while you're trying to watch *Emmerdale Farm.*

rat boy slim *n.* A youthful fellow, using his high-tech mobile phone to play a mash-up of his favourite clownstep songs at full volume in order to entertain his fellow commuters.

rat catcher's bait box *n.* An unpleasant tasting *fish pie.* A *nine volter, crabby patty.*

RATE/rate *acronym.* A description of the physical appearance of a person who does not come up to your exacting standards. Rough Around The Edges.

rat killer *n.* A foul *turd* capable of exterminating any pipe-dwelling rodent within a mile of the S-bend.

rat killer *n.* A *Tom tit* so bad that, when flushed, it will probably end all life in the local sewerage system.

rat nav *n.* A fellow's inbuilt propensity, when intoxicated, to scan his immediate locale for *fanny.* 'Don't mind me, pal. I'm on the rat nav at the moment, looking for the best rat in this here barn.'

rat packing *n.* The saucy act of storing an untold number of live rodent animals within a person's *back passage.*

rat's back *n.* A light brown, nicely curved *muff.*

rat's cocks! *exclam.* Expression of extreme disappointment. Drat, confound it, curses, *etc.* "My God!" the boatswain cried. 'What has happened to the ship?" "The Pequod has been stove in by a Leviathan, a Great White Whale!" replied the helmsman, scarce able to comprehend the enormity of his own words. "Rat's cocks," yelled Ahab. "That's fucking torn it!"' (from *Moby Dick* by Herman Melville).

rat's nose *n.* An inquisitive bit of *poo* poking out of the *nipsy* to see if the coast's clear. 'FX: DOOR OPENS, BUCKET CLANKS. Mrs Mopp: There you go, Mr Handley. Your smallest room's as clean as a Chinaman's chopsticks. Tommy Handley: Thank Christ for that, Mrs Mopp. I've been stood out here three quarters of a fucking hour with the rat's nose. FX: RUNNING FOOTSTEPS, DOOR OPENS AND CLOSES, ZIP, FOGHORN, SOUND OF LARGE SHIT HITTING WATER. Orchestra: Signature tune to finish.' (Script of *It's That Man Again*, broadcast on the BBC Home Service, March 1942).

rat stance *n.* Characteristic, hunched standing position adopted by a fellow who is having a spot of *hand to gland combat* in a shower. 'So there I was in the rat stance, I'd got to the jester's shoes and she walked in on the vinegar strokes. Nothing could *stop me by then.'*

rat tail *1. n.* In metalwork, a long, thin, cylindrical file. *2. n.* A very suspect eighties hairdo. *3. n.* A long, thin, cylindrical *Richard the Third.*

rattle and hum *1. n.* Title of a 1987 documentary about Bonio and his pop group. *2. n.* A loud and obnoxious-smelling visit to the *cackatorium* when, if it is the weekend and you have had a heavy night and a curry, you may find yourself singing *Sunday Bloody Sunday. 3. n.* The sound and fragrance of Bonio's *flatus.*

rattled more times than Banksy's spray can, she's been *exclam.* Descriptive of a woman who's been about a bit, s*xually speaking. See also *fingered more times than Bob Dylan's guitar, rogered more times than a policeman's radio, fucked more times than an Amstrad word processor, cocked more times than Davey Crockett's rifle etc.*

rattler, the *n.* A violent *April tart* released while on a bench, for example in the Wimpy on Southend seafront, to pick a location entirely at random, the force of which is felt through their buttocks by the other seated occupants.

rat trap *n.* A cheesy *snapper.*

rat van *n.* Specifically, the *kebabulance* parked on Christchurch Road outside Reading University, where undergraduate gastronomes are wont to go to "grab a rat" when sufficiently intoxicated.

Ratzinger's eye *n.* The winking *nipsy.* Named in honour of the ex-former late pontiff.

raver's ring *n.* Unpleasant symptom of dancing vigorously after failing to wipe *Robert Smith's gob* properly earlier in the evening.

Ravi Shankar *n. prop. rhym. slang.* A gentleman who plays a small, pink sitar.

raw child *n. Baby gravy,* concentrated *population paste.*

Ray Mears's nightmare *n.* A *bush* so overgrown and intimidating that even the roly-poly khaki-clad foliage-nibbler would think twice before he attempted to penetrate it. *Terry Waite's allotment, Stuart Hall's windowbox.*

Ray Mears trying to start a fire, going at it like *sim.* Descriptive of a very energetic and vigorous session of tugging and rubbing at one's *twig,* which is reminiscent of the tubby TV nettle-chomper attempting to instigate an *al fresco* conflagration without using matches. *'Oi, mind me bloody banjo string there love. You're going at it like Ray Mears trying to start a fire.'*

razor strops *n.* Long, thin, leathery, pendulous *baps* that would look more in place hanging off

the back of a barber's chair.

razz *v.* To *hoy up.*

Razzle *n. prop.* An unpretentious, no-nonsense *jazz mag.* In its own words "The magazine that makes your cock go big".

Razzle dazzle *1. n. Porn glare. 2. n.* Temporary blindness caused by a particularly nasty *growler shot* in a *self help book.*

Razzle jacket *n.* A newspaper used to conceal a *niff mag* when approaching the newsagent's till, in order to avoid embarrassment. Or a copy of *Readers' Wives Bums Special* used to conceal a copy of the *Daily Mail,* for the same reason. *Palmoflage.*

Razzle stack *n.* The fondly remembered, deeply erotic tableau in the said *art pamphlet,* featuring six vertically arranged *quims.* Now sadly banned due to health and safety following the regular near-suffocation of the lowermost participant.

Razzlet *n.* A slightly overweight, not too bright female, whose only hope of escaping her humdrum existence is to appear in cheap 'n' cheerful *bongo mags.*

razz, on the *adj.* Planning to *hoy up* later in the evening.

reach around *n.* In *botting,* pouring your partner a *hand shandy* while *ram shackled.*

reach for the baton *euph.* After taking a *Donald,* to grab behind for the toilet roll that you fervently hope is located on top of the cistern.

reading Cosmo *euph.* Of a lady, to be absorbed in one of her regular *monthly periodicals.* To be *dropping clots, up on blocks, on her rags etc. 'Fancy a quickie, babe?' 'Nah. I'm reading Cosmo this week,'* or indeed *'I'm getting worried, love. Cosmo hasn't been delivered yet. It's nearly a fortnight late.'*

Reading Hoover *n.* Foot used to clean the carpet by grinding in the dirt until it vanishes. Named after the houseproud Berkshire town. *'Oh no, I've knocked the ashtray over.' 'No problem, love. I'll use the Reading Hoover on it.'*

reading the Financial Times *n.* Performing *cumulonimbus* on a particularly large, loose-lipped, pink *clopper.*

reading the paper *v.* To examine one's used toilet tissue to catch up on the latest news of one's anal health. To peruse the *rusty bulletin.*

read the sport pages *v.* To flip over and concentrate on the *backside.*

ready brek glow *n.* The fuzzy, red outline surrounding everyone on a 6th generation copy of a *stick vid. Porn fuzz.*

ready brek ripper *n.* A stentorian *bubbly duck* that has the same audio characteristics as a petrol chainsaw being plunged into a bucket of porridge.

ready brek turd *n.* A *night watchman* that has been residing in the bottom of the *pan* for some time and has, consequently, acquired a ruddy aura not unlike the hot breakfast treat's trademark glow as seen on adverts in the last century. A *rusting copper pipe.*

ready my hawkmen! *exclam.* Bellowed at full Brian Blessed volume immediately prior to ejaculation, with the option of following with the exclamation "Die!" post emission.

Ready, Steady, Wank *n.* A game of skill based on the formerly popular, similarly named cookery show. The competitor has just half an hour and the most unpromising of materials (a month-old copy of *Chat, Murder She Wrote* on the telly, a Gideon Bible *etc.*) to *crack one out.*

reality wank *n.* A *toss* over someone one could *poke* in real life, therefore making it better and more realistic. Likely subjects include one's girlfriend or the local *bike.*

rear admiral *n.* A sailor who prefers to navigate the *windward passage.*

rear goggles *n.* Notably unreliable mechanism whereby one fondly imagines the front elevation of a woman merely by assessing her rearward appearance. See *crossword, teeth like a.*

rear-gripper *1. n.* In darts, someone who favours holding the back of his arrows when throwing. Well, presumably he lets go of them when he actually throws them. Unless he's got really bad dartitis like what killed Eric Bristow. *2. n.* In *wanking*, someone who favours a similar anterior *wanking spanner* position on the *knob* while *stabbing the cat.* Also *middle-gripper, front-gripper etc.*, as you might imagine.

rear gunner *n.* In aviation terms, a marksman who shoots one of his own side by firing his *lamb cannon* into their *bomb bay.*

rearotica *n.* Seed catalogues for *uphill gardeners* or *assmen.*

rear tits *n.* The fleshy parts of the body that hang over the *titpant lashing straps* of ladies with *nice personalities. Gwats.*

reavage *n.* The *decolletage*-revealing top worn to show an ex-boyfriend what he's missing. From revenge + cleavage.

rebellyon *n.* When a person's digestive system violently disagrees with the previous evening's choice of food or beverage, typically resulting in a mutinous stampede for the exits.

rebuttal *1. n.* A statement that a claim or criticism is false. *2. n.* A second attempt at the *south col.*

recalculating *exclam.* Said in a stilted, GPS-style voice after inadvertently *missing one's exit* during a spot of *back door action.*

recce the DZ *1. phr, milit.* What the army does to check that the landing ground for paras and/or helicopters is as safe as possible, *viz.* "reconnoitre the Drop Zone". *2. n. Ferkyfoodling* prior to performing *cumulonimbus*, and having a discreet sniff of the fingers to ensure there are no unpleasant surprises in store.

receiver of swollen goods *n.* Someone involved in a nefarious transaction with an *arse bandit.*

receive the rod of equity and mercy *1. exclam.* Said (with a straight face) by Archbishop of Canterbury Dr Justin Welby as he presented some gaudy, jewel-encrusted royal gewgaw or other to Camilla Parker-Bowels during the coronation service. *2. exclam.* Formal announcement made by a fully *erectitivated* chap immediately prior to *putting his missus to the sword.*

reconnaissance chip *n.* When making proper chips, the brave, lone pioneer bit of spud that enters the pan on his own to test whether the fat is hot enough.

recorded delivery *n.* Using a mobile phone to preserve the moment you post some first class *man-glue* onto a lady's *norks.*

rectal barometer *n.* The miraculous sensor that is situated in the anal tract and identifies whether the chamber is loaded with gaseous, liquid or solid matter, enabling the operator to decide whether or not to risk an *air biscuit.* The sensitive surfaces of the *rectal barometer* are prone to malfunction, giving erroneous readings uner certain circumstances, eg. When swamped with curry and lager.

rectal crude *n.* Distinctly unrefined *Tipperary tea*, a rich seam of which is typically struck the morning after an evening on the stout.

rectal retort *n.* A witty *fart* of the sort Oscar Wilde might have done.

rectoplasm *n.* A message from the other side which makes everybody's hair stand on end. Something that comes out of your *bum* which is so scary it makes you *shit* yourself. A *McArthur Park.*

rectospect *n.* The realisation that, with hindsight, something was a bit *arse.*

rectum scale, the *n.* Way of measuring the earthquake-like eruptions from one's *ringpiece* after a night on the White Lightning followed by a vindaloo in The Royal Bengal. *'Fuck me, your majesty, that's measured a straight eight on the rectum scale, and by the way it fucking stinks as well.'*

rectum spectrum *n.* The complete auditory range of which a person's *sub-whiffer* and *rusty bullet* *tweeter* are capable; all the way from a trouser-flapping *basso profundo* to a high-pitched *Tommy squeaker* that will annoy the neighbourhood dogs. *Shite noise.*

red alert *exclam.* Discreet *sotto voce* warning exchanged between males, advising each other to tread carefully around the lady of the house/office due to her having *women's things.* Also *code red.*

redbeard *n.* A piratical hue of facial hair obtained by performing *cumulonimbus* upon a lady who *has the painters in.* Also known as a *Henry the eighth* or *gorbie.*

red carpet *euph.* A ginger's *minge,* rolled out for special occasions.

red chef's hat *n.* A penis which has been polished within an inch of its life.

red diesel *1. n.* Low-duty fuel used in construction and agriculture. *2. n.* Popular in West Dorset, a luridly hued fermented apple beverage that exhibits explosive laxative effects after only 4 pints.

redecorate *v.* Of a male, to install a new girlfriend. *'How you getting on with your latest pneumatic blonde, then Rod?' 'To be honest, she's starting to get on me tits. I may have to redecorate.'*

red-glanded *adj.* Caught with one's pants down and one's *cock* in one's hand. *Wanking.*

red herring *n.* A lady's *maguffin* during *blob a job week.*

red hot chili paper *n.* The first tentative dab of *arsewad* against *raisin* after a spicy meal.

red leader *n.* A fellow who, during an attempt at penetrative sex, does not even manage to acquire the status of a *one pump chump.* From the *Star Wars* fighter pilot who took a pot shot at the Death Star but had to admit: "It didn't go in. It just impacted on the surface." Interestingly, the bloke who played the character in the film was married to Felicity Kendal between 1968 and 1979, so you can't really blame him.

red nose day *n.* An opportunistic *dip of the wick* taken during *rag week,* leaving a fellow's *herman jelmet* looking like late clown Charlie Cairoli's famously rubescent conk.

red ring *n.* Inflammation of the *chocolate starfish* as a result of being *skittered.* See *Japanese flag.*

red sauce shuffle *n.* The frantic ketchup bottle-style batting, shaking, pumping and tugging performed by a third party on a chap's *funny bone* in an attempt to get him to spill his *Daddy's sauce.* *'Okay everyone, let's cut there and have a cup of tea. That poor fluffer has been giving Gunther the red sauce shuffle for twenty minutes and there's still no sign of a money shot.'*

red sea scrolls *n.* The unexpected discovery of some ancient *jampax* that had been thought flushed away many hours before.

red sock, arse hanging out like a *sim. medic.* Descriptive of a full rectal prolapse. Such as one caused by a deliciously fatal plate of Curry Hell, the hottest curry in the world. Exclusively available at the Curry Capital, Bigg Market, Newcastle upon Tyne, the only restaurant to receive the coveted 5 Prolapses award in the *Viz Good Curry Guide.* Now closed.

red tee, play off the *1. v.* To be good with colours. *2. v.* To *put a long one into the hole* when the *front nine* has *fallen to the communists.*

red thunder *1. n.* Nickname of the Oklahoma State Guards 45th Fires Brigade field artillery division. *2. n.* A burst of flatulence so vigorous that it causes bleeding.

red tie *n.* To *finish oneself off* with a *sausage sandwich* after having had an elegant sufficiency of the *cranberry dip.*

redtooth technology *n.* The miraculous ability of females who are regularly in close proximity to synchronise their *clot-dropping* routines.

red wedding *1. n.* A disastrous event from the popular and impenetrable TV show *Game of Thrones,* a bit like the 1985 Moldavian massacre episode of *Dynasty,* but with *tits. 2. n.* A disastrous and impenetrable event whereby one's honeymoon night coincides with *rag week.* Also *honeymoon period.*

red wings *n.* Dubious honour bestowed upon one who doesn't mind a portion of *rag pudding.*

reedle *v.* To *piss* through an awkward opening or inconvenient gap, *eg.* Between the flaps of a tent (in or out), out of a partially opened Velux window, through Jacob Rees-Mogg's letterbox.

reef 'n' beef *adj.* Of a lady, *half rice half chips.* *'Marie-Antoinette was powerless to resist. The Scarlet Pimpernel's eyes burned into hers like sapphires. His muscular arms enfolded her body as she felt herself being swept away in a tai fung of passion. Suddenly, there was a knock at the door. "Oh no, it's the maid," he said. "'f she discovers us together, we'll be undone!" "Never mind," said the Queen. "I'm reef'n' beef. Let her in and I'll do her when I've finished with you."'* (from *The Lady and the Man and the Other Lady* by Barbara Cartland).

Reese Wetherspoons *n. prop.* A blonde with a *sticky carpet.*

Rees-Mogg *n. rhym. slang.* The *shitter.* *'Where's mom?' 'She's on the Rees-Mogg, John-Boy.'*

refecate *v.* To fill one's bowels by eating *crap.* *'The* *missus has had me on a veggie diet all week, so I'm just popping along to Maccy D's to refecate.'*

referee's coin, cock like a *sim.* A reference to a well-worn *tool* which has been subject to an inordiate amount of *tossing* over the years, *eg.* The one belonging to that *wanking* bloke who hides in a rhododendron bush in Heaton Park, Newcastle-upon-Tyne. Or the one belonging to Jonathan Ross, assuming they're not one and the same person.

referee's whistle *n.* Navigating an *Acme Thunderer* around a stubborn *malteser* lodged in the *shitbox.*

refer oneself to the watchdog *1. v.* What the police, politicians or the BBC do when they have *fucked up* or in some way *dropped a bollock. 'The prime minister has referred himself to the watchdog.' 2. v.* Similarly, to volunteer information to one's better half regarding one's internet history, gambling habits or attendance at an all-male *scrotal inflation* party in Stuttgart. *'The prime minister has referred himself to the watchdog.'*

refer one to the third umpire *v.* To cast a shrewd and experienced eye across one's *shreddies* to check for a *follow-through* that has fouled the crease. *'I tell thee what Blowers, it stinks that much, I might have to refer it to the third umpire, lad.'*

refleshment *n.* The energy boost gained by spotting a scantily clad young lady during an otherwise spirit-sapping episode.

refreshed *adj. Fucking mortal.*

refreshingly outspoken *euph.* Robustly opinionated in an extremely right wing sort of way. *'I do like that Katie Hopkins. She's refreshingly outspoken and not afraid to tell it like it is.'*

refusal *1. n.* In show-jumping, when a horse approaches the fence but only briefly puts its nose over the bar instead of jumping. *2. n.* In *shitting,* when a reluctant *German Byte* pokes its nose out of the *ringpiece* for a second before, notwithstanding Herculean efforts from the *toiletee,* returning back to the warmth and safety of the *dirt bakery.*

reggae like it used to be *n.* Masturbation. Wearing a bowler hat.

reggae strum *n.* A rather slow and laid back *wanking* technique consisting solely of up-strokes

Reggie *n.* Affectionate term for a registered sex offender. *'Yes, we've got three or four Reggies living in our street too, your majesty.'*

relaxation allowance *1. n.* Addition to the basic time allowed for a worker to recover after carrying out a particularly arduous task. *2. n.* Opportunistically *beating the meat* while the wife's eye is down.

relaxative *n.* Reading material that is taken to

the lavatory.

relaxed her fitness regime, she has *euph.* Of a svelte lady who has got married and evidently *found the key to the pie cupboard. 'I see that Claire out of off of Steps has relaxed her fitness regime again, then.'*

relax in a gentleman's way *v. euph.* To *interfere with oneself* down there. *'Scrooge pulled up his nightshirt, tucked it under his whiskery old chin and began relaxing in a gentleman's way, trying hard to conjure up a mental picture of Mrs Cratchit in the rik. Suddenly the room was filled with an eerie light, and there before him stood the second spirit, the spirit of Christmas Present.'* (from *A Christmas Carol* by Charles Dickens).

release some equity *v.* To *fart* and thereby *free up* your liquid assets.

release the chocolate hostage *v.* To liberate *Richard the Third* from his incarceration in your *chamber of horrors.*

release the Crayola catapult *v.* To propel a *motion* from the *Camillas* with such pressure that it leaves the U-bend looking *like a toddler's sketchbook.*

release the handbrake *v.* To *drop a gut* into your hand and then present it into a friend's face for their olfactory delectation. To proffer a *cupcake.*

release the hounds *n.* To empty one's *arse,* and thus...

release the hounds, Smithers *1. exclam.* Catchphrase of Mr Burns in *The Simpsons. 2. n.* Jocular instruction to one's *nipsy* when about to break cover.

release the Kraken! *exclam.* An announcement made when one is imminently expecting a *Chodzilla* movement of truly epic proportions.

release the mounds *v.* Of a well-endowed *piece* who is up on top, to remove her *tit pants. 'You've been riding at a fair pace for quite a time now, pet. Time to release the mounds, surely?'*

release the scorpions *v.* To produce a *wind of change* powerful enough to have brought down the Berlin Wall.

release your inner child *1. phr.* Some *bollocks* about the happy, imaginative, innocence that you used to have and still do have buried within, and you just need to tap into it again. *2. v. Letting one rip.*

releasing the flavour *1. n.* The act of adding water to whisky, or an Oxo cube to a stew. Or an Oxo cube to whisky. *2. n.* The act of *letting off* a meaty one. *Dropping a chum fart, opening the pork scratchings.*

relegation battle *euph. medic.* The rampant *shits.* As Jeff Stelling would say "it's all happening at the bottom".

relic hunter *n.* A young chap who desires the companionship of much older ladies. Also known as a *granny magnet, biddy fiddler, archaeologist, mothball diver* or *OAP-dophile*.

relief to hear that, it's a *exclam*. Humorous response to a longer-than-usual, albeit dry-sounding, *trouser cough*.

relief work, engaged in *1. euph*. Employed by – or volunteering for – an international aid agency such as the Red Cross or Medecin Sans Frontiers. *2. n*. Having a *Barclays*. 'Parcel to sign for down here, Mr Ross.' 'Sorry, I can't at the moment. I'm engaged in relief work.'

remaster the back catalogue *1. v*. In the world of pop music, to re-release an artiste's old records with slightly different covers and the loudness turned up. *2. v*. To enjoy a romantic interlude up an old flame.

reminder of home *n*. A *Miranda* performed in the workplace that is wistfully redolent of one's tea from the previous evening.

remould *n. Rubber, single finger Marigold glove, blob*.

rent boy's ringpiece, face like a *sim*. Descriptive of someone who looks like life has given them a regular, relentless and vigorous *shafting*. *'Ladies and gentlemen, our next guest needs no introduction from me. He's a musician, singer and songwriter and he's got a face like a rent boy's ringpiece. Let's have a big Alan Titchmarsh Show round of applause for Mr Mark E Smith!'*

reodorant *n*. Something that replaces one bad smell with another bad smell. *'I'd leave it ten minutes if I were you.' 'No time for that, Mr President. I'll just have to spray some reodorant around. Is there a can of Lynx in there?'*

re-offender *1. n*. In the world of probation officers and their clients, a little *shit* that keeps appearing over and over again. *2. n*. In the world of going to the toilet, a buoyantly recalcitrant *thirty-three-and-a-third* that re-surfaces repeatedly after flushing.

repeater Kay *n*. A man of low wit, who attempts to get laughs in the pub by lamely repeating comedy catchphrases, *eg*. "Garlic bread" *etc*.

replacement bus service *euph*. A substitute means of getting to one's intended destination during *planned engineering works*.

replacement hipster *n*. A gentleman who is well into his fifties, yet who mistakenly believes that he is rocking the flat cap, beard and tattoos look.

replicunt *n*. When your new boss is just like the old one.

rerack *1. v*. In snooker, pool or billiards, to use a triangular frame to re-arrange the balls on the table at the start of a game. *2. v*. To surgically improve a woman's *headlamps*. *'No way those bad boys are real, Detective Inspector. She's been reracked for sure.' 'You might be right, doctor. Anyway, let's cover them up and we'll get the husband in to see if he can positively identify her.'*

research a book *v*. To look at *Frankie Vaughan* that has been beamed in from the more *glittery* reaches of cyberspace.

researching a Greek holiday *euph*. Leisure activity which may well involve "looking at Lesbos on the internet". *Buying your better half an anniversary present; do your thing, clickety-click*.

research leave *euph*. In academia, a monastic months- or even years-long period of *working from home*, assisted by such periodicals as *Razzle, Knave* and *Women of the Swiss Reformation Go Wild*.

reserection *n*. The sure and certain hope that a seemingly deceased *cock* will rise from the dead. Generally takes about twenty minutes rather than three days.

reserve chute *1. n*. In the world of sky-diving, a secondary canopy which can be deployed in the event that the first one fails to open properly. *2. euph*. The *arsehole*. *'Woman in hotel bed wearing a corset and bridal veil, and with a 'Just Married' suitcase on the floor: 'Sorry, love. I'm on me rags. You'll have to use the reserve 'chute.' Red-nosed man in a top hat who is removing* his trousers: 'Geronimo!" (Bamforth's *Seaside Chuckles* postcard by Donald McGill, 1936).

reservoir dugs *n*. The nutritious *charms* of a lady who could nourish at least five neonates at a single sitting.

reshuffle the cabinet *v*. To re-arrange the *junk* for reasons of either comfort or public appeal. *'Botham there, confidently reshuffling the cabinet as he strides out to the crease.'*

resign! *exclam*. Shouted in the manner of a disgruntled backbencher following a loud *statement to the house*.

res ipsa loquitur *exclam. Lat*. In the common law of torts, whatever the fuck that is, "the thing speaks for itself". Often heard in robing rooms at Crown Courts up and down the country when a barrister takes ownership of an audible *flatus*.

restful service *1. n*. In computers, an architectural style that defines a set of constraints and properties based on HTTP. But you already knew that. *2. n*. Any sexual activity that aids tranquil repose, *eg*. Hand job, *horatio*.

resting Gazette face *n*. Cheerless mien traditionally worn, in photographs featured in popular Teesside newspaper *The Evening Gazette*, by members of the public who have suffered some form of mild injustice, *eg.* Changed wheelie bin collection schedules, newly imposed resident parking restrictions, or local youths on mopeds using their street as a bloody racetrack. May or may not be accompanied by folded arms.

rest in piss *phr.* Heartfelt eulogium delivered by a *turps nudger* over the prostrate form of his slumbering companion.

restless night *euph.* An evening filled with a lot of *tossing* and a lesser amount of turning. *'You've got terrible bags under your eyes, Jonathan.' 'I'm not surpwised. I had a vewy westless night.'*

restoration fund *1. n.* Appeal run by your local vicar who, despite the fact that the Church of England has an investment fund totalling several trillion pounds, has no money to fix a couple of tiles back on his vestry roof. *2. n.* Whatever's left in your wallet after a night *on the pop,* which can be used the next day to buy aspirins, water, a fry-up, the hair of the dog or whatever else is required so you can rejoin the human race. *'I went out with a hundred quid, but there's only sixteen pee in the restoration fund.'*

restore the factory settings *1. v.* To threaten to terminate a relationship unless your *big-boned,* frigid ladyfriend reverts to her slender, sexually adventurous former self. *2. euph. medic.* Hymenoplasty (also known as hymenorrhaphy, hymen reconstruction or hymen repair). Surgical restoration of the *Bill Wyman.*

restroom *n. US.* The toilet. *'I'd give it five minutes before you go in the restroom. I've just done a massive rest.'*

resurrection shuffle *1. n.* Title of a song by Ashton, Gardner and Dyke that reached number 3 in the UK charts in January 1971. *2. n.* A miraculous *second coming* while *working from home. Twice off the same hard.*

retain water *v.* Of a *plumper,* to eat lots of cake.

retch *v.* To vomit, but with more noise and less *puke.*

retire from the papacy *v.* To abandon an attempt to *pull the pope's hat off* halfway through as a result of laziness, ennui or simply being drunk.

retox *n.* The opposite of a detox, undergone by offshore workers after a two-week alcohol-free shift on the rigs. *'That trip was shit, Dave. I'm hitting the boozer for a retox.'*

retreat from Kabul, the *euph.* A catastrophic and out-of-control gastro-intestinal crisis. *'I thought I was going to be fine with the lamb phaal but after a couple of hours it was the retreat from Kabul.'*

retrobate *1. n.* A person stuck in the past who *knocks himself about* to 70s porn films/mags or Sam Fox topless shots *etc. 2. v.* To trawl Facebook one-handedly for old pictures of girls you used to fancy back when they didn't have two kids and were distinctly tidier.

retrosexual *n.* One who has sexual intercourse with someone from his or her past, *eg.* A former friend from school, college, prison, chapel of rest *etc.*

retro tug fodder *n.* A lady who, while a tad ropey now, was an absolute *shit hot wank* in her younger days.

return fire *n.* A cold, sniping splash of *chod bin* water that darts straight up one's *wrinkled penny* while *bombing China. Splashback.*

return serve *n.* The reappearance of a *copper bolt* you thought you had seen the last of.

return ticket *n.* Sheet of *lavatory tissue* that is still attached to the roll and bears the *imprimatur* of a previous user.

return to sender *1. exclam.* When someone has dropped a minging *bowel howl* and you "over-fart" it with an even fouler offering, thus *trumping it,* with interest. *2. exclam.* Elvis Presley's last words.

reveille *n.* An early morning *brass eye* fanfare delivered with military precision, that makes your company jump out of bed. A *breakfast maker.*

revenge porn *n.* Something to look at when the other half turns down the offer of *hanky panky.*

revenge, Turkish *n.* A *stab* up the *arse.*

reverse Churchill *n.* The finger position traditionally used by bare ladies in *art pamphlets* to hold their *snappers* open for their readers' delectation and perusal, an arrangement which is reminiscent of the "V for Victory" hand signal popularised by Britain's cigar-chomping wartime leader, albeit vertically transposed. And round a *fanny.*

reverse cowgirl *n.* A *cowgirl* who has been bucked through 180 degrees, a sexual position much favoured by *meat vid* cinematographers as one can see it *going in.* A *fucking bronco.*

reverse Doagan *n. NZ.* A *chocolate hostage* released into the *chod bin* while sitting the wrong way round, leaving a breathtaking *skidmark vista* for the next unfortunate lady patron of the toilet.

reverse eating *n.* Vomiting or *laughing at the carpet. 'I was up all night reverse eating. Must have been that dodgy catbab I had after those twelve pints.'*

reverse elephant *n.* What happens when one has *flown right past Dresden* without managing to locate a lavatory. A large *Thora* hanging out of one's *bomber aris,* creating the illusion when viewed from the rear of a pink-eared, brown-trunked pachyderm.

reverse midwife *n.* One who puts a baby into a woman.

reverse peach *n.* A rearward elevation of a lady's

parts of shame, such that they resemble a ripe and juicy, fuzzy pink fruit.

reverse Prince Andrew *n.* Sweating copiously at the slightest stimulus, such as climbing one flight of stairs, or eating a chicken dopiaza.

reverse rucksack *n.* A large *abdominal holdall,* used by the *lard of the manor* for storing all the pies.

reverse service charge *1. n.* How one must account for VAT on services bought from businesses based outside the UK. *2. n.* An additional fee requested by a *good time girl* for a spot of *back door work.* See also *council tax.*

reverse Tardis *euph.* A dimensionally transcendental *front bottom* that is massive on the outside but surprisingly snug on the inside.

reverse thrust *n.* The act of *getting off at Edge Hill.* The *interruptus* of one's *coitus.*

review, leave a *euph.* To drop a proper *stinker.* *'What's that terrible smell, Jay?' 'Sorry, I've just left a review.'*

revision *euph.* Masturbation. *'Just off to my room to do some revision, mam.'*

revision timetable *euph.* A student's carefully worked-out holiday roster of examination preparation which comprises sixteen hours per day of sleep, five hours per day of space invaders, and three hours per day of masturbation.

reward yourself *v.* To treat yourself to a *ham shank* after doing some housework, or any other type of work for that matter. *'What are you doing in the bedroom, Terry?' 'I cleaned the patio earlier so I'm just rewarding myself, June.'*

rewilding *n.* When a lady or gent gives up waxing for whatever reason; usually because they aren't getting *any.*

rewire *n.* That point reached during a Thai holiday when a s*x-crazed holidaymaker no longer cares whether the current is flowing *AC* or *DC.*

RFHTFH *abbrev.* Mildly sexist phrase applied to an eastern European lady shotputter, or a fat lass in a Sheffield bun shop. Rather Fuck Her Than Fight Her.

rhino horn *n.* A well-matted tarantula among *arse spiders.* Definitely not an aphrodisiac.

RHM sleep *acronym.* A peaceful snooze following Rapid Hand Movements.

rhoid rage *n.* The anger that wells up uncontrollably upon discovering a freshly swollen *arse grape.* *Seeing red, piling in.*

Rhyl jellyfish *n.* A used *jubber* washed up on the beach.

rhythm and blues *n.* Viagra-enhanced *art appreciation* for the mature gentleman.

rhythm mag *n. Jazz mag, scud book, art pamphlet,* one-handed reading material.

rhythm section *1. n.* In a pop group, the bass and the drums. *2. n.* In a newsagent, the shelf where they put the *jackage. 3. n.* In a *jazz mag,* the mucky pictures of bare ladies as distinct from the textual padding.

rhythm stick *n.* The late Ian Dury's *cock.* The *sixth gear stick, joy stick, copper stick, giggle stick, blood stick* or *slag bat.*

rib *n.* The missus, her indoors. From the children's fairy story *Adam and Eve.*

rib cushions *n. Dirty pillows.* Breasts.

rice krispies *n.* Genital warts that go snap, crackle and pop.

Richard *n. prop. rhym. slang.* A stool. From Richard the Third = turd. *'I've just given birth to a ten pound Richard and now I've got post-faecal depression.'*

Richard E Grants *n. rhym. slang.* Hughs, Brians, Gus Vans, Russells. *'When that big fuck off shark jumped out the water I fudged me Richard E Grants.'*

Richard Widmark *n. prop. rhym. slang.* A *skidmark.* Named after the American TV and film actor who looked like a cross between Frank Sinatra and Dickie Henderson.

Rich Tea quickie *n.* A solitary dunk followed swiftly by a disappointing collapse.

Rick Stein's bin *n.* Derogatory phrase implying that a lady's *bodily treasure* smells not unlike the celebrated fish-chef's kitchen refuse receptacle. *'No offence, Madge, but I'm going to have to call it a day. It's like Rick Stein's bin down here.'*

Rick Wakeman on two keyboards, go at it like *v.* To perform the multi-tasked act of a swain, perched on his knees, being *horatioed* by a reclining *piece* whilst managing to fiddle with her *flange* and *yabbos* with both hands at the same time. *'You remember that Ben Dover video you had, your holiness? He went at it like Rick Wakeman on two keyboards.'*

Rick Witter *n. rhym. slang.* The *crapper.* Named after the singer of York-based Brit-pop underachievers Shed Seven. *'Where's the band? The gig was supposed to start half an hour ago.' Keep your hair on. 'They're just getting changed in the Rick Witter.'*

ridden hard and put away wet *1. phr.* Descriptive of the worst way to treat an equestrian saddle. *2. phr.* Descriptive of a *lady of the night.*

riddle of the sphincter *n.* A mysterious *Bakewell tart* that could make your nose fall off.

ride *1. v.* That which one does to a *bike. 2. n.* She who is ridden. *3. n.* What a lady does to a reclining man. Very, very occasionally.

rider's block *n.* To irretrievably lose *wood* half way through intercourse as a result of a sudden, unexplained nasty sexual image entering the mind, *eg.* A vision of Jack Duckworth doing *oral* on his wife Vera while a post-*trout-pout* Ivy Tilsley *bobs* him with a *strap-on.*

ride the baloney pony *v. US.* To enjoy a *candy rush.*

ride the clutch *1. v.* To teeter on the brink of the *vinegar strokes* in an effort to prolong the act of congress. *2. v.* To maintain the hovering state between releasing the *pace car* and making *skidmarks* on one's underpants. To rein back the *turtle's head, fight a rearguard action.*

ride the dirtbike *v.* To be *on pillion duty.*

ride the great white knuckler *v.* To have *one o'er the thumb.*

ride the pink horse *1. n. prop.* Title of a 1947 film noir starring Robert Montgomery, Thomas Gomez and Rita Conde, remade for TV by Don Siegel in 1964 as *The Hanged Man.* The sort of thing that turns up on Talking Pictures TV, and looks like it's been transferred off Standard 8. *2. v.* To get *shagged.*

ride the porcelain bus *v. medic.* To be suffering from the *Engelberts.* *'Christ, I feel terrible. I was up riding the porcelain bus at five this morning, and I've been spewing up and shitting rusty water out me arse all day. Anyway, what was it you wanted again? Two haddock and chips, one mushy peas, a jumbo saveloy and chips and a pot of gravy? 'Scuse fingers.'*

ride the waves, slap the fat and *v.* To poke an amply proportioned partner. See also *moped.* *'It's not as bad as you might think if you just slap the fat and ride the waves.'*

ridge paste *n.* The sweaty, *smegma pâté* that collects under the *brim* of the *farmer's hat.*

riding a turtle *euph.* In possession of a full nappy. *'Seen that concert he did in Hawaii? I'm sure he's riding a turtle by the time he gets to the big "On" at the end of American Trilogy.'*

riding it out *1. phr.* Ingenious strategy for dealing with Omicron. *2. phr.* Heavily *sharting* oneself and then just proceeding with an important task such as getting married, performing *Hamlet* at the Globe, or piloting a transatlantic flight.

riding shotgun *euph. DVDA.* From the lyrics to the George Ezra song of the same name, *viz.* "(we got) two in the front, two in the back."

riding sidesaddle *n.* Descriptive of the *mincing* trot much favoured by men who are *good with colours.* The kind of gait adopted by Mr Humphries when he was summoned suddenly by Captain Peacock.

riding the goose *n.* Vigorous, two-handed male

masturbation technique. Often performed with the legs out-stretched up in the air, creating the illusion for a casual onlooker that the perpetrator is gripping onto an extremely short-necked goose like a jockey, while avoiding scuffing his shoes as his feathery steed gallops over rough ground. Also known as a *Bernie Clifton.*

riding the grog flume *n.* Falling down the stairs, on your *arse*, from top to bottom after necking a bottle of wine. Extra points if you still have dry clothes at the end of the ride.

riding the rapids *euph.* Intimate female freshening-up technique; flushing the *Rick Witter* while still seated followed by a quick dab dry. Also known as a *Barnsley bidet.*, *Neptune's delight.*

rift valley *1. n.* In geography, a linear-shaped lowland between highlands or mountain ranges, often volcanic. *2. n. medic.* In *bumology*, the low-lying territory between the buttocks; the cleft of the *arse*, which occasionally erupts, emitting clouds of sulphurous fumes and *piloclastic* magma.

rig for silent running *v.* To surreptitiously adjust one's sitting position when about to *step on a frog* so as to minimise one's sonar signature.

right hand cream *n. Vitamin S*-enriched hand and face moisturiser made from a special blend of *nut oils.*

right hand man *1. n.* A valuable colleague. *2. n.* A short, myopic and hairy-palmed pursuivant of *guru Palm and the five pillars of wisdom.*

right said Fred *euph.* A sudden image of the 1980s pop trio that flits unbidden into the mind while having one's head shaved at the barbers by a *bird* with massive *norks* in a low-cut top.

right side of the grass, on the *euph.* Alive. *'Princess Margaret brown bread? Are you sure? I could've sworn she was still the right side of the grass, your majesty.'*

rigid digit *n.* An erect *bone, bonk on.*

Rigsby *n.* A no-handed urination of such vigorous release and force that the hands can be safely placed on the hips for its duration.

Rigsby shag *n.* A sexual position favoured by male *Frankie Vaughan* stars, whereby they rest their hands on their lower backs so they don't get in the way of the camera "seeing it go in", in a style very reminiscent of the erstwhile *Rising Damp* landlord. The *exhibition position.*

rik, the *n.* That which a bare person is in. The *nuddy, nip, Billy bollocks.*

RILF/rilf *abbrev.* A term mainly used in small towns and island communities where they keep themselves very much to themselves; Relative I'd

Like to Fuck.

rim *1. n.* Circumference of the *anus*. *2. v.* To *go around the world.* Looking for a shop selling extra strong mints.

rimfire *1. n.* A small calibre ammunition round (usually.22) fired by means of the pin striking the edge of the casing. *2. n.* The state of the *tea towel holder* after an evening of highly spicy comestibles when it feels like you are trying to pass a marine distress flare. See *Johnny Cash.*

rim job *n.* A bout of *bummilingus.*

rim shot *1. n.* That thing the drummer does after an American late night chat show host has read out a joke. *Bahdumb bahdish. 2. n.* When having a *pony and trap,* the deeply regrettable experience of inadvertently directing a stream of urine under the seat, but over the rim of the *chod bin,* soaking one's *hoggers.*

rind *n.* Profuse build-up of hardened *knob-cheese* beneath a gentleman's *fiveskin.* The *dairy farmer's hatband.*

rind date *n.* An assignation with a lady who turns out to be not to your liking in the looks or weight department.

ring *1. n. Hole, jacksie, anus, brown eye, chocolate starfish. 2. n.* Confusingly, also the *fadge.*

ring bandit *n.* A *fruit feeler.*

ring-barer *n.* One who is predisposed, when excited or in a state of joyous inebriation, towards *mooning* an assembled company of friends, foes, or the fans of another footie club.

ringbinder *1. n.* A notebook containing spring-loaded clamps for the purpose of holding loose sheets of paper. *2. n.* An exceptionally tenacious *arse baby* which necessitates repeated wiping before the *freckle* is even vaguely free of *bum chutney.* A *Marmite pot. 3. n.* A meal designed to ensure minimal *foulage* in the ensuing 24 hours, *eg.* A dozen hard-boiled eggs and a double Immodium.

ring bling *n. Arse jewellery.* Haemorrhoids, *Adrian Chiles, Emma Freuds.* Oversized, ornamental decorations of the *nipsy; blood diamonds. Also Farmers, Keith Floyds, chuckle grapes, Rockfords, Steinbecks, arse chimes, four minute miles, Kurts, Bernards, Michaels etc.*

ring burner *n.* An exceptionally hot curry prepared for the entertainment of the waiters and kitchen staff in Indian restaurants.

ring clean *n.* A yearly buff-up of the *rusty sherrif's badge.*

ringcraft *1. n.* A generic term covering the multitude of techniques, moves and tactics associated with the ancient and noble art of boxing. *2. n.* A generic term covering the multitude of techniques, moves

and tactics associated with the ancient and noble art of *giving someone one up the council gritter.*

ring cycle *1. n.* An *arse*-numbingly over-long sequence of four operatic dramas by Richard Wagner (1813-83), based on characters from the Norse sagas, and involving a fat lady wearing a metal bra and a hat with horns on. The one they're always doing in *Bugs Bunny* cartoons. *2. n.* An *arse*-numbingly over-long sequence of *Peter O'Tooles,* which may leave one singing at the top of one's voice. A long and troubled *band practice* that is destined to last hours, if not days.

ring dragger *n.* A person whose legs are so short as to render their rear end perilously close to the ground. A sufferer from *duck's disease. 'Born on this day: Ted Nugent, musician and crazed gunman, 1948; Jim Davidson, cuntbubble, 1953; Gary Davies, former Radio 1 ring dragger, 1957.'*

ring Edward *n.* A well-baked *bum spud.*

ringerprints *n.* Overwhelming evidence of *bumcraft* detected on sheets, wallpaper, lampshades *etc.*

ringfence *1. v.* Something that chancellor of the exchequers do; protecting funding for essential things like health, education, defence and MPs' pensions. *2. v.* Of a polite, refined lady, to reserve her *council gritter* for only the most committed of romantic partners.

ring finger *1. n.* Typically the third digit of the left hand whereupon marriage is represented by a gold band. *2. n.* Any finger of either hand that has accidentally achieved *push through* during the *paperwork,* identifiable by a brown band. *3. n.* The digit – typically the middle finger of either hand – used to relieve the symptoms of an itchy *arse,* typically sniffed immediately before being washed or wiped hygienically on the curtain.

ringlets *n.* A young lady's anal beard. *4. n.* The digits that will end up the smelliest after a particularly sordid romantic interlude.

ring master *1. n.* The MC at a circus. *2. n.* An expert *botter. 3. n.* A person who rarely breaks wind, from the fact that they are "in control of their Billy Smarts".

ringmaster's dog *euph.* Said of a sexually experimental and enthusiastic lady who shocks even the most seasoned lover with her willingness to perform strange and exotic acts, *ie.* One who "knows more tricks than a ringmaster's dog".

ring of death *1. n.* The light display which indicates to a pasty-faced teenage troglodyte that his XBox has *had the dick* and he may have to venture out of his bedroom to summon help. *2. n.* A really stinky *dirtbox.*

ring of power *1. n.* In *Lord of The Rings,* one of

twenty magical rings forged in the Second Age, intended by Sauron to seduce the rulers of Middle-earth to evil. And grown-ups read this, you say? 2. *n.* A particularly loud *arsehole* that rattles the windows.

ring of shite water *n.* The brown halo that surrounds a *dead otter.*

ringpeace *n.* The uneasy truce finally called between you and your *scissor bone* after two hours of post-Madras nuclear fallout.

ringpiece *n.* A *Samantha Janus* or *Myleene Klarsehole.*

ringpiece de résistance *n. Fr.* A particularly clean and tidy *nipsy* which one would be proud to show off to one's GP or a couple of nuns driving a Morris Minor Traveller.

ringpiece roulette *n.* A good-humoured, bonding game in which one surreptitiously takes a cigarette from a friend's pack at random, inserts the filter end into one's *jacksie* and then replaces it, while neglecting to inform the smoker which one it was.

ring pirate *n.* A renegade *rear admiral.*

ringpull rugrat *n.* An unplanned child who was conceived while one or both of his parents were (or it might be was) intoxicated.

ring rusty 1. *adj.* Descriptive of an ageing pugilist who has not fought for quite some time. '*Prince Naseem Hamed, the ring-rusty boxer, was yesterday jailed for fifteen months by a judge at Sheffield Crown Court.*' (from the *Yorkshire Post,* May 13th 2006). 2. *adj.* Descriptive of someone who has abstained from giving or taking it *up the back garden* for a while. '*Prince Naseem Hamed of E-wing is no longer ring-rusty, according to sources close to the former boxer's showering companions.*' (from the gossip column, *Wakefield Prison News,* May 16th 2006). 3. *adj.* Descriptive of one who has gone through a prolonged period of constipation.

ringside seats, have *v.* To be *turtling* something rotten. To have a heavyweight *mole at the counter.*

rings of sat-on *n.* The bright red semi-circular marks left imprinted on a man's thighs and buttocks after a long and satisfying session of study in the *shittish library.*

ring's speech, the *n.* A staccato, stuttering and somewhat incoherent *anal announcement.*

ringstinct *n.* A mysterious seventh sense that tells a *farter* to wait until he is safely ensconced on the *chod bin,* thus preventing *follow through* in his *scads.*

ring sting *n. medic. Soreness* of the *seventh planet.*

ring stinger *n.* An exotic meal that induces *ring sting* and leaves one with an *arse* like *a Japanese flag.*

ring the bell *v. Pop the cork,* detonate the *fanny bomb.*

ring the waterboard *exclam.* A humorous announcement made following the birth of a particularly hefty *toilet baby.* '*Oi love. You'd better ring the waterboard and tell them to get the big knives out at the shit farm to chop that bastard up.*' '*Yes, Nigella.*'

ringtone *n.* A warning toot on the *trouser trumpet.*

ringtones *n.* The various options delineated on a *nipsy bleacher*'s colour sample chart.

ring was puckering like a toothless granny under the mistletoe, my *exclam.* Expression of trepidation coined in *The Moonstone* by Wilkie Collins.

ringwear 1. *n.* Damage or scuffing from handling a record sleeve that reduces its value in the vinyl marketplace, unless you want to buy it rather than sell it. 2. *n.* Signs of wear and tear on the *wrong 'un.*

ring worm *n.* A *backdoor worker's Jimmy Wonkle.*

ring wraiths *n.* Dark, shadowy creatures that inhabit a sinister netherworld. *Winnets, clagnuts, dangleberries.*

rinky dink 1. *n. rhym. slang.* A *Judi Dench,* that unpleasant odour created by a *fyst, Richard the Third's BO.* 2. *adj.* Descriptive of the Pink Panther.

rinse the lettuce *v.* To wash the *beef curtains in situ* as it were. Female equivalent of a *gentleman's wash.*

Rio Ferdinand's boxing career *euph.* Something that is over very quickly. '*How did it go last night, Bill?*' '*Not great, Jeff. Two pushes and it was over faster than Rio Ferdinand's boxing career.*'

riot coke *n.* Any tinned or bottled beverage that may incline the imbiber towards high-spirited behaviour in the street, *eg.* Strongbow.

riot hose *n.* When the *old man* delivers a powerful, out of control stream of *wazz* at the lavatory, soaking all and sundry in the style of a French police water cannon at a student demonstration.

rip a grumpy *v.* To *snip off a length of dirty spine.* '*Right, I'm off to rip a grumpy. Here's Daniel Corbett with the weather.*'

ripe as tripe *phr.* Descriptive of a pungent aroma '*Fuck me, what a ronk. Honestly, that's ripe as tripe, that is. I must get to the shitter right sharpish. Now here's Owain with the weather.*'

rip in a bear's back *n.* A *ragman's coat, butcher's dustbin, full Turkish, badly packed kebab, beaver's guts, untidy sock drawer; a pork pie that's been trodden on* or *an octopus climbing out of a wetsuit.*

rip in a werewolf's shin, like a *sim.* Descriptive of a vividly lycanthropous *snatch.*

rip one out *v.* To *squeak the breeze* slowly and painfully, in the style of a cowboy having an arrow pulled out of his shoulder.

rip out one's skeleton *v.* To attempt to remove your body's internal supporting framework by pulling repeatedly and viciously on the most visible *bone* about your person.

ripped mattress, fanny like a *sim.* A powerful literary metaphor for an unruly ginger *minge*.

ripped out fireplace *n.* A *butcher's dustbin*.

ripped shopping bag, arse like a *sim.* Descriptive of the unfortunate circumstances whereby the *foulage* is exiting one's *fundament* like groceries slipping out the bottom of a broken carrier in Tesco's car park.

ripped sofa *n.* A *badly packed kebab*.

ripped to the tits *adj.* Inebriated on drink and drugs. Also *whipped to the tits*, absolutely *bezzing*.

ripping up rags *sim.* Descriptive of the sound of a long drawn out *broken heart*.

ripple rider *n.* A swain who is not blind to the charms of the *bigger-boned* lasses in his manor. From the well known phrase "Slap her on the arse and ride the ripples".

rip snorter *n.* A *Bakewell* that sounds like Douglas Fairbanks Junior sliding down the canvas sail of a square-rigged pirate ship on his dagger.

Rip Van Tinkle *n. prop.* An inveterate bed wetter; one who *swamps*.

rise & shine *1. n.* Wholesome 1970s orange (the colour, not the fruit) drink which, if memory serves, came in a sachet and was possibly a by-product of the town gas industry. *2. n.* An early morning *wank*; a *squeeze* for the contents of the *fruitbowl*.

rise from the dead *v.* To achieve a *bone on* by looking at erotic pictures of women who have since passed on, *eg.* Marilyn Monroe, Jayne Mansfield, Peggy Mount *etc*.

rising main *n.* In pubic plumbing, the *tatty watta* supply pipe that is usually fed in through the *flange*. The *main cable*.

Ritz squits *n. medic.* The unedifying, though impressively thorough, purging of *drop zone two* which sometimes occurs following the over-enthusiastic consumption of foodstuffs one can't really afford. *'I knew I shouldn't of ate them swan canapes, Gillian. They've give me terrible Ritz squits.'*

Rives Gaucher *n. rhym. slang. Fr.* French cockney rhyming slang for a *twat*. From left banker = wanker. *'Cette Monsieur Michael McIntyre, il est un homme tres humereux, n'est-ce pas?' 'Pas du tout. Moi, je pense que le vagin unamusant est un veritable Rives Gaucher de l'eau premier.'*

rivet dance *n.* The uncoordinated, awkward, fast motioned-jig associated with those who are desperately trying to avoid *dropping their guts* on the hallway carpet. A *Michael Shatley*.

riveting stick *rhym. slang. Dick.* From the jeweller's instrument.

R Kelly weather *n.* A chill in the air during the summer. When the temperature is "dipping into the teens". From the singer's alleged, though we must stress completely unproven, penchant for cooling meteorological conditions.

road apples *n.* Horse *shit*.

roadhead *n. US.* Hitch hiker's currency. An act of *horatio* performed in return for a lift.

roadkill *n.* A rather flat, dry, *hedgehog*.

roadkill ruby *n.* A curry containing meat of dubious provenance.

roadkill soup *n.* The sanguinous *bearded clam chowder* produced in the process of *knobbing* a *tammy dodger*.

road less travelled, the *1. n.* Title of a poem by Robert Frost, which has been interpreted as a declaration of the importance of personal freedom. *2. euph.* The *back passage*. A tasteful and cultured turn of phrase which can usefully be employed while subtly suggesting to one's ladyfriend that she might like to *turn over a new leaf*. Also *do a Robert Frost*.

roadmap *n.* Unsightly stretchmarks after giving birth. *'Which way to Hastings?' 'Lift your top up love, and I'll have a look at the roadmap.'*

roadside risotto *n.* An appetising pile of *puke* on the kerb. A *pavement pizza, pigeon's buffet, Scotch pancake*.

roads scholar *n.* Someone with extensive experience of the country's highways and byways, acquired by dint of having no fixed abode; a *Harry Ramp*.

road thrill *n.* An *art pamphlet* which has been discarded in a layby by a trucker.

road to Grimsby *n.* The *farse, tinter, carse etc, etc*. The bit between a lady's *front* and *back bottoms*. So called because" there's always a whiff of fish and it's not far from a *shit-hole*".

Roalds *n. rhym. slang.* The male *gonads*. From Roald Dahls = baalls.

roast *1. n.* What a normal bloke has for his Sunday lunch when his missus is at home. *2. n.* What a professional footballer has when his missus is away climbing Mount Kilimanjaro for charity, to pick a completely hypothetical example entirely at random.

roast chicken *1. n.* A lady who lies motionless on her back with her legs apart, revealing a well-used *welly top*. *2. n.* Any member of a one-woman/

two-premiership-footballers configuration who gets cold feet at the last minute.

roast ghost *n.* An *air buffet* that is not suitable for vegetarians.

roasting joint *n.* A club or institution frequented by professional footballers, where they can experience *real end to end stuff.*

roasting over the coals *euph.* Phrase describing a particularly pungent blast of *negative feedback* which has spent some time internally in close proximity to faecal matter. *'I'm sorry about that one, your majesty. I'm afraid it spent some time roasting over the coals.'*

robbing the date locker *n.* The burgling of *turds.*

Robert Knobinson *n.* A few stray hairs slicked over a shiny, smooth, pink dome in the manner of the late 1970s *Call My Bluff/Ask The Family/ Brain of Britain* host. Also *Bobby Charltons, Demond Morrises.*

Robert Maxwell's swimming instructor, as much use as *sim.* Thoroughly ineffectual. *'This app for running my computer remotely from my iPad is about as much use as Robert Maxwell's swimming instructor.'*

Robert Plant *1. n.* prop. Erstwhile, big-choppered Brummie pop vocalist. *2. n.* An excessively large *lemon curd.* Named after the eponymous singer's 1982 single *Big Log. 3. n.* A marathon day of heroic multiple self pollution. Named after the eponymous singer's 1990 single *29 Palms.*

Robin Askwith button *n.* A social media icon depicting a clenched fist pumped into the crook of an elbow. Often used by men ogling holiday photos of the missus's sister/mother/gran *etc.* Named after the acclaimed RADA-trained thesp famous for portraying randy window cleaners and milkmen in the 1970s.

Robin Cook's beard *n.* A sparsely vegetated ginger *duff.* A *grated carrot, council twat.*

Robin's nest *n.* The kind of goood old-fashioned bushy *ladygardens* typically seen in the *Confessions* films starring erstwhile *bongo* thesp and Patricia Hayes-lookalike Robin Askwith.

Robinson Crusoe's trousers, arse like the bottom of *sim.* Descriptive of a *nipsy* that is hanging in tatters for whatever reason. *'Come to the Rupali Restaurant, Bigg Market, Newcastle upon Tyne, for a meal that will give you an arse like the bottom of Robinson Crusoe's trousers.'*

rob knot *n. medic.* A spooneristic *Doonican.*

robocrap *n.* The ominous feeling in the lower bowel which leaves a fellow in no doubt that he only has "twenty seconds to comply".

roboplop *n.* A person who decamps to the office/

works/submarine/aircraft *crapper* at the same time every day with machine-like regularity. Hopefully not leaving behind the aroma of melted electric insulation and hot hydraulic fluid, although some may say that would be preferable to the usual foetid *ronk.*

robot dick *n.* An e-cigarette. Also *douche flute.*

robot nipple *n.* The top of a battery.

rock around the cock *n.* For any number of reasons, none of which necessarily spring to mind, a quantity of seaside confectionary strewn about the male genitals.

rock candy *n.* An effeminate, yet intimidating fellow. A *muscle Mary.*

rocket *n.* A polite way of announcing that some herbert has drawn a *cock* and *balls* somewhere inappropriate, for example in a wedding book. A reference to the fact that the offending drawing can usually be changed into a depiction of a rocket blasting into the stratosphere, albeit one with big hairy engines at the bottom and a wiggly vein up the side. And *spunk* coming out the end of the command module.

rocket polisher *n.* An inveterate *wanker* who suffers an *explosion on the launchpad.*

rocket socket *n.* The *Edinburgh fringe.*

rocket strap *n.* The waistband of the *undercrackers* when used to tether the *old man* discreetly upwards to allow a be-*travel-fatted* fellow to alight decorously from the bus. *'You know I'm automatically attracted to beautiful—I just start kissing them. It's like a magnet. Just kiss. I don't even wait. And when you're a star, they let you do it. You can do anything. Grab 'em by the pussy. You can do anything. Hang on, Billy. Don't open the door yet, I'm just adjusting me rocket strap.'*

Rockfords *n. rhym. slang.* Arse grapes, Nobbies, Emmas, Michaels, farmers, ceramics, Chalfonts. From the TV series *The Rockford Piles.*

rock of ages *n.* A *feeshus* with the density and texture of solidified lava, which takes an eye-wateringly long time – and not a little water and blood – to *cleft.*

rock on Tommy! *exclam.* A snap of *undercracker* elastic against a *bollock* following the incorrect placing of a thumb while adjusting one's person, leading to an involuntary, shouted imprecation.

rock poodle *n.* A lightweight metallurgist, complete with long shaggy hair and puffed-up leather jacket.

rocks *1. n.* Masses of hard, stony matter, *esp.* an extensive formation of same. *2. n.* Big, hairy *bollocks. 3. n.* Those which one "gets off" while *on the job.*

Rocky Balboa's speedbag, clit like *sim.* A larger than normal *clematis*; a *bird's* oversized *wail switch*, which a chap might rapidly bat backwards and forwards while humming the chorus to *Eye of the Tiger*. Also (*clit like*) *a donkey's tongue, ~ a nurse's watch, ~ Rocky's speed bag.*

Rocky press-ups *n.* The act of *wanking* in the shower, pulling on one's genitalia with one hand while using the other one to lean against the wall for balance. The aquatic sinner ends up looking vaguely reminiscent of Mr Balboa doing one of his impressive one-armed, biceps-building exercises.

Rocky's lug *n.* A not particularly alluring *poke hole*.

rod *n. Spam sceptre.*

Roddies *rhym. slang.* The *Camillas*. From late *Planet of the Apes* monkey actor Roddy McDowalls = Enoch Powells. *'Ooh, doctor, me Roddies are giving me some gyp at the moment, I can tell you.'*

rodding point *1. n.* An aperture in a drainage system to allow the insertion of flexible shafts in order to clear blockages, and thus *2. n.* The female *parts of shame. 3. n.* The narrow window of opportunity during which an ageing fellow manages to attain a more or less useable level of *stonkage. 'I say, Camilla, it would appear that one has reached rodding point.' 'We'll go on then, Chaz. It won't bang itself.'*

rodeo sex *n.* A borderline-illegal bedroom game whereby the couple adopt the *doggy position*. The gentleman then calls out an ex-girlfriend's name and sees how long he can stay on for. Also *bronco sex.*

rodeo shit *n.* After a particularly spicy curry, sitting on the *jobby engine* with one hand under the front of the seat and the other one holding onto your hat, hanging on for dear life as the violent eruption from your *Samantha* tries to fling you wildly around the bathroom. Also *mucking bronco.*

Rod Hull's aerial *euph. Brewer's droop.* Named in honour of the late Antipodean ornithologist whose roof-mounted TV reception apparatus proved to be somewhat less rigidly attached than he might have hoped.

Rod Hull's roof, as wet as *adj.* Descriptive of a sexually excited lady; one who is *frothing like bottled Bass. 'Septicaemia was powerless to resist. His eyes burned into hers like 18-carrot diamond-cut Moissanites™. His muscular arms enfolded her body as she felt herself being swept away on an El Niño of passion. She could wait no longer. "Take me now, Kendo," she panted. "Me cunt's as wet as Rod Hull's roof."'* (from *The Lady and the All-In Wrestler* by Barbara Cartland).

Rodin's stinker *euph.* Time spent in sombre intro- spection on the *crapper* the morning after a night *on the pop*. From one's spent, naked, head-rest- ing-in-hands pose, which is reminiscent of the famous statue of Bruce Forsyth by the eponymous French sculptor (1840-1917). See *flatue.*

Rodney *n. prop. rhym. slang.* Convoluted term for a *shite*, named after the mediocre Australian fast bowler Rodney Hogg, whose name rhymes with *log. 'Where've you been, Olivia?' 'In the dunny having a Rodney, Cliff.'*

Rod Stewart's disease *n. medic. Rabbit tods.* Named after the gravel-throated veteran *crum- peteer's* early band the Small Faeces.

rod the drains *1. v.* To enjoy a spot of *bum fun. 2. n.* A Welsh plumber.

rod walloper *n.* One who *gives it six-nowt on the old walking stick.*

rofl rifle *n.* A small *mutton musket* that is a source of amusement to coarse, sexist women.

rogan nosh *n.* When your partner gives you a bit of spicy *fellatio* after having a curry. The female equivalent would, of course, be called a *quimdaloo*. Or possibly *currylingus.*

rogan splosh *n.* An incredibly runny *shit*, accompanied by a fusilade of splattering *tree monkeys* the morning after a *roadkill vindaloo.*

roger *v.* To *fuck*, in the style of a golf club bar bore.

roger and out *1. exclam.* In radio communications, something that *scuffers*, cabbies and airline pilots say at the end of their transmissions. *2. euph.* The gentleman's act of leaving extremely preve- niently following the successful conclusion of an act of intercourse. *'Honestly, darling. She didn't mean a thing to me. It was just roger and out, all twenty-three times.'*

Roger Daltrey's flip-flops *euph.* A particular- ly pungently odoured *fish slice*. Named after the hypothetical plastic footwear worn by the eponymous Who frontman and trout farmer.

roger dodger *n.* A frigid woman.

roger ramjet *n.* A *botter.*

Roger-Vasselin *1. n.* Surname of famed Gallic tennis ace Edouard. No, neither have we. *2. n.* Artificial sexual lubricant. *Granny batter, WD-over40.*

ROG/rog *acronym.* An ageing gent whose rampant libido belies his advancing years, *eg.* Sir Rod Stewart, Sir Mick jagger, Sir Ben Dover. Randy Old Git.

rogue's gallery *1. n.* A collection of photographs of known criminals, used by *the filth* to identify suspects. *2. n.* A person's collection of exes, many of whom wouldn't look out of place in a police lineup.

roider *n. medic. Flatus* of such velocity and force that it literally causes *Michael Miles*.

roid rage *1. n.* Sudden attack of *red mist* from a pumped-up bouncer when somebody's looked at him funny, or has tried to come in the club wearing the wrong sort of shoes. An outburst of anger caused by illicit body-building drugs. *2. n.* The violent anger exhibited by a haemorrhoid sufferer whose *bum grapes* have just been *twatted* with a *metal ruler*, for example. Any foul mood brought on by a sudden flare-up of the *Nobbys*.

Roland Kirk *1. n. prop.* A jazz musician (1936-1977) rightly lauded for his ability to get a tune out of two or more horns simultaneously, and thus *2. euph.* A *jazz actress* rightly lauded for her ability to get a tune out of two or more *horns* simultaneously.

Rolex fanny *n.* A *growler* of such spaciousness that one could easily mislay a wristwatch while giving it a bit of a *firkyfoodle*. Or, indeed, find one that has been mislaid by one of your ladyfriend's previous suitors. A *lucky dip, bran tub*.

Rolf Harris eating a banana *sim.* Descriptive of the close-up intercourse scenes in a very blurred, 200th generation *scruff video*.

Rolfies *n.* The pseudo-Aboriginal gasps and grunts produced when trying to pass an extremely large *didgeridoodoo*.

Rolf's house *n.* Prison. *'Where's Stuart Hall these days? I used to like him on It's a Knockout.' 'Hadn't you heard? He's staying at Rolf's house.'*

Rolf's paintbrush *euph.* Something stiff and not likely to get used in the foreseeable future.

roll back guarantee *n.* The unspoken arrangement between masseuse and client in a *rub-a-tug shop*.

roll call *n.* Desperate shout for help from the *smallest room* when the incumbent has run out of *arsewipe*.

rolling down the hill *euph.* Of a *custard*, to make its way under its own steam down the guts towards the *chuff*. *'I'd open a window if I was you, your holiness. Only I had Chicken Tonight and six pints of homebrew for tea yesterday, and I can feel one rolling down the hill.'*

rolling start *1. n.* Failing to successfully lower your *undercrackers* in time before the *pace car* makes a break for the pits. *Shitting* your pants. *2. n. rhym. slang.* A *Lionel Bart*.

rolling the dice *n. Feeding the ducks, spanking the monkey, flipping pancakes.*

rolling thunder *n.* An overlong *air buffet* served up while walking past a line of people, such as would be dropped by a well-fed monarch backstage at the Royal Variety Performance.

roll in the hay *n.* What everyone wanted to have with Julie Christie in *Far From The Madding Crowd*. And what Donald Sutherland actually had with her in *Don't Look Back*, according to a bloke in the pub.

roll model *n.* A *big-boned bird* who works behind the counter in a high street bakery and manages to sneak the occasional dozen sausage-filled pastry treats down her gullet when no-one's looking.

roll moip *n.* A fishy snack. Also known as a *Norwegian's lunchbox*.

roll mop *n.* A mature lady's rolled-up *mackerel flaps*.

roll of tarmac *n.* An enormous, thick, black, treacly, post-Guinness-session *digestive transit* that looks like it could be used to re-surface the driveway.

roll out the barrel *v.* To introduce your sizeable new girlfriend to your mates.

roll out the carpet *v.* To unpick the end of a fresh *bogroll* in order to impress an important visitor.

roll out the red carpet *1. v.* When hosting a ceremonial event, to make someone feel very welcome. *2. v.* When *hosting the decorators,* to make someone feel very unwelcome.

roll out the white carpet *v.* To lay a strip of lavatory tissue just next to the water in the *jobby engine* in a gallant attempt to prevent *dirty footprints* on the porcelain.

rollover jackpot *n.* A chap's champagne-cork-popping discovery that his latest female acquaintance takes it *up the Ronson*.

rollover week *n.* When the *painters are in*.

Rolls-Royce lifestyle on a rollerskate budget, have a *euph.* To live wildly beyond one's means.

roll the crevice *v.* To attempt to wipe one's *dot* with the coarse cardboard tube after exhausting the supply of *bumwad*.

roly poly *adj.* Tabloid prefix for any celebrity who's half an ounce overweight. For example, *'Roly poly funnyman Mark Watson...'*

romance lake *n.* A pool of *banana yoghurt* left on the sheet following a torrid interlude of some sort.

romancing the bone *n.* An evening in alone with a meal, a bottle of wine and some soft music, followed by a top shelf *stick vid*. *Everything but the girl*, a *one-man orgy*.

Romanian bidet *n.* The refreshing jet of water that hits one in the *nipsy* while depositing a *Bungle's finger* in the *shit pot*. A poor person's *bum washer*. Also *Neptune's kiss, Basildon bidet*.

Roman shower *n.* Term for the act favoured by *emetophiles,* ie. People who obtain sexual excitement by vomiting on one another. For fuck's sake.

Romford grapple *n.* The *Singapore handshake* or *Singapore grip*; an exotic sexual practice known as *pompoir* in French. Also, variously, the *Chelmsford hello, Rotherham toothpaste tube,* or *Colgate cowgirl.*

Romford Rolex *n.* A court-ordered electronic tag attached around the ankle of a feral youth. A popular *estatus symbol* in the salubrious Essex locale.

romosexual *n.* A *left-footed* priest, *cassock lifter.*

romp *v.* To chase a woman in a corset round and round a bedroom at about one-and-a-half times actual speed, lifting the knees very high and accompanied by "BOING!" noises when leaping onto the bed.

Ronaldo piss *n.* A *wazz* taken with the feet placed a yard apart in the style of the former Real Madrid/Portugal midfielder preparing to take a free kick. Usually by an inebriated fellow in a pub urinal or building society doorway.

Ronnie's cue *euph.* The gift of *spambidexterity*, that is to say the ability to *line up a long pink* with either your left or right hand.

Ronson *rhym. slang.* Arse. From Ronson lighter = shiter. *'What seems to be the problem, sir?' 'I've got a milk bottle stuck up me Ronson, doctor.'*

Roobarb and Custard moment *n.* A complete failure to *pull* where, in the style of the popular wobbly teatime animation, "the birds all laughed".

rook's nest *n.* An exceptionally untidy *faff*. *'Cor! Look at her. I bet she's got a minge like a rook's nest – all shit and sticks.'*

room clearer *n.* Of flatulent emissions, a rumble of *under thunder* which registers one notch higher than *breaking company* on the sphincter scale.

room for one more on top! *exclam.* A bus-conductor-esque exhortation employed by *jazz flick* directors when an actress is *gastight*, but an opportunity nevertheless exists for a further actor to essay a *diddy ride* until the scene's messy denouement.

room of doom *1. n.* Circle-shaped chamber inside Hogwarts Castle. *2. n.* The *crapper.*

room 237 bird *n.* A *lass* who looks like a supermodel at first glance, but on closer inspection turns out to be more like the cackling, sore-ridden hag from *The Shining.*

Rooneyed *adj.* Descriptive of one demonstrating an advanced case of sunburn, in the fashion of the scouse footballing wunderkind Wayne. *'Bugger the sunscreen, let's just get Rooneyed.'*

Rooney ramble *n.* A gentle stroll through a red

light district.

rooster *n.* A lady's *nether-wattle. Half a pound of liver.*

rooster tail *1. n.* In the world of Grand Prix motor racing, the characteristic plume of water which arcs up behind a Formula 1 car which is speeding around a waterlogged track. *2. n.* In the world of stomach upsets, a particularly spectacular, and wet, bout of the *Brads.*

root *v. Aus.* To *make love* to.

root beer *n. Aus. Spooge.*

root for truffles *v.* Of a gentleman, or indeed a *lady in tweed trousers*, to forage swinishly through the undergrowth in a *ladygarden* looking for a buried savoury nugget.

rope on a soap *n.* Someone else's *clockspring* embedded on your bar of Imperial Leather.

rope the pony *v.* To *gallop the lizard.*

ropey tit wank *n.* A less-than-satisfactory *diddy ride* off a *fenchested bird. 'Fancy a ropey tit wank, Pete?' 'No thanks, Kate. I'm just off out to buy some crack and a Jag.'*

rorschaching *n.* Idly examining your post-wipe *bum wad* to see if the *shite* smudge reminds you of anything.

Rory Delap *n.* The act of throwing one's *balls* into the *box* from a great distance, named after the erstwhile Stoke City and Ireland right back Rory "The Human Sling" Delap.

Roseberry Topping *1. n.* Frequently climbed hill offering unrivalled vistas over the magical petrochemical wonderland that is Middlesbrough. *2. n.* Put bluntly, the appearance of a chap's *bald man's hat* following a rampant session of *hide the sausage* while *Arsenal are playing at home.*

Rosemary's bum baby *n.* A particularly unsettling *Scooby Doo* which leaves you paranoid, confused and not even sure it happened in the first place.

rose-tinted testicles *n.* Those items through which one looks back fondly on all previous sexual encounters when trapped in a long-term relationship.

Rose West-tinted spectacles, seeing the world through *phr.* Idiomatic expression; taking an unreasonably optimistic and positive view of one's *other half*'s character and behaviour. *'Looking at the defendant in the dock, ladies and gentlemen of the jury, one might be excused from taking the view that his wife Lady Archer has spent the latter years of her marriage seeing the world through Rose West-tinted spectacles.'*

roshambo *n.* Light-hearted game apparently played by members of the Royal Marines, the Parachute Regiment, Red Arrows *etc.,* when they are competing for women, booze or sundry otherwise worthless items that somehow acquire value after a night out *on the piss*. The rules, such as they are, are as follows; Player 1 kicks Player 2 squarely in the balls. If Player 2 does not collapse in agony, he may kick Player 1 in the balls. The last man standing is the winner. It's hardly Mahjong.

Ross Kemp's cameraman, feel like *sim.* To be on the verge of *shitting* yourself over an extended period of time. *'Fuck me, I thought that meeting was never going to end. I've been like Ross Kemp's cameraman all morning.'*

Rotherham bobsleigh *euph.* Four individuals who are *dogging* in a small, upturned vehicle. *'Sgt Dixon told the court he approached the Ford Popular in Paddington Green Woods, and upon investigating it with his torch was able to identify Lord Archer of Weston super Mare as one of its naked occupants.'*

Rotherham railway station, wetter than *sim.* A topical reference to a ladyfriend who is in a heightened state of arousal, from February 2022 when the aforementioned station was submerged under floodwater. *'And I tell you something else, she came back from that Chippendales show wetter than Rotherham railway station. But enough about my weekend, let's play Popmaster.'*

rotoplooker *n.* US. Penis, *chopper.*

rotten bottom *1. n.* Sea-fishing terminology where a special rig is employed to fish over a reef or rocky bottom. Don't say we never learn you anything. *2. n.* A stinking *arsehole.*

Rotterdam roundhouse *n.* Similar to an *Amsterdam uppercut*, only the recipient is on all fours and the move is administered horizontally.

rotters *n.* Unpleasant looking *lungs*. The sort of saggy *tits* with *kneeshooter nips* normally encountered during amateur-style entertainment in the furthest reaches of the satellite television channel menu. *Nasty bags.*

Rottwifer *n.* A rough old *piece* mouthing off loudly when challenged for pushing into the queue for the tills in Lidl.

roughage *n.* Unkempt pubic foliage. High-fibre *holefood*. A portion of *gorilla salad* that counts towards your five-a-day.

rough as a three quid handjob *sim.* Used in reference to something or somebody unpleasantly coarse. *'Any chance you can fit my car in for a service? It's running as rough as a three quid handjob at the moment.'*

rough as guts and twice as smelly *phr.* *'How did you find your devilled quail in aspic, Lord Grantham?'* *'Rough as guts and twice as smelly, Mrs Patmore,*

thank-you for asking.'

roughing up the suspect *v.* What a vice squad copper tells his superiors he's doing when he's caught *polishing* his *bobby's helmet* in the seized *Frankie* store room.

rough wooing, the *1. n.* War between England and Scotland, 1543-1551, fought in an attempt to force a marriage between 6-year-old Edward and Mary (later Queen of Scots), aged 1. *2. n.* Descriptive of the behaviour of slapstick US President Donald Trump when he's out *on the sniff.*

round at Freddie's *adj.* To be *nicely poised, good with colours, light on one's feet.* *'That Duncan Norvelle – he's married with eight kids, you know.'* *'Never. I thought he was round at Freddie's.'* *'No. That's just an act.'*

roundhead *n.* A *pink Darth Vader* after the surgical removal of his *Kojak's rollneck*.

round of applause *n.* A dose of the *clap*. What a fellow might receive after appearing on stage at a nightclub stag-do in Benidorm.

round rubbin' *n.* A female *circle jerk*.

roundstretcher *n.* An outstandingly *lirthy* stool which dilates the *nipsy* as it makes its majestic progress south.

round the houses *1. rhym. slang.* A cockney fellow's trousers. *'Have you seen my round the houses, love? I need them to go for a piece of chalk down the frog and toad to the rub-a-dub for a kitchen sink and a kids from fame of horse and carts with my dinner plates.'* *'Aren't they in the Bobby Moore with your student grants, electric shocks and love really hurts? I'm sure I put them there after I Clarence the cross-eyed lionned them this four-minute warning.'* *2. n.* Prostitutes' argot for all-over erotic stimulation. *'How much for a spot of round the houses in a skip, love?'* *'Fifteen quid, Lord Archer. Or ten if I don't have to touch your disgusting spotty back.'*

round up the tadpoles *v.* To *wank, bash the bishop.*

rover's return *1. n.* Name of the fictional public house where every single resident of Coronation Street goes drinking three or four times a day. *2. n.* The act of stepping on a freshly laid *dog's egg* on the way back from the pub, and dragging it home on the sole of your shoe.

roving thighs *euph.* Telling expression used when referring to a woman who, one might think, may not be entirely faithful to her official partner. *'I wasn't at all surprised to see our Doris's email address turn up in that Ashley Madison database hack, you know. She's always had roving thighs, that one.'*

rowlocks *n.* British comedy staples. *'These contriv-*

ances on my boat serve as fulcrums for my oars.' *'Rowlocks.' 'No, it's true I tell you.'*

row the boat *v.* A dual *tug* boat, multiple *wanking*. Nautical variation on the *downhill skiing* position.

royal borough *1. euph.* The term insistently used, in the mystical twin towns of Maidenhead and Windsor, for what the rest of us would call "the council." *2. n.* The *tradesman's entrance*. *'Ah, Ambrosia, I see there is a mouse in the hole. Might I, before tennis, perchance venture into the Royal Borough?'*

royal carriage wave *n.* While lying in the bath and *blowing one's tanks*, the action of wafting the result towards the nose in order to check on the fragrance, in a style somewhat reminiscent of the current monarch's dropsical hand movements when greeting the great unwashed from within his hermetically sealed coach.

royal coffee table *n.* The act of depositing a *Richard the Third* onto the top of a glass occasional table for the erotic edification of a person lying underneath; a German custom, like Christmas trees, Christmas cards and *cock rings*, originally brought to Britain by Queen Victoria's *sex case* consort Prince Albert.

royal decrees *n. Movements* passed while sat on the *throne*.

Royal Enfield *euph.* A *ride* that goes through her life in a constant state of arousal, leaving small pools of lubricant wherever she settles, in the style of the erstwhile British motorbike of the 1950s and 1960s, whose various flanges were renowned for their lack of lubricant-retaining properties.

royal fanfare *n.* The *brass eye* trumpeting that heralds the imminent arrival of *George the Third*.

royal flush *n.* When a previous visitor to the *spam fritter* has flushed the bowl with, it would seem, a child's watering can, ensuring that the aftermath of their colonic extrusions remains all over the shop, and you have to clean up the mess lest any subsequent visitors think that the culprit was you. *Scraping one for the team.*

royal Iris *n.* A man who is *as tight as a bullfighter's pants* and, on a night out, always manages to be elsewhere or otherwise engaged when it is time for him to get a round in. So-called because, like the Mersey Ferry, he "turns around before he reaches the bar".

Royal Marine *n.* A *snatch* with a buzz cut.

royal peculiar *1. n.* An Anglican church which is, as we all know, out of diocesan jurisdiction and directly under that of the monarch. *2. n.* A member of the royal family who is unusual or a bit wrong. For instance, (name removed on legal advice), (name also removed on legal advice), or his highness Pr(name removed on legal advice)rew, Duke of York.

Royal premiere *n.* The act of menstruation, *ie. Rolling out the red carpet.*

royal Sheridan's *euph.* Named after the simultaneously poured "double bottle" drink, the ambitious yet rewarding act of *pulling oneself off* while concurrently squeezing out a length of *Guinness rope*.

royal wank *n.* A luxurious act of monomanual *personal pollution* enjoyed while watching *Frankie Vaughan* with the sound up high enough to hear what they're saying, *ie.* When the missus and kids won't be home for a good hour, or are at least two rooms away.

Roy Castle's kettle *n.* The use of a choked down *nipsy* in order to use a forcible *Exchange & Mart* to "scratch" an itchy *ringpiece*. A *Dutch cornet.*

Roy Castle's last blow *n.* A frankly unimpressive *trouser trumpet* that sounds like it's feeling very sorry for itself.

Royston Munt *n. rhym. slang.* The female *parts of shame*. From the uncredited actor in *A Room With a View, viz.* Royston Munt = Tristram Hunt.

Royston roulette *n.* The practice of coming home *heavily refreshed* and attempting to make chips, with a roughly 1-in-6 chance that you will set the house on fire. Developed as a pastime in the eponymous Bohemian Glasgow suburb.

Roy Walker moment *n.* A satisfying but morally dubious sexual encounter, *eg.* With a friend's wife or a woman old enough to be one's mother. Or a friend's mother. From the erstwhile *Catchphrase* personality-vacuum's TV catchphrase "it's good, but it's not right".

RPA *abbrev.* Recently Promoted Arsehole. *'This is Tony, the BBC's new DG and RPA.'*

RRSC *abbrev.* Affectionately descriptive of a lady of the ginger persuasion who, although proud of her flaming Pre-Raphaelite locks, can be relied upon to have a *clodge* that whiffs like Peterhead fish market during a heat wave. Rusty Roof, Smelly Cellar.

RSC *1. abbrev.* Royal Shakespeare Company. British theatre outfit boasting such thespish luminaries in its history as Sir John Gielgud, Dame Diana Rigg and Sir Daniel Dyer. *2. abbrev. medic.* Racing Shit Cramp. The debilitating spasms encountered when smashing out a *cable* far too rapidly so as not to miss too much of a match/film/all-you-can-eat buffet.

R2D2's cock *1. euph.* A battery-operated *neck massager*. *2. euph.* A vapist's overly complicated e-cigarette.

rub-a-tug shop *n.* Brothel, bordello, house of ill repute. A massage parlour supplying a rub down and a *tug off.*

rubber beer *n.* Booze bought with a return ticket. A pint one hasn't seen the last of. *Jesus beer, comeback Special Brew.*

rubber bomb *n.* An unrolled *jubber ray* left floating in lavatory pan at a party. A surefire conversation starter and source of amusing accusations and re-criminations amongst any group of pals. Probably a plot device in an episode of *Friends*, and if it wasn't, it should have of been.

rubber gash *n.* The sailor's favourite. A plastic *fanny* which the manufacturers claim is "better than the real thing". At £8.99 (including postage), that's got to be the bargain of the century.

rubber Johnny *n.* A *blob*, contraceptive, a *jubber ray*. Also *rubber, trojan, dunky.*

rubber kebab *n.* An item of fast food with a high coefficient of restitution which bounces back from the stomach onto the pavement or back of the taxi driver's head. See *abra-kebabra.*

rubber's rag *n.* A rigid piece of once-absorbent fabric kept conveniently close to a bachelor's computer workstation.

rubbie burns *n. Scots.* Chaffing of the *bell end* as a result of *going commando.* Originates in Scotland, where all men typically suffer from the affliction due to the scratchiness of their harsh, woollen kilts, which wear away the *wee heids* of their *boabies* while they are roaming in the gloaming.

rubbing one in *v.* The dirty lady's equivalent of *rubbing one out.*

Rubiks *n. rhym. slang. Gorilla salad, fusewire.* From Rubik cubic hair = pubic hair.

Rubik's cubes *1. n.* A far more common sight in the 1980s. *2. n. rhym. slang.* A far more common sight in the 1980s.

Rubik's pube *n.* A rogue strand of *flum* that wraps itself around the *pope's hat,* leaving a fellow with a perplexing mental puzzle to solve. Also *Bobby Charlton, cheese cutter, cock harp.*

rub roy *n.* Having one's *little freedom fighter tugged off* through one's *troos* by a lap dancer in a gentleman's club.

Ruby Murray *n. rhym. slang.* A *cuzza.* Named after the popular singer of the 1950s, who once had five hits in the Top Twenty in the same week, which made people's *arses* really sting.

Ruby splurry *n.* The abstract expressionist af-ter-effects of a previous night's injudiciously consumed comestibles.

Ruby Tuesday *1. n.* Rolling Stones song which was the 19th best-selling record of 1967. *2. n.* The day the missus goes *up on blocks.* Especially if it's a Tuesday.

Ruby worry *n.* Following a *spicy cuzza,* the usually justified fear that one might inadvertently *follow through* when *letting loose the dogs of war.*

rucksack *n.* A badly adjusted underpant or thong, hitched up a lady's back. With a tin mug and a frying pan hanging off it.

RUD *1. abbrev.* Rapid Unscheduled Disassembly; term used by billionaire alien-botherer Elon Musk to describe when another one of his SpaceX rockets explodes mid-launch, and similarly *2. abbrev.* The speedy collapse of all human evo-lutionary advances in a chap who has had a *bad pint. 'I'm sorry, Mrs Bosanquet. Your husband just experienced catastrophic RUD whilst reading the News at Ten.'*

rude awakening *n.* To rouse one's partner from her slumbers with an unexpectedly hearty *sausage breakfast.*

rude lodgings *n.* Somewhere to *drop the shopping* while on a road trip. *'Joseph, we must stop and seek rude lodgings, for I am heavy with mudchild and need shelter for thirty minutes or so. And have you got anything I can wipe my arse on?'*

rudimentary *n.* A late night TV *wanking* opportunity, thinly disguised as a factual programme, *eg.* A behind-the-scenes looks at the worlds of lap-dancing, the US hardcore porn industry or *tits* and *fannies.* Also *masturmentary, sockumentary. 'Are you coming up to bed?' 'In a minute, dear. I'm just watching a rudimentary. Do you know where there's any tissues?'*

Rudolf Nureyev *euph.* Used to describe the light-headed feeling of relief which one experiences after giving birth to a gigantic *arse baby* following a prolonged confinement, *viz.* "Light on one's feet and loose in the arse".

ruffle my lettuce *euph.* What a polite Canadian woman says when she is going to take a *Chinese singing lesson. 'If you would excuse me for a moment, gentlemen, I'm just going to ruffle my lettuce. In fact, fuck it. while I'm on the shitter I may as well snip off a length of dirty spine too.'*

rugby club shower plug hole, arse like a *sim.* The presence of a wad of unsightly, matted hair around a woman's *back body.*

rug doctor *1. n.* A trademarked brand of carpet cleaner. *2. n. medic.* A gynaecologist. Also *box doc, doctopussy, cunt dentist, dirty dentist, fanny mechanic, mingineer, snatch quack, bush doctor, minge miner etc.*

rugdoctor *1. n.* A large carpet-washing vacuum

that can be hired after elderly relatives have been staying. *2. n. medic.* A consultant gynaecologist. Also *doctopussy, box doc, fanny mechanic, mingineer* or *cunt dentist. 3. n.* A beautician specialising in feminine waxing of the *thighbrows.*

rug hugger *n.* Male version of a *fag hag.* A straight man who seeks out the company of women who are *on the bus to Hebden Bridge.*

rug munchers *n. Fanny noshers.*

rug of honour *n.* A carpet of indecent images strewn upon the bedroom floor of a hormonally advanced adolescent who is engaging in an act of *popular science. Also Jodrell banquet, pornorama, wank crescent, glandscape, wanquet, snatchwork quilt.*

ruined *adj.* A very attractive woman whose sex appeal has nonetheless been almost entirely nullified by her association with an unsuitable gentleman. *'Christ, that Billie Piper's a bit of alright.' 'Yeah, but that ginger twat Chris Evans has been there. That's ruined her for me.'*

rule of cock, the *n.* The gauge by which an overweight male notices he's slimming by looking down while standing to see if he can spot his *wedding vegetables. 'Hi Jeremy, how's the diet going? What do the scales say?' 'Don't use them, mate. The rule of cock is more accurate.'*

rule of six *1. n.* Some badly framed national Covid regulation restricting daily life that apparently didn't apply to the people who thought it up. *2. n.* A principle that regulated a fellow's lockdown routine, requiring him to *relax in a gentleman's way* half a dozen times every day.

rumble in the jungle, the *1. n.* Historic boxing match between George Foreman and Muhammad Ali, staged in Zaire in 1974. *2. n.* A deeply guttural *trouser cough* resonating through a disastrously overgrown *arse cleft.*

rumble strips *1. n.* A "cool" indie pop beat combo from Tavistock in Devon. *2. n.* The raised sections of bumps at the edges of the carriageway which are supposed to draw long distance lorry drivers' attention to the fact that they have fallen asleep at the wheel. *3. n.* The convoluted ripples of adipose tissue on girls with *big bones* who are crammed into cheap, one-size-fits-all leggings, and are often to be seen congregating around Great Yarmouth market's famous chip stalls.

rummage *n.* A jumble sale-style act of *self-delight* indulged in by a dirty lady.

rummage in the captain's pocket *v.* How one might end up getting *fish fingers.*

rump gully *n.* Viewed from *biffin bridge,* the gradually sloping valley beyond *kak canyon.*

rumpire *n.* A shrewd adjudicator of feminine beauty, for example the short, fat, bald proprietor of a central Newcastle office equipment shop standing on the pavement to have a fag, dispassionately judging the desirability or otherwise of passing women's *arses.*

Rumpleforeskin *n.* Penis, *John Thomas, junior.*

rumpo *n. Rumpy pumpy.*

Rumpole suntan *n.* An alcoholic red face as modelled by the late *Rumpole of the Bailey* actor Leo McKern.

rump ranger *n.* A *brokeback mountaineer.* One who takes a lively interest in *rusty sheriff's badges.*

rumpy pumpy *n.* Lightweight sexual shenanigans, slightly more erotic than *how's your father.*

rumpy thumpy *n.* Sado-masochistic *nookie.*

runners and riders *euph.* A slightly more to-the-point, binary version of *snog, marry, avoid. Fuck or chuck.*

runner's special *n.* A post-exercise *crap-up feast* of *bangers and mash* served with extra gravy in a special porcelain pot.

running a bit rich *1. phr.* Said of an engine running such that the stoichiometric ratio favours fuel over air, leaving deposits on the plugs. *2. phr.* Said of an over-rich *Lionel Bart* which leaves soot on the gusset.

running behind *euph.* Polite excuse which can be given when one is unable to stop and chat with a friend or colleague as a result of an overdue appointment to *drop a load of semi-viscid kids off at the pool. 'Film actor, director, grand old man of the British stage… Tonight, Sir John Geilgud, this is your life.' 'Sorry Eamonn, can't stop. I'm running late.'*

running in flip-flops *1. euph.* Description of the noise made by fleshy body parts walloping together during s*xual intercourse. *2. n.* Sound heard when sprinting to the finish of a *horizontal jog;* the *booty clap.*

running kick at a pork pie *euph.* A particularly unattractive *quim. 'Fuck me, this blurter looks like soemone's taken a running kick at a pork pie. Join us after the commercial break for more Embarrassing Bodies.'*

running on empty *euph.* Describing a lady who has not been in receipt of her fair share of *sausage* for some time. *'Your nan's been running on empty ever since Grandad copped it in the knackers at Monte Cassino.'*

running on red diesel *euph.* Said of a *bird* who has *got the painters in.* A reference to the low-duty agricultural fuel that is dyed to prevent it being used in road-going vehicles. *"Ere Rob, your missus has just tore me off a strip. Is she alright?' 'Sorry Jon. She's running on red diesel this week, so she's a bit temperamental.'*

running out the guns *n.* Sticking your *chuff* outside of the duvet in order to *drop your guts*, thus avoiding a *Dutch oven*, in the manner of the cannons being deployed on a warship from out of them little hatches.

run Shadowfax, show us the meaning of haste! *1. exclam.* In *The Lord of the Rings* (probably, we're certainly not looking it up) Gandalf the Wizard's encouragement to his horse when leaving for Minas Tirith. *2. exclam.* Shouted when attempting to *lay a cable* whilst your significant other is *braying* the bathroom door down as they have a case of the *Tom tits.*

runs, the *1. n.* What English cricketers get when they face fast bowlers. *2. n.* What English cricketers don't get when they face fast bowlers.

run the taps *v.* To take a *leak* following a spot of *bumfoolery.* From the practice of letting the taps run in a house with rusty pipes, in order to let out any unpleasant brown residue which may be present in the water.

runt of the litter *euph.* A sickly, unimpressive *poo* passed as an afterthought at the end of a proper *sit-down confinement.* Also *runt of the shitter.*

runtstable *n.* The kind of *short-arsed* police officer we have these days due to the old height restrictions being waived.

runway, taxiing down the *n.* The sensation experienced as you cross the last six feet towards the *crapper,* as your long-delayed stinky *passenger* slips into the *departure lounge* and makes a *break for the border.*

rush hour *n.* The race, first thing in the morning, to secure the last clean office toilet cubicle before heavy use causes damage that will not be rectified until the cleaner starts their next shift.

rushin' roulette *n.* A suicidally dangerous game whereby a gentleman attempts to *fire the one o'clock gun* when there is a fairly good chance that his wife may walk in on him.

Rusholme roulette *n.* *Farting* in the full knowledge that there is a one in six chance of *shitting* one's *kex.* Named after Rusholme, the district of Manchester famed for its curry houses.

rusketeers *n.* A group of self-proclaimed hard men who look like they've come straight from nursery school.

Ruskin's recoil *euph.* To be horrified at the sight of *Terry Waite's allotment.* A reference to the romantic poet, who was famously put off his

stroke on his wedding night by the sight of his missus's *gorilla salad.*

Russell Brand gig, as tense as a *sim.* Descriptive of an uneasy and unpleasantly fraught atmosphere. *'As the UN-imposed ceasefire deadline approached last night, the Gaza Strip remained as tense as a Russell Brand gig.'*

russet gusset *n.* *Skidmarks* or *dangleberrian* deposits on the *shreddies.* *Marmite stripe,* the *starting grid at Brands Hatch.*

Russian hamburger *n.* Popping one's *meat* between a bolshy *bird's top buns.* And adding a few squirts of *special sauce.* Up under her chin.

Russian poolette *1. n.* Firing off a *trouser burp* knowing full well that there is a significant risk of *gambling and losing.* Also *Rusholme roulette, brown roulette, twisting on nineteen.* *2. n.* Game of chance played when faced with a row of public lavatory cubicles; Trying to avoid choosing the one with a *full chamber.* *3. n.* A risky nocturnal shortcut along a darkened, *dogshit*-ridden path or alley.

Russian suicide *n.* A death caused by any number of bullet wounds greater than one.

Russian wedding ring *n.* Three different shades of gold. Found on close inspection of the missus's *tea towel holder* after she's had a good *curry-night crap.*

Russian yawn *n.* A *thirty-four-and-a-halfer, cannonball, jollyrancher.* A self-service *suck-off.* *'Call the ambulance mother. I just tried a Russian yawn and I can't feel my legs any more.'*

rusticles *n.* The orange *man spuds* of ageing, leathery, over-tanned gentlemen. The *pods* that might well be found in the cheap-as-chips *undercrackers* of David Dickinson, were one to sneak a crafty peek when he was otherwise engaged at an auction.

rusting copper pipe *n.* A *night watchman.* One of them stubborn *arse sausages* that sit in the *pan,* refusing to be flushed away, and giving off a Ready Brek-style brown aurora into the water.

rustler *n.* In a public lavatory environment, an occupant of a neighbouring *thunderbox* who seems to be making irregular and disconcerting noises which suggest they may be opening a bag of crisps.

Rustler's relish *n.* The kind of *man mayonnaise* typically guzzled down by the type of chap who *knows what's in his flowerbeds.* Named after the slightly less appetising condiment provided in a squeezable sachet for consumers of the eponymous microwavable burger.

rusty Brillo pad *n.* The pubular portions of a natural redhead. See also *brandy snap, fubes,* *fire down below,* grated carrot, *Noddy Holder's sideburns,* orangina, *orang utan salad* and *Robin Cook's beard. 'Blimey, Rula. It's like a rusty Brillo pad down here.'*

rusty door bolt *n.* A compacted *shit* that is extremely difficult to force out of the *nipsy.* *'What's up, Whitney?' 'Come in here and see if you can't get this rusty door bolt out my ass, Bobby.'*

Rusty Firmin *n.* A *rear entry specialist* of whatever stripe, named in honour of the erstwhile SAS legend and Blue Team commander who done in the Iranian embassy's back doors with no gloves on.

rusty fish hook *n.* An *erectivitation* that is covered in faecal matter.

rusty hoop *1. n.* Bow-legged cowboy actor of the 1940s. *2. n.* An inefficiently polished *ringpiece.* *Robert Smith's mouth.*

rusty knickers *n.* The aftermath of a *Turkish breakfast.*

rusty link *n.* That brown, *shitted* inch on a *salad dodger's* thong.

rusty nail *1. n.* A cocktail of Drambuie and Scotch. *2. n.* The inevitable result of inserting a digit into someone's *fifties tea towel holder,* for whatever reason. *'Paul, you just relax while Chris gives you the rusty nail. Coming up after the break, we're going to be talking to a man who's scared of sand and Gino's going to whip up a delicious Tiramisu.*

See you in a minute.'

rusty Norton *n.* The type of saucy care home resident that is only too delighted to pose for one of those mucky "mature" *grumble* mags. A filthy old *bike.*

rusty panda *n.* Like a *dirty Sanchez,* but using a two-handed rotary motion around the eyes.

rusty scone cutter *n.* A very unhygienic dough-shaping implement. The *arsehole.*

rusty sheriff's badge *n.* Ride south along *biffin bridge* from *John Wayne's hairy saddlebags* and there it lies, right in the middle of *kak canyon.* Just before you reach *rump gully*; the *anus.*

rusty trawler *n.* Similar to a *motorboat,* but performed with the face buried between a pair of *arse cheeks* instead of a lady's *chest plums.*

rusty trumpet, play the *v.* To perform *horatio* very shortly after having your *drains rodded. To pipe a rear admiral aboard.*

rusty water *n.* Liquid *feeshus* which is *pissed* out of the *arse.*

rusty zip *n.* An improperly wiped buttock cleft, where the *shite* has been spread about and then left to dry out. *Robert Smith's mouth.*

rut *1. v.* To *tup.* In the style of a deer or billy goat. *2. n.* Any single member from the pop band the Ruts, *eg.* John "Segs" Jennings or Gary Barnacle.

Ryan's palsy *n. medic.* The partial paralysis suffered following a flight on a budget airline.

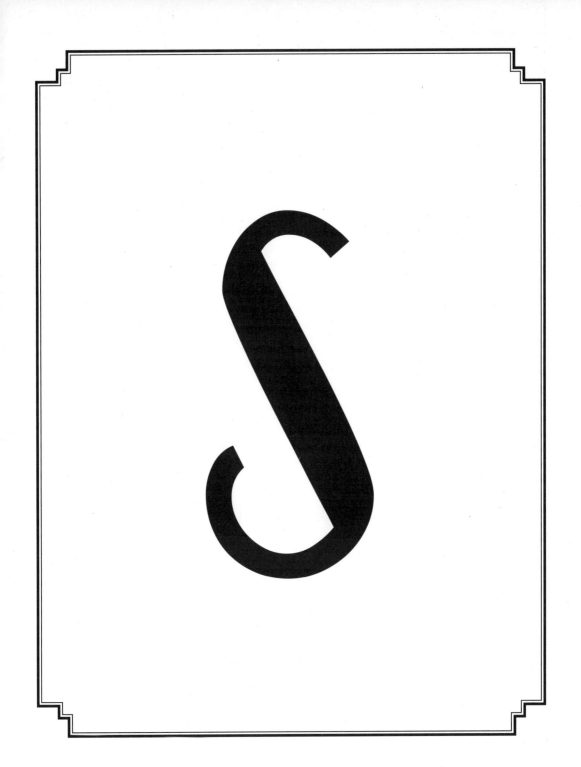

sachet of splendor *n.* A small limp bag which contains foul seed, carried between a bloke's legs and generally emptied by hand.

sack artist *n.* A womaniser, gigolo, *fanny rat, fanny hopper, crumpeteer.*

sack climber *n.* A bubble of *carbon dibaxide* that ascends the south face of the *tintis* from the depths of the bath.

sack dust *n.* Sand-fine scrotum particles collected in a pair of bachelor's *yellow-fronted brownbacks* that have done sterling service over a number of days.

sack nav *n.* While *rat-arsed*, relying on the inbuilt *fanny*-homing instincts of one's overladen *lower brain* in order to negotiate one's way around a dancefloor in search of *mackerel.*

sack race *n.* A *milk race.*

sack slap *n.* Of a gentleman who is *having it off* with a lady *con gusto,* the rhythmic percussive collision of his *clackerbag* against her *biffing plate.*

sacofricosis *n. medic.* A mental condition, the main symptom of which is the desire to cut a hole in one's pocket to facilitate *self-pollution* in public places. *'We've got your test results back, Mr Ross OBE, and it's bad news. You've got advanced sacofricosis.' 'Oh, cwumbs!'*

saddlebags *1. n.* Labia, *piss flaps*. *2. n.* Scrotum. *3. n.* Leathery receptacles wherein a cyclist's testicles are stored.

Saddleworth rabbit, hotter than a *sim. Hotter than a junkie's spoon. 'I tell you what, your holiness. That Rachel Riley on Countdown is hotter than a Saddleworth rabbit.'*

sad Max *n.* Owner of a £200 Honda Civic who has spent eighteen grand on accessories at Halfords so he can drive it round and round Lidl's car park at four in the morning, trying not to knock the exhaust pipe off on the speed bumps.

sadmin *n.* The dispiriting process of constantly checking all your social media accounts in the forlorn hope that someone – anyone – has interacted with you.

safe cracking *n.* The skilled task of simultaneously arousing a pair of nipples, possibly while wearing a stripy jersey. *Finding Radio Luxembourg, come in Tokyo, drawing a curve on an Etch-a-Sketch.*

safety catch *n.* Penile flaccidity employed by nature to offset the effects of industrial strength *beer goggles,* thus saving a *soused* gent from engaging in sexual intercourse while his judgement is impaired.

safety dance *1. n.* Song by Men Without Hats that reached number 6 in the UK hit parade back in 1983. *2. n.* The rhythmical *buttocky* shuffle performed while trying to find a position on the toilet seat that guarantees a smooth, efficient, smear-free and non-hazardous passage of one's *digestive transit.*

safety piss *n.* Sitting down for a *wee* whilst *heavily refreshed* in the early hours of the morning. See also *peemale, driving from the ladies' tee.*

safety wank *n.* A pressure-relieving act of *sexual outercourse* performed out of necessity rather than desire, and intended as a precaution against its lust-crazed perpetrator later going on some sort of politically incorrect spree or rampage. *'And now its time to see all our lovely contestants once again, this time wearing their bathing suits. Here they are now, parading onto the stage in their skimpy bikinis. What a mouth-watering parade of beauty from around the world, I'm sure you'll agree. I'll tell you what, ladies, it's a fucking good job I had that safety wank during the commercial break.'*

SAFOOMA/safooma *acronym.* Coded anilingual request when in polite company, or for use on an envelope when sending a love letter. Suck A Fart Out Of My Arse.

saga lager *1. n.* Sherry or mild, depending on gender. *2. n.* Geriatric *piss. 'I'd visit my granny more often if it wasn't for the smell of saga lager.'*

saga louts *n.* Packs of tea-fuelled pensioners travelling by coach who lay waste to garden centres, Edinburgh Woollen Mills and stately home gift shops.

Saharan shuffle *1. n.* A humorous sand dance of the sort performed by Wilson, Kepple and Betty. Eh kids? *2. n.* A dry and painful act of *self harm* of the sort performed by Wilson and Kepple.

sailor's ale *n.* The thick, salty, tangy beverage drunk by *sea bent* mariners while on long voyages. *'Adrift upon a glassy sea / No wind upon our sail / We pulled the boatswain's trousers off / And drank his sailor's ale'* (from *The Rime of the Ancient Mariner* by Samuel Taylor Coleridge).

sailor's handshake *n.* When two salty old dogs hoist each other's *jolly todgers*.

sailor's shot sock, fuller than a *sim.* Descriptive of when something is filled to bursting, *eg.* A post-Christmas binliner, the 4.24pm Newcastle to Prudhoe train, Tom Jones's skin, Cliff Richard's *saddlebags.*

sail through customs *v.* To enjoy a clean wipe despite having had *plenty to declare.* Also *draw an ace.*

Saint Wristopher *n. prop.* The patron saint of *self abusers.* He who watches over men in these uncertain times to bless them with an undisturbed bout of *autoerotic delight*.

salad bar at Butlins, quieter than the *sim.* Descriptive of a very, very quiet place indeed.

salad bowl at a barbecue, cunt like the *sim.* Something rather unappealing that, let's face it, is pretty much destined to remain uneaten.

salad cream *n.* The *man mayonnaise* of a vegan or vegetarian.

salad days *n.* Descriptive of the *lettuce-licking* past times of a woman who is now *back on solids* and chomping sausages like a good 'un.

salad dodger *n.* A contumelious epithet for a *fat bastard*. One who, at a buffet, sidesteps the lettuce and celery and heads straight for the pork pies. *'"Contrarywise," continued Tweedledee, "if it was so, it might be; and if it were so, it would be; but as it isn't, it ain't. That's logic." "That's not logic, that's bollocks, you salad dodger," said Alice.'* (from *Through The Looking Glass* by Lewis Carroll).

salad, Scottish *n.* The only vegetables that are ever spotted on a plate north of Carlisle, that is to say chips and beans.

salad tosser *n.* An annoying vegetarian.

salami slapper *n.* He who tolls upon his own *bell*. A *wanker*.

Salem slot *n.* An *egg hole* that is as frightening as a reasonably frightening 1970s TV mini-series starring David Soul.

Salford man o'war *n.* A gelatinous *Coney Island whitefish* found bobbing along the Manchester Ship Canal.

Salford snail *n.* Common species of mollusc (*Helix aspersalford*) that leaves a distinctive trail of thin horizontal lines scratched into the doors of 4x4s in inner city areas. Evidence of *Salford snail* activity is often found in the vicinity of groups of hooded youths.

saliva birds *n.* Lipstick lesbians *at it like knives*.

Sally Gunnell *n. prop.* A motor trade term to describe a used car, *ie.* "It's not much to look at but it's a fucking good runner".

Sally James, a *euph.* In the world of *grumble*, a comprehensive faceful of *spooge*. From the line that the eponymous *Tiswas* presenter (and member of the Four Bucketeers) sang in the *Bucket of Water Song*, viz. "But whatever the case, we take it in the face". Although she was presumably referring to a bucket of water, not the contents of some bloke's *nuts*.

Sally Morgan *1. n. prop.* A successful psychic who is genuinely in touch both with the spirits of those who have passed on and also with a team of expensive libel lawyers. *2. euph.* A person who wears clothes that are clearly far too small for

them, *ie.* One who "thinks they are a medium." *3. n. rhym. slang.* The male generative member or *Major Morgan*.

salmon *1. rhym. slang.* Sexual excitement. From salmon on prawn = the horn. *'I saw Pam Anderson's video on the internet last night. It didn't half give me the salmon, I can tell you.'* *2. rhym. slang. HMP.* Tobacco. From salmon and trout = snout. *"Ere, you don't half give me the salmon, Lord Archer. Fancy giving me a blow job for an ounce of salmon?'*

salmon canyon *n.* Piscatorial pass leading to *tuna town*.

salmon dust *n.* A light sprinkling of fishy residue that falls from a courting swain's hands when he rubs them together.

salmon fishing in the Yemen *1. n.* Title of a 2011 inspirational romantic drama starring Ewan McGregor. No, us neither. *2. n.* Yet another euphemism for *dining at the Y*.

salmon handcuffs *n. Pink handcuffs*. Invisible restraints that keep a gentleman from seeing any of his friends. The metaphorical restraints with which a *pussy-whipped* gentlemen is shackled. *'"This is quite rum do, Jeeves," I exclaimed. "I've met Piggy for cocktails every Friday for ten years. Where the pip can he be?" "If I may be so bold," intoned Jeeves in that way of his, "he has recently taken up with a soubrette from a London show, and I fear he has slapped the salmon handcuffs on the poor cunt."'* (from *What the Fuck, Jeeves?* by PG Wodehouse).

salmon's head *n.* A hatless *one-eyed zipper fish* as viewed from underneath.

salmon Wellington *1. n.* An oven-baked dish comprising of a generous fish fillet in white sauce, wrapped in puff pastry. *2. n.* A generously-proportioned *haddock pastie*.

saloon doors *n.* A pair of well-used, swinging *fanny flaps* that one's *cock* swaggers into, only to be thrown out three minutes later after a bit of frantic banging. Wild West-style *beef curtains*.

Salopian tube *n.* A *prick* from Shrewsbury or Ludlow or any other town in Shropshire.

salsa dip *n.* A splash about in the *crimson waves*.

salt *n.* 1960s Sexist mod term for a *bird*.

salt and pepper *n.* Horrible little *tits* where the nipple area is larger and more protruding than the rest of the breast, giving them the appearance of the silver-capped condiment shakers found in cafes.

salted caramel *1. n.* Ice cream flavour that nobody had heard of five years ago but is now fucking everywhere. *2. n. Shum, toffee yoghurt.*

salted slug, cock like a *sim.* A case of *shrinkage* so extreme that the afflicted *membrum virile* shrivels to near-invisibility.

salt'n'shake *n.* A crisp *one off the wrist* enjoyed in the salubrious surroundings of a public toilet.

salty towers *n.* The abode of an accomplished *onanist.*

Salvation Army are tuning up, the *exclam.* Another one of those humorous idiomatic apophthegms that can be usefully employed following a loudly *dropped gut.*

Samantha *n. rhym. slang.* An anus. From Samantha Jingpiece.

Samantha foxhole *n. arch.* A bucolic repository for relaxation-themed literature.

same day delivery *n.* Food which passes right through you on the day of consumption. *'Come and enjoy a meal at the Rupali Restaurant, Bigg Market, Newcastle upon Tyne. We offer same day delivery on all our meals.'*

Sam Plank *n. prop. rhym. slang. Stoke-on-Trent.* An act of *self abuse* named after the popular late Radio Stoke disc jockey. *'Did you manage to pull last night?' 'No. I went home for a Pot Noodle and a Sam Plank.'*

sample pants *n.* Underwear towards the end of a good night out when CSI-style forensic traces of semen, faeces, urine, and blood can all be identified in the gusset. *Neapolitan knickers.*

Sam Spoon's rhythm pole *n.* A male *Piers Morgan*, generously equipped with *Alberts, cock rings*, bolts, chains and what-have-you, such that the ensemble provides a musical accompaniment during intercourse or *rub-and-tuggage.* From the apparent aural similarity to the sound made by the be-belled "rhythm pole" played by erstwhile Bonzo Dog Doo-dah Band percussionist Sam Spoons. See also *the full Roger McGuinn. 'Ooh, Evan. I didn't realise you had a Sam Spoon's rhythm pole.'*

Samurai *n.* A fearsome, ceremonial *pork sword.*

sand hole *n.* Of crowded beaches, the hole caused by sunbathing on your stomach in order to conceal a *Jake.*

sandies *n. rhym. slang.* Pubic lice *(Phthirus pubis).* Named after the famous 1930s Scottish international midfielder Sandy McNabs = crabs.

sandjob *n.* A painfully abrasive *wristy* received at a beach, in a golf bunker or in the back of a builder's lorry.

S and M *n. Rub-a-tug shop* parlance for sado-masochism. *Mr Whippy, fladge and padge.*

Sandras *n.* The male testicles. Named after *Gravity*

actress Sandra Bollock.

sandrex *n.* Extremely low quality *shit tickets.* *'Can you thrown another roll of sandrex up onto the landing, dear, only my arse seems to have momentarily stopped bleeding.'*

sandwich, like a tramp on a *sim.* Enthusiastic – if not very hygienic – *noshing. 'Granted she's not much to look at, but get your Charlie out and she's like a tramp on a sandwich, your Honour. And I would hope that the court would take this mitigating factor into account when deciding upon its sentence. The defence rests its case.'*

sandworm *1. n.* In Frank Herbert's *Dune* trilogy, a desert-dwelling sci-fi creature that chased spice miners about on the planet Arrakis, or some such tosh. *2. n.* An unlubricated *membrum virile.*

Sandy Lyles *n. rhym. slang.* Haemorrhoids.

Sangatte, do a *v.* Of married men, to make a *bid for the tunnel* in the middle of the night, almost certainly only to get turned back by the wife.

sanitised *adj.* Descriptive of the trouble-free, rose-tinted view of the world induced by quaffing vast quantities of Spanish lager.

sansquit *n.* An obscure and ancient written language that appears in the underpants of a *heavy smoker.* See also *wind sketch, air tattoo, skidoo, gusset moth, phartoshop* and *knickertine stains.*

Santa's beard *n.* A festively voluminous example of *jelly jewellery* festooning a person's lower jaw. A *chin omelette.*

Santa's sack on Boxing Day, like *sim.* Something that is exceedingly empty. *'Look, Mr Davro, we're going to have to cancel half the dates on your tour. The theatres are going to be like Santa's sack on Boxing Day.'*

Santa stuck up the chimney *exclam.* A reference to *blobstopper* removal problems, often as a consequence of drunken intercourse.

Santorum *n.* Amongst people who are *nicely poised*, the frothy mix of lubricant and faecal matter that is sometimes the by product of their saucy carryings-on. Amusingly named after the anti-gay former US senator Rick Santorum. *Sexcrement, shum, toffee yoghurt.*

Sarah Jessica Porker *n.* She who wears all the right clothes from all the right labels, but not necessarily in the right sizes.

sargasm *n.* An insultingly unconvincing fake orgasm.

sarlacc pit *n.* A particularly angry-looking, frightening, voracious yet dry *minge.* Named after that big pink thing with all them teeth which was in that hole in the ground out of off of *Return of* *the Jedi* (1983).

sarson's nose *adj.* The condition of the *old fella,* post *vinegar strokes,* after leaving a *salty dressing* on the *pink lettuce salad.*

SAS *1. abbrev.* What your mate's dad was in: the Special Air Service. *'Don't mess with him, mate. He's SAS.'* 2. *abbrev.* Soft As Shit. *'Go ahead and fill your boots, nan. He's SAS.'*

Satan's banquet *n.* An unlikely sounding variation on the *devil's kiss,* whereby a saucy lady delivers a still-warm baguette from her *dirt bakery* into the waiting mouth of a *poovert* friend underneath, by way of a kinky treat.

Satan's chuckles *n.* The series of sulphurous *botty burps* that often presage *the Blue Peter tortoise coming out of hibernation.* Also *turtle's gurgles, string of pearls.*

Satan's claw *n.* The crabbed hand position adopted by a man in order to perform simultaneous digital stimulation of both the *freckle* and *kitten purse* on his ladyfriend.

Satan's piano, noises like *sim.* Descriptive of a prolonged eighty-eight note chromatic scale played on his *nipsy* by an unaccompanied virtuoso ensconced in the *sweet wrapper.* *'Bloody hell, Simon. I've just walked past the Rick Witter that Amanda's in and her arse is making noises like Satan's piano."*

Satan's salute *n.* Diabolical way your *piss stream* waves around if you *fart* while stood at the urinal.

Satan's smelling salts *n.* A *dropped hat* of such a noisome character that He Who Walks Backwards himself would feel moved to waggle his nostrils in disgust.

sat chav *n.* When you are lost in a strange town, a surly feral youth from whom you are forced to ask directions, in the full and certain knowledge that he will send you in entirely the wrong direction and then have a good laugh about it with all his *scratter* mates as soon as you have driven away.

Satchmo *n.* The technique of skillfully cupping your hand over the bell of your *muck trumpet* in order to elicit a more muted, jazz-infused timbre while *sounding the charge.* Named after Louis "Satchmo" Armstrong (1901-1971), whose charismatic, improvised approach to tonality and phrasing revolutionised the world of *farting.*

satiscraptory *adj.* Decriptive of something of a poor, but adequate standard, *eg.* BBC local radio, the Edge's guitar playing, McDonald's food.

sat-nag *n.* Expensive unit that barks orders at you on car trips, whether required or not.

sat-nav *1. n.* An in-car electronic device which allows reps to find their way to cheap hotels and massage parlours while avoiding areas of traffic congestion. *2. n.* An in-head device which allows *bladdered* gentlemen to find their way home on a Saturday night while they are unconscious with the drink.

sat'n'aving *phr.* Amusing way of declaring one's toilet activity to a curious interlocutor. *'Hey Tom! Tom! What you doing in there?' 'Not much dear, just sat'n'aving a dump.'*

Saturday night beaver *n.* Dancefloor fauna and, you would imagine, the title of a *grumble film* or two.

Saturday night diva *n.* Woman, dressed to the nines in the latest fashions and *ripped to the tits* on 2-for-1 cocktails, who steps up to the karaoke mic to take on a Whitney classic, and clears a packed pub in thirty seconds flat.

Saturday night fever *n. medic.* A *happy rash* contracted following an inebriated weekend quickie behind Atmospheres in Birkenhead. The *clap, a dose, cockrot.*

sauce *1. n.* Booze, usually when taken in large quantities. *'That Keith Floyd didn't half hit the sauce, you know.'* 2. *v.* To seduce. *3. n.* Cheek. *'He asked to borrow me motor, and then said could I bring it round and make sure the tank was full. What a fucking sauce!'*

saucepan tit *n.* A breast with an outline sadly reminiscent of a saucepan hanging by its handle. A *sock-full-o-beans.*

sauce, tramp *n.* The rancid, sticky substance painted over the tongue and on the corners of the mouth by elves while one is asleep following a night *on the piss.*

saucy *1. adj.* Of British seaside postcards; featuring busty young ladies, fat old ladies, hen-pecked husbands, frigid spinsters, honeymooning couples, nudist camp barbecues, people sticking their *cocks* through fences and getting them bitten by a goose *etc. 2. exclam.* The late Barbara Windsor's inevitable response to a sexual overture, whether intended or accidental.

Saul Hudson, I'm just going for a *exclam.* A means of explaining that you are going to take a *Chinese singing lesson.* From the real name of the straggly barnetted, top-titfered Guns'n'Roses plank spanker Slash.

sausage and doughnut situation *n.* Heterosexual intercourse. *'I did NOT engage in a sausage and doughnut situation with that woman. Miss Lewinsky. She merely sucked me off a bit and stuck my cigar up her cludge. Then I dropped my yop on her frock.'* (President Bill Clinton giving evidence to Special Prosecutor Kenneth Starr).

sausage casserole *n.* The insertion of more than one porky *banger* into a lady's *hotpot* for a warming winter treat. A *top hat.*

sausage cosy *n.* A snuggly nest of male *pubage* which keeps the *wife's supper* warm.

sausage derby *n.* A duel fought with a pair of *pork swords.*

sausage dock *n.* The *Bristol channel*, where which one may pop one's *porky iprod* to recharge.

sausage dodger *n.* A bird who is *off solids* and *on the bus to Hebden Bridge.*

sausage dog *n.* A woman who combines a *lovely personality* with a penchant for pork cylinders with all hot fat coming out of them.

sausage fat *n. Jitler.*

sausage grappler *n.* A *salami slapper.*

sausage jockey *n.* Any small Irish man who sits on a chipolata and then bounces up and down. A *sausage rider.*

sausage kennel *n.* The *rear quarters* of a *good listener.*

sausage maker *n.* The *arsehole.*

sausage pizza *n.* The closest thing to a *sausage sandwich* that *Miss Lincolnshire* is able to provide. A *diddy ride* on a lady with *stits, gilgai.*

sausage pocket *n.* A polite term for a lady's *parts of shame. 'Right then madam, if you'd just like to get on the table and pop your feet in the stirrups, we'll take a butcher's at your sausage pocket.'*

sausage pot *n.* A lady's privates.

sausage roll *1. n.* Prole-ish foodstuff. *2. n.* Sexual intercourse. *Jelly roll.*

sausage sandwich *n.* A juicy *salami frotted* between two pink *baps*, the end result of which is a *pearl necklace. Dutch.*

sausage sisters *n.* Female equivalent of *custard cousins.* Two or more ladies who have shared the same *banger, eg.* Lady Di, Camilla Parker-Bowels and the Th(name of female vocal group removed on legal advice)es.

sausages under the grill, have *v.* To be in imminent need of the lavatory for a sit down visit. To be *turtling* or *touching cloth. 'Mr Burrell regrets that he will not be able to accede to your request that he re-attend the hearing, your honour, as he informs me that he has sausages under the grill.'*

sausage supper *n.* Female equivalent of a *fish supper.* A *nosh* on a *giggling pin* sticking out of a pile of mashed potato.

sausage surprise *1. n.* A dubious dish cooked by Jean off *EastEnders. 2. exclam.* A humorous announcement uttered by bloke a while thrusting his erect penis against his wife's back first thing in the morning to get her in the mood. Or make her

get up and put the kettle on while he has a *wank.*

sausage wallet *n.* A wallet for putting sausages in. A *quimpiece.*

savanna *n.* A hot, grassy territory found *down south* on a female.

save some room for later Augustus *exclam.* A light-hearted and subtle means of suggesting to a *double sucker* that they might consider moderating their intake of comestibles, best delivered in a cod-German accent.

save the children *1. n.* A very worthy charity. *2. n.* A not particularly worthy abortive *wank.*

savilating *n.* Involuntary production of bodily fluids at inappropriate times. We'll put it no more strongly than that.

Savile Row *1. n.* Street in London famous for its bespoke male tailoring. *2. n.* A police line-up of *kiddie fiddlers*, named in honour of erstwhile *kiddie fiddler* Sir Jimmy OBE. *3. n.* A line of beds in a children's hospital ward or Intensive Care Unit, named in honour of erstwhile *philanthrapist* Sir Jimmy OBE. *4. n.* The *nonces* wing in one of His Majesty's Prisons, named in honour of erstwhile *nonce* Sir Jimmy OBE. *5. n.* Any queue of weirdos and middle-aged *sexcases* such as might be found at the end of a railway platform, named in honour of erstwhile weirdo and *sexcase* Sir Jimmy OBE. *6. n.* The Sex Offenders Register, named in honour of erstwhile sex offender Sir Jimmy OBE. *7. n.* The queue of "uncles" who congregate outside school gates despite the fact that they are not necessarily related to any specific member of the student body.

Savile servant *n.* A overly keen amateur youth worker or scoutmaster.

Savile-skip *n.* A bizarre "time-jump" phenomenon experienced when binge-watching re-runs of *Top of the Pops* on BBC4, whereby certain episodes have been omitted for reasons of taste, leading to sudden drastic changes in the charts from episode to episode. Also *Glitter gap.*

Savile's travels *n.* Wandering hands.

saving your ammo *n.* The act of withholding your *guffs* in order to release them later with somewhat more dramatic éclat, *eg.* During a job interview, court appearance, mother-in-law's funeral, while resigning as Prime Minister, doing the *Shipping Forecast etc.*

say again Broadsword you're breaking up *exclam.* Said in the style of Admiral Rolland out of *Where Eagles Dare*, in response to a particularly loud *bomber aris.*

say hello to my little friend *1. exclam.* A bedroom ice-breaker, delivered with distinctive Pacino accent. *2. exclam.* A witty announcement before a flatulatory release, delivered in the style of AR-15-assault-rifle-toting Tony Montana in *Scarface*.

SBD *abbrev.* Of *farts* and *farting*, Silent But Deadly. A subtly noiseless release of fatally noisome *botty gas*.

SBJ *abbrev. medic.* Doctor's notes terminology for a senior citizen or *coffin dodger, low flying angel, estate agent's dream.* Still Breathing, Just.

SBV *abbrev.* Of *farts* and *farting*, Silent But Violent. A *minging eruption* from the *cleftal horizon*.

scabbatical *n.* A self-imposed temporary break from *carnival* shenanigans taken while waiting for the *happy rash* pustules on your *bellend* to heal up.

scabby chic *n.* Fashionable interior design "look" achieved by letting your pets and feral children *crap* everywhere while the house falls down round your fucking ears.

scads *n.* Kicksies, dunghampers, thunderbags.

scaffolder's laptop *n.* A fruit machine. Also *Glasgow piano, Scouser's cashpoint.*

scalloped barrel *1. n.* A type of dart that has an indentation in it to aid the grip while throwing *2. n.* A type of dick that has an indentation in it due to excessive *web-browsing*.

scally's comet *n.* The fiery parabola described by a petrol bomb, thrown through the air by a member of the lower orders expressing dissatisfaction with his lot.

scallywagon *n.* A boxy white van with blacked-out square windows, the preferred mode of transport for guests of His Majesty. Also *Merthyr minibus*.

scamborghini *n.* A *doles Royce* parked up outside Wetherspoons.

scambulance *n.* Bogus emergency vehicle that makes an abrupt and unexpected stop, causing one to collide with its rear end, before conveying its occupants to the nearest Casualty department to be treated for imaginary injuries.

scampi flapper *n.* An unfortunate but hilariously ill-timed *fart* from a man who is being romantically spooned by his missus. A *love puff.*

scampi fries *n.* Small, piquantly flavoured twists of toilet paper found in a lady's *notcher* region. *Gashlycrumb tinies.*

scampi NikNak, cock like a *sim.* Said of a *clappy chappy* who has a *shaft* covered in various bumps and lumps, resembling nothing so much as the oddly shaped extruded corn crisp. See also *stinks like a fishmonger's bin*.

Scania scotch *n.* Dark yellow, pungent spirit found in old lemonade bottles at the side of motorways and A-roads, having been discarded there by the hitch-hiker-murdering HGV drivers who distil it

in their kidneys. An acquired taste. Also known as *wagon wine* or *trucker's Tizer.*

scared stiff *adj.* Aroused while watching a horror movie, for example by Drew Barrymore's jumper arangement in *Scream*.

scare the cat *n.* To produce a startlingly loud *trouser cough*.

scarlet emperor *n.* A red, rather bruised, male reproductive organ after an extended session of *self-help*.

scarlet wankernel *n.* When a lady awakens in the night to find her husband has vanished from the bed next to her and is elsewhere in the house, indulging in *the monomanual vice*. *'She seeks him here, She seeks him there, his missus seeks him everywhere. Is he in heaven, is he in hell? He's in the spare room having a wank.'* (from *The Scarlet Wankernel* by Baroness Emmuska Orczy).

scat *n.* Form of *shite*-fixated *grumble* particularly popular amongst our saucy Teutonic cousins.

scatastrophe *n.* Something dreadful, disastrous and horrific that happens during a spot of *shite*-based sex play. So that's anything that happens during a spot of *shite*-based sex play then, you would imagine.

scatman *1. n.* A jazz singer who improvises nonsense Bill and Ben-style lyrics because they've forgotten the proper words, *eg.* Sammy Davis Jnr., Cleo Laine, Nat Gonella. *2. n.* A German *poo-game enthusiast.*

scat nav *n.* The insistent voice in your head that is forever steering your life in a *shit* direction, *eg.* Ordering one more pint, texting an ex- after midnight, or managing Manchester United.

scatter cushions *n.* *Baps* that seem to be all over the place. See also *surprised frog*.

scentry *n.* A noxious gaseous entity standing guard over any space. A *dropped gut* left to deter interlopers.

Schatenfreude *n. Germ.* The vicarious pleasure felt when someone else *shits* themself.

scheisseberg *n. Germ.* A *digestive transit* of truly titanic proportions whose towering brown peak breaks through the waterline, hinting at an even greater mass lurking under the surface.

Scherzinger's sniffle *n.* A blob of low-fat *man yoghurt* on the end of a slightly surprised girlfriend's nose.

Schettino, do a *1. v.* To leave a pub before a round or a fight. Named in honour of the comedy captain of cruise liner the Costa Concordia, who claimed to have "fallen" into one of his stricken vessel's lifeboats. *2. n.* While wiping, to *breach the* *hull* disastrously.

schlong *n. Yiddish.* A large *putz.* A *schlonger* or *kosher dill.*

schlong shed *n.* Condom, *stopcock, stiffy stocking.*

schmeckie *n.* Opposite of a *schlong.*

scholar's bonus *n.* A rare, but cherished glimpse of a short-skirted young lady's intimate nethergarments as she pedals past in a cycle-heavy city such as Oxford or Cambridge. A *rabbit's tail.*

schoolboy error *n. Shooting one's load* far too early while *on the job.* Premature ejaculation. *'I admit it, I spent my money before I got to the shop. It was a schoolboy error, your honour.'*

school dinner *1. n.* A foul, brown mess, served in a large white bowl, the smell of which makes you heave. *2. n.* A toilet full of *shit.*

school gate mafia *n.* Social grouping of mams, nans and aunts who congregate in school playgrounds at drop-off and pick-up times, spending every available second networking with each other and ingratiating themselves with teachers and playground wardens. They probably know more about your kid than you do.

school night *n.* Any ill-advised evening out on the town till the early hours where you only get about three hours sleep despite knowing you'll have to be up for work in the morning. *'I shouldn't really, you know. It's a school night. Go on then, I'll have a pint of Absinthe with an Everclear chaser. And a bag of Mini Cheddars to line me stomach.'*

school of hard cocks, went to the *phr.* Said of one who's not too choosy. *'You know that bird off Atomic Kitten? No fancy Oxford degree for her, Theresa. She went to the school of hard cocks, she did.'*

school play curtain, fanny like a *sim.* A lady's *part* that has so many flaps and folds that it effectively obstructs and frustrates one's progress. From the familiar childhood experience of fumbling about behind a large curtain trying to make your way onto the stage to deliver your lines during a school play. A *labiarinth, hampton maze.*

school run *1. n.* Dropping one's kids off at the school at the same time every morning. *2. n. Dropping one's kids off at the pool* at the same time every morning.

schort *n.* Like a *schlong,* only shorter.

Schrodinger's arsehole *n.* A person who makes offensive comments and then decides whether it's actually a joke based on their audience's reaction.

Schrödinger's fart *n.* A philosophically paradoxical *guff* that is emitted while the perpetrator is walking along listening to music *via* headphones; in the absence of auditory observation, the *Bakewell* in question can be considered to be both audible and silent at the same time..

Schrödinger's immigrant *n.* Thought experiment carried out in the pages of the *Daily Mail,* where an Eastern European person can simultaneously be both "stealing our jobs" and "sponging our benefits".

Schrödinger's scat *1. n.* Liquid *foulage* that is simultaneously both inside and outside the *chod bin* bowl, *eg.* After eating dodgy shellfish. *2. n.* A self-contradictory *turd* which, upon exiting the *bomb bay,* appears to disappear into the ether without a trace and consequently both exists and doesn't exist.

Schrödinger's shat *n.* The feeling of dread experienced when approaching a shared toilet on which the lid has been left down.

Schubert *n. prop. euph.* In reference to the classical composer who famously wrote an unfinished symphony; the sensation one's *nipsy sometimes* gets after a lengthy *cable-laying* session that there is yet more to come.

schwanzstucker *n.* A sizeable *Piers Morgan.* From Mel Brooks's *Young Frankenstein.*

Schwarzenegger *n.* A lady's *tinter,* so-named because it lies "between her ARse and her fanNY".

scissor bone *n.* The nipsular guillotine which chops one's *logs* into manageable lengths. The *cigar cutter.*

scissor sack *n. medic.* A usually non-fatal genital injury in men caused by sitting down awkwardly in overly tight trousers. A *gentleman's discomfort, torsion of the testes.*

scissor sisters *n. Tennis fans bumping fur. Pasty bashers, pasty smashers, Siamese quims.*

scissors, paper, stone *1. n.* A traditional playground game. *2. n.* The hand motion used by German porn stars in *fisting* movies, *ie.* First two fingers, then four, then the full Monty. *'Get out of the pool and we'll have a game of scissors, paper, stone.'*

scissorwork *n.* Hot *quim-to-quim* clam-jousting *lezbo* action.

scleg *n.* The sweat-prone yet sensitive area of skin between a fellow's *haggis* and his leg. Not to be confused with the *barse.* From scrotbag + leg. Also *bluck leg.*

scobie *n.* The low-level urinal at the end of the row, used by children, midgets and Stephen Pound MP. From Scobie Breasley, the diminutive jockey of the 1960s and 70s.

scones out the oven, take one's *v.* To empty the *Simon Cowells* most urgently at the conclusion of a *Great British bake-off. 'Let's take a look* *through the round window. Oh, look children, it's a big liquorice allsorts factory. And what's that lady doing? That's right, she's off to the shitters to take her scones out the oven.'*

scooberty *n.* That period of adolescence when the male voice oscillates wildly and unpredictably between *basso profundo* and *soprano,* and thus resembles that of a popular, cheaply animated caretaker-hunting cartoon Great Dane.

scoobysnack *n.* Oral sex involving a dog and a very tall sandwich.

scooch *n.* A less vulgar term for a good old-fashioned *fuck*. *'Nowt on telly tonight. Fancy a scooch?'*

scooter *n.* A two-stroke *arse.*

scoots *n. medic.* An affliction characterised by morbid frequency and fluidity of faecal evacuations. The *Brads, Engelberts, Kurts, silly string.*

scorched earth *1. n.* Policy implemented by the Wehrmacht when retreating from the Soviet Union during WW2 whereby factories, infrastructure and houses were blown up to render lost territory uninhabitable by the enemy. *2. n. Dropping your hat* in a pub or club and making the area uninhabitable by anyone for a good twenty minutes.

score from a set piece *v.* To *pull* a *bird* who is a friend of a friend, or one on a blind date, *etc.*

score from open play *v.* To *pull* a *bird* one has never met before by simply bumping into her in a pub, club, chippie, funeral parlour, *etc.* and chatting her up.

scosser *n.* An annoying chap who hails from north of the border. A clever elision of the words Scotch + tosser.

Scotch egg *1. n.* Party foodstuff of absolute last resort. *2. n.* A *turd* which has rolled out of the trouser leg of a Caledonian *professional outdoorsman.*

scotchguard shite *n.* A *Brad* which, no matter how messy it feels on exit, leaves one's *brown eye* miraculously unsullied. Named after the 3M product sold to countless paranoid housewives by surly soft furnishing salesmen.

Scotch pancake *n.* A pool of *spew.* A *pavement pizza.*

Scotsman's lounge *1. n.* An historic pub in Cockburn Street, Edinburgh. *2. n.* The gutter. *'That's my 20th pint of the day. I'm just off for a wee lie down in the Scotsman's lounge.'*

Scottish bank holiday *n.* An *ad hoc* furlough that is called on an informal basis when excessive amounts of Sweetheart Stout have been consumed. A hangover.

Scottish bedwarmer *n.* See *wake up and cough the smelly.*

Scottish breakfast *n.* Two paracetamols.

Scottish enlightenment, the *1. n. hist.* A flourishing of philosophy, economics and the natural sciences that emerged in Scotland in the late eighteenth century. *2. n.* A temporary flourishing of Scottish culture as the inhabitants sober up, a cognitive renaissance that typically occurs between between 11am and 3.30pm most days.

Scottish penthouse *1. n.* A first floor flat. *2. n.* Unsuccessful, region-specific *grumble mag.*

Scottish play *1. euph.* Shakespearean drama (*Macbeth* or *Hamlet* or something), the title of which cannot be spoken by superstitious *chickenshit* actors in case ill fortune befalls them. *2. n.* Anal sex with an otherwise respectable partner.

Scottish sunshine *n.* Rain.

Scottish yoga *n.* A hot bath and a can of Tennent's Super.

scouse *v.* To misappropriate opportunistically. *'I say, what a poor show. I left my dressing room unlocked for five minutes and when I came back my gold and diamond cigarette holder had been scoused.'* (Terry-Thomas, *Liverpool Magistrates Court,* 1960).

Scouse cheeseboard *n.* Dairylea Lunchables.

Scouse gold *n.* Copper pipe.

Scouser's cashpoint *n.* A fruit machine. Also *Glasgow piano.*

scouser's library *n.* A job centre.

scouse sauna *n.* Being kettled and simultaneously tear-gassed by riot gendarmerie outside a French football stadium

scousework *n.* Burglary.

scout movement *n.* A wholesome act of defecation performed in the great outdoors. A *brown owl, bear chod* or *bear grill.*

scout's honour *euph.* The simultaneous use of the index, middle and third finger to stimulate a dirty lady's nether regions once a week in your local church hall. Also *scout's salute.*

scran *1. n.* That bit of a fellow's anatomy which falls between his *hairy swingers* and his *clackervalve.* The *barse, tintis, notcher, stinker's bridge.* The *perineum. 2. n.* Dinner, *snap.*

scrandemonium *n.* Life-threatening mayhem encountered at the self-service breakfast area of a Scottish hotel.

scrank *n.* An inadvertent scrape of the *clockweights* or *clackerbag* which turns, as sure is eggs is eggs, into an act of *personal pollution.* Typically occurs when watching television during the day, alone.

scranus *n.* The fucking *barse* again.

scrape one off *v.* To commit a filthy act of

unseemly *self-improvement*.

Scrapheap Challenge *1. n.* Old Channel 4 programme where teams competed to construct contraptions from scrap metal. *2. n.* The prospect of having to perform *cumulonimbus* on a *bird* who is *up on blocks*. So called because of the general messyness, metallic taste and all-pervading odour of dirty blood.

scraping the crisp packet *1. n.* Enjoying those last bits of healthful flavour that get trapped in the bottom corner of your favourite savoury snack bag, whilst other pub-goers to silently judge you. *2. n.* Licking the salty *juice* from the central digit after a successful *manual service* of one's betrothed.

scraping the roadkill from the tarmac *euph.* Peeling a sweaty *tackle bag* from the inner thigh. *'Sit still, Charles. The Archbishop of Canterbury has arrived.' 'Sorry Camilla. These tights are murder and I'm just trying to scrape the roadkill from the tarmac.'*

scrap iron! *exclam.* A loud shout delivered after a particularly impressive honk on the *back trumpet.*

scrappy doo *1. n.* Irritating nephew/cousin of ghost-hunting, economically animated, anthropomorphic canine Scooby. *2. n.* An untidy *follow through. 'Daddy. I think I just did a scrappy doo.' 'Me too, love. I think it must be that prawn vindaloo I got off the car boot sale that we had for tea.'*

Scrappy Doo moment *n.* The successful conclusion of a *titwank*, at which a gentleman might exclaim, in the style of the erstwhile cartoon canine: "Ta-da-da-da-da-da! Puppy power!"

scrapyard dog, going at it it like *sim.* Phrase evocative of a newly acquired inamorata administering a *chewy* in the romantic surroundings of a vandalised playground or other bit of hastily discovered abandoned wasteland.

scratch *v.* Of a Scouse fellow, to sign on. *'I can't fix your roof Thursday. I'm scratching.'*

scratchcard relative *n.* A *minted* family member who has unaccountably remembered you in their will.

scratcher *n.* Bed, *fart sack, wanking chariot.*

scratch 'n' sniff *1. n.* The method used since time immemorial to verify the freshness of a recently discovered *shite* stripe on a bathroom towel. *2. phr.* When comfy in bed, skilfully clenching the *bummocks* so that a hearty *Donald* provides hands-free relief of an itchy *ringpiece.*

scratch on *v.* To sign on the dole. A phrase used because none of the *fucking* pens work either.

scratter *n.* A person of limited finances, education and breeding.

scratter cushions *n.* The wipe-clean, blue mattresses found in police cells.

scrattering classes *n.* Social division populated by the lower class fodder upon which the *Jeremy Kyle Show* historically fed.

scrattersphere *1. n.* The clouds of pleasant, sociable youths that gather round amusement arcades, chip shop fruit machines and the doorways of bargain booze establishments. *2. n.* Extra-urban region surrounding a town that is populated by *scratters.*

scrattitude *n.* The refreshing self-confidence that members of the lower orders display by stepping off the kerb and causing traffic to slow down or stop while they take their time casually sauntering across the road. From scratter + attitude.

scrawnography *n.* The type of *Frankie Vaughan* eschewed by devotees of fuller figured ladies. *'That website you told me about was shite. Them birds on it didn't have a decent pair of tits between them. You know I don't like scrawnography, your holiness.'*

screamer *n.* A raving *good listener.*

scream for me, Long Beach! *exclam.* Iconic shout by vocalist Bruce Dickinson on Iron Maiden's classic *Live After Death* album. *2. n.* Something to be yelled hoarsely before dropping a Hammersmith Odeon-sized *guff.*

screamin' eagles *n. Stick vid* cinematography term for a scene where a man feeds his *cock* to two or more open-mouthed women who are on their knees, like a parent bird feeding a big purple worm to its hungry chicks. *Baby birding, passing the mic.*

screaming monkey *n.* A bit of female genitalia. Probably the bit which looks the most like a screaming monkey.

scree *1. n. coll.* Shale-like nuggets of *shit*, approximately the size of a marrowfat pea.

screensaver *1. n.* An animated scene on an idle computer, intended to prevent damage to the monitor. *2. n.* A hastily improvised protective clingfilm cover for an internet *art enthusiast's faptop* display. *'Jason, what's all this kitchen wrap on your computer screen?' 'Oh that? It's a screensaver from when I was on tour, love. I used to go back to the hotel and enthusiastically eat yoghurt while browsing the web for antiquarian books, you see.'*

screw *1. v.* To *fuck, bang, scuttle, poke, shag.* To *m*ke l*ve. 2. v.* To have sex piggy-style, rotating clockwise due to having a corkscrew-shaped *cock* like what pigs do. Look it up.

screwfix catalogue *n.* Tinder, or any other dating app.

screwly trumptious *n.* A *queefsome* lady whose *toot sweets* turn out to be slightly less tuneful and perfumed than might have been hoped.

screwnicorn *n.* A mythical and somewhat magical sex act whereby a lesbian puts a *strap-on dildo* on her forehead and goes at her partner like a bull at a gate.

scrincter *n.* The bit between the scrotum and the sphincter. The *tintis, scran, barse.*

script for a jester's tear *1. n.* Title track of a 1983 album by progressive rock band Marillion. *2. n.* The unnecessary plot-establishing footage that is routinely fast-forwarded through by the impatient viewers of adult-oriented cinematographic productions who are only really interested in seeing *it* going *up, in, out and off. Expresso bongo, foreporn, fist forward.*

scrobbing *n. onomat.* The sound made by a dog when licking its own genitalia.

scrogg *1. v.* To partake in in an act of penetrative sexual intercourse up a lady. To *fuck. 2. n.* An act of penetrative sexual intercourse partaken up a lady. A *fuck.*

scroggie meadow *n.* A *front lawn* that has been allowed to run to seed. *Terry Waite's allotment.*

scrogglings *1. n.* Olde English term for the small, irrelevant apples left on the tree after the main scrumpy crop has been harvested. *2. n. Spunk bubbles.*

scroll *1. v.* To apply the index finger to the central button on a computer mouse in order to move the page on the screen up or down. *2. v.* To apply the index finger to the central button of a female's *parts of shame* in order to achieve an *organism.*

scrolling the ipod *n.* Manually setting the missus's *playlist.* A more modern version of *finding Radio Luxembourg* or *drawing a curve on an Etch-a-Sketch* for the gent with a delicate touch.

Scrooge's shithouse, as cold as *sim.* Disparaging assessment of the current temperature. *'Fuck me, it's as cold as Scrooge's shithouse in here. Put another bar on, Camilla.'*

scroped *n.* A small motorbike ridden by *scrotes* when out making deliveries to their customers, mainly at night. Unlike properly licensed and insured motorbikes, scropeds can be ridden on pavements , where their small size, manoeverability and lack of headlights make them ideal for swerving round obstacles such as police officers.

scrotal recoil *n.* Involuntary retraction of the *clockweights* into the body in harsh winter climes, when swimming in cold water or when watching Neil Kinnock's "We're alright! We're alright!" speech at Labour's 1992 Sheffield election rally.

scrotal sack *n.* JD Sports or similar branded plastic duffle bag given away free with a pair of trainers and slung over the shoulder of a track-suited shaver.

scrote *1. n. Knacker, bollock brain. 2. n.* Someone who fails to match *Country Life's* preferred readership demographic profile.

scrote couture *n.* Clothing worn by the economically inactive denizens of the urban underclass. *Armani and Navy, Kyle style.*

scrote cuisine *n.* Fast food. *Cordon bleurgh.*

scrotee *1. n.* The sort of feeble, adolescent beard which appears to be composed principally of spare *nadbag* fluff. *2. n.* The clump of pretentious, tufted *jazz hair* growing off the lower slopes of one's *chicken skin handbag.* From scrotum + goatee.

scrotelifter *n.* A comprehensively well-plastered *bum sink* which results in gentleman users having to lift up their *scrotii* while *dropping off the shopping* to avoid getting them smeared with previous occupants' *Tom tit.* Particularly prevalent at music festivals. *'How was Glastonbury, John?' 'Well, Ghost Poet was spot on, but by day three every single bog was a Scrotelifter, Evan.'*

scrote rack *n.* Any civic amenity to which track-suited, baseball-hat-wearing ne'er-do-wells flock, in the style of the crows who congregate on the climbing frame in Alfred Hitchcock's movie *The Birds, eg.* Bus shelters, playgrounds, war memorials *etc.* A *scrotial club.*

scrotesque *adj.* Descriptive of a person or place which rarely features in the society pages of *Tatler. 'Of all the neighbourhood locales, the Bransholme Estate well earns its reputation as the most scrotesque.'* (from *A Guide to the Architecture of Humberside* by Sir Nikolaus Pevsner).

scrotiform *adj.* An actual, real dictionary word, meaning 'shaped like a ballsack'. Ask Susie Dent, she'll tell you. We'd ask her ourselves, but she unfollowed us on Twitter. *'Today's birthdays: Nadia Sawalha, EastEnders actress, 1963; Peta Wilson, Australian model, 1970; Therese Coffey, scrotiform politician, 1971.'*

scrotinise *v.* Of a female friend, to carefully and expertly examine a chap's *clockweights,* possibly on the lookout for *bollock jockeys* and/or *brothel sprouts.*

scrotobahn *n.* A busy main road and/or pavement used by feral youths riding unlicensed quad bikes and electric scooters. *Without helmets, we* might add.

scroto GP *n.* Parade of de-restricted mopeds piloted by tracksuited *asbolescents* racing around the local leisure centre car park.

scrotorbike *1. n.* Any child's motorcycle being wheeled along the pavement by a fat man wearing a vest and holding a can of lager. *2. n. n.* A rugged off-road or scooter-type two-wheeled vehicle ridden by an adolescent at night, without lights and on the wrong side of the road. *3. n.* The 48cc clown-sized scooters ridden by *ratboys* around the pedestrian thoroughfares of the country's less salubrious residential areas.

scrototype *n.* A one-off bespoke *scrotrod*.

scrotox *n.* The reduction in the visible signs of ageing upon one's *pod pouch* which occurs following a prolonged period of enforced celibacy, or an evening in a *fanny out* bar.

scrotozoa *n.* The *tadpoles* of the urban underclasses.

scrotrod *n.* A poverty-spec Corsa, Saxo or Golf that looks like it's been covered in Loctite and driven through Halfords.

scrotumnal *adj.* Describing anything *clackerbag*-related. As autumnal is to autumn, so *scrotumnal* is to scrotumn.

scrotum pole *n.* Old Native American erection with a frightening head, at the foot of which lie *John Wayne's hairy saddlebags*, and around which *Madam Palm and her five sisters* do short, ritual dances to precipitate *jizzle*.

scrotum ticklers *n.* The huge comedy moustaches favoured by the acutely observed *fruit feelers* who used to populate the cartoons illustrating Richard Littlejohn's columns in *The Sun*.

scroturboating *n.* The erotically charged act of a woman (or man in these modern, politically correct times) mooching his (or her in these modern, politically correct times) lips and blowing a big raspberry on a man's (or a woman's in these modern, politcally correct times) *nadbag*. From scrotum + motorboating.

scrub *n.* An exfoliant facial treatment bestowed upon the *licker out* of a *stubbly bush*.

scrubber *n.* A vulgar woman, *eg.* One who uses foul language.

scrubbery *n.* Any place where groups of coarse young ladies tend to gather, *eg.* By the tills in a 24-hour garage, round a night bus driver, on a shopping precinct bench, outside an off-licence, in Ben Dover's bedroom *etc*.

scrubbing the cook *n. milit. US.* Bashing the bishop, *cuffing the suspect, knocking off Patton's tin hat.*

scruburb *n.* A less than desirable area to live.

scrubweasel *n.* A sexually enthusiastic lady of low breeding, low moral standards and low intellectual capacity. *'Mater, pater, I'd like you to meet Sarah, my new scrubweasel.'*

scruff *n.* Pornography, *muck, grumble.* *'"Look what I've got," said William breathlessly, as he emptied the contents of his jumper at the Outlaws' feet. "It's a load of scruff. Jumble found it under a hedge."'* (from *William's Milk Race* by Richmal Crompton).

Scruggs style *1. n.* A popular approach to bluegrass playing popularised by aristocratic banjo player Earl Scruggs, which involves frenetic picking with the thumb, index and middle fingers. *2. n.* In the world of *invisible banjo playing*, to place one's thumb on a lady's *clematis* and one's index and middle fingers up her *blurtch* and *chuff* respectively, before trying to get a tune out of her. *3. n.* A lady *practising her fingerwork, perfecting her licks.*

scrump *n.* A simultaneous *shit*, cough and a *trump*. From shit + cough + trump.

scrumping *1. n. US.* Having sex. *2. n.* Playing the *botty bugle*. *3. n. UK.* Stealing apples.

scruncher *n.* One who stores his discarded vestments in his *floordrobe,*

scrunchies *1. n.* The colourful elasticated hairbands captured by rival teenage *slappettes* in battle. *2. n.* Excess batter in a chip shop. *Scraps, scranchions.*

scrunger *n.* Another name for one of those bike seat sniffers found lurking around the cycle racks of convents, nurses' homes and women's drop-in centres. A *garboon, snufty, snurglar, nurfer.*

scrunion *n. Aus. medic.* The wrinkly scrotal remnant immediately preceding the perineum. From scrotum + onion.

scrunt *1. n.* A scruffy *cunt*. From scruffy + cunt. *'Born on this day: Ashikaga Yoshihisa, Japanese Shogun, 1465; Nikki Sixx, Motley Crue bass player, 1958; Marco Pierre White, scrunt chef, 1961.' 2. n. coll. Blart, flange, gusset.* A group of attractive women. *'Suddenly, at the age of 25, the Prince was cast as the world's most eligible bachelor. On a Royal tour of New Zealand in 1973, he found himself having to batter off top-end scrunt with a shitty stick.'* (from *HRH The Prince of Wales* by Jim-Bob Dimbleby).

scrut *n.* Hardcore *oyster grumble* that would satisfy the curiosity of even the most ardent amateur gynaecologist. *Close up pink.*

scruttock *n.* The area of skin 'twixt *scrot* and *bot*. The *barse, tintis, notcher.*

scudaddle *v.* To *soil* yourself and then take your leave forthwith. From scud + skedaddle. *'Eeh, did you see Eamonn Holmes scudaddle when them Fathers for Justice protesters invaded the* *lottery show?'*

scud brothers *n.* Collective term describing the pair of male professional footballers taking part in a typical *threesome*. See also *Newton's cradle, prawn sandwich, two-pronged attack etc.*

scuddle *n.* Almost-extinct genre of comforting, life-affirming *erotica*, consisting largely of friendly-looking women in their *scads*.

scud marks *n.* Chalky residue left on a young *onanist's underchunders* after a large release of *gentlemen's relish.*

scud widow *n.* A woman who rarely or never gets a *portion* due to her husband having opted to exist permanently in a *porn vortex.*

scuffer *n.* A *cozzer, rozzer, tit-head,* a member of *the filth. 'Look out, it's the scuffers!'*

scuffers *n.* *Tits* that hang so low that the *nips* get carpet burns. *'Nice scuffers, Lord Owen.'*

scuffing *n.* Hands-free *self abuse* technique, which involves rubbing one's *cock* against the mattress until the job is done. Presumably the hands are then brought back into service in order to clean up the mess.

scuff it *1. v.* In football, to lose concentration at the critical moment, leading to a disappointing shot. *2. v.* In *fucking,* to lose concentration at the critical moment, leading to a disappointing *shot.* To *suffer a lack of composure in front of the goal.*

scufflink *n.* The resulting mess when, while wiping your *balloon knot* at the conclusion of a particularly stercoraceous *digestive transit,* the wrist of your shirt inadvertently comes into contact with the *Marmite pot.*

scumbag *n.* The ultimate term of abuse known to British tabloid journalists.

scumble *1. n.* A *shit,* heavily dated paint effect inflicted on the participants of TV room makeover programmes. *2. n.* A language spoken exclusively by *Harold Ramps.* From Scottish + mumble.

scumbrella *n.* Any item pressed into service to keep the rain off a poor person, in lieu of a genuine umbrella, *eg.* A Greggs carrier bag.

scum-dog millionaire *n.* Contumelious epithet applied to any female "celebrity" who somehow manages to amass a seven-figure fortune despite displaying no evidence that she possesses any talent whatsoever.

scummertime *n.* The start of the school holidays when a flood of teenage *ronkers* descends upon a town's unwitting shoppers.

scummy mummy *n.* The opposite of a *yummy mummy.* A coarsely plebeian materfamilias, if you will. A *miwlf.*

scumper *n.* Someone who lays sheets of *bog roll* on the seat of a public toilet so as his *arse* does not touch the same place as someone else's *arse* has touched. The late *Carry On* star Kenneth Williams was known to be a keen *scumper.*

scumpole *n.* Young offender-type whose impressive working knowledge of criminal law is often successfully put to use in avoiding the legal consequences that may otherwise result from his criminal *shenanigans.*

scum shovel *n.* Any form of public transport generally eschewed by the elite, *eg.* The no.11 Torry to Northfield bus in Aberdeen.

scumwad *n. US.* The ultimate term of abuse known to American tabloid journalists.

scungies *n.* Disreputable *scads.* *'What's the matter, Carol?' 'While I was onstage, performing a medley of my hits including China in Your Hand, some dirty bastards have been in the dressing room and wanked on my scungies.'*

scuns *n.* *Scads.*

scunt *n.* Like a *scosser,* but even worse.

scutter *n.* A lady of easy virtue.

scuttle *1. v.* To *sink the pink,* or *brown,* esp. in a hurried fashion from behind. *2. n.* A swift, frantic act of intercourse. Or something to keep the coal in.

scuttler *n.* A fellow who, for whatever reason, will not *piss* alongside another at a urinal, but instead *scuttles off* into a cubicle, usually locking the door too.

SDL *abbrev.* Shitting Dead Leg. *'The ostentatiously erudite Will Self's Brobdingnagian new tome is simply the ambrosial epitome of sesquipedalian reading. The first chapter alone gave me SDLs for 20 minutes.'*

sea bent *adj.* Descriptive of a matelot whose sexual tastes have been re-oriented due to a prolonged period of enforced abstinence while at sea. Of otherwise heterosexual sailors, tempted to have a *ride on the other ferry* while at sea. *'Kiss me Hardy, I'm feeling distinctly sea bent.'*

sea biscuit *1. n.* Legendary (not literally) US racehorse, recently immortalised (not literally) in a *shit* (literally) film. *2. n.* Nautical equivalent of an *air biscuit,* delivered while in an over-relaxing bath. *3. n.* A *turd* floating in the *briny.* *'Observant Admiral (Who has, through his extended telescope, spotted trouble in store for the heroic Channel swimmer half way through his heroic traversal of "La Manche" 'twixt Dover and Calais, and resolves to vouchsafe this important information "post-haste" to the natatorial half-man half-fish by hailing him at the top of his not inconsiderable voice): 'Look out, Captain Webb. There's a sea biscuit on* *the top of the next wave.' Captain Webb (With a big turd stuck in his mouth): 'Too late!"* (cartoon by Sir John Tenniel in *Punch*, 1875).

sea breeze *n.* A *fanny fart, queef* or *Lawley kazoo. Harry Secombe's last raspberry.*

seafood splatter *n.* The inevitable consequence of a night spent eating a big silver tray full of prawns, mussels, squid, *blobs etc.*

seafood taco *n.* A lady's *clout* that smells like a fishmonger's hands and could lead to an upset stomach.

seagulling *1. n.* The mischievous act of dropping *jizz* onto a passer-by from a height, *eg.* A tree, a roof or a Status Quo hotel room balcony. Could lead to *Graham Norton's hair. 2. n.* Amongst the *dogging* community, spattering the windscreen of a vehicle with *spongle,* in the manner of a passing kittiwake with loose *Camillas.* See *jizzle.*

seagull's breakfast *n.* A tempting full English smorgasbord of kebab, vomit, chips, pizza and used condoms, of the sort found at taxi ranks up and down the country every weekend.

seagulls' wellies *n.* Maritime used *dunkies. 'How was your swim, David?' 'Awful. I was only in the water ten minutes and I swallowed a turd and three seagulls' wellies. I'm going to write to the council.'*

seahorse *n.* A man doing a woman's job, *eg.* Arranging flowers, designing dresses, pushing a baby about in a pram. From the comedy fish the hippocampus, the male of which species carries its wife's young about like some sort of big girl's blouse.

Sealink salsa *n.* Cross-Channel ferry passenger vomit. *'Careful on your way to the bar, your majesty. There's Sealink salsa all over the fucking shop.'*

seal of Hades *n.* The boundary between our world and the *devil's kitchen.* The *ringpiece.*

seal's breath *euph.* A very fishy *fanny.* See also *adventure bay, anchovy alley, kipper's twat etc.*

sea monster *n.* Swamp donkey, hippocrocapig.

searchlights *n.* Dazzling *headlamps* which cause a driver to mount the kerb. *'I couldn't help myself officer. I was driving past the Further Education College and I was momentarily blinded by searchlights.'*

seaside bucket *n.* Often seen on Fraisthorpe Beach, a capacious vessel that smells of dead fish.

seaside shithouse, fuller than a *sim.* Descriptive of something that is replete to bursting point. Also *full as a fat bird's shoe, full as a parson's sack. 'Will somebody take that bin bag out? It's fuller than a seaside shithouse.'*

seasonal aisle *1. n.* Section of the supermarket only available at certain times of the year, *eg.* Christmas.

2. n. Section of the wife that is only available at certain times of the year, *eg.* Christmas.

season cliff hanger *1. n. US.* In TV drama series, the final show of a season which ends just at the exciting part, encouraging viewers to tune in next time. *2. n.* A large *shit* which cuts off at the exciting part, thus causing one to have to wait for what feels like an eternity to find out the ending.

seasoned diner *euph.* A fat *bastard* or *salad dodger.* One who has *ate all the pies.*

season of the witch *n.* When *the reds are playing at home* and the missus starts *showing off.*

sea toad *1. n.* A family of deep sea angler fishes known as the *chaunacidae. 2. n.* An amphibious *Thora* which crouches in the toilet bowl and is resistant to flushing.

seaweed *n.* The grimpen mixture of girl hair and *fanny batter* that needs to be extricated from the plughole every once in a while.

seaweed smuggler *n.* One who emerges from the ocean/swimming pool with what appears to be two pounds of loose kelp dangling out of their gusset.

secaturds *n. medic.* The muscles surrounding the *nipsy* that provide the power to operate the *turtle guillotine.*

second album *n.* Following an earlier successful release, a follow-up *poo* that proves more troublesome to produce than was originally anticipated. *'Are you alright in there, Lee? You've been making some terrible noises.' 'I'm working on my difficult second album, love, and I'm having musical differences.'*

second crop of tomatoes, a *n.* Unwelcome reappearance of the *Duke of Argylls,* just when it seems that the Anusol is kicking in.

second hand dart board, she's had more pricks than *phr.* Said non-judgementally of a lady who has been *cocked more times than Davy Crockett's rifle. 'I wouldn't say the Duchess of York is easy, but she's had more pricks than a second hand dartboard, your holiness.'*

second hand parrot's cage, she's got a mouth like a *sim.* Said of a woman of reputedly loose morals, from the fact that "it's had a cockatoo (sounds a bit like cock or two) in it".

second handrex *n.* The somewhat unlikely use of someone else's pre-*spangled* tissue for the purpose of cleaning up your own manly emissions, in the absence of anything else to hand, *eg.* Tea towel, sock, living room curtains, dog's ears *etc.*

second post *n.* A supplementary delivery of *anal parcels* which takes one by surprise half way through the morning.

second sitting *1. n.* An immediate, unavoidable

return visit to the *shitter* after wiping and washing.
2. n. One of those times when the first gush of
feculence smells so foul – and fills the bowl to
such an alarming depth – that one is forced to
flush before continuing, perhaps following a
delicious meal at Heston Blumenthal's Fat Duck
restaurant. *3. n.* The lavatorial act of adding one's
own serving on top of one left unflushed by the
previous customer; a double helping of *bangers
and mash* that might well put you off your dinner.

second that motion *v.* To take a *shit* into an
unflushed *bog*, like what Smokey Robinson
sang about.

second wind *n.* Vigorous flatulence even after
you've been to *drop the kids off the pool.*

secret lemonade drinker *1. n.* A good listener. *2. n.*
One with a hidden taste for midnight *watersports.*
*'Born on this day: Boy George, big-titfered singer,
1961; Rowan Williams, God-botherer, 1950; Donald
J Trump, American secret lemonade drinker, 1946.'*

secret men's business *phr.* An expression, it says
here, from Australian indigenous language.
Relaxing in a gentleman's way.

secrets *n. medic. rhym. slang.* Cockney haemorrhoids. From secret smiles = Johnny Giles.

secret smile *n.* A *cunt.*

secret speech *1. n.* Controversial address
denouncing Stalin, made by Nikita Krushchev
at the 1956 CPSU party congress. *2. n.* A particularly shocking *anal announcement* delivered
behind closed doors in a highly powered
committee environment.

section in defence, teeth like a *sim. milit.* The
dental status of many in this country, *viz.* "All
cammed up and spread out".

security check *1. n.* Rounds made last thing at
night to assure oneself that the front and back
doors are definitely locked. *2. n.* Last thing at
night grope of the missus to check that her *front*
and *back doors* are definitely locked.

sediment *n.* The *totty crud* that remains unsyphoned
when the *ugly lights* come on at chucking out time
in a night club. *Floor sweepings.*

see a friend to the coast *euph.* To answer a *call
of duty.*

see a man about a log *euph.* To politely excuse
yourself in order to empty your *chumhole. 'Where
there is discord, may we bring harmony. Where there
is error, may we bring truth. Where there is doubt,
may we bring faith. And where there is despair, may
we bring hope. But first I'm off to see a man about
a log.'*

seed *n.* That which was spilled upon the stoney croft

by Onan, and great was the wrath of the Lord.

seed catalogue *n.* A *flesh mag* for *onanists.*

seed demon *n.* An actress in an *art film* who enthusiastically imbibes the *spongle* from her thespian
partners' *clockweights.*

seeded baps *n. Tits* with all *spunk* on them.

seeded buns *n.* A nicely decorated pair of *savoury
delights,* between which one might decide to slip
a piece of meat. And some cheese. And a slice
of pickle.

seedless grapes *n.* Post-vasectomy *knackers.* As
swallowed by women who are languorously
reclining on *chaises longues.*

see full t's and c's on our website *1. exclam.* What
presenters on TV programmess say after a rip-off
competition has just been advertised. *2. exclam.*
An invitation to go online and look at *tits* and
cunts on internet *grumble and grunt* sites.

see her fillings *v.* For whatever reason, to get a view
of a lady's molars that is usually reserved for her
dental surgeon. Especially if she regularly *sucks
him off.*

seeing to *n.* Sexual servicing, a "jolly good" or
"proper" one of which is often said to have been
given to a woman by a man. And vice versa, occasionally. See *pegging.*

seesaw *n.* The act of *the other* with a *bird* who is *up
the duff* or heavily *greggnant.*

see the bishop *v.* To *talk to the boss. 'Oh, there's a
lovely pair of shoes in Russell & Bromley's window,
love. £39.99 down from £79.99. They're an absolute
bargain.' 'You'll have to see the bishop about that
one, dear.'*

see to Uncle Albert *euph.* To *knock one out.* A phrase
made popular by the character Ken Barlow in old
episodes of *Coronation Street. 'Ken (on phone):
What's that Deirdre? There's a big order to fill at
the factory and you've got to work late…? I see. And
after that, there's an emergency council meeting at
Weatherfield Town Hall…? (sigh) No, don't worry
about me, love. I'll just grab a hotpot at the Rovers,
then go home and see to Uncle Albert.'*

see you later masturbator *exclam.* Amusing
valedictory shout, most effectively delivered in
the sort of high-pitched shriek usually associated
with fish-faced Aerosmith warbler Steve Tyler.

see you next time *exclam.* A more useful valedictory
taunt that can be employed when you are going to
next see someone on a day other than a Tuesday.
'See you next time Lord Archer, you cunt.'

see you next Tuesday *sort of acronym.* Ingeniously
offensive parting pleasantry allowing you the satisfaction of calling someone a rude word (*cunt*

again) to their face without them knowing it.

self-arselating *n.* Taking oneself off to a quiet corner of the pub, bookies, restaurant *etc.* for a period of time, in order that others need not be in danger of inhaling your particularly noxious variant of *carbon-dibaxide.*

self-catering *n.* See *self discipline.*

self-censorship *n.* Tactfully muffling an *Exchange & Mart* with a well-timed cough.

self-cleaning oven *1. n.* In the world of kitchen appliances, a cooker which does not in any sense whatsoever clean itself. *2. n.* The *cludge* of a *Norris.*

self contact sport *n.* The exercise regimen of choice for the armchair athlete who lives alone.

self discipline *n.* Character-building regime engendered in the armed forces and public schools. *Masturbation, self improvement, self harm.*

self discovery *n. Self help, self catering, self discipline. Relaxing in a gentleman's way.*

self expression *euph.* Monomanual auto-erotic stimulation. *'What are you doing in there, Vincent? You're not cutting your ear off again, are you?' 'No mam. I'm just expressing myself. Into a sock.'*

self help manual *n.* An item of literature that aids *relaxation.* An *art pamphlet, flesh mag* or *bachelor's newsletter.*

selfie *1. n.* Something that all the newspapers have got inexplicably excited about in recent times. *2. n. Clearing the custard.*

selfie stick *1. n.* A *cunt pole* or *twat mirror.* *2. n.* A *dildo, fiddlestick, dolly dagger* or *neck massager.* *3. n.* The male forearm.

self improvement *euph.* Intellectually flavoured, autodidactic approach to masturbation, such as *tossing off* to the description of Helen of Troy in Marlowe's *Doctor Faustus, strangling Kojak* during a Bethany Hughes documentary on BBC4, or merely *throwing one over the thumb* while watching Rachel Riley on *Countdown.*

self indulgent *adj.* Prone to treating yourself to a brisk *rub down* from time to time.

self loaf *n.* Solo act of filthy unpleasantness carried out by a beastly male using a warm, unsliced sandwich loaf and an apple corer.

self-medicating *euph.* Relieving one's troubles in the standard way. *'Mr Skinner, you are severely dehydrated, you have lost six inches in height, you are practically blind and your hands are covered in coarse hair. Why haven't you been to see me before now?' 'I've been self-medicating, doctor.'*

self-partnered *1.adj.* Descriptive of being contendedly single, a phrase coined by Emma Watson off the films. *2. adj.* Descriptive of an uncouth male who is undergoing a rigorous course of *cockupational therapy* whilst thinking about, for example, Emma Watson.

self service station *n.* A computer desk.

self waxing *n.* Hair removal when a gent pulls back his crusted bed sheets the morning after a vigorous session of *making the bald man cry.*

selling Buicks *n. US.* Vomiting. From the similarity of the sounds made by a *chunderer* to the cries of the Buick street vendors of Detroit, *viz.* "Buick! Buick!"

semen *n. Aphrodite's Araldite, joy gloy, gunk, spunk, goo. Sailor's ale.*

semen-olina *n. Love porridge* of an especially lumpy nature.

sement *n.* Quick-drying, gloopy substance used for binding *hardcore. Sement* has to be mixed vigorously for a couple of minutes before it is applied. The main constituent of *cumcrete. Jazz glue.*

semetery *n.* A well-used tissue within the warp and weft of which are buried the corpses of a million *likely lads.*

semi *1. n.* A *lazy lob on,* a *dobber,* a half-erect penis. *2. n.* A house joined to one other house. See *semi-detached.*

semi circle *n.* The crescent of *synchronised swimmers* in a *gang bang scud* video who are all pulling at their *half-fat man-bats* while awaiting their turn at the *crease* and cinematic glory.

semi-demi-on *n.* A *quarter-on, half a lob on.* The first stirrings of *dobberdom.*

semi-detached *1. adj.* Of a house, completely attached to another house. *2. n.* A partial tumescence of the *giggle stick* which arises of its own accord and for no particular reason while one is daydreaming.

seminal *adj.* A highbrow, intellectual way of referring to something as being *wank. 'Surely the seminal sitcom of recent years must be Mrs Brown's Boys.'*

seminal text *1. n.* Any written tract that has acquired recognition sufficient to establish for itself an indisputable place in the literary or academic canon. *2. n.* Any printed material that has received so much critical attention that its pages can no longer be prized apart.

semi-on *n.* A partially tumescent *membrum virile. Half a teacake,* a *dobber.*

semi professional *1. adj.* In the olden days of *Opportunity Knocks,* a word that was used to describe the *shite* acts who appeared each week, such as impressionists who did all the same impressions as Mike Yarwood, and contrtionists who squeezed themselves into small perspex boxes. *1. n.* In the world of cinematographic *scud*, a male thespian who is evidently not quite as excited as the faces and noises he is making might imply. A *Frankie* actor whose spirit is willing, but whose flesh is weak. *3. n.* A female who possesses the necessary attributes and application to breathe life into the most reluctant of members.

semi-skinned *adj.* State of a festival goer's intellect after spending the evening puffing on a meticulously hand-rolled cigarette that contains a crumbled Oxo cube for which he paid the thick end of twenty quid.

send a sausage to the seaside *euph.* To *sink a few U boats.*

send for Sepp Maier! *exclam.* Shouted out in the presence of a lady with *outstanding qualifications.* A reference to the eponymous Bayern Munich goalkeeper who had big gloves which would have been suitable for fondling a large pair of breasts.

send for the namby-pambulance *exclam.* Facetious call for assistance when a Premier League footballer is making more of his "injury" than is strictly necessary.

send her to the Klondike *exclam.* An ungenerous vociferation pertaining to any reasonably pulchritudinous young lady adorning the arm of a more mature or sub-average looking man who just happens to be *caked.* Often prefixed with "Give her a pan and…"

sending back the toast *phr.* Of a fellow's *membrum virile* that presents in a less-than-ready state, resembling nothing so much as floppy, underdone toast. *'On the night in question I couldn't generate any lift at all, your honour. She was gagging for it but I ended up having to send back the toast.'*

sending in the Wolf *euph.* Embarking upon a lengthy clean-up of the back of the toilet-seat, one's cleft, one's wiping hand, one's shirt tails, and one's shirt cuffs following a really, really unpleasant lavatory misadventure. From Harvey Keitel's character in the movie *Pulp Fiction* and them insurance ads.

send in Major Kong *euph.* To ingest a powerful dose of laxative. Named after the character played by Slim Pickins in Stanley Kubrick's *Dr. Strangelove.* Just the thing to open them pesky *bomb-bay doors* and get that *payload* on its way.

senior-ita *n.* A vintage Spanish lass who is *pulled* by a desperate gent in the closing hours of his continental sojourn.

Senna *n. prop.* Named in honour of the eponymous, late racing driver's famously impressive performance in the rain-sodden 1984 Monaco Grand Prix, a bloke who is *good in the wet.*

senokot army *n.* The thick grey line of *gimmers* that stands between you and a first class stamp on pension day.

senorita beater *n.* Any Spanish lager, such as San Miguel *etc. Pedro's piss.*

sentimental *euph.* Descriptive of a chap who is *knowledgeable about the contents of his borders.*

sepia screenshot *n.* The charming vignette left on a sheet when a sweaty, ill-wiped *ringpiece* slides across its surface on the way out of the bed in the morning. An ochre-tinged print from the *bumhole camera.*

serpent socket *n.* That hole into which the *one-eyed trouser snake* is plugged.

serpent's tongue *n.* A forked *piss* caused by a *jazz egg* blocking the *hog's eye.* Twin jets. *'Jesus! You've pissed on the floor again.' 'Sorry, love, only I had the serpent's tongue this morning.'*

serve an ace *v.* To loose off a *back pocket rocket.* See also *bang! and the dirt is gone!*

serve and volley *1. n.* A dynamic form of tennis whereby, having served, a player makes his way directly to the net in order to despatch his return shot. *2. n.* When a drinker, having consumed an elegant sufficiency of alcohol, finds himself unable to take any more on board and immediately throws up on the spot. *'Terrific serve and volley there from Vegas. That shot went straight back into the glass.'*

serve for the match *v.* To complete an act of *self-pollution*, particularly while enjoying women's sports. *'I was watching Sharapova v Lisicki and my mum walked in just as I was serving for the match.'*

serves tea with doilies *euph.* Said of a *sensitive* gentleman who is always *first on the dancefloor* and *bakes a light cake.*

serving *n.* A single sitting's worth of *bumwad.*

serving it up *n. Having it off* with, or *slipping a length* to, someone. *'Throughout the early eighties, Prince Charles was plagued by persistent rumours that Major James Hewitt was serving it up to Princess Diana.'* (from *Charles the Biography* by Little Jimmy Dimbleby).

session ale *n. Piss-*weak beer.

set fire to the rain *1. n.* Adele song about some emotional *bollocks* or other. *2. n.* An unpleasant combination of *ring sting* and liquid diarrhoea, likely caused by Special Brew and a cheap chicken phall.

Seth Armstrong in a SARS mask *sim.* An erotically alluring description of a vaginally hirsute lady wearing a thong-style underpant.

set on fire and put out with a shovel, looks like she's been *sim.* Light-hearted expression which can be used to gently broach the subject of an *eight-pinter*'s appearance. *'I don't fancy yours much, mate. She looks like she's been set on fire and put out with a shovel.'* (Dr Rowan Williams, the Archbishop of Canterbury, while officiating at the wedding of His Royal Highness the Prince of Wales and Camilla Parker-Bowels in the function room of the Travelodge, Windsor, on 9th April 2005).

set the dog off *euph.* To achieve penile turgidity.

setting one's affairs in order *euph.* Paying the gas bill and unstacking the dishwasher before having a *wank*.

setting the video *v.* Sexual position, in which the lady is on her knees and elbows, with her *arse* in the air, tutting exasperatedly.

settle down now please *exclam.* To be uttered with authority after an inappropriately loud *backfire*, reminiscent of the instruction customarily given by a snooker referee when a member of the Crucible crowd disturbs the atmosphere at a tense moment in the championship.

sett point *n.* The critical moment during a bout of canoodling when a gent finally gets his *jazz bands* on his date's *badger.*

seven am angel *n.* When lighting an early morning *brown candle* while running out of time to catch a train, a benevolent *poo* that only requires only a couple of wipes. *'Please Lord, send me a seven am angel.'*

seven pint stunner *n.* A *bird* whose inner beauty only struggles to the surface after one has quaffed the best part of a gallon of *Nelson Mandela.* One pint better looking than a *gallon girl*; two pints worse looking than a *St Ivel lass.*

seven stepper *n.* An extended *Exchange & Mart* which, as its name suggests, lasts for a good few paces as one saunters down the street. A length-specific *string of pearls, duckwalk.*

seven/ten split *1. n.* In ten-pin bowling, a *pair of skittles* so far apart that hitting them both with a single shot is almost impossible. *2. n.* A really wide *fanny* that can only be taken on while wearing special shoes.

seven-thirty from Brownhill *euph.* A morning *four man bob* of enviable regularity. Unless, that is, one typically doesn't wake up until quarter to eight.

seventies football manager chewing gum, like a *sim. exclam.* Said of a skilled *fellatrix.* *'I wasn't sweating, your holiness, even though she was going at my Charlie like a seventies football manager chewing gum.'*

seventy-one *n.* A *soixante-neuf* with a couple of extra fingers stuck up the *lady's wrong 'un* for good measure.

seven wanks in to a six wank day *exclam.* An expression of utter exhaustion.

sews his own buttons on *euph.* Said of a *sensitive* man who is *good with colours, knows what's in his flowerbeds, bakes a light cake, doesn't play poker* and is *first on the dancefloor.* Put bluntly, a chap with *nice nails.*

sex *1. n.* It, the other, how's your father, nookie, slap and tickle, dirties. *2. v.* To pump someone full of *pineapple chunk.* *'Babe, I'm gonna sex you up.'* (*Sex You Up* song lyric, George Michael). *3. n.* A lady's *mingepiece.* *'I want your sex.'* (*I Want Your Sex* song lyric, George Michael).

sex act *1. n.* Versatile, vague tabloid term used to describe and denigrate specifically non-specific acts or *shenanigans* which have been "performed". Usually prefixed "vile", "lewd" or "sordid". *2. n.* Vile, lewd and sordid entertainments performed on a stage at Club Baghdad, Barcelona, to pluck an example out of thin air. *3. v.* To fake an *organism.*

sexaggerate *v.* To lie about the amount or quality of *the other* you are having.

sexaphone *n.* The horn section of a *bongo movie* score, typically accompanying a scene where Robin Askwith's *arse* is going up and down ten to the dozen between some *fat-titted* lovely's legs while a smiling Bob Todd is tripping up the stairs, wearing a bowler hat and carrying a bunch of flowers for his missus.

sex camel *n.* Her indoors. "After a hump or two she has the ability to go weeks or months without another". *'Have I introduced you to my sex camel, Lord Mayor?'*

sexcrement *n. medic.* The mix of bodily fluids that is passed through the *nipsy* after several sessions of *backdoor love. Santorum.*

sex drive *n.* A jolly motorised sojourn to a *dogging* site in one's shooting brake. *'I'm off for a sex drive, dear. Do you want anything bringing back while I'm out?' 'Ooh, can you get me Steve McFadden and Stan Collymore's autographs please, love?'*

sex fruit *n.* A baby. See also *fuck trophy.*

sexile *n.* A forlorn, lonely fellow in a bar, constantly checking his watch and desperately trying to make a half last all evening because his flatmate is *getting his end away.*

sex meringue *n.* The sticky, white, albuminious foam that's created after an over-aggressive bout of *stabbing the cat.*

sex offenders register *n.* Any mid-1970s copy of the

Radio Times.

sex pack *n.* Toned, ripped abdominal muscles as a result of lots of *how's your father.*

sex pat *n.* A chap of a certain age whose only reason for leaving the shores of Blighty to live abroad is his propensity for encounters with local ladies and/or *ladyboys* who are young enough to be his daughters and/or daughtersons.

sex pest buffet *n.* The male bodyspray section of the supermarket.

sex pipe *n.* A cock. *'Ow! I've got the end of me sex pipe caught in the dustbuster again, mum.'*

sex pistons *n.* The legs.

sex roses *n.* Romantic post-coital tissues left to harden into perfectly formed, albeit non-too-fragrant, flower petals on the bedside table.

sexual athlete's foot *n. medic. Happy rash.*

sexual harrisment *n.* Unwanted attention accompanied by heavy breathing and wobbleboard noises.

sexual outercourse *1. n.* Masturbation. *2. n. Dogging. 3. n. Dry humping.*

sex wee *1. n.* An ejaculation of *spongle. 2. n.* The *spongle* that is thusly *spoffed.*

SFW *1. abbrev.* Internet reassurance that the content being linked to is "Safe For Work". *2. abbrev.* Internet reassurance that the content being linked to is not safe for work. "Suitable For Wanking".

SFZ *abbrev.* The Southern Frigid Zone; everything south of the missus's belt which is a no-go area. Named after the similarly chilly geographical region located between the Antarctic Circle and the South Pole.

Shabba *1. n. rhym. slang.* Multiple acts of masturbation. From the name of the famous *puddlejumperphobic* Jamaican dancehall artiste Shabba Rultipleactsofmasturbation. *2. n. exclam.* Shouted catchphrase of former *Young Butcher of the Year* host George Lamb, during his thankfully short-lived stint as a morning radio presenter on BBC Radio 6Music.

shabby chick *n.* An older female who is still serviceable despite a somewhat distressed appearance.

shackered. *adj.* Exhausted. From shagged + knackered.

shackled *adj.* The condition of a man searching the house for *arse paper* with his trousers and underpants round his ankles. See *convict's shuffle, jailbreak, paperchase, penguin.*

shackles, arse like a bag of *sim. naut.* Charming maritime expression used to describe the *stern end* of a lady who has successfully *dodged* a significant quantity of *salad,* ie. One whose *back porch* resembles half a hundredweight of steel lumps in a sack.

Shackleton's shaft *n.* A dire state of genital hygiene resulting from a failure to clean one's *bellend* or change one's *undercrackers* every month as one is supposed to.

shadow on the wall *1. n.* Title of a song by Mike Oldfield off his *Crises* album, later covered by Swedish death metal band Arch Enemy. No, us neither. *2. n.* The result of a particularly violent *Kinder fart.*

Shadsworth six-seater *n.* An ambulance, named after the delightful area of Blackburn, where trips home after a night out are customarily taken in just such a conveyance. Also *Wetherspoon's taxi.*

shady milkman *n.* A seedy character who flogs his *man jam* down at the local *wham bank* on a daily basis.

shaft *1. v.* To *shag, screw. 2. n.* The mast on the *skin boat. 3. n. prop.* A black private dick that's a sex machine to all the chicks in town. Damn right. *4. v.* To screw someone over, in a financial sense. *'Ooh, you got shafted there.'*

shafterburn *n.* Painful friction-induced scorching of the *skinclad tube* caused by excessive and frantic *relaxation.*

shaftertaste *n.* After performing an act of oral horatio, that lingering flavour of foetid cheese that no amount of brushing and flossing will remove.

shaft sisters *n.* Two or more unrelated females who are concurrently getting a *rattling* off the same bloke, probably Boris Johnson. It usually is.

shag *1. v.* To copulate, to *fuck.* A once shocking term, now lame enough to be used by "right on" vicars and CBeebies presenters. *2. n.* A sexual encounter, a *screw. 3. n. US.* 1950s dance craze. *4. n.* Type of sea bird. *5. n.* Tobacco. *6. n.* Something to do with piles on carpets. *5. n.* A person with whom one is sexually involved. *'Have you met Roxxxy, vicar? She's my current shag.'*

shag bag *n.* A loose woman or *bike.*

shag bandy *n. medic.* Descriptive of a gait common amongst women who are *generous with their affections.*

shag dust *n. Fuck powder.* Make-up.

shag factory *n.* A joint that is heaving with *blit; knickerville, blart city.*

shaggability *n.* Measurement of how *prodworthy* a person is on an arbitrary, non-scientific scale.

shaggable *adj.* Worth a *one.*

shagged out *adj.* Exhausted, *jiggered, buggered, zonked, fucked.*

shagging a bike *sim.* Sex with an extremely thin

woman. *'These supermodels, nice faces, some of 'em, but get 'em in the fart sack and believe you me, it's like shagging a bike. I would imagine.'*

shagging a waterbed *sim.* To describe sex with an extremely *big-boned* woman. *Slapping the fat and riding the waves.*

shaggin' wagon *n.* A *passion wagon, fuck truck,* or *spambulance.*

shaggis *n.* A Scotsman's bloated, blotchy scrotum that is piped into the room on Burns Night.

shag lag *n.* Mild temporal disorientation brought on by an excess of sexual shenanigans.

shag monster *n.* A not necessarily ugly woman who has a voracious appetite for something to do with carpets, seagulls or pipe tobacco. A *nymphomentalist.*

shagnasty *n.* A *shag monster* who is also extremely ugly.

shagony aunt *n.* An Mrs Robinson-type older lady who gives comfort to suffering younger men. See also *punani granny, silver box, cougar, M&Ms.*

shag pile *1. n.* A subsidiary residence maintained principally as a venue for penetrative, extra-marital liaisons. A *fur trapper's cabin* or *stabbin' cabin.* *'Mr Plywood has been MP for Fulchester Sunnybrook since 1987, and was recently appointed Shadow Minister for Family Values. He lives in the constituency with his wife and three children, and has a small shag pile near the Palace of Westminster.'* *2. n.* The small heap of *Richards* typically left on a gentleman's mattress after he has *kicked* a particularly relaxed sexual partner's *back doors in.*

shag shed *n.* The boudoir.

shag slab *n.* Bed, *passion pit, cock block, anvil, fart sack, scratcher.*

shagstick *n.* An extremely thin – though nonetheless attractive – young lady.

shag tags *n.* Love bites, *hickies, suckers.*

shake and vac, do the *v.* To indulge in a cheeky toot of *bacon powder.*

shake a seven *v.* To *gamble and lose.*

shake a tit *v.* To defecate spooneristically.

shake hands with the French *v.* To push one's finger through the *bumwad* when wiping the *freckle.* To *breach the hull, push through.* From the similarity to the moment when the two bore drills met in the Channel Tunnel and the English bloke forced his hand through the thin divide to shake the hand of his Gallic counterpart. *'Did you wash your hands before kneading that dough, Nigella?'* *'Erm, no. But it's okay, it's not as if I've shaken hands with the French today.'*

shake hands with the mayor *1. v.* To greet the leading alderman in one's borough, perhaps while he is judging a sandcastle, snowman or large vegetable competition in a municipal park. Like they do. *2. v.* To manually interfere with your own *bits and bobs,* while paying scant regard to the medically documented risks that you run, *viz.* Going blind, insane, hairy-handed, bald and/or short.

shake hands with the wife's best friend *v.* To perform a shameful act of *self-pollution.*

shake hands with the Wookie *v.* Of those men blessed with eight-foot-long hairy *cocks* that make growling noises, to enjoy an *armbreaker.*

shake 'n' bake *1. n.* Some sort of proprietary breadcrumb-based coating for pork or chicken. *2. n.* The peculiar physiological phenomenon whereby a person who is on a jog or run feels the sudden, inexplicable need to *lay a cable.* *'Born on this day: Bob Guccione, dead US bongo magnate, 1930; Bernard Hill, late Yosser Hughes actor and Baxter's Beetroot Chutneys and Sauces ad voiceover man, 1944; Paula Radcliffe, Olympic Marathon-running shake 'n' bake champion, 1973.'*

shake shifter *n.* The first pint of the day. *'Good morning and welcome aboard flight BA 103 from Oslo. The captain's had a shake shifter, so we'll shortly be proceeding to the runway to commence our take-off.'*

shakes on a plane *n.* Joining the *mile I club.* Making like a *Chinese helicopter pilot* in an aeroplane toilet.

shake the bishop's hand *v.* To have a *piss,* as opposed to sticking your hand through a hole in the lavatory wall *and wanking* him off.

shake the lettuce *v.* Of females, to *pee* and give the *beef curtains* a quick tumble dry afterwards.

shake the snake *v.* Male equivalent of *shake the lettuce,* the object being to dislodge any post-*wazz forget-me-nots* before returning the *schlong* to the *shreddies.*

shaking hands with the unemployed *n.* Having *one off the wrist, rubbing one out* during a *doley's blackout.*

shaking like a flatpack wardrobe *sim.* Descriptive of the female equivalent of the *vinegar strokes.*

shaking like a shitting dog *sim.* A bad attack of *barrel fever* after a night on the *sauce.*

shaky, the *n.* Involuntary leg spasms achieved when *pulling the head off it* in the shower. At the point of the *vinegar strokes,* the legs perform in a similar manner to those of the eighties Fulchester Rovers striker and occasional pop musician.

shame glaze *n.* The shimmering crystalline sheen of ignominious varnish left upon one's person following an act of *self harm. Dutch polish.*

shammocks *n.* The low-slung jeans worn by youths,

that from the rear look like they said a *fond farewell to yesterday's sausages* without first taking the precaution of removing them first. From shit + hammocks.

shammy batter *n.* KY jelly. Also *phoney batter, I can't believe it's not batter, granny batter, fuck butter, pork pie jelly*. 'TERRY: Eurgh! June, this margarine tastes horrible. JUNE: That's not margarine, Terry. It's Great Aunt Lucy's tub of shammy batter.' (script of *Terry & June*, BBC TV, February 1832).

shampoo *n.* A pretend *shit*. A toilet break taken for the sole purpose of avoiding an unpleasant task. *'Where's Dave? I thought I told him to take the bins out.' 'I think he's gone to the bogs for a shampoo.'*

shampoo the rug *v.* To squirt one's *heir tonic* onto a *mapatasi*. Then rinse and repeat.

sham-rock *n.* Descriptive of a man who, despite talking the talk, couldn't knock the head off a half of shandy. *'Today's Birthdays: Jean Picard, French astronomer, 1620; Ernest Hemingway, Nobel Prize-winning American author, 1899; Isaac Stern, Ukrainian violin virtuoso, 1920; Ross Kemp, balding sham-rock Fruit & Fibre ad actor, 1964.'*

sham 69 *1. n.* Mid- to late-1970s punk band, who hailed from Hersham, Surrey, and were responsible for such songs as *If the Kids Are United, Angels With Dirty Faces* and *Hurry Up, Harry*. *2. n.* An episode of *soixante-neuf* in which one or both participants display insufficient enthusiasm.

Shamu *n.* An overly acrobatic *dreadnought* that splashes the spectating testicles. From the performing whale of the same name that lives (or lived) simultaneously in Florida, California and Texas. And occasionally manages (or managed) to take a bite out of its handlers.

shanarak *n.* A shamefully *shite* anorak. *'Look, Roy. I've bought you a shanarak off the indoor market. It's much nicer than the ones that all the other kids are wearing.'*

shandy andy *n.* A *jizzmop*.

shandydextrous *adj.* To be blessed with the ability to give one's *monkey* an equally vicious *spanking* with either hand.

shandygram *n.* A luridly worded SMS message, typically texted to a female acquaintance with the left hand after one has taken onboard a plethora of *love potion*. In 2004, the *News of the World* published several *shandygrams*, purported to have been sent to Channel 5 pig-*wanker* Rebecca Loos by simpleton billionaire ex-free kick merchant David Beckham.

shandylion *n.* A usually meek and quiet fellow who, upon imbibing any amount of alcohol, transmogrifies into a roaring king of the jungle. Also

drambo, two can Van Damme, half pint Harry, tinny mallet, two pint Tyson or *two pot screamer.*

shandy sunbed *n.* A bench in a park or a precinct. The *tramp grill.*

shandy tan *n.* The ruddy-red complexion sported by *professional outdoorsmen* after they have spent too long snoozing on *Frosty Jack's barbecue.*

shandy tickler *n.* One who has foolishly decided to *bang one out* while *Brahms & pissed.*

Shane *n.* A once grubby, rowdy mate who has formed a new relationship and simultaneously undergone a complete makeover of both appearance and behaviour. From late Australian cricketer Shane Warne, who apparently went all metrosexual when he started *banging* that Liz Hurley.

Shane McGowan's toothbrush, it looked like *sim.* Descriptive of a particularly heavily soiled *bogbrush* of the sort typically found in a bookies' toilet.

shaneurysm *n. medic.* Sequelae of profound constipation; a burst brain caused by pushing too hard. *'Elvis was found on the floor of the bathroom at Graceland, having succumbed to a shaneurysm some time in the early hours.'*

Shanghai/Shanghai finish *1. n.* In the world of darts, triple twenty; twenty; double top. *'I'll never forget the Shanghai finish I got at the Lakeside Country Club, Frimley Green.'* *2. n.* In the world of romance, *arse; fanny; double top (tits)*. *'I'll never forget the Shanghai finish I got in a layby near the Forth Road Bridge.'* *3. n.* Of a *Frankie Vaughan* presentation, having a woman simultaneously with a *prick* in all three orifices, *viz.* Mouth, *fanny,* and *bum.* See also *gastight, holy trinity.*

shank *n.* A multi-tasking lavatory adventure. From shit + wank.

Shanks Bay *n.* The natural habitat of the toilet duck and the *brown trout*. A natural harbour, flowing into the *China Sea,* which is noted for its high concentrations of effluent.

shanny *1. n.* A type of fish, specifically the smooth blenny. *2. n.* Appropriately enough, a *shaven haven.* From shaved + fanny.

shanty *1. n.* A crudely constructed house made of scrap wood. From £350,000. *2. n.* A sailor's work song, possibly involving *fucking* a mermaid. *3. n.* A fouled *undercracker*. From Shit + Panty.

shapeshifter *1. n.* A seven-foot-tall reptilian member of the royal family and/or Freemasons. *2. n.* A *dump* so large that it leaves the stomach visibly flatter.

share a tent *euph.* To be *on safari. 'Didn't you hear? (name removed on legal advice) off (programme* *removed on legal advice) used to share a tent with Princess (name removed on legal advice).'*

shark *v.* To go on the *pull*, using aggressive, sly or cunning tactics.

shark's arse, tight as a *1. sim.* Thrifty, frugal. Often used, offensively, in relation to Yorkshire folk who *wouldn't give you the steam off their turds. Also as tight as a bullfighter's pants; tighter than a teenage wanker's curtains. 2. sim.* Of a lady's *blurtch*, somewhat cramped. Also *tighter than a worm's belt; tighter than a mouse's waistcoat.*

shark's fin *n.* The profile of a neighbour's proud *beetle bonnet* viewed through a tight bikini bottom while sunbathing on the beach. *Pigeon's chest, tump, monkey's forehead.*

shark's mouth *n.* A somewhat unsettling term for a gentleman's urinal.

shark's nose *n.* A *clematis* when it is in an advanced state of arousal, to the extent that it would scare away all but the bravest *muffdivers.*

sharks sniffing, have the *euph.* Of a lady, afflicted with her monthly courses. *"'My darling, at last we are alone,'' murmured Heathcliffe, as he took Cathy in his arms. "I cannot wait a moment longer. I must have you now." "Sorry, love, I've got the sharks sniffing,''' she replied.'* (from *Wuthering Heights* by Tracey Brontë).

shark week *n.* That quarter of each month when there is "blood in the water". Also *rag week, blob week, rollover week, gypsy week, blow job week* and *cricket week.*

Sharon sixteen stone *n.* A *bird* who crosses her legs when she isn't wearing any knickers and you still can't see anything. See also *J-lower.*

shar-pei's nose *euph.* The appearance of an exotic, pedigree fighting *clopper* with numerous rolls of sagging flesh surrounding a *badly packed kebab.*

sharpen the morning spear *v.* To take advantage of your *motorcycle kickstand* by having a sneaky *tug* at *sparrowfart.*

sharp intake of breadth *phr.* A phenomenon prevalent amongst rotund middle-aged men, the art of sucking in the *beergut* when spying an attractive member of the opposite sex.

shart *v.* To *pass wind* with an unexpected non-gaseous component. To *follow through.*

shartburn *n. medic.* Internal charring of the *nipsy* after *gambling and losing* on a spicy *bonus ball.*

shartenfreude *n. Germ.* Taking pleasure in the certainty that someone who has been making you miserable with their flatulence has just pushed too hard and *followed through.*

shartex *n.* Textured public convenience wall render, or the unfortunate result of a personal

catastrophe, being licked off the wall by the patient's Alsatian.

shartisan *adj.* Descriptive of poor quality, over-priced goods that are manufactured locally by a heavily bearded man.

shartwork *1. n.* Expressionistic aesthetic oeuvre that resembles a load of *shit. 2. n.* Describing an aesthetically challenging load of *foulage*, possibly within one's underwear. *'Gavin dear, you've got shartwork all over your underkeks.' 'Yeah, I got a bit bothered defending meself in front of the Education Select Committee again, innit.'*

shaternity leave *n.* A statutory period of rest and recuperation after the difficult birth of a *mudchild*, during which one is not required to do any work. *'I'm afraid the doctor can't see you now. She's on shaternity leave.'*

shatinee *n.* A *sit-down performance* enjoyed in the afternoon or early evening.

shatin underwear *n.* The amusingly soiled *undercrackers* found up back alleys, in bushes in Hereford, and stuffed through building society letterboxes on Sunday mornings.

shatisfaction *n.* That unequalled feeling of relief and joy after *dropping* at least one minibus load of *kids off at the pool*, possibly following a nail-biting *photo finish.*

shatkins *n.* Rapid, astonishingly effective diet based on the somewhat controversial theory that the most effective way to lose weight is to acquire a bacterial stomach infection by the intake of meat only, especially 2am burger bar fayre. *'Good grief, you've lost weight since yesterday.' 'Yes, six stones. I've been on the shatkins.'*

shatmosphere *n.* A thick, toxic, colourless and pungently malodourous faecal fog that would arguably not enhance Russ Abbott's enjoyment of a social gathering.

shat nav *1. n.* The use of cutting-edge automotive GPS technology in order to locate a fast food restaurant where one can *go for a McShit. 2. n.* On the approach to the toilet, that moment when the *Simon Cowells* suddenly seize control of the situation.

shatoll *n.* An emergent isle of *foulage* protruding through the idyllic, sun-swept waters of the *crapper.* A *misty mountain top.*

shat on from a height *adj.* Badly exploited, humiliated, let down.

shatsy *n.* The poor sap in a crowded room who finds himself unfairly taking the blame for a rancid *guff.* A term that was first used by Lee Harvey Oswald as he was escorted out of the Rupali Restaurant (formerly the Curry Capital),

Bigg Market, Newcastle upon Tyne on November 22nd 1963.

shatthissen keks *n. slang. S. Yorks.* The fashion followed by *neds, scratters* and other denizens of the urban underclasses, whereby trousers are slung down around the *ringpiece*, giving the impression they are weighed down by *foulage. Shammocks. 'Pull 'em up, son. Tha's got shatthissen keks theer.'* (Michael Parkinson, introducing rapper 50 Cent at the Variety Club Showbiz Awards, 2009).

shattiato *n.* First double-strength coffee of the day that *pulls the pin on the arse grenade.*

shattoo *n.* A tattoo on the leg that, when exposed during good weather, looks from a distance as if the victim has had an inadvertent *Denis Howell movement.*

shat trick *n.* The professional goal of the salaried worker, *ie.* Three *Mr Browns* in one working day.

shave a horse *v.* To have a *piss, take a leak, turn your bike around, see a man about a dog.*

shaven haven *n.* A bald *monkey's forehead,* a shot-blasted *beetle bonnet.*

Shawshank *1. n.* A *number two* taken while flushing the *Rick Witter,* often to avoid embarrassment in a public restroom, much as the eponymous movie's protagonist Andy Dufresne uses a thunderstorm as cover for his own escape down a filthy, *shite*-filled pipe. Also *camouflush, covering fire. 2. n.* A *non-wiper.* From the moment in the eponymous movie where Andy Dufresne crawls through a river of convicts' *number twos* and comes out nipping clean on the other side.

SHAW/shaw effect *phr. acronym.* The unforgettable first impression an incredibly beautiful lady can make; having such a romantic effect on a gentleman as to make him go "Straight Home And Wank".

Shearer's Island *n.* That increasingly isolated patch of hair on the front of a balding chap's head. Named after now baldy former footballer Alan, who fought an increasingly desperate battle to retain a minuscule archipelago of *Barnet* on his *noggin* for many years. Neil Tennant out of the Pet Shop Boys for many years had one of the most impressive *Shearer's Islands* in Britain.

she-bass *n.* The fishy, female equivalent of *he-dam.*

she-bay *n.* Online retailing that is responsible for filling your dwelling with handbags, shoes, make-up, hairdryers, soft furnishings, food supplements and exercise bikes whilst you are out at work.

she can give it back to me as small as she likes *exclam.* Said by a sexist fellow in bawdy appreciation of a *trollop* that he would ideally like to *slip*

a length to.

she could shit on my chest and slap it with a cricket bat *exclam.* A romantic young man's declaration of his deep, undying love for the new girl in his life. *'Did my heart love 'till now? Forswear its sight. For I never saw true beauty 'till this night. 'Tis Juliet, and if she's not my true love I wouldst eat my hat. She could shit on my chest and slap it with a cricket bat.'* (from *Romeo and Juliet* by William Shakespeare).

shecycling *n.* Of a man, passing on a piece of moderately costly sports equipment (bike, paddleboard, fishing rod *etc.*) to his better half in order to justify a more expensive upgrade.

shed *n.* A large, promiscuous woman. Somewhere to stick *tools* and keep the lawnmower.

shedded *adj.* Trousered, cattled, wankered.

shedphones *n.* The medical condition that renders a married man unable to hear his wife's admonishments when he is at the bottom of the garden, happily fettling.

sheep dog trials *n. medic. rhym. slang.* Carpet tiles. *'I'm sorry to tell you that these are the worst sheep dog trials I have ever seen. I'm afraid that in my professional opinion, you have less than six weeks to live. Mind you, I'm a milkman not a doctor, so what do I know?'*

sheeps' cunts, eyes like *n. 'Appen my next guest is one of Britain's best loved poets, as well known for the stylistic variety of his prodigous output as for the fact that he has eyes like sheeps' cunts. A big Parkinson welcome, then, for WH Auden.'*

sheep's heart on a Vim tin *sim. Scots.* Descriptive of a *hard-on* to be proud of. A baby's arm holding an apple.

sheep sitting *adj.* On the blob, dropping clots.

sheeps' twats, eyes like *sim. medic.* The appearance of the eyes in the morning after a night on the sauce. Or, for that matter, the appearance of the eyes in the afternoon after a morning on the sauce. Also *eyes like sheeps' cunts, piss holes in the snow, David Davis eyes. 'Christ, Judy. You can't go on looking like that. You've got sheep's twats.'*

sheet music *n.* Aeolian emanations from beneath the covers as two lovers semi-consciously serenade each other with their *wind sections.* Usually performed at the break of day following a night *on the pop.*

sheezer *n.* A woman who exhibits a disproportionate number of male traits in her everyday behaviour, *eg.* Drinking beer, watching football, excessive masturbation, shagging *birds,* smoking a pipe. A *ladette.*

Sheffield hammer *n.* A rolled-up newspaper used as an *ad hoc* cudgel in a *pagga,* a weapon which can handily be unrolled before the *scuffers* arrive.

she-gulling *n.* The popular post-coital act whereby the lady scoops the *man fat* from out her *blurtch* and flings it back into her paramour's face.

sheik of saggy old labia *n.* A *quim fancier* whose reputation goes before him.

Sheila feeler *n.* An Antipodean *lady golfer.*

Sheila's wheels *n.* The *clockweights* of a *trolley dolly* who is *big down under.*

shejaculate *n.* The *love relish* that some women supposedly fire from their *fur burgers* when they suffer an organism.

shelf-employed *adj.* Currently seeking work.

shelfie *n.* A picture taken of one's *stool* to share with one's Facebook friends and Twitter followers. *'Here's today's shelfie. Blimey, last night's mixed grill with black pudding took some shifting. I feel a stone lighter! Join me, @Eamonnholmes, from 6am on #GBNews.'*

shelf restraint *n.* The admirable willpower which must be summoned by a fellow in order to resist the temptation to treat himself to a nice new *niff mag* at the newsagent. *'For God's sake Mr Larkin, show some shelf restraint. That ceiling's going to come through if you try to put any more cunt-books in the attic.'*

shelling *n.* Yet another supremely unlikely sounding practice, most probably cooked up in the fevered imagination of a popular tabloid columnist, which involves the removal of a snail from its shell and the insertion of said evicted mollusc into a *competent ironer's nipsy* in order that he can savour the wriggling sensation. Don't knock it till you've tried it.

Shelob's lair *sim.* Condition brought on by unsuccessful wiping, leaving the *nipsy* covered in a steely web of matted hair and *feeshus.* *'"Mr Frodo!" cried Sam. "You look uncomfortable. Are your nauticles playing up? Here's my cloak to sit upon." "No, Sam," replied Baggins. "I haven't had a wash since Rivendell and my arse is like the entrance to Shelob's lair."'* (from *The Lord of the Ringpieces* by JRR Tolkein).

shelter belter *n.* A damsel who specialises in *having it off* at bus stops.

she may be up on blocks but the boot's always open *phr.* Offensively sexist suggestion made by a boorish male to his *blue-balled* mate whose *tart* is *boiling beetroots.*

shenis *n.* What you need in order to make the most of a *mangina.*

Shepherd Neame *n.* A more extreme version of a *Kronenberg, viz.* A female who looks youthfully pulchritudinous from the back and senescently decrepit from the front. A reference to the eponymous brewer's "1698" ale.

shepherd's pie *n.* A main course in the *dirt oven;* a layer of hot brown *bum-mince,* topped with a fluffy white "mash" of *arsewipe* and finished off with a yellow "crust" of *Tweedledee.*

sherbet phantom *n.* A person responsible for traces of *Columbian marching powder* left on *bogs,* twenty pound notes and CBBC studio fittings.

Shergar, do a *v.* To mysteriously disappear during a night out, only to turn up later in a kebab shop.

sheriffs are coming, the *1. n.* Daytime BBC1 television programme about the work of High Court enforcers. Without having seen it, you'd assume it's probably quite a lot like *Can't Pay? We'll Take it Away* or *It's the Bailiffs. 2. exclam.* A declaration that one is in imminent need of a *burglar's dollop. 'Prime Minister, do you have a couple of moments to answer a few questions about your policies?' 'No, I'm afraid I have to dash to the shit pit. The sheriffs are coming.'*

Sherman *n. rhym. slang.* A *tug.* From Sherman tank = wank.

sherry monocle *n.* Upper class equivalent of *beer goggles. 'I know she's no oil painting, old boy, but I had my sherry monocle on, what what.'*

sherry shawl *n.* A metaphorical garment donned by an older lady to keep warm on the walk home from her local. See also *bacardigan.*

she's a bit bang! knock knock *exclam.* Humorous phrase used to describe a lady with a substantial *bow frontage.* Descriptive of a woman caller whose *generous provisions* inevitably make contact with the front door before her knuckles do.

shethane *n.* The gaseous content of a delightfully feminine *dropped gut.*

Shetland *n.* A *Tom tit* of little consequence. From the fact that it is, like the miniature horses famously drawn by the late Norman Thelwell, a "tiny *pony*".

Shetland fudge *n.* Stiff, caramel-coloured *feeshus* which comes in a Tartan tin and makes an ideal gift for an elderly relative.

Shetland pony and trap *n.* An under-sized *feeshus.*

Shetland pony's cock, sticks out like a *sim.* Useful expression descriptive of something which is conspicuously obvious. From the fact that the *blood sausages* of the popular miniature horses are noticeably sizeable in comparison to their diminutive stature. *'It's no good, Johnny. We're going to have to lose the syrup. It sticks out like a Shetland pony's cock under the studio lights.'*

Shetland rabbit, hung like a *sim.* Noticeably under-endowed in the *trouser department.* Also *hung* *like a Chinese mouse, hung like the Rt Hon Jack Straw MP.*

she-tox *n.* A period when a married gentleman's spouse is away, during which he cleanses his system of her wholesome influences. A welcome relapse into bachelorhood ways of drinking, *wanking* and curry-eating himself daft. A *total wifeout*.

shiatus *n.* The interval, when ensconced on the *khazi*, between crowning and the splash. *'Phew! I made it to the crapper in time, but the shiatus kicked in and it was a good thirty seconds before I could breathe again.' 'That's great, Dave. Now, let's see which Chaser you'll be playing.'*

shick *v.* To defecate and vomit at the same time, following a cracking night on the ale. From shit + sick.

shift *v.* To *bang, poke, screw.*

shift a round bale *1. v.* On a farm, to transport one of them big bundles of hay, usually tightly wrapped in black or white polythene, at 4mph during rush hour so as to cause the maximum annoyance to other road users. *2. v.* To *forklift* a lass *with a lovely personality* during *bush hour*, especially if she is wearing an ill-advisedly skintight black or white outfit.

shifting cement *n.* A fatiguing act of *one-handed filthy concrete* mixing. *'Anyone seen Dave with my copy of National Geographic?' 'Yeah, he's shifting cement with it in the crappers.'*

shifting furniture *euph.* To produce a loud, scraping *horse & cart* which sounds like people moving heavy objects around in the flat upstairs. *'Eat your lunch at the Curry Capital, Bigg Market, Newcastle upon Tyne (now closed) and I, the late Lord Abdul Latif of Harpole, personally guarantee that you'll be shifting furniture by teatime.'*

shift, put in a *v.* To have sexual intercourse with a partner when one can't really be *arsed*. *'What's up, George? Why the long face?' 'Oh, it's me and the missus's 34th wedding anniversary. She'll be expecting me to go home and put in a shift tonight.'*

shiggle *v.* To follow through while laughing. From shit + giggle. *'You watching ITV? I'm sure Osborne just shiggled when they announced the exit poll.'*

shight-seeing *n.* Enjoying a whistle-stop tour of a provincial northern town.

shilencer *1. n.* The piece of folded *bumwad* that is placed into the toilet before taking a massive *dump* when in a public convenience or while sharing a hotel room, in order to muffle the embarrassing splashdown of a *copper bolt* as it enters the water. From *shite* + silencer. *Pap baffle, crash mat, dump proof course. 2. n.* Device used by James Bond to deaden the noise when firing his Walther PPK, but only in the films in which he was played by Sean Connery.

shims *n.* Ladyboys, flippers. LGBLTs.

shinty *adj.* The aroma often found in campsite toilets in the morning when the fragrance of fresh morning *shit* mingles alluringly with that of the fresh mint toothpaste of people brushing their teeth.

Shipman, to do a *v.* To *inject* a lady much older than oneself. *Granny banging, biddy fiddling.*

shipyard hot *adj.* Descriptive of the only woman in a *cock-heavy* facility, who by default seems to look super hot and is the subject of every worker's fantasies during the day, but outside that environment is average at best.

shirt fly *n.* A "yes man". One who is always up the gaffer's *arse*. A *fart-sucker, brown noser* or *Penfold*.

shirtful *n.* A well-stocked *rack*. *'My, what a shirtful. You've got the job.' 'Thank-you Mr Berlusconi.'*

shirt lifter *n.* A tall man employed in a clothing shop to place stock on high shelves.

shirtlifter's arms *n.* Any pub frequented by *style conscious* gentlemen.

shirtos liftos *n. Span.* A jumper of Spanish puddles, if they have puddles in Spain.

shirt potatoes *n. Tits, melons, top bollocks, fat rascals, milky swingers.* Those glands that fill a blouse.

shirt potato salad *n.* A healthy, *tossed* mixture of *chest spuds* and *man mayonnaise*. A disarranged *solicitor's tie.*

shirt raiser *n.* A mighty zephyr from the *brass eye*. An enormous, *syrup*-floating *Bakewell*.

shirt snifter *n.* Of a normally red-blooded male, a brief, temporary foray into a previously unknown world of interior design, male grooming products or cookery.

shirt turnips *n.* Small, yet upwardly perky breasts. *Chest swedes, Sara Cox's orange pippins.*

shisotonic *adj.* Descriptive of some "sports drink" manufactured in Bulgaria that, when consumed in quantity, ensures you can run like *fuck*, especially to the *Rick Witter.*

shit *1. v.* To *shit, defecate, sink the Bismarck, build a log cabin, crimp one off, light a bum cigar. 2. n.* Crap, excrement, stools, assorted faecal matter. *3. n.* Git, sod, get, a *shitty* person, usually "little". *4. adj.* Crap, useless. *'Shit weather for this time of year, eh, vicar?' 5. exclam.* Oh dear.

shit a brick *1. interj.* A foul-mouthed exclamation of surprise. *2. v.* To be scared, to *papper* one's *trolleys. 3. v.* To be delivered of a frankly Brobdingnagian *mudchild.*

shit, all the *phr.* See *all the shit*. No, just kidding.

The full range of extra condiments, seasonings, and what-have-you added to a comestible item purchased from a 2am *kebabulance* by a *wankered* fellow. From the scene in the Bravo Channel's hard-hitting *Booze Britain* documentary series, in which an incoherent *Friday foal* in Hartlepool or Doncaster or somewhere was asked whether he wanted sauce or onions on his purchase and replied: "Oh aye, all the shit", while simultaneously losing his balance and falling sideways into the side of the burger van.

shit ambulance *n.* A municipal bin wagon, local authority dustcart *etc.*, making its way down the road with its yellow lights flashing.

shitamin *n.* Any form of over-the-counter laxative that stimulates the digestive tract walls or softens the surface tension of one's *Peter O'Tooles* in order to make them easier to pass. *'Nanny, can you get me some shitamins, please? Last evening's supper of savoury forcemeats followed by game pie with poached darioles of rabbit isn't sitting well on my family seat.' 'Certainly, master Jacob. Now let's get you out of that wet nightshirt before Helena eats all your Coco Pops.'*

shitamins *n.* Kebab-shop nutrients that ensure you enjoy a vigorously healthy morning movement just before you get up.

shit an angry squid *euph.* To pass a less-than-solid *Andrew.*

shit-and-run *1. n.* Fleeing from the scene of a beer and curry-fuelled *pile-up* in a public *biscuit wrapper* without first alerting the cleaning attendant on duty. *2. v.* To drop in on a friend or relative, on the pretence of seeing them, when in fact you just want to use their *bog* before making your excuses and leaving.

shitanium *n.* Something pretending to be better than it is, particularly plastic pretending to be metal. The opposite of *unobtainium*, the material you want but which doesn't exist, *shitanium* is a material that is readily available but that you want less than scabies. *'Hey Steve, I'm jealous of the gear knob in your Corsa.' 'Don't be, Dave. It's made of shitanium.'*

shitarette *n.* The first cigarette of the day, which wakes up your *Camillas*. A *player's number two*, *arse fuse.*

shitbat *n.* A small black bag of *dog toffee* that resembles a sleeping pipistrelle hanging off a tree.

shit bit *n.* What mainstream American comedy writers call that *yoff*-inducing little moral homily, expository sermon or hortatory discourse they are contractually obliged to include towards the end

of each script.

shitbit *n.* Non-branded wrist-worn exercise monitor typically found for sale out of a suitcase or on a market stall, notable for the extraordinarily small font utilised on its instruction leaflet.

shitbits *n.* Small pieces of *feeshus*-clad *bumwad*, the remnants of vigorous wiping, which have a habit of turning up in a variety of places, *eg.* On the toilet seat, in one's underwear, tastefully garnishing Piers Morgan's soup.

shitboy *n. Northumb.* Term of abuse for one engaged in menial employment. *'How, shitboy! Big Mac and chips, son!'*

shit brick house, built like a *sim.* Said of one who is not necessarily in the best physical shape. *'You seen that Shane MacGowan recently? He's built like a shit brick house.'*

shit bumpers *n.* Polite euphemism for the b*ttocks. *'Phwooar! That Serena Williams has got some rare old shit bumpers on her, eh Cliff?'*

shit butties, eat *v. euph.* To have bad breath, halitosis. *'I'd stay clear of Ted today, lads. He's been eating shit butties again.'*

shitch *n.* An annoying itch which is so far up your *bottle* that the only way to scratch it is to pass a *Thora* down past it.

shit chips *n.* The result of pushing a *turd* through the drain with your toes whilst in the shower.

shit chisel *n.* A stout tool used when *mining for gold* in *kak canyon.*

shitchy *adj.* How you might describe your *ringpiece* if you don't follow a sufficiently rigorous wiping regimen.

shitcloud *n.* A common meteorological phenomenon involving a silent movement of wind and a strong smell of bad eggs. See *SBD, beefy eggo.*

shitcoin *n. Bogroll.* The latest currency.

shitcom *n.* A lamentable situation comedy, such as that *Mrs Brown's Boys* or *Threads.*

shitcrumb *n.* A worthless item. *'So, let's see what auctioneer Philip Serrell has to say about the shitcrumbs that the tasteless bellends on the red team have bought.'*

shit diamonds *v.* The end result when one is desperate for a *number two*, but is nevertheless denied access to the *chod bin*, so that one's *feeshus* get packed tightly into the *bomb-bay. 'Hurry up in there, your holiness. I'm shitting diamonds out here.'*

shit down *1. n.* A trip to the works toilet with the sole intention of taking the weight off your feet, checking your phone *etc. 'Claude, hold the fort here for a bit, will you? I'm off for a shit down.' 2. v.* To kill two birds with one stone, *viz.* To take the weight off one's feet after a hard day's work while simultaneously *dropping a length of dirty spine.*

shit-down protest *euph.* Act of protest whereby a radicalised *tod* refuses to budge from the *cludgie pan*, even after several flushes.

shite *n. & v.* See shit.

shite alight *n.* A doorstep incendiary; a *Thora* in a burning paper bag, used as an offensive-smelling weapon against one's neighbour's slippers. *Pyropastie.*

shit-eating grin *n.* Exaggerated, smug, self-satisfied smile as worn by the likes of Noel Edmonds and Nigel Farage.

shite at the end of the tunnel *phr.* Obstruction encountered when travelling on the *Bakerloo line. One in the chutney locker.*

shitebulb *n.* A thoroughly disapppointing source of luminescence of the sort greatly prized by world-saving types for their eco-friendly properties. *'Have you noticed, love? I've put a shitebulb in at the top of the cellar steps.' 'Who said that? Aargh, I've fell down the stairs and broken my neck.' 'Who said that?'*

shite bulb moment *n.* A sudden notion that it would be a good idea to get out of bed and *feed the toilet.*

shitecap *n.* A swift *arse emptier*, just before bedtime. Handily.

shitecap *n.* A well-deserved *poo* just before bedtime.

shitegeist *n.* Collective consciousness or shared feeling that the world is *crap.*

shite-headed *adj.* A feeling of being ill after *picking up a virus* during a night *out on the town.* Symptoms may include headache/dizziness, upset stomach and loose movements.

shite house *1. n.* A poorly constructed abode. *2. n.* A well-constructed brick lavatory building with a door which is prone to oscillate percussively at times of velocitous atmospheric turbulence. *3. n.* The smallest room.

shitelight *n.* The big light that goes on in the bathroom when having a *sit down toilet adventure*, even on the sunniest days, due to its being wired to the same switch as the extractor fan.

shitemare *n.* A dream so scary it makes you *papper* your *fart sack.*

shitemove *n.* The impulse to sell up and move house rather than try to shift a *King Kong's finger* that is blocking the *khazi.*

shitened up *phr.* Of the weather, having taken a turn for the worse. *'It was sunny when we set off, but once we got into Wales it really shitened up.'*

shiten the mood *v.* To do the polar opposite of lightening the mood; to deliberately turn a con-

versation sour for one's own amusement. *'Way to shiten the mood your holiness. They fuckin' love it when you mention the war.'*

shite-off *n.* Any event, or indeed entire day, that is completely ruined by a miscalculated and entirely-liquid *trouser cough.* And it certainly would be.

shiter *n.* Arse, *kak cannon.* The *Ronson lighter.* That which *shites.*

shiter's block *n.* A codeine-related *Enoch* obstruction. *'How's it going, Mr Hemingway?' 'I've got shiter's block, so I think I might go and shoot meself.'*

shitesabre *n.* Mythical weapon used by wishful thinking young males to fight off hordes of adoring ladies on a night out. An updated version of the *shitty stick.*

shiteseeing *n.* While on holiday, being forced by the missus to visit museums, historic buildings and other places of interest when you should be getting *leathered* at the all-inclusive hotel you have already fucking paid for.

shite that killed Elvis, boaby like the *sim. Scots.* A rock hard big *cock. 'Maw! Maw! Come quick! Maggie's suckin' oaf the milkman an' he's got a boaby like the shite that killed Elvis!'*

shit-faced *n.* Arseholed, intoxicated, *wankered. Pissed as a bishop.*

shit fizz *n.* That heady cocktail of imodium and champagne drunk in the airport lounge at the end of a bibulous business trip to Indonesia.

shit-for-brainer *n.* A notion that is obviously stupid. *'Yes, I weighed up the options and that's how I voted. To me it was an absolute shit-for-brainer.'*

shit-for-brains *n.* One who is intellectually challenged. A *joskin, fuckwit, dolt.* Whoever designed the traffic system for getting in and out of the short-stay car park at Newcastle Central Station.

shit for purpose *adj.* When barely adequate is adequate. For example, a 23-year-old Perodua Nippa is no great *fanny magnet*, but if it gets you to Morrisons and back without catching fire, being stolen or more than one wheel falling off, it can be deemed *shit for purpose. Satiscraptory.*

shit Forsyth's eyes *v.* To suffer extreme constipation resulting in the expulsion of little more than a couple of tiny, hard *rabbit tods. 'Didn't she do well? She's shitted Forsyth's eyes.'*

shit glitter *n.* Dusting of faecal matter over the back of the toilet seat as a result of over-vigorous wiping.

shitgun! *exclam.* What you must be the first to say in order to bagsy the *biscuit wrapper* when you get home after a long drive.

shit house *n.* See *shite house.*

shithouse and Rastrick *euph.* A long and melodious series of parps, honks and toots from the *brass section.*

shithouse door on a trawler, stinks like the *sim.* Descriptive of a woman whose personal hygiene regimen may leave something to be desired. Also *stinks like the fishmonger's armpit.*

shithouse shin pad *n. nav.* A concealed *grumble mag* wrapped around a sailor's leg under his sock as he makes his way to the HMS Ark Royal *crappers* to *fire the one o'clock gun.*

shitificate *n.* Meaningless award that is literally not worth the *fucking* paper it is written on, *eg.* 5m swimming badge, Employee of the Month, Upper Second Class Honours in the School of Literae Humaniore at Oxford *etc.*

shit in a doorway, stand out like a *sim.* '"What do you think of my new trousers, Jeeves?" I expostulated. "These knee-length houndstooth twill bags are all the go at the Drones Club this season, you know. I thought I'd wear them for Tuppy Glossop's wake tomorrow, but I'm wondering if they might not be a little ostentatious for such a sombre bash." "Ostentatious isn't, if you'll excuse me for saying so, sir, the word," opined the perspicacious manservant. "If you wear them kecks for a funeral, I can guarantee that you'll stand out like a shit in a doorway."' (from *I Was Only Following Orders, Jeeves* by PG Wodehouse).

shitingale *n.* One who breaks into song while *dropping a length of dirty spine,* usually in order to shield their audience from the slightly less tuneful cacophony being produced by their *turtle guillotine.*

shit in my hair! *exclam.* An exclamation of surprise similar to "Oh my days!" or "I'll go to the foot of our stairs!"

shit in the pool *v.* To commit a petty *faux pas, eg.* Passing the port to the right, eating peas with a fork, tickling the King's *knackers* during your investiture *etc.*

shit in the Queen's handbag, it would be easier to *sim.* A measure of the difficulty of a task. *'Removing yourself from Facebook is theoretically possible, but to be frank, it would be easier to shit in the Queen's handbag.'*

shititch *n. medic.* Brass eye irritation suffered by one who has exited the *cludgy* without wiping properly. An attack of *arse wasps* or *wire spiders.* From shit + itch. *'Mr Glitter, will you please stand still while we take aim?' 'Sorry mate, only I had a dodgy plate of Tai Hea Ngam Chua for my final*

meal and then when I went off to drop me shopping there was no paper in the crapper. I've got terrible shititch here, I tell you.'

shit kiss *n.* A small, star-shaped brown mark left on the chin of a none-too-fussy *cumulonimbulist.*

shit-knitter *n.* One who weaves his *crap* into tall stories that we are expected to believe. Also *fliar.* See *away and take your face for a shite.*

shit knot *n.* A knot made by re-tying lots and lots of little knots in the vain hope that it will hold. Like a slip knot but *shit. 'I simply can't imagine why that Victorian wardrobe came loose from the roof of my car in the fast lane, officer. It was fastened securely with a length of stout garden twine which I tied to the radio aerial with a large shit knot.'*

shitleist *n.* The second hand, *wanked-out* golf kit used by one who is too tight to fork out for the proper equipment.

shit lips *n.* Affectionate term for a sycophantic person or *ass-kisser. 'Situations vacant: A national pop music radio station is looking to recruit an experienced shit lips to sit in the studio and agree with an overweight, sweating fuckwit on its breakfast show.'* (advert in *Broadcast* magazine, 2003).

shit locker *n.* Arse, bomb bay, chamber of horrors.

shit machine *n.* A dog. *'I fired three shots, and moments later the hellish, glowing beast, whatever it was, lay dead in the Grimpen Mire. If I had hesitated for a second, or had my aim been less than true, it would most certainly have killed Sir Henry where he stood, as Stapleton had intended. "My God, Holmes," I vociferated breathlessly. "What on earth is it?" The great detective stepped forward and examined the foul creature's still-luminous form through his eyeglass. "A simple trick, Watson," he announced presently. 'It is merely a large shit machine which has been coated with phosphorus.'"* (from *The Shit Machine of the Baskervilles* by Arthur Conan-Doyle).

shitmus test *n.* Like a litmus test, only instead of indicator paper in a laboratory there's *arse paper* in a lavatory, and instead of an acid/base there's an *anus* that might have let *something slip* while *stepping on a duck. 'Crikey, I think there was something in that. I'd better go and take a shitmus test.'*

shitnic *1. n.* A modern world solution to time pressures in the workplace, *viz.* Eating your packed lunch while sat on the works *Rick Witter. Logistics. 2. n.* An *al fresco Scooby Doo.* A *fly feast, forest dump* or *bluebottle banquet.*

shitoir *n. Fr.* A proper toilet, as opposed to a urinal. *'Je had to go allez pissoir, but then je realised je had* *to go allez shitoir aussi.'*

shit on a shingle *euph. US. milit.* Chipped beef on toast, whatever chipped beef is.

shit on a shot putt, like *sim.* A hefty, spherical *arse ball* that heralds a new beginning in an individual's battle with constipation. *'You might need to use the neighbour's bog, love. It finally came out... like shit on a shot putt.'*

shit on your own doorstep *euph.* To foul the nest, eg. *Shag* one's mother-in-law while totally *pissed*. Piss on your chips, fart on your Weetabix, cum on your faggots.

shitoris *n. medic.* The sensitive bundle of nerves up a fellow's *jacksie* that get stimulated during *bottery*. The male *dizzy button* or *prostrate gland*. The *tremble trigger* or *walnut*.

shitosomatic *adj. psych.* When you think you need a *poo* but it turns out you don't.

shitpickers *n.* Dog owners. *'Cruft's is the world's greatest dog show, and once again dishevelled shitpickers from all over the country have descended on the NEC here in Birmingham, all hoping to win the coveted trophy for Best in Show.'*

shit pit *n.* The lavatory.

shitpot *1. n.* A flushing, porcelain receptacle for one's *feeshus*, typically found in the bathroom. *2. n.* A contumelious epithet applied to an idiot or person of restricted intellectual capacity. *Fuckwit. 3. n.* The *back body* or *wrong'un*. *'Tell you what, love. It's your birthday, so just for a change I'll do you up the shitpot tonight.'*

shit pump *n.* The television. *'I'm off to bed. Don't forget to turn the shit pump off when you come up.'*

shitrous oxide *n. Bum gas.*

shitrus *n.* The charming aroma of *shit* mixed with lemon-scented air freshener.

shit sandwich *n.* A rhetorical suggestion, *viz.* That which someone afflicted with less than agreeable breath may be accused of eating. *'Oi, Turdbreath! Have you been at the shit sandwiches?' 'Just step out of the car please, sir, and blow into this bag.'*

shitscale *n.* Cause of mysterious brown staining in a student house toilet pan. *Turdigris.*

shit scrape *n.* Arse wipe, *bottery tickets, brown shield stamps,* bathroom tissue.

shit shadow *n.* A noisome *guff* smell that sticks tenaciously to a fellow like Bud Flanagan used to stick to Chesney Allen. Another reference for the youngsters there. A *velcro fart*.

shitshod *adj.* Wearing *Frenchman's shoes*.

shit shoveller's crack *n.* A less than fragrant *bottom burp. 'Jesus, your majesty. No offence, but that one smells like a shit shoveller's crack.'*

shitshower *n.* Turning on the bathroom shower

while having a *shite* to prevent your partner in the next room from having to listen to your groaning, straining, *farting*, weeping and splashing. Used mostly in the initial few months of a new romantic relationship. See also *turning Yoko's mic off*.

shit shy *adj.* Constipated. *'Strewth, doc. Can you squirt something up there, only I ate fifteen Scotch eggs and a big treacle tart for a bet and I've been shit shy for a fortnight.'*

shit-smuggler's rucksack *sim.* The *ne plus ultra* of halitosis. *'Fuck me, what have you been eating?' 'I don't know what you mean, Lord St. John.' 'Your breath smells like a shit-smuggler's rucksack, your majesty.'*

shitsophrenia *n. medic.* That distressing condition where the sufferer alternates between having wild *squirts* and normal *Simon Cowell* movements. See also *brown triathlon*.

shit splitter *n.* A G-string worn so tight on the lady's *heave-ho* that it will fillet the *brown trout* in the unlikely event that she *follows through* on a *cheese cracker*.

shit stabber *n.* A *stylish,* Errol Flynn-style *pork swordsman*.

shits that pass in the night *1. n.* A philisophical and stoical way of coming to terms with with nocturnal incontinence. *'The way I look at it, it's just a case of shits that pass in the night. But then again, I consider myself very much a mattress half full person, doctor.' 2. phr.* While *dropping the kids off at the pool,* particularly in a transportation hub, not caring if the person in the next cubicle can hear you because you're never going to see them again.

shits, the *n. medic.* Of *smallroom dancing,* those up-tempo *trots* which include the *Tijuana cha-cha,* the *sour apple quickstep* and the *Aztec two-step*.

shitstopper *n.* An unexpectedly large household bill, derived from the practice of reading the mail while on the toilet. *'And now we move onto the case of Mr Jack Trubshaw of St. Neots, who last winter received a right shitstopper from British Gas, even though his central heating is oil-fired.'* (Nicky Campbell, *Watchdog,* BBC TV).

shit stove *n.* The lavatory. *'Where's mam?' 'She's on the shit stove, son.'*

shitsworth *1. n.* SI unit. The quantity of toilet paper required for one sit-down visit to the cludgy. *2. n.* A particularly odious enforcer of petty rules.

shitsy-niner *n.* An unfortunate, intimate encounter with someone who recently ran out of Andrex at a critical point.

shittens *n.* Lingering odour on the hands and fingers that no detergent can shift, experienced in the aftermath of a particularly pasty, pestilential *Tom tit*. *'I'd shake your hand, your majesty, only I'm wearing shittens.'*

shitter *1. n.* Anus, *kakpipe, council gritter. 2. n.* A sit down lavatory, the *pan. 3. n.* One who *shits. 4. adj.* More *shit* than another thing or things. *'This final definition of the word is shitter than the other three.'*

shitteracy *n.* Basic measure of a person's ability to leave the *bum sink* in a more or less civilised state as a courtesy to others. *'The levels of shitteracy at the Guardian's head offices were found to be well below the average expected of adults aged 18-65.'*

shitterati *n. coll.* Collective term for the heroic figures of the age who turn up on programmes such as *I'm a Celebrity Get me Out of Here, Britain's Worst Celebrity Drivers' Pets from Hell, etc*. The kind of people who would happily fuck a pig if it were to get their face on TV. Those *plebrities* who aspire to join the D-list.

shitter chatter *n.* Long-winded anal babble emitted when a *mudchild* is expected.

shitter door seance *n.* Eerie scene enacted by a shambling *gimmer* in an inner city pub gents whereby he raps three times on the door and asks "is there anybody there?".

shittered *adj.* Extremely fatigued following a draining visit to the *chod pan*. *'That sounds like a nasty fall you've had, nan. I'd come over and help you up only I'm absolutely shittered.'*

shitter's ridge *n.* The *scranus etc.*

shitter's smirk *n.* The stoical rictus grin that accompanies the experience of squirting *dirty water* through a *Wigan rosette* that is hanging in tatters.

shit the alphabet in morse code *v.* To be suffering from a digestive upset that results in a dot-dash-dot-dot-dash type of *sit-down toilet adventure*.

shit the bed *1. euph.* To make a big mistake. *'Addressing the Parliamentary Committee on Culture, Media and Sport, BBC Director General George Entwistle admitted that he had really shit the bed over his handling of the Newsnight investigation into Jimmy Savile.' 2. exclam.* A sudden shout of alarm or frustration when one realises one has made a big mistake. *'Shit the bed! I've agreed to go and address the Parliamentary Committee on Culture, Media and Sport this afternoon.'*

shit the chart *v. medic.* To do assorted foulages of varying consistency such that the entire Bristol Stool Chart is represented in the *pan*.

shit the tub, I/he/she/they *phr.* Retrospective assessment of a situation an order of magnitude worse than one in which the participant(s) merely *shit the bed*; this by dint of the fact that the *foulage*

in question is not localised, but has broken up and performs a merry water-borne dance around the subject's prone, naked body.

shit thickener *n.* Any foodstuff taken on board in an attempt to stem the flow of *rusty water* from one's *red eye* following a night *on the lash*. *'Ooh, I feel terrible, your holiness. I must have had a bad pint or something.' 'Bless you my son. Here, have some of me scratchings as a shit thickener. Oi, not that many, you theiving cunt.'*

shit tickets *n.* Bumwad.

shit-tickler *n.* A *kidney wiper.*

shit tie *1. n.* The rather unsavoury end result of a spot of vigorous *back door work* followed by a *diddy ride* to finish. *2. n.* The sort of studiedly eccentric, garish neckwear typically worn by Jon Snow when he used to present the news on Channel 4.

shitting forecast *n.* A prediction of the number of lavatory visits that will be needed later in the day based on how things went in the morning.

shitting glass *n.* A morning-after *crap* that feels like half your torso is being stripped away from the inside.

shitting purple bricks *n.* Looking into the toilet and being momentarily terrified, before remembering that you ate a load of beetroots yesterday.

shitting through a sponge *n.* A novel toiletary ability gained after a night eating delicious curries at the Curry Capital.

shitting twiglets *n.* Especially furious at someone else's incompetence or treachery. *'Mr Sunak said he was shitting twiglets when he heard that senior officials had placed bets on the date of the forthcoming election.'*

shitting yellow *adj.* Very young. *'Listen, sunshine. Don't tell me how to do my fucking job. I've been painting covers for the People's Friend since you were shitting yellow.'*

shit-tinted spectacles *n.* Metaphorical misanthroptical corrective device that bestows upon the wearer the ability to only see the worst in everything and everyone.

shittish gas *n.* The early warning *bottom burp* that heralds the passing of a massive, foetid *Peter O'Toole*. Also *duck dastardly, fart buffer, turtle's breath.*

shittish gas *n.* The UK's leading supplier of methane to sofa cushions, underpants and duvets.

shittle *n.* A yob or vandal who is, annoyingly, too young and small to be thumped by the adults he is annoying.

shittoon *n.* The *thundermug* or *porcelain god*, especially when in receipt of something less-than-usually solid. From the other side of the room.

shit trigger *n.* The first cigarette of the day, which has the effect of pulling the pin out of the *chod grenade.* 'I Love Phillip Morris king size. It's not just because they're clean and fresh tasting. It's not just because their mellow taste gives me mouth and throat comfort and freedom from cigarette cough. And it's not just because they have a great shit trigger action and give me all day smoking enjoyment. I love them because they're the mildest high tar cigarette on the market.' (*I Love Philip Morris* advertisement featuring Lucille Ball, 1953).

shitty shitty gang bang *n.* A particularly messy *bumcraft fayre.*

shitty stick *n.* A stick, covered in *shit*, used by men with powerful cars and expensive aftershave to stave off advancing *scrunt.*

shituation *n.* A bad situation. 'Hello Houston, we've got a shituation here.' (Commander James Lovell, speaking from Apollo 13 when the main turd valve short-circuited during the Trans-Lunar Injection Phase of the troubled Moon mission, filling the Command Module with weightless *bangers and mash*).

shit ups *n.* Strenuous, repetitive abdominal exercises carried out in an attempt to keep one's *nipsy* tightly closed when one cannot access a *chocolate cabin.*

shitwhistler *1. n.* A high-pitched *trouser trumpet* released nervously around a *turtle's head.* *2. n.* An untrustworthy fellow, prone to making outrageous or untruthful claims. *'You only have to look at him stood there with his orange face and his stupid hair to see he's a fucking shitwhistler.'* (Hillary Clinton, US Presidential debate, 2016).

shitwreck *n.* The broken-up remnants of a scuttled *dreadnought*, lying in deep water by the S-bend.

shit-wrecked/shitwrecked *1. adj.* Laid waste by a terrible *arse*-related mishap just at the moment when everything seems to be going swimmingly. *2. adj.* Utterly sunk by *foulage.*

shit your pants *v.* To *drop a brick, cake your kecks, papper your trolleys.*

shitzkreig *n.* An unstoppable, hostile force which overwhelms one on the toilet.

shiver shit *v.* Of a constipated dog, to labour particularly hard while laying an *egg.* *2. n.* A disparaging monicker bestowed upon one who wimps out of a soft task, *eg.* Taking one's 5-year-old on the 'Ben 10 – Ultimate Mission' family rollercoaster at Drayton Manor.

shlong covid *n. medic.* The long term and still unknown after-effects of too much *working from home* during lockdown.

shnickers *n.* A lady's soiled *scads.* From shitty + knickers.

shniffle-piffler *n.* Somebody else who sniffs lady's bicycle seats. They're everywhere.

shnit *v. onomat.* To sneeze so violently that one loses control of one's rectum. Normally occurring when the pollen count is high and one has over-indulged in spicy provender the night before. *'Oh dear, I do declare I appear to have shnit myself. You've not got a clean pair of gruds about the place, have you, Bosey?'*

shocked hippo, fanny like a *sim.* Descriptive of a spaciously appointed *Rick Stein's dustbin.*

shocker *n.* A Mr Spock-style hand gesture which alludes to the practice of wedging one's middle and index fingers in a lady's *front bottom* while simultaneously interpolating one's pinkie into her *back bottom.* See also *two in the pink, one in the stink; the old shocker; Dagenham handshake.*

shock to the cistern *euph.* An uncomfortably large *copper bolt* that challenges the swallowing capabilities of the average *chod bin.*

shoebox special *n.* A magnificent *Thora*, exhibiting a length and girth of which one is so proud that one feels tempted to fish it out of the *bum sink*, put it in a shoebox and take it to work to show it off to one's colleagues.

shoe bun *n.* A profiterole of *hound cable*, a *barker's egg custard tart.* 'This is one small step for a man, one giant leap for…Fuck me, I've just stepped in a shoe bun.'

shoe horn *1. n.* Device for gently easing a foot into a piece of ill-fitting footwear. *2. n.* The glottal contortions apparent in the tongue of a *grot* actress when she is preparing to swallow a foot. *'Blimey, that's a broad fitting. No wonder she's doing the shoe horn.'* *3. n.* The state of spontaneous phallic turgidity which occurs when a *feet footishist* sees a stiletto or pair of Wellingtons. But not flip-flops.

shoelace view *n.* A gentleman's surreptitious glimpse of a *bird's* gusset gained while pretending to tie up his slip-ons.

shoe pastry *n.* Dried *dog egg* adhering to the sole of one's loafer.

shoe poisoning *n. medic.* The alarming symptons of one suffering the effects of a *fucking good kicking.*

shoe shiners *n.* Pendulous *spaniel's ears* that are in dire need of uplift and thus swing to and fro beneath the waistline. *Shoe shiners* can bring up a patent leather finish on a pair of matt slingbacks in the time it takes to dance the whole of *I Will Survive.* Also *low loaders, Gandhi's flip-flops,* socktits, Fred Bassets, beaver tails.

shoe show 1. n. US. A major American footwear retailer, apparently. 2. n. Erotic performance at a strip club during which the artiste only sports footwear, eg. High heels, a pair of wellies etc.

shoe-sizer n. A dog's egg of such gargantuan proportions that, when stepped in, it comfortably accommodates the entire area of the victim's shoe, thus providing a complete imprint from which a detective could, if necessary, gauge the exact size of their feet. 'Them from number seven have been past with their fucking St. Bernards again, leaving fucking shoe-sizers down the bottom of the drive.'

shog n. The choking brownhouse gases left in the littlest room after a particularly rough Tom tit. From shit + fog. 'I'd give it ten minutes for the shog to clear, nan. Make it twenty.'

shomit v. To shit and vomit at at same time. 'Granddad went down with the norovirus last winter. The poor old get was shomitting for days.'

shoogle v. At a pub quiz, to pretend you've gone for a number two, whereas you are actually in the bogs looking up all the answers on your phone.

shoot babies v. To ejaculate.

shooting boots on, to get one's 1. v. Football commentator's phrase, to describe the actions of a player who has excelled in the "kicking the ball at the goal" part of the game. 'Rooney's certainly got his shooting boots on for Manchester United today, Gary.' 2. v. Phrase describing the bizarre contortions a gentleman's feet go through in the moments leading up to a pop shot. 'Rooney's certainly got his shooting boots on up that raddled old prostitute today, Gary.'

shooting brake 1. n. What old people call estate cars, in an attempt to sound like they grew up at Downton Abbey. 2. n. A mental image conjured up by a chap in the throes of passion in an effort to stop himself going up and over like a pan of milk after a couple of pushes.

shooting bunnies n. Polite euphemism for letting rip. Passing wind, blowing off. Also killing the Easter bunny.

shooting jam adj. Menstruating, on the blob, dropping clots, up on blocks.

shooting times n. Self help literature, DIY mags, bachelors' newsletters.

shooting wax darts n. Unpleasantly evocative phrase describing a chap blowing the tanks following a long period of abstinence. 'Okay, whatever you want Cliff, but don't finish in my mouth. After this long it could be dangerous. You'll be shooting wax darts.'

shoot in your boot euph. To be so sexually excited as to lose one's mess into one's footwear.

shoot oneself in the cock v. To perform a self-destructive act that unintentionally scuppers your chances of scoring with a member of the opposite gender. 'With the benefit of hindsight, it was a definite error of judgement on our first date to tell my mother-in-law about the Rugby Club World Brothel Tour of 1986-2007 that took in Soho, Hamburg, Thailand, Amsterdam and Leeds. I definitely shot myself in the cock there.'

shoot putty at the moon v. To go off.

shoot the breeze 1. v. To chat in a casual, relaxed and friendly manner. 2. v. To blow off, in a casual, relaxed and friendly manner.

shoot your load/bolt/wad/stack v. To ejaculate, lose your mess, discharge the mutton musket.

shopkeeper 1. n. A sudden, movement of stoolage into the bomb bay, that occurs completely unexpectedly. Named after the proprietor of the fancy dress shop frequented by single man Mr Benn in the 1970s children's television series of the same name, who would materialise "as if by magic" when his sole customer entered his seemingly empty establishment. 2. n. Someone who is not in the vicinity of the bar when it is their round, but who miraculously appears when someone else is going to the bar.

shop'n'drop n. Hitting the Amazon website on the phone whilst parking your breakfast on the shitter.

shopping n. The underpant aftermath of follow through. 'Did I detect a twin tone there, your honour?' 'I'm afraid so. Court adjourned for fifteen minutes while I check my trolleys for shopping.'

shop round the corner 1. n. Film with James Stewart they show at Christmas. Not that one, the other one. 2. v. To be good with colours.

shoptimism n. Buying petrol station flowers and/or chocolate for the missus in the vain hope of a shot at stabbing the beaver or getting a blow job.

shorn bean n. Depilatory practice whereby the anterior portion of the vulva is denuded of hair in order to expose the erectile tissue of the clematis.

shortage n. coll. Collective term for a group of vertically challenged persons.

short arms inspection n. milit. Armed services slang for an under the bridge medical examination, specifically looking for evidence of cock rot or mechanical dandruff.

shortarseache n. medic. An affliction usually suffered by those of diminutive stature, whereby the victim feels the whole world is against them. 'What's up with Rishi now?' 'Oh nothing. He's just got the shortarseache.'

short back and sympathy euph. A cod haircut

performed by an indulgent barber upon the pate of a balding gent, which involves making clipping noises near the customer's ears while throwing a bit of hair about to add realism.

short back and wipe *n.* The latest cut for the more follicly challenged gent. *'What will it be today, Prince William?' 'Short back and wipe please, barber.'*

short-changed *adj.* Descriptive of the situation that obtains when a video clip one has downloaded stops just short of the *money shot*, so you have to phone Barclaycard and get them to cancel the transaction.

short measure *n.* The difference between the seven units of alcohol you tell your doctor that you consume each week and the vast amount you actually put away.

short-staffed *adj.* Lacking vigour in the *trouser department*. *'I'm afraid it won't be possible to organise a meeting for you with Mr Straw at the House of Commons, as he's very short-staffed. But you could go and talk to Stephen Pound if you like. He's hung like a fucking carthorse.'*

Short Stirling *n.* A perfect visit to the *chod bin*, which consists of a smooth sit-down, efficient opening of the *bomb-bay doors* and release of *payload*, and which concludes with the *drawing of an ace*, the whole operation taking place in the blink of an eye. Named after the famous British four-engined heavy bomber which saw service in the Second World War, dropping excrement onto Germany without needing to wipe its undercarriage.

shot across the bowels *n.* A cannon-like warning shot of *brownhouse gases* athwart the *poop deck* that heralds much worse to come as *Shanks's Bay* hoves into view.

shot at the title *n.* A do-or-die, last chance to have a go on a *bird's snatch*.

shot from the starter's gun *euph.* A *cock* up the wrong 'un. See *jockey's starting position*.

shotgun fart *n.* A sudden ballistic *poot* which peppers pellets of *crapnel* into the toilet bowl or underpants.

shotgun through a butcher's window, like someone fired a *sim.* Used to describe an upsettingly meaty set of female *pudenders*. *A fanny like the bottom of a ratcatcher's mallet.*

shoulder boulders *n.* Big breasts, *gazungas, bazingers.*

shoulder to cum on, have a *v.* To be blessed with a special friend who is there for you in times of need.

should've gone to Specsavers *exclam.* Amusing apophthegm said of a mate who has inexplicably chosen to *cop off* with a *right boiler*. *'Charles Philip Arthur George, will you take Camilla Rosemary to be your wife? Will you love her, comfort her, honour and protect her, and, forsaking all others, be faithful to her as long as you both shall live? You may lift the veil... Jesus Christ. If you don't mind me saying so, your royal highness, you should've gone to Specsavers.'*

shouty crackers *adj.* Descriptive of the understated acting/mountaineering style of *face-fannied* thesp Brian Blessed OBE (a term first coined in a *Nobby Piles* cartoon in *Viz*, unless we're very much mistaken).

shovel recce *euph. milit.* Used by members of HM Forces on manoeuvres when they wander off in search of somewhere quiet to *bid a fond farewell to yesterday's sausages.*

shoving paper down a Greek toilet *n.* Attempting to sort out a problem, but only succeeding in making things a whole lot worse. *'How long is the Prime Minister prepared to continue pursuing his current policy of forcible occupation, which is merely shoving paper down a Greek toilet?'* (Sir Mingice Campbell MP, quoted in *Hansard*, June 8th 2007).

showbiz shuffle of shame *n.* The decrepit gait adopted by celebrities for their daily walk to court during their assorted sex trials.

shower angling *n.* Fishing around the *winking walnut* with a hooked index finger to free a particularly stubborn tomato seed or sweetcorn kernel.

shower babies *n.* The clingy offspring born following a spot of *self delight* in the shower.

shower cock *n.* The ideal penis size when using a communal washing facility; neither too small nor too troublingly erect. A *quarter-on, Goldicock.* The effect that Alan Bates and Oliver Reed were aiming for during that wrestling scene in *Women in Love.*

showercrap *n.* The unfortunate situation whereby one suddenly gets the *turtle's head* straight after freshening up.

shower creme *1. n.* A more expensive version of shower gel. Which in itself is just a more expensive version of washing-up liquid. *2. n.* Hand-made unguent produced during a very long, relaxing shower.

show job *1. n.* The making of theatrically appreciative noises by a gentleman who is the recipient of a particularly artless act of oral *horatio*. *2. n.* The sort of transparently fake *nosh* typically performed in front of a roaring fire and filmed from behind a lace curtain in one of them glossy, softcore *spam vids* they used to show on satellite telly late at night, someone once told us, where a *bird* moves her head up and down in front of a bloke while he pulls a face like he's just shut his *knackers* in the car door.

shown the ropes *1. phr.* In the world of office work, of a new employee on their first day, having had the location of the kettle, teabags, cups, sugar and spoons pointed out to them. *'Well, I've shown you the ropes. I'll leave you to get on with it, Secretary of State.'* *2. phr.* Of a new bus garage employee on their first day, having been stripped naked, secured across an inspection pit using a broom handle and duct tape, and then had axle grease and sump oil smeared across their testicles. *3. phr.* In the world of romance, of a new sexual partner, having had their face and/or body ejaculated upon, but not yet their back.

show off *v.* Of a woman, to exhibit the hystrionic symptoms of pre-menstrual tension. See also *fanny fit, boiling beetroots.*

showroom finish *n.* The effect of rubbing your *naughty polish* into a ladyfriend's *bodywork* and then buffing her *headlamps* till they gleam.

showstop *1. n.* In the theatre world, a severe technical or safety issue that causes a halt to a production. *2. n.* In the *cottaging* world, anything that interrupts the festivities. Most likely the British Transport Police arriving with a mirror on the end of a long pole.

showstopper *1. n.* A round in *The Great British Bake Off* in which participants are required to create a dramatic and technically challenging confection in an attempt to impress Prue Leith. *2. n.* Any sudden and unexpectedly dramatic passage of *marsh gas* which momentarily stops all activity within a 200m radius. *3. n.* A *back forest gateau* of epic proportions. A *plumber's bonus* or *Hollywood loaf.* *4. n.* A big, fancy *cock* that might well earn you a handshake off Paul Hollywood.

shramp *v.* To pursue the incredibly common hobby of sniffing ladies' recently vacated bicycle seats. To *quumf, snudge, snurgle, snuftify.*

shredded wheat *n.* A large, wholesome, vigorous and surprisingly well-groomed blonde *landing strip* of the sort which is found on most German ladies of a certain vintage, apparently.

shreddie brek *n.* Found in the *undercrackers* of a fellow with a poorly moisturised *clacker bag,* a deposit of flaking roughage resembling porridge oats. *Scrote so simple.*

shreddies *1. n. Underchunders, scads, dunghampers, scuns. 2. n.* The tiny little threadbare Hitler *'taches* typically seen on videographic models.

Shrek *n.* A large, shaven-headed man with bad teeth and protruding ears found on low-brow, moron-baiting television programmes such as the *Jeremy Kyle Show* or *Question Time. 'Yes, you sir. No, not you. The man in blue sitting next to the Shrek. I'm sorry, the lady in blue. Go ahead. What's your question?'*

shrimp *v.* Of an American financial manager, to suck a ginger duchess's toes for purposes of sexual gratification.

shrine of our lady of Coors *n.* The healing power of a visit to Wetherspoons, whose patrons miraculously find themselves able to discard their *social sticks* and *Govan go-karts* as they pass though its doors.

shrinkflation *1. n.* Post-Brexit reduction in the size of common foodstuffs, *eg.* Toblerone, whilst their price remains the same. *2. n.* Common physiological shift amongst *salad-dodging* males whereby the size of their genitalia becomes inversely proportional to their body mass.

shrinkles *n.* The wrinkles that appear on a penis that has blenched due to extreme cold or from inadvertently looking at photos of Katie Hopkins. See also *cockordian.*

shrink-wrapped gammon *n.* A lady who wears clothing several sizes too small for her *lovely personality.*

shrivel me timbers *exclam.* Pirate-like phrase used by a fellow looking down at his *shrunken treasure* when getting out of a cold shower, cold bath, unheated swimming pool, cryogenic storage unit under Snow White's castle at Disneyland *etc.*

shrunken treasure *1. n.* Reduced circumstances in the *family jewels* brought about by chilly weather or immersion. *Shrinky-dinkage. 2. n.* A *laptop, midget gem* or *cock puppet.*

shtup *v. Yiddish.* To have sex, *fuck, bang.*

shuffling the deck *n. Winding the clock, sorting out the boys, nipping and rolling, re-shuffling the cabinet.* The dextrous act of manually relieving testicular torsion or *Betty Swallocks. 'Sorry madam, I was just shuffling the deck there. I'll take your order now.'*

shum *n.* That saucy mixture which is a by-product of certain practices which are frowned upon by readers of the *Daily Mail. Santorum.*

shump *v.* To *follow through* or *shart.* Derivation unknown. *'Have a look in me kegs, will you, nan? I think I might've just shumped.'*

shunt *1. v.* To *shtup. 2. v.* To push, as opposed to pull, a train.

shush *n. Dropping the shopping* at the same time as flushing in order to muffle the noise of *splashdown* in a busy public *crapper.* From shit + flush.

shushes *n.* One's early morning preparations for the day ahead. A *shag,* a shave, a *shit,* a shower and a shampoo. *'His Holiness will be out to canonise you in a moment, Mother Teresa. He's just finishing off his shushes.'*

shuttle cock *n.* One who *explodes* on re-entry. Or occasionally *goes off* a few seconds after lift-off.

shwank *n.* A multi-task-enabled showering experience.

shwee *n.* A watery *poo. Rusty water.*

shwiss *n.* Portmanteau term for a comprehensive trifecta of toilet functions performed by a person with a busy schedule. From shit + wank + piss. *'Raef, with regret, I have to tell you that you're fired. Right, are we all done? I'm off for a shwiss.'*

Siamese quims *n.* Scissor sisters. *Lezzas* who are constantly *bumping fur. Carpet bumpers.*

Siberian laundry, stiffer than *sim.* A state of intense arousal. *Stiff as a signalman's rag, stiff as a varnished eel, stiff as a bishop's dick.*

sicasso *n.* A colourful bit of pavement art in which can be seen figurative elements of diced carrots, peanuts and crisps. An example of *late night abstract expressionism* reminiscent of the action paintings of Jackson Pollock.

sickerette *n.* A *snout* smoked in an attempt to prevent the onset of *spewing* after a heavy drinking session. *'Quick, someone spark up a sickerette for Andrew. We're on air in ten minutes.'*

sick, my arse has just been *phr.* Overly information-rich particulars vouchsafed to one's colleagues when returning from a visit to the works *Ricks* after an explosive purge of the *Simons.*

sick-off *n.* A competitive event where contestants attempt to vomit the furthest, normally from a raised platform, balcony or dais. *'It's a good job his holiness finally won it on the cardinals' vote. The rest of the results were so close we thought at one point we were going to have to decide it with a sick-off from the Vatican roof.'*

sideburns *n.* The marks left on multi-storey car park walls by drivers who should either get power steering or trade down to a *witch's broom.*

side entrance to Debenhams *euph.* The *back passage. 'My brother's mate did her up the side entrance to Debenhams. You wouldn't think that when you see her sat there reading the news.'*

side hustle 1. *n.* A loss-making small business carried on in one's spare time. 2. *n.* The secret life of a married man who also *enjoys a good walk.*

side hustle *n.* For some married men, *cottaging.* And for some *cottagists,* being married.

sidepipe *n.* A semi-erect *cock* visible down one leg of a tight pair of trousers, as sported by *rock poodles* and *sex cases* in closely packed London Underground carriages.

sidesaddle 1. *n.* Title of chart-topping Russ Conway single from 1959. Remember that, kids? 2. *n.* A demure horse-riding style preferred by young ladies so as not to snap their *virgin strings* before their wedding night. 3. *n.* Non-conventional *porcelain pony*-riding style that finds favour with the more capaciously buttocked defecator.

sidesplitter 1. *n.* A joke that makes you laugh immoderately. 2. *n.* A *feeshus* of such girth that it feels like you're being torn asunder, although you're definitely not laughing. Also *splitter cable, Jack the ripper, knot splitter.*

sideways monkey mouth *n.* The female *flapdoodle. 'Phwooarr! If you freeze the frame at the exact right moment, you can see her pubes and her sideways monkey mouth and everything.'* (Barry Norman reviewing *Basic Instinct,* or possibly *Fatal Attraction,* on *Film '92,* BBC1).

sidewinder 1. *n.* Some sort of snake that is often seen in nature documentaries, scuttling across the desert sand like a scaly brace and bit. 2. *n.* Missile used by the Americans to shoot British reporters. 3. *n.* The elevation of one's left or right buttock in order to facilitate the surreptitious release of a *Judi Dench.* A *one cheek sneak* or *cushion creeper.*

side winders *n.* Spaniel's ears which appear to be gravitating towards the oxters. *Pit fillers.*

siesta with a Fiesta *n.* That relaxing afternoon interlude of *art pamphlet* perusal typically snatched by a married gentleman while his wife is paying a visit to the hairdresser. A *siesta with a Fiesta* is usually brought to an abrupt conclusion when the sound of the front door rudely rouses the siestee from his slumbers, and he finds that he has nodded off on the sofa with his trousers round his ankles and his *wanking spanner* glued to his forehead.

sigh of relief *n.* The first successful *Exchange & Mart* after a particularly vicious bout of the *trots.*

signalman's rag, stiff as a *sim.* A colourful turn of phrase dating from the days when a railway employee would spend all day alone with little to do except while away the hours frantically and repeatedly *polishing the brasswork* in his lonely box – a tradition still kept alive by volunteers at heritage railways throughout the country.

signalman's tea break *euph.* After the little white *jizz train* has passed, the necessary pause before the *big yellow express* can use the same bit of track. *'Can you use the downstairs bog, love? Only I'm trying to sluice the pipes in here but I'm on a two-fag* *signalman's tea break.'*

signature challenge *1. n.* A round on *The Great British Bake Off* during which the contestants are asked to bake something and they must put their own spin on it with various flavours and themes and so on. *2. n.* The production of a quite unusual sound accompanied by a uniquely acrid aroma, enabling passers by to easily identify who has just *guffed*. See also *technical challenge*.

signature dish *1. n.* A *poncy* chef's favourite recipe. *2. n.* A well *skid-marked chod pan.*

sign no dockets, tip the load and *euph.* Of a gentleman, to deposit his *filthy concrete* in a place where he wouldn't want anyone to find out about, *eg.* Up the *clopper* of a lady who his mates might regard as falling short of their rigorous quality control standards. From the habit of cheeky HGV drivers who, in order to avoid tedious form-filling and ridiculous red tape, prefer to empty skipfuls of rubble, asbestos, toxic clinical waste, dead hitch-hikers *etc.*, in remote lay-bys and under picturesque country hedgerows.

Signora Romero *n.* An apparently beautiful woman who, on closer inspection, is sporting a moustache under her makeup. From the natty facial hair visible in close-ups – and indeed mid- and long-shots – of Cesar Romero's Joker in the 1960s *Batman* TV series.

sign the visitors' book *v.* To leave a note of appreciation at the bottom of another's *skidpan. Sign the guest book.*

Sigourney Weaver *n. rhym. slang. Beaver.*

silencer *n.* A *pap-baffle.*

silent footstep *n.* The horrible moment when one's shoe lands in a *dog egg.* *"'My whiskers, Holmes!" I expostulated. "How did you know our quarry wasn't a huge, ravening beast?" "Elementary, my dear Watson," the great detective replied. "I have long made a systematic study of the sizes, shapes and consistencies of the shites produced by every breed of dog. I deduced from the viscosity and diameter of the silent footstep in question that it was from a small dog, probably a yappy fucker."'* (From *The Houndrope of the Baskervilles* by Sir Arthur Conan-Doyle).

silent movie, watch a *1. v.* To enjoy the slapstick, dialogue-free antics of Buster Keaton, Harold Lloyd, Fatty Arbuckle and friends. *2. v.* To anxiously thrash one's genitals within an inch of their lives while watching a *grumble vid* with the sound muted so as not to disturb the *bag for life* (who is *jilling herself daft* over a well-thumbed copy of *50 Shades of Grey* upstairs).

silent notification *1. n.* On your mobile phone, a message that shows up with no audible or visual alert to let you know it is there. *2. n.* A *fart* that makes its presence felt with no audible or visual alert.

silent partner *1. n.* An investor who plays no part in the running of the business. *2. n.* A bedfellow with a penchant for emitting *SBDs* under the cover of darkness.

silent performer *1. n.* A mime artist like your man Marcel Marceau there. *2. n.* A model of vacuum cleaner made by Electrolux. *3. n.* A person who excels at dropping aphonic *brews.*

silent release *1. n.* In IT, an upgrade that is unannounced and adeptly timed, such that it goes entirely unnoticed, in theory. *2. n.* A sulphurous *prairie wind* that is rolled out on a similarly speculative principle.

silent roar *1. n.* Trade name of the small pellets containing lion excrement, the smell of which apparently keeps zebras off your flower beds for up to six months. *2. n.* A *feeshus* dropped in the toilet, the smell of which keeps everyone out of the bathroom for up to six months.

silent running *euph.* The use of well-honed *bum gum* muscles to release a long but inaudible stream of *carbon dibaxide* exhaust gas whilst maintaining plausible deniability

silent wetness *n.* A tell-tale stain appearing on the front of a pair of light coloured *daks*; conclusive evidence that you have *pissed yourself.*

silent witness *n.* Upon visiting the *chod-bin* and carrying out a *CSI*-style recce of the *pan,* the sodden, *stool*-soiled and flush-resistant *bumwad* that offers compelling forensic evidence of a recent lavatorial crime.

silicone strap *n.* The strap of a shoulder or handbag which pulls tightly in between the *baps,* enhancing their size and profile without the need for costly cosmetic surgery. A *tit splitter.*

silicone valley *n.* The cleavage 'twixt adjoining, artificially enhanced *bazongers.* The *Bristol Channel, sausage dock, snooker rest.*

silly cones *n.* Implausible fake breasts.

silly mid on *1. n.* Cricket fielding position, on the leg-side forward of the batsman's wicket and very near to the batsman. *2. n.* A *lazy lob* or *plod*; a half-cocked *stonk-on* which is too big to hide, yet too soft to be of any practical use.

silly string *1. n.* A light-hearted novelty *shit* that squirts out in a rapid and erratic manner. Breaks the ice at parties. Occasionally incorporating small solid lumps, when it is known as a *bicycle chain. 2. n.* Sticky substance light-heartedly sprayed in the face of an actress in a slapstick *art film*. Kept in a handy cylindrical canister that requires vigorous shaking.

silver blurtch *n*. The withered fleece to be found 'twixt the legs of a *coffin dodger. Gash in the attic.*

silver box *n*. A comely and alluring older woman, *eg.* Dame Helen Mirren or Blanche off *Corrie.*

silver sandwich *n*. A group s*x session involving liberal-minded senior citizens.

Simba *1. n.* Holding one's mobile phone skywards like out of that bit in *the Lion King* in a vain attempt to to acquire a signal while in a rural area. Or, if you're on Vodafone, while anywhere at all, including standing on a ladder next to a Vodafone aerial mast. *2. n.* The act of ejaculating over a ladyfriend's face and then using your thumb to spread your *love porridge* across her forehead in a sweeping fashion similar to the red and blue-*arsed* baboon anointing the eponymous kitten in the aforementioned cartoon.

Simon Cowells *1. n. rhym. slang.* Bowels, *Enochs, ie.* Sometimes irritable and are usually full of *shit.* *2. n. rhym. slang.* Jamrags. From Simon Cowells = sanitary towels. *'Here's a fiver, son. Go and fetch some Simon Cowells for your nan.'*

Simon says *exclam.* Chucklesome preamble to the delivery of a crunchy *air biscuit.*

simpleston *n.* A dim-witted fellow who finds nothing more amusing than them fucking GoCompare meerkat adverts.

Sindy's dildo *n.* A particularly under-endowed *endowment*, that is to say a risibly small penis.

Sindy's tampon *n.* One of them things that smokers stick in the end of their roll-up *coffin nails* to make them even more healthy. A *Harry Wragg* filter.

sine trousers *phr. leg. Lat.* Archaic legal terminology. When a judge wishes to retire to his chambers in order to consider the evidence prior to sentencing in a case involving hardcore *Frankie*, he is said to *adjourn sine trousers.*

sing a rainbow *v.* To *shout soup.*

sing at St. Paul's *v.* To perform *cumulonimbus* on a *cathedral.* To *yodel in the canyon.*

singed tights *n.* Symptom suffered by over-excited middle-aged women in the audience at performances by Tom Jones, the Chippendales, the Wurzels, Gary Barlow *etc. 'BBC News reported that hundreds of female viewers experienced singed tights last night after seeing the video of Michael Gove dancing at Aberdeen's swish Bohemia nightclub.'*

Singer *n.* Sexual athlete, he or she who goes *at it* like a sewing machine.

sing first at Eurovision *euph.* To turn up early to the gents – or on *cottaging/dogging* night at the Thicket Roundabout, Maidenhead, to pick an example

entirely at random – and then find yourself sadly forgotten when the real action happens later in the evening. "Nil points" may result.

singing for your supper *n.* Of a *bog ostrich*, making those vocal noises from which a spectator could safely infer that he is shortly going to be reunited with his tea.

singing ginger *n. Scots.* Glaswegian slang for any beverage containing alcohol. *'An' gie me a bottle o' yer cheapest singing ginger, Jimmy.'*

singing into the mic *sim. Horatio* performed in the style of a *slag night* karaoke star.

singlie rosettes *n.* The discarded *jizzmops* that adorn the floors of unattached men's rooms. *Bedroom popadoms, wanker's crisps, porn crackers.*

sing sweet violets *v.* Airy version of *building a log cabin*, to *take a dump.*

sink a few U boats *v.* To *bid a fond farewell to yesterday's sausages.*

sink plunger *n.* A *tug* administered by an inexperienced woman where she appears to be attempting to snap your *banjo* and pull your *fiveskin* over your *clockweights;* the action she would use when unblocking a borstal kitchen plughole. Opposite of a *squid wank.*

sink the Bismarck *v.* To launch one *fucking* enormous *dreadnought*, deposit a *U-blocker.*

sink the sausage *v.* To get your *leg over.*

sink the skidmark *v.* To repeatedly flush in the hopes of dislodging from the *pan* a piece of *clippage* that is as resilient as a World War II German battleship .

sinky *n.* The *gentleman's wash* taken by a married man in preparation for his annual *Boris Johnson.*

sin lumps *n. Jubblies, kahunas, shirt potatoes, boobs, sweater fruit, knockers, cab man's rests, baps, funbags, bumpies, neddies, chichis, mambas, dirty pillows, chebs, charlies, diddies, doos, cajooblies, jugs, bubbies, zeps, bazongers, headlamps, whammies, norks, bangers, dumplings, hogans, thrupennies, assets, churns, whammers, yoinkahs, begonias, mumbas, pink pillows, top bollocks, melons, oomlaaters, nellies, choozies, chubblies, chumbawumbas, blimps, charms, baby's dinners, fun cushions, paps, bojangles, garbonzas, airbags, Gert Stonkers, puppies, Bristols.* That'll be tits, then.

siphon the python *v.* To take a *Chinese singing lesson*, see a *man about a dog*, turn your *bike around.* To go for a *gypsy's kiss.*

SIP/sip *acronym.* When you get home from work and everybody's out so you can have a Shit In Peace.

sip that off a spoon, you could *exclam. medic.*

Expression used in the medical profession to describe the more fluviatile *digestive transits* of a patient. *'How is the lady in bed five coming along, matron?' 'It's hard to tell really, Dr Nookey. One day you could bolt the door with her shits, the next day you could sip them off a spoon.'*

Sir Alan's lieutenants *n.* The sour-faced duo who hang around underneath one's *Lord Sugar*. *The gonk-faced Mother Teresa sisters, McSquirter twins.*

Sir Anthony *n. rhym. slang.* A proper *charlie*. From Sir Anthony Blunt = cunt.

Sir Cliff's neck *n.* The bit of taut, elongated *scrotum* just above the bit that's got your *knackers* in.

Sir Douglas *n. rhym. slang.* Shit. From Sir Douglas Turd.

Siri play me some James Blunt *exclam.* Announcement of the imminent arrival of a very loud and pungent *Bonfire Heart*. A reference to the former *short-arsed* tank driver turned warbler.

Siri, pull my finger *exclam.* See *and one from the bottom please, Rachel.*

sir lunchalot *n. prop.* An enthusiastic, salad-dodging expense account diner. A *Charlie two-dinners* or *Lord of the pies.*

SISO/siso *1. acronym.* A gentleman who suffers from premature ejaculation. A *two-push Charlie.* From Straight In Straight Out. *2. acronym.* Allowances claim protocol for members of the European Parliament, *viz.* Sign In, Sod Off.

sit down meal *n.* A relaxing four- or five-course *shit* that has a habit of spreading out into Sunday afternoon.

site box *1. n.* In the construction industry, a filthy, dented, cold and rattly receptacle that everybody is allowed to chuck their tools in at the end of the day. *2. n.* In a public house, a resident female with a filthy, dented, cold and rattly *box* that everybody is allowed to chuck their *tools* in at the end of the night. A *shed.*

sit on a mortar *v.* To suffer the catastrophic consequences of a *dirty bomb* detonation. *"'Unfortunately my dear Mrs Bennet, Mr Darcy had some dodgy prawn chimichongas for lunch and has sat on a mortar, thus I regret that he will not be able to attend tea at the parsonage.'"* (from *Pride and Sensibility* by Jane Austen).

sit-on job *n.* Term used in the construction industry referring to the hanging out of a contract. *'You want it finished in time for the opening ceremony, do you? Up your bollocks, this is a sit-on job, mate. We'll get eight more turkeys out of this power station, don't you worry.'*

sitting on a brown snake *n.* Having to stay seated so you don't let the *bowl constrictor* escape.

sitting on an elephant *adj.* To be highly *burbulent*, to have *brewed a massive one up.*

sitting on the stove *euph.* Of a lady, to have been *scuttled* from behind so hard and so often that she develops twin circular red glowing patches at the back and top of her thighs, as if she has been resting her *arse* on the two front rings of the cooker hob.

sitting on your balls, it's like *sim.* Descriptive of the unpleasant and distinctly sickening feeling experienced when watching the fake jollity and camaraderie between the hosts of BBC's breakfast programme.

sitting, standing, leaning *1. n.* One of the hilarious, totally improvised rounds in the hilarious, totally improvised gameshow *Whose Line is it Anyway?*, throughout which each of the three contestants was required to adopt one of the specified postures at all times. *2. n.* In any *troilistic* pornographic scenario, a common arrangement of the participating artistes, adopted in order to facilitate the filming of *DPs, spitroasts, anal titwanks, sticky belly flapcocks etc.*

situation room, the *n.* The *water closet.*

Sitzpinkler *n. Germ.* Old Teutonic term typically referring to a man who sits down in order to urinate.

six-back *n.* The not-overly attractive rolls of lard on the backs of fat grannies. *Back tits.*

six dwarf *n.* Wife or girlfriend that constantly changes her mood like Snow White's monomaniacal bachelor cohabitees, "but is never Happy". And so...

six dwarves *euph.* Not happy.

six knuckle shuffle *n.* An act of *personal pollution* enjoyed by one who lives in a rural community on the Norfolk, Lincolnshire and Cambridgeshire borders.

six nowt *euph.* Descriptive of something performed on the *old walking stick con gusto.*

six-pack grip *n.* See *tenpin.*

six-point-niner *n.* A *sixty-niner* which is "interrupted by a period", *viz.* "6.9".

sixteen valve *n.* A stunner, a proper *goer.*

sixth gear *n. Wanking*, especially in a parked car. See *stick shifter.*

sixtitty-nine *n.* A sort of splendid lesbian version of *looping-the-loop* which somehow involves four knockers. See also *clam 69.*

sixty-eight *n.* Oral sex undertaken on the understanding that the favour will be returned. *"Ere, give us a sixty-eight and I'll owe you one.'*

sixty grit *1. n.* The coarsest grade of sandpaper

available. *2. n.* The coarsest grade of woman available. *'Up betimes, and much perturbed to find a veritable piece of sixty grit alongside me in the fart sack. Resolv'd never again to mix the port and the stout.'* (from *The Diary of Samuel Pepys*).

sixty-nine *n.* *Soixante-neuf, loop the loop.* Also known as a *sixty-niner.* Put crudely, mutual simultaneous oragenitalism. Named after the atomic number of thulium.

60-second assassin *1. n.* New York-based affiliate of nine-man hip-hop troupe the Wu-Tang Clan. *2. n.* A gentleman who is *up and over like a pan of milk.* Also *Benjamin Button, fruit machine Freddy, Ikea bulb, one pump chump, two-push Charlie,* or *minuteman.*

size aero *euph.* The opposite of size zero. The dress size of a lady who has a tendency towards over-indulgence in the popular, eponymous bubble-filled chocolate confection.

size ten *euph.* How girls of sizes fourteen to eighteen describe themselves prior to going on a blind date.

skagamuffin *n.* A colourful street urchin with the impressive ability to transmute shoplifted goods, his landlord's furniture and friends' giros into narcotics.

skanky panky *1. n.* Scoring with a member of the lower orders. *2. n.* Relations with someone sufficiently attractive for one to overlook their poor personal hygiene.

skate wings *n.* Very large, fishy, pink *Keith Burtons.* Often served with a white, creamy sauce.

skeet *1. v. US.* To shoot clay pigeons. *2. v.* To *shoot your load.* To *come off at the Billy Mill roundabout.*

skeeze *v. US.* To *shag, shtup.*

Skeggie donkey *euph.* A *bint* who'll let anyone get their *leg over* for a quid. And has all flies round her *arse.*

skelpit erse *sim. Scots.* Descriptive of a face that looks like a *smacked arse.* A *torn-faced bint.*

sket vet *n.* The clinic where a fellow must take his *cocker* when it picks up a *Doonican* such as *happy rash,* the *pox* or *galloping knob rot.*

ski-ba bop-ba-dop bop *exclam.* Said as one is just about to *go down* on a partner's anal cavity. Aptly taken from the lyrics of the one-hit-wonder *I'm a Scatman* by Scatman John.

skiddy fiddler *n.* One with an arguably unhealthy interest in soiled undergarments.

skid games *n.* Gambling that a *fart* is not a *shit.* Poor play can lead to serious injury or even death.

skidmarks *n.* Severe *russet gusset, pebble dashing* of the *undercrackers,* the *turtle's brylcreem.*

skid-marquetry *n.* Decorative finish applied to ceramics and porcelain using a self-adhesive brown veneer.

skidmata *n.* The miraculous brown wounds which manifest themselves on the fingertips of one who is a martyr to thin *bumwad.* Also *taxi driver's tan, mechanic's fingernails.*

skid missile *n.* A large *grogan* which shoots round the U-bend in record time, leaving a smoking trail of unprecedented devastation in its wake.

skidnature *n.* That which is scribbled in *brown crayon* on the porcelain.

skidney stones *n.* The solid consequences of *netting a serve,* found rolling around in the *sump* of the *underchunders. Bonus balls.*

skidoo *n.* A Glühwein-fuelled *wind sketch* in the salopettes that is accompanied by a high-pitched buzz reminiscent of an over-revved two-stroke engine.

skid pan *n.* A *bum sink* that looks like the *starting line at Brands Hatch, eg.* One out of a student house.

skid pan alley *euph.* A row of poorly maintained public *chod bin* cubicles.

skid row *1. n.* A run-down district east of downtown Los Angeles where *Harold Ramps* have congregated in large numbers since the 1930s. *2. n.* In one's local area, a stretch of path, alley or ginnel where irresponsible dog owners allow their *shit machines* free expression.

skidzilla *n.* Someone who specialises in leaving monster-sized, smoking tracks on the toilet bowl. *'Looks like Skidzilla has been on the rampage again, your holiness. That bog looks like Richard Hammond's driveway.'*

skiff *v. RN.* A tradition of the Royal Navy and the Royal Marines, whereby a member of the other ranks rubs his *bellend* – or a finger that has been up his *jacksie* – over a cup or plate that is going to be used by an officer. Tableware on the Royal Yacht Britannia was apparently routinely *skiffed* until that vessel was decommissioned in 1997. *'Room service was good, although I noticed that my toothbrush, face flannel and shaving brush had been thoroughly skiffed by the maid while I was enjoying my splendid full English breakfast in the elegant Tudor dining room.'*

skiing position *n.* *Pulling off* two men at the same time while wearing only a *helmet, goggles and thick mittens. Crane operating, Madam twoswords.*

ski jump *n.* That challenging first *slash* of the day when one has woken up *piss proud.*

skimmed milk *1. n.* Horribly thin and weedy dairy produce that invariably spoils a perfectly good cup of tea. *2. n. Baby gravy* with all the goodness taken out. *Decaff spaff* that would also, to be fair, comprehensively spoil a cuppa.

skimming *n.* A discreet act performed by a gentleman who secretly wants to avoid getting his broody missus up the stick; regularly *beating his meat* in order to "skim off" the healthiest *tadpoles* from his *man milk.*

skin boat *n.* The male penis. *'I think I'll sail the old skin boat to tuna town.'*

skin chimney *n.* A flue that requires regular sweeping with a *womb broom.*

skin-clad tube *n.* A *live sausage*, a *girlometer.*

skin flick *n.* A *nuddy film* or *blue movie.*

skin flute *n.* A *fleshy flugelhorn, bed flute, pink oboe.*

skin grafts *n.* Somewhat unimpressively low relief *tits.*

skinny latte *n.* The runny, watery fluid typically released at the climax of a chap's third *glad-handing* of the day when he is *working from home.*

skinstick *n.* A tumescent *bum beater.*

skinternet *n.* Ceefax, teletext. From skint + internet.

skin the rabbit *v.* To forcefully pull the pelt off an *old friend.*

skin violin *n.* The *string section* counterpart to the *pink oboe. 'After 10,000 hours of rigorous study of his mam's Grattan catalogues and his dad's copies of Parade, he truly became the Yehudi Menuhin of the skin violin. How tragic that he wanked himself to death at such an early age.'*

skipper 1. *n.* A lady's elusive *clematis, love button, devil's doorbell* or *wail switch.* See *bald man in a boat*, if you can find it. 2. *v. naut.* In naval parlance, to wipe one's *arse* on a slice of bacon prior to presenting it to the captain in a sandwich. The bacon not your *arse.*

skipper's tablecloth *n.* Several sheets of *bumwad* laid carefully across a *self indulgent* chap's stomach and legs in order to contain and absorb any spillages which may occur while he is *tossing* in his bunk.

skippy *n.* A promiscuous male *crumpeteer* who jumps about from *bush* to *bush.* A *fanny hopper, stickman, bush ranger* or *harbour master.*

Skippy's tail *euph.* A preposterously large *turd*, emerging from down under the *chod-hopper* waterline and tapering to a whiplike point. Usually light brown in colour, with a fur-like appearance.

skips without a rope, he *euph.* Descriptive of a fellow who has *yet to find the right girl.*

skirt *n. coll.* Fanny, blart, toosh, talent, crumpet, tussage. *'I've got a pink ticket tonight. Let's get down the bar and pick up some skirt.'*

skirt lifter *n.* The female equivalent of a *shirt lifter.*

A *carpet muncher, lezza, Victorian photographer.*

ski slope *n.* A hair-raisingly elongated *pap baffle* that reaches the back of the seat.

skit *v.* To *shit* diarrhoea. To pour a bowl of hot *hoop soup.*

skittered *adj.* Afflicted with the *skitters.*

skitters, the *n. medic.* The *shits*, *s*quirts, *Earthas, Brads* or *Kurt Schwitters.*

Skittery Gussett 1. *n. prop.* Actual name – it says here – of a member of the Aucocisco Sagamore band of Native Americans who, in 1623, met English explorer Christopher Levett at the Presumpscot Falls in what is now Maine, USA. 2. *n.* The result of *unrest in the south.*

skittling *n. Dining at the Y* during *cricket week.* From the popular fruit-flavoured confectionery catchphrase, *ie.* "Taste the rainbow".

skittuin *n.* That which is produced when suffering from the *Engelberts*, especially in dogs; *canine paint stripper*, puddles of brown acidic gunge on the carpet.

Skoda going over a cattle grid, like a *sim.* Phrase used to describe the throes of female ecstasy. *Shaking like a flat-pack wardrobe. 'After some hours tramping across the remote glens beyond Cairnsmore of Fleet, I found myself hungry and tired at the door of a herd's cottage set in a nook beside a waterfall. The door swung open as I knocked, and stepping inside the lowly dwelling I was surprised to see the householder, a dour, elderly shepherd, up to his apricots in his wife. He was banging away like a steam-hammer as I entered, and, oblivious to my presence, the lady of the house was shaking like a Skoda going over a cattle grid.'* (from *The Sixty-Nine Steps* by John Buchan).

skull buggery *n. Pugwashing, salami-sucking.* Also *skull-fucking.*

skunking *n.* The rejection of a partner's amorous advances by one employing a defence mechanism similar to that of the American stink badger (*Mephitis mephitis*), namely the release of a noisome scent from the anal region. Usually an even more effective deterrent than claiming to have a headache.

skunk skin trousers *n.* A poor excuse for introducing a pungent odour into a room. Also *dog's arse. 'I do apologise, your holiness, only I'm wearing my skunk skin trousers today.'*

skunk stripe *n.* The characteristic white residue left by dried-up *bum sweat* in a pair of ladies' black *grundies.*

skunt *n.* A person what skis. From ski + cunt.

skwank *n.* A video-chat-fuelled act of

self improvement.

skwype *v.* To clean the screen of one's computer following a successful video conferencing session.

skyagra *n.* A quick flick through the satellite TV channels before bedtime, made by a middle-aged gentleman in search of something to boost his flagging *hard-drive.*

skydiver's mouth, fanny like a *sim.* A gaping *clunge* reminiscent of the late great John Noakes hitting terminal velocity with the Red Devils.

skydogs *n.* Seagulls that *crap* everywhere. *Tees ducks, sky rats.*

Skyrim *1. n.* A Space Invaders computer game for children. *2. n.* That pose in certain *noddy books* which shows a lady's tongue hovering a bare millimetre over the *balloon knot* of another nubile female without actually touching it so it doesn't contravene the Obscene Publications Act. Contactless form of *anilingus* as depicted in cheaper foreign *art pamphlets* with names like *Asshole Fucker – In Action!* (€3.99 from most kiosks in Jerez, Spain).

sky sports news, put it this way you'd never see her presenting *phr. Fugly.* A politely-teasing expression of the sort that Radio 5Live's John Inverdale might use to describe a female athlete that he wouldn't touch with yours.

slabber *n.* Someone of whom a fellow would have to drink a full slab of beer before he took them home. Also *double slabber*; a *coyote.*

slabberdash *v.* In fighting or romance, to slap one's opponent or lover upon the side of the face with a semi-erect penis. To *chap.*

slab cracker *n.* Affectionate term of endearment referring to a *digestively overqualified bird.*

slack handful *phr.* A generous helping of something that can be grabbed. *'Wooar, I'll have a slack handful of that alright, Mother Superior.'*

slack in the box *1. adj.* Of a female, possessing a *fanny like a builder's bucket. 2. adj.* Of a male, *hung like a hummingbird.*

slack mabbut *n.* A *hippo's mouth, beef Wellington.*

slacktivewear *n.* Sports clothes worn on the sofa, in the pub, on a bench in the precinct *etc.*

slacktivity *n.* Swinging the lead in the workplace, *eg.* Idly rating the women who walk past, stealing stationery, masturbating in the toilets, stealing toilet paper, masturbating in the stationery cupboard *etc.*

sladger *n.* A west country term for a lady's *minge.* A *Cornish konz.*

slag *1. n.* A woman of easy virtue. A *hingoot. 2. n.* Waste material from a mine. *3. n.* Term of abuse applied liberally to male criminals and other assorted *toe rags* in *The Sweeney.*

slag-a-pult *n.* An aircraft belonging to a budget airline. So called due to the fact that its primary function is to fire drunken young ladies across Europe.

slagazine *n.* Periodical that does not make too many intellectual demands on its female readership, *eg. Take a Break, Chat, Hello, OK, Spare Rib etc.*

slag bag *n.* The one bag for life in your kitchen that all your other bags for life get stuffed into.

slagbait *n.* Aftershave.

slag bat *n.* A crude term for the *rhythm stick.*

slaggle *1. n. coll.* Collective noun for a group of young ladies who are generous with their affections. From slag + gaggle. *2. v.* To barter with a *lady of the night* for a better value *knock up.*

slag hammer *n.* A stout *tool* that a *stickman* uses for *banging twats* rather than nails. Also *twat mallet.*

slag heap *1. n.* A run-down pub or nightclub in any northern town. *2. n.* See *Razzle stack. 3. n. Bike shed.*

slag night *n.* High-spirited female binge drinking excursion in a town centre. A *hen night* or *slag do.*

slag off *v.* To deprecate verbally.

slag pellets *n.* Small tablets used by women to ward away unwanted pests. The *Benny Hill, Harry Hill, Vince Hill.*

slag's breakfast *n.* A raging pre-breakfast *dawn horn* or early morning *drink on a stick. Morning wood, morning glory.*

slag stamp *n.* A tasteful *tartoo* applied to the small of a *salad dodger's* back in the mistaken belief that it will draw attention away from her enormous *shitlocker. See arse antlers,*

slagtime *n.* Type of music that gets every lass in the place up on the dancefloor. Popular *slagtime* numbers include Gloria Gaynor's *I Will Survive,* Whigfield's *Saturday Night* and *Eat Yourself Fitter* by the Fall.

slag wellies *n.* Knee-high boots.

slam dumping *n.* A light-hearted jape whereby the prankster *shits* in the cistern rather than the bowl. *Top decking, slam dunking, top loading.*

slam hound *n.* US. *Slapper, slut, slag, slattern.* See *tenpole tudor.*

slam in the lamb *v.* Bayonet manoeuvre involving the *mutton musket.* From the old New Zealand Lamb television advert slogan that will be immediately familiar to anyone currently approaching death from old age.

slam on the brakes *v.* To stop wiping one's *arse* for some reason, *such as* the house burning down, with the full knowledge that the process is incomplete, resulting in *skidmarks* or *russet gusset*.

slam spunk *v.* To *jump* and thus *empty your balls* into a *hoop*.

slap and tickle *n.* A sex act, a bit like *rumpy pumpy* or *how's your father*, whereby a man wearing a dress shirt and sock suspenders chases a giggling, scantily clad lady round a bed before playfully spanking her *buttocks*, tickling her ribs and *fucking* her up the *cunt* with his *cock*. A *romp*.

slap and trickle *n.* A perfunctory, routine act of *self abuse* that elicits only a half-hearted return on one's *wristy investment,* possibly as a result of the four *wanks* one has had in the previous couple of hours. A low budget *money shot*.

slap happy *adj.* The giddy, cheerful state of light-hearted jubilation a fellow occasionally experiences after *knocking himself about a bit*.

slaphead *n.* A *chrome dome*, a *baaldie*.

slaphood *n.* The prime of a *butcher's daughter's* life.

slapper *n.* An *old banger*. A *high miler* who has been around the block a few times.

slapperazzi *n. coll.* The humorous youths who use their mobile telephones to make amusing films of their friends committing acts of grievous bodily harm on innocent bystanders. *Pappy slappers*.

slappertite *n.* A hunger for loose women. *'Do you fancy a fuck, Donald?' 'No thanks, Stormy. I don't want to spoil my slappertite.'*

slapper trapper *n.* A man who, lacking the wherewithal to trap a *fox*, settles for hunting *swamp hogs* instead. A *pig-sticker.*

slappette *n.* A betracksuited, *hickied*, bubblegum-chewing, *scrunchie*-wearing fledgling *slattern*.

slapster *n.* One afflicted by male pattern baldness, alopecia or mange.

slapstick *n.* A light-hearted, comical *wank,* accompanied by frantic piano music and culminating in a small amount of custard getting thrown.

slap the monkey *v.* To *chimp oneself* till one is *blue in the arse*. To do a *Mary Chipperfield*.

slash *1. n.* A *piss, wee wee, number one*. *2. n.* Stoke-on-Trent-raised *Hatty Town* lookalike guitarist out of Guns'n'Roses.

slash and burn *1. n.* Impressively efficient third world deforestation technique. *2. n.* A painful symptom of the *pox* and the *clap*.

slashback *n.* A *wet penny in the pocket*. Visual evidence of *trouser rain* in the *honeymoon area* following a trip to *turn one's bike around.*

slash in the pan *n.* A quick and unexpected *number one*.

slash on a gorilla's back *n.* A particularly hirsute *growler* of the sort to be seen, apparently, in 80s German erotica.

slash palace *1. n.* Public lavatory. *2. n.* The ostentatious Hollywood home of the top-hatted guitarist out of Guns'n'Roses.

slash point *n.* Sheltered area in a town centre which affords privacy for the purpose of depositing urine, usually located in a bank doorway. *'Hang on lads, I've just got to nip to the slash point before I flood me Calvins.'*

slate layer's nailbag *sim.* Descriptive of very saggy or battered *labia*.

slats *1. n.* Ribs that are rattled. *2. Aus. Beef curtains* that are rattled.

sledge *n.* A bloke who constantly finds himself being *pulled* by *dogs*.

sledgehammering *n.* Violent masturbation. *'Jonathan! Will you keep the noise down? We can't hear ourselves think in here with you next door doing all that sledgehammering.'*

sledging *1. n.* Unsporting cricket match repartee designed to put batsmen off their stroke. *2. n. Aus.* Consenting impolite *rumpy pumpy*. Acts of intercourse during which one or both parties abuse each other with colourful profanities. Foul-mouthed pillow talk. *'August 6th. To the BBC for a recording of Call My Bluff with Frank (Muir), Ian (Ogilvy), Angharad (Rhys), Hannah (Gordon) and Joyce (Grenfell). Joyce afterwards invited me to take tea in her room at the Savoy. One thing led to another and we ended up sledging into the early hours. Gracious, what a potty-mouth she can be.'* (from *Fiddling in the Foliage*, the memoirs of Arthur Marshall).

sleep in a tent *v.* To have a large *bell end* with a *big top*.

sleeping beast *n.* A flaccid *trunk, marshmallowed main pipe*. A *dead budgie*.

sleeping cat *n. A brown beast slumbering contentedly in the U-bend. A night watchman, brown barge in the lock.*

sleeping fruit bat *n.* A vagina with *flaps* which are so big and leathery it appears that the lady has a mammal of the genus *Pteropus* napping between her legs. A *resting pterodactyl.*

sleeping head to toe *n.* Of two *women in comfortable shoes*, to take off their comfortable shoes and get into bed to perform an act of mutual gratification. *Lesbotic sardines. 'I bet there is plenty of sleeping head to toe going on in Style Prison tonight, Home Secretary.'*

sleeping policeman *1. n.* A hump in the road, designed to slow down traffic and remove exhaust pipes from sports cars. *2. n.* An officer of His Majesty's Constabulary in his pyjamas with his eyes shut. *3. n.* An *angry* penis, tucked up behind the belt in order to conceal it from family or friends. *A Kilroy, cruising at periscope depth, peeping over the garden fence.*

sleeping pull *n.* When a fellow is unable to sleep, he may have one or two of these to help him nod off. *Forty wanks, knuckle nightcap, wanker's cocoa, pullaby.*

sleep mode *n.* A married man's semi-somnolent state, whereby he appears to be awake and listening to his wife, even nodding and occasionally murmuring assent, while he is actually completely oblivious to every single word she has said for the last half hour. Just like the Amazon Echo, a man can be instantly awoken from *sleep mode* by the use of the phrase "What do you think?"

sleep on a chocolate *v.* To *shit the bed*. In upmarket hotels, it is common practice for the staff to place a posh chocolate on a turned down sheet, leading to distress and confusion in the morning. *'Can you taste this for me, luv? I'm reasonably sure I've been sleeping on a chocolate, but there's also the possibility that I've slept on a chocolate.'*

sleepover *n.* The sort of miraculous hangover enjoyed by students, jobseekers and bar personnel the world over whereby, following a surfeit of booze, they simply remain comatose throughout all the unpleasantness and wake up on the other side with a slightly dry mouth and feeling a bit hungry.

sleep vaulting *n.* Gentleman's nocturnal discomfort, which involves him growing a massive *pole* while asleep, only for it to jam into the sheet when he tries to turn over, thus startling him into pained wakefulness. A *motorcycle kickstand* complication.

sleep with *v.* To *fuck* someone, for example up against the side of a bus shelter or behind a skip.

slice *n.* A portion of *hairy pie*. *'Do you want some custard on that slice, madam?'*

slice of cheesecake *n.* A *plate* of *horatio*. *'Belgravia was powerless to resist. His eyes burned into hers like caborundums. His strong arms enfolded her tender body as she felt herself being swept away in an Aurora Australis of passion. Eagerly she fell to her knees, pulled down his scuds and helped herself to a slice of cheesecake.'* (from *The Lady and the Darts Player* by Barbara Cartland).

slice of wind & a fried snowball *euph.* Fuck all. *'What are you having off the two-course menu, Posh?' 'I'm absolutely starving, David, so I'll have a slice of wind and a fried snowball, please.'*

slick 50 *1. n.* An engine oil additive of debatable utility. *2. n.* A newly divorced middle-aged gent who drives a brand new convertible, goes to the gym (mainly the yoga classes) and, annoyingly, somehow manages to pull *top end scrunt* that is at least 30 years his junior.

slider *1. n. US.* A steam-grilled (it says here) sandwich that is usually two inches in size. *2. n.* British term for a *brown steamer* of similar dimensions, which has slid from the *ring* to splash down in the *chodhopper*.

Slimbridge, dawn chorus at *sim.* The cacophonous symphony of hooting, quacking, honking and whistling which emanates from a lavatory cubicle occupied by a person *paying in installments* for a particularly virulent and delicious *slip-up* feed. From the aural similarity to the early morning sounds heard at the late Sir Peter Scott's famous duck zoo.

slime *v. Aus.* To ejaculate, *chuck one's muck*. To reach *Lake Wendouree*.

Slim Pickens is waving his hat *exclam.* An expression of relief after the first *bombs away* moment following a spell of sluggish *digestive transit*, such as might be caused by a week on Cocodamol. From the famous last scene of the film *Dr Strangelove*.

slip a length *1. v.* To *give a good seeing-to to someone. 'I'd slip her a length any day of the week, your honour.' 2. v.* In the world of *saucy* seaside postcards, a conversational misunderstanding involving a landlady with a tenant who works at a linoleum factory.

slipcase *1. n.* Hard cover inside which a valuable book may be placed. *2. n.* A bird's *doo-dah* or *fufu*.

slip her a crippler *v.* A few notches up from *slip her a length*, to *shtup* someone so hard they can't walk. See also *kipper ripper, kidney wiper, appendix tickler*.

slip on *1. n.* A type of shoe worn by someone who doesn't know how to tie his laces. *2. n.* A petite lady whom a gent can lift easily and "slip on" his knob. A *fisherman's sock, throwabout*.

slippers, Scouse *n.* Prison-issue white training shoes. *Merthyr flipflops, Geordie brogues.*

slippers, shit in his *v.* To *do the dirty* with a good friend's missus. *'Are you going to poke me then, Eric? I'm absolutely gagging for it.' 'No, I can't Patti. It just wouldn't be cricket to shit in George's slippers like that.'*

slippery as a butcher's cock *sim.* Untrustworthy, sly. From the well known fact that most butchers take carnal advantage of the meat in the back room before selling it. That's why you should always cook it thoroughly or become a vegetarian. Mind you, greengrocers are just as bad. Always wash your hands after handling bananas.

slip the lead *1. v.* Of a dog, to escape from its owners while on a walk and run off, only to later turn up on the doorstep absolutely shagged out and covered in fox shit, chicken feathers and sheep blood. *2. v.* To have one's *jubber ray* fall off in the midst of a *bang*. '*Mick became a father for the eighth time after he slipped the lead during an encounter with a Columbian cocktail waitress following a whirlwind romance and a bunk up behind a skip in St. John's Wood.*'

slit *n. Blit, fanny, vertical bacon sandwich.*

slob *n.* A *slight lob*, not even a quarter of a teacake. Certainly nothing to write home about.

slobbatical, take a *v.* To enjoy an extended break from work in order to "find yourself" by eating junk food and sitting around in your pants and drinking whilst watching old episodes of *Top Gear* on Dave. Excuses for absence include Covid, long-Covid, Covid-like symptoms, and vague and difficult-to-diagnose back pain.

slobberchops *n.* The thin film of translucent *blip* secreted from the *bacon sandwich* that forms a crust in a *bird's dunghampers* after intercourse. '*How dare you accuse me of knocking one out in your scads while you were on holiday? That's the remnants of your slobber-chops, you cheeky cow.*'

Slobodan Milosevic *n. onomat.* The sound made by an explosive outburst of the *squitters*. Named in honour of the genocidal Serbian statesman who *carked it* in 2006.

Slobodan shot *n.* A powerful *shart* that leaves you slumped in a courtroom in The Hague.

slob's oven *sim.* Descriptive of an overused and undercleaned *divot*. With black, carbonized chips lying round the bottom of it. One that would benefit from a good scrubbing with Mr Muscle and a wire brush.

slo-mo-sexual *n.* A *bongo vid* viewer who fast forwards through the foreplay before pausing at the crucial moment and inching through the *money shot* frame by frame.

sloom *n. medic.* The lubricating secretion of the female Bartholin's glands. *Blip, moip, chin varnish.*

slop dodger *n.* A prudish or frigid lady who for some reason objects to getting her face *bespunkled* by a gentleman.

slop on *n.* A state of feminine sexual arousal. A *wide on. 'That bit in Pride and Prejudice where he comes out the pond gave your poor old nan a proper slop on, son.'*

sloppy Giuseppe *1. n.* A spicy, beef-based menu item at Pizza Express. *2. n.* A *well-buttered bun.*

sloppy seconds *n.* To *stir the porridge*. To stick one's

naughty paintbrush into a *billposter's bucket* filled with another chap's *population paste.*

slot *n. Slit.*

slot garnish *n.* A frilly bit of nothing which looks nice, but is quickly pushed to one side so one can tuck into the *meaty main course.* Any ladies' *farting crackers* bought from the Ann Summers shop.

slot machine *n.* A battery-powered *neck massager* that is shaped like a big nobbly *cock.* A fruity *vibrator, bob, AA member, dildo.*

slot-pants *n.* Overly short trousers that ride up the *crack* due to the porcine nature of their wearer.

slottery *n.* A *fucky dip* that may *come up trumps.*

slow cooker *n.* The lower reaches of one's *Simon Cowells,* where a wholemeal *loaf* may be left baking for many hours.

slow over rate *1. n.* Problem affecting Test Cricket whereby not enough overs are achieved per hour. *2. euph.* Problem affecting ugly blokes whereby not enough *leg-overs* are achieved per year.

slow puncture *1. euph.* One of those days when one seems to be constantly *losing gas.* '*I don't know what was in that fifteen pints of Younger's Scotch Bitter I had last night, but I seem to have a slow puncture today.*' *2. n.* The soul-destroying act of attempting to keep *shagging* after you have *chucked your muck.* From the fact that "you can keep it hard as long as you keep pumping, but as soon as you stop it's all over".

slow softie *1. n.* What cyclists call a gradually deflating tyre caused by a small puncture. *2. n.* What *pork swordsmen* call a gradually shrinking *erectivation* caused by drink.

sludge dredgers *n.* XXXL-sized feminine *nether apparel,* made of an absorbent (not shiny) material and cut in the *Bridget Jones* style.

sludge factory *1. n.* Titile of track 3 from grunge legends Alice In Chains's self-titled 1995 album. *2. n.* Your *dirt bakery* or *devil's kitchen.*

sludgie *n. medic.* The first non-liquid *jobby* enjoyed after a colonoscopy.

slug and lettuce *1. n.* Name of a chain of hilarious pubs where, you might think, it would be a good idea to avoid the salads. *2. n.* The post-*pop shot* state of a chap's *pocket rocket* wilting inside a woman's *man mayonnaise*-filled *cabbage.*

slugging/the slug *n.* The unholy act of dragging a dirty *tummy stick* across a lucky lady's forehead, leaving a big trail of glittering slime.

slug on a brillo pad *sim.* Poetic description of the result of *relaxing* rather too often and violently in a *gentleman's way. 'I tell you what, Natasha, I'm going to have to cancel my wank channel subscription. My cock looked like a slug on a brillo pad* this morning.' 'Thanks, Dermot. And now over to Everton Fox with the weather.'

sluice noose *n*. The string that hangs off the end of a *jam rag* which is *in situ* when *Arsenal are playing at home. The white mouse's tail, Fishwick*.

sluice the caboose *v*. To use the shower head to direct a high pressure jet of water up between one's buttocks in order to remove accumulated pubes, *winnits*, badger hair and other miscellaneous anal flotsam, jetsam, detritus and effluvium.

slumberjack *n*. An unbidden stirring of the loins that makes its appearance in the middle of the night and taps the missus insistently on the backside.

slumberlumber *n*. *Morning wood*. A timber kickstand for one's wrinkly, pink-wheeled hairy motorcycle. *Dawn horn*.

slumpiercer *n*. A rail service that carries passengers to and through some of a metroplitan area's less salubrious suburbs.

slurry mints *1*. *n*. Sugar-free sweets that have a laxative effect when eaten in any quantity, which rather undoes all the good work they've done freshening your breath. *2*. *n*. Proprietary branded medicaments for the treatment of acute diarrhoea. *'Can I have some slurry mints please, Mr Chemist? Only I've just ate four packets of slurry mints and I'm pissing rusty water out my arse here.'*

slush *n*. The hugely encouraging, early-stage defrosting of an *ice maiden*'s frosty gusset.

slut *n*. A woman who doesn't wash her nets often enough and has the milk bottle on the breakfast table. She who is no better than she ought to be. Also *slattern, trollop*.

slut hut *n*. An inner city pub, *bike shed*.

slutton *n*. A cross between a *slut* and a *slattern*. Which are both the same thing, if you think about it. *'Where do you think you are you going dressed like that, you dirty slutton?' 'Westminster Abbey. I'm going to get married to Prince Andrew.'*

slut-trotters *n*. High heels.

slybrarianship *n*. A chap's discreet stewardship of his *grumble* stash. *'Few people realise that the poet Philip Larkin was a slybrarian throughout his whole working life.'*

Sly TV *n*. Illegally accessed satellite television. *'Right love, I'm off to the boozer to watch the footie on the Sly TV. It's beamed in from Uzbekistan on the Eurobird, so the commentary will be all tits and thumbs.'*

smackanory *n*. The heart-rending tale of woe with which heroin addicts routinely regale passers-by in the hope of relieving them of their small change.

smackdonalds *n*. A residence in a less than

salubrious *scruburb* where money is deposited in one window and pharmaceuticals are dispensed at another.

smacket *n*. An opioid enthusiast's multi-pocketed coat worn when skulking round shops.

smack fairy *n*. A cheeky imp that gives you a right leathering. *'Fucking hell, Shane. What happened to you?' 'I don't know, I was like this when I woke up. I must've got a visit from the smack fairy in the night.'*

smack generator *n*. A retailer of second hand electrical goods which is used by thieves to convert stolen goods into cash to spend at *smackdonalds*.

smackhead special *n*. A nourishing bus station cafe feast, consisting of pie, chips, peas, two slices of buttered toast and a pot of tea, all for £1.25.

smackiavellian *adj*. Descriptive of the cunning and devious ways off those who enjoy getting *ripped to the tits*.

smack oneself about *v*. To *relax in a gentleman's way*.

smackpool illuminations *n*. Extremely premature and gaudy Christmas.

smacksuit *n*. A set of market-bought athletic clothes of the sort favoured by youngsters on Britain's more vibrant estates.

smack Tardis *n*. A public telephone box, if such a thing still exists, principally used for the purpose of calling heroin dealers in order to expedite multi-dimensional journeys through time and space.

smack tokens *n*. Items of electronic equipment, *eg*. Car radios, laptop computers, videos *etc*., with the plugs cut off.

small arms fire from the suburbs *exclam*. Used to describe a rapid staccato burst of *bottom bullets*, for example as a result of a previous evening's indulgence in dark ales and well-seasoned victuals.

small fanny footprint, he's got a *euph*. Said of an altruistic chap who does his bit to ensure there are more women available for his fellows by electing to *travel on the other bus*.

smank *n*. An act of self pleasurement which unaccountably involves hitting your own penis and testicles. From smack + wank.

smart fart *n*. A targeted act of flatulence that only affects its intended victim. A *bronze bullet*.

smarty pints *n*. The person in the pub who becomes possessed of great wisdom and knowledge after a few drinks. The *Dalai Lager, gintellectual*.

smash *1*. *n*. Brand of instant mashed potato popularised by tin Kermits with Dalek voices in the 1970s. *2*. *v*. *Grumble* channel-specific euphemism for "fuck" popularised by lycanthropic, unemancipated ex-Sky Sports presenter and offside rule expert Richard Keys. *3*. *v*. To succeed hyperbolically in carrying out a simple task.

'Myself headed up the creative team, Lord Sugar, and myself absolutely smashed it.' 'You're fired.'

smashed tarantula *n.* An hirsute *butcher's dustbin.* Also *stamped bat, bottom of a ratcatcher's mallet.*

smashing pumpkins *1. n.* US popular musical combo of some sort. *2. n.* Lady's secondary sexual characteristics.

smash it like a cheap glass, I'd *phr.* Humorous exclamation that signals a lecherous, overweight, impotent, sweating, purple-faced television football pundit's intention to engage in momentary, imaginary coitus with an attractive young lady.

smash or dash? *exclam. interrog.* Humorously rhyming question of the sort typically posed to one another by certain TalkSport presenters when they spot a female in the street.

smashturbate *v.* To *wank* so violently that you damage your *plums.*

smat *n.* The sort of person who drives his electric car to his second home in The Lakes and is constantly banging on about how well Tarquin and Jocasta are doing at "uni". From smug + twat.

smawning *n.* A combination of smirking and yawning; the expression that former Home Secretary Priti Patel typically seemed to adopt when announcing some national disaster or another.

smear campaign *1. n.* A series of verbal or written attacks deliberately intended to defame or discredit someone. *2. n.* What happens inadvertently when one has the *turtle's head. Fudging the issue. 'Oh come on, just answer the question, Mr Howard. In your capacity as Home Secretary, did you or did you not threaten to over-rule the head of the Prisons Service Derek Lewis? Yes or no.' 'I'm not going to answer that, Jeremy, but what I will say is this – if I don't pot the brown soon I'm going to embark on a smear campaign.'*

smear test *1. n.* Something what women get. 2. n. Something what blokes do. *'Where's Justin gone?' 'Oh he's just nipped to the bogs for a smear test, your majesty. He thinks he might have followed through during the first hymn.'*

smear test pizzas *n.* Budget supermarket foodstuff on which the toppings have been kept to a minimum for reasons of economy. *'What's for tea, mum? I hope it's not one of them fucking smear test pizzas again.'*

smedgie *n. Can.* An hilarious practical joke whereby a lady's *bills* are vigorously yanked up her *clopper.* From smeesh + wedgie. What's a

smeesh, you say? Allow us to elucidate.

smeesh *1. n. Can.* Female reproductive *farmyard area.* The *snapper.* 2. *n. Can.* A collective noun for ladies. *Blart, tussage, cabbage.* 3. *n. pej. Can.* A doltish fellow. A *fuckwit.*

smeesh hawk *n. Can.* A *clout* with the *gorilla salad* shaved into a mohican.

smeg *1. n.* Pungent *fromunder.* 2. *n. prop.* Amusingly named Swedish manufacturer of white goods. 3. *n.* A substitute for *fuck* overused in *Red Dwarf.*

smeg cup *n.* The cupped hand traditionally used by *wankers* as a receptacle to catch their *muck* when *pulling the Pope's cap off* in a standing position. A *wanker's chalice, poly grail.*

smeg farmer *n.* A fellow who gives the impression he does not pay particular attention to hygiene in the *fiveskinular* region. Also *tramp's mate, indoor hobo.*

smegma *n.* A slightly longer version of the fridge manufacturer.

smegma dome *n.* A baby *bell end*, with a waxy, red skin. The *lid, Dutch strawberry.*

smegma kazoo *n.* A male *membrum virile* from which it is difficult to get a tune notwithstanding the enthusiastic ministrations of an obliging *oboeist.*

smeg peg *n.* An unwashed penis, with a gamey aroma redolent of *spunk* and stale *blip.*

smeg pegs *n. pl.* Buck teeth which are particularly useful for grating the cheese off a chap's *herman gelmet. 'Don't forget to brush your smeg pegs before you go to bed, Janet.'*

smelegant *adj.* Descriptive of the sort of *honk* emanating from the *chuff* of a stylish or aristocratic person, such as Beau Brummell, Simon Sebag-Montefiore or Laurence Llewelyn Bowen.

smellbound *adj.* The feeling of having a particularly potent *Bakewell tart* fermenting in one's guts with release imminent. *'Are you okay, Louise? You look like you're in pain.' 'I'm just a bit smellbound, Dan, that's all. Anyway, here's the news, travel and weather wherever you're watching this morning.'*

smellend *n.* The piquant result of a chap attending to his personal hygiene regimen with insufficient dilligence.

smellfie *n.* An arms-length mobile phone photograph of one's own *tea towel holder. 'Ooh look. Your nan's posted another smellfie on Facebook.'*

smellibacy *n.* An involuntary state of total sexual abstinence caused by cleanliness issues. Up to seventy percent of *professional outdoorsmen* are believed to be effectively *smellibate* at any one time.

smelling a rat *n.* The result of an insufficiently rigorous feminine daintiness programme. Also *tuna bake.*

smelling mistake *n.* Emitting an unpleasant miasma and/or a comical sound from one's *fundament* at a time when one would be best advised to grit one's teeth and hang on for dear life in an attempt to keep it in, *eg.* At a funeral, while exchanging one's wedding vows, when being chased through a spaceship by an alien.

smellmet *n.* A smelly *helmet.* From smelly + helmet.

smellody *n. Chamber music* played on a *wind instrument.* A *botty bugle* solo of a particularly musical timbre.

smells like a Beach Boy's bird's fanny *sim.* Found wanting in matters of personal freshness. From the lyrics to the song *California Girls, viz.* "Those Southern girls with the way they talk, they knock me out when I'm down there".

smells like a big 'un *phr.* An expression of male bravado to make up for being *a bit lacking in the trouser department.* 'It may only be little, love, but it smells like a big 'un.'

smell that! *exclam.* Not, as one might imagine, an enthusiastic invitation to enjoy a rich *banker's draught.* Rather, a phrase used after announcing to colleagues that one has given the *bag for life* a right good *seeing to* before coming to work. Usually delivered in a loud voice, with one's boiler suit round the ankles and accompanied by a vigorous pointing action.

smell the toffee, wake up and *exclam.* Useful phrase which a married man can use when a *breakfast maker* has failed to rouse his missus from her slumbers.

smelly as a dog walker's van *sim.* A right whiffy *quimpiece.*

smellycopter *n.* Unflushable *number two* that simply rotates dizzily with each and every pull on the chain.

smig *n. W. Yorks.* A person of *shit* quality from Huddersfield. Subs please add joke here.

sminge *n.* The act of inserting a sugar-free mint into a *minge* for freshness. For the male alternative, see *smint shuffle.*

smint shuffle *n.* Allowing a small breath-freshening mint to dissolve under the *fiveskin* in order to make the *herman gelmet* cool and tingly in preparation for a subsequent *wank.* The technique can also be used by the more considerate *noshee* prior to receiving a *nosh* to mask the emetic aroma of *hedam* and thus make the experience

marginally less vile for his *noshatrix.*

Smithfield porter's cap *n.* A *clopper* deprived of its necessary monthly launder.

SMOG/smog *acronym.* Suck Me Off Gob. A lady's mouth which appears capable of drawing a golfball through 200 yards of garden hose, *eg.* Angelina Jolie, Sophie Marceau or any Brazilian *bird* one cares to mention.

smoke *n.* A *chewie,* a *nosh.* A *blow job.* 'Excuse me, Miss Taylforth, this is a no-smoking taxi.'

smoke a gadgee *v.* To take a few drags on a *fag.* Though not in a public place.

smoke it to the filter *v.* To *deep throat* a fellow's *gigglestick* all the way, like a seasoned professional.

smoke out the mole *v.* To avail oneself of the laxative effects of the first *coffin nail* of the day. To spark up an *Embassy number two.*

smoker's cough *n.* The phlegmy substance that the *bag for life* leaves in the *Rick Witter* after you have been *boffing* her up the *whispering Bob* all night.

smoke the bald man *v.* To light up a *salami cigarette, smoke the white owl.*

smoking bangers, looks like she's been *sim.* Descriptive of a woman *with a lovely personality, ie.* One who looks as though she's been sparking up fireworks.

smoo *n. Aus.* A *minge,* a *sportsman's gap.*

smoot *n. medic.* The *fufu.* 'The babysitter wanted me to go to bed after Big Brother, so I gave her a right kick up the smoot, mum.'

smooth as snake shit *sim.* A phrase used to describe a bloke who has unrivalled success chatting up the ladies, such as Callum Best, and which can also be used to describe the miraculous effect of Gillette's new 10-blade razor on one's chin. Also *smoother than silkworm shit.*

SMS **1.** *abbrev.* Something to do with text messages, probably. Fuck knows. Something messaging something, probably. **2.** *abbrev.* Saturday Morning Shag. 'No, I better not have another. The wife's promised me an SMS tomorrow.

smudger *n.* A press photographer. See also *craparazzi, pap.*

smug **1.** *adj.* Overly pleased and self-satisfied. **2.** *n.* An ephemeral morning *cock* blockage that causes a *piss* aimed north to actually emerge at all other points of the compass for just long enough to require the missus to fetch a mop and bucket. From smeg + plug.

smugget *n.* A *tittishly* self-satisfied pearl of erudite wisdom. On *Have I Got News For You,* Ian Hislop is wont to deliver a *smugget* at the end of each answer, before tapping his pen on the desk and pulling an expression like one of those squashable rubber faces with finger holes in the back.

smugglers' haven *1. n.* Club 18-30 campsite situated near Newquay. *2. n.* The *arsehole*. *'I can't wait to get some smugglers' haven at Smugglers Haven, Dave.'*

smuggling a brownie *n.* Being in possession of the *turtle's head*. *'He seemed quite anxious to get away, officer. I suspect he was smuggling a brownie.'*

smuggling Smarties *euph.* Of a lady, having her *fighter pilot's thumbs* visibly erectivated under her blouse.

smug shot *n.* One's favourite selfie.

smunt *1. n.* A freshening mint surreptitiously inserted into the folds of a particularly malodorous *furry hoop* prior to performing an act of *cumulonimbus* thereupon. May range in size and strength from a Tic-Tac to a Trebor Extra-Strong, depending on the relative aroma level and the space available. Also *bint imperial, crack bullet* and *sminge*. *2. n.* A smug *cunt*. From smug + cunt. *'Sebastian! Sebastian! Big smile over here for the Standard, you smunt.'*

smurfing *n. Blue surfing.* Trawling the information superhighway on the lookout for pictures of *tits, bums, fannies*, the lot.

smurf's hat *n.* A freshly filled *dunky*. *'Please dispose of sanitary napkins and smurf's hats in the receptacle provided.'*

smush piece *n.* The *faff.* A lady's *front bottom*, a *clopper*.

smut *n.* Mild *jazz. Porn lite* that would make a maiden aunt purse her lips like a dog's *ringpiece*.

smut butter *n. Man paste, jazz funk, baby gravy, Winner's sauce.*

smutton *adj.* Romantically smitten by a woman *with a lovely personality. 'He's inconsolable. He was smutton with Clarissa Dickson-Wright and now she's gone.'*

snaccident *n.* Eating an entire box of chocolates, a whole box of Ritz crackers or a family size bag of crisps by mistake. *'What can I say? It was a snaccident. These things happen.'*

snachos *n.* Crispy flakes of salty skin that fall from a scrofulous *mingepiece* when it is scratched.

snackered *adj.* Extremely fatigued consequent upon overconsumption of pastry-based comestibles. From snack + knackered.

snackspectations, great *n.* The feeling of searching through your cupboard for something, only to find that nothing meets your specific grazing needs.

snack whore *n.* A lady who *does it* for a Greggs vanilla slice, a steak bake or a bag of pickled onion Monster Munch rather than freebase cocaine.

snag your jeans on a nail *v.* To emit a high-pitched, rasping *ringtone*.

snail's doorstep *n.* A slippery area found just south of the *devil's doorbell*.

snail trail *n. Smoo juice* in a lassie's well-worn *scuns*.

snake *v.* To *fuck, poke, bang, futter*.

snake charmer *n.* A girl who has an uplifting effect on your *pant python*, such that it rises up and sways about in her face.

snakecharmer's basket *1. n.* A lavatory so heavily beturded by *bowl constrictors* that it resembles the inside of the popular bazaar entertainer's wickerware prop. *'Oh, and before you go for your doctor's appointment, can you give the upstairs snakecharmer's basket a thorough going over?' 2. n.* A roomy receptacle that is capable of accommodating a serpent of any size, possibly even accompanied by a cross-legged fakir playing a pungi (look it up).

snake eater *n.* A fearless *nosh artist* whose *deep-throating* skills rival those of a mongoose. A *sword swallower*.

snakeskin *1. n.* The clothing sloughed off in one piece and found at the bottom of the bed after a night *on the piss. 2. n.* The dried, flaky layer that tends to form overnight on the *gock* of an unhygienic male who nods off after commiting an act of *self-pollution*.

snake spit *n.* The clear fluid that precedes the *jizz bolt. Perseverance soup, ball glaze, preek. 'Get some snake spit on them boots, soldier. I want to be able to see my face in them. What do I want to be able to see in them, you horrible little royal highness?'*

snap and tickle *n.* Of an *earthing cable*, the phenomenon of it touching the bottom of the *chod bin* before snapping off at the *clackervalve*, and then striking the back of the *chicken skin handbag* as it falls.

snap, crackle, plop *onomat.* The sound made in the bowl during a particularly satisfying session of *parking one's breakfast*.

snapdragon *n.* A normally agreeable female who, under certain circumstances, *such as* when *up on blocks* or full of *tart fuel*, becomes a vicious, fire-breathing monster.

snap ET's neck *v.* To *crimp off a length of dirty back*.

snapped candles *sim.* Descriptive of the legs after a night *on the lash*, when one is wearing one's *wobbly boots*.

snapper *1. n.* North-east colloquialism for a thin fellow. *2. n. milit.* Royal Naval slang for one who is *nicely poised. 3. n.* A lady's *bodily treasure*.

snap the key off in the lock *v.* To suffer an unsatisfying *shit. 'Good dump, dear?' 'Sadly not, my petal. I'm afraid I've snapped the key off in the lock. I'll* *have this pine cone in all night now.'*

snaptwat *n.* A person who spends more time on their mobile, filming themselves and taking "selfies" for the amusement of people who don't give a *fuck*, than they do living in the real world.

snart *1. v.* To sneeze and *fart* at exactly the same moment, resulting in *nose jizz* on the face or *rabbit tods* in the *bills*. Or both, if you're lucky. *2. v.* To snore and *fart* at the same time. *'I couldn't get to sleep last night. The missus wouldn't stop snarting.'*

snatch *n. Quim*, vagina, *liver sock*.

snatch fence *n.* An invisible, *cock*-proof barricade erected down the centre of the matrimonial bed following a domestic argument. A *gash barrier*.

snatchfinder general *n.* One with a preternatural ability to track down *crumpet*.

snatch fit *adj.* Back on active service after a week on the *blob bench*.

snatch hatch *n.* Feminine version of the more traditional male public toilet *glory hole*.

snatchlings *n.* Up-and-coming *talent*.

snatchment area *n.* The geographical radius from which a drinking establishment draws its feminine clientele.

Snatchmo *n.* A *fanny* with lips strong enough to play *Basin Street Blues* on an E-flat trumpet.

snatch mouse *n.* A tampon, *cotton pony*, *Prince Charlie*, *chuftie plug*.

snatchoo *n. onomat.* A particularly violent gust from a lady's *tuppence* during, or just after, a frantic session. A sudden sneeze of air mid- or post-coitus. Also *queef, dropped hat, cunt grunt*. *'Snatchoo!' 'Bless you, Sue.'*

snatchos *n.* Dried flakes drizzled with sour cream and festooned with cheese, sometimes served with a spicy meat filling in the back row of the cinema.

snatch patch *n.* A feminine hygiene product. A *fanny nanny, beaver dam*.

snatchphrase *n.* A particularly successful chat-up line.

snatch ponytail *1. n.* A fancy plait that "snatches" the face, lifting the cheekbones, it says here. As worn by Kim Kardashian and Ariana Grande. *2. n.* High-maintenance *hairy knickers*.

snatch quack *n. medic.* One who has the sexy, enviable job of examining malfunctioning, diseased and infected *minges*. A *box doc, fanny mechanic*. A gynaecologist.

snatch rats *n.* Ladies' sanitary products. *Jampaxes, jam rags, etc*.

snatch scratcher *n.* The small, ineffectual *cock* of one who is *hung like a Shetland rabbit*. A *tenis, gnomon, grubscrew, meat stub* or *wurzel*.

snatchsquatch *n.* A particularly hirsute, aggressive,

and sexually-dominant lass.

snatch 22 *n.* An aesthetically unconventional woman who would, paradoxically, require so much beer to *scuttle* that you couldn't *get it up* anyway. Bit sexist.

snatch up TV *n.* Watching *Frankie* from where you left off after being interrupted by the missus, girlfriend, vicar, fire brigade *etc*.

snatchwork quilt *n.* An impressive display of *niff mags* arrayed across the duvet prior to indulging in a *five knuckle shuffle*.

snatch worms *n.* Tiny pieces of tightly rolled bog paper that lurk in the labial folds, normally only discovered when particularly expert *cumulonimbus* dislodges them from their hidey-holes.

sneaky blinder *n.* A silent *Lionel Bart* that brings tears to the eyes of everybody in the room.

sneaky Hitler *n.* The surreptitious slipping of one's index finger under one's nose in order to savour the aroma of one's ladyfriend's *blip*.

sneaky Keith *euph.* To surprise your *significant other* by unexpectedly *slipping them a length* up the *wrong 'un*. From the song *Losing My Touch*, as performed by leather-faced guitar zombie Keith Richards, *viz.* "Keep an eye on on your front door, baby/I'll be slipping in round the back".

sneaky Kiki *n.* A clump of pubular follicles protruding above the trouser line. A reference to the sexually provocative French frog who used to climb up a ladder and poke her head over the garden wall in *Hector's House*. A *hairy Kilroy*.

snedds *n. Lincs.* Flatlander argot for *winnits*.

snedge *1. n.* Snow. *2. n. Jism*.

snedgehog *n.* A person with a voracious appetite for *the white stuff*. *'Oh, so he's a snedgehog, is he, the lanky one? Who'd have thought it? Mind you, that would explain that whole hoo-ha in the hotel.'*

snedger *n. Snufty, snurglar, snudger, quumfer*. Another name for a smeller of ladies' bicycle seats.

sneeze in the cabbage *v. arch.* To *lick someone out* in the 18th Century. Also *dine at the Y, don the beard, clean behind the curtains, eat sushi off a barbershop floor*.

snicker stool *n.* A vegetarian's nut-enriched *arse bar*.

sniffers' row *n.* In a strip club, the seats that are closest to the stage. *'Quickly, Lord Longford. I've saved you a place in sniffers' row.' 'Thank-you Mrs Whitehouse.'*

sniff the air, kiddies. there's vitamins *exclam.* A Wildean apophthegm uttered by the purveyor of a particularly pungent *eggo*.

sniff the cork *v.* To check one's finger the morning after going *knuckle deep* up the missus's *bonus* *tunnel,* to determine whether your hand needs a proper wash with soap or whether a quick wipe on her flannel will suffice.

snifter *1. n.* A harmless daytime drink enjoyed by a hopeless alcoholic. *2. n.* A brief interlude of *working from home* snatched between conference calls taken from one's sofa. *3. n.* Any other convenient opportunity to swiftly *bash one out.* 'Sun's over the yard arm, dear. Time for a quick snifter.'

sniggerette *n.* A drug addict's *tab* containing a quantity of *happy baccy.* A *spliff.*

sniping *n.* Accidentally shooting a jet of *slash* through the gap between the rim of the *chod bin* and the underside of the seat and onto your *kex* while sat down having a *Tom tit.* A *Wee-Harvey Oswald, rim shot.*

snipper reflex *n. medic.* The counter-productive and inexplicable urge to cut a *cable* before it is fully *laid,* usually resulting in an *arse like a Marmite pot.*

snippit valve *n.* The *anal sphincter.* The *nipsy, cigar cutter, turtle guillotine.*

snish *n.* The result of a person with poor bladder control sneezing. From sneeze + pish. Also *a-pissue.*

snitches *n.* *Two aspirins on an ironing board, stits, fried eggs.*

snoaking *n.* The time-honoured pastime of putting a lady's used *dunghampers* up to one's face, covering the nostrils and mouth and inhaling the *fent* from her *smush piece.* 'I'm sorry Lord Archer. You'll have to leave the premises. This is a no snoaking brothel.'

snob sick *n.* Vomit with plenty of canapes and Chardonnay in it outside a wine bar.

snobtoss *n.* An act of cultured *self-pollution* committed while watching a sophisticated, subtitled movie on Film Four.

snog *v.* To *swap spit, tongue wrestle, play tonsil hockey.*

snogging water *n.* A male grooming lotion that smells like *Joan Collins's knickers. Fanny-magnetic* aftershave, such as Hi Karate, Brut 33 or Old Spice.

snood *1. n.* Some sort of peculiar scarfy-balaclava-cum-hat-type contrivance. *2. v.* To surreptitiously sniff the saddles in a ladies' bicycle shed. To *snuft, snudge, shramp, quumf, scrunge, pringle, snerge, snedge, snaffle, snarze, snerk, snerdle, shniffle-piffle, nurf, moomph, barumph, garboon, poon, snarf, snurdle* or *snurge. 3. n.* A *fiveskin* that bunches loosely around the neck of the *tallywhacker,* due to historic *banjo string* trauma.

snoodling *n.* An unlikely sounding sexual practice

reputedly favoured by gents who are *good with colours,* whereby one of them pulls his *fiveskin* over the *herman gelmet* of his chum. Also *docking,* a *clash of heads.*

snookered behind the red *adj.* Unable to *sink the pink* due to the time of month, and therefore faced with a *difficult brown.*

snooker rest *n.* The *Bristol channel* of an amply endowed lady, used to steady the *pink cue* as it slides back and forth before making a *shot.*

snoopies *n. Spaniel's ears, Ghandi's flip-flops.*

snooze control *n.* Tying to maintain composure when in bed next to a new partner, desperately holding in your *night-farts* and praying you don't dribble, snore or mutter a co-worker's name whilst sporting a *hard-on like a baby's arm holding an apple.*

snoregasm *n.* The culmination of a *wet dream.*

snorgasbord *n.* A filling buffet consisting of food which can effectively be prepared while in the arms of Morpheus through an excess of drink, *eg.* Chips. 'I was just knocking meself up a nice evening snorgasbord when I set the house on fire.'

snorkeller's lunch *n.* A moist fish dish which is a particular favourite amongst *muff divers.*

snorkelling *n.* The holding of a gentleman's *nollies* in the mouth while applying a repetitive stroke to his *favourite member.*

snorker *n.* A *sausage, porky banger, Cumberland.*

snot *n.* The perineum of the lady. Because "it's not" *etc. etc.* Also *tinter, werntfor.*

snot allotment *n.* A sleeve-based greenspace.

snot noodle *n.* A shred of nasal detritus rendered visible following a violent sneeze. 'Bless you, your holiness. Oh, and you've got a snot noodle. That's it, use the sleeve of your soutane there.'

snotty eye *n.* The result of a poorly-controlled male *stress relief exercise.*

snotty hammock *n.* The gusset area of a maiden's intimate apparel at the end of a long day. A *toddler's sleeve.*

snoutcasts *n.* Those poor unfortunates who are forced to huddle in pub, factory and office doorways to enjoy their *cancer sticks. Fag lepers.*

snout pout *n.* That haughty uptilt of the nose favoured by *pedigree ratters* with ideas somewhat above their stations, *eg.* Posh Spice, Candice who used to be *in Corrie.*

snowball *v.* To blow *salami cigarette* smoke back into the tobacconist's mouth.

snowcapping *n. milit.* while on manouevres, to lose one's *officer's mess* onto the summit of a mountain of ordure, Kilimanjaro-style. A bit like *icing the* *log*, but with a larger pile of *feculent*.

snowdrifts *n.* The extra *Keiths* that larger ladies have, which are crisp and white due to the fact that they never receive any sunlight.

snowdrop *v.* To *felch*. Or *feltch*, if you want to spell it like that.

snowdropper *1. n.* Underwear fetishist who steals to sniff, usually from washing lines. A *knicker bandit*. *2. n.* One who *snowdrops*.

snowman, do a *v.* To exit the water closet having completed a *Camillas*-emptying movement of such magnitude that one feels as if one is "walking in the air".

snozzling *n.* The practice of using your nose when *noshing out* a *piece*.

snudge *v.* To sniff a lady's bicycle seat after she leaves it chained to the railings. *To moomph*.

snuffling for truffles *sim.* Descriptive of a loud and somewhat messy performance of *cumulonimbus*. From the act's resemblance to the phenomenon of a large, wet-nosed pig rooting through the topsoil looking for a pungent, yet valuable actinomycete. Presumably without a large mob of excitable French peasants watching, though you never know. *Darth vulva*.

snufty *n.* One who *snudges*. A *garboon*.

snurge *v.* To *snudge, snurgle, barumph*.

snurglar *n. Quumfer, snudger,* bicycle *snufty*.

snurglar's delight *n.* A velocipede which offers double the *quumfing* opportunities for an enterprising *snufty, shniffle-piffler* or *shramper.* A tandem.

snurgle *v.* To *snuft, snudge, shramp, quumf, scrunge, pringle, snerge, snedge, snaffle, snarze, snerk, snerdle, shniffle-piffle, nurf, moomph, barumph, garboon, poon, snarf, snurdle* or *snurge*. To pursue a hobby that seems to be named more often than it is performed.

soap dropper *n.* One who is *light on his feet*. From the prison shower etiquette whereby, like a Georgian lady dropping her handkerchief in the park to attract the attention of an eligible suitor, a big, hairy psychopath with an erection drops the carbolic in the showers to woo a prospective companion.

soap-on-a-roper *n.* One who prefers not to bend down in communal washing facilities.

soapy carpenter *n.* A fellow who is *good with colours*. From the fact that he "lathers at the sight of wood".

soapy tit wank *n.* A *sausage sandwich* served in the bath or shower. *'Take two bottles into the shower? Not me. I just go in there with me bird and she gives me a soapy tit wank.'*

sob stopper *n.* A small present of little value that is acquired on the way home by a thoughtful man who has drunk too much and stayed out too late in the hope of stopping his missus turning the fucking waterworks on. Examples include cheap chocolates bought from all night garages and bunches of flowers stolen from cemeteries and railings.

social hand grenade *n.* A married man who comes out *on the pop* so infrequently that when he does he is a major liability to those around him.

social intercourse *n.* Group sex, typically enjoyed in a layby or Louis Theroux documentary.

socialising *n. Cottaging. 'Hobbies: interior design, going to the theatre, socialising.'*

social netwanker *n.* An opportunist who befriends an attractive female colleague *via* a web-based online community not because he is interested in receiving a constant stream of pithy, exclamation-mark-heavy updates about her life, but in order to *relax in a gentleman's way* over her scantily clad holiday snaps.

social sticks *n.* Crutches that are only used when the bearer is going for a medical, signing on, cashing his giros *etc.*, and not when he is refereeing a Premiership football match. See also *dole pole*.

sockbreaker *n.* A *strum* of such vim and vigour that the weft of one's chosen *jitler* receptacle is abraded.

sock full of sand *euph.* A *heavy dick*.

sock in a washing machine, like a *sim.* Descriptive of an unsatisfying act of intercourse. See also *throwing a Woodbine up Northumberland Street, waving a sausage in the Albert Hall, dipping a worm in a bucket, punching smoke etc.*

sock jock *n.* One who likes to *ride the baloney pony* harnessed with a trusty item of hosiery.

sock monkey *n.* A single man who is well-versed in the art of *self pollution*.

sockrifice *v.* To forfeit an item of clothing on the altar of *gentlemanly relaxation*.

SOCK/sock *abbrev.* Some Other Cunt's Kid.

sock starch *n.* Easily whipped-up starchy paste which has been used by generations of males to convert their hosiery into *bachelor's boomerangs, midget's surfboards, Wombles' toboggans etc.*

sock sucker *n.* A prudish woman who insists on one donning a *dunky* before deigning to *nosh* on one's *slag hammer*. A *French puritan*.

socksure *adj.* Guaranteed to *pull* – at the very least, *yourself off* – by the end of the evening.

socktator sport *n.* Any game played by scantily clad and copiously perspiring young ladies which is broadcast to a rhythmically appreciative male audience. Also *pullympics, quimbledon fortnight.*

socktits *n.* Very long, saggily pendulous *chichis. Spaniel's ears.*

sockumentary *n.* A *masturmentary, rudimentary, palmorama.* A TV programme best enjoyed while wearing an odd number of socks.

SOC/soc *acronym.* A.N. Other. Some Other Cunt. *'That wasn't me who put dog shit in the collection box, vicar. It was SOC.'*

sod *n.* A loose piece of turf in an *uphill garden.*

soda scream *n.* The unintelligible *pop shot* outburst of a chap who is *getting busy with the jizzy.*

soda stream *n.* An underwater bath-time *trump.* An *Edward Woodward, tottle, blooper* or *bottle of olives.*

sodcasting *n.* The act of a *scratter* relaying the ringtones, clownstep remixes and new monkey mash-ups off his mobile telephone for the benefit of the other passengers on the bus, train *etc.* A term coined by Radio 4 presenter Evan Davis on that station's flagship *Today* programme.

soddler *n.* From sod + toddler, the kind of life-ru-ining little *bastard* that makes his old man wish he'd been down the clinic to have his *guns spiked* when he had the chance, or at the very least used a *jubber ray.*

sodom eyes *n.* The look of love that one gives the missus at bedtime to let her know that there may be slightly more than a cuddle on the cards.

sofa scramble *n.* The rush to find the remote control when the theme music for *The One Show* starts.

sofa spud *n. US.* An enthusiastic televisual autodidact with square eyes. An American equivalent to the British *couch potato.*

SOFO *abbrev.* A polite way to tell someone to *shit or get off the pot.* Suck Off or Fuck Off.

soft brexit *n.* Some *freedom of movement* four hours after a Wetherspoon's Full English.

soft closer *n.* A *Peter O'Toole*, the last emerging part of which is cone-shaped, thus ensuring that the *gravy ring* doesn't snap shut with a bang. *Skippy's tail.*

soft launch *1 n.* The release of a product or service to a limited market prior to it being made available to the general public. *2 n.* An attempt at *intercourse* before being fully tumescent.

softly softly spankee monkey *euph.* The art of *relaxing in a gentlemanly manner* while lying next to a sleeping *bag for life.* Also *American beauty, silent running, swank, outrigger.*

soft on, have a *v.* To be confronted by a less-than-ex-citing amorous prospect.

soft play area *1. n.* A leisure facility allowing toddlers to play and explore safely. *2. n.* A bouncy pair of *bangers.*

soft reminder *1. n.* Stupid business-speak for a passive-aggressively polite email that basically means, "I hope you're going to send me that document on time, you cunt." *2. n.* A barely turgid prompt a lady may feel against her hip on the dancefloor, a signal that her male companion is hoping to attempt to initiate sexual congress after the taxi home.

soft skills *1. n. Wanky* management term for the general administration abilities of office pro-fessionals. *2. n.* When a kind gentleman bravely continues to plough away after he has *shot his bolt* in order to enable his partner to reach a satisfactory conclusion.

softwear *n.* Any item of clothing that protects its owner in any way from the effects of the winter weather, worn when out on the town by a *nesh* weakling in the North East of England, *eg.* A coat, jumper, gloves, or – in Newcastle on a Friday evening – a shirt with long sleeves.

soggy mag *n.* An *al fresco art pamphlet* found in a lay-by or under a hedge. *Grummer.*

soggy moggy *n.* A romantic epithet to describe the *back to front* of a lady who has reached a sufficient state of arousal so that it will *go in* without too much fuss. A *slop on, wide on.*

soggy pocket *n.* A lady's *minge* which is deep enough to stash your car keys and loose change in. Not as capacious as *Mary Poppins' bag.*

soiled for choice *adj.* Male condition encountered when a bloke is *private-browsing* a selection of internet videos for the purpose of *buying a present for his wife* and is unable to make up his mind about which clip to *pollute himself* over.

soilonoid valve *n.* The pressure-controlled mechanism which activates the *brown light.*

soil the air *v.* To *drop a gut.*

so it begins *1. exclam.* In *The Lord of The Rings*, a foreboding utterance by King Théoden before The Battle of Helms Deep. It says here, and we're not looking it up. *2. exclam.* A foreboding utterance by a bloke as he settles on the *crapper* the morning after sinking eight pints of Guinness and a mutton Vindaloo. See also *hello darkness my old friend.*

soixante-neuf *n. Fr.* Top-to-tail *horatio-cumulonimbus.*

soldier's toecap *n.* A very shiny, rounded thing that a Sergeant Major likes to be able to see his face in. A *bell end* which has been polished with a generous portion of spit and *guardsman's gloss.*

solicitor's office *n.* Something a person enters in a spirit of optimism, only to leave a short time later screwed, shafted and penniless.

solicitor's tie *n. Fr.* A *pearl necklace.* Costing £160 an hour plus disbursements.

solid air *1. n.* 1980s album by thirsty folk-bluesman John Martyn when he had two legs and was still alive. *2. n.* A *backdraft* resulting in *trouser shittage.*

solitaire *1. n.* A procrastinatory single-player card game featured in a 1973 song by disproportionately large-*noggined* late US crooner Andy Williams. *2. n.* A *procrasturbatory* game played by lonely gentlemen whereby they repeatedly *deal themselves a losing hand.*

solitary joy, the *euph.* The monomanual vice of monks, long distance lorry drivers and teenage boys.

solo dating *1. n.* Social media trend whereby individuals take themselves out, *eg.* To the cinema or for food. *2. n. Romancing the bone.*

sologamy *1. n.* Absurd new trend of "marrying oneself" in an attention-seeking ceremony costing several grand. *2. n.* Long-lasting commitment to a life of monastic *onanism,* perhaps celebrated with a quiet pot noodle and some sobbing.

someone else's mum *n.* When you are unable to use your dominant hand to *scrub the dirtbox,* usually due to some kind of shoulder injury, so a volunteer wiper has to step in. The closest thing to a *stranger* that the *nipsy* can experience.

someone let him in *exclam.* An amusing remark which can be used immediately after an audible *rectal report* has been filed. See also *more tea vicar; speak on, sweet lips that never told a lie.*

someone's moving in next door *exclam.* A witty rejoinder when someone *steps on a duck.* A reference to the sound of heavy furniture being dragged across bare wooden floorboards in an adjoining room. Also *ooh, get her!; language Timothy; that tuba needs tuning; that's all I have to say on the matter; thank-you for the music.*

someone's tinkered with Herbie *exclam.* A humorous riposte one delivers when one *backfires* unexpectedly. From the lines delivered in *The Love Bug* after the baddy has sabotaged the eponymous VW beetle, causing its engine to cough and splutter. See also *someone let him in; more tea vicar?*

something in the pipeline, got *phr.* Said of one who has the *turtle's head.*

something is rotten in the state of Denmark *exclam.* A Shakespearean declamation after the release of a notably *beefy eggo.* Also *ah, bisto; wonder how*

many calories there are in that; who's the daddy?

something to bite on *n.* After a prolonged bout of diarrhoea, the first green shoot of recovery, *viz.* Something vaguely solid that you take as a sign that you might be getting better. *'May 7th 1867. Lake Victoria. After eleven days of the ague, at last something to bite on! However, prudence dictates that I should forfend from coughing or sneezing for several days yet.'* (from *The Diary of David Livingstone*).

something to go on *1. phr.* What the police require in order to pursue an enquiry into a crime which has been committed, *eg.* Reliable forensic evidence which points to the perpetrator, a reliable eye-witness account linking a suspect with the crime scene, a local roller-skating simpleton who can be fitted up. *2. n.* Onanistic fodder. *'Come on, love. Just a quick flash, that's all I'm asking for. Only I've got a wank window this afternoon and I could do with something to go on.'*

something wicked this way comes *exclam.* A quote from Act 4 Scene 1 of Shakespeare's "Scottish play" (*Macbeth*), said by theatrical types (Johnny Gielgud, Larry Olivier, Ralphy-Walphy Richardson, Kenny Branagh and the like) the morning after they dine upon a flavoursome *Ruby Murray.* A line that comes just before the "Fire burn and cauldron bubble" bit.

some viewers may find this distressing *1. exclam.* Content warning given before a hard-hitting TV documentary, drama, or Christmas episode of *Mrs Brown's Boys.* *2. exclam.* Hilarious pre-*guff* exclamation delivered in the style of an earnest continuity announcer.

somewhere to park the Harley *euph.* A particularly massive *arse.* From the fact that the buttock cleft on just such an outsized posterior would be the ideal place to lodge the front wheel of a 700lb 1340cc Soft Tail Fatboy motorcycle in order to prevent it falling over.

songs from the big chair *1. n.* Title of a 1985 album by curly-haired Bath songsmiths Tears for Fears. *2. n.* A *pocket frog* chorus of tuneful anthems released while sat on the *bum sink.*

sonic & knuckles *1. n.* A mid-nineties Sega Mega Drive game starring a colourful hedgehog. *2. n. One off the wrist* performed at the speed of sound.

sonic bog lock *n.* The random assortment of whistles, coughs, hums and throat clearings that are made by the patron of a public *crapper* cubicle with no lock on the door.

SO19 officer *euph.* Any overly eager gentleman who, while in a state of excitement, prematurely pumps several rounds from his *mutton musket* into an innocent *Brazilian*.

SONPA/sonpa *acronym.* A *bit on the side* who knows her place. Sex Only No Public Appearances.

sons of accountancy *n.* Gang of middle-aged, midlife-crisis-torn, middle-management fat men, who spend their working weeks chained to a desk answering purchase ledger queries, but have saved enough to buy a Harley Davidson, on which they hit the two-lane blacktop every weekend, pretending to be outlaws.

sooker *n. Scots.* A *tit*.

sook the pish oot her knickers *exclam. Scots.* A colloquial phrase emphasising the attractiveness of a member of the opposite sex. '*Och, Granpaw. Did ye see yon tits on thae Sophie Raworth readin' the news last nicht?' 'Aye, Wullie a did. She's got a braw pair, thae lassie. Y'ken, ah'd sook the pish oot her knickers.'*

Sooty and Sweep moment *n.* The act of a female who indulges in an act of one-handed *self delight*, attempting to *bring herself off* in record time by means of the rapid movement of all four fingers and her thumb. Dedicated to the memory of famed Yorkshire entertainer Harry Corbett who could, through sheer manual dexterity, make his eponymous glove puppets clap their hands and nod their heads simultaneously.

Sooty and Sweep's frying pan *n.* Capacious women's genitalia.

Sooty's arse *n.* Something furry that you could stick your whole hand up.

Sophie's choice *n.* An insoluble dilemma: Upon entering the toilet to *drop off the shopping*, finding that some dirty *bastard* (possibly Lord Archer of Weston super Mare) has *pissed* all over the seat, and there is only enough *shitscrape* to wipe the throne, or your *arse. Catch twenty-poo.*

sophisticuffs *n.* A fight at the opera.

soporiflick *n.* Late night *strumming* technique employed by members of the fairer sex to stave off insomnia. A feminine equivalent of the *sleeping pull* beloved of bachelors the world over.

Soprendos *n.* A series of gentle *farts* which precede a *Thora*. From the catchphrase of the formerly obese magical faux-Spaniard Quaker: "Piff, paff, poof".

soreskin *n.* A sore *foreskin*.

sorry for your loss *1. exclam.* A touching phrase that can be proffered to a recently bereaved person. *2. exclam.* An amusing comment to make in the wake of a loudly *dropped gut.*

sorry, Greta! *exclam.* Jocularly apologetic exclamation to the formidable young Swedish environmental activist, upon the emission of a par-

ticularly toxic *brownhouse gas*.

sorry, I'm not media-trained *exclam.* A humorous statement to be made immediately after one has *let rip.* Also *who would live in a house like this? It's over to you David; can you tell what it is yet? etc.*

sorry, I thought I was on mute *exclam.* Humorous, quasi-apologetic declaration following the triggering of *farticle fifty.* Also *sniff the air, kiddies. there's vitamins; the Salvation Army are tuning up; fer-fetch a cloth, Granville.*

sorry, I was on mute *exclam.* Either something to say before letting rip with an audible *treacle tart*, or something to say after you've released a *silent but deadly.* Quite possibly in a board meeting.

sorry, the Amazon guy was at the door *exclam.* The Swiss army knife of Zoom/Teams call excuses when working from home; equally valid whether you're leaving the call for five minutes to make tea, failing to hear an important question, loudly breaking wind, or *choking the chicken* on your web camera.

sorting hat *n.* An older man's leathery-brown, wrinkled, *cock and balls.* '*Put your sorting hat away, Chris. Your show starts in five minutes.'*

SOS *abbrev.* A Shirt Off Shit. A proper blue collar act of defecation that makes you feel all manly like the bloke banging the gong at the start of a Rank film, an Icelandic strongman humping an Atlas Ball onto the top of an oil drum or a galley slave in *Ben Hur.*

so solid poo *n.* An extremely troublesome *dump* which feels like passing a handgun wrapped in a sock.

SOSPOS/sospos *abbrev. rhet.* A toilet dilemma, usually faced when one is in a hurry: Stand Or Sit, Piss or Shit?

soul of a Dad in Primark, as empty as the *sim.* Describing something that is chillingly devoid of content. '*Just looking at your life's work here, Eamonn, and I'm afraid it's as empty as the soul of a Dad in Primark.'*

soundcloud *1. n.* Website where musicians can display their wares. *2. n.* A tuneful *botty bugle* playlist.

sounded like the call of the Scotch woodcock, that *exclam. ornith.* A witty Chris Packham-esque remark said in response to an *eggy quack.* See also *speak up caller, you're through; taxi for Brown; that's working, now try your lights; well struck sir!; what's that, Sweep?; you'll have to buy that now, you've ripped it; sew a button on that; catch that one and paint it blue; good health!; pin a tail on that; there goes the elephant; my, that duck's got bad* *breath etc.*

sound of trumpets, going in to the *euph.* Undertaking a desperate, last-ditch cavalry charge to the *khazi to the accompaniment of* a stirring *brass eye* fanfare.

sounds like a problem with your SCART socket *exclam.* An amusing phrase used by techie types to mark the audible release of a *gravy*-soaked *air biscuit.* From scat + fart.

sounds like Dr Banner is changing again *exclam.* Phrase to be used when someone *blows off* so violently that it sounds like clothes being ripped. Named after troubled scientist-turned argumentative mental green muscle man, Dr Bruce Banner, aka the Incredible Hulk, who went through shirts like nobody's business.

sound the charge *v.* In a row of engaged toilet cubicles where *shit-shyness* prevents any and all occupants from performing their foul ablutions, to blow the first *botty bugle* blast. *'I was sat in there ages until someone sounded the charge.'*

soup but no croutons *adj. medic.* Descriptive of a low *springle count, spoogeless spaff. Firing blanks, derren.*

soup cooler *n.* A lipless *fart* that has the characteristics of a gourmand gently and silently blowing across a bowl of piping hot lobster bisque in a posh restaurant.

soup fork *n.* A completely useless *fuckwit, toolbag, thundercunt, dobber,* or *dickhead. 'Today's birthdays: Vincent Van Gogh, monaural Dutch artist, 1853; Albert Pierrepoint, hangman, 1905; Piers Morgan, soup fork, 1965.'*

soup kitchen *euph.* When *professional outdoorsfolk* hold an orgy inside a stolen/abandoned vehicle, in the style of *Theatre of Blood.*

sour apple quickstep *n.* Another diarrhoea dance. The *Tijuana cha-cha. 'Your wife is taking rather a long time in the powder room, vicar.' 'Yes, I'm afraid she's dancing the sour apple quickstep tonight.'*

sour mash *n.* A particularly soft morning *shit,* usually sponsored by Jack Daniels or Jim Beam.

sour trout *n.* Salty, fermented savoury garnish on some gorilla salad that is past its "best before" date.

South Beach Tow cameraman, shaking like a *sim.* To suffer severe tremors, in the style of the camera operators filming the eponymous, defunct, hard-hitting reality television series. *'Ah, what a beautiful morning, Mr Patel. Ten cans of Special Brew, if you please. I'm shaking like a South Beach Tow cameraman here.'*

south Cluanie *euph.* RAF. Scots. Put crudely, the *back passage.* From mountain rescue terminology,

referring to the north and south Cluanie ridges in the north of Scotland where, apparently, attempting to scale the south ridge is regarded as going "up the wrong 'un".

south col *n.* Confusingly, mountain climber's euphemism for a lady's *front bottom.*

southern comfort *n.* A *hand job* that brings solace.

southern corridor *1. n.* Mysterious place where that Malaysian Airlines Boeing 777 was thought to have gone missing without trace. *2. n.* Mysterious place where the *bag for life* lets you go if you've been particularly good.

southern sideburns *n. Thighbrows.*

south hams *1. n.* A district in Devon containing the towns of Totnes, Salcombe, and Dartmouth. *2. n.* A lengthy and protruding set of *gammon flaps.*

South London tapas *n.* The result of adding pork scratchings, peanuts and Mini Cheddars to an open packet of crisps, in order to *scrote-cuisine-ify* the consumption of the said snacks into a sociable, European-style, epicurean experience. *'Fancy a drink, Tel?' 'Yeah, pint of Nelson please, Dave. Oh, and get some South London tapas while you're at the bar, will you? Cheese and onion.'*

southmouth *n.* The *snatch, fadge, quim.*

Southport *1. n.* The *arsehole. 'Fancy a trip to Southport tonight, love?' 'Yeah, alright then.'* *2. n.* Lancashire town at the mouth of the Ribble Estuary. *'Fancy a trip to Southport tonight, love?' 'Eurgh! Certainly not. Don't be disgusting.'*

Southwark sellotape *n.* Police crime scene cordon tape. Named after the London borough where it is an ubiquitous item of street furniture. *Balham bunting, Hackney bunting.*

souvenir *n.* A troublesomely ithyphallic *membrum virile.* From the lyrics to the OMD song of the same name, *viz.* "It's so hard, it's leading me astray"

sovereign's entrance *1. n.* The gate of Victoria Tower at the Palace of Westminster, which is only accessed on very special occasions such as the State Opening of Parliament. *2. n.* The *bumhole.*

sovving *n.* The use, in a proper old-style Cockney punch-up, of one or more sovereign-ring-bedecked fists.

SOW/sow *abbrev.* Sexy Older Woman. A *gilf* one wouldn't ask to leave the bed, despite her advancing years.

soylent grey *n.* Any comestible of dubious provenance offered for sale by a thin, unhealthy-looking *beardy-weirdy* in a vegan food shop. *'What's in these pies?' 'Soylent grey, water, and egg substitute.'*

space clopper *n.* A large, capacious – and possibly

bright orange – *Jack and Danny.*

space docking *n.* Pooing into a ladyfriend's *furry hoop.* They should bring back hanging.

spacehopper *n.* A grinning *homely* lass with a fake tan.

spacehopper caught in a snare *n.* The upsetting *backside* of a larger *bird* who has unwisely decided to effect a thong. And has an orange *arse* with a big tattoo of Parsley the Lion on it.

spacehoppers and seafood *euph.* Big, bouncy *bollocks* teamed with a little, prawn-like *cock.* Also *button mushroom resting on a spacehopper.*

spaceman, do the *v.* Having unprotected *how's your father* with a lady who is riddled with *happy rash,* realising your mistake too late and carrying on regardless, *viz.* "Burning up on re-entry."

spaceman's helmet *n.* Glossy, thumb-polished sheen on a chap's *bell end* after he has *taken Herman to the circus.*

spacers *n.* A pair of breasts which, though large in size, exhibit no cleavage due to their distance apart. *East-westers.*

space shuttle *n.* A *shit* that has a tendency to break up on entry into the *bog bowl.* A *six million dollar man.*

SPAD *1. abbrev.* Signal Passed At Danger. To drive your *Interclitty 125* at full pelt into the *tomato tunnel,* despite seeing the red warning signs at the entrance. *2. euph.* Following through whilst *breaking wind,* having ignored all warnings that *the goods are rapidly approaching the station. 3. n.* Ordering a seventh pint despite "that look" from the her indoors who wanted to leave two hours ago. *4. n.* Someone who works in a government department. *'Where are all the SPADs today?' 'They've gone down William Hills, Prime Minister.'*

spaddel *n.* Spooge, spoff, spaff, spangle, gunk, jitler. *'Eugh! There's all spaddel in me sandwich.' 'Just leave that bit at the side of the plate, Lord Archer.'*

spadework *n.* The hard graft that must be undertaken before finally planting one's *seed* in the *ladygarden. Frigmarole, choreplay.*

spadger *n. Aus.* Vagina. *'I'm sure you can see her spadger when she crosses her legs, cobber.'*

spaff *1. v.* To *spoff* or *spod. 'No, no, no, Gunther! Be professional, spaff on the chest, not in the pussy.'* (from an unidentified grumble flick, circa 1980). *2. n.* Splid, splunt, sploffer, sprankle.

spaffa cake *n.* A middle class version of the classic *soggy biscuit* game.

spaff batteries *n.* A chap's reserves of sexual energy. *"'The false king Joffrey will bend the knee, or be destroyed," snarled Stannis Baratheon. "Plus, remind me not to shag the red witch again. It was*

awesome, but she seems to have permanently drained my spaff batteries."'* (From *A Veritable Feast of Norks and Clunge* by George RR Martin).

spaff gasket, blow one's *v.* To reach a dangerously extreme state of arousal. *'Have you seen Sunshine Cleaning, with Emily Blunt and Amy Adams? You get to see both of them in their underwear. I tell you, I nearly blew my spaff gasket. And now we'll all sing hymn number 352 – We Plough the Fields and Scatter.'*

spaghetti bollocknaise *n.* The multiple thin white strands draped over an actress's face in the final scenes of a *Frankie flick.*

spaghetti girl *euph.* She who can be persuaded into *lesbism* when sufficiently aroused. One who, like the popular bacilliform foodstuff is "straight until she is wet".

spaghetti spunk *n.* The impossible-to-remove residue which remains after straining the cylindrical Italian staple. *'Have you done the washing-up, Fanny?' 'Yeah, but I couldn't all get the spaghetti spunk out the sieve I'm afraid, Johnny.'*

spam alley *n.* The target zone for *meat javelin* throwers.

spambidextrous *adj.* Gifted with the ability to *beat your truncheon meat* with either *wanking spanner.*

spambulance *n.* A hellish mobile boudoir, *eg.* A city centre police van on a Friday night. *Also shaggin' wagon, fuck truck, stick transit, willibago.*

spam butterfly *n.* A finger-assisted *close-up pink* shot in a *bongo mag. A peel.*

spam castanets *n.* Percussive *scallops, clapping fish.*

spam chow mein *n. Popshot noodles* that you want another portion of after ten minutes. *Chopper suey, sour pork.*

spam danglers *n.* The sloppy, protruding inner *flaps* of a lady's *hooter.* Generously proportioned *bacon strips, gammon goalposts.*

spam dunk *n.* The act of gently ushering a romantic partner's head southwards, so that they may enjoy a short *reformed meat* snack.

spam folder *1. n.* The separate destination on a computer in which unwanted advertisements for enlargement of the male organ, re-vivification of dead batteries, proposals of marriage from lonely Ukrainian women, and important, time-sensitive work emails are automatically filed. *2. n.* A female crow's nest. *'I've frozen the frame, look. Just as she crosses her legs you can clearly see her spam folder. Then she just gets on with opening Parliament.'*

spam fritters *n.* Labia. *Dangly ham,* especially when served in *batter.*

spam javelin *n.* An 8-foot long *cock* with a sharpened end that'll have your eye out if you're not careful.

spam monkey *n.* An overly keen *self-improver.*

spamnesia *n. medic.* Condition that makes a fellow forgetful about how many *wanks* he may have had. *'The missus has been in hospital and I'm suffering from chronic spamnesia.'*

spamogram *n.* Stylised pictographic representation, or hieroglyph, of a disembodied set of male genitalia, usually seen scrawled on toilet walls, bus shelters, religious textbooks and the backs of photographs of washing machines posted to disc jockey Mike Read (you'll have to look that reference up). A *three-line pud, cockage, le cock spurtif, organogram.*

spamouflage *n.* Copies of *Time, The Economist, London Review of Books etc.,* picked off the lower shelves of newsagents in an effort to give the impression to the woman behind the till that one's copy of *Hot 'n' Horny* was merely an ironic afterthought. *Palmouflage.*

spampon *n.* A ball of absorbent *shitscrape* inserted under a chap's *fiveskin* during his *unclean times.* *'Did awaken late in the night and, unable to get back to my slumbers, did decide to perform an act of personal delight upon my turgid membrum virile. Thus resolv'd, I betook myself off to the earth closet with a tallow candle, my looking spectacles and the latest copy of Enrazzlement. I had been ensconced in there fully five minutes, vouchsafing it half a dozen to nothing on my aged knobkerrie over the most comely centrefold, and was at the praxiomatic point of discharging my foul seed when Jane banged on the earth closet door to tell me of a great fire that hadst been seen in the City. I was forced quickly to fashion myself a series of small spherules of vellum, or spampons, which I did insinuate round the brim of my farmer's hat to prevent any of my base spendings from leaking therefrom. By and by Jane did come and tell me that she heard that above 300 houses had been burned down in the night by the fire we saw, and that it is now burning down all Fish Street, by London Bridge. There was nothing to do, so I went and had another wank.'* (from *The Diary of Samuel Pepys,* September 2nd 1666).

spam purse *n.* A particularly unsightly *snapper,* usually found in the nether regions of women with *lovely personalities.*

spam sceptre *n.* The ceremonial *rod* that sits atop the *crown jewels.*

spamurai *n.* A fellow who waves his *pork sword* around somewhat over-melodramatically while *turning Japanese.*

spandrels *n. Men overboard, croutons, tiger nuts.*

General vaginal detritus.

spangle *1. n.* A sticky, unpleasant mouthful that is most often spat out. *2. n.* Old English-flavour *spunk.*

spangle bangle *n.* A hair band kept close to her bed by a keen *fellatrix* in order to keep her *barnet* out of her eyes as she performs *horatio.*

spangle dangle *n.* A lady's intimate jewellery item, hanging off her pierced *pygmy's thumb,* popular amongst actresses in *self help* films.

spaniel's ears *n.* Sagging, flat *thru'penny bits. Snoopies, Fred Bassets.*

Spanish archer *n.* The push, the "El Bow". *'I can't believe it. She's given me me the old Spanish archer. Tchoh! Women, eh? You can't live with them, you can't fuck their sisters and mums.'*

Spanish cravat *n.* A *pearl necklace.* Also *Dutch cravat, Chinese bow tie.*

Spanish lullaby *1. n.* A *fart.* From Madonna's *La Isla Bonita,* viz. "Ring through my ears and sting my eyes, your Spanish lullaby." *2. n.* A really stinky *digestive transit.*

Spanish omelette *n.* A vagina so slack, eggy and moist as to render it useless.

Spanish plumbers *n.* Ill-tailored trousers, from their tendency to pinch the base of the urethra and thus "always leave it dripping".

spank banks *n.* A mental reference library of erotic imagery, which can be consulted when *spanking the monkey.* See also *mammary banks, wank bank.*

spankerchief *n.* A tissue, or square of fabric used for mopping up *banana yoghurt* after you have *smacked yourself about.*

spankety plank *euph.* Popular single-handed game in which five contestants team up to take on a solitary, one-eyed competitor.

spanking *n.* A form of corporal punishment still practised in *rub-a-tug shops* on the Isle of Man. See *Mr Whippy, fladge and padge, S and M.*

spank manager *n.* A chap's *lady of the night* who furnishes him with dominatrix-style *how's your father,* culminating in the deposit of a large *wad* and a trip to Casualty.

spank plankton *n.* Bath-borne *tadpoles.* Also *diquid, lava lamp.*

spankrupt *adj.* Descriptive of a gentleman who, upon *advancing the manly meat,* finds himself bereft of *seed capital.*

spank the monkey *v.* To *bash the bishop, burp the worm.* See *Mary Chipperfield.*

spank the plank *1. v.* To play the electrical guitar in a "pop" beat combo. *2. v.* To *toss* oneself off.

spanky hanky *n. Jit gel rag, wank sock.* Anything used for clearing up *gunk* after a *tug.*

spanner *1. n.* Not the sharpest tool in the shed; a

right *fuckwit*. 2. *n.* Top *stoat*, one who "tightens one's nuts". A *monkey wench*.

Spaphrodite *n. prop.* The Greek goddess of *bukkake*. A sylvan sylph with a *face like a plasterer's radio*.

spare *n.* In a *meat market*, any *smeesh* which is not yet spoken for.

spare elbow skin *n.* The crinkled leather of which the scrotal sac comprises.

spare room offence *n.* Any minor misdemeanor that upsets a wife or girlfriend, *eg.* Coming home drunk, forgetting her birthday, *fucking* her mum and her sister *etc*.

sparf *n.* What comes up when a person's *vom toggle* gets activated while they are chowing down on a proper *slag bat*. From spunk + barf. See also *stroker's cough*.

Spar jellyfish *n.* Soft-bodied marine wildlife often seen floating in the waters off Britain's east coast; discarded carrier bags. Also *Londis jellyfish, Iceland man o' war*.

sparrowfart *n.* Early morning.

sparrowfuck *n.* A rapid act of *congress* between a man and a woman, reminiscent of the 1-second *spunk up* of the common house sparrow (*Borrius beckerensis*).

sparseholes *n.* Somewhat disparaging term for owners of hot tubs.

sparsley *adv.* Descriptive of a thinly garnished meal.

spasm chasm *n. Spam alley*.

spatchelor *n.* A single fellow who resorts to *floor-scraping* tactics in order to pick up the crusty bits of *sediment* off the dance floor when it's time to *put the bints out*.

spat-out toffee, face like a *sim.* Disparagingly descriptive of a person with a physiognomy somewhat reminiscent of a *stripper's clit*. *'Auden was noted for the stylistic and technical ingenuity of his poetry, his engagement with the eternal themes of love, politics and religion, and his face like a spat-out toffee.'*

spatterdash *n.* When you are just about to give an accommodating lady companion a *facial*, but her husband walks in and you're compelled to leg it with all *spongle* coming out the end of your *cock*.

spawning *v.* The saucy act of masturbating in a public swimming pool. *'Of course, his career was effectively over when he was caught spawning, and they killed him off in an off-screen motorway pile-up.'*

spawnography *n.* Semen-encrusted *jazz mags*, found secreted in attics and garden sheds years after the images within were first *photo-slopped*.

speak duck *v.* To communicate with pond-dwelling avians in a Dr Doolittle stylee while lowering yourself into the bath. To squeeze out an *apple tart* just as your *nipsy* touches the surface of the water, thus creating a noise that only a mallard would understand.

speaking clock *n.* He what is afflicted with premature *spoffage*. A *two-push Charlie*. From the fact that he "never gets past the third *stroke*". Another reference for the youngsters there. They've probably all got quartz watches now.

speak one's truth *v.* To emit a heartfelt, long-bottled-up *Exchange & Mart*.

speak on, sweet lips that never told a lie *exclam.* Poetic riposte which can be delivered to humorous effect after someone has *stepped on a frog*. See also *someone's tinkered with Herbie; keep shouting sir, we'll find you*.

speak to me oh toothless one *exclam.* Uttered prior to the release of a noisome *air biscuit*. Also *our survey said; I'll name that tune in one; I smell with my little nose, something beginning with…; fire up drop zone two*.

speak up caller, you're through *exclam. Can I quote you on that?; an excellent theory, Dr Watson etc*.

speak Welsh *v.* To *shout soup, blow chunks, yoff*. To *sing a rainbow* in a Brythonic fashion.

spearmint wino *n.* A *heavily refreshed* gentleman of no fixed abode who insists on undressing and gyrating in the street.

spear the bearded clam *v.* to perform a trick involving a *spam javelin* and an hirsute bivalve.

spear the blow hole *v.* To *make the beast with two backs* and about eight stomachs.

special ops otter *n.* A *poo* that noiselessly enters the water and disappears round the bend within a split second.

special resin *1. n.* The viscid fluid famously used by Gavin from the Autoglass adverts to fill chipped windscreens. *2. n.* A viscid fluid used to fill *cracks*.

specrackular *adj.* Of a *rack*, spectacular. *'Gosh, your worship. That new bicycle rack outside the Council offices is absolutely specrackular. As are your knockers.'*

speech! *exclam.* Humorous riposte to a clearing of the *nether throat* that rattles the wine glasses on the table.

speedballing *n.* Bizarre sexual practice whereby the female lies on her back and repeatedly punches a straddling fella's *knackersack*, bouncing it off his *arse* and *shaft* whilst building up a rhythm in the style of Rocky Balboa at Mighty Mick's gym.

speed bump *n.* A quickie, *knee-trembler* or *punch up the whiskers*. *'Ooh, that speed bump just knocked me glasses off, mother superior.'*

speed bump bird *n.* A sexually alluring young

lady walking along the pavement who causes male drivers to slow down dramatically, as if approaching a traffic calming measure, when in fact they are merely interested in having a good old ogle at her *tits* and *arse*. A staple trope of 1970s British sex comedies.

speed bumps *n.* An impressive set of *top bollards* on a new conquest which means that her paramour approaches the *yabba dabbas* somewhat more quickly than usual.

speed dating *1. n.* Something people probably do in bloody Richard Curtis films or them fucking Bridget Jones books. *2. n.* The use of the fast forward button while watching a *Baywatch* DVD in order to find a suitable lady with whom one can enjoy a brief yet torrid relationship. *3. n.* The act of looking out of a train or bus window into the bedroom windows of passing houses in the hope of seeing a nice pair of *milkers*.

speed hump *n.* The existing paramour of someone that you fancy. From the fact that "it doesn't stop you, it just slows you down".

speeding ticket *1. n.* Expensive piece of ephemera resulting from a minor motoring misdemeanour. *2. n.* A small *tod* which nevertheless entails an un-expectedly large amount of *paperwork*. A *shite of a thousand wipes.*

speed of shite, the *n.* Amusingly rhetorical expression implying that an object is travelling very slowly. *'Hello, is that the Gas Board? My boiler's not working and there's a very strong smell of gas in the house.' 'Don't worry, madam. We'll send an engineer round at the speed of shite.'*

speed of smell, the *n.* The distance travelled per unit time by a vile odour as it propagates through the atmosphere. The *speed of smell* is unaffected by temperature, atmospheric pressure and prevailing climatic conditions, though it can be enhanced by the consumption of cauliflower, boiled eggs, Brussels sprouts, beans, peas and draught Bass.

speedophile *n.* A suspicious-looking man in a swimming pool who does a lot of watching but very little swimming.

speem *n.* The fragrant mist which arises from the toilet bowls of poorly heated houses during cold weather. From steam + pee.

spegg *n.* An incredibly unappealing person who makes one ponder the 300 million-to-one miracle of human reproduction. From sperm + egg. *'Born on this day: Celine Dion, long-faced Canadian screecher, 1968; MC Hammer, low-gussetted US rapper, 1962; Piers Morgan, cuntish spegg, 1965.'*

Speke easy *adj.* Descriptive of the accommodating sexual morals exhibited by the young women who travel to Mediterranean resorts each summer from the eponymous Liverpool suburb's airport.

spelky fence *sim.* A *John Craven* that is in the early, stubbly stages of pubular regrowth. A *cuntry file. 'It was like running my hand across a spelky fence, nan.'*

Spencer Davis poop *n.* A motion that, in the words of the famous beat group's 1965 hit, "keeps on running".

spend a pound in pennies *v.* To play the *tuppenny waterfall,* to *shit the jackpot* and win a *flock of pigeons;* to suffer a *fall of old shoes from the loft.* Also *spend tuppence in ha'pennies and farthings, drop the jackpot.*

spend a shilling *v.* To visit to the *smallest room in the house* for a purpose which requires more time and investment than merely *spending a penny.*

spend one's money before one gets to the shop *euph.* Of an over-eager gentleman, to *spongle* his *spaff* before the *glebe end* has entered the *faff.* To suffer the enjoyable, time-saving affliction of premature ejaculation. See also *(like) tossing a softmint into a bottle of coke, approach shot, potting the black on the break.*

spenk *n.* The final, limited issue of *jipper* when one achieves one's *personal best.* The *spendings* generated by a pair of *knackers* that have been *wanked flat as a widow's batteries,* possibly during the Olympic Beach Volleyball competition. From spent + spunk.

spent fuel rod *1. n.* A limp bar of depleted uranium following its removal from a nuclear reactor. *2. n.* A sadly depleted and flaccid *giggle stick* following its removal from a *clunge.*

sperm *n. medic.* How doctors refer to *spunk.*

spermaid *n.* In the absence of a proper *fluff mag,* any depiction of a female which is pressed into service as inspiration during a bout of *monomanual self pleasure, eg.* Any half-decent image of feminity found on a holiday brochure, knitting pattern or Quality Street tin.

spermal underwear *n.* Y-fronts that are wet as well as (momentarily) warm, the result of *popping one's cork* recklessly.

sperm bank *n.* A chap's personal account, in which he invests in the days leading up to a night out, cutting back his reckless *spending* so that he can *blow it all* on a pretty lady.

sperm burper *n.* A sensible wench who isn't afraid to guzzle *spadge.*

sperm curdler *1. n.* A Victorian kitchen utensil made from copper. *2. n.* A satanically *fugly woman,* *eg.* Nora Battye, Ann Widdecombe.

sperm flag/cum flag *n.* To save his curtains, the bedside towel on which a fellow wipes his *twig* after *winching out the Chilean miners.*

sperminator *n.* Lady who is the subject of a mental image summoned by a gentleman to delay his delivery of *man milk* when the thought of a dead puppy isn't having the desired effect, *eg.* Erstwhile Dodd-alike art nun Sister Wendy.

spermint *n.* Diabolical flavour of tooth whitener, usually dispensed from a pink tube. With all blue veins up the side. And a big pair of hairy *bollocks* hanging down underneath.

spermit *1. n.* The licence given by one's partner that it is okay to eschew supplementary latex prophylaxis during a bout of *penetrative affection.* *2. n.* A particularly unsuccessful Muppet character which, inexplicably, never really caught on.

sperm noodle *n.* An airing cupboard-dried sleeping bag previously used by a sexually overactive male who has inadvertantly impregnated it with a quantity of *dream topping.* Best avoided by ovulating, damp females.

sperm perm *n.* Distinctive tonsorial style achieved by the application of glutinous *heir gel.* 'Ooh, I like your new sperm perm. It suits you, Cameron.'

sperm wail *n.* A low grunting noise emitted at the moment one's *moby dick spouts.* An ejaculatory ejaculation, if you will. See *spuphemism.*

sperm worm *n.* The male penis. See also *baby birding.*

spew *1. v.* To be sick; to vomit, *park a tiger, bowk, barf, shout soup, look for Burt.* *2. n.* The sick itself. 'Mum. This soup tastes like fucking tramp's spew.'

spewnami *n.* A tidal wave of *puke.* From spew + nami.

spewsical *n.* A lengthy, melodious vomiting session following a night *on the lash,* punctuated by short periods of unintelligible dialogue.

spew-sprayed shoes *n.* Vomit-encrusted Nikes following a smashing night out. 'I'm going to put these spew-sprayed shoes on eBay, nan.'

sphincter gnats *n. medic.* What feels like an army-sized infestation of belligerent, stinging *arse wasps.* 'Sort out your sphincter gnats with these wet wipes, now half price until April. Every little helps.'

sphinny *n.* The *nipsy.* 'I think we should stop, Rod. Me sphinny isn't what it used to be.'

spice girls *n.* Ladies of the road sparked out on a bench having had a cheeky puff or two of the popular, eponymous recreational synthetic cannabinoid.

spice island *n.* Stinkhole Bay, Dilberry Creek. A foul-smelling archipelago favoured by sailors on their *trips around the world.* The *arsehole.*

spicy duck *n.* An *Exchange & Mart* that sounds like Donald Duck throwing up, and probably presages a swift trip to Primark to buy some clean *underkecks.*

spiddle *n.* A term for the *Peters and Lee* a lady takes after intercourse. A mixture of *spunk* and *widdle.*

spider-man *n.* A chap who has white, sticky hands after spending all day "on the web".

spider-man, do a *v.* To *spunk up* into one's hand, then attempt to remove it by *flicking ropes* against the wall.

spider-man wank *n.* An act of *self-pollution* undertaken while wearing a pair of the missus's *bills* on the head, such that the *gusset* is directly over the nose, leaving eyeholes in the place normally filled by legs. See also *musk mask, fentilator.*

spiders' legs *n.* Of *muffs,* rogue pubic hairs which protrude beyond the knicker line, the hairs of a *pant moustache.*

spider wank *n.* A sneaky *five knuckle shuffle* using your fingers in arachnid fashion. Particularly in the Fens.

spigot *exclam.* Lancashire dialect exclamation of surprise when recognising a famous jockey.

spike the guns *v.* To have a vasectomy. To *domesticate the Mitchell brothers.*

spill one's beans on the worktop *v.* To *ice* a lady's *buns.* To *lob ropes, fling string.*

spill the beans *v.* To *blow off* thunderously.

spill the Brasso *v.* To *drop one's yop,* donate to the church fund. To ejaculate while *polishing the coal scuttle.* 'What's all this mess on the carpet?' 'Sorry mum, I spilled the Brasso. What's good for getting spunk out of tufted Wilton?'

spill the genes *v.* To complete of an *act of self delight,* possibly into a sock.

spinal crap *n.* A *motion* of such forceful velocity that it displaces a vertabra.

spin cycle *1. n.* The final phase of a bloke attaining *organism.* Derived from the frantic crescendo of noise and vibration produced by a washing machine, just before it loses all its energy and turns itself off. 'Tickets from Weston super Mare, please. First class tickets from Weston super Mare.' 'Give me a moment, my good man. I'm just on the spin cycle.' *2. n.* The final, frenzied stages of a proper *larrup,* when the floor starts to vibrate and nearby crockery starts to rattle and fall off shelves *etc.* A *wanker's vinegar strokes.* *3. n.* An inebriated person's *attack of the helicopters.*

spinnaker stiffy *n.* A majestic *erectivitation* that is sadly achieved too late to serve any useful purpose, for example after the wife has come back from the shops. Named after the tower built in Portsmouth to mark the new Millennium, which was opened in 2005.

spinner *1. n.* Member of that semi-religious, polo-neck wearing folk band without whom no variety programme in the 1970s was complete. *2. n.* A petite lady who can be spun on one's *cock* like the propellor on a beany hat. A *throwabout, cock puppet, laptop.*

spinnickers *n. Underchunders* as worn by more amply *arsed* women. Named after the large, baggy sails hoisted by yachtsmen on still days. Though a lack of wind's probably not so much of a problem round that particular stern.

spinning plates *n.* An old-fashioned novelty act in which the performer attempts to keep both of a lady volunteer's *Scammel wheelnuts* erect at the same time.

spinning silk *n. medic.* When a boulder of *foulage* pushes against your *muddy walnut* and a line of silky fluid shoots out of your *bell end*. Usually happens when constipated, it says here. Is that a thing? We're not a doctor, but you may need to see a doctor.

spinstergram *n.* Any social media outlet popular with single, middle-aged women.

spinster's Ginster's, drier than a *sim.* A *slice* that is notably lacking in moisture. The *pie* of a woman who is long past her best before date on the motorway services fridge shelf of life.

spinster's hand luggage, buzzing like a *sim.* '*Mr Rees-Mogg told reporters that he was already buzzing like a spinster's hand luggage at the prospect of post-Brexit Britain's return to the 1950s.*'

spin the jam/spread the jam *euph.* To *finger* a lady who's *on the blob.*

spirit level arse *n.* A little bubble of *fart* that lodges between the *arse cheeks* and acts as an indicator of one's inclination with regard to the horizontal.

spirit levelled *adj.* In the ultimate state of *refreshment.* As *refreshed as a fucking newt.*

spiss *n.* The mixture of sperm and urine produced during a post-coital *wee-wee. Spiddle.* '*That was a truly beautiful lovemaking experience, darling. Now keep toot for the scuffers while I have a spiss in Bradford & Bingley's doorway.*'

spit *v.* What fussy or frigid women do instead of *swallowing.*

spit a nut *v.* To *gamble and lose.* To *follow through, shoot the breeze.*

spite wank *n.* An ill-natured *act of self delight* perpetrated to *clear out the tanks* on one of the rare occasions when you know the missus is *choking for a bit,* so you can tell her you don't feel like it.

spit her rag out *v.* Of a lady during *cricket week,* to uncontrollably eject her *jammy dodger* onto the floor while undergoing a spontaneous and unnecessary bout of *showing off.* Also *pop a knocker.*

spit roast *n.* Someone simultaneously skewered at both ends by *pork swords.* A *sausage jockey* who plays a *pink oboe* while still *in the saddle.* Something like that, anyway. A *corn on the cob.*

spitwank *n.* A lazy or prudish lady's *horatio* avoidance technique; specifically a saliva-assisted *J Arthur* masquerading as a *blow job.* Normally experienced when the man has recently spent time shifting a heavy filing cabinet up or down a fire escape, imbibed several pints of export strength lager or when *EastEnders* is about to start.

spizm/spism *n.* Somewhat unsavoury mixture expectorated by *grot* actresses following a busy day at the *boffice.* From spit + jizm/jism.

spladge *n.* Vaginal juices, sloshing around and easing the entry of the *pork sword,* fingers, tongue, a wine bottle *etc.*

splashback *1. n.* An area of tiles behind a sink. *2. n.* Unfortunate tidal effect of a *depth charge* or *belly flopper* within the *pan,* resulting in splashing of the *arse* and *barse.* *3. n.* A woman's dorsal area upon which has been bestowed the *mark of Zorro.* Or maybe a vestigial '7' or half a hyphen. Or a small comma.

splash barrier *n.* Any *ad hoc,* improvised contrivance employed by a lavatory user, usually made from *bog roll* and constructed in order to counteract the uncomfortable sensation of *splashback* when taking a *dump.*

splashdeck *1. n.* A bit of a canoe, probably. *2. n.* The tastefully tattooed portion of a *grumble flick* actress's back that provides a convenient target at which her male co-star may aim his *spod* during the *money shot. Arse antlers.*

splash diet *n.* A weight loss programe that involves shedding pounds of unsightly excrement. A *dump.* '*I can't do these jeans up again. I'd best just go on a splash diet. See you in ten minutes.*'

splashdown *n. milit.* Official Parachute Regiment terminology for a *wetting of the bed* after a mammoth drinking session.

splash me boots *v.* To have a *piss,* take a *leak.*

splash 'n' dash *1. n.* In motor racing when they used to have them big pipes full of petrol, the act of heading to the pits for a quick fill when short on fuel within the last few laps of the race. *2. n.* In *dumping,* to head to the *crapper* when *touching cloth* while late for an important engagement.

'Where's Reginald? He's on air in forty-five seconds.' *'Don't worry. He's just gone for a splash'n'dash. 3. n. A squat 'n' squirt. 4. n. Shooting your muck* over or up a casual acquaintance before exiting as fast as humanly possible to avoid conversation and/or cuddling. *4. n.* Grabbing a quick pint before the bar closes.

splash one's clogs *v.* To have a *Peters and Lee.*

splash the mash *v.* To ejaculate onto your *bird's tits,* leaving a residue which looks like a bit of your grandad's dinner.

splash the pot *1. v.* More poker terminology. To throw one's chips down in a disorderly fashion. *2. v.* To *drop the kids off at the pool* in a disorderly fashion.

splat *n. medic. Bollock batter, fetch.*

splatisfaction *n.* The intense, almost euphoric feeling after finally dislodging a big, reluctant *pace car* and exploding the rest of the contents of your *Camillas* into the *bum sink* almost immediately afterwards.

splat screen TV *n.* Any tablet, laptop, personal computer or portable device used to sneakily *whack one out* over one's favourite *Frankie* site.

splattulence *n. medic.* A big wet *Lionel Bart* that sprays *Bovril bullets* everywhere.

spla water *n.* Semen, *gunk.*

splay *v. US.* To draw back the *beef curtains* and make a grand entrance.

splice *1. v.* British version of *splay. 2. v.* What a pirate does to his mainbrace.

splifty-fifty *phr. Lancs.* Amongst drug addicts in the red rose county, the correct ratio of ordinary tobacco to specially cultivated herbs in one of their hand-rolled organic cigarettes.

splinge *n.* A particularly lubricious *kipper mitten.* A *bag of slugs.*

split a kipper *v.* To *part the whiskers,* to *have it off.*

splitarse *n.* An offensive, sexist term for a *bird. 'Born on this day: TV and film actor Tom Selleck, 1945. Olympic Gold medalist diver Greg Louganis, 1960. Splitarse boffin Germaine Greer, 1939.'*

split bag of mince *n.* A *gutted rabbit, butcher's dustbin, stamped bat.*

split-flap display *n.* The technical name for one of those old-fashioned timetable boards they used to have in railway stations.

split from the peloton *euph.* After a prolonged period of severe constipation, to finally put some distance between oneself and one's *foulage.*

split me with your jism stick *exclam.* To be shouted Ian Dury-style whilst receiving an ardent gent's romantic attentions.

splitter cable *1. n.* An adaptor from Maplins for plugging two television sets into a single chipped satellite decoder. *2. n.* A *Thora Hird* which is so humungous that it rents one's *Japanese flag* in twain.

split the beard *v.* To *part the whiskers,* again. After 20 minutes or so. And a fag.

split the winnings *euph.* To stop *moving heavy furniture* halfway through. *'And after four days without movement Job took up his toilet and great was his relief. But even as he released his burden there came a voice and it was the Lord. And the Lord spake in a loud voice saying Come unto Me Job. And Job replied saying Oh God, what is it this time, for I have only just sat down. And great was the wrath of the Lord. And He commanded Job to split the winnings and come now unto Him. And great was Job's discomfort.'* (from *The Book of Job*).

splod *1. n. Sprag, spoff. 2. v.* To *sprag, spoff.*

splodge *v.* To *chuck muck* over a glossy magazine.

splodgenessabounds *1. n.* Lightweight British punk band, fronted by Max Splodge (real name Maxwell Splodgeworth), whose sole 1980 hit unwittingly provided the title for evergreen BBC3 shitcom *Two Pints of Lager and a Packet of Crisps. 2. n.* A massive ejaculation covering everyone and everything in the vicinity with *Harry Monk.*

splosh *1. n.* Money. *2. n.* Britain's leading periodical for those interested in genito-tinned-spaghetti pursuits.

spluff *1. v.* To *spunk up. 'She took her bra off and I spluffed in my pants.' 2. n.* Spunk. *'Nice tits, mother superior. By the way, is there anywhere I can put these pants? They're full off spluff.'*

splurry *n. Fizzy gravy.* Diarrhoea.

splutterbeans *n.* The *Eartha Kitts, plopsy.*

Spock *v.* To make a "V" with one's fingers and boldy go where no man has gone before, *ie.* Two up the *twat* and two up the *arse.*

spocks *n.* Socks that have been used as ejaculation receptacles or post-*bust off* clean-up devices. From *spodge, spadge, spoodge, spaff, spangle, spingle, spongle etc.* + socks.

spod *n.* See *spof.*

spof *n.* See *spod.*

spoilers *1. n.* Aerodynamic wing modifications that prevent Citroen Saxos from flying into the sky when being driven up and down in Burger King car parks. *2. n* Buttocks, *mudflaps.*

spoilsports bra *n.* An item of intimate apparel used by a woman who unaccountably wishes to suppress the natural motion of her *bangers.*

spoilt paper *n.* A saucy photogravure that has been

fouled with *jipper.*

spondle *n. Spooge, spluff, spangle, jitler, knob toffee.*

sponge *1. n.* In a *puddle jumping* couple, the one who has feathers stuck in his teeth. *2. n. prop.* A silent character played by the late Colin Bean in *Dad's Army.*

Spongebob's nose *n.* A distinctly unimpressive, yellow *cock.*

sponk *n. Fanny batter, milm.*

spooch *n. Spooge, spodge, spadge, splang etc. Jism.*

spoof is in the pudding *phr.* What waiters say to Piers Morgan.

spooge *n. US. Spoff.* See *spod.*

spooge scrooge *n. A trojan,* condom, *rubber policeman.*

spooge stick *n. Gut stick, fuck rod, slag hammer.* The p*nis.

spoogilist *n.* An overly enthusiastic advocate of the *five knuckle shuffle*; someone who *beats his old man* like he owes him money.

spoonatics *n.* The drink-crazed daytime denizens of certain high street pubs, particularly the one in Bishop Auckland.

spoonbenders *1. n.* Those blessed with the inexplicable ability to deform cutlery using merely the power of their minds and hands. It was all the go back in the 1970s. *2. n.* Lengthy periods of liquid *refreshment* enjoyed in a national pub chain's outlets. *Yates's wine lunch.*

spoonies *n.* Hardy 'spoons regulars who can essentially be classified as furniture-owning thanks to their presence from opening time to closing time, seven days a week.

spoonwalk *n.* Slow, heavy-footed gait, similar to that of a lunar astronaut, exhibited by patrons of high-street drinking establishments due to their feet sticking to the carpet.

spoot *n. Scots. Spunk.* Usage limited to Campbeltown on the Mull of Kintyre. If you went into the pub in Machrihanish and said the beer tasted like spoot, they wouldn't know what you were talking about.

sporran catalogue *n. Scots.* A *grot mag.* Specialising in ladies with snap-shut, shaggy grey *snatches, eg. Hoots Mon Only.*

sport relief *1. n.* A laudable charity whereby celebrities perform marathon feats of endurance. *2. n. Relaxing in a gentleman's way* while watching ladies' beach volleyball, ladies' tennis or ladies' crown green bowling.

sports bag *n.* A handy *cottaging* accessory in which one *cottager* stands to conceal his feet and avoid detection by lavatory attendants or *scuffers* looking under the door. See *bagging,* although

you'll not find out anything new.

Sports Direct mug, like a *sim. 'After all them years of shagging rock stars, that Pats(name obscured on legal advice)nsit must have a starfish like a Sports Direct mug, your majesty.'*

sports model *n.* A woman who has had her *tubes* tied and thus provides worry-free sexual fun for caddish males.

spot welding *n.* Process by which *bowl moles* resistant to even the strongest *golden power-washer* are fused onto the porcelain.

spouse *1. n.* One's marital partner. *2. n.* Her *fanny.*

sprag *1. n. Spoff, splod. 2. v.* To *spoff, splod.*

sprag *n.* Any handy cloth, such as a tissue, crusty sock or curtain, used to remove, dab at or mop up *jizz* after ejaculation. From spunk + rag. Also *frag*; a female version of the above.

spraint *n.* Otter *shit.* Now there's a word that's going to come in useful.

sprats *n. onomat.* A shoal of small, tightly packed *trouser coughs* emitted in quick succession, *eg.* When Olympic speed-walking the day after a vindaloo. Also *string of pearls, air croutons, ugly duckling, one stroke cylinder engine* or *seven stepper.*

spray bentos *euph.* The aftermath of a hot and loose emptying of the *caboose* that leaves the *smallest room* looking like someone has recklessly flung shepherd's pie all over the *bog* seat and up the walls.

spray egg *v.* Of an excitable *Norris,* to *ejillulate.*

spray the pine *v.* To go for a good *sit-down visit* which could endanger the ecosphere.

spread bet *1. n.* In the world of gambling, a bet whereby the eventual payout is dependent upon the accuracy of the wager rather than a simple "yes/no" outcome, whatever that means. For more details, have a look at Wikipedia, whence this definition was ham-fistedly précised. *2. n.* The perspicacious act of proceeding simultaneously with two or more concurrent courtships, thereby increasing the mathematical odds that at least one of your ladyfriends will "spread".

spreader *n.* A variation on a *moonie,* whereby the buttocks are manually pulled apart to reveal the *red eye.*

spreadsheet *n.* Shiny, crinkly toilet paper found in public lavatories which only succeeds in smearing the *shit* around one's *arse* like a plasterer's float.

spreadshite *n.* Useless information given to irritating people in order to temporarily placate them.

spread the good news *v.* To *drop a gut* whilst in motion, altruistically leaving a trail of joy as you go.

sprew n. Spongle, jitler, spragg. Spunk.

spring a coil v. To lay a cable, drop a copper bolt, build a log cabin, grow a tail, drop your fudge, pinch a loaf, crimp one off, drop the shopping, drown a copper, give birth to a dead otter, light a bum cigar, park your breakfast or drop off a length of dirty spine. 'Have you seen the new Viz kicking about anywhere, nan? I'm off to spring a coil.'

spring awakenings n. When a sleeping person blows off so hard that the mattress coils reverberate and wake up everybody in the building.

spring clean n. A gentleman's first morning visit to the crapper after a night on the lash, where he has a dump and a slash, blows his nose, picks the sleep from his eyes and generally begins the miraculous process of coming back to life like a Blue Peter tortoise after it's been taken out of the airing cupboard.

spring equinorks, the n. The most concise calculation of the beginning of Spring known to science. The initial period of heightened exposure of Gert Stonkers to sunlight. In many cultures this begins a season of rejoicing and thanksgiving that the deity has blessed his people with abundance: "Every good and perfect gift is from above, coming down from the Father of the heavenly lights." (James 1:17).

spring onion roots n. An elderly maiden's unruly gorilla salad. The welcome mat of a lady of advanced years.

spring roll euph. When one has more skin than meat on a cold day, due to shrinkage.

sprinklings n. Those suspicious-looking brown, black, or red particles on the seat of a public Rick Witter that a previous incumbent has left for you to clean up before your arse makes contact. Or not; depends on how fussy you are.

sprogdrop n. medic. Pregnancy/giving birth. Any state of current or recent up-the-duffness.

sprog-eared adj. Worn-out, stained and a bit knackered, specifically as a result of the ministrations of young children. 'For Sale: 2006 Ford Mondeo 2.0 LX TDCi. Silver, 204k miles, some service history, generally clean condition except for rear seats that are badly sprog-eared.'

sprogs or logs? phr. Mankind's eternal dilemma, viz. Whether to go for the easy pink or the difficult brown.

sprouts n. Children. Also fuck trophies.

sprout shout n. A loud, raucous and festively foetid Bronx cheer from the nether throat, typically yodelled post prandially during the King's Speech.

SPSM n. Ad hoc unit of measurement used by local councils and police forces to categorise certain economically challenged locales. Staffies Per Square Mile.

spuck n. Hybrid substance created via a session of vigorous backdoor action followed by subsequent pearl necklacing. From spunk + muck. Santorum, shum, bummus, Greek-style yoghurt.

spud v. To deliberately mess up a job interview in order not to jeopardize one's benefits. Named after the character in Trainspotting.

spud fumbler n. A puddle jumper. 'Born on this day: Angela Lansbury, actress, 1925; Edward Ardizzone, illustrator, 1900; Oscar Wilde, spud fumbler, 1854.'

spud grinder n. The cake-hole. 'Put that in your spud grinder, Mary.'

spud gun euph. Used in a spot of botting, a male Piers Morgan that eventually spunks out an earthy pellet in the manner of the popular Lone Star toy.

spuds deep adj. In up to the maker's nameplate, in up to the back wheels, in up to the apricots.

spuffer n. An extremely localised Tyne Dock colloquialism describing male ejaculate.

spuffing dust n. The plight of a gentleman working from home who is experiencing a jizzbolt drought, following a 6-hour wanking marathon.

spuff leach n. A small slug of coagulated jipper clinging tenaciously to the leg of a chap who has but recently gripped the lather. A lava lamprey.

spunch n. A forceful facial that causes the stunned recipient to recoil. A white hook.

spuncle n. A jitler donor who has altruistically fathered a child for a couple of women of the library. From spondle + uncle.

spunctual adj. Of a grumble thespian who is able to blow his beans on cue or to a pre-arranged schedule.

spuncture n. An incidence of latex failure at a critical moment while using a jubber ray. A leak in a beef wellington; a bursted blob.

spungle 1. n. Seed emitted prematurely or infelicitously; an ejaculatory misfire. 'I knew I should of got her to wash the spungle out of that frock.' 2. v. To achieve release at a time or in a manner probably not of one's choosing. 'I want to say one thing to the American people. I want you to listen to me. I'm going to say this again: I did not have sexual relations with that woman, Miss Lewinsky. But I may have spungled somewhere in her vicinity.'

spunk 1. n. Semen, seed. 2. n. Spirit, pluck. 3. n. Aus. A good-looking man, dish, hunk. 4. n. Tinder made from fungus. 5. v. To ejizzulate, to spooge, esp. vertically.

spunk cousin n. A member of a fellow's extended spam-ily tree who has slept with the same woman that he has. Also *custard cousin.*

spunk-curdling *adj.* Descriptive of a woman who can induce an instantaneous *derection* at a hundred paces. *'I must say, Compo, I cannot understand your seemingly insatiable lust for the spunk-curdling Mrs Battye at number twenty-eight.'*

spunk dado rail *n.* A crusty frieze-like excrescence at about waist-height on the bedroom wall of a single young man.

spunk double *n.* Ersatz *man milk,* fake semen. Any substance used on a pornographic film set when the lead actor has already *jizzed* his *balls* as *flat as a bat's wings, eg.* Yakult, wallpaper paste, Tippex, egg nog, Scott's emulsion, No More Nails, salad cream, toothpaste (not the stuff with a stripe in it).

spunk-drunk *adj.* Delirious as a result of the over-consumption of *root beer.*

spunk dustbin *n.* A *spooge bucket, box of assorted creams.* An exceptionally accommodating young lady who has a *twat like a billposter's bucket.*

spunkeyed *adj.* In such an extreme state of advanced *liquid refreshment* that your eyes struggle to open. Reminiscent of the appearance of a *grumble* thesp following a well-aimed *facial.*

spunk gurning *n.* The delightful faces a *niff flick* starlet pulls as she excitedly anticipates the *tipping* of the romantic lead's *cement* onto her face.

spunk gutters *n.* Crude term for those ridiculously oversized false eyelashes worn by young *Martini girls.*

spunk juggler *n.* An *onanist* on a unicycle.

spunkle *n.* Familial relationship that exists between an anonymous *jizz* donor and his resultant offspring. *Spunkles* are typically tracked down by the dogged research of Davina McCall and Nicky Campbell. Oh, and a big office filled with researchers.

spunkled *adj.* Besprinkled with *spunk.*

spunkling *adj.* Sparkling or glistening as a result of being *spunkled.*

spunk mail *n.* The lifelong postal monsoon of unsolicited pornographic brochures and catalogues received as a result of foolishly buying a Linsey-Dawn McKenzie video from an ad in the back of the *Sunday People* twenty years ago.

spunk oven *n.* A delightful term for the feminine *bower of pleasure.*

spunk rat *n.* A good looking bloke, as described by females.

spunk run *n. RN.* On His Majesty's warships, the 2-inch gap down the side of a sailor's bunk where he stows *pop-up books,* soiled *grundies* and tissues

on which he has blown his nose.

spunk's burning a hole in my scrotum, this *exclam.* Rhetorical statement said when a fellow is afflicted by the raging *horn.*

spunk shuffle *n.* The characteristic gait adopted by a chap's girlfriend as she tries to stop the *congregation leaving the cathedral* before she reaches the *bog.*

spunktastic *adj.* Erotically enervating. *'Have you seen Kylie's lingerie video? It's absolutely spunktastic.'*

spunkteneity *n.* Ad-*cock* premature ejaculation.

spunktrough *n.* The conveniently located elliptical depression found atop a lady's sternum at the base of her throat, which forms a convenient receptacle for any overflowing semi-viscid liquid which may dribble from her mouth for any reason.

spunk trunk *n.* A prehensile *cock* that could easily spray *spunk* all over Johnny Morris. Let's just stop and savour that mental image for a moment, shall we.

spunktuation *n.* The natural breaks taken during the reading of a work of erotic literature. Also *full pops, cummas, semi-on colons.*

spunktuation mark *n.* Commonly found in *bongo mags,* marking where a previous reader paused to reflect on what he had read.

spunky wrench *n.* A *wanking spanner* or *cunt scratcher.* A swain's hand.

spuphemism *n.* A humorous *sperm wail.* A jolly shout upon *spoffage, eg.* "There she blows!" "Timberrrrr!" or "Yabba Dabba Dooooo!"

Spurlock, Morgan *1. n. prop.* Late US documentary film maker. *2. n.* Any source of erotic stimulus, such as a *bongo mag, grumble flick* or *left-handed website,* which results in a fellow's *Hampton* becoming *supersized.*

spurt curses *n.* Involuntary profanities shouted out by a bloke as he arrives at the *Billy Mill roundabout. 'Sorry, Mrs Harris. That was just some spurt curses.' 'That's okay, Cliff. Now quick, get in the wardrobe. I just heard Jet's key in the front door.'*

Spurt Reynolds *n.* Pet name for the tearful *bald man* who sits atop the *hairy beanbags.*

spurtsmanship *n.* The enviable ability to project *spaff* a prodigious distance; typically into the eye on a receptive *bongo* movie co-star.

spurtual reality *n.* The act of pausing a *skin flick* before *lobbing ropes* onto the TV screen, in order to create the impression that you are involved in the action; a feeling that, one would imagine, very quickly gives way to a vivid sense of self-loathing, not to mention an urgent need to clean a load of *jitler* off the telly before the missus comes in.

spurt your curd *v.* To spread your *spunk*; perhaps

while stood next to a bouncing Seat Alhambra near the Thicket Roundabout, Maidenhead.

squack *n. onomat.* The sound of a male ejaculation. Also *frish.*

squaddie's delight *n.* A woman in the armed forces who is not *on the bus to Hebden Bridge.* A heterosexual Army, Navy or Air Force lady.

squaddie's mattress *n. milit.* Army version of the naval *matelot's mattress.* She who *spreads* for soldiers, especially round the back of Cheeks nightclub, Aldershot.

squaddie's sleeping bag *n.* A well-used and crusty *haddock pastie. 'Joan Hunter-Dunn was nothing like the bird in the poem, you know Michael. I licked her out once behind a skip in Camberley and she had a blurtch like a squaddie's sleeping bag, I can tell you.'* (Sir John Betjeman on *Parkinson,* BBC TV, 1975).

squander a child *v.* To commit the mortal *sin of Ona*n and *shed one's seed* upon the thorny croft. *'Bless me father, for I have squandered a child.' 'Me too, pal, just now.'*

squart *n. onomat.* A *fart* which has turned into a *squirt* halfway through.

squashed spuggy/spoggy/sparrow *n.* An elderly lady's *world of leather. Granny's oysters.*

squat chic *1. n. Guardian*-ese description of some sort of interior design *bollocks* that employs a riot of patterns and hues and looks like Pete Doherty's been cold-turkeying in it. *2. n.* A stylish and colourful unflushed *feeshus* exhibited in a *jobby pan.*

squat 'n' squirt *n.* A manoeuvre often performed up dark alleys by females returning from the pub, and filmed by *wanking* CCTV operators. A *splash 'n' dash.*

squatter *n.* An annoying little *turd* that takes up residence in one's *arse* and refuses to leave, unless threatened by Bermondsey Dave.

squatter's rights *n.* The unwritten rule that, when a man takes a newspaper into the *stink hut* to do some *bum rubbish,* not even the might of the British legal establishment can move him until he's finished. *'Winston, please do hurry up darling. Black Rod is waiting and his majesty has terrible cramps.' 'I have the News of the World, a cigar, and am about to drop a second H-bomb. So you can fuck off and tell them I've got squatter's rights.'*

squeak and bubble *n.* Cabbagey japes in the bath.

squeak the breeze *v. US.* To *fart, talk German, pass wind.*

squeaky blinder *n.* A high-pitched *Lionel* of such potency that it fair makes one's eyes water.

squeaky toy *n.* An *Exchange and Mart* which

sounds, and indeed occasionally smells, not unlike the popular, shrill-noise-producing dog amuser.

squeezebox *n.* A bellows-powered aerophonic instrument that issues rhythmic wheezing noises when played tunefully in the lavatory. *Pan pipes, bogpipes.*

squeeze the cheese *v.* To *stretch the sausage.*

squeeze the dog *euph.* To grab and hug the nearest pet/cushion/person in order to gain extra purchase when extraculating a particularly troublesome *Lionel.*

squeeze the fig *v.* When needing a *Tom tit* in a public place, to keep one's *nipsy* firmly clenched to prevent the *turtle's head* poking out. *'His majesty the king there, regally squeezing the fig as he sits down on this ancient throne at this historic moment, this moment of history, this historical moment of history. Will that do? Where's my money?'*

squeeze the lemon *v.* Of women, to urinate. Possibly onto a pancake.

squeeze your head *v.* To take a *Donald Trump.*

squeeze your swimmers out *1. v. Aus.* To wring the seawater from your bathing trunks. *2. n.* To wring the *taddies* from your *giggling pin.*

squeezure *n. medic.* Acute infarction or aneurism suffered while desperately trying to hold in a *bottom burp. 'Looks like grandad's having a squeezure trying to hold that fart in, nan.'*

squeezy beef oxo *n.* Rich *bum gravy* that requires intense abdominal clenching to expunge from the *Enochs.*

squelchy *n.* A *wide on, slop on, soggy moggy, squidge, throb on, wetty, fizzy knickers.*

squench *1. n.* A moist *fart* which feels like one has *gambled and lost. 2. n.* A character in Dickens's *The Old Curiosity Shop* who suffered a *fall of soot* during Little Nell's funeral.

squibble *n.* The second in a triumvirate of gentleman's *popshots,* the first of which is a squirt and the third of which is a dribble. Derivation unknown.

squidge *n.* A *fadge* with a *wide on.*

squid legs *n.* The thin, rubbery tentacles found floating on the water after a bath night session of *making nylon.*

squid marks *n.* Fishy *skids* in a lady's *fairy hammock.* Also *snail trail.*

squid wank *n.* The kind of *toss* received from a lady inexperienced in the provision of such things. Derived from the distinctive cuttlefish-like movement of the hand. A *tail of the unexpected, scuttlefish.*

Squidward's nose *n.* A sad and droopy-looking *cock.* From the miserable cephalopod/mollusc in the *Spongebob Squarepants* cartoons.

squinternet *1. n.* The eye-damagingly microscopic web pages to be found on the screen of a mobile telephone. *2. n.* The somewhat larger internet pages to be found on a full-size computer, which are nonetheless just as deleterious to the viewer's visual faculties.

squirrel covers *n.* A lady's *dunghampers*.

squirrel's nostril *n.* An exceptionally tight, tufty *ringpiece*.

squirter's alley *n. medic.* The *bodily treasure*.

squirtilizer *n.* Loose *stools* that *come out like bats at dusk.* Also *brown paratroopers, Ikeas, jungle jitters.*

squirting like a badly laid paving slab *sim. medic.* *Shitting* through the *eye of a needle, pissing rusty water* out of one's *arse,* in the style of an *affpuddle,* as defined in the *Meaning of Liff.*

squirt in the guts *n.* Making love. *'I don't want clever conversation / Just want to give you a squirt in the guts.'* (lyric to Just *the Way You Are* by Barry White).

squirts *n. medic.* In proctology, a series of fiery eruptions from the *chamber of horrors* resulting in a pyroclastic flow from the *back body.* A condition also known as the *skitters,* the *Earthas* or *the Engelberts.*

squirty dirt *n. medic.* Faeces of an extremely low viscosity. *'Come to the Curry Capital, Bigg Market, Newcastle upon Tyne, for an attack of squirty dirt you won't forget in a hurry.'*

squirt your dirty water pistol *v.* To *tip your filthy concrete, drop your yoghurt, lose your mess.* *'Aw, bloody hell. Who's been squirting their dirty water pistol into me knicker drawer?'*

squishpot *n. US.* The area right below the *devil's doorbell* and just above the *snail's doorstep.*

squits *n. medic.* Dangerously wet *farts,* constantly bordering on the *follow through.* Junior *squirts.*

squit thrusts *n.* During a bout of diarrhoea, involuntary spasms in the *nipsy* that precipitate a rapid and bountiful ejection of *fizzy gravy* and a *ringpiece like a Japanese flag* for afters. *Spurting superstars.*

squiz *n.* Having a *shit* while doing a puzzle in a tabloid newspaper. *'Just pull the nose up to the docking tower, will you number two? I'm off to the bogs for a squiz.'*

SSOBS *abbrev.* An abbreviation often used in the *Autotrader* and suchlike. Shit Stain On Back Seat. *'For sale 1973 Ford Capri. One careful owner, RWD, ABS, DFI, SSOBS £300 No tyre kickers or time wasters.'*

SSR *abbrev.* Sound, Smell and Residue. Useful three-factor scale for assessing how embarrass-

ing a *sit-down lavatory adventure* will be when in a confined and sensitive situation, such as in a cosy hotel room with a romantic partner, on an aeroplane or train, or being in a very small workplace with only one *khazi.*

SSSWSO *abbrev.* She Said She Was Sixteen, Officer.

STA *abbrev. Grumble* industry code denoting the job prospects of a starlet with somewhat less than conventional good looks. Straight To Anal.

stabbin' cabin *n.* A secondary residence kept for the sole purpose of discreet carnival encounters, *eg.* A discreet flat in Belgravia, a small cottage in the Cotswolds, or a 12-foot caravan on the cliffs at Scarborough.

stabbing the cat *n. Self discipline.* From the motion of knifing an invisible feline on one's lap. Similar to *feeding the ducks,* but with the emphasis on the downward stroke.

stabilisation wank *n.* A restorative act of *self-pollution* performed after a long session of viewing *grummer* or an intense, tiring day at work.

stab vest *n.* A *rubber Johnny.*

stab wound in a gorilla's back *sim.* A charmingly poetic evocation of an ungroomed *blurtch.* A *ripped sofa, badly packed kebab, beaver's guts.*

stack blow *n.* A gentleman's *organism.*

stacked *adj. Well qualified.*

stackwhacker *n.* A friend or colleague who possesses a phenomenally large and well-kept collection of *jazz periodicals.* A *slybrarian.* *'Today's birthdays: Lewis Caroll, English author, 1832; Elmore James, American blues musician, 1918; Frank Skinner, Brummie stackwhacker, 1957.'*

staffing issue *euph.* An internet-fuelled act of monomanual *self harm.* From the explanation proffered by Texas Senator Ted Cruz after he inadvertently "liked" a hardcore *grumble vid* on his Twitter account. *'I walked through the park this morning and there was a tramp in a bush having a staffing issue.'*

staff of life *1. n.* Bread, a very basic food that is found in some form in almost every society on Earth. *2. n.* The penis. *'The parson, walking along the road and meeting a young parishioner with a loaf of bread in one hand and his other hand in his pocket: "Oh, good day to you, Johnny. What is that you have there? Ah! The staff of life, I see. And what is in your other hand?" Johnny: "A loaf of bread, vicar".'* (cartoon by Leonard Raven-Hill in *Punch,* 1926).

stagalmites *n. medic.* Pubic lice acquired on a prenuptial grand tour of eastern European fleshpots.

stagecoach *n.* A cramped, filthy *ride* which leaves

you in need of a wash. Also *riding shotgun*.

stage door *n.* Round-the-back, semi-hidden entrance used by *Johnnies* of a theatrical bent.

staggered start *n.* A marathon *dump* session in which the release of *runners* is punctuated by distinct periods of frustrating inactivity. A *handicrapped* race to the beach.

staining in *n.* Having a quiet night at home, watching DVDs and leaving blotches on the living room upholstery.

stain, the *n.* The *freckle, rusty bullet hole*.

stalactits *n.* Historical hanging breasts of the long, thin variety. Also *socktits, bun-chukas, knee shooters, toe polishers, Basset hounds' ears, beaver tails, Gandhi's flip-flops, bingo baps*.

stalagshites *n.* Naturally occurring, upward-pointing turdiferous deposits which form in porcelain basins.

stale bait *n.* A *bit of stuff* that's gone slightly past its "best before" date.

stalk *n.* Erection, *stiffy*. A *third leg, middle stump*. *'Any suggestions? I just can't seem to get rid of this stalk this morning. Anyway, let's carry on. Ashes to ashes, dust to dust.'*

stalk fever *n. medic.* Serious condition affecting men. Symptoms include short-sightedness, stunted growth, insanity and palmar hypertrichosis.

Stallone's bottom lip *euph.* The way the *fiveskin* sags after a serious and prolonged bout of repeated *self harm* while *working from home*.

stall shy *1. adj.* An equestrian figure of speech referring to a racehorse that doesn't want to go into its box prior to the start of a race. *2. n.* A public lavatory figure of speech descriptive of a fellow's inability to make eye contact with the man who has just emerged from the next cubicle, after spending the last five minutes being forced to listen to what sounded like a Sumo wrestler giving birth to several catering-sized black puddings through a loud-hailer. Also *bogshy. 3. adj. medic.* Effect of the psychological condition that renders *scuttlers* unable to micturate in public lavatories unless there is vacant stall between them and the next customer. *Stage fright.*

stamped bat *euph.* One of the most horrific kinds of *ladypart* imaginable; a *bodily treasure* that resembles nothing so much as a flying rodent that has been subjected to a heavy shoeing. A *snatch* that not even Ozzy Osbourne would consider eating. *'Nostalgia was powerless to resist. His eyes bored into hers like zirconium-coated drill bits. His muscular arms enfolded her body as she felt herself being whisked away on a soufflé of passion. Gently he lowered her bloomers, and a thrill of forbidden excitement shot through her loins as she felt his hot Latin breath beginning to creep down her crab ladder towards her altar of Venus. But it was not to be. "Bloody Nora!" shouted Sextus Empiricus from between her legs. "I'm not licking that out. It looks like a stamped bat."'* (from *The Lady and the 2nd Century Pyrrhonic Skepticist Philosopher* by Barbara Cartland).

stamp licker *n.* A *bird's quimpiece* which is so wet that it could be usefully employed in the despatch department of a busy mail order business. Before stamps were self-adhesive, that would be.

stamp on the toothpaste *v.* To ejaculate in an over-excitable manner, *go off like a punched icing bag*.

standard eight *1. n.* More-or-less obsolete double-run home movie format which involved opening the side of the camera half-way through the exposure of the film in order to turn the spool over, thus ensuring that the mid-point of any domestic cine presentation in the early 1970s was characterised by flashing psychedelic orange lights. This was followed shortly by the splice, where the two twenty-five foot lengths of longitudinally split 16mm film had been joined together at the processing laboratory, snapping in the projector and the image on the screen melting before one's very eyes like something out of *The War Game*, then a bout of swearing while your dad tried to re-thread the melted end of the film through the white-hot gate with his fingers. *2. n.* Crapulent 1950s small family automobile, particularly suitable for the sort of small family that didn't require any boot space or a car that would climb any sort of gradient, and hence *3. n.* A gentleman equipped with a small, under-powered *trouser engine* which is inclined to conk out mid-journey.

standby on *n. Half a teacake.* A penis in a state of semi-tumescence, ready to leap into action if required.

standing on the fireman's hose *sim.* At the conclusion of the evening's fourth or fifth bout of *Jesuit boxing*, a complete failure to release *jaff.* An *air horn, chucking salt*.

standing ovation *1. n.* Mark of respect given to a *digestive transit* which is so impressive that one has to get to one's feet and have a good look at it. *2. n.* Characteristic posture taken up by someone attempting to lay a particularly recalcitrant *dog's egg*. Half standing up and hammering the knees in agony.

stand lunch *v.* To provide an *air buffet* which stops everyone in the room feeling hungry any more.

'It's alright, folks. Grandad's going to stand lunch.'

stand on *n.* A *bone on*, a *stalk*.

stanky *n.* The glaze that is left on the *shaft* of the *choad* after a bout of *kipper splitting*. May be *zuffled* on curtains or wiped on a *stankychief*.

Stannah stunna *n.* A *gilf*.

star baker *1. n.* Worthless honour awarded to the weekly winner of the *The Great British Bake Off*. *2. n.* An *arse* that produces hugely impressive chocolate cakes.

starboard bow *n. RN.* The *arse*.

starching your socks *euph. Relaxing in a gentleman's way* into a convenient item of hosiery. *'MARGO: Jerry! Jerry! Open this door immediately! What are you doing in there? JERRY: (pokes head round door) Just starching my socks, dear. Only Barbara's bending over to plant some spuds next door. And if I crouch on top of the wardrobe and angle the dressing table mirror just right, I can get a great view of her arse. It's like two hard boiled eggs in a hand-kerchief.'* (Extract from script of *The Good Life Easter Special*, BBC TV 1978).

starch pill *n.* A Viagra tablet, a *bluey, Bongo Bill's banjo pill.*.

starfish enterprise *n.* Guile and native cunning used when attempting "to boldly go where no man has gone before".

starfish trooper *n.* An *arsetronaut*.

starfucked *adj.* The loss of credibility suffered by a product as a result of its endorsement by a celebrity. *'I see Jaguar cars have been starfucked by Jimmy Carr, then.'*

stargate *1. n.* An Einstein–Rosen wormhole-style portal device that allows practical, rapid travel between two distant locations within the *Stargate* fictional universe. *2. n.* The *arsehole*.

stargazer *n.* A gentleman's *pork scimitar* with a pronounced upwards curve, allowing the *hog's eye* to scan the heavens.

staring at the sun *n.* An act which is apt to make one go blind. *'Oi, Gerald. What are you doing under your coat?' 'I'm just staring at the sun into my popcorn bucket, dear.'*

starter button *n.* The *clematis, wail switch*. The *clit*.

starter leads *n.* Suspenders, *giggle bands*.

starting line at Brands Hatch *1. sim.* Descriptive of severely *be-skidmarked undercrackers*. Guaranteed to cause embarrassment the first time they are handed to one's newly wedded bride for washing. *2. sim.* The *skid pan* of a student house or dysentery hospital *chod bin*. Also the *Ark Royal landing deck, thrush's chest*.

starting pisstol *n.* During a *sit down lavatory adventure*, the initial *Peters and Lee* which heralds the start of a marathon session.

star trek *n.* Any sexual encounter where one would be going (boldly or otherwise) "where no man has gone before", *eg. Getting tops and fingers* off Ann Widdecombe or *doing* Richard Littlejohn up the *shitter*.

Star Trek door *n.* The futuristic sound of the *turtle's breath* as it sweeps out of the *rusty sheriff's badge*.

start the car *exclam.* An announcement proclaiming the iminent arrival of a very loud *exchange and mart*.

start the horn mower *v.* To perform that particularly vicious upstroke which is often essayed by an inexperienced *masturbatrix*.

start up Guinevere *euph.* To pull the handle after dropping six brown balls and a bonus.

start with a clean slate *v.* To be the privileged first occupant of the works *biscuit wrapper* after the cleaner has been round, and thereby the person who can sit down with no hygiene concerns.

Star Wars door *sim.* In *backdoor work*, descriptive of the manner in which the *death star* closes after the *pink Darth Vader* is removed. See *hoob*.

Star Wars waiting room *euph.* A local *cantina* that is frequented by all manner of disreputable-looking lifeforms.

stash dash *n.* A married man's sprint from front room window to *grumble* collection once the front gate is securely fastened behind the wife as she pops out for a pint of milk.

stash in the attic *n.* Grandpa's legacy of vintage *jazz mags*; *Knave, Penthouse, Razzle, Health & Efficiency etc*.

statement piece *1. n.* A large, tasteless and garishly coloured piece of furniture that wants throwing on a bonfire. *2. n.* A genuinely massive *cock*. *3. n.* A *fuck-off pan blocker*.

state of the art *n. rhym. slang.* An act of rectal flatulation. A *broken heart*. *'Jesus! Is that your state of the art, Dot? I thought it was the bleeding Noggin the Nog.'*

Statue of Liberty, she's had more men up her than *sim.* A sexist and offensive insinuation that a *bird* may have been *rogered more times than a policeman's radio*.

stauner *n. Scots.* A dour, granite-hard *bone on*. An *Old man of Hoy*.

staying up to watch Family Guy *euph.* White lie told by a gent to his better half at bedtime, allowing him the opportunity for a spot of uninterrupt-ed *self pollution* over the ten-minute *fanny*-free free-view on the *fanny channel*.

stay in the shallow end *exclam.* A request made by

a female to a fledgling *snatch nosher.*

St. Bernard's chin *sim.* Descriptive of a *muff* that has had lots of *ropes lobbed* at it. A heavily *bespunkled mingepiece.* Also *bloodhound's jowls.*

St Crispin's Day, an arse like *sim.* A *twenty-four sheeter,* a *nipsy* that refuses to wipe clean. From the date of Shakespeare's *Henry V* Battle of Agincourt speech, *viz.* "Once more unto the breach, dear friends, once more". See also *scraping out the Marmite pot, ringbinder, clean up on aisle two etc.*

steak drapes *n. Gammon goalposts, beef curtains.*

steakwich *n.* The external pudenders of a lady of a certain age which resembles a traditional British pub snack. *'Would you like any sauce on your steakwich, madam?'*

stealing petrol, sucks cock like she's *sim.* Said of a *fellatrix* who goes at it enthusiastically like a *scratter* syphoning unleaded from a car in a lay-by.

steal mill *n.* Any place where industrious *neds* exchange purloined goods for money and/or drugs. *Crack converters.*

stealth bomber *n.* A subtle *leg lifter.* A *mystery benefactor* or *phantom raspberry blower.* An anonymous gaseous altruist.

stealth bummer *n.* An undercover, hard-to-detect *fruit feeler* who flies under the *gaydar.*

stealth moose *n.* A *long range fox.*

stealth shit *n.* An act of public lavatory defecation performed surreptitiously, that is to say under the *covering fire* of some sort of masking sound, *eg.* A toilet flush, somebody washing their hands vigorously or heavy, German-accented breathing from the adjoining cubicle.

stealth sites *n.* Football, car and DIY websites which can be quickly clicked on after *desktop dusting* in order, you would hope, to fool the more IT-literate missus.

steam off ma lash *phr. Scots.* An infinitesimal estimation of the value of someone or something. *'Och, ye paid how much to see yon Michael McIntyre in concert? I wouldnae gie him the steam off ma lash.'*

steam off one of his turds, wouldn't give you the *exclam.* Said of a fellow *who's tighter than a matador's trousers.*

steamroller effect *n.* Last resort of one who discovers that there is no *arse paper* left while suffering from severe post-curry *ring sting* in the *crapper.* The gentle rolling of the cool cardboard tube backwards and forwards across the anal cheeks to afford soothing, albeit extremely temporary, relief.

steam seeker *n.* The conscientious cleaner at work

who's in the *trap* inhaling the perfume of your most recent *Simon Cowell* movement before you've even had time to wash your hands.

steel steamer *n.* A foaming, rearing, thoroughbred *horse's handbrake* that appears to be giving off clouds of vapour like a Grand National winner.

steeped in theatrical tradition *euph.* Pissed as an astronaut. *'My next guest is steeped in theatrical tradition. Ladies and gentlemen, a big hand for Mr Oliver Reed.'*

steg *n.* A woman resembling a ferocious, spiny, squat, prehistoric dinosaur, *eg.* Extinct late TV harridan Rita Webb.

stegmata *n.* The piercings, tattoos, and facial hair sculpting effected by certain *homely* people in the mistaken belief that they will look attractive and trendy.

Steinbecks *n. Chalfonts, Tate & Lyles* or *farmers.* Named after the Pulitzer Prize-winning author of *The Grapes of Wrath,* not to mention *Of Mice and Haemorrhoids. 'Ooh, Jesus wept. These fucking Steinbecks are giving me some gyp today, I can tell you. The emergency exits are located here, here and here. Please take time to look around and locate the nearest one.'*

stellabate *adj.* Chaste, as a consequence of imbibing excessive quantities of *Nelson. Stellabacy* is a situation neatly summed up in the phrase "The spirit is willing but the flesh is weak because the export strength lager is strong".

stellacetamol *n.* A large amount of continental lager, the consumption of which anaesthetises the drinker, protecting him from any sensation of pain when falling through plate glass windows, being hit by cars or toppling off scaffolding while imitating a gibbon.

stellacide, commit *v.* To purposely down a *Keighley picnic* in order that one's sorrows choke on their own vomit.

stellanoia *n.* The state of aggressive paranoia which one attains shortly after imbibing one's tenth pint of *wifebeater.*

stella performance *1. euph.* A comprehensive act of spousal abuse. *2. n.* Any occasion enhanced by someone who is heavily *self-medicated,* be they recounting a self-aggrandising anecdote, singing a power ballad on the karaoke, settling an ongoing dispute at a family wedding or being interviewed by Michael Aspel.

stellaporter *n.* A futuristic form of instantaneous transportation which warps the time/space continuum, leaving one outside the front door mere moments after leaving the pub. Often with a wet trouser leg, a nasty head wound, a shoe full of *piss* and a half-eaten kebab.

stellarisation *n.* Process by which a man is rendered unable to father children. *'Sorry love, I can't do it. I've been stellarised, see.'*

stella stairlift *n.* Ascending to one's bedroom on one's hands and knees at the conclusion of a heavy night.

stellavision *n.* Premium strength, kaleidoscopic *beer goggles.*

stellify *1. n.* Title of two verses and a half-arsed chorus masquerading as a complete Ian Brown song. *2. v.* To imbibe a reassuringly excessive quantity of a certain Belgian beer.

stelloquence *n.* Term descriptive of a mightily *refreshed* late night kebab shop customer's witty, free-flowing banter and the fluent, well-informed discourse with which he regales his fellow prospective catmeat snack purchasers.

St Elmo's fire *1. n.* 1985 hit by Worksop-born American hairdresser John Parr. *2. n.* Luminous plasma due to a coronal discharge from a grounded object in an electric field, for example around the rigging of a ship, caused by the influence of Catholic martyr St. Erasmus of Formiae. *3. n.* The dramatic rectal side effects of a particularly devastating Indian meal, such as one prepared in the kitchens of the Rupali Restaurant, Bigg Market, Newcastle upon Tyne (now closed, as we may have mentioned previously).

stemmer *n.* A *chewie* in which the dirty lady is able to swallow the whole shebang. A *deep throat.*

stench coat *n.* The embarrassing result of *blowing off* while wearing a Crombie, thereby sealing the lighter-than-air *whiff* inside until it is taken off at one's genteel destination. *'Here, allow me to take your stench coat, archbishop.'*

stenching *n.* Deliberately refraining from *dropping the kids off at the pool* to add potency to your *air biscuits.*

stench manicure *n.* The result of a badly timed structural failure of one's lavatory tissue, leaving one with miasmatically abhorrent cuticles.

stench trench *n.* The *ha'penny.*

stench warfare *n.* That olfactory conflict which is played out between two workmates in adjoining *bog* cubicles.

Stephen Hawking's homework, as hard as *sim.* Said of something particularly unyielding. *'Effluvia was powerless to resist. Imbroglio's eyes burnt into hers like hydrogrossular garnets. His muscular business magnet's arms enfolded her softly yielding body as she felt herself being swept away in a tropical cyclone of passion. Holding her close, he put his lips close to her ear and whispered the words she had* longed to hear off him for so long. "Come and have a suck on me cock, love. It's as hard as Stephen Hawking's homework."' (from *The Lady and the Man* by Barbara Cartland).

step on a duck *v.* To create a quack, *fart. 'Pardon me, Ladies and Gentlemen. Do not adjust your wireless set, Mrs Simpson has just stepped on a duck.'* (from The Abdication Broadcast of Edward VIII, 1937).

step on a frog *v.* To *step on a duck.*

step on a rake *v.* To attain a particularly speedy erection.

step on one's dick *v.* To make a mistake or blunder. *'They say that all political careers ultimately end in failure, and it's hard to escape the conclusion that Mr Cameron has really stepped on his dick here.'*

stepping back from royal duties *euph.* Laying low for a while following a colossal *fuck up.*

stepping bone *n.* A s*xual conquest which a person hopes will lead to better things. *'I knobbed chubby Kerry with the lazy eye as a stepping bone to her mate Teresa with the big tits. I'm not proud of it but at least it pissed Ron off as he was engaged to Kerry at the time.'* (Excerpt from *Rod* by Rod Stewart, Random House, 2010).

Steptoe & Son *n.* A drab and depressing sexual position, whereby a solitary, clapped out old nag kneels on the bed, proffering her knackered back end up to her old man, who slowly and disgruntledly *bangs* her while gurning and muttering under his breath. And then stops to shovel her steaming dung into a bucket.

Steptoe's face *n.* A saggy non-too-fussy set of *flackets. ie.* "They will take in any old rag or bone".

Steptoe's yard, more crap than *sim.* Said of a proper *Boxing Day* stock *clearance.*

Steven and the twins *euph.* A fellow's *meat and two veg,* often referred to by Ian Beale in *EastEnders.* The *Kennedys, the boys.*

Steve Smith, harder to get out than *sim.* Said of a stubborn splinter, rusty screw or nail, possibly a reference to the Australian cricket captain rather than the similarly named twenty-fourth Adjutant General of Connecticut, born in 1836.

Stevie Nicks's tambourine, like *sim.* Descriptive of the rhythmic hand/wrist work performed by a lady practised at *Salvation armwork.*

Stevie Wonders, the *n. medic.* The involuntary wobbling of the head that one exhibits when desperately trying to stay awake, *eg.* A student in a Friday afternoon lecture or a lorry driver on the M6. From the erratic head movements of the Motown star. *'The trial of the Millennium Dome Jewel Robbers was held up today after Judge Michael Coombe was spotted having a severe attack* of the Stevie Wonders during the defence council's summing up.' 2. n. The act of rocking one's head from side to side while negotiating a particularly large and recalcitrant *turtle's head*, usually after several pints of Irish stout.

Stevie Wonder's toilet seat, wetter than *sim.* Dripping like a fucked fridge. 'Her twat was wetter than Stevie Wonder's toilet seat.'

stew *v.* To leave one's *lamb cannon* in the *hairy casserole* at a low heat while one has forty winks.

stewing in your own juice *n. Dropping a gut* in the car in a cold winter's day, with no possibility of ventilation. An automotive *Dutch oven.*

stew-pé *n. Fr.* A *faux* pie, typically bought as part of a pub meal. A dish of caserole that sports a pastry wig, but doesn't have any fucking pastry on the bottom or round the sides like a proper pie.

St. George *n.* The act of *lancing your old dragon* from behind.

St. Giro's day *n.* Regular fortnightly festival for those seeking gainful employment. 'It's St. Giro's day, so the drinks are on me.'

stick a long one in the slot *phr.* Humorous instruction to play a lengthy record given by an afternoon radio presenter to his "posse" when taking leave from his studio to *park his breakfast* in the radio station *shitters.* 'That lamb phaal I had last night is playing havoc with me Simons. I might be gone for some time, so I'd best stick a long one in the slot. Here's the twelve-inch mix of Autobahn by those cheeky Germans Kraftwerk.'

stick at 15 *v.* From the pontoon playing gambit, to settle for a low quality score; thus to go for the first half decent bit of *blart* who shows interest in a night club. See also *go ugly early.*

stickier than a library copy of Fifty Shades of Grey *sim.* Said of something that is upsettingly tacky to the touch.

sticking point *1. n.* A stumbling block which stalls or prevents an amicable agreement between two or more parties. *2. n.* Any permitted orifice.

sticking your hand into a nest full of bats' wings, like *sim.* Discovering a set of excessively large, warm, leathery *labia majorcas,* while fumbling about in a lady's *applecatchers.*

sticklebrick *n.* A particularly difficult and uncomfortable *tod.* A *pine cone.*

sticklebricking *n.* The unlikely – but nonetheless theoretically possible – act of being *noshed off* by a dwarf while returning the favour to another dwarf who is standing on the shoulders of the first one. It could happen. Frankly nothing would

surprise us any more.

stickman *n.* A *fanny hopper, skippy* or *crumpeteer.*

stick shifter *n. Wanker.*

sticky belly flap cock *n.* Post *curd-spurting* condition enjoyed by *monkey spankers.*

sticky Gomez *n.* Dabbing one's spent *Gonzo's nose* up a lady's arm as a romantic act of love and appreciation, much in the way Gomez Addams kissed Morticia.

sticky keys *1. n.* Some sort of annoying computer function on the Windows operating system which is activated by pressing the shift key five times, apparently. 'I was just messing about on the computer and I turned on sticky keys by accident.' 2. n. The inevitable result of an overenthusiastic and poorly aimed session of *one-handed web-surfing.* 'I was just messing about on the computer and I got sticky keys by accident. And spunk all over the mousemat and screen. And in the printer.'

stick your hand up my arse – I've got piles *phr.* A wittily epigrammatic rejoinder that can be employed whenever one is asked for change by carol singers, *Harold ramps* or *chuggers.*

sticky toffee pudding *n.* A thick, dense portion of *bum rubbish* that adheres to everything it touches, particularly one's *arse cress.*

sticky wicket *1. n.* A post-coitally limpening *middle stump. 2. n.* A well-used *crease* with all the bounce fucked out of it. A *box of assorted creams.*

stiff *n.* A corpse. 'Come on jerkwad, let's plant the motherfucking stiff and get out of here.' 'Very well, vicar. I'll tell the organist to miss out the last two verses of the Funeral March, shall I?'.

stiff drink *n.* A warming tot of *vitamin S* quaffed by females and *puddle jumpers.* A *drink on a stick.*

stiffener *1. n.* That which is added to something in order to increase its rigidity, such as starch for a collar, for example. *2. n.* A person who is apt to *stiffen a rod.* 'Today's birthdays: Arthur Scargill, seventies miners' union firebrand, 1936; Mary J Blige, US singer, songwriter, actress and philanthropist, 1971; Rachel Riley, stiffener, 1986.'

stiff enough for the wife *adj.* Descriptive of something which, while not optimal, is adequate for the job at hand. 'Is that plaster dry yet, Dave?' 'No mate, but I reckon it's stiff enough for the wife. Let's sling the wallpaper up and then we can piss off down the pub early.'

stifficult *adj.* Awkward as a consequence of unwanted tumescence in the generative member. 'Fuck me, look at the knockers on that stripper. By the way, it's your round.' 'I can't go to the bar just now. It's a bit stifficult.' 'Why are you frantically *looking for change in your trouser pockets, then?'*

stifficulty *n.* Trouble in the trouser department. *'Pass me a couple of blueys out the bedside drawer, will you, Marcia? I'm having stifficulty again.'*

stiff-legged deadlift *1. n.* A weight training exercise involving bending over and picking up a barbell while the legs are held straight. *2. n.* Bending over to pick up a dropped roll of *bum wad* while the legs are constricted by the trousers around one's ankles.

stiff lock *n.* A *piss-proud spooge stick.*

stiffy *n.* A *stalk.*

stiffy bag *1. n.* Receptacle used by undertakers for the transportation of a recently deceased person. *2. n.* A *jubber Ronnie.*

stiffy graph *n.* Scientific scale for the quantification of erectile function in males watching lady tennis players. The parameters of the *stiffy graph* range between zero (Betty Stove lumbering about with her bandaged leg) to ten (Anna Kournikova in a short skirt, bending over to receive a good hard service. Or even playing tennis).

stiffy stocking *n. Rascal wrapper, cheesepipe clingfilm, Spurt Reynolds's sickbag.*

stig *n.* One who is a little bit *council, common as shite.* A dump dweller.

stig of the dump *1. n.* A *turd* that makes a rapid exit, smells strongly of burning rubber and leaves plenty of *skidmarks. 2. n.* A turbo-charged *bum cigar* that whips round the U-bend faster than the eponanonymous white-suited *Top Gear* racing driver and registered trademark.

stigor mortis *n. medic.* Torpid condition affecting jobseekers, students and men who work from home, whereby they are regularly rendered completely immobile watching repeats of *Top Gear* on Dave all afternoon.

stillborn dachshund, cock like a *sim.* A deeply unpleasant simile used when describing a *membrum virile* which maintains impressive length, weight and girth, even while it is *on the slack.*

stillborn stoat *n.* A *dead otter* that slips silently under the water's surface.

still fighting *adj.* Of a curry or other spicy meal, to display the same or greater aggression on the way out as/than it did when it went in. *'Are you all right in there, June?' 'No. It's that chili I had last night, Terry. It's still fighting.'*

stilt on *n.* A long, thin, savoury erection.

stilton muffle *n.* A pungent and unwashed *fish mitten.* A particularly stenchsome *trench.*

stiltons *n. Lady dumplings* which don't get see a great deal of sunlight, and as a result are usually

very white and covered with prominent blue veins.

stinger *1. n.* A device used by the police to impale the tyres of cars driven by criminals and thus instantly slow down the pusuit. *2. n.* A mental image conjured up by a gentleman to instantly slow things down during a *scuttle.* See also *cock witch, globstopper. 3. n.* A small extra nugget of *foulage* that makes its presence felt only after one has patiently sat through the *end credits.* If this implies that one will need to visit the toilet again later for a tired retread of the whole thing, it is known as a *sequel hook.*

stinging minging pee, the *euph.* Tell-tale sign that last week's surprisingly advantageous business arrangement with that *good time girl* in Amsterdam might not have been the bargain it originally appeared to be.

stinging minging tree *n.* A mature lady's overgrown and ill-toped shrubbery.

stingpiece *n.* A *chocolate starfish* suffering the piquantly calefacient consequences of a phaal or similarly spicy curry that was ill-advisedly consumed the previous evening.

stingray *n.* A single, large, streamlined, high velocity *brown trout* that speeds from its base location into the ocean without touching the sides, in the manner of the eponymous vehicle from the Gerry Anderson series of the same name. *'That was quick, your majesty.' 'Yes Archbishop, it was a veritable stingray. I'd still give it ten minutes if I was you, though but.'*

Sting wank *n.* A post-pub act of *self- pollution* which, as a result of the amount of alcohol one has consumed, becomes a turgid marathon lasting many hours. From the lute-crazed former Police frontman's notoriously fruitless attempts to *go off* up his missus.

stinker, the *1. n. prop.* Title of a 1980 *Tales of the Unexpected* episode, where Denholm Elliott probably bakes Joss Ackland in a pie or minces him into fucking sausages or some such *shite. 2. n.* One who ponders the vicissitudes of life whilst perched naked and Rodin-like aboard the *crapper;* elbows on knees and head cupped in hands.

stink horn *1. n.* Foul-smelling comedy mushroom – *Phallus impudicus* – found on rotting trees. *2. n.* A ripe, unwashed *cock* that would even put the keenest *fellator* off their dinner.

stinking bishop *n.* The miasmatic result of poor *fiveskin* husbandry, that is to say, *smegma.* Also *brimula, foreskinzola, Fred Leicester, fromunder, helmetdale, knacker barrel, Hamish blue, he-dam, Lymeswold, knob stilton, bell end brie, trollop* snack, Wankashire cheese and willydelphia.

stinking thinking n. That time ensconced upon the bum sink when the brown muse is upon a fellow and he gets philosophical.

stink-pipe 1. n. A term used quite often in the construction trades to describe the snorkel that vents out your home's sewer gasses through your roof 2. n. The arsehole.

stink sponge n. A chair or bus seat into which someone has just dropped a gut.

stinky finger n. Having eaten up the captain's pie without a knife and fork. Stinky pinky.

stinky kitkat euph. To put four fingers up the arse and then in the mouth.

stinky Mervyn/Mervin n. The Finsbury bridge, biffin bridge, barse, carse, taint, notcher, etc.

stinky rooster n. A rousing report that wakes up the farmer as well as the rest of the household. A breakfast maker, dawn chorus, reveille.

stinky sailboat n. When your dog drags its arse across the carpet. Also known as yachting.

stinky toffee pudding n. A spot of distinctly unappetising, post-Sunday-dinner shopping with remarkable adhesive properties, meaning that it requires great perseverance to successfully polish it off.

stinky winky n. prop. Popular purple children's TV character of the 1990s, who suffered from poor genital hygiene.

Stirling n. rhym. slang. A Hilary. From Stirling Moss = Jonathan Ross.

stir porridge with a chop stick v. To stick a thin length of wood into a vastly over-sized billposter's bucket.

stirring the porridge n. Having sloppy seconds.

stir the gravy v. To agitate the marmite pot. 'How was your date with Big Sandra?' 'Great. She let me stir the gravy and everything.'

stir the stew 1. v. To arrange the orchestra, wind the clock, nip and roll, sort out the boys, tune the banjo, pop the mouse back in the house. To rearrange the trouser furniture. 2. v. To perform the anal sex, backdoor work.

stir the tanks v. To have a wank without ejaculating. From the routine procedure on the ill-fated Apollo 13 moonshot which inadvertently led to an explosion. As it would. See almosturbate.

stit pants n. A brassiere fitted out with FA cups. See AA.

stits n. Small tits, bee stings, Dutch Alps.

St. Ivel n. An imperial measurement of beer, equal to two-and-a-half quarts or five eigths of a gallon. Five pints. 'Mr Barratt appeared to be shaky as he got out of the car. I asked him if he had been

drinking and he replied: "Not really. I've only had a St. Ivel."'

stoat n. The furry prey of the one-eyed trouser snake.

stobart 1. n. An articulated humpty dumpty that jack-knifes in the pan. 2. v. To successfully deposit one's load having carefully manoeuvred one's semi up a particularly tight loading bay.

Stobby doorbell n. A handful of gravel directed at the window of an upper floor residence to alert the occupants as to one's presence below. Used extensively in the salubrious Stobwells district of Dundee.

Stockholm syndrome 1. n. Recognised psychological response whereby, after being held prisoner for a considerable period of time, captives begin to identify with their abductors. 2. n. Situation that can occur after a prolonged bout of constipation, when one's chocolate hostages start to sympathise with the Simon Cowells where they are being held, and begin actively wishing to stay in captivity.

Stockport overcoat n. A thick coating of glitter spray which, when combined with a boob tube and greyhound skirt, keeps the young ladies of the eponymous Cheshire town snug and toasty on the bitterest of winter evenings. A Bigg Market duffle coat, Whitley Bay parka, bacardigan, Pontefract puffa.

stock pubes n. Culinary flavour enhancer preferred by chefs when a difficult customer or particularly irritating food critic is dining at their establishment. 'This Tuscan Risotto has an unusually pungent, cheesy flavour.' 'That'll be the chef's stock pubes, Mr Coren.'

Stockton pizza n. Home made Mediterranean-style delicacy prepared using a slice of bread, a dollop of ketchup and a cheese slice.

Stoke chamois leather n. An orbital sander, used to remove grafitti from the boarded-up windows which are commonplace in the popular Potteries metropolis.

Stoke on Trent adj. rhym. slang. Colwyn Bay. 'Have you met Oscar, Bosie? I'm sure you two will get on like a house on fire. He's well Stoke on Trent too.'

stoke your arse v. To vigorously riddle one's bottom to the point of creating an unpleasant odour not entirely dissimilar to that of an old-fashioned town-gas works. 'Have you been stoking your arse in here again, Donny?' 'Sorry Marie.'

stomach statue n. Easter Island-quality morning wood.

stonads n. Testicles which have fossilized due to under-use. 'A lifelong celibate, Sir Isaac got the idea for his popular Newton's Cradle executive toy when his stonads banged together as he was sitting *down under an apple tree to invent gravity.'* (from *Connections* by James Burke).

stone *n.* The reason a *sponge* has got feathers stuck in his teeth.

stone cold stunner *1. n.* A wrestling move, actually a variation on the "ace cutter", made popular by redneck grapple fave "Stone Cold" Steve Austin. *2. n.* An actress in a vintage black and white movie who still manages to give one the *horn* despite the fact that she is almost certainly six feet under. See *rise from the dead.*

stone of contentment *n.* The excess 14lbs avoirdupois rapidly acquired by a bloke when he moves in with his ladyfriend and starts spending a significant proportion of his spare time sitting on his *arse* watching repeats of *Coronation Street* on ITV3.

stoner's grocer *n.* An all-night petrol station selling family sized chocolate bars, breakfast cereals and biscuits to narcotics enthusiasts at unsociable hours.

stoner's thumb *n. medic.* Repetitive strain injury brought about by repeatedly attempting to use a lighter to spark up a pipe of whatever herbal tincture takes your fancy in a windy park.

stones *n. arch.* Olde Worlde *balls. Bollocks, knackers, plums, orchestras.* 'He that is wounded in the stones, or hath his Charlie cut off, shall not enter into the congregation of the LORD.' (from *Deuternomy* 23:1).

stonka toy *n.* A virtually indestructible piece of hardware for use on the male person when there are no women about. A *pocket fanny.* 'Put that down, Shane. It's your grandad's stonka toy. It's not for playing with.'

stonker *1. n.* An erection, *hard-on, stiffy. 2. n.* Something big.

stool box *n.* Coarse epithet for a *bird's shit hopper.* 'Look at the stool box on that, your honour. It's like a violin case.'

stoolmate *n.* The situation that obtains when two persons are seated in adjacent public *crapper* cubicles, each desperate to *drop off their shopping* but waiting for the other to make the first "plop" noise. In a *stoolmate*, neither player is able to move their *Camillas*, and so, after about an hour-and-a-half, a draw is declared.

Stool-on-the-Wold, the right honourable member for *euph.* A *Sir Douglas Hurd.*

stool pigeon *n.* Person advancing with an odd, strutting, arms akimbo walk whilst attempting to get to the *crapper* in time.

stool reunion *1. n.* Unexpectedly encountering a *night watchman* that has been brewing in the *pot* through the hours of darkness. *2. n.* Finally meeting *yesterday's dinner*, which one has been *baking* for some time in the *devil's oven.*

stool shed *n.* Place where a chap can retire for a bit of quiet solitude. And a big *dump*. The *bog.*

stool shifter *n.* A sudden unpleasant shock, *eg.* Theresa May knocking on the door with a leaflet, and offering to do you one of her dances if you'll promise to vote for her.

stool softener *1. n.* Powder or liquid given to patients to ease stubborn digestive transit. *2. n.* Saturday night refreshments which assist in the *passing of motions* the following day. And perhaps on Monday, and in some cases the whole of the next week. And occasionally in the taxi on the way home.

stool stool *n.* An item of bathroom furniture that doubles up as a makeshift stirrup, enabling one to raise one's ankles while sat on the *bum sink* to ease the delivery of difficult *arse babies.*

stop at Boots *v.* Phrase expressing optimism about the outcome of a romantic interlude. 'You going to get in Tracey's knickers tonight, then Steve?' 'Well, I'll stop at Boots, put it that way'.

stopgash measure *n.* A *futter* with a woman who is just killing time between proper *fucks.*

stop press *n.* An explosive extra that won't wait for the next issue, an unexpected *front page splash* that hits the presses just as you've *put your paper to bed.*

store defective *n.* A retail store *fuckard.*

storm in a D-cup *n.* A particularly frantic *diddy ride.*

storming Batista's palace *euph.* An unexpectedly bloody episode of *falling to the communists.* Named after the events of March 13th 1957, when a group of revolutionary students attacked the Havana stronghold of Cuban dictator Fulgencio Batista, while his missus was *dropping clots.*

stout trout *n.* The impressively charcoal-hued *Eartha* that transpires following an eighteen-hour sampling of dark ales and burgundy pie.

stoutzheimers *n. medic.* Condition suffered by drinkers in Irish theme pubs, where the bar staff completely forget about waiting customers while half way through pulling their pint of Guinness, and wander off to serve someone else.

Stowford bottom *1. n.* A village in Somerset. *2. n.* What the Worzels get the morning after they've had a heavy night out imbibing cider.

stradivarious *adj.* Descriptive of the sundry miscellaneous techniques that may be employed by anyone having a *good old fiddle.*

straight and narrow, on the *adj.* Happily married.

Doing *penile servitude.*

straight as a shitting cow's tail *sim.* Said of a gent that likes engines, beer, football *etc.* *'He's a real man's man, my brother. Straight as a shitting cow's tail, your majesty.'*

straight as a shitting dog's tail *phr.* Descriptive of the tumescence of a randy lad's *membrum virile.* *'Come and see what I woke up with this morning, Carrie. It's as straight as a shitting dog's tail.'*

straight brown card, a *n. Following through.* *'And that's a straight brown card there for Lineker.'*

straightening the elephant man's bow tie, like *sim.* Setting about a pointless task, *eg.* Issuing a digitally re-mastered box set of Lou Reed's *Metal Machine Music.*

straightening your hat *n.* Raking one's kex out the crack of one's *arse.*

straighten your tie, let me *exclam.* Phrase used by a woman who is offering to give a man an erection in the *trouser department.* Or just possibly suggesting that she is about to re-arrange his neckwear.

straight from the whore's mouth *exclam. rhet.* A clever figure of speech which can be effectively employed as a rhetorical device during heated debates with members of the opposite sex. *'There you have it, ladies and gentlemen of the jury. Straight from the whore's mouth.'*

straight to main *1. euph.* In a restaurant setting, dispensing with any starters so as to get immediately to the good stuff. *2. euph.* In a romantic setting, for a similar reason dispensing with the need for foreplay.

strain a Penny Lane *v.* To perform an impressive *rumpet voluntary* that resembles nothing so much as the high-pitched brass solo from the eponymous Beatles song.

strain the potatoes *v.* To *strain your greens, see a man about a dog.*

strain your greens *v.* To *strain the potatoes, turn your bike around.*

strange *n.* Any woman of whom one has not had *carnival knowledge* of. An antidote to a *groundhog lay.* *'I know she's minging compared to the girlfriend, but you can't beat a bit of strange, can you?'*

strange Rover *n.* Favoured by the middle classes, one of them new types of dog that are hybrids of various, mismatched breeds, *eg.* A "St Bernork-shireterrier" or similar.

stranger, the *n.* Sitting on one's hand until it falls asleep before a bout of *self help,* giving the impression that one is getting a – presumably clumsy – *hand job* from someone else.

strangle Kojak *v.* To *make the bald man cry,* peel the carrot.

stranks *n.* The delightful "fridge magnet bunch of grapes"-style *shit* clusters one finds plastered to the porcelain in public convenience *chod bins.*

strapadictomy *n.* Routine operation to affix a *strap-on.*

strawberry Sunday *n.* The point when a man is so desperate for a *scuttle* that he no longer cares that *rag week* is not yet over.

straw pole/poll *1. n.* Something carried out for *Newsnight* when there isn't any proper news. *2. n.* A masculine *membrum virile* which, while of adequate length, is of such thin and reedy girth that it flops about and could be easily bent, snapped or tied in a reef knot.

stray spray *n.* Wayward urination caused by cheese-based occlusion of the *snake's eye. Twin jets.*

stray steaks *n.* Outsized flappage. *Beef curtains* of Brobdingnagian proportions.

streaker *1. n.* One who removes their clothes and runs about at sporting events while the BBC pretend they are not there, *eg.* That witless *twat* from Liverpool or Erica Roe with her big *tits.* *2. n.* A *Richard the Third,* slightly smaller than a *U-blocker* and with a slightly pasty consistency, which leaves behind a brown streak as it scuds around the *pan* while being flushed away. A *brown arrow.*

stream of unconsciousness *n.* Mystical body of fluid in which one's lower torso is dipped while asleep following a surfeit of *happy juice.* See *on golden pond, golden slumbers.*

street food *1. n.* Vibrant *al fresco* cuisine. *2. n.* A takeaway comestible that is eaten regardless of the fact that it has been dropped on the pavement.

street food *n.* Appetising Sunday morning gallimaufry prepared on the pavement specially for hungry pigeons by the previous evening's revellers.

streetmate *1. n.* Lighthearted TV dating show presented by that Scarlett Moffatt. Not been on for years. *2. n.* An act of wobbly legged *coitus* performed in an alley up against a wheelie bin. A *fork lift truck, the chinook position, a flying buttress.*

Stretch Armstrong *n.* One gifted with the ability to eat *gorilla salad* while simultaneously *finding Radio Luxembourg.* Also *Superman.*

stretched quimosine *1. n.* An extremely elongated *James Hunt* that has taken plenty of people for a ride. *2. n.* One of those ridiculously overlong deathtrap American cars, well stocked with wine, breezers, nibbles and plenty of *gash,* that are typically seen failing to negotiate corners in

British town centres on Friday nights.

strides *n.* Trousers. *'You ought to get yourself some longer strides, Rishi.'*

strike a burnt match *v.* To fruitlessly attempt to re-ignite one's *wood* immediately after *blowing one's load*. *'Sorry love, you'll have to give me another twenty minutes. It's like striking a burnt match at the moment.'*

strike a damp match *1. v.* To stimulate oneself illegally against an unwitting stranger in a crowd, *eg.* On a tube train, in a queue to see the Pope lying in state. To *frotter. 2. v.* To attempt to have a *wank* with a *soft on.*

strike gold *v.* While *pan-handling* up another's muddy *creek*, to get a lucky nugget of sweetcorn lodged in the *hog's eye*. To have a *kernel blink.*

strike oil *v.* When doing a *duty* on the lavatory, to eject a *feeshus* with such force that its impact causes a vertical spout of water which hits one squarely in the *jotter.*

strike up the colliery band *euph.* To produce a protracted *brass fanfare* from your *coal hole.*

strike while the iron's hot *v.* To have an opportunistic *Barclays* as a result of spotting something completely *wankworthy* when out and about, *eg.* In the bus station toilets after spotting a *cracker* on the number 38, or in a department store toilet after encountering a really sexy mannequin in the lingerie department.

striking north *n.* Light-hearted violation of Section 74 of the Sexual Offences Act 2003. Missing the target and taking the missus unawares, thus initiating an inadvertent game of *Bronco.*

string *n. Wood*, tumescence. *'Quick, everybody, Gunther's got string. Fluffer off set, please and roll camera.'*

stringback *1. adj.* Of a pair of gloves, suitable for use while driving a Sunbeam Alpine. *2. n.* while *talking to God on the great white telephone*, a thick strand of viscid saliva/vomit that makes contact with the contents of the bowl, thus allowing the *spew* germs to travel back to their progenitor.

stringbean *n.* A long, thin, probably green, penis that gets left at the side of your plate.

string of pearls *n.* A series of tiny *botty burps* released in quick succession while walking. *Air croutons.*

stringvestite *n.* Word coined in an episode of *Are You Being Served?*, describing a fellow that *electric-lawnmower-owning* menswear salesman Mr Humphries has met over the weekend at a party in Newcastle upon Tyne.

strip advisor *n.* Name given to the urbane chap in the pub who knows the locations of every lap-dancing bar and *knocking shop* in the local area.

stripper's clit, face like a *adj.* Of a woman, having a *charming personality.*

stripy laugh *n.* A *parked tiger*, a *Welsh monologue.*

stroke mag *n.* An item of top shelf literature, *art pamphlet, gentleman's interest magazine, noddy book.*

stroke of midnight *n.* A gratis *one off the wrist*, courtesy of the Adult Channel ten-minute freeview. A *discount wank.*

stroker *1. n.* A *wanker, ie.* One who masturbates, *eg.* Jonathan Ross. *2. n.* A *wanker, ie.* One who is a *twat, eg.* Jim Davidson.

stroker's cough *n.* The retching gag reflex of a lucky lady who has bitten off more than she can chew.

strokes of genius *n.* The deft hand movements of a seasoned masseuse. *'That will be ten pounds for the strokes of genius please, Lord Archer.'*

stroke the dog through the letterbox *euph.* To slide one's hand down the front of a lady's knickers.

Stromboweli *n.* Somewhat contrived alternative to *Vesuviarse*, describing a fumerole that ejects bursts of hot gas and high velocity debris on a regular basis.

strong and vigorous brushstrokes *1. euph.* A phrase used by Labour leader Kier Starmer to describe the life of the Duke of Edinburgh. *2. phr.* A particularly frenzied and enthusiatic bout of *self-pollution.*

strong favourite *n.* A *fart* that can be forced out as hard as you want with no risk of *following through*, because you have just been and went for a huge *shit*. A *banker.*

strop *1. n.* A sort of leather thing that old fashioned barbers use to sharpen their razors. *2. n.* A lady's, usually *tomato festival*-propelled temper tantrum. A *wobbly*, a *wendy. 3. n.* That which a bachelor has in order to *relax* while reading a *newsletter* or watching a *masturmentary.*

stroppy jam *euph. rhet.* Cause of a *period drama. 'My missus broke all the plates last night. She isn't Greek, so I think she must have opened a jar of stroppy jam.'*

strop sign *n.* A sometimes subtle indication that one's female partner *has the painters in*. If missed, a *strop sign* can lead to painful repercussions. *'Did you get any last night?' 'Nah. When I got back from the pub I went straight through a strop sign and had to sleep in the spare room with a bag of frozen peas on my bollocks.'*

struggle nugget *n.* A troublesome *duty* that only comes out after putting up a fight.

struggling with the overtime *euph.* Of a fellow

who's attempting in vain to continue *banging* his *bag for life* after having already prematurely *shot his bolt*.

strum *v.* A relaxed *tug* on the *one-string banjo*.

strumboli *n.* Any fast-fingered solo building to a crescendo that involves a dramatic eruption.

strum half *n.* A session of *polishing the coal scuttle* that is frustratingly interrupted at a crucial mid-way point.

strumming your plum *phr.* Usually said to a female who is dragging her heels, for instance the pay lady at work. *'For fuck's sake, love, stop strumming your plum and get the wages done. Don't you know it's Friday and the beers are calling?'*

strumpet *n.* *arch.* Olde Worlde *brass*. Also *strombone*.

strumping *n.* Predatory behaviour by a *bird of prey*, the female equivalent of *sharking*.

strum the hairy harp *v.* Of a disgustingly coarse lady, to essay a few arpeggios on her *upside down piano*. To *shuffle the Kit-Kat, gusset type, dial Australia, flap dabble*.

Stuart Hall's front lawn *n.* An unkempt, overgrown *ladygarden. Terry Waite's allotment, Rolf's window box, Max Clifford's shrubbery*.

stuba *n.* Like a *strumpet*, but much bigger.

stubbly gums *n.* A recently shaved *quimpiece*.

stuck in fist gear *n.* To spend all day slouched on the couch in crusty underwear, *relaxing* with the curtains drawn. Being overcome with lethargy and *ennui* in the style of Byron or someone like that.

student garden *n.* An uncared-for *fritter*. A scrubby area of *cunt turf*. With a fridge and an old sofa in it.

student knob *n. medic.* A *hampton* that has been *wanked* black and blue.

student's elbow *n. medic.* Undergraduate-specific repetitive strain injury resulting from a combination of excessive masturbation and attempting to knock out a 10,000 word dissertation in three hours using a biro nicked from Argos.

stuffing a marshmallow in a piggy bank *v.* Of those unfortunate situations involving *brewer's droop*, to attempt to force one's *loose sausage meat* into the *slot*.

stumbleweed *n.* Herbal infusion that can lead to a certain amount of unsteadiness on the old pins.

stumper *n.* A *coyote*.

stump grinder *1. n.* Lumberjacks' mechanical tool for removing the remains of felled trees and excess fingers. *2. n.* A gent who prefers to *relax* by gripping the base of his *timber column* rather than the *herman gelmet* end.

stump nest *n.* Another name for a fellow's pubulent

outcroppings. The *stump bed*.

stumpy tower *1. n.* The former gaol in the town of Girvan, Scotland. See also *hairy tree*. *2. n. 'Fancy a wee climb up the stumpy tower, love? Thought not.'*

stun grenades *n.* A pair of *flesh bombs* so impressive they make a man lose control of his senses. *Air bags*.

stunt cock *n.* In a *bongo vid*, when the leading thespian is unable to sustain *wood* or provide a *money shot*; cue the *stunt cock*, a fat ugly cameraman with a *concrete donkey* on a *hair trigger*.

stuntman's knee, face like a *sim.* A light-hearted, affectionate putdown for a lady with a *lovely personality*.

stuntman's tyre *sim.* Descriptive of the state of your *council gritter* after spicy food, *ie.* Like a tyre that has been doused in petrol and set on fire ready for a daredevil to jump through after jumping off the bonnet of a brush-painted Talbot Solara..

stupendulous *adj.* Superlative used to describe an impressive endowment in either the *shirt potato* or *trouser plum* department.

stupor glue *n.* Powerful adhesive which keeps a student stuck to his mattress until the morning's lectures have finished. *Booze, degreevostik, bed glue*.

stuporman *n.* One who is so inebriated that he believes himself in possession of superpowers. Also *ciderman, acrotwat*.

stupormarionation *n.* Stage of inebriation at which the person behaves as if he were under the control of a malicious *Thunderbirds* puppeteer, complete with involuntary lurching, confused expression and rubber legs.

stupor noodles *n.* Clod of cold, congealed starch found welded to a bowl next to the kettle the morning after a heavily *refreshing* night.

sty at night, the *n.* The last pickings of *salad dodging swamp hogs* hanging round the *swill* van outside a nightclub after the *two am bin rake*.

style conscious *adj.* A euphemistic term describing a fellow who is *good with colours*. Stylish. *'Has your youngest lad married yet, Maureen? He was very style conscious, as I recall.' 'No he hasn't. Well, he's not really found the right girl yet, you see. And he's very busy, too, of course, with his shop selling poppers, gimp masks and butt plugs.'*

subarus *n.* A pair of ladies' *undercrackers*. So named as you are quite likely to find a small, hairless *cunt* sat inside.

submarine *n.* A lady whose available holes are all being simultaneously bunged up by a variety of gentleman callers, resulting in her being, a-hem, "air tight and full of semen".

submarine after curry night, stinks worse than a *sim.* Descriptive of a particularly pungent miasma that *smells worse than a zookeeper's boots.* *'What's that scent you're wearing, my dear? It stinks worse than a submarine after curry night.' 'Oh this? It's Vindaloo Nights by Ricky Tomlinson.'*

sub-prime wine *n.* Late vintage alcoholic refreshment for the more economically challenged, *eg.* White Lightning, *spesh,* Wilko window polish. Also *credit crunch punch, prol-seco.*

subsidise the arts *v.* To pay a professional dancer to take her clothes off; to visit the *cock buskers.* *'Oi, what have you done with the children's lunch money, you dirty bastard?' 'Sorry love, I've been subsiding the arts with it.'*

subtitles *1. euph.* A triumvirate of *big-boned* ladies walking in a line abreast. From the Teletext page familiar to those who are hard of hearing, *viz.* 888. *2. n.* When engaged in conversation with a comely foreign *piece,* something to hold a non-polyglot gent's attentioneven though he can't really understand the words being spoken.

subtle Vader *n.* In a quiet situation when someone is unknowingly breathing like the Imperial tyrant from *Star Wars, eg.* Former Home Secretary Charles Clarke wheezing away sinisterly like he was in an iron lung while being asked a question on the *Today* programme.

subtract tare from gross *v.* To weigh oneself just prior to, and just after, performing the morning's alimentary ablutions, in order to ascertain the weight of the fruits of one's *arse labour.* A technique that eliminates the need for manual extraction and subsequent kitchen scale befoulment.

subway *1. n.* A fast food chain sandwich which harbours pretensions towards healthiness, with all sauce dripping out of it. *2. n.* A fellow in possession a *foot-long,* possibly with all sauce dripping out of it, *eg.* John Holmes, Ron Jeremy, Nicholas Parsons, Stephen Pound MP. *3. n.* A freshly prepared *footlong* in the toilet. *'I've just had a subway and now my ring hurts.'*

succubus *n.* A phantom night-time *cocksucker* once thought to be responsible for *nocturnal emissions.*

suckers *n. Shag tags.*

suck face *v. US.* To kiss.

suck her shit through a tramp's sock, I'd *exclam.* A romantic declaration of undying love. *'Then plainly know my heart's dear love is set / On the fair daughter of rich Capulet. Though lovers ever run before the clock / I'd suck Juliet's shit through a tramp's sock.'* (from *Romeo and Juliet* by William

Shakespeare, Act 2 scene iii).

suckhole *n.* In radio studios or on American late night chat shows, one who is employed to scream with laughter at everything the presenter says. A *brown noser, toady, arselick, sycophant, fart catcher.*

suckhole's dilemma *n.* Of a *shirt fly,* to be in a situation where they don't know whose *arse* to lick first, *eg.* A salesman in a room full of purchasing managers.

sucking a tramp's cock, like *sim.* The consumption of something which is unpleasant, or which leaves a foul taste in the mouth. *'How was your Pig Cheek and Aubergine with a Truffle jus, sir?' 'Like sucking a tramp's cock, thanks. Could we see the dessert menu, please, Heston?'*

sucking on a piss-flavoured gobstopper, face like she's *sim.* Descriptive of a particularly sour-looking, hatchet-faced harridan who can make milk sour from a mile away, *eg.* Pantomime trout and Brexit Party politician Ann Wid(the rest of this name has been obscured on legal advice)decombe MEP.

suck my Northern *exclam. rhym. slang.* A dismissive announcement. From Northern Rock, the now defunct bank. Unless they're still going.

suck off *v.* To relieve an attack of pancreatitis.

suck the chrome off a tow bar, she could *phr.* A somewhat hyperbolic review of a woman's ability to *perform a sex act.*

suck the poison out *v.* To conduct an altruistic act of *horatio* on a man who is suffering from a life-threatening erection. *'She clasped his neck, and for the first time Bertram learnt what an impassioned woman's kisses were like upon the lips of one whom she loved with all her heart and soul, as Tess loved him. 'There – now are you convinced of my true feelings?" she asked, flushed, and wiping her eyes. "I'm still not sure, love,' he replied, undoing his zip and withdrawing eight quivering inches of pink steel. "But I might believe you if you suck the poison out of this bastard."'* (from *Tess of the d'Urbervilles* by Thomas Hardon).

suddenly the door creaked open... *exclam.* Witty narration that is equally effective uttered before or after a particularly lengthy, creaky *trouser cough.*

sudoku wank *n.* Something that takes about ten minutes to finish, gives you a brief feeling of mild satisfaction when you complete it, but leaves you wondering why you bothered.

suds' law *n.* The immutable scientific principle whereby a quick pint after work inevitably descends into an all night session.

suetcide *n.* Self-inflicted death by cake.

Suez blocker *1. n.* A large steamer capable of

stopping all traffic between the Red Sea and the Mediterranean. *2. n.* A large *steamer* cabable of stopping all traffic between the U-bend and the local sewage works or area of oustanding natural beauty.

suffrajet *n.* A budget airline aircraft, packed with disenfranchised, badly-treated passengers who appear to have no rights.

sugar doughnut, the *n.* A lady's *ringpiece*, lightly dusted with talcum powder, which thusly delights her swain when she *drops a gut*. A romatic scene that must have been cut from the original cinema release of *Love Story*.

sugared almond *n.* The *clematis*. Also *peanut in a kebab*.

sugar-free spongle *n.* The ejaculate of a male who has had a *walnut whip*. *Australian gravy*.

sugar puff *n.* A diabetic.

sugarpuffs, mouth full of *euph.* A description of dentition that leaves something to be desired, cosmetically speaking. *Queen mum's teeth, English teeth, pan of burnt chips.*

sugars *n.* The *clockweights*. A reference to UK-based entrepreneur and *Apprentice* host Lord Sir Alan of Amstrad, whose gnarled, wrinkled face covered in wiry whiskers looks not unlike half a scrotum.

sugar walls *n.* Sheena Easton's *slice* sides.

suicycle *n.* Any massively overpowered sports motorbike purchased by a balding, paunchy middle-aged bloke in order to bring his mid-life crisis to a swift conclusion. See also *midlife cricycle*.

suitable advice *euph.* In police terminology, a *fucking* good kicking. *'Constable Penrose, the gentleman in cell three has been banging on the door all night. Go down and give him some suitable advice, will you?'*

suitcase handle, gusset like a *sim.* Descriptive of the petrified state of a dirty *bird*'s crusty 3-week-old *scuns.*

SUITED/suited *acronym.* Straight Up Into ThE Day. An even less rigorous personal hygiene regimen than a *Glasgow shower.*

summer assessments *n.* The first day in the year when ladies deem it opportune to leave their jumpers at home and venture forth wearing tight tops and loose blouses, so that men can review their *qualifications. 'Take the table outside the pub, lads, and don your examiners' sunglasses for the summer assessments.'*

Summer break in Southend-on-Sea *euph.* Taking a *shit* in the sea. The result of the beaches of the Essex resort currently being open whilst all the biscuit wrappers are closed.

summer poppy *n.* A young man whose intentions are obvious, *ie.* One who is "heavy with seed".

summoning Parcelforce *n.* The act of going for a *gypsy's kiss, Tom tit* or a *Sherman tank*, or indeed any other activity that leaves you incapable of getting to your front door in the three nanoseconds it takes for a Royal Mail Delivery operative to tickle your door with a hummingbird feather and ram a card through the letterbox saying "Sorry we missed you".

sump *n. medic.* The part between the *front* and *back bottoms* on a lady. The *manifold, rocker box, fire break, kerb, tinter* or *carse.*

sunblest loaf *n.* A festivalgoer's *shite* deposited in a bread bag, thus avoiding the long walk to the toilets.

sunburnt ginger, arse like a *sim.* Descriptive of one's *ringpiece* following a particularly piquant Indian repast. The reddest possible thing in the world.

sundance *n.* The fairer, *lipsticker* member of a *lesbidaceous* couple, *ie.* "The one who isn't Butch". A *mug runcher*.

Sunday joint without the string on *euph.* A *clunge* which has far too much flabby gristle, collapsed crackling and stubbly skin going on.

Sunday leaguer *n.* A toilet *pan* that looks like someone has cleaned their football boots in it after a match on Hackney Marshes.

Sunday night cyanide *n.* A heavy drinking session intended to combat the end-of-the-weekend blues, which leaves the celebrant feeling like death warmed up come Monday morning.

Sunday stopper *n.* A *mystery meat* kebab purchased and consumed on your way home from the pub on a Saturday night that effectively ruins all your plans for the Sabbath by keeping you ensconced on the *crapper* till well after *Antiques Roadshow* has finished.

Sunderland easter egg hunt *n.* A family event, where youngsters equipped with buckets and spades excitedly seek out and collect *dog eggs* which have been secreted around the garden over the past fortnight.

Sunderland hotdog *n.* A popular pastime in the north eastern holiday resort; a refined *Barclays* performed with the *giggling pin* wrapped in raw bacon. A *pig in a blanket, pork scratching.*

Sunderland's trophy cabinet, a fanny like *sim.* A large, empty void, based on the fact that the eponymous, notoriously unsuccessful football team owns a large, empty trophy cabinet shaped like a *vagina*. A simile which can be varied, depending on one's footballing allegiances and/or geographical prejudices.

sundowner *n.* A *dump* so large that you know you will not require a visit to the *crapper* for at least another twenty-four hours, perhaps even a week.

sung-through *1. n.* Theatrical terminology for a musical that is all songs and no breaks for talking, *eg. Les Mis, Hamilton, Cats,* and thus *2. n.* A wordless test of endurance in the *smallest room.*

Sun Hill ink pad, fingered more times than the *sim.* Said of a *lady of easy affections* who has had *more cocks in her than a pair of Moss Bros hire trousers.* From the fictional location of long-running former police drama *The Bill.*

sunnies *n. Aus.* Tits, baps.

sunnyside up *adj.* Of *top eggs* spotted while on *beach patrol,* frying gently in the sunshine.

sunscreem *n.* A *perfect motion, viz.* A *sit down toilet adventure* with no stresses, strains or even *foulage* on the paper after wiping. Named after the eponymous Essex techno house combo's best known track which reached number 18 in 1992. No, us neither.

suns of anarchy *n.* Lawless blasts of diarrhoea that sound like a Harley Davidson motorbike and fill the room with the smell of burning rubber.

superbeero *n.* The *alter ego* of an otherwise mild-mannered chap, revealed in all its glory after fifteen pints of *dizzyade.* Powers include *shitting* himself, dashing into a phonebox to *piss* all over the floor, being sick down his shirt and the ability to fall off scaffolding in a single bound.

super furry animal *n.* A *hairy axewound, biffer, sweep's brush, captain caveman, Judith* or *full Belgian.*

superfuzz bigmuff: deluxe edition *1. n.* 1992 re-issue of the classic album by Seattle grunge combo Mudhoney. *2. n.* A dead hairy *biffer, Judith. 'That's a superfuzz bigmuff: deluxe edition you've got there, your worship, look you. Isn't it.'*

super gran *n.* An older female adult film star (38 and above) who falls into the *GILF* category. From the theme song of the eponymous 1980s TV show, specifically the line "She does things that you'll never see your granny do".

Super League, last as long as a *v.* To *spill the Brasso* somewhat prematurely, and therefore conclude proceedings earlier than planned. *'Ah, sorry about that, love. I lasted as long as a Super League. Still, you take your time. Finish yourself off and then you can get me a cup of tea.'*

Superman *n.* Name given to the occasional consequences of a chap *tipping his filthy concrete* onto the bedsheet so that it adheres to his partner's back when she gets up in the morning to go for a *shit* and make his breakfast, thus mimicking the style of the erstwhile comic book superhero's cape.

supermarket bag *n.* A particularly secure pair of crinkly *cat flaps* that, in order to be opened, must first be blown on and/or rubbed together using a licked finger and thumb.

supermarket checkout *n.* A delusory game played by men while trundling round the local supermarket with a trolley full of cheap lager, white bread, sausages and pile ointment.

supermarket smack *n.* Special brew, *pagga starter, falling down juice.*

supermarket sweep *1. n.* A colonic irrigation that includes a whole fortnight's worth of *shopping. 2. n.* The inevitable, furtive look-around undertaken by a chap upon entering a large store in order to see if there's any quality *tussage* on view to enliven an otherwise mundane grocery shopping experience.

supermarket swipe *n.* Game played by local *scrotes* competing against security guards to secure *five finger discounts* on easily resaleable items such as steak, multiblade razors and spirits.

super spreader *1. n.* In the context of a human-borne illness, an individual who is more likely to infect others, compared with a typical infected person. *2. n.* A woman who *goes a bit. 3. n.* Someone who leaves the toilet bowl in a state of utter disarray.

super trouper *n.* A person who desperately needs to urinate, yet overcomes the urge by means of superior mental strength. From the lyric of the eponymous Abba song, *viz.* "Smiling, having fun / Feeling like a number one".

supperman *n.* A bloke who acts like a superhero but who carries rather too much weight to get airborne.

supreme champion *1. n.* That pedigree dog which has been raised on a diet of fillet steak and patty de fwar grar that gets paid thousands of pounds to sit by a big silver cup and advertise tinned kangaroo bollocks for a couple of weeks after it wins Cruft's. *2. n.* Offensive, sexist terminology describing the *best in show* out of a group of *hounds.*

surbrowned sound *n.* A burst of casement-rattling noise from one's *sub-woofer.*

surf and turd *euph.* Shitty *bog* water splashback.

surfboard *1. n.* A flat-chested female, *Miss Lincolnshire. 2. n. Aus.* A piece of equipment used by women to *catch the waves* when the *red flag is flying.* A *fanny nanny* for a heavy *aunt Flo.*

surfing the crimson wave *n. Riding the menstrual cycle.*

surf 'n' turf *1. n.* The act of orally probing a lady's *rusty sheriff's badge* during an act of *cumulonimbus*. 2. *n.* An 1980s-style meal served at a Berni Inn, consisting of a fish and steak combo that tasted, one might imagine, not unlike orally probing a lady's *rusty sheriff's badge* during an act of *cumulonimbus*.

surgeon's sink plug *n.* A used *clot mop*. Also *Dracula's tea bag, dangermouse, blood muppet*.

surprised frog *n.* A woman's discollimated *nips* when her *knockers* are released from her *tit pants*. Marty Feldmans.

surprise Jasmin *n.* When you have hurriedly closed down your online filth browser windows only to find a semi-clad *totty* from Live Jasmin still disinterestedly pleasuring herself on your monitor. *'Roger that, flight TZ5674. I think you're clear for landing on Runway 4. I can't actually see because I've got a surprise Jasmin blocking the screen.'*

surprise, sur-fucking-prise! *exclam.* Remark made at a depressingly predictable event, *eg.* England (the men's team anyway) losing on penalties.

Surtsey *n.* When you do a *poo* so big that it sits comfortably on the bottom of the *pan* whilst simultaneously breaching the water's surface. Named in honour of the small Icelandic volcanic atoll in the Vestmannaeyjar archipelago that broke the water's surface in 1963.

survivor *n.* A buoyant *stool* which resists all attempts to *send it to the beach*.

Susie Dent *n. prop. rhym. slang. Colwyn Bay.* From Susie Dent = Stoke on Trent.

suspect remains at large, the *exclam.* Euphemistic police speak for a post-coital *lob-on*. *'I took down her particulars and banged her in the back of the black maria, sarge, but the suspect remains at large.'*

suspicion *n. coll.* Collective noun for a group of television and radio stars from the 1970s.

Suthen 1. *n. prop.* An eleventh century Queen of Scotland who, according to Shakespeare, was "oftener on her knees than on her feet" and hence 2. *n.* Any lady who frequently provides *oral pleasure*. Don't say we never learn you any fucking culture.

Suzie Fletcher's fingers, seen more pricks than *exclam.* Said of a *bird* who's had more jabs than the digits of the resident leather restorer from BBC teatime show *The Repair Shop*.

Swaffham *v.* Of a lady, to practise the gentle art of cramming both a chap's *clockweights* in her mouth at the same time. Named after the town in Norfolk, where all the womenfolk, without exception, are experts in this procedure.

swaffling *n.* The act of a chap putting his flaccid member against a famous building, *eg.* The Berlin Wall, Buckingham Palace, the Taj Mahal *etc.,* taking a photo of it and displaying said snap on the internet. A popular pastime in the Netherlands, apparently, where they still have to make their own entertainment.

swagman's hat *n. medic.* Condition of the *anus* when infested with numerous *tagnuts*. *'Holmes surveyed the water closet cubicle before announcing, "The game is afoot, Watson, and our quarry has a bandy-legged gait." "How the devil do you know that, man?" I exclaimed. "Elementary," vouchsafed the esteemed detective. "The Izal toilet paper by the crapper means the miscreant will almost certainly have a ringpiece like a swagman's hat."'* (from *The Red-Ringed League* by Sir Arthur Conan-Doyle).

SWAG/swag 1. *n.* What is written on the sack in which a traditional, stripy-jerseyed burglar places candelabras and silver trays. 2. *acronym.* A *well-manicured* chap who always seems to have a female hanger-on, but who never seems to have a girlfriend. One who, it might be suspected, *bakes a light cake*. Secret Will And Grace.

swallow *v.* What proper women do.

swallows his toothpaste *euph.* Said of somebody who is *tighter than a penguin's ballbag*.

swallow the bear *v.* To perform *cumulonimbus* on a lady with a right old *biffer* on her. *Don the beard, impersonate Stalin.*

swallow the oysters *exclam.* A phrase of friendly encouragement to a *nosher* who is being a little too fussy about eating all her *porridge* up.

swallow your pride *euph.* Following oral sex, having your own *spinkle* passed back to you *via* a kiss, in the mistaken belief you might somehow find this erotic.

swamp *v. milit.* To *piss*, urinate, *esp.* the bed.

swamp donkey *n.* Female who is not overly endowed with physical beauty. A *tug boat, boiler, sea monster, steg.*

swan 1. *n.* Big posh duck that can break a man's arm with one flap of its wing. 2. *n.* The wife of a *pavilion end bowler,* whom he marries in order to mask his true sexual orientation. So-called because she's a "queen's bird". The *beard* in a *lavender marriage.* 3. *n.* Style of *wanking* that can break a chap's arm.

swank 1. *v.* To walk into a room like one is walking onto a yacht, *viz.* With your hat all cock-eyed and a pink scarf on. 2. *n.* A secretive *five knuckle shuffle* utilizing minimal wrist action, enjoyed while lying next to one's sleeping partner. Normally practised spitefully following the rejection of drunken sexual advances. Also *American beauty, outrigger.*

swans' feet *n.* Large, leathery flaps found tucked

away amongst the nether-plumage of a generously-proportioned *bird*, occasionally covered in algae.

swan shag *1. n.* The presumably treasonable practice of copulating with one of his majesty's favourite teatime waterfowl. *2. n.* The last, dying sexual act of a doomed relationship. *3. n.* A romantic dalliance with a *flapper* so beefy it could result in a fractured humerus.

swan strangler *n.* Stretchy piece of plastic which throttles large waterbirds. Can also be used to secure several cans of *wifebeater* together at once. A term coined on Armando Iannucci's *Charm Offensive* programme on the Home Service.

swap spit *v.* To *suck face.*

sward swallower *n.* The *bog, blatter closet, coil well, crap chute, rust rooms* or *slimmers. 'Where's your dad?' 'He's went to the sward swallowers.'*

sweater girl *n.* From Hollywood's golden era, a starlet with spectacular *twin peaks.*

sweatermeat *n.* Phrase used to alert friends to the presence of a nice pair of *tits.* Usually accompanied by clockface directional information. *'Sweatermeat at 3 o'clock.'*

sweater puppets *n. Fondleberries.* Particularly animated *howdy doodies* that keep a fellow entertained. *Milky swingers, puppies.*

sweats *n. rhym. slang.* An affectionate term for people of Caledonian extraction. From sweaty socks = jocks.

sweaty bullets *n.* Low calibre *slugs* that appear in the *grundies* while undertaking strenuous physical exercise, such as moving a filing cabinet up a fire escape or throwing twenty car batteries into a high skip while wearing a duffle coat during a heatwave.

sweaty Morph *n.* A *mudchild*, a *turd.*

swedge *n.* That piece of folded bogroll which a sweating *pie shifter* wedges in his *potty slot* in order to stop his *farting clappers* rubbing together. A *manpon, botcap, toffee rizla. 'Substantial Andrex swedge worn by Bad Manners frontman Buster Bloodvessel (Douglas Trendle) while performing Just a Feeling in a deep-sea diver's suit on Top of the Pops c. May 1981. Complete with certificate of authenticity. Estimate £3000 – £4000.'* (extract from Christie's Rock Memorabilia Auction Catalogue, August 2004).

Swedish *n. Greek.*

Swedish bake *1. n.* A multilayered pasty popular in Scandinavia, consisting of yellow onions, red cabbage and minced beef inside a sort of a tart. You can probably get them in that half-arsed food shop near the tills in Ikea, along with "Daim" bars, "Lingonberry" sauce and that odd gravy. *2. n.* The yellow, red and brown ingredients in a slovenly lady's *applecatchers.* Also *Neapolitan knickers.*

Swedish roulette *n.* An act of onanistic gambling in which the *wanksmith* plies his ancient and noble trade while watching an Abba video, hoping that – at the moment of truth – the screen will be displaying the blonde one, or maybe one of the girls.

Sweeney! *exclam.* A humorous utterance shouted out in the style of Flying Squad DI Jack Regan by a man who is *kicking a lady's back doors in.*

sweep's brush *n.* A *Judith. 'That's a proper sweep's brush you've got there, Germaine. It looks like you've been hit between the legs with a bag of soot.'*

sweep the chimney *v.* To inadvertently push toilet paper up the *flue* while overzealously wiping one's *bum.* See *fall of soot.*

sweep the special chimney *v.* To *have it off*; a phrase coined by Carol Midgley in *The Times*, which used to be known as the Paper of Record.

sweep the yard *v.* To loudly scratch your pubic area, making a sound like brushing paving slabs with a hard-bristled broom.

sweetbreads *n.* The testicular component of the *family jewels.* The *clockweights* or *knackers.* The *plums* in the *fruitbowl.*

sweetcorn bukkake *n.* When eating a corn on the cob, a jet of juice that shoots out and into the eye of the person sitting opposite.

sweetcorn itch *n.* A scratchy *ringpiece* caused by insufficient wiping. *IRS.*

sweet FA *acronym.* Sweet Fanny Adams, *fuck all*, absolutely nothing. Nowt. *Jack shit.*

sweetmeat *n.* A *gigglestick* dipped in honey or something similar to make it more palatable to a picky *fellatrix.*

sweet tits *n.* Affectionate male term of endearment for females. *'Goodnight, goodnight! Parting is such sweet sorrow / That I shall say goodnight until it be morrow, sweet tits.'* (from *Romeo and Juliet* by William Shakespeare).

sweet wrapper *n. rhym. slang.* The lavatory bowl or, indeed, the cubicle wherein it is typically situate.

swellington boots *n.* Footwear for those blessed with the bigger-boned *cankle.*

swervature of the earth *euph.* The naturally-occurring gravitational effect of the roundness of the spinning planet on *shit-faced* people *pinballing* home following a swift half at their local. The powerful pull of the planet's *swervature* often drags its helpless victims into privet hedges or leaves them slumped against the doorways of long-closed shops for up to four or five hours.

swift *n.* A bit like a *swallow,* only faster. So fast, in fact, that there isn't the option to spit.

swill out the trough *v.* Female equivalent of *cleaning inside the farmer's hat.*

Swilly salad *n.* A pasty and a blob of tomato sauce, as enjoyed by the health-conscious residents of Plymouth's swish North Prospect estate.

swim against the tide *v.* To take a *dip* while the *red flag* is flying. *To surf the crimson wave.*

swimming with turtles *1. n.* Cut-price alternative to swimming with dolphins done alongside the aquatic tortoises in Mexico, Barbados, Florida, *etc. 2. n.* Free activity currently available at most UK beaches.

swine flu *n. medic.* Mild nausea and cold sweats experienced upon waking up in bed with a right *pig.*

swing *1. n.* In musical theatre parlance, a performer with the versatility to fill in any number of roles or positions at short notice, or even to watch from the audience and critique subtle errors in the show. *2. n.* An entirely similar figure in the world of *cottaging. 3. n.* Likewise in *dogging.*

swing ball *n.* When a *miniature hero* clings to the *arse cress* for dear life. *A soft conker, crapeze artist.*

swing both ways *v.* To be a *switch hitter, happy shopper, half-rice half-chips.*

swingers *1. n.* Sinister, grim-looking couples who have uninhibited sex in suburban houses with other sinister, grim-looking couples. *Swingers'* homes can be spotted because they have pampas grass growing in the front garden, in amongst all the fat, middle-aged couples *fucking* each other. *2. n. Clockweights, knackers, pods, gourds. 3. n.* Big bangers, esp. milky~.

swinging a bat in the Holland Tunnel, like *sim. US.* Descriptive of performing the act of *concubinage* with a woman who has a *snatch like a builder's rubble tub.* Also *throwing a hot dog down a hallway, waving a stick in a field, waving a sausage in the Albert Hall.*

swinging grimp *n.* A tiny ball of *poo* hanging like grim death onto the tip of an *arse* hair. Named after the Playstation Network game *Pixel Junk Eden,* in which players control a plip-like "grimp", which tarzans on an *arse* hair from flower to flower in a pyschedelic garden.

swirly *n.* Bullies' lavatory game whereby the victim's head is pushed into the *crapper* and the flush pulled. *'I say you chaps, look out! Williamson and Smith are in the bogs and they've just given Hammond a swirly.'*

Swiss *adj.* Completely useless. *'Did you see England playing Germany? They were completely fucking Swiss.'*

Swiss army wife *n.* Rare and amazing lady who can work, bring up the kids, cook, push the hoover round a bit, open beer bottles and polish her husband's *family jewels* all at the same time.

Swiss chocolatier *n.* A cove who leaves his *pan* in a very messy condition.

Swiss finger *n.* An erect *todger* with a pink iced topping upon withdrawal from a lady on the eve of a week's *visit from the painters,* or in the 24 hours following their departure. From the similarity to the doughy confection of the same name to be found in the window of all Ainsley's branches.

Swiss kiss *n.* A *post-horatio spangle*-flavoured snog.

Swiss movement *n.* A *chod* dropped in the *pan* with almost nazi-like precision by a humourless person with disciplined and regular bowel habits.

Swiss roll *1. n.* A type of sponge cake confection filled with whipped cream and jam and that. *2. n.* A rolled-up length of *bog paper,* loaded with *spunk* following a rather vigorous session of *web browsing.*

Swiss seafood *euph.* Something fishy that hasn't been fresh for a while.

Swiss wank account *n.* An optimistic fellow's untraceable email account, created solely for the purpose of registering with *left-handed websites.*

swit *n.* An odious, yet distinctly sickly, sweet-smelling *shit* that one could imagine would be the result of consuming three tubs of salted caramel Haagen Dazs after downing a large can of cream of tomato soup.

switchcraft *n.* The magical ability of a woman to make incredible amounts of cash disappear into thin air while out shopping.

switch from ketchup to HP *1. euph.* Of a full English breakfast connoisseur, to make a gustatory decision. *2.* To *change at Oxford Circus* when the *Fairlop loop* is out of service.

switch from prawn cocktail to beef & onion *euph.* A crisp-based analogy for *changing at Baker Street. A last minute platform alteration, playing the B-side etc.*

switch hitter *n. US.* Person who *bats with both hands*; a bisexual. One who approaches the *oyster* and *snail buffet* with a broad plate.

switching to manual *n.* Solo completion of a bout of sexual activity due to the missus falling asleep before you've finished.

switch island *1. n.* Depressing no man's land on the outskirts of Liverpool. *2. n.* The *taint, gooch, barse, scranus, notcher, tintis, ploughman's, scruttock.*

swive *v. 17thC. Fuck. 'Swiving hell. I've had to take*

six chops at the King's neck and I've still not got his swiving head off.'

swizzjizz *n.* A synthetic, vegetarian alternative to genuine *baby gravy.* A mixture of icing sugar and warm water, *swizzjizz* is most often used as a cinematic aid or enhancement during the dénouement of lower budget *scud vids.* Also *fake man, spray-onnaise, spunk double.*

swoo *n.* The viscid emulsion of perspiration and excrement found in the *arse-crack* of one who has been exercising vigorously, for example an overweight bachelor attempting to manhandle a filing cabinet up a fire escape on a particularly clammy day. From sweat + poo.

swope *n.* The hairstyle affected by balding men whereby the remaining strands of hair on one side of the head are grown long and swept over the dome, giving the impression of a full, healthy head of hair, *eg.* Robert Robinson, Bobby Charlton, Desmond Morris.

sword heavy *adj.* Of a party or other social gathering, suffering from an evident plethora of male attendees, and consequently a marked dearth of *knob fodder. 'I reckon I'm going to stop going to the Masons, Chief Constable. The meetings are a bit too sword heavy.'*

swordsman's shelf *n.* The conveniently placed ledge, normally used for one's washing requisites, located in the corner of a hotel shower and upon which one's ladyfriend can place one foot or, in extreme cases, one knee, thus encouraging unfettered access to her *bodily treasure* during the sort of bouts of sexual intercourse which are normally encountered only when on holiday. *'Thoughtful gestures such as night-time chocolates, fluffy towelling robes and a swordsman's shelf make this hotel a winner with honeymooners.'*

sword swallower *n.* A circus *fellatrix.*

swotty totty *n.* The sort of female television personalities who know history or science and stuff, can do simple mental arithmetic, play a bit of piano or look *shit* up in a dictionary.

Syd 'n' Eddies *euph.* A pair of asymmetrical *knockers,* with one noticeably larger than the other. A frankly unsatisfactory and distinctly unamusing combination.

syllojism *n.* A logical argument about *wanking* that begins with the premise: "All men are human".

symphony *n.* A stirring trip to the *thunderbox* that consists of three separate and distinct movements. Also *symphony number two.*

symphony for the devil *euph.* A Stentorian blast from the *nether throat* that puts one in mind of the first two bars of Beethoven's Fifth.

syncronised swimmers *n.* In a *grumble flick* with a big cast, the queue of actors who are all *treading water* in an orderly line. See also *semi circle.*

synipsis *n.* A brief précis or pithy resumé of one's anal health, issued irrespective of whether anyone wants to hear it. Which they don't.

SYNT/synt *acronym.* Polite and lexicographically accurate pronunciation of "See You Next Tuesday". *'Lovely mass, father. See you next Tuesday, you synt.'*

syrup *n.* Hairpiece. From syrup of fig = Irish jig. *'Q: 'Just look at this, 007.' Bond: 'What is it, Q? Looks like an ordinary syrup to me.' Q: 'Yes, but one tug on the chinstrap and it turns into a miniature helicopter.' Bond: 'Hmm! Hair raising!'* (from *Never Say Never Again,* 1983).

syrup of pigs *n.* The sort of sour *blip* exuded by women of disagreeable countenance.

syruptitious *adj.* Of a balding gentleman, furtively and undetectably be-wigged.

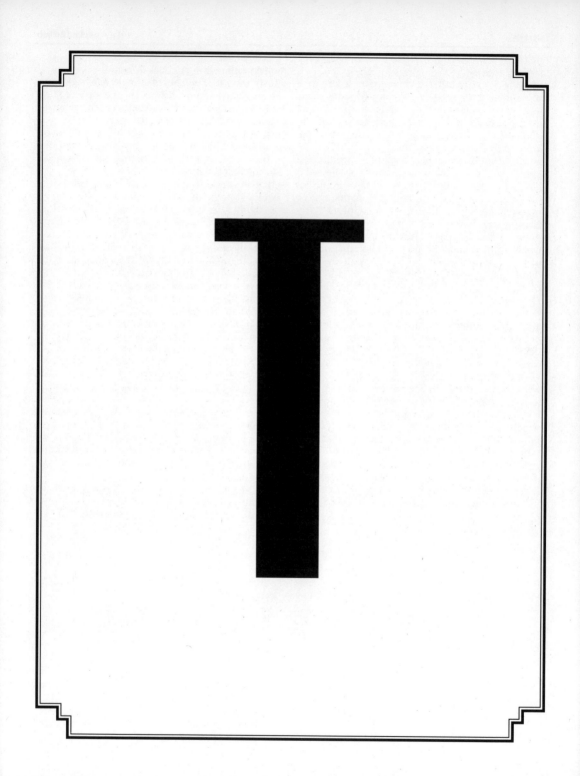

tabby afro *n.* A collection of differently hued *pubes* found blocking the plughole of the bath in a shared flat.

table a motion *1. v.* In the British political system, to begin consideration (or reconsideration) of a political proposal. *2. v.* In employment terms, to *drop a log* on the boss's desk after receiving one's P45. *3. v.* To partake in a saucy practice whereby a member of parliament lies under a glass coffee table whilst an obliging *lady of the night drops a log* onto it for their pleasure.

tablet bender *n.* An internet erotic tableau of such high quality that any attempt to push back the resulting tumescence by applying pressure to the groinal region will result in damage to one's iPad.

table tipping *1. n.* Supernatural furniture knocking and wobbling as seen on TV's *Most Haunted* when ghostly orbs are detected. *2. n.* A *bone on* which taps the underside of one's desk when orbs are detected.

tabs *1. n.* Cigarettes. *Also coffin nails, cancer sticks, oily rags. 2. n.* The external labia. *'Phwooar! I tell you what, I wouldn't mind getting my hands on her tabs. And it's a new Olympic Women's High Jump record! Now back to John Inverdale in the studio.'*

TAB/tab *acronym. milit.* Tactical Advance to Battle. How a squaddie might describe a march towards the enemy. *2. n.* A cigarette, *coffin nail, gasper. 3. acronym.* A mnemonic to remind a person of the minimum areas to be washed before, or possibly after, sexual congress, *viz.* Todger, Arse, Ballbag. Or indeed, Twat, Arse, Barse, in these forward-thinking days of female empowerment for the *splitarses*.

tacho break *n.* A lorry driver's four-and-a-half-hourly respite interval, during which he pulls over and has a hitch-hiker-strangling-fantasy-fuelled *wank* in his cab, before *shedding his load. 'I just come through the centre of Birmingham and after seeing all that blart I had to stop at Keele Services for a tacho break and a KFC.'*

tackle *n.* What you grip and fling around when you go *fly fishing*.

tackle bag *1. n.* Something that rugby players practise pummelling into submission, prior to drinking pints of vomit and lighting rectally inserted toilet paper. *2. n.* The *ball sack* or scrotum. Also *John Wayne's hairy saddlebags*, the *happy sack, raisin bag etc.*

tacklebags *n.* Underpants, *bills, scads, scuns, dunghampers*.

tackleshack *n. Tacklebags.*

taco tickler *n.* A *gusset typist, Kit-Kat shuffler,*

hairy harpist.

tactical chunder *n.* Student *refreshment* technique. A deliberate *technicolour yawn* performed to make a bit of extra beer room in the stomach, or to delay the arrival of a *helicopter attack*.

taddies wear armbands, I bet his *phr.* Said of a feeble or effeminate man; literally that his spermatozoans lack natatory expertise, and may need the assistance of water-wings or, indeed, the lifeguard.

tadger *n.* A thing that tadges. Also *todger,* so it presumably todges as well.

tadpole coulis *n.* The porridgey gloop of which *haroldite* is principally made.

tadpole net *n. Blob, rubber johnny, cheesepipe clingfilm.*

tadpole yoghurt *n. Gentleman's relish, man mayonnaise,* dressing for a *sausage sandwich.*

tagazzle *v.* Of an *asbolescent* youth, to personalize or otherwise decorate their electronic tag.

tagnuts *n. Toffee strings, winnets, clinkers, dangleberries, bead curtains.* Rectal hangers on, *arse cress Tarzans.*

tail *1. n. arch.* That which wags when it sees a pretty lady. The *veiny bang stick. 2. n. Fluff, totty, skirt, talent. 3. n.* Your *bum.*

tail ender *n.* A small dollop of *doings* that one must wait for after the main stool has been expelled, the finial on a *log cabin* roof. *Geetle.*

tail gunner *n.* A *style-conscious* fellow.

tailpipe *1. n.* The exhaust of a motor car. *2. n. US. Corybungo.*

tail sap *n.* Any sticky secretion from a man's *stem.*

tail shot *n.* A *change of heart.*

tail wind *n.* A *southern breeze* tending to push one forward. Unless you're following someone, in which case it will have the opposite effect.

taint *n. Niftkin's bridge.*

taint week *n.* The pointless period that falls between December 25th and January 1st. Because "it taint Christmas, it taint New Year and it taint worth going back to work". See also *the perineum, the festive perineum, merryneum, twixtmas. 'Hello. Is that the police? There's a masked man with an axe trying to smash the front door down.' 'Sorry love. I can't send anybody out till a week Tuesday at the latest, only it's taint week and there's no fucker here.'*

take a knee *v.* To avoid splashing the floor when *seeing a man about a dog* in the middle of the night, by adopting a respectful, genuflecting position in front of the *bum sink.*

take an air dump *v.* To *let rip, blow off.*

take a packed lunch *v.* To take a girlfriend on holiday to avoid all the *fucking about* and loss of drinking time that goes with finding a suitable female at one's destination. *'I went to Ibiza last year and wasted the first day and a half sorting myself out with someone to bang. I'm going to Agya Napa this year, and I'm going to take a packed lunch.'*

take a screenshot *v.* To burp and *fart* simultaneously.

take Captain Picard to warp speed *v.* To *make the bald man cry.* To *strangle Kojak, pull Paul Daniels' head off, cuff the suspect, box the Jesuit.*

take communion *v.* To kneel before the altar and partake of a portion of *haddock pie* during *rag week. Fish on Friday.*

take Herman to the circus *euph.* To engage in an *act of personal delight.*

take matters into your own hands *v.* To *finish yourself off* after your partner fails to successfully bring you to *organism. 'I'm sorry Trudie, but this has gone on long enough. It's reached the stage where I'm going to have to take matters into my own hands. Pass me that copy of Readers' Wives Bums Special. It's on the bedside table under my lute.'*

take me home button *1. n.* Convenient feature of these sat-navs they have nowadays. *2. n.* The *bipper, starter button, magic jelly bean, devil's doorbell, tremble trigger* or *trouser tonsil.*

take one in the company's time *v.* while at work, to hold in a *number two* until one's unpaid break is over, thus ensuring that one gets paid the full hourly rate for having a *shit.*

takeout *n.* A professional escort, whose door-to-door sexual services are ordered from a menu over the phone.

takes his decorations down on Boxing Day *euph.* Said of one who dresses and leaves almost immediately after delivering his presents.

takes his own bags to the supermarket *euph.* Said of a chap with *clean nails* who *bakes a light sponge* and *likes his peas minted. 'He's not fooling me. Fathering a baby's not going to convince me he doesn't take his own bags to the supermarket.'*

takes his time shopping *euph.* Descriptive of a *sentimental* chap who *sews his own buttons* and *likes to send thank-you notes.*

takes his time shopping *euph.* Said of he whom *bakes a light cake.*

take that with you missus *exclam.* What your old man would say after *trumping.* See also *get your dinner out of that; fer-fetch a cloth, Granville; someone let him in; someone's tinkered with Herbie; speak on, sweet lips that never told a lie; I'm ready for the question, Noel* and *mighty fine words, preacher.*

take the A train *1. n.* Title of a jazz classic penned by Duke Ellington and Billy Strayhorn, which was

famously covered by Dave Brubeck. *2. v.* To travel in the missus's *caboose, buffers* permitting.

take the bait *v.* Of one's lavatory U-bend, to successfully swallow a long, weighty *feeshus. 'Thank God for that, the bog took the bait on the eighth flush. I thought I was going to have to call the plumber out to deal with that fucker.'*

take the ball into the corner *v.* To go for a *shit* in the works *bogs* at about half past four on a Friday afternoon in order to kill time and wind down the clock until home time. *'Where's Lord Sugar, Claude?' 'He's taken the ball into the corner, Karren.'*

take the cat to the vet *euph.* To knock off work early. See *let the dog out, fire the one o'clock gun.*

take the crust off *v.* Nautical term describing the precautionary pre-disembarkation *wank* taken by trawlermen before they are reunited with their ladyfriends. See also *take the edge off.* Here it is now, look.

take the edge off *v.* To *relax in a gentleman's way* in order to prolong a putative *scuttle* with one's partner. To *put a wank in the bank. 'Got a big night with the missus planned, so I'd better go and take the edge off first.'*

take the glaze off *v.* To have a long-awaited and particularly powerful *slash.*

take the goalie off the pitch *v.* To withdraw protection in a positive attempt to conceive.

take the hotseat *v.* To be forced, through sheer desperation, to sit on a *crapper* while the seat is still at *bum* temperature from the previous occupant.

take the low offer *1. v.* To lame out on *The Chase,* bringing shame and disgrace upon your family for generations. *2. v.* To make a low denomination withdrawal from the *wankbank.*

take the minus offer *1. phr.* To take the Chaser's least lucrative offer in order to avail oneself of the best opportunity of taking anything home. *2. n.* In pulling, to plump for the least attractive prospect on offer in order to avail oneself of the best opportunity of taking anything home. Also *go ugly early.*

take them off so we can all shit in them *exclam.* Ribald suggestion uttered when someone emits a *trouser cough* amongst friends or colleagues.

take the scenic route *v.* To explore the sometimes forgotten areas of potential interest while *en route* to the main event. *'You can put those back on for the time being, darling. I'll be taking the scenic route tonight.'*

take up the flute *v.* To suddenly develop a taste for *cock,* seemingly overnight. *'She enthusiastically took up the flute after meeting Michael Hutchence.*

take your finger, touch your nose, blink three times and off it goes *exclam.* A Mr Tumble-style incantation, complete with actions, to be performed in the style of the popular CBeebies simpleton prior to the release of a *guff*. See also *listen to this, too good to miss, da-da da-da da; our survey said; please hold for the president; my next guest needs no introduction*.

take yourself to town *v.* To have a *five knuckle shuffle*. On the bus.

taking a shit in a sewer, like *sim.* Descriptive of performing an ultimately futile act. For example, sending a tweet to Southern Rail asking why their service is so terrible, a missive which will get lost in an ocean of identical questions.

taking in washing *euph.* Having the *gorilla's knuckles*. *'I see Kylie's taking in washing in her new video, then.'*

taking the brown bin out *1. n.* Moving your household's dry mixed recycling container onto to pavement, ready for collection the next morning. *'I'm just going to take the brown bin out, luv.' 'Make sure you wash your hands when you're done, dear.'* *2. euph.* Laying a cable, releasing a brown trout. *'I'm just going to take the brown bin out, luv.' 'For God's sake open a window this time. And wash your fucking hands when you're done.'*

taking the steps at Goodge Street *euph.* A lonely, last resort act of *self pollution*, only embarked upon to *get the boys out of the tube* in extreme circumstances. From the lonely, last resort means of exiting the eponymous London Underground station, which entails a life-sapping trudge up 136 steps.

talent *1. n.* What broadcasting companies call the talentless people who appear on screen. *2. n. coll. Crumpet, bush, scrunt.*

talented Mr Gripley, the *n.* Affectionate name for the hand one uses for *self-pleasure*, as its skills are multi-faceted, encompassing not merely *onanism* but also hastily grabbing tissues, turning off Babestation when you hear someone coming down the stairs, placing a pillow over the private parts, and many other, less useful functions.

talent scout *n.* A designated member of a group who looks round the pub door to check whether the *blart* inside is worth pushing your way to the bar for.

talk broken biscuits *v.* To speak in a somewhat unintelligible manner while *heavily refreshed*.

talk German *v.* To *fart, blow off,* puff on an imaginary *bum cigar*.

talk on the great white telephone *v.* To be sick into the lavatory. *Drive the porcelain bus, wear a Twyfords collar, call Huey.*

talk to the boss *exclam.* A married man's response to his wife's request for some of his hard-earned cash to fritter away on luxuries. An suggestion to perform an act of *horatio*. *'It's no good, love. I'm going to have to go shopping. We're right out of baby food and the twins need new shoes.' 'It's not up to me, you'd better talk to the boss.'*

talk to the judge *n.* To *suck a copper's helmet* by way of avoiding a speeding ticket. *'I know I was doing 75 in a 30 zone, officer, but is there any way we can work this out? Perhaps if I spoke to the judge behind that skip?' 'I'm not sure that's going to make any difference, sir.'*

talk turkey, let's *exclam.* A proposal made by a rural swain to his partner, involving some *gobbling*.

tallboy *1. n.* What your nan would have called a big chest of drawers. *2. n.* An 'earthquake' bomb designed by Neville Barnes Wallis, weighing some 12,000 lbs and deployed by the RAF to sink the Tirpitz in 1944. *3. n.* A piece of feculent ordnance that hits the water before it snaps off. An *earthing cable, walking stick, bridger* or *neck breaker*. A *Sir Douglas Hurd* of such impressive dimensions that it could fatally hole a Nazi battleship under the waterline.

tallywhacker *1. n. 18thC.* Penis, *old man. 2. n.* A not-overly attractive young lady with whom a bloke has *carnival relations* merely in order to increase his "tally" of sexual partners.

tammy dodger *n.* A gentleman forced to go to the pub, chippy, video shop, church, round the world balloon attempt *etc.*, to avoid his *blob-stropping bag for life*.

tammy huff *n.* A monthly feminine mood swing. A *rag rage* or *mad cow disease*.

tamnesia *n.* Male short term memory failure; accidentally forgetting that it is your partner's *cricket week*. Symptoms include being hit in the face with a pan and getting stabbed with a bread knife.

tampax dancing *n.* A cool new disco craze, as seen in countless *jam rag* adverts, that requires the carefree participant to be "Up tight, out of sight" and, indeed, "into the groove".

tamper proof *adj.* Descriptive of a lady with a *lovely personality* whose looks are enough to repel boarders.

tamper seal *1. n.* Any device or item of clothing that hampers access to a lady's *parts of shame*, eg. *Chuftie plug*, skims, spanx, crossed legs. *2. n. The Bill Wyman. 'I'm off down the dirty dentist to get me tamper seal put back in before the wedding.' 'Righto Megs.'*

tampoff *n.* That all too brief three or four days

of each lunar cycle when a lady is not *up on blocks,* not premenstrual, not neurotic, and not completely impossible to please.

tampon *1. n.* A small, highly sophisticated implant which enables women to play tennis. *2. n.* An injury-prone footballer, from the fact that he is "one week in, three weeks out", *eg.* Darren "Sicknote" Anderton, who didn't play for Spurs, Birmingham and England.

tampora *n.* A piquant *women's thing* that is covered in a light, crispy batter.

tampremental *adj.* Periodically over-dramatic. *Showing off.*

tam rag *n. Jampax.*

tamtrum *n.* A monthly exhibition of petulance. A *blobstrop* or *tammy huff.*

Tamworth *n.* Perjorative term for a ginger person, named after them pigs which have ginger bristles and funny-looking eyes.

tandem *n.* A *bike* of such prodigious sexual appetites that she would happily let two men *ride her* at the same time.

tandoor clay oven *n.* A post-curry, smoke-infused, under-duvet, miasmatic *blanket banquet* which one's better half is encouraged to enjoy. Like a *Dutch oven,* but particularly rich with the spicy aromas of the mystic east.

tandoori whisper *n.* A silent, yet exquisitely rancid, burst of *wind* following an Indian meal.

tango butter *n. Fanny slobber, sloom.*

tank drip tray, muckier than a *sim. milit.* A measure of the physical enthusiasm shown by ladies who enjoy the company of soldiers around Catterick and Tidworth, where the armoured fighting vehicles of the British Army are maintained.

tank driver's hat *n.* A particularly hairy *fanny* with flaps that fasten under your chin. A *biffer, bear trapper's hat, deerstalker.*

tanked up *1. adj.* Usefully drunk, sufficient to fight or drive a car very fast. *2. adj. milit.* To be sufficiently equipped with tanks.

tank slapper *1. n.* An exciting incident that happens to a motorcyclist shortly prior to a thrilling ride in an ambulance. *2. n.* An ugly biker's moll. *3. n.* Good-naturedly smacking the *arse* of a stout lady while attempting to swing your leg over her *pillion.*

tanorexia *n. medic.* Psychological disorder common in footballers' wives types who, despite daily *cancer shop* sessions, still believe they are pasty when in fact they have the skin tone of an Oompah-Loompah.

tantric drinking *n.* The shameful art of *babysitting* a pint in the pub so much that Sting would probably finish a *shag* faster.

tantric sex *n.* Five-and-a half-hours exactly. Every time.

tantric shit *n.* An extremely prolonged visit to the porcelain *chod bin,* where one sits for four hours, *humming.*

tapas, chav *n.* A selection of savoury morsels hurriedly purchased from a petrol station chiller cabinet by a rapscallion who is suffering from a hangover, *eg.* Dairylea Dunkers, Peperami and Matteson's Chicken Bites. Best enjoyed with a carafe of blue Powerade and a Nurofen chaser.

tapas, Scouse *n.* An appetising smorgasbord of assorted traditional Liverpudlian nibbles, such as *disco biscuits,* MDMA bombs and amphetamines.

tap in *n.* Any drinking venue where *pulling* presents little or no difficulty.

tapioca tash *n.* Facial ornamentation that is popular amongst *stick vid* starlets.

tapioca toothpaste *n.* Just the thing when *brushing the au pair's teeth.*

tap off *v.* To successfully *tap up.*

tapping on the high hat *v.* Rhythmic, percussive *jazz* masturbation.

tapping out *1. n.* In American wrestling, the point at which a combatant can't take any more and concedes that he has lost his bout. *2. n.* During a bout of *horatio,* the point at which the *noshee* can't take any more and *loses his mess.*

tapping the ash *n.* Refers to the vigorous shaking and pulling apart of the buttocks in an attempt to force out the final, troublesome bit of *bum rubbish* that ends a *shitting* session, but refuses to drop into the *pan.* Akin to tapping the end of a cigarette in order to encourage the ash to drop. *'Are you going to be long in the crapper, archbishop?' 'Shouldn't be long now, your majesty, I'm just tapping the ash.'*

tappit clearance *1. n.* Something on a motor car engine that a real man would understand, and possibly be able to adjust using a hammer. *2. n.* Measurement of the *Toblerone tunnel* between a lass's legs where her *beetle bonnet* resides.

TAPS/taps *acronym. medic.* Technical term used by doctors on medical notes, Thick As Pig Shit.

tap up *1. v.* Of football managers, to make an illegal approach to a player who is signed to another team. *2. v.* Of Football Association officials, to chat up and attempt to instigate a sexual liaison with a typist in a lift at FA headquarters in Soho Square.

Tarantino hangover *n.* The kind of hangover whereby one's memory behaves in the style of *Pulp Fiction, viz.* One's recollections of the night before appear in a seemingly random order and one has to wait until one has seen all of them to finally understand what happened.

tar baby *1. n.* Something that perennially challenged the powers of imagination of the various artists hired to illustrate *Brer Rabbit*. *2. n.* A loose *Tom tit* that could certainly not be picked up and held.

Tarbucks *n.* A set of *tits* so impressive that the viewer involuntarily shouts "ho-ho!" in the manner of the cheeky, gap-toothed scouser comedian and golf enthusiast Jimmy.

Tardis fanny *n.* A deceptively spacious *snatch*. Opening the *saloon doors* to find a disappointingly capacious *cathedral* when one was expecting a *priest's hole*.

tarmacing *n.* Like preparing a *Boston pancake*, but instead of your buttocks, you use a 14-ton Aveling & Porter steamroller to flatten your *turds* across your missus's *knockers*. And then knock on the neighbours doors to tell them you've got some left over if they're interested.

tarmac round the garage *sim.* Descriptive of a slightly grubby *path to the back door*, making *rear entry* an unpleasant prospect.

tarrantless *adj.* Even less talented than Chris Tarrant, *eg.* Steve Penk, Eamonn Holmes, that arsehole mate of Robbie Williams's who used to do *You've Been Framed* for a few weeks before they got Harry Hill in.

tart *n. Slapper, dolly bird,* a nice bit of *cheesecake.*

tart-an *n.* The traditional pattern worn by young ladies who are generous with their affections.

tart farmer *n.* A *pimp, flapmonger, fanny magnate.*

tart fuel *n.* Any alcoholic drink consumed by young women which gets them going. *Knicker oil. 'She's very light on tart fuel, sir. She'll go all the way to Cockfosters on three bottles of Hooch.'*

tart ink *n.* That which is used to draw a more attractive face onto a plain woman. Make-up, *fuck dust.*

tartoo *n.* Any permanently inked design located in a lady's lower lumbar region or *splashdeck.* A *tramp stamp, slag tag* or *whoremark.* Also *arse antlers.*

tart's window box, a *sim.* What one smells like when one has too much aftershave on. Also *Joan Collins's knickers.*

tart-throb *n.* A low-grade hunk who is unaccountably alluring to ladies from the lower echelons, *eg.* Peter Andre, Robson Green, Lord Mellor.

Tarzan cord *n.* The narrow lace which attaches *Kojak's roll-neck* to the *bobby's helmet.* The *guy rope,* the *banjo, Darth Vader's chinstrap.*

Tarzan's feet, as hard as *sim.* Said of someone who

is good with his fists. *'I wouldn't fuck about with that big bouncer on the door, Professor Hawking. He's as hard as Tarzan's feet, him.'*

tash *n.* Any one of a wide variety of vaginal topiary arrangements, ranging from Robert Mugabe to Nietzsche.

tassel *n.* Innocent schoolboy term for the penis. *Winkle, willie, winkie-woo, slag hammer.*

tasseline *n.* Any smooth, soft, grease-like product that can be pressed into service to reduce friction when a bachelor wishes to *knock himself about a bit, eg.* Butter, marge or liquid soap, but not Arkwright's No 6 valve grinding paste.

tassel tingler *n.* That woman, usually someone on television, who provoked the first, vague, fizzy twitch in a young swain's loins, *eg.* Wilma from *Buck Rogers,* Mel and Kim, Heather Locklear off *TJ Hooker,* Donna Summer, Molly Weir out the Flash adverts *etc.*

tassel twanger *n.* A pithy and inoffensive way to call an *onanist* a *wanker.*

taste of bigger things to come, a *euph.* A potentially chewy announcement that one's *brownies are nearly baked.*

taste of your own medicine *n.* An unwanted dose of *Vitamin S;* inadvertently receiving a savoury soupçon of your own *special sauce* when kissing goodbye to someone who has just *noshed you off.*

taste the rainbow *v.* To have a little mouthful of everything from the "All You Can Eat" *pant buffet.*

ta tas *n. Noinkers, jubblies, cajooblies, jugs, bubbies, charms.*

Tatchell satchel *n.* A man-bag.

'taters *n. Nads, balls, bollocks.* The testicles. Contraction of potatoes. *'We Englishmen are conscious of our status / Which is why the beastly foreigners all hate us / But it's always seemed to me / That it's simply jealousy / 'Cos they're envious of the size of English 'taters.'* (From *The Stately Genitals of England* by Noel Coward).

tatties *n.* The male *testii, love spuds, pods.*

tattivate *v.* To tattily tattoo one's body in the belief that it makes one more attractive.

tattoo tipp-ex *n.* While *back-scuttling* a young lady, the act of whipping out one's *chopper* at the onset of the *vinegar strokes* in order to *white out* the *tramp stamp* just above her *arse crack* with about 5ccs of *erection fluid.*

tat twat *n.* A snobbish term used to denigrate a member of the pond-level social class often to be seen swimming round car boot sales and *Car Booty* on daytime BBC1.

tatty watta *n. Nat. Am.* Red Indian word for *spud*

juice. Literally "potato water".

tavern tumour *n. medic.* Benign male abdominal growth believed to be linked to chronic, repetitive stress on the right elbow joint. A *beerby*.

tawdry Hepburn *n.* A fine-boned, porcelain-skinned beauty who, on closer inspection, is revealed to be cheaply constructed and of poor quality.

taxi *v.* To *come* late. Or never at all.

taxi driver's clutch *euph.* An overly eager *fellatrix*. An *Ikea bulb*. '*Fuck me, Dave. I brought that fucking howler who works in the fishmongers home the other night and she went down like a taxi driver's clutch.*'

taxi driver's minute *n.* Any period of time which is longer than half an hour.

taxi driver's tan *1. n.* An area of sunburn on the right index finger caused by hooking it on the top of the cab while driving along. *2. n.* A similar effect caused by *breaching the hull*. A *filter tip*, *mechanic's nails*.

taxi floor, dirtier than a *sim.* Sexually compliant. '*Phwooar! Have you seen that new girl with the massive tits they've got doing the weather on the local news? Bet she's dirtier than a taxi floor, her.*' '*Thank-you, Archbishop. Tomorrow's Thought for the Day will be from the Chief Rabbi, Dr Jonathan Sachs.*'

taxi for Brown *exclam.* A witty riposte to an *anal retort*, such as what Dorothy Parker or Oscar Wilde might have said after they *dropped a gut*.

taxi greyhound *n.* One who bolts out of a cab door like a whippet, leaving his mates to pay his fare.

taxi tiger *n.* A desperate last-chance lunger on the way home.

tax on the elderly *euph.* Any low quality, overpriced tat advertised in weekend newspapers with the sole intention of extracting pensioners' money from the biscuit tin behind the clock.

Taylback *n.* A traffic jam caused by an ill-timed *attack of pancreatitis* in a layby.

Taz *1. n. prop.* A hairy cartoon beast that dribbles, found in the Antipodes. *2. n.* A hairy *grotter* that dribbles, found *down under*.

TBS *abbrev.* Toxic Bott Syndrome. Severe noxious emissions or *brewer's farts* when someone is *burning bad powder*.

TCGR *abbrev. medic.* Toe Cap Gender Reassignment. An *ad-hoc* sex change procedure consisting of a hefty hoof in the *knackers*. '*Emergency crash call. Adult male with TCGR injuries, name of Kyle.*'

TCM *1. abbrev. medic.* Turd Cutting Muscle, *crimper, cigar cutter*, anal sphincter. The *nipsy, secaturds*. *2. abbrev.* A Two Cock Mouth.

Also *Wallace*.

TCP *1. abbrev.* A sterilizing ante-meridian routine that can lead to a certain amount of stinging, *viz.* Tea, Ciggy, Poo. *2. abbrev. medic.* Temporary Cock Paralysis. A morning after symptom of *Post Traumatic Sex Disorder*. '*What about a quickie before you go to work, Chief Constable?*' '*Sorry love, I've got TCP.*'

TCS *abbrev.* Traction Control System. When *farting* following a bellyfull of *dizzyade* and/or curry, the precise control of the *nipsy* required to allow one to *squeak one out* without producing any *wheelspin*, thus preventing *laying rubber* in the *banana hammock*.

TDS *abbrev.* Turd Dumping Session. '*Pull over whenever it is prudent to do so please, Miss Berryman, using the gears, brakes and making appropriate signals to other traffic. I'm off behind the fence for a TDS.*'

teabagged by the dentist, like being *sim.* Describes the experience of finding yourself in a situation over which you have little or no control, when you are unable to do anything about the grim outcome, *eg.* Having to use your hand when there is no *bog roll*, having to smell other people's *Exchange & Marts* in a crowded lift, going for a "friendly chat" with your bank manager.

teabagging *n.* Making a strong brew with *Fussell's Milk* and two lumps. A last-resort sexual practice whereby the man lowers his *saddlebags* into the lady's mouth.

teabag left in the pot *1. euph.* A *white mouse* still in its house. '*Not again, Gladys. There's a teabag left in the pot.*' *2. euph.* An *unexpected item in the bagging area*. '*Not again, Gladys. There's a teabag left in the pot.*' *3. euph.* The discovery of a *night watchman* on the *starting line at Brand's Hatch.* '*Not again, Gladys. There's a teabag left in the pot.*'

tea chicken *n.* Game played by severely hungover flatmates, whereby they all sit immobile waiting for the first one to bottle it and offer to put the kettle on.

teaching William a lesson *n.* Punishing Percy, pulling the Pope's cap off. '*"What's all this banging and groaning?" bellowed a puce-faced Mr Wilkins as he burst into the dorm. "Please, Sir," piped-up Venables. "It was Darbishire teaching Jennings a lesson."*' (from *Jennings and the Mysterious Body Hairs* by Anthony Buckeridge).

tea cosy *n.* A place to hide one's *spout* while thinking about the true object of one's affections. '*Deaths: Lady Diana Spencer, shopping enthusiast, landmines campaigner and Prince's tea cosy, 36.*'

tea fairy *n.* Term used to describe a rather poor

drinker. *'Come on, George, you big tea fairy. One drink won't hurt you.'*

teaking *n.* Act of eating and talking simultaneously, as practised by Americans.

teams are in the tunnel, the *1. exclam.* The sort of banal expression uttered by potato-faced football presenter Adrian Chiles before he used to hand over to Clive Tyldesley and Andy Townsend in the commentary box. *2. exclam.* The awkward, alarming feeling that often comes between *touching cloth* and *touching socks.*

teapot *1. n.* A male from the Larry Grayson school of posturing. *'You know that bloke at number thirty-three? Well I was talking to Edna in the butchers and, well, not to put too fine a point on it, let's just say he's a bit of a teapot, I'll put it no stronger than that.'* *2. n. Self harm* position. One hand pulling at the spout and the index finger of the other hand stuck up the nipsy to stimulate the *walnut.* Superficially resembles the "I'm a little teapot" nursery rhyme dance, though with somewhat less innocent overtones.

teapot shuffle *n.* Descriptive of the pose adopted by internet-fuelled *self-polluters, ie. Pulling themselves off* with the left hand, while the right arm is extended to faciltate control of the mouse.

teapot sucker *n.* A *bottom shelf drinker,* a teetotaller.

teapotting *n.* The rather unpleasant feeling experienced when a fellow's dangling *clockweights* are immersed in the rising water of an overfilled *chod bin.*

teaquilibrium *n. medic.* State of physiological balance reached when one has drunk so much tea that each further sip of the tasty tannin-rich beverage necessitates an immediate bathroom visit in order to *strain the greens.*

tearful wank *n.* A light-hearted taunt directed at a newly heartbroken male colleague. It involves sticking the bottom lip out, and doing a masturbating gesture with one hand and a "boo hoo" eye fist twist gesture with the other.

teargas has been deployed in the rotunda *exclam.* Humorous riposte to a *rectal retort.* See also *speak on sweet lips that never told a lie, ahoy there! etc.*

tear in a coalman's jacket *sim.* A large, raggy *blart.* A *ripped sofa, ragman's coat.*

tearing cloth *n.* The frankly alarming stage which immediately succeeds *touching cloth.*

tearjerker *1. n.* A particularly painful masturbation session. *2. n.* A particularly joyful masturbation session. *3. n.* A particularly poignant masturbation session. *4. n.* A *Camilla* movement that requires concentration and effort to the extent you leave the toilet looking like you've just sat

through the end of *ET, Titanic, Ghost* or some other such mawkishly overwrought tragedy-fest.

tear off a piece *v. US.* To have s*x. *Tear one off.*

tea spoon *n.* A cosy cuddle up behind the missus, when you want her to get out of bed and make a cuppa.

tea strainer *n.* An *Enoch* movement that is forcibly withheld during your teabreak so that you can later have a *Tom tit* while getting paid for the pleasure. *Time and a turd, taking one on the company's time.*

tea towel holder *n. Anus, ringpiece, freckle.* From the 1950s plastic "finger poke" cat's *arse-*style kitchen accessory. Also *old-fashioned fifties tea towel holder. 'Just bend over, sir, and I'll insert this camera up your tea towel holder.' 'Are you absolutely sure this is necessary when I'm being measured for a new hat?'*

teat-seeking missile *n.* A man who fails to maintain proper eye contact when talking to women.

teazle *n.* The alluring glimpse of luxuriant *faff* that is observable from the rear of a *bird* via her *Toblerone tunnel. Reverse peach, coconut husk, coffee bean.*

techie's perks *n.* While fixing a mate's PC, taking the opportunity to search his hard-drive for photographs of his missus in highly compromising positions. *"Ere, John. What's that pic of my Angie with a dildo up her Gary doing on your mobile phone?' 'Techie's perks, mate.'*

technical area *1. n.* In football, the designated space that a manager, other coaching personnel and team substitutes occupy during the course of a match. *2. n.* The *fruit bowl. 'Now look here, officer. You've got this all wrong. I was just taking the opportunity to re-arrange my technical area while the cinema lights were down.' 'Save it for the judge, Gerald.'* *3. n.* The missus's *bits and pieces.* Not to be confused with her *dugout,* unless you want to be *on the bench* for the rest of the season.

technical challenge *1. n.* A round on *The Great British Bake Off* during which the contestants are given a recipe at the last minute with no time for advance preparation, to test how they deal with pressure and how inventive they can be in a crisis. *2. n. Dropping fudge* when there is no viable toilet in the immediate vicinity. A test of how a person deals with pressure, and how inventive they can be in a crisis.

technical knockout *1. n.* Something in a boxing match that presumably doesn't include biting your opponent's ear off. *2. n.* A perfectly executed *hand shandy* below the belt that leaves no *spoff* on the knuckles.

technicolour yawn *n.* A *yoff*.

technology lessons *1. n.* What go-getting entrepreneur Jennifer Arcuri claimed that Boris Johnson was getting when he kept going round to her flat. *2. euph. The other.*

techno-tab *n.* An e-cigarette. Also *R2D2's cock*.

Tecwens *n. medic.* An attack of pathetic fake coughing that one effects at work the day before one throws a sickie. From the *Who Wants to be a Millionaire* coughing *knacker* Tecwen Whittock. *'The lads are playing Locomotiv Moscow tomorrow, live on Sky, only the kick off's at two in the afternoon. Cough! Cough! Ooh, dear. I can feel a touch of the Tecwens coming on.'*

Ted *1. n. rhym. slang.* The penis. From Teddington Lock = cock. *2. n. prop.* An abbreviation of *shithead*. *'President Ted says you can't look at them cardboard boxes of nuclear secrets he nicked from the White House and anyway he's got Presidential privilege and he definitely didn't show them to the Russians.'*

Ted Bundies *n. prop. rhym. slang. US.* Blood-soaked *undies*, named after the infamous American murderer. *'I do wish you'd occasionally pick your Ted Bundies up off the goldarn bathroom floor, Sue-Ellen.'*

Teddington *rhym. slang.* The penis. From the *Magpie* studio address Teddington Lock = corn on the cob.

teddy bear smile *n.* Condition affecting the *front bottoms* of ladies in leggings. Also *camel's foot, camel's lip, knicker sausages, Twix lips, cloven hoof, Cyclops' hoof, gorilla's knuckles, moose knuckles, the pig's trotter.*

teddy bear's nose *n.* The *clematis* or *devil's doorbell*.

teddy bear wank *n. Relaxing in a gentleman's way while wearing woolly gloves.*

teddy's leg *n.* State of stool expulsion somewhere beyond the *turtle's head*, but prior to *touching sock*. Point midway through *smoking a bum cigar*. *Bungle's finger.*

Ted Rogers *n. prop.* A special sort of *gusset typing* utilising the lightning fast, dextrous finger technique made famous by the eponymous, late, fast-talking host of erstwhile purgatorial Yorkshire TV dustbin-based gameshow *3-2-1*.

tee off *v.* To *wank* and/or *fart*. Not necessarily at the same time.

Tees duck *n.* A seagull. Also *sky rat, shitehawk, skydog*.

teeter meter *n.* Calibration scale assessing the attractiveness of women based on how far from sober one would have to be to *slip them a length*.

eg. Kylie Minogue would be 0 on the teeter meter, whereas Phyllis off *Coronation Street* would be 15 pints of Stella with whisky chasers, even when she was alive. More now.

teeth are in the bin, his/her *exclam.* Referring to *FFFA* media *nonebrities'* habit of getting their *gnashers* smashed out and replaced with a strip of white plastic at the first glimmer of limelight.

teeth like the holy commandments *phr.* Said of any person doing badly at their six-monthly dental check-up, because "there's only ten of them and every one is broke".

Tegel airport *1. n.* Berlin's busiest air transport hub, famous for having two hexagonal terminal buildings. *2. n.* Over-excited planespotter terminology for a lady's twin nether openings.

teggat *n.* A short-necked *turtle's head* which is unable to *touch cloth*, and retreats back into the *bomb bay*.

telegraph pole dancer *n.* A somewhat cumbersome erotic performer, as found cavorting clumsily about the stage of one's local *peppermint pig*.

telescoping *n.* Looking squarely into the end of a stiff *stalk*, waiting to get a proper eyeful. *'Admiral Fellatio Nelson lost his eye quite early in his naval career, following a telescoping accident below decks on HMS Dolphin.'*

telling bone *1. n.* What displaced 11th century wizard Catweazle called a telephone in the eponymous 1970s children's TV series. *2. n.* An errant *stiffy*; a twitching bulge in the front of a pair of speedos that indicates clearly that a fellow likes what he sees at the beach/swimming pool/Olympic Beach Volleyball event.

telly tuggy *n.* A jobseeker's hour-long morning *wank* over his favourite pulchritudinous daytime television presenters.

temazepalm *n. medic.* Hand-induced insomnia relief. *Forty wanks, knuckle nightcap*.

temperature, take her *n.* To insert one's finger into the missus's *Gary Glitter*.

temporary hole *1. n.* Addition to the golf course when the green keeper has been unable to do his job for whatever reason. *2. n.* Somewhere to *sink a few shots* during *rag week*.

tempura, lose your *v.* To lightly batter someone.

tena city *n.* Retirement community or old people's home.

tenapause *n.* The stage in a woman's life-cycle when she loses the ability to control her bladder effectively.

tenderise *1. v.* In cooking, to make meat more digestible by *knacking* it with a big *fuck-off* wooden mallet. *2. v.* In *cocking*, to *beat the meat.*

tender perennials *1. n.* Plants from warm climes that need protection from the frost in the British winter. *2. n.* The male testes. *'I trod on a garden rake today and the handle came up and smacked me right in the tender perennials.'*

TENFOLD/tenfold *abbrev. RAF.* A young lady who is blessed with smashing *eye magnets* while, somewhat off-puttingly, being cursed with the crumpled face of a 1970s northern club comedian. Tits Extremely Nice, Face Of Les Dawson.

ten gallon twat *n.* An *eggbox* like a bucket.

tenis *n.* A tiny *manhood. 'Welcome to the tenis club, Mr Davro.'*

ten metre board *n.* The toilet seat; the place from where a *Tom Daley* is launched.

ten minutes' peace and quiet *n.* An offensive term used by sexist men to describe getting a *chewie* off their *bit of fluff. 'Mr Campbell-Bannerman: Yes, Mrs Pankhurst, I agree that the introduction of universal suffrage is a worthy political objective, and I shall endeavour to include it in the King's speech at the beginning of the next parliamentary session… but only if you give me ten minutes peace and quiet. Mrs Pankhurst: Glub! Glub!'.* (Cartoon in *Punch* by Bernard Partridge, 1905).

Tennents association *n.* A group of widely travelled *Terence Stamps* enjoying a well-earned quaff of their favourite tipple on the *tramp grill.*

Tennents elbow *n. medic. Scots.* Chronic muscular/skeletal ailment caused by repetitive flexing of the *humeroulnar ginglymus.* Particularly prevalent amongst Glaswegian *professional outdoorsmen* the Monday after an Old Firm game. Also known as *tramp's cramp. 'I'm sorry Mr Floyd. I'm afraid you've got an advanced case of Tennents elbow.'*

Tennents poetry *n.* A moving sonnet of threats and expletives, usually *scumbled* by a dishevelled Caledonian while leaning forwards.

Tennents tan *n.* The reddish-purple glow that an ardent lager connoisseur acquires after years of wandering from bar to bar in a *pissed-up* frenzy of unquenchable thirst. Also *tramp's tan.*

tenner lady *1. n.* A female who is *pissed* after just ten quid's worth of *sauce. 2. n.* A cheap, incontinent *prossie. 'Excuse me, are there any tenner ladies in the area? I fancy a cheap, sordid poke with a tart who is the very antithesis of my own, fragrant missus who has full control of her bladder.' 'There's one over there by that skip, Lord Archer.'*

tennis elbow *n. medic.* A condition of the right arm caused by repeated games of *singles. 'Ooh, that's a nasty case of tennis elbow you've got there, Tim.'*

tennis fan *n.* A woman who is *fond of walking* holidays to Wimbledon. Also *lady golfer.*

ten o'clock to nine o'clock, move my *euph.* Humorous way to inform one's secretary that you'll be taking your morning *Tom tit* an hour earlier than usual. *'Joan, that double espresso you gave me means I'll need to move my ten o'clock to nine o'clock. Has the Washington Post arrived yet?'*

ten of clubs *n.* The polar opposite of *drawing an ace,* from the busy appearance of one's used *bumwad.* That is to say, the aftermath of a messy *chod* that leaves a person's *nipsy* like an open jar of Nutella, thus leading to a wiping job that is akin to the mythical Fifth Labour of Heracles.

ten of diamonds *n.* A cheeky trick played by one's *council gritter* when one is attempting to *sail through customs* at the end of a game of *craps* with *Famer Giles.*

tenpin *v.* To place digits simultaneously in the *tea towel holder* and the *fish mitten.* From the grip used in ten pin bowling. To *spock.*

ten pint princess *n.* A *donner.* Two pints *bubblier* than a *gallon girl;* twice as bubbly as a *St Ivel.*

ten points to Gryffindor *n.* Another witty riposte which can be delivered upon hearing a *botty burp.*

tenpole tudor *n.* A *dollymop,* ie. One who has had "the swords of a thousand men".

ten pounds of shit in a five pound bag *euph.* Useful phrase which can be used when referring to either a deceptively powerful motor car or a *generously boned* woman who has shoehorned herself into a dress which is several sizes too small for her. *'How do I look, Andrew?' 'Like ten pounds of shit in a five pound bag, Sarah. But we've got to get going. The Archbishop of Canterbury is waiting.'*

tension in the Balkans *1. euph.* Period of uncomfortable apprehension experienced by the residents of the eponymous geopolitical region in the period between the assassination of Archduke Franz Ferdinand and when it all kicked off. *2. euph.* A build-up of *spoffological* pressure in a chap's *bulgars* following a period of sexual inactivity. *'There's tension in the Balkans, Sue. I'm going to have to put on a larger pair of tennis shorts.'*

tentertainment *n.* Any recreational diversion that entails a small, cloth-covered erection being pitched.

tent flaps *n.* Dewy *Keith Burtons* that one pokes one's head through first thing in the morning.

ten-to-two shuffle *n.* A perfunctory dance that *pissed up* gentlemen engage in with the *floor sweepings* at the end of a long and unspectacular evening *on the pull. 'Any luck last night?' 'No. Ended up doing the ten-to-two shuffle with some dental receptionist. She gave me a bit of duck* *sausage and then I got the last bus home.'*

tent pole *n.* A *stiffy*, especially in bed. A *trouser tent, morning glory, dawn horn, dusk tusk.* Also the *motorcycle kickstand.*

tequila sunrise *n.* The awe-inspiring visual effect produced when a man's bright yellow urine flows into the *pan* where the previous (female) occupant has *blobbed.*

Terence Stamp *n. prop. rhym. slang.* A merry, carefree *gentleman of the road.*

terminal five *1. n.* The *landing strip* on a very large woman. Named after the biggest runway in the UK, which is at Heathrow Airport. *2. n.* A completely blocked system in which nothing moves. *'Pass me the Senokot tin, love. I haven't been able to park my breakfast from four days ago yet, or indeed any meal since. I've become the human equivalent of Heathrow Airport's terminal five on opening day. Only with turds instead of suitcases.'*

terminal two *n.* The *shitter. 'This won't hurt a bit, Mr Trubshaw. I'm just going to pop a rubber glove on and stick my finger up terminal two.' 'Is that strictly necessary? After all, I'm only applying for a Nectar card.'*

terminal viscosity *n.* Medical term to describe a dangerously sticky *digestive transit* that may initiate a near death experience for its creator.

terminate the call *v.* To cut short a *Lionel Bart* for fear of *following through.* To *reverse the charge.*

terms & conditions apply *exclam.* A jocose retort in response to the launch of a bewilderingly complex *air biscuit.*

terra firmer *n.* Following several days of post-curry *squits*, a return to somewhat more solid *Enoch* movements. *'Ah-haar, me hearties! 'Tis good to be back on terra firmer at last.'*

terrapin *n.* A firm *tod* that busts one's *Jeremy Kyles*, thus leaving livid red streaks along its neck in the style of one of the popular pond-dwelling tortoises.

terrorist's backpack, ticking like a *sim.* Of a woman with a very loud biological clock. *'I'd steer clear of her if I was you, mate. She's ticking like a terrorist's backpack.'*

Terry Funk *1. n. prop.* A popular Discotheque personality in the Midlands, circa 1970. *2. n. rhym. slang.* Marijuana cigarettes, from Terry Funk = skunk. *3. n. rhym. slang.* Spooge, from Terry Funk = spunk. *'Waiter. There's some Terry Funk in my soup'. 'Yes, Mr Coren That's because the chef, the entire kitchen and serving staff, and indeed the rest of the customers have all masturbated into it.'*

Terry Nutkin's finger *euph.* Descriptive of a less *well-endowed* man; perhaps one whose *cock*, like the late television wildlife favourite's digit, was

partially bitten off by a hungry otter.

Terry Waite *v.* To lock an item firmly to an immovable object, such as a radiator. *'Will your new bike be alright left out in the street?' 'Don't worry. I've Terry Waited it to a lamppost.'*

Terry Waite's allotment *sim.* Descriptive of a badly overgrown *ladygarden. 'Marriette was powerless to resist. His eyes burned into hers like emeralds. His muscular arms enfolded her body as she felt herself being swept away in a monsoon of passion. "Bloody hell! You've got a twat like Terry Waite's allotment!" the corporal cried, as he pulled out the waistband of her bloomers and peered inside.'* (from *The Peasant Girl and the First World War Soldier* by Barbara Cartland).

Tesco at midnight, like *sim.* Descriptive of a dirty lady's *clunge* during *rag week* which, while it is a mess of debris and reconstructive activity, remains nominally open for business.

Tesco bags full of piss, tits like two *sim.* A delightful turn of phrase that wouldn't have sounded out of place being enunciated in the cut-glass tones of Sir Noel Coward. Breasts that hang like saucepans.

Tesco finish *n.* In pornographic cinematography, the sort of *pop shot* where the over-enthusiastic gentleman actor vigorously attempts to squeeze every last drop of *spaff* out of his *gut stick.* From the all-conquering town centre-fucking supermarket's well-known advertising slogan; "Because every little helps".

Tesco's barcode fault *euph.* Named after the 2011 fiasco whereby the supermarket chain inadvertently mis-priced Terry's Chocolate Oranges at 29p instead of the usual £2.75, causing canny customers with an eye for a bargain to go into a frenzy of panic buying; thus, to "fill your trolleys with chocolate". *'Can you stick these in the boil wash please, pet? I've had a bit of a Tesco's barcode fault on me way back from the pub.'*

tescosexual *n.* A man whose incidence of sexual activity peaks during his wife's trips to the shops. A *home-alone-o-sexual.*

tescosterone *n.* Hormone which causes aggressive behaviour in males who are forced to queue up behind a long queue of lottery-ticket-buying OAPs just in order to buy themselves a packet of fucking fags.

Tessa Munt *n. rhym. slang.* A *Kenny Lunt.* Named in honour of the former Liberal Democrat MP for Wells in Somerset who, amusingly enough, was apparently a governor of the Hugh Sexey Middle School.

test and trace *v.* The forensic art of sniffing a *dropped gut* in the pub and trying to determine which of your mates produced it, based entirely upon what they are each drinking.

test card wank *n.* A *tug* one has, not because one is feeling particularly *fruity*, but simply because there is nothing else to do. A *loose end away*.

test cricket shit *euph.* A particularly troublesome *turd* which is played out over many sessions and involves multiple trips to the *crease*, halts for tea and follow-ons. See *test match*.

testicalia *n.* Any collection of items that are *bollocks* in general. *'They'd bought a right load of testicalia on Bargain Hunt today.'*

testicle test *n. medic.* An act of male *auto-eroticism* carried out for routine maintenance purposes. *'Have you seen my new Razzle, verger? I've got to carry out my mid-afternoon testicle test.'*

testing the Fray Bentos *n.* The unfortunate experience of *breaching the hull* while wiping, resulting in a finger end which is covered in gravy. From the eerie similarity to the act of pushing a digit through the pastry on one of them pies in a tin.

testing the internet *euph.* Masturbating. *'I'll be down in a minute, love. I'm just testing the internet into a sock.'*

testing the water *euph.* The moment during an innocent Thai massage when the massoose "accidentally" touches a chap's *bollocks*; depending upon his reaction, he may then be offered a *happy ending* (unless he's already just had one). Apparently. Not that we'd know.

test match *n.* An extremely long sit-down sojourn in the lavatory, which to the subject feels like it is taking five days to achieve any sort of conclusive result. So-named due to the similarity to the cricket competitions, *viz.* Long, silent periods of intense concentration broken by occasional grunts, cracks and thuds, irregularly interspersed with splatters from the *pavilion end* that sound not unlike bursts of applause.

test ride *n.* In the executive world, the act of taking the *office bike round the block* before deciding whether or not to dump one's missus for her.

Tetley trot *n.* Conveniently short bout of s*xual intercourse that happily finishes before your cup of tea has a chance to go cold.

Tewkesbury doorstep, wetter than a *sim.* A no-longer-topical description of a lady who is suffering a flash flood *down south*. *'I tell you what, Geoff, she can't have had it for a while. Her fanny was wetter than a Tewkesbury doorstep.'*

Tewkesbury postman's wellies, wetter than a *sim.* Said of a lady in an advanced state of arousal. Also *wetter than ~a turfer's knee, ~Stevie Wonder's toilet seat, ~an otter's neck, ~a bad plumber's mop, ~Lee Evans's suit, ~Whitney Houston's last joint etc.*

Texan *n.* A difficult *motion*. One that, in the words of the 1970s advert for the chocolate bar of the same name, "takes time a'chewin'".

Texas meal *n.* A massive pile of *shite*. *'Miss Ellie, was it you who was just in the cludgie? Only there's a proper Texas meal in there that won't flush away and I'm going to have to go and fetch JR to break it up with the potato masher.'*

Texas panhandle *1. n.* Area consisting of the 29 most northerly counties of the Lone Star State. *2. n.* A bigger than normal erection you feel the need to boast about.

Tex Ritter *n. rhym. slang.* The *cludgie*, named after the famous country music singer and film star. From Tex Ritter = Rick Witter.

textbook dog *n.* The recognition of an absolutely perfect *doggy-style* position seen in everyday situations, *eg.* A secretary crawling on the floor to find a contact lens.

texticles *n.* A modern gent's foolproof method of wooing casual female acquaintances *via* mobile picture messaging.

text sausages *v.* To send alluring photographs of one's semi-turgid *porky banger* to a lucky lady.

Tex Tucker's guns *euph.* From the 1960s children's television puppet show *Four Feather Falls*, where the sheriff was able to raise and fire his pistols without touching them. An involuntary *stonk-on* and *pop shot*.

TFFA *abbrev.* Initials never used as a catchphrase by erstwhile late syrup-topped Radio 2 disc geriatric Jimmy Young. Thanks For Fuck All.

TFTF *abbrev.* The sort of classily-turned-out *tussage* that rock up at Bonbar looking like they're footballers' wives, so all the blokes are too intimidated to approach them, even though they actually work at Boots. Too Fit To Fuck.

TGIG *abbrev.* Thank God It's Gas. Used when one has *gambled and won*.

Thaiarrhoea *n. medic.* A temporary loosening of the *foulage* as a result of eating delicious spicy delicacies from the faraway south-east Asian kingdom.

Thai lottery jackpot *n.* On an exotic holiday, the thrill and excitement felt after *picking up* a couple of far eastern *hotties* and, when you get them back to your hotel, discovering that, between you, you have "six matching balls".

Thaiphoon *n.* The gusty winds that follow a trip to one's local oriental eaterie for a plate of khao phat naem.

Thai stripper's scrotum, ugly as a *sim.* Graphic metaphor descriptive of that moment when something which seems to be going along swimmingly suddenly takes a distinctly uexpected turn. *'Senna's lap looked perfect until he ran wide into the Tamburello Curve, when things turned as ugly as a Thai stripper's scrotum.'*

Thames trout *n.* A fishy-smelling, rainbow-coloured, *spawn*-filled object with its tickling days now long behind it, typically found floating near one of London's major sewerage outlets. A spent *jubber.* A British variation on the American *Coney Island whitefish.*

Thames whale *n.* A large *turd* which appears in the *pan* without any explanation, and is reluctant to return to the sea.

thank *v.* From think + wank. *'What's the matter, Wills? You've went limp again. Is it Pippa?' 'Yes darling. I was just thanking about her before I came to bed. Especially her arse.'*

thank God, here's the cavalry! *exclam.* Said of an *arse trumpet* that starts off quietly but gets louder as it approaches its final destination.

thankles *n.* Thick ankles. From thick + ankles.

thanks for that, now can you please throw something? *exclam. interrog.* Another one of those phrases that can be employed to humorous effect after someone has *dropped* a high decibel *spare part.* From Yvette Fielding's risible satellite television programme *Most Haunted*, when the crew conjured up ghosts, unexplained thumps and groans *etc.*, prior to the makeup girl and the baldy cameraman getting scared, punched scratched or possessed.

thanksgiving dinner *n.* An act of *oral affection* performed on a *big bird* who has *got the painters in. Dinner at the Y* with extra ketchup. *Cranberry dip.*

thank-you for coming to my TED talk *exclam.* Humorous interjection following the release of a high-minded *idea worth spreading* following a five-hour marathon at the local carvery.

thank-you for the music *exclam.* The opening lines from Abba's melodious hit single of 1977, which can be pressed gnomically into service (to include as much of the rest of the song as may be deemed appropriate in the circumstances) as a tuneful expression of gratitude and enthusiasm following the release of a particularly harmonious *dropped hat.* Also *someone's moving in next door; that's how I attract the bitches; that's right Doodles* and *that's the chairs arranged then.*

thank-you for the opportunity, Lord Sugar *exclam.* Yet another thing to say in the wake of a loud *trouser cough.* See also *if that's not out I'm not playing; can I quote you on that?; fall out the officers; thanks for that, now can you please throw something?; is that Ziggy?; a bit more choke and she would have started; a confident appeal by the Australians there; an excellent theory, Dr Watson; anybody injured?; Alexa, open a window* and *you were only supposed to blow the bloody doors off.*

that bugger's going on my CV *exclam.* Something proudly announced to workmates after spending the last half hour on the *Rees-Mogg.*

that can be for the charity shop *exclam.* Announcement following a *number two* that sounds like you've just thrown a heavy plastic bag of old clothes from the landing to the bottom of the stairs.

thatched cottage *1. n. arch.* A delightfully picturesque half-timbered *cunt* with roses round the *pissflaps*, which would make a good jigsaw puzzle or tea tray. Also *thatched mottage. 2. n.* A picture postcard gents' bog.

Thatcher's funeral *1. n.* Any ludicrously expensive event, trip or occasion desired by a few but which, nevertheless, everyone has to pay for. *2. n.* Ten million quid. *'Bloke in the pub reckons Newcastle want James Milner back as a squad player, but Brighton want half a Thatcher's funeral for him.'*

thatch hatch *n.* A chocolate-boxy *box* with roses round the *saloon doors.*

thatch 22 *n.* Sexual dilemma faced by a gentleman considering committing *cumulonimbus* on a lady with an horrendous *clown's pie.*

that fart had back-up *exclam.* Phrase uttered as a plea of mitigation shortly after inadvertently *buttering one's cheeks, drawing mud from the well, dropping one's revels, preparing a portion of duck soup, failing one's driving test, suffering a fall of soot* or being the victim of a *jacksydent. 'Jesus Christ, Dame Margot! Do you mind?' 'Sorry, Rudolph. I was just trying to sneak it out during the grand jete, but that fart had back-up.'*

that is no orc horn *1. exclam.* A line said by Legolas in *The Lord Of The Rings* upon hearing the Elves arriving to join the Battle of Helms Deep. *2. exclam.* A line said by a gentleman just after *dropping his guts.*

that'll put lead in your shit! *exclam.* Something to say to someone who is sinking numerous pints of Guinness.

that one came with a prize *exclam.* Polite phrase acknowledging that an *air biscuit* has been accompanied by a *malteser* or two.

that one jumped the queue *exclam.* Said when one has inadvertently *dropped* an item of *shopping* while *stepping on a duck* in polite company.

that one's got a skin on it *exclam.* Humorous riposte following the release of a *Donald* that has been *stewing* in the *back boiler*. From the similarity to a milky coffee that has been left too long in the cup.

that one takes a few listens *exclam.* Connoisseurial advice given to listeners after emitting a sonically complex *piece of Musique concrète* with an unusual time signature. Also *it makes more sense in the context of the whole album.*

that one will itch when it dries *exclam.* Comment made after unsuccessfully *twisting on nineteen.*

that's a clear round for David Broome! *exclam.* Uttered when someone breaks wind. From the commentaries on TV showjumping back in the 1970s, when the horses always seemed to *step on a duck* after clearing the last fence. Also *four faults!; let's have a look at the scores on the doors.*

that's another fine mess you've got me into *exclam.* Said following a slapstick *trouser yodel*, accompanied by an exasperated look to an imaginary camera. Also *them's the breaks, horn of Gondor!* etc.

that's another marvellous delivery *exclam.* An amusing thing to say in the aftermath of a loud *appeal to the umpire*, preferably in the peculiar strangled Antipodean tones of Richie Benaud. Also *ease springs*; *back to bed Peppa; a confident appeal by the Australians there; an excellent theory, Dr Watson; anybody injured?; fer-fetch a cloth, Granville; that's numberwang!*

that's a signal for me, not for you *exclam.* Announced in the manner of a tired geography teacher following a loud *flies' dinner gong.* Also *can everybody smell that?; this claim about election fraud is disputed; Great Scott!; Does this meat smell off to you?; read the standing orders!* etc.

that's gone for a corner! *exclam.* When trapped in a football crowd, the cry that goes up when someone *drops his guts.*

that's music to my nose *exclam.* A witty riposte to musical sounds from a *bum-trumpet*, when you know it's going to be a right *rotter.*

that's my target weight achieved ... again *exclam.* Expression uttered when a cove exits the bathroom after a particularly impressive *Enoch* movement.

that's nothing, watch this *exclam.* When entering a stinking *Rick Witter* cubicle full of confidence that your own befoulment will be more than capable of overpowering the current stench.

that's not the Brexit I voted for *exclam.* Cast-iron defence after one has just thunderously *sharted.*

that's one for the purists *exclam.* Proclamation announcing that you have just played a distinctly pungent *smellody.*

that's the shit I'm talking about *exclam.* One of numerous phrases to say after *chuffing.*

that strimmer sounds broken *exclam.* Something to say after loudly *dropping a guff.* Also *another remark like that and you'll be in contempt of court!; steady on old boy; someone's not in bed, Iggle Piggle's not in bed; Well, you've got to give something back!; Sic transit gloria mundi* etc.

that's working, now try your lights *1. exclam.* Phrase shouted by a motor mechanic following the successful testing of a car's horn. *2. exclam.* Phrase shouted following the successful floating of an *air biscuit.* Also *sew a button on that; catch that one and paint it blue; good health;, pin a tail on that* and *you should put that on eBay.*

that was absolutely tremendous *phr.* When one has endured tedious company, an acronymious way to convey to your host, without fear of consequence, that you think he's a twat. *'Well, how did you enjoy your lap in the reasonably priced car?' 'That was absolutely tremendous, Jeremy.'*

that was a party political broadcast on behalf of the [insert name of political party here] *exclam.* Used to bring closure after a loud, wet-sounding *Bronx cheer.*

that won't get me to Monte Carlo! *exclam.* Said in the style of Terry-Thomas after noisily applying substantial choke to the *rattletrap* and possibly flooding it.

that won't get you there any faster! *exclam.* Ribald feedback offered to a walker audibly attempting to generate forward thrust by means of gas propulsion.

that would be lovely – milk and two sugars please *exclam.* Light-hearted witticism uttered when someone nearby *steps on a duck.* See *yes you did – you invaded Poland.*

that would cure bacon *n.* A throwaway quip uttered when a pal emits a particularly potent mole of intestinal *carbon dibaxide.*

Theakston's *rhym. slang.* The rear *fundament.* From Theakston's bitter = Gary Glitter. *'Jesus love, no offence, but your breath stinks. Tell you what, I'll do you up the Theakston's tonight, eh?'*

the ayes have it, the ayes have it, clear the lobby! *exclam.* Amusing warning shouted immediately prior to a *motion of very little confidence.*

the big O *n. prop.* Roy Orbison.

the buffet is now open *exclam.* Post-*hat drop* announcement that heralds a mass stampede into the next room.

the dark knight rises *1. n.* Batman film, featuring

very little actual Batman and a lot of Tom Hardy speaking into a bucket. *2. exclam.* Used when the speaker is about to *hoy up* an impressive quantity of Irish stout. *'He waits. That's what he does. And I'll tell you what, tick followed tock followed tick followed tock followed tick. Ahab says "I don't care who you are. Here's to your dream." And after eight pints the dark knight rises.'*

the following programme contains adult themes *exclam.* Announcement before an almighty *trouser cough* that doesn't start until after 9pm.

their face is made out of the same stuff as your arse *phr.* A refreshing apophthegm expressing the common bond of humanity that links us us all together. All things considered, it is unlikely that BBC royal correspondent Nicholas Witchell would ever conclude one of his reports with this phrase.

Thelonious *n. prop. rhym. slang.* Semen. Named after the jazz pianist Thelonious Spunk.

Thelonius junk *n. US.* What a jazz fan might nickname *big Jim and the twins.*

the one show *1. n.* BBC 1 programme broadcast at 7pm every weekday, and watched when the remote control can't be found. *2. n.* An *act of solo pleasure.* Also *hand party, heir flick.*

there goes the cockle train *exclam. S. Aus.* Said after a voluble blast on the *guardsman's whistle.*

there go the Maldives! *exclam.* A humorous rejoinder following a voluble release of *brownhouse gases.* The potent, climate-changing nature of *carbon dibaxide* is widely believed to contribute to rising sea levels, which currently threaten the eponymous low-lying, Indian Ocean-based chain of atolls.

there is a caller at the back gate, please attend *1. exclam.* Announcement made over the supermarket tannoy, alerting staff to the need to receive a delivery. *2. exclam.* Announcement that a nearby *chodbin,* (or one's nether-gussetry for that matter) will shortly be in receipt of a malodorous brown consignment.

there is unrest in the south, colonel *exclam.* Phrase used when suffering from untrustworthy *Simon Cowells,* and one dare not venture far from the *throne room* in case *the rebels should charge the gates.*

there'll be blood on the bog roll tomorrow *exclam.* A portentous augury of one's intentions to drink brown beer and consume spicy foodstuffs.

there's a fog out in the channel, Cap'n *exclam.* Witty maritime riposte following a *nautical chart* of a particularly deep and sonorous timbre.

Theresa May *1. n. rhym. slang.* Cockney argot for a delay or hold up, named in honour of the popular Prime Minister. *'Sorry love, I'm gonna be a bit late. There's been a right old Theresa May on the trains.'* *2. n.* A technique of delaying sexual gratification by picturing the former premier's embittered face. Or in extreme cases, her dancing.

there's an app for that *sim.* One of those humorous idiomatic apophthegms that can be usefully employed following a loud *bark from a red-eyed dog.*

there's Bully – you're out of time *exclam.* Humorous utterance to be employed when someone emits a low frequency, bovine *Exchange & Mart.* From late deputy-headmaster-turned-bottle-bottomed-standup Jim Bowen's gentle chastisement of slow-witted contestants on his erstwhile darts-themed eighties Sunday teatime gloomfest *Bullseye.*

there's some news coming in *exclam.* Said to pre-empt a breaking honk from the tuneless *nether trumpet.* Also *ladies and gentlemen, please give a warm welcome to Florence and the Machine. 'Quick, Charlie, turn the wireless up. There's some news coming in.'*

there's the thunder, where's the lightning? *exclam. rhet.* To be said after *letting off* an earth-shaking *egg McWhiff.*

there's Wally! *exclam.* Exclamation of surprise when inspecting the contents of the lavatory pan and spotting a *teddy's leg* reminiscent of the well-travelled Arctic pinniped Wally the Walrus.

there we are then *exclam. acronym.* Another covert way of calling another person a *twat.* See also *see you next Tuesday, can't understand new technology, that was absolutely tremendous.*

there will be blood *1. n.* Title of an Oscar-seeking epic film starring Daniel Day-Lewis. *2. exclam.* Statement made as one pushes one's chair back from the table following a particularly stodgy Christmas dinner, in reference to the inevitable *arse*-ripping *yule log*-based activities which will ensue on Boxing Day.

thesbian *n.* A *grumble flick* actress who does *girl on girl* professionally, but is not a *tennis fan* in real life.

these shares pay dividends *exclam.* One of many announcements to be made prior to *dropping a gut.* See also *our survey said; going once, going twice; I smell with my little nose, something beginning with; please hold for the president; I'll name that tune in one etc.*

the slot it's not *1. exclam.* On Real Radio North East's erstwhile *Gary and Lisa Breakfast Show,* the clue that told listeners which of the vending machine slots the prize money wasn't in; thus making winning the jackpot marginally easier for subsequent contestants. 2. n. The *bonus tunnel*.

the sustain – listen to it *exclam.* A quote from *This is Spinal Tap* where Nigel shows off one of his favourite guitars. 2. *exclam.* Something to say to pass the time while dropping a very long *Bakewell tart*.

they call the wind Mariah *exclam.* Jocose reference to the Lerner and Loewe song from *Paint Your Wagon*, made by someone who has just dropped a particularly melodious *Exchange and Mart*. See also *speak on sweet lips that never told a lie, better an eviction than a bad tenant etc.*

they never mentioned that in the forecast *exclam.* A humorous remark uttered after someone has *dropped a gut*.

they're firing Sir, they're firing! *exclam.* A humorous riposte to a *rumpet voluntary*. See also *well struck Sir.*

they're playing our tune again darling *exclam.* Sparkling repartee after *the band strikes up*. See also *an excellent theory Dr Watson, what's that Sweep?* and many, many more.

thick as a ghurka's foreskin *sim.* Descriptive of someone who is as *thick as a Welshman's cock.*

thickening up *adj.* To be in the early stages of erectile tumescence. The penile equivalent to that moment when you're stirring a pan of Bisto on the hob and it suddenly starts to look and behave a bit like gravy. *Getting a bit of blood in it. 'You'll have to excuse me sitting down while I read this next disgusting continental hardcore scan magazine, Mrs Whitehouse, only I'm definitely thickening up in spite of myself.' 'Feel free, Lord Longford. I'm as horrified as you at these explicit photographs of depraved behaviour, yet I am ashamed to admit that, against my better judgement, I'm dripping like a fucked fridge here.'*

thicker than a butcher's wrist *sim.* Notably girthsome. *'I swear on the Holy Bible, Mother Superior, his Charlie was thicker than a butcher's wrist. I could barely get it in my mouth, and I play the bass harmonica.'*

thicker than Jack Grealish's Calves *sim.* Said of an *intellectually challenged* individual spouting utter *bollocks*. A reference to the stoutly legged Manchester City pig-bladder-botherer.

thick lit *n.* Rabble-pleasing novels by the likes of Andy McNab, Dan Brown, Barbara Cartland *etc.*, that do not typically come within the purview of your Radio 4 literary bluestockings.

thick repeater *n.* A large bore, semi-automatic, single barrel *mutton musket*.

thick spunk *n.* Extremely fertile, high motility *spaff. Jitler* that requires factor 40 contraception. *'I've got eight brothers and six sisters thanks to Pop's thick spunk. Gee whiz, his sperm count is so high, I'll bet mom has to chew before swallowing.'* (Little Jimmy Osmond interviewed in *Look In*, 1972).

thigh breaker *n.* Having to hover over the porcelain in a filthy public *shithouse* after a *badger* unexpectedly makes its presence felt *at the back door*.

thighbrows *n.* A profusion of bikini overspill. *Loose baccy, whack-os, Jeremy Clarkson's eyebrows.*

thigh's the limit, the *exclam.* Said by a prudish young lady who will only allow her ardent suitor to touch the top of her leg and not her *stench trench*.

thightanic *n.* A lady whose upper legs have enormously *lovely personalities*.

thigh ticklers *n.* Bugger's grips, face fannies, sideboards. *'Ooh, Dr Rhodes Boyson. What a magnificent set of thigh ticklers.' 'Thank-you, your majesty.'*

thine *n.* The seamless blending of a lady's thighs into her spine without any intervening *bummocks* on a scrawny woman.

thin film of dust, all over the telly like a *sim.* Said of someone who is never off the fucking box. *'Bugger me. That Romesh Ranganathan is all over the telly like a thin film of dust, isn't he?'*

thinge, the *n.* A lady's *undersmile* so monstrous that it resembles an animatronic special effect from a 1980s horror film directed by John Carpenter.

think of the money shot *n.* In *bongo videography*, the less than enthusiastic expression on the lead actress's face as Ron Jeremy, Bill Margold or Ben Dover, or possibly all three, empty their *pods* into it.

think outside the box *1. v.* Yet another meaningless corporate buzzword expression commonly used by the sort of desperate utter *arseholes* who appear on programmes like *The Apprentice. 2. v.* The actions of a thoughtful gentleman in bed, *ie.* One who doesn't immediately focus his attentions on his ladyfriend's *cludge*, but considerately mashes her *tits* for a couple of minutes first.

think outside the box *v.* To consider anal sex.

thinkpod *1. n.* An individual, quiet oasis of contemplation provided for each Scottish MP in their parliamentary building. *2. n.* A works *bog* cubicle used as a place of solitude and relaxation, a base for formulating company policy, playing Angry Birds, or simply *wanking oneself blind*.

thin lizzy *n.* An undercracker *skidmark*. From the verse in that group's song *Dancing in the Moonlight (It's caught me in its spotlight)* which goes "I should have took that last bus home / But I asked you for a dance / Now we go steady to the pictures / I always get chocolate stains on my pants."

thinternet *n.* The diaphanously gossamer worldwide web which intermittently manages to squeeze asthmatically out of your router after you pay a major national telecommunications company for (insert unrealistically big number of MBs here) broadband. *Fraudband, lie-fi.*

third and bird *1. n.* Title, apparently, of a charming CBeebies programme. *2. n. rhym. slang.* A *feeshee.* *'Hold my calls please, Moneypenny. I'm off for a third and bird.'*

third leg *1. n.* Cricketing position between mid-off and gully. *2. n.* The *middle stump.*

third place, the *n.* Splaystation *2.* The *arse.*

third rail, the *1. n.* Means of providing electricity to a railway locomotive or train *via* a rigid, semi-continuous conductor placed alongside or between the rails of the track. And if you wee on it, you'll die, and that's true. *2. n.* A particularly well-wrought *hard-on.* An impressive length *of pink steel.*

third up, the *euph.* Building site terminology for a mistake. From the fact that in the construction industry there are three "ups", *ie.* "Muck up, tea up and fuck up".

third way, the *1. n.* Tony Blair's way of combining traditional socialist and conservative policies. *2. n.* Anal sex.

thirsty alsatian, lap it like a *sim.* To commit the filthy act of *cumulonimbus* with all the gusto of a parched *shit machine* with its nose in a puddle.

thirsty binman, faster than a *sim.* A classist description of someone doing something very hastily, in the manner of a sprinting refuse collector who is keen to finish his shift and tuck into a few jars and a farmhouse breakfast. *'Here's my column for the Sunday paper, Tony.'* *'Fucking hell, Tony. You've finished that faster than a thirsty binman.'*

thirty-four-and-a-halfer *n.* A hermit blessed with the miraculous ability to perform *horatio* upon himself. A *human cannonballer.*

this is the way *exclam.* Solemn Mandalorian declaration made after a thunderous *trump* rasps off their bescar *undercrackers.*

This Morning sickness *n. medic.* When you become so sick and tired of inane daytime television programmes that you start to seriously consider going out and getting a job.

thistle funnel *1. n.* A piece of laboratory glassware used by a chemist to add liquid to an existing system or apparatus. *2. n.* Name given to the *pudendas* of a rather rough member of the fairer s*x. *'Why are you chatting her up, Dave? She looks like she has a right thistle funnel on her.'*

this update will be installed later tonight *exclam.* A prediction following an excitingly spicy – or badly cooked – meal.

this will get you on your feet *exclam.* Something to announce before *the wind cries Mary. Also I'm just going to exercise my constitutional right.*

Thora bird *n.* A *nana Kournikova.*

thoracic park *n.* Any venue heaving with ladies who possess well-developed *chest-bumps.*

Thora Hird *1. n. prop.* Pelican-throated actress of stairlift testimonial fame, no longer alive at time of going to press. *2. n. rhym. slang.* A *Sir Douglas.*

Thoras *n. medic.* The *Brads, Kurts.*

thorn in my shite *euph.* A real *pain in the arse.*

Thorntons, little bit of *sim.* Euphemism used when attempting to talk the wife into a bit of *backdoor action.* From the famous gift toffee manufacturer's advertising slogan, *ie.* "Skilled in the ways of the chocolatier". *'Roll over, love. I fancy a little bit of Thorntons tonight.'*

thought for the day *1. euph.* Switching off the bedside wireless at about 7.45am and embarking on one's last bout of *how's your father* before getting up for work. *2. n.* A blast of *shitey* early morning *guff* that causes you to bury your head in the pillow.

thought shower *1. n.* Stupid business-speak term for a brainstorming session. Which is also a stupid business-speak term in itself. *2. n.* At the moment of *spaffing*, conjuring up mental images of attractive women from work.

thousand island dressing *n.* The sauce which coats one's *naughty spoon* after tossing the *gorilla salad* when *cranberry dip* is on the menu.

thousand mile service *euph.* A woman's *unclean time*, when she is *up on blocks.* A regular four-weekly *oil and filter change.*

thrap *v.* To masturbate furiously, to give it *six nowt* on the *Right Honourable Member for Pantchester.* Also *thrape, fap fap fap.*

thraptop *n.* A computer device used for trawling the worldwide web for the best/newest in *Frankie Vaughanographic* clips. *Filth machine, dirty mac, flaptop, faptop.*

thrashroom *n.* A word which, if mumbled sufficiently quickly, can sound a little like "bathroom".

thrash your hat *v.* To *relax in a gentleman's way.* From the lyrics of the unforgettable Paul Young hit, *viz.* "'Cos I'm the type of guy who is always on the road. Wherever I thrash my hat that's my home."

threadripper *n.* A very powerful *air-drop* that sounds like it has – and, indeed, may well have – torn the stitches of your underwear and/or trousers.

thread the lead *n.* To attempt to insert the *old chap* into a *mouse's ear*, usually while in an advanced state of refreshment and with one eye closed and the tongue stuck out in concentration.

thread the needle *v.* To go for a liquid *dump* after a powerfully spicesome *Ruby Murray*. *'I'm just going outside to thread the needle. I may be some time.'*

three bears shit *n.* A poo – typically but not exclusively a dog *shite* – that comes in three sections; rock solid at one end, runny at the other end but "just right" in the middle. Also known as a *Goldilocks dump*.

three-bed semi *1. n.* A medium-sized dwelling that would cost about eight quid in Middlesrough or £500 million in London. *2. n.* A *chopper* taking on such an excessive workload that its performance is being adversely affected.

three bells in a row *1. n.* A disappointingly low payout on a *Glasgow piano*. *2. n.* Finding all three urinals in a public lavatory unoccupied, thus allowing one the luxury of a comfortably relaxed *gypsy's kiss*.

three bogs full *n.* An impressive volume of *feeshus* that requires multiple flushes of the *jobby engine* before the water in the pan returns to its usual consistency. A *long haul shite*.

three card trick *n. rhym slang.* Prick, dick. *'She got her jazz bands round me three card trick and started giving it six nowt.'*

three cocks to the cunt *euph.* Con gusto. Doing anything to the extreme, *eg.* Driving at 180mph down a country lane, drinking vodka in pint glasses, driving at 180mph down a country lane while drinking vodka in pint glasses. *'Ferdinand Hiller remembered Sterndale Bennett's piano playing as "perfect in mechanism, and, while remarkable for an extraordinary delicacy of nuance in the quieter passages of the Mendelssohn Barcarolle, full of soul and fire in the finale, which he always played three cocks to the cunt".'* (Cecil Gaybody, writing in *Classic FM* Magazine).

three coiler *n.* A canine *turd*, the curled and crimped result of not having walked the dog, usually found on a carpet or light-coloured sofa cushion.

three counters Ben, I think I'm gonna risk it for *exclam.* Said before one breaks wind. Also *please hold for the president; our survey said.*

three-darter *n.* A person of such *big-boned-ness* that one couldn't hit their weight on a dartboard

with three arrows.

three-dayer *n.* A *dump* so large it looks like it could incorporate yesterday's, today's and tomorrow's *foulage*.

three day event *n.* A swift half after work on Friday, which lasts all weekend until you return to the office on Monday morning, much to the chagrin of the *bread knife*.

three dick gob *n.* A capacious mouth. *'The next record is You're So Vain by Carly Simon, the lady with the three dick gob. And it's for Terry, who is seven today. Lots of love from mummy, daddy, nana and granpa Johnson and nana Robins.'*

three D printer *n.* The *arse*.

three-fag omelette *n.* For a non-smoker, the satisfying yet unfamiliar pattie of phlegm coughed up the morning after having drunk enough to *ponce* a few fags off a mate at about ten past eleven.

three flush turd *1. n.* An *everlasting bog stopper.* *2. n.* A person that you simply can't get rid of. *'Today's birthdays: Emma Thompson, thesp, 1959; Marty Wilde, antediluvian pop star, 1939; Lord Jeffrey Archer of Weston-super-Mare, Parliamentary three flush turd, 1940.'*

three for a bob *rhym. slang.* The *corn on the cob*, the *Teddington Lock.*

three inch soilpipe, fanny like a *sim.* Charming plumber-speak to describe the genital accoutrements of a lady whose *bodily treasure* is very much at the other end of the tightness scale from a *mouse's ear*.

three-in-one oil *n.* Any expensive *tart fuel* that is pretty much guaranteed to ease access to all the important moving parts of a *bike*.

three-legged race *n.* When *fuckstruck*, to stumble up the stairs with a *bone on*.

three meals ahead and two shits behind *phr.* Said of a *Lord of the pies.*

three mile island *n.* An extremely noxious rectal meltdown with a half-life of about ten minutes. A *Smellafield*.

three-panter *n.* A horror film or experience so terrifying that you have to change your *undercrackers* at least twice.

three-pegger *n.* Someone who requires three pegs to hang their pants on the line. A *salad dodger.*

three piece suite *n.* That which has to be plumped up and rearranged on a regular basis to ensure seated comfort. The *Meat and two veg, wedding tackle.* The male *undercarriage*.

three pipe problem *1. euph.* A case so perplexing that Arthur Conan Doyle's great detective Sherlock Holmes was forced to retire and ponder it carefully while smoking. *2. euph.* Issues of complex familial infidelity and possible paternity so perplexing that they were only ever examined on *the Jeremy Kyle Show*.

three quarters of half a soft on *euph.* When a chap's cock has almost got a bit of a lazy lob on, but not quite. *'Sasparilla was powerless to resist. His eyes burnt into hers like lab-grown cristinites. His strong arms enfolded her softly yielding body as she felt herself being swept away on a vertically oriented, rotating atmospheric vortex of passion. "Take me, Figaro! Take me now!" she gasped. "Sorry, love," replied Doctor Fernando. "I just had one off the wrist over the bra pages of me mam's Freeman's catalogue, so I won't even be able to manage three quarters of half a soft on for at least another twenty minutes."'* (from *The Gypsy Ballerina Princess and the Tree Surgeon* by Barbara Cartland).

three S's, the *euph.* A chap's morning ablutions, *viz.* "A Shower, a Shit and a Shave". Not really sure about the apostrophe in there, but what can you do? And you'd probably want to have the shower *after* the shit, all things considered. Re-arrange them how you like, really. The *shushes*.

three times a lady *1. n.* Title of a heartfelt love song that Lionel Richie dedicated to his wife, who he later divorced. *2. n.* A female who will happily provide three ports of ingress to her happy beau.

three wank hangover *n.* Semi-terminal *brewer's flu;* an attack of *beer cancer* so brutal that the sufferer cannot even consider getting out of bed before he has committed a trio of *monomanual self-debasements*.

three-wheeler *n. rhym. slang. Lesbian.* From three-wheeled trike, which is a popular means of transport for *women in comfortable shoes*.

three wipe problem *euph.* When a trifecta of salvos from the *burly* are required in order to clear the *chocolate speedway* of all *clag, winnets, tagnuts* and *klingons*. Named in honour of Victorian detective Sherlock Holmes's favoured solution when faced with particularly complex mysteries. *'It is quite a three wipe problem and I beg you won't speak to me for fifty minutes, Dr Watson.'*

Thresher's shark *n.* An inebriate who circles around outside the town off-licence offering to buy drink for under-18s in return for a small commission.

thrilled to the marrow *adj.* Visibly delighted in one's trousers. *'Eeh by gum, Dame Helen, 'appen I'm thrilled to the marrow to have you on the show again.'*

thriller in manila *n.* Intriguing brown paper package with an Amsterdam postmark.

thripe *n.* The so-called "three-stroke method"

of wiping one's *arse*, as recommended by parsimonious parents, factory overseers, orphanage managers *etc.* That is to say, "one back, one forward, and one to polish."

throatmanship *n.* The noble art of gagless *horatio*, as practised by the late actress Linda Lovelace. Also *throatsmanship*.

throat singing *1. n.* Popular form of vocal entertainment in the Inuit community. Like Lee Marvin doing *I Was Born Under a Wonderin' Star* but by an Eskimo. *2. n.* Vomiting loudly after downing twelve pints of watered-down lager at a rock festival.

throbbin' hood *n. coll. Notts.* A sore *fiveskin*. A *Little John* that as been excessively "made merry on".

throbbledegook *n.* The rubbish a bloke promises his missus whilst he is nursing a *bone-on*. *'But you said you'd take me somewhere expensive.' 'Nah love, that was just a bit of throbbledegook. Nip out and get me a Yorkie, would you?'*

throb on *n.* A *wide on*, *slop on*.

throbservation *n.* When a fellow notices a particularly attractive prospect, and consequently experiences an involuntary palpitation amongst his *wedding vegetables*.

throne *n.* The monarch's *bum sink*.

throne bone *n.* The *bonk-on* that sometimes pops up temptingly while a young man is *dropping a length of dirty spine*.

throne call *n.* A mobile phone conversation during which the recipient is unaware that you are simultaneously *dropping the kids off at the pool*. Also *dirty phonecall*.

throne of games *n.* Male idea of multi-tasking. Combining a nice, sit-down *poo* with a few games of Candy Crush Saga.

throne room *n.* The downstairs *shit palace* at Windsor Castle. *'Now you're not taking them Leonardo da Vinci metalpoints in the throne room are you, Charles?'*

throng *adj.* Descriptive of a fashionably skimpy item of intimate apparel being worn by someone who really should have known better, *eg.* Women *with nice personalities* or oldies. From thong + wrong. *'Did you see what Bob's bird was wearing when she bent over?' 'Aye Joe, that's just throng, that.'*

throttle pit *n. Aus.* The *dunny*. Toilet, *cludgie, khazi*.

throttle the turkey *v.* To masturbate in Norfolk. *'I just throttled the turkey and it was boodiful, really boodiful.'*

througher *n.* A 24-hour drinking session. A *Leo Sayer, MGM*.

throw *v.* To *barf, hoy, chuck*.

throwabout *n.* A petite woman who can be easily

and casually "thrown about" from one position to another during sex. A *laptop.*

throw a brick down the well *v.* To pass a particularly solid *Douglas, causing* a loud splash in the *pan* that can be heard throughout the home or workplace.

throw air *v.* To play a bit of musique concrète on your *brass eye.*

throw a pot *v.* To *drop a log* that looks like something done against the clock on the *Generation Game* by a flustered middle-aged woman in a trouser suit.

throw ass *v. US.* To *take a dump, shit, defeesheate.* *'I'm afraid Barack can't come to the phone, Mrs Merkel. He's just throwing ass at the moment.'*

throwing a Woodbine up Northumberland Street, like *sim. NE.* A disparaging reference to unsatisfying sex with a *bucket-twatted* individual. Also *throwing a sausage up Briggate* (Leeds), *chucking a fag down Parliament Street* (Nottingham). *'Why man, it was like throwing a Woodbine up Northumberland Street.'*

throw in the brown towel *v.* To give up up trying to persuade the missus to let you *kick her back doors in.* *'It's me and your nan's golden wedding anniversary coming up, so I've decided to finally throw in the brown towel.'*

throw it in her, I'd *phr. US.* Decidedly offensive and sexist aside made to friends (typically at a party, the pub or the House of Commons debating chamber) in reference to an attractive young *piece of crumpet.*

throw me a clip *1. exclam.* Desperate request for more ammunition, often shouted heroically across the battlefield to a fellow soldier during big-budget action movies. *2. exclam.* Desperate request for more *shit scrape,* often shouted heroically across the landing and/or down the stairs.

throw meat at the problem *v.* Of a couple whose relationship is on the rocks, to engage in a last-ditch act of penetrative romance.

thrown off Love Island, get oneself *v. euph.* To have a *wank. 'Are you coming out for a drink after work?' 'Nah, I think I'll go home and get myself thrown off Love Island. Twice.'*

throw one's cap into the hangar *v. milit.* To have sex with a lady who is endowed with a *poacher's pocket.* From the naval act of throwing a rating's hat into the *Simon Cowells* of a through-deck cruiser. Also *throwing a kitbag in a dry dock.*

throw out the garbage *v.* To flush out one's *spooge pipe,* have a *pipecleaner.*

throw the clay *n.* To commence the construction of

a *coil pot* on the *potter's wheel.*

throw the meat dart at the brown bullseye *v.* To *bott,* hopefully not while Tony Green stands next to you, saying: "Okay, take your time. Nice and easy, nice and easy. Settle in now. You've got all the time in the world."

throw the towel in *1. v.* Of a boxing trainer, to concede defeat when his fighter is getting his *fucking* head kicked in. *2. v.* To give up trying to have a *poke* because the missus has *got the painters and decorators in. 3. v.* Of a lady, to casually insert a *mouse.*

throw your bollocks at the clock *exclam.* An exclamation of total exasperation. *'We've been talking about the future of power sharing in Northern Ireland for five weeks now, and they still won't sit in the same bloody room. It's enough to make you want to throw your bollocks at the clock.'* (Senator George Mitchell, Report on the Northern Ireland Peace Process).

thru'penny bits *1. rhym. slang.* Tits. *2. n. rhym. slang.* The *shits.*

thrushian roulette *n.* The risky practice of *slipping* the missus *a length* while she's cooking a small loaf of *cunt bread.*

thrush's chest *n.* The appearance of the *Ark Royal landing deck* following a visit from any bird of the genus *Turdus. The starting line at Brands Hatch.*

thruster *n. medic.* A muscle, somewhere in the neck or jaw, the tensing of which forces out stubborn *shits* and *farts.*

thrusties *n.* Delightful morning repast served tigerishly to an overnight guest.

thumb a ride on the rocket *adj.* To *take Captain Picard to warp speed.*

thumb bumming *v. Touching last night's tea.*

thumb in bum, mind in neutral *phr.* A vacant state of blissful ignorance of one's environment, *eg.* While queuing at the post office, waiting for a bus, or preparing one's Autumn Budget Statement.

thumbing in a slacky *n.* An optimistic bout of lovemaking for which the gentleman's spirit is willing, but his flesh is weak. *Pushing a marshmallow into a moneybox.*

thumbing the putty *1. n.* Glaziers' argot for running a line of linseed oil-based sealant around a new pane of glass with one's pollical digit. *2. euph.* Attempting to initiate possibly unsatisfactory intercourse following a night on the ale.

thumbrise *n.* The time of day at which a fellow in a loving relationship is allowed out of the house by his other half, to go for a quick drink with his mates. See also *thumbset.*

thumbrosis *n. medic.* A fatal condition caused by

vigorous overtwanging of the *banjo string*; a *grot* accident. See also *remote controlapse*.

thumbset *n.* Having left the house at *thumbrise*, the time by which a *birdseed* has to be back in the house with his *pink handcuffs* on.

thumper *1. n.* A big, pounding erection, a *stalk*, a *stiffy*. *2. n.* In the Walt Disney film *Bambi*, the annoying rabbit who, if the extracts shown every fucking week on *Screen Test* were anything to go by, spent the entire movie encouraging the lead character to walk out onto a frozen pond.

thumpology *n.* The resolution of disputes by recourse to physical argument. *Closing time counselling, chin music.*

thump one off *v.* To masturbate in a somewhat heavy-handed manner, in the style of the Honey Monster *knocking one out* over the *titpants* pages in his mum Henry McGee's *Grattan Catalogue*.

thunderarms *n.* Overdeveloped limbs as often seen on middle-aged female *salad dodgers*. Often adorned with masterpieces of the tattooist's art. Also *bingo wings, dinner ladies' arms.*

thunder bags *n.* Underpants, *trolleys.*

thunderbirds *n.* Women of ample proportions. *Barge arses, size aeros.*

Thunderbird two *1. n.* Virgil Tracey's heavy equipment transporter. *2. n.* A faecal bolus of such generous proportions that it could easily contain a miniature submarine, fire engines and assorted mining equipment.

thunderbolt *n.* A sudden *number two* which startles onlookers and scares birds.

thunderbox *n. arch.* Lavatory, *shitter.* Also *thunder bowl.*

thunderbox shuffle *1. n.* A song by short-arsed Skiffle king Lonnie Donnegan that reached no.3 in 1960. *2. n.* The *arse* dance performed while sitting on the *chod bin* trying to *get* the *pit bull out of the kennel.*

thundercrack *n.* The kind of *fart* that requires one to check one's *kex* for *thunderbolts*. A *squench.*

thunderdoming *n.* A *spitroast* which is prematurely curtailed due to one of the male participants pulling out after remembering he has left the gas on or similar. Named after the cage-fighting venue superintended by Tina Turner in the third *Mad Max* film where "two men enter – one man leaves".

thunder from down under, the *n.* Nickname for Aussie snooker giant Neil Robertson.

thunder handed *adj.* Descriptive of one who manually *pleasures* a lady with in a vigorous, aggressive and rough manner, like you would imagine an old-fashioned steam locomotive

fireman, all-in wrestler or shipyard plate riveter might.

thunder mug *n.* Chamber pot, *guzunda.*

thunderous applause *n.* The loud appreciation shown by your digestive system to last night's jalfrezi, that is enough to tear the roof off the place.

thunderslash *n.* A splendidly loud urination delivered *con gusto* directly into the water of the pot. A *dad's piss*, a *round of applause*, a *standing ovation.*

thunders of darkness *1. n.* Song by black metal band Immortal, founded by lead singer and guitarist Abbath Doom Occulta (real name Cedric Tinkle). *2. n.* Guinness-fuelled flatulence.

thunderthumbs *n. prop.* Nickname of Level 42 bassist Mark King.

thunderturds are go! *exclam.* Announced before launching a small, brown-coloured submersible that eventually settles on the sea-bed. Or in a nearby river.

thunt *n.* When fat thighs trick you into thinking you may have seen a bit of *flange.*

thus spake the coracle *exclam.* Dafydd's jocular rejoinder, when Myffanwy's *Welsh canoe* – in oratorical mode – emits a particularly rousing *queef*. Also *Hear this men of Harlech* or *hearken to the Bard.*

tiara, tramp's *n.* A bobble hat.

Tibetan blackbird *n.* A huge and voluminous *shite* of the kind experienced by impoverished student types after subsisting on a diet of lentils and brown rice for half a term. Derived from the Latin name for the aforementioned oriental fowl, viz. *Turdus maximus. 'Where are you off to, Chris? We're on air in thirty seconds.' 'Sorry Michaela. I'm off to the khazi to free a Tibetan blackbird.'*

tickets for the away end *n.* Anal sex. *'Arsenal are at home. So I might try and get tickets for the away end.'*

tickets to the dirt track *n.* Toilet paper. Also *bumwad, turd tokens, chocolate shark bait, burly, brown shield stamps, clag rag, job application forms.*

ticket to tottieville *euph.* See *token for the cockwash, pink ticket.*

tickle Fat Ed *v.* Of a fellow, to *pleasure himself* in a leisurely, almost lackadaisical manner. As one would do on a chaise-longue in a gazebo, or in a blazer and straw boater while drifting in a punt.

ticklers *n.* Corrugated condoms, amusing *French letters* which are ribbed for your pleasure.

tickle tackle *n.* Anteater's nose, cock collar, lace curtains. The *fiveskin* or a *Charlie* so equipped.

tickle the baby *v.* To engage in a spot of sexual

intercourse with a pregnant ladyfriend. *'What was the milkman doing upstairs?' 'Nothing love. He was just tickling the baby.'*

tickle the ivories *v.* To give someone a smack in the mouth, resulting in a sound like the lid being slammed shut on a badly tuned pub piano.

tickle the ovaries *v.* What Russ Conway used to do to Mrs Conway on a Friday night.

tickle the pickle *v.* To *jerk the gherkin.*

tickle your pip *v.* To be aroused sexually by Leslie Philips or Terry-Thomas.

tickling the scampi *v.* A means of getting *fish fingers.* Feminine *monkey spanking.*

tickling the turtle's nose *n.* A wipe which gets the *turtle's autograph* on the paper, but which doesn't, in any meaningful sense, get the job done.

TIC/tic *1. abbrev. legal.* Take Into Consideration. *2. abbrev. legal.* Thick Ignorant Cunt.

tiddle the wink *v.* To *flick the bean, stab the cat, smack the clam, play the gusset piano.*

tidemark *n.* The staining on a *gentleman's pickle* after it is withdrawn from the *rusty sheriff's badge.*

tied by the brown rope *adj.* To be confined to the *chod bin* by an intractable *Brad.*

tier three tapas *n.* Token Lockdown nourishment, *eg.* Scotch eggs, crisps, peanuts, served by public houses in order to circumvent strict lockdown regulations by claiming they were serving "substantial meals" to drinkers.

tiffin *n.* An afternoon *fuck* up the *cunt* off Sid James in a pith helmet.

tiffter *n.* An unwanted erection or *Jake.*

tiger bread *1. n.* Visually alluring but strangely flavourless loaf that is sold in supermarkets. *2. n.* Appearance of the sponge after giving one's inadequately wiped *ringpiece* a quick buff-up in the shower.

tiger's back *n.* The decorative striped effect left in the *pan* after a particularly sticky *Meat Loaf's daughter* has *gone to the beach.*

tiger's face *n.* The *wind sketch* inscribed in your *Bill Grundies* after a soggy *air biscuit* that would certainly make Siegfried and Roy jump. Well, Roy anway.

tight as a bullfighter's pants *sim.* Particularly parsimonious. Also *tight as a shark's arse. 'Don't expect my brother to get a round in. He's tight as a bullfighter's pants.'*

tighter than a ballet dancer's snatch *sim.* Descriptive of one whose wallet needs prizing open when it's their round.

tighter than airport security *sim.* Description of a frigid *bird;* one who "refuses to take any liquids

on board".

tighter than a teenage wanker's curtains *sim.* Descriptive of something which is very secure. *'And as the King's carriage glides majestically up to the steps of the Palace of Westminster, security is, of course, tighter than a teenage wanker's curtains.'*

tightie *n. medic. Scots.* The feeling of discomfort experienced when attempting to peel back the *fiveskin* due to it being stuck to the *helmet* with *cheese.* Possibly something to do with the humid atmosphere found inside a kilt.

Tijuana bible *n.* A *jazz mag.*

Tijuana cha-cha *n. medic.* The *trots.* See *sour apple quickstep, Mexican screamers.*

Tilbury triathlon *n.* A race to evade arrest when caught thieving at the picturesque Essex port, which alternately involves running, swimming and cycling. Also *rucking* and climbing fences.

tile hanger's nailbags *sim.* Sagging, lumpy *Charlies. 'She had tits like a tile hanger's nailbags.'*

till Wednesday at twelve *exclam.* A nifty and sneaky way of calling your boss a *twat* while ostensibly organising a meeting. Also *that was absolutely tremendous, there we are then.*

tilly tubbies *n.* The shaven-headed, morbidly-obese security staff in your local store who couldn't outrun Thora Hird, even after she was dead.

timber merchant *1. n.* Typically the man in a town who has the fewest number of complete fingers remaining on his hands. *2. n.* A person who gives you wood. *'That Claire in accounts, she's a right timber merchant she is.' 3. n.* A reliable male *grumble* thespian, a *woodsman, cocksmith, punctual plumber.*

time and a turd *n.* The art of having a *Tom tit* at work while being paid overtime by an unwitting employer. *Taking one in the company's time,* an *I'm alright cack.*

time and lotion study *n.* What many a red-blooded male gets up to when he's supposed to be working from home. Yes, it's *wanking* again.

time & tissues, I need some *phr.* A request from a man who needs people to give him some space so he can *pull himself together.*

timebomb fuse *n.* A length of string emanating from a lady's *bodily treasure,* from which a trained expert can infer that a violent, explosive outburst is imminent. Also known as a *party popper, mouse's tail, sluice noose, fishwick.*

time machine, the *n.* A cubicle device into which travellers lock themselves before emerging at some point in the future; the lavatory. The passage of time is not apparent while the subject sits on the seat, especially when engrossed in a copy of *AutoTrader, Razzle*, or *Viz*. '*I announced to my wife that I was going to test the time machine and that I knew not when, or indeed if, I would eventually emerge. Later, after I had opened a window, I checked my watch to find that a full two-and-a-half hours had elapsed, the washing up had been done, and my good lady had run off with the window cleaner.*'

time off in loo *n.* Industrial productivity lost due to *sweet wrapper* breaks during working hours.

time team *euph.* The regulars in your local pub to whom you invariably find yourself talking, even though you hate them. Much like watching the erstwhile Sunday tea-time television show of the same name, the experience is strangely depressing and you're not entirely sure why you started doing it in the first place. It's even more profoundly dispiriting when you realise that you are a member of your own *time team*'s *time teams* too.

Time Team bonus *n.* Special treat for the grub-by-minded fans of televised archaeological digs. Occured when an attractive female undergraduate was filmed working avidly at some compacted earth with her trowel or little brush, allowing the cameraman to frame an excellent shot of her unfettered breasts wobbling excitedly within her University of East Anglia T-shirt.

time team, do a *v.* To re-boot a casual sexual relationship with an ex-girlfriend. To *open up a second trench.*

time to water the cactus *euph. Women's things.* From the fact that a lazy man often uses his wife or girlfriend's *thousand mile service* interval as a reminder to perform his regular monthly chores. Also *time to to pay the rent, time to worm the cat, time to feed the ducks.*

Tim Henman *n.* A *penis* which promises great things but fails to achieve anything even vaguely resembling hardness, *ie.* It doesn't even get to the *semi* stage.

Tim Henman's trophy cabinet, as empty as *sim.* Wittily descriptive of something that has little or no contents. '*I'm going to have to go shopping soon. The fridge is as empty as Tim Henman's trophy cabinet.*'

Timmy twostroke *n.* A gentleman blessed with the enviable ability to *blow his stack* after a couple of *cock stabs*. A *two-push Charlie, speaking clock.*

Tim's dozen *n.* Generous portion of chips served with a Wetherspoons meal.

tincture *n.* An alcoholic drink taken for medicinal purposes, perhaps at breakfast time or during an early morning walk back from Boozebuster.

tinderbox *1. n.* A mature female with a *snatch* that has been lying fallow for so long that she has resorted to internet dating. *2. n.* A parched area of genital *scrub* that would go up like a rocket if someone were to accidentally discard a fag-end in it.

tinder eggs *1. n. medic.* Cause of itchiness around the groinal region after a one night stand arranged *via* a smartphone app. *2. n.* Those who have undergone significant hair loss and weight gain since their hirsute, svelte dating site profile pictures were taken.

Tinderella *n.* A female user of popular courtship software who cannot stay overnight due to undisclosed obligations, *eg.* She is married, turns into a pumpkin at midnight, is a chronic bed-wetter *etc.*

tinder miles *n.* An evaluation of the attractiveness of a prospective assignation, calculated according to how far one would be prepared to drive in order to *have it off* with them. '*She's reasonably fit, I suppose, but in tinder miles she's not really worth the petrol.*'

tinder surprise *1. n. medic.* An unexpected bout of *trench dick* contracted as a result of an intimate liaison organised through the eponymous smartphone application. *2. n.* The discovery that Natasha, the sexy, nymphomaniac, exotic, pouting Brazilian lingerie model on your smartphone, is actually Keith, a not-hugely-attractive dogfood factory worker from Grimsby.

tingler, the *1. n.* B-movie nasty featuring a spinal parasite which causes its screaming victims to fizz uncontrollably with horror. *2. n.* An *anal sphincter* with an eerily similar *modus operandi.*

tin, it does what it says on the *1. exclam.* Advertising slogan for a popular range of DIY timber treatments. *2. exclam.* A humorous remark made by a man to a person who is about to *polish his wood* while he lies back and observes.

Tinkerbell *n.* A delightfully delicate *dropped gut* of the sort that would follow a charming young lady round like a spangly cloud of iridescent glitter.

Tinkerbell's tampon *n.* A discarded filter from a roll-up cigarette.

tinker's curse *n.* An involuntary and highly ill-timed erection that somewhat takes the gloss off social occasions. '*Do you, Charles Philip Arthur George, take Diana Frances…oops, sorry about that. I've got the tinker's curse.*' (Dr Robert Runcie, speaking at the Marriage of Prince Charles and Lady Di, 1981).

tinker time *1. n.* On Channel 4's *Scrapheap*

678

Challenge, the extra hour that was allotted to the teams on the morning after the build, when they were allowed to make minor adjustments to their deathtraptions. *2. n.* Sunday afternoon televisual interlude enjoyed by bachelors when Lisa Rogers was on the screen.

tinkle on the ivories *1. v.* To play the piano, usually in a *half-arsed* sort of way, the opposite of going at it *three cocks to the cunt*. You could never accuse Oscar Peterson of *tinkling on the ivories*, for example, whereas it describes Richard *fucking* Clayderman's insipid noodlings to a tee. *2. v.* To participate in a particular sort of *watersport*. To take a *gypsy's* in a ladyfriend's *north and south*. Or on your piano keyboard.

tinny mallet *n.* A perfectly normal bloke, who turns into an utter, utter annoying *see you next Tuesday* after a couple of cans. A *halfpint Harry* or *two-pot screamer.*

tin of supermarket ham, like a *sim.* Said of the offspring of a *woman of easy virtue*, in that its origins are from "mystery meat".

tin of Vim with an apple on top *sim.* A fictitious penis measurement.

Tinsley flyover *1. n.* The M1 bridge that joins/divides glamorous Sheffield to/from dingy Rotherham and its sewage works, and hence *2. n.* The *taint, no man's land*, the *Baker Street concourse.*

tin-snip sisters *n.* Particularly butch *lezzers.*

tinter *1. n.* High class *totty,* top class *talent.* 'That Mick Hucknall's a jammy get. A face like his and he still gets all the top tinter.' *2. n.* A lady's *barse*, because "'tin't 'er arse and 'tin't 'er fanny". The *taint, werntfor.*

Tin-Tin *1. n. prop.* Boy detective hero of them books done by that Belgian. *2. n. prop.* Nickname for a chap who has a small *winky*. From northern lasses' plaintive cry of "'Ti'n't in, love. Try pushing a bit harder."

tip drip *n.* The final trickle of urine which cannot be unloosed by shaking and squeezing, preferring instead to wait until your member is safely tucked away before making a cheekily amusing cameo appearance in you boxer shorts and down your leg.

tip one's skip *v.* Term used in polite company when one needs to visit the bathroom for a *number two*. 'Where's Oates? He's been gone ages.' 'I think he's went out to tip his skip, Captain.'

tippexing *n.* The act of *whiting out* a tattoo on the small of an Essex lady's back. 'I had not intended to love Mr Rochester; the reader knows I had wrought hard to extirpate from my soul the germs of love there detected; and yet now, as he stood up and wiped his bell end on the curtains after tippexing my tramp stamp, they spontaneously revived, great and strong!' (from *Jane Eyre* by Charlotte Brontë).

tipping point *1. n.* Intellectually unchallenging tuppenny waterfalls-based television gameshow presented by Ben Shephard. *2. n.* Sudden moment of panic immediately following the *turtle's head*, when it instantly becomes a matter of the utmost urgency that you be seated on a *crapper*, ideally with your *trolleys* around your ankles and well out of harm's way. 'I'm at tipping point, dear, so I'm off to drop zone one.'

tipping point *n.* That critical moment during a bout of *firkyfoodling* when the clutch starts to bite.

tipping the barrow *n.* The minimum effort required in order to deposit one's *rubbish*. 'I thought I was just going to fart, but I accidentally overcooked it, tipped the barrow and dropped my shopping.'

tipping the teapot *n.* Situation which occurs when, owing to a fully or semi-erectivated state, a fellow is unable to aim his *tassel* at the toilet bowl for a *slash* and must therefore bend his whole body to attain the required angle of incidence.

tipping the velvet *n.* Of TV companies, the practice of promising *full-nutted* viewers explicit *lesbo cumulonimbus* in order to boost ratings.

tipple *n.* The very *tittermost* tip of the nipple.

tipsy nipsy *n. medic.* Alcohol-induced loosening of the *balloon knot*, usually resulting in the need for a boil-wash or bonfire.

tipsy-turvy *adj.* Characteristic of a *heavily refreshed* person's footing while promenading on *legs like snapped candles.*

tip-toe through the two lips *euph.* Of a lady, to gently strum her *invisible ukulele*, to *let her fingers do the porking.*

tip-toe tottie *n.* The various *wank pamphlets* adorning the top shelves of *Grumbelows*, thwarting the aspirations of shorter men such as "diddy" David Hamilton and "wee" Mrs Jimmy Krankie when he grows up.

tip-toe trap *n.* A public house lavatory which abstains from the operation of a regular cleansing regime, thus requiring the user to stand on tip-toes to avoid unpleasantness.

Tipton barbershop *n.* The harmonious chorus made up from the combined sirens of two police cars, an ambulance and a fire engine, all racing towards another "domestic incident" in the boisterous Black Country town of the same name. Usually heard at three in the morning, and typically followed by an hour-long *son et lumiere* courtesy of the West Midlands Police helicopter.

Tipton uppercut *n.* A knee in the *bollocks.*

TIPTOP/tiptop *abbrev.* A transsexual who has yet

to go the whole hog and is still mid-way through the gender re-alignment process. Tits In Place, Tackle Op Pending. A *bobby dazzler, flipper.*

tip your concrete *v.* A sophisticated term for ejaculation for when *cough your filthy yoghurt* seems inappropriately coarse. *'If you could just go into the booth and tip your concrete into this receptacle, sir.'*

tired dog's mouth, loose as a *sim. Aus.* A charmingly lyrical figure of speech which may be applied to the more accommodating maiden. *'Have you met my sister, Archbishop? I wouldn't say she's easy, but she's as loose as tired dog's mouth.'*

tired horse *n.* The situation whereby a lady's *nether regions* develop a sad, untidy and distressed appearance as she ages, eventually coming to resemble the sagging *mush* of Old Man Steptoe's nag Hercules. *'Until she turned the light on, your honour, I honestly thought I had been feeding a tired horse.'*

'tis a beast more bowel than man *exclam.* Dramatic proclamation upon the launch of a particularly animalistic *air biscuit.*

tisnae *n.* A scotch lassie's perineum. The *McSnarse.*

tisn'ts *n.* Very small, practically non-existent breasts. *Knockers* that barely merit the description *tits.*

tissent *n.* The *taint, tinter, tintis.*

tissue chrysanthemum *n.* Once dry, the shape of any piece of *bumwad* in which one has *caught the lads* at the culmination of a *ride on the great white knuckler. Porn cracker, wanker's crisp, discharge papers, bedroom popadoms.*

tissue of pies *n. medic. Greggcessive* bodily adiposity produced by the consumption of pastries.

tissue-tearer *n.* An explosive *pop shot.* Also known as a *sock wrecker.*

tit *n.* Small bird that likes nuts.

Titanic *n.* A lass who *goes down* first time out. An *Ikea bulb, taxi driver's clutch.*

titan punkvag *n.* One of them downward-pointing mohawks that you occasionally get between a woman's legs. See also *Ho Chi Minge.*

tit brisket *n.* The nourishing and flavoursome cut of meat that can be extracted from a man with a substantial set of *moobs. 'If we ever get trapped without food, I'm calling first dibs on Uncle Jim's tit brisket.'*

titcoins *n.* A currency popular with large-chested females that is regularly exchanged with weak-willed men in return for alcohol, meals, taxi fares *etc. Bouncing cheques.*

tit-dial *v.* Of a woman, or Lord Owen of the City of Plymouth, to accidentally call someone

from a smartphone while it is tucked inside their brassiere.

tit fairies *n.* Mythical visitors who magically transform the wife's *fried eggs* into *TNTs* during and after *sprogdrop.* Not that she'll let you on them for the next ten years.

titfer twat *n.* One of them hat-wearing celebrities such as Bonio, Jay Kay, Farrell or Olly Murs who think they look like Humphrey Bogart when, in actual fact, they look like *cuntish bellends.*

tit for brains *n.* A woman who makes up for her lack of intellectual capacity with a surfeit of *chesty substances. 'Born on this day: George Best, thirsty Northern Irish footballer, 1946; Dale Winton, late orange television presenter, 1955, Morrissey, daffodil-arsed miserablist, 1959; Katie Price, tit for brains Grattan Celebrity Mum of the Year and Face of Foxy Bingo, 1978.'*

tit for tat *1. phr.* Equal retaliation in kind, if you will. Like when your neighbour lights his barbecue when you've got the washing out and you break all his windows, tip sump oil into his prized koi pond and empty a bottle of clutch fluid on the bonnet of his new Jag. *2. n.* The gift of some cheap and meaningless piece of *Lizzie Duke* in exchange for the chance of *getting your tops* off the missus. *3. n.* Barter system by which a gentleman pays for a prostitute's services on another continent using fake Western designer goods, *eg.* A pair of Oaklie sunglasses or some nice Serjio Armani jeans.

tit for twat *1. n.* The act of fondling a woman's breast in the vain hope of getting her sufficiently aroused to permit one to have a shot on her *blurtch. 2. n.* A *lezzie* session. *3. phr. 'Fancy a shag, Pamela?' 'Sorry, Tommy. The tomato boat's docked in tuna town at the moment. But you can have tit for twat if you like.'*

titful *adj.* Impressively *qualified.*

titilate *v.* To excite with bosoms.

tit kit *n.* The depth of *Bristol channel* necessary to successfully *bring* a gentleman *off.* Doesn't have to be *that* deep, obviously. *'The vicar was delighted to see that his blind date had all the tit kit required for the night ahead.'*

tit kitten *n.* A diminutive lady who compensates for her small stature by having superior *leisure facilities.* A *midget gem.*

titlash *n. medic.* Medical condition afflicting young men visiting nudist beaches for the first time.

tit leech *1. n.* A baby. *'Births: Fforbes Hhamilton. 23rd November, at The Portland Hospital. To the Hon. Hector and Julia (nee Ffyffe-Lewerthwaite-Ffyffe), a 6lb 4oz tit leech, Tarquin Hector Sebastapol, brother for Semolina. Deo Gracias.' 2.*

n. A bloke who enjoys sucking on his wife's *jugs.*

titless wonder *n.* Female version of the male upper class chinless wonder.

tit man *n.* He who prefers *Bristols* to *arses* or *gams.*

tit mitts *n.* A brassiere. *'What's up, Carol?' 'Someone's broken into me dressing room and wanked on me tit mitts, Ronnie.'*

Titmuss paper *n.* The *spooged*-on tissues which are the residue of a solitary pleasure session involving images of the eponymous celebrity. That's Abi Titmuss, by the way. Not the Middlesex, Surrey and England cricketer who was the unwitting subject of the Half Man Half Biscuit song *Fuckin' 'Ell It's Fred Titmus.* His name wasn't even spelled the same.

titnotised *adj.* To be involuntarily mesmerised by a smashing pair of *churns. Nipnotised.*

tit nystagmus *n. medic.* Ophthalmological condition in red-blooded males, characterised by the involuntary rhythmic oscillation of the eyeballs from side to side while cycling or driving in summertime, due to the presence of scantily clad *blart* on either side of the thoroughfare.

tit on your own doorstep *v.* To buy *rhythmic literature* at one's own local newsagents, thus running the risk of being spotted by neighbours or loved ones.

titoris *n.* An unusually sensitive female nipple that doubles as an effective remote *wail switch.*

tit pants *n.* A bra.

tit pits *n.* The constantly moist area underneath the breasts of women packing more than a B-cup.

tit pizzas *n.* Big, round, mottled, crusty aereolae. With garlic bread for starters.

tit rank *n.* A *bunny rub* administered between a right pair of *rotters.*

titris *n.* When two women hug each other off-centre to allow their *norks* to fit together like the pieces in a Nintendo puzzle.

titroaster *n.* A modern smartphone such as the Samsung S6 which, when nestled in the shirt pocket, occasionally and randomly decides to emulate a Morphy Richards flat iron.

tits *1. n.* Breasts, *knockers. 'What a pair of tits.' 2. n.* Foolish or derisory people. *'What a bunch of tits.' 3. n.* Nerves. *'Christ, that Piers Morgan gets on my tits.' 4. exclam.* An expression of dismay. *'Tits. Mrs Brown's Boys is on again.'*

titscramble *n.* Quickly averting your eyes to focus on something else when you get busted looking at a woman's *jugs. 'I done a massive titscramble this morning when this bird caught me eyeing up her bojangles. Then I remembered I was a senior consultant gynaecologist and she was a patient attending my Harley Street surgery for a routine*

breast examination.'

tit scrap *n.* The fighting motion of the breasts of a very *big-boned* council estate woman who chooses not to wear *tit pants* as she walks to the bingo.

tits first, I ain't a tart *exclam.* A phrase heard in the back seat of a Ford Cortina in Bristol in the 1970s.

tit-shaped eyes *euph.* A grown-up version of square eyes; a consequence of watching too much porn. *'Jonathan, you've been sat looking at that computer all night. Honestly, you'll end up with tit-shaped eyes, you will.'*

tit shelf *n.* A voluminous gut.

tits in her handbag, she's got her *euph.* An amusing reference to a lady who has failed to attain a sufficiently impressive level of mammary development. *'I don't fancy that Kate Moss much, Dalai Llama. She's got her tits in her handbag, her.'*

tits on a fish *n.* Descriptive of a supremely useless thing. *'Did you see (insert name of striker currently having a run of bad form) play on Saturday? He was about as much use as tits on a fish.'*

tits on a stick *n.* An affectionate, informal epithet for a bony *tart* with big *churns.*

titsophrenia *n. psych.* A mental condition whereby a gentleman deviates from his habitual state of reason at the sight of a big pair of *wobblers.*

tits out for the lads, get your *exclam.* A compliment proffered by a large group of aggressively drunken men to any female above the age of puberty.

tit splitter *n.* A lady's fashion bag worn diagonally across the torso such that it bisects the *headlamps.*

tit spotters *n.* Sunglasses as used when holidaying with the missus, employed to save getting a boot in the *knackers* when a tasty *piece* pops them out beside you at the poolside. *Perv windows.*

tittage *n.* The average weight *avoirdupois* of the *knockers* on a group of women at a bus stop, for instance.

tit tap *n. medic.* A nipple. *'Camera three. Forget about the crazy paving, zoom in on her tip taps, quick.'*

titterati, the *n. coll.* The country's elite *jug* models.

titti politti *n. Ital.* The policy of the late Silvio Berlusconi's Forza Italia party regarding the recruitment of its female parliamentary representatives.

tittlish *adj.* Prone to laughing at ladies' secondary sexual characteristics for no apparent reason.

tittoo *n.* A small piece of body art found in the breastular region. A *tit* tattoo.

titty bar bill, big as a *sim.* Descriptive of something unexpectedly large. *'After being showered by milkshake once more whilst campaigning in Clacton, Nigel Farage claims that the dry cleaning costs for his suits this month will be as big as a titty* *bar bill.'*

tittybollocks *n. medic.* Women's breasts which are no bigger than a man's testicles.

titty fuck *n.* A *sausage sandwich*, a *diddy ride, breastbone.*

titty mustard *n. Daddy's sauce.*

titty skittles *n. medic.* Estradiol tablets used to treat gender dysphoria.

tittywings *n.* A saggy pair of *moobs* that meet at the back. A *pork waistcoat.*

titular *1. adj.* Of a woman, having the same name as something else, but also smashing *tits*. *'In chapter 12 of Jane Eyre, Mr Rochester bumps into the titular heroine and is instantly struck by her powerful charms.' 2. adj.* Descriptive of a man who not only has the same name as something else, but also likes *tits. 'Michael Caine in Alfie (1966) plays the part of the titular womanising young Cockney.'*

tit up *v.* To get one's *tops. 'The Man Who Titted Up the Lord Mayor's Mother During the Loyal Toast'.* (Cartoon in *Punch* by HM Bateman, 1926).

tit wank *n.* A *soapy tit wank*, without the soap.

titwicks *n. medic.* Ladies' nipples. *'When it comes to feeding baby, breast really is best. Mother's milk contains the perfect balance of nutrients that your child needs, and although the titwicks may be painful for the first few days, feeding quickly becomes a relaxing and bonding time for both.'*

tit winch *n.* A powerful brassiere. Also *tit pants.*

tit window *n.* When engaged in a serious conversation with a lady, that split second when her attention is momentarily diverted elsewhere and one has a chance to take a *sneaky peek* at her *rib cushions. 'When the doctor told me the outlook was bleak, I looked her straight in the eye and asked her how long I had left. It was at that moment that the phone rang and I knew I had my tit window.'*

titzkreig *n.* A group of buxom young *Frauleins* on the pavement, dazzling oncoming chaps with their *searchlights.*

TK man *n.* A gent with a *membrum virile* so long that it can comfortably accommodate "ten knuckles" gripping it at once.

TKO *abbrev.* A completed but ultimately unsatisfying *pud pull, eg.* One undertaken while one is concerned about the imminent return of the missus, distracted by the telly, or looking at old photos of Penelope Keith. A Technical Knock Out.

TMT *abbrev.* A desirable person; one who will, unbeknownst to them, be put into your *wank bank* for secret enjoyment later. That's Mine Tonight.

TNTs *abbrev.* Two Nifty Tits.

toad in the hole *1. n.* Alternative name for the s****l practice of dipping one's *banger* into a *batter*-filled *sausage pot.* Sort of thing. *2. n.* An ugly bloke accompanied by an absolute stunner, *eg.* Rupert Murdoch and the current Mrs Murdoch, Rod Stewart and the current Mrs Stewart.

toad of fuck all *euph.* A motorist who believes that his personalised numberplates are a symbol of esteem and influence.

toast a bum crumpet *v.* To *fart. 'Houston, we have a problem. We're down to our last two hours of oxygen and Fred has just toasted one hell of a bum crumpet.'* (Mission Control TX log. Transmission from Jim Lovell, Commander, Apollo 13).

toasted cheese sandwich, like a *sim.* Phrase used to describe a woman's *kitten purse* that hasn't seen any saucy action for an inordinately long time, if at all. *'Right then. Would you shag Ann Widdecombe for a grand?' 'I don't think it'd be possible. It would be like trying to pull apart a toasted cheese sandwich.'*

toaster *n.* A crumb-filled vagina with two slots and a spring mechanism that you have to fish your *cock* out of with a wooden spoon.

toaster sex *euph.* Polite expression describing *backdoor action.* From the fact that, like a slice of bread, "the longer you leave it in, the browner it gets". Also known as *the third way* or *bumcraft.*

toasticles *n.* Very hot, buttered testicles.

toast, Scottish *n.* Stale bread.

toast to the Queen *n.* Historically, a *rumpet voluntary* that scores highly in all three categories; volume, longevity and stench. Often followed by a round of applause. Also (currently and for the foreseeable future) *Toast to the King.*

tobleromeo *n.* A bloke who gives fat *birds* chocolate in the hope of getting his *leg over.*

Toblerone tunnel *n.* The gap, triangular in cross section, between the tops of a slender woman's thighs and her *skin gusset*, into which the popular confection would slide neatly. Also *Foyston gap, Barbie gap, Cumberland gap, quedge, f-duct.*

tockley *n. Aus.* The *gut stick. 'Ooyah! I've caught me tockley in me zip.'*

toddlers *n.* Collar bone decorations of the sort worn by *Miss Lincolnshire. Dutch Alps, stits, tisn'ts.*

toddler's arse *n.* A rather impressive cleavage on a comely lady.

toddler with a chocolate cake, like a *sim.* A heavily abused *khazi.*

todger *n.* That which todges. The penis. Also *tadger, tockley, tool. 'Ooyah! I've caught me todger in me zip.'*

todger dodger *n.* A *lady golfer* who is *off solids* and thus leaps out of the way of an on-coming male genital. A lesbian.

to do list *1. n.* In the workplace, a schedule or agenda of jobs yet to be completed. *2. n.* The mental list of workplace *tussage* that a sexually frustrated office employee would like to *do*, all things being equal.

toe bunger *1. n.* In football, a "hit & hope" power blast which exhibits little aim and zero placement. *2. n.* A *jam rag* used when *Liverpool are at home*.

toed in the hole *exclam.* Suffering a sharp boot up the *nick*.

toffee apple *1. n.* A cotton bud covered in excessive ear wax. *2. n.* The glans of the *slag hammer* after it's been dipped in something hot and sticky.

toffee Rizla *n.* An absorbent pad of toilet paper worn in the *arse cleft* of a *double sucker* to absorb moisture and guard against *buttering* of the *cheeks*. A *manpon, swedge, botcap*.

toffee strings *n.* See *bead curtains*.

toffee yoghurt *n.* That semi-viscous mixture of mingled bodily fluids which, one fondly imagines, dribbles down the backs of *puddle jumpers'* legs after they have successfully completed one of their randy romps. *Santorum, shum, sexcrement.*

toffice *n.* Homeworking premises; from toilet + office. *'Right, I'm just off to the toffice to drop off the kids off at the pool and email that invoice to facilities. Should be about ten minutes, then it's straight back to Grand Theft Auto for another eight hours, with three or four breaks for a wank.'*

TOFU/tofu *acronym.* Tastes Of Fucking Underpants.

togging *n.* Indulging in promiscuous, semi-public sex with middle-aged Radio 2 listeners in the car parks of Dobbies, National Trust properties and farm shops.

toggle and two *euph. Nav.* A jolly Jack Tar's *meat and two veg*.

toilet cluedo *euph.* Entertaining mystery game for several people staying in a large house, after an unpleasant length of rope or lead piping has desecrated the *pot* and the guilty party must be determined, arrested, and quite possibly imprisoned.

toilet dick *n.* A hand-held, nozzle-ended dispenser used by a bloke to clear *pebble-dashing* from his lavatory *pan*. Also known as the *yellow toilet brush* or *piss chisel*.

toilet duck *n.* An untimely and probably unwanted erection which manifests while one is sitting on the *pot*. Named after the well known brand of *chod bin* cleaner which boasts of "reaching under the rim". *Throne bone.*

toileteer *n.* A water closet patron. *'We were driving along the A303, and not only were my bottom teeth*

floating but there was also a mole at the counter. So we pulled the Super Snipe into a local beauty spot car park, only to find the facilities already occupied by fellow toileteers.'* (from *The Journals of Sir John Betjeman*).

toilet equinox *n.* The rare occasion, typically occurring just twice a year, when the time taken to actually perform your *dump* is exactly the same length as the subsequent wiping time.

toilet snails *n.* Cryptozoological molluscs that slither around the *bog pan* in student houses, leaving brown *skidmarks* for which no-one claims responsibility.

toilet stilt *n.* A particularly long and rigid *stool* which stands on one end and clears the water surface by at least three inches. A *bowl vault*.

toilet suicide *n.* A loud explosion followed by a low groan from a cubicle.

toilet truffles *n.* The pungent nuggets of *bum rubbish* found ensconced in the *earth closet* after *gurning out* a hot, dry curry.

token for the cockwash *n.* A romantic gift bestowed upon a lady by a man, (eg. Flowers, chocolates, bottle of *screwtop*) in the hope that it will secure him *a bit*. *'I'm just nipping down the off licence to get a token for the cockwash.'*

toley *n. Scots.* A *shite* or *jobby*. *'Och the noo, Eric. I just dropped a braw toley in your shoe.'*

tolly ring *n. medic.* Condition prevalent amongst employees in the printing industry, the chief symptom of which is soreness in the anal area. So-called because sufferers believe that inhalation of the aromatic hydrocarbon solvent toluene, which is used as a cleaning agent in their workplace, is what causes their *farts* to burn their *nipsies*. *'I'm sorry, Mr Caxton. You'll have to finish typesetting the 1475 edition of Recuyell of the Historyes of Troye yourself. I'm off home to put some ointment on me tolly ring.'*

tom *1. n.* Prostitute. *2. v.* To carry out prostitution. *'Are you tomming it?' 3. n. rhym. slang.* Tomfoolery = joolery. *3. n. Thai.* Comfortably shod *lesbian, carpet muncher etc.*

tomahawk *n.* A little penis, possibly one fitted with stabiliser wheels. From the smaller version of the "Chopper", the very popular 1970s Raleigh bicycle, which was named after a big *cock*. Also known as a *grifter*.

Tomatina, la *1. n. Sp.* Yearly festival held on the last Wednesday of August in the Spanish town of Buñol, during which locals and tourists spend a morning pelting each other with tomatoes, rendering the entire town centre a deep red colour. *2. n.* The missus's *cricket week.*

tomato boat has docked, the *euph.* Phrase used to put hubbie off his stroke when *Arsenal are playing at home.*

tomato varnish *n.* The Mozambican term for the clear, colourless solution secreted by the *plums*, which provides the *tadpoles* with something to swim in. Also *ball glaze, guardsman's gloss, perseverance soup, dew on the lily, clear smear.*

tomb raider *n.* A gent whose romantic preference lies at the more mature end of the scale. A *granny fucker, biddy fiddler.*

Tom Daley *euph.* A medal-winning expulsion of *biosolids* that gracefully enters the water without a hint of a splash, even though it has the weight of a sixteen-year-old boy.

Tom Daley's forehead *n.* A buoyant *floater* that bobs back up at the water's edge shortly after flushing.

tomfuckery *n.* Light-hearted dealings with a *lady of the night. 'I don't know what you're getting so cross about, darling. It was just a spot of drunken tomfuckery on a lads' trip to Amsterdam.'*

Tom Good's rotovator, arse like *sim.* Bad guts. Descriptive of a *ringpiece* that, like the eponymous self-sufficient sitcom horticulturalist's mechanical tiller, makes a dreadful racket, emits all manner of toxic fumes and turns everything in sight brown.

Tom Hank *n. rhym. slang.* A *Jonathan Ross.*

Tom Kite *n. rhym. slang.* A *shite. 'And the tension's really building up at the eighteenth hole here at Barnsley International Golf Course. Tiger Woods is lining up the birdie shot that could see him awarded the magnificent onyx and pewter trophy of the inaugural South Yorkshire Golf Championship. And… oh no. He's trod in a big pile of Tom Kite. Aw, fucking hell, the poor cunt. It's one of them orange, blancmangey ones and it's gone right over the top of his shoe.'*

Tommy Cooper, to do a *v.* To die on the big stage mid-performance. To lose *wood*, just like that. *'Sorry, love, we'll have to stop. I've done a Tommy Cooper.'*

Tommy's out! *n.* A light-hearted party game where one of the guests secretly *lays a cable* in the house and shouts "Tommy's out!", whereupon everyone else tries to find it. *'To Aldeborough for the weekend, as a guest of Benjamin [Britten]. What a hoot. Simply everyone was there including Larry [Olivier], Ivor [Novello], Terrence [Rattigan] and Alfie [Bass]. Charades in the orangery, then after supper we played a game of Tommy's out which ended at three in the morning when Kit [Hassall] found a dead otter in the piano stool, courtesy of Johnny [Gielgud].'* (From *The Diary of Noel Coward*).

Tommy squeaker *n.* A small, high-pitched *Daimler Dart* released unwittingly when lifting something heavy, such as a manhole cover, car battery or Dame Margot Fonteyn.

Tommy two-ways *n.* A *Betty both* or *happy shopper.* Coined by Stewie-voiced ex-MP Gyles Brandreth on *QI.*

Tom off *v.* To ejaculate immediately upon reaching full tumescence. Named in honour of the notoriously *trigger-happy* male of the cat species. *'Sorry love, I've just Tommed off. Giz twenty minutes and I'll have another go.'*

tomorrow's shit *n.* Food. *'Tomorrow's shit, glorious tomorrow's shit! Hot sausage and mustard. Who wouldn't like a bit, of plum pudding and custard?'* (Lyrics from the musical *Oliver!* by Lionel Bart).

Toms *n. medic. rhym. slang.* The *splatters.* From Tom tits = squits.

Tom Thumb's arsehole, a fanny like *sim.* The kind of *twat* one would imagine Emily Bishop off *Coronation Street* might have, if that's the sort of thing you are wont to imagine. A *mouse's ear., worm's belt.*

Tom Tom *1. n. prop.* A popular satellite navigation system used by motorists. *2. n.* Simultaneously *exorcising one's morning demon* while dropping a *copper bolt.* From *Tom tit* and *Tommy tank.*

tongue and groove *1. n.* Basic carpentry technique. *2. n.* Basic *carpet-munchery* technique.

tongue fu *n.* An over-zealous act of *cumulonimbus* which leaves the victim feeling like her *gammon flaps* have just gone five rounds with Jackie Chan.

tongue job *n.* A lick, as opposed to a *blow, job.*

tongue punchbag *n.* A *bald man in a boat, clematis.*

tongue shui *n.* The ancient, mystical art of knowing the most effective place to stick your tongue to get the best flow of energy through your missus's *snatch.*

tongue, tramp's *n.* A flash of pink poking out through a mass of unruly whiskers.

tongue wrestling *n.* Tonsil hockey.

tonight Matthew *euph.* A plain, ugly or indeed plain ugly, girl seen at the start of a drinking session, who returns later, magically transformed by one's *beer goggles* into a gorgeous celebrity lookalike.

tonk *v. onomat.* To *fuck, poke, shtup.*

tonsil hockey *n.* Snogging, spit swapping, sucking face.

tonto pronto *n. Sp.* Spanish lager enjoyed more for its cheapness and strength than for its flavour. See also *señorita beater, Pedro's piss.*

Tony Martin *n.* The act of *giving it* to someone from

behind with both barrels. A double *back scuttle*.

tookus *1. n. Bum. 2. n. coll. Tussage.*

tool *n.* Penis, *manhood*. All the *home handyman* needs, along with his *wanking spanners* and a couple of suitably sized *nuts*, to perform a spot of *DIY*.

tool of the trade *n.* The *twat* who everyone hates at a place of work.

tool station *1. n.* On an industrial estate near you, suppliers of tools to trade and DIY customers seven days a week. *2. n.* Any national chain pub on a Saturday night.

tool time *1. n.* A programme hosted by Tim Allen in the American sitcom *Home Improvement. 2. n.* Five minutes of *woodwork* in the shed.

too much chlorine in the pool *euph.* Implausible excuse proffered after arriving at work red eyed and hungover. *'Did you have one too many in the Strangers' Bar last night, minister?' 'Certainly not. I did forty lengths before I came into the office and there was too much chlorine in the pool. Now fetch me the EU27 Position Papers and a bottle of blue Powerade.'*

toosh *n. Totty, blart. 'There's not enough toosh on this oil rig.'*

toot *v.* A child and vicar-friendly term for a *parp*.

tooth coming through, have a *euph.* To be suffering from *IRS*. To have a *wire spider*, a *sweetcorn itch, pine cone*. To be the victim of a swarm of *arse wasps*.

tooth dryer *n.* Any repair required on your car, house, or a domestic appliance that requires the recruitment of a qualified tradesman and will thus, once the surly *bastard* has finished sucking air through his incisors, end up costing you a *fucking* packet.

tooth fairy *n.* A promiscuous person of either gender or persuasion. Because, like the eponymous nocturnal dental philanthropist, "they have seen more than their fair share of bedrooms".

toothless gibbon *n.* A *clapping fish*.

toothless granny's gob *phr.* Descriptive of a well serviced *arsehole* as might be seen in a niche *grumbleflick. 'She's gaping like a toothless granny's gob, your holiness. I'll lend it you when I've finished with it.'*

toothless kiss *1. n.* Something you got off your nan back in the old days, when all nans had had a dental clearance for their 18th birthday. *2. n.* Some sort of saucy *act of lesbitious romance*, according to people who've accidentally happened upon it on the internet. See also *clam jousting, carpet bumping*.

toothless sea lion *sim.* A smelly and unkempt *minge. 'I don't think I'll see her again, Paul. She had a fanny like a toothless sea lion.'*

toot meat *n.* Penis. From the fictional musical sweet of a similar name from *Chitty Chitty Bang Bang. Bed flute, meat flute, pink oboe.*

TOOTS/toots *acronym.* The toppest sort of *top bollocks* available. Ten Out Of Tens.

toot toot *1. n.* Risqué BBC parlance for vagina. *2. onomat.* The noise made by Mr Toad's car horn. Actually, that should be *poop poop. 3. onomat.* The noise made by the *spunk trumpet* during a *blow job. 4. n.* That part of Denise Lasalle with which one would be well advised not to mess.

top banana *exclam.* Give that man a coconut, whacko-the-diddle-oh. Jolly good.

top bollocks *n.* Breasts, *jubblies, breasticles*.

top bottom *n.* The mouth.

top bum *n.* An impressive *embonpoint* and *decolletage*.

top deck *v.* Of a house guest, to defecate in one's host's cistern, rather than, more conventionally, in the toilet, for comic effect. *'"I say, Jeeves, he was a bit of a rum cove, what? Did you see him pass the port from left to right?" I whispered. "Indeed I did, Sir," replied the sage retainer. "I took the liberty of top decking the servants' bathroom before leaving."'* (from *Heil Hitler, Jeeves!* by PG Wodehouse).

top dog *n.* An unattractive woman in a workplace whom one fancies simply because all the others are even worse. The least unattractive of a set of unattractive ladies. Default *blart, best in show.*

top dressing *n.* A term used in the catering industry for an *air crouton* dropped next to a table by a disgruntled waiter.

top fruit *1. n.* Botanical term describing cherries, plums, apples *etc.*, which grow on trees. *2. n.* A fine "pear". *'Excellent top fruit on page three today, Percy.'*

top gun *n.* In the works *bogs*, the honour awarded to the *porcelain pilot* whose *afterburner*, upon inhalation, literally "takes [one's] breath away".

top hat *n.* The implausible achievement of a lady with three blokes up her *wizard's sleeve*. After a explicitly erotic dish of the same name available in the restaurant on the Stenna Ferry, consisting of three pork sausages in mashed potato sitting in a Yorkshire pudding.

Topic pregnancy *n. medic.* Characteristic *flabdominal* swelling caused by excessive consumption of hazelnut-rich chocolate confectionery.

to play a wrong note is insignificant; to play without passion is inexcusable *phr.* Attributed to Ludwig van Beethoven; a cold dismissal of another man's *calling card*.

topless hand shandy *1. n.* A lemonade and beer drink, pulled from a pump by a barmaid who is naked from the waist up. *2. n.* A squirt of something fizzy pulled from a *love pump* by a masseuse who is naked from the waist up.

topless relief *n.* Happy hour offer in a *toss parlour.* Presumably exactly the same as a topless hand shandy.

toploader *n.* A shared marijuana joint, in which the roller has generously overfilled his own half in order to get himself more *whipped to the tits* than his sharee.

top of a coconut *n.* Descriptive of a *Hitler tash* which has been neglected. A *pieman's wig*.

to poo list *n.* That rollcall of *cuntish* celebrities to whom, in an ideal world, one would like to mail one's own *feeshus.*

top rack *1. n.* One's upper set of teeth. From the highest shelf of a newsagent's stand where the *jazz mags* at the top are covered in white covers to protect the models' modesty. *'I'm warning you, if you don't stop looking at my bird's tits, you're going to lose your top rack.'*

tops and fingers *adj.* Scale on which sexual achievement is measured by teenage males. See also *cloth tit. 'Get far last night?' 'Not bad. I got my tops and two fingers.'*

top secret files *n.* Sensitive material stashed in the lav.

top shelf *adj. Wankerish. 'Johnson? What a guy! Absolutely top shelf!'*

top shelf-harm *n. Jazz mag-*fuelled *bongo fury* that leaves a chap weak and full of self-loathing.

top shelf quick *adj.* Lightning fast. From the Zorro-like rapid reflexes of a man in a newsagents staring steadfastly at the *Radio Times* until the moment the shop empties, then reaching for a *Fiesta*, slapping it on the counter and in one smooth movement simultaneously proffering the exact change and slipping it into an opaque carrier bag before exiting. *'I tell you what, Brendan. Usain was top shelf quick out of the blocks there.'*

top shelf shit *n.* An explosive *Sir Douglas* that's on the runny side, and manages to paint the top rim of the toilet bowl and escape the flush.

top shelf tornado *n.* A purchaser of *bliff mags,* who blows into the shop, selects his quarry in the blink of an eye, swiftly secretes it within the covers of a daily newspaper and heads for the till with impressive haste.

top stealth *n.* The alternative approach of entering a newsagents, grabbing your desired *bongo mag,* paying and leaving with such *sang froid* that

no-one bats an eyelid.

top trumper *n.* A colleague who can beat any story you tell with one of his own crazier anecdotes. Also see *racunteur, twat o'nine tales, Bertie big bollocks, two shits* and *four ball Paul.*

top up a half-pint *euph.* Having *drawn an ace* in the *thunderbox,* to take the opportunity to have a *piss* before standing up. *'Have you finished in there, Jonny? Ravi's just gone out to bat.' 'I'm nearly done. I'm just topping up a half-pint, then I'll get me pads on.'*

top up the font *euph.* To have a quick *wank.* From the excuse given by Dr Chasuble the vicar in Oscar Wilde's *The Importance of Being Ernest,* when Miss Prism comes into the vestry and catches him looking at some mucky pictures. Don't say we never learn you any fucking culture.

tornado alley *1. n.* The area of the USA in which twisters are most frequent, encompassing the lowland areas of Mississippi, Ohio and the lower Missouri River valleys. *2. n.* The low-lying region between the *council gritter* and the *love spuds,* in which unusually fierce spiralling zephyrs run wild. The *taint, tintis, notcher, barse* etc. *Fartbreak ridge.*

torn pocket *n.* A particularly hammered *quimpiece* where all the stitching has come undone.

torpaedo *n.* A public swimming pool patron who, suspiciously, heads straight for the shallow end with all frothy bubbles coming off his feet.

torpedo cupcake *n.* A guided, deadly bubble of *sulphur dibaxide* released under the jacuzzi water to pop up under an unsuspecting fellow bather's nose.

torpedo in the water *1. exclam. nav.* Warning shouted by a submarine sonar operator on hearing the splash of an air-dropped ordnance. *2. exclam.* Warning shouted by people dwelling in a cheap, thin-walled (name of building company removed following legal advice) house upon hearing the splash of a large *Sir Douglas.*

torpoodo *n.* A *brown missile* launched with such ferocity it could sink the Bismarck or Tirpitz. Also known as a *pan cracker* or *Bedfordshire clanger..*

Torrey caviar *n.* A refined gastronomic delicacy named after one of Aberdeen's many cultural hotspots. Mince.

tortoise *n.* A *kiddy fiddler.* From the fact that he "gets there before the hair".

toss *1. v.* To *wank,* usually "oneself off". *2. n.* A Noel Coward-style act of casual *self-delight. 3. v.* To flip pancakes through 180° during cooking.

tossanova *n.* Any fellow that is celebrated for his prowess at wrist-intensive, bachelor-orientated pursuits.

tossed salad *n. US.* Anal sex between male prisoners. *'More tossed salad, Lord Archer?' 'No thanks, Mr Big, I'm completely stuffed.'*

tosser *n.* A contumelious epithet applied to one who is being rhetorically deprecated.

Tosser del Mar *1. n. prop.* Principal town on the Spanish Costa Brava. *2. n.* A discreet underwater *one off the wrist* at a topless beach, rendered undetectable thanks to the laws of refraction and Mediterranean murk.

tosser's twitch *n.* Nervous affliction suffered by *self-improvers* during periods of abstinence.

tossing a softmint into a bottle of coke, like *euph.* A description of a *fruit machine Freddie*'s premature ejaculation. See also *up and over like a pan of milk.*

tossing the caber *v.* Having *one off the wrist* with a massive length of *wood.*

toss parlour *n.* A *rub-a-tug shop.*

tosspitality *n.* The thoughtful facilities provided for hotel guests who wish to *relax in a gentlemanly manner, eg. Grumble* channels on the telly, box of tissues on the bedside table, curtains *etc.*

toss pot *1. n.* A jar for keeping *toss* in, esp. At a sperm bank, for example. No other examples spring immediately to mind. *2. n.* A drunk. *3. n.* One held in low esteem, a *fuckwit.*

tosstalgia *v.* The act of *smacking oneself about* while fondly remembering a former dalliance.

tossteopath *n.* A masseur or masseuse who offers a range of *stiffness*-relieving *extras.*

tosstesterone *1. n.* The primary *wanker* hormone. *'You've got to make allowances for the high jinks of these members of the Bullingdon Club. They are just young men with high tosstesterone levels, out enjoying themselves.' 2. n.* Sex hormone that makes young men *pull their puds* until their *knackers* go flat, catch fire or fall off.

tostoffalone *n.* The hormone a single male releases when viewing *gentleman's comics* in his bedsit. *'Hmm. There's traces of tosstoffalone on the duvet cover, sergeant.'*

total eclipse of the blart *n.* while eyeing up some *fit* piece of *mackerel* across the pub/street/nunnery, the phenomenon of having some vast, planet-sized *salad dodger* slowly drift into your line of sight, completely obscuring the object of your scrutiny.

total wifeout *n.* A one-man, against-the-clock *sexual assault course*, enjoyed while the missus is at the supermarket on a Saturday evening, which involves large red balls, squirting liquids and the risk of sustaining a serious back injury.

to the delight of David Attenborough *phr.* When something emerges from its burrow after a long wait. *'I was sat there with backed-up Simon Cowells for close to an hour when, to the delight of David Attenborough, a litter of arse-joeys came out for a swim.'*

to the tasting table! *1. exclam.* Instruction issued to contestants on the *Great British Menu* that their culinary efforts should be served up to the judge chef. *2. exclam.* Instruction issued to a chap's *inamorata*, informing her that a *drink on a stick* will shortly be served, and she might care to *assume the position* in order to enjoy a proper *gobful.*

TOTM pole *abbrev.* A man's *love length*, a *fanny mouse* or any other more or less cylindrical object which enters a woman's *teepee* during *rag week.* From Time Of The Month.

Tottenham millionaire *n.* Anyone who has a job of any sort in the picturesquely strife-torn North London locale.

totter frotter *n.* A *foot fetishist* or *feet footishist* who gets the *shoe horn*. Also *shrimper.*

Tottle *n.* A bath-time *air biscuit.* From the joke with the punchline "But, Sir I distinctly heard you say, 'What about a water bottle, Tottle?'". An *Edward Woodward, Bill Oddie.*

totty *n. coll.* Girls, *fanny. 'Hey, this Popemobile's an absolute fanny magnet. Since I bought it I've been beating off the totty with a shitty stick.'*

toucan's bill *n.* The firm, leathery and yellowed hood adorning a well-thumbed *starter button.*

touch *v.* To *fondle*, usually "up", *esp.* with a paintbrush.

touch and go *euph.* The phenomenon of premature ejaculation, the unfortunate affliction whereby the sufferer can barely *stick it in* before shooting his *population paste. 'HAMLET: What a piece of work is man! How noble in reason! How infinite in faculties! And yet, dear Rosencrantz, with narry a pregnant pause my accursed spongle did spray. Hardly did I tarry within dear Ophelia's sweet clout. ROSENCRANTZ: Verily, my Lord, her ladyship did lament that your congress was an ephemeral joy; a fleeting pleasure, fading afore 'twouldst be prehended. HAMLET: Aye, 'tis true. It was touch and go alright.'* (from *Macbeth* by William Shakespeare).

touch base *1. v.* Nonsensical corporate *twat* buzzword. *2. v.* To make a spatial awareness misjudgement while wiping one's *rusty sheriff's badge* following a *German Byte,* sometimes resulting in a *taxi driver's tan* or, in extreme cases, *beef palm.* A *masonic handshake.*

Touché Turtle *1. n. prop.* Eponymous hero of the

70s TV cartoon, which ran to 52 fucking episodes. *2. n.* A little more than just *the turtle's breath.*

touching a snail's face, like *sim.* The effect of cold *wanking spanners* on the *old chap* when popping behind a tree to *drain the lizard* in mid-winter.

touching ball *1. n.* In snooker, a situation where one ball is touching another, allowing the participant to shoot in any direction without a penalty. *2. n.* In pornography, exactly the same. *Newton's cradle.*

touching carpet *phr.* The result of ignoring the fact that one is *touching cloth* until it is too late. The stage after *touching socks.*

touching cloth *adj.* That stooling stage immediately after *turtle's head* when the *Sir Douglas* establishes contact with the *trolleys. 'Is there a bog round here mate? I'm touching cloth.'*

touching socks *adj.* The stage after *touching cloth* but before *touching carpet* by which time it is too late to look for a toilet. But it might be a good time to look for a trouser shop.

touching the void *1. n.* The unsettling sensation of wearing a dressing gown without any clothes on underneath. Also a successful film about falling down a hill. *2. n.* A lady's act of filthy self pollution.

touch last night's tea *v.* To insert a digit into the *ringpiece* of someone with loose morals.

touch on *n.* The first vague stirrings of a *panhandle,* caused by something like the swimwear pages of the Grattan catalogue, or the problem pages of a tabloid newspaper. A *twitch on. Getting a bit of blood in it.*

tough mudder *1. n. milit.* An arduous assault course. A test of a combatant's grit, spunk and determination to succeed. *2. n.* A difficult *rear entry. 3. n.* A reluctant anal sex participant.

tour de pants *n.* A gruelling and exhausting peregrination around the missus's knickers, taking in all the points of interest along the way.

tour de twats *n.* A high cholesterol *peloton* of fat, lycra-clad cyclists clogging up the road on their overpriced *push irons.*

tour down under *1. n.* Elite international cycling race in that takes place in Australia. *2. n.* Tentative suggestion of a bit of *head. 'Do you want to go for a tour down under, love?'*

Tourette's juice *n.* Freshly squeezed orange juice, of the sort that is so bitter it makes the drinker twitch and swear involuntarily.

tourist's touchpool *1. n.* In a marine wildlife complex, the much-visited but rarely cleaned crab section which smells of fish and in which members of the public are encouraged to dip their hands. *2. n.* A filthy *slattern's clout.*

towbar *n.* A bulbous *turtle's head.* With a 12 volt output.

towel hook *n.* A *hard-on* that's strong enough to support the weight of a damp bath towel.

TOWIE *abbrev.* A reference to the preferred style of congress enjoyed by the tangerine-faced denizens of the uncouth southern county. The Only Way Is Essex, *viz.* A *scuttle* up the *wrong 'un.*

town halls *n. rhym. slang.* Bollocks. Also *Henry Halls, Granby halls, orchestras, Egyptian halls etc.*

tow oneself round the cabin *v. naut.* To indulge in a bout of vigorous *self abuse.*

toxic socks syndrome *n. medic.* An allergic reaction to a room-mate's feet, principally symptomised by a tightening of the throat, involuntary gagging and watering eyes.

toxic waist *n.* A health-threatening *poond* resulting from a diet of Ginster's pasties, Fray Bentos pies and KFC party buckets, all washed down with a non-diet cola drink (Coke).

Toxteth airshow *n.* A low-level aeronautical spectacular performed by police helicopters chasing Scouse *twockers,* drug traffickers and other sundry Merseyside ne'er-do-wells. See also *Moss Side airshow.*

tracer bullets *n.* Hard, difficult-to-digest items, such as corn, peanuts or Lego, that show up in *Thoras* and provide a good estimate of the time it has taken for a meal to negotiate the digestive tract.

tracer fire *n.* Type of food that passes through the alimentary canal entirely unscathed (*eg.* Sweetcorn), and shows up the next day in the toilet as good as new.

Tracey Island *n. Bum rubbish* of such a volume and consistency that it forms a compelling simulacrum of the erstwhile International Rescue base as it rises majestically above the waves of the *chod pan.*

track and field *euph.* To stimulate a lady's *clematis* in a vigorous, two-fingered manner reminiscent of playing the eponymous classic 1980s "button-basher" arcade game.

track and trace that! *exclam.* Said after *dropping a gut* that could see you quarantined for fourteen days.

tractor pull *1. n.* A sophisticated entertainment enjoyed by inbred redneck Americans whereby a large block of concrete is dragged along some mud by a piece of souped-up farm machinery with thick black smoke billowing out of the exhaust and destroying the atmosphere. *2. n.* A romantic Italian lovemaking technique whereby the gentleman sticks his *Charlie* up his *bird's shitter* while he has his *pods* stuffed up her *clopper.*

tradesman's entrance *n.* The *back passage.* Also

tradesmen's entrance, where the *milkman* leaves his *yoghurt.*

tradesman's nudge *n.* A firm blow which is delivered with the intention of making a broken object operational again. *'Mission Control can now confirm that the crew of Space Shuttle Atlantis today visited the Hubble Space Telescope in order to give the malfunctioning Cosmic Origins Spectrograph and Wide Field Camera a tradesman's nudge with a big fuck-off hammer.'*

trade spit *v.* To osculate.

trad jazz *1. n.* Classic genre of early twentieth century popular music which actually had a tune and everything. *2. n.* Pre-internet *grumble,* consisting of magazines with naked ladies in them, as opposed to being up at 4.00am, unable to tear yourself away from yet another video of *lady-weaselling, Glaswegian sumo scat,* or *Vatican City hump-shunting.*

traff *1. v.* To *guff, pump, let off. 2. v.* To stifle a *fart,* and sort of swallow it back up one's bottom. *'I was sat next to this cracking bird on the train all the way from Doncaster to Manchester. I must've traffed eighty or ninety times.'*

traffic calming measure *n.* A *fly feast* in the road that could take your exhaust off. A *Radcliffe's sleeper.*

traffic Tourettes *n. psych.* State of *potty-mouthed* excitement that forces a driver to compulsively comment on the habits and road manners of his fellow fellow road users.

tragic marker *n.* Vaguely brown skidmark found on your *skants* or a white towel.

train horn *n.* A lady's party trick in which she firstly *drops a gut,* and then *drops her hat forwards* in quick succession, creating a tuneless, two-toned blast. Also known as a *Robson and Jerome.*

training lager *n.* Piss weak beer. *'As God is my witness, I'm as sober as a judge. I've been on the training lager all afternoon, officer.'*

trampadol *n.* Powerful prescription sedative used as a recreational drug by the financially challenged. *'We're out of vodka and faux-caine, so it's time to break out the trampadol left over from your whiplash, mam.'*

trampagne *n.* A homeless person's celebratory beverage, laid down for special occasions, *eg.* White Lightning, Red Label Thunderbird, Mr Muscle Drain Foamer. *'Break out the trampagne, boys. I've found an Embassy with ten left on it.'*

trampanzee *n.* A foliage-dwelling *Harold Ramp* sitting amongst the bushes in the park, furiously *feeding the ducks* and throwing his *shit* at passers-by.

trampari *n.* A turpentine substitute aperitif taken as an appetiser before a bin-rifling buffet.

tramp eating a kebab *sim.* An enthusiastic performance of *cumulonimbus.* The male equivalent of a *dog eating hot chips.*

trampede *n.* A stampede of tramps. From tramp + stampede.

tramp grill *n.* Any city centre area where *Harry Ramps* gather in the summer to soak up the sun. The *shandy sunbed.*

tramping *n.* The opposite of glamping, ie. Sleeping in a *crappy* little tent, waking up shivering in a wet sleeping bag at 5am and *shitting* in a bucket.

trampitheatre *n.* The arena chosen by a cohort of drunken *gentlemen of the road* to drink white cider, shout incoherent abuse at one another and engage in *mortal combat.* Especially applies to circular public spaces, such as the central areas of road underpasses, *eg.* The St. James Barton Roundabout in Bristol (*aka* The Bear Pit).

tramp l'oeil *n.* Refers to a cheap *dollymop* who looks *good from far, but far from good* at closer range. A *low resolution fox.*

trampoline *n.* Any petroleum-based beverage. *Trampari, trampagne, tramp's treacle.*

trampon *n.* A *dangermouse* that's been left in the *trap* long after it should have been taken out.

tramp's knapsack, ballbag like a *sim.* Descriptive of an ageing *chicken skin handbag* that has seen better days in terms of hygiene and sexual health.

tramp stamp *n.* Any tattoo on a slatternly *bird's* body, usually around the base of the spine or on the left *qualification.* A *tittoo.*

tramp's tan *n.* The healthy, ruddy complexion achieved by spending a lot of time in the fresh air. *Shandy sunburn.*

tramp steamer *1. n.* A ship which doesn't have any fixed schedule or published ports of call. *2. n.* A refreshingly *al fresco dreadnought* left for us all to enjoy by a cheery *professional outdoorsman.*

tramps' treacle *n. Supermarket smack.* Special Brew.

tramputee *n.* A *Terence Stamp* who has become separated from his can of *treacle.*

tramp Vegas *n.* Telephone booths, vending machines and parking meters that are regularly checked for rejected coins by passing *gentlemen of the road.*

trancock's half hour *n.* An errant thirty minutes spent surfing *flipper* pornography on the internet, before returning to normality.

tranny *1. n.* An old fashioned radio. *2. n.* Transvestite, transexual, transparency or transit van, *eg.* A fetish photographer might say *'Shit. I left that tranny of the tranny and the tranny in the back of* *the tranny.'*

tranny cranny *n. medic.* A bubble'n'squeak-style *minge* knocked up from leftover bits of *meat and two veg* as part of gender reassignment surgery. *'Bloody hell, love. Do we have to watch these Channel 4 documentaries about sex change operations while we're having our tea?' 'Yes we do, it's educational. That doctor's just made his patient a nice new tranny cranny, look. More sausage casserole, dear?'*

transalvite *n.* Peculiar term for a transvestite used by your grandad, who is not sure how to pronounce the word correctly as there weren't any around while he was busy winning two world wars. Mind you, he had a few close shaves in the brothels out east after the last lot, he can tell you.

transferred phallus *euph.* Adapted from the well known legal term "transferred malice", whereby a person receives a blow which is intended for another person. *Transferred phallus* is where a woman receives a *scuttling* which is likewise intended for another, *eg.* When her husband *gives her one* while fondly imagining he is *banging* that blonde who works in the fish shop.

transformer *1. n.* One who, on finally *coming out*, starts going on about Judy Garland a lot. *2. n.* Lou Reed album which includes the track *Walk on the Wild Side.*

Transit of Venus *1. n.* Small spot crossing the face of the Sun behind thick clouds four times every 243 years. *2. n.* A mobile boudoir, *ie.* A van containing a heavily stained mattress and the smell of *spunk.* A *shagging wagon, fuck truck, lust bus, spambulance, willybago.*

transporter bridge *1. n.* Petrochemical wonderland Middlesbrough's most famous landmark. *2. n.* The no-man's-land between the *freckle* and the *Mary Hinge.* Also, variously, the *Humber bridge, taint, tinter, notcher, carse, biffon, scran, twernt, Berlin Wall, Botley Interchange, Barry Gibb, Bosphorus, brink, crontis, clutch, joy division, Potsdamer Platz, butfer, snarse, biffin bridge, Checkpoint Charlie, varse* or *Wirral peninsula.*

trap *1. n.* A toilet cubicle in a line of toilet cubicles. *2. v. nav.* To *pull. 'I went down to Pompey docks last night and trapped the Commander's missus.' 3. n.* A *flipper.*

trapped in the Himalayas *adj.* To be mid-way through a *tit wank.*

trapper's delight *euph.* When washing one's hands in a public lavatory, the *schadenfroh* pleasure felt as an unfortunate victim enters the *trap* where one has just sent a spectacularly pungent *shit to*

the beach.

trap pirouette *n.* The light-footed, on-a-sixpence-style 180 degrees twirl performed when a fellow walks into an empty public lavatory cubicle only to find that it has been the subject of a *dirty protest*, been *pebbledashed* with *arse-gravy* or is full of *bangers and mash.*

trap three trepidation *n.* Understandable feeling of anxiety about what one is about to encounter upon venturing into the last operational cubicle in the *Rick Witters. Crapidation.*

travel dick *n.* Like an ordinary *dick*, only smaller. *'Put your travel dick away, will you, Nigel.'*

travel fat *n.* Unwanted *stalk* which sprouts on public transport. A *purple-headed gristle thistle* germinated by sitting on a seat located directly over the axles of a corporation omnibus. Also *travel fat, traveller's marrow, diesel dick, routemaster, Varney teacake.*

travel iron *1. n.* A small, hard thing that puts creases in one's trousers on holiday. *2. n.* A small, hard thing that puts creases in one's trousers on a bus.

travelled through shit *phr.* Said of a particularly smelly *toot* on the *trumpaphone. 'Christ on a fucking bike, that one had travelled through shit alright, your holiness.'*

Travelling Wilberries *1. n.* Short-lived pensioner supergroup. *2. n.* Time-served *clagnuts.*

travelodge kettle *n.* An extremely small, unimpressive object that is quick to *turn on* and occasionally emits steam out of its spout.

travel penis *n.* A particularly compact male member. *'Oh, I see, you've only brought your travel penis. Well, never mind, Mr Straw, you're here now.'*

trawlerman's welly, fanny like a *sim.* Descriptive of a commodious *snapper.* With the eye-stinging smell of dead kippers.

trawler's bilge *n.* Festering *moip*, stagnant *blip.*

trawler trash *n.* Lower class fisher-folk.

trawl of shame *n.* The sordid list of *strum sites* found on a gentleman's computer when he has neglected to clear his browser history.

traxedo *n.* Elegant evening wear sported by the *scratting* classes on a night out, consisting of a fake designer tracksuit purchased from a market stall.

Tray bentos *n. prop.* Nickname given to a lady with an obvious liking for cheap, tinned pastry delicacies.

treacle *1. n.* Term of affection used solely by Pete Beale in *EastEnders. 2. rhym. slang.* A *brew.* From treacle tart = Bakewell tart.

treading air *n.* Sitting on the *crapper* for an indefinite period, pushing tiny pockets of gas from one's *arse*.

treading bacon *n.* Depressing state of affairs whereby a chap has failed to bring his lady to a sufficient state of erotic rapture. *'I'm getting cramp in my hand here, Cleopatra. Can I just call it a day and go to sleep, love?' 'Aye, go on then, Mark Anthony. You've been at it for half an hour and you're still treading bacon.'*

treading water *n.* Light *strumming* on the *banjo* in order to keep one's interest up during the dull plot bits in a *grumble flick*, for example, or when queuing in *Dutch traffic.* Maintaining a *satiscraptory* level of *wood. 'You're under arrest.' 'But officer, I wasn't wanking, I was just treading water.'*

tread on a frog *v.* A wetter sounding version of *step on a duck.*

treasure trail *n.* The female equivalent of the *crab ladder.* The hairy line of fluff that joins the navel to what's buried down below.

tree hugger *n.* A magical *copper cable* which leaves your *nipsy* so clean you could eat your dinner off it. If you could reach. An environmentally friendly *faecee.*

tree log *n.* A *chocolate shark* whose snout is in the water before its tail leaves one's *arse*; a *Cuban bum cigar*, a *bridger, earthing cable, bottom log.*

tree monkey *n.* A *hand on heart.*

treen *n. Wood* of the sort that *Bargain Hunt's* car-boot-sale Terry-Thomas Tim Wonnacott might get while looking at Clarice Cliff's jugs.

tremble trigger *1. n.* In munitions, a booby trap or anti-handling device that explodes if tampered with. *2. n.* The *devil's doorbell, clown's hat, shark's nose, wail switch, love button* or *skipper. 3. n.* The male *G-spot*, lurking up the *chocolate starfish*, just behind the *doughnut. 'How about there, Edward?' 'That's it, Sophie, bit higher. Yes, that's me tremble trigger alright.'*

trench dick *n. medic.* The *clap. Happy rash.*

trench gooch *n. medic.* The degraded state of a chap's *biffin bridge* during a sustained period of hot weather, or simply after not washing his *undercarriage* properly for a few weeks.

trenchmates *n.* Multiple comrades who have had *carnival knowledge* of the same *bird*, whether simultaneously or otherwise. *Custard cousins, twatmates, brothers quim.*

treseme *n.* A lower-class *lady of the night*, ie. One who is, like the eponymous TV-advertised shampoo, "professional but affordable".

triage *n.* Mental process of a chap entering a nightclub, whereby he mentally sorts the attending *flap* into three groups; those that deserve attention immediately, those who can wait until after a few

pints and those who are beyond help.

triangle of success *1. n.* In root cause analysis, whatever that is, a schematic diagram outlining the current issue and the steps that must to be taken to address it before everyone falls asleep. *2. n.* A *ladygarden. 'How did you get on with that bird from the Feathers, Ian?' 'I achieved the triangle of success, mate.'*

tribe tribe tribe tribe *exclam.* Peer-pressurised chant which is shouted at a drinking companion who is imbibing a mind-bending lager against his better judgement. From adventurer Bruce Parry's erstwhile *Tribe* programme, during which he routinely got administered with poisonous frogs' anal bum juice and what-have-you.

trick *n.* Customer in a *rub-a-tug shop*, a *Hillman Hunter, gonk* or *John* who is "turned" by a *good time girl.*

trickle-down economics *n.* Calculation to work out the proportion of one's income which must be spent on incontinence products as advancing years wreak havoc on one's *waterworks* infrastructure.

trick or treat *n.* A *tree monkey* that could easily *drop a log.* A possible *follow through.*

triffid, the *n.* Bizarre and frankly pointless sexual act whereby a fellow presses the tip of his *referee's whistle* against his partner's forehead, then pinches the *fiveskin* between his finger and thumb while pulling back gently, causing a slight vacuum. Done correctly, this apparently leaves a lovebite-type circle on his victim's skin, it says here, as if they have been in a fight with a carnivorous tulip.

triffid wilter *n.* A *botty burp* of such rancid pungency that it would even poison a highly venomous and carnivorous extra-terrestrial plant.

trifle *n.* The multi-layered mess residing in the bottom of the *shit pot* after a bhuna too far.

trifucta *n. Aus.* A *three root* weekend, with three different *Sheilas.*

triggernobetry *n.* The ability to produce instant ejaculation in a man by prodding his prostrate gland with the finger, practised by pros, *joff clinic* nurses and Countesses of Wessexes. The *walnut manoeuvre.*

trilogy *n.* Also known as *brown Star Wars.* A *turd* of such epic proportions it has to be released in three instalments. The first can stand on its own as a complete adventure. The second links to the first, but has a dark, inconclusive feel generating an air of foreboding and leaving itself wide open for an unknown ending. The final chapter has drama, excitement and moments where you think all is lost. A grand battle is waged where good overcomes evil and peace is restored in your *arse*.

trim *n. coll.* Tidy *bush, talent* or *totty*. *'Plenty of trim in tonight, vicar.'*

trim the wax *v.* To clean the build-up of *hedam* from under the brim of the *bishop's mitre*.

trip advisor *1. n.* A website where you can *slag off* someone's restaurant or hotel. *2. n.* A name given to the person who can inform you of the best place to buy illicit psychoactive substances. *'Got any Charlie, Dave?' 'No mate, you'd be best talking to the Trip Advisor. He's that big cunt over by the bar.'*

tripe hound *n.* A sexist description of a *fugly dog*.

tripe stick *1. n.* Evil-smelling piece of chewable gristle which keeps the mouth of man's best friend occupied. *2. n.* A pet food treat.

triple crown *1. n.* The Holy Grail of Rugby Union players; to win matches against the other three home nations. *2. n.* The Holy Grail of Rugby Union players; to *shout soup, piss* and *shit* oneself in the back of a taxi. *3. n.* When the missus is kitted out in matching bra, panties and suspenders and you confidently anticipate spending the evening punting your *balls between her uprights*.

triple-jabbed *adj.* Descriptive of a recumbent lady who has just been *done front, gob and back*. Also *shanghaied*.

triple jump *1. n.* A soft playground sport as practised by *bespectable*, grinning sometime God-botherer Jonathan Edwards. *2. n.* To *have* all three available *holes* in one session.

triple point shite *n.* A far-from-sublime *feeshus* in the *Camillas* that exists simultaneously in the three known states of matter, *viz.* Gas, solid and liquid.

triple threat *1. n.* In showbusiness, a performer who can act, sing and dance, *eg.* Michael Caine, Vinnie Jones. *2. n.* A *Lionel Bart* that is not only noisy, but also smelly and wet.

trip to Trumpton *n.* A visit to the *cludgie* where you sit on the *Barney McGrew* and fart several times.

Tristram hand shandy *n.* An amusing, yet rambling and ultimately inconclusive, *wank*, named after the book by Laurence Sterne which nobody has ever finished, and what's more anybody who tells you they have is a liar. A *cock and balls story*.

triting *n.* The pseudo-meaningful *shite* written all over the soft furnishings, wallpaper and Twitter profiles of *fucking* idiots, *eg.* "Life isn't about waiting for the storm to pass – it's about learning to dance in the rain" and so on.

trogg *n.* A simpleton or *fuckwit*. See also *pranny*.

Trojan *n. US.* An American brand of war-like, Greek *French letters*. Although a brand name

which brings to mind the story of the Trojan horse is, if you think about it for a moment, a strange one for a *rubber Johnny* manufacturer to have chosen.

Trojan arse *n.* A toilet bowl invasion that takes one by surprise in the middle of the night and sends one back to bed in a state of sleepy bemusement. A somnambulodefecation.

Trojan fart *n.* A *cheek flapper* that conceals an unwanted passenger. A *shart, shump* or *brown cough*.

Trojan flick *n.* The act of removing the last globules of *love porridge* from one's *tackle* by firmly holding the penile shaft and applying a single firm shake in the style of a fly fisherman or hansom cab driver.

trolley bag *n.* A *fugly* stewardess working for a budget airline. The opposite of one of them *trolley dollies* off of the Virgin Airlines adverts.

trolley dash *n.* An urgent sprint towards the supermarket *crappers* in order to avoid an *unexpected item in the bagging area*. *2. n.* Of a *punter,* to chase a prostitute who has stolen his trousers down a back alley, wearing just his underpants, shoes and socks.

trolley dolly *1. n.* An air hostess. *2. n.* A *ladyboy, shim, bobby dazzler* or *tiptop*.

trolleys *1. n.* Kecks *2. n.* Underkecks.

trolleytubby *n.* An overweight airline stewardess, usually found working in the first class cabin because she's too wide to fit down the economy aisle.

troll factory *1. n.* A means of disseminating fake news and other disinformation via the internet, usually sponsored by Russian intelligence as a means of distracting and demoralising the Western world, as if that needed doing any more. *2. n.* A bad discotheque with a plethora of *bonekickers, eg.* Cheeks Nightclub, Aldershot.

trollop *n.* See *trull*.

trollop snack *n.* Helmet cheese, foreskinzola, babybellend.

trollstoy *n.* A prolific online commentator; one who wages *War and Peace* on social media, *eg.* That fucking poisonous *bint* who was on *The Apprentice*.

trombone fag *n.* The attempts made to light a cigarette when you are so *wankered* that all perception of distance and perspective has evaporated and you cannot locate the end of your *coffin nail*, giving the impression that you are playing a rather melancholy tune on a small sackbut.

trombone player *n.* Someone who gives *blowjobs*. Or plays the trombone. Best sort that one out before you go on a date.

tromboning *v.* A thoroughly impractical sex act in which a person *rims* a pal's *brass eye* while simultaneously reaching round the front to give it some elbow on his *horn*. A *George Jism*.

troop the colour *v.* To leave a *skidmark* down the right or left hand side of the *pan* as a result of sitting side-saddle on the *crapper*, like the late Queen on parade. Before she was late, obviously. That would be horrible.

troot's mooth *n. Scots.* The *meatus*, *hog's eye*. *'Och maw, come quick! Gran'paw's stuck the wee pencil aff his diary doon his troot's mooth!'*

trophy hives *n. medic.* Painful or itchy eruptions of the skin that act as mementos of a sexual conquest. The *clap, happy rash, cock rot, brothel sprouts.*

trots, the *n.* The rapid foot movement required to urgently convey a diarrhoea sufferer to the lavatory. See also *Tijuana cha-cha, sour apple quickstep, Turkish two-step.*

trotter's knot *n.* The anal twitching of one afflicted with *the runs* who is trying not to dramatically *drop the shopping* while availing themselves of a lavatory which is not theirs.

trouble Tripitaka *v.* To have *one off the wrist.* From the popular, badly dubbed-into-English, Japanese kids' serial *The Water Margin* of the late 1970s, where the androgynous monk regularly used to *punish the monkey* when he got out of order.

trouble trophies *n.* Flowers, choccies and what-not intended to get a bloke out of the *shit* with his significant other. See also *dragon food.*

trough out *v.* To romantically *lick out* your missus like a pig looking for truffles.

trouser a Cuban *v.* To *shit* oneself, *light a bum cigar.* *'That portrait of Cherie on the stairs at Number Ten gave me quite a fright. In fact I think I may have trousered a Cuban, prime minister.'*

trouser arouser *n.* A *fit* lass.

trouser bandit *n.* Slightly more polite version of *turd burglar.* A *puddle jumper* who steals trousers.

trouser browser *n.* In a lap-dancing establishment, public park or cinema specialising in continental "art" films, a gentleman engrossed in an increasingly agitated search for loose change in his pockets.

trouser butter *n. Spunk. 'I don't know what the blob is on my thigh, vicar. Perhaps it's some trouser butter that dripped off my toast.'*

trouser chuff *n.* A Cornish seagull that lives in some *kex.*

trouser cough *n.* A *clearing of the nether throat* or *cat scarer.*

trouser department *1. n.* Section of a store dealing

with men's legwear. *2. n.* Area of the store in which middle-aged men experience problems. *3. n.* Wher Mr Lucas, Mr Humphries and Mr Rumbold work.

trousered *1. adj.* Wearing trousers. *2. adj.* Wasted, arseholed, wankered, shit faced. *3. adj.* Of an amount of money, appropriated opportunistically.

trouser engine *n.* Gentleman's machinery which, when sufficiently fuelled with beer, can be cranked into life and will thenceforth run by itself with a vigorous reciprocating action until its *nuts* work loose.

trouser folder *n.* The sort of fastidious person who, one might imagine, would have to carefully fold their clothes after taking them off before they could indulge in sexual intercourse, *eg.* Sven Goran Ericsson, Simon Cowell, the late Bruce Forsyth.

trouser grouse *n.* The melodious/malodorous warbling which emanates from a fellow's pantaloons after a night spent drinking Guinness and eating fish balti. Evocative of the mating call of a moorland game bird. *'What was that, Jeeves?' 'A trouser grouse, sir.'*

trouser jazz *n.* A session of different-sounding be-bop blasts on the *bum trumpet* released in quick succession.

trouser leg trombonist *n.* Popular female musician who plays in the same ensemble as the *skin flautist, meat harpist* and *pink oboe* virtuoso.

trouser Mauser *n.* A small, rapid firing *porridge gun.* A *pump action mottgun, mutton musket.*

trouserpatch *1. n.* A colourfully contrasting repair on a *Harry ramp's* twills as he merrily makes his way along the highways and byways of the English countryside, taking his pleasures where he may. *2. n.* A urine stain on the front of a pair of light kegs.

trouser rain *n.* A small downpour in the *keg* region leading to some dampness in the south. See *wet penny in the pocket, slashback, bowser trouser.*

trouser rake *n.* A stiffer version of the *trouser snake.* Often pops up and hits women in the face when inadvertently stood upon in the undergrowth.

trouser rouser *n.* A *brass eye*-opener. A *Bronx cheer.*

trouser snake *n. One-eyed pant python.*

trouser sneeze *n.* Like a *trouser cough*, but much wetter.

trouser tent *n.* Embarrassing portable erection made from canvas or other material, with a zip up one side and supported by a rigid *wood shaft.* If *pitched* while one is seated, a *trouser tent* can easily be concealed with a bowler hat. Or a top hat if one is particularly well endowed.

trouser tits *n.* A large pair of prominent *testicles.*

Man marbles. 'Fuck me, have you seen Rudolf Nureyev's trouser tits, your majesty? Have a lend of me opera glasses, not that you'll need them.'

trouser tonsil n. A woman's *wail switch, panic button* or *clematis*.

trouser trout n. Something one tickles in one's *trolleys* before taking it out and banging its head against a rock.

trouser truffle n. Following an over-enthusiasic *Bronx cheer*, a small nugget of *feeshus* nestling between your cheeks or in your gusset that may attract the interest of passing pigs.

trouser trumpet *1. n.* A trad solo blown on the *botty bugle. 2. n.* The E-flat *anus*.

trouser truncheon n. The stout length of *wood* a bobby takes out in the back of his van on a Saturday night. A *turned-on copper's torch*.

trout v. To *pull*. 'I was out trouting last night. Ended up with a right old five-to-twoer. Had to chew me own arm off this morning.'

trout gout n. medic. An inflammation of the female genitals, causing a fishy-smelling discharge. Particularly prevalent amongst *good time girls* who ply their trade near ports and dockyards.

trout jelly n. Artificial sexual lubricant. *I can't believe it's not batter, Grandma's little helper, granny batter.*

trout pocket *1. n.* A large, secret, slimy, fishy pouch concealed inside a poacher's waxed cotton coat, and hence *2. n.* A lady's *minge* with a coshed salmon hidden inside.

trout's mouth n. The *down there part* of a proper hotty.

trout tickling *1. n.* The time-honoured country technique of rubbing a fish's underbelly with the fingers. The sort of thing Jack Hargreaves or Phil Drabble would have done. *2. n.* The art of fingering the *blurtch* of a lady with personal hygiene issues. The sort of thing Jack Hargreaves or Phil Drabble would have done.

trucker's apple n. As coined by him out of off of The Beautiful South; a Scotch egg.

trucker's cushions n. *Ker-nockers, cabman's rests. Manchester Cities.*

trucker's mate n. Someone who looks like he could be a sex case, *eg.* Roy off *Coronation Street.*

trucker's mudflap, face like a sim. A reference to a lady who has evidently fallen out of the ugly tree and hit every branch on the way down. And then landed face-first in a pile of ugly gravel. And then been *twatted* with an ugly frying pan.

trucker's Tizer n. Refreshing brownish-yellow or orange liquid found reposing in plastic bottles on the hard shoulders and central reservations of

motorways. *Scania Scotch, hedge coke.*

truffle euph. To *follow through* when posh. *'Fetch a cloth, Carson. I do believe Lady Grantham's just truffled.'*

truffle butter n. Milp, blip. The *fanny batter* of a woman who is *frothing like bottled Bass.* 'I must say dear, watching Alan Titchmarsh at the Chelsea Flower Show has got my truffle butter streaming and now my gusset is wetter than an otter's neck. I really need to see to myself.'

truffle, chav n. A pork pie.

truffle heart *1. n.* One of the chocolates in a box of Milk Tray. *2. n. rhym. slang.* A *dropped gut.* From truffle heart = Bakewell tart.

truffle hunter n. An unnecessarily contumelious epithet for a *right fugly salad dodger.*

truffle hunting v. Taking a *trip around the world. Rimming.* Have a box of Smints handy.

truffle pigs n. *Digestively overqualified* folk with their snouts pressed up against the counter in Greggs.

truffleshuffle n. The characteristic gait of one who has *split the winnings.*

truffles, tramps' n. Discarded chips.

trull n. 19thC. A prostitute, a *hoo-er.* With fat *tits* but not many teeth, as stabbed up by Jack the Ripper in Old London Town.

trump *1. v.* To *fart* or *pass wind* in a chair-shaking way. *2. v.* To do a noisier or smellier *fart* than the previous person.

trumpaphone *1. n.* One of the less classy instruments of the orchestra; a brass/woodwind hybrid which is basically a trumpet fitted with the mouthpiece from a saxophone. *2. n.* A windsome *freckle* put to musical use, making a sound not unlike *1.*

trump campaign n. An inexplicably well-received passing of noxious *flatus.*

trumped phr. When exiting a works *bog* cubicle and breathing deeply, encountering a flatulent miasma even worse than that which you have been holding your breath attempting to avoid.

trumpelstiltskin n. prop. Affectionate nickname in the pub for a *short-arsed* geezer who *farts* a lot.

trumpeteering n. Trying to keep a *fart* in with a wet finger. And failing, you might reasonably suppose.

trumpeter's lips n. The involuntary pursing of the *tea towel holder* at moments of extreme fear. *'Any man who tells you he is not afraid to go into battle is either a fool or a liar. It is the fear that makes him fight. I personally had the trumpeter's lips throughout the entire North African campaign.'* (from *The Memoirs of Field Marshal Montgomery*).

trumpet flower n. *Balloon knot, ringpiece,*

chocolate bassoon.

trumpet major, the *1. n.* Historical novel by Thomas Hardy, published in 1880. Never heard of it. *2. n.* A brassy, Pearl & Dean-style fanfare blast from the *fifties teatowel holder* that could easily tear a hole through your *undercrackers.*

trump force one *1. n.* Comical former US president's personal aircraft. *2. n.* A very slight *flatus,* detectable only by sensitive vicars, bloodhounds, and maiden aunts, that causes minor disturbance to a rising smoke plume.

trump landslide *n.* An unexpected and unfortunate event whereby a simple release of hot air from an *arsehole* escalates calamitously.

trump plaza *n.* A public restroom where a *craps tournament* takes place. Also ideal for the storage of *top secret files.*

Trump's fingers *n.* Distressing condition caused by the overconsumption of Tingly Prawn Skips and Scampi Fries.

Trump Turnberry *1. n.* An exclusive Scottish 'golf resort' where Irn Bru is banned. *2. n.* A forceful *air-biscuit* that prompts the release of an unexpected *clagnut.*

trump with a lump *n.* A *grime bubble* that has a hidden *easter egg.* *'Oops. That was a trump with a lump. Now let's go over to Carol Kirkwood in the Blue Peter Garden and see what the weather's got in store for us today.'*

truncheon *n.* A solid, one piece *turd* which, if grasped, firmly could be used to stun a miscreant.

truncheon voucher *n.* A *porking ticket* issued the missus in lieu of a present.

truncheon voucher *n.* A *ticket to the policeman's ball.* A constabulary bribe, a *cop tip.*

trunk *n.* A large *knob* which squirts water over Johnny Morris.

trunking *n.* An amusing gentleman's party trick whereby he pushes his *dobber* up his own *nipsy,* in a style that is charmingly reminiscent of the way an elephant pushes a bun into its mouth.

trunkles *n.* Ankles that are so big they look like arboreal boughs.

truth serum *1. n.* A synthetic psychoactive chemical such as sodium pentothal, flunitrazepam or amobarbital used by intelligence agencies to extract secrets from persons under interrogation. *2. n.* A quantity of alcohol sufficient to allow the imbiber to foolishly tell their nearest and dearest what they really think of them.

try a little Freddie *v.* To indulge in a spot of light *bumcraft,* out of curiosity more than anything. *'After Lancing, Evelyn Waugh went up to Oxford, where he read History at Hertford College. During* his three years there, he neglected his formal studies and threw himself into a vigorous social scene populated by artists, actors, poets and aesthetes. He later recalled: "Moving in such artistic circles in those heady, hedonistic days between the wars, one was inevitably tempted to try a little Freddie from time to time. I tried it at least twice, but found it most disagreeable as it tended to make my nipsy feel sore."' (from Waugh and Peas – The Novelist and his Allotment Produce by Michael Holroyd and Alan Titchmarsh, Macmillan Books).*

try and find a yankee candle made from that *exclam.* Humorous saying used after breaking wind. Also *fer-fetch a cloth, Granville; someone let him in; someone's tinkered with Herbie; speak on, sweet lips that never told a lie; I'm ready for the question, Noel* and *mighty fine words, preacher.*

trycoxagain *n. medic.* Treatment which may be efficacious when attempting to alleviate symptoms in short-tempered, overly emotional *splitarses. 'What's up with her, doctor?' 'Oh, nothing a dose of trycoxagain couldn't cure.'*

trying to catch a fart with a fishing net, like *sim.* Pursuing a futile endeavour. *'I've used a whole box of firelighters and about half a gallon of petrol attempting to get this Tesco Instant Light Barbecue going. It's like trying to catch a fart with a fishing net, your holiness.'*

trying to get the last pickled onion from the jar *euph.* Deep *gusset typing* while biting the tongue.

trying to open an oyster with a bus ticket, like *sim.* Descriptive of a fruitlessly flaccid attempt at intercourse. Also *like an elephant nudging a tree, stuffing a marshmallow in a piggy bank, pushing string, poking fog up a hill with a sharp stick.*

trying to separate two stubborn bacon rashers, like *sim.* Said of a properly tight *mouse's ear.* Also *trying to pull open a toasted cheese sandwich.*

trying to stamp a rugby ball down a golf hole *phr.* Descriptive of the painful experience of attempting to pass an *April fool* that is several sizes too big for one's *nipsy. 'I hate going to the bog on Boxing Day, Bing. It's like trying to stamp a rugby ball down a golf hole. Anyway, let's sing a duet. Do you know the Little Drummer Boy?'*

trying to start a Spitfire with the choke out *euph.* while enjoying a post beer and curry dump, the noise one's *chamber of horrors* makes as it expels a plethora of solids and slime.

try on the comedy beard *v.* To perform *cumulonimbus, impersonate Stalin.*

Ts and Cs apply *euph.* In a Situations Vacant ad, a hint that applications from female candidates will be particularly welcomed.

tubby chaser *n.* A man who thinks *thunderbirds* are go. Also a woman who prefers her *beefcakes* to be *salad dodgers*.

TUBER/tuber *1. acronym. medic.* Doctor's shorthand written on the notes of good-looking female patients. Totally Unnecessary Breast Examination Required. That one's not aged well. *2. acronym.* Descriptive of certain aesthetically upsetting breeds of dog, such as the Basenji, Beagle, Elkhound, Fox Terrier, Chow Chow and Bichon Frise. Tail Up, Brown Eye Revealed. *'Have you met my pedigree tuber, Portnoy Fauntleroy of Ballykissangel? Oh he likes you, look. He's got his lipstick out and ejaculated down your leg.'*

tubesteak *n. Beef bayonet on the bone.*

tube strike *n.* That time of the month.

TUBFUF/tubfuf *acronym.* Thumb Up Bum, Finger Up Fanny. All business.

tub thumper *n.* One who is not averse to the odd game of *up periscope* on bath night.

tucking [one's] shirt-tails in *euph.* Initiating a saucy *one-in-a-bed romp*. A phrase believed to have first been coined by mad-eyed US lawyer Rudi Giuliani whilst cooking up a *bonobo's breakfast in* his trousers in front of a teenaged female *Borat* stooge.

Tuesday, Wednesday and Thursday *phr.* Way of spelling out the word "twat" that can be used in response to someone saying they will "See you next Tuesday."

tufty club *n.* A *vertical bacon sandwich* surrounded by scraggy outcrops of *gorilla salad*. Named after the 1960s/70s schools road safety campaign fronted by a threadbare squirrel which was animated in a distinctly sub-Ray Harryhausen style repeatedly nearly stepping out in front of motor vehicles after buying an ice cream and so on.

tug *v.* To *pull*, as in a *pud*. A light-hearted *wank*. *'Dinner's ready, Sidney!' 'Down in a minute, dear. I'm just having a little tug.'*

tugboat *1. n.* A chunky *skiff* who is no oil painting but nevertheless provides an efficient *pulling* service. *2. n.* The small *frigspawn* vessels which navigate round the bath after a chap has *gripped the lather. 3. n.* A bachelor's crusty sock or other handy *spooge* receptacle.

tugbutt *n.* A saggy *caboose* that has lost its fight with the force of gravity and begun accelerating towards the centre of the earth at a rate of thirty-two feet per second squared.

tuggernaut *n.* A lorry driver *shedding his load* in his cab at Barton Park Services on the A1.

tugger's luck *n.* Fortuitously happening upon a stimulating sight which will come in handy when one is knocking out a few *knuckle children* later on. Coined in honour of the late erstwhile *Grange Hill* spin off in which Todd Carty drove around on a motorbike in search of fodder for his *wank bank*.

tugger's remorse *n. psych.* The more-or-less instant feeling of self-reproach experienced by a *merchant* who has just *banked with Barclays. Wangst, wanguish, Crying over spilt milk. 'There once was a man with a horse | Who found a jazz mag in some gorse | He went to his stable | Wanked all he was able | Then suffered the tugger's remorse.'* (from *Nonsense Rhymes I Tossed Off in Five Minutes* by Edward Lear).

tug interest *n.* An attractive person on an otherwise dull show who is there to hold the interest of long-term daytime TV viewers, *eg. Coutdown*'s Rachel Riley, *Good Morning*'s Holly Willoughby, *Real Deal*'s David Dickinson *etc.*

tugliatelly *n.* Italian pornography.

tug of bore *n.* A lethargic, half-hearted and uneventful *J Arthur* (for example inspired by a television weather forecaster's *frontal systems*) that is essayed simply to fill in the time between getting up and going back to bed.

tug of love *n. Pulling your string,* and really putting your heart into it.

tug of phwoar *n.* A spontaneous and urgent *one off the wrist* brought on by a particularly *horny* sight, *eg.* The bra adverts on London Underground escalators.

tug of raw *n.* The horrific tenth *Barclays* of the day for the gentleman who is *working from home.* A *blood wank.*

tug of war *1. n.* A notably hard and tiring act of *self pollution* undertaken while *heavily refreshed.* A *J Arthur Rank* which requires a lot of willpower to bring to a *satiscraptory* solution. *2. n.* A jobseeker or student's eighth *ham shank* of the day, enjoyed at about ten in the morning. *3. n.* A traditional rope-based contest for two teams of drunk, roaring rugby players at a village fete, whereby one team pulls the other over a central line to win. *4. n.* An urgent *act of self delight* practised by a man who is pressed for time, *eg.* One whose missus has just left the room to get her glasses. Also known as a *fist of fury* or a *race against the cock.*

tug pamphlet *n.* A *jazz magazine.*

tugpusher *n.* Of schools, workplaces and police stations, the individual who has taken on the responsibility for distributing hardcore *art pamphlets* amongst his colleagues. A *pornbroker, grumblemonger.*

tugs aft *exclam. marit.* An apposite response to the sound of a *Lionel Bart*. From the Merchant Navy practice whereby tugboats sound their foghorns when approaching the aft of a ship, which is usually acknowledged by the ship's mate announcing "tugs aft" over the tannoy. Which is a trade name, so it should be written with a capital 'T', but fuck that. And here's some more, portakabin, biro and hoover.

tug typing *n.* The ability to watch *grumble* on one's *jerk station* screen while simultaneously *glazing the knuckle*, without once averting the eyes down to one's turgid *old man*, even when it erupts a torrent of *hot fish yoghurt* onto the keyboard.

tugwax *n. Spongle, spadge, jitler.*

Tulisa's hanky, as wet as *sim.* A reference to a degree of moistness on a par with an *otter's pocket*, named in honour of the erstwhile NDubz singer's penchant for bursting into floods of tears when she was a judge on *The X Factor,* every time a contestant said their granny had piles.

tumblepube *n.* A fur ball of *clock springs* and other discarded pubic foliage which wafts around when the *bog* door opens.

tummy banana *n.* The most penis-shaped item in the *fruit bowl.*

tummy smile *n.* A glorious morning *boner* that rises once the *bag for life* has got up and gone off to work.

tummy Tetris *n.* The strange, yet not unpleasant, sensation whereby one's unborn *change of hearts* slot together satisfyingly in one's alimentary canal, before disappearing with an amusing noise.

tummy truncheon *n. Sixth gear stick, porridge gun,* penis.

tumnus *1. n. prop.* Surname of some hobbit or other out of *The Lion, the Witch and the Wardrobe.* 2. *n.* Portmanteau word describing the *tintis, notcher, barse etc.* From scroTUM = aNUS.

tump *n. Welsh.* The *beetle bonnet, monkey's forehead, monkey's chin, grassy knoll.*

tumwiper *n.* Any unfashionable item of clothing received as a gift from a well-meaning relative or friend that is immediately relegated to the function of wiping *spoof* off one's stomach after *self help.* A *jazz rag.*

tuna canoe *n.* A *bird's front bottom.* Also *Billingsgate box, adventure bay,* the *Bermuda triangle.*

tuna pruner *n.* Electric device for the removal of unwanted feminine hair; a machine that scythes mercilessly through a lady's *gorilla salad* with the vehemence of an angry 18th century crofter. Typically branded with a gentle sounding name to

give no clue as to the agony that awaits its user.

tuna taco *n.* A hot dish, not requiring cutlery, served when *dining at the Y*. If eaten with a side order of *cranberry dip*, it could lead to *Mexican lipstick*.

tuna town *n.* The female genitalia, *Billingsgate box.*

tuning up *1. n.* A series of discordant ascending and descending notes played on an instrument until an acceptable level of tunefulness is achieved, prior to the main performance, and thus *2. n.* A series of trombone-like *botty burps* of varying degrees of noise and odour prior to the ejection of *fudge* from the *tunnel.*

Tuns Lane interchange *1. n.* Roundabout junction on the M4 used to transit between touristic Windsor and the more utilitarian Slough, and thus *2. n.* The *taint, gooch, Humber Bridge, Tinsley Flyover, Luton-to-Dunstable busway, Potsdamer Platz, switch island* etc.

tup *1. v.* To have sex, *fuck.* 2. *v.* Of sheep-to-sheep *shagging*, red hot *horny* ram on ewe action.

tuppence licker *n.* A *bean flicker, carpet muncher, pelt lapper.* A wearer of *comfortable shoes.*

tuppenny all-off *1. n.* A cheap, no-nonsense haircut popular amongst national servicemen in the 1960s. 2. *n.* A no-nonsense *fannicure.* A *Brazilian.*

tupperware farty *n.* Dropping a *cupcake* into tight *undercrackers* and then, much later, breaking the airtight seal to share the still-fresh aroma with friends and neighbours.

tupperware tushe *n.* A gas-tight *rear box* that is very popular at parties.

tuppie *n. Scots.* A Dundonian term for a lady's *fluffit.* 'There's nae a kitten, moose or puppy / Ha'f sae soft as ma wife's tuppie.' (from *The Song O' the Dundee Growler* by Robbie Burns).

turbo shandy *n.* A male who is completely *shitfaced* after a couple of pints. A *two pot screamer* or *halfpint Harry.*

turbo shit *n.* The high-speed *dump* required to fool a ladyfriend into thinking you had only went for a *gypsy's kiss.* A *greyhound's egg.*

turbot for tea *exclam.* Announcement that *fish supper* is served. 'Never mind that tug, Sidney. It's turbot for tea.'

turd *n.* A cylindrical unit of *shit,* longer than a *tod.* A link of *feeshus.*

turdal wave *n.* The calamitous result of a giant *motion* dropping into the *bum sink.* A *poonami.*

turd bath *n.* The *bum sink.* 'Hello, this is Prince Harry in the Honeymoon Suite. Can you send someone up to unblock the turd bath please? It's all clogged up with Meghan's bangers and mash.'

turdberg *n.* A feculent shipping hazard of such deceptively gigantic proportions that ninety percent of its bulk typically remains underwater. A *growler.*

turdboggan *n.* A long, light, raft of *bumwad*, used to aid *number twos* sliding downhill over porcelain and reducing the likelihood of *skidmarks*.

turdbulimia *n.* Situation whereby your toilet eagerly swallows all your *bum rubbish* only to cough it back up shortly afterwards. *'Hello, is that Dyno-Rod? Can you send someone round, only our bog's suffering from turdbulimia.'*

turd burglar *n.* Stealthy thief who forces entry into the rear of a person's premises via the inside of the *chocolate drainpipe.*

turd clippers *n. US.* Buttocks.

turd degree burns *n. medic.* Post-curry *shitting* injuries. *'A man was taken to hospital last night after being found unconscious on the pavement outside a curry restaurant in Newcastle upon Tyne. He was suffering from shock, alcohol poisoning and had turd degree burns covering 90% of his anus. A spokesman for the restaurant said "Come to the Curry Capital, Bigg Market, Newcastle upon Tyne."'*

turd eagle *n. Aus.* A large *blowfly, dunny budgie* or *poobottle.*

turder *n.* The begetter of a *feeshus.*

turd eye *n.* The mystical sixth sense that usually, though not always, enables a pedestrian to avoid tripping over a length of *canine cable.*

turd fairies *n.* Mythological creatures that are thought to be the cause of the mysterious *ghost shit* phenomenon, ie. Those *Peter O'Tooles* of which there are no trace when one turns round to admire them in the *bum sink.*

turd fairies, visit from the *euph.* Descriptive of a sudden knock at the *back door* caused by the magical appearance of a large, explosive *payload* in the *bomb bay. 'Sorry I was late, General Custer, only I had a visit from the turd fairies. Did I miss anything?'*

turd girdle *n.* The feeling of uncomfortable abdominal tightness and cramping in the *Roddies* which is experienced when one's unborn *mudchild* is approaching full term. *Concraptions, turdle.*

turd hammock *n.* A looping piece of bathroom tissue dangling over the *bum sink*, held in place by the thighs of the sitter, which catches his or her *foulage* and suspends it mid-drop, allowing it to be gently lowered into the pan in a controlled fashion. For use at friends' and relatives' houses, or on caravan holidays, when a loud splash is simply not an option. Or you could even just do it for fun.

turd hernia *n. medic.* Brown *trout*-induced inability to walk upright. *'My client Mr Weinstein recently*

suffered a turd hernia, your honour, and therefore feels it would be unjust to make him go to prison for all them rapes he did.'

turd hurdling *n.* The sport of running in one's local municipal pleasure grounds. *'Mo Farah is a familiar figure to his Twickenham neighbours, and can often be seen turd hurdling through Strawberry Hill Park.'*

turdigo *n. medic.* Psychological condition, *viz.* In the *shitehouse*, the inability to look down at, or indeed to do anything about, the enormous *skidmarks* you've just left on the *pan*, which you then leave to the unalloyed delight of the next user.

turd immunity *n. medic.* The ability of a gentleman's *bag for life* who, after years of suffering, is no longer affected by the pungent aromas of her better half's particularly rancid *feeshii.*

turd in the hole *n.* Unpleasant, albeit compulsory, game played in rustic French campsite toilets, whereby the participant is required to *crimp off a length of dirty spine* while squatting over a hole the size of a coffee mug without *dropping his shopping* into his trousers.

turdis *1. n.* One of them detached, modern, portable, space-age-looking public conveniences that could well be a phonebox, bureau de change or small internet cafe. A *turd tardis. 2. n.* A disappointing *shit* that feels massive on the inside but is surprisingly tiny on the outside.

turdish delight *n.* The feeling of pride and well-being which results from an enjoyable and productive session on the *jobby engine.*

turdle *1. n.* A small but annoying obstacle in one's path when trying to accomplish something mundane. One *turdle* isn't too bad, but many everyday endeavours are wearingly replete with them, *eg.* Trying to speak to an actual person when calling the My Hermes helpline number to report a missing parcel, changing a forgotten iCloud password. *2. n.* Anything you mess about with on your phone while waiting for *a load of shoes to drop out the loft*, *eg.* Word games and such.

turdmoil *n.* A state of extreme perturbation, confusion, commotion, agitation or tummult occasioned by being in desperate need of a *nettie.*

turd'n'dickular *adj.* Said of someone who is both a *shit* and a *cock.*

turdo-prop *n.* A once-in-a-lifetime *Eartha* that presses down on the bottom of the U-bend while still firmly attached at the *nipsy*, thus providing its proud parent with much-needed support. A junior *neckbreaker.*

turdsearch *n.* The desperate hunt for reading

material one embarks upon when *Mr Brown is tapping at the window.*

turd's nest *n.* Before dropping a *shite*, arranging a baffle of folded toilet tissue in the hope of stopping – or at least minimising – *splashback. See also chocolate quilting, pap baffle, lilies on the pond.*

turd trimester *n.* Technical term describing the later stages of *mudchild birth. Concraptions.*

turdulence *n.* The area of dirty air affected by a particularly foulsome *trouser trumpet,* usually dispensed by a man walking in front of one in a tightly packed establishment, *eg.* The make-up section at John Lewis or when attempting to view the Rosetta Stone in the British Museum.

turd wallet *n.* The *arse.*

turd widow *n.* The lonesome mien of a one who is left on their own for extended periods of time while their partner *drops the shopping.*

turfer's knee, wetter than a *sim.* Descriptive of a lady's *clunge* in a state of preternatural excitement. A phrase that can be usefully employed when referring to a *fish drowner* that is *frothing like bottled Bass* or, indeed, *dripping like a fucked fridge.*

turf out *1. n.* An anal spring clean. A *shit* like a *butcher emptying his offal bin. 2. v.* To excrete *faceetious.*

Turin shroud *1. n.* Famous medieval sheet with Mick Fleetwood's face painted on it. *2. n.* A piece of *lavatory tissue* draped tastefully over a floating *log* that will not flush away. Also *coroner's cloth.*

turistas *n.* The *Turkish two-step.*

turk *v.* To *do* someone or something *up the council.* '*Sit down please, Lord Archer.*' '*If it's all the same with you, Governor, I'd rather stand. I've just been turked in the showers by Mr Big.*'

turkey *n.* The *cracker* you think you've pulled while drunk at the office Christmas party who turns out to be a rough old *bird* who only gets *stuffed* once a year.

turkey crown *n.* A recently shaved *cunt bone* that takes some *stuffing.*

turkey moss *n.* Serious *fluff* on a *bird's bodily treasure. Gorilla salad.*

turkey-neck *n.* That which is *throttled* in Norfolk.

turkey's wattle *n.* A *ragman's coat* or *club sandwich.*

turkey twizzler *1. n.* Unappetizing helix of nondescript brown matter of mysterious and sinister provenance, served to schoolchildren in lieu of real food. '*Minister, the current average cost of a primary school dinner is just fifty pence. That's not enough to provide pupils with a proper, balanced and nutritious meal.*' '*Fuck 'em. Just give the little cunts some turkey twizzlers or something.*' *2. n.* A thin, spiralling *turd* which retains its corkscrew shape even after it has been dropped into the *pan.*

Turkish *1. n.* Heterosexual *back door work,* while wearing curly slippers. *Irish. 2. rhym. slang.* An excrement. From Turkish delight = shite. '*What's the matter, Eric?*' '*Jocky Wilson done a Turkish in me shoe. Again.*'

Turkish barber's bin-bag *euph.* A particularly wiry-haired and well-stuffed lady's *clopper.*

Turkish delight *n.* Sweet, perfumey, chocolate-covered and exotic far-Eastern delicacy, manufactured in Birmingham. *2. n. Foulage.* '*Aw bollocks. Some dirty cunt's trod all Turkish delight into the hall carpet, June.*'

Turkish love letter *n.* A kebab posted through a letterbox on a drunken night out.

Turkish slippers *n.* The *jester's shoes.*

Turkish tumbleweed *n.* Kebab boxes, bits of uneaten salad and other cosmoplitan post-pub detritus blowing about the high street at 2am.

Turkish two-step *n. Smallroom dance* not dissimilar to the *sour apple quick step, Tijuana cha-cha,* or *Aztec twostep.* The *skitterbug.*

turned back at Timperley *euph.* Halted at *third base* by a lady due to timetabling issues or technical difficulties, obliging one to conclude one's journey manually. From the Altrincham line of the Manchester Metrolink, where trams will often eject all passengers at Timperley station, just short of the terminus.

turned-out trouser pocket, arsehole like a *sim.* A dropped *clacker valve,* resulting from either an excess of *Turkish,* or a red hot Indian.

Turner pants *euph.* Impressionistic image, quite possibly resembling an 18th century ship in fog, left on the underpants due to poor wiping prior to riding home on one's bike. '*Have you washed me Turner pants yet, mam?*'

turning the lawn into a nature reserve *euph.* Of a lady who refuses to tend to her *downstairs allotment,* letting it become as thick and unkempt as Epping Forest.

turning Yoko's mic off *euph.* Any intervention to attempt to mask an undesirable sound, *eg.* A modesty flush, a floating crashmat of *bog paper,* or closing the toilet door. See also *cough drop.*

turn it brown *v.* To eat something. '*Frances, your Midsummer Night's Dream wedding cake decorated with a confetti of beetroot hearts and dried pineapple flowers looks absolutely scrumptious. Paul and I can't wait to take a slice out of it and turn it brown.*'

turn Japanese *v.* To make like a *Chinese helicopter pilot,* gripping his *joystick* for grim life and concentrating on keeping his *chopper* up.

turn the air brown *euph.* To *cough* a cloyingly pungent *dead rat* which has the effect of lowering a sepia filter across the nasal passages.

turn your bike round *v.* To go to the lavatory. *'Excuse me, I'm just going to turn my bike round. Have you got any arse paper?'*

turpsichord *n.* A public house pianoforte, as played by rubber-fingered drunks.

turps nudger *n.* A *top shelf drinker. 'Have you seen that bloke who reads the local news? Jesus, what a fucking turps nudger.'*

turquoise *n.* A lady who allows the *dog in the bathtub*. One who doesn't object to being *turked* up the *bonus tunnel*.

turtle *1. n.* A passive sexual partner, *ie.* "Get her on her back and she's fucked". *2. n. coll. Blit, fanny, fluff, talent. 3. n.* One of the least sexy *bum games* a flatulent couple can play in the bedroom, the winner being the last one to poke their head out from under the duvet.

turtle beach *n.* The *bog*, where you drag yourself late at night to *lay your eggs*, hopefully without David Attenborough crouching next to you with a torch.

turtleberries *n. Winnets, dangleberries, Payne's Poppets.*

turtle bollix *exclam. NE.* Ashington dialect describing something substandard. *'Mam, this chicken oddments box from AFC is turtle bollix man. It's aal beaks and eyebrows.'*

turtle bungee *n.* The dangerous sport of releasing and retracting *turds* by clever use of the sphincter muscles just before they *touch cloth. Prairie dogging, gophering.*

turtle burps *n.* The sequence of small, soundless, foul-smelling *trouser coughs* emitted in the minutes immediately preceding the *monkey's toe.*

turtle charmer *n.* A person who overbakes their *Thoras* and leaves going for a *Tom tit* to the very last minute.

turtle guillotine *n.* The *nipsy, cigar cutter, clackervalve.*

turtle mat *1. n.* Revolutionary mud-trapping doormat as endorsed by digitally challenged beardy ice-plodder Sir Ranulph Fiennes. *2. n.* The *autographed jelly hammock* of the *dunghampers* when one is *clutching Bungle.*

turtle neck *n.* An advanced *peeping Tom.* So-called because it is "like a turtle's head but you know it's going to be a sweater".

turtle nudger *n.* A *fruit fumbler.*

turtle power *n.* The unstoppable superhero-like strength exhibited by a determined *chod* as it tries

to overcome a tightly clenched *nipsy.*

turtle recall *v.* The brief retraction of the *turtle's head* while en route to the *thunderbox.*

turtle's breath *n.* The very final warning *fart* before the *turtle* pokes its *head* out to *autograph the gusset.*

turtle scarer *n.* A pile of *bangers and mash* left by the previous occupant of a public lavatory cubicle, causing the *tortoise's leg* to withdraw in fear.

turtle's den *n.* The *bomb bay, dirt kitchen, devil's bakery.*

turtle's head *n.* The initial protrusion of a stool though the *tea towel holder*, the point at which contracts are exchanged for the construction of a *log cabin.* Not quite *touching cloth; the monkey's toe.*

turtle's head revisited *n.* A fond, nostalgic look back at an old pair of *autographed grundies.*

turtle soup *1. n.* Politically incorrect testudinoid delicacy served as a starter in certain, high-end Oriental restaurants. *2. n.* A very runny reminder of a meal in a low-end Oriental restaurant. *'Four score and seven years ago our fathers brought forth on this continent, a new nation, conceived in Liberty, and dedicated to the proposition that all men are created... I'm sorry, does anyone know where the bogs are? Only I've got the turtle soup.'* (text of address by Abraham Lincoln, Gettysburg, Pennsylvania, November 19th 1863).

turtle's shoulders *euph.* The *point of no return*, lavatorially speaking. *'Hey Gary, pass the ball!' 'I can't. I've got the turtle's sh-sh-shoulders. Aw bollocks.'*

turtle's tail *1. n.* The last bit of *Gladys* to drop out of the *back bottom* at the pleasingly relaxed end of a *sit-down toilet adventure* that began somewhat more urgently. *2. n.* The opposite of the *turtle's head*; the re-appearance of the tapered end of a *feeshus* from the U-bend after flushing. A *déjà poo.*

turtle stew *n.* A well-stocked *can* of *bum soup.*

turtle wax *1. n.* Car polish. *2. n. medic.* Haemorrhoid ointment. *3. n.* The peculiar-smelling clear lubricant which is all that remains to be wiped off your *cigar cutter* when you do one of those really satisfying, hard-but-clean *oily loafs* that descend *like an otter off a bank.*

turtle wipeout *n.* The careful removal of a small brown deposit from the *dot* of a chap who has *gambled and lost.*

tush *n. US. Bum* (but not a tramp), *ass* (but not a donkey). *'That's it, girls. Stick out your tushes!'* (Busby Berkeley on the set of *42nd Street Proctologist Scandals of 1933*).

tussage *n. coll. Talent*, female *buffage, blart, totty.*

Tutankhamen's nut sack *euph.* Something very

wrinkly, *eg.* Lord Sir Alan Sugar's forehead, Lord Sir Alan Sugar's *saddlebags.*

tutu *n.* A tissue paper bib placed around the base of the tumescent generative member to catch any *ropes* which get *lobbed* while *relieving stress.* Named after the famous Anglican Archbishop of Cape Town who popularised this practice.

TV *1. abbrev.* A television. *2. abbrev.* A *tranny.*

TWABs/twabs *abbrev. Scots.* Scrotal condition which principally affects oil workers who find themselves stranded on the rig beyond their usual fortnight working period due to bad weather. Three Week Away Baws.

twactor *n.* A tragedian of dubious thespolographical accomplishments.

TWAC/twac *abbrev.* The sort of person you don't want to get stuck behind on a Bank Holiday Friday driving over Kirkstone Pass. Tosser With A Caravan.

twambler *n.* A *twat* who ambles around. From twat + rambler. Normally found wandering in a vague direction while staring at their mobile phone.

twanger *1. n. Whanger. 2. n.* Half of a pair of *twangers.*

twangers *n. onomat.* Generic term for ladies' *undercrackers,* but more specifically those worn by dirty *scutters.* Named after the Etch-a-Sketch-like sound the gusset makes as it leaves the crotch when pulled hastily down from either side. *'And Lady Diana Spencer looks resplendent as she walks down the aisle, keeping up the age old traditions. She's wearing an old 18th century tiara, a magnificent new wedding dress, a diamond necklace borrowed from her friend the Duchess of Argyll, and a pair of blue twangers.'* (Sir Alastair Burnett, Royal Wedding commentary, ITN, 1981).

twangling *n.* The jaunty action of a lady's *independent front suspension* under a T-shirt, especially in the summer months.

twangs my banjo string *phr.* Said of a woman who *floats your boat. 'Did you see that fascinating documentary about medieval illuminations on BBC 4? It was an absorbing insight into something or other, I would imagine. And that hottie who presents it really twangs my banjo string and all, I can tell you.'*

twang the wire *v.* To pluck out a *jazz rhythm* on the one-stringed banjo.

twankunt *n.* Descriptive of someone who is not just a *twat,* but also a *wanker* and a *cunt* to boot. *'Today's birthdays: Sandro Botticelli, Italian painter of the Florentine school, 1445; Augustus Pugin, Gothic revivalist architect, 1812; Nick Griffin,* twankunt, 1959.'

twart *n.* At a disco, the quasi-terpsichorean practice of projecting the *mud-flaps* rearwards and oscillating seductively, whilst simultaneously taking advantage of the opportunity provided by the accompanying percussive pop music to release a *flock of excitable ducks.* From Twerk + Fart.

twastard *n.* A person who is not only a *twat,* but also a *bastard.* From twat + bastard. *'Today's birthdays: Sandro Botticelli, Italian painter of the Florentine school, 1445; Augustus Pugin, Gothic revivalist architect, 1812; Nick Griffin, twastard, 1959.'*

twaste *n.* The taste of a *twat.* From twat + taste, one would imagine. *'Come on, eat it all up.' 'I don't like the twaste.'*

twat *1. n.* A *minge. 2. n.* Stupid person. *3. v.* To hit, beat up. *'And Richard Dunn's getting fucking twatted here, ladies and gentlemen.'* (Harry Carpenter, BBC1, May 24th 1976). *4. v.* Past participle of the verb "to twitter". *'I just twat my followers and told them I was stuck in a lift.'*

twataclysm *n.* An horrific event involving *twats,* such as the celebrity-studded opening of a "fashionable London cupcake bakery".

twatalogue *n.* A magazine of *pornitholgical* interest. An *art pamphlet.*

twatapult *1. n.* A lady's skimpy elasticated undergarment. *'Aw, the decorator's jizzed in me twatapult drawer again, Terry. You'd best have a word with him.' 2. n.* A cheap flight to Prague, full of stag weekend revellers.

twat burger *euph.* A polite euphemism for an *act of oral affection* performed upon a woman's *bodily treasure.* Hopefully without too much ketchup on it.

twat burglar *n.* A man, presumably wearing a mask and stripy jersey, who steals another bloke's missus.

twat cap *n.* A flat or country cap when worn by a *scrote, pog, rat boy* or ne'er-do-well.

twatch *n.* An oversized, gaudy timepiece of the sort worn by a professional footballer, *Grand Tour* presenter, carpet warehouse owner or Formula One racing driver. From twat + ch.

twat clap *n.* A *fanny fart, frampton* or *queef.*

twaterpillars *n.* Female version of *willipedes. Cloppular crabs, mechanical dandruff.*

twatful *1. n.* A good *seeing to* in the sexual sense. *'Just 8 pints tonight, lads. Got to get home to give the rib a twatful.' 2. n.* An imperial measure of *spangle,* equal to 2 *nutsworths. 'Sister Amoeba was powerless to resist. His eyes burned into hers like a sort of stone. His papal arms enfolded her body as she felt herself being swept away in some sort of weather system of* *passion. Then he lifted his cassock and gave her a right twatful.'* (From *The Mother Superior and the Holy Father*, by Barbara Cartland).

twat hook *n.* Curved implement used to catch a *mackerel*. A chap's finger.

twat hour *n.* The times of day, typically around 8.30 am and 3.30 pm, when every road near any school in Britain is brought to a halt by large numbers of parents attempting to reverse their enormous off-road vehicles into 8-foot parking spaces. *'Sorry I'm so late. I hit twat hour just as I turned onto St. Paul's Road, Cambridge. I was stuck outside Sancton Wood School for two hours while some fuckwit drove a VW Touareg backwards and forwards 635 times without turning the steering wheel in the hope that it might somehow magic the thing into the fucking space.'*

twatire *n.* Type of low level topical humour of the sort popularised by sour-faced comedians on programmes such as *Mock the Week*. *'And the subject of the next round is "Things an audience would never laugh at". Let's have some twatire written by a large team of desperate programme associates on that subject.'*

twat like a jailor's keyring *sim.* A slack *mingepiece*. *'My client wouldn't say the plaintiff's easy, but she's got a twat like a jailor's keyring, your honour.'*

twatlings *n.* Juvenile offsprings of the lower orders who follow their (slightly) elders around whilst aping the dress, foul language, and poor behaviour of the adults. *'Welcome to Alton Towers. Admission £53 per adult, children £46, £60 per twatling. OAPs free.'*

twat mag *n. Bongo periodical,* noddy comic. *'You don't know anything about this half-hundredweight of twat mags I've just found on top of the wardrobe, do you, Frank?'*

twat mallet *n.* A *fanny hammer.* *'Need anything fetching from the shops, Mildred?' 'Just a loaf of bread and some new PP3s for me twat mallet, George.'*

twatmates *n.* Gentlemen who have both had a portion of the same *haddock pastie,* eg. Bryan Ferry, Mick Jagger and Rupert Murdoch; Michael Jackson & Nicholas Cage; Sir Donald Campbell & Claude Greengrass off *Heartbeat.* No, it's true. Look it up. *Custard cousins, brothers quim.*

twatmosphere *n.* The unpleasant feeling that develops in a room the moment a *twat* walks in.

twat nappy *n.* See *clot mop.*

twat nav *n.* Motoring terminology; the wife with a road atlas. *Sat nag.*

twat of nine tales *n.* The fellow office worker who always has a story that whips whatever it is that

you happen to be talking about. A *top trumper, raconteur* or *four ball Paul.*

twatois *n.* The sort of Chet Hanks-stylee fake West Indian dialect favoured by middle class youths wishing to enhance their street credibility. *Jafaican.*

twat pamphlet *1. n.* A *grumble book, noddy comic* or *flesh mag* purchased by men who aspire to *unblock the sink,* eg. *Razzle, Knave, Splosh* etc. *2. n.* An aspirational "lifestyle" magazine read by utter *wankers,* eg. *Dazed & Confused, Wonderland™, Wallpaper.*

twatplates *n.* Personalised car registration plates, especially those on which the numbers have been re-spaced or mutilated in order to make them spell out something from a distance, *eg.* Those on a white Fiat Punto 1.4 where the owner might place a black screw at the bottom of the two 1s in P11 NTO*. (*That number is actually on a Porsche 911, so what do we know?)

twat rats *n. Cunt mice* for ladies with a heavier quad-hebdomadal flow of *fanny jam.* Industrial strength *mott blotters.*

twat rattler *n.* A *plastic cock,* a vibrator, *neck massager, bob, AA member.*

twatriot *1. n. UK.* Someone who waved a Union Jack and shouted "Come on Tim!" between every point while Tim "Spoilt Bastard" Henman got thrashed at Wimbledon every fucking year between 1994 and 2007. Also to be found wearing a plastic Union Jack hat and singing *Land of Hope and Glory* at the Last Night of the Proms, or queueing up for a week to shuffle past her maj's casket. *2. n. US.* A proud American defender of the Second Amendment, asking for a room overlooking the park when booking into an hotel carrying ten wheeled suitcases filled with automatic weapons.

twat seats *n.* The back two rows on the upper tier of a double-decker bus or an EasyJet flight from Newcastle to Alicante, reserved for cap-headed *scratters* who wish to cycle through their ringtones, engage in foul-mouthed, shouted debates and/ or light-hearted vandalism, and otherwise *act the cunt.*

twat shack *n.* A cheap and porous pop-up tent of the sort bought by thousands of music fans for the summer festival season.

twatslapping *n.* The untraceable clapping noise generated *below the stairs* when a man and a lady are doing *thingy.* A *Blair's ovation.* The same sound there was after Liz Truss said "pork markets."

twat snap *1. n.* The female equivalent of a *dick pic,* and likewise something that no member of the opposite sex would care to receive unsolicited on his mobile phone. *2. n.* A selfie with a UK politician. *'I just got a twat snap with Suella Braverman.'*

twatsuma *n.* Any annoying, bright orange celebrity.

twattachino *n.* Any one of the multitude of ridiculously overpriced, pretentiously named variations on a cup of fucking coffee, as ostentatiously enjoyed by *man bag*-toting *arseholes* around the world. *'Could we take a latte macchiato, a mochaccino freddo, a double doppio Americano and a ristretto lungo please?' 'Right, I'll just check that order back. So, that's four twattachinos. That'll be twenty-eight pounds. Also, we won't be paying any tax on that, neither.'*

twatter *n.* In-your-face workplace version of the popular, pointless internet micro-blogging service, whereby you are unable to avoid the *twat* sat three seats away loudly announcing to everyone in the room absolutely everything they've done since leaving the office the night before.

twatters *n.* Smashing *churns*. The sort that Nell Gwynn would have sported, especially if she was being portrayed in a *Carry On* film, a Michael Winner historical epic, or a sketch on *The Two Ronnies*. *Fat rascals.*

twat tickler *n.* An RAF pilot-type top lip adornment, popular with Triumph Spitfire drivers, *Countdown* presenters, and – more latterly – Norwegian ski jumpers.

twattoo *1. n.* A badly conceived, situated, designed, executed and/or spelled piece of body art, *eg.* The word "Brooklyn" written above someone's *arsecrack* in Ye Olde English capital letters. *2. n.* A *flapdoodle.*

twattoria *n.* Poncy restaurant for *bellends.*

twat tractor *n.* Any large, black, four-wheel-drive vehicle of the type favoured by professional footballers and other *twats*. *'The new BMW X6 is as outstanding in performance as it is impressive in appearance. Powerful engines endow it with the dynamics of a sports car, while the chassis combines the athletic shapes of a coupé with the thirst for adventure of a thoroughbred twat tractor.'*

twatula *n.* A flat wooden paddle for spreading depilatory unguents on a *bird's clopper.*

twaturated *adj.* Saturated with *twats*. *'This place is twaturated. Let's knock these back quick and go to the Black Bull.'*

twat vat *n.* Hot tub.

twatwrapper *n.* A multi-pocketed garment of the sort worn by the *sex cases* who stand at the end of railway platforms spotting numbers written on the sides of diesel locomotives. An anorak.

twaxi *n.* A cab being driven in a selfish and *twattish*

manner; that is to say, more or less all of them.

tweedle *1. n. rhym. slang.* Male ejaculate, *jitler* or *Thelonious*. From Tweedledum = cum. *2. n. rhym. slang.* Urine, *wazz* or *piss*. From Tweedledee = Peters & Lee.

twee surgeon *n. medic.* One employed to "tidy up" and make presentable the various bits and pieces of the missus's *farmyard* in the wake of a particularly traumatic birth.

tweezerpleaser *n.* A two-fingered *wank*. A *Harvey Smith*, snapping the chick's neck.

twelve o'clock cock *n.* A *pop-up pirate* which points straight upwards and thus casts no shadow at midday.

twentieth century fox *n.* A *milf* or, indeed, *gilf*. A saucy piece of historical *crumpet* dating from the previous millennium.

twenty-eighth of Mayhem *n.* The day marking the start of *rag week*. *Ruby Tuesday.*

twenty-five yard screamer *1. n.* Some sort of long range kick in an association football match. *2. n.* A former ladyfriend whose only means of social interaction with you seems to involve yelling your sexual shortcomings at you from a distance while full of *bitch piss.*

twenty-four sheeter *1. n.* Printing terminology for one of those large billboard posters you find at railway stations. *2. n.* A woman whose attractiveness is inversely proportional to a viewer's proximity to her. An *LRF* – from the fact that, like *1.*, she is attractive from three platforms away, but covered in a patchwork of big, colourful spots close up. *3. n.* A *Marmite pot.*

twenty-one bum salute *n.* A rousing rear-end cannonade traditionally delivered to welcome certain Potusses.

twenty-one gunt salute *euph.* A hen-night in Doncaster.

20/20 vision *euph.* Overly optimistic visual appreciation of the opposite sex following an excessive intake of the eponymous, fruity, fortified wine. Fashionable *beer goggles* as prescribed by an *alcopoptician.*

twernt *n.* The *tinter.*

twhat *1. n.* Piece of self-consciously eccentric millinery sported by the sort of *cuntish* oik who thinks that such headgear marks them out as being someone special and wacky. George Galloway wears a *twhat*, as do certain pony-tailed "cultural historians" on BBC4 documentaries. *2. n.* One of those tea-cosy-style *titfers* worn by Subaru drivers.

twice off the same hard *1. n.* The once-in-a-lifetime phenomenon of achieving two orgasms from the same erectivation with no intervening *downtime*, and thus *2. euph.* Any once-in-a-life-time phenomenon. *'And what is there to look forward to in the night sky next year? Well of course, the big story is the return of Halley's Comet which is only visible every 76 years. So it's a real twice off the same hard for most astronomers.'* (Patrick Moore, *The Sky at Night*, 1985).

twig & giggle berries *n.* The *fruitbowl*, the *meat and two veg.*

twiglet factory *n.* A heaving dancefloor populated by sweaty-*arsed* women wearing G-strings or *throngs.*

twiglet tips *1. n.* The brown stains left on the fingertips after consuming the nation's favourite marmite-flavoured, timber-based party snack. *2. n.* Of similar appearance, but as a consequence of an inadvertent *hull breach.* Also *taxi driver's tan.*

twig toothbrush *n.* A *cock* with enough bristles to fight plaque, dental caries and gingivitis. The implement used to *brush the au pair's teeth.*

TWILF/twilf *abbrev.* Tena Women I'd Like to Fuck. A GILF with added age-related plumbing issues.

twilight at Dracula's castle *n.* A romantic version of *bats at dusk.* A cataract of small, foul-smelling, semi-solid stools, diarrhoea and hypersonic whistling noises that leaves one pallid, lifeless, a stone lighter and in no mood to look in a mirror.

twilight throne, the *n.* Visit to the water closet which results in two simultaneous phenomena, *viz.* A *ghost shit* and *drawing an ace*, resulting in the confused *toiletee* wondering, due to the lack of any physical evidence, whether the whole experience ever actually happened at all.

twilight zone *n.* Facility for *coffin dodgers* to live out their final years. A nursing home, *death nest.*

TWIM/twim *abbrev.* A lady who is sadly under-endowed in the *chesty substances* department. Tit Wank IMpossible.

twink *n.* A *fart* so potent that it makes the hairs on your *arse* curl. Named after the fondly forgotten home perm solution of the 1970s.

twinkie *1. n. US. Turd, chocolate log. 2. n.* An apprentice *mudhole plumber.*

twin peaks *1. n. prop.* An experimental television series first broadcast in the early 1990s, created by David Lynch and Mark Frost. *2. n.* Smashing *tits* like Audrey's in the aforementioned series. *Dunce's hats, sweatermeat.*

twinset *1. n.* Matching combination of cardigan and sweater as favoured by ladies of a certain age. *2. n. Biblically enjoying* two sisters concurrently, like what David Essex does in *Stardust.* Also *twinset with pearls*, and then a nap.

twins, the *1. n.* A fine pair of *milky swingers* that

could prevent a fellow getting a good night's sleep for months on end. *2. n.* The unsettling sensation, after a fairly good morning *digestive transit,* that there's "another identical one in there" (which will make its presence known shortly before the announcement that your flight is going to be held on the tarmac for a further forty-five minutes).

twin SUs *1. n.* Type of sexy, *tit*-shaped carburettors fitted to British Leyland automobiles. *2. n.* The *assets* of a well-endowed lady that need to be fiddled with to get the best out of them. Also *Strombergs. 'Phwooar! That's a nice pair of twin SUs, your highness.'*

twin tone *n.* A *fart* which suddenly and ominously drops in pitch, indicating something other than *marsh gas* may have been expelled. A *follow through, squench, Doppler shit.*

twin tub *n.* Back, then frontal penetration.

twirling the baton *n.* A glitzy *one off the wrist* preferably performed while promenading down the street in front of a delighted crowd with loads of floats following on behind.

twirly *n.* An affectionate term used by omnibus drivers to describe senior citizens who attempt to use their free passes before 9.00am. *ie,* They are "too early" and have to be rudely thrown off the bus despite having fought in two world wars.

twist *1. rhym. slang. US.* Girl. From twist and twirl. *2. n.* Of *carpet munching* relationships, the *carpet,* as opposed to the *hoover.* A passive *lesbo. 3. v.* From the pontoon playing gambit, to risk losing a scoring hand in the hope of getting a better one; thus to turn down the advances of a half decent lady in the hope that one will later *cop off* with something better. The opposite of *going ugly early.*

twister *n. US.* Pervert, a *nonce.*

twist on nineteen *1. v.* In the world of blackjack – which seems to be a bit like pontoon, but played for money instead of matches – to foolishly risk busting your hand by asking the dealer to turn over another card. To gamble when the odds are stacked against you. *2. v.* In the world of flatulence, to *fart* recklessly while *touching cloth. 'Open a window, love. I've had five Guinnesses and a prawn egg foo yung but I'm gonna twist on nineteen. By the way, just before I do, is there a twenty-four hour Tesco round here that sells underpants?'*

twitcher *n.* A *bird watcher,* ie. One who light-heartedly takes photographs of his female colleagues on his mobile phone in the full knowledge that he will later *wank his knackers flat* at home while viewing the snaps. So-called because of the involuntary twitches his *knob* makes while he's taking the pictures.

twitcher's chin *n.* A very scruffy, chronically untrimmed lady's *front bottom* which resembles the unkempt lower mandible of bino-toting TV ornithologist Bill Oddie.

twitching Buddah *n.* A short, fat, excitable erection that treads a path between sensual indulgence and severe asceticism.

twitching hour *n.* That strange pre-dawn period during which a somnolent man is wont to experience episodic turgidity.

twitching wurzel *n.* An early morning visitor to a corner shop or supermarket, getting in his daily supply of cut-price apple-based beverage before most people have thought about sparking up the kettle for their first cup of tea.

twitter *1. n.* Friendly social media platform where thoughts and ideas are exchanged and debated in a congenial manner. Now called "x" by vanishingly few users. *2. n.* A lady's perineum, that area of the anatomy between the *twat* and the *shitter. Duffy's bridge, biffin bridge, tinter, taint, carse.*

Twix lips *n.* A *front bottom* version of *hungry arse. Knicker sausages.* See *hiding denim.*

two! *exclam.* Humorous retort following the discharge of a loud *backfire.* Named for the number of remaining Coffman shotgun starter cartridges in the engine-firing sequence from the film *The Flight Of The Phoenix.* See also *one year out!.*

two am grab bag *n.* In a night club, the ropey assortment of frankly second-rate *knob fodder* which is all that is left to choose from at chucking out time. The *floor sweepings, bin rake, sediment.*

two aspirins on an ironing board *sim.* Descriptive of the bosoms of the slimmer-figured lady. Flat *stits, fried eggs, lung warts, TPTs, tisn'ts.*

two-bagger *n.* Someone with such a *lovely personality* that a brace of bags is required in order to go *quim wedging* with them; "one over their head and one over yours, just in case theirs falls off".

two-bean salad *n.* A *lady golfer's* packed lunch.

two bird stuff *1. n.* Culinary dish involving the insertion of a quail into a partridge before roasting the both of them, and thus *2. n.* A very, very lucky night indeed.

two-bob billionaire *n.* A young man in an £80 shirt who still lives with his mum and dad.

two-bottle Aristotle *n.* In the pub, that tiresome individual who, upon imbibing a most trifling amount of alcohol, insists on sententiously supplying unwilling listeners with his unsolicited philosophical theorisings. See also *gintellectual,*

Dalai lager.

2B2W *abbrev.* An internet or mobile telephone textual contraction, meaning "Too Busy To Wank". It is not thought that any male has ever actually been rushed off their feet to such an extent.

twoc *v.* From Take Without Owner's Consent. To borrow someone's car, not in order to steal it, but merely to drive it through Dixon's window and set it on fire. Also *twock/twocker* and so on. *'My son is not a thief, officer. He is a professional twocker.'*

two-can Jackie Chan *n.* A *pissive aggressive* person. See also *two-can Van Damme, two-pint Tyson, tinny mallet, halfpint Harry, two pot screamer.*

two-can Van Damme *n.* See *two-can Jackie Chan.* It's not far away, look. Same sort of thing.

two-car garage *n.* A particularly accommodating and capacious *fadge* that could add value to your home.

twocker *n.* A cheeky rapscallion who *twocks.* A loveable rogue, a lively urchin or scallywag.

two-cocker *n.* A *Thora Hird* of such extraordinary length and girth that it momentarily makes you wonder what your *hoop* might be able to accommodate if you were so inclined as to put its capabilities to the test.

two dollar steak, tougher than a *sim. US.* Said of something that looks like it could handle itself in a *barney,* or like it would take a bit of chewing.

two-flush Charlie *n.* A prodigious *dumper.*

two-flush push *n.* An obstinate *digestive transit* which requires a second pull on the *bog* handle before it will set off for the seaside.

two-hander *1. n.* A film or play where a pair of actors share the stage, *eg. The Dumb Waiter* by Harold Pinter; *Educating Rita* by Willy Russell; *The Stronger* by August Strindberg. *2. n.* A gigantic, tumescent *chopper* which requires the simultaneous deployment of both of a romantic suitor's hands. As seen only in extreme *whirlwind romance videos.*

two-hundred-yarder *n.* The kind of man who looks like he may be legally obliged to avoid public places frequented by minors.

two-inch bather *n.* Descriptive of a *salad-dodger* who only needs to run the specified minimal depth of bath water before getting in to fill up the tub. *'Jesus, look at the back tits on that two-inch bather. I bet she can shit, your holiness.'*

two-into-ones *n.* Impossibly tight trousers, of the style into which an overly optimistic *salad dodger* may attempt to squeeze their enormous *arse;* in flagrant contravention of the basic mathematical axiom that "two into one won't go". Even though it obviously does, because it's a half.

two little boys fighting under a blanket *n.* Alluringly unrestrained *fat rascals*. Also *two puppies fighting in a bag, dead heat in a Zeppelin race.*

two-man sniff test *1. n. milit.* Following a chemical or biological incident, when contamination is no longer detectable, a standardised routine whereby two squaddies remove their safety equipment and alternately take shallow breaths in order to detect symptoms (vomiting, dilating pupils, muscle spasms, excessive salivation/drooling *etc.*) in each other caused by the latent presence of toxic airborne agents. *2. n.* A similar routine following a *two's up* in the back lane behind Cheeks Nightclub, Aldershot.

two metre range *n. milit.* while on manoeuvres, a secluded area in which a squaddie might take the opportunity to *fire the one o'clock gun.*

two minutes please while I change my string *exclam.* Said after *tipping your hat forward.* Originally said by Jacqueline du Pre when she *stepped on a duck* during her famous 1968 performance of the Dvorak Cello Concerto.

two-nut shuffle *n.* Action of a man *going commando*, gently manoeuvring his hips from side to side so that his *clockweights* rock between his thighs, giving him a pleasant, swinging sensation. Normally practised while leaning on a counter of some sort; awaiting medicines, dry cleaning, a pint *etc.*

two padded coat hangers, a fanny like *sim.* A phrase that can be used to describe a luxurious-ly-appointed *mound of Venus.*

two-page charlie *n.* The literary equivalent of a *two push charlie.* An overexcited *one-handed reader* who foolishly doesn't take the opportunity to fully peruse his new *art pamphlet* in a leisurely manner before *squirting his curd.*

two pee peace *n.* A relaxing toilet break taken at work, which lasts so long that there is time to *piss* twice.

two-peggers *n.* Large ladies' *undercrackers* which require two pegs to hang them on the washing line. See also *three-peggers.*

two-piece jigsaw puzzle, easier than *sim.* Said of a lady who is particularly accommodating. *'I tell you, that bird I was with last night was a right little raver. She was easier than a two-piece jigsaw puzzle.' 'Did you get any, then?' 'Not as such, no.'*

two-pint Tyson *n.* A bloke who goes all fighty after a minimal amount of ale. Also *two can Van Damme, tinny mallet, halfpint Harry, two-pot screamer.*

two pit-stop strategy *1. n.* Something that Jeremy Hardy soundalike Formula 1 commentator

Martin Brundle gets implausibly excited about when you're trying to have a nice Sunday afternoon nap during a Grand Prix motor race. *2. n.* In a municipal *turdis*, breaking off a *copper bolt* mid-thread and moving to a different cubicle in order to prevent a blockage.

two-pot bechamel *n.* A thick, white *bollock sauce* produced by heating up one's *two-pots* without serving. *'The wedding was pukka, but straight after the honeymoon I had to spend a month away filming. By the time I saw Jools again, I was gasping to dish up a portion of the old two-pot bechamel.'* (from *Mockney Rebel*, the autobiography of Jamie Oliver).

two-pot screamer *n. Aus.* Someone who cannot hold their beer. A more reserved British equivalent would be *halfpint Harry.*

two-pronged attack *1. n.* Military manoeuvre. *2. n.* Two-on-one sexy shenanigans in a fancy hotel suite involving a pair of pop musicians, professional footballers, stand-up comedians or cabinet members, and someone who's just met them.

two puppies fighting in a bag *n.* Large, mobile and unrestrained breasts, like what Twickenham streaker Erica Roe had back in 1982.

two-ring circus *n.* The greatest show on earth. *Over the shoulder boulder holder, tit pants,* a bra.

two-seater *1. n.* A small motor car, usually a convertible. *2. n.* A *fat fuck* who regularly sidesteps salads and as a consequence occupies twice their allocated seating accommodation on planes, trains and automobiles.

two shits behind *phr.* The situation of being so ex-traordinarily busy at work than one is forced to forego the traditional daily brace of trips to the *smallest room* during office hours. *'Sorry madam. I'm afraid the dentist won't be able to give you an appointment till Thursday week at the earliest. He's two shits behind as it is.'*

twoskin *n.* Half a *fourskin.*

two-slice toaster *n.* A tragic person whose dishevelled appearance and evident social inadequacy leads one to conclude that they are unlikely ever to find themselves preparing a meal for anyone else.

two sniffs of that and you're greedy *exclam.* Said after dropping an *air biscuit* that *smells like Gillian McKeith's Tupperware cupboard.* Also *pull me through with a burning dufflecoat.*

two-stroke oil *1. n.* The type of lubricant used in mopeds, strimmers and other similar contraptions that are driven by crankcase compression engines. *2. n.* The type of lubricant used by a *two-push Charlie* in a desperate bid to *keep the wolf from the* *door. Stallion delay spray* or *buffering butter.*

two-stroke poke *n.* Similar to a *one pump chump,* only twice as sexually satisfying for his lucky missus. A *two-push Charlie.*

twos-up *n.* A *two-up,* a *threesome* with two blokes and a dirty lady. 2. *n.* A *two-up,* a threesome with one bloke and two dirty ladies.

two-thirtier *n.* After having missed all the *ten-to-twoers* at the nightclub *binrake,* a *two-thirtier* can usually be pulled in a kebab shop, taxi rank or hospital Accident & Emergency Department.

two-thrust bust *n.* An example of premature ejaculation.

two Tommies, the *1. n.* *Shit* music hall comedy act. 2. *phr.* A man-about-town's early morning routine, *viz.* A *Tommy tit,* followed by a *Tommy tank.*

TWOTS *acronym.* A time-management strategy of employees seeking a better work-life balance in the works *lavs, viz.* TWitter On The Shitter.

two-up *1. n.* A *twos-up,* a *threesome* with two blokes and a dirty lady. 2. *n.* A *twos-up,* a threesome with one bloke and two dirty ladies.

two wank minimum *phr.* Grading standard applied to high quality *grumble.*

two-way teaser *1. n.* A well-known daily newspaper's coffee break crossword puzzle which offers both easy and difficult clues, both ending in the same result. 2. *n.* A lady who, at the start of the evening, disingenuously implies that both an *easy pink* and a *difficult brown* may be on the cards.

two wombles looking over a balcony *sim.* Descriptive of *NGTs.*

twunt *n.* Useful, satisfying yet inoffensive combination of two very rude words which

can safely be spoken in the primmest and properest company.

Twyfords base jumper *n.* A daredevil *shit.*

tying down Gulliver *n.* The ineffably charming tableau of many men simultaneously *lobbing ropes* over one delighted young lady.

Tyne Bridge *adj.* Descriptive of the position adopted by a canine trying to lay a particularly tenacious *dog's egg.*

type a letter to Roy *euph.* Of a *gusset typist,* to quickly toss off a missive in the hope of reaching "the Big O".

types at arms' length *euph.* A cheeky reference to a *well-qualified* secretary.

typing pool *n.* Tell-tale patch of *moip* on a young woman's gusset, duvet or ceiling after she's been *looking for change in the hairy purse.*

tyrannosaurus *n. rhym. slang. The other.* From tyrannosaurus rex = s*x. *'Did you get any tyrannosaurus off your new bird last night, then?' 'No. I just went home for a pot noodle and a Luxembourg Franc.'*

tyrannosaurus kex *n.* Undergarmentry worn by the *bigger-boned* lady. *'I don't suppose you would consider taking your tyrannosaurus kex in off the line, would you Miss Widdecombe? Only I'm trying to grow tomatoes here.'*

tyre *n. medic.* Swollen condition of the *fiveskin* caused by over-zealous *relaxation. 'Did you get your internet sorted out, Clive?' 'Yes, I got it connected yesterday, and I've already got a tyre.'*

Tyson Brewery *n. prop.* A *pissive aggressive* person who, after a couple of beers, wants to fight the fucking world. Also *one can Van Damme, tinny mallet, half pint Harry, drambo, Hulk Höegarden.*

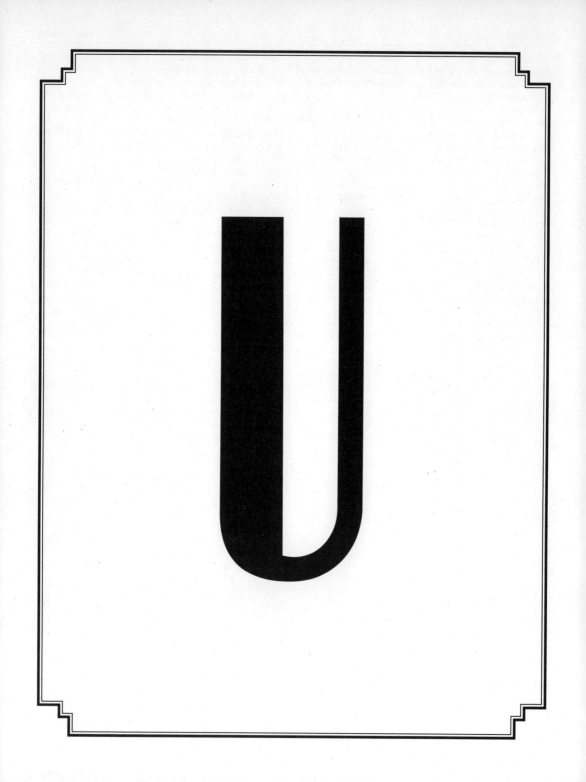

U-bend straightener *n.* A mighty powerful *depth charge*. A *rat killer* of such impressive length and tensile strength that it could push the kinks out of the *chod bin* pipework. See also *neckbreaker.*

uberade *n.* A bottle of yellow/green liquid found in a gutter after being discarded by a taxi driver desperately trying to keep to a tight schedule.

UB40 winks *n.* A mid-afternoon nap taken during *Doctors* after a hard morning at the telly face.

U-blocker *n.* A titanic *dreadnought* so big it causes a *jobbie* jam in the foul drainage system. The Moby Dick of *brown trouts, a plumber's bonus.*

U-boat *n.* A *Richard III* lodged in the bend of the *crapper foulage* pipe, enforcing a naval blockade against enemy *shitting.*

udderpants *n.* A utility brassiere in which function is more important than form.

udders *n.* Breasts with absolutely no erotic qualities whatsoever.

udder scudder *n.* An agricultural-grade *sausage sandwich.*

UDI *abbrev.* Unidentified Drinking Injury. Inexplicable damage sustained during a *bender* of which the victim has no recollection. A mystery *binjury.*

ugly Betty *n.* A particularly unsightly *grimquim;* an unholy hybrid of *Terry Waite's allotment* and a *snatchmo,* with an odour redolent of Whitby when the tide's out. And not in a good way.

ugly bus *n.* A vehicle that mysteriously turns up after one has had eight pints on a Friday night and takes all the *hippocrocapigs* home, leaving the pub full of beauties.

ugly duckling *n.* A long, protracted *Exchange & Mart* which is launched mid-perambulation, whereby the *benefactor* "walks with a quack and a waddle and a quack".

ugly lights *n.* A revealing illumination apparatus which is switched on in pubs at chucking out time.

ugly stripper, works harder than an *sim.* Descriptive of one who is extremely conscientious in the workplace. *'Don't get me wrong, I'm not condoning Fred West. But apparently when he was on the sites he worked harder than an ugly stripper.'*

ugly taxi *n.* The vehicle which mysteriously delivers an unattractive *bird* into one's *fart sack* on a Saturday morning.

ugly toe *n.* The male p*nis. *'The right honourable gentleman has made a both erudite and lengthy defence of his government's policy to fund tax cuts for the rich with a reduction in nursery budgets. However he has left his flies unbuttoned and his ugly toe is showing, so I am inclined to disagree.'*

UHEZ *abbrev.* Ultra High Emissions Zone. The area of dangerous, noxious pollutants which surround a person the day after enjoying several pints of real ale, pork scratchings, a Scotch egg and a vindaloo. May be picketed by protesters and placards.

'U' in cunt, no but there's a *exclam.* The only worthwhile response to a graduate of the firm's management training programme after they utter the well-used rallying call "There's no 'I' in team".

Ullswater steamer *1. n.* Beloved Victorian cruiser; one of the Lake District's most famous attractions. *2. n.* A *cable* laid by a rambler caught short on the chilly Cumbrian fells.

Ulrikas *n.* A pair of *kahoomas* that look smashing in clothing, but plummet earthwards like dropped car batteries when unleashed. *Metatarsal breakers.*

ultra-processed food *n.* Shite. *'Ah, bollocks, I've trod in some ultra-processed food, nan.' 'Keep your feet off the fucking carpet then.'*

Ultravox fart *n.* An *air biscuit* that causes those present to start "dancing with tears in their eyes".

ummfriend *n.* A *fuck buddy.* From the commonly heard introduction at parties: "Hi, Gillian. Have you met Kate? She's my... ummm... friend."

unable to find second gear *euph.* Being *sucked off* while driving, possibly to relieve the symptoms of chronic pancreatitis. *'Yes officer, I know I was only doing 10mph in the outside lane, but I was unable to find second gear. Wasn't I darling?'*

unblocking the sink *sim.* A vigorous and impatient *wank,* presumably using both hands. *Starting the hornmower.*

Uncle Albert's beard *n.* Jelly jewellery, *cumbledore.*

Uncle Bens *n.* Petite, flaccid *headlamps* which resemble the famous uncooked sachets of boil-in-the-bag rice, and should ideally be fluffed up with a fork before use.

Uncle Doug *rhym. slang. Self abuse.* From Uncle Doug = tug. *'I'm just off for an Uncle Doug, but if there's anything you need, just ask one of the stewardesses.'*

Uncle Fester *n.* A *bald-headed old man* from the old Adam family, who occasionally rises and puts the *willies* up your missus.

uncle mustard *n.* Playful term for *jitler. 'These plumbers are definitely not getting a very big tip, Terry. They've left all uncle mustard in my knicker drawer again.'*

uncomfortable *adj.* Of shoes, having "fuck me" written all over them.

uncork the brown champagne *v.* On the morning after a night of strong ale and spicy foodstuffs, to release the *pace car,* thus unleashing a frothy torrent of foul, effervescent liquid.

uncuntured *adj.* Descriptive of some *cunt* with no

culture. *'He's uncultured, darling. I bet he never watches BBC4.'*

undefuckable *adj. Bust*, damaged beyond repair. *'Oh, and there goes Barrichello's engine on the warm-up lap. He'll head straight for the pit lane, but that looks pretty undefuckable. It's certainly the end to his Portuguese Grand Prix, Martin.'* (Murray Walker, commentating as Frentzen's front left wheel came off on the final corner, Belgian Grand Prix 1999).

underbeard *n. Minge.*

undercard, the *n.* A small *poo* before the main event. Also *escort vehicle, gatekeeper, black rod.*

undercarriage *n.* Genitals, usually male. *The fruit bowl, family jewels, pudendas, wedding vegetables.*

underchunders *n. Underkeks.*

undercoat *n.* A soft drink ordered to accompany the first pint of a long session which prepares the stomach's surface for the later layers of alcoholic emulsion. Also *George Best undercoat, Winehouse lining paper, Keith Floyd's primer.*

undercover cop *1. n.* A plain clothes detective. *2. n.* A crafty spot of *DIY* under the bedsheets while the missus is in the ensuite. *3. n.* A trivial, opportunistic sexual assault committed on a crowded bus or underground train.

undercrackers *n. Underchunders.*

underdaks *n. Undercrackers.*

under house arrest *adj.* The official status of one who has had his pub privileges withdrawn. *'No, Noel. Liam will not be coming down The Feathers for last orders tonight. He's been a very naughty boy and I've put him under under house arrest.'*

underkecks *n. Underdaks.*

underkrakatoa *n.* A deafening and catastrophic eruption in the *East Undies* that reverberates around the globe.

underneath of a three-day ground mat, like the *euph.* A minge that is reminiscent of when you pack up a tent and the flattened grass underneath is a sickened yellow hue, with a few sunlight-starved slugs and beetles moving around.

under one's wing, take someone *v.* To perform a spot of *bagpiping*. To essay a *Hawaiian muscle fuck.*

underpants roulette *n.* Taking a chance with a *trouser cough* when one has *the shits*. Betting on whether or not there is *a bullet in the chamber.*

under starter's orders *1. adj.* Suffering from that uncomfortable rising pressure in the lower gastric tract that signals the onset of *arse labour. 'Christ, nan, hurry up and get out of there before I papper me trolleys, will you? I'm under starter's orders here.' 2. euph.* Crouched over the *porcelain saddle* and ready for the off.

under starter's ordures *euph.* To squat like a jockey in the stirrups in an attempt to shift an obdurate *feeshee* lodged stubbornly in the *Enochs. 'Sorry I'm late. I'm afraid I had extra scrambled eggs for breakfast, and I was under starter's ordures in the crappers for an hour this lunchtime.'*

undertaker, play the *v.* To bury a *stiff. 'Was it okay meeting up with your ex-wife?' 'Yeah, not bad. She let me play the undertaker, anyway.'*

undertaker's privileges *n.* Funeral director's perks, *viz.* Acts of carnality performed by a *corpse packager* on his recently deceased clients. *'Wanted. Hard-working young man to train as Mortuary Attendant in a busy London hospital. Must have 4 GCSEs at grade C or above. 35 hours per week, occasional weekends. Starting salary £10,000 plus use of company hearse, clothing allowance & undertaker's privileges.'*

undertaker's wind, the *1. n.* A nightly stiff breeze that blows across the island of Jamaica between 6pm and 6am, and the original title of Ian Fleming's James Bond novel *Live and Let Die. 2. n.* A *dustman's special* so noxious it smells as though you're standing next to a decomposing corpse.

under the bridge *1. n.* Dwelling place of easily dissuaded billygoat-gruff-eating trolls. *2. n. Down below.* You know, where your *unmentionables* are. That bit of the anatomy that gets a cursory wash during a *workman's plunge.*

under the Bush administration *1. adj.* Descriptive of the United States Senate between 2001 and 2009. *2. adj.* Descriptive of a lady who *knows her way around an engine.*

under the Wether *adj.* Not exactly firing on all cylinders following a night on the tiles at a well known cheap booze emporium. *Spooned.*

under thunder *n.* Ominous rumbles from the bowels of Hades.

underworld *n.* A post-binge *poo* that is about 90% lager. Because it is, like the title to the eponymous group's 1996 hit record, "Born Slippy".

undie fudge *n. Miniature heroes, clinkers, winnets.*

undieseal *n.* Viscous, fast-setting substance that can be applied to virtually any fabric to provide a tough, waterproof barrier.

undiewhelmed *adj.* Aroused in one's undergarmentry by the sight of a curvaceous young *piece* in hers. *'What do you think of the new Grattan catalogue, grandad?' 'Quite frankly, I was undiewhelmed by it.'*

undissolved stock cube *n.* The dozen or so fragments of *shite* discarded by a recent lavatory occupant, caught swirling gently in an eddy.

unexpected item in bagging area *1. exclam.* When a visit to the *chod-bin* has been overly delayed and an impromptu cough results in the inadvertant download of a *mud button* into the *applecatchers. 2. exclam.* The irritated vociferation of a ladyfriend when you inadvertently attempt to *pot the brown. 3. exclam.* Shout of a chap who has just, using only the sense of touch, inadvertently identified a *Bobby dazzler.*

unexpected item in the bagging area *exclam.* Statement to be proffered after a proper *arse-ripper.*

unfappable *adj.* Too *fugly* to *wank off* to under even the most desperate or drunk circumstances, *eg.* The *unfappable* Ann Noreen Widdecombe.

unfinished symphony *1. n.* Schubert's Symphony No. 8. in B Minor D759. *2. euph.* Of *crimping* and *laying cable,* the situation whereby one has to cut short a *sit-down toilet adventure,* with the intention of returning at a later date in order to complete the *final movement.*

unflappable *adj.* Exercising restraint in the face of *fanny.*

unforced error *n.* A rectal mis-step that makes it look as if one has taken a fall on a wet clay court. Also *failed parking test* or *shart.*

unfuckcessful *adj.* Of an evening out, or a person, sexually fruitless.

unibum *n.* Them jeans that make women's *arses* look like a single continuous buttock.

unisexual *1. adj.* Descriptive of one who is *self-sufficient* as long as he doesn't break his right wrist. *2. n.* A chap who lives the *good life.*

unit *1. n.* The genitals, usually male, particularly the *veiny bang stick. Pud. 2. n.* An individual piece of *talent. 3. n.* A right *twat.*

unit counter *n.* Someone who is scared stiff of drinking to a respectable level. A *budgie supper.*

unit move *1. n.* Film industry phrase describing the transfer of the crew and all their equipment to the next filming location. *2. n.* Toilet industry phrase describing a *Roddie motion.*

University of Edge Hill *1. n.* The trial-and-error process by which a young man learns to successfully time the *interruptus* of his *coitus. 2. n.* One of the country's most exclusive seats of higher learning, ranked 54th in the UK, one above Bournemouth.

unknown waters *n.* A friend or relative's *crapper.* Location of a *sailor's funeral.*

unleash the benefits of Brexit! *exclam.* Proclamation announcing the arrival of a violent and disturbingly pungent *beefy eggo.*

unleash the dobermans *v.* After a night on the stout, to let loose with a particularly savage and uncontrollable outburst of *black and tan* from the *back gate.* Also let out the *boys from the black stuff.*

unless I could piss petrol *phr.* A humorous codicil to the commonly used vituperative exclamation "I'd not piss on him if he was on fire," which can be used to rich comic effect, *viz. 'That Bono's a tosser. I'd not piss on him if he was on fire...unless I could piss petrol.'*

unload *v.* To drop a *depth charge* or launch an *air biscuit.* To empty one's *hatchback* of *shopping.*

unmentionables *n.* Roman Catholic word which enables mother-in-laws to mention genitals or underwear. *'Sweet Jesus mother of Mary, stop playing with your fecking unmentionables, will you father, and have another slice of cake.'*

unmown crease *1. n.* An unprepared cricket pitch. *2. n.* A particularly hirsute clopper. *Max Clifford's allotment,* a *biffer, Judith etc.*

unpacking a new memory foam mattress, like *sim.* Descriptive of the experience of removing tight clothing from a *lass* just before lights out, only to watch as she expands to three times her previous compact dimensions.

unpack your holiday luggage *v.* To unleash a gargantuan seven-day behemoth of a *Richard* when you get home from a week's all-inclusive. *'No, dear, we're not stopping on the way home to say hi to your parents. I need to get home to unpack the holiday luggage.'*

unpleasantness *n.* The triangular tuft of hair that inexplicably sprouts under the lower lip of certain men. The *moip mop, foof brush. 'How was your date last night? Do you think you'll see him again?' 'I don't think so. He sounded lush over the phone, but when he showed up in person, there was some unpleasantness.'*

unplugged *1. adj.* Of a popular beat combo, playing in the simple, old-fashioned way through a bewilderingly complicated system of microphones, passive pick-ups, mixing desks, amplifiers, compressors, speakers and recording equipment. *2. adj.* Descriptive of the act of congress with a menstruating woman who has kindly pulled out *Dracula's teabag* to facilitate the process.

unplumbtable *adj.* A feeling of generalised discomfort in the *fruitbowl,* usually experienced on long car journeys, which necessiates immediate re-adjustment. *'I can explain everything, officer. I was feeling unplumbtable after a prolonged period in the driving seat, so I simply asked my wife here to reach into my scads and wind the clock.'*

unsafe release *1. n.* At the conclusion of a Formula 1 pit-stop, for example, when a driver is waved back out into the pit lane just as another car is passing. *2. n.* What at first seems to be a simple *trouser cough*, but later turns into a *shart*. '*Oh my, that looked like an unsafe release for Hamilton there. And the stewards are going to be looking at that one very carefully.*'

unshit *v.* To retract a partially emerging *turd* back into the *cigar cutter* to facilitate the answering of the door or telephone.

unsinkable Molly Brown, the *1. n.* American socialite and philanthropist who survived the sinking of the *Titanic* and later became the subject of a Broadway musical. *2. n.* A buoyant *floater* left by the wife or a ladyfriend, for which one would be unlikely to receive backing to stage a sumptuous theatrical production.

unsponsored roundabout *n.* A *Busby Berkeley*. See also *Lord Winston's moustache, Paddy McGinty's goat, barber's floor, Bilbo Baggins's foot* and *Mary Hinge*.

unstipation *n.* Medical condition of the *back body* which necessitates trips to the *shitter* every five minutes or so. Usually caused by a heavy night. '*This fella goes to the doctor and he says, "Have you got anything for unstipation?" The doctor says yes, have this fucking bucket.*' (Routine by Bernard Stone-Age-Manning, Neanderthal stand-up comedian, 500,000 BC).

untertainment *n.* The opposite of entertainment.

untested *euph.* Description of an electrical item offered for sale on a popular internet auction site. Absolutely *fucked*.

untidy sock drawer *n.* A *ripped sofa, badly packed kebab, ragman's coat.*

unwrap a sprout *v.* To release a noisome blast on the *muck trumpet* that is rich in vitamins C, K and B6.

unwrap the meat *v.* To *let the twins out.* Of Lord Owen, to get *his tits out for the Liberal Democrats.*

up and down like a gambler's moods, his arse was *exclam.* Said of an enthusiastic *pork swordsman.*

up and down like a jockey's bollocks *1. sim.* Descriptive of an act of *making the beast with two backs* that makes up for what it lacks in technique with a surfeit of enthusiasm. *2. sim.* A colourful figure of speech. '*How many times has that fucking phone rang tonight? Honestly, I've been up and down like a jockey's bollocks, Lord Grantham.*' *3. sim.* A poetic phrase used when referring to something that varies considerably and often above and below a comfortable median value. '*Have you seen them pictures of Kerry Katona on the beach in the Daily Mail? Christ, her weight's up*

and down like a jockey's bollocks, your holiness.'

up and over like a pan of milk *euph.* Descriptive of a gentleman who is so good at *the other* that he can *blow his beans* before he's even got his *dunghampers* off.

up and twitchin' *adj.* The point at which the *old chap* is ready to engage in the courses of love.

up before me arsehole *phr.* An early start which disrupts one's *jobby clock.* '*The sky looks beautiful at this dawn hour, doesn't it your majesty?*' '*Fuck that, I'm off to the throne room. I was up before me arsehole.*'

up before the governor *euph.* '*How did your night out go with that bird from behind the bar at the Feathers, grandad?*' '*Smashing. I had her back at mine and up before the governor before lights out at eleven.*'

upchuck *v.* To *laugh at the carpet, chuck up.*

upcycle *v.* To paint something.

upgrade *v.* To go to the *chod bin* for a *number one,* but decide to take the opportunity to sir down for a *number two* while one is there. And a *wank,* time permitting.

upgrade a fart *v.* To go for a *shit.* '*I would love to stand here chatting all day, your majesty, but I really must go and upgrade a fart.*'

uphill gardener *n.* That vertiginously inclined horticulturalist who sows his *seed* on the *backyard allotment.* An enthusiastic *weeder of the lavender path.* A *crafty butcher.*

uphill wanking *n.* Masturbating over somewhat challenging *whack fodder,* for example a knitting pattern, hotel room Gideons Bible or Reform Party election leaflet.

up, in, out and off *phr.* Comprehensive plot synopsis or narrative arc that is essential to all *grumble flicks.*

uplifting *adj.* Descriptive of something stirring that circulates blood to the *old chap.* '*What do you think of the new Grattan catalogue, grandad?*' '*Quite frankly, I found it uplifting.*'

upload a file to the cloud *v.* To *blow off.*

up on blocks *adj.* Of a woman. A monthly *mott* failure due to a recurring leak under the *beetle bonnet.*

upper inflection *n.* A *Tommy squeaker* that rises in pitch as if it is asking a question or appearing in an Australian soap opera.

up periscope *n.* Bathtime game for up to one person. *Polishing the lighthouse, waxing the dolphin, making nylon.*

upside-down Christmas tree *euph.* Decorative little piece of female topiary with a present underneath.

upstairs *n.* The *rack, top bollocks, top bum.* '*What's* *she got upstairs?' 'Two knockers.'*

up the Beeston ginnel, one *n.* The act of *making love* up the *wrong 'un*, from the name of a narrow, malodorous passage in the environs of the notorious Leeds *shit hole*. *'Tamoshanta was powerless to resist. His eyes burnt into hers like agates. His muscular arms enfolded her body as she felt herself being swept away on a dustpan of passion. "I'm sorry, Your Grace," she gasped breathlessly in the throes of her passion, "but you'll have to give me one up the Beeston ginnel this morning as I am dropping clots at present."'* (from *The Milkmaid and the Bishop* by Barbara Cartland).

up the Burway *euph.* Up the arse. Named after the eponymous snicket in the Shropshire Hills. *'I took the missus up the Burway for an anniversary treat.'*

up the down staircase *1. n.* Title of a 1967 movie starring Sandra Dennis. *2. phr.* Reference to a spot of *backdoor work*, if you will.

up the duff *adj. medic.* Up the pasture, up the poke, up the stick, in the club.

up the gable end, do someone *v.* To *do it* up the *Myleene*, if you will.

up the Jimmy Savile, to take a lady *v.* To indulge in a session of *back door work*. So called because of the warbling "eeurgh!-eeurgh!-eeurgh! now then! now then!" noises made by the lucky recipient of one's romantic attentions.

up the pasture *adj. medic.* Up the poke, up the duff.

up the poke *adj.medic.* Up the stick, up the pasture.

up the stick *adj. medic.* In the club, up the poke.

up the Tregenna, take the missus *v.* To *poke* one's good lady up the *coal hole*. A phrase coined with reference to Merthyr's poshest restaurant, where the South Wales man-about-town takes his wife for birthdays or anniversaries. According to the website menulist.menu, the Tregenna offers the following ingredients: Pork Meat, Vegetables, Beef and Carrots. To have a *once a year special*.

up the wooden hill to Wankashire *phr.* Phrase a bloke proclaims before retiring to his bedroom for a session of *self pollution*. *'Fetch me one of my finest silk socks and the latest issue of Razzle, Carson, there's a good fellow. I'm about to head up the wooden hill to Wankashire.'*

up to her flaps in chaps *phr.* Offensively sexist female equivalent of a harmless bit of male locker room banter, *viz.* Up to your nuts in guts.

up to the apricots *adj.* Up to the back wheels, up to the maker's nameplate.

up to the back wheels *adj.* Up to the apricots, up to the buffers.

up to the buffers *adj.* Up to the bumper, up to the cannon wheels.

up to the bumper *adj.* Up to the cannon wheels, up to the eggs.

up to the cannon wheels *adj.* Up to the eggs, up to the buffers.

up to the eggs *adj.* Up to the maker's nameplate, up to the back wheels.

up to the maker's nameplate *adv.* An engineering term for being *conkers deep*. Also *up to the boilermaker's nameplate.*

up to the wrist, go for the elbow *phr.* A more imaginative alternative to "in for a penny, in for a pound," which is much in use amongst farm vets, gynaecologists and customs officers.

uptown girl *n.* A lady whose *rear entrance virgin string* is still intact. From the eponymous Billy Joel song of the same name, *viz.* "I bet she's never had a backstreet guy." Not from Sunderland, then.

uptown spunk *n.* That with which a chap fills a *jubber ray* when he indulges himself with a *posh wank.*

up to your nuts in guts *adj. Aus.* In a *sausage and doughnut situation*, to throw oneself fully into one's work.

up to your pots *adj.* Amazingly enough, not to be *up to the apricots, wheels, buffers, bumper, cannon wheels, eggs or maker's name plate* or whatever, but to be *ripped to the tits* on drink. *Pissed, wankered, shit-faced, arseholed, refreshed.* Also *in your pots. 'You were up to your pots reading the news last night, Mr Bosanquet.'*

up with the cock *1. n.* To rise from one's slumber at an early hour. *2. n.* To awaken with a fearsome *stalk* in your pants, *pitch a dawn tent.*

Urals, the *n.* Vague and tenuous British film comedy euphemism for the testicles. See also *the Balkans, Balearics, Trossachs.*

Uranus *1. n.* A large planet with brown rings around it. With a big smelly *shit* coming out a hairy hole in the middle of it. Sadly, these days it is usually pronounced "Ur-arn-us" to save the blushes of Brian Cox, or "Carx", as he probably prefers to say it. *2. n. Urarse.*

urban cockerel *n.* A loud, rasping reveille emitted from under the duvet around sunrise, with enough volume to wake everyone in the street. A *dawn chorus, breakfast maker.*

urban jellyfish *n.* A rubbery, semi-translucent, parazoological beast typically found drifting in the stagnant canals and waterways of our towns and cities. *Jubber ray, dunky, Coney Island whitefish.*

urban vibe *euph.* Term used by aristocratic house-flogger Kirsty Allsop on Channel Four's *Location, Location, Location* to describe an area steeped in stabbings, drugs and all manner of violent crime. *'Yeah, the Bransholme Estate certainly has quite an urban vibe, and at just eight pounds, this four-bedroom semi represents a great way to get your foot on the housing ladder. Ooh, Phil. I think I've been shot.'*

Uri *1. n. rhym. slang.* Premium Belgian lager. From cutlery-*fucking* man of mystery Uri Geller = Stella. Also *Nelson Mandela. 2. n.* A spontaneous erection. From the famous telekinetic paranormalist's catchphrase, *viz.* "Look, it's bending and I'm not even touching it."

Uri Geller smeller *n.* After one has dropped a major-league *nine inch nail* in the *pan*, the foulsome miasma that emanates from the smallest room and spreads round the house, bending spoons and stopping clocks as it goes.

Urinarnia *n. prop.* A *pisstical* destination at which you arrive during a drunken sleepwalk. A dream fantasy toilet that is in reality the back of the wardrobe.

urineapple chunks *n.* The unpleasantly flavoured, fruit-like yellow cubes that nestle around the plughole of a *shark's mouth. Kola cubes.*

urine shroud *n.* A cotton or nylon artefact, clearly showing the miraculous crusty image of a *bearded clam. ie,* A pair of discarded *scads* found sunny side up on a lady's bedroom floor.

urj *v. Corn.* To retch or heave. *'Here Bob, that overflowing dogshit bin up the road is fucking vile. Makes me urj every time I go past.'*

Usain Bolt *n.* That which is *shot* by a bloke who has a tendency to be *out of the blocks* before the starter has fired his gun.

Usain Dolt *n. prop.* Nickname bestowed upon someone who reaches idiotic conclusions very quickly indeed. *'The Usain Dolt with us today to discuss the newspapers is former Secretary of State for Digital, Culture, Media and Sport, Nadine Dorries.'*

use *v.* In broadsheet newspaper articles about the scourge of pornography, words meaning to *wank* over. *'Many men use pornography on a regular basis.'*

user friendly *1. adj.* Of an item of technology, such as a computer or similar, very easy to operate. *'Have you seen me new iPad? It's very user friendly. Even me grandad's had a go on it.' 2. adj.* Of a young lady, possessing the deeply attractive quality of requiring very little *end-user* input before satisfying a chap's beastly urges. *'Have you met me new bird? She's very user friendly. Even me grandad's had a go on her.'*

UTAH FD *1. abbrev.* The people who come to the rescue when the Osmonds catch *ahad. 2. abbrev.* An accommodating one-night-stand. Up The Arse Hole First Date.

UTBNB *abbrev.* A reliable, albeit malodorous, contraceptive system. Opposite of an IUD. Up The Bum, No Babies.

utility wank *n.* A masturbatory act carried out prior to a train journey, exam, Presidential Investiture *etc.*, purely to preclude the possibility of an unwanted erection taking place later. *'Tony, are you doing a speech at Lady Di's funeral tomorrow? If so, you'd best have a utility wank in the morning just in case you get a bone-on from all the excitement.' 'Don't worry, Cherie. I'll be stood behind a lectern, and if I start getting a heavy dick I'll do what I do at PMQs and look over at Margaret Beckett.'*

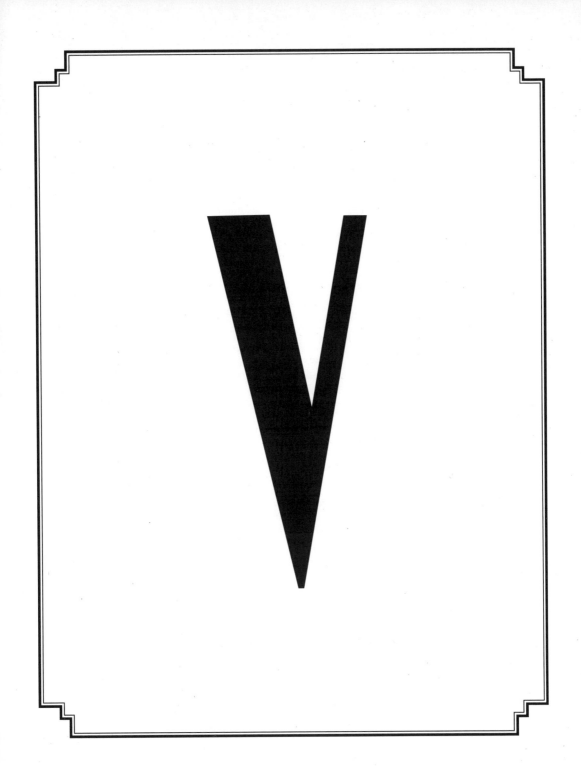

vadge *n.* A *fadge*.

vadge of honour *1. n.* The completely natural and wildly unkempt *minge* of a proud feminist, worn with pride. *'Yes, Germaine, we've all seen your vadge of honour. Now put it away, please. Time for our first question, which comes from Lionel Boothby, who is a baker. Mr Boothby.'* *2. n.* A conquest worth bragging about.

vadger farm *n.* An old folks' home.

vafrazzle *v.* To decorate one's ladyfriend's *vajayjay* with cheap, bacon-flavoured crisps. It could happen.

vafro *n.* A magnificently hairy 1970s *biffer.*

VAG *abbrev.* The Volkswagen Audi Group.

vag-a-bond *n.* An exceptionally adhesive *danny fishcharge.*

vagelfie *n.* An intimate self-portrait of a woman's *mixed grill;* the latest new word to be included in the *Oxford English Dictionary. 'I sent you a vagelfie. Did you get it?'*

vagenius *n.* A smart *cunt.*

vaggie *n.* An uncomfortable front-tuck for a lady. A vaginal *wedgie,* a *smedgie, vedgie, quedgie. 'A major diplomatic row errupted today after the Australian Premier gave the Queen a vaggie when she was attending the State Opening of Parliament in Melbourne.'*

vagging out *n.* Of a young lady, the act of relaxing at the beach with legs akimbo while wearing a bikini, affording any less reconstructed males who happen to be passing a smashing view of her lunch.

vag gnats *n. medic.* Pubic lice. Also *knackernits, crabs, pissnits, mechanical dandruff, mechanical dandruff, willipedes* and *twatterpillars.*

vagician *n.* One who uses *sleight of gland* to charm the ladies.

vagilant *adj.* On the sharp-eyed look out for *cunker.*

vagile *adj.* Of a female, unusually limber, supple or flexible about the nether regions.

vagimite *n.* Unpleasant-tasting yeast derivative, most commonly sampled *down under.*

vagimix *n.* Noisy electrical appliance which makes life easier for housewives. Usually has three speeds and is perfect for whipping up a light and frothy *batter.* A *fanny hammer, bob, neck massager.*

vagina crisis *n. Rag week, blob week, cricket week.* See also *red nose day.*

vagina decliner *n.* The male equivalent of a *todger dodger.* A *beaver leaver,* a *pie-shy guy.*

vagina monologues *1. n.* A play about *quims,* a bit like *Yes We Have No Pyjamas* was in the seventies, presumably. *2. n.* A series of *queefs* emitted while a young lady is *fapping* herself silly. *3. n.* The sound of a *cunt* talking.

vaginosaur *n.* A rather mature actress in a *meat flick.*

vaginyl *n.* Classic, analogue *clopper,* much sought after by connoisseurs.

vagitarian *n.* He who only eats *hairy pie, fur burgers,* and *vertical bacon sandwiches.* Plus the occasional *fish supper.* An inveterate *diner at the Y.*

vagitas *n.* Tex-mex *snatches.* Hopefully served without salsa and cheese.

vagitation *n.* Agitation of the *meat flower. Bean flicking, invisible banjo playing, gusset typing,* female masturbation.

vagitative state *adj.* The semi-comatose, *twatatonic* frame of mind resulting from a period of time spent fantasising over an attractive stranger. Often occurs on train journeys or while queueing at the tills in a supermarket. See also *norkolepsy, titnosis.*

vag patch *n.* A wholesome, well-ploughed *ladygarden* which should provide a chap with a fair percentage of his five-a-day.

vajanuary *1. n.* A lack of sex between December 31st and February 1st of the next year. Or the one after that, for that matter. *2. n.* Yearly pledge, rarely kept up for the full thirty-one days, to eat nothing but *hairy pie* for a month.

vajayjay *n.* A *John Craven.* That which is typically *vajazzled.*

vajazzle *1. v.* To gaudily decorate Jennifer Love Hewitt's *vajayjay* by pasting a selection of Swarovski crystals onto it. *2. n.* A high profile individual who, having *brown-nosed* their way on to the Birthday, New Year's, or Prime Minister's biennial Resignation Honours List, is subsequently found to be somewhat wanting in their behaviour, character and integrity. A "decorated cunt". *'So Sir Jimmy Savile was a vajazzle. Who'd have thought it, eh? And he always seemed such a nice man. It just goes to show, you just can't tell, can you?'*

vajazzle, Scouse *n. medic.* Herpes. Also *brothel sprouts, German cornflakes.*

vajillion *n.* In mathematics, an unspecified but very high number, specifically referring to an innumerable multitude of *fannies. 'Having now spent a time in excess of thirty years as the capital's leading gynaecologist, I have built up the London Surgical Home for Women into one of Europe's most pre-eminent establishments specialising in the treatment of feminine complaints. Indeed, it is scarcely an exaggeration to say that during my medical career, I have successfully treated countless ladies and performed medical procedures on a vajillion twats.'* (Preface to *On the Curability of*

Certain Forms of Insanity, Catalepsy and Hysteria in Females, by Dr Isaac Baker Brown, 1866).

vajism *n.* Female ejaculate. Also known as *bean soup, milp, moip, fanny batter, blip, truffle butter, birds' custard, parsley sauce* or *beef dripping.*

vajizzle *v.* To improvise the decoration of a special friend's *vajayjay* when there are no Swarovski crystals immediately to hand.

Valentine's day mascara *n. Eyelid glue.*

Valentine's day porridge *n. Semen-o-lina, spaff, spangle, snedge, gunk, liquid pearls.*

valet your hoop *n.* To give one's *ringpiece* a proper wipe round every month or so.

valley of decision *1. n.* A literary work penned by late 19th century author Edith Wharton; the story of a man who is forced to choose between two conflicting loyalties during an Italian revolution. *2. n.* The story of a man forced to choose between two conflicting loyalties during a romantic episode, *ie.* The *nipsy* or the *minge.*

valley of the deaf *n.* The *Bristol channel* of a generously *top-bollocked* woman, wherein a fellow might hope to experience a temporary loss of hearing.

valley parking *n.* Assistance provided by an accommodating lady in skilfully slotting one's *old chap* into the correct space.

valurian steel *n.* Finely wrought tumescence of impossible hardness and strength. Named after the eponymous material that was much sought after for weapon construction in *Game of Thrones. Pink steel.*

vampire *1. n.* A person who decides to start being a *fruit feeler* only in middle age; one who "comes out late". *2. n.* A *big-boned* female who forces her fat *arse* into tight jeans, because "she obviously can't see herself in the mirror".

vampire sandwich *n. Jam rag, zombie's napkin.*

vandal grease *1. n.* Substance used to deter Liverpudlians from climbing onto the tops of public buildings. *2. n.* Substance used by those who *know what's in their flowerbeds* to lubricate their *uphill gardening tools.*

vandalised bus seat *n.* A well-*shagged minnie-moo* which has been badly repaired using duct-tape. A *badly packed kebab* that has taken a proper hammering over the years.

vandaljism *n.* The wantom damage done to a lady's curtains, towels, bedsheets, cat *etc.*, when a chap elects to clean off his *pecker* after an amorous assignation.

V&A museum *1. n.* New, funny-shaped public building in Dundee where visitors can view familiar artifacts from a bygone age. *2. n.* Large *dunghampers* of the sort worn by ladies who have largely given up on intimacy.

V&A, the *n.* The *carse, tinter, butfer* or *Humber Bridge.* The fusty, little-used corridor between a woman's *Victoria* and her *Albert.*

vangina *n.* A high-mileage, untidy, battered yet capacious receptacle into which tradesmen put their *tools.* Although they don't keep them in there overnight, obviously.

vangina *n.* A *twat* in a white Transit who cuts you up at the roundabout.

Van Gogh's beard *euph.* The effect of enjoying a *clam chowdown* on a lady who's got the post impressionist *painters in.* Named after monaural Dutch artist Vincent (1853-1890), who painted a famous self-portrait in 1887 shortly after *licking out* his neighbour Madame Ginoux, who was *up on blocks* at the time.

van Halen *n.* A solo on the *one-string guitar,* either administered by oneself or an assistant, which involves "both hands on the neck". From the trademark "tapping" style of playing favoured by eponymous *rock poodle plank spanker* Eddie.

vanilla *adj. US.* A term used by sadomasochists to refer to normal, respectable people, *eg.* Doctors, lawyers *etc.,* who do not share their foul perversion. Also *civilians, muggles.*

vanilla strip *n.* The *tinter, carse* or *taint.* A lady's perineum, named after the pale-coloured vanilla flavour section which, in a tub of Neapolitan ice cream, is found precisely between the pink (strawberry flavour) and the brown (chocolate flavour).

vanity manitee *n.* A person of exceptional abdominal girth who takes excessive pride in his or her appearance.

vank *n.* A *wank* in a van. From van + wank.

vanta *n.* The orangey-looking liquid often found in bottles discarded on the central reservations of motorways. *Truckers' Tizer, kidney cider.*

VAR *abbrev.* What a naughty lady might allow her lucky partner to review on a night of erotic discovery. Vaginal And Rectal.

variant of Concern *euph.* That one bloke in the pub whose pint you definitely don't want to knock over.

varnished eel, stiff as a *sim.* Figure of speech which can be usefully employed when describing a long, hard thing. Such as a penis. *'I'm as disgusted, sickened, horrified and revolted by this live sex show as you are, Mrs Whitehouse. I'd walk out of the theatre too; however, I can't stand up as my nob's as stiff as a varnished eel.'*

varnish the cane *v.* To give the old *walking stick* a

one-handed waxing. To *oil the bat.*

varnish the chair *phr.* Hyperbolic reference to the succulence of an excitable lady's *nethers. See also froth at the gash, chomp at the clit. 'Ooh Sister Mary, when that man comes on screen during Homes Under the Hammer, I varnish the chair.'*

varse *n.* That strip of skin between a lady's *fanny* and her *shitter*, also variously referred to as the *taint, tinter, twernt, carse, biffon, Humber Bridge* etc. And it does get referred to a lot.

vart *n.* A *queef. Twatulence.* From vag + fart.

VAT 1. *abbrev.* Any *blurtch* which has been so adorned as to materially increase its appeal, *eg.* By the addition of some form of pubic topiary, *va-jazzlement* or by the addition of a piece of erotic ironmongery hammered through the *clematis.* Value Added Twat. 2. *abbrev.* Mammary glands which have been surgically enhanced, and are thus worth between fifteen and twenty percent more than they were originally. Value Added Tits.

VAT fighters *n.* Larger-boned folk who perhaps, it could be argued, were wont to protest a tad too much over any proposed imposition of a 20% tax on sausage rolls and pasties.

Vatican roulette *n. Pull out and pray.* A foolproof method of contraception practised by *left-footers* with extremely large families.

vault whiskey *n.* Liquor so strong it convinces the imbiber that he's a thoroughbred racehorse who can leap hedges on his way home from the pub.

vauxhall vivaro *n.* A woman who can "take a hefty load" according to the eponymous vehicle's advertising campaign. Also *industrial washing machine.*

V-bone steak *n.* A sumptuous, meaty meal, eaten off a *hairy plate.*

vedgie *n.* A vaginal *wedgie.* Also known as *splitting the twix.*

vegan quiche *euph.* Something that is an entirely underwhelming example of its kind, *eg.* The Rover 75 CDT "Connoisseur".

vegan sausage *n.* A *meat-free* lesbidaceous accessory. A *strap-on banger.*

vegan's fry-up *n.* Something that is extremely unsatisfying, *eg.* A *tit wank* off a lady with *bangers like two aspirins on an ironing board.*

veg for vag *phr.* Syndrome whereby one of your hitherto carnivorous male friends gets a new vegetarian or vegan girlfriend and suddenly declares that they will no longer eat meat. *'Is Nigel coming for a kebab?' 'No, haven't you heard? He's gone veg for vag.'*

veinish blue *n. Hedam.*

vein strainer *n.* A *hog's-eye*-popping *diamond cutter*

of potentially life-threatening proportions, which could quite easily place intolerable demands on one's circulatory system. *Pink steel* that looks like it's in danger of going off like that bloke's head in *Scanners.*

veiny bang stick *n.* The *slag hammer.* *'Mr Buonarroti? Can you hear me up there? The Holy Father was just wondering if you could make Adam's veiny bang stick a bit smaller.'*

veiny vuvuzela *n.* The latest addition to the *woodwind* ensemble, to be played alongside the *skin flute, one-eyed piccolo, American trombone, pink oboe, beef bugle, fleshy flugelhorn, hairy-bollocked ejaculating clarinet* and *purple-headed spam bassoon.*

velcro arse *n. medic.* Descriptive of the condition of a driving instructor's *bum cheeks* after a long, hot day in the passenger seat.

velcro special *n.* A particularly adhesive *shite* – popularly believed to be the result of a diet of crisps, chocolate and chips – that sticks immovably to the porcelain of the lavatory bowl. *Velcro specials* are typically unresponsive to bleach and other chemical treatments, and can only be removed by brute force, using a chisel and mallet.

velcro triangle *n. Minge, mott, mapatasi.*

Velma *n.* The act of deliberately or accidentally shooting *jitler* into the *bread knife*'s eyes, reproducing the disorientating effects suffered by the four-eyed character from *Scooby Doo* each time she lost her glasses. *Spunkblindness. St. Valentine's Day mascara, Gabrielle, King Harold.*

velocipedophile *n.* A *snufty, snudger, shramper, quumfer, scrunger, pringle, snerger, snedger, snaffler, snarze, snerk, snerdler, shniffle-piffler, nurfer, moompher, barumpher, garboon, pooner, snarfer, snurdle* or *snurge.* A harmless fellow who takes his olfactory pleasures while in close proximity to young ladies' recently vacated bicycle saddles.

velvet parachute 1. *n.* A new type of mushroom discovered recently in Madagascar. 2. *n.* A *fanny* you could fry up for breakfast.

velvet rope 1. *n.* Apparently seminal nineties album by Janet Jackson. 2. *n.* A lengthy chod that rates a luxurious 4 on the Bristol Stool Scale.

venerable bead *n.* The *clematis.*

venereal *n. rhym. slang.* How a Cockney refers to cheese. From venereal disease = cheese. *'What's for tea, Ange?' 'Venereal on toast, Den.'*

venetian bind *n.* An awkward situation in which a gentleman finds himself when there isn't a curtain available to *zuffle* his *cock* on.

Venezuela *euph.* A malodorous and dishevelled *minge.* From the line in the popular cartoon film

Avatar, where Colonel Quaritch says: "Venezuela, that was some mean bush".

venison blinds *n.* Posh *mutton shutters*, sirloin *beef curtains, Sir Keith Burtons.*

venison ram rod *1. n.* Luridly named meat product made by New Zealand-based butchers Beard Brothers (who also produce bangers called 'Sausage Party' and 'Sheep Thrill'). *2. n.* The male *w*lly.*

Venus *n.* A tiny *porky banger.* From the fact that, like the popular planet, it is rarely visible to the naked eye and women tend to point at it and laugh. A *gnomon.*

Venus pie trap *n.* A fat lass who lies in ambush for Greggs delivery drivers.

verandah *phr.* Arguably the best joke in the film *The Three Amigos. 'We could take a walk and you could kiss me on the verandah' 'That's OK... lips will be fine.'*

verandah over the toyshop *n. Aus.* An *ocker's* lovingly nurtured *greggnant* tummy. A *one-pack, party seven, Foster's child, beerby.*

verminillionaire *n.* A lottery winner who has a criminal record as long as your arm and spends all the money on helicopters and Ferraris. Mind you, the ones who say it won't change their lives are even worse. Bastards.

verminions*n.* Artful dodgers of indifferent pedigree.

verse from the Old Testament, like a *sim.* Description of horrid sounds emanating from a *trap* during the exorcism of a particularly malevolent *copper bolt*, viz. "...much wailing and gnashing of teeth".

versnatche *n.* A designer *cunt.*

vertical bacon sandwich *n.* That which is clearly visible in *hamburger shots.* Also *vertical smile, vertical taco, club sandwich, haddock pastie.*

vertical eyebrow *n.* A *bush* that has been trimmed to within a quarter of an inch of its life. A *Pires's chin.*

very tits off the Virgin Mary, thinks he's the *exclam.* Said of a person with a particularly high opinion of himself. *'Yeah, I met the tidy-bearded little shortarse at a helicopter show. Thinks he's the very tits off the Virgin Mary.'*

vesser *n.* A silent *fart, SBD.*

vesta *n.* A short, purple-ended length of *wood* that *goes off* when rubbed gently on the side of a *box.*

vestal virgin *n.* A person who has never worn a vest before.

vesta vespa *n.* The two-stroke engine-like noise one's *anus* makes the morning after eating a box of the foul, dried curry substitute. Accompanied

by a puff of blue smoke.

vested interests *n. Assets, competitive advantages, first impressions, qualifications, impressive CVs, leisure facilities.* An extensive *HR department* or splendid *set of references.*

vesti-boules *n. A French bird's knockers. 'You want to see Brigitte Bardot's vesti-boules in And Woman...Was Created, your holiness. You'll wank yourself daft.'*

vestosterone *n.* Middle-aged male hormone caused by drinking in the afternoon during summer, an excess of which leads to the wearing of sleeveless singlets and sudden bursts of manly violence.

vest stretchers *n. Leisure facilities* that are at the more generous end of the scale. Good old fashioned *oomlaaters. Gert stonkers.*

Vesuviarse *n.* A mighty eruption of sulphurous lava from your *fumerole* the morning after a hot curry. Named after Mount Vesuviarse, which erupted on August 24th A.D.79, burying the town of Pompeii under a superincumbent mass of hot diarrhoea. Also *Cackatoa, Stromboweli.*

Vesuvius sir! *1. exclam.* In the film *633 Squadron,* the radio signal sent to base to confirm that an overhanging rock has finally been bombed free. *2. exclam.* Said through the lavatory door to a concerned relative to announce that an over-baked *loaf* has successfully been extracted from the *mud oven.*

vet's dustbin *n.* A very nasty *clunge.* Also *vet's bin. 'You seen the centrefold in this month's Readers' Wives, your holiness? It's a proper vet's dustbin down there. Took me ages.'*

vext messaging *n.* Unreasonable, harshly worded SMS communications sent by a chap's wife/girlfriend enquiring after his current location and status, eg. "For fuck's sake Baz where are you? You only popped out for some milk and that was 3 days ago. PS I gave birth to a baby boy. WTF LMFAO. Not. :("

V festival *1. n.* An annual musical concert of some sort featuring electrically amplified guitars, which is no doubt very popular with the young people. *2. n.* A club or party which is notable for the unusually high number of nubile females in attendance. *3. n.* A lesbian *orgy.* A gathering of sweaty *twats* lip-synching.

VHS vixen *n.* A *stick vid* actress that one finds slightly less appealing when viewed on Blu-ray. A *low resolution fox.*

viaggro contretemps *n.* Low rent fisticuffs waged between gentlemen of more mature years goaded by their equally aged and vituperative wives, eg. A row over the last disabled parking bay in

Morrisons car park on Christmas Eve.

viagra falls *1. n.* The dispiriting moment when Pele's erectile enhancement medication finally wore off. *2. n.* A girl with such a *lovely personality* that she easily counteracts the stiffening effects of sildenafil citrate.

viagravated *adj.* The resignedly annoyed attitude of the *bag for life* when she realises you've popped a *Bongo Bill's banjo pill* and, thus, yet another unwelcome two-hour bedroom tussle followed by a heart attack is in the offing. *Bone-weary*.

viagravation *n.* Discomfort and frustration experienced by a chap who has recently ingested a *Bongo Bill's banjo pill* only to learn that his life partner's immediate plans do not necessarily coincide with his own.

vibration white fanny *n. medic.* A *plastic-coccupational* hazard. Semi-numbed condition of a *bird's farmyard area*, typically resulting from prolonged use of heavy duty *snatch plant*.

vibration white finger *1. n.* A medical condition which commonly affects miners and people who use powerful drilling machinery. *2. n.* Condition commonly suffered by teenage boys and monks.

vicar's bath *n.* An emergency Sunday morning wash; face, testicles and a quick go under each arm. Also *workman's plunge*.

vicar's calling card *n.* Sticking the *organ* up the *reredos*. A *sting in the tail*. *Bumming*.

vicar's piss *n.* Any particularly weak beer. *'I've already had six pints and I'm driving, so I'd better not.' 'Tell you what, Katie, I'll just get you a vicar's piss then.'*

vice crispy *n.* A contagious wart, boil or scab, occasionally spotted while enjoying a *full English breakfast*. A *brothel sprout*. *'Eurgh. What's this, love?' 'It's just a vice crispy. I've had it since that business trip to Amsterdam.'*

vicious circle *n.* An angry *ringpiece*. *'Come for a night at the Rupali Restaurant, Bigg Market, Newcastle upon Tyne, and wake up with a vicious circle you'll have to take to A&E.'*

Vicks shit *n.* A *number two* of such olfactory potency that it manages to unblock your nose and make your eyes water at the same time. *Olbas soil*.

Victorian photographer *n.* Any *cunning linguist* who performs under the skirts of a lady.

victory flush *n.* After many attempts, the deluge that finally clears the toilet bowl of a *bog-breaking* mass of *bum cigars* and damp *shit tickets*, following a nighttime session of lamb tindaloo, Harp, and Pringles.

Vi-curious *adj.* Mildly intrigued at the prospect of a spot of *biddy-fiddling*.

video ref, go to the *v.* Humorous, rugby-based expression; to check the back of one's shorts following a particularly violent *back pass*, when one is unsure whether one has *touched down* or not.

vidiot *n.* A translucent, spotty youth who spends most of his time cooped up in his bedroom kidding himself he's in the magical land of Zelda and not Basingstoke.

Vienna *1. n.* Title of a turgid 1981 Ultravox single that was happily kept off the top spot in the charts for a month by the Joe Dolce novelty song *Shaddap You Face*. *2. n.* A satisfyingly monumental *dump* that refuses to move despite endless flushing, prodding it with a stick and attempts to break it up using illegal fireworks left over from November 5th. A *non-moving number two*.

Viennetta *n.* A rich and satisfying multi-layered toilet pudding, consisting of several alternating layers of *bum rubbish* and *bumwad*. *Bangers and mash, lasagne*.

Vietnamese waltz *n.* Form of locomotion peculiar to those unfortunate enough to have consumed a bad prawn in last night's pho. Characterised by the rapid, scuttling gait of the sufferer as he reels from one stall to another in his search for a convenience that is not already full of *bangers and mash*.

viewrinal *n.* A stand-up lavatory at a club or night spot frequented by unusually well-groomed young men. Sometimes with a *water sports* enthusiast reclining in the trough, so they say. Mind you, anyone would look well-groomed next to someone who'd been lying down getting *pissed* on in a pub bog.

vihagra *n.* Extra-powerful *bongo Bill's banjo pills*.

Viking funeral *n.* Akin to the launch of a burning longboat in Norse times, a big, hot and florid *Meat Loaf's daughter* floated out towards the sea, *Up Helly Arse*-style, the morning after a red hot curry or chilli.

vile high club, join the *v.* During a commercial flight, to leave an aircraft *crapper* in such a state as to force the aircrew to make an emergency landing.

village pub's hanging baskets, dripping like the *sim.* Figure of speech describing a woman who is in a state of arousal. See also *(dripping like a) fucked fridge, (wetter than) Lee Evans's suit etc. 'As soon as Pete started singing Farmer Bill's Cowman, I was dripping like the village pub's hanging baskets.'*

vin blank *n.* A missing period of time caused by over-indulgence in certain grape-based beverages. *'SUE LAWLEY: Keith Floyd, you're* *one of Britain's most popular television celebrities, but you weren't always in the public eye, were you? Tell me about some of the formative experiences of your early life. KEITH FLOYD: Well Sue, I clearly remember going into the pub on my thirteenth birthday and I vaguely recall getting out of a taxi outside Broadcasting House about twenty minutes ago. Everything between those two events is pretty much a vin blank, I'm afraid.'* (Transcript of *Desert island Discs*, BBC Radio 4, broadcast on December 30th 1990).

Vince *1. n. prop. rhym. slang.* An excreta. From the name of Parker-out-of-*Thunderbirds* lookalike Lib Dem stalwart Vince Cable = *Auntie Mabel*. *2. n. prop. rhym. slang.* The contraceptive pill. From the name of 1970s Happy Shopper Andy Williams, Vince Hill = *the Benny Hill*.

vindaloose *adj.* Of the *Simon Cowells,* practically overwhelmed by the power of exotic spices.

vindaluminous *adj.* Descriptive of a super-heated *teatowel holder* whose proprietor has over-indulged in the culinary delights of the Orient, and which can be seen glowing in the dark as he gropes his way towards the bathroom for the tenth time of the night.

vin de van *n.* Plastic bottles of straw-coloured liquid of indeterminate vintage found in lay-bys and overnight parking spots.

Vin Diesel *1. n. prop.* Gravel-voiced, bald actor who always wears sunglasses. *2. n.* Happy Shopper wine costing less than £2 a bottle, which leaves one gravel-voiced, bald and wearing sunglasses. *Screwtop.*

vinegar dip *n.* A bout of penetrative affection with a lady who is sadly past her prime years of youthful ripeness, such that her *fanny* has went all wrong and caustic.

vinegar Joe *n.* The *stick vid* thespian responsible for causing *porn trauma.*

vinegar string *n.* The *banjo.*

vinegar strokes *n.* Of males *on the job*, the final climactic stages of intercourse or masturbation. From the similar facial expression associated with sipping non-brewed condiment. *'Would you believe it? The phone rang just as I was getting onto the vinegar strokes. I nearly ran into the car in front.'*

vinegar tits *n.* The sort of miserable, sour-faced woman that looks, one might unfairly judge, like her *lils* would deliver neat Sarson's into the mouth of any unfortunate suckling neonate, *eg.* Her off *Emmerdale* with the Jimmy Cricket hat.

vinegar trauma *n. psych.* Distressing condition that affects those whose parents/siblings/partners have walked in on them nearing the climax of an *act of monomanual personal delight.* Also affects those who, at a similar stage of the game, suddenly find their view of a *Frankie* starlet's *ladygarden* is obscured by the hairy *arse* of a fictional builder.

vinyl driver *n.* A traditional analogue motorist of advancing years who happily maintains a steady 45 under all circumstances.

Violet Elizabeth *n.* A loud and demonstrative female *organism*. Named after *Just William*'s nemesis, who famously threatened to "Thcream and thcream until I'm thick…"

V.I. Paedo *n.* A 1970s celebrity whose legacy of primetime family-friendly fun has since perforce been re-assessed.

VIP entrance *n.* The *back passage*, reserved for dignitaries.

viper's tongue *sim.* A figure of speech, or trope, illustrative of the bifurcated stream of micturant which issues from a urethral *meatus* that is partially occluded by post-coital *sponglement*, fossilised *smegma* or a piece of sweetcorn. *Twin jets.*

VIP lounge, chavs' *n.* The back seat upstairs on a double decker bus.

virgin oil *n.* The facial grease secreted by *scoobescent* teenagers.

virgin poo *n.* The first *turd* laid at work after the cleaning lady has scrubbed the rim.

virtual meat-up *n.* A sordid sexual encounter mediated by online video streaming technology. *'Could we delay dinner tonight, darling? Only I've got a couple of Zoom meetings and a virtual meat-up to do first. So don't come up to the loft, okay?'*

virtuoso *1. n.* A talented musician, *eg.* An oboe soloist capable of tackling Pasculli's fiendishly difficult *Le Api.* *2. n.* One whose *cherry* remains firmly intact, *eg.* See 1.

visible pantry line *n.* Phenomenon whereby a young lady's underwear is clearly struggling to hold in her *arse* due to the fact that she looks like she's scoffed the entire contents of the family food cupboard.

visibodies *n.* Hi-vis jacketed, officious jobsworths.

visit from aunt Flo *euph. Having the painters in. Sheep sitting, dropping clots.*

visit from the follow-through fairy *euph.* An evil manifestation that may cause distress to one's laundry maid.

visit from Zebedee *n.* An instantaneous erection so sudden that it should be accompanied by a 'boing' sound, much like that which heralded the appearance of the eponymous character on hallucinogenic 60s/70s children's TV show *The Magic Roundabout. 'Whenever that Alex Jones is on the telly, I get a visit from Zebedee.' 'That's fascinating,* *your holiness. And did you know there's a woman on British telly with the same name?'*

visiting day at Preston Prison *euph.* An assortment of rough-looking women, inexplicably dressed as if going to a discotheque at ten-thirty on a Monday morning.

visit Lord Turgleton *v.* To enjoy an aristocratic *digestive transit.*

visit the cash machine *v.* To make a withdrawal from the *poop-chute* followed immediately by a sizeable deposit in the *pie-hole*. *ATM.*

visit the graveyard *n.* To indulge in post break-up sexual shenanigans with a former girlfriend.

visit the V&A *v.* To spend a leisurely time exploring two or three of the more interesting exhibits *down south.*

visual disturbance *n.* An unwanted and very noticeable *hard-on*. *'Dear Pamela. I am a male Guardian reader who works in a laboratory. The air-conditioning broke last week and one of my colleagues told me she was only wearing underwear beneath her labcoat. I was so aroused that I actually had a visual disturbance. It's not really a problem as such; I just wanted to tell someone.'*

vital organs *euph.* Breasts. *'We've got a female, mid-twenties, been in an RTA. Irregular heartbeat, her breathing's erratic and shallow, she's semi-conscious with a weak radial pulse, but her vital organs are looking good.'*

vitaminge *n.* A handy source of essential fish oils and other *holesome* goodness.

vitamin M *n. medic.* Taken in daily doses when *dining at the Y*, *vitamin M* ensures that a chap has a healthy wet nose. *Moip.*

vitamin P *n.* The luminescent lime green *wazz* produced after one has consumed high dose multivitamins.

vitamin S *n.* A naturally occurring substance which men insist is very good for women when taken orally in 5ml doses.

vitamin T *n.* Essential dietary supplement north of the border. Tennent's lager.

vixen *n.* Wily *bird*, a young temptress, a foxy *chick, nymph, eg.* Stevie Nicks in about 1978.

Viz moment *n.* Time taken out of a busy day to *snap off a length of dirty spine* while perusing your favourite humorous magazine. Or *Viz*, for that matter.

VLT *abbrev.* In astronomy, a Very Large Telescope. *2. abbrev.* Dating ad terminology. *'Male, 58, seeking female, 18-24, with GSOH & VLT. GSOH not essential.'*

vogue *1. n.* A briefly fashionable pose-striking dance made popular by pointy-titted singer Madonna. *2. v.* To strike an artistic pose prior to *dropping one's guts* in order to amuse friends or charm young ladies into bed.

voice of Winehouse, face of shitehouse *n.* A cumbersome bit of terminology describing a local pub karaoke queen who, despite having a fair set of pipes on her, has a *face like a sack of broken bells*.

void the warranty *v.* To *jailbreak* one's partner in a matter that is clearly at odds with the manufacturer's intentions; an act which could result in a hefty bill for repairs should any damage arise.

vol au vent *n.* A light, savoury snack served as an appetiser before the main, sit-down event. A posh *air biscuit*. From the French meaning "a flight in the wind".

volcanic gash *n.* A *fanny* that explodes if you *poke* it too much. A *squirter.*

Voldemort *n.* Secret name for a chap's *thingie*. "Him who must not be named" or "you know who".

Volkswagen fart *n.* A noxious *backfire* you had hoped to slip out secretly, but which is so foul that your reputation is ruined.

Volvo, drop a *v.* To do a not particularly aerodynamic *poo* that keeps its headlamps on during daylight hours, and would score an easy 5 stars in the Euro/NCAP crash tests.

vombard *v.* To bombard with vomit from a high place. From vomit + bombard.

vomcano *n.* A spectacular eruption of beer and curry-based lava spewing upwards from the *cakehole* while lying on one's back.

vomelch *v. n.* A lusty belch with an unexpected *yoff* follow-through that must then be swallowed back down, especially if one finds oneself amongst polite company. *Vurp, Monkhouse syndrome.*

vomelette *n.* A bright yellow *pavement pizza*. Mushrooms 60p extra.

vomit comet *1. n.* NASA's zero gravity training plane that flies in alarming parabolas to create the temporary illusion of weightlessness and is usually full of BBC science documentary presenters doing pieces to camera whilst wearing blue boilersuits. *2. n.* The last train home.

vomiting milkman *n.* A whistling *chap* that *spunks up* on the doorstep early in the morning. Also *blue-veined junket pump, captain, chimney sweep's brush, pud etc.*

vommunition *n.* Anything eaten to line the stomach before a drinking session. *'Giz some of them scratchings, mate. I need some vommunition.'*

vom toggle *n.* The exact point at which a noisome *whiff* triggers the gag reflex.

Von Crapp family *n.* A huge brood of *scratters*

living in a big council house, who are likely to suddenly do a flit.

voodoo butter *n.* The raw material of *squid marks*. *Ghee*.

vowel and towel *n.* The daily pleasure of *relieving one's internal tensions* while watching quiz-show *arithmetrix* Rachel Riley going about her business.

vowel movement, have a *v.* To talk *shit*.

voyage of self discovery *n.* Yet another way of saying a *wank*. *'Ian arrived back at the house to find it empty. By his calculations he just had time for a quick voyage of self discovery with his favourite art pamphlet before the missus came home. With a smile of triumph, he unbuckled his belt and let his 501s hit the lino.'*

VPL *abbrev.* Visible Panty Line. A dead giveaway that a *bird* is wearing *Alans*, and is therefore frigid.

vragrance *n.* The signature perfume of a *gentleman of the road*.

V2 *1. n.* In aviation, the runway velocity at which a pilot is committed to completing a take-off. *2. n.* In *pooing*, the point at which there is no turning back, the *turtle's head* is fully engaged in the *dirt canal* and the *pooer* is committed to doing a *poo*. *'Oh bollocks. I'm at V2 and my belt buckle has jammed. Mayday! Mayday!' 2. abbrev.* That critical moment during the *vinegar strokes* at which a gentleman is irretrievably committed to *crashing the yoghurt lorry*. *'What's up, Sting?' 'I'm at V2, Trudi.'*

Vulcan bomb doors *sim. RAF.* Huge, gaping *piss flaps,* making the *hairy pie* resemble the underside of one of the eponymous delta-winged bombers making a low pass over the runway at Port Stanley.

Vulcan's kiss *n.* Named after the Roman god of fire; the burning sensation experienced around the *balloon knot* the morning after a particularly spicy *Ruby Murray*.

vulva eroders *n.* High-waisted denim shorts worn so high and tight that they abrade everything in their path. Also known as *clunge huggers, cooter cutters* or *Daisy Dukes*.

vulvaline *n.* The lubricant that keeps the missus's *cylinder* from seizing up during high speed reciprocating activity.

vulvarine *1. n.* A formidably powerful, grey, hairy *wolf bite* with a feral, bloody aroma. A hairy *growler* that can cut you to shreds when provoked. *2. n. Fanny batter* that spreads straight from the fridge.

vulvo *1. n.* A solidly built *snapper* which is unlikely to set your *heirbags* off, but could nevertheless withstand an offset frontal impact at 40mph and come out reasonably unscathed. *2. euph.* What the Swedes call a car that is a *fanny magnet*.

vulvuzela *n.* A *queef* that sounds like kick-off in a South African football match.

vurp *n.* A burp which brings up a foul-tasting slug of acrid stomach contents that is small enough to be gulped straight back down again. A *broat, Bob's full mouth*.

wab *n.* The *bald-headed hermit.*

WABOC/waboc *abbrev.* Shorthand terminology for a group of disagreeable people. What A Bunch Of Cunts.

wabs *n.* Tits. *'I hope you don't take this the wrong way, Lord Owen, but you've got a smashing set of wabs on you.'*

wacaday *1. n.* A morning television show for children, broadcast between the mid-80s and the early 90s, starring hyperactive, bespectacled *arsehole* Timmy Mallett. *2. n.* The sad and repetitive *Groundhog wank*-filled sexual routine enjoyed by a single male.

wactation *n.* The milky substance that emanates from the male organ during periods of sexual arousal. *Tatty watta.*

wad *1. n.* The large sum of money which Harry "Loadsamoney" Enfield waved around after he started getting advertising work. *2. n.* That featured in a *money shot.* A small package of *hot fish yoghurt* flying out the end of a *mutton musket.* A *jizzbolt.*

wad chomper *n.* A lady who is anxious to please. One who enjoys a portion of *man pop* and sees no reason to spit it out. A *swallower.*

wadding *n.* Poking a *Thora* down the plughole with one's toes following a natural delivery in the shower or bath. See *waffle stomper.*

wade in *1. v.* To *move in for the kill* immediately prior to *pulling.* *2. v.* To walk towards the centre of a *pagga*, with one's arms above one's head in order to join the fun.

waffle stomper *n.* One who disposes of an unwelcome *Sir Douglas* in the shower by forcing it down the plughole with the feet. See also *shit chips.* *'Born on this day: Geoffrey Boycott, Yorkshirish batsman, 1940; Mandy Rice-Davis, cabinet muse, 1944; Julian Cope, erstwhile waffle stomper, 1957.'*

waft ale *n.* Fart fuel. *'You've had nine pints of waft ale, your holiness. You'll be kipping on the sofa then.'*

wafty crank *n.* One off the wrist knocked out on the sly. *'Terry knew it would only take his missus ten minutes to pop the local corner shop to pick up her daily supplies of forty Embassy and eight cans of Natch, just enough time for a wafty crank. Or two.'*

wag bag *n.* A middle-aged woman who, despite her advancing years, elects to dress like the wife of a famous footballer.

wage against the machine *phr.* Feeding all your hard-earned *moolah* into a one-armed bandit during a once-in-a-lifetime trip to Las Vegas, a glamorous casino trip to Monte Carlo, or over the course of a wet February afternoon on Aberystwyth pier.

wagging a boxer dog's tail *euph.* So desperate to *visit Lord Turgleton* that one feels that one could actually wave one's *Bungle's finger* from side to side.

wagon weals *n.* The treadmarks left on a *bird's* back and buttocks after being *rogered* by an HGV driver up against one of his lorry's tyres.

Wagon Wheel *1. n.* A sickly, cream-filled confection that "observational" comedians are wont to ask if their audiences remember, even though they have failed to observe that they are still fucking make them. *2. n.* A large *cock.* From the 1980s advertising slogan for *1.* "You've got to grin to get it in".

wags to witches *euph.* The change in women from being attractive to *minging* over decades. Or overnight after a *piss up.*

Waikiki sneaky, the *n.* Surreptitiously slipping your *old fella* up the *wrong 'un* when you think nobody will notice.

wail switch *n.* An excitable lady's *clematis. The devil's doorbell, starter button.*

waist height delight *n.* A fun-size lady, ideal for vertical *horatio* or enthusiastic *cowboy.* A *laptop,* a *throwabout.*

wait for the wings *v.* To eagerly anticipate the demise of an elderly loved one to fund the purchase of luxury items in their memory. *'Sadly, my granny is very ill at the moment. I'm just waiting for the wings, then I'm going to get some 8 by 18-inch Wolfrace Spirit alloys for my Saxo. And an exhaust pipe like a fucking coal scuttle.'*

waiting for a fridge to be delivered *euph.* An excuse given when taking an entire day off work to endlessly *wank your knackers flat* over online filth. Craftily, there is always a reason to ignore or abruptly terminate any phone calls one receives, thanks to the ever-imminent arrival of the imaginary (and tardy) delivery folk. A *doley's blackout* that lasts all day and comes with the bonus of a salary.

waiting for Ben *euph.* Said of any saucily dressed young lady standing around at a train station. Based on the stereotypical opening scenes of all movies made by legendarily priapismic octogenarian UK *sticksman* Ben Dover (real name Linseed Honeybee) during his prolific career as an erotic *auteur* before his back went.

waiting for the red cheque to clear *euph.* Of a married man, to endure the monthly four to five day period of sexual limbo which occurs while *his missus's fanny account is overdrawn.*

waiting for the worms *1. n.* Title of a track by

Pink Floyd off their classic album *The Wall*. 2. *n.* When you've had a black coffee and/or prune juice first thing in the morning; the experience of killing time in anticipation of your morning *earth movement* before leaving the house. *'Thought you'd have left by now, love.' 'Not yet, dear. I'm still waiting for the worms.'*

wake the bishop *1. n.* Name of a coffee made by Dear Green of Glasgow, with tasting notes of chocolate, caramel, apricot and praline, it says here. 2. *euph.* To arouse oneself, or be aroused, in *the trouser department*.

wake the wife *v.* Of a sleeping gent, who has enjoyed a surfeit of brown ales and spicy provender, to *let the cat out of the bag* in the wee small hours. To somnolently light a *Dutch oven*.

wake up and cough the smelly *phr.* An encouragement to rouse oneself and flap the quilt a bit following a heavy night.

wake up and smell the cocky *exclam.* Motivational phrase which can be used to encourage a wavering *vagitarian* to get herself *back onto solids*.

wake up at the crap of dawn *euph.* When you're aroused from your slumbers because you need a *shit* and have to get up or else you'll end up rolling around in your own filth. See also *cock-a-doodle poo*.

wake up with Jake up *v.* To have a *dawn horn, morning glory, motorcycle kickstand*. To *pitch a tent*.

walking condom *n.* Descriptive of a breed of young male who is probably up to no good in a baggy tracksuit with a hood. An *asbolescent*. *'Hello, police? I've just seen a walking condom trying car doors down Falmouth Road.' 'Very good, sir. We'll send a potted plant round next Thursday with a customer satisfaction survey for you to fill in.'*

walking like you've done your back in *phr.* Bent-over stoop concealing a *chirp-on* when answering the door to the Amazon man. Not necessarily because you're particularly excited to see him.

walking on the Moon *1. n.* The feeling one experiences after depositing a particularly weighty *lemon curd*, similar to that encountered by astronauts in one-sixth gravity. 2. *n.* Autobiographical song written by Sting out of the Police after he'd just done a really big *shit*.

walking stick *1. n.* Long piece of nobbly wood wielded by senior citizens on buses. 2. *n.* That old object upon which a fellow gives it *six nowt* while *relaxing in a gentleman's way*. 3. *n.* A long, knobbly *motion* that has bottomed out on the pan while still connected to your *arse*. A *neckbreaker,* earthing cable, tallboy*.

walking the plank *n.* When having a *gypsy's kiss,* starting with a long, forceful stream far from the toilet and then, as the flow gradually weakens, advancing tentatively towards the bowl.

walking tripod *sim.* A well-endowed, *donkey-rigged* individual. When admiring *buffage*, a sexist lady might offensively remark *'Look at the third leg on that. Stephen Pound MP's a walking tripod.'*

walking wounded *n. milit.* Women who go out *on the pull* despite the fact that they are *bleeding from a shotgun wound*. *'I wouldn't bother buying her a drink, Geordie. She's walking wounded.' 'So? She's got a mooth, hasn't she?'*

walk in the country *n.* Taking a gentle stroll with the index and middle fingers through, in and around a woman's *ladygarden*. A pubic ramble, *tiptoe through the two lips*.

walk like a tinman *v.* To be so badly in need of a *Richard the Third* that while making your way to the *plopper* you are unable to even bend your knees.

walkman shit *n.* Pairs of dead AA or AAA batteries found on bus seats and in other public places.

walk of shame *n.* Crossing the campsite holding a toilet roll.

walk the line *v.* To go for a *Johnny Cash*. *'Watch runways three, four, five and seven for a minute, will you? I'm off to walk the line.'*

walk the plank *1. v. rhym. slang.* To *wallop* the *pirate of men's pants* while a jeering monocular unidexter jabs a cutlass in your *arse*. 2. *v.* To avoid *splashback* at a urinal when doing a high-pressure *gypsy's kiss* by standing three or four feet back, and advancing slowly towards the *shark's mouth* as the flow recedes.

walk the shiterope *v.* To skillfully pull and push at the same time in order to sneak out an urgent, pressure-relieving *air biscuit* while practically *touching cloth*.

Wallace *1. n.* A disappointingly flaccid penis. From sweaty, egg-headed *Masterchef* host Gregg Wallace's catchphrase; "It doesn't get harder than this". 2. *v. rhym. slang.* To vomit. From Wallace & Gromit. *'Aw shite. Ashley's Wallaced all over my new carpet.'*

wallet drains *n.* Bin lids, kids, offsprings, *cuntburps, fuck trophies, sprouts*.

wall of death *1. n. Attack of the helicopters*. 2. *n. Last hot dog in the tin*.

wallop *n. Cookin'*. Any beer bought by a hearty *twat* with an eggy beard who calls the barman Landlord, mine host or Squire.

wallpaper stripper *n.* A *government nation-wide*

emergency alert test of such vigorous potency that it saves its author the bother of a trip to B&Q.

Wallsend trim *n.* A haircut so short that you lose three layers of skin off your scalp in the process. Administered by all barbers in the eponymous leafy Tyneside suburb, irrespective of the style requested by the customer. A *tuppenny all-off, Geordie affro.*

walnut *1. n.* The leaky washer in an old man's *waterworks.* The prostrate gland, *doughnut, shitoris* or *tremble trigger.* 2. *n.* Those annoying, little bits of feculent that "walnut" come off. *Tagnuts, dangleberries.* 3. *n.* The balloon knot, *chocolate starfish, rusty bullet hole* or *rusty sheriff's badge.*

walnut lodge *n.* Resting place of the *clockweights.*

walnut manoeuvre *n.* The legendary method by which good looking nurses are trained to poke one's *tremble trigger* in order to obtain an instant *Thelonious* sample. See *triggernobetry.*

walnut whip *1. rhym. slang.* A minor operation which removes the *cream,* but leaves the *nuts* intact. The *snip.* 2. *n.* A firm, cone-shaped stool that has been hollowed out and filled with a sickly cream-like substance, usually while a couple is exploring *the third way.* 3. *n.* When a romantic partner – quite possibly from the Derby area – provides an added thrill whilst performing *horatio,* by sliding a finger up a fellow's *nipsy* and giving his *tremble trigger* a playful flick.

walnut whip, cock like a *sim.* A tragic condition that effects men in the chillier months of the year.

walrus fold *n.* On a young lady with a *lovely personality,* that insulating bulge of blubber that protrudes forwards further than her *headlamps* when she is seated.

walrus, the *n.* Another unlikely sounding – and hopefully illegal – sexual act whereby a fellow gets a friend to swallow his *mess* before karate chopping them on both sides of the neck, causing "tusks" of *jitler* to run out of their nostrils in a style reminiscent of the popular moustachioed underwater dog. *'Reader, I married him. A quiet wedding we had: he and I, the parson and clerk, were alone present. On the way back from church, I've gave Mr Rochester a nosh in the back of the carriage and he done the walrus on me.'* (from *Jane Eyre Does Milcote* by Charlotte Brontë).

Walter *n.* A particularly verdant, luxurious, deep-pile *cunt-rug.* From "Walter Wall carpets". A *Judith, biffer, sweep's brush. 'Nice Walter you got there, your worship. You look like you've been hit between the legs with a bag of soot, look you.'*

Walter Raleigh *n. prop.* The selfless act of a true gentleman, *viz.* Following a *scuttle,* laying his discarded *underkegs* on the wet patch for his lady to sleep on without undue discomfort. Named in honour of the erstwhile naval hero (1552-1618), who famously laid his cloak across a puddle of *spunk* so that Queen Elizabeth I wouldn't get any of it on her *Jimmy Choos.*

Walters *n. rhym. slang.* Breasts. From the eponymous character in James Thurber's 1942 short story *The Secret Life of Walter Mockers.*

wancave *n.* A "man cave" that is equipped with superfast broadband internet access and a door that can be locked from the inside. *'You in, Jonathan?' 'I'm up in my wancave, Miles.'*

wanctuary *n.* A place of refuge in which a hunched man might enjoy an intimate moment alone.

wancunian *1. n.* A *wanker* from Manchester, *eg.* Morrissey. 2. *adj.* Descriptive of a *wanker* from Manchester, *eg.* Morrissey.

wanderlust *n.* Masturbating while walking around the house, typically in order to combine the performance of mundane household chores with a nice *hand shandy. Wanderlust* can also be practised on its own, in the style of a heavy metal band lead guitar solo, accompanied by appropriately pained facial expressions and occasional crouches.

wand waver *n. Flasher,* sexual exhibitionist.

wang *n. Wab.*

wang commander *n.* Temporary, transient *willitary* rank enjoyed by a chap gripping his *joystick* in the *bogs* of an aeroplane.

wanger *n.* A turgid *membrum virile* that, when sharply whacked with a pencil, snooker cue or garden spade, creates a noise not dissimilar to that of a tuning fork.

wanger management *n. Winding the clock, shuffling the cabinet etc.*

wangle *v.* To *wank* oneself into an advantageous situation. Although, to be perfectly frank, it's not entirely clear under what circumstances this might be achieved.

wangst *n.* Post-masturbatory *wanguish.* Also *wank hangover, crying over spilt milk.*

wanic *n.* The state of perturbation that occurs when a wife or girlfriend returns home unexpectedly just as one is reaching the *vinegar strokes* in front of one's favourite *scud mags* or *grumble site.* A *wank panic, jazz funk.*

wank *1. n.* A bout of *self help. 'If you have a wank every day you'll go blind.'* 2. *n.* Rubbish. *'Don't talk wank.'* 3. *v.* To masturbate. *'Well my brother wanks all the time and he's gone blind.'*

wankache day *n.* A special day which a fellow spends gripping a throbbing *panhandle* while *tossing hot batter* towards the ceiling.

wank against time *n*. An anxious, *Tarzan cord*-chafing act of *self harm* indulged in during Television X's ten-minute freeview, in the hope of *dropping one's yop* before it becomes necessary to phone in one's credit card details to the topless *scrubber* on the screen.

wankaid *n*. Any item pressed into service as an accessory during an act of *relaxation, eg*. Fingerless gloves, bag of carrots, Bodyshop peppermint foot lotion, big pink electric neck massager with all wiggly veins up the side and a bit sticking out the side to go up your *arse etc*.

wankameters *n*. Optimistically self-administered moral, ethical and legal boundaries set and hopefully adhered to by single gentlemen, with the intention of precluding the development of undesirable habits and preoccupations.

wank and a cider *n*. A man's post-work plans for the evening. *'Doing anything tonight, Andrew?' 'Yeah. After This Week, it's a wank and a cider for me.'*

wank and file *n*. The queue of male thesps *treading water* and waiting to *empty their sacks* over a lucky young actress on a *Frankie Vaughan* movie set. *Bukkaktors, sextras*.

wankard *n*. A real ale *twat*. With a tankard.

wankarium *n*. A box room containing a chair, a computer and a sock drawer. Also *masturbatorium*.

Wankashire cheese *n*. A vintage delicacy matured in an unwashed *fiveskin*. Also *fromunder, stinking bishop, brimula, foreskinzola, Fred Leicester* and so on.

wankathon *n*. A single man's right arm exercise endurance test. Days of frenzied *self abuse* heralded by the arrival of a large brown envelope with a Dutch postmark. Often ends with a dehydrated and disorientated *self-harmer* being wrapped in a large sheet of tin foil and wheeled to an ambulance on a drip.

wank baffle *n*. The corner of a duvet cleverly folded to lessen the sounds of frantic *self harm* while trying not to wake one's sleeping partner.

wank bank *n*. A fellow's curated mental inventory of erotic material. *'You're going straight in the wank bank with that wimple, Mother Teresa.'*

wank chaser *n*. A swift *hand shandy* slipped in during a brief lull in proceedings after *dropping the kids off at the pool. Icing the log*.

wank cheques *n*. A limitless supply of tissues to use up while *working from home. Standing orders, wankers' drafts*.

wank clamp *n*. A hand, *spunky wrench, cunt scratcher*.

wank crank *n. medic*. The elbow.

wankend *n*. A well-earned period of uninterrupted *relaxation* enjoyed by a gentleman between Friday teatime and *sparrowfart* the following Monday. Also *wank holiday, wristuntide*.

wank engine *n*. Any computerised device used for finding *gentleman's relaxation material* on the world wide web.

wanker *1. n*. One who practises a secret vice. *2. n*. A fellow road user, a motorist at whom one waves.

wanker butter *n*. Salty, off-white spread usually eaten on cracker biscuits or toast at public schools. *'"" say, Brown," cries Flashman, catching Tom by the collar as he passes the older lad's study door. "These crumpets are dry, you cursed young skulk. You know perfectly well that I always have my fags put wanker butter on my crumpets, don't you?" But alas, before poor Tom can answer, he has been dragged into Flashey's dorm to get his cheeks roasted in front of the fire by every chap in the Remove.'* (from *Tom Brown's Schooldays* by Thomas Hughes).

wankerchief *n*. A *spanky hanky, jizz sock, toss rag, j-cloth*.

wankered *adj. Shit-faced* as a newt.

wanker's badge *n*. A moustache. From the fact that most people sporting moustaches tend also to be *wankers. 'The usual, is it, Miss Robinson? Not too much off the top and tapering at the neck? And would you like me to trim your wanker's badge too?'*

wanker's block *n*. A complete absence of imagination or inspiration when trying to stimulate a reaction in the *trouser department*. Often occurs when one has the *horn* but is too *pissed* to think of anything rude.

wanker's cocoa *n*. A late night *tug* that induces a restful night's sleep. *Temazepalm*, a *knuckle nightcap*.

wanker's colic *n. medic*. Of seasoned factory/warehouse workers, a humorous diagnosis of the cause of hiccups or burps in their younger colleagues.

wanker's crisps *n*. Brittle, ready-salted tissues found under any healthy gentleman's bed. *Porn crackers*.

wanker's fist, full as a *sim. Full as a fat bird's shoe. 'I wouldn't bother going up on the top deck if I was you, Blakey. It's full as a wanker's fist up there.'*

wanker's genie *n*. The irresistible force that resides inside one's *magic lamp* and regularly tempts one to release it via a quick *magic buff*.

wanker's hankie *sim*. Descriptive of something very brittle. *'Come along to the Curry Capital (formerly* *the Rupali Restaurant), Bigg Market, Newcastle upon Tyne (now closed), where the food is hot, the beer is cold and the popadoms are as brittle as a wanker's hankie.'*

wanker's rancour *n.* The festering resentment that curdles the milk of human kindness in an habitual *self-abuser.*

wanker's rickets *n. medic.* The wobbling movements of the legs caused by orgasmic weakening of the knees.

wanker's sock, as stiff as a *sim.* Rigid. *'Marley was dead: to begin with. There is no doubt whatever about that. The register of his burial was signed by the clergyman, the clerk, the undertaker, and the chief mourner. Scrooge signed it. And Scrooge's name was good upon 'change, for anything he chose to put his hand to. Old Marley was as stiff as a wanker's sock.'* (from *A Christmas Carol Vorderman* by Charles Dickens).

wanker's tache *n. medic.* The vertical line of hair between the navel and the top of the *Rubiks.* Develops as a consequence of masturbation, along with spots, hairy palms, shortsightedness, insanity and stunted growth. The *crab ladder.*

wanker's tan *n.* Ghostly pallor effected by *anoraksics* who spend far too much time alone in their rooms with the curtains shut. *'I've just got Need for Speed ProStreet for Christmas, so I'll be spending the next few months working on my wanker's tan.'*

wanker's wigwam *n.* Small tent under a duvet wherein onanism is performed.

wankety blank *n.* Psychological state of mental blockage during attempted masturbation when one's *mammary banks* are in the red. *Wanker's block.*

wankfurter *n.* A laughably unsatisfying *banger.*

wank handle *n. medic.* In sex, a male erection of the penile shaft and glans. A turgid *crank.*

wank hangover *n.* Post *self abuse* self-loathing. De-bilitating *wangst* which can only be assuaged by the hair of the dog.

wank hat *n.* The *titfer*-like remains on a chap's *helmet* after he has left his *nob turban* on for too long.

wank holiday *1. n.* An exhausting day off work spent doing *cockupational therapy. 2. n.* Contrari-wise, a period of self-imposed abstention, brought on through guilt and/or severe cramp.

wankier mâché *n.* The malleable sculputural compound produced when an onanist's *love glue* mixes with his cleaning-up material. *Bedroom popadoms* – also known as *wankerchiefs, porn crackers* or *wanker's crisps* – as well as *monks'*

trunks, crunchies and *midget's surfboards,* are made of *wankier mâché.*

wanking, agile *n.* Of a man, splitting his usual *self discipline* routine into smaller bite-sized sprints in order to achieve his goal in a quicker and more efficient manner.

wanking and banking *n.* What most males use the internet for.

wanking back to happiness *phr.* From Helen Shapiro's chart-topping hit of 1961. Indulging in copious *self-abuse* after your *significant other* has decided to *put the toys back in the cupboard.*

wanking chariot *n.* A single bed.

wanking ears *n.* Descriptive of the bat-like, heightened sensitivity of hearing achieved by a fellow indulging in a bit of *self discipline,* allowing him to detect the faint sound of a key entering the lock two floors below. *'September 2nd, 1666, Morning. Up betimes, and finding the house deserted, was minded to settle down with a hose for a brief strum over the corsetry pages of Mr Grattan's estimable catalogue. However, Mrs Pepys return'd unexpectly, and, had it not been for my wanking ears, would surely have discovered me in a most compromising situation. Afternoon. London burned down.'* (from *The Diary of Samuel Pepys).*

wanking glove *n.* A sexual partner to whom one feels no emotional attachment. *'Well, Martin, there were three of us in that marriage, so it was a bit crowded. To Charles I was no more than a wanking glove.'*

wanking gown *n.* A dressing robe made of absorbent towelling material, of the style favoured by bachelors at weekends, and those who are actively seeking work seven days every week. *'Aw, do I have to come down the morgue, Sergeant? I'm in my wanking gown.'*

wanking jacket *n.* Dressing gown.

wanking on thin ice *n.* The very risky practice of gingerly pulling the covers down past a sleeping wife or girlfriend's *tits* for a spot of late night visual stimulation, despite her having gone to bed in a distinctly frosty demeanour.

wanking parlour *n.* A brothel, house of ill repute; any club popular with *gonks.* A *toss parlour, rub-a-tug* shop.

wanking sabbatical *n.* A three-month tour of duty on a nuclear submarine.

wanking spanners *n. Spunky wrenches, cunt scratchers, dick skinners.*

wanking studs *n. medic.* Warts on the hands or fingers.

wanking to the same jazz mag *phr.* Middle management jargon – a somewhat coarser variant of "singing from the same hymn sheet".

wanking with sand, like *sim.* A reference to an act of penetrative afection performed up a particularly dry and barren *foofoo*. *'Christ, my roundhead is sore. Your clunge was so dry it was like wanking with sand.'*

wanking wrench *n.* A gentleman's forearm. *'Posh, I'm thinking of having your name tattooed in Sanskrit along my wanking wrench, only spelled wrong.'*

wank in progress *n.* A protracted *hand shandy* that somehow drifts into *water treading* territory and has to be put on hold in order to eat/wash/sleep/go to work *etc.*

wank into her pant drawer, I'd *exclam.* A charming tribute to an alluring public figure.

wankish *adj.* Slightly useless. *Mouse, Swiss. 'That Eamonn Holmes is a bit wankish, isn't he.'*

wank it dry *v.* To obsessively persevere with something long after it is clear that there is no more benefit to be gained.

wank it thin *v.* To overdo it.

wank jockey *n.* A chap who takes control of the arm which is providing him with *manual relief, eg.* While its owner is doing it all wrong or fast asleep.

wanklash *n.* A painful spinal injury sustained while *pulling off* without due care and attention. A *slipped dick.*

wankle *1. n.* A wrongly spelled type of rotary engine. *2. n. medic.* The wrist. From wank + ankle.

wank-life balance *n.* The logistical organisation of a *self-employed* bloke's day to allow him plenty of time to *bash the bishop.*

wank lyrical *v.* To praise someone or something so enthusiastically that an observer may gain the impression that the speaker is about to *knock one off* over them or it.

wank-me-downs *n. Bongo mags* inherited from an elder brother or friend. Also *one-hand-me-downs. Pubic hairlooms.*

wank nappy *n.* A small piece of tissue placed on the end of the *giggle stick* after a *solo session* in order to prevent tell-tale *slug trails* on the inside of the *dunghampers. 'I have to use a wank nappy, only the missus has got eyes like a shithouse rat.'*

wankohol *n.* Overpriced *bullshit* drinks like dark fruit cider, chocolate beer, martini spritzer, and most modern gins. *'Pint for me and a small wankohol for the missus, please.'*

wank or bank *n.* The quandary faced by a fellow who must decide whether to *knock himself about a bit* or conserve his fluids until his ladyfriend's next visit when he can *make a deposit.*

wank out a bollock *v.* To masturbate furiously until a *spud* is loosened.

wank outsider *n.* A chap who prefers the hedgerow to the bedroom as a location for a *five knuckle shuffle.* An *al fresco onanist. 'My husband's always been a wank outsider, vicar. He spends most days pulling himself off in a bush in Heaton Park.'*

wank pie *n.* Something third rate. *'Have you heard that Ed Sheeran record Galway Girl? It's a right load of wank pie.'*

wank pipe *n.* A vape device or e-cigarette which produces with each puff a cloud of steam reminiscent of the Sir Nigel Gresley pulling thirty fully laden coaches up the Lickey Incline. Also *nosh pipe. 'Oi, I told you sunshine. If you want to vape, do it outside. No wank pipes in the bar.'*

wank potholes *n.* Tell-tale knee-sized indentations on the bed suggesting that a bloke "working from home" may not be totally focused on his work.

wankquiliser *n.* One of them *sleeping pulls* that a gentleman essays not because he is bursting with sexual energy but because he can't nod off, and at least it might give him a brief respite from worrying about his *shitty* job if he manages to slip into a post-orgasmic forty winks. A *knockout yop.*

wank robber *n.* Onanistically speaking, a parent who, when returning home unexpectedly early, robs their teenage son of his *money shot.*

wankroll, put her on the *exclam.* Phrase used by a businessman when deciding to employ a pulchritudinous young female, despite the fact that her CV may not be quite as impressive as those of certain other candidates. *'Let's cut the bollocks, darling. You're a lightweight, you're a quitter, you're a schmoozer and you're a bullshitter. And let me tell you this, I don't like lightweights, I don't like quitters and I don't like bullshitters. But when I saw you bending over to open the filing cabinet I thought your Lordship, do yourself a favour. Put her on the wankroll. Michelle, you're hired.'*

wankrupt *adj.* Descriptive of one who has *spent his wad* and has an empty *pod purse.*

wank seance *n.* While *pulling one's pud,* the eerie feeling that one is being watched disapprovingly by dead relatives from beyond the grave. Also *Doris Strokes.*

wank side/bottom *n.* After a bedtime re-buff from one's somnolent *significant other,* the no doubt politically incorrect act of *bashing one out* over her lower back after she turns over and goes to sleep.

wank slacks *n.* Type of dirty tracksuit trousers, designed to afford the wearer easy and unencumbered manual access to his *fruit bowl* at short notice. Worn by students, jobseekers and other people who find themselves spending a lot of time lounging round the house. *'Have you seen my smart trousers, Jane? I've got an interview this afternoon.' 'They're in the wash, Jonathan. Why don't you just put your wank slacks on? Your legs will be behind your desk, and everybody will be looking at Madonna anyway.'*

wanksmith *n.* An enthusiastic or workmanlike *onanist.*

wank sock *n.* Cylindrical cloth item tied to a bedpost, designed to indicate when wind conditions are suitable for *monkey spanking.*

wank sprain *n. medic.* Any male wrist injury. *'World number one Novak Djokovic has been forced to pull out of the Davis Cup after suffering a severe wank sprain during the final of the Australian Open.'*

wank stain *n. Bum scrape, piss flap, dip shit, toss pot.* General purpose insult. *'Oi, I said a Crunchie McFlurry, you fucking wank stain.'*

wank stamp *n.* A saucy thumbnail image saved to a smartphone device as an aid to *self help.*

wankster's paradise *euph.* A situation or period in a man's life, for the duration of which all barriers to repeated acts of *self-pollution* are removed, *eg.* Solitary confinement, attending university, being trapped in a lift for a Bank Holiday weekend, accidentally getting locked overnight in a porn warehouse or a career in journalism. *'Ever since my wife was hospitalised / 'bin livin' in wankster's paradise.'*

wankstop *n. medic.* The flange that prevents the *wanking spanner* disengaging from the end of the *shaft* when revving your *single cylinder engine.* The brim of the *herman gelmet.* The *sulcus.*

wanksworth *n.* A volumetric measure equal to the average quantity of male ejaculate. *'How much hand sanitiser, love?' 'Just give us a wanksworth, pet.'*

wanksy *n.* Street art graffiti of the *cock & balls* variety. Sometimes enhanced with *jizz* spurts coming out the top. Also *pud, three-line pud etc.*

wank tank *n.* The portaloo on a building site. *'Where's the gaffer?' 'He's in the wank tank.'*

wank tanks *n. Balls, nads, knackers.*

wank Tardis *n.* A blue portable lavatory of the sort frequented by builders during their teabreaks.

wank throne *n.* A large and flashy office chair, purchased at the start of lockdown to ensure a comfortable and productive environment when *working from home.*

wankticipation *n.* Feeling of hollow, mounting excitement experienced by a man sitting in front of his computer with his trousers round his ankles and his *pink mouse* in his hand, while he waits for

his *cyber scud* to download.

wanktimonious *adj.* Descriptive of a person who denounces the practice of *self delight.*

wanktique *n.* An ancient *rhythm pamphlet,* such as a dog-eared 1978 *Whitehouse* found behind some tins of paint in your late grandfather's garage.

wankton *n.* A unicellular life-form that inhabits the shallow waters of the bath after a session of *dolphin waxing. Dutch jellyfish, nylon squid, frigspawn.*

wanktuary *n.* Pater's study where he is wont to disappear in the evenings to "check on some work emails".

wankupuncture *n.* Ancient, tried-and-tested alternative therapy self-administered by ailing gentlemen. The belief that the symptoms of an illness can be ameliorated, if not cured completely, by a quick *hand shandy.* The *placebone effect.*

wank wall *n.* The masturbatory equivalent of the marathon runner's "wall", whereby an over-achieving *self harmer* loses consciousness after biting off more than he can chew, if you will. *'Somehow, he must still have been in the porn warehouse when they locked up for the night. They reckon he must have hit his wank wall at about 3am. Anyway, ashes to ashes, dust to dust.'*

wank window *n.* An opportune moment during which a crafty gentleman can enjoy a swift bout of *relaxation. 'A woman tells her husband she is just popping to the shops to get a pint of milk and a loaf of bread. The shops are 4 miles away and her husand knows that his wife's car travels at an average speed of 22 mph. He also knows that his wife will spend ten minutes selecting each of the items from the shelves of the supermarket and a further twelfth of her total journey time queuing at the till. For how long is the man's wank window open?'* (Associated Examining Board GCE Applied Mathematics paper, Summer 1986). *2. n.* On modern internet browsers, the "Incognito" or "Private" browser tab that can be opened when *buying a present for the wife.*

wank xerox *1. n.* One who *knocks one out* repeatedly throughout the day, only to find the quality diminishes as his *toner* runs out. *2. n. Rubbing one out* over and over again to the same *jazz mag. Groundhog wanking.*

wanky *adj.* Self-indulgent, pretentious, *eg.* Them *bollocks* "tick followed tock" Guinness adverts that *cunts* used to pretend to like.

wankydextrous *n.* Blessed with the gift of being able to manually pleasure a gentleman using either hand with equal facility. *'Have you met my granny, your holiness? She's wankydextrous* *you know.'*

wanky panky *n.* Mutual masturbation. *'For crying out loud, Philip. If you suppose I'm going to get up to anything remotely athletic after that eight course state reception, you've got another think coming. A spot of wanky panky is the most you're getting tonight, matey.'*

wannocks *1. n.* The area of no-man's land between the *nuts* or the *fadge*, and the *ringpiece*. The *biffin bridge, notcher, barse, taint, tintis, twitter, scranus*. *2. n.* Range of hills on the Shropshire/Rutland border.

wanquet *n.* A magnificent spread in a *jazz mag.*

wanquility *n.* The all-too-brief post-*toss* period of serenity experienced immediately before the loathing, self-hatred, *wangst* and shame set in.

wanquilizer *n.* Frantically *thrapping one out* with the aim of gently sending oneself off to the land of nod.

want to hear my Joe Biden impersonation? *exclam. interrog.* Question asked before *letting off* with a gust of heroic, weapons-grade wet flatulence. The post-COP26 *pull my finger.*

want to join my bubble? *1. exclam. interrog.* An invitation for others to join your social circle. *2. exclam. interrog.* A witty remark following an audibly wet *gut drop.*

WAN/wan *acronym. medic.* Debilitating masculine affliction caused by an excess of testosterone as spring takes hold. Wanking All Night.

wanxious *1. adj.* Worried, nervous, or uneasy about getting caught *relaxing in a gentleman's way*. *'I was having one off the wrist in my hotel room, when suddenly I became wanxious about the possibility of hidden cameras in the ceiling.'* *2. adj.* Excited at the prospect of a forthcoming *five-knuckle shuffle* session that is as yet some hours in the future.

wap *n.* Afternoon shut-eye combined with a little light *relaxation*. From wank + nap. *'Look after the kids for a couple of hours, will you love? I'm off for a wap in the shed.'*

wap the baps *v.* To *get the tits oot* for the lads, the lasses or any other interested parties nearby.

wap-waps *n. medic.* A lady's mammary glands. *'Now, Mrs Johnson, if you'll just get your wap-waps out, I'll start the examination.'*

war and faece *n.* A substantial piece of *shiterature* taken into the *smallest room* to peruse during a lengthy *sit down adventure.*

war horse *n.* A "rearing steed" stance adopted while trying to pass an enormous *copper bolt* following two weeks of constipation. An ordeal that could possibly be ameliorated by imagining Benedict Cumberbatch shouting "Be brave!

Be brave!"

warm as The Broons's bog seat *sim.* Said of something that never gets the chance to grow cold. Also *warm as the Osmonds's bog seat, warm as the Waltons's bog seat.*

warmhole *n.* A *hairy split* in the space-time continuum.

warm Norman *n.* A *hotplate, Cleveland steamer.*

warm toilet seat, like sitting on a *sim.* Descriptive of the uncomfortable, dawning realisation that one may not necessarily be the exclusive beneficiary of one's current partner's affections.

warm up the choirboys' breakfast *n.* Of a vicar, to *relax in a gentleman's way.*

warning George and Gracie *n.* To emit a long, drawn-out *basso profundo Bakewell tart* that resembles plangent whalesong and hence could have been used to warn the two humpback cetaceans, George and Gracie, about the whaling vessel they were about to encounter in the film *Star Trek IV.*

warning shot across the bowels *n.* A *botty burp* signalling that your *arse* means business and a *brown torpedo* is about to be launched.

war of the noses *n.* An uneasy, stenchsome armistice between two occupants of adjacent public lavatory cubicles, each one sitting over their festering *copper bolts* in silence and waiting for the other to make the first move, clean up, flush and depart. A *Mexican shit-off.*

war paint *n.* Of *glamourpotamii* getting ready to go out at night, their make-up. *Fuck dust.*

warren *n. prop.* Generic term for one not blessed with conventionally attractive features. From "Warren ugly bastard".

Warrington spa *n.* A quick blast of deodorant, a stick of chewing gum and a *wank*. The traditional preparations for a night out in the vibrant Mancunian suburb.

warthog whammies *n.* Fantastic *chudleighs* on an ugly woman. *Hefferlumps.*

wartime searchlights *n.* Descriptive of the amusingly discollimated vision of one who is in an advanced *state of refreshment*, whose eyes appear to be independently raking the heavens for incoming Heinkel bombers. *'Look out everyone, Ronnie's got his wartime searchlights on.'*

Warwick Passage fayre *n.* Ugly, rough or slatternly women. A reference to the alley next to the Old Bailey where the wives and girlfriends of the accused traditionally await access to the public galleries of the courtroom, saying "My fella never done nothing, bless," and other lies.

wasbian *n.* In the world of *grumbular* entertainment, a *carpet muncher* over the age of about thirty who should probably start thinking about earning a living in a manner that better befits her advanced years, *eg.* Dinner lady. Also *hasbian, lesbeen.*

wash and go *n.* A sublime *sit down toilet adventure* that is a miraculous combination of a *ghost shit* and a *7 am angel, ie.* One that requires no flushing and no wiping, so you just "wash (your hands) and go". In fact, you might as well not bother washing your hands either, in the circumstances.

washing machine doors *n.* Swirling, export strength *beer goggles.*

Washington refill *n.* The type of night-time urination carried out in a rush in order to return to the warmth of one's bed as soon as possible. From the speedy nature of petrol station customers in Washington DC and surrounding districts during their 2002 Beltway sniper shenanigans.

wash the cosh *v.* To polish the *love truncheon, oil the bat.*

wasping *n.* Cruising well-known *dogging* hotspots around one's locale with a ready-made excuse to hand in case of unwelcome constabulary interest, *viz.* "But I'd just stopped to let a wasp out of the car, officer, honest."

wasp on an over-ripe plum, going at it like a *sim.* A measure of the extreme avidity with which a *randy* young chap performs *cumulonimbus* on his *significant other.*

waste *n.* An attractive feature on an otherwise unattractive individual. *'Jesus. Have you seen the chebs on that Kerry Katona, your grace?' 'I know, archbishop. What a fucking waste.'*

waste buds *n.* Sensitive spice receptors located in and around the *rusty sheriff's badge. 'Ooh, that prawn and Scotch bonnet vindaloo I had last night is really tickling my waste buds this morning, Rabbi.'*

waste of a good cock *adj.* A *hard-on* of impressive proportions which is tragically allowed to wither away to nought because the missus wants to go shopping, or to catch the *Big Brother Live Eviction. 'You'll be sorry. That's a waste of a good cock, is that. How far apart are the contractions anyway?'*

waste the morning *v.* To *relax in a gentleman's way. 'I wasted the lot of the morning and then felt guilty all afternoon.'* (from *Tony Benn's Diaries,* Sunday March 18th 2007).

watcha gonna do brother? *exclam.* Bellowed in the style of mulleted wrestler-turned-racist Hulk Hogan before performing a *back body drop* (which is an actual wrestling move, and if you don't believe us you can look it up on the internet).

watching something other than the news *euph.* Common euphemism used by high-ranking US politicians to describe watching internet *grummer.* Coined by Frank Underwood from *House of Cards, viz. 'Meecham just caught me watching something other than the news.'*

watchmaker's spanner, hung like a *sim.* Descriptive of a fellow who has not been blessed by nature.

water babies *1. n.* Aquatic fairies featured in the Victorian novel by Charles Kingsley. *2. n.* Floating clumps of semi-congealed *merry monk* in the bath, toilet, *Times* restaurant critic's drinking glass *etc. Frigspawn.*

water birth *n.* For those with a close affinity to nature, the act of pushing out a *dump* while partially or fully immersed in water, *eg.* In the sea, at the local swimming baths or – for the real enthusiast – while sitting in the bath at home. Preferably done with a few josticks and tealights burning nearby and a whale-song CD on the stereo.

waterboarding *1. n.* A brief drowning sensation experienced while *orally pleasuring* a *bird* who happens to be a profuse *Norris. 2. n.* Perverse *watersports* variation in which the young lady sits upon her partner's face and then proceeds to *piss* her *scads.*

waterboarding Donald Duck, like *sim.* Descriptive of the noise of a violently unpleasant *digestive transit.* A panicked, gurgling, storm of noise that sounds like the CIA are questioning the angry cartoon fowl on suspicion of terrorism using an enhanced coercive interrogation technique.

Waterboys *phr.* Large pasty *arses* that leave nothing to the imagination. Because, in the words of the eponymous group's 1985 single, you get to see "the whole of the Moon".

watering can wazz *n.* The uncontrollable multi-directional *gypsy's kiss* taken after a bout of *horizontal jogging* or a *five knuckle shuffle.*

watermark *1. n.* A subtle identifying image or overlay on a banknote or certificate. *2. n.* A *piss* stain on a mattress (or, for that matter, on John Bonham's first class plane seat).

water music, play Handel's *v.* To swish one's *tallywhacker* around while doing a *number one,* in order to create melodious sounds from the water, porcelain, toilet seat, adjacent carpet and pile of old copies of *Viz* which you are about to put on eBay. Best performed while *heavily refreshed* at 2.30 am.

water puppies *n.* Term used by swimming pool lifeguards to draw each other's attention to a large pair of *milky swingers* bobbing playfully up and down while their owner does the backstroke.

watershit brown *n. medic.* Feculence of a type referenced at the thinner end of the Bristol stool chart. *Bum gravy, rusty water.*

watersports *n. Recreational Chinese singing. Golden showers, dripteases* and the like.

water taxi *n.* A particularly buoyant *turd.*

Watford *n. medic.* The correct gynaecological term for a lady's *gap.*

wath *1. n.* A small town in the Dearne valley, just outside Rotherham. 2. n. A bout of *self delight* essayed while ostensibly enjoying a long, hot soak. From wank + bath.

Watkins *n. rhyming slang.* The *cigar cutter.* From the haulage company whose trucks are often to be seen along the A30 between the Clock House Roundabout and Hatton Cross; Watkins & Sole. *'Sit still will you, prime minister.' 'Sorry Nick, I've got an itchy Watkins.'*

Watney houston *n.* A *discount diva* who, after downing a few pints, will tunelessly belt out pompous tear-jerking anthems over the jukebox. A bit like Whitney Houston used to do, if you believe what you read in the papers.

wattle and daub *1. n.* A medieval building material consisting of a woven wooden lattice clagged up with straw and cow *shite.* 2. n. A situation that arises when the residue from a session of the *squirts* binds with one's *arse cress* and dries to form a sturdy and resilient parget. *3. n.* Appearance of some older ladies, characterised by dangling neck flesh overlaid with thick makeup.

waving a sausage in the Albert Hall *n.* Sticking one's *cock* in a *fanny* that can seat five thousand people and the London Symphony Orchestra. Also *waving a stick in a field, wall of death, dipping a worm in a bucket, last hotdog in the tin, throwing a woodbine up Northumberland Street, punching smoke, fucking the night.*

waving hello to Judith *euph.* Engaging in a spot of *firkyfoodling* with a woman who looks like she's *sitting on Phil Lynott's shoulders.* Named in honour of the hirsutely be-*fannied Life of Brian* character.

waving the evacuees off at the station *euph.* Topical wartime expression for *dropping the kids off a the pool.*

WAW/waw *abbrev.* Worth A Wank.

wax one's slats *v.* Of a woman, to *play the invisible banjo* until her *blip tap* begins to drip.

wax the bonnet *v.* To *spoff* over a *bird's* dry bodywork, then lean over and polish it with a clean, soft, lint-free cloth until the desired shine is achieved.

wax the dolphin *v.* To *polish the lighthouse.*

wazoo *n. Jacksie, anus, gazoo.*

wazz *v.* Variously to *piss,* to *puke,* to *wank.* *'Who's wazzed on the bathroom floor?' Erm…'It might be me, mum. In what sense are you using the word wazz?'*

wazzed *adj.* Pissed on, *puked* on and *wanked* off. And *pissed up,* come to think of it. *'Ollie, you're completely wazzed.'*

wazzock *n.* Mild northern insult for a great, useless, spawny-eyed, parrot-faced person.

wazz spangles *n.* Perfumed cubic confection found in urinals. Also *bog dice, urineapple chunks.*

WC Handy *1. n. prop.* Alabama-born African American jazz composer, who wrote *Saint Louis Blues.* 2. n. A *Fulham handshake.*

WD naughty *n.* Lubricant for mature adults.

WD over 40 *n.* KY jelly. Also *I can't believe it's not batter, phoney batter, trout jelly, Grandma's little helper.*

weakender *1. n.* One who frequently calls in sick on a Monday and/or a Friday. *2. n.* Any punch-line-free sketch – that is to say any sketch at all – on Radio 4's erstwhile topical comedy show *Weekending.*

wealth distribution *n.* Of a *grumble benefactor,* to apportion shares of his *money shot* equally onto the faces of multiple needy *beneficiaries.*

weapon *1. n.* See *mutton musket, spam cannon, bacon bazooka* etc. *2. n. pej.* An idiotic person. *'You absolute weapon, prime minister. Look what you've done.'*

weaponise *v.* To stimulate a *pork sword* into an erectivated state, ready to *go over the top* at a given signal.

weapon of ass destruction *1. euph.* A rather large, thick-cut *trouser torpedo,* capable of delivering significant harm to those who find themselves in its blast zone.

wear a Twyfords collar *v.* To *drive the porcelain bus,* to *shout soup,* to *yoff,* call Ralph on the great white telephone.

wears gloves at the garage *euph.* Said of a chap with nice nails who *takes his own bags to the supermarket* or *gives his car a name.*

wears his arse on his sleeve, he *exclam.* Said of one who, through a poor wiping technique, might be well advised to throw his shirt in the bin.

Wearside vines *n.* Exposed outcrop of *Valentines* which looks for all the world like an attractive bunch of Gamay grapes glistening on a sun-kissed slope.

wear the beard *1. v.* To perform *cunning linguistics*

on a woman. *To impersonate Stalin.* 2. *v.* Of *bean flickologists*, to be the *stone*, as opposed to the *sponge*. *'You can tell which one of them two wears the beard.'*

weather bomb *1. n.* A meteorological catastrophe that is the worst meteorological catastrophe since records began. 2. *n.* A change in wind direction while urinating outdoors that results in *piss*-drenched trousers.

weathered on *1. adj.* Of North Sea offshore workers, to be unexpectedly stranded on an oil rig due to poor meteorological conditions and have nothing to do but sit about and *wank*, and thus 2. *adj.* Descriptive of the dejected mien of a man whose missus has *fallen to the communists.*

weather-house shorts *n.* Dysfunctional breeches or swimming trunks of such a parsimonious cut that one *bollock* or the other is always hanging out, depending upon the weather. *'Come and look at this, nan. Ray Mears is wearing his weather-house shorts again and his right knacker's gone walkabout.'*

weatherman's jacket, tight as a *sim.* See also *as tight as a ~worm's belt; ~bullfighter's pants; ~shark's arse; ~mouse's waistcoat; ~teenage wanker's curtains.*

we 'avin' 'em or no? *exclam. Corn. dial.* Poetic prelude to the West Country act of love.

webbed tits *n.* *Frankentits* of elderly Hollywood actresses with a highly stressed membrane between, caused by the sheer weight of *blimplants*.

webcamouflage *n.* The use of cheaply available photo editing software to "clean up" low resolution internet-sourced images of rough women, thus making them suitable fodder for *relaxation.* Using the technique, superficial blemishes such as spots, scars, wrinkles, varicose veins, stretch-marks, bruises, boils, herpes and prison tattoos *etc.* become difficult, if not impossible, to detect. Especially if the perpetrator's eyesight isn't very good. And it won't be, all things considered.

wedding car shit *n.* Of a canine laying a length of *cable*, who is afflicted by an incomplete drop. When the movement has left the *nipsy* but continues to be attached by a length of grass, string or whatever the *fuck* it has been eating, so it ends up dragging its *turds* round behind it like the tin cans and boots behind a post-prandial automobile.

wedding milk *n.* Spingle, spangle, spint, spongle, spadge, spedge, spidge, spodge, spudge, *etc.* *Spunk.*

wedding ring polish *n.* Alternative name for male seminal fluid.

wedding sausage *1. n.* A small, limp piece of charcuterie served at a wedding breakfast. 2. *n.* A

small, limp penis served at a wedding night.

wedding tackle *n.* The male genitalia. Also *wedding furniture, wedding vegetables, family jewels.*

wedge *v.* To pull another's *bills* up the crack of their *arse.*

wedgehog *n.* A *fuller-figured* lady who affects tight-fitting leggings, thus showing off her generously proportioned *camel's toe* to great advantage.

wedgie *n.* Nickname of late politician Anthony Wedgwood Benn, who's *bills* were always getting pulled right up the crack of his *arse.*

wedgie, atomic *n.* The act of pulling someone's *bills* up the *crack* of their *arse* with a dockyard crane, while their shoes are bolted to the floor.

wedgiemite *n. Aus.* Organic ooze *down under* that collects in the *fairy hammock* on hot days. *Arse feta.*

wed zeppelin *n.* A former *looker* who, once she has got married, lets herself go and fills up with hydrogen. And then explodes in a ball of flame at Lakehurst Naval Air Station, New Jersey, killing 36 of the people on board.

weebles *n.* Large, pert non-fake *tits* that defy gravity, named after the popular 70s toy slogan, *viz.* "Weebles wobble, but they don't fall down."

wee heid rules the big heid *phr. Scots.* Descriptive of the moment when a fellow, usually wearing *beer goggles*, decides that sexual intercourse with the woman he has just met and whose name he does not know is the correct course of action to take.

wee-hole surgery *n.* Do-it-yourself medical experiments carried out by bored bachelors, involving the insertion of foreign objects into the urethra. *'Is there a man doctor I can see please, nurse? Only it's a bit delicate. I was doing a bit of wee-hole surgery and I've got a propelling pencil lead stuck in my hog's eye.' 'I'll just see if there's anyone available, Mr Brown. It is Mr Brown, isn't it? The former publisher?'*

weekend flat in Brighton, to have a *v.* Of a gentleman, to be a *good listener* on a part-time basis. Likewise of a woman, to be an occasional *consumer of tufted wilton.* To be *half-rice half-chips.*

weekend in Wales, wetter than a *sim.* Claggy in a romantic way. See also *wetter than a Tewkesbury doorstep, ~an otter's neck, ~a turfer's knee, ~a fat bird's armpit, ~Whitney Houston's last joint, ~Lee Evans's suit.*

weenie *n. US.* Penis. Also *wienie, wiener.*

weenie waggler *n.* A *wand waver, flasher* or *sexhibitionist.* *'Apparently he was well known as a bit of a weenie waggler back when he was on Channel 4.'*

weenis *n.* A minuscule *veiny bang stick*, such as those sported by jockeys, Channel swimmers, Arctic explorers and former Lord High Chancellor and Secretary of State for Justices.

weeze *v.* To experience a genital *organism* without producing any bodily fluid. To fire the *air pistol.*

weft *n.* Lady's *pubes,* which are all lying in one direction after she has been wearing particularly tight briefs, like a snooker table. *Twat nap.*

weggy *adj.* Of a flatulent emission, to be wet and eggy. From wet + eggy. *'Open the window, Buzz. That fucker was distinctly weggy.'*

weigh anchor *v.* To drop an immensely large *gick,* being careful not to break the porcelain.

weighing up the poos and cons *v.* The process by which a public lavatory visitor must compare the lamentable states of the various adjoining *shit-pots* available before deciding which one to patronise with his *arse's* custom.

weigh some scrap in *v.* To *drop a load off, go for a shit. 'Brian, keep an eye on my pint while I nip to to the gents and weigh some scrap in.'*

weightlifter's fart, breath like a *sim.* Halitosis. See also *necking turds, dung lung, shit smuggler's rucksack.*

weight off my hind, that's a *exclam.* A reference to the outcome of a successful diet or large *number two.*

weight off my mind, that's a *phr.* Said in the immediate aftermath of a *Richard the Third* of such diabolical, *nipsy*-bruising magnitude that it leaves one on generally very good terms with the world.

wein and stein *phr.* Abrupt form of courtship where, instead of taking a girl out for dinner and being charming, a man simply answers the door wearing only a towel and demands a *wank* with menaces.

weinstein *n.* One who becomes a fucking genius after downing a few drinks.

we just lost the moon *exclam.* Phrase used by Tom Hanks in the film *Apollo 13,* which can also be used to great effect in everyday life when something goes drastically wrong and you are unable to reach your objective but have to go through the motions nevertheless. For example, when a fellow is having to *bang* his *pissed* wife at her instigation and he knows that there's no way on God's earth that his *taddies* are going for a swim tonight.

welcomed with open flaps *exclam.* Following a period of separation, to be warmly greeted by a female companion who is in the throes of libidinousness.

welcome to Monkton Manor m'lady *exclam.* Useful phrase which can be usefully employed by a gentleman at the moment of ejaculation in order to maintain a composed and dignified facial expression.

welder's bench, face like a *sim.* An ugly woman. Also *blind cobbler's thumb, burglar's dog, box of frogs, sack of chisels, bag of spanners, bulldog licking piss off a nettle.*

welder's nod, quick as a *sim.* Said of a lass that "goes down" very quickly and willingly.

welder's shoelaces, fanny like a *sim.* Evocative phrase which is descriptive of the state of a particularly unkempt *ladygarden.* From the visual similarity to the said artisan's footwear fastening appurtenances, which have typically been frazzled and re-tied many times. *'Sorry pet, but I'm going to call it a day. You've got a fanny like a welder's shoelaces. It's like bobbing for sardines in a bucket of pipecleaners down here.'*

welder's wife *n.* A spouse whose aesthetic attributes are best appreciated while afflicted with a severe case of photokeratitis.

well appointed *adj.* Surveyor's appraisal of a *frontage,* especially with regard to good structural integrity, a generous balcony area, and prominent *nips.*

well done peloton, you smashed it! *exclam.* Jocular, self-congratulatory phrase enunciated following a really big *shit.*

well fair state *n.* The state of drunkenness only achievable for many on Giro day.

well hello! *exclam.* A simple greeting expertly turned into a double entendre so overt it might as well be wearing boxing gloves, as perfected by the actor Leslie Phillips. In the TV series *The Bidding Room,* the phrase seems to always be just on the lips of Nigel Havers when he is engaging with attractive ladies of a mature vintage.

well, here's one good thing that's come from Brexit *exclam.* Provocative pre-*guff* announcement that somewhat overstates the prospective benefits that subsequently ensue.

well man clinic *n.* The *smallest room, water closet* or *shite house.* From the fact that it is the only health check a real man ever needs. A *squaddie's medical.*

well-nourished *euph.* Descriptive of one who eschews salad.

well-presented *adj.* Of a large-breasted lady, wearing a low-cut top and, for example, riding a bike with low handlebars, so that she is leaning forwards as she pedals, thus giving a delightful prospect to any driver or pedestrian aproaching from the opposite direction.

well struck sir! *exclam.* An amusing remark which can be used immediately after someone has hit *a corker* for six with their *arse.* Also *what's* *that, Sweep?*

well that's my opinion! *exclam.* Announcement after expressing a forceful *point of view.* Also *more tea vicar?; fer-fetch a cloth, Granville etc.*

well, that's your breakfast sorted *exclam.* Said at the end of a highly romantic sexual encounter, after a gentleman provides his *inamorata* with a highly nourishing *protein shake* in bed. *'Well, that's your breakfast sorted, love. How about nipping down the kitchen to knock me up some bacon and eggs?'*

well thumbed *adj.* Much consulted or handled, *eg.* The state of Will Self's copy of *Roget's Thesaurus* and (reference to Ulrika Jonsson removed on legal advice).

welly full of custard *euph.* An over-full *cream pie.* *'She says she'll do the whole orchestra, string section first, then the woodwinds and finally the brass and percussion, which is fine as long as I can go first. After all, I'm the conductor and I don't want to stick my foot in a welly full of custard.'*

welly top *sim.* A term used to describe the larger *billy goat's mouth.* A *yawning donkey.* *'That (reference to Ulrika Jonsson removed on legal advice) must have a fluffit like a welly top.'*

welly tubbies *n.* Small, fat lasses squeezed into knee-high boots and out *on the lash.* So-called due to their similarity to the children's TV characters, in both their brightly coloured appearance and limited vocabulary.

Welsh *n. Self improvement* while listening to a male voice choir.

Welsh Champagne *n.* Vandal strength cider.

Welsh letter *n.* Same as a *French letter,* but "with a leak".

Welsh lighthouse *n.* The bright light that is beamed from the police helicopter over every town in the valleys on a Saturday night, searching for *doggers.*

Welshman's cock *sim.* Descriptive of someone who is short and thick, *eg.* Dennis Wise.

Welsh mist *n.* A particularly dense and clammy *fart* which hovers around ankle level and chills the bones.

Welsh salad, go for a *v.* To urinate, go for a *leak.* From the Welsh national vegetable, the pea.

Welsh shot *n.* The knocking back of the contents of a *smeg cup.* A *Dutch oyster.*

Welsh square *n.* A piece of toilet paper or tissue, saturated with either fresh or dried *likely lads.* From the Welsh for "Welsh", *viz.* "Cymraeg", which may or may not be pronounced a bit like "cum rag".

welt *n.* A Scottish penis. *'Tell me my good man, is anything worn under the kilt?' 'Awnlie ma welt, yir*

lairdship. The puir thing's red raw frae fuckin' yir missus up her airse.' (Bamforth's *Anal Chuckles* postcard by Donald McGill, 1926).

we may end up in the Hudson *exclam.* When you have reached *V2* but cannot make it to the nearest toilet. From *Miracle on the Hudson* pilot Chesley "Sully" Sullenberger III, who famously ditched his passengers in the water.

wenchmarking *n.* The practice amongst gentlemen of comparing the carnal performance of their repective inamoratae.

Wendy *n.* An uncomfortable front tuck for a lady. A vaginal *wedgie,* a *vaggie, vedgie.*

Wendy's melt *1. n. US.* A sandwich served at the popular eponymous fast-food restaurant, consisting of two prime strips of beef, bacon strips, cheese and mayonnaise in between. *2. n.* A *ladyburger.*

Wenlock *n.* An episode of extreme but temporary flatulence, as described in his poem *On Wenlock Edge* by AE Housman: "The gale, it plies the saplings double, It blows so hard, 'twill soon be gone." Don't say we never give you no fucking culture.

Wensleymale *n. Organzola, himula, felladelphia, veinish blue.*

went *v.* To nearly nod off; whereby one's head rolls forward before immediately jerking back awake. *'Christ, I'm absolutely knackered. I was out on the piss till two and then I had to be up in time to get to the airport by six. I've been wenting since before we took off.' 'Would you like me to fetch you a cup of coffee, captain?'*

werecow *n.* A nice, pleasant woman who mysteriously transforms into a right *fucking cow* once a month.

we're gonna need a bigger boat *exclam.* From the famous scene in the fish-based film *Jaws.* A witty apophthegm following the release of an ominous-sounding double-bass-like *Bakewell tart.*

wereminge *n.* A frighteningly hairy, bloody *twat,* occasionally glimpsed during a *full moon.*

we're over Dresden *exclam.* Phrase used by someone who is about to open his *bomb-bay doors* in advance of a *heavy drop,* in the certain knowledge that expediency must over-ride any ethical considerations.

werewolf whistle *n.* A two-part, audible signal of manly appreciation for a woman who appears attractive from behind but who, before the second note has been completed, turns round to reveal herself to be a monster, thus causing the finale to tail off pathetically.

werntfor *n.* A noun describing the skin between a

woman's *fanny* and her *arse*, *viz*. The *gooch, carse, taint, tinter, happy valley, tissent, crunk* or *Luton-to-Dunstable busway*. So-called because "if it weren't for that, her guts would fall out".

west coast shit *n*. An *airburst*. Taken from the lyrics to the popular hit parade foot-tapper *Xxplosive, West Coast Shit* (feat. Hitman, Kurupt, Nate Dogg and Six-Two), during which Dr Dre (real name Andre Romelle Young PhD) also vouchsafes "my shit's the bomb".

west country trim *n*. Yokel alternative to a *Brazilian* or *Hollywood wax* which is situated somewhere between a *landing strip* and *Terry Waite's allotment* on the feminine intimate grooming spectrum. A rudimentary trim of the *spider's legs* sticking out the sides of the large pants using the wallpaper scissors, before trotting off to the local barn dance. See *Luton airport*.

western grip *n*. Manner of *knocking one out* in which the *smeg peg* is held as a rodeo rider holds onto his steer, *ie*. With the fingers of one hand on top, the thumb underneath and the other hand waving a hat behind his head.

West Indian 80s pace attack *n*. Another somewhat contrived cricketing analogy for toilet troubles to file alongside *Harmison loosener*, *viz*. An explosive early morning burst from the *Pavilion end*, consisting of several fierce *deliveries*, followed up almost immediately by a renewed and more dangerous onslaught. A *West Indian 80s pace attack* could end up with your nose bones lying shattered on the lavatory floor.

West Kent Hunt *rhym. slang*. A lady's *bodily treasure*. Famously mispronounced as "cunt" by presenter Nicky Campbell on two separate occasions during the same breakfast programme on Radio 5Live.

wet and forget *1. n*. A magical detergent that promises to make your patio like new again. *2. n*. A drunken one-night dalliance that is better dismissd from the mind.

wet as a bus window *sim*. Descriptive of the *pudenders* of a friendly *bird* who finds herself in a somewhat amorous frame of mind.

wet as an otter's pocket *sim*. Descriptive of the moistness of an object, *eg*. A face flannel, a raincoat, a *frothing West Kent Hunt*.

wet cress, eat *v*. During an act of man-on-lady, or indeed lady-on-lady, oral-type s*x, to munch on a bit of exceptionally moist *gash garnish*.

wet dog's beard, flange like a *sim*. When a man's *bag for life* decides she needs a *gypsy's kiss* just before *having it off*. Also *soggy pasty*. '*I was right in the mood last last night until June returned from the bog with a flange like a wet dog's beard, Great Aunt Lucy.*'

wet dream *n*. A night-time reverie which leads to *milmed jim-jams*. Can be avoided either by having a cold bath or a right good *pull* into a sock before retiring.

wet dress rehearsal *1. n*. The process of fully charging a rocket with fuel. '*Sorry, Mr Bezos. Elon can't come to the phone as he's in the middle of a wet dress rehearsal.*' *2. n*. *Sharting* one's *kecks*. '*Sorry, Mr Bezos. Elon can't come to the phone as he's in the middle of a wet dress rehearsal.*'

wet fart in a whisky bottle, like a *sim*. Malodorous. See also *(smells like) Gillian McKeith's Tupperware cupboard*.

Wetherspoon's burger, moist as a *sim*. *Dry as a moth sandwich, an old dog's nose, a pilgrim's pocket* or *a budgie's tongue*.

Wetherspoon's, like waiting to get served at *sim*. Fruitlessly waving something in your hand, in the vain hope of catching the wife's or girlfriend's (or somebody else'e wife's or girlfriend's) eye.

Wetherspoon's run *n*. A trip to one's nearest Wetherspoon's pub for the sole purpose of *laying a cable* in one of their spotlessly clean, luxury cubicles, thus avoiding the *shit/puke/spunk*-covered seats of the average drinking house *bogs*. '*Watch me pint lads, taxi's here. I'm just off on a Wetherspoon's run.*'

Wetherspoon's taxi *n*. An ambulance parked outside a popular town centre pub in the afternoon, ready to assist any unfortunate customer who makes it onto the pavement only to get ruthlessly picked off by the *beer sniper*.

Wetherspoon's wurzel *n*. A turnip-headed drinker who habitually lingers in branches of the eponymous public house chain, frightening off any *birds* who enter. A *pub scarecrow*.

wet Hurst *n*. A *Wolstenholme*. The final bit of *piss* which waits until the *cock* is safely back in the trousers before dribbling out causing a *wet penny in the pocket*. From the famous commentary describing Geoff Hurst's final goal in the 1966 World Cup final. "They think it's all over… it is now".

wet Jeffrey *n*. Dubious sexual practice whereby a lady slowly lowers her *pissy fanny* onto a waiting gentleman's chin.

wetmare *n*. A dream that is both wet and a nightmare. A *wet scream*.

wet market *n*. A specialist retail establishment stocked with exotic delights that offer a brief moment of pleasure, albeit with the ever-present possibility of picking up a nasty virus. A *knocking shop.*

wet one *1. n.* A pre-moistened cleaning tissue. *2. n.* An untrustworthy *fart*, possibly a *twin tone* that would require the use of *1.* A pre-moistened *Bakewell tart.*

wet pattern *n.* A noticable cycle of *randiness* as observed in members of the fairer s*x.

wet penny in your pocket *n.* A circular *piss*-stain on the trouser frontage, caused by insufficient shaking of the *prong.*

wet season *n.* That time of the month when the *crimson tide* comes in. *Blow job week.*

wet signature *1. n. Twattish* business term for a signature made with pen on paper, as opposed to a fax, email *etc. 2. n.* An especially stylish autograph that a fellow may sign on a ladyfriend, usually across her *norks*, thighs or back, symbolising either the commencement of a personal relationship or the conclusion of a quasi-legal business transaction. *3. n.* The detritus left in one's underpants following a particularly risky *flutter.*

wetsuit *1. n.* In sub-aquatic pursuits, a protective rubber garment worn while one plumbs the murky depths. *2. n.* In *sub-bridge* pursuits, a protective rubber garment worn while one sticks one's *cock* in some sort of fishy *chasm.*

wet tea bags *n.* Small, saggy *tits*, usually found on the older woman. Or, on the fifth series of *I'm a Celebrity,* on Willie Carson.

wet the baby's head *v.* To have intercourse up a woman who has a *bun in the oven.* To *tickle the baby.* '*And so it was that Mary and Joseph came to an inn in Bethlehem. And Mary was heavy with child and the innkeeper spake unto them saying, Behold, there is no room at the inn. And Joseph replied unto him saying, Yea, we have travelled from Nazareth, and my wife is heavy with child, and I have great need to wet the baby's head. And he gave unto the innkeeper a wink. And lo the wink was cheeky.*'

wetty *n.* The feminine version of a *stiffy.* A *wide on, slop on.*

wet wipe *n.* The act of dabbing the *dewdrops* from one's damp *bellend* onto on a sleeping loved one's *aris* when returning to the *fart sack* after a nocturnal *slash.*

wet wish *n.* A fellow's fond desire, imagined in such a way as to require a tissue. '*Since this lockdown began, I've been home all day long, mostly wet-wishing.*'

wet your whistle *1. v.* To pop into the pub for a drink in order to stop your hands shaking. *2. v.* When *dropping the kids off at the pool,* to suffer an unexpected splash of water up your *nipsy.*

we've got her, sir! *1. exclam.* A shout in a 1940s black and white film starring Jack Hawkins or John Gregson, when they'd been dropping depth charges on an unseen U-boat. *2. exclam.* A shout in the bath when bubbles and debris break the surface.

Weymouths *n. Spaniel's ears. Bristol Cities* that have drifted due south over the years.

WFH *1. abbrev.* Business shorthand for Working From Home. *2. abbrev.* Wanking Furiously Hard. A common consequence of *1.* in your dressing gown with lots of unsupervised downtime to fill. *3. abbrev.* Wanking For Hours.

whackaday *n.* An early morning *pink steel wallop on the scrotal anvil* with the old *slag hammer.*

whackademy award *n.* Any of the various accolades which are conferred upon the makers of *bongo flicks* in recognition of excellence in a particular field, *eg.* The Palms d'Or. *Toscars.*

whackmail *n.* Procedure whereby devious hackers somehow switch on an unsuspecting gentleman's webcam and then demand large sums of money under threat of exposing him *beating his meat* over donkey porn.

whacknicolour *n.* The luridly alluring, garishly hued inks with which *seed catalogues* are printed.

whack off *v.* To pleasure oneself manually, for example onto a *TV's ass.*

whack pack *n.* The essential equipment taken by a chap heading off on a solo self-catering break in a cheap hotel, *ie.* A holdall full of *noddy comics,* five rolls of Andrex Extra Soft and a crate of Red Bull. '*Right then, mam. I'll be off.*' '*Don't forget your whack pack, son.*'

whackpot *n.* A windfall of *grumble* that unexpectedly comes the way of a lucky gentleman. '*I tell you what, I really hit the whackpot when I got the job of clearing the effects of the late poet and lifelong jazz enthusiast Philip Larkin from his house.*'

whack shack *n.* The smallest room. '*Is your Jeffrey in, Mrs Archer?*' '*He's in his whack shack.*'

whacksmith *n.* A workmanlike masturbator who seems intent on beating his *pork sword* into a *ploughshare.*

whackult *n.* A yoghurty drink that is rich in *Vitamin S* and plays an important role in the relief of Irritable Bollock Syndrome.

whale hunt *n.* A 3am trawl round the bar/nightclub/ Greggs in search of a tasty piece of *blubber.*

whalesong *n.* A melodic, though slightly eerie, sequence of whines, squeaks, clicks and whistles that emanate from a toilet cubicle.

whaletail *1. n.* A laughable aerodynamic feature favoured by the smaller-penissed car driver. *2. n.* The unsightly effect produced when the *throng* of a lady in ill-fitting jeans rides up her *arse crack*. See *crack hanger.*

whammers n. *Bazoomas, Gert Stonkers, big tits.*

whanger n. An extremely large *wang.*

what do you think of that, Mean Gene? Ooo yeah! *exclam.* Something to say, in the style of deceased bonkers wrestler "Macho Man" Randy Savage after *letting one rip*. Also *you've got to let it breathe.*

what hath God wrought? *exclam.* Used when looking back into the *bum sink* and seeing something terrifying in the water.

what should that go down as on my time sheet? *exclam. rhet.* A humorous thing to say after coming back from the *works shitters* following a relaxed *number two.*

what's in Mr Tumble's spotty bag? *1. exclam. interrog.* Question asked by popular children's entertainer Justin Fletcher on his television show *Something Special*. No, us neither. *2. exclam. interrog.* What someone with a proper old dose of the *clap* jocularly states before *making the beast with two backs.*

what sort of cheese was that? *exclam.* Another in the seemingly never-ending litany of amusing remarks to be uttered after someone has *dropped their guts*. Also *more tea vicar?; what's that, Skippy? The miners are in trouble?; what's that, Sweep?* and many more.

what's that you say, Sooty? *exclam. rhet.* To be said after a particularly noisy drop of *wuffle dust.*

what's the story n. *rhym. slang. Manc.* A *morning glory,* from the lyrics to the Oasis song, *What's the Story in Balamory. 'Giz a quick fiddle will you, love? Only I've woken up with a raging what's the story.'*

whatsthrapp *euph.* Making use of the saucy profile pictures on a popular messenger app for inspiration when *relaxing in a gentleman's way.*

what time would she be in the window? *exclam. interrog.* Discussion of a woman's attractiveness by rhetorical reference to the timing of her shift if she were a *hingoot* in Amsterdam; the later the shift, the more complimentary the assessment. *'I haven't seen that new assistant in accounts yet, what time would she be in the window?' '2pm and that's being generous, chairman.'*

what year is it?! Who's the president?! *exclam.* A useful rejoinder following a particularly miasmic and eye-watering *trouser cough* that leaves your hair standing on end and smoking. Also *what year is this?*

wheek v. *Scots.* To remove *jobbies* from an aeroplane toilet.

wheelbarrow, the n. When sat on the *bum sink,* holding onto the back of your legs above the bent knees while straining to evict a *bad tenant.* Making you look a bit like a man pushing a wheelbarrow. Actually, not much like a man pushing a wheelbarrow, if we're honest.

wheelie bin full of kelp, like a *sim.* Yet another term describing the sopping *parts of shame* of an *enfrothulated* lady. Also *otter's pocket, turfer's knee, gravel lorry at the lights, Whitney Houston's last joint, Lee Evans's suit.*

wheelie bint n. A woman so ugly that she only gets taken out once a week. In the dark.

wheelspins n. The brown *skidmarks* on the *starting line at Brands Hatch* caused by the sudden acceleration of a *high arsepower shoebox special* when the flush is pulled.

wheezy bagpipe n. A red-faced tartan-clad *bloater* who has a waistline in the high 40s and risks death every time he attempts intercourse.

where there's a wank there's a way *exclam.* The determined exclamation of a *self-harmer* who is intent on carrying on his filthy vice in spite of a marked lack of *grumble mags* or other suitable fodder.

where there's blame there's a claim *phr.* An up-to-date, topical version of the timeless poetic classic "He who smelt it dealt it".

whet oneself v. To perform the masochistic act of going to the pub bang on last orders, allowing time for one pint and one pint only.

whidgey n. *Front bottom.*

whiffhanger n. A *dropped gut* so pungent that it clings to your *duds*. A *velcro fart.*

whiff of lavender n. Of a marriage, the suspicion of a *beardsome* bride. *'I don't know about Edward. There's a distinct whiff of lavender about that marriage if you ask me, Phil.'*

whiff of nostalgia n. Having failed to wash around your *herman gelmet* for a week to remind you of your *pipe's* last romantic interlude, a wistful Condor moment.

whiff of the cat's breath n. A *fanny fart, crumpet trumpet* or *queef*. A fishy gust from the wife's *whiskers.*

whinge drinker n. An overly *refreshed* patron of licensed premises who insists upon sharing his problems – be they marital, financial, professional, medical or whatever – with any of his fellow drinkers who are unfortunate enough to inadvertantly make eye contact with hm.

whinge minge n. A disgracefully sexist and misogynistic expression for a woman's mouth that would never be acceptable for inclusion in a woke family publication such as this. *'This house has listened to the Shadow Secretary of State for Culture, Media* *and Sport at some length on this matter. However, Mr Speaker, she has equivocated for long enough. It is now time for my right honourable friend to shut her whinge minge and tell us which way her party intends to vote.'*

whinjury *n.* An agonising, potentially career-ending trauma suffered by a professional football player that causes him to scream in agony, but which can be instantly cured by spraying something onto the outside of his boot, awarding him a free kick or sending off a member of the opposing team.

whippy shit *n.* A soft *Sir Douglas* that is whirled stylishly into the *crapper* and nipped off at the top end. Possibly with monkey blood and crushed nuts, although you would hope not.

whip-round, to have a *v.* To *relax in a gentleman's way* into a coachdriver's hat.

whips *1. n.* Officials of a political party who are charged with making sure that *pissed-* and *coked-up* MPs vote for the correct side. *2. n.* Things you *twat* a horse with. *3. n.* The middle area on a *large-boned bird* which tends to blend into one inchoate coagulation. From Waist + Hips.

whirling pits *n.* Attack of the *helicopters, wall of death.*

whirlwind romance video *euph.* A short play with limited dialogue where the characters get on very well.

whirly wheel challenger *n.* Something which drops to the ground unexpectedly, *eg.* A small nugget of excrement which hits the landing carpet when you are shuffling across to the *bogroll* cupboard.

whisker biscuit *n.* A *fur burger.*

whisker pot *n.* Fanny, minge, whidgey.

whisky dick *n.* A *knob of butter* that's about *as rigid as Rod Hull's aerial. Distiller's droop.*

whisky tango foxtrot *exclam.* Internationally recognised phonetic alphabet phrasing of an expression of surprise, consternation or annoyance.

whispering gallery *n.* A *ringpiece* or *quimpiece* that exhibits considerable gape.

whistle down the Y-fronts *v.* To *fart,* pass wind.

whistling gorilla *n.* An inviting and voluptuous *toothless gibbon.*

whistling in the dark *n.* Muff diving, eating *hairy pie.*

Whitby kipper *n. rhym. slang.* Stripper. Possibly also a reference to the aroma released when an exotic early afternoon pub dancer cracks open her legs as the finale to her act.

white arrow angels *n.* Van-driving messengers who bring catalogue goods to those ill-equipped to afford them.

whitecastleassitis *n. medic.* Alimentary canal condition afflicting up to 90% of the US population, caused by consumption of that country's most infamous small burgers, six at a time, steamed and lavished with onions. *Whitecastleassitis* is principally symptomised by the passage of stools which are indistinguishable from the said burgers – affectionately known as *belly bombers* – in both appearance and odour.

white caviar *n.* A salty delicacy for the ladies that is rich in *brotein.*

Whitechapel hat peg *n.* A particularly prominent *clematis,* proudly protruding from the *pantry curtains* of a gin-soaked *pearly queen.*

white goods *1. n.* Fridges, cookers and that. *2. n.* A *special delivery* that can be offloaded up front or round the back. Or all over the missus's *tits.*

white knuckle ride *n.* A solo thrill which makes your eyes bulge and lasts about three minutes. *One off the wrist.*

white lightnin' Hopkins *n.* An *al fresco* beverage enthusiast who is wont to sing about his woes to the world in general. Also *blind drunk Lemon Jefferson.*

white mouse *n.* Tampon. A *cotton mouse, fanny mouse, chuftie plug, jampax.*

white-out! *exclam.* When two large, pale *hogans* are exposed.

white pointers *n.* Extremely impressive *doos* found inhabiting a wet T-shirt.

Whitesnake, going for a *n.* The act of sloping off to indulge in a bit of *one-handed worm-burping.* From the lyrics to the famous song by the erstwhile Middlesbrough-based *poodle rockers, viz.* "Here I go again on my own / Going down the only road I've ever known".

white stuff *1. n.* Boutique-style shop popular with middle-class mums. *2 n. Daddy's sauce* popular with middle-class mums.

whitewash the hall *v.* To *throw a bit of white himulsion round* up the *front entrance.* A far more fulfilling job than *painting the ceiling.*

whitewater wristing *v.* To rapidly paddle the *skin boat.* To *interrogate the prisoner.*

white wee-wee *n.* Planet Skaro Dalek term for semen. *Spiff, spaff, spoff, spuff.*

white whale *n.* A uniquely special pornographic clip that was happened upon in the distant past, and now can no longer be found, which has thus taken on such legendary status that one restlessly searches for it across the wide waters of the web. *The old man and the scene.*

white witch *1. n.* A believer in – and practitioner

of – magic, who uses her evil powers for good. *2. n.* An actress who doesn't mind getting covered in *spunk*. A willing *plasterer's radio, cock mess monster* or *quattro formaggio*.

Whitfield tan *n.* The blue and red tartan effect often seen on the legs of residents of Dundee's premier housing development, achieved by the simple expedient of sitting in front of a two-bar electric fire. *The Whitfield tan* is a look which is always in fashion amongst those who choose to opt out of the wage slave ratrace. This condition even has a medical term of *erythaema ab igne*, or "redness due to fire".

Whitney dressed as Britney *n.* Descriptive of a lady who's done a few miles, and is gamely attempting to turn the clock back. *Mutton dressed as lamb, Elsie Tanner Montana, nana Kournikova.*

Whitney Houston's last joint, wetter than *sim.* Offensively and disrespectfully descriptive of the moistness of a young lady in a state of excitement. *Wetter than Lee Evans's suit.*

Whitney, up the *euph.* Reference to anal sex. From the lyrics to the late diva's song, *viz.* "It's not right but it's okay". See *wrong 'un*.

whiztits *n.* Unusually conicular breasts. Named after the seldom-loved children's television show which featured a crudely animated magic cone with the voice of balding, now deceased confabulist Paul Daniels. *Dunce's hats.*

whizzer and chips *1. n.* A fondly remembered comic. *2. n.* The gentle art of unzipping and *slashing* with one hand while holding a hot takeaway with the other. *'Keep toot for the filth, Mr Mayor. I'm just off for a whizzer and chips in the Nationwide Anglia doorway.'*

whodungit *n.* A Hercule Poirot-style gathering of suspects to deduce which member of a household blocked the *biscuit wrapper* with a large, unflushable *Ingrid*.

who let the ducks in? *exclam. rhet.* A witty post-flatulence ice-breaker sung to the tune of *Who Let The Dogs Out* by Baha Men.

whoof *v.* To *fart* at a burglar.

whoof whoof! *1. exclam.* Term of friendly approval directed at passing *talent*, esp. from scaffolders, van drivers, former Minister of Defences *etc. 2. exclam.* Term of disapproval aimed at passing women who simply haven't made the effort.

whoopie pie *1. n.* Hand-sized cake treat popular in Maine, USA, it says here. *2. n.* The wet patch in the bed. *'No, it's definitely your turn to sleep in the whoopie pie, mother superior.'*

whoops a gaysy *n.* Of a gentleman, slipping over in an effeminate manner while emitting an unexpectedly girly whimper.

whoopsy *n.* A *piss* or *shit*, usually done by a cat in Frank Spencer's beret.

whopper with cheese *1. n.* A *buffet slayer* with a savoury fungal infection in her *club sandwich*. *2. n.* An unwashed *quarterpounder.*

who put 50p in the dickhead? *exclam. interrog.* Said when someone is being overdramatic or having an adult tantrum.

whore DERV *1. n.* A shameless strumpet who works at the local petrol station. *2. n. Tart fuel, hen petrol, whore star* or *knicker oil.*

whore d'oeuvres *n.* The unnecessary appetizers before the main course at a massage parlour, *ie.* The massage.

whore drawer *n.* Out of bounds area where Essex housewives keep their hooker heels, crotchless panties, anal lube, rampant rabbits and other sundry erotic miscellanea. *'What's that whirring noise from Mum's bedroom, Dad?' 'Don't go in there, son. I heard her opening the whore drawer earlier.'*

whoredrobe *n.* The special place where, in a bloke's opinion, his girlfriend keeps her best outfits.

whoreem *n.* A brothel. *Also known as a box office, brasserie, fanny farm, pop-up shop* or *cocking shop.*

whore from Fife *n. derrog.* A term of abuse that incorporates the two insults of being a whore and of coming from Fife. *'Hey, you've just taken my last fag, you whore from Fife.'*

whore frost *n.* A *good time girl's* sudden change of attitude once the *dirty deed* is done.

whoreganisation *n.* Of a commercial traveller, the practice of sorting out the order of his evening's entertainment using the contact ads section of the *Daily Sport* and a highlighter pen. Perhaps while sitting in a Vauxhall Vectra outside a Little Chef situated just off the A1 north of Newcastle upon Tyne.

whoregasm *n.* The unconvincing, appreciative noises made by a *lady of the night* to persuade her customer that he is getting his money's worth, despite sensory evidence to the contrary.

whoregeous *adj.* Descriptive of a particularly comely *Covent Garden nun. 'Look at these photos of the pro I knobbed in Amsterdam. That's my cock in her mouth there.' 'Fuck me, well done mate, she's absolutely whoregeous. Anyway, I'm going to prescribe you a some penicillin for the syphilis, antivirals for the genital herpes and a course of metronidazole for the trichomoniasis.'*

whorelage *n.* The stretch limo trade. *'I'm thinking of buying a 35-foot Hummer and going into the* *whorelage business.'*

whore licks *n.* Malty bedtime drink for a gentleman or lady, consisting of either warm *spongle* or a *furry cup* of *kitten tears.*

whoremark *n.* A small tattoo on a lady's lower back, aping the classy style originally adopted by *Frankie* actresses. A *tramp stamp*, *slag tag* or *arse antlers.*

whorendous *adj.* Of time spent in the company of a *good time girl*, bad. *'Well, what a whorendous evening I've had. It's almost a relief to be going home.' 'That'll be two thousand pounds in a brown envelope please, Lord Archer.'*

whoreovirus *n. medic.* A dose of *cock rot* contracted from a lady of the night.

whore's bath *n.* An act of personal hygiene practised by ladies of the lower orders; a brief, yet fulsome handwash of the *undercarriage* often performed at a sink. *Rinsing the lettuce.*

whore's brass *n.* The shiny Lizzie Duke *tack* found decorating women in southern pubs. *Bingo clink.*

whore's headboard, banging like a *sim.* Descriptive of the action of an improperly-secured lavatory entrance/egress that is being adversely affected by sustained surface winds of between 32 and 63 mph.

whoreshoes *n.* Fashionable pink stilettos. *Fuck me shoes* that are extremely uncomfortable.

whoresome *adj.* Heaving with easy *blart*. *'Hey lads, it's going to be a great night. I've heard this place is whoresome.'*

whoretumnal *adj.* Descriptive of the latter years of a *working girl*'s career, when her *foliage* begins to change colour and everything starts heading south.

whore wound *n.* Injury sustained when going into battle with a *trull*, usually in the form of grazed knees or a stabbed *arse.*

whorienteering *n.* The time-honoured bachelor's habit of following his genital compass and journeying to the exotic far east in search of a *new model in town.*

whorism *n.* The horizon-broadening practice of travelling the world to experience different and exotic cultures via the medium of *going with* prostitutes.

whorist *n.* A person who is prepared to trek to far-flung destinations in order to expand his cultural *whorizens*. That's probably enough entries beginning with the word "whore".

who's the daddy? *exclam. interrog.* Another one of those phrases which can be shouted after one has *dropped* a noisily noisome *gut.*

who-tree *n.* An alleged celebrity *nonce* from the 1960s and 70s whom, disappointingly, one has never heard of.

why, are you hungry? *exclam.* Humorous riposte to someone who asks if one has *farted.*

whybrows *n.* Eyebrows which, for unexplained reasons, have been shaved off and redrawn – evidently by a toddler with a sharpie – to create the appearance of a surprised clown. *'I like your whybrows, Cheryl.'*

whycon *n.* A celebrity who has achieved their status for reasons that are not entirely clear – perhaps even to them, *eg.* Kerry Katona, Andrea Leadsom, Joe Swash *etc.*

why not wipe your arse and call it a shit? *exclam. interrog.* Homespun advice to one who has just *let rip* with a loud and prolonged blast of *bum thunder. 'Why not wipe your arse and call it a shit, Miss Widdecombe?'*

why why why Delilah *exclam.* To be sung before *ripping* a series of rapid, staccato *Tony Harts.*

wibbly wobblies *n. Bristols. 'The marble statue of Venus, thought to date from the Hellenistic period, depicts an armless female figure, her lower half covered by drapery and with her wibbly wobblies out for the lads.'* (Kenneth Clark's Civilisation, BBC, 1969).

WIB/wib *abbrev.* Working In Bed; an extreme version of *working at home* whereby the employee makes little or no pretence that they actually intend to get up, let alone work, other than remotely logging on in case HR are doing a sweep.

wicca furniture *n.* Various items of necromantic bric-a-brac, such as dreamcatchers, black candles, pentagram coasters, frogs, and purple lipsticks, which appear in teenagers' bedrooms, indicating a lively interest in the occult or satanism. Parents may console themselves with the thought that they are unlikely to have to fork out for a prom dress and stretch limousine at the end of term.

wick *1. n.* Penis. See *dip your wick. 2. n.* Nerves, *tit ends. 'I wish that Chris Evans would fuck off. He really gets on my fucking wick.'*

wicked pisser *n. US.* A good egg or a good show, top notch person or experience. As in *'Thank you very much for your kindness and generosity. You really have been the most wicked pissers. My name's Bing Crosby. Goodnight.'*

wicker basket *n.* A matted and tangled *bush* in which the previous night's *clacker lacquer* has been allowed to dry out.

wicket-keeper *n.* A third *cottagist*, employed as a lookout while his two pals have a *knock up at the gasworks end.*

Widdecombe's hymen *euph.* Something that's

clearly never been touched. *'Carson, could you have a word with Mrs Patmore about the understairs maid? The library grate is like Widdecombe's hymen.'*

widdle *1. n.* Childish term for a *wee wee.* *2. v.* To do some *wee wee.* *3. n. prop.* Surname of the Private played by Charles Hawtrey in *Carry On Up the Khyber.*

wide awank *adj.* Roused from one's slumber and ready to *knock oneself about a bit.*

wide-mouthed frog *1. phr.* Subject of an old joke that breaks the ice at parties. *2. euph.* The act, which also breaks the ice at parties, of spreading one's buttock cheeks apart with both hands in order that a high pressure buildup of *flatus* be released discreetly.

wide on *n.* Female equivalent of a *hard-on; a slop on.*

widget *1. n.* Device in a can of beer that makes it go off like a hand grenade when opened. *2. n.* A small *widgy.*

widgy *n.* A large *widget.*

widower's tears *n.* The involuntary dribble of grey *spunk* from the end of a long-disused *cock.*

widower's tickle *n.* The short burst of pleasure a man experiences when he flushes while in a sitting position and his *three piece suite* is momentarily caught in the spray. A thrill of almost pound shop cheapness.

widow maker *1. n.* Nickname given to the Winchester model 1911 shotgun. *2. n.* A monstrous, high density *feeshus* of the sort that constipated *coffin dodgers* typically strain long and hard to pass, often with tragically fatal results. *'God's truth, it was a widow maker that did for Elvis. I've read the coroner's report.'*

widow's memories *n.* Penis-shaped sausages, cucumbers *etc.* Indeed, anything vaguely cylindrical in a supermarket which is fingered nostalgically by old ladies.

widow wanky *1. n.* A person who has lost their partner, due to death or other less dramatic circumstances, and who now enjoys unrestricted access to the internet. *2. n.* The first, despondent but necessary, *act of self violation* indulged in after the wife or girlfriend has left for good.

wife baiter *n.* Any borderline non-essential item purchased by a married man on the joint account he shares with his missus with the reasonable expectation that it might bring out the beast in her, *eg.* A new set of fancy, carbon fibre golf clubs to accompany the graphite-shafted ones he bought three months ago to replace the titanium ones he bought a couple of months before that.

wifebeater *1. n.* An unnecessarily strong lager. *Wreck the hoose juice.* *2. n. US.* A string vest or singlet, usually worn with a pair of shorts.

wifectomy *n.* An extremely painful divorce. One invariably experiences an *OPE* during the operation.

wife expectancy *n.* The amount of time a chap has while out shopping with his *last resort* – not usually very long – before she catches him perving at a huge pair of *jugs* on a mannequin or sneaking off to the pub.

wife eye *n.* That unmistakable look off the missus when she catches you viewing something dodgy on your mobile or laptop.

wife-fi *n.* The means by which married men log onto the internet in order to frantically *find a present for the wife* every time she leaves the house.

wifeguard *n.* A computer system that prevents a man being killed by his missus, *eg.* The "Incognito" function on Google Chrome. *'My heart stopped when I saw her crank up the laptop, but then I remembered I was protected by the wifeguard.'*

wifer *n.* A fellow who is imprisoned in his marriage with no hope of escape, parole or remission.

wife saver *n.* The new 4% Stella, as opposed to full-strength *wifebeater.*

wife's radar *n.* A lady's *old bat*-like ability to detect the merest rustle of a *jazz mag* from a hundred yards.

wifestyle *n.* The expensive and excessive level of comfort in which one must keep one's good lady, in order to ensure regular and unencumbered access to her *quim* and *charlies.*

wifetamer *n.* An impressive *weapon* that affords one the respect of one's spouse, like a whip and chair would on a lion in a circus. A *cuntbuster.*

wifetreater *n.* Alcohol-free version of the ever-popular aggression-inducing tipple. *'I'll have a pint of wifetreater, please, and whatever my good lady is having.' 'Certainly, vicar.'*

wifey hotspot *n.* Any place that is a magnet for *bingo-winged*, middle-aged females, *eg.* Iceland, Mecca or the box office at any venue where Michael Bolton, Daniel O'Donnell or Take That are appearing.

WIFI/wifi *abbrev. interrog.* Would I Fuck It?

Wigan didge *n.* Lancashire pastry- and meat-based foodstuff with a filling so volcanically hot that those who eat it risk third degree burns. Named after the circular breathing method practised by Australian didgeridooists.

Wigan rosette *n.* The state of the *freckle* after a particularly fierce *all nighter.* A *Johnny Cash, Japanese flag.*

Wigan wash *n.* A quick *up'n'under* spray with

deodorant. *'I'll be there in ten minutes. I'm just having a Wigan wash.'*

Wigan wet wipe *n.* The act of spitting on a wad of Poundland *shitscrape* in order to lessen its impact on a raw *ringpiece* after a hard night in the Royal Bengali.

Wiggins *n. Pubage* that carries on down the insides of a young lady's thighs. Named after the trademark sideburns of yellow-jerseyed mod bicyclist Sir Bradley. Also *Rhodes Boysons, inside burns, thighbrows, judge's eyebrows* and *whack-os*.

wil *n.* A lady's *snarse, tinter, taint, carse*, whatever. Her perineum. So-called because it is situated "between the *Gary* and the M*ott*".

Wilberforce *n.* An inoffensive term for one's *ladykiller*. *'Come through here and I'll introduce you to Wilberforce. You two would get on like a house on fire.'*

wild westing *n. Fingering* two women simultaneously, in a style reminiscent of a cowboy brandishing a couple of six-shooters.

Wilfrid *n.* The spontaneous retraction of the prepuce, exposing the *bellend*. Named after the character whose domed head pokes out the top of his pullover in *The Bash Street Kids*.

WILF/wilf 1. *abbrev.* Term used when referring to the sexier *chavettes*, office cleaners, burger van girls *etc.*, whom one encounters in the course of one's daily round. Wilkinson's shopper I'd Like to Fuck. 2. *acronym.* Weather presenter I'd Like to Fuck. Not a term much in use back in Bert Ford's time.

Wilkinson, to do a *v.* To perform a defecation from a hovering, squatting position over a *pissy*-seated pub *bog*. From the pose's similarity to the hands-clasped, sticky-out-*arsed* stance struck by rugby star Jonny before he took a kick and went off injured.

willically challenged *euph.* Descriptive of a chap who wishes that centimetres were inches *in the trouser department*. Normally rocks up serenaded by over-compensatory exhaust noise.

willie *n.* A ten-foot penis that has to be cut with a rake. *John Thomas, Percy the pork swordsman*, he who gives *Gert Stonkers* a *pearl necklace*. The *tassel*, the *Peter*, the *Charlie*. Also *willy*.

willie and the hand jive *n.* Rhythmic, throbbing cork-popping combo who perform the *Bologna bop* among other dances.

willie-litres/willie-metres *n.* Any flattering unit of measurement that enhances the teller's side of the story, *eg.* A sweating bloke recounting the quantity of drink he has thrown down his neck on a particular evening will invariably measure that amount in *willie-litres*; likewise any correspondent stating the length of his *cock* in a letter to a *jazz mag* will use the other designation. *Dog inches.*

willie weep *n.* The meagre tears that fall from a man's *tickle-tail* when trying to urinate in a bleary-eyed state of semi-tumescence.

willie welly *n. French letter, French safe, English overcoat* out of the packet. Later, a *Dutch jellyfish.*

willie woofter *n. Fruit feeler, spud fumbler.*

willipedes *n. medics.* Genital arthropods. *Mechanical dandruff.*

Willivander *v. rhym. slang.* To masturbate. From the 70s Dutch footballer Willi Van der Kerkhof = jerk off.

willnots *n. Tagnuts, dangleberries.* Toffee entwined in the *arse cress* which simply "will not" come off. *Walnuts.*

will o' the nipse *n.* A visible state of the art. For example, one released while bending over in the shower in a cold house, or while standing in one of those heat scanner things at an airport.

Will Smith assault, weaker than a *sim.* Decidedly lacking in strength. Descriptive of, for example, a cup of tea with way too much milk in it where the teabag was whipped out within 0.9 seconds, or an 'ad hoc' comedy routine on erstwhile "satirical" TV show *Mock the Week*. Named in honour of the Oscar-winning actor's post-gag slap across Chris Rock's chops.

willy *n.* The *tassel.*

willydelphia *n.* Soft, spreadable *knob cheese.* Often to be found on your *crackers.*

Willy Fog 1. *n. prop.* Eponymous hero of the 80s Spanish-Japanese animated television series *Around the World with Willy Fog*, based on the Jules Verne novel *Around the World in 80 Days*. Us neither. 2. *n. medic.* When you have *wanked* so much that you can't remember how many *wanks* you have had. Ah, with you now.

willy mid-on *n.* Amusing cricketer's term for a *semi*, such as like what might make it uncomfortably cramped in one's *box. 'I say Aggers, the batsman's Holding the umpire's Dickie. If I'm not much mistaken he's getting a willy mid-on.'*

willy milk monitor *n.* The person working on a *grumble-flick* set whose unenviable task is to mop up all the stray *man-muck* at the end of a shoot.

willy nilly *n.* A gent's *failure in front of an open goal* after one too many pints on a Friday night. Also *alehouse cock, knob of butter, brewer's droop, los lobos.*

willyonaire *n.* A man who has won the girth jackpot due to his larger than average *old man.*

will you start the fans please *exclam.* Announced

in the stentorian style of Richard O'Brien, Ed Tudor-Pole or Richard Ayoade introducing the climactic round of TV adventure gameshow *The Crystal Maze*, a *Protect & Survive*-style warning of impending flatulatory meltdown.

willy string *n.* Sticky substance that sprays everywhere after sufficient shaking.

willy welly *n.* A *jubber ray* that pulls your socks off.

Willy Wonka's river *n.* A never-ending cataract of liquid chocolate with the occasional green and orange *oompah lumpa* floating in it. *'Come to the Rupali Restaurant, Bigg Market, Newcastle upon Tyne, no longer open, for a top class dining experience that will leave you with an arse like Willy Wonka's river.'*

Wilmslow panzer *n.* A large 4-wheel-drive vehicle which is designed to operate in the harshest of terrain and to protect its occupants from the most inclement conditions, but which only ever gets used to drive the hundred yards from a 4-bedroom house on a Balfour-Beatty estate to a Montessori fucking primary school. The north-west equivalent of a *Chelsea tractor.*

WILSTAF/wilstaf *abbrev.* A polite term for a particularly alluring female. Woman I'd Like to Shag To A Frazzle.

Wilton to Stilton, prefer *v.* To be a woman suffering from *lesbicious* tendencies; specifically to be keener on *munching carpet* than chomping down on a savoury mouthful of *blue-veined cheese.* *'Sorry pal, you're wasting your time. I prefer Wilton to Stilton.' 'Fair enough, pet. I'll just sit over here and watch instead, then.'*

wilt or tilt *n.* Recreational pastime whereby a *mucky-minded* young swain works his way through a mental inventory of all the women he knows whilst imagining what it would be like to *have it off* with them. Or, indeed, what it would be like to *have it off.*

Wimbornes *n. rhym. slang.* Haemorrhoids. From the Dorset village of Wimborne St. Garsegrapes.

wimp wiper *n.* In an office or workplace environment, a big girl's blouse who takes in his/her own toilet tissue rather than use the 60-grit industrial type provided by the management.

winching out the Chilean miners *euph.* Manually hoisting one's *tadpoles* up a narrow tube and out into daylight.

windaloo *n.* Following a piquantly spicesome *Ruby Murray* and finding oneself without access to a suitable water closet, violently voiding the *dirt bakery oven* through the nearest convenient casement.

wind break *1. n.* Series of wooden poles held together with striped canvas which is arranged to prevent gentle winds, gusty sea breezes, horizontal Arctic sleet and what-have-you spoiling the enjoyment of beach-bound British holidaymakers. *2. n.* Intermission during a business meeting or similar which allows the attendees to leave the room in order to *drop their guts*, having politely refrained from doing so thus far. *'Well, ladies and gentlemen, I think we'll adjourn there for a fifteen minute wind break. When we re-convene, Mr Burrell will begin his evidence.'*

wind chime *n.* A *backdoor bell* that wakes you up.

windchimes *1. n. pl.* Gravitationally challenged breasts which sway gently in the morning breeze, occasionally clanging together in a restful and melodic manner. *2. n. pl.* Soothingly melodic noises in the middle of the night.

wind cries Mary, the *1. n.* Third UK single by the Jimi Hendrix Experience. *2. n.* A *fanny fart, queef, C-biscuit, flap raspberry, farkle, muff puff, sea breeze* or *frampton.*

wind farm *n. milit.* A barracks full of vigorously *farting* squaddies.

wind in the pillows *1. n.* Unlikely sounding bedtime practice, involving a squatting gentleman and his very accommodating prostrate ladyfriend. *2. n.* A laterally diffused *Dutch oven. 3. n.* Using one's feather-filled bolster to mask the sound and smell of a bedtime *botty burp* whilst sharing the divan with a new partner. Also *give her more sail, Mr Christian.*

wind in the willows *1. n. prop.* Anthropomorphic tale of woodland goings-on written by Kenneth Grahame. *2. n.* Expulsion of *flatus* in a Sylvan setting of such *puissance* that it causes the leaves of *Salix babylonica* to tremble and shimmer.

wind jammer *n.* A *style-conscious* chap.

windmills on a Dutch painting, that could start the *exclam.* Said to the deliverer of a particularly violent *Exchange and Mart.*

wind off the top of the iceberg *n.* A chilling *blast* that marks the impending arrival of something far bigger, more serious, and capable of ripping its way through your hull without any warning.

windowbox *n.* A pair of crotchless *dunghampers.*

window cleaner's pocket *n.* A large, sad, damp and dishevelled *fadge.*

window of opportunity *n.* The short period of time after someone has admitted *dropping a gut*, during which it is safe for others to do likewise, safe in the knowledge that the earlier confessor will take the rap.

window of plopportunity *n.* That brief period of time in the digestive process when a *turd* comes out just lovely.

window shopping *v.* Of a lady, to go out on the town and give blokes the impression that she is interested when she actually has no intention of opening her *purse*.

windscape *n.* The barely tolerable miasma of blended *carbon dibaxide* that persists in a shared workspace until everyone has had the chance to retire for their mid-morning *dump*.

wind sketch *n.* The masterpiece that's left in the *applecatchers* when a fine *fartist* inadvertently *follows through*. '*Lot 356. Scotch Jim (fl. 1990-2006). A fine wind sketch on purple Y-fronts gusset by this much sought-after morbidly overweight office furniture delivery man. This particular work was created while single-handedly manoeuvring a loaded filing cabinet up a narrow Middlesbrough fire escape on a very hot day. A fine sepia image which exhibits mild vignetting, approx. 65mm x 72mm. Est. £3500-£4000.*'

windsock *n.* A particularly low-hanging *fiveskin*. An *anteater's nose, lace curtains*.

wind that shakes the barley *1. n.* Title of a controversial Ken Loach film depicting the history of the English Black & Tans in Ireland in the early part of the century, and the formation of the IRA. Sounds like a laugh a minute. *2. n.* An *air biscuit* so strong that it blows all one's *arse cress* in the same direction, creating the appearance of a dark Irish wheat field in one's *cleft*.

wind the clock *n.* To perform a repetitive action with one's wrist shortly before going to sleep. '*Each night, Charlotte, Anne, Emily and Branwell would hear their father Parson Brontë pause on the landing to wind the clock.*'

wind triangle *1. n.* A graphical representation of the relationship between aircraft motion and atmospheric air velocity. *2. n.* See *kweef, Lawley kazoo, vulvuzela*.

Windy Miller's chimney, as dry and floury as *sim.* Descriptive of an orifice that hasn't seen any action in living memory; an arid, and heavily be-talcum-powdered *front bottom*. Named after the *Chigley* – or possibly *Camberwick Green* – character. See also *as dry as ~a budgie's tongue; ~a moth sandwich; ~an M&S low fat sausage; ~an old dog's nose*. Actually, it might of been *Trumpton* come to think of it.

wind your watch *euph.* To commit a disgusting act of *self delight* upon one's generative member. From the similarity of a *relaxing* chap's hand movements to the characteristic rapid flicks and rotations which must be performed in order to prime the mainspring of an automatic timepiece.

'*What were you doing in there?*' '*I was just winding my watch, love.*' '*But your watch is at the menders.*' '*I know. I meant having a wank.*' (Bamforth's *Seaside Chuckles* postcard, by Donald McGill, 1933).

windy pops *n.* *Arse tremblers, chuffs, trouser coughs.*

wine flu *n. medic.* Short-lived virus typically caught from a drinking glass, which leaves its victim suffering from a headache, stomach upset, fever, night sweats, vomiting, diarrhoea, dizzyness and a bright red nose. Also *beer ache, rumbago, brewmonia, ginfluenza, beer cancer*.

wine from the devil's cellar *euph.* Women's things.

wine glasses *n.* The female equivalent of *beer goggles*.

wine, having a glass of *euph.* A discreet reference to someone *sucking* someone else *off*. '*The Northern Ireland Secretary walked in the office without knocking and inadvertently caught them having a glass of wine.*'

wine-ker *n.* An aggravating and pretentious oenophile who can't glug a glass of Aldi screwtop without using words like "bouquet", "grape" and "nose".

winestein *n.* A person who, after consuming vast quantities of cheap plonk, becomes the font of all knowledge. Also *gintellectual*.

wing commander *n.* Rank given to those that have achieved distinction in all four of the major bedroom disciplines, *viz. Yellow, brown, green* and *red wings*.

wings at the speed of sound *1. n. prop.* Title of a successful Paul McCartney album released in the mid 70s. *2. n.* The flapping noise made at bingo halls by the *generously proportioned* patrons as they dash outside between games to wheeze their raddled way through a well-earned *coffin nail*.

wingspan *n.* A measure of manual spreadability in *meat mag* models posing for *spam butterfly* shots. '*Have you seen Irene from Walsall in this month's Readers' Wives? Just look at the wingspan she's achieved.*'

wing wank *n.* A pleasure only a true *18-wheeler* can really give. A *bagpipe* off a lass *with a lovely personality*.

winking *n.* When preparing to *hack off a lump*, the uncomfortable feeling of your *anus* twitching while you're still undoing your belt. The *point of no return*.

winking the hog's eye *n.* Cutting-short of an act of micturition in an emergency. Curtailing a *slash*, if such a thing is possible.

winking walnut *n.* *Brown eye, chocolate starfish, rusty bullet hole.*

Winkleman's thicket *n.* A *lady garden* that looks

like it's been trimmed with a laser.

winkle picker *1. n.* A fashionable, long, pointed shoe of the style favoured by 1950s rock and roll fans, magazine publishers and the erstwhile music hall entertainer Little Tich. *2. n.* A beautiful, *well-qualified* lady who can have any man she so desires.

winkle picking *1. v. medic.* Anal sex with one who is afflicted with *Chalfonts. 2. v.* Ancient seafarer's practice acheived using special pointed shoes.

winky *1. n.* A tiny *cock. 2. adj.* Having a tendency to wink a lot.

winkybag *1. n.* A tiny scrotum. *2. n.* An ugly old woman who has a tendency to wink a lot.

winner *n.* Unit in which *spunk* was traditionally measured in the catering industry until 2013. *'Boil 1 small tablespoon of sago in very little water till clear. Dissolve a teaspoonful of meat or vegetable extract in a cup of boiling water. Strain the cooked sago into the made broth. Season to taste, and lastly, if a red-faced cunt is coming to dine, stir in a generous winner of gentleman's spendings.'* (from *Household Management* by Mrs Beeton).

winner corner *n.* Secluded quarter of a restaurant kitchen, where staff members traditionally retire in order to discreetly prepare *perseverance soup* for their less popular customers.

winnered *adj.* Wanked dry. Term used to describe the *clockweights* of kitchen staff following a sudden rush on *chef's special sauce,* for example if *Times* restaurant critic Giles Coren is in.

winners' podium *n.* Sir Chris standing proudly in the middle and the Brownlee boys on either side. The *fruit bowl.*

winnet *n. Kling on, dag, dangleberry, willnot, brown room hanger on.* Also *winnit.*

winnet picker *n.* Someone of arguably lower social standing than a *jizz mopper. 'I only got three A's and a B at A-Level, so I'm working as a winnet picker in an old folks' home.'*

Winnie *1. n. prop.* A lesbian, she who licks the *honey pot. 2. n.* A "pooh" that has become so fat that it is stuck fast in the hole with only its head poking out, such that it cannot easily be pushed in either direction. Based on the much-loved AA Milne story where the eponymous honey-loving bear becomes lodged in the doorway of his proctologist's surgery.

winning a tenner on the fanny lottery *euph.* Having drunken *carnival knowledge* of a *hippocrocadogapig with a lovely personality.*

winnit *n.* See *winnet,* but not if you're eating.

winosaur *n.* A lady of advanced years who enjoys

a drink or two.

winotaur *n.* She who, after taking alcohol on board, turns in a violent, foul-mouthed beast that looks like something animated by Ray Harryhausen.

Winslet twins *n.* A proper pair of buoyant *nicebergs* as sported by *Titanic* actress Kate. *'As usual, the Winslet twins put in an excellent performance.'*

wintercourse *n.* Frosty s*x, the kind to be had with a lady who doesn't approve of that kind of carry on. One would imagine couples such as Margot and Jerry out of *The Good Life,* the Queen and Prince Philip, and Stanley and Evelyn Blunt in *Carry On Abroad* engaged in *wintercourse. Grumpy pumpy, how's your father-in-law.*

winter rules *1. n.* In golf, when a chap is given dispensation to advantageously place his ball a few inches away from its original landing spot because of the claggy conditions underfoot. *2. n.* When the missus deems it too cold in the bedroom for her hubby to *eat out to help out* due to the risk of the duvet being pulled any lower than her chin.

winter's bone *1. n.* Title of a 2010 Oscar-nominated movie starring Jennifer Lawrence. Never heard of it. *2. n.* An impressively robust *stonk-on* achieved on a particularly cold day.

winter warmer *n.* A particularly long, drawn out, hot and stinky *Miranda* emitted beneath the duvet at any time between October and February. *'That was quite a winter warmer, love. I think I'll turn down the electric blanket.'*

win the chocolate lottery *v.* To receive a particularly large *milkman's bonus.*

win the speedboat *v.* Having already secured a dead-cert *bang* while out *on the pull,* to go for – and miraculously get the go-ahead from – a much better option. From the closing round on TV quiz-show *Bullseye,* where the contestants could gamble their safe £60 winnings on scoring a hundred-and-one with six darts or fewer and thus win a mystery prize, which was invariably revealed as a speedboat full of *fat-titted,* bikini-clad blonde *birds* when they lost. Or, if they won, a trailer tent, hostess trolley or Etch-a-Sketch.

wipe my arse on that, I could *exclam.* A slightly more crude version of "That's so clean I could eat my dinner off it".

wipeout *1. n.* Surfing terminology describing the situation whereby a "dude" attempting to "hang ten" ends up *tits*-first in the briney. *2. n.* Underestimating the amount of *shit tickets* left on the roll. Running out of *arsewipe* when one's *ringpiece* is still *like a Marmite pot.*

wipes their arse like Robert Smith applies lipstick *sim.* Descriptive of a person's slapdash attempt at *nipsy* hygiene, reminiscent of the tousle-haired Cure frontman's shambolic cosmetics regimen. Also *Queen Amidala's lipstick.*

wipe the slate clean *euph.* To manually erase the image of a sexually-appealing woman so that one can concentrate on the task at hand.

wipe to beige *n.* In a situation where a person is low on time or toilet paper, a temporary hygiene technique employed until circumstances allow a more rigorous and effective regimen to be undertaken.

wipe your arse and call that a shit *exclam.* A witty retort to another person's foul *trouser cough.*

wipe your feet *v.* To vigorously *beskid* a lavatory pan. *"I is the only nice and jumbly giant in Giant Country! I is the Big Friendly Giant!" "I don't care who you are," replied Sophie. "I'm not using that crapper. It looks like you've wiped your feet in there, you mucky old cunt."'* (from *The BFFG* by Roald Dahl).

wiping the hard drive *euph.* In the interests of prolonging an impending bout of *carnival pleasure*, the process of *clearing the pipes* in order to *take the edge off* one's ardour. Restoring one's *mammary banks* to their factory settings.

wire spiders *n.* The hairs around the *chocolate starfish* that come to life when you are in a meeting or in the checkout queue at Asda. *Arse wasps, jerry in the trench, sphincter gnats.*

Wirral peninsula *1. n.* The area of land which falls between Chester and Liverpool. *2. n.* Them bits of skin that separate *cunts* and *arseholes.* The *taint, notcher, carse, snarse, biffin bridge, Humber Bridge, tinter etc.*

wise guy in concrete boots, go down like a *sim.* To embark on a marathon session of *cumulonimbus.* *'You should have seen her face when she caught me strangling Kojak over her sister's holiday pics. I had to go down like a wise guy in concrete boots to get away with that one. And now here's Liam Dutton with the weather.'*

WI-sexual *adj.* Descriptive of those with a penchant for *elepants*-clad middle-aged ladies.

wishbone *n.* The often-pulled penile consequence of an aspirational sexual fantasy.

witch doctor's necklace, mouth like a *sim.* A description of a particularly unimpressive set of pearly whites. See also *teeth like a crossword, English teeth, mouth full of sugarpuffs, Queen Mum's teeth* and *pan of burnt chips.*

witch doctor's rattle *n.* Descriptive of a woman with a *nice personality.* A *monk's pin-up.*

witches' knickers *n.* Thin plastic bags fluttering menacingly in the twigs of an urban tree.

Govan bunting.

witchettey grub *n. Aus.* The *clematis*, that is to say, the *bush-tucker* gourmand's prize delicacy.

Witch magazine *n.* A specialist *top shelf* periodical featuring the somewhat aesthetically challenged wives of its short-sighted, hairy-palmed readers.

witch's cave *n.* A *wizard's sleeve, clown's pocket, wall of death.* An enormous *fadge.* *'Soldier, soldier, would you marry me / For you are so strong and brave / Oh no, sweet maid, I cannot marry you / 'Cos your twat's like a witch's cave.'* (Traditional folk song).

witch's finger *n.* A gnarled, knobbly *feeshus*, hooked at one end, that could be used to beckon Snow White to come to her cottage door and look at a basket of apples.

witch's leg, cock like a *sim.* A crooked, knobbly-kneed *giggle stick* with all blue varicose veins up the side.

witch's lips *n.* The cold kiss of a porcelain toilet bowl on one's *bell end*, occasionally felt while *dropping off the shopping.*

witch's tit, flat as a *sim.* In the retail world, a reference to a period of slow sales. *Flat as a plate of cold piss. 'How's the C5 doing, Sir Clive?' 'Terrible. Business has been flast as a witch's tit for – ooh, let me see now – the last thirty-three years.'*

witch's trick *n.* The phenomenon of a *back beauty, backstabber* or *golden deceiver* who appears stunning from behind, only to reveal herself as looking like Grotbags off *Emu's World* from the front.

witch's wardrobe *n.* A tree with all bin bags and other detritus fluttering in its branches, *eg.* One growing in the car park of Asda at Queslett in North Birmingham.

witch switch *n.* The final glass of house red that turns a hitherto pleasant evening out with your other half into a fight in the taxi queue.

witch wagon *n.* Elongated white, left-hand-drive vehicle designed to shunt drunk harpies of limited vocal and cerebral capacity to and from, to pick a destination at random, The Black Sheep, Croydon CR0 1NA on a Saturday night. A stretch limo. *'Will you be having pissed-up sex in the back of the witch wagon, madam? Only we charge an extra fiver for the hire of a special sheet to keep spunk and vomit off the velour seats.'*

with bagpipes it's not the tune, it's the tone *exclam.* Humorous expression to be used after one *steps on a duck.* As originally coined by universally popular ex-royal Prince Harry about bagpipes rather than *farting.*

withdrawal agreement *n.* Unreliable, potentially

disastrous deal brokered by a chap who has negotiated a bit of *bareback nookie* off his lass by claiming he'll pull out before the *vinegar strokes*.

withdrawal symptoms *n. Spangle* on the stomach, *iced buns, iPod earphones, jelly jewellery* and other assorted evidence of *aerial jackrobatics*.

with one's cock out, do something *v.* To perform a task or action badly. *'My right honorable friend would have us believe that he can increase government spending in the health service while at the same time delivering tax cuts across the board. Well I'm afraid he must have written this budget with his cock out, because I can tell him that the figures simply do not add up.'*

witten *n.* See *winnet*.

Wittgenstein, do a *v.* Yet another classical piano-based term for a specific act of *self pollution*. To perform a few *five finger exercises* with the left hand on one's short, pink *upright,* possibly in front of a large audience in the Royal Albert Hall. Named after the unidextrous Austrian concert pianist Paul Wittgenstein (1887-1961), who lost his right arm in WWI, but nevertheless continued his musical career using his remaining limb to play a number of specially commissioned works. And it always felt like someone else was doing it.

wizards' hats *n. Dunces' hats, motorway cones, twin peaks, whiztits*.

wizard's sleeve *n.* A *witch's cave*. A generously appointed *sausage wallet. 'I can't feel a bloody thing, Mother Teresa. You must have a fanny like a wizard's sleeve.'*

WKR *abbrev.* Any male caught drinking WKD after the age of fourteen.

WLD *abbrev.* Weapon of Lass Destruction. An *ICBM* that would not leave a woman standing, a *cuntbuster*.

WMKO *abbrev.* Internet abbreviation. Wanking My Knob Off. *'@Real_Nana_Mouskouri: Just seen your new video. #WMKO.'*

WOAGST/woagst *abbrev.* Said of a *yummy mummy*. Worthy Of A Good Seeing To. Also *hagst,* said of a *goer* who is now *up the stick, viz.* Had A Good Seeing To.

WOAT/woat *abbrev.* A light-hearted, ironically male chauvinist term for a woman at a football, rugby or cricket match. Waste Of A Ticket.

wobbly boots *adj.* Uncontrollable alcoholic footwear. *Seven pint boots* worn when you've got *legs like snapped candles*.

wobbly landing *n.* Trying, when drunk, to manoeuvre your under-inflated *zipper Zeppelin* safely through your wife's *hangar doors*.

Wogan *n.* An impressively large *gut stick* (possibly half a teacake), poorly disguised by tight-fitting trousers), which causes middle-aged ladies to gasp. From the late Sir Terry's notoriously semi-priapismic *Points of View* appearance on October 14th 2007. No wonder he had such a deep voice.

wolfbagging *v.* To have sex with a wolf inside a large bag.

wolf bait *n.* An unusually meaty, pungent *fart,* similar to the smell encountered when opening a tin of Butcher's Tripe Mix. A *fyst, kangaroo-y eggo*.

wolf bite *n.* A really painful *arsehole, eg.* After a curry. *'"Would you care to ride with us to Wenlock Edge, Captain Tremaine?" she asked. The Captain winced. "I regret I must decline your kind offer, Mrs Dugdale," he replied. "I lately partook of a monstrous vindaloo with the Lord of Harpole, and I still have a wolf bite upon my postillion."'* (from *Middlemarch,* by George Eliot).

wolf pussy *n.* A nasty, exceptionally hairy *growler* that looks like it could inflict serious damage if provoked. *'Girl, you ain't coming no muthafucking way near me with that goddam muthafucking wolf pussy of yours and mess up my muthafucking dick, bitch. Shiiit.'* (Eddie Murphy in *Nutty Professor II The Klumps*).

wolverine wank *n.* An act of third party *manual relief* where the recipient is in fear of getting his *bell end* scratched by a lady with long, sharp nails.

woman in comfortable shoes *n.* A *tennis fan,* a *lady golfer.* A *gash badger* who is *fond of walking holidays*.

wombat hole *n.* An elegant way to describe a woman's *cunt*.

womberang *n. Aus.* A randy length of *wood* that keeps coming back for more.

womb fruit *n.* A baby. Also *fuck trophy, cunt cough*.

wombling *n.* When investigating a lady's *applecatchers*, the point when one's hand goes from exploring "overground" to exploring "underground", if you will.

womb service *n.* What a randy woman may request of her *fuck buddy* at 1am when she is alone and feeling a tad *peckerish*.

womb strudel *n.* An unsavoury *strawberry* dessert baked once a month in a *hairy pie-dish*.

women and children first! *1. exclam.* Shouted when a ship is sinking. *2. exclam.* Shouted when a *shit* is stinking. *3. exclam.* Amusing cry after *stepping* on a particularly wet *duck*.

women's game of pool, as long as a *sim.* Said of a particularly lengthsome member. *'And our final panel member tonight is Stephen Pound who has been MP for Ealing North since 1997. Prior to* *becoming an MP he worked as a bus conductor and hospital porter. In Tony Blair's government he was parliamentary private secretary to Hazel Blears, and he is well known in the House of Commons for having a Charlie as long as a women's game of pool.'*

women's things *n. medic. Flangina.*

womentating *n.* Feminine version of *mansplaining.* Continuing to go on about a poor fellow's failings despite the fact that he is not particularly interested, clearly no longer listening, or asleep.

womfer *n.* The female equivalent of a *barse.* A *chinrest* used to avoid getting cramp at a *hairy pie* tasting.

womit *n.* Dribbly sick.

womoaning *n.* Ladies' equivalent of mansplaining.

wonder how many calories are in that? *exclam.* A rhetorical exclamation in the wake of a particularly nourishing *air buffet.*

wonderlaps *n.* The impressive, swaying *headlamps* on an approaching lady cyclist wearing loose summer attire, which offer a pleasant diversion for gentleman road-users, providing them with a welcome respite from the dull business of observing the Highway Code, looking out for other traffic or pedestrians, and steering.

wonderwank *n.* An act of *self abuse* carried out without the use of visual stimulation. Named after the pop singer Stevie.

wonder woman *n.* A lady with a *lovely personality.* Derivation unknown.

wonga conga *n.* A Thursday night on the tiles funded by a payday loan.

wongle *v.* To rive one's *passion cosh* up and down the *bag for life*'s *arse* in an attempt to wake her up for a *poke.*

wonion *n.* One onion. See also *wunion.*

wonk *1. n.* A political researcher. Usually a young man with glasses and a *wanker's tan* who would fail the Turing Test. A *spod. 2. n.* A desperate and ultimately unsatisfying act of *self help* with multiple interruptions. *'Bless me Father for I have sinned.' 'Do you mind coming back in about ten minutes, my son? I'm half way through a wonk in here.'*

Wonkas *n.* Your *balls.* A-hem… "The bit between Willy and the chocolate factory."

Wonnacott wait, the *n.* When *working from home,* one *off the wrist* enjoyed in the recreational no-man's-land between *Ken Bruce's Popmaster* and *Bargain Hunt.*

woo *1. v.* To charm someone with your romantic behaviour, perhaps by buying them flowers and chocolates and that. *'Matron: I'm a simple woman with simple tastes, and I want to be wooed. Dr Cutting: You can be as 'wude' as you like with me. I'll happily fuck you up the cunt.'* (*Carry On Matron* screenplay by Talbot Rothwell). *2. v.* To wee and *poo* at the same time. From wee + poo. *3. v.* To charm a German by *weeing* and *pooing* at the same time. *3. n.* A *wee* that unexpectedly and unilaterally makes the decision that a *poo* has to follow it. From, not surprisingly, wee + poo.

wood *n.* Erectification of the peniculastical appendulation.

woodburner *n.* An enthusiastic close pal who gives it *six nowt* while *playing fives* on a fellow's *walking stick* to such an extent as to cause a certain amount of charring to his *wood.* Someone who goes at it *like Ray Mears starting a fire.*

wooden *1. adj.* Of a thespian, gifted with limited acting ability. *'That Ross Kemp's rubbish, isn't he. He's so wooden.' 2. n.* Of a male lead in a *stick vid,* gifted with the ability to get a *bone on. 'That Ben Dover's great, isn't he. He's so wooden.'*

wooden horse *n.* In a public *Rick Witter,* the act of releasing a noisy *chocolate hostage* at the exact moment when one's neighbour is flushing. Named after a famous Second World War prison escape which applied a similar subterfuginous stratagem.

wooden leg, draw the spunk from a *phr.* A somewhat hyperbolic assessment of a woman's attractiveness. *'Fuck me static, missus. You'd draw the spunk from a wooden leg, you would. Anyway, the reason I'm calling is to see if you have ever thought about joining the Church of Jesus Christ of Latter-day Saints.'*

wooden onesie *n.* Coffin.

wood glue *1. n.* Sticky white substance which is typically used for bonding timber. *2. n.* Sticky white substance which is not typically used for bonding timber, but might work in an emergency. *Population paste.* Also *cockidex, pyjama glue, sement, jazz glue, Aphrodite's evostick, gonad glue, prick stick, man mastic.*

woodland *n.* A *dogging* site, *eg.* The sylvan glades and copses near the Thicket Roundabout, Maidenhead.

wood morning *exclam.* Upon waking, a young chap's spoken greeting to his youthful *ante meridiem* tumescence.

woodpecker *n.* She who performs rapid, hands-free *horatio.* From the movement of the *bird's* head as she hammers a chap's *trunk.*

woodpecker, the *n.* The bizarre act of a woman *bobbing* her husband up the *cigar cutter* with a *dildo* that is strapped to her forehead. An impractical-sounding heterosexual variation on the fabled *screwnicorn*, which involves the purchase of similarly unlikely-sounding equipment. If you get it on Amazon, it'll play havoc with your "You might also like" suggestions.

woodsman *n.* In the *Frankie Vaughan* industry, a *chopper*-wielding actor who almost certainly will not be able to act, but who can be relied upon to get venous blood to flow into his *corpora cavernosa* just before the director shouts "Action!".

woodwind *n.* Open air playing of the *pink oboe*.

woodwork *n.* Creative and practical subject practised to O-level standard by schoolboys until their wrists ache.

woodwork chewer *n.* An arduous late night *dreadnought*; a laborious, supersized *moonlight flit*.

woodworker *n.* A person engaged in the trade of working with *wood*. A r*ub and tugstress, Tom* or *dicksmith*.

woodwrecker *n.* An inopportune thought that comes unbidden into a fellow's mind at a vital moment while entertaining a young lady, causing a catastrophic f*elling of timber, eg.* A train accident, a full nappy, the missus's tutting, disappointed face *etc.*

woody *n.* What a young American surfer dude takes to the beach.

wookiee hole *1. n.* Slightly uninspiring, mis-spelled Somerset tourist attraction consisting of a hole in the ground and a gift shop. *2. n.* A harticularly pairy *Mary Hinge*. A *biffer*, a *Judith*.

Wookiee's purse *n.* A particularly hirsute *growler. A smashed tarantula, Bluto's beard.*

wool *n. coll. US.* Fluff, *blart, fanny, totty.*

woolly bird *n. Aus.* A sheep.

woolly scooter *n.* A crinigerous, yet nonetheless tidy, *minge*. Perhaps with a load of mirrors sticking out the sides for good measure, and Phil Daniels sat on it in a fishtail parka.

woolly wardrobe *n.* A bulky, cavernous receptacle in the bedroom where gentlemen stuff their *roll neck sweaters* at night.

woolsack *1. n.* Large square cushion stuffed with horsehair, upon which the Speaker of the House of Lords dozes gently during debates. *2. n.* A particularly hairy *ball bag*, upon which the Speaker of the House of Lords sits, whilst dozing gently during debates.

Woolworths *n.* A plain *bird* that may not impress your mates, but who will do absolutely anything you can think of, though not to a particularly high standard.

woo-woo *n.* See *wu-wu.*

Wordle Gummage *n. prop.* The scarecrow-like appearance of a person unable to progress into

their day until they have solved a letter-based internet puzzle.

work a split shift *v.* Of a lovable, lucky, cheeky chappie, to have two *ladyfriends* on the go at the same time.

working from home *euph.* Spending the day *relaxing in a gentleman's way. Jerking from home, catching up with some paperwork.*

working on a dream *1. n.* Chart-topping album by Bruce Springsteen and the E-Street Band. *2. n.* A ferocious early morning *hand shandy*, essayed while desperately trying to recapture the essential details of what was going on in one's reverie just moments earlier. From the lyrics to the Boss's song of the same name, *viz.* "Out here the nights are long, the days are lonely / I think of you and I'm working on a dream... /... Rain pourin' down / I swing my hammer / My hands are rough from working on a dream".

working on his novel *euph.* Of a tortured artist, frittering away the limited time he has on this earth watching Jeremy Kyle, eating Quavers and *wanking* in his dressing gown.

working on my guns *euph.* Indulging in a gruelling, epic programme of *self improvement*, which will leave the arms aching.

working out loud *1. n. Bullshite* hipster management-speak term, apparently referring to the radical concept of talking to people and sharing documents for review, or some such *bollocks*. *2. n.* Sitting on a public or works *crapper* and letting everyone around know exactly what post-Guinness/vindaloo turmoil one is going through.

workman's plunge *n.* Before going out, a quick wash of your *parts* in the sink on the offchance that you *pull some cabbage*. A *gentleman's wash.*

work one's passage *1. v.* To pay for a voyage by one's on-ship labour. *2. v.* To monetise one's *Samantha.*

works microwave, filthier than a *sim.* Descriptive of an accommodating female who *bangs like a belt-fed mortar. Dirty as a zoo keeper's boot.'*

workwomanship *n.* Dents in the car, knives and forks put in the wrong drawers, overcooked vegetables, burnt toast.

world cup Willy *n.* Regular sexual intercourse with the missus, *ie.* Once every four years.

world number two *1. n.* A highly accomplished sports person. *2. n.* A highly accomplished *shit*, with few if any redeeming qualities.

world of inferiors *n.* Outdoor markets and boot fairs vending suspiciously low-priced designer label goods. *'Is that new Armani sports coat genuine?' 'If it's not, I've been cheated out of five* *quid by the world of inferiors down the plaza.'*

world of leather *n.* The *parts* of an aged lady. *Granny's oysters, grandma's Wolseley.*

wormhole *1. n.* A *cludge* into which a lucky gent could only fit the slenderest of *custard cannons*. A *mouse's ear, paper cut* or *Bugner's eye*. *2. n.* An inexplicable highway-based space/time phenomenon, whereby a taxi driver asks you if you're from round here, then takes a sharp turn-off from a supposedly straightforward route, and takes a short cut which inevitably ends up trebling the distance travelled and hence the fare.

worming the dog *1. n.* A three-monthly ordeal in which the man of the house attempts to cajole a reluctant hound into swallowing a pill. *2. n.* A three-monthly ordeal in which the man of the house attempts to cajole his missus into swallowing the contents of his *pills.*

worm's belt, tighter than a *sim.* Descriptive of a particularly unaccommodating *snatch*, a *butler's cuff, mouse's ear, mole's eye. 'DUCHESS OF BERWICK: My dear Lord Plymdale. I really do not understand why you associate with Mrs Erlynne. She is such a tiresome conversationalist. LORD PLYMDALE: Conversation is, I find, a somewhat over-rated virtue, your ladyship. Besides which, Mrs Erlynne kindly vouchsafed me tops and fingers in Lord Darlington's gazebo last night and believe you me, her twat's tighter than a worm's belt.'* (from *Lady Windermere's Fanny* by Oscar Wilde).

worries about his clothes *euph.* Said of a chap who *makes a good quiche.*

worth an empty *adj. W Yorks.* An expression of heartfelt appreciation for the charms of a young lady which is apparently common parlance in Bradford.

worth a squirt *adj.* Sexually desirable. *Prodworthy.*

worzel cummidge *n. prop.* The scarecrow-like appearance of one incapable of functioning until they have had *one off the wrist* or a *blowie* before leaving for work.

worzel gummage *1. n. Horatio* off elderly, toothless ladies of Cornish origin. *Flo jobs. 2. n.* Deeply unsatisfactory *nosh* performed by a toothless country bumpkin.

worzel gusset *n.* The *fairy hammock* of a girl with a *minge like a rook's nest*, with all bits of straw and twigs sticking out the sides and probably a robin or a cuckoo living in it.

worzel quimmage *n.* A dense, unkempt and rainforest-like *hairport* of *gorilla salad*. A *crow's nest*. Named after the badly stuffed scarecrow character played by Dr Who, who had a series of novelty hits about tractors and cider in the 1970s.

worzel rummage *n.* A wholesome, rural, bucolic outdoor *bum swizzle* in the bushes. *'You're late home, Terry' 'Yes, June. I've been at the police station. I got arrested having a worzel rummage in the rhododendrons by the bowling green steps.'*

worzel, the *n.* Carefully curated "eccentric" hairstyle preferred by certain turnip-headed comedy Prime Ministers.

WOT/wot *abbrev.* An aesthetically challenged person who nevertheless sports a fine pair of *eye magnets* on their chest. *Waste Of Tits.*

would anyone like a tea or coffee? *exclam. interrog.* When subjected to a lengthy and multi-voiced *trouser trumpet*, a polite indication that you would like the cacophony to stop. From the strained interjection frequently spoken by Radio 4 producer Simon Tillotson at the end of the extra bit on the *In Our Time* podcast, when it would seem he's possibly had enough of Melvyn Bragg and his A-level-heavy guests yammering on and he wants to get out to the pub.

would survive in the wild *euph.* Way of describing the size of the *larger-boned* lady in a positive manner.

would the in-store cleaner please make their way to the underwear department? *exclam.* A charming riposte declaimed in the style of a supermarket announcer after a voluble act of flatulence. Also *wretched neighbours; you'll be learning to shite next son; let's see if it's right and let's see how many people said Tuvalu; quick George, check the grassy knoll.*

would you kiss your mother with that arse? *exclam. interrog.* Humorous riposte to someone *stepping on a duck.*

would you like a VAT receipt as well? *exclam. interrog.* Light-hearted rhetorical statement proffered after audibly *breaking wind*. See also, *well struck, sir; you won't be able to get that after Brexit, etc.*

would you like some product in your hair? *1. exclam. interrog.* An innocent question asked by a barber at the end of one's haircut. *2. exclam. interrog.* A less innocent question asked by a bloke when he's near the *vinegar strokes. 3. exclam. interrog.* A distinctly less innocent question asked by a barber when he's near the *vinegar strokes.*

would you like to gift aid that? *exclam. rhet.* Another post-*air biscuit* saying. See also *what year is it? Who's the president?*

wounded soldier's walk *n.* The trip a gentleman makes to the bathroom after completing a messy act of *relaxation* when he has nothing to hand with which to clean up the resultant mess. From the fact that cupping a few teaspoonsful of rapidly cooling *spuffer* to his belly causes him to assume a hunched posture which is very reminiscent of a shot infantryman clutching his injured stomach as he hobbles off the battlefield.

WOW/wow *acronym. interrog.* Work Or Wank? The first decision of the day for any *home worker* as he fires up his laptop.

wozny *n. Scots/Ir.* A *bird's* perineum or *taint*, from the fact that "if it wozny there, you'd be in the shit". The *tinter, carse, Humber bridge, Niftkin's bridge, tisnae, snarse etc.*

WRAC/wrac 1. *abbrev. milit.* The Women's Royal Army Corps. 2. *abbrev. milit.* Coarse squaddies' argot for Weekly Ration of Army Cunt. *'Good news lads. The WRAC's arrived. Bagsy fog up.'* (General Bernard Montgomery addressing his troops on the eve of the battle of El Alamein, North Africa, October 29th 1942).

wrestle an alligator *euph.* After *dropping* a particularly large *dreadnought*, to use your hand to break it into smaller parts after it refuses to flush down the *pan* the first couple of times. *'If anyone is wondering what's happened to Judith, she'll be back with us in a minute, only she's still wrestling an alligator after eating a whole meat platter last night. Now over to Raymond, who's been over to Japan to see a revolutionary new machine for making toast.'*

wrestler's neck, stiffer than a *sim.* Notably inflexible. See also *as stiff as a varnished eel; a wanker's sock; a bishop's dick; a signalman's rag.*

wrestle with one's conscience *v.* To spend a sleepless night *tossing*, but not necessarily turning.

wrestling fan's virginity, as long as a *sim.* An incredibly lengthy space of time, with no sign of change on the horizon. *'Oh yes, the first charter was granted in the 12th Century, madam. There's been a Wednesday market in Tewkesbury Town Square for as long as a wrestling fan's virginity.'*

wrestling Sergeant Brown *euph.* Struggling to force out a particularly recalcitrant *pop.* From the film *Bear Man*, in which the protagonist describes a fight between two grizzlies thusly: "Crikey, what a horrible mess. It looks like someone's been wrestling Sergeant Brown."

wrestling the Balrog 1. *n.* In *The Lord of the Rings*, Gandalf the Grey's display of heroics in halting the advance of the eponymous flame-spewing behemoth. 2. *n.* The challenge a chap's *nipsy* faces when valiantly attempting to hold back a particularly foul and gruesome *bogstopper* as he makes his way home following an impressively ambitious curry. Often accompanied by the shouted avowal:

"You shall not pass."

wretch-a-sketch *n.* Any low quality tattoo shop where the design of the shopfront fails to fill one with confidence as regards the proprietor's artistic abilities.

wring a kidney *v.* To pass urine. *'Where's the gurgler, your majesty? I've just got to wring a kidney before I get knighted. I don't want to piss meself when I kneel down, do I?'*

wring the rattlesnake *v.* Siphon the python. To *piss*, *strain the greens*.

wrinkled penny *n. US.* The *ringpiece, balloon knot, tea towel holder, nipsy.*

wrist assessment *n.* Urgent mental calculation made by a fellow contemplating a *Max Planck* while his *bread knife* has nipped out to the shops.

wristeria *n.* The frantic, nerve-shredding conclusion to a fellow's *ferret milking* session when his *bread knife* returns home from the shops unexpectedly early.

wrist flick *n.* A *grumble vid*, a *stick film.*

wrist fodder *euph.* Any one-handed *art pamphlet*, website or film.

wristicuffs *n.* A bout of *knocking oneself about a bit. Boxing the Jesuit.*

wristing the night away *n.* Standard evening's entertainment for the impecunious undergraduate.

wrist oil *n.* Perseverance soup, guardsman's gloss, ball glaze, dew on the lily, balm before the storm, knuckle varnish, snake spit or French polish.

wristorative *n.* An act by which an otherwise dejected individual can be returned to a state of general well-being, thus enabling him to carry out a difficult task *eg.* Going to the post office to cash a giro, opening a bag of Tangy Cheese Doroitos, getting out of bed and waiting for *Homes under The Hammer* to come on.

wrist-strainer *n.* A female of such exquisite attractiveness that she can cause ligament damage in the scapholunate joint.

writer's cock 1. *n. psych.* Psychological condition whereby a scribe is unable to put pen to paper until he has had at least five *wanks.* A condition which is commonly suffered by journalists facing imminent deadlines, students with essays to complete and Ernest Hemingway. *'Ah, Herr Schubert. How is that Eighth Symphony of yours coming along?' 'Well, I was thinking of doing a nice scherzo section for it, and then maybe a big finale in B Minor in which all the themes of the earlier movements are brought together, only I've had terrible writer's cock for the last six years.'* 2. *n.* The excuse used by authors caught looking at illegal *grumble* while *researching a book. Writer's* *cock* can be so bad that some of the books being researched take many years to be completed, if they ever appear at all.

write the letter 'M' *v.* To inscribe the thirteenth letter of the alphabet in *arse* sweat on the toilet seat while having a *Queensway*.

wrongbow *n.* White cider. A tangy, refreshing apple-based alternative to *trampagne*, *supermarket smack* or metal polish.

wrong 'un *n.* The *coal hole*. To quote Roy Walker, "it's good, but it's not right."

wronk *n.* *Self harm* performed in morally dubious circumstances.

WTW/wtw *abbrev.* Supportive form of letters designed to help a friend feel better about the *munter* he is currently *scuttling*. A comforting reassurance that you have "Wanked To Worse".

wuffle dust *1. n.* Magical compound utilised by erstwhile aphasic bear Sooty and his original handler Harry Corbett, who spoke not unlike Norris off *Coronation Street*. *2. n.* The somewhat less-than-magical faecal matter that, in terms of collateral damage, falls somewhere between a crisp, clean *treacle* and a catastrophic *shart*. A junior *follow through*.

wuffle nuts *n.* The sour fruits of the *dangleberry* tree.

wugyu pork *1. n.* A piece of meat treated to regular massaging. *2. n.* A teenager's *cock*.

wuilty *adj.* Descriptive of the sense of shame a fellow experiences when he inadvertently bumps into a lady over the thought of whom he has *knocked himself about a bit* earlier that very day. *'Did you catch Jonathan Ross interviewing that stripper who's married to Marilyn Manson the other night? He didn't half have a wuilty expression on his face.'*

wunch *n. coll.* Collective noun for a group of those hard-working, public-spirited heroes who toil for our benefit in the financial sector, *viz.* "A wunch of bankers".

wunion *n.* One onion. See also *wonion*.

wurzel *1. n. prop.* A member of the English rock supergroup of the 1970s. *2. n.* A beet with a large root. *3. n.* An embarrassingly small penis. An *acorn*.

wurzel quimmage *n.* A dense, unkempt and rain-forest-like *hairport* of *gorilla salad*. A *crow's nest*. Named after the badly stuffed scarecrow character played by Dr Who, who had a series of novelty hits about tractors and cider in the 1970s.

wu-wu *1. n.* Childish name for a *fufu* or *toot-toot*. *2. n.* The noise a train makes.

WWOH/wwoh *1. abbrev.* Text-speak for "Writing With One Hand." *2. abbrev.* Text-speak for "Wanking With Other Hand." Which is more or less the same thing, really.

WWW/www *abbrev.* Usefully alliterative mantra for those engaged in a romantic dalliance; Whip it in, Whip it out, Wipe it on the curtains.

WYSINWYG/wysinwyg *1. abbrev.* What You See Is Not What You Get. Computer-talk for flirting on the internet with a pert bit of blonde, A-level *fluff* who turns out to be a 58-year-old *sex case* panel beater masturbating in his mum's spare room. *2. n.* Welsh for helicopter.

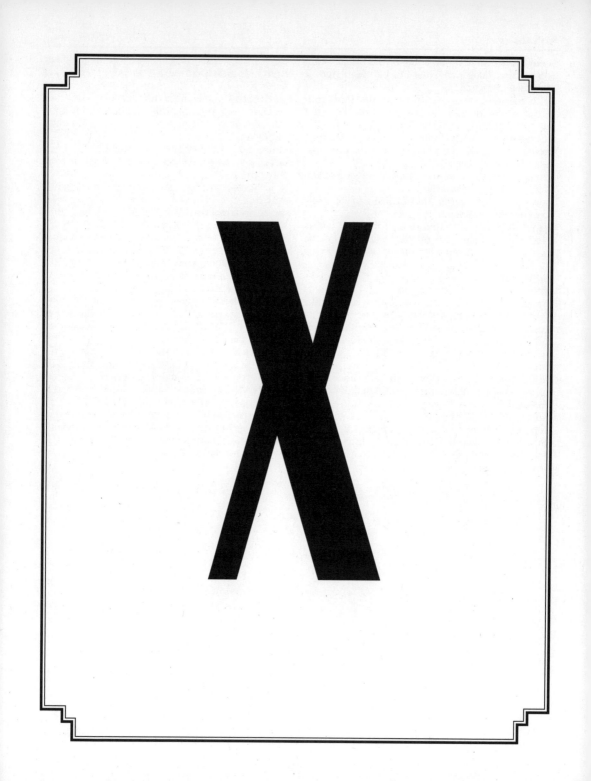

Xanadu *1. n.* Site of Kubla Khan's fabled pleasure dome, according to Samuel Taylor Coleridge. *2. n.* Title bestowed upon a public *crapper* that is too foul to use, no matter how great one's need. From the 1980 song by Olivia Newton-John: "A place, where nobody dares to go".

XBox legs *n. medic.* Doughy, atrophied lower limbs, as sported by pasty-faced teenagers with unusually well-developed thumbs.

X-flow, rough as a cold *sim.* A mechanic's term when referring to an aesthetically unconventional female. Named after Ford's notoriously noisy pushrod engine of the 1970s. *'No, but seriously though, fuck me, she's as rough as a cold X-flow.'* (Dr Rowan Williams, the Archbishop of Canterbury, addressing the reception following the wedding of His Royal Highness the Prince of Wales and Camilla Parker-Bowels, in the cafe of the Wacky Warehouse, Bracknell on April 9th 2005).

xiphoid *adj.* Sword-shaped. *'How pet? Do you like fencing? Suck me cock, it's xiphoid.'*

XL-men *n.* Thickset track-suited superhumans gifted with a range of amazing pie-, Scotch egg- and sausage roll-eating powers. Also *Greggs-men.*

Xmas tree light, weenie like a *sim.* An unnecessarily cutting reference to the diminutive dimensions of a fellow's *old chap*, as heard in kiddies' cartoon series *Family Guy.*

X-men *1. n.* Team of youthful superheroes recruited by the mysterious Professor X and brought to live with him at his secretive School for Gifted Youngsters. Probably all completely above board, but it might be worth a call to Social Services, just to be on the safe side. *2. n.* Those pale fellows in bottle-bottomed glasses who have a superfast broadband connection and never open their curtains. Full-time *pornithologists* who *work from home.*

X-piles *n.* Mysterious, unidentified throbbing objects from *Uranus.* That's pronounced "your anus", by the way. Like "your arsehole" sort of a thing.

X-ray specs *n.* Cheap, cardboard spectacles, available only by mail order from the backs of pubescent boys' comics, which enable the wearer to see through women's clothing. A more expensive version, advertised in the back of the *Lancet,* is used to diagnose fractures in hospital Accident & Emergency departments.

XX *adj.* Special video certificate awarded to pornographic films of poor sound and picture quality.

XXX *adj.* Special video certificate awarded to pornographic films of exceptionally poor sound and picture quality.

XXXX *adj.* Special brewing certificate awarded to Australian lager of *etc. etc.*

xylophone *1. n.* Like a piano, but you *twat it* with little sticks. From the Greek xylo = wood & phonnicus = to be hit tunelessly by a fat astronomer at a Royal Variety Performance. *2. v.* To move along a line of naked women who are all bending down, and spank their variously sized bottoms with one's penis. To play a tune on women's buttocks. See also *zylophone.*

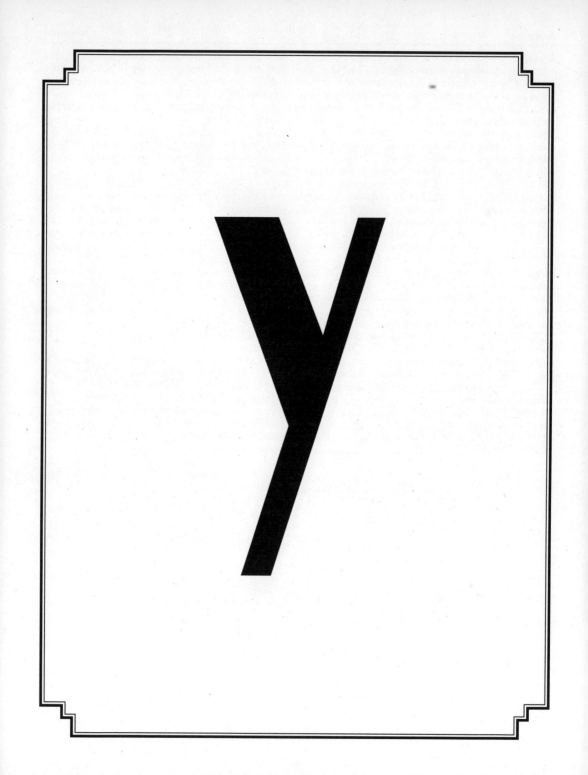

yabba dabbas *n.* In stone age cartoon intercourse, the climactic stages of *coitus* which immediately precede the *dooooooos*. The *vinegar strokes*.

yachting *n.* The stirring sight of a cocker spaniel in full sail, tacking its way across the living room carpet, attempting to remove the *barnacles* from its *keel*.

yaffle the yoghurt cannon *v.* To *nosh* voraciously, in the style of a woodpecker.

yak *1. n.* Big hairy animal of untidy appearance. Possibly the same as a gnu, but we can't be arsed to look it up. *2. n.* A big hairy *eskimo's glove* of untidy appearance. An ardent feminist's *beaver*, a *minge* with a *pant moustache*.

yambag *n.* The wrinkled retainer in which the *gourds* are kept.

yang *n. US.* A *wang*.

yank *1. n.* An inhabitant of the northern states of America. *2. n.* A "one-man-band"-type device with which a *sex case* attaches his *schlong* to his ankle in an attempt to *pull himself off* while walking about, Billy Dainty-style.

yank bias *1. n.* The sort of cultural imperialism which means that small numbers of unfortunate deaths in the USA receive infinitely more UK news and media coverage than disasters resulting in thousands of fatalities that occur somewhere where they don't speak English. *2. n.* A distinctly musatoid *love sausage* created by repeated and vigorous tugging with a sideways wrist-flick action.

yank fuel *n.* Onanistic *fodder. Frankie Vaughan. 'Mam, where did you put all me yank fuel when you tidied me bedroom?'*

yank off *v.* To *relax* vigorously *in a gentleman's way.*

yank the plank *v.* To *tug* one's *wood*, while running the risk of getting a hand full of splinters.

yarbles *n.* Testicles. *'He's lost his yarbles.'*

yard *1. n. arch.* Olde Worlde Penis. *2. n.* Confusingly, the *ladygarden* too.

yardbrush *n.* A bristly *fanny* one could sweep out the garage with.

yard high club *n.* The exclusive group of sexual adventurers who have made love in the lavatory of a static caravan.

yard of tripe *sim.* Descriptive of a capaciously-*flapped* lady. *'I got my hand up her skirt and it was like a yard of tripe, granddad.'*

yard-on *n.* An extra large *hard-on* achieved when particularly aroused, although probably still smaller than 3 feet, if we're being honest. A faint on.

Yaris fanny *euph.* A lady's *bodily treasure* which is, like the eponymous Toyota vehicle, "bigsmall". Something you think is going to be like a *mouse's*

ear which ends up being like the Albert Hall. A *twat* where you can fold down the seats and get your week's shopping, an Old English Sheepdog and four sets of skis in.

Yarmouth clam *n.* Similar to a *Viennese oyster,* only performed by a malodorous woman from the "Great" Norfolk seaside town.

Yasser *abbrev. US.* Erection. From "Yasser Crack-a-fat". A lame and pointless pun on the name of the late tea-towel-titfered Palestinian Ringo Starr lookalike.

yawning goldfish *n.* A particularly wide *hog's eye.*

yawning tabbycat *n.* Poetic term for the female *flangepiece*, particularly while in a state of post-coital relaxation.

yawnography *n.* Dull, uninspiring *grumble* of the sort shown on the telly, where they don't let you *see it going up, in, out or off,* or anything.

Y-bone steak *n.* Female opposite of a *tube steak.* The *beef curtains.*

Y-box *n.* Much more fun than an X-box, and only costs the price of a bunch of flowers from the 24-hour garage.

yearn *n.* A lengthy, wistful session on the *casserole pot,* awaiting the arrival of a *religious relic.* A bout of constipation. *'Derek's been a while in the gents.' 'Aye, he's having a yearn. His wife told me he's not been for a week.'*

yearning curve *n.* The parabola described by the movement of the *bell-end* as it progresses from dormancy to *full bonk.*

yeastiality *n.* Penchant for the fragrant blooms hidden among the lush undergrowth of *Max Clifford's* allotment.

yeast infection *n. medic.* A mild dose of *beer cancer.*

yeasty beasty *n.* A derogatory term for a lady with a dubious sexual hygiene regimen.

yeet *v.* To throw forcefully. Also *lob, hoy. 'Aw, for fuck's sake. Some cunt's just yeeted a full nappy over the fucking fence, your holiness.'*

yellow arrows display *n.* In a busy male public lavatory with a bank of urinals, the precisely co-ordinated positional exchange of *slashers.* As the first phalanx of blokes finish their *wees* and move out of the way, waiting men move smoothly into their vacated spaces with all the practised elegance of an RAF air display.

yellow Dick Turpin *n.* A speed camera.

yellow-fronted brown-backs *n. Nether garments* which are in need of a good wash. *'Eeh, we had a smashing night at the Arena. Tom Jones come on for his encore and did Delilah, and your nan got so excited she threw her yellow-fronted brown-backs up* *on the stage.'*

yellow noise *n.* Diffuse and unsatisfactory *pissing* stream, which can only be tuned out by careful of adjustment of the *knob*. Possibly caused by interference from Hilversum. *'I was suffering from terrible yellow noise this morning, and now I've got Dutch brogues.'*

yellow party *n.* A specialist German club night at which, instead of dancing, the participants *piss* on each other around their handbags.

yellow rope, to throw *v.* To urinate with force. *'Fuck me, Bobby. I've got five pints backed up here. I need to go and throw some yellow rope before I drown.'*

yellowstone *n.* The morning-after effect of a powerful *Ruby Murray* on one's digestive system. Named after the famous American National Park tourist attraction where, every so often, a brimstone-smelling gush of scalding liquid shoots out uncontrollably from a muddy, bubbling hole.

yellow toilet brush *euph.* The use of a skilfully controlled stream of high-pressure *wazz* to clean the *Bisto skids* off the sides of the *gravy bowl*.

ye-stenders *n.* Dismissive epithet for any period soap opera, *eg. Cranford, Downton Abbey, Upstairs Downstairs.*

yesterbeer *n.* Urine. *'Aw, you've got all splashes of yesterbeer on your shoes again, grandad.'*

yes you did – you invaded Poland *exclam.* Another bit of post-flatulatorial drollery. See also *that would be lovely – milk and two sugars please* and *you'll need to give her a little more throttle sir.*

yeti's welly *n.* A voluminous *fadge*, a *donkey's yawn*, a *hippo's mouth*.

yewdini *n.* A celebrity *wrongcock* who ingeniously escapes being taken in for questioning by the ever-vigilant *titheads* by having invincible lawyers or by being dead.

Yewtree, a touch of *euph.* A slight, indefinable sense that someone might be a tiny bit dodgy. *'I always thought there was a touch of Yewtree about him, you know. In retrospect, it probably might have been a mistake to give him an OBE and then a knighthood and then that Papal knighthood, and then an honorary doctorate of law and the Cross of Merit of the Order pro Merito Meritensi and also to appoint him as an honorary fellow of the Royal College of Radiologists and give him a solid gold set of keys to Broadmoor.'*

yimby *1. acronym.* Opposite of a *nimby*; a homeowner who wants even more housing constructed in their locale. From Yes, In My Back Yard. *2. acronym.* A person who is not averse to the odd round of *mud darts*.

yinyang *1. n. US. Arse, bum. 2. n. US. Fuckwit,*

jerkwad, asswipe, dicksplash.

yitney *n.* One who is *yitten*.

yitten *adj.* Scared of something very tame, *eg.* Donald Trump, when they put that eagle next to him and it flapped its wings and he fucking *shat* himself.

yobble *v.* To *defeesheeate* somewhere other than on a toilet, usually for the amusement of others. *eg.* Onto a cow from a tree.

Yoda's ears *n. Piss flaps* which conjure up the image of the erstwhile wisdom-filled mystical *Star Wars* Jedi Master, who spoke with the same voice as Fozzie Bear off *The Muppets*.

Yoda's gran *n.* A female senior citizen.

yodel *v.* To vomit, to *sing a rainbow*.

yodel in the canyon/valley *v.* To *growl* at a very *capacious badger* while wearing a small hat with a shaving brush stuck in it.

yoffy's finger *euph. Touching cloth.* From the 1970s children's show *Fingerbobs*. "Yoffy lifts a finger / and a mouse is there / puts his hands together / and a seagull takes the air / Yoffy lifts a finger / And a scampi darts about / Yoffy bends another / and a tortoise head peeps out".

yoga mat, she can use my face as a *exclam.* Complimentary comment as might be uttered about a *fit* young *piece* by a fellow who has not necessarily been keeping up with all the latest developments in sexual politics.

yoghurt weaver *n.* The sort of holistic, green, vegan, yurt-wearing right-on liberal who drives a G-Whizz.

yoinkahs *n.* A pair of *twin peaks* that cause a volcanic eruption in your *underkrakatoas*.

yokel anaesthetic *n. medic.* Industrial strength *scrumpy* that allows the imbiber to be dragged painlessly into a thresher. Popular in areas where family trees don't branch.

Yoko *n.* A *bird* who accompanies her boyfriend everywhere, *eg.* Down the pub with mates, fishing, recording sessions for the *Let It Be* album, the lot.

yongles *n. US. Clockweights*, testii, *nads, churns.*

yoni *n.* Ancient Hindu female genitals. How the mystic Karma Sutra refers to a *twat*.

yonic boom *n.* An especially thunderous *queef*.

yonks! *exclam.* Popular speech balloon reaction to finding a tenner on a cartoon pavement.

yoo poos, you lose *exclam.* A mordant aphorism uttered to one returning from a lengthy sojourn in the *cludgie*, only to find that the final glass of wine or share of spliff has been consumed in their absence.

york *exclam. onomat.* To vomit, *call Huey.*

Yorkie bar *n.* A *puddle jumper, botter* or *gaylord.*

From the popular chocolate confection advertising slogan. "It's not for girls".

Yorkshire caviar *n.* A refined delicacy enjoyed by sophisticated gourmands from the world's finest tri-ridingous county. Mushy peas. See also *Geordie hummus.*

Yorkshire dump *1. n.* Big piece of leftover glass used as a doorstop or paperweight. *2. n.* A right big *shite* that speaks as it finds.

Yorkshire flamingo *n.* A tired-looking, malnourished, pink-faced *bird* who, due to the sorry state of her even more shabby surroundings (*eg.* The Frontier Club, Batley), may erroneously appear exotic and alluring to the untrained eye.

you broke it, you bought it *exclam.* See *Alexa, open a window.*

you can't piss in the sink when it's full of teabags *phr. Yorks.* Profound, Confucious-like aphorism much used by denizens of the South Riding Shangri-La of Barnsley. *'Well, Geoffrey, he's pitched the ball up well wide of off-stump, and the batsman's nicked it to short leg.' 'Aye. That was woeful batting, that, especially on a turning wicket. But England need three hundred-and-six off the next four balls and, as we say in Fitzwilliam, you can't piss in the sink when it's full of teabags.'*

you can't stop there, Mr Derek *exclam.* Witticism said after a particularly long *fart* comes to an abrupt end. From the similar utterance of anthropomorphic fox Basil Brush when his human sidekick abruptly stopped reading the story at the end of the show. Also *you can't stop there, Mr Roy; you can't stop there, Mr Howard; you can't stop there, Mr Billy* or *you can't stop there, Mr Rodney,* according to preference.

you could hear a fly wank *exclam.* Literary phrase illustrating a scene of notable quietude. *"Twas the night before Christmas, and all through the house, not a creature was stirring, not even a mouse. The building lay silent, in fact to be frank, the house was so still, you could hear a fly wank.'*

you could make soup with her knickers *exclam.* Said of a woman who is not overly diligent about personal daintiness.

you couldn't have got all that on one shovel *exclam.* Statement made after someone serves up an impressively substantial *Texas meal.*

you could shove him/her in a flute and still hear the tune *phr.* Phrase which could be used to describe beanpole footballer Peter Crouch, malnourished comedian Mark Watson or any other ludicrously skinny person. *'Radcliffe on the starting line there, waiting for the signal to go. And there's not an ounce of excess flesh on her, is there Brendan?' 'That's*

right, Steve. You could shove her in a flute and still hear the tune.'

you could strike a match off that *exclam.* Cheeky comment to a *bird* who hasn't shaved the *monkey's forehead* for a couple of days.

You do not have to say anything, but it may harm your defence if you do not mention, when questioned, something which you later rely on in court *exclam.* Witty announcement preceeding an audible emission of wind from one's bottom. Also *this is Ripley, last survivor of the Nostromo, signing off; and the Thunderball is…; over to you, Esther; now back to Davina in the studio; observe, Mr Bond, the instruments of Armageddon; prisoner… show yourself!; my next guest needs no introduction; I'll name that tune in one* etc.

you got this, Peloton! *exclam.* Pre-*dump* motivational cry, stridently uttered whilst perched on the toilet, hunched forwards in the manner of someone on a glorified £4000 exercise bike, undertaking a virtual fitness class and bracing themselves for "the burn."

you got yourself a sandwich sir *exclam.* An advertising slogan used on commercials for Wendy's, an American burger restaurant, wittily pressed into service to describe a *bone-on* of notable length or girth, *ie.* A fat-filled half-pound of sweaty meat, preferably stuck between a couple of *baps.* With a cheesy topping.

you guessed today's Heardle! *exclam.* A witty riposte to a particularly short, sharp *horse and cart.*

youkakke *n.* The inadvertent practice of rendering oneself in one's own *nut butter.*

you'll have to buy that now, you've ripped it *exclam.* Humorous phrase which can be used to great effect after someone has *uploaded a file to the cloud* in a particularly resonant manner. See *keep shouting sir, we'll find you.*

you'll need to give her a little more throttle, sir *exclam.* Likewise *that would be lovely – milk and two sugars please; one year out!* and *yes you did – you invaded Poland.*

you might think that; I couldn't possibly comment *exclam.* Said in response to a powerful *statement in the chamber.*

you milk? *exclam. interrog.* A phrase used by far-eastern prostitutes to ascertain whether or not their client has *dropped his yop.*

you rebel bum *exclam.* A humorous *Star Wars*-style retort following a *nether cough.*

you're gonna hear me roar *1. exclam.* Lyric from the Katy Perry song *Roar. 2. n.* Something to say before ferociously *dropping a gut.* Also *what's that behind the brown door?; I smell with my little nose,* *something beginning with; our survey said; well, here's one good thing that's come from Brexit.*

You're only supposed to blow the bloody doors off *exclam.* More post-flatal repartee. See *you should put that on eBay.*

you're right Louis, it is a wonderful world *exclam.* Witty riposte to a rasping and gravel-voiced *postern blast.* Also *you won't find that one on the setlist tonight; a confident appeal by the Australians there; speech!*

you shall not pass! *1. exclam.* Iconic phrase intoned by Gandalf the Grey when battling the Balrog in *The Lord Of The Rings. 2. exclam.* Iconic phrase that can be intoned by anyone after loosing off an almighty *guff.*

you shop, we drop *1. phr.* Advertising slogan displayed on the sides of Tesco supermarket home delivery vans. *2. n.* Tempting overture delivered by one or more *ladies of the night* through the rolled-down window of a Premiership footballer's, or indeed his team manager's, motor car.

you should put that on eBay *exclam.* Something to say after somebody *drops a gut.* Also *if that's not out I'm not playing; can I quote you on that?; fall out the officers; thanks for that, now can you please throw something?; is that Ziggy?; a bit more choke and she would have started; an excellent theory, Dr Watson; anybody injured?; don't tear it, I'll take the whole piece; how much?; more tea vicar?; someone let him in; someone's tinkered with Herbie; speak on, sweet lips that never told a lie; speak up caller, you're through; taxi for Brown; that's working, now try your lights; well struck sir!; what's that, Sweep?; sew a button on that; catch that one and paint it blue; good health!; pin a tail on that; there goes the elephant; my, that duck's got bad breath* and many, many more.

you still have two wishes left! *exclam. hum.* Amusing phrase which can be used to lighten a ladyfriend's rancorous mien after you have used your *magic wand* to cover her face with *jizz*, for example.

you've solved the wall! *1. exclam.* Proclamation made by *Only Connect*'s Victoria Coren-Mitchell when a team of *four-eyed* weirdos solves one of the trickier parts of her high-brow quiz. *2. exclam.* Proclamation made by one who has just dropped a particularly foul *horned viper* through their *eye of Horus.*

yo-yo knickers *n.* A *bike*, loose woman; she whose *twangers* are *up and down more often than a jockey's arse.*

yule log *n.* The smoking centrepiece of festivities on December 26th. A monster *feeshus* with all the trimmings. And a robin sat on top of it.

yule tide *n.* The alarming, rising water level in a Boxing Day *crapper* that is thoroughly occluded.

yummy mummy *1. n.* A middle-aged woman who is worthy of a good *seeing to. 2. n.* A young materfamilias with a fantastic *arse* pushing a buggy. That's the young woman pushing the buggy, by the way, not her *arse. 3. n.* On a cannibal menu, either a delicious, well-cooked mother, or jerky made from the desiccated remains of an Egyptian pharaoh.

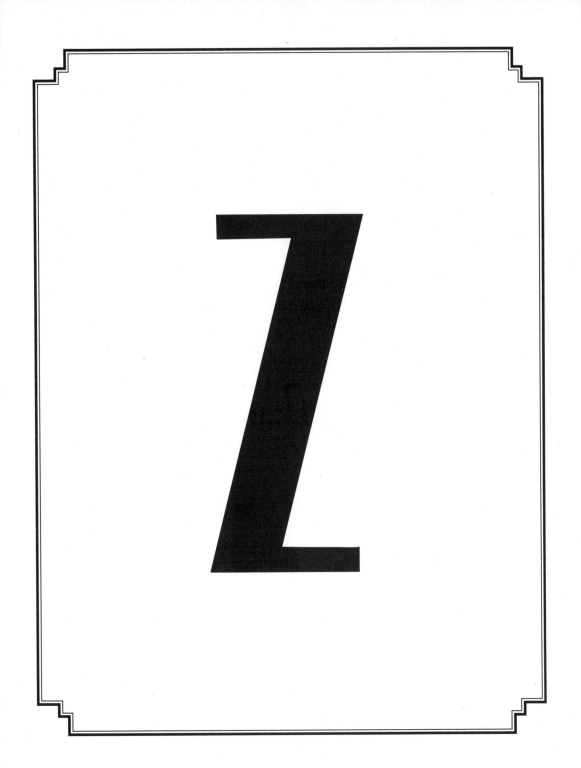

Zag's eyes *euph.* When a low budget *Frankie* artiste's *plastic fantastics* aren't quite symmetrical, with the left *tit-tap* going to the shop, and the right one coming back with the change, in the manner of the erstwhile, eponymous breakfast telly puppet's ocular organs. *Nips like a bucket of whelks.*

zasm *n.* The female equivalent of *jism*. *'Do you know where my other tie is, love? I can't read the Channel 4 News in this one, it's got all zasm down it.'*

Zebedee *1. n.* At school, a face – complete with "Julius Pringles"-type moustache – drawn onto the *glans* with a biro in order to amuse one's classmates or one's pupils. *2. n.* A tea-time erection that springs up unexpectedly, signalling that it is "time for bed".

zebra, splayed *euph.* See *lion's breakfast.*

Zee DT on FB *phr.* Tactical cessation of all activity on social network sites while off sick, in order to fool colleagues you may be genuinely ill as opposed to playing the PS3, *wanking*, drinking, *wanking*, watching *Bargain Hunt*, *wanking*, etc. Zero Dark Thirty on Facebook.

zelebrity *n.* Somewhat oxymoronically, a *Z-list* celebrity. *'This Autumn on Living TV sees the return of Zelebrity Most Haunted Live. Some cunt off Hollyoaks, Becki from Big Brother 4 and the Duchess of York attempt to spend the night in a darkened room with Yvette Fielding, her fat mate and the bald bloke who looks like Uncle Fester.'* (from *TV Times,* August 2009).

zendrex *n.* Cheap, impossibly thin *bog roll* that your fingers will definitely go through, thus putting you "in touch with your inner self".

zeps *abbrev.* Zeppelins. Large, hydrogen-filled, flammable spheroid *meat balloons. Hindenburgs, blimplants DDirigibles.* See also *dead heat in a Zeppelin race.*

zero flowers contract *n.* Tacit understanding, implicitly established from the moment a couple first meet, that this is a one-off sexual encounter and romantic involvement is neither warranted nor desired.

zero-hours contract *n.* A modern form of binding relationship in which, whilst the bloke is not guaranteed a minimum level of *shagging*, he must nevertheless remain on 24/7 call should his sexual, financial, emotional, DIY or spider-re-moval services be required.

zerotica *n. Wanking* material of the lowest imaginable potency, *eg.* A thermal underwear catalogue, a picture of a nuns' hockey team, a stamp with a picture of Florence Nightingale on it, or the letters page in the *People's Friend.*

zero worship *n.* The adoration of *Z-list* celebrities, such as *Big Brother* contestants, *Geordie Shore* cast members, or orange people off *Towie.*

zig-a-zig ahhhh! *onomat. arch.* The sound of a bloke having a bloody good *one off the wrist* while watching the Spice Girls on a mysteriously DLT-free *Top of the Pops* re-run on BBC2.

zilch *n. Fuck all, jack shit, sweet FA.*

zipper fish *n.* The *rod* part of the male *tackle;* the *trouser trout. 'I've caught my zipper fish, and it's a big one.'*

zipper sniffer *n.* A keen penis enthusiast of either gender.

zipper Zeppelin *n.* Shiny, cigar-shaped craft which occasionally explodes at its moorings. *'Watch it! Watch it! Oh, get out of the way of my zipper Zeppelin! Too late! Oh, the humanity! Oh, the humanity! Let me get you a tissue, Mother Teresa.'*

zippy *1. n. prop.* Annoying, one-armed character in children's series *Rainbow. 2. n.* A nasty accident suffered when trying to do up your trousers impetuously. See *angry rabbi.*

zip snip *n.* An unintentional circumcision and/or vasectomy operation performed using the flies of a chap's trousers. Usually carried out under about ten pints of general anaesthetic. *'Don't worry about that, love. I've had the zip snip.'*

zit *n.* A *pluke.*

zitwank *n.* A *bunny rub* into a pointlessly tiny pair of *norks.*

Z-lister *n.* See *zelebrity, eh?-lister.* Probably on ITV2.

Zoes *n. Balls, clockweights, gonads,* testicles. From the *Jersey-royalled Big Family Cooking Showdown* presenter Zoe Bollocks = orchestras.

zombie ashopolypse *n.* A mind-numbing afternoon spent trailing round after the *bag for life* at the retail park, where all the blokes are stumbling about with blank, empty expressions as if their souls have been sucked out of them.

zombie's fart *1. n.* A *food's ghost* so retchingly evil it could only have been summoned by the undead. See also *kexorcism. 2. sim.* A poetic evocation of the potent morning-after breath of one who has eaten more than his fair share of kebab meat and chili sauce the previous evening. And then come home and opened the Doritos.

zombie's napkin *n.* A *Dracula's teabag* or *twat rat* used by a lady who is *walking wounded. 'I thought I had a shot at the title, but when I got her knickers down she was wearing a fucking zombie's napkin, nan.'*

zonked *adj. Pissed, wankered, wazzed, trousered.*

zoo keeper's boot *1. euph.* A reduced state of oral

hygiene, for example, the morning after excessive alcohol consumption, eating out at a less than salubrious establishment, or *dining at the Y* on a lady who eschews feminine hygiene requisites. *2. sim.* Said of a woman who looks like she *goes a bit. 'I tell you what, though, her who does the business news, I bet she's as dirty as a zoo keeper's boot. Anyway, fingers on buzzers, here's your starter for ten.'*

zookkake *n.* A quite possibly made-up sexual practice whereby ten Japanese men wearing noh masks take turns to *wank* onto an otter's face. It's a good job Johnny Morris never lived to see this.

zoomorrhoids *n. medic.* Lockdown-fostered *Nobby Stiles* which start to twinge during the day's third or fourth online webcam meeting.

zopi clown *n.* A person comically attempting to carry out simple household tasks whilst slipping into a tranquilised state under the influence of quick-acting prescription sleeping tablet zopiclone. *'Maw, maw! Come quick. Gran'paw's deein' a shite in the neighbours' garden the noo!' 'Don't worry, oor Wullie. The daft auld cunt's just playin' the zopi clown. I'll fetch ma brush.'*

Zorro *v.* To wield one's tumescently *xiphoid manhood* as the fictional masked bandit would his trademark rapier, and with a skilful flick of the wrist *lob ropes* benevolently over a lucky slattern in a zig-zag fashion. *'Please don't spaff over my face, Harry. We're meeting your nan in twenty minutes.' 'Fine, pop your tits out and I'll Zorro them instead, Megs.'*

zounds *n. arch.* "God's wounds"; 17th century swear word banned by Act of Parliament in 1651, but okay now if used in moderation. Also *g*dzooks, fuckanory.*

zucchini *n. US. Cock.* Something stuck into burgers by disgruntled fast food preparation staff. *Dill,* the *man mayonnaise bottle, jerked gherkin.*

zuffle *v.* To wipe one's *Charlie* clean on the curtains after having a *fuck,* usually in a posh *bird's* house;

that is to say, one that has curtains. *To fly the flag, gloop the loop.*

zuffle bag *n.* She who is *no better than she ought to be,* whose soft furnishings show evidence of substantial previous *zuffling.*

zuffle cat *n.* An unfortunate pet that finds itself cornered in a curtainless bedroom.

zuffle coat *n.* The topmost item of clothing in the pile on a bed at a party. Used by a male guest to clean the *sloom* off his *three card trick* after a furtive *poke.*

zylophone *n.* Incorrect spelling of *xylophone.*

ZZ bottom *n.* An exceptionally long-haired *muff,* from the resemblance to the unsightly, unkempt beards sported by the remaining members of antediluvian Texan blues rock band ZZ Top. But not the drummer.

ZZ mott *n.* A badly overgrown *underbeard.* Also *Max Clifford's allotment, tank driver's hat, Taz, wookiee hole, yak, superfuzz bigmuff deluxe edition, Judith, eskimo's glove, granny's hat, gruffalo, guardsman's hat, busby berkeley, hairy knickers, Lord Winston's moustache, Paddy McGinty's goat, Rolf Harris's lawn, radar trap, barber's floor, beartrapper's hat, biffer, Bilbo Baggins's foot, wolf pussy, bushell, divot, Dougal* and *Mary Hinge.*

ZZ tops and fingers *n. Firkyfoodling* one's missus while she's dozing.

Z Zulu *euph.* A reference to a particular arrangement of nautical flags which means, variously, "I require a tug" and, apparently, "I am shooting nets". Also *flag zulu.*

ZZZ tops and fingers *n. Firkyfoodling* one's missus while she's in a coma.

ZZZZ-list *1. n.* Mental list of people with whom one would like to *sleep. 2. n.* In showbiz, the section of a celebrity booker's address book containing people who might be persuaded to *wank off* a pig in return for the chance of getting on television.

Acknowledgments

Roger Mellie OBE would like to express his sincere gratitude to all the *Viz* readers and visitors to *viz.co.uk* who continue to send in Profanisaurus definitions. It is thanks to their efforts over the years that he has been able to produce such a massive volume of foulage.

Mr Mellie also extends his grateful thanks to Caroline Addy, Richard Osman, Alex Collier, Chris Donald, Simon Donald, Davey Jones, Dave Saunders, Lee Boyman and all the scientists working at Pfizer who discovered the phosphodiesterase 5 blocker Sildenafil.

You can follow *Viz* at
twitter.com/vizcomic
and
facebook.com/vizcomic

Please send your suggestions for new entries to *profanisaurus@viz.co.uk*

The Profanisaurus is updated in every issue of *Viz*. Get it ten times a year by visiting *subscribe.viz.co.uk*

Now wash your hands.